WHO'S WHO IN

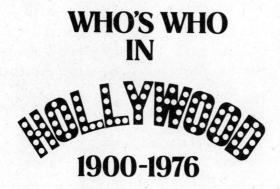

1900-1976

WHO'S WHO IN

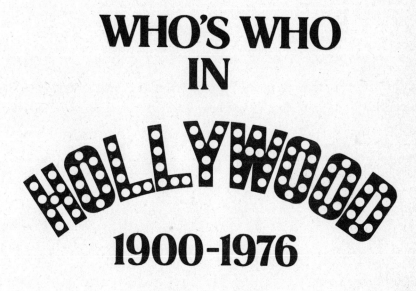

1900-1976

DAVID RAGAN

NEW ROCHELLE, NEW YORK

Library of Congress Cataloging in Publication Data

Ragan, David.
  Who's who in Hollywood, 1900-1976.

    1. Moving-picture actors and actresses—United States—Biog-
raphy. I. Title.
PN1998.A2R3   791.43′028′0922[B]   76-25542
ISBN 0-87000-349-6

This book is dedicated with love to
CLAIRE, DAVEY, SARAH and JENNIFER

. . . and with lasting affection to

Fay Bainter, Albert Bassermann, Charles Bickford, Walter Brennan, Pamela Brown, Harry Carey, Eduardo Ciannelli, Charles Coburn, Constance Collier, Patricia Collinge, Ronald Colman, Gladys Cooper, Frank Craven, Donald Crisp, Cecil Cunningham, Esther Dale, Harry Davenport, Philip Dorn, Emma Dunn, Frances Farmer, John Garfield, Gladys George, Sir Cedric Hardwicke, Samuel S. Hinds, Martita Hunt, Walter Huston, Frieda Inescort, Buck Jones, Roscoe Karns, Erich Korngold, Alma Kruger, Vivien Leigh, Carole Lombard, Miles Mander, Mae Marsh, Thomas Mitchell, Ona Munson, Maria Ouspenskaya, Lynne Overman, Mabel Paige, Elizabeth Patterson, Claude Rains, Marjorie Rambeau, Florence Rice, Stanley Ridges, May Robson, C. Aubrey Smith, Henry Travers, Queenie Vassar, Cheryl Walker, Lucile Watson, Virginia Weidler,

. . . and with continuing admiration to

Brian Aherne, Louise Allbritton, Muriel Angelus, Lew Ayres, Binnie Barnes, Lucille Benson, Beulah Bondi, Dorris Bowdon, Jane Bryan, Ellen Burstyn, Madeleine Carroll, Bette Davis, William Demarest, Robert De Niro, Faye Dunaway, Irene Dunne, Deanna Durbin, Albert Finney, Geraldine Fitzgerald, Connie Gilchrist, Lillian Gish, Gene Hackman, Wendy Hiller, Henry Hull, Victor Jory, Nancy Kelly, Leonid Kinskey, Priscilla Lane, Carolyn Lee, Andrea Leeds, Myrna Loy, Ida Lupino, Una Merkel, Ruth Nelson, Jack Nicholson, Lloyd Nolan, Barbara O'Neill, Al Pacino, Anne Revere, Lynne Roberts, Ginger Rogers, Norma Shearer, Barbara Stanwyck, Charles Starrett, Linda Stirling, Kent Taylor, Shirley Temple, Claire Trevor, Nella Walker, and Bobs Watson.

For assistance of various sorts, and encouragement, the author gratefully acknowledges his indebtedness to

WALTER MICHAEL KOREMIN

&

GARRET McCLUNG

and

Dora Albert
Alice Huldah Allen
Jimmy Allen
Penny Pence Anderson
Army Archerd
Fredda Dudley Balling
Marilyn Beck
Connie Berman
Mrs. Frank M. Blyth
Marcia Borie
Pat Canole
Roy Carlin
Bernadette Carroza
Kirk Crivello
Frank Edwards
Dean Gautschy
Gus Gazzola

Vic Ghidalia
Tom Grafton
Hank Grant
Hortense Hearn
John Howard
Katherine Parr Kuvula
Mrs. Elizabeth B. Loyd
Robert Lukas
John Marven
Ruth Pearce
Vivian Senise Poppenberg
Martha Greenhouse Sasmor
Lawrence B. Thomas
Ruth Waterbury
Mildred Watt
Earl Wilson

TABLE OF CONTENTS

Preface

This volume, despite its size, is incomplete.

Though the accomplishments of several thousand screen performers are noted here, there remain many hundreds of players the author would have liked to include so that a permanent record might exist of all who, in large parts and small, have made their contribution to motion picture history. In hopes of achieving this, a wide net was cast. All players who could be found, those still living and those not, are included. As for the rest, some of whom created indelible memories, one can but regret that they walked out of the frame and faded from view without receiving proper salutations.

A word should be said about the title of this volume, *Who's Who in Hollywood: 1900-1976*. It was selected in the interest of simplicity, to indicate the period of time covered, and in full awareness that Hollywood, the community itself, was not founded until several years after the turn of the century. Motion pictures were being made, and movie personalities being created, in the East, long before the existence of Hollywood. Those players, many of whom never worked in Hollywood, could not be ignored. Finally, since "Hollywood" in recent decades has become a global community, with films being made all over the world and films from all over the world being shown on American screens, players from many nations—some few, even, who have never appeared in a "Hollywood" movie—are to be found herein.

LIVING PLAYERS

Unless otherwise indicated, it may be assumed that the following performers remain active today, either fully or part-time, in some area of show business—motion pictures, television, night clubs, or the legitimate stage.

Motion picture credits cited for each player, except in rare instances, are not meant to be complete. Instead, they are to be construed as a telescoped sampling—beginning with the performer's early films and working forward sequentially.

In parentheses immediately following each player's name is to be found the state, country, or territory where he or she lives today.

A

AADLAND, BEVERLY (S. Cal.) A teenager at the time she was Errol Flynn's last real-life romantic interest, she was also his leading lady in 1959's *Cuban Rebel Girls*—his final film and, reportedly, her only one. After a brief career as a nightclub entertainer, she became the wife of an automobile salesman and at last report lived in Van Nuys.

ABBOTT, JOHN (S. Cal.) In Hollywood movies since *The Shanghai Gesture*, following an Old Vic career and English films, this gaunt Britisher remains, in his 70s (b. 1905), one of the industry's stalwart character actors. Often a guest on TV series, he has done cartoon voices for Disney, and in '75 was featured in *The Black Bird*, his 65th Hollywood picture. Onscreen in the U.S. from 1941. IN: *Missing Ten Days, Joan of Paris, Mrs. Miniver, Mission to Moscow, Jane Eyre, The Mask of Dimitrios, Summer Storm, Saratoga Trunk, Anna and the King of Siam, The Woman in White, Sombrero, Gigi, The Greatest Story Ever Told, Gambit, 2000 Years Later,* more.

ABBOTT, PHILIP (S. Cal.) Support. Onscreen from 1957. IN: *The Bachelor Party, Sweet Bird of Youth, The Spiral Road, Miracle of the White Stallions, Those Calloways,* more.

ABBOTT, RICHARD (N.Y.) Character. Onscreen from 1934. IN: *The Fountain, Action in the North Atlantic, The Moon Is Down, Green Dolphin Street, The Hucksters, The Manchurian Candidate, The World of Henry Orient,* more.

ABEL, WALTER (N.Y.) One of the screen's great farceurs, he has lived for over two decades in New York, where his acting career began. Silver-haired and in his 70s (b. 1898), he costars most often now on the legitimate stage. He was top-billed with Kim Hunter in stock in the summer of '75 in the play *In Praise of Love,* following it with a featured role in the New York revival of *Trelawny of the Wells.* The previous year he appeared opposite Sada Thompson on Broadway in *Saturday, Sunday, Monday.* On TV in '73, he shared billing with Cliff Robertson in the special *The Man Without a Country.* The actor and his wife of many years, Marietta, live in an apartment in the fashionable East 70s and have two grown sons—Michael, a film producer, and Jonathan, a Vietnam Marine veteran. Privately, Abel is active in the Episcopal Actors Guild and has occasionally been narrator of music programs at Alice Tully Hall. Onscreen from 1930. IN: *Liliom, Fury, Portia on Trial, Arise My Love, Skylark, Holiday Inn,*

Star-Spangled Rhythm, Fired Wife, So Proudly We Hail, Kiss and Tell, Dream Girl, That Lady in Ermine, Raintree County, Mirage; Silent Night, Bloody Night; more.

ABERG, SIVI (S. Cal.) Support. IN: *I'll Take Sweden, That Funny Feeling; Easy Come, Easy Go; The Killing of Sister George.*

ACKER, SHARON (S. Cal.) Leading lady. Onscreen from 1958. IN: *Lucky Jim, Point Blank,* more.

ACKERMAN, BETTYE (S. Cal.) Support. Onscreen from 1959. IN: *Face of Fire, Rascal, M*A*S*H,* more.

ACQUANETTA (Ariz.) For many years in Scottsdale, this handsome woman—her raven hair parted in the center and drawn severely back, as she always wore it on the screen—has been hostess of a popular television talk show. A sponsor of the program is Baschuck Auto Agency—Luciana Baschuck, its wealthy proprietor, having been the husband of the beautiful Cheyenne Indian actress since '46, the year she left the screen. Childless, they live in a ranch house that is a showplace of the local suburbs. Onscreen from the early '40s. IN: *Captive Wild Woman, Jungle Woman, Tarzan and the Leopard Woman,* more.

ADAMS, BEVERLY (N.Y.) Leading lady. Married to hair stylist Vidal Sassoon, and retired, she has a daughter, born in '70. Onscreen from 1964. IN: *The New Interns, The Silencers, Murderers' Row, The Ambushers, Torture Garden, Hammerhead,* more.

ADAMS, CASEY/now MAX SHOWALTER (N.Y.) Comic support. Onscreen from 1949. IN: *Always Leave Them Laughing, What Price Glory?, Niagara, Bus Stop, Designing Woman, Summer and Smoke, The Music Man; Move Over, Darling; How to Murder Your Wife, The Anderson Tapes,* more.

ADAMS, DOROTHY (S. Cal.) A character actress much in demand in the '40s and '50s, she appeared in dozens of films playing country women *(Shepherd of the Hills)* and maids *(Laura).* Less active in the '60s (just two movies: *From the Terrace, The Good Guys and the Bad Guys),* she became a lecturer in Theatre Arts on the staff at UCLA, near her Westwood home. A widow since the death of her character actor husband, Byron Foulger, in '70, she has two daughters, Amanda and Rachel Ames (a star of the ABC-TV serial *General Hospital),* and, by Rachel, a teenage granddaughter, Susan. The actress was seen late in '74 portraying the hillbilly mother of Dyan Cannon in the TV-

movie *Virginia Hill,* and in '75 had a supporting role in *Peeper,* starring Michael Caine. Onscreen from 1941. IN: *Bedtime Story, My Darling Clementine, So Proudly We Hail, The Best Years of Our Lives, Miss Susie Slagle's, Carrie, The Man in the Gray Flannel Suit, The Big Country,* more.

ADAMS, EDIE (S. Cal.) The widow of comedian Ernie Kovacs and later the wife of a photographer, the blonde singer is now married to trumpeter Pete Candoli, former husband of Betty Hutton. They costar in a nightclub act and, in the summer of '75, in various Ohio cities, were in a new comedy with music, *The Cooch Dancer,* which they hoped to take to Broadway. Onscreen from 1960. IN: *The Apartment, Lover Come Back, Under the Yum Yum Tree, The Best Man, Made in Paris, The Oscar, The Honey Pot,* more.

ADAMS, JILL (Eng.) Costar. Onscreen from 1954. IN: *The Young Lovers, Chance Meeting, Doctors at Sea, Private's Progress, The Green Man, Value for Money, Brothers in Law,* more.

ADAMS, JOEY (N.Y.) Comedian. IN: *Ringside, Singing in the Dark,* more.

ADAMS, JULIE (S. Cal.) Since leaving Universal-International in '58, after seven years and 22 costarring roles, the actress has opted for variety in her career. She has done much TV—daytime (a running lead in *General Hospital* in 1969–70) and nighttime (various TV movies, dramatic series such as *Marcus Welby,* and costarred as the wife in *The Jimmy Stewart Show).* On the stage in stock she has starred in *Forty Carats* and *The Prime of Miss Jean Brodie.* In '75 she costarred in two pictures, *The McCullochs* and *Psychic Killer.* The latter was directed by her husband of two decades, Ray Danton *(The George Raft Story),* who is now billed Raymond. The Dantons have two teenage sons, Steve and Mitchell. Fans of Westerns of the '40s (Don "Red" Barry's *The Dalton Gang* and other Lippert productions) will recall Julie as Betty Adams, and, of course, in her earliest pix at Universal she was Julia. Onscreen from 1948. IN: *Bright Victory, Bend of the River, Horizons West, Mississippi Gambler, Wings of the Hawk, Six Bridges to Cross, The Private War of Major Benson, Underwater City, The Valley of Mystery,* more.

ADAMS, MARLA (N.Y.) Support. IN: *Splendor in the Grass.*

ADAMS, MAUD (N.Y.) Leading lady. IN: *The Christian Licorice Store, The Man With the Golden Gun, Rollerball, Killer Force,* more.

ADAMS, NEILE (S. Cal.) Support. IN: *The Wonders of Aladdin, This Could Be the Night,* more.

ADAMS, PETER (S. Cal.) Support. IN: *Donovan's Brain, The Big Fisherman,* more.

ADAMS, STANLEY (S. Cal.) Character. Onscreen from 1956. IN: *Hell on Frisco Bay, The Young Savages, Breakfast at Tiffany's, Lilies of the Field, A House Is Not a Home, Nevada Smith, Thunder Alley,* more.

ADDAMS, DAWN (Sp.) Giving up her Hollywood career for a long (1954–71), sometimes stormy marriage to Italy's Prince Don Vittorio Massimo, the English-born actress continued to appear in European and British films. In '73 her then-18-year-old son, Prince Stefano, married Atalanta Foxwell, 17, daughter of a London movie producer, and was reportedly disinherited by his father from an estate worth many millions. The couple has since made the actress a young (she was born in '30) grandmother. She and her present (since '74) husband, Englishman James White, live most of the year at her villa in Malta. Onscreen from 1951. IN: *The Unknown Man, Singin' in the Rain, Plymouth Adventure, Young Bess, The Moon Is Blue, The Robe, A King in New York, House of Fright, Come Fly With Me, The Thousand Eyes of Dr. Mabuse,* more.

ADDY, WESLEY (N.Y.) Support. Onscreen from 1951. IN: *The First Legion, Dreamboat, The Big Knife, What Ever Happened to Baby Jane?, Hush . . . Hush . . . Sweet Charlotte, Seconds, Tora! Tora! Tora!,* more.

ADJANI, ISABELLE (Fr.) Leading lady. Nominated for Best Actress Oscar in *The Story of Adele H.* IN: *La Gifle, The Story of Adele H.*

ADLER, JAY (N.Y.) Character. Onscreen from 1938. IN: *No Time to Marry, The Mob, Vice Squad, Illegal, Lucy Gallant, The Killing, Sweet Smell of Success, The Brothers Karamazov, Story on Page One,* more.

ADLER, LARRY (Eng.) The world-famed American harmonica player, a "blacklist" victim, is in his 60s now (b. 1914) and a longtime British resident. In '75 he visited New York for the first time in more than two decades. He appeared triumphantly in concert at Carnegie Hall—reunited with tap dancer Paul Draper, the other half of a once-famous duo—and in a solo engagement at the Rainbow Room. With the musician was his fiancé, Lady Selina Hastings, age 30. By two previous wives, both English, he has four children: Carole (married and a London advertising executive), Peter (an art dealer in London and single), Wendy (married to a New Yorker), and Caitlin (of grammar-school age). In England, Adler is as occupied with writing as with music—reviewing books, writing articles for such magazines as *Punch* and *Tennis,* and doing his autobiography, *From Hand to Mouth.* Onscreen from 1937. IN: *The Singing Marine, Sidewalks of London, Music for Millions,* more.

ADLER, LUTHER (S. Cal.) Character. Onscreen from 1937. IN: *Lancer Spy, The Loves of Carmen, Wake of the Red Witch, House of Strangers, Kiss Tomorrow Goodbye, The Desert Fox, The Miami Story, The Girl in the Red Velvet Swing, The Last Angry Man, The Brotherhood, Live a Little, Steal a Lot, The Man in the Glass Booth,* more.

ADLER, STELLA (N.Y.) Character. Long one of New York's most illustrious drama instructors, she rarely acts professionally now. Onscreen from 1937. IN: *Love on Toast* (billed Stella Ardler), *Shadow of the Thin Man, My Girl Tisa.*

ADRIAN, IRIS (S. Cal.) Hollywood's favorite wisecracking, gum-chewing blonde, in her 60s now (b. 1913), she has been for many years the wife of "Fido" Murphy, former football star and later a consultant with the Chicago Bears. Besides owning and managing a number of apartment houses in Los Angeles, Iris does TV commercials (toothpaste, recently) and an occasional guest stint on television. When this veteran of 150 movies does her "loudmouth act" onscreen now, it's usually for Disney: *The Love Bug, The Barefoot Executive, The Apple Dumpling Gang, Gus,* etc. Loving children (and enjoying much fan mail now from young Disney buffs), and never having had any, she has for decades made the swimming pool of her hillside home available to all youngsters in the neighborhood. Also, avidly interested in astrology, she says, "My sign is Gemini (May 29), 'the twins'—the actress and the landlady." The latter role, thanks to California's earthquakes, causes her some concern, because, she fears, "One good shake and 'Mrs. Murphy the landlady' is out of business." Onscreen from 1934. IN: *The Freshman's Goat, Rumba, Our Relations, Road to Zanzibar, Lady of Burlesque, Roxie Hart, Rings on Her Fingers, It's a Pleasure, The Stork Club, Boston Blackie's Rendezvous, Paleface, My Favorite Spy, Stop That Cab!, Blue Hawaii,* more.

AGAR, JOHN (S. Cal.) Silver-haired and in his 50s now (b. 1921), he was last prominently featured in John Wayne's *Big Jake* in '71. Earlier he had been in many Wayne pix: *Fort Apache, Sands of Iwo Jima, Chisum,* etc. More recently he has been a salesman for a Los Angeles Mercedes-Benz firm and, following that, an insurance executive. He has been married for well over two decades to Loretta Combs, a former dancer. Active in the Hollywood Christian Group, they have two teenage sons, Martin and John Jr. He has a daughter, Susan, now in her late 20s, by first wife Shirley Temple. Long-haired and outgoing, Susan had been living in Africa with her mother, U.S. ambassador to Ghana, and her stepfather, Charles Black. Besides studying Ghanian culture and sometimes standing in for her mother at durbars (tribal chiefs' outdoor feasts), Susan—a college graduate—had assisted her in writing articles about their life in Africa for American magazines. On October 8, 1975, in a ceremony at the United Presbyterian Church in Portola Valley, Calif., John Agar's only daughter became the bride of Italian diplomat Roberto Falaschi, whom she had met in Ghana. Onscreen from 1948. IN: *She Wore a Yellow Ribbon, Adventure in Baltimore, Along the Great Divide, Bait, Shield for Murder, The Golden Mistress, Of Love and Desire, Johnny Reno, The Undefeated*, more.

AGUILAR, TONY (Mex.) Mexico's combination of John Wayne and Roy Rogers—two-fisted and musical—lives with his wife, Flor Silvestre, and two young sons, Tony Jr. and Pepito, on a 30,000-acre ranch in the state of Zacatecas where he has 5,000 head of cattle and breeds show horses. IN: *The Undefeated, La Cucaracha, The Important Man*, more.

AHERNE, BRIAN (Switz.) In his 70s (b. 1902), he remains one of the handsomest men of his time, and perhaps one of the most content. He and his second wife (married since '46), the former Eleanor de Liagre Labrot, a New York socialite, have lived for years in Vevey in a "beautiful but crumbling old chateau" (his words), overhanging the Lake of Geneva, with magnificent views of the surrounding mountains. "I play golf on the course at Lausanne and we travel about Europe from time to time. In the winter, we spend a few weeks at our New York apartment, hoping to find something worth seeing in the theatre, and we go over to London with the same object," he says. In '69 he published his self-written autobiography, *A Proper Job*. A witty, graceful recounting of his life, it contained many tales out of school—his first wife, Joan Fontaine (1939-43), did not go unscathed. When they met for the first time in years in '72 at a New York theatrical gathering, they were polite. His most recent activity as a performer was recording his book for the American Foundation for the Blind. *Rosie* ('68), with Rosalind Russell, a frequent co-star of yesteryear, was his latest movie, and

Dear Liar ('63), his last Broadway play. As for Hollywood, he says, "About once a year, we go out to Santa Monica, where I still own my great house on the beach [bought it from Barbara Hutton], which we rent furnished . . . but to me California is sad now, and Hollywood a ghost town. Everybody I knew seems to have either died or gone away." Onscreen from 1929. IN: *Underground, Song of Songs, Sylvia Scarlet, Beloved Enemy, The Great Garrick, Juarez; My Son, My Son; Vigil in the Night, My Sister Eileen, Forever and a Day, What a Woman, Green Dolphin Street, I Confess, Titantic, The Swan, The Best of Everything, Susan Slade, The Sword of Lancelot*, more.

AHN, PHILIP (S. Cal.) One of the most villainous "Japanese" in WW II movies, Ahn is actually Korean, the son of one of the founders of the Republic of Korea. A lifelong bachelor, in his 60s now (b. 1911), he lives on a one-acre "ranch" in the San Fernando Valley, where he owns a flourishing Chinese restaurant. Active in movies through '67, he more recently had a regular role, Master Kan, in TV's *Kung Fu*, and has played guest parts in a variety of television series. Except for an almost imperceptible limp, he is fully recovered from having been run down by a car in a crosswalk in Los Angeles in 1970. Onscreen from 1936. IN: *The General Died at Dawn, China Passage, Thank You, Mr. Moto, King of Chinatown, A Yank on the Burma Road, The Story of Dr. Wassell, Betrayal From the East, Back to Bataan, Japanese War Bride, Love Is a Many-Splendored Thing, Yesterday's Enemy, Diamond Head, Thoroughly Modern Millie*, more.

AIDMAN, CHARLES (S. Cal.) Support. Onscreen from 1959. IN: *Pork Chop Hill, War Hunt, Hour of the Gun, Countdown; Angel, Angel, Down We Go*; more.

AILEY, ALVIN (N.Y.) Dance star. IN: *Carmen Jones*.

AIMEE, ANOUK (Eng.) Star. Nominated for Best Actress Oscar in *A Man and a Woman*. Onscreen from 1948. IN: *The Lovers of Verona, Golden Salamander, Pot Bouille, The Journey, La Dolce Vita, Lola, 8½, Sodom and Gomorrah, White Voices, A Very Handy Man, Justine*, more.

AKINS, CLAUDE (S. Cal.) Character. Onscreen from 1953. IN: *From Here to Eternity, The Caine Mutiny, The Defiant Ones, Onionhead, Rio Bravo, Inherit the Wind, Merrill's Marauders, The Killers, Ride Beyond Vengeance, Waterhole #3, The Devil's Brigade, Nobody Loves Flapping Eagle*, more.

ALBERGHETTI, ANNA MARIA (S. Cal.) During her marriage to producer-director Claudio Guzman (they are now divorced), the singer-actress who, in her teens, was groomed by Paramount as a latterday Deanna Durbin, soft-pedaled her career. Now, as she enters her 40s (b. 1936), she is rebuilding it via college concert tours, TV commercials for an Italian sauce, guest appearances on such quiz shows as *Name That Tune*, and an occasional nightclub stint. In '75 she was announced to costar with Pat O'Brien in the movie *The Trial of Mother Cabrini*, portraying Sister Sarafini. The Italian-born star is the mother of a young son, Alexander, and daughter, Pilar. Onscreen from 1951. IN: *The Medium, Here Comes the Groom, Stars Are Singing, The Last Command, 10,000 Bedrooms, Cinderfella*, more.

ALBERONI, SHERRI (S. Cal.) A popular juvenile in the '50s, she is Mrs. Richard Van Meter and has a daughter, born late in '74. IN: *Dance With Me Henry, The Three Worlds of Gulliver*, more.

ALBERT, EDDIE (S. Cal.) Costar. Nominated for Best Supporting Oscar in *Roman Holiday* and *The Heartbreak Kid*. Onscreen from 1938. IN: *Brother Rat, Four Wives, Eagle Squadron, Out of the Fog, Smash-Up, The Fuller Brush Man, Carrie, Oklahoma!, The Joker Is Wild, Beloved Infidel, The Longest Day, Captain Newman, M.D., The Longest Yard, Devil's Rain, Escape to Witch Mountain, Whiffs, Hustle, Birch Interval*, more.

ALBERT, EDWARD (S.Cal.) Costar. Son of Eddie. IN: *Butterflies Are Free, Forty Carats*.

ALBERTSON, GRACE (N.Y.) Singer-dancer-actress. IN: *DuBarry Was a Lady, Girl Crazy, Best Foot Forward, Cover Girl*, more.

ALBERTSON, JACK (S. Cal.) Comedian/costar. Won Best Supporting Actor Oscar in *The Subject Was Roses*. Onscreen from 1954. IN: *Top Banana, The Harder They Fall, The Eddy Duchin Story, Monkey on My Back, Don't Go Near the Water, Lover Come Back, Days of Wine and Roses, How to Murder Your Wife, The Flim-Flam Man, Rabbit Run, Changes, The Poseidon Adventure, The Late Liz*, more.

ALBERTSON, MABEL (S. Cal.) Character. Onscreen from 1939. IN: *Mutiny on the Blackhawk, My Pal Gus, She's Back on Broadway; Forever, Darling; The Long Hot Summer, Home Before Dark, Don't Give Up the Ship, Barefoot in the Park, What's Up, Doc?*, more.

ALBRIGHT, LOLA (S. Cal.) Three times divorced (no children) and in her early 50s now (b. 1925), this actress, a still-trim-and-attractive blonde, has resumed her career via television. She has been seen in guest-star roles in episodes of *Police Story, Kojak, McMillan and Wife*, etc. During her most recent marriage (1961–75), to musician-restaurateur Bill Chadney, she appeared in just 10 films. More often, though she continued to do TV occasionally, she was to be found singing at Chadney's Restaurant in Sherman Oaks, accompanied at the piano by her husband. Shades of her costarring torch-singer role in the *Peter Gunn* television series of the late '50s. She was previously married (1952–58) to the late screen comedian Jack Carson, after a teenage marriage to a nonprofessional that lasted four years. Onscreen from 1949. IN: *Champion, The Good Humor Man, The Magnificent Matador, The Tender Trap, A Cold Wind in August, Lord Love a Duck, The Way West, The Impossible Years*, more.

ALBRIGHT, WALLY, JR. (S. Cal.) If "Our Gang" had a romantic lead, Wally, with his blond curls and sensitive face, was it in the early '30s. In features he also played the son of Irene Dunne, Swanson, Garbo and others. Following WW II service in the Navy, he returned to movies, finally quitting after playing a cyclist in Brando's *The Wild One*. Today, just past the half-century mark, ruggedly handsome and almost bald, Wally owns and operates a produce packing-shipping concern in Southern California, and is a successful real-estate investor. A great sportsman, he flies his own plane and has won several hundred trophies at golf, motorcycling and calf roping, and, in '57, won the Men's National Trick Ski Championship. He and wife Helen—married for over three decades—have an almost-teenage son, named after his father. Onscreen from 1929. IN: *Thunder, East Lynne, Salvation Nell, Sob Sister, Zoo in Budapest, The Count of Monte Cristo, Black Fury, The Woman I Love, What Price Vengeance, Sons of the Legion*, more.

ALCAIDE, CHRIS (S. Cal.) Character. Onscreen from 1950. IN: *The Glass Menagerie, The Big Heat, The Miami Story, Chicago Syndicate*, more.

ALDA, ALAN (S. Cal.) Star. Onscreen from 1963. IN: *Gone Are the Days!, The Extraordinary Seaman, Paper Lion, The Mephisto Waltz*, more.

ALDA, ROBERT (S. Cal.) The former star, now a character actor, has settled back in Hollywood again after almost a decade in Rome. There he made numerous European films, starred on TV and radio, ran an importing-exporting business on the continent, and commuted to the States for a variety of show business activities—a song-dance cafe act, wine commercials, stock performances, etc. With him in California is his second wife (since '56), the former Italian screen actress Flora Marino. In '75 their 18-year-old son, Antony, was married in New York, where he is the leader of a working rock band. One of Alda's early return appearances was with his only other son, Alan, in *M*A*S*H*. Besides guest stints in many other TV series (*Police Story*, *The Invisible Man*, and *Rhoda*, in which he has turned up often as Valerie Harper's swinging father-in-law), he has costarred in the movie *I Will, I Will ... For Now*. Onscreen from 1945. IN: *Rhapsody in Blue, Cinderella Jones, Cloak and Dagger, The Beast with Five Fingers, Nora Prentiss, Homicide, Mr. Universe, Imitation of Life, The Devil's Hand, Revenge of the Barbarians*, more.

ALDEN, NORMAN (S. Cal.) Character. Onscreen from 1960. IN: *The Walking Target, Portrait of a Mobster, Operation Bottleneck, Bedtime Story, The Wild Angels, Tora! Tora! Tora!, The Great Bank Robbery*, more.

ALDERSON, JOHN (S. Cal.) Character. Onscreen from 1953. IN: *The Desert Rats, Violent Saturday, Shoot Out at Medicine Bend, The Young Lions, Pork Chop Hill, The War Lord, The Molly Maguires*, more.

ALDON, MARI (S. Cal.) During her marriage to director Tay Garnett, this blonde leading lady, still lovely in her 40s (b. 1929), put aside her career while rearing their daughter, Tiela, a teenager now. She also completed a five-year course of study at the Los Angeles Church of Religious Science, qualifying her for ordination, but on which she did not follow through. Since their (most amicable) divorce, she has starred for Garnett in *The Mad Trapper* ('72) and is resuming her career fulltime. Onscreen from 1951. IN: *Distant Drums, The Tanks Are Coming, This Woman Is Dangerous, Tangier Incident, The Barefoot Contessa, Summertime*, more.

ALDREDGE, TOM (N.Y.) Support. IN: *The Mouse on the Moon, The Troublemaker*, more.

ALEJANDRO, MIGUEL (N.Y.) Juvenile. Onscreen from 1969. IN: *Popi, The Last Valley, Yuma*, more.

ALETTER, FRANK (S. Cal.) Support. IN: *Mister Roberts, Tora! Tora! Tora!*, more.

ALEXANDER, CHRIS (N.Y.) Character. IN: *Auntie Mame*.

ALEXANDER, JAMIE (N.Y.) Juvenile actor. Onscreen in the '70s. IN: *Midnight Cowboy, Carnal Knowledge, Believe in Me, Child's Play*, more.

ALEXANDER, JANE (N.Y.) Costar. Nominated for Best Actress Oscar in *The Great White Hope*. Onscreen from 1970. IN: *A Gunfight, The New Centurions*, more.

ALEXANDER, ROD (N.Y.) Dancer. IN: *The Heat's On*.

ALEXANDER, TERENCE (Eng.) Costar. Onscreen from 1951. IN: *The Gentle Gunman, The One That Got Away, A Doctor's Dilemma, The League of Gentlemen, The Long Duel, Only When I Larf*, more.

ALFARO, KEIVA (N.Y.) Juvenile actress. Onscreen in the '70s. IN: *Carnal Knowledge, Believe in Me*, more.

ALFARO, RHONDA (N.Y.) Juvenile. Onscreen in the '70s. IN: *Carnal Knowledge, A Safe Place*, more.

ALLAN, ELIZABETH (Eng.) Freddie Bartholomew's courageous, lovely young "mother" in *David Copperfield* returned to England in '37, after more than a dozen Hollywood films, and continued to have an active career—movies, TV, the stage—for another 25 years. She has been happily married since '32 to W.J. O'Bryen, once her manager, who is a partner in London's top firm of theatrical agents. In her late 60s (b. 1908), she rarely acts any more. Onscreen from 1930. IN: *Alibi, Michael and Mary, Men in White, The Mystery of Mr. X, A Tale of Two Cities, A Woman Rebels, Camille, Michael Strogoff, Slave Ship, No Highway in the Sky, The Heart of the Matter, Front Page Story*, more.

ALLAN, JED (S. Cal.) Support. IN: *Ice Station Zebra*.

ALLBRITTON, LOUISE (N.Y.) Had this blonde star, so gifted at screwball comedy, not left the screen, she might well have become what Universal promised she would be—the "new" Lombard. But she did give up her starring career, in '46, to marry CBS news correspondent Charles Collingwood, and remains happily married to him. When she returned to Hollywood at irregular intervals for six additional films—the last being 1950's *The Great Manhunt*—she only played secondary roles. For long periods of their marriage, the Collingwoods (they have no children) have lived in London—1957–59 and 1964–75. Her husband, during their most recent residence there, was chief European correspondent for his network. Before they last departed for New York, Queen Elizabeth, in recognition of Collingwood's contribution to Anglo-American friendship and understanding, named him an honorary commander of the Most Excellent Order of the British Empire. The appointment was officially awarded later at the British Embassy in Washington. Louise Allbritton, darker haired now, a most dignified matron in her 50s (b. 1920), and one of New York's most popular hostesses, has not acted since appearing on Broadway in a short-lived play over two decades ago. And, she says, she would not trade the life she has known as Mrs. Charles Collingwood for any number of great movie roles. Onscreen from 1942. IN: *Who Done It, Pittsburgh, Fired Wife, Her Primitive Man; San Diego, I Love You; Bowery to Broadway, That Night With You, Tangier, The Egg and I, Sitting Pretty, An Innocent Affair, Walk a Crooked Mile, The Doolins of Oklahoma,* more.

ALLEGRET, CATHERINE (Fr.) Support. IN: *L'Envers, Lady L, The Sleeping Car Murder,* more.

ALLEN, ADRIANNE (Switz.) On the threshold of her 70s now (b. 1907), this English star lives at Glion sur Montreux, and occupies herself with entertaining visiting friends, cooking, and interior decorating, but is otherwise quite retired. She last acted onstage in London in *Five Finger Exercise* in '58. Her farewell movie appearance was in *Meet Mr. Malcolm,* four years earlier. By her first marriage, to actor Raymond Massey, which lasted a decade and ended in divorce in '39, she has two famous children—actor Daniel Massey, who was nominated for an Oscar in *Star!,* and actress Anna, who gave a brilliant performance in Hitchcock's *Frenzy.* Miss Allen was married to attorney William Dwight Whitney in '39. Onscreen from 1930. IN: *Loose Ends, The Night of June 13th, Merrily We Go to Hell, The Morals of Marcus, The October Man, Vote for Huggett, The Final Test,* more.

ALLEN, COREY (S. Cal.) Support/occasional leading man. Onscreen from 1954. IN: *Rebel Without a Cause, The Big Caper, Darby's Rangers, Private Property, The Chapman Report, Sweet Bird of Youth,* more.

ALLEN, ELIZABETH (S. Cal.) Costar. Onscreen from 1960. IN: *From the Terrace, Diamond Head, Donovan's Reef, Cheyenne Autumn, The Undefeated,* more.

ALLEN, JONELLE (S. Cal.) Black leading lady. Onscreen from the '70s. IN: *Come Back,*

Charleston Blue; Cotton Comes to Harlem, Cross and the Switchblade, more.

ALLEN, JUDITH (S. Cal.) Leading lady, retired. Onscreen from 1933. IN: *This Day and Age, The Old-Fashioned Way, Bright Eyes, Behind Green Lights, Navy Spy, Boots and Saddles, Port of Missing Girls,* more, including 1940's *Framed,* her last.

ALLEN, PATRICK (Eng.) Costar. Onscreen from 1955. IN: *High Tide at Noon, The Traitors, The Night of the Generals, The Body Stealers, Puppet on a Chain,* more.

ALLEN, PENNY (N.Y.) Support. IN: *Dog Day Afternoon.*

ALLEN, RAE (S. Cal.) Comedienne. Onscreen from 1958. IN: *Damn Yankees, The Tiger Makes Out, Taking Off,* more.

ALLEN, REX (S. Cal.) Over two decades have passed since Rex was Republic's last major singing-yodeling cowboy. But he has hardly been idle. Much professional activity emanates from his 20-acre Diamond X ranch in Malibu Canyon, home to wife Bonnie, himself, and their two youngest—Mark, a teenager, and little Bonita Kae, who longs to be. They have two grown sons, singer Rex Jr., married, living in Nashville and recording hit C&W albums for Warners *(The Great Mail Robbery, Goodbye,* etc.), and Curt, a recent Wesleyan University journalism graduate. More than 200 days of the year Rex—in his 50s now (b. 1922)—is on personal appearance tours with trick pony Koko Jr., a chocolate-colored stallion with a honey mane exactly like his famous sire. (The original Koko, who galloped through 35 Westerns with his master, died at 28 in '64 and is commemorated today by a life-sized statue looking down from the highest hill in the valley.) Not seen on any screen since a '71 episode of TV's *Men from Shiloh,* the former cowboy star narrated the film *Vanishing Wilderness,* as well as the earlier *Charlotte's Web.* Onscreen from 1950. IN: *Arizona Cowboy, Thunder in God's Country, Silver City Bonanza, Old Oklahoma Plains, Iron Mountain Trail, The Phantom Stallion,* more.

ALLEN, ROBERT (N.Y.) In the '30s, when he was most popular, he juggled two entirely different careers. As a tall-dark-'n-handsome leading man, he was in *Love Me Forever,* with Grace Moore, *Night Nurse, Party Husband,* etc. But he was also one of Columbia's top cowboy stars, headlining in his own "Texas Ranger" series *(Ranger Courage, The Rangers Step In,* etc.). He's now in his 70s (b. 1906) and the division in his careers continues to exist. In

17

the New York *Player's Guide* there is *Robert Allen*—the accompanying photo being that of a rugged, pipe-smoking, genial gent in mod silver-rimmed specs. But in Hollywood's *Academy Players Directory*, beside the picture of an unsmiling man under a Stetson, the identification is *Bob "Tex" Allen*. By any name, the actor-cowboy-singer—privately a sophisticated resident of posh Oyster Bay—remains busy, acting on Broadway, off Broadway, in movies *(Dirty Mouth)*, in soap operas *(Somerset, First Love)*, and TV-movies *(Brimstone, The Amish Horse)*. His first wife, former MGM actress Evelyn Pierce, died in '60. They had been married almost three decades. He has been married since '64 to Frances Cookman, a Philadelphia socialite. Onscreen from 1934. IN: *Jealousy, I'll Love You Always; Ride, Ranger, Ride; Crime and Punishment, The Awful Truth, Craig's Wife, Fighting Thoroughbreds, Winter Carnival, City of Chance, Terror in the City*, more.

ALLEN, SETH (N.Y.) Support. IN: *Catch 22, Madigan, Jesus Christ Superstar, The Hot Rock.*

ALLEN, SIAN BARBARA (S. Cal.) Leading lady. Onscreen from 1972. IN: *You'll Like My Mother, Billy Two-Hats*, more.

ALLEN, STEVE (S. Cal.) Comedian/costar. Onscreen from 1949. IN: *I'll Get By, The Benny Goodman Story, The Burglar, The Big Circus, Warning Shot, Where Were You When the Lights Went Out?, The Sunshine Boys*, more.

ALLEN, WOODY (N.Y.) Comedy star. Onscreen from 1965. IN: *What's New Pussycat?; What's Up, Tiger Lily?; Casino Royale, Take the Money and Run, Bananas; Play It Again, Sam; Everything You Always Wanted to Know About Sex, Sleeper, Love and Death, The Front.*

ALLISON, MAY (Ohio) A devastatingly beautiful blonde from the South, she was onscreen for a dozen years, through 1927's *The Telephone Girl*, and was particularly noted for the eight movies in which she and the late Harold Lockwood costarred. In the early '20s, she was one of Metro's greatest box-office attractions. Today, in her 80s (b. 1895), she lives, as she has for many years, in well-off retirement in Cleveland. She remains what she has always been—an intelligent, gregarious, vital woman given to charm and easy laughter. Her friendly laugh is employed when, complimented on her still-youthful vigor, she comes back, "What should I seem like, a broken-down old lady?" Such a "today" person is she that she refuses to reminisce about her screen triumphs, saying,

"That was all such a long time ago." Happily married for years to former business man Carl N. Osborne, she reported as this was written, "He is well and just celebrated his 90th birthday." Early in the '20s she was married to and divorced from Robert Ellis, who costarred with her in *Peggy Does Her Darndest* and *In for Thirty Days*. Then, from '26 until his death in '32, she was the wife of James R. Quirk, editor of *Photoplay* in its heyday. Now, completely out of the limelight and happy to be, the star is anything but a recluse; she remains listed in the Cleveland phone book. Onscreen from 1915. IN: *A Fool There Was, The Secretary of Frivolous Affairs, Youth for Sale, I Want My Man, The Greater Glory, Men of Steel*, more.

ALLMAN, ELVIA (S. Cal.) Character. Onscreen from 1940. IN: *A Night at Earl Carroll's, Sis Hopkins; A Wave, a Wac and a Marine; Weekend with Father, You Can't Run Away From It, Breakfast at Tiffany's*, more.

ALLWYN, ASTRID (S. Cal.) Leggy, blonde, and beautiful heiresses—in the '30s and early '40s, no girl played them better than she. Today in her 60s (b. 1909), still blonde and striking, she has long since been a leading Beverly Hills socialite—the wife of Charles Fee, a top executive with Eastern Life Insurance—and active in such philanthropies as the Children's Hospital of Los Angeles. A while back, recovering from a cataract operation, she reflected without regrets on her long-departed movie career: "I feel very rich in having had the experiences I did in pictures. But I'll take my being at this time—in stride." She has traveled widely, most recently in the Orient. And she has reared four children. The eldest are a stepson, Charles Jr., and her daughter Kristine (by her first marriage, which ended in divorce, to late actor Robert Kent); a language scholar, Kristine attended college and lives now in Sweden. Two daughters were born to her and Mr. Fee, Melinda Fee, a dark-haired actress who was in TV's *The Guilding Light* and later was the leading lady in the *Invisible Man* series—and Vickie (actually named Astrid, she was always called Vickie). A stunningly beautiful girl, Vickie Fee Steele, once under contract to Seven Arts and Universal, died on December 13, 1975, after a lengthy illness. She was 28. In her grief Astrid Allwyn was conforted by the many Hollywood friends made during her long career. Onscreen from 1932. IN: *Lady With a Past, Night Mayor, Beggars in Ermine, The White Parade, Accent on Youth, Hands Across the Table, Dimples, Stowaway, Love Affair, Honeymoon in Bali, Mr. Smith Goes to Washington, The Lone Wolf Strikes Back*, and more, including *Hit Parade of 1943*, her last.

ALLYSON, JUNE (S. Cal.) Star. First onscreen in musical shorts in 1937. Onscreen in features from 1943. IN: *Best Foot Forward, Thousands Cheer, Girl Crazy, Two Girls and a Sailor, Her Highness and the Bellboy, Two Sisters from Boston, Till the Clouds Roll By, High Barbaree, Good News, Words and Music, Little Women, The Stratton Story, The Girl in White, The Glenn Miller Story, Executive Suite, Strategic Air Command, The Shrike, The McConnell Story, Stranger in My Arms, They Only Kill Their Masters,* more.

ALPERT, HERB (S. Cal.) Musician. IN: *The Ten Commandments.*

ALTMAN, FRIEDA (N.Y.) Support. IN: *Go, Man, Go.*

ALVIN, JOHN (S. Cal.) Support. Onscreen from 1944. IN: *Destination Tokyo, The Sullivans, Objective Burma, Roughly Speaking, Two Guys From Texas, Carrie, April in Paris, Irma La Douce,* more.

ALYN, KIRK (Ariz.) After starring in the title role in two *Superman* serials, he found that, despite his 40 movie features, producers could only envision him in that union suit emblazoned with the massive "S." He gave up movies, worked onstage a while, and retired. Today, in his late 60s (b. 1910), a handsome man with silver in his waves, he lives alone on a lakeside in Arizona. He has not married again since his 13-year marriage to actress-singer Virginia O'Brien ended in divorce in '55. By her he has a son and two daughters. The eldest of them, Theresa (Terri), tours with her own all-girl singing group, The Cover Girls. *Superman,* the former actor says, ruined his career. Admitting that "I was bitter for a number of years," he adds that now "a new interest in Superman is booming. College and nostalgia groups all around the country are inviting me to appear before them." He often accepts. And, he laughs, should Hollywood decide to resurrect the *Daily Planet* reporter, "Maybe, because of my age, they'll want me to play the father of Superman." Onscreen from the 1940s. IN: Features—*Pistol Packin' Mama,* more; serials—*Superman, Atom Man vs. Superman, Radar Patrol vs. Spy King, Blackhawk.*

AMECHE, DON (S. Cal.) Still married (since '32) to his original wife, Honore, and the father of five children—grown, and successful in non-show-business careers—he has spent most of the past two decades on the legitimate stage. On Broadway, *Silk Stockings* and *Holiday for Lovers* were his biggest hits. In '74 he toured with Evelyn Keyes and then Ruby Keeler in *No, No,*

Nanette, and was on TV in a *McCloud* episode. In the summer of '75, he teamed with Alice Faye in a tour of *Good News,* their first reunion since 1941's *That Night in Rio,* unfailingly playing to SRO audiences. Onscreen from 1936. IN: *Ramona, One in a Million, In Old Chicago, Alexander's Ragtime Band, The Story of Alexander Graham Bell, Swanee River, Four Sons, Lillian Russell, Kiss the Boys Goodbye, Heaven Can Wait, Happy Land, A Wing and a Prayer, Sleep My Love, A Fever in the Blood, Picture Mommy Dead, Suppose They Gave a War and Nobody Came, The Boatniks; Won Ton Ton, the Dog Who Saved Hollywood;* more.

AMES, LEON (S. Cal.) White-haired and in his 70s (b. 1903), this veteran character actor remains busy, not only as the owner of a lucrative Ford automobile agency in Studio City, but on the screen. In '72 he played top roles in *Hammersmith Is Out* and *The Timber Trap.* That same year he signed a five-year contract with Sun International Films, of which he also became a board member. For this company, he has narrated *Brother of the Wind* and starred in *Toklat.* On TV in '74 he guest-starred in an *Apple's Way* episode. Married since 1938 to former actress Christine Gossett, he has two children: Shelley, a Deb Star of '64 who later opted for an advertising career, and Lee (Leon Jr.), who, after a four-year stint in the Navy, became a Broadway actor. Ames, oldtimers will recall, began his screen career under his real name, Leon Waycoff, using it in his first 13 movies. Onscreen from 1932. IN: *Murders in the Rue Morgue, The Count of Monte Cristo, Mr. Moto in Danger Island, Man of Conquest, Crime Doctor, Thirty Seconds Over Tokyo, Meet Me in St. Louis, Week-End at the Waldorf, Yolanda and the Thief, They Were Expendable, Lady in the Lake, A Date with Judy, Little Women, Battleground, Crisis, On Moonlight Bay, From the Terrace, The Absent-Minded Professor, The Monkey's Uncle, The Meal,* more.

AMES, LIONEL (S. Cal.) Support. IN: *Why Must I Die?,* more.

AMES, RACHEL (S. Cal.) Support. IN: *Daddy's Gone A-Hunting.*

AMES, RAMSAY (Sp.) She and her playwright-husband, Dale Wasserman of *Man of La Mancha* fame, live in a villa (appropriately called "La Mancha") on the Costa del Sol. They travel extensively, frequently to London and New York where they have other residences. The still-beautiful actress, now in her 50s (b. 1919), gave up her leading lady career in B's with 1947's *Philo Vance Returns.* In the past two decades, though, she has played secondary roles in three: *Alexander the Great, The Running Man,* and *The Rampage.* Onscreen from 1943. IN: *Two Senoritas From Chicago, Calling Dr. Death, Ali Baba and the Forty Thieves, The Mummy's Ghost, The Gay Cavalier, Beauty and the Bandit,* more. Serials: *Black Widow, G-Man Never Forget, The Vigilante.*

AMOS, JOHN (S. Cal.) Black support. IN: *The World's Greatest Athlete,* more.

AMSTERDAM, MOREY (S. Cal.) Comedian. Onscreen from 1960. IN: *Murder, Inc., Beach Party, Muscle Beach Party, The Horse in the Gray Flannel Suit,* more.

ANDERS, GLENN (Mex.) Well into his 80s (b. 1889), he last acted onscreen in 1951's *Behave Yourself* and onstage in 1960's *The Visit.* Today he lives in luxurious retirement in Guadalajara. Onscreen from 1930. IN: *Laughter, Nothing but the Truth, The Lady From Shanghai, M,* more.

ANDERS, LUANA (S. Cal.) Costar. Onscreen from 1958. IN: *Life Begins at 17, The Pit and the Pendulum, Night Tide, Dementia 13,* more.

ANDERSON, CARL (S. Cal.) Black singer-support. IN: *Jesus Christ Superstar.*

ANDERSON, CLINTON (N.Y.) Support. IN: *The Quiet American.*

ANDERSON, DINA (N.Y.) Juvenile. Onscreen in the '70s. IN: *Up the Sandbox,* more.

ANDERSON, DONNA (S. Cal.) Besides movie work, this featured actress—a discovery of Stanley Kramer—is active in Los Angeles' Players Projects and The Players Theatre. She was also for two years, until '74, treasurer of the American National Theatre & Academy (ANTA-West). Onscreen from 1959. IN: *On the Beach, Inherit the Wind.*

ANDERSON, DUSTY (Sp.) She was one of the great dark-haired beauties of the '40s—famous cover girl and later one of Columbia's most decorative young actresses. She has, in her 50s, changed little. In '74 she and her husband, Jean Negulesco (married since '46; no children), sold their properties in Beverly Hills and settled on the Spanish island of Majorca. In retirement, as she did in L.A., she paints professionally, having had several exhibitions. Her husband, in his mid-70s now, was for years a top Hollywood director—of *Johnny Belinda, Humoresque,* etc., through 1970's *Hello—Goodbye.* He has lately assisted Iran in establishing a film industry in Teheran. Onscreen from 1944. IN: *Cover Girl, Tonight and Every Night, A Thousand and One Nights,* more.

ANDERSON, EDDIE "ROCHESTER" (S. Cal.) Retired after *It's a Mad Mad Mad Mad World* ('63), his first in many years, the raspy-voiced comedian attempted a comeback in '72. He did a nightclub act, opening in Houston, backed by two girl singer-dancers and a soft rock band. This led to his being signed for Broadway's *Good News,* but health reasons forced his resignation during rehearsals. Today, after cataract operations, the actor, who is in his 70s (b. 1905), wears dark glasses hiding his near blindness. This, however, did not prevent his being present at Oakland, Calif., in February 1975 to receive a coveted Oscar Micheaux Award presented him by the Black Filmmakers Hall of Fame committee. Jack Benny's death was a devastating blow to "Rochester": "It was more than just being an employee or just a member of the cast. There was a warmth, a closeness. There was a love between us." Onscreen from 1932. IN: *What Price Hollywood, The Green Pastures, You Can't Take It With You, Gone With the Wind, Thanks for the Memory, Kentucky, Man About Town, Buck Benny Rides Again, Love Thy Neighbor, Birth of the Blues, Cabin in the Sky, Brewster's Millions, The Sailor Takes a Wife,* more.

ANDERSON, ERNEST (S. Cal.) Black support. Onscreen from 1942. IN: *In This Our Life, The Well, 3 for Bedroom C, tick . . . tick . . . tick,* more.

ANDERSON, GIA (N.Y.) Juvenile. Onscreen in the '70s. IN: *Up the Sandbox, Class of '44,* more.

ANDERSON, HERBERT (S. Cal.) The bumbling, curly-haired gob, the hero, in 1941's *Navy Blues* has long been one of Hollywood's most dependable character actors. Besides playing the bespectacled, long-suffering dad in the *Dennis the Menace* TV series, he's been in scores of movies, and in '74 played Senator Kefauver in the TV-movie *Virginia Hill.* In his late 50s now (b. 1917) and long married, he has two grown children. Onscreen from 1940. IN: *'Til We Meet Again, No Time for Comedy, The Bride Came C.O.D., The Male Animal, Give My Regards to Broadway, Sunrise at Campobello, Rascal, Night Passage, Hold On,* more.

ANDERSON, JOHN (S. Cal.) Support. Onscreen from 1952. IN: *Against All Flags, Target Zero, Ride the High Country, The Hallelujah Trail, Welcome to Hard Times,* more.

ANDERSON, DAME JUDITH (S. Cal.) Character. Nominated for Best Supporting Actress

Oscar in *Rebecca*. Onscreen from 1933. IN: *Bloody Money, Rebecca, Lady Scarface, Kings Row, Laura, And Then There Were None, Tycoon, The Red House, The Furies, The Ten Commandments, Cat on a Hot Tin Roof, Cinderfella, Why Bother to Knock?, A Man Called Horse*, more.

ANDERSON, MARY (S. Cal.) This gentle-faced actress was last seen on TV in *Peyton Place* (as Catherine Harrington), made at 20th Century-Fox where, as a young leading lady, she did so many movies. There, too, her cinematographer was often Leon Shamroy, the four-time Oscar winner, who was two decades her senior. She married him in '53, when 31, remaining happily married until his death in '74. Besides his wife, Shamroy left a daughter, now Mrs. Patricia Freeman, and a son, Timothy. The actress still lives in their family home, a picturesque house filled with fine art objects that overlooks the Sunset Strip. Onscreen from 1939. IN: *Gone With the Wind, All This and Heaven Too, Cheers for Miss Bishop, Henry Aldrich for President, The Song of Bernadette, Wilson, Keys of the Kingdom, Lifeboat, To Each His Own, Whispering City, Passage West, Chicago Calling, Jet Over the Atlantic*, more.

ANDERSON, MICHAEL, JR. (S. Cal.) Costar. Onscreen from 1957. IN: *The Moonraker, The Sundowners, Reach for Glory, The Greatest Story Ever Told, The Glory Guys, A Hall of Mirrors, WUSA, The Last Movie*, more.

ANDERSON, RICHARD (S. Cal.) Support. Onscreen from 1949. IN: *Twelve O'Clock High, The Magnificent Yankee, Payment on Demand; Rich, Young and Pretty; Across the Wide Missouri, Escape from Fort Bravo, Hit the Deck, The Search for Bridey Murphy, Paths of Glory, The Long Hot Summer, Compulsion, A Gathering of Eagles, Seconds, Tora! Tora! Tora!, Doctors' Wives*, more. (See Norma Shearer.)

ANDERSON, THOMAS (N.J.) Black support. IN: *Jeremy Jones, Don't Play Us Cheap, Gordon's War; Tricks, Baby; The Learning Tree, The Legend of Nigger Charley*, more.

ANDERSON, WARNER (S. Cal.) Character. Onscreen from 1943. IN: *Destination Tokyo, Objective Burma, My Reputation. The Beginning or the End?, Destination Moon, Only the Valiant, Detective Story, The Star, A Lion Is in the Streets, The Blackboard Jungle, Rio Conchos*, more.

ANDERSSON, BIBI (Swe.) Swedish star. Onscreen from 1953. IN: *Smiles of a Summer Night, The Seventh Seal, Brink of Life, Wild Strawberries, Duel at Diablo, Persona, Le Viol, The Touch, It Is Raining on Santiago*, more.

ANDERSSON, HARRIET (Swe.) Swedish star. Onscreen from 1952. IN: *Summer with Monika, Smiles of a Summer Night, Through a Glass Darkly, The Deadly Affair, Cries and Whispers*, more.

ANDES, KEITH (S. Cal.) Costar. Onscreen from 1947. IN: *The Farmer's Daughter, Clash by Night, Split Second, The Second Greatest Sex, Away All Boats, Model for Murder; Surrender, Hell!; Tora! Tora! Tora!, Hell's Bloody Devils*, more.

ANDOR, PAUL/formerly WOLFGANG ZILZER (N.Y.) This German-born character actor works primarily on the New York stage now. As Zilzer he had supporting roles in many movies between '28 and '44, including *Mata Hari: The Red Dancer; Shadows of Fear, Behind the Rising Sun, In Our Time*, more. Onscreen as Andor from 1945. IN: *Hotel Berlin, Counter-Attack, Walk East on Beacon, Singing in the Dark*, more.

ANDRE, LONA (S. Cal.) Dimpled, and still as pretty as an ingenue, she gave up her decade-long career in '43, is a business woman, and lives in North Hollywood. Onscreen from 1932. IN: *The Woman Accused, College Humor, Take a Chance, Come on Marines, Murder at the Vanities, Under the Pampas Moon, Our Relations, Custer's Last Stand* (serial; lead opposite Rex Lease), *Crusade Against Rackets*, more, including *Taxi, Mister*, her last.

ANDRESS, URSULA (Switz.) Costar. IN: *Dr. No, 4 for Texas, What's New Pussycat?, She, The Blue Max, Casino Royale, Red Sun*, more.

ANDREWS, ANN (N.Y.) Support. IN: *The Cheat*.

ANDREWS, DANA (S. Cal.) Costar. Onscreen from 1940. IN: *Lucky Cisco Kid, The Westerner, Tobacco Road, Crash Dive, The Ox-Bow Incident, The Purple Heart, Laura, State Fair, A Walk in the Sun, Fallen Angel, The Best Years of Our Lives, Boomerang, The Iron Curtain, Sword in the Desert, My Foolish Heart, Elephant Walk, Duel in the Jungle, While the City Sleeps, The Crowded Sky, In Harm's Way, Crack in the World, The Loved One, Battle of the Bulge, The Devil's Brigade, Innocent Bystanders, Take a Hard Ride, Airport 1975, The Last Tycoon*, more.

ANDREWS, EDWARD (S. Cal.) Character. Onscreen from 1955. IN: *The Phenix City Story, The Harder They Fall, Tea and Sympathy, El-*

mer Gantry, The Young Doctors, Advice and Consent, Good Neighbor Sam, Youngblood Hawke, Send Me No Flowers, The Glass Bottom Boat, Tora! Tora! Tora!, more.

ANDREWS, HARRY (Eng.) Support. Onscreen from 1952. IN: Paratrooper, The Man Who Loved Redheads, A Hill in Korea, I Accuse, Solomon and Sheba, Nine Hours to Rama, Nothing but the Best, The Agony and the Ecstasy, Modesty Blaise, The Hill, Dandy in Aspic, Nicholas and Alexandra, Man of La Mancha, The Internecine Project, The Last Days of Man on Earth, more.

ANDREWS, JULIE (Eng.) Music-dramatic star. Won Best Actress Oscar in Mary Poppins. Nominated in the same category for The Sound of Music. Onscreen from 1964. IN: The Americanization of Emily, Torn Curtain, Hawaii, Thoroughly Modern Millie, Star!, Darling Lili, The Tamarind Seed.

ANDREWS, MAXENE & PATTI (S. Cal.) Surviving members of the musical Andrews Sisters trio, which also included sister LaVerne. Onscreen from 1940. IN: Argentine Nights, In the Navy, Buck Privates, Hold That Ghost; Give Out, Sisters; Swing Time Johnny, Make Mine Music, Road to Rio, Melody Time, more. Patti Andrews later made a solo guest appearance in The Phynx.

ANDREWS, TIGE (S. Cal.) Support. Onscreen from 1955. IN: Mister Roberts, Until They Sail, Imitation General, Onionhead, China Doll, more.

ANDROSKY, CAROL (S. Cal.) Support. IN: Funnyman, more.

ANGEL, HEATHER (S. Cal.) Widowed by the murder (still unsolved) of her husband, director Robert Sinclair, in their Santa Barbara home, Heather mostly lives now in a Beverly Hills apartment. A veteran of 60 movies, the actress, now in her 60s (b. 1909), has been more active in TV in recent years—playing housekeepers in Peyton Place (Mrs. Dowell) and Family Affair (Miss Havisham). Her most recent movie was Premature Burial ('62). She only works, she has said, "when the spirit moves me." She has two children, Barbara and Anthony Robert, both in their 20s. Onscreen from 1930. IN: City of Song, Frail Women, After Office Hours, Berkeley Square, Charlie Chan's Greatest Case, Orient Express, The Mystery of Edwin Drood, The Informer, The Perfect Gentleman, Portia on Trial, Bulldog Drummond in Africa, Pride and Prejudice, That Hamilton Woman, Suspicion, Cry Havoc, Lifeboat, The Saxon Charm, more.

ANGELA, JUNE (N.Y.) Juvenile. Onscreen from 1966. IN: Any Wednesday, Twinky, more.

ANGELUS, MURIEL (N.Y.) Her career as a leading lady at Paramount (1939–40), after a few British pictures and a long stage career, encompassed just four movies. But few who ever saw her—and heard her melodious speaking voice—ever forgot this classic-featured blonde. She was particularly memorable in The Light That Failed, as Colman's ambitious girl friend, and The Great McGinty, as the gentle, on-consignment wife to phony politician Brian Donlevy who effects his reformation. Now she is a slender, glasses-wearing woman in her 60s (b. 1909), with her gray-blonde hair worn in a matronly upsweep, given to easy, friendly laughter, informality, and wearing pantsuits. For over three decades she has been married to famous music conductor Paul Lavalle, formerly the baton-wielder at Radio City Music Hall and more recently the guiding spirit behind McDonald's nationally known band for teenagers. The Lavalles keep an apartment in Manhattan, have a handsome Colonial house in Wilton, Conn., and a daughter, Suzanne, who has made them proud. Graduating summa cum laude from Briarcliff, dark-haired Suzanne is now a behind-the-scenes reporter for NBC. Coincidentally, it was with an NBC musical radio program in the '40s, Presenting Muriel Angelus, that the actress-singer phased out her career. (Hollywood never let her sing, but she was noted for her stage musicals in England. And it was as the star of Broadway's The Boys from Syracuse, in which she introduced "Falling in Love with Love," that Hollywood producers discovered her.) Her only professional work since becoming Mrs. Lavalle in '46 was a recitation-with-music album she did, more than a decade ago, with her husband conducting the orchestra—Muriel Angelus Expresses the Lyrics of Oscar Hammerstein II with Music of Richard Rodgers. Shortly before making the album, Richard Rodgers, a longtime friend, pleaded with her to audition for the Mother Superior role in his show The Sound of Music. After hearing her he said, "Muriel, you sound so young. Could you sing a little older?" That is when she laughed and decided to stay retired. Onscreen in England from 1930. IN: The Ringer, Night Birds, Hindle Wakes, more. Onscreen in America from 1939. IN: The Light That Failed, The Way of All Flesh, Safari, The Great McGinty.

ANKA, PAUL (Nev.) Singer-actor. IN: Girls' Town, Look in Any Window, The Longest Day.

ANKERS, EVELYN (Hawaii) A charming fixture and an excellent actress in Universal B's of the '40s, this leading lady stopped acting after

1950's *The Texan Meets Calamity Jane*. Since '68 she has lived with actor-husband Richard Denning (they married in '42) in a luxurious, beach-fronting condominium on the island of Maui in Hawaii. Tanned, and still shapely and blonde in her late 50s (b. 1918), the English-born beauty skin-dives, golfs, sails, and collects sea shells. She also assists her husband in managing their considerable investments in real estate and plastics. The Dennings have one child, daughter Dee, still single in her early 30s, who divides her time between California and Hawaii. Richard Denning's only acting now is in the TV series *Hawaii Five-O*, filmed in Honolulu, in which—on a part-time basis—he plays the handsome governor. His wife usually accompanies him on the 20-minute jet flight from Maui to Honolulu. "We stay at the Kahala-Hilton," she says, "and while Richard is working on the show, I do my 'big city' shopping and sightseeing. After a few days in Honolulu, we're always ready to leave the freeways and big-city atmosphere and return to the peace and quiet of our beloved Maui." Onscreen in England from 1933. IN: *The Villiers Diamond, Rembrandt, Over the Moon*, more. Onscreen in America from 1941. IN: *Hit the Road, Hold That Ghost, The Wolf Man, Eagle Squadron, Sherlock Holmes and the Voice of Terror, Son of Dracula, Hers to Hold, The Invisible Man's Revenge, Jungle Woman, Bowery to Broadway, Black Beauty, The Lone Wolf in London, Tarzan's Magic Fountain*, more. (See Richard Denning.)

ANN-MARGRET (S. Cal.) Star. Nominated for Best Supporting Actress Oscar in *Carnal Knowledge*. Nominated for Best Actress Oscar in *Tommy*. Onscreen from 1961. IN: *A Pocketful of Miracles, Bye Bye Birdie, Kitten With a Whip, Once a Thief, The Cincinnati Kid, The Swinger, Murderer's Row, The Train Robbers, Tommy, The Twist*, more.

ANNABELLA (Fr.) In her 60s (b. 1909) and little changed in looks, she is completely retired from acting. Her final Hollywood movie was *13 Rue Madeleine*, after which she made just one more French film, *Dernier Amour* ('48). She is mainly occupied now, as a volunteer, with prison welfare work in her native France. She has two residences—a splendid apartment in Paris and a farm in the French Pyrenees. Her only near relation is her daughter, Anna, who is in her 40s; of Annabella's marriage to actor Jean Murat, she was adopted by Tyrone Power in the '40s—and was then known as Anne—while the actress was married to Power. Anna also was later married to an actor, Oskar Werner, for a dozen years, but has no children. Anna secured a divorce from Werner in '71 in Hanover, N.H., and was accompanied on that occasion—their most recent trip to the States—by her mother. Annabella herself has not remarried since her divorce from Tyrone Power in '48. Onscreen from 1931. IN: *Le Million, Wings of the Morning, Under the Red Robe, Dinner at the Ritz, The Baroness and the Butler, Suez, Bridal Suite, Tonight We Raid Calais, Bomber's Moon*, more.

ANSARA, MICHAEL (S. Cal.) Support. Onscreen from 1944. IN: *Action in Arabia, Soldiers Three, Diplomatic Courier, White Witch Doctor, The Saracen Blade, Diane, Voyage to the Bottom of the Sea, . . . And Now Miguel, Texas Across the River, Stand Up and Be Counted, The Bears and I, It's Alive*, more.

ANSPACH, SUSAN (S. Cal.) Leading lady. IN: *Five Easy Pieces; Play It Again, Sam; Blume in Love*.

ANTHONY, JOSEPH (N.Y.) Support. IN: *Hat, Coat and Glove; She; Shadow of the Thin Man; Joe Smith, American*. Now a director.

ANTHONY, RAY (S. Cal.) Orchestra leader-actor. IN: *The Girl Can't Help It, High School Confidential, The Five Pennies*.

ANTHONY, TONY (It.) Leading man. IN: *A Stranger in Town, The Stranger Returns, The Blind Man*, more.

ANTONIO, LOU (N.Y.) Support. IN: *America, America; Hawaii; Cool Hand Luke*.

APLON, BORIS (N.Y.) Support. IN: *Citizen Saint*.

APPLEBY, DOROTHY (Eng.) Former leading lady. Onscreen from 1931. IN: *Under Eighteen, As the Earth Turns, Charlie Chan in Paris, The Flying Irishman, Convicted Woman*, more.

APPLEGATE, EDDIE (S. Cal.) Support. IN: *Ticklish Affair*.

ARCHER, ANNE (S. Cal.) Young leading lady. IN: *Cancel My Reservation*.

ARCHER, JOHN (S. Cal.) Support. Onscreen from 1938. IN: *Flaming Frontier, Scattergood Baines, Guadalcanal Diary, Roger Touhy—Gangster, Destination Moon, My Favorite Spy, Best of the Bad Men, The Big Trees, Emergency Hospital, 10,000 Bedrooms, Apache Rifles, I Saw What You Did, How to Frame a Figg*, more.

ARCHERD, ARMY (S. Cal.) *Daily Variety* columnist-TV emcee-actor. Onscreen from the '60s. IN: *Wild in the Streets* (as himself), *Escape From the Planet of the Apes* (as the Referee), *The Outfit*, more.

ARDEN, EVE (S. Cal.) Comedienne/costar. Nominated for Best Supporting Actress Oscar in *Mildred Pierce*. Onscreen from 1937. IN: *Oh, Doctor, Stage Door, A Letter of Introduction, Eternally Yours, At the Circus, Comrade X, That Uncertain Feeling, Ziegfeld Girl, She Knew All the Answers, Manpower, Cover Girl, The Doughgirls, Night and Day, My Reputation, Voice of the Turtle, Tea for Two, Goodbye My Fancy, Our Miss Brooks, Anatomy of a Murder, The Dark at the Top of the Stairs; Sgt. Deadhead, the Astronaut; The Strongest Man in the World*, more.

ARDEN, ROBERT (Eng.) Support. IN: *The Man from Morocco, Mr. Arkadin, No Orchids for Miss Blandish, Confidential Report*, more.

ARINBASAROVA, NATALIA (Rus.) Leading lady. IN: *The First Teacher*, more.

ARKIN, ALAN (N.Y.) Star. Nominated for Best Actor Oscar in *The Russians Are Coming, The Russians Are Coming* and *The Heart Is a Lonely Hunter*. Onscreen from 1966. IN: *The Last Mohican, Woman Times Seven, Wait Until Dark, Inspector Clouseau, Popi, Catch-22, Little Murders, Last of the Red Hot Lovers, Freebie and the Bean, Rafferty and the Gold Dust Twins, Hearts of the West*, more.

ARLETTY (Fr.) This glorious French actress is no longer young (b. 1898) and is almost blind. Partial vision in one eye was restored only after three operations. While ending her screen career with 1962's *Maxime*, she did return to the stage six years later in Cocteau's *Montres Sacres*. She has been retired since. Onscreen from 1931. IN: *Un Chien Qui Rapporte, Hotel du Nord, Extenuating Circumstances, Les Enfants de Paradis, The Devil's Own Envoy, Fric-Frac, The Longest Day*, more.

ARLING, JOYCE (S. Cal.) Character. IN: *The Romance of Rosy Ridge, Ruthless*, more.

ARMS, RUSSELL (S. Cal.) Singer-actor. Onscreen from 1942. IN: *The Man Who Came to Dinner, Captains of the Clouds, Always in My Heart, Wings for the Eagle, By the Light of the Silvery Moon*, more.

ARMSTRONG, R. G. (S. Cal.) Character. Onscreen from 1957. IN: *Garden of Eden, From Hell to Texas, Never Love a Stranger, The Fugitive Kind, Ride the High Country, He Rides Tall, Race with the Devil, White Line Fever*, more.

ARNAZ, DESI (S. Cal.) Musician-comedian. Onscreen from 1940. IN: *Too Many Girls, Father Takes a Wife, The Navy Comes Through, Bataan, Holiday in Havana; The Long, Long Trailer; Forever, Darling*, more.

ARNAZ, DESI, JR. (S. Cal.) Actor-son of Desi Arnaz and Lucille Ball. Onscreen from 1966. IN: *Murderers' Row, Billy Two-Hats*, more.

ARNESS, JAMES (S. Cal.) Star. Onscreen from 1947. IN: *The Farmer's Daughter, Battleground, Wagonmaster, The Thing, The People Against O'Hara, Carbine Williams, Big Jim McLain, Lone Hand, Island in the Sky, Them, Many Rivers to Cross, The Sea Chase, Flame of the Islands*, more.

ARNGRIN, STEVAN (S. Cal.) Juvenile. IN: *The Way West*.

ARNOLD, DOROTHY (S. Cal.) Divorced from Joe DiMaggio in the early '40s (married in '39), and long offscreen, the blonde former actress has a business in Palm Springs and a grown son, Joe Jr. Onscreen from 1938. IN: *The Storm, Secrets of a Nurse, Unexpected Father*, and the serial *The Phantom Creeps*.

ARNOLD, EDDIE (Tenn.) C&W song star. IN: *Feudin' Rhythm, Hoedown*.

ARNOLD, JEANNE (S. Cal.) Support. Onscreen from 1966. IN: *Munster, Go Home; What's So Bad About Feeling Good?*, more.

ARNOUL, FRANCOISE (Fr.) Costar. Onscreen from 1950. IN: *Companions of the Night, The Sheep Has Five Legs, French Can-Can, No Sun in Venice, The Cat*, more.

ARNT, CHARLES (Wash.) Last onscreen in 1962's *Sweet Bird of Youth*, the veteran character actor, now in his late 60s (b. 1908), lives in retirement with his wife, Pat, on the island of Orcas in the San Juans of Washington State. Onscreen from 1934. IN: *Ladies Should Listen; Swing High, Swing Low; Remember the Night, Pot O' Gold, Ball of Fire, The Lady Has Plans; Take a Letter, Darling; Christmas in Connecticut, Somewhere in the Night, Sitting Pretty, That Wonderful Urge, Wild in the Country*, more.

ARTHUR, BEA (S. Cal.) Star comedienne. IN: *Lovers and Other Strangers, Mame*.

ARTHUR, CAROL (N.Y.) Support. IN: *Making It, The Sunshine Boys*.

ARTHUR, GEORGE K. (Eng.) In his 70s (b. 1899), the onetime star and later supporting actor is now a movie producer-distributor. Onscreen from 1921. IN: *Kipps, The Salvation Hunters, Lady of the Night, Sun Up, Irene, Kiki, Tillie the Toiler, The Gingham Girl, Spring Fever, Circus Rookies, Looking Forward, Blind Adventures, Vanessa: Her Love Story*, more.

ARTHUR, JEAN (N. Cal.) Comedienne/star. Nominated for Best Actress Oscar in *The More the Merrier*. Following her last movie, 1953's *Shane*, she retired for a decade to her cliffside, ocean-fronting, old-fashioned house at Carmel. She was seen onstage in '63 when she appeared with University of California at Berkeley students in a production of Shaw's *Saint Joan*, playing the title role. A guest-star role in a 1965 episode of *Gunsmoke* led, the following year, to the short-lived TV series *The Jean Arthur Show*. Scheduled to return to the New York stage during the 1967–68 season in *The Freaking Out of Stephanie Blake,* she withdrew from the play during its Broadway previews. Between then and '73, when the actress again returned to Carmel, she taught drama at both Vassar and the North Carolina School of Arts. In '75, the star, who is slender and silver-haired in her 70s (b. 1905), still publicity-shy and quirkily humorous, came out of retirement once more, briefly. It was announced that she would return to Broadway, opposite her sometimes screen leading man Melvyn Douglas, in *First Monday in October*. During the show's pre-New York tryout in Cleveland, she left the play, as she had four prior legitimate productions since '45, because of alleged illness. As she retired once again to Carmel, admirers recalled what movie director Frank Capra had said of her in his book *The Name Above the Title:* "Never have I seen a performer plagued with such a chronic case of stage jitters. . . . When the cameras stopped she'd run to her dressing room, lock herself in —and cry. . . . When called for another scene she would come out looking like a mop; walk aimlessly around muttering a torrent of non-sequitur excuses for not being ready. And it wasn't an act. Those weren't butterflies in her stomach. They were wasps. But push that neurotic girl forcibly, but gently, in front of the camera and turn on the lights—and that whining mop would magically blossom into a warm, lovely, poised, and confident actress." Still, Jean Arthur was for Capra "my favorite actress"—as she was for many thousands of moviegoers. Onscreen from 1923. IN: *Cameo Kirby, Seven Chances, The Cowboy Cop, Sins of the Father, The Canary Murder Case, The Return of Fu Manchu, The Past of Mary Holmes, The Whole Town's Talking, Diamond Jim, Mr. Deeds Goes to Town, The Plainsman, History is Made at Night, You Can't Take It With You, Only Angels Have Wings, Mr. Smith Goes to Washington, Too Many Husbands, Arizona, The Devil and Miss Jones, A Lady Takes a Chance, Foreign Affair,* more.

ARTHUR, MAUREEN (S. Cal.) Leading lady. Onscreen from 1967. IN: *How to Succeed in Business Without Really Trying, The Wicked Dreams of Paula Schultz, Thunder Alley, A Man Called Dagger, The Love God, How to Commit Marriage,* more.

ARTHUR, ROBERT (S. Cal.) Entering his 50s (b. 1925), he retains that boy-next-door face that kept him playing juveniles for 15 years in 32 films. Leaving movies after 1960's *Wild Youth*, he was in more than 100 TV shows before dropping out of acting completely. He operated a book-gift shop, a business called Home Owners' Services (furniture repairing and refinishing, etc.), then sold life insurance. Today, still single, he has established the "Robert Arthur Workshop," in which he coaches newcomers in the principles of movie and TV acting. He has also announced plans, in association with the Marvin Paige Independent Casting Agency, to coproduce and direct feature films. Onscreen from 1945. IN: *Roughly Speaking, Too Young to Know, Mother Wore Tights, Green Grass of Wyoming, Yellow Sky, Mother Is a Freshman, September Affair, Belles on Their Toes, Just for You, Take the High Ground,* more.

ARVAN, JAN (S. Cal.) Support. IN: *The Other Woman, The Cobweb, Curse of the Faceless Man, Three Came to Kill, The Brass Bottle, The Spy with My Face,* more.

ASHCROFT, DAME PEGGY (Eng.) Character. Onscreen from 1935. IN: *The Thirty-Nine Steps, Rhodes, The Nun's Story, Sunday Bloody Sunday, The Pedestrian,* more.

ASHER, JANE (Eng.) Leading lady. IN: *Loss of Innocence, The Model Murder Case, Alfie, Deep End,* more.

ASHERSON, RENEE (Eng.) Olivier's charming "French" princess in *Henry V*, in her 50s now (b. 1920), remains active in British movies. Onscreen from 1944. IN: *The Way Ahead, The Small Back Room, The Malta Story, The Day the Earth Caught Fire, Theater of Blood,* more.

ASHLEY, EDWARD (S. Cal.) A handsome man still, in his 60s, this Australian who was once one of Hollywood's busiest second leads in A's and frequent star of B's (*Love, Honor and Goodbye*) is today an active character player. *Herbie the Love Bug Rides Again* and *Genesis II* are among his recent movies. Besides doing much TV work and many commercials, he has costarred on stage in many places in the States, as well as the rest of the globe. Most often playing dapper David Niven-type roles, he has in the past decade or so appeared opposite Carolyn Jones in *The Second Man*, Dorothy Collins in *The Moon Is Blue*, Sylvia Sidney in *Kind Lady*, Dyan Cannon in *The Firebrand*, etc. Onscreen in America from 1940. IN: *Pride and Prejudice, Maisie Was a Lady, Come Live With Me, The Black Swan; Love, Honor and Goodbye; The Other Love, Dick Tracy and Gruesome, Elephant Walk, The Court Jester*, more.

ASHLEY, ELIZABETH (S. Cal.) Costar. Onscreen from 1964. IN: *The Carpetbaggers, Ship of Fools, The Marriage of a Young Stockbroker, Rancho Deluxe, 92 in the Shade, The Great Scout & Cathouse Thursday*, more.

ASHLEY, JOHN (S. Cal.) Support. Onscreen from 1957. IN: *Motorcycle Gang, Zero Hour, Frankenstein's Daughter, Hud, Beach Party, How to Stuff a Wild Bikini, Young Dillinger, Brides of Blood*, more.

ASKEW, LUKE (S. Cal.) Support. IN: *Posse*, more.

ASKIN, LEON (S. Cal.) Character. Onscreen from 1953. IN: *Road to Bali, South Sea Woman, The Robe, Secret of the Incas, Valley of the Kings, One Two Three, What Did You Do in the War Daddy?, Guns for San Sebastian*, more.

ASNER, EDWARD (S. Cal.) Character. Onscreen from 1965. IN: *The Satan Bug, The Slender Thread, The Venetian Affair, The Todd Killings*, more.

ASTAIRE, FRED (S. Cal.) Dancer/star. Received a special Academy Award (statuette) in 1949 "for his unique artistry and his contributions to the technique of musical pictures." Nominated for Best Supporting Oscar in *The Towering Inferno*. Onscreen from 1933. IN: *Dancing Lady, Flying Down to Rio, Top Hat, Swing Time, Shall We Dance?, The Story of Vernon and Irene Castle, Broadway Melody of 1940, Holiday Inn, You Were Never Lovelier, Ziegfeld Follies, Blue Skies, Easter Parade, The Barkleys of Broadway, Royal Wedding, The Band Wagon, Funny Face, Silk Stockings, On the Beach, Pleasure of His Company, Finian's Rainbow, Midas Run, That's Entertainment*, more.

ASTAR, BEN (S. Cal.) Character. Onscreen from 1952. IN: *Five Fingers, Marriage-Go-Round, The Honeymoon Machine, Bye Bye Birdie, Dead Heat on a Merry-Go-Round*, more.

ASTHER, NILS (Swe.) In 26 years in American movies, he went from star to "also in the cast" bits. The character he played in *Samson and Delilah* ('49) did not even have a name—a far cry from the days when he had twice costarred with Garbo, in *The Single Standard* and *Wild Orchids*. He was known in Hollywood as "the masculine Garbo," not merely for his strong, handsome face which, in its male way, was as beautiful as hers; like Garbo, his countrywoman (he was born in Malmo), he was fond of solitude, was thrifty, and had simple tastes. The last may have been fortunate. While staying on in Hollywood almost a decade past his final picture, he had earlier earned enough to live well. Back in Sweden since '60, he still lives comfortably, though he rarely works now, in a small apartment. Twice married, he has been single since the early '30s. His first wife, a Swedish woman, died. He was later married to Vivian Duncan, with whom he costarred in 1927's *Topsy and Eva*, and by whom he has a daughter, Evelyn Rosetta, now in her 40s and living in California. This marriage ended in divorce. When he acts now on Stockholm stages, the roles—usually small—are those of a very old, large-framed, silver-haired man. He is in his late 70s now (b. 1897) and the once widely admired handsome features now seem austere and stern. Onscreen from 1927. IN: *Topsy and Eva, Sorrell and Son; Laugh, Clown, Laugh; Our Dancing Daughters, The Wrath of the Seas, But the Flesh Is Weak, The Bitter Tea of General Yen, Madame Spy, Dr. Kildare's Wedding Day, Sweater Girl, Night Monster, The Hour Before the Dawn, Son of Lassie*, more.

ASTIN, JOHN (S. Cal.) Support. Onscreen from 1961. IN: *West Side Story, That Touch of Mink, Move Over Darling, The Wheeler Dealers, Candy, Prelude, Viva Max , Every Little Crook and Nanny*, more.

ASTOR, GERTRUDE (S. Cal.) One of the most popular leading ladies in Universal silents (under contract there 1914–25), she continued her career, in supporting roles, for many more years before leaving the screen after 1961's *All in a Night's Work*. This veteran of more than 300 movies is in her late 80s now (b. 1889), and in '75 her old studio honored her with a luncheon. Present to salute her were numerous directors for whom she had worked over the years, including George Cukor, Allan Dwan, and Henry Hathaway. In a speech laced with humor, she told many tales of film-making in Hollywood's early days that kept her full-house audience enthralled. Of her own movies, she cited 1927's *Uncle Tom's Cabin* as her favorite. But, she added, laughing, "I paid for that part. The director [Harry Pollard] didn't want me, and he didn't like me, so he made me kneel for three

weeks by the side of the girl's bed, crying."
Accepting a bouquet of roses, she brought a
tear or two among listeners by saying, "I am
very proud. I thought life was over and I should
just crawl in a corner and die. I have no family.
I haven't a soul on earth to enjoy this with, but
I'm going to do plenty of that." Onscreen from
1914. IN: *The Concert, The Wall Flower, Ru-
pert of Hentzau, Flaming Youth, The Wife Who
Wasn't Wanted, Satan in Sables, The Taxi
Dancer, The Irresistible Lover, The Butter and
Egg Man, The Fall of Eve, Dames Ahoy, Western Limited; Wine, Women and Song; My Dear
Secretary*, more.

ASTOR, MARY (S. Cal.) Entering her 70s (b.
1906), the onetime Supporting Oscar winner
(*The Great Lie*) resides at the Motion Picture
and TV Country Home—she has a chronic
heart condition—where she has completed her
seventh book. Among her published works are
several novels (*The Incredible Charlie Carewe,
A Place Called Saturday*, etc.) and two best-
selling autobiographies, *Mary Astor My Story*
and *A Life on Film*. Son Anthony del Campo
has made her a grandmother once and daughter
Marylyn (over whom she once fought a headlined custody battle), four times. Also, late in
'74, courtesy of Marylyn's eldest daughter,
Mrs. Clare Reiley, the actress became for the
first time a great-grandmother—of a little boy.
You get the impression she treasures him more
than the Oscar statuette she was belatedly pre-
sented—supporting winners in '42 receiving
plaques instead of Oscars—in April 1972. On-
screen from 1920. IN: *The Beggar Maid, Beau
Brummell, Don Q Son of Zorro, Two Arabian
Knights, New Year's Eve, Holiday, Runaway
Bride, White Shoulders, Lost Squadron, Red
Dust, Jennie Gerhardt, The Case of the Howling
Dog, Dinky, Page Miss Glory, Dodsworth, The
Prisoner of Zenda, The Hurricane, Midnight,
Brigham Young—Frontiersman, The Maltese
Falcon, Across the Pacific, The Palm Beach
Story, Thousands Cheer, Meet Me in St. Louis,
Claudia and David, Desert Fury, Little Women,
So This Is Love, A Kiss Before Dying, This
Happy Feeling, Return to Peyton Place, Young-
blood Hawke, Hush . . . Hush . . . Sweet Char-
lotte*, more.

ASTREDO, HUMBERT ALLEN (N.Y.) Support. IN: *House of Dark Shadows*.

ATHERTON, WILLIAM (N.Y.) Leading man.
IN: *The New Centurions, Class of '44, The Sug-
arland Express, The Day of the Locust, The
Hindenburg*.

ATKINS, EILEEN (Eng.) Support. IN: *Inadmissible Evidence*.

ſTAWAY, RUTH (N.Y.) Support. IN: *The
President's Lady, The Young Don't Cry, Porgy
and Bess, Terror in the City*, more.

ATTENBOROUGH, SIR RICHARD (Eng.)
Costar. Knighted by Queen Elizabeth in 1976.
Onscreen from 1942. IN: *In Which We Serve,
Stairway to Heaven, Dulcimer Street, Glory at
Sea, Private's Progress, Brothers in Law, Dun-
kirk, I'm All Right Jack, The League of Gentle-
men, The Great Escape, Seance on a Wet After-
noon, Guns at Batasi, The Flight of the
Phoenix, The Sand Pebbles, Doctor Dolittle,
The Bliss of Mrs. Blossom, 10 Rillington
Place, Brannigan, Ten Little Indians, Rosebud*,
more.

ATTERBURY, MALCOLM (S. Cal.) Charac-
ter. Onscreen from 1954. IN: *Dragnet, Crime in
the Streets, Toward the Unknown, From Hell to
Texas, Rio Bravo, Wild River, Summer and
Smoke, Seven Days in May, Hawaii, The
Chase, The Learning Tree*, more.

ATWATER, BARRY (S. Cal.) Character. Onscreen from 1956. IN: *The Rack, Nightmare,
Pork Chop Hill, The Battle at Bloody Beach,
Sweet Bird of Youth, Return of the Gunfighter*,
more.

ATWATER, EDITH (S. Cal.) Character. On-
screen from 1936. IN: *The Gorgeous Hussy, We
Went to College, The Body Snatcher, C-Man,
Sweet Smell of Success, Strait-Jacket, Strange
Bedfellows*, more. (See Kent Smith.)

AUBERJONOIS, RENE (S. Cal.) Character.
IN: *M*A*S*H, McCabe and Mrs. Miller, Pete
'n Tillie, The Hindenburg*, more.

AUBREY, SKYE (S. Cal.) Support. Daughter of
Phyllis Thaxter. IN: *Skyjacked*.

AUDLEY, ELEANOR (S. Cal.) Support. IN:
*Pretty Baby, Prince of Players, Cell 2455—
Death Row, Full of Life, Home Before Dark, A
Summer Place, The Second Time Around;
Hook, Line and Sinker*; more.

AUDLEY, MAXINE (Eng.) Support. IN: *The
Sleeping Tiger, The Vikings, Our Man in Havana, The Agony and the Ecstasy, The Battle of
the Villa Fiorita, The Looking Glass War*,
more.

AUDRAN, STEPHANE (Fr.) Costar. Onscreen
from 1963. IN: *Landru, The Third Lover, The
Champagne Murders, Les Biches, The Discreet
Charm of the Bourgeoisie, Ten Little Indians,
The Black Bird, The Twist*, more.

27

AUGER, CLAUDINE (Fr.) Leading lady. IN: *Thunderball, Triple Cross, The Devil in Love,* more.

AUMONT, JEAN-PIERRE (Fr.) Star. IN: *Maria Chapdelaine; Bizarre, Bizarre; Assignment in Brittany, The Cross of Lorraine, Heartbeat, Song of Scheherazade, Siren of Atlantis, Lili, Hilda Crane, Royal Affairs in Versailles, John Paul Jones, The Devil at 4 O'Clock, Castle Keep, Day for Night, The Happy Hooker, Mahogany, Turn the Other Cheek,* more. (See Marisa Pavan.)

AUMONT, TINA (It.) Leading lady. Daughter of Jean-Pierre Aumont and Maria Montez. IN: *Partner, Torso, A Matter of Time,* more.

AUSTIN, PAMELA (S. Cal.) Support. IN: *Kissin' Cousins, Hootenanny Hoot, The Phynx,* more.

AUSTIN, TERRY/VIVIAN AUSTIN (S. Cal.) (See Vivian Coe.)

AUTRY, GENE (S. Cal.) Cowboy star. Now a business man. Was #1 Western star at the box-office from 1937 through 1942, and was #2 (behind Roy Rogers) from 1947 through 1954, the year he retired from movies. Was among the Top Ten of all box-office stars in 1940, 1941, and 1942. Onscreen from 1934. IN: *In Old Santa Fe, Melody Trail, Red River Valley, The Singing Cowboy, The Man from Music Mountain, Gold Mine in the Sky, Mexicali Rose, South of the Border, Back in the Saddle, Stardust on the Sage, Strawberry Roan, Beyond the Purple Hills, Mule Train, Blue Canadian Rockies, Apache Country, On Top of Old Smoky,* more.

AVALON, FRANKIE (S. Cal.) A teenage heartthrob of the '60s, the singer-actor is in his late 30s now (b. 1939), performs in nightclubs and on TV, and has costarred of late in the movie *The Take,* in a nonsinging role—his character self-described as "a punk, a wise guy who is really a terrible coward." Married just once (since '63), he and his wife Kay have eight children, the newest arriving in '74. Onscreen from 1957. IN: *Jamboree, Guns of the Timberland, The Alamo, Sail a Crooked Ship, Muscle Beach Party, I'll Take Sweden, Ski Party, Fireball, How to Stuff a Wild Bikini,* more.

AVEDON, DOE (S. Cal.) Last in movies two decades ago, the onetime leading lady has long been married to *Dirty Harry* director, Don Siegel (formerly the husband of Viveca Lindfors), and is the mother of four children. IN: *The High and the Mighty, Deep in My Heart, The Boss.*

AVERY, PHYLLIS (S. Cal.) Divorced years ago from actor-director Don Taylor, she has two grown daughters by him, Avery and Ann. The former leading lady retired from acting a decade ago after costarring in the TV series *The Ray Milland Show* and *Mr. Novak.* More recently she has been a real estate agent for the William Justice Company in West Los Angeles —William Justice being the real name of former actor Richard Travis. IN: *Queen for a Day, Ruby Gentry, The Best Things in Life Are Free,* more.

AVERY, VAL (S. Cal.) Character. Onscreen from 1956. IN: *The Harder They Fall, Edge of the City, The Long Hot Summer, Hud, Hombre, Faces, Russian Roulette,* more.

AVON, VIOLET (S. Cal.) The sister of star Laura La Plante, this Wampas Baby Star of 1925 retired for marriage after a few minor roles, and later worked as a receptionist at a Los Angeles business firm.

AYARS, ANN (Eng.) After her brief Hollywood career, the singer-actress was featured in the British-made *Tales of Hoffmann,* but is now, in her 50s, retired. Onscreen from 1942. IN: *Nazi Agent, The Human Comedy, Reunion in France, The Youngest Profession,* more.

AYLMER, FELIX (Eng.) Character. Onscreen from 1930. IN: *The Temporary Wife, Nine Days a Queen, The Mill on the Floss, Victoria the Great, The Citadel, Sixty Glorious Years, The Ghost of St. Michael's, The Wicked Lady, Henry V, The Magic Bow, Hamlet, Edward My Son, Prince of Foxes, Quartet, Trio, Quo Vadis, Ivanhoe, Anastasia, Separate Tables, From the Terrace, Exodus, The Road to Hong Kong, The Chalk Garden, Becket, Masquerade,* more.

AYRES, GORDON (S. Cal.) Long retired from movies, the former juvenile actor—popular as a freckle-faced member of "Our Gang"—has lately been a ballroom dance instructor.

AYRES, LEW (S. Cal.) On December 27, 1968, the day before his 60th birthday, he became a father for the first time—of a son, Justin Bret Ayres. This most welcome child is the product of his marriage (since '64) to a most attractive English woman, Diana Hall, many years his junior. Previously, he was married to Lola Lane (1931–33) and Ginger Rogers (1934–41). In 1941 he had spoken of his desire to have children, principally for "their companionship— their association and enjoyment." Now, finally a father, he says: "This has so altered the structure of my life, changed it completely. Most men have this experience of fatherhood when they are younger, so it is like I have gone back in time. I take Justin *everywhere*—to museums, great churches, parks. It recaptures for me *my* youth." A star from age 20, even before *All Quiet on the Western Front*, Lew deliberately wrote finis to his starring career in 1953—just five years after being nominated for a Best Actor Oscar in *Johnny Belinda*. He spent the next decade on a spiritual quest—traveling the world over making a series of documentaries on all the world's religions other than Christianity. He says still, "It was the most meaningful thing I have ever done." Gray now, he has long since resumed his career as a low-key, much-in-demand character actor—stepping, rather, in the shoes of Samuel S. Hinds, who portrayed his father in all the "Kildare" movies. Besides much TV work (*Streets of San Francisco, Kung Fu*, etc.), he has costarred in such movies of the '70s as Disney's *The Biscuit Eater, Genesis II, Battle for the Planet of the Apes*, and *The Man*. Home, from the time he married Diana, has been a charming house on a one-acre estate in Brentwood. There he mentions he is compiling notes for his autobiography while admitting to one hesitating factor: "One always feels, I suppose, that one still has to come to the great adventure which will be worth the recording." Onscreen from 1929. IN: *The Kiss, The Shakedown, Compromised, The Spirit of Notre Dame, State Fair, She Learned About Sailors, Silk Hat Kid, The Last Train from Madrid, King of the Newsboys, Holiday* (his personal favorite role), *Young Doctor Kildare, Ice Follies of 1939, Broadway Serenade, These Glamour Girls, Remember?, Maisie Was a Lady, Fingers at the Window, The Dark Mirror, The Unfaithful, Johnny Belinda, New Mexico, Donovan's Brain, Advise and Consent, The Carpetbaggers*, more.

AZNAVOUR, CHARLES (Fr.) Costar. IN: *The Chasers, Shoot the Piano Player, Testament of Orpheus, Taxi for Tobruk, Paris in the Month of August, Candy, The Adventurers, Ten Little Indians*, more.

AZZARA, CANDY (N.Y.) Support. IN: *They Might Be Giants, Made for Each Other, Who Is Harry Kellerman . . . ?*, more.

B

BABBITT, HARRY (S. Cal.) The former Kay Kyser band singer, retired from show business, has long been associated with a real estate firm in Laguna. Onscreen from 1939. IN: *That's Right, You're Wrong; You'll Find Out, Playmates, My Favorite Spy, Around the World, Carolina Blues*—all with Kay Kyser.

BABY LE ROY (S. Cal.) A ruggedly handsome man in his 40s (b. 1932), and out of movies since age four, he was at last report serving in the merchant marine. Onscreen from 1933. IN: *A Bedtime Story, Torch Singer, Tillie and Gus, Miss Fane's Baby Is Stolen, The Old-Fashioned Way, The Lemon Drop Kid, It's a Gift*, more.

BABY MARIE (S. Cal.) A costume designer now, this great young favorite of silents has received Wardrobe screen credits—women's clothes only—on such films as *How to Murder Your Wife* and *Spartacus*. Four times a grandmother and in her 60s, Marie Osborne Yeats lives near Universal where she often works. Onscreen from the teens. IN: *Joy and the Dragon, Little Mary Sunshine*, more.

BABY PEGGY (S. Cal.) An adorable tyke, she was the Shirley Temple of her day (the '20s), with her chubby face and short black hair with bangs. She continued on in movies into her teens, a charming young beauty, but no longer a star, in such films as *Eight Girls in a Boat*—and billed Peggy Montgomery. Never caring much for her given name, she long ago changed it to Diana. And she changed her last one, in '54, to Cary when she became the wife of painter Robert Cary. (Her only previous marriage, to "Our Gang's" Gordon "Freckles" Ayres, ended in divorce over three decades ago.) In her late teens, she turned to historical research and became a successful free-lance writer of articles for such magazines as *American Heritage, Esquire, Saturday Evening Post, Reader's Digest*, and, a convert to this faith, *Catholic Digest*. She has also worked as a newspaper staff correspondent, a store manager, and owner-operator of a nationwide greeting card company. For several years she lived in Spain with her husband and their only child, Mark (b. 1960). Today, younger than many oldtime fans realize (b. 1918), her black hair swept back into a chignon, she is general book buyer for the trade book department of the University Bookstore at the University of California at San Diego, and lives with her family in Encinitas. Though long away from Hollywood, Baby Peggy's memories of the place that was, but is no more, linger on. In '75, under the byline Diana Serra Cary, she published a fascinating book: *THE HOLLYWOOD POSSE: The Story of a Gallant Band of Horsemen Who Made Movie History* (Houghton Mifflin). It was a tribute to those little-heralded real-life cowboys who rode in Westerns, of whom her father was one. The fortune Baby Peggy earned as a child star, she concedes, is gone now—the stock market crash of '29 wiping out most of it when she and her family lost their investment in a ranch in Wyoming. But her life has been—and remains—a busy and happy one, and she would be horrified if anyone so much as mentioned a movie comeback. Onscreen from 1922. IN: *Peggy Behave, Hollywood, The Darling of New York, Captain January*, more.

BABY SANDY (S. Cal.) Universal's tiny, bright-eyed 1939-40 pot o' gold has lived a life untouched by glamour since her starring days. In her late 30s (b. 1938), the former Sandra Lee Henville is a sweet-faced dark blonde, small, with a tendency to plumpness, and is a legal secretary in the office of the County Counsel in Los Angeles. Twice-married, she is presently the wife of carpet layer William Magee. They have a son, Duane, just now of grammar school age; by her previous marriage she has a teenage son, Scott, and her husband also has a son by an earlier marriage. Home is a pleasant, nondescript house in Highland Park, one of Los Angeles' less fashionable suburbs. It is, as Sandy's fond mother-in-law once noted, "at all times a home. She is a real homemaker. Family and friends are always welcome. Sandy is never too busy to lend a hand, serve tea, or just be there." As for her life after her brief fame (which she does not recall), Sandy—who is still called that—says, "I attended high school in South Pasadena [where her parents still live], graduated from Pasadena City College and went to Arizona State University for one semester." Then came marriage and a business career. Today she says, "My job, children, husband, and dog and cat (a poodle and Siamese) keep me hopping and quite busy." And, she adds, she remains "surprised and delighted to know that there are still people outside of my family and friends who still remember Baby Sandy." Onscreen from 1939. IN: *East Side of Heaven, Unexpected Father, Little Accident, Sandy Is a Lady, Johnny Doughboy*, more.

BACALL, LAUREN (N.Y.) Star. Onscreen from 1944. IN: *To Have and Have Not, The Big Sleep, Key Largo, Young Man With a Horn, Bright Leaf, How to Marry a Millionaire, The Cobweb, Written on the Wind, Designing Woman, Shock Treatment, Sex and the Single Girl, Harper, Murder on the Orient Express, The Shootist*, and more.

BACHELOR, STEPHANIE (Nev.) The *Lady of Burlesque* role of raven-haired, black-hearted Princess Nirvana, stripper queen, set the pattern for the 30-picture career of this tall (5'8"), fascinating "lady heavy" with the soprano cello voice. As Republic's ace villainess, in B after B (*Port of Forty Thieves* through 1948's *Homicide for Three*), she was sophisticatedly malicious—even, once, planting a black widow spider in a boyfriend's bed. Long retired and happily married to business man Conrad Hurley, she is in her 50s, lives in Las Vegas, and devotes herself to writing (fiction) and such hobbies as illuminated Gothic hand-printing. She remains a stunning woman, but oldtime fans would not recognize her; her hair is completely white. It always was—throughout her entire career. "Premature white hair is a family characteristic. Mine began turning from Dutch blonde to white after I turned 14," she says. "We could put a black wig on her," director William Wellman said when he decided only she could play Princess Nirvana. They did, and she never took it off—in movies. Onscreen from 1943. IN: *The Man from Frisco, Earl Carroll Vanities, Lake Placid Serenade, Scotland Yard Investigator, The Magnificent Rogue, Passkey to Danger, The Undercover Woman, King of Gamblers*, more.

BACKES, ALICE (S. Cal.) Support. IN: *I Want to Live!, It Started With a Kiss*, more.

BACKUS, HENNY (S. Cal.) Support. IN: *The Great Man*, more.

BACKUS, JIM (S. Cal.) Comic support. Onscreen from 1942. IN: *The Pied Piper, Father Was a Fullback, Half Angel, Bright Victory, I'll See You in My Dreams, Pat and Mike, I Love Melvin, Meet Me in Las Vegas, Ask Any Girl, Boys' Night Out, My Six Loves, Sunday in New York, Where Were You When the Lights Went Out?, Crazy Mama, Friday Foster*, more.

BADDELEY, HERMIONE (S. Cal.) Character. Nominated for Best Supporting Actress Oscar in *Room at the Top*. Onscreen in England from 1928. IN: *The Guns of Loos, No Room at the Inn, Passport to Pimlico, Tom Brown's School Days, A Christmas Carol, The Pickwick Papers, Expresso Bongo*, more. Onscreen in America from 1960. IN: *Midnight Lace, The Unsinkable Molly Brown, Mary Poppins, Marriage on the Rocks, Do Not Disturb, The Adventures of Bullwhip Griffin, The Happiest Millionaire*, more.

BADEL, ALAN (Eng.) Support. IN: *Salome, Three Cases of Murder, Will Any Gentleman?, This Sporting Life, Arabesque, The Day of the Jackal*, more.

BADHAM, MARY (S. Cal.) Former juvenile. Nominated for Best Supporting Actress Oscar in *To Kill a Mockingbird*. Onscreen from 1962. IN: *This Property Is Condemned, Let's Kill Uncle*, more.

BAER, BUDDY (S. Cal.) Character. IN: *Two Tickets to Broadway, Quo Vadis, Flame of Araby, The Big Sky, Fair Wind to Java, Giant from the Unknown, Magic Fountain, Ride Beyond Vengeance*, more.

BAER, JOHN (S. Cal.) Support. IN: *About Face, Mississippi Gambler, The Miami Story, We're No Angels, Huk!*, more.

BAER, MAX, JR. (S. Cal.) Costar. IN: *The Long Ride Home, The McCullochs*, more.

BAER, PARLEY (S. Cal.) Character. Onscreen from 1950. IN: *Union Station, The Frogmen, Deadline U.S.A., The Young Lions, A Fever in the Blood, Gypsy, Those Calloways, The Ugly Dachshund, Day of the Evil Gun, Counterpoint*, more.

BAILEY, DAVID (S. Cal.) Support. IN: *The Subterraneans*, more.

BAILEY, PEARL (N.Y.) Black singer-comedienne. Onscreen from 1947. IN: *Variety Girl, Carmen Jones, St. Louis Blues, Porgy and Bess, All the Fine Young Cannibals*, more. Announced her retirement in '75.

BAILEY, RAYMOND (S. Cal.) Character. Onscreen from 1939. IN: *Secret Service of the Air, Hell's Kitchen, The Girl in the Red Velvet Swing, Picnic, Band of Angels, No Time for Sergeants, Vertigo, I Want to Live!, The Gallant Hours, Five Weeks in a Balloon, The Strongest Man in the World*, more.

BAILEY, ROBIN (Eng.) Character. Onscreen from the '40s. IN: *Private Angelo, Glory at Sea, Sailor of the King, Having a Wild Weekend, The Whisperers*, more.

BAIN, CONRAD (S. Cal.) Character. IN: *Bananas, Up the Sandbox, I Never Sang for My Father, Lovers and Other Strangers*, more.

BAIRD, JEANNE (S. Cal.) Support. IN: *Andy Hardy Comes Home*, more.

BAKER, BENNY (S. Cal.) His bespectacled, fun-filled face (far rounder than in those 75 comedy movies) continues—happily—to be much in evidence both onscreen (in *Jory* lately) and onstage. On Broadway recently, he co-starred with Ruby Keeler and Patsy Kelly in *No, No, Nanette*. It was a reunion for Patsy and himself—laughmates in so many Hal Roach two-reelers in the early '30s. Prior to *Nanette*, he supported Zero Mostel in the play *The Latent Heterosexual* at the Huntington Hartford Theater in Hollywood, was in the movie *Paint Your Wagon*, and toured in *The Music Man*. He has long been married to the former Betty Jane

Rase, the girl from Alabama who was the second of Mickey Rooney's tall wives. As B. J. Baker she has been the dubbed-in singing voice for several stars in movies, such as Nancy Kwan in *The Flower Drum Song*. Onscreen from 1934. IN: *The Hell Cat, Belle of the Nineties, The Big Broadcast of 1936, Thanks a Million, Rose of the Rancho, Rose Bowl, Champagne Waltz, Up in Arms, My Girl Tisa, The Inspector General, Public Pigeon No. 1, Boy, Did I Get a Wrong Number*, more.

BAKER, CARROLL (Eng.) Star. Nominated for Best Actress Oscar in *Baby Doll*. Onscreen from 1953. IN: *Easy to Love, Giant, The Big Country, Something Wild, How the West was Won, The Carpetbaggers, Cheyenne Autumn, Sylvia, Harlow, Paranoia, Captain Apache, The Sky Is Falling, Baba Yaga, Journey Into Fear*, more.

BAKER, DIANE (S. Cal.) Costar. IN: *The Diary of Anne Frank, The Best of Everything, Hemingway's Adventures of a Young Man, Nine Hours to Rama, Strait-Jacket, Marnie, Mirage, The Horse in the Gray Flannel Suit*, more.

BAKER, FAY (S. Cal.) The character actress whose personal stationery once carried the whimsical slug "Bitches by Baker" gave up acting a dozen years ago to follow her husband, Arthur Weiss, into movie and TV scriptwriting —and has been most successful at it. Casting directors, recalling her taut performances in *The Star* (as Davis' sponging sister), *The House on Telegraph Hill* (semimenace), *Notorious* (drunken party girl), *Deadline U.S.A.*, etc., have to date been unsuccessful in luring her back to the other side of the camera. Onscreen from the '40s. IN: *No Minor Vices, Chain Lightning, The Company She Keeps, Don't Knock the Rock*, more.

BAKER, GEORGE (Eng.) Costar. Onscreen from 1952. IN: *The Intruder, The Ship That Died of Shame, A Hill in Korea, The Feminine Touch, The Moonraker, The Extra Day, Justine*, more.

BAKER, JOBY (S. Cal.) Comic support. Onscreen from 1959. IN: *The Last Angry Man, The Wackiest Ship in the Army, Gidget Goes to Rome, When the Boys Meet the Girls, Blackbeard's Ghost*, more.

BAKER, JOE DON (S. Cal.) Costar. IN: *Wild Rovers; Welcome Home, Soldier Boys; Junior Bonner, Walking Tall, Framed, Mitchell*, more.

BAKER, KENNY (S. Cal.) Retired since the late '40s, the singer lives with his family on a ranch north of Hollywood. Onscreen from

1935. IN: *Metropolitan, King of Burlesque, A Day at the Races, The King and the Chorus Girl, Turn Off the Moon, 52nd Street, Radio City Revels, The Goldwyn Follies, The Mikado, The Hit Parade of 1941, Silver Skates, The Harvey Girls, The Calendar Girl*, more.

BAKER, STANLEY (Eng.) Costar. Onscreen from 1941. IN: *Undercover* (juvenile role), *The Cruel Sea, Hell Below Zero, The Good Die Young, Knights of the Round Table, Helen of Troy, Richard III, Alexander the Great, Campbell's Kingdom, Accident, The Guns of Navarone, Sodom and Gomorrah, Zulu, Sands of Kalahari, Robbery, Innocent Bystanders, Pepita Jimenez, Zorro*, more. (Died June 28, 1976.)

BAKEWELL, WILLIAM (S. Cal.) Leading man; now a character. Onscreen from 1925. IN: *The Heart Thief, Mother, West Point, Harold Teen, Hot Stuff, The Gold Diggers of Broadway, Lummox, All Quiet on the Western Front; Dance, Fools, Dance; Daybreak, The Spirit of Notre Dame, Back Street, Quality Street, Gone With the Wind, Seven Sinners, Cheers for Miss Bishop, The Bachelor and the Bobby-Soxer, Come Fill the Cup, Davy Crockett, King of the Wild Frontier, The Strongest Man in the World*, more.

BALDWIN, BILL (S. Cal.) Support. IN: *Once a Thief, The Day of the Locust*, more.

BALDWIN, DICK (S. Cal.) Leading man. Onscreen in the '30s. IN: *Life Begins at College, Love and Hisses, International Settlement, Mr. Moto's Gamble, One Wild Night, Spring Madness*, more. Retired. (See Cecilia Parker.)

BALDWIN, PETER (S. Cal.) A member of Paramount's "Golden Circle" of newcomers in the early '50s, he forsook acting more than a decade ago to become a director. He has helmed numerous episodes of TV's *Chico and the Man, Joe and Sons*, etc., and has recently formed his own company to produce movies and TV shows. IN: *The Girls of Pleasure Island, Stalag 17, Houdini, Little Boy Lost, The Tin Star, Teacher's Pet*, more.

BALDWIN, WALTER (S. Cal.) Character. Onscreen from 1941. IN: *The Devil Commands, Mr. Winkle Goes to War, The Best Years of Our Lives, Cry of the City, Come to the Stable, Cheaper by the Dozen, Carrie, Interrupted Melody*, more.

BALFOUR, BETTY (Eng.) In her 70s now (b. 1903), the comedienne has not appeared in films in more than two decades. Onscreen from the '20s. IN: *Paradise, Evergreen, Born for Glory, The Facts of Love*, more.

BALFOUR, KATHARINE (N.Y.) Support. IN: *Music for Millions, America America*.

BALFOUR, MICHAEL (Eng.) Character. Onscreen from the '40s. IN: *Johnny on the Run, The Sea Shall Not Have Them, Three Steps to the Gallows, Track the Man Down, Gentlemen Marry Brunettes, Double Jeopardy*, more.

BALIN, INA (N.Y.) Costar. Onscreen from 1958. IN: *Compulsion, The Black Orchid, From the Terrace, The Young Doctors, The Greatest Story Ever Told, Charro!*, more.

BALL, JANE (Pa.) The delicate, "All American-Girl" blonde who, in her 20s, was one of 20th Century-Fox's most promising young leads, is in her early 50s now and the widow of the famous impresario of New York's Copacabana nightclub, Monte Proser (d. 1973). She went into movies as a graduate of the chorus line at this club, then gave up acting to marry her "boss." They had five sons: Charles, William, Michael, Timothy, and James—the eldest born in '46. She lives in Newtown, and since her husband's death at 69 (he had been retired several years), she has worked as a nurse. Onscreen from 1944. IN: *Winged Victory, The Keys of the Kingdom, Forever Amber*.

BALL, LUCILLE, (S. Cal.) Star. Onscreen from 1933. IN: *Roman Scandals, Nana, Kid Millions, Murder at the Vanities, Bulldog Drummond Strikes Back, Broadway Bill, Carnival, I Dream Too Much, Follow the Fleet, Stage Door, Joy of Living, Having Wonderful Time, Room Service, The Affairs of Annabel, Five Came Back, You Can't Fool Your Wife; Dance, Girl, Dance; Too Many Girls, The Big Street, Best Foot Forward, Du Barry Was a Lady, Without Love, Ziegfeld Follies, The Dark Corner, Easy to Wed, Lured, Sorrowful Jones, Fancy Pants, The Fuller Brush Girl; The Long, Long Trailer; Critic's Choice; Yours, Mine and Ours; Mame*, more.

BALLANTINE, CARL (S. Cal.) Comic support. IN: *McHale's Navy, Penelope, Speedway, The Shakiest Gun in the West*, more.

BALLARD, KAYE (S. Cal.) Comedienne. IN: *The Girl Most Likely, A House Is Not a Home, The Ritz*, more.

BALLEW, SMITH (Tex.) Blond, rangy (6'5") and an excellent baritone, he was one of Hollywood's first singing cowboys. By '38 he was also one of the Top Ten Western Box-Office Stars, in addition to emceeing NBC's hour-long weekly radio show *Shell Chateau*. But few stars ever did such a total fade-out as he; by '43 he was finished, reduced to playing bits in other stars' pix. Today, a deceptively youthful-looking man in his 70s (b. 1902), lean and handsome still, Smith Ballew lives in a bachelor apartment in one of Fort Worth's better areas. "After those lean years during the 1940s," he said recently, "I chose to desert the movies and joined Howard Hughes Aircraft in 1950." He was with the company's missile division two years, in Culver City and Tucson, where his wife, Justine, developed an allergy from the desert air, requiring a move. Convair in Fort Worth offered the actor an excellent job in management. "So we moved back home, after our 10 years in New York with my band and 15 years in Hollywood." Their daughter and only child, also named Justine, married a young Texas business man and became the mother of two daughters of her own. On January 2, 1960, the wife who had been Smith Ballew's helpmate for 36 years died suddenly of a heart occlusion. Near the end of that year, he adds, "I married another wonderful woman, Mary Ruth, who had been a widow for 16 years, and was Consultant of Home Economics and Family Life for the Fort Worth Public Schools." He acquired by this marriage a stepdaughter, who, as the wife of a Houston lawyer, has since made the actor four times a step-grandfather. Soon after both he and his second wife retired from their respective careers, she became desperately ill, cancer eventually claiming her life in '72. "We had a most wonderful life together," he says. Unwilling then to live alone in the beautiful big house they owned on Spanish Oak Drive, he moved into his present apartment. He visits his daughters and grandchildren now, plays golf, and travels. "I am not a very happy man for the nonce," he admits. "However, I'm not throwing in the towel; even at my age, I still have hopes for the future." Onscreen from 1931 in two-reel musicals made in the East. Onscreen in Hollywood from 1935. IN: *Palm Springs, Roll Along Cowboy, Racing Lady, Hawaiian Buckaroo, Western Gold, Panamint's Badman, Driftin' Along, Gaucho Serenade, Under Arizona Skies, I Killed Geronimo, The Man Who Walked Alone,* more.

BALSAM, MARTIN (N.Y.) Costar. Won Best Supporting Actor Oscar in *A Thousand Clowns.* Onscreen from 1954. IN: *On the Waterfront, Twelve Angry Men, Middle of the Night, Psycho, Breakfast at Tiffany's, Seven Days in May, Hombre, 2001, The Good Guys and the Bad Guys, Tora! Tora! Tora!, The Anderson Tapes; Summer Wishes, Winter Dreams; The Man, Murder on the Orient Express, Mitchell, All the President's Men,* more.

BANCROFT, ANNE (N.Y.) Star. Won Best Actress Oscar in *The Miracle Worker;* nominated in the same category in *The Pumpkin Eater* and *The Graduate.* Onscreen from 1952. IN: *Don't Bother to Knock, Tonight We Sing, Demetrius and the Gladiators, New York Confidential, Walk the Proud Land, The Girl in Black Stockings, Girl on the Via Flaminia, Seven Women, The Slender Thread, The Public Image, Young Winston, The Hindenburg, Lipstick,* more.

BANG, JOY (S. Cal.) Support. IN: *Messiah of Evil,* more.

BANKY, VILMA (S. Cal.) "We wanted to make it stick," said husband Rod La Rocque. So they did—from the day of their 1927 wedding (one of Hollywood's great mob-scene spectacles) until his death in 1969. The one regret of the Catholic couple was that they did not have children. Today, many decades since Vilma and Ronald Colman were Goldwyn's great "love team," the Hungarian-born (1903) actress remains beautifully blonde and charming, and has never completely lost the accent that silent-film fans finally got to hear in just a few early talkies (*A Lady to Love, This Is Heaven,* etc.). For several years in the '40s she was undefeated golf champion (women's division) of the Wilshire Country Club. Not quite so physically active in her 70s, she lives quietly, and quite rich (her husband's astute investments), with a beautiful home in Beverly Hills and a ranch in the San Fernando Valley, still surrounded by friends—mostly from the "old days." Onscreen from 1925. IN: *The Dark Angel, The Eagle, The Son of the Sheik, The Winning of Barbara Worth, The Magic Flame, The Night of Love, The Lady From Paris, Two Lovers, The Awakening, The Rebel,* more.

BANNARD, ROBERT (N.Y.) Support. IN: *The Incident,* more.

BANNEN, IAN (Eng.) Costar. Nominated for Best Supporting Actor Oscar in *The Flight of the Phoenix.* Onscreen from 1955. IN: *Private's Progress, Man in a Cocked Hat, A French Mistress, The World in My Pocket, Station 6 Sahara, Rotten to the Core, The Hill, Mr. Moses, Penelope, Sailor from Gibraltar, Lock Up Your Daughters, Too Late the Hero, The Deserter,* more.

BANNON, JIM (S. Cal.) Leading man/cowboy star. Onscreen from 1944. IN: *Sergeant Mike, The Soul of a Monster, The Gay Senorita, Renegades, Johnny O'Clock, The Man From Colorado; Ride, Ryder, Ride; Sierra Passage, They Came to Cordura, A Gathering of Eagles,* more. Retired.

BARASH, OLIVIA (N.Y.) Juvenile. Onscreen in the '70s. IN: *Who Is Harry Kellerman . . . ?,* more.

33

BARCLAY, JOHN (S. Cal.) Character. IN: *The Mikado, Dr. Jekyll and Mr. Hyde, Aloma of the South Seas,* more.

BARD, KATHARINE (S. Cal.) Rarely active now, this supporting actress is the wife of TV-movie-stage director Martin Manulis. Onscreen from 1958. IN: *The Decks Ran Red, The Interns, Johnny Cool, Inside Daisy Clover, How to Save a Marriage—And Ruin Your Life,* more.

BARDETTE, TREVOR (S. Cal.) Character. Onscreen from 1937. IN: *White Bondage, They Won't Forget, The Great Garrick, Abe Lincoln in Illinois, Topper Returns, Wild Bill Hickok Rides, None Shall Escape, The Sea of Grass, Hellfire, Lone Star, Thunder Over the Plains, The Mating Game, The Way West,* more.

BARDOT, BRIGITTE (Fr.) Star. Onscreen from 1954. IN: *Act of Love, Helen of Troy, The Grand Maneuver, And God Created Woman, Please Mr. Balzac, La Parisienne, The Girl in the Bikini, Love Is My Profession, Babette Goes to War, Crazy for Love, A Very Private Affair, Love on a Pillow, Dear Brigitte, Viva Maria, Shalako,* more.

BARI, LYNN (S. Cal.) Now in her 60s (b. 1915), 20th Century-Fox's onetime "Queen of the B's" is stylish, long-limbed, and slim, with short reddish-brown hair. And, as cello-voiced as ever, she is resuming her career, hopefully onscreen, but for now on the stage. She recently completed a lengthy tour in the play *The Gingerbread Lady,* receiving rave reviews in each city she played. She lives alone in a chic, antique-furnished apartment in Beverly Hills, and says, "Now is the first time in my life that I've ever been able to feel free to do what I want to do. I'm not lonely. Believe me, nobody has to feel sorry for me. I'm living life to the hilt." She has no desire to remarry, having been married and divorced three times. Husband #1 was agent Walter Kane, now a Howard Hughes aide. Husband #2 was Sid Luft who later married Judy Garland. The son, John Michael, over whom they fought bitter, headlined custody battles, is now in his late 20s (b. 1948) and a successful painter-sculptor. Husband #3 (1955 –72), whose young daughter she also reared, was Dr. Nathan Rickles, a Beverly Hills psychiatrist. He practiced from an office in their home, with Lynn as his secretary and nurse, and the severe emotional problems of many of his patients created, she has said, a finally untenable household atmosphere. "I stood it all as long as I could; then, to preserve what was left of my sanity, decided I'd better get a divorce." The star who made a million dollars before she was 30—and lost most of it, she says, on bad investments—is raring to start on her second million. Onscreen from the early '30s. IN: *Stand Up and Cheer, The Baroness and the Butler, Mr. Moto's Gamble, Always Goodbye, I'll Give a Million, Speed to Burn, The Return of the Cisco Kid, News Is Made at Night, Hotel for Women, Charlie Chan in City in Darkness; Free, Blonde and 21; Lillian Russell, Kit Carson, Blood and Sand, Moon Over Her Shoulder, Sun Valley Serenade, Secret Agent of Japan, The Magnificent Dope, Orchestra Wives, The Falcon Takes Over, The Bridge of San Luis Rey, Captain Eddie, Home Sweet Homicide, Nocturne, I'd Climb the Highest Mountain, Francis Joins the Wacs, Damn Citizen, The Young Runaways,* more.

BARKER, JESS (S. Cal.) Now in his 60s (b. 1915), and after several years in Midwest radio, the former star has returned to Hollywood as a character actor. Associated with Caruth C. Byrd Productions, he has been on such TV shows as *Tenafly,* played a small role in the movie *Live a Little, Steal a Lot* (initially released as *Murph the Surf*), and has been announced to appear in *Monkeys.* Divorced wife, Susan Hayward, pointedly left him out of her will (this item from the April 15, 1975, *New York Times:* "Susan Hayward left $750,000 jointly to her 30-year-old twins, Timothy Barker of Los Angeles and Gregory Barker of Neptune Beach, Fla., but stipulated that they not share it with their father, Jess Barker, a former actor"). Via Timothy, called Ted and a theatrical publicist, Jess is the grandfather of two, a boy and a girl. Son Gregory, still a bachelor at last report, is a veterinarian. Onscreen from 1943. IN: *Government Girl, Cover Girl, Keep Your Powder Dry, This Love of Ours, The Daltons Ride Again, Scarlet Street, The Time of Their Lives, Reign of Terror, Dragonfly Squadron, Three Bad Sisters, The Night Walker,* more.

BARNES, BINNIE (S. Cal.) Married to producer Mike Frankovich since 1940, this still-highly-sophisticated blonde costarred for him in 1973's *Forty Carats,* her first movie since *Where Angels Go—Trouble Follows* ('68). And, said *Variety* of the actress just then about to enter her 70s (b. 1905), who portrayed Liv Ullmann's swinging mom, "She returns in a very delightful characterization, including a wild discotheque dancing turn that would exhaust a teenager." She and Frankovitch (Joe E. Brown reared him as his son) are well known in Los Angeles for their extensive philanthropies. They have three children: Mike Jr. (the unit manager on *Kojak;* he has presented them with a grandson, Michael John III), Peter (literary assistant for Frankovich Productions), and Michele (married and the mother of two). Onscreen from 1931. IN: *Murder at Covent Garden, The Private Life of Henry VIII, The Lady Is Willing, Diamond Jim, Sutter's Gold, Three Smart Girls, Broadway Melody of 1938, The Adventures of Marco Polo, Three Blind Mice, Holiday; Wife, Husband and Friend; Man About Town, 'Til We Meet Again, Skylark, I Married an Angel, The Hour Before the Dawn, The Spanish Main, The Pirates of Capri, Fire Over Africa,* more.

BARNES, JOANNA (S. Cal.) Active when she wishes to be, this blonde leading lady has written and published several Jacqueline Susann-type novels about Hollywood. Onscreen from 1958. IN: *Home Before Dark, Auntie Mame, Spartacus, The Parent Trap; Goodbye, Charlie; Don't Make Waves,* more.

BARNES, MAE (N.Y.) Support. IN: *Odds Against Tomorrow.*

BARNETT, VINCE (S. Cal.) The bald veteran comic (b. 1903) toured in '72 with Allan Jones and the late Cass Daley in the nostalgic revue *The Big Show of 1936*—getting big laughs with a ribald monologue—and still turns up in an occasional movie. Onscreen from 1930. IN: *Queen of Scandal, Night Mayor, Scarface, The Prizefighter and the Lady, Silk Hat Kid, The Woman I Love, East Side Kids, Seven Sinners, The Falcon's Alibi, Brute Force, Springfield Rifle, The Rookie, Zebra in the Kitchen, Dr. Goldfoot and the Bikini Machine,* more.

BARNEY, JAY (S. Cal.) Character. IN: *The Shrike, Mister Rock and Roll, Blueprint for Robbery,* more.

BARON, LITA (S. Cal.) Divorced from Rory Calhoun, this fiery leading lady, offscreen since '56, lives with their daughters in Palm Springs. Onscreen from 1945. IN: *The Gay Senorita, Pan-Americana, Club Havana, Jungle Jim, Savage Drums, Jesse James' Woman, Red Sundown, The Broken Star,* more.

BARONOVA, IRINA (Switz.) Fabled in the '30s as the "baby ballerina" of the Ballets Russe de Monte Carlo, she made her movie debut in MGM's *Florian* ('40) with Robert Young. She never worked in Hollywood again but those who saw this glorious little Russian in it never forgot her. She lives in Zurich now, and in '75 made her first visit to America in 23 years to be one of several famous ballerinas who were "walk-on" guests in the finale of the American Ballet Theater's 35th Anniversary Gala. Old-time admirers could see for themselves that she is still slender and beautiful, still brown-haired in her early 50s (b. 1922). What they could not see is that much of her life has been sad. For several years she was the wife of American Ballet Theater manager Gerry Sevastianov, during and after her time in Hollywood. Living in New York for a time, and then much longer in London, they had no children and were eventually divorced. While living in England she also worked in two more films, *Toast to Love* and *Train of Events*. She was then most happily married to famous English agent (for Olivier, etc.) Cecil Tennent, bore him three children—two girls and a boy—and in the mid-'60s was shattered by his death in an automobile accident. Later her previous husband came back into her life, and they had moved to Switzerland to live when, with no prior warning, he died suddenly. She has contemplated resuming her career—her children being grown now—but as an actress, not as a dancer.

BARR, PATRICK (Eng.) Support. IN: *The Return of the Scarlet Pimpernel, Frightened Lady, Golden Arrow, Black Orchid, The Intruder, Duel in the Jungle, The Brain Machine, The Dam Busters, It's Never Too Late, Billy Liar,* more.

BARRAULT, JEAN-LOUIS (Fr.) Star. Onscreen from the '30s. IN: *Helene, The Pearls of the Crown, Orage; Bizarre, Bizarre; Les Enfants du Paradis, Blind Desire, Street of Shadows, La Ronde, The Longest Day, Chappaqua,* more.

BARRETT, JUDITH (S. Cal.) Leading lady. Onscreen 1936–40. IN: *Flying Hostess, Good Old Soak, I'm from Missouri, The Gracie Allen Murder Case, The Great Victor Herbert, Road to Singapore, Women Without Names, Those Were the Days,* more. Retired.

BARRETT, LAURINDA (N.Y.) Support. IN: *The Wrong Man, The Heart Is a Lonely Hunter.*

BARRETT, LESLIE (N.Y.) Support. IN: *Career.*

BARRETT, MAJEL (S. Cal.) Support. IN: *Track of Thunder.*

BARRIE, BARBARA (N.Y.) Leading lady. IN: *One Potato, Two Potato.*

BARRIE, ELAINE (BWI) The onetime Mrs. John Barrymore has been a business woman in recent years. IN: *Midnight.*

BARRIE, WENDY (N.Y.) Before she became ill and entered the Lynwood Nursing Home in Manhattan—where she has continued to live—she was enjoying one of the great successes of her career. That was as the star of the nationally syndicated (360 stations) radio show *The*

Wendy Barrie Celebrity Parade. What listening audiences could not know was that she no longer was the pencil-slim, elegantly lovely star of the '30s. She had put on considerable weight and, wearing little makeup, had long since given up any pretense to beauty. All had been different, of course, in her heyday (1935–43) in Hollywood when she played leads in so many. That career ended abruptly; studios grew leery of hiring her almost assuredly because of her association with mobster "Bugsy" Siegel. Always gregarious, as well as garrulous, she found it easy to build a new career in broadcasting in the East. When *The $64,000 Question* went on TV she was—until replaced by Barbara Britton— Revlon's on-air spokeswoman. For almost a dozen years her *Wendy Barrie Show* (different versions of it) was one of the most popular local TV programs in New York, and her daily sign-off, "Be a good bunny," became a byword with her housewife audiences. (She also lived in Ohio for three years, doing a version of this program there.) The hallmarks of her shows were her wit, British charm, and a most disarming, riotous sense of humor. Often referring to herself as an "old bag"—and in her later TV shows she had begun to change appreciably—she loved it when her crew kiddingly insisted she had been "baby sitter for the Marx Brothers." On camera once, a production assistant surprised her with a huge blowup of a glamor pose of Wendy Barrie vintage 1937. She donned her specs, studied the image of the stars-in-her-eyes girl with her false lashes, chiseled features laden with Max Factor, hair shimmering gold under a halo light—and laughed like hell. In the '60s she had small roles in two movies, *Summer Holiday* and *The Moving Finger,* which did not lead, as she had hoped, to more parts. But then came her radio show—and her desperate illness. She is quite alone, having no immediate family, and not remarried since her five-year (and only) marriage, to New York manufacturer David L. Meyers, ended in divorce in '50. And it is a certainty that the star, in her 60s now (b. 1913), will never act again. Visitors to the nursing home where she lives, as a semi-invalid, are warned before seeing her: "We hope she recognizes you." Onscreen from 1933. IN: *The Private Life of Henry VIII, The Big Broadcast of 1936, Wings Over Honolulu, Dead End, Pacific Liner, The Hound of the Baskervilles, Five Came Back, The Saint in Palm Springs, A Date With the Falcon, Eyes of the Underworld, Forever and a Day,* more.

BARRY, DON "RED" (S. Cal.) Cowboy star/ character. Onscreen from the '30s. IN: *The Woman I Love, Sinners in Paradise, Only Angels Have Wings, Remember Pearl Harbor, The Adventures of Red Ryder, Red-Headed Justice, Carson City Cyclone, Outlaws of Santa Fe, Fugitive from Sonora, I Shot Billy the Kid, Warlock, I'll Cry Tomorrow, Twilight of Honor, Alvarez Kelly, Bandolero, The Shakiest Gun in the West, Blazing Stewardesses, Hustle,* more.

BARRY, GENE (S. Cal.) Costar. Onscreen from 1952. IN: *The Atomic City, The War of the Worlds, Red Garters, Naked Alibi, Soldier of Fortune, China Gate, Thunder Road, The Second Coming of Suzanne,* more.

BARRY, PATRICIA (S. Cal.) Leading lady. First billed as Patricia White. IN: *Safe at Home, Kitten With a Whip, Send Me No Flowers, Dear Heart,* more.

BARRY, PAUL (N.Y.) Support. IN: *Battle Cry, The Body Is a Shell,* more.

BARRY, WESLEY (S. Cal.) Now entering his 70s (b. 1906), the silent screen's favorite freckle-faced teenager with the big grin, whose career as a supporting player continued through the '30s, became in the '40s the assistant director of such B's as *Mr. Hex*—after WW II service in the Navy. Long retired from movies, he has lately operated a successful turkey ranch in Southern California and retains fondly expressed memories of late director Marshall Nielan, who discovered him and came to regard him as his son. Onscreen from the teens. IN: *The Unpardonable Sin, Dinty, Bits of Life, Penrod, The Country Kid, In Old Kentucky, Wild Geese, Sunny Skies, The Life of Vergie Winters, Night Life of the Gods, The Plough and the Stars.* more.

BARRYMORE, JOHN DREW/JOHN BARRYMORE, JR. (S. Cal.) The clean-cut youth of the '50s has long since been supplanted by a gaunt-faced, bearded man with shoulder-length gray hair—premature, for he is only in his mid-40s (b. 1932). In the '60s he played psychopathic killers in several European films until he became a disciple of antiviolence. After a period of meditation in India, he lived five years alone in a shack on the California desert—subsisting on wild lettuce, sunflower seeds, lamb's quarters (a plant), and watercress. Destitute, he returned to Hollywood in '74 when a friend, David Carradine, offered him a role on TV in *Kung Fu.* Late in that year he was arrested—his second such arrest— for possession of marijuana, to which he pleaded guilty, being fined $250 and placed on three-years probation. His most recent movie, in which he has the starring role, is *The South American Connection.* He has been married and divorced twice. By first wife, Cara Williams, he has an almost-grown son, John Blyth, who sports his carrot-red hair long like his father and was announced to star in the David Carradine-produced and -directed movie *Around*. There were no children by his second marriage, to Italian actress Gaby Pallazoll. Looking more like his famous father, John Barrymore, than ever, the tall, thin actor answers this way when asked if he is going back to acting for good: "Not going back—going forward." Onscreen from 1950. IN: *The Sundowners, High Lonesome, Quebec, The Big Night, While the City Sleeps, High School Confidential, Never Love a Stranger, Night of the Quarter Moon, The Cossacks, The Pharaoh's Woman, War of the Zombies,* more.

BARTEL, JEAN (S. Cal.) Support. IN: *Sanctuary.*

BARTHOLOMEW, FREDDIE (N. J.) At the Manhattan advertising agency of Benton & Bowles, the sign on one door reads: Fred L. Bartholomew, Vice President/Program Manager. Enter that plush suite and you will find a horn-rimmed, smallish, strong-featured superexecutive with thinning wavy hair who looks just vaguely familiar. And from his fine-tailored suit, staff, and surroundings, you know he has done well for himself. Among other agency chores, Fred(die) Bartholomew has lately been producer of the TV soap opera *As the World Turns*. His own private world centers around an estate in New Jersey where he lives with his wife (since '53) Aileen Paul. They have a college-age daughter, Kathleen Myllicent (named for the late aunt who was Freddie's guardian in Hollywood), and a son, Frederick Robert, in high school. The former actor was married once previously (1946–53) to a publicist, Maely Daniele, who was several years his senior, and has a grown daughter by her. This daughter, Celia, is now a teacher in Pittsburgh. On agency business, Freddie still spends time in Hollywood occasionally, and has even revisited MGM where his juvenile star shone so brightly. But at his present age (b. 1924), the thought of acting has no appeal for him. After Air Force service in WW II, he briefly essayed a movie career as a young adult, worked in just three pix, and gave it up after 1951's *St. Benny the Dip*. He was a TV director for a while, then, two decades ago, began his executive-ladder climb at Benton & Bowles. At their rambling Leonia, N.J., home, Freddie's wife—once the star of a local TV show in Manhattan, *New York Cook*—enjoys her own career. She gives lessons in cooking and indoor gardening to 7-to-12-year-olds, and out of this has written two books, *Kids Cooking* and *Kids Gardening*. Also, as a direct outgrowth of the Bartholomew family's favorite weekend pastime, camping, she has recently published a third, *Kids Camping*. Logically, you might expect that she could also write a book called *Kids Starring*—except for one

small hitch. That is a subject about which her agency-executive husband, Fred L. Bartholomew, who should know a great deal, amost never talks. Onscreen from 1935. IN: *David Copperfield, Anna Karenina, Little Lord Fauntleroy, The Devil Is a Sissy, Captains Courageous, Kidnapped, Lord Jeff; Listen, Darling; Spirit of Culver, Swiss Family Robinson, Tom Brown's School Days, Naval Academy, A Yank at Eton, The Town Went Wild,* more.

BARTLETT, MARTINE (S. Cal.) Support. IN: *Splendor in the Grass, The Prize, No Way to Treat a Lady,* more.

BARTOK, EVA (Hawaii) The brunette actress, now in her 40s (b. 1929), who was once the wife of Curt Jurgens, gave up her career while she spent three years near Jakarta, Indonesia, studying with the Pak Subuh sect. She has more recently taught this philosophy in a school she opened in Honolulu. From Hawaii, this veteran of 38 Hollywood films journeyed, in '74, to Rio and Mexico to costar with soccer star Pele in the picture, rather oddly titled, *Pele, King of Football*. Onscreen from 1952. IN: *The Crimson Pirate, A Tale of Five Women, The Assassin, Front Page Story, Ten Thousand Bedrooms, Circus of Love, SOS Pacific, Blood and Black Lace,* more.

BARTON, MARGARET (Eng.) Support. IN: *Brief Encounter, Temptation Harbor, Good Time Girl, Mr. Lord Says No!, Landfall, The Romantic Age, The Happy Family, The Gay Dog,* more.

BARTON, ROBERT "BUZZ" (Mo.) Support. IN: *In the Heat of the Night, In Cold Blood,* more.

BARTY, BILLY (S. Cal.) The '70s have been a bonanza for the little (3'9") man who has been an enjoyable fixture in Hollywood movies for four decades. In the summer of '70 he became the father of a son, and in the summer of '75, in the dream role of his career—the irascible dwarf in the cockfight episode of *The Day of the Locust* —he found critics exulting over his "brilliant performance." Onscreen from 1933. IN: *Alice in Wonderland, Gift of Gab, A Midsummer Night's Dream,* more.

BASEHART, RICHARD (S. Cal) Costar. Onscreen from 1947. IN: *Repeat Performance, Cry Wolf, He Walked by Night, The Black Book, Fourteen Hours, The House on Telegraph Hill, Decision Before Dawn, Titanic, Moby Dick, La Strada, The Brothers Karamazov, Portrait in Black, Hitler, The Satan Bug,* more.

BASQUETTE, LINA (Pa.) No longer the great raven-haired beauty she was onscreen—as early as '16 when, as a child, she was billed Lena Baskette—she is now, on the threshold of her 70s (b. 1907), a strong-featured, heavy woman with silver hair who lives on a Bucks County estate and breeds championship Great Danes. Single now, she has been married six times—to Sam Warner (of the Brothers; died 1927), Henry Mollison, a prizefight trainer, etc. —with most of her marriages ending in divorce. She has a son, a business man in Arizona, who has made her a grandmother, and a daughter, Lita (b. 1927), by her first husband, whom the other *freres* Warner successfully prevented her rearing; Lita grew up in Hollywood as the daughter, officially adopted, of Harry Warner. Mother and daughter have never had the opportunity to be close. The dancer-actress continued to be sultrily beautiful in movies—Westerns (*Rose of the Rio Grande*, etc.) and B's (*A Night for Crime, The Final Hour*)—through '42. IN: *Serenade, The Noose, Wheels of Chance, Show Folks, The Godless Girl, Goldie, Morals for Women, The Midnight Lady, Ebb Tide, Four Men and a Prayer*, more.

BASS, ALFIE (Eng.) Character. Onscreen from the '40s. IN: *It Always Rains on Sunday, The Hasty Heart, Pool of London, The Lavender Hill Mob, Brandy for the Parson, The Angel Who Pawned Her Harp*, more.

BATALOV, ALEXEI (Rus.) Costar. IN: *My Beloved, The Cranes Are Flying, The Lady With the Dog*, more.

BATES, ALAN (Eng.) Star. Nominated for Best Actor Oscar in *The Fixer*. Onscreen from 1960. IN: *The Entertainer, A Kind of Loving, Whistle Down the Wind, The Caretaker, Nothing But the Best, Zorba the Greek, Georgy Girl, King of Hearts, Far from the Madding Crowd, Women in Love, The Go-Between, A Day in the Death of Joe Egg, Butley, Royal Flash*, more.

BATES, JEANNE (S. Cal.) Leading lady. Onscreen in the '40s. IN: *Shadows in the Night, The Soul of a Monster*, more. Active on TV now.

BATTEN, TOM (N.Y.) Support. IN: *Rationing.*

BAUR, ELIZABETH (S. Cal.) Leading lady. IN: *The Boston Strangler.*

BAVIER, FRANCES (S. Cal.) Character. Onscreen from 1951. IN: *The Day the Earth Stood Still, Bend of the River, Horizons West, The Stooge, The Man in the Attic, It Started With a Kiss, Benji*, more.

BAXLEY, BARBARA (N.Y.) Support. IN: *The Savage Eye, All Fall Down, No Way to Treat a Lady, Countdown, Nashville*, more.

BAXTER, ANNE (S. Cal.) Star. Won Best Supporting Actress Oscar in *The Razor's Edge*. Nominated for Best Actress Oscar in *All About Eve*. Onscreen from 1940. IN: *Twenty Mule Team, The Great Profile, Swamp Water, The Magnificent Ambersons, Five Graves to Cairo, The Sullivans, Eve of St. Mark, Guest in the House, Yellow Sky, A Ticket to Tomahawk, I Confess, Carnival Story, The Ten Commandments, Three Violent People, Summer of the 17th Doll, A Walk on the Wild Side, Stranger on the Run, The Busy Body, The Comic, Fools' Parade, The Late Liz*, more.

BAXTER, JANE (Eng.) Support. IN: *We Live Again, Enchanted April, The Clairvoyant, Chinese Den, Ships With Wings*, more.

BAXTER, KEITH (Eng.) Support. IN: *The Barretts of Wimpole Street* ('57), *Falstaff: Chimes at Midnight*, more.

BAY, SUSAN (S. Cal.) Support. IN: *The Big Mouth.*

BAYNE, BEVERLY (Ariz.) She retains, in her early 80s (b. 1895), much of the beauty that left silent fans awestruck. And she is the personification of elegance—her figure slender and erect, her hair kept jet-black, and her voice low and resonant. Most famous during her marriage to (and costarring days with) Francis X. Bushman, she went into vaudeville after their divorce in the '20s, and later on the New York stage. She replaced Ina Claire as the mother in *Claudia*, then did a nationwide tour in the play, and was in *The Cup of Trembling* with Elisabeth Bergner. Her acting swan song came in '46 when, receiving excellent notices, she costarred with Bert Lytell in *I Like It Here*. Her second marriage (in '37), to a New York business executive, Charles T. Hvass, also ended in divorce, in '44. But the great tragedy of her life came in '67 when her only child, Richard (by Francis X. Bushman), died suddenly in his early 40s. For more than two decades she has lived alone in Scottsdale, where her main activity is working with civic and philanthropic organizations. It has been many a year since she had a custom-built, gold-monogrammed yacht at her command or lived on a vast California estate with kennels holding 300 Great Danes—that being during the Bushman era. But her own earnings have been wisely invested. She lives well, and she doesn't miss all that. Onscreen from 1912. IN: *The Magic Wand, The Snare, One Wonderful Night, Under Royal Patronage,*

Graustark, Romeo and Juliet, The Great Secret; Red, White and Blue Blood; Social Quicksands, Age of Innocence, Passionate Youth, more.

BEAIRD, BARBARA (S. Cal.) Support. IN: *The Man in the Net, Toby Tyler,* more.

BEAL, JOHN (S. Cal.) Leading man/character. Married to actress Helen Craig since 1934, he is the father of two grown daughters (Tita and Tandy) and, in his 60s (b. 1909), still stars in all media. He has been top-cast in such recent movies as *The Bride* (released in certain sectors as *The House That Cried Murder).* On radio he appears often in *CBS Radio Mystery Theatre,* and on TV, besides starring for many years (in the role of Jim Matthews) in the daytime serial *Another World,* he is frequently the guest star in shows such as *Kojak.* Also in the recent past, this veteran of countless Broadway successes, hailed by critic Brooks Atkinson as "one of the best actors in our theatre," starred in the East in two Eugene O'Neill plays, *The Iceman Cometh* and *Long Day's Journey Into Night.* In the latter, playing the father, James Tyrone, he was acclaimed by yet another critic—Emory Lewis —as "the most significant actor in New York." In addition, this actor who has been busy in pictures finds time to paint and teach acting. Onscreen from 1933. IN: *Another Language, The Little Minister, Laddie, Break of Hearts, We Who Are About to Die, Madame X, The Arkansas Traveler, The Cat and the Canary, Atlantic Convoy, Edge of Darkness, Chicago Deadline, My Six Convicts, The Vampire, The Sound and the Fury,* more.

BEAN, ORSON (N.Y.) Comedian. IN: *How to be Very, Very Popular; Anatomy of a Murder.*

BEARD, MATTHEW "STYMIE" (S. Cal.) "Our Gang's" little black boy with the bald head under the derby spent his movie adolescence in wide-eyed anticipation of disaster, and, later, several years of his adulthood in the vortex of its actuality—in prison. Sentenced to 10 years as a drug pusher, he served six—at Fort Worth and Minnesota's Sandstone Federal Prison—before being released as a model prisoner. Earlier he had been in and out of jail often —"petty thief with a prior record." Being a has-been in his teens was the trauma that led to marijuana and a $100-a-day heroin habit supported by thievery and pushing. Out of prison, and having kicked his drug habit there, Stymie sought rehabilitation at Santa Monica's Synanon House. He is today—a stocky, friendly man in his 50s (b. 1925)—an official there, helping others. There, too, he met a fine woman who had been rescued from the life of a "hopeless" alcoholic. Marrying Anne in '68, he became the stepfather of three sons, the eldest studying to be a lawyer. And Stymie's career as an actor, dormant since 1943's *Stormy Weather,* has been reactivated. On TV several times recently, he has played Monty in *Good Times* and Cleon in *Sanford and Son.* In movies he has been in *Truck Turner* with Isaac Hayes and Disney's *The Pond* with Moses Gunn. And, of course, the nostalgic boom for "Our Gang" (or "The Little Rascals," as the series is called on TV) continues unabated, with resultant sentimental dividends for Stymie. In November '74, at the Capitol Cinema in Passaic, N.J., the First Annual Our Gang Comedy Reunion was held, with Stymie and Spanky McFarland in attendance, meeting for the first time in many years. But the dedicated part of his life today is at Synanon. There, he and Anne are members of its choir, famous all over California's Southland. Often the choir sings at the Holiness Church near Watts, where the pastor is the elderly Matthew Beard Sr. "My father just *glows* when we come to sing," says Matthew Jr., looking not unlike the little boy named Stymie who remains so eternally young on television. Onscreen from the late '20s. IN: *Kid Millions, Rainbow on the River, Jezebel, Beloved Brat, Way Down South, The Return of Frank James,* more.

BEARDSLEY, ALICE (N.Y.) Support. IN: *Where the Lilies Bloom.*

BEATTY, NED (S. Cal.) Support. IN: *Deliverance, The Thief Who Came to Dinner, Nashville, W.W. and the Dixie Dancekings,* more.

BEATTY, ROBERT (Eng.) Costar. Onscreen from the '40s. IN: *Odd Man Out, The Girl in the Painting, Captain Horatio Hornblower, Man on a Tightrope, The Horse's Mouth, Tarzan and the Lost Safari, 2001: A Space Odyssey,* more.

BEATTY, WARREN (S. Cal.) Star. Nominated for Best Actor Oscar in *Bonnie and Clyde.* Onscreen from 1961. IN: *The Roman Spring of Mrs. Stone, Splendor in the Grass, All Fall Down, Lilith, Promise Her Anything, The Only Game in Town, $, McCabe and Mrs. Miller, The Parallax View, Shampoo, The Fortune,* more.

BEAUMONT, HUGH (S. Cal.) Leading man/character. Onscreen from 1940. IN: *Michael Shayne, Private Detective; South of Panama, The Fallen Sparrow, Murder Is My Business, Night Without Sleep, Night Passage, The Human Duplicators,* more.

BEAUMONT, SUSAN (Eng.) Leading lady. IN: *Eye Witness, High Tide at Noon, Carry on Nurse,* more.

BECAUD, GILBERT (Fr.) Singer. IN: *Le Pays d'ou Je Viens, Casino de Paris, Croquemitoufle.*

BECHER, JOHN C. (N.Y.) Support. IN: *Up the Sandbox.*

BECK, BILLY (S. Cal.) Support. IN: *Irma la Douce.*

BECK, JOHN (S. Cal.) Support. IN: *Rollerball.*

BECK, KIMBERLY (S. Cal.) Juvenile. IN: *Marnie.*

BECK, VINCENT (S. Cal.) Support. IN: *Santa Claus Conquers the Martians.*

BECKER, TERRY (S. Cal.) Support. IN: *Compulsion, The Fiend That Walked the West, Killer's Cage.*

BECKLEY, TONY (Eng.) Support. IN: *The Penthouse, The Lost Continent, Get Carter,* more.

BECKMAN, HENRY (S. Cal.) Support. IN: *Niagara, The Bramble Bush, The Caper of the Golden Bulls, Marnie, Kiss Me Stupid,* more.

BEDDOE, DON (S. Cal.) In August '74 this veteran character actor became the groom of blonde Joyce Mathews, former actress and former wife of Billy Rose and Milton Berle (she had married and divorced each twice). Joyce's grown-up daughter, Vicki Berle, was matron-of-honor. Perennially active in films, Beddoe is now in his 80s (b. 1888) and Joyce, in her late 50s (b. 1919). Onscreen from 1938. IN: *There's That Woman Again, Golden Boy, The Lone Wolf* series, *Unholy Partners, O.S.S., The Best Years of Our Lives, They Won't Believe Me, Another Part of the Forest, Cyrano de Bergerac, The Iron Mistress, Warlock, Pillow Talk, Papa's Delicate Condition, Generation,* more.

BEDELIA, BONNIE (S. Cal.) Leading lady. IN: *The Gypsy Moths; They Shoot Horses, Don't They?; Lovers and Other Strangers,* more.

BEDFORD, BRIAN (N.Y.) Leading man. IN: *The Angry Silence, The Pad (And How to Use It), Grand-Prix,* more.

BEE, MOLLY (S. Cal.) Singer-leading lady. IN: *Summer Love, Going Steady, The Chartroose Caboose.*

BEERS, FRANCINE (N.Y.) Support. IN: *A New Leaf.*

BEERS, JACK (Conn.) Support. IN: *Nobody Waved Goodbye.*

BEERY, NOAH, JR. (S. Cal.) Leading man/character. Onscreen from the early '20s. IN: *Father and Son, Tailspin Tommy* (and many other serials), *Girls School, Of Mice and Men, Only Angels Have Wings, Sergeant York, Gung Ho!, Corvette K-225, We've Never Been Licked, What a Woman, The Will Rogers Story, War Arrow, Jubal, Little Fauss and Big Halsy, Walking Tall, Walking Tall Part 2,* more.

BEGLEY, ED, JR. (S. Cal.) Comic support. IN: *Charlie and the Angel; Now You See Him, Now You Don't; The Computer Wore Tennis Shoes, Showdown,* more.

BEL GEDDES, BARBARA (N.Y.) Costar. Nominated for Best Supporting Actress Oscar in *I Remember Mama*. Onscreen from 1947. IN: *The Long Night, Caught, Panic in the Streets, 14 Hours, Vertigo, The Five Pennies, Five Branded Women, By Love Possessed, Summertree, The Todd Killings,* more.

BELAFONTE, HARRY (N.Y.) Star. Onscreen from 1953. IN: *Bright Road, Carmen Jones, Island in the Sun, Odds Against Tomorrow, Buck and the Preacher,* more.

BELASCO, LEON (S. Cal.) Character. Onscreen from the '30s. IN: *Broadway Serenade, Lucky Partners, The Mummy's Hand, Holiday Inn, The Gang's All Here, Yolanda and the Thief, Love Happy, Nancy Goes to Rio, Please Believe Me, Can-Can, My Six Loves, Ice Station Zebra,* more.

BELFORD, CHRISTINE (S. Cal.) Leading lady. IN: *Banacek.*

BELGRAVE, CYNTHIA (N.Y.) Support. IN: *The Hospital.*

BELITA (Eng.) Multitalented, she confused American audiences by her versatility—as an ice-skating star (*Ice-Capades*; an Olympic champ, she always professed to dislike skating), as a dramatic actress (*Suspense, The Gangster*), and as a ballerina (*Silk Stockings*). After this last film she danced in the Off Broadway production of *Ulysses in Nighttown* in '58, then returned to England where she appeared in one movie, *The Terrace* ('64), and retired. Previously married for many years to writer Joel McGinnis, she is now, in her early 50s (b. 1924), the wife of American actor James Berwick. They live in Fulham, some miles outside London, where they own and operate a successful greenhouse. Onscreen from 1941. IN: *Silver Skates, The Man on the Eiffel Tower, Never Let Me Go, Invitation to the Dance* ("Ring Around the Rosy" episode), more.

BELL, ARNOLD (Eng.) Character. IN: *Josser in the Army, Jack of All Trades, No Time for Jennifer, Star of India, Svengali, As Long As They're Happy, An Alligator Named Daisy, Seance on a Wet Afternoon,* more.

BELL, MARIE (Fr.) Costar. Onscreen from the '20s. IN: *Innocents of Paris, Figaro, The Night Is Ours, Un Carnet de Bal, La Charrette Fantome, La Bonne Soupe, Sandra, Hotel Paradiso,* more.

BELL, MARY (N.Y.) Support. IN: *The Shrike.*

BELLAMY, MADGE (S. Cal.) A major star (and a beauty) for many years after 1921's *Blind Hearts,* she remained active onscreen through 1936's *Under Your Spell.* Now in her 70s (b. 1900), she has lately been working on her autobiography, *I Was Madge Bellamy,* and, soliciting any assistance that might be forthcoming from long-memoried contemporaries, has made available her address: 1362 E. Holt Road, Ontario, California, 91761. IN: *Hail the Woman, Lorna Doone, The Hottentot, Love's Whirlpool, Love and Glory, The Iron Horse, The Parasite, Lightnin', Summer Bachelors; Bertha, The Sewing Machine Girl; The Telephone Girl, Silk Legs, The Play Girl, White Zombie, Charlie Chan in London, The Daring Young Man,* more.

BELLAMY, RALPH (S. Cal.) Costar. Nominated for Best Supporting Actor Oscar in *The Awful Truth.* Onscreen from 1931. IN: *Forbidden Company, The Secret Six, West of Broadway, Woman in Room 13, Parole Girl, Flying Devils, Spitfire, Hands Across the Table, The Man Who Lived Twice, Fools of Scandal, Carefree, Trade Winds, Boy Meets Girl, His Girl Friday, Ellery Queen, Dive Bomber, Lady in a Jam, Guest in the House, Lady on a Train, The Court-Martial of Billy Mitchell, Sunrise at Campobello, Rosemary's Baby, Cancel My Reservation,* more.

BELLAVER, HARRY (N.Y.) Character. Onscreen from 1939. IN: *Another Thin Man, Perfect Strangers, No Way Out, The Tanks Are Coming, From Here to Eternity, Miss Sadie Thompson, Love Me or Leave Me, The Birds and the Bees, The Old Man and the Sea, Madigan,* more.

BELMONDO, JEAN-PAUL (Fr.) Star. Onscreen from 1959. IN: *A Bout of Souffle, Trapped by Fear, Breathless, Two Women, Monkey in Winter, That Man from Rio, A Woman is a Woman, Male Hunt, Up to His Ears, Is Paris Burning?, Casino Royale, The Thief of Paris, The Tender Scoundrel, Stavisky, The Night Caller,* more.

BELMONT, TERRY (S. Cal.) Using this name in *Men Against the Sky,* he later acted in many under his real name, Lee Bonnell. (See Gale Storm.)

BENEDICT, BILLY (S. Cal.) The humorous Whitey in the first 24 of "The Bowery Boys" pix (1946–51), he is now entering his 70s (b. 1906) and, now billed William, plays supporting roles in many. Onscreen from 1935. IN: *College Scandal, Show Them No Mercy, Libeled Lady, Little Tough Guys in Society, My Little Chickadee, Confessions of Boston Blackie, The Ox-Bow Incident, Funny Girl, Homebodies, The Sting,* more.

BENEDICT, DIRK (S. Cal.) Leading man. IN: *Georgia, Georgia; W,* more.

BENET, BRENDA (S. Cal.) Leading lady. IN: *Track of Thunder.*

BENGAL, RICHARD (N.Y.) Support. IN: *The Window.*

BENJAMIN, RICHARD (N.Y.) Costar. Onscreen from 1953. IN: *Thunder Over the Plains, Goodbye Columbus, Diary of a Mad Housewife, The Steagle, Marriage of a Young Stockbroker, Portnoy's Complaint, Westworld, The Sunshine Boys,* more.

BENNETT, BRUCE (S. Cal.) In 1970, after a C picture, *Lost Island of Kioga,* and after an 80-movie career—begun under his real name, Herman Brix—this leading man called it quits and became a partner in the West Los Angeles firm of Helen Meigs Realty. He felt he'd had it all—played Tarzan twice *(New Adventures of Tarzan, Tarzan and the Green Goddess),* starred in the first ('38) *Lone Ranger* serial, co-starred in a great many A's in the '40s *(Nora Prentiss, The Man I Love,* etc.). Since then the only roles in which he has been seen were three guest-star stints in *Lassie.* Many months ago, he also costarred with Alan Arkin in an offbeat comedy for Paramount, *Deadhead Miles,* playing what seemed to be a dream role—a phantom truck driver dressed all in black, driving a black rig, who appears out of nowhere to help when another trucker—such as Arkin—is in distress. Those who have seen the picture in studio projection rooms have hailed his performance, but the movie has not been released to date and the story is that, for some obscure reason, it may never be. Meanwhile Bruce and his wife of more than four decades, Jeannette, continue to buy older houses and remodel them for sale. Their own West Hollywood home is one they redid and decided to keep. Socially active, the actor, who is now in his 70s (b. 1906) and still chisel-featured and lean, though gray, plays golf and tennis and attends play openings regularly. The Bennetts have two grown children—Christina, a manager of J. Magnin's department store in Beverly Hills, and Christopher, a mortgage broker. Onscreen from 1931. IN: *Touch Down, Million Dollar Racket, Silk and Saddles, The Man with Nine Lives, Phantom Submarine, Sahara, Danger Signal, A Stolen Life, Cheyenne, Dark Passage, The Treasure of Sierra Madre, To the Victor, Undertow, The Second Face, Angels in the Outfield, Sudden Fear, Bottom of the Bottle, Flaming Frontier, The Outsider*, more.

BENNETT, FRAN (Tex.) Support. IN: *Giant, That Night.*

BENNETT, HYWEL (Eng.) Costar. IN: *The Family Way, The Virgin Soldiers, Percy, The Love Ban*, more.

BENNETT, JILL (Eng.) Costar. Onscreen from 1951. IN: *The Long Dark Hall, Moulin Rouge, Aunt Clara, Lust for Life, The Extra Day, The Nanny, Inadmissible Evidence, Mr. Quilp*, more.

BENNETT, JOAN (N.Y.) She remains, in her 60s (b. 1910), an attractive brunette—and busy. Since her long run as the star of the TV soap opera *Dark Shadows*, she has mainly acted onstage—one week here, three weeks there—in such plays as *Butterflies Are Free, Janus* with Dana Andrews, *Never Too Late* with Robert Cummings, etc. After three marriages and divorces (John Fox, Gene Markey, Walter Wanger), and a longtime romance with actor John Emery that ended with his death in '64, she lives alone in a spacious house in Scarsdale. She has, though, a close male friend who spends much time with her there. Five times a year, regularly, she visits Hollywood, though she hasn't made a movie since appearing in a B in '67, *Blast-Off*. In '73 she was scheduled to make her comeback in the made-in-Australia film *Inn of the Damned*, but when she asked for script rewrites—not given—the role went to Judith Anderson. She has published her (and her family's) life-career history, *The Bennett Playbill*, and a book on beauty care. Yes, she says, "I still enjoy acting though every once in a while I talk of quitting. But then my children say, 'Mother, you wouldn't know what to do with yourself if you weren't working,' and, of course, they're right." She has four grown daughters, ranging in age from their late 20s to their late 40s, and 11 grandchildren of assorted ages—some in their mid-20s. Of her grandchildren, she says, "I'm not one of those doting grandmothers. I'm inclined to be stern. I have taken them for two weeks and then I'm done. I can't take the little ones too long. The big ones

—OK." Still, cozily perched in her lap on the day in '73 when the actress was named "Mother of the Year" by the Talbot Perkins Children Service—for her work with foster children—was Stephanie Guest, one of the "little ones." "I don't think of myself as a grandmother," says the star. "The children seem just an extension of me. No, they don't call me Grandmother. The younger ones call me Nona, the Italian word. The older group call me Sweetie." Onscreen from 1928. IN: *Power, Bulldog Drummond, Disraeli, Scotland Yard, The Trial of Vivienne Ware, LittleWomen, The Man Who Reclaimed His Head, Private Worlds, Vogues of 1938, The Texans, Trade Winds, The Man in the Iron Mask, The House Across the Bay, Twin Beds, The Wife Takes a Flyer, Margin for Error, The Woman in the Window, Scarlet Street, The Macomber Affair, Secret Beyond the Door, Father of the Bride, We're No Angels, Desire in the Dust*, more.

BENNETT, MARJORIE (S. Cal.) Character. Onscreen from 1947. IN: *Monsieur Verdoux, June Bride, Limelight, The Cobweb, Home Before Dark, What Ever Happened to Baby Jane?, Mary Poppins, Games, Coogan's Bluff, Charley Varrick*, more.

BENNETT, TONY (N.Y.) Singer. IN: *The Oscar.*

BENSON, GEORGE (Eng.) Character. Onscreen from the '30s. IN: *Convoy, The Man in the White Suit, Cage of Gold, Mother Riley Meets the Vampire, Take a Number, Doctor in the House, Aunt Clara*, more.

BENSON, JOHN (N.Y.) Support. IN: *The Blob.*

BENSON, LUCILLE (S. Cal.) Character. IN: *The Fugitive Kind, Little Fauss and Big Halsy, Cactus in the Snow, Huckleberry Finn*, more.

BENSON, MARTIN (Eng.) Character. IN: *I'll Get You for This, The Night Without Stars, The Frightened Man, West of Zanzibar, Knave of Hearts, The King and I, 23 Paces to Baker Street, Cleopatra, Goldfinger*, more.

BENSON, ROBBY (N.Y.) Leading man. IN: *Jeremy, Ode to Billy Joe.*

BENSON, ROBIN (BOBBY) (N.Y.) Juvenile. Onscreen in the '70s. IN: *Jory* (title role), *The Apple War*, more.

BENTLEY, JOHN (Eng.) Costar. Onscreen from 1947. IN: *The Hills of Donegal, Hammer the Toff, Tread Softly, Black Orchid, Men Against the Sun, Istanbul, Stolen Assignment, Escape in the Sun*, more.

BERADINO, JOHN (S. Cal.) Support. First on-screen in "Our Gang." IN: *The Kid from Cleveland, The Killer Is Loose*, more.

BERENSON, MARISA (N.Y.) Leading lady. IN: *Cabaret, Barry Lyndon.*

BERGEN, CANDICE (S. Cal.) Costar. Onscreen from 1966. IN: *The Group, The Sand Pebbles, The Magus, The Adventurers, The Executioner, Getting Straight, Soldier Blue, Carnal Knowledge, T. R. Baskin, The Wind and the Lion, Bite the Bullet*, more.

BERGEN, EDGAR (S. Cal.) Comedian/ventriloquist. Received a special Academy Award (wooden statuette) in 1937 "for his outstanding comedy creation, Charlie McCarthy." Onscreen from 1938. IN: *The Goldwyn Follies; Charley McCarthy, Detective; You Can't Cheat an Honest Man, Look Who's Laughing, Here We Go Again, Song of the Open Road, I Remember Mama, Captain China, The Hanged Man, Don't Make Waves, The Phynx*, more.

BERGEN, JERRY (N.Y.) Support. IN: *This Way Please, College Swing, The Pirate*, more.

BERGEN, POLLY (N.Y.) Costar. Onscreen from 1950. IN: *At War With the Army, Warpath, The Stooge, Cry of the Hunted, Half a Hero, Escape from Fort Bravo, Cape Fear, Move Over Darling, Kisses for My President*, more. Now a Manhattan business woman.

BERGER, HELMUT (It.) Costar. Onscreen from the late '60s. IN: *The Damned, Dorian Gray, Ash Wednesday, Conversation Piece, The Romantic Englishwoman*, more.

BERGER, SENTA (Ger.) Costar. IN: *The Victors, Major Dundee, The Glory Guys, The Quiller Memorandum; Bang, Bang, You're Dead; The Poppy Is Also a Flower, The Ambushers, Swiss Conspiracy*, more.

BERGERAC, JACQUES (Fr.) The former husband of actresses Ginger Rogers and Dorothy Malone, he was married in '75 to the former Edith Brennan—and, retired from acting, is president of Revlon in Paris. Onscreen from 1954. IN: *Twist of Fate, Strange Intruder, Les Girls, Gigi, A Sunday in Summer, Thunder in the Sun, Fear No More, Fury of Achilles, A Global Affair, The Emergency*, more.

BERGHOF, HERBERT (N.Y.) Character. Onscreen from 1952. IN: *Five Fingers, Diplomatic Courier, Assignment—Paris, Cleopatra, An Affair of the Skin*, more.

BERGMAN, JOEL (N.Y.) Juvenile. Onscreen from the '60s. IN: *The Arrangement; Me, Natalie; Midnight Cowboy, The People Next Door*, more.

BERGMAN, INGRID (Fr.) Star. Won Best Actress Oscars in *Gaslight* and *Anastasia*. Nominated in same category in *For Whom the Bell Tolls, The Bells of St. Mary's*, and *Joan of Arc*. Won Best Supporting Actress Oscar in *Murder on the Orient Express*. Onscreen in Sweden from 1934. IN: *Munkbrogreven, Swedenhielms, En Kvinnas Ansikte*, more. Onscreen in America and internationally since 1939. IN: *Intermezzo, Adam Had Four Sons, Dr. Jekyll and Mr. Hyde, Casablanca, Spellbound, Saratoga Trunk, Notorious, Arch of Triumph, Under Capricorn, Stromboli, Europa, Elena et les Hommes, Paris Does Strange Things, Indiscreet, Inn of the Sixth Happiness, The Visit, The Yellow Rolls-Royce, A Walk in the Spring Rain, Cactus Flower, A Matter of Time*, more.

BERGNER, ELISABETH (Eng.) Star. Nominated for Best Actress Oscar in *Escape Me Never*. The Austrian actress, the toast of London in the early '30s, is in her 70s now (b. 1900), a widow (her famous producer-director husband, Paul Czinner, to whom she was married for many years, died in '72), and has resumed her career after a self-imposed retirement. Deserting movies after her only Hollywood film—1941's *Paris Calling*, with Randolph Scott—she had continued to act onstage, in New York, London, and on the continent, until '63. In this decade, she has starred onstage, in London, in *Catsplay* (receiving critical raves), and, in Zurich, in *Liberty in Bremen* (playing, with conviction and restraint—not always her forte—a murderess). Scheduled to star in London in a revival of Eugene O'Neill's *More Stately Mansions* in '74, she withdrew before the opening. In films, making no attempt to be the great blonde beauty with page-boy hairdo that she was in her heyday, she costarred in '70 with Vincent Price in the horror flick *Cry of the Banshee* and in '74 did a cameo in *The Pedestrian*, produced-directed-written by Maximilian Schell. She appeared in an episode with such other noted, elderly actresses as Lil Dagover and Peggy Ashcroft. Reviewing this, *New York Times* critic Vincent Canby wrote: "Six grande dames in various stages of decay and expensive repair sit at a tea table talking at the top of their voices in a mixture of German, French and English. They trade muddled cliches . . . and wonder whether Verdun was in World War I or II." Confusion and bewilderment she can portray, accomplished actress that she is. They are not, however, characteristics to be found in her private life. Onscreen from 1934. IN: *Ariane, Miss Else, Catherine the Great, As You Like It,*

Dreaming Lips, A Stolen Life (British film pre-dating the Bette Davis film of the same title), more.

BERKELEY, BALLARD (Eng.) Support. IN: East Meets West, The Saint in London, In Which We Serve, Circumstantial Evidence, The Blue Parrot, Men of Sherwood Forest, more.

BERLE, MILTON (S. Cal.) Comedian/charac-ter. Onscreen from 1937. IN: New Faces of 1937, Over My Dead Body, The Dolly Sisters, Always Leave Them Laughing, The Bell Boy, The Loved One; Don't Worry, We'll Think of a Title; The Oscar, The Happening, The Silent Treatment, For Singles Only, The April Fools, Lepke, more.

BERLIN, JEANNIE (N.Y.) Costar. Nominated for Best Supporting Actress Oscar in The Heartbreak Kid. Onscreen from 1972. IN: Sheila Levine Is Dead and Living in New York.

BERLINGER, WARREN (S. Cal.) Support. IN: Three Brave Men, Blue Denim, The Wackiest Ship in the Army, Because They're Young, Bil-lie, Spinout, Lepke, I Will, I Will . . . For Now, more.

BERMAN, SHELLEY (S. Cal.) Comedian/char-acter. IN: The Best Man, Divorce American Style, more.

BERNARD, BARRY (S. Cal.) Character. IN: The Two Mrs. Carrolls, Cry Wolf, The Woman in White, Kind Lady, Titanic, Houdini, The Virgin Queen, more.

BERNARDI, HERSCHEL (S. Cal.) Character. IN: Stakeout on Dope Street, Murder by Con-tract, The Savage Eye, A Cold Wind in August, The George Raft Story, Love With the Proper Stranger, The Honey Pot, more.

BERRY, ERIC (Eng.) Character. IN: Edge of the World, Contraband, The Red Shoes, The Story of Gilbert and Sullivan, Miss Robin Hood, The Intruder, Double Exposure, The Constant Husband, more.

BERRY, KEN (S. Cal.) Leading man. IN: Two for the Seesaw, Hello Down There.

BERSELL, MICHAEL (N.Y.) Juvenile. On-screen from 1968. IN: Paper Lion, more.

BERSELL, SEAN (N.Y.) Juvenile. Onscreen from 1967. IN: Tony Rome, Pigeons, more.

BERTI, MARINA (It.) Leading lady. Onscreen from 1949. IN: The Earth Cries Out, Prince of Foxes, Up Front, Quo Vadis, The Queen of Sheba, Ben Hur, Jessica, Damon and Pythias, Cleopatra, Made in Italy, more.

BERTRAM, BERT (N.Y.) Support. IN: How to Steal a Million.

BESSELL, TED (S. Cal.) Support. IN: Don't Drink the Water, Lover Come Back, The Outsi-der; Captain Newman, M.D.; Billie, more.

BEST, JAMES (S. Cal.) One of Universal-Inter-national's promising stars of '49, he left the starting gate at the same time as Hugh O'Brian, Barbara Rush, and Rock Hudson. Though he appeared in 58 movies and more than 200 TV shows, first-class stardom did not come. In 1970 he relocated in Jackson, Miss., where a local millionaire bankrolled two independent movies produced by Best. Also, he played a supporting role in Sounder, made on nearby location. To-day Best is back in Hollywood and has co-starred in such recent TV-movies as The Runa-way Barge with Bo Hopkins and Savages with Andy Griffith. IN: Winchester 73, Comanche Territory, The Cimarron Kid, Apache Drums, Column South, Seminole, The Caine Mutiny, Come Next Spring, Last of the Badmen, The Naked and the Dead, Black Spurs, Shenan-doah, First to Fight, more.

BETHENCOURT, FRANCIS (N.Y.) Support. IN: This Earth Is Mine.

BETHUNE, ZINA (S. Cal.) Support. IN: Sun-rise at Campobello, Who's That Knocking at My Door?

BETTGER, LYLE (S. Cal.) A bit heavier in his 60s (b. 1915) than when he was Paramount's best blond menace, this still-forceful actor plays guest-star roles (often as a police com-mander) on TV (Hawaii Five-O, Police Story, etc.), appears in commercials (Grape Nuts, Texaco), and does much "voice-over" work in TV commercials. "I am not as active as I was, say, 10 or 15 years ago," admits the now-gray actor, "but then neither is anyone else, with rare exceptions." While not suffering finan-cially himself, he is greatly concerned about his fellow actors and Hollywood's movie and TV industry in general. Citing the far fewer films and TV episodes made, Bettger adds, "This is slow but steady strangulation." A part of the Hollywood scene since his debut in 1950's No Man of Her Own, he professes a growing disen-chantment with it, saying, "Most men can re-main reasonably happy or content if their busi-ness continues to stimulate their interest, but ours today is so dismaying, there is little love or fun left in it." The latter, for Bettger, is derived from his family. He and his wife of more than three decades, the former actress Mary Rolfe, have two grown sons, Franklin and Lyle Jr., who have chosen non-show-business careers, and a college-age daughter. Hawaii would seem his destined location when he retires. "Some years ago," he says, "I managed to acquire a lovely spot on the island of Maui, and ever since we have spent as much time as we could over there." IN: *Union Station, Dear Brat, The Greatest Show on Earth, The Denver and the Rio Grande, The Vanquished, The Great Sioux Uprising, Carnival Story, Drums Across the River, Gunfight at the O.K. Corral, Nevada Smith, Return of the Gunfighter, Golden Bullet, Impasse*, more.

BETTIS, VALERIE (N.Y.) Dancer-actress. IN: *The Dance of Life, Affair in Trinidad, Let's Do It Again*.

BETZ, CARL (S. Cal.) Costar. Onscreen from 1953. IN: *Powder River, The President's Lady, Vickie, Inferno, Dangerous Crossing, City of Bad Men, The Meal*, more.

BEUTEL, JACK (Ore.) Howard Hughes' Western extravaganza *The Outlaw* made a lasting star of Jane Russell but did nothing of the sort for the slim-hipped, curly-haired Texan who played the title role. It was not, incidentally, his first time onscreen, though heralded as his debut; he had previously played bits in *Gone With the Wind* and *Congo Maisie*. After *The Outlaw*, first released in '43 (though "officially" in '47), Hughes kept his discovery sitting on the bench for eight years. Finally, in the '50s, he appeared (sometimes billed Buetel) in *White Witch Doctor* and five Westerns (*Rest of the Badmen, Rose of Cimarron*, etc.). After 1959's *Mustang*, he tossed in his acting spurs for good. Today, in his late 50s (b. 1917), a good deal heavier and a marriage or two later (among his wives: actress Jill Meredith and Gloria Jean Bailey), Jack Beutel is an investment counselor in Portland. Discoverer Howard Hughes was reportedly not one of his accounts. Onscreen from 1939. ALSO IN: *The Half Breed* and *Jesse James' Women*.

BEVERLEY, HELEN (S. Cal.) Support. IN: *The Light Ahead, Overture to Glory, The Master Race, The Robe*, more.

BEY, TURHAN (Austria) In his 50s now (b. 1920), considerably heavier than in his Hollywood days, quite bald, and at last report still unmarried, he owns and operates "Glamour Travel," a travel agency located on Paradisgasse in Vienna. He has also achieved a considerable reputation as a photographer. And he is known now by his full name: Turhan Selahettin Schultavy Bey. One of his best friends from his years in California is actor Hurd Hatfield. They have occasionally vacationed together in Spain. Onscreen from 1941. IN: *Burma Convoy, Footsteps in the Dark, Arabian Nights, Danger in the Pacific, White Savage, Dragon Seed, Follow the Boys, The Climax, Ali Baba and the Forty Thieves, Sudan, Frisco Sal, The Mummy's Ghost, Adventures of Casanova; Parole, Inc.; Song of India*, more, including 1953's *Prisoners of the Casbah*, his last.

BEYMER, RICHARD (S. Cal.) Leading man. IN: *The Diary of Anne Frank, West Side Story, The Longest Day, Hemingway's Adventures of a Young Man, The Stripper*, more. Now a producer.

BHASKAR (N.Y.) Character lead. IN: *I Drink Your Blood*.

BIANCHI, DANIELA (It.) Leading lady. IN: *From Russia With Love; Weekend, Italian Style;* more.

BIBERMAN, ABNER (S. Cal.) Character. Onscreen from 1919. IN: *Each Dawn I Die, Another Thin Man, Gunga Din, Singapore Woman, Enemy Agent, Beyond the Blue Horizon; Little Tokyo, U.S.A.; The Leopard Man, The Bridge of San Luis Rey, Keys of the Kingdom, Back to Bataan, Winchester 73, Elephant Walk, Knock on Wood*, more.

BIKEL, THEODORE (N.Y.) Costar. Nominated for Best Supporting Actor Oscar in *The Defiant Ones*. Onscreen from 1951. IN: *The African Queen, Never Let Me Go, The Little Kidnappers, A Day to Remember, The Pride and the Passion, The Enemy Below, I Want to Live!, A Dog of Flanders, My Fair Lady, Sands of Kalahari; The Russians Are Coming, The Russians Are Coming; My Side of the Mountain, Nobody Loves a Drunken Indian, The Little Ark, Two Hundred Motels*, more.

BILL, TONY (S. Cal.) Leading man. Onscreen from 1963. IN: *Come Blow Your Horn, None But the Brave, You're a Big Boy Now, Never a Dull Moment, Ice Station Zebra, Castle Keep, Shampoo, Las Vegas Lady*, more. Now also a producer.

BILLINGSLEY, BARBARA (S. Cal.) Leading lady. Onscreen from 1950. IN: *Shadow on the Wall, Trial Without Jury, Three Guys Named Mike, The Tall Target, Woman in the Dark, The Careless Years*, more.

BILLINGSLEY, JENNIFER (S. Cal.) Leading lady. IN: *Lady in a Cage, The Young Lovers*.

BINNEY, CONSTANCE (Pa.) Greatly popular in silents—well into the '20s—she is in her 70s now, lives in Philadelphia, and has been married to socialite Henry Wharton Jr. since '32. Onscreen from the teens. IN: *Sporting Life, The Test of Honor, Stolen Kiss, Erstwhile Susan, The Case of Becky, Such a Little Queen*, more.

BINNS, EDWARD (S. Cal.) Support. Onscreen from 1951. IN: *Teresa, Without Warning, Vice Squad, Twelve Angry Men, Compulsion, The Man in the Net, North by Northwest, Judgment at Nuremberg, Fail Safe, The Americanization of Emily, Patton, Night Moves*, more.

BIRD, BILLIE (S. Cal.) Support. IN: *The Mating Season, Just Across the Street, Somebody Loves Me, Secret of Deep Harbor*, more.

BIRD, NORMAN (Eng.) Support. IN: *An Inspector Calls, Man in the Moon, Victim, Whistle Down the Wind, Cash on Demand, The Hill*, more.

BIRKIN, JANE (Eng.) Leading lady. IN: *Seven Deaths by Prescription*, more.

BIRNEY, DAVID (S. Cal.) Leading man. IN: *Trial by Combat*.

BISHOP, JOEY (S. Cal.) Comedian. Onscreen from 1958. IN: *Onionhead, The Deep Six, Ocean's 11, Pepe, Johnny Cool, Valley of the Dolls*, more.

BISHOP, JULIE (S. Cal.) Slender and extraordinarily lovely in face and figure, in her 60s (b. 1914), Julie has been the wife of a well-to-do Beverly Hills surgeon, Dr. William Bergin, since '68. In 1939 Julie was first married to, and shortly divorced from, Walter Brooks, whose socialite mother, Mrs. Louise Cromwell Brooks MacArthur Atwill, had once been the wife of Gen. Douglas MacArthur and was then married to actor Lionel Atwill. In '44 the actress married Lt. Col. Clarence Shoop (later General); theirs was a long and happy marriage—much of it spent in Europe—lasting until his death in the '60s. In those years Julie soft-pedaled the career that began when she was nine in 1923's *Maytime*. (Billed Jacqueline Wells, her real name, she continued to use this in dozens of pix, through 1941's *Back in the Saddle*. Warners then signed her to a star-making contract and she became Julie Bishop. She does not relish conversation about this long 74-film career, saying, "It does tend to date one.") By General Shoop she has two children: Stephen, an Air Force jet pilot, and Pamela. An actress, blonde Pamela has been in many TV series, in the movie *Changes*, and costarred, in the role of Allison (replacing Kathy Glass), in the now-departed daytime TV show *Return to Peyton Place*. She was also presented on a Bob Hope show in the spring of '75 as one of Hollywood's "Stars of Tomorrow." For herself, Julie Bishop paints still lifes (has had exhibitions) and devotes much time to ARCS (Achievement Rewards for College Scientists), an organization that presents scholarships to outstanding students in science and engineering; she recently completed a two-year term as its national president. As for her screen career—she hasn't been seen since 1957's *The Big Land*. While admitting, "My husband does not want me to work," Julie Bishop also confesses, "There are times when I long to return to the work I love . . . and someday I might." Onscreen as Jacqueline Wells from 1923. IN: *Maytime, Tarzan the Fearless, The Black Cat, Happy Landing, Coronado, Paid to Dance, Torture Ship, The Girl in 313*, more. Onscreen as Julie Bishop from 1941. IN: *International Squadron, Lady Gangster, Busses Roar, The Hard Way, Action in the North Atlantic, Princess O'Rourke, Rhapsody in Blue, Cinderella Jones, Murder in the Music Hall, Sabre Jet, The High and the Mighty, Headline Hunters*, more.

BISSELL, WHIT (S. Cal.) Character. Onscreen from 1943. IN: *Destination Tokyo, Brute Force, A Double Life, He Walked by Night, Anna Lucasta, The Killer That Stalked New York, Red Mountain, The Caine Mutiny, Riot in Cell Block 11, Not As a Stranger, Invasion of the Body Snatchers, The Defiant Ones, Birdman of Alcatraz, The Manchurian Candidate, Airport, Psychic Killer*, more.

BISSET, JACQUELINE (S. Cal.) Costar. Onscreen from 1965. IN: *The Knack, Casino Royale, Two for the Road, The Detective, Bullitt, Airport, The Thief Who Came to Dinner, Day for Night, Murder on the Orient Express, St. Ives, Murder on the Bridge*, more.

BIXBY, BILL (S. Cal.) Leading man. Onscreen from 1962. IN: *Lonely Are the Brave, Ride Beyond Vengeance; Doctor, You've Got to be Kidding; Clambake, The Apple Dumpling Gang*, more.

BJORK, ANITA (Swe.) Star. Onscreen from 1942. IN: *Himlaspelet, Kvinna utan Ansikte, Miss Julie, Night People, Of Love and Lust, Loving Couples, Adalen 31*, more.

BJORNSTRAND, GUNNAR (Swe.) Star. Onscreen from 1931. IN: *The False Millionaire, Frenzy, Smiles of a Summer Night, Wild Strawberries, The Magician, A Lesson in Love, Through a Glass Darkly; My Sister, My Love; Persona, Here's Your Life*, more.

BLACK, CILLA (Eng.) Singer. IN: *Work . . . Is a Four-Letter Word*.

BLACK, KAREN (S. Cal.) Costar. Nominated for Best Supporting Actress Oscar in *Five Easy Pieces*. Onscreen from 1969. IN: *Easy Rider, A Gunfight; Drive, He Said; Born to Win, Cisco Pike, Portnoy's Complaint, Hard Contract, You're a Big Boy Now, Law and Disorder, The Great Gatsby, The Day of the Locust, Airport 1975, Family Plot, Crime and Passion*, more.

BLACKBURN, CLARICE (N.Y.) Support. IN: *The Violators, Pretty Poison.*

BLACKBURN TWINS, THE (N.Y.) Perhaps best recalled as June Allyson's male dance partners in the "Thou Swell" number in *Words and Music*, they now own and operate a dancing school on Long Island. ALSO IN: *She's Working Her Way Through College.*

BLACKMAN, DON (S. Cal.) Support. IN: *On the Waterfront, Santiago.*

BLACKMAN, HONOR (Eng.) Leading lady. Onscreen from the late '40s. IN: *Quartet* ("The Alien Corn" episode), *The Conspirator, So Long at the Fair; Come Die, My Love; The Glass Tomb, A Night to Remember, Jason and the Argonauts, Goldfinger, Life at the Top, Captain Remo and the Floating City*, more.

BLACKMAN, JOAN (S. Cal.) Leading lady. Onscreen from 1958. IN: *Good Day for a Hanging, Career, Visit to a Small Planet, Blue Hawaii, The Destructors, Moonrunners*, more.

BLAIN, GERARD (Fr.) Costar. IN: *Deadlier Than the Male, Crime and Punishment, The Cousins, Hatari, Run With the Devil, The Eye of the Needle*, more.

BLAINE, MARTIN (S. Cal.) Support. IN: *The Satan Bug.*

BLAINE, VIVIAN (N.Y.) In '75 the singer-actress costarred with Milton Berle in the play *The Best of Everybody* that, headed for Broadway, closed during its Chicago tryout. 20th Century-Fox's onetime "Cherry Blonde" is in her 50s now (b. 1924) but the zing in her performing is still abundantly there. She has been married since '73 to real estate executive Stuart Clark. Onscreen from 1942. IN: *It Happened in Flatbush, He Hired the Boss, Nob Hill, Greenwich Village, Something for the Boys, State Fair, Doll Face, Come Back to Me, Three Little Girls in Blue, Skirts Ahoy!, Guys and Dolls*, more.

BLAIR, BETSY (Eng.) Costar. Nominated for Best Supporting Actress Oscar in *Marty*. In her 50s (b. 1923), she remains active—particularly in films made abroad. And her daughter Kerry (by former husband Gene Kelly), married since

'70 to Dr. John Novick and living in London, has twice made her a grandmother. Onscreen in American movies from 1947. IN: *The Guilt of Janet Ames, The Snake Pit, A Double Life, Kind Lady, Public Pigeon No. 1*, more. Onscreen in movies made abroad since 1956. IN: *Calle Mayor, Il Grido, The Halliday Brand, All Night Long; Marry Me! Marry Me!; A Delicate Balance*, more.

BLAIR, JANET (S. Cal.) Columbia's perkiest second-string star of the '40s (Hayworth was always first), this still-beautiful redhead remains just as vivacious in her 50s (b. 1921). Costarred with Henry Fonda in the TV series *The Smith Family* (1971–72), she has lately starred on tour in such musicals as *Irene, Mame* (longtime pal Jeff Donnell, from *My Sister Eileen* days, "babysat" her children while she was away for this), and *Follies*. The director of the Los Angeles Shubert Theatre, incidentally, at which she assumed the *Follies* role created by Dorothy Collins, is Nick Mayo, Janet's most recent ex-husband. (She had previously been married to musician Lou Busch.) Married 20 years, and divorced in '72, she and Nick Mayo have two teenage children—Amanda and Andrew. Living alone with them now in a house far less grand than the Bel Air mansion she previously owned, Janet says she gives her children a long leash: "I have to let them grow and fall down and take their own bruises." Her own most bruising experience, she says, was this latest divorce: "The whole thing came as a shock to me. I was distraught. I went into complete isolation—ran the house, scrubbed floors, watched television with the children. Sometimes we were just alone. I had custody of them, of course, but who gets custody of the friends? You know," she adds with that Irish fire that has long been her trademark, "no one called me for three months." She also fired off this cannonade at certain well-meaning friends who eventually did call: "If one more person says to me, 'Honey, you must go out and make a life for yourself,' I'll spit. It's like you just got out of surgery, still bleeding, and you're expected to run a 100-yard dash." For now, for her children, and to be near them, she has forsaken touring in musicals—her preferred professional activity—to remain in Hollywood where she frequently guests on such TV series as *Marcus Welby*. She is waiting, she admits, for something splendid and unexpected to occur in her life, and she says, "What I want while I'm waiting is to make myself smooth, clear, calm and all together." Onscreen from 1941. IN: *Three Girls About Town, My Sister Eileen, Something to Shout About, Once Upon a Time, Tonight and Every Night, The Fabulous Dorseys, The Fuller Brush Man, Boys' Night Out; Burn, Witch, Burn*; more.

BLAIR, JOAN (S. Cal.) Leading lady. IN: *The Murder of Dr. Harrigan, Mr. District Attorney, The Strange Death of Adolf Hitler, Deadline for Murder*, more.

BLAIR, JUNE (S. Cal.) Leading lady. Onscreen from 1957. IN: *Hell Bound, Island of Lost Women, The Lone Texan, The Fiend Who Walked the West, The Rabbit Trap, Mardi Gras*, more. Retired.

BLAIR, LINDA (S. Cal.) Juvenile star. Nominated for Best Supporting Actress Oscar in *The Exorcist*. Onscreen from 1971. IN: *Airport 1975, The Exorcist II*.

BLAIR, NICKY (S. Cal.) Support. IN: *Viva Las Vegas*.

BLAKE, AMANDA (Ariz.) Leading lady. Onscreen from 1950. IN: *Stars in My Crown, Battleground, On the Sunny Side of the Street, The Smuggler's Girl, Scarlet Angel, Cattle Town, Lili, About Mrs. Leslie, Adventures of Hajji Baba, The Glass Slipper*, more.

BLAKE, LARRY (S. Cal.) Character. Onscreen from 1937. IN: *The Road Back, Nurse From Brooklyn, They Made Her a Spy, Smash-Up, Holiday Affair, Sunset Boulevard, High Noon, Inside Detroit*, more.

BLAKE, MARIE/a.k.a. BLOSSOM ROCK (S. Cal.) The wisecracking switchboard operator in the "Kildare" movies, elder sister of the late Jeanette MacDonald, and, as Blossom Rock, the Granny in TV's *The Addams Family*, has resided for some years at the Motion Picture and TV Country Home. A stroke has deprived her of her speech and the use of her right hand, but she is still up and about and most active. The best illustration of this is the song-and-dance act she and brother-in-law Gene Raymond—a faithful, frequent visitor—did at a recent open house. (He did the singing, and together they did the dancing.) The resultant applause was like that she and her late husband, Clarence W. Rock, who died in '60, used to get when they were vaudeville headliners. The only time she leaves the Home today is to go for long drives with Gene Raymond. Explaining her professional names, when she still possessed speech, the actress said she was born Blossom MacDonald. Then she became Blossom Rock by marriage. And she became Marie Blake—under which name she made dozens of movies between 1938's *Everybody Sing* and 1952's *The Brigand*—on the advice of a numerologist (for a $5 fee). She eventually settled on Blossom Rock as both her professional and legal name, she said then, "because my bank accounts got all mixed up." Her age? She has never said;

perhaps because sister Jeanette's age was always a closely guarded studio secret. "Just say," said Marie/Blossom, in one of the last interviews she was ever able to give, "that I'm in pretty good shape for a gal of my years." So she was, and so—all considered—she remains, smiling and cheerful as always. Onscreen from 1938. IN (as Marie Blake): *Love Finds Andy Hardy, Mannequin, Dramatic School, The Women, Calling Dr. Kildare, They Knew What They Wanted, Caught in the Draft, Remember the Day, Small Town Deb, I Married a Witch, The Major and the Minor, Mourning Becames Electra, Love Nest*, more. IN (as Blossom Rock): *Hilda Crane, From the Terrace, The Second Time Around, The Best Man*, more.

BLAKE, ROBERT/a.k.a. BOBBY BLAKE/ a.k.a. MICKEY GUBITOSI (S. Cal.) As child actor Mickey Gubitosi he appeared, from the late '30s, in 40 "Our Gang" comedies. From 1942 to the '50s he was billed Bobby Blake. IN: *Mokey, Andy Hardy's Double Life, China Girl, Lost Angel, The Woman in the Window, The Horn Blows at Midnight, Cheyenne Rider, Dakota, In Old Sacramento, Treasure of Sierra Madre, The Black Rose*, more. Billed Robert Blake from 1958. IN: *Revolt in the Big House, Pork Chop Hill, Town Without Pity, The Greatest Story Ever Told, This Property Is Condemned, In Cold Blood, Tell Them Willie Boy Is Here, Electra Glide in Blue*, more.

BLAKE, WHITNEY (S. Cal.) Leading lady. IN: *-30-*.

BLAKELY, COLIN (Eng.) Support. IN: *The Hellions, This Sporting Life, Underworld Informers, A Man for All Seasons, Charlie Bubbles, The Private Life of Sherlock Holmes, Something to Hide*, more.

BLAKELY, JAMES (S. Cal.) Leading man. Onscreen from 1934. IN: *Broadway Bill, Paris in Spring, Two for Tonight, She Couldn't Take It, The Shadow Strikes*, more. Later a movie studio executive. (See Mary Carlisle.)

BLAKELY, SUSAN (N.Y.) Leading lady. IN: *The Way We Were, The Lords of Flatbush, Report to the Commissioner, Capone, The Towering Inferno, Shampoo*.

BLAKLEY, RONEE (S. Cal.) Leading lady. Nominated for Best Supporting Actress Oscar in *Nashville*.

BLANC, MEL (S. Cal.) Famous cartoon voice/ character. IN: *Neptune's Daughter; Kiss Me, Stupid*; more.

BLANCHARD, "DOC" (Tex.) His one movie, *Spirit of West Point* with Glenn Davis, was of course the offshoot of their being West Point's unbeatable gridiron combination in the '40s. In his 50s now (b. 1925), Felix "Doc" Blanchard, a retired Air Force colonel, lives with his wife, Jody, beside a lake in Burnet. They have two daughters in college, Jo and Theresa, and a businessman son in Atlanta, Tony, who is married and has two youngsters.

BLANE, SALLY (S. Cal.) Married to actor-director Norman Foster since 1934, and still slim and attractive in her 60s (b. 1910), the former leading lady has a grown son and a daughter, Gretchen, named after sister Loretta Young—Gretchen being Loretta's real name. Leaving movies after 1939's *Charlie Chan at Treasure Island*, Sally has played only one brief role since, in 1955's *A Bullet for Joey* with Edward G. Robinson. Onscreen from the late '20s. IN: "The Collegians" series, *Vanishing Pioneer, Tanned Legs, Eyes of the Underworld, X Marks the Spot, The Star Witness, I Am a Fugitive from a Chain Gang, No More Women, Night of Terror, This Is the Life, Numbered Women, Way Down South, The Story of Alexander Graham Bell*, more. (See Norman Foster.)

BLEIFER, JOHN (S. Cal.) Character. Onscreen from the '20s. IN: *We Americans, Captured, Black Fury, Les Miserables, Charlie Chan at Monte Carlo, Mr. Moto Takes a Vacation, The Mark of Zorro, In Our Time, The Juggler, The Hook*, more.

BLETCHER, BILLY (S. Cal.) One of Sennett's funniest Keystone comics and later one of Hal Roach's—costarring with Billy Gilbert in two-reelers and appearing in "Our Gang" (most often as Spanky McFarland's dad)—this little old baldie is still going strong in his 80s (b. 1894). Besides doing voices for Disney and children's records, he is seen regularly in supporting roles in features. Still married (since '15) to his original wife, the former Arline Roberts, he has one daughter. Onscreen from the teens. IN: *Branded Men, Diplomaniacs, The Lost City; High, Wide and Handsome; Buck Benny Rides Again, Chatterbox*, more.

BLONDELL, GLORIA (S. Cal.) Support. IN: *The Daredevil Drivers, Accidents Will Happen, Four's a Crowd, Don't Bother to Knock, White Lightning*, more. Retired.

BLONDELL, JOAN (S. Cal.) Costar. Nominated for Best Supporting Actress Oscar in *The Blue Veil*. Onscreen from 1930. IN: *Sinner's Holiday, Public Enemy, Night Nurse, The Greeks Had a Word for Them, Three on a Match, Gold Diggers of 1933, Dames, Three Men on a Horse, The King and the Chorus Girl, Stand-In, East Side of Heaven, Good Girls Go to Paris, Model Wife, Topper Returns, Cry Havoc, A Tree Grows in Brooklyn, Nightmare Alley, The Desk Set, Will Success Spoil Rock Hunter?, The Cincinnati Kid, The Trouble with Angels, Waterhole #3, The Delta Factor, The Phynx, Support Your Local Gunfighter*, more.

BLOOM, CLAIRE (N.Y.) Costar. Onscreen from 1948. IN: *The Blind Goddess, Limelight, The Man Between, Richard III, The Brothers Karamazov, Look Back in Anger, The Chapman Report, The Spy Who Came in From the Cold, Charly, The Illustrated Man, Islands in the Stream*, more.

BLOOM, VERNA (S. Cal.) Leading lady. IN: *Medium Cool, The Hired Hand, High Plains Drifter*.

BLYE, MAGGIE/a.k.a. MARGARET BLYE (S. Cal.) Leading lady. IN: *Hombre, Any Wednesday, Waterhole #3, Every Little Crook and Nanny, Hard Times*, more.

BLYTH, ANN (S. Cal.) Star. Nominated for Best Supporting Actress Oscar in *Mildred Pierce*. For a "retiree"—last onscreen in 1957's *The Helen Morgan Story*—this singer-dramatic actress is indeed active. Besides doing TV commercials (one for cupcakes recently), she each year plays the Light Opera circuit (Milwaukee, St. Louis, Sacramento, etc.) in musical productions. In '75 it was in *Bittersweet* and, as for several seasons, *The Sound of Music*. Starring in *South Pacific*, a year or so previous, she was awarded the "Show Stopper Plaque," given only when a show sells out its complete run in all cities played. So her movie "name," as does her performing, remains potent. It is because of her children and her wish to be with them that Ann Blyth continues to refuse movie offers. It is also because the youngest of them can travel with her in the summer that she has chosen this "substitute" career. Ann and her husband (since '53), Dr. James McNulty, an obstetrician, have five youngsters: Timothy Patrick (born 1954), Maureen Ann ('55), Kathleen Mary ('57), Terence Grady ('60), and Eileen Alana ('63). The youngest, she feels, is likely to be the only one of them to follow in her professional footsteps. As for the others, Timothy has already chosen a medical career, Maureen is domestically inclined, Kathleen has spoken of a desire to work with deaf children, and the youngest boy, Terry, she laughs, "is at that marvelous age when he just wants to have fun." The McNulty home in Toluca Lake (near both Warners and Universal, where she began her career) is a large establishment that manages to be both homey and extraordinarily glamorous—in its furnishings and Olympic-size pool. Frequent visitors are Dennis Day and his family, Dennis being James McNulty's brother. Dennis was also proudly present the day in 1973, in New York City, when Ann and her husband were invested with the rank of Lady and Knight of the Holy Sepulchre by Cardinal Cooke. Ruling out the likelihood of returning to the screen, at least in the foreseeable future, Ann Blyth—looking stunning enough in her 40s (b. 1928) to play leads for another decade—says: "Hollywood has been very good to me. I was never hurt by the town or the profession. I have only a deep appreciation for all the joy it has brought me. I have my husband, my children, my religion, my home, my work when I want it. I consider myself a blessed woman." Onscreen from 1944. IN: *Chip Off the Old Block, The Merry Monahans, Brute Force, Killer McCoy, Mr. Peabody and the Mermaid, Another Part of the Forest, Once More My Darling, Our Very Own, The Great Caruso, All the Brothers Were Valiant, Rose Marie, The Student Prince, Kismet, Slander, The Buster Keaton Story,* more.

BLYTHE, ERIK (N.Y.) Support. IN: *Invasion U.S.A.*

BLYTHE, JOHN (Eng.) Support. Onscreen from the '40s. IN: *This Happy Breed, Dear Murderer, Easy Money, The Huggetts Abroad, Lilli Marlene, Meet Mr. Malcolm, Three Steps to the Gallows, Doublecross,* more.

BOARDMAN, ELEANOR (S. Cal.) On the screen eight years and in more than 30 movies, through 1931's *The Squaw Man,* she always had intelligence and class. Today, in her late 70s (b. 1898), looking remarkably unchanged—tall, slender, and gently blonde—she is living proof that the cameras caught her exactly as she was. Wealthy and socially gregarious, she lives alone in a beautiful house near Santa Barbara, in the exclusive community of Montecito. Onetime husband (1926–33) director King Vidor (he was frequently her director) lives nearby on his great ranch, and visits often. They have two daughters, Antonia and Belinda, and several grandchildren, all married. Eleanor has no children by her second marriage, to French director Henri (Harry) D'Arrast, dead since '68. They lived several years in France in his family chateau at Etienne de Baigorry in the Pyrenees, which he willed to her though they had by then long since been divorced. For some time in the '50s, courtesy her friendship with both Marion Davies and William Randolph Hearst, she was the Paris fashion correspondent for *Harper's Bazaar* and the Hearst newspapers. Fashion has been a compelling, lifelong interest of hers. She was a high-fashion model prestardom, and today still designs and makes all her own clothes. A contented woman, she admits to few regrets, but one is surely that her final movie, *It Happened in Spain* ('34), made abroad and directed by D'Arrast, has never been shown in the States. Onscreen from 1923. IN: *Souls for Sale, Vanity Fair, The Day of Faith, Wine of Youth, So This Is Marriage, Proud Flesh, The Circle, Exchange of Wives, The Crowd, Redemption, The Great Meadow, Women Love Once,* more.

BOAZ, CHUCK (N.Y.) Support. IN: *My Gun Is Quick.*

BOCHNER, LLOYD (S. Cal.) Support. Onscreen from 1963. IN: *Drums of Africa, Sylvia, Tony Rome, Point Blank, The Detective, The Horse in the Gray Flannel Suit, Tiger by the Tail, Dunwich, Ulzana's Raid, The Man in the Glass Booth,* more.

BODDEY, MARTIN (Eng.) Support. Onscreen from the '40s. IN: *State Secret, Seven Days to Noon, The Franchise Affair, Rob Roy, Doctor in the House, Svengali, How to Murder a Rich Uncle, The Kitchen,* more.

BOEHM, KARL (Ger.) Costar. IN: *The Magnificent Rebel, Forever My Love, The Wonderful World of the Brothers Grimm, Come Fly With Me, Rififi in Tokyo, Cross of the Living, The Venetian Affair, Court Martial,* more.

BOGARDE, DIRK (Fr.) Star. Onscreen from the late '40s. IN: *Quartet* ("The Alien Corn" episode), *So Long at the Fair, Penny Princess, Doctor in the House, The Sea Shall Not Have Them, The Spanish Gardener, A Tale of Two Cities, The Doctor's Dilemma, Libel, Song Without End, Victim, I Could Go on Singing, The Servant, Darling, Modesty Blaise, Accident, Justine, The Damned; Oh, What a Lovely War; Death in Venice, Permission to Kill,* more.

BOIS, CURT (S. Cal.) Character. First onscreen in Germany. IN: *Der Schlemihl,* more. Onscreen in America from 1937. IN: *Tovarich, Gold Diggers in Paris, The Amazing Dr. Clitterhouse, He Stayed for Breakfast, That Night in Rio, Hold Back the Dawn, Princess O'Rourke, Cover Girl, Saratoga Trunk, Arch of Triumph, The Woman in White, Caught, A Kiss in the Dark, Joe Palooka Meets Humphrey,* more.

BOLES, JIM (S. Cal.) Character. IN: *The Tattooed Stranger, The Man With My Face, The Trouble With Angels, The Love God?, P.J.,* more.

BOLGER, RAY (S. Cal.) Comedian-dancer. Onscreen from 1936. IN: *The Great Ziegfeld,*

Rosalie, The Wizard of Oz, Sunny, The Harvey Girls, Make Mine Laughs, Look for the Silver Lining, Where's Charley?, April in Paris, The Entertainer, more.

BOLKAN, FLORINDA (Brazil) Leading lady. Onscreen from the late '60s. IN: *Candy, The Damned, The Last Valley; Metti, Una Sera a Cena; The Island, Royal Flash, A Brief Vacation, Assassination in Sarajevo,* more.

BOLLING, TIFFANY (S. Cal.) Support. IN: *The Marriage of a Young Stockbroker, The Wild Party,* more.

BOLOGNA, JOSEPH (N.Y.) Costar. IN: *Made for Each Other, Cops and Robbers.*

BOND, DAVID (S. Cal.) Character. Onscreen from the '40s. IN: *That Lady in Ermine, We Were Strangers, Song of India, Sirocco, Lust for Life, The Silencers,* more.

BOND, DEREK (Eng.) Costar. Onscreen from 1946. IN: *The Captive Heart, Nicholas Nickleby, Scott of the Antarctic, Tony Draws a Horse, The Caretaker's Daughter, Trouble in Store, High Terrace, Black Tide,* more.

BOND, LILLIAN (S. Cal.) Brunette, dimpled, and curvaceous, and with that charming English accent, she was one of the best "other women" in many in the '30s. She continued to act during her marriage (1935–44) to millionaire Sidney Smith, retiring soon after their divorce and after playing a supporting role in *The Picture of Dorian Gray.* She returned for minor parts in three in the '50s: *Man in the Attic, The Maze,* and *The Pirates of Tripoli.* In her 60s now (b. 1910), married again and living in Northridge—an exclusive mountainous Los Angeles suburb—she devotes herself to gardening and painting. Onscreen from 1931. IN: *Stepping Out, The Squaw Man, Union Depot, The Trial of Vivienne Ware, The Old Dark House, When Strangers Marry, Hell Bent for Love, China Seas, The Bishop Misbehaves, A Desperate Chance for Ellery Queen,* more.

BOND, RUDY (N.Y.) Character. Onscreen from 1950. IN: *With These Hands, A Streetcar Named Desire, Miss Sadie Thompson, On the Waterfront, 12 Angry Men, Middle of the Night, The Mountain Road,* more.

BOND, SHEILA (N.Y.) Support. IN: *The Marrying Kind.*

BOND, SUDIE (N.Y.) Support. IN: *A Thousand Clowns, Guns of the Trees, Andy, Cold Turkey, Jump, They Might Be Giants,* more.

BOND, TOMMY "BUTCH" (S. Cal.) Now entering his 50s but still easily recognizable as "Our Gang's" tough little "Butch," Tommy is Property Master for Metromedia Television in Hollywood, having dropped out of acting 25 years ago. He has been married since 1953, soon after he graduated from Los Angeles State College, to blonde singer Polly Ellis (Miss California of 1945). They have a son, Tommy Jr., a young teenager, who looks greatly like the "Butch" of four decades ago. Onscreen from the early '30s. IN: *Kid Millions, Hideaway, City Streets, A Little Bit of Heaven, Man From Frisco, Call Me Mister,* more.

BONDARCHUK, SERGEI (Rus.) Star. Onscreen from 1949. IN: *Young Guard, Dream of a Cossack, Taras Schevchenko, The Grasshopper, Era notte a Roma, Othello, Fate of Man, A Summer to Remember, War and Peace, Uncle Vanya,* more. Was the first Soviet actor to act outside Iron Curtain countries.

BONDI, BEULAH (S. Cal.) Seeing this superlative character actress at Hollywood social gatherings, one is apt to observe that finally, in her 80s (b. 1892), she almost looks the age of the characters they've been powdering her up to play since *Street Scene.* One party she would not have missed for anything was Henry Fonda's 70th birthday party—at which she had the chance to renew acquaintance with dozens of stars with whom she has acted over the years. She has not been seen in a film since 1963's *Tammy and the Doctor,* and for eight years she did not perform at all. In this decade, though, she has begun to make sporadic guest-star appearances on television. In '71 she was seen in an episode of *The Jimmy Stewart Show;* she had played Stewart's mother several times in movies. The following year she appeared in the CBS TV-movie *She Waits.* She starred, in '74, in a two-hour special episode of *The Waltons,* playing an old hill-country woman who fights a losing battle to keep the government from taking over her farm and running a highway through it. More than one contemporary "star" learned much about the art of acting the evening it was shown. And, early in '76, she costarred with Hal Holbrook in *Crossing Fox River,* based on Sandburg's Pulitzer Prize-winning biography of Lincoln. To remain free to travel is the principal reason this two-time Supporting Oscar nominee (*The Gorgeous Hussy* and *Of Human Hearts*) has turned down many acting offers in the past decade. "My last few years," she says, "have been filled with travel by ship and plane and car—around the world twice and many return trips to Europe, Africa, and Asia." When she is home—home being a lovely old Spanish house atop a Hollywood hill with a 360° view of Los Angeles and the Valley—her interests, she says, are "theater, music, art, books, museums, and philanthropic work—concerning children and the Motion Picture Relief Fund." Her favorite role? "It has always been the one I am playing at the moment. Perhaps there were some which were greater challenges, when I played elderly women—when I was much younger than their ages—and in playing age, changing from young to old. But I don't think I have a favorite." It is the same with the many countries to which she has journeyed. "How can one say which contributed the most? Each moment lived was an addition to life. It is good." Onscreen from 1931. IN: *Arrowsmith, Christopher Bean, Finishing School, The Good Fairy, Bad Boy, The Trail of the Lonesome Pine, Maid of Salem, Make Way for Tomorrow, The Buccaneer, Vivacious Lady, On Borrowed Time, Mr. Smith Goes to Washington, Remember the Night, Our Town, Penny Serenade, The Shepherd of the Hills, One Foot in Heaven, Watch on the Rhine, And Now Tomorrow, Sister Kenny, It's a Wonderful Life, The Snake Pit, So Dear to My Heart, The Furies, Track of the Cat, The Big Fisherman, A Summer Place, Tammy Tell Me True*, more.

BONERZ, PETER (S. Cal.) Comic support. IN: *Catch-22, Medium Cool, Funnyman, Jennifer on My Mind, Fuzz*, more.

BONNELL, JAY (N.Y.) Support. IN: *The World of Henry Orient.*

BONNELL, LEE (S. Cal.) Former leading man. Onscreen in the '40s. IN: *Lady Scarface, Look Who's Laughing, Army Surgeon, The Navy Comes Through, Criminal Court, San Quentin*, more. Appeared in a few earlier films as "Terry Belmont," the screen name he won on Jesse L. Lasky's radio program, *Gateway to Hollywood.* Now a California insurance executive. (See Gale Storm.)

BONO, SONNY (S. Cal.) Singer-actor. IN: *Good Times.*

BONOMO, JOE (S. Cal.) Severely crippled by arthritis, the strongest of all daredevil stars of silent serials could no longer, as he did in *The Great Circus Mystery*, hold up the main pole of a circus tent during a storm. But he remains in many ways *The Strongman*, which is the title he gave his 1968 autobiography. Extremely rich via various commercial enterprises, owned and operated, he flies regularly between Los Angeles and New York attending these businesses. He is now in his 70s (b. 1898) and still married to the wife he wed decades ago. Onscreen from 1921. IN SERIALS: *The Eagle's Talons, Beasts of Paradise, Perils of the Wild, The Golden Stallion, Heroes of the Wild, The China-town Mystery*, more. IN FEATURES: *The Flaming Frontier, You Never Know Women, Noah's Ark, The Sign of the Cross*, more.

BONYNGE, LETA (N.Y.) Support. IN: *The Group.*

BOOKE, SORRELL (S. Cal.) Character. Onscreen from 1963. IN: *Gone Are the Days!, Fail Safe, Joy House, Up the Down Staircase, Bye Bye Braverman, The Manchu Eagle Murder Caper Mystery*, more.

BOON, ROBERT (S. Cal.) Support. IN: *The Tanks Are Coming, Affair in Trinidad, The Last Blitzkrieg, Queen of Blood*, more.

BOONE, PAT (S. Cal.) Singer-actor. Onscreen from 1957. IN: *Bernardine, April Love, Journey to the Center of the Earth, State Fair, The Yellow Canary, Goodbye Charlie, The Greatest Story Ever Told, The Perils of Pauline*, more.

BOONE, RANDY (S. Cal.) Support. IN: *Backtrack*, more.

BOONE, RICHARD (S. Cal.) Costar. Onscreen from 1950. IN: *The Halls of Montezuma, The Desert Fox, Kangaroo, Man on a Tightrope, The Robe, Beneath the 12-Mile Reef, Dragnet, Man Without a Star, The Garment Jungle, The Alamo, Rio Conchos, The War Lord, Hombre, The Kremlin Letter, The Arrangement, Little Big Man, Madron, Big Jake, Against a Crooked Sky*, more.

BOOTH, ADRIAN (S. Cal.) Entering her 50s (b. 1924) and a most attractive woman still, she has long been married to actor David Brian and retired completely from the screen after 1951's *The Sea Hornet.* Onscreen from 1945. IN: *Home on the Range, The Man from Rainbow Valley, Valley of the Zombies, Exposed, Under Colorado Skies, The Plunderers, Brimstone, Rock Island Trail, Oh! Susanna*, more.

BOOTH, EDWINA (S. Cal.) Not, as many believe, a "one-picture" star, *Trader Horn's* exotic blonde leading lady appeared in at least three movies before this jungle epic and one after it. Now in her mid-60s (b. 1909), and divorced from producer Anthony E. Schuck since '33, she was last reported as working at the Mormon Temple in West Hollywood—and refusing all interviews. Onscreen from 1928. IN: *Manhattan Cocktail, Our Modern Maidens, The Last of the Mohicans, Midnight Patrol.*

BOOTH, SHIRLEY (S. Cal.) Star. Won Best Actress Oscar in *Come Back, Little Sheba.* Onscreen from 1952. IN: *Main Street to Broadway, About Mrs. Leslie, The Matchmaker, Hot*

Spell. Inactive since starring in the 1973 TV series *A Touch of Grace.*

BORCHERS, CORNELL (Ger.) Leading lady. First in German-language movies in the late '40s, she has been onscreen in English-speaking roles since 1950. IN: *The Big Lift, The Divided Heart, Istanbul, Oasis, Alone Together,* more.

BORG, SVEN-HUGO (S. Cal.) Character. IN: *Mystery Sea Raider,* more.

BORGE, VICTOR (N.Y.) Pianist-comedian. IN: *Higher and Higher, The Daydreamer.*

BORGNINE, ERNEST (S. Cal.) Star. Won Best Actor Oscar in *Marty.* Onscreen from 1951. IN: *Whistle at Eaton Falls, The Mob, From Here to Eternity, Vera Cruz, Bad Day at Black Rock, Run for Cover, Violent Saturday, The Catered Affair, Jubal, The Best Things in Life Are Free, The Vikings, Man on a String, Go Naked in the World, Barabbas, McHale's Navy, The Flight of the Phoenix, The Dirty Dozen, The Wild Bunch, The Adventurers, The Desperate Ones, Willard, Bunny O'Hare, The Poseidon Adventure, Emperor of the North Pole, The Neptune Factor, Law and Disorder, The Devil's Rain, Hustle, Shoot,* more.

BOSLEY, TOM (S. Cal.) Character. IN: *Call Northside 777, Love With the Proper Stranger, The Secret War of Harry Frigg; Yours, Mine and Ours;* more.

BOSWELL, CONNEE (N.Y.) The well-remembered singer was bereaved in '75 by the death of her husband, Harry Leedy. They had been married exactly 40 years. He had been her personal manager and, until they ceased trouping as an act, manager of The Boswell Sisters. Also, since Connee, crippled by polio as a child, had to get around in a wheelchair, Leedy had devised the stage technique that allowed his wife to get by on her talent rather than on sympathy—letting her be found seated on a darkened stage with the spotlight coming slowly up. In her 60s now, and childless, Connee lives in a beautiful apartment overlooking Central Park. Inactive in show business in recent years, she devotes her time to painting and seeing friends. Onscreen from 1932. IN: *The Big Broadcast, Transatlantic Merry-Go-Round,* and *Moulin Rouge* with her sisters, and, as a solo, in *Artists and Models, Kiss the Boys Goodbye, Syncopation.*

BOSWELL, VET (N.Y.) She was onscreen in three (see above) with sisters Connee and Martha (d. 1958). Also a widow (since '58), she has one grown daughter, lives on the Hudson River 50 miles north of Manhattan, and visits Connee regularly.

BOTTOMS, JOSEPH (S. Cal.) Young lead. IN: *The Dove, Crime and Passion,* more.

BOTTOMS, SAM (S. Cal.) Young support. IN: *The Last Picture Show.*

BOTTOMS, TIMOTHY (S. Cal.) Young lead. IN: *Johnny Got His Gun, The Last Picture Show, The Paper Chase, The Crazy World of Julius Vrooder,* more.

BOUCHEY, WILLIS (S. Cal.) Character. Onscreen from 1951. IN: *Red Planet Mars, Million Dollar Mermaid, Pickup on South Street, The Big Heat, The Bridges at Toko-Ri, The McConnell Story, The Man Who Shot Liberty Valance, The Love God?, Support Your Local Gunfighter,* more.

BOUCHIER, CHILI (Eng.) When James Stewart starred onstage in London in '75 in a revival of *Harvey,* this onetime movie sexpot played the sedate supporting role of a doctor's wife, She is now in her 60s (b. 1909). Onscreen from the late '20s. IN: *The Silver King, Mr. Cohen Takes a Walk, Murder in Reverse, Mrs. Fitzherbert,* more.

BOUDREAUX, JOSEPH (La.) Like the oil-riggers he so admired in the Robert Flaherty classic *The Louisiana Story,* his only film, the bayou boy is now himself—in his 40s—an oil-rigger.

BOULEY, FRANK (N.Y.) Support. IN: *Mr. Music.*

BOULTING, INGRID (S. Cal.) Leading lady from England introduced in 1976. IN: *The Last Tycoon* (as Kathleen).

BOURNEUF, PHILIP (S. Cal.) Character. Onscreen from 1944. IN: *Winged Victory, Joan of Arc, The Big Night, Beyond a Reasonable Doubt, Hemingway's Adventures of a Young Man, Chamber of Horrors, The Molly Maguires,* more.

BOUTON, JIM (N.Y.) Support. IN: *The Long Goodbye.*

BOVA, JOSEPH (N.Y.) Support. IN: *The Young Doctors, Pretty Poison,* more.

BOVASSO, JULIE (N.Y.) Support. IN: *Tell Me That You Love Me, Junie Moon.*

BOWDON, DORRIS (S. Cal.) They said it wouldn't last when, in her mid-20s, the Memphis-born leading lady who played Rosasharn in *The Grapes of Wrath* married its two-decades-older screenwriter Nunnally Johnson. But in

February 1976, back in Hollywood after several years' residence in London, she and Johnson (now producer-director-writer) celebrated their 36th wedding anniversary surrounded by children (three in all, two by his previous marriage) and grandchildren. Onscreen from 1939. IN: *Young Mr. Lincoln, Drums Along the Mohawk, The Grapes of Wrath, The Moon Is Down.* Retired.

BOWE, ROSEMARIE (S. Cal.) Leading lady. Onscreen from 1954. IN: *The Adventures of Hajji Baba, The Golden Mistress, The View From Pompey's Head.* Retired. (See Robert Stack.)

BOWEN, ROGER (S. Cal.) Character. IN: *Funnyman, Deadlock, Petulia, M*A*S*H, Move,* more.

BOWIE, DAVID (Eng.) Rock star. IN: *The Man Who Fell to Earth.*

BOWMAN, LEE (S. Cal.) Somewhat plumper now in his 60s (b. 1914), and having long since doffed the toupee he sported in many of those playboy roles in the '40s, Lee was until recently the radio-TV consultant for the Republican Senatorial and Congressional Committee in Washington. His assignment—helping these elected officials polish their style for radio and TV broadcasts. Filling this role, he says he had been "commuting between my house in West Los Angeles and Washington—spending two weeks of the month in the Capitol. The rest of my time has been spent handling my own business interests in New York and California." Celebrating their 36th wedding anniversary in '76, Lee and his wife, Helene, have two children—Lee Jr., a California businessman, and a college-age daughter. Lee hung up his acting spurs after 1964's *Youngblood Hawke*, in which he played a supporting role, and which was then his first movie in a decade. Yes, he admits, "I miss my profession, and I hope my friends miss me—so maybe, just maybe, I'll do another picture sometime in the future." Onscreen from 1937. IN: *Internes Can't Take Money, Sophie Lang Goes West, A Man to Remember, Love Affair, Stronger Than Desire, Dancing Co-Ed, The Great Victor Herbert, Model Wife, Design for Scandal, We Were Dancing, Bataan, Cover Girl, The Impatient Years, Tonight and Every Night, Smash-up, Desert Fury, My Dream Is Yours, There's a Girl in My Heart,* more.

BOXER, JOHN (Eng.) Character. IN: *Millions Like Us, The Half-Way House, The October Man, The Blue Lagoon, The Happiest Days of Your Life, Mr. Drake's Duck, The Red Beret,* more.

BOYAR, SULLY (N.Y.) Support. IN: *Dog Day Afternoon.*

BOYD, BETTY (Tex.) Happily married and the mother of several grown children, the onetime leading lady has been retired from acting since 1930. IN: *The Green Goddess, Under a Texas Moon,* more.

BOYD, JIMMY (S. Cal.) Singer-actor. Onscreen from 1956. IN: *The Second Greatest Sex, Platinum High School, High Time, Inherit the Wind, That's the Way of the World,* more.

BOYD, STEPHEN (S. Cal.) Costar. Onscreen from 1955. IN: *An Alligator Named Daisy, The Man Who Never Was, Abandon Ship, Island in the Sun, The Best of Everything, Ben Hur, Lisa, Jumbo, The Fall of the Roman Empire, The Oscar, Fantastic Voyage, The Poppy Is Also a Flower, Shalako,* more.

BOYER, CHARLES (Fr.) Star. Nominated for Best Actor Oscar in *Conquest, Algiers, Gaslight, Fanny. Stavisky,* in 1974, was proof that, while a "continental lover" may fall by the wayside, a superb actor can go on forever. Boyer is in his 70s (b. 1899), has never slackened his professional pace, and must have been pleased by the *New York Times* critic who wrote of his performance in this film: "Charles Boyer is effortlessly elegant and supple as a baron who enjoyed Stavisky's company. The eyebrows rise delicately above those knowing eyes, and it's a treat to watch him." The role also won him the New York Film Critics Circle's award as best supporting actor of the year. He has been happily married since '36 to English actress Pat Paterson, who was in many Hollywood movies before retiring when they married. In her 60s (b. 1911), she is still blonde and most attractive. Since '70 they have lived in a village in the south of France, high on a hill six miles from Cannes. They also spend part of the year in a house in Geneva, Switzerland, and visit Paris often to see plays and their friends. Their only child, Michael, then 21, died suddenly in '65. First newspaper accounts of his death were headlined: "Boyer's Son Takes Own Life"—followed by reporters' assertions that the young man, a Hollywood dialogue director, had "shot himself to death when his fiancee broke their engagement." A few weeks later, the actor made his only statement to the press, saying, "I don't expect anyone to believe me but it was a tragic accident." Onscreen from 1920. IN: *L'Homme du Large, L'Amour, La Bastille, Liliom, The Magnificent Lie, Red-Headed Woman, The Man from Yesterday, Caravan, Private Worlds, Shanghai, Garden of Allah, Tovarich, Mayerling, Love Affair, All*

This and Heaven Too, Hold Back the Dawn, Tales of Manhattan, The Constant Nymph, Together Again, Cluny Brown, Madame de . . ., Around the World in 80 Days, La Parisienne, The Four Horsemen of the Apocalypse, Is Paris Burning?, How to Steal a Million, Casino Royale, Barefoot in the Park, The Madwoman of Chaillot, Lost Horizon, A Matter of Time, more.

BOYLAN, MARY (N.Y.) Support. IN: *The Night of the Iguana.*

BOYLE, PETER (S. Cal.) Character costar. IN: *Joe, T. R. Baskin, Steelyard Blues, Slither, The Candidate, The Friends of Eddie Coyle,* more.

BRACKEN, EDDIE (N.Y.) In his 50s now (b. 1920), and looking much the same but for a touch of gray in his curls, this inimitable movie comic acts exclusively on the stage now. His last movie was 1953's *A Slight Case of Larceny.* In '75 he did a cross-country tour of one-nighters in *The Sunshine Boys.* Quite often in dinner theaters, he costars in such comedies as *Never Too Late* with his daughter Susie and his wife, Connie. He and his wife, the former Connie Nickerson, met in '39—when both were appearing on Broadway—at Gallagher's restaurant. In '74 they again had dinner at Gallagher's, celebrating the 35th anniversary of their marriage. They are parents of five—three girls and two boys—and live in Scarsdale. Financially, the actor was considerably better off in 1970 than he has been since. That year, with a partner, he attempted to create a circuit of 10 winter and summer stock theaters on the East Coast. Less than two years later, though, by his own estimation, he had lost most of the playhouses and more than $2 million invested by himself and his associate. On the day one of the theaters, the Coconut Grove Playhouse in Miami, was placed in the hands of a receiver, the actor admitted, "Dramawise, I'm playing the most tragic role of my life." Then, looking like an older version of the lovable, befuddled schnook he was so often at Paramount, he smiled and added: "My agent once said an actor is not a very good business man. So far he's been dead right." He has since announced his intention of making a movie musical of the book *Mama Was a Ballerina,* which he would film through his Major Studio Productions company in England. Of his old movies, the two dozen he starred in at Paramount, the actor says he liked only two—*Hail the Conquering Hero* and *The Miracle of Morgan's Creek.* But the latter, in which he was Norval Jones, established more strongly than any other the stereotype that eventually caused him to give up movies for the stage. "They thought Norval Jones was Eddie Bracken, and he is not. I was Eddie Bracken playing Norval Jones. So for versatility's sake I went out to prove they were wrong, and I think I succeeded." Onscreen from 1940. IN: *Too Many Girls, Caught in the Draft, The Fleet's In, Star Spangled Rhythm, Sweater Girl, Rainbow Island, Bring on the Girls, Duffy's Tavern, Hold that Blonde, Out of This World, Ladies' Man, Summer Stock, Two Tickets to Broadway, About Face, We're Not Married,* and, last to date, 1953's *A Slight Case of Larceny.*

BRADBURY, ALLAN (N.Y.) Juvenile. Onscreen in the 70s. IN: *The War Between Men and Women, Little Murders,* more.

BRADFORD, RICHARD (S. Cal.) Support. IN: *The Chase,* more.

BRADLEY, GRACE (S. Cal.) The widow of William "Hopalong Cassidy" Boyd (d. 1972), to whom she was married for 35 years, the still-blonde actress is now in her 60s (b. 1913) and lives quietly, wealthily, and alone (they had no children) in Newport Beach. She has not appeared in a movie since 1943's *McGuerins from Brooklyn,* with William Bendix. Onscreen from 1933. IN: *Too Much Harmony, Six of a Kind, Come On Marines!, She Made Her Bed, Redhead, The Gilded Lily, Rose of the Rancho, Anything Goes, Three Cheers for Love, Wake Up and Live, Big Broadcast of 1938, The Invisible Killer, Sign of the Wolf, Brooklyn Orchid,* more.

BRADLEY, LESLIE (S. Cal.) Character. Onscreen from the '40s. IN: *The Young Mr. Pitt, No Orchids for Miss Blandish, The Crimson Pirate, Kiss of Fire; Good Morning, Miss Dove; The Buccaneer,* more.

BRADNA, OLYMPE (N. Cal.) The dainty French actress, last seen in 1941's *International Squadron,* gave up her career to marry a handsome young millionaire, Douglas Wilhoit. More than three decades later, the erstwhile leading lady, a beautiful charmer still in her 50s (b. 1920), remains happily his wife. They live—luxuriously—in Carmel, where they are leaders in the community's society. Onscreen from 1936. IN: *Three Cheers for Love, College Holiday, Last Train From Madrid, Souls at Sea, Stolen Heaven, South of Pago Pago, Highway West,* more.

BRADY, SCOTT (S. Cal.) Leading man/character. Onscreen from 1948. IN: *Canon City, He Walked by Night, Undertow, I Was a Shoplifter, Montana Belle, Bloodhounds of Broadway, Gentlemen Marry Brunettes; John Goldfarb, Please Come Home; Fort Utah, Satan's Sad-*

ists, *Hell's Bloody Devils, Dollars, Five Bloody Graves*, more.

BRAEDEN, ERIC/formerly HANS GUDE-GAST (S. Cal.) Leading man. IN: *Dalton's Devils, 100 Rifles, Colossus, The Forbin Project, Escape Fron the Planet of the Apes*, more.

BRAGGIOTTI, FRANCESCA (Conn.) Retired leading lady. IN: *Scipio Africanus*. (See John Davis Lodge.)

BRAMLEY, FLORA (Eng.) After her brief career in American movies, which ended in 1930, this English-born beauty did stage plays on Broadway and in London. Long married, now retired and in her 60s, she lives in the country with her husband and gardens. Onscreen from 1927. IN: *College, We Americans, The Flirting Widow*, several Westerns.

BRAMLEY, RAYMOND (N.Y.) Character. Onscreen from 1930. IN: *The Vagabond King, The Scoundrel, Broken Arrow, The Sun Sets at Dawn*, more.

BRAMLEY, WILLIAM (S. Cal.) Character. IN: *West Side Story, Getting Straight, Suppose They Gave a War and Nobody Came?, Bless the Beasts and Children*, more.

BRAND, NEVILLE (S. Cal.) Character. Onscreen from 1949. IN: *D.O.A., Where the Sidewalk Ends, Only the Valiant, Red Mountain, Stalag 17, Riot in Cell Block 11, The Prodigal, The Way to the Gold, The Scarface Mob, The George Raft Story, Alcatraz Express, Birdman of Alcatraz, Tora! Tora! Tora!, Psychic Killer*, more.

BRANDEIS, RUTH (N.Y.) Support. IN: *Harry*.

BRANDO, JOCELYN (N.Y.) Support. IN: *The Big Heat, Ten Wanted Men, Step Down to Terror, The Ugly American, Bus Riley's Back in Town, The Chase, The Appaloosa*, more.

BRANDO, MARLON (Tahiti) Star. Won Best Actor Oscars in *On the Waterfront* and *The Godfather*. Nominated in the same category in *A Streetcar Named Desire, Viva Zapata!, Julius Caesar, Sayonara, Last Tango in Paris*. Onscreen from 1950. IN: *The Men, The Wild One, Guys and Dolls, Teahouse of the August Moon, The Young Lions, Mutiny on the Bounty, The Ugly American, Bedtime Story, Morituri, The Chase, The Appaloosa, Reflections in a Golden Eye, Candy, The Night of the Following Day, The Nightcomers, The Missouri Breaks*, more.

BRANDON, HENRY (S. Cal.) Perhaps the handsomest hissable villain in serials of the '30s

(*Jungle Jim, Secret Agent X-9, Buck Rogers*) and '40s (*Drums of Fu Manchu*, in which he was the sinister Oriental lead), he is in his mid-60s now and still up to movie evil. Onscreen from 1934. IN: *Babes in Toyland, The Trail of the Lonesome Pine, Black Legion, Beau Geste, Nurse Edith Cavell, Underground, Bad Man of Deadwood, Joan of Arc, Tarzan's Magic Fountain, War of the Worlds, Pony Express, Vera Cruz, Omar Khayyam, The Big Fisherman, Captain Sinbad*, more.

BRANDON, MICHAEL (S. Cal.) Leading man/former juvenile. Onscreen from 1947. IN: *The Arnelo Affair, The Gunfighter, Jennifer on My Mind, Lovers and Other Strangers*, more.

BRANDS, X (S. Cal.) Indian character. IN: *Young and Dangerous, Escort West, Where the Hot Wind Blows, Oklahoma Territory*, more.

BRASCIA, JOHN (S. Cal.) Character. IN: *White Christmas, Meet Me in St. Louis, The Ambushers, The Wrecking Crew*, more.

BRASSELLE, KEEFE (S. Cal.) Starred in the recent *If You Don't Stop It, You'll Go Blind* (an R-rated movie, not an X, he points out, despite its title), Keefe made headlines of various sorts in the first half of the '70s. In the summer of '71 he was arrested on the charge of "assault with intent to commit murder." He was accused of shooting a North Hollywood man in the chest during an argument in a San Fernando Valley bar. The case has since been settled and all charges dropped. He has authored two sensational best-selling novels: *The CanniBals* (an inside TV expose) and *The Barracudas* (similar on the movie industry). And, late in '74, after his divorce that year from the former Arlene DeMarco, mother of his two daughters who live with her in New York, he was sued by her. She contended, in Federal Court in Los Angeles, that the actor still owed her $266,417, plus interest of 7 percent, in alimony and other payments granted her by the State Supreme Court in New York when they were divorced. He may remain single a long while. Onscreen from 1944. IN: *Janie, River Gang, Railroaded, Not Wanted, Dial 1119, A Place in the Sun, It's a Big Country, The Eddie Cantor Story, Bring Your Smile Along, Battle Stations, The Fighting Wildcats*, more.

BRAY, ROBERT (S. Cal.) Retired since the early '70s, this former leading man in action pix lives with his family at Lake Arrowhead. Onscreen from 1948. IN: *Arizona Ranger, Return of the Bad Men, The Stagecoach Kid, The Man from the Black Hills, My Gun Is Quick, Never So Few, A Gathering of Eagles*, more.

BRAZZI, LIDIA (It.) Support. Wife of Rossano. IN: *After the Fox, The Christmas That Almost Wasn't.*

BRAZZI, ROSSANO (It.) Star. Onscreen in Italy from the mid '40s. IN: *The King's Jester, The Great Dawn, The Story of Tosca, Furia,* more. Onscreen in America and internationally from 1949. IN: *Little Women, Three Coins in the Fountain, The Barefoot Contessa, Summertime, South Pacific, The Ten Commandments, A Certain Smile, Light in the Piazza, Rome Adventure, The Battle of the Villa Fiorita, Woman Times Seven, The Italian Job, The Great Waltz, Political Asylum,* more.

BRECK, PETER (S. Cal.) Support/leading man. Onscreen from 1958. IN: *Thunder Road, I Want to Live!, Portrait of a Mobster, The Crawling Hand, The Glory Guys, Benji,* more.

BREEN, BOBBY (Fla.) Short, curly-haired, a tenor now and in his late 40s (b. 1927), he lives in Miami with his wife of two decades, Audre, who is also his manager. He is the stepfather of two young adults, Paul and Ronald, and the father of college-age son, Keith. He appears in nightclubs all over the country (did his first N.Y. engagement in years in '75) and occasionally does a musical in stock. He recently starred in an out-of-town production of *The Jazz Singer.* Said one Florida critic: "Breen has that indefinable star quality that lights up the stage. He has charm. He has a unique and superb singing voice." Reported another: "Bobby Breen, the big drawing card in the title role, is fine. His speaking voice is pleasant to listen to. . . . He made some in the audience think of Red Buttons, both in his appearance and his impish manner." His life between his boyhood stardom in movies and now? He graduated from U.C.L.A., majoring in music and drama; was California State oratorical champ six successive times and, as guest pianist, played with the National Broadcasting Company Symphony Orchestra on radio. He served in the Infantry in WW II, received the Bronze Star, and after his discharge in '48 studied at the American Academy of Dramatic Arts. Following this, he had a local TV show in New York, married, and launched his successful nightclub career. His wife, Audre, says that, besides getting him bookings, her major contribution has been that of changing his image. "He used to appear in a suit and tie. I made him put on sport clothes and throw away his elevator shoes." Onscreen from 1936. IN: *Let's Sing Again, Rainbow on the River, Make a Wish, Hawaii Calls, Fisherman's Wharf, Way Down South,* and more, including 1942's *Johnny Doughboy,* his last.

BREEN, MARY (N.Y.) Juvenile. Onscreen in the '70s. IN: *The Honeymoon Killers,* more.

BREL, JACQUES (Fr.) Singer-actor. IN: *A Pain in the A. . ., Jacques Brel Is Alive and Well and Living in Paris.*

BREMEN, LEONARD (S. Cal.) Character. Onscreen from 1949. IN: *The Inspector General, M,* more.

BREMER, LUCILLE (S. Cal.) One of the best dance partners Fred Astaire ever had, this MGM star left the screen in '48 to become the wife of Abelardo Louis Rodriguez, son of the former president of Mexico. After living in La Paz and Mexico City, they moved eventually to La Jolla, Calif. There, today, the former actress, now in her 50s (b. 1923) and the mother of five daughters, owns and operates a children's dress shop. Still a redhead and slender, she admits no wish to return to the career she dropped after *Behind Locked Doors.* Onscreen from 1944. IN: *Meet Me in St. Louis, Yolanda and the Thief, Till the Clouds Roll By, Ziegfeld Follies, Adventures of Casanova, Ruthless,* more.

BRENNAN, EILEEN (S. Cal.) Support. Onscreen from 1971. IN: *The Last Picture Show, At Long Last Love, Hustle, Murder by Death,* more.

BRENNAN, MICHAEL (Eng.) Support. Onscreen from the early '30s. IN: *Blackout, The Clouded Yellow, Tom Brown's Schooldays, The Lady With a Lamp, Ivanhoe, Personal Affair, See How They Run,* more.

BRENNAN, TERI (N.Y.) Support. In: *John and Mary.*

BRENT, EVE (S. Cal.) Leading lady/support. Onscreen from 1957. IN: *Forty Guns, Tarzan's Fight for Life, Cage of Evil, The Barefoot Executive,* more.

BRENT, GEORGE (S. Cal.) The actor whom some still insist was the "great love" of Bette Davis' life is today, in his 70s (b. 1904), quite heavy, totally white-haired, and, he insists, completely retired. Married and divorced four times (to non-pro Helen Campbell, Ruth Chatterton, Constance Worth, Ann Sheridan), he has been most happily married since December 18, 1947, to the former Janet Michael. Except for a year spent in Ireland, the actor's birthplace and where he had attended the University of Dublin after growing up in the States, they have resided during most of their married life in Rancho Santa Fe, an exclusive community south of Los Angeles. (A nearby neighbor of the Brents there: actor Robert Young.) They have two grown children: Susanne (b. 1951) and Barry (b. 1955). The actor made the last of his 110 movies, *Mexican Manhunt*, in 1953. He later ('56) starred in the TV series *Wire Service*, in addition to doing many guest-star roles, the last-recorded one being in the summer of '60 on *NBC Mystery Show.* Onscreen from the late '20s. IN: *Fair Warning, Charlie Chan Carries On, So Big, Miss Pinkerton, 42nd Street, Lily Turner, The Painted Veil, Front Page Woman, The Case Against Mrs. Ames, God's Country and the Woman, Jezebel, Wings of the Navy, Dark Victory, The Old Maid, The Rains Came, The Fighting 69th, In This Our Life, The Great Lie, Twin Beds, The Gay Sisters, My Reputation, Tomorrow Is Forever, The Spiral Staircase, Red Canyon, Bride for Sale, Montana Belle,* more.

BRENT, ROMNEY (Mex.) A widower since his actress-wife Gina Malo died in '63 after 26 years of marriage, he is now in his 70s (b. 1902), has one grown daughter, retired after 1958's *Screaming Mimi*, and lives in Mexico City. Onscreen from 1936. IN: *East Meets West, Head Over Heels in Love, Dreaming Lips, Dinner at the Ritz, His Lordship Goes to Press, School for Husbands, Adventures of Don Juan, Dream Ballerina, The Virgin Queen, Don't Go Near the Water,* more.

BRETT, JEREMY (Eng.) Leading man. Onscreen from 1956. IN: *War and Peace, The Model Murder Case, My Fair Lady, Young and Willing,* more.

BREWER, TERESA (N.Y.) Singer-actress. IN: *Those Redheads From Seattle.*

BREWSTER, MARGARET (N.Y.) Support. IN: *My Cousin Rachel, Second Chance.*

BRIALY, JEAN-CLAUDE (Fr.) Costar. Onscreen from the '50s. IN: *Elena and the Men, The Cousins, The 400 Blows, Paris Belongs to Us, A Woman Is a Woman, Circle of Love, How Not to Rob a Department Store, King of Hearts, The Bride Wore Black, Claire's Knee,* more.

BRIAN, DAVID (S. Cal.) Gray now in his 60s (b. 1914), the suave actor who was once one of Crawford's favorite leading men *(The Damned Don't Cry, Flamingo Road)* has lately put on a cruel face to play smooth criminals of the most despicable variety, in such TV shows as *Police Story. The Seven Minutes* ('71) was one of his most recent movies. He has been married to former actress Adrian Booth since 1949. Onscreen from 1949. IN: *Intruder in the Dust, Beyond the Forest, Fort Worth, This Woman Is Dangerous, Springfield Rifle, The High and the Mighty, Accused of Murder, How the West Was Won, The Girl Who Knew Too Much, Tora! Tora! Tora!,* more.

BRIAN, MARY (S. Cal.) "I am the Perpetual Ingenue. I shall never escape and, by this time, I know it. If I violated every decency of every morality code in the country, no one would believe it." The pretty girl who said this in 1934 is still extremely pretty though no longer a girl (b. 1908). And what she said about the "morality code" still holds true, though acquaintances have never held their breath awaiting any violations. In the summer of '75 she was one of Pat O'Brien's "wives" who turned up to salute him —together with hundreds of other friends—at a Beverly Hills fete tendered him for his humanitarianism. (Among his other ex-"movie wives" there: Margaret Lindsay, Ruth Hussey, Jane Wyatt, Ann Doran, and Jane Wyman.) She has not acted on TV since playing the mother in the *Corliss Archer* series in the '50s or in a movie since *Dragnet* in '47, the year she became the wife of film editor George Tomasini. (She had previously been married, briefly, to magazine illustrator Jon Whitcomb.) A widow since 1964, and childless, she now paints celebrity portraits (on commission) and often attends Hollywood events on the arm of Dick Clayton, the former juvenile actor who is now a Hollywood agent. Onscreen from 1924. IN: *Peter Pan, The Air Mail, A Regular Fellow, Beau Geste, Knockout Reilly, Forgotten Faces, Varsity, The Marriage Playground, The Virginian, The Royal Family of Broadway, The Front Page, The Run Around, Song of the Eagle, Shadows of Sing Sing, College Rhythm, Man on the Flying Trapeze, Affairs of Cappy Ricks, Passport to Heaven, I Escaped From the Gestapo,* more.

BRICKELL, BETH (S. Cal.) Leading lady. IN: *Posse.*

BRIDGES, BEAU (S. Cal.) Costar. In movies from childhood. Onscreen from 1948. IN: *Force of Evil, The Red Pony, No Minor Vices, Zamba, Gaily Gaily, The Landlord, The Other Side of the Mountain, Dragonfly, The Blarney Cock, Two-Minute Warning,* more.

BRIDGES, JEFF (S. Cal.) Costar. Nominated for Best Supporting Actor Oscar in *The Last Picture Show* and *Thunderbolt and Lightfoot.* Onscreen from 1970. IN: *Halls of Anger, Fat City, Bad Company, The Last American Hero, Hearts of the West, Rancho Deluxe,* more.

BRIDGES, LLOYD (S. Cal.) Star. Father of Beau and Jeff. Onscreen from 1941. IN: *Harmon of Michigan, The Lone Wolf Takes a Chance, Flight Lieutenant, Sahara, The Master Race, A Walk in the Sun, Ramrod, The Trouble*

With Women, Calamity Jane and Sam Bass, Colt .45, Three Steps North, The Whistle at Eaton Falls, High Noon, The Kid From Left Field, The Rainmaker, The Goddess, Around the World Under the Sea, To Find a Man, more.

BRIGGS, DONALD (S. Cal.) Character. IN: Love Before Breakfast, They Won't Forget, Captains Courageous, Fit for a King, more.

BRIGHT, RICHARD (N.Y.) Support. IN: Lions Love, The Panic in Needle Park, The Getaway, more.

BRIGHT, ROBERT (S. Cal.) Support. IN: Odds Against Tomorrow.

BRILL, MARTY (S. Cal.) Support. IN: Angel, Angel, Down You Go.

BRIND, TESSA (See Vanessa Brown.)

BRINEGAR, PAUL (S. Cal.) Support. IN: Larceny, The Captive City, Human Desire, Charro!, more.

BRISSAC, VIRGINIA (S. Cal.) Character. Onscreen from 1936. IN: White Bondage; Torchy Blane, the Adventurous Blonde; Dark Victory, Hired Wife, Strike Up the Band, The Great Lie, The Little Foxes, One Foot in Heaven, Phantom Lady, Captain From Castile, Summer Holiday, Cheaper by the Dozen, Harriet Craig, Executive Suite, About Mrs. Leslie, Rebel Without a Cause, more. Rarely active in the past two decades.

BRITT, MAY (S. Cal.) Formerly the wife of Sammy Davis Jr., the leading lady is remarried, retired, and living in Beverly Hills. Onscreen from 1952. IN: Affairs of a Model, The Young Lions, The Hunters, The Blue Angel; Murder, Inc.; A Matter of Morals, Secrets of a Woman, The Ship of Condemned Women, more.

BRITTON, BARBARA (N.Y.) Giving up movies in '55, the leading lady, now in her 50s (b. 1920), is married to a professor, the mother of a grown son and daughter, acts regularly in stock, and in '75 was starring in a cable-TV show (local) bearing her name. Onscreen from 1942. IN: Louisiana Purchase, Wake Island, So Proudly We Hail, Till We Meet Again, Captain Kidd, The Virginian, The Great John L., I Shot Jesse James, Bandit Queen, Bwana Devil, Dragonfly Squadron, Night Freight, more.

BRITTON, TONY (Eng.) Support. IN: Loser Takes All, Operation Amsterdam, The Risk, Portrait of a Sinner, There's a Girl in My Soup, Sunday Bloody Sunday, more.

BRIX, HERMAN (See Bruce Bennett.)

BROCCO, PETER (S. Cal.) Character. Onscreen from 1946. IN: The Lone Wolf in Mexico, The Gallant Blade, Jolson Sings Again, The Boy With Green Hair, The Big Knife, The Killer That Stalked New York, The Great Caruso, The Tall Target, Duffy of San Quentin, Spartacus, Our Man Flint, Games, What's the Matter with Helen?, Johnny Got His Gun, A Time for Dying, more.

BRODERICK, JAMES (S. Cal.) Support. Onscreen from 1960. IN: Girl of the Night, The Group, Alice's Restaurant, The Tree, The Todd Killings, Dog Day Afternoon, more.

BRODIE, STEVE (S. Cal.) In '75, after several years offscreen, he returned to costar with Barbara Hale in The Great Spider Invasion. Onscreen from 1944. IN: Follow the Boys, Thirty Seconds Over Tokyo, A Walk in the Sun, Crossfire, Station West, Home of the Brave, Kiss Tomorrow Goodbye, The Steel Helmet, The Charge at Feather River, Donovan's Brain, The Caine Mutiny, Sierra Baron, A Girl Named Tamiko, Roustabout, more.

BROLIN, JAMES (S. Cal.) Costar. Onscreen from 1965. IN: Von Ryan's Express, Take Her She's Mine, Goodbye Charlie; John Goldfarb, Please Come Home; Morituri, Fantastic Voyage, Our Man Flint, Class of '63, Gable and Lombard, more.

BROMFIELD, JOHN (S. Cal.) Leading man, retired. Onscreen from 1948. IN: Sorry, Wrong Number; Rope of Sand, The Furies, The Cimarron Kid, Ring of Fear, Revenge of the Creature, Three Bad Sisters, Quincannon—Frontier Scout, more.

BROMILOW, PETER (S. Cal.) Support. IN: Camelot.

BROMLEY, SHEILA/a.k.a. SHEILA MANNERS, SHEILA MANNORS, SHEILA FULTON (S. Cal.) Splendid talents do get lost in the Hollywood shuffle, this excellent actress being a case in point. Though such a beautiful blonde that she was chosen Miss California, it may be that she started "too late"—at 26 in 1937's Idol of the Crowds—and thus was never a typical "newcomer." Instead, until '42, in two dozen pix, she was a superlative second-string Davis, but featured in some of the worst movies ever made: Reformatory, Midnight Interlude, etc. Leaving the screen for more than a decade for the stage, where she played still more tough girls, she returned as a character actress—in Judgment at Nuremberg, Hotel, etc. Today television is her primary showcase and she has turned up regularly in such dramas as *Adam-12*. But you must look sharp to recognize her—she's that charming matron with the upswept hairdo and the pearl earrings and choker—the one who's acting the show's stars right off the screen. Onscreen from 1937. IN: *West of Shanghai, Missing Witness, Making the Headlines, King of the Newsboys, Accidents Will Happen, Girls on Probation, Torture Ship, Waterfront, Calling Philo Vance, Time to Kill, Spoilers of the Forest, Young Jesse James, For Those Who Think Young*, more.

BRON, ELEANOR (Eng.) Leading lady. IN: *Help!, Alfie, The Sailor From Gibraltar, Bedazzled, Thank You All Very Much, Women in Love*, more.

BRONSON, CHARLES (S. Cal.) Star. Onscreen (first under his real name, Charles Buchinski) from 1951. IN: *You're in the Navy Now, Red Skies of Montana, My Six Convicts, Miss Sadie Thompson, Vera Cruz; Big House, U.S.A.; Run of the Arrow, The Magnificent Seven, The Great Escape, Four for Texas, Battle of the Bulge, The Dirty Dozen, Villa Rides, The Valachi Papers, The Mechanic, Mr. Majestyk, Death Wish, Hard Times, Breakheart Pass, Breakout, St. Ives*, more.

BRONSON, LILLIAN (S. Cal.) Character. Onscreen from 1943. IN: *Happy Land, What a Man, In the Meantime Darling, A Tree Grows in Brooklyn, Junior Miss, Sentimental Journey, The Hucksters, Sleep My Love, In the Good Old Summertime, The Next Voice You Hear, Excuse My Dust, No Room for the Groom, Walk on the Wild Side, Spencer's Mountain, Fail Safe, The Americanization of Emily*, more.

BROOKE, HILLARY (S. Cal.) When this blonde dynamo from Brooklyn starred in B's she was charm meltingly incarnate and when she curled her lip as the menace in such as *Ministry of Fear*, she was a force to be reckoned with. In short, a consummate actress. Her English accent? Starring in a play in London before coming to Hollywood, she picked it up and never altogether lost it. In several dozen pix between *New Faces of 1937* and 1957's *Spoiler of the Forest* (being particularly effective as Blanche in Fontaine's *Jane Eyre*), she also costarred on TV in *My Little Margie*. In '60 she married Ray Klune, an MGM executive, wrapped her career in cellophane and never intends to reopen it. Her husband also retired now, they live in a seaside community south of Los Angeles, enjoy the sun and travel. Dark-haired now with a touch of gray (she was born in '14), and looking not at all like the girl with the cool blonde waves "fixed" in that upswept do that was her trademark, Hillary allows that she is content for the second generation to take over. That is, her son, Donald Klune (he uses his stepfather's name though he is by Hillary's former marriage to assistant director Jack Voglin). Donald, married to actress Maria Korda (*The Fastest Guitar Alive*), is an assistant director, most recently employed at MGM. Onscreen from 1937. IN: *Eternally Yours, Sherlock Holmes, Standing Room Only, The Crime Doctor's Courage, The Enchanted Cottage, Earl Carroll's Sketchbook, The Strange Woman, I Cover Big Town, The Fuller Brush Man, Alimony, Vendetta, Lucky Losers, Lost Continent, Never Wave at a Wac, The Lady Wants Mink, The Maze, The Man Who Knew Too Much*, more.

BROOKE, WALTER (S. Cal.) Character. Onscreen from 1942. IN: *Bullet Scars, Conquest of Space, The Party Crashers, The Graduate, Sergeant Ryker, How Sweet It Is, Zigzag, The Landlord, Tora! Tora! Tora!, The Return of Count Yorga, Lawman*, more.

BROOKS, GERALDINE (N.Y.) Leading lady. Onscreen from 1947. IN: *Possessed, Cry Wolf, Embraceable You, An Act of Murder, The Reckless Moment, The Green Glove, Johnny Tiger, Mr. Ricco*, more.

BROOKS, HAZEL (S. Cal.) Widowed when her husband, frequent Oscar-winning art director Cedric Gibbons, died in '60 after 16 years of marriage, the actress lives in retirement in Bel Air. Her home is a one-story hillside mansion with a pool featuring a 25-foot cascading waterfall, one of her husband's final designs. Onscreen from 1947. IN: *Body and Soul; Sleep, My Love; The Basketball Fix*.

BROOKS, IRIS (N.Y.) Support. IN: *Up the Sandbox*.

BROOKS, LESLIE (S. Cal.) The blonde who in the '40s was one of Columbia's loveliest second leads has long since been married (her second marriage) to Russ Vincent, president of Hollywood's Mount Olympus Housing Development, and has three grown daughters. When the girls were small she several times did TV commercials with them for her husband's business. Still most attractive in her 50s (b. 1922), Leslie does not anticipate working in movies again; her last, *Blonde Ice*, was released in '48. Onscreen from 1942. IN: *You Were Never Lovelier, Two Senoritas From Chicago, City Without Men, Cover Girl, Nine Girls, I Love a Bandleader, Tonight and Every Night, Cigarette Girl, Secret of the Whistler, The Corpse Came C.O.D., Hollow Triumph*, more.

BROOKS, LOUISE (N.Y.) Last in 1938's *Overland Stage Raiders*, a John Wayne Western and one of her least representative movies, this most excellent actress is now in her 70s (b. 1905) and has long been at work on a book about film. This is an outgrowth of several astute articles she has written about motion pictures for magazines such as England's *Sight and Sound*. She divides her time between New York City and Rochester, home of George Eastman House, the famous film institute, where she is researching her book. She is unmarried, having been divorced in '28 from director Eddie Sutherland. He was, according to most sources, her only husband. Yet in a '43 issue of *Photoplay*, writing about the wedding of Dorothy Lamour, "Cal York" said that Miss Lamour's husband, Captain William Ross Howard, was a "member of a famous Baltimore family and former husband of Louise Brooks, cute movie star who rose to fame during silent film days." Perhaps Miss Brooks will clarify matters in her book. Onscreen from 1926. IN: *The American Venus, A Social Celebrity, Love 'Em and Leave 'Em, Evening Clothes, The City Gone Wild, A Girl in Every Port, Pandora's Box, It Pays to Advertise, The Public Enemy*, more.

BROOKS, MARY (See Phyllis Brooks.)

BROOKS, PHYLLIS (N.J.) Universal changed the beautiful blonde's name from Phyllis Weiler to Mary Brooks in '34, but the next year she went to another studio and became and stayed Phyllis Brooks in dozens of pix (many leads in B's), through 1945's *High Powered* and *The Unseen*. Cary Grant's "best girl" for years, it was expected that they would marry. Instead, in '45, she became the wife of Harvard football star Torbert MacDonald, now a most successful business man, and moved to New Jersey. Now in her 60s (b. 1914), still happily married and a popular hostess in her fashionable community, she is the mother of a grown son, Torbert Jr. (b. 1946), and looking forward to being a grandmother. Onscreen from 1934. IN: *I've Been Around, Dangerously Yours, You Can't Have Everything, In Old Chicago, Little Miss Broadway, Charlie Chan in Honolulu, Bring on the Girls, Lady in the Dark, The Unseen*, more.

BROOKS, RAND (S. Cal.) Scarlett O'Hara's ill-fated young first husband in *Gone With the Wind*, this wavy-haired blond was, for 14 years in movies—through 1952's *Waco*—one of the better juvenile leads. He came back in the '60s for two Westerns—*Stagecoach to Danger's Rock* and *Comanche Station*—then quit acting for good. Now in his 50s (b. 1918) and known as A. R. Brooks, he owns and operates an ambulance service in Glendale. He resides in nearby

Tarzana and is the father of two grown children. Lois, his wife of many years, is the only child of the late Stan Laurel; she has lately collaborated with writer Carl Schroeder on an "official" Laurel and Hardy biography. Onscreen from 1938. IN: *Dramatic School, The Old Maid, Babes in Arms, Cheers for Miss Bishop, Cowboy Serenade, High Explosive, The Devil's Playground* (first of 12 "Hopalong Cassidy" movies—the final ones filmed—in which he played Lucky Jenkins), *Kilroy Was Here, Ladies of the Chorus, The Cimarron Kid*, more.

BROTHERS, CASSANDRA F. (N.Y.) Support. IN: *Bananas*.

BROWN, BARRY (S. Cal.) Young co-lead. IN: *Bad Company*.

BROWN, DOROTHY (S. Cal.) Support. IN: *The Girl from Havana*.

BROWN, GEORG STANFORD (S. Cal.) Black support. IN: *The Comedians, Bullitt, God Bless You Uncle Sam*, more.

BROWN, GEORGIA (Eng.) Singer-actress. IN: *A Study in Terror, The Fixer, Lock Up Your Daughters, Galileo*, more.

BROWN, JAMES (S. Cal.) In the '40s, thanks to such comedies as *Our Hearts Were Young and Gay* and GI roles in WW II epics like *Air Force*, he was momentarily a bobby-soxers' delight. Now in his 50s (b. 1920) and graying at the temples, the rangy actor has made a comeback in the most unexpected fashion. More than a decade ago, after 50 movies and the long-running *Rin-Tin-Tin* TV series, he gave up his career to become a manufacturer of body-building equipment—and made a fortune. In '69, Faberge Inc. bought him out and hired him as veepee in charge of customer relations, which he continued to be for three years, after which he retired. But in '75 Brut put the movie *Whiffs* before the cameras, starring Elliott Gould and Jennifer O'Neill, and this former Texan was the first supporting actor signed. Married more than two decades to his present wife, Betty, the actor has—by first wife, former model Verna Knopf—three grown daughters, Beverly, Barbara, and Carol, and is a grandfather. Onscreen from 1942. IN: *The Forest Rangers, Corvette K-225, Going My Way, Objective Burma, The Younger Brothers, Sands of Iwo Jima, Montana, The Groom Wore Spurs, The Pride of St. Louis, The Charge at Feather River, Black Spurs, Town Tamer*, more.

BROWN, JIM (S. Cal.) Black costar. Onscreen from 1964. IN: *Rio Conchos, The Dirty Dozen, Ice Station Zebra, El Condor, 100 Rifles,*

Slaughter, Black Gunn, Take a Hard Ride, more.

BROWN, JOE, JR. (S. Cal.) Support. Onscreen from 1940. IN: *High School, La Conga Nights, Naval Academy, Juke Box Jenny, The Wild Blue Yonder, The Fugitive Kind,* more.

BROWN, JOHNNY (N.Y.) Black singer-actor-comedian. IN: *A Man Called Adam, The Lost Man, The Out of Towners,* more.

BROWN, LEW (S. Cal.) Character. IN: *Crime and Punishment U.S.A.*

BROWN, PETER (S. Cal.) Leading man. Onscreen from 1958. IN: *Darby's Rangers, Merrill's Marauders, Ride the Wild Surf, Kitten With a Whip, Three Guns for Texas, Backtrack, Chrome and Hot Leather,* more.

BROWN, PHILIP (S. Cal.) Juvenile. IN: *Fitzwilly.*

BROWN, TOM (S. Cal.) Well into his 60s now (b. 1913) and almost bald, this blue-eyed actor still retains much of the youthful charm that made him—in more than 125 pictures—Hollywood's #1 boy-next-door. *Gentle Julia, Navy Blue and Gold, Margie,* and *The Duke of West Point* were among those that epitomized the image. Last onscreen in 1962's *The Choppers,* he has been doubly busy on TV. For several years he was featured concurrently in two series on competing channels. In CBS' *Gunsmoke* he was rancher Ed O'Connor who sometimes served as a catalyst for mischief but could usually be counted on for level-headed wisdom at the showdown. In ABC's daytime serial *General Hospital,* he has long been the loudmouthed, sometimes coarse, Al Weeks. Off TV, Tom Brown, who is bright and humorous, is neither loud, nor a rancher, nor married. Now living in a memento-filled Hollywood apartment, the actor, who saw military service as an infantry officer in two wars (WW II and Korea) has been married to and divorced from three wives. The first, the exquisite Natalie Draper, he married twice in a 10-day period in '37—first on a yacht, then on land; they were divorced in '39. Tom has, by a later wife, three grown children of whom he is enormously proud: younger son, Tuttle, lives in Tulsa; elder son, Christopher, handsome enought to be a screen star himself, has lately been a ski instructor near Sacramento; and daughter, Cathleen, who has made the actor a grandfather, is married to a Denver businessman. Admitting that after each of his tours of military duty he had difficulty getting started again as an actor, Tom Brown gives great credit to those who helped him. After

WW II, ex-actress Helen Mack, then a producer, gave him much work in radio dramas. After the Korean War, Don "Red" Barry and the late Lou Costello helped him break into the character-actor field. When not busy on TV, this actor writes, sails, and helps run the "Lady Sierra Mine," a pitchblende mine in Olancha, Calif., owned cooperatively by the cast and crew of *General Hospital.* Onscreen from 1924. IN: *The Hoosier Schoolmaster, Queen High, The Famous Ferguson Case, This Side of Heaven, Judge Priest, Anne of Green Gables, Annapolis Farewell, Rose Bowl, Merrily We Live, Swing That Cheer, These Glamour Girls, Sandy Is a Lady, Adventures of Smilin' Jack* (serial), *Slippy McGee, Ringside, The Naked Gun,* more.

BROWN, VANESSA (S. Cal.) One of the most fetching young leads in the '40s and early '50s, dark-haired Vanessa left the screen after 1952's *The Bad and the Beautiful.* But she never retired. "Quiz Kids" never quit—and, as Smylla Brind, long before becoming an actress, she was one of the most prominent of them. She married —and stayed married to—Mark Sandrich Jr., director of movies and TV (*The Mary Tyler Moore Show*), and composer of Broadway shows (*Ben Franklin in Paris.*) She has two children, Lisa and David Michael, both young teenagers now. She wrote newspaper and magazine articles, a novel, a nonfiction book (*The Manpower Policies of Secretary of Labor Willard Wirtz*), and for eight years was freelance correspondent for *The Voice of America*—doing scripts and on-the-air interviews. She played supporting roles in two movies: *Rosie* ('67) and *Bless the Beasts & Children* ('71). And, while not at all as active on TV as she had been in the '50s and '60s, she occasionally did a guest role on such shows as *Arnie* and *Police Story.* Now, on what she expects to be a full-time basis, she has resumed her screen career—costarring with Millie Perkins and Rick Jason (both, like herself, 20th Century-Fox veterans) in *The Witch Who Came Out of the Sea.* Despite these numerous "careers," Vanessa is still only in her 40s—born 1928. Onscreen from 1944. IN: *Youth Runs Wild* (billed Tessa Brind), *I've Always Loved You, The Late George Apley, The Ghost and Mrs. Muir, The Foxes of Harrow, The Heiress, The Secret of St. Ives, Tarzan and the Slave Girl, Three Husbands, The Fighter,* more.

BROWNE, CORAL (S. Cal.) Support. Onscreen from 1936. IN: *The Amateur Gentleman, We're Going to Be Rich, Piccadilly Incident, Auntie Mame, The Roman Spring of Mrs. Stone, The Night of the Generals, The Killing of Sister George, The Drowning Pool,* more.

BROWNE, KATHIE (S. Cal.) Leading lady. IN: *Man's Favorite Sport, Come Blow Your Horn, The Brass Bottle, Brainstorm*, more.

BROWNE, ROSCOE LEE (S. Cal.) Black co-star. Onscreen from 1962. IN: *The Connection, Black Like Me, Terror in the City, The Comedians, The Liberation of Lord Byron Jones, The Cowboys, Cisco Pike, The World's Greatest Athlete*, more.

BROWNELL, BARBARA (N.Y.) Support. IN: *Going Home.*

BRUBAKER, ROBERT (S. Cal.) Support. IN: *Seconds, The Bus Is Coming*, more.

BRUCE, BRENDA (Eng.) Support. IN: *I Live in Grosvenor Square, Night Boat to Dublin, While the Sun Shines, Carnival, When the Bough Breaks, Don't Ever Leave Me, The Uncle, The Virgin Soldiers*, more.

BRUCE, CAROL (N.Y.) The sultry singer-actress gave up her brief career as a leading lady at Universal in the early '40s. In the years since she has starred in many Broadway musicals, perhaps most notably in *Do I Hear a Waltz?* In the summer of '75 she costarred—still slender and dark-haired—with Edie Adams at theaters in Ohio in the pre-Broadway tryout of a new play with music, *The Cooch Dancer.* She played a vengeful clairvoyant, Madame Serena, in this carnival story. In her mid-50s now, she has been married to and divorced from (1945–63) manufacturer's representative Milton Nathanson, and is the mother of a grown daughter, Julie. Onscreen from 1941. IN: *This Woman Is Mine, Keep 'Em Flying, Behind the Eight Ball.*

BRUCE, SHELLEY (N.Y.) Juvenile actress. Onscreen in the '70s. IN: *The Godfather*, more.

BRUCE, VIRGINIA (S. Cal.) Now in her 60s (b. 1910), the actress who was once one of Metro's loveliest blonde stars still has a beautiful home in the Pacific Palisades, but various illnesses and mishaps have forced her to spend long periods at the Motion Picture and TV Country Home and Hospital. She was most recently readmitted there early in '73 following a fall in which she fractured her hip. She has not been seen onscreen since playing Kim Novak's mother in *Strangers When We Meet* ('60) and it is not likely she will ever act again. The former actress has had a traumatic marital life. She was first married ('32) to John Gilbert, divorcing him in '34, shortly before his death; by him, she has a daughter, Susan Ann (b. 1933). Married to MGM director J. Walter Ruben in '37, and after giving birth to a son, Christopher, she was wid-owed in '41. In '46 she married Turkish-born Ali Ipar, who was 13 years her junior. The following year, after visiting Turkey, he was refused permission to re-enter the United States as he was not an American citizen. After the actress made numerous trips to Washington, then-Secretary of State George Marshall personally arranged Ipar's re-entry—but, within months, her luckless husband had been conscripted into the Turkish Army. The actress was forced to divorce him—a technicality—because Turkish law forbade a commission to any man married to a foreigner. She joined him in Turkey in '52, remarried him, and starred there in a movie, *Istanbul*, that Ipar wrote and directed. After they had lived several years in Hollywood, Ipar returned to Istanbul where he was imprisoned for almost two years by the military junta that had taken over his country—during which time his American visa expired. The actress remains unreconciled to the series of misfortunes with which she has been plagued these decades. Onscreen from 1929. IN: *Why Bring That Up?, The Love Parade, The Miracle Man, The Wet Parade, The Mighty Barnum, Society Doctor, The Great Ziegfeld; Wife, Doctor and Nurse; Bad Man of Brimstone, Yellow Jack, There Goes My Heart, Stronger Than Desire, Hired Wife, The Invisible Woman, Butch Minds the Baby, Brazil, The Night Has a Thousand Eyes, State Department File 649, The Reluctant Bride*, more.

BRUNETTI, ARGENTINA (S. Cal.) Character. Onscreen from 1947. IN: *California, Man-Eater of Kumaon, Broken Arrow, My Cousin Rachel, King of the Khyber Rifles, The Rains of Ranchipur, The George Raft Story, The Appaloosa*, more.

BRYAN, DORA (Eng.) Support. Onscreen from the '40s. IN: *The Fallen Idol, No Room at the Inn, Glory at Sea, The Intruder, As Long as They're Happy, The Green Man, Carry on Sergeant, A Taste of Honey*, more.

BRYAN, JANE (S. Cal.) Fresh-faced, freckled, most beautiful, and vastly talented, she was Bette Davis' protegee at Warners. Particularly did her performance opposite Muni in *We Are Not Alone* give evidence she would be "another" Davis. But in 1940, after *Brother Rat and a Baby* (her 18th pic in five years), and with Davis' blessing, she quit the screen—for good. A few months earlier, in '39, age 21, she had become the wife of a handsome young Walgreen executive, Justin Dart, who was well on his way to becoming a millionaire. Today, looking much as she always did, Jane is still Mrs. Dart—and recently, speaking of her chief booster at Warners, she expressed the regret

63

that "while Bette Davis and I are still friends, our separate travels and different lives have not allowed us to see each other often." (It will be remembered that Davis married her second husband, Arthur Farnsworth, at the Darts' Arizona ranch in 1940.) Jane and her husband, a rugged, heartily gregarious man, are the parents of two sons, Michael (b. 1942), Steve (b. 1952), and a daughter, Jane; in 1972 their daughter, then 28, became the wife of John Campbell, who was an assistant to John D. Ehrlichman in the Nixon Administration. Both the actress and her husband are ardent Republicans, Dart having been a key Republican fund-raiser for two decades, while Jane has been on a federal arts commission in Washington. Also, in the living room of their magnificent, sprawling New England-style house in Bel Air (stone and shingle and white clapboard), on prominent display, is a framed photograph of Nancy and Ronald Reagan. Reagan, besides his political persuasion, costarred with Jane Bryan in several movies, including her last, and has remained her friend through the years. A life of adventure, Jane concedes, is what she has experienced as the wife of Justin Dart, who has converted Rexall into Dart Industries, maker of Tupperware, etc. Licensed pilots both, they have flown company planes all over the nation on business. On commercial flights, they have journeyed together to every part of the globe, he on business, she on archeological expeditions. (She has been governor of the Los Angeles Natural History Museum.) Indeed, they travel so much they have a house in London and an apartment in Manhattan. Travel, she says, is what she does best, adding, "To go somewhere and discover a new scene is like sending an arrow into the future." What she does least well, she insists, is public speaking because "I'm very shy. I think the shyness is caused by my being inarticulate. And I'm plagued by a lack of self-confidence." One of the few things that bores Jane Bryan is talk about her long-ago movie career. Shrugging with disinterest, she says, "I gave that all up when I married and began my new career." Onscreen from 1936. IN: *The Captain's Kid, The Case of the Black Cat, Marked Woman, Kid Galahad, A Slight Case of Murder, Girls on Probation, The Sisters, Brother Rat, The Old Maid, Invisible Stripes, Each Dawn I Die,* more.

BRYANT, JOHN (S. Cal.) Character. IN: *From Here to Eternity, Strangers When We Meet,* more.

BRYAR, CLAUDIA (S. Cal.) Support. IN: *I Was a Teenage Frankenstein.*

BRYAR, PAUL (S. Cal.) Character. Onscreen from 1938. IN: *Tenth Avenue Kid, Paris Call-*ing, Jungle Siren, Walk a Crooked Mile, Under My Skin, Dangerous When Wet, Inside Detroit, The Killer Is Loose, Butch Cassidy and the Sundance Kid,* more.

BRYNNER, YUL (Switz.) Star. Won Best Actor Oscar in *The King and I.* Onscreen from 1949. IN: *Port of New York, The Ten Commandments, Anastasia, The Brothers Karamazov, The Journey, Solomon and Sheba, The Magnificent Seven, Taras Bulba, Flight From Ashiya, Morituri, Return of the Seven, The Long Duel, Villa Rides, The Madwoman of Chaillot, The Light at the Edge of the World, Catlow, Fuzz, Westworld,* more.

BRYSON, BETTY (S. Cal.) Married in '36 to dance director LeRoy Prinz, who won an Oscar for directing the short *Boy and His Dog,* she is retired and the mother of several children. IN: *Shine on Harvest Moon.*

BUA, GENE (N.Y.) Leading man. IN: *Hot Rod Hullabaloo.*

BUCHANAN, EDGAR (S. Cal.) Character. Onscreen from 1940. IN: *Too Many Husbands, Arizona, Penny Serenade, Texas, The Talk of the Town, The Desperadoes, The Impatient Years, Bandit of Sherwood Forest, Sea of Grass, Coroner Creek, Any Number Can Play, Cheaper by the Dozen, It Happens Every Thursday, Shane, Wichita, Come Next Spring, It Started with a Kiss, Ride the High Country, Donovan's Reef, Welcome to Hard Times, Angel in My Pocket, Benji,* more.

BUCHHOLZ, HORST (Switz.) Costar. Onscreen from 1957. IN: *Confessions of Felix Krull, Marianne, Montipi, Sky Without Stars, Tiger Bay. The Magnificent Seven, Fanny, One Two Three, The Young Rebel, The Empty Canvas, That Man in Istanbul, The Great Waltz,* more.

BUCKINGHAM, ROBERT (N.Y.) Support. IN: *Return to Peyton Place.*

BUCKLEY, HAL (S. Cal.) Support. IN: *Kelly's Heroes.*

BUJOLD, GENEVIEVE (S. Cal.) Costar. Nominated for Best Actress Oscar in *Anne of the Thousand Days.* Onscreen from 1967. IN: *La Guerre est Finie, King of Hearts, Isabel, The Thief of Paris, An Act of the Heart, The Trojan Women, Earthquake, The Blarney Cock,* more.

BUKA, DONALD (N.Y.) The actor who played Bette Davis's teenage son in *Watch on the Rhine*—though he was then in his early 20s—is in his 50s now (b. 1921), has been married since '72 to casting director Joy Weber, and is the father of a son, born in '74. Last onscreen in 1964's *Shock Treatment*, he has directed a number of plays and frequently stars in the *CBS Radio Mystery Theater*. Onscreen from 1943. IN: *The Street with No Name, Between Midnight and Dawn, Vendetta, New Mexico, Operation Eichmann*, more.

BULIFANT, JOYCE (S. Cal.) Support. IN: *The Happiest Millionaire.*

BULL, PETER (Eng.) Character. Onscreen from 1934. IN: *The Silent Voice, As You Like It, The African Queen, Oliver Twist, Beau Brummel, The Three Worlds of Gulliver, The Scapegoat, Goodbye Again, Tom Jones, Dr. Strangelove, Dr. Dolittle, The Executioner*, more.

BULOFF, JOSEPH (N.Y.) Character. Onscreen from 1941. IN: *Let's Make Music, Carnegie Hall, To the Victor, The Loves of Carmen, A Kiss in the Dark, Somebody Up There Likes Me, Silk Stockings*, more.

BUNDY, BROOKE (S. Cal.) Leading lady. IN: *Firecreek, The Young Runaways, The Gay Deceivers*, more.

BUONO, VICTOR (S. Cal.) Character. Nominated for Best Supporting Actor Oscar in *What Ever Happened to Baby Jane?* Onscreen from 1962. IN: *Four for Texas, Robin and the Seven Hoods, The Strangler, Hush . . . Hush . . . Sweet Charlotte, Young Dillinger, The Greatest Story Ever Told, The Savage Season, Beneath the Planet of the Apes, The Wrath of God, Moon Child*, more.

BURDEN, HUGH (Eng.) Character. Onscreen from 1942. IN: *One of Our Aircraft Is Missing, Sleeping Car to Trieste, The Malta Story, Funeral in Berlin*, more.

BURGHOFF, GARY (S. Cal.) Comic support. IN: *M*A*S*H, B.S. I Love You.*

BURKE, PAUL (S. Cal.) Costar. Onscreen from 1951. IN: *Call Me Mister, South Sea Woman, Francis in the Navy, Disembodied, The Valley of the Dolls, Sudden Death, The Thomas Crown Affair, Psychic Killer*, more.

BURKE, WALTER (S. Cal.) Character. Onscreen from 1949. IN: *All the King's Men, Mystery Street, The Guy Who Came Back, The Wreck of the Mary Deare, Let No Man Write My Epitaph, The Wheeler Dealers, The President's Analyst, Support Your Local Gunfighter*, more.

BURNETT, CAROL (S. Cal.) Comedienne-actress. IN: *Who's Been Sleeping in My Bed?, Pete 'n Tillie, The Front Page.*

BURNS, BART (S. Cal.) Support. IN: *Fear Strikes Out, Seven Days in May.*

BURNS, CATHERINE (S. Cal.) Costar. Nominated for Best Supporting Actress Oscar in *Last Summer*. ALSO IN: *Red Sky at Morning.*

BURNS, EDMUND (S. Cal.) Claire Windsor's handsome leading man in the silent *To Please One Woman*, he is still dapper in his 80s (b. 1892) and lives in quiet retirement in Hollywood. But when there is a reunion of oldtimers, such as the last one at Mary Pickford's Pickfair in '64, or the '72 opening of the renovated Alexandria Hotel (a favorite haunt of silent stars in the '20s), he is certain to be invited and on hand. "Creative people have a zip and a zing to them and I want to be around them," he says. Onscreen from 1921. IN: *The Manicure Girl, Hell's Highroad, Simon the Jester, The Chinese Parrot, Phyllis of the Follies, Children of the Ritz, She Goes to War, Tanned Legs, Western Limited, The Death Kiss, Dangerously Yours*, more, including 1936's *Hollywood Boulevard*, his last.

BURNS, EILEEN (N.Y.) Support. IN: *Up the Sandbox.*

BURNS, GEORGE (S. Cal.) Star comedian. Won Best Supporting Actor Oscar in *The Sunshine Boys*. Onscreen from 1931. IN: *The Big Broadcast, International House, College Humor, Six of a Kind, We're Not Dressing, Love in Bloom, College Holiday, A Damsel in Distress, Honolulu, Many Happy Returns, The Sunshine Boys*, more.

BURNS, MICHAEL (S. Cal.) Young lead. Onscreen from 1960. IN: *The Wizard of Baghdad, Mr. Hobbs Takes a Vacation, The Raiders, Stranger on the Run, The Private Navy of Sgt. O'Farrell, That Cold Day in the Park*, more.

BURNS, RONNIE (S. Cal.) Support. George's son; now a business man. IN: *Anatomy of a Psycho, Bernardine.*

BURR, RAYMOND (S. Cal.) Character star. Onscreen from 1946. IN: *Without Reservations, I Love Trouble, Pitfall, Ruthless, Station West, Criss Cross, Key to the City, A Place in the Sun, New Mexico, Meet Danny Wilson, Serpent of the Nile, Rear Window, You're Never Too Young, Count Three and Pray, Secret of Treasure Mountain, Ride the High Iron, Affair in Havana*, more.

BURRUD, BILL (S. Cal.) The child actor who was in a dozen pix between his 11th and 13th birthdays is now a handsome man in his early 50s (b. 1925) and the producer of the award-winning TV series *Animal World*. Late in '75 he was married (his second marriage) to Marlene Dorman, a production aide on his show. He formed the Bill Burrud Company in '52 after Navy service in WW II and graduation from the Harvard Business School. Onscreen from 1935. IN: *Three Kids and a Queen, His Night Out, Pride of the Marines, The Magnificent Brute, Girl Overboard, Captains Courageous, It Happened in Hollywood, Idol of the Crowd, Night Hawk*, more.

BURSTYN, ELLEN (N.Y.) Star. Nominated for Best Supporting Actress Oscar in *The Last Picture Show*. Nominated for Best Actress Oscar in *The Exorcist*. Won Best Actress Oscar in *Alice Doesn't Live Here Anymore*. Onscreen from 1964. IN: *Goodbye, Charlie; For Those Who Think Young* (billed Ellen McRae in both), *Tropic of Cancer* (her first billed as Ellen Burstyn), *Alex in Wonderland, Pit Stop, The King of Marvin Gardens, Harry and Tonto*, more.

BURSTYN, NEIL (N.Y.) Support. IN: *Alex in Wonderland*.

BURTON, JULIAN (S. Cal.) Support. IN: *The Young Lions*.

BURTON, MARGARET (Eng.) Support. IN: *The Comedy Man*.

BURTON, RICHARD (Switz.) Star. Nominated for Best Supporting Actor Oscar in *My Cousin Rachel*. Nominated for Best Actor Oscar in *The Robe, Becket, The Spy Who Came in From the Cold, Who's Afraid of Virginia Woolf?, Anne of the Thousand Days*. Onscreen from 1948. IN: *The Last Days of Dolwyn, Waterfront, Green Grow the Rushes, The Woman With No Name, The Desert Rats, The Rains of Ranchipur, Alexander the Great, Look Back in Anger, Ice Palace, The Longest Day, Cleopatra, The V.I.P.s, Night of the Iguana, The Taming of the Shrew, The Comedians, Where Eagles Dare, Candy, Staircase, Under Milk Wood, The Assassination of Trotsky, Bluebeard, The Klansman*, more.

BUSH, BILLY GREEN (S. Cal.) Character. IN: *Five Easy Pieces, Monte Walsh, The Organization, The Jesus Trip, Alice Doesn't Live Here Anymore, Mackintosh & T.J.*, more.

BUSHELL, ANTHONY (Eng.) The former leading man, now in his 70s (b. 1904), acts only occasionally now, but was highly active through 1963. Onscreen from 1929. IN: *Disraeli, Green Stockings, Journey's End, The Flirting Widow, Three Faces East, The Royal Bed, Five Star Final, Vanity Fair, Soldiers of the King, Channel Crossing, The Scarlet Pimpernel, Troopship, The Miniver Story, The Small Back Room, The Red Beret, The Black Knight, The Purple Plain, Bhowani Junction, The Black Tent, Pursuit of the Graf Spee, A Night to Remember, The Queen's Guard*, more.

BUTLER, DAVID (S. Cal.) A major star for 10 years on the silent screen, he turned director in '27 and became one of Hollywood's most successful (*The Little Colonel, The Road to Morocco, My Wild Irish Rose*, etc.). Now in his 80s (b. 1894), he has been retired for several years. Onscreen from 1918. IN: *The Greatest Thing in Life, Upstairs and Down, The Sky Pilot, The Village Blacksmith, The Temple of Venus, In Hollywood with Potash and Perlmutter, Private Affairs, His Majesty Bunker Bean, The Man on the Box, Nobody's Widow, Seventh Heaven, Salute*, more.

BUTTON, DICK (N.Y.) The skating champ-turned-actor has lately been a TV commentator for *ABC's Wide World of Sports*. IN: *The Young Doctors*.

BUTTONS, RED (S. Cal.) Comedian/costar. Won Best Supporting Actor Oscar in *Sayonara*. Onscreen from 1944. IN: *Winged Victory, Imitation General, The Big Circus, One Two Three, Hatari!, Five Weeks in a Balloon, Your Cheatin' Heart, Harlow, Stagecoach, They Shoot Horses, Don't They?, Who Killed Mary What's 'er Name?, The Poseidon Adventure, Gable and Lombard*, more.

BUTTRAM, PAT (S. Cal.) The year 1975 brought great sorrow to the comedian—the death of his wife, actress Sheila Ryan. Married 23 years, they had met in '50 when working together in a Gene Autry pic, *Mule Train*. Buttram, of course, was Autry's screen sidekick for several years. In the '40s brunette Sheila Ryan had been one of 20th Century-Fox's loveliest young leading ladies, appearing in *Something for the Boys, Dressed to Kill, The Gang's All Here*, etc. After the birth of their only child, Kathleen Kerry, in '54, she had dropped out of movies, returning only for one final film, *Street of Darkness* in '58. She had been in delicate health—spending much time in hospitals—for more than a decade before succumbing to a lung ailment. But her husband's increasing success as a comedian had continued to the last to be a source of great pleasure to her. During his long run in the TV series *Green Acres*, Buttram became Hollywood's "sophisticated rube" and most-in-demand after-dinner speaker. His string ties and country-boy ways would leave audiences, if they were among the uninitiated, unprepared for the wise and witty Will Rogers-type zingers he delivered. Financially one of Hollywood's most astute citizens, Buttram owns horses, a radio station in Alabama, his home state, and a five-acre ranch in the fashionable Northridge section of the San Fernando Valley. The showpiece of his home, furnished in authentic Early American antiques, is the den—filled with books, relics of the Civil War, and a priceless (literally) collection of button hooks, believed to be the largest in the world. Onscreen from 1944. IN: *National Barn Dance, Strawberry Roan, Riders in the Sky, Hills of Utah, Twilight of Honor, Roustabout; Sgt. Deadhead, the Astronaut; The Sweet Ride,* more.

BUZZELL, EDDIE (S. Cal.) After starring in the '30 version of *Little Johnny Jones,* the musical comedy actor became one of Metro's most noted directors—of *Best Foot Forward, At the Circus, Go West,* etc. Retired now in his late 70s (b. 1897), he still plays golf, remains a candid camera buff, and attends the Philharmonic.

BYGRAVES, MAX (Eng.) Singer-comedian-actor. IN: *Bless 'Em All, Tom Brown's Schooldays, Charley Moon* (first starring role), *A Cry From the Streets,* more.

BYRNE, EDDIE (Eng.) Character. Onscreen from the '40s. IN: *Captain Boycott, Saints and Sinners; Time, Gentlemen, Please; Trouble in the Glen, The Divided Heart, Abandon Ship, Dunkirk, The Mark, Where's Jack?, Sinful Davey,* more.

BYRNES, EDD (S. Cal.) Support. Onscreen from 1958. IN: *Marjorie Morningstar, Yellowstone Kelly, The Secret Invasion, Any Gun Can Play,* more.

BYRON, JEAN (S. Cal.) Leading lady. Onscreen from the '50s. IN: *The Magnetic Monster, Wall of Noise, Flareup,* more.

BYRON, KATHLEEN (Eng.) Leading lady/character. Onscreen from the early '40s. IN: *Stairway to Heaven, Black Narcissus, Prelude to Fame, The Reluctant Widow, Tom Brown's School Days, Young Bess; Burn, Witch, Burn;* more.

C

CAAN, JAMES (S. Cal.) Star. Nominated for Best Supporting Actor Oscar in *The Godfather.* Onscreen from 1963. IN: *Irma La Douce, Lady in a Cage, Red Line 7000, The Glory Guys, Moon Shot, Games, El Dorado, The Rain People, Rabbit Run, T.R. Baskin, Slither, Freebie and the Bean, Funny Lady, Rollerball, The Killer Elite,* more.

CABAL, ROBERT (S. Cal.) Support. IN: *Maru Maru, Hell's Island,* more.

CABOT, SEBASTIAN (S. Cal.) Character. Onscreen in England from 1936. IN: *Secret Agent, Pimpernel Smith, Laughter in Paradise, Tony Draws a Horse, The Captain's Paradise,* more. Onscreen in America from 1953. IN: *Julius Caesar, Westward the Women, Kismet, Omar Khayyam, Black Patch, Say One for Me, Seven Thieves, The Family Jewels,* more.

CABOT, SUSAN (S. Cal.) Leading lady. Onscreen from 1950. IN: *On the Isle of Samoa, Tomahawk, Son of Ali Baba, Gunsmoke, Machine Gun Kelly, The Wasp Woman,* more.

CADY, FRANK (S. Cal.) One of Hollywood's best bald character actors for 30 years, in several dozen films, he spent eight years playing Sam Drucker on both *Green Acres* and *Petticoat Junction* on TV. Later, a resident member of the Mark Taper Forum's repertory company in Los Angeles, he had major roles in such Shakespearean productions as *Henry IV, Part 1.* Onscreen from 1947. IN: *Violence, The Checkered Coat, The Great Rupert, Dear Brat, Ace in the Hole, When Worlds Collide, Rear Window, The Bad Seed, The Tin Star, Seven Faces of Dr. Lao,* more.

CAESAR, SID (N.Y.) Star comedian. Onscreen from 1946. IN: *Tars and Spars, The Guilt of Janet Ames, It's a Mad Mad Mad Mad World, The Busy Body, Airport 1975,* more.

CAGNEY, JAMES (N.Y.) Stockier than he was ever seen on the screen, and in his 70s (b. 1899), he lives on a 500-acre "working" farm (millionaire-style) near Stanfordville in Dutchess County, with Billie, the wife he married in '22. They have two children, James Jr. and Mrs. Casey Cagney Thomas, and four grandchildren. Last onscreen in 1961's *One Two Three,* the actor says he will never make another picture and that he never watches his old ones on TV. But he admits that *Yankee Doodle Dandy,* which won him his Oscar, remains his favorite. (He had earlier been nominated in *Angels With Dirty Faces* and later in *Love Me or Leave Me.*) He says he still tap dances every morning to shake out the aches and pains, runs the 300 yards uphill to his painting studio, and jogs during TV commercials. Why did he give up moviemaking? "I was psychologically finished," he says. "I'd been at it 30 or 40 years. After a while, it gets down to essential needs. You need a wife, need friends, you need some money, good talk, and you need the laughs. I had it all." He now says that there aren't enough hours in the day to accomplish all the things he wants to do—paint, breed horses and prize cattle, collect fine art, and, when he's at his other estate on Martha's Vineyard, sail. Onscreen from 1930. IN: *Sinners' Holiday, The Public Enemy, Taxi, Winner Take All, The Mayor of Hell, Footlight Parade, Here Comes the Navy, Devil Dogs of the Air, G Men, A Midsummer Night's Dream, Ceiling Zero, Boy Meets Girl, Each Dawn I Die, The Roaring Twenties, The Fighting 69th, Strawberry Blonde, Johnny Come Lately, Blood on the Sun, The Time of Your Life, White Heat, Kiss Tomorrow Goodbye, A Lion Is in the Streets, Run for Cover, Mister Roberts, Tribute to a Bad Man, Man of a Thousand Faces, Never Steal Anything Small, Shake Hands With the Devil, The Gallant Hours,* more.

CAGNEY, JEANNE (S. Cal.) James' younger sister, she played major roles in many for 17 years—leads in B's, supporting parts in A's—through 1957's *Man of a Thousand Faces.* Since then she has been in just one, 1965's *Town Tamer.* For years she lived in New Hyde Park, N.Y., where she assisted a friend, the widow of James Barton, in writing a book about the great character actor's life. In '72, in New York, she received her divorce decree from Dr. Jack Morrison, after almost 20 years of marriage, and has since relocated in Newport Beach. The father of the actress's two daughters, Morrison was dean of the School of Fine Arts at Ohio University and is now an executive with the John D. Rockefeller 3d Fund. Now in her 50s (b. 1919), Jeanne is considering resuming her career in character roles. Onscreen from 1940. IN: *Queen of the Mob, Golden Gloves, Rhythm on the River, Yankee Doodle Dandy, The Time of Your Life, Quicksand, Don't Bother to Knock,* more.

CAILLOU, ALAN (S. Cal.) Character. IN: *Clarence, the Cross-Eyed Lion; The Losers, Hellfighters,* more.

CAINE, HOWARD (S. Cal.) Character. IN: *Pay or Die, The Man From the Diners' Club, Alvarez Kelly, Watermelon Man,* more.

CAINE, MICHAEL (Eng.) Star. Nominated for Best Actor Oscar in *Alfie* and *Sleuth.* Onscreen from 1956. IN: *How to Murder a Rich Uncle,*

The Two-Headed Spy, Zulu, The Ipcress File, Gambit, The Wrong Box, Funeral in Berlin, Hurry Sundown, The Magus, Too Late the Hero, The Battle of Britain, Kidnapped, Pulp; X, Y and Zee; Peeper, The Wilby Conspiracy, The Romantic Englishwoman, The Man Who Would Be King, more.

CALHOUN, RORY (S. Cal.) With graying temples and almost as handsome as in his peak days as a screen star, this actor has become in his 50s (b. 1922) one of the suavest villains on TV: *Petrocelli, Alias Smith and Jones, Owen Marshall,* etc. He has also costarred in a number of relatively recent movies: *Night of the Lepus, Blood Black and White.* For almost two years after his 1970 divorce from Lita Baron after 21 years of marriage—not one of the town's "amicable" divorces—Calhoun chose not to work at all, because, as he told a *New York Times* correspondent, "I figured the more I worked, the more alimony I had to pay her. So I stayed idle." To her charges that he committed adultery with 79 women, he grinned and said to the same reporter, "Heck, she didn't include even half of them." By Lita Baron, retired and living in Palm Springs, Calhoun has three daughters, now all in their teens: Cindy Frances, Tami Elizabeth, and Lorri Marie. On April 20, 1971, in Las Vegas, he married Susan K. Langely (a former newspaper woman from Australia, much younger than he; she met the actor when she interviewed him in London). Later that same year, they welcomed a daughter, Rory. Recently, Calhoun spoke of Catholic priest Rev. Donald Kanally, who took him in hand and changed his life when he had been sent to the Federal Reform School at El Reno, Okla., for a series of thefts as a youth. "He put me on the straight and narrow by teaching me to pray and respect myself," Calhoun said. "He taught me values I hadn't learned as a youngster. Today, he's a monsignor. And I hope that anyone who needs a helping hand will be as lucky as I was in having a Father Kanally." Onscreen from 1944. IN: *Sunday Dinner for a Soldier, The Great John L., The Red House, That Hagen Girl, Sand, A Ticket to Tomahawk, I'd Climb the Highest Mountain, How to Marry a Millionaire, River of No Return, Red Sundown, Ride Out for Revenge, Black Spurs, Apache Uprising, Operation Cross Eagles,* more.

CALLAHAN, JAMES (S. Cal.) Support. Onscreen from 1959. IN: *The Battle of the Coral Sea, All Fall Down, Experiment in Terror, Tropic of Cancer,* more.

CALLAN, MICHAEL (S. Cal.) Leading man. Onscreen from 1958. IN: *They Came to Cordura, Pepe, Gidget Goes Hawaiian, 13 West*

Street, Bon Voyage!, The Victors, The New Interns, Cat Ballou, Lepke, more.

CALLAS, CHARLIE (S. Cal.) Comedian. IN: *The Big Mouth.*

CALLAS, MARIA (It.) Opera star-actress. IN: *Medea.*

CALLOWAY, CAB (Ill.) Black orchestra leader. Onscreen with his band from 1932. IN: *The Big Broadcast, The Singing Kid, Manhattan Merry-Go-Round, Stormy Weather, Sensations of 1945.* Onscreen as a solo performer from 1958. IN: *St. Louis Blues, The Cincinnati Kid,* more.

CALVERT, PHYLLIS (Eng.) Hers is a name that generations of English audiences have grown up with, though she is now only in her early 60s (b. 1915). From age 10 she was popular on London stages. During the '40s and well into the '50s she was in the top 5 movie actresses. In the '60s, her beauty fading, she played major character roles in such films as *The Battle of the Villa Fiorita* and *Oh, What a Lovely War!* With fewer screen roles to pick from, she began, early in the '70s, to star in the TV serial *Kate*, playing an aging columnist. And, in '73, when Wendy Hiller left the cast after a year's run, she replaced her in the dramatic stage hit *Crown Matrimonial.* From '41 until his death in '57, she was the wife of actor-turned-publisher Peter Murray-Hill; the mother of a grown daughter by him, Auriol, she has not remarried. Onscreen from 1939. IN: *His Brother's Keeper, Inspector Hornleigh Goes to It, Kipps, The Young Mr. Pitt, Fanny by Gaslight, The Man in Grey, Madonna of the Seven Moons, The Magic Bow, My Own True Love, Appointment with Danger, Mandy, Indiscreet, Oscar Wilde,* more.

CALVET, CORINNE (S. Cal.) In her 50s now (b. 1925), this French actress, ex-sexpot once hailed as the "new" Hayworth, does not work as frequently as in her heyday. On TV in '74, in the pilot episode of *Police Woman,* she turned up, with short dark hair, playing an obviously aging gambling den queen. That same year, sans dialogue, she appeared in the TV-movie *The Phantom of Hollywood.* Her life since she was one of Hal Wallis' most promising stars has not been without drama. She has been married and divorced four times. Her husbands were actor John Bromfield, actor-writer Jeff Stone, movie producer Albert Gannaway, and a photographer, whose name she seldom mentions, who was 25 when she married him. There was also a five-year romantic liaison with a millionaire, Donald P. Scott, that ended in headlines when he sued to recover $750,000 in gifts he said he had given her while they were together. Corinne says she had little left after the settlement. During a low period in New York City, she worked for a while as a sales demonstrator in a toy shop. "I did whatever I could to survive," she has said. She has two sons—Robin, by Jeff Stone, who is grown now, and an adopted son, Michael, just entering his teens. Back in Hollywood today, the star, who once lived in a mansion in Trousdale Estates, lives in a rundown section in a rented frame house that is almost as old as Hollywood itself. She has lately studied (and taught) at the Arica Institute, a school of esoteric spiritualism, which she explains is "not a religion; it is a science." Her consciousness level-changing experiences there, besides bringing her "inner peace," have taught her "not to depend on anyone for happiness; that you have to look within yourself." As for her future, Corinne says, "Now I will take anything that God sends my way." Onscreen from 1949. IN: *Rope of Sand, My Friend Irma Goes West, Quebec, On the Riviera, Sailor Beware, What Price Glory, Thunder in the East, Powder River, The Far Country, One Step to Eternity, Hemingway's Adventures of a Young Man, Apache Uprising,* more.

CAMBRIDGE, GODFREY (Conn.) Black comedian/costar. Onscreen from 1959. IN: *The Last Angry Man, The Troublemaker, The President's Analyst, Bye Bye Braverman, Watermelon Man, Cotton Comes to Harlem, The Biscuit Eater, Come Back Charleston Blue, Whiffs, Friday Foster,* more.

CAMERON, ROD (S. Cal.) In his 60s (b. 1912) as lanky and leathery as ever, this actor from Canada still costars in movies. Recent ones: *Jessie's Girls, Redneck.* Curiously, on TV, where he works often, he is usually seen in minor roles—in the *Evel Knievel* dramatic special, an aging rodeo star who died early in the story; in *Police Story,* a desk-bound police lieutenant in a desert city, with but two lines of dialogue. In the '60s he starred in a number of movies made in Germany (*Old Firehand*) and Italy (*Bullets Don't Argue*), Westerns all. The actor has been married three times, first, prefame, to a nonprofessional by whom he has a grown daughter. In 1950 he married Anela Alves-Lico, and when that union ended 10 years later, he married her mother, Dorothy, who is a few years older than he. That marriage, at last report, still flourished. Onscreen from 1940. IN: *The Quarterback, Christmas in July, The Fleet's In, The Forest Rangers, Gung Ho!, Secret Service in Darkest Africa* (and other serials), *The Kansan, Salome Where She Danced, Panhandle, River Lady, Stampede, Dakota Lil, Cavalry Scout, Steel Lady, Hell's Outpost, Yaqui*

Drums, The Man Who Died Twice, Requiem for a Gunfighter, The Last Movie, Psychic Killer, more.

CAMP, HAMILTON (S. Cal.) Support. Onscreen from 1967. IN: *The Perils of Pauline, The Cockeyed Cowboys of Calico County,* more

CAMPANELLA, FRANK (S. Cal.) Character. IN: *Who Killed Teddy Bear?, Stage Struck, Seconds, What's So Bad About Feeling Good?, The Gang That Couldn't Shoot Straight,* more.

CAMPANELLA, JOSEPH (S. Cal.) Costar. IN: *Murder Inc., The Young Lovers, The St. Valentine's Day Massacre,* more.

CAMPBELL, BEATRICE (Eng.) Onscreen from the '40s. IN: *Meet Me at Dawn, My Brother Jonathan, The Mudlark, The Last Holiday, No Place for Jennifer, Laughter in Paradise, I'll Never Forget You, The Master of Ballantrae, Wicked Wife, The Cockleshell Heroes,* more.

CAMPBELL, GLEN (S. Cal.) Singer-leading man. IN: *Baby, the Rain Must Fall; The Cool Ones, True Grit, Norwood.*

CAMPBELL, JIM (N.Y.) Support. IN: *The Golden Gloves Story, Eternal Flame.*

CAMPBELL, JUDY (Eng.) Leading lady/support. Onscreen from the '40s. IN: *Convoy, Green for Danger, Bonnie Prince Charlie, There's a Girl in My Soup,* more.

CAMPBELL, LOUISE (Conn.) The lovely redhead who was one of Paramount's favorite leading ladies in the late '30s lives—as she has for decades—in a big house in Rowayton, and is enjoying a thriving career in TV commercials. Happily married to character actor Horace McMahon from '38 until his death in '71, she gave up acting after 1941's *Bowery Boy,* devoting herself to rearing a family. She has three grown children, Thomas, Kate, and Missy (Martha). Both daughters are actresses—Missy working in the New York theatre, and Kate in TV-movies. Devoutly religious, Louise Campbell is a parishioner of St. Joseph's Roman Catholic Church in South Norwalk—that being the church that she and her late husband attended, and the one in which he, as a youth, was confirmed. Onscreen in 1937. IN: *Bulldog Drummond Comes Back* (and two others of this series), *Night Club Scandal, The Buccaneer, Scandal Sheet, Men With Wings, The Star Maker, Emergency Squad, Anne of Windy Poplars,* more.

CAMPBELL, SHAWN (N.Y.) Juvenile actor. Onscreen from 1968. IN: *Rachel Rachel, Ask My Name* (documentary), more.

CAMPBELL, WILLIAM (S. Cal.) Support. Onscreen from 1950. IN: *Breakthrough, Battle Circus, Code 2, The High and the Mighty, Cell 2455—Death Row, Battle Cry, Love Me Tender, The Naked and the Dead, The Sheriff of Fractured Jaw, Hush . . . Hush . . . Sweet Charlotte, Track of the Vampire, Dirty Mary Crazy Larry,* more.

CAMPEAU, GEORGE (S. Cal.) Long retired from movies, he is the widower of June Harrison (d. 1974), who had been a screen child actress, and the father of four. Onscreen in the '40s. IN: *The Nurses's Secret,* more.

CAMPOS, RAFAEL (S. Cal.) Support. IN: *Blackboard Jungle, Trial, The Light in the Forest, Lady in a Cage, The Appaloosa, Mister Buddwing, The Drug Set, Hangup,* more.

CAMPOS, VICTOR (S. Cal.) Support. Onscreen from 1970. IN: *The Adversary, Newman's Law,* more.

CANALE, GIANNA MARIA (It.) Leading lady. Onscreen from the '40s. IN: *Rigoletto, A Dead Woman's Kiss; Theodora, Slave Empress; The Sword and the Cross, The Mighty Crusaders, The Slave, The Adventurers of Scaramouche,* more.

CANARY, DAVID (S. Cal.) Support. IN: *Hombre, The St. Valentine's Day Massacre, Posse,* more.

CANFIELD, MARY GRACE (S. Cal.) Support. IN: *Pollyanna.*

CANNON, DYAN (S. Cal.) Costar. Nominated for Best Supporting Actress Oscar in *Bob & Carol & Ted & Alice.* Onscreen from 1959. IN: *The Rise and Fall of Legs Diamond, This Rebel Breed, The Anderson Tapes, The Love Machine, Such Good Friends, Shamus, The Last of Sheila,* more.

CANNON, J. D. (S. Cal.) Support. IN: *An American Dream, Cool Hand Luke, Heaven With a Gun, Cotton Comes to Harlem, The Thousand Plane Raid; Krakatoa, East of Java;* more.

CANOVA, JUDY (S. Cal.) The yodeling hillbilly gal is gone; in her place there is a matronly redheaded woman, just entering her 60s (b. 1916), who has been seen on TV as Aunt Vivian in the Joy dish detergent commercials and, smartly coiffured, in mother roles on such shows as *Police Woman.* Also, in '72, she toured with June Allyson in *No, No, Nanette,* playing the comic maid role created on Broadway by Patsy Kelly. The actress has been married four times—to William Burns (divorced in '39), Cpl. James H. Ripley (their '41 marriage was annulled the same year), Chester England (divorced in '49), and, since '50, to Philip Rivero, a Cuban importer who later went into real estate. She has two grown children—Julietta, by England, and, by Rivero, Diana. Diana Canova—she uses her mother's surname professionally—is beginning her own acting career; introduced in a regular role in *Ozzie's Girls,* she has lately been seen in *Chico and the Man* and *Happy Days.* Onscreen from 1935. IN: *Going Highbrow, Artists and Models, Sis Hopkins, Puddin' Head, True to the Army, Sleepy Lagoon, Chatterbox, The Wac from Walla Walla, Untamed Heiress, Lay That Rifle Down,* more, including 1960's *The Adventures of Huckleberry Finn,* her most recent picture.

CANOVA, ZEKE (S. Cal.) Judy's comedian brother; he rarely acts now. IN: *In Caliente,* more.

CANTINFLAS (Mex.) Star comedian. Onscreen in Mexico in several dozen films from the early '40s. Onscreen in the U.S. from 1956. IN: *Around the World in 80 Days, Pepe.*

CANUTT, YAKIMA (S. Cal.) Stuntman/support. Received special Oscar in 1966 "for achievements as a stunt man and for developing safety devices to protect stunt men everywhere." Onscreen from silent days. IN: *Captain Cowboy, Hurricane Horseman, Dawn Rider, Stagecoach, Gone With the Wind, Ghost Valley Raiders, Prairie Schooners, Hidden Valley Outlaws, Rocky Mountain, The Far Horizons, In Love and War,* more.

CAPERS, VIRGINIA (N.Y.) Black character. IN: *Norwood, Support Your Local Gunfighter, Big Jake,* more.

CAPOTE, TRUMAN (N.Y.) Author-actor. Onscreen in 1976. IN: *Murder by Death.*

CAPRI, AHNA (S. Cal.) Formerly Anna. Leading lady. Onscreen from 1964. IN: *Kisses for My President, The Girls on the Beach, One of Our Spies Is Missing, Darker Than Amber, The Brotherhood of Satan,* more.

CAPUCINE (Fr.) Costar. Onscreen from 1960. IN: *Song Without End, North to Alaska, Walk on the Wild Side, The Lion, The Pink Panther, What's New Pussycat?, Tale of the Fox, Fraulein Doktor, The Exquisite Cadaver,* more.

CARBONE, ANTONY (S. Cal.) Character. IN: *The Pit and the Pendulum, Newman's Law,* more.

CARDI, PAT (S. Cal.) Former juvenile; young lead. Onscreen from 1958. IN: *The Naked and the Dead, Youngblood Hawke, And Now Miguel* (title role), *Let's Kill Uncle, Horror High;* more.

CARDINALE, CLAUDIA (It.) Costar. Onscreen from 1958. IN: *Il Bell Antonio, Big Deal on Madonna Street, Girl with a Suitcase, The Leopard, 8½, The Pink Panther, Circus World, Bebo's Girl, The Centurions, The Professionals, The Lovemakers, Don't Make Waves, Once Upon a Time in the West, The Red Tent; Libera, My Love; Midnight Pleasures,* more.

CARERE, CHRISTINE (Fr.) Leading lady. Onscreen in America from 1957. IN: *A Certain Smile, Mardi Gras,* more.

CAREY, HARRY, JR. (S. Cal.) Son of the great star, and once a favorite John Ford second lead, he now, in his 50s (b. 1921), plays hardbitten character roles in Hollywood. In Italy, though, he has continued to star in Westerns such as 1974's *A Man From the East.* Onscreen from 1947. IN: *Pursued, Red River, Three Godfathers, She Wore a Yellow Ribbon, Wagonmaster, Warpath, Mister Roberts, The Searchers, The Great Locomotive Chase, Kiss Them for Me, Alvarez Kelly, Big Jake, Take a Hard Ride,* more.

CAREY, JOYCE (Eng.) Character. Onscreen from the '20s. IN: *Because, God and the Man, Colonel Newcome, In Which We Serve, Blithe Spirit, Johnny in the Clouds, Brief Encounter, The Astonished Heart, Cry the Beloved Country, Street Corner, Stolen Assignment, The Black Windmill,* more.

CAREY, MACDONALD (S. Cal.) Leading man. Starring in recent years in the TV soap opera *Days of Our Lives,* he has not appeared in a movie in a decade. Onscreen from 1942. IN: *Take a Letter Darling, Wake Island, Star Spangled Rhythm, Shadow of a Doubt, Bride of Vengeance, The Great Gatsby, The Great Missouri Raid, Excuse My Dust, Meet Me After the Show, Fire Over Africa, John Paul Jones, These Are the Damned,* more.

CAREY, MICHELE (S. Cal.) Leading lady. Onscreen from 1967. IN: *El Dorado, The Sweet Ride, Changes, Dirty Dingus Magee, Scandalous John, The Animals,* more.

CAREY, OLIVE (S. Cal.) Married once, to the great Harry Carey, from 1913 until his death in

1947, she is in her 80s now and lives in retirement at her seaside ranch in Carpinteria. She has two children, actor Harry Carey Jr. and married daughter Ellen, and numerous grandchildren. One of the major events of her recent life was the wedding, held in the spring of '76 at the ranch, of grandson, Douglas Taylor, a singer, to actress Judy Norton ("Mary Ellen" in TV's *The Waltons*). During her long career, Olive Carey has acted under two names other than her married one: Olive Fuller Golden (as a leading lady in silents) and Olive Deering. Onscreen from 1914. IN: Pickford's *Tess of the Storm Country*, many silent Universal Westerns (often opposite her husband), *Trader Horn* (with Carey also), more. Onscreen as a character actress from 1949. IN: *Samson and Delilah, Caged, The Ten Commandments* (all billed Olive Deering), plus (as Olive Carey) *The Bride Comes to Yellow Sky, Affair With a Stranger, Rogue Cop, I Died a Thousand Times, The Searchers, Gunfight at the O.K. Corral*, more, including 1957's *Run of the Arrow*, her last.

CAREY, PHILIP (S. Cal.) Previously married (from '49) to college sweetheart, Maureen Peppler, by whom he has three grown children—Linda, Jeffrey, and Lisa Ann—the leading man, in '75, announced his engagement to Colleen Welch. Now in his 50s (b. 1925), he has been seen regularly in such TV shows as *Police Woman*. Onscreen from 1949. IN: *Daughters of the West, I Was a Communist for the FBI, Cattle Town, This Woman Is Dangerous, Calamity Jane, The Long Gray Line, Count Three and Pray, Shadow in the Window, Dead Ringer, Three Guns for Texas, Sudden Death, The Seven Minutes*, more.

CARGILL, PATRICK (Eng.) Costar. Onscreen from the early '60s. IN: *Help!, A Countess From Hong Kong, Inspector Clouseau, Hammerhead, Up Pompeii*, more.

CARLE, FRANKIE (S. Cal.) Band leader. IN: *My Dream Is Yours*.

CARLETON, CLAIRE (S. Cal.) The blonde character actress who could always be counted on for the quick, funny answer—particularly in B comedies of the '40s—continued in films for 17 years, but has seldom acted in the past two decades. Still living in Hollywood, she has been a widow since her character actor-husband, Fred E. Sherman, died in '69. Onscreen from 1940. IN: *Girl from Havana, Sing Dance Plenty Hot, Melody and Moonlight, Lady of Burlesque, Rookies in Burma, Gildersleeve on Broadway, A Double Life, Born Yesterday, Death of a Salesman, Witness to Murder, The Buster Keaton Story*, more.

CARLIN, GEORGE (S. Cal.) Comedian-support. IN: *With Six You Get Eggroll*.

CARLIN, LYNN (S. Cal.) Costar. Nominated for Best Supporting Actress Oscar in *Faces*. Onscreen from 1968. IN: *Tick Tick Tick, Taking Off, Wild Rovers, Dead of Night*, more.

CARLISLE, KITTY (N.Y.) Singer-actress. Onscreen from 1934. IN: *Murder at the Vanities, Here Is My Heart, A Night at the Opera, Larceny With Music*, more.

CARLISLE, MARY (S. Cal.) She was and she is—this blonde with the sweet smile, blue eyes, and fetching long lashes—as pretty as a picture. Since '51 the manager of Beverly Hills' Elizabeth Arden Salon, she is easily the beauty establishment's best recommendation. Now in her 60s (b. 1912), she entered movies at 10, costarred a bit later in "The Collegians" series, and then played femme leads in dozens of pictures through 1943's *Dead Men Walk*, after which she left her career without a backward glance. For more than three decades she has been the wife of socialite James Blakely, a tall, dapper man of great charm who was briefly an actor in the '30s and later a 20th Century-Fox executive. They live most elegantly in Beverly Hills and have one son, now a businessman. In his autobiography, *Wide-Eyed in Babylon* ('74), telling of his screen test in Hollywood, Ray Milland wrote: "To work with me they had assigned the cutest, prettiest little Dresden doll I had ever seen. Her name was Mary Carlisle." Someone should tell Milland—nothing, but nothing, has changed. Onscreen from 1922. IN: *Madame Satan, Sweetheart of Sigma Chi, Handy Andy, Kentucky Kernels, Champagne for Breakfast, Kind Lady, Double or Nothing, Hold 'Em Navy, Hunted Men, Dr. Rhythm, Touchdown Army, Hawaiian Nights, Dance Girl Dance, Rags to Riches, Torpedo Boat*, more.

CARLSON, KAREN (S. Cal.) Leading lady. Onscreen from 1970. IN: *Shame, Shame, Everybody Knows Her Name; The Student Nurses*, more.

CARLSON, RICHARD (S. Cal.) Yesterday's leading man is in his 60s now (b. 1914), has remained married (since '39) to model Mona Mayfield, is the father of two grown sons, Christopher and Richard Henry, and plays character roles. Concentrating on TV, he has been seen in recent months in *Cannon, Khan*, and *Owen Marshall*, for which he also wrote scripts. Writing is not a new occupation for him. It was as a writer that David Selznick originally brought him to Hollywood, to work on

Janet Gaynor's *The Young in Heart*. After meeting him, however, Miss Gaynor urged that he appear in the film instead, launching him on a 50-picture career that continued through *The Valley of Gwangi* and *Change of Habit*, both in '69. During WW II military service he wrote and directed numerous films for the government. After the war he made his living for several years by writing articles for *Ladies' Home Journal*, *McCall's*, and *Reader's Digest*. And during the '50s and '60s, concurrent with his acting career, he continued to direct—helming *Four Guns to the Border*, *The Saga of Hemp Brown*, and *Kid Rodelo*, in which he also acted. And he collaborated with Curt Siodmak on the scripts of two science-fiction films in which he starred—*The Magnetic Monster* and *Riders to the Stars*. Today, besides being a card-carrying member of the Screen Actors, Screen Writers, and Screen Directors Guilds, he does TV commercials (for Union Electric) and is president of the benevolent Actors & Others For Animals organization. Onscreen from 1938. IN: *The Duke of West Point, Dancing Coed, These Glamour Girls, Too Many Girls, The Howards of Virginia, The Little Foxes, The Magnificent Ambersons, King Solomon's Mines; Retreat, Hell!; Flat Top, Seminole, It Came From Outer Space, The Last Command, The Helen Morgan Story, Tormented, Della,* more.

CARLSON, STEVE (S. Cal.) Leading man. Onscreen from 1967. IN: *Deadlier Than the Male, The Young Warriors, Rascal,* more.

CARLSON, VERONICA (Eng.) Leading lady. Onscreen from the late '60s. IN: *Hammerhead, Dracula Has Risen From the Grave, The Horror of Frankenstein,* more.

CARLYLE, RICHARD (S. Cal.) Support. Not the character actor of the same name who began in silents. Onscreen from 1951. IN: *Target Unknown, The Iron Mistress, The Gallant Hours, Harper,* more.

CARMEL, ROGER C. (S. Cal.) Character comedian. Onscreen from 1964. IN: *Goodbye Charlie, Alvarez Kelly, The Venetian Affair, Myra Breckinridge, Skullduggery, The Telephone Book,* more.

CARMEN, JEAN (Conn.) (See Julia Thayer.)

CARMICHAEL, HOAGY (S. Cal.) The composer-singer-actor whose drolleries added so much to movies for almost two decades is in his well-preserved 70s now (b. 1899) and semiretired—devoting himself to golf at Palm Springs and working on his coin collection. But he has made news three times in this decade. In '70 he journeyed to Boston to star on public service television in a 15-episode children's musical series titled *Hoagy Carmichael's Music Shop*, featuring his original compositions for children. He did the show at the urging of its producer, Hoagy Jr., former manager of a Wall Street brokerage office, and one of his two sons; the other, Randy, has chosen a non-show-business career. In '72 Hoagy guest-starred, playing a composer, on the TV show *Owen Marshall*—his first acting role in six years. That same year saw him on the campus of his alma mater, Indiana University (he'd written "Stardust" on a previous visit there in 1927), where he received an honorary degree in music at the dedication of the school's $11-million Musical Arts Center. Following the ceremony was a reception in the building's Hoagland (his proper name) Carmichael Grand Foyer. There he expressed regret he'd had no opportunity to make a speech. "I was going to tell them," he said in that inimical dry way, "what a shocker it was for a guy to get a degree of Doctor of Music who can't sight-read music. I've always played by ear." Onscreen from 1937. IN: *Topper, To Have and Have Not, Johnny Angel, Canyon Passage, The Best Years of Our Lives, Night Song, Johnny Holiday, The Las Vegas Story,* and more, including 1955's *Timberjack*, his last.

CARMICHAEL, IAN (Eng.) Costar. Onscreen from 1947. IN: *Ghost Ship; Time Gentlemen, Please; Meet Mr. Lucifer, Betrayed, Simon and Laura, Private's Progress, Lucky Jim, I'm All Right Jack, School for Scoundrels, Heavens Above!,* more.

CARNE, JUDY (S. Cal.) Leading lady. IN: *A Pair of Briefs, The Americanization of Emily,* more.

CARNEY, ART (N.Y.) Comedian/star. Won Best Actor Oscar in *Harry and Tonto*. Onscreen from 1941. IN: *Pot O' Gold, The Yellow Rolls-Royce, A Guide for the Married Man, W. W. and the Dixie Dancekings; Won Ton Ton, The Dog Who Saved Hollywood;* more.

CARNOVSKY, MORRIS (N.Y.) Character. Onscreen from 1937. IN: *The Life of Emile Zola, Edge of Darkness, Cornered, Rhapsody in Blue, Dead Reckoning, Dishonored Lady, Man-Eater of Kumaon, Deadly Is the Female, Gun Crazy, Cyrano de Bergerac, The Second Woman, The Gambler,* more.

CAROL, CINDY (S. Cal.) Former juvenile; support. IN: *Good Morning, Miss Dove; Gidget Goes to Rome, Dear Brigitte,* more.

CAROL, SUE (S. Cal.) Plump and pretty in her late 60s (b. 1908), the actress who was one of the most popular ingenues in early talkies lives in Palm Springs where she operates the "Alan Ladd—Hardware & Gifts" store. This is the three-story, architecturally classic, $500,000-a-year enterprise founded by husband, Alan Ladd, several years before his death in 1964. Enjoying the success of this business, she takes even greater pride in the accomplishments of her children. Stepson Alan Ladd Jr.—dark-haired and looking not at all like his famous father—is, in his 30s (b. 1938), production chief of 20th Century-Fox, happily married since '59, and the father of three small children. Daughter Alana (b. 1943), who was briefly in movies (*Young Guns of Texas*) has been married for several years to a popular television personality in Los Angeles and has also made her a grandmother. Son David (b. 1947), who was married to Louise Hendricks and then to TV actress Cheryl Ladd, welcomed his first child, a daughter, on January 14, 1975. Still a busy young actor, David, a few months back, was obliged to terrorize Joan Crawford in the TV drama *We're Going to Scare You to Death.* During a break in filming, Miss Crawford reminded David she had attended his fourth birthday party. Onscreen from 1927. IN: *Slaves of Beauty, Soft Cushions, Skyscraper, Beau Broadway, The Air Circus, Win That Girl, Captain Swagger, Why Leave Home?, Exalted Flapper, Straightaway,* more. Retired from the screen in the mid-'30s and was for years a successful Hollywood agent.

CARON, LESLIE (S. Cal.) Star. Nominated for Best Actress Oscar in *Lili* and *The L-Shaped Room.* Onscreen from 1951. IN: *An American in Paris, Story of Three Loves, The Glass Slipper, Daddy Long Legs, Gigi, Fanny, Father Goose, A Very Special Favor, Promise Her Anything, Is Paris Burning?, Madron,* more.

CARPENTER, CARLETON (N.Y.) Still lanky, breezy, and single in his early 50's (b. 1926), the former juvenile lives alone in a small house at the extreme tip of Long Island, where he writes paperback mysteries. Of the six published to date (*Cat Got Your Tongue, Games Murderers Play,* etc.), one, *Deadhead,* has been optioned for a Broadway musical. Rarely in movies now —1971's *Some of My Best Friends Are* being his most recent credit—he appears regularly on the stage. In 1976 he was announced to costar with Julie Wilson in a Broadway revival of *Roberta,* playing the role that made Bob Hope famous. And a few seasons back, starring Off Broadway in *The Greatest Story Ever Told,* he proved he has not lost his sense of humor by quipping: "The part's a natural for me. I play an ancient Chinese philosopher." Onscreen from 1949.

IN: *Lost Boundaries, Three Little Words, Father of the Bride, Two Weeks with Love, The Whistle at Eaton Falls, Fearless Fagan, Take the High Ground, Up Periscope,* more.

CARPENTER, CONSTANCE (N.Y.) Less active now, in her 70s (b. 1906), she was a major name on the stage before her brief starring career in movies of the early '30s, and continued to be well into the '60s. IN: *Two Worlds, Just for a Song,* more.

CARPENTER, JOHN (S. Cal.) Disabled since an operation a decade ago, this actor who produced and starred in several low-budget Westerns in the '50s owns and operates—at his own expense and with outside contributions—a most unusual ranch near Los Angeles. Called "Heaven on Earth," the ranch is a place where mentally and physically handicapped children learn to ride horseback. The charge to them? Free. The former actor began this philanthropy several years before becoming handicapped himself.

CARR, DARLEEN (S. Cal.) Leading lady. IN: *The Impossible Years, Beguiled, Death of a Gunfighter, Monkies Go Home,* more.

CARR, PAUL (S. Cal.) Leading man. Onscreen from 1957. IN: *The Young Don't Cry, Brute Corps, The Bat People, Truck Stop Women,* more.

CARRADINE, DAVID (S. Cal.) Leading man. Onscreen from 1964. IN: *Taggart, The Violent Ones, Young Billy Young, The Good Guys and the Bad Guys, Boxcar Bertha, Death Race 2000, Bound for Glory,* more.

CARRADINE, JOHN (S. Cal.) Character. Father of actors David, Keith, and Robert. Onscreen from 1930. IN: *Tol'able David, The Invisible Man, Of Human Bondage, Les Miserables, The Crusades, Prisoner of Shark Island, Captain January, A Message to Garcia, The Hurricane, Four Men and a Prayer, Of Human Hearts, The Hound of the Baskervilles, Stagecoach, The Grapes of Wrath, The Return of Frank James, Swamp Water, The Mummy's Ghost, House of Dracula, Johnny Guitar, The Ten Commandments, The Court Jester, The Proud Rebel, The Adventures of Huckleberry Finn, The Man Who Shot Liberty Valance; Munster, Go Home!; The McMasters, The House of Seven Corpses; Silent Night, Bloody Night; Moon Child; Mary, Mary, Bloody Mary;* more.

CARRADINE, KEITH (S. Cal.) Costar. IN: *McCabe and Mrs. Miller, Thieves Like Us, Idaho Transfer, Nashville,* more.

CARRADINE, ROBERT (S. Cal.) Juvenile. IN: *The Cowboys.*

CARRERA, BARBARA (S. Cal.) Leading lady. IN: *The Master Gunfighter, Embryo.*

CARRICART, ROBERT (S. Cal.) Support. IN: *The Black Orchid, Robin and the Seven Hoods, Follow That Dream, Fun in Acapulco,* more.

CARRIER, ALBERT (S. Cal.) Support. IN: *Desert Sands, Tender Is the Night, Do Not Disturb, Thoroughly Modern Millie, The Secret Life of an American Wife,* more.

CARRILLO, CELY (S. Cal.) Support. IN: *Rampage,* more.

CARROLL, DIAHANN (N.Y.) Black star. Nominated for Best Actress Oscar in *Claudine.* Onscreen from 1954. IN: *Carmen Jones, Porgy and Bess, Goodbye Again, Paris Blues, Hurry Sundown, The Split,* more.

CARROLL, GEORGIA (Mass.) Leading lady. Onscreen in the '40s. IN: *Navy Blues, Around the World, Carolina Blues,* more. Retired. (See Kay Kyser.)

CARROLL, JANICE (S. Cal.) Support. IN: *Shane; How to be Very, Very Popular; How to Seduce a Woman, Three the Hard Way,* more.

CARROLL, JOHN (Fla.) After 1959's *The Plunderers of Painted Flats,* and after 24 years of movie fame, the curly-haired, actor-singer felt he'd had enough. He also had enough money—800 San Fernando Valley acres bought in the "old days" saw to that. He promptly retired to Bayway Isles in St. Petersburg with his wife, Lucille Ryman—they have now been married over three decades. (She was for many years Head of Talent at MGM.) Retirement soon palled. Fishing and golf weren't enough. He built a shrimp boat and a thriving business in shrimping; began buying—at auction—heavy equipment for resale, then, needing a storage place for the equipment, bought a steel mill. Finally, fate took him back into the movie business, as a producer. By accident, he stumbled upon an atmospheric rural Florida town, Rubonia, population 1,200 (black, Mexican, Puerto Rican, white), that resembled an MGM set. He decided, on the spot, to make a movie there. He had a script written, tailored to suit the community, had "country" music specially composed, signed up his stars—Glenn Corbett and Morgan Woodward—and, in Rubonia, he produced *Ride in a Pink Car.* Today, when not home in St. Petersburg, the former actor is to be found in the offices of his Clarion Pictures,

Inc., at the old Warners Studio lot in Burbank, where he is planning an additional six productions. In his 60s now (b. 1908), with silver in his black curls, and heavier than in his starring days, John Carroll is full of zest over his new career. He doubts he will ever again just sit on the dock and watch the porpoises lazily roll by on their way to Boca Ciega Bay. Onscreen from 1935. IN: *Hi Gaucho!, Murder on the Bridle Path, Zorro Rides Again* (serial), *Only Angels Have Wings, Congo Maisie, Susan and God, Hired Wife, Lady Be Good, This Woman Is Mine, Rio Rita, Hit Parade of 1943, Bedside Manner, Wyoming; I, Jane Doe; The Avengers, Two Grooms for a Bride,* more.

CARROLL, JUNE (N.Y.) Singer-actress. IN: *New Faces* ('54), *An Angel Comes to Broadway.*

CARROLL, MADELEINE (Fr.) She was a success in every medium in this country—in movies (until her last in Hollywood, *My Favorite Blonde* in '42), on Broadway (*Goodbye, My Fancy*), radio (last starred in the 1958 soap opera *The Affairs of Dr. Gentry*), TV ("live" dramas in New York in the '50s and filmed dramas such as *GE Theater*). Her four marriages — American and otherwise—fared badly, all ending in divorce. She was married to English attorney Philip Astly (1931–39); actor Sterling Hayden (1942–46)—he penned a bitter account of their marriage in his autobiography, *Wanderer;* French film producer Henri Lavorel (1946–49); LIFE Magazine publisher, Andrew Heiskell (1950–65), who sued her for divorce in '64 charging "desertion" and "intolerable cruelty." By Heiskell, she is the mother of Anne-Madeleine, her only child, who attended fashionable schools in New York and Paris, and is in her 20s now. The star, entering her 70s (b. 1906), with reddish-brown hair and no longer bothering to hide her freckles, lives on a magnificent farm near Paris. Still besieged by offers for movies (she doesn't even consider them; 1949's *The Fan* was her last) and plays (she would say "yes" to a great role), she has done no performing of any sort since '64—when she narrated a Berlioz music program abroad. Instead of her past accomplishments, she prefers talking about her successful orchards, saying, "As you see, I sell apples." Her closest companion in recent years, until his death in '70, was French star Fernand Gravet. And mention of him, even now, brings tears to her eyes. Onscreen in England 1928–35. IN: *The Gun of Loos, Atlantic, Young Woodley, Escape, The Sleeping Car, The 39 Steps,* more. Onscreen in America from 1936. IN: *The General Died at Dawn, Lloyds of London, On the Avenue, The Prisoner of Zenda, Blockade, Cafe Society, Honeymoon in Bali; My Son, My Son; North-*

west Mounted Police, Virginia, Bahama Passage, more.

CARROLL, PAT (S. Cal.) Comedienne. IN: *With Six You Get Eggroll.*

CARSON, CHARLES (Eng.) Character. He is in his 90s now (b. 1885) and retired. Onscreen from 1931. IN: *The Dreyfus Case, The Broken Melody, Sanders of the River, Scrooge, Secret Agent, Fire Over England, Dreaming Lips, Sixty Glorious Years; Cry, the Beloved Country; Beau Brummell, A Touch of Larceny,* more.

CARSON, JEANNIE (N.Y.) Comedienne-singer. Onscreen from the early '50s. IN: *Love in Pawn, Mad Little Island, As Long As They're Happy, An Alligator Named Daisy,* more.

CARSON, JOHN DAVID (S. Cal.) Young support. IN: *Pretty Maids All in a Row, Day of the Dolphin, The Savage Is Loose.*

CARSON, ROBERT (S. Cal.) Support. Onscreen from 1950. IN: *The Fighting Stallion, The Greatest Show on Earth, Actors and Sin, For Men Only, Gang Busters, You're Never Too Young,* more.

CARSON, SUNSET (Ken.) After playing the GI from Texas in *Stage Door Canteen* under his real name, Michael Harrison, this Texan found himself a real-life GI before achieving Western stardom—as Sunset Carson—at Republic later in the '40s. In '46 he was the eighth-ranking cowboy star at the box-office. He was no phony cowboy. The son of rodeo performers, he was, as a teenager, featured as a trick rider and bronc-buster with the Tom Mix Circus. He next was a working cowboy in Argentina and for two consecutive years, '41 and '42, won the title of All-Round Champion Cowboy of South America. When Hollywood phased out B Westerns, he took his buckskins to TV for two series—*The Black Bandit* and *The Ghost Rider*—and starred in the Wild West show of Clyde Beatty's Circus. Next he toured the world for years with his riding and sharpshooting act—headlining in Nationalist China, Australia, Japan, Egypt, Alaska, Russia, etc. Lately, 6'6" Sunset Carson—now a bulky bear of a man in his 50s (b. 1922)—has resurrected his movie career by moving to a little town in Kentucky, Middletown, where he directs, coauthors, and stars in Westerns. *Outlaw Grizzly* and *The Marshal of Windy Hollow* are just two that his company, Trail Blazers, has produced. He has also hosted a Western TV series for children on Louisville station WLKY-TV. Too, he is president of the Western Movie Collectors Association, helped establish the Cowboy Movie Hall of Fame at Owensboro, and influenced the making of more Hollywood movies in his adopted state. As a consequence, the governor recently made the star a Kentucky Colonel. Married—his brunette wife, Carol, acts in his movies too—Sunset Carson says, "I have five fine children, two of my own—Tim and Sue—and three stepchildren, Michelle, John, and Vicki." They are all, at this writing, in the 10-to-20 age range. And they, too—riders all—have acted in his Kentucky-made cowboy pix. Onscreen in 1943 as Michael Harrison. IN: *Stage Door Canteen, Janie,* more. Onscreen from 1944 as Sunset Carson. IN: *Firebrands of Arizona, Border Town Trails, Call of the Rockies, Bandits of the Badlands, Sheriff of Cimarron, Days of Buffalo Bill, Rio Grande Raiders,* more.

CARTER, JACK (S. Cal.) Comedian. IN: *Miracle in Harlem, The Horizontal Lieutenant, The Resurrection of Zachary Wheeler, Hustle,* more.

CARTER, JANIS (Fla.) Blonde and aristocratic-looking in her 50s (b. 1921), the former leading lady—she gave up her career after 1952's *The Half Breed*—has been married for two decades to wealthy Julius Stulman. She has a magnificent house in Sarasota and, in New York, where she is always to be found during the opera season, a Park Avenue penthouse. Onscreen from 1941. IN: *Cadet Girl, Who Is Hope Schuyler, I Married an Angel, Girl Trouble, One Mysterious Night, The Mark of the Whistler, Framed, And Baby Makes Three, My Forbidden Past, Flying Leathernecks,* more.

CARTER, JUNE (Tenn.) Singer. IN: *Johnny Cash! The Man, His World, His Music.*

CARTER, LYNNE (Ariz.) Leading lady. IN: *Port of New York.* Retired.

CARTER, TERRY (N.Y.) Black support. IN: *Black on White.*

CARTWRIGHT, ANGELA (S. Cal.) Leading lady/former juvenile. IN: *Something of Value, Lad: A Dog, The Sound of Music,* more.

CARTWRIGHT, VERONICA (S. Cal.) Leading lady/former juvenile. IN: *The Children's Hour, The Birds, One Man's Way, Spencer's Mountain, Inserts,* more.

CARUSO, ANTHONY (S. Cal.) Character. Onscreen from 1940. IN: *Tall, Dark and Handsome; And Now Tomorrow, Pride of the Marines, To the Victor, Anna Lucasta, Saskatchewan, Cattle Queen of Montana, Baby Face Nelson, Never Steal Anything Small, Where Love Has Gone, Young Dillinger,* more.

CARY, CHRISTOPHER (S. Cal.) Leading man. IN: *Marlowe, Raid on Rommel,* more.

CASARES, MARIA (Fr.) Costar. Onscreen from 1943. IN: *Children of Paradise, The Wench, Orpheus, Testament of Orpheus, Les Dames du Bois de Boulogne (Ladies of the Park),* more.

CASE, ANNA (N.Y.) The Metropolitan Opera star (1910–16) headlined in just one feature, 1918's *The Hidden Truth,* but appeared as a soprano soloist in several 1927 Vitaphone shorts. Now well into her 80s (b. 1889), she lives in a posh hotel on upper Fifth Avenue. From '31 until his death in '38, she was the wife of millionaire Clarence H. Mackay. By virtue of this marriage, she is the stepmother of Mrs. Irving Berlin, the former Ellin Mackay, to whom she remains close.

CASEY, BERNIE (S. Cal.) Black leading man. IN: *Guns of the Magnificent Seven, Tick Tick Tick, Black Chariot, Dr. Black-Mr. Hyde,* more.

CASEY, LAWRENCE (S. Cal.) Leading man. Onscreen from the late '60s. IN: *The Gay Deceivers, The Student Nurses,* more.

CASEY, SUE (S. Cal.) Support. Onscreen from the '60s. IN: *Camelot, Paint Your Wagon,* more.

CASH, JOHNNY (Tenn.) Singer-actor. Onscreen from the '60s. IN: *Hootenanny Hoot, Five Minutes to Live, Festival, A Gunfight, Johnny Cash! The Man, His Words, His Music.*

CASH, ROSALIND (S. Cal.) Black costar. Onscreen in the '70s. IN: *Klute, The Omega Man, The New Centurions, Hickey and Boggs, An All-American Boy, Melinda, Uptown Saturday Night, Amazing Grace; Cornbread, Earl and Me; Dr. Black-Mr. Hyde,* more.

CASON, BARBARA (S. Cal.) Character. Onscreen in the '70s. IN: *The Honeymoon Killers, Cold Turkey,* more.

CASS, PEGGY (N.Y.) Comedienne. Nominated for Best Supporting Actress Oscar in *Auntie Mame.* Onscreen from 1952. IN: *The Marrying Kind, Gidget Goes Hawaiian, The Age of Consent; If It's Tuesday, This Must Be Belgium; Paddy,* more.

CASS, RAY (N.Y.) Juvenile. Onscreen in the '70s. IN: *Carnal Knowledge, The French Connection, Believe in Me,* more.

CASSAVETES, JOHN (S. Cal.) Star. Nominated for Best Supporting Actor Oscar in *The Dirty Dozen.* Onscreen from 1954. IN: *Taxi, Crime in the Streets, Edge of the City, Saddle the Wind, The Devil's Angels, Rosemary's Baby, Faces, Husbands, Capone, Two-Minute Warning,* more.

CASSEL, JEAN-PIERRE (Fr.) Costar. Onscreen from 1960. IN: *The Love Game, The Five Day Lover, The Joker, Candide, The Elusive Corporal, Those Magnificent Men in Their Flying Machines, High Infidelity, Is Paris Burning?, The Killing Game, The Three Musketeers, The Four Musketeers, Murder on the Orient Express, That Lucky Touch,* more.

CASSEL, SEYMOUR (S. Cal.) Costar. Nominated for Best Supporting Actor Oscar in *Faces.* Onscreen from 1960. IN: *Murder, Inc., Too Late Blues, Juke Box Racket, Coogan's Bluff, The Revolutionary, Minnie and Moskowitz,* more.

CASSELL, WALLY (S. Cal.) For 15 years this rugged, dimpled, wavy-haired actor was one of Hollywood's top young character players, being seen often as not in military uniform (*Sands of Iwo Jima, The Wild Blue Yonder,* etc.). He gave up acting in '62, after *The Scarface Mob,* entering the printing business. In '75, he was elected president of Law Printing Company in Los Angeles. Onscreen from 1947. IN: *Gallant Bess, Ramrod, Saigon, We Were Strangers, White Heat, Little Big Horn, The City That Never Sleeps, Princess of the Nile, Until They Sail,* more.

CASSIDY, JACK (S. Cal.) Costar. Onscreen from 1962. IN: *Look In Any Window, Guide for the Married Man, The Cockeyed Cowboys of Calico County, Bunny O'Hare, The Eiger Sanction, W.C. Fields and Me* (as John Barrymore), more.

CASSIDY, JOANNA (S. Cal.) Leading lady. Onscreen in the '70s. IN: *Bullitt, Fools, The Laughing Policeman, The Outfit, Bank Shot, The Stepford Wives,* more.

CASTELLANO, RICHARD (S. Cal.) Character. Nominated for Best Supporting Actor Oscar in *Lovers and Other Strangers.* IN: *The Godfather.*

CASTELNUOVO, NINO (It.) Costar. Onscreen from 1960. IN: *Escapade in Florence, The Umbrellas of Cherbourg, Psychout for Murder,* more.

CASTLE, MARY (S. Cal.) Retired from movies since 1960's *The Threat,* this blonde former

77

leading lady married Edward Frezza in May 1971. Onscreen from 1950. IN: *The Tougher They Come, Prairie Roundup, Gunsmoke, The Lawless Breed, White Fire, Yaqui Drums, Crashing Las Vegas*, more.

CASTRO, FIDEL (Cuba) In his late teens, as a beardless youth, today's Premier of Cuba lived and worked in Hollywood, as an actor in movies. This is according to an interview with bandleader Xavier Cugat who was featured in the "South American" musicals in which he says Fidel appeared "quite a lot in crowd scenes because he was a typical Latin American boy," and "a ham." Cugat continued: "He was young. Ambitious. Very talented. An attractive boy. And he had aspirations for being discovered as an actor. All the Latins wanted to be 'discovered.' They are proud people. They work not for just the few dollars a day." Onscreen from the early '40s. IN: (definitely, as scene stills exist showing him in it) *Holiday in Mexico*, plus other Cugat movies—he cannot recall the exact ones—which include *You Were Never Lovelier, The Heat's On, Bathing Beauty*, etc.; and, in '71, Castro was featured in the documentary *Cuba: Battle of the 10,000,-000*.

CATES, MADLYN (N.Y.) Support. IN: *The Producers*.

CAULFIELD, JOAN (S. Cal.) Last starred in 1973's *The Doberman Heist*, then her first movie since 1968's *Buckskin*. The blue-eyed actress is most likely to be found now starring on resident stock company stages in Chicago, Texas, or Florida. Sometimes her vehicles are new plays (*Your Daughter Is Rated X*), but generally they are revivals of such hit comedies as *Forty Carats, Butterflies Are Free*, or *Plaza Suite*. A guest role in one episode of Bill Bixby's *The Magician* in '73 was one of her rare, relatively recent TV appearances. Privately, still strikingly blonde in her 50s (b. 1922) and retaining the nursery-pink, Technicolor-ready complexion, the ingenuous look that made her so appealing in *Blue Skies* and other Paramount hits, has vanished. Disappointment sometimes seems etched in her features, as though the Peggy Lee song "Is That All There Is?" contains sentiments not entirely alien to her own. The actress has been married and divorced twice. Her first husband, who produced two pictures in which she starred after their marriage (*The Rains of Ranchipur* and *The Lady Says No*) and both her TV series in the '50s (*My Favorite Husband* and *Sally*), was Frank Ross —previously married to Jean Arthur. They married in '50, with Joan filing for divorce in the spring of '59; their only child, a son, Caulfield, was born later that year. By her second hus-

band (1960–66), a Los Angeles dentist, Dr. Robert Peterson, she has another son, John, born in '62. Having started on the stage, on Broadway in her 20s, the actress is not at all unhappy that her greatest opportunities now seem to be in the legitimate theater. Onscreen from 1946. IN: *Miss Susie Slagle's, Monsieur Beaucaire, Dear Ruth, Welcome Stranger, The Unsuspected, Larceny, Dear Wife, Red Tomahawk*, more.

CAZALE, JOHN (N.Y.) Costar. Onscreen in the '70s. IN: *The American Way, The Godfather, The Conversation, The Godfather II, Dog Day Afternoon*.

CELI, ADOLFO (It.) Character. Onscreen from 1949. IN: *Guaglio, A Target for Killing, That Man From Rio, Von Ryan's Express, The Agony and the Ecstasy, Thunderball, Grand-Prix, King of Hearts, Woman Times Seven; Danger: Diabolik; Libera, My Love;* more.

CHAKIRIS, GEORGE (S. Cal.) Costar. Won Best Supporting Actor Oscar in *West Side Story*. Onscreen as a dancer from 1954. IN: *White Christmas, Meet Me in Las Vegas, Brigadoon*, more. Onscreen in acting roles from 1957. IN: *Under Fire, Two and Two Make Six, Kings of the Sun, Diamond Head, Flight From Ashiya, 633 Squadron, Bebo's Girl, Is Paris Burning?; McGuire, Go Home!; The Young Girls of Rochefort, The Big Cube, The Heroes*, more.

CHALLEE, WILLIAM (S. Cal.) Character. Onscreen from 1944. IN: *Days of Glory, None But the Lonely Heart, The Black Book, Port of New York, Outrage, Chicago Syndicate, Five Easy Pieces, Zachariah, Moon Child*, more.

CHAMBERLAIN, RICHARD (S. Cal.) Costar. Onscreen from 1960. IN: *The Secret of the Purple Reef, Joy in the Morning, Petulia, The Madwoman of Chaillot, The Music Lovers, Lady Caroline Lamb, The Three Musketeers, The Towering Inferno, The Four Musketeers*, more.

CHAMBERLAIN, HOWLAND (N.J.) This bald character actor, in more than 30 films prior to 1952's *The Big Night*, lives in Fairlawn, does much TV still, and, 1968–71, was artist in residence at Brandeis University. Onscreen from 1947. IN: *The Web, A Song Is Born, Force of Evil, Francis, House by the River, Edge of Doom, Mister 880, Pickup, The Racket*, more.

CHAMBERS, MARILYN (S. Cal.) Star of pornographic films. IN: *The Owl and the Pussycat*.

CHAMPION, GOWER (N.Y.) Last in a movie in 1955—in *Three for the Show*—he is in his 50s (b. 1921) and directs one prize-winning Broadway musical after another—*Hello Dolly!, Irene,* etc. Onscreen from 1946. IN: *Till the Clouds Roll By, Mr. Music, Show Boat, Lovely to Look At, Everything I Have Is Yours, Jupiter's Darling.*

CHAMPION, MARGE (S. Cal.) In 1975 the dancer-actress, divorced from dance partner Gower in '71 after 24 years of marriage, won a well-deserved Emmy for choreographing the Maureen Stapleton TV special, *Queen of the Stardust Ballroom.* Quite a different sort of endeavor, to which she is truly dedicated now, is one she undertakes almost every Sunday evening at the Bel Air Presbyterian Church. There she presents, and sometimes dances in, religious music-and-dance programs, several of which have later been presented at other churches. As has been noted by one who has attended and been moved by these services, "The church swings with everything from Yemenite dancers performing a 2500-year-old Hebrew wedding dance to the choreography of the Lord's Prayer." Another friend of the star has observed: "This work seems to have been a particular consolation to her since the death of her father in 1973." (Ernest Belcher—Belcher being Marge's real name—a noted Hollywood dance instructor, was also the stepfather of Lina Basquette, Marge's half-sister.) While giving up dancing professionally, Marge Champion has also taught ballet—free—at Los Angeles' black ghetto, Watts, and—not free—choreographed the dances for the movie *Day of the Locust.* And she has completed a book, *God Is a Verb,* comprised of poetry by friend Marilee Zdenik and photographs by herself. A beautiful woman still, in her 50s (b. 1919), Marge is the mother of two sons—Gregg Ernest, now in college, and Blake, in high school—by Gower Champion. When she attended and modeled in a recent nostalgic fashion show in Hollywood, she appeared in a gown she had worn in *Lovely To Look At,* starring Marge and Gower Champion; it was a memory-evoking moment. In movies from 1937, beginning as the model for Snow White in *Snow White and the Seven Dwarfs,* and as the voice of The Blue Fairy in *Pinocchio.* Onscreen with Gower Champion from 1950; credits cited in his entry. Onscreen in supporting roles from 1967. IN: *The Swimmer, The Party,* and her last, 1970's *The Cock-eyed Cowboys of Calico County.*

CHANDLER, CHICK (S. Cal.) The wonderfully dry and comic Chick, veteran support in more than 100—through 1963's *It's a Mad Mad Mad Mad World*—reports: "The reason I have sort of disappeared from the screen and TV is because I have retired. What do I do? I get up in the morning and start doing nothing and by noon I have it half done. Kidding aside, most actors tell you how much fun they have when making a picture. In time, if they are honest, they realize it is hard work—work they like, but it gets harder because you are judged by the last part you played. Will the next part be a good one? How do you make it a better part? If you are lucky, and some actors are, you can walk away from it. I was lucky, I decided to quit and really have fun, and now I enjoy going to the theater and watching TV." Privately, says the actor who is now entering his 70s (b. 1905), "I have been happily married for over 45 years to the same beautiful actress, Jean Frontai, who is also retired. We now live in Laguna and love it." Onscreen from 1933. IN: *Sweepings, Harold Teen, Love and Kisses, One Mile From Heaven, Portia on Trial, Alexander's Ragtime Band, Mr. Moto Takes a Chance, Hollywood Calvacade, Swanee River, The Bride Came C.O.D., I Wake Up Screaming, The Magnificent Dope, Hi Diddle Diddle, Captain Eddie, Mother Wore Tights, Blondie's Reward, Three Ring Circus, There's No Business Like Show Business, Battle Cry,* more.

CHANDLER, GEORGE (S. Cal.) 1975's *Escape to Witch Mountain* was sufficient evidence that this veteran character actor, now in his 70s (b. 1902), is still going strong. Onscreen from 1930. IN: *Only Saps Work, In Gay Madrid, Too Many Cooks, The Country Doctor, Libeled Lady, Woman Chases Man, Nothing Sacred, Second Fiddle, The Return of Frank James, The Great Man's Lady, Since You Went Away, Lover Come Back, Perfect Strangers, Across the Wide Missouri, Apache Uprising, The Ghost and Mr. Chicken, One More Train to Rob,* more.

CHANDLER, JAMES (S. Cal.) Support. IN: *Sweet Bird of Youth, Jumbo,* more.

CHANDLER, JOHN DAVIS (S. Cal.) Character. Onscreen from 1961. IN: *The Young Savages, Mad Dog Coll, Once a Thief, Shootout, The Ultimate Thrill,* more.

CHANDLER, MIMI (Ken.) She is married and retired. IN: *And the Angels Sing.*

CHANDOS, JOHN (Eng.) Character. Onscreen from 1942. IN: *The Invaders, Next of Kin, The Ship That Died of Shame, The Green Man, Pursuit of the Graf Spee, The Little Ones,* more.

CHANEY, FRANCES (N.Y.) Support. IN: *The Men.*

CHANG, TISA (N.Y.) Support. IN: *Ambush Bay.*

CHANNING, CAROL (S. Cal.) Comedienne. Nominated for Best Supporting Actress Oscar in *Thoroughly Modern Millie*. Onscreen from 1950. IN: *Paid in Full, The First Traveling Saleslady, Skidoo, Shinbone Alley* (cartoon voice), more.

CHANNING, STOCKARD (S. Cal.) Leading lady. Onscreen in the '70s. IN: *The Fortune*, more.

CHAPLIN, CHARLES (Switz.) Immortal comedy star. Nominated for Best Actor Oscar in *The Circus* and *The Great Dictator*. Received a special Oscar in 1927–28 "for versatility and genius in writing, acting, directing and producing *The Circus*." Received a special Oscar in 1972 "for the incalculable effect he has had in making motion pictures the art form of this century." Onscreen in shorts from 1914. Onscreen in features from 1920. IN: *The Kid, The Pilgrim, The Gold Rush, City Lights, Modern Times, The Great Dictator, Monsieur Verdoux, Limelight, A King in New York, A Countess from Hong Kong*.

CHAPLIN, GERALDINE (Sp.) Costar. Onscreen from 1965. IN: *Doctor Zhivago, Stranger in the House, Innocent Bystanders, The Three Musketeers, Nashville, The Four Musketeers, Buffalo Bill and the Indians*, more.

CHAPLIN, SYDNEY (S. Cal.) Leading man. Son of Charles, half-brother of Geraldine. Onscreen from 1952. IN: *Limelight, Land of the Pharaohs, Pillars of the Sky, The Deadlier Sin, Quantez, A Countess From Hong Kong, The Adding Machine, The Sicilians*, more.

CHAPMAN, LONNY (N.Y.) Support. Onscreen from 1955. IN: *Young at Heart, East of Eden, Baby Doll, Where the Red Fern Grows*, more.

CHAPMAN, MARGUERITE (S. Cal.) At first glance you would not recognize her. Her naturally dark hair is blonde now. Maturity has rounded her once finely chiseled features, and her face is not unlined. But her figure and those long legs, though she is in her 50s (b. 1920), are unchanged. Marguerite herself acknowledges the change, referring to Herself Then as "The Girl" and to Herself Now as "The Woman." Married previously to Beverly Hills attorney G. Bentley Ryan, she was most recently divorced ('74) from director J. Richard Bremerkamp. She has no children. Not seen in a movie since 1960's *The Amazing Transparent Man* (not one of her better efforts like *Counter Attack* or *Destroyer*), she has made recent efforts to reactivate her career. A step in this direction was a guest-star role in *Hawaii Five-O* on TV. Prior to this, she had guested in *Marcus Welby* with Robert Young, her costar in 1948's *Relentless*. Just before that she had done a number of out-of-town plays, her best role being perhaps that of Sylvia in *The Women*, the bitchy character played by Rosalind Russell in the long-ago movie. Seeing her in this Fort Worth revival, one critic hailed her "ribald comic flair," while another declared, "Here is another great performer with versatility spilling over in ebullient delight with every line and movement on stage." Interestingly, until the '60s, she had never so much as set foot onstage. An active woman, she paints (her pictures have been exhibited at the Beverly Hills Art League Gallery), golfs, decorates the house she recently bought in Woodland Hills, and writes. Of her two white French toy poodles, to whom she lightly refers as "my kids," Marguerite said recently, they "are busy trying to do their autobiography—which I am, of course, 'ghosting'." Onscreen from 1940. IN: *Four Sons, Navy Blues, Daring Young Man, Appointment in Berlin, My Kingdom for a Cook, Strange Affair, Pardon My Past, Gallant Blade, Sign of the Ram, The Green Promise, Sea Tiger, Bloodhounds of Broadway, The Seven Year Itch*, more.

CHAPMAN, RICHARD (S. Cal.) Support. IN: *There's Magic in Music*.

CHARISSE, CYD (S. Cal.) Star. Onscreen from 1943. IN: *Thousands Cheer, Something to Shout About, Till the Clouds Roll By, The Harvey Girls, Unfinished Dance, Fiesta, Words and Music, The Kissing Bandit, East Side West Side, Singin' in the Rain, Sombrero, The Band Wagon, Brigadoon, Deep in My Heart, It's Always Fair Weather, Silk Stockings, Party Girl, Two Weeks in Another Town, The Silencers, Maroc 7, No Place for Lovers*, more. Offscreen since 1969, she now stars in a nightclub act with singer-husband, Tony Martin.

CHARLES, LEWIS (S. Cal.) Support. IN: *Panic in the Streets, The Rose Tattoo, Sweet Smell of Success, Al Capone, Birdman of Alcatraz, Soldier in the Rain, A House Is Not a Home*, more.

CHARLESON, LESLIE (N.Y.) Leading lady. IN: *A Lovely Way to Die*, more.

CHARLITA (S. Cal.) Support. IN: *Brimstone, The Brave Bulls, Come Fill the Cup, Ride Vaquero, Green Fire*, more.

CHARNY, SUZANNE (S. Cal.) Leading lady. IN: *The Steagle*, more.

CHARRIER, JACQUES (Fr.) Leading man. Onscreen from 1960. IN: *The Chasers, Babette*

Goes to War, The Cheaters, La Belle Americaine, Seven Capital Sins, The Third Lover, Les Creatures, Winter Wind, more.

CHASE, BARRIE (S. Cal.) The girl who was Astaire's favorite dance partner on television, and had costar roles in several films, is now married to Dr. James Kaufman, retired, and the mother of a son born on December 12, 1973, the year she turned 39. Onscreen from 1958. IN: *Mardi Gras, The George Raft Story, Cape ear, It's a Mad Mad Mad World.*

CHASE, ILKA (N.Y.) It matters little that she is no longer young (b. 1905), she continues on her globe-trotting adventures, deriving a new book from them every second year or so. She has been happily married since '46 to Dr. Norton Brown, and their swank East Side apartment is veritably a salon of writers, actors, and artists. *Oceans 11*, in '60, was her last movie, though she has continued to act on television until as recently as '72, when she appeared in a *Cool Million* episode. And a "cool million" is about what this sophisticated character actress has earned from her many books since her first, the autobiographical *Past Imperfect*, in '41. Onscreen from 1929. IN: *Paris Bound, The Careless Age, The Big Party, Rich People, Let's Go Places, Once a Sinner, The Animal Kingdom, The Lady Consents, Stronger Than Desire, Now Voyager, Miss Tatlock's Millions, It Could Happen to You, The Big Knife*, more.

CHASE, STEPHEN (S. Cal.) Character. Onscreen from 1949. IN: *Bad Boy, Cavalry Scout, My Favorite Spy, When Worlds Collide, No Room for the Groom, The Great Sioux Uprising, Appointment with a Shadow*, more.

CHASTAIN, DON (S. Cal.) Leading man. IN: *Flareup, C. C. and Company, Black Godfather*, more.

CHAUVIN, LILYAN (S. Cal.) Support. IN: *The Perfect Furlough, The Mephisto Waltz*, more.

CHECCO, AL (S. Cal.) Character. Onscreen from 1967. IN: *Hotel, The Party, I Love My Wife*, more.

CHECKER, CHUBBY (N.J.) Black singer. Onscreen in the '60s. IN: *Twist Around the Clock, Don't Knock the Twist*. Now does records and personal appearances.

CHEIREL, MICHELINE (Fr.) Leading lady. Onscreen from 1936. IN: *La Kermesse Heroique, They Were Five, Hold Back the Dawn, Cornered, So Dark the Night, Jewels of Brandenburg*, more.

CHER (S. Cal.) Music star. IN: *Good Times, Chastity.*

CHERRILL, VIRGINIA (S. Cal.) Voluntarily or not, her beautiful face, gently framed by blonde waves, remains fixed in the memory of all who saw this Chaplin film. She is no stranger —since *City Lights* stills have been so widely reproduced—even to the few who never saw her performance as the blind flower-seller. And Cary Grant, whose first wife she was (1934–35), will never forget her. "During my last divorce [from Dyan Cannon]," he has said, "Virginia called and said, 'If you need a character witness, I'll come right down there and give you one.' " Earlier, more than a decade ago, in a magazine article bearing his byline, Grant revealed the cause of their own divorce: "My possessiveness and fear of losing her brought about the very condition it feared: the loss of her." Born in 1908, the former actress appeared in 10 talkies, the last, *What Price Crime?*, made the year she divorced Grant. A Chicago divorcee before she married him, she later lived in England as the wife of the Earl of Jersey. Today, says Cary Grant affectionately, "Virginia is happily remarried. She lives in Santa Barbara now, but every once in a while she comes to Los Angeles and we have a long chat, gabbing about one thing and another." Onscreen from 1931. IN: *Girls Demand Excitement, The Brat, Delicious, Fast Workers, The Nuisance, Charlie Chan's Greatest Case, Ladies Must Love, He Couldn't Take It, White Heat* ('34).

CHERRY, HELEN (Eng.) Support. Onscreen from 1947. IN: *The Courtneys of Curzon Street, The Mark of Cain, Last Holiday, Operation Disaster, Her Panelled Door, Run for the Sun, The Naked Edge, 11 Harrowhouse*, more.

CHEW, VIRGILIA (N.Y.) Support. IN: *The Fugitive Kind.*

CHI, GRETA (S. Cal.) Support. IN: *Fathom*, more.

CHIARI, WALTER Leading man/now support. Onscreen from the early '50s. IN: *Bellissima, The Little Hut, Bonjour Tristesse, The Sucker, Those Daring Young Men in Their Jaunty Jalopies, The Valachi Papers*, more.

CHILES, LINDEN (S. Cal.) Support. Onscreen from 1965. IN: *A Rage to Live, Texas Across the River, Marnie, Counterpoint, Eye of the Cat*, more.

CHILES, LOIS (N.Y.) Model/leading lady. IN: *The Way We Were, The Great Gatsby*, more.

CHING, WILLIAM (S. Cal.) Support. Onscreen from 1947. IN: *Something in the Wind, D.O.A., In a Lonely Place, The Wild Blue Yonder, Pat and Mike, Terror in the Haunted House,* more.

CHISSELL, NOBLE 'KID' (S. Cal.) In his 60's now (b. 1910), this veteran character actor still performs in movies occasionally but more regularly contributes show business articles to Los Angeles newspapers. Onscreen from the '30s. IN: *Ex-Champ, Home in Indiana; They Shoot Horses, Don't They?; The Last of the American Hoboes,* more.

CHOUREAU, ETCHIKA (Fr.) Leading lady. On American screens 1957–58. IN: *Lafayette Escadrille, Darby's Rangers.* Retired.

CHOW, DAVID (S. Cal.) Support. IN: *Samurai, Three the Hard Way,* more.

CHRIS, MARILYN (N.Y.) Support. IN: *Love With the Proper Stranger, Rhinoceros,* more.

CHRISTIAN, LINDA (It.) Leading lady. Onscreen from the '40s. IN: *Holiday in Mexico, Tarzan and the Mermaids. The Happy Time, Slaves of Babylon, The Devil's Hand, The VIPs, The Moment of Truth, Contest Girl,* more.

CHRISTIAN, MICHAEL (S. Cal.) Support. IN: *2,000 Years Later, Violent Young Hood; Where Angels Go, Trouble Follows;* more.

CHRISTIAN, PAUL (Ger.) Beginning his career in the '40s, this leading man acted first under his real name, Paul Hubschmid, in *Maria Ilona,* etc. For more than a decade, beginning in '49, he was billed Paul Christian. In recent years, in films such as *Funeral in Berlin,* and living again in Germany, he has reverted to Hubschmid. IN (as Paul Christian): *Rommel's Treasure, Bagdad, The Beast from 20,000 Fathoms, The Thief of Venice, No Time for Flowers, Journey to the Lost City.*

CHRISTIE, AUDREY (S. Cal.) Character. Onscreen from 1943. IN: *Keeper of the Flame, Deadline U.S.A., Carousel, Splendor in the Grass, The Unsinkable Molly Brown, Harlow, The Ballad of Josie, Mame,* more.

CHRISTIE, JULIE (S. Cal.) Star. Won Best Actress Oscar in *Darling.* Nominated in same category in *McCabe and Mrs. Miller.* Onscreen from 1963. IN: *Crooks Anonymous, The Fast Lady, Billy Liar, Dr. Zhivago, Young Cassidy, Fahrenheit 451, The London Scene, Far from the Madding Crowd, Petulia, In Search of Gregory, The Go-Between, Don't Look Now, Shampoo,* more.

CHRISTINE, VIRGINIA (S. Cal.) The blonde character actress, veteran of more than 400 movies and TV shows, is in her 50s (b. 1920), and has been the wife of character actor Fritz Feld since 1940. Iowa-born and of Swedish descent, she has been identified with Folger Coffee TV commercials for more than a dozen years, lately as "Mrs. Olson." Recently, with her husband, she made a long-anticipated trip to Scandinavia. It was, she reports, " 'Mrs. Olson's first visit to the country of her heritage. My grandparents were born there." Following that, she and Feld made a two-month photographic safari to India, Nepal, and Burma. The rest of the world these inveterate travelers have covered on prior journeys. The Felds have reared four children—two nieces of hers, as well as their own grown sons, Danny and Steven. The actress has most recently costarred in the TV-movie *Woman of the Year.* Onscreen from 1942. IN: *Truck Busters, Edge of Darkness, Mission to Moscow, Women at War, The Killers, The Gangster, Cyrano de Bergerac, Not as a Stranger, Three Brave Men, Judgment at Nuremberg, One Man's Way, Guess Who's Coming to Dinner,* more.

CHRISTOPHER, JORDAN (S. Cal.) Leading man. Onscreen from 1966. IN: *The Return of the Seven, The Tree; Angel, Angel, Down We Go; Pigeons,* more.

CHRISTY, ANN (Tex.) Harold Lloyd's lovely leading lady in *Speedy,* she retired in 1932, married a Texas business man that same year and remains happily married to him, has two sons, and is now in her 70s (b. 1905). Onscreen from 1928. IN: *The Water Hole, The Fourth Alarm, Behind Stone Walls,* more.

CHURCH, SANDRA (N.Y.) Brando's leading lady in 1963's *The Ugly American,* her only movie, she gave up her career (she had also starred on Broadway and TV) the following year. Happily married, to Norman Twain, she later decided to attend college. In '75, and in her mid-30s, she received her degree in art history, which will be her new career.

CHURCH, STANLEY (S. Cal.) Character. IN: *The Great Jewel Robbery,* more.

CHURCHILL, DIANA (Eng.) Leading lady. Onscreen from the '30s. IN: *School for Husbands, Eagle Squadron, Scott of the Antarctic,* more.

CHURCHILL, MARGUERITE (Port.) Married to cowboy star George O'Brien in '33 and divorced from him in '48—neither has remarried and they continue to be friends—she is now in her 60s (b. 1909) and has made her home in Lisbon for many years. She has, by O'Brien, a musician daughter, Orin (plays bass violin with the New York Philharmonic), and a son, Darcy (a Princeton graduate who later studied at Cambridge and is now a professor of English at Pomona College in California). She last played a role of consequence in 1936's *Legion of Terror*, but did appear in a supporting role in 1950's *Bunco Squad*, her last acting to date. Onscreen from 1929. IN: *They Had to See Paris, The Valiant, Good Intentions, The Big Trail, Ambassador Bill, Alibi for Murder, Dracula's Daughter, Murder by an Aristocrat, Penthouse Party*, more.

CHURCHILL, SARAH (Eng.) Leading lady. Onscreen from 1940. IN: *He Found a Star, Royal Wedding, A Touch of Hell*, more. Retired from the screen more than a decade ago.

CIDONI, JOMAR (N.Y.) Juvenile actor. Onscreen from 1969. IN: *Popi, Midnight Cowboy, Bananas, The Panic in Needle Park*, more.

CIOFFI, CHARLES (Conn.) Support. IN: *Klute, Shaft, The Thief Who Came to Dinner*, more.

CILENTO, DIANE (Eng.) Costar. Nominated for Best Supporting Actress Oscar in *Tom Jones*. Onscreen from 1954. IN: *The Angel Who Pawned Her Harp, A Woman for Joe, Jet Storm, Stop Me Before I Kill!, The Naked Edge, I Thank a Fool, Rattle of a Simple Man, The Agony and the Ecstasy, Hombre, Negatives, The Wicker Man*, more.

CLAIR, ETHLYNE (S. Cal.) Retired, now in her 70's, the former leading lady in Hoot Gibson Westerns left the screen when she married makeup man Ernest Westmore, from whom she was later divorced. Married a second time, to business man Merle Frost, she has been a widow for a number of years.

CLAIRE, INA (N. Cal.) Sophisticated she was and is, in her 80s now (b. 1892). Today, as she has been since '39, she is the wife of San Francisco attorney William R. Wallace Jr. She had earlier been married to newspaper reporter James Whitaker (1919–25), then to star John Gilbert (1929–31). She has no children by any of her marriages. First onscreen in 1915's *The Wild Goose Chase*, she did not appear in movies with any regularity—thanks to her great career onstage—until the '30s. She left the screen in a burst of glory, as the valiant, doomed mother of Dorothy McGuire in *Claudia*. As chic and blonde as ever, she starred on Broadway twice thereafter, in *The Fatal Weakness* and, in '54, to rave notices, in *The Confidential Clerk*. Retiring then, to devote herself to her home and various philanthropies, she has never acted again. She wavered in '57 when Vincente Minnelli offered her the role of Tante Alicia, the greatest courtesan in Paris, in *Gigi*, but at the last minute decided to remain in retirement. Onscreen (in talkies) from 1929. IN: *The Awful Truth, The Royal Family of Broadway, Rebound, The Greeks Had a Word for Them, Ninotchka, Stage Door Canteen*, more.

CLARK, ALEXANDER (N.Y.) Character. IN: *The Man Without a Country*.

CLARK, CANDY (S. Cal.) Young leading lady. Nominated for Best Supporting Actress Oscar in *American Graffiti*. Onscreen in the '70s. IN: *Fat City, Report to the Commissioner*.

CLARK, DANE (S. Cal.) Warners' popular and pugnacious (on the screen) Brooklyn-type leading man in the '40s, and active at other studios in the '50s, was away from Hollywood the entire next decade. He starred on Broadway in *Tchin-Tchin* and *A Thousand Clowns*, directed documentary films, and made pictures in England and France. Late in the '60s, his wife of many years, Margot, died. In '72, when he was 59, he married Geraldine Frank, a young stockbroker, while starring in the stage play *A Conflict of Interest*. Returning to Hollywood with his new bride, the actor picked up his film career—on TV—as though he had never been away. Besides guesting in *The Rookies, Night Gallery, Ironside*, etc., he has been seen in a number of well-received TV-movies (*The Family Rico, Say Goodbye, Maggie Cole*, among others). After costarring as Lt. Tragg in *The New Perry Mason*, he assumed a running role in *Police Story*. He has lately optioned the novel *Neighbors* with the intention of becoming a movie producer. Onscreen from 1942. IN: *The Glass Key, Pride of the Yankees, Action in the North Atlantic, Destination Tokyo, The Very Thought of You, Pride of the Marines, God Is My Co-Pilot, A Stolen Life, Dark Passage, Embraceable You, Moonrise, Backfire, Fort Defiance, Paid to Kill, The Toughest Man Alive, The Massacre, Time Running Out, The McMasters*, more.

CLARK, DICK (S. Cal.) TV emcee-actor. Onscreen from 1960. IN: *Because They're Young, The Young Doctors, Wild in the Streets, Killers Three*, more.

CLARK, KEN (S. Cal.) Support. Onscreen from 1955. IN: *Six Bridges to Cross, The Shrike, On the Threshold of Space, Love Me Tender, South Pacific, None But the Lonely, Apache Fury, A Man Called Sledge*, more.

CLARK, LON (N.Y.) Support. IN: *The Gentle Rain*.

CLARK, MARILYN (N.Y.) Support. IN: *Too Late Blues, The Horror of Beach Party, Shadows*, more.

CLARK, PETULA (Switz.) Singer-leading lady. Onscreen from 1944. IN: *Medal for a Coward, The Huggetts Abroad, Strawberry Roan, My Heart Goes Crazy, Track the Man Down, City after Midnight, Finian's Rainbow; Goodbye, Mr. Chips;* more.

CLARK, SUSAN (S. Cal.) Leading lady. Onscreen from 1967. IN: *Banning, Madigan, The Challengers, Coogan's Bluff, Tell Them Willie Boy Is Here, The Forbin Project, Skullduggery, Valdez Is Coming, Skin Game, Showdown, Night Moves, Airport 1975, The Apple Dumpling Gang*, more.

CLARKE, ANGELA (S. Cal.) Character. Onscreen from 1949. IN: *The Undercover Man, Mrs. Mike, Captain Carey U.S.A., The Gunfighter, The Great Caruso; Darling, How Could You!; The Miracle of Our Lady of Fatima, House of Wax, Houdini, The Seven Little Foys, Blindfold, The Harrad Summer*, more.

CLARKE, DAVID (N.Y.) Character. Onscreen from 1947. IN: *The Long Night, The Boy With Green Hair, The Set-Up, Thieves' Highway, Intruder in the Dust, The Narrow Margin, Edge of the City, The Great St. Louis Bank Robbery*, more.

CLARKE, JOHN (S. Cal.) Character. IN: *Operation Bottleneck, The Satan Bug*, more.

CLARKE, MAE (S. Cal.) James Cagney treated her mean—and gave her an immortal screen moment. He (and director William Wellman) told her the "big scene" in *The Public Enemy* would be faked. It wasn't. He ground that grapefruit into her face and twisted it, making her nose bleed, and provoking her to scream at him—when the scene was finished: "Oh you son of a bitch, look what you did to me!" What he did to her next, two years later in *Lady Killer*, was drag her, in satin pajamas, across the floor by her hair. She has long since forgiven him. She took a bow as an honored guest at the highly publicized "James Cagney Night" in Hollywood in the spring of '72, looking, in her 60s (b. 1910), stunningly beautiful—slender, with reddish-brown hair, her features altered little by time. That evening, referring to the "citrus massage" (his words), Cagney told her, "Mae, I'm glad we didn't use the omelette. It was called for in the earlier scripts." What distresses Mae most today is encountering news articles referring to her as "the late Mae Clarke" and giving 1968 as the year she "passed away," when, in fact, the writers mean Mae Marsh. Extremely active onscreen between 1929's *Big Time* opposite Lee Tracy and 1958's *Voice in the Mirror*, Mae still does an occasional supporting role in a movie (such as *Watermelon Man*) or on TV. But, living not far from Hollywood in semiretirement now, she is generally content writing fiction, painting, golfing, and teaching drama for the Parks and Recreation Department in Pico-Rivera, Calif. Married and divorced three times, she has no children. What Mae didn't know until 1974, when author Anita Loos confessed it finally, is that she was the inspiration for Lorelei Lee in *Gentlemen Prefer Blondes.* "I've never written this, never told it before," said Miss Loos, "but Lorelei was born full-blown in 1924. I patterned her on a cute little blonde H. L. Mencken was escorting at the time. Her name was Mae Clarke . . . Mae Clarke certainly added something to my experience. Mencken was a beau of mine. . . . It amused me to see how such a brilliant man could be amused by Mae, a cutie-pie blonde." It is not inconceivable that Mae Clarke, in lovely maturity, could still add something to Miss Loos' "experience." Onscreen from 1929. IN: *Nix on Dames, The Front Page, Waterloo Bridge, Three Wise Girls, Final Edition, Made on Broadway, The Man with Two Faces, Hearts in Bondage, Flying Tigers, And Now Tomorrow, King of the Rocket Men* (serial), *Thunderbirds, Not as a Stranger, Come Next Spring, The Catered Affair, Voice in the Mirror*, more.

CLARKE, RICHARD (N.Y.) Leading man/now character. IN: *Charlie Chan in City of Darkness, The Man Who Wouldn't Talk, Pigeons*, more.

CLARKE, ROBERT (S. Cal.) Leading man. Married to one of the singing King Sisters, he performs on TV and on tour with The King Family and rarely acts in films. Onscreen from 1944. IN: *The Falcon in Hollywood, San Quentin, Return of the Bad Men, Ladies of the Chorus, Outrage; Hard, Fast and Beautiful; The Man from Planet X, The Fabulous Senorita, Captive Women, The Incredible Petrified World, Beyond the Time Barrier, Zebra in the Kitchen*, more.

CLARY, ROBERT (S. Cal.) Comedian-character. Onscreen from 1954. IN: *New Faces, A New Kind of Love, Ten Tall Men, The Hindenburg*, more.

CLAYBURGH, JILL (N.Y.) Leading lady. Onscreen in the '70s. IN: *The Thief Who Came to Dinner, Portnoy's Complaint, The Terminal Man, Gable and Lombard.*

CLAYTON, DICK (S. Cal.) Jane Withers' juvenile leading man in *Small Town Deb*, the former actor, a handsome bachelor still, has been an agent for many years and recently formed Clayton Enterprises for the exclusive management of the career of Burt Reynolds. ALSO IN: *Our Neighbors—The Carters*.

CLAYTON, JAN/a.k.a. JANE CLAYTON (S. Cal.) Leading lady. Onscreen from the late '30s. IN: "Hopalong Cassidy" Westerns, *Flight Angels, This Man's Navy, The Snake Pit*, more. Starred on Broadway in *Carousel* and other musicals, later playing the mother in TV's *Lassie*, and still later had a supporting role in the touring company of *Follies*.

CLAYWORTH, JUNE (S. Cal.) A widow since the 1973 death of Oscar-winning producer Sid Rogell, her husband for many years, the former leading lady lives near Hollywood, has a grown son, and is retired. Onscreen from 1935. IN: *The Good Fairy, Two-Fisted Gentleman, Married Before Breakfast, Between Two Women; Live, Love and Learn; The Truth about Murder, Dick Tracy and Gruesome, The White Tower, Dream Wife, Marriage-Go-Round*, more.

CLEMENTS, JOHN (Eng.) The handsome leading man in *Four Feathers* has been Sir John since his knighting in '68, and for decades was an actor-manager-director, associated with many of the finest productions presented on English stages. His motion picture career has long been of secondary importance to him. In the past three decades he has acted in just four: *Train of Events* ('52), *The Silent Enemy* ('57), *The Mind Benders* ('63), and *Oh What a Lovely War!* ('69). Twice married—to Inga Maria Lillemor Ahlgren and to actress Kay Hammond—he is in his 60s now (b. 1910). Onscreen from 1935. IN: *Things to Come, Rembrandt, Knight Without Armor, Convoy, Ships With Wings, At Dawn We Die, They Came to a City*, more.

CLEMENTS, STANLEY (S. Cal.) Perhaps the screen's best young toughie in the '40s, "Stash," as friends still call him, has matured —busted nose, gargled vowels and all—into one of Hollywood's finer journeyman character actors. Still specializing in baddies, the actor who is now at the half-century mark (b. 1926) does occasional movies *(The Timber Tramp)* but is most often seen on TV—guesting in *Cannon* and such television specials as *Nobody's Perfetc*. He has also written a comic movie script, *A Man and His Lion*, that he plans to produce and direct. The script is based on the real-life experiences of animal trainer Klaudius Blaszak who, with his pet lion Asik, defected from the Polish circus while on tour for the government of Poland, eventually making their way to Hollywood. Twice married, first to actress Gloria Grahame (married in '45, divorced in '48), and now, for years, to an attractive woman named Marysia, the movies' perennial juvenile delinquent is the proud adoptive father of a college-age son. "In 1964," he says, "we adopted Sylvester from Poland. He was nine when he came to us and was the first child allowed for adoption from behind the Iron Curtain." Onscreen from 1941. IN: *Accent on Love; Tall, Dark and Handsome; The More the Merrier, Sweet Rosie O'Grady, Going My Way, Salty O'Rourke, The Babe Ruth Story, Racing Luck, Johnny Holiday, Boots Malone, White Lightning, The Rocket Man, Spook Chasers, Sniper's Ridge, That Darn Cat*, more.

CLIFFORD, RUTH (S. Cal.) The former leading lady of silents is a handsome, smiling character actress, now in her 70s (b. 1900), who still does an occasional movie role but is most often to be seen in television commercials. Onscreen from 1917. IN: *A Kentucky Cinderella, The Dangerous Age, Daughters of the Rich, Ponjola, The Dramatic Life of Abraham Lincoln, As Man Desires, The Love Hour, Only Yesterday, Elmer and Elsie, Not Wanted, Slattery's Hurricane, Wagonmaster, The Man in the Gray Flannel Suit, Two Rode Together*, more.

CLOONEY, ROSEMARY (S. Cal.) Singer-leading lady. Onscreen from 1953. IN: *The Stars Are Singing, Here Come the Girls, Red Garters, White Christmas, Deep in My Heart*. Retired to rear a family of five children by divorced husband Jose Ferrer, she has lately resumed her singing career in nightclubs.

CLOUTIER, SUZANNE (Fr.) Leading lady. Onscreen from the '40s. IN: *Temptation, Doctor in the House, Othello, Romanoff and Juliet*, more.

CLUTE, SIDNEY (S. Cal.) Character. IN: *Crime and Punishment U.S.A., Cry of Battle*, more.

CLYDE, JUNE (Eng.) The once-popular RKO leading lady left Hollywood after 1934's *Hollywood Party* and, with her husband (since '30), director Thornton Freeland, moved to England. Besides starring in such stage musicals as *The Flying Trapeze* and *Lucky Break*, she was in such British films as *Forbidden Music* ('38) and *School for Husbands* ('39). In the early '40s she was in two at Universal: *Unfinished Business* and *Hi 'Ya Chum* with the Ritz Brothers. She last had a supporting role in '57 in *The Story of Esther Costello*. In her 60s now (b. 1909), and still attractively blonde, the American-born actress no longer acts, but continues to live in

England, spending part of each year at her second home in Florida. Onscreen from 1929. IN: *Tanned Legs, Hit the Deck, The Cuckoos, Men Are Like That, The Mad Parade, The Secret Witness, The Cohens and Kellys in Hollywood, Radio Patrol, Back Street, Tess of the Storm Country, Hold Me Tight, Only Yesterday, Dance Band, She Shall Have Music*, more.

COATES, CAROLYN (N.Y.) Support. IN: *The Hustler.*

COATES, PHYLLIS (S. Cal.) Leading lady. Onscreen in the '50s. IN: *The Man from Sonora, Flat Top, Canyon Ambush, Wyoming Roundup, Topeka, The Claw Monsters, I Was a Teenage Frankenstein, Chicago Confidential, Blood Arrow*, more. Retired.

COBB, JOE "WHEEZER" (S. Cal.) The first fat lad in the "Our Gang" comedies of the '20s went into business after his juvenile career ended. Retired now, he still lives in Los Angeles.

COBURN, JAMES (S. Cal.) Star. Onscreen from 1959. IN: *Ride Lonesome, The Magnificent Seven, Hell Is for Heroes, The Great Escape, Charade, The Americanization of Emily, Major Dundee, Our Man Flint, Waterhole #3, Candy, The President's Analyst, Hard Contract, The Carey Treatment, Pat Garrett and Billy the Kid, The Internecine Project, Bite the Bullet, Hard Times, Sky Rider, The Last Hard Man*, more.

COCA, IMOGENE (S. Cal.) Star comedienne. IN: *Under the Yum Yum Tree, Promise Her Anything.*

COCO, JAMES (N.Y.) Costar. Onscreen in the '70s. IN: *A New Leaf, Such Good Friends, Man of La Mancha, The Wild Party, Murder by Death*, more.

CODY, IRON EYES (S. Cal.) Famous now for TV's public service commercial "Keep America Beautiful," the Indian actor (part Cherokee), in movies for five decades and now in his late 60s, devotes all his free time to Indian affairs. Besides his extensive collection of Indian artifacts, costumes, books, and paintings, housed in his private Moosehead Museum, he has published two books (*How Indians Sign Talk* and *Indian Talk*) and is writing two more, on Indian legends and rituals. He is on the board of directors of the Los Angeles Indian Center, the Southwest Museum, and the Los Angeles Library Association. Also he is vice-president of the Little Big Horn Indian Association, a Life Member of the Verdugo Council of the Boy Scouts of America, and serves as Grand Marshal of Indian pow-wows all over the nation. For his efforts on behalf of the American Indian, he has lately been presented a scroll by the City of Los Angeles in a special ceremony held in Council Chambers in the City Hall. Privately, he lives a simple life in a residential area in a modest home shared with his wife of many years, GaYeawas, and their youngest son, Arthur (Little Eagle), who has studied printing at the L.A. Technical College. The father of his wife was a famous anthropologist, Dr. Arthur C. Parker, founder of National Indian Day. A Seneca Indian—not a squaw, Iron Eyes points out—Ga Yeawas is also a descendant of General Ely S. Parker (under U.S. Grant), who was the first Commissioner of Indian Affairs and who was himself an Indian. The Codys' eldest son, Robert (Iron Eyes Jr.), a recent graduate of Colorado's Fort Lewis College as a Phys Ed major, is 6'9", and is a champion Indian dancer (as is his brother) who has performed his ritual dances before the Queen of England. Continuing to play top roles in numerous TV shows and movies (*El Condor, Cock-eyed Cowboys of Calico County, A Man Called Horse*, etc.), Iron Eyes Cody stepped out of Indian character for the first time since 1931's *Cimarron* when he accepted a costar role in the recent *Hearts of the West*—to play a cowboy. First onscreen in the '20s, as a youngster, in Westerns. Onscreen in talkies from the mid-'30s. IN: *Crashin' Thru, Northwest Mounted Police, Unconquered, Blood on the Moon, Broken Arrow, Red Mountain, Sitting Bull, The Light in the Forest, Nevada Smith*, more.

CODY, KATHLEEN (S. Cal.) Leading lady. IN: *Superdad*, and other Disney films.

COE, BARRY (S. Cal.) Leading man. Onscreen from 1956. IN: *Love Me Tender, Peyton Place, The Bravados, But Not for Me, One Foot in Hell, Fantastic Voyage, The Cat*, more.

COE, PETER (S. Cal.) Character. Onscreen from 1943. IN: *Gung Ho!, Gypsy Wildcat, Alaska Seas, Smoke Signal, The Ten Commandments, Desert Legion, Snow White and the Three Stooges, Tobruk*, more.

COE, VIVIAN (S. Cal.) During her marriage to the late Glenn Austin, an automobile dealer, by whom she has a grown daughter, Angela, this leading lady used the screen names of Vivian Austin and Terry Austin. Today the wife of Dr. Kenneth Grow, she lives in Palm Springs, is quite social, and has no plans to resume her career. IN: Numerous Westerns, including the 1940 serial *Adventures of Red Ryder*.

COFFIN, TRISTRAM (S. Cal.) Character. Onscreen from 1939. IN: *Queen of the Yukon, Fa-*

ther Steps Out, Cowboy Serenade, Meet the Mob, Bells of Capistrano, The Mysterious Mr. Valentine, Under Arizona Skies, Louisiana, Undercover Girl; Fireman, Save My Child!; The Creature with the Atom Brain, Good Neighbor Sam, Zebra in the Kitchen, The Barefoot Executive, more.

COGHLAN, JUNIOR (S. Cal.) The freckled popular juvenile lead who, a bit later, as Frank Coghlan Jr., played Billy Batson in the serial Adventures of Captain Marvel ('41), was bereaved in 1974 when his wife, Betty, died in her sleep. He has three daughters, Mary Elizabeth, Cathleen, and Judith, and two sons, Michael and Patrick. Born in 1917, Coghlan was active on the screen from childhood until he entered the Navy during WW II. Today, a retired lieutenant commander who serves as coordinator of special events with the Los Angeles Harbor Department, he is still listed in the Hollywood Academy Players Directory as being available for screen assignments. He most recently had a featured role in The Sand Pebbles, his first movie in more than two decades. Onscreen from the '20s. IN: Slide, Kelly, Slide; Let 'Er Go, Gallagher; River's End, It Pays to Advertise, Penrod and Sam, Union Depot, Racetrack, Drum Taps, In the Money, Kentucky Blue Streak, Boys' Reformatory, Henry Aldrich for President, more.

COHAN, HELEN (Fla.) The ingenue in Will Rogers' Lightnin' ('30), her only movie, and the daughter of the late George M., she has been in delicate health in recent years and is retired.

COLBERT, CLAUDETTE (B.W.I.) Star. Won Best Actress Oscar in It Happened One Night. Nominated in the same category in Private Worlds and Since You Went Away. Unchanged in looks or manner, though now in her early 70s (b. 1905), this actress resumed her career with a nationwide tour in the play A Community of Two in '74, following it with a briefer tour in Marriage-Go-Round. This was her first professional activity since a Broadway play in '63. (Her last movie, Parrish, was released in '61.) A widow (her husband of 33 years, Dr. Joel Pressman, died in 1968), she lives seven months of the year—alone, except for women servants and her dogs, a Yorkshire terrier and a whippet —on the sun-drenched island of Barbados. Her home, Bellerive, is a 200-year-old house she has owned for 15 years. A former plantation house, facing a white-sand crescent-shaped beach, it has been renovated by the actress—she did all the interior decorating—to look "like New Orleans" with wrought-iron grillwork. There is a separate guest house, a renovated stable, for visiting friends from New York and Hollywood. Bellerive was originally planned as the retirement home of the star and her husband. He is now buried in a small cemetery nearby, which she visits regularly. As recreation the actress paints—usually "memory portraits" of children. Twice married—first to actor-director Norman Foster—she has no children. And she travels. She keeps an apartment in Paris (she was born and lived there until her family moved to New York when she was 7), in the Passy section, and journeys there at least twice a year. She has another apartment in New York, to which she flies regularly to see friends and shows (fashion and Broadway) and to visit art galleries. And that charming sense of humor remains intact. At a charity benefit in New York a while back, she was asked by a photographer to go over to a table to be photographed with Joan Bennett, Alexis Smith, and Myrna Loy. After complying, that world-familiar Colbert laughter rippled and she said, "They really should have come over to me—I'm the oldest!" Onscreen from 1927. IN: For the Love of Mike, The Big Pond, Manslaughter, The Smiling Lieutenant, Secrets of a Secretary, The Sign of the Cross, Tonight Is Ours, Cleopatra, Imitation of Life, The Gilded Lily, Under Two Flags, Maid of Salem, Bluebeard's Eighth Wife, Drums Along the Mohawk, Arise My Love, Boom Town, Remember the Day, The Palm Beach Story, So Proudly We Hail, Practically Yours, Tomorrow Is Forever, The Egg and I, Sleep My Love, Three Came Home, Thunder on the Hill, Texas Lady, Royal Affair in Versailles, Parrish, more.

COLBERT, ROBERT (S. Cal.) Support. IN: Claudelle Inglish, A Fever in the Blood, The Lawyer, more.

COLBY, ANITA (N.J.) Called "The Face" because she was easily the most famous magazine cover girl in the '30s, she was featured in 10 movies between 1936's Mary of Scotland and 1947's Brute Force. She was later an assistant to David O. Selznick, a TV panelist, and a beauty expert, writing a nationally syndicated newspaper column and a book, Anita Colby's Beauty Book. Devoutly Catholic, she did not marry until she was 56. A highly glamorous matron now, she and her millionaire, textile-executive husband, Palen Flagler, live at Round Hill Farm in New Jersey's horse country. In '75, inviting 100 celebrity guests, she tossed herself a birthday party. There were four cakes, each iced with one word from "Happy Birthday to Me," and each cake bore one candle and three zeroes "because I'm a thousand years old," she said. But she was really just 61. Onscreen from 1936. IN: Walking on Air, The Bride Walks Out, China Passage, Cover Girl, more.

COLE, CORINNE (S. Cal.) Support. IN: *The Swinger, The Party*, more.

COLE, DENNIS (S. Cal.) Leading man. Onscreen first as an extra, double, stuntman, and chorus dancer (in *Bye Bye Birdie*). Onscreen as an actor from 1964. IN: *Palm Springs Weekend, A Distant Trumpet*, more.

COLE, GEORGE (Eng.) Support. Onscreen from the early '40s. IN: *Henry V, Quartet* ("The Kite" episode), *Laughter in Paradise, A Christmas Carol, Mr. Potts Goes to Moscow, The Bells of St. Trinian's, Quentin Durward, Too Many Cooks, Cleopatra, Gone in 60 Seconds*, more.

COLE, MICHAEL (S. Cal.) Leading man. IN: *The Bubble, Chuka*, more.

COLE, TINA (S. Cal.) Singer-support. IN: *Palm Springs Weekend*.

COLEMAN, DABNEY (S. Cal.) Support. IN: *The Slender Thread, This Property Is Condemned, I Love My Wife, The Dove, The Other Side of the Mountain*, more.

COLEMAN, MARGRET (N.Y.) Support. IN: *Little Murders*.

COLEMAN, NANCY (N.Y.) Tall (5'9"), thin, and redheaded, she was in the '40s one of Warners' most dynamic young dramatic stars. Today, in her 60s (b. 1914), changed little by time's passage, a kinetic, too-thin redhead still, she is one of the outstanding actresses of the theater. To her regret, most of the work she does—in *Another Part of the Forest, The Miracle Worker, The Glass Menagerie*, etc.—is in out-of-town playhouses where Broadway producers rarely get to see her perform. It was when her husband, writer-critic Whitney Bolton, died in '69 (they had been married since '43) that she decided to resume her career full-time. Their children, twin daughters Charla Elizabeth and Grania Theresa (b. '44), who still live on Long Island, were married with families of their own. So the actress closed up her big Sea Cliff house, from which she had commuted to do an occasional role on Broadway (*The Desperate Hours*) or a soap opera (*Valiant Lady*). And she moved into town—into a fine new apartment house on Manhattan's grubby Eighth Avenue, famous for its strip joints, porno houses, pimps, and prostitutes. But it is also—which is why she chose it—in the heart of the theater district. Her daughters, who frequently come in from the Island to lunch with her, remain horrified—and so was the actress herself the night an undershirted madman pounded on her door demanding to be let in—until the cops took him

away. Still she stays. And she keeps pounding on producers' doors, praying for another hypertense role in a smash hit such as she had in *The Desperate Hours*. Not unmindful that that was more than 20 years ago, she observes, "The minute one is off the screen, or not on the New York stage, people assume your career is over. That is one of the unfortunate things about our theater today." A total realist, she also adds, "I don't believe in Fate. You just have to be ready when a chance comes—have the background, the training and the spirit, or you lose the chance, and all the luck in the world won't do you any good. Work is the answer." And it's work she is after—on Broadway. Onscreen from 1941. IN: *Kings Row, Dangerously They Live, The Gay Sisters, Desperate Journey, Edge of Darkness, In Our Time, Devotion, Her Sister's Secret, Violence, Mourning Becomes Electra, The Man from Tangier, Slaves*.

COLEY, THOMAS (N.Y.) Support. IN: *Dr. Cyclops*.

COLIN, JEAN (Eng.) Leading lady. Now retired. Onscreen from 1930. IN: *The Hate Ship, The Mikado, Last Holiday, Scotch on the Rocks*, more.

COLLIER, LOIS (S. Cal.) The wife of a prominent Los Angeles lawyer, she has been retired for several years. Onscreen from 1938. IN: *A Desperate Adventure, West of Cimarron, Riders of the Range, Cobra Woman, Jungle Woman, Ladies Courageous, Weird Woman, Jungle Queen* (serial), *The Cat Creeps, Slave Girl, Humphrey Takes a Chance, Flying Disc Men from Mars* (serial), and more, including 1958's *Missile Monsters*, her last.

COLLINGS, ANN (S. Cal.) Leading lady. IN: *Seven Alone*.

COLLINS, GARY (S. Cal.) Leading man. IN: *Cleopatra, The Pigeon That Took Rome, The Longest Day, Greek Islands, Stranded, Airport, Angel in My Pocket*, more.

COLLINS, JACK (S. Cal.) Support. IN: *Emperor of the North Pole, The Other*, more.

COLLINS, JACKIE (Eng.) Joan Collins' beautiful sister, she has given up her screen career to write, and has published several sensational best sellers in the Jacqueline Susann vein. Onscreen in the '50s. IN: *All at Sea, The Safecracker*, more.

COLLINS, JOAN (S. Cal.) Costar. Onscreen from 1953. IN: *Judgment Deferred, The Slasher, Turn the Key Softly, Land of the Pharaohs, The Girl in the Red Velvet Swing, Island in the Sun*,

Stopover Tokyo; Rally Round the Flag, Boys; Esther and the King, Road to Hong Kong, Warning Shot, Besieged, Dark Places, Fear in the Night, Oh Alfie, more.

COLMAN, BOOTH (S. Cal.) Support. IN: *The Big Sky, Scandalous John,* more.

COLMANS, EDWARD (S. Cal.) Support. IN: *Sirocco, Thief of Damascus, The Iron Mistress, Secret of the Incas, The Third Voice,* more.

COLON, MIRIAM (S. Cal.) Support. IN: *Crowded Paradise, One-Eyed Jacks, Battle at Bloody Beach, The Outsider, The Appaloosa, Joaquin Murieto,* more.

COLONNA, JERRY (S. Cal.) Now in his 70s (b. 1904), this great walrus-moustachioed comedian was the victim of a stroke a decade ago. While generally inactive since, he made a guest appearance on *The Merv Griffin Show* late in '74. Onscreen from 1937. IN: *52nd Street, Rosalie, Garden of the Moon, Comin' Round the Mountain, Priorities on Parade, Atlantic City, Make Mine Music, Road to Rio, Meet Me in Las Vegas,* and more, including *Road to Hong Kong,* his last.

COMEGYS, KATHLEEN (Fla.) Unmarried, and in her 80s (b. 1895), the character actress is retired, having given up her career after playing Aunt Ev in *The Miracle Worker* ('62). IN: *Mr. Belvedere Rings the Bell,* more.

COMER, ANJANETTE (S. Cal.) Leading lady. Onscreen from 1964. IN: *Quick Before It Melts, The Loved One, The Appaloosa, Funeral in Berlin, Banning, Guns of San Sebastian, Rabbit Run, Lepke, The Manchu Eagle Murder Caper Mystery,* more.

COMI, PAUL (S. Cal.) Support. Onscreen from 1958. IN: *In Love and War, Pork Chop Hill, The Outsider, Cape Fear, Blindfold,* more.

COMO, PERRY (N.Y.) Singer-actor. Onscreen from 1944. IN: *Something for the Boys, Doll Face, If I'm Lucky, Words and Music.*

COMPTON, FAY (Eng.) Character. Earlier a leading lady. Onscreen from the teens. IN: *One Summer's Day, The Old Wives' Tale, Fashions in Love, Love Storm, The Battle of Gallipoli, Autumn Crocus, Strauss's Great Waltz, Wedding Group, Odd Man Out, Dulcimer Street, Nicholas Nickleby, Britannia Mews, Blackmailed, Laughter in Paradise, Othello, The Story of Esther Costello,* more.

COMPTON, FORREST (N.Y.) Support. IN: *Inherit the Wind, The Children's Hour, The Outsider, Kings Go Forth,* more.

COMPTON, JOYCE (S. Cal.) This fine, fluttery "Southern Belle" comedienne, still a perky blonde in her late 60s, who entered movies in the '20s and appeared in more than 100, quit the screen in 1949 after *Grand Canyon.* In '57–58 she came back for small roles in three—*Jet Pilot, The Persuader,* and *Girl in the Woods*—and that was it. In '56 she also was married for the first and only time—for three months. Today she lives alone (her parents, to whom she was deeply devoted and who always lived with her, having died some years back) in an old-English farmhouse in Van Nuys. She decorated it herself, filling it with paintings—landscapes and portraits. "I did them all," she says. "If my movie career hadn't materialized, art would have been my vocation." The inanities that script writers always gave her to say, incidentally, are not part of her natural personality, but that inimitable, quirky little voice is. A deeply religious woman, from a long line of Kentucky ministers, she attends a nearby church regularly, prays daily for guidance, and actively serves others—having been for many years a part-time practical nurse. The favorite of her many movies? She answers without a moment's hesitation: "*Sky Murder*"—in which she played the femme lead opposite Walter Pidgeon. Onscreen from 1926. IN: *Syncopating Sue, Sky Hawk, Annabelle's Affairs, Up Pops the Devil, Lena Rivers, If I Had a Million, Go Into Your Dance, Love Before Breakfast, Top of the Town, The Awful Truth, Kid Galahad, Rose of Washington Square, Turnabout, Manpower, Christmas in Connecticut, Dark Alibi, A Southern Yankee,* more.

CONDE, RITA (S. Cal.) Support. IN: *Ride the Pink Horse, Barquero,* more.

CONDOS, STEVE (S. Cal.) Actor-dancer; of the Condos Brothers. Works alone now on Broadway (*Sugar; Say, Darling;* etc.), on TV, in dinner theaters, and dubbing foreign films. Onscreen from 1937. IN: *Wake Up and Live, Happy Landing, In the Navy, Moon Over Miami, Pin-Up Girl; The Time, the Place and the Girl; She's Back on Broadway, Meet Me After the Show,* more.

CONGDON, JAMES (N.Y.) Support. Onscreen from 1958. IN: *The Left Handed Gun, The Group, Three Hundred Year Weekend,* more.

CONKLIN, PEGGY (N.Y.) In her 60s now (b. 1912), she continued her starring career on Broadway and TV into the '60s but has not appeared in a movie since 1938's *Having Wonderful Time.* Onscreen from 1934. IN: *The President Vanishes, One Way Ticket, Her Master's Voice, The Devil Is a Sissy.*

CONLEY, DARLENE (S. Cal.) Support. IN: *Faces.*

CONNELL, JANE (N.Y.) Comedienne. Onscreen from 1963. IN: *Ladybug, Ladybug; Trilogy* ("Miriam" episode), *Mame*, more.

CONNELLY, CHRISTOPHER (S. Cal.) Leading man. IN: *A Ticklish Affair, What a Way to Go!, They Only Kill Their Masters, Benji*, more.

CONNELLY, MARC (N.Y.) Playwright-character. IN: *The Spirit of St. Louis.*

CONNER, BETTY (S. Cal.) Support. IN: *The Man From Galveston.*

CONNERY, NEIL (Eng.) Leading man. Sean's brother. IN: *Operation Kid Brother, The Body Stealers*, more. Now works as a plasterer.

CONNERY, SEAN (Sp.) Star. A millionaire by virtue of the "James Bond" films, he lives, with second wife, Micheline, in a villa in Marbella. Onscreen from 1955. IN: *No Road Back; Another Time, Another Place; The Longest Day, Dr. No, From Russia With Love, Goldfinger, Thunderball, You Only Live Twice, Diamonds Are Forever, Murder on the Orient Express, The Wind and the Lion, The Man Who Would Be King, Ransom, Robin and Marian*, more.

CONNOLLY, NORMA (S. Cal.) Support. IN: *The Wrong Man*, more.

CONNOR, KENNETH (Eng.) Comic support. IN: *The Black Rider*, the "Carry On" series (*Carry On Sergeant*, etc.), *Ladykillers, Captain Nemo and the Underwater City*, more.

CONNOR, WHITFIELD (Conn.) Married to actress Haila Stoddard since '41, this leading man has just entered his 60s (b. 1916), and lives in South Weston. Onscreen from 1948. IN: *Tap Roots, Scarlet Angel, The President's Lady, City of Bad Men, The Saracen Blade, Butterfield 8*, more.

CONNORS, CHUCK (S. Cal.) Costar. Onscreen from 1952. IN: *Pat and Mike, Trouble Along the Way, The Human Jungle, Old Yeller, The Big Country, Flipper, Move Over Darling, Night of the Tiger, Tony Rome, Soylent Green, 99 44/100% Dead*, more.

CONNORS, MIKE (S. Cal.) Star of TV's *Mannix*, he was previously known as Touch Connors. Onscreen from 1953. IN: *Sudden Fear, Five Guns West, Jaguar, Panic Button, Where Love Has Gone, Harlow, Stagecoach*, more.

CONNORS, SHARON (N.Y.) Support. IN: *Blue Hawaii.*

CONRAD, MICHAEL (S. Cal.) Character. Onscreen from 1962. IN: *Requiem for a Heavyweight, Castle Keep; They Shoot Horses, Don't They?; Monte Walsh, The Todd Killings, Head On, The Longest Yard, "W,"* more.

CONRAD, ROBERT (S. Cal.) Costar. Onscreen from 1963. IN: *Palm Springs Weekend, Hotel Madrid, Young Dillinger; Live a Little, Steal a Lot;* more.

CONRAD, WILLIAM (S. Cal.) Character star. Onscreen from 1946. IN: *The Killers, Body and Soul, To the Victor; Sorry, Wrong Number; Any Number Can Play, Dial 1119, The Racket, The Desert Song, Five Against the House, The Conqueror, -30-, The Brotherhood of the Bell, The D.A.: Conspiracy to Kill; O'Hara, United States Treasury;* more.

CONRIED, HANS (S. Cal.) Character comedian. Onscreen from 1937. IN: *Dramatic School, Dulcy, The Wife Takes a Flyer, The Big Street, A Lady Takes a Chance, Summer Stock, Nancy Goes to Rio, The Birds and the Bees, Bus Stop, Jet Pilot, My Six Loves, Magic Fountain,* more.

CONSIDINE, JOHN (S. Cal.) Support. IN: *The Greatest Story Ever Told, Buffalo Bill and the Indians,* more.

CONSIDINE, TIM (S. Cal.) Young leading man; former juvenile. Onscreen from 1953. IN: *The Clown, Executive Suite, Her Twelve Men, Unchained, The Private War of Major Benson, The Shaggy Dog, Sunrise at Campobello, Patton,* more. Also he and brother John coauthored the screenplay of *Tarzan's Deadly Silence.*

CONSTANTIN, MICHEL (Fr.) Costar. IN: *The Night Watch, A Very Curious Girl,* more.

CONSTANTINE, MICHAEL (S. Cal.) Character. Onscreen from 1954. IN: *Cyanamide, The Last Mile, The Hustler; Quick, Before It Melts; Hawaii, Don't Drink the Water, The Reivers, Peeper,* more.

CONTINO, DICK (S. Cal.) Accordion player-actor. IN: *The Big Night.* Appears now in nightclubs.

CONVERSE, FRANK (S. Cal.) Leading man. IN: *Hurry Sundown, Hour of the Gun,* more.

CONVERSE, PEGGY (S. Cal.) Support. Onscreen from 1950. IN: *Father Is a Bachelor, Miss Sadie Thompson, They Rode West, Day of the Bad Man, The Thing That Couldn't Die,* more.

CONVY, BERT (S. Cal.) Leading man. Onscreen from the '60s. IN: *Gunman's Walk, Susan Slade, Act One,* more.

CONWAY, GARY (S. Cal.) Leading man. Onscreen from 1958. IN: *I Was a Teenage Frankenstein, Young Guns of Texas, Black Gunn, Once Is Not Enough,* more.

CONWAY, MORGAN (N.J.) Near the end of his Hollywood career he became the screen's first Dick Tracy, playing the role twice—in *Dick Tracy* ('45) and *Dick Tracy vs. Cueball* ('46). Records indicate that the latter was his last film. Photographs of the actor, which would appear to have been taken about that time, appear still in the New York *Players' Guide,* together with his Cranford address and phone number. But when contacted (a woman identifying herself as Mrs. Conway first answering the phone), the actor, who would be in his late 60s or early 70s now, declined to give additional private or career information. "Check Screen Actors Guild," he said, hanging up. Onscreen from 1934. IN: *Looking For Trouble, Nurse From Brooklyn, Crime Ring, Blackwell's Island, Charlie Chan in Reno, The Saint Takes Over, Brother Orchid, Jack London, Badman's Territory, The Truth About Murder,* more.

CONWAY, PAT (S. Cal.) Leading man. Onscreen from 1952. IN: *Invitation, Above and Beyond, An Annapolis Story, Flight to Hong Kong, Brighty of the Grand Canyon, Destination 60,000,* more.

CONWAY, RUSS (S. Cal.) Character. Onscreen from 1948. IN: *Larceny, My Six Convicts, Love Me Tender, Fort Dobbs, Our Man Flint,* more.

CONWAY, SHIRL (N.Y.) Support. IN: *You Can't Fool an Irishman.*

CONWAY, TIM (S. Cal.) Star comedian. Onscreen from 1964. IN: *McHale's Navy, McHale's Navy Joins the Air Force, The World's Greatest Athlete, The Apple Dumpling Gang, Gus,* more.

CONWELL, CAROLYN (S. Cal.) Support. IN: *Torn Curtain.*

COOGAN, JACKIE (S. Cal.) Bald, beefy, gregarious, and in his 60s (b. 1914), he is one of Hollywood's most in-demand character actors, appearing regularly on TV (where he costarred in the '60s in *The Addams Family*) and in movies (*The Manchu Eagle Murder Caper Mystery* recently). He has been married four times and divorced three. His first wives were Betty Grable (1936–39), Flower Parry (divorced in '43; she is the mother of the eldest of his four chil-

dren, who was named Anthony but lately, a Hollywood cameraman, has been called Jackie Jr.), and Anne McCormick (1946–50; she is the mother of his grown daughter, Joan, and by her Coogan also was the stepfather of actor Don Stroud). Married to his fourth wife, Dorothy (Dodie), since '52, Coogan has two youngsters by her: a college-age daughter, Leslie, and a son, Christopher, born in '67. This lad was the cause of grave concern to his parents in 1974 when he had to undergo surgery for removal of a growth on his leg—mercifully nonmalignant. Coogan's wife, too, has had surgery, nine times, since an automobile accident that almost cost her life in 1967. It has been a long time since 1923 when little Jackie Coogan of the Buster Brown haircut, the first major child star, was #1 at the box-office. He has 50 huge scrapbooks of those years to remind him, as well as prints of several of his best pictures that he shows often at home—to the particular fascination of his youngest, who looks much as Jackie did then. It has also been a long time since 1937 when he sued—and lost—to recover from his mother and stepfather the $1 million he had earned as a youngster. (The suit did result in the creation of the so-called "Coogan Law" in California that has protected all child stars since from a similar victimization.) His mother was still living at last report, an old lady in a wheel chair, and, Coogan insisted, the bitterness between them had long since been dissolved. As an adult he has made a great deal of money—so much, in fact, that he now only works about half the year. "Now I have a home in Palm Springs," Coogan says, referring to their main residence, "and another down in La Paz, Baja California, where I enjoy the fishing and the sun and the pure air. I've found great happiness with my wife Dorothy . . . So call me lucky. I've had a colorful career, beautiful wives, and four healthy kids. If that doesn't spell happiness, what does?" Onscreen from 1920. IN: *The Kid, Peck's Bad Boy, Oliver Twist, Daddy, A Boy of Flanders, Old Clothes, Buttons, Tom Sawyer, Huckleberry Finn, Million Dollar Legs, French Leave, Skipalong Rosenbloom, The Joker Is Wild, The Buster Keaton Story, Lonely Hearts, Night of the Quarter Moon; John Goldfarb, Please Come Home; Girl Happy,* more.

COOGAN, ROBERT (S. Cal.) Jackie's younger brother. Former juvenile. Now support. Onscreen from 1930. IN: *Skippy, Sooky, The Miracle Man, Johnny Doughboy, Kilroy Was Here, Joe Palooka Meets Humphrey, Here Come the Marines, Third of a Man,* more.

COOK, CAROLE (S. Cal.) Comedienne. Onscreen from 1963. IN: *Palm Springs Weekend, The Incredible Mr. Limpet,* more.

COOK, ELISHA, JR. (S. Cal.) Character. Onscreen from 1930. IN: *Her Unborn Child, Pig-*

*skin Parade, He Married His Wife, Tin Pan Al-
ley, The Maltese Falcon, Casanova Brown,
Phantom Lady, Dark Mountain, Up in Arms,
Dillinger, The Big Sleep, The Falcon's Alibi,
The Long Night, The Gangster, Don't Bother to
Knock, Baby Face Nelson, Plunder Road, Day
of the Outlaw, One-Eyed Jacks, The Glass
Cage, Rosemary's Baby, The Outfit, Messiah of
Evil, The Black Bird, St. Ives*, more.

COOK, FRED (N.Y.) Support. IN: *The Hot
Rock*, more.

COOK, PETER (Eng.) Half of the comedy
team of Dudley Moore and Peter Cook. Onscreen from 1966. IN: *The Wrong Box, Bedazzled, Those Daring Young Men in Their Jaunty
Jalopies, The Bed Sitting Room*, more.

COOK, TOMMY (S. Cal.) A popular child actor of the '40s (*The Gay Senorita, Michael
O'Halloran*, etc.) and teenager in the '50s (*The
Vicious Years, Battle Cry*, others), he acts only
on occasion now—appearing, for instance, as a
hood recently on TV in *Streets of San Francisco*. Principally, as one of California's best-
known tennis pros, his occupation is arranging
and promoting celebrity tennis tournaments—
that and producing concert appearances for
such music stars as Glen Campbell and Alice
Cooper in such far-flung locations as Tokyo and
Acapulco. Onscreen from 1942. IN: *The Tuttles
of Tahiti; Hi, Buddy; Wanderer of the Wasteland, Gallant Journey, Tarzan and the Leopard
Woman, Humoresque, Panic in the Streets, Mohawk, Alaska Passage, King Gun*, more.

COOKSON, PETER (N.Y.) Leading man. Onscreen in the '40s. IN: *Swingtime Johnny, The
Scarlet Horseman* (serial), more.

COONAN, DOROTHY (S. Cal.) This freckle-
faced gamine of the early '30s was happily married for four decades to famed director William
Wellman who died in '75. She lives near Hollywood on a six-acre estate with a pool and an
orange orchard, and with two of her seven children—Mike, of college age, and Maggie, a
young actress. Interestingly, and neatly, the
Wellman offspring arrived in girl-boy-girl-boy
order. From the top, the others are: Pat (once a
TWA stewardess), William Jr. (the actor),
Kitty, Tim, and Cissy. Except for Cissy, who at
last report lived nearby in a bachelor-girl apartment, all the older children are married—Kitty
to actor James Franciscus—and have made
Dorothy a 13-time grandmother. Dorothy—
whom Wellman always called "Mommy"—is,
in her early 60s, as vivacious and pretty as any
of her daughters. Onscreen in the early '30s.
IN: *Wild Boys of the Road*, more.

COOPER, BEN (S. Cal.) Support. Onscreen
from 1952. IN: *Thunderbirds, Flight Nurse, The
Rose Tattoo, War Drums, Duel at Apache
Wells, Waco, The Fastest Gun Alive, Support
Your Local Gunfighter, One More Train to
Rob*, more.

COOPER, EDWIN (Conn.) Character. IN: *The
Guilt of Janet Ames*.

COOPER, GEORGE A. (Eng.) Character. Onscreen from the '50s. IN: *Violet Playground,
Tom Jones, Life at the Top, The Black Windmill*, more.

COOPER, JACKIE (S. Cal.) Former juvenile/
now costar. Nominated for Best Actor Oscar in
Skippy. Onscreen from 1925. IN: "Lloyd Ham-
ilton" comedies, *Sunny Side Up*, "Our Gang,"
*Sooky, Donovan's Kid, When a Fellow Needs a
Friend, Treasure Island, Peck's Bad Boy,
Dinky, The Devil Is a Sissy, White Banners,
That Certain Age, What a Life, Seventeen, Re-
turn of Frank James, Ziegfeld Girl, Glamour
Boy, Syncopation, Where Are Your Children?,
Kilroy Was Here, The Joker Is Wild, Every-
thing's Ducky, The Love Machine, Chosen Sur-
vivors*, more.

COOPER, JEANNE (S. Cal.) Leading lady. Onscreen from 1953. IN: *The Redhead From Wyoming, The Man From the Alamo, Let No Man
Write My Epitaph, House of Women, The Intruder, Black Zoo*, more.

COOPER, MIRIAM (Va.) Six decades ago, a
girl with haunting dark eyes and chestnut hair
was one of D.W. Griffith's brightest stars. Playing a leading role in *Intolerance*—a gangster's
moll—she was paid $35,000 a week, she has
said. She earned huge salaries in many pix after
that, through 1923's *The Broken Wing*. Today,
frail, old (b. 1893), and bedridden, she is almost
penniless. Under treatment for arthritis and a
heart condition, the white-haired actress said
not long ago, "I can't afford to pay $100 a week
for the day and night nurses the doctor says I
have to have . . . I have some money of my
own, but not that much . . .I'm going to have to
go on relief." Since '52 she has lived in Charlottesville in a small white bungalow, that she
has had to sell. A devout Catholic, she has not
remarried since her divorce in '26 from director
Raoul Walsh. They were married exactly one
decade, adopted two sons, and parted bitterly.
In '74 two interesting books were published—
her autobiography (*Dark Lady of the Silents*)
and his (*Each Man in His Time*). In her book
she had a good deal to say about Walsh; in his
there is not one mention of her, his first wife.
For many years after leaving Hollywood ("It
was no life. I got out of the business because I

couldn't take it any more," she has said) she lived well. Thanks to her savings and alimony, she led a highly social life in New York and Florida (winters there for golf, which she played until two decades ago). And for a number of years she owned a 1,000-acre estate on the fashionable eastern shore of Maryland (her home state) before settling in obscurity in Charlottesville. Gradually her failing health, and lawyers' fees for legal skirmishes with her former husband, began to eat away at her bank balance. Not long ago, desperately determined not to go into a nursing home, she said, "I've had a lot of money and I've been very, very foolish with it." Then the faded star, but with unfaded gallantry, faced the spectre of bankruptcy—and the welfare rolls. Onscreen from 1910. IN: *The Duke's Plan, The Birth of a Nation, Intolerance, The Mother and the Law, Evangeline, The Deep Purple, The Oath, Kindred of the Dust, Daughters of the Rich,* more. (Died April 12, 1976.)

COOPER, TERENCE (Eng.) Leading man. IN: *Casino Royale.*

COOTE, ROBERT (Eng.) Character. Onscreen from the '30s. IN: *A Yank at Oxford, Gunga Din, Commandos Strike at Dawn, Stairway to Heaven, Forever Amber, The Ghost and Mrs. Muir, The Desert Fox, The Constant Husband, The Swan, The Horse's Mouth, The League of Gentlemen, A Man Could Get Killed, Prudence and the Pill,* more.

COPELAND, JOAN (N.Y.) Support. IN: *The Goddess, Middle of the Night.*

COPLEY, PETER (Eng.) Character. Onscreen from the '50s. IN: *The Promoter, The Sword and the Rose, Time Without Pity, Victim,* more.

COPPOLA, TALIA (S. Cal.) The first screen (and real) name of Academy Award nominee Talia Shire. Acted under this name, in '70, in *The Dunwich Horror* and *Gas-s-s-s!* (See Talia Shire.)

CORBETT, GLENN (S. Cal.) Leading man. Onscreen from 1950. IN: *The Fireball, The Crimson Kimono, The Mountain Road, All the Young Men, The Pirates of Blood River, Shenandoah, Big Jake, Ride in a Pink Car, Dead Pigeon on Beethoven Street,* more.

CORBY, ELLEN (S. Cal.) Character. Nominated for Best Supporting Actress Oscar in *I Remember Mama.* Onscreen from 1946. IN: *The Dark Corner, Strike It Rich, Little Women, Rusty Saves a Life, Madame Bovary, The Gunfighter, Caged, Harriet Craig; Goodbye, My Fancy; Shane, A Lion Is in the Streets, About*

Mrs. Leslie, Sabrina, Night Passage, Vertigo, Visit to a Small Planet, Hush . . . Hush . . . Sweet Charlotte, The Glass Bottom Boat, The Gnome-Mobile, The Legend of Lylah Clare, Angel in My Pocket, Support Your Local Gunfighter, more.

CORCORAN, BRIAN (S. Cal.) Former juvenile. Of the large Corcoran clan (see following entries), nearly all of whom were featured in movies as youngsters. Onscreen from 1961. IN: *Babes in Toyland, Cat on a Hot Tin Roof.* He is in his 20s now (b. 1951) and retired from acting.

CORCORAN, DONNA (S. Cal.) She was the first of the Corcoran family to become a contract player, being signed by MGM when she was six. In her 30s now (b. 1942), she is Mrs. Luis Newman, and retired from pictures. Onscreen from 1948. IN: *Angels in the Outfield, Young Man with Ideas, Don't Bother to Knock, Million Dollar Mermaid, Scandal at Scourie, Dangerous When Wet,* more.

CORCORAN, HUGH (S. Cal.) Giving up acting, he has become a producer—of *Welcome Home, Johnny* ('74).

CORCORAN, KELLY (S. Cal.) Teen support (b. 1958); he is the youngest member of the troup. IN: *The Courtship of Eddie's Father, Picture Mommy Dead, This Savage Land,* more.

CORCORAN, KEVIN (S. Cal.) One of Disney's most popular juvenile actors—for seven years —he is in his 20s (b. 1949) and pursuing other professional interests. Onscreen from 1955. IN: *Violent Saturday, Old Yeller, The Shaggy Dog, The Rabbit Trap, Toby Tyler, Pollyanna, Swiss Family Robinson, Bon Voyage!, Savage Sam, A Tiger Walks,* more.

CORCORAN, NOREEN (S. Cal.) She is in her 30s now (b. 1943) and retired. Onscreen from 1953. IN: *I Love Melvin, Young Bess, So This Is Love, Tanganyika, Violent Saturday, Band of Angels, Gidget Goes to Rome, The Girls on the Beach.*

CORD, ALEX (S. Cal.) Leading man. Onscreen from 1965. IN: *Synanon, Stagecoach, The Prodigal Gun, The Brotherhood; A Minute to Pray, a Second to Die; Stiletto, Chosen Survivors,* more.

CORDAY, MARA (S. Cal.) Widowed when her actor-husband, Richard Long, died in 1974, she has three children and has talked of resuming her career. Onscreen from 1952. IN: *The Lady Wants Mink, Drums Across the River, Playgirl, Dawn at Socorro, Francis Joins the Wacs, Raw*

Edge, The Girl on Death Row, The Giant Claw, Girls on the Loose, more.

CORDAY, PAULA (S. Cal.) The lovely blonde actress who was onscreen for over a decade through 1954's *The French Line*, and was sometimes billed Rita Corday or Paule Croset, has been married more than two decades to producer Harold Nebenzal, has two children, and is now in her early 50s (b. 1924). Onscreen from 1943. IN: *The Falcon Strikes Back, The Body Snatcher, The Exile, Sword of Monte Cristo, Because You're Mine?, You for Me, The Black Castle*, more.

CORDELL, CATHLEEN (S. Cal.) Support. IN: *Angel Street*, more.

CORDEN, HENRY (S. Cal.) Character. Onscreen from 1947. IN: *The Secret Life of Walter Mitty, Behave Yourself, Carbine Williams, King Richard and the Crusaders*, more.

COREY, JEFF (S. Cal.) Character. Onscreen from 1941. IN: *Small Town Deb, All That Money Can Buy, The Killers, Miracle on 34th Street, Ramrod, Brute Force, Joan of Arc, City Across the River, Home of the Brave, The Next Voice You Hear, Fourteen Hours, Lady in a Cage, In Cold Blood, The Boston Strangler, Butch Cassidy and the Sundance Kid, Beneath the Planet of the Apes, The Premonition, Paper Tiger*, more.

COREY, IRWIN (S. Cal.) Comedian. IN: *Thieves*.

CORIO, ANN (N.Y.) Stripper-actress. Onscreen in the '40s. IN: *Swamp Woman, Jungle Siren, Sarong Girl*. She has presented her stage revue, *This Was Burlesque*, with success in various cities in the past decade, and she remains a stunningly beautiful woman.

CORNTHWAITE, ROBERT (S. Cal.) Character. Onscreen from 1951. IN: *The Thing, His Kind of Woman, Monkey Business, War of the Worlds, Kiss Me Deadly, On the Threshold of Space, What Ever Happend to Baby Jane?, Waterhole #3, The Peace Killers*, more.

CORNWALL, ANNE (S. Cal.) The charmer of Christie comedies of the '20s still appears onscreen occasionally, e.g., an unbilled bit in *Inherit the Wind*. Married and living near Hollywood, she was first the wife of director Charles Maigne, who died in '29. Onscreen from 1923. IN: *Dulcy, The Roughneck, Introduce Me, The Rainbow Trail, The Flaming Frontier, College*, more.

CORRI, ADRIENNE (Eng.) Leading lady. Onscreen from 1951. IN: *The River, The Little*

Kidnappers, 3 Men in a Boat, Sword of Lancelot, Doctor Zhivago, A Study in Terror, Africa —Texas Style!, A Clockwork Orange, Madhouse, Rosebud, more.

CORRIGAN, DOUGLAS "WRONG WAY" (S. Cal.) Approaching his 70th birthday (b. 1907), the redhead who starred in one movie after achieving fame in '38 by landing his monoplane Lizz in Ireland when he "thought" he was bound for Los Angeles from New York lives in retirement in Santa Ana. Was his famous transatlantic flight in the government-deemed-"unsafe" plane an honest mistake or a planned defiance of official orders? Says Corrigan: "I really can't remember." Onscreen in 1939. IN: *The Flying Irishman*.

CORRIGAN, RAY "CRASH" (S. Cal.) Rugged still, though no longer young enough (b. 1907) to take on a dozen Western heavies, this famous cowboy star lives with his wife, the former Elaine DuPont, on a ranch at Corriganville, Calif. This is an authentic Western town, used for years as a movie location. There, besides inventing electronic devices (he holds more than two dozen patents), Ray manages his numerous business enterprises—a swimming pool concern, a soft drink franchise, real estate, etc. Considering himself "officially" retired after the last of his "Range Rustlers" Westerns (*Black Market Rustlers*) in '44, Ray continued to play occasional supporting roles until the end of the '50s—in *Killer Ape, Zombies of Mora-Tau, It! The Terror from Outer Space*, etc. Yes, Ray admits, he still sees one of his old "Three Mesquiteers" movies on TV once in a while, and gets a kick out of it, but has no hankering at all to go back to movie acting. Onscreen from 1934. IN: *Mystery Ranch, Roarin' Lead, Riders of the Whistling Skull, Call of the Mesquiteers, The Painted Stallion* (serial), *Pals of the Saddle, The Range Busters, Renegade Girl, Zamba, The Domino Kid*, more.

CORSARI, FRANCO (S. Cal.) Character. IN: *The Heavenly Body, Dangerous Millions, Black Magic, Pay or Die*, more.

CORSAUT, ANETA (S. Cal.) Leading lady. IN: *The Blob*.

CORT, BUD (N.Y.) Young character lead. IN: *M*A*S*H, The Strawberry Statement, Brewster McCloud, Harold and Maude, The Traveling Executioner, Gas-s-s-s!*

CORTESE, VALENTINA (It.) Costar. Nominated for Best Supporting Actress Oscar in *Day for Night*. Onscreen from 1941. IN: *A Yank in Rome, The Glass Mountain, The House on Telegraph Hill, Thieves' Highway, Malaya, Secret People, The Barefoot Contessa, Magic Fire,*

Barabbas, The Visit, Juliet of the Spirits, The Legend of Lylah Clare, First Love, Give Her the Moon, more.

CORTEZ, RICARDO (N.Y.) In his 70s (b. 1899), he is still swarthy and suave (though his hairline has receded). In the '60s he became a bridegroom for the third time when he married decades-younger Margarette Belle. (His first wife, star Alma Rubens, died in '31, and he had been divorced for years from the New York society woman, Mrs. Christine Lee, whom he had married in '34.) Essentially retired from his second career, which he entered upon in his 50s —that of a Wall Street broker—he now travels widely, to Paris, the Cannes Film Festival, etc. And he remains close to the friends made during his 28-year Hollywood career that ended in '48. (He played, later, in New York, a supporting role in 1958's The Last Hurrah, which for him it was.) When director pal Raoul Walsh was honored at the Museum of Modern Art in '74, this star of yesteryear was on hand with contemporaries like Blanche Sweet, Gloria Swanson, and others, to salute him. When home, Cortez lives in a swank townhouse a few doors off Fifth Avenue. Onscreen from 1920. IN: Children of Jazz, A Society Scandal, Feet of Clay, Argentine Love, The Torrent, Ladies of the Night Club, The Maltese Falcon, Thirteen Women, Flesh, Mandalay, The Man With Two Faces, A Lost Lady, The White Cockatoo, The Case of the Black Cat, Charlie Chan in Reno, Who Is Hope Schuyler?, The Locket, more.

COSBY, BILL (S. Cal.) Black comedy star. Onscreen in the '70s. IN: Hickey and Boggs, Let's Do It Again.

COSTA, MARY (S. Cal.) Leading lady. Onscreen from 1957. IN: The Big Caper, The Great Waltz.

COSTELLO, ANTHONY (S. Cal.) Support. IN: Blue, The Molly Maguires, more.

COSTELLO, DIOSA (Nev.) The fiery actress-dancer has changed careers—she is a blackjack dealer in one of Las Vegas' fanciest casinos. IN: The Bullfighters, Miss Sadie Thompson, more.

COSTELLO, DOLORES (S. Cal.) Garson Kanin has said in his book Hollywood that John Barrymore was intensely jealous when this beautiful wife of his was pregnant with their son, John Barrymore Jr., and accused her of being infatuated with her obstetrician, Dr. John Vrumink. The Barrymore-Costello marriage produced yet another child, Dolores (b. 1933), before they were divorced in '35. Four years later the actress—perhaps Barrymore had planted the idea?—did marry her obstetrician,

and remained married to him until they were divorced (no children) in '51. In 1942 The Magnificent Ambersons was her last starring appearance, though she did play a small role in the following year's This Is the Army. Dolores lives in quiet retirement on a ranch 100 miles south of Los Angeles. No longer quite the great beauty she was, she remains, in her 70s (b. 1905), an attractive, though perhaps a trifle disenchanted, blonde. She has not acted since appearing in a play, The Great Man, over two decades ago. One's impression is that she does not miss performing—or Hollywood—one bit. Onscreen from 1923. IN: Lawful Larceny, The Sea Beast, The Little Irish Girl, The College Widow, Madonna of Avenue A, Hearts in Exile, Outside These Walls, Expensive Women, Little Lord Fauntleroy, Beloved Brat, Breaking the Ice, Whispering Enemies, King of the Turf, more.

COSTELLO, WARD (S. Cal.) Character. IN: The Gallant Hours, more.

COSTER, NICOLAS (N.Y.) Support. Onscreen from 1965. IN: My Blood Runs Cold, The Sporting Club, more.

COTSWORTH, STAATS (S. Cal.) Character. IN: Peyton Place, They Might Be Giants, more. (See Josephine Hutchinson.)

COTTEN, JOSEPH (S. Cal.) Star. Onscreen from 1940. IN: Citizen Kane, Lydia, The Magnificent Ambersons, Shadow of a Doubt, Gaslight, Since You Went Away, Love Letters, Duel in the Sun, The Farmer's Daughter, Portrait of Jennie, Beyond the Forest, The Third Man, The Man with a Cloak, Niagara, Hush . . . Hush . . . Sweet Charlotte, The Oscar, Tora! Tora! Tora!, Soylent Green, Roots of the Mafia, more.

COULOURIS, GEORGE (Eng.) After his 20-year residence in Hollywood, this superlative character actor returned to his native England to live and work following 1954's Duel in the Jungle. Now in his 70s (b. 1903), he still flies back to the U.S. when beckoned for TV roles, but primarily he works—constantly—in English-or Italian-made films (Murder on the Orient Express, The Antichrist, Mahler, etc.). And he gave a particularly distinguished performance as crusty Mr. Grimethorpe in the five-part mystery drama Clouds of Witness, the Masterpiece Theatre production filmed in England and shown on TV here via PBS. Onscreen from 1933. IN: Christopher Bean, All This and Heaven Too, Citizen Kane, Assignment in Brittany, For Whom the Bell Tolls, Watch on the Rhine, None But the Lonely Heart, Mr. Skeffington, Lady on a Train, Nobody Lives Forever, Beyond Glory, The Assassin, Doctor at

Sea, Beasts of Marseille, King of Kings, Arabesque, Last Days of Man on Earth, more.

COURCEL, NICOLE (Fr.) Leading lady. Onscreen from the '40s. IN: Marie du Port; Mama, Papa, the Maid and I; The Case of Dr. Laurent, Sundays and Cybele, Stop Train 349, more.

COURT, HAZEL (S. Cal.) Leading lady. Onscreen from the '40s. IN: Dear Murderer, Meet Me at Dawn, Ghost Ship, Dr. Blood's Coffin, Mary Had a Little, The Premature Burial, The Raven, more. (See Don Taylor.)

COURTENAY, TOM (Eng.) Costar. Nominated for Best Supporting Actor Oscar in Doctor Zhivago. Onscreen from 1962. IN: Loneliness of the Long Distance Runner, Billy Liar, King Rat, King and Country, Operation Crossbow, The Night of the Generals, A Dandy in Aspic, Otley, One Day in the Life of Ivan Denisovich, more.

COURTLAND, JEROME (S. Cal.) Handsome still as he enters his 50s (b. 1926), but no longer the gangling Southern youth who made such a hit in Irene Dunne's Together Again or romanced Shirley Temple in Kiss and Tell, he is today one of Disney's most successful producers. Escape to Witch Mountain ('75), starring Eddie Albert and Ray Milland, was one of his. Courtland's Disney association dates back to the '50s, when he starred for the studio in the TV series The Saga of Andy Burnett, sang (offscreen) the title song for Old Yeller, did all the male voices for the Noah and the Ark cartoon, and narrated and sang for the TV show The Boy and the Falcon. There was a six-year gap while he went to Germany and Italy and—in the languages of those countries, both of which he speaks fluently—starred in a number of films never shown in the States. He returned to Hollywood—and Disney—in the mid-60s to become associate producer of The Gnome-Mobile and Follow Me Boys. Married a while, two decades ago, to Polly Bergen, he has been happily married for many years to a lovely girl named Janet. Parents of five young children—three sons and two daughters—they live on a ranch at Thousand Oaks. Onscreen from 1944. IN: Together Again, The Walking Hills, Battleground, Woman of Distinction, When You're Smiling, On the Sunny Side of the Street, Cripple Creek, Take the High Ground, Black Spurs, more.

COURTNEIDGE, CICELY (Eng.) This fine character actress, now in her 80s (b. 1893), published her biography in England in '75—The Little Woman's Always Right, written by her husband, Jack Hulbert. (Her autobiography,

Cicely, was published in '53.) The new volume appeared exactly 74 years after she made her stage debut as Peablossom in A Midsummer Night's Dream. As recently as '70, she toured South Africa and the United Kingdom in the comedy Oh, Clarence. Her most recent movie was 1973's Not Now Darling. Onscreen from the early '30s. IN: The Ghost Train, The Woman in Command, Along Came Sally, The Imperfect Lady, The Perfect Gentleman, The L-Shaped Room, Those Magnificent Men in Their Flying Machines, The Wrong Box, more.

COURTNEY, DAN (Pa.) The actor who supported Pearl White in The Perils of Pauline and was also in The Clutching Hand, is, in his late 70s, still active—often journeying from his home in Philadelphia to reminisce about the "old days" as a guest on The Joe Franklin Show or Johnny Carson's TV show.

COWLES, MATHEW (N.Y.) Support. IN: Me, Natalie; The People Next Door, They Might Be Giants.

COX, RONNY (S. Cal.) Support. IN: Deliverance, more.

CRABBE, BUSTER (Ariz.) A handsome man easily belying his years (b. 1907), he has bounced back from the illness—the nature of which was not disclosed—that hospitalized him in '74. He still acts occasionally; in '72 he co-starred with Ina Balin in the comedy Comeback Trail. And in '70, muscles rippling still, he did an underwater commercial seen on local New York TV stations. But he looks back with greatest pleasure on the TV series of the '50s, Captain Gallant, in which he costarred with his tow-headed son, "Cuffy" (Cullen). Besides "Cuffy," now in business after graduating from the University of Arizona, the actor and his wife Adah (married since '33) had two daughters, Caren and Susan. One is now deceased; the other, married and living in Los Angeles, has made them grandparents. A longtime resident of Scottsdale, the '32 Olympic swimming-champ-turned-actor finds himself caught up—and enjoying it—in the current nostalgia craze. In recent months, he has journeyed to Hollywood (for the Edgar Rice Burroughs Centennial: a consequence of his "Tarzan" pix); to New Orleans (dedicating a "Tarzan" memorial at the Morgan City Swamp Gardens where the first "Tarzan" pic, starring Elmo Lincoln, was filmed in '18); to Nashville (saluted at the annual Western Film Festival on behalf of his many cowboy pix), and to New York (for the Nostalgia Convention; hailed there as "Tarzan," "Buck Rogers," and "Flash Gordon." Asked how he stays in shape, the actor—dapper in a beige safari suit—answered that he watches his diet, takes food supplements and vitamins, swims, and runs a little. Onscreen from 1933. IN: *Tarzan the Fearless, Sweetheart of Sigma Chi, The Thundering Herd, Sophie Lang Goes West, Red Barry* (serial), *Million Dollar Legs, Flash Gordon Conquers the Universe* (serial), *Billy the Kid Trapped, Swamp Fire, Pirates of the High Seas* (serial), *Badman's Country*, more.

CRAFTS, GRIFFIN (N.Y.) Support. IN: *I Passed for White.*

CRAIG, CATHERINE (Conn.) Married to actor Robert Preston since '40—they have no children—she continued her career through 1950's *No Man of Her Own,* when she retired from acting. They live on a wooded, eight-acre estate near Greenwich, in a house more than a century old. She has sometimes written magazine articles (published) on film. Why did she give up acting? Preston answers for her: "She used to be an actress and a good one. She submerged her career to her marriage. In marriage, someone has to be a giver and someone, a taker. I am a taker who married a giver." Onscreen from 1940. IN: *Doomed to Die, Louisiana Purchase, Parachute Nurse, Lady in the Dark, Seven Were Saved, The Pretender, Albuquerque, Appointment with Murder*, more.

CRAIG, HELEN (S. Cal.) Character. Most active now in TV dramas such as *Kojak*. Onscreen from 1944. IN: *The Keys of the Kingdom, The Snake Pit, They Live by Night, The Sporting Club*, more. (See John Beal.)

CRAIG, JAMES (S. Cal.) The jet-black hair that made him such a ringer for Gable during his decade at MGM has turned to silver (though he still has every curl of it). And, while in his 60s (b. 1912) he looks a bit worn and slightly heavier, he remains a good-looking man. He still costars occasionally in little-publicized movies: *The Doomsday Machine; Educated Heart; If He Hollers, Let Him Go.* And a couple of years ago, in a 90-minute daytime drama on ABC-TV, *This Child Is Mine,* he and actor Stephen Young costarred as father-son courtroom attorneys. "In the past," says the actor whose career has encompassed 80 pictures, "there were many opportunities for character actors to obtain good roles. No longer. And that's what I am now, a character actor. I hope the pendulum swings, because I sure as hell know my business." While waiting, he continues to be employed, as he has been since '68, by a large southern California firm in the building and real estate business. "If I didn't enjoy it, I wouldn't be doing it," he remarks. "Salesmanship is something I've been doing all my life—selling myself to audiences." While he considers Hun-

tington Beach home, he has a mountain house at Big Bear Lake to which he retreats often. To keep in condition, he hikes and hunts (pheasant and quail), but, mentioning this, he adds, "I used to hunt deer and antelope. No more. I figure we should save some of them for posterity." The actor has been married and divorced several times. His first wife (1939–54) was non-professional Mary Ray. They have two grown children—Diane and James Jr., who is president of the Long Beach Wine & Food Society. (Their third child, Robert, died of a kidney malfunction in '48, age three.) Starlet Jill Jarmyn was his next wife (1959–62). He was married thereafter (1964–65) to Jane Valentine, who had a little boy by a previous marriage. Two years after their divorce, in a tragedy that seemed to have no connection at all with the actor, she shot the child and then herself in a California motel. He has since married again. A few months ago, leveling a blast at the permissiveness of movies today, James Craig mentioned a recent picture he and his present wife—he did not mention her name—went to see. "When my eyes adjusted to the light," he said, "there was a nude girl riding a motorcycle across the desert. Three little boys were sitting near us and I was embarrassed for my profession." Onscreen from 1937. IN: *Pride of the West, Seven Sinners, Kitty Foyle, All That Money Can Buy, Seven Miles to Alcatraz, The Human Comedy, Swing Shift Maisie, The Heavenly Body, Marriage Is a Private Affair, Code 2, Massacre, Naked in the Sun, Arizona Bushwhackers,* more.

CRAIG, JOHN (S. Cal.) Character. Onscreen from the '60s. IN: *Shock Corridor, The One and Only Genuine Original Family Band, Homebodies, How to Seduce a Woman*, more.

CRAIG, MICHAEL (Eng.) Costar. Onscreen from 1953. IN: *The Malta Story, Campbell's Kingdom, Sapphire, Doctor in Love, Payroll, Life at the Top, Modesty Blaise, A Funny Thing Happened on the Way to the Forum, Star!, Royal Hunt of the Sun, A Town Called Hell,* more.

CRAIG, WENDY (Eng.) Leading lady. Onscreen from the '60s. IN: *The Servant, The Nanny, I'll Never Forget What'shisname,* more.

CRAIG, YVONNE (S. Cal.) Leading lady. Onscreen from 1960. IN: *Gidget, The Gene Krupa Story, By Love Possessed, It Happened at the World's Fair, Quick Before It Melts, Ski Party, In Like Flint, How to Frame a Figg,* more.

CRAIN, JEANNE (S. Cal.) Star. Nominated for Best Actress Oscar in *Pinky.* Onscreen from

1944. IN: *Home in Indiana, Winged Victory, State Fair, Leave Her to Heaven, Margie, Centennial Summer, Apartment for Peggy, Letter to Three Wives, Cheaper by the Dozen, People Will Talk, Belles on Their Toes, Vicki, Gentlemen Prefer Brunettes, The Joker Is Wild, Queen of the Nile, Madison Avenue, Hot Rods to Hell, Skyjacked, The Night God Screamed, Michele,* more.

CRANE, BOB (S. Cal.) Leading man. IN: *Return to Peyton Place, Mantrap, The Wicked Dreams of Paula Schultz, Superdad,* more.

CRANE, DAGNE (N.Y.) Support. IN: *Bananas,* more.

CRANE, STEVE (S. Cal.) One of Lana Turner's ex-husbands, he owns and operates a successful Los Angeles restaurant where their daughter, Cheryl, still single at this writing, works as hostess. Onscreen 1944–45. IN: *Cry of the Werewolf, The Crime Doctor's Courage, Tonight and Every Night.*

CRAVAT, NICK (S. Cal.) Character. Onscreen from 1950. IN: *The Flame and the Arrow, The Crimson Pirate, Kiss Me Deadly, The Way West, Airport, The Midnight Man,* more.

CRAWFORD, ANDREW (Eng.) Character. Onscreen from the '40s. IN: *The Brothers, Dulcimer Street, Broken Journey, Operation Disaster, Julius Caesar,* more.

CRAWFORD, BRODERICK (S. Cal.) Star. Won Best Actor Oscar for *All the King's Men.* Onscreen from 1937. IN: *Submarine D-1, Ambush, Island of Lost Men, Beau Geste, Seven Sinners, The Trail of the Vigilantes, Tight Shoes, The Black Angel, The Time of Your Life, Sealed Verdict, Born Yesterday, Lone Star, The Last Posse, Night People, Convicts Four, The Swindle, A House Is Not a Home, Kid Rodelo, Hell's Bloody Devils,* more.

CRAWFORD, CHRISTINA (S. Cal.) Support. Eldest daughter of Joan Crawford. Onscreen from 1961. IN: *Force of Impulse, Wild in the Country,* more.

CRAWFORD, JOAN (N.Y.) Star. Won Best Actress Oscar in *Mildred Pierce.* Nominated in the same category for *Possessed* and *Sudden Fear.* Onscreen from 1925. IN: *Pretty Ladies, Old Clothes; Sally, Irene and Mary; Tramp Tramp Tramp, Rose Marie, Our Dancing Daughters, Our Modern Maidens, Paid, Grand Hotel, Rain, Dancing Lady, Chained, No More Ladies, The Gorgeous Hussy, The Bride Wore Red, The Women, Strange Cargo, Susan and God, A Woman's Face, Reunion in France, Hu-*

moresque, Daisy Kenyon, Flamingo Road, The Damned Don't Cry, Harriet Craig; Goodbye, My Fancy; Torch Song, Female on the Beach, Autumn Leaves, What Ever Happened to Baby Jane?, Strait-Jacket, I Saw What You Did, Circus of Blood, Berserk, Trog, more.

CRAWFORD, JOHN (S. Cal.) Character. Onscreen from 1945. IN: *Thoroughbreds, Cyrano de Bergerac, Actors and Sin, Conquest of Cochise, John Paul Jones, Solomon and Sheba, Exodus, The Americanization of Emily, Red Line 7000, Return of the Gunfighter, El Dorado, Night Moves,* more.

CRAWFORD, JOHNNY (S. Cal.) Leading man; former juvenile. Onscreen from 1965. IN: *Village of the Giants, Indian Paint,* more.

CRAWFORD, MICHAEL (Eng.) Costar. Onscreen from 1950. IN: *Blow Your Own Trumpet, Two Left Feet, The War Lover, The Knack, A Funny Thing Happened on the Way to the Forum, Nick the Click; Hello, Dolly!;* more.

CREAMER, JOHN (La.) Character. IN: *Live and Let Die.*

CRENNA, RICHARD (S. Cal.) Costar; former juvenile. Onscreen from 1952. IN: *The Pride of St. Louis, Red Skies of Montana, Our Miss Brooks, The Sand Pebbles, Wait Until Dark, Star!, Marooned, Doctors' Wives, Five Against Texas, Catlow,* more.

CRESPI, TODD (S. Cal.) Support. IN: *The Possession of Joel Delaney,* more.

CRIPANUK, MICHAEL (N.Y.) Support. IN: *Topaz.*

CRISTAL, LINDA (S. Cal.) Leading lady. First onscreen in Mexico in *When the Fog Lifts,* etc. Onscreen in the U.S. from 1956. IN: *Comanche, The Last of the Fast Guns, The Perfect Furlough, The Alamo, Legions of the Nile, Two Rode Together, Mr. Majestyk,* more.

CROFT, MARY JANE (S. Cal.) Support. IN: *Kathy O.*

CROMWELL, JOHN (Conn.) A Paramount leading man of the late '20s, following a career on Broadway, he quickly became one of Hollywood's most noted directors. Among the films he directed: *Of Human Bondage, Little Lord Fauntleroy, Abe Lincoln in Illinois, Dead Reckoning,* and 1961's *A Matter of Morals,* his last to date. He continued as a stage actor during and after his Hollywood career, last appearing in *Volpone* in '64. Previously married to actresses Alice Indahl, Marie Goff, and Kay Johnson, he has been married since '46 to movie character actress Ruth Nelson. They live in Wilton. Retired now, he is in his 80s (b. 1887). Onscreen from 1929. IN: *The Dummy*, more.

CRONKITE, KATHY (S. Cal.) Support. Daughter of CBS newscaster Walter Cronkite. Onscreen in the '70s. IN: *The Trial of Billy Jack, Network*, more.

CRONYN, HUME (N.Y.) Character. Nominated for Best Supporting Actor Oscar in *The Seventh Cross*. Onscreen from 1943. IN: *Shadow of a Doubt, Phantom of the Opera, Lifeboat, Main Street After Dark, The Green Years, Brute Force, The Beginning or the End?, The Postman Always Rings Twice, Under Capricorn, People Will Talk, Sunrise at Campobello, Cleopatra; Gaily, Gaily; There Was a Crooked Man, The Arrangement, The Parallax View, Conrack*, more.

CROSBY, BING (N. Cal.) Star. Won Best Actor Oscar in *Going My Way*. Nominated in the same category for *The Bells of St. Mary's* and *The Country Girl*. He hasn't made a movie since 1966's *Stagecoach* but, in his 70s (b. 1904) he remains active—doing his annual TV Christmas show with his family, and numerous television commercials for an orange juice company he owns. In '76 it was announced that he and Bob Hope would make yet another "Road" movie. Onscreen from 1930. IN: *King of Jazz, College Humor, We're Not Dressing, Here Is My Heart, Mississippi, Big Broadcast of 1936, Rhythm on the Range, Pennies from Heaven, Waikiki Wedding; Sing, You Sinners; East Side of Heaven, The Star Maker, The Road to Singapore, If I Had My Way, Holiday Inn, Dixie, Blue Skies, Welcome Stranger, The Emperor Waltz, Top O' the Morning, Riding High, Here Comes the Groom, White Christmas, High Society, Man on Fire, High Time, The Road to Hong Kong, Robin and the Seven Hoods, Stagecoach*, more. (See Kathryn Grant.)

CROSBY, BOB (S. Cal.) Orchestra leader-actor. Bing's brother. Onscreen (usually with his "Bobcats," with whom he still makes personal appearances) from 1940. IN: *Sis Hopkins, Rookies on Parade, Presenting Lily Mars, Thousands Cheer, Pardon My Rhythm, The Singing Sheriff*, more.

CROSBY, CATHY (S. Cal.) Bob's singer-actress daughter. Retired. Onscreen from 1959. IN: *Girls Town, Night of the Quarter Moon, The Beat Generation, College Confidential*.

CROSBY, CATHY LEE (S. Cal.) Leading lady. No relation to the famous Crosby clan. IN: *The Laughing Policeman, Call Me by My Rightful Name*.

CROSBY, DENNIS (S. Cal.) Support. One of Bing's twin sons (the other is Phillip). IN: *Sergeants Three, The Glory Stompers*, more.

CROSBY, GARY (S. Cal.) Support. Bing's eldest. Onscreen from 1942. IN: *Star Spangled Rhythm, Out of This World, Mardi Gras, Holiday for Lovers, Battle at Bloody Beach, Two Tickets to Paris, Girl Happy, Morituri, Which Way to the Front?*, more. More recently in TV dramas.

CROSBY, LINDSAY (S. Cal.) Support. Bing's youngest. Onscreen from 1962. IN: *Sergeants Three, Free Grass, Bigfoot; Live a Little, Steal a Lot;* more.

CROSBY, PHILLIP (S. Cal.) Support. Bing's other twin son. Onscreen from 1962. IN: *Sergeants Three, Robin and the Seven Hoods, None But the Brave*.

CROSET, PAULE (S. Cal.) Most often billed Paula or Rita Corday, she acted under this name in *The Exile*. (See Paula Corday.)

CROSS, DENNIS (S. Cal.) Support. IN: *Crime of Passion, Mrs. Pollifax—Spy*, more

CROSS, JIMMY (S. Cal.) Support. IN: *The Amazing Colossal Man*.

CROTHERS, SCATMAN (S. Cal.) Black character. IN: *Bloody Mama, Black Belt Jones, Truck Turner, Coonskin, One Flew Over the Cuckoo's Nest, Friday Foster*, more.

CROWLEY, KATHLEEN (S. Cal.) Leading lady. Onscreen from 1953. IN: *The Farmer Takes a Wife, Sabre Jet, City of Shadows, The Quiet Gun, The Rebel Set, Curse of the Undead, The Lawyer, The Downhill Racers*, more.

CROWLEY, MATT (N.Y.) Support. IN: *The Mob, Somebody Up There Likes Me*, more.

CROWLEY, PATRICIA (S. Cal.) Leading lady. Onscreen from 1953. IN: *Forever Female, Money from Home, Red Garters, Walk the Proud Land, The Scarface Mob, The Wheeler Dealers, The Biscuit Eater*, more.

CRUICKSHANK, ANDREW (Eng.) Character. Onscreen from the '30s. IN: *Eye Witness, The Reluctant Widow, Richard III, John and Julie, Grayfriars' Bobby, El Cid, Come Fly with Me*, more.

CRUTCHLEY, ROSALIE (Eng.) Support. Onscreen from 1949. IN: *Take My Life, Prelude to Fame, Quo Vadis, The Sword and the Rose, Flame and the Flesh, The Nun's Story, Sons and Lovers, The Haunting, Creatures the World Forgot, Wuthering Heights,* more.

CRUZON, VIRGINIA (N. Cal.) Support. IN: *The Trouble with Girls.*

CUGAT, XAVIER (S. Cal.) Now in his 70s (b. 1900) and married to pepperpot singer Charo, one of his several much younger wives, the orchestra leader-actor suffered a stroke in '71. Partially paralyzed on the left side, he walks with a cane—and flies with Charo to her out-of-town club engagements. Onscreen from 1936. IN: *Go West Young Man, You Were Never Lovelier, Tropicana, Bathing Beauty, The Heat's On, Weekend at the Waldorf, No Love No Leave, Luxury Liner, The Phynx,* more.

CULLUM, JOHN (N.Y.) Singer-actor. IN: *All the Way Home, 1776.*

CULP, ROBERT (S. Cal.) Costar. Onscreen from 1963. IN: *Sunday in New York, PT-109, The Hanged Man, Bob & Carol & Ted & Alice, Hickey and Boggs, Inside Out, Sky Rider, The Great Scout & Cathouse Thursday,* more.

CULVER, ROLAND (Eng.) Character. Onscreen from 1932. IN: *77 Park Lane, Night Train, The Avengers, Spitfire, The Life and Death of Colonel Blimp, To Each His Own, Dead of Night, Down to Earth, Singapore, The Emperor's Waltz, Hotel Sahara, Encore, Folly to be Wise, The Man Who Loved Redheads, Bonjour Tristesse, Mad Little Island, The Yellow Rolls-Royce, Thunderball,* more.

CUMMINGS, CONSTANCE (Eng.) Character; former leading lady. Onscreen from 1931. IN: *Traveling Husbands, The Lost Parade, Night After Night, Washington Merry-Go-Round, Billion Dollar Scandal, The Mind Reader, Glamour, The Haunted Honeymoon, Blithe Spirit, John and Julie, In the Cool of the Day, A Boy Ten Feet Tall,* more.

CUMMINGS, ROBERT (S. Cal.) Hollywood's perennial juvenile, he is now in his 60s (b. 1910), looks far younger (perhaps due to the heavy vitamin regimen to which he has subscribed for decades), and has been married since '71 to a lovely Oriental girl, Regina Fong, who was formerly his secretary, by whom he has a young son. His first two marriages—to hometown (Joplin, Mo.) sweetheart Edma Emma Myers and to Broadway actress Vivian Janis—did not produce children. His third, to Hollywood actress Mary Elliott, the wedding ceremony being performed by his mother who was a minister, lasted from '45 to '69 and resulted in five. The youngest, Anthony, was born in 1957. The others in ascending order are: Laurel, Patricia, Melinda and Robert Jr. (A young doctor now, Robert Jr. earned part of his medical expenses by working as his father's stand-in on the remake of *Stagecoach*.) The Cummings-Elliott divorce was acrimonious, she alleging, among other things in her cross-complaint for separate maintenance (he having filed for divorce earlier), that the actor has been using methadrine since 1965. Cummings' most recent wedding date (March 27), even the time (between 11:34 and 11:44 A.M.), was chosen, he says, by three famous astrologers he consulted, who worked independently. "I've run my whole life by astrology," he volunteers. Lately, besides acting, he has been vice-president of Holiday Magic, a 34-corporation conglomerate that produces cosmetics, among other things, and has schools teaching "mind dynamics," or clairvoyance. Frequently seen as a guest star on TV (*The Great American Beauty Contest,* etc.), he takes time out regularly to star at dinner theaters across the country in comedies such as *Never Too Late.* This play's plot, of course, is about a man who becomes a father again at a later-than-usual age. An appropriate vehicle for a man who not only wrote a book titled *How to Stay Young and Vital,* but has done just that. Onscreen from 1935. IN: *So Red the Rose, Sophie Lang Goes West, Wells Fargo, The Texans, Three Smart Girls Grow Up, The Devil and Miss Jones, Kings Row, Saboteur, Flesh and Fantasy, Forever and a Day, Princess O'-Rourke, You Came Along, The Accused, The Petty Girl, Dial M for Murder, How to be Very Very Popular, The Carpetbaggers, Promise Her Anything, Five Golden Dragons,* more.

CUMMINS, PEGGY (Eng.) The delicate-faced blonde 20th Century-Fox announced to star in *Forever Amber,* before giving the role to Linda Darnell, returned to London in '48 where she continued to play leading roles for years. Married to Derek Dunnett, she is the mother of a daughter born in '62, the year her most recent movie, *In the Doghouse,* was released. She is now in her 50s (b. 1925) and still lovely. Onscreen from 1939. IN: *Salute John Citizen, Old Mother Riley Detective, The Late George Apley, Moss Rose, Escape, Green Grass of Wyoming, That Dangerous Age, Street Corner, Always a Bride, Meet Mr. Lucifer, Both Sides of the Law, To Dorothy a Son, The March Hare, Cash on Delivery,* more.

CUNNINGHAM, SARAH (N.Y.) Support. IN: *Black Like Me.*

CUNY, ALAIN (Fr.) Support. Onscreen from 1942. IN: *Visitors of the Night, The Devil's Own*

Envoy, The Lovers, La Dolce Vita, Banana Peel, Satyricon, Emmanuelle, more.

CURRIE, LOUISE (S. Cal.) Popular in the '40s as the blonde leading lady in B's and serials (The Masked Marvel and Adventures of Captain Marvel), she owned, until recently, a clothes designing shop in Beverly Hills where she lives. Married to antiques dealer John V. Good, she is now retired. Onscreen from 1941. IN: Backlash, Second Chance, The Crimson Key, And Baby Makes Three, more.

CURTIS, BILLY (S. Cal.) Midget supporting actor. Onscreen from 1942. IN: Saboteur, Wings for the Eagle, Three Wise Fools, April Showers, The Incredible Shrinking Man, more.

CURTIS, KEENE (N.Y.) Stage-TV actor rarely in films. IN: Macbeth.

CURTIS, KEN (S. Cal.) Support; former cowboy star. Onscreen from 1945. IN: Song of the Prairie, Singing on the Trail, Over the Santa Fe Trail, Mister Roberts, The Searchers, Spring Reunion, The Last Hurrah, Escort West, The Young Land, The Alamo, Two Rode Together, Cheyenne Autumn, more.

CURTIS, TONY (S. Cal.) Star. Nominated for Best Actor Oscar in The Defiant Ones. Onscreen from 1949. IN: City Across the River, Criss Cross, Francis, Winchester 73, The Prince Who Was a Thief, Son of Ali Baba, Houdini, Beachhead, The Black Shield of Falmouth, Six Bridges to Cross, The Square Jungle, Trapeze, Sweet Smell of Success, Kings Go Forth, Some Like It Hot, Operation Petticoat, Spartacus, The Rat Race, Taras Bulba; Captain Newman, M.D.; Goodbye Charlie, The Great Race, Don't Make Waves, The Boston Strangler, Those Daring Young Men in Their Jaunty Jalopies, Suppose They Gave a War and Nobody Came, Lepke, The Last Tycoon, more.

CURTWRIGHT, JORJA (S. Cal.) The pencil-slim brunette whose kinetic dramatics in 1946's Whistle Stop left costar Ava Gardner waiting at the station, is now a kinetic redhead, a bit more curvy, and married to a very rich Beverly Hills man. Her husband of many years (since '51) is Oscar-winning scriptwriter (The Bachelor and the Bobby Soxer), TV producer (I Dream of Jeannie), Broadway play author (Redhead), and best-selling novelist (The Other Side of Midnight) Sidney Sheldon. They have not one mansion but three, their longtime family home in Bel-Air, which they now lease to visiting stars, a house in Palm Springs, and a Rodeo Drive estate in Beverly that they recently purchased from George Murphy. Business affairs, though, sometimes keep them from enjoying any of them for long periods of time—such as the year they lately spent in London. There, they did have the pleasure of watching their teenage daughter (b. 1956), Mary, their only child, make her acting debut in the lead in The Threepenny Opera at the Oxford Playhouse. Extremely social, Jorja and her husband regularly give the most glamorous parties, which she, a night person, enjoys to the end, but which her husband, an avowed day person, escapes as early as he appropriately can. Privately, they play backgammon, which he taught her on their honeymoon and at which she invariably wins. They are now considering buying yet another house, in the south of France, probably Cap Ferrat, and just possibly a jaunt to Poland. It seems that his novel, which sold to the movies for $250,000 and a paperback company for $400,-000, was serialized in Poland, earning him a total there of about $600—and these zlotys can only be spent in that country. "Well," says Jorja Curtright Sheldon, pondering the matter, "we've never been to Poland." Onscreen from 1946. IN: Whistle Stop, Heaven Only Knows,· M, Love Is a Many-Splendored Thing, The Revolt of Mamie Stover, more.

CUSACK, CYRIL (Eng.) Character. Onscreen from 1947. IN: Odd Man Out, Oliver Twist, Gone to Earth, The Blue Veil, The Secret of Convict Lake, Saadia, Gideon's Day, The Man Who Never Was, Shake Hands with the Devil, I Thank a Fool, The Spy Who Came in From the Cold, Fahrenheit 451, The Taming of the Shrew, The Abdication; Run, Run, Joe!; Children of Rage, more.

CUSHING, PETER (Eng.) Character star. Onscreen from 1939. IN: The Man in the Iron Mask, Vigil in the Night, Laddie, A Chump at Oxford, Hamlet, The End of the Affair, Time Without Pity, The Horror of Dracula, The Revenge of Frankenstein, John Paul Jones, Sword of Sherwood Forest, The Naked Edge, Dr. Terror's House of Horrors, She, The Man Who Finally Died, Harold and Maude, The Day of the Jackal, The Ghoul, The Devil's Men, more.

D

DA SILVA, HOWARD (N.Y.) Character. Onscreen from 1936. IN: Once in a Blue Moon, Golden Boy, Sergeant York, Blues in the Night, Keeper of the Flame, Tonight We Raid Calais, The Lost Weekend, Two Years Before the Mast, Blaze of Noon, Unconquered, Tripoli, Fourteen

Hours, David and Lisa, Topkapi, 1776, The Great Gatsby (both the '49 and '74 versions), more.

DABNEY, AUGUSTA (N.Y.) Support. IN: *That Night.*

DAGOVER, LIL (Ger.) In Maximilian Schell's *The Pedestrian* ('74), this great German favorite was—with Elisabeth Bergner, Francoise Rosay, etc.—one of the grande dames discussing war over tea. She is in her 70s (b. 1897), is married to playwright Fritz Daghofer, and this was her first return to the screen since 1939's *Fredericus.* In '75 she acted in another Schell-directed film, *Murder on the Bridge,* starring Jon Voight. Onscreen from 1919. IN: *The Cabinet of Dr. Caligari, Between Worlds, Tartuffe, Love Makes Us Blind, Discord, The White Devil, The Woman from Monte Carlo, Congress Dances, Madame Blaubart, The Kreutzer Sonata, Strife Over the Boy,* more.

DAHL, ARLENE (N.Y.) A Manhattan business woman now (cosmetics), the lovely redheaded leading lady has not appeared in a movie since 1970's *Land Raiders* with George Maharis. She does still act occasionally in stock and several years ago replaced Lauren Bacall on Broadway in the musical *Applause.* Onscreen from 1947. IN: *My Wild Irish Rose, Reign of Terror, Three Little Words, Watch the Birdie, Desert Legion, Here Come the Girls, Sangaree, Woman's World, Bengal Brigade, Journey to the Center of the Earth, Kisses for My President,* more.

DAHL, TESSA (Eng.) Young support, Patricia Neal's daughter. IN: *Happy Birthday, Mother . . . Love, George;* more.

DAHLBECK, EVA (Swe.) Leading lady. Onscreen from 1952. IN: *The Village, Smiles of a Summer Night, Brink of Life, A Lesson in Love, A Matter of Morals, The Counterfeit Traitor, Les Creatures, Loving Couples,* more.

DAILEY, DAN (S. Cal.) Star. Nominated for Best Actor Oscar in *When My Baby Smiles at Me.* Onscreen from 1940. IN: *The Mortal Storm, Dulcy, Ziegfeld Girl, Panama Hattie, Mother Wore Tights, Give My Regards to Broadway, You Were Meant for Me, Chicken Every Sunday, When Willie Comes Marching Home, My Blue Heaven, Call Me Mister, The Pride of St. Louis, What Price Glory?, There's No Business Like Show Business, Meet Me in Las Vegas, The Best Things in Life Are Free, Oh Men! Oh Women!, Hemingway's Adventures of a Young Man,* more.

DAILEY, IRENE (S. Cal.) Support. Onscreen from 1968. IN: *No Way to Treat a Lady,*

Daring Game, Five Easy Pieces, The Grissom Gang, more.

DAILY, BILL (S. Cal.) Support. IN: *The Barefoot Executive,* more.

DALE, DANA (Fla.) Leading lady. IN: *Ladies Must Live.* (See Maggie Hayes.)

DALE, JIM (Eng.) Star comedian. Onscreen from 1962. IN: *Raising the Wind,* the "Carry On" series (*Carry On Cleo,* etc.), *Lock Up Your Daughters; Digby, the Biggest Dog in the World;* more.

DALIO, MARCEL (Fr.) One of Hollywood's most popular character actors for three decades, from '41, he returned to Paris to live several years ago, is in his 70s (b. 1900), remains highly active, and in '75 was completing his memoirs. Onscreen from 1937. IN: *La Grande Illusion, The Shanghai Gesture, Casablanca, The Pied Piper, The Constant Nymph, To Have and Have Not, Wilson, A Bell for Adano, Lovely to Look At, Gentlemen Prefer Blondes, Sabrina, Tip on a Dead Jockey, Pillow Talk, Donovan's Reef, The List of Adrian Messenger, Cartouche, How to Steal a Million, Catch 22, The Mad Adventures of "Rabbi" Jacob,* more.

DALLAS, CHARLENE (S. Cal.) Leading lady. Onscreen in 1975. IN: *Rancho Deluxe.*

DALLESANDRO, JOE (N.Y.) Leading man. Former Andy Warhol star. Onscreen from 1968. IN: *Flesh, The Loves of Ondine, Trash, Andy Warhol's Frankenstein, Andy Warhol's Dracula, Black Moon,* more.

DALTON, ABBY (S. Cal.) Leading lady. Onscreen from 1956. IN: *Rock All Night, Stakeout on Dope Street, Girls on the Loose, The Viking Women and the Sea Serpent,* more.

DALTON, AUDREY (S. Cal.) Still pretty and dark-haired, this starlet of the '50s now plays middle-aged wives in such TV shows as *Police Woman.* Onscreen from 1952. IN: *The Girls of Pleasure Island, Dreamboat, My Cousin Rachel, Titanic, Drum Beat, The Prodigal, The Monster That Challenged the World, Separate Tables, Thundering Jets, Kitten with a Whip,* more.

DALTON, TIMOTHY (Eng.) Leading man. Onscreen from 1968. IN: *The Lion in Winter, Wuthering Heights; Mary, Queen of Scots; Permission to Kill,* more.

DALTREY, ROGER (Eng.) Rock star. Onscreen in 1975. IN: *Tommy, Lisztomania.*

DALY, JAMES (S. Cal.) Character. Onscreen from 1955. IN: *The Court-Martial of Billy Mitchell, Return of the Fly, I Aim at the Stars, The Big Bounce, Planet of the Apes, The Resurrection of Zachary Wheeler*, more.

DALY, JONATHAN (S. Cal.) Support. Onscreen from 1968. IN: *The Young Warriors, Rascal, $1,000,000 Duck*, more.

DALY, TYNE (S. Cal.) Support. James Daly's daughter. IN: *John and Mary, Angel Unchained*, more.

DALYA, JACQUELINE (S. Cal.) Long retired, this raven-haired beauty who played second leads in many pix in the '40s has resumed her career in this decade in pix such as *Love Me Like I Do*, in which she had a character role. She has been a widow since '71, when her songwriter-husband, Robert Hilliard, died of a heart attack at 52. They had no children. Hilliard was the lyricist of "Dear Hearts and Gentle People," the Broadway hit *Hazel Flagg*, Disney's *Alice in Wonderland*, etc. For a while, Jacqueline lived alone in their mansion atop one of Hollywood's highest hills, on a one-acre lot shaped like a grand piano, with a heated pool and recording studio. She eventually put it up for sale, along with her Rolls-Royce Silver Shadow, moving to a splendidly decorated smaller place. Lovely still, she is, as in former days, popular with Hollywood's leading bachelors. Onscreen from 1940. IN: *One Million B.C., The Gay Caballero, The Lady from Louisiana, Voice in the Wind, Bathing Beauty, Adventures of Casanova, Treasure of Sierra Madre, Wabash Avenue*, more.

D'AMBOISE, JACQUES (N.Y.) His screen work was, of course, only a sideline to his real career, which is that of a principal dancer with the New York City Ballet. Now in his 40s (b. 1934), he has been married since '56 to former dancer Carolyn George and is the father of two sons and twin daughters. Onscreen from 1954. IN: *Seven Brides for Seven Brothers, Carousel, The Best Things in Life Are Free, A Midsummer Night's Dream*.

DAMITA, LILI (S. Cal.) In her 70s now (b. 1904), she has been married since '62 to Allen B. Loomis, lives in Beverly Hills, and is retired. Her son, Sean Flynn (by Errol), who was briefly an actor, became a war correspondent on assignment in Vietnam. Missing in action for many months before the war's end, he still has not been found—though his mother has spent a fortune in her search for him. Onscreen from the late '20s. IN: *Forbidden Love, Scandal in Paris, The Bridge of San Luis Rey, Dancer of Barcelona, The Cockeyed World, Fighting Car-*

avans, Madame Julie, This Is the Night, Goldie Gets Along, The Devil on Horseback, more.

DAMON, MARK (It.) Possibly the busiest American actor in Italy during the past decade, he lives in Rome, is married to actress Barbara Frey (since '70), stars in many (*They Called Him Truth, A Scaffold for Django*, etc.), and produces still others (*The Great Chihuahua Treasure Hunt, The Arena*). Onscreen from 1955. IN: *Inside Detroit, Screaming Eagles, Young and Dangerous, Life Begins at 17, The Rebel Breed, The Longest Day, Johnny Yuma, Anzio*, more.

DAMONE, VIC (S. Cal.) Singer-actor. Onscreen from 1951. IN: *Rich, Young and Pretty; Athena, Deep in My Heart, Hit the Deck, Kismet, Hell to Eternity, Spree*, more.

DANA, BARBARA (N.Y.) Support. IN: *P.J., Popi, The Monitors*, more.

DANA, BILL (S. Cal.) Comedian. IN: *The Busy Body, The Harrad Summer*.

DANA, LEORA (N.Y.) Support. Onscreen from 1957. IN: *3:10 to Yuma, Kings Go Forth, Some Came Running, The Group, The Boston Strangler, Tora! Tora! Tora!, Wild Rovers*, more.

DANA, MARK (S. Cal.) Support. IN: *Thunder Over the Plains, The Big Fisherman, Tarzan Goes to India*, more.

DANA, VIOLA (S. Cal.) It has been many a year since she danced the Charleston on Aubusson rugs at Hearst's San Simeon, but, in her silver-haired 70s (b. 1897), Viola remains as merrily effervescent as in her lengthy heyday as a silent star. Childless, she has been married to and divorced from silent cowboy star Maurice "Lefty" Flynn (d. 1959) and golf pro James Thompson. Living for years in an ocean-front apartment in Santa Monica, she works sometimes as hostess at a popular restaurant in West Los Angeles, and can usually be counted on to appear at the "Silent Screen Stars" parties Hollywood tosses from time to time. At a recent one, she and longtime pal Laura La Plante, equally young at heart, were the real hits of the evening—stopping just short of dancing the Charleston. Onscreen from the teens. IN: *Rosie O'Grady, The Willow Tree, Revelation, Merton of the Movies, Forty Winks, Bigger Than Barnum's, Winds of Chance, Kosher Kitty Kelly, The Ice Flood, The Silent Lover*, more.

D'ANDREA, TOM (S. Cal.) Support. Onscreen from 1943. IN: *This Is the Army, Pride of the Marines, Night and Day, Humoresque, Dark*

Passage, To the Victor, Fighter Squadron, A House Is Not a Home, more. Inactive in movies since 1965.

DANDRIDGE, RUBY (S. Cal.) Black character. Onscreen from 1942. IN: *Tish, Cabin in the Sky, Junior Miss, Three Little Girls in Blue, Tap Roots, A Hole in the Head*, more. In her 70s (b. 1902), she has been inactive in movies since 1960.

DANGCIL, LINDA (S. Cal.) Support. IN: *Tropic Zone, Miss Sadie Thompson, Apache, The Magnificent Seven, West Side Story, El Dorado*, more.

DANGERFIELD, RODNEY (N.Y.) Comedian. IN: *The Projectionist.*

DANIEL, TAMARA (N.Y.) Support. IN: *A New Leaf.*

DANIELS, BILLY (S. Cal.) Black singer-actor. Onscreen from 1944. IN: *Frenchman's Creek, Masquerade in Mexico, The Beat Generation, Sunny Side of the Street, Cruising Down the River*, more.

DANIELS, LISA (S. Cal.) Support. Onscreen from 1953. IN: *Princess of the Nile, Man in the Attic, The Glass Slipper, The Virgin Queen, Curse of the Voodoo*, more. She now acts under the name Lise Lewiss.

DANIELS, MARK (S. Cal.) Giving up acting almost two decades ago, the former leading man has long since been one of the most successful directors in television. He has also sometimes lately used the billing Mark O'Daniels. Onscreen from 1942. IN: *Joe Smith, American; Fingers at the Window, Grand Central Murder, The War Against Mrs. Hadley, Whistling in Dixie, Winged Victory, Bury Me Dead*, more.

DANIELS, MICKEY (S. Cal.) The freckle-faced favorite in the very first bunch of "Our Gang" kids in the '20s, Mickey continued on the screen in many features *(Roaring Roads, Magnificent Obsession*, etc.), through 1941's *Miss Polly*. In his 60s now (b. 1914), and still considering Los Angeles home, he has long been a construction engineer whose work has taken him—often for long periods—all over the globe. He was greatly saddened by the death of Mary Kornman (in '73), the lifelong friend whose recommendation had originally gotten him into "Our Gang" with her, and who was later his young leading lady in the "Boy Friends" comedy shorts.

DANIELS, WILLIAM (N.Y.) Support. Onscreen from 1949. IN: *Family Honeymoon;*

Ladybug, Ladybug; A Thousand Clowns, Two for the Road, The President's Anyalst, The Graduate, 1776, The Parallax View, more.

DANIELY, LISA (Eng.) Leading lady. Onscreen from 1950. IN: *Lilli Marlene, Hindle Wakes, Operation Diplomat, Tiger by the Tail, The Man in the Road, Cop-Out*, more.

DANNER, BLYTHE (S. Cal.) Leading lady. Onscreen in the '70s. IN: *1776, Lovin' Molly, Hearts of the West*, more.

DANO, ROYAL (S. Cal.) Character. Onscreen from 1950. IN: *Undercover Girl, Red Badge of Courage, Bend of the River, The Far Country, Moby Dick, Never Steal Anything Small, The Adventures of Huckleberry Finn, Welcome to Hard Times, Death of a Gunfighter, The Undefeated, The Wild Party*, more.

DANOVA, CESARE (S. Cal.) Leading man. Onscreen from 1947. IN: *The Captain's Son, King of Kings, Tender Is the Night, Cleopatra, Gidget Goes to Rome; Boy, Did I Get a Wrong Number!; Che!*, more.

DANTE, MICHAEL (S. Cal.) Leading man. Onscreen from 1958. IN: *Fort Dobbs, Seven Thieves, Kid Galahad, Operation Bikini, Apache Rifles, Harlow, Willard*, more.

DANTINE, HELMUT (S. Cal.) When he had a corner on the market of young Nazi roles in the '40s, he was darkly handsome and unsmiling, lean, with finely chiseled features and an Austrian accent. Nothing, except for a touch of silver at the temples, has changed about this apparently ageless (b. 1917) actor. The silver could have been induced by the critical reception of the '74 movie *Bring Me the Head of Alfredo Garcia*, of which he was executive producer and in which he played a small role—a private detective. Cried one critic, Gene Shalit: "Bring me the head of the studio that released this one." Earlier, Dantine had coproduced *Stuntmen* ('71). He has occasionally appeared on TV in the '70s—in *Night Gallery* (as a Nazi general) and the mystery comedy *Call Holme*, both on NBC. Since January 1, 1958, he has been the husband of actress-heiress Nicola Schenck, who uses the professional name of Niki Dantine and is the daughter of Nicholas M. Schenck, former president of Loew's Inc. They have two daughters, the elder in college, the younger in high school. Dantine was previously married to and divorced from actress Gwen Anderson and oil heiress Charlene Wrightsman, by whom he also has a child. Prominent Beverly Hills socialites, Dantine and his wife own considerable California real estate, spend much of the winter skiing at Sun Valley, and are famed as hosts of lavish parties attended by such intimates as the James Stewarts, Andy Williams, and Kay Gable. The young "Nazi" who stumbled into the kitchen of *Mrs. Miniver* and, wounded, vulnerable, and arrogant, became an overnight star, has done well. Onscreen from 1941. IN: *International Squadron, Casablanca, Edge of Darkness, The Mask of Dimitrios, Hotel Berlin, Escape in the Desert, Call Me Madam, Alexander the Great, War and Peace, Hell on Devil's Island, Operation Crossbow, The Wilby Conspiracy*, more.

DANTON, RAY (S. Cal.) Leading man. Also now a director. Onscreen from 1955. IN: *Chief Crazy Horse, I'll Cry Tomorrow, Onionhead, Too Much Too Soon, Tarawa Beachhead, Yellowstone Kelly, The Rise and Fall of Legs Diamond, Portrait of a Mobster, The George Raft Story, A Majority of One, The Chapman Report, The Last Mercenary, The Centerfold Girls*, more. (See Julie Adams.)

D'ANTONIO, CARMEN (S. Cal.) Support. Onscreen from 1940. IN: *The Long Voyage Home, Arabian Nights, Coney Island, Cobra Woman, Salome, World for Ransom, Cheyenne Autumn*, more.

DARBY, KIM (S. Cal.) Leading lady. Onscreen from 1965. IN: *Bus Riley's Back in Town, True Grit, Norwood, Generation, The Grissom Gang*, more.

DARC, MIREILLE (Fr.) Leading lady. Onscreen from 1964. IN: *Male Hunt, The Great Spy Chase, Galia, Weekend, The Man in the Trunk, Where There's Smoke*, more.

DARCEL, DENISE (Fla.) Blonde still, and in her early 50s (b. 1925), she has two children (by her second marriage), has been married since '72 to Richard Vance, and acts in dinner theatres. She also flies often to Hollywood to do TV commercials (Cresthaven furniture, etc.). Her husband, a wealthy Iowan who owns a health spa in Des Moines, is also an executive of TV Channel 51 in Florida, where they live in Fort Lauderdale. Onscreen from 1947. IN: *To the Victor, Thunder in the Pines, Battleground, Westward the Women, Young Man with Ideas, Dangerous When Wet, Vera Cruz*, more.

D'ARCY, ALEX (S. Cal.) In his late 60s, and his fourth decade in movies, this actor who was for years Hollywood's favorite "gigolo" still plays dapper supporting roles—such as the victimized politician in *Dead Pigeon on Beethoven Street.* Onscreen from 1928. IN: *Paradise, Stolen Holiday, The Awful Truth, Topper Takes a Trip, Good Girls Go to Paris, Three Sons, Marriage Is a Private Affair, How to Marry a Millionaire, The St. Valentine's Day Massacre, The Seven Minutes*, more.

DARCY, GEORGINE (S. Cal.) Support. IN: *Rear Window, Don't Knock the Twist*, more.

DARCY, SHEILA (S. Cal.) A widow since the 1970 death of husband Preston Foster, by whom she has a grown daughter, Stephanie, she lives in retirement in San Diego. There, she owns an interest in a marina, plays golf, and occasionally sings for the entertainment of elderly patients in nearby hospitals. She recalls most fondly, not her movie career of the '30s, but the years in the '50s when she, her husband, and daughter had a family musical act—Preston Foster at the guitar—with which they barnstormed the country, at fairs, auto shows, and auditoriums, several months of each year. Onscreen from 1937. IN: *Wells Fargo, Union Pacific*, more.

DARDEN, SEVERN (S. Cal.) Support. Onscreen from 1965. IN: *Goldstein, Dead Heat on a Merry-Go-Round, Luv, The President's Analyst, Fearless Frank, The Hired Hand, Cisco Pike, The Last Movie, Werewolves on Wheels, Conquest of the Planet of the Apes, Legend of Hillbilly John*, more.

DARLING, JEAN (N.Y.) After her fame as a child actress—besides being in "Our Gang" she was featured in 1934's *Babes in Toyland* and *Jane Eyre*—she did much TV until the '60s, twice having local shows bearing her name. She also had a lead in the Broadway production of *Carousel*, followed by personal appearances as a singer in South Africa and South America. Since '54 she has been married to Reuben Bowen, known professionally as "Kajar the Magician," has a teenage son, is in her early 50s (b. 1925), seldom performs any more, and lives in an apartment on New York's fashionable East Side.

DARLING, JOAN (S. Cal.) Support. In '76 she was also the director of the nighttime TV soap opera *Mary Hartman, Mary Hartman*. Onscreen from 1964. IN: *The Troublemaker, The President's Analyst, Fearless Frank, Kansas City Bomber*, more.

DARNAY, TONI (N.Y.) Support. IN: *The Swimmer.*

DARREN, JAMES (S. Cal.) Leading man. Onscreen from 1956. IN: *Rumble on the Docks, The Brothers Rico, Gunman's Walk, Gidget, The Gene Krupa Story, All the Young Men, Let No Man Write My Epitaph, Gidget Goes Hawaiian, The Guns of Navarone, Under the Yum Yum Tree, Venus in Furs*, more.

DARRIEUX, DANIELLE (Fr.) During the German occupation of France in WW II, the Maquis placed her, France's most famous female star, on the execution list. She was charged with entertaining German troops and exposing, unwittingly, French Resistance fighters. The sentence, for which the French film industry must be grateful, was not carried out. She remains—apparently ageless, though born in 1917 —one of its most marketable exports. In '75 her movie *Divine* opened in Paris, to this comment from *Variety's* critic: "Danielle Darrieux, still looking well and in good singing voice, who hasn't made a film in some time, deserved better than this indifferent musical . . ." Never a successful star in Hollywood movies, excepting *Five Fingers*, she triumphed on Broadway in '70 when she followed Katharine Hepburn in the starring role in the musical *Coco*. She was back two years later in another musical, *Ambassador*, with Howard Keel, and with the critics it was a case of hated-it-loved-her. Said the *Times'* Clive Barnes: "Miss Darrieux . . . wears charm like a perfume, a heady scent like Mitsouko. She is totally feminine and highly adorable. She has a flutter of steel, a determined laugh, and . . . she sang deliciously and acted with grace." The actress has been married three times and divorced twice, her early husbands having been director Henri Decoin (1934 –40) and Porfirio Rubirosa (1942–47). For well over 25 years now, she has been the wife of George Mitsinkides, a Greek-born producer-writer (he wrote the screenplay for *Marie Octobre*, one of her great movies), and they have one son, Mathieu, of university age now. Their fulltime residence is a country house about 60 kilometers outside Paris. But family holidays, she reports, are spent at a private island they own off the coast of Brittany. "It is very simple," she says. "We use kerosene lamps and candles. Propane to make the refrigerator work and to cook . . . I'm a very family woman. I'm not an actress at all outside a movie studio or a theater." With no thought of retiring, ever, though, she says of age, "I don't think about it at all. I think in this business people look and stay younger. You know, when I am 70, it will be even better." Onscreen from the early '30s. IN: *Mayerling, Rage of Paris, Club de Femmes, Katia, Ruy Blas; Rich, Young and Pretty; Le Plaisir, La Ronde, The Earrings of Madame De, Alexander the Great, Le Rouge et le Noir, Loss of Innocence, Landru, Friend of the Family, The Young Girls of Rochefort, 24 Hours in a Woman's Life,* more.

DARRIN, DIANA (S. Cal.) Still active in movies, she is the wife of business man Norman Richard and the mother of a son born in '70. Onscreen from 1957. IN: *The Amazing Colossal Man, Reform School Girl,* more.

DARRO, FRANKIE (S. Cal.) Pint-sized and wizened as he enters his sixth decade (b. 1917),

the actor who, from the mid-20s to the mid-50s in more than 100 movies, was the screen's great little tough guy, takes a shrugging, whimsical view of life's vicissitudes. He's been down, he's been up. At the moment, he's not greatly in demand—his last movie credit was 1968's *Hook, Line and Sinker*—but there's always tomorrow. Divorced from his first wife, Betty Marie, in '47, and his second, dancer Aloha Wray (died 1968), he has been married for over 25 years to his third, Aloha Carroll. They live in a tiny Hollywood apartment, where Frankie waits for the phone call that would mean a great comeback role. With his proven track record—no pun, though he practically made a career at playing jockeys—it could happen. Onscreen from 1924. IN: *The Cowboy Cop, Little Mickey Grogan, Hearts and Spangles, The Lightning Warrior* (serial), *Tugboat Annie, Little Men, Broadway Bill, Wild Boys of the Road, Saratoga, Thoroughbreds Don't Cry, Boys' Reformatory, The Gang's All Here, Sarge Goes to College, Pride of Maryland, Across the Wide Missouri, The Lawless Rider,* more.

DARROW, BARBARA (S. Cal.) Support; former ingenue. Onscreen from 1954. IN: *The French Line, Tall Story,* more.

DARROW, HENRY (S. Cal.) Support. IN: *Cancel My Reservations, Badge 273,* more.

DARROW, JOHNNY (S. Cal.) In his 60s, a bachelor, and retired, he gave up his career as a popular young leading man in '38 and was, for over three decades, one of Hollywood's better-known agents. Onscreen from 1927. IN: *High School Hero, Prep and Pep, The Argyle Case, Hell's Angels, The Midnight Lady, The All American, Midshipman Jack, Flirtation Walk, Crime Over London,* more.

DASSIN, JULES (Greece) Director-actor. IN: *Never on Sunday, Phaedra, Promise at Dawn,* more.

DAUPHIN, CLAUDE (Fr.) Costar. Onscreen from 1931. IN: *La Fortune, Voyage Imprevue, Les Hommes Sans Peur, Innocents in Paris, Le Plaisir, April in Paris, Little Boy Lost, The Quiet American; Stop, You're Killing Me; The Visit, Grand-Prix, The Sleeping Car Murder, Is Paris Burning?, Two for the Road, The Madwoman of Chaillot, Rosebud,* more.

DAVALOS, RICHARD (S. Cal.) In his late 40s and graying, the actor who (with James Dean) was one of the cojuvenile leads in *East of Eden* now plays character roles, mostly on TV. Onscreen from 1955. IN: *All the Young Men, The Cabinet of Dr. Caligari, Pit Stop, Cool Hand Luke,* more.

DAVENPORT, DORIS (S. Cal.) She was Doris Jordan when she arrived in Hollywood and was given not one but two screen tests as Scarlett O'Hara. In November 1938 producer David O. Selznick noted in one of his famous memos: "Concerning Scarlett, I think that at the moment our best possibilities are: Paulette Goddard, Doris Jordan, Jean Arthur, Katharine Hepburn, and Loretta Young . . . It must be borne in mind that Jordan is a complete amateur who had not even had a single day's experience . . . at the time she made this scene . . ." Three days later he said in another: "I am anxious about Doris Jordan because I think . . . her new test is even more promising than the first . . . No pains should be spared in connection with this girl, since she is certainly one of our four or five final possibilities." Failing to become Scarlett, she never acted in any Selznick film. Two years later, though, Goldwyn made her Gary Cooper's leading lady in *The Westerner*, changing her name to Doris Davenport and promoting her as his next big star. Yet she appeared in just one more movie, a B titled *Behind the News*. Instead of stardom, she chose marriage—to a leading still photographer. She is in her 50s now, still lives in Hollywood, is still happily married, and still feels she made the right decision.

DAVENPORT, DOROTHY (S. Cal.) The daughter of beloved character actor Harry Davenport, the wife and frequent leading lady of star Wallace Reid from '13 until his death in '23, and an important star of silents herself, she lives now—in her 80s—in a small house in North Hollywood. She has not been seen onscreen since 1925's *Broken Laws*, a cautionary film about drugs, which caused her husband's death. But her association with movies continued for many years afterward, as producer-director Arthur (*Francis Joins the WACs*) Lubin's assistant and occasional writer. Until recently, she also wrote newspaper and magazine articles. Never remarried, she has, by Reid, two children. William Wallace Reid Jr., who briefly tried acting, is a leading Los Angeles architect. Daughter, Betty Ann, a local real estate agent and divorced, has three grown children—two sons and a daughter. Dorothy Davenport Reid's principal role today is that of great-grandmother, and she likes it fine. Onscreen from 1911. IN: *The Best Man Wins, His Only Son, The Crackman's Reformation, The Lightning Bolt, A Hopi Legend, The Countess Betty's Mine, The Heart of the Hills, The Fruit of Evil, Human Wreckage*, more.

DAVENPORT, NIGEL (Eng.) Costar. Onscreen from the late '50s. IN: *In the Cool of the Day, Sands of the Kalahari, A Man for All Seasons, The Virgin Soldiers, The Royal Hunt of the Sun, Living Free, The Last Valley; Mary, Queen of Scots; Phase IV*, more.

DAVID, THAYER (S. Cal.) Character. Onscreen from 1958. IN: *A Time to Love and a Time to Die, Journey to the Center of the Earth, The Story of Ruth, The Eiger Sanction, Peeper*, more.

DAVIDSON, JAMES (S. Cal.) Support. IN: *The Long Ride Home*.

DAVIDSON, JOHN (S. Cal.) Singer-actor. IN: *The Happiest Millionaire, The One and Only Genuine Original Family Band*.

DAVIES, JOHN HOWARD (Eng.) The juvenile actor who starred in several British films in the '50s is in his 30s now (b. 1939) and a successful director of television dramas in London. IN: *The Rocking Horse Winner, Oliver Twist, Tom Brown's School Days*, more.

DAVIES, RUPERT (Eng.) Character. Onscreen from the '50s. IN: *The Key, The Spy Who Came in From the Cold, The Uncle, The Conqueror Worm, Zeppelin, The Night Visitor*, more.

DAVION, ALEXANDER (Eng.) Support. Onscreen from 1960. IN: *Song Without End, Rattle of a Simple Man, Man in the Dark, Valley of the Dolls, The Royal Hunt of the Sun*, more.

DAVIS, ANN B. (S. Cal.) Character. IN: *A Man Called Peter, Pepe, All Hands on Deck, Lover Come Back*, more.

DAVIS, ANNETTE (S. Cal.) Support. IN: *What's the Matter with Helen?*, more.

DAVIS, BETTE (Conn.) Star. Won Best Actress Oscar in *Dangerous* and *Jezebel*. Nominated in the same category in *Dark Victory, The Letter, The Little Foxes; Now, Voyager; Mr. Skeffington, All About Eve, The Star, What Ever Happened to Baby Jane?* Onscreen from 1931. IN: *Bad Sister, Seed, The Man Who Played God, Cabin in the Cotton, So Big, Three on a Match, Of Human Bondage, Bordertown, The Petrified Forest, Marked Woman, The Sisters, The Private Lives of Elizabeth and Essex, Juarez, The Old Maid, All This and Heaven Too, The Great Lie, The Man Who Came to Dinner, In This Our Life, Old Acquaintance, Watch on the Rhine, The Corn Is Green, Deception, June Bride, Payment on Demand, The Star, The Catered Affair, The Scapegoat, A Pocketful of Miracles, Hush . . . Hush . . . Sweet Charlotte, The Nanny, The Anniversary, Bunny O'Hare*, more.

DAVIS, CHARLES (S. Cal.) Support. Onscreen from 1953. IN: *The Desert Rats, Five Steps to Danger; Oh Men! Oh Women!; The Young Stranger, The Savage Wild,* more.

DAVIS, CLIFTON (S. Cal.) Black leading man. Onscreen in the '70s. IN: *Lost in the Stars,* more.

DAVIS, DONALD (N.Y.) Support. Onscreen from 1957. IN: *Oedipus Rex, Joy in the Morning,* more.

DAVIS, GAIL (S. Cal.) The leading lady in Westerns and star of TV's *Annie Oakley* series is now a manager of other celebrities. Onscreen from 1950. IN: *Sons of New Mexico, Cow Town, Take Care of My Little Girl, Yukon Manhunt, Blue Canadian Rockies, On Top of Old Smoky, Winning of the West,* more.

DAVIS, GLENN (S. Cal.) In his early 50s, this West Point football great of the '40s was, with teammate Felix "Doc" Blanchard, a one-picture star. Married to and divorced from actress Terry Moore ('52), he has been married for years to second wife, Harriet, and has a college-age son, Ralph, who doesn't go in for sports. Living in North Hollywood, Davis is the director of special sports events for the Los Angeles *Times.* IN: *Spirit of West Point.*

DAVIS, JACK (S. Cal.) After playing "Toughie" in the original (early '20s) "Our Gang," he gave up movie acting and has been for many years a leading physician in Beverly Hills. Actress Mildred Davis, who was the wife of late comedian Harold Lloyd, and died in 1969, was his sister.

DAVIS, JIM (S. Cal.) This rugged 6'3" actor, silver-haired now in his 60s (b. 1915), may not have been much of a performer when young but he has developed into one of Hollywood's best and busiest characters. His three-decade-plus "seasoning"—onscreen since 1942's *Strange Cargo*—has paid off. Davis has lately had top supporting roles in such movies as *The Parallax View* (the Senator assassinated in the L.A. Coliseum), *Bad Company, Fireeaters,* and *The Honkers,* and such TV shows as *Streets of San Francisco* and *Caribe,* in addition to the 1974–75 series *The Cowboys,* in which he costarred as U.S. Marshal Bill Winter. He and his wife, Blanche, a former professional swimmer, married since '49, live in a ranch-type house in the San Fernando Valley and have a college-age daughter, Tara. Onscreen from 1942. IN: *White Cargo; What Next, Corporal Hargrove?; Romance of Rosie Ridge, Winter Meeting, Hellfire, The Sea Hornet, Ride the Man Down, The Bot-*

tom of the Bottle, Apache Warrior, Zebra in the Kitchen, El Dorado, more.

DAVIS, NANCY (S. Cal.) In her 50s (b. 1924), she has been married to Ronald Reagan for more than two decades and actively assists him in his political campaigns. Onscreen from 1949. IN: *The Doctor and the Girl, East Side West Side, The Next Voice You Hear, Talk About a Stranger, Donovan's Brain,* more, including 1958's *Crash Landing,* her last.

DAVIS, OSSIE ((N.Y.) Black star. Onscreen from 1950. IN: *No Way Out, The Joe Louis Story, The Cardinal, Shock Treatment, The Hill, A Man Called Adam, The Scalphunters, Slaves, Let's Do It Again,* more.

DAVIS, ROBERT (N.Y.) Character. IN: *Confessions of a Nazi Spy,* more.

DAVIS, SAMMY, JR. (S. Cal.) Black star-singer. Onscreen from 1955. IN: *The Benny Goodman Story, Porgy and Bess, Ocean's 11, Sergeants Three, Robin and the Seven Hoods, A Man Called Adam, Salt and Pepper, Sweet Charity, The Trackers,* more.

DAVIS, STRINGER (Eng.) Actress Margaret Rutherford's elderly (b. 1896) widower, he has been inactive in movies for the past decade. Onscreen from 1949. IN: *Miranda, The Happiest Days of Your Life, Castle in the Air, The Runaway Bus, The March Hare, The Smallest Show on Earth, Murder She Said, Murder at the Gallop,* more.

DAVIS, SYLVIA (N.Y.) Support. IN: *Alice's Restaurant,* more.

DAVISON, BRUCE (S. Cal.) Leading man. Onscreen from 1969. IN: *Last Summer, Willard, Been Down So Long It Looks Like Up to Me, Ulzana's Raid, Mame,* more.

DAVISON, DAVEY (S. Cal.) Ingenue. IN: *Angel, Angel, Down We Go;* more.

DAWN, HAZEL (N.Y.) The screen career of the lovely Broadway musical star (*The Pink Lady,* etc.) was long ago and brief—just six pictures. Today, in her 80s (b. 1894), she remains a startlingly beautiful woman and an active one—painting, theatergoing, taking long walks along the East River near her Stuyvesant Town apartment. A widow since her engineer-husband Edward Gruelle died in '41, she lives alone. She has two children: Hazel Jr. and a son, who is a business man living in the South. Onscreen from 1914. IN: *Heart of Jennifer, One of Our Girls, Saleslady, Under Cover, My Lady Incog, Devotion,* her last in 1921.

DAWN, HAZEL, JR. (N.Y.) After a few minor roles in Hollywood in the '40s, including that of Vi, a high school flapper, in Jeanne Crain's *Margie*, the daughter of the star above had a career on Broadway. Married for many years now to a physician, she lives in Scarsdale, and has made Hazel Dawn Sr. a grandmother five times.

DAWSON, ANTHONY (Eng.) Character. Onscreen from the '40s, IN: *The Way to the Stars, The Wooden Horse, Valley of the Eagles, Dial M for Murder, The Haunted Strangler, Tiger Bay, Midnight Lace, Dr. No, Battle of Neretva*, more.

DAWSON, DORIS (Fla.) Once the wife of Pat Rooney III, she was later the wife of a business man who died in '71. The pretty, dark-haired ingenue is in her early 60s now, and raises and shows dogs throughout Florida. Onscreen from the late '20s. IN: *Kentucky Courage, Naughty Baby, Hot Stuff, Broadway Scandals*, more, including 1935's *The Silver Streak*, her last.

DAWSON, HAL K. (S. Cal.) Character. Onscreen from 1933. IN: *Another Language, Dr. Socrates, Libeled Lady; Wife, Doctor and Nurse; Wells Fargo, Rose of Washington Square, Tin Pan Alley, Coney Island, Guest Wife, The Fabulous Dorseys, Chicken Every Sunday, Three for the Show*, more.

DAWSON, NANCY JUNO (N.Y.) Support. IN: *The Iceman Cometh.*

DAWSON, RICHARD (S. Cal.) Support. IN: *The Devil's Brigade, King Rat, Munsters Go Home*, more.

DAY, ALICE (S. Cal.) Last onscreen in 1932's *Two-Fisted Law Gold*, she is now in her 70s (b. 1905), has been married since 1930, has several children and grandchildren, lives in quiet retirement near Los Angeles, and takes no part in present-day Hollywood. Onscreen from 1923. IN: *The Temple of Venus, Secrets, The Gorilla, Night Life, The Smart Set, Red Hot Speed, Is Everybody Happy?, Little Johnny Jones, Let Us Be Gay*, more.

DAY, DENNIS (S. Cal.) Some of those who still think of him as Jack Benny's kid singer were taken aback a few months ago when he appeared in Las Vegas in the play *The Mind With the Dirty Man*, costarring with the queen of X-rated movies, Marilyn Chambers. But, entering his sixth decade (b. 1917), long and happily married, the father of a houseful of children, and a grandfather, it's been a while since the famous tenor was a kid. It has taken years, though, to shake the lamebrained adolescent role he played for 25 radio-TV seasons with Benny and he's happy to forget it. Jack Benny himself, however, he says he will never forget. "I was a green kid out of college when I joined the show in October 1939, and I was scared stiff. But he was like a father to me, so kind and gentle." Their association continued after the show ended in the '60s. "He kept in touch," Dennis Day said at the time of Benny's death in '74. "I saw him about six months ago at my daughter's wedding reception. This was the beauty of this man." Onscreen from 1940. IN: *Buck Benny Rides Again, Sleepy Lagoon, Melody Time, I'll Get By, Golden Girl, The Girl Next Door*, more.

DAY, DORIS (S. Cal.) Star. Nominated for Best Actress Oscar in *Pillow Talk*. In 1976 she published her autobiography, *Doris Day: Her Story*, including in it private life revelations that considerably altered her girl-next-door image. Onscreen from 1948. IN: *Romance on the High Seas, My Dream Is Yours, Young Man with a Horn, Tea for Two, Lullaby of Broadway, I'll See You in My Dreams, April in Paris, Calamity Jane, Young at Heart, Love Me or Leave Me, The Man Who Knew Too Much, Pajama Game, Teacher's Pet, Please Don't Eat the Daisies, Midnight Lace, That Touch of Mink; Move Over, Darling; The Glass Bottom Boat, Where Were You When the Lights Went Out?, With Six You Get Egg Roll*, more.

DAY, FRANCES (Eng.) Leading lady; retired. Onscreen from the '20s. IN: *The First Mrs. Fraser, The Girl From Maxim's, The Girl in the Taxi, Fiddlers Three*, more.

DAY, JOSETTE (Fr.) Leading lady. Onscreen from 1932. IN: *Le Barbier de Seville, Lucrezia Borgia, The Man of the Hour, The Well-Digger's Daughter, Beauty and the Beast, Les Parents Terribles, Stolen Affections*, more.

DAY, LARAINE (S. Cal.) A few months back Laraine Day returned to MGM for the first time since her contract there ran out after 1945's *Keep Your Powder Dry*. She found herself there as the guest star in a *Medical Center* episode, back in the operating room. But progress had been made. Instead of dewy-eyed Nurse Mary Lamont (which she played seven times in the "Dr. Kildare" movies), the actress, now in her late 50s (b. 1919), played a hardbitten surgeon. For a reserved woman, she has lived much of her life in surprisingly dramatic headlines. When she divorced her first husband (1942–47), musician Ray Hendricks, and quickly married baseball's Leo Durocher, newspapers and gossip magazines had a field day. As Mrs. Durocher, she became the Brooklyn Dodgers' famous #1 fan, wrote a syndicated sports column for newspapers, and, with Durocher, did a husband-wife radio show. They adopted two children—Michele, who married (happily, it has turned out) six months before her high school graduation and has made Laraine a grandmother, and son Christopher, who works now in Los Angeles for Continental Airlines. Both remain close to her and visit often. New headlines ensued when Durocher and Laraine were divorced in '60. In the spring of '61, in a three-hour ceremony in the Latter-Day Saints (Mormon) Temple in Hollywood, she became the wife of TV executive Mike Grilikhes. It was her first marriage in the faith in which she was reared, her new husband, reared Quaker, having converted to her religion. She next found herself in court—and in headlines—when she joined Grilikhes in '67 as he petitioned the Supreme Court in New York for permission to see his son and daughter by a previous marriage. The actress has given birth to two daughters by Grilikhes—Dana Laraine (born in '62, she is a brunette and looks like her father) and Gigi (born in '65, she is blonde, looks like her mother, and wishes to be an actress like her). Author of the inspirational book *The America We Love*, the actress, in the early '70s, was the official salaried spokeswoman for the Make America Better program of the National Assn. of Real Estate Boards. In this capacity she traveled all over the country speaking against pollution, crime, etc. Besides infrequent TV roles, she acts occasionally in short-run stage plays— *The Time of the Cuckoo* for six weeks in Chicago, for instance—and several months back starred in *House of Dracula's Daughter*, her first movie in a dozen years. What does she think of Leo Durocher's recent autobiography, *Nice Guys Finish Last?* Don't ask. Onscreen from 1937. IN: *Stella Dallas, Painted Desert, Tarzan Finds a Son, Calling Dr. Kildare; My Son, My Son; Foreign Correspondent, And One Was Beautiful, Kathleen, Journey for Margaret, Mr. Lucky, The Story of Dr. Wassell, The Locket, My Dear Secretary, Woman on Pier 13, The High and the Mighty, Toy Tiger, The Third Voice*, more.

DAY, LYNDA/now LYNDA DAY GEORGE (S. Cal.) Leading lady. Most popular on TV. IN: *Chisum*.

DAY, MARCELINE (S. Cal.) In her 60s now (b. 1908), the former leading lady—and younger sister of Alice Day—left the screen after 1937's *Damaged Lives*. She married well, she retired, she's happy, and she has never looked back. Onscreen from 1926. IN: *The Barrier, The Beloved Rogue, Rookies, Captain Salvation, London After Midnight, The Jazz Age, The Wild Party, Temple Tower, Sunny Skies, The Mad Parade, The Crusader, The Fighting Parson*, more.

DAY, SHANNON (N.Y.) The popular Paramount leading lady of the '20s is now in her early 70s and has lately been a drama coach in Manhattan. Onscreen from 1923. IN: *Marriage Morals, So This Is Marriage, The Vanishing American, The Barrier*, more.

DAYAN, ASSAF (Israel) Leading man. Onscreen from 1969. IN: *A Walk with Love and Death, Promise at Dawn*.

DE BANZIE, BRENDA (Eng.) Character star. Onscreen from 1951. IN: *The Long Dark Hall, Hobson's Choice, Doctor at Sea, As Long As They're Happy, Don't Blame the Stork, The Man Who Knew Too Much, Triple Deception, Too Many Crooks, The Entertainer, The 39 Steps, Come September, A Pair of Briefs, The Pink Panther, A Matter of Innocence*, more.

DE BANZIE, LOIS (N.Y.) Support. IN: *The Witches of Salem*.

DE BORD, SHARON (S. Cal.) Leading lady. IN: *The Reivers, The Cheyenne Social Club, That Tennessee Beat*, more.

DeCAMP, ROSEMARY (S. Cal.) Character. Onscreen from 1941. IN: *Hold Back the Dawn, Cheers for Miss Bishop, The Jungle Book, Yankee Doodle Dandy, Practically Yours, Pride of the Marines, Rhapsody in Blue, Weekend at the Waldorf, Nora Prentiss, Look for the Silver Lining, So This Is Love, Strategic Air Command, Many Rivers to Cross, Tora! Tora! Tora!*, more.

DE CARLO, YVONNE (S. Cal.) Star. Onscreen from 1942 in bits, first under her real name, Peggy Middleton. IN: *Youth on Parade, This Gun for Hire, The Story of Dr. Wassell*, more. Onscreen in major roles from 1945. IN: *Salome Where She Danced, Frontier Gal, Brute Force, Casbah, Criss Cross, Calamity Jane and Sam Bass, The Buccaneer's Girl, Hotel Sahara, The San Francisco Story, Sombrero, Fort Algiers, The Captain's Paradise, Flame of the Islands, The Ten Commandments, Raw Edge, McLintock!, A Global Affair, Munster Go Home, Huntsville, The Seven Minutes, Blazing Stewardesses*, more.

DE CICCO, PAT (N.Y.) Support. Later an agent. IN: *Night Life of the Gods*.

DE CONDE, SYN (Braz.) In a half-dozen Hollywood silents this handsome Brazilian was extremely popular. He is perhaps best recalled for appearing with Nazimova in *Revelation*. Returning to Brazil—his socially prominent family disapproved of his career—he never acted again. Instead, he resumed his true name (Sinesio Mariano de Aguiar), married, and for over four decades was an officer of the Ministry of Agriculture. Today, in his 70s, retired and living in Rio, he still regrets the abrupt end of his screen career. Onscreen from 1918 to 1921. IN: *The Girl Who Stayed Home, Revelation, Mary Regan, Out of the Shadows,* more.

DE FORE, DON (S. Cal.) Costar. Onscreen from 1937. IN: *Submarine D-1, We Go Fast, The Male Animal, The Human Comedy, A Guy Named Joe, Thirty Seconds Over Tokyo, You Came Along, Without Reservations, One Sunday Afternoon, My Friend Irma, Dark City, No Room for the Groom, Susan Slept Here, A Time to Love and a Time to Die,* more.

DE HAVEN, GLORIA (S. Cal.) Costar. Onscreen from 1936. IN: *Modern Times, Susan and God, Two-Faced Woman, Best Foot Forward, Two Girls and a Sailor, Between Two Women, Step Lively, Manhattan Serenade, Summer Holiday, The Yellow Cab Man, Summer Stock, Three Little Words, Down Among the Sheltering Palms, So This Is Paris, Girl Rush,* more. Now appears in nightclubs and on TV where, in '74, she costarred in the *Nakia* series.

DE HAVILLAND, OLIVIA (Fr.) Star. Nominated for Best Supporting Actress Oscar in *Gone With the Wind.* Nominated for Best Actress Oscar in *Hold Back the Dawn* and *The Snake Pit.* Won Best Actress Oscar in *To Each His Own* and *The Heiress.* Onscreen from 1935. IN: *Alibi Ike, Captain Blood, A Midsummer Night's Dream, Anthony Adverse, Adventures of Robin Hood, Private Lives of Elizabeth and Essex, Strawberry Blonde, In This Our Life, The Male Animal, Princess O'Rourke, Devotion, The Dark Mirror, My Cousin Rachel, Not as a Stranger, The Ambassador's Daughter, The Proud Rebel, Light in the Piazza, Lady in a Cage, Hush . . . Hush . . . Sweet Charlotte, The Adventurers, Waterloo,* more.

DE KOVA, FRANK (S. Cal.) Character. Onscreen from 1951. IN: *The Mob, Viva Zapata!, The Big Sky, The Robe, Santiago, The Ten Commandments, The Brothers Karamazov, The Rise and Fall of Legs Diamond, Those Calloways, The Greatest Story Ever Told, The Wild Country,* more.

DE LACEY, PHILIPPE (S. Cal.) Last onscreen in two 1930 pix (*Sarah and Son* and *One Romantic Night*), this once-popular juvenile who is entering his 60s now (b. 1917) directed the movie *Cinerama Holiday* and has long been an executive of the J. Walter Thompson advertising agency in Hollywood. "The ten years I spent in movies," he says, "were a wonderful experience. I feel fortunate to have had them." Onscreen from 1924. IN: *Peter Pan, Is Zat So?,*

The Student Prince, Mother Machree, 4 Devils, Napoleon's Barber, The Marriage Playground, more.

DE LUCE, VIRGINIA (N.Y.) Support. IN: *Hello, Frisco, Hello.*

DE LUISE, DOM (S. Cal.) Star comedian. Onscreen from 1966. IN: *The Glass Bottom Boat, The Busy Body, What's So Bad About Feeling Good?, Every Little Crook and Nanny, The 12 Chairs, Blazing Saddles, The Adventures of Sherlock Holmes' Smarter Brother, Mel Brooks' Silent Movie,* more.

DE MARNEY, DERRICK (Eng.) Character. Onscreen from the '30s. IN: *Things to Come, Victoria the Great, The Pearls of the Crown, Sixty Glorious Years, Suicide Squadron, Spitfire, Sleeping Car to Trieste, The Inheritance, The March Hare,* more.

DE MAVE, JACK (S. Cal.) Support. IN: *Blindford,* more.

DeMILLE, KATHERINE (S. Cal.) Long divorced from Anthony Quinn, father of her grown children, the adopted daughter of Cecil B. DeMille is in her 60s (b. 1911) and retired from acting. She lives in Bel Air and devotes herself to the study of philosophy. Onscreen from 1930. IN: *Madam Satan, The Crusades, The Black Room Mystery, Charlie Chan at the Olympics, In Old Caliente; Ellery Queen, Master Detective; Dark Streets of Cairo, Black Gold,* more.

DE NIRO, ROBERT (N.Y.) Costar. Won Best Supporting Actor Oscar in *The Godfather II.* Onscreen from the late '60s. IN: *Greetings, The Wedding Party, Bloody Mama; Hi, Mom!; Born to Win, The Gang That Couldn't Shoot Straight, Bang the Drum Slowly, Mean Streets, The Last Tycoon, Taxi Driver,* more.

DE RITA, JOE (S. Cal.) Comedian. One of "The Three Stooges" from '58. Onscreen from 1944. IN: *The Doughgirls, The Bravados,* more.

DE SALES, FRANCIS (S. Cal.) Character. Onscreen from 1957. IN: *Apache Territory, Return to Warbow, Face of a Fugitive, Let No Man Write My Epitaph, A Majority of One, The Outfit,* more.

DE SANTIS, JOE (S. Cal.) Character. Onscreen from 1949. IN: *Slattery's Hurricane, Deadline U.S.A., I Want to Live!, Al Capone, The George Raft Story, A Cold Wind in August, The Venetian Affair, The Brotherhood,* more.

DE WIT, JACQUELINE (S. Cal.) Character. Onscreen from 1944. IN: *Dragon Seed, Men in*

Her Diary, Saratoga Trunk, Something in the Wind, The Snake Pit, The Damned Don't Cry, Carrie, Tea and Sympathy, Harper, more.

DEL REY, PILAR (S. Cal.) Character. Onscreen from 1950. IN: *The Kid From Texas, Siege at Red River, Giant, And Now Miguel,* more.

DEL RIO, DOLORES (Mex.) Frankly in her 70s (b. 1905), she is, equally truthfully, still a gorgeous woman. She had been scheduled to return to Hollywood in '75, for the first time in years, to costar with Jason Miller in the TV-movie *Who'll See to the Children?,* but had to bow out because of a back injury—from which she has recovered. Heretofore enjoying buoyant health, she has never stopped acting since making her screen debut at 20 in *Joanna.* Leaving Hollywood in '47, she starred in dozens of Spanish-language films, returned occasionally for such pictures as *Cheyenne Autumn,* and—in this decade alone—has been a hit onstage in Mexico City in the musical *Applause* and the drama *Camille.* Previously married to and divorced from Jaime Martinez Del Rio and Hollywood art director Cedric Gibbons, she has been married since '59 to American motion picture producer Lewis Riley. They live in a Xanadu-like, million-dollar estate in Coyoacan, a suburb of Mexico City. The colonial hacienda is famed for its gardens and pre-Columbian art. A warm, gracious woman, the actress recalls with joy her years in Hollywood. But she says, "I am very much a person of today. I am not much for yesterday except for the lessons it has taught. As the years have gone by, I have become more and more interested in today. There is so little time left and I still want to do so many things. My time has become very precious to me." Much of the time of this woman who has never had children is devoted now to a project she worked years to establish. This is the Estancia Infantil, a nursery, open 24 hours a day, for the children of working actresses—the only one of its kind in the world, says she, the president of its board. "The children," she explains, "live there for many weeks, sometimes many months, while their mothers are on location." Asked repreatedly the secret of her beauty, she sometimes answers lightly, "So long as a woman has twinkles in her eyes, no man notices whether she has wrinkles under them." More practically, she neither smokes nor drinks (never has), sleeps long hours, and drinks 40 glasses of water daily. More esthetically, she subscribes to this philosophy: "Take care of your inner beauty, your spiritual beauty, and that will reflect in your face. We have the face we created over the years. Every bad deed, every bad fault will show on your face." On reflection, she adds, "I don't think I have ever

done anything bad, bad in the sense of wrong." Onscreen from 1925. IN: *Joanna, What Price Glory, Evangeline, Flying Down to Rio, Madame Du Barry, In Caliente, I Live for Love, The Devil's Playground, Lancer Spy, The Man from Dakota, Journey into Fear, Maria Candelaria, The Pearl, The Fugitive, Torero!, Flaming Star, La Dama Del Alba, Rio Blanco,* more.

DEACON, RICHARD (S. Cal.) Character. Onscreen from 1954. IN: *Desiree; Good Morning, Miss Dove; The Kettles in the Ozarks, The Solid Gold Cadillac, The Young Philadelphians, Lover Come Back, That Darn Cat, Enter Laughing, Lady in Cement,* more.

DEAN, DINKY (S. Cal.) The bratty little kid Chaplin booted across the room in *The Pilgrim* has long gone by his real name, Dean Riesner (son of the late Charles/Chuck), is now in his 50s, last appeared onscreen in 1950's *Traveling Saleswoman,* and was the screenwriter on *The Helen Morgan Story, The Man from Galveston,* and *Coogan's Bluff,* among many others.

DEAN, EDDIE (S. Cal.) The singing cowboy who was one of the Top Ten Western Stars 1946–47, still trim and handsome in his 60s, lives in Hollywood and reports, "I'm still playing nightclubs, rodeos, anything that comes along. I paint as a hobby. Outside that I'm just living, man." Onscreen from 1936. IN: *Law of the Pampas, Rolling Home to Texas, Song of Old Wyoming, Colorado Serenade, The Caravan Trail, Driftin' River, The Range Beyond the Blue, The Black Hills,* more, including 1951's *Varieties on Parade,* his last.

DEAN, ISABEL (Eng.) Support. Onscreen from the '40s. IN: *One Woman's Story, Twice Upon a Time, Gilbert and Sullivan, The Woman's Angle, Light in the Piazza, A Man Could Get Killed, Inadmissible Evidence,* more.

DEAN, JIMMY (N.C.) Singer-actor. IN: *Diamonds Are Forever.*

DEAN, MARGIA (S. Cal.) Now retired, the former leading lady lives in Beverly Hills. Onscreen from 1944. IN: *Call of the South Seas, Shep Comes Home, Rimfire, Savage Drums, The Baron of Arizona, Bandit Queen, The Creeping Unknown, Frontier Gambler, Secret of the Purple Reef, Seven Women From Hell,* more.

DEAN, PRISCILLA (N.J.) The leading lady who so memorably played Cigarette in 1922's *Under Two Flags* quit the screen after 1926's *Outside the Law* and is now in her 70s, retired, and living in Leonia. Onscreen from 1918. IN: *Two-Soul Woman, Paid in Advance, Wild*

Honey, Drifting, The Siren of Seville, A Cafe in Cairo, The Crimson Runner, more.

DEAN, SHERRY (N.Y.) Juvenile. Onscreen in the '70s. IN: *Honor Thy Father, Badge 373,* more.

DECKERS, EUGENE (Eng.) Character. Onscreen from the '40s. IN: *Woman to Woman, Sleeping Car to Trieste, Captain Horatio Hornblower R.N., Madeleine, So Long at the Fair, Tony Draws a Horse, Hotel Sahara, The Colditz Story, Doctor at Sea, Flame Over India,* more.

DEE, FRANCES (S. Cal.) Star; retired. Onscreen from 1930. IN: *Along Came Youth, Follow Through, June Moon, If I Had a Million, The Silver Cord, Little Women, Of Human Bondage, Souls at Sea, Wells Fargo, If I Were King, Coast Guard, So Ends Our Night, I Walked with a Zombie, Happy Land, Payment on Demand, Because of You, Mr. Scoutmaster,* more, including 1954's *Gypsy Colt,* her last. (See Joel McCrea.)

DEE, RUBY (N.Y.) Black leading lady. Onscreen from 1950. IN: *No Way Out, The Jackie Robinson Story, Edge of the City, St. Louis Blues, A Raisin in the Sun, Gone Are the Days, The Incident, The Betrayal, Deadlock, Buck and the Preacher,* more.

DEE, SANDRA (S. Cal.) The former juvenile star, so popular in the '50s and '60s, has not appeared in a movie since 1970's *The Dunwich Horror.* She is in her 30s (b. 1942) and has not remarried since her long-ago divorce from late singer Bobby Darin. Onscreen from 1957. IN: *Until They Sail, The Restless Years, The Reluctant Debutante, Gidget, A Summer Place, Stranger in My Arms, Romanoff and Juliet, Tammy Tell Me True, If a Man Answers, Take Her She's Mine, I'd Rather Be Rich, Rosie!; Doctor, You've Got to Be Kidding; The Man Hunters,* more.

DEEL, SANDRA (S. Cal.) Support. IN: *La Dolce Vita,* more.

DEERING, OLIVE (S. Cal.) (See Olive Carey.) Character. Onscreen from 1949. IN: *Samson and Delilah, Caged, Rogue Cop, The Cobweb, The Searchers, The Ten Commandments, The Alamo, Two Rode Together, Shock Treatment,* more.

DEGERMARK, PIA (Swe.) Leading lady. IN: *Elvira Madigan, The Looking Glass War,* more.

DELAIR, SUZY (Fr.) Leading lady. Onscreen from 1947. IN: *The Murderer Lives at Number 21, Jenny Lamour, Confessions of a Rogue, Fernandel the Dressmaker, Gervaise, Rocco and His Brothers, Is Paris Burning?, The Mad Adventures of "Rabbi" Jacob,* more.

DELL, GABRIEL (S. Cal.) The credits of the '75 movie *The Manchu Eagle Murder Caper Mystery* are revealing: Screenplay by Dean Hargrove and Gabriel Dell; Starring Gabriel Dell. Then, eight names down the cast list: Deputy—Huntz Hall. Rank notwithstanding, it was a grand reunion for the only two Dead End Kids still fully occupied with acting; pals since they were in the Broadway play of *Dead End* in 1935, they had not acted together since Dell dropped out of the "Bowery Boys" pix in '50. But together, recently, they bought an old abandoned church in Topanga Canyon, announcing plans to convert it into a restaurant called The Church. The 1970s have been bonanza years for Gabriel ("T.B.") Dell, a handsome man now in his 50s (b. 1921). Broadway plays in which he has starred: *Where Do We Go From Here?, Fun City, Prisoner of Second Avenue.* In '74 he co-starred in the movie *Framed* and had a major role in *Earthquake.* He starred on TV in '72 in the series *The Corner Bar,* playing a bartender (privately, he's a teetotaler). And he has guest-starred on television in *McCloud, Sanford and Son,* etc. Why did he hang on as his *Dead End* buddies dropped out one by one? "I didn't know anything else to do," says the man who was a kid actor on Broadway even before the play that made him world-famous. A native New Yorker, he still keeps an apartment on Manhattan's Upper West Side, even though Sherman Oaks has long been his home. There was, he frankly admits, a long rough period after he left movies to return to the stage: Actors Studio ("I had to learn technique"), stock, industrial shows, unemployment lines. He was also married to and divorced from the late ballerina Viola Essen (she had starred in the film *Spectre of the Rose*); their son, Beau, was born in '56. The 1964 play *The Sign in Sidney Brustein's Window* turned the tide of bad luck into good. He is married now to a beautiful girl 20 years his junior, Allyson Daniell, daughter of the late character actor Henry Daniell, and they have one son, born in '67, Gabriel Dell Jr. (It's actually del Vecchio, Gabriel Sr. never having legally adopted his professional monicker.) An easygoing man, a serious student of the philosophy of Zen ("Life is right here at the moment, and how can you make it work?"), Gabriel Dell, ex-*Dead End* kid who was then the toughest of the lot, grows furious over today's dope situation and the fact that little has been done to cut off the supply at its source. He thinks of actor friends he has seen lost to dope, so often when their careers were at low ebb, and says: "I'm convinced that's how a person gets hooked. A sense of unproductivity and unworthiness takes over and they try to make something happen to them." He intends to keep fighting until "they" listen. His one unfulfilled dream, he says, is this: "I saw some places around the world, like Kwajalein and Ceylon, when I was in the Merchant Marine for three years during World War II. Now I want to take the family." Onscreen from 1937. IN: *Dead End, Crime School, Little Tough Guy, They Made Me a Criminal, Angels Wash Their Faces, Mob Town, Tough as They Come, Bowery Champs, Million Dollar Kid, Hard-Boiled Mahoney, Jinx Money, Fighting Fools, Blonde Dynamite, Triple Trouble, 300 Year Weekend, Who Is Harry Kellerman . . .?*, more.

DELL, MYRNA (S. Cal.) One of RKO's most promising young stars in the '40s, and then a longtime—"platonic," she inserts—friend of Howard Hughes, she has recently launched a party-planning business in Hollywood—and is still, in her early 50s, a whistle-worthy woman. Onscreen from 1944. IN: *Arizona Whirlwind, The Falcon's Adventure, Nocturne, The Locket, Fighting Father Dunne, Roughshod, The Judge Steps Out, The Lost Tribe, The Furies, The Strip, The Bushwackers, Here Come the Marines*, more, including 1960's *Ma Barker's Killer Brood,* her last.

DELMAR, KENNY (Conn.) Comedian. IN: *Strangers in the City.*

DELON, ALAIN (Fr.) Star. Onscreen from 1959. IN: *Purple Noon, Rocco and His Brothers, Christine, The Leopard, Joy House, The Yellow Rolls-Royce, Is Paris Burning?, Texas Across the River, Spirits of the Dead, Red Sun, Scorpio, No Way Out, Zorro, Flic Story, Icy Breasts, The Gypsy,* more

DELON, NATHALIE (Fr.) Leading lady. Onscreen in the '70s. IN: *The Tender Moment, When Eight Bells Toll, The Romantic Englishwoman,* more.

DELORME, DANIELE (Fr.) Leading lady. Onscreen from 1948. IN: *Gigi* (French version), *Miquette, Pit of Loneliness, House of Ricordi, Royal Affairs in Versailles, Deadlier Than the Male, The Seventh Juror, The Crook,* more.

DEMAREST, WILLIAM (S. Cal.) Character. Nominated for Best Supporting Actor Oscar in *The Jolson Story.* Onscreen from 1927. IN: *The Jazz Singer, The Butter and Egg Man, Broadway Melody, Diamond Jim, Hands Across the Table, Charlie Chan at the Opera, Wake Up and Live, Easy Living, Rebecca of Sunnybrook* Farm, Rosalie, The Great Man Votes, Mr. Smith Goes to Washington, The Great McGinty, Christmas in July, The Palm Beach Story, My Favorite Spy, Hail the Conquering Hero, Salty O'Rourke, Sorrowful Jones, When Willie Comes Marching Home, Excuse My Dust, Jupiter's Darling, Lucy Gallant, The Mountain, Son of Flubber, It's a Mad Mad Mad Mad World, That Darn Cat, The McCullochs,* more.

DEMICK, IRINA (Fr.) Leading lady. Onscreen from 1962. IN: *The Longest Day, The Visit, Those Magnificent Men in Their Flying Machines, Male Companions, Prudence and the Pill, The Sicilian Clan,* more.

DEMONGEOT, MYLENE (Fr.) Leading lady. Onscreen from 1956. IN: *The Witches of Salem, Bonjour Tristesse, The Crucible, Under Ten Flags, Time Bomb, Rape of the Sabines, The Singer Not the Song, Doctor in Distress, The Tender Scoundrel,* more.

DEMPSEY, JACK (N.Y.) The "Manassa Mauler," immortal boxing champ who won additional fans as the star of several silents, celebrated his 80th birthday in '75. Still powerful-looking and erect, though he must walk with a cane (arthritis in both hips), he lives in a plush apartment in the East 50s with his wife of many years, Deanna. Their daughter, Barbara, has written his memoirs, and the book, he says, contains "everything I've never told before." His landmark restaurant on Broadway has been closed since '74, because of a huge rent hike he refused to pay. On its last night, near tears, the champ said, "I'm heartbroken and I'm disgusted. This is my second home and I have lost it." Onscreen from 1920. IN: *Daredevil Jack* (serial), *Fight and Win, The Prizefighter and the Lady, Off Limits, Requiem for a Heavyweight,* more.

DEMPSTER, CAROL (S. Cal.) D. W. Griffith's last "discovery," she was rarely a favorite with film critics, or, it seems with the director's cameramen who photographed her. In recently published books, both the famous Billy Bitzer (in his *Billy Bitzer: His Story*) and his assistant, Karl Brown (in his *Adventures with D. W. Griffith*), had a separate "go" at her. So far removed from the Hollywood of today is Carol Dempster that it is doubtful she even knows this, and if she does, scarcely cares. Gray-haired and vital in her 70s (b. 1902), she has been married for decades to a very wealthy man, financier Edwin Larsen, now retired, has no children, travels all over the world, and has two homes—in Palm Springs and La Jolla—and lives part of the year in each. Hollywood is not one of the waystops as she journeys from one to the other. Onscreen from 1919. IN: *The Girl Who Stayed Home, The Love Flower, Sherlock Holmes, One Exciting Night, The White Rose, America, Isn't Life Wonderful?, That Royle Girl, The Sorrows of Satan,* more.

DEMPSTER, HUGH (Eng.) Character. Onscreen from the '30s. IN: *The Student's Romance, April Romance, Waltz Time, Anna Karenina, The Fan, Happy Go Lovely, Babes in Bagdad, Moulin Rouge, Father Brown,* more.

DENEUVE, CATHERINE (Fr.) Star. Onscreen from 1958. IN: *La Vie du Chateau, The Umbrellas of Cherbourg, Repulsion, Male Companions, Les Creatures, Belle de Jour, Maroc 7, Mayerling, The April Fools, Act of Aggression, Drama of the Rich, The Savage, Hustle,* more.

DENHAM, MAURICE (Eng.) Character. Onscreen from the '40s. IN: *Jassy, The Smugglers, Blanche Fury, The Blue Lagoon, Man With a Million, The Purple Plain, Doctor at Sea, Our Man in Havana, The Mark, Loss of Innocence, Operation Crossbow, The Nanny, The Long Duel, Nicholas and Alexandra, Sunday Bloody Sunday, Some Girls Do, Luther,* more.

DENISON, MICHAEL (Eng.) Leading man. Onscreen from the '40s. IN: *Hungry Hill, The Blind Goddess, My Brother Jonathan, The Franchise Affair, The Importance of Being Earnest, The Truth about Women, Contraband Spain,* more.

DENNING, RICHARD (Hawaii) His face—one of the most photogenically perfect male faces in movies—always told such lies about blond Richard Denning. It proclaimed him to be a playboy—self-centered, concerned with shallow pleasures. This was the essential impression given from his first (1937's *Hold 'em Navy*) through his 90th and last (1963's *Twice Told Tales*). The real Richard Denning is something different—devoted husband (married once) and father, a "solid citizen," an executive director of the Boy Scouts of America, an active member of the Wailuku Union Church in Maui, where he lives. Speaking for himself and wife, Evelyn Ankers, he says, "Our country, God, and the entertainment industry have been exceptionally good to our family and we are most humbly grateful for our blessings." In his early 60s now (b. 1914), and looking far younger, he refers to himself as "semiretired." But he is often seen on TV as the governor in *Hawaii Five-0,* filmed in Honolulu. Though he still visits Hollywood, he has not acted there in more than a decade. At that time, he says, "My wonderful wife suggested that, since we had worked and saved together since our marriage, perhaps the time had come to do the things we really enjoyed, and at a comfortable tempo. We reviewed all the places we had visited and lived, and decided that Hawaii would be our goal. We analyzed and valued our assets and equities, projected our potential longevity, and estimated the standard of living we'd be contented with; it all looked favorable with God's help and blessing. We've found that life has many other values besides our careers, making a living, and keeping up with the Joneses. Our faith and relationship with God has taken on new dimensions." Often tagged the Honorary President of Maui's Chamber of Commerce, the actor says by way of explanation, "I just can't resist showing my love, appreciation and enthusiasm for a place that Evelyn and I always dreamed about—but didn't know actually existed. For us, it's about as close to Paradise as we could find on earth—and we love it more each day." Onscreen from 1937. IN: *Daughter of Shanghai, Her Jungle Love, Give Me a Sailor, Zaza, Million Dollar Legs, The Gracie Allen Murder Case, Geronimo, Disputed Passage, Those Were the Days, Northwest Mounted Police, Adam Had Four Sons, Beyond the Blue Horizon, Quiet Please Murder, The Glass Key, Fabulous Suzanne, When My Baby Smiles at Me, Okinawa, The Glass Web, The Magnificent Matador, The Day the World Ended, An Affair to Remember, The Lady Takes a Flyer, Desert Hell,* more. (See Evelyn Ankers.)

DENNIS, DANNY (N.Y.) Character. IN: *The Blackboard Jungle; Murder, Inc.;* more.

DENNIS, JOHN (S. Cal.) Character. Onscreen from 1953. IN: *From Here to Eternity, The Naked Street; Too Much, Too Soon; Mister Buddwing, Earthquake,* more.

DENNIS, NICK (S. Cal.) Character. Onscreen from 1951. IN: *A Streetcar Named Desire, Anything Can Happen, Eight Iron Men, East of Eden, The Big Knife, Spartacus, Birdman of Alcatraz, 4 for Texas,* more.

DENNIS, SANDY (N.Y.) Costar. Won Best Supporting Actress Oscar in *Who's Afraid of Virginia Woolf?* Onscreen from 1961. IN: *Splendor in the Grass, Three Sisters, Up the Down Staircase, The Fox, Sweet November, Images, That Cold Day in the Park, The Out-of-Towners, A Touch of Love, Thank You All Very Much, Mr. Sycamore, God Told Me To,* more.

DENNY, IKE (N.Y.) Juvenile. Onscreen from 1969. IN: *Generation, On a Clear Day You Can See Forever, Cotton Comes to Harlem, The Owl and the Pussycat, Pigeons,* more.

DENVER, BOB (S. Cal.) Comedy star. On-screen from 1959. IN: *A Private's Affair, For Those Who Think Young, Did You Hear the One About the Traveling Saleslady?, Who's Minding the Mint?, The Sweet Ride*, more.

DEPARDIEU, GERARD (Fr.) Leading man. Onscreen in the '70s. IN: *Going Places (Les Valeuses), 1900*, more.

DEREK, JOHN (S. Cal.) Silver-haired and still extraordinarily handsome as he enters his 50s (b. 1926), Derek now writes, photographs, and directs movies—four is the most recent being *And Once Upon a Time*, which he filmed in Greece. On this location he met the girl, 18-year-old Cathleen Collins, who became his constant companion. She is younger than his son and daughter by his first wife, starlet Patti Behrs. He has had two other marriages (child-less) and divorces: actresses Ursula Andress and Linda Evans. Something of a movieland recluse, by choice, and a well-heeled one, De-rek says, "I have very few friends and almost no acquaintances." Onscreen from 1945. IN: *I'll Be Seeing You, Knock on Any Door, All the King's Men, Rogues of Sherwood Forest, Satur-day's Hero, Thunderbirds, Prince of Pirates, The Annapolis Story, Run for Cover, The Ten Commandments, Massacre at Sand Creek, Omar Khayyam, Exodus*, more.

DERN, BRUCE (S. Cal.) Star. Onscreen from 1960. IN: *Wild River, Hush . . . Hush . . . Sweet Charlotte, The St. Valentine's Day Massacre, Waterhole #3, Psych-Out, Will Penny, Castle Keep; They Shoot Horses, Don't They?; Bloody Mama, Drive He Said, Silent Running, The Cowboys, The King of Marvin Gardens, The Great Gatsby, Posse, Smile, Family Plot, The Twist, Black Sunday; Won Ton Ton, the Dog Who Saved Hollywood;* more.

DERR, RICHARD (S. Cal.) Character; former leading man. Onscreen from 1941. IN: *Charlie Chan in Rio, Castle in the Desert, Ten Gentle-men from West Point, The Man Who Wouldn't Die, Tonight We Raid Calais, The Bride Goes Wild, Luxury Liner, When Worlds Collide, In-visible Avenger, Rosie, Three in the Attic, The Drowning Pool*, more.

DESMOND, FLORENCE (Eng.) Comedy char-acter. Onscreen from 1931. IN: *Sally in Our Alley, Mister Skitch, Accused, Three Came Home, Charley Moon*, more.

DESMOND, JOHNNY (N.Y.) Singer-actor. On-screen from 1957. IN: *Calypso Heat Wave, Es-cape from San Quentin, China Doll, Caribbean Hawk*, more.

DESNI, TAMARA (Eng.) Leading lady. On-screen from 1932. IN: *Der Schrecken der Garni-son, Jack Ahoy, Fire Over England, Murder on Diamond Row, Dick Barton at Bay*, more.

DESNY, IVAN (Fr.) Leading man. Onscreen from 1950. IN: *Madeleine, Anastasia, The Re-spectful Prostitute, Song Without End, Bon Voyage!, Guns for San Sebastian, Lola Montes, Mayerling*, more.

DESPO (N.Y.) Singer-actress. IN: *Never on Sunday, Something for Everyone, Promise at Dawn, The Horsemen*, more.

DEVANE, WILLIAM (S. Cal.) Leading man. Onscreen in the '70s. IN: *The Pursuit of Happi-ness, McCabe and Mrs. Miller, 300 Year Week-end, My Old Man's Place, Family Plot, Mara-thon Man*, more.

DEVI, KAMALA (S. Cal.) Leading lady; re-tired. Onscreen from 1958. IN: *Harry Black and the Tiger, Geronimo, The Brass Bottle*, more.

DEVINE, ANDY (S. Cal.) Character. Onscreen from 1928. IN: *Red Lips, Tom Brown of Culver, Dr. Bull, Wake Up and Dream, The Farmer Takes a Wife, In Old Chicago, Men with Wings, Yellow Jack, Stagecoach, Little Old New York, Torrid Zone, Flame of New Orleans, South of Tahiti, Corvette K-225, Ali Baba and the Forty Thieves, Sudan, Springtime in the Sierras, Never a Dull Moment, Red Badge of Courage, The Marauders, The Man Who Shot Liberty Valance, How the West Was Won, Ballad of Josie, The Road Hustlers, Myra Breckinridge; Won Ton Ton, the Dog Who Saved Hollywood;* more.

DEVON, RICHARD (S. Cal.) Character. On-screen from 1960. IN: *Battle of Blood Island, The Comancheros, Kid Galahad, Cattle King, The Silencers, Three Guns for Texas*, more.

DEVORE, DOROTHY (S. Cal.) Now in her 70s, this veteran who starred in more than 200 (many of them the two-reel "Dorothy Devore Comedies"), and is the widow of a wealthy theater magnate, lives at the Motion Picture and TV Country Home, and made a fleeting appear-ance—with Beverly Bayne, Laura La Plante, Viola Dana, etc.—on *The Merv Griffin Show* in '71. Onscreen from the teens. IN: *45 Minutes From Broadway, Winter Has Come, The Nar-row Street, How Baxter Buttered In, His Maj-esty Bunker Bean, The Social Highwayman, Senior Daredevil*, more.

DEWHURST, COLLEEN (N.Y.) Leading lady. Onscreen from 1959. IN: *The Nun's Story, Man* on a String, A Fine Madness, The Last Run, McQ., more.

DEXTER, ALAN (S. Cal.) Character. Onscreen from 1953. IN: *It Came From Outer Space, Forbidden, Time Limit, The Enemy Below*, more.

DEXTER, BRAD (S. Cal.) Going into his 60th year (b. 1917), and still good-looking, he is married to Star-Kist tuna heiress Mary Bogdonovich and, in '75, announced plans to produce the movie *Bad News* in Mexico. Onscreen from 1950. IN: *The Asphalt Jungle, The Las Vegas Story, 99 River Street; Run Silent, Run Deep; Vice Raid, The Magnificent Seven, The George Raft Story, Invitation to a Gunfighter, None But the Brave, Von Ryan's Express, Shampoo*, more.

DEY, SUSAN (S. Cal.) Ingenue. IN: *Skyjacked.*

DHIEGH, KHIGH (S. Cal.) Character. Onscreen from 1962. IN: *The Manchurian Candidate, 13 Frightened Girls, Seconds, The Hawaiians, The Mephisto Waltz*, more.

DI LEVA, ANTHONY J./formerly ANTHONY GARDELL (N.Y.) Character. IN: *A View From the Bridge.*

DI MAGGIO, JOE (N.Y.) The great baseball star has long been the TV spokesman for a leading Manhattan bank. IN: *Manhattan Merry-Go-Round.*

DIAMOND, DON (S. Cal.) Character. IN: *Borderline, Mrs. Pollifax—Spy, Viva Max!*, more.

DIAZ, RUDY (S. Cal.) Character. IN: *Hellfighters, McKenna's Gold, Che!, The Undefeated, Flap, Pieces of Dreams*, more.

DICK, DOUGLAS (S. Cal.) Still baby-faced in his 50s (b. 1920), though he's a bit heavier and his wavy locks are thinning, the actor who came close to an Oscar nomination—as the crippled young soldier in *The Searching Wind*, his first pic—keeps busy on the Hollywood scene. Seldom seen on the screen since the late '50s, he is a TV triple threat—as guest star ("I've done somewhere around 200," he ventures), pitchman in commercials (often in horn rims and a pipe clenched in his executive-type face), and script writer. He and his present wife—he was formerly married, briefly, to Ronnie Cowan—have collaborated on scripts for many shows: *Bewitched, Family Affair, Mothers-in-Law*, etc. His other interests today, he says, are politics, tennis, music, and camping. And, while he doesn't say it, he must think it—getting other movie roles like he enjoyed in *The Searching Wind* and, as the schizophrenic college Romeo,

in *The Accused*. Onscreen from 1946. IN: *Saigon, Casbah, Rope, Home of the Brave, The Red Badge of Courage, Something to Live For, The Iron Mistress, So This Is Love, North to Alaska, Flaming Star*, more.

DICKINSON, ANGIE (S. Cal.) Costar. Onscreen from 1954. IN: *Lucky Me, Tennessee's Partner, China Gate, Cry Terror, Rio Bravo, The Bramble Bush, Ocean's 11, A Fever in the Blood, Rome Adventure, Captain Newman M.D., The Killers, The Chase, Point Blank, Sam Whiskey, Pretty Maids All in a Row, Big Bad Mama*, more.

DICKSON, DOROTHY (Eng.) Leading lady. She is in her 70s now (b. 1902) and retired. Onscreen from the teens. IN: *Money Mad, Channel Crossing, Danny Boy*, more.

DIERKOP, CHARLES (S. Cal.) Character. IN: *The Sweet Ride, Butch Cassidy and the Sundance Kid, The Thousand Plane Raid, Pound*, more.

DIETRICH, MARLENE (N.Y.) Star. Nominated for Best Actress Oscar in *Morocco*. Onscreen in Germany from 1923. IN: *The Tragedy of Love, Manon Lescaut, The Blue Angel*, more. Onscreen in America from 1930. IN: *Dishonored, Shanghai Express, Desire, The Garden of Allah, Destry Rides Again, Seven Sinners, Manpower, The Spoilers, Pittsburgh, Kismet, Golden Earrings, A Foreign Affair, Around the World in 80 Days, Witness for the Prosecution, Touch of Evil, Judgment at Nuremburg*, more.

DIFFRING, ANTON (Eng.) Support. Onscreen from 1950. IN: *State Secret, The Colditz Story, The Black Tent, Reach for the Sky, Lady of Vengeance, Fahrenheit 451, The Blue Max, Where Eagles Dare, The Beast Must Die, Dead Pigeon on Beethoven Street*, more.

DIGGS, JOHN (S. Cal.) Character. IN: *Corvette K-225*, more.

DIGNAM, BASIL (Eng.) Character. Onscreen from the '50s. IN: *Touch and Go, Brothers in Law, Room at the Top, The Risk, Victim, Walk in the Shadow, Laughter in the Dark, 10 Rillington Place*, more.

DIGNAM, MARK (Eng.) Character. Onscreen from the '50s. IN: *Murder in the Cathedral, High and Dry, Beau Brummell, Sink the Bismarck!, Sword of Lancelot, Hamlet*, more.

DILLER, PHYLLIS (S. Cal.) Star comedienne. Onscreen from 1961. IN: *Splendor in the Grass; Boy, Did I Get a Wrong Number!; Eight on the*

Lam, *The Fat Spy, Did You Hear the One About the Traveling Saleslady?, The Silent Treatment, The Sunshine Boys,* more.

DILLMAN, BRADFORD (S. Cal.) Leading man. Onscreen from 1958. IN: *A Certain Smile, In Love and War, Compulsion, Crack in the Mirror, Sanctuary, A Rage to Live, Sergeant Ryker, Jigsaw, The Bridge at Remagen, Escape from the Planet of the Apes, The Resurrection of Zachary Wheeler, The Iceman Cometh, The Way We Were, Chosen Survivors, 99 44/100% Dead, Gold, Bug,* more.

DIX, ROBERT (S. Cal.) Leading man. Son of Richard Dix. Onscreen from 1955. IN: *Interrupted Melody, Screaming Eagles, Thundering Jets, Young Jesse James, King of the Road, Blood of Dracula's Castle, Satan's Sadists, Five Bloody Graves,* more.

DIXON, GLENN (S. Cal.) Support. IN: *Untamed Youth, The Barefoot Executive,* more.

DIXON, IVAN (S. Cal.) Black support. Onscreen from 1957. IN: *Something of Value, Porgy and Bess, A Raisin in the Sun, Nothing But a Man, A Patch of Blue, Clay Pigeon,* more.

DIXON, JEAN (N.Y.) Often the blonde and appealingly witty society woman in comedies of the '30s (*Joy of Living, She Married Her Boss,* etc.), she is indeed a society woman in real life. Married since '36 to Manhattan businessman Edward S. Ely, she lives in a beautiful apartment on Fifth Avenue. Now entering her 80s (b. 1896), she acted only on the stage after leaving the screen, last appearing on Broadway in 1959's *The Gang's All Here.* Onscreen from 1934. IN: *Sadie McKee, Dynamite, My Man Godfrey, To Mary With Love, You Only Live Once; Swing High, Swing Low; Holiday,* more.

DIXON, MARCIA (N.Y.) Juvenile. Onscreen in the '70s. IN: *Klute, The Magic Garden of Stanley Sweetheart, Born to Win, The Possession of Joel Delaney, The Hot Rock, They Might Be Giants,* more.

DO QUI, ROBERT (S. Cal.) Black support. IN: *The Devil's Eight, Uptight, The Fortune Cookie, The Cincinnati Kid, The Man,* more.

DOBKIN, LARRY (S. Cal.) Character. Onscreen from 1949. IN: *Twelve O'Clock High, People Will Talk, Five Fingers, Above and Beyond, The Ten Commandments, Sweet Smell of Success, The Defiant Ones, Patton, Underground, The Midnight Man,* more.

DOBSON, JAMES (S. Cal.) Character. Onscreen from 1940. IN: *Those Were the Days,*

Boomerang, Flying Leathernecks, The Tanks Are Coming, I Dream of Jeannie, Jet Attack, Armored Command, Mutiny in Outer Space, The Undefeated, What's the Matter With Helen?, more.

DOBSON, TAMARA (S. Cal.) Black star. Onscreen in the '70s. IN: *Cleopatra Jones, Cleopatra Jones & The Casino of Gold,* more.

DOLAN, JOANN (N.Y.) Support. IN: *The Eve of St. Mark.*

DOLENZ, MICKEY (S. Cal.) Singer-comedian. IN: *Head.*

DOLL, DORA (Fr.) Support; former leading lady. Onscreen from the '50s. IN: *Pardon My French, Savage Triangle, The Young Lions, The Lovemaker, Grisbi, Any Number Can Win; Cool, Calm and Collected* (or, *Calmos*); more.

DOMERGUE, FAITH (S. Cal.) Howard Hughes had her under contract between her 16th and 25th years. And in '72, the year of the Clifford Irving "autobiography" of the reclusive billionaire, a New York publisher announced he would issue a book by Faith Domergue, *My Life with Howard Hughes.* The publisher's statement, published in *Variety,* heralded this as "the first time one of his ladies really talked about the intimate relationship she had" with Hughes. The book never appeared and, when checked, a representative of the publisher said, "We doubt that it ever will be." Twice recently, for the first time since '69, the raven-haired actress—now in her early 50s (b. 1925)—has costarred in movies: *So Evil My Sister* and *The House of Seven Corpses.* Previously married to and divorced from restaurateur Ted Stauffer and director Hugo Fregonese (by whom she has a grown son, John, and daughter, Diana), she has been married since '66 to agent Paul Cossa. They have homes in Beverly Hills and in Italy, where the actress spent many of her offscreen years, and live part of the year in each. Onscreen from 1946. IN: *Young Widow, Where Danger Lives, Vendetta, The Great Sioux Uprising, It Came from Beneath the Sea, The Atomic Man, Escort West, The Gamblers, Besieged, Legacy of Blood,* more.

DON, CARL (N.Y.) Character. IN: *Zotz!*

DONAHUE, ELINOR (S. Cal.) As a juvenile, billed Mary Eleanor Donahue, she entered movies in 1943 and appeared in *Mister Big, The Unfinished Dance, Three Daring Daughters,* among others. Today, long married to producer Harry Ackerman, and the mother of five, she rarely acts. Onscreen (as Elinor Donahue) in the '50s. IN: *Her First Romance, Love Is Better Than Ever, Girls' Town,* more.

DONAHUE, TROY (S. Cal.) Support; former juvenile lead. Onscreen from 1957. IN: *Tarnished Angels, Summer Love, This Happy Feeling, A Summer Place, Imitation of Life, Parrish, Susan Slade, Rome Adventure, Palm Springs Weekend, My Blood Runs Cold, Come Spy with Me, Seizure, Born to Kill; The Godfather, Part II; Cockfighter,* more.

DONALD, JAMES (Eng.) Leading man. Onscreen from 1941. IN: *In Which We Serve, The Way Ahead, Edward My Son, The Gay Lady, Cage of Gold, Brandy for the Parson, The Pickwick Papers, Glory at Sea, Beau Brummell, Lust for Life, The Bridge on the River Kwai, The Great Escape, King Rat, The Jokers, Conduct Unbecoming,* more.

DONAT, PETER (S. Cal.) Support. Onscreen in the '70s. IN: *My Old Man's Place; The Godfather, Part II; Russian Roulette, The Hindenburg,* more.

DONLAN, YOLANDE (Eng.) Leading lady. Onscreen from 1941. IN: *Turnabout, Mr. Drake's Duck, Penny Princess, Tarzan and the Lost Safari, Expresso Bongo, Jigsaw,* more.

DONNELL, JEFF (S. Cal.) Comic support. Onscreen from 1942. IN: *My Sister Eileen, Eadie Was a Lady, Power of the Whistler, Tars and Spars, Mr. District Attorney, Easy Living, The Fuller Brush Girl, Three Guys Named Mike, Skirts Ahoy!, Because You're Mine, So This Is Love, The Blue Gardenia, Gidget Goes to Rome, Tora!, Tora!, Tora!, Stand Up and Be Counted,* more.

DONNELLY, RUTH (N.Y.) Pretending there is no such thing as age—she was born in 1896—this grand comedienne, mistress of the wisecrack and double-take, goes sailing on. In the recent past she has costarred on tour in *No, No, Nanette* with Don Ameche and Evelyn Keyes, playing the hilarious maid role created on Broadway by Patsy Kelly. She hasn't made a movie since 1957's *The Way to the Gold.* From '32 until his death in '58 she was the wife of Basil de Guichard, onetime president of A.C. Spark Plug Co. and later a missile executive with Lockheed. Childless, she lives alone, and between engagements has been working on her autobiography, *Tripping Along,* and writing songs. Her published patriotic peace-song "Hi There, Everybody!" was recently performed at a memorial for John Philip Sousa at Damrosch Park in New York's Lincoln Center. "This song has become a mission with me," the actress says, "as I feel it would be of great help in lifting up the morale of the country." Though she would like to do movies still, she has turned down several roles. "They were unsuitable to my talents," she says. "I have the gift of laughter and have worked hard all of my life to be an actress worthy of the name. The vulgar trend of today's movies is not to my liking. So, unless something of value comes along, where I can continue to uplift and bring some cheer, I prefer to devote myself to other interests." A religious woman, she lives her life with the thought "Never a 'has-been'—but an always 'will be.' The illumined walk without fear—by Grace." On a lighthearted note, when she recently moved into a well-known residential hotel for women, she cracked to pal Patsy Kelly, "We inmates call it 'Chock Full of Nuts'!'" That sounds like the movies' Ruth Donnelly. Onscreen from 1927. IN: *Rubber Heels, The Spider, Make Me a Star, 42nd Street, Goodbye Again, Hands Across the Table, Metropolitan, Mr. Deeds Goes to Town, Cain and Mabel, Portia on Trial, Holiday, Affairs of Annabel, A Slight Case of Murder, Mr. Smith Goes to Washington, Model Wife, Bells of St. Mary's, Little Miss Broadway, Fighting Father Dunne, The Snake Pit, Where the Sidewalk Ends, The Secret of Convict Lake, Autumn Leaves,* more.

DONNER, ROBERT (S. Cal.) Character. IN: *Cool Hand Luke, The Private Navy of Sgt. O'-Farrell, Skidoo, The Undefeated, Chisum, Rio Lobo, Vanishing Point,* more.

DONOVAN (Ire.) Singer-actor. Onscreen from 1967. IN: *Don't Look Back, Festival, Superstars in Film Concert,* more.

DONOVAN, KING (S. Cal.) Character. Onscreen from 1948. IN: *The Man from Texas, Alias Nick Beal, Angels in the Outfield, The Merry Andrew, Forever Female, Broken Lance, Invasion of the Body Snatchers, The Birds and the Bees, The Defiant Ones, The Thrill of It All,* more.

DOOHAN, JAMES (S. Cal.) Support. IN: *The Wheeler Dealers, The Satan Bug, Bus Riley's Back in Town, Pretty Maids All in a Row,* more.

DOOLEY, RAE (R.I.) The Scottish-born actress-comedienne was onscreen just once, in 1931's *Honeymoon Lane* with her late husband actor-producer-director Eddie Dowling. She has a daughter, Mary; her son, John, who was a *Time* magazine reporter, was killed in a plane crash in South America several years ago. In her late 70s now, the actress lives in retirement in Saylesville.

DORAN, ANN (S. Cal.) Character. Onscreen from 1936. IN: *Little Red Schoolhouse, Ring Around the Moon, You Can't Take It With You, Blind Alibi,* numerous "Three Stooges" two-reelers, *Penny Serenade, Air Force, I Love a Soldier, Pride of the Marines, Roughly Speaking, The Strange Love of Martha Ivers, Magic*

Town, My Dog Rusty, Beyond the Forest, No Sad Songs for Me, The High and the Mighty, Rebel Without a Cause, The Female Animal, Where Love Has Gone, Topaz, There Was a Crooked Man, The Hired Hand, more.

DORN, DOLORES (S. Cal.) Leading lady. Onscreen from 1954. IN: *The Bounty Hunter, Phantom of the Rue Morgue, Uncle Vanya, Underworld U.S.A., 13 West Street, Truck Stop Women,* more.

DORNE, SANDRA (Eng.) Support. Onscreen from 1945. IN: *Happy Go Lovely, The Clouded Yellow, The Beggars' Opera, The Yellow Balloon, The Iron Petticoat, Orders to Kill, The Secret Door,* more.

DORR, LESTER (S. Cal.) In his 70s, this veteran character actor remains highly active in TV and movies. Onscreen from 1931. IN: *Riders of the Purple Sage, Criminals of the Air, The Main Event,* more.

DORS, DIANA (Eng.) Yesteryear's blonde, bikini-clad bombshell remains blonde. The shape has changed. A guess at her weight, which she does not divulge, would be 175 pounds. In her 40s (b. 1931), she still stars. She was opposite Jack Palance in '74 in *Craze,* about which *The Hollywood Reporter* critic wrote: "Diana Dors pulls humor and credibility from her role as an over-the-hill chippie." In '75 she costarred in *The Amorous Milkman* with Alan Lake, her decade-younger husband, and the father of her youngest son, Jason (b. 1969). Her husband made headlines in '70 when he was sent to jail to serve an 18-month sentence for seriously wounding a man in a tavern brawl. And, in '72, after his release, the actress—once denounced by the Archbishop of Canterbury as a wayward hussy—made additional headlines. She joined a campaign aimed at allowing prisoners to have sexual intercourse with their wives in jail. Married twice previously, she has two teenage sons, Mark and Gary, by TV emcee Richard Dawson (her second husband), who live with their father in Hollywood. Onscreen from 1946. IN: *The Shop at Sly Corner, Oliver Twist, The Saint's Girl Friday, A Kid for Two Farthings, I Married a Woman, An Alligator Named Daisy; Tread Softly, Stranger; Ladies' Day, Berserk, Danger Route, Hammerhead, Baby Love, Deep End, Hannie Caulder,* more.

D'ORSAY, FIFI (S. Cal.) Leading lady. Onscreen from 1929. IN: *They Had to See Paris, Three French Girls, The Life of Jimmy Dolan, Going Hollywood, Three Legionnaires, Submarine Base, The Gangster, What a Way to Go!, The Art of Love, Assignment to Kill,* more. In 1971, in her 70s, she costarred on-

stage in the musical *Follies,* making her Broadway debut.

DOTRICE, KAREN (Eng.) Juvenile. Onscreen from 1963. IN: *The Three Loves of Thomasina, Mary Poppins, The Gnome-Mobile,* more. Now in her 20s (b. 1955), she has not acted for several years.

DOTRICE, MICHELE (Eng.) Leading lady. Onscreen in the '70s. IN: *And Soon the Darkness, The Blood on Satan's Claw,* more.

DOTRICE, ROY (Eng.) Character. Onscreen from 1965. IN: *The Heroes of Telemark, Lock Up Your Daughters, Nicholas and Alexandra, One of Those Things,* more.

DOUCETTE, JOHN (S. Cal.) Character. Onscreen from 1947. IN: *Road to the Big House, Canon City, Criss Cross, Broken Arrow, Winchester 73, The Breaking Point, Warpath, Strangers on a Train, Only the Valiant, High Noon, Beachhead, The Last Time I Saw Paris, The Maverick Queen, The Big Land, Cleopatra, The Sons of Katie Elder, True Grit, Patton, Big Jake, One More Train to Rob,* more.

DOUGLAS, DIANA (S. Cal.) Support. Onscreen from 1948. IN: *Sign of the Ram, House of Strangers, The Whistle at Eaton Falls, Monsoon, The Indian Fighter,* more.

DOUGLAS, DONNA (S. Cal.) Leading lady. Onscreen from the '50s. IN: *Career, Li'l Abner, Lover Come Back, Frankie and Johnny.* Later popular in the TV series *The Beverly Hillbillies,* she has been inactive of late.

DOUGLAS, GORDON (S. Cal.) From being one of the most popular juveniles in the Hal Roach stock company, he went on to become a prop man, gag man, film editor, assistant director, and, finally, director—his first effort, an "Our Gang" titled *Bored of Education,* winning an Academy Award. Years later, now in his 60s (b. 1909), and an erect, athletic man with rather tough good looks and a rasping voice, he remains one of Hollywood's busiest directors. Among his many credits, *Kiss Tomorrow Goodbye, Tony Rome, Lady in Cement,* and *The Detective.* Onscreen in the '20s. IN: "The Boy Friends" two-reelers, more.

DOUGLAS, JAMES (S. Cal.) Leading man. Onscreen from 1957. IN: *Time Limit, G.I. Blues, A Thunder of Drums, Sweet Bird of Youth.* Later popular in the TV series *Peyton Place,* he has since starred in a TV soap opera.

DOUGLAS, JOSEPHINE (Eng.) Leading lady. Onscreen from the '50s. IN: *Angels One Five,*

Lady in the Fog, Will Any Gentlemen . . . ?, Three Cornered Fate, more.

DOUGLAS, KIRK (S. Cal.) Star. Nominated for Best Actor Oscar in *Champion, The Bad and the Beautiful, Lust for Life.* Onscreen from 1946. IN: *The Strange Love of Martha Ivers, I Walk Alone, Mourning Becomes Electra, Letter to Three Wives, The Glass Menagerie, Ace in the Hole, Detective Story, The Big Sky, Ulysses, Gunfight at the O.K. Corral, Paths of Glory, Spartacus, Lonely Are the Brave, Seven Days in May, The Heroes of Telemark, Is Paris Burning?, The Way West, The Brotherhood, The Arrangement, There Was a Crooked Man, Once Is Not Enough, Posse,* more.

DOUGLAS, MARIAN (S. Cal.) (See Ena Gregory.)

DOUGLAS, MELVYN (Vt.) Star/character. Won Best Supporting Actor Oscar in *Hud.* Nominated for Best Actor Oscar in *I Never Sang for My Father.* Not even a heart attack suffered in '73 has slowed down this sophisticated leading man of yesteryear, now in his 70s (b. 1901), who turned character actor two decades back. Making fewer big-screen movies now, he works constantly in TV-movies (*Death Squad, The Champions, The Statesman,* in which he played elderly Benjamin Franklin in the last of four episodes on this man of history). And, in '75, he costarred with Jean Arthur (his *Too Many Husbands* vis-a-vis) in the play *First Monday in October.* Scheduled for an extensive tour before its Broadway debut, the show opened in Ohio and Miss Arthur withdrew from the cast. The actor made the first of his 75 movies, *Tonight or Never,* with Gloria Swanson in a role that had been played on Broadway by actress Helen Gahagan. That same year ('31), Miss Gahagan became—and remains—Mrs. Douglas. They live in Fairlee, Vt., on Lake Morey, in a big, bright-yellow, turn-of-the-century New England house with a vast circular porch and a breath-taking view. It is, his wife laughs, "so ugly it's beautiful. My family bought it in 1911. We're a whole compound here now. We're all relatives. Five houses." The other houses are occupied by Mrs. Douglas' younger brother, the actor's son Gregory (by a previous marriage), and the Douglases' two children, Peter and Mary. This second generation is, respectively, a painter, a psychotherapist, and a teacher. There are also six Douglas grandchildren—four boys, two girls. The actor and his wife also have an apartment in Manhattan, overlooking the Hudson, but their trips to New York are infrequent now. When they do travel, it is usually to Hollywood (their home for many years) for his work, or to Cuernavaca or Taxco for vacations. Melvyn Douglas says

now of old Hollywood: "I came to hate Hollywood so much that I enlisted in the Army again to get out of town. When I came out in 1945, I decided to get out of pictures." He was discharged as a major after three years' service in the China-Burma-India theatre. Though he has made 20 movies since, he has never again lived in Hollywood, and the emphasis in his career has been on the stage and television. Of his early movies, he insists, "I never watch any of them on the late show because they fill me with horror." And of his many famous colleagues at MGM, Melvyn Douglas says forthrightly, "Myrna Loy is the only one from that period I'd really still enjoy seeing today as a friend." Onscreen from 1931. IN: *As You Desire Me, Counsellor-at-Law; Mary Burns, Fugitive; She Married Her Boss, The Lone Wolf Returns, Theodora Goes Wild, I Met Him in Paris, Captains Courageous, The Shining Hour, That Certain Age, Ninotchka, Third Finger Left Hand, We Were Dancing, Two-Faced Woman, They All Kissed the Bride, Mr. Blandings Builds His Dream House, The Great Sinner, Inherit the Wind, The Best Man, The Americanization of Emily, Hotel, The Strangers, The Candidate, One Is a Lonely Number,* more.

DOUGLAS, MICHAEL (S. Cal.) Leading man. Son of Diana and Kirk Douglas. Onscreen from 1969. IN: *Where's Jack?; Hail, Hero!; Adam at 6 A.M., Summertree,* more.

DOUGLAS, MIKE (Pa.) TV emcee-singer. In 1950 he sang the role of Prince Charming in the Disney cartoon *Cinderella.* Onscreen as an actor in '76. IN: *'Gator.*

DOUGLAS, ROBERT (S. Cal.) Warners' suave, toupeed British villain of the '40s and '50s hasn't acted in a movie since 1959's *The Young Philadelphians.* Lately, though, he has appeared several times on TV— smooth as ever and generally villainous—in *The Woman I Love* (story of the Windsors) and episodes of *Columbo* and *Medical Center.* But he has not lacked for employment. Now in his 60s (b. 1910), he has, since 1961, directed more than 200 television shows. A bit earlier, he also directed one movie, *Night Train to Paris,* starring Leslie Nielsen, and several Broadway plays: *The Ponder Heart, Uncle Willie,* and *The Loud Red Patrick* among them. He does not, he says, greatly miss acting. Previously married to and divorced from British actress Dorothy Hyson (1935–43), he lives in Beverly Hills with his wife of more than three decades, the former Sue Weldon, and is, by her, the father of two grown children—Lucinda and Giles. Onscreen in England from 1931. IN: *P.C. Josser, Many Waters, The Blarney Stone, Over the Moon,* more. Onscreen in America from 1948. IN: *The Decision* of *Christopher Blake, The Adventures of Don Juan, The Fountainhead, The Buccaneer's Girl, The Flame and the Arrow, Kim, Thunder on the Hill, At Sword's Point, The Prisoner of Zenda, The Desert Rats, Saskatchewan, The Virgin Queen; Good Morning, Miss Dove; Helen of Troy,* more.

DOUGLAS, SHARON (S. Cal.) Popular in teen-age roles in the '40s, she is, in her early 50s, most active in television commercials now. IN: *A Gentleman After Dark. Our Hearts Were Growing Up,* more.

DOURIF, BRAD (N.Y.) Young character. Support. Nominated for Best Supporting Actor Oscar in *One Flew Over the Cuckoo's Nest.*

DOVE, BILLIE (S. Cal.) No matter that she is now in her 70s (b. 1904 most references say, but some still insist on 1900), this star is still a fascinatingly beautiful woman. And a positive, forward-looking one. The tell-all books about Howard Hughes that invariably recap their flaming love affair—even the one by his long-time associate Noah Dietrich, which really laid it on the line—rate no more than a shrug from her. That was yesterday. After that came her long marriage to millionaire Robert Kenaston, which, beginning in '33, ended in divorce in '71. (She had earlier been divorced from director Irwin Willat.) More recently came reports she would marry architect John Miller. Palm Springs was her home for years but today she lives on her estate in the Pacific Palisades. By Kenaston, the actress has two grown children of whom she is inordinately proud—a son, in business, and a daughter, Gail Kenaston Bertoya. Gail, besides currently following in her mother's acting footsteps, is an entrepreneur of considerable talents. She has operated a Beverly Hills shop, Bertoya Ltd. and, a few months back, on the old Columbia Studios lot (now vacated), she staged "The Greatest Antique Auction Show of the Century," which just about lived up to its billing. For the show, among other things, she had shipped intact from London a complete English pub. Turning out for both the opening of the shop and the antiques show was Gail's publicity-shy, but proud, mother—making her first public appearances in a decade. Last starred on the screen in 1932's *Blondie of the Follies,* and last seen onscreen in a fleeting appearance as a nurse in *Diamond Head* (a friendship gesture to the producer), Billie Dove is disinclined to feel she gave up much when she left the movies. Admirers still exist, though, who maintain that *they* did. Onscreen from 1922. IN: *Polly of the Follies, The Air Mail, The Light of the Western Stars, The*

Lucky Horseshoe, The Black Pirate, Kid Boots, Sensation Seekers, The Stolen Bride, American Beauty, The Heart of a Follies Girl, The Night Watch, A Notorious Affair, Sweethearts and Wives, The Lady Who Dared, Cock of the Air, more.

DOW, MAREE (N.Y.) Support. IN: *Pigeons.*

DOW, PEGGY (Okla.) Universal-International shortened the name of its clean-scrubbed, greatly talented young star from Louisiana to Dow, from Varnadow. In '51, after leads in nine pictures in three years, she lengthened it again—to Mrs. Walter Helmerich III. She wears it proudly still, as the wife of this wealthy Tulsa oil man, and as the mother of their five sons. In her late 40s now (b. 1928), she looks scarcely older than when she first arrived on the Universal lot, and remains too busy caring for her family and managing an active social life to give a thought to "days that were." Onscreen from 1949. IN: *Undertow, Woman in Hiding, Harvey, Shakedown, The Sleeping City, Bright Victory, I Want You, Reunion in Reno, You Never Can Tell.*

DOWD, HARRISON (N.Y.) Character. IN: *When New York Sleeps.*

DOWD, KAYE (N.Y.) Support. IN: *An Angel Comes to Brooklyn.*

DOWD, M'EL (N.Y.) Supporting actress. IN: *The Wrong Man, 300 Year Weekend,* more.

DOWLING, DORIS (S. Cal.) Support. Active lately on TV. Onscreen from 1945. IN: *The Lost Weekend, The Blue Dahlia, The Crimson Key, Bitter Rice, The Running Target, Party Chasers, Wink of An Eye, Birds Do It,* more.

DOWNEY, MORTON (Conn.) In this decade, the musical star has been attending weddings—his own (in '70) to socialite Ann Van Gerbig, and that of his granddaughter, Melissa Ellen Downey (in '73), to John Loesser, son of the late Broadway musical composer Frank Loesser. Onscreen 1929–30. IN: *Mother's Boy, Syncopation, Lucky in Love, The Devil's Holiday.* Later ('44) guested in *Ghost Catchers.*

DOWNS, JOHNNY (S. Cal.) Hollywood's one-time favorite singing-tap dancing collegian (he never really went to college; no time) is in his 60s now (b. 1913), the father of five, and a grandfather. But time's passage has changed him little. He's still lean, dapper, and light-hearted. For several recent years he has sold residential income property for Strand-Crown Real Estate in Coronado, Calif., adjacent to San Diego. Coronado has always been a part of his life. When he was eight his Navy officer-father settled the family there a while. One of his first adult movies, after "Our Gang" and many young juvenile leads, was *Coronado*, made partially on location there. Johnny and his brood moved there in '54 and stayed. Professionally, he learned long ago to swim with the tide. In the mid-40s, as the steam went out of B-movie musicals, which had become his chief province, Johnny Downs turned first to Broadway, where he starred in *Are You With It?* and *Hold It*, then performed in nightclubs and on "live" TV. Back in L.A., finding only secondary parts in a few pix such as 1953's *Cruising Down the River*, he hosted an afternoon local TV show. Then a friend, starting up a new TV station in Tijuana, Mexico (just across the California border), offered him the announcer's spot. "The pay wasn't much but at least it was steady," says Johnny, "and it's a decision I've never regretted." Fifteen months later came the move to Coronado as Johnny was offered the star spot on a new afternoon children's show, *The Magic Key*, on San Diego's KOGO-TV. In slipover sweater, strawhat, and nonerasable smile, he was phenomenally successful—the show winning many awards, lasting 17 years. Most recently Johnny has been working on the format for a new one. He and nonpro wife, June (married well over three decades), spend much time with their children—Mary, Claudia and John (they're married but nearby), and Maureen and Mollie, who still live at home. A while back, he and his two youngest, tennis buffs all, walked off with both the Coronado Father-Daughter and Mixed Doubles championship trophies. Active in church affairs (a devout, lifelong Catholic), Johnny participates in charity programs (has been a leading promoter of the Muscular Dystrophy Drive for a decade), entertains at local hospitals, and makes his vegetable garden grow. He has been so long a friendly, familiar face in the San Diego community, that, when he starred in a local stage production of *The Wizard of Oz* and, as the Tin Man, sang "If I Only Had a Heart," one citizen observed: "Wrong song for a right guy." Onscreen in the '20s in "Our Gang." Onscreen in talkies from 1934. IN: *Babes in Toyland, So Red the Rose, College Scandal, Pigskin Parade, College Holiday, The Plainsman, Clarence, Hold That Coed, Hawaiian Nights; I Can't Give You Anything But Love, Baby; A Child Is Born, Adam Had Four Sons, Moonlight in Hawaii, The Mad Monster, Rhapsody in Blue, The Kid from Brooklyn, Square Dance Jubilee, Column South*, more.

DOYLE, DAVID (S. Cal.) Character. Onscreen from 1963. IN: *Act One, No Way to Treat a Lady, Paper Lion, The Pursuit of Happiness, A New Leaf, Making It, Who Killed Mary What's'ername?*, more.

DOYLE, MIMI (S. Cal.) Support. IN: *Mister Roberts, The Baby Maker*, more.

DRAKE, ALFRED (N.Y.) Costar singer-actor. Onscreen from 1946. IN: *Tars and Spars, Strange Victory, Hamlet* (the '64 filmed stage play with Richard Burton). He has starred in numerous Broadway musicals, most notably in *Kiss Me, Kate*.

DRAKE, BETSY (S. Cal.) Once married to Cary Grant (1949-62)—and still friendly with him—she gave up movie acting after 1965's *Clarence, the Cross-Eyed Lion*. Now in her 50s (b. 1923), she has not married again, but she has created two new careers for herself. One is that of novelist. Her first book, *Children, You Are Very Young*, appeared in '71 to a warm critical reception, and the author's name on the jacket was revealing: Betsy Drake Grant. (And she still signs notes to friends: "Betsy G.") Her second full-time career is that of a psychodrama therapist. For the past decade she has been director of this field of research at UCLA Neuropsychiatric Institute. In addition, she has done similar work at the Los Angeles' Mount Sinai Hospital and Central City Community Mental Health Center, while also teaching psychodrama at Pepperdine College and UCLA Extension. "I have worked mostly with psychotics," she says, "mostly adolescents of fourteen and up and adults, in a group of ten to twelve people... I am fascinated by the poetry in the thinking of some schizophrenic patients, which is very like that of children . . . if you can really make an attempt to understand what the patients are trying to say, then everything opens up. In society in general, and even among some doctors and nurses in mental hospitals, there is so much fear, so much dislike of this kind of 'different, crazy talk' that no communication is possible." Her novel, which grew out of this work, took her three years. "I write in the mornings, work in the hospital in the afternoons, and teach at night," she says. She has recently been working on another novel and a nonfiction book about her experiences as a therapist. Little changed in looks—same rosy complexion, same soft hairdo, though with a hint of gray—she says this of today's motion pictures: "I think movies are better than ever. I wish I were young and making movies now." Onscreen from 1948. IN: *Every Girl Should Be Married, Dancing in the Dark, Pretty Baby, The Second Woman, Room for One More, Will Success Spoil Rock Hunter?, Intent to Kill, Next to No Time.*

DRAKE, CHARLES (S. Cal.) In movies more than 35 years, he still, in his 60s (b. 1914), has curly blond hair and looks fully ten years older than at his career's beginning. One of his favorite pix was *Now, Voyager* with Bette Davis and Claude Rains. In '73 he was reunited with Davis in an "ABC Suspense Movie," *Scream, Pretty Peggy*, and also in the cast was Jessica Rains—daughter of Claude. Still in an occasional movie, he most often guests on TV: *Marcus Welby, Harry O, The Rookies*, etc. Onscreen from 1941. IN: *I Wanted Wings, The Maltese Falcon, The Male Animal, The Gay Sisters, Mr. Skeffington, Conflict, You Came Along, Winchester 73, Little Egypt, Bonzo Goes to College, Female on the Beach, Jeanne Eagels, Tammy Tell Me True, Valley of the Dolls, The Counterfeit Killer, The Swimmer*, more.

DRAKE, DONA (S. Cal.) Retired, she has long been married to the Hollywood fashion designer Travilla. Onscreen from 1941. IN: *Louisiana Purchase, Star-Spangled Rhythm, Let's Face It, Without Reservations, Hot Rhythm, Another Part of the Forest, The Girl from Jones Beach, Beyond the Forest, Kansas City Confidential, Down Laredo Way*, more, including 1954's *Princess of the Nile*, her last.

DRAKE, DOROTHY (S. Cal.) A 1934 Wampas Baby Star, she is in her early 60s now, has three children by the late screenwriter Cyril Hume (d. 1966), and lives in retirement on a ranch near Los Angeles.

DRAKE, FABIA (Eng.) Character. Onscreen from the '30s. IN: *Meet Mr. Penny, White Corridors, London Belongs to Me, The Hour of Thirteen, Isn't Life Wonderful, All for Mary, My Wife's Family, A Nice Girl Like Me*, more.

DRAKE, FRANCES (S. Cal.) Last onscreen in 1942's *The Affairs of Martha* (a.k.a. *Once Upon a Thursday*), she is now in her late 60s (b. 1908), has been married since 1939 to the Hon. Cecil John Arthur Howard, son of the Earl of Suffolk of England, and lives—most socially—in Beverly Hills. Onscreen from 1934. IN: *Bolero, Ladies Should Listen, Les Miserables, The Invisible Ray, I'd Give My Life, Midnight Taxi, You Can't Have Everything, She Married an Artist, The Lone Wolf in Paris, It's a Wonderful World, I Take This Woman*, more.

DRAKE, PAULINE (S. Cal.) Character. IN: *Jam Session, Willard*, more.

DRAKE, TOM (S. Cal.) In his 50s (b. 1918), MGM's once-popular juvenile lead costars occasionally in such movies as *The Spectre of Edgar Allan Poe* and regularly plays character roles on TV. He has been seen in *Banacek*,

Night Stalker, etc., and was especially effective as a drunken ex-cop in a *Police Story* episode. Married to and divorced from singer-actress Christopher Curtis in the '40s, he has remained single since. But, at least twice, he and Jeannette Mazurki, former wife of actor Mike Mazurki, who have been steadily together for years, have announced their engagement. Onscreen from 1944. IN: *The White Cliffs of Dover, Two Girls and a Sailor, Marriage Is a Private Affair, Meet Me in St. Louis, Mrs. Parkington, The Green Years, The Courage of Lassie, Cass Timberlane, Words and Music, Mr. Belvedere Goes to College, Sangaree, Raintree County, The Bramble Bush, The Singing Nun, Warkill*, more.

DRAPER, PAUL (Pa.) Now a Professor of Liberal Arts at Carnegie Tech, and in his 60s (b. 1909), the inimitable tap dancer was reunited—for a single performance—with his oldtime partner, harmonica virtuoso Larry Adler, at New York's Carnegie Hall in June '75. It was the first time they had appeared together in 27 years. The *New York Times* critic said: "Mr. Draper's dancing remains impeccably musical and—at age 66—impressively limber . . . (He) seemed barely to be touching the floor at times . . . One thinks, naturally, of Astaire or Bolger when Mr. Draper is in full flight, but his style is so intense and serious that comparisons are not really to the point." Onscreen from 1936. IN: *Colleen, The Time of Your Life*.

DRESDEL, SONIA (Eng.) Character. Onscreen from the '40s. IN: *The Fallen Idol, The Clouded Yellow, The Trials of Oscar Wilde, Secret Tent, Lady Caroline Lamb*, more.

DREW, DAVID (N.Y.) Support. IN: *Fun and Games, Some of My Best Friends Are . . ., The Long Afternoon*, more.

DREW, ELLEN (S. Cal.) Married since '71 to James Edward Herbert, a retired Motorola corporation officer, and still a tanned, beautiful woman in her early 60s (b. 1915), Ellen lives near Palm Springs and only rarely visits Hollywood. Her three previous marriages, all of which ended in divorce, were to movie makeup man Fred Wallace (they have a grown son, David), writer-producer Sy Bartlett, and socialite William T. Walker. Though she continued to act on TV until '60, Ellen has not made a movie since 1957's *The Outlaw's Son* with Dane Clark, and there is only the remotest chance she will ever act again. Onscreen from 1935. IN: *Rhythm on the Range, Sing You Sinners, If I Were King, Buck Benny Rides Again, Christmas in July, Reaching for the Sun, The Parson of Panamint, The Remarkable Andrew, My Favorite Spy, Dark Mountain, Isle of the Dead,*

The Crime Doctor's Manhunt, Johnny O'Clock, Stars in My Crown, The Baron of Arizona, more.

DREW, GENE (S. Cal.) Character. IN: *Truck Stop Women,* more.

DREW, ROBERT J. (N.Y.) Character. IN: *Pretty Boy Floyd,* more.

DREYFUSS, RICHARD (S. Cal.) Costar. Onscreen from 1967. IN: *The Graduate, Valley of the Dolls, American Graffiti, Dillinger, The Second Coming of Suzanne, The Apprenticeship of Duddy Kravitz, Jaws, Inserts,* more.

DRISCOLL, PATRICIA (Eng.) Leading lady. Onscreen from the '60s. IN: *Timeslip, The Wackiest Ship in the Army, Charley Moon,* more.

DRIVAS, ROBERT (S. Cal.) Leading man. Onscreen from 1968. IN: *The Illustrated Man, Where It's At, Cool Hand Luke, True Grit, Road Movie,* more.

DRU, JOANNE (S. Cal.) Leading lady; retired. Onscreen from 1946. IN: *Abie's Irish Rose, Red River, She Wore a Yellow Ribbon, All the King's Men, Wagonmaster, 711 Ocean Drive, The Pride of St. Louis, Duffy of San Quentin, Hell on Frisco Bay, Sincerely Yours, The Warriors, The Light in the Forest, The Wild and the Innocent, Sylvia,* more.

DRUMMOND, ALICE (N.Y.) Support. IN: *Where's Poppa?, Man on a Swing,* more.

DRURY, JAMES (S. Cal.) Costar. Onscreen from 1955. IN: *The Tender Trap, Love Me Tender, Good Day for a Hanging, Pollyanna, Ten Who Dared, Ride the High Country, Third of a Man, The Young Warriors, Backtrack,* more.

DUBBINS, DON (S. Cal.) Support. Onscreen from 1953. IN: *From Here to Eternity, Tribute to a Bad Man, The D I, The Prize, The Illustrated Man,* more.

DUCHIN, PETER (N.Y.) Pianist-actor. IN: *The World of Henry Orient.*

DUDLEY, DORIS (Tex.) As a dramatic actress, this blonde was a powerhouse; today, in her 60s, still blonde and living in Dallas, she remains a dynamo as a most successful developer and builder of homes. Twice married and divorced, and a grandmother, she has two sons— "Skipper" Dudley, who has lived in Honolulu for years and is a free-lance writer using the pen name Theodore Dudley Curtis, and Jackie

"Butch" Jenkins (see below). Giving up her acting career in 1950, she moved with her sons upcoast toward San Francisco and lived there before settling in Dallas in '54. From a ceramic tile company has sprung the "Doris Dudley Jenkins" homes empire that has made her a very rich woman. Onscreen from 1936. IN: *A Woman Rebels, The Moon and Sixpence, The Secret Fury,* more.

DUDLEY-WARD, PENELOPE (Eng.) Leading lady; retired. Onscreen from 1935. IN: *Escape Me Never, I Stand Condemned, Major Barbara,* more.

DUERING, CARL (Eng.) Support. Onscreen from the '50s. IN: *The Red Beret, Beautiful Stranger, The Divided Heart, The Colditz Story, Arabesque, Duffy,* more.

DUFF, HOWARD (S. Cal.) Costar. Onscreen from 1947. IN: *Brute Force, All My Sons, Naked City, Red Canyon, Johnny Stool Pigeon, Lady from Texas, Private Hell No. 36, Blackjack Ketchum—Desperado, Broken Star, While the City Sleeps, War Gods of Babylon, Panic in the City,* more.

DUGGAN, ANDREW (S. Cal.) Character. Onscreen from 1956. IN: *Patterns, Three Brave Men, Westbound, Merrill's Marauders, Palm Springs Weekend, Seven Days in May, The Glory Guys, Skin Game, It's Alive, The Bears and I,* more.

DUKAKIS, OLYMPIA (N.Y.) Character. Onscreen from 1969. IN: *John and Mary, Made for Each Other,* more.

DUKAS, JAMES (N.Y.) Character. IN: *The Great St. Louis Bank Robbery,* more.

DUKE, PATTY (S. Cal.) Former juvenile/now costar. Won Best Supporting Actress Oscar in *The Miracle Worker.* Onscreen from 1958. IN: *The Goddess, Country Music Holiday, Happy Anniversary, 4-D Man, Billie, Valley of the Dolls; Me, Natalie; You'll Like My Mother,* more. Since her marriage to actor John Astin she has been billed Patty Duke Astin.

DULLEA, KEIR (Can.) Leading man. Onscreen from 1961. IN: *The Hoodlum Priest, David and Lisa, Bunny Lake Is Missing, Madame X, The Fox, 2001: A Space Odyssey, De Sade, Paul and Michelle, Black Christmas,* more.

DUMONT, PAUL (N.Y.) Support. IN: *The Lost Command,* more.

DUNA, STEFFI (S. Cal.) After 1940's *The Girl from Havana,* this Hungarian-born actress married its leading man, Dennis O'Keefe, left the movies, and stayed most happily married to him until his death in '68. She quit because her attitude toward marriage was totally European. As O'Keefe once explained with pride and affection: "Keep the husband well-fed, and the house beautifully manicured, and devote all your time and energy to the home—this was the attitude of my Hungarian idiot. So that's what she became—the perfect wife, European style. She never stopped waiting on me. She refused to hire any help, because she wanted to do everything herself." Today, as Steffi O'Keefe, her son and daughter grown and on their own, she still devotes herself to homes—selling them to others, working as a realtor for Stan Herman & Assoc. of Beverly Hills—and says she loves every minute of her new career. She last acted in a minor role in one episode of the departed *Nancy* TV series several seasons ago, but admits no desire to continue as an actress. Onscreen in England in 1931. IN: *The Iron Stair, The Indiscretions of Love.* Onscreen in America from 1934. IN: *Man of Two Worlds, La Cucaracha, One New York Night, Anthony Adverse, Hi Gaucho!, Panama Lady, The Magnificent Fraud, Law of the Pampas, Beasts of Berlin, The Marines Fly High, Waterloo Bridge, Phantom Raiders, The Great McGinty,* more.

DUNAWAY, FAYE (N.Y.) Star. Nominated for Best Actress Oscar in *Chinatown.* Onscreen from 1966. IN: *The Happening, Hurry Sundown, Bonnie and Clyde, The Thomas Crown Affair, The Arrangement, Little Big Man, Puzzle of a Downfall Child, The Extraordinary Seaman, Doc, The Deadly Trap, The Three Musketeers, The Towering Inferno, The Four Musketeers, Three Days of the Condor,* more.

DUNBAR, DIXIE (Fla.) "Cute as a button," she was and— in her 60s—is. *Alexander's Ragtime Band* was the last of her dozen movies at 20th Century-Fox. But in the '50s she was "anonymously famous" on TV as the dancing girl within the Old Gold pack. She's completely out of show business now, but her husband will have you know she's "still got pretty legs." He is Miami Beach millionaire Jack L. King. The actress is not known now as Dixie, but as Christina, or "Chris." And she is president of her Miami Beach church. Onscreen from 1934. IN: *George White's Scandals, King of Burlesque, Girls' Dormitory; Sing, Baby, Sing; Pigskin Parade, One in a Million, Life Begins at College, Rebecca of Sunnybrook Farm, Walking Down Broadway,* more.

DUNCAN, ANDREW (S. Cal.) Support. IN: *The Rain People, Loving, Love Story, The Crazy World of Julius Vrooder,* more.

DUNCAN, ANGUS (S. Cal.) Leading man. IN: *Simon, King of the Witches; How to Seduce a Woman,* more.

DUNCAN, ARCHIE (Eng.) Character. Onscreen from the '40s. IN: *The Bad Lord Byron, The Brave Don't Cry, Rob Roy, Trouble in the Glen, Saint Joan, John Paul Jones, Sword of Lancelot, Ring of Bright Water, The Man Outside,* more.

DUNCAN, MARY (Eng.) The former leading lady is in her 70s now (b. 1903) and retired. Onscreen from 1927. IN: *Very Confidential, Soft Living, 4 Devils, The River, Kismet, The Boudoir Diplomat, Men Call It Love, Five and Ten, State's Attorney, Thirteen Women, The Phantom of Crestwood,* more, including 1933's *Morning Glory,* her last.

DUNCAN, SANDY (S. Cal.) Comic leading lady. Onscreen in the '70s. IN: *The $1,000,000 Duck, Star-Spangled Girl.*

DUNCAN, TODD (D.C.) The singer-actor last starred on Broadway in *Lost in the Stars* ('49). He received his Ph.D. in Music at Howard University in '58. Today, in his 70s (b. 1903), he lives in the North West section of Washington with his wife (since '34), Gladys, and still does concerts. IN: *Syncopation, Unchained.*

DUNCAN, VIVIAN (N. Cal.) Still occasionally active in nightclubs and still attractively blonde, in her 70s (b. 1899), she lives just south of San Francisco in Burlingame with her husband, Frank Herman, a retired building contractor. Married three decades, they have no children. By previous husband, actor Nils Asther, she has one daughter, Evelyn Rosetta (b. 1930), who bears the names of Vivian's two sisters—both now deceased. Sister Evelyn (McClelland) died at 79 in '72, in Bellflower, near Los Angeles; a stage actress, and the eldest, she had assisted Vivian and Rosetta in entering show business but was never part of their act. Sister Rosetta, Vivian's partner in vaudeville and in movies, died in an automobile accident in '59. Onscreen from 1927. IN: *Topsy and Eva, Imperfect Ladies, It's a Great Life.*

DUNHAM, KATHERINE (N.Y.) Black dancer-actress. Onscreen from 1942. IN: *Star-Spangled Rhythm, Casbah, Mambo,* more.

DUNLAP, FLORENCE (N.Y.) Character. IN: *The Night They Raided Minsky's, The Group, The Producers, The Way We Were,* more.

DUNN, JOSEPHINE (S. Cal.) In 40 pictures in her short screen career, the popular leading

126

lady is in her 70s now (b. 1906), happily married, and has been retired since '33. Onscreen from 1926. IN: *Fascinating Youth, Love's Greatest Mistake, She's a Shiek, The Singing Fool, We Americans, Sonny Boy, Our Modern Maidens, Melody Lane, Big Time, Safety in Numbers, Madonna of the Streets, One Hour with You, Big City Blues*, more, including *Between Fighting Men*, her last.

DUNN, RALPH (N.Y.) Character. Onscreen from 1938. IN: *Tenth Avenue Kid, Tail Spin, The Lady from Cheyenne, Moontide, Laura, The Babe Ruth Story, Crowded Paradise, The Pajama Game, Black Like Me*, more.

DUNN, VIOLET (N.Y.) Character. Onscreen from 1931. IN: *The Black Camel, Doctors' Wives; Rachel, Rachel;* more.

DUNNE, IRENE (S. Cal.) Star. Nominated for Best Actress Oscar in *Cimarron, Theodora Goes Wild, The Awful Truth, Love Affair, I Remember Mama*. Onscreen from 1930. IN: *Leathernecking, Married in Haste, Melody of Life, Symphony of Six Million, Back Street, The Silver Cord, Ann Vickers, Stingaree, Roberta, Magnificent Obsession, Showboat; High, Wide and Handsome; Joy of Living, My Favorite Wife, Penny Serenade, A Guy Named Joe, The White Cliffs of Dover, Over 21, Anna and the King of Siam, Life with Father, The Mudlark, It Grows on Trees*, more. Retired in '52.

DUNNE, STEVE (S. Cal.) Support. Former leading man, he has had three screen names. Onscreen as Michael Dunne from 1945. IN: *Col. Effingham's Raid, Doll Face, Junior Miss, Mother Wore Tights, Kiss of Death*, more. Onscreen as Stephen Dunne from 1948. IN: *The Dark Past, Lady Possessed, Above and Beyond*, more. Onscreen as Steve Dunne from 1957. IN: *Ten Thousand Bedrooms, I Married a Woman, Home Before Dark, The Explosive Generation, The Late Liz*, more.

DUNNING, RUTH (Eng.) Character. Onscreen from the '50s. IN: *The Woman in the Hall, Save a Little Sunshine, Intimate Relations, The Weak and the Wicked*, more.

DUNNOCK, MILDRED (N.Y.) Character. Nominated for Best Supporting Actress Oscar in *Death of a Salesman* and *Baby Doll*. Onscreen from 1945. IN: *The Corn Is Green, Kiss of Death, I Want You, Viva Zapata!, The Trouble with Harry, Cat on a Hot Tin Roof, Story on Page One, The Nun's Story, Butterfield 8, Sweet Bird of Youth, Behold a Pale Horse, Youngblood Hawke, Seven Women, Whatever Happened to Aunt Alice?*, more.

DUPEREY, ANNY (Fr.) Leading lady. IN: *Stavisky.*

DUPREZ, JUNE (It.) After costarring in numerous Hollywood pix of the '40s, the last of which was 1947's *Calcutta*, she became—in '48—the wife of socialite George Moffett Jr. She has acted only once since—in the 1961's exploitation movie *One Plus One (Exploring the Kinsey Reports)*. In her 50s now (b. 1918), she and her husband, parents of two grown daughters, live in Rome. Onscreen in England from 1936. IN: *The Cardinal, The Spy in Black, The Lion Has Wings, Four Feathers, The Thief of Bagdad.* Onscreen in America from 1941. IN: *Don Winslow of the Coast Guard* (serial), *Little Tokyo U.S.A., Forever and a Day, Tiger Fangs, None But the Lonely Heart, And Then There Were None, That Brennan Girl*, more.

DUPUIS, PAUL (Eng.) Leading man; retired. IN: *Bad Sister, Sleeping Car to Trieste, Against the Wind, Passport to Pimlico, Madness of the Heart*, more.

DURANTE, JIMMY (S. Cal.) Star comedian. In his 80s (b. 1893) and ill, he has been retired for more than a decade. Onscreen from 1929. IN: *Roadhouse Nights, New Adventures of Get-Rich-Quick Wallingford, Blondie of the Follies, Broadway to Hollywood, Meet the Baron, She Learned About Sailors, Start Cheering; Sally, Irene and Mary; The Man Who Came to Dinner, Her Cardboard Lover, Two Girls and a Sailor, Ziegfeld Follies, On an Island With You, The Yellow Cab Man, Pepe, It's a Mad Mad Mad Mad World*, more.

DURBIN, DEANNA (Fr.) In the village of Neauphle-le-Chateau, some 50 miles from Paris, Mme. Charles-Henri David (pronounced, of course, Da-veed) lives, well-off but simply, in a two-story, six-room house with her elderly husband, a cultivated man of enormous charm but in the eyes of almost no one a handsome one. Their small estate, its gardens leaf-strewn and gloomy in the winter, alive with flowers in the summer, is one-quarter mile from the center of the village. Mme. David regularly walks this distance to deal with local tradesmen, always in French. Though bi-lingual, she rarely speaks English now. Mme. David is a beautiful woman —slender (about 130 lbs.), blue-eyed, smiling, with gently waved shoulder-length hair that is reddish-brown. In Paris, at a university, she has a son, Peter David, in his mid-20s, studying to be a doctor. In Los Angeles she has a daughter, Jessica, in her early 30s, who is now Mrs. Jay Davies—her second marriage—and has yet to make her a grandmother. Mme. David and her husband (her third), married since Dec. 21,

127

1950, live like the retired couple they are—always together, overseeing their land holdings, going to Paris often to concerts and movie premiers (he was a director), flying across the Channel to London to art galleries and theaters, entertaining close friends at home. Often, on evenings when they are alone, accompanied by her son at the piano, she sings for her husband's pleasure—operatic arias sometimes but more often modern songs, particularly those made popular by the Beatles, whom she greatly admires, as she does Barbra Streisand. Mme. David—lovely woman, superlative singer that she is—has never sung in public, appeared on radio, starred in a movie, or made a record. Deanna Durbin, on the other hand, who shared the same parents and the same birthdate (Dec. 4, 1921), did all these. Not only that, she starred in one movie, *Lady on a Train*, in '45, directed by Charles-Henri David. But Deanna Durbin, who made $300,000 a year as a star, was accorded a special (miniature) Oscar in 1938, and saved Universal Studios from bankruptcy, made her last movie, *For the Love of Mary*, in '48. She has never lived at Neauphle-le-Chateau. She ceased to exist, except in memory, in December 1950. And, in fact, now, the woman who "played" Deanna Durbin on the screen refers to her as a "fairytale character." Mme. David, a woman of wit and determination, who neither poses for photographs nor grants interviews, has given the author an amusing account of "what happened to Deanna Durbin," saying: "When we married, we made a deal . . . My husband would protect me from spiders, mosquitos and reporters whilst my job is to protect him from lions, tigers and dinosaurs. And we both came through. For years I have not had to give an interview, or pose for pictures, whilst it's ages since a dinosaur breathed down my husband's neck. . . . I have succeeded in attaining privacy and peace only through being most uncooperative in meeting press and photographers. . . . Please let my fans enjoy the Deanna Durbin of years ago and keep this fairytale character free from any 'what's happened to her' story. I have found my fans wonderfully understanding in my happily shedding Deanna Durbin to live the wonderful and exciting private life of Deanna Durbin David." In 1972, in Seal Beach, Calif., where they lived in comfortable retirement on an annuity established for them by their daughter, Deanna Durbin's aged parents, James and Ada, celebrated their 64th wedding anniversary. Two months later, Ada was dead. After the funeral, James Durbin went to France then to visit his daughter. She received him lovingly, with tears in her eyes. In that moment of private sorrow, Deanna Durbin was at Neauphle-le-Chateau. Onscreen from 1936. IN: *Every Sunday* (short), *Three Smart Girls, One Hundred Men and a*

Girl, Mad About Music, That Certain Age, Three Smart Girls Grow Up, First Love, It's a Date, Spring Parade, Nice Girl?, It Started with Eve, The Amazing Mrs. Holliday, His Butler's Sister, Hers to Hold, Christmas Holiday, Can't Help Singing, Lady on a Train, Because of Him, I'll Be Yours, Something in the Wind, Up in Central Park, For the Love of Mary.

DURNING, CHARLES (N.Y.) Character costar. Onscreen from 1965. IN: *Harvey Middleman, Fireman, I Walk the Line, The Pursuit of Happiness, The Front Page, The Sting, Dog Day Afternoon, The Hindenburg*, more.

DUVALL, ROBERT (S. Cal.) Costar. Nominated for Best Supporting Actor Oscar in *The Godfather*. Onscreen from 1963. IN: *To Kill a Mockingbird, The Chase, Bullitt, True Grit, M*A*S*H, Lawman, The Godfather II, Breakout, The Killer Elite, Network*, more.

DUVALL, SHELLEY (S. Cal.) Leading lady. Onscreen in the '70s. IN: *McCabe and Mrs. Miller, Brewster McCloud, Thieves Like Us, Nashville, Buffalo Bill and the Indians*.

DVORAK, ANN (Hawaii) Living in Honolulu, she is in her 60s (b. 1912), happily married, and has not acted since appearing in three movies released in 1951: *Mrs. O'Malley and Mr. Malone, I Was an American Spy*, and *The Secret of Convict Lake*. Onscreen from 1929. IN: *Hollywood Revue, Scarface, The Crooner, Love Is a Racket, Midnight Alibi, Murder in the Clouds, Dr. Socrates, Bright Lights, G-Men, Manhattan Merry-Go-Round, Midnight Court, Stronger Than Desire, Girls of the Road, Flame of the Barbary Coast, Masquerade in Mexico, Out of the Blue, The Private Affairs of Bel Ami, Walls of Jericho, Our Very Own*, more.

DWYER, HILARY (Eng.) Leading lady. Onscreen from the late '60s. IN: *The Conqueror Worm, Two Gentlemen Sharing, The Oblong Box, Cry of the Banshee, Wuthering Heights, The Body Stealers*, more.

DWYER, LESLIE (Eng.) Character. IN: *The Way Ahead, Piccadilly Incident, Bond Street, The Little Ballerina, Laughter in Paradise, Wall of Death, Double Confession, Midnight Episode, The 39 Steps*, more.

DYALL, VALENTINE (Eng.) Character. Onscreen from 1944. IN: *The Yellow Canary, Life and Death of Colonel Blimp, Henry V, Frenzy, I Know Where I'm Going, Corridor of Mirrors, Ivanhoe, Horror Hotel, The Haunting*, more.

DYER, CHARLES (Eng.) Support. IN: *The Knack, Rattle of a Simple Man*, more.

DYNELEY, PETER (Eng.) Character. IN: *Beau Brummell, Chance Meeting, Call Me Bwana, The Executioner*, more.

DYSART, RICHARD A. (S. Cal.) Costar. Onscreen from 1968. IN: *Petulia, The Lost Man, The Sporting Club, The Hospital, The Terminal Man, The Crazy World of Julius Vrooder, The Day of the Locust, The Hindenburg*, more.

E

EASTHAM, RICHARD (S. Cal.) Character. Onscreen from 1954. IN: *There's No Business Like Show Business, Man on Fire, That Darn Cat, Murderer's Row, McQ*, more.

EASTMAN, PETER (N.Y.) Character. IN: *What's Up, Doc?, The Way We Were*.

EASTON, JOYCE (S. Cal.) Support. Onscreen from 1969. IN: *Bob & Carol & Ted & Alice, Billy Bright, The Brotherhood of Satan, Memory of Us*, more.

EASTON, ROBERT (S. Cal.) Character. Onscreen from 1949. IN: *Undertow, Drums in the Deep South, Belles on Their Toes, O. Henry's Full House, Somebody Up There Likes Me, Voyage to the Bottom of the Sea, The Loved One, One of Our Spies Is Missing, Johnny Got His Gun, Mr. Sycamore*, more.

EASTWOOD, CLINT (N. Cal.) Star. Onscreen from 1955. IN: *Francis in the Navy, The First Traveling Saleslady, Lafayette Escadrille, Two Magnificent Rogues, A Fistful of Dollars, For a Few Dollars More, Hang 'em High; The Good, the Bad and the Ugly; Coogan's Bluff, Where Eagles Dare, Paint Your Wagon, Two Mules for Sister Sara, The Beguiled, Play Misty for Me, Dirty Harry, High Plains Drifter, Magnum Force, The Eiger Sanction, Outlaw—Josey Wales*, more.

EATON, SHIRLEY (Eng.) Leading lady. Onscreen from 1954. IN: *You Know What Sailors Are, Doctor in the House, The Love Match, 3 Men in a Boat*, the "Carry On" series (*. . . Sergeant, . . . Constable, . . . Nurse*), *No Place Like Homicide, Goldfinger, Rhino!, Around the World Under the Sea, Ten Little Indians, Kiss and Tell*, more.

EBEN, AL (Hawaii) Character. He lives in Honolulu now where he has been playing the recurring role of Doc, the medical examiner, in the TV series *Hawaii Five-O*. Onscreen from 1940. IN: *Citizen Kane, A Tree Grows in Brooklyn, The Brasher Doubloon, City Across the River, Sirocco*, more.

EBERLE, BOB (N.Y.) Singer. He remains a popular attraction in nightclubs. IN: *I Dood It*.

EBSEN, BUDDY (S. Cal.) Character star; former dancer. Onscreen from 1935. IN: *Broadway Melody of 1936. Banjo on My Knee, Born to Dance, Yellow Jack, My Lucky Star, Under Mexicali Stars, Silver City Bonanza, Red Garters; Davy Crockett, King of the Wild Frontier; Breakfast at Tiffany's, The Interns, Mail Order Bride*, more.

EBSEN, VILMA (S. Cal.) Brother Buddy's dance partner in *Broadway Melody of 1936* (after they had achieved stage fame in the *Ziegfeld Follies*), she left the screen for marriage. Now in her late 60s, she operates the Ebsen Studio of Dancing in the Pacific Palisades, in which Buddy also is a partner.

EBY-ROCK, HELEN (S. Cal.) Character. Onscreen from 1933's *Ann Vickers*, she remains active.

ECCLES, AIMEE/formerly **AMY** (S. Cal.) Young leading lady. Onscreen from 1968. IN: *No More Excuses, Little Big Man, Pretty Maids All in a Row, Marco*, more.

ECCLES, TED (S. Cal.) Juvenile lead. Onscreen in the '70s. IN: *My Side of the Mountain, The Phynx*, more.

ECKSTINE, BILLY (S. Cal.) Black singer-actor. IN: *Skirts Ahoy!, Let's Do It Again*.

EDELMAN, HERB (S. Cal.) Character. Onscreen from 1967. IN: *In Like Flint, Barefoot in the Park, The Odd Couple; I Love You, Alice B. Toklas; P.J., The Way We Were, The Front Page*, more.

EDEN, BARBARA (S. Cal.) Leading lady. Onscreen from 1956. IN: *The Wayward Girl, From the Terrace, All Hands on Deck, Voyage to the Bottom of the Sea, Double Trouble, Five Weeks in a Balloon, The Yellow Canary, The Brass Bottle, The New Interns, Ride the Wild Surf*, more.

EDERLE, GERTRUDE (N.Y.) After swimming the English Channel in 1926, she followed up by costarring with Bebe Daniels in one movie. In the spring of 1976, aged 69, and a lifelong resident of New York, she was guest of honor at the 50th anniversary dinner of the Boys Athletic League—being saluted as the "greatest swimmer ever developed in New York City." Onscreen in 1927. IN: *Swim, Girl, Swim.*

EDMUND, LADA, JR. (S. Cal.) Support. Onscreen from the '60s. IN: *The Devil's 8, Out of It, Jump, Act of Vengeance*, more.

EDWARDS, BILL (S. Cal.) The lanky leading man of the '40s is in his 50s now (b. 1918) and principally occupied as a reporter for a movie industry trade paper, but occasionally plays character roles on such TV shows as *Hawaii Five-O.* Onscreen from 1942. IN: *The Bugle Sounds, Our Hearts Were Young and Gay, You Can't Ration Love, Hail the Conquering Hero, Miss Susie Slagle's, Our Hearts Were Growing Up,* more.

EDWARDS, JENNIFER (Eng.) Juvenile. Daughter of director Blake Edwards. IN: *Heidi; Hook, Line and Sinker.*

EDWARDS, JIMMY (Eng.) Character. Onscreen from the '40s. IN: *Trouble in the Air, Helter Skelter, Innocents in Paris, 3 Men in a Boat,* more.

EDWARDS, MEREDITH (Eng.) Character. Onscreen from the '40s. IN: *The Last Page, Gift Horse, Ivory Hunter, Glory at Sea, The Third Key, Dunkirk, Tiger Bay,* more.

EDWARDS, PENNY (S. Cal.) Youthful-looking in her 40s (b. 1928), the former leading lady of Westerns gave up her decade-long career after 1957's *Ride a Violent Mile.* She has been long and happily married to Universal casting director Ralph Winters. Besides homemaking, she works actively in her church. She and her husband have a daughter, Deborah Winters, who is now an actress. She was seen in *The People Next Door*—as the doomed drug-addicted teenager—and in *Kotch.* Deborah gave her parents quite a turn in 1970 when, aged 14, she announced her intentions of marrying actor Richard Shelfo, then exactly twice her age. "My parents went right through the roof" is the way Deborah has described their reaction. And, Penny Edwards agrees, they did indeed. But because, as Deborah has said of herself, "Some people are born mature and I am one of them," they eventually gave their reluctant consent and the wedding took place. At last report, all had worked out well. Looking back on that traumatic moment, Penny Edwards laughs, "And I thought some of my movie roles were dramatic!" Onscreen from 1947. IN: *That Hagen Girl, My Wild Irish Rose, Two Guys from Texas, Tucson, North of the Great Divide, Sunset in the West, Trail of Robin Hood, In Old Amarillo, The Wild Blue Yonder, Heart of the Rockies, Missing Women, Utah Wagon Train, Pony Soldier, Powder River,* more.

EDWARDS, SAM (S. Cal.) Character; former juvenile. Onscreen from 1940. IN: *East Side Kids, The Street With No Name, Twelve O'-Clock High, The Sun Sets at Dawn, Gang Busters, Revolt in the Big House, Scandalous John,* more.

EDWARDS, VINCE (S. Cal.) Leading man. Onscreen from 1951. IN: *Sailor Beware, Hiawatha, Cell 2455—Death Row, The Three Faces of Eve, Island Women, Too Late Blues, The Outsider, The Victors, The Devil's Brigade, Sole Survivor, Fall Out,* more.

EGAN, JENNY (N.Y.) Support. IN: *That Kind of Woman, Pollyanna, They Might Be Giants,* more.

EGAN, RICHARD (S. Cal.) TV guest roles keep him principally occupied now—in series such as *Streets of San Francisco* and *Police Story,* and in such TV "Movies of the Week" as *Throw Out the Anchor* and *Shootout in a One Dog Town.* These, plus tours in plays like the comedy *No Hard Feelings.* He's been generally inactive in movies since 1971's *The Big Cube;* the actor says, "because I won't accept parts that would embarrass my kids." He and wife (since '58), former actress Patricia Hardy, have five. Their first daughter was born in '59, their newest in '74, and in between came two other daughters and a son. All were baptized by Egan's brother, Jesuit priest Willis E. Egan. The family lives in a rambling ranch-style house in Brentwood. He will remain off the screen, he says, as long as nudity and explicit sex trend continues. He does not subscribe to the theory that at his age (b. 1921) his ideas could be "old-fashioned." Instead, he insists, "There are other sides to life. There is someplace where man is trying to succeed, to do right, to live right." And Richard Egan, his friends say, lives in that "someplace." Onscreen from 1950. IN: *The Killer That Stalked New York, The Damned Don't Cry, Bright Victory, Up Front, The Hunters, Khyber Patrol, The View from Pompey's Head, Revolt of Mamie Stover, Voice in the Mirror, A Summer Place, Pollyanna, The Lion of Sparta, Heavens Above, Chubasco, Valley of Mystery,* more.

EGE, JULIE (Eng.) Leading lady. Onscreen from 1969. IN: *On Her Majesty's Secret Service, Creatures the World Forgot, Craze, Last Days of Man on Earth, The Mutations,* more.

EGGAR, SAMANTHA (S. Cal.) Costar. Nominated for Best Actress Oscar in *The Collector.*

Onscreen from 1963. IN: *Doctor in Distress, Dr. Crippen, Return from the Ashes; Walk, Don't Run; Dr. Dolittle, The Molly Maguires, The Light at the Edge of the World,* more.

EGGERTH, MARTA (N.Y.) Her career has been of secondary importance to her since the death in '66 of her husband, Jan Kiepura, the famous Polish tenor with whom she had co-starred in movies and in light operas all over the world. They had been married since '37. But, in '73, she was one of many stars who assisted in celebrating the 30th anniversary of New York's City Center. "There were many magic moments in the City Center gala," wrote one critic, "but the most magic of all was when Marta Eggerth sang a couple of songs from *The Merry Widow,* and then waltzed off on the arm of Donald Saddler." She has also recently done a 45-minute color TV show, for European viewing, about her husband's and her own careers onstage and in movies, and about her life today. The interview portion was filmed at the actress's beautiful estate in Rye, N.Y. She lives there with her two sons, both in their 20s. "My oldest son, Jan. Jr., is very handsome and has a beautiful voice," she says. "He studied opera in Milano, but did switch to pop and legit singing. He not only sings in four languages, he speaks all of them fluently." He was, at last report, concluding negotiations for European distribution of his recordings. "My younger son, Marjan," she adds, "has studied journalism. A pilot as well, he has a multi-engine license, and is very active writing about aviation. Several of his articles have been published by major aviation magazines. He also composes and plays the piano. As you can see, I am a proud mother." Among Marta Eggerth's other presentday activities is the management of an 18-story luxury apartment house she has long owned in New York, just off Fifth Avenue. Not only does she run it personally, she sometimes even types up its tenants' leases. Onscreen from 1933. IN: *Traum von Schoenbrunn, Kaiserwalzer, Unfinished Symphony, My Heart Is Calling, The World's in Love, For Me and My Gal, Presenting Lily Mars, Her Wonderful Lie,* more.

EHRHART, BARBARA (N.Y.) Juvenile. Onscreen in the '70s. IN: *Pound,* more.

EILERS, SALLY (S. Cal.) She's in her late 60s now (b. 1908), and it's been a while since she was a beauty, but Sally Eilers, hillside dweller of Beverly Hills, keeps her outrageous sense of humor. Example: On tour with the play *Butterflies Are Free,* a couple of years back, star Gloria Swanson was visited backstage by a well-dressed, sunburned, and not unwrinkled woman who greeted her most effusively. Swanson knew she knew her, but who, exactly, *was* she? The problem was compounded when this woman asked her to autograph her program. Playing for time, Swanson asked, "How shall I sign it?" The answer came, with a roaring laugh, "Oh, just sign it to Mrs. Hoot Gibson from Mrs. Wallace Beery!" Sally Eilers—dropping her first married name and Swanson's. Since Hoot Gibson, Sally has been married to and divorced from the late (d. '72) producer Harry Joe Brown (their son, her only child, Harry Joe Brown Jr., was born in '34), Navy Captain Howard Barney, and director John Hollingsworth Morse. Her last movie was 1951's *Stage to Tucson,* produced by Harry Joe Brown. Onscreen from 1928. IN: *Trial Marriage, Sailor's Holiday, Let Us Be Gay, Bad Girl, Hat Check Girl, Parlor Bedroom and Bath, Dance Team, Made on Broadway, Sailor's Luck, Three on a Honeymoon, Remember Last Night?, Florida Special, Condemned Women, They Made Her a Spy, I Was a Prisoner on Devil's Island, Strange Illusion,* more.

EISLEY, ANTHONY (S. Cal.) Leading man. Onscreen from 1964. IN: *The Naked Kiss, Frankie and Johnny, The Navy vs. the Night Monsters, Star!, The Witchmaker, The Blood Seekers, The Doll Squad,* more.

EKBERG, ANITA (It.) Leading lady. Onscreen from 1953. IN: *The Golden Blade, Blood Alley, War and Peace, Man in the Vault, Pickup Alley, Valerie, The Screaming Mimi, Paris Holiday, La Dolce Vita, Boccaccio, Call Me Bwana, Four for Texas, Woman Times Seven, The Cobra, Devil's Dolls, The Clowns, Fangs of the Living Dead,* more.

EKLAND, BRITT (S. Cal.) Leading lady. Onscreen from 1963. IN: *Il Commandante, After the Fox, The Bobo, Triple Cross, The Night They Raided Minsky's, McCain, Stiletto, At Any Price, Get Carter, Baxter, Asylum, The Ultimate Thrill, The Man with the Golden Gun, Royal Flash,* more.

ELAM, JACK (S. Cal.) Character star. Onscreen from 1950. IN: *High Lonesome, A Ticket to Tomahawk, High Noon, Shane, Ride Vaquero!, Cattle Queen of Montana, Kismet, Jubal, Gunfight at the O.K. Corral, Pocketful of Miracles, The Way West, Support Your Local Gunfighter, The Wild Country, The Last Rebel, A Knife for the Ladies,* more.

ELCAR, DANA (S. Cal.) Character. Onscreen from the '60s. IN: *Pendulum, The Maltese Bippy, The Learning Tree, The Fool Killer, Soldier Blue, Adam at 6 A.M., Zigzag, The Sting,* more.

ELDRIDGE, FLORENCE (N.Y.) Since husband Fredric March's death in '75 she has sold their country home, Firefly Farm, in New Milford, Conn., and moved into their city apartment. Now in her 70s (b. 1901), the actress is looking for a new play in which to star. Onscreen from 1929. IN: *The Greene Murder Case, The Divorcee, The Matrimonial Bed, Thirteen Women, The Great Jasper, The Story of Temple Drake, A Modern Hero, Les Miserables, Mary of Scotland, Another Part of the Forest, An Act of Murder (Live Today for Tomorrow), Christopher Columbus, Inherit the Wind,* more.

ELG, TAINA (N.Y.) Leading lady who, in this decade, has acted only on the New York stage. Onscreen from 1955. IN: *The Prodigal, Diane, Gaby, Les Girls, Imitation General, The 39 Steps, The Bacchantes, The Great Experiment,* more.

ELIZONDO, HECTOR (N.Y.) Character. Onscreen in the '70s. IN: *Valdez Is Coming, Born to Win, Stand Up and Be Counted, The Taking of Pelham One Two Three, Report to the Commissioner,* more.

ELLENSTEIN, ROBERT (N.Y.) Character. Onscreen from 1955. IN: *Rogue Cop, 3:10 to Yuma, North by Northwest, The Gazebo, Deathwatch, The Legend of Lylah Clare,* more.

ELLERBE, HARRY (Ga.) After his long screen and stage career he has been retired since 1964 and living in Atlanta, on Peachtree Street. Onscreen from 1932. IN: *Misleading Lady, Murder on a Honeymoon, So Red the Rose, The Magnetic Monster, Desk Set, The House of Usher, The Haunted Palace,* more.

ELLIMAN, YVONNE (N.Y.) Singer-actress. IN: *Jesus Christ Superstar.*

ELLIOT, BIFF (S. Cal.) Character; former leading man. Onscreen from 1953. IN: *I, the Jury; House of Bamboo; Good Morning, Miss Dove; Pork Chop Hill, The Story on Page One, The Hard Ride, The Front Page,* more.

ELLIOTT, DAVID (N.Y.) Juvenile. Onscreen in the '70s. IN: *The Possession of Joel Delaney,* more.

ELLIOTT, DENHOLM (Eng.) Costar. Onscreen from 1949. IN: *Dear Mr. Prohack, Breaking the Sound Barrier, The Cruel Sea, The Holly and the Ivy, The Man Who Loved Redheads, Station Six Sahara, Nothing But the Best, King Rat, Alfie, The Spy with a Cold Nose, The Night They Raided Minsky's, Too Late the Hero, The House That Dripped Blood, The Apprenticeship of Duddy Kravitz, Russian Roulette, Robin and Marian,* more.

ELLIOTT, LEONARD (N.Y.) Character. Onscreen from 1940. IN: *Overture to Glory, Buck Privates, It Started with Eve, Weddings and Babies,* more.

ELLIOTT, ROSS (S. Cal.) Character; former leading man. Onscreen from 1948. IN: *Chinatown at Midnight, Woman on the Run, I Can Get It for You Wholesale, Chicago Calling, The Beast from 20,000 Fathoms, Tarantula, Tammy Tell Me True, Watusi, Day of the Evil Gun, Kelly's Heroes, Act of Vengeance,* more.

ELLIOTT, SAM (S. Cal.) Leading man. Onscreen from 1969. IN: *Butch Cassidy and the Sundance Kid, The Games, Frogs, Molly and Lawless John,* more.

ELLIOTT, STEPHEN (N.Y.) Character. Onscreen from 1954. IN: *Three Hours to Kill, The Hospital, Death Wish, The Hindenburg,* more.

ELLIOTT, WILLIAM (S. Cal.) Black leading man. Onscreen from 1968. IN: *Change of Habit, Hangup,* more.

ELLIS, MARY (Eng.) In her 70s now (b. 1899) and long a widow, the singer-actress last played a character role in *The Three Worlds of Gulliver* ('60). Onscreen from 1935. IN: *Bella Donna, All the King's Horses, Paris in Spring, Glamorous Night, Fatal Lady,* more.

ELLISON, JAMES (S. Cal.) Long and happily married (since '37) to Gertrude Durkin, by whom he has a grown son and daughter, Ellison is now in his 60s (b. 1910), sells real estate in California, hasn't made a movie since 1952's *Dead Man's Trail* or appeared onstage since doing summer stock with daughter True in 1962. Onscreen from 1932. IN: *The Play Girl, Death on the Diamond, Reckless, Hitchhike Lady, The Plainsman, Annapolis Salute, Vivacious Lady, Mother Carey's Chickens, Hotel for Women, Zenobia, Anne of Windy Poplars, They Met in Argentina, Dixie Dugan, I Walked with a Zombie, Johnny Doesn't Live Here Any More, The Ghost Goes Wild, I Killed Geronimo, Sudden Death, Kentucky Jubilee, The Man from Black Hills,* more.

ELSOM, ISOBEL (S. Cal.) Last in *My Fair Lady* in '64, the noted character actress is in her 80s (b. 1894) and retired. Onscreen in America, after a long screen career in England, from 1941. IN: *Ladies in Retirement, Eagle Squadron, Seven Sweethearts, You Were Never Lovelier, Forever and a Day, First Comes Courage, Casanova Brown, The Unseen, Two Sisters from Boston, Escape Me Never, The Ghost and Mrs. Muir, Monsieur Verdoux, The Two Mrs. Carrolls, The Paradine Case, The Secret Garden, Love Is a Many-Splendored Thing, Lust* for Life, *The Bellboy, Who's Minding the Store?, The Pleasure Seekers*, more.

ELY, RON (S. Cal.) Leading man who became famous playing Tarzan in a long-running TV series. Onscreen from 1958. IN: *South Pacific, The Fiend Who Walked the West, The Remarkable Mr. Pennypacker, The Night of the Grizzly, Once Before I Die, Doc Savage—The Man of Bronze*, more.

EMAN, DAWN (N.Y.) Juvenile, Onscreen in the '70s. IN: *Carnal Knowledge, The People Next Door, Little Murders*, more.

EMAN, TRACEY (N.Y.) Juvenile actress. Onscreen in the '70s. IN: *The Boys in the Band, Husbands, The Kremlin Letter*, more.

EMERSON, FAYE (Sp.) In '63, at the height of the TV fame that followed her years of stardom at Warners, she said, "I just want to think and study and write and put my feet up and assess my whole life." She was rich, and she was weary of putting makeup on and taking weight off. She sailed to Spain, finally putting down roots at Majorca, and there she has remained. And now, sailing into her 60s (b. 1917)—silver-haired, suntanned, and heavy (somewhere between 160 and 180)—she has done the things she set out to do. Among other things, she has written a book about the Roosevelt clan. She was a member when married to Elliott Roosevelt, the second of her three ex-husbands—the last being bandleader Skitch Henderson. Of her marriages, she still says the one to FDR's son was the happiest, adding that if she had it to do over she "might have been wiser." When first on Majorca, she lived quite alone in the craggy, mountainous part of the island, in the village of Galilea, where she owned much land. Reportedly, she suffered a heart attack while living there and was not found for several days. She has since moved to a more populous area, the village of Establishment, where she has a beautiful, whitewashed house on a hillside, and—thanks to a network of young friends in the village's shops and cafes—successfully avoids reporters and photographers. "I might want marriage again for my sunset years," she has said, laughing. "It would be marvelous then to have a wonderful companion and great friend. But right now my life is very full. I'm never lonely." Onscreen from 1941. IN: *Bad Men of Missouri, Nine Lives Are Not Enough, Manpower, Lady Gangster, The Hard Way, The Desert Song, Air Force, Destination Tokyo, The Very Thought of You, Between Two Worlds, Uncertain Glory, The Mask of Dimitrios, Hotel Berlin, Nobody Lives Forever, Her Kind of Man, Guilty Bystander*, more.

EMHARDT, ROBERT (S. Cal.) Character. Onscreen from 1952. IN: *The Iron Mistress, The Intruder, The Big Knife, 3:10 to Yuma, The Badlanders, Underworld U.S.A., The Group, Hostile Guns, Rascal, Change of Habit, It's Alive*, more.

ENGEL, ROY (S. Cal.) Character. Onscreen from 1950. IN: *The Flying Saucer, Outrage, Rogue River, The Man from Planet X, M, Vickie, The Last Movie*, more.

ENGEL, SUSAN (Eng.) Leading lady. Onscreen in the '70s. IN: *King Lear, Butley*, more.

ENGLAND, SUE (S. Cal.) One of the better (and prettier) moppets of the '40s, she has lately played nurse roles in both *Marcus Welby, M.D.* and *Cannon* on TV. Onscreen from 1945. IN: *This Love of Ours, Kidnapped, City Across the River, Teenage Crime Wave, Women of Pitcairn Island, Funny Face, The Devil's Hairpin, Clambake*, more.

ENGLUND, PATRICIA (N.Y.) Support. IN: *Stage Struck.*

ERDMAN, RICHARD (S. Cal.) Warners discovered this freckled, rubber-faced comic at 19 and rushed him through 28 pictures in four years during WW II. Fans warmed up to his hijinks and homely puss from his first, *Janie*, which was followed later by *Janie Gets Married*. Last onscreen in Disney's *Rascal*, the actor, now in his 50s (b. 1925) and a few months back in support in *Kate McShane* and in the TV special *The Great Man's Whiskers*, says that for years "acting has been more of a sideline than a profession." After more than 100 movies and twice that many TV shows, he has found he prefers directing. He begun this second career on *The Dick Van Dyke Show*, following this debut with countless episodes of other television series as well as the feature film *BLEEP*, which he wrote, produced and directed. Now he is also producing TV commercials for his own company in Los Angeles. Married since '53 to former actress Sharon Randall, he has a college-age daughter, Erica, and lives in Pacific Palisades. Onscreen from 1944. IN: *The Very Thought of You, Danger Signal, Too Young to Know, Nobody Lives Forever, That Way with Women, The Time of Your Life, Easy Living, You're in the Navy Now, Jumping Jacks, The Happy Time, The Stooge, Stalag 17, The Power and the Prize, The Brass Bottle, Tora! Tora! Tora!*, more.

ERICKSON, LEIF (S. Cal.) Character; former leading man. Onscreen from 1935. IN: *Nevada, Waikiki Wedding, Conquest, One Third of a Nation, The Blonde from Singapore; H. M. Pulham, Esq.; The Fleet's In, Pardon My Sarong,*

Arabian Nights, The Gangster; Sorry, Wrong Number; Johnny Stool Pigeon, Three Secrets, Mother Didn't Tell Me, The Tall Target, With a Song in My Heart, Carbine Williams, Tea and Sympathy, Kiss Them for Me, The Young Lions, The Carpetbaggers, Strait-Jacket, I Saw What You Did, Abduction, more.

ERICSON, JOHN (S. Cal.) Leading man. Onscreen from 1951. IN: *Teresa, Rhapsody, Bad Day at Black Rock, The Return of Jack Slade, Day of the Bad Men, Pretty Boy Floyd, Under Ten Flags, Slave Queen of Babylon, The Money Jungle,* more.

ERSKINE, MARILYN (S. Cal.) Leaving the screen after 1953's *The Eddie Cantor Story,* in which she costarred as the comedian's wife, Ida, she has worked steadily in television ever since. Onscreen from 1951. IN: *Westward the Women, Just This Once, Above and Beyond, The Girl in White, A Slight Case of Larceny,* more.

ERWIN, BARBARA (N.Y.) Support. IN: *The Getaway.*

ESMOND, CARL (S. Cal.) Urbane, cultivated, and charming as ever as he enters his 70s (b. 1906), this Viennese actor is comfortably at home any place in the world. That is all to the good, as movie and TV assignments continue to take him to far-flung spots. "Like so many other Hollywood actors, I was in Europe," he noted a few months back, "doing a film in Italy and Germany," adding that he was leaving for Rome shortly to discuss another similar coproduction deal. Because of Esmond's extended stays abroad, it was rumored that he and his wife of three decades, former literary agent Ruth Taub, would give up their Brentwood home and move permanently to Europe. To the relief of such intimates as Joseph Cotten, Patricia Medina, and actor-director Don Taylor, among dozens more, this report proved erroneous. Esmond, an American citizen for more than 30 years, has lately done numerous TV commercials (for Columbia Records among others) and guested on such shows as *McMillan and Wife.* "In between acting chores," he says, "I am working with a well-known writer on two film scripts, one a comedy Western, the other a spoof on a smuggling ring." Esmond also adds, tongue in cheek, "Although I've had offers to play in some second-rate sex films, so far I have avoided doing so." Onscreen in America, after films made in England, from 1938. IN: *Dawn Patrol, Little Men, Sergeant York, Panama Hattie, Seven Sweethearts, Margin for Error, First Comes Courage, The Story of Dr. Wassell, Ministry of Fear, The Master Race, Experiment Perilous, Her Highness and the Bellboy, This Love of Ours, Lover Come Back, The Desert Hawk, From the Earth to the Moon, Brushfire, Morituri, Agent for H.A.R.M.,* more.

ESMOND, JILL (Eng.) Character; former leading lady. Inactive for the past two decades. Onscreen from 1931. IN: *Thirteen Women, Ladies of the Jury, State's Attorney, Is My Face Red?, No Funny Business, Eagle Squadron, This Above All, Random Harvest, Journey for Margaret, The Pied Piper, Casanova Brown, The White Cliffs of Dover, Bandit of Sherwood Forest, Night People, A Man Called Peter,* more.

ESPOSITO, GIANCARLO (N.Y.) Juvenile. Onscreen in the '70s. IN: *The Landlord,* more.

ESPOSITO, VINCENT (N.Y.) Juvenile. Onscreen in the '70s. IN: *Cancel My Reservation, The Landlord,* more.

ESPY, WILLIAM GRAY (S. Cal.) Leading man. IN: *Kansas City Bomber.*

ESSEX, DAVID (Eng.) Rock singer-actor. Onscreen in the '70s. IN: *That'll Be the Day, Stardust.*

ETTING, RUTH (Col.) With snow-white hair in her late 70s (b. 1897), the singer is vinegary, peppery, and humorous—despite the fact that she has spent a recent birthday or two at St. Francis Hospital in Colorado Springs, her home for decades. Childless, she is a widow—her husband, Myrl Alderman, died in '68. They had been married since '39. He was the Hollywood musician for whose shooting the singer's first husband, Chicago mobster Moe Snyder, did time in jail. Of Alderman and their years together, she says, "I've always considered myself the luckiest woman in the whole world to have had a man like him. He was so good to me, and we had a fine life." She shrugs off the movie, *Love Me or Leave Me,* based on her life. To reporter W. Franklyn Moshier, the star, who swears like a trucker, albeit good-naturedly, said: "Oh, what a —— mess that was. Can you imagine giving those two guys Academy Awards for writing that picture? I was *never* at any time a dance-hall girl. It was just a means of working in 'Ten Cents a Dance.' They took a lot of liberties with my life." In '72 she was greatly pleased to be invited—and to go for the first time in two decades—back to her home town, David City, Neb. (population 2,380), to help celebrate its centennial. She was saluted that June day as the town's most famous daughter. Onscreen 1933–34. IN: *Roman Scandals; Hips, Hips, Hooray; Gift of Gab.*

EVANS, BRUCE (Conn.) Character. IN: *Back Door to Heaven.*

EVANS, CLIFFORD (Eng.) Character; former leading man. Onscreen from 1936. IN: *River of Unrest, The Tenth Man, The Voice in the Night, Somewhere in France, Courageous Mr. Penn, Love on the Dole, The Straw Man, The Case of the Bogus Count, Kiss of the Vampire, The Long Ships,* more.

EVANS, DALE (S. Cal.) Married to Roy Rogers for three decades, she is in her 60s (b. 1912), has published a dozen inspirational books, and, except for TV commercials with her husband, has been retired from acting since '51. Onscreen from 1940. IN: *The East Side Kids, Hoosier Holiday; San Diego, I Love You; Lights of Old Santa Fe, Don't Fence Me In, Along the Navajo Trail, Rainbow Over Texas, Bells of San Angelo, The Golden Stallion, South of Caliente, Queen of the West,* more.

EVANS, DAME EDITH (Eng.) Character star. Nominated for Best Supporting Actress Oscar in *The Chalk Garden* and *Tom Jones.* Nominated for Best Actress Oscar in *The Whisperers.* Onscreen first in early silents. Onscreen in talkies from 1948. IN: *The Queen of Spades, The Importance of Being Earnest, The Nun's Story, Look Back in Anger, Young Cassidy, Fitzwilly, Prudence and the Pill, Trog, Scrooge, Craze,* more.

EVANS, EVANS (S. Cal.) Leading lady. Onscreen from 1962. IN: *All Fall Down, Bonnie and Clyde, Impossible Object.*

EVANS, GENE (S. Cal.) Costar. Onscreen from 1947. IN: *Under Colorado Skies; Larceny, Inc.; Force of Arms, The Steel Helmet, Fixed Bayonets, I Was an American Spy, Ace in the Hole, Cattle Queen of Montana, Revolt in the Big House, The Bravados, Shock Corridor, Nevada Smith, The War Wagon, Waco, There Was a Crooked Man, Support Your Local Gunfighter, A Knife for the Ladies, People Toys,* more.

EVANS, JOAN (S. Cal.) Last in 1960's *The Walking Target,* Goldwyn's teenage discovery is now in her early 40s (b. 1934), has been married to one husband, auto dealer Kirby Weatherley, since '52, has a grown daughter and a teenage son, and is the principal of an experimental elementary school in the San Fernando Valley. Onscreen from 1949. IN: *Roseanna McCoy, Our Very Own, Skirts Ahoy!, It Grows on Trees, Column South, The Outcast, The Flying Fontaines, No Name on the Bullet,* more.

EVANS, LINDA (S. Cal.) Leading lady. Onscreen from 1963. IN: *Twilight of Honor, Those*

Calloways, Cock-a-Doodle-Do, The Klansman, more.

EVANS, MADGE (N.J.) Still a beauty in her 60s (b. 1909), she began her career as a child star in 1915's *Zaza* with Pauline Frederick. Actually, she had been in movies from age 3 but this was the picture that "made" her. She ended her movie career in '38, starring in *Sinners in Paradise* and *Army Girl*—not of the caliber of her earlier *Dinner at Eight, David Copperfield,* etc. Since '39 she has been happily married (no children) to award-winning playwright Sidney *(Dead End)* Kingsley. She has not acted since '43, when she starred on Broadway in her husband's *The Patriots.* Still highly active in the New York theatrical social scene, they live in a magnificent house in Oakland, N.J., and keep an "in town" apartment-studio on lower Fifth Avenue in Manhattan. (A party sequence in *Serpico* was filmed in it.) Despite her long retirement, the star admitted recently, "I'm like anybody else. I would love to do something really great today . . . something that would be exciting to do." Specifically? "I would like to work with Stanley Kubrick." Onscreen in adult roles from 1930. IN: *Sporting Blood, Guilty Hands, West of Broadway, The Greeks Had a Word for Them, When Ladies Meet, What Every Woman Knows, Stand Up and Cheer, Age of Indiscretion, Moonlight Murder, Pennies from Heaven,* more.

EVANS, MAURICE (N.Y.) Character star. Onscreen from 1930. IN: *White Cargo, Wedding Rehearsal, Scrooge, Kind Lady, Androcles and the Lion, Gilbert and Sullivan, Macbeth, The Warlord, One of Our Spies Is Missing, Planet of the Apes, Rosemary's Baby, Beneath the Planet of the Apes,* more.

EVANS, MIKE (S. Cal.) Black leading man. Onscreen in the '70s. IN: *Now You See Him, Now You Don't; The House on Skull Mountain.*

EVANS, RICHARD (S. Cal.) Support. Onscreen from 1965. IN: *Synanon, Return of Mr. Moto, Macho Callahan, The Nickel Ride,* more.

EVANS, ROBERT (S. Cal.) Giving up acting after *Too Soon to Love* ('60), he became the head of production at Paramount, where he was in charge of *Love Story* and *Chinatown,* and is now an independent producer. Several times married (last to Ali MacGraw) and divorced, he is in his 40s now (b. 1930), and single. Onscreen from 1957. IN: *Man of a Thousand Faces, The Sun Also Rises, The Fiend Who Walked the West, The Best of Everything.*

EVANS, WILBUR (Pa.) The tenor, onetime husband and musical stage costar of Susanna

Foster, is in his 60s now (b. 1908) and reportedly operates a music school in Philadelphia. IN: *Her First Romance, Man with a Million.*

EVANSON, EDITH (S. Cal.) The movies have seen little of this fine character actress, in her 70s now, for the past decade, but she remains busy in television. Onscreen from 1942. IN: *Orchestra Wives, Reunion in France, Woman of the Year, I Remember Mama, Rope, The Damned Don't Cry, The Magnificent Yankee, Shane, It Happens Every Thursday, Storm Center, The Young Stranger, Toby Tyler, Marnie,* more.

EVERETT, CHAD (S. Cal.) Leading man. Onscreen from 1961. IN: *Claudelle Inglish, Rome Adventure, The Chapman Report, First to Fight, The Singing Nun, Made in Paris, Johnny Tiger, Return of the Gunfighter, The Impossible Years,* more.

EVERS, ANN (S. Cal.) One of the prettiest girls in movies of the '30s, she gave up her career for a long, happy marriage to writer-producer Seton I. Miller (d. 1974), by whom she has a grown son and daughter. Onscreen from 1936.

IN: *Forgotten Faces, A Son Comes Home, Frontier Town, Gunga Din, The Mad Miss Manton, Beauty For the Asking,* more.

EVERS, JASON (S. Cal.) Leading man. Onscreen from 1960. IN: *Pretty Boy Floyd, The Brain That Wouldn't Die, P.J., House of Women, The Illustrated Man, A Man Called Gannon, Escape from the Planet of the Apes,* more.

EWELL, TOM (S. Cal.) Character; former costar. Onscreen from 1939. IN: *The Kansas Kid, They Knew What They Wanted, Adam's Rib, Mr. Music, Up Front, Willie and Joe Back at the Front, The Seven Year Itch, The Lieutenant Wore Skirts, The Girl Can't Help It, Tender Is the Night, State Fair, Suppose They Gave a War and Nobody Came?, They Only Kill Their Masters, The Great Gatsby,* more.

EWING, ROGER (S. Cal.) Support. Onscreen from the '60s. IN: *Ensign Pulver, None But the Brave,* more.

EYRE, PETER (Eng.) Leading man. Onscreen in the '70s. IN: *Julius Caesar, Hedda.*

F

FABARES, SHELLEY (S. Cal.) Leading lady; former juvenile. Onscreen from 1956. IN: *Never Say Goodbye, Rock Pretty Baby, Summer Love, Ride the Wild Surf, Girl Happy, Clambake, A Time to Sing, UMC,* more.

FABIAN (S. Cal.) Singer-actor. Onscreen from 1959. IN: *Hound-Dog Man, High Time, North to Alaska, Five Weeks in a Balloon, Ride the Wild Surf, Dear Brigitte, Thunder Alley, Candy, Pretty Boy Floyd, The Inferno Road,* more.

FABIAN, FRANCOISE (Fr.) Leading lady. Onscreen from 1954. IN: *La Sacree Gamine, Fernandel the Dressmaker, Mam'zelle Pigalle, The Thief of Paris, L'Americain, My Night at Maud's,* more.

FABRAY, NANETTE (S. Cal.) Singer-actress. Onscreen at seven—in 1927—in "Our Gang." Returned to the screen in 1939. IN: *The Private Lives of Elizabeth and Essex* (billed Fabares), *A Child Is Born, The Band Wagon, The Happy Ending,* more.

FABRIZI, ALDO (It.) Character. Onscreen from 1946. IN: *Open City, To Live in Peace, Three Steps North., Flowers of St. Francis, Times Gone By, The Angel Wore Red, The Wonders of Aladdin, Three Bites of the Apple, Those Were the Days,* more.

FADDEN, TOM (Fla.) A widower—his beloved wife, Genevieve, died in '59—this superb character actor lives at Vero Beach. He is in his 80s now (b. 1895), and hasn't appeared in a movie since 1970's *Dirty Dingus Magee.* But by no means does he consider himself retired. He still has an agent, is still listed in the *Academy Players Directory,* and is ready to hop a plane back to Hollywood any time—for a short time. Onscreen from 1939. IN: *Destry Rides Again, I Stole a Million, The Shepherd of the Hills, Kiss the Boys Goodbye, The Remarkable Andrew, Edge of Darkness, A Lady Takes a Chance, The Hairy Ape, Tomorrow the World, State Fair, The Big Sleep, Cheyenne, State of the Union, Badmen of Tombstone, Prince of Players, Invasion of the Body Snatchers, Baby Face Nelson, Pocketful of Miracles; They Shoot Horses, Don't They?;* more.

FAIRBANKS, DOUGLAS, JR. (Fla.) English residents for decades, he and wife, Mary Lee, have sold their London home and settled in Palm Beach. From there the star journeys to stage engagements all over the States and, for television roles, to Hollywood where he unfailingly visits Mary Pickford, his onetime stepmother. Onscreen from 1920. IN: *Party Girl, Air Mail, Stella Dallas, The Barker, The Jazz Age, Our Modern Maidens, Little Caesar, Morning Glory, The Prisoner of Zenda, Having*

Wonderful Time, Joy of Living, Gunga Din, The Sun Never Sets, Angels Over Broadway, The Corsican Brothers, Sinbad the Sailor, That Lady in Ermine, The Fighting O'Flynn, Mr. Drake's Duck, more.

FAITHFULL, MARIANNE (Eng.) Leading lady. Onscreen from 1967. IN: *I'll Never Forget Whatshisname, Girl on a Motorcycle, Hamlet.*

FALANA, LOLA (S. Cal.) Black leading lady. IN: *The Liberation of Lord Byron Jones, The Klansman, Lady Coco,* more.

FALK, PETER (S. Cal.) Costar. Nominated for Best Supporting Actor Oscar in *Murder, Inc.* and *Pocketful of Miracles.* Onscreen from 1958. IN: *Wind Across the Everglades, The Rebel Set, The Secret of the Purple Reef, Pretty Boy Floyd, Pressure Point, Robin and the Seven Hoods, The Great Race, Penelope, Anzio, Castle Keep, Husbands, A Woman Under the Influence, Murder by Death,* more.

FALKENBURG, JINX (N.Y.) Still a beauty in her 50s (b. 1919), she remains happily married (since '45) to Tex McCrary, has two grown sons, lives in Manhasset on Long Island. Also a vice president for Marian Bialac Cosmetics (one of Jock Whitney's firms), she stages fashion shows to benefit such organizations as the Child Study Association, and, in '75, proving she's still a sensational tennis player, she was a member of the celebrity team playing a preopening match at Forest Hills. She has talked about returning to show business, but on TV, not the screen—where she has not been seen since 1946's *Meet Me on Broadway.* Onscreen first as Jinx Falken, leading lady in the 1939 serial *The Lone Ranger Rides Again.* That same year she also was in *Song of the Buckaroo* and *Professional Model,* which she had been (#1). Onscreen as Jinx Falkenburg from 1941. IN: *Two Latins from Manhattan, Sing for Your Supper, Sweetheart of the Fleet, Lucky Legs, Two Senoritas from Chicago, Nine Girls, Cover Girl, Tahiti Nights, The Gay Senorita, Talk About a Lady,* more.

FANTONI, SERGIO (It.) Costar. Onscreen from 1960. IN: *The Giant of Marathon, The Prize, Von Ryan's Express, High Infidelity, Do Not Disturb; What Did You Do in the War, Daddy?; Hornets' Nest,* more.

FARENTINO, JAMES (S. Cal.) Costar. Onscreen from 1964. IN: *Psychomania, Ensign Pulver, The War Lord, The Pad, Wings of Fire, Banning, Ride to Hangman's Tree, Rosie; Me, Natalie;* more.

FARLEY, MORGAN (Conn.) This fine character actor continued his career into this decade when he appeared in Disney's *The Barefoot Executive.* Now in his 70s (b. 1898), he lives in retirement in Stamford. Onscreen from 1929. IN: *The Greene Murder Case, The Love Doctor, Slightly Scarlet, The Devil's Holiday, A Man from Wyoming, Beloved, Gentleman's Agreement, Hollow Triumph, Top O' the Morning, The Man Who Cheated Himself, Sealed Cargo; Goodbye, My Fancy; The Wild North, Julius Caesar, Jivaro,* more.

FARMER, MIMSY (It.) The blonde American actress, whose Hollywood career amounted to little, is now (in her early 30s) one of the most popular stars in Italian movies. Onscreen from 1963. IN: *Spencer's Mountain, Bus Riley's Back in Town, Riot on Sunset Strip, The Wild Racers, Move, Road to Salina,* more.

FARR, DEREK (Eng.) Costar. Onscreen from 1940. IN: *The Voice in the Night, Wanted for Murder, Conspiracy in Teheran, Murder Without Crime, Double Confession, Front Page Story, Doctor at Large, The Circle,* more.

FARR, FELICIA (S. Cal.) Leading lady. Onscreen from 1956. IN: *The Reprisal, Jubal, 3:10 to Yuma, Onionhead; Kiss Me, Stupid; Charley Varrick, Kotch,* more.

FARR, JAMIE (S. Cal.) Character. Onscreen from 1955. IN: *The Blackboard Jungle, No Time for Sergeants, The Greatest Story Ever Told, Who's Minding the Mint? With Six You Get Egg Roll,* more.

FARRAR, DAVID (Eng.) Leading man. In his 60s (b. 1908), he has been inactive in movies for more than a dozen years. Onscreen from the late '30s. IN: *Danny Boy, The Dark Tower, Night Invader, The Lisbon Story, Black Narcissus, Frieda, Gone to Earth, Obsessed, Cage of Gold, Night Without Stars, The Hooded Terror, Duel in the Jungle, The Black Shield of Falworth, The Sea Chase, Woman and the Hunter, I Accuse!, Watusi, Solomon and Sheba, Lion of Sparta,* more.

FARRELL, CHARLES (S. Cal.) In his 70s (b. 1902), fast-receding white hairline or no, he remains a vital athletic figure—playing 18 holes of golf each and every day. Tennis? Still the major-domo of Palm Springs' "Charlie Farrell Racquet Club," as he has been for more than four decades, though he now no longer owns it, he plays "only occasionally" now. Regular visitors at the club are his many-times costar Janet Gaynor and her husband, stage producer Paul Gregory, who live between Palm Springs and Desert Hot Springs. They were also among the many scores of oldtime Hollywood friends who did all they could to console him at the time of the death of his wife, Virginia Valli, in 1968. He and the beautiful actress, who had no children, had been married since 1931. One of the best-loved members of the community, Farrell has twice—in '48 and again in '52—been mayor of Palm Springs. Act again? Thanks, but no. Onscreen from 1923. IN: *Wings of Youth, Old Ironsides, Seventh Heaven, Red Dance, Sunny Side Up, City Girl, Lucky Star, Happy Days, Liliom, Merely Mary Ann, Heartbreak, Delicious, The First Year, Our Daily Bread, Forbidden Heaven, Just Around the Corner, Tail Spin, Convoy,* more.

FARRELL, MIKE (S. Cal.) Leading man. Onscreen from the '60s. IN: *Captain Newman, M.D.; Targets, The Americanization of Emily, The Graduate,* more.

FARRELL, SHARON (S. Cal.) Leading lady. Onscreen from 1966. IN: *The Spy with My Face, A Lovely Way to Die, The Reivers, The Little Sister, The Love Machine, It's Alive, The Premonition,* more.

FARRELL, TOMMY (S. Cal.) Support. Onscreen from 1950. IN: *Pirates of the High Seas* (serial), *Duchess of Idaho, At War with the Army, A Yank in Korea, Meet Danny Wilson,* more.

FARROW, MIA (Eng.) Costar. Onscreen from 1964. IN: *Guns at Batasi, A Dandy in Aspic, Rosemary's Baby, Secret Ceremony, John and Mary, See No Evil, The Public Eye, The Great Gatsby,* more.

FARROW, TISA (N.Y.) Leading lady. Like Mia, a daughter of Maureen O'Sullivan. Onscreen in '70. IN: *Homer.*

FASSETT, JAY (Idaho) After *My Sin* and *The Cheat,* both in '31, he continued his career on Broadway before retiring after 1947's *Command Decision.* Well into his 80s now (b. 1889), he and wife Dorothy live in retirement at River's Edge Ranch in Sun Valley.

FAULK, JOHN HENRY (Tex.) Radio personality. Support. IN: *The Best Man.*

FAULKNER, EDWARD (S. Cal.) Support. Onscreen from 1965. IN: *Tickle Me, Chisum, Rio Lobo, The Barefoot Executive, Something Big, Scandalous John,* more.

FAULKNER, JAMES (Eng.) Leading man. Onscreen in the '70s. IN: *The Abdication, Conduct Unbecoming,* more.

FAULKNER, RALPH (S. Cal.) A vigorous man in his 80s (b. 1891), this character actor who almost always appeared in swashbucklers owns and operates a flourishing fencing school in Los Angeles. Onscreen from the '30s. IN: *The Three Musketeers, The Prisoner of Zenda,* more.

FAVERSHAM, PHILIP (N.Y.) Leading man. Onscreen in the '30s. IN: *Captured, The World Changes, The House on 56th Street, The Big Shakedown, Jimmy the Gent, Gambling Lady,* more.

FAWCETT, FARRAH /now **FARRAH FAWCETT-MAJORS** (S. Cal.) Leading lady. Onscreen in the '70s. IN: *Myra Breckinridge, Love Is a Funny Thing,* more.

FAY, BRENDAN (N.Y.) Character. IN: *The Hustler, Juke Box Racket, Man on a Swing,* more.

FAY, DOROTHY (Tenn.) In the '30s she was the blue-eyed leading lady of cowboys "Wild Bill" Elliott, Bob Baker, and Tex Ritter. She became Ritter's wife in '41, remaining most happily married to him until his death in '73. Retiring at the time of her marriage, she became the mother of two sons—John, now a successful non-Western Hollywood actor, and Tom, a Berkeley graduate student who has been active in Tennessee politics. During their last decade together, the Ritters lived in a big ranch house on Franklin Road in Nashville, where she has remained. Tex Ritter carved a new career for himself after his Hollywood days, in Nashville's C&W world (he also ran for U.S. Senator, but lost), and his wife enjoyed being of it, but not in it. IN: *Prairie Justice,* many more Westerns.

FAY, EDDY (N.Y.) Character. IN: *My Brother,* more.

FAYE, ALICE (S. Cal.) Married to comedian Phil Harris for more than three decades, this musical star has two daughters, several grandchildren, and lives in Palm Springs. Retired from the screen after 1945's *Fallen Angel,* she returned once, to play the mother in 1962's *State Fair.* In the '70s she starred in the stage musical *Good News* with two of her former leading men from the movies—John Payne on Broadway, Don Ameche on tour. Onscreen from 1934. IN: *George White's Scandals, She Learned About Sailors, King of Burlesque, Poor Little Rich Girl, Wake Up and Live, You're a Sweetheart, In Old Chicago, Alexander's Ragtime Band; Sally, Irene and Mary; Rose of Washington Square, Little Old New*

York, Lillian Russell, Tin Pan Alley, That Night in Rio, The Great American Broadcast; Hello, Frisco, Hello; The Gang's All Here, more.

FAYE, HERBIE (S. Cal.) Character. Onscreen from 1954. IN: *Top Banana, The Shrike, The Harder They Fall, Requiem for a Heavyweight, Thoroughly Modern Millie*, more.

FAYE, JOEY (N.Y.) Comedian. Onscreen from 1948. IN: *Close-Up, Top Banana, The Tender Trap, That Touch of Mink*, more.

FAYLEN, FRANK (S. Cal.) On the threshold of his 70s (b. 1907), he continues to be a much-in-demand character actor. Long married to serial leading lady Carol Hughes (Dale Arden in *Flash Gordon Conquers the Universe*), he has two grown daughters, Kay and Carol Faylen, both of whom have been actresses. In '64, when 15, Carol was featured as the elder daughter in the TV series *The Bing Crosby Show*. Onscreen from 1936. IN: *Bullets or Ballots, They Won't Forget, Marked Woman, No Time for Comedy, Silver Skates, Mission to Moscow, The Canterville Ghost, The Lost Weekend, The Blue Dahlia, To Each His Own, Two Years Before the Mast, California, Blood on the Moon, Francis, Fourteen Hours, 99 River Street, The McConnell Story, Gunfight at the O.K. Corral, North to Alaska, Fluffy*, more.

FEARS, PEGGY (S. Cal.) She still lives in Hollywood but is completely retired from acting. IN: *Lottery Lover*, more.

FEHMIU, BEKIM (It.) Leading man. Onscreen from 1968. IN: *The Feverish Years, I Even Met Happy Gypsies, Do Not Mention the Cause of Death, The Adventurers; Libera, My Love; Permission to Kill*, more.

FELD, FRITZ (S. Cal.) 1975 marked this most versatile character actor's 55th anniversary in the entertainment field. Born in 1900, he has appeared in 400 major movies, more than 300 "live" TV shows, and, he estimates, in excess of 500 TV films. Feld came to the States from Austria in '23 to play The Piper in Max Reinhardt's stage production *The Miracle*. (In '73, as the only survivor of the original Reinhardt ensemble, he was the principal guest speaker at New York State University in Binghamton, during its Max Reinhardt Centennial Symposium.) Following *The Miracle's* tour, he was signed by Hollywood, making 30 silents as a "heavy" with Barrymore, Jannings, and Norma Talmadge, before becoming one of the most recognizable faces in talkies. As a film comedian, he is perhaps best known for his "pop!" trick—a distinctive bit of oral punctua-

tion accomplished by bringing the flat of his palm sharply against his rounded mouth, the gimmick he has used in many roles: as butler, chef, movie director, foreign spy, etc. In '71, on photographic safari in Africa, he became an honorary member of Kenya Reserve's Masai tribe after teaching them this stunt. Fritz Feld and his wife, actress Virginia Christine, live in Brentwood, in a very modern house high on a bluff overlooking the Pacific, and filled with books (his vast Strindberg collection in all languages being his special joy), Bach recordings, and artifacts and rare plants from the many lands they have visited. Onscreen in talkies from 1929. IN: *Black Magic, Tovarich, True Confession, Bringing Up Baby, Gold Diggers in Paris, Idiot's Delight, Little Old New York, Victory, Maisie Gets Her Man, Phantom of the Opera, I've Always Loved You, Carnival in Costa Rica, Julia Misbehaves, Call Me Madam, Pocketful of Miracles, The Errand Boy; Promises, Promises; Barefoot in the Park; Hello, Dolly!; The Love Bug Rides Again, The Strongest Man in the World, The Sunshine Boys*, more. (See Virginia Christine.)

FELDMAN, MARTY (S. Cal.) Star comedian. Onscreen from 1969. IN: *Every Home Should Have One, Young Frankenstein, The Adventure of Sherlock Holmes' Smarter Brother*, more.

FELDON, BARBARA (S. Cal.) Leading lady. Onscreen from 1967. IN: *Fitzwilly, Smile*, more.

FELIX, MARIA (Mex.) Offscreen since the early '60s, the actress, one of Mexico's most famous and beautiful, announced in '75 that she would resume her career in a television series in Mexico City. Onscreen from the '40s. IN: *Enamorado, Hidden River, The Devil Is a Woman, French Can-Can, Les Heros Sont Fatigues (Heroes and Sinners), La Cucaracha, The Empty Star*, more.

FELL, NORMAN (S. Cal.) Character. Onscreen from 1960. IN: *Inherit the Wind, PT-109; Quick, Before It Melts; Fitzwilly, The Graduate, The Secret War of Harry Frigg, Bullitt, Catch 22, Airport 1975, Cleopatra Jones & the Casino of Gold*, more.

FELLOWS, EDITH (S. Cal.) In her early 50s (b. 1923) and looking younger, this greatly talented former juvenile star left the screen after making *Her First Romance* in 1947, and appeared for the next 15 years in musicals on Broadway and in stock, with some "live" TV while living in New York's Greenwich Village. Back in Hollywood, where she grew up as the ward of her long-deceased grandmother, Edith has lately admitted contemplating a return to the screen. Married and divorced twice, she has a grown daughter, Kathie Fields, an actress, who spent much time in her growing-up years with her father, agent Freddie Fields, and his then-wife, Polly Bergen. Onscreen from 1931. IN: *Daddy Long Legs, Huckleberry Finn, Cimarron, Kid Millions, Mrs. Wiggs of the Cabbage Patch, Keeper of the Bees, Dinky, Black Fury, Pennies from Heaven, Tugboat Princess, Little Miss Roughneck, Five Little Peppers, Music in My Heart, Nobody's Children, Her First Beau, Stardust on the Sage*, more.

FENEMORE, HILDA (Eng.) Character. Onscreen from the '50s. IN: *The End of the Road, The Large Rope, Saturday Island, Room in the House, Johnny You're Wanted*, more.

FENNELLY, PARKER (N.Y.) Character; retired. Onscreen from 1957. IN: *The Kettles on Old McDonald's Farm, It Happened to Jane, The Russians Are Coming . . ., Angel in My Pocket*, more.

FERDIN, PAMELYN (S. Cal.) Juvenile lead. Onscreen from the '60s. IN: *What a Way to Go!, Never Too Late, Beguiled, The Mephisto Waltz; Happy Birthday, Wanda June*; more.

FERGUSON, FRANK (S. Cal.) Character. Onscreen from 1940. IN: *They Died with Their Boots On, Boss of Big Town, Rhapsody in Blue, Canyon Passage, Fort Apache, Rachel and the Stranger, Roseanna McCoy, The Furies, Bend of the River, Million Dollar Mermaid, The Big Leaguer, Battle Cry, Tribute to a Bad Man, Sunrise at Campobello, Pocketful of Miracles, Hush . . . Hush . . . Sweet Charlotte*, more.

FERGUSON, HELEN (S. Cal.) Before her recent lengthy illness, she had long been—after her screen career—one of Hollywood's best-known publicity agents, representing Loretta Young, Barbara Stanwyck, etc. Onscreen in the '20s. IN: *Miss Lulu Bett, Hungry Hearts, The Famous Mrs. Fair, Within the Law, The Unknown Purple*, more.

FERNANDEZ, EMILIO (Mex.) Character. Onscreen in Mexico from 1934. Onscreen in America from 1965. IN: *The Reward, The Appaloosa, Return of the Seven, A Covenant with Death, Political Asylum*, more.

FERNANDEZ, ESTHER (Mex.) Leading lady. Onscreen in Mexico from 1936. Onscreen in America only in 1946's *Two Years Before the Mast*.

FERNANDEZ, PETER (N.Y.) Character. IN: *City Across the River*, more.

FERRADAY, LISA (Mich.) Remembered primarily for her B's, this beautiful leading lady gave up her career after 1956's *Death of a Scoundrel*. She has been married for a number of years to wealthy Wenslow Anderson of Grosse Point and is not only a popular hostess at this residence but also at their other homes in New York City and Acapulco, where they spend part of each year. Onscreen from 1951. IN: *Flame of Istamboul, China Corsair, I Was An American Spy, Belle of New York, Last Train from Bombay, The Snows of Kilimanjaro, The Merry Widow, The Kentuckian*, more.

FERRARE, CRISTINA (S. Cal.) Leading lady. Onscreen from 1968. IN: *The Impossible Years, J.W. Coop; Mary, Mary; Bloody Mary*, more.

FERRER, JOSE (S. Cal.) Character star. Nominated for Best Supporting Actor Oscar in *Joan of Arc*. Won Best Actor Oscar in *Cyrano de Bergerac*. Onscreen from 1948. IN: *Whirlpool, Crisis, Moulin Rouge, The Caine Mutiny, The Shrike, The Great Man, I Accuse!, Lawrence of Arabia, The Greatest Story Ever Told, Ship of Fools, Enter Laughing*, more.

FERRER, MEL (It.) Costar. Onscreen from 1949. IN: *Lost Boundaries, Born to Be Bad, The Brave Bulls, Scaramouche, Lili, Knights of the Round Table, War and Peace, Paris Does Strange Things, The Sun Also Rises, Blood and Roses, The Longest Day, Sex and the Single Girl, Paris When It Sizzles, El Greco, A Time for Loving, Night Visitor, The Anti-Christ, Brannigan*, more.

FERRIS, AUDREY (S. Cal.) Offscreen since 1930, the onetime Wampas Baby Star lives in retirement in North Hollywood. Onscreen from 1927. IN: *The Silver Slave, Beware of Married Men, Women They Talk About, The Little Wildcat, The Glad Rag Doll*, more.

FERRIS, BARBARA (Eng.) Leading lady. Onscreen from 1964. IN: *The Girl Getters, Children of the Damned, Having a Wild Weekend, Interlude, A Nice Girl Like Me*, more.

FETCHIT, STEPIN (Ill.) Now in his 80s (b. 1892), the comedian—a Chicago resident—resumed his movie career with a supporting role in 1974's *Amazing Grace*. Three years before that he had done a cameo on TV in the "NBC Mystery Movie" *Cutter*. Several years ago producer Joseph E. Levine announced plans for a film biography of Stepin Fetchit (r.n. Lincoln Theodore Perry) that, produced-written-directed by Ossie Davis, would star Godfrey Cambridge; to date, the movie has not been made. Of the roles he has played onscreen, the comedian has said, "Like Chaplin, I played the part of a simple, sincere, honest, and lovable character who won sympathy from an audience by being tolerant of those who hurt him so that he could do good for those he loved." He has most recently been in *Won Ton Ton, the Dog Who Saved Hollywood.* Onscreen from 1927. IN: *In Old Kentucky, Show Boat, Hearts in Dixie, The Galloping Ghost, Stand Up and Cheer, Carolina, David Harum, Judge Priest, County Chairman, Helldorado, Charlie Chan in Egypt, Steamboat 'Round the Bend, the Virginia Judge, Dimples, Love Is News, Zenobia, Miracle in Harlem, Bend of the River, The Sun Shines Bright,* more.

FEUILLERE, EDWIGE (Fr.) Star. Onscreen from 1930. IN: *Topaze, Lucrezia Borgia, The Idiot, Blind Desire, The Eagle with Two Heads, Pit of Loneliness, The Game of Love, Adorable Creatures, Fruits of Summer, Love Is My Profession,* more.

FICKETT, MARY (N.Y.) Leading lady. Onscreen 1957–58. IN: *Man on Fire, Kathy O.*

FIDLER, JIMMIE (S. Cal.) Retired now, this famous gossip columnist and newscaster, who was onscreen in a few, married Kathryn Davis on August 30, 1972, at 72. IN: *Garden of the Moon,* more.

FIEDLER, JOHN (S. Cal.) Character. Onscreen from 1957. IN: *12 Angry Men, Raisin in the Sun, That Touch of Mink, The World of Henry Orient; Kiss Me, Stupid; A Fine Madness, The Odd Couple, True Grit,* more.

FIELD, MARGARET/now MAGGIE MAHONEY (S. Cal.) Leading lady; retired. Onscreen as Margaret Field from 1948. IN: *Beyond Glory, My Friend Irma, The Man from Planet X, For Men Only, So This Is Love, Inside Detroit,* more. Onscreen as Maggie Mahoney (after marriage to Jock Mahoney) from 1956. IN: *Blackjack Ketchum Desperado, Desire in the Dust,* more.

FIELD, MARY (S. Cal.) Character. Onscreen from 1937. IN: *The Prince and the Pauper, White Banners, Dancing Coed; My Son, My Son; The Major and the Minor, You Were Never Lovelier, Frenchman's Creek, Sentimental Journey, Miracle on 34th Street, Life with Father, Chicken Every Sunday, Dear Wife, Lucy Gallant, Ride a Crooked Trail,* more.

FIELD, SALLY (S. Cal.) Leading lady. Daughter of Margaret Field/Mahoney. Onscreen from 1967. IN: *The Way West,* more.

FIELD, SHIRLEY ANN (Eng.) Leading lady. Onscreen from 1956. IN: *It's Never Too Late,*

Yield to the Night, The Silken Affair, The Good Companions, Horrors of the Black Museum, Once More With Feeling, The Entertainer, Saturday Night and Sunday Morning, The War Lover, Kings of the Sun, These Are the Damned, Doctor in Clover, Alfie, more.

FIELD, SYLVIA (S. Cal.) The widow of Ernest Truex, she lives in Fallbrook, south of Los Angeles, where she has an avocado orchard. Though in her 70s now and not in a movie in recent years, she still journeys to Hollywood occasionally for roles in TV series such as *Harry O.* Onscreen from 1929. IN: *The Voice of the City, Her Primitive Man, Junior Miss, All Mine to Give,* more.

FIELD, VIRGINIA (S. Cal.) Leading lady. Long offscreen, she is presently resuming her career. Onscreen from 1937. IN: *Lloyds of London, Mr. Moto's Last Warning, The Sun Never Sets, Eternally Yours, Waterloo Bridge; Dance, Girl, Dance; Singapore Woman, The Crystal Ball, The Imperfect Lady, Christmas Eve, Dream Girl, John Loves Mary, Weekend with Father, Veils of Bagdad, The Earth Dies Screaming,* more. (See Willard Parker.)

FIELDING, FENELLA (Eng.) Leading lady. Onscreen from 1961. IN: *Foxhole in Cairo, Follow a Star, No Love for Johnnie, The Old Dark House, Doctor in Distress; Arrivederci, Baby!;* more.

FIELDS, GRACIE (It.) The inimitable English actress-singer's four Hollywood films were her last. Now in her 70s (b. 1898), and still given to laughter and blonde locks, she lives in a villa in Capri where she owns and runs a combined restaurant-swimming club. Divorced from Archie Pitts, she was married for many years to comedian Monty Banks until his death in '50. Since '52, she has been married to Boris Alperovici, a few years her junior, who is her business partner. She has published her autobiography, *Sing As We Go* ('60). And, earlier this decade, the "pride of Lancashire," who insists she is retired, came out of retirement long enough to tape several singing appearances for *Stars on Sunday,* a British TV variety show. At that time she also recorded a new 12-track album of her greatest hits for York Records. Onscreen in England from 1931. IN: *Sally in Our Alley, Sing As We Go, The Show Goes On, Smiling Along, Shipyard Sally,* more. Onscreen in America 1943–45. IN: *Stage Door Canteen, Holy Matrimony, Molly and Me,* and *Paris Underground.*

FIELDS, KATHY (S. Cal.) Leading lady. Daughter of Edith Fellows. Onscreen in the '70s. IN: *Johnny Got His Gun,* more.

141

FIELDS, ROBERT (S. Cal.) Support. Onscreen from 1967. IN: *The Incident; They Shoot Horses, Don't They?; The Sporting Club, Rhinoceros,* more.

FIELDS, SHEP (S. Cal.) Yesterday's orchestra leader of "Rippling Rhythm" fame is now a senior vice president of a top talent agency in Hollywood. IN: *The Big Broadcast of 1938.*

FIERRO, PAUL (S. Cal.) Character. Onscreen from 1948. IN: *Red River, Amazon Quest, Abbott and Costello in the Foreign Legion, Wings of the Hawk, The Creature Walks Among Us,* more.

FIGUEROA, RUBEN (N.Y.) Juvenile. Onscreen from 1969. IN: *Pepi, Who Says I Can't Ride a Rainbow,* more.

FINCH, JON (Eng.) Costar. Onscreen from 1971. IN: *Macbeth, Sunday Bloody Sunday, Frenzy, Lady Caroline Lamb, The Last Days of Man on Earth,* more.

FINCH, PETER (Switz.) Star. Nominated for Best Actor Oscar in *Sunday Bloody Sunday.* Onscreen from 1937. IN: *Red Sky at Morning, The Power and the Glory, The Miniver Story, The Wooden Horse, Fighting Rats of Tobruk, Gilbert & Sullivan, Elephant Walk, The Heart of the Matter, Pursuit of the Graf Spee, A Town Like Alice, Windom's Way, The Nun's Story, The Sins of Rachel Cade, I Thank a Fool, In the Cool of the Day, Girl with Green Eyes, The Pumpkin Eater, Judith, The Spy Who Came in from the Cold, The Flight of the Phoenix, Far from the Madding Crowd, Lost Horizon, The Abdication, Network, Something to Hide,* more.

FINDLATER, JOHN (S. Cal.) Support. Onscreen from 1968. IN: *With Six You Get Egg Roll; Where Angels Go, Trouble Follows; Airport,* more.

FINK, JOHN (S. Cal.) Support. IN: *Loving.*

FINLAY, FRANK (Eng.) Nominated for Best Supporting Actor Oscar in *Othello.* Onscreen from the '60s. IN: *Doctor in Distress, Walk in the Shadow, Robbery, The Deadly Bees, I'll Never Forget What's 'Is Name, Inspector Clouseau, The Shoes of the Fisherman, Twisted Nerve, The Virgin Soldiers, Cromwell, Gumshoe, Shaft in Africa, The Three Musketeers, The Four Musketeers,* more.

FINNEY, ALBERT (Eng.) Star. Nominated for Best Actor Oscar in *Tom Jones* and *Murder on the Orient Express.* Onscreen from 1960. IN: *The Entertainer, Saturday Night and Sunday Morning, The Victors, Night Must Fall, Two for the Road, Charlie Bubbles, Madame de Pompadour, Scrooge, Gumshoe,* more.

FIRESTONE, EDDIE (S. Cal.) Character. Onscreen from 1950. IN: *Jackpot, With a Song in My Heart, One Minute to Zero, The Revolt of Mamie Stover, Bail out at 40,000, The Mountain Road, Two for the Seesaw, A Man Called Cannon, Suppose They Gave a War and Nobody Came?,* more.

FISCHER, MAX (N.Y.) Character. IN: *Grand Illusion, The Search.*

FISHER, CARRIE (S. Cal.) Newcomer daughter of Eddie Fisher and Debbie Reynolds. IN: *Shampoo.*

FISHER, EDDIE (S. Cal.) Singer-actor. Onscreen from 1950. IN: *All About Eve, Bundle of Joy, Butterfield 8.*

FISHER, "SHUG" (S. Cal.) Character. IN: *Mister Roberts, The Castaway Cowboy,* more.

FITZGERALD, GERALDINE (N.Y.) Costar. Nominated for Best Supporting Actress Oscar in *Wuthering Heights.* Now, in her 60s (b. 1914) and heavier than during her Hollywood years, she plays mothers in occasional movies but is principally one of New York's major character actresses—starring, as the mother, in the '75 revival of *Ah, Wilderness!,* etc. The mother of two—Michael Lindsay-Hogg (by her first marriage; now a top director of British TV) and Susan Scheftel—she has been married since '46 to Stuart Scheftel, cofounder of the Pan-Am Building and Chairman of the New York City Youth Board. Onscreen in England from 1934. IN: *The Turn of the Tide, Radio Parade of 1935, Mill on the Floss,* more. Onscreen in America from 1939. IN: *Dark Victory, A Child Is Born, Till We Meet Again, Shining Victory, The Gay Sisters, Watch on the Rhine, Wilson, The Strange Affair of Uncle Harry, Three Strangers, Nobody Lives Forever, O.S.S., So Evil My Love, 10 North Frederick, The Pawnbroker, Rachel Rachel. The Last American Hero,* more.

FITZGERALD, NEIL (N.Y.) Character. Onscreen from 1935. IN: *The Informer, The Bride of Frankenstein, Charlie Chan in Shanghai, Mary of Scotland, The Plough and the Stars, Parnell, Arrest Bulldog Drummond, Bulldog Drummond's Secret Police, Mirage,* more.

FITZGERALD, WALTER (Eng.) Character. Onscreen from 1930. IN: *This England, In Which We Serve, Blanche Fury, Edward My Son, The Fallen Idol, The Winslow Boy, Something of Value, Darby O'Gill and the Little People, Third Man on the Mountain,* more.

FITZPATRICK, PAT (S. Cal.) Character. Onscreen from 1940. IN: *Mozart, The Strongest Man in the World,* more.

FIX, PAUL (S. Cal.) One of the most commanding character actors ever in movies, he is, in his 70s (b. 1902), more likely to be found in such TV series as *Barnaby Jones* than in pictures. Onscreen from 1928. IN: *First Kiss, Bad Girl, Back Street; Little Man, What Now?; The Road to Glory, The Prisoner of Shark Island, Winterset, After the Thin Man, The Buccaneer, Mannequin, Penitentiary, Dr. Cyclops, Virginia City, Pittsburgh, Tall in the Saddle, Back to Bataan, Wake of the Red Witch, Red River, Fair Wind to Java, Island in the Sky, The Bad Seed, To Kill a Mockingbird, The Sons of Katie Elder, Welcome to Hard Times, Shoot Out,* more.

FLAGG, FANNIE (N.Y.) Comedienne. IN: *Five Easy Pieces, The Bar.*

FLANAGAN, FIONNUALA (S. Cal.) Leading lady. Onscreen from 1967. IN: *Ulysses, Sinful Davey,* more.

FLANAGAN, KELLIE (S. Cal.) Former juvenile. IN: *Wild in the Streets.*

FLANNERY, SUSAN (S. Cal.) Leading lady. Onscreen in the '70s. IN: *The Towering Inferno, The Gumball Rally,* more.

FLAVIN, JAMES (S. Cal.) Character. Onscreen from 1932. IN: *King Kong, Baby Take a Bow, G-Men, West Point of the Air, My Man Godfrey, League of Frightened Men, Queen of the Mob, Belle Starr, Gentleman Jim, Air Force, Corvette K-225, So Proudly We Hail, Conflict, Sentimental Journey, The Strange Love of Martha Ivers, The Big Sleep, Nora Prentiss, Fury at Furnace Creek, South Seas Sinner, Apache Ambush, Wild Is the Wind, The Last Hurrah, In Cold Blood, The Barefoot Executive,* more. (Died 1976.)

FLEMING, ART (S. Cal.) TV emcee-actor. IN: *A Hatful of Rain.*

FLEMING, ERIN (S. Cal.) Leading lady. IN: *Everything You Wanted to Know About Sex.*

FLEMING, RHONDA (S. Cal.) Costar. Onscreen from 1944. IN: *Since You Went Away, Spellbound, Abilene Town, The Spiral Staircase, A Connecticut Yankee in King Arthur's Court, The Eagle and the Hawk, Hong Kong, Pony Express, Those Redheads from Seattle, Jivaro, Yankee Pasha, Tennessee's Partner, While the City Sleeps, The Buster Keaton Story, Gunfight at the O.K. Corral, The Crowded Sky, Revolt of the Slaves, The American Wife,* more.

FLEMING, SUSAN (S. Cal.) Married to Harpo Marx from '36 until his death in '64, she lives in retirement in Beverly Hills and is the mother of four grown adopted children: Bill Woollcott, Alexander (both named for critic Alexander Woollcott, Harpo's lifelong friend and biographer), and twins Minny and Jimmy. Onscreen from 1931. IN: *Men Are Like That, Million Dollar Legs, My Weakness, Call It Luck, Break of Hearts, Star for a Night, Gold Diggers of 1937, God's Country and the Woman,* more.

FLEMYNG, ROBERT (Eng.) Character. Onscreen from 1937. IN: *Head Over Heels, Blackmailed, The Man Who Never Was, Funny Face, Cast a Dark Shadow, Windom's Way, Rapture, The Spy with a Cold Nose, The Quiller Memorandum, Oh, What a Lovely War!, Young Winston,* more.

FLETCHER, BRAMWELL (N.H.) The former leading man from England is in his 70s now (b. 1904), lives outside the village of Marlborough, has been divorced three times (Helen Chandler, Diana Barrymore, Susan Robinson), is presently married to writer Lael Wertenbaker and is the father of three grown children. It has been three decades since he appeared in a movie but after his screen career he went into television (over 200 leads) and resumed starring on the stage, which he continues to do. In 1975 he was seen in Kansas City in the leading role of the Missouri Repertory Theatre's presentation of *In the Well of the House.* Onscreen in America from 1930. IN: *Raffles, Svengali, Millionaire, Daughter of the Dragon, A Bill of Divorcement, The Silent Witness, The Mummy, The Monkey's Paw, Only Yesterday, Random Harvest, White Cargo, The Immortal Sergeant,* more.

FLETCHER, JACK (S. Cal.) Character. Onscreen from the 60s. IN: *The Tiger Makes Out, Any Wednesday,* more.

FLETCHER, LESTER (S. Cal.) Character. IN: *Operation Eichmann,* more.

FLETCHER, LOUISE (S. Cal.) Leading lady. Won Best Actress Oscar in *One Flew Over the Cuckoo's Nest.* Onscreen in the '70s. IN: *Thieves Like Us, One Flew Over the Cuckoo's Nest, Russian Roulette.*

FLON, SUZANNE (Fr.) Leading lady. Onscreen from 1953. IN: *Moulin Rouge, Mr. Arkadin, Monkey in Winter, The Trial, Castle in Switzerland, Zita,* more.

FLOWERS, BESS (S. Cal.) Retired now and in her 70s (b. 1900), this tall, dignified woman who was Hollywood's "Queen of Dress Extras" with shingled hair—dark, and later iron-gray—

143

looks exactly as she did in almost every movie anyone ever attended. Beginning in the '20s as a leading lady in Art Acord Westerns, she later—in addition to all her "extra" work—played supporting roles in many dozens, such as that of the society dowager in *All About Eve* who says to Anne Baxter, at the Sara Siddons Awards, "I'm so happy for you, Eve." There were of course, many beefier parts. Last on-screen in *Good Neighbor Sam* ('64), she has a residence in Hollywood, just south of Sunset, and has on occasion spent time at the Motion Picture and TV Country Home. Twice wid-owed, by director Cullen B. Tate and studio manager William S. Holman, she has a daugh-ter, by her first husband, who is a Hollywood script girl. Onscreen from the '20s. IN: *The Ghost Talks, Bachelor Apartment, The Golden Arrow, Marry the Girl, The Shadow, Paid to Dance, Women in Prison, The Lone Wolf in Paris, Deception, Song of the Thin Man, The View from Pompey's Head*, more.

FLUELLEN, JOEL (S. Cal.) Black character. Onscreen from 1950. IN: *The Jackie Robinson Story, Duffy of San Quentin, Sitting Bull, Friendly Persuasion, The Decks Ran Red, Porgy and Bess, A Raisin in the Sun, The Great White Hope, Thomasine and Bushrod*, more.

FOCH, NINA (S. Cal.) Bordered in black, this one-inch ad appears with some regularity in Hollywood trade papers: "Will accept a limited number of private students, professional or semiprofessional, for new Friday afternoon class starting (date). Tuition $200/quarter." The name at the top of the little ad, in caps: NINA FOCH. The actress once nominated for a sup-porting Oscar (*Executive Suite*) still acts, but sporadically now—in such TV "Movies of the Week" as *Female Artillery* and theatrical films like *Mahogany*. Working on the other side of the camera has long been more to her liking. She discovered this in '58 when she was direc-tor George Stevens' aide on the movie *The Di-ary of Anne Frank*, helping Millie Perkins and other youngsters in the cast develop the proper concepts of their roles. She became a movie dropout for eight years after costarring in *Spar-tacus* ('60). Living in Manhattan, she studied choreography, taught acting, acted on TV, was director John Houseman's assistant on the TV special *A Night at Ford's Theater*, and, in '62, when she was 38, gave birth to her only child: Schuyler Dirk Brite. *Prescription: Murder* brought her back to Hollywood in '68. The ac-tress has been married three times—to TV actor James Lipton (1954–58), to several-years-youn-ger writer Dennis Brite (1959–63), father of her son, and (in '67) to Michael Dewell. Onscreen from 1943. IN: *Return of the Vampire, Nine Girls, She's a Soldier Too, Strange Affair, A Song to Remember, My Name Is Julia Ross, Boston Blackie's Rendezvous, The Guilt of Janet Ames, The Dark Past, An American in Paris, St. Benny the Dip, Scaramouche, Som-brero, The Ten Commandments, Spartacus, Prescription: Murder, Such Good Friends*, more.

FONDA, HENRY (S. Cal.) Star. Nominated for Best Actor Oscar in *The Grapes of Wrath*. On-screen from 1935. IN: *The Farmer Takes a Wife, Trail of the Lonesome Pine, The Moon's Our Home, Wings of the Morning, You Only Live Once, Blockade, Jezebel, The Mad Miss Manton, I Met My Love Again, Jesse James, The Story of Alexander Graham Bell, Young Mr. Lincoln, Drums Along the Mohawk, Lillian Russell, The Lady Eve, The Big Street, The Im-mortal Sergeant, The Ox-Bow Incident, My Darling Clementine, The Fugitive, Fort Apache, Mister Roberts, War and Peace, The Wrong Man, Twelve Angry Men, Advise and Consent, The Longest Day, Fail Safe, The Best Man, Battle of the Bulge, Welcome to Hard Times, Firecreek, Madigan; Yours, Mine and Ours; The Boston Strangler, The Cheyenne Social Club, Sometimes a Great Notion, The Serpent, Ash Wednesday*, more.

FONDA, JANE (S. Cal.) Star. Nominated for Best Actress Oscar in *They Shoot Horses, Don't They?* Won in the same category in *Klute*. Onscreen from 1960. IN: *Tall Story, Walk on the Wild Side, Period of Adjustment, In the Cool of the Day, Sunday in New York, La Ronde, Cat Ballou, Any Wednesday, Barefoot in the Park, Barbarella, Steelyard Blues, Intro-duction to the Enemy, The Blue Bird, Fun with Dick and Jane*, more.

FONDA, PETER (S. Cal.) Leading man. On-screen from 1963. IN: *Tammy and the Doctor, The Victors, The Young Lovers, Lilith, Make Me an Offer, The Wild Angels, Easy Rider, Spirits of the Dead, Man Without Mercy, The Last Movie, The Hired Hand, Two People, Race with the Devil, 92 in the Shade, Killer Force, Fighting Mad*, more.

FONG, BENSON (S. Cal.) Character. Onscreen from 1943. IN: *Behind the Rising Sun, Charlie Chan in the Secret Service, The Purple Heart, Thirty Seconds Over Tokyo, Keys of the King-dom, First Yank in Tokyo, Calcutta, Boston Blackie's Chinese Adventure, His Majesty O'-Keefe, The Flower Drum Song, Our Man Flint, The Love Bug, The Strongest Man in the world*, more.

FONG, BRIAN (S. Cal.) Support. Onscreen from the '60s. IN: *The Unbelievers, Too Late the Hero, The Hawaiian, The Computer Wore Tennis Shoes, The Love Bug*, more.

FONG, KAM (Hawaii) Character. Onscreen from the '60s. IN: *Gidget Goes Hawaiian, Ghost of the China Sea, Seven Women from Hell, Diamond Head*, more.

FONTAINE, EDDIE (S. Cal.) Singer-actor. IN: *The Girl Can't Help It.*

FONTAINE, FRANK (Mass.) Comedian. Onscreen from 1950. IN: *Nancy Goes to Rio, Stella, Call Me Mister, The Model and the Marriage Broker.*

FONTAINE, JOAN (N.Y.) Star. Nominated for Best Actress Oscar in *Rebecca* and *The Constant Nymph*. Won in same category in *Suspicion*. Onscreen from 1935. IN: *No More Ladies, Quality Street, A Damsel in Distress, Duke of West Point, Man of Conquest, Gunga Din, The Women, This Above All, Frenchman's Creek, Jane Eyre, Ivy, The Emperor Waltz, Kiss the Blood Off My Hands, Letter from an Unknown Woman, September Affair, Ivanhoe, Casanova's Big Night, Serenade, Island in the Sun, A Certain Smile, Voyage to the Bottom of the Sea, Tender Is the Night*, more.

FONTANNE, LYNN (Wis.) Legendary stage star. Nominated for Best Actress Oscar in *The Guardsman*, one of two talkies in which she appeared. The other: *Stage Door Canteen*. She was also in one silent, *Second Youth*. (See Alfred Lunt.)

FORAN, DICK (S. Cal.) In his 60s now (b. 1910), heavier than in his starring days but nonetheless a fine-looking man, he lives in the San Fernando Valley. He is long and happily married, has grown sons and is a grandfather, takes an occasional supporting role on TV, and has profitable business interests. Onscreen from 1934. IN: *Stand Up and Cheer, Accent on Youth, Dangerous, The Petrified Forest, Song of the Saddle, Boy Meets Girl, Four Daughters, The Sisters, The Fighting 69th, My Little Chickadee, Unfinished Business, Keep 'Em Flying, The Mummy's Tomb, Guest Wife; Easy Come, Easy Go; Fort Apache, Thundering Jets, Studs Lonigan, Donovan's Reef*, more.

FORBES, BRENDA (Ill.) The character actress-daughter of the late Mary Forbes, she lives in Chicago now, is in her 60s (b. 1909), and remains active onstage, particularly in regional theaters. Onscreen from 1935. IN: *The Perfect Gentleman, Vigil in the Night, Miss Polly, Mrs. Miniver, The White Cliffs of Dover.*

FORBES, BRYAN (Eng.) Giving up his acting career after *The Guns of Navarone*, he has since been one of England's finest writer-directors (*Seance on a Wet Afternoon, The L-Shaped Room, The Whisperers*, etc.). Onscreen from 1948. IN: *The Small Back Room, The Wooden Horse, An Inspector Calls, Satellite in the Sky, House of Secrets, Enemy from Space, The Baby and the Battleship, The Colditz Story*, more.

FORBES, MERIEL (Eng.) Long and happily married to Sir Ralph Richardson, she is in her 60s now (b. 1913), continued her stage career well into the '60s, and last appeared onscreen in *Oh, What a Lovely War!* Onscreen from 1935. IN: *Mr. Cohen Takes a Walk, The Captive Heart, The Long Dark Hall, Home at Seven, Murder on Monday*, more.

FORBES, SCOTT (S. Cal.) Leading man. Onscreen from 1950. IN: *Rocky Mountain, Inside the Walls of Folsom Prison, Raton Pass, Operation Pacific, Subterfuge*, more.

FORD, BARRY (S. Cal.) Support. Onscreen from the '60s. IN: *Counterpoint, Tobruk, The Scorpio Letters, Von Ryan's Express, The Longest Day, Bridge to the Sun, Winning*, more.

FORD, CONSTANCE (N.Y.) Support. Onscreen from 1956. IN: *The Last Hunt, Bailout at 43,000, The Goddess, A Summer Place, Home from the Hill, All Fall Down, Claudelle Inglish, Rome Adventure, The Caretakers, 99 44/100% Dead*, more.

FORD, GLENN (S. Cal.) Star. Onscreen from 1939. IN: *Heaven with a Barbed Wire Fence, The Lady in Question, Blondie Plays Cupid, So Ends Our Night, Texas, The Adventures of Martin Eden, Destroyer, A Stolen Life, Gilda, The Loves of Carmen, Lust for Gold, The White Tower, Follow the Sun, Affair in Trinidad, The Big Heat, The Blackboard Jungle, Interrupted Melody, Teahouse of the August Moon, The Cowboy, It Started with a Kiss, Cimarron, A Pocketful of Miracles, The Courtship of Eddie's Father, The Rounders, Luv, Is Paris Burning?, Day of the Evil Gun, Smith!, Santee*, more.

FORD, HARRISON (S. Cal.) Support. Not the silent star of the same name. Onscreen from 1965. IN: *Luv, Getting Straight, The Long Ride Home, Zabriskie Point, The Conversation*, more.

FORD, ROSS (S. Cal.) Character; former leading man. Onscreen from 1943. IN: *The Adventures of Mark Twain, The Fuller Brush Man, Sign of the Ram, Night Unto Night, Challenge to Lassie, The Flying Missile, Force of Arms, Blue Canadian Rockies, Reform School Girl*, more.

FORD, RUTH (N.Y.) Character; former leading lady. Onscreen from 1942. IN: *The Lady Is*

Willing, Murder in the Big House, The Lady Gangster, The Hidden Hand, The Gorilla Man, Princess O'Rourke, Wilson, Circumstantial Evidence, Dragonwyck, Act One, more.

FOREST, MARK (It.) Leading man. Onscreen from 1960. IN: Goliath and the Dragon, The Revenge of Hercules, Goliath and the Giant, Son of Samson, more.

FOREST, MICHAEL (S. Cal.) Support. Onscreen from 1967. IN: Deathwatch, The Last Rebel, more.

FORMAN, JOEL (S. Cal.) Comedian. Onscreen from 1958. IN: Andy Hardy Comes Home, The Wheeler Dealers, The Wicked Dreams of Paula Schultz, more.

FORQUET, PHILIPPE (S. Cal.) Leading man. Onscreen from the '60s. IN: The Menace, Take Her She's Mine, In the French Style, Camille 2000, more.

FORREST, FREDRIC (S. Cal.) Leading man. Onscreen in the '70s. IN: Futz, When the Legends Die, The Conversation, Permission to Kill, more.

FORREST, HELEN (S. Cal.) The famous band singer remains a potent attraction in clubs as a solo performer. Onscreen in 1944. IN: Two Girls and a Sailor, Bathing Beauty.

FORREST, SALLY. (S. Cal.) Happily married to writer-producer Milo Frank since '51 (her only husband; no children), Sally remains beautifully blonde in her late 40s (b. 1928), lives in Beverly Hills (after residing for long periods in Spain and England), raises show dogs, and says, "I still take dancing lessons every day, because I enjoy it—and also because something one has done all her life is hard to drop." (Long before she costarred at MGM in such movies of the '50s as Excuse My Dust, Sally was a teenager in the chorus of musicals like Fiesta and The Pirate. Also, she was Ricardo Montalban's dance coach on The Kissing Bandit—before costarring with him two years later in Mystery Street.) Off the screen since 1956's While the City Sleeps, she admits, "I miss working and would love to do a film, but there is not much going at the moment." Onscreen from 1949. IN: Mr. Belvedere Goes to College, Not Wanted, Mystery Street, Valentino, Vengeance Valley; Hard, Fast and Beautiful; Bannerline, Code 2, Ride the High Iron, Son of Sinbad, more.

FORREST, STEVE (S. Cal.) Leading man. Onscreen from 1951. IN: Geisha Girl, Battle Circus, The Clown, Dream Wife, So Big, Take the High Ground, Rogue Cop, It Happened to Jane, Heller in Pink Tights, Five Branded Women, Flaming Star, The Second Time Around, Rascal, The Wild Country, The Late Liz, more.

FORREST, WILLIAM (S. Cal.) Character. Onscreen from 1940. IN: The Lone Wolf Meets a Lady, In This Our Life, Joe Smith American, The Masked Marvel (serial), So Proudly We Hail, Abroad with Two Yanks, Captain Eddie, The Road to Alcatraz, The Jolson Story, Dead Reckoning, The Senator Was Indiscreet, Race Street, I'll See You in My Dreams, A Man Called Peter, Band of Angels, Good Neighbor Sam, more.

FORSTER, ROBERT (N.Y.) Leading man. Onscreen from 1968. IN: Reflections in a Golden Eye, The Stalking Moon; Run, Shadow, Run; Medium Cool, Justine, Journey Through Rosebud, Cover Me Babe, more.

FORSYTH, ROSEMARY (S. Cal.) Leading lady. Onscreen from 1965. IN: Shenandoah, The War Lord, Texas Across the River, Where It's At, Whatever Happened to Aunt Alice?, Some Kind of a Nut, How Do I Love Thee, Black Eye, more.

FORSYTHE, JOHN (S. Cal.) Leading man. Onscreen from 1944. IN: Destination Tokyo, The Captive City, It Happens Every Thursday, The Glass Web, Escape from Fort Bravo, The Trouble with Harry, The Ambassador's Daughter, See How They Run, Madame X, In Cold Blood, The Happy Ending, Topaz, more.

FOSSE, BOB (N.Y.) Dancer-actor. Onscreen from 1953. IN: Affairs of Dobie Gillis, Give a Girl a Break, Kiss Me Kate, My Sister Eileen, The Little Prince, Thieves.

FOSSEY, BRIGITTE (Fr.) Leading lady; former juvenile lead. Onscreen from 1951. IN: Forbidden Games, The Happy Road, The Wanderer, Going Places, The Goodbye Singing, more.

FOSTER, BARRY (Eng.) Leading man. Onscreen from the '60s. IN: King and Country, The Family Way, Robbery, Ryan's Daughter, Frenzy, more.

FOSTER, BUDDY (S. Cal.) Former juvenile. IN: An Angel in My Pocket.

FOSTER, DIANNE (S. Cal.) Leading lady. Onscreen from 1951. IN: Drive a Crooked Road, The Big Frame, Bad for Each Other, The Violent Men, Monkey on My Back, The Last Hurrah, The Deep Six, Gideon of Scotland Yard, more.

FOSTER, FRANCES (N.Y.) Black support. Onscreen from 1961. IN: *Take a Giant Step, Cops and Robbers*, more.

FOSTER, GLORIA (S. Cal.) Black leading lady. Onscreen from 1964. IN: *The Cool World, Nothing But a Man, The Comedians, The Angel Levine*, more.

FOSTER, HELEN (S. Cal.) Going into her 70s (b. 1907), she last played leads in the early '30s, last played small roles (such as the telephone operator in *Call Northside 777*) in the '40s, but —a widow now—she loves moviemaking so she has continued to work as an extra. Onscreen from 1928. IN: *Hell-Ship Bronson, Gentlemen of the Press, Should a Girl Marry?, Linda, Hoofbeats of Vengeance, Gold Diggers of Broadway, Painted Faces, So Long Letty, Ghost City, The Big Flash, Lucky Larrigan, The Road to Ruin, School for Girls*, more.

FOSTER, JODIE (S. Cal.) Juvenile actress. Onscreen in the '70s. IN: *Tom Sawyer, Alice Doesn't Live Here Anymore, Taxi Driver*, more.

FOSTER, JULIA (Eng.) Leading lady. Onscreen from the '60s. IN: *The Loneliness of the Long Distance Runner, The Girl-Getters, Alfie, Half a Sixpence*, more.

FOSTER, NORMAN (S. Cal.) This star of the '30s gave up acting after 1942's *Journey Into Fear*, becoming a well-known director. Now, in his 70s (b. 1900), he has resumed acting—featured recently in an episode of *Cannon* and costarring on PBS in playwright Robert Anderson's *Double Solitaire*. Not altogether finished with directing, he recently directed for Orson Welles (a friend for decades) certain made-in-Hollywood scenes for *The Other Side of the Wind*; Welles has been shooting this film, all over the globe for several seasons. Once married to, and divorced from, Claudette Colbert (1928-35), he has long been the husband of Sally Blane, sister of Loretta Young. He has directed Sally Blane (*Charlie Chan at Treasure Island*), Loretta Young (*Rachel and the Stranger*), Polly Ann Young (*I Cover Chinatown*, in '36, which was the last movie in which Foster starred), as well as Ricardo Montalban (*Sombrero*), the husband of the fourth Young sister, Georgianna. In the '30s, Foster directed most of the "Mr. Moto" pix (also scripting several); in the '40s he directed *Kiss the Blood Off My Hands*, etc.; in the '50s, *Woman on the Run*, plus several for Disney, including *Davy Crockett, King of the Wild Frontier*; in the '60s, abroad, he was featured in *Murder Ahoy* and both produced and played a major role in *The Merry Wives of Windsor*. Onscreen from 1928. IN: *The Dove, Young Man of Manhattan, Up Pops the Devil,*

Confessions of a Coed, Play Girl, Working Wives, Smilin' Through, State Fair, Strictly Dynamite, Orient Express, Escape from Devil's Island, Ladies Crave Excitement, A Son Comes Home, Fatal Lady; Ride, Kelly, Ride; Scotland Yard, more.

FOSTER, PHIL (N.Y.) Comedian. Onscreen in 1955. IN: *Conquest of Space*.

FOSTER, RON (S. Cal.) Support. Onscreen from 1961. IN: *Operation Bottleneck, Secret of Deep Harbor*, more.

FOSTER, SUSANNA (N.Y.) Still an attractive blonde in her 50s (b. 1924), she is a business woman, working for a Wall Street firm. She now shuns the spotlight—which she deserted after 1945's *That Night with You*, as far as movies are concerned, and, in the mid-'50s, after costarring in light opera with her husband, Wilbur Evans. The parents of two grown sons, they have been divorced for years. The former star lives quietly in a West Side apartment and rarely sees anyone from her Hollywood days. Onscreen from 1939. IN: *The Great Victor Herbert, There's Magic in Music, Glamour Boy, Top Man, The Phantom of the Opera, The Climax, Follow the Boys, This Is the Life, Frisco Sal*, more.

FOULK, ROBERT (S. Cal.) Character. Onscreen from 1957. IN: *Last of the Badmen, The Tall Stranger, The Left-Handed Gun, Cast a Long Shadow, Tammy and the Doctor, Robin and the Seven Hoods, Bunny O'Hare*, more.

FOWLER, HARRY (Eng.) Character. Onscreen from 1942. IN: *Hue and Cry, I Was Monty's Double, She Shall Have Murder, The Pickwick Papers, A Day to Remember, Lucky Jim, The Blue Peter, Crooks Anonymous, Start the Revolution without Me*, more.

FOWLEY, DOUGLAS (S. Cal.) Character in more than 200 and still going strong. Onscreen from 1934. IN: *Gift of Gab, Old Man Rhythm, Ring Around the Moon, This Is My Affair, One Mile from Heaven, Alexander's Ragtime Band, Lucky Night, Charlie Chan at Treasure Island, Twenty Mule Team, The Devil with Hitler, Stand by for Action, Minesweeper; See Here, Private Hargrove; Undercover Maisie, Coroner Creek, Mighty Joe Young, Killer Shark, Across the Wide Missouri, This Woman Is Dangerous, Singin' in the Rain, The Naked Jungle, Miracle of the White Stallions, The Good Guys and the Bad Guys, Homebodies*, more.

FOX, BERNARD (S. Cal.) Character. Onscreen from 1964. IN: *Honeymoon Hotel, Bamboo Saucer*, more.

FOX, EDWARD (Eng.) Leading man. Onscreen from 1967. IN: *The Jokers, The Naked Runner, Oh, What a Lovely War!, Skullduggery, The Go-Between, The Day of the Jackal, Galileo,* more.

FOX, JAMES (Eng.) The young actor gave up his career in movies to become an evangelist, and has been married since '73 to Mary Piper. Onscreen from 1950. IN: *The Magnet, The Servant, Those Magnificent Men in Their Flying Machines, King Rat, The Chase, Thoroughly Modern Millie, The Loves of Isadora, Performance,* more.

FOX, JANET (N.Y.) Character. IN: *They Knew What They Wanted.*

FOXX, REDD (S. Cal.) Star comedian. IN: *Cotton Comes to Harlem.*

FOY, CHARLES (S. Cal.) One of the "Seven Little Foys," he is in his 70s now, retired, and living in Los Angeles. Onscreen from 1936. IN: *Hot Money, Polo Joe, Dance Charlie Dance; Torchy Blane, the Adventurous Blonde; King of the Underworld, Blackwell's Island, Mutiny in the Big House,* more, including 1944's *The Woman of the Town,* his last.

FOY, EDDIE, JR. (S. Cal.) The comedian who was the most famous of the "Little Foys" is also a retired Los Angeles resident and in his 70s (b. 1905). His last screen appearance was in 1968 in *Thirty Is a Dangerous Age, Cynthia* with English actress Suzy Kendall. Onscreen from 1929. IN: *Queen of the Night Clubs, Broadway Thru a Keyhole, Turn Off the Moon, Secret Service of the Air, Frontier Marshal, Lillian Russell* (the first of four movies in which he portrayed his famous comedian father), *Scatterbrain, Puddin' Head, Rookies on Parade, Yankee Doodle Dandy, Joan of Ozark, Dixie, And the Angels Sing, The Pajama Game, Bells Are Ringing, Gidget Goes Hawaiian,* more.

FOY, EDDIE, III (S. Cal.) Actor-son of the above. Now a business man. Onscreen in the '50s. IN: *Outlaw's Son; Run Silent, Run Deep; When Hell Broke Loose,* more.

FOY, MARY (S. Cal.) Also one of the "Seven Little Foys," she is retired and lives near Hollywood, as do sister Madeline and brother Bryan. Their brother Irving resides in New Mexico, and the last brother died in 1947. Onscreen from 1924. IN: *The Hoosier Holiday, The Manicure Girl, Irish Luck, Ankles Preferred, Slaves of Beauty, The Mad Hour, Dumbbells in Ermine, Ladies of the Big House, Love in Bloom,* more, including 1935's *Little Big Shot,* her last.

FRANCEN, VICTOR (Fr.) For 15 years in Hollywood this character actor from Belgium, with the deep-set eyes and sophisticated presence, played scoundrels so coolly and commandingly that he often acted stars like Bogart right off the screen. Since 1955 he has been living in Paris, where he began his movie career in the '20s. He is in his late 80s now (b. 1888), and as recently as a decade ago was still working in pictures—such as *Top-Crack,* with Terry-Thomas, made in Italy in '66. He still receives, and appreciates, fan letters from America praising his performances of Grodek in *The Mask of Dimitrios* and the dismembered piano virtuoso in *The Beast with Five Fingers.* Onscreen in Hollywood from 1941. IN: *Hold Back the Dawn, Ten Gentlemen from West Point, Tales of Manhattan, Mission to Moscow, Passage to Marseilles, The Conspirators, In Our Time, Confidential Agent, Devotion, The Desert Song, Madame Curie, The Beginning or the End?, To the Victor, Hell and High Water, Bedevilled, A Farewell to Arms* (filmed in Italy), *Fanny* (filmed in France),* more.

FRANCHI, SERGIO (N.Y.) Singer-leading man. IN: *The Secret of Santa Vittoria.*

FRANCINE, ANNE (N.Y.) Support. IN: *Juliet of the Spirits.*

FRANCIOSA, ANTHONY (S. Cal.) Costar. Nominated for Best Actor Oscar in *A Hatful of Rain.* Onscreen from 1957. IN: *A Face in the Crowd, Wild Is the Wind, The Long Hot Summer, Career, Story on Page One, Period of Adjustment, Assault on a Queen, Fathom, A Man Called Gannon, Across 110th Street, The Drowning Pool,* more.

FRANCIS, ANNE (S. Cal.) Leading lady. Onscreen from 1948. IN: *Summer Holiday, Elopement, Lydia Bailey, A Lion Is in the Streets, Susan Slept Here, Bad Day at Black Rock, Battle Cry, The Blackboard Jungle, The Great American Pastime, Don't Go Near the Water, The Crowded Sky, The Woman Who Wouldn't Die, Funny Girl; Hook, Line and Sinker; The Love God?,* more.

FRANCIS, ARLENE (N.Y.) Character. Onscreen from 1943. IN: *Stage Door Canteen, All My Sons, With These Hands; One, Two, Three; The Thrill of It All.*

FRANCIS, CONNIE (N.Y.) Singer-actress. Onscreen in the '60s. IN: *Where the Boys Are, Follow the Boys, Looking for Love, Where the Boys Meet the Girls.*

FRANCIS, EUGENE (N.J.) Character; former juvenile. Now in television. Onscreen in the '40s. IN: *Pride of the Bowery, Flying Wild.*

FRANCIS, IVOR (S. Cal.) Character. Onscreen in the '70s. IN: *I Love My Wife, Pieces of Dreams, The Steagle, The Late Liz, Busting, Superdad*, more.

FRANCIS, WILMA (S. Cal.) Character; former second lead. Onscreen from 1936. IN: *Sudden Death; Lady, Be Careful; Hideaway Girl, Trade Winds, Guest Wife*, more.

FRANCISCUS, JAMES (S. Cal.) Leading man. Onscreen from 1957. IN: *Four Boys and a Gun, The Outsider, The Miracle of the White Stallions, Youngblood Hawke, Trial Run, Hell Boats, Marooned, Beneath the Planet of the Apes*, more.

FRANCKS, DON (N.Y.) Leading man. Onscreen 1967–68. IN: *The Circle, Finian's Rainbow.*

FRANKEN, STEVE (S. Cal.) Leading man. Onscreen from 1964. IN: *The Americanization of Emily; Follow Me, Boys!; The Party, Which Way to the Front?*, more.

FRANKHAM, DAVID (S. Cal.) Character. Onscreen from 1961. IN: *Master of the World, Tales of Terror*, more

FRANKLIN, BONNIE (S. Cal.) Support. IN: *The Wrong Man.*

FRANKLIN, HUGH (N.Y.) Character. Onscreen from 1964. IN: *The Curse of the Living Corpse, The Borgia Stick, The Swimmer, What's So Bad About Feeling Good?*, more.

FRANKLIN, PAMELA (Eng.) Leading lady; former juvenile lead. Onscreen from 1961. IN: *The Innocents, The Lion, The Nanny, The Prime of Miss Jean Brodie, Sinful Davey, Necromancy, The Food of the Gods*, more.

FRANKOVICH, MIKE (S. Cal.) One of Hollywood's best-known producers now (*Forty Carats*, etc.), long the husband of Binnie Barnes, and in his 60s (b. 1910), but in his 30s he played second leads in several. Onscreen 1940–41. IN: *Yesterday's Heroes, Meet John Doe, Buck Privates, The Great American Broadcast*, more.

FRANZ, ARTHUR (S. Cal.) Character; former leading man. Onscreen from 1948. IN: *Red Stallion in the Rockies, Flight to Mars, The Sniper, A Member of the Wedding, The Eddie Cantor Story, Bad for Each Other, Battle Taxi, Beyond a Reasonable Doubt, The Young Lions, The Atomic Submarine, Alvarez Kelly, The Sweet Ride, The Human Factor*, more.

FRANZ, EDUARD (S. Cal.) This superb character actor, still going strong in his 70s (b.

1902), costarred in '75 on ABC-TV with teenager Jodie Foster in a special, *The Secret Life of T. K. Dearing*—advertised thusly by the networks: "She's joined her grandfather's crazy adventures, instead of keeping an eye on him." Yes, spirited still. Onscreen from 1947. IN: *Killer at Large, Wake of the Red Witch, Madame Bovary, Whirlpool, The Magnificent Yankee, The Great Caruso, The Desert Fox, Latin Lovers, Sign of the Pagan, The Ten Commandments, Day of the Bad Man, A Certain Smile, Francis of Assisi, The President's Analyst*, more.

FRASER, BILL (Eng.) Character. Onscreen from 1952. IN: *Meet Me Tonight, The Captain's Paradise, The Barefoot Contessa, The Americanization of Emily, Masquerade, Up Pompeii*, more.

FRASER, BRYANT (N.Y.) Juvenile. Onscreen in the '70s. IN: *Child's Play, The Panic in Needle Park*, more.

FRASER, ELIZABETH (S. Cal.) Fredric March's beautiful blonde daughter in *One Foot in Heaven* is still blonde, but, now in her 50s and having gained considerable weight, she usually plays character comediennes on such TV shows as *Maude*. She will be recalled also for having played, in the '50s, the continuing role of a WAC in *The Phil Silvers Show*. Her career would surely have gone further but for Russian Ambassador Maxim Litvinov. In the '40s she starred in the play *The Russian People*, which opened in Washington when the ambassador was there. He invited the entire cast to a party—strictly nonpolitical—at the Russian embassy. More than a decade later the director of that show, Harold Clurman, encountered the actress in Paris. As he reported in his recent book, *All People Are Famous:* "I asked her what progress she had made in her acting career. She had done well, she said, except for one hitch. She had contracted to appear in a Hollywood movie. Just before she was to go before the cameras, her agent called to say the contract had been canceled. No explanation. She asked her agent to inquire into the matter. A vigilant investigator had come upon a photograph of her in the company of the Soviet ambassador. It had been taken on the pleasant occasion of that opening night in Washington." She has long since resumed her Hollywood career with supporting roles in *The Graduate, Tony Rome, Seconds*, etc. Onscreen from 1941. IN: *The Man Who Came to Dinner, All My Sons, Hills of Oklahoma, Death of a Salesman, So Big, Young at Heart, The Steel Cage, Tunnel of Love, Two for the Seesaw, A Patch of Blue, The Glass Bottom Boat*, more.

FRASER, JOHN (Eng.) Leading man. Onscreen from 1951. IN: *Valley of Song, The*

Good Beginning, Lady Fair, Touch and Go, Tunes of Glory, The Trials of Oscar Wilde, El Cid, Operation Crossbow, The Loves of Isadora, more.

FRASER, MOYRA (Eng.) Character. Onscreen from 1950. IN: *Madeleine, The Man Who Loved Redheads; Left, Right and Center; Here We Go Around the Mulberry Bush, The Boy Friend*, more.

FRASER, PHYLLIS (N.Y.) Formerly the wife of Bennett Cerf, the late publisher-wit, she is presently married to Robert F. Wagner, once the mayor of New York. Onscreen from 1933. IN: *Lucky Devils, Little Men, Fighting Youth, Every Saturday Night*, more, including 1936's *The Harvester*, her last.

FRASER, RONALD (Eng.) Character. Onscreen from 1959. IN: *The Sundowners, Jungle Fighters, The V.I.P.s, The Model Murder Case, The Flight of the Phoenix, The Whisperers, Fathom, Sebastian, The Killing of Sister George, The Magnificent Seven, Deadly Sins, Paper Tiger*, more.

FRASER, SHELAGH (Eng.) Character. Onscreen from the '40s. In: *I Live in Grosvenor Square, Esther Waters, The History of Mr. Polly, The Second Mrs. Tanqueray, Raising a Riot, The Body Stealers*, more.

FRASER, STANLEY (S. Cal.) Character. Onscreen from 1953. IN: *The Maze*, more.

FRAZEE, JANE (S. Cal.) Her freckle-faced charm and excellent singing brightened countless B musicals of the '40s at Universal, Columbia, and Republic. She wound up her career with a Monogram feature, *Rhythm Inn*, in '51, and the "Joe McDoakes" shorts (playing comic George O'Hanlon's wife) in the mid-50s. Married for several years in the '40s to former star Glenn Tryon (d. 1970), she divorced him in '47, winning custody of her son, Timothy, who is a business man now in his early 30s. Still a most attractive blonde in her late 50s (b. 1918), and still single, she has been for more than 15 years a successful real estate agent in Newport Beach, the town south of Los Angeles where she lives. She has a theory as to why she never progressed beyond leads in B's: "I wasn't bad-looking, but I was never a beautiful girl, and in those days you had to look great." Furthermore, she adds: "I had a drive to do better things than I was doing, but not that great inner drive that very successful people have." Her later offscreen success would indicate she acquired it. Onscreen from 1940. IN: *Moonlight and Melody, Buck Privates, San Antonio Rose, Hellzapoppin', When Johnny Comes Marching*

Home, Kansas City Kitty, Rosie the Riveter, Calendar Girl, Springtime in the Sierras, more.

FRAZER, DAN (S. Cal.) Character. Onscreen from the '60s. IN: *Lord Love a Duck, Counterpoint, Tick Tick Tick, Bananas, The Stoolie*, more.

FRAZIER, SHEILA (S. Cal.) Black leading lady. Onscreen in the '70s. IN: *Three the Hard Way, Superfly, T.N.T., The Super Cops*, more.

FREBERG, STAN (S. Cal.) Comedian. IN: *Callaway Went Thataway*.

FREDERICK, HAL (S. Cal.) Black leading man. Onscreen from 1968. IN: *Two Gentlemen Sharing*, more.

FREED, BERT (S. Cal.) Character. Onscreen from 1957. IN: *Paths of Glory, The Goddess, Shock Treatment, Invitation to a Gunfighter, The Swinger, Wild in the Streets, There Was a Crooked Man, Evel Knievel, Billy Jack*, more.

FREEMAN, AL, JR. (S. Cal.) Black leading man. Onscreen from 1960. IN: *This Rebel Breed, Ensign Pulver, Black Like Me, The Troublemaker, The Dutchman, The Detective, Finian's Rainbow, Castle Keep, A Fable*, more.

FREEMAN, ARNIE (N.Y.) Character. Onscreen from 1954. IN: *Phffft, Popi, The Super Cops*, more.

FREEMAN, JOAN (S. Cal.) Leading lady. Onscreen from 1961. IN: *Come September, Tower of London, Roustabout, The Rounders, The Reluctant Astronaut*, more.

FREEMAN, KATHLEEN (S. Cal.) Character comedienne. Onscreen from 1949. IN: *Mr. Belvedere Goes to College, The Reformer and the Redhead, Kid Monk Baroni, Affairs of Dobie Gillis, Artists and Models, North to Alaska, The Nutty Professor, The Rounders, The Good Guys and the Bad Guys, Stand Up and Be Counted*, more.

FREEMAN, MONA (S. Cal.) Tiny (5'1"), spunky, and a honey blonde—and more beautiful now as she enters her 50s (b. 1926) than when a star—she has not made a movie since *The World Was His Jury* ('58). Since '61 she has been the wife of Los Angeles business man H. Jack Ellis. Formerly she was married to, and divorced from, wealthy auto dealer Pat Nerney (1945–52), father of her daughter, Monie. Born in '47 and now an actress, using the name Monie Ellis, Mona's daughter looks like a teenager and in '71 played one, as the star of TV's *Gidget Gets Married*. Always, Mona Freeman found her own extremely youthful face working against her efforts to win mature roles. Even as she racked up leads in some 80 TV shows, she lamented: "How old do you have to be to be grown up? I would like to play wildcats, brazen women, the menacing side of the triangle." Even if she came back to the screen today (she won't), she would most assuredly find herself confronted by her lifelong handicap. So she's a dedicated homemaker now, with no further dream of movie glory, exercising her artistic talents via canvas and brush—painting portraits and landscapes. And privately praying that Monie Ellis "ages" well. Onscreen from 1944. IN: *Till We Meet Again, Junior Miss, Roughly Speaking, Black Beauty, That Brennan Girl, Dear Ruth, Mother Wore Tights, Isn't It Romantic?, Streets of Laredo, Dear Wife, I Was a Shoplifter, Copper Canyon, Dear Brat, Jumping Jacks, Angel Face, Hold Back the Night, War Drums*, more.

FREEMAN, PAM (S. Cal.) Leading lady. Onscreen from the '60s. IN: *Girl Happy, Pajama Party, The Swinger, Fireball 500*, more.

FREES, PAUL (S. Cal.) Character. Onscreen from 1949. IN: *Red Light, A Place in the Sun, The Big Sky, War of the Worlds, Riot in Cellblock 11, Suddenly, The Raven, Wild in the Streets*, more.

FRENCH, ARTHUR (N.Y.) Character. IN: *Blade, The Super Cops*, more.

FRENCH, LEIGH (S. Cal.) Leading lady. Onscreen in the '70s. IN: *WUSA, Norwood, White Line Fever*, more.

FRENCH, LESLIE (Eng.) Character. Onscreen from 1941. IN: *This England, Orders to Kill, The Singer Not the Song, The Leopard, Death in Venice*, more.

FRENCH, SUSAN (S. Cal.) Leading lady; former juvenile. Onscreen from 1968. IN: *The Impossible Years*, more.

FRENCH, VALERIE (S. Cal.) Leading lady. Onscreen from 1956. IN: *Jubal, The 27th Day, The Garment Jungle, The Hard Man, Shalako*, more.

FRENCH, VICTOR (S. Cal.) Character. Onscreen from the '60s. IN: *Charro!, Rio Lobo, Flap, Wild Rovers, The House on Skull Mountain, The Nickel Ride*, more.

FREY, LEONARD (N.Y.) Character. Nominated for Best Supporting Actor Oscar in *Fiddler on the Roof*. Onscreen from 1970. IN: *The Boys in the Band; Tell Me That You Love Me, Junie Moon*.

FRID, JONATHAN (N.Y.) Character lead. Onscreen from the '60s. IN: *House of Dark Shadows, Seizure*, more.

FRIEND, PHILIP (Eng.) Leading man. Onscreen from 1941. IN: *Pimpernel Smith, Next of Kin, Sword in the Desert, My Own True Love, The Buccaneer's Girl, Sky Hunt, Thunder on the Hill, Desperate Moment, Web of Suspicion, Son of Robin Hood, The Vulture*, more.

FRIZZELL, LOU (S. Cal.) Support. IN: *Summer of '42, Lawman, The Front Page, The Crazy World of Julius Vrooder, The Nickel Ride*, more.

FROBE, GERT (Eng.) Character. Onscreen from 1952. IN: *The Berliner, Mr. Arkadin, Rosemary, He Who Must Die, The Longest Day, The Threepenny Opera, Goldfinger, High Wind in Jamaica, Is Paris Burning?, Triple Cross, Chitty Chitty Bang Bang, Those Daring Young Men in Their Jaunty Jalopies, Ten Little Indians*, more.

FROEHLICH, GUSTAV (Ger.) Character star. Onscreen from 1927. IN: *Metropolis, Homecoming, Temptation, Asphalt, The Immortal Vagabond, Gloria, What Women Dream, Barcarole, The Abduction, A Devil of a Fellow, Secrets of a Soul*, more.

FROMAN, JANE (Mo.) A Missouri native, she has been happily married since the early '60s (her third marriage) to a University of Missouri official, and has not sung professionally in more than 15 years. She is in her late 60s (b. 1907) and lives in Columbia. Onscreen in 1935 in *Stars Over Broadway* and in 1938 in *Radio City Revels*. Susan Hayward portrayed her in *With a Song in My Heart*.

FROME, MILTON (S. Cal.) Character. Onscreen from 1939. IN: *Ride 'em, Cowboy!; The Birds and the Bees, Public Pigeon No. 1, The Lonely Man, Short Cut to Hell; Go, Johnny, Go!; Bye Bye, Birdie; The Nutty Professor, Way Way Out, Enter Laughing, With Six You Get Egg Roll, The Strongest Man in the World*, more.

FUCHS, LEO (S. Cal.) Character. Onscreen from 1937. IN: *I Want to Be a Mother, American Matchmaker, The Story of Ruth*.

FUJIKAWA, JERRY (S. Cal.) Character. Onscreen from 1959. IN: *The Journey, Nobody's Perfect, Chinatown*, more.

FULLER, BARBRA (now **BARBARA**) (S. Cal.) Character; former leading lady. Onscreen from 1949. IN: *The Red Menace, Flame of Youth,*

Rock Island Trail, Harbor of Missing Men, Trial Without Jury, City of Bad Men, more.

FULLER, FRANCES (N.Y.) Gary Cooper's leading lady in *One Sunday Afternoon*, she is now President of the American Academy of Dramatic Art. The mother of two grown daughters by producer-director Worthington C. Miner, whom she married in '29, she lives on lower Fifth Avenue. In 1974, in her late 60s (b. 1907), she starred—as an eccentric recluse—in the movie *Homebodies*. Onscreen from 1933. IN: *Elmer and Elsie, The Girl in the Red Velvet Swing*.

FULLER, LANCE (S. Cal.) Support; former leading man. Onscreen from 1954. IN: *Cattle Queen of Montana; Taza, Son of Cochise; Apache Woman, Pearl of the South Pacific, Girls in Prison, Secret of Treasure Mountain, Voodoo Woman, God's Little Acre, The Longest Yard, Hustle*, more.

FULLER, ROBERT (S. Cal.) Leading man. Onscreen from 1957. IN: *Teenage Thunder, Return of the Seven, What Ever Happened to Aunt Alice?, King Gun, The Hard Ride*, more.

FULTON, EILEEN (N.Y.) Leading lady. IN: *Girl of the Night*.

FULTON, JOAN (now **JOAN SHAWLEE**) (S. Cal.) Supporting actress Joan Shawlee used this name when a starlet in the '40s. IN: *House of Horrors, The Runaround, Inside Job, White Tie and Tails, Buck Privates Come Home, The Vigilantes Return*, more.

FUNICELLO, ANNETTE (S. Cal.) Former juvenile; retired. Onscreen from 1959. IN: *The Shaggy Dog, Babes in Toyland, Beach Party, Pajama Party, How to Stuff a Wild Bikini, Head*, more.

FURNEAUX, YVONNE (Fr.) Costar. Onscreen from 1952. IN: *The Master of Ballantrae, The Beggar's Opera, Lisbon, The Mummy, La Dolce Vita, Slave Queen of Babylon, Repulsion, Night Train to Milan, The Champagne Murders*, more.

FURNESS, BETTY (N.Y.) Happily married to her third husband, and the mother of a grown daughter, Barbie (by musician Johnny Green), she is Director of Consumer Affairs for NBC-TV. And, entering her 60s (b. 1916), she looks exactly as she did when opening refrigerator doors on TV and saying, "You can be sure if it's Westinghouse." Onscreen from 1933. IN: *Professional Sweetheart, Emergency Call, Midshipman Jack, Lucky Devils, Beggars in Ermine, The Life of Vergie Winters, Gridiron Flash, Keeper of the Bees, Magnificent Obsession, Swing Time, The President's Mystery, Good Old Soak, Mama Steps Out*, more, including 1939's *North of Shanghai*, her last.

FURSE, JUDITH (Eng.) Character. Onscreen from 1939. IN: *Goodbye, Mr. Chips; Black Narcissus, While the Sun Shines, Dear Mr. Prohack, The Browning Version, The Heart of the Matter, Cockleshell Heroes, Blue Murder at St. Trinian's, Scent of Mystery, Sinful Davey*, more.

FURSTENBERG, IRA (N.Y.) Leading lady. Onscreen from 1966. IN: *Matchless, Caprice, At Any Price, The Battle of El Alemein, The Vatican Story, Hello—Goodbye*, more.

FURTH, GEORGE (S. Cal.) Character. Onscreen from 1961. IN: *The Best Man, A Rage to Live, A Very Special Favor, Tammy and the Millionaire, Games, Butch Cassidy and the Sundance Kid, Blazing Saddles*, more.

FURY, ED (S. Cal.) Leading man. Onscreen from 1960. IN: *Hercules in the Land of Fire, The Mighty Ursus, Samson Against the Sheik, The Seven Revenges*, more.

FURY, LORETTA (N.Y.) Support. IN: *Requiem for a Heavyweight, Man on a Swing*, more.

G

GABEL, MARTIN (N.Y.) Character. Onscreen from 1951. IN: *Fourteen Hours, Deadline U.S.A., Marnie, Goodbye Charlie, The Lady in Cement, There Was a Crooked Man, The Front Page*, more.

GABIN, JEAN (Fr.) Star. Onscreen from 1936. IN: *Grand Illusion, Pepe le Moko, Moontide, The Impostor, Stormy Waters, French Can-Can, Four Bags Full, Deadlier Than the Male, Razzia, Inspector Maigret, Monkey in Winter, Any Number Can Win, The Upper Hand, The Sicilians, Le Chat, Verdict*, more.

GABOR, EVA (S. Cal.) Leading lady. Onscreen from 1941. IN: *Forced Landing, The Countess of Monte Cristo, The Last Time I Saw Paris, Artists and Models, Don't Go Near the Water, Gigi, It Started with a Kiss, Wake Me When the War's Over*, more.

GABOR, ZSA ZSA (S. Cal.) Leading lady. On-screen from 1952. IN: *We're Not Married, Moulin Rouge, The Story of Three Loves, Three-Ring Circus, Lili, For the First Time, The Most Wanted Man in the World, Boys' Night Out, Picture Mommy Dead; Arrivederci, Baby!*; more.

GABRIEL, JOHN (S. Cal.) Leading man. On-screen from 1958. IN: *The Hunters, The Story of Ruth, Stagecoach, Oh! What a Lovely War, Hell's Bloody Devils*, more.

GADD, RENEE (Eng.) Leading lady; now inactive. Onscreen from 1932. IN: *Aren't We All?, White Face, The Love Captive, The Crimson Circle, They Came to a City, Frieda*, more.

GAHAGAN, HELEN (Vt.) In that exotic movie *She*, she was the 500-year-old queen of a lost kingdom who retained her youthful beauty by bathing in a miraculous flame—until she did it once too often. Said one critic: "Helen Gahagan gives a most impressive performance. She brings a stateliness to her acting and can recite the most ordinary dialogue in a way that makes it sound vital and important. I shall watch for this actress's next performance with more than ordinary interest." He could still be waiting. *She* was released in '35 and "she"—starring onstage both before and after it—never made another movie. But in the '40s she was twice elected (in '44 and '46) a U.S. Congresswoman from California. Her decision to run for the Senate in '50 pitted her against Richard M. Nixon. It was a heated battle, in which she was defeated. She left politics "because of the family." "I felt then it was time for the children to waste their mother's time . . . not to have to see their mother by appointment." Later, occasionally, she gave concerts (she was an opera star, here and abroad, as well as an actress), poetry readings, and lectures. "I wound up speaking almost wholly at colleges and universities," she says. Today, she is a handsome, big-boned, white-haired woman in her 70s (b. 1900) who has not let illness (breast surgery in '71) diminish her tempo. From the sidelines, she still takes an avid interest in politics, and, on errands pertaining to her family, she races about the Vermont countryside in her Volvo as though there is no tomorrow. (See Melvyn Douglas.)

GALE, DAVID (N.Y.) Support. Onscreen in the '50s. IN: *Legend of the Lost, Encounter.*

GALE, EDDRA (S. Cal.) Support. Onscreen from 1963. IN: *8½, What's New Pussycat?, The Maltese Bippy, A Man Called Gannon, The Strawberry Statement*, more.

GALE, JEAN (S. Cal.) Long divorced from agent Matty Rosen, this leading lady of the '30s has worked as an extra on such movies as *The Day of the Locust*. IN: *The Miracle Rider* (serial), more.

GALE, JUNE (S. Cal.) Another of the singing Gale Sisters (Jean, June, Jane, and Joan), she was married to Oscar Levant from '39 until his death in '72, and by him has three grown daughters: Marcia, Lorna, and Amanda. She lives in Beverly Hills and has been retired since her marriage to Levant. Onscreen from 1938. IN: *Time Out for Murder, While New York Sleeps, It Could Happen to You, Hotel for Women, Charlie Chan at Treasure Island, The Honeymoon's Over, City of Chance*, more.

GALENTO, TONY (S. Cal.) The famous heavyweight boxer who appeared in movies in the '50s is in his late 60s (b. 1910) and retired. Onscreen from 1954. IN: *On the Waterfront, The Best Things in Life Are Free, Wind Across the Everglades.*

GALVIN, KATHY (N.Y.) Juvenile. Onscreen from 1972. IN: *Lady Liberty*, more.

GALVIN, ROBBY (N.Y.) Juvenile actor. Onscreen in the '70s. IN: *Jenny*, more.

GALLAGHER, HELEN (N.Y.) Broadway musical star. IN: *Strangers When We Meet.*

GALLOWAY, DON (S. Cal.) Support. Onscreen from 1966. IN: *The Rare Breed, Rough Night in Jericho, Gunfight in Abilene.*

GALLOWAY, MORGAN (N.Y.) Character. Onscreen in 1932. IN: *Ladies of the Jury, Lena Rivers.*

GAM, RITA (N.Y.) Leading lady. Onscreen from 1952. IN: *The Thief, Saadia, Sign of the Pagan, Sierra Baron, Atilla, Hannibal, King of Kings, No Exit, Klute, Law and Disorder*, more.

GAMBARELLI, MARIA (N.Y.) The ballerina-actress, now in her 70s, teaches ballet, does voice-overs on countless TV commercials, and has acted in soap operas—*Secret Storm, Love Is a Many-Splendored Thing.* Long crippled by arthritis, she underwent a dramatic operation in '73—the revolutionary Charnley hip-joint replacement—that completely restored her ability to dance and play golf with a sweeping, hip-swiveling swing. "I feel like a marvelous car," says the slender, still-blonde star. "They have put in a new part, and I am like a brand-new Cadillac or Rolls-Royce." Onscreen in the '30s.

IN: *Here's to Romance, Il Dottor Antonio*, more.

GARBER, MATTHEW (Eng.) Former juvenile lead. Now in his 20s (b. 1956) and momentarily retired from acting. Onscreen from 1963. IN: *The Three Lives of Thomasina, Mary Poppins, The Gnome-Mobile.*

GARBO, GRETA (N.Y.) Legendary star. Nominated for Best Actress Oscar in *Anna Christie* and *Romance* (same year: 1929–30), *Camille, Ninotchka*. Awarded a special Oscar (statuette) in 1954 "for her unforgettable screen performances." Onscreen in Europe from 1922. IN: *Peter the Tramp, The Legend of Gosta Berling, Joyless Street (Streets of Sorrow)*. Onscreen in America from 1926. IN: *The Torrent, The Temptress; Love, Flesh and the Devil; The Divine Woman, The Mysterious Lady, A Woman of Affairs, Wild Orchids, The Single Standard, The Kiss, Inspiration, Susan Lenox: Her Fall and Rise, Mata Hari, Grand Hotel, As You Desire Me, Queen Christina, The Painted Veil, Anna Karenina, Conquest, Two Faced Woman*. Retired in 1942.

GARDE, BETTY (N.Y.) The character actress noted for several spellbinding performances—particularly as the hardbitten "key" to the mystery in *Call Northside 777*—lives in Brooklyn, is in her 70s (b. 1905), and, though not in movies since '62, remains active in the theater. In '75 she flew to Atlanta to costar with E. G. Marshall and Eli Wallach in the Peachtree Playhouse presentation of *The Sponsor*. Onscreen from 1929. IN: *The Lady Lies, Damaged Love, Secrets of a Secretary, Caged, Cry of the City, The Prince Who Was a Thief, One Desire, The Wonderful World of the Brothers Grimm*, more.

GARDENIA, VINCENT (N.Y.) Character. Nominated for Best Supporting Actor Oscar in *Bang the Drum Slowly*. Onscreen from 1958. IN: *Cop Haters; Murder, Inc.; The Hustler, A View from the Bridge, Where's Poppa?, Little Murders, Jenny, Cold Turkey, Hickey and Boggs, The Front Page, The Manchu Eagle Murder Caper Mystery, Death Wish*, more.

GARDINER, REGINALD (N.Y.) Character. Inactive in the past decade. Onscreen in Hollywood (after British pix) from 1936. IN: *Born to Dance, A Damsel in Distress, Marie Antoinette, The Doctor Takes a Wife, A Yank in the R.A.F., The Man Who Came to Dinner, Claudia, The Dolly Sisters, I Wonder Who's Kissing Her Now, That Wonderful Urge, Androcles and the Lion, The Barefoot Contessa, What a Way to Go!*, more, including 1965's *Sgt. Deadhead, the Astronaut*, his most recent to date.

GARDNER, AVA (Sp.) Star. Nominated for Best Actress Oscar in *Mogambo*. Onscreen from 1941. IN: *Highway to Freedom; Joe Smith, American; Calling Dr. Gillespie, Pilot No. 5, Lost Angel, DuBarry Was a Lady, Three Men in White, Reunion in France, Whistle Stop, The Killers, The Hucksters, One Touch of Venus, The Great Sinner; East Side, West Side; Pandora and the Flying Dutchman, Show Boat, The Snows of Kilimanjaro, Knights of the Round Table, The Barefoot Contessa, Bhowani Junction, The Sun Also Rises, On the Beach, 55 Days at Peking, Seven Days in May, The Night of the Iguana, The Life and Times of Judge Roy Bean, Earthquake, Permission to Kill, The Blue Bird, The Cassandra Crossing*, more.

GARDNER, JOAN (Eng.) After marrying director Zoltan Korda, she appeared in only a few more movies before leaving the screen after 1939's *The Rebel Son*. She is in her 60s (b. 1914) and has been a widow since 1961. Onscreen from 1934. IN: *Catherine the Great, The Private Life of Don Juan, The Scarlet Pimpernel, The Man Who Could Work Miracles, Forever Yours, The Challenge*, more.

GARFIELD, ALLEN (N.Y.) Character costar. Onscreen from the '60s. IN: *Greetings, Putney Swope, The Owl and the Pussycat, Hi, Mom!, Taking Off, Cry Uncle, The Organization, Roommates, You've Got to Walk It Like You Talk It or You'll Love That Beat, Believe in Me, The Front Page, Busting, The Conversation, Gable and Lombard*, more.

GARFIELD, JOHN DAVID (S. Cal.) Support. Son of John Garfield. Onscreen as John Garfield Jr. from 1963. IN: *The Victors, Warning Shot, That Cold Day in the Park, The Swimmer, McKenna's Gold*, more. Onscreen as John David Garfield from the early '70s. IN: *Candy Stripe Nurses, The Golden Voyage of Sinbad, White Line Fever*, more.

GARFIELD, JULIE (N.Y.) Support. Daughter of John Garfield. Onscreen from 1969. IN: *John and Mary, Goodbye Columbus, Coming Apart, The Revolutionary*, more.

GARGAN, WILLIAM (S. Cal.) Costar. Nominated for Best Supporting Actor Oscar in *They Knew What They Wanted*. Onscreen from 1932. IN: *Rain, Misleading Lady, The Animal Kingdom, Sweepings, Night Flight, Black Fury, Bright Lights, Alibi for Murder, The Milky Way, Wings Over Honolulu, You Only Live Once, Some Blondes Are Dangerous, Crime of Dr. Hallet, The Crowd Roars, Adventure of Jane Arden, Joe and Ethel Turp Call on the President, Three Sons, Sporting Blood, Star*

Dust, Cheers for Miss Bishop, I Wake Up Screaming, Desperate Chance for Ellery Queen, Follow That Woman, The Bells of St. Mary's, Behind Green Lights, Murder in the Music Hall, Waterfront at Midnight, Dynamite, Miracle in the Rain, Rawhide Years, The Best Man, more. Retired from acting in 1960 after losing his voice to cancer. He has since learned to speak again and is popular on the lecture circuit.

GARLAND, BEVERLY (S. Cal.) Leading lady. Onscreen from 1949. IN: *D.O.A., Killer Leopard, Bitter Creek, New Orleans Uncensored, The Steel Jungle, The Joker Is Wild, Chicago Confidential, Bombers B-52, Saga of Hemp Brown, Airport 1975,* more.

GARNER, JAMES (S. Cal.) Star. Onscreen from 1956. IN: *The Girl He Left Behind, Sayonara, Darby's Rangers, Up Periscope!, The Children's Hour, Boys' Night Out, The Great Escape, The Thrill of It All, Move Over Darling, The Americanization of Emily, Mr. Buddwing, Grand-Prix, Hour of the Gun, Support Your Local Gunfighter, Skin Game, They Only Kill Their Masters, The Castaway Cowboy,* more.

GARNER, PEGGY ANN (S. Cal.) In '45, as the child star of *A Tree Grows in Brooklyn,* she received a special Academy Award. She was 13 then and already a veteran of eight movies, dating from *Little Miss Thoroughbred* ('38). And she starred in a great many more, finally giving up movies altogether after 1966's *The Cat.* It has now been many years since she was a teenager at 20th Century-Fox, stalking every step of her idol, Betty Grable, and pestering the wardrobe department for costumes exactly like Betty's. She left Hollywood before she was 20, spending the entire decade of the '50s in New York, doing TV, flying back to Hollywood for an occasional movie role or to Germany (once) to star in *Black Forest,* and starring in four Broadway shows. In one play, the touring company of *Bus Stop,* her leading man was Albert Salmi, whom she married in '56. She had previously married and divorced ('53) actor Richard Hayes. Her marriage to Salmi, which also ended in divorce several years later, produced a daughter, her only child, Cassandra (Cas), a statuesque blonde now in her late teens who lives with Peggy Ann in an apartment in Brentwood. Later, the actress was married to and divorced from realtor Kenyon Foster Brown. For a while, having learned the business from him, she was a California real estate agent. But since '70, the still slim, trim, and blonde Peggy Ann Garner has worked for General Motors in Los Angeles—as a fleet car executive, selling, en masse, automobiles to major companies. And occasionally she has done a TV commer-

cial for her employer. Her offices are just a few blocks from RKO. There, when not quite 10, her high-powered emoting in two—*Abe Lincoln in Illinois* and *In Name Only*—led directly to her contract at 20th Century-Fox. "I didn't quit movies," she says. "I don't consider myself out of the business. Every time I've taken a job with a car dealership [this is her second], one of my stipulations has been that if a role was offered to me that I wanted to do, I'd have carte blanche to do it." Why did she choose the automobile business? "I've always been hung up on cars," she laughs. "I love them. I can take a car apart and, more important, put it back together again." As for acting, she insists, "I'm not through with show business. I have an agent who is busy scouting the right parts for me. I'm confident that something will come up." Onscreen from 1938. IN: *Blondie Brings Up Baby, Eagle Squadron, The Pied Piper, Jane Eyre, Keys of the Kingdom, Junior Miss, Home Sweet Homicide, Thunder in the Valley, Sign of the Ram, Teresa, Black Widow,* more.

GARR, TERI (S. Cal.) Leading lady. Onscreen in the '70s. IN: *The Conversation, Young Frankenstein,* more.

GARRALAGNA, MARTIN (S. Cal.) Character. Onscreen from 1939. IN: *Juarez, For Whom the Bell Tolls, The Laramie Trail, The Purple Heart, Voice in the Wind, The Cisco Kid Returns, Rogues' Regiment, Holiday in Havana, The Fortunes of Captain Blood, Lonely Are the Brave, Island of the Blue Dolphins, Whatever Happened to Aunt Alice?,* more.

GARRETT, BETTY (S. Cal.) The widow of Larry Parks, the mother of two grown sons, and now in her 50s (b. 1919), the comedienne has been out of pictures for two decades. She has, however, done much stage work in Los Angeles and for several TV seasons has played Archie Bunker's neighbor in *All in the Family.* Onscreen from 1945. IN: *Anchors Aweigh, The Big City, Words and Music, Take Me Out to the Ball Game, On the Town, Neptune's Daughter, My Sister Eileen, The Shadow on the Window,* more.

GARRETT, HANK (N.Y.) Character. Onscreen from the '50s. IN: *Never Steal Anything Small, The Producers, Richard, A Lovely Way to Die, Death Wish,* more.

GARRICK, JOHN (Eng.) The former leading man is in his 70s (b. 1902) and retired. Onscreen from 1929. IN: *Married in Hollywood, Song o' My Heart, Just Imagine, Charlie Chan Carries On, Always Good-Bye, The Broken Melody, Two Who Dared, The Great Victor Herbert, Suicide Legion,* more.

GARRISON, SEAN (S. Cal.) Leading man. On-screen from 1958. IN: *Onionhead, Up Periscope!, Bridge to the Sun, Splendor in the Grass, Moment to Moment, The Challengers,* more.

GARSON, GREER (N.M.) Star. Won Best Actress Oscar in *Mrs. Miniver.* Nominated in the same category in *Goodbye, Mr. Chips; Blossoms in the Dust, Madame Curie, Mrs. Parkington, The Valley of Decision, Sunrise at Campobello.* For over a decade, she and her very wealthy husband, Col. E. E. (Buddy) Fogelson (married since '49), have lived on a magnificent ranch near Santa Fe. They have been, since moving there, benefactors of the College of Santa Fe. In the fall of '75, passing up a Neil Simon movie and a Los Angeles play, the actress starred on campus there in a five-performance run of *The Madwoman of Chaillot.* The name of the playhouse in which she appeared: The Greer Garson Theater. A lovely redhead still, in her 60s (b. 1908), she has not been seen onscreen since 1967's *The Happiest Millionaire,* but she makes annual appearances on TV. In '74 she gave a sterling performance as Queen Mary in NBC's *Crown Matrimonial,* and in '75 costarred with Kirk Douglas and Ossie Davis in the documentary *My Father Gave Me America.* Onscreen from 1939. IN: *Remember?, Pride and Prejudice, When Ladies Meet, Random Harvest, Adventure, Desire Me, Julia Misbehaves, That Forsyte Woman, The Miniver Story, Scandal at Scourie, Julius Caesar, Strange Lady in Town, The Singing Nun,* more.

GARSON, JOHN (N.Y.) Character. Onscreen from the '40s. IN: *Peddlin' in Society, Werewolf of Washington, Black Magic,* more.

GARVER, KATHY (S. Cal.) Leading lady; former juvenile. Onscreen from 1956. IN: *The Ten Commandments, Monkey on My Back, I'll Cry Tomorrow; Kiss Me, Stupid;* more.

GARWOOD, JOHN (S. Cal.) Support. Onscreen from 1967. IN: *Hell's Angels on Wheels, The Savage Seven, Freebie and the Bean,* more.

GARY, HAROLD (N.Y.) Character. Onscreen from 1950. IN: *Undercover Girl, The French Connection,* more.

GARY, JOHN (S. Cal.) Singer. Onscreen as a juvenile. IN: *The Time of Your Life.*

GARY, LORRAINE (S. Cal.) Leading lady. Onscreen in the '70s. IN: *Jaws.*

GASSMAN, VITTORIO (It.) Star. Onscreen from 1946. IN: *Daniele Cortis, Anna, Bitter Rice, Sombrero, The Glass Wall, Rhapsody,* *Big Deal on Madonna Street, The Miracle, The Easy Life, The Best House in Naples, The Black Sheep, Thirteen Chairs, Scent of Woman, Midnight Pleasures, Those Were the Years,* more.

GATES, LARRY (S. Cal.) Character. Onscreen from 1952. IN: *Above and Beyond, Francis Covers the Big Town, The Brothers Rico, Cat on a Hot Tin Roof, Some Came Running, Underworld U.S.A., The Spiral Road, Toys in the Attic, In the Heat of the Night, Airport, Death of a Gunfighter, Funny Lady,* more.

GATES, MAXINE (S. Cal.) Character. Onscreen in small "tough gal" roles in many from the '40s on. *FLAP* is among her more recent pix.

GATES, NANCY (S. Cal.) One of RKO's perkiest brunette starlets in the '40s, with costar roles in many in the '50s, she left the screen after 1960's *Comanche Station,* soon after the birth that year of twin daughters. She and business executive husband, William Hayes, also have two sons: Jeff (b. 1953), a recent graduate of the University of Colorado, and Chip (b. 1957), a Harvard student who recently played the lead in the college's production of *Godspell.* Entering her 50s (b. 1926), Nancy Gates is just as pretty as when at RKO, but doubts she will ever resume her career. Onscreen from 1941. IN: *Come On, Danger; The Tuttles of Tahiti, The Great Gildersleeve, This Land Is Mine, Hitler's Children, The Master Race, Bride by Mistake, At Sword's Point, The Member of the Wedding, Hell's Half Acre, Suddenly, Stranger on Horseback, Top of the World, Some Came Running, Gunfight at Dodge City,* more.

GATESON, MARJORIE (N.Y.) In her 80s (b. 1891), this fine character actress suffered a stroke some years back that rules out all possibility of her acting again. Onscreen from 1931. IN: *The Beloved Bachelor, Society Girl, Silver Dollar, The King's Vacation, Lily Turner, Let's Fall in Love, Chained, Happiness Ahead, Down to Their Last Yacht, His Family Tree, The Milky Way, Vogues of 1938, Gateway, The Duke of West Point, Stablemates, Till Me Meet Again, Back Street, International Lady, You'll Never Get Rich, Rhythm of the Islands, The Sky's the Limit, I Dood It, No Time for Love, Seven Days Ashore, One More Tomorrow,* more, including 1953's *The Caddy,* after which she made a new career in soap operas in New York.

GAUTIER, DICK (S. Cal.) Comic leading man. Onscreen in the '70s. IN: *Wild in the Sky, The Manchu Eagle Murder Caper Mystery,* more.

GAVIN, JOHN (S. Cal.) Leading man. Onscreen from 1956. IN: *Four Girls in Town, Quantez, A Time To Love and a Time to Die, Spartacus, Psycho, Midnight Lace, Romanoff and Juliet, Tammy Tell Me True, Back Street, Thoroughly Modern Millie, The Madwoman of Chaillot*, more.

GAY, GREGORY/formerly GAYE (S. Cal.) Character. Onscreen from 1929. IN: *They Had to See Paris, What a Widow, Once in a Lifetime, Affairs of a Gentleman, Handy Andy, Dodsworth, Charlie Chan at the Opera, Lancer Spy, Tovarich, Paris Honeymoon, Ninotchka, Down Argentine Way, The Purple Heart, Cornered, The Bachelor and the Bobby-Soxer, The Unfinished Dance, Black Magic, The World in His Arms, Bailout at 43,000*, more.

GAYE, LISA (S. Cal.) Leading lady. Onscreen from 1954. IN: *Drums Across the River, Rock Around the Clock, 10,000 Bedrooms, Face of Terror, The Violent Ones, Castle of Evil*, more.

GAYNES, GEORGE (N.Y.) Support. Onscreen from the '60s. IN: *The Group, Marooned, Doctors' Wives*, more.

GAYNOR, JANET (S. Cal.) *Bernardine*, in 1957, her first in two decades, was and will remain her one "comeback" movie, insists this first-ever Academy Award-winning actress. She received the Best Actress Oscar in 1927–28 for her performances in three films—*Seventh Heaven, Street Angel*, and *Sunrise*. Her only other nomination came in 1937 in *A Star Is Born*. She has been married three times. Her first marriage, to Lydell Peck, ended in divorce in '33 after four years. Then, for exactly 20 years, until his death in '59, she was the wife of famous designer Gilbert Adrian—living most of that time on a magnificent ranch in Brazil. She has been married since '64 to stage impresario Paul Gregory. Still a feisty little redhead, with a touch of gray, the star recently turned 70 (b. 1906) and she keeps busy. With Gregory, on their lavish 100-acre desert estate between Desert Hot Springs and Palm Springs called Singing Trees Ranch, she raises squab—one 5,-000-member flock after another—for the gourmet market. And Jenny and Pablo, as they fondly call one another, occasionally find time to enjoy their huge pool, fed by an underground lake providing 105-degree mineral water. And always time to entertain the steady flow of famous guests from Hollywood and New York. One occasional, always welcome, guest, from Chicago where he is midwest director of spot sales for CBS-TV, is Janet's only son, Robin Adrian. Happily married and in his mid-30s, Robin has not, at this writing, made her a grandmother, to Janet Gaynor's regret. Vastly content on their ranch, the actress says she never plans to leave it—permanently. On summer nights, she and her husband sleep on rollaway beds under the stars, awaking at four to take long walks in the desert. For recreation (profit, too, it has turned out), she paints—Grandma Moses-type primitives—in an open-air gazebo one flight above the desert floor. In '73, in her first one-woman show at the Gregg Juarez Gallery in Beverly Hills, she exhibited 30 paintings —all sold. No recluse, the star lends her name and presence to many worthy causes. Recently, for instance, she and her long-ago costar Charles Farrell participated in fund-raising activities in Southern California for the Foster Grandparents program of Anchorage, Alaska. And she finds herself in Los Angeles for such events as the Oscars or, in '75, the huge (420 guests) 70th birthday party given Henry Fonda —her leading man in his first picture, 1935's *The Farmer Takes a Wife*. Today Janet Gaynor, truly a one-of-a-kind star, sums up her career like this: "I had a glorious 12 years in movies, a happy career, strange as it may seem. Most people stress the unhappiness in their careers. But it ended and I went into another life." Onscreen first as Laura Gainor—her real name— from 1924. IN: two-reelers starring Glenn Tryon, and Westerns starring Ben Corbin and Peewee Holmes. Onscreen as Janet Gaynor from 1926. IN: *The Johnstown Flood, The Midnight Kiss, The Return of Peter Grimm, Seventh Heaven, Two Girls Wanted, Sunny Side Up, Happy Days, Delicious, The Man Who Came Back, Daddy Long Legs, Merely Mary Ann, State Fair, Carolina, Change of Heart, Small Town Girl, Ladies in Love*, more, including two in 1938—*Three Loves Has Nancy* and *The Young in Heart*—after which she left the screen.

GAYNOR, MITZI (S. Cal.) Last in a movie in '69, this musical star now performs in the better nightclubs and does an annual TV special. Onscreen from 1950. IN: *My Blue Heaven, Golden Girl, Bloodhounds of Broadway, Down Among the Sheltering Palms, There's No Business Like Show Business, Anything Goes, The Joker Is Wild, Les Girls, South Pacific, Surprise Package, For the First Time*, more.

GAZZARA, BEN (S. Cal.) Star. Onscreen from 1957. IN: *The Strange One, Anatomy of a Murder, The Young Doctors, Reprieve, A Rage to Live, The Bridge at Remagen, Faces, Husbands, The Neptune Factor, Capone, The Voyage of the Damned*, more.

GAZZO, MICHAEL V. (N.Y.) Character. Nominated for Best Supporting Actor Oscar in *The Godfather, Part II*. Original author of *A Hatful of Rain*, the play and the movie. IN: *The*

Gang That Couldn't Shoot Straight, The Godfather.

GEAR, LUELLA (N.Y.) Character. Onscreen from 1938. IN: *Carefree, The Perfect Marriage, Jigsaw, Phffft,* more.

GEER, ELLEN (S. Cal.) Leading lady. Daughter of Will. Onscreen from the '60s. IN: *Petulia, The Reivers, Kotch, Harold and Maude, Silence, Memory of Us,* more.

GEER, LENNIE (S. Cal.) Support. IN: *The Great Locomotive Chase, The High Powered Rifle,* more.

GEER, WILL (S. Cal.) Character. Onscreen from 1932. IN: *The Misleading Lady, Intruder in the Dust, Anna Lucasta, Lust for Gold, The Kid from Texas, Winchester 73, Broken Arrow, To Please a Lady, Bright Victory, Advise and Consent, Seconds, In Cold Blood, The President's Analyst, The Reivers, Jeremiah Johnson, The Manchu Eagle Murder Caper Mystery,* more.

GEESON, JUDY (Eng.) Leading lady. Onscreen from 1967. IN: *To Sir With Love, Berserk!, Hammerhead, Prudence and the Pill, Three Into Two Won't Go, Two Gentlemen Sharing, Doomwatch, Brannigan,* more.

GELIN, DANIEL (Fr.) Star. Additionally famous now as the father of Maria Schneider who was with Brando in *Last Tango in Paris.* Onscreen from the early '40s. IN: *Children of Paradise, Edward and Caroline, La Ronde, Dirty Hands, Le Plaisir, Adorable Creatures, The Man Who Knew Too Much, The Snow Was Black, Woman of Rome, Royal Affairs in Versailles, Please Mr. Balzac, Testament of Orpheus, La Bonne Soupe, Is Paris Burning?,* more.

CELMAN, LARRY (S. Cal.) Character. Onscreen in the '70s. IN: *The Christian Licorice Store, Superdad,* more.

GENN, LEO (Eng.) Costar. Nominated for Best Supporting Actor Oscar in *Quo Vadis.* Already in movies more than a decade when he went to Hollywood, he spent four years there (1947–50), starring with inimitable low-key elan in *Mourning Becomes Electra, The Velvet Glove, The Miniver Story,* etc. Returning to England, he continued to star in numerous pix while headlining in a lengthy roster of plays. During the '60s he also appeared on Broadway in *The Devil's Advocate* and, as Caesar, in *Caesar and Cleopatra.* At the end of the decade, this scholarly man—a lawyer before becoming an actor—spent two additional years in Amer-

ica, but far from Hollywood. In '68 he was appointed Distinguished Visiting Professor of Theatre Arts at Pennsylvania State University, and, while on campus, appeared in various student productions. The following year, he was Visiting Professor of Drama at the University of Utah, where he also did the title role in *Dr. Faustus.* In England again, he costarred with Bette Davis in *Connecting Rooms.* More recently, in addition to writing his memoirs, he has costarred in the French-made *The Silent One,* with Suzanne Flon, which he did in both the French and English versions, and the West German-Israeli film *The Martyr.* Now in his 70s (b. 1905), the actor has been married for many years to Marguerite van Praag. Onscreen from 1935. IN: *Immortal Gentleman, When Thief Meets Thief, Drums, Immortal Battalion, Henry V, Caesar and Cleopatra, Green for Danger, The Snake Pit, The Plymouth Adventure, Girls of Pleasure Island, Affair in Monte Carlo, Personal Affair, Moby Dick, Steel Bayonet, Lady Chatterley's Lover, The Longest Day, 55 Days at Peking, Circus of Fear,* more.

GENTLE, LILI (S. Cal.) Divorced from producer Richard Zanuck, by whom she has two children, this starlet of the '50s has long been retired. Onscreen from 1956. IN: *Teenage Rebel, Will Success Spoil Rock Hunter?, Young and Dangerous, Mr. Hobbs Takes a Vacation,* more.

GEORGE, ANTHONY (N.Y.) Leading man. Lately active in TV soap operas. Onscreen in the '50s. IN: *Love That Brute, Where the Sidewalk Ends, Under My Skin, The Folsom Story, You Never Can Tell, Three Bad Sisters, Chicago Confidential,* more.

GEORGE, CHRISTOPHER (S. Cal.) Leading man. Onscreen from 1966. IN: *Gentle Rain, El Dorado, The Captive, The Thousand Plane Raid, The Devil's Eight, The Delta Factor, The Train Robbers, Grizzly,* more.

GEORGE, CHIEF DAN (Can.) Character. Nominated for Best Supporting Actor Oscar in *Little Big Man.* Onscreen from 1969. IN: *Smith!, Cancel My Reservation, Harry and Tonto, The Bears and I,* more.

GEORGE, ISABEL (Eng.) Leading lady. Onscreen from the '50s. IN: *Death Is a Number, Street Corner, The Beggar's Opera, The Love Match,* more.

GEORGE, LYNDA DAY (S. Cal.) Actress-wife of Christopher George. (See Lynda Day.)

GEORGE, SUSAN (Eng.) Leading lady. Onscreen from 1968. IN: *All Neat in Black Stock-*

ings, *The Looking Glass War, The Strange Affair, The Straw Dogs, Mandingo, Out of Season,* more.

GERMAINE, MARY (Eng.) Leading lady. Onscreen from the '50s. IN: *Laughter in Paradise, Cloudburst, Where's Charley?, The Night Won't Talk, House of Blackmail, Devil's Point,* more.

GERRITSEN, LISA (S. Cal.) Juvenile. IN: *Airport.*

GERRY, ALEX (S. Cal.) Character. Onscreen from 1950. IN: *Whirlpool, The Reformer and the Redhead, Excuse My Dust, The Jazz Singer, Lili, The Eddie Cantor Story, Funny Face, This Happy Feeling, Pillow Talk, The Brass Bottle,* more.

GERSON, BETTY LOU (S. Cal.) Support. Married Warren Berlinger and retired. Onscreen in the '50s. IN: *An Annapolis Story, The Green-Eyed Blonde, The Miracle of the Hills.*

GETTMAN, LORRAINE (S. Cal.) (See Leslie Brooks.)

GEVA, TAMARA (N.Y.) Actress-dancer. Onscreen from 1929. IN: *Night Club, The Girl Habit, Manhattan Merry-Go-Round, Orchestra Wives, Night Plane from Chunking, The Gay Intruders,* more.

GHOLSON, JULIE (Ala.) Juvenile lead. Onscreen in the '70s. IN: *Where the Lilies Bloom.*

GHOSTLEY, ALICE (S. Cal.) Comedienne. Onscreen from 1954. IN: *New Faces, To Kill a Mockingbird, My Six Loves, The Graduate, The Flim Flam Man, Vivi Max!,* more.

GIALLELIS, STATHIS (Greece) Leading man. Onscreen from 1963. IN: *America America, The Eavesdropper, Blue,* more.

GIAMI, GUILIANO (It.) (See Montgomery Wood.)

GIANNINI, GIANCARLO (It.) Star. Onscreen from the '60s. IN: *Anzio, The Secret of Santa Vittoria, Fraulein Doktor, Arabella, Love and Anarchy, The Seduction of Mimi, Swept Away . . ., Drama of the Rich, Midnight Pleasures, The Innocent, Seven Beauties,* more.

GIBBS, SHEILA SHAND (Eng.) Leading lady. Onscreen from the '50s. IN: *Mr. Denning Drives North, A Killer Walks, The Great Game, The Maggie,* more.

GIBSON, HELEN (Ore.) Famous for her daredevil stunts, this invincible actress—in her 80s now (b. 1892)—worked in movies from '12 until the late '50s. The first wife (married in '13) of cowboy star Hoot Gibson, who came out of rodeos as she did, she replaced Helen Holmes in the "Hazards of Helen" pix (she had been Rose Gibson, but for obvious reasons her name was changed to Helen). She then starred in countless silent Westerns (*The Wolverine,* etc.), railroad pix (*The Giant Swing*), and straight dramas (*No Man's Woman*). From '27, she doubled for other women stars, did minor character roles, worked in department stores for a firm specializing in nostalgia (photos of oldtime stars), and was highly active as an extra. Long divorced from Hoot Gibson, she became, in '35, the wife of Navy gunner Clifton Johnson, to whom she remains happily married. They live now in retirement in Roseburg, Ore. Despite a minor stroke suffered two decades ago, Helen Gibson remains as spunky as ever and, loving movie work, just wishes she could do it all over again. Some of the talkies in which she appeared: *Human Targets, Law and Lawless, Cheyenne Cowboy, The Crooked River, The Hollywood Story,* more.

GIBSON, HENRY (S. Cal.) Comedian-character star. Onscreen in the '70s. IN: *The Long Goodbye, Nashville.*

GIBSON, VIRGINIA (N.Y.) The dancer-actress, away from the screen since 1957's *Funny Face,* appeared on Broadway with Ethel Merman in the musical *Happy Hunting* and later was the hostess of a children's show on ABC-TV. Onscreen from 1950. IN: *Tea for Two; Goodbye, My Fancy; Painting the Clouds with Sunshine, About Face, She's Back on Broadway, Seven Brides for Seven Brothers, Athena,* more.

GIBSON, WYNNE (N.Y.) Following her long, busy movie career—1943's *The Falcon Strikes Back* was last—this actress enjoyed thriving careers in radio (*When a Girl Marries, Modern Romances, Whispering Streets,* etc.) and television (*Studio One, Martin Kane, Valiant Lady, Producers Showcase,* many more). She also served as a member of the board of both Television Authority and AFTRA. In her 70s now (b. 1905), still single, she lives in the country 20 miles north of Manhattan and, though she has done no acting in the past two decades, she is still listed in both the New York *Players' Guide* and *Hollywood Players Directory* as being available for work. Onscreen from 1929. IN: *Nothing But the Truth, Molly Magdalene, June Moon, City Streets, The Road to Reno, If I Had a Million, Ladies of the Big House, The Devil Is Driving, The Crosby Case, Sleepers East, The Captain Hates the Sea, Gangs of New York, Cafe Hostess, A Miracle on Main Street,* more.

GIELGUD, SIR JOHN (Eng.) Character. Nominated for Best Supporting Actor Oscar in *Becket.* Onscreen in a few silents of the '20s. Onscreen in talkies from 1932. IN: *Insult, The Good Companions, Julius Caesar, Romeo and Juliet, Richard III, Around the World in 80 Days, The Barretts of Wimpole Street, The Loved One, The Shoes of the Fisherman, Oh! What a Lovely War, Lost Horizon, Gold, Murder on the Orient Express, 11 Harrowhouse, Galileo,* more.

GIERASCH, STEFAN (N.Y.) Support. Onscreen from the '60s. IN: *The Hustler, The Traveling Executioner, Jeremiah Johnson, Claudine,* more.

GIFFORD, ALAN (Eng.) Character. Onscreen from 1952. IN: *It Started in Paradise, Satellite in the Sky, The Iron Petticoat, Across the Bridge, A King in New York, Screaming Mimi, Town Without Pity, Phase IV,* more.

GIFFORD, FRANCES (S. Cal.) There has been no further word about this lovely actress since 1958 when she was admitted to California's Camarillo State Hospital (for the mentally ill). She would be in her 50s now (b. 1920). Onscreen from 1937. IN: *New Faces of 1937, Woman Chases Man, West Point Widow, The Remarkable Andrew, The Glass Key, Cry Havoc, Marriage Is a Private Affair, Our Vines Have Tender Grapes, The Arnelo Affair, Luxury Liner,* more, including 1953's *Sky Commando,* her last.

GIFFORD, FRANK (N.Y.) The handsome football star who seemed a sure bet for screen stardom became, instead, one of television's best known sportscasters. IN: *Up Periscope!, Paper Lion.*

GIFTOS, ELAINE (S. Cal.) Leading lady. Onscreen in the '70s. IN: *On a Clear Day You Can See Forever, The Lovely Leggy World, Gas-s-s!, The Student Nurses,* more.

GILBERT, JOANNE (S. Cal.) Singer-actress. Daughter of late (d. 1976) Oscar-winning composer Ray ("Zip-a-Dee-Doo-Dah") Gilbert, who had a brief vogue in movies and still sings in clubs. Onscreen in the '50s. IN: *Red Garters, The Great Man, Ride Out for Revenge, The High Cost of Loving.*

GILBERT, JODY (S. Cal.) Character actress. Onscreen from 1939. IN: *Everything Happens at Night, Little Old New York, Hudson's Bay, Wild Geese Calling, Never Give a Sucker an Even Break, The Tuttles of Tahiti, The Hard Way, Blondie's Holiday, Albuquerque, My Dear Secretary, Gene Autry and the Mounties, Actors and Sin, The Big Fisherman, Butch Cassidy and the Sundance Kid, Willard,* more.

GILBERT, LAUREN (S. Cal.) Character actor. Onscreen from 1948. IN: *Close-Up, Girls of the Night, X-15, The Unsinkable Molly Brown,* more.

GILBERT, LEATRICE JOY (Conn.) The daughter of stars Leatrice Joy and John Gilbert, she has been working on a book about her father. On a research trip to Hollywood, she interviewed, among others, Virginia Bruce (also once married to John Gilbert), Eleanor Boardman, King Vidor, and Colleen Moore. In '74, in an "Author's Query" published in the *New York Times Book Review,* she stated: "I would appreciate any information, correspondence, remembrances or other material." She gave her name and address as Leatrice Gilbert Fountain, 24 Gilliam Lane, Riverside, Conn. 06878. Onscreen in 1938. IN: *Of Human Hearts.*

GILBERT, LOU (N.Y.) Character. Onscreen from 1962. IN: *Requiem for a Heavyweight, Across the River, Juliet of the Spirits, Petulia, The Great White Hope, Jennifer on My Mind,* more.

GILBERT, PHILIP (S. Cal.) Character. Onscreen from 1957. IN: *Checkpoint, The Frozen Dead,* more.

GILBERT, RONNIE (S. Cal.) Character actress. Onscreen from 1967. IN: *Festival, Windflowers, The Loves of Isadora,* more.

GILBERT, RUTH (N.Y.) Character. Onscreen in 1931. IN: *Alice in Wonderland.*

GILCHRIST, CONNIE (S. Cal.) In her 70s (b. 1901), this character actress still possesses the infectious gusto that made her such a joy in 76 pictures, the last of which was 1969's *Some Kind of a Nut.* And she has no objection to working again, if the right role presents itself. Married to her original husband, director-playwright Edwin O'Hanlon, since '22, she lives with him in a hillside house in Hollywood. They have one daughter, Dorothy, who lives and works in New York—to their regret. Onscreen from 1940. IN: *Hullabaloo, Whistling in the Dark, A Woman's Face, Johnny Eager, Tortilla Flat, Presenting Lily Mars, Cry Havoc, The Heavenly Body, Music for Millions, The Valley of Decision, Junior Miss, Good News, Chicken Every Sunday, A Letter to Three Wives, Stars in My Crown, Here Comes the Groom, It Should Happen to You, Auntie Mame, Some Came Running, The Misadventures of Merlin Jones, The Monkey's Uncle,* more.

GILFORD, JACK (N.Y.) Character. Nominated for Best Supporting Actor Oscar in *Save the Tiger*. Onscreen from 1944. IN: *Hey, Rookie!; The Reckless Age, Main Street to Broadway, Mister Buddwing, A Funny Thing Happened on the Way to the Forum, Enter Laughing, The Incident, Catch 22, They Might Be Giants*, more.

GILL, TOM (Eng.) Leading man. Onscreen from 1937. IN: *Midshipman Easy, The First Gentleman, Dr. Drake's Duck, Hotel Sahara, Lady Godiva Rides Again, The Steel Key, The Weak and the Wicked, Simon and Laura*, more.

GILLETTE, RUTH (S. Cal.) The actress who portrayed Lillian Russell in *The Great Ziegfeld*, and golden-haired still, in her 60s, has returned to Studio City to live after a long residence in New York. There, she was featured on Broadway in *70 - Girls - 70* and *The Gazebo*, and on tour in the national company of *Mame*, as well as in many TV shows. Last onscreen in *In a Lonely Place*, she hopes to get her screen career into motion again. Yes, she still sings—beautifully. Onscreen from 1934. IN: *Frontier Marshal, Wild Gold, Life Begins at 40, Off to the Races, In Old Chicago, Rebecca of Sunnybrook Farm, Josette, The Return of the Cisco Kid*, more.

GILLIAM, STU (S. Cal.) Black support. Onscreen in the '70s. IN: *The $1,000,000 Duck, The Mack, Dr. Black-Mr. Hyde*, more.

GILLIS, ANN (Eng.) David O. Selznick's charming little Becky Thatcher in *The Adventures of Tom Sawyer*, a beautiful redhead still as she heads into her 50s (b. 1927), has long been a British resident. For many years this "little girl from Little Rock" was married to actor Richard Fraser, now deceased, by whom she has a grown son. Since her divorce from him, she has been the wife of an English theatrical agent and lives in Epsom, Surrey, some 15 miles outside London. Last on Hollywood screens in 1947's *Big Town After Dark*, she acts occasionally on British television and sometimes does small roles in films. She is said to have done a walk-on in *2001*, but her name appears nowhere in this movie's cast list. Onscreen from 1937. IN: *The Singing Cowboy, The Garden of Allah, Little Orphan Annie, Beau Geste, Edison the Man, All This and Heaven Too, My Love Came Back, Nice Girl?, Meet the Stewarts; A Wave, a Wac and a Marine; Janie, Since You Went Away, The Time of Their Lives, Sweetheart of Sigma Chi*, more.

GILLMORE, MARGALO (N.Y.) This splendid character actress, now in her 70s (b. 1897), gave up her acting career after 1966's *The Trouble with Angels*. She had published her autobiography, *Four Flights Up*, two years previously. Onscreen first in 1932's *Wayward*. Onscreen regularly from 1950. IN: *The Happy Years, Perfect Strangers, Elopement, Cause for Alarm, Behave Yourself, Scandal at Scourie, Woman's World, High Society, Gaby*, more.

GILMAN, SAM (S. Cal.) Character. Onscreen from 1957. IN: *Full of Life, The Young Lions, One-Eyed Jacks, Sometimes a Great Notion, Wild Rovers, Gator Bait, Macon County Line*, more.

GILMORE, PETER (Eng.) Support. Onscreen from the '60s. IN: The "Carry On" series, *Oh! What a Lovely War, The Abominable Dr. Phibes*, more.

GILMORE, VIRGINIA (N.Y.) Giving up her movie career after 1952's *Walk East on Beacon*, the former leading lady has not acted in more than a decade, since appearing in stock in *Sweet Bird of Youth*. Single now, and in her late 50s (b. 1919), she was married to Yul Brynner for 16 years, until their divorce in '60. During much of her married life she lived abroad. And in '55 she completed her formal education (begun as a teenager at the University of California) and graduated from the University of Vienna where she majored in cytology (the branch of biology dealing with the study of cells). Today, in Manhattan, where she lives in an apartment on the West Side, she is a leading drama coach. Except that she is slightly heavier, and there is a gray streak in her blonde hair, she looks much as she did in her costarring days. By Brynner, she is the mother of a grown son, Roc, an actor-playwright. Onscreen from 1939. IN: *Winter Carnival, Manhattan Heartbeat, Laddie, Western Union; Tall, Dark and Handsome; Berlin Correspondent, The Pride of the Yankees, The Loves of Edgar Allan Poe, Orchestra Wives, That Other Woman, Chetniks, Wonder Man*, more.

GING, JACK (S. Cal.) Support. Onscreen from 1955. IN: *Desire in the Dust, The Ghost of Dragstrip Hollow, Sniper's Ridge, Intimacy, Play Misty for Me, Where the Red Fern Grows*, more.

GINGOLD, HERMIONE (N.Y.) Character star. Onscreen in England from 1936. IN: *Someone at the Door, Meet Mr. Penny, The Pickwick Papers, Mary Goes to Town, Adventures of Sadie*, more. Onscreen in America from 1956. IN: *Around the World in 80 Days; Bell, Book and Candle; Gigi, The Naked Edge, The*

Music Man, Harvey Middleman, Fireman; Promise Her Anything, Those Fantastic Flying Fools, more.

GIRARDIN, RAY (S. Cal.) Support. IN: *Star!*, more.

GIRARDOT, ANNIE (Fr.) Star. Onscreen from the '50s. IN: *Inspector Maigret, Speaking of Murder, Love and the Frenchwoman, Rocco and His Brothers, The Organizer, Male Companion, Live for Life, Dillinger Is Dead, To Die of Love, Where There's Smoke, It Is Raining on Santiago, The Gypsy, The Slap*, more.

GIROTTI, MASSIMO (It.) Leading man. Onscreen from the '40s. IN: *Woman Trouble, Iron Crown; Rome, 11 O'Clock; The Ten Commandments, The Cossacks, Head of a Tyrant, Marco the Magnificent, Senso*, more.

GISH, LILLIAN (N.Y.) Legendary star. Nominated for Best Supporting Actress Oscar in *Duel in the Sun*. In 1970 she received a special Academy Award "for superlative artistry and distinguished contribution to the progress of motion pictures." In 1975 this actress, now in her 80s (b. 1896), still a fine-looking woman and one of seemingly boundless energy, opened on Broadway in the Theatre Guild's *Musical Jubilee*. In it, among other things, she danced and sang Helen Kane's boop-boop-a-doop song, "I Wanna Be Loved by You." She can always be counted on to appear as guest speaker at retrospective showings of the works of her discoverer, D.W. Griffith, and was successful in lobbying for the issuance of a postage stamp bearing his likeness. She has not appeared in a movie since 1968's *Follow Me, Boys* but there has been no letup in her career since she made her stage debut at age five. Onscreen in silents from 1912. IN: *An Unseen Enemy, The Musketeers of Pig Alley, The New York Hat, The Unwelcome Guest, A Cry for Help, The Mothering Heart, Judith of Bethulia, The Birth of a Nation, Intolerance, Broken Blossoms, Way Down East, Orphans of the Storm, The Scarlet Letter*, more. Onscreen in talkies from 1930. IN: *One Romantic Night, His Double Life, Commandos Strike at Dawn, Miss Susie Slagle's, Portrait of Jennie, Night of the Hunter, The Cobweb, The Unforgiven, Warning Shot, The Comedians*, more.

GIVNEY, KATHRYN (S. Cal.) The character actress is in her 70s now and retired. Her last movie was 1962's *The Four Horsemen of the Apocalypse*. Onscreen from 1931. IN: *Lover Come Back, Isn't It Romantic?, My Friend Irma, Ma and Pa Kettle Go to Town, A Place in the Sun, Lightning Strikes Twice, Three Coins in the Fountain, Guys and Dolls, A Certain*

Smile, The Man in the Net, From the Terrace, more.

GLASER, DAREL (N.Y.) Juvenile actor. Onscreen in the '70s. IN: *Bless the Beasts & Children*, more.

GLASER, MICHAEL (N.Y.) Support. IN: *Fiddler on the Roof, Butterflies Are Free*.

GLASS, NED (S. Cal.) Character. Onscreen from 1938. IN: *Give Me a Sailor, He's a Cockeyed Wonder, Storm Warning, The Steel Cage, West Side Story, Experiment in Terror, Charade, A Big Hand for a Little Lady, The Fortune Cookie, Never a Dull Moment, The Love Bug*, more.

GLASS, SEAMON (S. Cal.) Character. Onscreen in the '70s. IN: *Deliverance, Slither, Bootleggers, Winterhawk*, more.

GLEASON, JACKIE (Fla.) Star comedian. Nominated for Best Supporting Actor Oscar in *The Hustler*. Onscreen from 1941. IN: *Navy Blues, Larceny, Inc., All Through the Night, Springtime in the Rockies, Life of Riley, Blood Money, Soldier in the Rain, Requiem for a Heavyweight, Papa's Delicate Condition, How to Commit Marriage, Skidoo, Don't Drink the Water, How Do I Love Thee?*, more.

GLOVER, BRUCE (S. Cal.) Support. Onscreen in the '70s. IN: *C.C. and Company, Scandalous John, Bless the Beasts & Children, Diamonds Are Forever, Walking Tall, Black Gunn, Chinatown*, more.

GLOVER, JULIAN (Eng.) Support. Onscreen from 1963. IN: *Tom Jones, The Alphabet Murders, Time Lost and Time Remembered, Five Million Years to Earth, The Magus, Nicholas and Alexandra, Luther, The Internecine Project, Juggernaut*, more.

GOBEL, GEORGE (S. Cal.) Star comedian. Onscreen in the '50s. IN: *The Birds and the Bees, I Married a Woman*.

GODDARD, MARK (S. Cal.) Support. Now an agent. Onscreen in the '60s. IN: *The Monkey's Uncle, A Rage to Live*.

GODDARD, PAULETTE (Switz.) Star. Nominated for Best Supporting Actress Oscar in *So Proudly We Hail*. Onscreen from 1931. IN: *City Streets, Roman Scandals, Modern Times, Dramatic School, The Women, The Cat and the Canary, Northwest Mounted Police, The Great Dictator, Hold Back the Dawn, Reap the Wild Wind, The Lady Has Plans, The Crystal Ball, I Love a Soldier, Standing Room Only, Kitty*,

Unconquered, An Ideal Husband, Anna Lucasta, Vice Squad, Sins of Jezebel, more. Retired.

GODFREY, ARTHUR (Va.) Rich, retired, and living in Paeonian Springs where he raises show horses, he is now in his 70s (b. 1903). Onscreen in the '60s. IN: *The Glass Bottom Boat, Where Angels Go Trouble Follows.*

GODSELL, VANDA (Eng.) Character. Onscreen from the '50s. IN: *Hour of Decision, Hell Is a City, This Sporting Life, A Shot in the Dark,* more.

GOFF, NORRIS (S. Cal.) Recovered from his cancer operation of two decades ago, "Abner" of "Lum 'n Abner" is in his 70s (b. 1906) and lives in well-off retirement in Palm Desert. Onscreen from 1940. IN: *Dreaming Out Loud, Bashful Bachelor, Two Weeks to Live, So This Is Washington, Goin' to Town,* more.

GOLAN, GILA (N.Y.) One of the lost refugee children of WW II, this brunette leading lady of the '60s has no knowledge of her real parents, birthplace, year or date of birth, or her true name. Found wandering in a small town in Poland, she was taken in by a large Catholic family named Zavatski, living with them for several years. A Jewish women's organization, looking for lost children, then accepted her and placed her in a boarding school in Aix-les-Bains, France, where she was given the name Miriam Goldenburg. Eventually sent with other refugee youngsters to Israel, she lived in a kibbutz and, in '61, was named Miss Israel. Taking the name Gila Golan ("Gila means joy; Golan is the name of a beautiful mountain in Israel"), she placed second in that year's Miss World competition in London. There she met Columbia Pictures executive William Cohan and his wife Selma. Coming to regard the young beauty as their foster daughter, and having no children of their own, they sponsored her entry into the United States and movies. Today, living in New York and having long since given up her career, Gila Golan not only has a real name, Mrs. Matthew Rosenhaus (her husband is a major Columbia stockholder), but three beautiful young daughters. And to Selma Cohan—her husband, William, died early in '76—these are indeed her "grandchildren." Onscreen from 1965. IN: *Ship of Fools, Our Man Flint, 3 on a Couch, Catch as Catch Can, The Valley of Gwangi,* more.

GOLDEN, BOB (S. Cal.) Character. Onscreen in the '70s. IN: *Willard, The Sugarland Express, Chinatown,* more.

GOLDEN, MICHAEL (Eng.) Character. Onscreen from 1947. IN: *Hungry Hill, The Blue Lamp, Cry the Beloved Country, Pool of London, Track the Man Down, Murder She Said,* more.

GOLDEN, OLIVE FULLER (S. Cal.) (See Olive Carey.)

GOLDINA, MIRIAM (N.Y.) As a young woman she made a vivid impression in her one movie, 1932's *Ladies of the Big House.* She continued her career in many roles on the Broadway stage and in television, and, in her 70s (b. 1898), remains professionally active.

GOLDONI, LELIA (S. Cal.) Leading lady. Onscreen from 1959. IN: *Faces, Hysteria, Alice Doesn't Live Here Anymore, The Day of the Locust.*

GOLONKA, ARLENE (S. Cal.) Leading lady. Onscreen from 1965. IN: *Harvey Middleman, Fireman; Penelope, Welcome to Hard Times, The Busy Body, Diary of a Bachelor, Hang 'Em High,* more.

GONZALEZ-GONZALES, PEDRO (S. Cal.) Comedy character. Onscreen from 1953. IN: *Wings of the Hawk, Ring of Fear, The High and the Mighty, Strange Lady in Town, The Sheepman, Rio Bravo, The Adventures of Bullwhip Griffin, The Love Bug, Support Your Local Gunfighter,* more.

GOODMAN, BENNY (N.Y.) Orchestra leader. Onscreen with his band from 1936. IN: *The Big Broadcast of 1937, Hollywood Hotel, Stage Door Canteen, The Powers Girl, The Gang's All Here, Sweet and Low Down, A Song Is Born.*

GOODMAN, DODY (S. Cal.) Comedienne. In 1976 she was one of the stars of the nighttime TV soap opera *Mary Hartman, Mary Hartman.* Onscreen from 1964. IN: *Bedtime Story,* more.

GOODNER, CAROL (N.Y.) The leading lady of the '30s is in her 70s now (b. 1904) and continued her career in radio (*Wendy Warren and the News*) and on the Broadway stage, where she last appeared in 1961's *A Man for All Seasons.* Onscreen from 1932. IN: *The Ringer, There Goes the Bride, Just Smith, Mimi, The Dominant Sex, The Student's Romance, The Frog, La Vie Parisienne,* more.

GOODWIN, HAROLD (Eng.) English character actor, not the American actor of the same name who was active from the '20s into the '50s but whose present whereabouts are unknown. Onscreen from 1950. IN: *Dance Hall, The Magnet, The Man in the White Suit, The Ladykillers, The Ship That Died of Shame, Prince and the Showgirl, All at Sea, Law and Disorder, The Bushbaby,* more.

GOODWIN, JIM (S. Cal.) Character. Onscreen from 1956. IN: *Attack!, Second to Hell,* more.

GORDON, BRUCE (S. Cal.) Character. Onscreen from 1949. IN: *Love Happy, Make Me an Offer, The Curse of the Undead, Key Witness, Alcatraz Express, The Scarface Mob, Hello Down There,* more.

GORDON, CLARKE (S. Cal.) Character. Onscreen from the '60s. IN: *A Cold Wind in August, Impasse; Gaily, Gaily; More Dead Than Alive,* more.

GORDON, DANIEL (N.Y.) Character. Onscreen from the '50s. IN: *The Wrong Man, The Hustler, Street of Sinners, Cancel My Reservation, The Godfather,* more.

GORDON, DON (S. Cal.) Character. Onscreen from the '50s. IN: *Force of Arms, Girls in the Night, Cry Tough, Bullitt, The Education of Sonny Carson, The Towering Inferno,* more.

GORDON, DOROTHY (Eng.) Character. Onscreen from 1945. IN: *The Silver Fleet, The Dummy Talks, Love in Pawn, Hobson's Choice, Tonight at 8:30* ("Fumed Oak" sequence), *The Haunted Strangler,* more.

GORDON, DOUGLAS (N.Y.) Character. Now a stage and TV actor. Onscreen in 1940. IN: *Adventure in Diamonds.*

GORDON, GALE (S. Cal.) Character actor. Onscreen from 1942. IN: *Here We Go Again, Here Come the Marines, Francis Covers the Big Town, Our Miss Brooks; Rally 'Round the Flag, Boys!; Visit to a Small Planet, All in a Night's Work, All Hands on Deck, Speedway,* more.

GORDON, GRANT (N.Y.) Character. IN: *The Subject Was Roses.*

GORDON, LEO (S. Cal.) Character. Now billed Leo V. Gordon. Onscreen from 1953. IN: *Gun Fury, Hondo, Riot in Cell Block 11, Soldier of Fortune, The Steel Jungle, The Man Who Knew Too Much, Great Day in the Morning, Baby Face Nelson, Apache Territory, Noose for a Gunman, Tarzan Goes to India, McLintock!, Kitten with a Whip, The Night of the Grizzly, St. Valentine's Day Massacre, Tobruk, You Can't Win 'Em All, My Name Is Nobody,* more.

GORDON, RUTH (N.Y.) Character. Nominated for Best Supporting Actress Oscar in *Inside Daisy Clover.* Won the Oscar in the same category in *Rosemary's Baby.* Her life story was dramatized in 1953's *The Actress* with Jean Simmons portraying her. Onscreen in a few silents from 1915. IN: *Camille, The Wheel of Life.* Onscreen in talkies from 1940. IN: *Abe Lincoln in Illinois, Dr. Ehrlich's Magic Bullet, Two-Faced Woman, Action in the North Atlantic, Edge of Darkness, Lord Love a Duck, Whatever Happened to Aunt Alice?, Harold and Maude.*

GORDONE, CHARLES (S. Cal.) Support. Onscreen in 1975. IN: *Coonskin.*

GORE, LESLEY (N.J.) Teen record star of the early '60s. Dropping out of music, she graduated from Sarah Lawrence College. In 1975, attempting a comeback, she sang at a rock 'n roll festival at Madison Square Gardon, her first such in eight years. Onscreen in 1965 in *Ski Party.*

GORING, MARIUS (Eng.) Character star. Onscreen from 1936. IN: *Consider Your Verdict, Rembrandt, Stairway to Heaven, The Red Shoes, Whirlpool, Pandora and the Flying Dutchman, The Barefoot Contessa, Quentin Durward, The Truth About Women, The Angry Hills, Exodus, The 25th Hour, The Girl on the Motorcycle, Zeppelin,* more.

GORMAN, CLIFF (N.Y.) Costar. Onscreen from 1968. IN: *Justine, The Boys in the Band, Class of '63, Cops and Robbers, Rosebud,* more.

GORNEY, KAREN (N.Y.) Leading lady. Onscreen from the '60s. IN: *David and Lisa, The Magic Garden of Stanley Sweetheart, Social Conscience,* more.

GORSHIN, FRANK (S. Cal.) Comedian. Onscreen from 1956. IN: *Between Heaven and Hell, Invasion of the Saucer Men, Warlock, Bells Are Ringing, Where the Boys Are, The Great Impostor, The George Raft Story, Sail a Crooked Ship, That Darn Cat, Batman, Skidoo,* more.

GORTNER, MARJOE (S. Cal.) Character lead. Former boy evangelist. Onscreen from 1972. IN: *Marjoe, Earthquake, Bobbie Jo and the Outlaws, The Food of the Gods,* more.

GOSDEN, FREEMAN (S. Cal.) Now in his 80s (b. 1896), "Amos" of radio's and movies' "Amos 'n Andy," a very rich man still, lives in retirement in Beverly Hills, goes fishing once in a while, and still misses his longtime pal and partner, Charles Correll (d. 1972). They began their blackface comedy act in 1919, continued in it for 32 years—becoming, along the way, a national institution on radio in the 30s—and never was there a trace of discord between them. Onscreen in 1930. IN: *Check and Double Check.*

GOSS, HELEN (Eng.) Character. Onscreen from the '40s. IN: *The Wicked Lady, Pink String and Sealing Wax, Outpost in Malaya, My Sister and I, The Pickwick Papers, The Sword and the Rose,* more.

GOSSETT, LOU (S. Cal.) Black costar. Onscreen from the '60s. IN: *A Raisin in the Sun, The Bush Baby, The Landlord, The Skin Game,* more.

GOTHIE, ROBERT (S. Cal.) Support. IN: *Kings Go Forth, Sanctuary,* more.

GOUDAL, JETTA (S. Cal.) "That consummate she-devil" of the silent screen—the words are S. J. Perelman's—who privately, until recently, did such "wicked" deeds as work on behalf of the Los Angeles Orphanage and Braille Institute, is in her 70s now (b. 1898). And, to the distress of this woman who was born for creative activity, she is incapacitated. Besides having a heart condition, a fall in her Los Angeles home in '73 has forced curtailment of most charitable and social endeavors. And to get about within her home she must use a wheelchair or walker. But, just as in her movie heyday, she is a strong-willed woman (gossips called it temperament then, but artistic integrity might be closer to the truth); she wants to walk again and probably will. Her husband, since '30, noted interior decorator Harold Grieve—they have no children—attends to her every need. The charming French accent that audiences heard in only a couple of talkies, *Business and Pleasure* with Will Rogers and *Tarnished Youth* with Gilbert Roland, she still has. Onscreen from 1923. IN: *The Bright Shawl, The Green Goddess, Salome of the Tenements, The Road to Yesterday, Three Faces West, White Gold, Lady of the Pavements,* more.

GOUGH, LLOYD (S. Cal.) Character. Onscreen from 1948. IN: *Black Bart, All My Sons, A Southern Yankee, Roseanna McCoy, Tulsa, Sunset Boulevard, Storm Warning, Valentino, Rancho Notorious, Tony Rome, Madigan, Earthquake,* more.

GOUGH, MICHAEL (Eng.) Costar. Onscreen from 1946. IN: *Blanche Fury, The Man in the White Suit, Rob Roy, The Sword and the Rose, Richard III, The Horse's Mouth, Tamahine, The Skull, They Came from Beyond Space, Berserk, Galileo,* more.

GOULD, DOROTHY (S. Cal.) Retired, she has been for many years wife of well-known motion picture exhibitor Sherrill C. Corwin. Onscreen from 1930. IN: *Ladies in Love,* more.

GOULD, ELLIOTT (S. Cal.) Costar. Nominated for Best Supporting Actor Oscar in *Bob & Carol & Ted & Alice.* Onscreen from 1966. IN: *The Confession, The Night They Raided Minsky's, M*A*S*H, Getting Straight, I Love My Wife, The Touch, Little Murders, The Long Goodbye, Busting, California Split, S*P*Y*S, Whiffs; I Will, I Will . . . For Now; Harry and Walter Go to New York, Mean Johnny Barrows* (cameo), more.

GOULD, HAROLD (S. Cal.) Character. Onscreen from 1963. IN: *The Yellow Canary, Harper, Mrs. Pollifax—Spy, The Front Page, The Strongest Man in the World,* more.

GOULD, SANDRA (S. Cal.) Character. Onscreen from 1948. IN: *June Bride, Honeymoon Hotel, Imitation of Life; Boy, Did I Get a Wrong Number!; The Ghost and Mr. Chicken, The Barefoot Executive,* more.

GOULD, SID (S. Cal.) Character. Onscreen from 1962. IN: *Teenage Millionaire,* more.

GOULET, ROBERT (S. Cal.) Singer-actor. Onscreen from 1964. IN: *Honeymoon Hotel, I'd Rather Be Rich, His and Hers, I Deal in Danger, Underground,* more.

GOYA, MONA (Fr.) Popular in early English and French talkies, this former leading lady, in her 70s now and a bit heavier, was at last report still starring on provincial stages in France. Onscreen from 1930. IN: *The Flame of Love, Coiffeur Pour Dames, Juggernaut, Francis the First,* more.

GRACIE, SALLY (N.Y.) Character. Onscreen from 1956. IN: *Patterns, Stage Struck, The Fugitive Kind,* more.

GRADY, DON (S. Cal.) Young lead. Formerly in TV's *My Three Sons.* Onscreen in the '70s. IN: *The McCullochs,* more.

GRAHAM, FRED (Ariz.) The former supporting actor is now director of the Arizona Motion Picture Development Office in Phoenix. Onscreen from the '40s. IN: *The Fighting Kentuckian, The Woman on Pier 13, Angels in the Outfield, 20,000 Leagues Under the Sea, The Last Hunt,* more.

GRAHAM, JOHN (S. Cal.) Character. Onscreen from the '60s. IN: *The Lost World,* more.

GRAHAM, RONNY (N.Y.) Comedian. Onscreen in 1954. IN: *New Faces.*

GRAHAME, GLORIA (S. Cal.) The blonde sexpot who was nominated for a Best Supporting Actress Oscar in *Crossfire* and won one in the same category in *The Bad and the Beautiful* is now a middle-aged woman (b. 1925) with dark hair shot through with gray, and still an actress to be reckoned with. On ABC-TV in '76 she costarred with Dorothy McGuire and Ray Milland in Irwin Shaw's *Rich Man, Poor Man*, a six-part (12-hour) TV-movie. About the same time she starred in the movie *Mama's Dirty Girls*, and, a bit earlier, costarred on TV in *The Girl on the Late, Late Show* (title role) and onstage with Henry Fonda in *The Time of Your Life*. She has been married four times: to actor Stanley Clements (1945–48), director Nick Ray (1948–52; they have a son, Timothy, who lives and works in New York), writer Cy Howard (1954–57; she has a grown daughter, Mariana, by him), and (since 1961) to Tony Ray, son of Nick Ray (once her stepson, of course), and by him she has four children. Tony Ray, who is a few years younger than the actress, was associate producer of *Blume in Love* and assistant director of *Harry and Tonto*. They live quietly, unglamorously, in a small house in Van Nuys. In her youth Gloria Grahame was easily—without nudity or vulgarity—the most blatantly sensual girl on the screen. Explaining this quality recently, she said, "It wasn't the way I looked at a man, but the thought behind it." Onscreen from 1943. IN: *Cry Havoc, It's a Wonderful Life, It Happened in Brooklyn, Song of the Thin Man, In a Lonely Place, Macao, The Greatest Show on Earth, Sudden Fear, The Glass Wall, Man on a Tightrope, The Big Heat, Human Desire, The Naked Alibi, The Cobweb, Not As a Stranger, Oklahoma!, Ride Out for Revenge, Odds Against Tomorrow, The Todd Killings,* more.

GRAHAME, MARGOT (Eng.) In her 60s (b. 1911), she remains a sophisticated, stunning redhead with a whistle-worthy figure and lives in a luxurious flat at Lancaster Gate. The widow of top literary agent A. D. Peters (and earlier divorced from actor Francis Lister and from Alan MacMartin), she was, in '75, reportedly engaged to former Hollywood actor Alexander Kirkland, who now lives in Mexico. Today she is almost as noted for her extensive jewel collection as she was for the great performance she gave in John Ford's *The Informer*. She gave up her screen career after 1957's *Saint Joan* in which she had a supporting role. Onscreen from 1930. IN: *Sorrell and Son, Two in the Dark, Trouble Ahead, Make Way for a Lady, The Three Musketeers, Criminal Lawyer, Michael Strogoff, The Buccaneer, Black Magic, Lucky Nick Cain, The Crimson Pirate, The Assassin, The Beggar's Opera,* more.

GRANER, GERTRUDE (S. Cal.) Character. Onscreen from the '50s. IN: *The Glass Menagerie, Witness to Murder,* more.

GRANGE, RED (Fla.) "The Galloping Ghost," one of football's immortals, starred heroically in the 1926 feature *One Minute to Play* and in the '31 serial *The Galloping Ghost*—billed in the latter as Harold "Red" Grange. Wry and spry in his 70s (b. 1903), with silver threads among the red, he still carries his exact playing-starring weight of decades ago—170 pounds. After writing books on football, and a career as a sportscaster, he went into insurance—and did well. Retired now, he lives quietly with his wife in Indian Lakes, near Orlando, and says, "I'm financially sound. I don't do much. A little fishing. I mostly throw them back. I hate to clean fish. If I get up in the morning and decide I don't want to do anything, then I just don't do anything."

GRANGER, DOROTHY (S. Cal.) Character. Onscreen from the late '20s. IN: *Love, Honor and Oh Baby!; I'll Tell the World, Dramatic School, When the Daltons Rode, The Lady from Cheyenne, One Body Too Many, The Southerner,* Leon Errol two-reelers (as his wife), *Westward the Women, New York Confidential, Raintree County, Dondi,* more.

GRANGER, FARLEY (S. Cal.) A bachelor still as he enters his 50s (b. 1925), he returned to Hollywood in '75 after a decade of picture-making in Italy. Onscreen from 1943. IN: *The North Star, The Purple Heart, Rope, Enchantment, Roseanna McCoy, Our Very Own, Strangers on a Train, I Want You, The Story of Three Loves, Small Town Girl, The Naked Street, The Girl in the Red Velvet Swing, The Wonderful World of the Brothers Grimm, The Serpent, The Man Called Noon,* more.

GRANGER, STEWART (Sp.) Single (after three divorces) and in his 60s (b. 1913), he lives in a mansion on 300 acres of Spain's Costa del Sol—and dreams of making a movie comeback. He has not appeared in a picture since 1969's *The Trygon Factor*, nor appeared on TV since playing Sherlock Holmes in *The Hound of the Baskervilles* in '71. The white-haired actor has been quoted: "It's very sad to grow old. It's depressing to watch anything deteriorate—particularly yourself." To see an old movie of his, he has said, is painful. "I feel like blowing my brains out. There I am, jumping around with a sword and winning all the battles and I know that physically I can't do that anymore. I'd do anything, give anything, to be young again." Onscreen from the '30s. IN: *So This Is London, Convoy, The Man in Grey, Caesar and Cleopa-*

*tra, Blanche Fury, King Solomon's Mines, Sol-
diers Three, Scaramouche, The Prisoner of
Zenda, Young Bess, Salome, All the Brothers
Were Valiant, Beau Brummell, Bhowani Junc-
tion, The Last Hunt, Harry Black and the Tiger,
Sodom and Gomorrah, The Crooked Road,
Rampage at Apache Wells, The Last Safari,
Red Dragon, Flaming Frontier,* more.

GRANT, CARY (N.Y.) Star. Nominated for
Best Actor Oscar in *Penny Serenade* and *None
But the Lonely Heart.* In 1969 he received a
special Oscar "for his unique mastery of the art
of screen acting with the respect and affection
of his colleagues." Onscreen from 1932. IN:
*This Is the Night, Blonde Venus, The Devil and
the Deep, She Done Him Wrong, I'm No Angel,
Spitfire, Ladies Should Listen, Sylvia Scarlet,
Topper, The Awful Truth, Holiday, Bringing
Up Baby, Only Angels Have Wings, Gunga
Din, His Girl Friday, My Favorite Wife, The
Philadelphia Story, Suspicion, Talk of . the
Town, Destination Tokyo, Mr. Lucky, Arsenic
and Old Lace, Night and Day, Notorious, The
Bishop's Wife, I Was a Male War Bride, People
Will Talk, Room for One More, Monkey Busi-
ness, To Catch a Thief, An Affair to Remember,
Kiss Them for Me, Indiscreet, North by North-
west, That Touch of Mink, Charade; Walk,
Don't Run;* more. Retired in 1966. Now a cor-
porate executive with Brut, a cosmetics and
film-producing company.

GRANT, KATHRYN (N. Cal.) Married to Bing
Crosby since '57—and the mother of his teenage children: Mary Francis, Nathaniel, and
Harry Lillis Jr.—she has lately starred in a daily
award-winning celebrity-interview program,
The Kathryn Crosby Show, on KPIX-TV in San
Francisco. She is in her 40s (b. 1933) and professes not to miss the screen career she gave up
after 1959's *The Big Circus.* The Crosby family
lives on a magnificent estate in Hillsborough
near San Francisco. Onscreen from 1953. IN:
*Forever Female, Casanova's Big Night, Un-
chained, Cell 2455—Death Row, Five Against
the House, Guns of Fort Petticoat, The Night
the World Exploded, Operation Mad Ball, The
Seventh Voyage of Sinbad, Anatomy of a Murder,* more.

GRANT, KIRBY (Fla.) The star of many Westerns for Universal and Monogram in the '40s
and '50s, and then famous as star of the TV
serial *Sky King,* he is presently in real estate in
Florida. As this is written, though, he has announced plans to produce and star in a syndicated, updated version of *Sky King*—and reportedly has heavy backing for it. For several
years after his Hollywood days he lived and
worked in Texas—where he was public rela-

tions director for an insurance company in Austin—and interested investors in his filming
plans. The new serial, he says, will be shot in
Florida. Plans are also on the drawing boards
for an actual Flying Crown Ranch to be constructed as a tourist attraction. A still-handsome man in his 60s (b. 1911), the actor has
been long and happily married and is the father
of two grown children. Onscreen from 1939.
IN: *Three Sons, Bullet Code, The Stranger from
Pecos, In Society, Babes on Swing Street, I'll
Remember April, Bad Men of the Border, Rustler's Roundup, Northwest Territory, Rhythm
Inn, Yukon Manhunt, Fangs of the Arctic,
Northern Patrol,* more.

GRANT, LEE (S. Cal.) Costar. Won Best Supporting Actress Oscar in *Shampoo.* Nominated
in the same category in *Detective Story,* (her
debut), and *The Landlord.* Onscreen from 1950.
IN: *Storm Fear, Middle of the Night, The Balcony, An Affair of the Skin, Pie in the Sky, Terror of the City, In the Heat of the Night, Divorce
American Style, Valley of the Dolls, The Big
Bounce, Marooned; Buona Sera, Mrs. Campbell; There Was a Crooked Man, Portnoy's
Complaint, The Internecine Project, Shampoo,
The Voyage of the Damned,* more.

GRANT, SHELBY (S. Cal.) Leading lady. Onscreen from 1964. IN: *The Pleasure Seekers,
Our Man Flint,* more.

GRANVILLE, BONITA (S. Cal.) Only 13 when
nominated for a Best Supporting Oscar in *These
Three* ('35), she had already been in movies
over three years. After 1949's *Guilty of Treason,* her 55th picture, she stopped acting. Two
years before, she had become the wife of young
oil-millionaire-producer Jack Wrather and she
wanted to rear a family. She has made just one
movie since, 1956's *The Lone Ranger,* and she
made it only at her husband's urging—he was
the producer. For almost two decades she devoted herself to behind-the-scenes activities on
Wrather's *Lassie* television series—first as associate producer, finally as producer. Still happily married to Wrather, her only husband,
Bonita is the mother of two children: Linda,
who is married to businessman Donald Billings
Brown and has made her a grandmother, and
Christopher, a Harvard graduate who has lately
done post-grad work at the University of California at Berkeley. Though home base is a magnificent establishment in Los Angeles, because
of Wrather's worldwide business interests, they
also have homes in London and Palm Springs,
in addition to permanent apartments in San
Francisco, at the Balboa Bay Club in Newport
Beach, and at the Pierre Hotel in New York,
plus a family cruiser, The Lone Ranger III,

berthed in Florida. Besides having served on the Board of Trustees of the John F. Kennedy Center in Washington, Bonita is on the Board of Directors of the Los Angeles Orphanage Guild (also past president), a founder-member of the Los Angeles Music Center, an active member of the Church of the Good Shepherd in Beverly Hills, and a trustee of Loyola Marymount University. No, the screen's best teenage brat didn't "reform," she just left behind those roles that rarely let the "real" Bonita Granville shine through. Onscreen from 1932. IN: *Silver Dollar, Cavalcade, The Life of Vergie Winters, Ah Wilderness!, Poppy, The Plough and the Stars, The Life of Emile Zola, The Beloved Brat, White Banners*, the "Nancy Drew" series *(Nancy Drew and the Hidden Staircase*, etc.), *Forty Little Mothers, The Mortal Storm; H. M. Pulham, Esq.; Syncopation, Now Voyager, Hitler's Children, Andy Hardy's Blonde Trouble, Breakfast in Hollywood, Suspense, The Truth About Murder, Strike It Rich*, more.

GRAVES, ERNEST (N.Y.) Character. IN: *Walk East on Beacon.*

GRAVES, PETER (S. Cal.) Costar. Onscreen from 1950. IN: *Rogue River, Stalag 17, East of Sumatra, The Long Gray Line, Wichita, Night of the Hunter, Death in Small Doses, The Stranger in My Arms, Texas Across the River, The Ballad of Josie, Five-Man Army, Sidecar Racers*, more.

GRAVES, PETER (Eng.) Character; former leading man. Onscreen from 1941. IN: *Kipps, Give Us the Moon, Waltz Time, Gaiety George, Spring in Park Lane, The Lady with a Lamp, Encore* ("The Ant and the Grasshopper" sequence), *The Jokers, I'll Never Forget What's 'Is Name, Paul and Michelle*, more.

GRAVES, TERESA (S. Cal.) Black star. Onscreen in the '70s. IN: *Vampira, That Man Bolt, Black Eye, Old Dracula*, more.

GRAY, BILLY (S. Cal.) Leading man; former juvenile. Onscreen from 1943. IN: *Man of Courage, Spectre of the Rose, Fighting Father Dunne, On Moonlight Bay, The Day the Earth Stood Still, By the Light of the Silvery Moon, The Seven Little Foys, The Explosive Generation, Two for the Seesaw, Werewolves on Wheels, Dusty and Sweets McGee*, more.

GRAY, CHARLES (Eng.) Character. Onscreen from 1957. IN: *Ride a Violent Mile, I Accuse!, Cattle Empire, Desert Hell, The Entertainer, The Night of the Generals, The Devil's Brigade, Charro!, Cromwell, Diamonds Are Forever, Wild Rovers, The Beast Must Die*, more.

GRAY, COLEEN (S. Cal.) Leading lady. Onscreen from 1947. IN: *Kiss of Death, Nightmare Alley, Red River, Riding High, Father Is a Bachelor, Apache Drums; Models, Inc.; Las Vegas Shakedown, Tennessee's Partner, The Killing, Death of a Scoundrel, Star in the Dust, The Mark of the Vampire, Johnny Rocco, Phantom Planet, P.J., The Late Liz*, more.

GRAY, DOLORES (N.Y.) Musical costar. Onscreen in the '50s. IN: *Always Fair Weather, Kismet, The Opposite Sex, Designing Woman.*

GRAY, DONALD (Eng.) Leading man. Onscreen from the '30s. IN: *Four Feathers, Well Done Henry, Murder in the Family, Sword of Honor, We'll Meet Again, Burnt Evidence, Secret Tent, Flame in the Sky*, more.

GRAY, DULCIE (Eng.) Leading lady. Onscreen from the '40s. IN: *Madonna of the Seven Moons, They Were Sisters, Wanted for Murder, The Years Between, Mine Own Executioner, A Man About the House, My Brother Jonathan, The Franchise Affair, A Man Could Get Killed*, more.

GRAY, NADIA (N.Y.) Berlin-born (1923; of a Russian father and a Bessarabian mother), Rumanian-reared, and an international star, this actress has lived a life of high drama, which is also a Cinderella story in reverse. She married the handsome prince first. But it was as the pilot of a commercial Rumanian airliner that he first attracted her attention. When an engine caught fire during a flight, Pilot Cantacuzino went back to reassure the passengers—actress Nadia Gray being one—of their safety. Fate. She became the wife of a flier who was, authentically, Prince Constantin Cantacuzino. Eventually, since Rumania was a Communist country, they felt compelled to flee. She went to France for a theater engagement, and he, hijacking his own plane—then turning it over to a copilot to return to Rumania—joined her in Paris. They lived happily there—she making many movies in Italy, France, and England—until her husband became ill and died. *La Dolce Vita* contained perhaps her most famous role, that of the bored, rich beauty at the orgy who does the mink-coated striptease. In 1967 the actress made two movies and went to New York for the Christmas holidays, disappearing from the screen and into a new life as an American citizen. She met and married—and remains contentedly married to—a New York lawyer named Herbert Silverman. Finally, in the spring of '76, in a somewhat surprising fashion, she resumed her career—not in movies, but as the headlined song star of a cabaret act that she opened at Manhattan's Spindletop Restaurant. Why this instead of pictures? "I really cut my bridges," she answers, "and being always the

168

star, it would be very difficult for me to start at this point in my life to play small roles." Onscreen from 1949. IN: *The Spider and the Fly, Valley of the Eagles, Night Without Stars, House of Ricordi, Sins of Casanova, Folies Bergere, La Parisienne, Holiday Island, The Captain's Table, Neapolitan Carousel, Candide, Maniac, The Adventure of Tortuga, The Crooked Road, Two for the Road, The Naked Runner, The Oldest Profession*, more.

GRAY, SALLY (Eng.) Leading lady. Onscreen from the '30s. IN: *The Saint in London, The Saint's Vacation, Lady in Distress, Suicide Squadron, Green for Danger, The Hidden Room*, more.

GRAY, VERNON (Eng.) Leading man. Onscreen from the '50s. IN: *A Day to Remember, To Paris With Love, Now and Forever*, more.

GRAYSON, KATHRYN (S. Cal.) Musical star. Onscreen from 1941. IN: *Andy Hardy's Private Secretary, Rio Rita, Thousands Cheer, Anchors Aweigh, Two Sisters from Boston, Till the Clouds Roll By, It Happened in Brooklyn, The Kissing Bandit, That Midnight Kiss, Toast of New Orleans, Show Boat, Lovely to Look At, The Desert Song, So This Is Love, Kiss Me Kate, The Vagabond King*, more.

GRAZIANO, ROCKY (N.Y.) Prizefighter-actor. Onscreen from 1957. IN: *Mister Rock and Roll, Teenage Millionaire, Tony Rome*, more.

GRECO, JOSE (Sp.) Giving his final performance in the States in the spring of '75, the great Spanish dancer has retired to Marbella, where he owns and operates a dance school. Onscreen from the '50s. IN: *Sombrero, Around the World in 80 Days, Holiday for Lovers, Ship of Fools*, more.

GRECO, JULIETTE (Fr.) Singer-leading lady. Onscreen from the '40s. IN: *The Green Glove, Paris Does Strange Things, The Sun Also Rises, Bonjour Tristesse, The Roots of Heaven, The Naked Earth, Crack in the Mirror, The Big Gamble, The Night of the Generals*, more.

GREEN, DANNY (Eng.) Character. Onscreen from the '20s. IN: *The Crooked Billet, Crime Over London, The Smugglers, A Tale of Five Cities, Whispering Smith Hits London, The Ladykillers, Abandon Ship, In the Wake of a Stranger, The Old Dark House*, more.

GREEN, DOROTHY (S. Cal.) Support. Not the actress of the same name who appeared in silents. Onscreen from the '60s. IN: *Critic's Choice, Palm Springs Weekend, It Happened at the World's Fair, Zebra in the Kitchen*, more.

GREEN, GILBERT (S. Cal.) Support. Onscreen from the '60s. IN: *By Love Possessed, Experiment in Terror, Dark Intruder*, more.

GREEN, HUGHIE (Eng.) Former juvenile. Now active in television in London. Onscreen in the '30s and '40s. IN: *Little Friend, Tom Brown's School Days, If Winter Comes, Hills of Home*, more.

GREENE, ANGELA (S. Cal.) In '75, after 30 years of marriage, the actress who was one of Warners' prettiest blonde second leads in the '40s separated from her millionaire husband, Stuart Martin (of New York's Strauss family). Leaving their palatial house in Coldwater Canyon, she took an apartment in Beverly Hills where, at last report, she was expected to become the wife of Richard de la Vega, a wealthy Spaniard. Onscreen from 1942. IN: *Hollywood Canteen, Too Young to Know; The Time, the Place and the Girl; Stallion Road, Wallflower, At War with the Army, Jungle Jim and the Forbidden Land, Spoilers of the Forest, The Cosmic Man, Tickle Me, The Good Guys and the Bad Guys*, more.

GREENE, LORNE (S. Cal.) Character star. Onscreen from 1954. IN: *The Silver Chalice, Tight Spot, Autumn Leaves, The Hard Man, Peyton Place, The Buccaneer, The Last of the Fast Guns, The Gaunt Woman, Earthquake*, more.

GREENE, REUBEN (N.Y.) Support. Onscreen in the '70s. IN: *Bye, Bye, Braverman; The Boys in the Band*, more.

GREENE, RICHARD (Ire.) He is not, in his 50s (b. 1918), the spectacularly handsome man he was in his 10 Hollywood movies or in the five-year (1955–60) British-made TV series *Adventures of Robin Hood*. His latest (and possibly last) picture, a B thriller, *Tales from the Crypt*, revealed yesterday's heartthrob to be considerably weathered, with modishly long hair and sideburns, several folds beneath that square chin, and his fabled dimples. How he looks does not concern the actor today as much as how well his stud horses perform. For years, he has owned and run a massive breeding farm in South Ireland, with fine assistance from his wife (since '60), the former Mrs. Beatrix Robledo Summers. From Colombia, she is knowledgeable about such a business as this—being one-quarter owner of her family's 33,000-acre ranch in South America. The actor was previously married (until '51) to actress Patricia Medina. He has no children by either marriage. Keeping his hand in the movie business, he announced plans to become a producer, with *Jonas Clint*. He looks back on his time in Hollywood with pleasure and laughter. He recalls that on the morning he arrived, he was whisked to a 20th Century-Fox soundstage where he was to costar in *Four Men and a Prayer*. There, facing a movie camera for the first time in his life, excepting his test, he found himself looking fondly into the eyes of Loretta Young, whom he had never in his life met before, and saying, "I love you, you know, I love you." Onscreen from 1938. IN: *Kentucky, My Lucky Star, The Hound of the Baskervilles, The Little Princess, Stanley and Livingstone, Here I Am a Stranger, Little Old New York, I Was an Adventuress, Flying Fortress, Forever Amber, The Fan, The Flying O'Flynn, The Desert Hawk, The Black Castle, Rogue's March, Captain Scarlett, Island of the Lost, Sword of Sherwood Forest, Assignment: Istanbul, Kiss and Kill*, more.

GREENE, SHECKY (N.Y.) Comedian. IN: *Tony Rome, The Love Machine*, more.

GREENE, STANLEY (N.Y.) Black support. IN: *For Love of Ivy, Cotton Comes to Harlem*, more.

GREENHOUSE, MARTHA (N.Y.) Support. Onscreen from the '60s. IN: *The Group, Up the Down Staircase, Bananas*, more.

GREENWOOD, CHARLOTTE (S. Cal.) In her 80s now (b. 1893), and last onscreen in 1956's *The Opposite Sex*, this inimitable character comedienne lives in quiet retirement in a beautiful house in Beverly Hills. She has been married since '24 to composer Martin Broones. Her primary interest is her Christian Science religion. For years a "reader" in this church, she has sometimes served in this capacity for stars such as Doris Day when they have adopted this faith. Her sense of humor has not deserted her. She was vastly amused recently to read this anecdote told on Groucho Marx: "Who else, one wonders, would go to a White House show, watch comedienne Charlotte Greenwood do a high kick that involved wrapping one leg around her neck, then turn to Mrs. Roosevelt and say, 'You could do that if you'd just put your mind to it'?" Onscreen (after a few silents) from 1928. IN: *So Long Letty, Stepping Out, Ritz Revue, Flying High, Moon Over Miami, Down Argentine Way, Springtime in the Rockies, The Gang's All Here, Home in Indiana, Up in Mabel's Room, The Great Dan Patch, Oh, You Beautiful Doll, Dangerous When Wet, Oklahoma!, Glory*, more.

GREENWOOD, JOAN (Eng.) Costar. Onscreen from 1940. IN: *John Smith Wakes Up, The October Man, Frenzy, The Smugglers, Saraband, Tight Little Island, Kind Hearts and Coronets, The Bad Lord Byron, The Man in the White Suit, The Importance of Being Earnest, The Detective, Moonfleet, Mysterious Island, Tom Jones, The Moonspinners*, more.

GREER, DABBS (S. Cal.) Character. Onscreen from 1948. IN: *The Black Book, House of Wax, Affair with a Stranger, Riot in Cell Block 11, Bitter Creek, Invasion of the Body Snatchers, The Vampire, Baby Face Nelson, I Want to Live!, The Lone Texan, Roustabout, Shenandoah*, more.

GREER, JANE (S. Cal.) Once the wife of Rudy Vallee, she married attorney Edward Lasker in '47, is the mother of three grown sons (Albert, Lawrence, and Stephen), and came out of retirement in '74 to costar on TV in a *Columbo* episode and the movie *The Outfit* (a.k.a. *The Good Guys Always Win*), in which she played petty crook Robert Duvall's grieving, angry sister-in-law. This was her first professional work since 1965's *Billie*. The actress, now in her 50s (b. 1924), was ill for some time with a heart condition that has been surgically corrected. Onscreen in 1945 as Bettyjane Greer. IN: *Two O'Clock Courage, George White's Scandals*. Onscreen as Jane Greer from 1946. IN: *Sunset Pass, The Falcon's Alibi, They Won't Believe Me, Out of the Past, Sinbad the Sailor, Station West, You're in the Navy Now, The Prisoner of Zenda, The Clown, Down Among the Sheltering Palms, Man of a Thousand Faces, Where Love Has Gone*, more.

GREER, MICHAEL (S. Cal.) Leading man. Onscreen in the '70s. IN: *Fortune and Men's Eyes, Messiah of Evil*, more.

GREGG, HUBERT (Eng.) Support. Onscreen from the '40s. IN: *In Which We Serve, Once Upon a Dream, The Facts of Love, The Story of Robin Hood, High and Dry, Svengali, Doctor at Sea*, more.

GREGG, VIRGINIA (S. Cal.) Character. Onscreen from 1947. IN: *Body and Soul, Dragnet, I'll Cry Tomorrow, The D.I., Twilight for the Gods, Operation Petticoat, House of Women, Spencer's Mountain, A Big Hand for a Little Lady, Madigan, A Walk in the Spring Rain*, more.

GREGORY, DICK (Ill.) Black comedy star. Onscreen in 1967. IN: *Sweet Love, Bitter*.

GREGORY, ENA (S. Cal.) Divorced from director Albert Rogell many years ago, and more recently widowed by her second husband, this blonde favorite from the '20s, now in her late 60s, has lately been a real estate agent in South Laguna. It will be recalled that she also acted in Tim McCoy Westerns and in 1928's *Shepherd of the Hills* under the name Marian Douglas. IN: *The Better Man*, more.

GREGORY, JAMES (S. Cal.) Character. Onscreen from 1948. IN: *The Naked City, The*

Young Stranger, Onionhead, Al Capone, The Manchurian Candidate, Twilight of Horror, The Great Escape, PT-109; Captain Newman, M.D.; Quick, Before It Melts; The Sons of Katie Elder, The Ambushers, The Secret War of Harry Frigg, Beneath the Planet of the Apes, The Late Liz, The Strongest Man in the World, more.

GREGORY, THEA (Eng.) Leading lady. Onscreen in the '50s. IN: *The Magnet, The Weak and the Wicked, The Case of the Second Shot, The Golden Link, Flame in the Sky,* more.

GRENFELL, JOYCE (Eng.) Star comedienne. Onscreen from 1942. IN: *The Demi-Paradise, While the Sun Shines, Stage Fright, Laughter in Paradise, The Magic Box, The Pickwick Papers, Genevieve,* the "St. Trinian's" series (*The Bells of . . . , Blue Murder at . . . , The Pure Hell of . . .), The Man with a Million, The Americanization of Emily, The Yellow Rolls-Royce,* more.

GREY, JOEL (N.Y.) Costar. Won Best Supporting Actor Oscar in *Cabaret.* Onscreen from 1952. IN: *About Face, Calypso Heat Wave, Come September, Man on a Swing, Buffalo Bill and the Indians,* more.

GREY, LITA (S. Cal.) Three times married and divorced (first to and from Charlie Chaplin), she lives in Hollywood and, though financially well off, works in a Beverly Hills department store. Son Sydney Chaplin, who remains close to his father and costarred for him in *A Countess from Hong Kong* ('67), has long been a well-established actor; her only other son, Charles Jr., died in '68. Lita, an attractive blonde now, is in her late 60s (b. 1909).

GREY, NAN (S. Cal.) Pretty and blonde she was when she starred in Universal B's; pretty and silver-blonde she is as the wife (since '50) of singer Frankie Laine. The major difference in her looks is that, long-bobbed then and almost translucently pale onscreen, she today wears her hair quite short and her complexion is an outdoorsey deep tan. Though her marriage to Laine has been childless, she has two grown daughters, Pam and Jananna, by her first marriage, to jockey Jackie Westrope. They were married in '39, divorced a decade later, and he was killed in a racetrack accident in '58. Nan has acted only once since the last of her 28 movies (*Under Age* in '41). That was in '60 when she and Frankie Laine both played dramatic roles in a single episode of TV's *Rawhide;* it was also his voice, incidentally, that was heard each week singing the theme song of this show. For a while Nan Grey tried—but has long since given up—a business career. She was president of "Nan's Close-Up Mirror/Lens, Inc.," which manufactured and marketed a cosmetic mirror for women with eyesight problems. The actress and her husband have a palatial home near San Diego but have little time to spend there. Frankie Laine's musical engagements take him all over the globe, and wherever he goes, she—an inveterate traveler—goes. Gladly. Onscreen from 1934. IN: *Babbitt, Crash Donovan, Sutter's Gold, Three Smart Girls, The Black Doll, Girls' School, Danger in the Air, The Under-Pup, The House of Seven Gables, The Invisible Man Returns, Sandy Is a Lady, Margie, You're Not So Tough, A Little Bit of Heaven,* more.

GREY, VIRGINIA (S. Cal.) A bachelor girl still, as she goes into her 60th year (b. 1917), she lives in a lovely house in Encino, is still slim and a "looker," acts occasionally on TV in *General Hospital,* and in '74 costarred with John Ireland in a new play, *Sugar and Spice,* that tried out (and fizzled) in Toronto. Signed with a new agent for both movies and TV, she expects to get her career into high gear again. Frank and honest as always, the girl who "almost" married Gable says, "I consider myself a professional who acts—not to express my soul or elevate the cinema—but to entertain and get paid for it." Onscreen as a child in the '20s. Onscreen in adult roles from 1931. IN: *Misbehaving Ladies, She Got Her Man, Old Hutch, Dramatic School, Idiot's Delight, The Women, Another Thin Man, Thunder Afloat, The Hardys Ride High, Three Cheers for the Irish, Keeping Company, The Big Store, Mr. and Mrs. North, Whistling in the Dark, Tarzan's New York Adventure, Tish, The Bells of Capistrano, Sweet Rosie O'Grady, Wyoming, So This Is New York, Mexican Hayride, The Bullfighter and the Lady, A Perilous Journey, The Rose Tattoo, All That Heaven Allows, Portrait in Black, Bachelor in Paradise, Back Street, The Naked Kiss, Madame X, Airport,* more.

GRIEM, HELMUT (Ger.) Leading man. Onscreen from 1969. IN: *The Damned, Cabaret, Ludwig, Children of Rage,* more.

GRIER, PAM (S. Cal.) Black star. Onscreen in the '70s. IN: *Black Mama, White Mama; Scream, Blacula, Scream; Coffy, The Arena, Foxy Brown, Bucktown, Friday Foster, Drum,* more.

GRIER, ROSEY (S. Cal.) Black support. Onscreen from the '60s. IN: *The Liberation of Lord Byron Jones, Joaquin Murietta, In Cold Blood, The Thing with Two Heads,* more.

GRIFFIN, JOSEPHINE (Eng.) Leading lady. Onscreen in the '50s. IN: *The House of the Arrow, The Weak and the Wicked, The Purple Plain, The Crowded Day, Room in the House, Portrait of Alison, The Man Who Never Was, The Extra Day, The Spanish Gardener.*

GRIFFIN, MERV (S. Cal.) Singer-actor. Now a TV talk-show host. Onscreen from 1952. IN: *Cattle Town, So This Is Love, The Boy from Indiana, Phantom of the Rue Morgue,* more.

GRIFFITH, ANDY (S. Cal.) Star comedian. Onscreen from 1957. IN: *A Face in the Crowd, No Time for Sergeants, Onionhead, The Second Time Around, Angel in My Pocket, Hearts of the West.*

GRIFFITH, CORINNE (S. Cal.) In a '74 interview, Adele Whitely Fletcher, editor of *Photoplay* in its heyday and a lifelong friend of this star, said, yes, it was true that the Corinne Griffith of today claims not to be the Corinne Griffith of the silent screen. Said Miss Fletcher: "She says her sister was Corinne Griffith and died, and that because she was a money-maker, Corinne stepped in. It could be true. I don't know that it isn't true, but I know the Corinne Griffith who was a very young woman at the Vitagraph studios and was married to Webster Campbell, is the same Corinne Griffith that I know today." It was in '66, when suing for divorce from her husband of a few days, Broadway actor Danny (*Call Me Mister*) Scholl, that Corinne Griffith testified in a Los Angeles court that "the other Corinne Griffith" was the silent star. But actresses Betty Blythe and Claire Windsor both declared in the same court that she was indeed she. Corinne Griffith's marriages, which also ended in divorce, were to actor Webster Campbell (1920–23), producer Walter Morosco (1924–34), and George Preston Marshall (1936–58), who was owner of the Washington Redskins football team. Today's Corinne Griffith is a frail, vastly rich (via real estate) woman whose primary occupation is writing books. In '72 she published *This You Won't Believe!*, and in '74, another amusing anecdotal book, *I'm Lucky—At Cards.* Previously, she had written almost a dozen others, including two best-sellers—one about the Washington Redskins, the other, *Papa's Delicate Condition*, made into a movie starring Jackie Gleason. She lives alone, with servants, in a Beverly Hills mansion. Though her starring career officially ended after 1932's *Lily Christine*, sometime in the '50s she appeared for producer-director Hugo Haas in a film, *Stars in Your Backyard*, that was never released. In the late '50s she was chairman of The Committee for Honoring Motion Picture Stars, which sponsored bronze statuary, to be erected in Beverly Hills, depicting luminaries who had been Beverly Hills residents: Valentino, Fairbanks, Mix, Will Rogers, etc. But not Corinne Griffith. The Corinne Griffith who appeared in court in 1966 gave her age as "approximately 51." The Corinne Griffith who starred in *Black Oxen, Classified*, and *The Divine Lady* was born in 1899, or,

other sources insist, 1896. It strains credibility that two women of not *similar*, but *identical*, beauty could have been born. Onscreen from 1916. IN: *Miss Ambition, A Girl at Bay, Deadline at Eleven, The Single Track, Six Days, The Common Law, Lilies of the Field, Single Wives, Love's Wilderness, Declassee, The Marriage Whirl, Into Her Kingdom, The Lady in Ermine, Three Hours, The Garden of Eden, Saturday's Children, Back Pay,* more.

GRIFFITH, HUGH (Eng.) Character. Won Best Supporting Actor Oscar in *Ben Hur.* Nominated in the same category in *Tom Jones.* Onscreen from 1940. IN: *Neutral Port, The Weird Sisters, So Evil My Love, The Last Days of Dolwyn, A Run for Your Money, Kind Hearts and Coronets, Laughter in Paradise, The Galloping Major, Gone to Earth, The Titfield Thunderbolt, The Beggars' Opera, The Sleeping Tiger, Lucky Jim, Exodus, The Counterfeit Traitor, Mutiny on the Bounty, How to Steal a Million, Oliver!, The Fixer, Two Times Two, Wuthering Heights, The Abominable Dr. Phibes, Who Slew Auntie Roo?, Luther, Canterbury Tales, Last Days of Man on Earth, The Passover Plot,* more.

GRIFFITH, JAMES (S. Cal.) Character. Onscreen from 1948. IN: *Appointment with Murder, Pardon My Rhythm; Oh, You Beautiful Doll; The Breaking Point, Red Skies of Montana, Eight Iron Men, Dragnet, Count Three and Pray, Omar Khayyam, Return to Warbow, Seven Guns to Mesa, The Big Fisherman, Advance to the Rear, A Big Hand for the Little Lady, Day of the Evil Gun,* more.

GRIFFITH, KENNETH (Eng.) Character. Onscreen from 1941. IN: *Love on the Dole, The Farmer's Wife, The Prisoner, Private's Progress, Lucky Jim, Tiger Bay, I'm All Right Jack, The Risk, Only Two Can Play, Track the Man Down, The Baby and the Battleship, Rotten to the Core, The Whisperers, S*P*Y*S,* more.

GRIFFITH, MELANIE (S. Cal.) Leading lady. Daughter of actress Tippi Hedren. Onscreen in 1975. IN: *The Drowning Pool, Night Moves, Smile.*

GRIFFITHS, JANE (Eng.) Leading lady. Onscreen from the '50s. IN: *The Man with a Million, The Green Scarf, Shadow of a Man,* more.

GRIMES, GARY (S. Cal.) Young leading man. Onscreen in the '70s. IN: *Summer of '42, Class of '44, The Culpepper Cattle Co.,* more.

GRIMES, TAMMY ((N.Y.) Leading lady. Onscreen from the '60s. IN: *Three Bites of the Apple; Arthur, Arthur.*

GRIZZARD, GEORGE (N.Y.) Leading man. Onscreen from 1960. IN: *From the Terrace, Advise and Consent, Warning Shot; Happy Birthday, Wanda June; more.*

GRODIN, CHARLES (N.Y.) Costar. Onscreen from the '60s. IN: *Rosemary's Baby, The Heartbreak Kid, 11 Harrowhouse, Thieves, King Kong,* more.

GROH, DAVID (S. Cal.) Leading man. Onscreen in the '70s. IN: *Two-Minute Warning,* more.

GRUENER, ALLAN (S. Cal.) Character. Onscreen from the '60s. IN: *Underworld U.S.A.,* more.

GUARDINO, HARRY (S. Cal.) Costar. Onscreen from 1951. IN: *Flesh and Fury, Hold Back Tomorrow, Houseboat, Pork Chop Hill, Five Branded Women, King of Kings, The Pigeon That Took Rome, Hell Is for Heroes, Rhino!, Jigsaw, Madigan, Lovers and Other Strangers, Dirty Harry, Capone, St. Ives,* more.

GUDEGAST, HANS (S. Cal.) Now known as Eric Braeden.

GUDRUN, ANN (Eng.) Leading lady. Onscreen from the '50s. IN: *Man With a Million, Doctor in the House, The Diamond, Trouble in the Glen, Thirty Six Hours, To Dorothy a Son, They Shall Not Have Them,* more.

GUETARY, GEORGES (Fr.) Singer-actor. Onscreen from 1948. IN: *Loves of Casanova, An American in Paris.*

GUILD, NANCY (N.Y) 20th Century-Fox's answer to Lauren Bacall, still trim and blonde as she enters her 50s (b. 1925), has been married for two decades to Broadway producer Ernest Martin (he coproduced such hits as *Guys and Dolls* and *Cabaret*). In the '40s she was married for a while to actor Charles Russell, by whom she has a daughter, born in '49. By Martin she has two daughters, plus one of New York's most chic apartments and a house in the south of France. When not traveling (often to Hollywood) or gardening, she serves on the Board of Memorial Sloan Kettering Cancer Center and works with the patients there. In '71 she did a cameo in *Such Good Friends,* her first movie work since *Francis Covers the Big Town* in '53. She says now, "I want to go back to work, and it's really quite remarkable because when I worked before, the only thing I liked about my work was lunch. Now I love the camaraderie of just working. If I could do something other than acting, I would. But acting is the only thing I ever made any money at, so I'm trying that

first. And you know something? Now that I'm older, I like acting." She doesn't say, though, she would like going back to such pictures as *The Brasher Doubloon.* Onscreen from 1946. IN: *Somewhere in the Night, Give My Regards to Broadway, Black Magic, Little Egypt, Abbott and Costello Meet Dr. Jekyll and Mr. Hyde.*

GUINNESS, SIR ALEC (Eng.) Star. Nominated for Best Actor Oscar in *The Lavender Hill Mob.* Won in the same category in *The Bridge on the River Kwai.* Onscreen from 1933. IN: *Evensong, Great Expectations, Kind Hearts and Coronets, Last Holiday, The Mudlark, Oliver Twist, The Cardinal, The Man in the White Suit, The Promoter, The Captain's Paradise, The Detective, The Prisoner, The Ladykillers, The Swan, The Horse's Mouth, The Scapegoat, Tunes of Glory, A Majority of One, Lawrence of Arabia, Dr. Zhivago, The Quiller Memorandum, The Comedians, Cromwell, Murder by Death,* more.

GUIZAR, TITO (Mex.) Last on Hollywood screens in '48, he is in his 60s now, married, with one grown daughter, and lives in Mexico City. He remains vastly popular in his homeland, in movies and, particularly, in musical concerts. In the summer of '74, for the San Diego Civic Theatre, he starred with Cantinflas, Miguel Mejia, and others in the variety show "Evening With the Stars"—playing to an SRO audience. Onscreen from 1938. IN: *The Big Broadcast of 1938, St. Louis Blues, Blondie Goes Latin, Brazil, Mexicana, Thrill of Brazil, On the Old Spanish Trail, The Gay Ranchero,* more.

GULAGER, CLU (S. Cal.) Costar. Onscreen from 1960. IN: *The Sam Spicer Story, The Killers, And Now Miguel, Winning, The Last Picture Show, McQ,* more.

GULLIVER, DOROTHY (S. Cal.) The delightful dark-haired little leading lady in "The Collegians" shorts, who was in many features in the '30s, has been married for years to second husband, Jack Proctor, a Hollywood publicist. (In the '20s she was married to and divorced from an assistant director.) Leaving the screen after 1933's *Cheating Blondes,* she returned for one in the '40s (*Borrowed Hero*), before dropping out for stage work in California. She came back strong in '68 in a character role—that of the blowsy Florence—in *Faces* with Gena Rowlands. She is hopeful of finding more gutsy supporting parts, preferably comedy. Onscreen from 1927. IN: *Shield of Honor; Good Morning, Judge; King of the Campus, College Love, Painted Faces, Night Parade, Troopers Three, Under Montana Skies, Honor of the Press, The Fighting Marshal, Revenge at Monte Carlo; Won Ton Ton, the Dog Who Saved Hollywood;* more.

GUNN, MOSES (S. Cal.) Black star. Onscreen in the '70s. IN: *WUSA, The Great White Hope, The Wild Rovers, Shaft, Shaft's Big Score, Eagle in a Cage, The Hot Rock, Amazing Grace, The Iceman Cometh, Rollerball; Cornbread, Earl & Me; Aaron Loves Angela*, more.

GUTHRIE, ARLO (Mass.) Singer-actor. IN: *Alice's Restaurant*.

GWYNN, MICHAEL (Eng.) Support. Onscreen from the '50s. IN: *Dunkirk, The Camp on Blood Island, A Doctor's Dilemma, Revenge of Frankenstein, Village of the Damned, Barabbas, Cleopatra, Scars of Dracula*, more.

GWYNNE, ANNE (S. Cal.) In her 50s (b. 1918) and still beautifully blonde, this leading lady of dozens of B's in the '40s—mostly Universal— married Beverly Hills attorney Max Gilford in the mid-'40s and has a daughter (b. '46) and a son (b. '48). Anne has not appeared onscreen since the '50s when she had secondary roles in four: *The Blazing Sun, The Breakdown, Call of the Klondike*, and, last, *Teenage Monster* ('57). A year or two ago, though, her photograph appeared in the *Academy Players Directory*, an indication she was available again to work.

Onscreen from 1939. IN: *Unexpected Father, Little Accident, Sandy Is a Lady, Spring Parade, The Black Cat, Tight Shoes, Mob Town, Melody Lane; Ride 'Em, Cowboy; Broadway, You're Telling Me, We've Never Been Licked, Top Man, Murder in the Blue Room, Ladies Courageous, Babes on Swing Street, I Ring Doorbells, Panhandle, The Enchanted Valley*, more.

GWYNNE, FRED (N.Y.) Character. Onscreen from 1954. IN: *On the Waterfront; Munster, Go Home*.

GWYNNE, MICHAEL C. (S. Cal.) Support. Onscreen in the '70s. IN: *The Terminal Man, Special Delivery*, more.

GYNT, GRETA (Eng.) Leading lady. Inactive in movies in the past decade but she has done stage work in both New York and London. Onscreen from 1937. IN: *The Road Back, The Human Monster, Dark Eyes of London, Mr. Emmanuel, The Common Touch, Soldiers Three, Lucky Nick Cain, Whispering Smith vs. Scotland Yard, My Heart Goes Crazy, Forbidden Cargo, The Strange Case of Dr. Manning, The Blue Peter, My Wife's Family*, more.

H

HAAS, DOLLY (N.Y.) In her 60s now (b. 1910), this fine German actress has been married since '43 to famous theatrical caricaturist Al Hirschfield, and their daughter Nina's name—as has been well publicized—is "hidden" someplace in all his work. She lives with her husband in a townhouse on East 95th Street and has not acted since starring off Broadway in '62 in *Brecht on Brecht*. Onscreen in Germany from 1930. IN: *Dolly's Way to Stardom, Dolly Macht Karriere, Der Brave Suender, Ein Maedel der Strasse*, more. Onscreen in English-speaking roles from 1937. IN: *Broken Blossoms* (talkie made in England), *Spy of Napoleon, I Confess*.

HACKETT, BUDDY (N.J.) Star comedian. Onscreen from 1953. IN: *Walking My Baby Back Home; Fireman, Save My Child; God's Little Acre, All Hands on Deck, Everything's Ducky, The Music Man, The Wonderful World of the Brothers Grimm, Muscle Beach Party, The Love Bug, The Good Guys and the Bad Guys*, more.

HACKETT, JOAN (N.Y.) Leading lady. Onscreen from 1966. IN: *The Group, Support Your Local Sheriff!, The Last of Sheila, Class of '63, Mackintosh & T.J.*, more.

HACKMAN, GENE (S. Cal.) Star. Nominated for Best Supporting Actor Oscar in *Bonnie and*

Clyde and *I Never Sang for My Father*. Won Best Actor Oscar in *The French Connection*. Onscreen from 1964. IN: *Lilith, Hawaii, Banning, A Covenant with Death, First to Fight, The Split, The Gypsy Moths, The Riot, Marooned, The Downhill Racers, The Stranger, Cisco Pike, Prime Cut, Scarecrow, The Poseidon Adventure, The Conversation, Zandy's Bride, Young Frankenstein, Bite the Bullet, Lucky Lady, The French Connection II, Night Moves*, more.

HADEN, SARA (S. Cal.) "Aunt Milly" is rounding out her 70s now (b. 1897), is gray but otherwise looks just the same, has not appeared in a movie since *Andy Hardy Comes Home* ('58), and lives alone in retirement in Santa Monica. She was married for many years, from '21 until they were divorced in '48, to actor Richard Abbott, who lives now in New York; they had no children. Abbott's real name is Simon Vandenberg. Acquaintances who knew Sara Haden during her marriage still refer to her as Mrs. Vandenberg. She is also, of course, the daughter of the beautiful late silent star Charlotte (*Kindling*) Walker. Onscreen from 1934. IN: *Anne of Green Gables, Spitfire, The White Parade, Black Fury, Way Down East, Captain January, Poor Little Rich Girl, Four Girls in White, The Shop Around the Corner, Woman of the Year*, 14 "Hardy Family" pix (all except

174

Judge Hardy's Children and *Love Finds Andy Hardy*), *Our Hearts Were Growing Up, Rachel and the Stranger, The Big Cat, Roughshod, A Lion Is in the Streets, The Outlaw's Daughter,* more.

HAGEN, JEAN (S. Cal.) A prolonged illness forced her retirement; she was for a long while a resident at the Motion Picture and TV Country Home, but is now resuming her career in character roles on TV. Onscreen from 1949. IN: *Adam's Rib, The Asphalt Jungle, A Life of Her Own, Shadow in the Sky, Singin' in the Rain, Latin Lovers, The Big Knife, Spring Reunion, The Shaggy Dog, Sunrise at Campobello, Dead Ringer,* more.

HAGEN, KEVIN (S. Cal.) Character; former leading man. Onscreen from 1964. IN: *The Man from Galveston, The Last Challenge,* more.

HAGEN, ROSS (S. Cal.) Leading man. Onscreen from 1968. IN: *Speedway, The Mini-Skirt Mob, The Devil's 8, Five the Hard Way, The Hellcats, The Organization,* more.

HAGEN, UTA (N.Y.) Broadway star. Onscreen just once, in the '70s. IN: *The Other.*

HAGERTHY, RON (S. Cal.) Leading man. Onscreen from 1951. IN: *I Was a Communist for the F.B.I., Starlift, The Charge at Feather River, City That Never Sleeps, Eighteen and Anxious, Saintly Sinners,* more.

HAGGARD, MERLE (N. Cal.) C&W singer-actor. Onscreen from 1968. IN: *Killers Three,* more.

HAGGERTY, DON (S. Cal.) Character. Onscreen from 1948. IN: *Train to Alcatraz, The Sundowners, The Kid from Texas, Quebec, Angels in the Outfield, Cry Vengeance, The Desperate Hours, Strategic Air Command, Day of the Bad Man, The Man Who Died Twice, Hell Is for Heroes, The Killers, The Great Sioux Massacre, The Life and Times of Grizzly Adams,* more.

HAGGERTY, H. B. (**"HARDBOILED"**) (S. Cal.) Character. Onscreen from the '60s. IN: *Paint Your Wagon, A Dream of Kings, The Wrestler, Earthquake,* more.

HAGMAN, LARRY (S. Cal.) Leading man. Onscreen from 1964. IN: *Ensign Pulver, Fail Safe, The Cavern, The Group, In Harm's Way, Up in the Cellar, Harry and Tonto,* more.

HAHN, JESS (Fr.) Character. Onscreen from the '50s. IN: *The Happy Road, Cartouche, Topkapi, What's New Pussycat?, Up to His Ears, The Great Spy Chase, The Postman Goes to War, The Night of the Following Day, Wise Guys,* more.

HAHN, PAUL (S. Cal.) Character. IN: *The Angry Red Planet,* more.

HAIG, SID (S. Cal.) Character. Onscreen from the '60s. IN: *The Hell with Heroes, Pit Stop, Che!, C. C. and Company, The Big Doll House, Busting, Foxy Brown,* more.

HAIGH, KENNETH (Eng.) Leading man. Onscreen from 1956. IN: *High Flight, Saint Joan, Cleopatra, A Hard Day's Night, Weekend at Dunkirk, A Lovely Way to Die, Eagle in a Cage, Man at the Top,* more.

HAINES, CONNIE (S. Cal.) Singer-actress. Still active in clubs she has not been seen in a movie in more than two decades. Onscreen from 1944. IN: *A Wave, a Wac and a Marine; The Duchess of Idaho,* more.

HAIRSTON, JESTER (S. Cal.) Character. IN: *The Alamo,* more.

HALE, ALAN, JR. (S. Cal.) Character. Onscreen first as a juvenile in 1933's *Wild Boys of the Road.* Onscreen in adult roles from 1940. IN: *I Wanted Wings, Spirit of West Point, It Happens Every Spring, The West Point Story, Lady in the Iron Mask, Springfield Rifle, Destry, Many Rivers to Cross, The Sea Chase, The True Story of Jesse James, Bullet for a Bad Man, Hang 'Em High, Dead Heat, There Was a Crooked Man,* more.

HALE, BARBARA. (S. Cal.) Leading lady. Onscreen from 1943. IN: *Gildersleeve's Bad Day, Higher and Higher, The Falcon Out West, West of the Pecos, Lady Luck, The Boy with Green Hair, Jolson Sings Again, The Window, Clay Pigeon, Seminole, A Lion Is in the Streets, The Houston Story, The Oklahoman, Desert Hell, Once More with Feeling, Buckskin, Airport, The Great Spider Invasion,* more.

HALE, BINNIE (Eng.) Comedienne. She is in her 70s now and retired. Onscreen in the '30s. IN: *The Phantom Light, Hyde Park Corner, Love from a Stranger,* more.

HALE, CHANIN (S. Cal.) Supporting actress. Onscreen from the '60s. IN: *Synanon, Will Penny, The Night They Raided Minsky's, The Wicked Dreams of Paula Schultz,* more.

HALE, GEORGIA (S. Cal.) Chaplin's pretty and talented leading lady in *The Gold Rush,* her second pic (she had previously played the femme lead in George K. Arthur's *The Salvation Hunters*), made only a few other silents before quitting the screen. In her 70s now, she is retired and living near Hollywood. Onscreen from 1925. IN: *The Rain Maker, The Great Gatsby, The Last Moment.*

HALE, JEAN (S. Cal.) Support. Onscreen from 1964. IN: *Psychomania, In Like Flint, The St. Valentine's Day Massacre*, more.

HALE, MONTE (S. Cal.) One of the last two singing cowboy stars developed by Republic—the other was Rex Allen—he made his last series of Westerns in '51 and has since been a top C&W songwriter and star attraction at rodeos and with circuses. He also played a supporting role in *Giant*, Still a ruggedly handsome man in his 50s (b. 1921), this Los Angeles resident made his movie comeback in '73 when he starred in two: *The Drifter* and *Guns of a Stranger* with Marty Robbins and Chill Wills. Onscreen from 1944. IN: *Steppin' in Society, California Gold Rush, Yukon Vengeance, Law of the Golden West, Prince of the Plains, Ranger of Cherokee Strip, Trail of Robin Hood, South of Rio, Along the Oregon Trail*, more.

HALE, RICHARD (S. Cal.) Character. Onscreen from 1944. IN: *None Shall Escape, Counter-Attack, A Thousand and One Nights, Badman's Territory, The Other Love, All the King's Men, Kim, Scaramouche, Springfield Rifle, Julius Caesar, Friendly Persuasion, Sergeants 3, Scandalous John*, more.

HALEY, JACK (S. Cal.) Star comedian. Onscreen from 1930. IN: *Follow Through, Redheads on Parade, Coronado, Pigskin Parade, Poor Little Rich Girl, Wake Up and Live, Alexander's Ragtime Band, The Wizard of Oz, Navy Blues, Higher and Higher, Scared Stiff, Sing Your Way Home, People Are Funny, Make Mine Laughs, Norwood*, more.

HALL, ELLA (S. Cal.) This leading lady of silents was last onscreen in *The Bitter Tea of General Yen* and now lives in retirement in Burbank. Onscreen from 1915. IN: *The Master Key* (serial), *The Bugler of Algiers, Under the Top, In the Name of the Law, The Third Alarm*, more.

HALL, GRAYSON (N.Y.) Character. Nominated for Best Supporting Actress Oscar in *The Night of the Iguana*. Onscreen from 1962. IN: *Satan in High Heels, That Darn Cat, Night of Dark Shadows*, more.

HALL, HUNTZ (S. Cal.) Now in his 50s (b. 1920), this happy-go-lucky veteran of 25 "Dead End Kids" pix (as Dippy), 26 "East Side Kids" pix (as Glimpy), and 48 "Bowery Boys" pix (as Satch), is sitting on top of the world. He gets around Hollywood in a brand-new Rolls-Royce (struck it rich with offshore oil wells). He acts constantly in movies (*The Manchu Eagle Murder Caper Mystery* recently) and on TV. He is planning to produce a movie series, "The Ghetto Boys," similar to "The Bowery Boys," and—that which makes him proudest of all—his son Gary, an honor graduate from Yale, has entered the Catholic priesthood. Huntz himself is active in lay Catholic affairs. In '73 he participated in Princess Grace of Monaco's Council for Drug Abuse, which is part of the Catholic Office of Drug Education. He lives in Toluca Lake with wife (# 3) Lee, who, on a recent birthday of his, presented this alleged tough guy with a gold plaque inscribed "Honorary Senior Citizen." He reacted just as he has through all the ups and downs of his career—he laughed. Onscreen from 1937. IN: *Dead End, They Made Me a Criminal, Angels Wash Their Faces, Angels with Broken Wings, Mr. Wise Guy, Wonder Man, A Walk in the Sun, Docks of New York, Bowery Battalion, Tell It to the Marines, Fighting Trouble, Hold That Hypnotist, Gentle Giant, The Phynx, The Love Bug Rides Again*, more.

HALL, JON (S. Cal.) A business man now and in his 60s (b. 1913), and considerably blockier than when he was the movies' #1 muscle man, he lives in Santa Monica with his third wife (since '59), former leading lady Raquel Torres. Several years ago he coproduced (with its star Ross Hagen) the picture *Five the Hard Way*, for which he also served as cinematographer. Onscreen from 1936. IN: *Hurricane, Kit Carson, Aloma of the South Seas, The Tuttles of Tahiti, Arabian Nights, Lady in the Dark, Gypsy Wildcat, Cobra Woman, Sudan, The Men in Her Diary, The Vigilantes Return, Prince of Thieves, Zamba, China Corsair, Ramar of the Jungle Secrets* (and five others in this series), *White Goddess, Phantom of the Jungle, Beach Girls and the Monster*, more.

HALL, LOIS (S. Cal.) She had an adventurous life as leading lady in such 1949–50 serials as *Adventures of Sir Galahad* and *Pirates of the High Seas*. Her private life has not been without its own exciting moments, but different. She and her husband, businessman Maurice Willows (they married in '52), are back in their Benedict Canyon house after a decade away from Hollywood. These 10 years were spent mainly serving their Baha'i Faith—first, three years in the Western desert, then, seven years in Hawaii where the actress did public relations for their religion. "Our stay in the islands was punctuated by mainland visits, a trip to London and, later, a trip around the world, visiting Baha'i holy places in Israel and Iran," she relates. Lois and her husband have a grown daughter, Debbie, and two younger ones, Kimberly and Christina; all are interested in dramatics and the youngest has modeled for Eastman Kodak. Lois herself has done some modeling lately, plus commercials and a small role in *Marcus*

Welby, and expects to resume her career full-time. Onscreen from 1949. IN: *The Duke of Chicago, Daughter of the Jungle, The Squared Circle, Slaughter Trail, Frontier Outpost, Colorado Ambush, Texas City*, more.

HALL, MARK (N.Y.) Juvenile. Onscreen from 1970. IN: *The Cross and the Switchblade, Child's Play*, more.

HALL, RUTH (S. Cal.) One of John Wayne's long-ago favorite leading ladies, Ruth is in her 60s now (b. 1912), married Oscar-winning (*Shanghai Express*) cinematographer Lee Garmes more than four decades ago, and devotes herself to philanthropic works. Onscreen from 1931. IN: *Monkey Business; Her Majesty, Love; Local Boy Makes Good, The Heart of New York, Miss Pinkerton, Blessed Event, The Kid from Spain, Laughing at Life, Beloved*, more.

HALL, ZOOEY (S. Cal.) Support. Onscreen from 1968. IN: *Born Wild, The Learning Tree, I Disremember Mama*, more.

HALLAM, JOHN (Eng.) Character. Onscreen in the '70s. IN: *The Last Valley, Nicholas and Alexandra, Villain, Murphy's War*, more.

HALLATT, MARY (Eng.) Character. Onscreen from the '30s. IN: *The Lambeth Walk, Black Narcissus, The Pickwick Papers, The Girl in the Canal, The Spider and the Fly, Separate Tables, Make Mine Mink*, more.

HALOP, BILLY (S. Cal.) Confronted with certain of his problems, lesser men would have given up. Alcoholism, several years ago, threatened to defeat him; Halop conquered it and has lately written his autobiography, *There's No "Dead End,"* emphasizing this aspect of his life. After the '40s, when he was no longer a juvenile toughie, Hollywood had few roles for him; he has recently tried for a comeback, as a character actor, with roles in TV's *All in the Family* and the television movie *The Phantom of Hollywood*. (Scrawny as a kid, he is a large man now in his 50s—he was born in '22—with a battle-worn face and a bit of a belly. It has been many a year since he was referred to as a "young Paul Muni"; he has no great expectation of ever again being compared to Muni—he just wants to make a living once more as an actor.) His marriages have not ended happily. Late in '60, already twice divorced, he was married to the former Suzanne Roe, whom he had known since they both were teenagers. Halop was then working for Leonard Appliance Company in Los Angeles, as an electric-dryer salesman, and had won the National Association of Manufacturers' award as the most crea-tive salesman in the U.S. When it was discovered that his wife was suffering from multiple sclerosis, Billy gave up his sales career and contemplated a medical career, but doctor friends—citing his age—convinced him, instead, to become a male nurse. So this became (and is today) his primary career; he has worked, ever since his training in this field, at St. John's in Los Angeles. Under his personal supervision at home, his wife's condition showed improvement. But, for reasons he does not discuss, in '71 he and his wife were divorced and he moved into a trailer court. And he was confronted by his own health problems. After two coronaries, he underwent open-heart surgery in the fall of '71. "I know too much about it," he said stoically then. "I have no choice between surgery or becoming an invalid. I have no intention of becoming an invalid." The operation was a success and today Billy Halop has every hope that "operation comeback" will be one too. Onscreen from 1937. IN: *Dead End, Angels with Dirty Faces, Hell's Kitchen, Dust Be My Destiny, Tom Brown's School Days, You're Not So Tough, Give Us Wings, Blues in the Night, Tough as They Come, Gas House Kids, Dangerous Years, For Love or Money, Fitzwilly*, more.

HALOP, FLORENCE (S. Cal.) Billy's sister, she is in her 60s now and is still active on TV in such as *The Mary Tyler Moore Show*. Onscreen from the '30s. IN: *Nancy Drew—Reporter*, more.

HALPIN, LUKE (S. Cal.) Former juvenile. Onscreen from 1961. IN: *Island of the Lost, Flipper, Flipper's New Adventure*, more.

HALPRIN, DARIA (N.M.) Married to actor Dennis Hopper and living on a ranch near Taos, the leading lady—discovered by Antonioni—is retired. Onscreen in the '70s. IN: *Zabriskie Point, The Jerusalem File*.

HALSEY, BRETT (S. Cal.) Leading man. Onscreen from 1954. IN: *Ma and Pa Kettle at Home, To Hell and Back, Desire in the Dust, The Best of Everything, Return of the Fly, The Atomic Submarine, Jet Over the Atlantic, Return to Peyton Place, War and Peace, Espionage in Lisbon, Anyone Can Play*, more.

HAMER, RUSTY (S. Cal.) This juvenile actor left the screen to become a business man. Onscreen in the '50s. IN: *Dance With Me Henry*, more.

HAMILTON, BERNIE (S. Cal.) Black character. Onscreen from 1950. IN: *The Jackie Robinson Story, Let No Man Write My Epitaph, The Devil at 4 O'Clock; One Potato, Two Potato;*

Synanon, *The Swimmer, The Losers, The Organization*, more.

HAMILTON, BIG JOHN (S. Cal.) Character. Onscreen from the '60s. IN: *Bandolero!, The Undefeated, The Sugarland Express, Ride in a Pink Car*, more.

HAMILTON, DRAN (S. Cal.) Formerly billed Dran Seitz—in 1953's *I, the Jury*—she has resumed her career under this new name.

HAMILTON, GEORGE (S. Cal.) Leading man. Onscreen from 1959. IN: *Crime and Punishment U.S.A., Home from the Hill, Where the Boys Are, All the Fine Young Cannibals, Light in the Piazza, Two Weeks in Another Town, Act One, The Victors, Your Cheatin' Heart, Viva Maria!, The Power, Evil Knievel, The Man Who Loved Cat Dancing, Once Is Not Enough*, more.

HAMILTON, KIM (S. Cal.) Black leading lady. Onscreen from 1959. IN: *Odds Against Tomorrow, The Leech Woman, The Wild Angels*, more.

HAMILTON, KIPP (S. Cal.) Leading lady. Onscreen from 1959. IN: *Good Morning, Miss Dove; Bigger Than Life, Never So Few, The Unforgiven, Harlow*, more.

HAMILTON, MARGARET (N.Y.) Her grandchildren can tell you that making Judy Garland's life miserable in *The Wizard of Oz*, as the cackling Wicked Witch, was completely out of character. Today, spry and spunky in her 70s (b. 1902), she lives in Gramercy Park, flies all over the country to star in regional theater productions (sometimes, even, in staged versions of *The Wizard of Oz*), and is on TV almost hourly—as Cora, the New England storekeeper, who promotes Maxwell House coffee. Her most recent movies were two in '71: *The Anderson Tapes* and *Brewster McCloud*. But in the later-released cartoon feature *Journey Back to Oz*, she recreated—voice only—her Wicked Witch role, with Liza Minnelli, Judy Garland's daughter, as Dorothy. Onscreen from 1933. IN: *Another Language, Broadway Bill, The Farmer Takes a Wife, Way Down East, You Only Live Once, Nothing Sacred, Saratoga, The Adventures of Tom Sawyer, Babes in Arms, My Little Chickadee, Journey for Margaret, Guest in the House, Janie Gets Married, The Sun Comes Up, The Red Pony, People Will Talk, Rosie, Angel in My Pocket*, more.

HAMILTON, MURRAY (S. Cal.) Character. Onscreen from 1951. IN: *The Whistle at Eaton Falls, Toward the Unknown, The Spirit of St. Louis, Jeanne Eagles; Too Much, Too Soon;*

Anatomy of a Murder, The Hustler, The Cardinal, Seconds, The Graduate, No Way to Treat a Lady, The Brotherhood, The Way We Were, The Drowning Pool, Jaws, more.

HAMILTON, NEIL (S. Cal.) The screen never boasted a handsomer leading man. Or a man of higher principles. In his vigorous 70s (b. 1899), he lives south of Los Angeles in Escondido with his wife Elsa; in 1976 they celebrated their 55th wedding anniversary. Travel is their primary interest now. When last heard from the star reported: "After nearly 50 years out there in front of that little piece of glass, with 265 features behind me, plays of all kinds, heaven only knows how many TV appearances, plus 120 *Batman* episodes, and an army of charming people, male and female, that I have worked with, I'm finally calling it quits." Onscreen from 1923. IN: *The White Rose, Isn't Life Wonderful?, The Little French Girl, Golden Princess, Beau Geste, The Great Gatsby, The Music Master, Mother Machree, Three Week Ends, Mysterious Dr. Fu Manchu, The Cat Creeps, The Sin of Madelon Claudet, What Price Hollywood?, The Animal Kingdom, Ladies Must Love, Fugitive Lady, Portia on Trial, Father Takes a Wife, Too Many Women, When Strangers Marry, Good Neighbor Sam, The Patsy, The Family Jewels*, more, including his final one, *Which Way to the Front?*, released in 1970.

HAMMER, ALVIN (S. Cal.) Character. Onscreen from 1946. IN: *A Walk in the Sun, Hollow Triumph, Ma and Pa Kettle, The Grissom Gang*, more.

HAMMER, BEN (N.Y.) Character. Onscreen in the '70s. IN: *Zabriskie Point, Johnny Got His Gun*, more.

HAMMOND, KAY (Eng.) The actress who was Mary Todd in Griffith's *Abraham Lincoln* is the wife of Sir John Clements, the actor-director, is now in her 60s (b. 1909), and has not appeared onscreen since 1961's *Five Golden Hours*. In '75 her son, John Standing (Standing was her family name and he uses it professionally), co-starred on Broadway in *Private Lives* with Maggie Smith as Amanda—the role Kay Hammond had played in '44. Onscreen from 1929. IN: *The Trespasser, Her Private Affair, Racetrack, Double Harness, Eight Girls in a Boat, Bitter Sweet, Jeannie, Call of the Blood*, more.

HAMPSHIRE, SUSAN (Eng.) Leading lady. Onscreen from 1949. IN: *The Woman in the Hall* (juvenile role), *During One Night, The Three Lives of Thomasina, Night Must Fall, The Fighting Prince of Donegal, The Trygon Factor, The Monte Carlo Rally, Those Daring Young Men in Their Jaunty Jalopies, Living*

Free, A Time for Loving, A Room in Paris, Neither the Sea Nor the Sand, more.

HAMPTON, HOPE (N.Y.) Well into her 70s and long a widow, this actress who made her debut in 1920's *A Modern Salome* is still buxom and blonde, still incredibly rich, still going to the theater and/or parties (dancing every dance) almost nightly. She has been called by Earl Wilson—not without reason—the "Duchess of Park Avenue." IN: *Star Dust, Lawful Larceny, The Price of a Party, The Road to Reno*, more.

HAMPTON, JAMES (S. Cal.) Support. Onscreen in the '70s. IN: *Soldier Blue, The Longest Yard, W.W. and the Dixie Dancekings, Hustle, Hawmps*, more.

HAMPTON, LIONEL (N.Y.) The famous bandleader became, in '76, the director of special (entertainment) events for President Gerald Ford's election campaign. Onscreen from 1948. IN: *A Song Is Born, The Benny Goodman Story, Mister Rock and Roll*, more.

HAMPTON, PAUL (S. Cal.) Support. Onscreen from 1959. IN: *Senior Prom, More Dead than Alive, Lady Sings the Blues*, more.

HAMPTON, RAPHIEL (N.Y.) Juvenile actor. Onscreen in the '70s. IN: *Klute, The War Between Men and Women*, more.

HANDL, IRENE (Eng.) Character. Onscreen from 1941. IN: *The Girl in the News, The Perfect Woman, The Belles of St. Trinians, Brothers in Law, The Key, I'm All Right Jack, Man in a Cocked Hat, Make Mine Mink, A Week-End with Lulu, Morgan, The Wrong Box, On a Clear Day You Can See Forever, The Private Life of Sherlock Holmes*, more.

HANIN, ROGER (S. Cal.) Support. Onscreen from 1958. IN: *He Who Must Die, The Cat, Tamango, Rocco and His Brothers, Night Affair, Riff Raff Girls*, more.

HANSEN, JANIS (S. Cal.) Support. Onscreen from 1967. IN: *Oh Dad, Poor Dad, Mamma's Hung You in the Closet and I'm Feeling So Sad; Airport*, more.

HANSEN, PETER (S. Cal.) Character; former leading man. Onscreen from 1950. IN: *Branded, Molly, When Worlds Collide; Darling, How Could You!; Something to Live For, A Bullet for Joey, Hell on Frisco Bay, Three Violent People, The Proud and the Profane, The Deep Six, Apache Rifles*, more.

HANSLIP, ANN (Eng.) Leading lady. Onscreen from the '50s. IN: *Gilbert and Sullivan, Face*

the Music, Knights of the Round Table, Fabian of the Yard, Where There's a Will, Three Cases of Murder, more.

HARDIN, TY (Sp.) The young (b. 1930) Texan, veteran of war pix *(Battle of the Bulge)* and big-budget Westerns *(Custer of the West)*, hasn't faced a camera since 71. Living at Los Boliches, now single—several times married and divorced—he operates a chain of laundromats and a bar, the Los Alamos. In the summer of '74, he was jailed for a month in Madrid on a drug-trafficking charge, Spanish police claiming they had found 25 kilos of hashish hidden in his automobile. Tried in court in the spring of '75, after having been released on bail, he was given a $9,200 fine. Onscreen from 1962. IN: *Merrill's Marauders, The Chapman Report, PT-109, Palm Springs Weekend, Berserk!, Circus of Blood, Death on the Run, The Last Rebel*, more.

HARDING, ANN (Conn.) A star of considerable magnitude in her time, she was nominated for the Best Actress Oscar in 1930–31 in *Holiday*. Today, unmarried since her divorce in 1963 from symphony conductor Werner Janssen, after 27 years of marriage, she is in her 70s (b. 1902), lives in Westport, and devotes herself exclusively to gardening, knitting, reading, and travel. Various playwrights have tried to induce her out of retirement but she is adamant on the subject. She made her last movie, *Strange Intruder*, in '56, and was last seen on the Broadway stage, in *Abraham Cochrane*, in '64. She later appeared in a few TV series *(Burke's Law, The Defenders, Dr. Kildare*, etc.) before retiring completely. Her daughter, Jane Bannister, has been married for more than two decades to stockbroker Alfred Otto Jr., is the mother of children, and lives near San Francisco. Onscreen from 1929. IN: *Paris Bound, Girl of the Golden West, East Lynne, Devotion, Westward Passage, The Animal Kingdom, The Life of Vergie Winters, The Fountain, Biography of a Bachelor Girl, Peter Ibbetson, Love from a Stranger, Stella Dallas, Eyes in the Night, The Male Animal, Mission to Moscow, The North Star, Janie, Christmas Eve, Two Weeks with Love, The Magnificent Yankee, The Man in the Gray Flannel Suit, I've Lived Before*, more.

HARDING, JOHN (S. Cal.) Character. Onscreen from 1955. IN: *Love Me or Leave Me, Please Don't Eat the Daisies, This Property Is Condemned, Hawaii, The Impossible Years*, more.

HARDING, JUNE (S. Cal.) Support. IN: *The Trouble with Angels*.

HARDT, ELOISE (S. Cal.) Support. Onscreen from 1967. IN: *Games, The Gay Deceivers, The Late Liz*, more.

HARDY, FRANCOISE (Fr.) Leading lady. Onscreen from the '60s. IN: *Castle in Switzerland, Grand Prix*, more.

HARDY, JOSEPH (N.Y.) Character. Onscreen from the '60s. IN: *Husbands, For Pete's Sake, Cops and Robbers*, more.

HARDY, ROBERT (Eng.) Support. Onscreen from 1958. IN: *Torpedo Run, The Spy Who Came in from the Cold, Berserk!, The Death Wheelers, Dark Places, Escape to Nowhere*, more.

HARE, DORIS (Eng.) Character; inactive in recent years. Onscreen from the '40s. IN: *Luck of the Navy, Here Come the Huggetts, The History of Mr. Polly, Dance Hall, Double Exposure, Tiger by the Tail, Another Time Another Place*, more.

HARE, ROBERTSON (Eng.) Comic character. Onscreen from the '30s. IN: *Rookery Nook, Friday the 13th, It's a Boy, Are You a Mason?, One Wild Oat, The Adventures of Sadie, Three Men in a Boat, Hotel Paradise*, more.

HARENS, DEAN (S. Cal.) Yesterday's young leading man is, in his 50s (b. 1921), today's character actor—frequently playing stuffy businessmen in *Barnaby Jones, Streets of San Francisco*, and other TV shows. Onscreen from 1944. IN: *Christmas Holiday, The Suspect*, more.

HARGITAY, MICKEY (S. Cal.) Muscleman support. Onscreen from 1957. IN: *Will Success Spoil Rock Hunter?, Revenge of the Gladiators; Promises, Promises; Bloody Pit of Horror*, more.

HARMON, JOHN (S. Cal.) Character. Onscreen from 1939. IN: *Gambling Ship, Gangs of Chicago, Devil's Island, Dangerously They Live, The Lady Gambles, The Crooked Way, Man in the Dark, Jack Slade*, more.

HARMON, TOM (S. Cal.) The football great of the '40s who starred in the biographical *Harmon of Michigan*. Onscreen from 1941. IN: *Spirit of West Point, That's My Boy, Off Limits*. (See Elyse Knox.)

HARNETT, SUNNY (N.Y.) The famous blonde model-actress is now in the cosmetics business. Onscreen just once, in 1957's *Funny Face*.

HARPER, VALERIE (S. Cal.) Television star. Onscreen in the '70s. IN: *Freebie and the Bean*.

HARRIGAN, NEDDA (N.Y.) Married for many years to director Josh Logan, she is completely retired from acting. Onscreen from 1930. IN: *The Laughing Lady, Charlie Chan at the Opera, The Case of the Black Cat; Thank You, Mr. Moto; Men Are Such Fools, Castle on the Hudson, Devil's Island*, more.

HARRINGTON, KATE (N.Y.) Character. IN: *Rachel Rachel, The Hospital, Child's Play*, more.

HARRINGTON, PAT, JR. (S. Cal.) Comic support. Onscreen from 1958. IN: *Stage Struck, The Wheeler Dealers, Move Over Darling; Easy Come, Easy Go; The President's Analyst, The Computer Wore Tennis Shoes*, more.

HARRIS, BARBARA (N.Y.) Leading lady. Nominated for Best Supporting Actress Oscar in *Who Is Harry Kellerman . . .?* Onscreen from 1965. IN: *A Thousand Clowns; Oh Dad, Poor Dad, Mamma's Hung You in the Closet and I'm Feeling So Sad; Plaza Suite, The War Between Men and Women, Nashville, The Fu Manchu Eagle Murder Caper Mystery, Family Plot*, more.

HARRIS, BRAD (S. Cal.) Support. Onscreen from 1957. IN: *Monkey on My Back, It Happened in Athens, Goliath Against the Giants, The Fury of Hercules, Black Eagle of Santa Fe, High Commissioner, The Mad Butcher, The Mutations*, more.

HARRIS, JONATHAN (S. Cal.) Character. Onscreen from the '50s. IN: *Botany Bay, The Big Fisherman*.

HARRIS, JUDY (S. Cal.) Support. Onscreen from 1960. IN: *Wild River*, more.

HARRIS, JULIE (N.Y.) Costar. Nominated for Best Actress Oscar in *The Member of the Wedding*, her debut film. Onscreen from 1952. IN: *East of Eden, I Am a Camera, The Truth about Women, The Poacher's Daughter, Requiem for a Heavyweight, The Haunting, Harper, You're a Big Boy Now, Reflections in a Golden Eye, The Split, The People Next Door, The Hiding Place, The Voyage of the Damned*, more.

HARRIS, JULIUS (N.Y.) Black character. Onscreen from 1964. IN: *Nothing But a Man, Redneck, Black Caesar, Live and Let Die, Trouble Man, Shaft's Big Score, The Taking of Pelham One Two Three*, more.

HARRIS, PHIL (S. Cal.) Star comedian. Onscreen from 1933. IN: *Turn Off the Moon, Buck Benny Rides Again, Dreaming Out Loud, I Love a Bandleader, Wabash Avenue, The High and the Mighty, The Patsy, King Gun*, more.

HARRIS, RICHARD (S. Cal.) Star. Nominated for Best Actor Oscar in *This Sporting Life*. Onscreen from 1958. IN: *Alive and Kicking, Shake Hands with the Devil, The Wreck of the Mary Deare, The Guns of Navarone, Mutiny on the Bounty, The Red Desert, Major Dundee, The Heroes of Telemark, The Bible, Hawaii, Camelot, The Molly Maguires, A Man Called Horse, Cromwell, Man in the Wilderness, Riata, Robin and Marian, The Return of a Man Called Horse, The Cassandra Crossing, Echoes of a Summer*, more.

HARRIS, ROBERT (Eng.) English character. Onscreen from 1931. IN: *How He Lied to Her Husband, The Life and Death of Colonel Blimp, Undercover, The Bad Lord Byron, For Them That Trespass, Laughing Anne, That Lady, Abandon Ship, The Model Murder Case, Oscar Wilde*, more.

HARRIS, ROBERT H. (S. Cal.) Hollywood character. Onscreen from the '50s. IN: *The Big Caper, No Down Payment, The Fuzzy Pink Nightgown, Peyton Place, Convicts 4, America America, Valley of the Dolls, Evel Knievel*, more.

HARRIS, ROSEMARY (N.Y.) Leading lady. Onscreen from 1954. IN: *Beau Brummell, A Flea in Her Ear*, more.

HARRIS, VIOLA (S. Cal.) Character. Onscreen from the '60s. IN: *The Children's Hour, The Greatest Story Ever Told, The Slender Thread, Funny Girl*, more.

HARRISON, GEORGE (Eng.) One of the Beatles. Onscreen from 1964. IN: *A Hard Day's Night, Help!, Let It Be*, more.

HARRISON, KATHLEEN (Eng.) After appearing as Mrs. Terence in 1937's *Night Must Fall*, her only American movie, the character actress returned home to England where she—in her late 70s now (b. 1898)—has remained much in demand both in films and on the stage. Onscreen from 1931. IN: *Hobson's Choice, Bank Holiday, Kipps, In Which We Serve, The Winslow Boy, Oliver Twist, The Huggetts Abroad, A Christmas Carol, The Pickwick Papers, Turn the Key Softly, Alive and Kicking, Lock Up Your Daughters*, more.

HARRISON, LINDA (S. Cal.) The former leading lady is married to producer Richard (*Jaws*) Zanuck and retired. Onscreen from the '60s. IN: *Way Way Out, A Guide for the Married Man, Planet of the Apes, Beneath the Planet of the Apes*, more.

HARRISON, MICHAEL (Ky.) (See Sunset Carson.)

HARRISON, NOEL (S. Cal.) Singer-actor. Son of Rex. Onscreen from 1962. IN: *The Best of Enemies, Agent 8 3/4, The Amorous Adventures of Moll Flanders, Where the Spies Are*, more.

HARRISON, REX (It.) Star. Nominated for Best Actor Oscar in *Cleopatra*. Won in the same category in *My Fair Lady*. Onscreen from 1930. IN: *The School for Scandal, Storm in a Teacup, The Citadel, Sidewalks of London, Over the Moon, Night Train, Blithe Spirit, Anna and the King of Siam, Notorious Gentleman, The Ghost and Mrs. Muir, The Foxes of Harrow, Unfaithfully Yours, The Four Poster, King Richard and the Crusaders, The Constant Husband, The Reluctant Debutante, Midnight Lace, The Yellow Rolls-Royce, The Agony and the Ecstasy, The Honeypot, Doctor Dolittle, A Flea in Her Ear, Staircase*, more.

HARRON, DONALD (N.Y.) Support. Onscreen from 1959. IN: *The Best of Everything, The Hospital*, more.

HART, DIANE (Eng.) Leading lady. Onscreen from the '40s. IN: *The Forbidden Street, Happy Go Lovely, You're Only Young Twice, The Pickwick Papers, One Jump Ahead, My Wife's Family*, more.

HART, DOLORES (Conn.) A convert to Catholicism in '48, she gave up her movie career after 1963's *Come Fly With Me* to enter the cloistered convent of Regina Laudis in Bethlehem, Conn. In her late 30s (b. 1938), she remains there, as Mother Dolores. In '71, Hollywood producer David Wolper filmed segments of her life there for inclusion in a television documentary he did on her. Onscreen from 1957. IN: *Loving You, Wild Is the Wind, Lonely Hearts, Where the Boys Are, Francis of Assisi, Sail a Crooked Ship, Come Fly with Me, Lisa*, more.

HART, DOROTHY (S. Cal.) Leading lady. Onscreen from 1947. IN: *The Naked City; Larceny, Inc.; Take One False Step, Calamity Jane and Sam Bass, Undertow, Raton Pass, I Was a Communist for the FBI, Tarzan's Savage Fury*, more.

HART, JOHN (S. Cal.) The actor who starred in the serial *Adventures of Captain Africa* and occasionally portrayed "The Lone Ranger" is a white-haired—and busy—character actor now. Onscreen from 1938. IN: *Prison Farm, King of Alcatraz, Disbarred, Champagne for Caesar, The Crooked Web, The Phynx; Simon, King of the Witches;* more.

HART, MARY (S. Cal.) Actress Lynne Roberts was billed this way at the beginning of her career—in 1937's *Love Is On the Air*, 1939's *Everything's on Ice*, etc. (See Lynne Roberts.)

HART, SUSAN /now **SUSAN HART NICHOLSON** (S. Cal.) Leading lady. Onscreen from 1964. IN: *A Global Affair, Ride the Wild Surf, Pajama Party, Dr. Goldfoot and the Bikini Machine, The Ghost in the Invisible Bikini*, more.

HARTFORD, DEE (S. Cal.) A famous fashion model before becoming the leading lady in 1952's *A Girl in Every Port*, she married its director, Howard Hawks, and gave up her career. Returning to modeling after their divorce ('59), she is back in Hollywood now—smashingly beautiful on the brink of 50 (b. 1927)—and is resuming her screen career.

HARTFORD, EDEN (S. Cal.) The leading lady-sister of Dee, she is divorced from Groucho Marx (since '69) and retired. Onscreen in 1961. IN: *When the Clock Strikes, The Flight That Disappeared, The Gambler Wore a Gun*.

HARTLEY, MARIETTE (S. Cal.) Leading lady. Onscreen from 1962. IN: *Ride the High Country, Drums of Africa, Marnie, Marooned, Barquero, The Return of Count Yorga*, more.

HARTLEY, TED (S. Cal.) Support. Onscreen from 1966. IN: *Walk, Don't Run; Barefoot in the Park*, more.

HARTMAN, DAVID (S. Cal.) Leading man. Onscreen from 1968. IN: *The Ballad of Josie, Nobody's Perfect, Ice Station Zebra, The Island at the Top of the World*, more.

HARTMAN, ELIZABETH (N.Y.) Costar. Nominated for Best Actress Oscar in *A Patch of Blue*, her debut movie. Onscreen from 1965. IN: *The Group, You're a Big Boy Now, The Fixer, The Beguiled, Walking Tall*.

HARTMAN, MARGOT (N.Y.) Support. Onscreen from 1964. IN: *Psychomania, The Curse of the Living Corpse*, more.

HARVEY, HARRY, SR. (S. Cal.) Character. Onscreen from 1942. IN: *The Pride of the Yankees, Trail Street, They Won't Believe Me, They Live by Night, Ace in the Hole, Outcasts of Poker Flat*, more.

HASKELL, PETER (S. Cal.) Leading man. Onscreen from 1967. IN: *Passages from James Joyce's Finnegans Wake, Christina*, more.

HASSETT, MARILYN (S. Cal.) Leading lady. Onscreen in the '70s. IN: *The Other Side of the Mountain, Two-Minute Warning*, more.

HASSO, SIGNE (N.Y.) Leading lady. Steadily active now in guest-star roles in television. Onscreen in Sweden from 1933. IN: *House of Silence, Money from Heaven, Emelie Hogquist*, more. Onscreen in America from 1942. IN: *Journey for Margaret, Heaven Can Wait, The Story of Dr. Wassell, The Seventh Cross, The House on 92nd Street, Dangerous Partners, A Double Life, To the Ends of the Earth, Crisis, Picture Mommy Dead, A Reflection of Fear, The Black Bird*, more.

HASTINGS, BOB (S. Cal.) Support. Onscreen from 1964. IN: *McHale's Navy, Did You Hear the One About the Traveling Saleslady?, The Bamboo Saucer, Angel in My Pocket, The Boatniks, How to Frame a Figg; No Deposit, No Return;* more.

HATFIELD, HURD (N.Y.) Just like the role that made him a star, he seems ageless. In his late 50s (b. 1918), he looks a good 15 years younger. A bachelor still, he owns a house on Long Island and another in Ireland, and acts with some regularity on TV but only occasionally in movies now. Onscreen from 1944. IN: *Dragon Seed, The Picture of Dorian Gray, Diary of a Chambermaid, The Unsuspected, Joan of Arc, Chinatown at Midnight, Tarzan and the Slave Girl, El Cid, King of Kings, Mickey One, The Boston Strangler, Von Richthofen and Brown*, more.

HAUSNER, JERRY (S. Cal.) Character. Onscreen from 1950. IN: *Outrage, Just This Once, Off Limits, Private Hell 36, Paths of Glory, Who's Minding the Store?*, more.

HAVER, JUNE (S. Cal.) Married to Fred MacMurray for more than two decades and the mother of twin daughters, she is retired. Onscreen from 1944. IN: *Home in Indiana, Irish Eyes Are Smiling, The Dolly Sisters, Wake Up and Dream, I Wonder Who's Kissing Her Now, Scudda-Hoo! Scudda-Hay!, Look for the Silver Lining; Oh, You Beautiful Doll; I'll Get by, The Daughter of Rosie O'Grady*, more, including 1953's *The Girl Next Door*, her last.

HAVOC, JUNE (N.Y.) The legitimate stage has been for the past two decades the primary interest of this actress. She writes plays, produced in New York and at various regional theaters, and stars in others such as *Habeas Corpus*, in which she appeared on Broadway 1975–76. Originally onscreen as a child in 1918–24 Hal Roach comedies. Onscreen in adult roles from 1941. IN: *Four Jacks and a Jill, Powder Town, My Sister Eileen; Hello, Frisco, Hello; Hi Diddle Diddle, Sweet and Low Down, Brewster's Millions, Gentleman's Agreement, The Iron*

Curtain, When My Baby Smiles at Me, Chicago Confidential, Once a Thief, Mother Didn't Tell Me, Follow the Sun, more, including 1956's *Three for Jamie Dawn,* her most recent to date.

HAWK, JEREMY (Eng.) Support. Onscreen from 1940. IN: *In Which We Serve, Who Done It?, Lucky Jim,* more.

HAWN, GOLDIE (S. Cal.) Costar. Won Best Supporting Actress Oscar in *Cactus Flower.* Onscreen from 1968. IN: *The One and Only Genuine Original Family Band, There's a Girl in My Soup, Butterflies Are Free, Dollars, The Sugarland Express, The Girl from Petrovka, Shampoo, The Duchess and the Dirtwater Fox,* more.

HAWORTH, JILL (N.Y.) Leading lady. Onscreen from 1960. IN: *Exodus, Your Shadow Is Mine, The Cardinal, In Harm's Way, It, Horror on Snape Island, The Mutation,* more.

HAWTREY, CHARLES (Eng.) Character. Onscreen from 1937. IN: *Good Morning Boys, A Canterbury Tale, Brandy for the Parson, Passport to Pimlico, Dark Secret, To Dorothy a Son, As Long as They're Happy, Timeslip, Simon and Laura,* the "Carry On" series (*Carry on Sergeant, . . . Nurse, . . . Jack, . . . Cleo,* etc.), *The March Hare,* more.

HAY, ALEXANDRA (S. Cal.) Leading lady. Onscreen from 1968. IN: *Guess Who's Coming to Dinner, Model Shop, Skidoo, The Love Machine, 1000 Convicts and a Woman, How to Seduce a Woman,* more.

HAY, AUSTIN (N.Y.) Character. Onscreen from the '60s. IN: *Pretty Boy Floyd, The April Fools, The Landlord, Child's Play,* more.

HAYDEN, LINDA (Eng.) Leading lady. Onscreen from the '60s. IN: *Baby Love, Taste the Blood of Dracula, The Blood on Satan's Claw, Madhouse, Something to Hide, Confessions of a Window Cleaner,* more.

HAYDEN, MARY (N.Y.) Character. Onscreen from the '60s. IN: *No Way to Treat a Lady, The Fourth Victim, The Night They Raided Minsky's, A Lovely Way to Die,* more.

HAYDEN, MELISSA (N.Y.) Ballerina. IN: *Limelight.*

HAYDEN, NORA (N.Y.) Leading lady. Onscreen from 1960. IN: *The Angry Red Planet,* more.

HAYDEN, RUSSELL (S. Cal.) "Lucky" was his nickname in the dozens of "Hopalong Cas-

sidy" he made, starting in '37, and lucky the actor considers himself. He says it despite the fact his eyesight is failing and, late in '74, he spent long weeks at the Eisenhower Hospital in Palm Springs—near his desert home in Pioneer Town—recuperating from a heart attack. He says it because of recalled pleasures on the "Cassidy" Westerns: "We were one big family. I really enjoyed getting up and going to work. We worked from sunup to sunset every single day but we had many weeks off between pictures. It was—every bit of it—a real pleasure." He says it because, since '46, he has had one of Hollywood's happiest marriages—to Lillian Porter, a promising 20th Century-Fox actress who gave up her career when they married. His only previous marriage—to Jan (then Jane) Clayton, several times a "Hopalong Cassidy" leading lady—ended in divorce. Now in his 60s (b. 1912), Hayden made his last movie in '51 (*Texans Never Cry*), and later produced two TV series (*Judge Roy Bean* and *26 Men*). He has, in recent years, twice been an honored guest at the Western Film Festival in Tennessee (attendees there have not forgotten that he was among the Top Ten Cowboy Stars in 1943–44), and—illnesses or not—he is today in the process of establishing a western museum at his ranch. "I've got everything to live for," says "Lucky." Onscreen from 1937. IN: *Hopalong Rides Again, Bar-20 Justice, Silver of the Sage, Three Men from Texas, Two in a Taxi, Down Rio Grande Way, Minesweeper, Wyoming Hurricane, Albuquerque, Where the North Begins, Sudden Death, Marshal of Heldorado,* more.

HAYDEN, STERLING (S. Cal.) At the beginning, in *Virginia* and *Bahama Passage* with Madeleine Carroll, who became the first of his four wives, he was billed Stirling and labeled "Hollywood's handsomest." Now in his 60s (b. 1916), he has long since been grizzled, barrel-chested and (often) bearded—and one of the screen's most unsavory, dependable character actors. Onscreen from 1940. IN: *Blaze of Noon, The Asphalt Jungle, Hellgate, Flat Top, The Star, Fighter Attack, Naked Alibi, Suddenly, Battle Taxi, Untamed, The Killing, Five Steps to Danger, Dr. Strangelove, Ten Days to Tulara, Hard Contract, Loving, The Godfather, The Long Goodbye, The Last Days of Man on Earth,* more.

HAYDN, RICHARD (S. Cal.) The character actor whose prim, tight-lipped comedy style and "typed" wardrobe—perfect fashion plate of 1909—were ever a joy, said long ago: "I'm a bachelor with all the typical traits—and I intend to stay a bachelor." He has. Now in his 70s (b. 1905), he still lives in Pacific Palisades in solo contentment with his dogs and birds, and, after

1967's *The Adventures of Bullwhip Griffin*, considered himself "retired." However, in '75, he did come back—just the same—in *Young Frankenstein*. And, as he has signed with a new agent, it would appear he has returned to stay. Onscreen from 1941. IN: *Charley's Aunt, Ball of Fire, Are Husbands Necessary?, No Time for Love, And Then There Were None, Tonight and Every Night, The Green Years, Cluny Brown, The Late George Apley, Forever Amber, The Merry Widow, The Emperor Waltz, Sitting Pretty, Please Don't Eat the Daisies, Five Weeks in a Balloon, The Sound of Music,* more.

HAYDON, JULIE (Minn.) The blonde dramatic actress, who so resembled Ann Harding in numerous pictures in the '30s, left the screen in '37 after a curious (for her) bit of casting. She played, in the first "Andy Hardy" movie, *A Family Affair,* the elder sister of both Mickey Rooney and Cecilia Parker—this character being dropped when it became a series. She was greatly famous on Broadway later as Laura in *The Glass Menagerie.* Recalling the unique qualities that rendered her performance so memorable, playwright Tennessee Williams wrote in his *Memoirs* ('75) that she "has never been in any mental or spiritual state short of ecstasy, at least none apparent to me." She continued acting onstage until '62, and even made one additional movie, 1948's *Citizen Saint.* She was married from '55 until his death in '58 to drama critic George Jean Nathan, later making a tour of university campuses reading from his works. Today, in her 60s (b. 1910), and looking exactly as she always has, the actress lives at the College of Teresa nunnery in Winona, not as a novitiate, but as a teacher of drama. Incidentally, only lately has it been disclosed that she provided—on the soundtrack—the scream for Fay Wray in *King Kong.* Onscreen from 1932. IN: *Thirteen Women, Lucky Devils, Their Big Moment, The Age of Innocence, The Scoundrel, A Son Comes Home, The Longest Night,* more.

HAYES, ALLISON (S. Cal.) Leading lady. Onscreen from 1954. IN: *Francis Joins the Wacs, Sign of the Pagan, Chicago Syndicate, Count Three and Pray, The Steel Jungle, The Undead, Attack of the Fifty-Foot Woman, The Hypnotic Eye,* more.

HAYES, BILL (S. Cal.) Singer-actor. He now stars in a TV soap opera. Onscreen from 1952. IN: *Stop, You're Killing Me; The Cardinal,* more.

HAYES, BILLIE (S. Cal.) Comedienne. Onscreen from 1959. IN: *Li'l Abner, Pufnstuf,* more.

HAYES, HAZEL (N.Y.) A Wampas Baby Star of 1934, she was a radio singer after her brief movie career but is now retired.

HAYES, HELEN (N.Y.) Star. Won Best Actress Oscar in *The Sin of Madelon Claudet.* Won Best Supporting Actress Oscar in *Airport.* She is the only actress to be nominated just once in each category and win on both occasions; Ingrid Bergman, with many Best Actress nominations, is the only other actress to win in both categories. Onscreen from the teens in a few silents. Onscreen in talkies from 1931. IN: *Arrowsmith, The Son-Daughter, A Farewell to Arms, The White Sister, Another Language, Night Flight, What Every Woman Knows, Vanessa—Her Love Story, My Son John, Anastasia, Third Man on the Mountain, The Love Bug Rides Again, One of Our Dinosaurs Is Missing,* more.

HAYES, ISAAC (Tenn.) Black singer-actor. The *Shaft* theme, which he wrote, won him an Oscar. Onscreen from 1975. IN: *Truck Turner.*

HAYES, JIMMY (S. Cal.) Support. Onscreen from 1956. IN: *Tea and Sympathy,* more.

HAYES, MARGARET (MAGGIE) (Fla.) Dana Dale she was at the beginning, at Paramount, then Margaret Hayes in other movies and on Broadway, and finally, since the '60s, Maggie Hayes. As Maggie, the former actress who is in her 50s (b. 1924), owns and operates the swank Maggie Hayes Jewelry Boutique in Palm Beach, on Worth Avenue. For years she has been an outstanding jewelry designer, her work sold in major department stores throughout the country, and has published an arrestingly beautiful book, *Maggie Hayes Jewelry Book,* on designing and making pendants, pins, necklaces, etc. Married in '42 for one month to actor Leif Erickson, she was later married for 26 years—until their amicable divorce in '73—to wealthy Herbert Bayard Swope Jr. They have a grown son, Rusty, and a daughter, Tracy Brooks Swope, who starred on TV in the soap opera *Where the Heart Is,* and is now acting in Hollywood. Maggie Hayes has not appeared in a movie since 1963's *13 West Street* and has no desire to perform again. She remains, though, without trying, a dramatically theatrical woman—with finely chiselled features, neatly coiffed reddish-brown hair, with long, manicured fingernails, and always-in-motion hands. And what her hands have found to do with silver and gemstones—that is what she has discovered to be more exciting than donning makeup. Onscreen from 1940. IN (as Dana Dale): *Ladies Must Live.* IN (as Margaret Hayes): *Sullivan's Travels, The Night of January 16th, The Lady*

Has Plans, *The Glass Key, They Got Me Covered, Violent Saturday, The Blackboard Jungle, The Bottom of the Bottle, Omar Khayyam, Fraulein, A Good Day for a Hanging, The Beat Generation, Girls' Town, House of Women*, more.

HAYES, PETER LIND (Nev.) The comedian-actor is in his 60s (b. 1915), lives in Las Vegas, participates in celebrity golf tournaments, makes an occasional movie, and travels much. In '75, he and wife, Mary Healy, made an extended excursion through the Soviet Union, Finland, and Scandinavia. Onscreen from 1938. IN: *Outside of Paradise, These Glamour Girls, Seventeen, Playmates, Seven Days' Leave, The Senator Was Indiscreet, The 5,000 Fingers of Dr. T., Sudden Death, Once You Kiss a Stranger*, more. (See Mary Healy.)

HAYES, RON (S. Cal.) Support. Onscreen from the '60s. IN: *Face of a Fugitive, Around the World Under the Sea*, more.

HAYMAN, LILLIAN (N.Y.) Black character. Onscreen from the '60s. IN: *The Night They Raided Minsky's, Mandingo*, more.

HAYMES, DICK (S. Cal.) Happy in his fourth marriage, the singer-actor is back in Hollywood (after a lengthy residence in England) and his career in clubs and on records is in high gear once more. He turned 60 in 1976. Onscreen from 1944. IN: *Four Jills in a Jeep, Irish Eyes Are Smiling, State Fair, Billy Rose's Diamond Horseshoe, Carnival in Costa Rica, One Touch of Venus, Up in Central Park, Cruisin' Down the River*, more.

HAYNES, HILDA (N.Y.) Black support. Onscreen from 1963. IN: *Gone Are the Days! The Pawnbroker, Home from the Hill*, more.

HAYNES, LLOYD (S. Cal.) Black leading man. Onscreen from the '60s. IN: *Ice Station Zebra, Madigan, The Mad Room*, more.

HAYNES, ROBERTA (S. Cal.) The statuesque brunette who shared those sizzling love scenes with Gary Cooper in *Return to Paradise* is divorced from screenwriter Larry Ward and works behind the scenes now in Hollywood. She wrote and coproduced an ABC TV-movie on Harriet Tubman, was production assistant on the movie *Rebel Jesus* and assistant casting director on *Mandingo*, and is a published novelist. Until recently she had lived in Rome for years. Onscreen from 1952. IN: *The Fighters, The Nebraskan, Hell Ship Mutiny, Point Blank, The Adventurers*, more.

HAYS, KATHRYN (N.Y.) Leading lady. She has lately starred in TV soap operas. Onscreen from 1963. IN: *Ladybug, Ladybug; Ride Beyond Vengeance, Counterpoint*, more.

HAYTER, JAMES (Eng.) Character. Onscreen from 1936. IN: *Sensation, Nicholas Nickleby, Tom Brown's School Days, Four Sided Triangle, The Pickwick Papers, Beau Brummell, Land of the Pharaohs, Abandon Ship!, The 39 Steps, Oliver!, David Copperfield, Song of Norway, The Blood on Satan's Claw*, more.

HAYTHORNE, JOAN (Eng.) Character. Onscreen from the '40s. IN: *Jassy, Svengali, Three Men in a Boat, A Coming-Out Party*, more.

HAYWARD, LOUIS (S. Cal.) In his 60s now (b. 1909), and off the screen after 1969's *The Phynx*, he reactivated his career in '73 with a co-star role in *Terror in the Wax Museum*, following it the next year with an appearance in the now-departed TV series *The Magician*. Married a third time, he has no children and lives in Palm Springs. Onscreen from 1933. IN: *Sorrell and Son, A Feather in Her Hat, Anthony Adverse, Duke of West Point, The Man in the Iron Mask; My Son, My Son; The Son of Monte Cristo, Ladies in Retirement, And Then There Were None, Ruthless, Walk a Crooked Mile, Black Arrow, Captain Pirate, The Saint's Girl Friday, The Search for Bridey Murphy, Chuka*, more.

HAYWORTH, RITA (S. Cal.) Star. Onscreen from 1935. IN: *Dante's Inferno, Charlie Chan in Egypt, Who Killed Gail Preston?, Only Angels Have Wings, The Lady in Question, Susan and God, The Strawberry Blonde, Blood and Sand, You'll Never Get Rich, My Gal Sal, You Were Never Lovelier, Cover Girl, Gilda, The Lady from Shanghai, The Loves of Carmen, Affair in Trinidad, Salome, Miss Sadie Thompson, Pal Joey, Separate Tables, They Came to Cordura, The Story on Page One, Circus World, The Rover, Sons of Satan*, more, including 1972's *The Wrath of God*, her most recent to date.

HEAD, MURRAY (Eng.) Leading man. Onscreen from 1967. IN: *The Family Way, Sunday Bloody Sunday*, more.

HEAL, JOAN (Eng.) Character. Onscreen from the '40s. IN: *Flesh and Blood, Happy Go Lovely, The Pickwick Papers, The Good Die Young, Svengali, Tiger by the Tail*, more.

HEALEY, MYRON (S. Cal.) One of the movies' busiest supporting players since the '40s, he is now in his early 50s (b. 1922), occasionally writes screenplays (*Colorado Ambush*), has a beauty-queen daughter, Ann, by a previous marriage, and in '71 married actress Adair Jameson. Onscreen from 1946. IN: *The Man from Colorado, Laramie, Law of the Panhandle, Slaughter Trail, Storm Over Tibet, Montana Territory, Monsoon, White Lightning, Combat Squad, Cattle Queen of Montana, African Manhunt, Running Target, Convicts Four, Journey to Shiloh,* more.

HEALY, MARY (Nev.) The beautiful (more so each year) singer-actress gave up her movie career after 1943's *Strictly in the Groove* to become the partner of her husband (married since '40), Peter Lind Hayes, in a club act, on radio and TV, and on Broadway in the hit comedy *Who Was That Lady I Saw You With?* She came back just once, exactly a decade later, when she and he costarred in Columbia's ill-fated musical *The 5,000 Fingers of Dr. T.* For years they lived in a Tudor castle-style mansion in New Rochelle, N.Y., just off the third hole of the Pelham Country Club's golf course (they're both golfers), kept a 36-foot Chriscraft at the marina, and reared two youngsters. Both Cathy and Michael are in their 20s now and making careers (nonshowbiz) of their own. Now Peter and Mary live in Nevada, a state with a decided sentimental association for them; they broke in the club act that made them mutually rich and famous at CalNeva Lodge in Lake Tahoe. They make their home in the desert of Las Vegas, but, the actress adds, "We spend a great deal of time traveling—partially for business. Peter does lectures for the Keedick Lecture circuit, is consultant to the President of Joseph E. Seagram Co., and does an occasional movie—one, a while back, in Hong Kong with James Mason. I go with him whenever it is possible. We also travel to do charity benefits, very often on the Celebrity Golf Tournament circuits—for the Cancer Society in Belleair, Florida, etc." In her late 50s now (b. 1918), she went from being a typist in 20th Century-Fox's branch office in New Orleans to fledgling stardom at 20th Century-Fox in Hollywood, with no opportunity to go to college. It is with some pride that she says now, "I am taking courses at the University of Nevada whenever it fits into our busy schedule." Her best friend in Hollywood remains former actress Dorris Bowdon (Mrs. Nunnally Johnson); they went West together on the train in 1939. For both it was the beginning of a long, interesting journey. Onscreen from 1939. IN: *Second Fiddle, Hotel for Women, 20,000 Men a Year, He Married His Wife, Star Dust, Hard Guy; Ride, Kelly, Ride; The Yanks Are Coming,* more.

HEARNE, RICHARD (Eng.) Comic character. Onscreen from 1935. IN: *Dance Band, One Night with You, Captain Horatio Hornblower,* *Miss Robin Hood, The Time of His Life, Stolen Time,* more.

HEATH, DODY (S. Cal.) Support. Onscreen from 1954. IN: *Brigadoon, The Diary of Anne Frank, Ask Any Girl, Seconds, Welcome to Arrow Beach,* more.

HEATHCOTE, THOMAS (Eng.) Character. Onscreen from the '50s. IN: *Dance Hall, The Red Beret, The Sword and the Rose, Doctor at Sea,* more.

HEATHERTON, JOEY (N.Y.) Leading lady. Onscreen from 1963. IN: *Twilight of Honor, Where Love Has Gone, My Blood Runs Cold, Bluebeard,* more.

HECKART, EILEEN (N.Y.) Character. Nominated for Best Supporting Actress Oscar in *The Bad Seed.* Won in the same category in *Butterflies Are Free.* Onscreen from 1956. IN: *Miracle in the Rain, Somebody Up There Likes Me, Bus Stop, Hot Spell, Heller in Pink Tights, Up the Down Staircase, My Six Loves, No Way to Treat a Lady, Zandy's Bride, The Hiding Place,* more.

HEDIN, JUNE (S. Cal.) Support; former juvenile. Onscreen from 1948. IN: *I Remember Mama, The Thirteenth Letter, The Member of the Wedding,* more.

HEDISON, DAVID (S. Cal.) Leading man. Onscreen from 1957. IN: *The Enemy Below, The Fly, The Lost World, The Greatest Story Ever Told, Live and Let Die,* more

HEDREN, TIPPI (S. Cal.) Costar. Onscreen from 1950. IN: *The Petty Girl* (in which she was the model "Miss Ice Box"), *The Birds, Marnie, A Countess from Hong Kong, The Man with the Albatross, Tiger by the Tail, Satan's Harvest, The Harrad Experiment,* more.

HEFFERNAN, JOHN (N.Y.) Support. Onscreen in the '70s. IN: *Puzzle of a Downfall Child, The Sting,* more.

HEFFLEY, WAYNE (S. Cal.) Support. Onscreen from 1962. IN: *The Outsider, Johnny Got His Gun,* more.

HEFLIN, FRANCES (N.Y.) Support. Sister of Van Heflin. A TV soap opera lead. Onscreen in the '70s. IN: *The Molly Maguires.*

HEFLIN, KATE (S. Cal.) Support. Onscreen in the '70s. IN: *Killer Elite.*

HEFLIN, NORA (N.Y.) Support. Daughter of Frances. Onscreen from 1974. IN: *Our Time.*

HEGIRA, ANNE (N.Y.) Support. Onscreen from the '50s. IN: *On the Waterfront, Love with the Proper Stranger, The Arrangement,* more.

HEIDT, HORACE (S. Cal.) Bandleader; retired. Onscreen in 1941. IN: *Pot O' Gold.*

HEIFETZ, JASCHA (S. Cal.) Violinist. Onscreen from 1939. IN: *They Shall Have Music, Carnegie Hall, Of Men and Music.*

HEIGH, HELENE (S. Cal.) Support. Onscreen from 1947. IN: *Her Sister's Secret, What's the Matter with Helen?,* more.

HELDABRAND, JOHN (N.Y.) Character. Onscreen from the '50s. IN: *On the Waterfront, The Wrong Man,* more.

HELM, ANNE (S. Cal.) Leading lady. Onscreen from 1955. IN: *Desire in the Dust, The Magic Sword, The Interns, Honeymoon Hotel, The Swingin' Maiden,* more.

HELM, BRIGITTE (Ger.) This German star is in her 60s (b. 1906), married to industrialist Hugh Kunheim, lives in West Berlin, gave up her career with 1937's *Gilgi Eine Von Uns.* Onscreen from 1926. IN: *Metropolis, The Love of Jeanne Ney, L'Argent, At the Edge of the World, The Wonderful Life, The Wonderful Lies of Nora Petrova, L'Atlantide, Gloria, Blue Danube,* more.

HELM, FRANCES (N.Y.) Support. IN: *The Ugly American.*

HELMORE, TOM (S. Cal.) One of the screen's better "other men," he is still dapper in his silver-haired 70s (b. 1916) and plays character roles now. Onscreen from 1930. IN: *White Cargo, Three Daring Daughters, Malaya, Let's Do It Again, The Tender Trap, Designing Woman, Vertigo, Count Your Blessings, The Time Machine, Advise and Consent, Flipper's New Adventure,* more.

HELPMANN, SIR ROBERT (Eng.) The great ballet star, and accomplished actor, last appeared in movies in 1972's *Alice's Adventures in Wonderland.* He was then, until late in '75, artistic director of the Australian Ballet in Melbourne, but has since returned to England. Onscreen from 1942. IN: *In Which We Serve, Henry V, The Red Shoes, Caravan, Tales of Hoffmann, The Iron Petticoat, 55 Days at Peking, The Quiller Memorandum, Chitty Chitty Bang Bang,* more.

HEMING, VIOLET (N.Y.) The widow of U.S. Senator Bennett Champ Clark (they were married from '45 until his death in '54), this excel-

lent English actress divides her time between her New York apartment (winters) and her big house in Gloucester, Mass. (summers). Now in her 80s (b. 1895), she has no children and last appeared on the stage in '52, though she appeared on TV—in the soap opera *From These Roots,* etc.—for a few years later. Onscreen from 1918. IN: *Turn of the Wheel, Everywoman, The Man Who Played God,* more.

HEMINGWAY, MARGAUX (S. Cal.) Leading lady. Granddaughter of novelist Ernest Hemingway. Onscreen from 1976. IN: *Lipstick.*

HEMMINGS, DAVID (Eng.) Costar. Onscreen from 1959. IN: *No Trees in the Street, Sing and Swing, The Girl-Getters, Blow-Up, Camelot, The Best House in London, The Charge of the Light Brigade, Alfred the Great, The Magic Christian, Barbarella, Only When I Larf, The Walking Stick, Mr. Quilp, Islands in the Stream,* more.

HENDERSON, DOUGLAS (S. Cal.) Character. Onscreen from 1953. IN: *Eight Iron Men, From Here to Eternity, Sniper's Ridge, The Manchurian Candidate, The Americanization of Emily, The Sandpiper,* more.

HENDERSON, FLORENCE (N.Y.) Musical star. Onscreen in 1970. IN: *Song of Norway.*

HENDRIX, WANDA (S. Cal.) Doll-faced still, in her 40s (b. 1928), she acts occasionally—sometimes in middle-aged mother roles—on TV (*Police Story*) and in B movies (*The Oval Portrait, Mystic Mountain Massacre*). She has been married three times—to the late Audie Murphy, millionaire James L. Stack Jr. (Robert's brother), and, in '69, to Italian financier Steve LaMonte. At that time, explaining what had happened to her career, she said, "After two marriages failed I just withdrew into myself and didn't care whether I worked or not." She attributed her renewed interest in acting to LaMonte. Lately she has been working on her autobiography—much of it, she says, dealing with her marriage to Audie Murphy. An 8' bronze statute of the war hero-actor was unveiled at the Audie L. Murphy Memorial Veterans' Hospital in San Antonio in '75, but she did not attend the ceremony. Onscreen from 1945. IN: *Confidential Agent, Ride the Pink Horse, Nora Prentiss, Welcome Stranger, Miss Tatlock's Millions, My Own True Love, Prince of Foxes, Sierra, Captain Carey U.S.A., Saddle Tramp, Montana Territory, The Golden Mask, Johnny Cool, Stage to Thunder Rock,* more.

HENDRY, GLORIA (S. Cal.) Black leading lady. Onscreen in the '70s. IN: *Black Belt Jones, Savage Sisters,* more.

HENDRY, IAN (Eng.) Leading man. Onscreen from 1960. IN: *In the Nick, Children of the Damned, The Model Murder Case, Repulsion, The Hill, Get Carter, The Jerusalem File, Theater of Blood, The Internecine Project*, more.

HENNING, LINDA KAYE (S. Cal.) Actress-dancer. IN: *Bye Bye Birdie*.

HENREID, MONIKA (S. Cal.) Support. Daughter of Paul Henreid. IN: *Blues for Lovers, Airport 1975*, more.

HENREID, PAUL (S. Cal.) Suave as ever in his late 60s (b. 1908), he still acts once in a while. In '75 he starred on NBC in the TV-movie *Death Among Friends*—as an aristocratic killer. And in '72–73 he costarred on Broadway (and on tour) in *Don Juan in Hell*. But now, in addition to being on the board of the San Fernando Valley Theatre of Performing Arts, he is principally a director—of movies (*Dead Ringer, Blues for Lovers*, etc.) and numerous TV shows (such as Anthony Quinn's 1972–73 series *Man and the City*). Onscreen in England—as Paul Von Henreid—from 1937. IN: *Jersey Lily, Victoria the Great, Goodbye Mr. Chips, Night Train, Under Your Hat*, more. Onscreen in America from 1942. IN: *Joan of Paris, Now Voyager, Casablanca, The Spanish Main, Devotion, Deception, Song of Love, A Stolen Face, Deep in My Heart, Meet Me in Las Vegas, Holiday for Lovers, Never So Few, Operation Crossbow, The Madwoman of Chaillot*, more.

HENREY, BOBBY (Eng.) This outstanding juvenile, now in his 30s (b.1939), is in business now, He appeared in just two—1949's *The Fallen Idol* and 1951's *Wonder Boy*.

HENRITZE, BETTE (N.Y.) Character. Onscreen in the '70s. IN: *Rage, The Happiness Cage, The Hospital*, more.

HENRY, BILL/WILLIAM HENRY (S. Cal.) Character; former juvenile lead. Onscreen from 1934. IN: *China Seas, Jezebel, Yellow Jack, Geronimo, Blossoms in the Dust, Johnny Come Lately, Sarong Girl, The Adventures of Mark Twain, Women in the Night, Streets of San Francisco, Secret of the Incas, The Last Hurrah, The Horse Soldiers, Sergeant Rutledge, The Man Who Shot Liberty Valance, Taggart!*, more.

HENRY, BUCK (S. Cal.) Support. Onscreen from 1964. IN: *The Troublemaker, The Graduate, Taking Off, The Man Who Fell to Earth*, more.

HENRY, CHARLOTTE (S. Cal.) Now in her 60s (b. 1913), she retired from the screen after 1942's *She's in the Army*, and today lives and works in San Diego. Onscreen from 1930. IN: *Courage, Huckleberry Finn, Arrowsmith, Lena Rivers, Alice in Wonderland, Babes in Toyland, Laddie, The Hoosier Schoolmaster, Hearts in Bondage, Charlie Chan at the Opera, Jungle Menace* (serial), *Bowery Blitzkrieg*, more.

HENRY, GLORIA (S. Cal.) Leading lady. Onscreen from 1947. IN: *Bulldog Drummond Strikes Back, The Strawberry Roan, Port Said, Johnny Allegro, Feudin' Rhythm, Rusty Saves a Life, Kill the Umpire!, Al Jennings of Oklahoma, Rancho Notorious, Gang War*, more.

HENRY, HANK (S. Cal.) Comedian. Onscreen from 1957. IN: *Pal Joey, Pepe, Sergeants 3, The Only Game in Town*, more.

HENRY, MIKE (S. Cal.) Support. Was the movies' most recent Tarzan. Onscreen from 1965. IN: *Tarzan and the Valley of Gold, Tarzan and the Great River, More Dead Than Alive, Tarzan and the Jungle Boy, Number One, Rio Lobo, The Longest Yard, Adios Amigos*, more.

HENSON, GLADYS (Eng.) Character. Onscreen from the '40s. IN: *The History of Mr. Polly, Frieda, The Happiest Days of Your Life, Happy Go Lovely, Cage of Gold, Prince and the Showgirl, Doctor at Large*, more.

HENVILLE, SANDRA LEE (S. Cal.) (See Baby Sandy.)

HEPBURN, AUDREY (It.) Star. Won Best Actress Oscar in *Roman Holiday*, her first Hollywood movie. Nominated in the same category in *Sabrina, The Nun's Story, Breakfast at Tiffany's*, and *Wait Until Dark*. Onscreen in England from 1951. IN: *One Wild Oat, Young Wives' Tale, Laughter in Paradise, The Lavender Hill Mob*, more. Onscreen in Hollywood (and internationally) since 1953. IN: *War and Peace, Funny Face, Love in the Afternoon, Green Mansions, The Unforgiven, The Children's Hour, Charade, Paris When It Sizzles, My Fair Lady, How to Steal a Million, Two for the Road, Robin and Marian*, more.

HEPBURN, KATHARINE (N.Y.) Star. Winner of three Best Actress Oscars—in *Morning Glory, Guess Who's Coming to Dinner*, and *The Lion in Winter*. Nominated in the same category in *Alice Adams, The Philadelphia Story, Woman of the Year, The African Queen, Summertime, The Rainmaker, Suddenly Last Summer*, and *Long Day's Journey Into Night*. No other screen performer, at this writing, has been nominated 11 times. In 1975 she costarred with John Wayne in *Rooster Cogburn*, her 40th motion picture. And in '76 she starred on Broadway, aged 69, in the play *A Matter of Gravity.* Onscreen from 1932. IN: *A Bill of Divorcement, Christopher Strong, Little Women, Spitfire, The Little Minister, Sylvia Scarlett, Break of Hearts, Mary of Scotland, A Woman Rebels, Quality Street, Stage Door, Bringing Up Baby, Holiday, Keeper of the Flame, Stage Door Canteen* (cameo), *Dragon Seed, Without Love, Undercurrent, Song of Love, Sea of Grass, State of the Union, Adam's Rib, Pat and Mike, The Iron Petticoat, Desk Set, The Madwoman of Chaillot, The Trojan Women, A Delicate Balance.*

HERBERT, DIANA (S. Cal.) Support. Former ingenue in movies of the '40s such as *Margie.*

HERBERT, PERCY (Eng.) Support. Onscreen from 1956. IN: *The Cockleshell Heroes, Bridge on the River Kwai, All at Sea, Tunes of Glory, Mutiny on the Bounty, Call Me Bwana, Becket, Guns at Batasi, Tobruk, Man in the Wilderness, Craze,* more.

HERBERT, PITT (S. Cal.) Character. Onscreen from 1963. IN: *Hud, The Trouble with Girls, How to Frame a Figg,* more.

HERD, DICK (S. Cal.) Support. Onscreen in the '70s. IN: *All the President's Men,* more.

HERLIE, EILEEN (Eng.) Character star. Onscreen from 1947. IN: *Hungry Hill, Hamlet, Gilbert and Sullivan, Freud, She Didn't Say No, The Sea Gull,* more.

HERMAN, WOODY (S. Cal.) The popular bandleader remains a stellar attraction in nightclubs and in concert. Onscreen from 1942. IN: *What's Cookin', Wintertime, Sensations of 1945, Earl Carroll Vanities, Hit Parade of 1947, New Orleans,* more.

HERN, PEPE (S. Cal.) Character. Onscreen from 1950. IN: *Borderline, Make Haste to Live,* more.

HERON, JOYCE (Eng.) Leading lady. Onscreen from the '40s. IN: *Women Aren't Angels, Don Chicago, She Shall Have Murder, The Weak and the Wicked, Three Cornered Fate,* more.

HERREN, ROGER (S. Cal.) Leading man. Onscreen in the '70s. IN: *Myra Breckinridge,* more.

HERSHEY, BARBARA/a.k.a. BARBARA SEAGULL (S. Cal.) Leading lady. Onscreen from 1968. IN: *With Six You Get Egg Roll, Last Summer, The Baby Maker, The Liberation of Lord Byron Jones, Boxcar Bertha, Dealing, The Last Hard Man,* more.

HERVEY, GRIZELDA (Eng.) Character; former leading lady. Onscreen from the '30s. IN: *The Informer, Girl in the Street, Kiss the Blood Off My Hands, The Yellow Canary, Trouble in the Glen, Gideon of Scotland Yard,* more.

HERVEY, IRENE (S. Cal.) In her 60s, she is a laughing, slender, and elegantly beautiful woman with a stylish gray coiffure who has lately worked at Valley Oaks Travel Agency in Sherman Oaks. Like so many in today's Hollywood, her career is a "sometime thing." Highly active on TV in the '50s and '60s, she won an Emmy nomination for a guest role she did in *My Three Sons* and was a regular—Aunt Meg—in the *Honey West* series. But she has been in just three movies in the last 15 years: *How to Commit Marriage* (a cameo), *Cactus Flower,* and *Play Misty for Me* ('71), in which she was a wealthy San Franciscan who offered Clint Eastwood a big-time job in network radio. It was filmed at Universal where she and former husband Allan Jones made many pix in the '40s. Married 21 years, they were divorced—his idea, she says—in '57. Their only child, famous singer Jack Jones, has himself been married and divorced three times, and has made Irene Hervey—by his first marriage—the grandmother of a teenage girl. Irene's other child, by her first marriage, Gail Fenderson, was legally adopted by Allan Jones; she is now married to James Christensen, writer and editor of documentary films, and has several children. Irene lives in North Hollywood and flies regularly—one advantage to being with a travel agency—to attend son Jack's more glamorous nightclub openings all over the world. Onscreen from 1930. IN: *The Count of Monte Cristo, The Winning Ticket, Charlie Chan in Shanghai, Along Came Love, League of Frightened Men, Society Smugglers, East Side of Heaven, The Boys from Syracuse, Mr. Dynamite, Bombay Clipper, Frisco Lil, Destination Unknown, Mickey, Mr. Peabody and the Mermaid, The Lucky Stiff, A Cry in the Night, Teenage Rebel, Crash Landing,* more.

HESTON, CHARLTON (S. Cal.) Star. Won Best Actor Oscar in *Ben Hur.* Onscreen from 1950. IN: *Dark City, The Greatest Show on Earth, Ruby Gentry, The President's Lady, Bad for Each Other, The Naked Jungle, The Far Horizons, The Private War of Major Benson, The Ten Commandments, Touch of Evil, The Big Country, The Buccaneer, El Cid, 55 Days at Peking, The Greatest Story Ever Told, The Agony and the Ecstasy, Major Dundee, Khartoum, Planet of the Apes, Will Penny, The Hawaiians, Beneath the Planet of the Apes, Julius Caesar, The Omega Man, Antony and Cleopatra, Skyjacked, Soylent Green, The Three Musketeers, Airport 1975, The Four Musketeers,*

Earthquake, Two-Minute Warning, The Last Hard Man, more.

HEWITT, ALAN (S. Cal.) Character. Onscreen from 1949. IN: *A Private's Affair, Bachelor in Paradise, That Touch of Mink, How to Murder Your Wife, The Monkey's Uncle,* more.

HEYMAN, BARTON (N.Y.) Character. Onscreen in the '70s. IN: *Valdez Is Coming, Let's Scare Jessica to Death, The Super Cops,* more.

HEYWOOD, ANNE (Eng.) Costar. Onscreen from 1955. IN: *The Brain, Violent Playground, Heart of a Man, A Terrible Beauty, Upstairs and Downstairs, The Fox, The Midas Run, The Chairman, The Siege of San Felice, I Want What I Want, The First Time, On the Grass,* more.

HIATT, RUTH (S. Cal.) Last onscreen in 1941's *Double Trouble,* the blonde comedienne of silents is in her 60s (b. 1908), a widow (since '72), and a California business woman. Onscreen from 1927. IN: *His First Flame, The Missing Link, Night Work, Her Man, The Big Flash, Sunset Trail, Riding Through,* more.

HICKEY, WILLIAM (N.Y.) Character. Onscreen from 1957. IN: *A Hatful of Rain; Happy Birthday, Wanda June; 92 in the Shade,* more.

HICKMAN, DARRYL (N.Y.) Under the gray-flecked full beard the former juvenile lead has sported of late, you will find a "new" character actor. In 1976 he returned to the screen in *Network,* his first movie since 1959's *The Tingler.* He was, after that, a television executive—CBS' director of daytime shows, and then executive producer of the soap opera *Love of Life.* But he kept his acting skills sharp by appearing in occasional Off Broadway productions such as *Mind With a Dirty Man* ('74), which he codirected as well. And he has written a musical based on Sardi's, the famous theatrical restaurant, for which he hopes to find backing. A longtime resident of upper Park Avenue, he is in his 40s now (b. 1931), the husband of the former Pamela Lincoln (since '59), and the proud father of teenage sons, Damian and Justin, who have evinced no interest in acting—preferring sports. Onscreen from 1939. IN: *The Star Maker, The Grapes of Wrath, Men of Boys Town, Northwest Rangers; Joe Smith, American; Keeper of the Flame, The Human Comedy, Song of Russia, Captain Eddie, Leave Her to Heaven, The Sainted Sisters, A Kiss for Corliss, Destination Gobi, Tea and Sympathy,* more.

HICKMAN, DWAYNE (S. Cal.) Famous as TV's "Dobie Gillis," Darryl's younger brother gave up his acting career for several years to be a Las Vegas public relations man but has recently resumed it. Onscreen from 1945. IN: *Captain Eddie, The Secret Heart, Return of Rusty* (and five others in the series), *The Boy with Green Hair, Cat Ballou, Ski Party; Doctor, You've Got to be Kidding;* more.

HICKOX, HARRY (S. Cal.) Character. Onscreen from 1962. IN: *The Music Man, Hotel, The Ghost and Mr. Chicken, Hot Rods to Hell,* more.

HICKS, HILLY (S. Cal.) Black character. Onscreen from the '60s. IN: *Halls of Anger, They Call Me Mister Tibbs, The New Centurions,* more.

HICKS, MAXINE ELLIOTT (S. Cal.) One of the silent screen's most famous juveniles, she is in her 70s, still lives in Hollywood, and has been retired from moviemaking for decades. She is especially well recalled for having played Mary Pickford's bratty nemesis in 1917's *Poor Little Rich Girl.* Their "enmity" was exclusively onscreen. The actresses have remained close friends throughout the years. And, in the spring of '76, when Filmex presented an award for Mary Pickford's "unparalleled contribution to the art form of this century," and the star was unable to attend the affair personally, it was Maxine Elliott Hicks who accepted the honor for her. Onscreen from the teens. IN: *The Eternal Mother* (as Ethel Barrymore's daughter), *Babbitt, Enticement, Ladies in Love,* more.

HICKSON, JOAN (Eng.) Character. Onscreen from the '30s. IN: *Love from a Stranger, This Was a Woman, Seven Days to Noon, The Promoter, The Man Who Never Was, Law and Disorder, The 39 Steps, A Day in the Death of Joe Egg, Confessions of a Window Cleaner,* more.

HIGGINS, JOE (S. Cal.) Character. Onscreen from the '60s. IN: *Geronimo, Kid Galahad, Flipper's New Adventure, Thrill of It All,* more.

HIGGINS, MICHAEL (S. Cal.) Leading man. Onscreen from 1966. IN: *Terror in the City, Wanda, The Arrangement, Desperate Characters, Holding On, The Conversation,* more.

HIKEN, GERALD (S. Cal.) Character. Onscreen from 1958. IN: *The Goddess, Uncle Vanya, Funnyman, Invitation to a Gunfighter,* more.

HILARY, JENNIFER (Eng.) Leading lady. Onscreen from 1963. IN: *Becket, The Heroes of Telemark, The Idol, One Brief Summer,* more.

HILL, ARTHUR (S. Cal.) Character lead. Onscreen from 1949. IN: *I Was a Male War Bride,*

The Deep Blue Sea, The Young Doctors, In the Cool of the Day, The Ugly American, Harper, Petulia, Don't Let the Angels Fall; Rabbit, Run; The Chairman, The Other Man, The Andromeda Strain, The Killer Elite, more.

HILL, BENNY (Eng.) Character. Onscreen from the '50s. IN: *Light Up the Sky, Those Magnificent Men in Their Flying Machines, Chitty Chitty Bang Bang, The Italian Job,* more.

HILL, DORIS (Ariz.) She left the screen in 1934, married (twice), and now, in her 60s, paints landscapes and is retired, living near Phoenix. Onscreen from 1927. IN: *Rough House Rosie, Tell It to Sweeney, Take Me Home, The Studio Murder Mystery, His Glorious Night, Men Are Like That, South of the Rio Grande, Spirit of the West, Galloping Romeo, Texas Tornado,* more.

HILL, MARIANNA (S. Cal.) Leading lady. Onscreen from 1965. IN: *Red Line 7000, The Traveling Executioner, El Condor, The Mad Mad Movie Makers, The Godfather II, Messiah of Evil,* more.

HILL, PHYLLIS (S. Cal.) Support. Onscreen from 1956. IN: *Singing in the Dark,* more.

HILL, STEVEN (S. Cal.) Leading man. Onscreen from 1950. IN: *A Lady Without a Passport, Storm Fear, The Goddess, A Child Is Waiting, The Slender Thread,* more.

HILL, TERENCE (It.) Leading man. Extraordinarily handsome star of Italian-made Westerns, whose pictures, when shown in the United States, have been dubbed. German-born, he speaks English, says actor Burt Reynolds who knows him, with "an accent that sounds exactly like Otto Preminger. He makes a million dollars a picture. Everyone asks him why he doesn't come to America to work. He says, 'Vy should I?! To play a Nazi?! For cheese und crackers?!'" Onscreen in the '70s. IN: *A Man From the East, My Name Is Nobody* (billed above Henry Fonda), more.

HILLAIRE, MARCEL (S. Cal.) Character. Onscreen from 1954. IN: *Sabrina, Seven Thieves, The Honeyoon Machine, The Wheeler Dealers, A Very Special Favor, Made in Paris,* more.

HILLER, WENDY (Eng.) Character star. Nominated for Best Actress Oscar in *Pygmalion.* Won Best Supporting Actress Oscar in *Separate Tables.* Nominated in the same category in *A Man for All Seasons.* Onscreen from 1937. IN: *Lancashire Luck, Major Barbara, I Know Where I'm Going, Outcast of the Islands,*

Sailor of the King, Something of Value, Sons and Lovers, Toys in the Attic, David Copperfield, Murder on the Orient Express, more.

HILLERMAN, JOHN (S. Cal.) Character. Onscreen in the '70s. IN: *Paper Moon, At Long Last Love, The Day of the Locust, Lucky Lady,* more.

HILLIARD, HARRIET (S. Cal.) Leading lady; now retired. Onscreen from 1936. IN: *Follow the Fleet, New Faces of 1937, Cocoanut Grove, Confessions of Boston Blackie, Juke Box Jenny; Hi, Buddy!; The Falcon Strikes Back, Swing time Johnny, Here Come the Nelsons,* more.

HILO HATTIE (Hawaii) Somewhere between 70 and 80, and more ample than ever, she remains a headlined attraction at the better clubs in Honolulu. "When Hilo Hattie Does the Hula Hop" is, naturally, always part of her act, along with other numbers she made famous during her long career. Onscreen in the '40s. IN: *Song of the Islands, Miss Tatlock's Millions,* more.

HINCKLEY, ALFRED (N.Y.) Character. Onscreen in the '70s. IN: *The Boston Strangler, Mortadella, Child's Play,* more.

HINGLE, PAT (N.Y.) Character. Onscreen from 1954. IN: *On the Waterfront, No Down Payment, Splendor in the Grass, All the Way Home, Inivitation to a Gunfighter, Hang 'Em High, Sol Madrid, Norwood, WUSA, The Carey Treatment, The Super Cops,* more.

HINWOOD, PETER (Eng.) Leading man. Onscreen in the '70s. IN: *Tam Lin, The Rocky Horror Show.*

HIRD, THORA (Eng.) Character. Onscreen from 1940. IN: *Next of Kin, 48 Hours, Corridor of Mirrors, Madness of the Heart, Maytime in Mayfair, Turn the Key Softly, Personal Affair, The Entertainer, A Kind of Loving, Term of Trial,* more.

HIRSCH, ELROY "CRAZY LEGS" (Wis.) Not only did the blond football hero (popularizer of the "bomb"—the long touchdown pass) play himself in the '53 movie biography *Crazy Legs, All-American,* but he stuck around to star in two other dramatic pix. Retiring simultaneously from movies and pro football then, he became —and remains—Director of Athletics at the University of Wisconsin where, as an undergrad, he began his climb to the Football Hall of Fame. He is in his 50s now (b. 1924), still visits Hollywood on occasion (recently for the Champs of Sports dinner benefitting Multiple Sclerosis), and, in '75, was the subject of a syndicated TV tribute, *Greatest Sports Legend.*

Also, little changed in looks and in great physical shape, he could still face movie cameras again on a moment's notice if he wished—which he doesn't. Onscreen from 1953. IN: *Unchained, Zero Hour!*

HITCHCOCK, PAT (S. Cal.) The actress-daughter of Alfred Hitchcock, she is married, the mother of several children, and while she has not acted in a movie for some years, she is still listed in the Hollywood *Academy Players Directory* as available for work. Onscreen from 1950. IN: *Stage Fright, Strangers on a Train, Psycho,* more.

HOAG, MITZI (S. Cal.) Support. Onscreen from 1963. IN: *Tammy and the Doctor, Cover Me Babe, Pieces of Dreams,* more.

HOBART, ROSE (S. Cal.) In 41 movies, with her glacial, blue-eyed, dark-blonde beauty, she was the ultimate "other woman," always magnificently dressed but at her sophisticated best in gold lame. Her career ended abruptly after 1949's *Bride of Vengeance.* Some have blamed this on her liberal politics, for Hollywood nabobs were running scared in those days. The only time she has faced Hollywood cameras in the decades since occurred in the mid-'60s when, for a short time, she played a maid in the nighttime *Peyton Place* series. Entering her 70s (b. 1906), long and happily married to architect Barton H. Bosworth, the mother of a grown son, Judson, and living in Sherman Oaks, Rose Hobart has no further interest in movie acting. "I am now a Practitioner of Science of Mind," she says. "I spend two days a week at our church center, and one day a week recording master tapes for the Braille Institute, plus teaching Sunday School." She also writes articles, such as "Daily Guide to Richer Living," for *Science of Mind* magazine. In addition, she has traveled widely and particularly enjoyed, she says, a recent long trip throughout the Orient. Onscreen from 1930. IN: *Liliom, East of Borneo, Dr. Jekyll and Mr. Hyde, Susan and God, Lady Be Good, Mr. and Mrs. North, Swingshift Maisie, Salute to the Marines, Conflict, The Cat Creeps, Claudia and David, The Farmer's Daughter, Cass Timberlane, Bride of Vengeance,* more.

HOBBS, PETER (S. Cal.) Character. Onscreen from 1964. IN: *Good Neighbor Sam, The Andromeda Strain, Star Spangled Girl,* more.

HOBSON, VALERIE (Eng.) This elegant actress, once married to English producer Anthony Havelock-Allan, gave up her 20-year career as a screen star in '54—after appearing in *Lovers, Happy Lovers*—when she married John D. Profumo. In '63, involved in the political-sexual scandal that came to bear his name, Pro-

fumo confessed an improper liaison with call-girl Christine Keeler and resigned as the British minister of war. He then began working at Toynbee Hall, a welfare organization for the poor and victims of alcohol and drugs, and has been there ever since. In '75 Valerie Hobson, who remained with him throughout his troubles, was enormously gratified when her 60-year-old husband was honored by the Crown. In recognition of his public service with the poor, Profumo was awarded, by the Queen, the title of Commander of the British Empire. Onscreen from 1934. IN: *Bride of Frankenstein, The Mystery of Edwin Drood, Life Begins at 40, Werewolf of London, Drums, The Spy in Black, Clouds Over Europe, The Adventures of Tartu, Great Expectations, Kind Hearts and Coronets, The Rocking Horse Winner, The Promoter, Tonight at 8:30* ("Ways and Means" episode), *Murder Will Out, The Passionate Sentry,* more.

HODGES, EDDIE (S. Cal.) Support; former juvenile. Onscreen from 1959. IN: *A Hole in the Head, The Adventures of Huckleberry Finn, Advise and Consent, Summer Magic, The Happiest Millionaire; Live a Little, Love a Little;* more.

HODGES, JOY (N.Y) In her 60s now, happily married and living in the exclusive community of Pound Ridge, the singer-actress is primarily a real-estate agent now. But she takes time off for singing stints in clubs and, earlier in this decade, returned to Broadway to star in *No, No, Nanette,* when Ruby Keeler left the show. Onscreen from 1935. IN: *Old Man Rhythm, Follow the Fleet, Merry-Go-Round of 1938, Personal Secretary, The Family Next Door, Unexpected Father, Little Accident, Laughing at Danger,* more, including 1940's *Margie,* her last.

HOFFMAN, BERN (S. Cal.) Character. Onscreen from 1946. IN: *Nocturne, The Man Who Understood, Li'l Abner, The Outfit,* more.

HOFFMAN, DUSTIN (N.Y) Star. Nominated for Best Actor Oscar in *The Graduate, Midnight Cowboy, Lenny.* Onscreen from 1967. IN: *Madigan's Millions* (his first, actually made in '66 but released in '69 after he had become a star), *The Tiger Makes Out, John and Mary, Little Big Man, Who Is Harry Kellerman . . .?, The Straw Dogs, Papillon, All the President's Men, The Marathon Man.*

HOFFMAN, FERDI (N.Y.) Character. Onscreen from 1963. IN: *All the Way Home,* more.

HOFFMAN, JANE (N.Y.) Character. Onscreen from 1957. IN: *A Hatful of Rain; Ladybug, Ladybug; They Might Be Giants,* more.

HOFFMAN, STAN (S. Cal.) Character. Onscreen from 1956. IN: *Singing in the Dark*, more.

HOGAN, JACK (S. Cal.) Support. Onscreen from 1956. IN: *Man from Del Rio, Paratroop Command, The Legend of Tom Dooley, The Bonnie Parker Story, Decoy*, more.

HOGAN, ROBERT (S. Cal.) Leading man. Onscreen from 1963. IN: *Greenwich Village Story, Memory of Us*, more.

HOGG, IAN (Eng.) Support. Onscreen from 1971. IN: *King Lear, The Last Valley, Macbeth*, more.

HOLBROOK, HAL (S. Cal.) Leading man. Onscreen from 1966. IN: *The Group, Wild in the Streets, The People Next Door, The Great White Hope, They Only Kill Their Masters, All the President's Men*, more.

HOLCOMBE, HARRY (S. Cal.) Character. Onscreen from 1962. IN: *The Couch, Bird Man of Alcatraz, The Unsinkable Molly Brown, Kisses for My President, There Was a Crooked Man, Foxy Brown*, more.

HOLDEN, JAN (Eng.) Support. Onscreen from the '50s. IN: *I Am a Camera, The Best House in London*, more.

HOLDEN, JOYCE (N.Y.) Since her conversion as a Jehovah's Witness, Universal's onetime singer-dancer-actress has worked in this religious organization's main office in Brooklyn. Still pretty and blonde in her 40s, she is so involved in her mission that she never gives a thought to those long-ago times when she was Miss Southern California of 1949 and, the next year, costarring with Donald O'Connor in *The Milk Man*. Onscreen from 1950. IN: *The Iron Man, Target Unknown, You Never Can Tell, Girls in the Night, Murder Without Tears, The Werewolf, Terror from the Year 5000*, more.

HOLDEN, SCOTT (S. Cal.) Support. Son of William Holden. Onscreen in the '70s. IN: *Breezy*, more.

HOLDEN, WILLIAM (Switz.) Star. Nominated for Best Actor Oscar in *Sunset Boulevard*. Won in the same category in *Stalag 17*. Onscreen from 1939. IN: *Golden Boy, Invisible Stripes, Our Town, Arizona, I Wanted Wings, The Remarkable Andrew, The Fleet's In, Dear Ruth, Rachel and the Stranger, Apartment for Peggy, Streets of Laredo, Born Yesterday, The Turning Point, The Moon Is Blue, Escape from Fort Bravo, Executive Suite, Sabrina, The Bridges of Toko-Ri, The Country Girl, Love Is a Many-Splendored Thing, Picnic, The Bridge on the* River Kwai, *The Horse Soldiers, The Counterfeit Traitor, Alvarez Kelly, The Wild Bunch, Wild Rovers, The Revengers, Breezy, The Towering Inferno, Network*, more.

HOLDER, GEOFFREY (N.Y.) Black dancer-actor. Onscreen from the '60s. IN: *All Night Long, Dr. Dolittle, Live and Let Die*, more.

HOLE, JONATHAN (S. Cal.) Character. Onscreen from 1954. IN: *Riot in Cell Block 11, The Opposite Sex*, more.

HOLIDAY, HOPE (S. Cal.) Support. Onscreen from 1960. IN: *The Apartment, The Ladies' Man, Irma La Douce, The Rounders, How to Seduce a Woman*, more.

HOLIDAY, LEILA (N.Y.) Support. IN: *Vacancy*, more.

HOLLAND, ANTHONY (S. Cal.) Support. Onscreen from 1965. IN: *Goldstein, The Last Mohican, Bye Bye Braverman, The Out-of-Towners, Lovers and Other Strangers, Fearless Frank, The Anderson Tapes*, more.

HOLLAND, BETTY LOU (N.Y.) Support. Onscreen from 1958. IN: *The Goddess, The Man in the Net*, more.

HOLLAND, EDNA (S. Cal.) Character. Onscreen from 1939. IN: *Bachelor Mother, Between Two Women, Kiss and Tell, Intrigue, Criss Cross; Once More, My Darling;* more.

HOLLAND, GLADYS (S. Cal.) Character. Onscreen from 1952. IN: *Lydia Bailey*, more.

HOLLAND, JOHN (S. Cal.) Character; former leading man. Onscreen from 1929. IN: *She Goes to War, The College Coquette, Eyes of the World, Dance Band, The Voice of the Turtle, Rock Island Trail, My Fair Lady, The Naked Brigade, Chinatown, Lost in the Stars*, more.

HOLLIDAY, FRED (S. Cal.) Actor-TV host. Onscreen from the '50s. IN: *Wind Across the Everglades, Odds Against Tomorrow, Middle of the Night, The Prize, A Patch of Blue, The New Interns, A Guide for the Married Man, Airport, The Man*, more.

HOLLIMAN, EARL (S. Cal.) Costar. Onscreen from 1952. IN: *Pony Soldier, East of Sumatra, The Bridges at Toko-Ri, Broken Lance, Giant, The Rainmaker, Don't Go Near the Water, Gunfight at the O.K. Corral, Hot Spell, Visit to a Small Planet, Summer and Smoke, The Sons of Katie Elder, The Power, Joaquin Murietta, The Biscuit Eater*, more.

HOLLOWAY, STANLEY (Eng.) Character. Nominated for Best Supporting Actor Oscar in

My Fair Lady. Onscreen from 1930 (after one silent). IN: *The Co-Optimists, Sleeping Car, Sing As We Go, The Vicar of Bray, Major Barbara, This Happy Breed, Caesar and Cleopatra, Brief Encounter, Nicholas Nickleby, Hamlet, The Winslow Boy, Passport to Pimlico, The Lavender Hill Mob, The Magic Box, The Titfield Thunderbolt, No Love for Johnnie, It's a Mad Mad Mad Mad World, Operation Snafu, In Harm's Way, Ten Little Indians; Mrs. Brown, You've Got a Lovely Daughter; The Private Life of Sherlock Holmes, Flight of the Doves,* more.

HOLLOWAY, STERLING (S. Cal.) In his 70s now (b. 1905), he does "voices" for countless TV commercials and Disney cartoon features. In '76 he did a comic cameo for the movie *Won Ton Ton, the Dog Who Saved Hollywood.* Onscreen from 1927. IN: *Casey at the Bat, Elmer the Great, Gold Diggers of 1933, Gift of Gab, Down to Their Last Yacht, Maid of Salem, Varsity Show, Remember the Night, Cheers for Miss Bishop, The Lady Is Willing, Twilight on the Rio Grande, The Adventures of Huckleberry Finn, Batman; Live a Little, Love a Lot;* more.

HOLLY, ELLEN (N.Y.) Black leading lady. IN: *Take a Giant Step.*

HOLM, CELESTE (N.Y.) Costar. Won Best Supporting Actress Oscar in *Gentleman's Agreement.* Nominated in the same category in *Come to the Stable* and *All About Eve.* Onscreen from 1946. IN: *Three Little Girls in Blue, Carnival in Costa Rica, The Snake Pit, Road House, Chicken Every Sunday, Champagne for Caesar, The Tender Trap, High Society; Doctor, You've Got to Be Kidding; Tom Sawyer,* more.

HOLM, ELEANOR (Fla.) "I got money for it, but I won't discuss how much," the swim star said in '75 after permitting the movie *Funny Lady* to show her (portrayed by a young actress) caught by "Fanny Brice" Streisand in the kip with "Billy Rose" James Caan. Eleanor Holm says the dramatized incident never actually occurred. In actual life, she was married—for 14 years—to the real Billy Rose after his divorce from Fanny Brice. She had previously been married to singer Art Jarrett, and in '74, then aged 60, became the wife of Tommy Whalen. She lives in Miami Beach and works on occasion as an interior decorator. Onscreen in 1938. IN: *Tarzan's Revenge* (as Jane).

HOLM, IAN (Eng.) Support. Onscreen from 1968. IN: *The Bofors Gun, The Fixer, A Severed Head, Nicholas and Alexandra; Mary, Queen of Scots; Young Winston, The Homecoming, Juggernaut,* more.

HOLM, JOHN CECIL (R.I.) Actor and author (original author of *Three Men on a Horse, Best Foot Forward,* etc.). Onscreen from 1958. IN *It Happened to Jane,* more.

HOLM, SONIA (Eng.) Leading lady. Onscreen from the '40s. IN: *The Loves of Joanna Godden, When the Bough Breaks, Miranda, The Bad Lord Byron, 13 East Street, The Crowded Day,* more.

HOLMES, MARIAN (S. Cal.) Support. IN *Miracle in the Rain.*

HOLMES, RICHARD G. (N.Y.) Character. IN *Scorpio.*

HOLT, CHARLENE (S. Cal.) Leading lady. Onscreen from 1962. IN: *If a Man Answers For Love or Money, Man's Favorite Sport, Red Line 7000, El Dorado,* more.

HOLT, JENNIFER (N.Y.) The daughter of the late star Jack Holt and the sister of the late Tim Holt, she gave up her career as leading lady in Westerns (more than 30) and serials in '48. She has been married for many years to business executive Richard A. Feldon, lives on Park Avenue not far from the Waldorf, and is very retired. Onscreen from 1942. IN: *Deep in the Heart of Texas, The Old Chisholm Trail, Cheyenne Roundup, Oklahoma Raiders, Marshal of Gunsmoke, Song of Old Wyoming, Hop Harrigan* (serial), *Moon Over Montana, Buffalo Bill Rides Again,* more.

HOLT, PATRICK (Eng.) Character; former leading man. Onscreen from 1938. IN: *Sword of Honor, Hungry Hill, Frieda, The October Man, The Girl in the Painting, Marry Me, Ivanhoe, The Unholy Four, Guns at Batasi, Thunderball, Genghis Khan, Hammerhead, The Death Wheelers,* more.

HOMEIER, SKIP (S. Cal.) Yesteryear's monster kid, as Skippy, he is now, in his 40s (b. 1930), as Skip, one of the best character leads in TV-movies (*The Voyage of the Yes*), television series (*Police Woman*), and B pix (*Starbird and Sweet William*). Onscreen from 1944. IN: *Tomorrow the World, The Big Cat, The Gunfighter, The Halls of Montezuma, The Black Widow, Cry Vengeance, The Burning Hills, Between Heaven and Hell, Stranger at My Door, Decision at Durango, Bullet for a Badman, Tiger by the Tail,* more.

HOMOLKA, OSCAR (Eng.) The fine character actor from Vienna, who was Oscar-nominated as Best Support in *I Remember Mama,* is in his 70s (b. 1898) and still going strong—getting "also starring" billing in movies such as *Fu-*

neral in Berlin and The Tamarind Seed. A long-time British resident, he returned to Hollywood in '75 for two television stints. He had a major role in the "NBC Monday Night Movie" One of Our Own, which was the on-air pilot for the series Doctors' Hospital. And, with his wife, Joan Tetzel (b. 1921), to whom he has been married for over two decades, he costarred in a CBS TV-movie, The Legendary Curse of the Hope Diamond. A New York native, Miss Tetzel was once one of Selznick's young contractees. In England she has played leads in The Red Dress, Meet Mr. Jones, etc., and in the recent past costarred onstage in London with Robert Morley in How the Other Half Loves. The Homolkas have no children although, by his former marriage, which ended in divorce, the actor has twin sons, Vincent and Laurence, both grown. Onscreen from 1927. IN: Aftermath, The Trial of Donald Westhof, Women Without Men, The Prince of Rogues, Hocuspocus, 1914: The Last Days Before the War, Rhodes, The Woman Alone, Ebb Tide, Seven Sinners, The Invisible Woman, Ball of Fire, Hostages, Mission to Moscow, The White Tower, Prisoner of War, The Seven Year Itch, A Farewell to Arms, Boys' Night Out, The Happening, Song of Norway, Assignment to Kill, The Madwoman of Chaillot, more.

HONG, JAMES (S. Cal.) Character. Onscreen from 1955. IN: Love Is a Many-Splendored Thing, China Gate, One Spy Too Many, The Sand Pebbles, more.

HOOD, DARLA (S. Cal.) Petite and perky in her 40s (b. 1933), "Our Gang's" Darla has been married since '57 to Jose Granson, a top California music publisher, lives in Studio City, and is the mother of two teenage children, Brett and Darlo Jo. Also, she relates, "When I married Jose, I got a darling six-year-old girl, Robin, in the bargain, and raised her plus my own. Robin is now married and she and her husband both recently graduated from UCLA." In show business from age three, Darla has never stopped working. She does commercials, "voices" for "talking toys," records for the Acama label, writes published songs, and a few months back appeared with Ken Murray in a stage-and-movie show presented in Anaheim. (Long ago, for three years, she was Ken Murray's singing-dancing leading lady on his CBS-TV show, followed by more months with his nightclub act in top clubs across the country.) She has also been caught up in the current "Our Gang" (or, as TV labels the series, "The Little Rascals") nostalgia craze, and enjoys every minute of it. Not long ago she guested with Spanky McFarland on The Mike Douglas Show, their first reunion in many years. And in '75 a firm in Pennsylvania announced that Darla, Spanky and "Stymie" Beard would be presented by it in shows at theaters across the land. Also, Darla adds, "I'm still getting fan letters from little boys who write things like, 'I've loved you since I was 6, I'm now 9.' They request pictures of me and I don't know whether to send them one of me now, or then." Of all the "Our Gang" members, she says her happiest relations were with Spanky, her least pleasant with "Alfalfa." In a recently published book, You Must Remember This, for which she was interviewed, Darla said: "The worst kid in the Gang was Alfalfa. His dad told him he was God's gift to the world, and he thoroughly believed it. In a way I feel guilty talking about him because he's dead. . . . But he was an awful problem on the set. Alfalfa said to me once, 'Reach in my pocket. I've got something for you.' I reached in, and he had an open knife in there, and I cut a couple of fingers. . . . He was just a misguided prankster." She admits a regret that the present generation does not have "Our Gang" to see at the movies. "All the Gang's fun," she says, "was harmless. No one got hurt, there was no violence. I wish my own children could grow up with 'Our Gang' instead of some of the things they watch on television." Onscreen from 1936. IN (besides the 154 "Our Gang" shorts): The Bohemian Girl, Born to Sing, Happy Land, The Pajama Game, The Helen Morgan Story, and, her most recent to date, 1959's The Bat.

HOOKS, DAVID (N.Y.) Character. Onscreen from 1961. IN: Dark Odyssey, The Hospital, more.

HOOKS, KEVIN (N.Y.) Young black lead. Son of Robert Hooks. Onscreen in the '70s. IN: Sounder, Aaron Loves Angela, more.

HOOKS, ROBERT (N.Y.) Black costar. Onscreen from 1966. IN: Sweet Love, Bitter; Hurry Sundown, Last of the Mobile Hot-Shots, Aaron Loves Angela, more.

HOOPES, ISABELLA (N.Y.) Character. Onscreen from the '60s. IN: The Producers, Move, The Boston Strangler, Cancel My Reservation, more.

HOPE, BOB (S. Cal.) The screen's most durable comedy star, he has received four special Academy Award citations. In 1940 he was given a silver plaque "in recognition of his unselfish services to the Motion Picture Industry"; in 1944, a Life Membership in the Academy of Motion Picture Arts and Sciences "for his many services to the Academy"; in 1952, an Oscar statuette "for his contribution to the laughter of the world, his service to the motion picture industry, and his devotion to the American premise"; and, in 1965, a gold medal "for unique and distinguished service to our industry and the Academy." Onscreen from 1938 (after shorts made in '34). IN: *The Big Broadcast of 1938* (his debut), *Thanks for the Memory, College Swing, The Cat and the Canary, The Road to Singapore, The Ghost Breakers, Caught in the Draft, Nothing But the Truth, My Favorite Blonde, Star-Spangled Rhythm, They Got Me Covered, Let's Face It, The Princess and the Pirate, Monsieur Beaucaire, The Paleface, Sorrowful Jones, Fancy Pants, The Lemon Drop Kid, Casanova's Big Night, The Seven Little Foys, That Certain Feeling, Beau James, Paris Holiday, The Facts of Life, Critic's Choice, I'll Take Sweden; Boy, Did I Get a Wrong Number; Eight on the Lam, The Private Navy of Sergeant O'Farrell, more.*

HOPKINS, ANTHONY (Eng.) Costar. Onscreen from 1968. IN: *The Lion in Winter, The Looking Glass War, When Eight Bells Toll, Young Winston, The Girl from Petrovka, A Doll's House, QB VII, Juggernaut,* more.

HOPKINS, BO (S. Cal.) Costar. Onscreen in the '70s. IN: *The Day of the Locust, Posse, The Nickel Ride, The Killer Elite,* more.

HOPKINS, LINDA (N.Y.) Black singer-actress. Onscreen in the '70s. IN: *The Education of Sonny Carson.*

HOPPER, DENNIS (N.M.) Costar. Onscreen from 1954. IN: *Johnny Guitar, Rebel Without a Cause, From Hell to Texas, The Young Land, Giant, Cool Hand Luke, Panic in the City, Hang 'Em High, Easy Rider, True Grit, The Last Movie, Dime Box Texas,* more.

HORDERN, MICHAEL (Eng.) Character. Onscreen from 1939. IN: *The Girl in the News, Mine Own Executioner, Passport to Pimlico, El Cid, The Spy Who Came in from the Cold, A Funny Thing Happened on the Way to the Forum, Where Eagles Dare, Theater of Blood, Mr. Quilp, Barry Lyndon* (narration only), *Lucky Lady,* more.

HORGAN, PATRICK (N.Y.) Support. Onscreen from 1968. IN: *The Thomas Crown Affair,* more.

HORN, CAMILLA (Ger.) John Barrymore's blonde love in the silent *Tempest* is in her 70s (b. 1906), has not made a movie since 1939's *Red Orchids,* and lives in retirement in West Germany. Onscreen from 1926. IN: *Faust, Eva and the Grasshopper, Eternal Love, The Royal Box, The Return of Raffles, Luck of a Sailor, Die Grosse Chance, Mother Love,* more.

HORNE, GEOFFREY /now **MICHAEL JEFFREY HORNE** (S. Cal.) Support. Onscreen from 1957. IN: *The Bridge on the River Kwai, The Strange One, Bonjour Tristesse, The Corsican Brothers, Joseph and His Brethren, Three Good Men, The Baby Maker,* more.

HORNE, LENA (N.Y.) Black star-singer. Onscreen from 1942. IN: *Panama Hattie, Cabin in the Sky, Stormy Weather, Thousands Cheer, Broadway Rhythm, Two Girls and a Sailor, Ziegfeld Follies, Till the Clouds Roll By, Meet Me in Las Vegas, Death of a Gunfighter,* more.

HORNE, VICTORIA (S. Cal.) Character. Onscreen from 1944. IN: *The Unseen, Pillow to Post, Key Witness, The Snake Pit, The Return of October, The Good Humor Man, Joe Palooka in Humphrey Takes a Chance, Harvey,* more. (See Jack Oakie.)

HORNEY, BRIGITTE (Ger.) Character; former leading lady. Onscreen from the '30s. IN: *Winter Storms, Tumult in Damascus, Goal in the Clouds, Dead Melody, The Glass Tower, Miracle of the White Stallions,* more.

HORSBRUGH, WALTER (Eng.) Character. Onscreen from the '40s. IN: *All Over the Town, Top Secret, Innocents in Paris, The Green Scarf, You Can't Escape, 23 Paces to Baker Street,* more.

HORSLEY, JOHN (Eng.) Character. Onscreen from the '40s. IN: *Encore* ("Winter Cruise" episode), *Sailor of the King, Night People, Sink the Bismarck!, Operation Amsterdam,* more.

HORTON, LOUISE (N.Y.) The former leading lady has been married since '51 to famous movie director George Roy Hill, has two sons and two daughters (one of whom, Frances, became a bride in '75). And, in '75, the actress signed to appear in Universal's *Swashbuckler,* her first movie in 25 years. Onscreen from 1948. IN: *All My Sons, Walk East on Beacon.*

HORTON, ROBERT (S. Cal.) Leading man. Now costars with his wife, Marilyn, in stock musical productions throughout the U.S. Onscreen from 1951. IN: *The Tanks Are Coming, Return of the Texan, Pony Soldier, Code 2, Arena, Men of the Fighting Lady, Private Eye, The Green Slime,* more.

HORVATH, CHARLES (S. Cal.) Character. Onscreen from 1951. IN: *Cave of the Outlaws, Voodoo Tiger, His Majesty O'Keefe, Vera Cruz, Francis in the Haunted House, The Thing That Couldn't Die, Twilight for the Gods, War Party, Kenner, A Woman Under the Influence,* more.

HOSKINS, ALLEN CLAYTON (N. Cal.) "Farina," the pigtailed delight of "Our Gang" for 11 years—just two when he started—appeared later in a few features before giving up movie acting at 15. He continued his education, receiving his certificate as a Psychiatric Technician, and is today, in his 50s (b. 1920), director of a workshop for a psychiatric agency near San Francisco. He works primarily with youngsters with drug problems. Onscreen from the '20s. IN: *The Life of Jimmy Dolan, The Mayor of Hell, Reckless,* more.

HOSKINS, BOB (S. Cal.) Support. Onscreen in the '70s. IN: *Inserts,* more.

HOSSEIN, ROBERT (Fr.) Costar. Onscreen from the '50s. IN: *Rififi, Crime and Punishment, Nude in a White Car, Paris Pick-Up, Love on a Pillow, Enough Rope, Marco the Magnificent, The Burglars,* more.

HOTCHKIS, JOAN (S. Cal.) Support. Onscreen in the '70s. IN: *The Late Liz,* more.

HOUGHTON, KATHARINE (N.Y.) Leading lady. Onscreen from 1967. IN: *Guess Who's Coming to Dinner, The Gardener.*

HOUSEMAN, JOHN (N.Y.) Character. Won Best Supporting Actor Oscar in *The Paper Chase.* He had previously been one of the screen's more astute producers—of *The Blue Dahlia, Letters from An Unknown Woman, The Bad and the Beautiful, Executive Suite, The Cobweb, Lust for Life,* etc. Onscreen from 1964. IN: *Seven Days in May, Three Days of the Condor, Rollerball, St. Ives,* more.

HOUSTON, DONALD (Eng.) Character; former leading man. Onscreen from 1949. IN: *The Blue Lagoon, A Run for Your Money, Paratrooper, Doctor in the House, Battle Hell, Room at the Top, The Man Upstairs, The Mark, Maniac, Doctor in Distress, My Lover My Son,* more.

HOUSTON, GLYN (Eng.) Character. Onscreen from 1950. IN: *The Blue Lamp, The Clouded Yellow, The Cruel Sea, Hell Below Zero, Turn the Key Softly, The Sleeping Tiger,* more.

HOUSTON, RENEE (Eng.) Character. Onscreen from the '30s. IN: *Their Night Out, Radio Parade, Fine Feathers, Lady Godiva Rides Again, The Belles of St. Trinian's, A Town Like Alice, The Horse's Mouth, Cul de Sac,* more.

HOVEY, ANN (Ariz.) A widow, she lives near Phoenix and is now a freelance magazine writer. Onscreen from 1933. IN: *Wild Boys of the Road, Annapolis Salute, Danger Patrol,* more.

HOWARD, ALAN (Eng.) Support. Onscreen from the 1960s. IN: *Victim, Work Is a Four-*

Letter Word, War and Peace, Little Big Man, more.

HOWARD, ARTHUR (Eng.) Character. Onscreen from 1934. IN: *The Lady Is Willing, Dulcimer Street, Passport to Pimlico, The Happiest Days of Your Life, Knave of Hearts, The Constant Husband, Joy House, Zeppelin,* more.

HOWARD, CLINT (S. Cal.) Juvenile. Onscreen from the '60s. IN: *The Courtship of Eddie's Father, Gentle Giant,* more.

HOWARD, JASON (N.Y.) Juvenile. Onscreen from 1969. IN: *Me, Natalie; Carnal Knowledge,* more.

HOWARD, JEAN (S. Cal.) Still a beauty in her 60s, she was married for years to the late agent-producer Charles K. Feldman and now lives in well-off retirement in Beverly Hills. Onscreen from 1934. IN: *Broadway to Hollywood, The Prizefighter and the Lady, Break of Hearts, We're on the Jury, Claudia, Bermuda Mystery,* more.

HOWARD, JOHN (S. Cal.) Yesterday's leading man is a character actor now and, in his 60s (b. 1913), a handsome one. Mostly he works in television. Besides playing a running character, Cliff Patterson, in NBC's *Days of Our Lives* soap opera, he has done supporting roles in many nighttime TV shows. Privately, he has long been married to Eva Ralf, formerly a soloist with the Berlin State Opera Ballet, and is the father of four—two grown sons and a daughter, and a teenage daughter. They live in Encino. Onscreen from 1939. IN: *Millions in the Air, Valiant Is the Word for Carrie, Lost Horizon, Bulldog Drummond Comes Back* (and five others in the series, in which he starred), *Disputed Passage, The Philadelphia Story, The Invisible Woman, Father Takes a Wife, Submarine Raider, Love from a Stranger, Radar Secret Service; Models, Inc.; The High and the Mighty, Destination Inner Space, The Destructors,* more.

HOWARD, JOYCE (Eng.) Leading lady; retired. Onscreen from 1940. IN: *The Voice in the Night, Love on the Dole, Mrs. Fitzherbert, Appointment with Crime,* more.

HOWARD, KEN (S. Cal.) Leading man. Onscreen from 1970. IN: *Tell Me That You Love Me, Junie Moon; Such Good Friends, 1776,* more.

HOWARD, MARJORIE (N.Y.) Character. Onscreen from the '50s. IN: *A View from the Bridge, The Hustler,* more.

HOWARD, MARY (N.Y.) Once one of MGM's most promising young stars, a certainty to inherit Shearer-type roles, she gave up her career in '42 after *Who Is Hope Schuyler?* and *The Loves of Edgar Allan Poe.* Since '45 she has been the wife of stage producer-director and socialite Alfred di Liagre Jr., and is the mother of a grown son and daughter. She is also by marriage the sister-in-law of Brian Aherne—the actor being married to Mr. di Liagre's sister. Their permanent residence is a beautiful apartment in the East 50s, but their summers are spent in East Hampton or abroad. Onscreen from 1938. IN: *Fast Company, Love Finds Andy Hardy, Four Girls in White, Nurse Edith Cavell, Abe Lincoln in Illinois, Billy the Kid, Riders of the Purple Sage, Swamp Water, Through Different Eyes,* more.

HOWARD, MICHAEL (Eng.) Character. Onscreen from the '40s. IN: *The Adventuress, It Always Rains on Sunday, Front Page Story, Out of the Clouds,* more.

HOWARD, RANCE (S. Cal.) Character. Father of Clint and Ron (Ronny). Onscreen from the '50s. IN: *Gentle Giant, Where the Lilies Bloom, Chinatown,* more.

HOWARD, RON (RONNY) (S. Cal.) Leading man; former juvenile. Onscreen from 1958. IN: *The Journey, The Music Man, The Courtship of Eddie's Father, Wild Country, Mother's Day, American Graffiti, Harry Spikes, The Shootist,* more.

HOWARD, RONALD (Eng.) Character. Son of the late Leslie Howard, nephew of Arthur Howard. Onscreen from 1946. IN: *While the Sun Shines, My Brother Jonathan, The Browning Version, Gideon of Scotland Yard, Naked Edge, Come September, Murder She Said, Africa—Texas Style!, The Hunting Party,* more.

HOWARD, TREVOR (Eng.) Star. Nominated for Best Actor Oscar in *Sons and Lovers.* Onscreen from 1945. IN: *The Way Ahead, Brief Encounter, Green for Danger, So Well Remembered, The Third Man, Outcast of the Islands, The Clouded Yellow, The Heart of the Matter, Glory at Sea, Cockleshell Heroes, Around the World in 80 Days, The Key, Roots of Heaven, Mutiny on the Bounty, The Lion, Father Goose, Operation Crossbow, Von Ryan's Express, The Long Duel, The Charge of the Light Brigade, Ryan's Daughter, The Night Visitor; Mary, Queen of Scots; Pope Joan, Ludwig, Persecution, Conduct Unbecoming, The Passover Plot,* more.

HOWARD, VINCE (S. Cal.) Black support. Onscreen in the '70s. IN: *Where It's At, Suppose They Gave a War and Nobody Came?, The Barefoot Executive,* more.

HOWAT, CLARK (S. Cal.) Character. Onscreen from 1953. IN: *The Glass Web, Airport, Billy Jack,* more.

HOWELLS, URSULA (Eng.) Leading lady. Onscreen from the '50s. IN: *I Believe in You, The Horse's Mouth, The Constant Husband, Track the Man Down, The Third Key, Dr. Terror's House of Horrors,* more.

HOWERD, FRANKIE (Eng.) Star comedian. Onscreen from 1954. IN: *The Runaway Bus, Ladykillers, Further Up the Creek, The Great St. Trinian's Train Robbery, Carry On Doctor, Up Pompeii, The House in Nightmare Park,* more.

HOWES, SALLY ANN (Eng.) Costar. Onscreen from 1943. IN: *Thursday's Child* (her debut at 13), *Half-Way House, Dead of Night, Nicholas Nickleby, The History of Mr. Polly, Pink String and Sealing Wax, The Admirable Crichton, Chitty Chitty Bang Bang,* more.

HOYOS, RODOLFO (S. Cal.) Character. Onscreen from 1951. IN: *Raton Pass, Second Chance, The Americano, The First Texan, The Brave One, Villa!, Toughest Gun in Tombstone, Operation Eichmann, Return of a Gunfighter,* more.

HOYT, JOHN (S. Cal.) Character. Onscreen from 1946. IN: *O.S.S., The Unfaithful, Brute Force, Winter Meeting, The Great Dan Patch, The Desert Fox, When Worlds Collide, Julius Caesar, The Girl in the Red Velvet Swing, Baby Face Nelson, Spartacus, Cleopatra, Young Dillinger,* more.

HSUEH, NANCY (S. Cal.) Leading lady. Onscreen from 1945. IN: *China's Little Devils* (as a child), *Intrigue, Cheyenne Autumn, Adventures of Robin Crusoe, Targets,* more.

HUBBARD, JOHN (S. Cal.) Character; former leading man. Onscreen from 1938. IN: *The Buccaneer, The Housekeeper's Daughter, Turnabout, One Million B.C., Topper Returns, Road Show, She Knew All the Answers, Our Wife, You'll Never Get Rich, The Mummy's Tomb, Chatterbox, Up in Mabel's Room, The Bullfighter and the Lady, Soldier in the Rain, Fate Is the Hunter, The Family Jewels, The Love Bug Rides Again,* more.

HUBER, GUSTI (N.Y.) Character; former leading lady. Onscreen from 1936. IN: *Tanzmusik, The Cabbie's Song, The Girl of Last Night, Between the Parents, The Diary of Anne Frank,* more.

HUBLEY, SEASON (S. Cal.) Leading lady. Onscreen in the '70s. IN: *Catch My Soul,* more.

HUBSCHMID, PAUL (Ger.) (See Paul Christian.)

HUDDLESTON, DAVID (S. Cal.) Character. Onscreen from 1964. IN: *Black Like Me, Slaves, Norwood, Rio Lobo, Something Big, Fools' Parade, Bad Company, The Klansman,* more.

HUDSON, JOHN (S. Cal.) Leading man. Onscreen from 1951. IN: *Bright Victory, Return to Paradise, Many Rivers to Cross, The Marauders, Fort Yuma, The Screaming Skull, All in a Night's Work, Sinai Commandos, Candy Stripe Nurses,* more.

HUDSON, ROCK (S. Cal.) Star. Nominated for Best Actor Oscar in *Giant.* Onscreen from 1948. IN: *Fighter Squadron, One Way Street, Winchester 73, The Iron Man, Bright Victory, Bend of the River, Seminole, The Golden Blade, Magnificent Obsession, Captain Lightfoot, All That Heaven Allows, Written on the Wind, Something of Value, A Farewell to Arms, Pillow Talk, Come September, Lover Come Back, The Spiral Road, A Gathering of Eagles, Send Me No Flowers, Strange Bedfellows, Seconds* (his personal favorite role)*, Tobruk, Ice Station Zebra, Darling Lili, The Undefeated, Hornet's Nest, Pretty Maids All in a Row, Showdown, Embryo,* more.

HUEBING, CRAIG (S. Cal.) Support. Onscreen in the '70s. IN: *Marooned, The Comic,* more.

HUGHES, ARTHUR (N.Y.) Character. Onscreen from 1951. IN: *Hue and Cry, Bananas,* more.

HUGHES, BARNARD (S. Cal.) Character. Onscreen from 1964. IN: *Hamlet* (the Richard Burton filmed-on-stage version)*, Midnight Cowboy, Cold Turkey, The Hospital,* more.

HUGHES, CAROL (S. Cal.) Buster Crabbe's dark-haired "Dale Arden" in the 1940 serial *Flash Gordon Conquers the Universe* is blonde and attractive in her 60s (b. 1915) and plays character parts (usually of an Iris Adrian "type") on television. The child bride, literally, of character actor Frank Faylen, she has been married to him—most happily—since 1928. Onscreen from 1936. IN: *The Golden Arrow, The Case of the Velvet Claws, Polo Joe, Three Men on a Horse, Renfrew of the Royal Mounted, Under Western Stars, Scattergood Baines, The Bachelor and the Bobby-Soxer, Scaramouche,* more. (See Frank Faylen.)

HUGHES, HAZEL (Eng.) Character. Onscreen from 1938. IN: *Ireland's Border Line,* more.

HUGHES, KATHLEEN (S. Cal.) Blonde now, she had a supporting role in 1975 in the TV special *Babe*—about golf star Babe Didrikson Zaharias. Onscreen from 1949. IN: *Mr. Belvedere Goes to College, Mother Is a Freshman, Take Care of My Little Girl, The Golden Blade, The Glass Web, It Came from Outer Space, Dawn at Socorro, Cult of the Cobra, The President's Analyst,* more.

HUGHES, MARY BETH (S. Cal.) Little changed in looks though in her 50s (b. 1919), she still stars in movies usually seen in small towns, such as 1975's *The Working Girls.*. Mainly, though, in recent years she earned her living in nightclubs—singing and playing the electric bass—more often than not in second-rate suburban bistros where the clientele cared more about getting the bartender's attention than listening to anyone's songs. "One day I told myself," she recently related, laughing, "that I either had to quit or become an alcoholic so I could stand that kind of life." She quit, got herself an agent, and leads in such B's as *Tanya* and *How's Your Love Life?* No longer pursuing bigtime stardom, this realistic veteran of 56 movies describes herself now as a "working girl making ends meet." Twice married and divorced—to ex-actor Ted (Michael) North, now an agent, and late singer David Street—she has been married since late '73 to Nicky Stewart, her personal manager, and lives with him in a rambling ranch house in Sepulveda, with many cats and an enormous pool. Her only child, Donald North, teaches scuba diving and owns a business selling sophisticated underwater equipment; married several years, he lives nearby. From time to time recently, because inactivity ill becomes her and she has been unsuccessful in getting what she really wants—a running role in a TV series—Mary Beth has resumed her nightclub act. This time in the better Southern California boites. "I have been asked in the clubs we work," she relates, "if I am the mother of the actress, Mary Beth Hughes. At first I would become angry, then I realized it was a compliment." Onscreen from 1939. IN: *These Glamour Girls; Free, Blonde and 21; Four Sons, The Great Profile, The Great American Broadcast, The Cowboy and the Blonde, Charlie Chan in Rio; Blue, White and Perfect; Orchestra Wives, The Ox-Bow Incident, Timber Queen, The Great Flamarion, Inner Sanctum, El Paso, Young Man with a Horn, Close to My Heart, Highway Dragnet, Las Vegas Shakedown, Dig That Uranium,* more.

HUGHES, RODDY (Eng.) Character. Onscreen from 1935. IN: *The Old Curiosity Shop, The Stars Look Down, Quiet Wedding, Hatter's Castle, So Well Remembered, Nicholas Nickleby, The Hidden Room, A Christmas Carol, The Man in the White Suit,* more.

HUGO, LAURENCE (N.Y.) Character. Primarily a TV soap opera stalwart and Broadway actor. Onscreen from 1954. IN: *Three Hours to Kill*, more.

HUGUENY, SHARON (S. Cal.) Formerly married to actor-producer Robert Evans, she is retired from the screen. Onscreen in the '60s. IN: *Parrish, A Majority of One, The Caretakers, The Young Lovers*.

HULBERT, JACK (Eng.) Character. Onscreen from 1930. IN: *Elstree Calling, The Ghost Train, Jack's the Boy, Bulldog Jack, Under Your Hat, The Magic Box, Not Now Darling*, more.

HULL, DIANNE (S. Cal.) Leading lady. Onscreen in the '70s. IN: *Aloha, Bobby and Rose, Man on a Swing*, more.

HULL, HENRY (Conn.) The venerable, great character actor gave up his 51-year career after 1967's *Covenant with Death*. Now in his 80s (b. 1890), the father of two sons, he lives in retirement on a farm near Old Lyme. Onscreen from 1916. IN: *The Little Rebel, One Exciting Night, The Hoosier Schoolmaster, The Man Who Came Back, Werewolf of London, Yellow Jack, Boys Town, Three Comrades, Jesse James, Stanley and Livingstone, Babes in Arms, Spirit of Culver; My Son, My Son; High Sierra, Lifeboat, Objective Burma, Deep Valley, High Barbaree, Mourning Becomes Electra, The Fountainhead, El Paso, The Great Gatsby, Thunder over the Plains, The Sheriff of Fractured Jaw, The Fool Killer, The Chase, Violent Journey*, more.

HULSWIT, MARTIN (N.Y.) Support. Onscreen in the '70s. IN: *Doc, Loving, A Lovely Way to Die, Come Spy with Me*, more.

HUME, DOUGLAS (S. Cal.) Support. Onscreen from 1960. IN: *This Rebel Breed, The Gay Deceivers*, more.

HUMPHREY, CAVADA (N.Y.) Character. Onscreen from 1948. IN: *The Naked City, Thoroughly Modern Millie*, more.

HUNNICUTT, ARTHUR (S. Cal.) Character. Nominated for Best Supporting Actor Oscar in *The Big Sky*. Onscreen from 1942. IN: *Wildcat, Fall In, Robin Hood of the Range, Johnny Come Lately, Abroad with Two Yanks, Pinky, The Great Dan Patch, Stars in My Crown, Broken Arrow, Two Flags West, A Ticket to Tomahawk, The Red Badge of Courage, Distant Drums, The Lusty Men, Split Second, The French Line, The Kettles in the Ozarks, The Cardinal, Cat Ballou, El Dorado, Adventures of Bullwhip Griffin, The Revengers, Moonrunners, Winterhawk*, more.

HUNNICUTT, GAYLE (Eng.) Leading lady. Onscreen from 1966. IN: *The Wild Angels, P.J., Marlowe, Eye of the Cat, Fragment of Fear, The Legend of Hell House*, more.

HUNT, MARSHA (S. Cal.) Once one of the screen's busiest and most popular actresses, she has appeared in just one movie—1971's *Johnny Got His Gun* —in more than a decade. But on TV she is to be seen every few weeks in character roles on shows such as *Barnaby Jones* and *Police Story*. Privately, she has been married for three decades to movie-TV scriptwriter Robert Presnell Jr. She divides her private-life energies among a variety of organizations concerned with such issues as peace, poverty, population, and pollution. An active and ardent worker, she serves on nearly a dozen Boards of Directors and is a frequent speaker on behalf of her favorite concerns. Onscreen from 1935. IN: *The Virginia Judge, Gentle Julia, Annapolis Salute, Irene, Pride and Prejudice, Flight Command, Cheers for Miss Bishop, I'll Wait for You, Blossoms in the Dust, Unholy Partners; Joe Smith, American; The Kid Glove Killer, Panama Hattie, Seven Sweethearts, The Human Comedy, Pilot No. 5, Cry Havoc, None Shall Escape, A Letter for Evie, The Valley of Decision, Smash-Up, Carnegie Hall, Actors and Sin, Bombers B-52, Blue Denim, The Plunderers*, more.

HUNTER, IAN (Eng.) In his 70s (b. 1900) and a grandfather—he has two adult sons, Jolyon and Robin—he lives in a fine flat in the heart of London and is completely retired. After playing major roles in many English films following his years in Hollywood (*Pursuit of the Graf Spee, Flame Over India, Mad Little Island*, etc.), he gave up his career after 1965's *Door in the Wall*. Onscreen from the '20s. IN: *Not for Sale, Confessions, There Goes the Bride, A Summer Night's Dream, The Girl from 10th Avenue, Jalna, The White Angel, The Devil Is a Sissy, Another Dawn, The Adventures of Robin Hood, The Sisters, Always Goodbye, The Little Princess; Yes, My Darling Daughter; Maisie, Tower of London, Strange Cargo, The Long Voyage Home, Billy the Kid, Come Live with Me, Ziegfeld Girl, Smilin' Through, Dr. Jekyll and Mr. Hyde, A Yank at Eton, Forever and a Day, Bedelia, Edward My Son, Eight O'Clock Walk, Northwest Frontier, Flame Over India, Dr. Blood's Coffin, The Queen's Guards*, more.

HUNTER, KIM (N.Y.) Costar. Won Best Supporting Actress Oscar in *A Streetcar Named Desire*. Soon afterward, though, her career suffered a grievous setback when her name appeared—without cause—in *Red Channels* and, blacklisted, she did not work in movies for four years. Later, when radio personality John Henry Faulk was similarly blacklisted and fought back in a celebrated trial, she became the heroine in the case. It was her testimony in court that broke the back of *Red Channels*, making it possible for many dozens of performers unjustly accused of Communist connections to resume their careers. (When this trial was dramatized on TV in 1975 she permitted herself to be portrayed, but under a fictitious name.) Today, long married to writer Robert Emmett and the mother of grown children, she acts steadily—on Broadway (the '73 revival of *The Women*), on TV (*Marcus Welby, M.D.*, *Medical Center*, such TV-movies as *Unwed Father*), and in movies. And in '75 she published a book titled *Loose in the Kitchen* and subtitled, "Kim Hunter's Autobiographical Cookbook"—as it contained not only the story of her life but dozens of recipes marking the major milestones of her life. Onscreen from 1943. IN: *The Seventh Victim, Tender Comrade, When Strangers Marry, You Came Along, Stairway to Heaven, Anything Can Happen, Deadline U.S.A., Storm Center, The Young Stranger, Lilith, Planet of the Apes, The Swimmer, Beneath the Planet of the Apes*, more.

HUNTER, ROSS (S. Cal.) Giving up acting for producing, he has been responsible for many major hits, including *Airport*. Entering his 60s (b. 1916), he is still a bachelor. Onscreen from 1945. IN: *A Guy, a Gal and a Pal; Sweetheart of Sigma Chi, Hit the Hay, Out of the Depths, The Bandit of Sherwood Forest*, more.

HUNTER, TAB (Va.) Still single in his 40s (b. 1931), he flies to Hollywood for an occasional movie (*The Life and Times of Judge Roy Bean*) or TV show (*Six Million Dollar Man*), and he acts onstage in stock and dinner theaters. His home, though, is the farm in Virginia that he purchased in '74 and where he trains horses—Mrs. Jock Whitney being one of his famous clients. Onscreen from 1950. IN: *The Lawless, Island of Desire, Gun Belt, Track of the Cat, Battle Cry, The Girl He Left Behind, Lafayette Escadrille, Damn Yankees, Gunman's Walk, That Kind of Woman* (his personal favorite), *They Came to Cordura, The Pleasure of His Company, Ride the Wild Surf, The Loved One, Hostile Guns*, more.

HUNTLEY, RAYMOND (Eng.) Character. Onscreen from 1934. IN: *Knight Without Armor, The Way Ahead, The Adventuress, So Evil My Love, Scotch on the Rocks, Hobson's Choice, Doctor at Sea, Wee Geordie, Brothers in Law, Room at the Top, Our Man in Havana, I'm All Right Jack, Man in a Cocked Hat, Waltz of the Toreadors, That's Your Funeral*, more.

HURLOCK, MADELINE (N.Y.) Mack Sennett called her the wittiest of his famous bathing beauties (reportedly, she also was the best paid). Her wit and beauty almost assuredly were the combination that caused two famous writers to fall in love with and marry her—Marc (*The Green Pastures*) Connelly and, after they were divorced, Robert E. (*Idiot's Delight*) Sherwood. The former actress has been a widow since Sherwood's death in '55, has long been retired, would now be in her 70s, and her late husband's biographers have not always been kind. Onscreen from the teens. IN: Sennett comedies such as *Don Juan's Three Nights*.

HURST, DAVID (S. Cal.) Support. Onscreen from the '50s. IN: *Tony Draws a Horse, So Little Time, Always a Bride; Hello, Dolly!;* more.

HURST, VERONICA (Eng.) Leading lady. Onscreen from the '50s. IN: *Laughter in Paradise, The Maze, The Girl on the Pier, Don't Blame the Stork, Storm Over Africa, The Boy Cried Murder, The 2nd Best Secret Agent in the Whole Wide World*, more.

HURT, JOHN (Eng.) Support. Onscreen from the '60s. IN: *A Man for All Seasons, Sinful Davey, 10 Rillington Place, The Ghoul*, more.

HUSH, LISABETH (S. Cal.) Leading lady. Onscreen from 1962. IN: *X-15, Thoroughly Modern Millie*, more.

HUSMANN, RON (S. Cal.) Leading man. Onscreen from 1965. IN: *Love Has Many Faces*, more.

HUSSEY, OLIVIA (S. Cal.) Leading lady. Onscreen from 1965. IN: *Cup Fever, The Battle of the Villa Fiorita, Romeo and Juliet, All the Right Noises, Hot Shot, Lost Horizon, Black Christmas, The Great Friday*, more.

HUSSEY, RUTH (S. Cal.) Costar. Nominated for Best Supporting Actress Oscar in *The Philadelphia Story*. She has not appeared in a movie since 1960's *The Facts of Life*—preferring to devote her professional energies to dramatized readings at women's clubs and on university campuses—but she remains well connected with the movie industry. Her husband (since '42) is actors' agent Robert Longenecker. And one of her sons, John William Longenecker, has produced many short films, one of which, *The Resurrection of Broncho Billy*, won an Oscar a few seasons back. Her other son, George, is a jet pilot, a Navy career officer. Her daughter, Mary Elizabeth, is a college student. The actress, in her 60s (b. 1914), remains an exceedingly attractive woman, but one not at all attracted to moviemaking now. Onscreen from 1937. IN: *The Big City, Marie Antoinette, Time Out for Murder, Honolulu, The Women, Blackmail, Another Thin Man, Northwest Passage, Susan and God, Flight Command; H.M. Pulham, Esq.; Our Wife, Bedtime Story, Tennessee Johnson, Tender Comrade, The Uninvited; I, Jane Doe; The Great Gatsby, Mr. Music, Woman of the North, Stars and Stripes Forever, The Lady Wants Mink,* more.

HUSTON, ANJELICA (S. Cal.) Leading lady. Onscreen from 1969. IN: *A Walk with Love and Death, Sinful Davey, The Last Tycoon,* more.

HUSTON, JOHN (Ire.) Director and character actor. Nominated for Best Supporting Actor Oscar in *The Cardinal.* Onscreen from 1948. IN: *The Treasure of the Sierra Madre, The List of Adrian Messenger, The Bible, Casino Royale, Candy, A Walk with Love and Death, De Sade, The Life and Time of Judge Roy Bean, Man in the Wilderness, Chinatown, Breakout, The Wind and the Lion,* more.

HUSTON, PATRICIA (S. Cal.) Support. Onscreen from 1962. IN: *Experiment in Terror, Synanon,* more.

HUSTON, PHILIP (N.Y.) Character; former leading man. Onscreen from 1936. IN: *The Big Game, We're on the Jury, The Man Who Found Himself, Behind the Headlines, Close-Up,* more.

HUSTON, TONY (S. Cal.) Support. Son of John, brother of Anjelica. Onscreen from 1963. IN: *The List of Adrian Messenger,* more.

HUTCHESON, DAVID (Eng.) Character. Onscreen from 1930. IN: *Fast and Loose, Next of Kin, The Life and Death of Colonel Blimp, Madness of the Heart, Operation X, Encore* ("Gigolo and Gigolette" episode), *Something Money Can't Buy, Law and Disorder, The National Health,* more.

HUTCHINS, WILL (S. Cal.) After playing Dagwood Bumstead in the short-lived *Blondie* series on TV in '68 (he had earlier starred in *Sugarfoot*), this movie-TV leading man turned to other areas of show business. In '76 when he returned for a guest role—that of a clown—in TV's *Streets of San Francisco,* he explained: "I was in a circus in 1974 as a ringmaster in this country and Canada. And in 1973 I was in two circuses, traveling around as a clown. Now I'm working for the theater-arts program of Los Angeles. We do free shows all over L.A. for schools, recreation centers, hospitals, libraries, senior-citizen homes." Divorced, the father of a teenage daughter, and in his 40s (b. 1932), he

returned to movies in 1976's *Teenage Slumber Party.* Onscreen from 1958. IN: *No Time for Sergeants, Claudelle Inglish, Merrill's Marauders, The Shooting, Spin-Out, Clambake.*

HUTCHINSON, HARRY (Eng.) Character. Onscreen from 1936. IN: *The Adventuress, Up the Junction, Salt and Pepper,* more.

HUTCHINSON, JOSEPHINE (S. Cal.) This splendid actress is, in her 70s (b. 1904), still going strong. Since the '69 movie *Rabbit, Run,* in which she was James Caan's mother, she has concentrated on TV, with episodes of *Little House on the Prairie* being among her most recent credits. On September 23, 1972, she became the wife of actor Staats Cotsworth. They had first met in '32 when, as members of New York's Civic Repertory Theatre, they had toured in *Alice in Wonderland.* In the years between, Cotsworth, star of radio's *Casey, Crime Photographer,* had been married to actress Muriel Kirkland, who died in '71. And Josephine had been married to Washington newspaperman Robert Bell and then to agent James Townsend. Onscreen from 1934. IN: *Happiness Ahead, Oil for the Lamps of China, The Story of Louis Pasteur, I Married a Doctor, The Crime of Dr. Hallett; My Son, My Son; Tom Brown's School Days, Cass Timberlane, Adventure in Baltimore, Many Rivers to Cross, North by Northwest, Nevada Smith,* more.

HUTTON, BETTY (S. Cal.) Early in '75 the "blitzkrieg blonde" comedienne, now in her 50s (b. 1921) and last onscreen in 1957's *Spring Reunion,* had gone back to live and work as a domestic at St. Anthony's Rectory in Portsmouth, R.I. After her conversion to Catholicism she had lived there earlier, before attempting a show business comeback—which came to naught—in New York. Returning to the rectory, she told a *Variety* reporter that she attended mass each morning and "the happiness is even greater." She added: "I love Rhode Island and the people here. It's wonderful how they love me—not because I'm Betty Hutton—but because I'm *me.*" It was not enough, apparently. Late in '75, she was back in Hollywood trying once more for a comeback. Then she told reporter Aaron Gold, "I've had a facelift and I look fabulous, and my figure (a size 10) is great. Nostalgia is in, and I think I'm nostalgia No. 1. I'm busy working with a pianist on a cabaret act for L.A.'s Studio One, but it's so expensive, and I really don't have any money. Of course, I'm also writing a book and if I get the front money from that, it would be enough." She added that MGM had invited her to tour the world for *That's Entertainment II* as it included scenes of her in *Annie Get Your Gun.* The actress has been married and divorced four times

—to Ted Briskin (1945–51), Charles O'Curran (1952–55), Alan Livingston (1955–58), and Pete Candoli (1961–66). By her first husband she has two grown daughters, Lindsay and Candice, but their relations have not always been amicable. She has a teenage daughter, Carolyn, by Candoli. Onscreen from 1942. IN: *The Fleet's In, Star-Spangled Rhythm, The Miracle of Morgan's Creek, Here Come the Waves, Incendiary Blonde, The Stork Club, The Perils of Pauline, Dream Girl, Let's Dance, The Greatest Show on Earth, Somebody Loves Me,* more.

HUTTON, JIM (S. Cal.) Leading man. Onscreen from 1960. IN: *Where the Boys Are, The Honeymoon Machine, Period of Adjustment, The Horizontal Lieutenant, Major Dundee, Never Too Late; Walk, Don't Run; The Trouble With Angels, Who's Minding the Mint?, The Green Berets, Psychic Killer,* more.

HUTTON, LAUREN (N.Y.) Model-leading lady. Onscreen from 1968. IN: *Paper Lion, Little Fauss and Big Halsy, Pieces of Dreams; Excuse Me, My Name Is Rocco Popaleo; The Gambler, Welcome to L.A.,* more.

HUTTON, LINDA (N.Y.) Leading lady. Niece of Dina Merrill. Onscreen from 1975. IN: *Shampoo, The Man Who Fell to Earth.*

HUTTON, MARION (S. Cal.) Singer-actress; retired. Onscreen from the '40s. IN: *Orchestra Wives, In Society, Crazy House, Love Happy,* more.

HUTTON, ROBERT (N.Y.) Well-married (after a failure or two), he lives in a nice community perhaps an hour's drive north of New York and, as Robert B. Hutton, writes screenplays. He is undaunted that one recent effort, the Gothic horror pic *Persecution,* turned out poorly. Made in England in '74, it starred Lana Turner, a decades-ago flame of his. When she made a '75 appearance in New York—as one of the screen's Legendary Ladies—the actress referred to the picture disparagingly, urging her admirers to avoid it. Until recently, the actor-turned-author—called in '43, by *Life* magazine, the "new" Jimmy Stewart—had resided in England for a dozen years and worked steadily as an actor. Compared to his spotlighted career as a young leading man at Warners, particularly in the "Janie" comedy series, his English career was decidedly low profile. Besides guesting in such British-made TV series as *Persuaders,* he was in many pix—including *Trog, House of a Thousand Dolls, Finders Keepers,* and *You Only Live Twice,* in which, billed 14th, he was the "President's Aide" (the American President being former star Alexander Knox). Moustachioed, in his 50s (b. 1920), and no longer rail-thin as in his youth, Hutton returned to Hollywood in '74 and signed with an agent to resume his acting career. Almost immediately changing his mind, he relocated in New York, and has been back at his typewriter since. Onscreen from 1943. IN: *Destination Tokyo, Roughly Speaking, Janie Gets Married, Love and Learn, Wallflower, The Younger Brothers, The Man on the Eiffel Tower, Paris Model, Yaqui Drums, The Colossus of New York, Cinderfella, The Vulture,* more.

HYAMS, LEILA (S. Cal.) In her 70s (b. 1905), she last appeared onscreen in 1936's *Yellow Dust* and has been married for many years to Phil Berg, a top Hollywood agent. Onscreen from 1924. IN: *Sandra, The Brute, Honor Bound, Alias Jimmy Valentine, Masquerade, The 13th Chair, The Big House, Sins of the Children, The Richest Man in the World, The Phantom of Paris, Saturday's Millions, The Big Broadcast, Freaks, The Constant Woman, Island of Lost Souls, Ruggles of Red Gap, $1,000 a Minute, No Ransom,* more.

HYDE-WHITE, WILFRID (S. Cal.) Character. Onscreen from 1936. IN: *Rembrandt, Trio* ("Mr. Knowall" sequence), *The Browning Version, Gilbert and Sullivan, Man with a Million, Tarzan and the Lost Safari, Libel, Let's Make Love, Carry On Nurse, In Search of the Castaways, My Fair Lady, Ten Little Indians, You Only Live Twice, P.J., His and Hers, Skullduggery, Gaily Gaily,* more.

HYER, MARTHA (S. Cal.) Married to producer Hal Wallis since '66, she has lately written for his movies (assisted on the *Rooster Cogburn* script) and for *Good Housekeeping* magazine—a reminiscence of her first Christmas away from home. Though nominated for a Best Supporting Actress Oscar in *Some Came Running* ('58), she gave up her screen career after 1970's *Once You Kiss a Stranger* to be free to travel wherever her husband's movies are shooting. She has no children, is one of Hollywood's leading hostesses, and, in her 50s (b. 1924), looks exactly as she always did in pictures. Onscreen from 1946. IN: *The Locket, Born to Kill, Roughshod, The Judge Steps Out, Sabrina, Lucky Me, Cry Vengeance, Kiss of Fire, Desire in the Dust, Battle Hymn, The Delicate Delinquent, Paris Holiday, The Big Fisherman, The Best of Everything, The Man from the Diner's Club, The Carpetbaggers, Blood on the Arrow, The Sons of Katie Elder, Picture Mommy Dead, House of a Thousand Dolls,* more.

HYLAND, DIANA (S. Cal.) Married to Joseph Goodson, the leading lady has a son, born in '73. Onscreen from 1964. IN: *One Man's Way, The Chase, Smoky, Jigsaw,* more.

HYLTON, JANE (Eng.) Leading lady. On-screen from 1947. IN: *The Upturned Glass, Dear Murderer, My Brother's Keeper, Passport to Pimlico, Here Come the Huggetts, Secret Venture, Circus of Horrors, One Man's Navy,* more.

HYMAN, EARLE (N.Y.) Black leading man. Onscreen from 1954. IN: *The Bamboo Prison,* more.

I

IGDALSKY, ZVIAH (N.Y.) Character. On-screen from the '60s. IN: *The Adventurers, Generation, The Angel Levine, Harry, The Night They Raided Minsky's,* more.

IGLESIAS, EUGENE (S. Cal.) Support. On-screen from 1951. IN: *The Brave Bulls, Duel at Silver Creek, Hiawatha, East of Sumatra; Taza, Son of Cochise; Walk the Proud Land, Cowboy, Apache Rifles, Harper,* more.

IMRIE, KATHY (S. Cal.) Black leading lady. Onscreen in the '70s. IN: *Shaft's Big Score, Go for Broke,* more.

INGELS, MARTY (S. Cal.) Comedian. On-screen from 1960. IN: *Armored Command, Ladies' Man, The Busy Body, A Guide for the Married Man, For Singles Only, The Pushover, How to Seduce a Woman,* more.

INNES, GEORGE (Eng.) Character. Onscreen from 1963. IN: *Billy Liar, Before Winter Comes, The Italian Job, The Last Valley,* more.

INNES, JEAN (S. Cal.) Character actress. Wife of Victor Jory. Onscreen from 1950. IN: *Edge of Doom, Mrs. Mike, The Gunfighter, I'd Climb the Highest Mountain, Sign of the Pagan, The Night Runner, Gun Fever,* more.

IRELAND, JILL (S. Cal.) Leading lady. On-screen from 1955. IN: *Oh, Rosalinda!* (dance solo); *The Woman for Joe, Simon and Laura, The Big Money, Three Men in a Boat, Carry On Nurse, Villa Rides!, Rider on the Rain, Someone Behind the Door, Cold Sweat, The Mechanic, Hard Times, Breakout,* more.

IRELAND, JOHN (S. Cal.) Costar. Nominated for Best Supporting Actor Oscar in *All the King's Men.* Onscreen from 1945. IN: *A Walk in the Sun, My Darling Clementine, I Love Trouble, Red River, A Southern Yankee, I Shot Jesse James, Little Big Horn, Red Mountain, Combat Squad, The Steel Cage, Queen Bee, Gunfight at the O.K. Corral, Spartacus, Wild in the Country, 55 Days at Peking, The Fall of the Roman Empire, Fort Utah; Run, Man, Run;*

The House of the Seven Corpses; Farewell, My Lovely; Welcome to Arrow Beach, more.

IRVING, CHARLES (S. Cal.) Character. On-screen from 1957. IN: *A Face in the Crowd, Countdown, Head, Project X,* more.

IRVING, GEORGE S. (N.Y.) Actor-singer. Onscreen from 1975. IN: *Foreplay.*

IRWIN, WYNN (S. Cal.) Character. Onscreen from the '70s. IN: *Dirtymouth, Willie Dynamite,* more.

ITO, ROBERT (S. Cal.) Support. Onscreen from the '60s. IN: *Some Kind of a Nut, The Terminal Man, Special Delivery,* more.

ITURBI, JOSE (S. Cal.) The famous pianist-actor, living still in Beverly Hills, remains, in his 80s (b. 1895), a top box-office attraction on the concert stage. *That Midnight Kiss,* in '49, was his last movie. Onscreen from 1943. IN: *Thousands Cheer, Two Girls and a Sailor, Anchors Aweigh, Holiday in Mexico, Three Daring Daughters.*

IVASHOV, VLADIMIR (Rus.) Star. Onscreen from 1960. IN: *Ballad of a Soldier,* more.

IVES, BURL (S. Cal.) Character star. Won Best Supporting Actor Oscar in *The Big Country.* Onscreen from 1946. IN: *Smoky, Green Grass of Wyoming, So Dear to My Heart, East of Eden, Cat on a Hot Tin Roof, Desire Under the Elms, Wind Across the Everglades, Let No Man Write My Epitaph, The Spiral Road, Summer Magic, Ensign Pulver, The Daydreamer, Those Fantastic Flying Fools, The McMasters, The Only Way Out Is Dead,* more.

IVES, GEORGE (S. Cal.) Character. Onscreen from the '60s. IN: *The Secret War of Harry Frigg,* more.

IZAY, VICTOR (S. Cal.) Character. Onscreen from the '60s. IN: *Wounded in Action, The Astro-Zombies, Billy Jack, The Trial of Billy Jack, The Single Girls,* more.

J

JACKSON, ANNE (N.Y.) Costar. Onscreen from 1950. IN: *So Young So Bad, The Journey, Tall Story, The Tiger Makes Out, How to Save a Marriage, The Secret Life of an American Wife, The Angel Levine, Lovers and Other Strangers, Zigzag, Dirty Dingus Magee,* more.

JACKSON, BARRY (Eng.) Support. Onscreen from 1968. IN: *The Bofors Gun, Alfred the Great, Ryan's Daughter, Long Ago Tomorrow,* more.

JACKSON, EDDIE (Nev.) Jimmy Durante's song-and-dance partner for 57 years, and a Las Vegas resident for over a decade, suffered a stroke in '74, aged 78, and was at last report "improving." Onscreen from 1930. IN: *Roadhouse Nights,* more.

JACKSON, EUGENE (S. Cal.) The hair that stood straight up, making "Pineapple" such a memorable delight in "Our Gang" in the '20s, is all gone, but the endearing smile remains. This you know if you saw him in the regular role of "Uncle Lou" in the now-departed TV series *Julia.* The actor lives in Compton with his wife of many years, Sue; they have a grown son and daughter, Gene III and Hazel Lee, and a teenage daughter, Sue Carol. Besides running a stage workshop there for musically inclined youngsters, he does TV guest appearances and commercials. Onscreen from 1925. IN: *Little Annie Rooney, Hearts in Dixie, Dixiana, Sporting Blood, Sporting Chance, The Lady's from Kentucky,* more.

JACKSON, FREDA (Eng.) Character. Onscreen from 1942. IN: *Henry V, Great Expectations, No Room at the Inn, Bhowani Junction, The Flesh Is Weak, A Tale of Two Cities, The Shadow of the Cat, Tom Jones, House at the End of the World,* more.

JACKSON, GLENDA (Eng.) Star. Won Best Actress Oscars in *Women in Love* and *A Touch of Class.* Nominated in the same category in *Sunday Bloody Sunday, Hedda.* Onscreen from 1966. IN: *The Persecution and Assassination of Jean-Paul Marat . . ., Negatives, The Music Lovers, The Boy Friend; Mary, Queen of Scots; The Triple Echo, A Bequest to the Nation, The Devil Is a Woman, The Maids, The Romantic Englishwoman, Hedda,* more.

JACKSON, GORDON (Eng.) Support. Onscreen from 1942. IN: *The Foreman Went to France, The Captive Heart, Tight Little Island, Happy Go Lovely, Abandon Ship, Tunes of Glory, Greyfriars' Bobby, Mutiny on the Bounty, The Great Escape, The Ipcress File, Danger Route, The Prime of Miss Jean Brodie,* more.

JACKSON, KATE (S. Cal.) Leading lady. Onscreen in the '70s. IN: *Night of Dark Shadows, Limbo,* more.

JACKSON, LEONARD (N.Y.) Black character star. Onscreen in the '70s. IN: *Super Spook, Blood Couple,* more.

JACKSON, MARY (S. Cal.) Character. Onscreen from 1968. IN: *Targets, Airport, Wild Rovers, Our Time,* more.

JACKSON, SAMMY (S. Cal.) Support. Onscreen from 1965. IN: *None But the Brave, The Night of the Grizzly, The Fastest Guitar Alive, Norwood, The $1,000,000 Duck,* more.

JACKSON, SHERRY (S. Cal.) Leading lady; former juvenile. Onscreen from 1950. IN: *The Breaking Point, The Miracle of Our Lady of Fatima, The Lion and the Horse, Trouble Along the Way, Come Next Spring, Wild on the Beach, Gunn, The Silent Treatment, The Mini-Skirt Mob,* more.

JACOBI, DEREK (Eng.) Support. Onscreen from 1965. IN: *Othello, Three Sisters, The Odessa File,* more.

JACOBI, LOU (S. Cal.) Character. Onscreen from 1956. IN: *A Kid for Two Farthings, The Diary of Anne Frank, Song Without End, Irma La Douce, The Last of the Secret Agents, Penelope,* more.

JACOBSSON, ULLA (Swe.) Leading lady. Onscreen in the '50s. IN: *One Summer of Happiness, Smiles of a Summer Night, Crime and Punishment, Love Is a Ball, Zulu, The Heroes of Telemark,* more.

JACOBY, SCOTT (S. Cal.) Juvenile. Came to prominence on TV in special dramas such as *That Summer.* Onscreen in 1976. IN: *The Little Girl Who Lives Down the Lane.*

JACQUES, HATTIE (Eng.) Character. Onscreen from the '40s. IN: *Chance of a Lifetime, Oliver Twist, Nicholas Nickleby, The Spider and the Fly, The Gay Lady, The Adventures of Sadie, Carry On Sergeant, Carry On Nurse, School for Scoundrels, Make Mine Mink, The Bobo,* more.

JAECKEL, RICHARD (S. Cal.) Costar; former juvenile. Nominated for Best Supporting Actor Oscar in *Sometimes a Great Notion*. Onscreen from 1944. IN: *Guadalcanal Diary, Wing and a Prayer, Battleground, Sands of Iwo Jima, The Sea Hornet, My Son John; Come Back, Little Sheba; Cowboy, The Naked and the Dead, Flaming Star, The Gallant Hours, Four for Texas, Nightmare in the Sun, The Dirty Dozen, The Devil's Brigade, Chisum, Chosen Survivors, Ulzana's Raid, The Drowning Pool, Walking Tall Part II, Grizzly*, more.

JAFFE, SAM (S. Cal.) Character. Nominated for Best Supporting Actor Oscar in *The Asphalt Jungle*. Onscreen from 1934. IN: *We Live Again, The Scarlet Empress, Lost Horizon, Gunga Din, 13 Rue Madeleine, Gentleman's Agreement, Accused, Rope of Sand, The Day the Earth Stood Still, I Can Get It for You Wholesale, Ben-Hur, A Guide for the Married Man, The Great Bank Robbery, The Dunwich Horror, Bedknobs and Broomsticks*, more.

JAGGER, DEAN (S. Cal.) Character. Won Best Supporting Actor Oscar in *12 O'Clock High*. Onscreen from 1929. IN: *Handcuffed, You Belong to Me, Wings in the Dark, Thirteen Hours by Air, Pepper, Star for a Night, Brigham Young—Frontiersman, Western Union, The Men in Her Life, Valley of the Sun, Sister Kenny, Pursued, Driftwood, C-Man, My Son John, Executive Suite, White Christmas, Bad Day at Black Rock, Three Brave Men, The Nun's Story, Elmer Gantry, Jumbo, Firecreek, Smith!, The Kremlin Letter, Vanishing Point*, more.

JAGGER, MICK (Eng.) Rock star. Onscreen from 1969. IN: *Ned Kelly; Performance; Ladies and Gentlemen, the Rolling Stones.*

JAMES, CLAIRE (S. Cal.) The knockout who was Alura in the serial *Jack Armstrong*, and had been one of director Busby Berkeley's wives as well as a member of Warners' "Navy Blues" Sextette, is still a fine-looking woman and works constantly—as an extra. Onscreen from 1940. IN: *Navy Blues*, more.

JAMES, CLIFTON (S. Cal.) Character. Onscreen from 1957. IN: *The Strange One, Experiment in Terror, David and Lisa, Black Like Me, The Happening, The Caper of the Golden Bulls, Cool Hand Luke, Will Penny, Rancho Deluxe, From Hong Kong with Love*, more.

JAMES, EMRYS (Eng.) Support. Onscreen from 1963. IN: *Darling*, more.

JAMES, HARRY (Nev.) The famous bandleader, a Las Vegas resident, is still to be seen and heard at the better nightclubs across the country. Onscreen from 1942. IN: *Private Buckaroo, Springtime in the Rockies, Best Foot Forward, Two Sisters and a Sailor, Bathing Beauty, If I'm Lucky, Carnegie Hall, The Benny Goodman Story, The Big Beat, Ladies' Man*, more.

JAMES, OLGA (S. Cal.) Black singer-actress. Onscreen in 1954. IN: *Carmen Jones.*

JAMES, SHEILA (S. Cal.) Support. Onscreen from 1953. IN: *Those Redheads from Seattle, Seven Brides for Seven Brothers, Teenage Rebel*, more.

JAMES, SIDNEY (Eng.) Character. Onscreen from the '40s. IN: *Last Holiday, The Lavender Hill Mob, The Assassin, The Detective, Crest of the Wave, Trapeze, The Iron Petticoat, The Sheriff of Fractured Jaw, Too Many Crooks, Campbell's Kingdom, The Pure Hell of St. Trinian's, No Place Like Homicide, Carry On Cleo, Bless This House*, more. (Died 1976.)

JAMESON, JOYCE (S. Cal.) Leading lady. Onscreen from 1955. IN: *Gang Busters, Tip on a Dead Jockey, The Apartment, The Balcony, The Comedy of Terrors, Good Neighbor Sam, The Split*, more.

JAMESON, PAULINE (Eng.) Support. Onscreen from 1948. IN: *Esther Waters, The Queen of Spades, The Millionairess, Crooks Anonymous*, more.

JANIS, CONRAD (N.Y.) Yesteryear's boy-next-door now plays, in his late 40s (b. 1928), bald business men and senators, on TV (*Virginia Hill*) and in movies. Onscreen from 1945. IN: *Snafu, Margie, The Brasher Doubloon, That Hagen Girl, Beyond Glory, Keep It Cool, Airport 1975, The Happy Hooker*, more.

JANNEY, LEON (N.Y.) Character; former juvenile star. Onscreen from 1929. IN: "Our Gang," *Father's Son, Courage, Old English, Doorway to Hell, Penrod and Sam, Police Court, Should Ladies Behave?, Son of Mine, The Last Mile, Charly*, more.

JANSSEN, DAVID (S. Cal.) Costar. Onscreen from 1946. IN: *Swamp Fire* (teen role), *Yankee Buccaneer, The Private War of Major Benson, Francis in the Navy, Away All Boats, Lafayette Escadrille, King of the Roaring Twenties, Ring of Fire, My Six Loves, Warning Shot, The Shoes of the Fisherman, Generation, Where It's At, Marooned, Once Is Not Enough, The Swiss Conspiracy*, more.

JANUARY, LOIS (S. Cal.) Character; former leading lady. Onscreen from 1934. IN: *By Can-*

dlelight, Affair of Susan, Society Fever, Rogue of the Range, Lightnin' Bill Carson, The Trusted Outlaw, Courage of the West, The Little Shepherd of Kingdom Come, more.

JARMAN, CLAUDE, JR. (N. Cal.) The blond Tennessee youngster, winner of a special Oscar in *The Yearling,* his debut movie, made 11 more pictures before retiring from the screen after 1956's *The Great Locomotive Chase.* Today, in his 40s (b. 1934), a dynamic, fast-talking man, he is manager of the San Francisco Opera House. But he wears many other hats. He holds the nonsalaried position of vice-chairman and treasurer of the San Francisco Film Festival. Previously, from '67, on the appointment after the city's mayor, he had served as Director of the Festival and had guided it from an insecure status into one of the most prestigious events of its kind in the world. He had earlier received his degree at Vanderbilt University, served in the Navy, and become a public relations expert. He has also been for almost a decade a partner in a San Francisco film production company, Medion, Inc. This firm has made over 100 films—documentaries, TV commercials, major political campaign films, and the feature-length rock-music movie *Fillmore* (he was executive producer). He has also lately assisted in founding Tucson's annual Western Film Festival. Round-faced, charmingly unflappable, and suggestive of a slightly older Jon Voight, the former actor has been married twice. By his first marriage, which ended in divorce, he has three children. He and his present wife, Vanessa (married since '68), have two little girls—the first adopted, the second born in '72. Onscreen from 1946. IN: *The Sun Comes Up, Roughshod, Intruder in the Dust, Rio Grande, Hangman's Knot, Fair Wind to Java,* more.

JARMIN, JILL/formerly JARMYN (S. Cal.) Leading lady. Onscreen from 1955. IN: *Lay That Rifle Down, War Drums, Tarzan's Fight for Life,* more.

JAROSLOW, RUTH (N.Y.) Character. IN: *Harvey Middleman, Fireman.*

JASON, MITCHELL (N.Y.) Support. IN: *The Heartbreak Kid,* more.

JASON, RICK (S. Cal.) Leading man. Onscreen from 1953. IN: *Sombrero, The Lieutenant Wore Skirts, The Wayward Bus, Sierra Baron, Color Me Dead,* more.

JASON, SYBIL (S. Cal.) In the '30s she was Warners' tiny brunette answer to 20th Century-Fox's Shirley Temple. Finally, in 1940's *The Blue Bird,* the second picture in which she had acted with Temple (first, *The Little Princess*),

the little freckle-face nosed out such competition as May Robson to win the New York Critics' award as the year's Best Supporting Actress. You will find the silver tray commemorating this performance, as an adorable Cockney lackey—and her last movie role—on the mantel above the fireplace in her English-style home in Hollywood today. Yesterday's juvenile star, still a vivacious, petite (5') brunette with a British accent, lives there with her scriptwriter husband of two decades, Anthony Drake, and their only child, teenage daughter Toni. Kinetic, and suggestive of a youngish Sylvia Sidney—she is in her 40s (b. 1929)—Sybil attributes the abrupt end to her career to "circumstances." In '41 the studio sent their moppet star on a worldwide personal appearance tour that, on December 7, found her in Johannesburg, South Africa, with no possible chance to return to America. The irony of it is that she was born in Capetown, where her parents still lived. (An older sister had taken Sybil to England years before, where she got her into movies, and almost immediately to Hollywood.) Sybil remained there with her parents throughout the war years, and only in '47 was she able to get on a plane that would take her as far as Canada. Though an American citizen (since '37), she had been born a British subject and found herself ensnarled in red tape and denied readmission to the States, until former employer Jack Warner and Louella Parsons prevailed upon her behalf. Back in Hollywood, she found no work except in a little-theater production of *The Wizard of Oz*—where she met Anthony Drake. "I had lived such a sheltered life before I married Tony," she says, "that he had to teach me how to cook and keep house." To this, he adds, "I also had to iron her blouse for her before our first date." But housekeeping, the P.T.A., and Beverly Hills Women's Club activities became—by happenstance—her new career. Lately, she has been doing a series of benefit lectures on motion pictures and acting for Senior Citizen groups. "It never ceases to amaze me," she says, "how they hold one in such special regard when all the time one is thrilled by the length of their memories. The things they bring you to sign! Besides the usual photographs and music sheets that I'm on, one gentleman had a beautiful case. Inside, it was lined with plush, and centered in an indentation was a small photograph autographed in my childish handwriting that I had sent him originally years ago. He had me re-sign it, then very carefully placed it back in its case, and I saw him in the audience each of the three nights I was appearing at that particular date." Of the legion of fans that obviously remembers, Sybil says, "Bless them all!" She also says: "What I'd love to be is a second banana on a TV series. I can't wait to act again. Every single second of my acting career was the high point of my life. I'm an insomniac to this day because, then, I was so anxious to get to the studio to *play* the next day." Onscreen from 1935. IN: *Little Big Shot, Barnacle Bill, I Found Stella Parrish, The Singing Kid, The Captain's Kid, Comet Over Broadway, The Great O'Malley, Woman Doctor,* more.

JAYNE, SUSAN (N.Y.) Juvenile. Onscreen in the '70s. IN: *Baxter, The Rivals, To Find a Man,* more.

JAYSTON, MICHAEL (Eng.) Leading man. Onscreen from 1968. IN: *A Midsummer Night's Dream, Cromwell, Nicholas and Alexandra, A Bequest to the Nation, Tales That Witness Madness, The Homecoming, Craze, The Internecine Project,* more.

JEAN, GLORIA (S. Cal.) In a small house in Canoga Park, this former child star gives her teenage son, Angelo, breakfast and an off-to-school kiss, sees to the last-minute needs of her elderly mother, then drives to a manufacturing company in Van Nuys, a few miles away. There, for the next eight hours, she operates a switchboard, takes messages, smiles prettily, and assists all who approach her receptionist's cubicle. It is perhaps 15 minutes from this desk to Universal where, for six years (1939–45) and 18 musical movies, her star shone so brightly. But, like the nearest quasar, Universal—and the other studios where she worked—is millions of light years away. She still sings beautifully—as a member of the choir at Canoga Park's Church of the Valley. But Hollywood calls her "uncastable" now: a bit overweight, not young enough for ingenue roles (b. 1928), too baby-faced for older roles. Her life savings wiped out (by Uncle Sam; someone erred in figuring her childhood income tax), she has stood in unemployment lines, worked as a restaurant hostess, had a bit role in a Jerry Lewis picture, suffered a disastrous one-year marriage (her husband, who worked for the Italian government in Los Angeles, went back to Italy before their son was born and didn't return), and shed a tear or two over the way the beautiful dream turned sour. "My advice to young stars today is, make sure you have some other skill to fall back on," she says. "Be prepared for the day Hollywood may reject you." Does the hope of a return to show business linger on? It does, she admits. "I can still act, I can still sing," she volunteers, adding with no apparent bitterness, "but no one, not even the people I had helped, will even see me any more." Onscreen from 1939. IN: *The Under-Pup, If I Had My Way, A Little Bit of Heaven, Never Give a Sucker an Even Break, When Johnny Comes Marching Home, Get Hep to Love, The Ghost Catchers, Destiny, I'll Re-* member *April, Copacabana, An Old-Fashioned Girl, I Surrender Dear,* more, including 1961's *Ladies' Man,* her most recent to date.

JEANMAIRE (Fr.) Sometimes billed Renee or Zizi Jeanmaire, the ballerina-actress lives in Paris and has been long married to choreographer Roland Petit and long retired. But early in '75, it was announced that she would dance again, after 15 years, in the Paris Opera Ballet's *The Fantastic Symphony,* to be staged by her husband. A bit later, though, came the news that a sprained tendon had forced her to withdraw, but that she still hoped to resume her career. Onscreen from 1952. IN: *Hans Christian Andersen, Anything Goes, Folies Bergere, Black Tights.*

JEANS, ISABEL (Eng.) Character; former leading lady. Onscreen from the '20s. IN: *Downhill, Tovarich, Fools for Scandal, Garden of the Moon, Secrets of an Actress, Good Girls Go to Paris, Man About Town, Suspicion, Gigi, Heavens Above, The Magic Christian,* more.

JEFFORD, BARBARA (Eng.) Leading lady. Onscreen from 1967. IN: *Ulysses, The Bofors Gun, The Shoes of the Fisherman, Lust for a Vampire,* more.

JEFFREY, PETER (Eng.) Support. Onscreen from 1964. IN: *Becket, The Abominable Dr. Phibes, Dr. Phibes Rises Again, The Odessa File,* more.

JEFFREYS, ANNE (S. Cal.) If ever a star had an all-media career, it is she—now only in her early 50s (b. 1923) and still a great blonde beauty. A famous John Robert Powers model, she has played leads in 47 movies; giving up her screen career after 1948's *Return of the Badmen,* she has been seen but once since, in 1962's *Boys' Night Out.* She has sung grand opera—*La Boheme* with the New York City Opera Co., *La Tosca* with the Los Angeles Philharmonic and at Brooklyn's Academy of Music. She has starred in 28 plays, on Broadway and on tour—musicals, comedies, light operas (*Bitter Sweet; Kiss Me, Kate; Happy Anniversary, The Most Happy Fella,* etc.). On TV she has done more than 100 guest-star roles (*Police Story* in '75 for instance); costarred in one successful series (*Topper,* in 1952–53, with husband Robert Sterling) and one unsuccessful series (1972's *The Delphi Bureau*); and in 1971 she was a regular, as a femme fatale, in the soap opera *Bright Promise.* First married to Navy Captain Joseph Serena in '45 (the marriage was annulled), she has been married since '51 to former actor Robert Sterling, whose previous wife was Ann Sothern. They have frequently costarred onstage as well as on TV. Now successful as a computer expert, the former actor took time out from this career in '72 to appear with his wife in an episode of ABC-TV's *Love, American Style*. He has no intention, however, of resuming his acting career fulltime. The Sterlings have three sons—Jeffreys and Robert, young adults now, and high-schooler Tyler. They live in Westwood Village. Onscreen from 1942. IN: *X Marks the Spot, I Married an Angel, Calling Wild Bill Elliott; Dick Tracy, Detective; Nevada, Those Endearing Young Charms, Dillinger, Step Lively, Sing Your Way Home, Vacation in Reno, Step by Step, Trail Street, Riffraff*, more.

JEFFRIES, FRAN (S. Cal.) Singer-actress. Onscreen from 1958. IN: *The Buccaneer, The Pink Panther, Sex and the Single Girl, A Talent for Loving*, more.

JEFFRIES, LANG (It.) Leading man. Onscreen from 1961. IN: *The Revolt of the Slaves, Sword of the Empire, The Spy Strikes Silently, The Hotheads, Mission Stardust*, more.

JEFFRIES, LIONEL (Eng.) Character. Onscreen from 1952. IN: *High Terrace, Bhowani Junction, Lust for Life, The Nun's Story, Two-Way Stretch, Fanny, The Notorious Landlady, Murder Ahoy, The Spy with a Cold Nose, Camelot, Those Fantastic Flying Fools, Chitty Chitty Bang Bang, Who Slew Auntie Roo?, Royal Flash*, more.

JENKINS, JACKIE "BUTCH" (Tex.) During WW II and just after, when he was between the ages of 5 and 10, "Butch" Jenkins was America's authentic "little brother." Enormous freckles; guileless grin; bright, natural, humorous, sensitive. (How complex and deep was the expression on his kindergarten face in *The Human Comedy*, his first picture, as he watched an old Negro hobo on a railroad flatcar ride slowly by while playing on his harmonica the plaintive "Weep no more my lady . . . ") He also had straw-colored hair that never saw a comb, a genius for malapropisms, and a stammer—and he still has all three. At five, his announced ambition was to become a "real cowboy." He almost made it. Today, in Quinlan, Tex., 60 miles east of Dallas, in a modern-rustic cedar house beside Lake Tawakoni, there lives a good-looking, rugged (6'3", 195-pound) outdoorsman named Jack B. Jenkins. Anyone would recognize him immediately as "Butch." He's in his late 30s (b. 1938), and now for more than a decade he has been owner of the East Texas Water Systems. ("I pump water out of Lake Tawakoni, process it, put it up in storage tanks, and pipe it around the lake—it has a shoreline of about 1200 miles—to the different developments.") He also owns water systems

on other lakes, three self-service car washes, and a pig farm called the "J&B Beautiful Pig Farm." ("Butch" Jenkins still lives.) "I will assure you," he laughs, "you've really got to love pigs to go in the pig business . . . unless you're like a silent partner and can live far away from the odor." He also likes dogs (keeps seven) and travel. Six months of the year, during his "off" season, he says, he boards his motorcycle and heads for Mexico or Baja for some deep-sea fishing. Hollywood? "I visit there occasionally—though I never see the people I worked with—and I'm really glad I'm out of there. I visited MGM about three years ago and it was just like a morgue. No, I don't have any desire to get back into movies again." Divorced, he lives alone in his three-bedroom house, furnished with early American antiques and equipped with a pool. His former wife, remarried, lives in Dallas with their three daughters—Deborah Ann, Christina Elizabeth, and Tammy Lynette, all still under age 16. He keeps an apartment in Dallas so that he can see them often. Commuting between Dallas and the lake, he runs his business via the phone in his car. His obvious business success contradicts the reason he gives for dropping out of the State University of Iowa before getting his business degree: "I was just too goddam dumb." At his rustic hideaway, one may safely assume the well-off young man does not lack female companionship. A while back, a New York editor wrote asking for current information on his life. Instead of writing (which he hates to do), the former actor made a tape for him, starting early on a given evening ("I'm sittin' here relaxin', drinkin' Scotch, in front of a big log fire . . ."). He had a leg of lamb going on the rotisserie outside, he said. He would stop the tape, tend it, and resume. Then, "Here comes some comp'ny. I'll be talkin' into this thing later . . . I guess." And finally, "It's now about four hours later. There's a lady here with me. (A giggle in the background.) She's very attractive . . . got a lot of polka dots on right now . . . great big bosoms. (She giggles.) . . . And, as for what we're doin' right now, ah guess you might call it an X-rated scene." (Jackie "Butch" Jenkins *does* still live—he just calls himself Jack now.) Onscreen from 1943. IN: *National Velvet, An American Romance, Our Vines Have Tender Grapes, Boys Ranch, Little Mr. Jim, My Brother Talks to Horses, Summer Holiday, Stork Bites Man, The Big City, The Bride Goes Wild*.

JENKINS, MEGS (Eng.) Character. Onscreen from 1939. IN: *Green for Danger, The Brothers, The History of Mr. Polly, Ivanhoe, Saraband, Personal Affair, No Place for Jennifer, The Cruel Sea, The Innocents, Bunny Lake Is Missing, Oliver!*, more.

JENNINGS, CLAUDIA (S. Cal.) Leading lady. Onscreen in the '70s. IN: *Jud, The Single Girls, Gator Bait, Truck Stop Women*, more.

JENNINGS, WAYLON (Tenn.) C&W star. Onscreen in 1974. IN: *Moonrunners*.

JENS, SALOME (N.Y.) Leading lady. Onscreen from 1961. IN: *Angel Baby, The Fool Killer, Seconds, Violent Journey; Me, Natalie;* more.

JENSEN, KAREN (S. Cal.) Leading lady. Onscreen from the '60s. IN: *Out of Sight, The Ballad of Josie,* more.

JENSEN, STERLING (N.Y.) Character. Onscreen from the '60s. IN: *Guns of the Trees,* more.

JENSON, ROY (S. Cal.) Character. Onscreen from 1964. IN: *Law and the Lawless, Harper, Red Tomahawk, Waterhole No. 3, Face to the Wind,* more.

JEPSON, HELEN (N.J.) The great, blonde Metropolitan Opera soprano is now in her 70s (b. 1905), attends the opera regularly, and is always a guest attraction at the Met's special events. Married to Walter Dellera (her second marriage), she is a grandmother and lives in Orange. A voice teacher at Fairleigh Dickinson University after her starring days, she has lately done volunteer work as a speech therapist in her hometown's Cerebral Palsy Rehabilitation Center. Onscreen in 1938. IN: *The Goldwyn Follies.*

JERGENS, ADELE (S. Cal.) Leading lady. Onscreen from 1944. IN: *Black Arrow* (serial), *Tonight and Every Night, A Thousand and One Nights, Down to Earth, I Love Trouble, The Prince of Thieves, Ladies of the Chorus, The Fuller Brush Man, The Crime Doctor's Diary, The Treasure of Monte Cristo, Pirate Ship, Abbott & Costello Meet the Invisible Man, Somebody Loves Me, The Cobweb, Strange Lady in Town, Girls in Prison,* more, including 1958's *The Lonesome Trail,* her most recent to date. (See Glenn Langan.)

JERGENS, DIANE (S. Cal.) Married to musician Randy Sparks, the former ingenue is the mother of a daughter born in '70. She has been inactive in show business since the early '60s. Onscreen from 1954. IN: *The Bob Mathias Story, Teenage Rebel, Desk Set; Sing, Boy, Sing; High School Confidential, Island of Lost Women, Teenage Millionaire,* more.

JESSEL, GEORGE (S. Cal.) In 1975, at 77, the four-times married and divorced (last in '42) ac-tor-producer published his (second) autobiography, *The World I Lived In,* and several well-known Hollywood women wish he hadn't. It "might as easily have been called 'The Beds I Slept In,'" said *Variety*. His first autobiography, which appeared in '43, was *So Help Me.* Onscreen from 1911. IN: *Widow at the Races* (with Eddie Cantor), *Private Izzy Murphy, Ginsberg the Great, George Washington Cohen, Lucky Boy, Happy Days, Four Jills in a Jeep, Valley of the Dolls, The Busy Body, The Phynx,* more.

JOBERT, MARLENE (Fr.) Leading lady. Onscreen from 1966. IN: *Masculine Feminine, The Thief of Paris, Rider on the Rain, Catch Me a Spy, Ten Days' Wonder,* more.

JOHANN, ZITA (N.Y.) The beauty from Hungary, and still a good-looking woman in her 70s (b. 1904), has been married and divorced three times, has no children, lives on a country estate on the Hudson, and devotes herself to charitable works, particularly those concerned with helping the physically handicapped. Onscreen from 1931. IN: *The Struggle, The Mummy, Tiger Shark, The Man Who Dared, Luxury Liner, The Sin of Nora Moran,* and 1934's *Grand Canary,* her last.

JOHANSSON, INGEMAR (Swe.) Fat now, the once-handsome prizefighter-actor owns and operates a bar in Stockholm. Onscreen in 1960. IN: *All the Young Men.*

JOHN, ELTON (Eng.) Rock star. Onscreen in 1975. IN: *Tommy.*

JOHN, ROSAMUND (Eng.) This greatly popular star, in her 60s now (b. 1913), gave up her movie career in '56 after *Operation Murder.* Onscreen from 1934. IN: *The Secret of the Loch, The Gentle Sex, The Lamp Still Burns, The Tawny Pipit, The Way to the Stars, Fame Is the Spur, When the Bough Breaks, Never Look Back,* more.

JOHNS, GLYNIS (Eng.) Costar. Nominated for Best Supporting Actress Oscar in *The Sundowners.* Onscreen from 1938. IN: *South Riding, Prison Without Bars, The Invaders, The Adventures of Tartu, An Ideal Husband, Mine Own Executioner, Miranda, No Highway in the Sky, The Promoter, The Sword and the Rose, Rob Roy, Personal Affair, The Beachcomber, The Court Jester; Another Time, Another Place; The Chapman Report, Papa's Delicate Condition, Mary Poppins, Lock Up Your Daughters, Under Milk Wood,* more.

JOHNS, HARRIETTE (Eng.) Support. Onscreen from 1944. IN: *An Ideal Husband, Ed-*

ward My Son, Meet Mr. Callahan, The Two-Headed Spy, more.

JOHNS, MERVYN (Eng.) Oak-sturdy in his 70s (b. 1899), the Welsh character actor-father of Glynis retired to a farm in South Africa a decade ago. Since his wife's death, though, he has closed up his house there and returned to London, announcing he was resuming his career. Onscreen from 1934. IN: *Lady in Danger, Jamaica Inn, Convoy, Dead of Night, The Captive Heart, Quartet* ("The Kite" episode), *Edward My Son, Tony Draws a Horse, A Christmas Carol, The Master of Ballantrae, The Horse's Mouth, Romeo and Juliet, Moby Dick, The Sundowners, Day of the Triffids, The Victors, The Heroes of Telemark,* more.

JOHNSON, ARCH (S. Cal.) Character. Onscreen from 1956. IN: *Somebody Up There Likes Me, Gun Glory, G.I. Blues, Sullivan's Empire, The Liberation of Lord Byron Jones, The Cheyenne Social Club,* more.

JOHNSON, ARTE (S. Cal.) Comedian. Onscreen from 1960. IN: *The Subterraneans, The Third Day, The President's Analyst,* more.

JOHNSON, BEN (S. Cal.) Costar. Won Best Supporting Actor Oscar in *The Last Picture Show.* Onscreen from 1948. IN: *Three Godfathers, She Wore a Yellow Ribbon, Mighty Joe Young, Wagonmaster, Rio Grande, Shane, War Drums, Ten Who Dared, One-Eyed Jacks, Major Dundee, The Wild Bunch, Hang 'Em High, The Undefeated, Junior Bonner, Dillinger, The Train Robbers, The Sugarland Express, Bite the Bullet, Hustle,* more.

JOHNSON, CELIA (Eng.) Character; former costar. Nominated for Best Actress Oscar in *Brief Encounter.* In her late 60s (b. 1908), she is rarely active on the screen now. Just twice has she been seen in the past two decades—in *The Good Companions* ('57) and *The Prime of Miss Jean Brodie* ('69), in which, in wimple and of stern visage, she was the unfeeling headmistress and not at all reminiscent of the English housewife who loved Trevor Howard in *Brief Encounter.* Onstage in London, in '75, she starred in the title role of *The Dame of Sark.* Married to Peter Fleming, she lives in Nettlebed, Oxon. Onscreen from 1942. IN: *In Which We Serve, The Happy Breed, The Astonished Heart, I Believe in You, The Captain's Paradise, The Holly and the Ivy, A Kid for Two Farthings,* more.

JOHNSON, DON (S. Cal.) Leading man. Onscreen from 1970. IN: *The Magic Garden of Stanley Sweetheart, Zachariah, A Boy and His Dog,* more.

JOHNSON, DOTTS (N.Y.) Black character. Onscreen from 1948. IN: *Paisan, No Way Out, The Joe Louis Story, The Grissom Gang,* more.

JOHNSON, FRED (Eng.) Character. Onscreen from 1942. IN: *Native Land, Adam and Evelyn, Martin Luther, The Saint's Return, The Naked Heart, The Brides of Dracula, Scream of Fear, Von Richthofen and Brown,* more.

JOHNSON, HELEN (S. Cal.) (See Judith Wood.)

JOHNSON, LAMONT (S. Cal.) Actor-director. Onscreen from 1952. IN: *Retreat, Hell!, The Glory Brigade, The Human Jungle, Please Murder Me, The Brothers Rico,* more

JOHNSON, LARAINE (S. Cal.) Laraine Day's real name, which she used in Westerns and B's before her MGM contract. Onscreen in 1938. IN: *Scandal Street, Painted Desert,* more. (See Laraine Day.)

JOHNSON, MELODIE (S. Cal.) Leading lady. Onscreen from 1968. IN: *Coogan's Bluff, Gaily Gaily; Rabbit, Run; The Moonshine War,* more.

JOHNSON, PAGE (N.Y.) Support. Onscreen from 1967. IN: *Passages from James Joyce's Finnegans Wake,* more.

JOHNSON, RAFER (S. Cal.) Black leading man. Onscreen from 1961. IN: *Pirates of Tortuga, Wild in the Country, The Sins of Rachel Cade, None But the Brave, Tarzan and the Great River, The Games, The Lion, The Last Grenade,* more.

JOHNSON, RICHARD (Eng.) Costar. Onscreen from 1951. IN: *Captain Horatio Hornblower, Saadia, Never So Few, The Haunting, The Other Woman, Operation Crossbow, The Amorous Adventures of Moll Flanders* (co-starred with Kim Novak, who became his wife and from whom he has since been divorced), *Khartoum, Deadlier Than the Male, Oedipus the King, Trajan's Column, Julius Caesar, Some Girls Do, Hennessy, Beyond the Door,* more.

JOHNSON, RUSSELL (S. Cal.) Leading man. Onscreen from 1952. IN: *For Men Only, Seminole, Back at the Front, It Came from Outer Space, Column South, Ma and Pa Kettle at Waikiki, Many Rivers to Cross, Attack of the Crab Monsters, A Distant Trumpet, The Greatest Story Ever Told,* more.

JOHNSON, VAN (N.Y.) Entering his 60s (b. 1916), and looking far younger, this great, freckled favorite of the '40s lives in a bachelor apartment on the East Side in Manhattan and still makes an occasional movie, such as 1973's *Eagles Over London,* filmed in Italy. He also appears frequently on TV; in '74 he costarred with Gloria Grahame and Walter Pidgeon in the TV-movie *The Girl on the Late Late Show* and did a *McMillan & Wife* episode. But for ten years his real career has been on the stage—in dinner theaters. The acknowledged "king of supper-theaterland," he plays the circuit 50 weeks a year, earning over $250,000 annually. He appears mostly in comedies (*6 Rms Rv Vu*) and musicals (*Bells Are Ringing, I Do! I Do!, The Music Man*). Of this career he says, "I'm happier than I've ever been. Now I don't do anything if I don't enjoy it." There has been no recurrence of the cancer for which he had two operations on his leg, in '63 and '65. A member of Dr. Norman Vincent Peale's Marble Collegiate Church in Manhattan, he credits the minister with rescuing him from despair at the time of his illness. Actively practicing the power of positive thinking, he says, "Now I start each day by 'painting a perfect picture'—and though I can never be certain that I've beaten cancer for good, I don't worry about it any more." His divorced wife, Evie, by whom he has a grown daughter—Schuyler (b. 1948)—lives in Beverly Hills still and has lately been on staff at the Wally Findlay Art Galleries there. Onscreen from 1940. IN: *Too Many Girls, Murder in the Big House, The War Against Mrs. Hadley, Dr. Gillespie's New Assistant, A Guy Named Joe, Two Girls and a Sailor, Thirty Seconds Over Tokyo, Weekend at the Waldorf, Easy to Wed; No Leave, No Love; Romance of Rosy Ridge, State of the Union, Command Decision, In the Good Old Summertime, Battleground, Duchess of Idaho, Plymouth Adventure, Remains to be Seen, The Caine Mutiny, Brigadoon, Miracle in the Rain, Action of the Tiger, Wives and Lovers; Where Angels Go, Trouble Follows; Yours, Mine and Ours; Battle Squadron, Spider on the Wall,* more.

JOHNSTON, ERNESTINE (N.Y.) Black support. Onscreen from 1968. IN: *Midnight Cowboy, A Lovely Way to Die, The Tiger Makes Out, The Great White Hope, Cotton Comes to Harlem, The Landlord, Johnny Got His Gun,* more.

JOHNSTON, JOHNNY (Ariz.) The singer lives in Phoenix, owns a plant manufacturing sporting goods, and sometimes talks of doing stage musicals on tour. The early '70s were years of tragedy for him. His four-year-old son died in his arms after a sudden bronchial attack. Also, his daughter, then not quite two, was seriously injured in an automobile accident and lay unconscious for weeks before beginning a slow recovery. And there were other crises: he and

his third wife, Carol, separated, and he himself underwent an operation for the removal of a lung tumor—mercifully, benign. But 1974 brought good news. His daughter by Kathryn Grayson, Patti Kate—happily married for several years to Bob Towers, a Los Angeles business man—made him a first-time grandfather, of a little girl. Onscreen from 1942. IN: *Sweater Girl, Priorities on Parade, Star-Spangled Rhythm, You Can't Ration Love, Unchained, Rock Around the Clock,* more.

JOHNSTON, JULANNE (Mich.) "She has everything," Douglas Fairbanks exulted of his princess in 1924's memorable *Thief of Bagdad.* "She's beautiful and she moves—let's just say she glides about. There's something sinuous about her that looks seductive. On top of that, she can act." So she flew on The Thief's magic carpet (in truth she didn't; that part was doubled) and on Hollywood's, for another ten years, through 1934's *The Scarlet Empress.* In 1931 she married a well-to-do electrical engineer, Don Rust, and moved with him to Michigan. They lived, and live still, happily ever after in Detroit. He, as well as she, is retired now—and the princess, remaining forever young on film, is in her 70s (b. 1906) and lovely yet. Onscreen from 1924. IN: *Aloma of the South Seas, Twinkletoes, Venus of Venice, Good Time Charley, Her Wild Oat; Oh, Kay!; Synthetic Sin, Smiling Irish Eyes, Strictly Modern, General Crack, Golden Dawn, Madam Satan,* more.

JOHNSTON, MARGARET (Eng.) Costar. Onscreen from 1940. IN: *The Prime Minister, Notorious Gentleman, A Man about the House, Portrait of Clare, The Magic Box; Lovers, Happy Lovers; The Model Murder Case, Life at the Top, The Psychopath, Sebastian,* more.

JOHNSTONE, WILLIAM (N.Y.) Character. Onscreen from the '50s. IN: *Titanic, Fallen Angel, Down Three Dark Streets,* more.

JOLLEY, I. STANFORD (S. Cal.) Character. Onscreen from 1940. IN: *Midnight Limited, Rolling Home to Texas, A Gentleman from Dixie, Corregidor, The Chinese Cat, Fighting Bill Carson, Dangers of the Canadian Mounted,* (and 13 other serials), *West of Dodge City, The Prince of Thieves, The Long Hot Summer, The Haunted Palace,* more.

JONES, ALLAN (N.Y.) Singer-actor. He is presently active onstage and in nightclubs. Onscreen from 1935. IN: *A Night at the Opera, Rose Marie, Showboat, A Day at the Races, The Firefly, Honeymoon in Bali, The Great Victor Herbert, The Boys from Syracuse, One Night in the Tropics, Moonlight in Havana,*

Crazy House, The Singing Sheriff, The Senorita from the West, Stage to Thunger Rock, A Swingin' Summer, more.

JONES, ANISSA (S. Cal.) The former juvenile actress (b. 1958), popular on TVs *Family Affair,* is a college student now and retired from acting. Onscreen in 1969. IN: *The Trouble with Girls.*

JONES, BARRY (Eng.) Character. Onscreen from 1931. IN: *Arms and the Man, Spring Cleaning, Seven Days to Noon, The Bad Lord Byron, The Clouded Yellow, Plymouth Adventure, Return to Paradise, Demetrius and the Gladiators, The Glass Slipper, Saint Joan, The 39 Steps, The Heroes of Telemark, Appointment with Venus,* more.

JONES, CAROLYN (S. Cal.) Costar. Nominated for Best Supporting Actress Oscar in *The Bachelor Party.* After 1969's *Color Me Dead,* she gave up acting to become a published novelist, but in '76 she announced the resumption of her movie career. Onscreen from 1952. IN: *The Turning Point, Off Limits, The Big Heat, House of Wax, Three Hours to Kill, The Seven Year Itch, Invasion of the Body Snatchers, The Tender Trap, The Man Who Knew Too Much, Baby Face Nelson, Marjorie Morningstar, King Creole, The Last Train from Gun Hill, Man in the Net, A Hole in the Head, Career, Sail a Crooked Ship, How the West was Won, A Ticklish Affair,* more.

JONES, CHARLOTTE (N.Y.) Character. IN: *Lovers and Other Strangers,* more.

JONES, CHRISTOPHER (S. Cal.) The leading man so reminiscent of James Dean has been inactive since the '70 release of *Ryan's Daughter*—in which much of his dialogue was dubbed by an English actor. Onscreen from 1968. IN: *Wild in the Streets, Chubasco, Three in the Attic, The Looking Glass War,* more.

JONES, DEAN (S. Cal.) Leading man. Onscreen from 1956. IN: *The Great American Pastime, These Wilder Years, Jailhouse Rock, Imitation General, Under the Yum Yum Tree, The New Interns, That Darn Cat, The Monkey's Uncle, Any Wednesday, The Ugly Dachshund, The Horse in the Gray Flannel Suit, The Love Bug, The $1,000,000 Duck, Snowball Express, Mr. Superinvisible,* more.

JONES, DICK(IE) (N. Cal.) The buckskinned lad from Texas, who was featured in dozens of Westerns in the '30s and '40s, and later starred, until '60, in the TV series *Buffalo Bill Jr.,* knew his own mind at 12. He said then: "When I finish high school I want to go to Agricultural College to study animal husbandry because I want to buy a ranch and then know how to run it." That is why he is to be found today on a working ranch, which he owns, not far from Salinas, where he lives with his wife, Betty. Married young, they have four grown children: twins Jeffrey and Jennifer (b. 1956), and Melody (b. 1950) and Ricky "Buck" (b. 1953). Still a ruggedly handsome, easily recognizable, youthful-looking man (b. 1927), this veteran of over 150 movies—and also the voice and model of Disney's *Pinocchio*—hasn't actively pursued his movie career in several years. But his photograph, meaning he is available for assignments, still appears in Hollywood's *Academy Players Directory.* In it he wears (what else?) buckskins. Onscreen from 1934. IN: *Little Men, Moonlight on the Prairie, Daniel Boone, Black Legion, Renfrew of the Royal Mounted, Wild Bill Hickok* (serial), *A Man to Remember, Young Mr. Lincoln, Destry Rides Again, Virginia City, Brigham Young—Frontiersman, The Howards of Virginia, Strawberry Roan, Rocky Mountain, Last of the Pony Riders, The Wild Dakotas,* more.

JONES, FREDDIE (Eng.) Support. Onscreen from 1968. IN: *The Bliss of Mrs. Blossom, Frankenstein Must Be Destroyed, Antony and Cleopatra, Sitting Target, Son of Dracula, In the Devil's Garden, Juggernaut,* more.

JONES, GEMMA (Eng.) Leading lady. Onscreen from 1971. IN: *The Devils,* more.

JONES, GRIFFITH (Eng.) Character; former leading man. Onscreen from 1932. IN: *The Faithful Heart, Escape Me Never, A Yank at Oxford, The Avengers, Henry V, Notorious Gentleman, The Wicked Lady, Miranda, Once Upon a Dream, The Sea Shall Not Have Them, Strangler's Web,* more.

JONES, HENRY (S. Cal.) Character. Onscreen from 1943. IN: *This Is the Army, The Bad Seed, Will Success Spoil Rock Hunter?, The Rise and Fall of Legs Diamond, Angel Baby, Never Too Late, Rascal, Butch Cassidy and the Sundance Kid, Angel in My Pocket; Rabbit, Run; The Cockeyed Cowboys of Calico County, Dirty Dingus Magee, The Outfit,* more.

JONES, JACK, (S. Cal.) Singer-actor. Son of Allan Jones and Irene Hervey. Onscreen in 1959. IN: *Juke Box Rhythm.*

JONES, JAMES EARL (N.Y.) Black star. Nominated for Best Actor Oscar in *The Great White Hope.* Onscreen from 1964. IN: *Dr. Strangelove, The Comedians, The End of the Road.*

JONES, JENNIFER (S. Cal.) Star. Won Best Actress Oscar in *The Song of Bernadette.* Nominated for Best Supporting Actress Oscar in *Since You Went Away*. Nominated for Best Actress Oscar in *Love Letters, Duel in the Sun*, and *Love Is a Many-Splendored Thing*. Onscreen in 1939 under her real name, Phyllis Isley. IN: *New Frontier* and *Dick Tracy's G-Men*. Onscreen from 1943 as Jennifer Jones, the name given her by producer David O. Selznick, whom she later married. IN: *Cluny Brown, Portrait of Jennie, We Were Strangers, Madame Bovary, Carrie, Gone to Earth, Ruby Gentry, Indiscretion of an American Wife, Beat the Devil; Good Morning, Miss Dove; The Man in the Gray Flannel Suit, The Barretts of Wimpole Street, A Farewell to Arms, Tender Is the Night, The Idol; Angel, Angel, Down We Go* (a.k.a. *Cult of the Damned*); *The Towering Inferno*.

JONES, L. Q. (S. Cal.) Character. Onscreen from 1955. IN: *Target Zero, Annapolis Story, Toward the Unknown, Men in War, Operation Mad Ball, The Naked and the Dead, Warlock, Ride the High Country, Hell Is for Heroes, The Wild Bunch, The Ballad of Cable Hogue, The Petty Story, White Line Fever*, more.

JONES, MARCIA MAE (S. Cal.) Brats and spiteful adolescents—in the '30s she had a monopoly on them, perhaps because she had a round freckled face and curly red hair. In her 50s (b. 1924), her face is round still, and freckled, but the hair is short, straight, and blonde. And when she gets the chance to work, in small roles on TV *(Streets of San Francisco, Barnaby Jones)* and in movies *(The Way We Were, The Spectre of Edgar Allan Poe)*, she is one of Hollywood's better character actresses. Onscreen from age 7, and in more than three dozen pictures, she dropped out after 1951's *Chicago Calling*, not returning for 17 years, until she played a minor role in *Rogue's Gallery*, which was followed by several on TV *(Peyton Place, Mr. Ed*, etc.). "For many years," she says, "I was attorney Greg Bautzer's PBX receptionist and he allowed me to work on TV in order to raise my sons." This was after her first marriage and before her second, to television writer Bill Davenport, which also ended in divorce, in '65. By her first husband, a merchant marine officer, she has two sons, both tall, dark-haired, good-looking young men. Her eldest, Robert Dennis Chic, was stage manager of TV's *The Dean Martin Show* and has been married for several years to Rosetta Cox, one of the show's original "Golddiggers." Her other son, Tim Jordan Chic, recently worked his way through Europe, seeing the world on his own. Before she moved back to Hollywood recently, the actress had lived several years at the beach in Venice, Calif., where she worked with the youth of that community in their Free Theatre, sometimes performing in their stage produc-

tions. Taking a candid look at herself as she is now, Marcia Mae says, "I am one of the child actresses who has survived, and I am happy. I feel younger today than I did when I played in *Heidi*, and who knows, I may make it back as a good character actress." But, at the moment, she laughs, "like most of the actors in Hollywood, I am out of work—and wondering whether I should get a steady job or continue on with my career. Time will tell. For now, I do a lot of charity work to occupy my time until I make the final decision about my career." Onscreen from 1931. IN: *The Champ, King of Jazz, These Three, Garden of Allah, The Life of Emile Zola, The Adventures of Tom Sawyer, Mad about Music, The Little Princess, Anne of Windy Poplars, The Old Swimmin' Hole, The Gang's All Here, Secrets of a Coed, Top Man, The Youngest Profession, Lady in the Death House, Snafu, Tucson, Daughter of Rosie O'-Grady*, more.

JONES, MARY (Eng.) Character. Onscreen from 1938. IN: *The Promise, Trottie True, Black Orchid, Fatal Journey, The Magic Box, Valley of Song, One Jump Ahead, A Time to Kill, Doublecross*, more.

JONES, PAUL (Eng.) Singer-actor. Onscreen from 1966. IN: *Privilege, Demons of the Mind, Superstars in Film Concert*, more.

JONES, PETER (Eng.) Character. Onscreen from 1944. IN: *Fanny by Gaslight, The Blue Lagoon, Time Gentlemen Please, The Browning Version, Miss Robin Hood, Private's Progress, School for Scoundrels, Charley Moon, Romanoff and Juliet*, more.

JONES, ROBERT EARL (N.Y.) Character actor-father of James Earl Jones. Onscreen from 1960. IN: *Wild River; One Potato, Two Potato; Terror in the City, Odds Against Tomorrow, The Sting*, more.

JONES, SAMANTHA (S. Cal.) Leading lady. Onscreen from 1967. IN: *Wait Until Dark, The Way We Live Now*, more.

JONES, SHIRLEY (S. Cal.) Costar. Won Best Supporting Actress Oscar in *Elmer Gantry*. Onscreen from 1955. IN: *Oklahoma!, Carousel, April Love, Never Steal Anything Small, Pepe, Two Rode Together, The Music Man, The Courtship of Eddie's Father, Bedtime Story, Fluffy, The Happy Ending, The Cheyenne Social Club*, more.

JORDAN, DOROTHY (S. Cal.) One of MGM's most popular leading ladies, she left the screen in '33 when she became the wife of *King Kong* producer, Merian C. Cooper, by whom she has a son, Major Richard Cooper, USAF, and two grown daughters. In the '50s, at the request of director John Ford—a family friend—she played supporting roles in three of his films: *The Sun Shines Bright*, *The Searchers* (her husband was also its executive producer), and *The Wings of Eagles*. Shortly before Merian Cooper's death in 1973, they had just completed a year's trip around the world visiting spots where he had been during his Air Force years and location sites of several of his early movies. Returning to their home in Coronado, where the actress still lives, she assisted him in completing his autobiography. In her 60s now (b. 1908), she does not anticipate a return to the screen. Onscreen from 1929. IN: *The Taming of the Shrew*, *Devil May Care*, *In Gay Madrid*, *Min and Bill*, *A Tailor-Made Man*, *Shipmates*, *The Beloved Bachelor*, *The Lost Squadron*, *The Wet Parade*, *Roadhouse Murder*, *Cabin in the Cotton*, *Bondage*, *Strictly Personal*, *One Man's Journey*, more.

JORDAN, JIM (S. Cal.) "Fibber McGee" retired in '61 when his beloved wife, Marian ("Molly"), died. But he found that idleness, at least for him, "Tain't funny." In recent months, Johnson's Wax, his old radio sponsor, came after him to do a series of TV commercials, and he said yes. He was asked to host a syndicated radio series, *Good Old Days of Radio*, and he found it impossible to refuse. Besides which, he operates a home remodeling business, and, with his son, Jim Jr., he owns a construction firm in Nevada. Now entering his silver-haired 80s (b. 1896), Jordan lives with his second wife in Beverly Hills and he's happy doing something "Fibber McGee" never believed in at all—keeping busy. Onscreen from 1937. IN: *This Way Please*, *Look Who's Laughing*, *Here We Go Again*, *Heavenly Days*.

JORDAN, PATRICK (Eng.) Character. Onscreen from the '50s. IN: *The Man Upstairs*, *Play Dirty*, *Too Late the Hero*, *The Last Escape*, *In the Devil's Garden*, more.

JORDAN, RICHARD (S. Cal.) Support. Onscreen in the '70s. IN: *Lawman*, *Valdez Is Coming*, more.

JORY, VICTOR (S. Cal.) Character. Onscreen from 1932. IN: *Pride of the Legion*, *Madame DuBarry*, *Escape from Devil's Island*, *Bulldog Drummond at Bay*, *First Lady*, *The Adventures of Tom Sawyer*, *Blackwell's Island*, *Gone With the Wind*, *The Light of the Western Stars*, *Charlie Chan in Rio*, *The Loves of Carmen*, *South of St. Louis*, *Caribou Trail*, *Son of Ali Baba*, *Blackjack Ketchum—Desperado*, *The Fugitive Kind*, *The Miracle Worker*, *Cheyenne Autumn*, *Jigsaw*, *Mackenna's Gold*, *Flap*, more.

JOSEPH, JACKIE (S. Cal.) Comedienne. Onscreen from the '60s. IN: *With Six You Get Egg Roll*, *The Cheyenne Social Club*, *Who's Minding the Mint?*, *A Guide for the Married Man*, more.

JOSLYN, ALLYN (S. Cal.) Retired and in his 70s (b. 1905), this great farceur lives in Beverly Hills with his wife, Dorothy, to whom he has been married since '35; they have a grown daughter. *Nightmare in the Sun* ('65) was the last of his 100-plus movies. Onscreen from 1937. IN: *They Won't Forget*, *Hollywood Hotel*, *The Shining Hour*, *Sweethearts*, *Only Angels Have Wings*, *Cafe Society*, *If I Had My Way*, *No Time for Comedy*, *The Great McGinty*, *Spring Parade*, *Bedtime Story*, *My Sister Eileen*, *The Wife Takes a Flyer*, *Heaven Can Wait*, *Dangerous Blondes*, *Col. Effingham's Raid*, *It Shouldn't Happen to a Dog*, *The Lady Takes a Sailor*, *Harriet Craig*, *I Love Melvin*, *Island in the Sky*, *You Can't Run Away from It*, *Public Pigeon No. 1*, more.

JOSTYN, JAY (S. Cal.) Character. Onscreen from 1947. IN: *Kiss of Death*, more.

JOURDAN, LOUIS (Fr.) Costar. Onscreen from 1939. IN: *La Vie de la Boheme*, *L'Arlesienne*, *The Paradine Case*, *Letter from an Unknown Woman*, *No Minor Vices*, *Madame Bovary*, *Anne of the Indies*, *The Happy Time*, *Three Coins in the Fountain*, *Julie*, *The Swan*, *Gigi*, *The Best of Everything*, *Can-Can*, *The V.I.P.s*, *Disorder*, *Made in Paris*, *A Flea in Her Ear*, *To Commit a Murder*, more.

JOY, LEATRICE (Conn.) Her long career, beginning in the teens, ostensibly ended with 1930's *Love Trader*. But she has occasionally come back for supporting roles—in Deanna Durbin's *First Love* ('39), in 1949's *Red Stallion in the Rockies*, and in 1951's *Love Nest*. First married (1920–24) to John Gilbert, father of her daughter, Leatrice Joy Gilbert, she was later married to Los Angeles business man William Spencer Hook and to A. W. Westermark. Now in her 70s (b. 1899), and a handsome-featured woman still, she lives in Riverside, and most recently visited Hollywood in '71 to attend the Los Angeles International Film Expo, where *The Ten Commandments*—one of her several starring pictures for DeMille—was screened and roundly applauded. Onscreen from 1915. IN: *Just a Wife*, *Bunty Pulls the Strings*, *A Tale of Two Worlds*, *Manslaughter*, *Ladies Must Live*, *The Silent Partner*, *Changing Husbands*, *Vanity*, *Man Made Women*, *The Bellamy Trial*, *Strong Boy*, *A Most Immoral Lady*, more.

JOYCE, BRENDA (N. Cal.) In '39, when she played Fern in *The Rains Came*, the gorgeous blonde U.C.L.A. coed was 20th Century-Fox's cinderella girl. She continued onscreen a full decade, finally playing Jane five times in "Tarzan" pix—and was the only actress to do the role with two different Tarzans, Weissmuller and Lex Barker. She bowed out after 1949's *Tarzan's Magic Fountain*. She had then been married several years to college sweetheart Owen Ward; their daughter, Pamela Ann, born in '43, was Hollywood's first wartime baby. Today, dark-haired and in her 50s (b. 1918), divorced for some time from Ward, the actress is a leading social figure in Carmel. She is now Mrs. Betty Bemis. Still avidly interested in sports, she keeps in shape by playing tennis regularly, and retains much of the All-American-girl look that made her so appealing onscreen. She also devotes much of her time to charitable works. Tyrone Power once called her "the girl with the undazzled charm." The description still applies—as does her determination never to act again. Onscreen from 1939. IN: *Here I Am a Stranger, Little Old New York, Maryland, Elsa Maxwell's Public Deb No. 1, Private Nurse, Right to the Heart, The Postman Didn't Ring, The Enchanted Forest, Little Giant, The Spider Woman Strikes Back, Danger Woman, Springtime in the Sierras, Shaggy*, more.

JOYCE, ELAINE (S. Cal.) Leading lady. Onscreen in the '70s. IN: *The Christine Jorgensen Story, How to Frame a Figg*, more.

JOYCE, JAMES (S. Cal.) Character. Onscreen from 1962. IN: *Too Late Blues, The Swimmer, A Woman Under the Influence*, more.

JOYCE, NATALIE (S. Cal.) Long a resident of San Diego, she is happily married and the mother of a grown son. Onscreen from the '20s. IN: *The Circus Ace, A Girl in Every Port, Dance Hall, Cock O' the Walk*, more.

JOYCE, YOOTHA (Eng.) Character. Onscreen from the '60s. IN: *Sparrows Can't Sing, The Pumpkin Eater, Having a Wild Weekend, A Man for All Seasons, Stranger in the House, Fragment of Fear, The Night Digger*, more.

JUDD, EDWARD (Eng.) Support. Onscreen from 1959. IN: *The Man Upstairs, The Day the Earth Caught Fire, It Takes a Thief, Stolen Hours, Strange Bedfellows, The Vengeance of She*, more.

JULIA, RAUL (S. Cal.) Supporting actor. Onscreen in the '70s. IN: *The Panic in Needle Park, The Organization, Been Down So Long It Looks Like Up to Me, The Gumball Rally*, more.

JULIEN, MAX (S. Cal.) Black leading man. Onscreen from 1968. IN: *Psych-Out, The Savage Seven, Up Tight, Getting Straight, Thomasine and Bushrod*, more.

JUNG, ALLEN (S. Cal.) Character. Onscreen from 1943. IN: *China Girl, Night Plane from Chunking, The Party, Star Spangled Girl*, more.

JURADO, KATY (Mex.) Leading lady. Nominated for Best Supporting Actress Oscar in *Broken Lance*. Onscreen from 1951. IN: *The Bullfighter and the Lady, High Noon, San Antone, Arrowhead, The Racers, Trial, Trapeze, The Man from Del Rio, One-Eyed Jacks, Barabbas, A Target for Killing, A Covenant with Death; Stay Away, Joe!; The Bridge in the Jungle*, more.

JURGENS, CURT (Switz.) Costar. Onscreen from the '50s. IN: *The Enemy Below, The Devil's General, And God Created Woman, This Happy Feeling, Me and the Colonel, Inn of the Sixth Happiness, House of Intrigue, I Am at the Stars, Michael Strogoff, Duel in the Jungle, The Longest Day, Miracle of the White Stallions, Of Love and Desire, Hide and Seek, Lord Jim, The Assassination Bureau, Legion of the Damned, Hello and Goodbye, Nicholas and Alexandra, Vault of Horror, Kill Kill Kill, Undercover Hero*, more.

JUSTICE, KATHERINE (S. Cal.) Leading lady. Onscreen from 1967. IN: *The Way West, 5 Card Stud, Limbo*, more.

JUSTIN, JOHN (Eng.) As handsome—in 1940's *The Thief of Bagdad*—as any prince ever on the screen, he remains, in his late 50s (b. 1917), a splendid-looking man—and one almost totally dedicated to the stage. In the past 15 years he has been seen on English stages in such diverse plays as *Death of a Salesman* (played Willy Loman), *As You Like It, The Mousetrap*, and *Lulu* —in which he played, not surprisingly, Prince Escerny. But, since 1960, he has appeared in only three movies: *The Spider's Web, Candidate for Murder*, and *Savage Messiah*. He has not been married since his divorce, years ago, from actress Barbara Murray. Onscreen from 1940. IN: *The Gentle Sex, Angel With the Trumpet, Breaking the Sound Barrier, Melba, King of the Khyber Rifles, The Village, Crest of the Wave, Untamed, The Man Who Loved Redheads, The Teckman Mystery, Island in the Sun*, more.

KAAREN, SUZANNE (N.Y.) Until his death in '73, she had been (since '42) long and happily married to actor Sidney Blackmer. The mother of two grown sons by him, she lives alone in a beautiful apartment on Central Park South. Onscreen from 1934. IN: *Bottoms Up, When's Your Birthday?*, more.

KABIBBLE, ISH (Hawaii) Kay Kyser's comic with the pre-Beatle long hairdo is in his 60s (b. 1908) and is in real estate in Honolulu. Onscreen from 1939. IN: *That's Right, You're Wrong; You'll Find Out, Playmates, My Favorite Spy, Around the World*, more.

KAHN, MADELINE (S. Cal.) Costar. Nominated for Best Supporting Actress Oscar in *Paper Moon* and *Blazing Saddles*. Onscreen from 1972. IN: *What's Up Doc?, At Long Last Love, Young Frankenstein, The Adventure of Sherlock Holmes' Smarter Brother; Won Ton Ton, the Dog Who Saved Hollywood;* more.

KALLEN, KITTY (S. Cal.) The singer-actress is married to publisher-TV producer Budd Granoff and retired from performing. Onscreen in 1956. IN: *The Second Greatest Sex.*

KALLIANIOTES, HELENA (S. Cal.) Support. Onscreen in the '70s. IN: *Five Easy Pieces, The Baby Maker*, more.

KALLMAN, DICK (S. Cal.) Comic lead. Onscreen from 1957. IN: *Hell Canyon Heroes, Verboten!, Back Street; Doctor, You've Got to Be Kidding!;* more.

KAMEN, MILT (S. Cal.) Character. Onscreen in the '70s. IN: *Me, Natalie; Believe in Me*, more.

KAMINSKA, IDA (Israel) Character. Nominated for Best Actress Oscar in *The Shop on Main Street.* The tiny, superb Polish actress settled in New York in 1969 just as she became world-famous as the star of the above-mentioned movie—and found it a lonely place. In 1975, aged 75, with her husband, she emigrated to Israel. Their announced dream was to start an Israeli-Yiddish Theater there. Onscreen abroad from 1924. IN: *Without a Home, A Vilna Legend*, more. Onscreen in America in 1970. IN: *The Angel Levine.*

KANE, BYRON (S. Cal.) Character. Onscreen from 1954. IN: *Gog*, more.

KANE, CAROL (N.Y.) Leading lady. Nominated for Best Actress Oscar in *Hester Street.* Onscreen in the '70s. IN: *Carnal Knowledge, Desperate Characters, Wedding in White, The Last Detail, Dog Day Afternoon, Hester Street, Harry and Walter Go to New York*, more.

KANE, MICHAEL (N.Y.) Support. Onscreen from 1965. IN: *The Bedford Incident*, more.

KANE, SID (S. Cal.) Character. Onscreen from the '50s. IN: *Twelve Hours to Kill*, more.

KANN, LILLY (Eng.) Character. Onscreen from 1943. IN: *Escape to Danger, The White Unicorn, Woman to Woman, Frenzy, The Woman in the Hall, The Clouded Yellow, Betrayed, Nowhere to Go*, more.

KANN, SYLVIA (N.Y.) Character. Onscreen in the '70s. IN: *The Anderson Tapes, Mortadella, Born to Win, The Hospital, The Hot Rock, Portnoy's Complaint*, more.

KANNER, ALEXIS (Eng.) Support. Onscreen from 1968. IN: *Goodbye Gemini, Connecting Rooms*, more.

KAPLAN, MARVIN (S. Cal.) Character. Onscreen from 1949. IN: *Adam's Rib, The Reformer and the Redhead, Criminal Lawyer, Angels in the Outfield, The Fabulous Senorita, The Nutty Professor, Wake Me When It's Over, The Great Race*, more.

KAREN, ANNA (S. Cal.) Support. Onscreen in the '70s. IN: *The Ski Bum*, more.

KARIN, RITA (N.Y.) Character. IN: *The Gang That Couldn't Shoot Straight.*

KARINA, ANNA (Fr.) Costar. Onscreen from 1961. IN: *Cleo from Five to Seven, Three Fables of Love, My Life to Live, A Woman Is a Woman, Sweet and Sour, Circle of Love, Alphaville, Peter the Crazy, Made in U.S.A., La Religieuse, The Oldest Profession, The Magus, Justine, The Salzburg Connection*, more.

KARLAN, RICHARD (S. Cal.) Character. Onscreen from 1950. IN: *Union Station, The Racket; Wait Till the Sun Shines, Nellie; Blowing Wild, Star!*, more.

KARLIN, MIRIAM (Eng.) Character. Onscreen from the '50s. IN: *The Entertainer, Hand in Hand, The Millionairess, Heavens Above!, The Small World of Sammy Lee, A Clockwork Orange*, more.

KARNILOVA, MARIA (N.Y.) Ballerina-actress. Principally a Broadway leading lady. Onscreen in 1964. IN: *The Unsinkable Molly Brown.*

KARRAS, ALEX (N.Y.) Actor-TV sportscaster. Former pro football star. Onscreen from 1968. IN: *Paper Lion, Blazing Saddles.*

KARTALIAN, BUCK (S. Cal.) Character. Onscreen from 1955. IN: *Mister Roberts, Planet of the Apes; Stay Away, Joe; Myra Breckinridge,* more.

KASEM, CASEY (S. Cal.) Support. Onscreen from the '60s. IN: *The Glory Stompers, 2000 Years Later, Cycle Savages, The Incredible Two-Headed Transplant,* more.

KASHFI, ANNA (S. Cal.) The former wife of Marlon Brando, she married business man James Hannaford in January 1974, lives in Los Angeles, and hasn't worked in a movie in more than a decade. Onscreen from 1956. IN: *The Mountain, Battle Hymn, Cowboy, Night of the Quarter Moon.*

KASKET, HAROLD (Eng.) Character. Onscreen from 1947. IN: *One Good Turn, The House of the Arrow, Moulin Rouge, Beau Brummell, Saadia, Stowaway Girl, The Boy Who Stole a Million, Return of Mr. Moto, Arabesque,* more.

KASTNER, PETER (S. Cal.) Leading man. Onscreen from 1965. IN: *Nobody Waved Goodbye, You're a Big Boy Now, B.S. I Love You,* more.

KASZNAR, KURT (N.Y.) Character. Onscreen first in 1926 in two silents with Max Linder made in his native Vienna. Onscreen in America from 1951. IN: *The Light Touch, Anything Can Happen, Lovely to Look At, The Happy Time, Lili, Kiss Me Kate, The Last Time I Saw Paris, Valley of the Kings, Fanny, Anything Goes, A Farewell to Arms, The Journey, 55 Days at Peking, The Thrill of It All, The Ambushers, The Perils of Pauline,* more.

KATCHER, ARAM (S. Cal.) Character. Onscreen from 1950. IN: *Spy Hunt, Flight to Hong Kong, The Girl in the Kremlin, Do Not Disturb,* more.

KAUFMANN, CHRISTINE (Fr.) Leading lady. Second wife (divorced) of Tony Curtis. Onscreen from 1959. IN: *Embezzled Heaven, Last Days of Pompeii, Silent Angel, Town Without Pity, Constantine and the Cross, Taras Bulba, Sword of Siena, Escape from East Berlin, Murders in the Rue Morgue,* more.

KAUFMANN, MAURICE (Eng.) Support. Onscreen from 1964. IN: *A Shot in the Dark, Die! My Darling, The Abominable Dr. Phibes,* more.

KAY, BEATRICE (S. Cal.) The comedienne-singer and her mother, then 93, who had been managing on Social Security and unemployment insurance, were devastated when a fire in '71 destroyed their Hollywood apartment and all their possessions. Alone now—her mother died the following year—Beatrice has lately been singing her oldtime songs at a club in Santa Monica. Onscreen in 1945 in *Billy Rose's Diamond Horseshoe* and 1961's *Underworld, U.S.A.*

KAY, BERNARD (Eng.) Support. Onscreen from the '60s. IN: *The Shuttered Room, Interlude, Darling Lili, Trog, The Hunting Party,* more.

KAY, CHARLES (Eng.) Support. Onscreen from 1958. IN: *Bachelor of Hearts, The Deadly Affair,* more.

KAY, RICHARD (Eng.) Support. Onscreen from 1970. IN: *Three Sisters,* more.

KAYE, CELIA (S. Cal.) Leading lady. Onscreen in the '70s. IN: *Island of Blue Dolphins,* more.

KAYE, DANNY (N.Y.) Star comedian. In 1954 he was awarded a special Oscar (statuette) "for his unique talents, his service to the Academy, the motion picture industry, and the American people." In his 60s now (b. 1913) and retired from movies—1969's *The Madwoman of Chaillot* was his last—he has dedicated himself to serving the children of the world. Married to writer Sylvia Fine for almost four decades, he is the father of a daughter, Dena Kaye, who is herself an established writer of articles for various New York magazines. Onscreen from 1944. IN: *Up in Arms, Wonder Man, The Kid from Brooklyn, The Secret Life of Walter Mitty, A Song Is Born, Inspector General, On the Riviera, Hans Christian Andersen, Knock on Wood, White Christmas, The Court Jester, Merry Andrew, Me and the Colonel, The Five Pennies, On the Double, The Man from the Diner's Club.*

KAYE, SAMMY (S. Cal.) Bandleader. Onscreen in the 40s. IN: *Iceland, Song of the Open Road,* more.

KAYE, STUBBY (N.Y.) Comedian. Onscreen from 1955. IN: *Taxi!, Guys and Dolls, You Can't Run Away from It, Li'l Abner, Sex and the Single Girl, Cat Ballou, The Way West, Sweet Charity, Can Hieronymus Merkin Ever Forget Mercy Humppe and Find True Happiness?,* more.

KAZAN, ELIA (N.Y.) Before becoming a noted director he was an actor. Onscreen from 1940. IN: *City for Conquest, Blues in the Night.*

KAZAN, LAINIE (S. Cal.) Leading lady. Onscreen in 1968. IN: *Dayton's Devils, Lady in Cement.*

KEACH, STACY, JR. (S. Cal.) Costar. Onscreen from 1968. IN: *The Heart Is a Lonely Hunter, End of the Road, The Traveling Executioner, Brewster McCloud, Doc, Fat City, The New Centurions, Luther, The Life and Times of Judge Roy Bean, Conduct Unbecoming,* more.

KEAN, BETTY (N.Y.) Comedienne-leading lady. Onscreen in the '40s. IN: *Gals, Inc.; Murder in the Blue Room.*

KEAN, MARIE (Eng.) Character. Onscreen from 1958. IN: *Great Catherine, Broth of a Boy, Rooney, Home Is the Hero, Girl With Green Eyes, Cul de Sac,* more.

KEARNEY, CAROLYN (S. Cal.) Leading lady. Onscreen from 1958. IN: *The Thing That Wouldn't Die,* more.

KEARNEY, MICHAEL (N.Y.) Support. IN: *All the Way Home, The Swimmer,* more.

KEATON, DIANE (N.Y.) Leading lady. Onscreen from 1972. IN: *Lovers and Other Strangers; Play It Again, Sam; The Godfather, Sleeper, The Godfather II, Love and Death; I Will, I Will . . . for Now; Harry and Walter Go to New York,* more.

KEATS, STEVEN (N.Y.) Leading man. Onscreen in the '70s. IN: *Death Wish, The Gambler, Hester Street,* more.

KEATS, VIOLA (Eng.) Character. Onscreen from the '30s. IN: *Mister Hobo, Two Who Dared,* more.

KEDROVA, LILA (Fr.) Character. Won Best Supporting Actress Oscar in *Zorba the Greek.* Onscreen from 1955. IN: *No Way Back, Razzi, The Lovemaker, The Female, Human Cargo, Modigliani of Montparnasse, A High Wind in Jamaica, Torn Curtain, Penelope, The Runaround, Tenderly, The Kremlin Letter, Escape to the Sun, Undercovers Hero, The Tenant,* more.

KEEFE, ZEENA (Mass.) This popular actress of early silents was at last report living in retirement in Belmont. Onscreen from 1915. IN: *La Boheme, The Hero of Submarine D2,* more.

KEEFER, DON (S. Cal.) Character. Onscreen from 1951. IN: *Death of a Salesman, The Girl in White, Riot in Cell Block 11, The Private War of Major Benson, Torpedo Run, R.P.M.; Rabbit, Run; The Grissom Gang, Candy Stripe Nurses,* more. (See Catherine McLeod.)

KEEL, HOWARD (S. Cal.) In '75 at 57, and already a grandfather—thanks to daughter Kaija, eldest of his three grown children—the singer-actor became a father again, of a daughter who was named Leslie. Keel's present wife (3) is the former Judy Magamoll, who was an airline stewardess prior to their marriage in '71. The actor, whose last Hollywood pic was 1968's *Arizona Bushwackers,* stays busy. Prior to a '75 concert tour, in which he sang only Cole Porter songs, he played music fairs in *I Do, I Do* and *The Unsinkable Molly Brown,* did a long nightclub tour in Australia, and played the Palladium in London where he also did a new album of *Annie Get Your Gun* with Ethel Merman. He also sometimes plays Las Vegas with his former Metro costar Kathryn Grayson. Onscreen first in England in 1948. IN: *The Small Voice.* Onscreen in America from 1949. IN: *The Hideout* (supporting role, at Republic), *Annie Get Your Gun, Pagan Love Song, Show Boat, Callaway Went Thataway, Love to Look At; Ride, Vaquero!; Kiss Me Kate, Calamity Jane, Rose Marie, Seven Brides for Seven Brothers, Jupiter's Darling, Kismet, The Big Fisherman, Armored Command, Waco, The War Wagon, Red Tomahawk,* more.

KEELER, ELISHA C. (N.Y.) Character. IN: *Square Dance Tonight, Country Rhythm.*

KEELER, RUBY (S. Cal.) Early in '75, two months after surgery in Montana for a brain aneurysm, this great favorite—well enough to walk on her own—was able to return to her home in Laguna Beach. In her 60s now (b. 1909), the dancer-actress has five children. When married to Al Jolson, they adopted a son and called him Al Jr.; today he is called Peter and is a California landscape contractor. She was then married to Pasadena broker John Lowe, from '41 until his death in '69, and bore him four children: Kathleen (married and a sociologist, she has presented Ruby with two grandsons), Christine (a recent graduate of the University of California at Berkeley), John Jr. (a stage manager and married), and Theresa (she lives in Montana where the actress was visiting when she became ill). When Ruby left her long-run comeback hit on Broadway, *No, No, Nanette,* in the fall of '72, she said she was retiring this time "for keeps." She still holds to that. Onscreen from 1933. IN: *42nd Street, Gold Diggers of 1933, Footlight Parade, Dames, Flirtation Walk, Go Into Your Dance, Shipmates Forever, Colleen; Ready, Willing and Able; Mother Carey's Chickens,* and *Sweetheart* *of the Campus*, her last starring pic in '41; in '59 she did a cameo in the little-seen *The Phynx*, and in '69, visiting the set of *They Shoot Horses, Don't They?*, she was pressed into service as an extra.

KEEN, DIANE (Eng.) Support. Onscreen in the '70s. IN: *Here We Go Round the Mulberry Bush, The Sex Thief*, more.

KEEN, GEOFFREY (Eng.) Character. Onscreen from 1947. IN: *Odd Man Out, The Third Man, The Fallen Idol, Treasure Island, Cry the Beloved Country, Rob Roy, Genevieve, High and Dry, Doctor in the House, The Man Who Never Was, The Key, The Scapegoat, Doctor Zhivago, Born Free, Berserk!*, more.

KEEN, NOAH (S. Cal.) Support. Onscreen from 1967. IN: *The Caper of the Golden Bulls, Black Starlet*, more.

KEENER, HAZEL (S. Cal.) Popular as a leading lady in silent Westerns, particularly those of Fred Thomson, she is now in her late 60s and a minister in the Church of Religious Science. She was last onscreen in a supporting role in *Murder By Invitation* ('41), starring Wallace Ford. Onscreen from the early '20s. IN: *Empty Hands, The Freshman, Ports of Call*, more.

KEIM, BETTY LOU (S. Cal.) She is married to Warren Berlinger and retired. Onscreen from 1956. IN: *These Wilder Years, Teenage Rebel, The Wayward Bus, Some Came Running.*

KEIR, ANDREW (Eng.) Character. Onscreen from the '50s. IN: *Scotch on the Rocks, High and Dry, Cleopatra, Lord Jim, The Long Duel, Five Million Years to Earth, Attack on the Iron Coast, Zeppelin, Blood from the Mummy's Tomb*, more.

KEITEL, HARVEY (S. Cal.) Leading man. Onscreen in the '70s. IN: *Alice Doesn't Live Here Anymore, That's the Way of the World, Buffalo Bill and the Indians, Welcome to L.A.*, more.

KEITH, BRIAN (Hawaii) Costar. Onscreen from 1953. IN: *Arrowhead, Jivaro, Tight Spot, Storm Center, Chicago Confidential, The Parent Trap, The Pleasure Seekers, Moon Pilot, Those Calloways; The Russians Are Coming, The Russians Are Coming; Reflections in a Golden Eye, Way Way Out, With Six You Get Egg Roll, Gaily Gaily, Scandalous John, The Wind and the Lion*, more.

KELLER, HIRAM (N.Y.) American leading man who has worked exclusively in European pictures to date. Onscreen from 1968. IN: *Fellini Satyricon, Orestes, Michael Strogoff, The Night of the Flowers, In the Eyes of the Cat, Rosina Comes to the City, It Was I, Orlando Furioso, The Life Span Code, Rome Wants Another Caesar, Noah Noah.*

KELLER, MARTHE (S. Cal.) Leading lady from Switzerland. Onscreen in 1976. IN: *Marathon Man, Black Sunday, White Dog.*

KELLERMAN, SALLY (S. Cal.) Costar. Nominated for Best Supporting Actress Oscar in *M*A*S*H*. Onscreen from 1957. IN: *Reform School Girl, The Third Day, The Boston Strangler, The April Fools, Brewster McCloud, Last of the Red Hot Lovers, Lost Horizon, Slither, Rafferty and the Gold Dust Twins, Welcome to L.A.* more.

KELLEY, DE FOREST (S. Cal.) Support; former leading man. Onscreen from 1947. IN: *Fear in the Night, House of Bamboo, The View from Pompey's Head, Illegal, Gunfight at the O.K. Corral, Where Love Has Gone, Black Spurs, Marriage on the Rocks, Apache Uprising, Waco*, more.

KELLIN, MIKE (S. Cal.) Character. Costarred on Broadway in '75 in the musical *The Ritz*. Onscreen from 1949. IN: *So Young So Bad, At War with the Army, Lonely Hearts, The Great Impostor, The Wackiest Ship in the Army, Invitation to a Gunfighter, Banning, The Boston Strangler, The Maltese Bippy, Fools' Parade, Freebie and the Bean*, more.

KELLINO, PAMELA/now PAMELA MASON (S. Cal.) Actress, first wife of James Mason (divorced), later a gossip columnist for *Photoplay*. Onscreen from the '30s. IN: *I Met a Murderer, They Were Sisters, Pandora and the Flying Dutchman*, more.

KELLOGG, JOHN (S. Cal.) Character. Onscreen from 1940. IN: *Young Tom Edison, Johnny O'Clock, The Gangster, House of Strangers, Twelve O'Clock High, The Enforcer, Come Fill the Cup, The Greatest Show on Earth, Edge of the City, Go Naked in the World, Convicts Four, A Knife for the Ladies*, more.

KELLY, BARBARA (Eng.) Leading lady; rarely active now. Onscreen from 1953. IN: *A Tale of Five Cities, Castle in the Air, Glad Tidings, Love in Pawn*, more.

KELLY, BRIAN (S. Cal.) The good news is that he and actress-wife, Valerie Ann Romero—married since '72—welcomed their first child, a daughter, Hale O'Brien, in the spring of '75. The unfortunate news is that the handsome actor will never be able to resume his acting career. A motorcycle accident in '71 permanently impaired the movement of one leg, both arms, and his speech—for which a lawsuit settlement of $750,000 is small recompense. He has announced plans to become a motion picture producer. Onscreen from 1963. IN: *Thunder Island, Flipper's New Adventure, Around the World Under the Sea, Not Buried But Dead,* more.

KELLY, EMMETT (Fla.) He remains active clowning, as does his son, Emmett Kelly Jr. Onscreen in the '50s. IN: *The Fat Man, The Greatest Show on Earth, Wind Across the Everglades.*

KELLY, GENE (S. Cal.) Star. Nominated for Best Actor Oscar in *Anchors Aweigh.* In 1951 he received a special Oscar (statuette) "in appreciation of his versatility as an actor, singer, director and dancer, and specifically for his brilliant achievements in the art of choreography on film." Onscreen from 1942. IN: *For Me and My Gal, Pilot No. 5, Thousands Cheer, The Cross of Lorraine, Christmas Holiday, Cover Girl, Ziegfeld Follies, The Pirate, The Three Musketeers, Words and Music, On the Town, Take Me Out to the Ball Game, Summer Stock, Black Hand, An American in Paris, Singing in the Rain, Brigadoon, It's Always Fair Weather, Invitation to the Dance, The Happy Land, Les Girls, Inherit the Wind, What a Way to Go!, The Young Girls of Rochefort, Forty Carats, That's Entertainment!,* more.

KELLY, GRACE (Monaco) Star; retired. Nominated for Best Supporting Actress Oscar in *Mogambo.* Won Best Actress Oscar in *The Country Girl.* Onscreen from 1951. IN: *Fourteen Hours, High Noon, Dial M for Murder, Rear Window, Green Fire, The Bridges at Toko-Ri, To Catch a Thief, The Swan, High Society.*

KELLY, JACK (S. Cal.) Character; former leading man. Brother of Nancy Kelly. Onscreen from 1949. IN: *Fighting Man of the Plains, The Wild Blue Yonder, The Stand at Apache River, Column South, The Night Holds Terror, Julie, Cult of the Cobra, A Fever in the Blood, FBI Code 98, Dr. No,* more.

KELLY, JIM (S. Cal.) Black star. Onscreen in the '70s. IN: *Enter the Dragon, Black Belt Jones, Three the Hard Way, Golden Needles, Take a Hard Ride,* more.

KELLY, JUDY (Eng.) Leading lady. Rarely active now. Onscreen from the '30s. IN: *At the Villa Rose, At Dawn We Die, Dead of Night,* more.

KELLY, NANCY (N.Y.) She is, in her 50s (b. 1921), no longer the beautiful girl she was when 20th Century-Fox began starring her at 17. But she is a handsome, if a trifle overweight, woman with just a touch of gray in her dark hair —and a superlative actress. This anyone knows who saw her in the nationwide tour of the play *The Gingerbread Lady,* or on television in *The Impostor* ('74)—her first TV-film appearance— or a *Medical Center* episode in which she portrayed a famous woman scientist. The actress gave up her decade-long movie career after 1948's *Disaster,* an accurate description of what that career had become. During her Hollywood years she was twice married and divorced—her husbands being actor Edmond O'Brien and cameraman Fred Jackman Jr. She returned to the stage where, at 16, she had scored sensationally with Gertrude Lawrence in *Susan and God.* History repeated itself as she won accolades for her performances in *The Big Knife, Season in the Sun,* and, particularly, *The Bad Seed.* Playing the mother in this, she won a Tony Award, repeated her role in the '56 screen version, and was nominated for the Oscar as Best Actress. Onstage in Chicago, in *The Bad Seed* and *Who's Afraid of Virginia Woolf?,* she twice won the coveted Sarah Siddons Award. From '55 until they were divorced in '68, she was married to Theatre Guild executive Warren Caro, by whom she has a grown daughter, Kelly, lately in Hollywood studying at the Actors Studio to follow in her mother's footsteps. When the actress and her husband separated in '65, she took a five-year vacation from her career, she has said, "to give Kelly a feeling of security." She resumed acting in '70 in the play *Remote Asylum* and, she adds, she is back to stay. Onscreen in juvenile roles in 1929 in *Girl on the Barge* and 1935 in *Convention Girl.* Onscreen in adult roles from 1938. IN: *Jesse James, Submarine Patrol, Stanley and Livingstone, Tailspin, Frontier Marshal, He Married His Wife, One Night in the Tropics, To the Shores of Tripoli, Tarzan's Desert Mystery, Show Business, The Woman Who Came Back, Murder in the Music Hall,* more.

KELLY, PATSY (N.Y.) Show business miracles can occur—when talent is involved. Until 1943 she was one of the screen's most beloved comediennes, delivering wry, matter-of-fact laugh lines like no other. "Queen of the wisecrackers," they called her. And she was, this loudmouth from Brooklyn (b. 1910). But for almost two dismal decades she disappeared from the scene. "Personal problems," it was said, but what they might have been, if the report was true, has never been spelled out. During much of that time her benefactor was Tallulah Bankhead who, among other things, found a small role for her in the touring summer stock company of *Dear Charles.* In the '60s she began getting small parts in pictures again—*Please*

Don't Eat the Daisies, The Ghost in the Invisible Bikini, and particularly Rosemary's Baby, in which she was a witch—but nothing of the "old" Patsy Kelly was in evidence. In 1971 the "real" Patsy Kelly returned in full panoply, costarring on Broadway with Ruby Keeler—her pal from childhood—in No, No, Nanette. "Patsy Kelly takes full and rich advantage of the part of the outspoken maid in a glorious display of pure ham," wrote Douglas Watt. All the other critics unanimously agreed—and she won a Tony. After that show's long run, lightning struck again. She costarred with Debbie Reynolds in Irene, after which she delighted her old movie fans with a nationwide tour of the same musical. She was then the costar of the '76 TV series The Cop and the Kid. "You know," said the still-single comedienne recently, "in 40-odd years in show business—some of them I could do no wrong and some I could do nothing right—I haven't been so excited. It's a miracle. I think people are starved for happy endings. I know I was." Onscreen from 1933. IN: 40 Hal Roach short subjects with Thelma Todd, Pert Kelton, and finally Lyda Roberti; The Girl from Missouri, Go Into Your Dance, Every Night at Eight; Sing, Baby, Sing; Pigskin Parade, Pick a Star, Wake Up and Live, There Goes My Heart, The Cowboy and the Lady, Road Show, Topper Returns, Playmates, Sing Your Worries Away, In Old California, The Crowded Sky, The Naked Kiss; Come On, Let's Live a Little; more.

KELLY, PAULA (S. Cal.) Black dancer-leading lady. Onscreen from 1969. IN: Sweet Charity, The Andromeda Strain, Soylent Green, Uptown Saturday Night, Lost in the Stars, Drum, more.

KELLY, TOMMY (S. Cal.) Selznick's boy star of The Adventures of Tom Sawyer is in his early 50s now (b. 1925) and reportedly a teacher in a Southern California high school. Onscreen from 1938. IN: Peck's Bad Boy with the Circus, They Shall Have Music, Military Academy, Gallant Sons, Nice Girl?, more, including 1943's Mugtown, his last.

KELSALL, MOULTRIE (Eng.) Character. Onscreen from the '40s. IN: Last Holiday, Captain Horatio Hornblower, High and Dry, The Barrets of Wimpole Street, Abandon Ship, The Inn of the Sixth Happiness, Light in the Piazza, The Birthday Party, more.

KEMMER, ED (S. Cal.) Support. Onscreen from 1956. IN: Calypso Joe, The Spider; Too Much, Too Soon; Hong Kong Confidential, Giant from the Unknown, The Crowded Sky, more.

KEMP, JEREMY (Eng.) Leading man. Onscreen from 1961. IN: Cleopatra, Dr. Terror's House of Horrors, Operation Crossbow, The Blue Max, The Games, Sudden Terror, The Blockhouse, more.

KEMPSON, RACHEL (Eng.) Character; former leading lady. The wife of Michael Redgrave, she is the mother of all the acting Redgraves—Vanessa, Lynn, and Corin. Onscreen from 1943. IN: Jeannie, The Captive Heart, A Woman's Vengeance, Tom Jones, The Third Secret, Georgy Girl, The Charge of the Light Brigade, The Virgin Soldiers, Jane Eyre, more.

KEMP-WELCH, JOAN (Eng.) Character. Onscreen from 1938. IN: Sixty Glorious Years, Girl in the Street, The Citadel; Goodbye, Mr. Chips; School for Husbands, Haunted Honeymoon, and last, Jeannie, released here in 1943; since which she has devoted herself exclusively to the English stage and directing—since '54—such prize-winning television productions as A View from the Bridge and The Birthday Party.

KENDALL, SUZY (Eng.) Leading lady. Onscreen from 1966. IN: The Liquidator; To Sir, With Love; Up the Junction, The Penthouse, Fraulein Doktor, Darker Than Amber, Tales That Witness Madness, In the Devil's Garden, Craze, Torso, more.

KENDALL, WILLIAM (Eng.) Character; former leading man. Onscreen from 1932. IN: Magic Night, This'll Make You Whistle, One-Way Ticket to Hell, Dance Little Lady, A Touch of Larceny, The Jokers, more.

KENNEALLY, PHILIP (S. Cal.) Support. Onscreen from 1953. IN: Man on a Tightrope, Little Big Man, The Outfit, more.

KENNEDY, ADAM (S. Cal.) Former support. Now a scriptwriter—coauthor of 1974's The Dove. Onscreen from 1957. IN: Men at War, Bailout at 43,000, Until They Sail, more.

KENNEDY, ARTHUR (S. Cal.) Costar. Nominated for Best Actor Oscar in Bright Victory. Nominated for Best Supporting Actor Oscar in Champion, Trial, Peyton Place, and Some Came Running. Onscreen from 1940. IN: City for Conquest, High Sierra, They Died with Their Boots On, Desperate Journey, Air Force, Devotion, Boomerang, Too Late for Tears, The Window, The Glass Menagerie, Bend of the River, Rancho Notorious, The Lusty Men, The Desperate Hours, A Summer Place, Elmer Gantry, Barabbas, Murder She Said, Lawrence of Arabia, Cheyenne Autumn, Nevada Smith, Fantastic Voyage, Day of the Evil Gun, Anzio; Hail, Hero!; My Old Man's Place, more.

KENNEDY, CHERYL (Eng.) Support. Onscreen from 1965. IN: Doctor in Clover, more.

KENNEDY, GEORGE (S. Cal.) Costar. Won Best Supporting Actor Oscar in *Cool Hand Luke*. Onscreen from 1961. IN: *Little Shepherd of Kingdom Come, Lonely Are the Brave, Charade, Strait-Jacket, Island of Blue Dolphins; Hush ... Hush ... Sweet Charlotte; In Harm's Way, Mirage, Shenandoah, The Sons of Katie Elder, The Flight of the Phoenix, The Dirty Dozen, The Legend of Lylah Clare, The Ballad of Josie, The Guns of the Magnificent Seven, Gaily Gaily, The Good Guys and the Bad Guys, Tick Tick Tick, False Witness, Lost Horizon, Airport, The Human Factor, Earthquake, The Eiger Sanction*, more.

KENNEDY, MADGE (S. Cal.) In '75 this great favorite from silent days appeared, to rave notices, as the Old Tenant at the shabby rooming house in *Day of the Locust*. It was her first screen role since she appeared in support in *The Baby Maker* ('70). Now in her 80s (b. 1892), she lives alone in Los Angeles, a widow since the '59 death of her husband, William B. Hanley Jr., who was a radio producer at the time of their marriage in '34. Of Samuel Goldwyn's first group of femme stars—Geraldine Farrar, Mabel Normand, Mae Marsh, Pauline Frederick, and herself—she is the sole survivor. Onscreen from 1916. IN: *Baby Mine, The Danger Game, The Fair Pretender, Friendly Husband, A Perfect Lady, The Kingdom of Youth, Leave It to Susan, Three Miles Out, Bad Company, Lying Wives*, more, including 1926's *Oh Baby!*, after which she was off the screen until she returned as a character actress in 1952; *The Marrying Kind, The Rains of Ranchipur, The Catered Affair, Lust for Life, A Nice Little Bank That Should Be Robbed, Let's Make Love; They Shoot Horses, Don't They?*; more.

KENNEY, JAMES (Eng.) Support. Onscreen from 1941 (at age 11). IN: *Circus Boy, Captain Horatio Hornblower, Outcast of the Islands, Doctor at Sea*, more.

KENT, BARBARA (Idaho) Harold Lloyd's charming brunette leading lady in his first two talkies, *Feet First* and *Welcome Danger*, she continued in pix through 1941's *Under Age*. Long the wife of actors' agent Harry E. Eddington (d. 1948), she has remarried and, entering her 70s (b. 1906), lives in retirement near Sun Valley. Onscreen from 1928. IN: *Modern Mothers, Retribution, Lonesome, Welcome Danger, Night Ride, Indiscreet, Chinatown After Dark, Dumbbells in Ermine, Emma, Vanity Fair, Pride of the Legion, Marriage on Approval, Old Man Rhythm*, more.

KENT, CHRISTOPHER (S. Cal.) (See Alf Kjellin.)

KENT, JEAN (Eng.) Former leading lady. Now in her 50s (b. 1921), she has been far more active on the English stage than in movies. Onscreen from 1934 in juvenile roles. Onscreen in adult roles from 1942. IN: *It's That Man Again, Madonna of the Seven Moons, Notorious Gentleman, The Wicked Lady, The Magic Bow, The Smugglers, Sleeping Car to Trieste, Caravan, The Gay Lady, The Browning Version, Prince and the Showgirl, Bonjour Tristesse, Bluebeard's Ten Honeymoons, Please Turn Over*, more, including, in '76, a cameo in *Shout at the Devil*.

KENT, MARSHALL (S. Cal.) Character. Onscreen from 1960. IN: *The Last Voyage, Ring of Fire*, more.

KENYON, DORIS (S. Cal.) Rounding out her 70s (b. 1897), she remains an extraordinarily beautiful, warm, and outgoing woman. Until his death in '71 she had been married for 24 years to musicologist Bronislaw Mylnarski. Previously, she had been married to Milton Sills, with whom she made many pictures, for three years, until he died in '30, and then, briefly, to broker Arthur Hopkins and to Albert Lasker. Her only child, Kenyon Sills, who was a well-known California geologist, died in April 1971, leaving a son—a teenager now—who lives with her in Beverly Hills. Financially well off, she is active in various charities. Onscreen from 1916. IN: *The Traveling Salesman, The Hidden Hand* (serial), *The Conquest of Canaan, Get-Rich-Quick Wallingford, Monsieur Beaucaire, A Thief in Paradise, Men of Steel, Loose Ankles, Burning Daylight, Beau Bandit, The Ruling Voice, The Man Called Back, Counsellor-at-Law, Voltaire, Whom the Gods Destroy, Girls' School*, more, including 1939's *The Man in the Iron Mask*, her last.

KERMAN, DAVID (N.Y.) Character. IN: *Putney Swope, Cry Uncle*, more.

KERMOYAN, MICHAEL (N.Y.) Support. Onscreen from the '50s. IN: *With a Song in My Heart*, more.

KERNAN, DAVID (Eng.) Support. Onscreen from 1964. IN: *Gaolbreak, Zulu, Otley*, more.

KERR, BILL (Eng.) Character; former leading man. Onscreen from 1934. IN: *Penny Points to Paradise, Appointment in London, The Night My Number Came Up, The Wrong Arm of the Law, A Pair of Briefs*, more.

KERR, DEBORAH (Switz.) Star. Nominated for Best Actress Oscar in *Edward My Son, From Here to Eternity, The King and I; Heaven Knows, Mr. Allison; Separate Tables*, and *The Sundowners*. Onscreen in England from 1939.

IN: *Contraband, Major Barbara, The Avengers, Courageous Mr. Penn, The Life and Death of Colonel Blimp, Love on the Dole, Vacation from Marriage, The Adventuress, Black Narcissus*, more. Onscreen in America and internationally since 1947. IN: *The Hucksters, King Solomon's Mines, Quo Vadis, The Prisoner of Zenda, Dream Wife, Julius Caesar, Young Bess, The Proud and the Profane, Tea and Sympathy, An Affair to Remember, Bonjour Tristesse, The Journey, Beloved Infidel, The Grass Is Greener, The Innocents, The Naked Edge, The Chalk Garden, The Night of the Iguana, Prudence and the Pill, The Gypsy Moths, The Arrangement*, more.

KERR, GEOFFREY (Eng.) The English actor-playwright, father of American actor John Kerr, is in his 80s now (b. 1895), retired and living in Hampshire, where he devotes himself to the hobby of photography. After his career in Hollywood movies, he returned to England where he wrote plays and pictures *(The Tenth Man, Break the News, Jassy)*, and acted on the stage until 1958's *The Elder Statesman*. Onscreen from 1922. IN: *The Man from Home, Just Suppose, Women Love Once, The Runaround*, and *Once a Lady*, his last in 1931.

KERR, JOHN (S. Cal.) Costar. Now a practicing attorney with a Beverly Hills law firm, he acts only on television—in *Police Story*, TV-movies *(The Longest Night)* and *Streets of San Francisco*, in which he has played the running role of plainclothes detective Gerald O'Brien. He and his wife, Priscilla, live in Westwood and are the parents of three—twins Rebecca and Jocelyn, who are in their early 20s, and college student Michael. In his 40s (b. 1931), the actor still looks young enough to play juvenile leads. Onscreen from 1955. IN: *The Cobweb, Gaby, Tea and Sympathy, South Pacific, Girl of the Night, The Crowded Sky*, more, including 1962's *Seven Women from Hell*, his most recent to date.

KERRIDGE, MARY (Eng.) Character. Onscreen from 1935. IN: *Paradise for Two, Anna Karenina, The Blue Peter, Richard III, The Duke Wore Jeans, The Gaunt Woman*, more.

KERSH, KATHY (S. Cal.) The former ingenue, after her divorce from Vince Edwards, married TV actor Burt (Robin in *Batman*) Ward in 1967 and retired. IN: *The Americanization of Emily*.

KERT, LARRY (S. Cal.) Actor-singer, primarily on Broadway. He began his professional career as a juvenile stuntman doubling for Roddy McDowall in *Lassie Come Home*. Onscreen from 1965. IN: *Synanon*, more.

KESTELMAN, SARA (Eng.) Leading lady. Onscreen in the '70s. IN: *Zardoz, Lisztomania*, more.

KETCHUM, DAVID (S. Cal.) Support. Onscreen from 1964. IN: *Good Neighbor Sam, Bless the Beasts & Children*, more.

KEYES, DANIEL F. (N.Y.) Character. Onscreen in the '70s. IN: *I Never Sang for My Father, 1776, Stiletto; Me, Natalie; Lovers and Other Strangers*, more.

KEYES, EVELYN (N.Y.) The reissue of *The Jolson Story* and her nationwide tour in *No, No, Nanette* with Don Ameche have revitalized the career of this still-beautiful-in-her-50s (b. 1919) actress. Childless, she has been married four times, presently—and for two decades—to Artie Shaw (she is # 8). Theirs would seem a "modern" marriage. Shaw has said, "I'm incapable of jealousy, and I want the same freedom I give her . . . We see each other when we want to. In her I've got something important . . . friendship—and trust . . . I'm very concerned about her. Is that love? I don't know what that word means. But that's what we've got going for us." Gray-blonde now, the onetime Columbia star is a true cosmopolite, having lived for long periods in France, England, and Mexico, and speaking Spanish and French fluently. In '75 she published her somewhat sensational autobiography. And, several years ago, she authored a novel, *I Am a Billboard*, about a Southern girl who becomes, not without pain, an overnight star in Hollywood. She herself is from Atlanta, and after Cecil B. DeMille discovered her at 19, much the same happened to her. Onscreen from 1938. IN: *The Buccaneer, Union Pacific, Gone With the Wind, The Lady in Question, The Face Behind the Mask, Here Comes Mr. Jordan, Ladies in Retirement, The Desperadoes, Nine Girls, Strange Affair, A Thousand and One Nights, Thrill of Brazil, The Mating of Millie, Enchantment, Mr. Soft Touch, Mrs. Mike, The Prowler, The Iron Man, Shoot First, 99 River Street, The Seven Year Itch, Around the World in 80 Days* (cameo), *Across 110th Street* (in which both she and Artie Shaw made cameo appearances).

KHAMBATTA, PERSIS (Eng.) Leading lady from India. Onscreen in 1975. IN: *The Wilby Conspiracy, Conduct Unbecoming*.

KIAMOS, ELENI (N.Y.) Support. Onscreen from 1956. IN: *Patterns*, more.

KIDD, JONATHAN (N.Y.) Support. IN: *Macabre*, more.

KIDD, MICHAEL (N.Y.) Costar/dancer. Onscreen from 1955. IN: *It's Always Fair Weather, Smile.* He choreographed *Where's Charley?, The Band Wagon, Seven Brides for Seven Brothers,* and *Knock on Wood,* and directed *Merry Andrew* and *Star!*

KIDDER, MARGOT (S. Cal.) Leading lady. Onscreen in the '70s. IN: *Gaily Gaily, Quackser Fortune Has a Cousin in the Bronx, Sisters, 92 in the Shade, Black Christmas, The Reincarnation of Peter Proud,* more.

KIEL, RICHARD (S. Cal.) Character. Onscreen from 1952. IN: *The Magic Sword, House of the Damned, A Man Called Dagger, The Human Duplicators, The Longest Yard,* more.

KILBURN, TERRY (Mich.) The London cockney lad's most memorable roles were his first 1938–39): *Lord Jeff, A Christmas Carol* (as Tiny Tim), and *Goodbye, Mr. Chips,* especially, in which he played the fresh-faced Peter Colleys I, II, III, as well as the young John Colley. Today, as Terence Kilburn (his actual name is Kilbourne), a bachelor still as he enters his youthful-looking 50s (b. 1926), he lives in Rochester where he teaches drama at Oakland University and is director of the school's Meadow Brook Theater. His mother, who is ill now, lives with him; his father died more than two decades ago. Many believe his career ended in his teens. Not true. Until the mid-'50s, even while working on his drama degree at U.C.L.A., he averaged one picture a year (*Bulldog Drummond at Bay, Fortunes of Captain Blood, Only the Valiant,* etc.). In New York in his late 20s, besides doing much "live" TV, he was onstage in four plays: *Candida* (with Olivia de Havilland), *Teahouse of the August Moon* (was one of several who played Sakini), *Charley's Aunt,* and *Sherlock Holmes.* Turning director, he staged many successful plays both in London (*Look Homeward, Angel* as a major triumph there) and in Los Angeles. He acts occasionally now in one of his university productions, but he has not been onscreen since playing a minor role in *Lolita* ('62). Onscreen from 1934. IN: *No Greater Glory, Sweethearts, They Shall Have Music, The Adventures of Sherlock Holmes, Swiss Family Robinson, A Yank at Eton, National Velvet, Keys of the Kingdom, Song of Scheherazade, The Fan, Slaves of Babylon,* more.

KILEY, RICHARD (N.Y.) Costar. Onscreen from 1951. IN: *The Mob, The Sniper, Eight Iron Men, The Blackboard Jungle, The Phenix City Story, Pendulum, The Little Prince,* more.

KILGALLEN, ROB (S. Cal.) Support. IN: *The Glass Bottom Boat,* more.

KILIAN, VICTOR (S. Cal.) Noted for his earthy, jaundiced portrayals of the common man (as well as leathery villains), this moustachioed veteran of 150 movies looks back on a career containing some of Hollywood's best— *The Ox-Bow Incident, Only Angels Have Wings, They Knew What They Wanted,* etc.— and picks as his favorite *The Happiest Man on Earth,* a short he did long ago with Paul Kelly. In his 80s now (b. 1891), this fine character actor has been a widower since '61 when his wife, Daisy, died just one month after their 45th wedding anniversary. "I have a son (Victor Kilian Jr., a TV scriptwriter) and daughter-in-law who live out here," he says, "and three grandsons scattered all over the continent, *and* a great-granddaughter." Last onscreen in 1951's *The Tall Target,* he returned to Hollywood to live in '70 after 13 years in New York, where he appeared in such hit plays as *Look Homeward, Angel; Gideon,* and *All the Way Home.* A while back, he lamented, "Now I'm trying to get somebody out here"—producers he meant— "to remember me." Someone obviously did. In '76 he turned up as one of the stars of TV's first nighttime soap opera, *Mary Hartman, Mary Hartman,* delighting all as the quirky grandfather known to the police in the fictional small town in Ohio as "the Fernwood Flasher." Onscreen from 1929. IN: *Valley Forge, Bad Boy, Riffraff, The Road to Glory, The Adventures of Tom Sawyer, Boys' Town, Virginia City, Dr. Cyclops, Young Tom Edison, All This and Heaven Too, Blood and Sand, Western Union, Hitler's Hangman, The Adventures of Mark Twain, The Spanish Main, Spellbound, Yellow Sky, Colorado Territory, The Flame and the Arrow, One Too Many,* more.

KILLY, JEAN-CLAUDE (Fr.) Ski champion-actor. Onscreen in the '70s. IN: *Snow Job.*

KILPATRICK, LINCOLN (N.Y.) Black support. Onscreen in the '70s. IN: *The Lost Man, Generation, Stiletto, The Omega Man, Brother John, Chosen Survivors, Uptown Saturday Night, Together Brothers,* more.

KIMBROUGH, CLINT (N.Y.) Leading man. Onscreen from 1958. IN: *Hot Spell, Bloody Mama, The Last Movie, Von Richthofen and Brown, Night Call Nurses, Crazy Mama,* more.

KINCAID, ARON (S. Cal.) Leading man. Onscreen from 1963. IN: *Palm Springs Weekend, Ski Party, Beach Ball, The Ghost in the Invisible Bikini, The Happiest Millionaire,* more.

KING, ALAN (N.Y.) Star comedian. Onscreen from 1955. IN: *Hit the Deck, Miracle in the Rain, The Girl He Left Behind, The Helen Morgan Story, Operation Snafu, Bye Bye Braverman, The Anderson Tapes,* more.

KING, ANDREA (S. Cal.) At Warners for four years and nine pictures in the '40s, this actress with the clipped, breathy speech and volatile acting style gave bigger-name Ida Lupino a run for her money. But gradually, though she continued to do one or two supporting roles a year, marriage took precedence over her career—particularly after the birth of her only child, Deborah Anne, in '55. For 30 years, until his death in '70, after a three-year illness, she was happily married to attorney Nat Willis, who managed her career. During the 1960s, except for one picture in '69 (*Daddy's Gone A-Hunting*), she was completely out of movies but very active in TV roles that took only a day or two each to shoot—in *Maverick, Perry Mason,* etc. Today, happily married again—to a businessman from South America—and living in Beverly Hills, the actress, still a handsome, slender blonde in her 50s (b. 1918), does television commercials and hopes to reactivate her movie career. Onscreen from 1944. IN: *The Very Thought of You, God Is My Co-Pilot, Roughly Speaking, Hotel Berlin, The Man I Love, The Beast with Five Fingers, Ride the Pink Horse, My Wild Irish Rose, Mr. Peabody and the Mermaid, Dial 1119, Mark of the Renegade, The World in His Arms, Band of Angels, Outlaw Queen,* more.

KING, CAMMIE (S. Cal.) After a later career as an airline stewardess, *GWTW's* "Bonnie Butler" married and is now retired from both acting and flying.

KING, DENNIS, JR. (Eng.) Support. IN: *Let's Make Love.*

KING, DAVID (Eng.) Support. Onscreen in the '60s. IN: *Pirates of Tortuga, Strange Bedfellows,* more.

KING, EDITH (Fla.) Entering her 80s (b. 1896), the noted stage character actress gave up her career a decade ago and lives in retirement now in Riviera Beach. Onscreen from 1945. IN: *Blaze of Noon, Calcutta, Gallant Blade, Belle Starr's Daughter,* more.

KING, JOHN "DUSTY" (S. Cal.) At a thriving waffle shop in La Jolla, drop-in patrons often are surprised to recognize its owner—a lanky (6'2"), athletically lean, friendly man named Miller MacLeod Everson. He lives upcoast a bit, at Del Mar, but is almost always at the shop. Because he has changed so little in the

three decades he's been out of pictures—he's i his 60s (b. 1909)—they spot him immediately a John King. Some remember him from the be ginning, when he was a singer with Ben Be nie's orchestra. Serial buffs know him as th star of *Ace Drummond* ('36). B-pic aficionadc recall him as the romantic lead in *Mr. Mo Takes a Vacation* and *Charlie Chan in Honc lulu.* To all these he is John King. But to Wes ern fans, who perhaps hold him in greatest e teem, he is John "Dusty" King, slugging singing-hard riding cohero (with Ray "Crash Corrigan and Max Terhune) of Monogram "Range Busters" series of the early '40s. Ye he tells them, the movie career was fun but so his business one, adding that he seldom se anyone he knew in Hollywood, and no, sorr he hasn't been near a horse in years. Onscree from 1936. IN: *Crash Donovan, The Hard Ride High, The Range Busters, West of Pin Basin, Trail of the Silver Spurs, Wrangler Roost, Rock River Renegades, Law of the Ju gle, Boot Hill Bandits, Two-Fisted Justic* more.

KING, KIP (S. Cal.) Support. Onscreen fro 1956. IN: *Tea and Sympathy,* more.

KING, MORGANA (S. Cal.) Character actres singer. Onscreen in the '70s. IN: *The Go father, The Godfather II.*

KING, PEGGY (S. Cal.) Singer-actress. O screen in 1957. IN: *Zero Hour.*

KING, PERRY (N.Y.) Leading man. Onscre in the '70s. IN: *Slaughterhouse-Five, The Pe session of Joel Delaney, The Wild Party, T Lords of Flatbush, Lipstick,* more.

KING, TONY (S. Cal.) Support. Onscreen the '70s. IN: *Bucktown, Report to the Comm sioner, Sparkle,* more.

KING, WALTER WOOLF (S. Cal.) The tim when he set femme hearts aflame as the singi star of such as 1930's *Golden Dawn* are jus pleasant memory now. He is in his 70s (b. 189 a much-in-demand character actor, especia for TV dramas, and, in '75, he and wife, Ern tine, celebrated their Golden Anniversary. C screen from 1930. IN: *Lottery Lover, One Me Spring, Ginger, Spring Tonic, A Night at Opera, Walking Down Broadway, Big To Czar, Balalaika, Melody for Three, A Yank Libya, Bottom of the Bottle, The Helen Morg Story, Hong Kong Confidential, Rosie,* more.

KING WRIGHT (S. Cal.) Support. Onscre from 1951. IN: *A Streetcar Named Desire, Pl et of the Apes, Finian's Rainbow,* more.

KING, ZALMAN (S. Cal.) Leading man. On-screen from the '60s. IN: *Stranger on the Run, The Dangerous Years of Kiowa Jones, Whiskey Flats, The Ski Bum, You Gotta Walk It Like You Talk It or You Lose the Beat, The Passover Plot*, more.

KING SISTERS, THE (S. Cal.) Now part of the musical King Family act, Alyce, Donna, Luise, and Yvonne sang in a number of movies for MGM, RKO, and Universal in the '40s. They are all married, with children, and most with grandchildren. Alyce is married to actor Robert Clarke and Yvonne is the mother of actress Tina Cole. All live in the Los Angeles area. IN: *Sing Your Worries Away*, more.

KING-WOOD, DAVID (Eng.) Character. On-screen from the '40s. IN: *The Blakes Slept Here, Men of Sherwood Forest, Break in the Circle, Private's Progress*, more.

KINGSTON, NATALIE (N. Cal.) Another of Tarzan's "Janes" (she was twice in serials with Frank Merrill), she ended her decade-long career by retiring after 1933's *His Private Secretary*—for marriage to a Los Angeles realtor. A widow now, in her late 60s, she lives in quiet retirement in San Francisco. Onscreen from 1923. IN: *Wet Paint, Kid Boots, The Silent Lover, The Night of Love, Lost at the Front, The Harvester, A Girl in Every Port, Street Angel, The Port of Missing Girls, The River of Romance, Her Wedding Night, Under Texas Skies*, more.

KINNEAR, ROY (Eng.) Character. Onscreen from 1961. IN: *Sparrows Can't Sing, Heavens Above!, The Small World of Sammy Lee, Tiara Tahiti, The Hill, The Deadly Affair, A Funny Thing Happened on the Way to the Forum, Willy Wonka and the Chocolate Factory, Juggernaut*, more.

KINSKEY, LEONID (S. Cal.) He would raise his wrinkled brow while a wide half-moon grin all but encircled his Pinocchio nose, and movie-goers laughed—hundreds of times in scores of pictures between 1932's *Trouble in Paradise* and 1956's *Glory*. It would be his pleasure to do it all again—play once more those bartenders, professors, and ballet masters of the pixilated look and Russian accent (authentic; he was born in St. Petersburg in 1903). But the roles are not there now. Just once in recent years has he found a part that pleased him, on TV, in *Mayberry R.F.D.*, in which he guested twice as Alice Ghostley's harp teacher-suitor, Prof. Wolfgang Radetsky, a tragi-comic character. Movies? He still makes them, but not for theater audiences. Operating out of his studio-home, this inimitable comedian writes and di-rects industrial films for major corporations. "To dramatize a machine or product," he says, "requires a great deal more ingenuity to keep it going than a well-written scene played by able actors." His round-the-clock companion in his North Hollywood home is Lady Bug, a four-pound Yorkie, inherited from his wife, who died in 1963. Mrs. Kinskey was Iphigenia Castiglioni, a great beauty from Vienna who was frequently cast in movies—in *The Story of Louis Pasteur*, etc.—as Empress Eugenie. The actor and she were married four times—to one another. "It started in Mexico City," he relates, "and then over 20 years of our happy marriage we celebrated every five years by taking a new marriage license in a different country." With few ties and obligations now, he travels much—to Palm Springs (to visit old friends from Hollywood's "Russian colony"), to New York (on business), and thinks nothing of hopping on a plane on a moment's impulse, as he recently did, for a pleasure jaunt to Moscow. But, being an ever-youthful man of action, what he would really like is for Hollywood to be the center of action it used to be. Onscreen from 1932. IN: *Duck Soup, Three-Cornered Moon, Les Miserables, Peter Ibbetson, The Road to Glory, Rhythm on the Range, The General Died at Dawn, Cafe Metropole, The Great Waltz, Three Blind Mice, The Story of Vernon and Irene Castle, On Your Toes, He Stayed for Breakfast, Down Argentine Way, That Night in Rio, So Ends Our Night, Weekend in Havana, Ball of Fire, I Married an Angel, Casablanca, Presenting Lily Mars, Can't Help Singing, Monsieur Beaucaire, Gobs and Gals, The Man with the Golden Arm*, more.

KIRGO, GEORGE (S. Cal.) Character. Now a screenwriter. IN: *The Best Man*.

KIRIENKO, ZINAIDA (Rus.) Star. IN: *And Quiet Flows the Don, Destiny of a Man*, more.

KIRK, PHYLLIS (S. Cal.) Happily married to TV producer Warren Bush, she rarely acts now —a hip injury, suffered in a fall several years ago, severely restricting her activities and sometimes forcing her to get about on crutches. She remains, in her 40s (b. 1929), a most attractive woman. Onscreen from 1950. IN: *Two Weeks with Love, A Life of Her Own, Our Very Own, Three Guys Named Mike, About Face, The Iron Mistress, House of Wax, Johnny Concho, Back from Eternity, The Sad Sack*, more, including 1959's *City After Midnight*, her most recent to date.

KIRK, TOMMY (S. Cal.) Former juvenile star. Onscreen from 1957. IN: *Old Yeller, The Shaggy Dog, The Absent-Minded Professor, Moon Pilot, Savage Sam, Son of Flubber, Pa-*

jama Party, The Monkey's Uncle, Village of the Giants, It's a Bikini World, more.

KIRKLAND, ALEXANDER (Mex.) Popular in movies of the early '30s, he then returned to the stage where, as producer-director-actor, he enjoyed a distinguished career. Later he wrote for "live" television. After '50, he became an art dealer and lecturer, and for several years operated a gallery in Palm Beach. He is in his 60s now (b. 1908), has long resided in Mexico City, and in '75 was reported engaged to English star Margot Grahame. He was previously married to Greta T. Baldridge; Phyllis Adams, by whom he has a grown daughter; and Gypsy Rose Lee. In '46, while he and Gypsy Rose Lee were estranged, the stripper-actress-author gave birth to a son, who, until he was 26, was known as Erik Kirkland, the name by which he married and became the father of a son. In '71, producer-director Otto Preminger, for whom Erik had worked for several years as a casting director, revealed that he was the boy's father—after which, in New York Surrogates Court, he legally adopted Erik, changing his name to Preminger. Onscreen from 1931. IN: *Tarnished Lady, Surrender, Passport to Hell, Strange Interlude, Almost Married, Black Beauty, Humanity,* more.

KIRKLAND, SALLY (S. Cal.) Leading lady. Onscreen first in three Andy Warhol skinflicks in the '60s. Onscreen elsewhere from 1968. IN: *Blue, Futz, Coming Apart, Brand X, Going Home, Big Bad Mama, Bite the Bullet,* more.

KIRKWOOD, JOE, JR. (S. Cal.) He owns and operates various sports enterprises, including a bowling alley in North Hollywood. Onscreen from 1946. IN: *Joe Palooka—Champ, Joe Palooka in the Big Fight, Joe Palooka Meets Humphrey,* etc., and, in 1961, *Marriage-Go-Round,* his last.

KIRKWOOD, PAT (Eng.) The English singer-actress who costarred with Van Johnson in *No Leave, No Love* made a few more films when she returned to the British Isles, but has mainly enjoyed a thriving career in stage musicals and comedies, on TV, and in cabarets. During the '50s, she starred with her husband, Hubert Gregg, in the TV series *From Me to You,* played leads in such English television specials as *Pygmalion* and *Our Marie,* and had her own radio show, *My Patricia.* In the past decade she has starred onstage in *Lock Up Your Daughters, The Constant Wife, The Rumpus,* and a revival of *Hay Fever.* She remains, in her 50s (b. 1921), a most attractive brunette. Onscreen from 1938. IN: *Save a Little Sunshine; Come On, George; Flight from Folly, Band Wagon, Once a Sinner, Stars in Your Eyes,* more.

KIRSTEN, DOROTHY (S. Cal.) On the last night of 1975, with much media fanfare, the great soprano ended her 30-year reign—unrivaled—at the Metropolitan Opera by singing *Tosca.* She made it plain, however, that she would be singing opera and giving concerts elsewhere, saying, "I will sing as long as I sing well." Still an attractive, shapely blonde, on the threshold of 60 (b. 1917), she expressed a wish to spend more time with her husband, Dr. John French, head of the Brain Research Institute at U.C.L.A., and to paint. She has already had two one-woman shows in Los Angeles, where they live. Onscreen in 1950 in *Mr. Music* and in 1951 in *The Great Caruso.*

KITT, EARTHA (S. Cal.) Black singer-actress. Onscreen from 1954. IN: *New Faces, St. Louis Blues, Anna Lucasta, Mark of the Hawk, The Saint of Devil's Island, Synanon, Friday Foster,* more.

KJELLIN, ALF (S. Cal.) Producer David O. Selznick saw the tall, thin, taciturn, and handsome, Swede in 1947's *Torment,* imported him to Hollywood to costar with Jennifer Jones, and changed his name to Christopher Kent. He did eventually costar with Miss Jones, but at MGM in *Madame Bovary.* And he remains exactly as described above, except that in his 50s (b. 1920) he is silver-haired now, and he is no longer Christopher Kent. Nor is he primarily an actor. He still acts once in a while, as in a '74 episode of *Cannon,* in which he starred, chillingly, as a Nazi-hunter. After *Madame Bovary,* he says, "I changed my name back to Alf Kjellin, made a lot of lousy pictures here, and went home to Sweden to act and direct." He has been back in Hollywood since '59, directing TV shows— *Alfred Hitchcock Presents, Hawaii Five-0, The Six Million Dollar Man, Columbo,* etc. In '74 he was awarded the Royal Order of Vasa, with the rank of Knight First Class, by King Carl XVI Gustav of Sweden. The honor was in recognition of his "most excellent contribution to the arts of the theatre and film as actor, writer, director and producer of plays and film" and for the "very favorable image you have given Swedish talent in these areas." Divorced, the actor-director lives in a mountaintop home above Beverly Hills with his five children, all, at this writing, under the age of 17. Onscreen in Hollywood as Alf Kjellin from 1952. IN: *My Six Convicts, Affairs of a Model, The Iron Mistress, The Juggler, Illicit Interlude, Ship of Fools, Assault on a Queen,* and, his most recent to date, *Ice Station Zebra.*

KLAVUN, WALTER (N.Y.) Character. Onscreen from 1951. IN: *The Mob, It Should Happen to You,* more.

KLEEB, HELEN (S. Cal.) Character. Onscreen from 1952. IN: *Kansas City Confidential, Witness to Murder, Magnificent Obsession, Friendly Persuasion, Curse of the Undead, the Gazebo, The Manchurian Candidate, Seven Days in May, The Hallelujah Trail, The Fortune Cookie, Blue, Halls of Anger, Star Spangled Girl*, more.

KLEIN, ADELAIDE (N.Y.) Character. Onscreen from 1948. IN: *The Naked City, C-Man, The Enforcer, Splendor in the Grass*, more.

KLEMPERER, WERNER (S. Cal.) Character. Onscreen from 1956. IN: *Flight from Hong Kong, Istanbul, Kiss Them for Me, Houseboat, Operation Eichmann, Judgment at Nuremberg, Ship of Fools, The Wicked Dreams of Paula Schultz*, more.

KLUGMAN, JACK (S. Cal.) Character star. Onscreen from 1956. IN: *Timetable, Twelve Angry Men, Cry Terror, The Days of Wine and Roses, I Could Go On Singing, Act One, Hail Mafia!, The Detective, Goodbye Columbus, Two-Minute Warning*, more.

KNAPP, DAVID (S. Cal.) Support. Onscreen from 1961. IN: *Parrish, The Pledgemasters*, more.

KNAPP, EVALYN (S. Cal.) In her 60s now (b. 1908), she lives in retirement in Beverly Hills, the widow—since the early '70s—of a prominent physician, Dr. George A. Snyder, whom she married in '34. She seldom gives a thought to her 70-picture career on which she closed the book after 1943's *Two Weeks to Live*. Onscreen from 1930. IN: *Sinners' Holiday, River's End, Gentlemen of the Evening, Big Time Charlie, Fifty Million Frenchmen, You and I, Big City Blues, Madame Racketeer, Fame, Sporting Widow, Night Mayor, Air Hostess, His Private Secretary, The Perils of Pauline* (serial), *Speed Wings, Ladies Crave Excitement, Three of a Kind, Hawaiian Buckaroo, The Lone Wolf Takes a Chance*, more.

KNIGHT, CHRISTOPHER (S. Cal.) Former juvenile. IN: *The Narrow Chute*.

KNIGHT, DAVID (Eng.) Leading man. Onscreen from 1955. IN: *The Young Lovers, Out of the Clouds, Eyewitness, Chance Meeting, Tears for Simon, Across the Bridge, Nightmare*, more.

KNIGHT, DON (S. Cal.) Support. Onscreen from 1967. IN: *Kill a Dragon, Too Late the Hero, The Hawaiians, Something Big*, more.

KNIGHT, ESMOND (Eng.) Character; former leading man. Onscreen from 1931. IN: *The Ringer, A Clown Must Laugh, Blackout, This England, Half-Way House, Henry V, Black Narcissus, Hamlet, The Red Shoes, A Canterbury Tale, The River, Helen of Troy, Richard III, Prince and the Showgirl, The Spy Who Came in from the Cold*, more.

KNIGHT, JACK (S. Cal.) Support. Onscreen from the '60s. IN: *Plaza Suite, Rosemary's Baby; Wicked, Wicked; The Long Goodbye*, more.

KNIGHT, PATRICIA (S. Cal.) The former leading lady and ex-wife of Cornel Wilde does supporting roles now. Onscreen from 1947. IN: *Roses Are Red, The Fabulous Texas, The Second Face*, more.

KNIGHT, ROSALIND (Eng.) Character. Onscreen from 1963. IN: *Tom Jones, Start the Revolution without Me*, more.

KNIGHT, SANDRA (S. Cal.) Formerly married to Jack Nicholson, and the mother of his teenage daughter, Jenifer, she currently does TV commercials. Onscreen from 1958. IN: *Frankenstein's Daughter, Blood Bath*, more.

KNIGHT, SHIRLEY (N.Y.) Leading lady. Nominated for Best Supporting Actress Oscar in *The Dark at the Top of the Stairs* and *Sweet Bird of Youth*. She left Hollywood in 1962 to study at the Actors Studio in New York. Though she has returned since to appear in a few movies, and has made still others in New York, she has mainly starred on Broadway. Notably, she has been seen in *The Three Sisters* and, in the 1975–76 season, in the lead in *Kennedy's Children*. For several years she also lived and worked in England, where she met and married her second husband, playwright John Hopkins, by whom she has a daughter, Sophie (b. 1967). By first husband, Gene Persson, the young movie producer, she also has a daughter, Katlyn (b. 1964). She and her family live now in the suburban community of Chappaqua. A particularly outspoken individual, the Kansas-born (1937) actress said in '74: "I will *not* do some Hollywood garbage again, ever, for any salary. I'd rather stay home with my husband and children." Somewhat mellower the following year, reflecting on the Hollywood career she rejected, she admitted: "Yes, I've regretted it at times. I could be both rich and famous now, but I'm neither." Onscreen from 1959. IN: *Flight From Ashiya, The Group, The Dutchman, The Counterfeit Killer, The Rain People, Petulia*, more.

KNIGHT, TED (S. Cal.) Character. Onscreen from the '60s. IN: *Countdown*, more.

KNOTTS, DON (S. Cal.) Star comedian. Onscreen from 1958. IN: *No Time for Sergeants, The Last Time I Saw Archie, Move Over Darling, The Incredible Mr. Limpet, The Ghost and Mr. Chicken, The Reluctant Astronaut, The Shakiest Gun in the West, The Love God?, The Apple Dumpling Gang; No Deposit, No Return;* more.

KNOWLES, PATRIC (S. Cal.) The Errol Flynn look-alike—besides being best friends, they occasionally played brothers—is white-haired, still handsome in his 60s (b. 1911), and acts only once in a while. In '73 he supported Roddy McDowall in *Arnold*, just as he had 32 years earlier in *How Green Was My Valley*. That same year he was also in *Terror in the Wax Museum*. But there is little slack time in his life as he has numerous business interests—apartments, gas docks, and rental houses in Balboa. He and his wife, Enid—English like himself; they married in '35 just before he came here to make *The Charge of the Light Brigade*—have recently moved into a new townhouse in Woodland Hills. "We sold the 'big-house-on-the-hill' as it was just too much for us," he reports, "and now I have no lawn to mow or pool to clean, it's all done for us—very comfortable way of life." He speaks often and with pride of his children, saying, "Our son, Michael [Flynn was his godfather], is married, has two children—a boy and a girl—and is managing a plant for Container Corp. in Milano, Italy. Our daughter, Toni, who gave us two marvelous boys by her previous marriage, has remarried and is living near here with her new husband, Gary, and the boys—I take them fishing and I've taught them to swim." Besides this, the actor is a community leader (onetime Honorary Mayor of Tarzana); a published novelist *(Even Steven);* a guest lecturer on writing, directing, and acting at various Southern California colleges; a Shakespeare scholar; and a student of horticulture and history. Friends who should know refer to him as a "compleat man." His life has been—and obviously still is—a full and fulfilled one. His friend Flynn should have been so lucky. Onscreen in England from 1934. IN: *Royal Jubilee, A Student's Romance, Mister Hobo,* more. Onscreen in America from 1936. IN: *Give Me Your Heart, It's Love I'm After, The Adventures of Robin Hood, The Sisters, Torchy Blane in Panama, Another Thin Man, A Bill of Divorcement, The Mystery of Marie Roget, Crazy House, Forever and a Day, Chip Off the Old Block, Kitty, O.S.S., Dream Girl, Quebec, Khyber Patrol, Auntie Mame, From the Earth to the Moon, The Way West, Chisum,* more.

KNOX, ALEXANDER (Eng.) In '54, after a dozen years in Hollywood, many major roles, and one Oscar nomination as Best Actor in *Wilson*, this Canadian-born actor moved back to England. It had become his "second home" when he was an aspiring actor in his 20s. In the years since his departure, he has played supporting roles in more than 40: *Khartoum, Puppet on a Chain, Nicholas and Alexandra, You Only Live Twice* (playing a character designated as the "American President," he ranked 13th in the credits). As he enters his 70s (b. 1907), he has given no thought to retiring. His wife, though, actress Doris Nolan, intends never to perform again. Perhaps best recalled as the blonde society girl in *Holiday* who lost Cary Grant to her screen sister, Katharine Hepburn, she was in *Top of the Town, Irene, Follies Girl,* and many other Hollywood movies. Still a stunning woman, in her early 60s (b. 1916), she has long been a business associate of the Eric Esterick art galleries in London. Her actor-husband's own "second career"—not really new—is writing. A newspaper man before he was an actor, he coauthored two of the Hollywood pix in which he appeared: *Sister Kenny* and *Sign of the Ram.* In this decade, working in solitude at their country house in Northumberland, he has turned out—to date—two critically acclaimed adventure novels: *Night of the White Bear* and *Totem Dream,* of which *Publishers Weekly's* critic said: "The actor-author . . . returns with another beautifully written novel of wild country (the Canadian Great Lakes region in 1770) and the people who struggle to survive in it." Reviews such as this seem to mean most to the actor today. Onscreen in England from 1938. IN: *Four Feathers, The Phantom Strikes,* more. Onscreen in America and internationally from 1941. IN: *The Sea Wolf, Commandos Strike at Dawn, None Shall Escape, Over 21, Indian Summer, Tokyo Joe, The Judge Steps Out, The Night My Number Came Up, The Vikings, Oscar Wilde, In the Cool of the Day, Modesty Blaise, Shalako, Fraulein Doktor, How I Won the War,* more.

KNOX, ELYSE (S. Cal.) She is, in her sixth decade (b. 1917), still one of the great blonde beauties, as all know who have seen her in those TV Geritol commercials with her grandchildren. At last count she had five—four by eldest daughter, Kristin, wife of actor-singer Rick Nelson. Second daughter, Kelly, adopted a son, Zachary Thomas (called Z.T.), during her marriage to young G.M. executive John DeLorean; the boy lives now in Washington with DeLorean and his present wife. Elyse Knox's third child is ex-UCLA football star Mark Harmon, now preparing to be a lawyer working in the sports contract field. For over three decades, the actress (veteran of 45 movies) has been happily married to a "football hero" of her own—the great All-American halfback at Michigan in '39 and '40, Tom Harmon. He, too, starred in one movie, 1941's *Harmon of Michigan*. White-haired now, and deeply tanned, Harmon is sports director for Mutual Broadcasting in Los Angeles. (Just for the fun of it, in '73, he also did a guest-star stint in one episode of TV's *Mannix*, just as son Mark did about the same time in *Ozzie's Girls*. The latter constituted an "in family" lark—Harriet and the late Ozzie Nelson being Kristin Harmon Nelson's parents-in-law.) The Harmons live, as they have for years, in a Brentwood mansion presided over by Elyse—lovingly nicknamed "The Boss" by her family. Despite the appellation, daughter Kristin has said, "In my parents' house, everything was very traditional. My father worked, my mother took care of the children . . . but it was my father's opinions that *really counted.*" The Knox-Harmon combination obviously has been a successful one. Son Mark, looking forward to marriage and his own family, recently paid his parents the supreme compliment, saying, "I'd love to be able to know I could raise my kids the way they did. We have no major hassles." Onscreen from 1940. IN: *Lillian Russell; Free, Blonde and 21; Footlight Fever, Tanks a Million, The Mummy's Tomb, Mr. Big, Don Winslow of the Coast Guard* (serial), *Hit the Ice, So's Your Uncle; A Wave, a Wac and a Marine; Moonlight and Cactus, Gentleman Joe Palooka, Sweetheart of Sigma Chi, Linda Be Good*, more, including 1949's *There's a Girl in My Heart*, her last.

KNUDSEN, PEGGY (S. Cal.) First onscreen in 1946's *The Big Sleep* and last in 1957's *Istanbul*, the once stunning blonde starlet, longtime best friend of Jennifer Jones (they were together in *Good Morning, Miss Dove*), lives in Hollywood where she is waging a valiant battle against a crippling arthritic condition. Now in her early 50s (b. 1923), she has had, to date, five operations for this. IN: *Never Say Goodbye, Shadow of a Woman, A Stolen Life, Stallion Road, The Unfaithful, Half Past Midnight, Perilous Waters, Copper Canyon, Unchained, The Bottom of the Bottle, Hilda Crane*, more.

KOBART, RUTH (N. Cal.) Onscreen from 1966. IN: *How to Succeed in Business Without Really Trying*, more.

KOBE, GAIL (S. Cal.) Support. Onscreen from 1956. IN: *The Ten Commandments, La Notte, Eclipse*, more.

KOGAN, MILT (S. Cal.) Character. Onscreen in the '70s. IN: *Dr. Black-Mr. Hyde*, more.

KOHNER, SUSAN (N.Y.) Leading lady. Nominated for Best Supporting Actress Oscar in *Imitation of Life*. An elegant, raven-haired beauty in her early 40s (b. 1936), she does not expect ever to act again. She has been happily married since '64 to John Weitz, and is the mother of two young sons, Paul and Chris. Her husband is, of course, the big, ruggedly masculine, and vastly successful menswear designer. He also writes best-selling books—the novel *The Value of Nothing* and the nonfiction *Man in Charge* ("The Executive's Guide to Grooming, Manners and Travel"). The actress (his third wife) and he have a magnificent apartment in the city but, when not traveling all over the globe, live mainly on their 50-foot yacht Milagros (Spanish for miracles), moored intermittently at Palm Beach or Sag Harbor, Long Island. She does not miss the limelight, the former young star says. "I'm just the kind who prefers the man to be the focus of attention professionally—it may be my Latin upbringing." She is, it will be recalled, the daughter of former Mexican actress Lupita Tovar and Hollywood agent Paul Kohner. "I'm happy," she adds. "I don't feel a need to work. And I like to be with John." Onscreen from 1955. IN: *To Hell and Back, The Last Wagon, Dino, Trooper Hook, The Gene Krupa Story, The Big Fisherman, All the Fine Young Cannibals, By Love Possessed, Freud*.

KOMACK, JIMMIE (JAMES) (S. Cal.) Support. Now producer of TV's *Chico and the Man*. Onscreen from 1958. IN: *Damn Yankees, A Hole in the Head*, more.

KONRAD, DOROTHY (S. Cal.) Character. Onscreen from 1962. IN: *Sweet Bird of Youth, Blue*, more.

KOPELL, BERNIE (S. Cal.) Support. Onscreen from 1965. IN: *The Loved One*, more.

KORDA, MARIA (S. Cal.) Leading lady. Onscreen from 1967. IN: *The Fastest Gun Alive*, more. (See Hillary Brooke.)

KORJUS, MILIZA (S. Cal.) Late in '72, at the Hollywood premiere of *The Great Waltz* remake, Miliza Korjus, the legendary coloratura soprano from Poland, was an honored guest. All other celebrities present were forgotten as photographers converged upon her. Except for rare appearances on the concert stage, she had not been seen in public in decades. A large woman in her 70s (b. 1902), and rather heavy, she wore white furs and an ill-fitting blonde wig. Unchanged, though, was the gaiety and humor that had made her so unforgettable in *The Great Waltz*, her only Hollywood movie, which brought her an Academy Award nomination as

Best Supporting Actress. Madame Korjus' screen career was jinxed by an automobile accident in 1940 which hospitalized her for almost a year. She next moved to Mexico for several years. Reportedly she made one other movie there, *Caballeria del Imperio,* but locating anyone who has seen it is difficult. She returned to the States, made her concert debut at Carnegie Hall in '44, and, in the years since, while continuing to concertize occasionally, she has primarily recorded. Venus Recordings of Beverly Hills—she is reportedly a stockholder—lists seven Korjus LPs. Formerly married to Kuno Foelsch, by whom she has a grown daughter, also named Miliza, the singer became the wife of Dr. Walter Schecter in 1952 and lived happily with him until his death a few years ago. For many years she has lived in a beautiful house in West Los Angeles, only a few miles from MGM, scene of her great movie triumph. Sometimes she has talked of making a screen comeback—*Salome,* she has said, would be the ideal vehicle. But friends believe she will be content to let fans remember her as she was in *The Great Waltz.*

KORMAN, HARVEY (S. Cal.) Comedian. Onscreen from 1966. IN: *Lord Love a Duck, Don't Just Stand There, Last of the Secret Agents, Three Bites of the Apple, The April Fools, Blazing Saddles, Huckleberry Finn,* more.

KORVIN, CHARLES (N.Y.) He had black wavy hair, smoldering eyes, rugged masculinity (though not a brawny man), a deeply clefted chin guaranteed to provoke excitement in the opposite sex, a strong handsome face, and a deep accented (Hungarian) speaking voice. Universal was certain it had discovered "another" Charles Boyer. They paired him with Merle Oberon in two romantic melodramas, *This Love of Ours* and *Temptation.* Despite the sizzling impression he made, he apparently decided he would rather be Charles Korvin, Actor, than Charles Korvin, the "new" anyone. Succeeding movies emphasized qualities other than his romantic appeal. Today, physically, the actor is naturally different than he was, as he is entering his 70s (b. 1907). His hair is thin—as he is—and silver, but his potency as an actor is unchanged. Reviewing a movie in which he recently appeared, in a character role, *Variety*'s critic observed that the director had "the benefit of some smooth performances, particularly from Charles Korvin." Leaving Hollywood almost 25 years ago, though returning at intervals for roles, the actor devoted his energies to the stage and TV. He toured the country in leading roles in *Tiger at the Gates, The King and I, The Fourposter,* etc. He starred on television in the '59 series *Interpol Calling,* and acted on *Studio One, Playhouse 90,* etc. Stage acting was not

new to him. Born Geza Kaiser, he had arrived in New York in '37, changed his name to Geza Korvin and, under that name, starred on Broadway in the early '40s in *Winter Soldiers* and *Dark Eyes.* It was in the latter show that Hollywood discovered him and changed his name again—first to George Korvin, as he was billed in his first picture, *Enter Arsene Lupin,* and then to Charles. In '57 he became both a naturalized American citizen and the husband of Anne Bogy—his second wife—after a seven-year courtship. He is the stepfather of a son, Edward, a recording studio executive in Manhattan. He and his wife divide their time between New York City, where they have a West Side apartment, and Switzerland, where they have a condominium. Besides being an in-demand character actor, he has photographed and directed two documentaries. And he has no regrets, none at all, that he did not become the "new" Charles Boyer. Onscreen abroad in 1937 in *Hearts of Spain.* Onscreen in America and internationally from 1944. IN: *Berlin Express, The Killer That Stalked New York, Lydia Bailey, Tarzan's Savage Fury, Sangaree, The Blackwell Story, Interpol Calling, Ship of Fools, The Man Who Had Power Over Women,* and, in '75, *Inside Out.*

KOSCINA, SYLVA (It.) Leading lady. Onscreen from 1957. IN: *The Mighty Crusaders, Hercules, Swordsman of Siena, Jessica, Love on the Riviera, Juliet of the Spirits, Agent 8 3/4, That Man in Istanbul, Judex, Three Bites of the Apple, The Private War of Harry Frigg, The Charge of the Light Brigade, He and She, Battle of Neretva,* more.

KOSLECK, MARTIN (S. Cal.) With his high cheekbones, Teutonic accent, and wickedly slanted eyes, not to mention his icy-hearted demeanor, he was the nastiest movie "Nazi" of them all. For years, in the '40s, he had audiences spitting venom at the screen, particularly when he portrayed—five times—Hitler's Dr. Goebbels. Going into his 70s (b. 1907) and unchanged in looks, he still plays bad guys, as in the recent *A Day at the White House,* but he acts less frequently now. He has been back in Hollywood for several years after more than a decade in New York, where he did plays, radio, TV, and three movies including *Something Wild.* His wife died while they lived in Manhattan and he has remained single since. "She was the Baroness Eleonora von Mendelssohn," he says, "named after her godmother, Eleonora Duse. She was a Reinhardt star and also appeared in starring parts on Broadway as Eleonora Mendelssohn." Much of the actor's performing in recent years has been on TV. "When I am not acting," he says, "I paint. I have had a number of exhibits here and in New

232

York; Bette Davis and Marlene Dietrich own some of their portraits. And I am translating into English a book my sister wrote. She is all the family I have now—living in my house in West Germany, which I had built for my mother. My sister conducts a flourishing Scotch Terrier kennel. The book, which I hope will be a success here, is a story of love for all the kindred animals—pets or wild ones—amongst whom she lives or has lived.'' This is Martin Kosleck—the man everyone loved to hate? Onscreen abroad from the '30s. IN: *Napoleon auf St. Helena*, more. Onscreen in America from 1939. IN: *Confessions of a Nazi Spy, Espionage Agent, Foreign Correspondent, The Mad Doctor, Underground, All Through the Night, Berlin Correspondent, Manila Calling, Chetniks, Bomber's Moon, The North Star, The Hitler Gang, The Spider, She-Wolf of London, The Beginning or the End?, Smuggler's Cove, Morituri, The Agent from H.A.R.M., Which Way to the Front?*, more.

KOSSOFF, DAVID (Eng.) Character. Onscreen from 1950. IN: *Svengali, The Bespoke Overcoat, The Iron Petticoat, Count Five and Die, Indiscreet, The Mouse That Roared, The House of the Seven Hawks, The Mouse on the Moon, Ring of Treason*, more.

KOTKIN, EDWARD S. (N.Y.) Character. Onscreen in the '70s. IN: *Cops and Robbers, The Filthiest Show in Town, The Mating Chase*, more.

KOTTO, YAPHET (S. Cal.) Black star. Onscreen from 1968. IN: *Nothing But a Man, Five Card Stud, The Thomas Crown Affair, The Liberation of Lord Byron Jones, Across 110th Street, Sharks' Treasure, Report to the Commissioner, Friday Foster, Drum, The Shootist*, more.

KOVACK, NANCY (S. Cal.) Married to famous conductor Zubin Mehta, she no longer acts. Onscreen from 1960. IN: *Strangers When We Meet, Cry for Happy, Jason and the Argonauts, Sylvia, The Silencers, The Great Sioux Uprising, Enter Laughing, Marooned*, more.

KOVE, MARTIN (N.Y.) Support. Onscreen in the '70s. IN: *Last House on the Left, Janis, Cops and Robbers, Savages, Little Murders*, more.

KRESKI, CONNIE (S. Cal.) Leading lady. Onscreen from the '60s. IN: *Can Heironymus Merkin Ever Forget Mercy Humppe . . .?, The Black Bird*, more.

KREUGER, KURT (S. Cal.) On the threshold of his 60s (b. 1917), his blond hair is thinning and he wears the face—ruddy, smiling—of a once-handsome man. Unchanged is Kreuger's European charm and athletic physique, which perhaps is due to spending many weeks each year on the ski slopes at Aspen, Colo. Still living in Hollywood, in a magnificent house above the Sunset Strip, Kreuger still acts, on TV's *Barnaby Jones*, etc., but so irregularly that longtime fans are often surprised to learn this. They are the ones who recall the 6-foot Swiss-German, usually in Nazi uniform, in so many movies of the '40s. Perhaps, too, they wrote some of the fan mail that made him 20th Century-Fox's #3 male pinup, just behind Tyrone Power and John Payne. Those were the days when he urged his ski-buddy and studio boss, Darryl F. Zanuck, to give him better roles, and was told: "What's your hurry? With your looks you'll be good at fifty." He never got the star-making parts. Three decades later, his European accent still pronounced, the actor laughs and volunteers his present credo for accepting TV or movie roles: "Either the part or the money has to be good." His home and its expensive furnishings are evidence that he can afford to be selective. The walls of his living room, furnished in massive dark woods, are filled with the best French Impressionist and Oriental art. Through the glass doors, a pool shimmers under a sunny blue sky. Pointing beyond a row of pepper trees, he says, "This house is part of a complex. I own four others on the same street. It's an outlet for my creative talent. I take an old house and revamp it—do my own designing and decorating—then furnish and lease it. I paint them all the same putty color. Friends joke that they can drive past a property of mine and recognize at once that it's been 'Kreugerized.' Over the years, 33 properties have gone through my hands." Kreuger has lived in America since he was 20—except for six years in the '50s when he lived and made movies in Europe. He has been married once, in '51 to a woman whose mother was Swiss and whose father was South American. "Three years of bliss, three years of hell," the actor says succinctly. They had a son, they divorced, and there was a custody battle, which he lost. The son, also named Kurt, goes by his mother's name, is a graduate of the University of Lausanne—his father's school—and has been to New York but never to Hollywood. Reflecting on his life and careers, Kurt Kreuger says: "I would have preferred success in acting to success in other areas, and with the right breaks at the right time I could have become a major star." The weather-tanned man smiles and shrugs, his blue eyes rueful, and says, "Hardly anyone has complete happiness. You make do with what you have. Who knows? One day I may come back as a character actor." It seems a promise to yesteryear fans who come upon a bronze star on the sidewalk on Vine Street emblazoned with his name and remember a smiling young blond who was charming even in his screen villainy, and wonder, Where is he now? Onscreen from 1943. IN: *The Purple V, The Moon Is Down, None Shall Escape, Sahara, The Strange Death of Adolf Hitler, Mademoiselle Fifi* (his favorite), *Escape in the Desert, Paris Underground, The Dark Corner, Sentimental Journey, The Enemy Below, Legion of the Doomed; What Did You Do in the War, Daddy?; more, including 1967's The St. Valentine's Day Massacre, his most recent to date.*

KRISTEL, SYLVIA (Holland) Leading lady. Onscreen in the '70s. IN: *Emmanuelle, Madame Claude.*

KRISTEN, MARTA (S. Cal.) Leading lady. Onscreen from 1963. IN: *Savage Sam,* more.

KRISTOFFERSON, KRIS (S. Cal.) Singer-songwriter-leading man. Onscreen in the '70s. IN: *Cisco Pike, Bring Me the Head of Alfredo Garcia, Alice Doesn't Live Here Anymore, The Sailor Who Fell from Grace with the Sea, A Star Is Born,* more.

KROEGER, BERRY (S. Cal.) Character. Onscreen from 1948. IN: *The Iron Curtain, Act of Violence, Cry of the City, Chicago Deadline, Deadly as the Female, Down to the Sea in Ships, Guilty of Treason, Blood Alley, Man in the Vault, Seven Thieves, Hitler, Youngblood Hawke, Chamber of Horrors, The Mephisto Waltz, Pets, The Man in the Glass Booth,* more.

KRUEGER, LORRAINE (S. Cal.) Still living in Los Angeles, she rarely acts now. Onscreen from 1937. IN: *New Faces of 1937, I'm from the City, Exposed, Idiot's Delight, He's My Guy,* more.

KRUGER, HARDY (Ger.) Costar. Onscreen from 1956. IN: *As Long As You're Near Me, The Rest Is Silence, Taxi for Tobruk, Sundays and Cybele, Hatari!, The Flight of the Phoenix, The Uninhibited, The Secret of Santa Vittoria, The Red Tent, Battle of Neretva, Paper Tiger, Barry Lyndon,* more.

KRUGMAN, LOU (S. Cal.) Character. Onscreen from 1948. IN: *To the Ends of the Earth, I Want to Live!,* more.

KRUSCHEN, JACK (S. Cal.) Character. Nominated for Best Supporting Actor Oscar in *The Apartment.* Onscreen from 1949. IN: *Woman from Headquarters, Confidence Girl, The War of the Worlds, Blueprint for Murder, Money from Home, Tennessee Champ, Soldier of Fortune, Julie, Cry Terror, Fraulein, The Decks*

Ran Red, The Buccaneer, The Last Voyage The Angry Red Planet, Ladies' Man, Love Come Back, Cape Fear, Convicts Four, McLin tock!, The Unsinkable Molly Brown, The Hap pening, Caprice, Freebie and the Bean, more.

KULP, NANCY (S. Cal.) Character comedi enne. Onscreen from 1952. IN: *The Model an the Marriage Broker, Shane, Sabrina, Foreve Darling, The Three Faces of Éve, The Paren Trap, Who's Minding the Store?, Strange Bed fellows, The Night of the Grizzly,* more.

KULUVA, WILL (S. Cal.) Character. Onscreen from 1949. IN: *Abandoned Woman, Th Shrike, Crime in the Streets, Odds Against To morrow, Go Naked in the World, The Spira Road, The Christine Jorgensen Story,* more.

KURTZ, SWOOSIE (N.Y.) Support. Onscree in the '70s. IN: *Jenny, The Tiger Makes Ou* more.

KUTER, KAY E. (S. Cal.) Character. Onscree from 1955. IN: *Guys and Dolls, The Steel Jur gle, The Big Night, A Time for Killing, Wate melon Man,* more.

KWAN, NANCY (S. Cal.) Leading lady. Or screen from 1960. IN: *The World of Suzi Wong, Flower Drum Song, The Main Attra tion, Honeymoon Hotel, Fate Is the Hunter, T mahine, The House of Seven Joys, The Wrec ing Crew, The McMasters, Fortress in the Su* more.

KYDD, SAM (Eng.) Character. Onscreen fro 1945. IN: *The Captive Heart, The Rainbo Jacket, The Detective, The End of the Roa Treasure Island, Pool of London, Murder W Out, Ladykillers, Trent's Last Case, Law an Disorder, I'm All Right Jack, The Last Gre ade, Too Late the Hero, 10 Rillington Plac Confessions of a Window Cleaner,* more.

KYO, MACHIKO (Jap.) Leading lady. Or screen from 1951. IN: *Rasho-Mon, Ugets Gate of Hell, Yang Kwei Fei, The Teahouse the August Moon, Street of Shame, Buddh Face of Another,* more.

KYSER, KAY (Mass.) In '47, when the famo bandleader had a radio show near the top of th ratings and his sponsors inexplicably cancele he threw down the script, said "That's it," a left bigtime show business for good. Retiring Chapel Hill, in his native state of North Car lina, the "Ol' Professor of Musical Know edge" was accompanied into noncelebrityho by his wife (since '44), Georgia Carroll. Besid being the nation's #1 cover girl—there was period when no issue of *Redbook* went to pre without this honey-blonde on the cover—she had been used decoratively in many movies, and then was Kyser's lead singer ("And here's Gorgeous Georgia Carroll!"). They parented three stunningly blonde "cover girls," all replicas of Georgia—Kimberly Ann and Carroll, both married now, and Amanda. For a while, in his early "retirement," Kay Kyser served as technical adviser for his community's television station. But, troubled by an arthritic condition and, later, a slight heart condition, he gave up all such professional activities and began devoting himself fulltime to his religion, Christian

Science, as an authorized practitioner. Late in '74, the "Kollege of Musical Knowledge" maestro, then 69, and accompanied by Georgia, moved without fanfare to Christian Science headquarters in Boston. There now, as manager of the film and broadcasting department of the church, he produces films to be shown in churches and at meetings of church officials. Onscreen from 1939. IN: *That's Right, You're Wrong; You'll Find Out, Playmates, My Favorite Spy, Thousands Cheer, Swing Fever, Around the World, Carolina Blues.*

L

LA PERA, SAM (N.Y.) Character. Onscreen in the '70s. IN: *Lovers and Other Strangers, Believe in Me, Who Is Harry Kellerman . . . ?,* more.

LA PLANCHE, ROSEMARY (S. Cal.) Miss America of 1941, who appeared in numerous pix in the '40s, she was married for almost three decades to radio emcee-TV producer Harry Koplan, until his death in '73. By him, she has two grown children, a son, Terry, and a daughter, Carol. Since she left the screen in '49, Rosemary, a beauty still, has been a professional painter. Starting as a total amateur, with a dime-store tin of water colors, she has had regular one-woman showings of her oils both in Los Angeles and Laguna. To date she has sold more than 500 paintings, two of which, during the Nixon Administration, hung in the Western White House. She lives in Sherman Oaks where she faithfully attends services at St. Francis de Sales Church. Onscreen from 1943. IN: *Prairie Chickens, Manhattan Serenade, Strangler in the Swamp, Swing Your Partner, Betty Coed, Angel's Alley, An Old-Fashioned Girl,* more.

LA PLANTE, LAURA (S. Cal.) The effervescence and blonde beauty that made her, in the '20s, the "Doris Day" of Universal comedies remain her chief characteristics in her 70s (b. 1904). She has been married since 1934 to producer Irving (*Blossoms in the Dust*) Asher. Her previous marriage, to director William Seiter, lasted six years: 1926–32. The Ashers have two children—Jill, who is married to a California attorney, and Tony, a Hollywood ad man and, at last report, still a bachelor. The actress and her husband live in a desert mansion near Palm Springs. This has been their home since they returned from a six-year (1934–40) residence in England where Asher was a movie exec for, successively, Warner, London Films, and Columbia. He was later executive producer of 20th Century-Fox in Hollywood. Laura has acted before cameras just three times since giving up

her starring career of more than 75 pictures in '31. In '46 she supported Jackie "Butch" Jenkins in *Little Mister Jim.* Then, in the '50s, she starred in one drama on CBS-TV's *Telephone Time* and in the movie *Spring Reunion* played Betty Hutton's mother. Of most of her movies she laughs, "That was so long ago I cannot even remember doing them." *Finders Keepers,* though, she does recall as her personal favorite. Anyone holding fond memories of Laura La Plante had best cherish them—she won't be back. Onscreen from 1921. IN: *The Old Swimming Hole, Perils of the Yukon, Sporting Youth, Dangerous Innocence, The Midnight Sun, Skinner's Dress Suit, Butterflies in the Rain, Beware of Widows, The Cat and the Canary, Finders Keepers, Scandal, Show Boat, Hold Your Man, Captain of the Guard, King of Jazz, God's Gift to Women, Meet the Wife, Men Are Like That,* more.

LA ROCHE, MARY (S. Cal.) Former leading lady; retired. Onscreen from 1950. IN: *Catskill Honeymoon, Operation Mad Ball; Run Silent, Run Deep* (as Gable's wife); *Gidget, Bye Bye Birdie, The Swinger,* more.

LA ROY, RITA (S. Cal.) A chic woman in her late 60s (b. 1907), she has long owned one of Hollywood's most noted model agencies. Onscreen from the '20s. IN: *Dynamite, Children of the Ritz, Fashions in Love, Check and Double Check, The Gay Diplomat, Playthings of Hollywood, While Paris Sleeps, Bachelor's Affairs, So Big, Blonde Venus, Sinners in the Sun, Fugitive Lady, The Mandarin Mystery, Condemned Women,* more, including 1940's *Hold That Woman,* her last.

LA RUE, JACK (S. Cal.) He began his movie career as a mobster and, 150 pictures later, in his most recent outing (1973's *A Voice in the Night*), he was still up to his old bad deeds. In his 70s (b. 1900), living in a posh apartment in North Hollywood, the actor considers himself

235

essentially retired and emphatically a single man—after several marriages and a couple of expensive divorces. He has one son, Jack Jr., an actor, a handsome young man in his 20s with a modified hippie hair style, who is a strong-faced look-alike—even to the cleft chin—of his famous father. La Rue rarely makes the Hollywood scene now, but in '73 he did turn out for "Mae Day," to assist pal George Raft and others in the Masquers Club's toast to Mae West, whose leading man he was in the play *Diamond Lil*. Onscreen from 1932. IN: *When Paris Sleeps, Three on a Match, A Farewell to Arms, Gambling Ship, The Kennel Murder Case, Miss Fane's Baby Is Stolen, Waterfront Lady, Dancing Pirate, Go West Young Man, Trapped by G-Men, Valley of the Giants, Charlie Chan in Panama, Ringside Maisie, X Marks the Spot, The Spanish Main, Murder in the Music Hall, My Favorite Brunette, Robin and the Seven Hoods, Those Who Think Young*, more.

LA RUE, LASH (S. Cal.) Washed up as a cowboy star by 1950, he later, he has said, worked in a porn film—as a gray-bearded heavy. "Oh yes, it was a hard-core job and I was definitely in it," he admitted. "The title was *Hard on the Trail*, but it should've been *Hard-on the Trail*... I wasn't connected with the shooting of the dirty stuff. They spliced that in around me." Of this assignment, which meant two days' work, he said, "It was an honest mistake on my part. I was duped. I'm sorry I made it, but I'm glad, too, in a way. I got paid for it." The years since stardom have been hard scrabble. He coasted on his black-garbed fame a while as a King of the Bullwhip attraction at carnivals. Two headlined arrests killed what was left of his career. One was in Memphis in '56, when he was arrested while appearing at the fairground there on charges of buying and receiving three stolen sewing machines and a calculating machine. Pleading innocent, stating that he did not know they were stolen, he was cleared in a Criminal Court trial in '57. But the damage was done, and was compounded four years later when, in Miami, he was arrested for vagrancy with just 35 cents in his pocket. Later, for a while, he toured the South as a Bible-thumping evangelist, emphasizing his life's misdeeds and his reformation. There was, still later, a rancorous split-up with the evangelical outfit in Florida that had promoted his preaching career, and he returned to the Los Angeles area. He lives alone after 10 marriages and divorces (his figure), one wife having been actress Barbara Fuller, and the most recent being Reno Brown, who was a leading lady in Westerns and is the mother of his two sons. Grizzled and in his 50s (b. 1921), seeming, actually, far older than his years, and known to like a drink, he contemplates reincarnation and astrology—and seems

a sadly disillusioned man. A letter received by the author from the star little boys once idolized, tells much. "I have been preparing all my life for a one-night stand and I'm not yet booked," he wrote, adding the belief that he had already lived and died in another area of time. The letter continued: "Since we are coming to the time of my demise again it is my desire to share what I know to be true. Between the Masons and the Catholics there is such a confusion you can't die one time and find out which side you're on. If the world can't conform you or control you it will kill you, and if you don't die when they try—you will be degraded till you would welcome death. That's where I am, in abject poverty waiting the relief of death . . . I am writing a story, 'The Prophet from Hell,' which may be worth something after I get an acknowledged funeral." Onscreen from 1945. IN: *Song of Old Wyoming, Law of the Lash, Return of the Lash, Mark of the Lash, Prairie Outlaws, Son of Billy the Kid, Dead Men's Gold, Frontier Revenge*, more.

LA STARZA, ROLAND (S. Cal.) Support. Onscreen from the '60s. IN: *Reprieve, The Outfit*, more.

LA TORRE, CHARLES (S. Cal.) Character. Onscreen from 1942. IN: *Louisiana Purchase, My Sister Eileen, Casablanca, Passage to Marseille, Enter Arsene Lupin, A Double Life, 711 Ocean Drive*, more.

LA TOURNEAUX, ROBERT (N.Y.) Support. IN: *The Boys in the Band*.

LAAGE, BARBARA (Fr.) Leading lady. Onscreen from 1948. IN: *B.F.'s Daughter, Act of Love, The Happy Road, The Respectful Prostitute, Paris Blues, Therese and Isabelle, Bed and Board*, more.

LACEY, CATHERINE (Eng.) Character. Onscreen from 1938. IN: *The Lady Vanishes, I Know Where I'm Going, Tight Little Island, Pink String and Sealing Wax, Mad Little Island, Crack in the Mirror, Another Sky, The Servant, The Sorcerers* (won her the Best Actress award at the 1968 Trieste Film Festival), *The Private Life of Sherlock Holmes*, more.

LACK, SIMON (Eng.) Character. Onscreen from 1941. IN: *Proud Valley, The Bushbaby*, more.

LACY, JERRY (N.Y.) Support. Onscreen in the '70s. IN: *Play It Again, Sam* (as Bogart), more.

LADD, ALANA (S. Cal.) Daughter of Alan Ladd. Onscreen in the '60s IN: *Guns of the*

Timberland, Young Guns of Texas. (See Sue Carol.)

LADD, DAVID (S. Cal.) Support; former juvenile lead. Son of Alan Ladd. Onscreen from 1957. IN: *The Big Land, The Proud Rebel, A Dog of Flanders, Misty, R.P.M., Catlow, The Klansman,* more. (See Sue Carol.)

LADD, DIANE (S. Cal.) Support. Nominated for Best Supporting Actress Oscar in *Alice Doesn't Live Here Anymore.* Onscreen from 1966. IN: *The Wild Angels, The Reivers, WUSA, Macho Callahan, Rebel Rousers, Chinatown, Embryo,* more.

LAFFAN, PATRICIA (Eng.) Character. Onscreen from 1936. IN: *One Good Turn, Caravan, Quo Vadis, Old Mother Riley at Home, Death in High Heels, Rough Shoot, Escape Route, 23 Paces to Baker Street,* more.

LAGARDE, JOCELYNE (Hawaii) Character. Nominated for Best Supporting Actress Oscar in *Hawaii* ('66), her only film.

LAINE, FRANKIE (S. Cal.) Singer-actor. Onscreen from 1950. IN: *When You're Smiling, On the Sunny Side of the Street, Rainbow 'Round My Shoulder, Bring Your Smile Along, Meet Me in Las Vegas,* more. (See Nan Grey.)

LAIRD, JENNY (Eng.) Character. Onscreen from the '30s. IN: *Wanted for Murder, Black Narcissus, The Girl in the Canal, Eye Witness, Village of the Damned,* more.

LAIRE, JUDSON (N.Y.) Character. Onscreen from 1963. IN: *The Ugly American, Shock Treatment, John Paul Jones,* more.

LAKE, ARTHUR (S. Cal.) This item, appearing in *Variety* early in 1974, gladdened many hearts: "Penny Singleton and Arthur Lake open in Milwaukee next June in *No, No, Nanette.* Penny and Arthur made their very first 'Blondie' film in 1939 for Harry Cohn's Columbia Pictures, then heading for bankruptcy. The film cost $85,000 and grossed $9 million." Professional appearances such as this are a rarity now for the comedian, though spry as ever in his 70s (b. 1905). The records, in fact, show nothing else for him since the *Blondie* TV series he did opposite Pamela Britton in '57 was canceled. Lately, though, there has been talk of a TV special he would do with Penny Singleton. Whenever the actor works now it's not just for the money. Ever careful with investments, he is financially well fixed. Also, he has been married since '37 to former actress Patricia Van Cleve. (They costarred in TV series, *Meet the Family,* in the mid-'50s.) Beyond that, she was Marion Davies' only niece and one of her principal heirs. The Lakes have two grown children, Arthur Jr. and Marion, live as they have for decades in a veritable showplace in Santa Monica, when not in Palm Springs, and travel widely. One long journey to Guatemala resulted in a travelogue, made for theatrical release. It was reported a while back that Lake was negotiating to open a chain of Dagwood Sandwich restaurants, an indication the "Bumstead" connection has in no way been severed. Except for this, the actor's offscreen life (he has been offscreen since 1950's *Blondie's Hero*) has been so private his name rarely appears in Hollywood papers. Of course, there was the brief newspaper report of a few months back, that he and Hoagy Carmichael had locked horns—legally—after an automobile accident in the parking lot of a Palm Springs restaurant. There was no follow-up account in the papers. But the scene of the suit was Small Claims Court. The amount involved—$127.75. Onscreen from the teens—first as a boy actor. IN (besides the three dozen "Blondie" pix): *Cradle Snatchers, The Air Circus, Harold Teen, Tanned Legs, Dance Hall, The Silver Streak, Annapolis Salute, Topper, Double Danger, There Goes My Heart, Footlight Glamour, Sailor's Holiday, 16 Fathoms Deep,* more.

LAKE, FLORENCE (S. Cal.) She has lately played spunky old ladies in many TV shows: *The Mary Tyler Moore Show, The Family Holvak, Apple's Way, Adam-12, Banyon,* the "ABC Suspense Movie" *Live Again, Die Again,* etc. Onscreen from the '20s. IN: *Thru Different Eyes, The Rogue Song, Ladies of the Jury, The Sweetheart of Sigma Chi, Quality Street, I Met My Love Again, Condemned Woman, Stagecoach, Crash Dive; San Diego, I Love You;* more, including of course the two dozen comedy shorts with Edgar Kennedy in which she was the daffy wife.

LAKE, JANET (S. Cal.) Former ingenue. Now married, the mother of two daughters, living in Holmby Hills, and retired. Onscreen from the '50s. IN: *The Fastest Gun Alive, Raintree County, The Opposite Sex, Two Weeks in Another Town,* more.

LALLY, WILLIAM (S. Cal.) Character. Onscreen from 1949. IN: *The Red Menace,* more.

LAMARR, HEDY (N. Y.) Attractive still, in her 60s (b. 1915), she lives—unmarried now—in an apartment on Riverside Drive, has recovered from cataract operations, and has announced plans to open an 'Ecstasy' boutique in New York. Onscreen abroad from 1929. IN: *One Doesn't Need Money, Storm in a Water Glass, Ecstasy,* more. Onscreen in America from

1938. IN: *Algiers, I Take This Woman, Lady of the Tropics, Boom Town, Comrade X, Come Live with Me, Ziegfeld Girl;* H. M. Pulham, Esq.; *Tortilla Flat, White Cargo, Her Highness and the Bellboy, The Strange Woman, Samson and Delilah, Copper Canyon, My Favorite Spy,* more, including 1958's *The Female Animal,* her most recent to date.

LAMAS, FERNANDO (S. Cal.) Dashingly handsome still in his early 60s (b. 1915), the silvery Argentinian appears often on TV talk shows as guest host or guest, still acts once in a while (a recent *McCloud* episode), but is primarily a director of movies (*The Scavengers,* for which he also did the screenplay) and TV shows (*S.W.A.T., The Rookies,* etc.). He has been married since '69 to Esther Williams, with whom he costarred in *Dangerous When Wet;* they have no children. His first wife was Argentine actress Pearla Mux; his second, Uruguayan heiress Lydia Babachi (they have a daughter, Alexandra, b. 1947); his third, Arlene Dahl, with whom he costarred in *Sangaree* (married 1954–60, they have a son, Lorenzo, b. 1958). Of his present wife, he says, "She is *not* a Liberated Woman—thank heaven. She has had all of that career success and now is content. Maybe that's why our marriage works." He was distressed by 1974 headlines involving his daughter, whom he rarely sees as she has been for some time a naturalized Australian living Down Under. She was visiting in Chile when she was expelled from the country. Military authorities, who escorted Alexandra Lamas aboard a Peru-bound plane, en route to Australia, stated that she was deported from Chile because she was caught carrying "Communist propaganda." Onscreen in Spanish-language pix such as *Historia de una Mala Mujer* from 1945. Onscreen in America from 1950. IN: *Rich, Young and Pretty; The Merry Widow, Diamond Queen, Jivaro, Rose Marie, Duel of Fire, The Revenge of the Musketeers, Kill a Dragon, 100 Rifles, Valley of Mystery, Backtrack,* more.

LAMB, CHARLES (Eng.) Character. Onscreen from the '40s. IN: *The Galloping Major, Curtain Up, The Intruder, Raising a Riot, John and Julie, The Extra Day, Life at the Top,* more.

LAMB, GIL (S. Cal.) Now in his 70s (b. 1906), Paramount's yesteryear comedian with the bobbing Adam's apple and long limber legs keeps moving. "I'm tall at my age," he laughs, "so it comes naturally." On TV in 1975's *Queen of the Stardust Ballroom,* he was glimpsed whirling about the dance floor with a partner—had billing but no lines. Two years before, Lamb had feature billing in the movie *Terror Circus,* and a bit before that was prominently cast in the short-lived Broadway musical *70 - Girls - 70.*

Onscreen from 1941. IN: *The Fleet's In, Star-Spangled Rhythm, Riding High, Practically Yours, Make Mine Laughs, The Boss, The Gnome-Mobile, The Love Bug, Norwood, The Boatniks,* more.

LAMBERT, JACK (Eng.) Character. Onscreen from the '30s. IN: *The Ghost Goes West, The Master of Ballantrae, Twice Upon a Time, Companions in Crime, The Sea Shall Not Have Them, Track the Man Down, Storm Over the Nile, Neither the Sea Nor the Sand,* more.

LAMBERT, PAUL (S. Cal.) Support. Onscreen from 1960. IN: *Spartacus, The Big Mouth, Planet of the Apes, All the Loving Couples, Mama's Dirty Girls,* more.

LAMBLE, LLOYD (Eng.) Character. Onscreen from the '50s. IN: *Curtain Up, White Fire,* the "St. Trinian's" series, *The Green Buddha, The Straw Man, Private's Progress, The Man Who Never Was,* more.

LAMBRINOS, VASSILI (S. Cal.) Support. Onscreen from the '60s. IN: *Island of Love, The Unsinkable Molly Brown, Female Animal,* more.

LAMONT, DUNCAN (Eng.) Character. Onscreen from the '50s. IN: *The Man in the White Suit, The Intruder, The Teckman Mystery, Quentin Durward, A Touch of Larceny, The 39 Steps, Mutiny on the Bounty, The Devil's Own, The Battle of Britain,* more.

LAMOUR, DOROTHY (S. Cal.) Star. Onscreen from 1936. IN: *Jungle Princess, The Last Train from Madrid, Hurricane, Jungle Love, Spawn of the North, Disputed Passage, Johnny Apollo* (her personal favorite), *The Road to Singapore* (and many other "Road" pix), *Aloma of the South Seas, The Fleet's In, Beyond the Blue Horizon, They Got Me Covered, A Medal for Benny, Wild Harvest, On Our Merry Way, Lucky Stiff, The Greatest Show on Earth, Donovan's Reef, Pajama Party,* more.

LAMPERT, ZOHRA (N.Y.) Leading lady. Onscreen from 1959. IN: *Odds Against Tomorrow, Posse from Hell, Splendor in the Grass, A Fine Madness, Bye Bye Braverman, Let's Scare Jessica to Death,* more.

LAMPKIN, CHARLES (S. Cal.) Black character. Onscreen from 1951. IN: *Five, Toys in the Attic, Watermelon Man,* more.

LANCASTER, BURT (S. Cal.) Star. Won Best Actor Oscar in *Elmer Gantry.* Nominated in the same category in *From Here to Eternity* and *Bird Man of Alcatraz.* Onscreen from 1946. IN:

The Killers, Desert Fury, Brute Force; Sorry, Wrong Number; All My Sons, Mr. 880, The Flame and the Arrow; Come Back, Little Sheba; Vera Cruz, The Rose Tattoo, Trapeze, Gunfight at the O.K. Corral, Separate Tables, Judgment at Nuremberg, The Leopard, Seven Days in May, The Swimmer, Castle Keep, Airport, Valdez Is Coming, Ulzana's Raid, Scorpio, The Midnight Man, Buffalo Bill and the Indians, The Cassandra Crossing, more.

LANCASTER, LUCIE (N.Y.) Character. Onscreen from the '50s. IN: The Vagabond King, 23 Paces to Baker Street, more.

LANCASTER, STUART (S. Cal.) Character. Onscreen from 1968. IN: Good Morning and Goodbye!, Wilbur and the Baby Factory, The Sex Life of Romeo and Juliet, more.

LANCHESTER, ELSA (S. Cal.) Character. Nominated for Best Supporting Actress Oscar in Come to the Stable and Witness for the Prosecution. Onscreen in England from 1928. IN: The Constant Nymph, Day Dreams, The Love Habit, The Private Life of Henry VIII, Rembrandt, more. Onscreen in America from 1935. IN: David Copperfield, Naughty Marietta, Bride of Frankenstein, Ladies in Retirement, Forever and a Day, Lassie Come Home, The Razor's Edge, The Bishop's Wife, The Secret Garden, Dreamboat, The Glass Slipper; Bell, Book and Candle; Mary Poppins, That Darn Cat, Rascal, Willard, Terror in the Wax Museum, Murder by Death. more.

LANDAU, LUCY (N.Y.) Character. Onscreen from 1963. IN: The Thrill of It All, Strange Bedfellows, more.

LANDAU, MARTIN (S. Cal.) Costar. Onscreen from 1959. IN: Pork Chop Hill, North by Northwest, Cleopatra, The Greatest Story Ever Told, Stagecoach to Dancers' Rock, Nevada Smith, They Call Me Mister Tibbs, Black Gunn, more.

LANDEN, DINSDALE (Eng.) Support. Onscreen from 1961. IN: The Valiant, Every Home Should Have One, Mosquito Squadron, more.

LANDERS, HARRY (S. Cal.) Character. Onscreen from 1949. IN: C-Man, Guilty Bystander, Drive a Crooked Road, The Indian Fighter, The Wild One, Cease Fire, Rear Window, The Ten Commandments, The Gallant Hours, Charro!, more.

LANDERS, MURIEL (S. Cal.) Character. Onscreen from 1952. IN: Pony Soldier, Doctor Dolittle, more.

LANDGARD, JANET (S. Cal.) Leading lady. Onscreen from the '60s. IN: The Swimmer, Moon Child, more.

LANDI, MARLA (Eng.) Leading lady. Onscreen from 1957. IN: Across the Bridge, The Hound of the Baskervilles, The Murder Game, more.

LANDOLFI, TONY (Mass.) Character. Onscreen from the '50s. IN: Home Before Dark, The Thomas Crown Affair, Charly, Love Story, The Boston Strangler, more.

LANDON, MICHAEL (S. Cal.) Star. Onscreen from 1957. IN: I Was a Teenage Werewolf, Maracaibo, God's Little Acre, The Legend of Tom Dooley, The Errand Boy (cameo), more.

LANDONE, AVICE (Eng.) Character. Onscreen from the '40s. IN: Guilt Is My Shadow, The Franchise Affair, White Corridors, Love in Pawn, Operation Diplomat, The Embezzler, Windfall, The Blood on Satan's Claw, more. (Died 1976.)

LANE, ABBE (S. Cal.) Singer-actress. Onscreen from 1953. IN: Wings of the Hawk, Ride Clear of Diablo, Chicago Syndicate, The Americano, more.

LANE, CHARLES (S. Cal.) Character. Onscreen from the '20s. IN: Sadie Thompson, The Milky Way, Ali Baba Goes to Town, Kentucky, You Can't Take It With You, Mr. Smith Goes to Washington, Johnny Apollo, Ellery Queen and the Perfect Crime, Never Give a Sucker an Even Break, The Farmer's Daughter, State of the Union, Call Northside 777, The Mating Game, The Music Man, The Ugly Dachshund, The Ghost and Mr. Chicken, more.

LANE, JOCELYN (JACKIE) (Eng.) Leading lady. Onscreen as Jackie Lane from 1957. IN: These Dangerous Years, Fra Diavolo, Men of Sherwood Forest, Goodbye Again, Operation Snatch, more. Onscreen as Jocelyn Lane from 1964. IN: Tickle Me, How to Seduce a Playboy, Hell's Belles, A Bullet for Pretty Boy, Land Raiders, more.

LANE, KENT (S. Cal.) Leading man. Son of Rhonda Fleming. Onscreen in the '70s. IN: Changes, The Sandpit Generals, more.

LANE, LENITA (S. Cal.) Until his death in '73, this leading lady of the '30s had been married for 36 years to Crane Wilbur, a greatly popular star of silents (was "Handsome Harry" in Pearl White's The Perils of Pauline) and later a screenwriter (House of Wax) and director (Solomon and Sheba); they had no children. In her

60s now, retired and living in Toluca Lake, the actress last appeared onscreen in support in two in the '50s—*The Mad Magician* and *The Bat*, which her husband directed. Onscreen from 1931. IN: *Murder by the Clock, We're Rich Again, The Gay Deception, Dead Men Tell*, more.

LANE, LOLA (S. Cal.) Heavier than in her starring days, and retired from the real estate business, the actress is entering her 70s (b. 1906), lives in the Pacific Palisades and has been married for many years to lawyer Robert Hanlon. Childless in this and four previous marriages— to Lew Ayres, Henry Dunham, and directors Roland West and Alexander Hall—she is devoted to the grown daughter (Bridgette Anderson) and three young grandsons of sister Rosemary, whose '74 death she still mourns. Older sister, Leota, who never appeared in pictures with the Lane Sisters, died in '60. Younger sister, Priscilla, lives with her family in New Hampshire, and while they remain close, they rarely see one another. Onscreen from 1929. IN: *Speakeasy, The Girl from Havana, Let's Go Places, Public Stenographer, Burn 'Em Up Barnes* (serial), *Murder on a Honeymoon, Marked Woman, The Sheik Steps Out, Torchy Blane in Panama, Four Daughters, Daughters Courageous, Four Wives, Four Mothers, Buckskin Frontier, Steppin' in Society*, more, including 1946's *Deadline at Dawn*, her last.

LANE, MARYON (Eng.) The ballerina featured in one movie two decades ago still dances with the Royal Ballet, has twin daughters in their teens, and is the widow of dance star-choreographer David Blair (d. 1976). Onscreen in 1955. IN: *Dance Little Lady.*

LANE, MIKE (S. Cal.) Character. Onscreen from 1956. IN: *The Harder They Fall*, more.

LANE, PRISCILLA (N.H.) Her long-ago movies (*The Roaring Twenties, Brother Rat*, etc.) made in her vibrant 20s, are all over the TV dials. Almost never shown are the two she came out of retirement to make: *Fun on a Weekend* ('47) and *Bodyguard* ('48). Since then the actress has almost totally avoided the limelight. Two exceptions: years ago, she had her own local television show in Boston and, more than a decade back, she filmed a hosiery commercial seen mainly in the Eastern states. Her sole career since has been that of wife and mother. Her husband, since '43, is Joseph A. Howard. A bombardier pilot when they wed, he later became a wealthy building contractor in Andover, Mass. The actress' only other marriage, to screenwriter Oren Haglund, reportedly lasted one day, was annulled in '40. The Howards have four children, all now in their 20s:

Larry, Hannah, Judith and James. Hannah, the actress said not long ago, "looks very much like I did when I was her age." Whether one would recognize Priscilla Lane today would depend on the acuteness of one's observation. Certain factors have not changed—her wide smile, her slender figure, her gentle blue eyes. Other things have altered. Her blonde hair—darker and graying—is worn now in a short feather bob, with bangs. Her face—she is on the threshold of her 60s (b. 1917)—is not unlined. And, cherishing her privacy, she seems far less outgoing than before—avoiding reporters, always wearing dark glasses when she goes out, generally sitting in the back row at church. Their church—they are devoutly Roman Catholic—is an important part of the Howards' life; affixed to the front door of their home is, symbolically, a small plaque of the Christ figure. When her children were younger, the actress was active in school affairs and was for a time a Girl Scout leader, much loved and admired by her young charges. Today, in retirement, Priscilla Lane and her husband have moved permanently from their longtime home in Andover to their former summer residence in Derry, N.H. They swim, fish, and live quietly beside their private bay. Onscreen from 1937. IN: *Varsity Show, The Cowboy from Brooklyn, Four Daughters*, etc., *Brother Rat, The Roaring Twenties, Brother Rat and a Baby, Three Cheers for the Irish, Million Dollar Baby, Ladies Must Live, Blues in the Night, Saboteur, Baby, Ladies Must Live, Blues in the Night, Saboteur, Silver Queen, Arsenic and Old Lace*, more.

LANE, RICHARD (S. Cal.) For 15 years and in more than 250 movies, this big, broad-shouldered, square-jawed actor—usually seen in uniform, police or military—was one of Hollywood's toughest characters. He gave up that career in '51, after *I Can Get It for You Wholesale* and, except for a cameo in 1972's *Kansas City Bomber*, he hasn't appeared in a movie since. A wealthy man, with a beautiful home in Newport Beach and properties in Palm Springs and Colorado, he says, in that friendly (offscreen), gravelly bark, "I'm still offered movie roles, but I turn them all down. I don't want to be taking the place of somebody who really needs the dough." Besides, since the late '40s, he's had a steady, two-days-a-week career as a sports announcer in Los Angeles. On Saturday nights he broadcasts wrestling matches for KCOP, and on Sundays he moves downtown to the Olympic Auditorium to do similar duty on the syndicated TV show *Roller Game of the Week*. A vigorous man in his 70s (b. 1900), and long and happily married, he has a son, a daughter, and a granddaughter, and terms himself "probably the luckiest actor I ever knew." It's been many a year since he was the jut-jawed commanding officer ordering Randolph Scott into the North Atlantic in *Corvette K-225*, but Richard Lane still looks like he could play such a role any time—if he wished. Onscreen from 1937. IN: *You Can't Buy Luck, The Outcasts of Poker Flat, Blind Alibi, Charlie Chan in Honolulu, Mutiny on the Blackhawk, I Wanted Wings, Navy Blues, To the Shores of Tripoli, Air Force, Gung Ho!*, the "Boston Blackie" series, *Tenth Avenue Angel*, more.

LANE, SARA (S. Cal.) Former ingenue. Married and retired. Onscreen in 1965. IN: *I Saw What You Did*.

LANG, BARBARA (S. Cal.) Leading lady. Onscreen from 1957. IN: *House of Numbers, Party Girl*, more.

LANG, DOREEN (S. Cal.) Support. Onscreen from 1956. IN: *The Wrong Man, The Cabinet of Dr. Caligari*, more.

LANG, JUNE (S. Cal.) Gorgeous was—and is— the operative word. No matter that she is in her early 60s (1915), she came gifted with a face and figure that nothing could change. And nothing has. But there is a dignified reserve about her that is surprising to find in so lovely a woman. Though born under the sign of Taurus the Bull, the leading lady of 32 movies admits, "I am easily discouraged. I would so love to act in pictures again, even in small parts, but I don't know how to go about it. I don't have the right contacts in motion pictures any more. And there are so *many* talented younger people around." June quit her career in utter discouragement in '46 after a dismal B, *Lighthouse*, made on Hollywood's Poverty Row—a long way from 20th Century-Fox where she had her best opportunities in the '30s. A decade ago there were two TV commercials and, for two weeks she was the on-the-air "telephone girl" on a local TV talk show in Los Angeles. Now, she laughs, "I just rake leaves and garden a bit; I do pretty much what I want to do and I guess it's nothing!" She lives in a house she's owned for years in North Hollywood, an attractive one-story wood-and-gray-stucco dwelling ("a nice female house," she describes it). Living with her are her elderly mother, Mrs. Vlaskek (June's real name, under which she began her career), and her only child, Patricia Morgan. Patricia, in her mid-20s, has lately worked at the Lowman School for Handicapped Children in the Valley and, her mother inserts, "is looking for a nice policeman or fireman to marry." June herself has been married three times. "The dumbest thing I ever did in my life was marry—each time," she vigorously insists. "I did not choose wisely in my husbands. I do not, though, like being *unmarried*." She was married first, briefly, to agent-playboy Vic Orsatti, and then, again for a short time, to John Roselli. Finally, for several years, until they were divorced in '54, she was married to Mr. Morgan, father of her daughter. Now, she says, "Actually, I don't have to work. I've always taken care of my money. And, except when I had a big house in Beverly Hills, I've always lived frugally. But for the last few years, I've wanted to be creative. I even wrote the outline for a TV series that a studio—yes, 20th—seriously considered, but it didn't sell. Now that my daughter is grown, I would like to work again. I have wonderful memories of my acting years. But I'm not fiercely ambitious, never pushed to get parts, never even had an agent." She ponders the future for a moment, her incredibly lovely blue eyes lighting up, and she adds with a smile, but little conviction, "Maybe I'll get an agent" Onscreen from 1931. IN: *Young Sinners, Music in the Air, Captain January, The Country Doctor, The Road to Glory, Nancy Steel Is Missing, Ali Baba Goes to Town, Wee Willie Winkie, One Wild Night, Zenobia, Captain Fury, Isle of Destiny, Too Many Women, Footlight Serenade, Up in Arms* (in which she, a near-star for a decade, was a Goldwyn Girl), *Three of a Kind*, more.

LANG, ROBERT (Eng.) Support. Onscreen from the '60s. IN: *Interlude, A Walk with Love and Death, Othello, Dance of Death*, more.

LANGAN, GLENN ((S. Cal.) The former actor roared with laughter when he heard about it— this passage in a book, *Don't Say Yes Until I Finish Talking*, about his long-ago studio boss, Darryl F. Zanuck: "Glenn Langan was one of the several faceless players who popped up with regularity in Fox products in usually interchangeable parts. One measure of this facelessness, even with Zanuck's biggest names, is how many have been forgotten, even by Zanuck. 'Who's Glenn Langan?' he asks." Many thousands of Langan fans are still walking around who could not only tell him but cite the movies in which he costarred. Langan himself comes back with this, still smiling, "Regardless of what Darryl had to say, due to my inbred love of animals, I have always liked him!" Today, as he heads into his 60s (b. 1917), the gray-eyed and graying, 6'4" actor remains a rugged, handsome man who keeps himself in tiptop physical shape. He has been happily married since '54 to actress Adele Jergens. She was the tall, buxom silver-blonde beauty (her hair is dark blonde now) featured in so many Technicolor extravaganzas at Columbia in the '40s. She gave up her career after 1958's *The Lonesome Trail*. Now in her early 50s (b. 1922), and still possessed of an exceptionally fine figure (she credits swimming and daily dance practice), as well as a positive, outgoing personality, Adele gives the impression her movie career was something of a happy adventure and she wouldn't mind doing it all again. But, to her husband's dismay, knowing how much she enjoyed the work, she hesitates. "A large commercial agency has been after her several times in the last months to interview for TV commercials," he says, "but she feels she isn't ready. This could be a whole, new and very satisfying career for her." The Langans live in a fine house in Encino and are the proud parents of a son, Tracy, a recent college graduate. "He has moved into his own diggings in a 'swinging singles complex' about five miles from us, in Woodland Hills," his dad reports, "and has a good job with Panavision." As for himself, Glenn Langan says: "I am now associated with National Utility Service of San Francisco, as Divisional Sales Manager. I handle the 11 Western States plus Hawaii. I spend over 60% of my time on the road or in San Francisco and try to commute weekends back to Encino. It is a good job in a steadily growing company, but it has been very difficult on both Adele and me, as we have always been so close to one another. It is especially lonesome for Adele since Tracy struck out on his own. However, it is a good and honest living and, at the moment, it is the only game in town. We are both looking forward to the day when it will be economically feasible for both of us to have enough cushion so that we can do an occasional picture, or play, or TV commercial, and still continue some kind of life style." Onscreen from 1939. IN: *The Return of Dr. X, Riding High, Something for the Boys, Wing and a Prayer; In the Meantime, Darling; A Bell for Adano, Hangover Square, Sentimental Journey, Margie, Dragonwyck, Homestretch, Forever Amber, Fury at Furnace Creek, The Snake Pit, Iroquois Trail, 99 River Street, Jungle Heat*, more, including 1965's *Mutiny in Outer Space*, his most recent to date.

LANGDON, SUE ANE (S. Cal.) Leading lady. Onscreen from 1961. IN: *The Great Impostor, The New Interns, Roustabout, The Rounders, When the Boys Meet the Girls, Frankie and Johnny, A Guide for the Married Man, The Cheyenne Social Club*, more.

LANGE, HOPE (S. Cal.) Costar. Nominated for Best Supporting Oscar in *Peyton Place*. Onscreen from 1956. IN: *Bus Stop, The True Story of Jesse James, The Young Lions, In Love and War, The Best of Everything, Pocketful of Miracles, Wild in the Country, How the West Was Won, Love Is a Ball, Jigsaw, Death Wish*, more.

LANGE, JESSICA (S. Cal.) Leading lady. Onscreen from 1976. IN: *King Kong*.

LANGELLA, FRANK (N.Y.) Leading man. Onscreen from 1970. IN: *The Twelve Chairs, Diary of a Mad Housewife, The House Under the Trees, The Deadly Trap, The Wrath of God*, more.

LANGFORD, FRANCES (Fla.) She and her millionaire husband, outboard-motor tycoon Ralph Evinrude, own and operate at Jensen Beach, where they live, the Frances Langford Outrigger Resort. It has 40 motel units located on a lush 200-acre estate flecked with citrus groves, and is adjacent to its own marina, where their 118-foot yacht, the *Chanticleer*, lies at anchor. A major part of the complex is the Outrigger Restaurant, where she still sings now and then, backed up by Tony Romano, who accompanied Langford and Hope on all those WW II USO tours to battlefronts the world over. The Frances Langford seen by her restaurant patrons is, in her 60s (b. 1914), little changed from the singer who was in so many movie musicals. Still blonde, pretty, and singing like a southern lark (she is a Florida native), she is also still the possessor of the most incredibly fine figure ever seen on a small (5') woman. She and her husband live near their resort in a mostly glass mansion with a spectacular view of the St. Lucie River as it meets the Atlantic. She last appeared onscreen in 1954's *The Glenn Miller Story*, and last entertained in public—except at the Outrigger—in '66 when she took her own troupe to Vietnam. Onscreen from 1935. IN: *Broadway Melody of 1936, Collegiate, Born to Dance, The Hit Parade, Too Many Girls, Romance and Rhythm, All-American Coed, This Is the Army, Career Girl, Follow the Band, Cowboy in Manhattan, Never a Dull Moment, Dixie Jamboree, Radio Stars on Parade, Melody Time, Make Mine Laughs, The Purple Heart Diary*, more.

LANGTON, PAUL (S. Cal.) Character; former leading man. Onscreen from 1943. IN: *Destination Tokyo, Thirty Seconds Over Tokyo, The Hidden Eye, They Were Expendable, My Brother Talks to Horses, For You I Die, Jack Slade, The Snow Creature, To Hell and Back, The Incredible Shrinking Man, The Cosmic Man, Three Came to Kill, Shock Treatment*, more.

LANSBURY, ANGELA (Ire.) Costar. Nominated for Best Supporting Actress Oscar in *Gaslight* (her first picture), *The Picture of Dorian Gray*, and *The Manchurian Candidate*. Besides their Santa Monica residence, where she and actor-agent husband Robert Shaw go less often now, they own a farm in Ireland and consider it home. Onscreen from 1944. IN: *National Velvet, The Harvey Girls, Till the Clouds Roll By, Private Affairs of Bel Ami, State of the*

Union, The Three Musketeers, Samson and De-
lilah, Remains to be Seen, The Court Jester, The
Long Hot Summer, The Dark at the Top of the
Stairs, All Fall Down, In the Cool of the Day,
The Out-of-Towners, The World of Henry Ori-
ent, The Greatest Story Ever Told, Mister
Buddwing, Bedknobs and Broomsticks, more.

LANSING, ROBERT (S. Cal.) Leading man.
Onscreen from 1959. IN: The 4-D Man, The
Pusher, A Gathering of Eagles, Under the Yum-
Yum Tree; Namu, the Killer Whale; Danger
Has Two Faces, It Takes All Kinds, The Gris-
som Gang, more.

LANTEAU, WILLIAM (S. Cal.) Character. Onscreen from 1959. IN: Li'l Abner, The Facts of
Life, Hotel, more.

LARABEE, LOUISE (N.Y.) Character. Onscreen from the '60s. IN: Act One, Fail Safe,
more.

LARCH, JOHN (S. Cal.) Character; former
leading man. Onscreen from 1954. IN: Bitter
Creek, The Phenix City Story, Seven Men from
Now, Written on the Wind, Quantez, Hell to
Eternity, Miracle of the White Stallions, The
Wrecking Crew, Hail Hero!, Play Misty for Me,
Dirty Harry, Framed, more.

LARRAIN, MICHAEL (S. Cal.) Support. Onscreen from 1968. IN: Rosemary's Baby, Buckskin, more.

LARSEN, KEITH (S. Cal.) Leading man. On-
screen from 1949. IN: Son of Belle Starr, The
Rose Bowl Story, War Paint, Fort Vengeance,
Chief Crazy Horse, Badlands of Montana,
Apache Warrior, Women of the Prehistoric
Planet, more.

LARSON, CHRISTINE /now **CHRISTINE
LARSON COOK** (S. Cal.) Leading lady. Onscreen from 1950. IN: The Well, Last Train
from Bombay, Brave Warrior, Valley of the
Headhunters, more.

LARSON, PAUL (N.Y.) Character. Onscreen
from 1968. IN: The Detective, Pretty Poison,
more.

LASSER, LOUISE (S. Cal.) Leading lady.
Since '76 she has starred in the title role in the
nighttime soap opera Mary Hartman, Mary
Hartman. Onscreen from 1965. IN: What's
New Pussycat?, Take the Money and Run, Ba-
nanas, Slither, more.

LATHAM, LOUISE (N.Y.) Leading lady. Onscreen from 1964. IN: Marnie, Firecreek, Adam
at 6 A.M., 92 in the Shade, more.

LATIMER, HUGH (Eng.) Character. Onscreen
from 1946. IN: Corridor of Mirrors, The
Cosmic Monster, more.

LATIMORE, FRANK (It.) One of 20th Century-Fox's most popular curly-haired young leading men in the '40s, he relocated in Rome in
'50s. He has played supporting roles there ever
since, usually in American pictures made on
European location. Patton, in which he played
a Lieutenant Colonel—a rise in rank since he
was a 2nd Lieutenant in In the Meantime, Darling with Jeanne Crain—is among his more recent films. Onscreen from 1944. IN: The Dolly
Sisters, The Razor's Edge, Three Little Girls in
Blue, 13 Rue Madeleine, Black Magic, Three
Forbidden Stories, John Paul Jones, Blazing
Sun, Cast a Giant Shadow, The Sergeant,
more.

LAUCK, CHESTER (Tex.) As the famous radio
team of "Lum 'n' Abner"—he was Lum—he
and partner, Norris Goff, costarred in five movies in the '40s. Their last was 1944's Going to
Town. Now in his 70s (b. 1902), he lives in
Houston and for over two decades has been the
goodwill ambassador (with high executive rank)
for the Continental Oil Company. Onscreen
from 1940. IN: Dreaming Out Loud, Bashful
Bachelor, Two Weeks to Live, So This Is
Washington.

LAUGHLIN, TOM (S. Cal.) Star. Onscreen
from 1956. IN: Tea and Sympathy, South Pacific, Gidget, Tall Story, The Born Losers, Billy
Jack, The Trial of Billy Jack, The Master Gunfighter, more.

LAURIE, JOHN (Eng.) Character. Onscreen
from 1930. IN: Juno and the Paycock, The 39
Steps, Nine Days a Queen, Four Feathers, Convoy, Henry V, Jassy, Hamlet, Mine Own Executioner, Madeleine, Laughter in Paradise, Pandora and the Flying Dutchman, Encore
("Winter Cruise" episode), Richard III, Kidnapped, Murder Reported, more.

LAURIE, PIPER (N.Y.) Former leading lady.
Nominated for Best Actress Oscar in The Hustler. Universal's redheaded teenage sexpot remains a redhead (her hair worn waist-length
now, and straight), but in her 40s (b. 1932) plays
down the glamour. Last in a movie in the
above-mentioned, released in '61, she acted in
'73 in the play Marco Polo Sings a Solo, which
tried out in stock but did not make it to Broadway. In '76 she made her screen comeback as
the co-star of United Artists' Carrie. Married
since '62 to writer Joseph Morgenstern, she
lives with him and their only child, Anna Grace
(b. 1971), in rural Woodstock, in a 250-year-old
farmhouse on a mountain side. Totally domes-

tic, she is usually to be found in her magnificently appointed kitchen—marble-topped counters, three ovens, etc.—surrounded by flour, yeast, and rising dough. Loaves of bread of all shapes and descriptions roll out of her kitchen virtually every day of the week. And so adept has she become at bread-making that friends urge her to write a cookbook. With a potential collaborator right in the house, she's listening. Onscreen from 1950. IN: *Louisa, The Milkman, Francis Goes to the Races, The Prince Who Was a Thief, Son of Ali Baba, Has Anybody Seen My Gal?, No Room for the Groom, Mississippi Gambler, The Golden Blade, Johnny Dark, Dawn at Socorro, Smoke Signal, Until They Sail, Kelly and Me*, more.

LAUTER, HARRY (S. Cal.) Character. Onscreen from the '40s. IN: *Trader Tom of the China Seas* (serial), *Experiment Alcatraz, Thunder in God's Country, Night Stage to Galveston, Prince of Pirates, Yankee Pasha, It Came from Beneath the Sea, The Creature with the Atom Brain, The Toughest Gun in Tombstone, Tarzan's Fight for Life, Good Day for a Hanging, Fort Utah*, more.

LAVI, DALIAH (S. Cal.) Leading lady. She has been married since '73 to yacht builder Peter Rittmaster and, while still living in Beverly Hills, no longer actively pursues her career. Onscreen from the '60s. IN: *Two Weeks in Another Town, Lord Jim, The Silencers, The Spy with a Cold Nose, Casino Royale, Those Fantastic Flying Fools, The High Commissioner, Catlow, Some Girls Do*, more.

LAVIN, LINDA (N.Y.) Leading lady. Onscreen in 1976. IN: *Bogart Slept Here*.

LAW, JOHN PHILLIP (It.) Leading man. Onscreen from 1965. IN: *High Infidelity; The Russians Are Coming, The Russians Are Coming; Hurry Sundown, Barbarella, The Sergeant, The Hawaiians, Death Rides a Horse, Von Richthofen and Brown, The Love Machine, Open Season, The Golden Voyage of Sinbad*, more.

LAWFORD, PETER (S. Cal.) Costar. Onscreen in America (after a few English movies) from 1938. IN: *Lord Jeff, A Yank at Eton, Sherlock Holmes Faces Death, Paris After Dark, Mrs. Parkington, The White Cliffs of Dover, Son of Lassie, My Brother Talks to Horses, Cluny Brown, Two Sisters from Boston, Good News, On An Island With You, Easter Parade, Julia Misbehaves, Little Women, Royal Wedding, You for Me, It Should Happen to You, Exodus, Ocean's Eleven, Dead Ringer, The Oscar, Salt and Pepper, The April Fools, They Only Kill Their Masters, Rosebud*, more.

LAWLOR, MARY (Eng.) The peppy leading lady of early talkies is in her late 60s now and has long been retired. Onscreen from 1930. IN: *Shooting Straight, Good News*, more.

LAWRENCE, CAROL (S. Cal.) Leading lady. Onscreen from 1954. IN: *New Faces, A View From the Bridge*, more.

LAWRENCE, DELPHI (N.Y.) Leading lady. Onscreen from the '50s. IN: *Meet Mr. Callahan, Duel in the Jungle, Murder by Proxy, The Feminine Touch, Doublecross, The Last Challenge*, more.

LAWRENCE, ELIZABETH (N.Y.) Support. Onscreen from the '60s. IN: *Lilith, The Borgia Stick*, more.

LAWRENCE, MARC (S. Cal.) Character. Onscreen from 1933. IN: *White Woman, Road Gang, San Quentin, I Am the Law, Dust Be My Destiny, Invisible Stripes, Charlie Chan at the Wax Museum, Lady Scarface, This Gun for Hire, The Ox-Bow Incident, Cloak and Dagger, Key Largo, Unconquered, Jigsaw, The Asphalt Jungle, Black Hand, Johnny Tiger, The Man With the Golden Gun*, more.

LAWRENCE, MARY (S. Cal.) Support. Onscreen from 1949. IN: *The Stratton Story, Night Into Morning, The Lady Says No, Back Street, The Best Man*, more.

LAWRENCE, STEVE (N.Y.) Singer-actor. Onscreen in 1972. IN: *Stand Up and Be Counted*.

LAWRENCE, VICKI (S. Cal.) Comedienne-singer. Onscreen in 1967. IN: *The Young Americans*.

LAWS, SAM (S. Cal.) Black character. Onscreen from the '60s. IN: *The Pawnbroker, Truck Turner, Dirty O'Neil*, more.

LAWSON, LINDA (S. Cal.) Leading lady. Onscreen from 1963. IN: *Night Tide, The Threat, Let's Kill Uncle, Sometimes a Great Notion*, more.

LAWSON, SARAH (Eng.) Leading lady. Onscreen from the '50s. IN: *Both Sides of the Law, The Devil's Bride, The Browning Version, Three Steps in the Dark, Meet Mr. Malcolm, The Blue Peter, The Battle of Britain*, more.

LAWTON, ALMA (S. Cal.) Character. Onscreen from the '50s. IN: *My Cousin Rachel, Mary Poppins*, more.

LAYE, DILYS (Eng.) Leading lady. Onscreen from 1951. IN: *The Gay Lady, Doctor at Large,*

The Bridal Path, Please Turn Over, Carry On Camping (and others in the "Carry On" series), more.

LAYE, EVELYN (Eng.) In her 70s now (b. 1900), she is the widow of actor Frank Lawton (d. 1969), who was so memorable in *David Copperfield*. She continues to have a full, active career. In this decade she has been onstage in plays such as *The Amorous Prawn* and films such as *Say Hello to Yesterday*, with Jean Simmons. Onscreen from 1929. IN: *Luck of the Navy, Queen of Scandal, One Heavenly Night, Waltz Time, Evensong, The Night Is Young, Princess Charming*, more.

LAYTON, DOROTHY (Md.) The blonde leading lady in Hal Roach comedies left the screen in '33 for marriage and in recent years has been a recreation director in Baltimore. IN: *Pick Up*, more.

LAZENBY, GEORGE (Eng.) Leading man. Onscreen from 1969. IN: *On Her Majesty's Secret Service, The Dragon Flies*, more.

LE BEAU, MADELINE (It.) Support. Onscreen from 1941. IN: *Hold Back the Dawn, Casablanca, Paris After Dark, Music for Millions, Cage of Gold, Sins of Paris, La Parisienne, 8½*, more.

LE GALLIENNE, EVA Stage star. On Broadway in 1976, age 77, she starred in a revival of *The Royal Family*. Onscreen in the '50s. IN: *Prince of Players* and *The Devil's Disciple*.

LE MASSENA, WILLIAM (N.Y.) Character. Onscreen from 1956. IN: *Carousel, The Wrong Man, The World of Henry Orient, Where's Poppa?*, more.

LE MAT, PAUL (S. Cal.) Leading man. Onscreen in the '70s. IN: *Graffiti; Aloha, Bobby and Rose;* more.

LE MESURIER, JOHN (Eng.) Character. Onscreen from the '40s. IN: *Death in the Hand, Brothers in Law, Law and Disorder, Too Many Crooks, Man in a Cocked Hat, The Day They Robbed the Bank of England, The Mouse on the Moon, The Main Attraction, Salt and Pepper, The Adventures of Sherlock Holmes' Smarter Brother*, more.

LE NOIRE, ROSETTA (N.Y.) Black character. Onscreen from 1959. IN: *Anna Lucasta, The Sunshine Boys*, more.

LE ROY, KEN (N.Y.) Character. Onscreen from the '30s. IN: *Back Door to Heaven*, more.

LEACHMAN, CLORIS (S. Cal.) Leading lady. Won Best Supporting Actress Oscar in *The Last Picture Show*. Onscreen from 1955. IN: *Kiss Me Deadly, The Rack, The Chapman Report, Blood Fiend, The Steagle, Dillinger, Charlie and the Angel, Daisy Miller, Crazy Mama*, more.

LEARY, NOLAN (S. Cal.) Character. Onscreen from 1937. IN: *Make Way for Tomorrow, Ten North Frederick, Pollyanna, Sweet Charity*, more.

LEAUD, JEAN-PIERRE (Fr.) Leading man; former juvenile lead. Onscreen from 1959. IN: *The 400 Blows, Testament of Orpheus, Love at Twenty, Masculine Feminine, Made in U.S.A., La Chinoise, Weekend, Stolen Kisses, Bed and Board, Two English Girls, The Mother and the Whore, Day for Night, Last Tango in Paris*, more.

LEAVER, PHILLIP (Eng.) Character. Onscreen from the '30s. IN: *This Man Is News, The Lady Vanishes, Inspector Hornleigh on Holiday, The Silver Fleet, Tales of Hoffmann, Martin Luther, Double Jeopardy, The Gamma People*, more.

LEAVITT, NORMAN (S. Cal.) Character. Onscreen from 1946. IN: *The Harvey Girls, The Spider Woman Strikes Back, Slattery's Hurricane, The Inspector General, Stars and Stripes Forever, Inside Detroit, Jumbo*, more.

LECLERC GINETTE (Fr.) Character; former leading lady. Onscreen from 1937. IN: *The Late Mathias Pascal, Prison Without Bars, Louise, The Baker's Wife, Two Women, The Raven, Le Plaisir, Gas-Oil, Lover's Net; Money, Money, Money; Tropic of Cancer*, more, including 1974's *Rampart of Desire* and *Popsy Pop*.

LEDERER, FRANCIS (S. Cal.) Yesterday's leading man is today's civic leader, involved in countless activities of Hollywood and nearby communities. "I am so busy that I wish there were fifteen of me in order to fulfill all the obligations I have put upon myself," says the actor who came to California from Czechoslovakia in '34, "but due to the fact that there are not fifteen of me, I am behind in practically everything I do or intend to do." Besides being Honorary Mayor of Canoga Park (the community where he invested in real estate in the '30s that has made him many times a millionaire), he has lately been president of the Southern California chapter of the American National Theatre and Academy and the Director of the ANTA Academy of Performing Arts, teaching there four times a week. He also writes (did a recent script for ABC Motion Pictures), directs and occa-

245

sionally produces movies, and, more rarely now in his 70s (b. 1902), acts. In '72, on TV's *Night Gallery*, he—whose darkly handsome looks (he still has them) caused swoons in the '30s—portrayed Count Dracula and won an acting award doing it. Hollywood counts on him in many ways. In '74 he was the speaker at memorial services for Tyrone Power held on the 16th anniversary of the star's death. When Ginger Rogers received the "Heart of Hollywood" award, her leading man in 1935's *Romance in Manhattan* was on hand to present it to her. And long an active participant in the national program to aid American Indians, he recently pledged four one-year scholarships in the American National Academy of Performing Arts. Also, he and his wife, Marion (married since '41), own and operate the Canoga Mission Gallery, and have been responsible for first gallery showings by many now-celebrated Mexican and young American artists. On a broader canvas, he has recently spearheaded a campaign named "National Taxpayers Lib," its membership comprised of property owners fearful of losing their homes because of skyrocketing real estate taxes. In 1937, when his idealistic "cause" was world peace—he lost unfortunately—Francis Lederer was the greatest employer of secretaries in Hollywood. He had then no fewer than five. How many must he have on staff today! Onscreen in Europe from 1929. IN: *Pandora's Box, Refuge, Her Majesty of Love*, more. Onscreen in America from 1934. IN: *Man of Two Worlds, The Gay Deception, One Rainy Afternoon, My American Wife, The Lone Wolf in Paris, Confessions of a Nazi Spy, Midnight, The Man I Married, Puddinhead, The Bridge of San Luis Rey, Voice in the Wind, The Madonna's Secret, Diary of a Chambermaid, Captain Carey U.S.A., Surrender, The Ambassador's Daughter, Maracaibo, The Curse of Dracula, A Breath of Scandal*, more.

LEE, ANN (Ariz.) Character. Onscreen in 1955. IN: *Trial.*

LEE, ANNA (S. Cal.) Since 1970 this blonde English actress—whose looks do not change—has been the seventh wife of famous novelist Robert (*Portrait of Jenny*) Nathan. She is in her 60s (b. 1914), he is 20 years her senior, and they live above the Sunset Strip in an English manor house that is like a transplanted corner of Middlesex. At the time of their meeting, the author has said, he felt he had stopped living and started getting ready to die. Anna has changed all that. In the summer of '74 they motored through New England, he showing her Truro on Cape Cod where he wrote *Portrait of Jenny*. And in '75 he published yet another of his mystical novels. Several times married and divorced, Anna Lee has two children—a daugh-

ter, actress Venetia Stevenson, and a son now in his early 20s, Timothy Stafford, who has taken the screen name of Jeffrey Byron and had a small role in *At Long Last Love*. She herself has acted only on TV in recent years, and then in only about one each season—in *Marcus Welby, Mannix, The FBI*—which takes only a few days to do. Up on the hill there is a role more to her liking. That is, as her devoted husband has said, being "a painter, plumber and paperhanger"—and his inspiration. Onscreen in England from 1935. IN: *First a Girl, The Man Who Changed His Mind, King Solomon's Mines*, more. Onscreen in America from 1940. IN: *Seven Sinners, My Life with Caroline, How Green Was My Valley, Flying Tigers, Commandos Strike at Dawn, Forever and a Day, Flesh and Fantasy, Hangmen Also Die, Summer Storm, Bedlam, The Ghost and Mrs. Muir, Fort Apache, Boots Malone, The Last Hurrah, This Earth Is Mine, The Horse Soldiers, Jet Over the Atlantic, Two Rode Together, What Ever Happened to Baby Jane?, For Those Who Think Young, The Sound of Music, Seven Women, Picture Mommy Dead, In Like Flint*, more.

LEE, AVALON (N.Y.) Character. IN: *Shadows*, more.

LEE, BERNARD (Eng.) Character. Onscreen from the '30s. IN: *Let George Do It, The Fallen Idol, The Third Man, Last Holiday, Glory at Sea, Sailor of the King, Beat the Devil, The Detective, Crest of the Wave, Fire Down Below, Across the Bridge, The Key, The L-Shaped Room, Dr. No* (and all other "James Bond" pix, as M), *Long Ago Tomorrow*, more.

LEE, CAROLYN (N.Y.) Paramount's adorable brunette tot of 1940 has grown up but she hasn't grown much. In her early 40s (b. 1935), she stands 5' and weighs 105 lbs. Since '69 she has been happily married—her only marriage—to William G. McCollum, an attorney in international and foreign tax for Bankers Trust, and lives just across the East River in a Brooklyn Heights townhouse. When she was onscreen she was so appealingly "real" and lovable that one New York critic exulted, "I wanted to grab her right off the screen and squeeze her." Her sudden disappearance from the screen went unexplained. But she came from a "normal" family background. Her father, the late Warren F. Copp, was an executive with the Wheeling-Pittsburgh Steel Corp. in their hometown, Wheeling, W. Va., and could not be with Carolyn and her mother in California. And Mrs. Copp, as war clouds threatened in '41, became fearful that they might be separated for the duration. It was her reluctant decision then to terminate the youngster's contract with Paramount and return to Wheeling. Completing her schooling there, Carolyn went on to get her master's degree at the University of Virginia. She later studied art in Pittsburgh, worked as a professional artist for the Mellon Bank there, and illustrated a book published by the University of Virginia. She has recently received her Ph.D. in Education at Columbia University and is writing a textbook on reading disability and its correction. With it all, Carolyn Lee's long ago admirers may be interested to know, she has continued to be humorous, and candid, and, yes, "lovable." Onscreen from 1939. IN: *Rhythm on the River, Honeymoon in Bali, Virginia, Birth of the Blues*, more.

LEE, CHRISTOPHER (Eng.) Star. Onscreen from the '40s. IN: *Corridor of Mirrors, Hamlet, Scott of the Antarctic, Valley of the Eagles, The Crimson Pirate, That Lady, Storm Over the Nile, Moby Dick, Dracula* and *The Curse of Frankenstein* (both in '57; first of his dozens of horror films), *Bitter Victory, City of the Dead, Two Faces of Dr. Jekyll, Terror in the Crypt, Castle of the Living Dead, The House of Blood, Dr. Terror's House of Horrors, She, Circus of Fear, Three in the Attic, The Oblong Box, Julius Caesar, The Private Life of Sherlock Holmes, Killer Force*, more.

LEE, DOROTHY (Ill.) The leading lady who was once married to columnist Jimmie Fidler lives in Chicago now, is in her 60s (b. 1911), and retired. Onscreen from 1929. IN: *Syncopation, Rio Rita, Dixiana, Half Shot at Sunrise; Hook, Line and Sinker; Laugh and Get Rich, Too Many Cooks, Local Boy Makes Good, Peach O'Reno, Take a Chance, Cockeyed Cavaliers*, more, including 1939's *SOS Tidal Wave*, her last.

LEE, FRAN (N.Y.) Character. Onscreen from the '60s. IN: *Splendor in the Grass, Up the Down Staircase, Goodbye Columbus, The Producers, Funny Girl*, more.

LEE, FRANCES (S. Cal.) She made her last movie in '34, *These Thirty Years*, when she married Enid Bennett's insurance broker-brother. And, these 40-years-plus later, they are still happily together. Onscreen from the late '20s. IN: *Chicken a la King, The Carnation Kid*, more.

LEE, LAURA (N.Y.) Character; former leading lady. Onscreen from 1930. IN: *Top Speed, Maybe It's Love, Going Wild, Jesse James' Women*, more.

LEE, MADELINE (N.Y.) Character. Onscreen in the '70s. IN: *Save the Tiger*, more.

LEE, MICHELE (S. Cal.) Leading lady. Onscreen from 1967. IN: *How to Suceed in Business Without Really Trying, The Love Bug, The Comic*, more.

LEE, PALMER /now **GREGG PALMER** (S. Cal.) Leading man. Onscreen from 1951. IN (as Palmer Lee): *The Cimarron Kid, Battle of Apache Pass, Red Ball Express, Francis Goes to West Point, Son of Ali Baba, Back at the Front, It Happens Every Thursday, Column South*, more, up to 1953. (See Gregg Palmer.)

LEE, PEGGY (S. Cal.) Singer-actress. Nominated for Best Supporting Actress Oscar in *Pete Kelly's Blues*. Onscreen from 1950. IN: *Mr. Music, The Jazz Singer*. She has also written songs for *The Jazz Singer, Lady and the Tramp*, and *Tom Thumb*.

LEE, PINKY (S. Cal.) The lisping little comic from burlesque with the funny checkered hat lives, with his wife, in an apartment in Culver City. He is in his late '60s but only semi-retired. In '74 he costarred in clubs around the country in *Las Vegas Laugh-In*, and in '75 was a guest on *The Mike Douglas Show* on TV. A serious sinus condition cut short his career in the '50s, requiring a stay of several years in Arizona to cure it—which it did. Now he would like to be busier than he is. "People keep asking, 'Pinky, when are you coming back?'" And, he adds simply, "My heart aches to perform." Onscreen in the '40s. IN: *Lady of Burlesque, Earl Carroll Vanities*, more.

LEE, RUTA (S. Cal.) Leading lady. Onscreen from 1955. IN: *Twinkle in God's Eye, Funny Face, Marjorie Morningstar, Operation Eichmann, Sergeants 3, Hootenanny Hoot, Gun Hawk, Bullet for a Badman*, more.

LEE, TOMMY (S. Cal.) Character. Onscreen from the '40s. IN: *The Sand Pebbles*, more.

LEE, WILL (N. Y.) Character. Onscreen from the '40s. IN: *Ball of Fire, Almost Married, Casbah, The Little Fugitive*, more.

LEECH, RICHARD (Eng.) Character. Onscreen from the '50s. IN: *Lease of Life, The Third Key, A Night to Remember, The Wind Cannot Read, Tunes of Glory, Desert Attack*, more.

LEEDS, ANDREA (S. Cal.) Between '36 and '40 she played major roles in ten well-recalled movies including *Stage Door*, for which she was Oscar-nominated as Best Supporting Actress. And on moviegoers she made an indelible impression—auburn-haired, full-lipped, brown-eyed, gentle-faced. The description remains apt. She had said at the outset she would leave the screen at the appropriate time for marriage and children. When she made good on this promise, one would have predicted two things about her—for she was that kind of person: that she would not be back and that, having chosen well, her married life would be a happy one. And it was. But it also contained areas of deep shadows and immeasurable sorrow. Her young husband was the extremely wealthy Robert Stewart Howard of Palm Springs. They had 31 years of happiness together before his death in '62. Recently, in Palm Springs, Andrea said, "I have a wonderful, handsome son, R. S. Howard Jr. My beautiful daughter, Leann, passed away with cancer in January 1971. So I have had a share of unhappiness but have also been blessed in many ways." Somehow it reminded one—the unspoken emotion, the quiet courage of it—of the characteristics that never failed to come across on the screen, and of something she had said about herself long ago. That was, "I didn't know I was reticent till I became a movie actress. I knew I was a little shy, a little reluctant to express my feelings. But that was just me—the way I was made." The way Andrea Leeds was "made" was, obviously, to accept life's bounties with gratitude and its severest blows with indomitable grace. Today, still lovely in her early 60s (b. 1914), with—as she once foretold in her youth—a "few lines in her face," she owns and operates a jewelry shop, Andrea of Palm Springs, a short drive from the luxurious home she shares with her elderly mother. Besides being a thriving business, the shop is a therapeutic hobby. "With this, friends, and various charities, I keep busy," she says. Much is left unvoiced, or unadorned, in simple statements. But there is deep emotional implication. That was true, too, of her most memorable performances. Onscreen from 1936. IN: *Come and Get It, It Could Happen to You, Stage Door, The Goldwyn Follies, Letter of Introduction, Youth Takes a Fling, They Shall Have Music, The Real Glory, Swanee River, Earthbound.*

LEEDS, PETER (S. Cal.) Character. Onscreen from 1942. IN: *Treat 'Em Rough, The Lady Gambles, 99 River Street, Tight Spot, Interrupted Melody, I'll Cry Tomorrow, The Facts of Life, Eight on the Lam, With Six You Get Egg Roll*, more.

LEEDS, PHIL (N.Y.) Character. Onscreen from the '60s. IN: *Rosemary's Baby, Don't Drink the Water*, more.

LEGGATT, ALISON (Eng.) Character. Onscreen from the '40s. IN: *This Happy Breed, Waterloo Road, The Miniver Story, Encore* ("The Ant and the Grasshopper" episode), *The*

Promoter, Touch and Go, Day of the Triffids, One Way Pendulum, Far From the Madding Crowd; Goodbye, Mr. Chips; more.

LEHMAN, TRENT (S. Cal.) Juvenile. Onscreen in the '70s. IN: *The Christine Jorgensen Story, The Love God?*, more.

LEHMANN, BEATRIX (Eng.) Character. Onscreen from 1935. IN: *The Passing of the Third Floor Back, Strangers on a Honeymoon, The Key, The Spy Who Came in from the Cold, Staircase*, more.

LEHMANN, CARLA (Eng.) Former leading lady; inactive in recent years. Onscreen from the late '30s. IN: *So This Is London, Flying Fortress, Candlelight in Algeria, The Facts of Love, Fame Is the Spur*, more.

LEIBMAN, RON (N.Y.) Leading man. Onscreen from 1970. IN: *Where's Poppa?, Slaughterhouse-Five, The Hot Rock, The Super Cops*, more.

LEIGH, BARBARA (S. Cal.) Leading lady. Onscreen in the '70s. IN: *The Student Nurses, Pretty Maids All in a Row, The Christian Licorice Store, Junior Bonner*, more.

LEIGH, GILBERT (N.Y.) Leading man. Onscreen from the '60s. IN: *Mad Dog Call, Felicia*, more.

LEIGH, JANET (S. Cal.) Costar. Nominated for Best Supporting Actress Oscar in *Psycho*. In 1975 she costarred with Jack Cassidy on Broadway in the play *Murder Among Friends*, her debut on stage. Onscreen from 1947. IN: *The Romance of Rosy Ridge, Hills of Home, Words and Music, Little Women, That Forsyte Woman, Holiday Affair, Two Tickets to Broadway, Angels in the Outfield, Scaramouche, The Naked Spur, Houdini, Prince Valiant, My Sister Eileen, Pete Kelly's Blues, The Vikings, Touch of Evil, Who Was That Lady?, The Manchurian Candidate, Bye Bye Birdie, Wives and Lovers, Harper, The Moving Target, Where Were You When the Lights Went Out?, Hello Down There, One Is a Lonely Number*, more.

LEIGH, JENNIFER (S. Cal.) Leading lady. Onscreen in the '70s. IN: *Lialeh*, more.

LEIGH, SUZANNA (Eng.) Leading lady. Onscreen from 1965. IN: *Boeing Boeing, The Pleasure Girls; Paradise, Hawaiian Style; The Deadly Bees, The Lost Continent, Son of Dracula*, more.

LEIGH-HUNT, BARBARA (Eng.) Support. Onscreen from 1961. IN: *A Midsummer Night's*

Dream, Frenzy, Henry VIII and His Six Wives, more.

LEIGH-HUNT, RONALD (Eng.) Support. Onscreen from the '50s. IN: *Shadow of a Man, Sink the Bismarck, Oscar Wilde, Hostile Witness, Le Mans,* more.

LEITH, VIRGINIA (N.Y.) The leading lady of the '50s has been married to stage-screen actor Donald Harron since 1959, lives in an apartment just off Central Park West, and is retired. Onscreen from 1953. IN: *Fear and Desire, Black Widow, Violent Saturday, On the Threshold of Space, Toward the Unknown, White Feather, A Kiss Before Dying,* more.

LEMBECK, HARVEY (S. Cal.) Character. Onscreen from 1951. IN: *You're in the Navy Now, Fourteen Hours, Back at the Front, Girls of the Night, Stalag 17, The Last Time I Saw Archie, Sail a Crooked Ship, A View from the Bridge, Love with a Proper Stranger, The Unsinkable Molly Brown, Pajama Party; Sgt. Deadhead, the Astronaut; The Ghost in the Invisible Bikini, Hello Down There,* more.

LEMMON, JACK (S. Cal.) Star. Won Best Supporting Actor Oscar in *Mister Roberts.* Won Best Actor Oscar in *Save the Tiger.* Nominated for Best Actor Oscar in *Some Like It Hot, The Apartment,* and *Days of Wine and Roses.* Onscreen from 1954. IN: *It Should Happen to You, Phffft!, My Sister Eileen, Operation Mad Ball; Bell, Book and Candle; Cowboy, It Happened to Jane, The Wackiest Ship in the Army, The Notorious Landlady, Irma la Douce, Under the Yum-Yum Tree, Good Neighbor Sam, The Great Race, How to Murder Your Wife, The Fortune Cookie, The Odd Couple, The April Fools, The Out-of-Towners, The War Between Men and Women, The Front Page, The Entertainer,* more.

LENARD, GRACE (S. Cal.) Character. Onscreen from 1940. IN: *Girls of the Road, Paris Calling,* more.

LENARD, MARK (S. Cal.) Support. Onscreen from 1966. IN: *The Greatest Story Ever Told, Hang 'Em High,* more.

LENIHAN, DEIDRE (N.Y.) Support. Onscreen in the '70s. IN: *Glass Houses,* more.

LENNON, JOHN (N.Y.) Of the Beatles. Onscreen from 1964. IN: *A Hard Day's Night, Help!, How I Won the War; Diaries, Notes and Sketches; Let It Be, Superstars in Film Concert,* more.

LENSKY, LEIB (N.Y.) Character. Onscreen from the '30s. IN: *Grand Illusion, The Pawnbroker, Goodbye Columbus, The Arrangement, The Night They Raided Minsky's, Bye Bye Braverman,* more.

LENYA, LOTTE (N.Y.) Character-singer. Nominated for Best Supporting Actress Oscar in *The Roman Spring of Mrs. Stone.* Onscreen in Germany from 1930. IN: *The Threepenny Opera,* more. Onscreen in America from 1960. IN: *From Russia with Love, The Appointment,* more.

LENZ, KAY (S. Cal.) Leading leady. Onscreen in the '70s. IN: *Breezy, White Line Fever, The Great Scout & Cathouse Thursday,* more.

LENZ, RICK (S. Cal.) Leading man. Onscreen from 1969. IN: *Cactus Flower, How Do I Love Thee, Scandalous John, Where Does It Hurt?, The Shootist,* more.

LEON, JOSEPH (N.Y.) Character. Onscreen from the '50s. IN: *Sweet Smell of Success, Act One, The People Next Door, Shaft,* more.

LEONARD, QUEENIE (S. Cal.) Besides continuing to lend her quirky charm to movies, this inimitable character actress does voices for such Disney cartoon features as *A Hundred and One Dalmatians.* Onscreen from 1938. IN: *Moonlight Sonata* (in England), *Ladies in Retirement, Confirm or Deny, This Above All, Forever and a Day, The Lodger, Molly and Me, And Then There Were None, Cluny Brown, Life with Father, Thunder on the Hill, The Narrow Margin, 23 Paces to Baker Street,* more.

LEONARD, SHELDON (S. Cal.) He gave up being the screen's most ominous hood after 1961's *Pocketful of Miracles* and became one of TV's most successful (and wealthiest) producers. *I Spy* was just one of his hit shows. In 1975, a vigorous, silver-haired 68, he returned to acting in the disastrously unsuccessful TV series *Big Eddie,* as a Runyon-style gambler gone legit—and a grandfather. The last he is in private life; in '76 he and wife Frances celebrated their 45th wedding anniversary surrounded by children and grandchildren. Onscreen from 1939. IN: *Another Thin Man; Tall, Dark and Handsome; Tortilla Flat, Lucky Jordan, The Falcon in Hollywood, To Have and Have Not; Crime, Inc.; The Last Crooked Mile, It's a Wonderful Life, The Gangster, Sinbad the Sailor, My Dream Is Yours, Come Fill the Cup, Diamond Queen, Guys and Dolls,* more.

LEONTOVICH, EUGENIE (S. Cal.) Playing the long-suffering mother of Don Ameche, Alan Curtis, *et al.,* in 1940's *Four Sons,* her first picture, this Russian actress seemed such a small, frail old woman. That was an acting job—call it sleight of hand—of the first rank; she had not been a student of the Moscow Art Theater's Vsevolod E. Meyerhold for naught. Today, in her 80s (b. 1894), she is petite as always (and most often to be found clad in blue jeans), but frail and old she is not. Even yet. But a dynamo in the theater, yes. She lives alone in a house in the Pacific Palisades left her by her late husband, director-actor Gregory Ratoff (d. 1960), though they had been divorced in '49, after 26 years of marriage. Much of her time, though, is spent elsewhere—in some theatrical capacity. In '75 in New York she directed the Off Broadway comedy *And So to Bed.* The year before it was the play *Medea and Jason,* which she had also adapted from the *Medea* of Euripides by Robinson Jeffers. In '72, she directed *Anna K.,* her own conception of Tolstoy's *Anna Karenina,* in which she portrayed two separate old aristocrats; "riveting theater," wrote Clive Barnes of the New York *Times.* Prior to these activities, she had costarred on Broadway in the '50s (winning a Tony) in *Anastasia,* spent seven years in Chicago with the Goodman Theater as actress-teacher-director, and owned and operated two legitimate theaters in Los Angeles. "My husband was making very big money as a moving-picture director, and I spent it, to my pleasure." And, she adds with a casual shrug, "I lost every penny." What she has left is her house. "I didn't sell that yet." And her memories—of fleeing the revolution; of 50 years in the theater in Russia, France and the U.S., and in movies; and of her tumultuous life with Gregory Ratoff. She is writing her memoirs. Onscreen from 1940. IN: *Four Sons, The Men in Her Life, Anything Can Happen, The World in His Arms, The Rains of Ranchipur, Homicidal,* more.

LeROY, GLORIA (S. Cal.) Support. Onscreen in the '70s. IN: *Cold Turkey, The Gang That Couldn't Shoot Straight, Welcome to Arrow Beach,* more.

LeROY, HAL (N.J.) In '34, Fred Astaire was *his* rival as a movie dancer. He continued his fancy stepping onscreen (in addition to playing the title role in *Harold Teen*) through 1940. After that he did Broadway musicals (as he had before) and danced on TV. In his 60s now (b. 1913), just as tall and lithe, but no longer rail-thin and with silver in his curly sideburns, he still dances. But not professionally. He hasn't set foot onstage in two decades. Instead, he turns up regularly, unpublicized and as a volunteer, to dance for and entertain shut-ins at such as the DeWitt Nursing Home. His career in recent years has been that of director-choreographer-producer of industrial shows. He and his wife, former model Ruth Dodd, live in Maywood, and have been happily married since the year the famous "boy dancer" got out of his teens. Onscreen from 1934. IN: *Wonder Bar, Start Cheering, Too Many Girls,* more.

LESCOULIE, JACK (N.Y.) TV personality. Onscreen from the late '30s. IN: B Westerns.

LESLIE, BETHEL (S. Cal.) Leading lady. Onscreen from 1959. IN: *The Rabbit Trap, Captain Newman M.D., A Rage to Live, The Molly Maguires,* more.

LESLIE, JOAN (S. Cal.) Yesterday's girl-next-door remains a redhead—slender, freckled, and delightful. She is not a girl any more (b. 1925), no longer looks 19, and there are wrinkles at the corners of her eyes and next to her dimples. But you would recognize her in an instant and might even congratulate yourself for having liked her so three decades back. She has been married since '50 to Dr. William G. Caldwell, a leading obstetrician and gynecologist. Devout Catholics both, they live in a two-story yellow brick house in the fashionably old-fashioned Los Feliz area of Hollywood, and are proud parents of identical twins, Patrice and Ellen, described by their mother as "wonderful girls—warm, down-to-earth, very bright." Honor graduates of USC, they have also received their master's degrees in English, and now both write and teach. Some of Dr. Caldwell's medical-profession idealism, which Joan will proudly cite for you at the least urging, has rubbed off on her. "I'm very much involved with the St. Anne's Home for Unwed Mothers," she says. "I'm on the Board of Directors, assisting in raising funds to help with their medical and educational program which aids so many young girls in trouble and gives them a new start in their somewhat confused lives." She is also resuming the acting career she gave up two decades ago when her daughters were small. "I never 'retired' officially," she says. "My husband has always said that as long as it wasn't hard for me, and was something I enjoyed, I should work if I wanted to. Now that the girls are grown, I want to." The parts she has been offered and accepted have been on TV and have been, as she knew they would be, character actress roles. In a *Police Story* episode in '75, she played the plain, middle-aged wife of drunken cop Howard Duff. And in the more recent TV-movie *The Keegans,* she was the mother in a contemporary Irish family with Mafia connections. Reminiscing, she looks back on the role of Mary in *Yankee Doodle Dandy* with Cagney as "the thrill of my life." Not unnaturally, she was on hand the night of Hollywood's big fete for Cagney. Looking to the future, since she was Cagney's leading lady in the picture that won him an Oscar, and Cooper's in *Sergeant York*, which brought him his first, there could still be one ahead for Joan Leslie herself. Onscreen from 1936. IN: *Camille, Winter Carnival, Laddie; Nancy Drew, Reporter* (and others in which she was a juvenile); *High Sierra, The Wagons Roll at Night, The Male Animal, The Hard Way, The Sky's the Limit, Hollywood Canteen, Rhapsody in Blue, Where Do We Go from Here?, Two Guys from Milwaukee, Janie Gets Married, Repeat Performance, Born to Be Bad, The Skipper Surprised His Wife, Hellgate, Flight Nurse, Hell's Outpost*, more, including 1956's *The Revolt of Mamie Stover*, her most recent to date.

LESLIE, NAN (S. Cal.) Leading lady. Onscreen from 1946. IN: *Sunset Pass, Woman on the Beach, Wild Horse Mesa, Western Heritage, Pioneer Marshal, Miracle of the Hills, The Crowded Sky, The Bamboo Saucer*, more.

LESSER, LEN (S. Cal.) Character. Onscreen from 1956. IN: *Shack Out on 101; Crime and Punishment, U.S.A.; Kelly's Heroes, Blood and Lace*, more.

LESSMAN, HARRY (N.Y.) Character. Onscreen from the '50s. IN: *The Wrong Man, Twelve Angry Men, The Fugitive Kind, Stage Struck, Something Wild, Midnight Cowboy, The Night They Raided Minsky's, Mirage, Penelope*, more.

LESSY, BEN (S. Cal.) Character. Onscreen from 1943. IN: *Thousands Cheer, Her Highness and the Bellboy, The Pirate, The Purple Heart Diary, Just for You, Gypsy, Pajama Party, That Funny Feeling, The Last of the Secret Agents, The Fastest Guitar Alive, The Love Machine*, more.

LESTER, BUDDY (S. Cal.) Support. Onscreen from 1960. IN: *Ocean's Eleven, Sergeants 3, Three on a Couch, The Nutty Professor, The Big Mouth, The Party*, more.

LESTER, JACK (S. Cal.) Character. Onscreen from the '50s. IN: *No Orchids for Miss Blandish*, more.

LESTER, JERRY (N.Y.) Comedian. Onscreen from 1960. IN: *The Rookie*, more.

LESTER, MARK (S. Cal.) Former juvenile (b. 1958). Onscreen from 1964. IN: *Spaceflight IC-1, Our Mother's House, Oliver!; Run Wild, Run Free; Sudden Terror, Who Slew Auntie Roo?, The First Time, On the Grass*, more.

LESTER, TOM (S. Cal.) Support. Onscreen in the '70s. IN: *Benji*, more.

LESTOCQ, HUMPHREY (Eng.) Character. Onscreen from the '50s. IN: *Once a Sinner, Angels One Five, Come Back Peter, Meet Mr. Lucifer, The Good Beginning*, more.

LETTS, PAULINE (Eng.) Character. Onscreen from 1950. IN: *Pink String and Sealing Wax*, more.

LETZ, GEORGE (S. Cal.) (See George Montgomery.)

LEVENE, SAM (N.Y.) On Broadway, in the 1975–76 season, this inimitable character actor who is now in his 70s (b. 1905) costarred with Eva LeGallienne in *The Royal Family*. Onscreen from 1936. IN: *Three Men on a Horse, After the Thin Man, Yellow Jack, The Shopworn Angel, Golden Boy, The Big Street, Gung Ho!, Action in the North Atlantic, The Killers, Brute Force, Boomerang, Killer McCoy, Crossfire, Dial 1119, The Opposite Sex, Designing Woman, Sweet Smell of Success, A Farewell to Arms, Act One, Such Good Friends*, more.

LEVERSEE, LORETTA (S. Cal.) Support. Onscreen from 1965. IN: *The Playground*, more.

LEWIS, ABBY (N.Y.) Character. Onscreen from the '60s. IN: *The Miracle Worker, The Young Doctors*, more.

LEWIS, AL (S. Cal.) Character. Onscreen from 1964. IN: *The World of Henry Orient; Munster, Go Home; They Shoot Horses, Don't They?; The Boatniks, They Might Be Giants*, more.

LEWIS, ALLAN (N.Y.) Support. Onscreen from the '50s. IN: *Comanche*, more.

LEWIS, ARTIE (S. Cal.) Character. Onscreen from 1951. IN: *Pickup; What Did You Do in the War, Daddy?; Which Way to the Front?, Star Spangled Girl*, more.

LEWIS, BOBO (N.Y.) Support. Onscreen from 1962. IN: *The Interns, It's a Mad Mad Mad Mad World, Way . . . Way Out, Hootenanny Hoot, Which Way to the Front?*, more.

LEWIS, DAVID (S. Cal.) Character. Onscreen from 1956. IN: *That Certain Feeling, The Apartment, Honeymoon Hotel; John Goldfarb, Please Come Home; Generation*, more.

LEWIS, DIANA (S. Cal.) Ever since she married William Powell in '40, the onetime MGM starlet has lived in Palm Springs. Though, unbelievably, she is in her early 60s now (b. 1915), she is a bouncy, trim, tanned, and most social woman who plays championship (local) tennis and golf. Asked if she has ever regretted giving up her career—after 1943's *Cry Havoc*—she is likely to laugh and ask, "What career?" Onscreen from 1934. IN: *It's a Gift, Enter Madame, Gold Diggers in Paris, Forty Little Mothers, Bitter Sweet, Andy Hardy Meets a Debutante, Go West, The People vs. Dr. Kildare, Johnny Eager, Whistling in Dixie, Seven Sweethearts*, more.

LEWIS, ELLIOTT (S. Cal.) Character; now a producer. One of radio's most famous leading men, he was often teamed with his former wife, Cathy Lewis, now deceased. Onscreen from the '40s. IN: *The Story of Molly X* (with Cathy Lewis), *Ma and Pa Kettle Go to Town, Saturday's Hero, Let's Do It Again*, more.

LEWIS, FIONA (Eng.) Leading lady. Onscreen from the '60s. IN: *The Fearless Vampires* (or, *Pardon Me But Your Teeth Are in My Neck*), *Otley, Where's Jack?, Villain, Lisztomania, Drum*, more.

LEWIS, GEOFFREY (S. Cal.) Support. Onscreen in the '70s. IN: *Thunderbolt and Lightfoot, Macon County Line, My Name Is Nobody, Lucky Lady*, more.

LEWIS, JERRY (S. Cal.) Star comedian. Onscreen from 1949. IN: *My Friend Irma, At War with the Army, That's My Boy, Jumping Jacks; Sailor, Beware!; The Caddy, Scared Stiff, Money from Home, Living It Up, Three-Ring Circus, Artists and Models, Pardners, The Delicate Delinquent, The Sad Sack, The Geisha Boy, Visit to a Small Planet, Cinderfella, Ladies' Man, The Errand Boy, The Nutty Professor, The Patsy, The Big Mouth, Which Way to the Front?*, more.

LEWIS, JERRY LEE (Tenn.) C&W singer. Onscreen in 1958. IN: *High School Confidential*.

LEWIS, MARY RIO (N.Y.) Black character. Onscreen from the '60s. IN: *The Pawnbroker, The Hospital, A Place Called Today*, more.

LEWIS, MONICA (S. Cal.) The singer-actress has been married for a number of years to agent Jennings Lang, and, after a 17-year absence from movies, played a secretary in *Earthquake* ('74). Onscreen from 1951. IN: *Inside Straight, Excuse My Dust, Everything I Have Is Yours, Affair with a Stranger, The D.I.*, more.

LEWIS, ROBERT (N.Y.) Character. One of the founders of Actors Studio, with Elia Kazan and Cheryl Crawford, he gave up his movie acting career three decades ago. Since, he has directed movies (*Anything Goes*), produced and directed Broadway shows, acted on Broadway and taught drama. Onscreen from 1942. IN: *Tonight We Raid Calais, Paris After Dark, Dragon Seed, Son of Lassie, Ziegfeld Follies, Monsieur Verdoux*, more.

LEWIS, ROBERT Q. (S. Cal.) Comedian. Onscreen from 1957. IN: *An Affair to Remember, Good Neighbor Sam, Ski Party, Ride Beyond Vengeance, How to Succeed in Business Without Really Trying*, more.

LEWIS, RONALD (Eng.) Leading man. Onscreen from the '50s. IN: *The Square Ring, The Beachcomber, Storm Over the Nile, Helen of Troy, Panic in the Parlor, Conspiracy of Hearts, Stop Me Before I Kill, Scream of Fear, Billy Budd, Paul and Michelle*, more.

LEYTON, JOHN (Eng.) Leading man. Onscreen from 1962. IN: *The Great Escape, Guns at Batasi, Von Ryan's Express, The Idol, Every Day Is a Holiday, Seaside Swingers, Krakatoa —East of Java*, more.

LIBERACE (S. Cal.) Pianist-actor. Onscreen from 1950. IN: *South Sea Sinner, Footlight Varieties, Sincerely Yours, When the Boys Meet the Girls, The Loved One*, more.

LIEB, ROBERT P. (S. Cal.) Character. Onscreen from 1956. IN: *Somebody Up There Likes Me, Myra Breckinridge, How to Frame a Figg*, more.

LIGON, TOM (N.Y.) Leading man. Onscreen from 1969. IN: *Paint Your Wagon, Jump*, more.

LILLIE, BEATRICE (N.Y.) The great British comedienne, in her 70s now (b. 1898), suffered a stroke several years ago and has been desperately ill since. Onscreen from 1927. IN: *Exit Smiling, The Show of Shows, Dr. Rhythm, On Approval, Around the World in 80 Days, Thoroughly Modern Millie*, more.

LIME, YVONNE (S. Cal.) The former Paramount starlet has been married for a decade to TV producer Don Fedderson and has a daughter (b. 1970). Onscreen from 1956. IN: *The Rainmaker, Untamed Youth, I Was a Teenage Werewolf, Dragstrip Riot, Speed Crazy*, more.

LINCOLN, ABBEY (S. Cal.) Black leading lady. Onscreen from 1957. IN: *The Girl Can't Help It, Nothing But a Man, For Love of Ivy*, more.

LINCOLN, CARYL (S. Cal.) She lives now, in her late 60s, at the Motion Picture and TV Country Home with happy memories of the days when she was a popular heroine in Westerns and later a character actress. Even the still-later times when she worked as an extra are pleasant to recall, for she loved the movie business. From '34, until his death from a heart attack in '64, she was married to actor Byron Stevens, brother of Barbara Stanwyck. She has a devoted son, Brian, happily married, and a teenage grandson, Michael. The kind of life she had with Byron Stevens was summed up once by Barbara Stanwyck, who said to her brother: "*You* are the lucky one. You have a wonderful wife who loves you. You have a fine son and daughter-in-law who adore you and stay close to you. And you have the pleasure of your grandson. There aren't enough marquee lights with my name on them to add up to what you have." Onscreen from 1928. IN: *A Girl in Every Port, The Lost Special* (serial), many B Westerns.

LINCOLN, STEVE (N.Y.) Character. Onscreen in the '70s. IN: *The Hot Rock, The Gang That Couldn't Shoot Straight, The Hospital, Such Good Friends, Mortadella,* more.

LIND, DELLA (S. Cal.) In her 60s now, the former Hal Roach leading lady—retired for four decades—lives near Hollywood and is a widow, her husband, musical director-composer Franz Steininger, having died in 1974. Onscreen from 1938. IN: *Swiss Miss,* more.

LIND, GILLIAN (Eng.) Character actress. Onscreen from 1932. IN: *Condemned to Death, The Oracle, The Heart of the Matter, Aunt Clara, The Horse's Mouth,* more.

LINDEN, ERIC (S. Cal.) Almost 20 years ago, concerned that the actor was becoming a "recluse," a man professing to be a close friend wrote a magazine, giving Linden's address, and urging its readers to write him. No such recommendation would be needed now. The actor, in his 60s today (b. 1909), still lives quietly in South Laguna Beach—enjoying his daily hikes on the beach and working in his garden. But he also has a lively young family—a lovely wife named Joanne and three teenage children: David, Andrea, and Karen. Linden still evinces little interest in his 40-picture career that began in '31 and ended in '41 after *Criminals Within.* Once he expressed his incompatibility with Hollywood like this: "The first year changed me; the second year I realized that change and if I'd stayed . . . I'd have grown used to it and accepted it—along with all that Hollywood is made of—as natural. But when I realized what was happening to me I left. . . ." He still stands by that. Onscreen from 1931. IN: *Are These Our Children?, The Crowd Roars, Young Bride, Roundhouse Murder, Age of Consent, Life Begins, The Phantom of Crestwood, The Silver Cord, Sweepings, Flying Devils; Ah, Wilder-*

ness!; Ladies Crave Excitement, The Voice of Bugle Ann, Old Hutch, Accent on Love, Sweetheart of the Navy, A Family Affair, Girl Loves Boy, Here's Flash Casey, Everything's On Ice, Gone With the Wind, more.

LINDEN, JENNIE (Eng.) Leading lady. Onscreen from the '60s. IN: *Nightmare, Women in Love, A Severed Head, Old Dracula, Hedda,* more.

LINDFORS, VIVECA (N.Y.) Costar. Onscreen in Sweden from 1940. IN: *In Paradise, The Crazy Family, Appassionata, Interlude,* more. Onscreen in America from 1948. IN: *To the Victor, The Adventures of Don Juan, Night Unto Night, No Sad Songs for Me, Dark City, Somewhere in the City, Run for Cover, I Accuse!, Weddings and Babies, The Story of Ruth, King of Kings, An Affair of the Skin, Sylvia, The Way We Were, Welcome to L.A.,* more.

LINDLEY, AUDRA (S. Cal.) Character. Onscreen in the '70s. IN: *Taking Off,* more.

LINDSAY, JOHN V. (N.Y.) Former mayor of New York City. Onscreen as an actor in 1975. IN: *Rosebud.*

LINDSAY, MARGARET (S. Cal.) Nothing external about her has changed. She looks, in her 60s (b. 1910), just as she did in her 30s—except for a very few gray hairs she did not have then. And she remains a "bachelor girl." Onscreen for 31 years, in more than 100 pictures following *The All-American,* she quit in '63 after a supporting role in *Tammy and the Doctor.* "I decided I was going to stop acting," she explains, "so I said goodbye to my agent, and booked a flight to Europe. I just wanted to take it easy for a while." After Europe, she traveled to the mid-East and to Hawaii. "And in my years of spare time, I redecorated my house several times," she laughs. She also discovered that, thanks to TV's Late Shows, she had a new crop of fans. "People were stopping me in the market, on the street, at the beauty parlor wanting to know what it was like working with a Bogart or Cagney. And always concluded by asking why I wasn't still acting." And sometimes, especially when attending a Hollywood fete for one of her still-active costars of the past, such as Pat O'Brien, she would ask herself the same question. At a party in '74 her dinner partner was an agent. Next day he phoned saying he had landed her an interview at Universal for the role of secretary to Fred MacMurray in a TV-movie, *The Chadwicks.* It was just a one-day job, but. . . "Two days later I was on the stage, in makeup and raring to go," she says. "I didn't realize how much I missed the excitement on a happy set." She was particularly pleased when members of the crew—old friends from her Warners days—greeted her and a commissary waitress rushed over to say hello. Describing this exhilarating experience, the actress adds, "After lunch one of the young players looked wistfully out of the soundstage door and sighed, 'Oh, it's such a wonderful day. How I wish I were outside.' I just thought to myself, how nice it is to be on a set again—*Inside*.'" Onscreen from 1932. IN: *The All-American; Paddy, the Next Best Thing; Cavalcade, Voltaire, The House on 56th Street, The Dragon Murder Case, Bordertown, Devil Dogs of the Air, Dangerous, The Case of the Curious Bride, G-Men, Public Enemy's Wife, Slim, Green Light, Gold Is Where You Find It, Garden of the Moon, Jezebel, Hell's Kitchen, The Under-Pup; Ellery Queen, Master Detective* (and six others in this series in which she was Nikki Porter to Ralph Bellamy's and William Gargan's Ellery Queen); *The Spoilers, Crime Doctor, Adventures of Rusty, Louisiana, Seven Keys to Baldpate, B.F.'s Daughter, Cass Timberlane, The Bottom of the Bottle, Please Don't Eat the Daisies*, more.

LINDSAY, MARY (S. Cal.) Leading lady. Onscreen from 1968. IN: *Pamela, Pamela, You Are . . .* , more.

LINDSEY, GEORGE (S. Cal.) Character. Onscreen from the '60s. IN: *Ensign Pulver, Snowball Express*, more.

LINDSTROM, PIA (N.Y.) Daughter of Ingrid Bergman. Now a TV news reporter for NBC. Onscreen in 1964. IN: *Marriage Italian Style*.

LINKLETTER, ART (S. Cal.) TV personality. Onscreen from 1946. IN: *People Are Funny, Champagne for Caesar*, more.

LINN, BAMBI (Conn.) Divorced from dancer Rod Alexander, she is married to Joseph de Jesus and lives in Westport, where she is director of a dance school, teaching ballet and modern dance. She has one daughter by her first husband and two by her second. Onscreen in 1955. IN: *Oklahoma!*

LINVILLE, ALBERT (N.Y.) Character. Onscreen in 1958. IN: *Damn Yankees*.

LINVILLE, JOANNE (S. Cal.) Leading lady. Onscreen from 1950. IN: *Copper Canyon* (bit as a dance hall girl), *The Goddess, Scorpio, Gable and Lombard*, more.

LINVILLE, LARRY (S. Cal.) Support. Onscreen in the '70s. IN: *Kotch, Vanished, The Night Stalker*, more.

LIPTON, PEGGY (S. Cal.) TV leading lady. Onscreen in 1968. IN: *Blue*.

LIPTON, ROBERT (S. Cal.) Support. Onscreen from 1968. IN: *Blue, Bullitt, Tell Them Willie Boy Is Here*, more.

LISI, VERNA (It.) Costar. Onscreen in Europe from 1963. IN: *Duel of the Titans, The Doll That Took the Town, Eva*, more. Onscreen in America and internationally from 1965. IN: *How to Murder Your Wife, Casanova 70, Assault on a Queen; Not With My Wife, You Don't; Made in Italy; The Birds, the Bees and the Italians; The Girl and the General, Kiss the Other Sheik, The Secret of Santa Vittoria, The Statue*, more.

LISTER, MOIRA (Eng.) Character; former leading lady. Onscreen from 1943. IN: *The Shipbuilders, A Lady Surrenders, So Evil My Love, A Run for Your Money, White Corridors, The Cruel Sea, The Deep Blue Sea, Trouble in Store, Abandon Ship, The Yellow Rolls-Royce, The Double Man*, more.

LITTLE, CLEAVON (S. Cal.) Black leading man. Onscreen from 1969. IN: *Three, What's So Bad About Feeling Good?, John and Mary, Vanishing Point, Blazing Saddles*, more.

LITTLEFEATHER, SACHEEN (S. Cal.) American Indian support. Onscreen in the '70s. IN: *The Trial of Billy Jack, Winterhawk*, more.

LIVINGSTON, BARRY (S. Cal.) Former juvenile. Onscreen in the '60s. IN: *The Errand Boy, My Six Loves*, more.

LIVINGSTON, MARGARET (Pa.) Onscreen for 15 years, she left movies after 1934's *Social Register*. In her 70s now (b. 1900), she lives in well-off retirement in Doylestown. She told portly, famous bandleader Paul Whiteman in '31 that, if he would lose weight, she would marry him. He did (more than 100 pounds) and she did (becoming his fourth and last wife); she later collaborated on a humorous book about his dieting experiences, *Whiteman's Burden*. They had one daughter, Margot. The actress remained happily married to the noted musician until his death in '67; she has not remarried. Onscreen from the early '20s. IN: *Divorce, Love's Whirlpool, I'll Show You the Town, Best People, The Yankee Senor, Slaves of Beauty, Sunrise, Streets of Shanghai, The Mad Hour, The Bellamy Trial, Innocents of Paris, Seven Keys to Baldpate, What a Widow, Kiki, God's Gift to Women, Smart Money*, more.

LIVINGSTON, ROBERT (S. Cal.) Robust and ruggedly handsome in his 60s (b. 1908), yesterday's great cowboy favorite has darkened his snow-white hair and come back in this decade —after 15 years offscreen—to costar in a series of R-rated, soft-core porn films. In them, he stays fully clothed; the girls, however, do not. First off the assembly line was *The Naughty Stewardesses*. "It was a dirty picture, but that was fine with me," he laughs, "because I'm a dirty old man." Next was *Girls for Rent*—with Georgina Spelvin, no less. And then, in '75, *Blazing Stewardesses* opposite Yvonne De Carlo, who also remained clothed. It is, of course, as "Stony Brooke"—the character he played 29 times in "The Three Mesquiteers" pictures—that Robert Livingston's fans will always think of him. The "Mesquiteers" series was among the Top Ten Western Box-Office attractions for seven consecutive years, 1937 through 1943. Before and during this series, the actor had made a specialty of portraying "masked hero" roles: as "The Eagle" in the '36 serial *The Vigilantes Are Coming*, in the '38 serial *The Lone Ranger Rides Again*, and as "Zorro" in Republic's first color feature, *The Bold Caballero*, in '36. When he left Republic and the "Mesquiteers," Livingston starred for PRC as the "Lone Rider" in another profitable Western series. By the mid-1940s he had begun to do character roles in both Westerns and B's such as *Valley of the Zombies* and *Undercover Woman*. After more than a decade of supporting roles, he bade the screen farewell in '58, when he completed a small part in Rowan and Martin's first comedy, *Once Upon a Horse*. Financially well off, with a beautiful home in Beverly Hills, he declared himself retired. He wrote, raised prize roses, and read in the garden, sitting on a small bench placed under a sign with the legend *I Hate People*. He granted no interviews, refused to pose for fans who invaded his privacy. Why did he decide to come back? He answers simply that producer Sam Sherman "wanted me to do it, so I did." He has been married twice. In 1947 he was briefly wed to Margaret Roach, the blonde starlet-daughter of producer Hal Roach. They were divorced, and she has been deceased since 1964. His present marriage, to a nonprofessional, has been a long, happy one. He has one son, in his 20s, actor-write Addison—named for Livingston's late cowboy star-brother, Addison Randall. Onscreen from 1929. IN: *Public Enemy No. 2, Enlighten Thy Daughter* (he also wrote the screenplay), *Death on the Diamond, West Point of the Air, Murder in the Fleet, Absolute Quiet, Larceny on the Air, Wild Horse Rodeo, Riders of the Whistling Skull, Renfrew of the Royal Mounted, Heroes of the Saddle, Covered Wagon Days, Brazil, Lake Placid Serenade, Dakota, The Feathered Serpent, Riders in the Sky, Mule Train, Winning of the West*, more.

LIVINGSTON, STANLEY (S. Cal.) Young leading man; former juvenile (b. 1950). Onscreen from the '60s. IN: *Rally Round the Flag Boys!, Peck's Bad Girl, How the West Was Won, X-15*, more.

LIVINGSTONE, MARY (S. Cal.) Jack Benny's widow and inimitable partner. She has long been retired. Onscreen in 1937. IN: *This Way Please*.

LLOYD, NORMAN (S. Cal.) The former character actor gave up his career more than two decades ago and is now a television producer. Onscreen from 1942. IN: *Saboteur, Within These Walls, The Southerner, A Walk in the Sun, A Letter for Evie, Young Widow, No Minor Vices, Calamity Jane and Sam Bass, The Black Book, Buccaneer's Girl, M, He Ran All the Way, Limelight, The Light Touch*, more.

LLOYD, SHERMAN (N.Y.) Character. Onscreen from 1968. IN: *Pamela, Pamela, You Are . . .*, more.

LLOYD, SUE (Eng.) Leading lady. Onscreen from 1964. IN: *Nothing But the Best, Hysteria, The Ipcress File, Percy*, more.

LO BIANCO, TONY (N.Y.) Leading man. Onscreen from 1969. IN: *The Honeymoon Killers, The French Connection, The Seven Ups*, more.

LOCANTE, SAM (N.Y.) Character. Onscreen from the '50s. IN: *The Wrong Man, Public Energy No. 1, Middle of the Night, Happy Anniversary*, more.

LOCKE, HARRY (Eng.) Character. Onscreen from the '40s. IN: *The Naked Heart, The Undefeated, Time Bomb, Paratrooper, Doctor in the House, The Teckman Mystery, Reach for the Sky, Treasure Island, Carry On Nurse*, more.

LOCKE, KATHARINE (S. Cal.) Married to writer Norman Corwin since '47, she has a grown son and daughter, and lives in Sherman Oaks. Onscreen from 1944. IN: *The Seventh Cross, The Snake Pit, Try and Get Me, People Will Talk, Flesh and Fury, A Certain Smile*, more.

LOCKE, SONDRA (S. Cal.) Leading lady. Nominated for Best Supporting Actress Oscar in *The Heart Is a Lonely Hunter*. Onscreen from 1968. IN: *The Lovemakers; Run, Shadow, Run; Cover Me Babe, Willard, The Second Coming of Suzanne*, more.

LOCKE, TERRENCE (S. Cal.) Leading man. Onscreen in 1976. IN: *Goodbye, Norma Jean.*

LOCKHART, ANNE (S. Cal.) Support. Daughter of June, granddaughter of the late Gene. Onscreen from 1972. IN: *Jory*, more.

LOCKHART, CALVIN (S. Cal.) Black star. Onscreen from 1968. IN: *Joanna, Cotton Comes to Harlem, Myra Breckinridge, Halls of Anger, Leo the Last, Uptown Saturday Night; Honeybaby, Honeybaby; The Beast Must Die, Let's Do It Again*, more.

LOCKHART, JUNE (S. Cal.) Leading lady. She has acted only on TV and the legitimate stage in the past decade. Onscreen from 1938. IN: *A Christmas Carol, Sergeant York, All This and Heaven Too, Adam Had Four Sons, Miss Annie Rooney* (all juvenile roles), *Meet Me in St. Louis, Son of Lassie, Keep Your Powder Dry, She-Wolf of London, Easy to Wed, The White Cliffs of Dover, The Yearling, T-Men; It's a Joke, Son; Red Light, Lassie's Great Adventure*, more.

LOCKHART, KATHLEEN (S. Cal.) This noted character actress, widow of Gene Lockhart and mother of June, has been retired since 1960. Onscreen from 1936. IN: *The Devil Is a Sissy, Career Woman, Something to Sing About, Penrod's Double Trouble, Men Are Such Fools, A Christmas Carol, Sweethearts, Our Leading Citizen, All This and Heaven Too, Mission to Moscow, Wilson, The Seventh Cross, Lady in the Lake, I'd Climb the Highest Mountain, Walking My Baby Back Home, The Glenn Miller Story*, more.

LOCKWOOD, ALEXANDER (S. Cal.) Character. Onscreen from 1941. IN: *Flight from Destiny, Just Off Broadway, Jigsaw, The Tattered Dress, The Tarnished Angels*, more.

LOCKWOOD, GARY (S. Cal.) Leading man. Onscreen from 1960. IN: *Tall Story, Wild in the Country, Splendor in the Grass, The Magic Sword, It Happened at the World's Fair, Firecreek, 2001: A Space Odyssey, The Model Shop, They Came to Rob Las Vegas, R.P.M., Stand Up and Be Counted*, more.

LOCKWOOD, JULIA (Eng.) Leading lady. Onscreen from 1947. IN: *The White Unicorn* (child's role), *My Teenage Daughter, Please Turn Over*, more. (See below.)

LOCKWOOD, MARGARET (Eng.) Briefly in Hollywood in '39 (after five years in British pix) to play the romantic interest in *Susannah of the Mounties* and Fairbanks Jr.'s *Rulers of the Sea*, she returned to England. There, in many films, she quickly became the #1 Most Popular Actress, a position she held for years—thanks to *The Man in Grey, Hungry Hill, Bedelia*, etc. In '57, after costarring with Dirk Bogarde in *Cast a Dark Shadow*, she gave up her movie career, and has only lately, two decades later, resumed it—signing to costar as The Stepmother in the musical movie *The Slipper and the Rose*. In the interim, she starred on British TV—as the woman barrister in the *Justice* series, followed by another series, *The Flying Swan*. Onstage, she had a long run in an Agatha Christie mystery, starred in Wilde's *An Ideal Husband*, and, late in '75, after a two-year absence from West End stages, opened in the suspense thriller *Double Edge*—still, at 59 (b. 1916), a stunning, auburn-haired beauty. Her one marriage, to steel broker Rupert W. Leon, entered into when she was 21, ended in divorce when she was 39. She has one child, daughter Julia Lockwood (b. 1941), the actress, now married to British actor Ernest Clark, who, in '70, made her the grandmother of a boy. At home, Margaret Lockwood seems the unlikeliest of stars. She lives at Kingston-upon-Thames, Surrey, in a small suburban house that is exactly like hundreds of others around it. She admits no liking for *The Wicked Lady*, the movie that made her notorious overnight. But she knows that, to fans, she will ever remain "the wicked Lady Skelton, with low necklines and lower tastes, the lady of the manor who turned parttime highwayman for the hell of it and got seduced by James Mason." As she said recently to a friend, "It's a label I'll carry round my neck to the day I die." Onscreen from 1935. IN: *Lorna Doone, Dr. Syn, The Lady Vanishes, The Stars Look Down, Gestapo, Night Train, The Girl in the News, Alibi, Dear Octopus, Love Story, A Place of One's Own, Jassy, The Bad Sister, Madness of the Heart, The White Unicorn, Trent's Last Case, Laughing Anne, Trouble in the Glen*, more.

LODEN, BARBARA (N.Y.) Actress-director (*Wanda*) who was discovered by Elia Kazan and has since become his wife. Onscreen from 1960. IN: *Wild River, Splendor in the Grass.*

LODER, JOHN (Eng.) Heavier than in his Hollywood heyday, the actor is still, in his 70s (b. 1898), a notably good-looking man. He made his first movie in a decade in '70, in England, *Cause for Alarm*, but has not acted since and possibly won't again. Financially, he is well off from carefully invested movie earnings (and his present wife, whom he married in '58, owns an enormous cattle ranch in Argentina, where they lived until '71). He is also a man "rich" in ex-wives. By his first wife, an English woman, has a son, Robin, now middle-aged. He later was married to and divorced from French star

Micheline Cheirel (1937–41), Hollywood star Hedy Lamar (1943–48), and non-pro Evelyn Auffmordt (1949–55). By Miss Cheirel, he is the father of a daughter, Danielle (b. 1938). By Hedy Lamarr, he has two grown children, Denise Hedy and Anthony. Denise, a raven-haired, green-eyed beauty—and look-alike for her famous mother—has been married since '65 to Lawrence Colton, once-famous Philadelphia Phillies pitcher; they met as students at the University of California at Berkeley. Son Anthony has lately been a professional photographer working in Mexico. Still the tweedy, pipe-smoking sort that he often portrayed onscreen, John Loder lives in the English countryside, works on his memoirs, and often runs in to own for a bit of "actor talk" with fellow members of the Garrick Club. Onscreen from 1927. IN: *Madame Wants No Children* (his debut, made in Germany), *The Doctor's Secret, Wedding Rehearsal, The First Born, You Made Me Love You, The Private Life of Henry VIII, The Man Who Lived Again, King Solomon's Mines, Non-Stop New York, Mademoiselle Docteur, Adventure in Diamonds, Scotland Yard, How Green Was My Valley, Confirm or Deny, One Night in Lisbon, Now Voyager, Eagle Squadron, Gentleman Jim, The Male Animal, Old Acquaintance, Passage to Marseilles, Abroad with Two Yanks, The Woman Who Came Back, One More Tomorrow, Dishonored Lady* (with wife Hedy Lamarr), *The Story of Esther Costello, Gideon of Scotland Yard,* more.

LODGE, DAVID (Eng.) Character. Onscreen from the '50s. IN: *The Cockleshell Heroes, The League of Gentlemen, Kill or Cure, Trial and Error, A Shot in the Dark, Having a Wild Weekend,* more.

LODGE, JEAN (Eng.) Character. Onscreen from the '40s. IN: *Dick Barton Strikes Back, White Corridors, Brandy for the Parson, Glad Tidings, The Black Knight, Final Appointment,* more.

LODGE, JOHN DAVIS (Conn.) A popular leading man—often billed simply John Lodge—he was onscreen in many in the '30s. In the '40s, after starring on Broadway in *Watch on the Rhine,* he entered politics, eventually becoming (1950–51) governor of Connecticut. Appointed U.S. Ambassador to Spain in '55, he served here until '61, in what was the longest term of any American ambassador to that country. Later, for almost five years, until late '73, he was the U.S. Ambassador to Argentina. At his side through all his several careers has been his actress-wife (since '29) Francesca Braggiotti, who, while they lived in Argentina, became the only woman ever named "Woman of the Year" by that country. They have two daughters, Lilly

Lodge, an actress, and Beatrice, married to Antonio de Oyarzabal, first secretary in the Spanish Embassy in London; they have made the Lodges grandparents several times. The former actor, a stolidly handsome, silver-haired but balding man in his 70s now (b. 1903), has not entirely lost his dramatic flair. As an active member of Westport's Bicentennial Committee, it was his happy duty to mount an outdoor rostrum on a church green and recite "Paul Revere's Ride"—while bells from 13 churches pealed and the town cannon boomed. Not even having tiny "daughter" Shirley Temple sit on his lap in *The Little Colonel* gave him such a thrill. Onscreen from 1932. IN: *The Woman Accused, Murders in the Zoo, Under the Tonto Rim, Little Women, The Scarlet Empress, Ourselves Alone, Bulldog Drummond at Bay, The Tenth Man, River of Unrest, Just Like a Woman, Lightning Conductor, White Cargo, The Pasha's Wives,* more.

LOGAN, JACQUELINE (N.Y.) Three times married and divorced, she is in her 70s (b. 1904), lives in Bedford Hills, and is retired. Onscreen from the early '20s. IN: *Ebb Tide, A Blind Bargain, Salomy Jane, The Light That Failed, The Dawn of a Tomorrow, Manhattan, Playing with Souls, Thank You, The King of Kings, The Blood Ship, Leopard Lady, Stocks and Blondes, The Cop, Power, General Crack,* more, including 1930's *The Middle Watch,* her last.

LOGAN, JAMES (S. Cal.) Character. Onscreen from 1947. IN: *Blonde Savage, Mr. Peabody and the Mermaid,* more.

LOGGIA, ROBERT (S. Cal.) Leading man. Onscreen from 1956. IN: *Somebody Up There Likes Me, The Garment Jungle, Cop Hater, The Greatest Story Ever Told, The Lost Missile, The Nine Lives of Elfego Baca, Che!,* more.

LOLLOBRIGIDA, GINA (It.) Less active on the screen now, in her late 40s (b. 1927), this star has embarked on a successful new career as a photographer-journalist. Besides having had a famous interview with Fidel Castro, she has published books of her photographs. Onscreen from 1947. IN: *Pagliacci, Times Gone By, Fanfan the Tulip, Beat the Devil, Crossed Swords, Beauties of the Night, Trapeze, Woman of Rome, Never So Few, Solomon and Sheba, Where the Hot Wind Blows, Go Naked in the World, Come September, Strange Bedfellows, Hotel Paradiso, Cervantes, The Private Navy of Sgt. O'Farrell, Assassination Bureau; Buona Sera, Mrs. Campbell;* more.

LOM, HERBERT (Eng.) Character star. Onscreen from 1939. IN: *Mein Kampf, The Sev-*

enth Veil, The Mark of Cain, The Brass Monkey, The Black Rose, Whispering Smith vs. Scotland Yard, Rough Shoot, Star of India, Ladykillers, War and Peace, Fire Down Below, I Accuse!, Roots of Heaven, The Big Fisherman, Third Man on the Mountain, Spartacus, El Cid, Phantom of the Opera, A Shot in the Dark, Gambit; Bang! Bang! You're Dead!; The Happy Ending, Asylum, Ten Little Indians, The Return of the Pink Panther, more.

LONCAR, BEBA (It.) Leading lady from Yugoslavia. Onscreen from 1964. IN: The Long Ships, The Boy Cried Murder; The Birds, the Bees and the Italians; The Sucker; Listen, Let's Make Love; Some Girls Do, more.

LONDON, BABE (S. Cal.) The big funny girl of the silent screen, in her late 60s now, married composer Phil Boutelje in '75. They are both residents of the Motion Picture and TV Country Home. Onscreen from the early '20s. IN: Christie Comedies (Winter Has Come, etc.), The Boob, All Aboard, The Fortune Hunter, more.

LONDON, BARBARA (S. Cal.) Support. Onscreen from 1966. IN: The Pad (And How to Use It), Psych-Out, California Split, more.

LONDON, JULIE (S. Cal.) Singer-leading lady. Onscreen from 1944. IN: Jungle Woman, A Night in Paradise, The Red House, Tap Roots, Task Force, The Fat Man, The Girl Can't Help It, Drango, Voice in the Mirror, Saddle the Wind, Night of the Quarter Moon, A Question of Adultery, The George Raft Story, more.

LONDON, STEVE (S. Cal.) Support. Onscreen from 1957. IN: Zero Hour, more.

LONG, AVON (N.Y.) Black actor-dancer. Onscreen from 1946. IN: Centennial Summer, Harry and Tonto, more.

LONG, RONALD (S. Cal.) Character. Onscreen from 1961. IN: Two Loves, The Notorious Landlady, more.

LONG, SALLY (S. Cal.) Last onscreen in 1930's Cock O' the Walk, the former leading lady of Buck Jones and Bob Custer in silent Westerns is happily married and still living near Hollywood in Sherman Oaks. For over two decades, until his death in '56, she was the wife of composer Jean (Chinatown, My Chinatown) Schwartz. Onscreen in the '20s. IN: King of the Jungle (serial), in addition to Westerns.

LONGDEN, JOHN (Eng.) Character; former leading man. Onscreen from the '20s. IN: Blackmail, The Flame of Love, Juno and the Paycock, Clouds Over Europe, Bonnie Prince Charlie, Pool of London, The Elusive Pimpernel, The Magic Box, The Ship That Died of Shame, Count of Twelve, Alias John Preston, more.

LONGDON, TERENCE (Eng.) Leading man. Onscreen from 1951. IN: Angels One Five, Helen of Troy, Another Time Another Place, Ben Hur, Carry On Nurse (others in the comedy series), more.

LONGET, CLAUDINE (Colo.) Leading lady. Onscreen from 1964. IN: McHale's Navy, The Party, more.

LONSDALE, MICHEL (Fr.) Costar. Onscreen from the '60s. IN: The Trial, The Bride Wore Black, Stolen Kisses; Destroy, She Said; Murmur of the Heart, Galileo, The Romantic Englishwoman, more.

LOO, BESSIE (S. Cal.) This supporting actress has long operated one of Hollywood's most successful actors' agencies, primarily for Oriental performers. Onscreen in the '30s. IN: Mr. Wong in Chinatown, more.

LOO, RICHARD (S. Cal.) The Hawaii-born Chinese actor who was one of the most hated "Japs" in WW II movies is in his 70s (b. 1903), married, has grown twin daughters, was most recently a regular—Master Sun—in TV's Kung Fu, and is looking forward to his next 250 movies. Onscreen from 1932. IN: War Correspondent, The Bitter Tea of General Yen, The Good Earth, Daughter of the Tong; Little Tokyo U.S.A.; Bombs Over Burma, Flight for Freedom, China, The Purple Heart, The Story of Dr. Wassell, God Is My Co-Pilot, Betrayal from the East, Back to Bataan, Tokyo Rose, The Cobra Strikes, Malaya, The Steel Helmet, Five Fingers, Soldier of Fortune, Battle Hymn, The Quiet American, A Girl Named Tamiko, The Sand Pebbles, more.

LOPEZ, PERRY (S. Cal.) Support. Onscreen from 1954. IN: Drum Beat, Battle Cry, Mister Roberts, Hell on Frisco Bay, The Steel Jungle, Cry Tough, Flaming Star, Taras Bulba, McLintock!, Sol Madrid, Che!, Chinatown, more.

LOPEZ, TRINI (S. Cal.) Singer-actor. Onscreen from 1965. IN: Marriage on the Rocks (as himself), The Poppy Is Also a Flower, The Dirty Dozen.

LORD, JACK (Hawaii) Star. Onscreen from 1950. IN: Cry Murder, The Court-Martial of Billy Mitchell, The Vagabond King, Tip on a Dead Jockey, Man of the West, God's Little Acre, The Hangman, Dr. No, The Counterfeit Killer, The Name of the Game Is Kill, more.

LORD, MARJORIE (S. Cal.) After her divorce from John Archer, this leading lady, a spirited redhead, was asked if she would marry another actor. "Only if he has a *visible* halo," she replied. Instead, in '58, she married stage producer Randolph Hale, and remained happily married to him until his death in 1974. By her first marriage she has two grown children—Gregg Archer, a business man, and Anne Archer, a greatly talented leading lady in movies (*The All-American Boy*) and on TV, who is married and has made Marjorie a grandmother of a boy. A Broadway actress before her movie career (in *The Old Maid*) and after it (*Happy Anniversary*), she now performs in dinner theaters across the land—in *Wait Until Dark; Mary, Mary; How the Other Half Loves*, etc. Her only movie in the past 20 years was 1966's *Boy, Did I Get a Wrong Number!*, and she rarely performs on TV any more, though in the early '60s she was popular as Danny Thomas' wife in *Make Room for Daddy*. In her 50s (b. 1921), she remains a beauty and a redhead. Onscreen from 1937. IN: *Hideaway, Border Cafe, Escape from Hong Kong, Moonlight in Havana, Shantytown, Johnny Come Lately, Sherlock Holmes in Washington, Air Hostess, Masked Raiders, Riding High, The Lost Volcano, Stop That Cab!, Rebel City, Down Laredo Way*, more.

LOREN, DONNA (S. Cal.) Singer-actress. Onscreen from the '60s. IN: *Muscle Beach Party, Bikini Beach Party, Pajama Party, Beach Blanket Bingo; Sgt. Deadhead, the Astronaut;* more.

LOREN, SOPHIA (Fr.) Star. Won Best Actress Oscar in *Two Women*. Nominated in the same category in *Marriage Italian Style*. Onscreen from 1950. IN: *A Husband for Cynthia, Africa Beneath the Seas, Village of the Bells, Aida, Too Bad She's Bad, Gold of Naples, The Pride and the Passion, Legend of the Lost, Boy on a Dolphin, Desire Under the Elms, Houseboat, The Key, Black Orchid, That Kind of Woman, Heller in Pink Tights, It Started in Naples, El Cid, The Millionairess; Yesterday, Today and Tomorrow; Operation Crossbow, Arabesque, Lady L, The Countess from Hong Kong, The Best House in Naples, Man of La Mancha, Verdict, The Cassandra Crossing*, more.

LORIMER, LOUISE (S. Cal.) Character. Onscreen from 1938. IN: *Gangster's Boy, Flying Cadets, Gentleman's Agreement, The Glass Menagerie, The Prowler, The People Against O'-Hara, Japanese War Bride, Night Without Sleep, Compulsion, The Impossible Years*, more.

LORING, ANN (N.Y.) Character; former leading lady. She now appears on TV and the stage. Onscreen in 1936. IN: *The Robin Hood of El Dorado* and *Absolute Quiet*.

LORING, EUGENE (N.Y.) The well-known choreographer has appeared in movies twice as a performer. Onscreen in 1944 in *National Velvet* and 1953 in *Torch Song*.

LORING, LYNN (S. Cal.) Support. Onscreen from the '60s. IN: *Splendor in the Grass, Pressure Point*, more.

LORMER, JON (S. Cal.) Character. Onscreen from the '50s. IN: *I Want to Live!, The Matchmaker, Career, The Gazebo, Pollyanna, Where the Boys Are, The Wonderful World of the Brothers Grimm, Dead Ringer, Zebra in the Kitchen, A Fine Madness, The Singing Nun, The Sand Pebbles*, more.

LORNE, CONSTANCE (Eng.) Character. Onscreen from 1948. IN: *Curtain Up*, more.

LORRAINE, GUIDO (Eng.) Character. Onscreen from the '40s. IN: *One Woman's Story, Hotel Sahara, The Detective, The Colditz Story, Paratrooper, Encore* ("Gigolo and Gigolette" episode), *Gentlemen Marry Brunettes, The Village, Port Afrique, Blue Murder at St. Trinian's*, more.

LORRAINE, LOUISE (S. Cal.) After her divorce from silent cowboy star Art Acord, the actress who was Elmo Lincoln's "Jane" in 1921's *The Adventures of Tarzan* married again and retired. Long widowed, she has grown children and lives in the San Fernando Valley. In the summer of '75 she made an appearance at a Tarzan reunion in Hollywood with Johnny Weissmuller and Buster Crabbe. Still beautifully blonde—and dimpled, of course—she was a slender knockout in a dark silk pantsuit. Onscreen from 1921. IN: *The Jade Box* (serial), *The Great Circus Mystery* (serial), *Rookies, Legionnaires in Paris, Baby Mine, Circus Rookies*, more.

LORRE, PETER, JR. (S. Cal.) Character—and a look-alike of his famous father. Onscreen from 1966. IN: *Torn Curtain*, more.

LORRING, JOAN (N.Y.) The actress who was nominated for a Supporting Oscar in *The Corn Is Green*, and later costarred in several at Warners, made her first screen appearance in more than two decades in '74 in a Burt Lancaster movie, *The Midnight Man*, in which she portrayed the wife of Cameron Mitchell. She also is heard regularly on radio in the *CBS Radio Mystery Theater*, and in '75 became a star of the new (first to be produced in 15 years) daytime radio soap opera *Radio Playhouse*. She has been married for many years to a well-known New York endocrinologist, Dr. Martin Sonenberg, is the mother of two daughters, and lives in the fashionable East 60s. She is now in her 40s (b. 1931), and her consuming passion is breadbaking, about which she has written articles for such magazines as *Vogue*. "You might say that I'm a breadmaking nut," she laughs, "but breadmaking is a most rewarding occupation. Since my first successful loaf, twenty-one years ago, I've baked at least once a week and in some fairly odd situations." She explains that once she even "raised a batch of bread while traveling at fifty miles per hour in a house trailer along the Skyline Drive in Virginia." The actress plans no full-scale renewal of her career in Hollywood; she prefers the yeasty life she has found in New York. Onscreen from 1944. IN: *Song of Russia, Bridge of San Luis Rey, Three Strangers, The Verdict, The Other Love, The Gangster, The Lost Moment, Good Sam, The Big Night, Stranger on the Prowl*, more.

LOTIS, DENNIS (Eng.) Singer-actor. Onscreen from the '50s. IN: *The Extra Day, It's a Wonderful World, Horror Hotel*, more.

LOUGHERY, JACKIE (S. Cal.) The leading lady who was Miss USA of 1952 and is one of Jack Webb's former wives has been retired from movies since 1958, though she still lives near Hollywood. Onscreen from 1955. IN: *The Naked Street, Pardners, Eighteen and Anxious, The D.I.* (with Webb), *The Hot Angel*.

LOUISE, TINA (S. Cal.) Leading lady. Onscreen from the '50s. IN: *God's Little Acre, The Hangman, The Trap, The Warrior's Empress, Armored Command, The Wrecking Crew, House of Seven Joys, The Happy Ending, The Good Guys and the Bad Guys, How to Commit Marriage, The Stepford Wives*, more.

LOVE, BESSIE (Eng.) The Texas-born star of the silent screen made such an easy transition to talkies, in *The Broadway Melody*, which was MGM's first sound musical, that she was nominated for an Oscar as Best Actress. She consolidated her renewed glory by starring in another 11 in Hollywood: *Morals for Women, Chasing Rainbows, Good News*, etc. She next starred in plays on Broadway. Then, in '35, she moved to England with her husband, director William Ballinger Hawks, from whom she was divorced the following year. (Their daughter, Patricia Hawks, after a brief acting career, married a Briton, and has made her a grandmother.) During the war years, the star served with the American Red Cross in England, was for a while a film technician at Ealing Studios, and acted in an occasional picture. At war's end she began performing on British TV and resumed the stage career she had begun in New York in '31—only now in character roles. She was with Olivier in *Born Yesterday* and with Muni in *Death of a Salesman*. She also starred onstage in *The Glass Menagerie, The Children's Hour* and *The Homecoming*, which she wrote. Today, in her 70s (b. 1898), as merry and sprightly as she was in her best comedies, diminutive Bessie Love plays cameo roles without cease in British films. She has been seen in *Sunday Bloody Sunday* (the busybody telephone operator shocked by Peter Finch's homosexual dalliances), *Loves of Isadora, Catlow, Hot Millions*, etc. In '74 she was in the TV-movie *Mousey* filmed in England, starring Kirk Douglas. And a couple of seasons before that she scored a personal triumph as Aunt Pittypat in the hit stage musical version of *Gone With the Wind*. Long a British subject (though still referring to America as "home"), and a lifelong Christian Scientist, the gray-haired actress moves with the spring of an Olga Korbut. She attributes her perennial bounce to keeping busy all her life and attending dance movement classes "whenever I've got the time for it." Onscreen from 1915. IN: *Intolerance, Reggie Mixes In, Hell-to-Pay Austin, Forget Me Not, The Village Blacksmith, Human Wreckage, Slave of Desire, The Woman on the Jury, Those Who Dance, Tongues of Flame, The King on Main Street, New Brooms, Lovey Mary, Rubber Tires, The Matinee Idol, Sally of the Scandals, Good News, See America Thirst, Journey Together, The Barefoot Contessa, Touch and Go, Next to No Time, Loss of Innocence, Vampyres*, more.

LOVE, PHYLLIS (N.Y.) The award-winning young stage actress who gave a memorable debut performance as Gary Cooper's daughter Mattie Birdwell, in *Friendly Persuasion*, is in her 50s now (b. 1925), has been happily married to teacher-playwright James Vincent McGee since '48, and has not acted on either stage or screen since '61. ALSO IN: *The Young Doctors*.

LOVEGROVE, ARTHUR (Eng.) Character. Onscreen from the '40s. IN: *Noose, The Steel Key, Three Steps to the Gallows, A Kid for Two Farthings, They Can't Hang Me, Dial 999, Safari*, more.

LOVELACE, LINDA (S. Cal.) Star of porno films. Onscreen in the '70s. IN: *Deep Throat, Deep Throat Part II*, more.

LOVSKY, CELIA (S. Cal.) The venerable character actress, in her 70s now, remains professionally active. In '73 she was featured in *Soylent Green*, and the following year gave a memorable performance, as an old lady in a wheelchair, in an episode of TV's *Streets of San Francisco*, in which she costarred with Sam Jaffe and Luther Adler. Onscreen from 1947. IN: *The Foxes of Harrow, Sealed Verdict, The Killer That Stalked New York; Captain Carey,*

U.S.A.; *The Scarf, Because You're Mine, Rhapsody, The Last Time I Saw Paris, The Garment Jungle, Man of a Thousand Faces, Me and the Colonel, The Gene Krupa Story, Hitler, 36 Hours, The St. Valentine's Day Massacre, The Power,* more.

LOW, CARL (N.Y.) Character. Onscreen in the '60s. IN: *Hud, America America.*

LOWE, ARTHUR (Eng.) Character. Onscreen from 1947. IN: *London Belongs to Me, Kind Hearts and Coronets, This Sporting Life, If, The Bed-Sitting Room,* more.

LOWENS, CURT (N.Y.) Character. Onscreen from 1961. IN: *Francis of Assisi, Werewolf in a Girls Dormitory, Two Women, The Pawnbroker, Torn Curtain, Tobruk, Counterpoint, The Secret of Santa Vittoria, The Mephisto Waltz,* more.

LOWRY, JUDITH (S. Cal.) Character. Onscreen from 1963. IN: *Ladybug, Ladybug; Cold Turkey, The Anderson Tapes, Superdad,* more.

LOY, MYRNA (N.Y.) She's still a humorous redhead, still enchanting, still lovely in her 70s (b. 1905), and still active in movies (*Airport 1975*) and on the stage (*Don Juan in Hell,* on tour in '74). The movies' "perfect wife" has been divorced four times, and has no children, but she has three step-grandchildren who adore her and call her Grandma. Her stepson, in his 40s now and a doctor, was six when she married his father, Arthur Hornblow Jr., and they have remained close. (Hornblow, who was her first husband, lives in New York, is married to the former Mrs. Wayne Morris, and with her writes children's books.) Politically active, the actress moved to New York from Hollywood in 1952 and for almost a decade was a member-at-large of the U.S. Commission to UNESCO. She lives alone in a penthouse in Manhattan's East 60s and, socially, is one of the city's most sought-after women. Asked about William Powell, with whom she costarred in all the "Thin Man" movies and others, she says, "It's been twenty years since we saw each other, but we still talk on the phone." Onscreen from 1926. IN: *Don Juan, Beware of Married Men, The Midnight Taxi, The Desert Song, Rogue of the Rio Grande, Skyline, A Connecticut Yankee, Arrowsmith, Love Me Tonight, The Mask of Fu Manchu, The Prizefighter and the Lady, Men in White, Wife versus Secretary, The Great Ziegfeld, Libeled Lady, Parnell, Test Pilot, Too Hot to Handle, The Rains Came, Love Crazy, The Best Years of Our Lives, The Bachelor and the Bobby-Soxer, Mr. Blandings Builds His Dream House, The Red Pony, Cheaper by the Dozen, Belles on Their Toes, The Ambassador's Daughter, Lonelyhearts, From the Terrace, Midnight Lace, The April Fools,* more.

LUCAS, NICK (S. Cal.) Inimical to the '20s and '30s, the guitar-playing "Singing Troubadour" has been rediscovered in this decade by Hollywood, as Hollywood discovered the nostalgic value of its past. The crooner singing all the songs on the soundtracks of *The Day of the Locust, The Great Gatsby,* and *Hearts of the West* was the "Tiptoe Through the Tulips" man himself. On the threshold of 80 now (b. 1897), and a widower since '70, after more than five decades of marriage, he is several times a grandfather by his one daughter. He lives alone in an apartment in central Hollywood when not elsewhere appearing in nightclubs, which he most often is. Onscreen from 1929. IN: *The Gold Diggers of Broadway, The Show of Shows,* numerous musical shorts, and *Disc Jockey.*

LUCAS, WILLIAM (Eng.) Leading man. Onscreen from the '50s. IN: *Breakout, Crack in the Mirror, Sons and Lovers, The Shadow of the Cat, Payroll,* more.

LUCCI, SUSAN (N.Y.) Leading lady in TV soap operas. Onscreen from 1969. IN: *Me, Natalie; Goodbye, Columbus* (bits); *The Breakstone Story* (lead).

LUCE, CLAIRE (N.Y.) A widow now, she paints (has had several one-woman shows at Manhattan galleries, and pictures by her are on permanent display in museums in Rochester and Southhampton), and records numerous dramatic and poetry-reading albums (often designing their covers as well). She has not been onscreen in decades and last acted, in the mid-sixties, in a one-woman dramatic program that toured university campuses across the country. Onscreen in 1930. IN: *Up the River,* in which she costarred with Spencer Tracy.

LUCKHAM, CYRIL (Eng.) Character. Onscreen from the '50s. IN: *How to Murder a Rich Uncle, Invasion Quartet, The Pumpkin Eater, The Alphabet Murders,* more.

LUCKINBILL, LAURENCE (S. Cal.) Leading man. Onscreen in the '70s. IN: *The Boys in the Band, Such Good Friends.*

LUDDY, BARBARA (S. Cal.) The great radio favorite, star of the long-running *First Nighter* series, is in her 60s now, lives in Hollywood, and has lately done voices for Disney cartoon features. Onscreen in 1925. IN: *Rose of the World.*

LUDLAM, HELEN, (N.Y.) Character. Onscreen from the '50s. IN: *Patterns, The Miracle*

*Worker, Pigeons, Is There Sex After Death?,
The Hospital; Summer Wishes, Winter Dreams;*
more.

LUDLOW, PATRICK (Eng.) Character. On-screen from the '30s. IN: *Evergreen, Gangway,*
more than 50 others in England and Hollywood.

LUDWIG, SALEM (N.Y.) Character. Onscreen
from 1936. IN: *Sweet Surrender* (as a dancer),
*Never Love a Stranger, America America; I
Love You, Alice B. Toklas;* more.

LUISI, JAMES (N.Y.) Support. Onscreen in
the '70s. IN: *The Tiger Makes Out, Ben,* more.

LUKAS, KARL (S. Cal.) Character. Onscreen
from 1958. IN: *Onionhead, There Was a
Crooked Man; Tora! Tora! Tora!;* more.

LUKE, KEYE (S. Cal.) Beginning with 1935's
Charlie Chan in Paris, he was ten times Charlie
Chan's Number One Son, Lee Chan—eight
times with Warner Oland and twice with Roland
Winters (the final two: *The Feathered Serpent*
and *Sky Dragon,* in '49), but never with the in-between Chan, Sidney Toler. Though he was in
his 30s (b. 1904) when he began playing this
role, he still looked so youthful in his 70s—
when featured as the ancient monk, Master Po,
in the TV series *Kung Fu*—that it required two
hours each morning to apply the makeup. But
he has aged sufficiently to play Charlie Chan
himself, or at least be his voice, in the TV car-toon series for children *The Amazing Chan and
the Chan Clan.* A native of Canton, though he
grew up in Seattle, Keye Luke has been a part
of the Hollywood scene since his youth. Prior
to his acting career, he had been an artist for the
Fox theaters, an RKO publicity aide, and a
technical advisor on movies about China. The
only time he has not been steadily occupied as
an actor in Hollywood was when he took three
years out, 1958–61, to star on Broadway as Fa-ther Wong in the musical *Flower Drum Song,*
which he still plays in various summer theaters.
"In my spare time," he says, "I am continuing
with my art studies—as I was and still am an
artist, specializing in black and white pen-and-ink drawings and oil paintings. I also do a lot of
recording—reading selections from Shake-speare, Keats, Coleridge and *The Rubaiyat,* as
well as excerpts from art histories." He works
as assiduously on his singing. "My voice stud-ies find me singing Schubert lieder, Mozart bari-tone and bass arias, and Verdi arias. This helps
me when I lecture on Oriental art, as singing has
greatly strengthened my voice." Privately, he
lives in Hollywood and, happily married for
well over three decades, is the stepfather of
several children, one of whom, he says

proudly, "has made me a great-grandfather."
Onscreen from 1933. IN: Leon Errol and Edga(r)
Kennedy shorts, *The Painted Veil, Oil for th(e)
Lamps of China, Shanghai, Disputed Passage(,)
Burma Convoy, Across the Pacific, The Fal(-)
con's Brother, Dr. Gillespie's New Assistan(t)
Dragon Seed, First Yank in Tokyo, Sleep M(y)
Love, Fair Wind to Java, Love Is a Many
Splendored Thing* (which featured four Charli(e)
Chan "sons": Luke, Benson Fong, James
Hong, and Victor Sen Yung), *Battle Hell, No(-)
body's Perfect, The Chairman,* more.

LULU (Eng.) Singer-actress. Onscreen from
the '60s. IN: *To Sir, With Love; The Cherry
Picker,* more.

LUMET, BARUCH (S. Cal.) The character ac-tor-father of director-actor Sidney Lumet, he
wrote and starred in a play, *Autumn Fever,*
staged in Hollywood in '75. Onscreen from
1939. IN: *One Third of a Nation, The Pawnbro-ker,* more.

LUMET, SIDNEY (N.Y.) Yesterday's juvenile
actor is one of today's major directors (*Serpico,*
etc.), long and happily married to Lena Horne's
daughter, Gail, and the father of two children.
Onscreen from 1939. IN: *One Third of a Na-tion,* more.

LUMMIS, DAYTON (S. Cal.) Character. On-screen from the '50s. IN: *Return to Treasure
Island, Prince of Players, The Prodigal, High
Society, The View from Pompey's Head, The
First Texan, The Wrong Man, Monkey on My
Back, Spartacus, Jack the Giant Killer,* more.

LUNA, BARBARA (S. Cal.) Leading lady. On-screen from 1959. IN: *Cry Tough, The Devil at
4 O'Clock, Five Weeks in a Balloon, Dime with
a Halo, Mail Order Bride, Synanon, Ship of
Fools, Firecreek, Che!,* more.

LUNA, DONYALE (N.Y.) Model-actress. On-screen in 1968. IN: *Skidoo.*

LUND, ART (S. Cal.) Character. Onscreen
from 1968. IN: *The Molly Maguires, Ten Days
Till Tomorrow; Decisions, Decisions; Head On,
Bucktown,* more.

LUND, DEANNA /now **DEANNA LUND
MATHESON** (S. Cal.) Support. Onscreen from
1965. IN: *Hawaiian Paradise, Tony Rome,*
more.

LUND, JOHN (S. Cal.) In his 60s now, and
looking much the same as in his starring days,
he is retired from acting, still happily married
(no children), and is a Hollywood business man
now. Onscreen from 1946. IN: *To Each His*

Own, *The Perils of Pauline, Variety Girl, The Night Has a Thousand Eyes, A Foreign Affair, Bride of Vengeance, My Friend Irma Goes West, No Man of Her Own, The Mating Season, Steel Town, Battle of Apache Pass, Latin Lovers, Five Guns West, Hell's Outpost, High Society, The Dakota Incident, The Wackiest Ship in the Army,* more, including 1962's *If a Man Answers,* his last.

LUND, LUCILLE (S. Cal.) Offscreen since 1937's *A Fight to the Finish,* she is still attractively blonde. Long married to radio producer Kenneth Higgins, she lives in retirement near Hollywood. Onscreen from 1933. IN: *Saturday's Millions, The Black Cat, Pirate's Treasure* (serial), *Kiss and Make-Up, What Price Vengeance,* more.

LUNG, CLARENCE (S. Cal.) Character. Onscreen from the '40s. IN: *Dragon Seed, Prisoner of War, World for Ransom,* more.

LUNSFORD, BEVERLY (S. Cal.) Support; former juvenile. Onscreen from the '50s. IN: *That Night, The Intruder, Tender Grass, The Cobweb,* more.

LUNT, ALFRED and **LYNN FONTANNE,** (Wis.) Together, this greatest of all Broadway teams, and husband and wife since '22, starred in the sophisticated 1931 comedy *The Guardsman*—receiving Best Actor and Best Actress Oscar nominations. They had costarred earlier in a silent, *Second Youth* ('24), and later did cameos in *Stage Door Canteen* ('43). They also appeared in silents separately—he in *Backbone, The Ragged Edge,* and *Lovers in Quarantine* with Bebe Daniels; she in *The Man Who Found Himself* with Thomas Meighan. They last acted together, onstage, in a revival of *The Visit,* one of their great stage vehicles, which played both New York and London in '60. Three years later, they said farewell to acting, on television, in *The Old Lady Shows Her Medals*—in which she starred and he was the Narrator. Since, they have lived in complete retirement on their farm at Genesee Depot in Wisconsin, the actor's home state, entertaining a steady stream of famous visitors from both coasts. The actor is in his 80s now (b. 1892), and the actress, exactly one decade older. Among their closest friends is Helen Hayes, who costarred on Broadway with Alfred Lunt in 1919's *Clarence.* In the summer of '75, reflecting on growing older, the venerable Miss Hayes recounted: "Alfred Lunt called from Wisconsin the other day. He had been up in the garden. He leaned on his cane trying to bend over, and the cane slowly sank in the ground and Alfred had to lie there until someone came to pick him up. He made it sound funny, but I said, 'Oh, Alfred, we should not

laugh about this. Isn't it awful what age has done to us?' "

LUPINO, IDA (S. Cal.) Star who, in 1972's *Junior Bonner,* resumed the movie career she had surrendered voluntarily in '56. In the interim she starred in a TV series with former husband Howard Duff, *Mr. Adams and Eve,* directed countless TV shows, guest-starred in occasional ones, and directed the movie *The Trouble with Angels.* Onscreen from 1932. IN: *Money for Speed; Come On, Marines!; Peter Ibbetson, The Gay Desperado, Coast Patrol, Artists and Models, The Lady and the Mob, The Light That Failed, The Adventures of Sherlock Holmes, They Drive by Night, High Sierra, Ladies in Retirement* (her personal favorite), *Moontide, The Hard Way, In Our Time, The Very Thought of You, Devotion, Escape Me Never, Deep Valley, Lust for Gold, Beware My Lovely, The Bigamist, The Big Knife, While the City Sleeps, Strange Intruder,* more, including the recent *The Devil's Rain* and *The Food of the Gods.*

LUPTON, JOHN (S. Cal.) Leading man. Onscreen from 1951. IN: *Shadow in the Sky, Rogue's March, Escape from Fort Bravo, Prisoner of War, Battle Cry, Diane, The Great Locomotive Chase, Gun Fever, The Man in the Net, Three Came to Kill, The Greatest Story Ever Told,* more.

LUPUS, PETER (S. Cal.) Support. Onscreen from 1964. IN: *Muscle Beach Party, Hercules and the Tyrants of Babylon, The Gladiator Who Challenged an Empire,* more.

LUTTER, ALFRED (N.J.) The juvenile actor lives with his parents in Ridgewood. Onscreen in 1975. IN: *Alice Doesn't Live Here Anymore, Love and Death.*

LUXFORD, NOLA (S. Cal.) This leading lady of the early '30s lives in La Canada, one of Los Angeles' more posh neighboring mountainside communities. Besides authoring children's books *(Kerry Kangaroo),* she is now a fashion director, news commentator, and foreign correspondent for overseas publications. Onscreen from 1932: IN: *A Successful Calamity, The Iron Master,* more.

LYDON, JIMMY (S. Cal.) Yesterday's juvenile star is now, in his 50s (b. 1923), a character actor—usually playing business men—in such TV shows as *Rockford Files.* But he still wears Henry Aldrich's funny, friendly, freckled face. When he sported a moustache in a *Cannon* episode, one Hollywood critic noted: "Behind the adornment was the face of the worrisome teenager known to moviegoers of the 1940s, unchanged." But acting is only one string in his bow now. Besides directing such TV shows as *McHale's Navy* and *77 Sunset Strip*, he has been associate producer of movies *(The Learning Tree)* and numerous television series *(M*A*S*H, Roll Out, Anna and the King of Siam*, etc.) And he recently optioned the play *My Husband's Wild Desires Almost Drove Me Mad* for motion picture production. "To be the best producer-director of my era" has long been his professional goal. Yes, he looks back with affection on the "Henry Aldrich" movies. "The series really became a family affair," he says. "The late Olive Blakeney, who played my mother, eventually became my mother-in-law in real life." Her daughter, Betty Lou Nedell, and Jimmy were married on May 1, 1952. (For a while in the '40s, he had been married to Patricia Pernetti, by whom he has one child.) Jimmy and Betty Lou have two grown daughters, Cathy Ann and Julia Jaye, and live in a three-level English-style house in the Hollywood Hills. Observing that the movie industry today is "in such lousy shape," he adds, "but I'm still in love with this business that I've given over 40 years of my life to—in spite of everything." And how does Jimmy Lydon, producer, see Jimmy Lydon actor? "He's strictly a centerville character man, USA. I'd hire him as a bank clerk, neighbor next door, or the jovial best friend of the hero. Actually, I think he'd make a pretty good 'heavy' if somebody would give him a chance." Onscreen from 1939. IN: *Two Thoroughbreds, Back Door to Heaven, Tom Brown's School Days, Bowery Boy, 9* "Henry Aldrich" pix *(Henry Aldrich for President, Henry Aldrich Gets Glamour*, etc.), *Cadets on Parade, My Best Gal, Twice Blessed, Cynthia, Life With Father, The Time of Your Life, Joan of Arc, An Old-Fashioned Girl, When Willie Comes Marching Home, The Magnificent Yankee, Gasoline Alley, Corky of Gasoline Alley, Island in the Sky, Desperado, The Hypnotic Eye, The Last Time I Saw Archie, Death of a Gunfighter, Scandalous John*, more.

LYN, DAWN (S. Cal.) Juvenile (b. 1963). Onscreen in the '70s. IN: *The Love God?, Cholla Three, Walking Tall, Walking Tall Part II*, more.

LYN, JACQUIE (S. Cal.) (See Jackie Lynn Taylor.)

LYNAS, JEFF (S. Cal.) Leading man. Onscreen in 1976. IN: *Breaking Point*.

LYNCH, ALFRED (Eng.) Character. Onscreen from the '60s. IN: *Two and Two Make Six, 55 Days at Peking, The Hill, The Taming of the Shrew, The Blockhouse*, more.

LYNCH, KEN (S. Cal.) Character. Onscreen from 1958. IN: *Voice in the Mirror; Run Silent,*

Run Deep; Pork Chop Hill, Anatomy of a Murder, North by Northwest, The Dark at the Top of the Stairs, Portrait of a Mobster, Walk on the Wild Side, The Days of Wine and Roses, Dear Heart, Mister Buddwing, Hotel, Willie Dynamite, "W," more.

LYNDE, PAUL (S. Cal.) Comedian. Onscreen from 1954. IN: *New Faces, Son of Flubber, Bye Bye Birdie, Under the Yum Yum Tree, For Those Who Think Young, Send Me No Flowers, Beach Blanket Bingo, The Glass Bottom Boat, The Silent Treatment, How Sweet It Is*, more.

LYNLEY, CAROL (S. Cal.) Leading lady. Onscreen from 1958. IN: *Light in the Forest, Holiday for Lovers, Blue Denim, Return to Peyton Place, Under the Yum Yum Tree, The Cardinal, The Pleasure Seekers, Bunny Lake Is Missing, Harlow, Sudden Death, The Maltese Bippy, Norwood, The Poseidon Adventure*, more.

LYNN, ANN (Eng.) Leading lady. Onscreen from the '60s. IN: *Flame in the Streets, The Girl-Getters, The Uncle, Separation, I'll Never Forget What's 'Is Name?*, more.

LYNN, BETTY (S. Cal.) Support; former ingenue. Onscreen from 1948. IN: *June Bride, Sitting Pretty, Mother Is a Freshman, Father Was a Fullback, Cheaper by the Dozen, Payment on Demand, Take Care of My Little Girl, Meet Me in Las Vegas, Behind the High Wall, Gun for a Coward*, more.

LYNN, CYNTHIA (S. Cal.) Leading lady. Onscreen from 1964. IN: *Bedtime Story*, more.

LYNN, JEFFREY (S. Cal.) His lean, handsome looks belying his years (b. 1909), he is a San Fernando Valley realtor now, having retired from acting in '73. In the autumn of '75 he returned to New York for the wedding of his only daughter, Letitia Chandler Lynn, which was one of the society events of the season. He also has one son, Jeffrey Jr., a bearded, good-looking young artist living in Greenwich Village. They are the children of his first marriage ('46), to Robin Chandler Tippett, which ended in divorce in '57. His former wife is presently married to millionaire Angier Biddle Duke, Commissioner of Civic Affairs and Public Events in New York City. Daughter Letitia became the bride of Dominicus Rytis Valiunas, president of Neris Transatlantic Minerals, Inc., at St. Luke's Chapel of Trinity Parish in Greenwich Village, and was given away by her father. A young career woman, she is a director at the Odyssey House residence in Manhattan, which assists in the rehabilitation of former drug addicts. From '67 until their divorce in '74, Jeffrey Lynn was married to actress Patricia Davis and was the stepfather of her seven children by a former marriage. His screen career flourished between '38 and '51, with four years out for service in the RAF. During the '50s and '60s he starred onstage in many plays: *Mary, Mary; Any Wednesday, Two for the Seesaw, Dinner at 8,* others. He also headlined for several seasons, as wealthy newspaper editor Charles Clemens, in the daytime serial *The Secret Storm.* Since 1960 he has played minor roles in two films—*Butterfield 8* and *Tony Rome.* Before deciding to retire from acting, he played guest star roles in such TV series as *Matt Lincoln* and *Barnaby Jones.* Onscreen from 1938. IN: *Cowboy from Brooklyn, Four Daughters, Daughters Courageous; Yes, My Darling Daughter; Four Wives, It All Came True, The Fighting 69th, My Love Came Back, All This and Heaven Too, Four Mothers, Law of the Tropics, Underground, For the Love of Mary, Black Bart, Washington Girl, A Letter to Three Wives, Captain China, Home Town Story. Up Front,* more.

LYNN, LENI (Eng.) The teenaged soprano once highly publicized by MGM moved to England in the '40s and played leads in a number of musical movies: *Showtime, Happy Go Lovely, Give Me the Stars, Spring Song, Heaven Is Round the Corner.* Entering her 50s now (b. 1925), she no longer appears onscreen but still sings in clubs. Onscreen in Hollywood from 1939. IN: *Babes in Arms, Hullabaloo,* more.

LYNN, MARA (N.Y.) Leading lady. Onscreen from 1950. IN: *Prehistoric Women, Last Train from Gun Hill, Let's Make Love, Wild 90, Beyond the Law,* more.

LYON, BARBARA (Eng.) Actress-daughter of Ben Lyon and Bebe Daniels. Now retired. Onscreen in the '40s. IN: *Life With the Lyons, The Lyons in Paris.* (See Ben Lyon.)

LYON, BEN (S. Cal.) Happily married to Bebe Daniels from '30 until her death early in '71, this veteran star became, on April 1, 1972, the husband of Marian Nixon. He is retired now, in his 70s (b. 1901), and they live in Beverly Hills. During much of the time he was married to Bebe Daniels they lived in England. Besides being greatly popular as a duo in music halls (song-dances-monologues), they each made a number of British movies. After they costarred in *Hi Gang* in '41, she gave up movie acting, which he also did the following year, after *This Was Paris,* becoming a lieutenant colonel in the U.S. Army Air Force. (They never gave up their American citizenship despite their long English residence.) In addition to his military service, the actor continued to costar with his wife in a morale-boosting radio show *Hi Gang.* After the war they returned to Hollywood for three years, Ben becoming executive talent director for 20th Century-Fox. In that period, their son, Richard Lyon, became a quite popular juvenile actor in a number of pictures. He was particularly fine as Irene Dunne's sensitive-faced lad in *Anna and the King of Siam.* In his early 40s now, Richard lives in England and works behind the scenes in the movie industry there. Also in London is the Lyons' daughter, Barbara (Mrs. Colin Burkett), who, at 39, made Ben Lyon a first-time grandfather with the birth of a son in May 1971—sadly, just six weeks after Bebe Daniels died. Barbara herself became desperately ill in the spring of '73 when she suffered a cerebral hemorrhage, with her father flying from California to be at her hospital bedside. Her recovery from this has been complete. On a happier, more recent visit to England, Ben Lyon took the occasion to donate all his and Bebe Daniels' scrapbooks and kindred show business memorabilia to the National Film Archive in London. Considering the long, illustrious careers of each, film scholars should find this a treasure for years to come. Onscreen from the '20s. IN: *Potash and Perlmutter, Painted People, The White Moth, Wine of Youth, So Big, The Reckless Lady, The Great Deception, The Air Legion, The Flying Marine, Lummox, Hell's Angels, Queen of Main Street; Her Majesty, Love; Night Nurse, A Soldier's Plaything, Hat Check Girl, Rackety Rax, I Cover the Waterfront, Crimson Romance, Lightning Strikes Twice, Dancing Feet, He Loved an Actress, Down Under the Sea, I Killed the Count, Treachery on the High Seas,* more.

LYON, RICHARD (Eng.) Former juvenile. Son of Bebe Daniels and Ben Lyon. Onscreen from 1945. IN: *The Unseen, The Green Years, Anna and the King of Siam, The Boy with Green Hair, The Great Lover, Life With the Lyons, The Lyons in Paris,* more. (See Ben Lyon.)

LYON, SUE (S. Cal.) Though she appeared in movies for a full decade after *Lolita,* her subsequent roles brought her fewer headlines than her personal life. She has been married and divorced three times. She was married first, for five years, to actor Hampton Fancher, and then to a black sports figure by whom she has a daughter. The wedding that raised eyebrows was her third. "LOLITA" TO WED KILLER, headlines blazed. On November 4, 1973, in a cream-colored floor-length dress and veil, and with her 20-month-old daughter as flower girl, she became the wife of Gary "Cotton" Adamson, 33. The ceremony was held behind bars in the Colorado State Penitentiary in Canon City where Adamson, a maximum security prisoner, in prison since '64, was serving a 20-to-40 year term for crimes including second-degree murder and armed robbery. They had met in '72 through an unnamed mutual friend who was once jailed with the groom in Los Angeles. During neither their courtship nor marriage did they ever have a private hour together. "Our relationship is not based on sex," said the actress, who later campaigned unsuccessfully for changes in prison regulations that would allow conjugal rights. "We have a common bond of friendship. We're willing to wait because we love each other." She waited one year before filing for divorce. In that year she worked as a cocktail waitress at the Ramada Inn in Denver —until she was fired by manager Michael Murphy who said she had been the subject of customers' complaints of poor service, and that she had created friction with other employes by insisting on special treatment. Despite the divorce, the actress said she still loved her husband, but this was the one way she might get to work again in movies. "I've been told by people in the movie business, specifically producers and film distributors, that I won't get a job because I'm married to Cotton. Therefore, right now we can't be married. But that doesn't mean love has died. I'll always love him." The actress, who turned 30 in 1976, had, at last report, returned to live in Los Angeles and look for a comeback role. Onscreen from 1962. IN: *Lolita, The Night of the Iguana, Seven Women, The Flim-Flam Man, Tony Rome,* and, her most recent to date, 1972's *Evel Knievel.*

LYONS, ROBERT F. (S. Cal.) Leading man. Onscreen from 1969. IN: *Pendulum, Getting Straight, The Todd Killings, Shoot Out,* more.

M

MacARTHUR, JAMES (Hawaii) Costar. He has lived for several years in Honolulu while playing a lead in the TV series *Hawaii Five-O.* Onscreen from 1957. IN: *The Young Stranger, The Light in the Forest, Third Man on the Mountain, Swiss Family Robinson, Cry of Battle, Spencer's Mountain, Battle of the Bulge, The Bedford Incident, Ride Beyond Vengeance, The Angry Breed, Hang 'Em High,* more.

MacDONALD, WALLACE (S. Cal.) A cowboy star who became a character actor and then a producer, he is in his 80s (b. 1891) and retired. Onscreen from 1919. IN: *Leave It to Susan, The Spoilers, The Sea Hawk, Roaring Rails, The Bar C Mystery, Fighting with Buffalo Bill, Breaking Thru, Whispering Smith Rides, Gunmen from Laredo, Hell's 400,* more.

MacGIBBON, HARRIET (S. Cal.) Character. Onscreen from 1961. IN: *Cry for Happy, A Majority of One, The Four Horsemen of the Apocalypse,* more.

MacGINNIS, NIALL (Eng.) Character star. Onscreen from 1935. IN: *Turn of the Tide, The Invaders, Henry V, Hamlet, No Highway in the Sky, Martin Luther, Hell Below Zero, Alexander the Great, Lust for Life, Tarzan's Greatest Adventure, Sword of Sherwood Forest, Billy Budd, Becket, The War Lord, The Spy Who Came in from the Cold, The Shoes of the Fisherman, Darling Lili, The Kremlin Letter,* more.

MacGRATH, LEUEEN (N.Y.) Support. Onscreen from 1938. IN: *Pygmalion, The Saint's Vacation, Edward My Son, Three Cases of Murder,* more.

MacGRAW, ALI (S. Cal.) Star. Nominated for Best Actress Oscar in *Love Story.* Onscreen from 1968. IN: *A Lovely Way to Die, Goodbye Columbus, The Getaway.*

MacKENZIE, JOYCE (S. Cal.) The former leading lady teaches journalism now in a Los Angeles high school. Onscreen from 1950. IN: *Mother Didn't Tell Me, Broken Arrow, Stella, A Ticket to Tomahawk, The Racket, Deadline U.S.A., Tarzan and the She-Devil,* more.

MacLACHLAN, JANET (S. Cal.) Black leading lady. Onscreen from 1968. IN: *Up Tight, Sounder, The Man,* more.

MacLAINE, SHIRLEY (N.Y.) Star. Nominated for Best Actress Oscar in *Some Came Running, The Apartment, Irma la Douce.* Living in Manhattan, she has in this decade starred in a brief-run TV series, *Shirley's World,* and written two books: her autobiography, *Don't Fall Off the Mountain,* and *You Can Get There From Here,* based on her tour of the People's Republic of China. This journey also resulted in a documentary movie, *The Other Half of the Sky: A China Memoir,* that she produced, codirected, and narrated. Onscreen from 1955. IN: *The Trouble With Harry, Artists and Models, Hot Spell, The Matchmaker, Ask Any Girl, Can-Can, All in a Night's Work, My Geisha, The Children's Hour, Two for the Seesaw, What a Way to Go!, The Yellow Rolls-Royce, Gambit, Sweet Charity, The Bliss of Mrs. Blossom, Two Mules for Sister Sara, Desperate Characters, The Possession of Joel Delaney,* more.

MacLANE, KERRY (S. Cal.) Former juvenile actor. Onscreen in 1971. IN: *Johnny Got His Gun.*

MacLAREN, MARY (S. Cal.) White-haired now and in poor health—she is in her 80s (b.

1896)—the actress who was Douglas Fairbanks' lovely young Queen Anne in 1921's *The Three Musketeers* lives in the center of Hollywood. And in the hope—and positive expectation—that tomorrow will bring better news than today. Her house is the one she bought when she first became a star in '16, though, in the name of survival, she has sold at auction certain of its most treasured furnishings. Small and frail she is, but her cornflower-blue eyes twinkle with merriment, her mind is sharp, and she talks at a mile-a-minute clip. On many a subject. "No, thank God, I never had any children," she says. "Is that an awful thing to say? Capricorn is a barren sign, and I had my moon in Virgo—they're both barren signs. My mother paid a terrible price with each of my sisters (one was the late star Katherine MacDonald), and with me." The actress was married in '24 to Col. George Herbert Young, of England's Indian Army, and they lived several years in India. After her starring career she played character parts. "I did hundreds of talking pictures," she says, "but I was forced to retire in 1952. I had so many auto accidents and so many broken bones. I just couldn't go on." In retirement, she has written a novel—published two decades ago —dabbled in numerology and astrology, studied and talked to all who would listen about nutrition and proper diet, and lectured against tobacco. She also, in '74, flew to New York to help publicize the Raquel Welch version of *The Three Musketeers*—and enjoyed everything about it except the pipe of the man who sat behind her on the plane. Humor—often directed at herself—is perhaps her most essential characteristic, but she also grows reflective, saying, as she did on one recent occasion, "It's a great responsibility just to be alive." Onscreen from 1916. IN: *Shoes, Under the Red Robe, The Black Swan, King of the Pecos, A Lawman Is Born, Duke of West Point, Misbehaving Husbands, Prairie Schooners, Lady in the Dark, Navajo Trails, Frontier Feud*, more.

MacLEOD, GAVIN (S. Cal.) Character. Onscreen from 1958. IN: *I Want to Live!, Compulsion, Operation Petticoat, McHale's Navy, The Sand Pebbles, Deathwatch, The Party, Kelly's Heroes*, more.

MacMAHON, ALINE (N.Y.) Character. Nominated for Best Supporting Actress Oscar in *Dragon Seed*. In her silver-haired 70s now (b. 1899), she has not acted in a movie since 1963's *All the Way Home*. But, a regular member of The Repertory Theater of Lincoln Center, just around the corner from her home in Manhattan, she costarred there in '75 in a revival of *Trelawny of the Wells*. A widow (her husband, architect Clarence Stein, died early in '75) and, to her personal regret, childless, she does not have

to work. Besides investments and her monthly Social Security check, she has well-earned pensions coming in from both Screen Actors Guild and Actors Equity. But when a suitable role turns up, she eagerly dons greasepaint. "I've been acting ever since I graduated from college in 1920," she says in that fine, still-firm voice. "It's a delightful profession if you have a measure of success." And that she has had. But, these many years later, she still laments losing the role of O-lan in *The Good Earth*—for which she had been scheduled—to Luise Rainer. Recalling that loss, she says, "So my husband told me, 'We'll get even with them,' and we went to China . . . My husband and I had hoped to spend our later years in Peking. We thought it the most beautiful city in the world. We never went back, of course, after they stopped allowing Americans to visit. And my husband just grew older and sicker and sicker, until he died." Onscreen from 1931. IN: *Five-Star Final, One Way Passage, The Mouthpiece, Silver Dollar, Once in a Lifetime, Gold Diggers of 1933, The Life of Jimmy Dolan, Babbitt, Kind Lady; Ah, Wilderness!; Back Door to Heaven, Tish, The Lady Is Willing, Guest in the House, The Search, Roseanna McCoy, The Eddie Cantor Story, The Young Doctors, Diamond Head, I Could Go on Singing*, more.

MacMURRAY, FRED (S. Cal.) Star. Onscreen from 1935. IN: *The Gilded Lily, Hands Across the Table, Alice Adams, The Trail of the Lonesome Pine, The Princess Comes Across, Maid of Salem, True Confession, Champagne Waltz; Swing High, Swing Low; Men With Wings, Sing You Sinners, Cafe Society, Honeymoon in Bali, Too Many Husbands, Remember the Night, Virginia, Dive Bomber; Take a Letter, Darling; Above Suspicion, Practically Yours, Double Indemnity, Captain Eddie, The Egg and I, Miracle of the Bells, Callaway Went Thataway, The Caine Mutiny, Good Day for a Hanging, The Shaggy Dog, The Apartment, The Absent-Minded Professor, Bon Voyage, Kisses for My President; Follow Me, Boys!; The Happiest Millionaire, Charley and the Angel*, more.

MacRAE, ELIZABETH (S. Cal.) Leading lady. Onscreen from 1961. IN: *Everything's Ducky, For Love or Money, The Conversation*, more.

MacRAE, GORDON (S. Cal.) Away from movies since 1956's *The Best Things in Life Are Free*, the musical star, in his 50s now (b. 1921), started up his Hollywood career again in '74 via a straight dramatic role in an episode of TV's *McCloud*. That same year he became a first-time grandfather when daughter Meredith and her actor-husband, Greg Mullavey, had a little girl, named Allison Lee. Onscreen from 1948. IN: *The Big Punch, Look for the Silver Lining,*

Daughter of Rosie O'Grady, Tea for Two, The West Point Story, On Moonlight Bay, By the Light of the Silvery Moon, The Desert Song, Oklahoma!, Carousel, more.

MacRAE, MEREDITH (S. Cal.) Actress-daughter of Gordon. Onscreen from 1963. IN: *Beach Party, Bikini Beach, Footsteps in the Snow,* more.

MACK, HELEN (N.Y.) The once highly popular leading lady gave up her movie career after 1946's *Strange Holiday,* became a successful radio producer (*A Date with Judy*), and later ('65), coauthored a Broadway play, *The Mating Dance,* that starred Van Johnson but was not a success. From '42 until his death in '72, she was the wife of radio-TV executive Tom McAvity, by whom she has a grown son. Semiretired now, in her 60s (b. 1913), she lives in the East 50s. Onscreen from 1930. IN: *Pied Piper Malone, Under the Red Robe, The Struggle, Sweepings, Melody Cruise, Kiss and Make-Up, The Lemon Drop Kid, Captain Hurricane, She, The Return of Peter Grimm, I Promise to Pay, The Milky Way, King of the Newsboys, Secrets of a Nurse, Mystery of the White Room, Girls of the Road, Power Dive, And Now Tomorrow,* more.

MACKAILL, DOROTHY (Hawaii) Sunbronzed and quite rich—thanks to long-ago real estate investments in Hollywood on now-exclusive Wilshire Boulevard, she has lived for almost two decades in a suite at the Waikiki Beach Hotel in Honolulu. She voluntarily, and permanently, retired from movies after 1937's *Bulldog Drummond at Bay.* A Britisher who began making movies in England at a tender age, she emigrated to America at—the records say 18, but she laughingly explains now that the records are wrong. "My passport read 18 years, so I'm stuck with it. I couldn't enter the U.S.A. unless I was 18. That's why I sailed from France—50 million can't be wrong! But I really was 15½. Now I would like to claim those 2½ years!" So in 1976 she became an extraordinarily youthful-looking 70, retaining her fine figure and dancer's grace. After being one of Ziegfeld's most celebrated chorines, the blue-eyed blonde was summoned to Hollywood where she quickly became one of the most popular silent stars, often costarring with Jack Mulhall. She was particularly effective in siren and flapper roles, and, with a well-modulated British accent, made an easy transition into talkies, starring in 23 before retiring. A very popular member of the Hawaii social circuit, she lives alone. "I do not have any family," she reports. "My dear mother died 20 years ago. And I have been married and divorced thrice—all of my husbands, incidentally, being my very *good* friends." Her husbands were, sequentially, Lothar Mendes, crooner Neil Miller, and famous New Jersey orchid grower Harold Patterson. There was a certain poignancy in her reply to a Honolulu columnist who recently asked her to cite the three greatest moments in her life. She answered: "The times I got married . . . when I thought the marriages would work." She travels each year to New York and San Francisco but is always delighted to return to the Islands. Her love affair with Hawaii is long standing—dating back to her first visit in 1929, when *His Captive Woman* was filmed at Kalapana. Hawaii reciprocates her affection. A few months back, 22 top civic leaders in Honolulu declared it "Dorothy's Day in Hawaii" and tossed a gala surprise luncheon in her honor. Their mutual affection for her was the sole justification for the occasion. Seating her in a throne-like wicker chair, they serenaded her with "A Pretty Girl Is Like a Melody," made her pretty speeches, presented her with long-stemmed red roses, and crowned her with a tiara of pikakes. At one point, her tiara slipped and one of her court quipped: "I hope that's not all you're doing to drop today." Tossing her short blonde hair, she laughed, "Watch yourself, or you won't be here long!" Hollywood's gay flapper of long ago is still in good form. Onscreen from 1921. IN: *Bits of Life, Mighty Lak a Rose, The Bridge of Sighs, Shore Leave, The Dancers of Paris, Man Crazy, Ladies' Night in a Turkish Bath, Lady Be Good, The Barker* (her personal favorite), *Two Weeks Off, Strictly Modern, The Office Wife, Bright Lights, Party Husband, Safe in Hell, Lost Lady, The Chief, Cheaters, Curtain at Eight,* more.

MACKAY, BARRY (Eng.) Character; former leading man. Onscreen from 1934. IN: *The Private Life of Don Juan, Evergreen, Born for Glory, The Great Barrier, Sailing Along, A Christmas Carol, Grand National Night, The Pickwick Papers, Timeslip, Orders Are Orders,* more.

MACNEE, PATRICK (S. Cal.) Character. Onscreen from the '40s. IN: *Hamlet, Three Cases of Murder, Les Girls, Incense for the Damned,* more.

MACY, BILL (S. Cal.) Character. Television personality. Onscreen in the '70s. IN: *Oh! Calcutta!*

MADDEN, PETER (Eng.) Character. Onscreen from the '40s. IN: *Tom Brown's School Days, Fiend Without a Face, The Road to Hong Kong, The Loneliness of the Long Distance Runner, Nothing But the Best, Doctor Zhivago, He Who Rides a Tiger,* more.

MADDERN, VICTOR (Eng.) Character. Onscreen from 1949. IN: *Seven Days to Noon, Sailor of the King, Court Martial, The Night My*

Number Came Up, Saint Joan, All at Sea, Dunkirk, Exodus, Damn the Defiant, Carry On Cleo, more.

MADISON, GUY (S. Cal.) His movies may not be blockbusters but Hollywood's golden boy of the '40s still stars. In '73 he starred in *War Devils*, and in '75, almost unrecognizable with shoulder-length white hair and neat gray beard, in *The Pacific Connection*. That year he was also announced to appear in *The Thin Line* and *They Couldn't Kill Sullivan*. Nearly all of his current pictures are made on faraway location, such as the Philippines, and he is accustomed to that; for several years in the '60s he lived in Italy making "spaghetti Westerns." In his 50s now (b. 1922), twice divorced (from actresses Gail Russell and Sheila Connelly) and the father of three grown daughters, he recently endorsed a Los Angeles dating service. Beneath his photograph in its newspaper ads was this quote: "Discovering theatrical talent is not a job for amateurs, and discovering a compatible human partner is also not a job for amateurs. In the field of compatibility matching, there is really only ONE professional that comes to my mind . . . Do yourself a favor, call the professionals." This testimonial could have been a shock to millions of now-aging bobby-soxers who had feverish dreams over the muscular, curly-locked sailor first glimpsed in *Since You Went Away*. Onscreen from 1944. IN: *Till the End of Time, Honeymoon; Texas, Brooklyn and Heaven; Drums in the Deep South, On the Threshold of Space, Hilda Crane, Jet Over the Atlantic, Sword of the Conqueror, Adventures of Tortuga, Duel at Rio Bravo, Shatterhand*, more.

MAGEE, PATRICK (Eng.) Support. Onscreen from the '60s. IN: *The Young Racers, Dementia 13, The Servant, Zulu, Marat/Sade, The Birthday Party, Hard Contract, A Clockwork Orange, The Last Days of Man on Earth, Barry Lyndon*, more.

MAGGIORANI, LAMBERTO (It.) Director Vittoria De Sica, discovering this laborer and starring him in *The Bicycle Thief*, later set him up in business with a shoe shop in Rome, which has continued to be a successful enterprise. Onscreen in 1949 and 1951. IN: *The Bicycle Thief* and *Women Without Names*.

MARGARO, POLLI (N.Y.) Character. Onscreen from the 60s. IN: *Popi, The Brotherhood, The Cross and the Switchblade, The Anderson Tapes, Lovers and Other Strangers, Across 110th Street, Godspell*, more.

MAGUIRE, KATHLEEN (N.Y.) Leading lady. Onscreen from 1957. IN: *Edge of the City, Flipper*, more.

MAHAN, BILLY (S. Cal.) The youngest in the "Jones Family" series—Bobby he was called by "mom" Spring Byington—is now in his 40s (b. 1933) and still a part of show biz. One of his occupations, as Bill, is that of nationally syndicated columnist. For the Des Moines *Register and Tribune* Syndicate, he writes, from Hollywood, two columns—*Inside the Tube* (thrice-weekly) and *Outside Hollywood* (weekly). The other role this slender, exuberant man plays, with riotous humor, is that of lecturer. He is one of the stellar attractions of the Keedick Lecture Bureau in New York, touring the country spieling on such head-spinning topics as "Everything You Always Wanted to Know about Failure . . . but didn't have time to find out the hard way," and "Why You Should Go Ahead and Do Whatever It Is You Always Wanted to Do." Bill's columns and lectures are based on his personal experience and delivered with his refreshing point of view—which often depicts himself as the born loser, enjoying every minute of it, but ultimately "managing." The keynote of all he says or writes, with unquenchable optimism, is, "Live. Because there's not time to merely exist." After his movie career, and service in the Navy, he says that "funny things happened on the way to oblivion." For a while he was David O. Selznick's Man in South America—managing a segment of the movie business he didn't understand (he says), selling films he hadn't seen to people whose language he couldn't speak. He wrote a play that didn't sell and produced an underwater treasure film that did—to ABC. He also was assistant film editor on the movie *Gigi*. His wife, Patte, has written a novel on child abuse, *By Sanction of the Victim*, that, at last report, he was planning to produce as a film. They live in Woodland Hills and have three young children: Kerrigan Patrick, Colleen Shannon, and Erin Kelly. They have two to go to "keep up with the Joneses." Incidentally, his mother, Madge, is in her 70s, secretary to a producer at 20th Century-Fox—as is his sister—and "loves it." And Bill Mahan himself often visits this studio, where decades ago he romped to fame as little Bobby Jones—looking, not for a movie role, but for items for his columns. Onscreen from 1936. IN: *Every Saturday Night, Educating Father, Off to the Races, Big Business, Hot Water, A Trip to Paris, Safety in Numbers, Young As You Feel*, more.

MAHARIS, GEORGE (S. Cal.) Costar. Onscreen from 1960. IN: *Exodus, Quick Before It Melts, The Satan Bug, Sylvia, A Covenant with Death, The Happening, The Desperadoes*, more.

MAHONEY, JOCK (S. Cal.) Character. Former "Tarzan" and cowboy star. Onscreen from 1945. IN: *Rough Rider of Durango, South of the*

Chisholm Trail, The Doolins of Oklahoma, Cow Town, Showdown at Abilene, Battle Hymn, Last of the Fast Guns, Tarzan the Magnificent, Tarzan Goes to India, Moro Witch Doctor, The Glory Stompers, Bandolero!, more

MAILER, NORMAN, (N.Y.) Famous novelist and biographer of Marilyn Monroe. Onscreen in 1971. IN: *Maidstone* (starred and produced).

MAIN, LAURIE (S. Cal.) Character. Onscreen in the '70s. IN: *On a Clear Day You Can See Forever, Darling Lili*, more.

MAITLAND, MARNE (Eng.) Character. Onscreen from the '50s. IN: *Outcast of the Islands, Flame and the Flesh, The Detective, Bhowani Junction, The Mark of the Hawk, Tiger Bay, Cleopatra, Lord Jim, Return of Mr. Moto, Khartoum, The Bobo, The Statue, The Man with the Golden Gun*, more.

MAITLAND, RUTH (N.Y.) Still active, the singer-dancer succeeded Ruby Keeler, a few seasons back, in the leading role in *No, No, Nanette* on Broadway. Onscreen from 1934. IN: *Heart Song*, more.

MAJORS, LEE (S. Cal.) TV star. Onscreen from 1964. IN: *Strait-Jacket, Will Penny, The Liberation of Lord Byron Jones*, more.

MAKO (S. Cal.) Character. Nominated for Best Supporting Actor Oscar in *The Sand Pebbles*. In 1976 he starred on Broadway in the Kabuki-style musical *Pacific Overtures*. Onscreen from 1966. IN: *The Ugly Dachshund, The Private Navy of Sgt. O'Farrell, The Great Bank Robbery, The Hawaiians, Tora! Tora! Tora!, The Killer Elite*, more.

MALDEN, KARL (S. Cal.) Character star. Won Best Supporting Actor Oscar in *A Streetcar Named Desire*. Nominated in the same category in *On the Waterfront*. Onscreen from 1940. IN: *They Knew What They Wanted, Boomerang, Kiss of Death, The Halls of Montezuma, Diplomatic Courier, Ruby Gentry, I Confess, The Desperate Hours, Baby Doll, Fear Strikes Out, Bombers B-52, The Hanging Tree, Pollyanna, One-Eyed Jacks, How the West Was Won, All Fall Down, Gypsy, Birdman of Alcatraz, Cheyenne Autumn, Blue, Patton, Wild Rovers*, more.

MALINA, JUDITH (N.Y.) Character. Onscreen in the '70s. IN: *Dog Day Afternoon*, more.

MALLORY, DRUE (N.Y.) Retired from acting, she is the wife of the very rich John Henry Heinz 2d, with an East River apartment and a dozen homes scattered all over the world. And she is just as beautifully auburn as in her last movie. Onscreen from 1950. IN: *Three Came Home, Please Believe Me*, more.

MALLORY, EDWARD (S. Cal.) TV soap opera star. Onscreen from 1963. IN: *Diamond Head*, more.

MALLORY, JOHN (S. Cal.) (See John Mitchum.)

MALONE, DOROTHY (Tex.) Costar. Won Best Supporting Actress Oscar in *Written on the Wind*. In 1968, after starring for four years in television's *Peyton Place*, she packed her belongings and daughters Mimi and Diane (both teenagers now), rented a trailer and moved back to Dallas, her hometown. The Oscar, she felt, had been a jinx, the movies following it had all been duds, and she saw little future for herself in Hollywood. Living in a bright yellow house on a tree-lined street in the exclusive Turtle Creek section, the actress said, "I didn't realize how weary I was of sound stages, hot lights and hard work until I got away from it." But she didn't get entirely away. She shortly flew back to Hollywood for one picture, *The Pidgeon*, and to Rome for another, *The Drug of Success*. She costarred with Harvey Korman at the Dallas State Fair in the musical *Little Me*, and did *Goodbye, My Fancy* in summer stock. And she did live "interpretive news features" four times daily on local FM radio station KNUS. "I'm not financially secure enough to stop working forever," she said. Also, she acquired her second and third husbands. (Former actor Jacques Bergerac, father of her daughters, was her first.) On Easter weekend in '69, in Las Vegas, she was married to New York-Dallas stock broker Robert Tomarkin. But a few days later she testified before a Dallas judge that her new husband tried to swindle her out of her savings and the marriage was annulled. Then, in the autumn of '71, she married motel-chain executive Charles Huston Bell. Now, commuting from Dallas, she continues to act. In '75 she costarred with Leif Erickson in the exploitation movie *Abduction*, which appeared to be patterned on the Patty Hearst kidnap. Despite her own success, the actress, entering her 50s now (b. 1925), is anxious that her daughters not become actresses. "I know all teenagers go through it," she says. "But you pay too big a price. I hope my girls won't get into that." Onscreen from 1943. IN: *The Falcon and the Coeds* (billed under her real name, Dorothy Maloney), *Too Young to Know, The Big Sleep, Night and Day, Two Guys from Texas, To the Victor, One Sunday Afternoon, Colorado Territory, South of St. Louis, The Killer That Stalked New York, Scared Stiff, Torpedo Alley, Private Hell No. 36, Babble Cry,*

270

Five Guns West, Sincerely Yours, Man of a Thousand Faces, Tip on a Dead Jockey, Tarnished Angels, Too Much Too Soon, Warlock, The Last Voyage, Fate Is the Hunter, more.

MALONE, NANCY (S. Cal.) Leading lady. Onscreen from 1959. IN: *The Violators, An Affair of the Skin, Intimacy,* more.

MAMAKOS, PETER (S. Cal.) Character. Onscreen from 1950. IN: *Cargo to Capetown, The Adventures of Hajii Baba, Desert Sands, The Conqueror, The Heart Is a Lonely Hunter, A Dream of Kings, For Pete's Sake,* more.

MAMO, JOHN (S. Cal.) Character. Onscreen from the '50s. IN: *A Girl Named Tamiko, The Island at the Top of the World,* more.

MAN, CHRISTOPHER (N.Y.) Juvenile. Onscreen in the '70s. IN: *Child's Play,* more.

MANCINI, RIC (S. Cal.) Support. Onscreen from the '60s. IN: *The Honeymoon Killers, Turn On to Love,* more.

MANFREDI, NINO (It.) Star. Onscreen from the '50s. IN: *Wild Love, Fiasco in Milan, Not on Your Life, High Infidelity, Made in Italy, Treasure of San Gennaro, The Female Is the Deadliest of the Species,* more.

MANGANO, SILVANO (It.) Star. Onscreen from 1949. IN: *Elixir of Love, Bitter Rice, Anna, The Brigand, Mussolini, Ulysses, Gold of Naples, This Angry Age, Five Branded Women, The Great War, Barabbas, . . . And Suddenly It's Murder!, The Witches, The Decameron, Death in Venice,* more.

MANN, HOWARD (N.Y.) Character. Onscreen from the '60s. IN: *The World of Henry Orient, Blast of Silence,* more.

MANN, LARRY D. (S. Cal.) Character. Onscreen from the '60s. IN: *The Appaloosa, Caprice, The Wicked Dreams of Paula Schultz, Black Eye,* more.

MANN, PAUL (N.Y.) Actor-director-teacher. Onscreen from 1963. IN: *America America, Fiddler on the Roof,* more. In 1976 he was appointed full Professor in the Theater Arts Department of City College in New York.

MANNE, SHELLY (S. Cal.) Musician-actor. Onscreen from 1959. IN: *The Five Pennies, The Subterraneans,* more.

MANNERS, DAVID (S. Cal.) Still a bachelor in his 70s (b. 1900), he has not made a movie since 1936's *A Woman Rebels*—though he did appear on Broadway in two plays in '46 (*Truckline Cafe, Hidden Horizon*)—lives in a most elegant ocean-view home in the Pacific Palisades, and, as David J. Manners, has written several published mystery novels. Onscreen from 1930. IN: *Journey's End, Troopers Three, Kismet, He Knew Women, The Miracle Woman, Dracula, The Greeks Had a Word for Them, Beauty and the Boss, A Bill of Divorcement, Cock of the Air, The Mummy, The Devil's in Love, Roman Scandals, The Black Cat, The Moonstone, Jalna, Hearts in Bondage,* more.

MANNERS, SHEILA (S. Cal.) (See Sheila Bromley.)

MANNHEIM, LUCIE (Eng.) Character. Onscreen from 1931. IN: *Danton, The 39 Steps, East Meets West, The Yellow Canary, Tawny Pipit, Confess, Dr. Corda, Bunny Lake Is Missing,* more.

MANNING, HOPE (See below.)

MANNING, IRENE (N. Cal.) As Hope Manning, when first onscreen in '37, she was Gene Autry's leading lady in three Westerns, including *The Old Corral*, and then was at MGM. But it was at Warners in the '40s, as Irene Manning, that the blonde actress-singer became a star—in *The Desert Song* with Dennis Morgan, *The Doughgirls,* and, particularly, in *Yankee Doodle Dandy* as the lovely Fay Templeton. In '74, when Hollywood staged its mammoth American Film Institute tribute to Cagney, his costar made a special trip to Hollywood—her first such in years—from her home in San Carlos to add her respects. Except that she is a brunette now, and entering her 60s (b. 1916), she has changed little in looks. Semiretired, though still listed in New York's *Players' Guide*, she has been married since '64 to engineer Maxwell W. Hunter II. She was previously married to writer-producer Het Manheim (1940–44), L.A. police department special investigator Keith Kolhoff (1944–46), and newspaper man Clinton Green (1948–51). Though she last starred in Hollywood in 1945's *Escape in the Desert*, she later appeared in two British films, *I Live on Grosvenor Square* and *Bonnie Prince Charlie* ('48). Living several years in London, she also had her own radio show and wrote a weekly newspaper column on show business, "Girl About Town." Back in the States, and a longtime resident of Manhattan, she played summer theaters and toured in musicals (*The King and I*) and comedies (*Holiday for Lovers*). Also, an accomplished abstract painter, she had exhibitions of her work both in Washington and New York. She last acted on television in '63, in *Dodsworth*, as the wife of the industrialist. Onscreen from 1937. IN: *Two Wise Maids, The*

Big Shot, Spy Ship, Shine On Harvest Moon, Make Your Own Bed, Hollywood Canteen, Escape in the Desert, more.

MANNING, JACK (S. Cal.) Character. Onscreen from 1952. IN: *Walk East on Beacon, The Owl and the Pussycat, The Great Northfield Minnesota Raid, Superdad*, more.

MANOR, CHRIS (N.Y.) Character. Onscreen from the '50s. IN: *Butterfield 8, West Side Story, Fail Safe, Love Story, On a Clear Day You Can See Forever, The Owl and the Pussycat*, more.

MANSON, ALAN (S. Cal.) Character. Onscreen from the '60s. IN: *The Rain People, Let's Scare Jessica to Death*, more.

MANSON, MAURICE (S. Cal.) Character. Onscreen from 1948. IN: *Close-Up, The Creature Walks Among Us, Autumn Leaves, The Girl in the Kremlin, Hell's Five Hours*, more.

MANTEE, PAUL (S. Cal.) Leading man. Onscreen from 1964. IN: *Robinson Crusoe on Mars, Blood on the Arrow, An American Dream, A Man Called Dagger; They Shoot Horses, Don't They?*; more.

MANTELL, JOE (S. Cal.) Character. Nominated for Best Supporting Actor Oscar in *Marty*. Onscreen from 1949. IN: *Barbary Pirate, Storm Center, Beau James, The Sad Sack, Onionhead, The Crowded Sky, The Birds, Mister Buddwing, Chinatown*, more.

MANZA, RALPH (S. Cal.) Character. Onscreen from 1957. IN: *The Enemy Below, Three Guns for Texas*, more.

MARA, ADELE (S. Cal.) In her 50s (b. 1923) and looking a beautiful 15 years younger, she has been married for almost three decades to a very successful TV producer, Emmy-winning Roy Huggins, and is the mother of three sons: Thomas Roy, John Francis, and James Patrick —one grown, the others "almost." She has not been seen in a movie since 1959's *The Big Show*, but in '73 she did a guest stint, as starprivate eye James Farentino's lovely assistant, in the TV show *Cool Million*—produced by Roy Huggins. Onscreen from 1942. IN: *You Were Never Lovelier, Shut My Big Mouth, Alias Boston Blackie, Reveille with Beverly, Atlantic City, Song of Mexico, The Vampire's Ghost, The Magnificent Rogue, I've Always Loved You, The Last Crooked Mile, Wake of the Red Witch; I, Jane Doe; The Sands of Iwo Jima, Rock Island Trail, The Sea Hornet, The Black Whip*, more.

MARAIS, JEAN (Fr.) This extravagantly handsome star, now in his 60s (b. 1913) and only occasionally active on the screen in the past decade, published his autobiography *(Stories of My Life)* in France in '75. It became an immediate best seller, not least because in it he told the inside story of his love for the late Jean Cocteau who shaped him into one of France's greatest screen idols. Onscreen from 1943. IN: *Eternal Return, Beauty and the Beast, The Eagle Has Two Heads, Orpheus, Paris Does Strange Things, The Secret of Mayerling, Royal Affairs in Versailles, White Nights, Testament of Orpheus, The Hunchback of Notre Dame, Friend of the Family, Napoleon, The Reluctant Spy*, more, including 1975's *Donkey Skin (Peau d'Ane)*.

MARCEAU, MARCEL (Fr.) Mime star. Onscreen from 1968. IN: *Barbarella, Shanks*.

MARCH, ELSPETH (Eng.) The former leading lady, and first wife of Stewart Granger, is in her 60s now and remains in demand as a character actress. Onscreen from 1944. IN: *Mr. Emmanuel, Quo Vadis, His Excellency, The Miracle, The Playboy of the Western World, Dr. Crippen, The Rise and Fall of Michael Rimmer, Promise at Dawn; Goodbye, Mr. Chips*; more.

MARCH, LORI (N.Y.) Star of TV soap operas and the wife, since '43, of character actor Alexander Scourby. Onscreen from 1956. IN: *Ransom, Lovers and Lollipops*, more.

MARCHAND, COLETTE (Fr.) Nominated for Best Supporting Actress Oscar in *Moulin Rouge*. Generally inactive since that year, 1953.

MARCHAND, CORINNE (Fr.) Leading lady. Onscreen from 1962. IN: *Cleo from 5 to 7, Seven Deadly Sins ("Lust" episode), Rider on the Rain, Borsalino*, more.

MARCHAND, NANCY (N.Y.) Character. Onscreen from 1957. IN: *The Bachelor Party; Ladybug, Ladybug; Me, Natalie; Tell Me That You Love Me, Junie Moon*; more.

MARDEN, ADRIENNE (S. Cal.) Character. Onscreen from 1936. IN: *13 Hours by Air, F-Men, Star for a Night, Dangerous Crossing, The Shrike, Birdman of Alcatraz, Kisses for My President*, more.

MARFIELD, DWIGHT (N.Y.) Character. Onscreen from 1955. IN: *The Trouble with Harry, Studs Lonigan*, more.

MARGO (S. Cal.) Appointed Commissioner of Social Service in Los Angeles in 1974, by

272

Mayor Tom Bradley, was this actress who will never be forgotten for her performances in *Winterset* and the original *Lost Horizon*. She is in her late 50s now (b. 1918), has not acted since 1965's *Taffy and the Jungle Hunter*, and misses it not at all. But she sometimes conducts acting classes—on the lawn of her Pacific Palisades estate. Once the wife of actor Francis Lederer, she has been married since '44 to Eddie Albert, and is the mother of two grown children—Maria and actor Edward Albert. Many have wondered why the career of this greatly talented Spanish-born actress never flourished as it should. Recently her son explained: "My mom was blacklisted for appearing at an anti-Franco rally; she was branded a Communist, was spat upon in the streets, and had to have a bodyguard. She didn't work on the screen for many years. And my dad found himself unemployable at several major studios, just when his career was gathering momentum. But, growing up, I wasn't aware of the difficulties my mother and dad were having with their careers. Their spirits at home were always the same—high." Onscreen from 1934. IN: *Crime Without Passion, Rumba, A Miracle on Main Street, Behind the Rising Sun, The Leopard Man, The Falcon in Mexico* (after this '44 movie she did not work again until '52), *Viva Zapata!, I'll Cry Tomorrow, From Hell to Texas*, more.

MARGO, GEORGE (Eng.) Character. Onscreen from the '50s. IN: *The Saint's Return, Paratrooper, Lilacs in the Spring, Circle of Danger, Windom's Way, The Mouse That Roared*, more.

MARGOLIN, JANET (S. Cal.) Leading lady. Onscreen from 1962. IN: *David and Lisa, Bus Riley's Back in Town, Morituri, The Greatest Story Ever Told, Nevada Smith, The Eavesdropper, Enter Laughing, Take the Money and Run*, more.

MARGOLIN, STUART (S. Cal.) Support. Onscreen in the '70s. IN: *Kelly's Heroes, The Gambler, Death Wish*, more.

MARICLE, LEONA (S. Cal.) The widow of character actor Louis Jean Heydt, she is in her 70s now (b. 1905), and has been retired from acting since her early 60s. Onscreen from 1935. IN: *O'Shaughnessy's Boy, Theodora Goes Wild, Woman Chases Man, The Lone Wolf in Paris, Comet Over Broadway, Judge Hardy and Son, The Hard Way, My Reputation, A Scandal in Paris*, more.

MARICLE, MARIJANE (S. Cal.) Character. Onscreen in the '70s. IN: *Our Time*, more.

MARIELLE, JEAN-PIERRE (Fr.) Costar. Onscreen from the '60s. IN: *Sweet and Sour, Banana Peel, Backfire, How Not to Rob a Department Store, Male Companion, Tender Scoundrel; Cool, Calm and Collected*; more.

MARIHUGH, TAMMY (Nev.) The former juvenile actress, in many in the '60s, lives in Las Vegas and has lately worked downtown at the Union Plaza, selling real estate. What she would like, she says, is to get back into pictures. Onscreen from 1960. IN: *The Last Voyage, A Thunder of Drums, Back Street, The Wonderful World of the Brothers Grimm*, more.

MARIN, JACQUES (S. Cal.) Character. Onscreen from the '50s. IN: *Forbidden Games, Gates of Paris, The Roots of Heaven, Gigot, The Train, How to Steal a Million, Charade, The Night of the Following Day, Darling Lili, S*P*Y*S, The Island at the Top of the World*, more.

MARION, PAUL/now PAUL MARIN (S. Cal.) The lean young supporting actor, reminiscent of Lindbergh in his early films, is now a heavy, balding character actor, with a slight change in name. Onscreen from 1944. IN: *To Have and Have Not, So Dark the Night, Sword in the Desert, The Lost Tribe, Ten Tall Men, Scared Stiff, Green Fire, Law of the Six Gun, Circle of Fear, A Bullet for Joey*, more.

MARIS, MONA (Peru) The Argentine actress returned to Buenos Aires after her last Hollywood pic, *Heartbeat*, in '46—following 17 years of sultry roles on American screens—and made several more films. Her last was 1952's *La Mujer de las Camelias*. Once the wife of Hollywood director Clarence Brown, she has been married since '60 to a Dutch millionaire and living in Lima. A lifelong globetrotter, she still travels extensively, frequently to New York. When encountered in a swank Fifth Avenue shop, one discovers with pleasure that the years have been kind; she is yet, in her 70s (b. 1903), raven-haired and beautiful. Onscreen in America from 1929. IN: *Under a Texas Moon, The Spy of Madame de Pompadour, The Arizona Kid, One Mad Kiss, A Devil with Women, The Man Who Called Back, Once in a Lifetime, Secrets, Flight from Destiny, Law of the Tropics, A Date with the Falcon, My Gal Sal, I Married an Angel, Cairo, Berlin Correspondent, The Falcon in Mexico, The Desert Hawk* (serial), *Monsieur Beaucaire*, more.

MARIS, ROGER (Fla.) The New York Yankees home run hero—hit 61 homers in '61 to break Babe Ruth's season record—costarred in one movie. He lives now with his wife and four children in Gainesville, Fla., where he has a Budweiser distributorship—courtesy August Busch Jr., owner of the beer firm and of the St. Louis Cardinals where Maris played last. Onscreen in 1962 in *Safe at home*.

MARKEN, JANE (Fr.) The noted character actress is in her 80s now (b. 1895) and has been inactive in movies for the past decade. Onscreen from the teens. IN (since talkies): *Hotel du Nord, Children of Paradise, The Eternal Husband, Dedee, The Cheat, Sins of Paris, Dr. Knock, And God Created Woman, Pot Bouille, The Mirror Has Two Faces, La Bonne Soupe, Friend of the Family*, more.

MARKEY, ENID (N.Y.) Elmo Lincoln's "Jane" in *Tarzan of the Apes* ('18) is in her 80s now (b. 1896) and still recovering from a broken hip suffered in '73, but remains a witty woman and one anxious to get well and get back to the character roles she was enjoying onstage before her injury. Onscreen from 1915. IN: *The Darkening Trail* (with William S. Hart), *The Aztec God, Civilization, The Yankee Way, Romance of Tarzan, Snafu, The Naked City*, more.

MARKEY, MELINDA (S. Cal.) The actress-daughter of Joan Bennett and producer Gene Markey (a Kentucky resident now), she is married and retired. Onscreen 1954–55. IN: *The Adventures of Hajii Baba, The Other Woman, Crashout*, and *Prince of Players*.

MARKHAM, MONTE (S. Cal.) Leading man. Onscreen from 1967. IN: *Hour of the Gun, Guns of the Magnificent Seven, Project X, One Is a Lonely Number*, more.

MARKS, ALFRED (Eng.) Character. Onscreen from 1953. IN: *Penny Points to Paradise, Johnny You're Wanted, There Was a Crooked Man, A Week-End With Lulu, Scream and Scream Again*, more.

MARKS, GUY (S. Cal.) Support. Onscreen in the '70s. IN: *Peeper, Train Ride to Hollywood*, more.

MARLEY, JOHN (S. Cal.) Character. Nominated for Best Supporting Actor Oscar in *Love Story*. Onscreen from 1952. IN: *My Six Convicts, The Joe Louis Story, The Square Jungle, Timetable, I Want to Live!, America America, Cat Ballou, Faces, In Enemy Country, A Man Called Sledge, The Godfather, Framed, W. C. Fields and Me, Fifty-Two Pickup*, more.

MARLOWE, ANTHONY (Eng.) Character. Onscreen from the '50s. IN: *Saadia, Doctor in the House, Room in the House*, more.

MARLOWE, DON "PORKY" (S. Cal.) A supporting actor now, the former child actor also writes books. Onscreen from the '30s. IN: "Our Gang," more.

MARLOWE, HUGH (N.Y.) Leaving Hollywood after 1969's *The Last Shot You Hear*, the former leading man moved to New York and began a new career as a costar in the soap opera *Another World*. Now in his 60s (b. 1911), he is married to a much younger wife, former actress Rosemary Tory, and the father of a young son, Hugh Michael II, born the same year his father's serial career began. The actor was previously married to actresses Edith Atwater and K. T. Stevens (from '46 to '66), by whom he has two grown sons, Jeff and Chris. "Parenthood, late in life, is better," he says. "The first time, you're so involved with your career and getting established you don't have time to really enjoy your children." He asserts he feels much the same about his most recent occupation. Onscreen from 1936. IN: *It Could Have Happened, Married Before Breakfast, Marriage Is a Private Affair, Mrs. Parkington, Murder in the Blue Room, Come to the Stable, Twelve O'-Clock High, All About Eve, Night and the City, Mr. Belvedere Rings the Bell, The Day the Earth Stood Still; Wait Till the Sun Shines, Nellie; Bugles in the Afternoon, Monkey Business, Garden of Evil, Elmer Gantry, The Long Rope, 13 Frightened Girls, Seven Days in May*, more.

MARLOWE, JUNE (S. Cal.) Well-recalled for playing Jackie Cooper's teacher in "Our Gang" and as the femme lead in numerous Rin-Tin-Tin silents, she had better roles in many: Barrymore's *Don Juan* (as Trusia), *A Lost Lady, The Foreign Legion* with Norman Kerry, etc. Now in her 70s (b. 1903), and last onscreen in 1935's *Riddle Ranch*, she has been married for years to business man Rodney S. Sprigg. She lives in retirement in San Diego, enjoys her gardening and charities, and rarely sees anyone from Hollywood. Onscreen from the '20s. IN: *When a Man's a Man, Tracked in the Snow Country, The Wife Who Wasn't Wanted, The Clash of the Wolves, The Branded Men, Their Hour, Free Lips, Grip of the Yukon, Pardon Us, Devil on Deck*, more.

MARLOWE, NORA (S. Cal.) Support. Onscreen from the '50s. IN: *Designing Woman, North by Northwest, An Affair to Remember, The Brass Bottle, Texas Across the River, The Thomas Crown Affair*, more.

MARLOWE, SCOTT (S. Cal.) Leading man. Onscreen from 1956. IN: *Gaby, The Young Guns, Men in War, The Restless Breed, Young and Wild, The Subterraneans, A Cold Wind in August*, more.

274

MARLY, FLORENCE (S. Cal.) Paramount's exotic Czechoslovakian discovery of '48 is still a "looker" in her 50s (b. 1918) and still plays leads, but in "programmers." In this decade she has been in *Queen of Blood*, *Lady from Hell*, and *Doctor Death, Seeker of Souls*. She also wrote, produced, and starred in a musical short, *Spaceboy: A Cosmic Love Affair*, which received a diploma when presented at the Cannes Film Festival in '73. She has been twice married and divorced. Her most recent husband was Count von Wurmbrand, whose name she still uses; copyright on the ballad she did for *Spaceboy* reads "Words and Music by Florence Marly von Wurmbrand." She was previously married for many years to French director Pierre Chenal, who discovered her and starred her in a number of films, one of the first being *The Postman Always Rings Twice*, the French version of the James M. Cain novel made in 1940. "Brilliant," said the *Picturegoer* critic of her performance. Another movie by Chenal, starring his wife, *Voyage Sans Retour*, led directly to her playing the lead for Rene Clement in *Les Maudits* (*The Damned*). The Best Actress award she won for it at Cannes then led to her Paramount contract and her first costarring role here, opposite Ray Milland in *Sealed Verdict*. Her American career was going strong until 1952, when she disappeared from the Hollywood scene for five years. She went to South America to do a picture for a Hollywood company, and on its completion was refused permission to re-enter the United States. Another actress with a name remarkably like hers, she learned years later, was on the "subversive" list and Immigration had confused her with this other person. When she finally made it back to the States in '57 she was approaching her middle years and found the best roles going to younger stars. She never had another chance at first-class stardom in Hollywood. Onscreen in America from 1948. IN: *Sealed Verdict*, *Tokyo Joe*, *Tokyo File 212*, *Gobs and Gals*, *Undersea Girl*, *Planet of Blood*, *Games*, more.

MARMONT, PATRICIA (Eng.) She is the actress-daughter of Percy. Onscreen from 1946. IN: *Loyal Heart*, *Front Page Story*, *The Crowded Day*, *Helen of Troy*, more.

MARMONT, PERCY (Eng.) The famous actor is in his 90s at this writing (b. 1883), and retired. But his decades-long movie career continued well into the '50s, when he was in *Lisbon*, *Footsteps in Fog*, *Knave of Hearts*, etc. Onscreen from 1913. IN: *Turn of the Wheel*, *The Branded Woman*, *If Winter Comes*, *The Light That Failed*, *The Shooting of Dan McGrew*, *The Street of Forgotten Men*, *Fine Clothes*, *Lord Jim*, *San Francisco Nights*, *The Silver King*,

Ariane, *The Pearls of the Crown*, *Courageous Mr. Penn*, *No Orchids for Miss Blandish*, *Four Sided Triangle*, more.

MAROSS, JOE (S. Cal.) Character. Onscreen from 1958. IN: *Run Silent, Run Deep*; *Zigzag*, *Sometimes a Great Notion*, more.

MARQUAND, CHRISTIAN (Fr.) Former leading man. Has been a director for the past decade. Onscreen from the early '50s. IN: *The Doctors*, *And God Created Woman*, *No Sun in Venice*, *The Longest Day*, *I Spit on Your Grave*, *Behold a Pale Horse*, *Lord Jim*, *The Flight of the Phoenix*, more.

MARQUAND, TINA (Fr.) Leading lady. Onscreen from the '60s. IN: *Modesty Blaise*, *Texas Across the River*, *The Game Is Over*, more.

MARQUES, MARIA ELENA (Mex.) After her young actor-husband, Miguel Torruco, died in '56, she made only a few more films before retiring after completion of *The Marriage Came Tumbling Down*. Now in her 50s, the former actress is a congresswoman in Mexico. And, says one who knows her well, "She works terribly hard and is up at 6, not to go to a studio, but to work for the people of her district." Onscreen from the '40s. IN: *The Pearl*, *Across the Wide Missouri*, *The Doctors*, *Royal Affairs in Versailles*, *Made in Paris*, *Landru*, more.

MARR, EDWARD (S. Cal.) Character. Onscreen from 1937. IN: *Forty Naughty Girls*, *Mr. Moto's Gamble*, *The Affairs of Annabel*, *Tail Spin*, *Charlie Chan at the Wax Museum*, *The Glass Key*, *Rhapsody in Blue*, *On Moonlight Bay*, *The Steel Trap*, *20,000 Leagues Under the Sea*, more.

MARR, SALLY (S. Cal.) Support. Onscreen from 1967. IN: *The Drifter* (billed Sadia), *Star!*, *The Grasshopper*, *The Christian Licorice Store*, more.

MARRIOTT, JOHN (N.Y.) Black character. Onscreen from 1940. IN: *The Little Foxes*, *The Joe Louis Story*, *Dear Dead Delilah*, *The Court-Martial of Billy Mitchell*, *The Cool World*, *Black Like Me*, more.

MARS, KENNETH (S. Cal.) Support. Onscreen from 1968. IN: *The Producers*, *The April Fools*, *Butch Cassidy and the Sundance Kid*, *Viva Max*, *Desperate Characters*, *What's Up Doc?*, *Night Moves*, more.

MARSAC, MAURICE (S. Cal.) Character. Onscreen from 1944. IN: *This Is the Life*, *The*

Happy Times, How to Marry a Millionaire, China Gate, King of Kings, What a Way to Go!, The Pleasure Seekers, Gambit, Caprice, more.

MARSDEN, BETTY (Eng.) Character. Onscreen from 1941. IN: Ships With Wings, Chance Meeting, The Lovers, Let's Get Married, The Big Day, more.

MARSH, CAROL (Eng.) Support. Onscreen from the '40s. IN: Brighton Rock, A Christmas Carol, Marry Me, Horror of Dracula, more.

MARSH, GARRY (Eng.) Character. Onscreen from 1929. IN: The Dreyfus Case, The Man They Couldn't Arrest, Fires of Fate, Scrooge, Break the News, When Knights Were Bold, Notorious Gentlemen, The Adventuress, Pink String and Sealing Wax, Murder Will Out, Camelot, more.

MARSH, JEAN (Eng.) Support. Also creator and star of television's Upstairs, Downstairs. Onscreen from the '50s. IN: Where's Charley?, Tales of Hoffman (bits), The Horsemasters, Cleopatra, Frenzy, Dark Places, more.

MARSH, JOAN (S. Cal.) Still attractively blonde in her 60s (b. 1913), the leading lady so reminiscent of Harlow lives in Los Angeles and has long owned and operated Paper Unlimited, a thriving stationery business. She married (second time) in '43, the year before she made a Monogram B titled Follow the Leader and left the screen. She had then been "Joan Marsh" for 14 years (since Whiteman's King of Jazz) and in three dozen movies. As a little girl, billed Dorothy Rosher, her real name, she had been in Mary Pickford's Pollyanna and Daddy Long Legs—her father, Charles Rosher, being a famous Pickford cameraman. Onscreen as Joan Marsh from 1930. IN: Little Accident, All Quiet on the Western Front; Dance, Fools, Dance; A Tailor-Made Man, Shipmates, Are You Listening?, The Wet Parade, Rainbow Over Broadway, Anna Karenina, Life Begins at College, Charlie Chan on Broadway, The Man in the Trunk, Police Bullets, more.

MARSH, LINDA (S. Cal.) Leading lady. Onscreen from 1963. IN: America America, Hamlet (the Richard Burton filmed-stage-play version, in which she was Ophelia), Che!, Freebie and the Bean, more.

MARSH, MARIAN (S. Cal.) Warners, her studio, put her name above the title of Under Eighteen and took full-page ads in magazines "Introducing the First Star of 1932." Despite talent and blonde good looks, she slipped into B's (Black Room Mystery, etc.), then support-

ing roles before she quit after 1942's House of Errors. She's in her 60s now (b. 1913) and, still pretty, has long been married to millionaire Cliff Henderson and lives in Palm Desert. High-rankers in the Palm Springs social swim, they golf, attend all major parties of the community, and travel widely. Previously married to stockbroker Albert Scott (once wed to Colleen Moore), she also had a previous screen name—Marilyn Morgan—when in Cantor's Whoopee. Onscreen from 1930. IN: Hell's Angels, Svengali, Five Star Final, Beauty and the Boss; Free, White and 21; Daring Daughters, Notorious but Nice, Girl of the Limberlost, Crime and Punishment, The Man Who Lived Twice, The Great Gambini, The Hound of the Baskervilles, The Man I Married, Adam Had Four Sons, Sleepers West, more.

MARSHALL, BRENDA (S. Cal.) Friends in Palm Springs, where she has lived for years, are convinced she will not act again or remarry. She divorced William Holden in '71 after exactly 30 years of marriage. By him she has two sons: West (b. 1943), married and a business man, and Peter (b. 1946), still single and an actor—was a veterinarian in his father's pic Breezy. By previous husband, actor Richard Gaines, she is the mother of a daughter, Virginia (adopted by Holden after Brenda married him), who is married, after trying an acting career (Walk East on Beacon), and living in Los Angeles. Brenda, who gave up her career after 1950's Iroquois Trail, and is now in her early 60s (b. 1915), is known to friends as Ardis Holden—Ardis being her real name. Onscreen from 1939. IN: Espionage Agent, South of Suez, The Sea Hawk, Footsteps in the Dark, Captains of the Clouds, You Can't Escape Forever, The Constant Nymph, Paris After Dark, Background to Danger, Something for the Boys, Strange Impersonation, more.

MARSHALL, DODIE (S. Cal.) Leading lady. Onscreen from the '60s. IN: Easy Come, Easy Go; Spinout, more.

MARSHALL, DON (S. Cal.) Black support. Onscreen from the '60s. IN: The Interns, Sergeant Ryker, Uptown Saturday Night, more.

MARSHALL, E. G. (S. Cal.) Character. Onscreen from 1945. IN: The House on 92nd Street, 13 Rue Madeleine, Call Northside 777, The Caine Mutiny, Broken Lance, The Left Hand of God, The Mountain, Twelve Angry Men, Man on Fire, The Bachelor Party, Compulsion, Is Paris Burning?, The Bridge at Remagen, Tora! Tora! Tora!, more.

MARSHALL, MARION (S. Cal.) Married to and divorced from director Stanley Donen and actor Robert Wagner, she has three children, is retired from acting, and lives in Palm Springs. Onscreen from 1948. IN: *Sitting Pretty, Street With No Name, I Was a Male War Bride, A Ticket to Tomahawk, My Blue Heaven, Stella, I Can Get It for You Wholesale, That's My Boy, The Stooge, Gunn,* more.

MARSHALL, MORT (N.Y.) Character. Onscreen from the '50s. IN: *Go, Man, Go; The Silver Chalice, Kiss Me Deadly,* more.

MARSHALL, PAT (S. Cal.) The singer-actress has been married to TV writer Larry Gelbart since '56 and is the mother of three sons and two daughters. Onscreen from 1947. IN: *Good News,* more.

MARSHALL, PENNY (S. Cal.) Support. Onscreen from the '60s. IN: *The Savage Seven,* more.

MARSHALL, PETER (S. Cal.) Comedian-television personality. Onscreen from 1960. IN: *The Rookie, Swingin' Along, Ensign Pulver, The Cavern,* more.

MARSHALL, SARAH (S. Cal.) Support. The daughter of Herbert Marshall and Edna Best. Onscreen from 1958. IN: *The Long Hot Summer, Wild and Wonderful,* more.

MARSHALL, TRUDY (S. Cal.) If possible, she is more of a knockout now in her 50s (b. 1922) than when playing second leads at 20th Century-Fox in the '40s. Well married to meat brokerage executive Philip Raffin for almost three decades, she lives in a posh section of West Los Angeles and is the mother of three grown children: Judy (married), Bill, and Deborah Raffin. Deborah, of course, is the young actress who made a considerable splash as January in *Once Is Not Enough.* Married, since '74, to writer-producer Michael Viner, who is also her manager, Deborah lives in nearby Beverly Hills. Indicative that Trudy Marshall has not forgotten her days at 20th-Fox is that guests at Deborah's engagement party included such old pals as Cesar Romero and Mary Anderson. Recognizing Deborah's acting talents early, Trudy coached her from the time she began appearing in high school plays and was instrumental in the high-fashion modeling career that led to leading roles in *Forty Carats* and *The Dove.* Still much a part of the Hollywood scene, Trudy has been president of The Smart Set, a charitable organization comprised of screen luminaries and local socialites. She has also been chairwoman for benefit premieres—proceeds going to the Motion Picture and Television Relief Fund. Last onscreen in 1957's *Full of Life,* the beauty with the reddish-blonde hair is content now to leave the acting to daughter Deborah. Onscreen from 1942. IN: *Secret Agent of Japan, Heaven Can Wait, The Dancing Masters, The Purple Heart, The Sullivans, Roger Touhy—Gangster, Circumstantial Evidence, The Dolly Sisters, Dragonwyck, Sentimental Journey, Joe Palooka in The Knockout, Key Witness, The Fuller Brush Man, Shamrock Hill, Mark of the Gorilla, Full of Life,* more.

MARSHALL, WILLIAM (Fr.) The former husband of Michele Morgan and Ginger Rogers, he is a film producer and novelist now. Onscreen from 1940. IN: *Flowing Gold, Santa Fe Trail, Belle of the Yukon, State Fair, Murder in the Music Hall, Earl Carroll Sketchbook, That Brennan Girl,* more.

MARSHALL, WILLIAM (Ind.) This fine black actor-singer still uses Gary, his birthplace, as home base—flying to New York, Hollywood, or abroad for acting or (stage) directing assignments. Onscreen from 1952. IN: *Lydia Bailey, Demetrius and the Gladiators, Something of Value, Blacula, Abby.*

MARSHALL, ZENA (Eng.) Leading lady. Onscreen from the '40s. IN: *Snowbound, Sleeping Car to Trieste, The Lost People, So Long at the Fair, The Caretaker's Daughter, Let's Be Happy, Dr. No.* more.

MARSTON, JOEL (S. Cal.) Support. Onscreen from the '40s. IN: *Mississippi Rhythm, There's a Girl in My Heart, Jiggs and Maggie in Jackpot Jitters, Just for You, Battle Taxi, The Night Holds Terror, The Last Voyage, Ring of Fire,* more.

MARTEL, WILLIAM (S. Cal.) Character. Onscreen from 1949. IN: *The Red Menace; Simon, King of the Witches;* more.

MARTELL, DONNA (S. Cal.) Support. Onscreen from the '40s. IN: *Bomba and the Elephant Stampede, Last Train from Bombay, Hills of Utah, The Egyptian, Law of the Six Gun, Ten Wanted Men, Love Is a Many-Splendored Thing,* more.

MARTH, FRANK (S. Cal.) Support. Onscreen from the '60s. IN: *Madigan, Pendulum, Marooned, The Lost Man,* more.

MARTIN, ANDRA (S. Cal.) The former leading lady—once married to actor Ty Hardin—still lives in Los Angeles but has been inactive professionally in the past decade. Onscreen from 1958. IN: *The Big Heat, The Lady Takes a Flyer, The Thing That Couldn't Die, Yellowstone Kelly, Up Periscope!, Fever in the Blood,* more.

MARTIN, CHARLES (S. Cal.) Character. On-screen from the '60s. IN: *Gentle Giant*, more.

MARTIN, CLAUDIA (S. Cal.) Dean Martin's daughter. Onscreen in 1968. IN: *Ski Fever.*

MARTIN, DEAN (S. Cal.) Star. Onscreen as half of the Jerry Lewis-Dean Martin comedy team 1949–56. IN: *My Friend Irma, At War with the Army, That's My Boy, The Stooge, Jumping Jacks, The Caddy, Scared Stiff, Living It Up, Three-Ring Circus, Pardners*, more. On-screen as a starred leading man from 1957. IN: *Ten Thousand Bedrooms, Some Came Running, Rio Bravo, Who Was That Lady?, Bells Are Ringing, Toys in the Attic, Four for Texas, Kiss Me Stupid, The Sons of Katie Elder, The Silencers, Bandolero, The Wrecking Crew, Airport, Something Big, Showdown, Mr. Ricco*, more.

MARTIN, DEANA (S. Cal.) Dean Martin's daughter. Onscreen in 1969. IN: *Young Billy Young.*

MARTIN, DEWEY (S. Cal.) A rugged hand-some man still, in his 50s (b. 1923), he is starring again in such pix as *Seven Alone*—after four years as a movie dropout. He lived in Mexico, Canada, Alaska, Japan, and Italy, making his way by working at odd jobs—in a lumbermill, a cannery, on a fishing boat, teaching conversational English. "I found I can always make a buck, but I like to act and good parts are coming my way," says the actor who wanted to learn—and did—about the "real" world. "I think I'll stick around a while." He has been twice married and divorced, most recently, a decade ago, from singer Peggy Lee. Onscreen from 1949. IN: *Knock on Any Door, The Golden Gloves Story, The Thing, The Big Sky, Tennessee Champ, Men of the Fighting Lady, The Desperate Hours, The Proud and the Profane, Savage Sam, Flight to Fury*, more.

MARTIN, DICK (S. Cal.) Half of the Rowan and Martin comedy team. Onscreen from the '50s. IN: *Once Upon a Horse, The Glass Bottom Boat, The Maltese Bippy*, more.

MARTIN, DINO, JR. (S. Cal.) Dean Martin's actor son. Onscreen from 1967. IN: *Rough Night in Jericho, A Boy . . . A Girl*, more.

MARTIN, FREDDY (S. Cal.) The famous band-leader, on the threshold of 70 (b. 1907), is still leading his orchestra in playing "Tonight We Love" in nightclub engagements throughout the land. Onscreen in the '40s. IN: *Seven Days' Leave, The Mayor of Forty-Fourth Street, What's Buzzin' Cousin, Hit Parade of 1943, Stage Door Canteen*, more.

MARTIN, JARED (S. Cal.) Character. On-screen from the '60s. IN: *Murder a la Mod, The Second Coming of Suzanne*, more.

MARTIN, KIEL (S. Cal.) Leading man. His screen name was chosen before he became, for a while, Dean Martin's son-in-law. Onscreen from the '60s. IN: *The Undefeated, The Panic in Needle Park, Moonrunners*, more.

MARTIN, MARCELLA (S. Cal.) Character. Onscreen from 1939. IN: *Gone With the Wind*, more.

MARTIN, MARION (S. Cal.) In her sixth decade (b. 1916) she remains a statuesque platinum blonde with a high bosom and a low voice, just as in *Lady of Burlesque, The Big Store*, and another 55 features. But the blowzy beauty of the screen and the real Marion Martin are, always have been, blondes of a different hue. Actually a well-bred girl from one of Philadelphia's Main Line families (her father was a top executive at Bethlehem Steel), and educated in the best European schools, the real Marion Martin has been married for many years to a successful Southern California physician. In retirement, and childless, she devotes much of her time to the charities of a Beverly Hills Catholic church. She admits no desire to kick up her heels again as a movie dance-hall hostess, but, should she change her mind, she still has the equipment. Onscreen from 1939. IN: *Invitation to Happiness, Boom Town, The Lady from Cheyenne, Mexican Spitfire's Baby, The Big Street, Woman of the Town, Irish Eyes Are Smiling, It Happened Tomorrow, Eadie Was a Lady, Penthouse Rhythm, Angel on My Shoulder, Deadline for Murder, Come to the Stable*, more, including 1950's *Dakota Lil* and *Key to the City*, her last.

MARTIN, MARY (S. Cal.) Sleek, snowy-haired, and lovely, the song star is in her 60s (b. 1913), a widow (husband Richard Halliday died in '73), several times a grandmother via her two children—Heller Halliday De Merritt and actor Larry Hagman, and lives in solitary splendor in Palm Springs. In '76 she published her autobiography, *My Heart Belongs*, and was planning a return to the stage, in a musical version of *Life With Father*. Onscreen from 1939. IN: *The Great Victor Herbert, Rhythm on the River, Love Thy Neighbor, New York Town, Kiss the Boys Goodbye, Birth of the Blues, True to Life, Happy Go Lucky, Night and Day*, and, last, 1953's *Main Street to Broadway*, in which she did a cameo.

MARTIN, MILLICENT (Eng.) Singer-actress. Onscreen from 1960. IN: *The Horsemasters, Invasion Quartet, Nothing But the Best, Those*

Magnificent Men in Their Flying Machines, Stop the World I Want to Get Off, Alfie, more.

MARTIN, NAN (S. Cal.) Character. Onscreen from 1957. IN: *The Buster Keaton Story, The Mugger, 3 in the Attic, For Love of Ivy; Goodbye, Columbus; The Other Side of the Mountain,* more.

MARTIN, PAMELA (S. Cal.) Ingenue. Onscreen in the '70s. IN: *To Find a Man, The Poseidon Adventure,* more.

MARTIN, PEPPER (S. Cal.) Character. Onscreen from the '60s. IN: *Angels from Hell; If He Hollers, Let Him Go; The Wrecking Crew, The Animals,* more.

MARTIN, ROSS (S. Cal.) Character. Onscreen from 1955. IN: *Conquest of Space, Underwater Warrior, Geronimo, Experiment in Terror, The Ceremony, The Great Race,* more.

MARTIN, STROTHER (S. Cal.) Character. Onscreen from 1950. IN: *The Asphalt Jungle, Strategic Air Command, Attack!, Copper Sky, Sanctuary, The Man Who Shot Liberty Valance, McLintock!, Invitation to a Gunfighter, Shenandoah, Harper, Cool Hand Luke, The Wild Bunch, True Grit, Butch Cassidy and the Sundance Kid, Pocket Money, Hard Times, Rooster Cogburn,* more.

MARTIN, TODD (S. Cal.) Support. Onscreen from the '60s. IN: *The Thomas Crown Affair; If He Hollers, Let Him Go;* more.

MARTIN, TONY (S. Cal.) He and dancer-wife Cyd Charisse—married since '48 and parents of a grown son, Tony Jr. (b. 1950)—do an act now that plays the finer supper clubs. Onscreen from 1936. IN: *Pigskin Parade; Sing, Baby, Sing; Follow the Fleet, You Can't Have Everything; Sally, Irene and Mary* (with first wife Alice Faye); *Ziegfeld Girl, Casbah, Two Tickets to Broadway, Easy to Love, Hit the Deck,* more.

MARTIN, VIVIENNE (Eng.) Support. Onscreen from the '50s. IN: *The Belles of St. Trinian's,* more.

MARTINELLI, ELSA (It.) The Italian star, who acts less frequently now, arrived in New York in the autumn of '75 to promote her new career —fashion designer. Her first showing in New York was a 20-piece collection of young casual styles. "I found myself getting bored and restless between pictures," said the onetime model, now in her 40s (b. 1933). "That's why two years ago I decided to go back to fashion." A success at designing, she has her own factories in Bologna and Perugia, and has had four collections shown abroad. But, she added, "I'm not giving up making movies." She is the wife of fashion photographer-interior designer Willie Rizzo, and has four homes—in Paris, St. Tropez, and Rome, and a country house in Italy. Onscreen from 1955. IN: *The Indian Fighter, Four Girls in Town, Blood and Roses, Hatari!, The Pigeon That Took Rome, The Trial, The V.I.P.s, The Tenth Victim, Rampage, Maroc 7, Woman Times Seven, The Oldest Profession,* more.

MARTINEZ, JOAQUIN (S. Cal.) Support. Onscreen from the '60s. IN: *The Stalking Moon, Ulzana's Raid,* more.

MARTINS, ORLANDO (Eng.) Black character who, in his 70s (b. 1899), acts less often now. Onscreen from 1934. IN: *Sanders of the River, The Man from Morocco, Men of Two Worlds, The Hasty Heart, American Guerrilla in the Philippines, Ivory Hunter, The Heart of the Matter, West of Zanzibar, Tarzan and the Lost Safari, Sapphire, Call Me Bwana,* more.

MARVIN, LEE (S. Cal.) Star. Won Best Actor Oscar in *Cat Ballou.* Onscreen from 1951. IN: *You're in the Navy Now, Eight Iron Men, Seminole, The Big Heat, The Wild One, The Caine Mutiny, Bad Day at Black Rock, Not As a Stranger, Shack Out on 101, Attack!, The Comancheros, Donovan's Reef, The Killers, Ship of Fools, The Dirty Dozen, Hell in the Pacific, Paint Your Wagon, Monte Walsh, Prime Cut, Emperor of the North Pole, The Klansman, Shout at the Devil, Great Scout and Cat-House Thursday,* more.

MARX, GROUCHO (S. Cal.) Star comedian. Onscreen from 1929. IN: *The Cocoanuts, Animal Crackers, Monkey Business, Horsefeathers, Duck Soup, A Night at the Opera, A Day at the Races, Room Service, At the Circus, Go West, The Big Store, A Night in Casablanca, Copacabana, Love Happy, Mr. Music, Double Dynamite, A Girl in Every Port, Will Success Spoil Rock Hunter, The Story of Mankind,* and, last, 1968's *Skidoo!*

MARX, ZEPPO (S. Cal.) In his 70s (b. 1901), twice married and divorced, he lives in retirement in Palm Springs. Onscreen as one of the four Marx Brothers from 1929, in their first five films: *The Cocoanuts, Animal Crackers, Monkey Business, Horsefeathers,* and *Duck Soup.* He then left the act and became a highly successful Hollywood agent.

MASE, MARINO (It.) Leading man. Onscreen from the '60s. IN: *Arialda, The Soldiers, Between Two Worlds, Le Gendarme a New York, Love and Marriage (One Moment Is Enough), Les Carabiniers, Fist in His Pocket,* more.

MASINA, GIULIETTA (It.) Fellini's wife, she has not been seen in a film since 1969's *The Madwoman of Chaillot*. Onscreen from the '40s. IN: *Without Pity, Behind Closed Shutters, The Greatest Love, The White Sheik, La Strada, Angels of Darkness, Cabiria, Il Bidone, Variety Lights, Juliet of the Spirits*, more.

MASLOW, WALTER (S. Cal.) Support. Onscreen from 1961. IN: *Francis of Assisi*, more.

MASON, BERYL (Eng.) Support. Onscreen from 1936. IN: *Accused*, more.

MASON, BREWSTER (Eng.) Support. Onscreen from the '50s. IN: *The Dam Busters, Private Potter*, more.

MASON, JAMES (Switz.) Star. Nominated for Best Actor Oscar in *A Star Is Born*. Onscreen from 1935. IN: *Late Extra, Fire Over England, The Return of the Scarlet Pimpernel, Hatter's Castle, Thunder Rock, Candlelight in Algeria, The Man in Grey, They Met in the Dark, Fanny by Gaslight, They Were Sisters, Wicked Lady, The Seventh Veil, Odd Man Out; East Side, West Side; Madame Bovary, Pandora and the Flying Dutchman, The Desert Fox, Five Fingers, The Prisoner of Zenda, Julius Caesar, The Desert Rats, 20,000 Leagues Under the Sea, North by Northwest, Lolita, The Pumpkin Eater, Lord Jim, Georgy Girl, The Blue Max, Mayerling, The Sea Gull, Child's Play, The Last of Sheila, Mandingo, Inside Out, The Voyage of the Damned*, more.

MASON, MARLYN (S. Cal.) Leading lady. Onscreen from 1968. IN: *The Trouble with Girls, Making It, Christina*, more.

MASON, MARSHA (S. Cal.) Costar. Nominated for Best Actress Oscar in *Cinderella Liberty*. Onscreen from 1973. IN: *Blume in Love, more*.

MASON, MARY (N.Y.) The former leading lady gave up her movie career four decades ago and her stage career after 1942's *Cafe Crown*. Happily married for years to theatrical attorney John F. Wharton, she lives in Manhattan, and is known as Betty Wharton. She has long been, and remains, a New York City librarian—with time out in 1975 for cataract and retina surgery. Onscreen in the early '30s. IN: *Wall of Gold, The Mad Game*, more.

MASON, MORGAN (S. Cal.) James Mason's son. Onscreen in 1965. IN: *The Sandpiper* (juvenile role).

MASON, PAMELA/formerly PAMELA KELLINO (S. Cal.) James Mason's former wife.

Onscreen as Pamela Mason from 1951. IN: *Lady Possessed, Sex Kittens Go to College, College Confidential, Door to Door Maniac, Voices*, more.

MASON, PORTLAND (S. Cal.) James Mason's daughter. Onscreen in 1956. IN: *The Man in the Gray Flannel Suit* (juvenile role).

MASON, SHIRLEY (S. Cal.) After her famous director-husband, Sidney Lanfield, retired—1952's *Skirts Ahoy!* was the last of his dozens of films—they lived for two decades in Palm Springs where they reared their family. A widow now (since '72, after more than four decades of marriage), and a grandmother, Shirley has moved to Marina Del Rey to be closer to sister Viola Dana. She is in her 70s (b. 1900), financially well off, and retired. Onscreen from 1915. IN: *Vanity Fair, Come On In, Treasure Island, The Eleventh Hour, The Talker, What Fools Men Are, Lord Jim, Desert Gold, Sweet Rosie O'Grady, Let It Rain, Show of Shows*, more.

MASON, SYDNEY L. (S. Cal.) Character. Onscreen from the '50s. IN: *Paula, Creature from the Black Lagoon, Blackjack Ketchum Desperado*, more.

MASSARI, LEA (It.) Leading lady. Onscreen from the '60s. IN: *L'Avventura, From a Roman Balcony, The Colossus of Rhodes, Paris Pick-Up, Made in Italy, Murmur of the Heart, Impossible Object, Escape to Nowhere, Allonsanfan*, more.

MASSEY, ANNA (Eng.) Support. Daughter of Raymond Massey and Adrianne Allen. Onscreen from 1957. IN: *Gideon of Scotland Yard, Bunny Lake Is Missing, David Copperfield, The Looking Glass War, Frenzy, A Doll's House*, more.

MASSEY, DANIEL (Eng.) Costar. Son of Raymond Massey and Adrianne Allen. Nominated for Best Supporting Actor Oscar in *Star!* Onscreen from 1942. IN: *In Which We Serve* (juvenile role), *Girls at Sea, The Entertainer; Upstairs, Downstairs; The Amorous Adventures of Moll Flanders, The Jokers; Mary, Queen of Scots; Vault of Horror*, more.

MASSEY, RAYMOND (S. Cal.) Character star. Nominated for Best Actor Oscar in *Abe Lincoln in Illinois*. Most recently in 1968's *Mackenna's Gold*, he costarred in Los Angeles in '75 in the play *The Night of the Iguana*, as the half-senile old poet, Nonno. Said *Variety*'s critic of the actor, now entering his 80s (b. 1896), "Massey is simultaneously foolish and grandiloquent, quite an achievement." Onscreen from

1931. In: *The Speckled Band, The Scarlet Pimpernel, Things to Come, The Prisoner of Zenda, Hurricane, Drums, Reap the Wild Wind, Santa Fe Trail, Action in the North Atlantic, The Woman in the Window, Arsenic and Old Lace, Stairway to Heaven, Possessed, Mourning Becomes Electra, The Fountainhead, Roseanna McCoy, David and Bathsheba, Prince of Players, East of Eden, The Naked and the Dead, The Great Impostor, How the West Was Won,* more.

MASSIE, PAUL (Eng.) Leading man. Onscreen from the '50s. IN: *Orders to Kill, Libel, Sapphire, House of Fright, Call Me Genius, 20,000 Eyes,* more.

MASSINE, LEONID (N.Y.) Unforgettable as the satanic dancing shoemaker who lured Moira Shearer to her tragic fate in *The Red Shoes,* the Moscow-born dancer-choreographer became 80 in 1976. Of course he no longer dances, but as befits one trained by Diaghilev over six decades ago to be Nijinski's replacement, he remains a seminal force in the world of ballet. In this decade, the naturalized American citizen (since '39) has published a book (*Massine on Choreography*), been honored with an all-Massine program by the New York City Ballet (an evening in which four of his most famous ballet creations were danced), founded a choreographic center in England, and established a ballet company in the Diaghilev tradition in Prato, Italy. And, while New York remains his home base, he travels constantly, all over the globe. He has had "several" wives and has two children—Leonide Jr., who lives in Paris and is a choreographer, and Tatyana, a partner in a Manhattan art gallery. Onscreen from 1929. IN: *Versailles, The Red Shoes, Tales of Hoffmann, Neapolitan Carousel,* more.

MASTERSON, MARY STUART (N.Y.) Daughter of actor Peter. Onscreen in 1975. IN: *The Stepford Wives* (juvenile role).

MASTERSON, PETER (N.Y.) Leading man. Onscreen from 1966. IN: *Ambush Bay, Counterpoint, Tomorrow, Von Richthofen and Brown, Man on a Swing, The Exorcist, The Stepford Wives,* more.

MASTROIANNI, MARCELLO (It.) Star. Nominated for Best Actor Oscar in *Divorce Italian Style.* Onscreen from 1947. IN: *I Miserabili, Sunday in August, Too Bad She's Bad, The Miller's Beautiful Wife, White Nights, Where the Hot Wind Blows, The Big Deal on Madonna Street, La Dolce Vita, 8½, The Organizer; Yesterday, Today and Tomorrow; Marriage Italian Style, Casanova 70, Kiss the Other Sheik, Man with the Balloons, Sunflower, Leo the Last,* *Down the Ancient Stairs, Sunday Woman,* more.

MASURAT, THERESA (N.Y.) Support. IN: *The Naked Runner,* more.

MATCHETT, CHRISTINE (S. Cal.) Former juvenile (b. 1957). Onscreen from 1967. IN: *The Reluctant Astronaut, The Illustrated Man,* more.

MATHERS, JERRY (S. Cal.) The former child actor, now in his late 20s (b. 1948), works behind the scenes in Hollywood and has been married since September '74 to the former Diana Platt. Onscreen from 1954. IN: *This Is My Love, The Trouble with Harry, Bigger Than Life, That Certain Feeling,* more.

MATHESON, DON (S. Cal.) Leading man. Onscreen in the '70s. IN: *Live a Little, Steal a Lot,* more.

MATHESON, MURRAY (Can.) Living on Otter Lake in Ontario, this Australian-born character actor, in his 60s now (b. 1912), still flies to Hollywood for an occasional movie assignment. Onscreen from 1940. IN: *The Way to the Stars, Journey Together, Hurricane Smith, Plymouth Adventure, Botany Bay, King of the Khyber Rifles, Love Is a Many-Splendored Thing, Signpost to Murder, In Enemy Country,* more.

MATHESON, TIM (S. Cal.) Leading man. Onscreen from 1968. IN: *Yours, Mine and Ours; How to Commit Marriage, Divorce American Style,* more.

MATHEWS, CARMEN (N.Y.) Character. Onscreen from 1960. IN: *Butterfield 8; Rabbit, Run; Sounder,* more.

MATHEWS, CAROLE (S. Cal.) Support; former leading lady. Onscreen from 1944. IN: *Swing in the Saddle, The Monster and the Ape* (serial), *Massacre River, Cry Murder, Swamp Woman, Shark River, Treasure of Ruby Hills, Betrayed Women, Showdown at Boot Hill,* more.

MATHEWS, GEORGE (N.Y.) Character. Onscreen from 1944. IN: *Up in Arms, The Eye of St. Mark, Pat and Mike, City Beneath the Sea, The Man with the Golden Arm, The Proud Ones, Heller in Pink Tights,* more.

MATHEWS, JOYCE (S. Cal.) Former support. Famous beauty. Onscreen from 1937. IN: *Artists and Models, The Big Broadcast of 1938, Tip-Off Girls, Million Dollar Legs, $1,000 a Touchdown, Mr. Universe,* more. (See Don Beddoe.)

MATHEWS, KERWIN (N. Cal.) The big handsome swashbuckler, beginning his 50s now (b. 1926), gave up his long career in '74, and became an antiques dealer in San Francisco. Onscreen from 1955. IN: *Five Against the House, The 7th Voyage of Sinbad, The Three Worlds of Gulliver, Man on a String, The Devil at 4 O'-Clock, Pirates of Blood River, The Battle Beneath the Earth, A Boy . . . A Girl*, more.

MATHIAS, BOB (N. Cal.) The Olympic decathlon champion made his debut in 1954's *The Bob Mathias Story*, in which he portrayed himself, and his charming wife, Melba, herself. He continued his acting career for several years, starring on TV (the '59 series *Troubleshooters*) and in movies. He was later, as Robert B. Mathias, until losing his seat in the 1974 elections, a U.S. Congressional Representative (Rep.) from California. He lives now, with his wife and several children, on a ranch near his home town, Tulare. IN: *China Doll, The Minotaur, It Happened in Athens*, more.

MATHIES, CHARLENE (N.Y.) Support. Onscreen from the '60s. IN: *Lady in Cement; Me, Natalie;* more.

MATTHAU, WALTER (S. Cal.) Costar. Won Best Supporting Actor Oscar in *The Fortune Cookie*. Nominated for Best Actor Oscar in *Kotch* and *The Sunshine Boys*. Onscreen from 1955. IN: *The Kentuckian, Bigger Than Life, A Face in the Crowd, Voice in the Mirror, Strangers When We Meet, Lonely Are the Brave, Charade, Fail Safe, Mirage, A Guide for the Married Man, The Odd Couple, Candy; Hello, Dolly!; Cactus Flower, A New Leaf, Plaza Suite, Pete 'n Tillie, The Front Page, The Taking of Pelham One Two Three, Earthquake, The Sunshine Boys, The Bad News Bears*, more.

MATTHEWS, CHRISTOPHER (Eng.) Leading man. Onscreen in the '70s. IN: *Scream and Scream Again, See No Evil, Scars of Dracula*, more.

MATTHEWS, ERIC (S. Cal.) Leading man. Onscreen in the '70s. IN: *End of August*, more.

MATTHEWS, FRANCIS (Eng.) Leading man. Onscreen from the '50s. IN: *Bhowani Junction, Murder Ahoy; Dracula, Prince of Darkness; Just Like a Woman*, more.

MATTHEWS, GLORIA/formerly GLORIA TO-FANO (N.Y.) Support. Onscreen from the '60s. IN: *The Brotherhood, Stiletto, Lovers and Other Strangers, The Hospital, The Gang That Couldn't Shoot Straight*, more.

MATTHEWS, JESSIE (Eng.) The song-and-dance star of many musicals of the '30s, known as the "lady with the loveliest legs in London," may no longer be young (b. 1907)—and is indeed a bit rounder than in her prime—but her indomitable zip remains. In the '60s she starred on radio in the serial *The Dales*, playing the motherly Mrs. Dale. In '73, long absent from the stage, she headlined in the children's play *The Water Babies* at the Royalty Theatre. And, in '74, she published her autobiography, the rather sensational *Over My Shoulder*. Three times married and divorced, she has an adopted daughter and, by her, is several times a grandmother. Onscreen from 1923. IN: *This England, The Beloved Vagabond, There Goes the Bride, The Good Companions, Evergreen, First a Girl, It's Love Again, Head Over Heels in Love, Gangway, Sailing Along, Climbing High, Forever and a Day, Tom Thumb*, more.

MATTHEWS, LESTER (S. Cal.) The popular English-born character actor, in his 70s (b. 1900) but looking far younger, does almost as many TV commercials now as movies. But old-time fans may have to look twice to recognize him. Instead of the familiar bald pate, there's a handsome silver toupe with a matching (real) moustache. His commanding presence, though, remains unmistakable. A resident of Hollywood since 1934, he still lives there. Onscreen from 1931. IN: *Creeping Shadows* (English film), *Fires of Fate, Lloyds of London, Lancer Spy, The Adventures of Robin Hood, If I Were King, Across the Pacific, Tonight We Raid Calais, Ministry of Fear, Salty O'Rourke, Bulldog Drummond at Bay, Niagara, Sangaree, King Richard and the Crusaders, Flame of the Islands, Mary Poppins*, more.

MATTHEWS, WALTER (Conn.) Character. Onscreen from the '60s. IN: *Not With My Wife, You Don't*, more.

MATTINGLY, HEDLEY (S. Cal.) Character. Onscreen from the '60s. IN: *The Thrill of It All, Five Weeks in a Balloon, Torn Curtain*, more.

MATTOX, MATT (N.Y.) The nimble dance star, one of the brothers (Caleb) in *Seven Brides for Seven Brothers*, a bachelor still in his 50s (b. 1921), lives in Long Island City, just across the river from Manhattan. No longer a professional dancer—he gave up that career in the '60s—he has been choreographer of such Broadway musicals as *Jennie* and *What Makes Sammy Run?*, in addition to teaching dance. Onscreen from 1945. IN: *Yolanda and the Thief* (chorus dancer), *Easy to Wed, Good News, Something in the Wind, The Merry Widow, The I Don't Care Girl, Gentlemen Prefer Blondes, The Band Wagon, Brigadoon, The Girl Rush, Pepe*, more.

MATURE, VICTOR (S. Cal.) In the spring of '75, aged 59 and in his fifth marriage, he became a father for the first time; he and wife, Lorey, named her Victoria. On January 1, 1976, came the announcement of their expecting a second. His first marriage, to non-pro Frances Evans, was annulled and his subsequent ones—to Martha Stephenson Kemp, socialite Dorothy Berry, and Joy Urwick—ended in divorce. Though the actor officially "retired" after 1962's *The Tartars*, he has appeared in four pix since: *After the Fox* ('66), *Head* ('68), *Every Little Crook and Nanny* ('72), and, most recently, *The Escape of Nicholas and Alexandra* with Joan Fontaine and Rossano Brazzi. He also did, as a lark, a cameo role in *Won Ton Ton, the Dog Who Saved Hollywood*. As for future movies, Mature says, "I'm in no hurry. I'll do something if it's good." He can afford to wait. Living a life of luxury in Rancho Santa Fe (golfing, hunting), he is a very rich man from many business interests—restaurants, real estate, electronics—as well as from his earnings as a star. In addition, a dozen years ago he came into a considerable inheritance. He also can afford to—and does—eat five meals a day. And if the result is a heftier physique than before, perhaps that is what makes critics take him more seriously than in the past. Said the one on *Esquire*, after *Every Little Crook and Nanny*: "As Mafia boss Carmine Ganucci, he is massive, vigorous, vulgar, authentic, and splendid." The actor, who drives only Cadillacs, admits he really does not like to work. "I loaf very gracefully. There's a lot to be said for loafing if you know how to do it gracefully." A movie he would like to make, he adds, would be *The Black Knight*, in which he would star in full armor throughout. His double would do all the action scenes. But when the camera came in for a closeup, the visor would be lifted, and there would be the Mature phiz. Onscreen from 1939. IN: *The Housekeeper's Daughter, One Million B.C., Captain Caution, I Wake Up Screaming, My Gal Sal, Seven Days' Leave, My Darling Clementine, Kiss of Death, Moss Rose, Fury at Furnace Creek, Samson and Delilah, Easy Living, Wabash Avenue, Androcles and the Lion, Million Dollar Mermaid, Affair With a Stranger, The Robe, Demetrius and the Gladiators, Chief Crazy Horse, Zarak, Tank Force, China Doll, The Big Circus, Hannibal*, more.

MAUCH, BILLY (S. Cal.) Balding in his early 50s, just like identical twin brother Bobby (they were born in '24), Billy—or William, as his screen credit reads now—has been happily married for many years, has an almost-grown son, and lives in the San Fernando Valley. Today he is one of Hollywood's better-known sound editors. The winner of a Motion Picture Sound Editors' Golden Reel award for his work on *The Wild Bunch*, he often works at Warners where he and his brother were juvenile stars in the '30s. Little realized is that his acting career be-

gan earlier than Bobby's and continued longer. *Anthony Adverse*, in which he was the Fredric March character as a youngster, was his first. He was also in *Penrod and Sam* and *White Angel* without Bobby, and later, as a young adult (1948–51), in *The Accused, Street With No Name, Roseanna McCoy,* and *Bedtime for Bonzo*.

MAUCH, BOBBY (S. Cal.) This other half of the movies' most famous male-twin act appeared "officially" in just three pictures—all with brother Billy: *Penrod and His Twin Brother, The Prince and the Pauper,* and *Penrod's Double Trouble*. Unofficially, he played more than one of Billy's scenes in *Anthony Adverse*. After WW II service—they were together in the Air Force—Bobby never returned to acting. For a while he was a makeup man at Warners before switching to a career in film editing, working for several years for Jack Webb's Mark VII productions. He has been married and divorced, is now, of course, known as Bob, has a house in the Valley, and he and Billy remain as close as ever.

MAUDE, MARGERY (N.Y.) In her 90s now (b. 1889), the English character actress remained professionally active through a 1968 revival of *My Fair Lady* in New York, in which she played Mrs. Higgins. Onscreen from the '50s. IN: *You're Never Too Young, The Birds and the Bees*, more.

MAUDE-ROXBY, RODDY (Eng.) Support. Onscreen from 1960. IN: *The Bliss of Mrs. Blossom*, more.

MAULDIN, BILL (N.M.) The real-life GI whose cartoons of mud-slogging foot soldiers, "Willie and Joe," in WW II catapulted him to fame—and a Pulitzer Award—resides in Santa Fe (with third wife, Chris), is in his bearded 50s (b. 1922), and does political cartoons (five per week) for the Chicago *Sun-Times* and 250 other papers. A high school dropout, he has won a second Pulitzer for his editorial cartoons, holds five honorary doctorates from as many universities, and, in '74, taught a seminar on cartooning at Yale. He commuted between New Haven, his Chicago office, and Santa Fe in a twin-engine plane that he pilots himself. There has been, besides success, tragedy and misfortune. His second wife was killed in an automobile accident several years ago, and, while he has been undaunted by this, he himself has suffered an alarming and melancholy disability—severe arthritis in both hands. Onscreen from 1951. IN: *Teresa, The Red Badge of Courage, Up Front*.

MAUNDER, WAYNE (S. Cal.) Leading man. Onscreen in the '70s. IN: *The Seven Minutes*, more.

MAUR, MEINHART (Eng.) Character. Onscreen from the '30s. IN: *Rembrandt, Dr. Syn, Candlelight in Algeria, The Wooden Horse, The Tales of Hoffmann, Decameron Nights, Never Let Me Go, Malaga*, more.

MAUREY, NICOLE (Fr.) Former leading lady. Inactive in this decade in movies. Onscreen in France from the '40s. IN: *Blondine, Diary of a Country Priest*, more. Onscreen in America and internationally from 1953. IN: *Little Boy Lost, Secret of the Incas, The Bold and the Brave, Me and the Colonel, The Scapegoat, The Jaywalkers, High Time, The Most Wanted Man in the World, Day of the Triffids, Why Bother to Knock?*, more.

MAX, EDWIN (S. Cal.) Character. Onscreen from the '40s. IN: *Stairway to Heaven, The Set-Up, Thieves' Highway, Side Street, Love That Brute, The Well, Bloodhounds of Broadway*, more.

MAXWELL, FRANK (S. Cal.) Character. Onscreen from 1959. IN: *Lonelyhearts, By Love Possessed, Ada, The Intruder, The Haunted Palace*, more.

MAXWELL, JENNY (S. Cal.) Former ingenue; inactive now. Onscreen from 1959. IN: *Blue Denim, Blue Hawaii*, more.

MAXWELL, LOIS (Eng.) The Warners' starlet of the '40s has lived and worked in England since 1950, notably as Miss Moneypenny in the James Bond movies. Onscreen from 1947. IN: *That Hagen Girl, The Big Punch, The Decision of Christopher Blake, The Dark Past, The Crime Doctor's Diary, Scotland Yard Inspector, Satellite in the Sky, Lolita, The Haunting, Dr. No, From Russia with Love, Goldfinger, Thunderball, The Man with the Golden Gun*, more.

MAY, DONALD (N.Y.) Leading man. Onscreen from 1961. IN: *The Crowded Sky, Kisses for My President; Follow Me, Boys!;* more.

MAY, ELAINE (N.Y.) Comedienne-director. Onscreen from 1967. IN: *Enter Laughing, Luv, A New Leaf.*

MAYAMA, MIKO (S. Cal.) Leading lady. Onscreen from the '60s. IN: *Impasse, The Hawaiians*, more.

MAYEHOFF, EDDIE (S. Cal.) Character. Onscreen from 1951. IN: *That's My Boy!, The Stooge, Artists and Models, How to Murder Your Wife, The Military Policeman*, more.

MAYER, CHARLES (N.Y.) Character. Onscreen in the '70s. IN: *Mister Buddwing, The Night They Raided Minsky's*, more.

MAYNE, FERDY (Eng.) Character. Onscreen from the '40s. IN: *The Blue Parrot, Hotel Sahara, The Divided Heart, Gentlemen Marry Brunettes, Abandon Ship, Blue Murder at St. Trinian's, Third Man on the Mountain, The Fearless Vampire Killers (or, Pardon Me but Your Teeth Are in My Neck), Innocent Bystanders*, more.

MAYO, VIRGINIA (S. Cal.) The widow of Michael O'Shea (d. 1973), she continued to act on the stage in stock and dinner theatres after giving up her screen career in '67. The mother of a grown daughter, she remains a most attractive woman in her 50s (b. 1922), with reddish-brown hair now, and has lately resumed her Hollywood career via cameo roles in TV dramas. Particularly effective was her performance in an episode of *Police Story* seen late in '75—as a tipsy trollop arrested for speeding, and simultaneously sexy, amusing, and touching. Onscreen from 1944. IN: *Jack London, Up in Arms, The Princess and the Pirate, The Kid from Brooklyn, The Best Years of Our Lives, The Secret Life of Walter Mitty, Colorado Territory, Always Leave Them Laughing, White Heat, The Flame and the Arrow, Painting the Clouds with Sunshine, The Iron Mistress, She's Back on Broadway, King Richard and the Crusaders, The Proud Ones, The Big Land, Jet Over the Atlantic, Fort Utah*, more.

MAYRON, MELANIE (N.Y.) Support. Onscreen in the '70s. IN: *Gable and Lombard*, more.

MAZURKI, MIKE (S. Cal.) Yesterday's sinister menace is today's heroically admirable character star, as in 1975's *Challenge to Be Free*. Twice married and the father of two married daughters, he still looks, in his 60s (b. 1909), like a man who could whip his weight in wildcats. And, despite his old screen image, he is one of Hollywood's most scholarly gentlemen —university educated, speaking several Slavic languages, reading and writing Russian and Ukrainian. Totally compatible with his past movie reputation is that he, a former professional wrestler, has for the past 20 years enjoyed a second highly active career—refereeing championship wrestling matches in the States, Europe, and the Orient. Onscreen from 1941. IN: *The Shanghai Gesture, Behind the Rising Sun, Summer Storm; Murder, My Sweet; The Spanish Main, I Walk Alone, Nightmare Alley, Unconquered, Come to the Stable, Samson and Delilah, Night and the City, The Dark City, The Egyptian, Blood Alley, Hell Ship Mutiny, Some Like It Hot, Pocketful of Miracles, Four for Texas, Requiem for a Heavyweight, The Adventures of Bullwhip Griffin, Mad Trapper of the Yukon*, more.

MAZURSKY, PAUL (N.Y.) Director of *I Love You Alice B. Toklas!, Taxi Driver*, etc. Initially an actor. Onscreen from 1953. IN: *Fear and Desire, Blackboard Jungle, Deathwatch*, more.

McALISTER, MARY (S. Cal.) In her 60s now, she has not acted on the screen since *On the Level*, made in 1930 just before she married a successful young businessman. But, still living near Hollywood, the onetime leading lady (and earlier child actress) has occasionally participated in little-theater productions—just for the fun of it. Onscreen from the early '20s. IN: *Ashes of Vengeance, The Boomerang, One Minute to Play, The Waning Sex, Singed, Loves of An Actress*, more.

McANALLY, RAY (Eng.) Support. Onscreen from 1957. IN: *She Didn't Say No, The Naked Edge, Shake Hands with the Devil, Billy Budd*, more.

McANDREW, MARIANNE (S. Cal.) Leading lady. Onscreen from 1969. IN: *Hello, Dolly!; The Seven Minutes, The Bat People*, more.

McAVOY, MAY (S. Cal.) The sweetness in her face, ever apparent onscreen, was no lie. And in her white-haired 70s (b. 1901) it is still there, the gentle purity that made her so appealing in all her films, and particularly so in her two best silents: *Sentimental Tommy* and *The Enchanted Cottage*. They are her favorites also, together with *The Jazz Singer* with Al Jolson. The '75 reissue of *The Jolson Story*, in which she did not appear, of course, brought her considerable pleasure, for she holds an abiding affection for her onetime costar. Even before it was brought back, she had said, "I saw *The Jolson Story* four times, and I thought Al's voice was greater then than it was when he was in his prime." She also recalls that, not long before his death, when Jolson did *The Jazz Singer* on the radio, "I listened with tears in my eyes." May left her starring career when she married Maurice G. Cleary, then vice-president and treasurer of United Artists. He is retired now and they live unpretentiously in Beverly Hills on, she carefully points out, laughing, "the wrong side." They have a son, Patrick, who has given them several grandchildren. Until two decades ago, May continued to act, at the studio where she had starred in the first *Ben Hur*, in minor roles, simply because she enjoyed being a part of it all. She did not need the money and it mattered not a bit to her that producers feared featuring her too prominently, knowing that the sight of a familiar face to oldtime fans would set them buzzing, detracting from the picture. She was enormously pleased when, in his book *The Movies in the Age of Innocence*, film historian Edward Wagenknecht noted the frequent comparisons between Marguerite Clark and May McAvoy and said of the latter: "But she was a far greater artist, with a far greater imagination —one of the most sensitive actresses indeed that our screen has known." May McAvoy reflects on this and observes—predictably— "Well, Marguerite Clark was awfully good." Onscreen from 1918. IN: *A Perfect Lady, A Private Scandal, The Top of New York, Clarence, Kick In, Grumpy, West of the Water Tower, Tarnish, The Mad Whirl, Lady Windemere's Fan, Fire Brigade, Matinee Ladies, If I Were Single, The Lion and the Mouse, The Terror, Caught in the Fog, No Defense, Stolen Kisses*, more.

McBAIN, DIANE (S. Cal.) When the screen career of this blonde leading lady, popular at Warners in the '60s, waned, she returned to school in Hollywood and became an executive secretary. She took a leave of absence in '72 when her former studio boss (and former actor), William Orr, costarred her at MGM in *Wicked, Wicked*, which he produced. Since then she has graduated to being a real estate agent, and for some time has been associated with Lakeworld Enterprises, a land development company near Victorville. In her 30s (b. 1941), she is still beautiful and still single. Onscreen from 1960. IN: *Ice Palace, Claudelle Inglish, Parrish; Mary, Mary; A Distant Trumpet, Spin-Out, Thunder Alley, The Mini-Skirt Mob, The Delta Factor, The Savage Season*, more.

McBRIDE, PATRICIA (N.Y.) Ballet star. Onscreen in 1967. IN: *A Midsummer Night's Dream*.

McCALL, MITZI (S. Cal.) Leading lady. Onscreen from 1955. IN: *You're Never Too Young*, more.

McCALLA, IRISH (S. Cal.) The leggy star of the TV series of the '50s *Sheena, Queen of the Jungle*, she is now a painter, having had several exhibitions in Los Angeles, and having had her pictures bought by—among others—Mrs. Richard Nixon. Onscreen from 1959. IN: *Five Gates to Hell, She Demons, The Beat Generation, Five Bold Women, Hands of a Stranger*, more.

McCALLISTER, LON (S. Cal.) The wavy locks are just a memory, but the boyish smile remains, as does his determination to remain a bachelor. In his 50s (b. 1923) and independently wealthy from early-career real estate investments, McCallister says: "I wouldn't make a good husband. I like the freedom to get on a boat and go across the seas [something he's done more than once, sometimes as a crew member on merchant ships]. I also have a motor home, and I usually spend several months each year just driving and stopping wherever my desires lead me. That isn't the picture of an ideal family man, now is it?" When in California, he lives in a splendid beach house he has owned at Malibu for 30 years. Growing up in Hollywood, he was an extra and small-parts player before landing his star-making role in *Stage Door Canteen*. He remained a star for exactly one decade and was one—and still only 30—when he quit after 1953's *Combat Squad*. While actually no longer of Hollywood, the former actor maintains close ties with many associates from his past. One is director George Cukor. In '36 Cukor directed the then 13-year-old in a small role in *Romeo and Juliet*; in '44, in a leading role in *Winged Victory*; and in '74, when the director flew to Moscow to discuss production details of the Russian-American production of *The Blue Bird,* McCallister accompanied him there. One thing he has no further desire to do is act. "Being a movie star was great," says the round-faced, graying man who looks now like an investment broker, "but I never considered doing it for a lifetime. I always thought of retiring, of going to sea, of writing. I loved being in pictures, but I love privacy more. I wanted to blend into a crowd. To be myself. To go where I pleased without causing a traffic jam. I've succeeded in this and I'm happy." Onscreen from 1936. IN: *Souls at Sea, Babes in Arms, Henry Aldrich for President, Home in Indiana, Thunder in the Valley, The Red House; Scudda Hoo! Scudda Hay!; The Story of Seabiscuit, The Big Cat, The Boy from Indiana, A Yank in Korea, Montana Territory*, more.

McCALLUM, DAVID (S. Cal.) Leading man. Onscreen in England from 1956. IN: *Hell Drivers, The Secret Plan, Robbery Under Arms, A Night to Remember*, more. Onscreen in America from 1963. IN: *The Great Escape, The Greatest Story Ever Told, Around the World Under the Sea, One Spy Too Many, The Spy with My Face, Three Bites on the Apple, Mosquito Squadron*, more.

McCALLUM, JOHN (Australia) After almost a decade of starring in English movies, this native of Brisbane returned to Australia where he stars in—and often directs—stage shows (*Roar Like a Dove, Relatively Speaking*, etc.). He and his wife, British star Googie Withers, live near Melbourne. Onscreen from 1944. IN: *Joe Goes Back, Bush Christmas, It Always Rains on Sunday, Miranda* (with Googie Withers), *Valley of the Eagles, Melba, The Long Memory, Trent's Last Case, Lady Godiva Rides Again, Trouble in the Glen*, more.

McCALLUM, NEIL (Eng.) Support. Onscreen from the '50s. IN: *The Devil's Disciple, Lisa, The Woman Who Wouldn't Die, The Lost Continent, Quest for Love*, more. (Died 1976.)

McCAMBRIDGE, MERCEDES (S. Cal.) Support. Won the Best Supporting Actress Oscar in *All the King's Men*, her debut movie. Nominated in the same category in *Giant*. Onscreen from 1949. IN: *Lightning Strikes Twice, The Scarf, Inside Straight, Johnny Guitar, A Farewell to Arms, Touch of Evil, Suddenly Last Summer, Angel Baby, The Counterfeit Killer, 99 Women, The Exorcist* (voice of Satan on the soundtrack), *Thieves*, more.

McCANN, CHUCK Character lead. Onscreen from 1968. IN: *The Heart Is a Lonely Hunter, The Projectionist, The World of Hans Christian Andersen, Jennifer on My Mind, Herbie Rides Again*, more.

McCARTHY, KEVIN (N.Y.) Costar. Nominated for Best Supporting Actor Oscar in *Death of a Salesman*. Onscreen from 1951. IN: *Drive a Crooked Road, Nightmare, An Annapolis Story, Invasion of the Body Snatchers, The Misfits, A Gathering of Eagles, The Best Man, An Affair of the Skin, Mirage, A Big Hand for the Little Lady, A Time for Heroes; If He Hollers, Let Him Go; Kansas City Bomber, Buffalo Bill and the Indians*, more.

McCARTHY, LIN (S. Cal.) Support. Onscreen from the '50s. IN: *Yellowback, The D I*, more.

McCARTHY, NEIL (Eng.) Support. Onscreen from the '60s. IN: *Zulu, Where Eagles Dare*, more.

McCARTHY, NOBU (S. Cal.) Leading lady. Jerry Lewis picked this young beauty—Canadian-born but reared in Japan during WW II—as his leading lady in *The Geisha Boy*. Her popularity with casting directors lasted for two more years and five more pictures. Involuntarily "retired" after 1961, she married (divorced now) and had two children. Good roles for Oriental actresses, she found, came seldom. She did not get another major career opportunity for 15 years. In 1976, she costarred in the NBC-TV special *Farewell to Manzanar*, about Japanese-Americans interned in detention camps in WW II. Personally still exquisitely beautiful, and only in her 40s, she gladly deglamorized herself to play the mother role, a woman in her mid-50s, saying hopefully: "The drama could open up more opportunities." Onscreen from 1958. IN: *The Geisha Boy, Tokyo After Dark, Five Gates to Hell, Wake Me When It's Over, Walk Like a Dragon, Two Loves*, more.

McCARTNEY, PAUL (N.Y.) Of the Beatles. Onscreen from 1964. IN: *A Hard Day's Night, Help!*, more.

McCARTY, MARY (N.Y.) A bit heavier, but funnier than ever, the singer-comedienne has starred only on Broadway in recent years. She was in *Follies* and returned in the 1975–76 season in the musical *Chicago* with Gwen Verdon. Critics, hailing her performance in the latter, said: "Mary McCarty is impressive as a bulky [prison] matron on the take." Onscreen from 1938. IN: *Rebecca of Sunnybrook Farm, Keep Smiling, The Sullivans, The French Line, My Six Loves*, more.

McCAY, PEGGY (S. Cal.) Leading lady. Onscreen from 1958. IN: *Uncle Vanya, Lad: A Dog, FBI Code 98*, more.

McCLANAHAN, RUE (S. Cal.) Supporting actress. Onscreen in the '70s. IN: *The People Next Door, The Pursuit of Happiness, They Might Be Giants, Some of My Best Friends Are.* . . .

McCLENDON, ERNESTINE (N.Y.) Black character actress. Retired from acting, she has been an actors' agent since 1962. Onscreen from 1957. IN: *A Face in the Crowd, The Last Angry Man, The Apartment, The Rat Race, The Young Doctors, The Young Savages*, more.

McCLORY, SEAN (S. Cal.) Character. Onscreen from 1949. IN: *Beyond Glory, The Daughter of Rosie O'Grady, Storm Warning, Anne of the Indies, The Quiet Man, Botany Bay, Island in the Sky, Them, The Long Gray Line, Cheyenne Autumn; Follow Me, Boys!; The Happiest Millionaire, Bandolero*, more.

McCLURE, DOUG (S. Cal.) Costar. Onscreen from 1957. IN: *The Enemy Below, Gidget, Because They're Young, The Unforgiven, The Lively Set, Shenandoah, Beau Geste, Nobody's Perfect, The Land That Time Forgot*, more.

McCONNELL, GLADYS (S. Cal.) In her 60s now, she has been married (second husband) since '32, hasn't worked in pictures since *Parade of the West* ('30) and, enjoying retirement, lives near Hollywood. Onscreen from the '20s. IN: *Three's a Crowd, The Chaser*, more.

McCONNELL, KEITH (S. Cal.) Character. Onscreen from the '50s. IN: *Kind Lady, Mutiny on the Bounty, Breakheart Pass*, more.

McCORD, KENT (S. Cal.) Leading man from television. Onscreen from the '60s. IN: *The Young Warriors*, more.

McCORMACK, PATTY (S. Cal.) The pigtailed girl who was so "bad" she was great in *The Bad Seed* (nominated as Best Supporting Actress at age 11) is now in her early 30s (b. 1945), lives in Woodland Hills, and is the mother of two youngsters. She has been married since '67 to childhood sweetheart Robert Catania (they met

in the fourth grade in a Hollywood Catholic school), who owns an Italian restaurant in the San Fernando Valley. Patty's acting schedule is still a busy one—onstage in Los Angeles (in *Time of the Cuckoo* with Jean Stapleton), in movies (*The Hephaestus Plague*), and particularly on TV. In the '74–75 season alone she was in *Police Story, Manhunter, Barnaby Jones, Streets of San Francisco*, and the ABC "Wide World Mystery" *Murder Impossible*. Onscreen from 1951. IN: *Two Gals and a Guy, All Mine to Give, Kathy O', The Adventures of Huckleberry Finn, Maryjane, The Mini-Skirt Mob, The Young Runaways, Born Wild, Bugs*, more.

McCOWEN, ALEC (Eng.) Character star. Onscreen from 1952. IN: *The Cruel Sea, Time Without Pity, A Midsummer Night's Dream, The Loneliness of the Long Distance Runner, The Agony and the Ecstasy, The Devil's Own, The Hawaiians, Frenzy, Travels With My Aunt*, more.

McCOY, SID (S. Cal.) Black support. Onscreen from the '60s. IN: *The One With the Fuzz, Medium Cool, Colossus, The Lost Man*, more.

McCOY, TIM (Ariz.) Col. Tim McCoy, Cowboy Star. The title, at this writing, remains current. Asked what he's up to these days, he replies, "I stay in shape cracking Australian bull whips while I'm headlining Tommy Scott's Country Music Circus. We play 300 days a year." The great Western favorite's one regret is that they won't let him ride a horse in the show, because of his age (b. 1891). When home —Thanksgiving Day to February—he's at his ranch near Nogales, where he lives with wife, Inga Arvad, the noted Danish journalist he married in '45. They have two sons, Ronnie and Terry, business men who are active in Arizona politics. Their house is a magnificent Spanish Colonial affair with windowless walls turned to the outside world, sunlit patio within and fireplaces in almost every room. The Colonel (authentic military title that he bore in both World Wars—and in the second of which he won the Bronze Star) was married once before—to Agnes Miller of the New York theatrical-society family. This marriage of contrasting cultures produced two sons, much friction, and ended in divorce in '28. Col. Tim McCoy, the last of the fabled cowboys of the silent (and talkie) screen, and still going strong. Onscreen from 1925. IN: *The Thundering Herd, Winners of the Wilderness, The Frontiersman, Law of the Range, Wyoming, Beyond the Sierras, Sioux Blood, The Desert Rider, The Indians Are Coming* (serial), *The Riding Tornado, The End of the Trail, Square Shooter, Roarin' Guns, Texas Wildcats, Outlaws of the Rio Grande, Ghost Town Law, Riders of the West, Around the*

World in 80 Days, Run of the Arrow, Requiem for a Gunfighter, more.

McCREA, ANN (S. Cal.) Leading lady. Onscreen from 1955. IN: *Artists and Models, Kiss Them for Me, China Doll; Girls! Girls! Girls!; Welcome to Hard Times*, more.

McCREA, JODY (N. M.) Former leading man. Son of Joel McCrea. Onscreen from 1956. IN: *The First Texan, Lafayette Escadrille, Beach Party, Muscle Beach Party, The Glory Stompers*, more. (See below.)

McCREA, JOEL (S. Cal.) Joe, his friends call him. They are legion and they agree with this recent summation of Ginger Rogers, his *Primrose Path* costar: "Joe embraces everybody with his heart the first time he meets them. Few of us would dare be as open with our friendship as he. One of the nicest, warmest, most generous of heart men in the world, he truly loves everybody. You must have a very genuine love for humanity to risk having your feelings taken advantage of like this." In 1975 the star, who is now in his 70s (b. 1905), laughingly agreed that "somebody" had taken advantage of him—talked him into making a comeback in the picture *Mustang Country*. "I wake up in the morning wondering why I said yes," he said on the Calgary location. "I'm torn between hoping it's a hit or a flop. I've decided I'm not going to read any more scripts." This, in which he is a retired rodeo rider, is his first since 1962's *Ride the High Country*. He had been quite content running his two ranches (about 100 miles from Hollywood), officiating as president of the board of directors of the National Cowboy Hall of Fame, working with the YMCA and various boys clubs, and narrating such rodeo films as *Great American Cowboy* ('74). A veteran of 82 movies (not counting silents in which he was an extra or stunt double), he does not find it difficult to do without them. He has been married since '33 to his former leading lady Frances Dee —silver-haired now but still a great beauty as she rounds out her 60s (b. 1907). They have three sons: Jody (b. 1934), David (b. 1935), and Peter (b. 1955), a recent college graduate. Both Jody, a former actor, and David are ranchers, living near Roswell, N.M. Married a number of years, David has four times made the senior McCreas grandparents. His youngest is named Robert Joel, for his dad. Besides ranching, bachelor Jody participates in rodeos throughout the Southwest. Jody and David both learned ranching firsthand, growing up as they did on the vast McCrea homestead near Camarillo—so sprawling, in fact, that it takes 25 miles of barbed wire to encircle it. And they grew up hearing authentic tales of the Old West—for Joel McCrea's grandfather, as a stagecoach driver in the Pacific Southwest, survived more than one Apache Indian attack. "Joe's first love was ranching," recalls Dorothy Mackaill, his *Kept Husbands* ('31) leading lady, and a friend ever since. "Stardom was really a means to an end so that he could afford to own a ranch. Will Rogers, his friend and mentor, kept telling Joel, 'Get yourself a piece of land and you'll never have to worry.' He even helped Joel pick out choice ranchland in Simi Valley." There you will find him today—and only there in the future, if the actor holds firm to his decision to make no more pictures. Onscreen from 1923. IN: *Penrod and Sam, The Jazz Age, Dynamite, The Silver Horde, The Plutocrat, Lost Squadron, Bird of Paradise, Our Betters, The Silver Cord, The Richest Girl in the World, Private Worlds, Our Little Girl, Barbary Coast, These Three, Come and Get It, Banjo on My Knee, Interns Can't Take Money, Dead End, Wells Fargo, Three Blind Mice, Union Pacific, Foreign Correspondent, Sullivan's Travels, The Great Man's Lady, The Palm Beach Story, The More the Merrier, Buffalo Bill, The Unseen, Ramrod, Four Faces West, Colorado Territory, Stars in My Crown, Cattle Drive, The San Francisco Story, Lone Hand, Black Horse Canyon, The Oklahoman, Trooper Hook, Fort Massacre*, more.

McCREERY, BUD (N.Y.) Singer-actor-composer. Onscreen in 1950. IN: *The West Point Story*.

McCULLOCH, ANDREW (Eng.) Character. Onscreen from the '60s. IN: *Cry of the Banshee, The Last Valley, Kidnapped, Macbeth*, more.

McCULLOUGH, PHILO (S. Cal.) In his 80s now (b. 1893), this fine Western heavy, widower of actress Laura Anson (d. 1968), played a cameo role in *They Shoot Horses, Don't They?* ('69), which was his first in two decades, then retired again. Onscreen from the teens. IN: *Soldiers of Fortune, Trilby, Dick Turpin, The Boomerang, Easy Pickings; Smile, Brother, Smile; The Night Flyer, The Leatherneck, On the Border, The Sky Spider, The Lawless Nineties, Defenders of the Law, Sunset Trail, Wheels of Destiny, Thunder over Texas, Texas Trail, The Buccaneer, That Way with Women, Stampede*, more.

McCURRY, JOHN (N.Y.) Black support. Onscreen from 1959. IN: *The Last Mile, The Pawnbroker, The Landlord, Little Murders, Where's Poppa?*, more.

McCUTCHEON, BILL (N.Y.) Character. Onscreen from 1964. IN: *Santa Claus Conquers the Martians, Viva Max!*, more.

McDEVITT, RUTH (S. Cal.) Character. On-screen from 1951. IN: *The Guy Who Came Back, The Parent Trap, Boys' Night Out, The Birds, Love Is a Ball, Dear Heart, The Out-of-Towners, The Shakiest Gun in the West, Angel in My Pocket, Change of Habit*, more. (Died 1976.)

McDONALD, WILLIAM (N.Y.) Character. Onscreen from 1927. IN: *Twinkletoes*, more.

McDOWALL, RODDY (N.Y.) Costar; former juvenile. Onscreen in England from 1936. IN: *Murder in the Family, Scruffy, Dead Man's Shoes, This England*, more. Onscreen in America from 1941. IN: *How Green Was My Valley, Man Hunt, Confirm or Deny, Son of Fury, The Pied Piper, My Friend Flicka, Lassie Come Home, The White Cliffs of Dover, Keys of the Kingdom, Molly and Me; Thunderhead, Son of Flicka; Holiday in Mexico, Green Grass of Wyoming, Tuna Clipper, The Steel Fist, Midnight Lace, Cleopatra, That Darn Cat, Inside Daisy Clover, The Loved One, Planet of the Apes* (and its sequels), *The Midas Run; Angel, Angel, Down We Go; Hello Down There, The Poseidon Adventure, Funny Lady*, more.

McDOWELL, MALCOLM (Eng.) Star. On-screen from 1969. IN: *If, Figures in a Landscape, A Clockwork Orange, Long Ago Tomorrow, O Lucky Man, Royal Flash, The Voyage of the Damned*, more.

McEACHIN, JAMES (S. Cal.) Black star. On-screen from the '60s. IN: *True Grit; Hello, Dolly!; The Undefeated, Play Misty for Me, Buck and the Preacher, Fuzz*, more.

McENERY, JOHN (Eng.) Leading man. On-screen from the '60s. IN: *Romeo and Juliet, Bartleby, Nicholas and Alexandra, Galileo, The Land That Time Forgot*, more.

McENERY, PETER (Eng.) Leading man. On-screen from 1960. IN: *Tunes of Glory, The Moonspinners, The Game Is Over, Negatives, Entertaining Mr. Sloane, The Atlantic Wall, Better a Widow, Tales That Witness Madness*, more.

McEWAN, GERALDINE (Eng.) Support. On-screen in the '70s. IN: *Escape from the Dark*, more.

McFARLAND, PACKY (N.Y.) Character. On-screen from the '60s. IN: *A Fine Madness, Any Wednesday, A Man Called Adam, Sweet November, Wait Until Dark, The Night They Raided Minsky's*, more.

McFARLAND, SPANKY (Tex.) Short and roly-poly still, in his 40s (b. 1928), George (Robert Phillips) McFarland has been happily married since '56 (his second), has two youngsters, and, sporting horn-rim glasses, is a sales-training supervisor who teaches agents in the Dallas area to sell the consumer products of Philco-Ford. Coincidentally, he was born in Dallas, where his elderly mother also lives now, but was taken to Hollywood at an early age. From '31 until the series ended in '45, "Spanky" was easily the most famous of all "Our Gang" kids. He also was featured in numerous full-length films. His childhood fame, thanks to TV's "The Little Rascals" (the "Our Gang" shorts under a different label), refuses to fade away. Only recently has he surrendered to the inevitable and decided to go with the nostalgic tide. In the summer of '74 he guested with Darla Hood (their first meeting since '54) on *The Mike Douglas Show* in Philadelphia. Five months later, seeing one another for the first time in three decades, "Spanky" and "Stymie" Beard were honored guests at the *Our Gang Comedy Reunion* in Passaic, N.J. In '75 he did a "special guest" cameo in the movie *Moonrunners*, starring James Mitchum. And a promoter in Pennsylvania, Rick Saphire, has stated in *Variety* that his firm handles "The Little Rascals"— "Spanky," Darla, and "Stymie"—for personal appearances. The former child actor also says of the phony "Spanky McFarlands" who appear at fairs and in clubs around the country, cashing in on his name: "I do everything I can to locate them and have them prosecuted." Prior to his present position in Dallas, he held a similar one for the same firm in Philadelphia. And before that he was the state sales manager for a wine company in Oklahoma, after hosting a children's TV show in Tulsa, operating a restaurant, etc. These various occupations he pursued after trying free-lancing in movies as a young man after service in the Army. While asserting that the "Our Gang" kids had a "lack of formal education," he adds, "But we got a good education. You can get a good education even if you don't go to college." A formal education, though, is what he wants for his children. He has a son, Verne (b. 1957), a college student now, and a daughter, Betsy (b. 1962). "My son is interested in science and my daughter in acting," he says. "I guess some of it just rubbed off on her. They're both very outgoing kids, very gregarious, especially Betsy." Of his wife, he says, "Her name is Doris and she comes from Pawnee, Oklahoma. Though we lived in the East several years, we've always considered Oklahoma 'home'—especially Oklahoma City, where I lived for 11 years." And the McFarlands' life today, he says, is "just a very normal family life." As for fan mail, he adds, a trifle wearily, that, yes, it still rolls in. "But fan mail is an ego-feeding thing and I don't need that. I'm a man lucky enough to have a life that is both satisfying and fulfilling." Onscreen from 1930. IN: "Our Gang" (89 episodes), *Kidnapped, Kentucky Kernels, The Trail of the Lonesome Pine, Peck's Bad Boy with the Circus*, more, including 1943's *Johnny Doughboy*, his last principal role.

McGAVIN, DARREN (S. Cal.) Costar. Onscreen from 1945. IN: *A Song to Remember, Counter-Attack, Queen for a Day, Summertime, The Man with the Golden Arm, Beau James, The Great Sioux Massacre, Ride the High Wind, Mission: Mars, Mrs. Pollifax—Spy, No Deposit No Return*, more.

McGEE, VONETTA (S. Cal.) Black star. Onscreen in the '70s. IN: *Melinda, Blacula, Hammer, Shaft in Africa, Detroit 9000, The Eiger Sanction, Thomasine and Bushrod*, more.

McGINN, WALTER (S. Cal.) Support. Onscreen in the '70s. IN: *The Parallax View*, more.

McGOOHAN, PATRICK (Eng.) Costar. Onscreen from 1955. IN: *Passage Home, I Am a Camera, Zarak, Hell Drivers, Elephant Gun, Three Lives of Thomasina, Walk in the Shadow, Ice Station Zebra, The Moonshine War; Mary, Queen of Scots; The Genius*, more.

McGRATH, PAUL (N.Y.) Character. Onscreen from 1938. IN: *The Parole Fixer, This Thing Called Love, Dead Men Tell, No Time for Love, A Face in the Crowd, Advise and Consent, Pendulum*, more.

McGRAW, CHARLES (S. Cal.) Character. Onscreen from 1943. IN: *The Mad Ghoul, They Came to Blow Up America, The Moon Is Down, The Killers, The Long Night, T-Men, The Threat, The Narrow Margin, War Paint, The Bridges at Toko-Ri, Joe Butterfly, Twilight for the Gods, The Defiant Ones, Man in the Net, Spartacus, The Horizontal Lieutenant, In Cold Blood, Hang 'Em High, Tell Them Willie Boy Is Here, A Boy and His Dog*, more.

McGUIRE, BIFF (N.Y.) Former leading man. Now primarily a stage character actor, on Broadway and elsewhere. Onscreen from 1955. IN: *The Phenix City Story, Station Six–Sahara, The Thomas Crown Affair, The Heart Is a Lonely Hunter*, more.

McGUIRE, DON (S. Cal.) The leading man of the '40s gave up his acting career in 1951 and has since been a movie director (*Johnny Concho, The Delicate Delinquent*, more) and writer (*Three Ring Circus, Bad Day at Black Rock,*

Suppose They Gave a War and Nobody Came?, others). Onscreen from 1945. IN: *Pride of the Marines, Pillow to Post, Shadow of a Woman, My Wild Irish Rose, Nora Prentiss, The Man I Love, Possessed, The Fuller Brush Man, Boston Blackie's Chinese Venture, Armed Car Robbery, Three Guys Named Mike, Double Dynamite*, more.

McGUIRE, DOROTHY (S. Cal.) Costar. Nominated for Best Actress Oscar in *Gentleman's Agreement*. In the past decade she has appeared in just one movie, 1971's *Flight of the Doves*, in which she portrayed a grandmother. But she was the voice of the mother in *Jonathan Livingston Seagull* and has often been featured in TV specials (*She Waits, The Runaways, Another Part of the Forest* and, in '76, *Rich Man, Poor Man*). Also, she takes great pride in the successful screen career of her daughter, leading lady Topo Swope. Onscreen from 1943. IN: *Claudia, A Tree Grows in Brooklyn, The Enchanted Cottage, The Spiral Staircase, Mister 880, Three Coins in the Fountain, Friendly Persuasion, A Summer Place, The Dark at the Top of the Stairs, Susan Slade, Summer Magic, The Greatest Story Ever Told*, more.

McGUIRE, KATHRYN (S. Cal.) Keaton's lovely young leading lady in *The Navigator*, etc., is in her 70s now (b. 1897), long retired, and living near Hollywood with happy memories of her brief career and her 28-year marriage to studio publicist George Landy, which only ended with his death in '55. Onscreen from the early '20s. IN: *The Silent Call, The Crossroads of New York, The Shriek of Araby, Sherlock Jr., Naughty But Nice, Lilac Time; The Long, Long Trail; Children of the Ritz, Synthetic Sin, The Lost Zeppelin*, more.

McGUIRE, MAEVE (N.Y.) Support. Onscreen in the '70s. IN: *End of the Road, For Love of Ivy*.

McHUGH, FRANK (Conn.) Playing the comic lead in the out-of-town tryouts of *No, No, Nanette* (he did not come into town with the show) constituted this grand character star's only acting in recent years. In more than 150 pix between the silent *M'lle Modiste* and 1967's *Easy Come, Easy Go*, he is in his 70s (b. 1898), and most comfortably retired in Cos Cob. He has been married since '33 to Dorothy Margaret Spencer, has two sons and one daughter, numerous grandchildren, and no further interest in performing. Onscreen from 1926. IN: *Bright Lights, Little Caesar, The Front Page, One Way Passage, 42nd Street, Elmer the Great, Fashions of 1934, Six Day Bike Race, Page Miss Glory, Gold Diggers of 1935, Bullets or Ballots, Three Men on a Horse, Boy Meets Girl, Four*

Daughters, Wings of the Navy, The Roaring Twenties, Till We Meet Again, Back Street, Manpower, Going My Way, A Medal for Benny, State Fair, The Velvet Touch, It Happens Every Thursday, The Last Hurrah, Say One for Me, more.

McINTIRE, JOHN (S. Cal.) Character. Onscreen from 1948. IN: *Black Bart, Call Northside 777, Command Decision, An Act of Murder, Red Canyon, Francis, Winchester 73, No Sad Songs for Me, Westward the Women, Glory Alley, Mississippi Gambler, Stranger on Horseback, The Light in the Forest, Elmer Gantry, Psycho, Summer and Smoke, Two Rode Together, Challenge to be Free, Rooster Cogburn,* more.

McINTIRE, TIM (S. Cal.) Support. Son of John McIntire and his wife, actress Jeanette Nolan. Onscreen from the '60s. IN: *The Sterile Cuckoo; Aloha, Bobby and Rose; The Gumball Rally,* more.

McKAY, ALLISON (S. Cal.) Support. Onscreen from the '60s. IN: *Doctor, You've Got to Be Kidding; The Lost Man, Airport, Superdad,* more.

McKAY, GARDNER (S. Cal.) Leading man from TV. Now a writer. Onscreen in 1964. IN: *The Pleasure Seekers.*

McKAY, SCOTT (S. Cal.) Character; former leading man and the widower of Ann Sheridan. Costarred on Broadway, 1975–76, in *Absurd Person Singular.* Onscreen from 1944. IN: *Thirty Seconds Over Tokyo, Guest in the House, Kiss and Tell, Duel in the Sun,* more.

McKAYLE, DONALD (N.Y.) Dancer-actor-choreographer. Onscreen from 1957. IN: *Edge of the City, Jazz on a Summer's Day, On the Sound,* more.

McKECHNIE, DONNA (N.Y.) Leading lady. Broadway dance star (*A Chorus Line, Company,* etc.). Onscreen in 1974. IN: *The Little Prince.*

McKEE, LONETTE (S. Cal.) Leading lady. Onscreen in the '70s. IN: *Sparkle,* more.

McKELLEN, IAN (Eng.) Leading man. Onscreen from 1969. IN: *Alfred the Great, The Promise, Thank You All Very Much,* more.

McKENNA, PEGGY (N.Y.) Support. Onscreen from the '60s. IN: *Bananas, Carnal Knowledge, Lovers and Other Strangers, Diary of a Mad Housewife,* more.

McKENNA, SIOBHAN (Eng.) Character star. Onscreen from 1946. IN: *Hungry Hill, Daughter of Darkness, The Adventurers, King of Kings, The Playboy of the Western World, Dr. Zhivago,* more.

McKENNA, T. P. (Eng.) Support. Onscreen from 1964. IN: *Girl with Green Eyes, Young Cassidy, Ulysses, Anne of the Thousand Days, Villain, Straw Dogs,* more.

McKENNA, VIRGINIA (Eng.) *Born Free,* in which she and her husband, Bill Travers, costarred, brought both greater popularity than they had previously enjoyed. Since, the actress has appeared in just three movies: *Ring of Bright Water, An Elephant Called Slowly,* and 1970's *Waterloo.* She has, instead, devoted herself to writing (two books, outgrowths of *Born Free: On Playing with Lions, Some of My Friends Have Tails*), rearing their four children, and making occasional appearances on TV or the stage in England. Onscreen from 1952. IN: *The Cruel Sea, A Town Like Alice, The Smallest Show on Earth, The Barretts of Wimpole Street, The Wreck of the Mary Deare; Two Living, One Dead;* more.

McKENNON, DALLAS (S. Cal.) Character. Onscreen from the '50s. IN: *Tom Thumb, The Misadventures of Merlin Jones,* more.

McKENZIE, ELLA (S. Cal.) Retired character actress. Widow of comedian Billy Gilbert, to whom she was married 35 years. Onscreen from the '30s. IN: *Alice Adams,* more.

McKENZIE, FAY (S. Cal.) For well over two decades this popular leading lady in Gene Autry Westerns and Republic B's of the '40s has been the wife of writer-producer Thomas Waldman. They live in Beverly Hills and have a grown son. She was once, briefly, married to the late Steve Cochran, by whom she had no children. Except that her raven locks of yore are reddish brown now, she has changed scarcely at all. Onscreen from 1941. IN: *When the Daltons Rode, Sierra Sue, Down Mexico Way, Remember Pearl Harbor, Heart of the Rio Grande, The Singing Sheriff, Murder in the Music Hall,* more, including 1968's *The Party,* in which she agreed to do a cameo because the script was coauthored by her husband.

McKENZIE, LOUIS (N.Y.) Black support. Onscreen in the '70s. IN: *Shaft, The Anderson Tapes, The Hospital,* more.

McKERN, LEO (Eng.) Character costar. Onscreen from 1952. IN: *Murder in the Cathedral, Time Without Pity, A Tale of Two Cities, The Mouse That Roared, Scent of Mystery, Lisa,*

They All Died Laughing, The Amorous Adventures of Moll Flanders, A Man for All Seasons, The Shoes of the Fisherman, Ryan's Daughter, The Adventures of Sherlock Holmes' Smarter Brother, more.

McKINLEY, J. EDWARD (S. Cal.) Character. Onscreen from the '60s. IN: *A Thunder of Drums, The Impossible Years, The Party, Charro!*, more.

McKINNEY, BILL (S. Cal.) Support. Onscreen in the '70s. IN: *Thunderbolt and Lightfoot, The Parallax View, For Pete's Sake, The Outfit, Breakheart Pass*, more.

McKUEN, ROD (S. Cal.) Singer-songwriter-poet-actor. Onscreen in 1958. IN: *Summer Love.*

McLAUGHLIN, GIBB (Eng.) Venerable character actor, now in his 90s (b. 1884), and retired since the late '50s. Onscreen from 1920. IN: *Nell Gwyn, The Farmer's Wife, The White Sheik, Congress Dances, Catherine the Great, Little Friend, Alias Bulldog Drummond, The Old Curiosity Shop, Juggernaut, Courageous Mr. Penn, The Black Rose, Oliver Twist; The Lavender Hill Mob, The Promoter, The Pickwick Papers, The Deep Blue Sea, The Man Who Never Was, Hobson's Choice*, more.

McLEAN, WILLIAM (S. Cal.) Character. Onscreen from 1948. IN: *Fighter Squadron*, more.

McLEOD, CATHERINE (S. Cal.) Republic, rather half-heartedly, since Vera Hruba Ralston always came first there, sent this beauty to the stardom starting gate four times—in *I've Always Loved You* with Philip Dorn, *That's My Man* with Don Ameche, and two B-plus Westerns with "Wild Bill" Elliott, *The Fabulous Texan* and *Old Los Angeles*. That was 1946-48. She has been ever since, as she was before, a second lead—with a pleasant shrug and no complaints. "I had a couple of halcyon days in the '40s as a little movie starlet," she says, "and by now find it boring to be identified only as the actress who did 'that piano picture' [*I've Always Loved You*, in which she 'played' Rachmaninoff's Piano Concerto # 2 at least a dozen times]—and received the dubious honor of being voted Worst Actress of the Year by *Harvard Lampoon.*" The other identification, which she finds as wearisome, is that of the nameless actress who won an international TV award for saying, "Mother, please! I'd *rather* do it myself!" Yes, in that famous, oft-imitated television commercial, the grouch at the sink was Catherine. Besides commercials, she has been a regular on the soap opera *Days of Our Lives* and acted consistently on the nighttime

shows. Also she works on the other side of the screen writing for fan magazines—as the longtime West Coast editor of a leading daytime television magazine, reporting on the doings of other performers. Married since '50 to character actor Don Keefer (her second marriage), she is the proud mother of the "three greatest sons in the world": Tom, a teenager; John, a college student and a gifted classical guitarist; and Don. The last, an "all honors" student, won a full scholarship at—and recently graduated from—Yale. Guess Harvard didn't know a good thing when it saw it—*twice*. Onscreen from 1945. IN: *They Shall Have Faith, Courage of Lassie; So Young, So Bad; My Wife's Best Friend, A Blueprint for Murder, Sword of Venus, The Outcast, Return to Warbow, Tammy Tell Me True, The Sergeant and the Lady, Ride the Wild Surf*, more.

McLEOD, DUNCAN (S. Cal.) Character. Onscreen from the '60s. IN: *Finders Keepers, Losers Weepers; Beyond the Valley of the Dolls*, more.

McLERIE, ALLYN ANN (S. Cal.) Character; former leading lady in musicals. Onscreen from 1948. IN: *Words and Music, Where's Charley?, The Desert Song, Calamity Jane, Phantom of the Rue Morgue, Battle Cry, The Reivers; They Shoot Horses, Don't They?; Monte Walsh, The Entertainer*, more.

McLIAM, JOHN (S. Cal.) Character. Onscreen from 1967. IN: *My Fair Lady, Cool Hand Luke, In Cold Blood, The Reivers, Riverrun* (lead), *R.P.M., Monte Walsh, Halls of Anger, The Dove*, more.

McMAHON, ED (S. Cal.) TV personality. Character. Onscreen in 1967. IN: *The Incident.*

McMARTIN, JOHN (S. Cal.) Leading man. Onscreen from 1968. IN: *What's So Bad About Feeling Good?, Sweet Charity*, more.

McMULLAN, JIM (S. Cal.) Leading man. Onscreen from 1965. IN: *Shenandoah, The Raiders, The Happiest Millionaire, Windsplitter, The Downhill Racer, Extreme Close-Up*, more.

McMURRAY, RICHARD (S. Cal.) Character. Onscreen from the '60s. IN: *David and Lisa, The Swimmer, Zigzag*, more.

McNAIR, BARBARA (S. Cal.) Black singer-leading lady. Onscreen from 1968. IN: *If He Hollers, Let Him Go; Stiletto, Change of Habit, They Call Me Mr. Tibbs, Venus in Furs, The Organization*, more.

McNALLY, ED (S. Cal.) Character. Onscreen from 1957. IN: *Time Limit, The Naked and the Dead, Never Steal Anything Small, Charly,* more.

McNALLY, STEPHEN (HORACE) (S. Cal.) Character; former leading man. Onscreen as Horace McNally from 1942. IN: *Grand Central Murder, Eyes in the Night, The War Against Mrs. Hadley, Keeper of the Flame, Thirty Seconds Over Tokyo, Bewitched, Up Goes Maisie, Magnificent Doll,* more. Onscreen as Stephen McNally from 1948. IN: *Johnny Belinda, Criss Cross, The Lady Gambles, Sword in the Desert, Iron Man, Battle Zone, Split Second, Violent Saturday, Tribute to a Bad Man, Requiem for a Gunfighter, Black Gunn,* more.

McNAMARA, MAGGIE Former leading lady whose present whereabouts are a mystery. Nominated for Best Actress Oscar in *The Moon Is Blue.* Onscreen from 1953. IN: *Three Coins in the Fountain, Prince of Players, The Cardinal.*

McNAUGHTON, JACK (Eng.) Character. Onscreen from the '40s. IN: *She Shall Have Murder, High Treason, The Man in the White Suit, Secret People, The Pickwick Papers, Trent's Last Case, Rough Shoot, Man With a Million, The Detective, The Purple Plain, Men of Sherwood Forest,* more.

McNEIL, CLAUDIA (N.Y.) Black character. Onscreen from 1959. IN: *The Last Angry Man, A Raisin in the Sun, There Was a Crooked Man, Black Girl,* more.

McNULTY, DOROTHY (S. Cal.) (See Penny Singleton.)

McQUEEN, BUTTERFLY (N.Y.) "Prissy," then 64, received her bachelor's degree in political science in '75 at New York's City College. Living in Harlem, she does community relations and recreation work for the City Parks system. In '74 she also appeared in the film *Amazing Grace.* Except for a cameo in the scarcely released *The Phynx* ('69), this was her first movie role since *Duel in the Sun.* But in recognition of her comedy performances in *GWTW* and the numerous pix following it, she was, in '75, one of the 20 artists honored at the second annual Black Filmmakers Hall of Fame dinner in Oakland, Calif. One offscreen role she has several times played for New York City's Department of Recreation is that of visiting Santa Claus—in white beard and full regalia—at children's hospitals in Harlem. The children, she says, readily accept a black, female Santa Claus, but the real problem has been her distinctive, high-pitched voice, which she has had to consciously lower for the role. Heftier now than when she played (at 28) the teenage role in *GWTW,* she is a forceful figure indeed as she talks about the part that made her famous. "I was the only unhappy one in that film," she says now. "Mr. Selznick understood. He was a very understanding man. He knew it was a stupid part and I was an intelligent person . . . and it wasn't a very pleasant part to play. I didn't want to be that little slave. I didn't want to play that stupid part. I was just whining and crying. However, I did my best. My very best." But she is well aware of her permanent identification with that role. A note recently received from the actress was signed "Prissy Butterfly McQueen." Onscreen from 1939. IN: *Affectionately Yours, Cabin in the Sky, I Dood It, Flame of the Barbary Coast, Mildred Pierce,* more.

McQUEEN, STEVE (S. Cal.) Star. Nominated for Best Actor Oscar in *The Sand Pebbles.* Onscreen from 1956. IN: *Somebody Up There Likes Me, Never Love a Stranger, The Blob, Never So Few, The Magnificent Seven, The Honeymoon Machine, Hell Is for Heroes, The Great Escape, Love With the Proper Stranger, Soldier in the Rain, The Cincinnati Kid, Nevada Smith, The Thomas Crown Affair, Bullitt, The Reivers, Le Mans, Junior Bonner, The Getaway, The Towering Inferno,* more.

McRAE, ELLEN (N.Y.) (See Ellen Burstyn.)

McSHANE, IAN (Eng.) Leading man. Onscreen from 1962. IN: *Young and Willing, The Pleasure Girls, If It's Tuesday This Must Be Belgium; Pussycat, Pussycat, I Love You; Tam Lin, Villain, The Last of Sheila, Ransom,* more.

McVEAGH, EVE (S. Cal.) Character. Onscreen from the '50s. IN: *High Noon, Tight Spot; Crime and Punishment, U.S.A.; 3 in the Attic, The Liberation of Lord Byron Jones,* more.

McVEY, TYLER (S. Cal.) Character. Onscreen from 1951. IN: *The Day the Earth Stood Still, A Blueprint for Murder, The Come On, Hot Car Girl, Terror in a Texas Town, The Giant Leeches, The Gallant Hours, The Best Man, Dead Heat on a Merry-Go-Round,* more.

MEACHAM, ANNE (N.Y.) Support. Onscreen from 1964. IN: *Lilith, Dear Dead Delilah,* more.

MEAD, TAYLOR (N.Y.) Star of pornographic movies who also acts in other types of films. Onscreen from the '60s. IN: *The Flower Thief, Lemon Hearts, Hallelujah the Hills, Open the Door and See All the People, The Nude Restaurant, The Illiac Passion,* more.

MEADE, JULIA (N.Y.) Leading lady. Onscreen from 1959. IN: *Pillow Talk, Tammy Tell Me True, Zotz!*, more.

MEADOWS, AUDREY (S. Cal.) Support. Onscreen from 1962. IN: *That Touch of Mink, Take Her She's Mine, Rosie*, more.

MEADOWS, JAYNE (S. Cal.) Support. Wife of Steve Allen, sister of Audrey Meadows. Onscreen from 1946. IN: *Undercurrent, Dark Delusion, Lady in the Lake, Song of the Thin Man, Luck of the Irish, Enchantment, David and Bathsheba, It Happened to Jane, College Confidential*, more.

MEARA, ANNE (S. Cal.) Leading lady. Onscreen in the '70s. IN: *Lovers and Other Strangers, The Out-of-Towners*, more.

MEARS, MARTHA (S. Cal.) Character. Onscreen from 1940. IN: *Our Neighbors—The Carters, My Foolish Heart*, more.

MEDFORD, KAY (S. Cal.) Comedienne. Nominated for Best Supporting Actress Oscar in *Funny Girl*. Onscreen from 1942. IN: *The War Against Mrs. Hadley, Swing Shift Maisie, Adventure, A Face in the Crowd, The Rat Race, Butterfield 8, Two Tickets to Paris, Ensign Pulver, A Fine Madness, Angel in My Pocket, Twinky*, more.

MEDIN, HARRIET/formerly HARRIETTE WHITE MEDIN (S. Cal.) Character. Onscreen from the '60s. IN: *Blood and Black Lace*, more.

MEDINA, PATRICIA (S. Cal.) A dark-haired beauty still, in her 50s (b. 1919), the former wife of Richard Greene has been married for years to Joseph Cotten and appears opposite him at dinner theaters all over the country, in plays such as *The Reluctant Debutante*. Onscreen in England from 1938. IN: *Double or Quit, Secret Journey, Kiss the Bride Goodbye, Don't Take It to Heart*, more. Onscreen in America from 1947. IN: *Moss Rose, The Foxes of Harrow, Francis, Valentino, The Lady and the Bandit, Botany Bay, Plunder of the Sun, The Black Knight, Miami Expose, The Beast of Hollow Mountain, Snow White and the Three Stooges*, more.

MEDWIN, MICHAEL (Eng.) Character. Onscreen from the '40s. IN: *The Root of All Evil, Mr. Know-All, The Gay Lady, The Long Dark Hall, Both Sides of the Law, The Horse's Mouth, The Green Scarf, Doctor at Sea, Crooks Anonymous, Night Must Fall, The Dream Maker, A Countess from Hong Kong, Law and Disorder*, more.

MEEHAN, DANNY (S. Cal.) Character. Onscreen from 1961. IN: *Blast of Silence, Don't Drink the Water*, more.

MEEKER, RALPH (S. Cal.) Character; former leading man. Onscreen from 1951. IN: *Teresa, Four in a Jeep, Somebody Loves Me, The Naked Spur, Jeopardy, Kiss Me Deadly, Battle Shock, Run of the Arrow, The Fuzzy Pink Nightgown, Paths of Glory, Something Wild, Wall of Noise, The Dirty Dozen, The Detective, The Devil's Eight, The Anderson Tapes*, more.

MEGNA, JOHN (N.Y.) Former juvenile. Onscreen in the '60s. IN: *To Kill a Mockingbird, Blindfold*, more.

MEGOWAN, DON (S. Cal.) Support. Onscreen from 1951. IN: *The Kid from Amarillo; Davy Crockett—King of the Wild Frontier; The Creature Walks Among Us, Gun the Man Down, Hell Canyon Outlaws, The Man Who Died Twice, Valley of the Doomed, Creation of the Humanoids, The Devil's Brigade, Blazing Saddles*, more.

MEHRA, LAL CHAND (S. Cal.) Character. Onscreen from 1931. IN: *Friends and Lovers, Singapore, Hellfighters*, more.

MEILLON, JOHN (Eng.) Character. Onscreen from the '50s. IN: *On the Beach, The Sundowners, Jungle Fighters, Billy Budd, 633 Squadron, Guns at Batasi, Walkabout*, more.

MEISER, EDITH (N.Y.) Character. Onscreen from 1941. IN: *Glamour Boy; Go West, Young Lady; Queen for a Day, It Grows on Trees, Middle of the Night.*

MELATO, MARIANGELA (It.) Star. Onscreen in the '70s. IN: *The Seduction of Mimi, Love and Anarchy, Swept Away, La Poliziotta, Guernica, The Female Is the Deadliest of the Species*, more.

MELFORD, JACK (Eng.) Character. Onscreen from the '30s. IN: *When Thief Meets Thief, It's in the Air, The October Man, No Room at the Inn, My Brother Jonathan, Fatal Journey, Ladykillers*, more.

MELFORD, JILL (Eng.) Leading lady. Daughter of Jack Melford. Onscreen from 1951. IN: *Will Any Gentleman . . . ?, Out of the Clouds, Murder by Proxy, Abandon Ship, The Constant Husband, The Vengeance of She, The Servant*, more.

MELL, MARISA (S. Cal.) Leading lady. Onscreen from the '60s. IN: *Soldat Schweijk, French Dressing, Casanova 70, Masquerade,*

Train D'Enfer, Che Notte Ragazzi, Anyone Can Play; Danger: Diabolik!; Mahogany, more.

MELLY, ANDREE (Eng.) Support. Onscreen from 1951. IN: *The Belles of St. Trinian's, The Secret Tent, Brides of Dracula*, more.

MELTON, SID (S. Cal.) Comic character. Onscreen from 1942. IN: *Blondie Goes to College, Suspense, Kilroy Was Here, Close-Up, Knock on Any Door, Radar Secret Service, Holiday Rhythm, The Steel Helmet, The Lemon Drop Kid, Stop That Cab!, Leave It to the Marines, The Lost Continent, Beau James, Thundering Jets, The Atomic Submarine, The Girl from Peking, Sheila Levine Is Alive and Living in New York*, more.

MELVILLE, SAM (S. Cal.) Leading man. Onscreen from the '60s. IN: *Hour of the Gun, The Thomas Crown Affair*, more.

MELVIN, DONNIE (N.Y.) Juvenile. Onscreen in the '70s. IN: *Ladybug, Ladybug;* more.

MELVIN, MURRAY (Eng.) Support. Onscreen from 1959. IN: *The Criminal, A Taste of Honey, HMS Defiant, The Ceremony, Alfie, The Fixer, The Devils, The Boy Friend*, more.

MENGES, JOYCE (S. Cal.) Former ingenue; now inactive. Onscreen in the '60s. IN: *The Gnome-Mobile.*

MENKEN, SHEPARD (S. Cal.) Character. Onscreen from the '40s. IN: *The Red Menace, The Great Caruso, The Merry Widow, Man in the Dark, The Juggler, The Benny Goodman Story*, more.

MENUHIN, YEHUDI (N.Y.) Violinist. Onscreen in 1943. IN: *Stage Door Canteen.*

MERCER, FRANCES (S. Cal.) Raven-haired, with a center part, she was one of the loveliest girls in movies of the late '30s—and had one of the shortest (two years), busiest (nine movies), strangest careers as a Hollywood leading lady. In B's, the former Powers Girl was the love interest opposite Richard Dix in *Blind Alibi* and opposite Allan Lane in *Crime Ring*. In A's, she was the star's best friend (Stanwyck's in *The Mad Miss Manton*) or sophisticated young rival (Ginger Rogers' in *Vivacious Lady*). Her brief time at RKO constituted her season of glory in Hollywood, and most people believe her sole appearances before the camera. Not true. In London just after WW II she "lucked in" on an excellent featured role in Anna Neagle's *Piccadilly Incident*—that of a beautifully dressed American girl. She filled the bill in all particulars, having just arrived in England with a splendid wardrobe and, equally in her favor, as the wife of a Lieutenant Commander in the British Navy. No work permit necessary. (He, William Gillett, was the second of three husbands from whom she has been divorced. First, in the early '40s, was a Manhattan socialite; third was Robert Fleming, whose business career required their living in Japan during several years of their marriage.) Back in Hollywood since the '50s, where she has lately worked as a bank teller, medical assistant, or antiques dealer, she had a successful decade or so in television. Commercials; a soap opera (*For Better or Worse*—as a vituperative mother-in-law); a supporting role in a long-running series (*Dr. Hudson's Secret Journal*). And there have been bits—sometimes unbilled—in many movies. She was in *There's Always Tomorrow*, starring longtime acquaintance Barbara Stanwyck; MacMurray's *Bon Voyage!* (a crowd scene), *The Rise and Fall of Legs Diamond, Pardners* (brief role in the opening as Dean Martin's wife), etc. Not long ago, this slender cosmopolite who looks considerably younger than her years—late 50s—expressed the desire to return to New York and resume her career on the stage. New York is where it all began for this native of New Rochelle, and where she enjoyed several successes greater than those found in Hollywood. Immediately after her leading-lady period, she costarred on Broadway in two musicals: *Very Warm for May* (introduced "All the Things You Are") and *Something for the Boys*; was the headlined attraction as a singer in the best supper clubs; had her own radio program (*Sunday Night at Nine*) and, during WW II, with the Co-ordinator of Inter-American Affairs, did another radio series for South America. She looks back on these as the halcyon years of her life and career, not her stint at RKO, and feels confident that, given a break, it could all happen again. Onscreen from 1938. IN: *Vivacious Lady, Smashing the Rackets, Annabel Takes a Tour, Beauty for the Asking, The Story of Vernon and Irene Castle, Society Lawyer*, more.

MERCER, JOHNNY (S. Cal.) In 1975, at 67, the Oscar-winning songwriter ("Laura," "That Old Black Magic," etc.) underwent brain surgery. Onscreen in 1935. IN: *Old Man Rhythm.* (Died June 25, 1976.)

MERCER, MAE (S. Cal.) Black leading lady. Onscreen from the '60s. IN: *The Hell with Heroes, The Beguiled, The Swinging Cheerleaders*, more.

MERCER, MARIAN (N.Y.) Singer-actress. Onscreen in 1969. IN: *John and Mary.*

MERCHANT, VIVIEN (Eng.) Character. Nominated for Best Supporting Actress Oscar in *Alfie*. Onscreen from the '40s. IN: *The Way Ahead, Accident, Frenzy, Under Milk Wood, The Homecoming, The Maids*, more.

MERCIER, LOUIS (S. Cal.) Character. Onscreen from 1937. IN: *Charlie Chan at Monte Carlo, Bulldog Drummond's Bride, This Woman Is Mine, Sahara, Passage to Marseille, The Conspirators, Attack!, An Affair to Remember, Will Success Spoil Rock Hunter?, Darling Lili*, more.

MERCIER, MICHELE (Fr.) Leading lady. Onscreen from 1960. IN: *The Nights of Lucretia Borgia, Goodbye Again, The Wonders of Aladdin, Shoot the Piano Player, A Global Affair, Casanova, The Oldest Profession*, more.

MERCOURI, MELINA (Greece) Star. Nominated for Best Actress Oscar in *Never on Sunday*. Onscreen from the '50s. IN: *Stella, He Who Must Die, Where the Hot Wind Blows, Phaedra, The Victors, Topkapi, A Man Could Get Killed, The Uninhibited, Gaily Gaily, Promise at Dawn, Once Is Not Enough*, more.

MEREDITH, BURGESS (N.Y.) Costar. Nominated for Best Supporting Actor Oscar in *The Day of the Locust*. Onscreen from 1936. IN: *Winterset, Of Mice and Men, Idiot's Delight, Second Chorus* (with then wife Paulette Goddard), *Castle on the Hudson; Tom, Dick and Harry; The Story of G.I. Joe, Diary of a Chambermaid* (also with Goddard), *The Magnificent Doll, Mine Own Executioner, The Man on the Eiffel Tower, Advise and Consent, The Cardinal, In Harm's Way, A Big Hand for the Little Lady, Batman, Hurry Sundown, MacKenna's Gold, The Torture Garden, There Was a Crooked Man, Such Good Friends, The Man, The Hindenburg, 92 in the Shade, Day of the Locust*, more.

MEREDITH, JOAN (S. Cal.) The brunette leading lady in silent Westerns retired for marriage and, a grandmother now, still lives near Hollywood. Onscreen in the '20s. IN: *Gun Justice*, more.

MEREDITH, JO ANNE (S. Cal.) Leading lady. Onscreen in the '70s. IN: *The Loving Touch, How to Seduce a Woman, The Last Porno Flick*, more.

MEREDITH, JUDI (S. Cal.) Leading lady. Onscreen from 1958. IN: *Summer Love, Jack the Giant Killer, The Night Walker, Dark Intruder, Something Big*, more.

MEREDITH, LEE (N.Y.) Leading lady. Onscreen from the '60s. IN: *The Producers, Hello Down There, Welcome to the Club, The Sunshine Boys*, more.

MEREDITH, LU ANNE (S. Cal.) After playing several second leads in the early '30s, she married and retired. Still a Los Angeles resident, she is the mother of two grown daughters.

MERIVALE, JOHN (Eng.) Character; former leading man. Son of the late Philip Merivale. Onscreen from 1933. IN: *The Invisible Man* (juvenile role: newsboy), *If Winter Comes, Battle of the River Plate, A Night to Remember; Caltiki, the Immortal Monster; Circus of Horrors, The List of Adrian Messenger, 80,000 Suspects*, more.

MERIWETHER, LEE (S. Cal.) Leading lady; former Miss America. Onscreen from 1959. IN: *The 4-D Man, Batman; Namu, the Killer Whale; The Legend of Lylah Clare, The Courtship of Eddie's Father, Angel in My Pocket, The Undefeated*, more.

MERKEL, UNA (S. Cal.) In her 70s (b. 1903), she is as she has always been, blonde, full of blue-eyed zip and good humor. A "bachelor girl" since her one marriage and divorce (she was married to Ronald Burla 1932–47; no children), she lives at the beach, surrounded by friends, and wishes casting directors would call more often. In the '50s, when Hollywood was making scant use of her proven (since the early '20s) talents, she turned to Broadway and scored a great hit in Eudora Welty's *The Ponder Heart*. It led to one splendid character role in movies, as Geraldine Page's embittered mother in *Summer and Smoke*. (Incredibly, to get it, she not only had to make a personal bid for it, but submit to a screen test.) This won her a first-time Supporting Oscar nomination—but only four more roles followed: *The Parent Trap, Summer Magic, A Tiger Walks*, and, last, in '67, *Spin-Out*. She has done a bit of stage work since but she would like to be active in movies again. Onscreen from 1921. IN: *The White Rose* (as an extra), *Love's Old Sweet Song* (a '24 two-reel talkie, in which she played the lead), *Abraham Lincoln, The Bat Whispers, The Maltese Falcon, Private Lives, Red-Headed Woman, 42nd Street, Bombshell, Broadway to Hollywood, Paris Interlude, Evelyn Prentice, Broadway Melody of 1936, Riffraff, Born to Dance, Saratoga, Test Pilot, On Borrowed Time, Destry Rides Again, The Bank Dick, Twin Beds; It's a Joke, Son!; The Bride Goes Wild, Kill the Umpire, With a Song in My Heart, The Merry Widow, Bundle of Joy, The Kettles in the Ozarks, The Mating Game*, more.

MERLIN, JAN (S. Cal.) Leading man. Onscreen from 1955. IN: *Six Bridges to Cross, Illegal, Running Wild, Screaming Eagles, Cole Younger—Gunfighter, Gunfight at Comanche Creek, The St. Valentine's Day Massacre,* more.

MERMAN, ETHEL (N.Y.) Legendary singer-actress. Onscreen from 1930. IN: *Follow the Leader, The Big Broadcast of 1932, Kid Millions, We're Not Dressing, Happy Landing, Strike Me Pink, Alexander's Ragtime Band; Straight, Place and Show; Call Me Madam, There's No Business Like Show Business, It's a Mad Mad Mad Mad World, The Art of Love,* more.

MERRICK, LYNN (N.Y.) She has lately been a representative for a leading modeling agency in New York. Onscreen from 1940. IN: *Flight Angels* (as Marilyn Merrick), *Death Valley Outlaws, Sis Hopkins, The Gay Vagabond, The Cyclone Kid, Youth on Parade, Mountain Rhythm, The Crime Doctor's Strangest Case, Swing Out the Blues, Nine Girls, The Blonde from Brooklyn, Boston Blackie Booked on Suspicion; A Guy, a Gal and a Pal; The Voice of the Whistler, A Close Call for Boston Blackie,* more, including 1947's *I Love Trouble,* her last.

MERRILL, BARBARA (N.Y.) Bette Davis' daughter. Onscreen in 1962. IN: *What Ever Happened to Baby Jane?*

MERRILL, DICK (Fla.) Famed aviator. Married to former actress Toby Wing, he lives in Miami. Onscreen in 1937. IN: *Atlantic Flight.*

MERRILL, DINA (N.Y.) Costar. Onscreen from 1957. IN: *Desk Set, Operation Petticoat, Don't Give Up the Ship, Butterfield 8, The Young Savages, The Courtship of Eddie's Father, I'll Take Sweden, The Meal,* more.

MERRILL, GARY (Me.) Single since his second marriage, to Bette Davis (1950–60), ended in divorce, he lives alone at Cape Elizabeth, in a century-old, cast-iron lighthouse called "West Light." He has living quarters on all six levels of the converted tower, with a winding iron staircase leading to a glassed-in bedroom at the top with a 360-degree sweeping view of the Atlantic and the mainland. And, in '68, he ran unsuccessfully for Congress in Maine. He still flies regularly to Hollywood for acting assignments on TV (*Movin' On,* etc.) and in movies (1976's *Thieves*). Onscreen from 1944. IN: *Winged Victory, Twelve O'Clock High, Where the Sidewalk Ends, All About Eve* (in which he met Bette Davis), *Another Man's Poison* and *Phone Call from a Stranger* (both also with Davis), *Decision Before Dawn, Blueprint for Murder, The Wonderful Country, The Savage Eye, The Pleasure of His Company, A Girl Named Tamiko, Around the World Under the Sea, Ride Beyond Vengeance, The Incident, Clambake, The Last Challenge, A Wrong Kind of Love, Huckleberry Finn,* more.

MERRITT, GEORGE (Eng.) Character. Onscreen from 1931. IN: *The W Plan, The Dreyfus Case, Mr. Cohen Takes a Walk, Rembrandt, The Return of the Scarlet Pimpernel, Clouds Over Europe, The Smugglers, Nicholas Nickleby, Hatter's Castle, Don't Take It to Heart, A Canterbury Tale; I, Monster;* more.

MERRITT, THERESA (S. Cal.) Black character. Onscreen in the '70s. IN: *They Might Be Giants,* more.

MERROW, JANE (Eng.) Leading lady. Onscreen from the '60s. IN: *The Woman Who Wouldn't Die, The Girl-Getters, The Lion in Winter,* more.

MERVYN, WILLIAM (Eng.) Character. Onscreen from 1946. IN: *The Blue Lamp, The Third Key, Murder Ahoy, Hammerhead, Salt & Pepper, The Railway Children,* more.

MESKILL, KATHERINE (N.Y.) Character. Onscreen from 1951. IN: *The House on Telegraph Hill, Hollywood Story, Diary of a Mad Housewife,* more.

MESTRAL, ARMAND (Fr.) Character. Onscreen from the '50s. IN: *Gervaise, Morgan the Pirate, They Came to Rob Las Vegas,* more.

METRANO, ART (S. Cal.) Character. Onscreen from the '60s. IN: *They Shoot Horses, Don't They?; Dirty O'Neil,* more.

MEYER, EMILE (S. Cal.) Character. Onscreen from the '50s. IN: *Shane, Riot in Cell Block 11, The Blackboard Jungle, The Tall Men, Man With the Golden Arm, Sweet Smell of Success, Paths of Glory, Revolt in the Big House, Good Day for a Hanging, Young Jesse James, Taggart, Young Dillinger, Hostile Guns,* more.

MEYERINCK, VICTORIA (S. Cal.) Former child actress; inactive now. Onscreen in 1968. IN: *Speedway.*

MEYERS, MICHAEL (N.Y.) Support. Onscreen from 1969. IN: *Goodbye, Columbus; Parachute to Paradise, The Incident, What Do You Say to a Naked Lady?,* more.

MEYERS, MICHAEL (N.Y.) Juvenile. Onscreen from 1969. IN: *Generation, Little Murders,* more.

MICHAEL, RALPH (Eng.) Character. Onscreen from 1937. IN: *John Halifax, Gentleman; Dead of Night, The Hasty Heart, Abandon Ship, Murder Most Foul, The Heroes of Telemark, Khartoum, Grand Prix, Assassination Bureau,* more.

MICHAELS, BEVERLY (S. Cal.) Large in size and talent, she was, in the early '50s, one of producer-director-star Hugo Haas' two favorite leading ladies—the other being the late Cleo Moore. Retired for over two decades, she has long been married to her own producer-director, Russell Rouse (he was associated with Haas), and lives in Beverly Hills. Onscreen from 1949. IN: *East Side, West Side; Pickup, The Girl on the Bridge, Wicked Woman, Betrayed Women, Blonde Bait,* more.

MICHEL, FRANNY (N.Y.) Juvenile. Onscreen in the '70s. IN: *Diary of a Mad Housewife,* more.

MICHELL, KEITH (Eng.) Costar. Onscreen from 1956. IN: *Dangerous Exile, The Hellfire Club, Prudence and the Pill, House of Cards, The Executioner, Henry VIII and His Six Wives,* more.

MIDDLETON, NOELLE (Eng.) Support; former leading lady. Onscreen from the '50s. IN: *Tonight's the Night, Court Martial, The Iron Petticoat, John and Julie, The Circle, 3 Men in a Boat,* more.

MIDDLETON, RAY (S. Cal.) In '71 the singer-actor returned to Hollywood, where he had not lived since his starring years at Republic in the '40s and early '50s, to work in *1776.* In the interim he had starred in many Broadway musicals. Most particularly there was a six-year run in *Man of La Mancha,* during which two dramatic events in his personal life took place. He had to take time out for heart surgery—removal of 10 inches of his aorta and substitution of a dacron sleeve, which saved his life. And, for the first time, he married. His wife is the lovely Patricia Dinnell, a choreographer. It was she, seeing California for the first time, who convinced the actor that this should be their permanent home, rather than New York or the cliffside modern-rustic mansion he had built in the northern Michigan forests overlooking Lake Michigan. The latter he had constructed over a dozen years ago, premarriage, in anticipation of eventual retirement. Today the Middletons live in Panorama City on an acre of land—big enough for a thriving vegetable garden—in a bright yellow house ("Disneyland Yellow," he says) with blue shutters and white trim. A happy house for a happy, involved couple. The nearby Unitarian Church is at the center of their lives. For special occasions, they have arranged "Sermons in Dance" at the church—Ray planning the music and doing the narration, and his wife handling the choreography. (A Middle Westerner, from Illinois, with his roots firmly in the soil, the actor does frequent, short tours throughout the country in his one-man program "America in Song and Story"—dramatic readings and music. And he unfailingly closes with a passage from the Bible.) No longer even thinking of retirement, though his seventh decade looms (b. 1907), the actor does much work as a guest-star on TV, and, he adds, "I have discovered the new world of TV commercials. Thus far, I have spoken for wine, dog food, milk, and salad dressing." That's par for the course for an actor who has shunned the glitter of show business for the "basics." Onscreen from 1940. IN: *Gangs of Chicago, Lady from Louisiana, Lady for a Night, Hurricane Smith, Mercy Island, Girl from Alaska, I Dream of Jeannie, Jubilee Trail, I Cover the Underworld, The Road to Denver,* more.

MIDDLETON, ROBERT (S. Cal.) Character. Onscreen from the '50s. IN: *The Silver Chalice, The Desperate Hours, Friendly Persuasion, The Proud Ones, Tarnished Angels, Day of the Bad Man, Don't Give Up the Ship, The Great Impostor, Cattle King, A Big Hand for the Little Lady, The Cheyenne Social Club,* more.

MIDDLETON, TOM (S. Cal.) Support. Onscreen from the '60s. IN: *Twist Around the Clock,* more.

MIDLER, BETTE (N.Y.) Singer-actress. Onscreen in the '70s. IN: *The Divine Mr. J.*

MIFUNE, TOSHIRO (Japan) Japan's #1 star, still making many films (*Paper Tiger, The Red Sun,* etc.), owns and runs his own studio in a Tokyo suburb where he produces and stars in Japanese-language TV series. He has at this writing completed three 52-episode, one-hour programs. In one, *Chushingura,* he starred as a Samurai detective; the other two were straight Samurai action dramas. The actor, who is in his 50s (b. 1920), has a son, Shiro, who studies English at Cambridge, and in '75 played a supporting role with his father and David Niven in *Paper Tiger.* Onscreen from 1948. IN: *The Drunken Angel, Rasho-Mon, Samurai, The Magnificent Seven, Throne of Blood, Yojimbo, The Idiot, High and Low, Grand-Prix, The Sword of Doom, Rebellion, Whirlwind, Red Beard, Hell in the Pacific,* more.

MILES, BERNARD (Eng.) Character. Onscreen from 1937. IN: *Channel Crossing, Pastor Hall, One of Our Aircraft Is Missing, The Avengers, In Which We Serve, Great Expecta-*

tions, Tawny Pipit, Nicholas Nickleby, Fame Is the Spur, The Magic Box, The Man Who Knew Too Much, Moby Dick, Zarek, Saint Joan, Tom Thumb, Sapphire; Run Wild, Run Free; more.

MILES, JOANNA (S. Cal.) Leading lady. Onscreen from 1960. IN: *Butterfield 8, Splendor in the Grass, Girl in the Dark* (bit roles), *The Way We Live Now, Bug,* more.

MILES, LILLIAN (S. Cal.) Married and retired, she lives near Hollywood. Onscreen in the early '30s. IN: *Man Against Woman, Moonlight and Pretzels,* more.

MILES, PETER (S. Cal.) The appealing lad who starred in *The Red Pony,* and is the brother of former moppet Gigi Perreau (their real family name), is in his late 30s now, writes for the screen, and is a published novelist. Onscreen from 1944. IN: *Passage to Marseille, Heaven Only Knows, Enchantment, Family Honeymoon, The Good Humor Man, California Passage, Quo Vadis,* more.

MILES, ROSALIND (S. Cal.) Black leading lady. Onscreen in the '70s. IN: *Shaft's Big Score, Girls for Rent, The Black Six,* more.

MILES, SARAH (Eng.) Costar. Nominated for Best Actress Oscar in *Ryan's Daughter.* Onscreen from 1962. IN: *Term of Trial, The Ceremony, The Servant, Those Magnificent Men in Their Flying Machines, Blow-Up, Time Lost and Time Remembered, Lady Caroline Lamb, The Hireling, The Man Who Loved Cat Dancing, Pepita Jimenez, The Sailor Who Fell from Grace with the Sea,* more.

MILES, SHERRY (S. Cal.) Leading lady. Onscreen in the '70s. IN: *The Phynx, Making It, The Velvet Vampire, Calliope, The Harrad Summer,* more.

MILES, SYLVIA (N.Y.) Support. Nominated for Best Supporting Actress Oscar in *Midnight Cowboy* and *Farewell, My Lovely.* Onscreen from 1961. IN: *Parrish; Murder, Inc.; Black Autumn, Terror in the City, The Truant, The Last Movie, Who Killed Mary What'sername?, Heat; Farewell, My Lovely; 92 in the Shade, Great Scout and Cat-House Thursday,* more.

MILES, VERA (S. Cal.) Leading lady. Onscreen from 1952. IN: *For Men Only, The Rose Bowl Story, Tarzan's Hidden Jungle, Wichita, The Searchers, Autumn Leaves, Beau James, The Wrong Man, The FBI Story, Five Branded Women, A Touch of Larceny, Psycho, Back Street, The Man Who Shot Liberty Valance, Those Calloways, Gentle Ben, It Takes All Kinds, Hellfighters, The Wild Country, The Castaway Cowboy,* more.

MILIAN, TOMAS (It.) Costar. Onscreen from the '60s. IN: *The Big Gundown, The Ugly Ones, A Fine Fair, The Last Movie, Sonny and Jed, The Cop in Blue Jeans,* more.

MILLAN, VICTOR (S. Cal.) Character. Onscreen from 1956. IN: *Giant, The Ride Back, Touch of Evil, The FBI Story, The Pink Jungle,* more.

MILLAND, RAY (S. Cal.) Star. Won Best Actor Oscar in *The Lost Weekend.* Published his autobiography, *Wide-Eyed in Babylon,* in 1974. Onscreen in England from 1929. IN: *The Flying Scotsman, The Plaything,* more. Onscreen in America from 1931. IN: *Ambassador Bill, Polly of the Circus, We're Not Dressing, Charlie Chan in London, Return of Sophie Lang, Jungle Princess, Ebb Tide, Men With Wings, Beau Geste, Irene, The Doctor Takes a Wife, Arise My Love, I Wanted Wings, Reap the Wild Wind, The Major and the Minor, The Uninvited, Lady in the Dark, Kitty, California, Golden Earrings, The Big Clock, Copper Canyon, Close to My Heart, Bugles in the Afternoon, Dial M for Murder, Three Brave Men, Premature Burial, Hostile Witness, Love Story, Frogs, The Thing with Two Heads, The House in Nightmare Park, Escape to Witch Mountain, Swiss Conspiracy, The Last Tycoon,* more.

MILLER, ANN (S. Cal.) Tap dancer/costar. Published her autobiography, *Miller's High Life,* in 1972. Onscreen from 1937. IN: *New Faces of 1937, Life of the Party, Stage Door, Room Service, You Can't Take It With You, Too Many Girls, Priorities on Parade, Reveille with Beverly, Eadie Was a Lady, The Thrill of Brazil, Easter Parade, The Kissing Bandit, On the Town, Watch the Birdie, Lovely to Look At, Small Town Girl, Kiss Me Kate, Deep in My Heart, Hit the Deck, The Opposite Sex,* more.

MILLER, BUZZ (N.Y.) Actor-dancer. Onscreen from 1951. IN: *On the Riviera, There's No Business Like Show Business, Anything Goes, The Pajama Game,* more.

MILLER, CHERYL (S. Cal.) Leading lady. Onscreen from 1965. IN: *Clarence, the Cross-Eyed Lion; The Monkey's Uncle,* more.

MILLER, COLLEEN (S. Cal.) In 1975 the brunette former leading lady, once one of Universal's most popular, and husband, Ted Brisking (formerly wed to Betty Hutton), announced they were divorcing after 21 years of marriage and two children. Still a beauty in her early 40s (b. 1932), she has considered resuming her career. Onscreen from 1952. IN: *The Las Vegas Story, Playgirl, Four Guns to the Border, The Rawhide Years, Hot Summer Night, The Night*

Runner, more, including 1963's *Gunfight at Comanche Creek*, her most recent to date.

MILLER, DEAN (S. Cal.) MGM's former young leading man is in the production end of TV now. Onscreen 1952–53. IN: *Skirts Ahoy!, Everything I Have Is Yours, Because You're Mine, Dream Wife, Small Town Girl*.

MILLER, DENNY (S. Cal.) The muscular blond who played the title role in 1959's *Tarzan of the Apes* is now, in addition to being a supporting actor, an advertising exec in Los Angeles. Onscreen from 1959. IN: *Love in a Goldfish Bowl, The Party, Armageddon, Making It, The Island at the Top of the World, Gravy Train*, more.

MILLER, FRED (N.Y.) Character. Onscreen from 1934. IN: *Gambling, Sophie Lang Goes West, Star!, The Night They Raided Minsky's*, more.

MILLER, JAN (Eng.) Leading lady. Onscreen from 1957. IN: *Raising a Riot, The Secret, The Body Stealers*, more.

MILLER, JASON (S. Cal.) Costar and Pulitzer Prize-winning playwright *(That Championship Season)*. Nominated for Best Supporting Actor Oscar in *The Exorcist*. Onscreen in the '70s. IN: *The Nickel Ride*, more.

MILLER, JOAN (Eng.) Character. Onscreen from 1948. IN: *Cry of the City, The Woman in the Hall, Criss Cross, Caged, The Jackpot, Hans Christian Andersen, Fire Down Below, Blonde Sinner, Heavens Above!*, more.

MILLER, JONATHAN (Eng.) Comic leading man. Onscreen from 1964. IN: *One Way Pendulum, Take a Girl Like You*, more.

MILLER, MANDY (Eng.) The former child star, in her 30s now (b. 1944), no longer acts. Onscreen from 1953. IN: *The Story of Mandy, Edge of Divorce, Dance Little Lady, The Snorkel*, more.

MILLER, MARK (S. Cal.) Leading man. Onscreen from 1963. IN: *The Hook, Youngblood Hawke, Mr. Sycamore*, more.

MILLER, MARVIN (S. Cal.) Character. Onscreen from 1945. IN: *Blood on the Sun, Deadline at Dawn, The Brasher Doubloon, Dead Reckoning, The Prince Who Was a Thief, Hong Kong, Red Planet Mars, Jivaro, The Day the Earth Froze, A Trip to Terror, Is This Trip Necessary?, How to Seduce a Woman*, more.

MILLER, PATSY RUTH (Conn.) One of the most popular players throughout the last decade of silent movies, she wrote finis to her movie career after 1931's *Lonely Wives*. Except for a minor supporting role in 1951's *Quebec*, she never acted onscreen again. In the decades between, she did not lack for careers. She appeared on Broadway, wrote prize-winning short stories, was seen in vaudeville, owned an exclusive beauty parlor in Hollywood, and penned a novel, *That Flanagan Girl*. Divorced from both Tay Garnett, the director, and scriptwriter John Lee Mahin, she has been happily married since the early '50s to New York businessman E. S. Deans. They live in a beautiful, rambling house in Stamford and travel extensively. Both fashionable and highly social, the star, dark-haired still, is in her 70s (b. 1905). Onscreen from the teens. IN: *Judgment, Remembrance, The Girl I Loved, The Hunchback of Notre Dame, The Yankee Consul, Red Hot Tires, Rose of the World, Hell-Bent for Heaven, So This Is Paris, Private Izzy Murphy, The White Black Sheep, Painting the Town, South Sea Love, We Americans, Hot Heels, Marriage by Contract, The Aviator, So Long Letty*, more.

MILLER, PEGGY (S. Cal.) Support. Onscreen from 1947. IN: *Pursued*, more.

MILLER, ROGER (Tenn.) C&W singer-songwriter. Onscreen in 1966. IN: *The Big T.N.T. Show*.

MILLER, SCOTT (S. Cal.) Support. Onscreen from 1968. IN: *Run Like a Thief, Play Dirty, Open Season*, more.

MILLER, SIDNEY (S. Cal.) No sprig now, and progressively balding, yesteryear's humorous teenager continues to be one of Hollywood's all-round talents. Besides having been music arranger and director of *The Bobby Darin Show* on TV, and director of Jean Arthur's short-lived series, he still acts on most of the major television dramas—*Columbo, Marcus Welby, M.D.*, etc. He has long been married to actress Dorothy Green, who was '''Jennifer Brooks'' on the soap opera *The Young and the Restless*. And it is second-generation time—his son, Barry, then 16, played Tony Curtis as a teenager in the movie *Lepke* ('75). Onscreen from 1933. IN: *Mayor of Hell, The Band Plays On, Dinky, Boys Town, Streets of New York, Andy Hardy Gets Spring Fever, What a Life, Golden Gloves, Men of Boys Town, Moonlight in Vermont, Babes on Swing Street, The Lucky Stiff, The Sniper, Walking My Baby Back Home, Experiment in Terror, Which Way to the Front?* (as Hitler), *For Pete's Sake*, more.

MILLETAIRE, CARL (S. Cal.) Character. Onscreen from 1950. IN: *Black Hand, 711 Ocean Drive, The Great Caruso, Young Man with*

Ideas, The Miracle of Our Lady Fatima, New York Confidential, Shadow on the Window, Inside the Mafia, more.

MILLHOLLIN, JAMES (S. Cal.) Character. Onscreen from 1958. IN: *No Time for Sergeants, Everything's Ducky, Zotz!, Bon Voyage!, The Swingin' Set, Never a Dull Moment*, more.

MILLI, ROBERT (S. Cal.) Character. Onscreen from 1964. IN: *The Curse of the Living Corpse, Act One, Hamlet* (Burton filmed-stage version), more.

MILLIGAN, SPIKE (Eng.) Actor-director-playwright. Onscreen from the '50s. IN: *Watch Your Stern, The Risk, Invasion Quartet, The Magic Christian, Alice's Adventures in Wonderland*, more.

MILLOT, CHARLES (Fr.) Support. Onscreen from the '60s. IN: *The Train, The Great Spy Chase, Trans-Europ-Express*, more.

MILLS, DONNA (S. Cal.) Leading lady. Onscreen from the '60s. IN: *The Incident, Play Misty for Me; Live a Little, Steal a Lot*; more.

MILLS, HAYLEY (Eng.) Leading lady; former juvenile. Daughter of John Mills. Received a special Oscar (miniature statuette) "for *Pollyanna*, the most outstanding juvenile performance during 1960." Onscreen from 1959. IN: *Tiger Bay, The Parent Trap, In Search of the Castaways, Summer Magic, The Moonspinners, The Chalk Garden, That Darn Cat, The Trouble with Angels, The Family Way, A Matter of Innocence, Take a Girl Like You, Endless Night*, more.

MILLS, JOHN (Eng.) Costar. Won Best Supporting Actor Oscar in *Ryan's Daughter*. Onscreen from 1932. IN: *The Midshipmaid, River Wolves, Born for Glory, Nine Days a Queen; Goodbye, Mr. Chips; Young Mr. Pitt, In Which We Serve, This Happy Breed, The Way to the Stars, Great Expectations, Scott of the Antarctic, The Rocking Horse Winner, The Colditz Story, Hobson's Choice, War and Peace, I Was Monty's Double, Tiger Bay* (with daughter Hayley), *Tunes of Glory, The Desert Hawk, The Chalk Garden* (again with Hayley), *Operation Crossbow, King Rat, Africa—Texas Style, Chuka, Oh! What a Lovely War* (with daughter Juliet Mills), *Young Winston, Lady Caroline Lamb, Oklahoma Crude, The Human Factor*, more.

MILLS, JULIET (S. Cal.) Leading lady. Daughter of John Mills. Onscreen from 1942. IN: *In Which We Serve* (at the age of 11 weeks she was seen as the infant of Ordinary Seaman Shorty Blake, played by her father), *So Well Remembered* (juvenile role in '47, again with her father), *The History of Mr. Polly* (another juvenile role in this film, produced by John Mills, who also starred); *No, My Darling Daughter* (first leading role, in '61); *Twice Around the Daffodils, Nurse on Wheels; Carry On, Jack; The Rare Breed, Wings of Fire, Oh! What a Lovely War, The Challengers, Avanti!, Riata, Beyond the Door*, more.

MILLS, MORT (S. Cal.) Character. Onscreen from the '50s. IN: *Affair in Trinidad, The Farmer Takes a Wife, Cry Vengeance, Desert Sands, The Name of the Game Is Kill*, more.

MILLS BROTHERS, THE (S. Cal. and Nev.) Just the titles of the songs this incomparable singing act has recorded (and the total by 1975 was 1,264) bring back glorious memories to millions: "Tiger Rag" (their first), "Dinah," "Goodbye Blues" (their theme), "Paper Doll" (their greatest success: 6 million copies), "I'll Be Around," "You Always Hurt the One You Love," etc. In '75 they celebrated their 50th anniversary in show business and were saluted at various industry functions. The most sentimental affairs were two held in Los Angeles. One was a banquet tendered by the Pacific Pioneer Broadcasters. Calling them to the stand to present them gold cuff links was a tearful Harry Von Zell, their first radio announcer on what was a history-making program, the first commercially sponsored network show for black artists. The other particularly nostalgic tribute was a supergala at the Dorothy Chandler Pavilion. On the program with them was Bing Crosby, with whom they made their first movie, *The Big Broadcast of 1932*. The Mills Brothers, in their 60s and still working six months each year here and abroad, are three now, and have been for almost a decade. Harry (whose eyesight is failing) and Don (the youngest, with the beard) live in Los Angeles; Herb (the plump one, and now eldest) lives in Las Vegas. Oldest brother, John Jr., from the time they began as children on a local radio station in Piqua, Ohio, in 1925, was the original fourth member of the group. After his death in 1936, his place was taken by John Mills Sr., their father, until his own death in 1968. Entertaining no thoughts of retiring, and making only one small concession to time's passage—they no longer do one-nighters—they are unique in the annals of show business. Perhaps no other singing group has successfully endured for a half-century with its original members. Their 1975 album was titled simply *The Mills Bros. Story*. And quite a story it has been—and continues to be. Onscreen from 1932. IN: *The Big Broadcast of 1932, Broadway Gondolier, He's My Guy, Reveille With Beverly, Chatterbox*, more.

MILNER, MARTIN (S. Cal.) Leading man. Television star. Onscreen from 1947. IN: *Life With Father, The Halls of Montezuma, Destination Gobi, Francis in the Navy, Marjorie Morningstar, Too Much Too Soon, Compulsion, Sex Kittens Go to College, 55 Days at Peking, The V.I.P.s, The Pink Panther, Zebra in the Kitchen, Valley of the Dolls, Three Guns for Texas, Ski Fever,* more.

MILO, SANDRA (It.) Leading lady. Onscreen from the '50s. IN: *The Mirror Has Two Faces, General Della Rovere, The Green Mare, 8 1/2, Juliet of the Spirits, The Visit; Weekend, Italian Style;* more.

MILTON, BILLY (Eng.) Character. Onscreen from 1930. IN: *Young Woodley, The Man from Chicago, Along Came Sally, Yes Madam, License to Kill, Hot Millions, Heavens Above! The Black Windmill,* more.

MIMIEUX, YVETTE (S. Cal.) Costar. Onscreen from 1960. IN: *Platinum High School, The Time Machine, Light in the Piazza, The Wonderful World of the Brothers Grimm, Diamond Head, Toys in the Attic, Joy in the Morning, The Reward; Monkeys, Go Home; The Mercenaries, Three in the Attic, Skyjacked, The Neptune Factor, Journey Into Fear,* more.

MIMS, WILLIAM (S. Cal.) Support. Onscreen from the '60s. IN: *Sanctuary, Wild in the Country, The Day Mars Invaded Earth, Flap, The Ballad of Cable Hogue, Johnny Got His Gun,* more.

MINARDOS, NICO (S. Cal.) Leading man. Onscreen from 1955. IN: *Desert Sands, Istanbul, Holiday for Lovers, Twelve Hours to Kill, It Happened in Athens, Samar, Day of the Evil Gun, Daring Game, Assault on Agathon,* more.

MINER, JAN (N.Y.) TV-radio-stage character actress. Onscreen from 1968. IN: *The Swimmer, Lenny.*

MINKUS, BARBARA (S. Cal.) Support. Onscreen from the '60s. IN: *What's So Bad About Feeling Good?,* more.

MINNELLI, LIZA (S. Cal.) Star. Nominated for Best Actress Oscar in *The Sterile Cuckoo.* Won in the same category in *Cabaret.* Onscreen from 1968. IN: *Charlie Bubbles; Tell Me That You Love Me, Junie Moon; Lucky Lady, A Matter of Time.*

MINOT, ANNA (N.Y.) Character. Onscreen from the '50s. IN: *Teresa, Odds Against Tomorrow,* more.

MINTER, MARY MILES (S. Cal.) Heavier now than she was ever seen on the screen or even in the tabloids, this great silent favorite—once Pickford's closest rival at portraying innocents—lives in solitary retirement in a big house in Santa Monica. She is in her 70s now (b. 1902), sees almost no one from the "old days," and has small fondness for conversation about her 50-picture, 1912–23 career. Perhaps because such talk inevitably leads to the 1922 murder—one of Hollywood's classic, unsolved cases—of William Desmond Taylor, the much older director with whom she was in love. Mary Miles Minter was never a suspect in the case. But in her book *The Honeycomb,* ace reporter Adela Rogers St. John, mentioning no names, intimates strongly that the star's overly possessive mother might well have committed the deed—to protect her daughter from any further involvement with Taylor. A maid of the mother, Mrs. Charlotte Shelby, told police that Mrs. Shelby had once gone to the director's home and threatened him—adding that Mrs. Shelby had a gun and practiced with it regularly. No one was ever charged with the crime, though tabloids had a decades-long field day with the drama. As recently as November 17, 1974, New York's *Sunday News* recapped the whole lurid story. Mary Miles Minter, rigidly under the thumb of her archetypal "movie mother" until adulthood, was involved in strenuous court battles with Mrs. Shelby—later in the '20s—over her earnings as a star. But they eventually reconciled, and it was in the actress's home that Mrs. Shelby was living at the time of her death in '57. Mary Miles Minter made only four more movies after William Desmond Taylor's murder (*Drums of Fate, The Cowboy and the Lady, South of Suva,* and *The Trail of the Lonesome Pine*), her studio then settling her contract for more than $300,000. At 21 she was through. She never acted again in any medium and, since she always maintained the screen career had been her mother's idea, it's doubtful she ever missed performing. Instead, she became a most astute business woman, particularly enterprising in real estate, which made her very rich. And finally, at 55, she married for the first and only time. Her husband was Brandon O'Hildebrandt, who had been her associate in various commercial ventures for almost two decades. They had only seven years as husband and wife before his death in '65. The passage of time has not diminished Mary Miles Minter's sensitivity about the William Desmond Taylor murder case. In February 1970, a segment of the TV series *Rod Serling's Wonderful World Of . . .* recapped the Taylor murder. In May, Mary Miles Minter, who had successfully fled the spotlight for decades, filed a $350,000 suit for invasion of privacy, contending that in this segment dealing with famous crimes Serling had mentioned the still-unresolved murder of Taylor and had implied she was a suspect in the case. The lawsuit came before the court in March 1973, and she lost. Los Angeles Superior Court Judge Benjamin Landis, after hearing the case, delivered the verdict himself without even permitting the case to go to the jury. If photos of the former star were made at the time of the suit, they did not appear in the press. And if they had, her oldtime admirers would not have found recognizing her an easy matter. Onscreen from 1912. IN: *The Nurse, Emma of Stork's Nest, Barbara Frietchie, Dimples, Lovely Mary, A Dream or Two Ago, The Gentle Intruder, Melissa of the Hills, Her Country's Call, The Mate of the Sally Ann, A Bit of Jade, The Ghost of Rosy Taylor, Rosemary Climbs the Heights, A Bachelor's Wife, Anne of Green Gables, Judy of Rogue's Harbor, Nurse Marjorie, Jenny Be Good, Eyes of the Heart, The Little Clown, Moonlight and Honeysuckle, Tillie, The Heart Specialist,* more.

MINTZ, ELI (N.Y.) Character. Onscreen from 1951. IN: *Molly, The Proud Rebel; Murder, Inc.;* more.

MIONI, FABRIZIO (S. Cal.) Leading man. Onscreen from the '50s. IN: *Hercules, The Blue Angel, The Venetian Affair, The Secret War of Harry Frigg, The Pink Jungle,* more.

MIOU-MIOU (Fr.) Leading lady. Onscreen in the '70s. IN: *Going Places, The Genius,* more.

MIRANDA, ISA (It.) Gabriele D'Annunzio, long ago, hailed her as "the most glamorous woman in the world." But Paramount, hoping she would prove another Dietrich, concluded—after *Hotel Imperial, Zaza,* and *Adventure in Diamonds*—she wasn't. The English language, which she has since mastered, gave the Italian star enormous difficulty. Returning to Europe, she enjoyed a starring heyday lasting another 15 years, including several successful roles. One was as The Actress in France's elegant *La Ronde;* another was in *The Walls of Malapaga,* which won her the Cannes Film Festival's Best Actress award in '50. Then came the supporting roles, some quite small, averaging about one a year—in *The Yellow Rolls-Royce, Summertime, The Empty Canvas,* etc. In '74 there was a strong one, as the domineering Countess in the Dirk Bogarde exercise in sado-masochism, *The Night Porter.* In a blonde wig reminiscent of Shearer's in *Idiot's Delight,* she looked younger than her years; she was then 65. Between acting jobs these days, perhaps to fill her hours, perhaps to earn extra income, she sometimes works as a seamstress, making and dressing

dolls and puppets. There is irony here. As a child, daughter of a streetcar motorman, she went to work in a dressmaker's shop, and by 12 was a skilled seamstress. To break away from the sewing machine, she took typing lessons and became a secretary. With those earnings, she studied acting at Milan's Dramatic Arts Academy. She became a star overnight in her first two movies, *Tenebre* and *Darkness,* and was in truth the Sophia Loren of her day. Italian fans, recalling this, spearheaded a drive a while back to change the name of the street on which the former star lives, Via St. Angela de Merici, to Isa Miranda Street. Today, her star no longer soaring as it did so long, Isa Miranda acts whenever there is a job; when there isn't she occupies herself with costuming her puppets and dolls. Onscreen from 1934. IN: *Everybody's Lady, Red Passport, Malcombra, Mistake to be Alive, Pact with the Devil, Senza Cielo, The Seven Deadly Sins, Before the Deluge, Defeat of Hannibal, Rommel's Treasure, A Young World, The Great Britain Train Robbery, Caroline Cherie, The Shoes of the Fisherman, Marta,* more.

MIRANDA, SUSANA (S. Cal.) Support. Onscreen from 1969. IN: *Bob & Carol & Ted & Alice, Flap,* more.

MIRREN, HELEN (Eng.) Leading lady. Onscreen from 1969. IN: *Age of Consent, Savage Messiah, O Lucky Man,* more.

MITCHELL, BELLE (S. Cal.) Character. Onscreen from the '20s. IN: *Flying Romeos, The Firefly, The Mark of Zorro, That Lady in Ermine,* more.

MITCHELL, CAMERON (S. Cal.) Costar. Onscreen from 1945. IN: *What Next, Corporal Hargrove?; They Were Expendable, Tenth Avenue Angel, High Barbaree, Cass Timberlane, Outcasts of Poker Flat, Pony Soldier, Man on a Tightrope, How to Marry a Millionaire, Hell and High Water, Garden of Evil, Love Me or Leave Me, Carousel, Monkey on My Back, No Down Payment, Three Hours to Kill, Attack of the Normans, Hombre, Knives of the Avenger, Buck and the Preacher, The Midnight Man, The Klansman, Political Asylum,* more.

MITCHELL, DON (S. Cal.) Black star. Onscreen in the '70s. IN: *Blacula II,* more.

MITCHELL, GUY (S. Cal.) A prolonged illness from which he has recovered kept the red-headed singer-actor, so popular in the '50s, professionally inactive for a decade. In 1975 he attempted a comeback via the recording "Learn to Love Again." Onscreen 1953–54.

IN: *Those Redheads from Seattle* and *Red Garters*.

MITCHELL, GWENN (S. Cal.) Black leading lady. Onscreen in the '70s. IN: *Shaft, Chosen Survivors*, more.

MITCHELL, JAMES (N.Y.) Still a handsome bachelor in his 50s (b. 1920), the actor-dancer who seemed certain to become a star at MGM has not acted in a movie for two decades. Instead he has starred on Broadway in such dramas as *The Deputy* and such musicals as *Carnival!* and, in 1974, *Mack & Mabel* with Robert Preston. He has also been highly popular playing the role of "Julian Hathaway" in the TV soap opera *Where The Heart Is*. Onscreen from 1949. IN: *Colorado Territory, Border Incident, Stars in My Crown, The Band Wagon, Deep in My Heart, The Prodigal, Oklahoma!, The Peacemaker*.

MITCHELL, SHIRLEY (S. Cal.) Support. Onscreen from 1943. IN: *Jamboree, Mr. Lord Says No!*, more.

MITCHELL, STEVE (S. Cal.) Support. Onscreen from 1955. IN: *It's Always Fair Weather, China Doll, Once a Thief*, more.

MITCHELL, WARREN (Eng.) Character. Onscreen from 1956. IN: *Stowaway Girl, The Crawling Eye, Surprise Package, Moon Zero Two, The Boy Who Stole a Million, The Small World of Sammy Lee; Arriverderci, Baby!; The Jokers, Innocent Bystanders*, more.

MITCHELL, YVONNE (Eng.) Support; former leading lady. Onscreen from 1948. IN: *The Queen of Spades, Turn the Key Softly, Blonde Sinner, Woman in a Dressing Gown, Sapphire, Tiger Bay, Conspiracy of Hearts, The Trials of Oscar Wilde, Johnny Nobody, The Great Waltz, Demons of the Mind*, more.

MITCHUM, CHRIS (S. Cal.) Leading man. Robert Mitchum's son. Onscreen in the '70s. IN: *Suppose They Gave a War and Nobody Came?, Chisum, Rio Lobo, Big Jake, Cactus in the Snow, Once, The Great Friday*, more.

MITCHUM, CINDY (S.. Cal.) Support. Wife of

Chris Mitchum. Onscreen in 1969. IN: *Changes*.

MITCHUM, JIM (S. Cal.) Leading man. Robert Mitchum's son. Onscreen from 1958. IN: *Thunder Road* (with his father), *The Beat Generation, Girls Town, The Last Time I Saw Archie, The Victors, Ride the Wild Surf, In Harm's Way, The Money Trap, The Heroes, Bigfoot, Moonrunners*, more.

MITCHUM, JOHN (S. Cal.) Character. Robert Mitchum's younger brother. Onscreen first as "John Mallory" in 1951's *Flying Leathernecks*. Onscreen under his own name from 1962. IN: *Hitler, Cattle King, Bandolero!, Paint Your Wagon, Chisum, Breakheart Pass*, more.

MITCHUM, ROBERT (S. Cal.) Star. Nominated for Best Supporting Actor in *The Story of G.I. Joe*. Onscreen from 1943. IN: *Hoppy Serves a Writ* (billed Bob Mitchum), *Bar 20, The Dancing Masters, Gung Ho!, When Strangers Marry, Undercurrent, The Locket, Pursued, Desire Me, Crossfire, Rachel and the Stranger, The Red Pony, The Racket, Macao, The Lusty Men, Angel Face, White Witch Doctor, River of No Return, Track of the Cat, Night of the Hunter; Heaven Knows, Mr. Allison; Home Before Dark, Thunder Road, The Wonderful Country, Home from the Hill, The Sundowners, Cape Fear, The Longest Day, Two for the Seesaw, What a Way to Go!, El Dorado, Anzio, Secret Ceremony, Villa Rides, The Good Guys and the Bad Guys, Ryan's Daughter, The Wrath of God, The Friends of Eddie Coyle, Going Home; Farewell, My Lovely; The Last Tycoon*, more.

MITO, MITSUKO (Japan) Leading lady. Onscreen from the '50s. IN: *Ugetsu, Samurai, Golden Demon*, more.

MOBLEY, MARY ANN (S. Cal.) Leading lady. Onscreen from 1964. IN: *Get Yourself a College Girl, Harum Scarum, Young Dillinger, Three on a Couch, The King's Pirate*, more.

MOFFAT, DONALD (S. Cal.) Support. Onscreen from 1957. IN: *Pursuit of the Graf Spee, Rachel Rachel, The Great Northfield Minnesota Raid*, more.

MOFFATT, JOHN (Eng.) Character. Onscreen from 1955. IN: *Loser Take All, Tom Jones, Julius Caesar, Murder on the Orient Express*, more.

MOFFO, ANNA (N.Y.) Opera star-actress. Onscreen from 1968. IN: *La Traviata, The Adventurers*.

MOHNER, CARL (Eng.) Character. Onscreen from 1955. IN: *Rififi, The Last Bridge, The Camp on Blood Island, He Who Must Die, Sink the Bismarck!, The Kitchen, It Takes a Thief, Carmen Baby*, more.

MOHYEDDIN, ZIA (Eng.) Character actor from Pakistan. Onscreen from 1961. IN: *Lawrence of Arabia, Deadlier Than the Male, Sammy Going South, The Sailor from Gibraltar*, more.

MOLINA, CARLOS (S. Cal.) A top orchestra leader during the big-band era. Came out of retirement to play a nonmusical character role, his debut, in 1976. IN: *The Gumball Rally.*

MOLINARI, DOREEN (N.J.) Juvenile. Onscreen in the '70s. IN: *Made for Each Other*, more.

MOLINAS, RICHARD (Eng.) Character. Onscreen from the '40s. IN: *Gaiety George, Snowbound, The Bad Lord Byron, Brandy for the Parson, The Sword and the Rose, A Day to Remember, Track the Man Down*, more.

MOLL, GEORGIA (It.) Leading lady. Onscreen from the '50s. IN: *The Quiet American, The Cossacks, The White Warrior, Island of Love, Dark Purpose, The Devil in Love, Beyond Control*, more.

MOLLISON, CLIFFORD (Eng.) Character; former leading man. Onscreen from the '30s. IN: *Jaws of Hell, Almost a Honeymoon*, more.

MOLLOT, YOLANDE (Eng.) Actress who used this billing in 1940's *Turnabout*, later changing her name. (See Yolande Donlon.)

MONCION, FRANCISCO (N.Y.) Ballet star. Onscreen in 1967. IN: *A Midsummer Night's Dream.*

MONDO, PEGGY (S. Cal.) Support. Onscreen from 1963. IN: *Who's Minding the Store?, The Man from the Diner's Club, Girl Crazy, The Patsy, The Shakiest Gun in the West, Angel in My Pocket*, more.

MONK, JULIUS (N.Y.) Cabaret impresario. Onscreen in 1960. IN: *Girl of the Night.*

MONKHOUSE, BOB (Eng.) Comic character. Onscreen from the '50s. IN: *Carry On Sergeant, A Weekend with Lulu, The Bliss of Mrs. Blossom*, more.

MONKS, JAMES (N.Y.) Support. Has acted mainly on TV and the stage since his brief Hollywood career. Onscreen from 1941. IN: *How Green Was My Valley* (as one of the brothers, Owen), *Joan of Paris*, more.

MONTAGUE, LEE (Eng.) Support. Onscreen from 1952. IN: *Moulin Rouge, Billy Budd, The Horse Without a Head, How I Won the War, Eagle in a Cage*, more.

MONTALBAN, CARLOS (N.Y.) Character. Onscreen from 1956. IN: *The Harder They Fall, Crowded Paradise, Pepe, Love Has Many Faces*, more.

MONTALBAN, RICARDO (S. Cal.) Costar. Onscreen in Spanish-speaking movies from 1941. IN: *El Verdugo de Sevilla, La Fuga, La Casa de la Zorro, Pepita Jimenez*, more. Onscreen in American movies from 1947. IN: *Fiesta, On an Island with You, Neptune's Daughter, Mystery Street, Two Weeks with Love, Across the Wide Missouri, Sombrero, Latin Lovers, The Saracen Blade, Sayonara, Let No Man Write My Epitaph, Cheyenne Autumn, The Money Trap, The Singing Nun, Sweet Charity, Conquest of the Planet of the Apes, The Train Robbers*, more.

MONTANA, MONTIE (S. Cal.) In 1975, age 65, the cowboy actor famed for his stunt riding and lasso tricks celebrated his 50th anniversary in show business. Rarely seen in movies now, he is on the road eight to ten months a year, performing at rodeos and in Wild West shows— keeping in shape between engagements by swinging from the roof of his San Fernando Valley ranch-house on a trapeze. Touring and performing with him is the former Eleanor Orlando, the attractive young woman who became his bride in '72. His catchy professional name he got by chance, incidentally. Starting out as Owen Harlan Mickel, of Wolf Point, Mont., he says, "During the Buck Jones show in 1929, the announcer couldn't remember my name—so he called me 'Montie from Montana,' " and the monicker stuck. Onscreen from the '30s. IN: Many Tom Mix and Buck Jones Westerns, followed by *Circle of Death, Riders of the Deadline, Down Dakota Way, Arizona Bushwhackers*, more.

MONTAND, YVES (Fr.) Costar. Onscreen from 1946. IN: *Star Without Light, Gates of the Night, The Wages of Fear, Witches of Salem, Heroes and Sinners (Les Heros Sont Fatigues), Let's Make Love, Where the Hot Wind Blows, Sanctuary, My Geisha, The Sleeping Car Murder, La Guerre est Fini, Is Paris Burning?, Grand-Prix, Live for Life, On a Clear Day You Can See Forever, Cesar and Rosalie, Delusions of Grandeur, The Savage*, more.

MONTENEGRO, CONCHITA (Sp.) Last on Hollywood screens in '35 in *He Trusted His Wife*, the sultry Spanish beauty, now in her 60s (b. 1912), made several more in Italy, Spain, and France before retiring in '48. The wife of actor Raul Roulien at the time she left California, she has since been married to a Spanish diplomat, Gimenez Arnau, and lives in Madrid. Onscreen from 1931. IN: *The Cisco Kid, Never the Twain Shall Meet, Strangers May Kiss, The Gay Caballero, Laughing at Life, Handy Andy, Hell in the Heavens*, more.

MONTEVECCHI, LILIANE (It.) Leading lady. Onscreen from 1955. IN: *The Glass Slipper,*

Moonfleet, Meet Me in Las Vegas, The Sad Sack, The Young Lions, King Creole, Me and the Colonel, more.

MONTGOMERY, BELINDA J. (S. Cal.) Leading lady. Onscreen in the '70s. IN: *Running Scared, The Other Side of the Mountain, Breaking Point,* more.

MONTGOMERY, EARL (N.Y.) Character. Onscreen in 1963. IN: *Act One* (as Alexander Woollcott).

MONTGOMERY, ELIZABETH (S. Cal.) Leading lady. Onscreen from 1955. IN: *The Court-Martial of Billy Mitchell, Johnny Cool, Who's Been Sleeping in My Bed?,* more.

MONTGOMERY, GEORGE (S. Cal.) Costar. Onscreen from 1938. IN: *The Lone Ranger* (serial; billed under his real name, George Letz), *Stardust, The Cowboy and the Blonde, Cadet Girl, Roxie Hart, Ten Gentlemen from West Point, China Girl, Orchestra Wives, Coney Island, Bomber's Moon; Davy Crockett—Indian Scout; The Iroquois Trail, Cripple Creek, Seminole Uprising, Toughest Gun in Tombstone, Watusi, Samar, Battle of the Bulge, Hostile Guns, Warkill,* more.

MONTGOMERY, PEGGY (S. Cal.) (See Baby Peggy.)

MONTGOMERY, RAY (S. Cal.) Still there is the engaging grin of the leading man of the '40s —the young groom in *June Bride,* and often a G.I. Gone are the wavy locks and slender physique. Now, looking well-fed and with shiny dome, he plays middle-aged government agents or business men. The latter he has long been off the screen—the owner and operator of one of the movie colony's most successful real estate agencies. Onscreen from 1942. IN: *The Hard Way, Action in the North Atlantic, Johnny Belinda, Task Force, House Across the Street, People Will Talk, Ramar and the Jungle Secrets* (and other "Ramar" pix), *Down Among the Sheltering Palms, Bombers B-52, A Private Affair, A Gathering of Eagles,* more.

MONTGOMERY, ROBERT (N.Y.) Star. Nominated for Best Actor Oscar in *Night Must Fall* and *Here Comes Mr. Jordan.* In his 70s now (b. 1904), and dapper still, the former star has in recent years served as president of New York's Lincoln Center Repertory Theater and as a trustee of the National Citizens Committee for Broadcasting—advocating a strengthened public broadcasting system. Previously married (1928–50) to socialite Elizabeth Allan (not the English star), he has been married since a divorce was granted in '50 to the former Eliza-

beth Grant Harkness. By his first wife he has two children, Elizabeth Montgomery, the actress, and Robert Jr., a telephone company executive in Milwaukee; they have made him five times a grandfather. The Montgomerys have an elegant townhouse on Manhattan's East 72nd Street and a summer house off the coast of Maine. They visit Hollywood on occasion, but he says he has no further interest in acting. Onscreen from 1929. IN: *College Days, Father's Day, Our Blushing Brides, The Divorcee, Sins of the Children, Let Us Be Gay, The Big House, Shipmates, Letty Lynton, Blondie of the Follies, When Ladies Meet, Night Flight, Private Lives, The Mystery of Mr. X, Riptide; Vanessa —Her Love Story; No More Ladies, Biography of a Bachelor Girl, Petticoat Fever, The Last of Mrs. Cheyney, Yellow Jack, Three Loves Has Nancy, The Earl of Chicago, Mr. and Mrs. Smith, The Rage of Heaven, Unfinished Business, They Were Expendable, Ride the Pink Horse, The Saxon Charm, June Bride, Once More My Darling,* his last, in 1949.

MONTIEL, SARITA (Sp.) Popular in Hollywood movies in the early '50s at the time she was married to (the late) director Anthony Mann, the actress-singer has not appeared in a film since 1963's *A Girl Against Napoleon,* made abroad. An idol in Spain, her homeland, she has long since returned there, making records and starring in stage shows such as the recent *Saritisima.* In '75 she made a two-month tour of North and South America. Opening in New York, she worked her musical way south to Miami, Mexico City, Panama, Caracas, Bogota, Rio de Janeiro and Buenos Aires. Onscreen from the '50s. IN: *Vera Cruz, Serenade, Run of the Arrow, Circle of Death,* more.

MONTOYA, JULIA (S. Cal.) Character. Onscreen from the '50s. IN: *One Way Street,* more.

MOODY, KING (S. Cal.) Support. Onscreen from the '60s. IN: *Sweet November, The Strawberry Statement,* more.

MOODY, RON (Eng.) Character. Nominated for Best Actor Oscar in *Oliver!* Onscreen from 1953. IN: *Davy, Make Mine Mink, Follow a Star, The Mouse on the Moon, Murder Most Foul, Ladies Who Do, A Pair of Briefs, Seaside Swingers, Flight of the Doves,* more.

MOORE, ADRIENNE (S. Cal.) Character. Onscreen from 1956. IN: *Patterns,* more.

MOORE, ALVY (S. Cal.) Character. Onscreen from 1952. IN: *Okinawa, The Glory Brigade, Riot in Cell Block 11, Susan Slept Here, Five Against the House, Designing Woman, The*

Wackiest Ship in the Army, Everything's Ducky, Move Over Darling, Three Nuts in Search of a Bolt, The Witchmaker, The Brotherhood of Satan, A Boy and His Dog, more.

MOORE, ARCHIE (S. Cal.) Black character. Onscreen from 1960. IN: *The Adventures of Huckleberry Finn, The Carpetbaggers, The Fortune Cookie, Breakheart Pass*, more.

MOORE, CHARLES (N.Y.) Black support. Onscreen from the '60s. IN: *Where Were You When the Lights Went Out?, You're a Big Boy Now, Who Killed Teddy Bear?*, more.

MOORE, CLAYTON (Nev.) The rugged star of dozens of Westerns and almost as many serials (*Perils of Nyoka, Jungle Drums in Africa*, etc.) retired from movies after 1959's *The Ghost of Zorro*. His long-running (seven years) TV series of *The Lone Ranger* bit the dust a bit earlier, in '56. Until '72 he toured in a stage act at fairs and rodeos, after which he, his wife, and teenage daughter settled at Lake Tahoe, Nev. The actor, now in his 60s (b. 1914), considered himself retired. But Hollywood has continued to call him back, off and on, for TV commercials —automobiles (for which he did wear the "Lone Ranger" mask) and after-shave (for which he didn't). A bonus item for nostalgia-quiz buffs: he and Jay Silverheels ("Tonto") twice acted together in pictures in which they were *not* in costume as "The Lone Ranger" and "Tonto"—the movies were *Black Dakotas* and *The Cowboy and the Indians*. Onscreen from 1940. IN: *Kit Carson, International Lady, Along the Oregon Trail, G-Men Never Forget, Riders of the Whistling Pines, Night Stage to Galveston, Buffalo Bill in Tomahawk Territory, Montana Territory, Barbed Wire, Kansas Pacific, Down Laredo Way*, more.

MOORE, COLLEEN (S. Cal.) Perhaps the silent screen's most insouciant—and delightful— flapper, she is well into her 70s (b. 1900) and into a new career—writing. In less than a decade she has published three books: *Silent Star* (her autobiography, and as fetching as its subject), *Colleen Moore's Doll House* (the million-dollar miniature viewed by millions in the past four decades), and *How Women Can Make Money in the Stock Market*. Justifiably proud of this achievement in publishing, she has papered the powder room in her new house in Paso Robles with the jackets of these books. And as for that book on the stock market, it is not to be overlooked that its author is an exceedingly rich woman, and Wall Street is one of the avenues by which she got to that plateau. Her third husband, from '37 until his death in '67, was Homer Hargrave, a partner in one of New York's most estimable brokerages, which she also

eventually joined. He taught her the "inside" of money, saying, "If you're going to handle it, you may as well understand it." Mr. Hargrave, a widower when they married, also gave her the only children she has "had," a son and a daughter. It is of no consequence that she did not bear them, they are "hers"; today there are five grandchildren and they too are "hers." There is much new about Colleen Moore now. She wears tinted horn-rim glasses, so there are fewer comments on her eyes—one blue, one brown. Instead of her familiar bangs, she wears her dark hair, parted on the left, almost shoulder-length and straight. And she is unabashedly in love. Her "beau" is famed director King Vidor, a vigorous, handsome man a few years her senior. They first met and fell in love 55 years ago, but each of them continued to marry others—Colleen marrying and divorcing studio executive John McCormick and stockbroker Albert P. Scott before her third, happy, marriage. Fate brought them together again a few years ago. Today they live on neighboring ranches near Paso Robles—his, a huge spread of over 1,200 acres. "We have the same sense of humor, and we both love to travel," he says. So, together, they have journeyed throughout the Far East, Europe, and the South Pacific. One of Vidor's former wives, Eleanor Boardman, living near Santa Barbara, told a Hollywood friend not long ago, "They stopped off to see me recently on their way back from Europe. I hope that King will be able to marry Colleen. She's the nicest girl he ever had." Onscreen from 1917. IN: *Bad Boy, An Old-Fashioned Young Man, A Hoosier Romance, The Busher, The Egg Crate Wallop, The Wall Flower, Flaming Youth, Painted People, The Perfect Flapper, So Big, Sally, We Moderns, Irene, Ella Cinders, Twinkletoes, Orchids and Ermine, Her Wild Oat, Lilac Time; Oh, Kay!; Smiling Irish Eyes, Footlights and Fools, The Power and the Glory, Success at Any Price*, more, including 1934's *The Scarlet Letter*, her last.

MOORE, CONSTANCE (S. Cal.) Stylish and attractive in her 50s (b. 1920), she has been married since '39 to John Maschio, former actors' agent and more recently a real estate executive. They live in a rambling house overlooking Beverly Hills, have a daughter, Gina (b. 1942), a son, Michael (b. 1947), and are grandparents. Onscreen steadily through 1948's *Hats Off to Rhythm*, the singer-actress has appeared in two B's since—1951's *The 13th Letter* and 1967's *Spree*. Also, in the mid-1960s, she costarred with Robert Young in the short-lived TV series *Window on Main Street*, followed, in '67, by a single guest stint in *My Three Sons* on television. She devotes herself now to family, hobbies—gardening and painting still lifes—and favorite charities. In 1975 she served as Chairman of the Braille Institute's Auxiliary in Beverly Hills. Onscreen from 1938. IN: *A Letter of Introduction, The Crime of Dr. Hallet, Swing That Cheer, You Can't Cheat an Honest Man, Mutiny on the Blackhawk, Hawaiian Nights; Charlie McCarthy, Detective; Framed, I'm Nobody's Sweetheart Now, La Conga Nights, Argentine Nights, I Wanted Wings; Take a Letter, Darling; Show Business, Mexicana, Earl Carroll's Sketchbook, In Old Sacramento, Hit Parade of 1947*, more.

MOORE, DENNIE (N.Y.) The blonde so amusing as daffy servant girl Maudie Tilt in *Sylvia Scarlett*, her debut, is retired, lives alone at an excellent hotel on Park Avenue, and is in her late 60s (b. 1907). This does not stop her, however, from citing roller skating as one of her pet recreations. Before, during, and after her movie career she was featured on Broadway, appearing first ('24) in the *Ziegfeld Follies* and last ('55) as Mrs. Van Daan in *The Diary of Anne Frank*. Onscreen from 1935. IN: *The Perfect Specimen, Boy Meets Girl, The Women, Saturday's Children, Dive Bomber, Anna Lucasta, The Model and the Marriage Broker*, more.

MOORE, DICKIE (N.Y.) Famous in more than 100 features for his cherubic face, big dark eyes, and pout, this talented boy actor of yesteryear, just entering his 50s (b. 1925), is now head of Dick Moore and Associates on West 57th Street, which produces industrial shows. Formerly married (1949–54) to Patricia Dempsey, by whom he has a grown son, he is now married (since '59) to Eleanor Donhowe Fitzpatrick, and is the father of a teenage son by her. Living at an excellent address on the West Side, the actor has taught acting, written published books on the subject, edited *Equity* magazine, performed on Broadway, in stock, and on TV (for which he has also written and directed), produced a short film—*The Boy and the Eagle*—that was nominated for an Oscar, and until recently was still listed in the *Players' Guide* as being available for acting assignments. Those wise child's eyes should have been a tipoff to his multitalented future. Onscreen from 1926. IN: *The Beloved Rogue*, "Our Gang," *Seed, Manhattan Parade, So Big, When a Fellow Needs a Friend, Blonde Venus, Union Depot, Oliver Twist, The Cradle Song, Gallant Lady, A Man's Castle, This Side of Heaven, Little Men, The Story of Louis Pasteur, Timothy's Quest, My Bill, A Dispatch from Reuters, Sergeant York, Are These Our Children?, Miss Annie Rooney* (gave Shirley Temple her first screen kiss), *Heaven Can Wait, The Song of Bernadette, Youth Runs Wild, The Eve of St. Mark, Together Again, Bad Boy, Tuna Clipper, Eight Iron Men*, more, including 1952's *The Member of the Wedding*, his last.

MOORE, DUDLEY (S. Cal.) Star comedian. Now married to actress Tuesday Weld. Onscreen from 1966. IN: *The Wrong Box, Bedazzled, 30 Is a Dangerous Age, Cynthia, The Bed Sitting Room, Those Daring Young Men in Their Jaunty Jalopies*, more.

MOORE, EILEEN (Eng.) Leading lady. Onscreen from the '50s. IN: *Mr. Denning Drives North, An Inspector Calls, Men of Sherwood Forest, The Green Man, A Town Like Alice*, more.

MOORE, ERIN O'BRIEN (S. Cal.) Character. Onscreen from 1934. IN: *His Greatest Gamble, Destination Moon, The Long Gray Line*, more.

MOORE, GAR (S. Cal.) Acclaimed as the young GI in *Paisan* and in *To Live in Peace*, both made in Italy, he later made several in Hollywood including, last, in '52, *The Girl in White*. Since then he has been a successful business man in Palm Springs. Now in his 50s, he has been married to and divorced from comedienne Nancy Walker, and in '71 he married millionairess Marge Sinek, of Palm Springs, who is reportedly of the Oscar Meyer weiner family. Onscreen from 1947. IN: *Illegal Entry, Johnny Stool Pigeon, The Underworld Story*, more.

MOORE, JOANNA (S. Cal.) Leading lady. Formerly married to Ryan O'Neal, she is the mother of Oscar-winning juvenile Tatum O'Neal. Onscreen from 1957. IN: *Slim Carter, Appointment with a Shadow, Touch of Evil, The Last Angry Man, Son of Flubber, The Man from Galveston, Never a Dull Moment, Countdown, The Hindenburg*, more.

MOORE, JUANITA (S. Cal.) Black character. Onscreen from 1952. IN: *Affair in Trinidad, Lydia Bailey, Women's Prison, Imitation of Life, Tammy Tell Me True, A Raisin in the Sun, Papa's Delicate Condition, The Singing Nun, Rosie, Up Tight, The Mack*, more.

MOORE, KIERON (Eng.) Leading man. Onscreen from 1944. IN: *The Voice Within, Anna Karenina, Saints and Sinners, David and Bathsheba, The Naked Heart, The Green Scarf, The Angry Hills, Darby O'Gill and the Little People, League of Gentlemen, Lion of Sparta, I Thank a Fool, The Main Attraction, Crack in the World, Bikini Paradise, Custer of the West*, more.

MOORE, LAURENS (N.Y.) Character. Onscreen from the '60s. IN: *North by Northwest*, more.

MOORE, MARJORIE (S. Cal.) (See Marjorie Reynolds.)

MOORE, MARY TYLER (S. Cal.) Television star. Onscreen from 1961. IN: *X-15, Thoroughly Modern Millie, What's So Bad about Feeling Good?, Don't Just Stand There, Change of Habit.*

MOORE, MELBA (N.Y.) Singer-actress. Onscreen in the '70s. IN: *Pigeons*, more.

MOORE, MICHAEL (S. Cal.) Leading man who gave up acting and became a director—of *Paradise, Hawaiian Style; The Fastest Guitar Alive*, etc. Onscreen from 1952. IN: *The Atomic City, Pony Express, Stalag 17, Little Boy Lost, Sabre Jet*, more.

MOORE, ROBERT (N.Y.) Actor-director. Onscreen in 1970. IN: *Tell Me That You Love Me, Junie Moon.*

MOORE, ROGER (Eng.) Star. Onscreen from the '50s. IN: *The Last Time I Saw Paris, The King's Thief, Interrupted Melody, Diane, The Sins of Rachel Cade, Gold of the Seven Saints, Rape of the Sabines, Crossplot, Live and Let Die, Gold, The Man with the Golden Gun, That Lucky Touch, Shout at the Devil*, more.

MOORE, STEPHEN (Eng.) Support. Onscreen from 1961. IN: *A Midsummer Night's Dream*, more.

MOORE, TERRY (S. Cal.) Leading lady. Nominated for Best Supporting Actress Oscar in *Come Back, Little Sheba*. Off the screen since 1967's *A Man Called Dagger*, the actress, who is now in her 40s (b. 1929), figured in the news at various times in the '70s. In 1970 she filed for divorce from third husband, millionaire Stuart Cramer III, father of her sons, Stuart IV and Lamar, both teenagers now. They had married in 1959. Previously she had been married to football hero Glenn Davis and wealthy real estate man Eugene McGrath, both marriages ending in divorce. Also in '70, she announced formation of a movie-TV production company, Starcross, and the titles of three films in which she would costar; none to date has been produced. In 1971 she and her mother, Mrs. Luella Koford, were engaged in a legal battle in Los Angeles. Mrs. Koford filed suit to have a Los Angeles Superior Court name her temporary conservator of her daughter's $190,000 estate. She asserted that the actress, despondent over the failure of her marriage to Cramer, had once taken an overdose of sleeping pills. Additionally, she testified that her daughter had fallen under the influence of a young man—unnamed —who wished to become an actor. Terry Moore's mother withdrew the suit in '72 after the actress agreed to the appointment of a neutral third party to assist in managing her prop-erty. This agreement was reached in September, two weeks after the star had been arrested in New Orleans. She was charged with possession of marijuana while deplaning there for a brief stopover on a trip to Los Angeles where, she told authorities, she was to make an anti-drug recording. The star, a member of the Nixon Administration Antidrug Committee, and then one of Henry Kissinger's favorite dinner dates, maintained—successfully—that someone had planted the marijuana on her before the arrest in the lobby of New Orleans International Airport. In 1974 she starred, to excellent notices, at various dinner theaters in the musical *No, No, Nanette*. Also in 1975, having been one of Howard Hughes' frequent dates in the '50s, she appeared on TV—and looking remarkably attractive—when ABC's *Wide World* did "an unauthorized biography" on the billionaire. Then, in 1976, after the billionaire's death, she claimed she was once secretly married to him. Now, except for occasionally making the Hollywood social scene, sometimes with former costar Glenn Ford, she lives quietly with her children in a magnificent Spanish-French castle in Brentwood. Onscreen—under four different names—from 1940, beginning in child roles. IN: *The Howards of Virginia* (as Helen Koford, her real name), *My Gal Sal, Gaslight, Son of Lassie, Sweet and Low Down* (billed in some of the pictures of this period as Judy Ford), *The Devil on Wheels* (billed, when under contract to Eagle-Lion, as Jan Ford), *The Return of October* (her first as Terry Moore, when under contract to Columbia), *Mighty Joe Young, The Great Rupert, The Barefoot Mailman, Man on a Tightrope, Beneath the 12-Mile Reef, King of the Khyber Rifles, Daddy Long Legs, Shack Out on 101, Bernardine, Peyton Place, A Private's Affair, Platinum High School, Why Must I Die?, Black Spurs, Waco*, more.

MORAN, DOLORES (S. Cal.) Divorced from (the late) producer Benedict Bogeaus in '64, after 15 years of marriage, the girl who was one of Warners' more promising starlets in the '40s lives alone in North Hollywood. She has not acted since 1954's *The Silver Lode*. A slimmer, more sophisticated-looking blonde than in her buxom teenage heyday, she has entered her 50s (b. 1926) and is the mother of a son who, educated at the University of London, is a successful young business man. Onscreen from 1941. IN: *Yankee Doodle Dandy, The Hard Way, Old Acquaintance, To Have and Have Not, The Horn Blows at Midnight, The Man I Love, Christmas Eve, Johnny One-Eye, Count the Hours*, more.

MORAN, ERIN (S. Cal.) Juvenile. Onscreen from the '60s. IN: *How Sweet It Is, 80 Steps to Jonah*, more.

MORAN, LOIS (Ariz.) A widow, she lives in retirement in Sedonia. Her husband—from '35 until his death—was Col. Clarence M. Young, onetime assistant U.S. Secretary of Commerce and later vice president of Pan Am. She has a grown son, Timothy. Still dark-blonde and attractive as she enters her seventh decade (b. 1907), she last acted over two decades ago, co-starring in the TV series *Waterfront* with the late Preston Foster. Immediately before that she had done an occasional stage role at Stanford University, where she was artist-in-residence for a while in the '50s when she and her family lived in Palo Alto. She has not been seen onscreen since 1932's *West of Broadway*. Onscreen from 1925. IN: *Stella Dallas, Just Suppose, The Road to Mandalay, God Gave Me Twenty Cents, The Music Master, The Whirlwind of Youth, Sharp Shooters, Love Hungry, The River Pirate, Behind That Curtain, Mammy, The Dancers, Transatlantic, The Spider, The Men in Her Life*, more.

MORAN, PEGGY (S. Cal.) Universal, in the '40s, had no pin-up more squeaky-clean sighable, no young leading lady more devastatingly vivacious than this photogenic brunette. When she left the screen in '43, the veteran of nearly three dozen pix made in a six-year span, it was because she had just become (in '42) the wife of German-born director Henry (*Three Smart Girls*) Koster. The first time he saw her, the day he (and producer-partner Joe Pasternak) decided to sign her to a Universal contract, he told her she was too pretty to be an actress. These decades later, when her svelte figure has filled out quite regally and her hair is graying, he still tells her. Peggy is now not far from her 60th birthday (b. 1918) and her husband is 15 years older, though certain sectors in Hollywood still maintain the fiction that she married a "much older" man. They live in a splendid house in Pacific Palisades, have a wide circle of Hollywood friends, and two sons: Nicolas (b. 1943), a San Francisco psychiatrist, and Peter (b. 1946), who works for the Los Angeles Police Department as a probation officer. Koster is retired now, the uplifting type of movie for which he was famous (musically talented youngsters/symphony orchestras) having gone out of vogue. So he paints, they entertain often, and Peggy and he travel widely—to music festivals in Europe, and to New York to catch the latest plays. She is content, she says, to watch other actors do the work now. Onscreen from 1938. IN: *Girls' School, Little Accident; Oh Johnny, How You Can Love; Alias the Deacon; I Can't Give You Anything But Love, Baby; Trail of the Vigilantes, The Mummy's Hand, Argentine Nights, Spring Parade, One Night in the Tropics, Flying Cadets, Drums of the Congo, Seven Sweethearts*, more, including 1943's *King of the Cowboys*, her last.

MORE, KENNETH (Eng.) Star. Onscreen from 1948. IN: *Scott of the Antarctic, The Clouded Yellow, No Highway in the Sky, Brandy for the Parson, Genevieve, The Deep Blue Sea, Doctor in the House, Reach for the Sky, A Night to Remember, The Sheriff of Fractured Jaw, The 39 Steps, Loss of Innocence, The Collector, Oh! What a Lovely War, The Battle of Britain, Scrooge*, more.

MOREAU, JEANNE (Fr.) Star. Onscreen from 1952. IN: *Three Sinners, The Doctors, Demoniaque, The Lovers, Five Branded Women, Les Liaisons Dangereuses, La Notte, Jules and Jim, The Trial, The Victors, Diary of a Chambermaid, The Train, The Yellow Rolls-Royce, Viva Maria, The Sailor from Gibraltar, The Bride Wore Black, Monte Walsh, Alex in Wonderland, The Last Tycoon*, more.

MOREL, GENEVIEVE (Fr.) Support. Onscreen from the '40s. IN: *Man to Men, The Thirst of Men, Dr. Knock*, more.

MORELL, ANDRE (Eng.) Character. Onscreen from 1938. IN: *Thirteen Men and a Gun, Missing Ten Days, Stage Fright, Madeleine, Trio* ("Sanitorium" sequence), *Seven Days to Noon, Summertime, His Majesty O'Keefe, Bridge on the River Kwai, Ben Hur, The Moonspinners, Judith, The Wrong Box, The Vengeance of She, Dark of the Sun*, more.

MORENO, RITA (N.Y.) Leading lady. Won Best Supporting Actress Oscar in *West Side Story*. Onscreen from 1950. IN: *Pagan Love Song, The Toast of New Orleans, Latin Lovers, El Alamein, Jivaro, Yellow Tomahawk, Garden of Evil, Seven Cities of Gold, The Lieutenant Wore Skirts, The King and I, Summer and Smoke, Cry of Battle, Popi, The Night of the Following Day, The Ritz*, more.

MORENO, ROSITA (S. Cal.) She has long been married to movie agent Melville Shauer. Onscreen from 1930. IN: *Her Wedding Night, The Santa Fe Trail, Walls of Gold, Ladies Should Listen, The Scoundrel, Tango-Bar, A Medal for Benny; So Young, So Bad*; more.

MORFOGEN, GEORGE (N.Y.) Character. Onscreen in the '70s. IN: *What's Up Doc?*, more.

MORGAN, CLARK (N.Y.) Black support. Onscreen from the '60s. IN: *Something Wild, Shadows*, more.

MORGAN, DAN (N.Y.) Character. Onscreen from the '60s. IN: *Charly, The Gang That Couldn't Shoot Straight*, more.

MORGAN, DENNIS (N. Cal.) In 1975 this veteran actor-singer, fully as handsome in his 60s (b. 1910) as in his starring days at Warners, turned down $10,000 a week to star in *The Vagabond King*. Instead he devotes his services fulltime, as he has for over a decade, as a volunteer for the American Cancer Society. Besides traveling throughout the country on speaking engagements, he has been chairman of the crusade in California, and was recently president of the Cancer Society unit in Fresno, near the ranch to which he retired many years ago. Living with him there is his wife (since 1933), Lillian, who has long been in delicate health. Their two sons and daughter—Stanley, James, and Kristin—are all grown and on their own, and have made them grandparents. The actor, who was Warner Brothers' highest-paid star for a decade, gave up his movie career after 1956's *Uranium Boom* and has acted on the screen only once since, in 1967's *Rogue's Gallery*. Late in the '50s he starred in the TV series *21 Beacon Street*, guest-starred in many others, and did supper club singing engagements that took him all over the world, including Hawaii and Australia. Rarely seen at social events in Hollywood now, he did appear at the premiere of *That's Entertainment*. Also, in '74, he was seen on TV for the first time in a decade when he was a guest on the music-variety special *Grammy Salutes Oscar*—in which, instead of singing, he reminisced about the WW II years. Onscreen from 1936. IN: *Suzy, The Great Ziegfeld, Navy Blue and Gold, Waterfront, The Fighting 69th, River's End, Kitty Foyle, The Male Animal, Affectionately Yours, In This Our Life, Wings for the Eagle, The Hard Way, The Desert Song, Shine On Harvest Moon, The Very Thought of You, Christmas in Connecticut, God Is My Co-Pilot, Two Guys from Milwaukee, My Wild Irish Rose, One Sunday Afternoon, It's a Great Feeling, Perfect Strangers, This Woman Is Dangerous, Cattle Town, Pearl of the South Pacific*, more.

MORGAN, HARRY (S. Cal.) Character. Onscreen from 1942—billed as Henry Morgan for the first 13 years of his movie career. IN: *Orchestra Wives, To the Shores of Tripoli, Crash Dive, The Ox-Bow Incident, Wing and a Prayer, A Bell for Adano, The Big Clock, All My Sons, Down to the Sea in Ships, Madame Bovary, Dark City, Bend of the River, My Six Convicts, Strategic Air Command*, more. Onscreen as Harry Morgan from 1955. IN: *Not As a Stranger, Inherit the Wind, How the West Was Won; John Goldfarb, Please Come Home; Charley and the Angel, Snowball Express, The Apple Dumpling Gang, The Shootist*, more.

MORGAN, HENRY (N.Y.) TV panelist-comedian. Onscreen in 1948. IN: *So This Is New York*.

MORGAN, JAYE P. (N.Y.) Singer-actress. Onscreen in 1973. IN: *The All-American Boy*.

MORGAN, MARILYN (S. Cal.) Billing originally used by Marian Marsh in pix such as 1930's *Whoopee*. (See Marian Marsh.)

MORGAN, MICHELE (Fr.) In 1975 this actress —with Danielle Darrieux, the most enduringly popular femme star of the French screen— came out of a self-imposed eight-year absence from movies to star for director Claude Lelouch in *The Cat and the Mouse*. Her immediately previous movie had been Paramount's *Benjamin* in which she costarred with Catherine Deneuve. In 1976 she wrote her memoirs and made her first record, "If I Talk of Her," a bittersweet love talk-poem with musical backing. During her years off the screen she painted, and enjoyed several successful exhibitions in Paris, where she lives. During her Hollywood years she was married ('42) to American actor William Marshall—later the husband of Ginger Rogers—by whom she has a son, Michael (b. 1946), and from whom she has long since been divorced. Next the wife of French star Henri Vidal, she has not remarried since his death in 1959. She is in her 50s (b. 1920) and looks decades younger. Onscreen from 1937. IN: *Gribouille, Orage, Port of Shadows, Joan of Paris, Higher and Higher, Passage to Marseilles, Two Tickets to London, The Chase, Symphonie Pastorale* (perhaps her greatest role), *The Fallen Idol, The Naked Heart, The Grand Maneuver, There's Always a Price Tag, The Mirror Has Two Faces, Maxime, Landru, Lost Command*, more.

MORGAN, READ (S. Cal.) Support. Onscreen from the '50s. IN: *Ask Any Girl, Marlowe, Kelly's Heroes, The Cheyenne Social Club, Shanks*, more.

MORGAN, ROBIN (ROBYN) (N.Y.) Support. Former juvenile actress on TV's *Mama*. Onscreen from 1948. IN: *Citizen Saint; Me, Natalie;* more.

MORGAN, TERENCE (Eng.) Leading man. Onscreen from 1948. IN: *Hamlet, Encore* ("Gigolo and Gigolette" episode), *Turn the Key Softly, Svengali, Dance Little Lady; Tread Softly, Stranger; Mission of the Sea Hawk, The Flame and the Sword, The Penthouse*, more.

MORI, TOSHIA (N.Y.) Married, retired, and now in her early 60s, this beautiful Japanese actress was for a decade after her screen career an assistant on the staff of Robert L. Ripley's "Believe It or Not." Onscreen from 1932. IN: *The Hatchet Man, The Bitter Tea of General Yen, Blondie Johnson, Chinatown Squad, Charlie Chan on Broadway*, more.

MORIARTY, MICHAEL (N.Y.) Costar. Onscreen from 1972. IN: *My Old Man's Place;*

Shoot It: Black, Shoot It: Blue; Bang the Drum Slowly, The Last Detail, Report to the Commissioner, more.

MORIN, ALBERTO (S. Cal.) Character. Onscreen from the '30s. IN: *Wings of the Navy, Gone With the Wind, The Desert Song, House of Strangers, The Gunfighter, Tripoli, Lydia Bailey, Rio Grande, My Sister Eileen, An Affair to Remember, Will Success Spoil Rock Hunter?, Hellfighters, Two Mules for Sister Sara, The Cheyenne Social Club, Chisum, The Mephisto Waltz,* more.

MORISON, PATRICIA (S. Cal.) Nothing has changed—neither her looks, hair style, nor marital status—still single in her 60s (b. 1915). She has not made a movie since 1960's *Song Without End,* in which she played George Sand. On TV in '74, she had a supporting role in *The Ambassador* (the Eddie Albert segment of CBS' four-part series on Benjamin Franklin). But it is on the civic light opera circuit, in Los Angeles and cities across the country, that she unflaggingly stars in musicals: *Gigi* (as "Mamita"), *Company, The Sound of Music* (as glamorous, wealthy widow Frau Schraeder who almost snares the hero), and, of course, *Kiss Me, Kate,* which she created on Broadway in '48 and has played countless times since. (It is ironic that in 30 movies, from '39, Hollywood made use of her magnificent mezzo-soprano voice just three times, and then only fleetingly, in *Sofia, Are Husbands Necessary,* and *Return of Wild Fire,* a Western with Richard Arlen.) After *Kiss Me, Kate,* she scored a second theater coup when Rodgers and Hammerstein selected her to succeed the late Gertrude Lawrence in *The King and I,* in which she costarred for two years with Yul Brynner. Not given to gratuitous praise of his leading ladies, Brynner said of her recently: "Then Pat Morison came to the show. She was marvelous. I could do anything with her." And he glowingly recalled that when, two decades later, the two of them did "Shall We Dance?" at the Tony Awards in New York, "the house came down. She was perfect." Today, between musical engagements, Patricia Morison paints professionally. There have been many showings of her work in Los Angeles where she is an attractive figure on the social scene, known for her stylish clothes and, most particularly, conversational ability. In Hollywood's halcyon days, admiringly observing her on the dance floor at Ciro's, Norma Shearer told all in earshot, "There goes a girl who should be a star." Patricia Morison never made it in Hollywood—but she made it. Onscreen from 1938. IN: *Persons in Hiding, The Magnificent Fraud, Untamed, Rangers of Fortune, Romance of the Rio Grande, One Night in Lisbon, Beyond the Blue Horizon, Night in New Orleans, Silver Skates, Hitler's Hangman, The Fallen Sparrow, Without Love, Lady on a Train, Dressed to Kill, Tarzan and the Huntress, Song of the Thin Man, Prince of Thieves,* more.

MORLEY, KAREN (S. Cal.) In her 70s now (b. 1905) and looking far younger, this actress—always one of the screen's best—made a tentative return to acting a few TV seasons ago, when she played the secretary of star Robert Forster in the short-lived series *Banyon.* A victim of the notorious "Hollywood blacklist," she has not made a movie since 1952's *M.* Married to character actor Lloyd Gough, she has a grown son, Michael Vidor, by her previous marriage (1932–43) to late director Charles Vidor. Onscreen from 1931. IN: *Daybreak, The Sin of Madelon Claudet, Lullaby, Cuban Love Song, Scarface, Mata Hari, Arsene Lupin, The Mask of Fu Manchu, Dinner at Eight, The Crime Doctor, Our Daily Bread, Black Fury, The Littlest Rebel, Last Train from Madrid, Kentucky, Pride and Prejudice, The 13th Hour, Framed, Code of the Saddle,* more.

MORLEY, KAY (S. Cal.) The widow of Richard Crane, she has two grown daughters and is retired. Onscreen in the '40s. IN: *Campus Honeymoon,* more.

MORLEY, ROBERT (Eng.) Character star. Nominated for Best Supporting Actor Oscar in *Marie Antoinette.* Onscreen from 1938. IN: *Major Barbara; Edward, My Son; The African Queen, Outcast of the Islands, Melba, Beat the Devil, Beau Brummel, Quentin Durward, The Sheriff of Fractured Jaw, The Journey, Oscar Wilde, The Road to Hong Kong, Joseph and His Brethren, Take Her She's Mine, Topkapi, The Loved One, Life at the Top, Way Way Out, Finders Keepers, Hot Millions, The Song of Norway, Doctor in Trouble, Cromwell,* more.

MORONEY, E. J. (N.Y.) Character. Onscreen from the '60s. IN: *The Hustler, Requiem for a Heavyweight, Star!, The Night They Raided Minsky's,* more.

MORRELL, VALERIE (N.Y.) Character. Onscreen from the '60s. IN: *Midnight Cowboy; Me, Natalie; Bananas, The Hospital,* more.

MORRIS, DOROTHY (Fla.) MGM's delicate-faced, dark-haired ingenue of the '40s—always cast as the daughter or chum (Donna Reed's in *The Human Comedy*) of a star, she gave up her career in '46 when she married math instructor Marvin Moffie. The marriage, lasting a decade before they were divorced, produced two sons. She resumed acting then and continued, in minor supporting roles, on TV (*Marcus Welby,*

Rawhide, Name of the Game, etc.), and in two movies (*Macabre* and *Seconds,* in '66, which was her last role). In her 50s (b. 1922), slender and lovely, but now a blonde, she has been married since '70 to the Reverend Roger E. Miller of the Church of Religious Science in Fort Lauderdale. Her interest in acting now does not extend beyond amateur theatricals. Onscreen from 1942. IN: *Seven Sweethearts, The War Against Mrs. Hadley, The Youngest Profession, Cry Havoc, None Shall Escape, Rationing, Main Street After Dark, Our Vines Have Tender Grapes,* more.

MORRIS, FRANCES (S. Cal.) An active member of the North Hollywood Church of Religious Science, she was married for many years, until his death in '72, to silent leading man Antrim Short (later a top Hollywood agent). She has one son, Michael Antrim Short, a business man in Paso Robles. Onscreen from the '20s. IN: *Thunder, Our Leading Citizen, Over My Dead Body, The Unfaithful, Mrs. Mike, Edge of Doom, The Captive City, The Miracle of Our Lady Fatima, Miss Sadie Thompson,* more.

MORRIS, GREG (S. Cal.) Black leading man. Onscreen from 1964. IN: *The New Interns, The Lively Set, The Sword of Ali Baba,* more.

MORRIS, HOWARD (S. Cal.) Comedian. Onscreen from 1962. IN: *Boys' Night Out, 40 Pounds of Trouble, The Nutty Professor, Fluffy, Way . . . Way Out,* more.

MORRIS, LANA (Eng.) Leading lady. Onscreen from the '40s. IN: *The Weaker Sex, Spring in Park Lane, Trio* ("The Verger" episode), *Operation Disaster, The Gay Lady, Paratrooper, Trouble in Store,* more.

MORRIS, MARY (S. Cal.) The lovely and excellent actress who was under MGM contract for a while in the '30s returned to England and made a number of movies. But the major portion of her career has been on the stage. She has starred in *Mourning Becomes Electra, The Maids, Caligula,* and many more, a number of which she has produced. She is in her 60s now (b. 1915), and records do not show that she has ever married. Onscreen from 1938. IN: *Prison Without Bars, Victoria the Great, U-Boat 29, The Thief of Bagdad, Mister V, The Man from Morocco, The Agitator, Train of Events,* more.

MORRIS, PHYLLIS (Eng.) The character actress is in her 80s (b. 1894) and makes fewer movies now, but at last report she was still going strong on British stages. Onscreen from 1935. IN: *Non-Stop New York, The Life and Death of Colonel Blimp, The Adventures of Tartu, Master of Lassie, Julia Misbehaves, My*

Own True Love, Three Came Home, Black Hand, That Forsyte Woman, Top Secret, The Embezzler, Kind Lady, The Angel Who Pawned Her Harp, more.

MORRIS, RUSTY (S. Cal.) Support. Onscreen in the '70s. IN: *Pretty Maids All in a Row,* more.

MORRISON, ANN (S. Cal.) Character. Onscreen from the '40s. IN: *The Walls of Jericho, Caught, House of Strangers, People Will Talk, Violent Saturday, The Brothers Karamazov,* more.

MORRISON, BARBARA (S. Cal.) Character. Onscreen from the '50s. IN: *From Here to Eternity, These Thousand Hills, Do Not Disturb, The Wicked Dreams of Paula Schultz,* more.

MORRISON, BRET (S. Cal.) Character. Famous radio star ("The Shadow": 1944–56). Onscreen in the '70s. IN: *Black Eye,* more.

MORRISON, ERNIE (S. Cal.) As "Sunshine Sammy," he was the first black youngster in "Our Gang" in silent days. Today, just as happy-go-lucky as in his days of fame, he lives still in Los Angeles, works in the missile industry, is well married, and says he has great memories of the movies but no burning urge to be a part of them now. After he left the Gang, he appeared for years onstage as a singer-dancer-comedian, was leader of a popular dance band, and—billed Sunshine Morrison—was featured in several movies in the early '40s. Onscreen from the early '20s. IN: *Flying Wild, Spooks Run Wild, Mr. Wise Guy,* more.

MORRISON, SHELLEY (S. Cal.) Support. Onscreen from the '60s. IN: *The Interns, The Greatest Story Ever Told, Band of Gold, Divorce American Style, Mackenna's Gold, Funny Girl,* more.

MORROW, JEFF (S. Cal.) Highly active for a decade, up to '63, the handsome leading man—in his 60s now (b. 1913)—acts far less often now. Onscreen from 1953. IN: *Flight to Tangier, The Robe, Tanganyika, Sign of the Pagan, Captain Lightfoot, The World in My Corner, Pardners, The Creature Walks Among Us, The First Texan, Copper Sky, Kronos, Five Bold Women, The Story of Ruth,* more.

MORROW, JO (S. Cal.) Leading lady. Onscreen from 1956. IN: *Because They're Young, The Legend of Tom Dooley, Juke Box Rhythm, Our Man in Havana, 13 Ghosts, The Three Worlds of Gulliver, Sunday in New York, He Rides Tall, The Strangler,* more.

313

MORROW, PATRICIA (S. Cal.) Television leading lady (*Peyton Place, Return to Peyton Place*) who gave up acting and became a lawyer. Onscreen from 1944. IN: *Marriage Is a Private Affair* (played Lana Turner's baby at the age of two weeks), *Roar of the Crowd* (juvenile role), *Surf Party* (leading lady).

MORROW, SUSAN (S. Cal.) One of the loveliest redheads ever on the screen, this leading lady made her last movie, *Macabre*, in 1958. In her 40s now, she is happily married to a Los Angeles dentist and is the mother of two. Two previous marriages—to comedian Gary Morton and agent Bill Robinson—ended in divorce. Newspapers mentioned her name for the first time in years in 1975. That was when her sister, Mrs. Judy Campbell Exner, made headlines with the admission that she (Mrs. Exner) had once had a relationship of a "close, personal nature" with President John F. Kennedy—at the same time she was associating with underworld figures Sam (Momo) Giancana and John Rosselli. Onscreen from 1951. IN: *Gasoline Alley, Corky of Gasoline Alley, On the Loose, The Savage, The Blazing Forest, Man of Conflict, Cat-Women of the Moon, Battle Cry,* more.

MORROW, VIC (S. Cal.) Costar. Onscreen from 1955. IN: *Blackboard Jungle, Tribute to a Bad Man, God's Little Acre, Hell's Five Hours, King Creole, Portrait of a Mobster, Posse from Hell, Last Year at Malibu, Dirty Mary Crazy Larry, The Take,* more.

MORSE, BARRY (Can.) Character star from England who has long lived in Montreal, commuting to Hollywood and London for movies and TV (*Space: 1999*). Onscreen from 1942. IN: *When We Are Married, Daughter of Darkness, Mrs. Fitzherbert, Kings of the Sun, Justine, Puzzle of a Downfall Child, Asylum, The Telephone Book,* more.

MORSE, ELLA MAE (S. Cal.) Singer-actress; now retired. Onscreen in 1944. IN: *Ghost Catchers.*

MORSE, HAYWARD (N.Y.) Support. Onscreen from the '60s. IN: *Sebastian,* more.

MORSE, ROBERT (N.Y.) Costar. Onscreen from 1956. IN: *The Proud and the Profane, The Matchmaker, The Cardinal, Quick Before It Melts, The Loved One, How to Succeed in Business Without Really Trying; Oh Dad, Poor Dad, Mama's Hung You in the Closet and I'm Feeling So Sad; A Guide for the Married Man, Where Were You When the Lights Went Out?, The Boatniks,* more.

MORSELL, FRED (N.Y.) Black support. Onscreen in the '70s. IN: *The Hospital, The Delta Factor,* more.

MORTON, GARY (S. Cal.) Comedian. Husband of Lucille Ball. Onscreen in 1974. IN: *Lenny.*

MORTON, GREGORY (S. Cal.) Character. Onscreen from 1956. IN: *The Vagabond King, Bye Bye Birdie, The New Interns, Synanon, The Mephisto Waltz,* more.

MORTON, MICKEY (Fla.) Support. Lives in Miami. Onscreen from the '60s. IN: *Nobody's Perfect, Head On,* more.

MOSLEY, ROGER (Eng.) Leading man. Onscreen in the '70s. IN: *Drum,* more.

MOSS, ARNOLD (N.Y.) In '73, then aged 63, this veteran character actor received his Ph.D. from New York University. Still highly active on stage (*Follies*) and TV (an endless string of soap operas), he has performed as narrator-soloist with the Boston, Milwaukee, and Detroit Symphonies. Between engagements he has taught drama for almost a decade at Brooklyn College. He has a grown son and daughter by writer Stella Reynolds, to whom he has been married since '33. Onscreen from 1946. IN: *Temptation, The Loves of Carmen, Reign of Terror, Salome, Kim, Quebec, My Favorite Spy, Viva Zapata!, Casanova's Big Night, Bengal Brigade, Hell's Island, The Fool Killer, Gambit, The Caper of the Golden Bulls,* more.

MOSS, STEWART (S. Cal.) Support. Onscreen from 1965. IN: *In Harm's Way, Chubasco, Pendulum, Zigzag, The Bat People* (lead), more.

MOSTEL, JOSH (JOSHUA) (N.Y.) Support. Son of Zero Mostel. Onscreen in the '70s. IN: *Going Home, Harry and Tonto,* more.

MOSTEL, ZERO (N.Y.) Star comedian and character. Onscreen from 1943. IN: *Du Barry Was a Lady, Panic in the Streets, Sirocco, Mr. Belvedere Rings the Bell, The Model and the Marriage Broker. A Funny Thing Happened on the Way to the Forum, The Producers, The Great Bank Robbery, The Hot Rock, Rhinoceros, Marco, Foreplay,* more.

MOUNT, PEGGY (Eng.) Comedienne. Onscreen from 1956. IN: *Sailor Beware, The Embezzler, Panic in the Parlor, Your Past Is Showing, One Way Pendulum, Hotel Paradiso!, Oliver!,* more.

MOUSTACHE (Fr.) France's most gloriously lovely model of the '30s and '40s who, grown ample of girth, has appeared in movies as a character. Onscreen from 1961. IN: *Paris Blues, How to Steal a Million, A Flea in Her Ear, Mayerling,* more.

MOVITA (S. Cal.) Once married to Brando, and the mother of a son by him, she rarely acts now, but did appear as an extra in *Day of the Locust*. Onscreen from 1935. IN: *Mutiny on the Bounty, Paradise Isle, Rose of the Rio Grande, Wolf Girl, Tower of Terror, Wild Rose Ambush, Dream Wife, Apache Ambush*, more.

MUIR, JEAN (Mo.) Missouri, the "Show Me State"—it's appropriate that this actress, in her 60s now (b. 1911) and the mother of three grown children, should elect to live and work there. In the '30s at Warners, she was nicknamed, with grudging admiration, The Studio Pest because, with a brilliant, steel-trap mind, she had questions about everything from camera angles to publicity practices. No more avid student of motion pictures ever worked in them. But, in '43, when she still had never been given a strong role, she finished a supporting part in *The Constant Nymph* and quit. She married attorney Henry Jaffe (they have long since been divorced), acted on radio (*Nick Carter*), and in '50 was signed to play the mother in the TV series *The Aldrich Family*. Before the first episode went on the air she was fired. Her name, with the names of 150 other celebrities, appeared—without foundation—in *Red Channels*, the vicious, shockingly irresponsible "anti-Communist" pamphlet. Finally, on June 15, 1953, she had the chance to clear her name. Voluntarily appearing before the House Committee on Un-American Activities in Washington, she stated that she was not, nor had she ever been, a Communist. But the damage done to her career was irrevocable. She had become "controversial." The acting jobs she found were few, far between, and generally inconsequential. She did "live" TV (*Philco Playhouse* and one or two others), filmed TV (an episode each in *Route 66* and *Naked City*), and found a supporting role on Broadway in *Semi-Detached* in '60. Her troubles led to a bout with alcoholism—an illness over which she long ago triumphed. Finally, she began to teach drama and direct in community playhouses in Manhattan. Then there was a most serious illness. Told by physicians that she had only six months to live, that she would never see Christmas again, she refused to accept their prognosis. "Suddenly I became aware of every blade of grass and every little thing in life," she said later. "I realized how important every person was to me." She fought back—and staged a miraculous recovery, enjoying excellent health to this day. When in her mid-50s, the actress accepted an offer to teach two summers at Perry-Mansfield, a summer drama school in Colorado run by Missouri's Stephens College. In '68, Stephens' famed theater department (once under the guidance of the renowned Maude Adams) instituted a new program—to train young women students as professional actresses. The logical candidate to head this department was Jean Muir, whose scholarly exploration of Warner Bros. Studio in her 20s had given her, besides a nickname, a profound knowledge of motion pictures. In '71, accompanied by 10 of her students, the actress went back to Hollywood for the first time in years—to launch a building fund campaign among girl graduates of Stephens now working in the movie industry. Hollywood found Jean Muir little changed—older, of course, and a bit fuller of figure—but still charged with energy, opinions, spunk—and curiosity. Onscreen from 1933. IN: *The World Changes, As the Earth Turns, Desirable, Dr. Monica, A Modern Hero, Oil for the Lamps of China, The White Cockatoo, A Midsummer Night's Dream, Orchids to You, Stars Over Broadway, Fugitive in the Sky, Her Husband's Secretary, White Bondage, The Outcasts of Poker Flat, Dance Charlie Dance, And One Was Beautiful, The Lone Wolf Meets a Lady*, more.

MULDAUR, DIANA (S. Cal.) Leading lady. Onscreen from 1968. IN: *The Swimmer, The Lawyer, Number One, The Other, McQ, Chosen Survivors*, more.

MULHALL, JACK (S. Cal.) Dapper still, in his 80s (b. 1894), he continued to appear in movies through 1959's *The Atomic Submarine*. More recently he has worked in the Hollywood office of the Screen Actors Guild, lives near the center of Hollywood, and, after more than a half-century, is still happily married to his "original" wife. It's been many a year since he owned a 16-room Beverly Hills mansion or was a star earning $3,000 a week. That all ended, in fact, in 1930. Then came the decades of small roles and matching salaries. But, as he once said, "I have nothing tragic, pitiful or tear-jerking to recall. My real friends didn't drop me when my money was gone and no doors were slammed in my face." So he has smiled and gone right on, as though nothing has changed. And nothing "important," he says, has. Onscreen from the teens. IN: *Mickey, Should a Woman Tell? Dulcy, The Breath of Scandal, Folly of Vanity, The Mad Whirl, We Moderns, Joanna, Sweet Daddies, Subway Sadie, Orchids and Ermine; Smile, Brother, Smile; The Crystal Cup, Lady Be Good, The Butter and Egg Man, Children of the Ritz, Twin Beds, Show of Shows, Her Golden Calf, Reaching for the Moon, The Old-Fashioned Way, Mississippi, Beloved Enemy, Tim Tyler's Luck* (serial), *Cheers for Miss Bishop, The Man from Headquarters, Deadline for Murder, Around the World in 80 Days, Up in Smoke*, more.

MULHARE, EDWARD (Conn.) Leading man. Onscreen from 1955. IN: *Hill 24 Doesn't An-*

swer, *Signpost to Murder, Von Ryan's Express, Our Man Flint, Caprice, Eye of the Devil*, more.

MULLANEY, JACK (S. Cal.) Leading man. Onscreen from 1957. IN: *The Young Stranger, The Vintage, Kiss Them for Me, All the Fine Young Cannibals, The Honeymoon Machine, The Absent-Minded Professor, Seven Days in May, Tickle Me, Spinout, Little Big Man, George!*, more.

MULLAVEY, GREG (S. Cal.) Leading man. Costar, in '76, in the nighttime TV soap opera *Mary Hartman, Mary Hartman*. Onscreen from the '60s. IN: *Bob & Carol & Ted & Alice, The Shakiest Gun in the West, C.C. and Company, Raid on Rommel, The Love Machine, The Christian Licorice Store, The Single Girls, The Hindenburg*, more.

MULLEN, BARBARA (Eng.) Former leading lady, in her 60s (b. 1914), who in recent years has starred mostly on the legitimate stage and TV in Great Britain. The Boston-born actress has also been, since '54, a director of Pilot Films, Ltd. Onscreen from 1941. IN: *Jeannie, Thunder Rock, Welcome Mr. Washington, The Trojan Brothers, A Place of One's Own, Corridor of Mirrors, My Sister and I, You Can't Beat the Irish, So Little Time, The Gentle Gunman, Innocent Sinners, Kidnapped, It Takes a Thief*, more.

MULLIGAN, GERRY (N.Y.) Jazz saxophonist-actor. Onscreen in 1960. IN: *The Rat Race, Jazz on a Summer's Day*, and *The Subterraneans*.

MULLIGAN, RICHARD (S. Cal.) Leading man. Onscreen from 1964. IN: *One Potato, Two Potato; The Group, A Change in the Wind, The Undefeated, Little Big Man, Visit to a Chief's Son*, more.

MUMY, BILLY (S. Cal.) Former juvenile (b. 1954). Onscreen from 1960. IN: *The Wizard of Baghdad, Tammy Tell Me True, A Child Is Waiting, A Ticklish Affair, Palm Springs Weekend, Dear Brigitte, Rascal, Bless the Beasts & Children*, more.

MUNKER, ARIANE (N.Y.) Juvenile. Onscreen from 1971. IN: *Ace Eli and Roger of the Sky*, more.

MUNRO, NAN (Eng.) Character. Onscreen from 1938. IN: *Black Limelight, Morgan!, A Suitable Case for Treatment, Song of Norway, Games That Lovers Play, Jane Eyre, The Walking Stick*, more.

MUNSEL, PATRICE (N.Y.) A Metropolitan Opera star from age 17, the coloratura soprano is in her early 50s (b. 1925), has been married since '52 to TV producer Robert Schuler, is the mother of two sons and two daughters, and in the 1975–76 Broadway season costarred with John Raitt in *A Musical Jubilee*. Onscreen in 1953. IN: *Melba* (starring role).

MURCELL, GEORGE (Eng.) Character. Onscreen from 1960. IN: *Campbell's Kingdom, A Walk with Love and Death, The Horsemen*, more.

MURDOCH, RICHARD (Eng.) Character. Onscreen from 1934. IN: *The Ghost Train, Golden Arrow, The Gay Adventure, Strictly Confidential*, more.

MURDOCK, GEORGE (S. Cal.) Character. Onscreen in the '70s. IN: *Willie Dynamite, Earthquake, Thomasine and Bushrod, Hangup*, more.

MURDOCK, JACK (N.Y.) Support. Onscreen in the '70s. IN: *Newman's Law, The Crazy World of Julius Vrooder*, more.

MURDOCK, KERMIT (S. Cal.) Character. Onscreen from the '60s. IN: *In the Heat of the Night, Blackbeard's Ghost, On a Clear Day You Can See Forever, The Andromeda Strain*, more.

MURPHY, BEN (S. Cal.) Leading man. Onscreen from 1968. IN: *Yours, Mine and Ours; The Thousand Plane Raid, Sidecar Racers*, more.

MURPHY, BRIAN (Eng.) Character. Onscreen from the '60s. IN: *The Activist, The Boy Friend, The Devils, The Ragman's Daughter*, more.

MURPHY, CHARLES (N. Cal.) The veteran character actor (*not* the oldtime comedian, Charlie, now deceased) lives in San Francisco and remains active. Onscreen from the '20s. IN: *Spell of the Circus* (serial), *Two-Fisted Stranger*, more.

MURPHY, EILEEN (Eng.) Support. Onscreen from the '60s. IN: *A Walk with Love and Death, Sinful Davey*, more.

MURPHY, GEORGE (S. Cal.) In 1950 this popular MGM hoofer and dramatic star received a special Oscar (statuette) "for his services in interpreting the film industry to the country at large." Shortly thereafter he gave up his screen career and became a politician. Now, in his 70s (b. 1904), this former U.S. Senator (Rep.) from California is not entirely done with politics. He heads and partly owns a public relations firm called Washington Consultants Inc. Until its expulsion from the United Nations, Nationalist China was one of his largest accounts. Nor is he entirely done with show biz. For showing in 1976, he produced the TV special *The All-American Bicentennial Minstrels*. When it was being filmed, the former hoofer of stage and screen was asked if he would appear on his own show, and he smiled and said, "I hadn't planned to, but . . ." With this reemergence into the entertainment limelight, he finds he is no longer asked the question that became the title of his 1970 autobiography, "*Say . . . Didn't You Used To Be George Murphy?*" He considered retiring, but decided against it, at the time of the death of his wife, Juliette, in 1973. They had been married since '26, and she had not only been his dance partner in vaudeville, but had been the one who taught him how to dance. By her, the actor has a son, Dennis (b. 1939), a public relations expert now, and a daughter, Melissa (b. 1943), who is now Mrs. Robert Ellis of Beverly Hills and has presented him with two granddaughters. Since his wife's death, Murphy has sold their Beverly Hills mansion—too many memories—and moved into an apartment. There has been no recurrence of the cancer that threatened his life in 1966, when a malignant growth was removed from his vocal cord. Onscreen from 1934. IN: *Kid Millions, I'll Love You Always, Choose Your Partner, The Navy Steps Out, Top of the Town, Broadway Melody of 1938, A Letter of Introduction, Two Girls on Broadway, Little Nellie Kelly, Public Deb No. 1; Tom, Dick and Harry; For Me and My Gal, The Powers Girl, This Is the Army, Bataan, Show Business, Having a Wonderful Crime, Up Goes Maisie, Cynthia, Battleground, It's a Big Country, Walk East on Beacon,* more.

MURPHY, JIMMY (S. Cal.) Support. Onscreen from the '50s. IN: *Curse of the Dead, Paratroop Command, Platinum High School, The Good Guys and the Bad Guys,* more.

MURPHY, MARY (S. Cal.) The "good girl" in *The Wild One,* the brunette young waitress whose love redeemed Brando, later married actor Dale Robertson and gave up her career. Now, long since divorced, she has resumed it on TV. An attractive woman in maturity (b. 1931), she has played wives and mothers in series such as *Streets of San Francisco* and TV-movies such as *Born Innocent* and *The Stranger Who Looks Like Me.* The *Hollywood reporter* said of her in the latter: "Mary Murphy gives an incredible performance as a birth parent who gives up her child [Meredith Baxter]." Onscreen from 1949. IN: *The Lemon Drop Kid, When Worlds Collide, Carrie; Come Back, Little Sheba; Houdini, Main Street to Broadway, The Mad Magician, Sitting Bull, The Desperate Hours, Maverick Queen; Live Fast, Die Young;*

Crime and Punishment, U.S.A.; The Electronic Monster, 40 Pounds of Trouble, more.

MURPHY, MATT (S. Cal.) Character. Onscreen from 1956. IN: *The Harder They Fall,* more.

MURPHY, MICHAEL (S. Cal.) Leading man. Onscreen from the '60s. IN: *The Arrangement, M*A*S*H, Brewster McCloud; Count Yorga, Vampire; McCabe and Mrs. Miller, Phase IV,* more.

MURPHY, PAMELA (S. Cal.) Leading lady. Onscreen from 1970. IN: *Zigzag,* more.

MURPHY, ROSEMARY (N.Y.) Leading lady. Onscreen from 1948. IN: *Berlin Express, Der Ruf, The Last Illusion, That Night, To Kill a Mockingbird, Any Wednesday, Ben, You'll Like My Mother, Walking Tall, Forty Carats,* more.

MURRAY, BARBARA (Eng.) Leading lady. Onscreen from 1948. IN: *Passport to Pimlico, Tony Draws a Horse, Another Man's Poison, Both Sides of the Law, The Dark Man, Mystery Junction, Death Goes to School, Meet Mr. Lucifer, A Cry from the Streets, Campbell's Kingdom, Doctor in Distress, Up Pompeii,* more.

MURRAY, BRIAN (Eng.) Support. Onscreen from 1959. IN: *The Angry Silence, The League of Gentlemen,* more.

MURRAY, DON (S. Cal.) Costar. Nominated for Best Supporting Actor Oscar in *Bus Stop,* his debut. Onscreen from 1956. IN: *The Bachelor Party, A Hatful of Rain, Shake Hands with the Devil, From Hell to Texas, One Foot in Hell, The Hoodlum Priest, The Hustler, Advise and Consent, One Man's Way; Baby, the Rain Must Fall; Sweet Love Bitter, Conquest of the Planet of the Apes; Happy Birthday, Wanda . . .; Deadly Hero, Damien,* more.

MURRAY, JAN (S. Cal.) Star comedian. Onscreen from 1965. IN: *Who Killed Teddy Bear?, The Busy Body, Thunder Alley, Tarzan and the Great River, A Man Called Dagger,* more.

MURRAY, KEN (S. Cal.) In his 70s (b. 1903), the comedian whose Hollywood stage show, *Ken Murray's Blackouts,* was a must-see during WW II is still going strong. For years his much-publicized hobby has been shooting candid offscreen movies of celebrities. In '74 he launched a new career as humorist-narrator of these assembled films, presented at California theaters together with a vaudeville stage show. That same year one of his two daughters, Pam, became the wife of film editor Steve Bushleman, causing the comedian—thinking of the vintage home movies stored in his vault—to crack: "I'm not losing a daughter; I'm gaining a film editor." There is a second generation Murray in show business now, too. His son, Cort, has become a well-received popular singer. Onscreen from 1929. IN: *Half Marriage, Leathernecking, Ladies of the Jury, Crooner, From Headquarters, You're a Sweetheart, A Night at Earl Carroll's, Juke Box Jenny, The Marshal's Daughter, The Man Who Shot Liberty Valance, Son of Flubber, The Way West,* more, including 1968's *The Power,* his most recent.

MURRAY, PEG (N.Y.) Support. Onscreen from 1968. IN: *The Illiac Passion, Some of My Best Friends Are . . .,* more.

MURRAY, STEPHEN (Eng.) Character. Onscreen from 1941. IN: *The Prime Minister, Dulcimer Street, My Brother Jonathan, Silent Dust, For Them That Trespass, The End of the Affair, The Nun's Story, Master Spy, Door in the Wall,* more.

MURTAGH, KATE (S. Cal.) Character. Onscreen in the '70s. IN: *Farewell, My Lovely; Deceit,* more.

MURTON, LIONEL (Eng.) Character. Onscreen from the '40s. IN: *Meet the Navy, The Long Dark Hall, Night People, The Pickwick Papers, Raising a Riot, Pursuit of the Graf Spee, Surprise Package, A Touch of Larceny, The Captain's Table, The Last Shot You Hear, The Revolutionary, Patton, Welcome to the Club,* more.

MUSANTE, TONY (S. Cal.) Costar. Onscreen from 1965. IN: *Once a Thief, The Incident, The Detective, The Mercenary, The Bird with the Crystal Plumage, The Last Run, The Grissom Gang, The Anonymous Venetian, One Night at Dinner,* more.

MUSE, CLARENCE (S. Cal.) No longer young (b. 1889), this fine black character actor keeps moving right along. And he takes no guff from anyone. In 1973 he was among the artists honored in Oakland, Calif., at the first Black Filmmakers Hall of Fame awards. This was in tribute both to the longevity of his career and to his many outstanding performances. At a Q&A symposium in Oakland that day, certain audience members, aware that the actor holds a degree in international law and has written and starred in excellent pictures (*Broken Strings,* etc.) made specifically for black audiences, were openly critical of his many Uncle Tom roles. They were referring to *Maryland, Show Boat* ('36), *Heaven Can Wait, Way Down South,* etc. Muse listened and replied: "A lot of you people called me Uncle Tom, but I have

something to call you. You were as dumb as was. You were the audience and you laughed a what I did." Then he flew back to Hollywoo where he made his 150th movie, Disney's *Th World's Greatest Athlete.* Onscreen from 1928 IN: *Hearts in Dixie, Huckleberry Finn, Th West Parade, Is My Face Red?, Cabin in th Cotton, The Count of Monte Cristo, Broadwa Bill, So Red the Rose. Follow Your Heart, Zan zibar, Adam Had Four Sons, Love Crazy, In visible Ghost, The Black Swan, Watch on th Rhine, Shadow of a Doubt, Night and Day, Th Great Dan Patch, Riding High, Apache Drums Jamaica Run, Porgy and Bess,* more.

MUSTIN, BURT (S. Cal.) Character. Onscreen from 1951. IN: *Detective Story, The Lusty Men The Thrill of It All, The Witchmaker, A Tim for Dying,* more.

MYERS, CARMEL (S. Cal.) Just as Scarlet O'Hara went back to Tara, so has this grea silent favorite returned to Hollywood. Her hus band, Al Schwalberg, died, and New York their home for decades, was no longer th same. So she found a buyer for the perfum enterprise, Zizanie, she had created and oper ated successfully for years, knowing she mus go back "home" to California. Her family wer all there—her son, Ralph Blum (author of th non-fiction best-seller *Beyond Earth*), her tw daughters, and her grandchildren. And perhaps she told herself, she could resume the caree she had given up after 1934's *Countess c Monte Cristo.* (She had also appeared, but no in starring roles, in two in the '40s: *Lady for Night* and *Whistle Stop.*) It has been accom plished. In '75, she found herself back on soundstage at MGM, where *Ben Hur* was made her first time on the lot in more than 40 years She was there to play a supporting role, a mur der suspect, in an ABC-TV movie, *The Thi Man.* And she has since followed this up wit an appearance on *The Tonight Show* and a cam eo role in the movie *Won Ton Ton, the Do Who Saved Hollywood.* The actress remains most attractive woman in her 70s. Reference give her birthdate as 1899; she says it was later She says she was tall for her age and got he first movie role at 13 by assuring the producer she was 18. And, she adds, "Mother was right She warned me: 'Someday you'll look franti cally for those five lost years.'" This all cam back to her at a party in Hollywood, given i honor of actress Jean Stapleton, at which sh was a guest. Meeting Carmel Myers, wit whom she had struck up an immediate, warn friendship, said Miss Stapleton, was a peak mo ment she would never forget. Then, in Carmel presence, she added: "She must be about hundred years old but she's so vital and aliv and beautiful, it's the big thrill of my life." In stead of "looking frantic," though, Carmel Myers kept sampling the cheese dip, laughing like hell. Onscreen from 1923. IN: *The Famous Mrs. Fair, Slave of Desire, Reno, Beau Brummell, Broadway After Dark, Babbitt, Ben Hur, Tell It to the Marines, Sorrell and Son, A Certain Young Man, Dream of Love, The Ghost Talks, Carless Age, Broadway Scandals, The Ship from Shanghai, Svengali, The Mad Genius, Nice Women,* more.

MYERS, PAULENE (S. Cal.) Black character. Onscreen from 1961. IN: *Take a Giant Step, Shock Treatment, The Comic, Tick Tick Tick, Lost in the Stars,* more.

MYHERS, JOHN (S. Cal.) Character. Onscreen from 1960. IN: *Weddings and Babies, How to Succeed in Business Without Really Trying, The Private Navy of Sgt. O'Farrell, The Wicked Dreams of Paula Schultz, Willard,* more.

MYLES, MEG (N.Y.) Leading lady. More recently a star of the TV soap opera *Where the Heart Is.* Onscreen from 1955. IN: *The Phenix City Story, Battle Cry, New York Confidential, Dragnet, Calpyso Heat Wave, Satan in High Heels, A Lovely Way to Die, Coogan's Bluff,* more.

MYRTIL, ODETTE (Pa.) The forceful, French-accented character actress (and how could such WW II pix as *Reunion in France, The Pied Piper, Forever and a Day,* and *Uncertain Glory* have managed without her?) vanished from the Hollywood scene in '52. *Lady Possessed* was her last. She was possessed—with the idea of having her own restaurant. She has had it, Chez Odette, since '60, on South River Road in New Hope, which is antiques-and-theater country. The zestful player, who made her American debut on Broadway in '17, certainly qualifies in the second category, and perhaps in the first—if one heeds a recent, well-known patron who saluted her as "ageless and outrageous." She is actually, with her saucy wink and *joie de vivre,* despite her ever-present Malacca walking stick, most youthfully in her 70s (b. 1898). After Hollywood, she continued her career onstage, as Bloody Mary in *South Pacific.* Following that, one finds by reading the back of the menu at Chez Odette, the actress "like Washington, crossed the Delaware and there on the shores of New Hope, she discovered her Bali Hai." Her 18th-century inn, indeed on the banks of the Delaware, is a mixture of pewter plates, assorted modern and antique French travel posters, and old Quaker fireplaces. It is homey, and, it is obvious, it is her true home. "We are all friends here. Everybody talks to everybody else in my joint," she says. "And once in a while I sing to my audience." All of her oldtime Hollywood friends come there to see her. One, character actress Marjorie Gateson, though she suffered a stroke years back, is often driven out from New York for a visit with her. And, perennially insouciant Odette Myrtil glories in the *laissez-faire* of her adopted village. "In New Hope," she says, "you can keep even a goat in your bedroom and nobody cares!" Onscreen from 1936. IN: *Dodsworth, The Girl from Scotland Yard, Kitty Foyle, Out of the Fog, I Married an Angel, Yankee Doodle Dandy, Assignment in Brittany, Forever and a Day, Dark Waters, Devotion, The Fighting Kentuckian, Here Comes the Groom,* more.

N

NADER, GEORGE (S. Cal.) Universal's handsome leading man of the '50s has returned to Hollywood after a decade of moviemaking abroad and, considerably aged in appearance (b. 1921), has lately played character roles on TV. He remains a bachelor. Onscreen from 1950. IN: *Rustlers on Horseback, Take Care of My Little Girl, Sins of Jezebel, Down Among the Sheltering Palms, Carnival Story, Six Bridges to Cross, Four Guns to the Border, Lady Godiva, The Unguarded Moment, Away All Boats, Appointment with a Shadow, The Female Animal, The Great Space Adventure, House of 1,000 Dolls, Death in a Red Jaguar, Operation Hurricane,* more.

NAIL, JOANNE (S. Cal.) Leading lady. Onscreen from 1976. IN: *The Gumball Rally* (debut).

NAISMITH, LAURENCE (Eng.) Character. Onscreen from 1947. IN: *High Treason, I Believe in You, Mogambo, The Black Knight, The Man Who Never Was, Lust for Life, The Barretts of Wimpole Street, I Accuse!, The Naked Earth, Third Man on the Mountain, Solomon and Sheba, The Angry Silence, The World of Suzie Wong, Greyfriars' Bobby, The Long Duel, Camelot, Deadlier Than the Male, Fitzwilly, The Bushbabies, Diamonds Are Forever,* more.

NAMATH, JOE (N.Y.) Football star-actor. Onscreen from 1970. IN: *Norwood, C.C. and Company, The Last Rebel.*

NAPIER, ALAN (S. Cal.) Of all the elegant British character actors who strongly bolstered Hollywood movies during the '40s, none was finer than 6'5" Alan Napier. "Indeed," he remarks of his height, "I was for 25 years the tallest actor in the world. Then Jim Arness came along and topped me by an inch." Napier continued steadily in pictures through the 1966 big-screen version of *Batman*, in which he recreated the Alfred the Butler role he played in the television series. He lives now, as he has for years, in a charming house in the Pacific Palisades overlooking the ocean—and in an interesting family set-up. "Some years ago when my dear and wonderful wife was dying she would urge me to remarry," he says. "But I knew no one could ever take her place. So after a sad year of living alone I invited my daughter, Jennifer, and her husband, actor Robert Nichols, who had been going great guns in London, to come back to California and share my home. They and the grandchildren, Christie and David [both of college age], have lived with me since. The experiment has been a tremendous success. The five of us find no obtrusive generation gaps to mar our mutual understanding." The actor, white haired and in his 70s now (b. 1903), keeps extraordinarily fit—swimming in summer, running on the beach in winter, and gardening all the year round. Of his career, he says, "At present I am involuntarily retired since the makers of entertainment seem to think that the public is only interested in the activities and problems of the young. Our family life suggests to me that this is a narrow view of the American scene. I feel quite ready to resume my career when stories of wider interest are once more in the making. In the meantime I am writing an autobiographical book, because it seems to me that the life of an actor who has lived from hand to mouth for 40 years, yet survived despite enormous difficulties, could be quite interesting. I take some pride in the fact that I have played in theatre, films and television, every conceivable type role from Shakespeare to low comedy. Who can say that I shall not return to Shakespeare yet?" Onscreen in England from 1930. IN: *In a Monastery Garden, Wings Over Africa, Premier Stafford, The Revenge of General Ling*, more. Onscreen in America from 1939. IN: *We Are Not Alone, The Invisible Man Returns, Confirm or Deny, Cat People, Random Harvest, Lassie Come Home, The Uninvited, The Hairy Ape, Hangover Square, Isle of the Dead, Three Strangers, Forever Amber, The Lone Wolf in London, Macbeth, Joan of Arc, Johnny Belinda, The Hills of Home, The Great Caruso, The Blue Veil, Julius Caesar, Until They Sail, Tender Is the Night, Signpost to Murder, The Loved One*, more.

NAPIER, CHARLES (S. Cal.) Leading man. Onscreen from the '60s. IN: *Cherry, Harry and Raquel; Beyond the Valley of the Dolls, The Seven Minutes*, more.

NAPIER, DIANA (Eng.) Former leading lady, in her late 60s now (b. 1908) and retired since the late 1940s. Onscreen from 1933. IN: *Catherine the Great, Mimi, Heart's Desire, A Clown Must Laugh, Forbidden Music*, more.

NAPIER, JOHN (S. Cal.) Support. Onscreen from the '60s. IN: *The Slender Thread, The Gypsy Moths*, more.

NAPIER, PAUL (S. Cal.) Support. Onscreen from the '60s. IN: *The Secret Life of an American Wife*, more.

NAPIER, RUSSEL (Eng.) Character. Onscreen from the '40s. IN: *Blind Man's Buff, Stolen Face, Black Orchid, The Saint's Return, 36 Hours, The Brain Machine, The Blue Peter, The Unholy Four, The Angry Silence, Francis of Assisi, The Mark, Twisted Nerve, The Black Windmill*, more.

NARDINI, TOM (S. Cal.), Support. Onscreen from 1965. IN: *Cat Ballou, Africa—Texas Style!, Born Wild, The Young Animals, The Devil's Eight*, more.

NASH, BRIAN (S. Cal.) Former juvenile (b. 1956). Onscreen in 1963. IN: *The Thrill of It All*.

NASH, NOREEN (S. Cal.) Last in 1960's *Wake Me When It's Over*, the former leading lady is married to Dr. Lee Siegel of Beverly Hills, and is retired. Onscreen from 1945. IN: *The Southerner, Red Stallion, The Big Fix, The Tender Years, Adventures of Casanova, The Checkered Coat, Storm Over Wyoming, The Lone Ranger and the Lost City of Gold*, more.

NATHAN, VIVIAN (N.Y.) Character. Onscreen from 1958. IN: *Teacher's Pet, The Young Savages, The Outsider, Klute*, more.

NATWICK, MILDRED (N.Y.) Character. Nominated for Best Supporting Actress Oscar in *Barefoot in the Park*. A "bachelor girl" in her 60s (b. 1908), she lives in a splendid duplex on Park Avenue, flying regularly to Hollywood for movies and TV stints. Onscreen from 1940. IN: *The Long Voyage Home, The Enchanted Cottage, Yolanda and the Thief, The Late George Apley, Three Godfathers, She Wore a Yellow Ribbon, The Quiet Man, The Trouble with Harry, The Court Jester; If It's Tuesday, This Must Be Belgium; Daisy Miller, At Long Last Love*, more.

NAUGHTON, JAMES (S. Cal.) Leading man. Onscreen in the '70s. IN: *The Paper Chase*, more.

NAZZARI, AMEDEO (It.) Leading man. Onscreen from the '30s. IN: *La Grande Luce, The*

Life of Donizetti, Times Gone By, We Are All Murderers, The Ten Commandments, The Naked Maja, The Little Nuns, The Valachi Papers, more.

NEAGLE, ANNA (Eng.) In her 70s now (b. 1904), she has been Dame Anna since '70, is still happily married to producer Herbert Wilcox, has no children, remains beautiful and blonde, and stars constantly onstage—in musicals, comedies, and dramas. Onscreen from 1930. IN: *The Little Damozel, Bitter Sweet, Nell Gwyn, Peg of Old Drury, Victoria the Great, Girl in the Street, Sixty Glorious Years, Nurse Edith Cavell, Irene; No, No, Nanette; Sunny, Forever and a Day, The Yellow Canary, A Yank in London, The Courtneys of Curzon Street, Spring in Park Lane, Odette, The Lady with a Lamp, Maytime in Mayfair, My Teenage Daughter, The Man Who Wouldn't Talk*, more.

NEAL, FRANCES (S. Cal.) The widow of actor Van Heflin, she became in '72 the wife of Los Angeles business man Lionel Talbot. Her daughter, Kate Heflin, is now following both parents into the acting profession. Onscreen from 1941. IN: *Lady Scarface, Powder Town*, more.

NEAL, PATRICIA (Eng.) Costar. Won Best Actress Oscar in *Hud*. Nominated in the same category in *The Subject Was Roses* (her first film after recovering from a stroke suffered in the '60s). Her husband, Roald Dahl, frequently writes for the screen (*You Only Live Twice*) and one of her daughters, Tessa Dahl, is now also an actress. Onscreen from 1949. IN: *John Loves Mary, The Fountainhead, The Hasty Heart, Bright Leaf, The Breaking Point, The Day the Earth Stood Still, Diplomatic Courier, A Face in the Crowd, Breakfast at Tiffany's, In Harm's Way, Mother's Day*, more.

NEAR, HOLLY (S.Cal.) Leading lady-folk singer. Onscreen from the '60s. IN: *Angel, Angel, Down We Go; The Magic Garden of Stanley Sweetheart, Minnie and Moskowitz, The Todd Killings*, more.

NEELEY, TED (S. Cal.) Leading man. Onscreen in the '70s. IN: *Jesus Christ Superstar* (lead).

NEFF, HILDEGARDE (Austria) The German-born actress, now in her early 50s (b. 1925) and using the proper spelling of her name, Hildegard Knef, made *The Lost Continent* in '68 and said she would never act again. In '75 she changed her mind and signed to star, opposite Gert Frobe, in a German film about WW II, *Death Always Comes Alone*. Since '62 she has been married (her second marriage) to English

actor-producer David Cameron, who is her manager, and is the mother of a daughter, Christina (b. 1968). They live in Salzburg but also spend much time in St. Moritz and the south of France. As a singer, she has lately made several greatly popular records abroad—one selling three million copies. As an autobiographical writer in this decade, she has published two books that have made her better known than all her movie roles, and extremely rich. Her first bestseller, issued here in '71, was *The Gift Horse*, about her young-life experiences (many of them shocking) in Germany, Hollywood, and New York. *The Verdict*, her newest, treats principally the attack of cancer that hospitalized her for more than two years, requiring more than 50 operations, one of them a radical mastectomy. Onscreen from 1946. IN: *Between Yesterday and Tomorrow, The Sinner, Decision Before Dawn, Diplomatic Courier, The Snows of Kilimanjaro, Sunderin, Svengali, Holiday for Henrietta, Port of Desire, Catherine of Russia, Valley of the Doomed, Landru, The Threepenny Opera, Escape from Sahara, Mozambique*, more.

NEGRI, POLA (Tex.) In her 70s (b. 1897), unmarried for many years, and still with jet-black hair, the great star from Poland lives quietly—though she has many local friends—in San Antonio. Active in civic affairs, she is on the board of the city symphony. In '70 she published her autobiography, *Memoirs of a Star*. Publicizing the book then, though declining to be photographed, she told reporters that she has never had a face lift . . . that she would like to see her life story filmed (with Vanessa Redgrave) . . . that she disapproves of nudity and obscenity in present-day movies . . . that she shops in New York twice yearly . . . that, even though she has sold much of her famous jewel collection, she still has enough left to "dazzle" when the occasion requires it . . . and that—speaking of Rudolph Valentino—"I regret that I met him so late. We had only one year of happiness." And reporters found her to be a small woman with long bright-red fingernails, given to turtle-neck sweaters (black, of course, which "has always been my favorite color") and shocking pink trousers, smoking filtered cigarettes extracted from a gold case. They also could not help noting that "her throaty, fascinatingly harsh voice retains the full flavor of her Polish accent." Far from a recluse, as often stated in print, the green-eyed star with the gardenia-white complexion (still) travels widely. In '73 she paid her first visit to Hollywood in almost a decade. She was offered, then, a role in *The Sugarland Express*, which was filmed in Texas, but she declined it—as she does other movie offers, regularly received. In '75 director Vincente Minnelli was most anxious that she costar with his daughter Liza in the romantic fantasy *A Matter of Time;* when she demurred, Ingrid Bergman accepted the role. On Hollywood screens steadily through '32 (*A Woman Commands*), she has made three widely spaced comebacks: in 1937's *Madame Bovary,* 1943's *Hi Diddle Diddle,* and 1964's *The Moonspinners.* She figures that is sufficient. A deeply religious woman, attending services faithfully, she also supports San Antonio's St. Mary's University in numerous ways and has lately given its drama department prints of several of her films. There has been much drama, as well as tragedy, in her personal life. Childless, she has been married twice. She married Polish Count Eugene Domski in '19, but divorced him a year later. In '27, in the aftermath of Valentino's sudden death, she married Russian Prince Serge Mdivani, who was killed in a Florida polo game in '36. Aware of these and other traumatic events in her life, one ventures to ask, would she do it all over again, or change any of it? Pola Negri answers: "I would relinquish neither inner scars nor external glories. I have wept and laughed, been foolish and wise. There is even a certain edge of triumph in the peacefulness of my present life." Onscreen in Germany from the teens. Onscreen in Hollywood from 1922. IN: *The Red Peacock, Bella Donna, Passion, The Spanish Dancer, Shadows of Paris, Men, Forbidden Paradise, East of Suez, Flower of the Night, A Woman of the World, Crown of Lies, The Woman on Trial, Loves of an Actress, The Woman from Moscow, Forbidden Paradise,* more.

NEHER, SUSAN (S. Cal.) Ingenue. Onscreen in 1967. IN: *Divorce, American Style.*

NEIL, HILDEGARDE (Eng.) Leading lady. Onscreen in the '70s. IN: *The Man Who Haunted Himself, Antony and Cleopatra* (as Cleopatra), *A Touch of Class,* more.

NEILL, NOEL (S. Cal.) Long retired, the Paramount starlet of the '40s and later famous as "Lois Lane" in TV's *Superman,* she is, in her 50s, resuming her career. Onscreen from 1943. IN: *Are These Our Parents?, Here Come the Waves, Are You With It?,* more.

NEILSON, PERLITA (Eng.) Support. Onscreen in 1963. IN: *She Didn't Say No.*

NEILSON-TERRY, PHYLLIS (Eng.) In her 80s now (b. 1892), this character actress has been retired since 1960. Onscreen from 1955. IN: *Doctor in the House, Look Back in Anger, Conspiracy of Hearts,* more.

NEISE, GEORGE (S. Cal.) Character. Onscreen from 1944. IN: *Experiment Perilous, One Sunday Afternoon, The Three Stooges in*

Orbit, Did You Hear the One About the Trave *ing Saleslady?, The Barefoot Excutive,* more.

NELSON, BARRY (N.Y.) Leading man. Or screen from 1941. IN: *Johnny Eager, Shado of the Thin Man, Dr. Kildare's Victory, Stan By for Action, Eyes in the Night, A Yank on th Burma Road, The Human Comedy, Bataan, Guy Named Joe, Undercover Maisie, Tenth A enue Angel, The Man with My Face, Fort Guns, Mary Mary, The Only Game in Towr Airport, Pete 'n Tillie,* more.

NELSON, DAVID (S. Cal.) The son of Harrie Hilliard and the late Ozzie Nelson, he gradu ated from teen roles to young leading man Now in his 40s (b. 1936), he has been a TV director for several years. Onscreen from 1952 IN: *Here Come the Nelsons, Peyton Place, Th Remarkable Mr. Pennypacker, Day of the Ou law, The Big Circus, -30-, The Big Show,* more.

NELSON, ED (S. Cal.) Leading man. Onscreer from 1955. IN: *Attack of the Crab Monsters New Orleans Uncensored, Hell on Devil's Is land, Invasion of the Saucer Men, Street Darkness, The Young Captives, Soldier in th Rain, Judgment at Nuremberg, Elmer Gantr The Man from Galveston, Time to Run, Airpo 1975, That's the Way of the World,* more.

NELSON, GENE (S. Cal.) Nimble as always i his 50s (b. 1920), the singer-dancer-actor hasn acted in a movie since 1963's *Thunder Islanc* preferring to direct. And he is one of TV's bus est. But twice in this decade he has costarred i musicals on Broadway—in *Follies* and *Goo News* with Alice Faye (replacing John Payn who withdrew). Onscreen from 1943. IN: *Th Is the Army, I Wonder Who's Kissing Her No* (chorus dancer), *Daughter of Rosie O'Grady Tea for Two, The West Point Story, Lullaby o Broadway, Painting the Clouds with Sunshine Three Sailors and a Girl, So This Is Paris, Okl homa!, The Atomic Man, 20,000 Eyes,* more.

NELSON, KENNETH (N.Y.) Leading man. On screen from 1970. IN: *The Magic Christiar The Boys in the Band.*

NELSON, KRISTIN (S. Cal.) Former ingenue Wife of Rick Nelson, daughter of Elyse Kno: and Tom Harmon. Inactive now. Onscreen i 1965. IN: *Love and Kisses.*

NELSON, LORI (S. Cal.) Still a youthful-look ing blonde in her 40s (b. 1933), she is divorce from Johnny Mann (of the Johnny Mann Sing ers) and has two teenage daughters, Susie an Jennifer. She lives on a rustic estate in Chats worth, is active in the nearby Catholic Church and says she would like to work again, bu adds, "This is not as easy as it sounds, though, after having been inactive for so long." Onscreen from 1952. IN: *Francis Goes to West Point, Bend of the River, All I Desire, The All-American, Walking My Baby Back Home, Destry, Ma and Pa Kettle at Waikiki, Revenge of the Creature, Sincerely Yours, The Day the World Ended, Pardners*, more, including 1957's *Untamed Youth*, her last to date.

NELSON, PORTIA (N.Y.) Singer-actress. Onscreen from 1965. IN: *The Sound of Music, Doctor Dolittle*, more.

NELSON, RICK (S. Cal.) The son of Harriet Hilliard and the late Ozzie Nelson, he is in his 30s (b. 1940), has not pursued his movie career since 1965, but as a singer he remains highly popular on records and in club appearances. Onscreen from 1952. IN: *Here Come the Nelsons, The Story of Three Loves, Rio Bravo, The Wackiest Ship in the Army, Love and Kisses*.

NELSON, RUTH (Conn.) With her unique, warm speaking voice, and *simpatico* style of acting, she was one of the most memorable of all character actresses of the '40s—and particularly appealing when playing mothers, such as William Eythe's in *The Eve of St. Mark*. She wound up her Hollywood career in 1947's *Mother Wore Tights*. Married for more than three decades to actor-director John Cromwell, she lives in Wilton, is in her 70s, and is retired. Onscreen from 1943. IN: *The North Star, None Shall Escape, Wilson, The Keys of the Kingdom, A Tree Grows in Brooklyn, Sentimental Journey, Till the End of Time, Humoresque, The Sea of Grass*, more.

NELSON, TRACY (S. Cal.) Daughter of Rick Nelson. Onscreen in 1968. IN: *Yours, Mine and Ours* (child role).

NERO, FRANCO (It.) Leading man. Onscreen from 1966. IN: *The Bible, The Hired Killer, Camelot* (as Lancelot, his most memorable role), *The Mercenary, The Virgin and the Gypsy, Pope Joan, Confessions of a Police Captain, Don't Turn the Other Cheek*, more.

NESBITT, CATHLEEN (Eng.) Only Estelle Winwood, her senior by six years, is the rival of this aristocratic woman as the busiest elder character actress around. In her late 80s (b. 1889), she lives in London but spends much of her time on jets flying wherever her work calls her. She has, in this decade, appeared in *Villain, French Connection II* and Hitchcock's *Family Plot*; acted Off Broadway with George C. Scott in *Uncle Vanya* and starred onstage in Chicago in *The Royal Family*; been on TV in the *George Sand* series and the ABC afternoon special *The Mask of Love* (winning, in '74, the best actress of the year Emmy); she also found time to write and publish ('73) her autobiography, *A Little Love and Good Companions*. She has been married since 1922 to C. B. Ramage, a former stage actor who became a barrister and is now retired. They have two children: Mark, an advertising executive in London, and Jennifer, a psychiatrist who is also author of the novel *Proud Adversary*. Onscreen from 1932. IN: *The Case of the Frightened Lady, The Passing of the Third Floor Back, Nicholas Nickleby, Desiree, Three Coins in the Fountain, So Long at the Fair, Black Widow, An Affair to Remember, Separate Tables, The Parent Trap, Promise Her Anything, The Trygon Factor, Staircase*, more.

NESBITT, DERREN (Eng.) Character. Onscreen from the '60s. IN: *Kill or Cure, The Amorous Adventures of Moll Flanders, Underworld Informers, The Naked Runner, Innocent Bystanders*, more.

NESMITH, MICHAEL (S. Cal.) Of "The Monkees." Onscreen in 1968. IN: *Head*.

NESOR, AL (N.Y.) Character. Onscreen from 1959. IN: *Li'l Abner, Andy, Where Were You When the Lights Went Out?, Requiem for a Heavyweight, A Lovely Way to Die, No Way to Treat a Lady*, more.

NESS, ED (EDDIE) (S. Cal.) Character. Onscreen in the '70s. IN: *The Outfit*, more.

NETTLETON, JOHN (Eng.) Support. Onscreen from 1966. IN: *A Man for All Seasons, And Soon the Darkness, Black Beauty*, more.

NETTLETON, LOIS (S. Cal.) Leading lady. Onscreen from 1962. IN: *Period of Adjustment, Come Fly With Me, Mail Order Bride, The Good Guys and the Bad Guys, Valley of Mystery, The Bamboo Saucer, Dirty Dingus Magee, The Honkers, The Man in the Glass Booth, Echoes of a Summer*, more.

NEUMANN, DOROTHY (S. Cal.) Character. Onscreen from 1948. IN: *Sorry, Wrong Number; My Blue Heaven, Latin Lovers, A Man Called Peter, Anything Goes, Spring Reunion, The Thrill of It All, The Man from the Diner's Club, Get Yourself a College Girl*, more.

NEVENS, PAUL (N.Y.) Character. Onscreen in the '70s. IN: *Bananas, Shaft, Come Back Charleston Blue*, more.

NEVILLE, JOHN (Eng.) Leading man. Onscreen from 1960. IN: *Oscar Wilde, Billy Budd, I Like Money, Topaze, A Study in Terror, The Adventures of Gerard*, more.

NEVINS, CLAUDETTE (S. Cal.) Leading lady. Onscreen from 1961. IN: *The Mask*, more.

NEWARK, DEREK (Eng.) Character. Onscreen from the '60s. IN: *The Little Ones, Oh! What a Lovely War, Fragment of Fear, The Black Windmill*, more.

NEWHALL, PATRICIA (N.Y.) Support. Now a stage producer-director. Onscreen from 1949. IN: *Prince of Foxes, Metamorphosis*, more.

NEWHART, BOB (S. Cal.) Star comedian. Onscreen from 1962. IN: *Hell Is for Heroes, Hot Millions, Catch-22, On a Clear Day You Can See Forever, Cold Turkey, Thursday's Game*, more.

NEWILL, JAMES (S. Cal.) He began as a singer in movies (*Something to Sing About*: '37) then became a popular star of Westerns (the "Texas Rangers" series) and serials. Retiring from movies in '47, after *Thundergap Outlaws*, he appeared for a while on the musical stage. For the past two decades this actor who is now in his 60s (b. 1911) has owned and operated a plastics business in Southern California. Onscreen from 1937. IN: *Renfrew of the Royal Mounted, Crashing Through, Young People, Murder on the Yukon, The Great American Broadcast, The Falcon's Brother, Bombardier, Riders of Mystery Mountain, Return of the Rangers, Brand of the Devil, Gunsmoke Mesa*, more.

NEWLAN, PAUL (S. Cal.) Character. Onscreen from 1951. IN: *David and Bathsheba, Against All Flags, Pirates of Tripoli, The Americanization of Emily, The Slender Thread*, more.

NEWLAND, JOHN (S. Cal.) Support. Now a director. Onscreen from 1947. IN: *Gentleman's Agreement, The Challenge, 13 Lead Soldiers*, more. He has directed *The Violators, The Spy With My Face, Legend of Hillbilly John*, more.

NEWLAND, MARY/a.k.a. LILIAN OLDLAND (Eng.) Support. IN: *The Silent Passenger*, more.

NEWLEY, ANTHONY (S. Cal.) Costar and composer. Onscreen from 1946. IN: *Adventures of Dusty Bates* (at age 15), *Little Ballerina, Oliver Twist, Vote for Huggett, Madeleine, The Weak and the Wicked, Above Us the Waves, Fire Down Below, How to Murder a Rich Uncle, Killers of Kilimanjaro, The Small World of Sammy Lee, Doctor Dolittle, Sweet November, Mr. Quilp*, more.

NEWMAN, BARRY (N.Y.) Leading man. Onscreen from 1960. IN: *Pretty Boy Floyd, The Lawyer, Vanishing Point, The Salzburg Connection*, more.

NEWMAN, MELISSA (S. Cal.) Leading lady. Onscreen from the '60s. IN: *The Undefeated*, more.

NEWMAN, NANETTE (Eng.) Costar. Onscreen from the '50s. IN: *The League of Gentlemen, The Wrong Arm of the Law, Seance on a Wet Afternoon, The Whisperers, Deadfall, Captain Nemo and the Underwater City, Long Ago Tomorrow, The Stepford Wives*, more.

NEWMAN, PAUL (Conn.) Star. Nominated for Best Actor Award in *Cat on a Hot Tin Roof, The Hustler, Hud, Cool Hand Luke.* Onscreen from 1954. IN: *The Silver Chalice, Somebody Up There Likes Me, The Helen Morgan Story, The Long Hot Summer; Rally Round the Flag, Boys; The Left-Handed Gun, Exodus, From the Terrace, Sweet Bird of Youth, The Prize, Harper, Torn Curtain, Lady L, Hombre, The Secret War of Harry Frigg, Butch Cassidy and the Sundance Kid, Winning, W.U.S.A., Sometimes a Great Notion, Pocket Money, The Mackintosh Man, The Life and Times of Judge Roy Bean, The Sting, The Towering Inferno, The Drowning Pool, Buffalo Bill and the Indians*, more.

NEWMAN, PHYLLIS (N.Y.) Leading lady. Onscreen from 1956. IN: *Picnic, The Vagabond King, Let's Rock, Bye Bye Braverman, To Find a Man*, more.

NEWMAN, ROGER (S. Cal.) Support. Onscreen from the '60s. IN: *Marlowe, Too Late the Hero*, more.

NEWMAN, SCOTT (S. Cal.) Support. Paul Newman's son. Onscreen in the '70s. IN: *Breakheart Pass*, more.

NEWMAN, THOMAS (N.Y.) Character. Onscreen from the '50s. IN: *Never Steal Anything Small, North by Northwest, Cape Fear, Horror at Party Beach*, more.

NEWMAR, JULIE (N.Y.) Leading lady. Onscreen from 1954. IN: *Seven Brides for Seven Brothers* (billed Julie Newmeyer), *Li'l Abner, The Rookie, Marriage-Go-Round, For Love or Money, Mackenna's Gold*, more.

NEWTON, JOHN (N.Y.) Character. Onscreen from the '60s. IN: *This Rebel Breed, The Satan Bug, The Man from the Diner's Club*, more.

NEWTON, WAYNE (Nev.) Singer-actor. Lives in Las Vegas, where he is reportedly a more potent nightclub attraction than Elvis Presley. Onscreen in 1969. IN: *80 Steps to Jonah*.

NEY, MARIE (Eng.) Character. Onscreen from 1930. IN: *Escape, The Wandering Jew, Scrooge, Jamaica Inn, Conspirator, Seven Days to Noon, Simba, Yield to the Night*, more.

NEY, RICHARD (S. Cal.) He is, in his 60s (b. 1916), slender, sleek, sensationally handsome— and rich. A Rolls-Royce-driving Bel-Air investment counselor, representing many of the most affluent people in show business, he is also the author of three explosive best-selling books: *The Wall Street Jungle, The Wall Street Gang,* and *Making It in the Market*. Besides wielding a heavy hatchet on the Eastern money establishment, the books were written with the purpose of showing the reader "how to attack the financial conspiracy with its own weapons: buy when the insiders buy and sell when they sell." The former actor has also been appointed Honorary Professor of Investments at USC's School of Business Administration. Onscreen for a decade after his debut in *Mrs. Miniver* (as the son of Greer Garson, to whom he was later married for several years), he went into the investment arena on a part-time basis in the '50s. After two films in the early '60s (*Midnight Lace* and *Premature Burial*), he became a full-time counselor, and achieved national prominence in this area when *Time* magazine included him in its June 1962 cover story on the stock market and cited him as having "called" the market crash of that year. Other, later forecasts of his have also been provably accurate. Ney operates from his elegant home in Bel Air. He also has a richly furnished co-op on Fifth Avenue in New York, overlooking Central Park, filled with Monets and Degas line drawings. His second wife of several years—they have no children—is the former Pauline McMartin, a gentle, charming woman once married to a wealthy Canadian. She may be, like Greer Garson, a bit his senior, but then, he has always looked younger than his years. They describe theirs as a "commuting" marriage. Mrs. Ney lives in New York ("She loves the social life," he says) and Ney lives in California, coming East every six weeks or so. "For a man, work always comes first," he explains. "My wife understands this, but loves New York, so this works best for us." It's most unlikely he will ever return to acting. "I loved being an actor," he has said. "It was a marvelous holiday." But, he adds, "All this is much more exciting than being an actor. I feel for the first time that I'm alive." Proof of his present contentment is this statement: "Recently I came into a lot of money, and I thought to myself, 'Gee, do I want anything?' And I couldn't think of a thing." Onscreen from 1942. IN: *The War Against Mrs. Hadley, Ivy, The Late George Apley, The Fan, Joan of Arc, The Lovable Cheat, Miss Italy, Babes in Bagdad, The Sergeant and the Spy*, more.

NICHOLAS BROTHERS, THE (S. Cal.) Black acrobatic dancers, Harold and Fayard, who comprised the most energetic and almost certainly greatest dance team ever to work in American movies. They remain active in clubs. Harold was married to the late Dorothy Dandridge, by whom he has a grown daughter. Onscreen from 1935. IN: *The Big Broadcast of 1936, Down Argentine Way, The Great American Broadcast, Tin Pan Alley, Sun Valley Serenade, Orchestra Wives, Stormy Weather, Carolina Blues* (Harold only), *The Pirate*, more. In 1974 Harold played a supporting role, "Little Seymour," in *Uptown Saturday Night*.

NICHOLAS, DENISE (S. Cal.) Black leading lady. Onscreen in the '70s. IN: *Blacula, Let's Do It Again, Mr. Ricco*, more.

NICHOLAS, PAUL (Eng.) Leading man. Onscreen in the '70s. IN: *Lisztomania*, more.

NICHOLLS, ANTHONY (Eng.) Character. Onscreen from 1948. IN: *The Hasty Heart, No Place for Jennifer, High Treason, Both Sides of the Law, Tonight's the Night, Dunkirk, Victim, Othello, If, The Battle of Britain*, more.

NICHOLS, BARBARA (S. Cal.) Support. Onscreen from 1956. IN: *The King and Four Queens, Manfish, Sweet Smell of Success, Pal Joey, The Pajama Game, The Naked and the Dead, Who Was That Lady?, The Scarface Mob, The Loved One, The Human Duplicators, The Power*, more.

NICHOLS, DANDY (Eng.) Character actress. Onscreen from the '40s. IN: *The Fallen Idol, The Winslow Boy, Tony Draws a Horse, Blonde Sinner, Georgy Girl, The Birthday Party, Confessions of a Window Cleaner*, more.

NICHOLS, JOSEPHINE (N.Y.) Support. Onscreen from the '60s. IN: *Petulia, Riverwind*, more.

NICHOLS, JOY (Eng.) Support. Onscreen from the '40s. IN: *Not So Dusty, Pacific Adventure, The King in New York*, more.

NICHOLS, MIKE (Conn.) Comedian, Oscar-winning director (*The Graduate*), and actor. Onscreen in 1957. IN: *Bed of Grass*.

NICHOLS, NICHELLE (S. Cal.) Black leading lady. Onscreen from 1966. IN: *Mister Buddwing, Truck Turner*, more.

NICHOLS, ROBERT (S. Cal.) Character. Onscreen from the '50s. IN: *The Thing, Eight Iron Men, Giant, Don't Go Near the Water, Call Me Bwana, Man in the Middle*, more.

NICHOLSON, JACK (S. Cal.) Star. Won Best Actor Oscar in *One Flew Over the Cuckoo's Nest.* Nominated for Best Supporting Actor Oscar in *Easy Rider.* Nominated for Best Actor Oscar in *Five Easy Pieces, The Last Detail, Chinatown.* Onscreen from the '50s. IN: *Little Shop of Horrors, The Cry-Baby Killer, Back Door to Hell, Too Young to Love, Studs Lonigan, The Raven, Hells Angels on Wheels, Flight to Fury, The Trip, On a Clear Day You Can See Forever, Carnal Knowledge, The King of Marvin Gardens, The Passenger, The Fortune, Tommy, One Flew Over the Cuckoo's Nest, The Missouri Breaks, The Last Tycoon,* more.

NICKERSON, DAWN (N.Y.) Leading lady; inactive now. Onscreen in 1961. IN: *Hey, Let's Twist.*

NICKERSON, DENISE (N.Y.) Juvenile. Onscreen from 1971. IN: *Willy Wonka and the Chocolate Factory* (as "Violet"), more.

NICOL, ALEX (S. Cal.) Character; former leading man. Onscreen from 1950. IN: *The Sleeping City, Air Cadet, Tomahawk, Lone Hand, Heat Wave, About Mrs. Leslie, Strategic Air Command, Great Day in the Morning, Five Branded Women, Under Ten Flags, The Sleeping Skull, Run With the Devil, Bloody Mama,* more.

NIELSEN, LESLIE (S. Cal.) Leading man. Onscreen from 1956. IN: *The Vagabond King, The Opposite Sex, The Sheepman, See How They Run, The Reluctant Astronaut, Rosie, Gunfight in Abilene, Counterpoint, Dayton's Devils, How to Commit Marriage, Four Rode Out, The Poseidon Adventure,* more.

NIGH, JANE (S. Cal.) She lives in Beverly Hills and is retired. Onscreen from 1944. IN: *Something for the Boys, Fighting Man of the Plains, Blue Grass of Kentucky, Rio Grande Patrol, Disc Jockey, Rodeo,* more, including 1957's *Hold That Hypnotist,* her last to date.

NILSSON, BIRGIT (N.Y.) Opera star. Onscreen in 1954. IN: *Rhapsody.*

NILSSON, HARRY (Eng.) Popular music singer-composer and actor. Onscreen in 1974. IN: *Son of Dracula.*

NIMMO, DEREK (Eng.) Comedian. Onscreen from 1958. IN: *The Millionairess, Tamahine, Murder Ahoy, Casino Royale,* more.

NIMOY, LEONARD (S. Cal.) Character star. Onscreen from 1951. IN: *Rhubarb, The Balcony, Seven Days in May, Deathwatch, Catlow,* more.

NINCHI, AVE (It.) Support. Onscreen from the '40s. IN: *To Live in Peace, The Walls of Malapaga, Teresa, Tomorrow Is Too Late, The Bigamist, Purple Noon, House of Cards, Murmur of the Heart,* more.

NIVEN, DAVID (Switz.) Star. Won Best Actor Oscar in *Separate Tables.* In the '70s he has published two best-selling autobiographies, *The Moon's a Balloon* and *Bring On the Empty Horses.* Onscreen from 1935. IN: *Splendor; Thank You, Jeeves; Rose Marie, Dodsworth, The Charge of the Light Brigade, The Prisoner of Zenda, Four Men and a Prayer, Three Blind Mice, Dawn Patrol, Eternally Yours, Wuthering Heights, Raffles, Spitfire, Stairway to Heaven, The Magnificent Doll, The Bishop's Wife, Enchantment, The Moon Is Blue, Around the World in 80 Days; Oh Men! Oh Women!; Bonjour Tristesse, The Guns of Navarone, The Pink Panther, The Impossible Years, Prudence and the Pill, The Kremlin Letter, The Statue, Paper Tiger, Old Dracula, No Deposit No Return, Murder by Death,* more.

NIVEN, KIP (S. Cal.) Leading man. No relation to David Niven. Onscreen in the '70s. IN: *Newman's Law, Airport 1975, Earthquake,* more.

NIXON, MARIAN (S. Cal.) Now in her 70s (b. 1904), and beautiful still, she last appeared onscreen in 1936's *Tango,* after having starred in 44 talkies and countless silents. She was widowed in 1964, after a marriage spanning exactly 30 years, when her husband, director William Seiter, passed away. (He had once been married to Laura La Plante.) On April 1, 1972, she was married to former star Ben Lyon at the Westwood Methodist Church. Attending the happy event were many Hollywood friends and relatives including Marian's daughter and two young grandchildren, a boy and a girl. Onscreen from 1925. IN: *Riders of the Purple Sage, I'll Show You the Town, Devil's Island, Out All Night, The Chinese Parrot, Red Lips, The Rainbow Man, Say It With Songs, General Crack, Courage, College Lovers, Women Go on Forever, Charlie Chan's Chance, Madison Square Garden, Best of Enemies, Doctor Bull, Strictly Dynamite, We're Rich Again,* more.

NIXON, MARNI (S. Cal.) Singer-actress. Well-publicized "dubber" of stars' singing voices (Natalie Wood's in *West Side Story,* etc.). Onscreen in 1965. IN: *The Sound of Music.*

NOBLE, EULALIE (N.Y.) Leading lady. Onscreen from the '60s. IN: *Alice's Restaurant,* more.

NOBLE, JAMES (N.J.) Leading man. Costar of the TV soap opera *A World Apart.* Onscreen in the '70s. IN: *What's So Bad About Feeling Good?*, *The Sporting Club*, *Dragonfly*, more.

NOBLE, RAY (N.Y.) Famous orchestra leader. Onscreen from 1937. IN: *A Damsel in Distress*, *Here We Go Again*, more.

NOEL, CHRIS (N.Y.) Leading lady. Onscreen from 1963. IN: *Soldier in the Rain*, *Honeymoon Hotel*, *Get Yourself a College Girl*, *Joy in the Morning*, *Girl Happy*; *John Goldfarb, Please Come Home*; *Wild Wild Winter*, *The Glory Stompers*, *For Singles Only*, more.

NOEL, MAGALI (It.) Leading lady. Onscreen from the '50s. IN: *Rififi*, *The Grand Maneuver*, *Passionate Summer*, *Razzi*, *Lovers and Thieves*, *La Dolce Vita*, *All the Other Girls Do!*, *Tropic of Cancer*, *Fellini Satyricon*, *The Man Who Had Power Over Women*, *Amarcord*, more.

NOEL-NOEL (Fr.) Character. Onscreen from the '30s. IN: *Bouquets from Nicholas*, *A Cage of Nightingales*, *The Seven Deadly Sins*, *The Spice of Life*, *The French They Are a Funny Race*, *Jessica*, more.

NOIRET, PHILIPPE (Fr.) Comic character star. Onscreen from the '60s. IN: *Zazie*, *Crime Does Not Pay*, *Therese*, *Lady L*, *The Night of the Generals*, *The Other One*, *Tender Scoundrel*, *Alexander*, *Justine*, *Topaz*, *Mister Freedom*, *Give Her the Moon*, *Murphy's War*, more.

NOLAN, DORIS (Eng.) Leading lady; retired. Onscreen from 1936. IN: *The Man I Marry*, *Top of the Town*, *As Good as Married*, *Holiday* (perhaps her most memorable role), *One Hour to Live*, *Irene*, *Moon Over Burma*, more. (See Alexander Knox.)

NOLAN, JAMES (S. Cal.) Character. Onscreen from the '30s. IN: *Girls on Probation*, *Torchy Blane in Panama*, *Dick Tracy Meets Gruesome*, *Miracle of the Bells*, *Fighting Father Dunne*, *Death Valley Gunfighter*, *Alias the Champ*, *The Big Caper*, *Portrait in Black*, *Airport*, more.

NOLAN, JEANETTE (S. Cal.) Character. Wife of character John McIntire, mother of Tim McIntire. Onscreen from 1948. IN: *Words and Music*, *Macbeth*, *No Sad Songs for Me*, *The Big Heat*, *Tribute to a Bad Man*, *April Love*, *The Great Impostor*, *Two Rode Together*, *The Man Who Shot Liberty Valance*, *My Blood Runs Cold*, *The Reluctant Astronaut*, *Did You Hear the One about the Traveling Saleslady?*, more.

NOLAN, JOHN (S. Cal.) Support. Onscreen from 1961. IN: *The Last Time I Saw Archie*, more.

NOLAN, KATHLEEN (KATHY) (S. Cal.) In 1975 the redheaded leading lady—better known for the TV series *The Real McCoys* than for her movies—was elected the first woman president of the Screen Actors Guild. Onscreen from the '50s. IN: *The Desperadoes Are in Town*, *No Time to be Young*, *Benjie Gault*, *Limbo*, more.

NOLAN, LLOYD (S. Cal.) Character star. Onscreen from 1934. IN: *Atlantic Adventure*, *The Devil's Squadron*, *Texas Rangers*, *Interns Can't Take Money*, *Wells Fargo*, *Hunted Men*, *King of Alcatraz*, *Ambush*, *The House Across the Bay*, *Johnny Apollo*, *Sleepers West*; *Blue, White and Perfect*; *It Happened in Flatbush*, *Guadalcanal Diary*, *Bataan*, *A Tree Grows in Brooklyn*, *Captain Eddie*, *The House on 92nd Street*, *Somewhere in the Night*, *Green Grass of Wyoming*, *The Sun Comes Up*, *Island in the Sky*, *A Hatful of Rain*, *Peyton Place*, *Portrait in Black*, *Susan Slade*, *Circus World*, *Never Too Late*, *Sergeant Ryker*, *Ice Station Zebra*, *Airport*, *Earthquake*, more.

NOLAN, MARGARET (S. Cal.) Support. Onscreen from the '60's. IN: *Promise Her Anything*; *Don't Raise the Bridge, Lower the River*; *Can Heironymus Merkin Ever Forget Mercy Humppe . . . ?*, more.

NOLAN, TOM (MY) (S. Cal.) Onscreen from the '60s. IN: *Kiss Me Stupid*, *Chastity*, more.

NOLTE, CHARLES (Minn.) After his debut in *Warpaint*, this blond, extraordinarily handsome actor—widely acclaimed in his starring role on Broadway in *Billy Budd*—appeared in several more. Then, turning playwright, he wrote and starred onstage in London in *The Summer People*. Entering his 50s now (b. 1926), still a most handsome man, he has been in Minneapolis for several years, writing and directing plays (*Alexander's Death*, etc.) for the University of Minnesota, where his father was dean and he himself received his master's in drama. Onscreen from 1963. IN: *The Steel Cage*, *Ten Seconds to Hell*, *Under Ten Flags*, *Armored Command*, more.

NOONE, PETER (BLAIR) (Eng.) Singer-actor. Of "Herman's Hermits." Onscreen from 1966. IN: *Hold On!*; *Mrs. Brown, You've Got a Lovely Daughter*; more.

NORDEN, TOMMY (N.Y.) Former juvenile; inactive now. Onscreen in 1963. IN: *Five Miles to Midnight*.

NORLUND, EVY (S. Cal.) Leading lady from Denmark. She has been married for two decades to actor James Darren and is retired. Onscreen in 1959. IN: *The Flying Fontaines*.

NORMAN, MAIDIE (S. Cal.) Black character. Onscreen from 1948. IN: *The Burning Cross, The Well, Bright Road, About Mrs. Leslie, What Ever Happened to Baby Jane?*, more.

NORMINGTON, JOHN (Eng.) Support. Onscreen from 1967. IN: *Inadmissible Evidence, A Midsummer Night's Dream, The Reckoning*, more.

NORRIS, CHRISTOPHER (S. Cal.) Ingenue. Onscreen in the '70s. IN: *Summer of '42, Airport 1975*, more.

NORRIS, EDWARD (S. Cal.) Still living in the Los Angeles area, where he has business interests, the former leading man is in his 60s now (b. 1910) and has been inactive in movies for the past two decades. Onscreen from 1934. IN: *Murder in the Fleet, Show Them No Mercy, They Won't Forget, Tail Spin, The Lady in Question, Angels with Broken Wings, The Mystery of Marie Roget, I Live on Danger, Murder in the Music Hall, Trapped by Boston Blackie, Killer Shark, I Was a Communist for the FBI, Murder Without Tears*, more.

NORRIS, KAREN (S. Cal.) Support. Onscreen from 1957. IN: *The Bachelor Party, Back Street, Lover Come Back, The Impossible Years*, more.

NORTH, JAY (S. Cal.) The former juvenile star —most famous for his two TV series, *Dennis the Menace* and *Maya*—is in his 20s now (b. 1952), has been married and divorced, and has most recently starred in touring productions of plays such as *Butterflies Are Free*. Onscreen from 1959. IN: *The Big Operator, Pepe, Zebra in the Kitchen, Maya*.

NORTH, MICHAEL (TED) (S. Cal.) He is now a vice president of International Creative Management, perhaps Hollywood's largest talent agency, and the father of two young daughters. His wife, Leona, passed away in 1975. Once married to Mary Beth Hughes, he has a grown son by her. Onscreen as Ted North from 1940. IN: *Chad Hanna, The Bride Wore Crutches, To the Shores of Tripoli, Manila Calling, Girl Trouble, Thunder Birds, Roxie Hart, Margin for Error, The Ox-Bow Incident*, more. Onscreen as Michael North from 1947. IN: *The Unseen*, more. (See Mary Beth Hughes.)

NORTH, SHEREE (S. Cal.) Her platinum-blonde starring roles at 20th Century-Fox in the '50s, as a pseudo-Marilyn Monroe, prepared no one for the superlative dramatic performances this now-dark-haired actress has given in this decade on TV (where she has been tellingly present every few weeks) and in movies. Critics, seriously regarding her work and growth, foresee Emmys and/or Oscars for her, the only performer of her era to have achieved such a total metamorphosis. Still youthful in looks (b. 1930), she has been married and divorced three times, and has a grown daughter, Dawn, by first husband, Fred Bessire, and a teenage daughter, Erica, by third husband, Dr. Gerhart Sommer; her second husband was music publisher Bud Freeman. Onscreen from 1945. IN: *An Angel Comes to Brooklyn* (adolescent role), *Excuse My Dust* (dancing role), *Living It Up* (based on the Broadway musical *Hazel Flagg* in which she was starring when actually "discovered" by Hollywood, her home town), *How to Be Very Very Popular, The Lieutenant Wore Skirts, The Best Things in Life Are Free, No Down Payment, Mardi Gras, In Love and War, The Gypsy Moths, The Trouble with Girls, The Outfit, Lawman, The Organization, Charley Varrick, Breakout, The Shootist*, more.

NORTH, ZEME (S. Cal.) Supporting actress. Onscreen from the '60s. IN: *Zotz!, Palm Springs Weekend*, more.

NORTON, CLIFF (S. Cal.) Character. Onscreen from the '60s. IN: *It's a Mad Mad Mad Mad World; The Russians Are Coming, The Russians Are Coming; Won Ton Ton, the Dog Who Saved Hollywood*; more.

NORTON, JUDY (S. Cal.) Former juvenile. Popular as "Mary Ellen" in TV's *The Waltons*. Onscreen in 1967. IN: *Hotel*.

NORTON, KEN (S. Cal.) Leading man. Onscreen in the '70s. IN: *Drum*, more.

NOURSE, ALLEN (N.Y.) Character. Onscreen from the '50s. IN: *The Long Gray Line, Pushover, Tight Spot, Cell 2455—Death Row, The Phenix City Story, Odds Against Tomorrow*, more.

NOVA, LOU (S. Cal.) The heavyweight-turned-actor (after his career in the ring in the '30s and '40s) is in his 60s now and lives in semiretirement in Los Angeles. He was last onscreen in two in the '60s: *What a Way to Go!* and *Thoroughly Modern Millie*. Onscreen from 1944. IN: *Swing Fever; Joe Palooka, Champ; Somewhere in the Night, Love and Learn, World for Ransom, The Leather Saint*, more.

NOVACK, SHELLY (S. Cal.) Pro football player-turned-actor. Onscreen from 1969. IN: *Tell Them Willie Boy Is Here, Airport, Kansas City Bomber, Toke*, more.

NOVAK, EVA (S. Cal.) In her 70s (b. 1899), she lives in retirement in Van Nuys, having last played small roles in two movies in the '60s: *Sergeant Rutledge* (as a courtroom spectator) and *Wild Seed*. Onscreen from the '20s. IN: *O'Malley of the Mounted, The Tiger's Claw, Sally, Irene, For the Term of His Natural Life, The Medicine Man, The Topeka Terror, Apology for Murder, Blackmail, Four Faces West, Ride a Violent Road*, more.

NOVAK, JANE (S. Cal.) Also retired, like her star-sister Eva, she lives near her in neighboring Sherman Oaks. Jane, who is entering her 80s (b. 1896), phased out her career with minor roles in three Hal Wallis productions in the late '40s: *Desert Fury, Paid in Full*, and *Thelma Jordan*. Onscreen from 1914. IN: *From Italy's Shore, Roads of Destiny, String Beans, The Money Corporal, The Rivers End, Divorce, Closed Gates, Redskin, Hollywood Boulevard, Foreign Correspondent, Prison Girls, Man of Courage*, more.

NOVAK, KIM (N. Cal.) Friends predicted that after the disillusionment of her first marriage—to British actor Richard Johnson—she would not try matrimony again. Married on March 15, 1965, they separated the following February, and on May 26, 1966, the star was awarded a divorce—in Salinas, Calif. Almost exactly one decade later, on March 12, 1976, she did remarry, becoming the wife of a Salinas resident, Dr. Robert Malloy, the veterinarian who tended the many animals—horses, dogs, etc.—at her ranch in Carmel. The marriage was also the second for Dr. Malloy, who is seven years younger than his bride (the actress was born 1933); his previous, 12-year marriage had ended in divorce a short time before he and Kim Novak were united in a small outdoor ceremony. The couple's honeymoon was spent horseback-riding and camping along the Big Sur coastline. The star has lived for several years in luxurious semiretirement in one of the most spectacular mountain-top houses in this area. There now, as before, she paints, writes poetry, and cares for a burgeoning menagerie—with live-in help. Life at the ranch, for the affluent actress, who remains blonde and lovely, looking years younger than her age, is Spartan. She retires by 9:30 P.M., arises each morning at 5, and her customary attire is blue jeans and tennis shoes. Her social life involves but a few longtime close friends. Her only professional activity in this decade to date was the co-star role, in '73, in an ABC "Movie of the Week," *Third Girl From the Left*, her performance being harshly received by critics. Said *Variety*: "The movies found out that Kim Novak couldn't act in a series of fiascos in the mid-50s, but television didn't find out until her TV debut last week." She still reads movie scripts but says she has found none she wishes to do. Her last big-

screen effort was *The Great Train Robbery*. *Vertigo* and *The Legend of Lylah Clare*, neither made at Columbia, still rank as her favorites among her films. When she looks back on her days at the studio, where she became a major star, she recalls it as "a heavy number." Onscreen from 1953. IN: *The French Line* (secondary role), *Pushover* (her first lead), *Five Against the House, Picnic, The Man With the Golden Arm, The Eddy Duchin Story, Jeanne Eagels, Pal Joey; Bell, Book and Candle; Middle of the Night, Strangers When We Meet, The Notorious Landlady, Boys' Night Out, Kiss Me, Stupid; The Amorous Adventures of Moll Flanders*, more.

NOVELLO, JAY (S. Cal.) Character. In his 70s now (b. 1904), he has been inactive in this decade. Onscreen from 1938. IN: *Tenth Avenue Kid, Calling All Marines, They Met in Bombay, Phantom Lady, Hotel Berlin, Kiss the Blood Off My Hands, Sirocco, The Sniper, The Robe, Beneath the Twelve-Mile Reef, The Mad Magician, The Prodigal, Lisbon, A Pocketful of Miracles, Escape from Zahrain, Sylvia, The Caper of the Golden Bulls*, more, including 1969's *The Comic*, his most recent to date.

NUGENT, CAROL (S. Cal.) Married to and divorced from actor Nick Adams, now deceased, she has not appeared in a movie since '59. Onscreen from the '40s. IN: *Little Mr. Jim* (adolescent role), *Cheaper by the Dozen, Belles on Their Toes, The Lusty Men, Fast Company, Vice Raid*, more.

NUGENT, EDWARD "EDDIE" (Tex.) Now in his late 60s, he left the screen after 1938's *Meet the Mayor*, and today, quite retired, lives in San Antonio. Onscreen from 1928. IN: *Our Dancing Daughters, Our Modern Maidens, The Vagabond Lover, The Duke Steps Out, Loose Ankles, Clancy in Wall Street, War Nurse, Shipmates, Bright Lights, Up Pops the Devil, The Crooner, 42nd Street, College Humor, Dance Hall Hostess, This Side of Heaven; Ah, Wilderness!; Dancing Feet, The Harvester, Pigskin Parade, Speed to Spare, Two Minutes to Play*, more.

NUGENT, ELLIOTT (N.Y.) Writing has been the career in recent years for this former leading man, now in his 70s (b. 1899). In '62 he published the novel *Of Cheat and Charmer*, and in '65 his autobiography, *Events Leading Up to the Comedy*. The latter, besides covering the world of show business from the early '20s to the date of publication, was a chronicle of his emotional breakdown and recovery. Now semiretired, he devotes himself, in addition to writing, to golf and photography. He last appeared onscreen in 1951's *My Outlaw Brother*, last directed a movie, *Just for You*, in '52, and last acted—that same year—in a New York revival of the play *The Male Animal* (with James Thurber, he was its coauthor as well). He was later (1952–57) the producer of numerous Broadway shows including *The Seven Year Itch*. He and his wife, Norma Lee, married since '21, have two daughters and numerous grandchildren; their third daughter, Barbara, an actress, died in a freak accident near her home in Princeton, N.J., in 1974, leaving her husband and three sons. Onscreen from 1929. IN: *So This Is College, Not So Dumb, The Unholy Three, Sins of the Children, Romance, Virtuous Husband, The Last Flight, Stage Door Canteen*, more.

NUNN, ALICE (S. Cal.) Comic character. Onscreen in the '70s. IN: *Johnny Got His Gun*, more.

NUREYEV, RUDOLF (N.Y.) It was announced in 1976 that this great ballet star from Russia would star in the title role in *Valentino*, making his dramatic debut. Onscreen in dance movies from the 60s. IN: *An Evening With the Royal Ballet, Romeo and Juliet, I Am a Dancer, Don Quixote*.

NUYEN, FRANCE (S. Cal.) Leading lady. Onscreen from 1958. IN: *South Pacific, In Love and War, The Last Time I Saw Archie, Diamond Head, A Girl Named Tamiku, Man in the Middle, Dimension 5*, more.

NYE, CARRIE (N.Y.) The wife of TV talk-show host Dick Cavett, she is primarily a New York stage actress. Onscreen in 1966. IN: *The Group*.

NYE, LOUIS (S. Cal.) Comedian. Onscreen from 1960. IN: *The Facts of Life, The Last Time I Saw Archie, The Stripper, The Wheeler Dealers, Who's Been Sleeping in My Bed?, Good Neighbor Sam, A Guide for the Married Man*, more.

NYE, PAT (Eng.) Character actress. Onscreen from the '40s. IN: *Mr. Perrin and Mr. Traill*, more.

NYPE, RUSSELL (N.Y.) Singer-actor most famous for his juvenile lead on Broadway in *Call Me Madam*. Onscreen in 1970. IN: *Love Story*.

O

OAKIE, JACK (S. Cal.) Nominated for Best Supporting Actor Oscar in *The Great Dictator*, his portrayal of Mussolini being one not soon to be forgotten. White-haired and in his 70s (b. 1903), jovial and an inveterate Hollywood partygoer, this great comedian has been writing—and selling—magazine articles lately. One of them, in *Modern Maturity* magazine, was a reminiscence piece, "The Times I Saw Garbo"—he having been one of her close friends at Metro. He gets paid for his work but he hardly needs the money. Thanks to San Fernando Valley real estate, purchased in his early days as a star, he has long been a multimillionaire. It is the mark of the man that among his closest friends today are those who were his closest friends then—Mary Brian, Buddy Rogers, Laura La Plante, Carmel Myers, Dorothy Lamour, et al. Work now? He made his first picture, *Finders Keepers*, in '28, and his last (roughly #150), *Daughter of Tugboat Annie*, in '69. He says that's enough. The offers come in by the week—for movies or TV series (these he doesn't even consider; "too much work")—but Oakie grins and says no. Once in a while he makes a TV guest appearance, but always one that requires "no work." He opts for the parties, where he has been known to do an impromptu buck 'n' wing or convulse pals with long-forgotten tunes, such as "The Klopstock-ian Love Song" from *Million Dollar Legs*. He not only remembers every picture he ever made, but every star and bit player—even the names of the animals he worked with. Married for over 30 years to character actress Victoria Horne, he lives in a beautiful English manor (bought decades ago from Barbara Stanwyck), situated behind electric gates, on a ten-acre estate in Northridge. To keep his weight down (to 200 at least), he exercises daily—starting with a morning swim in his Olympic-sized pool, followed by several sets of tennis. (The court also serves as a roller rink for him to practice his skating.) The Oakies, who have no children, hold open house for their close friends, who number in the hundreds, every Sunday—beginning in the afternoon and running late into the evening. Gregarious and friendly, Jack Oakie lives life to the hilt and sums up his philosophy in a revealing four-word catch phrase he has employed for years: "It's all in fun!" Onscreen from 1928. IN: *The Fleet's In, Chinatown Nights, The Dummy, Sweetie, The Sap from Syracuse, Hit the Deck, Let's Go Native, June Moon, The Touchdown, Once in a Lifetime, Million Dollar Legs, Too Much Harmony, Alice in Wonderland, Murder at the Vanities, College Rhythm, Call of the Wild, Collegiate, Champagne Waltz, The Toast of New York, Affairs of Annabel, The Great Dictator, Little Men, The*

Great American Broadcast, Navy Blues, Song of the Islands; Hello, Frisco, Hello; Wintertime, Sweet and Lowdown, Bowery to Broadway, She Wrote the Book, When My Baby Smiles at Me, Northwest Stampede, Tomahawk, The Wonderful Country, The Rat Race, Lover Come Back, more.

OAKLAND, SIMON (S. Cal.) Character. Onscreen from 1958. IN: *The Brothers Karamazov, I Want to Live!; Murder, Inc.; Psycho, The Rise and Fall of Legs Diamond, West Side Story, The Raiders, The Sand Pebbles, Tony Rome, Bullitt, On a Clear Day You Can See Forever, Chato's Land,* more.

OATES, WARREN (S. Cal.) Costar. Onscreen from 1959. IN: *Up Periscope!, Private Property, Ride the High Country, Major Dundee, The Rounders, Return of the Seven, Welcome to Hard Times, In the Heat of the Night, The Wild Bunch, The Split, Trog, There Was a Crooked Man, The Hired Hand, Two-Lane Blacktop, The Thief Who Came to Dinner, Dime Box, Dillinger, White Dawn, Bring Me the Head of Alfredo Garcia, Cockfighter, Race With the Devil, Born to Kill, 92 in the Shade, Drum, Dixie Dynamite,* more.

OBER, PHILIP (Mex.) Formerly married to actress Vivian Vance, he has remarried—his wife, Jane, was previously an NBC press agent in Hollywood—and, retired from acting, lives in Puerto Vallarta. There he acts as Emergency U.S. Representative for the American Consul in Guadalajara. The character actor, in his 70s now (b. 1902), receives a steady stream of Hollywood visitors at his Casa Juanita. Onscreen from 1950. IN: *Never a Dull Moment, The Magnificent Yankee; Come Back, Little Sheba; The Washington Story, The Clown, From Here to Eternity, Broken Lance, About Mrs. Leslie, 10 North Frederick, North by Northwest, Beloved Infidel, Elmer Gantry, Go Naked in the World, The Ugly American, The Brass Bottle,* more.

OBERON, MERLE (S. Cal.) Star. Nominated for Best Actress Oscar in *The Dark Angel.* In 1973, still extraordinarily youthful for her age (b. 1911), she came out of retirement to do *Interval,* the story of a young man's love for a considerably older woman. Opposite her was actor Robert Wolders, perhaps 15 years her junior; they have been married since 1975. He is her fourth husband. She was previously married to and divorced from Sir Alexander Korda, famous British producer, cinematographer Lucien Hubbard, and millionaire Bruno Pagliai. By her marriage to the latter, lasting 17 years, most of them spent in Mexico, she has two teenage children—Bruno Jr. and Francesca. Onscreen from 1930. IN: *Wedding Rehearsal,*

Thunder in the East, The Private Life of Henry VIII, Folies Bergere (her first in Hollywood, in '35), *These Three, Beloved Enemy, The Cowboy and the Lady, Wuthering Heights, Till We Meet Again, That Uncertain Feeling, Affectionately Yours, Lydia, First Comes Courage, Forever and a Day, The Lodger, Dark Waters, A Song to Remember, Hangover Square, This Love of Ours, Berlin Express, Desiree, Deep in My Heart, The Oscar, Hotel,* more.

O'BRIAN, HUGH (S. Cal.) Costar. Onscreen from 1950. IN: *Young Lovers, Rocketship X-M, Vengeance Valley, Sally and St. Anne, Meet Me at the Fair, The Man from the Alamo, Saskatchewan, Drums Across the River, Broken Lance, There's No Business Like Show Business, Twinkle in God's Eye, Come Fly with Me, In Harm's Way, Strategy of Terror, Killer Force, The Shootist,* more.

O'BRIEN, CHET (N.Y.) Dancer-actor. Now a stage director. Onscreen from 1930. IN: *Heads Up* and numerous musical shorts for Warners in the '30s.

O'BRIEN, CLAY (S. Cal.) Juvenile. Onscreen in the '70s. IN: *The Apple Dumpling Gang, Mackintosh & T.J.,* more.

O'BRIEN, EDMOND (S. Cal.) Costar. Won Best Supporting Actor Oscar in *The Barefoot Contessa.* Nominated in the same category in *Seven Days in May.* Onscreen from 1939. IN: *The Hunchback of Notre Dame; A Girl, A Guy and a Gob; Parachute Battalion* (with Nancy Kelly who became his first wife), *The Amazing Mrs. Holliday, The Killers, A Double Life, Fighter Squadron, White Heat, D.O.A., 711 Ocean Drive, The Turning Point, Julius Caesar, Pete Kelly's Blues, 1984, The Big Land, The Last Voyage, Moon Pilot, Bird Man of Alcatraz, The Longest Day, Synanon, Fantastic Voyage, The Wild Bunch, They Only Kill Their Masters, 99 44/100% Dead, RE: Lucky Luciana,* more. (See Olga San Juan.)

O'BRIEN, ERIN (S. Cal.) Ingenue; retired. Onscreen 1958–59. IN: *Onionhead, Girl on the Run, John Paul Jones.*

O'BRIEN, FRANK/a.k.a. GERALD FRANK O'BRIEN (N.Y.) Support. Onscreen from the '60s. IN: *Wait Until Dark,* more.

O'BRIEN, GEORGE (S. Cal.) This well-remembered cowboy star follows the wind now. Rugged, friendly, and as vital as ever, in his 70s (b. 1900), he has globe-trotted to every corner of the planet. And scarcely a season passes that he isn't packing his bags and setting off from his Brentwood home for some faraway spot no one else ever heard of. A bachelor since his '49 divorce (after 16 years of marriage) from actress Marguerite Churchill, and having given up acting after playing a character role for director-friend John Ford in 1964's *Cheyenne Autumn* (then his first in 13 years), he is free to come and go as he pleases. He has two children. Son, Darcy, teaches English at Pomona College. And daughter, Orin, a tall (5'9"), black-haired beauty (and look-alike for her famous mother) who is still single in her early 40s, plays bass fiddle with the New York Philharmonic. *The Iron Horse*, his first starring picture, remains his favorite, says George O'Brien. Onscreen from 1923. IN: *The Ne'er Do-Well, Woman Proof, Shadows of Paris, The Dancers, Is Zat So?, Sunrise, Salute, The Gay Caballero, Robbers' Roost, Whispering Smith Speaks, Border Patrolman, The Arizona Legion, Racketeers of the Range, The Marshal of Mesa City, Bullet Code, My Wild Irish Rose, Fort Apache, She Wore a Yellow Ribbon*, more.

O'BRIEN, JOAN (S. Cal.) Leading lady; retired. Onscreen from 1958. IN: *Handle with Care, Operation Petticoat, The Alamo, The Comancheros, Samar, 6 Black Horses, It's Only Money, It Happened at the World's Fair*, more, including 1965's *Get Yourself a College Girl*, her most recent to date.

O'BRIEN, MARGARET (S. Cal.) In the summer of 1972 a plump, rather matronly looking young woman arrived with little fanfare on a set at Universal. There to guest-star in a *Marcus Welby* episode, she found herself warmly embraced by the star of the TV show, Robert Young. It was a moment of sentiment and instant nostalgia. The last time the actress had received such demonstrable affection from Robert Young, she had been five years old. That was in 1942 when, in her second film (she'd earlier had a bit in *Babes in Arms*), she became Hollywood's moppet star of the decade, sharing billing with Young in the wartime tear jerker *Journey for Margaret*. By the end of the '40s she had made a mint for MGM, earned a personal fortune (at 21 she came into an estate valued at a quarter of a million, which she has continued to invest well), been honored with a special Oscar at 7 (after *Meet Me in St. Louis*), and starred in another 16 movies. Until she reached her teens she remained the favorite movie tyke of everyone in America. Almost. One notable exception was Mary Astor, who played her mother in *Meet Me in St. Louis*. Writing of that experience in one of her books, Mary Astor said, "Margaret O'Brien was at her most appealing (I might say 'appalling') age. And she could cry at the drop of a cue. Real tears, an endless flow, with apparently no emotion drain whatsoever. She was a quiet, almost too-well-behaved child, when her mother was on the set. When Mother was absent, it was another story and she was a pain in the neck." Five years later, Miss Astor again played the young star's mother, Marmee, in *Little Women* —a film she did not enjoy making and "Maggie O'Brien looked at me as though she were planning something very unpleasant." But Margaret O'Brien's public, which was legion, cherished her—as long as she remained young. Between the ages of 14 and 23, she made only three movies, the last being 1960's *Heller in Pink Tights*, and she has not appeared to date in another in Hollywood. In this melodramatic 19th-century Western, she was seen as a sly, somewhat fiendish young actress touring the Old West with stage mom Eileen Heckart. These many years later, this movie's director, George Cukor, still recalls Margaret O'Brien with admiration, saying: "She was our technical expert on certain things, because she was a famous child actress. She'd tell me, 'When I'm having a row with my mother, I break off to smile very sweetly to anyone who passes, then back back to the row . . .' She's a real movie actress, she looks at the dead bodies and you know they're dead, she feels cold and makes you feel the cold." Since she is a "born" actress, thus compelled to act, she spent most of the next decade plying her trade in TV dramas and touring in plays like *Under the Yum-Yum Tree* and *Barefoot in the Park*. She also tried Broadway in two plays, both flops, despite glowing personal reviews. And she was married for nine years (1959-68) to a California advertising art director, Robert Allen Jr. As this marriage was ending, the actress, who has no children, took up residence in Lima, Peru, and became a local celebrity. She starred (in English) in two films made there, both based on Edgar Allan Poe works: *Annabel Lee* and a horror movie, *Diabolical Wedding*. Also she became the hostess (speaking Spanish) of a daily soap opera based on the second picture. And she fell in love with one of Lima's wealthiest socialite-business men, Julio Tijero, and, with him, returned to Southern California. For several years they lived in a splendid house in the San Fernando Valley furnished with priceless Peruvian and Spanish art. Her return to acting in the *Marcus Welby* episode was a type-cast role—that of a too-plump young woman who sought the doctor's aid in weight reduction. In the years since, the actress has herself recaptured her slender, youthful look. The great "comeback" movie role she has yet to find. But she has continued to be active in dinner theaters—in *Star-Spangled Girl* and similar plays—and in television. One recent role was in the ABC "Wide World Mystery" *Death in Space*. Married again, since May 5, 1974, to Scandinavian steel executive Roy Thorvald Thorsen, and living in Los Angeles, she says she has no intention of ever retiring. "Actresses often say that they're going to give up acting, but I always stare at them open-eyed when they say it," she told a reporter recently. "I could never say I'll never act again. I always loved acting and I still do." Early in 1976, she announced that in July her first child would be born. Onscreen from 1941. IN: *Lost Angel, Dr. Gillespie's Criminal Case, Madame Curie, Jane Eyre, The Canterville Ghost, Our Vines Have Tender Grapes, Bad Bascomb* (with Wallace Beery, the only star she recalls as having been unkind to her: "He pinched my bottom because he thought I was stealing a scene, and one day he even stole my lunch."), *Three Wise Fools, The Unfinished Dance, Tenth Avenue Angel, The Secret Garden, Her First Romance, Glory,* more.

O'BRIEN, MARIA (S. Cal.) Leading lady. Daughter of Edmond O'Brien and Olga San Juan. Onscreen in the '70s. IN: *When Dinosaurs Ruled the Earth, Smile,* more.

O'BRIEN, MARIANNE (S. Cal.) The Warner starlet of the '40s married businessman Lee Meyers in '70 and no longer acts. Onscreen from 1944. IN: *The Very Thought of You,* more.

O'BRIEN, PAT (S. Cal.) In his 70s (b. 1899), this great favorite remains highly active in dinner theatres (usually costarring with wife Eloise) and on TV. Onscreen from 1929. IN: *Freckled Rascal, Determination, The Front Page, The Final Edition, Arm of the Law, Air Mail, I've Got Your Number, Twenty Million Sweethearts, Flirtation Walk, Here Comes the Navy, Oil for the Lamps of China, Ceiling Zero, China Clipper, San Quentin, Submarine D-1, Boy Meets Girl, Angels With Dirty Faces, Garden of the Moon, The Fighting 69th; Knute Rockne—All-American* (his personal favorite); *Till We Meet Again, Flight Lieutenant, Bombardier, His Butler's Sister, Marine Raiders, Having a Wonderful Crime, Crack-Up, Fighting Father Dunne, The Boy with Green Hair, The People Against O'Hara, Ring of Fear, The Last Hurrah, Some Like It Hot, Town Tamer,* more, including 1969's *The Phynx,* his most recent to date.

O'BRIEN, RICHARD (S. Cal.) Character. Onscreen in the '70s. IN: *Pieces of Dreams, The Andromeda Strain,* more.

O'BRIEN, RORY (S. Cal.) Former juvenile (b. 1955). Onscreen in 1964. IN: *One Man's Way.*

O'BRIEN, SYLVIA (N.Y.) Support. Onscreen in the '70s. IN: *The Molly Maguires, The Exorcist,* more.

O'BRIEN, TEDDY (N.Y.) Juvenile. Onscreen in the '70s. IN: *On a Clear Day You Can See Forever, The Kremlin Letter, Pigeons,* more.

O'BRIEN, VINCE (N.Y.) Character. Onscreen from 1961. IN: *The Hoodlum Priest,* more.

O'BRIEN, VIRGINIA (S. Cal.) The deadpan singer is happily married to wealthy building contractor Harry B. White and the mother of a son and a trio of daughters (the eldest three of her children being by her marriage to actor Kirk Alyn). She lives in a showplace home atop a small mountain in Woodland Hills, and in Disney's *Gus* played her first movie role since one in 1955's *Francis in the Navy.* Onscreen from 1940. IN: *Hullabaloo, Lady Be Good, The Big Store, Ringside Maisie, Ship Ahoy, Panama Hattie, Du Barry Was a Lady, Meet the People, Two Girls and a Sailor, Ziegfeld Follies, The Harvey Girls, The Show-Off, Till the Clouds Roll By, Merton of the Movies,* more.

O'BRIEN-MOORE, ERIN (S. Cal.) In her 60s (b. 1908), the former leading lady is still professionally active, now as a character actress. Onscreen from 1934. IN: *His Greatest Gamble, Little Men, Our Little Girl, Seven Keys to Baldpate, Two in the Dark, Ring Around the Moon, The Ex-Mrs. Bradford, The Plough and the Stars, Green Light, Black Legion, The Life of Emile Zola;* after this '37 film she was off the screen 13 years; *Destination Moon, The Family Secret, Phantom of the Rue Morgue, The Long Gray Line, Peyton Place, John Paul Jones, How to Succeed in Business Without Really Trying,* more.

O'BYRNE, BRYAN (S. Cal.) Comic character. Onscreen from the '60s. IN: *Two for the Seesaw, Who's Minding the Mint?, Marnie, Gunfight at Abilene, $1,000,000 Duck,* more.

O'CALLAGHAN, ED (Eng.) Support. Onscreen in the '70s. IN: *Ryan's Daughter,* more.

O'CALLAGHAN, RICHARD (Eng.) Support. Onscreen from 1968. IN: *The Bofors Gun, Butley,* more.

OCASIO, JOE (N.Y.) Support. Onscreen from the '60s. IN: *The Out-of-Towners, Plaza Suite,* more.

OCKO, DAN(IEL) (N.Y.) Character. Onscreen from 1943. IN: *Mission to Moscow, Background to Danger, Stage Struck, Taras Bulba, Who's Been Sleeping in My Bed?, Judith,* more.

O'CONNELL, ARTHUR (S. Cal.) Character. Nominated for Best Supporting Actor Oscar in *Picnic* and *Anatomy of a Murder.* Onscreen from 1938. IN: *Murder in Soho* (made in England), *Citizen Kane* (bit as a reporter), *Man from Headquarters, Countess of Monte Cristo, The Solid Gold Cadillac, The Proud Ones, Bus Stop, The Monte Carlo Story, April Love, Voice in the Mirror, Operation Petticoat, Cimarron, Misty, Your Cheatin' Heart, The Great Race, The Third Day, Fantastic Voyage, A Covenant with Death; If He Hollers, Let Him Go; There Was a Crooked Man, Ben, The Poseidon Adventure, They Only Kill Their Masters, The Hiding Place,* more.

O'CONNELL, BOB (N.Y.) Character. Onscreen from the '50s. IN: *Marty, Strangers in the City, Jack of Diamonds, Act One, Violent Women, Where Were You When the Lights Went Out?, Cop Hater, No Way to Treat a Lady, Madigan; Harvey Middleman, Fireman; Joe, Love Story,* more.

O'CONNELL, HELEN (S. Cal.) Singer. Onscreen in 1943. IN: *I Dood It.*

O'CONNELL, PATRICK (Eng.) Onscreen in the '70s. IN: *Cromwell, The McKenzie Break, The Ragman's Daughter,* more.

O'CONNELL, WILLIAM (S. Cal.) Support. Onscreen from the '60s. IN: *Way . . . Way Out, Ice Station Zebra, The Happy Ending, Paint Your Wagon, Scandalous John, Big Bad Mama,* more.

O'CONNOR, CARROLL (S. Cal.) Character star. Most famous as "Archie Bunker" in TV's *All in the Family.* Onscreen from 1961. IN: *By Love Possessed, Belle Sommers, Lonely Are the Brave; Lad: A Dog; Cleopatra; Not With My Wife, You Don't; Hawaii, Point Blank, Waterhole #3, Warning Shot, Marlowe, The Devil's Brigade, For Love of Ivy, Death of a Gunfighter, Doctors' Wives, Law and Disorder,* more.

O'CONNOR, DARREN (N.Y.) Young lead. Brother of actress Glynnis O'Connor. Onscreen in 1972. IN: *To Find a Man.*

O'CONNOR, DONALD (S. Cal.) Concentrating on nightclub appearances in the past decade, he starred in the 1976 Broadway-bound out-of-town flop *Weekend With Feathers.* This same year, his daughter, Donna O'Connor, made her movie debut in a small role in *All the President's Men,* acting alongside another newcomer, Kerry Sherman—daughter of Peggy Ryan, Donald O'Connor's long ago dance partner at Universal. Onscreen from 1937. IN: *Melody for Two* (his first, age 12); *Sing, You Sinners; Men With Wings, Million Dollar Legs, Beau Geste, On Your Toes, Get Hep to Love, What's Cookin'?, Strictly in the Groove, Private Buckaroo, Mr. Big, The Merry Monahans, Something in the Wind, Francis* (and five more "Francis" pix), *Singin' in the Rain, I Love Melvin, Call Me Madam, There's No Business Like Show Business, The Buster Keaton Story, Cry for Happy, That Funny Feeling,* more.

O'CONNOR, GLYNNIS (N.Y.) Leading lady. Daughter of actress Lenka *(Panic in the Streets)* Peterson, sister of actors Darren and Kevin O'Connor. Onscreen in the '70s. IN: *Jeremy, Ode to Billy Joe, Vendetta.*

O'CONNOR, KEVIN (N.Y.) Young supporting actor who has managed a screen career while completing law studies at Fordham University. Onscreen from 1969. IN: *Coming Apart, Let's Scare Jessica to Death, Welcome to the Club, The Passover Plot,* more.

O'CONOR, JOSEPH (Eng.) Character. Onscreen from 1950. IN: *Gorgo, Oliver!, Anne of the Thousand Days, The Black Windmill,* more.

O'DAY, ANITA (S. Cal.) Fabled jazz singer. Onscreen from the '60s. IN: *The Gene Krupa Story* (as herself), *Jazz on a Summer's Day* (as herself in this documentary), *Zigzag* (character), *The Outfit* (as herself).

O'DAY, DAWN (S. Cal.) This was Anne Shirley's name as a movie moppet from 1923 through 1934. IN: *The Spanish Dancer, The Man Who Fights Alone, 4 Devils, Rich Man's Folly, So Big,* more. (See Anne Shirley.)

O'DAY, MOLLY (S. Cal.) Long married, the mother of four, and now in her 60s (b. 1911), the star-sister of the late Sally O'Neil has been a successful California real estate agent for years. When she was a young star she was a favorite of George Raft. In his authorized biography, *George Raft,* by Lewis Yablonsky, published in '74, the actor tells his version of what happened to her screen career: "She was a gorgeous girl, and one of the sweetest, most gentle women I've ever met. . . . She was doing pretty well in films but she loved to overeat and that weight proved to be her downfall. She tried some weird plastic surgery, where she paid quack doctors a fortune for an operation in which they tried to cut the fat off her body. When they sewed her up she had seam scars running up the sides of her formerly beautiful body. The operation ruined her health, her career, and damn near killed her." Onscreen from 1927. IN: *The Patent-Leather Kid, Hard-Boiled Haggerty, The Lovelorn, The Shepherd of the Hills, Kentucky Courage, Sob Sister, Devil on Deck, Gigolettes of Paris, The Life of Vergie Winters,* more, including 1935's *Skull and Crown* and *Lawless Border,* her last.

O'DEA, DENIS (Eng.) Character; former leading man. Onscreen from 1935. IN: *The Informer, The Plough and the Stars, Odd Man Out, Under Capricorn, The Fallen Idol, The Long Dark Hall, Captain Horatio Hornblower, Never Take No for an Answer, Niagara, Sea Devils, Mogambo, The Rising of the Moon, Darby O'Gill and the Little People, Esther and the King,* more.

ODETTA (N.Y.) Singer-actress. Onscreen from the '50s. IN: *The Last Time I Saw Paris, Sanctuary, Festival,* more.

ODETTE, MARY (Eng.) A popular child star, later seen in adult roles, she is in her 70s (b. 1901) and retired. Onscreen from 1914. IN: *Dombey and Son, With All Her Heart, Mr. Gilfil's Love Story,* more, including 1927's *Edmund Kean: Prince Among Lovers,* her last.

O'DONNELL, GENE (S. Cal.) Character. Onscreen from 1940. IN: *The Ape, Corvette K-225, The Lawyer,* more.

O'DONNELL, MAIRE (Eng.) Character. Onscreen from 1961. IN: *Home Is the Hero, Paddy, Wedding Night,* more.

O'DONOVAN, ELIZABETH (Eng.) Character. Onscreen in 1968. IN: *Doctor Faustus.*

O'DOWD, MIKE (N.Y.) Character. Onscreen from 1954. IN: *On the Waterfront, The Goddess, Take the Money and Run,* more.

O'DRISCOLL, MARTHA (Ill.) On July 20, 1947, she became the wife of business man Arthur Appleton, to whom she remains happily married, and became a young matron on Chicago's elegant North Shore. Her husband is chairman and president of the Appleton Electric Company. The only evidence of the actress' continuing interest in drama is that she served a while as president of Chicago's Sarah Siddons Society, whose annual acting awards are as coveted as Broadway's Tonys. She also was Ways and Means Chairman of the Chicago Junior League, president of the Women's Board of the Chicago Boys Clubs, and Treasurer of the local chapter of W.A.I.F. Onscreen for 11 years, through 1947's *Carnegie Hall* (in 37 movies), she was a spectacularly lovely blonde. Today, in her 50s (b. 1922), she is an equally spectacularly lovely brunette. And the mother of four fine-looking children, all in their 20s—Jim (married, he completed graduate school at Tulane), John (a graduate of Southern Methodist University), Linda (a graduate of Wellesley, where, in '71, she was Dartmouth Winter Carnival Queen), and Bill (a graduate of Massachusetts' Babson College). Though the family's permanent residence is in a swank suburb of Chicago, they spend winters at their home in Miami, and they travel—often as a family—extensively. "My life," says Martha O'Driscoll, "has been very full since I left Hollywood." Onscreen from 1937. IN: *Collegiate, Champagne Waltz, Mad about Music, Girls' School, Forty Little Mothers, Laddie, Midnight Angel, Reap the Wild Wind, Young and Willing, The Fallen Sparrow, We've Never Been Licked, Crazy House, Hi Beautiful!, The Daltons Ride Again, Here Come the Coeds, Shady Lady, Blonde Alibi, Down Missouri Way,* more.

O'FARRELL, BERNADETTE (Eng.) Leading lady. Inactive in movies in the past 15 years. Onscreen from 1947. IN: *Captain Boycott, The Happiest Days of Your Life, Gilbert and Sullivan, The Bridal Path,* more.

O'FLYNN, DAMIAN (S. Cal.) Character. Inactive since 1963's *Gunfight at Comanche Creek.* Onscreen from 1937. IN: *Marked Woman, Lady Scarface, So Proudly We Hail, Wake Island, Crack-Up, Philo Vance Returns, The Snake Pit, The Miami Story, Daddy Long Legs, Drango, Apache Warrior,* more.

O'FLYNN, PHILIP (Eng) Support. Onscreen from the '50s. IN: *Broth of a Boy, The Poacher's Daughter, Home Is the Hero, Young Cassidy, Ryan's Daughter,* more.

OGILVY, IAN (Eng.) Support. Onscreen from the '60s. IN: *The Day the Fish Came Out, Cop-Out, The Conqueror Worm, Wuthering Heights, Waterloo,* more.

O'HANLON, GEORGE (S. Cal.) The star of all the "Joe McDoakes" comedy shorts (63 of them) went on to direct movies (*The Rookie*) and write the screenplays of others (*Benny, For Those Who Think Young,* etc.). He has also written for TV (*Gilligan's Island, Barefoot in the Park*) and guested in such series as *Adam-12; Mission: Impossible;* and *The Odd Couple.* In this decade he has also had supporting roles in three Disney features: *$1,000,000 Duck* (as the parking lot attendant), *Charley and the Angel,* and *The World's Greatest Athlete.* Further, he is understandably proud of the screen success of his son, George O'Hanlon Jr., and feels certain that his teenage daughter, Laurie, will eventually follow in his acting footsteps too. Onscreen from the early '30s as a chorus boy and bit player in Warner Bros. musicals. Onscreen as an actor from 1941. IN: *New Wine, The Man from Headquarters, Corvette K-225, Spirit of West Point, Are You With It?, June Bride, Triple Cross, The Lion and the Horse, Park Row, Kronos, The Rookie,* which he also wrote.

O'HANLON, GEORGE, JR. (S. Cal.) Young comic support. Onscreen from 1974. IN: *Our Time*, more.

O'HARA, BARRY (S. Cal.) Character. Onscreen from the '50s. IN: *World Dances, Chuka*, more.

O'HARA, JILL (N.Y.) Leading lady from Broadway. Onscreen from 1971. IN: *Pigeons*, more.

O'HARA, JIM (JAMES) (S. Cal.) Character. Onscreen from 1957. IN: *Garden of Eden, The Deadly Companions, Death of a Gunfighter*, more.

O'HARA, MAUREEN (Virg. Is.) The Irish redhead, in her 50s (b. 1920) and still an outstanding beauty, lives now in a round house with two circular towers at the top of the island of St. Croix. Twice married before—pre-Hollywood, to George Brown (their '38 marriage was annulled in '41); in Hollywood, to dialogue director Will Price (divorced in '53 after 12 years)—she has been the wife of Charles Blair since '68. A retired Air Force brigadier general and former chief pilot for Pan Am, Blair is famous as the first pilot to make a solo flight over the Arctic Ocean and the North Pole and for his subsequent best-selling autobiography, *Red Ball in the Sky*. Today, in the Virgin Islands, he owns and operates Antilles Air Boats Company, a passenger and cargo airline, of which his actress-wife is vice-president. She says she sits in on board meetings, does public relations, checks the accounts, and interviews employees. "I've flown over a million miles with my husband since our marriage," she says, "and I'm still scared to death of flying." No pilot herself, she proved her mettle in '74. In Sydney, Australia, then, she and her husband set forth on a 12,000-mile flight across the Pacific to Long Beach, Calif., aboard an old British Sunderland flying boat that dated back to World War II, which they had bought from an Australian line. With the aid of four crewman, making rest and refueling stops in Samoa and Hawaii, they successfully flew the ancient craft to California—and then on to the Virgin Islands, where it became the 23rd plane in their fleet. Enjoying her real-life experiences in the islands—and particularly the visits of her young grandson (by her only child, daughter Bronwyn, by Will Price)—the actress admits no anxiety to return to acting. In '71 she was seen in *Big Jake*, opposite John Wayne, which was their fifth pic together. She has turned down many roles since, saying, "I will not do dirty pictures. And Hollywood is making so many of them now." She would most readily accept a directing assignment. "I want to direct a Western," she

says. "And why not? I think I'd be good at it. I seem to have a facility for telling other people what to do, even things I can't do myself. Directing is one of my three ambitions. The other two are to have a smash musical on Broadway and to write a best seller." (She has contemplated writing a book about her life with Blair.) Of her 52 Hollywood movies she mentions only four with pride: *How Green Was My Valley, The Quiet Man, The Long Gray Line* (all directed by John Ford), and *Sentimental Journey*. Calling herself now "the happiest woman alive," she admits that throughout her Hollywood career she was intensely jealous of Jennifer Jones. "When she was married to Selznick," she explains, "they'd shoot a scene 40 times, and he'd look at all the film, and print the stuff she looked best in. Whenever *I* made a picture, if the horse didn't you-know-what in the middle of the shot, it was a take!" Onscreen from 1938. IN: *Kicking the Moon Around, Jamaica Inn, A Bill of Divorcement; Dance, Girls, Dance; To the Shores of Tripoli, The Black Swan, This Land Is Mine, The Immortal Sergeant, The Fallen Sparrow, Buffalo Bill, The Spanish Main, Miracle on 34th Street, Sinbad the Sailor, Sitting Pretty, Father Is a Fullback, Rio Grande, At Sword's Point, War Arrow, The Wings of Eagles, The Parent Trap, Mr. Hobbs Takes a Vacation, McLintock!, Spencer's Mountain, The Battle of the Villa Fiorita, How to Commit Marriage, How Do I Love Thee*, more.

O'HARA, QUINN (S. Cal.) Leading lady. Onscreen in the '70s. IN: *Cry of the Banshee*, more.

O'HARA, SHIRLEY (S. Cal.) In a '75 episode of *The Bob Newhart Show* on TV, the ingenue of yesteryear played a temporary replacement receptionist—a youthful-looking, sweet but addled, gray-haired woman who made numerous office mistakes, all hilarious. Onscreen from 1927. IN: *A Gentleman of Paris, The Wild Party, Tarzan and the Amazons, The Chase*, more.

O'HERLIHY, DAN (S. Cal.) Costar. Nominated for Best Actor Oscar in *The Adventures of Robinson Crusoe*. After several years in Ireland, his birthplace, he now lives in Malibu eight months of the year and four in his homeland. He and his wife, Elsa, have five children —ranging from young teenagers to young adults. Onscreen from 1947. IN: *Odd Man Out, Macbeth, Kidnapped, The Blue Veil, Soldiers Three, At Sword's Point, Sword of Venus, The Black Shield of Falworth, The Virgin Queen, Cry After Midnight, Home Before Dark, Imitation of Life, The Young Land, One Foot in Hell, King of the Roaring Twenties, Fail Safe, 100*

Rifles, The Big Cube, Waterloo, The Carey Treatment, The Tamarind Seed, more.

OHMART, CAROL (S. Cal.) By choice she became "invisible" in 1962. She, the chestnut-blonde sexpot on whom Paramount spent $2,-000,000 in a publicity build-up to make her its own "Marilyn Monroe." She, of the cool blue eyes and chiseled features, who smiled secretively, seductively from the covers of *Newsweek* and *Life* the same week. But being that girl she found unreal and unsatisfying. For the following ten years, by choice, she acted just enough to survive, playing a few secondary roles on TV in *Get Smart* and *Branded*, which went almost unnoticed. And by choice she returned as a committed actress in 1972—a middle-aged woman, a trifle buxom, her face fuller and not unlined, her hair dark and streaked with gray—to play character roles. She has since done numerous TV roles, including a *Mannix* episode, "The Crimson Halo," that won an Edgar Allan Poe award, and—coincidentally—she acted in the movie *The Spectre of Edgar Allan Poe*, playing Cesar Romero's lunatic, violent wife. She dropped out, she says, to search "for a higher Truth, which some call metaphysics. For me, it was God." She gave away most of her possessions, reduced her life to its essentials, and "I locked up with a Bible in a small place in Van Nuys. No calls, no outside life at all. I studied all the sacred mystery teachings— of Jesus, Lao Tse, Gautama the Buddha, and Confucius." Dedicated only to her studies, she moved constantly—each time friends discovered her whereabouts—finally returning to Salt Lake City, her home town. There she taught speech and, continuing her studies, acquired a doctorate in metaphysics. The return address on letters received from her is: Dr. C. Ohmart, Box__, Beverly Hills. It was a performance of Patricia Neal's that reawakened her interest in acting—the role of the mother in the TV special *The Homecoming*, which developed into *The Waltons*. "That made me miss acting, and I knew it was time to come back," she says serenely. "This is the beginning of a new cycle. I know there will be character roles for me, which I always wanted to play." Between acting assignments, she is writing. Lately she has been working on three books simultaneously ("As a triple Gemini I'm allowed . . ."), one of them a Love-Spiritual volume. This work involves her daily, six days of the week, but not the seventh, for she reports, "I take a faithful full Sabbath each week." The actress-writer—in her late 40s and unmarried—sees no conflict between acting and her continuing search for Truth. "We all play a role, and carry the character through the play which is Life," she says. "We are lucky when we do our acting consciously. Doing both things should cause no confusion if you have proper guidance." Onscreen from 1955. IN: *The Scarlet Hour, The Wild Party, House on Haunted Hill, Born Reckless, Wild Youth, The Scavengers, One Man's Way, Caxanbu* (unreleased), more.

O'KEEFE, PAUL C. (N.Y.) Support. Onscreen in the '70s. IN: *Child's Play, The Daydreamer*, more.

OLAF, PIERRE (N.Y.) Support. Onscreen from 1946. IN: *Devil in the Flesh, Virgile, French Can–Can, Wild and Wonderful, The Art of Love, The Counterfeit Constable, Camelot*, more.

O'LEARY, JOHN (N.Y.) Character. Onscreen from the '60s. IN: *The Group, The Heart Is a Lonely Hunter, A New Leaf*, more.

OLIVER, ANTHONY (Eng.) Support. Onscreen from 1948. IN: *The Clouded Yellow, The Magnet, Glory at Sea, Both Sides of the Law, Tears for Simon, Checkpoint*, more.

OLIVER, ROCHELLE (N.Y.) Support. Onscreen in the '70s. IN: *Next Stop, Greenwich Village*, more.

OLIVER, STEPHEN (S. Cal.) Leading man. Onscreen from 1968. IN: *Angels From Hell, Werewolves on Wheels*, more.

OLIVER, SUSAN (S. Cal.) Leading lady. Onscreen from 1957. IN: *The Green-Eyed Blonde, The Gene Krupa Story, Butterfield 8, The Caretakers, The Disorderly Orderly, Your Cheatin' Heart, The Monitors, A Man Called Gannon, Ginger in the Morning*, more.

OLIVER, THELMA (N.Y.) Black support. Onscreen from 1964. IN: *Black Like Me, The Pawnbroker*, more.

OLIVIER, SIR LAURENCE (Eng.) Star. Won Best Actor Oscar in *Hamlet*. Nominated in the same category in *Wuthering Heights, Rebecca, Henry V, The Entertainer, Richard III, Othello, Sleuth*. Onscreen from 1930. IN: *Too Many Crooks, As You Like It, Fire Over England* (with the late Vivien Leigh, second of his three wives; first married to actress Jill Esmond, he is presently married to actress Joan Plowright), *The Divorce of Lady X, Pride and Prejudice, That Hamilton Woman, The Invaders, The Magic Box, Carrie, The Beggar's Opera, Prince and the Showgirl, The Devil's Disciple, Spartacus, Term of Trial, Bunny Lake Is Missing, Khartoum, The Shoes of the Fisherman, The Battle of Britain; Oh! What a Lovely War; Three Sisters, Nicholas and Alexandra, Lady Caroline Lamb, Marathon Man, A Bridge Too Far*, more.

O'LOUGHLIN, GERALD S. (S. Cal.) Support. Onscreen from 1956. IN: *Lollipops and Lovers, A Hatful of Rain, Cop Hater, Ensign Pulver, A Fine Madness, In Cold Blood, Ice Station Zebra, The Riot, Desperate Characters, The Organization,* more.

OLSEN, CHRISTOPHER (S. Cal.) The former juvenile actor (b. 1947) is resuming his theatrical career. During his years out of movies, he received his bachelor's degree from Pierce College in California and his master's in dramatic arts from Valley State College. He is the brother of Larry Olsen and Susan Olsen. Onscreen from 1947. IN: *The Iron Curtain* (at 14 months), *I'll See You in My Dreams, The Marrying Kind, Above and Beyond, The Man Who Knew Too Much* (as James Stewart's kidnapped son), *Bigger Than Life, Tarnished Angels,* more.

OLSEN, LARRY (S. Cal.) Former juvenile (b. 1939) who gave up acting and now, living in Tarzana, is an aircraft engineer. Onscreen from 1943. IN: *Happy Land, Address Unknown, Sitting Pretty, Isn't It Romantic, Room for One More,* more.

OLSEN, SUSAN (S. Cal.) Teenager (b. 1961) who was popular on TV as Cindy in *The Brady Bunch.* Onscreen in the '70s. IN: *The Boy Who Stole an Elephant,* more.

OLSON, JAMES (S. Cal.) Leading man. Onscreen from 1956. IN: *The Strange One, Rachel Rachel, Moon Zero Two, The Andromeda Strain, Wild Rovers,* more.

OLSON, NANCY (S. Cal.) Leading lady. Nominated for Best Supporting Actress Oscar in *Sunset Boulevard.* Onscreen from 1949. IN: *Canadian Pacific, Union Station, Mr. Music, Force of Arms, Big Jim McLain, So Big, Donovan's Brain, The Boy from Oklahoma, Pollyanna, The Absent-Minded Professor, Smith!, Snowball Express, Airport 1975,* more.

O'MALLEY, J. PAT (S. Cal.) Character. Onscreen from 1957. IN: *Courage of Black Beauty, The Long Hot Summer, A House Is Not a Home, Apache Rifles, Gunn, Star!; Hello, Dolly!; The Gumball Rally,* more.

O'MALLEY, KATHLEEN (S. Cal.) Support. Onscreen from 1947. IN: *Down to Earth, Wagonmaster, Mister Roberts,* more.

O'MALLEY, REX (N.Y.) Robert Taylor's friend Gaston in *Camille,* his first movie in Hollywood, he became part of an anecdote—concerning Garbo's famous feet—still being told. There is the Hollywood version, as related by veteran actress Dorothy Gulliver, also in *Camille:* "The English actor Rex O'Malley was dancing around with Garbo during the rehearsal for one scene. She trips, and he very gallantly helps her up and says, 'Oh, I'm sorry, Miss Garbo, did I step on your dainty little feet?' In all seriousness. One by one, you saw the cameramen disappear, and everybody cleared the set because they all cracked up." (This was in an interview with Leonard Maltin.) O'Malley's own version, related to Garbo biographer Norman Zierold, is: "Once when we were dancing in a scene she started giving way, and over she went. I fell too, as gently as possible, right on top of her. She burst into laughter. 'It's my little feet,' she said." The actor was citing this as an example of her little-known sense of humor. O'Malley remained in Hollywood for numerous other pix but, preferring the stage, returned to Broadway where he has been featured in and directed many plays. Now in his 70s, a bachelor still, he is seen today in numerous TV commercials, in which he has specialized for a decade. Onscreen in England from 1924. Onscreen in Hollywood from 1937. IN: *Zaza, Midnight, The Thief, Taxi,* more. (Died 1976.)

O'MARA, KATE (Eng.) Leading lady. Onscreen from the '60s. IN: *Corruption, The Desperados, The Vampire Lovers, The Tamarind Seed,* more.

OMENS, ESTELLE (N.Y.) Character. Onscreen from 1968. IN: *The Secret Cinema, Joe,* more.

O'MOORE, PATRICK (S. Cal.) Character. Onscreen in Hollywood (after British pix) from 1941. IN: *Smilin' Through, Sahara, Conflict, Cloak and Dagger, Bulldog Drummond at Bay, The Two Mrs. Carrolls, Moss Rose, Kind Lady, Bwana Devil, Trooper Hook, Copper Sky, Cattle Empire, The Rookie, How to Succeed in Business Without Really Trying, The Resurrection of Zachary Wheeler,* more.

ONDRA, ANNY (Ger.) She lives in Hamburg with her husband of many years, Germany's greatest boxer, former world heavyweight champion Max Schmeling. In '75, one of West Germany's best-loved figures, he celebrated his 70th birthday, receiving a flood of telegrams, including a congratulatory note from President Walter Scheel. The actress, also in her 70s (b. 1903), gave up her career decades ago, after 1950's *Schon Muss Man Sein.* Though greatly popular in English silents such as Hitchcock's *The Manxman,* she lost out—except in European films—when sound came in. To those who contend that she spoke perfect English in Hitchcock's *Blackmail,* the director has explained: "The star was Anny Ondra, the German actress, who, naturally, hardly spoke any English. We couldn't dub in the voices then as we do today. So I got around the difficulty by calling on an English actress, Joan Barry, who did the dialogue standing outside the frame, with her own microphone, while Miss Ondra pantomimed the words." Onscreen from the '20s. IN: *Chorus Girls, Versuchen Sie Meine Schwester, Die von Rummelplatz, Eine Nacht im Paradies, Klein Dorrit, Knock-Out, Der Junge Graf,* more.

O'NEAL, FREDERICK (N.Y.) Black character. Onscreen from 1949. IN: *Pinky, No Way Out, Something of Value, Anna Lucasta* (his personal favorite), *Take a Giant Step, The Sins of Rachel Cade; Free, White and 21;* more.

O'NEAL, KEVIN (S. Cal.) Support. Younger brother of Ryan O'Neal. Onscreen from 1959. In: *The Blue Angel, Young Fury, Kisses for My President, Cheyenne Autumn, The Big Bounce,* more.

O'NEAL, PATRICK (N.Y.) Leading man. Onscreen from 1954. IN: *The Black Shield of Falworth, From the Terrace, A Matter of Morals, In Harm's Way, A Fine Madness, Alvarez Kelly, A Big Hand for the Little Lady, Where Were You When the Lights Went Out?, Castle Keep, Stiletto, The Kremlin Letter, The Way We Were, The Stepford Wives,* more.

O'NEAL, RON (S. Cal.) Black star. Onscreen in the '70s. IN: *The Organization, Super Fly, Super Fly, T.N.T., The Master Gunfighter,* more.

O'NEAL, RYAN (S. Cal.) Star. Nominated for Best Actor Oscar in *Love Story.* Onscreen from 1969. IN: *The Big Bounce, The Games, Wild Rovers; What's Up, Doc?; The Thief Who Came to Dinner, Paper Moon, Barry Lyndon, Nickelodeon, A Bridge Too Far,* more.

O'NEAL, TATUM (S. Cal.) Juvenile. Daughter of Ryan O'Neal and Joanna Moore. Won Best Supporting Actress Oscar in *Paper Moon,* her debut. Onscreen from 1973. IN: *Nickelodeon, The Bad News Bears.*

O'NEIL, BARBARA (Conn.) Character. Nominated for Best Supporting Acress Oscar in *All This and Heaven Too.* But she is perhaps best recalled for playing Scarlett O'Hara's tragic mother in *Gone With the Wind.* She made her last four movies in the '50s: *Whirlpool, Angel Face, Flame of the Islands,* and *The Nun's Story.* For two years (1958–60), she was artist-in-residence at the University of Denver. Since then, this daughter of an extremely wealthy and social family has lived in complete retirement at the family home in Cos Cob. In her 60s now (b.

1909), she was once married, briefly in the '40s, to' director Josh Logan. She has not talked about this for publication, but her former husband has. To a *New York Post* writer, in '73, Logan said, "I decided to get married just on the spur of the moment. She was so beautiful and lovely that I practically forced her to say yes to me—and suddenly we had a loveless marriage and that had to be broken up immediately." Onscreen from 1937. IN: *Stella Dallas, The Toy Wife; Love, Honor and Behave; The Sun Never Sets, Tower of London, When Tomorrow Comes, Shining Victory, The Secret Beyond the Door, I Remember Mama, Whirlpool,* more.

O'NEILL, DICK (S. Cal.) Character. Onscreen from the '60s. IN: *Pretty Poison, Some of My Best Friends Are . . . , The Front Page, The Taking of Pelham One Two Three,* more.

O'NEILL, EILEEN (S. Cal.) Support. Onscreen from 1964. IN: *Kiss Me, Stupid; A Man Called Danger, The Loved One, Loving,* more.

O'NEILL, JENNIFER (N.Y.) Costar. Onscreen from 1970. IN: *Rio Lobo, Summer of '42, Such Good Friends, The Carey Treatment, The Reincarnation of Peter Proud, The Flower in the Mouth, The Intruder,* more.

O'NEILL, JIMMY (S. Cal.) TV personality. Onscreen in 1964. IN: *Surfer Go-Go.*

O'NEILL, SHEILA (Eng.) Actress-dancer. Onscreen from 1963. IN: *Summer Holiday, Half a Sixpence,* more.

ONTKEAN, MICHAEL (S. Cal.) Leading man. Onscreen in the '70s. IN: *Bayou Boy, The Peace Killers, Hot Summer Wind, A Time to Every Purpose,* more.

OPATOSHU, DAVID (S. Cal.) Character. Onscreen from 1939. IN: *The Light Ahead, The Naked City, Thieves' Highway, Molly, The Brothers Karamazov, Cimarron, Exodus, King of Kings, Sands of Beersheba, Torn Curtain, One Spy Too Many, Tarzan and the Valley of Gold, Enter Laughing, Death of a Gunfighter, Romance of a Horsethief,* more.

OPPENHEIMER, ALAN (S. Cal.) Character. Onscreen from the '60s. IN: *How to Save a Marriage—And Ruin Your Life; Star!, Little Big Man,* more.

ORBACH, JERRY (N.Y.) Leading man. Onscreen from 1961. IN: *Mad Dog Coll; John Goldfarb, Please Come Home; The Gang That Couldn't Shoot Straight, Foreplay,* more.

ORBISON, ROY (Tenn.) C&W music star. Onscreen in 1968. IN: *The Fastest Guitar Alive.*

ORCHARD, JOHN (S. Cal.) Character. Onscreen from 1953. IN: *I Believe in You, The Thomas Crown Affair, Ice Station Zebra, Raid on Rommel, Bedknobs and Broomsticks*, more.

ORCHARD, JULIAN (Eng.) Character. Onscreen from the '50s. IN: *Crooks Anonymous, The Spy with the Cold Nose, Can Heironymous Merkin Ever Forget Mercy Humppe . . . ?*, more.

O'REARE, JAMES (S. Cal.) Character. Onscreen from 1949. IN: *Criss Cross, Mister Buddwing, Conrack, Chinatown*, more.

O'REILLY, ERIN (S. Cal.) Leading lady. Onscreen in the '70s. IN: *Little Fauss and Big Halsey, T.R. Baskin*, more.

ORLANDI, FELICE (S. Cal.) Leading man. Onscreen from 1956. IN: *The Harder They Fall, Bullitt; They Shoot Horses, Don't They?; The Outfit*, more.

ORMAN, ROSCOE (S. Cal.) Black star. Onscreen in the '70s. IN: *Willie Dynamite*, more.

ORR, MARY (N.Y.) Actress-author. She wrote the *Cosmopolitan* short story on which *All About Eve* was based. Onscreen in 1971. IN: *Pigeons*.

ORR, WILLIAM (S. Cal.) Still a good-looking blond as he enters his 60s (b. 1917), the former actor is a TV and movie producer now. Onscreen from 1939. IN: *The Hardys Ride High, The Mortal Storm, My Love Came Back, Honeymoon for Three, Navy Blues, Three Sons O'Guns, Unholy Partners, The Gay Sisters, The Big Street, He Hired the Boss*, more.

OSBORN, ANDREW (Eng.) Character; former leading man. Onscreen from 1938. IN: *Who Goes Next? Poet's Pub, Dark Interval, The Lady With a Lamp, Blackout, Blood Orange, Murder by Proxy*, more.

OSBORNE, JOHN (Eng.) Oscar-winning screenplay writer (*Tom Jones*), playwright (*Look Back in Anger, The Entertainer*, etc.) and actor. Onscreen in 1970. IN: *First Love*.

OSBORNE, MARIE (S. Cal.) (See Baby Marie.)

OSCARSSON, PER (Sweden) Leading man. Onscreen from the '60s. IN: *The Doll; My Sister, My Love; A Dandy in Aspic, Here's Your Life, The Last Valley, The Night Visitor, The Emigrants, The Blockhouse*, more.

O'SHEA, MILO (Eng.) Character. Onscreen from the '50s. IN: *You Can't Beat the Irish, Carry On Cabby, Ulysses, Romeo and Juliet, Barbarella, The Angel Levine, Sacco and Vanzetti; Digby, the Biggest Dog in the World;* more.

O'SHEA, TESSIE (Fla.) Character. Onscreen from the '50s. IN: *The Russians Are Coming, The Russians Are Coming; Bedknobs and Broomsticks*, more.

OSMOND, CLIFF (S. Cal.) Character. Onscreen from 1963. IN: *Irma la Douce; Kiss Me, Stupid; The Fortune Cookie, Three Guns for Texas, The Devil's Eight, The Front Page*, more.

OSMOND, HAL (Eng.) Character. Onscreen from the '40s. IN: *Hell Is Sold Out, The Story of Robin Hood, Stolen Face, The Brave Don't Cry, The Steel Key, The Sword and the Rose, Cash on Delivery, Simon and Laura*, more.

OSTERLOH, ROBERT (S. Cal.) Character. Onscreen from 1948. IN: *The Dark Past, City Across the River, White Heat, 711 Ocean Drive, The Fat Man, The Prowler, The Day the Earth Stood Still, The Wild One, Riot in Cell Block 11, Wicked Woman, Violent Saturday, Rosemary's Baby*, more.

OSTERWALD, BIBI (N.Y.) Character. Onscreen from 1961. IN: *Parrish, The World of Henry Orient, A Fine Madness, The Tiger Makes Out, They Might Be Giants*, more.

OSTROVE, MICHELE CHRISTINE (N.Y.) Juvenile. Onscreen in the '70s. IN: *The War Between Men and Women*, more.

O'SULLIVAN, MAUREEN (N.Y.) Incredible though it may seem, she is almost as well known now as "the mother of Mia Farrow" as for her own long and notable screen career. That career, besides her Jane role in the Weissmuller *Tarzan* series, included performances in some of Hollywood's most illustrious movies: *The Barretts of Wimpole Street, The Thin Man, Anna Karenina, Pride and Prejudice*, etc. During her long marriage to director John Farrow, she became the mother of four daughters (another of whom, Tisa Farrow, has also become an actress) and three sons (one of whom, Michael, was killed in a private plane crash a number of years ago). In 1962, the year her husband died, she scored a triumph on Broadway in *Never Too Late*, her New York debut. Three years later she repeated her role in this comedy when it was filmed. Between, in a case of serious miscasting, she did a rather unhappy stint as the "Today Girl" on TV's *Today Show*. Her only recent movie appearance was a cameo role in a little-seen 1969 comedy, *The Phynx*. In this decade, except for costarring with Douglas Fairbanks Jr. in an ABC "Movie of the Week," *Lonelyheart 555* ('72), she has acted exclusively on the stage. In New York she has been seen in a revival of *Charlie's Aunt* and *No Sex Please, We're British* and, on out-of-town stages, in *The Pleasure of His Company*, *The Glass Menagerie*, *Butterflies Are Free*, etc. She has also initiated other careers—as a writer (she has been working on a novel and her autobiography) and as executive director of Wediquette International, an agency that licenses complete bridal services. She lives alone in a Manhattan penthouse and has gone on record as saying that she herself would like to marry again. A while back, the actress—still highly attractive in her 60s (b. 1911)—observed that "children don't take the place of a husband. Many women —and I'm one of them—need both. I'd like to find a strong, wonderful, brilliant man who'd be everything to me and consider me everything to him." Shortly afterward she met actor Robert Ryan. Friends were certain that they would marry. Then he became ill and died in 1973— with Maureen O'Sullivan at his bedside. Onscreen from 1930. IN: *Song O' My Heart*, *Just Imagine*, *A Connecticut Yankee in King Arthur's Court*, *Tarzan the Ape Man*, *Tugboat Annie*, *David Copperfield*, *Cardinal Richelieu*, *The Voice of Bugle Ann*, *A Day at the Races*, *A Yank at Oxford*, *The Crowd Roars*, *Let Us Live*, *Sporting Blood*, *The Big Clock*, *Bonzo Goes to College*, *All I Desire*, *Duffy of San Quentin*, *The Steel Cage*, more.

O'SULLIVAN, RICHARD (Eng.) Support. Onscreen from the '50s. IN: *The Green Scarf* (one of numerous adolescent roles), *The Stranger's Hand*, *It's Great to be Young*, *Cleopatra*, *A Dandy in Aspic*, *Terror House*, more.

OTTAWAY, JAMES (Eng.) Character. Onscreen from 1938. IN: *In the Wake of a Stranger*, *Inadmissible Evidence*, *That'll Be the Day*, more.

O'TOOLE, PETER (Eng.) Star. Nominated for Best Actor Oscar in *Lawrence of Arabia*, *Becket*, *The Lion in Winter*; *Goodbye, Mr. Chips*; *The Ruling Class*. Onscreen from 1960. IN: *Kidnapped*, *The Day They Robbed the Bank of England*, *What's New Pussycat?*, *Lord Jim*, *How to Steal a Million*, *The Bible*, *The Night of the Generals*, *Murphy's War*, *Under Milk Wood*, *Man of La Mancha*, *Rosebud*, *Man Friday*, more.

OTT, WARRENE (S. Cal.) Supporting actress. Onscreen from 1962. IN: *If a Man Answers*, *Where It's At*, *The Witchmaker*, more.

OULTON, BRIAN (Eng.) Character. Onscreen from 1938. IN: *Miranda*, *Man with a Million*, *Will Any Gentleman?*, *Doctor in the House*, *Young Wives' Tale*, *The Deep Blue Sea*, *Private's Progress*, *The Man Who Never Was*, *Carry On Cleo*, more.

OURY, GERARD (Fr.) Character. Onscreen from the '30s. IN: *Duguesclin*, *Antoine and Antoinette*, *The Sword and the Rose*, *The Detective*, *The Heart of the Matter*, *Those Who Dare*, *House of Secrets*, *Heroes and Sinners (Les Heros Sont Fatigues)*, *Young Girls Beware*, *Woman of the River*, *Back to the Wall*, *The Prize*, more.

OUSLEY, TIMMY (N.Y.) Juvenile. Onscreen from 1969. IN: *Goodbye, Columbus; Jenny, Husbands*, more.

OWEN, BILL (Eng.) Character. Onscreen from 1945. IN: *Way to the Stars* (billed under his real name, Bill Rowbotham), *My Brother's Keeper*, *Easy Money*, *Daybreak*, *The Weaker Sex*, *The Gay Lady*, *A Day to Remember*, *The Story of Robin Hood*, *The Ship That Died of Shame*, *Carry On Sergeant*, *Georgy Girl*, *The Fighting Prince of Donegal*, more.

OWENS, BONNIE (S. Cal.) Support. Onscreen in 1968. IN: *Killers Three*.

OWENS, GARY (S. Cal.) Comic support. Onscreen from the '60s. IN: *McHale's Navy Joins the Air Force*, *The Love Bug*, *Midnight Cowboy*, more.

OWENS, PATRICIA (S. Cal.) One of 20th Century-Fox's promising stars of the late '50s, she is married, a mother, and retired. Onscreen in England from the '40s. IN: *The Happiest Days of Your Life*, *The Good Die Young*, more. Onscreen in America from 1957. IN: *Island in the Sun*, *No Down Payment*, *Sayonara*, *The Law and Jake Wade*, *The Fly*, *These Thousand Hills*, *Hell to Eternity*, *X-15*, *Walk a Tightrope*, *Black Spurs*, more, including 1967's *The Destructors*, her most recent to date.

OXLEY, DAVID (Eng.) Support. Onscreen from the '50s. IN: *Bonjour Tristesse*, *Saint Joan*, *Night Ambush*, *Yesterday's Enemy*, more.

P

PAAR, JACK (N.Y.) Wealthy and retired, the TV comedian and wife, Miriam, live most of the year at their estate in Westchester, the rest at their apartment in Key Biscayne, Fla. Onscreen from 1948. IN: *Variety Time, Easy Living; Walk Softly, Stranger; Footlight Varieties, Down Among the Sheltering Palms.*

PACE, JUDY (S. Cal.) Black leading lady. Onscreen from 1966. IN: *The Fortune Cookie, The Thomas Crown Affair, 3 in the Attic, Cotton Comes to Harlem, Up in the Cellar, Cool Breeze, Frogs,* more.

PACKER, DORIS (S. Cal.) Character. Onscreen from 1967. IN: *The Perils of Pauline,* more.

PACINO, AL (N.Y.) Star. Nominated for Best Supporting Actor Oscar in *The Godfather.* Nominated for Best Actor Oscar in *Serpico, The Godfather Part II,* and *Dog Day Afternoon.* Onscreen from 1969. IN: *Me, Natalie; Panic in Needle Park; The Godfather, Scarecrow, Dog Day Afternoon,* more.

PADILLA, MANUEL, JR. (S. Cal.) Former juvenile (b. 1956); inactive now. Onscreen from 1963. IN: *Dime With a Halo, The Young and the Brave, Taffy and the Jungle Hunter, Robin and the Seven Hoods, Sylvia, Tarzan and the Valley of Gold, Tarzan and the Great River,* more.

PADOVANI, LEA (It.) Leading lady. Onscreen from the '40s. IN: *Eyes of the Sahara, Three Steps North, Scandal in Sorrento, The Naked Maja, Anatomy of Love, The Reluctant Saint, The Empty Canvas, Candy,* more.

PAGE, ANITA (S. Cal.) In her 60s (b. 1910) and still an exceedingly beautiful blonde, she lives in Coronado, has been married for four decades to Rear Admiral Herschel A. House (U.S. Navy, Ret.), and is the mother of two daughters, both—no surprise—lovely blondes. The eldest, Anita Sandra, married to a Lockheed electrical engineer, Joseph Eaton Young, lives in Burbank and has a teenage daughter. The Houses' youngest is Linda, lately a drama student at San Diego State College and now embarking on an acting career. Both Anita and her husband are active in local civic and cultural affairs. She has served as social director of the Coronado Community Theater and chairman of the Coronets' Art Ball. In 1970 she was feted in Hollywood at a film festival of early talkies, where her *Broadway Melody* (first musical to win a Best Picture Oscar) was screened and cheered anew. The event was held at MGM, scene of her eight-year, 32-picture starring career, and there was a particularly nostalgic lunch at the Metro commissary where she dined with long-ago friends. Asked why she gave up her career at 26, she replies: "I enjoyed making pictures and always felt it was a fabulous experience. But the ultimate goal was a happy marriage, and when this came along, it took priority over and replaced everything else." Onscreen from 1928. IN: *Telling the World, Our Dancing Daughters, The Flying Ensign, Hollywood Revue of 1929, Our Modern Maidens, Navy Blues, War Nurse, Our Blushing Brides, Sidewalks of New York, Under Eighteen, Are You Listening?, Skyscraper Souls, Night Court, Jungle Bride, Soldiers of the Storm, The Phantom Broadcast,* more, including 1936's *Hitchhike to Heaven,* her last.

PAGE, GALE (S. Cal.) She is married, in her 60s (b. 1913), the mother of grown children, and long retired. Her son, Luchino Solito de Solis (Jr.) was featured on Broadway in a juvenile role in 1956's *Waiting for Godot.* Onscreen from 1938. IN: *Crime School, The Amazing Dr. Clitterhouse, Four Daughters, Daughters Courageous, Four Wives, Indianapolis Speedway, A Child Is Born, They Drive by Night; Knute Rockne—All-American; Four Mothers, The Time of Your Life, Anna Lucasta,* more, including 1954's *About Mrs. Leslie,* her last.

PAGE, GENEVIEVE (Fr.) Leading lady. Onscreen from 1953. IN: *Fanfan the Tulip, The Silken Affair, Michael Strogoff, Song Without End, El Cid, The Day and the Hour, Youngblood Hawke, Grand-Prix, Tender Scoundrel, Belle de Jour, The Private Life of Sherlock Holmes,* more.

PAGE, GERALDINE (N.Y.) Costar. Nominated for Best Supporting Actress Oscar in *Hondo* (her first film), *You're a Big Boy Now, Pete 'n Tillie.* Nominated for Best Actress Oscar in *Summer and Smoke* and *Sweet Bird of Youth.* Onscreen from 1953. IN: *Toys in the Attic, Dear Heart, The Out-of-Towners, Three Sisters, Monday's Child, The Happiest Millionaire, What Ever Happened to Aunt Alice?, The Beguiled, Day of the Locust,* more.

PAGE, JOY ANN (S. Cal.) Remarried after her divorce from actor-producer William Orr, she is now retired. Onscreen from 1942. IN: *Casablanca, Kismet, Man-Eater of Kumaon, The Bullfighter and the Lady, The Shrike,* more, including 1959's *Tonka,* her most recent to date.

PAGE, PATTI (S. Cal.) Singer-actress. Onscreen in the '60s. IN: *Elmer Gantry, Dondi,* and *Boys' Night Out.*

PAGET, DEBRA (Tex.) In '58 she became the fifth wife of the late singer David Street (d. 1971), and in '60, the third wife of movie director Budd Boetticher; both marriages ended in divorce. Since '64 she has been the wife of Chinese oil man Louis C. Kung and living, most reclusively, on a palatial estate—her husband's worth is estimated in the billions—near Houston. The mother of several children by him, the actress, now in her 40s (b. 1933), remains a slender and beautiful woman—one given, not surprisingly perhaps to mandarin-style fashions. Onscreen from 1948. IN: *Cry of the City, House of Strangers, Broken Arrow, Bird of Paradise, Anne of the Indies, Belles on Their Toes, Stars and Stripes Forever, Demetrius and the Gladiators, The Gambler from Natchez, White Feather, The Ten Commandments, Omar Khayyam, Journey to the Lost City, Most Dangerous Man Alive,* more, including 1963's *The Haunted Palace,* her last.

PAGET-BOWMAN, CICELY (Eng.) Character. Onscreen from 1936. IN: *Conspirator, The Miniver Story, The Trials of Oscar Wilde,* more.

PAGETT, GARY (S. Cal.) Support. Onscreen from 1955. IN: *Good Morning, Miss Dove; The Front Page,* more.

PAIGE, JANIS (S. Cal.) One of Warners' busiest young actresses in the '40s, she went on to star on Broadway in musicals (*The Pajama Game*) and comedies (*Remains to be Seen*), and on television in her own situation-comedy series, *It's Always Jan.* In no movies of this decade to date, the redhead, who is now in her 50s (b. 1922), has been highly active in television: *Columbo, Mannix, Hec Ramsey,* and, in '75, in a series pilot, *The Prime of Life,* that did not sell. She has also starred in summer theaters in such musicals as *Annie Get Your Gun* and, in '71, played a lengthy tour in South Africa in *Applause.* Childless after three marriages, the actress lives alone in a modest bungalow in the Hollywood Hills. Her first two marriages—to restaurateur Frank Martinelli, when in her 20s, and later to TV writer-producer Arthur Stander (now deceased) ended in divorce. Her next, to bearded, soft-spoken, Oscar-winning songwriter ("Zip-a-Dee-Doo-Dah") Ray Gilbert, which took place on August 30, 1962, was a long and happy one. She had met Gilbert—father of singer-actress Joanne Gilbert—two years earlier. Shortly after they were married, she said, "Love is supposed to stem from mutuality and shared growth. You're not supposed to say that you can love someone with constancy after knowing them only a few minutes. But I did." She had gone to the composer's apartment in Hollywood to discuss a nightclub act she was planning. She had found him both understanding and astute about "show business, careers or just life. He was so mature. I was in love with him before I left his apartment." Their life together lasted until Gilbert's death, following heart surgery, in March 1976. To assuage her grief, the actress began then to accelerate her professional activities. Onscreen from 1944. IN: *Bathing Beauty* (bit), *Hollywood Canteen, Of Human Bondage* (Eleanor Parker version); *The Time, the Place and the Girl; Two Guys from Milwaukee, Her Kind of Man, Love and Learn, Wallflower, Winter Meeting, One Sunday Afternoon, Romance on the High Seas, The Younger Brothers, Two Guys and a Gal, Silk Stockings, Please Don't Eat the Daisies, Bachelor in Paradise, The Caretakers* (regarded by many as her best dramatic performance), *Follow the Boys,* more, including 1967's *Welcome to Hard Times,* her most recent to date.

PAIGE, ROBERT (S. Cal.) One of Deanna Durbin's most memorable leading men—in *Can't Help Singing*—and a Universal stalwart throughout the '40s, he is now in his 60s (b. 1910), little changed in looks, and a senior executive with the Hollywood public relations firm of McFadden, Strauss & Irwin. Onscreen 37 years, this veteran of 62 movies turned to TV in the '50s. For a long while the cohost, with Bess Myerson, of the network game show *The Big Payoff,* beamed from New York, he returned to Hollywood and was for years—until '70—an on-the-air newscaster for local station KABC-TV. He later formed a business partnership with his artist-wife, Jo Anne Ludden, Paige-Ludden Enterprises, that did sales promotion for TV shows. The Paiges, married in '61, have a teenage daughter, Colleen; Mrs. Paige also has another daughter, Suzanne, by a previous marriage, who lived with them until she entered college. They live on a comfortable estate in one of the more rustic sections of Beverly Hills. Robert Paige has not been seen on the screen since he played supporting roles in two in the early '60s *(Marriage-Go-Round* and *Bye Bye Birdie),* and professes not to miss acting. Socially active, he still sees such former Universal colleagues as Andy Devine and Peggy Moran and her director-husband Henry Koster. Onscreen from 1937. IN: *Smart Blonde, Murder in Swingtime, Who Killed Gail Preston?, Flying G-Men* (serial). *Women Without Names, Opened by Mistake, The Mobster and the Girl, Melody Lane, Hellzapoppin, What's Cookin'?, Pardon My Sarong, Crazy House, Mr. Big, Fired Wife, Her Primitive Man, You Can't Ration Love, Shady Lady, Tangier, Red Stallion, Blonde Ice, Split Second, It Happened to Jane,* more.

PAISNER, DINA (N.Y.) Support. Onscreen from the '60s. IN: *A Thousand Clowns, Pretty Boy Floyd, Lilith,* more.

PALANCE, JACK (S. Cal.) Costar. Nominated for Best Supporting Actor Oscar in *Sudden Fear* and *Shane*. Onscreen from 1950. IN: *Panic in the Streets, Arrowhead, Man in the Attic, Kiss of Fire, The Big Knife, Attack!, The Lonely Man, Sword of the Conqueror, Once a Thief, The Professionals, They Came to Rob Las Vegas, The Mercenary, Che!, Legion of the Damned, The McMasters, Monte Walsh, The Horsemen, The Getaway, Oklahoma Crude, The Cop in Blue Jeans,* more.

PALFI, LOTTA/a.k.a. LOTTA ANDOR (N.Y.) Character. Onscreen from 1940. IN: *Confessions of a Nazi Spy, Underground, Above Suspicion, The Seventh Cross, In Our Time, Walk East on Beacon,* more.

PALMER, ANTHONY (N.Y.) Support. Onscreen in the '70s. IN: *My Sweet Charlie, Comforts of Home,* more.

PALMER, BELINDA (S. Cal.). Ingenue. Onscreen in the '70s. IN: *Clay Pigeon, Chinatown.*

PALMER, BETSY (N.Y.) Leading lady. She acts mostly in stock and dinner theaters now. Onscreen from 1955. IN: *Mister Roberts, The Long Gray Line, Queen Bee, The Tin Star, The True Story of Lynn Stuart, The Last Angry Man, It Happened to Jane,* more.

PALMER, BYRON (S. Cal.) Actor-singer. In 1974 he was married to actress Georgine Darcy. Onscreen from 1953. IN: *Tonight We Sing, Man in the Attic, Ma and Pa Kettle at Waikiki, Glory, Emergency Hospital, The Best Things in Life Are Free,* more.

PALMER, GREGG/formerly **PALMER LEE** (S. Cal.) Support. Onscreen as Palmer Lee (his real name) from 1951. IN: *The Cimarron Kid, Francis Goes to West Point, The Redhead from Wyoming, Son of Ali Baba, Veils of Bagdad,* more. Onscreen as Gregg Palmer from 1954. IN: *Playgirl, Magnificent Obsession, To Hell and Back, The Creature Walks Among Us, Hilda Crane, Thundering Jets, Most Dangerous Man Alive, 40 Pounds of Trouble, The Quick Gun; If He Hollers, Let Him Go;* more.

PALMER, LILLI (Switz.) Formerly the wife of Rex Harrison, she has been married for two decades to leading man-turned-writer Carlos Thompson, lives at Gstaad when not at their Spanish villa in Costa del Sol, and remains beautiful in her early 60s (b. 1914). She acts mainly in films made in her native Germany now (*The Return of the Beloved* in '74) and, in 1975, published a most candid autobiography. Written in German and issued abroad as *Fat Lilly—Good Child,* she translated it into English before it was published here as *Change Lobsters and Dance*—to high acclaim from critics, if not Rex Harrison. Onscreen in England from 1934. Onscreen in America and internationally from 1946. IN: *Cloak and Dagger, My Girl Tisa, Body and Soul, No Minor Vices, The Fourposter, But Not for Me, The Pleasure of His Company, The Counterfeit Traitor, The Miracle of the White Stallions, Operation Crossbow, Maedchen in Uniform, Sebastian, Hard Contract, Murders in the Rue Morgue,* more.

PALMER, MARIA (S. Cal.) Actress-sister of Lilli Palmer. Well remembered for her performance in Stanwyck's *The Other Love,* she is in her 50s (b. 1924) and has been inactive in movies since 1958's *Outcasts in the City.* But she appears frequently in television commercials. Onscreen from 1943. IN: *Mission to Moscow, Days of Glory, Lady on a Train, The Web, Thirteen Lead Soldiers, Strictly Dishonorable, By the Light of the Silvery Moon, City of Women, Three for Jamie Dawn,* more.

PALMER, PETER (S. Cal.) He plays supporting roles on TV now. Onscreen in 1959. IN: *Li'l Abner* (title role).

PALMER, ROBERT (S. Cal.) Support. Onscreen from the '60s. IN: *The Desperate Ones,* more.

PALUZZI, LUCIANA (S. Cal.) Leading lady. Early billed as Paoluzzi. Onscreen from 1954. IN: *Three Coins in the Fountain, Tank Force, Journey to the Lost City, Return to Peyton Place, Muscle Beach Party, Thunderball, To Trap a Spy, The Venetian Affair, A Black Veil for Lisa, Captain Nemo and the Underwater City, Mean Mother, The Klansman,* more.

PAN, HERMES (S. Cal.) Oscar-winning choreographer (*Damsel in Distress*). Onscreen in 1950. IN: *A Life of Her Own.*

PANCAKE, ROGER (S. Cal.) Character. Onscreen in the '70s. IN: *Tender Loving Care,* more.

PANI, CORRADO (It.) Leading man. Onscreen from the '60s. IN: *Rocco and His Brothers, Girl With a Suitcase, Run With the Devil, Bora Bora, Kama Sutra,* more.

PANVINI, RON (N.Y.) Support. Onscreen in the '70s. IN: *The People Next Door,* more.

PAPAS, IRENE (Greece) Leading lady. Onscreen from the '70s. IN: *The Man from Cairo, Tribute to a Bad Man, Attila the Hun, The Guns of Navarone, Antigone, Zorba the Greek,*

The Moonspinners, Z, The Brotherhood, A Dream of Kings, Anne of the Thousand Days, The Trojan Women, Moses, more.

PARFITT, JUDY (Eng.) Leading lady. Onscreen from the '60s. IN: *Hide and Seek, The Mind of Mr. Soames*, more.

PARFREY, WOODROW (S. Cal.) Character. Onscreen from the '60s. IN: *Madigan; How to Save a Marriage—And Ruin Your Life; Planet of the Apes, Cold Turkey*, more.

PARIS, JERRY (S. Cal.) Giving up his acting career after 1959's *No Name on the Bullet*, he has since been one of Hollywood's busiest directors of movies (*Star Spangled Girl*, etc.) and TV series (*Happy Days*). Onscreen from 1950. IN: *Outrage, Cyrano de Bergerac, Sabre Jet, Drive a Crooked Road, Marty; Good Morning, Miss Dove; The View from Pompey's Head, Zero Hour!, Man on the Prowl, The Naked and the Dead*, more.

PARKER, CECILIA (S. Cal.) She came out of retirement to play "Andy Hardy's" older sister, Marian, again in 1958's *Andy Hardy Comes Home* (then her first in exactly 12 years), and promptly retired again—for good. Today she and her husband are real estate agents in Ventura County (about 50 miles upcoast from Hollywood), and formerly owned and operated a rather sumptuous motel there. He is former actor Dick (*Life Begins in College*) Baldwin. They have been married since '38, have grown children—two sons and a daughter—and are grandparents. Suntanned, a bit heavier than in her movie days, and still attractively blonde, the actress is now in her —. Her age is subject to debate; some sources say 1915 was her birth year, others insist on 1912, while still others maintain—but it's most unlikely—it was 1905. The actual date, Cecilia Parker Baldwin laughs, is her secret. Onscreen from 1931. IN: *Young As You Feel, Mystery Ranch, The Rainbow Trail, The Painted Veil* (her personal favorite; as Garbo's sister), *Enter Madame, High School Girl; Ah, Wilderness!; The Mine With the Iron Door, A Family Affair* (followed by 11 more appearances in the 16 "Andy Hardy" movies), *Sweetheart of the Navy; Burn 'Em Up, O'-Connor; Gambling Daughters, Seven Sweethearts, Grand Central Murder, Suicide Squadron*, more.

PARKER, ELEANOR (S. Cal.) Costar. Nominated for Best Actress Oscar in *Caged, Detective Story*. Onscreen from 1941. IN: *They Died With Their Boots On, Mission to Moscow, Mysterious Doctor, Between Two Worlds, The Very Thought of You, Pride of the Marines, Of Human Bondage, Escape Me Never, The Woman in White, The Voice of the Turtle, Chain Lightning; Valentino, Scaramouche, Above and Beyond, Escape from Fort Bravo, Many Rivers to Cross, The Man With the Golden Arm, The King and Four Queens, A Hole in the Head, Home from the Hill, Return to Peyton Place, The Sound of Music, Warning Shot, The Tiger and the Pussycat, Eye of the Cat*, more.

PARKER, FESS (S. Cal.) Costar. Onscreen from 1952. IN: *Untamed Frontier, Springfield Rifle, The Kid from Left Field, Them, Battle Cry; Davy Crockett—King of the Wild Frontier; The Great Locomotive Chase, Old Yeller, The Light in the Forest, Alias Jesse James, The Jayhawkers, Hell Is for Heroes, Smoky*, more.

PARKER, JANET LEE (N.Y.) Support. Onscreen from the '60s. IN: *David and Lisa, Act One*, more.

PARKER, JEAN (S. Cal.) At Hollywood press parties now, those few that she attends, she seems a wistful, albeit still lovely ghost of Hollywood Past. Her auburn hair, in an upsweep, is a charming pile of curls. Her curvy figure, once the most whistle-worthy in town, remains astonishingly good; it would become a woman of 40 and she has entered her 60s (b. 1915). But her dark hazel eyes, then so flashing and teasing, or beguilingly innocent, seem to hold a melancholy secret. It could be nothing more than the self-acknowledgment that, while she has survived, "her" Hollywood is gone forever. Occasionally, she admits she would like to be part of the "new" Hollywood. Where, though, does one begin? It is generally more difficult to make movie moguls take a second look than a first. Meanwhile Jean Parker, who gave up her career after 1966's *Apache Uprising*, stays busy. She lives five miles east of Hollywood in an attractive small house in Eagle Rock, a middle-class suburb of Los Angeles. Sharing this home with her until he went away to law school was her only child, Robert Lowery Hanks Jr., now in his mid-20s, who remains devoted and attentive. His father was the late actor Robert Lowery, last of the actress's husbands. Jean Parker's most active employment today is coaching young performers, sent to her by old studio friends, who are being groomed for movie roles. She finds great satisfaction in this occupation. "Sometimes I work with them on an individual basis, sometimes I hold classes," she says. "It's marvelous and stimulating, and I adore sharing my experience and craft. One day I'd love to have a school, one that would feature Pre-preparation for Acting." She has lately been writing an actors' textbook on this theme. "Acting," she says, "is truly a glorious and noble profession. When anyone can give other people a few hours of escape, or enchantment, away from the ills of the world and their own personal lives, well, that's a very worthwhile occupation." Few actresses are better qualified to know. In 34 years and 68 movies, she was a glowing talent, with a range greater than Hollywood ever acknowledged, She played everything and did it well—ingenues (*Little Women, Lady for a Day*), gypsies (*Caravan*), society girls (*The Ghost Goes West*), country girls (*Sequoia, The Arkansas Traveler*), comedy (*The Flying Deuces*), pathos (*Have a Heart*), heavy drama (*Lady in the Death House*), crisp and dauntless career girls in a slew of Pine-Thomas thrillers (*High Explosive, Power Dive*), and, finally, when older, brittle tough-girls (*The Gunfighter, Black Tuesday*). As her movie career waned, she turned to the legitimate stage, on Broadway and on tour, winning high critical praise in plays like *Dream Girl, Born Yesterday,* and *Burlesque*. In recent years, though, the only "acting" she has done was in a series of commercials for Hollywood's First Federal Savings and Loan Association, taped in 1974. She has been married and divorced four times. Her husbands were New York newspaperman George MacDonald (1936–40), radio news commentator Douglas Dawson—real name H. Dawson Sanders (1941–43), foreign correspondent-movie executive Dr. Curtis Grotter (1944–49), and actor Robert Lowery (1951–57). After her son was born she made only five more films before deciding she preferred being a fulltime mother to being an actress. Of her son she says now: "He has a keen mind and a great natural interest in political science. I wouldn't be surprised if he winds up in politics someday." This late in her career, there are two things Jean Parker would like her admirers to know the truth about. Her real name is not Lois Mae Green, as was so highly publicized for years; it is—she's of Polish-French descent—Luis Stephanie Zelinska. And, born in Montana (though she grew up in Pasadena, Calif.), she hails not from that state's Deer Lodge, but from Butte. These items were studio publicity phoniness, and Jean Parker says she has had enough of that. What she has not had enough of is acting. She wants to be back in front of the cameras. Onscreen from 1932. IN: *Divorce in the Family, What Price Innocence?, Rasputin and the Empress, You Can't Buy Everything, Murder in the Fleet, The Texas Rangers, Romance of the Redwoods, Zenobia, The Pittsburgh Kid, Flying Blind, Torpedo Boat, Alaska Highway, Dead Men's Eyes, Toughest Man in Tombstone, Those Redheads from Seattle, The Parson and the Outlaw,* more.

PARKER, LARA (N.Y.) Leading lady. Star of TV soap operas. Onscreen in the '70s. IN: *Hi, Mom!, Night of Dark Shadows, Race With the Devil,* more.

PARKER, LEONARD (N.Y.) Black character. Onscreen from the '60s. IN: *Nothing But a Man, Sweet Love Bitter, Stiletto, Child of Anger,* more.

PARKER, MARY (Eng.) British leading lady. Not the American actress (deceased) of the same name. Since her movie career she has been a TV-radio announcer in England. Onscreen in the '50s. IN: *Triple Blackmail, The Deception, Third Party Risk, You Lucky People,* more.

PARKER, SHIRLEY (S. Cal.) Support. Onscreen from the '60s. IN: *Mission Mars, The Minx,* more.

PARKER, SUZY (S. Cal.) Since her marriage (#3) to actor Bradford Dillman in 1963, by whom she has two children, the #1 model-turned-actress has appeared in just two movies: *Flight from Ashiya* ('64) and *Chamber of Horrors* ('66). Late in 1975, aged 42 and still a beautiful redhead, she came down from their Santa Barbara home for a guest-star role in TV's *Joe Forrester*—in which she played a model. Onscreen from 1957. IN: *Funny Face, Kiss Them for Me, 10 North Frederick, The Best of Everything, Circle of Deception, The Interns,* more.

PARKER, WARREN (S. Cal.) Character. Onscreen from the '60s. IN: *Too Soon to Love, The Hoodlum Priest,* more.

PARKER, WILLARD (S. Cal.) Recovering from a stroke suffered in '74, the former swashbuckling star, who was later a successful realtor, is now in his 60s (b. 1912) and lives near Palm Springs. He has been married since '51—his second marriage, her third—to English actress Virginia Field. This beautiful blonde had many major roles in Hollywood between *Little Lord Fauntleroy* in '36 and *The Earth Dies Screaming* in '64, and was especially effective in *The Sun Never Sets* and *Waterloo Bridge,* as Vivien Leigh's ballerina friend. Though she and Willard Parker have no children, her daughter, Margaret Douglas (by actor Paul Douglas), who was small when they married, lived with them until she grew up and moved to England where she works for an advertising agency and occasionally acts on television. Parker's only child, a son by his previous marriage to actress Marion Pierce, is now a banker. With her husband's illness, Virginia Field, who had owned and operated a motel and boutique near their desert home, decided to resume her career. She signed with a top Hollywood agency and in '75 appeared before cameras for the first time in a decade in an episode of the TV series *Adam-12.* It is her hope that there will now be many more roles. Considering that, as she enters her sixth decade (b. 1917) she remains a most attractive

—albeit darker haired—woman, and was always one of Hollywood's more accomplished actresses, there is every expectation that her hopes will be fulfilled. Many are cheering for her, including her devoted husband. Onscreen from 1937. IN: *Over the Goal, That Certain Woman, Love Is on the Air, A Slight Case of Murder, What a Woman, The Fighting Guardsman, Relentless, Renegades, The Mating of Millie, Calamity Jane and Sam Bass, Bandit Queen, The Vanquished, Kiss Me Kate, The Naked Gun, The Lone Gunman, Young Jesse James, Air Patrol*, more, including 1966's *Waco*, his last.

PARKES, GERARD (S. Cal.) Support. Onscreen from the '60s. IN: *Isabel, The First Time*, more.

PARKINS, BARBARA (Eng.) Single still, the Hollywood actress now lives and works in England. Onscreen from 1967. IN: *Valley of the Dolls, The Kremlin Letter, The Mephisto Waltz, Puppet on a Chain, Asylum, Christina, Shout at the Devil*, more.

PARKS, HILDY (N.Y.) The leading lady once married (1950–51) to actor Jackie Cooper has been married since 1956 to Broadway producer Alexander H. Cohen. In her 50s she seldom acts now, but each year she helps her husband stage the Tony Awards show, which she also writes. Onscreen from 1955. IN: *The Night Holds Terror, Fail Safe*, more.

PARKS, MICHAEL (S. Cal.) Leading man. Onscreen from 1964. IN: *Bus Riley's Back in Town, Wild Seed, The Bible, The Idol, The Happening*, more.

PARNELL, EMORY (S. Cal.) In his 80s (b. 1894), this noted character actor has been inactive in movies for almost two decades. Onscreen from 1938. IN: *Call of the Yukon, Doctor Rhythm, If I Had My Way, So Ends Our Night, They All Kissed the Bride, Mission to Moscow, The Falcon in Mexico, Wilson, The Crime Doctor's Courage, Deadline for Murder, Mr. Blandings Builds His Dream House, Key to the City, Ma and Pa Kettle at the Fair, How to Be Very Very Popular*, more, including 1961's *The Two Little Bears*, his most recent to date.

PARR, KATHERINE (Eng.) Character. Onscreen from the '60s. IN: *This Sporting Life, A Severed Head*, more.

PARRISH, GIGI (S. Cal.) A pretty brunette still, she has long been the wife of novelist John Weld and, she says, permanently retired. Onscreen in the early '30s. IN: *20th Century, Down to Their Last Yacht, A Girl of the Limberlost*, more.

PARRISH, JULIE (S. Cal.) Leading lady. Onscreen from 1961. IN: *It's Only Money, The Nutty Professor, Boeing Boeing; Paradise, Hawaiian Style; Fireball 500*, more.

PARRISH, LESLIE (S. Cal.) The screen's most recent "Daisy Mae," in 1959's *Li'l Abner*, she still plays an occasional lead on TV but works most regularly for the Hall Bartlett company as production assistant—on such movies as *Jonathan Livingston Seagull* and *The Children of Sanchez*. Onscreen from 1959. IN: *Portrait of a Mobster, The Manchurian Candidate, Sex and the Single Girl, 3 on a Couch, The Money Jungle, The Devil's Eight, The Candy Man*, more.

PARRY, NATASHA (Eng.) Support; former leading lady. Onscreen from 1949. IN: *Dance Hall; Lovers, Happy Lovers; Midnight Episode, The Golden Arrow, Midnight Lace, Portrait of a Sinner, The Model Murder Case, Romeo and Juliet, Oh! What a Lovely War*, more.

PARSONS, ESTELLE (N.Y.) Character. Won Best Supporting Actress Oscar in *Bonnie and Clyde*. Nominated in the same category in *Rachel Rachel*. Onscreen from 1963. IN: *Ladybug, Ladybug; Don't Drink the Water, I Never Sang for My Father, Watermelon Man, I Walk the Line, Two People, For Pete's Sake, Foreplay*, more.

PARSONS, MICHAEL J. (S. Cal.) Leading man. Onscreen from 1963. IN: *Cry of Battle, The Walls of Hell, Too Late the Hero*, more.

PARSONS, MILTON (S. Cal.) Character. Onscreen from 1939. IN: *When Tomorrow Comes, Edison the Man, Roxie Hart, The Remarkable Andrew, The Great Man's Lady, Life Begins at 8:30, The Cry of the Werewolf, Dick Tracy vs. Cueball, The Secret Life of Walter Mitty, The Senator Was Indiscreet; How to Be Very, Very Popular*; more.

PARSONS, NICHOLAS (Eng.) Support. Onscreen from 1949. IN: *Master of Bankham, Too Many Crooks, Man in a Cocked Hat; Don't Raise the Bridge, Lower the River*; more.

PARTEN, PETER (Fr.) Support. Onscreen from the '60s. IN: *And So to Bed, Le Mans*, more.

PASCAL, GISELLE (Fr.) Leading lady. Onscreen from the '40s. IN: *La Vie de Boheme, The Naked Woman, Fire Under Her Skin, Secret World*, more.

PASCO, RICHARD (Eng.) Support. Onscreen from the '50s. IN: *Yesterday's Enemy, Room at the Top, Sword of Sherwood Forest, 6 Black Horses*, more.

PASSANTINO, ANTHONY (N.Y.) Support. Onscreen in the '70s. IN: *The Hospital, A Change in the Wind*, more.

PATACHOU (Fr.) Chanteuse. Onscreen from 1936. IN: *Maedchenraeuber, Song of the Street, French Can-can*.

PATAKI, MICHAEL (MIKE) (S. Cal.) Support. Onscreen in the '70s. IN: *The Return of Count Yorga*, more.

PATE, MICHAEL (Australia) One of Hollywood's strongest, busiest young character actors for 16 years, he gave up his acting career in 1967 after the movie *Return of the Gunfighter* and the TV series *Hondo*, in which he again played the Apache Indian chief Vittoro that he had portrayed in the '53 movie. With his family —former movie actress Felippa Rock and their now-grown son, Christopher—he returned to his native Sydney, Australia. (They still maintain their California home in Woodland Hills and spend part of each year there.) The former actor was first, in Sydney, associate producer of the James Mason film *Age of Consent*. In '69 he became Executive Producer in charge of production for Amalgamated Television Network in Sydney, and the following year published his book *The Film Actor: Acting for Motion Pictures and Television*. He has since devoted himself exclusively to producing movies and TV series, as well as writing. But he is still young enough (b. 1920) to resume his acting career at any time, and the offers come in steadily. Onscreen in Australia from 1941. IN: *Forty Thousand Horsemen, The Rugged O'Riordans* (made by Universal in Australia in '49, in which he starred), more. Onscreen in Hollywood from 1951. IN: *Thunder on the Hill, Five Fingers, Face to Face* ("The Secret Sharer" episode), *Julius Caesar, El Alamein, King Richard and the Crusaders, A Lawless Street, Something of Value, The Tall Stranger, Desert Hell, Sergeants Three, PT-109, McLintock!, California, Major Dundee, The Great Sioux Massacre, The Singing Nun*, more.

PATERSON, PAT (Fr.) Blonde leading lady, long married to Charles Boyer and retired. Onscreen in the '30s. IN: *Bitter Sweet, Bottoms Up, Call It Luck, Charlie Chan in Egypt, 52nd Street, Idiot's Delight*, more. (See Charles Boyer.)

PATRICK, BUTCH (S. Cal.) Juvenile. Onscreen from 1966. IN: *Munster, Go Home; The Phantom Tollbooth, The Sandpit General, 80 Steps to Jonah*, more.

PATRICK, DENNIS (S. Cal.) Character. Onscreen from 1969. IN: *Daddy's Gone A-Hunting, Joe, House of Dark Shadows*, more.

PATRICK, GAIL (S. Cal.) Her raven locks are silver now. That is the extent and total of any change in the actress who, between 1933's *If I Had a Million* and 1948's *Inside Story*, was without equal as the screen's perennial "other woman." That, and the fact that in the autumn of '74 she married her fourth husband, Illinois business man John Velde Jr. Her previous husbands: Bob Cobb (famous Brown Derby owner, now dead), Navy lieutenant Arnold White, and agent Cornwall Jackson. She and Jackson adopted two children, both grown now, Jennifer and Tom. The latter grew into a handsome blond giant of 6'3" and is now an actor-model. When he was 16 he served as Youth Ambassador for the Christmas Seal campaign, while his mother was national chairman—the two of them touring the country on behalf of the drive. During her marriage to Jackson, Gail Patrick changed careers and became a very rich woman. That was via the *Perry Mason* TV series, on which she was executive producer. It was Jackson who, as author Erle Stanley Gardner's agent and business partner, executed the sale to CBS, but it was the actress who handled the production reins. The show was a great hit for almost a decade. "Then Erle died, and Gail and I broke up and got a divorce," Jackson recalled not long ago when the program was brought back—unsuccessfully—as *The New Perry Mason*. "It was an interesting situation, since we're still partners together in Erle's company, Paisano Productions"—with members of the Gardner family. "The estrangement between Gail and me led to some real battles in Paisano, but the conflict got *Perry Mason* moving again." This time, Jackson served as executive producer, while his former wife held the title "executive consultant." Now in her 60s (b. 1912), with that all behind her, and with a new marriage to build, Gail Patrick has yet to decide what, if any, her next career should be. One thing she knows most definitely—it won't be acting. Onscreen from 1933. IN: *The Cradle Song, Mysterious Rider, Death Takes a Holiday, Murder at the Vanities, Rumba, Mississippi, Early to Wed, My Man Godfrey, The Lone Wolf Returns, Stage Door, Mad About Music, King of Alcatraz, Man of Conquest, The Doctor Takes a Wife, My Favorite Wife, Love Crazy, We Were Dancing, Hit Parade of 1943, Up in Mabel's Room, Brewster's Millions, Claudia and David, King of Wild Horses*, more.

PATRICK, LEE (S. Cal.) In the Bogart version of *The Maltese Falcon* ('41), the actress who always had the funny, sardonic answer, played his secretary; in the comic remake, *The Black Bird* ('75), starring George Segal, she came out of self-imposed retirement to play—that's right. Long and happily married—to newsman-writer Tom Wood (author of the book *The Lighter Side of Billy Wilder*)—she quit movies after 1964's

The New Interns. She had then been in more than 75 pictures in 35 years, and she was weary of greasepaint—on herself. And she was still only in her 50s (b. 1911). It was time, she told herself, to do those things she had long wanted to do—paint and travel. So each year she and her husband have gone to both New York and London, seeing all the new shows and visiting friends, and, when at home in Beverly Hills, she has painted. If she has a regret, it's that, loving the theater, she spent too few of her years on the stage and too many in movies. "I started on Broadway and found a camaraderie, professionalism, and generosity there that was rarely found in films," she has said. She remains somewhat surprised at herself for having agreed to work again in *The Black Bird*—the only explanation being she thought it would be fun to play "Effie" once more. She has no intention of saying "yes" again any time soon. Onscreen from 1937. IN: *Music for Madame, Danger Patrol, Condemned Women, The Sisters, Invisible Stripes, Strange Cargo, City for Conquest, South of Suez, Footsteps in the Dark, Honeymoon for Three, Now Voyager, In This Our Life, George Washington Slept Here, Somewhere I'll Find You, A Night to Remember, Mrs. Parkington, Mildred Pierce, Keep Your Powder Dry, Wake Up and Dream, The Snake Pit, The Fuller Brush Girl, Take Me to Town, Vertigo, Auntie Mame, Pillow Talk, Visit to a Small Planet, Goodbye Again, Summer and Smoke, Wives and Lovers*, more.

PATRICK, LORY (S. Cal.) The former ingenue has been married for several years to actor Dean Jones and is retired. Onscreen from the '60s. IN: *Surf Party*, more.

PATRICK, NIGEL (Eng.) Costar. Onscreen from 1939. IN: *Mrs. Pym of Scotland Yard, Spring in Park Lane, The Browning Version, Trio* ("Mr. Know-All" episode), *Pandora and the Flying Dutchman, Breaking the Sound Barrier, The Pickwick Papers, Tonight at 8:30* ("Ways and Means" episode), *How to Murder a Rich Uncle, Count Five and Die, Sapphire, The Green Carnation, The League of Gentlemen, Underworld Informers, The Virgin Soldiers, The Great Waltz*, more.

PATTEN, LUANA (S. Cal.) The adorable Disney moppet, inactive for the past decade, lives near Los Angeles and is in her late 30s (b. 1938). A two-time divorcee (actor John Smith was her second husband), she had two careers, beginning the first and ending the second at Disney. Dropping out as a child star, she returned in young leading lady roles, the latest of which was 1966's *Follow Me, Boys*. Onscreen from 1946. IN: *Song of the South, Fun and Fancy Free, Melody Time, So Dear to My Heart, Joe Dakota, Johnny Tremain, The Restless Years,*

Home from the Hill, Go Naked in the World, A Thunder of Drums, more.

PATTEN, ROBERT (S. Cal.) Support. Formerly Bob. Onscreen from the '40s. IN: *The Street With No Name, Mr. Belvedere Goes to College, Twelve O'Clock High, The Frogmen, Riot in Cell Block 11, Unchained, Return from the Sea, Airport, Zigzag*, more.

PATTERSON, ALBERT (N.Y.) Character. Onscreen from the '60s. IN: *Act One, The Daydreamer, Fail Safe, Stay Tuned for Terror*, more.

PATTERSON, DICK (S. Cal.) Support. Onscreen from the '60s. IN: *A Matter of Innocence*, more.

PATTERSON, LEE (N.Y.) Leading man. Most recently he has starred in the TV soap opera *One Life to Live.* Onscreen from 1951. IN: *36 Hours, The Story of Esther Costello, Reach for the Sky, Third Man on the Mountain, Jack the Ripper, The Three Worlds of Gulliver, The Ceremony, Search for the Evil One, Chato's Land*, more.

PATTERSON, MELODY (Hawaii) Married to actor James MacArthur, she lives in Honolulu and is inactive now. Onscreen from the '60s. IN: *The Angry Breed, Cycle Savages, Blood and Lace*, more.

PATTERSON, NEVA (S. Cal.) Support. Onscreen from 1953. IN: *Taxi, The Solid Gold Cadillac, Desk Set, An Affair to Remember; Too Much, Too Soon; The Spiral Road, David and Lisa, The Out-of-Towners, Counterpoint* (the screenplay of which was written by her husband, James Lee), more.

PATTERSON, PAT (S. Cal.) Character actor. Onscreen from the '60s. IN: *The Traveling Executioner, Gas-s-s!*, more.

PATTON, MARY (S. Cal.) Character. Onscreen from the '40s. IN: *The Search, Please Don't Eat the Daisies, Marriage-Go-Round, The Outsider*, more.

PAUL, BETTY (Eng.) Singer-dancer-actress who, retired from movies and the stage, has lately written scripts for British television. Onscreen from 1947. IN: *Out of the Blue* and *Oliver Twist.*

PAUL, JOHN (Eng.) Character. Onscreen from the '60s. IN: *The Desperados, Cromwell*, more.

PAUL, LEE (S. Cal.) Support. Onscreen in the '70s. IN: *The Island at the Top of the World*, more.

PAUL, LES (N.J.) Famous guitarist. Onscreen with The Les Paul Trio in 1944. IN: *Sensations of 1945.*

PAUL, MIMI (N.Y.) Ballerina. Onscreen in 1967. IN: *A Midsummer Night's Dream.*

PAUL, STEVEN (N.Y.) Juvenile. Onscreen in the '70s. IN: *Happy Birthday, Wanda June* (repeating his stage role of "Paul Ryan"), more.

PAULL, MORGAN (S. Cal.) Leading man. Onscreen in the '70s. IN: *Patton, Dirty O'Neil; Live a Little, Steal a Lot; Mitchell,* more.

PAULSEN, ALBERT (S. Cal.) Character. Onscreen from the '60s. IN: *The Manchurian Candidate, Gunn, Che!, Mrs. Pollifax–Spy,* more.

PAULSEN, PAT (S. Cal.) Comedian. Onscreen from 1968. IN: *Where Were You When the Lights Went Out?, Foreplay,* more.

PAVAN, MARISA (Fr.) Leading lady. Nominated for Best Supporting Actress Oscar in *The Rose Tattoo.* The twin of the late star Pier Angeli (d. 1971), she has been married since '56—with time out for a divorce and remarriage—to actor Jean-Pierre Aumont. They have two teenage sons, Jean-Claude and Patrick, both sufficiently "Americanized" (though, like both parents, they are French citizens) to dress exclusively in jeans and Texas cowboy boots. "They've even developed those 'male ego' swaggers," reports the actress. The Aumonts have a home in Paris and a farm house on the island of Ibiza, but she agrees with her husband's contention that "the best place to be is on an airplane, you have to be ready to fly. That's the way the work is now." The actress—still lovely in her early 40s (b. 1932)—makes an occasional movie now, usually in Europe. And in '74 she had a hit record overseas, her French-language version of Bacharach's "Green Grass Starts to Grow." Singing is not a new career for her or her husband. In the '60s they starred in a supper club act at the Plaza Hotel in New York that they took on tour in the States, Canada, and Mexico, and did several times on TV. Aumont remains continually busy, in movies (*The Happy Hooker, Day for Night,* etc.), touring in the U.S. in such plays as *Janus* with Joan Bennett, and acting on European TV. Now in his 60s (b. 1913), he is the father—by his late first wife, Maria Montez—of Tina Aumont, a well-established star of Italian films. Onscreen from 1952. IN: *What Price Glory, Down Three Dark Streets, Drum Beat, Diane, The Man in the Gray Flannel Suit, The Midnight Story, Solomon and Sheba, John Paul Jones,* more, including 1974's *The Most Important Event Since Man First Set Foot on the Moon,* opposite Mastroianni.

PAVLOW, MURIEL (Eng.) The leading lady, married to actor Derek Farr, has acted only on the British stage in the past decade. Onscreen from 1936. IN: *A Romance in Flanders, Project M 7, It Started in Paradise, Fuss Over Feathers, Simon and Laura, Reach for the Sky, Doctor at Large, Murder She Said,* more.

PAYN, GRAHAM (Eng.) Singer-actor. Onscreen from 1932 as a boy soprano (age 14). Primarily a stage performer, often seen opposite Gertrude Lawrence, his movie appearances as an adult have been few. Most memorable was his performance in 1950's *The Astonished Heart.*

PAYNE, JOHN (S. Cal.) Rich from Malibu real estate (as well as a flourishing ranch in Montana), the star gave up movie acting after 1957's *Hidden Fear.* Between then and '71 he was seen only on TV—a total of six guest appearances on *Gunsmoke,* etc.—and, for a while on Broadway and on tour in the early '60s, on stage in the play *Here's Love.* Mainly, instead of acting, he wrote—numerous TV scripts and a play that interested Broadway producers once but has yet to be produced. And, in '72, he even attended a secretarial college to learn typing, as he was writing his autobiography. In 1973 John Payne, lean, pipe-smoking, and handsome still in his early 60s (b. 1912), surprised many by signing a one-year contract to costar with Alice Faye on stage in the musical *Good News.* The Payne-Faye combo had made movie-musical history by teaming romantically in four pictures, the last being 1943's *Hello, Frisco, Hello.* It was Alice Faye, though she had not seen him in 17 years, who asked that Payne be cast opposite her in *Good News.* History repeated itself; the show played to nationwide SRO audiences for months before its New York opening. In a jocular mood when he arrived in New York alone, the actor said, "I told my family the last half of my life is gonna be for me. Everybody off the boat." Married since '53 to his present wife, Sandy, he was previously married to actresses Anne Shirley (1937–43) and Gloria De Haven (1944–50). By Anne Shirley he has an actress-daughter, Julie (b. 1940); and by Gloria De Haven, a son, Thomas (b. 1948), now in business in San Francisco, and a daughter, Kathie (b. 1945), who has operated a health shoppe in Hollywood and has lately launched a singing career. All, he reports, are married and Julie has made him a grandfather. During the run of *Good News,* in which he played the football coach and sang "You're the Cream in My Coffee" with his costar, Payne confessed, "I didn't exactly know what I was signing up for. At this period of my life, let's face it, I'm in the foot-hills of old age." Particularly, he found the attention of fans discomfiting. "The whole scene," he said, "surprises the bejesus out of me. People come backstage and look at you as if you were something in amber." He was relieved, when his contract ended, to return to Malibu to "buying, selling, investing and trading." Still only semiretired, in '75 he guested in a *Columbo* episode ("Forgotten Lady"), in which he and Janet Leigh played dancing stars of early movie musicals. So the beat goes on. Onscreen from 1936. IN: *Dodsworth, Garden of the Moon, Wings of the Navy, Indianapolis Speedway, Maryland, Tin Pan Alley, The Great American Broadcast, Moon Over Miami, Sun Valley Serenade, Footlight Serenade, Iceland, The Dolly Sisters, Sentimental Journey, Miracle on 34th Street, Larceny, The Eagle and the Hawk, 99 River Street, The Vanquished, The Silver Lode, Tennessee's Partner, Hold Back the Night, Bail Out at 43,000*, more.

PAYNE, JULIE (S. Cal.) Actress-daughter of John Payne and Anne Shirley. Onscreen from 1963. IN: *Irma la Douce, Island of Blue Dolphins, Celebration at Big Sur*, more.

PAYNE, LAURENCE (Eng.) Leading man. Onscreen from the '50s. IN: *Night Ambush, The Crawling Eye, Ben Hur, Barabbas*, more.

PAYNE, SALLY, (S. Cal.) Character. Onscreen from 1940. IN: *La Conga Nights*, more.

PAYTON-WRIGHT, PAMELA (N.Y.) Broadway leading lady. Onscreen in the '70s. IN: *Corky.*

PEABODY, RICHARD (DICK) (S. Cal.) Support. Onscreen from the '60s. IN: *Support Your Local Sheriff, The Good Guys and the Bad Guys, The Moonshine War*, more.

PEACH, MARY, (Eng.) Leading lady. Onscreen from the '50s. IN: *Room at the Top, A Pair of Briefs, A Gathering of Eagles, Blues for Lovers, The Projected Man, Scrooge*, more.

PEAKER, E. J. (S. Cal.) Support. Onscreen from 1969. IN: *Hello, Dolly!*, more.

PEARL, BARRY (N.Y.) Support. Onscreen from the '60s. IN: *A Fine Madness, P.J.*, more.

PEARL, JACK (N.Y.) In his 80s now (b. 1895), the "Baron von Munchausen" lives on the fashionable East Side in well-off retirement. Onscreen 1933-34. IN: *Meet the Baron* and *Hollywood Party.*

PEARL, MINNIE (Tenn.) Country music star comedienne. Onscreen in 1966. IN: *That Tennessee Beat.*

PEARSON, BEATRICE (N.Y.) Former leading lady. Now retired. Onscreen in 1948 and 1949. IN: *Force of Evil* and *Lost Boundaries.*

PEARSON, BRETT (S. Cal.) Support. Onscreen from the '60s. IN: *This Property Is Condemned, Stagecoach*, more.

PEARSON, JESSE (S. Cal.) Leading man. Onscreen from 1963. IN: *Bye Bye Birdie, Advance to the Rear*, more.

PEARSON, RICHARD (Eng.) Character. First in movies in 1938 but more active since the '60s. IN: *Charlie Bubbles, Inspector Clouseau, Sunday Bloody Sunday, Macbeth*, more.

PEARSON, SUSAN G. (N.Y.) Support. Onscreen in 1969. IN: *Goodbye, Columbus.*

PEARY, HAROLD (S. Cal.) "The Great Gildersleeve" of movie and radio fame (played the role a total of 16 years) is in his late 60s now (b. 1908), celebrated his 55th year of continous employment in show business in 1976, and notes with that inimitable chuckle: "Like old-fashioned ice cream freezers, I'm back in style. And why not? Men are wearing mustaches again and even women are smoking cigars! So I'm swamped with offers to make personal appearances and radio and TV commercials." Until recently, he also did many TV guest spots—in *The Ghost and Mrs. Muir, The Doris Day Show, The Brady Bunch, That Girl*, etc. Since 1964 he has been married to the former Juanita Parker-Lawson, now retired, who was for 15 years an electronics engineer with Douglas and Hughes Aircraft. One newspaper headlined their marriage as GILDERSLEEVE WEDS ENGINEER and, he laughs, "We got some awful funny mail at our house for a while after that." By his previous marriage, he has a son, Page Peary, a U.S. Army Medical Corp. veteran of Vietnam. The actor and his wife live in the seaside community of Manhattan Beach, about 15 miles from Hollywood, where he owns considerable real estate and is Honorary Mayor. Onscreen from 1940. IN: *Comin' Round the Mountain, Look Who's Laughing, Country Fair, Here We Go Again, Seven Days' Leave, The Great Gildersleeve, Gildersleeve's Bad Day, Gildersleeve on Broadway, Gildersleeve's Ghost*, more, including 1967's *Clambake*, his most recent to date.

PEATTIE, YVONNE (S. Cal.) Character. Onscreen from the '50s. IN: *Dangerous Crossing, The Private War of Major Benson, Donovan's Reef*, more.

PECK, GREGORY (S. Cal.) Star. Won Best Actor Oscar in *To Kill a Mockingbird.*

Nominated in the same category in *The Keys of the Kingdom, The Yearling, Gentleman's Agreement, Twelve O'Clock High*. Onscreen from 1944. IN: *Days of Glory, The Valley of Decision, Spellbound, Duel in the Sun, The Macomber Affair, The Paradine Case, Yellow Sky, The Gunfighter, Only the Valiant, David and Bathsheba, The Snows of Kilimanjaro, Roman Holiday, Night People, The Man in the Gray Flannel Suit, The Big Country, Pork Chop Hill, On the Beach, The Guns of Navarone, How the West Was Won, Mirage, Arabesque, Mackenna's Gold, The Chairman, Marooned, The Stalking Moon, I Walk the Line, Billy Two Hats, MacArthur*, more.

PECK, STEVEN (S. Cal.) Character. Onscreen from the '50s. IN: *Some Came Running, A House Is Not a Home, Lady in Cement*, more.

PEDI, TOM (N.Y.) Character. Onscreen from 1942. IN: *Native Son, The Naked City, State of the Union, Up in Central Park, Criss Cross, Sorrowful Jones, The Taking of Pelham One Two Three*, more.

PEEL, EILEEN (Eng.) Character. Onscreen from 1932. IN: *The First Mrs. Fraser, Bad Sister*, more.

PEERCE, JAN (N.Y.) Opera star. Onscreen from 1946. IN: *Hymn of the Nations, Carnegie Hall, Something in the Wind, Of Men and Music*.

PEINE, JOSH (S. Cal.) Leading man. Onscreen from the '60s. IN: *Mr. Hobbs Takes a Vacation*, more.

PEISLEY, FREDERICK (Eng.) Character. Onscreen from 1933. IN: *The Scotland Yard Mystery*, more.

PELISH, THELMA (S. Cal.) Comedienne. Onscreen from 1957. IN: *The Pajama Game, Up Pompeii*, more.

PELLEGRINI, EUGENE (N.Y.) Leading man in TV soap operas. Onscreen in 1957. IN: *8 × 8*.

PENBERTHY, BEVERLY (N.Y.) Leading lady in TV soap operas. Onscreen in 1970. IN: *I Never Sang for My Father*.

PENDLETON, AUSTIN (S. Cal.) Comedian. Onscreen from the '60s. IN: *Skidoo, Catch-22, Petulia, What's Up, Doc?, Every Little Crook and Nanny, The Front Page*, more.

PENDLETON, STEVE (GAYLORD) (S. Cal.) Character; former leading man. Onscreen from

1923. IN: *Success* (juvenile role), *Up the River, The Last Parade, The Informer, Internes Can't Take Money, The Duke of West Point, Geronimo, One Crowded Night, Untamed Fury, Beyond Glory, Rio Grande*, more.

PENDLETON, WYMAN (N.Y.) Character. Onscreen in the '70s. IN: *Pigeons*, more.

PENNELL, LARRY (S. Cal.) Support. Onscreen from 1955. IN: *Seven Angry Men, The Far Horizons, The Vagabond King, The Devil's Hairpin, The F.B.I. Story, Flaming Frontier, The Great White Hope*, more.

PEPPARD, GEORGE (S. Cal.) Costar. Onscreen from 1957. IN: *The Strange One, Pork Chop Hill, Home from the Hill, Breakfast at Tiffany's, How the West Was Won, The Victors, The Carpetbaggers, Operation Crossbow, The Blue Max, P.J., What's So Bad About Feeling Good?, Pendulum, House of Cards, The Executioner, The Groundstar Conspiracy, Newman's Law*, more.

PEPPER, BUDDY (S. Cal.) In his 50s now (b. 1922), the once popular juvenile gave up acting over three decades ago to become a songwriter. He first did the tunes for pal Donald O'Connor's *Mister Big* ('43), and has since written the title songs for such pictures as *Pillow Talk* and *Portrait in Black*, plus many "singles" ("Vaya con Dios," "What Good Would It Do?," "Don't Tell Me," etc.). He still lives in Hollywood and in the past has been piano accompanist for Marlene Dietrich and Margaret Whiting. Onscreen from 1937. IN: *Streets of New York, Seventeen, The Reluctant Dragon*, more.

PEPPER, CYNTHIA (S. Cal.) Leading lady. Onscreen from 1963. IN: *Take Her, She's Mine; Kissin' Cousins*, more.

PERDUE, DERELYS (S. Cal.) Married, she has long been retired. Onscreen from the '20s. IN: *Small Town Idol, The Last Man on Earth*, more.

PERETZ, SUSAN (N.Y.) Support. Onscreen in the '70s. IN: *Dog Day Afternoon*, more.

PEREZ, JOSE (N.Y.) Support. Onscreen from the 50's. IN: *A Life in the Balance, The Young Savages, Born to Win*, more.

PERIER, FRANCOIS (Fr.) Character lead. Onscreen from the '30s. IN: *Man About Town, A Lover's Return, Loves of Colette, The Bed, Gervaise, Demoniaque, The Five Day Lover, Testament of Orpheus, The Organizer, Sweet and Sour, The Visit*, more.

PERKINS, ANTHONY (N.Y.) Costar. Nominated for Best Supporting Actor Oscar in *Friendly Persuasion*. Onscreen from 1953. IN: *The Actress, Fear Strikes Out, The Lonely Man, The Tin Star, Desire Under the Elms, The Matchmaker, Green Mansions, On the Beach, Tall Story, Psycho, Goodbye Again, The Trial, The Fool Killer, Is Paris Burning?, Pretty Poison, Catch-22, Play It As It Lays, The Last of Sheila, Murder on the Orient Express, Mahogany*, more.

PERKINS, CARL (Tenn.) C&W star and composer ("Blue Suede Shoes"). Onscreen in 1969. IN: *Johnny Cash!*

PERKINS, GIL (S. Cal.) Character. Onscreen from the '50s. IN: *Hans Christian Andersen*, more.

PERKINS, MILLIE (S. Cal.) Leading lady. Introduced in the principal role in *The Diary of Anne Frank*, she still plays leads but in less auspicious movies. Onscreen from 1959. IN: *Wild in the Country, Ensign Pulver, Wild in the Streets, Born to Kill, Lady Coco*, more.

PERKINS, VOLTAIRE (S. Cal.) Character. Onscreen from the '50s. IN: *The Far Horizons, A Man Called Peter, Over-Exposed, Macabre, Compulsion*, more.

PERREAU, GERALD (S. Cal.) The real name of former child star Peter Miles which he used in his earliest movies: *San Diego, I Love You; Possessed*, more. He is, of course, the brother of Gigi Perreau. (See Peter Miles.)

PERREAU, GIGI (S. Cal.) As lovely a little girl —and as talented—as was ever on the screen, she now has four youngsters of her own, two girls, two boys: Gina (the eldest, b. 1964), Tony, Danielle, and Keith (b. 1972). She was first married, at 19, to Frank Gallo, handsome heir of the famous California vineyards, and the father of Gina and Tony. She is now the wife of Gene deRuelle, who was an assistant director on the *Kung Fu* TV series. They live in Studio City in a modest three-bedroom house. She has only the pleasantest memories of her life as a movie moppet, saying, "I had a happy childhood. My parents never pushed me and they kept me in line by reminding me that acting was just my job, like any other job—a plumber or pipe fitter. I'm glad I had it and grateful for the opportunities I enjoyed." Last onscreen in 1967's *Hell on Wheels* (her 36th film), in an ingenue role, Gigi Perreau is in her mid-30s now (b. 1941), and an exceptionally beautiful dark-haired suburbanite. Lately she has signed with an agent for the resumption of the career that

began at 2 in *Madame Curie*. Meanwhile she acts—gratis—in the Theater Arts Program of Los Angeles. This federally funded repertory group performs free at hospitals, churches, and senior-citizen centers in Southern California, and the only word for it, she says, is "Exciting." Onscreen from 1943. IN: *Dark Waters, Two Girls and a Sailor, Mr. Skeffington, The Master Race, Yolanda and the Thief, High Barbaree, Green Dolphin Street, Song of Love, Enchantment* (perhaps her best role), *Roseanna McCoy, My Foolish Heart, Weekend with Father, Bonzo Goes to College; Dance With Me, Henry; Girls Town, Tammy Tell Me True*, more.

PERREAU, JANINE (S. Cal.) Former child actress, now retired, sister of Gigi Perreau. Onscreen from 1947. IN: *Song of Love, The Red Danube, The Redhead and the Cowboy, M, 3 for Bedroom C*, more.

PERRIN, JACQUES (Fr.) Leading man. Onscreen from the '60s. IN: *Girl With a Suitcase, Family Diary, The Sleeping Car Murder, Almost a Man, All the Other Girls Do!, The Young Girls of Rochefort, Z, Donkey Skin*, more.

PERRIN, VIC (S. Cal.) Character. Onscreen from the '50s. IN: *Forever Female, Dragnet, Black Tuesday, The Klansmen*, more.

PERRINE, VALERIE (S. Cal.) Leading lady. Nominated for Best Actress Oscar in *Lenny*. Onscreen in the '70s. IN: *Slaughterhouse-Five, W. C. Fields and Me*, more.

PERRY, BARBARA (S. Cal.) Still active, she now does TV commercials. Onscreen from the '30s. IN: *Counsellor-At-Law*, more.

PERRY, DESMOND (Eng.) Character. Onscreen from the '60s. IN: *Ulysses, Brotherly Love, Paddy*, more.

PERRY, FELTON (S. Cal.) Black support. Onscreen in the '70s. IN: *Medium Cool, The Towering Inferno, Night Call Nurses*, more.

PERRY, FRANK (N.Y.) Director of *David and Lisa, Last Summer*, etc. Onscreen in a character role in 1969. IN: *My Side of the Mountain*.

PERRY, JOAN (S. Cal.) Rich, blonde, and social, she was widowed by Columbia studio chief Harry Cohn, and later was married to and divorced from the late actor Laurence Harvey. There was still later a published report that she and Tab Hunter were engaged, but nothing came of that. Onscreen from 1935. IN: *The*

Case of the Missing Man, Meet Nero Wolfe, The Devil Is Driving, Blind Alley, Good Girls Go to Paris, The Lone Wolf Strikes Out, Maisie Was a Lady, Strange Alibi, Nine Lives Are Not Enough, more, including 1941's *International Squadron,* her last.

PERRY, JOSEPH (S. Cal.) Character. Onscreen from the '60s. IN: *Don't Just Stand There,* more.

PERRY, MARGARET (Colo.) Just 23 when she left the screen, she continued on Broadway until '50—as actress (*The Greatest Show on Earth*), production assistant (*Craig's Wife*), and director (*The Shop at Sly Corner* and *Love Me Long*). Daughter of the famous director Antoinette Perry (for whom the Tony Awards are named), she has two sons and two daughters, all grown. Her three marriages, all ending in divorce, were to newspaper columnist Winsor B. French, actor Burgess Meredith, and artist Paul P. Fanning. Retired now, she lives in Pueblo. Onscreen from 1932. IN: *New Morals for Old; Go West, Young Man;* more.

PERRY, ROGER (S. Cal.) Support. Onscreen from the '60s. IN: *Follow Me, Boys; Heaven With a Gun; Count Yorga, Vampire; The Return of Count Yorga,* more.

PERRY, SCOTT (S. Cal.) Support. Onscreen in the '70s. IN: *Getting Straight,* more.

PERSCHY, MARIA (Fr.) Leading lady. Onscreen from the '60s. IN: *The Password Is Courage, Man's Favorite Sport?, 633 Squadron, The Desperate Ones, Murders in the Rue Morgue,* more.

PERSKY, MARILYN S. (N.Y.) Support. Onscreen in the '70s. IN: *The Effect of Gamma Rays on Man-in-the-Moon Marigolds; Summer Wishes, Winter Dreams;* more.

PERSOFF, NEHEMIAH (N.Y.) Character lead. Onscreen from 1948. IN: *The Naked City, A Double Life, The Harder They Fall, The Wrong Man, Al Capone, Green Mansions, Day of the Outlaw, Fate Is the Hunter, A Global Affair, The Greatest Story Ever Told, Day of the Owl, The Power, Red Sky at Morning, Mrs. Polifax—Spy, Psychic Killer,* more.

PERSSON, ESSY (Swe.) Leading lady. Onscreen from 1966. IN: *I, A Woman; Therese and Isabelle, Mission Stardust, Cry of the Banshee,* more.

PERSSON, MARIA (Swe.) Leading lady. Onscreen in the '70s. IN: *Pippi in the South Seas,* more.

PERTWEE, JON (Eng.) Character. Onscreen from 1939. IN: *Miss Pilgrim's Progress, Murder at the Windmill, Mr. Drake's Duck, Dear Mr. Prohack, The Body Said No, Will Any Gentleman . . .?, Carry On Cleo, The House That Dripped Blood,* more.

PERTWEE, ROLAND (Eng.) British playwright-scriptwriter. Onscreen in the '40s. IN: *The Secret Four, Mister V, They Were Sisters.*

PETERS, AUDREY (N.Y.) Leading lady in TV soap operas. Onscreen in 1959. IN: *Middle of the Night.*

PETERS, BERNADETTE (N.Y.) Comic leading lady. Onscreen in the '70s. IN: *The Longest Yard, Silent Movie.*

PETERS, BROCK (N.Y.) Black character. Onscreen from 1954. IN: *Carmen Jones, Porgy and Bess, To Kill a Mockingbird, Major Dundee, The Pawnbroker, The Incident, P.J., Daring Game, Ace High, The McMasters, Black Girl, Soylent Green, Framed,* more.

PETERS, GEORGE J. (N.Y.) Character. Onscreen from the '60s. IN: *Teenage Mother, The Borgia Stick, Midnight Cowboy, Stiletto, Little Murders, Where's Poppa?, The Hot Rock, Puzzle of a Downfall Child, The Godfather,* more.

PETERS, GORDON (S. Cal.) Support. Onscreen from the '60s. IN: *A Lovely Way to Die,* more.

PETERS, HOUSE, JR. (S. Cal.) Character. Onscreen from the '30s. IN: *Public Cowboy No. 1, Under California Stars, Sheriff of Wichita, Cow Town, Gene Autry and the Mounties, Red Planet Mars, Waco, Black Patch, Inside the Mafia, The Big Night, The Great Sioux Massacre,* more.

PETERS, JEAN (S. Cal.) Less beautiful as she enters her 50s (b. 1926) than when she gave up her career to be Mrs. Howard Hughes—for 14 years—she resumed acting in 1973. Then she starred on Public Television in the Hollywood Television Theatre's production of *Winesburg Ohio,* in a mother role. ("Beautifully realized performance," said the *Hollywood Reporter.* "I don't know if I would want to do a film," she said during the taping, "but this is perfect. Only a few weeks long, right here in Los Angeles—and a marvelous role." To date, she has not acted since. She devotes herself instead to charitable works (was national honorary chairwoman of the Society for Autistic Children recently) and homemaking. Since 1971 she has been married to 20th Century-Fox production executive Stanley L. Hough, whom she met when making her first movie. Plucked from the campus of Ohio State after inadvertently winning a photographic beauty contest (a friend had entered her picture) in 1947, she found herself catapulted to overnight stardom in *Captain From Castile* opposite Tyrone Power. In 18 subsequent movies she played only leads. For two years (1954–56) she was married to young millionaire Stuart Cramer III, who later married Terry Moore, who had been a favorite date of Howard Hughes, whom Jean Peters had dated before marrying Cramer. Of her marriage to the reclusive Hughes, which took place in '57, Jean Peters could assuredly write a book. Almost as certainly she won't. The report—neither confirmed nor denied—is that in the eventual divorce settlement she received a hotel. After she became Mrs. Hughes at 31, she not only retired but dropped completely out of sight. No photograph was ever published of the actress and the billionaire, and in all those years only one was seen of her. That was in 1969 when *Life* magazine managed to snap one of her alone at the opera in Los Angeles. During most of her marriage to Hughes she lived in a heavily guarded mansion near Beverly Hills, spending certain weekends in Las Vegas where Hughes lived. To fill her hours (she has had no children by any of her marriages), she took art courses at U.C.L.A., did door-to-door political polling, and read textbooks for taping by the Braille Institute until "I couldn't stand the sound of my own voice any more." Only columnist Jack Anderson has ever printed intimate details of this strange marriage. In May 1974 he informed his readers: "Hughes kept his last wife, movie actress Jean Peters, on a yo-yo string. He would disappear for long stretches and send her endearing but false messages through his aide William Gay . . . In 1965, he promised to have Thanksgiving dinner with her. But because of his fear of germs, he told her to sit across the room from him. She walked out in a huff. The following year, he persuaded her to join him in Boston where he promised they would settle down. But again, he kept her at across-the-room distance. She put up with it for three days. But when the marriage broke up, he blamed Gay who had merely carried the messages back and forth. Hughes complained bitterly: 'Bill's total indifference and laxity to my pleas for help in my domestic area, voiced urgently to him . . . have resulted in a complete, I am afraid irrevocable loss of my wife . . . I blame Bill completely for this unnecessary debacle.' " Recently the actress was asked what it was *really* like to be married to Howard Hughes. "That," she said, "was and shall remain a matter on which I will have no comment." At this same meeting, reflecting on her life before Howard Hughes, before Hollywood, she said, "I come from East Canton, Ohio,

which had all of 800 population. I liked m small town. I often wonder what my life woul have been like if I had remained there." On screen from 1947. IN: *Deep Waters, It Happen Every Spring, Anne of the Indies, Take Care o My Little Girl, As Young As You Feel, Viv Zapata!, Niagara, Pickup on South Street Blueprint for Murder, Three Coins in the Foun tain, Broken Lance, Apache,* more, includin 1955's *A Man Called Peter,* her most recent to date.

PETERS, KAY (S. Cal.) Support. Onscreen from the '60s. IN: *Flareup, The Seven Minutes, How to Seduce a Woman,* more.

PETERS, KELLY JEAN (S. Cal.) Support. Onscreen in the '70s. IN: *Little Big Man,* more.

PETERS, LAURI (S. Cal.) Support. Onscreen from 1962. IN: *Mr. Hobbs Takes a Vacation, For Love of Ivy,* more.

PETERS, LYNN (S. Cal.) Leading lady. Onscreen in the '70s. IN: *Grave of the Vampire,* more.

PETERS, ROBERTA (N.Y.) Opera star. Onscreen in 1953. IN: *Tonight We Sing.*

PETERS, SCOTT (S. Cal.) Leading man. Onscreen from 1957. IN: *The Amazing Colossal Man, Invasion of the Saucer Men, The Outlaw's Son, Motorcycle Gang, Suicide Battalion, The Canadians, The Girl Hunters,* more.

PETERSEN, PAUL (Conn.) In his 30s now (b. 1944), the former child star of movies and TV (for eight years the son in *The Donna Reed Show*) lives with his wife, Hallie, and small son Brian in a frame house in Westport, and has given up acting. Now he is a successful paperback novelist. Creating a James Bond-type hero, Eric Saveman ("The Smuggler"), he has published eight books to date. When interviewed, he asserted that writing had saved him from drugs, a trap he fell into when fame passed him by. Speaking of his drug-induced "purple haze" years, he said, "I was a full freak. I did all the things that you might expect someone to do who thought his life was over." His life, it seems to him now, has just begun. Onscreen from 1957. IN: *This Could Be the Night, The Monolith Monsters, Houseboat, The Happiest Millionaire, A Time for Killing, Journey to Shiloh,* more.

PETERSON, ARTHUR (S. Cal.) Character. Onscreen from the '60s. IN: *Targets, The Young Animals, Born Wild,* more.

PETERSON, DOROTHY (N.Y.) The "mother" of Edith Fellows, et al., in the "Five Little Peppers'' series of movies, and top support in more than 100 other pix in 17 years in Hollywood, she moved to New York after *The Hagen Girl* in '47 and hasn't been onscreen since. In her 70s now, and looking the same as when in pictures, she lives in Greenwich Village, spends her summers on Fire Island, and acts regularly in soap operas —*As the World Turns, Secret Storm, Edge of Night,* etc. Onscreen from 1930. IN: *Mother's Cry, The Plutocrat, Penrod and Sam, Cabin in the Cotton, So Big, Life Begins, I'm No Angel, Beloved, As the Earth Turns, Peck's Bad Boy, Treasure Island, Society Doctor, The Country Doctor, 52nd Street, Hunted Men, Girls on Probation, Dark Victory, Sabotage, Too Many Husbands, Lillian Russell, Cheers for Miss Bishop, Saboteur, The Moon Is Down, Air Force, Mr. Skeffington, Woman in the Window, Sister Kenny,* more.

PETERSON, GIL (S. Cal.) Support. Onscreen from the '60s. IN: *The Cool Ones,* more.

PETERSON, LENKA (N.Y.) Character. The real-life mother of screen players Glynnis, Kevin, and Darren O'Connor. Onscreen from 1950. IN: *Panic in the Streets, Take Care of My Little Girl, The Phenix City Story, Black Like Me, Homer,* more.

PETERSON, MONICA (S. Cal.) Black leading lady. Onscreen from the '60s. IN: *Changes,* more.

PETIT, PASCALE (Fr.) Leading lady. Onscreen from the '50s. IN: *Witches of Salem, Women Are Weak, The Cheaters, Cross of the Living, Julie the Redhead, A Mistress for the Summer,* more.

PETIT, ROLAND (Fr.) Ballet star and choreographer. Husband of Zizi Jeanmaire. Onscreen from 1952. IN: *Hans Christian Andersen, Black Tights.*

PETRIE, GEORGE (N.Y.) Character. Onscreen from 1944. IN: *Winged Victory, Four Days' Leave, Gypsy, Hud, Wall of Noise,* more.

PETROVA, OLGA (Fla.) Entering her 90s (b. 1886), the English-born *femme fatale* lives luxuriously in Clearwater with husband, Lewis Willoughby, her leading man in plays she did after leaving the screen. Onscreen from 1914. IN: *The Vampire, The Black Butterfly* (one of her first for Louis B. Mayer's new Metro Pictures Corporation, where she was the first star), *The Soul Market, The Eternal Question, The Life Mask* (billed Mme. Petrova), *Tempered Steel,* more.

PETTERSSON, BRIGITTA (Swe.) Leading lady. Onscreen from the '50s. IN: *The Magician, The Virgin Spring, Les Creatures,* more.

PETTERSSON, HJORDIS (Swe.) Support. Onscreen from the '30s. IN: *Froeken Blir Piga, Frustration, Of Love and Lust (A Doll's House), "2," The Cats, The Passion of Anna,* more.

PETTET, JOANNA (S. Cal.) Leading lady. Onscreen from 1966. IN: *The Group, The Night of the Generals, Casino Royale, Blue, The Best House in London, The Long Day's Dying, Catch a Pebble, Welcome to Arrow Beach,* more.

PEVNEY, JOSEPH (S. Cal.) One of the screen's best young "tough" supports, he gave up his acting career in '50 and has since been one of Hollywood's most-in-demand directors —of *Man of a Thousand Faces, Portrait of a Mobster, The Crowded Sky,* etc. Onscreen from 1946. IN: *Nocturne, Body and Soul, The Street With No Name, Thieves' Highway, Outside the Wall,* more.

PFLUG, JO ANN (S. Cal.) Leading lady. Onscreen in the '70s. IN: *M*A*S*H, Catlow, Where Does It Hurt,* more.

PHELAN, BRIAN (Eng.) Support. Onscreen from the '60s. IN: *The Kitchen, Accident; Honeybaby, Honeybaby;* more.

PHELPS, ELEANOR (N.Y.) The beautiful "Charmian" in DeMille's *Cleopatra* ('34) is still regally lovely and blonde in her 70s, and still active professionally. Since her brief movie career, she has appeared in many Broadway plays, including, in recent years, *Garden District, The Disenchanted, Color of Darkness.* Onscreen in the '30s. ALSO IN: *The Count of Monte Cristo* (as "Haydee").

PHILBIN, MARY (S. Cal.) This lovely leading lady of silents, never married, is in her 70s (b. 1903), and lives in quiet seclusion near Hollywood, taking small interest in the community of which she was once such an important part. Onscreen from 1921. IN: *The Blazing Trail, The Temple of Venus, Fifth Avenue Models, The Phantom of the Opera, Surrender, Drums of Love, Love Me and the World Is Mine, Affairs of Hannerl, The Last Performance, The Shannons of Broadway,* more.

PHILBROOK, JAMES (S. Cal.) Support. Onscreen from the '50s. IN: *I Want to Live!, Warlock, The Thin Red Line, Fingers on the Trigger, Drums of Tabu, Son of a Gunfighter,* more.

PHILIPPE, ANDRE (S. Cal.) Support. Onscreen in the '70s. IN: *Alex in Wonderland, Black Belt Jones; Goodbye, Norma Jean*; more.

PHILIPS, LEE (S. Cal.) 20th Century-Fox's young leading man quickly gave up acting and has become one of TV's busiest directors. Onscreen from 1957. IN: *Peyton Place, The Hunters, Middle of the Night*, more, including 1964's *Psychomania*, his most recent to date.

PHILLIPS, BARNEY (S. Cal.) Character. Onscreen from 1953. IN: *Eight Iron Men, A Blueprint for Murder, The Square Jungle, Cry Terror, The Decks Ran Red*, more.

PHILLIPS, CONRAD (Eng.) Leading man. Onscreen from the '50s. IN: *Sons and Lovers, Circus of Horrors, The Shadow of the Cat, Murder She Said, The Murder Game*, more.

PHILLIPS, GORDON (N.Y.) Character. Onscreen from the '60s. IN: *Lilith, Something Wild, Von Richthofen and Brown*, more.

PHILLIPS, JEAN (N.Y.) The Paramount leading lady of the '40s has been married since '44 to playwright Francis (*Out of the Frying Pan*) Swann, has a grown son, is now in her late 50s, and hasn't acted in many years. Onscreen from 1941. IN: *Among the Living, Dr. Broadway, Night in New Orleans*, more.

PHILLIPS, JOBYNA (N. Cal.) Character. Now living and performing in San Francisco. Onscreen from the '60s. IN: *The Boston Strangler, They Call Me Mr. Tibbs, Take the Money and Run, Harold and Maude, Dirty Harry; What's Up, Doc?; The Candidate, The Conversation*, more.

PHILLIPS, JOHN (Eng.) Character. Onscreen from the '40s. IN: *So Goes My Love, Black Angel, Richard III, Romanoff and Juliet, Man in the Moon, The Mouse on the Moon*, more.

PHILLIPS, LESLIE (Eng.) Character. Onscreen from 1936. IN: *The Citadel, Train of Events, The Woman with No Name, Pool of London, As Long As They're Happy, Breaking Through the Sound Barrier, The Barretts of Wimpole Street, Les Girls, Please Turn Over, Doctor in Love, A Coming-Out Party, Crooks Anonymous, Doctor in Trouble*, more.

PHILLIPS, MacKENZIE (S. Cal.) Young leading lady. Daughter of popular music composer John Phillips. Onscreen in the '70s. IN: *American Graffiti, Rafferty and the Gold Dust Twins*.

PHILLIPS, MARGARET (N.Y.) This actress from South Wales was a leading lady on the stage long before her brief movie career, and

continues to be. Onscreen from 1950. IN: *A Life of Her Own* (a commanding performance as the crippled wife of Ray Milland), *The Nun's Story*.

PHILLIPS, MICHELLE (S. Cal.) Leading lady. She has been married to and divorced from both musician John Phillips (hence was MacKenzie Phillips' stepmother a while) and actor Dennis Hopper. Onscreen in the '70s. IN: *The Last Movie, Dillinger*.

PHILLIPS, PAUL (S. Cal.) Character. Onscreen from 1940. IN: *Brother Orchid, Strange Alibi, Nine Lives Are Not Enough*, more.

PHILLIPS, ROBERT (S. Cal.) Support. Onscreen in the '70s. IN: *Darker Than Amber, Gravy Train, The Killing of a Chinese Bookie*, more.

PHILLIPS, ROBIN (Eng.) Leading man. Onscreen from 1967. IN: *Decline and Fall, David Copperfield*, more.

PHILLIPS, SIAN (Eng.) Support. Often in movies starring her husband, Peter O'Toole, she appears in others as well. Onscreen from the '60s. IN: *Becket, Young Cassidy, Laughter in the Dark; Goodbye, Mr. Chips; Murphy's War, Under Milk Wood*, more.

PHILLIPS, WENDELL K. (N.Y.) Character. Onscreen from the '60s. IN: *The Glass Cage*, more.

PHILLPOTS, AMBROSINE (Eng.) Character actress. Onscreen from the '40s. IN: *The Duke Wore Jeans, The Captain's Paradise, Room at the Top, Expresso Bongo, Life at the Top*, more.

PHIPPS, NICHOLAS (Eng.) Supporting actor and screenwriter. Onscreen from 1940. IN: *Spring in Park Lane, Maytime in Mayfair, The Captain's Paradise, Doctor in Love, A Pair of Briefs*—all of which he wrote; also in: *The Intruder, The Iron Petticoat, Orders to Kill, The Pure Hell of St. Trinian's*, more.

PHIPPS, SALLY (N.Y.) Married to and divorced from an heir of the Gimbel's fortune, this leading lady of the late '20s is now in her 60s and has long been retired from acting. Onscreen from 1927. IN: *Bertha, The Sewing Machine Girl; High School Hero, Why Sailors Go Wrong, The News Parade, The One Woman Idea*, more.

PHIPPS, WILLIAM (S. Cal.) Character. Onscreen from 1947. IN: *Crossfire, Desperadoes* of Dodge City, The Man on the Eiffel Tower, Five, War of the Worlds, Julius Caesar, Riot in Cell Block 11, Smoke Signal, Lust for Life, The Brothers Rico, Escape from Red Rock, Gunfight at Abilene, more.

PIAZZA, BEN (S. Cal.) Support. Onscreen from the '50s. IN: The Hanging Tree, No Exit; Tell Me That You Love Me, Junie Moon; more.

PIAZZA, JIM (N.Y.) Support. Onscreen from the '60s. IN: Goodbye, Columbus; Generation; Me, Natalie; more.

PICCOLI, MICHEL (Fr.) Leading man. Onscreen from the '50s. IN: Foxiest Girl in Paris, Sinners of Paris, Contempt, Masquerade, The Sleeping Car Murder, Lady L, Les Creatures, Is Paris Burning?, La Guerre est Fini, Benjamin, Belle de Jour, The Young Girls of Rochefort, Danger Diabolik, La Chamade, The Things of Life, more.

PICERNI, PAUL (S. Cal.) Character; former leading man. Onscreen from 1950. IN: Breakthrough, I Was a Communist for the F.B.I., Force of Arms, Cattle Town, The System, House of Wax, To Hell and Back, Flight to Hong Kong, Miracle in the Rain, Operation Mad Ball, Marjorie Morningstar, The Man Who Died Twice, Torpedo Run, The Young Philadelphians, Che!, Airport, Land Raiders, more.

PICKARD, JOHN (S. Cal.) Character. Onscreen from the '50s. IN: The Gunfighter, Stage to Tucson, Flight to Tangier, Human Desire, The Lone Ranger, The Oklahoman, A Gathering of Eagles, Charro!, Act of Vengeance, more.

PICKENS, SLIM (S. Cal.) Character. Onscreen from the '40s. IN: Border Saddlemates, South Pacific Trail, The Will Rogers Story, The Last Command, The Sheepman, Escort West, A Thunder of Drums, Savage Sam, Dr. Strangelove (as Major T. J. "King" Kong, the bomber pilot; perhaps his best role), Major Dundee, In Harm's Way, The Flim Flam Man, Will Penny, The Ballad of Cable Hogue, The Apple Dumpling Gang, Rancho Deluxe, White Line Fever, Hawmps, more.

PICKFORD, MARY (S. Cal.) Legendary star. Won the Best Actress Oscar in Coquette, her first talking picture, after which she made but three more before retiring: The Taming of the Shrew, Kiki, and, in 1933, Secrets. At the Academy Awards ceremony in the spring of 1976, she received a special honorary award "in recognition of her unique contribution to the film industry and the development of film as an ar-

tistic medium." She is in her 80s now (b. 1893), frail and ailing, no longer the vivacious spirit who was the movies' first great woman star, who reigned unchallenged as Queen of the Screen for more than two decades. She has a nurse in constant attendance at Pickfair. And she sees almost no one—except husband (since 1937) Buddy Rogers. Exceptions are Lillian Gish, whose introduction into movies she engineered, and Douglas Fairbanks Jr., once her stepson and to whom she remains deeply devoted. During a recent visit of his, she allowed Fairbanks to give the first party in many years at Pickfair. Only one of the famous guests, Pearl Bailey, was admitted to her bedroom for a chat. She remains secluded in her upstairs room with its five windows overlooking all of Los Angeles, thankful she can again enjoy this view and read—with heavy glasses—her favorite book, The Runner's Bible. "I had an operation. Double cataracts," she said not long ago. "That was upsetting. More to my nerves than to my eyes." In 1971, while granting no person-to-person interviews, she did for a while accept phone calls from reporters, brief ones, each day. Film festivals, comprised of 11 of her greatest hits, were then being held all over the world. Oddly, of her three personal favorites— Suds, Secrets and Little Lord Fauntleroy—only the latter was among those included in the festival films. Nor was Coquette. Some of those shown: Pollyanna, Daddy Long Legs, Sparrows, and her last silent film, My Best Girl, co-starring Buddy Rogers. ("She was My Best Girl in 1927 and she's still my best girl," says Rogers today.) To launch the Los Angeles film festival, Buddy Rogers invited members of the press on three occasions to Pickfair where Mary Pickford greeted them—via a tape-recorded speech, her voice so fragile as to leave the reporters shaken. One, Aljean Harmetz, described it as "cracked and faded, like a piece of velvet ruined by the sun. It has a musty, unused sound that is painful to hear." But this reporter, and others, speaking with her on the phone, found that while her voice may be pallid, her views and personality are as astringent as ever. On Hollywood—"I saw Hollywood born and I've seen it die . . . We didn't know it would change so drastically. And now Hollywood is dead." On TV—"I like The Beverly Hillbillies and Bonanza. That Lorne Greene on Bonanza looks a lot like my Buddy." On her dissatisfaction with most of her films—"I can't stand that sticky stuff. I got so tired of being a Pollyanna." Also, "I never liked any one of my pictures in its entirety." On actors performing nude—"The public wants spectaculars, nudity. But I'm pretty disgusted with it . . . And where do they go from here?" On Charlie Chaplin (he, Douglas Fairbanks, and she founded United Artists)—"That obstinate, suspicious, egocentric, maddening, and lovable genius of a problem child." *On her thwarted intention to destroy all her films* (those which she personally owns) —"Lillian Gish and I had the only argument we ever had. 'Don't you dare do that, Mary. They don't belong to you; they belong to the public. The public will be very upset.' I said, 'Well, time's passing and people will compare me to modern actresses, and I just don't want them to do it.' I felt the films had served their purpose and I just wanted to get rid of them and I decided to burn them." (Instead, with Buddy Rogers' aid, Mary Pickford spent a Fortune restoring 29 of her 78 feature films, and 28 of her shorts, and donated another 51 shorts to the Library of Congress, which promised to restore them also.) *On Women's Lib*—"I don't go along with the women's liberation movement. Not at all. I don't see why women aren't happy just being feminine. Let the men take care of things." (Libbers, though, might rightfully answer back that it wasn't by relying on men that Mary Pickford, a brilliant business woman, became the multimillionaire she is.) *On her reluctance now to see her old films*—"It made me so sad to look at them, you know. Because so many . . . so many . . . had died. Including my own family. And my friends." Furthermore, "I know every one of my films inch by inch." *On her stature as an actress*—"I know I'm an artist, and that's not being arrogant, because talent comes from God." *On her retirement*—"I always said I would retire when I couldn't play little girls any more, when I couldn't do what I wanted to." So, at 40, Mary Pickford, "America's Sweetheart," by far the greatest female star of silents, walked away from her career. Born Gladys Smith in Toronto, she had acted onstage at 5, had no real childhood or formal education (one winter's schooling), became a screen player at 16, and, under D. W. Griffith's tutelage, an almost immediate star. Though she made a lifelong career of playing children and very young adults (with exceptions), she experienced two unsuccessful marriages, which ended in divorce, to stars Owen Moore and Douglas Fairbanks. Four years after retirement, she embarked on her long-lasting third one. In the decades since leaving the screen, she has devoted herself to her husband, her house, her countless charities, particularly the Motion Picture Relief Fund—"my baby." Today, her health failing, though she remains philosophical and cheerful, grievously disillusioned by the industry she adored, tiny Mary Pickford rests quietly in her upstairs room, or sometimes, when the weather is fine, takes the sun in the garden of her fabled estate. Wherever she is, "America's Sweetheart," its beloved "little girl" now grown old, is surrounded by golden memories—many of them, she must know, shared by millions the world over. On-screen from 1909. IN: *Her First Biscuits* (debut), *The Lonely Villa, The Little Darling, The Broken Locket, Ramona, Muggsy's First Sweetheart, Wilful Peggy, The Dream, For Her Brother's Sake, The Mender of Nets, The New York Hat, A Good Little Devil, Tess of the Storm Country, Such a Little Queen, Cinderella; Fanchon, the Cricket; A Girl of Yesterday, Madame Butterfly, Poor Little Peppina, Hulda from Holland, The Poor Little Rich Girl, The Little American, Rebecca of Sunnybrook Farm, A Little Princess, Stella Maris, M'Liss, Captain Kidd Jr., The Heart O' The Hills, Pollyanna, Through the Back Door, Dorothy Vernon of Haddon Hall, Little Annie Rooney,* more.

PICKLES, CHRISTINA (N.Y.) Leading lady. Onscreen in 1974. IN: *Seizure.*

PICKLES, VIVIAN (Eng.) Character. Onscreen from the '60s. IN: *Sunday Bloody Sunday, Nicholas and Alexandra, Harold and Maude,* more.

PICKLES, WILFRED (Eng.) Character. Onscreen from the '60s. IN: *Billy Liar, The Family Way,* more.

PICKUP, RONALD (Eng.) Support. Onscreen from 1970. IN: *Three Sisters,* more.

PICON, MOLLY (N.Y.) The beloved character star of the Yiddish theater became a widow in 1975 when her husband (since 1919), stage producer-writer-star Jacob Kalich, died at 83. Onscreen from 1937. IN: *Yiddle with His Fiddle* and *Mamele: Little Mothers* (both made in Poland), *Come Blow Your Horn, Fiddler on the Roof, For Pete's Sake.*

PIDGEON, WALTER (S. Cal.) Star. Nominated for Best Actor Oscar in *Mrs. Miniver* and *Madame Curie.* Handsome still as he approaches his 80s (b. 1897), he remains active in movies. Onscreen from 1925. IN: *Old Loves and New, The Gorilla, Turn Back the Hours, Melody of Love, Bride of the Regiment, Kiss Me Again, Big Brown Eyes, Saratoga, Shopworn Angel, Too Hot to Handle, Stronger Than Desire; Nick Carter, Master Detective; It's a Date, Man Hunt, How Green Was My Valley, Blossoms in the Dust* (the first of many in which he costarred with Greer Garson), *White Cargo, Mrs. Parkington, Holiday in Mexico, If Winter Comes, Command Decision, That Forsyte Woman, The Bad and the Beautiful, Executive Suite, Men of the Fighting Lady, Hit the Deck, The Rack, Voyage to the Bottom of the Sea, Advise and Consent, Funny Girl, Skyjacked, Harry in Your Pocket, Two Minute Warning,* more.

PIERCE, JAMES (S. Cal.) The man who played Tarzan just once onscreen, in 1927's *Tarzan and the Golden Lion*, produced by Joseph Kennedy, says nothing would please him more than to see this movie again. But it is, he has found, one of Hollywood's "lost" films—no print is known to exist. He says his best memories of it are that the censors, refusing to let him go barechested, forced him to wear a strap across his upper torso—and that he was paid $75 a week to star in it. He made more in other movies. And he did considerably better when for five years he starred on a syndicated radio show as Edgar Rice Burroughs' world-famous Apeman. For many years, until her death, he was also married to Burroughs' daughter, Joan. It is by virtue of this family connection that Pierce's Tarzan association continues to this day—he is an active member of the board of directors of Edgar Rice Burroughs Inc., the exclusive licensing agency for any item utilizing the Tarzan name. Said to be the oldest living movie Tarzan —he was born in 1905—Pierce is today big, erect, white-haired, and, as the phrase went when he was young, still a "fine figure of a man." Onscreen from the mid-20s. IN: *Jesse James, Ladies of the Mob, Horsefeathers*, more.

PIERCE, MAGGIE (S. Cal.) Leading lady. Onscreen from 1962. IN: *Cattle King, Tales of Terror, The Fastest Guitar Alive*, more.

PILBEAM, NOVA, (Eng.) England's greatest teen female star is in her 50s (b. 1919), has enjoyed an active stage career, but has made no movies since the 1950s. Her first husband, Penrose Tennyson, was killed in WW II; she has since been married to Alexander Whyte. Onscreen from 1934. IN: *Little Friend* (her first and best performance), *The Man Who Knew Too Much, Tudor Rose, Nine Days a Queen, The Girl Was Young, Spring Meeting, Pastor Hall, Banana Ridge, Next of Kin, The Yellow Canary, This Man Is Mine, Three Weird Sisters, The Devil's Plot*, more.

PINE, PHILIP (S. Cal.) Support. Onscreen from 1949. IN: *The Set-Up, My Foolish Heart, Under the Gun, The Wild Blue Yonder, Hoodlum Empire, Dead Heat on a Merry-Go-Round, Project X; Hook, Line and Sinker;* more.

PINE, VIRGINIA (N.Y.) As publicized for having been George Raft's long-term girl friend as for her roles, this actress—real name Virginia Peine—has been married since '72 to Gen. John B. Coulter, USA-Retired, now a stockbroker, who was the widower of actress Constance Bennett. At their marriage in Palm Springs, their attendants were Miss Pine's daughter, Joan (often photographed as a little girl with Raft and her mother), and her husband, young real estate tycoon David Muss. The wedding was the fifth for the former actress. Among her previous husbands were Richard Lehmann, owner of the Fair department store in Chicago; the late writer Quentin Reynolds; and the late Byron C. Foy, a Chrysler Corporation vice president, whose widow she was. The actress and her present husband have homes in both New York City and Southampton. Onscreen in the '30s. IN: *Dr. Monica*, more.

PINNEY, CHARLES (N.Y.) Character. Onscreen in the '70s. IN: *Cold Turkey*, more.

PINSENT, GORDON (S. Cal.) Support. Onscreen from the '60s. IN: *The Thomas Crown Affair, The Forbin Project, Newman's Law*, more.

PINTA, PAMELA (N.Y.) Juvenile. Onscreen in the '70s. IN: *The War Between Men and Women*, more.

PIPER, FREDERICK (Eng.) Character. Onscreen from the '30s. IN: *Jamaica Inn, The October Man, My Brother's Keeper, Pink String and Sealing Wax, The Lavender Hill Mob, Brandy for the Parson, The Stranger in Between, One Way Pendulum*, more.

PITHEY, WENSLEY (Eng.) Character. Onscreen from the '40s. IN: *Guilt Is My Shadow, Oliver!, Oh! What a Lovely War*, more.

PITLIK, NOAM (S. Cal.) Support. Onscreen from the '60s. IN: *The Hallelujah Trail, The Big Bounce, The Front Page*, more.

PITT, INGRID (Eng.) Leading lady. Onscreen from the '60s. IN: *Where Eagles Dare, The Vampire Lovers, Countess Dracula*, more.

PIZZA, PATT (N.Y.) Character. Onscreen from the '60s. IN: *The Hustler*, more.

PLANCO, GEORGE (N.Y.) Leading man in TV soap operas. Onscreen in the '70s. IN: *Hi, Mom!*, more.

PLANK, MELINDA (N.Y.) Leading lady in TV soap operas. Onscreen from the '60s. IN: *Greenwich Village Story*.

PLATT, ALMA (S. Cal.) Character. Onscreen from the '50s. IN: *Johnny Holiday*, more.

PLATT, HOWARD (S. Cal.) Support. Onscreen in the '70s. IN: *T.R. Baskin, Newman's Law, Three the Hard Way, The Great Scout & Cathouse Thursday*, more.

PLATT, LOUISE (N.Y.) The actress who made an indelible impression as the pregnant Mrs. Mallory in the John Ford classic *Stagecoach* gave up her movie career in 1942. Divorced from stage director-producer Jed Harris in '44, by whom she has a married daughter, she last acted on Broadway in a play, *The Traitors* ('49), produced by her ex-husband. Except for some "live" TV work in the '50s, she has not performed since. For well over two decades she has been married to Stanley Gould, who was Jed Harris' stage manager and later taught drama at a Long Island college. By him she also has a grown daughter, a professional painter. Retired now, in her early 60s (b. 1915), the former actress lives with her husband in Cutchogue, Long Island. Onscreen from 1938. IN: *I Met My Love Again, Spawn of the North, Tell No Tales, Captain Caution, Forgotten Girls, Street of Chance.*

PLATT, MARC (Fla.) The redheaded dancer-actor, popular in the '40s, has lately lived in Cape Coral, is in his 60s (b. 1913), and has been professionally inactive for some time. Onscreen from 1945. IN: *Tonight and Every Night, Tars and Spars, Down to Earth, The Swordsman, When a Girl's Beautiful, Seven Brides for Seven Brothers, Oklahoma!*, more.

PLAYTEN, ALICE (N.Y.) Comic leading lady. Onscreen in the '70s. IN: *Who Killed Mary What'sername?*, more.

PLEASENCE, ANGELA (Eng.) Support. Daughter of Donald Pleasence. Onscreen from the '60s. IN: *Here We Go Round the Mulberry Bush*, more.

PLEASENCE, DONALD (Eng.) Character. Onscreen from 1952. IN: *The Big Day, 1984, A Tale of Two Cities, Look Back in Anger, Sons and Lovers, The Horsemasters, Lisa, The Inspector, The Caretaker, The Great Escape, Fantastic Voyage, You Only Live Twice, Night of the Generals, Will Penny, Outback, Escape to Witch Mountain, Hearts of the West, The Devil Within Her, The Devil's Men, The Passover Plot, The Last Tycoon*, more.

PLESHETTE, JOHN (S. Cal.) Support. Onscreen in the '70s. IN: *End of the Road*, more.

PLESHETTE, SUZANNE (S. Cal.) Costar. Onscreen from 1958. IN: *The Geisha Boy, Rome Adventure* (with Troy Donahue who became her first husband; she is now married to businessman Tom Gallagher), *The Birds, A Distant Trumpet, A Rage to Live, Youngblood Hawke, The Ugly Dachshund, Mister Buddwing, The Adventures of Bullwhip Griffin, Bluebeard's Ghost, The Power, Suppose They Gave a War and Nobody Came?; If It's Tuesday, This Must Be Belgium; Support Your Local Gunfighter*, more.

PLIMTPON, GEORGE (N.Y.) Writer-TV personality-editor-actor. Onscreen in 1968. IN: *Beyond the Law.*

PLIMPTON, SHELLEY (N.Y.) Leading lady. Onscreen in the '70s. IN: *Glen and Randa*, more.

PLISETSKAYA, MAYA (Rus.) Ballet star. Onscreen from 1954. IN: *Stars of the Russian Ballet, Swan Lake, Khovanshchina, The Little Humpbacked Horse, Anna Karenina*, more.

PLOWRIGHT, HILDA (Eng.) Character. Onscreen from the '30s. IN: *Partners of the Plains, Cafe Society, Raffles, Separate Tables*, more.

PLOWRIGHT, JOAN (Eng.) Leading lady. Wife of Sir Laurence Olivier and the mother of his three young children. Onscreen from the '50s. IN: *Moby Dick, Time Without Pity, The Entertainer* (with her husband, playing his daughter), *Three Sisters*, more.

PLUMLEY, DON (N.Y.) Support. Onscreen in the '70s. IN: *The Hospital, A Change in the Wind*, more.

PLUMMER, CHRISTOPHER (N.Y.) Leading man. Onscreen from 1958. IN: *Wind Across the Everglades, Stage Struck, The Sound of Music, Inside Daisy Clover, Night of the Generals, Oedipus the King, Lock Up Your Daughters, Nobody Runs Forever, The Battle of Britain, The Royal Hunt of the Sun, Waterloo, Conduct Unbecoming, The Return of the Pink Panther, The Man Who Would be King, Assassination in Sarajevo*, more.

PLUNKETT, PATRICIA (Eng.) Leading lady. Inactive in movies now. Onscreen from the '40s. IN: *It Always Rains on Sunday, Murder Without Crime, The Story of Mandy, Landfall, Dunkirk*, more.

PODESTA, ROSSANA (It.) The Italian leading lady starred by Warners in *Helen of Troy* didn't make it big in the States, but, still beautiful (and brunette now) in her 40s (b. 1934), remains highly popular in films made in her homeland. Onscreen from 1953. IN: *Luxury Girls, Ulysses, Raw Wind in Eden, Temptation, The Slave of Rome, Sodom and Gomorrah, Alone Against Rome, The Golden Arrow, Seven Golden Men, Man of the Year (Homo Eroticus)*, more.

361

POHLMANN, ERIC (Eng.) Character. Onscreen from 1950. IN: *State Secret, Mogambo, Flame and the Flesh, Gentlemen Marry Brunettes, Quentin Durward, Lust for Life, Fire Down Below, I Accuse!, Across the Bridge, Elephant Gun, John Paul Jones, Cairo, 55 Days at Peking, Those Magnificent Men in Their Flying Machines, The Horsemen, The Return of the Pink Panther*, more.

POITIER, SIDNEY (Bahamas) Black star. Won Best Actor Oscar in *Lilies of the Field*. Nominated in the same category in *The Defiant Ones*. When not working or "seeing the world and meeting people," the actor makes his home in the Bahamas, not far from his boyhood home. In 1976, in Los Angeles, he was married (his second time) to actress Joanna Shimkus, his leading lady in *The Lost Man*, by whom he has two young children. Onscreen from 1949. IN: *No Way Out, Cry the Beloved Country; Go, Man, Go; The Blackboard Jungle, Edge of the City, Something of Value, Porgy and Bess, A Raisin in the Sun, Paris Blues, Pressure Point, The Greatest Story Ever Told, The Bedford Incident, A Patch of Blue, The Slender Thread, In the Heat of the Night, To Sir With Love, Guess Who's Coming to Dinner, For the Love of Ivy, They Call Me Mr. Tibbs, The Organization, Buck and the Preacher, Let's Do It Again, The Wilby Conspiracy*, more.

POLANSKY, ROMAN (Eng.) The famous director (*Rosemary's Baby, Chinatown*, etc.) began as an actor and still performs occasionally. Onscreen in his native Poland from 1953. IN: *Three Stories, The Magic Cycle, Wrecks, See You in the Morning, A Generation, Innocent Sorcerers, Samson*, more. Onscreen internationally from the '60s. IN: *The Fearless Vampire Killers, or Pardon Me But Your Teeth Are in My Neck; Chinatown, The Tenant*, more.

POLEN, NAT (N.Y.) Character; former bigband jazz drummer. Now popular in the TV soap opera *As the World Turns*. Onscreen as a drummer in 1942. IN: *Seven Days' Leave, Behind the Eight Ball*. Onscreen as an actor in the '70s. IN: *Across 110th Street*, more.

POLITE, CHARLENE (S. Cal.) Support. Onscreen in the '70s. IN: *Memory of Us*, more.

POLLARD, MICHAEL J. (S. Cal.) Costar. Nominated for Best Supporting Actor Oscar in *Bonnie and Clyde*. Onscreen from 1962. IN: *Hemingway's Adventures of a Young Man, The Stripper, Summer Magic, The Wild Angels, Caprice, Enter Laughing; The Russians Are Coming, The Russians Are Coming; Jigsaw, August/ September, Hannibal Brooks, Little Fauss and Big Halsy, Dirty Little Billy*, more.

POLLOCK, DEE (S. Cal.) Supporting actor. Onscreen from 1952. IN: *Beware My Lovely, It Grows on Trees, Park Row, Carousel, The Wayward Bus, Take a Giant Step, Kelly's Heroes*, more.

POLLOCK, ELLEN (Eng.) Character. Onscreen from 1927. IN: *Moulin Rouge, The Street Singer, Non-Stop New York, Sons of the Sea, Kiss the Bride Goodbye, Something in the City, To Have and to Hold, The Galloping Major, The Time of His Life*, more.

POLLOCK, NANCY R. (N.Y.) Character. Onscreen from 1959. IN: *The Last Angry Man, Go Naked in the World, The Pawnbroker, The Best of Friends*, more.

PONDEROSO, LOUIS (N.Y.) Support. Onscreen from the '60s. IN: *Charly*, more.

POOLE, ROY (S. Cal.) Character. Onscreen from the '60s. IN: *Experiment in Terror, Up the Down Staircase*, more.

POOLEY, OLAF (Eng.) Character. Onscreen from 1945. IN: *Penny and the Pownall Case, The Huggetts Abroad, She Shall Have Murder, Hell Is Sold Out, Gift Horse, The Woman's Angle, Top Secret, The Gamma People, Windom's Way*, more.

POPE, PEGGY (S. Cal.) Support. Onscreen in the '70s. IN: *Made for Each Other; Hail, Hero;* more.

POPWELL, ALBERT (S. Cal.) Black support. Onscreen from the '60s. IN: *Journey to Shiloh, The Peacekillers, The Single Girls*, more.

POPWELL, JOHNNY (Ga.) Black support. Life sometimes imitates art. In the movie *The Heart Is a Lonely Hunter*, this actor played Cicely Tyson's kid brother Willie, who was sent to prison in Georgia on an assault with a deadly weapon conviction. In real life, in 1975, he was convicted of involuntary manslaughter (the charge growing out of a street shooting in Atlanta in '72) and sentenced to 10 years in prison —in Georgia. Onscreen from the '60s. ALSO IN: *Challenge*, more.

PORCELLI, FRED (N.Y.) Character. Onscreen from the '50s. IN: *A Face in the Crowd, Four Boys and a Gun, Middle of the Night*, more.

POREL, MARC (S. Cal.) Leading man. Onscreen from the '60s. IN: *Secret World, The Sicilian Clan, Road to Salina*, more.

PORTER, DON (S. Cal.) Character; former leading man. Onscreen from 1942. IN: *Eagle*

Squadron, Who Done It?, Eyes of the Underworld, Danger Woman, She-Wolf of London, Wild Beauty, Buck Privates Come Home, 711 Ocean Drive, The Turning Point, Cripple Creek, Our Miss Brooks, Bachelor in Paradise, Gidget Goes to Rome; Live a Little, Steal a Lot; The Candidate, Forty Carats, White Line Fever, more.

PORTER, ERIC (Eng.) Support. Onscreen from the '60s. IN: The Pumpkin Eater, The Fall of the Roman Empire, The Heroes of Telemark, Kaleidoscope, Anthony and Cleopatra, Nicholas and Alexandra, The Day of the Jackal, more.

PORTER, J. ROBERT (S. Cal.) Character. Onscreen from the '60s. IN: Firecreek, Mackenna's Gold, The Klansmen, more.

PORTER, JEAN (S. Cal.) In her 50s she is much as she was when one of MGM's most promising young stars in the '40s—a vivacious half-pint, five feet tall and weighing just a bit over 100 pounds. She has been married since '48 to ace director Edward Dmytryk—they met when she had a supporting role in his Till the End of Time—and her life with him has not been without drama. Appearing before the House Committee on Un-American Activities in '47, and refusing to answer whether he was or had been a Communist, Dmytryk was labeled one of the "Hollywood Ten." No Hollywood studio would hire him then so he and Jean moved to England where he could still work. There, in '49, the first of their three children, Richard Edward, was born. In '50, after a trial in Washington, Jean's husband was convicted of contempt of Congress, fined $1,000, and sentenced to six months in prison. She stood staunchly by him through this, giving up their home and moving with the baby into a small rented apartment. Dmytryk appeared before the committee again in the spring of '51 as a "friendly" witness, and has since explained his change of heart by saying: "I learned more about communism in the three and a half years I was one of the 'Hollywood Ten' than I ever learned when I was actually a party member. And what I learned wasn't good." The second of his and Jean's children, Victoria Jean, was born in the autumn of '51, with their other daughter, Rebecca, coming along exactly 10 years later. The director has long since been able to resume his career—directing Raintree County, Shalako, etc.—as though there had been no interruption. But those early years of his and Jean's marriage were dark ones and it is unlikely they will ever forget them. The Dmytryks maintain a beautiful permanent home in Bel Air but they have continued to spend long periods in Rome, London, and other cities

abroad where he has made films. And somehow, the perky actress from Cisco, Texas, who has not been onscreen since 1955's The Left Hand of God (directed by her husband), has found time recently to write a published novel, Wake the Devil. Onscreen from 1942. IN: Heart of the Rio Grande, Fall In!, The Youngest Profession, That Nazty Nuisance, San Fernando Valley, Andy Hardy's Blonde Trouble, Bathing Beauty, Thrill of a Romance, Twice Blessed; What Next, Corporal Hargrove?; That Hagen Girl, Two Blondes and a Redhead, Little Miss Broadway, Cry Danger, G.I. Jane, Kentucky Jubilee, Racing Blood, more.

PORTER, LILLIAN (S. Cal.) The dark-haired beauty who played second leads in many has been married for many years to former cowboy star Russell Hayden, and is retired. Onscreen from 1938. IN: Josette; Stop, Look and Love; Tin Pan Alley, That Night in Rio, Song of the Islands, more. (See Russell Hayden.)

PORTER, LULU (S. Cal.) Singer-actress; inactive lately. Onscreen in 1964. IN: The Brass Bottle.

PORTER, NYREE DAWN (Eng.) Leading lady. Onscreen from the '60s. IN: Two Left Feet, Jane Eyre, The House That Dripped Blood, more.

POST, WILLIAM, JR. (N.Y.) In his 60s and living in New York, the leading man of movies returned to the stage—where he had begun his career in 1924—and has since been a character actor both on Broadway and in TV dramas. Onscreen from 1931. IN: The Black Camel, Secret Service, Mr. and Mrs. North, Ship Ahoy, Pacific Rendezvous, Sherlock Holmes and the Secret Weapon, The Moon Is Down; Roger Touhy, Gangster; Bride by Mistake, Experiment Perilous, The House on 92nd Street, more, including Call Northside 777, his most recent to date.

POSTA, ADRIENNE (Eng.) Support; former juvenile (b. 1948). Onscreen from the '50s. IN: No Time for Tears, To Sir With Love, Up the Junction, Percy, Up Pompeii, more.

POSTON, TOM (N.Y.) Support. Onscreen from 1953. IN: The City That Never Sleeps, Zotz!, The Old Dark House, Soldier in the Rain, Cold Turkey, The Happy Hooker, more. (See Jean Sullivan.)

POTTER, BETTY (Eng.) Support. Onscreen in the '40s. IN: Stairway to Heaven, more.

POTTER, BOB (S. Cal.) Support. Onscreen in the '70s. IN: Dirty O'Neil, more.

POTTER, MARTIN (Eng.) Leading man. On-screen in the '70s. IN: *Fellini Satyricon, Goodbye Gemini, Nicholas and Alexandra, Craze*, more.

POTTER, MAUREEN (Eng.) Support. Onscreen from the '50s. IN: *The Rising of the Moon, Gideon of Scotland Yard, Ulysses*, more.

POTTS, NELL (Conn.) The screen name used by the adolescent daughter of Paul Newman and Joanne Woodward when she made her debut playing the daughter of her real-life mother. Onscreen in 1968. IN: *Rachel, Rachel*.

POULTON, MABEL (Eng.) The former leading lady is in her 70s (b. 1905) and has been retired for decades. Onscreen from 1924. IN: *The Heart of an Actress, Palais de Dance, Not Quite a Lady, The Constant Nymph, Escape, Children of Chance*, more.

POVAH, PHYLLIS (N.Y.) The character actress who was Phyllis Potter in *The Women*, and was later in several pix in addition to her long stage career, retired from acting after the '59 movie *Happy Anniversary*. Now in her 70s, she leads a highly social life in Port Washington, Long Island. Long married to business executive Henry E. Drayton, she is the mother of a son and daughter, and the grandmother of several children. Onscreen from 1939. IN: *Let's Face It, The Marrying Kind, Pat and Mike*, more.

POWELL, ADDISON (N.Y.) Character. Onscreen from the '50s. IN: *The Mating Game, In the French Style, The Thomas Crown Affair*, more.

POWELL, DICK, JR. (S. Cal.) Support. Son of June Allyson and Dick Powell. Onscreen in 1975 portraying his crooner-actor father. IN: *Day of the Locust*.

POWELL, ELEANOR (S. Cal.) The movies' nonpareil tap dancer is in her 60s (b. 1910 or 1912; reference sources differ), heavier than in her prime and the once-chestnut locks are silver-blonde now, but the twinkle in her blue eyes and the warmth of her dimpled smile—nothing changes her. Though she still rehearses daily, it's been well over a decade since "The World's Greatest Female Tap Dancer" (title accorded her in 1928 by the Dancing Masters of America) put away her tap shoes. But 1964, the last year she danced professionally, was a very good year for Eleanor Powell. She did an SRO nightclub engagement at Manhattan's Latin Quarter, a guest-star stint in hometown Springfield, Mass. (at the Storrowton Mu-

sic Fair), another on TV's *Hollywood Palace*, and gave a command performance in Monaco for Princess Grace. Her "retirement" has not stopped the producers of *No, No, Nanette*, who had offered her the lead in the touring company of that musical, from urging her to star in a projected revival of *Pal Joey*. Causing her to hesitate is that she has gone into real estate in Los Angeles, as an equal partner with her onetime press agent Jimmy Juris in the Crestview Escrow firm. Besides, she has already staged one greatly successful comeback. That was in 1961, at the behest of her then-15-year-old son Peter, who had never seen her dance professionally. She was then two years divorced from Glenn Ford after a marriage (her only one) spanning 16 years (1943–59). The moment was "right" for her to get back into action. Peter had his opportunity to see her perform at the top of her sensational form in the better clubs in Las Vegas and New York, as well as on several leading TV shows. During her years as Mrs. Glenn Ford she seldom worked. She did two movies and three brief stage engagements. That was it, except for a religious TV series she did for NBC (1953–56), *Faith of Our Children*, which won five Emmys and the National Conference of Christians and Jews Seventh Annual Brother Award. This program, though, an outgrowth of her real-life role of a Presbyterian Sunday School teacher, she never regarded as "work." It was for home and family that she gave up her career. Son Peter, married now, is a Hollywood dialogue director, after having tried acting and a recording career, and deciding against them. Considering his heritage, it would have been unusual for Peter to have rejected a show business career totally. In their teens, his parents both were already professional entertainers—indeed, Eleanor Powell, who had begun as a child dancer, was already a Broadway star. As for their movie careers, it may come as a surprise to Powell fans when they realize that, in contrast to Glenn Ford's 140-plus movies to date, their favorite appeared in only 13 motion pictures—and two of those (*Thousands Cheer* and *The Duchess of Idaho*) were mere guest-star stints. Perhaps it proves what a lasting impression one can make by tapping away on a set of mammoth drums—if one is certifiably "The Greatest." Onscreen from 1935. IN: *George White's Scandals of 1935, Broadway Melody of 1936, Born to Dance, Rosalie, Broadway Melody of 1938, Honolulu, Broadway Melody of 1940, Lady Be Good, Ship Ahoy, I Dood It, Sensations of 1945*, and the two mentioned above.

POWELL, JANE (S. Cal.) Petite, pretty, and incredibly youthful in her 40s (b. 1929), the song star, three times married and divorced and the mother of three, staged a sensational comeback in this decade on Broadway. That was when she replaced Debbie Reynolds in the musical *Irene*. Onscreen from 1944. IN: *Song of the Open Road, Holiday in Mexico, Three Daring Daughters, Luxury Liner, A Date with Judy, Nancy Goes to Rio, Two Weeks with Love, Royal Wedding; Rich, Young and Pretty; Small Town Girl, Seven Brides for Seven Brothers, Deep in My Heart, Athena, Hit the Deck*, more, including 1958's *Enchanted Island*, her most recent to date.

POWELL, LOVELADY (N.Y.) Support. Onscreen in the '70s. IN: *I Never Sang for My Father*, more.

POWELL, MEL (S. Cal.) The musician-husband of Martha Scott. Onscreen in 1948. IN: *A Song Is Born*.

POWELL, ROBERT (Eng.) Leading man. Onscreen in the '70s. IN: *Running Scared, Asylum*, more.

POWELL, WILLIAM (S. Cal.) Star. Nominated for Best Actor Oscar in *The Thin Man, My Man Godfrey, Life With Father*. He is old now (b. 1892), not in the best of health, and entitled to be a bit testy. Last onscreen in 1955's *Mister Roberts*, he is still married to third wife (since 1940) Diana Lewis, and lives in somewhat reclusive retirement in Palm Springs. He and Myrna Loy, his colleague in all those "Thin Man" movies as well as others, who haven't met face to face in years, still talk occasionally on the phone reexperiencing "the good old days." Onscreen from 1922. IN: *Sherlock Holmes, Under the Red Robe, Too Many Kisses, Sea Horses, Aloma of the South Seas, Beau Geste, The Great Gatsby, Special Delivery, Senorita, The Last Command, Beau Sabreur, Forgotten Faces, The Canary Murder Case, The Greene Murder Case, For the Defense, Man of the World, Dishonored, One Way Passage, Manhattan Melodrama, Evelyn Prentice, Reckless* (with his lost love, Jean Harlow), *Libeled Lady, The Great Ziegfeld, The Emperor's Candlesticks, The Baroness and the Butler, Love Crazy, Crossroads, The Heavenly Body, The Hoodlum Saint, The Senator Was Indiscreet, Mr. Peabody and the Mermaid, Dancing in the Dark, It's a Big Country, The Girl Who Had Everything, How to Marry a Millionaire*, more. (See Diana Lewis.)

POWER, ROMINA (It.) Leading lady in Italian-made films. Daughter of Tyrone Power and Linda Christian. Onscreen from 1968. IN: *24 Hours in a Woman's Life*, more.

POWERS, BEVERLY (S. Cal.) Leading lady. Onscreen from the '60s. IN: *More Dead Than Alive, Like a Crow on a June Bug*, more.

POWERS, MALA (S. Cal.) *The Doomsday Machine* ('73) and *Six Tickets to Hell*, filmed in Buenos Aires in '75, marked her return to the screen after several years in television. A brunette knockout still, in her 40s (b. 1931), she has been married since '70 (her only marriage) to young millionaire book publisher—and New York Social Register-listed—M. Hughes Miller. They live on a woodsy estate in Toluca Lake. Her husband recently optioned dramatic rights to the book *Madame de Stael* and announced plans to present it on Broadway as a starring vehicle for her. Onscreen from 1942. IN: *Tough As They Come* (juvenile role), *Outrage, Edge of Doom, Cyrano de Bergerac, City That Never Sleeps, Geraldine, Yellow Mountain, Tammy and the Bachelor, The Unknown Terror, Man on the Prowl, Sierra Baron, Flight of the Lost Balloon, Rogue's Gallery, Daddy's Gone A-Hunting*, more.

POWERS, STEFANIE (S. Cal.) Leading lady. Onscreen from 1961. IN: *Among the Thorns, Experiment in Terror, The Interns, If a Man Answers, McLintock!, Tammy Tell Me True; Die! Die! My Darling; Stagecoach, Love Has Many Faces, Warning Shot, The Love Bug Rides Again*, more.

PRATT, JUDSON (S. Cal.) Character. Onscreen from the '50s. IN: *I Confess, Somebody Up There Likes Me, Man Afraid, Monster on the Campus, The Rise and Fall of Legs Diamond, Sergeant Rutledge, The Ugly American, A Distant Trumpet, Cheyenne Autumn, The Barefoot Executive*, more.

PRATT, MICHAEL (Eng.) Support. Onscreen from the '60s. IN: *A Dandy in Aspic, Goodbye Gemini*, more.

PREJEAN, ALBERT (Fr.) The comic character lead, featured in many of Director Rene Clair's best, is in his 80s (b. 1894), lives in Paris, and is retired. Onscreen from 1920, first as an extra. IN: *La Fantome du Moulin Rouge, Le Miracle des Loups, An Italian Straw Hat, Under the Roofs of Paris, Theodore & Co., L'Opera de Quat' Sous, Dede, La Crise est Finie, Jenny, L'Alibi, Hatred, Shop-Girls of Paris*, more, including 1951's *Le Desir et L'Amour*, his last.

PRELLE, MICHELINE (Fr.) (See Micheline Presle.)

PREMINGER, OTTO (N.Y.) The ever-villainous, shiny-domed character actor from Austria gave up movie acting over two decades ago and has since been one of the most successful—if not always most tasteful—directors (*Hurry Sundown, Such Good Friends*, etc.). Onscreen in Hollywood from 1942. IN: *The Pied Piper,*

They Got Me Covered, Margin for Error, Stalag 17.

PRENTICE, KEITH (N.Y.) Support. Onscreen in 1970. IN: *The Boys in the Band.*

PRENTISS, ANN (S. Cal.) Leading lady. Younger sister of Paula Prentiss. Onscreen from the '60s. IN: *Any Wednesday; If He Hollers, Let Him Go; The Out-of-Towners,* more.

PRENTISS, ED (S. Cal.) Character. Onscreen from the '50s. IN: *The F.B.I. Story, Man on a String, Project X,* more.

PRENTISS, PAULA (S. Cal.) Costar. Wife of Richard Benjamin. Onscreen from 1961. IN: *Where the Boys Are, Bachelor in Paradise, The Horizontal Lieutenant, Follow the Boys, Man's Favorite Sport?, The World of Henry Orient, In Harm's Way, What's New Pussycat?, Catch-22, Move, Born to Win, Last of the Red Hot Lovers, The Parallax View, The Stepford Wives,* more.

PRESLE, MICHELINE (Fr.) Though already a star when imported by 20th Century-Fox, she allowed (under protest) the spelling of her name to be changed to "Prelle"—which she continued to use for a few years after returning to France. She resumed its proper spelling in '57. Today, living in Paris, stunningly beautiful in her 50s (b. 1922), she continues to costar—though often in mother roles. In 1974–75 alone, she was seen in *The Most Important Event Since Man First Set Foot on the Moon* opposite Mastroianni, *Donkey Skin, Trompe L'Oeil,* and *The Butcher, The Star and the Orphan.* Onscreen from 1938. IN: *Je Chante, Seul Amour, Boule de Suif, The Devil in the Flesh, Under My Skin, American Guerrilla in the Philippines, Adventures of Captain Fabian, The French Way, Royal Affairs in Versailles, The Five Day Lover, If a Man Answers, 7 Capital Sins, The Prize, Dark Purpose, King of Hearts, To Be a Crook,* more.

PRESLEY, ELVIS (S. Cal.) Star-singer. Onscreen from 1956. IN: *Love Me Tender, Jailhouse Rock, Loving You, G.I. Blues, Wild in the Country, Blue Hawaii, Follow That Dream, It Happened at the World's Fair, Viva Las Vegas!, Roustabout, Kissin' Cousins, Girl Happy, Harum Scarum, Paradise Hawaiian Style, Spin-out; Easy Come, Easy Go; Clambake, Double Trouble, Speedway, Charro!, The Trouble with Girls,* more, including 1969's *Change of Habit,* his most recent to date.

PRESNELL, HARVE (S. Cal.) Leading man-singer. Onscreen from 1964. IN: *The Unsinkable Molly Brown, Where the Boys Meet the Girls, The Glory Days, Paint Your Wagon.*

PRESSMAN, LAWRENCE (S Cal.) Leading man. Onscreen in the '70s. IN: *Making It, The Hellstrom Chronicle, Shaft, The Crazy World of Julius Vrooder, The Man in the Glass Booth,* more.

PRESTON, ROBERT (Conn.) Vigorous as ever in his late 50s (b. 1918), he lives in Greenwich with wife, Catherine Craig, still enjoys a booming career in Broadway musicals (*Mack and Mabel,* etc.) and, when he wishes, in movies. Onscreen from 1938. IN: *King of Alcatraz, Union Pacific, Beau Geste, Typhoon, Northwest Mounted Police, New York Town* (with Mary Martin, his decades-later costar in the Broadway musical *I Do! I Do!*), *The Night of January 16th, This Gun for Hire, Reap the Wild Wind, Wake Island, Wild Harvest, The Macomber Affair* (regarded by many as his best performance), *The Lady Gambles, Tulsa, The Sundowners, Best of the Bad Men, Face to Face* ("The Bride Comes to Yellow Sky" episode), *The Dark at the Top of the Stairs, The Music Man, How the West Was Won, All the Way Home, Child's Play, Junior Bonner, Mame,* more.

PRESTON, WAYDE (It.) A minor-league leading man in Hollywood, better known for a TV Western series than his movies, he has lived for several years in Rome. There, starring in "spaghetti Westerns" seldom shown here, he has become highly affluent—living in a well-staffed villa that he owns. Onscreen from 1963. IN: *The Man on the Spying Trapeze, Anzio, A Long Ride from Hell; Today We Kill, Tomorrow We Die!; A Man Called Sledge,* more.

PRETTY, ARLINE (S. Cal.) Leading lady; retired. Onscreen from the teens. IN: *In Again—Out Again; The Secret Kingdom* (serial), *Barriers Burned Away,* more.

PREVIN, ANDRE (Eng.) Composer-conductor. Married to Mia Farrow. Onscreen in the '60s. IN: *The Subterraneans, Pepe.*

PREVOST, FRANCOISE (Fr.) Leading lady. Onscreen from the '60s. IN: *The Enemy General, Bon Voyage!, The Girl with the Golden Eyes, Paris Belongs to Us, Time Out for Love, The Condemned of Altona, Galia, The Other One, A Woman on Fire,* more.

PRICE, ALAN (Eng.) Rock star-actor. Onscreen in the '70s. IN: *O Lucky Man, Oh Alfie.*

PRICE, ROGER (S. Cal.) Character. Onscreen in the '70s. IN: *Mixed Company,* more.

PRICE, SHERWOOD (S. Cal.) Character. Onscreen from the '60s. IN: *The Man from Galveston, Ice Station Zebra,* more.

PRICE, VINCENT (S. Cal.) Character star. Married now to English actress Coral Browne. Onscreen from 1938. IN: *Service de Luxe, Tower of London, The Private Lives of Elizabeth and Essex, The Invisible Man Returns, The Song of Bernadette, Buffalo Bill, Laura, The Keys of the Kingdom, Leave Her to Heaven, A Royal Scandal, Dragonwyck, Moss Rose, The Three Musketeers, Up in Central Park, The Baron of Arizona, House of Wax, Casanova's Big Night, The Mad Magician, The Ten Commandments, The Fly, The Tingler, The Pit and the Pendulum, Convicts Four, The Raven, The Last Man on Earth, Dr. Goldfoot and the Bikini Machine, House of a Thousand Dolls, The Conqueror Worm, Scream and Scream Again, The Abominable Dr. Phibes, The Devil's Triangle, Madhouse,* more.

PRICE, WALTER (S. Cal.) Character. Onscreen in the '70s. IN: *Sugar Hill,* more.

PRICKETT, OLIVER (S. Cal.) Character who has also often been billed Oliver Blake (as when playing the Indian "Geoduck" in the "Ma and Pa Kettle" movies). Onscreen from 1940. IN: *New York Town, Shadow of the Thin Man, Saboteur, Casablanca, Sweet Rosie O'Grady, The Mask of Dimitrios, The Enchanted Cottage, A Medal for Benny, Out of the Past, Nightmare Alley, Summer Holiday, Moonrise, The Lemon Drop Kid, The Long Long Trailer, Brigadoon, Lust for Life, Raintree County, Onionhead, Bells Are Ringing,* more.

PRIEST, DAN (S. Cal.) Character. Onscreen from the '60s. IN: *Black Like Me,* more.

PRIEST, NATALIE (N.Y.) Character. Onscreen from the '50s. IN: *The Wrong Man,* more.

PRIEST, PAT (S. Cal.) Leading lady. Onscreen from the '60s. IN: *Easy Come, Easy Go; The Incredible Two-Headed Transplant,* more.

PRIMA, LOUIS (S. Cal.) Late in 1975, age 62, the bandleader-comedian was reported still in a coma weeks after surgery for a brain tumor. Previously married to his professional partner, singer Keely Smith, he has been married since 1963 to the former Gia Miles, by whom he has two small children. Onscreen from 1937. IN: *Manhattan Merry-Go-Round, Start Cheering, You Can't Have Everything, Rose of Washington Square; Hey Boy! Hey Girl!;* more.

PRIMROSE, DOROTHY (Eng.) Support. Onscreen from 1943. IN: *S.S. San Demetrio,* more.

PRIMUS, BARRY (N.Y.) Leading man. Onscreen from the '60s. IN: *The Brotherhood,*

Puzzle of a Downfall Child, Von Richthofen and Brown, Been Down So Long It Looks Like Up to Me, Gravy Train, more.

PRINCE, WILLIAM (N.Y.) Silver-haired and in his 60s (b. 1912), the actor who played romantic GIs for Warners in the '40s flies to Hollywood often now to play character roles—on TV *(Cannon)* and in such movies as *The Stepford Wives, Blade,* and Hitchcock's *Deceit.* Long off the screen until lately, he has starred in many stage productions. He gave a particularly notable performance in 1973's *The Caretaker,* of which the *Times* critic said: "Mr. Prince, a gifted actor, stars as the shuffling old derelict. A once handsome man is apparent through those white, scraggly bristles." He has also done much work in TV soap operas. In one, *Another World,* he played for months the husband of actress Augusta Dabney; he assumed the role in real life in '65. From '34 to '64, he was married to the former Dorothy Huass; they have four grown children—two sons and two daughters—and are now grandparents. Onscreen from 1943. IN: *Destination Tokyo, Hollywood Canteen, The Very Thought of You, Pillow to Post, Objective Burma, Cinderella Jones, Shadow of a Woman, Carnegie Hall, Dead Reckoning, Lust for Gold, Cyrano de Bergerac, Secret of Treasure Mountain, The Vagabond King, Macabre,* more.

PRINCIPAL, VICTORIA (S. Cal.) Leading lady. Onscreen in the '70s. IN: *The Life and Times of Judge Roy Bean, The Naked Ape, Earthquake, I Will, I Will . . . For Now,* more.

PRINE, ANDREW (S. Cal.) Leading man. Onscreen from 1958. IN: *Kiss Her Goodbye, The Miracle Worker, Advance to the Rear, Texas Across the River, Bandolero!, The Devil's Brigade, Generation, This Savage Land, Grizzly,* more.

PRINGLE, AILEEN (N.Y.) Sophisticated and smartly dressed, she was one of Metro's great stars throughout the '20s. Nothing has changed except that she is now in her 80s (b. 1895) and hasn't starred in decades. (She did continue in movies, because she enjoyed acting, long past her days of fame, through a small role in 1944's *Since You Went Away.*) Anyone who has ever been entertained by her in her East Side apartment, or even encountered her at a play opening (she is an inveterate theatergoer), can attest that she is still slender, chic, and a fashionplate. She has no children and has not remarried since her second marriage—to novelist James M. *(Mildred Pierce)* Cain—ended in divorce, after less than a year, three decades ago. Onscreen from 1919. IN: *Redhead, The Tiger's Claw, In the Palace of the King, Three Weeks, A Kiss in the Dark, A Thief in Paradise, The Wilderness*

Woman, The Great Deception, Tea for Three, Beau Broadway, Night Parade, Puttin' on the Ritz, Murder at Midnight, Fame Street, The Phantom of Crestwood, The Unguarded Hour, The Last of Mrs. Cheney, The Hardys Ride High, The Night of Nights, Happy Land; A Wave, a Wac and a Marine; more.

PRINGLE, BRYAN (Eng.) Support. Onscreen from the '60s. IN: *Saturday Night and Sunday Morning*, more.

PRINGLE, JOAN (S. Cal.) Black leading lady. Onscreen in the '70s. IN: *J.D.'s Revenge*, more.

PRINTEMPS, YVONNE (Fr.) The popular singer-actress, now in her 80s (b. 1895) and long retired, has been a widow since 1975 when her star-husband Pierre Fresnay died at 77. Onscreen from the '30s. IN: *La Dame aux Camelias, Adrienne Lecouvreur, Three Waltzes, Le Duel, The Paris Waltz, Voyage to America*, her last, in 1952.

PRITCHETT, PAULA (N.Y.) Leading lady. Onscreen from the '60s. IN: *Chappaqua, Adrift*, more.

PROCHNICKA, LIDIA (N.Y.) Leading lady. Onscreen from the '60s. IN: *The Group, Dante's Inferno*, more.

PROCTOR, MARLAND (S. Cal.) Support. Onscreen in the '70s. IN: *Chrome and Hot Leather, The Dark Side of Tomorrow, Curse of the Headless Horseman, Garden of the Dead*, more.

PROCTOR, PHILIP (N.Y.) Support. Onscreen from the '60s. IN: *The Thousand Plane Raid, A Safe Place*, more.

PROFANATO, GENE (N.Y.) Juvenile. Onscreen in the '70s. IN: *Twinky*, more.

PROKHOVENKO, SHANNA (Rus.) Leading lady. Onscreen from the '60s. IN: *Ballad of a Soldier, Italiano Brava Gente, The Marriage of Baezaminov*, more.

PROVINE, DOROTHY (S. Cal.) Leading lady. Onscreen from 1958. IN: *The Bonnie Parker Story, Riot in Juvenile Prison, The Thirty Foot Bride of Candy Rock, It's a Mad Mad Mad Mad World, Good Neighbor Sam, That Darn Cat, The Great Race, One Spy Too Many, Who's Minding the Mint?, Never a Dull Moment*, more.

PROVOST, JON (S. Cal.) The former boy actor —most famous as one of "Lassie's" young masters on TV—still looks like a juvenile, in his

20s (b. 1949), is financially well off, still single, and hopeful of making a comeback as a leading man. Onscreen from 1953. IN: *So Big, The Country Girl, Back from Eternity, Escapade in Japan, Lassie's Great Adventure, This Property Is Condemned, The Computer Wore Tennis Shoes*, more.

PROWSE, JULIET (S. Cal.) Dancer-actress. Onscreen from 1960. IN: *Can-Can, G.I. Blues, The Second Time Around, The Right Approach, Who Killed Teddy Bear?, Dingaka, Run for Your Wife, Spree*, more.

PRYOR, MAUREEN (Eng.) Character. Onscreen from the '60s. IN: *Walk in the Shadow, Passages from James Joyce's Finnegan's Wake, The Music Lovers, The Black Windmill*, more.

PRYOR, NICHOLAS (S. Cal.) Leading man. Onscreen in the '70s. IN: *The Way We Live Now, Man on a Swing, Smile, All the President's Men, The Gumball Rally*, more.

PRYOR, RICHARD (S. Cal.) Black star. Onscreen from the '60s. IN: *The Busy Body, Wild in the Streets, The Green Berets, The Phynx, You've Got to Walk It Like You Talk It or You'll Lose That Beat, Uptown Saturday Night, Adios Amigos, The Silver Streak*, more.

PULVER, LISELOTTE (LILO) (Switz.) Leading lady. She has resumed the use of her real name, Liselotte, which she had used in movies before Hollywood dubbed her Lilo. Onscreen from 1953. IN: *The White Hell of Pitz Palu, The Confessions of Felix Krull, Reaching for the Stars, A Time to Love and a Time to Die; One, Two, Three; Arms and the Man, Lafayette, A Global Affair, The Nun*, more.

PUNSLEY, BERNARD (S. Cal.) "Milty," the overweight lad in the "Dead End Kids," always considered his life in films that of a "sheep in wolf's clothes." "Sure I can dish it out and I can take it," he said back then, "but most people don't understand I'm only tough when I'm acting." Now in his 50s, Punsley is the only "Dead End" guy to make a clean, complete break with acting. After serving in the Army, he attended the University of Georgia Medical School, where he graduated at the top of his class. He is today an outstandingly successful physician in Huntington Beach. Several years ago when working in Florida in the *Gentle Ben* TV series, his "Dead End" pal Huntz Hall was talking about him and said: "I'd like him to be my personal physician but I live in Miami— and that's a long way for a house call." Huntz is back in Hollywood now, thus nearer, but Huntington Beach is still a long way down the coast. Which is how Dr. Punsley feels about his boyhood career in Hollywood—that it was a "long way" back. Onscreen from 1937. IN: *Dead End, Crime School, Little Tough Guy, Angels with Dirty Faces, They Made Me a Criminal, Hell's Kitchen, Angels Wash Their Faces, Give Us Wings, Hit the Road, Mob Town,* more.

PURCELL, LEE (S. Cal.) Leading lady. Onscreen in the '70s. IN: *Adam at Six A.M., Mr. Majestyk,* more.

PURCELL, NOEL (Eng.) Character actor, in his 70s (b. 1900) and still going strong. Onscreen from 1939. IN: *Ireland's Border Line, Captain Boycott, Saints and Sinners, Encore* ("Winter Cruise" sequence), *The Crimson Pirate, Moby Dick, Lust for Life, Mad Little Island, The Millionairess, Mutiny on the Bounty, The Ceremony, Lord Jim; Arrivederci, Baby!; Sinful Davy,* more.

PURDOM, EDMUND (It.) Handsomer now, in his early 50s (b. 1924), than when costarring at Metro, this Englishman left Hollywood in '55 and has since played secondary roles in a number of pix—*The Yellow Rolls-Royce, The Man in the Golden Mask, The Beauty Jungle,* etc. But his primary role in Rome, where he has lived for years, is not acting. He is a top produc-

cer of classical records for RCA Victor, overseeing symphonic recordings both in Italy and England. Successful in this field, he lives in a villa. And he still flies to London on occasion to guest-star on BBC-TV's *Movie Quiz* program and to discuss movie roles, most recently the lead in a horror flick for Hammer Productions. Onscreen from 1953. IN: *Titanic, Julius Caesar, The Egyptian, Athena, Moment of Danger, The Prodigal, Strange Intruder, Trapped in Tangiers, Loves of Salambo, Malaga, Last of the Vikings, Lafayette, Suleiman the Conqueror, Last Ride to Santa Cruz,* more, including 1969's *Sweden—Heaven and Hell,* an Italian-made documentary about Sweden that he narrated.

PURNELL, LOUISE (Eng.) Leading lady. Onscreen from 1970. IN: *Three Sisters,* more.

PYLE, DENVER (S. Cal.) Character. Onscreen from 1948. IN: *Marshal of Amarillo, Hellfire, Streets of San Francisco, Hills of Utah, The Maverick, Ten Wanted Men, The Lonely Man, Jet Pilot, The Left-Handed Gun, A Good Day for a Hanging, The Alamo, Mail-Order Bride, The Great Race, Bonnie and Clyde, Welcome to Hard Times, Bandolero!, Escape to Witch Mountain, Buffalo Bill and the Indians,* more.

Q

QUADFLIEG, WILL (Ger.) Character. Onscreen from the '30s. IN: *Der Maulkorb, Faust, Lola Montes,* more.

QUADE, JOHN (S. Cal.) Character. Onscreen in the '70s. IN: *The Swinging Cheerleaders,* more.

QUAID, RANDY (S. Cal.) Support. Nominated for Best Supporting Actor Oscar in *The Last Detail.* Onscreen in the '70s. IN: *The Last Picture Show, The Apprenticeship of Duddy Kravitz, Breakout,* more.

QUALEN, JOHN (S. Cal.) This great character actor is now in his 70s (b. 1899), still happily married (since '24) to the former Pearle Larson, and still going strong. Almost any week on TV, since he has appeared in more than 1300 shows, you can catch him guesting in series such as *Streets of San Francisco* or *Movin' On,* or, if you prefer the neighborhood Bijou, find him prominent in the cast of *Frasier, the Loveable Lion,* among others. Once famous onscreen as the "father" of the Dionne Quintuplets (*Five of a Kind, The Country Doctor*), Qualen is actually the father of three married daughters: Meredith, Kathleen, and Elizabeth. "Our first

grandchild," he says with that familiar wide smile, "was a boy and born on my birthday at that (December 8). Never having had a son, you can imagine what a thrill that was." He now has, he adds collectively, as though there's entirely too many to count, "umpteen grandchildren." Onscreen from 1931. IN: *Street Scene* (his first), *Arrowsmith, Counsellor-At-Law, Our Daily Bread, Charlie Chan in Paris, Road to Glory, Nothing Sacred, Joy of Living, Four Wives, The Long Voyage Home, The Shepherd of the Hills, All That Money Can Buy (The Devil and Daniel Webster), Tortilla Flat, Roughly Speaking, My Girl Tisa, Goodbye My Fancy, The Big Land, Anatomy of a Murder, Cheyenne Autumn, A Patch of Blue, P.J.,* more.

QUALTINGER, HELMUT (Ger.) Support. Onscreen from the '60s. IN: *Castle Keep,* more.

QUARRY, ROBERT (S. Cal.) Leading man. Onscreen from 1955. IN: *House of Bamboo, Agent for H.A.R.M., Winning; Count Yorga, Vampire; W.U.S.A., The Return of Count Yorga, Sugar Hill, The Midnight Man,* more.

QUAYLE, ANNA (Eng.) Comedienne. Onscreen from 1964. IN: *A Hard Day's Night;*

Arrivederci, Baby!; Smashing Time, Chitty Chitty Bang Bang, Mistress Pamela, more.

QUAYLE, ANTHONY (Eng.) Star. Nominated for Best Supporting Actor in *Anne of the Thousand Days.* Onscreen from 1948. IN: *Hamlet, Oh Rosalinda!, The Wrong Man, Woman in a Dressing Gown, Pursuit of the Graf Spee, Tarzan's Greatest Adventure, The Guns of Navarone, Damn the Defiant, Lawrence of Arabia, It Takes a Thief, Operation Crossbow, A Study in Terror, Mackenna's Gold, A Bequest to the Nation, The Tamarind Seed, Moses,* more.

QUEDENS, EUNICE (S. Cal.) Eve Arden's real name which she used in 1929. IN: *The Song of Love.* (See Eve Arden.)

QUENSEL, ISA (Swe.) Character. Onscreen from the '30s. IN: *Petersson & Bendel; Raggen, Det Aer Jag Det; To Love, Swedish Wedding Night, The Cats,* more.

QUESTEL, MAE (N.Y.) Character. Onscreen from the '60s. IN: *A Majority of One, It's Only Money, Funny Girl, Move,* more.

QUIGLEY, DON (N.J.) Character. Onscreen in the '70s. IN: *The Hot Rock,* more.

QUIGLEY, GODFREY (Eng.) Character. Onscreen from the '50s. IN: *The Rising of the Moon, Rooney, Broth of a Boy, Nothing But the Best, A Clockwork Orange, Get Carter.*

QUIGLEY, JUANITA (Pa.) One of the screen's most enormously appealing child stars (the original "Baby Jane"—but not *that* one—before being billed under her own name), she continued in pictures through the '40s. As a youngster, she was a bright-eyed, precocious doll, with her hair in bangs and a phenomenal I.Q. As an adult (b. 1931), happily married, the mother of a boy and a girl, Erik (b. 1966) and Marta (b. 1969), and a teacher, she is down-to-earth, greatly likable, brainy—and nobody's pushover. Not long ago, and reluctantly, for she shies away from publicity now, she granted an editor a story about her later life. There was a proviso; it was not to be titled *The Child Star Who Became a Nun,* though that, too, was true. This was honored. The title used was innocuous: *The Child Star Who Found the Happiest Life.* But, on the fifth page of the published article, the editor weakened and, unable to resist the drama of it, inserted the blurb "Leaving the convent after so long as a teaching nun, the one-time actress never guessed that marriage and motherhood awaited her." A kind and charming note of thanks soon afterward arrived at the editor's desk. But one line in it—a velvet-gloved slap—disquieted his conscience: "You

are almost a man of your word. (The 'almost' refers to the article's mid-way caption.)'' At 18, Juanita Quigley stopped the movie career that had begun when she was 2½, entered college, played leads in a couple of campus plays, and thought that, possibly, the stage would be her next career. "I'm glad that I acted in movies, but in a sense it's an empty life," she says now. "As I got older, I wanted to be liked for what I was, not for what I did." In '51, though, four months short of her 20th birthday, she gave up Hollywood to enter a Roman Catholic convent in Pennsylvania. For years she was a dedicted nun and teacher. With the many changes that came about in her order and the church in general, she then asked for and received Papal dispensation to renounce her vows and return to the laity. She left the convent 13 years to the day from the time she entered it. "The sisterhood," she says, "became a restrained kind of life for me. I was teaching in a high school, but I wanted to have more scope." Outside, she worked for her Master's in English and met Donald "Dutch" Schultz, who, interestingly, had once studied to be a priest. Their mutual interest, now, was in the field of education. They have been married for well over a dozen years, Juanita teaching English at Delaware County Community College in Media, Pa., and her husband being a Professor of theology at Villanova University, not far from their home in Philadelphia. "I am trying to teach my students," she says, "something about the problems of being a parent, of getting older, and of the needs of older persons"—and her own youngsters "to be unselfish, to think of other people." And, as for herself, the woman who was the little girl all America loved says, "I think of myself as Juanita Quigley Schultz, who expresses herself as a wife, as a mother and as a teacher. I am Juanita—in the process of becoming." Onscreen from 1933. IN: *Gimme My Quarter Back* (short), *In Love With Life, Invincible, We're Rich Again, Have a Heart, Imitation of Life, The Man Who Reclaimed His Head, I've Been Around, The Great Ziegfeld, Straight from the Heart, Riffraff, The Devil Doll, Born to Dance, Hawaii Calls, Having a Wonderful Time, Woman Against Woman, Men With Wings, That Certain Age, The Blue Bird, The Vanishing Virginian, A Yank at Eton, Assignment in Brittany, The Lady and the Monster, National Velvet,* more.

QUIGLEY, RITA (S. Cal.) Certain movie youngsters do find happiness in their postcareer lives. Proof is classic-featured Rita Quigley, petite, auburn-haired, and beautiful in her 50s (b. 1923), long and happily married to a successful Culver City merchant, and the mother of six. She came on the movie scene seven years later than baby sister Juanita. At 17, she won the plum ingenue role of the season—that of the daughter in *Susan and God*, who is neglected when her socialite mother, Joan Crawford, discovers "religion." Though she won glowing notices in this and later movies, she retired in '44 when she married Arthur Goehner (pronounced Gaynor), then a Navy lieutenant. Rita's children, their ages ranging from the mid-teens to the late twenties, are, in youngest-to-oldest order: Patrick (he has done commercials and industrial films), Andre (known professionally as Andy Gaynor, he too does TV commercials), Theresa (an aspiring actress), Paul (in college), Martin (a Navy man who served in Vietnam), and Judy (married to a young Naval officer). As for herself, Rita says: "Now that most of our children are grown I work part-time as an actors' agent. If the opportunity presented itself I would love to return to acting." Onscreen from 1940. IN: *The Howards of Virginia, The Human Comedy; Henry Aldrich, Editor; Blonde Inspiration, Women in Bondage*, more.

QUILLAN, EDDIE (S. Cal.) In movies from his 20s, and now entering his still-active 70s (b. 1907), he has run the acting gamut—campus hero, light leading man, the hero's pal, comedian, supporting roles, and now character parts. There's still an occasional movie role, as in the recent Disney comedy *The Strongest Man in the World*, but, as with most performers in Hollywood, now with so few pictures made, his steady employment is in television. In this decade, Eddie Quillan has been seen in most of the series (*Julia, Columbo, Mannix, Police Story*, etc.) and in such TV-movies as *Hitchhike!* (as a diner counterman), *Melvin Purvis, G-Man* (hotel clerk), and *She Lives* (janitor). A lifelong bachelor, Quillan lives in the San Fernando Valley with his sisters, Peggy and Roseanne, also unmarried, in a charming three-bedroom, California-style ranchhouse with a pool and colorful garden. Sharing the home with them, until her death in 1969, was their actress-mother, Sarah Quillan. Living nearby are three married sisters and two brothers. "With all the changes that have taken place in this industry," Eddie Quillan says, "one of the biggest has been the new people who are running it today. So many of the great producers and directors are no longer being hired. And I must admit that some of the producers and directors I have worked with in the past few years seem to have no knowledge of who I am or what I've done. I realize that some of these people weren't even born when I was doing (some people said, even some critics) great things on that old silvery screen. [Among other things, for his role in the 1935 version of *Mutiny on the Bounty*—as Smith, victim of the gang—he received the first Screen Actors Guild Award accorded an actor in a supporting role. For the same portrayal he

also won *Box Office* Magazine's Blue Ribbon Award.] On the other hand, there are some left in the business who know me and my work through the years. One of them is Hal Kanter." This producer-writer rarely turns out a show in which Eddie Quillan is not featured: *Valentine's Day, Julia, The Jimmy Stewart Show*, etc. "Hal Kanter is probably one of my greatest boosters and it makes me very proud," he adds. The slim little guy with the familiar, beguiling expression loses his broad grin momentarily as he laments the changes in the movie industry, saying, "The way things have gone to pot out here I wouldn't be surprised if in the very near future people will wonder what you're talking about when you mention movies." While "things won't ever be the same again," he says, ". . . I still enjoy working in a studio and on a sound stage. There's a camaraderie you can't find anyplace else." The genial Eddie Quillan smile returns as he tells of his one unfulfilled movie ambition—"to work with Barbara Stanwyck—just once." Eddie has known the star for some 40 years, but even though their professional careers ran parallel to each other, they have met only socially. "She's such a great gal, both on and off the screen," he says, "that I don't care what kind of part is involved, as long as I could say that I worked with Barbara Stanwyck." Onscreen from 1928. IN: *Show Folks, The Sophomore, The Godless Girl, Sweepstakes, The Optimist, Girl Crazy, The Gridiron Flash, Made for Each Other, Young Mr. Lincoln, Allegheny Uprising, The Grapes of Wrath, La Conga Nights, The Flame of New Orleans, It Ain't Hay, Dark Mountain, Mystery of the River Boat* (serial), *Twilight on the Prairie, Jungle Queen* (serial), *Sensation Hunters Brigadoon, Promises Promises, Move Over Darling, Angel in My Pocket, How to Frame a Figg*, more.

QUILLEY, DENIS (Eng.) Support. Onscreen from the '60s. IN: *Life at the Top, Anne of the Thousand Days, The Black Windmill, Murder on the Orient Express*, more.

QUINE, RICHARD (S. Cal.) The onetime leading man has been, since giving up his acting career more than two decades ago, one of Hollywood's top directors—of *Operation Mad Ball; Bell, Book and Candle; How to Murder Your Wife*, etc. He is now in his 50s (b. 1920). Onscreen from 1932. IN: *The World Changes, Counsellor-At-Law, Jane Eyre, Little Men, A Dog of Flanders, Dinky* (all adolescent roles), *Babes on Broadway, Tish, My Sister Eileen* (the remake of which, in 1955, he directed), *For Me and My Gal, Stand By for Action, Dr. Gillespie's New Assistant, We've Never Been Licked, Command Decision, Words and Music, No Sad Songs for Me*, more, including 1950's *The Flying Missile*, his last as an actor.

QUINN, ANTHONY (S. Cal.) Star. Won Best Supporting Actor Oscar in *Viva Zapata!* and *Lust for Life*. Nominated for Best Actor Oscar in *Wild Is the Wind, Zorba the Greek*. Onscreen from 1936. IN: *Parole, The Plainsman, The Last Train from Madrid, Daughters of Shanghai, The Buccaneer* (the remake of which, in 1958, he directed), *Bulldog Drummond in Africa, Island of Lost Men, Union Pacific, The Road to Singapore, The Ghost Breakers, City for Conquest, They Died with Their Boots On, The Black Swan, Guadalcanal Diary, The Ox-Bow Incident, Back to Bataan, Black Gold* (opposite first wife, Katherine De Mille), *The Brave Bulls, Against All Flags; Ride, Vaquero!; Blowing Wild, Seminole, The Magnificent Matador, Ulysses, La Strada, The Story of Esther Costello, Attila the Hun, Last Train from Gun Hill, Heller in Pink Tights, Portrait in Black, The Guns of Navarone, Barabbas, Lawrence of Arabia, Requiem for a Heavyweight, The Visit, Behold a Pale Horse, A High Wind in Jamaica, Marco the Magnificent, The Happening, Guns for San Sebastian, The Shoes of the Fisherman, The Secret of Santa Vittoria, Dream of Kings, A Walk in the Spring Rain, Flap, Across 110th Street, The Destructors,* more.

QUINN, BILL (S. Cal.) Character. Onscreen from the '60s. IN: *Love Is a Funny Thing, How to Frame a Figg,* more.

QUINN, LOUIS (S. Cal.) Character. Onscreen from the '50s. IN: *Al Capone, Gypsy, Welcome to the Club,* more.

QUINN, PAT (S. Cal.) Leading lady. Onscreen from 1969. IN: *Alice's Restaurant, Zachariah, Shoot Out,* more.

QUINN, TEDDY (S. Cal.) Former juvenile (b. 1959). Onscreen from 1966. IN: *Madame X, 80 Steps to Jonah, Black Hooker,* more.

QUO, BEULAH (S. Cal.) Character. Onscreen from the '60s. IN: *The Seventh Dawn, The Sand Pebbles, Chinatown,* more.

R

RABAL, FRANCISCO (It.) Leading man. Onscreen from the '60s. IN: *The Mighty Crusaders, Viridiana, Belle du Jour, Nazarin, Exorcism's Daughter,* more.

RACIMO, VICTORIA (VICKI) (S. Cal.) Leading lady. Onscreen from the '60s. IN: *What's So Bad About Feeling Good?, The Magic Garden of Stanley Sweetheart, Red Sky at Morning, Journey Through Rosebud,* more.

RADD, RONALD (Eng.) Character. Onscreen from the '50s. IN: *The Camp on Blood Island, Where the Spys Are, The Sea Gull, The Kremlin Letter, Operation Daybreak,* more. (Died 1976.)

RADER, GENE (S. Cal.) Support. Onscreen in the '70s. IN: *The Sugarland Express,* more.

RADER, JACK (S. Cal.) Leading man. Onscreen from 1968. IN: *The Edge, Barbara,* more.

RAE, CHARLOTTE (N.Y.) Comedienne. Onscreen from the '60s. IN: *Hello Down There, Jenny, The Hot Rock, Bananas,* more.

RAE, JOHN (Eng.) Character. Onscreen from the '50s. IN: *The Brave Don't Cry, The Little Kidnappers, Reach for Glory* (he also wrote it), *Morgan!, Fragment of Fear,* more.

RAEBURN, HENZIE (Eng.) Character actress. Onscreen from the '50s. IN: *The Policewoman, Orders to Kill,* more.

RAFFERTY, FRANCES (S. Cal.) Married and retired, she has not been in a movie since 1961's *Wings of Chance*, or on TV since *December Bride*. Onscreen from 1942. IN: *The War Against Mrs. Hadley, Seven Sweethearts, Dr. Gillespie's Criminal Case, Girl Crazy, Dragon Seed, Mrs. Parkington, Bad Bascomb, Lost Honeymoon, An Old-Fashioned Girl, The Shanghai Story,* more.

RAFFIN, DEBORAH (S. Cal.) Leading lady. Daughter of retired actress Trudy Marshall. Onscreen in the '70s. IN: *The Dove, Once Is Not Enough,* more.

RAFT, GEORGE (S. Cal.) In his 70s (b. 1903) and single (unable to divorce his long-estranged wife, he never married again after her death), he lives in an apartment in Westwood's Century City and takes part in many nostalgia events in L.A. His life was filmed in 1961 as *The George Raft Story*, with Ray Danton portraying him. And two hardcover books about the actor have been published. In 1973 there was *The George Raft File: The Unauthorized Biography*, by James Robert Parish with Steven Whitney, and in 1974, his authorized biography by Lewis Yablonsky, *George Raft*. Onscreen from 1929. IN: *Queen of the Night Clubs, Palmy Days, Scarface* (the famous coin trick that became his trademark, seen here for the first time, originated with director Howard Hawks. Author Lewis Yablonsky writes: "Hawks was clever enough to know that the coin-flipping would cover a lot of Raft's lack of acting experience.

'When he didn't have anything else to do, he would flip a coin. It worked. From beginning to end he looked as if he'd been acting for years.''' He further quotes Hawks: "Having George flip the coin made him a character. The coin represented a hidden attitude—a kind of defiance, a held-back hostility, a coolness—which hadn't been found in pictures up to that time; and it made George stand out. It probably helped make him a star.''), *Undercover Man, If I Had a Million, Night World, Midnight Club, Bolero, Limehouse Blues, Rumba, The Glass Key, Souls at Sea, You and Me, Spawn of the North, Each Dawn I Die, I Stole a Million, They Drive by Night, Manpower* (costar Edward G. Robinson, in his posthumously published autobiography *All My Yesterdays,* recalled of this picture: "Raft was touchy, difficult, and thoroughly impossible to play with. He threw a punch at me, and I was ready to walk; Hal Wallis had to act as peacemaker . . . I was in the hospital lately, and the first flowers I received carried a card that read: 'Get well, your pal, George Raft.' I guess he forgave me for whatever infraction caused him to clop me on the 'chops.'"), *Broadway, Nob Hill, Mr. Ace, Nocturne, Whistle Stop, Race Street, Outpost in Morocco, Lucky Nick Cain, The Man from Cairo, Black Widow, Some Like It Hot, The Ladies' Man, The Patsy, Casino Royale,* more, including 1972's *Hammersmith Is Out,* his most recent to date, in which he did a cameo.

RAGIN, JOHN S. (S. Cal.) Support. Onscreen from the '60s. IN: *Earthquake,* more.

RAGNO, JOSEPH (N.Y.) Support. Onscreen in the '70s. IN: *Law and Disorder,* more.

RAIN, DOUGLAS (Eng.) Support. Onscreen from the '50s. IN: *Oedipus Rex, 2001: A Space Odyssey* (voice of "Hal 9000"), more.

RAINE, JACK (S. Cal.) Character, in his 70s and still active. Onscreen from 1930. IN: *The Hate Ship, The Middle Watch, Fires of Fate, Mine Own Executioner, Above and Beyond, Dangerous When Wet, Rhapsody, Prince of Players, Not As a Stranger, Woman Obsessed, Scandalous John,* more.

RAINER, LUISE (Eng.) The Viennese actress who was the first star to win two Oscars back to back, in *The Great Ziegfeld* and *The Good Earth,* married British publisher Robert Knittel in '45 and has lived in England since. She was previously (1937–40) married to and divorced from playwright Clifford Odets. She has not appeared in a movie since 1943's *Hostages,* though in '65 she did return to Hollywood to guest-star in one episode of the TV series *Combat.* By coincidence, it was filmed at MGM where she had reigned supreme in the '30s. She recalled then her differences with studio chief Louis B. Mayer. "Why should I have any love for Mayer?" she asked. "After I had won an Academy Award for the studio on *Ziegfeld,* I was still only making $250 a week on *The Good Earth.*" The last thing Mayer said to her when she left the studio, she related, was: "We made you and we're going to kill you." To which she retorted: "God made me." She went to New York where she starred on Broadway and, before her second marriage, studied medicine and journalism. Her last stage appearance in America was in '52 when she returned to star, at a Hollywood theater, in *Joan of Lorraine.* In '74 the actress found herself visiting in California. "I came here running after my daughter who suddenly decided she wanted to live in Los Angeles," she said. Her daughter, the former Patricia Knittel (b. 1946), had made her professional acting debut the previous year in Princeton, N.J., in a production of *The Tempest,* and wished to try her luck in Hollywood. She uses her married name as an actress, Patricia Norsa, and she and her husband—a young Italian-born architect, Alda Norsa—are parents of a grammar-school-age youngster. Luise Rainer, in her 60s (b. 1910), has changed imperceptibly in appearance. Trim (perhaps due to her chief avocation, mountain-climbing) and petite, she still wears her brown hair in the familiar modified page-boy style, and she remains a dramatic conversationalist—her dark eyes flashing, her hands in constant motion. Often queried about the famous "telephone scene" in *The Great Ziegfeld,* a contributing factor in the winning of her first Oscar, she confessed recently the underlying emotion of it. "My little dog was sick and I was very unhappy," she said. "I had taken him to the vet the night before the scene. There I saw a beautiful little cocker spaniel, which I was told would have to be destroyed. In the telephone scene, I was thinking, not of Flo Ziegfeld, but of that little dog." Her only performing in recent years has been in narrating, on rare occasions, the Honegger oratorio *Judith.* But, she insists, "I haven't retired even though I may not work continuously. No one ever retires." Of herself, she says, "I always consider myself the world's worst actress." She lives with her husband in a house in Belgravia, takes art classes three days a week, and spends every moment she can manage in the Alps. Onscreen from 1935. IN: *Escapade, The Emperor's Candlesticks, The Big City, The Toy Wife, The Great Waltz, Dramatic School.*

RAINES, CHRISTINA (S. Cal.) Leading lady. Onscreen in the '70s. IN: *Nashville, Russian Roulette,* more.

RAINES, ELLA (Colo.) Now in her 50s (b. 1921), the former leading lady lives in Colorado Springs, where, for several years, her husband,

Brigadier General Robin Olds, has been Commandant of the Air Force Academy. Visitors to their 24-room house on the Academy grounds include senators, generals, heads of state, and, more rarely, friends from her movie days such as Forrest Tucker and Douglas Fairbanks Jr. Married to General Olds, her second husband, since '47, she has two grown daughters, Christina and Susan. Christina, a recent graduate of Vassar, majoring in drama, is following in her mother's acting footsteps; she is not, of course, the Christina Raines, who has already been in several movies. As for Ella Raines, she hasn't made a movie since 1957's *Man in the Road*, but she has lately admitted that she would not be averse to making an occasional picture now "if the part was right." Onscreen from 1943. IN: *Corvette K-225, Cry Havoc, Phantom Lady, Hail the Conquering Hero, Tall in the Saddle, The Suspect, The Strange Affair of Uncle Harry, White Tie and Tails, Brute Force, The Web, The Senator Was Indiscreet, Impact, The Second Face, The Singing Guns, Fighting Coast Guard, Ride the Man Down,* more.

RAINEY, FORD (S. Cal.) Character. Onscreen from 1949. IN: *White Heat, Perfect Strangers, 3:10 to Yuma, The Badlanders, John Paul Jones, Two Rode Together, Parrish, 40 Pounds of Trouble, Kings of the Sun, The Sand Pebbles, Johnny Tiger, The Gypsy Moths, My Old Man's Place, Like a Crow on a June Bug,* more.

RAINS, JESSICA (S. Cal.) Support. Daughter of the late Claude Rains. Onscreen in the '70s. IN: *Stand Up and Be Counted, Kotch,* more.

RAITER, FRANK (N.Y.) Support. Onscreen from the '60s. IN: *Lady in Cement, The McMasters,* more.

RAITT, JOHN (S. Cal.) Singer-leading man. In 1975–76 he costarred on Broadway in *A Musical Jubilee*, and his daughter, Bonnie Raitt, is now a song star. Onscreen from 1940. IN: *Flight Command, Ziegfeld Girl, Minstrel Man, The Pajama Game.*

RAKI, LAYA (S. Cal.) Leading lady. Onscreen from the '50s. IN: *Up to His Neck, The Seekers, Quentin Durward, Land of Fury, The Poppy Is Also a Flower,* more.

RALLI, GIOVANNA (It.) Leading lady. Onscreen from the '40s. IN: *Lights of Variety, La Lupa, It Happened in the Park, The Bigamist, The Most Wonderful Moment, General Della Rovere; What Did You Do in the War, Daddy?; A Very Handy Man, The Caper of the Golden Bulls, Deadfall, The Mercenary, Cannon for Cordoba,* more.

RALSTON, ESTHER (N.Y.) Classically blonde, this star was in more than 150 pix (1918–40) before she left the screen after supporting roles in *Tin Pan Alley* and *San Francisco Docks*. Famous in her heyday as "The Paramount Clotheshorse," she lived in a mansion and drove about in a Rolls-Royce with liveried chauffeur—his uniform matching the color of her dress of the hour. Today, in her 70s (b. 1902), still vivacious and pretty, with silver-blonde hair, but no longer rich, the actress lives in Glens Falls, N.Y.—about 175 miles north of Manhattan—where she works as a lighting consultant for the Glens Falls Electrical Supply Co. It is by choice; she likes her independence. She has not been married since her third divorce—from newspaper man Ted Lloyd, in '54, by whom she has two children, Ted Jr. and Judy, both in their late 20s. Her previous husbands were actor-producer George Webb (their daughter, Mary, was tabbed "the $100,000 baby" because the actress turned down a contract in that amount when she became pregnant), and Will Morgan, a Fred Waring musician. After her divorce from Lloyd, she moved from California to New York, where she reared her three children. She acted onstage a while, then worked 10 years in a Long Island department store before returning to acting in a soap opera. She was later a vice president in a New York talent agency. Then she moved to Salem, N.Y., to live with daughter Mary and her husband and their three children, in an apartment attached to their home, and finally migrated farther north to Glens Falls. She often flies to Setauket, L.I., to visit daughter Judy Callahan, a folksinger, who also has presented her with a granddaughter. No, the actress laughs, she no longer stands on her head five minutes a day to keep slender—this habit being a once-publicized "beauty secret" of hers. But she can still do it, she adds, to amuse her teenage grandson, Daniel. She is also completing her autobiography, *Someday We'll Laugh*. There will be no shocking revelations or complaints in it, she promises. For, says Esther Ralston today, "I've had a good life." Onscreen from 1918. IN: *Oliver Twist, Peter Pan, The Goose Hangs High, The Little French Girl, Beggar on Horseback, The Lady Who Lied, Best People, A Kiss for Cinderella, Womanhandled, The American Venus, The Quarterback, Old Ironsides, Children of Divorce, Love and Learn, The Case of Lena Smith, The Wheel of Life, Lonely Wives, The Prodigal, After the Ball, Sadie McKee, The Marines Are Coming, Mr. Dynamite, Shadows of the Orient,* more.

RALSTON, VERA HRUBA (S. Cal.) Last onscreen in 1958's *The Man Who Died Twice*, made, as were all her 26 starring pix, at Republic

374

where her husband, Herbert J. Yates, was studio chief, she lives on a lavish estate in Santa Barbara and is retired. In a letter to the author in '72 she wrote: "I have been ill after my husband's death, which is now six years. The late Mr. Herbert Yates was a great man and we have spent many happy years together. I have been with him to his last breath for I loved him so very much." She also wrote, with great affection, of her mother who was then hospitalized after suffering several strokes and has since passed away. "Due to my concern for her," she added, "I have lost a lot of weight, from size 12 to size 8. My brother, Rudy Ralston [a Hollywood production executive], my mother and I are very close." She has since begun a new happy life—as the wife, since the summer of '73, of Santa Barbara business man Charles Luciano Alva. She also reports that once more she is in the best of health. During the years the Czechoslovakian-born actress starred on the screen, she was not unaware that she was a sitting target for critics. It is to her credit, however, that among her co-workers she made many lasting friendships, including those with actor John Carroll and the celebrated character actress Blanche Yurka. The latter, now dead, appeared with her in *The Flame* and years later still spoke of her with admiration, saying, "Vera worked so seriously and so hard to be a good actress that she won everyone's empathy." Several years after her first husband's death, she considered returning to the screen—"if just maybe the right part comes along." Today, still attractively blonde in her 50s (b. 1919), she says, "I decided not to make a comeback. I'd rather spend my time tending avocado trees and painting—not pictures—but walls and furniture." Onscreen from 1941. IN: *Ice Capades* (billed merely Vera Hruba), *The Lady and the Monster*, *Lake Placid Serenade*, *Storm Over Lisbon*, *Murder in the Music Hall* (billed Vera Hruba Ralston), and, after 1946 (billed Vera Ralston), *The Plainsman and the Lady*, *The Flame*, *Wyoming; I, Jane Doe; The Fighting Kentuckian*, *The Wild Blue Yonder*, *Belle la Grande*, *Hoodlum Empire*, *Fair Wind to Java*, *Jubilee Trail*, *Timberjack*, *Accused of Murder*, more.

RAMBO, DACK (S. Cal.) Leading man. Onscreen in the '70s. IN: *Which Way to the Front?*, *Deadly Honeymoon*, more.

RAMIREZ, CARLOS (N.Y.) MGM's Mexican minstrel still sings in such New York night spots as Chateau Madrid. Said *Variety*, after one recent appearance, "After more than a couple of decades, the pipes still hold up in power and timbre . . . He is melodic and romantic . . . " Onscreen from 1944. IN: *Two Girls*

and a Sailor, Bathing Beauty, Where Do We Go From Here?, Anchors Aweigh, Easy to Wed, Night and Day.

RAMOS, RICHARD (N.Y.) Support. Onscreen in the '70s. IN: *Klute, Bananas, Believe in Me*, more.

RAMPLING, CHARLOTTE (Eng.) Leading lady. Onscreen from 1965. IN: *The Knack, Rotten to the Core, Georgy Girl, The Long Duel, Sequestro di Persona, The Damned, Three, Corky, The Ski Bum, Henry VIII and His Six Wives, Asylum, Zardoz, The Night Porter; Farewell, My Lovely; Caravan to Vaccares*, more.

RAMSEY, ANNE (N.Y.) Character. Onscreen in the '70s. IN: *For Pete's Sake*, more.

RAMSEY, LOGAN (S. Cal.) Character. Onscreen from the '60s. IN: *The Hoodlum Priest, Head, The Traveling Executioner, What's the Matter with Helen?, The Sporting Club, Jump, Busting*, more.

RAND, SALLY (S. Cal.) This amazing woman, Queen of the Fan Dancers, is in her 70s (b. 1903), but she keeps her shape and her dates with her public: "I have *never* retired—I have averaged 40 working weeks a year since 1933." She also keeps her equilibrium, except when labeled an "exotic" dancer. "The dictionary," she is apt to remind you, "defines 'exotic' as that which is strange and foreign. I am not 'strange'; I like boys. I am not foreign; I was born and raised in Hickory County, Mo." Her act hasn't changed. In clubs she usually does two numbers—the fan dance and her famous five-foot bubble dance; at outdoor theaters, usually just the bubble because of a long-ago experience—"when I first came out with my fans and the wind hit me, I almost took off." How good her act is at this late date is indicated by *Hollywood Reporter* critic Sue Cameron, who reviewed a 1974 performance in L.A. and found the fan dance "glorious" ("The way she moves those fans is an art") and the bubble number "remarkable" ("The audience loved her"). Sally Rand says she does "exactly the same" dance she did that made her the sensation of the 1933 Chicago World's Fair because, "Why not? I'm the original." As for keeping that small (she's only 5'1"), firm, fantastic (35-22-35) shape, she says, "If you love living, you try to take care of the equipment." But, having dieted much of her life, she finds she now can eat whatever she wishes, and her dance rehearsals and performances are the only exercise she needs to stay trim. Her special campaign today is "the value of senior citizens," and in the cities where she plays she oftens addresses local Kiwanis Clubs on the topic. "I'm not the type to sit on the porch and watch life go by," she says, and, given the choice, she thinks most other senior citizens would not be either. As difficult as it may be to believe now, Sally Rand began in movies, after attending Missouri's Christian College, as an ingenue—and as a protegee of Cecil B. De Mille (in *The King of Kings*, she was The Slave to Mary Magdalene). Having already been an artist's model and a successful cafe dancer, this Wampas Baby Star of 1927 rebelled against playing "sweet young things," and, after 1934's *Bolero*—in which at least she danced—she never again appeared in movies. Privately, Sally Rand is petite, bouncy, and miniskirted, and lives in a Frank Lloyd Wright-designed mansion in Glendora, Calif. In 1974 she became a grandmother when her son Sean and his wife Linda, who live nearby in Alta Loma, had a daughter and named her Shawna Michele, whose photograph Sally flashes often and proudly. At Christmas time 1975 she interrupted a $1,500-a-week booking in Seattle to fly to California where she prepared a "huge crown-roast Christmas dinner" for members of her church and spent the holidays with her family. Then, flying off again on her appointed rounds, she laughed, "What in heaven's name is strange about a grandmother dancing nude? I'll bet lots of grandmothers do it." Onscreen from 1924. IN: *The Dressmaker from Paris, Man Bait, The Night of Love, Getting Gertie's Garter, His Dog, The Fighting Eagle, A Girl in Every Port*, more.

RANDALL, ANNE (S. Cal.) Leading lady. Onscreen in the '70s. IN: *A Time for Dying, The Christian Licorice Store*, more.

RANDALL, JERRY (S. Cal.) Support. Onscreen from the '60s. IN: *Hell's Belles, Angel Unchained*, more.

RANDALL, LESLIE (Eng.) Comic character. Onscreen from 1948. IN: *The Small Back Room, Billy Liar, Mystery Submarine*, more.

RANDALL, PAT (S. Cal.) Supporting actress. Onscreen from the '60s. IN: *The Reivers, Adam at 6 A.M.*, more.

RANDALL, STUART (S. Cal.) Character. Onscreen from 1950. IN: *Storm Warning, Bells of Coronado, Tomahawk, The Hoodlum, Bugles in the Afternoon, This Woman Is Dangerous, Kid Monk Baroni, Carbine Williams, Rancho Notorious, Pony Soldier, They Rode West, Run of the Arrow, Frontier Uprising, Taggart!, Fluffy, From the Terrace*, more.

RANDALL, TONY (N.Y.) Costar comedian. Onscreen from 1957. IN: *Oh Men! Oh Women!; Will Success Spoil Rock Hunter?, No Down Payment, The Mating Game, Pillow Talk, Let's Make Love, Lover Come Back, Boys' Night Out, The Brass Bottle, The Seven Faces of Dr. Lao, Send Me No Flowers, The Alphabet Murders, Where Were You When the Lights Went Out?, Hello Down There, Everything You Always Wanted to Know About Sex*, more.

RANDAZZO, TEDDY (N.Y.) Rock singer-actor. Onscreen in 1957 and 1962. IN: *Mister Rock and Roll* and *Hey, Let's Twist*.

RANDELL, RON (S. Cal.) In 1976, after a six-month stage tour in his native Australia in *The Champagne Complex*, this movie leading man costarred on Broadway with Lynn Redgrave in a revival of *Mrs. Warren's Profession*. Onscreen from 1947. IN: *It Had to be You, Bulldog Drummond Strikes Back, The Sign of the Ram, The Mating of Millie, The Loves of Carmen, The Lone Wolf and His Lady, China Corsair, Mississippi Gambler, Kiss Me Kate, Desert Sands, I Am a Camera, The Gold Virgin, The Story of Esther Costello, The Girl in Black Stockings, Most Dangerous Man Alive, King of Kings, Follow the Boys, Legend of a Gunfighter, Electra Glide in Blue*, more.

RANDOLPH, DON (S. Cal.) Character. Onscreen from 1950. IN: *Rogues of Sherwood Forest, The Desert Hawk, Fourteen Hours, The Prince Who Was a Thief, Gunsmoke, Dream Wife, Khyber Patrol, Phffft, Son of Sinbad, The Rawhide Years, My Gun Is Quick, Cowboy*, more.

RANDOLPH, ELSIE (Eng.) Singer-actress. Onscreen from the '30s. IN: *Rise and Shine, That's a Good Girl, This'll Make You Whistle, Sky Riders* (in Poland), *Lord Arthur Saville's Crime, Larceny Street, Frenzy*, more.

RANDOLPH, JANE (Sp.) The tall, dark-haired all-American beauty who, in *The Cat People*, stood by Kent Smith through his travail with "Irena" (Simone Simon) left Hollywood after 1948's *Abbott and Costello Meet Frankenstein*. Now a stately beauty in her 50s (b. 1919), the former Ohio girl has for years been a leader in Madrid society, as the wife of wealthy Jaime del Amo. She paints, attends openings, travels widely, and has no further interest in performing. Onscreen from 1942. IN: *The Falcon's Brother, The Falcon Strikes Back, The Curse of the Cat People, Jealousy, T-Men, Open Secret*, more.

RANDOLPH, JOHN (N.Y.) Character. On-screen from the '60s. IN: *Seconds, Pretty Poison, Number One, There Was a Crooked Man, Escape from the Planet of the Apes, Little Murders, Earthquake,* more.

RANDOLPH, LILLIAN (S. Cal.) Black character actress. Onscreen from 1940. IN: *Little Men, West Point Widow, Mexican Spitfire Sees a Ghost, The Great Gildersleeve, Gildersleeve's Bad Day, The Adventures of Mark Twain, A Song for Miss Julie, It's a Wonderful Life, The Bachelor and the Bobby-Soxer, Sleep My Love; Once More, My Darling; Dear Brat, That's My Boy; Hush . . . Hush, Sweet Charlotte; Once Is Not Enough, Rafferty and the Gold Dust Twins,* more.

RANDOM, BOB (S. Cal.) Leading man. Onscreen from the '60s. IN: *The Restless Ones, This Property Is Condemned, Tick Tick Tick, A Time for Dying,* more.

RANDONE, SALVO (It.) Character. Onscreen from the '60s. IN: *Family Diary, Magnificent Cuckold, The 10th Victim, We Still Kill the Old Way, Investigation of a Citizen Above Suspicion, Fellini Satyricon, Machine Gun McCain,* more.

RANKIN, GIL (S. Cal.) Character. Onscreen from the '60s. IN: *Midnight Cowboy,* more.

RANSOME, PRUNELLA (Eng.) Leading lady. Onscreen from the '60s. IN: *Far From the Madding Crowd, Alfred the Great, Man in the Wilderness,* more.

RAPHEL, JEROME (N.Y.) Character. Onscreen from the '60s. IN: *The Connection, The Cool World,* more.

RAPP, RICHARD (N.Y.) Ballet Star. Onscreen in 1967. IN: *A Midsummer Night's Dream.*

RAS, EVA (Fr.) Leading lady. Onscreen from the '60s. IN: *An Affair of the Heart, Man Is Not a Bird,* more.

RASP, FRITZ (Ger.) Character who, in his 80s (b. 1891), is now retired. Onscreen from the '20s. IN: *Metropolis, The Last Waltz, The Loves of Jeanne Ney, Spies, By Rocket to the Moon, The Beggar's Opera, Karamazof, Klein Dorrit; So, You Don't Know Korff Yet?; Passion, Somewhere in Berlin,* more.

RASULALA, THALMUS (S. Cal.) Black star. Onscreen in the '70s. IN: *Cool Breeze, Bucktown, Mr. Ricco, Friday Foster, Adios Amigo,* more.

RAUCH, SIEGFRIED (Ger.) Leading man. On-screen from the '60s. IN: *Patton, Le Mans,* more.

RAVEN, ELSA (N.Y.) Character. Onscreen in the '70s. IN: *The Honeymoon Killers, The Gang That Couldn't Shoot Straight, Such Good Friends,* more.

RAVEN, MIKE (Eng.) Support. Onscreen in the '70s. IN: *Lust for a Vampire; I, Monster,* more.

RAWLEY, JAMES (S. Cal.) Character. Onscreen from the '50s. IN: *The Creature Walks Among Us, The Thomas Crown Affair,* more.

RAWLINGS, ALICE (S. Cal.) Support. Onscreen from the '60s. IN: *Where Angels Go, Trouble Follows,* more.

RAWLINGS, MARGARET (Eng.) Character. Onscreen from the '50s. IN: *Roman Holiday, Beautiful Stranger, No Road Back,* more.

RAWLINS, LESTER (N.Y.) Support. Onscreen from 1951. IN: *Mr. Congressman, Within Man's Power, Diary of a Mad Housewife, They Might Be Giants,* more.

RAWLS, LOU (S. Cal.) Black singer-actor. On-screen from the '60s. IN: *Angel, Angel, Down We Go* (or, *Cult of the Damned),* more.

RAY, ALDO (S. Cal.) Character; former leading man. Onscreen from 1951. IN: *Saturday's Hero, The Marrying Kind, Pat and Mike, Miss Sadie Thompson, Battle Cry, We're No Angels, The Naked and the Dead, God's Little Acre, Dead Heat on a Merry-Go-Round; What Did You Do in the War, Daddy?; Welcome to Hard Times, The Violent Ones, The Green Berets, Deadlock, Inside Out, Seven Alone, Psychic Killer,* more.

RAY, ANDREW (Eng.) Support; former juvenile lead (b. 1939). Onscreen from 1950. IN: *The Mudlark, The Yellow Balloon, A Prize of Gold, Woman in a Dressing Gown, Gideon of Scotland Yard, The Girl-Getters,* more.

RAY, ANTHONY (S. Cal.) Former supporting actor. Now an assistant director. Son of director Nicholas Ray. Husband of actress Gloria Grahame (once married to his father). Onscreen from the '50s. IN: *Men in War, Shadows, War Hunt.*

RAY, ELLEN (N.Y.) Dancer-actress. Onscreen from 1948. IN: *The Pirate, Take Me Out to the Ball Game, Meet Me After the Show, On the Riviera, The Merry Widow,* more.

RAY, JOHNNIE (Eng.) Popular singer ("Cry"), still active in clubs. Onscreen in 1954. IN: *There's No Business Like Show Business.*

RAY, LEAH (N.Y.) The brunette singer-actress, offscreen since 1938's *Walking Down Broadway*, has been married for many years to socialite Sonny Werblin and, with him, is a racetrack devotee. Onscreen from 1933. IN: *A Bedtime Story, One in a Million, The Holy Terror, Wake Up and Live, Sing and Be Happy, Thin Ice*, more.

RAY, MICHEL (Eng.) Former juvenile. Onscreen from 1955. IN: *The Divided Heart, The Brave One, The Tin Star, Lawrence of Arabia,* etc.

RAY, RENE (Eng.) Support; former leading lady. Onscreen from 1930. IN: *Young Woodley, The Passing of the Third Floor Back, Man of Affairs, The Rat, Troopship, Crime Over London, Housemaster, The Green Cockatoo, If Winter Comes, The Galloping Major, The Circle,* more.

RAY, TED (Eng.) Comedian. Father of former juvenile Andrew Ray. Onscreen from the '30s. IN: *Radio Parade of 1935, A Ray of Sunshine, Meet Me Tonight (Red Peppers), Please Turn Over,* more.

RAYE, CAROL (Eng.) Leading lady. Inactive in movies for two decades. Onscreen from the '40s. IN: *Strawberry Roan, Waltz Time,* more.

RAYE, MARTHA (S. Cal.) The great comedienne's only movie to date in this decade was 1970's *Pufnstuf*, based on the kiddie TV series *H.R. Pufnstuf*, in which she starred. She has not been idle, however. Her South Vietnam war-zone service as a nurse and entertainer endeared her to thousands of American men and women in uniform. Since that combat ended she has starred on tour in such plays as *Everybody Loves Opal, Hello, Dolly!* (which she had done on Broadway), and *No, No, Nanette.* She also, in 1975, made her TV dramatic debut in a two-hour segment of *McMillan & Wife*, titled "Greed." In her 60s now (b. 1916) and single, she has been six times married and divorced. Her husbands: makeup man Buddy Westmore, composer-conductor David Rose, hotel man Neal Lang, dancer Nick Condos (father of her only child, Melodye, b. 1945), dancer Edward Thomas Begley, and policeman Robert O'Shea. Back in Hollywood now, she says, "I've been away from this business for so many years some people in the industry don't know that Martha the Mouth is still around. Well, I am. And I want security. I want money. I want my own TV series—and I'm going to do everything

I can to get it." Onscreen from 1934. IN: Short subjects first, *Rhythm on the Range* (in which her musical rendition of "Mr. Paganini" shot her to stardom), *Big Broadcast of 1937, Waikiki Wedding, Mountain Music, Double or Nothing, Artists and Models, College Swing, Give Me a Sailor, $1,000 a Touchdown, The Boys From Syracuse, Navy Blues, Keep 'Em Flying, Hellzapoppin, Pin-Up Girl, Four Jills in a Jeep, Monsieur Verdoux, Jumbo, The Phynx,* more.

RAYMOND, GARY (S. Cal.) Leading man who was briefly popular in America in the TV series *The Rat Patrol.* Onscreen from 1957. IN: *The Moonrakers, Look Back in Anger, Suddenly Last Summer, El Cid, The Millionairess, The Playboy of the Western World, The Greatest Story Ever Told* (as St. Peter), *Traitor's Gate,* more.

RAYMOND, GENE (S. Cal.) Handsome still in his late 60s (b. 1908), and unmarried since the death of his only wife, Jeanette MacDonald, he lives alone in Brentwood and remains professionally active. In this decade he has worked in such movies as *Five Bloody Graves* (as the Voice of Death), the TV series *Invisible Man, Apple's Way,* and *The D.A.,* and such TV specials as *The First Woman President* with Eva Marie Saint. Onscreen from 1931. IN: *Personal Maid, Ladies of the Big House, Red Dust, If I Had a Million, Zoo in Budapest, The House on 56th Street, Transatlantic Merry-Go-Round, Sadie McKee, The Woman in Red, Love on a Bet, The Life of the Party, Mr. and Mrs. Smith, Smilin' Through* (his only film with Jeanette MacDonald), *The Locket, Sofia, Hit the Deck, Plunder Road, I'd Rather Be Rich, The Best Man,* more.

RAYMOND, GUY (S. Cal.) Character. Onscreen from 1958. IN: *Marjorie Morningstar, Sail a Crooked Ship, Gypsy; The Russians Are Coming, The Russians Are Coming; The Reluctant Astronaut, The Ballad of Josie, Bandolero!,* more.

RAYMOND, PAULA (S. Cal.) Leading lady. Onscreen from 1948. IN: *Racing Luck, Rusty Leads the Way, The Duchess of Idaho, Crisis, Inside Straight, The City That Never Sleeps, King Richard and the Crusaders, The Human Jungle, The Flight That Disappeared, The Spy With My Face, Five Bloody Graves,* more.

RAYMOND, ROBIN (S. Cal.) One of the loveliest girls on the screen in the '40s, and who remained active until the recent past, she underwent eye surgery in the spring of '75 and it is believed she will be able to resume her career. Onscreen from 1941. IN: *Johnny Eager, Moontide, Arabian Nights, Secrets of the Under-*

378

ground, *Are These Our Parents?*, *A Letter for Evie*, *Men in Her Diary*, *The Web*, *Wabash Avenue*, *There's No Business Like Show Business*, *Beyond a Reasonable Doubt*, *Wild in the Country*, *Pendulum*, more.

RAYNER, JOHN (S. Cal.) Leading man. Onscreen from the '60s. IN: *Countdown*, more.

REA, PEGGY (S. Cal.) Character. Onscreen in the '70s. IN: *Cold Turkey*, *What's the Matter with Helen?*, more.

READ, DOLLY (S. Cal.) Leading lady. Former wife of comedian Dick Martin. Onscreen in the '70s. IN: *Beyond the Valley of the Dolls*, more.

READER, RALPH (Eng.) This supporting actor is in his 70s (b. 1903) and retired. Onscreen from 1924. IN: *The Red Robe*, *The Gang Show*, *Derby Day*, *Lilacs in the Spring*, *Limelight*, more.

REAGAN, MAUREEN (S. Cal.) Singer-actress, mainly on the legitimate stage and in TV guest roles. Daughter of Ronald Reagan and Jane Wyman. Onscreen from 1949. IN: *It's a Great Feeling* (juvenile role), more.

REAGAN, RONALD (S. Cal.) Well-preserved in his 60s (b. 1912), the former Warner Bros. star was, before his 1976 Presidential campaign, Governor of California. By his first marriage, to Jane Wyman, he has two children: Maureen, a twice-divorced singer and former TV talk-show hostess, and Michael (adopted), married and a boat dealer in Los Angeles. He also has two by his present, second, wife, former actress Nancy Davis: Patti, a songwriter and singer who goes by the professional name Patti Davis, and Ron Jr., a college student. Financially, the actor did well both at Warners and since; his declared worth in 1976—$1,400,000. Onscreen from 1937. IN: *Love Is on the Air*, *Submarine D-1*, *Boy Meets Girl*, *Brother Rat* (with Jane Wyman), *Dark Victory*, *Secret Service of the Air*, *Angels Wash Their Faces*; *Knute Rockne—All-American*; *Million Dollar Baby* *Kings Row* (perhaps his finest performance), *Juke Girl*, *Desperate Journey*, *This Is the Army*, *Stallion Road*, *The Voice of the Turtle*, *John Loves Mary*, *The Girl From Jones Beach*, *The Hasty Heart*, *Storm Warning*, *Bedtime for Bonzo*, *She's Working Her Way Through College*, *The Winning Team*, *Law and Order*, *Cattle Queen of Montana*, *Hellcats of the Navy*, *Bombs Over China*, more, including 1964's *The Killers*, his most recent to date.

REARDON, MICHAEL (S. Cal.) Leading man. Onscreen from the '60s. IN: *The Syndicate*, *A Death in the Family*, more.

REASON, REX (S. Cal.) Leading man. Inactive in movies for more than a decade. Onscreen from 1952. IN: *Storm Over Tibet*, *Mission Over Korea*, *Salome*, *Yankee Pasha* (billed Bart Roberts), *Smoke Signal*, *Kiss of Fire*, *The Creature Walks Among Us*, *The Desperadoes Are in Town*, *Badlands of Montana*, *A Band of Angels*, *Thundering Jets*, *The Miracle of the Hills*, more.

REASON, RHODES (S. Cal.) Leading man. Onscreen from 1956. IN: *Flight to Hong Kong*, *Emergency Hospital*, *Voodoo Island*, *The Big Fisherman*, *Yellowstone Kelly*, *A Fever in the Blood*, more.

REDD, MARY-ROBIN (S. Cal.) Support. Onscreen in 1966. IN: *The Group*.

REDDY, HELEN (S. Cal.) Grammy-winning singer ("I Am Woman") and actress. Onscreen in 1974. IN: *Airport 1975*.

REDEKER, QUINN (S. Cal.) Support. Onscreen from the '60s. IN: *The Three Stooges Meet Hercules*, *The Christine Jorgensen Story*, *The Midnight Man*, more.

REDFIELD, WILLIAM (N.Y.) Support. Author of the book *Letters From an Actor*. Onscreen from 1939. IN: *Back Door to Heaven* (his debut, in a leading role, at 12), *Conquest of Space*, *The Proud and Profane*, *I Married a Woman*, *The Connection*, *Hamlet* (filmed-on-stage version with Richard Burton), *Morituri*, *Fantastic Voyage*, *A New Leaf*, *Such Good Friends*, *Pigeons*, *One Flew Over the Cuckoo's Nest*, more.

REDFORD, ROBERT (N.Y.) Star. Nominated for Best Actor Oscar in *The Sting*. Onscreen from 1962. IN: *War Hunt*, *Inside Daisy Clover*, *This Property Is Condemned*, *The Chase*, *Barefoot in the Park*, *Tell Them Willie Boy Is Here*, *Butch Cassidy and the Sundance Kid*, *Downhill Racer*, *The Hot Rock*, *Jeremiah Johnson*, *The Candidate*, *The Way We Were*, *The Great Gatsby*, *The Great Waldo Pepper*, *Three Days of the Condor*, *All the President's Men*, more.

REDGRAVE, CORIN (Eng.) Support. Onscreen from 1963. IN: *When Eight Bells Toll*, *A Man for All Seasons*, *A Deadly Affair* (with sister Lynn Redgrave), *The Charge of the Light Brigade* (with sister Vanessa Redgrave), *Oh! What a Lovely War* (with his father, Michael Redgrave, and mother, Rachel Kempson), *The Magus*, *Von Richthofen and Brown*, more.

REDGRAVE, LYNN (N.Y.) Costar. Nominated for Best Actress Oscar in *Georgy Girl*. Daughter of Michael Redgrave. She has been living in

New York for some time as a "resident alien." Onscreen from 1963. IN: *Tom Jones, Girl With Green Eyes, Smashing Time, The Virgin Soldiers, Last of the Mobile Hot-Shots, Every Little Crook and Nanny, Everything You Always Wanted to Know About Sex, Don't Turn the Other Cheek, The Happy Hooker*, more.

REDGRAVE, SIR MICHAEL (Eng.) Star. Nominated for Best Actor Oscar in *Mourning Becomes Electra*. Onscreen from 1938. IN: *The Lady Vanishes, The Stars Look Down, The Remarkable Mr. Kipps, Jeannie, Thunder Rock, The Way to the Stars, Dead of Night, The Captive Heart, Fame Is the Spur, The Smuggler, The Secret Beyond the Door, The Browning Version, The Importance of Being Earnest, The Dam Busters, The Night My Number Came Up, 1984, Time Without Pity, The Quiet American, Shake Hands With the Devil, The Wreck of the Mary Deare, The Innocents, The Loneliness of the Long Distance Runner, Young Cassidy, The Hill, The Heroes of Telemark, The Battle of Britain; Goodbye, Mr. Chips; Goodbye Gemini, Nicholas and Alexandra*, more.

REDGRAVE, VANESSA (Eng.) Star. Nominated for Best Actress Oscar in *Morgan!; Isadora; Mary, Queen of Scots*. Onscreen from the '60s. IN: *A Man for All Seasons, Blow-Up, The Sailor From Gibraltar, The Charge of the Light Brigade, Camelot, A Quiet Place in the Country, Oh! What a Lovely War, The Seagull, Out of Season, The Devils, The Trojan Women, Murder on the Orient Express*, more.

REDMAN, JOYCE (Eng.) Support. Nominated for Best Supporting Actress Oscar in *Tom Jones* and *Othello*. Onscreen from 1942. IN: *One of Our Aircraft Is Missing, The Amorous Adventures of Moll Flanders, Prudence and the Pill*, more.

REDMOND, LIAM (Eng.) Character. Onscreen from 1945. IN: *I See a Dark Stranger, Sword in the Desert, The Divided Heart, Tonight's the Night, 23 Paces to Baker Street, The Curse of the Demon, Under Ten Flags, Kid Galahad, The Luck of Ginger Coffey, The Ghost and Mr. Chicken, Tobruk, The Adventures of Bullwhip Griffin*, more.

REDMOND, MARGE (S. Cal.) Character. Onscreen from 1961. IN: *Sanctuary, The Trouble With Angels, The Fortune Cookie, Adam at 6 A.M., Johnny Got His Gun*, more.

REDMOND, MOIRA (Eng.) Leading lady. Onscreen from 1957. IN: *Jigsaw, Doctor in Love, Kill or Cure, Nightmare*, more.

REED, ADAM (N.Y.) Juvenile. Onscreen from 1968. IN: *Star!, Where's Poppa?, Pigeons*, more.

REED, ALAN, SR. (S. Cal.) Character. Onscreen from 1944. IN: *Days of Glory, The Postman Always Rings Twice, Perfect Strangers, The Redhead and the Cowboy, Viva Zapata!, Actors and Sin, Woman's World, The Far Horizons, The Desperate Hours, Timetable, The Tarnished Angels, Marjorie Morningstar, Breakfast at Tiffany's, A Dream of Kings*, more.

REED, ALAN, JR. (S. Cal.) Support. Son of the above actor. Now in business. Onscreen from 1956. IN: *Rock, Pretty Baby; Peyton Place, Going Steady, The New Interns*, more.

REED, DONNA (S. Cal.) Costar. Won Best Supporting Actress Oscar in *From Here to Eternity*. Beautiful still in her 50s (b. 1921), she lives in Beverly Hills, is completely retired from acting, and, since August 1974, has been the wife of U.S. Army Colonel Grover Asmus, her third husband. She was previously married for two decades to TV producer Tony Owen, with whom she had four children, and earlier—briefly—to MGM makeup man Bill Tuttle. Never entirely satisfied with her movie career, the Iowa-born actress (real name Donna Belle Mullenger) recently expressed the opinion that it might have been different under a name other than "Donna Reed." "A studio publicist hung the name on me, and I never did like it," she said. "I hear 'Donna Reed' and I think of a tall (she is 5'4"), chic, austere blonde that isn't me. 'Donna Reed'—it has a cold, forbidding sound." At that, she concedes, it's an improvement over the first name MGM gave her, changing it just before her first movie was released—Donna Adams. Onscreen from 1941. IN: *The Get-Away, The Bugle Sounds, The Human Comedy, The Courtship of Andy Hardy, Calling Dr. Gillespie, Eyes in the Night, Thousands Cheer; See Here, Private Hargrove; The Picture of Dorian Gray, They Were Expendable, It's a Wonderful Life, Green Dolphin Street, Beyond Glory, Saturday's Hero, Hangman's Knot, Trouble Along the Way, Three Hours to Kill, The Last Time I Saw Paris, The Benny Goodman Story, Ransom, Backlash, Beyond Mambosa*, more, including 1960's *Pepe*, her last.

REED, GEOFFREY (Eng.) Support. Onscreen from the '60s. IN: *The File of the Golden Goose, Macbeth*, more.

REED, JORDAN (N.Y.) Juvenile. Onscreen from 1968. IN: *Star!, Lovers and Other Strangers* (as "Junior"), more.

REED, MARSHALL (S. Cal.) Support; former leading man. Onscreen from 1944. IN: *Mojave Firebrand, Gentleman from Texas, Angel and the Badman, The Gallant Legion, Stampede, Radar Secret Service, Oh! Susanna, Purple Heart Diary, Night Raiders, Cow Country, The Night the World Exploded, The Lineup, A Time for Killing, The Hard Ride,* more.

REED, OLIVER (Eng.) Star. Onscreen from 1960. IN: *The Rebel, Curse of the Werewolf, Paranoic, The System, The Crimson Blade, The Trap, The Girl-Getters, The Jokers, Oliver!, Hannibal Brooks, Women in Love, The Shuttered Room, The Assassination Bureau, The Devils, Sitting Target, Days of Fury, The Three Musketeers, The Four Musketeers, Tommy, Ten Little Indians, Royal Flush, Blood in the Streets, Great Scout & Cathouse Thursday,* more.

REED, PAUL (N.J.) Support. Onscreen from the '60s. IN: *Did You Hear the One about the Traveling Saleslady?,* more.

REED, PHILIP (S. Cal.) Still suavely handsome, married, and Beverly Hills-social, he is a successful business man. Though in his 70s (b. 1900) he looks, easily, two decades younger. Onscreen from 1933. IN: *Female, A Lost Lady, Dr. Monica, Glamour, The Case of the Curious Bride, The Girl from Tenth Avenue, Klondike Annie, Merrily We Live, A Gentleman After Dark, Her Sister's Secret, Big Town After Dark, Song of the Thin Man, Bodyguard, Bandit Queen; Davy Crockett—Indian Scout; The Girl in the Red Velvet Swing, The Tattered Dress,* more, including 1965's *Harum Scarum,* his most recent to date.

REED, REX (N.Y.) Columnist-actor. Onscreen in 1970. IN: *Myra Breckinridge.*

REED, ROBERT (S. Cal.) Costar. Onscreen from 1967. IN: *Hurry Sundown, Star!, The Maltese Bippy.*

REED, SUSAN (N.Y.) Folksinger-actress. Onscreen in 1941. IN: *Glamour Boy.*

REED, TRACY (S. Cal.) Black leading lady. Onscreen from 1964. IN: *Dr. Strangelove, A Shot in the Dark, 1,000 Convicts and a Woman, Percy, The Take,* more.

REED, WALTER (S. Cal.) Leading man. Onscreen from 1942. IN: *Seven Days' Leave, Mexican Spitfire's Elephant, Bombardier, Night Song, Fighter Squadron, The Lawless, Young Man with a Horn, The Eagle and the Hawk, Flying Disc Man from Mars* (serial), *Government Agents vs. Phantom Legion* (serial), *The Clown, War Paint, The Yellow Tomahawk, The Far Horizons, Slim Carter, Sergeant Rutledge, Where Love Has Gone, Moment to Moment, Tora! Tora! Tora!,* more.

REES, LLEWELLYN (Eng.) Character. IN: *Salt & Pepper, Cromwell,* more.

REESE, DELLA (N.Y.) Grammy-winning black singer. Onscreen in 1975. IN: *Psychic Killer.*

REESE, TOM (S. Cal.) Character. Onscreen from the '60s. IN: *Flaming Star; Marines, Let's Go!; The Greatest Story Ever Told, Murderers' Row, Vanishing Point,* more.

REEVES, STEVE (Switz.) Graying as he enters his 50s (b. 1926), Mr. America of 1947 lives in Berne with his blonde-countess wife, Aline, and still displays that rippling muscled physique in Italian-made epics like *A Long Ride to Hell.* His wife (his first and only), who speaks several languages, is his business manager, handling all his contracts, and the actor says, "I have enough money to last me 60 years." And the shape he is in he could live so long. When living in Italy, he said what he missed most about America was: "Rib steak. All beef in Italy is cooked to death. To get a good rib steak you have to go to Switzerland." That problem has been solved. Onscreen from 1954. IN: *Athena, Hercules, Goliath and the Barbarian, The Giant of Marathon, Hercules Unchained, The Last Days of Pompeii, The White Warrior, Morgan the Pirate, The Thief of Bagdad, The Trojan Horse, Duel of the Titans, The Slave, The Last Glory of Troy, The Pirate Prince, Sandokan the Great,* more.

REGAN, PATTI (S. Cal.) Comedienne. Onscreen from the '60s. IN: *How Sweet It Is,* more.

REGAN, PHIL (S. Cal.) The hearts of his Hollywood friends, and they are legion, broke on April 16, 1975. That day, 68 years old and gray, he appeared before an unyielding Santa Barbara judge and wept. "I'm not ready to go—I hadn't planned on it," said the "Singing Policeman" of radio fame who went on to star in many pictures of the '30s and '40s. The judge had just ordered him to begin serving a 1-to-14 year prison sentence. The charge, to which he had pleaded innocent in his '73 trial, was attempted bribery. The actor had been convicted then of trying to bribe a Santa Barbara County supervisor—to influence a zoning change for a lavish ocean-front residential-recreational complex. During the trial his attorney kept Regan from going on the stand in his own defense and maintained a prison term would kill him. And a diagnostic study by the California Institute for Men at Chino also recommended that he not be sent to prison because of medical reasons. After his conviction, while free on $10,000 bond, the former star attempted to live as normally as before—he and his wife, Jo, spending all the time possible with their four grown children (Joseph, Phil Jr., Joan Anne, and Marilyn) and grandchildren. He took little or no part in the political activities—Democratic—in which he had always previously been engaged. He had sung his theme song, "Happy Days Are Here Again," at numerous Democratic National Conventions and had sung the national anthem at the inauguration of President Harry S. Truman. As recently as February 1972, when President Nixon left for Peking, and the Vietnam conflict still raged, he and his wife had circulated a "call for International Peace." And *Variety* noted then that his "homes in Palm Springs, Santa Barbara and Pasadena have been crossroads for top political and labor leaders when they come to the coast." The actor's last public appearance in Hollywood was in February 1975, when he joined with dozens of Friars Club colleagues in a "Roast" of pal George Raft. Two months later, he stood in court hearing a judge order that he begin serving his prison term immediately. Phil Regan, who had come a long way from the time he was a young cop on a beat in New York, sobbed. Pointing to his wife, who was in the courtroom, he cried, "I've been married 51 years—who's going to take care of her?" No one answered. A door closed. The long winter of his life began. Onscreen from 1934. IN: *Dames, The Key, Housewife, Student Tour, The Girl From Tenth Avenue, Go Into Your Dance, Stars Over Broadway, We're in the Money, Broadway Hostess, Laughing Irish Eyes, The Hit Parade, Manhattan Merry-Go-Round, She Married a Cop, Flight at Midnight, Tugboat Annie Sails Again, Las Vegas Nights, Sweet Rosie O'-Grady, Sunbonnet Sue, Sweetheart of Sigma Chi*, more, including 1950's *Three Little Words*, his last.

REGGIANI, SERGE (Fr.) Leading man. Onscreen from the '40s. IN: *Star Without Light, Gates of the Night, Children of Chaos, The Sinners, Manon, Act of Love, La Ronde, Marie Octobre, Paris Blues, The Leopard; Doulos—The Finger Man; Vincent, Francois, Paul and the Others;* more.

REID, BERYL (Eng.) Character. Onscreen from 1954. IN: *The Belles of St. Trinian's, Trial and Error, Inspector Clouseau, Star!, The Killing of Sister George, The Assassination Bureau, Entertaining Mr. Sloan, Dr. Phibes Rises Again, The Death Wheelers*, more.

REID, ELLIOTT (S. Cal.) Support; former leading man. Onscreen from 1940. IN: *The Ramparts We Watch, The Story of Dr. Wassell, A Double Life, Gentlemen Prefer Blondes, Vickie, Woman's World, Inherit the Wind, The Absent-Minded Professor, The Thrill of It All, The Wheeler Dealers, Move Over Darling, Blackbeard's Ghost, Some Kind of a Nut*, more.

REID, FRANCES (S. Cal.) Character. Popular on TV soap operas. Onscreen from 1966. IN: *Seconds*, more.

REID, KATE (S. Cal.) Support. Onscreen from 1961. IN: *One Plus One, This Property Is Condemned, Pigeons, The Andromeda Strain*, more.

REID, MILTON (Eng.) Character. Onscreen from the '60s. IN: *The Wonders of Aladdin, Deadlier Than the Male, The Horsemen*, more.

REID, SHEILA (Eng.) Support. Onscreen from the '60s. IN: *Othello, The Alphabet Murders, The Touch, Three Sisters*, more.

REID, WALLACE, JR. (S. Cal.) Support; inactive in movies now. Onscreen in 1940. IN: *Gold Rush Maisie*. (See Dorothy Davenport.)

REID, MRS. WALLACE (S. Cal.) Leading lady Dorothy Davenport used this, her married name, in numerous silents: *Human Wreckage, Broken Laws, The Satin Woman, Hell-Ship Bronson*, more. (See Dorothy Davenport.)

REILLY, CHARLES NELSON (N.Y.) Comic support. Onscreen from 1957. IN: *A Face in the Crowd, Let's Rock, Two Tickets to Paris, The Tiger Makes Out*, more.

REILLY, HUGH (S. Cal.) Leading man. Inactive in movies in recent years, he has appeared regularly in the TV soap opera *Edge of Night*. Onscreen from 1949. IN: *Johnny Stool Pigeon, Bright Victory, Chuka*, more.

REILLY, JANE (N.Y.) Support. Onscreen from 1967. IN: *Passages From James Joyce's Finnegans Wake.*

REIMERS, ED (N.Y.) Actor-TV announcer (Allstate). Onscreen from the '50s. IN: *Hard, Fast and Beautiful; On the Loose, The Barefoot Executive*, more.

REINDEL, CARL (S. Cal.) Support. Onscreen from the '60s. IN: *Bullitt, Speedway, The Gypsy Moths, The Thousand Plane Raid, The Cheyenne Social Club, Tora! Tora! Tora!*, more.

REINER, CARL (S. Cal.) Character comedian. Onscreen from 1959. IN: *Happy Anniversary, The Gazebo, It's a Mad Mad Mad Mad World, The Thrill of It All, The Art of Love; The Russians Are Coming, The Russians Are Coming; A Guide for the Married Man, Generation,* more.

REINER, ROB(ERT) (S. Cal.) Comic leading man. Son of Carl Reiner. Onscreen from 1967. IN: *Enter Laughing, Where's Poppa?, Halls of Anger, Summertree,* more.

REMICK, LEE (Eng.) Costar. Nominated for Best Actress Oscar in *Days of Wine and Roses.* Married (her second marriage) to an Englishman, assistant movie director Kip Gowans, the American actress lives in London now. Onscreen from 1957. IN: *A Face in the Crowd, The Long Hot Summer, Anatomy of a Murder, These Thousand Hills, Wild River, Sanctuary, Experiment in Terror, The Wheeler Dealers, The Running Man; Baby, the Rain Must Fall; No Way to Treat a Lady, The Detective, Hard Contract, Sometimes a Great Notion, A Delicate Balance, Hennessy, The Omen,* more.

REMSEN, BERT (S. Cal.) Character. Onscreen from the '60s. IN: *Moon Pilot, The Strawberry Statement, Brewster McCloud, Thieves Like Us, California Split,* more.

RENALDO, DUNCAN (S. Cal.) When he last portrayed "The Cisco Kid"—after 12 movies and 156 half-hour TV shows—he was 53. He is well into his 70s now (b. 1904), but, at his public's insistence, he has never been able to stop "playing" the Kid. Ostensibly retired, he says, "My wife and I are living on my ranch, Rancho Mi Amigo, here in Santa Barbara and enjoying the blessings of our country." But the cowboy star's retirement is not a sedentary one. In '73, for instance, a rock group named War recorded a hit song beginning with the line "Cisco Kid was a friend of mine," and, naturally, Renaldo was summoned to make—and gladly did—TV promotional spots for the record. Furthermore, he says, "I am called upon to do many personal appearances at service clubs and community events, and to give lectures at schools. Simultaneously, I am on the board of directors of Hope Ranch Association, the Old Spanish Days of Santa Barbara, and the Research Park Association here. Also I have written scripts for a new TV production, *Son of Cisco Kid,* in which we plan to star one of my sons." The Renaldos have two grown sons, Richard and Jeremy, and a daughter, Stephanie, who teaches music. The actor adds: "We still have both horses I used in the series. Both are named Diablo and both exhibit all the attributes of motion picture horses." A recent visitor to Rancho Mi Amigo

reports of Duncan Renaldo: "Wrinkles of age etch his face, the once coal-black hair is now snow white and the Argentine gaucho costume no longer fits. But the Cisco Kid still lives within Duncan Renaldo." Onscreen from 1925. IN: *Fifty-Fifty* (his first lead after many bits), *Romany Love, Marchetta, Bridge of San Luis Rey, Trader Horn, Moonlight Murder, Crime Afloat, Rose of the Rio Grande, Spawn of the North, Covered Wagon Days, Secret Service in Darkest Africa* (serial), *For Whom the Bell Tolls, The Fighting Seabees, Sheriff of Sundown, The Cisco Kid Returns, In Old Mexico, Sword of the Avenger, Bells of San Fernando, The Daring Caballero, We Were Strangers, The Capture, Zorro Rides Again,* more.

RENARD, DAVID (S. Cal.) Support. Onscreen from the '60s. IN: *The Counterfeit Killer, Change of Habit, Hangup,* more.

RENARD, KEN (S. Cal.) Character. Onscreen from the '50s. IN: *Lydia Bailey, Something of Value, These Thousand Hills, Home From the Hill,* more.

RENAY, LIZ (S. Cal.) Support. Onscreen from the '60s. IN: *The Hard Road, Refinements of Love,* more.

RENELLA, PAT (S. Cal.) Supporting actor. Onscreen from the '60s. IN: *Dayton's Devils, Moon Child,* more.

RENN, KATHARINA (Fr.) Leading lady. Onscreen from the '60s. IN: *The Rise of Louis XIV,* more.

RENNICK, NANCY (S. Cal.) Support. Onscreen from the '60s. IN: *The Young Lovers,* more.

RENNIE, GUY (S. Cal.) Support. Onscreen from the '50s. IN: *Grounds for Marriage, Lenny,* more.

RENOIR, JEAN (Fr.) One of the screen's great directors (*Grand Illusion, The Southerner,* etc.), he also has appeared in numerous pictures as an actor. IN: *The Human Beast, The Rules of the Game, A Day in the Country,* more.

RENOUDET, PETE (S. Cal.) Character. Onscreen from the '60s. IN: *The Love Bug, The Computer Wore Tennis Shoes, $1,000,000 Duck, The Barefoot Executive,* more.

RENZI, EVA (Ger.) Leading lady. Onscreen from the '60s. IN: *Funeral in Berlin, That Woman, The Pink Jungle, The Bird with the Crystal Plumage,* more.

RESIN, DAN (N.Y.) Support. Onscreen in the '70s. IN: *Hail, Crazy Joe*, more.

RETTIG, TOMMY (S. Cal.) Early in 1976 *Variety* published a news story about the former boy actor (b. 1941) under the headline: LASSIE WOULD SAY: 'SAY IT AIN'T SO, JOE.' The reference, of course, was to the fact that in the '50s on TV, Tommy Rettig had portrayed the young master of the famous canine. Now he had made news of a different sort. He had been arrested in Los Angeles in '75—his second arrest on California drug charges—and accused of smuggling liquid cocaine from Peru into the United States in liqueur bottles. Rettig maintained he had been writing a book about cocaine smuggling when the real smugglers framed him. But, finding him guilty, a Los Angeles judge sentenced him to five and a half years in Federal prison. The former actor said he would appeal even though he and his wife were flat broke. A public defender was assigned to handle the appeal. Onscreen from 1950. IN: *Panic in the Streets, The Jackpot, Two Weeks with Love, For Heaven's Sake, Elopement, Weekend With Father, Paula, The Lady Wants Mink, The 5,000 Fingers of Dr. T, So Big, River of No Return, The Raid, The Eygptian, The Cobweb, At Gunpoint*, more, including 1956's *The Last Wagon*, his most recent to date.

REVERE, ANNE (N.Y.) Character. Won Best Supporting Actress Oscar in *National Velvet*. Nominated in the same category in *The Song of Bernadette* and *Gentleman's Agreement*. Hollywood kept this dominant actress incredibly busy for a full decade—36 movies between 1940's *The Howards of Virginia* and *The Great Missouri Raid*, filmed in 1950 and released the following year. And, as noted above, it honored her, reserving its highest praise for her mother roles. But in 1951 the town turned its back on her. Eighteen years passed before she again faced motion picture cameras—in *Tell Me That You Love Me, Junie Moon*. Following that came *Macho Callahan*, described by the actress as "an ill-fated Western which I did on a fabulous location in Mexico; unfortunately, the picture didn't match the location." There was then a guest role on TV in *Six Million Dollar Man*, and, in 1976, finally, a major role in an important movie, *Birch Interval*. What happened that kept Anne Revere away from the screen for so many years was the House Un-American Activities Committee. She "took the Fifth," refusing to answer questions regarding alleged Communist affiliations. She has long since maintained that the photocopy of her alleged Communist Party registration card, which bore no signature, was a "plant." A dyed-in-the-wool Yankee and a direct descendant of Paul Revere, she has also pointed out with

some fervor that in 1948 she had signed a United States loyalty oath and has not since changed her ideology. Still, Hollywood—running scared in those days—shut the door on Anne Revere and cost her two decades of what should have been her prime years on the screen. When this professional tragedy occurred she was only 48, and at the peak of her powers as a performer. Her unique essence as a character actress was finely captured by Doug McClelland in his book *The Unkindest Cuts*: "There was something about Anne Revere—her long Yankee face, her rigid, even stern stoicism that was not without a certain humor, her golden silences, the repressed emotion only a nick beneath the surface. . '. her strength, her presence. Miss Revere could fasten down the flightiest screenplay, toss security blankets to an entire audience." After her blacklisting, Paramount scissored her finished performance in *A Place in the Sun*, as Montgomery Clift's Salvation Army mother, until it was no more than a bit—leaving a considerable hole in the film. Broadway, where the actress had enjoyed a long career between graduation from Wellesley and her Hollywood years, provided her then with several outstanding roles. She received a Tony for her performance in 1960's *Toys in the Attic*. Between Broadway plays she appeared in many stock productions throughout the country. New York, though, was—and is—home base. For years it was Manhattan. She and her husband, director-writer Samuel Rosel (married since 1935), kept a big apartment on the upper West Side, nearby the Hudson River. Now, she says, "I live with my husband on the North Shore of Long Island less than half a mile from some of the best swimming on the Sound. We live on a two-acre—shall I say estate? I shall because when there are just two of us [they do not have children] to care for it, it seems immense. But it is our pride and joy and we delight in working on it." Truth to tell, she enjoys work itself—and exploring new fields. In 1939 she had appeared in an experimental television production and found it challenging. In 1950 she had been set to star in a TV series when fate canceled that. Finally, in the early 60s, she did a few educational TV dramas and discovered not only that she enjoyed the medium, but how much she had missed working before cameras. Plunging into the world of daytime serials, she played running roles in *Edge of Night, A Time for Us*, and, for all of 1970, *Search for Tomorrow*. A friendly, warm woman, and homely elegant, decidedly unlike the austere characters she most often played on the screen, Anne Revere admits she is most interested in working steadily in pictures again, but, she adds. "in the meantime I don't lack for pleasurable work and magnificent surroundings." Onscreen once in 1934 in *Double Door*.

Then onscreen regularly from 1940. IN: *One Crowded Night, Men of Boys Town, Remember the Day, The Flame of New Orleans, The Gay Sisters, Star-Spangled Rhythm, Old Acquaintance, Standing Room Only, The Keys of the Kingdom, Sunday Dinner for a Soldier, The Thin Man Goes Home, Fallen Angel, Dragonwyck, Forever Amber, Body and Soul, The Secret Beyond the Door; Scudda Hoo! Scudda Hay!; Deep Waters,* more.

REVIER, DOROTHY (S. Cal.) Now in her 70s (b. 1904) and married a second time—after a long-ago divorce from director Harry Revier— she gave up her career after a 1936 Western with Buck Jones, *The Cowboy and the Kid.* Living in semiretirement near Hollywood, she paints as a hobby and seldom gives a thought to the years in which she was one of the silent screen's best blonde vamps. Onscreen from 1922. IN: *Just a Woman, Poker Faces, The Drop Kick, The Red Dance, Beware of Blondes, The Siren, The Iron Mask, Tanned Legs, The Donovan Affair, The Dance of Life, Hold Everything, The Way of All Men, The Black Camel, Night World, By Candlelight, Unknown Blonde, Circus Shadows, The Lady in Scarlet,* more, including 1936's *The Cowboy and the Kid,* her last.

REVILL, CLIVE (Eng.) Costar. Onscreen from the '50s. IN: *The Headless Ghost, Bunny Lake Is Missing, Kaleidoscope, The Double Man, A Fine Madness, Modesty Blaise, The Shoes of the Fisherman, The High Commissioner, Nobody Runs Forever, The Assassination Bureau, The Private Life of Sherlock Holmes, Avanti, The Little Prince, Galileo, One of Our Dinosaurs Is Missing,* more.

REY, ALEJANDRO (S. Cal.) Leading man. Onscreen from 1959. IN: *Solomon and Sheba, The Battle at Bloody Beach, Fun in Acapulco, Blindfold, Synanon, The Sandpit Generals, Breakout,* more.

REY, ANTONIA (N.Y.) Character. Onscreen from the '60s. IN: *Popi, The Lords of Flatbush,* more.

REY, FERNANDO (Sp.) Costar. Onscreen from the '40s. IN: *Don Quixote, The Mad Queen, The Last Days of Pompeii, Viridiana, The Running Man, The Ceremony, Return of the Seven, El Greco, Navajo Joe, The Desperate Ones, Villa Rides, Guns of the Magnificent Seven, The Discreet Charm of the Bourgeoisie, The French Connection, Drama of the Rich, The French Connection II, Seven Beauties, A Matter of Time,* more.

REYNOLDS, BURT (S. Cal.) Star. Onscreen from 1961. IN: *Angel Baby, Armored Command, Navajo Joe, Sam Whiskey, Shark, The Golden Bullet, 100 Rifles, Skullduggery, Shamus, Fuzz, Deliverance, The Man Who Loved Cat Dancing, The Longest Yard, At Long Last Love, Lucky Lady, W.W. and the Dixie Dancekings, Hustle, Nickelodeon,* more.

REYNOLDS, DALE (N.Y.) Leading man. Onscreen in the '70s. IN: *Hail,* more.

REYNOLDS, DEBBIE (S. Cal.) Star. Nominated for Best Actress Oscar in *The Unsinkable Molly Brown.* In this decade she starred on Broadway in the musical *Irene.* Onscreen from 1948. IN: *June Bride, Daughter of Rosie O'-Grady, Three Little Words, Two Weeks with Love, Mr. Imperium, Singin' in the Rain, I Love Melvin, Give a Girl a Break, Susan Slept Here, Athena, Hit the Deck, The Catered Affair, Bundle of Joy* (with singer Eddie Fisher, first of her two husbands—the other was tycoon Harry Karl—and the father of her children, Carrie and Todd), *Tammy and the Bachelor* (introduced the song "Tammy" which sold a million copies, winning her a Gold Record), *The Mating Game, It Started With a Kiss, The Gazebo, The Rat Race, The Pleasure of His Company, How the West Was Won, Mary Mary, My Six Loves, Goodbye Charlie, The Singing Nun, Divorce American Style, What's the Matter with Helen?,* more.

REYNOLDS, GENE (S. Cal.) One of the screen's better juvenile leads from the '30s and well into the '40s—in more than 30 pix—he has long since worked on the other side of Hollywood cameras. And with spectacular results. Now a wiry, slender man in his 50s (b. 1925), he is executive producer (and sometimes director) of the TV series *M*A*S*H,* winning Emmys and Directors Guild awards right and left. He has done similar chores also on such other series as *The Ghost and Mrs. Muir, Room 222,* and *Anna and the King of Siam.* The still dark-haired (but graying) former actor—his last role a supporting one in Lana Turner's *Diane* in '55 —is married to ex-actress Bonnie Jones. She also switched careers in mid-course with happy consequences. Her novel *The Truth About Unicorns,* published in '72, won an Oppie as "Best First Novel of the Year." It was then optioned for a movie to be produced and directed by— Gene Reynolds. Onscreen from 1936. IN: *Sins of Man; Thank You, Jeeves; Let's Sing Again, Madame X, Heidi, In Old Chicago, Of Human Hearts, Boys Town, Love Finds Andy Hardy, The Spirit of Culver, They Shall Have Music* (a particularly outstanding performance), *The Blue Bird, Edison the Man, The Mortal Storm, The Tuttles of Tahiti, Eagle Squadron, 99 River Street, The Country Girl, The Bridges at Toko-Ri,* more.

REYNOLDS, JOSEPH (N.Y.) Support. Onscreen from the '60s. IN: *How to Murder Your Wife, Mirage,* more.

REYNOLDS, KAY (N.Y.) Support. Onscreen from the '60s. IN: *How to Succeed in Business Without Really Trying,* more.

REYNOLDS, MARJORIE (S. Cal.) If Hollywood producers have a job for this actress—onscreen from age 3 right through a 1964 B, *The Silent Witness*—she may be easily found. She's still a member of Screen Actors Guild, has a good agent, her photo appears regularly under "Leading Women" in the *Hollywood Players Directory,* and she's just a phone call away in the San Fernando Valley. If the phone calls don't come, Marjorie Reynolds—or Marjorie Moore as she was billed in many early movies, including 1934's *Wine, Women and Song*—can afford to shrug. She's comfortably set up, having invested her earnings wisely, and she's happy. Since '46 she has been married to film editor John Hafen, by whom she has a married daughter, Linda. (Marjorie was earlier—1936-45—the wife of Signal Corps Captain Jack Reynolds.) Besides their home and other plots of real estate, Marjorie and her husband own a five-unit apartment building in Beverly Hills that she personally supervises. Now in her 50s (b. 1921) and no longer a blonde—brown-haired with an attractive gray streak—Marjorie Reynolds is still lighthearted, trim, and pretty, and looks fit (thanks to golf and swimming) to face the cameras on a moment's notice. Onscreen from the mid-'20s. IN: *Scaramouche, Revelation, The Broken Wing, Svengali, College Humor, Murder in Greenwich Village, Champagne Waltz, Tailspin Tommy* (serial), *Overland Express* (one of 30 Westerns in which she was the leading lady), *Mr. Wong in Chinatown, Midnight Limited, Up in the Air, Tillie the Toiler, Holiday Inn* (the '42 movie in which she danced with Astaire—the beginning of her Paramount contract and her best screen period), *Star-Spangled Rhythm, Dixie, Ministry of Fear, Up in Mabel's Room, Duffy's Tavern, Bring on the Girls, Monsieur Beaucaire, Heaven Only Knows, That Midnight Kiss, The Great Jewel Robbery, His Kind of Woman; Mobs, Inc.; Juke Box Rhythm,* more.

REYNOLDS, PETER (Eng.) Character. Onscreen from the '40s. IN: *The Captive Heart, Smart Alec, The Guinea Pig, Adam and Evalyn, The Woman's Angle, The Silver Chalice, It Takes a Thief,* more.

REYNOLDS, WILLIAM (S. Cal.) Leading man. Onscreen from 1951. IN: *Dear Brat, No Questions Asked, The Desert Fox, Has Anybody Seen My Gal?, Carrie, Son of Ali Baba, Francis Goes to West Point, The Mississippi Gambler, Away All Boats, Mister Cory, The Thing That Couldn't Die, A Distant Trumpet; Follow Me, Boys!;* more.

RHETT, ALICIA (S.C.) She was in her early 20s in '39 when she played Leslie Howard's stern young spinster sister, "India Wilkes," in *Gone With the Wind,* her only movie. After it, she returned to her native city, Charleston, S.C., and has never again been back to Hollywood, though critics praised her performance and she could easily have continued as an actress. Today, in her 50s, she is a petite, friendly, rather shy gentlewoman with a salt-and-pepper feather bob who wears mod wire-rimmed specs, and who has a total aversion to publicity. She lives graciously in a fine old house (inherited) in downtown Charleston. Asked what she has been doing in the many years since *GWTW,* she answers with a gay, lilting laugh—and in an accent far more delicate even than the "Georgia" one employed in the movie: "Oh, I've been painting and having a good time." During WW II she used her artistic talent as an avocation, sketching servicemen's portraits at the Charleston USO. Later, after a stint as a radio news commentator on local station WTMA, she worked as a commercial artist with Bradham Advertising. She has long since been one of the South's finest and most successful portrait painters, some of her work hanging in the Charleston Museum. She works at home in a second-floor studio that captures the northern light. Despite her shyness, Alicia Rhett (her real name, incidentally) is a gregarious woman, highly social, with many close friends. Trapped in an interview, she answers with a smile—a charming, wide smile showing perfect teeth—and gives brief answers. Her age now? "I'm not going to tell you!" A brief bit of background information? "I think we'll just let it go. I don't want to go into any life history or anything." *GWTW?* "A delightful memory. I enjoyed it." Director George Cukor who did her test and directed the Twelve Oaks barbecue scenes? "A charming man." Has she seen the movie in recent years? "Oh-h, I don't want to talk about *Gone With the Wind.* I'm tired of it!" Why didn't she continue in Hollywood? With both hands she outlines an airy Mae West shape and says she didn't have what it took to succeed there. Did she have a new photograph? "No." One final question: Did she marry? "No!"—said with that smile. She guards her privacy well—charmingly.

RHOADES, BARBARA (S. Cal.) Leading lady. First billed Barbara Rhodes. Onscreen from the '60s. IN: *Don't Just Stand There, The Shakiest Gun in the West, There Was a Crooked Man, Harry and Tonto,* more.

RHODES, BILLIE (S. Cal.) The charming brunette of early silents, now in her late 70s, has long been retired but still lives in Hollywood. Onscreen from 1913. IN: *Perils of the Sea, A Seminary Scandal* (the very first of the Al E. Christie Comedies, released in '16, in which she and Harry Ham costarred), *Some Nurse, Beware of Blondes, Dad's Knockout*, more.

RHODES, CHRISTOPHER (Eng.) Character. Onscreen from the '50s. IN: *Betrayed, The Colditz Story, Naked Earth, El Cid, Becket*, more.

RHODES, DONNELLY (S. Cal.) Support. Onscreen from the '60s. IN: *Butch Cassidy and the Sundance Kid*, more.

RHODES, ERIK (N.Y.) The comedian who, with Eric Blore, was often in Astaire-Rogers movies, dropped out of movies after 1939's *On Your Toes*. Following service in the Pacific as a captain in the Air Force in WW II, he played leads in many Broadway musicals: *Shinbone Alley, Dance Me a Song, A Funny Thing Happened on the Way to the Forum*, etc. In addition to doing still more musicals on tour (*1776* recently) and at civic light opera playhouses across the country, he acted in the soap opera *The Secret Storm*. Long and happily married, the actor, now in his 70s (b. 1906), lives with his wife, Emmala, in a townhouse in the East 50s. He was highly incensed when, in a recent *New York Times* article on actors who had portrayed homosexuals on the screen, his name was included. In a letter dispatched at once to the *Times*, he said, among other things, "On the ground of invasion of personal privacy, the ghosts of Franklin Pangborn and Eric Blore, and I, who happen to be still on this planet, take great exception to his [the author] including us in patently homosexual roles such as he describes . . . The roles we appeared in were not conceived along those lines . . ." Onscreen from 1934. IN: *The Gay Divorcee, A Night at the Ritz, Charlie Chan in Paris, The Nitwits, Old Man Rhythm, Top Hat, Two in the Dark, One Rainy Afternoon, Second Wife, Criminal Lawyer, Woman Chases Man, Music for Madame, Meet the Girls, Dramatic School, Mysterious Mr. Moto of Devil's Island*, more.

RHODES, GRANDON (S. Cal.) This veteran character actor is retired and in bereavement for his wife of many years, actress Ruth Lee, who died in 1975. He was last onscreen in 1960's *The Bramble Bush*. Onscreen from 1944. IN: *Follow the Boys, Sensations of 1945, The Magnificent Doll, Ride the Pink Horse, Walk a Crooked Mile, It Happens Every Spring, All the King's Men, Tucson, Born Yesterday, Detective Story, Revenge of the Creature, Earth vs. the Flying Saucers, These Wilder Years*, more.

RHODES, HARI (S. Cal.) Black leading man. Onscreen from the '60s. IN: *Drums of Africa, The Satan Bug, Taffy and the Jungle Hunter, Return to Peyton Place, Mirage, Shock Corridor, The Sins of Rachel Cade, Let No Man Write My Epitaph, Blindfold, Conquest of the Planet of the Apes*, more.

RHODES, JORDAN (S. Cal.) Support. Onscreen in the '70s. IN: *Angel Unchained, The Terminal Man, Mr. Majestyk*, more.

RHODES, MARJORIE (Eng.) Character. Onscreen from 1939. IN: *Poison Pen, Love on the Dole, On Approval, Enchantment, The Inheritance; Time, Gentlemen, Please; Both Sides of the Law; Mrs. Brown, You've Got a Lovely Daughter;* more.

RHODES, VIVIAN (N.Y.) Character. Onscreen in the '70s. IN: *Watermelon Man*, more.

RHUE, MADLYN (S. Cal.) Leading lady. Onscreen from 1959. IN: *Operation Petticoat, A Majority of One, Escape from Zahrain, He Rides Tall, Stranger on the Run, Stand Up and Be Counted*, more.

RICE, DARLENE (S. Cal.) Black juvenile. Onscreen in the '70s. IN: *Brother John*, more.

RICE, HOWARD (S. Cal.) Black juvenile. Onscreen in the '70s. IN: *Brother John, The Liberation of Lord Byron Jones*, more.

RICE, JOAN (Eng.) Character; former leading lady. Onscreen from 1950. IN: *One Wild Oat, The Story of Robin Hood* (as Maid Marian), *The Crowded Day, Glory at Sea, His Majesty O'-Keefe, Women in Prison, A Day to Remember, Blonde Bait, The Long Knife, Payroll, Horror of Frankenstein*, more.

RICH, ALLAN (N.Y.) Character. Onscreen in the '70s. IN: *The Gambler*, more.

RICH, CLAUDE (Fr.) Character. Onscreen from the '50s. IN: *Mitsou, Love and the Frenchwoman, Male Hunt, Is Paris Burning?, The Bride Wore Black, Stavisky*, more.

RICH, FRANCES (S. Cal.) The daughter of star Irene Rich, she had a brief movie career before giving it up to become a sculptor—which she still is. At last report she was unmarried and living with her mother. Onscreen in 1933. IN: *Zoo in Budapest* and *Pilgrimage*.

RICH, IRENE (S. Cal.) In her 80s now (b. 1891 —a date well publicized when she was featured for years in Welch's Grape Juice advertisements), she is silver-haired, well preserved, and living in quite wealthy retirement in Santa Barbara. "I have been through aitch-ee-double-ell," she has said, "and I think that that kept me looking young. Trying experiences are the best character builders and you can keep young if you take your blows with your chin up." She did. And it obviously worked. Onscreen from 1918. IN: *Stella Maris, Jes' Call Me Jim, Brass, Lucretia Lombard, Beau Brummell, Cytherea, Behold This Woman, A Lost Lady, Silken Shackles, Beware of Married Men, Craig's Wife, Ned McCobb's Daughter, They Had to See Paris, Father's Son, So This Is London, The Champ, Her Mad Night, Manhattan Tower, That Certain Age* (her comeback movie after six years in radio in New York), *The Mortal Storm, The Lady in Question, This Time for Keeps, Angel and the Badman, New Orleans,* more, including her last two in 1948, *Joan of Arc* and *Fort Apache.*

RICH, RON (S. Cal.) Support. Onscreen from the '60s. IN: *The Fortune Cookie, Chubasco,* more.

RICHARD, CLIFF (Eng.) Singer-actor who gave up show business and is now an evangelist. Onscreen in 1960. IN: *Expresso Bongo.*

RICHARD, LITTLE (N.Y.) Black singer. Onscreen in 1957. IN: *Don't Knock the Rock* and *Mister Rock and Roll.*

RICHARDS, ANN (S. Cal.) The Australian actress who made a vivid impression in *An American Romance, Love Letters,* and *The Searching Wind,* as well as others of the '40s, has been married since early in '49 to Edmond Angelo. A onetime play producer, and author of the college textbook *Curtain, You're On!,* he directed her last film, 1952's *Breakdown.* For more than 25 years he has been a space engineer with a major California firm. The Angelos have two grown sons, Christopher and Mark, and a teen-age daughter, Juliet. Besides their large house in Los Angeles, they have a mountain house near Big Bear where they ski on weekends in the winter. In her 50s now (b. 1919), the former actress is today a poet—author of the book of poems *The Grieving Senses* and the verse play *Helen of Troy,* which she and her husband have occasionally presented on college campuses. As a poet she has been a panelist at—among others—the California Writers Conference at California State University. She has also been, for more than a decade, International Chairman of the International Senior League. This organization, sponsor of Teacher Remembrance Day, presents awards annually to outstanding educators, both national and foreign. Her only acting now, she says, is giving readings—usually at schools—of poetry, her own and that of others.

But she does not rule out a return to motion pictures. Onscreen in Australia from 1937. IN: *Come Up Smiling, Tall Timber, The Woman in the House,* more. Onscreen in America from 1942. IN: *Dr. Gillespie's New Assistant, Random Harvest, Badman's Territory, A Scandal in Paris, Lost Honeymoon, Love From a Stranger; Sorry, Wrong Number;* more.

RICHARDS, AUBREY (Eng.) Character. Onscreen from the '60s. IN: *The Ipcress File,* more.

RICHARDS, BEAH (S. Cal.) Black character. Nominated for Best Supporting Actress Oscar in *Guess Who's Coming to Dinner.* Onscreen from 1961. IN: *Take a Giant Step, The Miracle Worker, Gone Are the Days!, Hurry Sundown, In the Heat of the Night, The Biscuit Eater, Mahogany,* more.

RICHARDS, BURT (N.Y.) Character. Onscreen from the '60s. IN: *Mortadella, Sisters, Shamus, Loving, The Godfather, The French Connection, Badge 373, The Hot Rock, Godspell,* more.

RICHARDS, FRANK (S. Cal.) Character. Onscreen from 1940. IN: *Before I Hang, No Way Out, Carbine Williams, Pat and Mike, The Savage, A Woman Under the Influence,* more.

RICHARDS, JON (N.Y.) Character. Onscreen from the '60s. IN: *I Never Sang for My Father, Plaza Suite, The Boston Strangler, Shaft,* more.

RICHARDS, KEITH (S. Cal.) Support; former leading man. Onscreen from 1942. IN: *The Forest Rangers, So Proudly We Hail, Queen of the Amazons, Aerial Gunner, Where the North Begins, Walk a Crooked Mile, Captain China, Spoilers of the Plains, Yaqui Drums, The Buster Keaton Story, Incident in an Alley,* more.

RICHARDS, KEN (N.Y.) Support. Onscreen from the '50s. IN: *The Last Angry Man,* more.

RICHARDS, KIM (S. Cal.) Juvenile actress. Onscreen in the '70s. IN: *The Monster of Strawberry Cove, Kotch, Escape to Witch Mountain, No Deposit No Return,* more.

RICHARDS, STEPHEN (S. Cal.) The screen name of Mark Stevens in his earliest pictures. Onscreen from 1944. IN: *Passage to Marseille, The Doughgirls, Objective Burma, God Is My Co-Pilot,* more. (See Mark Stevens.)

RICHARDS, SUSAN (Eng.) Character. Onscreen from the '50s. IN: *The Rocking Horse Winner, The Devil Within Her,* more.

RICHARDS, VINCENT (S. Cal.) The screen name of Vincent Edwards in his first picture—1952's *Hiawatha*. (See Vincent Edwards.)

RICHARDSON, IAN (Eng.) Support. Onscreen from the '60s. IN: *Marat/Sade*, more.

RICHARDSON, JOHN (Eng.) Leading man. Onscreen from 1958. IN: *Bachelor of Hearts, Black Sunday, She, One Million B.C.; On My Way to the Crusades, I Met a Girl Who . . .; On a Clear Day You Can See Forever, Duck in Orange Sauce*, more.

RICHARDSON, SIR RALPH (Eng.) Character star. Nominated for Best Supporting Actor Oscar in *The Heiress*. Onscreen from 1933. IN: *The Ghoul, The Return of Bulldog Drummond, Things to Come, The Man Who Could Work Miracles, The Citadel, Four Feathers, The Avengers, Anna Karenina, The Fallen Idol, An Outcast of the Islands, Breaking the Sound Barrier, The Holly and the Ivy, Richard III, Oscar Wilde, Our Man in Havana, Exodus, Long Day's Journey Into Night, Doctor Zhivago, Khartoum, The Midas Run, The Battle of Britain, Oh! What a Lovely War, The Looking Glass War, Eagle in a Cage, Lady Caroline Lamb, Tales From the Crypt, A Doll's House, O Lucky Man*, more.

RICHFIELD, EDWIN (Eng.) Support. Onscreen from the '50s. IN: *Up the Creek*, more.

RICHMAN, PETER MARK/formerly MARK RICHMAN (S. Cal.) Support. Onscreen from 1956. IN: *Friendly Persuasion, The Strange One, The Black Orchid, Crime Busters, Dark Intruder, A Dandy in Aspic, For Singles Only*, more.

RICKLES, DON (S. Cal.) Comedian-actor. Onscreen from 1958. IN: *Run Silent, Run Deep; The Rabbit Trap, The Rat Race, Muscle Beach Party, Enter Laughing, Where It's At, Kelly's Heroes*, more.

RICO, MONA (S. Cal.) Last onscreen in a supporting role in the '37 serial *Zorro Rides Again*, this Mexican actress—particularly popular in silents—lives in retirement in Los Angeles. Her husband for over four decades, also retired now, is a well-to-do sportsman. Onscreen from the '20s. IN: *Eternal Love, Shanghai Lady, A Devil With Women, Thunder Below*, more.

RIDDLE, HAL (S. Cal.) Character. Onscreen from the '50s. IN: *Cop Hater*, more.

RIDGELY, ROBERT (S. Cal.) Support. Onscreen in the '70s. IN: *Chrome and Hot Leather*, more.

RIEFENSTAHL, LENI (Ger.) The German actress-director who was Hitler's favorite maker of documentaries (*The Olympiad* and *Triumph of the Will*) was later tried and acquitted several times for collaboration with the Nazi regime. After the war, though she had moviemaking offers from France, she was not permitted to leave Germany—nor work in pictures there. Today, an athletic (fond of scuba diving), white-haired woman in her 70s (b. 1902), and once more able to travel and to work, she again works in film—but as a still photographer. In this decade a book of her pictures was issued here, *Last of the Nuba*, based on her two expeditions in Africa with the Nubian tribe. In 1974 she was feted at film festivals in the United States—and was a figure in ongoing dispute at each. Onscreen from the mid-'20s. IN: *Peaks of Destiny, The White Hell of Pitz Palu, Storms on Mont Blanc, The White Ecstasy, Avalanche, S O S Iceberg, The Blue Light* (said to be the film that attracted Hitler to her; she both starred in and directed it), more.

RIEHL, KATE (S. Cal.) Character. Onscreen from the '40s. IN: *The Red Menace, The Star*, more.

RIESNER, DEAN (S. Cal.) The real name of silent juvenile "Dinky Dean"—now a producer-director-writer—that he used when acting in 1950's *Traveling Saleswoman*. (See Dinky Dean.)

RIETTY, ROBERT (Eng.) Character. Onscreen from 1938. IN: *Emil* (juvenile role), *Give Us This Day, Prelude to Fame, The Story of Joseph and His Brethren, The Bible*, more.

RIFKIN, RON (S. Cal.) Support. Onscreen from the '60s. IN: *The Devil's Eight, Flareup*, more.

RIGAUD, GEORGE (Fr.) Character. Onscreen from the early '30s. IN: *Fantomas, The Living Corpse, Paris Underground, Masquerade in Mexico, I Walk Alone, Native Son, The Happy Thieves, A Place Called Glory, Grand Slam, Guns of the Magnificent Seven, The Last Mercenary*, more.

RIGBY, ARTHUR (Eng.) Character. Onscreen from 1927. IN: *Q Ships*, more.

RIGBY, TERENCE (Eng.) Support. Onscreen from the '60s. IN: *Accident, Get Carter*, more.

RIGG, DIANA (Eng.) Costar. Onscreen from 1968. IN: *The Assassination Bureau, On Her Majesty's Secret Service, The Hospital, Theatre of Blood*, more.

RIHA, BOBBY (S. Cal.) Former juvenile (b. 1958). Onscreen from the '60s. IN: *The One and Only Genuine Original Family Band, Countdown, The Good Guys and the Bad Guys*, more.

RILEY, JACK (S. Cal.) Support. Onscreen in the '70s. IN: *Bank Shot*, more.

RILEY, JEANNINE (S. Cal.) Leading lady. Onscreen from 1962. IN: *Five Finger Exercise* (bit), *The Big Mouth, Fever Heat, The Comic*, more.

RILEY, MARIN (N.Y.) Character. Onscreen from the '60s. IN: *Midnight Cowboy, Husbands, The Anderson Tapes; Summer Wishes, Winter Dreams; The French Connection, The Last Detail*, more.

RILLA, WALTER (Eng.) Character. Onscreen from the '20s. IN: *Sajenko, The Soviet, Rendez-Vous, The Scarlet Pimpernel, Victoria the Great, Candlelight in Algeria, Mr. Emmanuel, State Secret, Lucky Nick Cain, The Confessions of Felix Krull, Song Without End, Day of Anger*, more.

RIPLEY, HEATHER (Eng.) Juvenile. Onscreen from the '60s. IN: *Chitty Chitty Bang Bang*, more.

RIPPER, MICHAEL (Eng.) Character. Onscreen from the '40s. IN: *Captain Boycott, Eye Witness, Gilbert and Sullivan, Richard III, 1984, Woman in a Dressing Gown, The Brides of Dracula, A Matter of Who, Inspector Clouseau*, more.

RIPPY, RODNEY ALLEN (S. Cal.) Black juvenile. Onscreen in the '70s. IN: *Blazing Saddles*.

RISSO, ROBERTO (It.) Leading man. Onscreen from 1951. IN: *Tomorrow Is Another Day* (his first), *Forbidden Woman; Bread, Love and Dreams; One Step to Eternity; Bread, Love and Jealousy; Paris Hotel, A Breath of Scandal, The Valiant*, more.

RIST, ROBBIE (S. Cal.) Juvenile. Onscreen in the '70s. IN: *Memory of Us*, more.

RITCHARD, CYRIL (N.Y.) Character star. Onscreen from 1929. IN: *Piccadilly, Blackmail, Reserved for Ladies, Half a Sixpence*, more.

RITCHIE, CLINT (S. Cal.) Leading man. Onscreen from 1967. IN: *The St. Valentine's Day Massacre, Bandolero!, Patton, The Peace Killers, Against a Crooked Sky*, more.

RITCHIE, JUNE (Eng.) Leading lady. Onscreen from the '60s. IN: *A Kind of Loving, The Mouse on the Moon, The Syndicate*, more.

RITCHIE, LARRY (N.Y.) Support. Onscreen from the '60s. IN: *The Connection*, more.

RITT, MARTIN (S. Cal.) The producer-director (*Hud*) appeared onscreen as a serviceman-performer in 1944's *Winged Victory*.

RITTER, JOHN (S. Cal.) Supporting actor, son of late cowboy star Tex Ritter and actress Dorothy Fay. Onscreen from 1971. IN: *The Barefoot Executive, Scandalous John, The Other*, more.

RITZ BROTHERS, THE (S. Cal.) Al is dead now ('65), but Jimmy (b. 1905) and Harry (b. 1908) are still a team and still going strong. In '76, in their first screen appearances since 1943's *Never a Dull Moment*, they did comic cameos in *Won Ton Ton, the Dog Who Saved Hollywood* and *Blazing Stewardesses*. In recent years the brothers—their real family name, incidentally, is Joachim—have continued to star in nightclubs all over the country and occasionally have done a guest stint on TV. And Harry's son, Phil Ritz, a bullfighter living in Mexico City, has announced plans to make a motion picture based on the lives of The Ritz Brothers. Onscreen from 1933—first in comic shorts. IN: *Sing, Baby, Sing; One in a Million, On the Avenue, Life Begins in College, You Can't Have Everything, Kentucky Moonshine, The Goldwyn Follies, The Three Musketeers, Argentine Nights, Pack Up Your Troubles; Hi Ya, Chum!*; more.

RIVA, EMMANUELE (Fr.) Leading lady. Onscreen from the '50s. IN: *Hiroshima, Mon Amour; Therese, The Hours of Love, Thomas the Impostor, Lover a la Carte*, more.

RIVA, MARIA (N.Y.) Marlene Dietrich's daughter who, in 1934's *The Scarlet Empress*, and under her maiden name, Maria Sieber, portrayed her mother as a child. Later she assumed her married name for a successful career as a TV dramatic actress in New York, where she lives now—still happily married, retired from acting, the mother of three sons, and a grandmother.

RIVAS, CARLOS (S. Cal.) Support. Onscreen from the '50s. IN: *The King and I, The Black Scorpion, The Unforgiven, True Grit, The Undefeated*, more.

RIVERA, CHITA (N.Y.) Singer-actress. Onscreen in 1969. IN: *Sweet Charity*.

RIVERA, LUIS (S. Cal.) Support. Onscreen from the '60s. IN: *Guns of the Magnificent Seven, Murders in the Rue Morgue*, more.

RIVERO, JORGE (Mex.) Leading man. Onscreen in the '70s. IN: *Rio Lobo, Soldier Blue*, more.

RIVERS, JOAN (N.Y.) Comedienne-actress. Onscreen in 1968. IN: *The Swimmer*.

RIX, BRIAN (Eng.) Support. Onscreen from 1951. IN: *Reluctant Heroes, Up to His Neck, Nothing Barred*, more.

RIXON, BENJAMIN R. (N.Y.) Black support. Onscreen in the '70s. IN: *The Possession of Joel Delaney, The Hot Rock, Believe in Me, The Gang That Couldn't Shoot Straight*, more.

RIXON, MORRIS L. (N.Y.) Character. Onscreen from the '50s. IN: *Never Steal Anything Small, That Kind of Woman, From the Terrace, The Mugger, What's So Bad About Feeling Good?*, more.

RIZZO, ALFREDO (It.) Character. Onscreen from the '50s. IN: *Roman Holiday, Three*, more.

RIZZO, GIANNI (It.) Character actor. Onscreen from the '50s. IN: *Three Steps North, Head of a Tyrant, Sabata, Adios Sabata*, more.

ROAD, MIKE (S. Cal.) Leading man. Onscreen from the '60s. IN: *Destination Inner Space*, more.

ROARKE, ADAM (S. Cal.) Leading man. Onscreen from the '60s. IN: *Hell's Angels on Wheels, Psych-Out, The Savage Seven, Hell's Belles, Play It As It Lays*, more.

ROBARDS, JASON (S. Cal.) Costar. He has lately dropped the Jr. from his name. Onscreen from 1959. IN: *The Journey, By Love Possessed, Tender Is the Night, Long Day's Journey Into Night, A Thousand Clowns, A Big Hand for the Little Lady, Any Wednesday, The St. Valentine's Day Massacre, The Night They Raided Minsky's, The Loves of Isadora, The Ballad of Cable Hogue, Johnny Got His Gun, The War Between Men and Women, Pat Garrett and Billy the Kid, Play It As It Lays, A Boy and His Dog, Mr. Sycamore, All the President's Men*, more.

ROBB, LORI (Pa.) Juvenile. Onscreen in the '70s. IN: *Husbands*, more.

ROBBIN, PETER (S. Cal.) Former juvenile (b. 1956). Brother of actress Anna Capri. Onscreen from 1963. IN: *A Ticklish Affair, Moment to Moment, . . . And Now Miguel, Good Times*, more.

ROBBINS, CINDY (S. Cal.) The former young leading lady is married and retired. Onscreen from 1959. IN: *This Earth Is Mine*, more.

ROBBINS, GALE (S. Cal.) This singer-actress, a lovely blue-eyed redhead, began at 20th Century-Fox at exactly the same time as Jeanne Crain and June Haver but never enjoyed their professional luck. In many pictures through *Quantrill's Raiders* in 1958, and happily married, she phased out her movie career and concentrated on TV guest appearances (*Gunsmoke*, etc.) and a supper club career. Not until 1972, in a very small role in *Stand Up and Be Counted*, did she again face movie cameras. In the interim, in 1968, her construction-engineer husband was killed in a building accident. Following that tragedy, she took her two teenage daughters and went on a trip around the world. A chance encounter in Munich made her, she says, decide to stop "running away" and resume her career as a singer. An American Army officer, recognizing her on the streets of that German city, invited her to sing at army hospitals in the area—which she did, though she had not sung in years. Returning home, she prepared an act and did a prolonged nightclub tour of the Far East, followed by others all over the United States. Recently the actress, still a great beauty in her early 50s (b. 1924), said, "I have decided to go at a career again full-time and I have an agent and I'm going out on calls—though the pace is a lot faster today than I remember." No sooner was her decision made than, in 1975, she found herself starring on stages throughout California in Civic Light Opera productions of the Broadway musical *Company*. Movie roles will surely follow. Onscreen from 1944. IN: *In the Meantime, Darling; Mr. Hex, My Girl Tisa, My Dear Secretary, Race Street; Oh, You Beautiful Doll; Three Little Words, The Barkleys of Broadway, The Fuller Brush Girl, Strictly Dishonorable, The Belle of New York, Calamity Jane, The Girl in the Red Velvet Swing*, more.

ROBBINS, JANE MARLA (N.Y.) Ingenue. Onscreen from the '60s. IN: *Coming Apart*, more.

ROBBINS, SHEILA (Eng.) Support. Onscreen from the '50s. IN: *Suddenly, Last Summer*, more.

ROBERSON, CHUCK (S. Cal.) Character. Onscreen from the '60s. IN: *Shock Corridor, 99 44/100% Dead*, more.

ROBERT, YVES (Fr.) Character; former leading man. Onscreen from the '50s. IN: *The Grand Maneuver, Folies Bergere, The Green Mare, The Man With Connections, The Crook*, more.

ROBERTS, BART (S. Cal.) (See Rex Reason.)

ROBERTS, BEVERLY (N.Y.) Now in her 60s (b. 1914) and considerably heavier than she ever was in movies, but still with close-cropped auburn curls, this outdoorsy actress has been for well over two decades the Executive Secretary of Theatre Authority, Inc. This is a union clearing house of which all 12 actors' unions are members. She had starred in two dozen pictures before closing out her movie career in '40 in *Buried Alive*. During that decade she enjoyed a singing career in the better supper clubs (New York's Versailles, Chicago's Chez Paree) and starred in various radio soap operas—*Portia Faces Life, Light of the World, Our Gal Sunday*, etc. Until she assumed her present position in '54, she played leads in such "live" TV dramatic programs as *Kraft, Westinghouse*, and *Schlitz Playhouse*. Still single, she shares a house north of New York City, on the Henry Hudson Parkway, with former star Wynne Gibson, and commutes to her Fifth Avenue office. She remains fond of such athletic recreations as undersea exploration and mountaineering, and such hobbies as sculpting, astronomy, and painting. Onscreen from 1936. IN: *The Singing Kid, Two Against the World, China Clipper, Hot Money, God's Country and the Woman, Her Husband's Secretary, The Perfect Specimen, West of Shanghai, Outside the Law, Call of the Yukon, Tenth Avenue Kid, I Was a Convict*, more.

ROBERTS, CHRISTIAN (Eng.) Support. Onscreen from the '60s. IN: *To Sir, With Love; The Anniversary, The Desperados, The Adventurers, The Mind of Mr. Soames, The Last Valley*, more.

ROBERTS, DAVIS (S. Cal.) Black character. Onscreen from the '60s. IN: *Hotel, Willie Dynamite*, more.

ROBERTS, DESMOND (Eng.) Character. Onscreen from the early '30s. IN: *The Squaw Man, Cavalcade, Christopher Strong, Tarzan and His Mate, Of Human Bondage, The Count of Monte Cristo, Clive of India, Beau Brummell, Scott of the Antarctic*, more.

ROBERTS, DORIS (N.Y.) Support. Onscreen from 1968. IN: *No Way to Treat a Lady, A Lovely Way to Die, The Honeymoon Killers, Something Wild, Little Murders, A New Leaf, Such Good Friends, Hester Street*, more.

ROBERTS, EWAN (Eng.) Character. Onscreen from 1946. IN: *Castle in the Air, The Titfield Thunderbolt, Day of the Triffids, The Traitors, Brotherly Love, The Internecine Project*, more.

ROBERTS, HI (S. Cal.) Character actor for well over three decades and still active. Onscreen from 1940. IN: *Adventure in Diamonds, The Cheyenne Social Club*, more.

ROBERTS, KEITH (Eng.) Character. Onscreen from the '60s. IN: *Oliver!*, more.

ROBERTS, LOIS (S. Cal.) Onscreen from the '60s. IN: *Gypsy, Island of Love*, more.

ROBERTS, LUANNE (S. Cal.) Leading lady. Onscreen in the '70s. IN: *The Dark Side of Tomorrow, How to Succeed with Sex*, more.

ROBERTS, LYNNE (S. Cal.) One of the prettiest, most charmingly talented, and least appreciated girls ever on the screen—she never got the breaks under either her first screen name, Mary Hart, or this one. Happily married now, after a failure or two, she lives in retirement in the San Fernando Valley. In her 50s (b. 1919), and still lovely, she has not appeared onscreen since 1953's *Port Sinister*. Onscreen as Mary Hart from 1937. IN: *Love Is on the Air, Everything's on Ice*, more. Onscreen as Lynne Roberts from 1939. IN: *The Mysterious Miss X, My Wife's Relations, Romance of the Rio Grande, Moon Over Miami, Riders of the Purple Sage, The Man in the Trunk, Dr. Renault's Secret; Quiet Please, Murder* (a particularly effective performance); *The Port of Forty Thieves, Behind City Lights, Girls of the Big House, The Magnificent Rogue, Sioux City Sue, Winter Wonderland, Robin Hood of Texas, Madonna of the Desert, Call of the Klondike, The Great Plane Robbery, Because of You*, more.

ROBERTS, MARILYN (N.Y.) Support. Onscreen in the '70s. IN: *Futz*, more.

ROBERTS, MARK (S. Cal.) Support; former leading man. Onscreen from the '50s. IN: *Taxi, Onionhead, Once Is Not Enough*, more.

ROBERTS, MEADE (S. Cal.) Screenwriter (*Summer and Smoke*) who played a character role in 1976's *The Killing of a Chinese Bookie*.

ROBERTS, PERNELL (S. Cal.) Character; former leading man. Onscreen from 1957. IN: *Desire Under the Elms, The Sheepman, Ride Lonesome, The Errand Boy, Four Rode Out*, more.

ROBERTS, RACHEL (Eng.) Costar. Nominated for Best Actress Oscar in *This Sporting Life*. Onscreen from 1952. IN: *Valley of Song, The Weak and the Wicked, Our Man in Havana, Saturday Night and Sunday Morning, Girl on Approval, A Flea in Her Ear, The Reckoning, Wild Rovers, Doctors' Wives, O Lucky Man, Murder on the Orient Express, Belstone Fox*, more.

ROBERTS, RALPH (N.Y.) Character. Onscreen from the '60s. IN: *Bells Are Ringing, Gone Are the Days!*, more.

ROBERTS, RUTH (N.Y.) Character. Onscreen from 1951. IN: *Native Son, The Windsplitter*, more.

ROBERTS, STEPHEN (S. Cal.) Character. Onscreen from 1951. IN: *Rogue River, Gog, The Wild and the Innocent, Diary of a Madman,* more.

ROBERTS, TOM (N.Y.) Support. Onscreen in the '70s. IN: *Love Story, Lovers and Other Strangers,* more.

ROBERTS, TONY (N.Y.) Leading man. Onscreen in the '70s. IN: *The $1,000,000 Duck, Star-Spangled Girl; Play It Again, Sam; Serpico, The Taking of Pelham One Two Three, The Savage,* more.

ROBERTS, TRACEY (S. Cal.) Supporting actress and Hollywood drama coach. Onscreen from 1952. IN: *Actors and Sin, The Prodigal, Murder Is My Beat, Anything Goes, Hollywood or Bust, The Wayward Girl, Go Naked in the World,* more.

ROBERTSON, CLIFF (N.Y.) Star. Won Best Actor Oscar in *Charly.* Married to actress Dina Merrill. Onscreen from 1955. IN: *Picnic, Autumn Leaves, The Naked and the Dead, Battle of the Coral Sea, Gidget, All in a Night's Work, The Interns, My Six Loves, PT-109, Sunday in New York, The Best Man, Masquerade, The Honey Pot, The Devil's Brigade, Too Late the Hero, The Great Northfield Minnesota Raid, J. W. Coop, Three Days of the Condor, Out of Season, Shoot,* more.

ROBERTSON, DALE (S. Cal.) Costar. Onscreen from 1949. IN: *Fighting Man of the Plains, Caribou Trail, Call Me Mister, Take Care of My Little Girl, Golden Girl, Lydia Bailey, The Outcasts of Poker Flat, The Farmer Takes a Wife, Gambler from Natchez, Sitting Bull, Son of Sinbad, Dakota Incident, Hell Canyon Outlaws, Blood on the Arrow, Coast of Skeletons,* more.

ROBERTSON, DENNIS (N.Y.) Support. Onscreen from the '60s. IN: *Marooned,* more.

ROBERTSON, DORIS S. (N.Y.) Support. Onscreen from the '50s. IN: *A Face in the Crowd, Sweet Smell of Success,* more.

ROBERTSON, WILLIAM (N.Y.) Veteran character actor. In his late 70s now, and still professionally active. Onscreen from 1939. IN: *Jesse James,* many more.

ROBIN, DANY (Fr.) Leading lady. Onscreen from the '40s. IN: *Man About Town, Gates of the Night, Act of Love, Holiday for Henrietta, Maid in Paris, Love and the Frenchwoman, Waltz of the Toreadors, Tales of Paris, Follow the Boys, The Best House in London, Topaz,* more.

ROBINS, BARRY (N.Y.) Juvenile. Onscreen in the '70s. IN: *Bless the Beasts & Children,* more.

ROBINS, TOBY (Eng.) Supporting actress. Onscreen from the '60s. IN: *The Naked Runner, Friends, Paul and Michelle,* more.

ROBINSON, ANDY (S. Cal.) Support. Onscreen in the '70s. IN: *Dirty Harry,* more.

ROBINSON, ANN (S. Cal.) Former leading lady; now retired. Onscreen in the '50s. IN: *The War of the Worlds, The Glass Wall, Bad for Each Other, Dragnet, Julie, Imitation of Life.*

ROBINSON, BARTLETT (S. Cal.) Character. Onscreen from the '50s. IN: *Toward the Unknown, Battle Hymn, The Spirit of St. Louis, No Time for Sergeants, I Want to Live!, Warlock, Where Love Has Gone, A Distant Trumpet, The Fortune Cookie, The Bamboo Saucer,* more.

ROBINSON, CHARLES KNOX/formerly CHARLES ROBINSON (S. Cal.) Leading man. Onscreen from 1965. IN: *Dear Brigitte, The Singing Nun, The Sand Pebbles, Shenandoah, The Flim Flam Man, For Singles Only; Drive, He Said; The Brotherhood of Satan, The Bridge in the Jungle,* more.

ROBINSON, CHRIS (S. Cal.) Leading man. Onscreen from 1959. IN: *Diary of a High School Bride, Because They're Young, The Long Rope, The Young Savages, Birdman of Alcatraz, The Hawaiians, Darker Than Amber, Cycle Savages, Ace of Hearts,* more.

ROBINSON, DAVID (Eng.) Support. Onscreen from the '60s. IN: *Damn the Defiant,* more.

ROBINSON, JAY (S. Cal.) At 23 he played the mad emperor Caligula so brilliantly in *The Robe,* his debut movie, that *New York Times* critic Bosley Crowther hailed it as "one of the best ten performances in the history of film." His studio, 20th Century-Fox, rushed him into a repeat performance as Caligula—almost as successful—in 1954's *Demetrius and the Gladiators.* But the star's youthful fame collapsed abruptly four years and just three pictures later. With his trained actor's memory, he recalls the exact date this golden time in his life ended—November 13, 1958. Six policemen from Los Angeles broke into his Bel Air mansion and, he says, "found a small quantity of methadon in my bathroom. They handcuffed me, and booked me for possession of narcotics." Of his lost fame, he says now, "I thought it would last forever. It didn't. And when it was stripped away, I was a man in terror." Adding to his despair was that movie industry friends failed to come to his assistance—and, on the morning of his preliminary hearing, his father, with no history of heart trouble, dropped dead of a seizure. Sentenced to a year in Los Angeles jail, Robinson was freed on bail, pending an appeal. Hollywood closed its doors to him. He held onto his house a while, though all the furniture except the bed had to be sold to keep him going, but when he was truly penniless, he lost the house too. It was on January 19, 1960, he says, that he gave up drugs—permanently—and, "from that day to this, I've had nothing stronger than a couple of aspirin tablets." That same year he met and married—and remains most happily married to—the former Pauline Flowers, who was then a doctor's assistant. "My reconstruction started when I married Pauline," he says simply. But the first ten years of their married life were not untroubled ones. For a while the actor, whose movie salary had been $3,000 a week, worked at a zoo—"training chimps and cleaning cages . . . for three hundred dollars a month." Shortly before their son, Jay Paul, was born in 1961, a newspaper story appeared stating that his narcotics conviction had been reversed by the courts. Concluding—erroneously—that he had been exonerated and the case was closed, he moved his family to New York. There he tried for a fresh start as an actor but found the best he could get was a bus-and-truck tour of high schools in New York State. And, for an entire year, his wife was desperately ill with acute pulmonary tuberculosis—until a miracle drug worked and she was pronounced well again. Moving back to California, Robinson held a series of demeaning jobs—fry cook in a Santa Ana cafe ($1.25 an hour), veterinarian's assistant, skid-row rooming house manager. When he innocently applied for a job in a state hospital as a psychiatric technical assistant, which required fingerprints and a routine check, he found himself entangled once more with the law. He was served with a warrant that police said dated back to his original narcotics arrest in 1958. After a jury trial in Santa Monica, Robinson was sentenced to state prison—for a minimum of six months, a maximum of 10 years. At the California prisons in Tracy and Chino he served 15 months before he was finally paroled in 1968. Back in Hollywood he discovered, to his great pleasure, that the doors were open to him once more. Thin and graying, and looking older than his years (b. 1930), he did a long series of guest-star roles on television—in *Bewitched*, *Planet of the Apes*, *Mannix*, etc. And in 1971, Bette Davis, with whom he had acted in 1955 in *The Virgin Queen*, and who respected his talents greatly, paved the way for his return to movies by demanding that he be given a major role in her *Bunny O'Hare*. That role—billed "Also Starring"—has since led to many others. Living with his family in a small house in the San Fernando Valley, Jay

Robinson has written—in collaboration with United Press correspondent Vernon Scott—a book about his life. And, should it be made into a movie, he has every hope of playing the leading role himself. Surely, no one could play it better. Onscreen from 1953. IN: *The Robe, Demetrius and the Gladiators, The Virgin Queen, The Wild Party*; and, in this decade, *Bunny O'Hare, Three the Hard Way, Shampoo* (as owner of the beauty salon where Warren Beatty works), *Zorc, Train Ride to Hollywood*, more.

ROBINSON, JOE (Eng.) Character; former leading man. Onscreen from 1956. IN: *A Kid for Two Farthings, East of Barcelona, The Loneliness of the Long Distance Runner, Diamonds Are Forever*, more.

ROBINSON, JOHN (Eng.) Character. Onscreen from 1936. IN: *The Heirloom Mystery, All That Glitters, Farewell to Cinderella, The Lion Has Wings, The Story of Shirley Yorke, Hundred Hour Hunt, Emergency Call, Ghost Ship, The Constant Husband, A Doctor's Dilemma*, more.

ROBINSON, SHARI (S. Cal.) The curly-haired little girl 20th Century-Fox introduced in 1949's *You're My Everything* as the "new" Shirley Temple is now a big—and sexy—girl, and a star dancer in clubs and on the stage. Some months back, she costarred in New York with Allan Jones and others in the nostalgic revue titled *The Big Show of 1936* (she wasn't born, though, until '42). And, observed the admiring critic of the *New York Post*: "When was the last time you saw a dancer doing handstands and turning cartwheels? Shari Sue Robinson, a trim youngster in the nostalgic game, Charlestoned and boop-boop-ee-dooed, besides." The *Times* also hailed her as "a gifted youngster." She could get her second crack at movie stardom. Onscreen in 1949 and 1951. IN: *You're My Everything* and *Molly*.

ROBINSON, SUGAR RAY (S. Cal.) Former middleweight and welterweight prize fighting champion and actor. Onscreen from 1968. IN: *Paper Lion, The Detective, Candy*.

ROBINSON, SUGARCHILE (Mich.) The diminutive boy jazz pianist—still small in his 30s (b. 1940)—owns and operates a food mart in Detroit, his native city. Onscreen in 1946. IN: *No Leave, No Love*.

ROBLES, WALTER (S. Cal.) Support. Onscreen from the '60s. IN: *The Savage Seven, Cycle Savages*, more.

ROBSON, DAME FLORA (Eng.) Character. Nominated for Best Supporting Actress Oscar in *Saratoga Trunk*. An actress since age 5, she is, in her 70s (b. 1902), still busily at her trade. Earlier in this decade, in addition to her movie work, she starred at the Edinburgh Festival in the title role of *Elizabeth Tudor, Queen of England*. And on BBC-TV in '74, she played the blind grandmother in a six-week serialized version of *Heidi*. She has not acted in Hollywood, where she lived for seven years, since 1945, nor in America since starring on Broadway in 1950 in *Black Chiffon*. Never married, she lives outside London and, in her free time, makes tapestries. Onscreen from 1931. IN: *Dance Pretty Lady, Catherine the Great, Fire Over England, Farewell Again, Wuthering Heights, The Lion Has Wings, We Are Not Alone, Invisible Stripes, The Sea Hawk, Bahama Passage, Caesar and Cleopatra, Black Narcissus, Frieda, Saraband, Romeo and Juliet, 55 Days in Peking, Guns at Batasi, Young Cassidy, Those Magnificent Men in Their Flying Machines, 7 Women, Eye of the Devil, Day of the Arrow, The Beloved, Fragment of Fear, The Beast in the Cellar*, more.

ROBY, LAVELLE (S. Cal.) Support. Onscreen from the '60s. IN: *Finders Keepers, Losers Weepers; Beyond the Valley of the Dolls*, more.

ROC, PATRICIA (Eng.) The blonde leading lady who came to Hollywood for just one picture, 1946's *Canyon Passage*, is in her 50s now (b. 1918) and more active in theater and TV than movies. Onscreen from the '30s. IN: *The Gaunt Stranger, Three Silent Men, Madonna of the Seven Moons, Johnny Frenchman, The Wicked Lady, So Well Remembered, Jassy, The Brothers, The Man on the Eiffel Tower, Circle of Danger, Captain Black Jack, Something Money Can't Buy*, more, including 1960's *Bluebeard's Ten Honeymoons*, her most recent to date.

ROCCA, DANIELA (It.) Leading lady. Onscreen from the '50s. IN: *The Giant of Marathon, Esther and the King; Divorce—Italian Style; The Empty Canvas, Behold a Pale Horse, The Sucker*, more.

ROCCO, ALEX (S. Cal.) Support. Onscreen in the '70s. IN: *Freebie and the Bean, Brute Corps, Three the Hard Way*, more.

ROCHE, EUGENE (N.Y.) Character. Onscreen in the '70s. IN: *Cotton Comes to Harlem, They Might Be Giants, Newman's Law, "W," Mr. Ricco*, more.

ROCHEFORT, JEAN (Fr.) Character actor. Onscreen from the '60s. IN: *Cartouche, Symphony for a Massacre, Up to His Ears, La Fantome de la Liberte; Cool, Calm and Collected* (or *Calmos*); *Salut L'Artiste*, more.

ROCHESTER (S. Cal.) (See Eddie "Rochester" Anderson.)

ROCK, BLOSSOM (S. Cal.) (See Marie Blake.)

ROCK, FELIPPA (Australia) Support. Onscreen in the '40s. IN: *Moss Rose*, more. (See Michael Pate.)

ROCKLAND, JEFFREY (Eng.) Support. Onscreen from the '60s. IN: *Doctor Zhivago*, more.

ROCKWELL, ROBERT (S. Cal.) Leading man; lately inactive in movies. Onscreen from 1948. IN: *You Gotta Stay Happy, The Red Menace, Belle of Old Mexico, Blonde Bandit, Destination Big House, The Frogmen, The War of the Worlds, Our Miss Brooks* (in his TV role of "Mr. Boynton"), *Sol Madrid*, more.

RODANN, ZIVA (S. Cal.) Leading lady; lately inactive in movies. Onscreen from 1957. IN: *The Story of Mankind, Courage of Black Beauty, Last Train from Gun Hill, The Big Operator, Macumba Love, The Story of Ruth, Samar, Three Nuts in Search of a Bolt*, more.

RODD, MARCIA (N.Y.) Leading lady. Onscreen from 1971. IN: *Little Murders, T.R. Baskin*, more.

RODERICK, GEORGE (Eng.) Support. Onscreen from the '60s. IN: *Rattle of a Simple Man, The 25th Hour*, more.

RODGERS, ANTON (Eng.) Character. Onscreen from 1965. IN: *Rotten to the Core, The Man Who Haunted Himself, Scrooge, The Day of the Jackal*, more.

RODGERS, ILONA (Eng.) Support. Onscreen from the '60s. IN: *Salt and Pepper*, more.

RODGERS, JOHN WESLEY (N.Y.) Black support. Onscreen from the '60s. IN: *Uptight*, more.

RODGERS, PAMELA (S. Cal.) Leading lady. Onscreen from 1965. IN: *The Silencers, Three on a Couch, Doomsday Flight, The Oscar, The Big Cube*, more.

RODGERS, RICHARD (N.Y.) Illustrious composer (*South Pacific, The Sound of Music*, etc.). Onscreen as himself in 1953 in *Main Street to Broadway*.

RODMAN, NANCY (S. Cal.) Support. Onscreen from the '60s. IN: *The Candy Man, Chosen Survivors*, more.

RODRIGUEZ, CHARLES J. (N.Y.) Support. Onscreen in the '70s. IN: *The Possession of Joel Delaney, Mortadella, The Hospital*, more.

RODRIGUEZ, PERCY (S. Cal.) Black character. Onscreen from 1967. IN: *The Plainsman, The Sweet Ride, The Heart Is a Lonely Hunter, Who Fears the Devil*, more.

RODWAY, NORMAN (Eng.) Support. Onscreen from 1958. IN: *The Quare Fellow, This Other Eden, A Question of Suspense, Four in the Morning; Falstaff: Chimes at Midnight; The Penthouse, I'll Never Forget What's 'Isname*, more.

ROE, PATRICIA (N.Y.) Stage actress. Onscreen from 1941. IN: *It Happened to One Man* and *A Face in the Crowd*.

ROERICK, WILLIAM (Mass.) The character actor lives in a 200-year-old farmhouse at "Lost Farm," near Tyringham, and commutes to Broadway and Hollywood. Onscreen from 1943. IN: *This Is the Army, The Harder They Fall, Flight to Hong Kong, Not of This Earth, The Sporting Club, The Love Machine, A Separate Peace*, more.

ROGAN, BETH (S. Cal.) Leading lady; lately inactive in movies. Onscreen from 1958. IN: *Count Five and Die, Mysterious Island*, more.

ROGAN, JOHN (Eng.) Support. Onscreen in the '70s. IN: *The Molly Maguires*, more.

ROGER, LEE (N.Y.) Character actress. Onscreen in the '70s. IN: *Loving, The French Connection*, more.

ROGERS, BLAKE (S. Cal.) Support. Onscreen from 1962. IN: *13 West Street*, more.

ROGERS, BROOKS (N.Y.) Support. Onscreen from 1969. IN: *Trilogy*, more.

ROGERS, CHARLES "BUDDY" (S. Cal.) A handsome silver-haired man in his 70s (b. 1904), and still the husband of Mary Pickford after four decades, he journeys to film festivals all over the globe where her films are honored. Onscreen from 1926. IN: *Fascinating Youth, So's Your Old Man, Wings, My Best Girl* (opposite Mary Pickford), *Abie's Irish Rose, Varsity, Close Harmony, The River of Romance, Half Way to Heaven, Young Eagles, Heads Up, The Road to Reno, Best of Enemies, Dance Band, Sing for Your Supper, The Mexican Spitfire* (and five others in the series), *That Nazty Nuisance, An Innocent Affair*, more, including 1957's *The Parson and the Outlaw*, his most recent to date. (See Mary Pickford.)

ROGERS, GIL (N.Y.) Support. Onscreen from the '60s. IN: *A Fan's Notes, The Panic in Needle Park, Pretty Poison*, more.

ROGERS, GINGER (S. Cal.) Star. Won Best Actress Oscar in *Kitty Foyle*. She is in her mid 60s (b. 1911), but nothing about her has changed —neither the smile, nor the shoulder-length blonde hair, nor the legs. Nor the genuine friendliness. Nor her religion—Christian Science. Nor the zeal for work. Oscar or no Hollywood—as it's apt to do with its female stars when no longer young—put her out to pasture in 1957, after *Oh Men! Oh Women!* But she showed them there are other places for an authentic star to shine. On Broadway, for instance, where she enjoyed a long run after taking over in *Hello, Dolly!* And on the London stage where she starred triumphantly in the musical *Mame*, under a 56-week contract at $12,000 a week—after dazzling reporters by disembarking the ocean liner with 118 pieces of luggage. Then in 1971 she starred in music fairs in *Coco*. In 1972 she signed a seven-year contract to act as fashion consultant for J. C. Penney—touring the country several times visiting many stores, appearing in the spring catalogue in the smart women's section, the clothes for which she personally selects. J. C. Penney describes her salary as "substantial." That same year, besides appearing in summer theaters in *Auntie Mame*, she received an honorary Ph.D in Arts from Austin College in Sherman, Texas (her native state), and a divorce—after 11 years of marriage—from former actor William Marshall. It was her fifth marriage, all of them childless. "I have been very glad I haven't had children," she said recently, "seeing what's happened to the majority of youngsters who've taken to a rather unfortunate mode of thought, embedded in false satisfactions." Previous husbands: Edward Culpepper—or Jack Pepper as he was known in show business (1929–31); Lew Ayres (1934–41); former actor Jack Briggs, then a U.S. Army private, age 22, to her 31 (1943-49); former actor Jacques Bergerac, also considerably younger than she (1953–57). After the divorce from William Marshall, she said of marriage, with an appropriate gesture: "I've had it up to here." (As a "bachelor girl," she lives with her mother Lela—"my best friend"—in Palm Springs, when not at the 600-acre, million-dollar Rogue River ranch they have owned in Oregon for many years.) 1973 was the year of gala tributes to Fred Astaire—solo—to most of which she was invited as a special audience-guest. Film clips shown at these affairs, many culled from the 11 great Astaire-Rogers musicals, invariably proved anew that he had not danced alone. Just as regularly, Astaire graciously included his former partner in his appreciatory comments, bringing her onstage to tumultuous applause. Also in '73, she "took her act"—as a singer—to Europe. *Variety* headlined it: GINGER ROGERS CLICKS WITH A SOCKO NEW ACT AT ITALO SEASIDE CLUB. In a one-hour song recital at Viarregio's dinner club La Bussolo, she clearly captivated "an SRO audience of haute spenders, at $40 a head"—and "took numerous curtain calls and dropped a tear or two between the wings and stage as Italy's cafe society spectators covered the footlights with flowers." Taped, the show was later seen on Italian television. 1974 brought a successful tour in *No, No, Nanette;* 1975, another in *Forty Carats.* With a brand-new nightclub act in '76, in which she was backed up by four young male dancers, she sang and danced her way across the country, finally appearing triumphantly at the Waldorf-Astoria. Calling her "the golden Ginger," the *New York Times'* Howard Thompson reported: "Miss Rogers still dances . . . like an angel." Onscreen from 1930. IN: *Young Man of Manhattan, The Sap from Syracuse, Hat Check Girl, Professional Sweetheart, 42nd Street, Gold Diggers of 1933, Flying Down to Rio, Sitting Pretty, The Gay Divorcee, Twenty Million Sweethearts, Roberta, Top Hat, Follow the Fleet, Swing Time, Shall We Dance, Stage Door, Having a Wonderful Time, Vivacious Lady, Carefree, Bachelor Mother* (one of her two personal-favorite movies; the other being *Kitty Foyle), Fifth Avenue Girl, The Story of Vernon and Irene Castle, Primrose Path, Roxie Hart, The Major and the Minor, Tender Comrade, Lady in the Dark, I'll Be Seeing You, Weekend at the Waldorf, The Magnificent Doll, The Barkleys of Broadway* (her last with Astaire), *Storm Warning, We're Not Married, Monkey Business, Black Widow, Tight Spot, Harlow* (the Magna version in which she portrayed the star's mother), more, including her most recent to date, a 1964-filmed picture, *The Confession* (retitled *Let's Get Married),* produced by her former husband William Marshall, which has been seen on TV but rarely in theaters.

ROGERS, HARRIET (S. Cal.) Character. Onscreen in the '70s. IN: *Dragonfly,* more.

ROGERS, JEAN (S. Cal.) Entering her 60s (b. 1916), the widow of agent Danny Winkler (d. 1970), and a grandmother, Jean models and does TV commercials now. Blue-eyed and still blonde, she is a bit heavier (145 lbs.) than she ever was in movies, and there is an infectious warmth about her that her leading-lady roles almost never permitted her to reveal. "She is the perfect candidate," someone at the model agency representing her has accurately observed, "for grandmother, club woman, and hostess-type roles." Her last movie work was in 1951's *The Second Woman,* but she is ready and eager to act in pictures again. Onscreen from 1934. IN: *Eight Girls in a Boat, The Great Air Mystery* (serial), *Flash Gordon* (serial; as Dale Arden), *Ace Drummond* (serial) *My Man Godfrey, While New York Sleeps, The Mysterious Mr. Moto, Heaven With a Barbed Wire Fence, Viva Cisco Kid!, Charlie Chan in Panama, Dr. Kildare's Victory, Pacific Rendezvous, Whistling in Brooklyn, Gay Blades, Undercover Maisie, Speed to Spare,* more.

ROGERS, JOHN (S. Cal.) Character. Onscreen from 1929. IN: *Behind That Curtain, Raffles, Charlie Chan Carries On, Limehouse Blues, Klondike Annie; Think Fast, Mr. Moto; Typhoon, Lassie Come Home, Moss Rose, Thunder in the Valley, A Lovely Way to Die,* more.

ROGERS, KASEY (S. Cal.) Leading lady. Onscreen from 1949. IN: *Special Agent, My Favorite Spy, A Place in the Sun, Denver and the Rio Grande, Union Station, Strangers on a Train,* more.

ROGERS, LELA (S. Cal.) Ginger Rogers' talent scout-screenwriter-actress mother, who played her mother in 1942 in *The Major and the Minor.* (See Ginger Rogers.)

ROGERS, PAUL (Eng.) Costar. Onscreen from 1950. IN: *Murder in the Cathedral, Beau Brummell, The Beachcomber, Our Man in Havana, The Trials of Oscar Wilde, The Mark, Billy Budd, Young and Willing, Walk in the Shadow, The Looking Glass War, The Reckoning, The Homecoming, Mr. Quilp,* more.

ROGERS, ROY (S. Cal.) In 1975 the "King of the Cowboys" starred in *Mackintosh & T.J.,* in which he did not ride a horse, his first movie since 1952's *Son of Paleface.* Onscreen from 1935—first in bit roles and short subjects. IN: *The Old Corral, Under Western Stars, Frontier Pony Express, In Old Caliente, The Arizona Kid, Colorado, Robin Hood of the Pecos, Red River Valley, Idaho, Silver Spurs, The Cowboy and the Senorita, Bells of Rosarita, My Pal Trigger, The Gay Ranchero, Susanna Pass, Trigger Jr., Heart of the Rockies, Pals of the Golden West,* more.

ROGERS, ROY, JR. (S. Cal.) Son of the above. Now a business man. Onscreen in 1968. IN: *Arizona Bushwhackers.*

ROGERS, VICTOR (S. Cal.) Support. Onscreen from the '60s. IN: *Thoroughly Modern Millie,* more.

ROGERS, WAYNE (S. Cal.) Leading man. Onscreen from 1959. IN: *Odds Against Tomor-*

row, *Cool Hand Luke, Chamber of Horrors, Pocket Money, WUSA, Matalan,* more.

ROGERS, WILL, JR. (S. Cal.) The son of the late star, he has not appeared in a movie since 1958, but has recently toured the West with a solo stage show titled "My Father's Humor." Onscreen from 1949. IN: *Look for the Silver Lining, The Story of Will Rogers, The Eddie Cantor Story* (portraying his father in these three), *The Boy from Oklahoma, Wild Heritage.*

ROHM, MARIA (Eng.) Leading lady. Onscreen in the '70s. IN: *Venus in Furs, Eugenie, Dorian Gray, Black Beauty, Count Dracula,* more.

ROJO, GUSTAVO (Sp.) Leading man. Onscreen from 1948. IN: *Tarzan and the Mermaids, Alexander the Great, The Buccaneer, It Started with a Kiss, The Miracle, Ghengis Khan, The Tall Woman, Salt and Pepper, The Valley of Gwangi, El Condor,* more.

ROKER, RENNY (S. Cal.) Black leading man. Onscreen in the '70s. IN: *Tough,* more.

ROLAND, GILBERT (S. Cal.) Leading man, now in his 70s (b. 1905), still handsome, still active. Onscreen from the '20s. IN: *The Plastic Age, The Campus Flirt, Camille, The Dove, New York Nights, Life Begins, She Done Him Wrong, The Last Train from Madrid, Juarez, The Sea Hawk, Captain Kidd, Pirates of Monterey, The Other Love, Malaya, We Were Strangers, The Bullfighter and the Lady, My Six Convicts, Diamond Queen, That Lady, The Midnight Story, The Big Circus, Cheyenne Autumn, The Reward, The Christian Licorice Store, Run Wild, Islands in the Stream,* more.

ROLAND, GYL (S. Cal.) Leading lady. One of Gilbert Roland's two daughters—the other is Lynda, a sculptor—by his marriage (1941–46) to the late Constance Bennett, the first of his two wives. Onscreen in the '70s. IN: *Terror Circus,* more.

ROLAND, KATHLEEN (N.Y.) Character. Onscreen in the '70s. IN: *The Molly Maguires,* more.

ROLAND, STEVE (N.Y.) Support. Onscreen from the '60s. IN: *Some Kind of a Nut,* more.

ROLFE, GUY (Eng.) Costar. Onscreen from 1945. IN: *Hungry Hill, Nicholas Nickleby, Ivanhoe, King of the Khyber Rifles, Yesterday's Enemy, The Strangler of Bombay, King of Kings, Taras Bulba, The Fall of the Roman Empire, The Alphabet Murders, The Land Raiders, Nicholas and Alexandra,* more.

ROLLER, CLEVE (N.Y.) Character actress. Onscreen in the '70s. IN: *The Exorcist,* more.

ROMAIN, YVONNE (Eng.) Leading lady. Onscreen from the '50s. IN: *Corridors of Blood, The Curse of the Werewolf, Frightened City, Devil Doll, The Swinger, Double Trouble,* more.

ROMAN, GREG (S. Cal.) Support. Onscreen from 1958. IN: *The Naked and the Dead,* more.

ROMAN, LETICIA (S. Cal.) Leading lady. Onscreen from 1958. IN: *G.I. Blues, Gold of the Seven Saints, Fanny Hill, Flaming Frontier,* more.

ROMAN, RIC (S. Cal.) Support. Onscreen from 1952. IN: *Lone Star, Appointment in Honduras, Lizzie, Nevada Smith,* more.

ROMAN, RUTH (S. Cal.) One of Hollywood's more dynamic talents, she let her career slide for several years in the '60s. In this decade she has come back strong, playing character leads in numerous TV series (*Medical Center, Cannon, Marcus Welby,* etc.) and movies. She is in her 50s now (b. 1923), and in 1956 was married to agent Buddy Moss, her third husband. She was previously married to and divorced from Jack Flaxman (1940–41) and publisher Mortimer Hall (1950–55), by whom she has a grown son, Richard (b. 1953). Onscreen from 1943. IN: *Stage Door Canteen, Since You Went Away, Gilda, The Big Clock;* many others in which she played bits; *Champion* (bringing her first strong notices), *The Window, Beyond the Forest* (beginning, in '49, her Warner's contract and her best starring period), *Three Secrets, Colt 45, Dallas, Lightning Strikes Twice, Strangers on a Train, Mara Maru, Blowing Wild, Down Three Dark Streets, The Far Country, Bottom of the Bottle, Bitter Victory, Look in Any Window, Love Has Many Faces, The Killing Kind, A Knife for the Ladies, Dead of Night; Want a Ride, Little Girl?;* more.

ROMANCE, VIVIANE (Fr.) In 1974 in Paris, aged 65, France's memorable *Carmen* (seen here in '46) reactivated her career, as a chanteuse, at the Left Bank nightclub La Belle Epoque—to fine reviews. She has not appeared in a movie since 1963's *Any Number Can Win.* Onscreen from 1931. IN: *La Chienne* (bit), *Dark Eyes, The Pasha's Wives, It Happened in Gibraltar, Sirocco, The Queen's Necklace, Panic, The Seven Deadly Sins, Flesh and Desire,* more.

ROMANO, ANDY (S. Cal.) Support. Onscreen from the '60s. IN: *The Ghost in the Invisible Bikini, Bamboo Saucer,* more.

ROMANUS, RICHARD (S. Cal.) Support. Onscreen in the '70s. IN: *Gravy Train, Bogart Slept Here*, more.

ROMAY, LINA (S. Cal.) Absolutely unchanged in looks or voice, the raven-haired singer lives in Los Angeles and would like to be working fulltime once more. In the summer of '75 she was the femcee—dynamic as ever—when the Pacific Pioneer Broadcasters tossed a 700-guest dinner in honor of 17 all-time-great female vocalists. Saluted, besides Lina, were: Loyce Whiteman, Aileen Stanley, Rosemary Clooney, Kay Starr, Gogo Delys, Frances Wayne, Carmene Ennis, Patsy Garrett, Marion Holmes, Nellie Lutcher, Ann Richards, Paula Kelly, Ella Mae Morse, Kay St. Germain, Helen Greco, and Margaret Whiting. One of the honorees, Patsy Garrett, said with a laugh, "This group should be called the 'is-was'—has-beens who are still working." In the audience, cheering, were many of the famous bandleaders for whom the singers had worked—including Lina's longtime boss and friend, Xavier Cugat. She was upfront with his orchestra, you will recall, in many musicals. Branching out as an actress later, she worked steadily in pix through 1952's *Man Behind the Gun*. At the Broadcasters event, a spokesman announced the possibility of the affair being restaged and filmed for network television. Onscreen from 1942. IN: *You Were Never Lovelier, The Heat's On, Stage Door Canteen, Tropicana, Bathing Beauty, Two Girls and a Sailor, Weekend at the Waldorf* (all with Cugat); then in *Adventure, Love Laughs at Andy Hardy, Honeymoon, Embraceable You, Cheyenne Cowboy, The Big Wheel, The Lady Takes a Sailor*, more.

ROMERO, CARLOS (S. Cal.) Character. Onscreen from 1958. IN: *The Gun Runners, They Came to Cordura, The Deadly Duo, Island of Blue Dolphins, The Professionals*, more.

ROMERO, CESAR (S. Cal.) Vital—and still a bachelor—in his white-haired 70s, this popular actor continues to play prominent roles in many. Onscreen from 1934. IN: *The Thin Man, Clive of India, The Devil Is a Woman, Diamond Jim, Love Before Breakfast, Wee Willie Winkie, Happy Landing, The Little Princess, Charlie Chan at Treasure Island, Cisco Kid and the Lady; Tall, Dark and Handsome; Weekend in Havana, Orchestra Wives, Springtime in the Rockies, Captain from Castile, Julia Misbehaves, Vera Cruz, Ocean's Eleven, Donovan's Reef, Marriage on the Rocks, Batman, Skidoo, The Midas Run, Madigan's Millions, The Computer Wore Tennis Shoes; Now You See Him, Now You Don't; The Spectre of Edgar Allan Poe, The Strongest Man in the World, Carioca Tiger*, more.

ROMERO, NED (S. Cal.) Support. Onscreen from 1964. IN: *The Talisman, Paradise Road, The Savage American, The Violent Ones, Winchester 73, Hang 'Em High, Tell Them Willie Boy Is Here*, more.

ROMNEY, EDANA (Eng.) The former leading lady is in her 50s (b. 1919) and retired. Onscreen from 1941. IN: *East of Piccadilly, Alibi*, and *Corridor of Mirrors*.

RONAY, EDINA (Fr.) Leading lady. Onscreen from the '60s. IN: *Night Train to Paris, A Study in Terror, He Who Rides a Tiger, Three*, more.

RONET, MAURICE (Fr.) Leading man. Onscreen from the '40s. IN: *The Seven Deadly Sins, Sins of the Borgias, La Sorciere, He Who Must Die, Purple Noon, The Victors, The Champagne Murders, How Sweet It Is!, Birds in Peru, La Femme Infidele, The Swimming Pool, The Destructors*, more.

ROOK, HEIDI (S. Cal.) Former juvenile. Onscreen in 1968. IN: *The One and Only Genuine Original Family Band*.

ROOKS, CONRAD (N.Y.) Producer-director-writer-actor. Onscreen in 1967. IN: *Chappaqua*.

ROONEY, MERCY (S. Cal.) Leading lady. Onscreen in the '70s. IN: *The Single Girls*, more.

ROONEY, MICKEY (Fla.) Star. Received a special juvenile Oscar in 1938. Nominated for Best Actor Oscar in *Babes in Arms, The Human Comedy*. Nominated for Best Supporting Actor Oscar in *The Bold and the Brave*. In 1975, after his seventh wife, 31-year-old Carolyn Zack, filed for divorce, asking for considerable support and alimony, the actor's accountant testified in court that Rooney owed $250,000 in back taxes to the Federal government and the state of California. And, further, that his Fort Lauderdale home had mortgages on it totalling $108,000. That same year, one of his earlier wives, Elaine Mahnken, sued him for $14,350 in back alimony. His wives, divorces, and offspring are as follows: Ava Gardner (1942–43); Betty Jane Rase (1944–47), mother of Mickey Jr. and Timothy (son Mickey Jr. is now an evangelist for the First Church of God and The Father in Hollywood); the late actress Martha Vickers (1949–51), mother of Teddy; Elaine Mahnken (1952–59); the late Barbara Thomason (wed in 1959, they were still married in 1966 at the time of her murder by an alleged lover), mother of Kelly, Kerry, and Kimmy—whose custody was awarded by the courts to the parents of this wife; Margaret Lane (1966–67); Carolyn Zack (1969–74), mother of Jonelle—the actor also legally adopted her son by a previous marriage, Jimmy. So Rooney—the # 1 box-office star in 1939, '40, and '41—still goes from picture to picture, in addition to working steadily on the stage. *George M!*, a Bicentennial musical about George M. Cohan, with Rooney in the title role, was announced to open on Broadway in the winter of 1976, after a nationwide tour. Onscreen as Mickey Rooney (after his child career as Mickey McGuire) from 1932. IN: *Fast Companions; My Pal, the King; Broadway to Hollywood, Manhattan Melodrama, Chained, A Midsummer Night's Dream; Ah, Wilderness!; The Devil Is a Sissy, A Family Affair* (first of 16 "Andy Hardy" pix), *Boys Town, Stablemates, Young Tom Edison, Strike Up the Band, A Yank at Eton, Girl Crazy, National Velvet, Killer McCoy, Summer Holiday, Words and Music, Quicksand, Off Limits, Drive a Crooked Road, The Bridges at Toko-Ri, Operation Mad Ball, Baby Face Nelson, Breakfast at Tiffany's, Requiem for a Heavyweight, It's a Mad Mad Mad Mad World, Skidoo!, 80 Steps to Jonah, The Projectionist, Pulp, The Godmothers, Ace of Hearts, Rachel's Man, From Hong Kong with Love*, more.

ROONEY, TEDDY (S. Cal.) Mickey Rooney's son. No longer acting. Onscreen 1958–60. IN: *Andy Hardy Comes Home, It Happened to Jane, Seven Ways from Sundown.*

ROONEY, TIM(MY) (S. Cal.) Mickey Rooney's son. Onscreen from 1965. IN: *Village of the Giants, Riot on Sunset Strip; Storyville, New Orleans;* more.

ROONEY, WALLACE (N.Y.) Character. Onscreen in the '70s. IN: *Desperate Characters,* more.

ROOS, JOANNA (N.Y.) Support. Onscreen in 1961. IN: *Splendor in the Grass.*

ROOSEVELT, BUDDY (S. Cal.) A favorite Western star in the '20s for Artclass Productions and Universal, he continued to star in cowboy movies until 1933, when he began playing supporting parts and character roles. Now in his 70s (b. 1898), and still living in Hollywood, he has rarely been professionally active in the past decade. Onscreen (first in bits) from 1922. IN: *Walloping Wallace, Biff Bang Buddy, Gold and Grit, Galloping Jinx, Twin Triggers, Bandit Buster, Way Out West, Lightnin' Smith's Return, Wild Horse Mesa, The Fourth Horseman, The Old Corral, The Buccaneer, Boss Cowboy, Fury at Showdown, Flesh and the Spur, Buck Privates Come Home, The Belle of New York, Around the World in 80 Days,* more.

ROOT, ROBERT (N.Y.) Support. Onscreen in the '70s. IN: *Prism,* more.

ROPER, BRIAN (Eng.) Support. Onscreen from the '40s. IN: *Just William's Luck, William Comes to Town, The Secret Garden, The Naked Heart; Time, Gentlemen, Please; The Girl on the Pier, The Blue Peter,* more.

RORY, ROSSANA (It.) Leading lady. Onscreen from the '50s. IN: *The Big Boodle, The Angel Wore Red, Robin Hood and the Pirates, The Big Deal on Madonna Street, Come September, Jessica, Eclipse, Captain Falcon,* more.

ROSADO, PEGGY MORAN (N.Y.) Support. Onscreen in 1961. IN: *Back Street.*

ROSCOE, LEE (N.Y.) Support. Onscreen from the '60s. IN: *Beyond the Law, Events,* more.

ROSE, AL (La.) Author-actor. Onscreen in the '70s. IN: *Storyville, New Orleans* (based on his book of the same title; in which he played Alderman Sidney Story; after whom New Orleans' red-light and jazz district was named).

ROSE, ALEXANDER (N.Y.) Character. Onscreen in 1961. IN: *The Hustler.*

ROSE, CLIFFORD (Eng.) Support. Onscreen from 1967. IN: *Marat/Sade,* more.

ROSE, GEORGE (Eng.) Character. Onscreen from 1952. IN: *The Pickwick Papers, The Night to Remember, The Devil's Disciple, Jack the Ripper, Hamlet, Hawaii, The Pink Jungle, A New Leaf, Believe in Me,* more.

ROSE, JANE (S. Cal.) Character. Onscreen from 1955. IN: *Summertime, The Monte Carlo Story, One Plus One, Flipper, I Walk the Line,* more.

ROSE, JENNIFER (N.Y.) Juvenile. Onscreen in the '70s. IN: *Carnal Knowledge, The Mixed-Up Files of Mrs. Basil E. Frankenweiler,* more.

ROSE, LAURIE (S. Cal.) Ingenue. Onscreen in the '70s. IN: *The Working Girls,* more.

ROSE, NORMAN (S. Cal.) Character. Onscreen from the '60s. IN: *The Anderson Tapes, Who Killed Mary What's 'Ername?, Jump, The Telephone Book,* more.

ROSE, REVE (S. Cal.) Support. Onscreen from the '60s. IN: *3 in the Attic; If It's Tuesday, This Must Be Belgium; Bunny O'Hare,* more.

ROSE, VIRGINIA (S. Cal.) Character. Onscreen from the '60s. IN: *Waterhole #3,* more.

ROSE MARIE (S. Cal.) Comedienne. Onscreen from 1954. IN: *Top Banana, The Big Beat; Don't Worry, We'll Think of a Title; Dead Heat on a Merry-Go-Round, Dick and Jane,* more.

ROSHER, DOROTHY (S. Cal.) (See Joan Marsh.)

ROSQUI, TOM (N.Y.) Support. Onscreen in the '70s. IN: *The Godfather,* more.

ROSS, BETSY KING (S. Cal.) With smalltowners in the '30s, this spunky little girl with the Buster Brown haircut, a championship trick rider, was greatly popular for a while. In tomboy roles, she was prominently cast in Western features with Gene Autry (*Radio Ranch*), Ken Maynard (*In Old Santa Fe,* in which she also sang), and George O'Brien (*Smoke Lightning*). Besides the serial *Fighting With Kit Carson,* which was released in some places as *The Return of Kit Carson* with Johnny Mack Brown, she was in another with Autry and Frankie Darro, *Phantom Empire.* Dropping out of movies, she went to college, received her M.S. degree at Northwestern, and became an anthropologist in Mexico. Marriage to engineer David Day took her eventually to a 10,000-acre ranch in Colombia. After her young husband's death there in a landslide in the Andes, she returned with her son, Rusty, to Los Angeles. She has gone back to school to win her Ph.D. and is now a medical writer. In her 50s (b. 1923), she is a slender, most attractive, outdoorsy-looking woman, and—it will be of interest to Betsy King Ross' long-ago fans to know—she remains an avid horsewoman. Onscreen from 1931; all her pictures are listed above.

ROSS, CHRISTOPHER (S. Cal.) Support. Onscreen from the '60s. IN: *How Sweet It Is!, Viva Max, Celebration at Big Sur,* more.

ROSS, DIANA (S. Cal.) Black star-singer. Nominated for Best Actress Oscar in *Lady Sings the Blues.* ALSO IN: *Mahogany.*

ROSS, DON (S. Cal.) Character. Onscreen from the '50s. IN: *Anatomy of a Murder,* more.

ROSS, ED (S. Cal.) Character. Onscreen in the '70s. IN: *How Sweet It Is!,* more.

ROSS, JOE E. (S. Cal.) Comedian. Onscreen from the '60s. IN: *All Hands on Deck, Maracaibo, Hear Me Good, The Love Bug, The Boatniks, The Godmothers, How to Seduce a Woman,* more.

ROSS, JULIE (Eng.) Support. Onscreen from the '60s. IN: *Young Cassidy,* more.

ROSS, KATHARINE (S. Cal.) Leading lady. Nominated for Best Supporting Actress Oscar in *The Graduate.* Onscreen from 1965. IN: *Shenandoah, The Longest Hundred Miles, The Singing Nun, Mister Buddwing, Games, The Ski Bums, A Nice Girl Like Me, Bullitt, Hellfighters, Butch Cassidy and the Sundance Kid, Tell Them Willie Boy Is Here, Fools, They Only Kill Their Masters, The Stepford Wives,* more.

ROSS, LANNY (N.Y.) Well-off and still a fine-looking man as he enters his 70s (b. 1906), he no longer takes professional engagements. Instead, the singer who was "the idol of the airwaves" devotes much of his time to working—gratis—for the TV-radio actors' guild, AFTRA. He and his wife, the former Olive A. White, married since '35, have one granddaughter, now grown; their daughter—only child—died a number of years ago. Onscreen from 1934. IN: *Melody in Spring, College Rhythm, The Lady Objects, Gulliver's Travels* (singing voice of Gulliver), *Home in Oklahoma.*

ROSS, MARION (S. Cal.) Leading lady. Not the supporting actress of the same name who died in 1966. Onscreen in the '70s. IN: *The Forbin Project,* more.

ROSS, MICHAEL (S. Cal.) Character. Onscreen from 1950. IN: *Blonde Dynamite, The Well, Don't Bother to Knock, Those Redheads from Seattle, Tarzan and the She-Devil, The Return of Jack Slade, Artists and Models, The Lieutenant Wore Skirts, The Buster Keaton Story, Kiss Them for Me, The Disorderly Orderly,* more.

ROSS, MYRNA (S. Cal.) Support. Onscreen from the '60s. IN: *Ghost in the Invisible Bikini, The Swinger, 2000 Years Later,* more.

ROSS, STAN (S. Cal.) Character. Onscreen from the '40s. IN: *The Pretender, Requiem for a Heavyweight, How to Murder Your Wife, Beyond the Valley of the Dolls,* more.

ROSS, WILLIAM (N.Y.) Character. Onscreen from the '60s. IN: *The Green Slime,* more.

ROSSELLINI, ISABELLA (It.) One of Ingrid Bergman's and director Roberto Rossellini's twin daughters. Onscreen from 1976. IN: *A Matter of Time* (starring her mother; her twin sister, Isotta Ingrid, assisted on wardrobe and makeup for this film).

ROSSELLINI, RENZO (It.) Roberto Rossellini's composer brother. Onscreen in 1963. IN: *Love at Twenty.*

ROSSEN, CAROL (S. Cal.) Leading lady. Daughter of the late director Robert Rossen and wife of actor Hal Holbrook. Onscreen from the '60s. IN: *The Arrangement, The Stepford Wives*, more.

ROSSI, ALFRED (S. Cal.) Support. Onscreen in the '70s. IN: *Dealing*, more.

ROSSI, STEVE (S. Cal.) Singer-actor. Onscreen from the '60s. IN: *The Last of the Secret Agents?, The Man from O.R.G.Y. and the Real Gone Girls*, more.

ROSSI-DRAGO, ELEANORA (It.) Leading lady. Onscreen from the '40s. IN: *Pirates of Capri, Sensualita, Hell Raiders of the Deep, The Awakening, Under Ten Flags, Violent Summer, Love at Twenty, The Facts of Murder, The Bible, Camille 2000*, more.

ROSSINGTON, NORMAN (Eng.) Character. Onscreen from the '50s. IN: *Carry On Sergeant, Saturday Night and Sunday Morning, Tobruk, Negatives, Deathline*, more.

ROSSITER, LEONARD (Eng.) Character. Onscreen from 1961. IN: *A Kind of Loving, This Sporting Life, Billy Liar, King Rat, Hotel Paradiso, The Whisperers; 2001: A Space Odyssey; Luther*, more.

ROTH, ANDY (S. Cal.) Support. Onscreen in the '70s. IN: *Double Initiation, The Stewardesses*, more.

ROTH, GENE (S. Cal.) Character. Onscreen from the '50s. IN: *The Baron of Arizona, Red Planet Mars, The Farmer Takes a Wife*, more.

ROTH, LILLIAN (N.Y.) Unmarried since her '63 divorce from Burt McGuire (he figured prominently in her autobiography, *I'll Cry Tomorrow)*, she lives in an apartment on the West Side, and still sings in nightclubs. She is in her 60s now (b. 1910). Onscreen from 1929. IN: *The Love Parade, Illusion, The Vagabond King, Sea Legs, Animal Crackers, Madam Satan, Honey, Take a Chance, Ladies They Talk About*, more.

ROTHA, WANDA (Eng.) Supporting actress-daughter of writer-director Paul Rotha. Onscreen from the '50s. IN: *Delire a Deux, Mrs. Fitzherbert, Saadia, Circus World*, more.

ROTHWELL, MICHAEL (Eng.) Support. Onscreen in the '70s. IN: *Fragment of Fear*, more.

ROTHWELL, ROBERT (S. Cal.) Support. Onscreen in the '70s. IN: *Fools, The Last Movie*, more.

ROUDE, NEIL (N.Y.) Support. Onscreen from the '60s. IN: *Harvey Middleman, Fireman;* more.

ROUGAS, MICHAEL (S. Cal.) Support. Onscreen from the '60s. IN: *Flareup*, more.

ROULIEN, RAUL (Sp.) He continued to make movies in Spain after leaving Hollywood in the mid-'30s, but is now, in his 70s, retired and living in Madrid. Onscreen from 1931. IN: *Delicious, Careless Lady, State's Attorney, The Painted Woman, It's Great to be Alive, Flying Down to Rio, The World Moves On, Granaderos del Amor, Asegure a su Mujer*, more.

ROUNDS, DAVID (N.Y.) Support. Onscreen from 1972. IN: *Child's Play*, more.

ROUNDTREE, RICHARD (S. Cal.) Black star. Onscreen from 1970. IN: *What Do You Say to a Naked Lady?, Parachute to Paradise, Shaft, Embassy, Shaft's Big Score, Shaft in Alaska, Charlie One-Eye, Earthquake, Man Friday*, more.

ROUSE, SIMON (Eng.) Character. Onscreen in the '70s. IN: *Butley, The Ragman's Daughter*, more.

ROUTLEDGE, PATRICIA (Eng.) Leading lady. Onscreen from the '60s. IN: *To Sir, With Love; A Matter of Innocence, 30 Is a Dangerous Age, Cynthia; Don't Raise the Bridge, Lower the River; The Bliss of Mrs. Blossom*, more.

ROUVEROL, JEAN (S. Cal.) The former actor has more recently been a screenwriter—of *The Legend of Lylah Clare*, etc. Onscreen from 1934. IN: *It's a Gift, Bar-20 Rides Again, Private Worlds, Fatal Lady, The Road Back, Stage Door, Annabel Takes a Tour, The Law West of Tombstone*, more.

ROUX, JACQUES (S. Cal.) Support. Onscreen from the '60s. IN: *The List of Adrian Messenger, The Secret War of Harry Frigg*, more.

ROVERE, GINA (It.) Support. Onscreen from the '50s. IN: *Hercules, Love a la Carte, All the Other Girls Do!, Catch-22*, more.

ROWAN, DAN (S. Cal.) Comedian. Onscreen from 1958. IN: *Once Upon a Horse* (reissued as *Hot Horse), The Maltese Bippy*.

ROWE, EARL (N.Y.) Support. Onscreen from 1958. IN: *The Blob*, more.

ROWE, MISTY (S. Cal.) Leading lady. Onscreen in 1976. IN: *Goodbye, Norma Jean*.

ROWLAND, GERALD (Eng.) Juvenile. Onscreen in the '70s. IN: *Cromwell*, more.

ROWLAND, HENRY (S. Cal.) Character. Onscreen from 1940. IN: *Safari, The Pied Piper,*

Berlin Correspondent, The Moon Is Down, Paris After Dark, Winged Victory, Rogue's Regiment, Sealed Cargo, All the Brothers Were Valiant, Prince of Pirates, Topeka, Kiss of Fire, Women of Pitcairn Island, Chicago Confidential, Gun Duel in Durango, Wolf Larson, Street of Darkness, Diamonds Are Forever, more.

ROWLAND, STEVE (S. Cal.) Leading man, lately inactive in movies. Onscreen from the '50s. IN: *The Student Prince, Gun Glory, Gunfighters of Casa Grande,* more.

ROWLANDS, DAVID (S. Cal.) Character. Brother of actress Gena Rowlands. Onscreen in the '70s. IN: *Husbands, Minnie and Moskowitz, 11 Harrowhouse,* more.

ROWLANDS, GENA (S. Cal.) Leading lady and wife of actor John Cassavetes, her frequent director. Nominated for Best Actress Oscar in *A Woman Under the Influence,* which he directed. Onscreen from 1958. IN: *The High Cost of Loving, Lonely Are the Brave, The Spiral Road, A Child Is Waiting, Tony Rome, Faces, The Happy Ending, Minnie and Moskowitz, Two-Minute Warning,* more.

ROWLANDS, LADY (S. Cal.) Character. Mother of actress Gena Rowlands. Onscreen in the '70s. IN: *Minnie and Moskowitz, A Woman Under the Influence.*

ROWLANDS, PATSY (Eng.) Support. Onscreen from 1960. IN: *Tom Jones, Carry On Loving,* more.

ROWLES, POLLY (N.Y.) Stage-TV character. Onscreen from 1937. IN: *Wings Over Honolulu, Some Blondes Are Dangerous, Vogues of 1938, Springtime in the Rockies.*

ROXANNE (N.Y.) TV personality. Inactive in movies now. Onscreen in the '50s. IN: *The Seven Year Itch, The Young Don't Cry.*

ROYCE, RIZA (S. Cal.) Character. Onscreen from the '60s. IN: *Good Neighbor Sam,* more.

ROYE, PHILLIP (S. Cal.) Black support. Onscreen from the '60s. IN: *The Sergeant,* more.

ROYLE, SELENA (Mex.) This superb character actress, noted for her wise and kindly mother roles, *The Sullivans* being the supreme example, withdrew from the screen after 1955's *Murder Is My Beat.* Now in her 70s (b. 1904), as the acknowledged *doyenne* of Guadalajara, she "mothers" painters, writers, and composers who people the artistic salon that her beautiful hacienda has become. She retired to this community two decades ago with her husband, character actor George Renavent, who has

since died ('69), and is buried in a nearby cemetery. Socially, she sees much of fellow actor Glenn Anders, whose own house is close, and frequently visits actor Romney Brent in Mexico City. And she has recently authored a book, *A Gringa's Guide to Mexican Cooking.* Onscreen from 1932. IN: *The Misleading Lady, Stage Door Canteen, Main Street After Dark, 30 Seconds Over Tokyo, Mrs. Parkington, The Green Years, The Harvey Girls, Night and Day, Till the End of Time, Courage of Lassie, The Romance of Rosy Ridge, Cass Timberlane, Summer Holiday, You Were Meant for Me, Moonrise, You're My Everything, Bad Boy, The Heiress, The Damned Don't Cry, He Ran All the Way, Come Fill the Cup,* more.

ROZAKIS, GREG (N.Y.) Leading man in TV soap operas. Onscreen in 1963. IN: *America America.*

RUBIN, BENNY (S. Cal.) The career of this funny man rolls right along. In '75 he did a cameo in *Won Ton Ton, the Dog Who Saved Hollywood.* He is in his 70s now (b. 1899), unmarried, and lives in Hollywood. Onscreen from 1929. IN: *Naughty Baby, Marianne, Lord Byron of Broadway, Montana Moon, Sunny Skies, George White's Scandals of 1935, Go Into Your Dance, Sunny, Here Comes Mr. Jordan, Mr. Wise Guy, Just This Once, Yankee Pasha, Meet Me in Las Vegas, A Hole in the Head, A Pocketful of Miracles, The Patsy, That Funny Feeling, Thoroughly Modern Millie, Airport,* more.

RUBIN, RONALD (Eng.) Support. Onscreen from the '60s. IN: *The Sergeant, Can Heironymus Merkin Ever Forget Mercy Humppe . . . ?,* more.

RUBINSTEIN, ARTUR (N.Y.) Classical pianist. Onscreen from 1944. IN: *Follow the Boys, Carnegie Hall, Night Song, Of Men and Music.*

RUBINSTEIN, JOHN (N.Y.) Leading man—son of Artur Rubinstein. Onscreen in the '70s. IN: *Getting Straight, The Sandpit Generals, Zachariah,* more.

RUBY, THELMA (Eng.) Character. Onscreen from 1955. IN: *Room at the Top; Live Now, Pay Later; Invasion Quartet,* more.

RUDD, PAUL (N.Y.) Stage and TV (*Beacon Hill*) leading man. Onscreen in the '70s. IN: *Tell Me That You Love Me, Junie Moon.*

RUDDOCK, JOHN (Eng.) Character, now in his 70s (b. 1897) and still going strong. Onscreen from 1938. IN: *Lancashire Luck, Waltz Time, Meet Me at Dawn, Under Capricorn, The Fallen Idol, Quo Vadis, Ivanhoe, Martin Luther, Lust for Life, Lawrence of Arabia, Cromwell,* more.

RUDIE, EVELYN (S. Cal.) Yesterday's child prodigy (TV's "Eloise") now operates a theater workshop in Los Angeles. She is now in her 30's (b. 1947). Onscreen from 1955. IN: *The View from Pompey's Head, The Wings of Eagles, The Restless Breed, The Gift of Love.*

RUDLEY, HERBERT (S. Cal.) Character. Onscreen from 1940. IN: *Abe Lincoln in Illinois, Marriage Is a Private Affair, The Master Race, The Seventh Cross, A Walk in the Sun, Rhapsody in Blue, Hollow Triumph, Joan of Arc, The Silver Chalice, The Court Jester, That Funny Feeling, The Young Lions, Beloved Infidel, Who Was That Lady?, The Great Impostor,* more.

RUEHMANN, HEINZ (Ger.) Character. Onscreen from 1931. IN: *Die Drei von der Tankstelle, Man Braucht Kein Geld, Der Brave Suender, If We All Were Angels, The Captain from Koepenick, It Happened in Broad Daylight, The Judge and the Sinner, Ship of Fools,* more.

RUIZ, ANTONIO (Mex.) Support. Onscreen in Hollywood from the '60s. IN: *The Long Duel, Villa Rides,* more.

RULE, JANICE (S. Cal.) This leading lady, long married to actor Ben Gazzara, is still in an occasional movie but her acting career has taken second place to her new one—psychoanalyst. After commuting regularly from Hollywood to Chicago, to attend classes at the Institute for Psychoanalysis, she completed her graduate studies in Los Angeles, and is now a member of the Southern California Psychoanalytic Institute. As a speaker, in conjunction with this profession, she sometimes delivers papers on subjects such as "The Actor's Identity Crisis." Onscreen from 1951. IN: *Goodbye, My Fancy; Starlight, Holiday for Sinners, Rogues' March, A Woman's Devotion; Bell, Book and Candle; Invitation to a Gunfighter, The Chase, Alvarez Kelly, Welcome to Hard Times, The Swimmer, Gumshoe,* more.

RUSH, BARBARA (S. Cal.) Leading lady. Onscreen from 1951. IN: *The First Legion, Molly, Quebec, When Worlds Collide, It Came from Outer Space, Magnificent Obsession, The Black Shield of Falworth, Captain Lightfoot, Kiss of Fire, Bigger Than Life; Oh Men! Oh Women!; No Down Payment, The Young Lions, The Young Philadelphians, Strangers When We Meet, Come Blow Your Horn, Robin and the 7 Hoods, Hombre, The Man, Superdad,* more.

RUSKIN, SHIMEN (N.Y.) Character. Onscreen from the '20s. IN: *Beau Brummel* (silent), *Having Wonderful Time, Lady from Louisiana, Dance Hall, Body and Soul, Fiddler on the Roof, The Producers, Shaft.* (Died 1976.)

RUSSEL, DEL (S. Cal.) Former juvenile actor (b. 1952). Onscreen from 1954. IN: *Riders to the Stars; Tammy, Tell Me True; Cleopatra,* more.

RUSSEL, TONY (S. Cal.) Support. Father of the above. Onscreen from the '50s. IN: *War Is Hell; Wild, Wild Planet; The Hard Ride,* more.

RUSSELL, ANDY (Argentina) The singer whose last Hollywood pic was 1947's *Copacabana* has lived and worked for years in Buenos Aires, where he emcees a popular TV variety show and, in Spanish, makes recordings. Many of them—"Love Story" was one—become #1 on the local hit parade. Onscreen in the '40s. IN: *The Stork Club, Make Mine Music, Breakfast in Hollywood,* and *Copacabana.*

RUSSELL, ANNA (Eng.) Comedienne. Was the voice of the Witch in the 1954 cartoon feature *Hansel and Gretel.*

RUSSELL, BING (S. Cal.) Support. Onscreen from the '60s. IN: *Journey to Shiloh, The Computer Wore Tennis Shoes,* more.

RUSSELL, CONNIE (S. Cal.) Singer. Inactive in movies now, she still sings in clubs. Onscreen in the '40s. IN: *Lady Be Good, Nightmare.*

RUSSELL, ELIZABETH (N.Y.) In the '40s at RKO she all but made a career of leads in Val Lewton's classic horror pix. She was featured in no fewer than five, including *Bedlam,* her last movie, in '46. Since then, living in New York, she has done supporting roles in summer stock and occasionally on TV, and written short stories published in the better magazines. In her early 60s now and long divorced from Rosalind Russell's brother John, she has one son, John Knight Russell, and, by him, several grown grandchildren. Onscreen from 1936. IN: *Girl of the Ozarks, Hideaway Girl, Cat People* (her first for Lewton), *Hitler's Madman, The Seventh Victim, The Curse of the Cat People, Youth Runs Wild, Weird Woman,* more.

RUSSELL, HAROLD (Mass.) The handless ex-paratrooper who acted in *The Best Years of Our Lives* became the only performer in history to receive two Academy Awards for the same role. He won as Best Supporting Actor and was accorded a special one, by Academy members wanting to make sure that his splendid portrayal of Homer Parrish did not go unhonored. In his 60s now (b. 1914), the onetime actor and Boston University graduate lives in Wayland, is head of a major company (Tag-A-Bag) that employs many handicapped individuals, and, in his spare time, works with the handicapped. He and his wife, married more than three decades, have two grown children, Adele and Jerry, and are grandparents. On March 10, 1976, when *Best Years* director, William Wyler, was honored in Los Angeles and received the fourth Life Achievement Award of the American Film Institute, Harold Russell was among the 1,200 celebrities present for the ceremony. He paid moving tribute to the director, praising Wyler for his decision to cast a nonactor in *Best Years* and suggested the role had given others with a handicap a determination "not to give up."

RUSSELL, JACKIE (S. Cal.) Supporting actress. Onscreen from the '60s. IN: *A Guide for the Married Man, The Cheyenne Social Club,* more.

RUSSELL, JANE (S. Cal.) Ironically, considering the volume of publicity about Howard Hughes' invention of a "specially engineered" bra for her when she made her debut in his *The Outlaw*, she has lately and often been seen on TV—doing a bra commercial. In her 50s (b. 1921), her beauty remains, but she rarely does movies now. Instead she stars onstage, appearing in 1974 and '75, in dinner theaters and music fairs, in such shows as *Mame* and *Catch Me If You Can*. The mother of three grown children, adopted during her first, 25-year, marriage, to football star Bob Waterfield, she has been married three times. Her second husband, actor Roger Barrett, died three months after their marriage in 1968. On January 31, 1974, in a "kaftan ceremony" in a seaside chapel in Santa Barbara, where she now lives, she became the wife of real estate man John Calvin Peoples, who is three years younger than she. All six members of the wedding party wore kaftans, hers made of green sari cloth, his of green velvet. Onscreen from 1945. IN: *The Outlaw* (though because of censorship problems its "official" release was held up until '47, it was shown in certain parts of the country two years earlier), *Young Widow, The Paleface, His Kind of Woman, Double Dynamite, The Las Vegas Story, Gentlemen Prefer Blondes, The French Line, The Tall Men, Gentlemen Marry Brunettes, The Revolt of Mamie Stover, Fate Is the Hunter, Johnny Reno, Born Losers, Darker Than Amber,* more.

RUSSELL, JOHN (S. Cal.) Leading man. Onscreen from 1937. IN: *The Frame Up, Always Goodbye, Mr. Smith Goes to Washington, Sabotage;* more in which he appeared as a teenager; *A Bell for Adano, Somewhere in the Night, Forever Amber, Yellow Sky, The Story of Molly X, Slattery's Hurricane, Undertow, Saddle Tramp, The Fat Man, Hoodlum Empire, Fair Wind to Java, The Last Command, Yellowstone Kelly, Rio Bravo, Fort Utah; If He Hollers, Let Him Go; Buckskin, Cannon for Cordoba,* more.

RUSSELL, KURT (S. Cal.) Popular young actor (b. 1951) in Disney movies. Onscreen from 1963. IN: *It Happened at the World's Fair; Follow Me, Boys!; The One and Only Genuine Original Family Band, The Horse in the Gray Flannel Suit, Charley and the Angel; Now You See Him, Now You Don't; The Strongest Man in the World, Superdad,* more.

RUSSELL, REB (Kan.) In Nowata County, in northern Oklahoma just below the Kansas line, you will find a huge ranch and on it, its owner, Fay H. Russell, a big, genial, well-muscled man. He spends every waking hour here, but his home is a few miles away in the little town of Coffeyville, Kansas. He is a cowboy and looks it—sunbrowned, in plaid shirt, faded jeans, and Western boots. There's no mistaking it, this is Reb Russell, one of those great football heroes who became, in the '30s, great Western movie cowboys. Only when he sweeps off his rancher's hat in greeting does one realize this is no longer 1930, or even 1937, the last year he and his stallion "Rebel" galloped through a horse opera. That distinctive coal-black hair—wavy still, but cotton-white now. Catching you up on what happened after his movie-starring days, the cowboy, now in his 70s (b. 1905), reveals that an old football injury —he had been All-American fullback at Northwestern—caused him to forsake the fisticuffs and hard riding. For a short while then he starred on radio in Chicago in a Western drama. But he gave that up to become a real-life rancher, first in southern Missouri. He finally settled in Coffeyville, where he raised his family, and bought the farm-ranch in Nowata County where he concentrates on improving livestock and farming methods. He delights in talking about his Hollywood days and remains surprised at fans' continued interest in him and his Stetsoned colleagues. "You know, us old-timers had lots of fun makin' them Westerns," he says, "but we figured they took us for granted. Shucks, we practically always used the same story, the same actors and the same horses. All we really did was change hats." Onscreen from 1932. IN: *All-American* (as a football star), *Outlaw Rule, Arizona Badman, Fighting Thru, Border Vengeance, Man From Hell, Lightning Triggers, Rough and Tough,* more.

RUSSELL, ROSALIND (S. Cal.) Star. Nominated for Best Actress Oscar in *My Sister Eileen, Sister Kenny, Mourning Becomes Electra, Auntie Mame.* Severely stricken with arthritis, and heavier now because of the medication she must take, the actress devotes most of her time to working on behalf of the Arthritis Foundation. She has not appeared in a movie since 1971's *Mrs. Pollifax—Spy*, and was most recently on TV the following year with Douglas Fairbanks Jr. in the special *The Crooked Hearts*. Recently it was announced she would resume her career in a Broadway play. Married to stage producer Fred Brisson (her only marriage) since 1941, she has a grown son, magazine reporter Lance Brisson. Onscreen from 1934. IN: *Evelyn Prentice, The President Vanishes, Reckless, China Seas, Under Two Flags, Craig's Wife, Night Must Fall; Live, Love and Learn; The Citadel, The Women, His Girl Friday, Hired Wife, No Time for Comedy, They Met in Bombay; Take a Letter, Darling; Flight for Freedom, Roughly Speaking, What a Woman, The Guilt of Janet Ames, The Velvet Touch, Never Wave at a Wac, Picnic, A Majority of One, Five Finger Exercise, Gypsy, The Trouble with Angels, Rosie, Where Angels Go Trouble Follows*, more.

RUSSELL, THERESA (S. Cal.) Leading lady. Introduced in 1976. IN: *The Last Tycoon.*

RUSSELL, WILLIAM (Eng.) Support. Onscreen from 1954, first as Russell Enoch, in *Intimate Relations*, etc. Changed his name in 1955 to William Russell. IN: *The Saint's Return, They Who Dare, One Good Turn, Above Us the Waves, The Man Who Never Was*, more.

RUSSO, MATT (N.Y.) Character. Onscreen from the '50s. IN: *On the Waterfront, A Face in the Crowd, A Man Called Adam, Stiletto, Splendor in the Grass, The Arrangement*, more.

RUST, RICHARD (S. Cal.) Support. Onscreen from 1960. IN: *This Rebel Breed, Underworld U.S.A., Comanche Station, The Legend of Tom Dooley, Walk on the Wild Side, Taras Bulba, The Student Nurses*, more.

RUTHERFORD, ANN (S. Cal.) In the summer of '72 "Polly Benedict" went home to MGM for the first time in exactly 30 years. It was in 1942 that, after *Andy Hardy's Double Life* (her 17th "Hardy" pic) and *Whistling in Dixie*, she checked off the lot and forever stopped being Andy's beloved "Polly." Or so she thought—TV's "Late Show" being a gleam in no one's eye in that year. She became a freelance. At a variety of studios, she appeared in another 10 movies before retiring after a B picture, *Operation Haylift*, in 1950. Only once in the years since had she broken her vow never to act again. That was in 1969 when she guest-starred in a single episode of ABC-TV's *Love American Style*. She had returned to MGM, still perkily youthful and brunette (but graying), in her 50s (b. 1920), to appear in *They Only Kill Their Masters*. Billed as "costars" in it was a triumvirate that had once loomed large at Metro—June Allyson, Peter Lawford, and Ann. Her role—not large—was, as she described it, "A fun role with shades of Thelma Ritter in the character." She was, in this comedy-mystery, a fast-talking switchboard operator who was essentially the major-domo of a police station. But if her part was small, the reception she was given by the studio was huge—and sentimental. Strung across the front gate was a banner: WELCOME HOME POLLY. Tipped off about her return, a throng of admirers was on hand to greet her. As was then-studio chief, James Aubrey, with a bouquet of red roses. As was Andy Hardy's—the genuine, the original—jalopy. All that was missing was Mickey Rooney, and he was halfway around the world, in Sardinia, making *Pulp*, in which he played an aging Hollywood has-been. She had accepted the part, she said, because the producer was a personal friend and wanted her—"And because I wanted, one last time, to walk on the Carvel Street which was home to me for all those years in the 'Andy Hardy' series." She knew that *They Only Kill Their Masters* was the last picture that would ever be shot on the old MGM backlot. That part of the studio had even then already been sold to a real estate outfit. If this made her weep, another discovery left her laughing. The famous "Little Red Schoolhouse" on the lot, where she, Lana Turner, Elizabeth Taylor, et al., slaved at lessons between scenes, was now the office of her current producer. When she asked if she might use her old dressing room, she was told, sorry, it had been sold at the big MGM auction two years before. So Ann Rutherford's home studio—for six years and 34 movies—was not as she had left it. She said at the time that her return to moviemaking was not just a one-shot affair, but that she had hired an agent with the intention of resuming her career fulltime. To date, though, she has not acted since. The actress, born in Toronto of show-business parents, has lived in Hollywood since she was 11. In radio first, she became a leading lady in Westerns (an even dozen) at 15. She has been married twice. In 1942 she became the wife of David May, young heir of Los Angeles' famous May Co. They adopted a child, Gloria, who has opted for a private life rather than show business. Divorced from May in 1953, she married producer William Dozier that same year and remains married to him. On the set of *They Only Kill Their Masters*, Ann Rutherford gave evidence that her humor had not changed. "Can you imagine," she asked, "how today's young people would howl over the father-and-son dialogues between Lewis Stone and Mickey Rooney when 'The Judge' warns Andy about respecting the girl next door, and not engaging in any heavy smooching!" Onscreen from 1935. IN: *Melody Trail, The Singing Vagabond, The Harvester, Public Cowboy No. 1, Annie Laurie* (short subject; her first role at MGM at '37), *The Devil Is Driving, Of Human Hearts, Judge Hardy's Children, Four Girls in White, These*

Glamour Girls, Gone With the Wind, Andy Hardy Gets Spring Fever, Pride and Prejudice, Whistling in the Dark, Orchestra Wives, Happy Land, Bermuda Mystery, Bedside Manner, Murder in the Music Hall, The Secret Life of Walter Mitty, Adventures of Don Juan, more.

RYAN, EDMON (S. Cal.) Character. Onscreen from 1938. IN: *Crime Over London, The Human Monster, Mystery Street, The Breaking Point, Three Secrets, The Guy Who Came Back, Two for the Seesaw, The Americanization of Emily, The Playground, Topaz, Tora! Tora! Tora!,* more.

RYAN, FRAN (S. Cal.) Character. Onscreen in the '70s. IN: *Scandalous John, How to Seduce a Woman,* more.

RYAN, JOHN (S. Cal.) Leading man. Onscreen in the '70s. IN: *It's Alive,* more.

RYAN, KATHLEEN (Eng.) Leading lady. She is still active on the London stage but has not worked in movies for almost two decades. Onscreen from 1947. IN: *Odd Man Out, Christopher Columbus, Prelude to Fame, Try and Get Me, Captain Lightfoot, Scotch on the Rocks, The Yellow Balloon, Jacqueline,* more.

RYAN, MADGE (Eng.) Character. Onscreen from 1960. IN: *Upstairs and Downstairs, Summer Holiday, Strange Affair, I Start Counting, A Clockwork Orange,* more.

RYAN, MICHAEL M. (N.Y.) Popular leading man in the TV soap opera *As the World Turns.* Onscreen in 1968 in *The Stranger.*

RYAN, MITCHELL (S. Cal.) Leading man. Onscreen from 1970. IN: *Monte Walsh, The Hunting Party, High Plains Drifter, My Old Man's Place, The Honkers, The Entertainer,* more.

RYAN, PEGGY (Hawaii) The teenager who tapped her way to stardom alongside Donald O'Connor in those WW II musicals at Universal is in her auburn-haired 50s now (b. 1924), and lives in Hawaii with her third husband, Eddie Sherman. A striking-looking man, he was until recently the noted columnist of the Honolulu *Advertiser* and is still more recently famous for his best-selling novel, *Mention My Name in Hawaii.* In '76 they celebrated their 18th wedding anniversary. The actress has a grownup songwriter-son, James ("Chris"), by James Cross; a daughter, Kerry, by the late movie dance star Ray McDonald; and she and her present husband have an adopted son, Shawn Edward Arthur (for godfather Arthur Godfrey) Kalaii Sherman (b. 1963), who is part Hawaiian, Chinese, and Caucasian. This youngster, undergoing a slight name change to Sean Sherman, made his movie debut in '74 with Keenan Wynn in *He Is My Brother.* In Hawaii, Peggy Ryan has choreographed such stage productions as *Funny Girl* and *The Music Man.* She has taught dancing at the University of Hawaii and currently conducts classes for emotionally and physically handicapped children. Seen often as Jack Lord's secretary in *Hawaii Five-0,* she hung up her professional dancing shoes when she became Mrs. Sherman. She says she has no desire to return to fulltime activity in show business. But her husband said a while back, "If someone asked her to do *No, No, Nanette* in London, I think she'd put on her tap shoes again." While waiting, she is busy in a boutique she recently opened in Honolulu. She and Donald O'Connor remain the best of friends, always see one another when she and her husband visit Hollywood, and there, in '72, for the first time in decades, they celebrated their birthdays—August 28 for her, August 30 for him—together. And, as before, he rubbed it in that he is one year younger than she. As of 1976, the O'Connor-Ryan professional association had resumed, via the second generation. Anyone seeing *All the President's Men* and observing closely can spot two young actresses, secretaries working side by side—his daughter Donna and her daughter Kerry making their movie debuts together. Onscreen from 1937. IN: *Top of the Town, Women Men Marry, She Married a Cop, The Flying Irishman, Miss Annie Rooney, Private Buckaroo, Get Hep to Love, When Johnny Comes Marching Home, Mister Big, Top Man, Chip Off the Old Block, The Merry Monahans, Follow the Boys, This Is the Life, Patrick the Great, Here Come the Coeds, That's the Spirit, Men in Her Diary, Shamrock Hill, There's a Girl in My Heart,* more, including 1953's *All Ashore,* her most recent to date.

RYDELL, BOBBY (N.Y.) Singer-actor. Onscreen in 1963. IN: *Bye Bye Birdie.*

RYDELL, MARK (S. Cal.) He is a director now —of John Wayne's *The Cowboys,* etc., is married to actress Joanne Linville, and they have a daughter, born in '71. Onscreen from the '50s. IN: *Crime in the Streets,* more, including 1973's *The Long Goodbye,* his only acting role in more than a decade.

RYDER, ALFRED (S. Cal.) Former leading man who now alternates between directing plays and doing character roles in movies. Onscreen from 1944. IN: *Winged Victory, T-Men, The Story on Page One, Invitation to a Gunfighter, True Grit, Who Fears the Devil, "W," Escape to Witch Mountain,* more.

S

SAAD, MARGIT (Fr.) Leading lady. Onscreen from the '50s. IN: *The Gypsy Baron, The Chasers, Call Me Genius, The Last Escape,* more.

SABATO, ANTONIO (It.) Leading man. Onscreen from the '60s. IN: *Grand-Prix, The Lady of Manza, When Women Played Ding Dong,* more.

SABRINA (Eng.) Leading lady; lately inactive in movies. Onscreen from the '50s. IN: *The Belles of St. Trinian's, Satan in High Heels,* more.

SACHS, DAVID (S. Cal.) Support. Onscreen in the '70s. IN: *Road to Salina,* more.

SACHS, LEONARD (Eng.) Character. Onscreen from 1936. IN: *Gentlemen Marry Brunettes, Oscar Wilde, Scream of Fear,* more.

SACK, ERNA (Bavaria) Coloratura soprano. Retired since 1955, she lives on the shores of the Staffelsee in Upper Bavaria. Onscreen 1938–39. IN: *Manon, Flowers from Nice.*

SACKS, MICHAEL (N.Y.) Leading man. Onscreen in the '70s. IN: *Slaughterhouse Five, The Sugarland Express,* more.

SADLER, BARRY (S. Cal.) Support. Onscreen from the '60s. IN: *Dayton's Devils,* more.

SADOFF, FRED E. (Eng.) Actor-stage producer-director. Onscreen in the '50s. IN: *Viva Zapata!, The Quiet American.*

SADUSK, MAUREEN (S. Cal.) Character. Onscreen in the '70s. IN: *Sticks and Stones,* more.

SAHL, MORT (S. Cal.) Comedian. Onscreen from 1958. IN: *In Love and War, All the Young Men, Johnny Cool; Doctor, You've Got to be Kidding; Don't Make Waves,* more.

SAINT, EVA MARIE (S. Cal.) Costar. Won Best Supporting Actress Oscar in *On the Waterfront,* her first film. Onscreen from 1954. IN: *That Certain Feeling, Raintree County, A Hatful of Rain, North by Northwest, Exodus, All Fall Down, 36 Hours, The Sandpiper; The Russians Are Coming, The Russians Are Coming; The Stalking Moon, Grand-Prix, Loving, Cancel My Reservation,* more.

ST. ANGEL, MICHAEL (S. Cal.) The former leading man, playing character roles on TV in recent years, has been a widower since the death of his wife, actress-dancer Marjorie Holliday, in 1969. Onscreen from the '40s. IN: *Marine Raiders, Bride by Mistake, The Brighton Strangler, The Truth About Murder, The French Line,* more.

ST. CLAIR, ELIZABETH (S. Cal.) Support. Onscreen in the '70s. IN: *Welcome to Arrow Beach,* more.

ST. CLAIR, MICHAEL (S. Cal.) Support. Onscreen from the '60s. IN: *Von Ryan's Express, Thoroughly Modern Millie,* more.

ST. CYR, LILI (S. Cal.) Many times married and divorced, the exotic dancer—as shapely and blonde as ever in her 50s (b. 1920)—still does her act in clubs. Onscreen in the '50s. IN: *Son of Sinbad, The Naked and the Dead; I, Mobster;* more.

ST. JACQUES, RAYMOND (S. Cal.) Black star. Onscreen from 1964. IN: *Black Like Me, The Pawnbroker, Mister Moses, Mister Buddwing, The Comedians, Madigan, The Green Berets; If He Hollers, Let Him Go; Betrayal, Up Tight, Change of Mind, Cotton Comes to Harlem, Cool Breeze; Come Back, Charleston Blue; Lost in the Stars,* more.

SAINT JAMES, SUSAN (S. Cal.) Leading lady. Onscreen from 1967. IN: *Where Angels Go, Trouble Follows; P. J., New Faces in Hell, Jigsaw, What's So Bad About Feeling Good?,* more.

ST. JOHN, BETTA (Eng.) Leading lady; lately inactive in movies. Onscreen from 1953. IN: *Dream Wife, All the Brothers Were Valiant, The Robe, The Saracen Blade, The Naked Dawn, Tarzan and the Lost Safari, Corridors of Blood, Horror Hotel,* more.

ST. JOHN, CHRISTOPHER (S. Cal.) Black leading man. Onscreen from 1968. IN: *For Love of Ivy, The Awakening, Shaft, Top of the Heap,* more.

ST. JOHN, JILL (Colo.) Rich, childless after three marriages and divorces, still beautiful and young (b. 1940), she lives in a magnificent chalet in Aspen and declares she has little further interest in a movie career. But, in the spring of 1976, in her first part in some time, she acted on TV in the title role of ABC's "Monday 'Night Movie" *Brenda Starr.* Onscreen from 1958. IN: *Summer Love, The Remarkable Mr. Pennypacker, Holiday for Lovers, The Roman Spring of Mrs. Stone, Tender Is the Night, Come Blow Your Horn, Who's Been Sleeping in My Bed?,*

Honeymoon Hotel, The Oscar, Fame Is the Name of the Game, Banning, The King's Pirate, Tony Rome, Diamonds Are Forever, more.

ST. JOHN, RICHARD (S. Cal.) Support. Onscreen from the '50s. IN: Kisses for My President, more.

ST. JOHN, VALERIE (Eng.) Leading lady. Onscreen in the '70s. IN: The Swappers, The Wife Swappers, more.

SAIRE, DAVID (Eng.) Support. Onscreen from the '60s. IN: Loss of Innocence, Rattle of a Simple Man, more.

SAIS, MARIN (S. Cal.) Long retired, this leading lady of the silent action pix of True Boardman and Jack Hoxie still lives in Hollywood. She is in her late 80s (b. 1888). Onscreen from 1910. IN: Twelfth Night, The Social Pirates, Thunderbolt Jack (serial), many more silents; talkies: Pioneer Trail, Phantom Gold, Wild Horse Range, Enemy of Women, Border Badmen, Terrors on Horseback; Ride, Ryder, Ride; more, including 1950's The Fighting Redhead, her last.

SAITO, BILL (S. Cal.) Character. Onscreen from the '60s. IN: The Wrecking Crew, more.

SAKATA, HAROLD "ODDJOB" (S. Cal.) Character. Onscreen from the '60s. IN: The Poppy Is Also a Flower, Goldfinger, The Phynx, Dead of Night, The Wrestler, more.

SAKS, GENE (S. Cal.) Director of Mame, Barefoot in the Park, etc. Husband of comedy star Beatrice Arthur. Onscreen as a supporting actor in 1965 A Thousand Clowns.

SAKS, MATTHEW (S. Cal.) Juvenile. Son of Beatrice Arthur and Gene Saks. Onscreen in 1969. IN: Cactus Flower.

SALE, VIRGINIA (S. Cal.) This character actress, in her 80s now, fulfilled a lifelong ambition in this decade. She took time out from movies to do a nationwide tour of her one-woman comedy-drama act, playing theaters, schools, and local clubs. Her goal of 3,000 personal appearances reached, she has returned to Hollywood to resume her career and has lately appeared on TV, in dramatic series and commercials. Onscreen from the '20s. IN: Legionnaires in Paris, Harold Teen, The Cohens and the Kellys in Atlantic City, Fancy Baggage, Lovin' the Ladies, Bright Lights, Moby Dick, Gold Dust Gertie, Union Depot, Oliver Twist, The Man with Two Faces, Madame Du Barry, Topper, Gold Rush Maisie, Miss Annie Rooney, Dark Mountain, The Thin Man Goes Home,

When Strangers Marry, Badman's Territory, Trail Street, The Hat Box Mystery, How to Succeed in Business Without Really Trying, more.

SALES, SOUPY (N.Y.) Comedian. Onscreen in 1961 and 1966. IN: The Two Little Bears and Birds Do It.

SALLAS, DENNIS (N.Y.) Support. Onscreen from 1961. IN: Faces, more.

SALLIS, PETER (Eng.) Character. Onscreen from 1952. IN: Anastasia, Saturday Night and Sunday Morning, The V.I.P.s, The Scapegoat, The Mouse on the Moon, Inadmissible Evidence, The Night Digger, Wuthering Heights, more.

SALLIS, ZOE (Eng.) Support. Onscreen from the '60s. IN: The Bible, The Statue, more.

SALMI, ALBERT (S. Cal.) Support. Former husband of Peggy Ann Garner. Onscreen from 1958. IN: The Brothers Karamazov, The Bravados, Wild River, The Unforgiven, The Flim Flam Man, The Ambushers, Lawman, Something Big, The Deserter, The Take, The Crazy World of Julius Vrooder, more.

SALT, JENNIFER (S. Cal.) Leading lady. Daughter of screenwriter Waldo Salt. Onscreen from 1969. IN: Midnight Cowboy; Hi, Mom!; Brewster McCloud, The Revolutionary, Sisters, more.

SALVATORI, RENATO (It.) Support. Onscreen from the '50s. IN: Three Girls from Rome, The Big Deal on Madonna Street, Two Women, Rocco and His Brothers, The Organizer, How to Seduce a Playboy, more.

SAMOILOVA, TATYANA (Rus.) Leading lady. Onscreen from the '50s. IN: The Mexican, The Cranes Are Flying, The Letter That Was Never Sent, Italiano Brava Gente, more.

SAMPSON, ROBERT (S. Cal.) Leading man. Onscreen from 1962. IN: Look in Any Window, more.

SAN JUAN, OLGA (S. Cal.) Paramount's saucy little Latin from Manhattan married actor Edmond O'Brien in '48 and quit the screen. Except for a small role in his The Third Voice ('60), she hasn't been seen in a movie since. Happily married still, the O'Briens live in a Brentwood hacienda called, naturally, "San Juan Hill," and are parents of two daughters, Bridget (b. 1949) and Maria (b. 1950), and a son, Brendan (b. 1962). Maria began her own acting career on TV in '74 and the following year had a top supporting role—that of a beauty contestant

—in the movie *Smile*. Hailing the film, the *New York Times* critic said: "Three young actresses stand out . . . Maria O'Brien as a pushy, driving contestant who sells her Mexican-American heritage for all its worth," etc. She has chosen to follow both parents into the profession despite this warning from her Supporting Oscar-winning (*The Barefoot Contessa*) father: "Nobody achieves a real lasting reputation as an actor. Acting is a highly transient art form. There isn't as much satisfaction in a good performance as in a good book." Both Olga San Juan and Edmond O'Brien have suffered serious illnesses in recent years—she from a stroke, from which she is recovering; he from a seizure that occurred on a movie location in '71. When admitted to San Bernardino Community Hospital then, his condition was listed as "guarded"; a few days later, as "fair"; today it would seem to be "excellent." Years before this traumatic time, the actor—a lifelong practicing Catholic, like his wife—had said: "I don't know what keeps other people going, but for me, the so-called joy of living isn't enough. What keeps me going is faith in an afterlife . . . faith is what I have chosen." Perhaps not insignificantly, the title of the movie on which he was working when later taken ill was *The Faith Healer*. And faith, the entire O'Brien family believes, is what will make still-young (b. 1927) Olga San Juan well again; they all are praying. Onscreen from 1944. IN: *Rainbow Island, Blue Skies, Out of the World, Duffy's Tavern, Variety Girl, Are You With It?, One Touch of Venus, Countess of Monte Cristo, The Beautiful Blonde from Bashful Bend*, more. (See Edmond O'Brien.)

SANCHEZ, JAIME (S. Cal.) Support. Onscreen from 1962. IN: *David and Lisa, The Pawnbroker, Heroina, Beach Red, The Wild Bunch*, more.

SANCHEZ, PEDRO (It.) Character. Onscreen from the '60s. IN: *Any Gun Can Play, Sabata, Adios Sabata*, more.

SANCHO, FERNANDO (It.) Character. Onscreen from the '60s. IN: *Backfire, A Pistol for Ringo, The Big Gundown*, more.

SAND, PAUL (S. Cal.) Comic support. Onscreen from 1969. IN: *Viva Max!; The Hot Rock, The Second Coming of Suzanne*, more.

SANDA, DOMINIQUE (It.) Leading lady. Onscreen from 1970. IN: *Une Femme Douce, The Conformist, The Garden of the Finzi-Continis, Without Apparent Motive, 1900*, more.

SANDER, IAN (S. Cal.) Support. Onscreen in the '70s. IN: *Beyond the Valley of the Dolls, The Swinging Cheerleaders*, more.

SANDERS, ANITA (S. Cal.) Leading lady. Onscreen from the '60s. IN: *The Tenth Victim, Black on White*, more.

SANDERS, ANN (N.Y.) Support. Onscreen from the '50s. IN: *A View from the Bridge*, more.

SANDERS, SHEPHERD (S. Cal.) Support. Onscreen in the '70s. IN: *Kelly's Heroes*, more.

SANDFORD, CHRISTOPHER (Eng.) Character. Onscreen from the '60s. IN: *Half a Sixpence, Before Winter Comes, Deep End*, more.

SANDOR, STEVE (S Cal.) Support. Onscreen from the '60s. IN: *If He Hollers, Let Him Go; The Bridge at Remagen, Hell's Angels, One More Train to Rob*, more.

SANDREY, IRMA (N.Y.) Support. Onscreen from the '60s. IN: *The Best Man*, more.

SANDRELLI, STEFANIA (It.) Leading lady. Onscreen from the '60s. IN: *Divorce—Italian Style; Seduced and Abandoned, The Climax, Tender Scoundrel, Partner, The Conformist*, more.

SANDRI, ANNA-MARIA (It.) Leading lady; rarely active in movies now. Onscreen from the '50s. IN: *The Black Tent, Reaching for the Stars*, more.

SANDS, BILLY (S. Cal.) Character. Onscreen from the '60s. IN: *McHale's Navy, How to Frame a Figg*, more.

SANDS, JOHNNY (Hawaii) The blond lad from Texas who played Shirley Temple's basketball-playing beau so engagingly in 1947's *The Bachelor and the Bobby-Soxer* that he ranked second in *Photoplay's* "Most Promising Newcomer" poll, gave up movies in 1952. Today, a rugged, handsome man entering his 50s (b. 1927), and a longtime resident of Honolulu, he is married (reportedly his third) to a beautiful girl named Donella, has a houseful of kids, and is a business man. Onscreen from 1946. IN: *Till the End of Time, Blaze of Noon, The Fabulous Texan, Adventure in Baltimore, Massacre River, The Lawless, Two Flags West, The Admiral Was a Lady, Target Unknown, The Basketball Fix*, more, including *Aladdin and His Lamp*, his last.

SANDS, LESLIE (Eng.) Character. Onscreen from 1960. IN: *The Deadly Affair, Walk in the Shadow, One More Time, The Ragman's Daughter*, more.

SANDS, TOMMY (Hawaii) The singer-actor who in the '50s was ballyhooed to replace Presley, and was for a while Frank Sinatra's son-in-law, lives in Honolulu, has remarried—his wife was the former Sheila Wallace, a non-pro—and is the stepfather of two youngsters. Recovered from breakdowns and a near-fatal kidney ailment, he now has three careers. He acts occasionally in the locally produced TV series *Hawaii Five-O*, conducts nightclub tours for tourists, and sings in local clubs and TV. Last onscreen in 1965's *None But the Brave*, with Sinatra, he is in his 40s (b. 1936). Onscreen from 1958. IN: *Sing Boy Sing, Mardi Gras, Love in a Goldfish Bowl, Babes in Toyland, The Longest Day, Ensign Pulver*, more.

SANFORD, ISABEL (S. Cal.) Black character. Costar of TV's *The Jeffersons*. Onscreen from 1967. IN: *Guess Who's Coming to Dinner, The Young Runaways, Pendulum*, more.

SANTON, PENNY (S. Cal.) Character. Onscreen from 1955. IN: *Interrupted Melody, Full of Life, Dino, West Side Story, Cry Tough, Love With the Proper Stranger; Captain Newman, M.D.; Don't Just Stand There, Funny Girl, Kotch*, more.

SANTONI, RENI (S. Cal.) Leading man. Onscreen from 1967. IN: *Enter Laughing, Anzio, Guns of the Magnificent Seven, Dirty Harry*, more.

SANTOS, BERT (S. Cal.) Support. Onscreen from the '60s. IN: *Cherry, Harry & Raquel; Mr. Majestyk*, more.

SANTOS, JOE (S. Cal.) Support. Onscreen from the '60s. IN: *Moonlighting Wives, The Panic in Needle Park, The Gang That Couldn't Shoot Straight, Zandy's Bride, A Knife for the Ladies*, more.

SARANDON, CHRIS (N.Y.) Leading man. Nominated for Best Supporting Actor Oscar in *Dog Day Afternoon*. Husband of actress Susan Sarandon. Onscreen in the '70s. IN: *Lipstick*, more.

SARANDON, SUSAN (N.Y.) Leading lady. Onscreen from 1970. IN: *Joe, The Great Waldo Pepper, The Front Page, The Rocky Horror Picture Show, Dragonfly*, more.

SARDO, COSMO (S. Cal.) Character. Onscreen from the '40s. IN: *Amazon Quest*, more.

SARDOU, FERNAND (Fr.) Support. Onscreen from the '50s. IN: *Savage Triangle, Letters from My Windmill, The Wild Oat, Forbidden Fruit, Picnic on the Grass*, more.

SARGENT, DICK (S. Cal.) Leading man. Onscreen from 1957. IN: *Bernardine, Mardi Gras,*

Operation Petticoat, The Great Impostor, That Touch of Mink; Captain Newman, M.D.; The Ghost and Mr. Chicken, The Private Navy of Sgt. O'Farrell, The Young Runaways; Live a Little, Love a Little; more.

SARGENT, LEWIS (N. Cal.) Retired, the actor who played "Huck" in 1920 in *Huckleberry Finn* lives in San Francisco. Onscreen from 1920. IN: *The Soul of Youth, The New Adventures of Tarzan* (serial), more.

SARNE, MICHAEL (Eng.) Director of *Myra Breckinridge*, etc. Formerly a supporting actor. Onscreen in the '60s. IN: *Sodom and Gomorrah, The Guns of Navarone, Every Day's a Holiday*, more.

SARNO, JANET (N.Y.) Support. Onscreen in the '70s. IN: *Bananas, The People Next Door, The Hospital*, more.

SAROYAN, LUCY (N.Y.) Supporting actress-daughter of novelist-playwright William Saroyan. Onscreen from 1969. IN: *Some Kind of a Nut, The Taking of Pelham One Two Three*, more.

SARRACINO, ERNEST (S. Cal.) Character. Onscreen from 1960. IN: *Strangers When We Meet, A Dream of Kings*, more.

SARRAZIN, MICHAEL (S. Cal.) Leading man. Onscreen from 1967. IN: *The Flim Flam Man, Gunfight in Abilene, The Sweet Ride, Journey to Shiloh, In Search of Gregory; They Shoot Horses, Don't They?; The Pursuit of Happiness, Sometimes a Great Notion, Believe in Me, The Groundstar Conspiracy, The Reincarnation of Peter Proud, The Gumball Rally, The Loves and Times of Scaramouche*, more.

SASSARD, JACQUELINE (Fr.) Leading lady. Onscreen from the '50s. IN: *Guendalina, Women Are Weak, Violent Summer; My Son, the Hero; White Voices, Accident, Les Biches*, more.

SASSOLI, DINA (It.) Leading lady; inactive in movies in recent years. Onscreen from the '40s. IN: *The Loves of Don Juan, The Mill on the Po, The Life of Donizetti*, more.

SATO, REIKO (S. Cal.) Singer-actress; now married and retired from movies. Onscreen from 1950. IN: *Mother Didn't Tell Me, Woman on the Run, Kismet, Flower Drum Song, The Ugly American*, more.

SATTERLEE, BRUCE (S. Cal.) The boy actor of the '30s attended the Pasadena Playhouse as a young man but has since opted for a career in

411

business. Onscreen from 1937. IN: *Stella Dallas*, more.

SATTON, LON (S. Cal.) Support. Onscreen from 1969. IN: *For Love of Ivy; Hello—Goodbye; Welcome to the Club*, more.

SAUNDERS, LORI (S. Cal.) Leading lady. Onscreen from the '60s. IN: *Girls on the Beach, Myra in the Wilderness, Shadows Reach Out, Head On*, more.

SAUNDERS, MARY JANE (S. Cal.) This child actress later did a few ingenue roles but is now retired. Onscreen from 1949. IN: *Sorrowful Jones, Father Is a Bachelor, A Woman of Distinction, The Girl Next Door*, more.

SAVAGE, ANN (S. Cal.) Still a beautiful blonde and now in her 50s (b. 1921), she is married to business man Vern Lawrence (since '62), and retired. Her last movie was 1953's *The Woman They Almost Lynched*.

SAVAGE, BRAD (S. Cal.) Leading man. Onscreen in the '70s. IN: *Echoes of a Summer*, more.

SAVAGE, JOHN (Conn.) Leading man. Onscreen in the '70s. IN: *Bad Company, The Killing Kind, Steelyard Blues, No Deposit No Return*, more.

SAVAL, DANY (Fr.) Leading lady; lately inactive in movies. Onscreen from 1961. IN: *The Cheaters, Moon Pilot, 7 Capital Sins, The Devil and the 10 Commandments; Boeing, Boeing;* more.

SAVALAS, GEORGE (S. Cal.) Character actor-brother of Telly Savalas. Onscreen in the '70s. IN: *A Dream of Kings, Kelly's Heroes*, more.

SAVALAS, TELLY (S. Cal.) Star. Nominated for Best Supporting Actor Oscar in *Bird Man of Alcatraz*. Onscreen from 1960. IN: *The Interns, Mad Dog Coll, The Young Savages, Cape Fear, Love Is a Ball, Johnny Cool, Genghis Khan, Battle of the Bulge, The Greatest Story Ever Told, The Slender Thread, The Dirty Dozen, The Scalphunters, Sol Madrid, MacKenna's Gold, The Assassination Bureau, On Her Majesty's Secret Service, Pretty Maids All in a Row, Kelly's Heroes, Land Raiders, Clay Pigeon, A Town Called Hell, Horror Express, Sonny and Jed, Inside Out, Killer Force*, more.

SAWYER, CONNIE (S. Cal.) Character. Onscreen from the '50s. IN: *A Hole in the Head, Ada*, more.

SAWYER, JOE (S. Cal.) Character who, early in his career, was sometimes billed under his real name, Joseph Sauers. Inactive in movies for the past 15 years. Onscreen from 1933. IN: *College Humor, Jimmy the Gent, I Found Stella Parish, The Petrified Forest, Crash Donovan, The Leathernecks Have Landed, Black Legion, Slim, San Quentin, They Gave Him a Gun, Confessions of a Nazi Spy, I Stole a Million, The Grapes of Wrath, The Long Voyage Home, Sergeant York, They Died With Their Boots On, The Outlaw, Let's Face It, Gilda; Joe Palooka—Champ; Christmas Eve, A Double Life, Coroner Creek, Lucky Stiff, Red Skies of Montana, Johnny Dark, The Kettles in the Ozarks, The Killing*, more, including *North to Alaska*, his most recent to date.

SAXON, JOHN (S. Cal.) Leading man. Onscreen from 1955. IN: *Running Wild, Rock Pretty Baby, The Reluctant Debutante, This Happy Feeling, Cry Tough, The Big Fisherman, Portrait in Black, The Unforgiven, War Hunt, Mr. Hobbs Takes a Vacation, The Cardinal, The Appaloosa, Winchester 73, For Singles Only, Death of a Gunfigher, Black Christmas, Metraleta Stein, Mitchell, The Swiss Conspiracy*, more.

SAYERS, JO ANN (N.J.) The lovely blonde MGM leading lady of the late '30s next starred on Broadway in the title role of *My Sister Eileen*. That was essentially the end of her career except for a bit of summer stock, a few TV talk shows, and one "live" TV drama with Lloyd Nolan. In '42, she became the wife of a very rich and social young New Yorker, Anthony A. Bliss, to whom she was married for many years. They lived on Long Island as do, now, all three of their children: John (a young Amherst graduate, single, an inventor, works on documentary films); Anthony Jr. (in his early 30s, divorced, works for the *New York Times*, attends graduate school at NYU); Eileen Andahazy (named for her mother's famous stage role, divorced, has two little girls). For nine years, while living on Long Island, the actress was on the board of trustees of Hofstra University. She later returned to college herself, and in '66 received her degree in French at Columbia. While there, she made a single stage appearance—in the 50-minute monologue, *Le Voix d'Humaine*, by Jean Cocteau. Her only other recent dramatic activity—"the most exciting thing I have ever done"—was in '72. She narrated then, at Long Island University, Stravinsky's *Persephone*, with a full symphony and a chorus of 200. Divorced from Anthony Bliss, she has been married since '68 to Charles K. Agle, an architect and city planner. They live in Princeton and she is the stepmother of his three married sons. And, in her late 50s (b. 1918) is still a very beautiful woman. Onscreen from 1938. IN: *Young Doctor Kildare, Honolulu,*

Huckleberry Finn, Fast and Loose, Within the Law, The Man With Nine Lives, more.

SAYLOR, KATIE (S. Cal.) Leading lady. Onscreen in the '70s. IN: *Dirty O'Neil*, more.

SAYRE, C. BIGELOW (S. Cal.) Character. Onscreen from the '50s. IN: *Union Station*, more.

SCALES, PRUNELLA (Eng.) Leading lady. Onscreen from 1952. IN: *Scotch on the Rocks, Hobson's Choice, Room at the Top, Waltz of the Toreadors, Escape from the Dark*, more.

SCANNELL, FRANK (S. Cal.) Character. Onscreen from the '40s. IN: *Shadow of Suspicion, An Angel Comes to Brooklyn, Hit Parade of 1947, I Wonder Who's Kissing Her Now, Kilroy Was Here, Apartment for Peggy, When My Baby Smiles at Me, Ladies of the Chorus, The Country Girl, The Incredible Shrinking Man, The Screaming Mimi, High Time, The Disorderly Orderly*, more.

SCARDINO, DON (N.Y.) Leading man. Onscreen in the '70s. IN: *Homer*, more.

SCHAFER, NATALIE (N.Y.) Character. Onscreen from 1944. IN: *Marriage Is a Private Affair, Keep Your Powder Dry, Masquerade in Mexico, The Other Love, Repeat Performance, The Secret Beyond the Door, The Snake Pit, Caught, Payment on Demand, Callaway Went Thataway, Female on the Beach, Forever Darling, Anastasia; Oh Men! Oh Women!; Bernardine, Back Street, Susan Slade, The Day of the Locust*, more.

SCHAFER, REUBEN (N.Y.) Character. Onscreen from the '60s. IN: *Goodbye, Columbus* (as "Uncle Max"), more.

SCHALLERT, WILLIAM (S. Cal.) Character. Onscreen from 1950. IN: *The Man from Planet X, Flat Top, The Red Badge of Courage, Riot in Cell Block 11, Gog, Bigger Than Life, Written on the Wind, Friendly Persuasion, Cry Terror, Pillow Talk, In the Heat of the Night, Will Penny, The Computer Wore Tennis Shoes, The Strongest Man in the World*, more.

SCHEIDER, ROY (N.Y.) Leading man. Nominated for Best Supporting Actor Oscar in *The French Connection*. Onscreen from 1964. IN: *The Curse of the Living Corpse* (billed Roy R. Sheider), *Stiletto, Klute, The Outside Man, Sheila Levine Is Dead and Living in New York, Jaws, Marathon Man*, more.

SCHELL, CATHERINE (Switz.) Leading lady. Of the acting Schell family—Maria, Maximilian, and Karl. Onscreen in the '70s. IN: *The*

Black Windmill, The Return of the Pink Panther, more.

SCHELL, KARL (CARL) (Switz.) Leading man. Onscreen from the '60s. IN: *Escape from East Berlin, Werewolf in a Girls' Dormitory, The Blue Max*, more.

SCHELL, MARIA (Switz.) Costar. Onscreen from the '40s. IN: *Steinbruch, Angel With the Trumpet, The Magic Box, So Little Time, Gervaise, The Brothers Karamazov, The Hanging Tree, Cimarron, The Mark, As the Sea Rages, White Nights, End of Desire, Duel in the Forest, 99 Women, Tiger by the Tail, The Odessa File, The Twist*, more.

SCHELL, MAXIMILIAN (Switz.) Costar and director. Won Best Actor Oscar in *Judgment at Nuremberg*. Nominated in the same category in *The Man in the Glass Booth*. Onscreen from the '50s. IN: *The Young Lions, Five Finger Exercise, The Reluctant Saint, The Condemned of Altona, Topkapi, Return from the Ashes, The Deadly Affair, Counterpoint, The Desperate Ones, The Castle; Krakatoa—East of Java; The Odessa File, St. Ives, Assassination in Sarajevo, A Bridge Too Far*, more.

SCHIAFFINO, ROSANNA (It.) Leading lady. Onscreen from the '60s. IN: *The Minotaur, La Notte Brava, Two Weeks in Another Town, Crime Does Not Pay, Lafayette, The Victors, The Long Ships, The Cavern; Arrivederci, Baby!; El Greco, Red Dragon, The Man Called Noon*, more.

SCHILLER, NORBERT (Switz.) Character. Onscreen from the '40s. IN: *Sealed Verdict, The Girl in the Kremlin, Torn Curtain, The Pedestrian* (as himself), more.

SCHMIDT, PEER (Ger.) Support. Onscreen from the '50s. IN: *The Confessions of Felix Krull, The Gypsy Baron, Those Daring Young Man in Their Jaunty Jalopies*, more.

SCHMIDTMER, CHRISTIANE/a.k.a. CHRISTINE MERR (S. Cal.) Leading lady. Onscreen from the '60s. IN: *Stop Train 349, Fanny Hill; Boeing, Boeing; Ship of Fools, The Big Doll House*, more.

SCHMELING, MAX (Ger.) Retired heavyweight boxing champ. Married to Anny Ondra. Onscreen in the '30s. IN: *Liebe im Ring* and *Knock-Out*. (See Anny Ondra.)

SCHNABEL, STEFAN (N.Y.) Character. Most active in recent years in TV soap operas. Onscreen from 1942. IN: *Journey Into Fear, The Iron Curtain, The Barbary Pirate, Diplomatic Courier, Houdini, Crowded Paradise, The*

Counterfeit Traitor, Two Weeks in Another Town, The Ugly American, Rampage, The Happy Hooker, more.

SCHNEIDER, MAGDA (Ger.) Leading lady, later a character actress, now retired. Mother of actress Romy Schneider. Onscreen from the early '30s. IN: *Longing, Be Mine Tonight, Tales from the Vienna Woods, Rendezvous in the Black Forest, The Right to Love, The Story of Vickie, The House of Three Girls*, more.

SCHNEIDER, MARIA (Fr.) Leading lady. The illegitimate daughter, she has said, of French star Daniel Gelin. Onscreen from 1973. IN: *Last Tango in Paris, The Passenger*, more.

SCHNEIDER, ROMY (Fr.) Leading lady. Onscreen from 1958. IN: *The Story of Vickie, Christine, Boccaccio '70, The Trial, The Cardinal, The Victors, Good Neighbor Sam, What's New Pussycat?, Maedchen in Uniform, Triple Cross, Otley, The Assassination of Trotsky, Cesar and Rosalie, A Woman in the Window*, more.

SCHOLL, DANNY (N.Y.) Broadway singer, once married to Corinne Griffith, who, lately beset by physical problems, works for the President's commission to aid the handicapped. Onscreen in 1954. IN: *Top Banana*.

SCHREIBER, AVERY (S. Cal.) Support. Onscreen from the '60s. IN: *Don't Drink the Water*, more.

SCHREIBER, SALLY (N.Y.) Character. Onscreen from the '60s. IN: *Madigan, Rivals, Who Is Harry Kellerman and Why Is He Saying Those Terrible Things About Me?*, more.

SCHRODER, ERNST (Ger.) Character. Onscreen from the '50s. IN: *The Last Illusion, The Man Between, The Counterfeit Traitor, The Visit, Heidi*, more.

SCHUCK, JOHN (S. Cal.) Character. Onscreen in the '70s. IN: *M*A*S*H, Brewster McCloud, McCabe and Mrs. Miller, Thieves Like Us*, more.

SCHUMANN, ERIK (Ger.) Support. Onscreen from the '50s. IN: *Reaching for the Stars, The Two-Headed Spy, Question 7, The Counterfeit Traitor*, more.

SCHWARTZ, SAM (N.Y.) Character. Onscreen from the '50s. IN: *The Vagabond King, The Hustler*, more.

SCHWARTZKOPF, ELISABETH (It.) The opera star, a soprano from Germany, lives in Milan. Onscreen in 1952 and 1962. IN: *St. Matthew Passion* and *Der Rosenkavalier*.

SCOB, EDITH (Fr.) Support. Onscreen from the '60s. IN: *The Burning Court, Therese, Judex, The Milky Way*, more.

SCOFIELD, PAUL (Eng.) Costar. Won Best Actor Oscar in *A Man for All Seasons*. Onscreen from 1954. IN: *Carve Her Name with Pride, That Lady, The Train, King Lear, Scorpio, A Delicate Balance*, more.

SCOLLAY, FRED J. (S. Cal.) Support. Onscreen from the '50s. IN: *A View from the Bridge, Odds Against Tomorrow, Stage Struck, Death Wish*, more.

SCOOLER, ZVEE (N.Y.) Character. Onscreen from the '60s. IN: *The Pawnbroker, Fiddler on the Roof* ("The Rabbi"), *The Detective, No Way to Treat a Lady, A Dream of Kings, The Apprenticeship of Duddy Kravitz*, more.

SCORSESE, MARTIN (N.Y.) Director of the '70s (*Mean Streets*, etc.). Onscreen in a supporting role ("Weird Passenger") in 1975 *Taxi Driver* (which he directed).

SCOTT, ALAN (Fr.) Leading man. Onscreen from the '60s. IN: *Lola, Paris in the Month of August*, more.

SCOTT, ALEX (Eng.) Character. Onscreen from the '60s. IN: *Darling, Fahrenheit 451, The Abominable Dr. Phibes*, more.

SCOTT, AVIS (Eng.) Former leading lady; inactive in movies in recent years. Onscreen from the '40s. IN: *Millions Like Us, Brief Encounter, To Have and to Hold, Hundred Hour Hunt, It Started in Paradise, Storm Over the Nile*, more.

SCOTT, BARRY (Eng.) Support. Onscreen in the '70s. IN: *Goodbye Gemini*, more.

SCOTT, BONNIE/a.k.a. BONNIE SCOTT HUTCHINS (S. Cal.) Support. Onscreen from the '60s. IN: *Vicki, Beware My Love, Love Is Better Than Ever, Dondi*, more.

SCOTT, BRENDA (S. Cal.) Leading lady. Niece of the late star May Busch. Onscreen from the '60s. IN: *Johnny Tiger, Journey to Shiloh, This Savage Land; Simon, King of the Witches* (with Andrew Prine, to whom she was married); more.

SCOTT, BRUCE (S. Cal.) Support. First husband of comedienne Sandy Duncan. Onscreen in the '70s. IN: *The People Next Door*, more.

SCOTT, CONNIE (N.Y.) Leading lady. On-screen from the '60s. IN: *Flipper, The Brotherhood*, more.

SCOTT, DAVID (S. Cal.) In numerous pix of the '30s, he has long been a film editor, married to scriptwriter Evelyn F. Scott, and the father of a grown daughter, Ursula. His wife, daughter of one of DeMille's most noted continuity writers, Beulah Dix Flebbe, is author of a charming book about the movies' early years, *Hollywood When Silents Were Golden*. On-screen from 1930. IN: *In Gay Madrid, The Melody Lingers On*, more.

SCOTT, DEBRALEE (S. Cal.) Ingenue. On-screen in the '70s. IN: *Our Time, The Crazy World of Julius Vrooder*, more.

SCOTT, EVELYN (S. Cal.) Support; former leading lady. Onscreen from the '50s. IN: *Wicked Woman, I Want to Live!*, more.

SCOTT, FRED (S. Cal.) One of the most popular cowboy stars of the '30s, billed "The Silvery-Voiced Buckaroo"—after leads in *The Grand Parade* with Helen Twelvetrees, followed by many musicals—he left the screen in the early '40s. For the rest of that decade, he was a singer in the "Florentine Gardens Revues" presented by Nils T. Granlund in his club on Hollywood Boulevard. He also worked for a brief period in MGM's sound department. For more than 25 years he has been a successful Hollywood realtor. Considerably heavier now than in his prime, and with his coal-black hair turned to silver (he was born in 1902), he lives with wife, Marietta (she was in *George White's Scandals*), in the hills in the San Fernando Valley; they have two daughters and five grandchildren. On-screen from 1920. IN: *The Bride of the Storm, Rio Rita, Swing High, Beyond Victory, The Last Outlaw, Make a Wish, Romance Rides the Range, Singing Buckaroo, Moonlight on the Range, Melody of the Plains, Roaming Cowboy, Knight of the Plains, Song of the Prairie*, more.

SCOTT, GEORGE C. (N.Y.) Star. Won Best Actor Oscar in *Patton* (saying in advance he would refuse to accept it, he did not; it is still in a vault at the Motion Picture Academy). Nominated in the same category in *The Hospital*. Nominated for Best Supporting Actor Oscar in *The Hustler* and *Anatomy of a Murder*. On-screen from 1959. IN: *The Hanging Tree, The Power and the Glory, The List of Adrian Messenger, Dr. Strangelove, The Yellow Rolls-Royce, The Bible; Not With My Wife, You Don't; The Flim Flam Man, Petulia, The Last Run, They Might Be Giants, The Day of the Dolphin, Rage, Oklahoma Crude, The Savage Is Loose, The Hindenburg, Islands in the Stream*, more.

SCOTT, GORDON (It.) Making swashbucklers and "spaghetti Westerns" in Italy has made the former Tarzan—and former husband of actress Vera Miles—hugely successful and wealthy. As ruggedly handsome as ever as he enters his 50s (b. 1927), he lives in princely fashion in a villa. Onscreen from 1955. IN: *Tarzan's Hidden Jungle* (with Vera Miles), *Tarzan and the Lost Safari, Tarzan the Magnificent, The Lion of St. Mark, Coriolanus, Hero Without a Country, Beast of Babylon vs. the Son of Hercules, Goliath and the Vampires, Hero of Rome, Samson and the Seven Miracles of the World, The Tramplers*, more.

SCOTT, HAZEL (N.Y.) The black jazz pianist-singer, famous for her boogie-woogie, lives in Manhattan, journeys regularly to Israel for extended concert tours, and remains a steady, SRO attraction at Jimmy Weston's club in New York. In 1973 she did an acting stint in the TV soap opera *One Life to Live*, in which she performed a song of the same title that she wrote. She has also written two books—her autobiography and a biography of her former husband, the late (d. 1972) Adam Clayton Powell Jr., congressman and pastor of Harlem's Abyssinian Baptist Church. By him she has a son, Adam Clayton Powell III, news editor at radio station WINS and Executive Editor of the black community weekly newspaper *New York Age*. He is married to socialite Beryl Slocum, whose noted Newport family traces its ancestry back to Miles Standish, and has made Hazel Scott a grandmother of two young boys. For a decade, beginning in the mid-'50s, the performer lived and worked in France. While abroad, after divorcing Powell in 1960, she was briefly married to Swiss entertainer Ezio Bedin. She was also, in that period, under personal contract to Orson Welles as an actress. Returning to the States in '67, she lived in Hollywood again, guest-starred in a single dramatic episode of TV's *The Bold Ones*—playing a terminal cancer patient—and attempted to make a career as an actress. Today, a dramatically attractive woman in her 50s (b. 1920), the Trinidad-born star still has acting aspirations. "I'm dying to get a good, meaty role," she says. "It could be serious or it could be comedy. I like both. I like comedy and I'm also a good crier." Onscreen from 1943. IN: *Something to Shout About, I Dood It, The Heat's On, Broadway Rhythm, Rhapsody in Blue, Night Affair*, more.

SCOTT, JACQUELINE (S. Cal.) Leading lady. Onscreen from the '50s. IN: *Macabre, Firecreek, Death of a Gunfighter*, more.

SCOTT, JANETTE (S. Cal.) The English leading lady—and former child star— has been married for years to singer Mel Torme and is the mother of three young children, a daughter and two sons, the most recent born in '73. Onscreen from 1945. IN: *Spellbound, No Place for Jennifer, No Highway in the Sky, The Magic Box, The Good Companions, The Devil's Disciple, School for Scoundrels, Day of the Triffids, Paranoiac, The Old Dark House, Crack in the World*, more, including 1968's *His and Hers*, her most recent to date.

SCOTT, JAY (S. Cal.) Support. Onscreen in the '70s. IN: *Grave of the Vampire*, more.

SCOTT, JOAN (Eng.) Character. Onscreen in the '70s. IN: *The Mutations*, more.

SCOTT, KATHRYN LEIGH (N.Y.) Leading lady. Popular in TV soap operas. Onscreen in the '70s. IN: *House of Dark Shadows*, more.

SCOTT, KEN (S. Cal.) Support. Onscreen from 1957. IN: *The Three Faces of Eve, Stopover Tokyo, The Bravados, This Earth Is Mine, Beloved Infidel, Desire in the Dust, The Second Time Around, The Naked Brigade, The Murder Game, Psych-Out*, more.

SCOTT, KEVIN (Eng.) Support. Onscreen in the '70s. IN: *The Internecine Project*, more.

SCOTT, LEE (S. Cal.) Support. Onscreen from the '50s. IN: *Excuse My Dust*, more.

SCOTT, LINDA (S. Cal.) Leading lady. Onscreen from the '60s. IN: *Don't Knock the Twist, Little Fauss and Big Halsy, Psych-Out*, more.

SCOTT, LIZABETH (S. Cal.) Producer Hal Wallis dropped her option in '57 after *Loving You*. He had been the guiding force behind her career for a dozen years, and at one time Hollywood had expected that they would marry. Now in her 50s (b. 1922), slender and deeply suntanned, she still has not married though she dates some of the town's most eligible men, including Henry Berger who was the husband of late actress Anita Louise. For several years, until his death in '69, she was constantly with Texas millionaire William Lafayette Dugger Jr. In a handwritten codicil to his will, in which he referred to the star as "my fiancee," Dugger left equal shares of his oil-rich estate to the actress and to his sister, Sarah Dugger Schwartz, of San Antonio. The sister, who had been the sole heir in the original will, contested the revision. Though the actress had fought her way out of the Czech ghetto in Scranton, Pa., to become a major star at 23, she lost this battle.

San Antonio District Judge Eugene C. Williams ruled in '70, and the following year the Court of Civil Appeals upheld his decision, that the star was not entitled to share in the estate. She has been similarly luckless in her career. She has been seen in just two movies in 20 years, *Quantrill's Raiders* in '58 and *Pulp* in '73. In the latter, a bizarre mystery-comedy with Michael Caine and Mickey Rooney, she had the outré role of Princess Betty Cippola, an aging, ex-Hollywood star, gave an excellent performance, and it was expected that it would prove the beginning of a new career for her. Onscreen from 1945. IN: *You Came Along, The Strange Love of Martha Ivers, Dead Reckoning, I Walk Alone, Desert Fury, Pitfall, Easy Living, Too Late for Tears, Paid in Full, Dark City, The Company She Keeps, The Racket, A Stolen Face, Scared Stiff, Bad for Each Other, The Weapon*, more.

SCOTT, MARGARETTA (Eng.) The screen career of this lovely leading lady, and lately a character actress, which began with *The Private Life of Don Juan*, always took second place to her work on the stage. The latter—long and illustrious—included many Shakespearean roles (Portia in *The Merchant of Venice*, the Queen in *Hamlet*, etc.), as well as many popular hits, and has continued to the recent past. Less active in all areas of performing now—an occasional TV role or, more rarely, a character role in a movie such as 1971's *Percy*—she lives on fashionable Molyneux Street in London and takes frequent motoring trips in the English countryside. She is in her 60s now (b. 1912) and a widow, her one husband having been the late John de Lacey Wooldridge. Onscreen from 1934. IN: *Things to Come, The Return of the Scarlet Pimpernel, The Girl in the News, Quiet Wedding, Fanny by Gaslight, The Man from Morocco, Man of Evil, Mrs. Fitzherbert, Where's Charley?, Landfall, Devil's Plot, The Last Man to Hang, An Honorable Murder, Crescendo*, more.

SCOTT, MARTHA (S. Cal.) Character, former costar. Nominated for Best Actress Oscar in *Our Town*, her debut. In 1969, after many years in the East, this actress cast her lot—permanently she said—with Hollywood. She appears in an occasional movie, such as *Airport 1975*, but is seen far more regularly on TV—in *The Bob Newhart Show* (in which she plays the comedian's flighty mother) and specials such as the one on President Harry Truman (in which she was his elderly mother). Moreover, she stars frequently on the legitimate stage, in plays like *The Skin of Our Teeth*, almost always under the auspices of the Plumstead Playhouse, of which she is a founder-director. Originated years ago on Long Island, this company now operates out of the old Pasadena Playhouse.

She and her associates decided to move this production unit west because she believes Los Angeles will be the Broadway of the future. There is irony in her decision to settle in California, because Martha Scott is one star Hollywood never quite knew what to do with. Movie moguls, after her success as the tragic Emily in *Our Town*, pondered over how to cast her, for she was not dazzlingly lovely as they counted beauty. Though she was then only 26, there was already a decided maturity in her features, particularly her haunting, deep-set eyes. There was, they decided, even in her speech, something prim, proper and schoolmarmish about her. So they twice cast her as a schoolteacher—first as a young smalltown teacher who, bypassing love in her dedication, grows honorably ancient in her profession; then, as a frontier schoolmarm who wages a spirited battle to win back her job after writing a daring book. And as an aristocratic Early Virginia plantation wife. And as a Methodist minister's wife who goes from youth to old age. In each she was splendid, but an actress, not a star. One producer, desperate to change this, cast her in a farce with Dennis O'Keefe, *Hi Diddle Diddle*, with unfortunate results. By then it was only 1943, but Martha Scott concluded the one way to salvage her career was to return to Broadway where, in the following three decades, she had numerous successes. She did much "live" TV, was for three years (1954–57) the narrator-hostess of daytime's *Modern Romances*, and infrequently would fly to Hollywood for a picture or a filmed-TV guest appearance (*Route 66, The Nurses*, etc.). Often a screen wife, the actress has twice been one offscreen. Presently, as she has been since July 23, 1946, she is the wife of pianist-composer Mel Powell, who is almost a decade her junior (she was born 1914). They married in Las Vegas on the same day the actress received her divorce, after six years of marriage to Carleton Alsop. By Alsop she has a son, Scott. And by Powell she has two grown daughters, Mary Mark and Kathleen Ellen. At the time of their marriage, Powell was most famous as Benny Goodman's star pianist. But he has long since made his mark as a music scholar. Besides having received a Guggenheim Fellowship, he taught music at Yale for eight years and is currently dean of the School of Music at the California Institute of Arts in Los Angeles. It was her husband's career as well as her own that prompted their return to Hollywood from Connecticut, where they lived for years. Martha Scott says she is glad to be back, but adds that it was not a pursuit of security that was behind their decision. "When you've been in the business as long as I have," she says, "you learn to live with this thing actors call insecurity. If you become so preoccupied with security that you permit it to dictate your professional future, then you're lost . . . You can't take money with you, but you can take satisfaction." Onscreen from 1940. IN: *Cheers for Miss Bishop, The Howards of Virginia, They Dare Not Love, One Foot in Heaven, War of the Wildcats* (released in some areas as *In Old Oklahoma*), *So Well Remembered, Strange Bargain, When I Grow Up, The Desperate Hours, The Ten Commandments, Sayonara, Ben-Hur*, more.

SCOTT, PIPPA (S. Cal.) Leading lady. Onscreen from 1956. IN: *The Searchers, Auntie Mame, Petulia, Some Kind of a Nut, Cold Turkey*, more.

SCOTT, RANDOLPH (S. Cal.) *Badman's Territory*, made in 1946 when Scott was 43, was a box-office bonanza—and the turning point in his career. Earlier he had played heroes of every stripe—military men (*To the Shores of Tripoli, Bombardier*, etc.) and adventurers (*The Spoilers, Captain Kidd*). He had done romantic comedies (*My Favorite Wife, Follow the Fleet*, etc.). He'd even lent his strong-jawed, smiling, blond, hazel-eyed presence to a long string of Westerns without becoming a box-office goldmine. But the surprise success of *Badman's Territory* prompted him to devote the balance of his screen career to Westerns—with three exceptions: *The Assassin, Christmas Eve*, and the all-star *Starlift* in which he did a cameo. It may have been the wisest decision the 6'2" Southern-accented gentleman ever made. In the subsequent 16 years, he starred in 39 big-budget Westerns and was for four successive years (1950–53) among the 10 Top Box-Office Stars. He made a fortune for his producers—and himself. Today, with investments—still personally supervised from an office on Hollywood Boulevard—in real estate, gas and oil wells, and securities, he is reportedly worth $50 to $100 million. Money is nothing new to the amiable Virginian. Born Randolph Crane Scott, the son of an administrative engineer, he was educated in private schools and at the University of North Carolina. After graduation he became a textile manufacturer and, in his 20s, the husband of one of the world's richest women, Mariana Somerville DuPont (of the Maryland DuPonts), whose hobby was race horses and who, in photographs, seemed considerably older than the actor. Illness forced him to go to California in 1929 to recuperate. There he admitted a deep-seated desire to become an actor. A game of golf—still his recreation—with young millionaire Howard Hughes proved fortunate. Hughes helped him get a small role in a silent movie, *Far Call*. This was followed by two years of study at the Pasadena Playhouse. In 1931, in *Women Men Marry*, he was "officially" launched on a career that spanned the next 31 years and more than 100 movies. The actor and his wife were seldom seen together after he went to Hollywood, and were eventually divorced. For a long while he shared bachelor's digs with good pal—and still his friend—Cary Grant. He has been married to former actress Pat Stillman since 1944 and has two grown children, Christopher and Sandra, both adopted. Home is a mansion in Beverly Hills. In his 70s—his only concession to age being a slight deafness—Randolph Scott remains an extraordinarily handsome, athletic man, and, as he always has been, highly leery of publicity about his private life. He swims, rides horseback and golfs—usually with pals Bob Hope and Bing Crosby. His favorite companions, though, are the cowboys with whom he worked in his early films. He doesn't consider himself retired, not with his financial empire to oversee, but he does admit "enjoying my role as an ordinary Joe." Onscreen from 1929. IN: *Far Call, Island of Lost Souls; Hello, Everybody!; Wild Horse Mesa, Murders in the Zoo, Home on the Range, Roberta, She, So Red the Rose; High, Wide and Handsome; Rebecca of Sunnybrook Farm, The Texans, Virginia City, Western Union, Belle Starr, Paris Calling, Pittsburgh, Corvette K-225, Gung Ho!, China Spy, Home Sweet Homicide, Trail Street, Coroner Creek, Albuquerque, Fighting Man of the Plains, Colt '45, Fort Worth, Man in the Saddle, The Bounty Hunter, Tall Man Riding, Decision at Sundown, Ride Lonesome, Comanche Station,* more, including 1962's *Ride the High Country* (perhaps his finest performance), his last.

SCOTT, SIMON (S. Cal.) Character. Onscreen from the '50s. IN: *Man of a Thousand Faces, Compulsion, Moon Pilot, Dead Heat on a Merry-Go-Round, In Enemy Country, Cold Turkey,* more.

SCOTT, SONDRA (S. Cal.) Leading lady. Onscreen in the '70s. IN: *The Christine Jorgensen Story; Rabbit, Run;* more.

SCOTT, TIMOTHY (S. Cal.) Support. Onscreen from the '60s. IN: *The Ballad of Josie, The Party, Vanishing Point, One More Train to Rob, Macon County Line, Vendetta,* more.

SCOTTI, VITO (S. Cal.) Character. Onscreen from 1960. IN: *Where the Boys Are, The Explosive Generation, Two Weeks in Another Town; Captain Newman, M.D.; Rio Conchos, The Pleasure Seekers, Von Ryan's Express; What Did You Do in the War, Daddy?; The Caper of the Golden Bulls, The Secret War of Harry Frigg, How Sweet It Is, Head, Cactus Flower, The McCullochs,* more.

SCOULAR, ANGELA (Eng.) Leading lady. Onscreen from the '60s. IN: *A Countess from Hong Kong, Casino Royale, Here We Go Around the Mulberry Bush,* more.

SCOURBY, ALEXANDER (N.Y.) Character-narrator. Married to TV soap opera star Lori March. Onscreen from 1952. IN: *Affair in Trinidad, Because of You, The Big Heat, The Glory Brigade, Giant, Ransom, Me and the Colonel, The Big Fisherman, The Shaggy Dog, The Man on the String, The Devil at 4 O'Clock,* more. Perhaps his most famous narration was that for 1954's *Victory at Sea.*

SCOURBY, HELEN (N.Y.) Support. Onscreen in the '70s. IN: *Cops and Robbers,* more.

SCRUGGS, LINDA (S. Cal.) Leading lady. Onscreen in the '70s. IN: *Shoot It: Black, Shoot It: Blue;* more.

SEAFORTH, SUSAN (S. Cal.) Leading lady in TV soap operas. Onscreen from 1959. IN: *The Five Pennies, Billie; If He Hollers, Let Him Go;* more.

SEAGRAM, LISA (Eng.) Leading lady. Onscreen from the '60s. IN: *A House Is Not a Home, Caprice, 2000 Years Later,* more.

SEAGULL, BARBARA/formerly BARBARA HERSHEY (S. Cal.) Leading lady. Onscreen as Barbara Hershey from 1968. IN: *With Six You Get Egg Roll,* more. She became Barbara Seagull in the '70s. IN: *Boxcar Bertha, The Crazy World of Julius Vrooder,* more.

SEAL, ELIZABETH (Eng.) Leading lady-dancer. Onscreen from 1955. IN: *Town on Trial, Cone of Silence, Trouble in the Sky, Vampire Circus,* more.

SEARLE, JACKIE (S. Cal.) The once greatly popular boy star is in his 50s now (b. 1920) and is the owner of a small manufacturing plant near Hollywood. The pint-sized and balding dad of two grown children, he hasn't been in a movie since 1948's *The Paleface,* but every once in a while he does a TV role—usually villainous—just to keep his hand in. Onscreen from 1929. IN: *Daughters of Desire, Tom Sawyer, Skippy, Sooky, Daybreak, Huckleberry Finn, The Miracle Man, Lovers Courageous, Oliver Twist, Alice in Wonderland, Topaze, The World Changes, Peck's Bad Boy, Ginger, Gentle Julia, Little Lord Fauntleroy, Little Tough Guy, That Certain Age, Angels Wash Their Faces, Military Academy, My Little Chickadee, Small Town Deb, The Fabulous Dorseys,* more.

SEARLE, JUDITH (N.Y.) Leading lady in TV soap operas. Onscreen in the '70s. IN: *To Find a Man,* more.

SEARS, HEATHER (Eng.) Leading lady. Onscreen from 1956. IN: *Dry Rot, The Story of Esther Costello, Room at the Top, Four Desperate Men, Sons and Lovers, Phantom of the Opera, Black Torment,* more.

SEAY, JAMES (S. Cal.) Character; former leading man. Onscreen from 1940. IN: *Women Without Names, Those Were the Days, The Way of All Flesh, The Face Behind the Mask, Two in a Taxi, The Man from Cheyenne, Highways by Night, The Secret Beyond the Door, Slippy McGee, I Cheated the Law, Union Station, The Day the Earth Stood Still; Models, Inc.; Fort Ti, Phantom from Space, The Steel Cage, Vera Cruz, Kiss Me Deadly, The Amazing Colossal Man, The Threat, What Ever Happened to Baby Jane?, There Was a Crooked Man,* more.

SEBASTIAN, JOHN (S. Cal.) Character. Onscreen from the '50s. IN: *Cry Tough,* more.

SEBASTIAN, JOHN (S. Cal.) Musician-singer. Onscreen in the '70s. IN: *Woodstock. Celebration at Big Sur,* more.

SEBERG, JEAN (Fr.) Otto Preminger's *Saint Joan* star discovery from Iowa became and remains a major star in France where, three times married, she lives. Her popularity in the United States has always been considerably less. Onscreen from 1957. IN: *Bonjour Tristesse, The Mouse That Roared, Let No Man Write My Epitaph, Breathless* (it made her reputation in France), *The Five Day Lover, Lilith, Backfire, Moment to Moment, A Fine Madness, Birds in Peru, Pendulum, Paint Your Wagon, Airport, Macho Callahan, Dead of Summer, Kill Kill Kill,* more.

SECOMBE, HARRY (Eng.) Character-singer. Onscreen from 1949. IN: *Penny Points to Paradise, Svengali, Oliver!, Song of Norway, The Bed Sitting Room, Doctor in Trouble, Rhubarb,* more.

SECREST, JAMES (N.Y.) Support. Onscreen from the '60s. IN: *Fate Is the Hunter, Fear No Evil,* more.

SEDGWICK, EILEEN (S. Cal.) The silent actress lives alone in retirement in Westwood now since the death in '73 of her star-sister, Josie, who had resided with her. Onscreen from the '20s. IN: *In the Days of Daniel Boone,* more.

SEEGAR, MIRIAM/now MIRIAM SEEGAR WHELAN (S. Cal.) The leading lady of the '30s is active again, mostly in TV commercials. Onscreen from 1929. IN: *Fashions in Love, The Love Doctor, Seven Keys to Baldpate, Clancy in Wall Street, Big Money, The Famous Ferguson Case, Strangers of the Evening, False Faces,* more.

SEEGAR, SARA (S. Cal.) Character. Wife of Ezra Stone. Onscreen from 1939. IN: *Dead Men Tell No Tales, Room 13, Smash and Grab, The Shrike, The Music Man, The Boatniks,* more.

SEEGER, PETE (N.Y.) Folksinger-actor. Onscreen from 1964. IN: *The Inheritance, Festival; Tell Me That You Love Me, Junie Moon;* more.

SEEGER, SANFORD (N.Y.) Character. Onscreen from the '50s. IN: *Uncle Vanya, Never Steal Anything Small,* more.

SEEL, CHARLES (S. Cal.) This veteran character actor, still active in his 70s, has been a widower since the death of his wife, Jeanne, in 1964. Onscreen from the '40s. IN: *Not Wanted, Lady in a Cage, Mister Buddwing, This Savage Land,* more.

SEELY, TIM (Eng.) Support. Onscreen from the '60s. IN: *The Poacher's Daughter, Please Turn Over, Mutiny on the Bounty,* more.

SEGAL, ERICH (Conn.) Novelist, author of *Love Story,* who was onscreen as an actor in 1972 in *Without Apparent Motive.*

SEGAL, GEORGE (S. Cal.) Costar. Nominated for Best Supporting Actor Oscar in *Who's Afraid of Virginia Woolf?* Onscreen from 1961. IN: *The Young Doctors, The Longest Day, Act One, The New Interns, Ship of Fools, King Rat, Lost Command, The Quiller Memorandum, The St. Valentine's Day Massacre, Bye Bye Braverman, No Way to Treat a Lady, The Bridge at Remagen, Where's Poppa?, Loving, The Owl and the Pussycat, The Hot Rock, Born to Win, A Touch of Class, Blume in Love, Russian Roulette, The Black Bird, The Duchess and the Dirtwater Fox, Dick and Jane,* more.

SEGAL, VIVIENNE (S. Cal.) She is in her 70s (b. 1897), lives alone in Hollywood, is retired. Her second husband, Hubbell Robinson, former CBS-TV vice president—they were long separated but still friendly—died in September '74. The singer-actress figures prominently in his autobiography, *Wanderer in the Wasteland,* completed shortly before his death. Onscreen from 1930. IN: *Song of the West, Bride of the Regiment, Golden Dawn, Viennese Nights,* and *The Cat and the Fiddle,* her last in 1934.

SEITZ, DRAN/now DRAN HAMILTON (S. Cal.) Leading lady, long offscreen, now resuming her career. One of the Seitz Twins, the other being Tani. Onscreen (together) in 1953 in *I, the Jury*.

SEITZ, TANI (N.Y.) Leading lady; inactive in movies now. Besides the above, she was (alone) in 1963's *Greenwich Village Story*.

SEKKA, JOHNNY (S. Cal.) Black support. Onscreen from the '60s. IN: *Flame in the Streets, Woman of Straw, Khartoum, The Southern Star, Uptown Saturday Night, Visit to a Chief's Son*, more.

SELBY, DAVID (N.Y.) Leading man from TV soap operas. Onscreen in the '70s. IN: *Night of Dark Shadows, Up the Sandbox, The Super Cops, The Girl in Blue*, more.

SELBY, NICHOLAS (Eng.) Character. Onscreen from the '60s. IN: *A Midsummer Night's Dream, Macbeth*, more.

SELBY, SARAH (S. Cal.) Character. Onscreen from 1944. IN: *San Diego, I Love You; The Beautiful Cheat, Stork Bites Man, Trapped by Boston Blackie, Beyond the Forest, The McConnell Story, Battle Cry, Stopover Tokyo, An Affair to Remember, Moon Pilot, Taggart!, Don't Make Waves*, more.

SELBY, TONY (N.Y.) Support. Onscreen from 1951. IN: *The Lonely Night* (documentary; juvenile role, age 13), *Mr. Lincoln* (documentary), *The Big Fisherman, The Greatest Story Ever Told, Villain*, more.

SELDES, MARIAN (N.Y.) Support. Daughter of Gilbert Seldes. Onscreen from 1951. IN: *The Lonely Night, Mr. Lincoln, The True Story of Jesse James, The Young Stranger, The Light in the Forest; Crime and Punishment, U.S.A.; The Greatest Story Ever Told*, more.

SELLARS, ELIZABETH (Eng.) Leading lady. Onscreen from 1949. IN: *Floodtide, Madeleine, The Stranger in Between, Recoil, Desiree, The Barefoot Contessa, Prince of Players, Forbidden Cargo, Law and Disorder, The Day They Robbed the Bank of England, 55 Days at Peking, Never Let Go, The Chalk Garden, The Hireling*, more.

SELLECK, TOM (S. Cal.) Leading man. Onscreen in the '70s. IN: *Myra Breckinridge, The Seven Minutes*, more.

SELLERS, CATHERINE (Fr.) Leading lady. Onscreen in the '70s. IN: *Destroy, She Said; Woman of the Ganges*, more.

SELLERS, PETER (Eng.) Star. Nominated for Best Actor Oscar in *Dr. Strangelove*. Onscreen from the '50s. IN: *Orders Are Orders, Ladykillers, Tom Thumb, The Mouse That Roared; I'm All Right, Jack; Battle of the Sexes, The Millionairess, Waltz of the Toreadors, Only Two Can Play, Lolita, Trial and Error, The Wrong Arm of the Law, Heavens Above, The World of Henry Orient, The Pink Panther, A Shot in the Dark, What's New Pussycat?, Wrong Box, After the Fox, Casino Royale, The Bobo, The Party; I Love You, Alice B. Toklas!; The Magic Christian, There's a Girl in My Soup, Where Does It Hurt?, The Optimists, The Blockhouse, Return of the Pink Panther, Murder by Death*, more.

SELLERS, RONNIE (N.Y.) Black support. Onscreen in the '70s. IN: *Shoot It: Black, Shoot It: Blue*; more.

SELWART, TONIO (N.Y.) In his 80s (b. 1896), the veteran character actor from Munich—long a fixture in Hollywood movies—lives in mid-Manhattan and remains active, particularly on TV and the stage. Onscreen in the United States from 1943. IN: *Edge of Darkness, Hangmen Also Die, The North Star, The Cross of Lorraine, The Hitler Gang, Wilson, My Favorite Spy, The Barefoot Contessa, Congo Crossing, The Naked Maja, Romanoff and Juliet, The Sign of Zorro*, more.

SELZER, MILTON (S. Cal.) Character. Onscreen from the '60s. IN: *The Young Savages, The Yellow Canary, In Enemy Country, The Legend of Lylah Clare, Blood and Lace*, more.

SERNA, PEPE (S. Cal.) Support. Onscreen in the '70s. IN: *Red Sky at Morning, Shoot Out, Hangup*, more.

SERNAS, JACQUES (It.) The muscular, handsome blond from Lithuania didn't make it in the United States when Warners costarred him (with Rossana Podesta) in *Helen of Troy*, but he has continued to be a stellar attraction abroad. He lives in Rome, remains, in his early 50s (b. 1925), a most attractive man, has been married since he was 20 to Maria Signorini, and is the father of a grown daughter (b. 1957). Onscreen from 1946. IN: *Miroir, Il lupo della Sila, Lost Youth, The Mill on the Po, Golden Salamander, The Sky Is Red, Sign of the Gladiator, The Nights of Lucretia Borgia, La Dolce Vita, Duel of the Titans, 55 Days at Peking, The Slave, Goliath and the Vampires, The Balearic Caper, Midas Run, Hornets' Nest*, more.

SEROFF, MUNI (N.Y.) Character. Acts mainly on the stage now. Onscreen from the '30s. IN: *Two Sisters, Two Senoritas from Chicago, Phantom of the Opera, Call of the Jungle, Copacabana, Mr. Imperium*, more.

SEURAT, PILAR (S. Cal.) Leading lady. Onscreen from the '60s. IN: *The Young Savages, Battle at Booody Beach, Seven Women from Hell*, more.

SEVEN, JOHNNY (S. Cal.) Character. Onscreen from the '50s. IN: *The Last Mile, The Apartment, Guns of the Timberland, The Greatest Story Ever Told; What Did You Do in the War, Daddy?; Gunfight at Abilene, The Destructors, The Love God?, Hangmen from Hell*, more.

SEVEREN, MAIDA (S. Cal.) Character. Onscreen from the '60s. IN: *Nobody's Perfect*, more.

SEWELL, GEORGE (Eng.) Character. Onscreen from the '60s. IN: *Sparrows Don't Sing, This Sporting Life, Robbery, The Vengeance of She, Journey to the Far Side of the Sun*, more.

SEYLER, ATHENE (Eng.) Character actress, in her 80s (b. 1889), who gave up acting in movies in the early 1960s (*Nurse on Wheels* was one of her last) and on the stage in 1966, after starring in London in *Arsenic and Old Lace*. Onscreen from the '20s. IN: *This Freedom, The Perfect Lady, Be Mine Tonight, The Private Life of Don Juan, Scrooge, Sailing Along, The Citadel, The Mill on the Floss, Nicholas Nickleby, The Beggar's Opera, The Pickwick Papers, Doctor at Large, Inn of the Sixth Happiness, Francis of Assisi, I Thank a Fool*, more.

SEYMOUR, ANNE (N.Y.) Character. Onscreen from 1949. IN: *All the King's Men* (her debut, as "Willie Stark's" wife), *The Whistle at Eaton Falls, The Gift of Love, Desire Under the Elms, Home from the Hill, Pollyanna, Misty, Good Neighbor Sam, Mirage, Fitzwilly; Stay Away, Joe;* more.

SEYMOUR, CAROLINE (Eng.) Leading lady. Onscreen in the '70s. IN: *There's a Girl in My Soup; Unman, Wittering and Zingo;* more.

SEYMOUR, DAN (S. Cal.) Character. Onscreen from 1942. IN: *Bombs Over Burma, Casablanca, To Have and Have Not, Confidential Agent, The Searching Wind, Cloak and Dagger, Slave Girl, Key Largo, Johnny Belinda, Mara Maru, The Bride Comes to Yellow Sky, Human Desire, Beyond a Reasonable Doubt, The Buster Keaton Story, The Sad Sack, The Return of the Fly*, more.

SEYMOUR, JOHN D. (N.Y.) Character. Onscreen from the '50s. IN: *Patterns, The Producers, The Sporting Club*, more.

SEYRIG, DELPHINE (Fr.) Leading lady. Onscreen from 1958. IN: *Pull My Daisy, Last Year at Marienbad, La Musica, Accident, Stolen Kisses, Mister Freedom, The Milky Way, The Discreet Charm of the Bourgeoisie, The Day of the Jackal, Donkey Skin*, more

SHAFTER, BERT (N.Y.) Support. Onscreen in the '70s. IN: *The Godfather*, more.

SHALET, DIANE (S. Cal.) Leading lady. Onscreen from 1969. IN: *The Reivers, Deadhead Miles*, more.

SHANE, SARA, (S. Cal.) No longer acting, she has lately published, under the name Elaine Hollingsworth, two novels, *Zulma* and *Ain't Life Cold-Blooded?* Onscreen from 1954. IN: *Magnificent Obsession, Sign of the Pagan, Daddy Long Legs, Affair in Havana, The King and Four Queens*, more, including 1959's *Tarzan's Greatest Adventure*, her most recent to date.

SHANKAR, RAVI (S. Cal.) Musician-actor. Onscreen from the '60s. IN: *Kanchenjungha, Chappaqua, Raga*, more.

SHAPS, CYRIL (Eng.) Character. Onscreen from the '60s. IN: *The Little Ones, The Kremlin Letter, The Looking Glass War, The Odessa File, 11 Harrowhouse*, more.

SHARBUTT, DEL (S. Cal.) Radio announcer; retired. Onscreen in 1947. IN: *Hit Parade of 1947.*

SHARIE, BONNIE (N.Y.) Support. Onscreen from the '50s. IN: *A Face in the Crowd, The Bachelor Party, That Kind of Woman*, more.

SHARIF, OMAR (Fr.) Costar. Nominated for Best Supporting Actor Oscar in *Lawrence of Arabia*. Onscreen from 1953. IN: *The Blazing Sun* (an Egyptian film opposite Egypt's movie queen Faten Hamama, who became and remains his wife, though long separated; he was billed Omar El Sharif), other Egyptian films, the best of which was *Goha; The Fall of the Roman Empire, Behold a Pale Horse, The Yellow Rolls-Royce, Genghis Khan, Doctor Zhivago, Marco the Magnificent, The Night of the Generals, Funny Girl, Mackenna's Gold, Che!, The Last Valley, The Horsemen, The Tamarind Seed, Funny Lady, Crime and Passion*, more.

SHARIF, TAREK (It.) Omar Sharif's son, who lives in Rome with his mother and played a juvenile role in 1965's *Doctor Zhivago*.

SHARP, ANTHONY (Eng.) Character. Primarily a stage actor. Onscreen in the '70s. IN: *A Clockwork Orange*, more.

SHARP-BOLSTER, ANITA (Eng.) Support. Onscreen from the '40s. IN: *Love From a Stranger, The Woman in White, The Rising of the Moon, The Boy Cried Murder*, more.

SHARPE, ALBERT (Eng.) Character; inactive in movies in recent years. Onscreen from the '40s. IN: *Up in Central Park, Portrait of Jennie, Adventure in Baltimore, Royal Wedding, Brigadoon, Darby O'Gill and the Little People, The Day They Robbed the Bank of England*, more.

SHARPE, CORNELIA (N.Y.) Leading lady. Onscreen in the '70s. IN: *Diana, Kansas City Bomber, The Way We Were, Busting, Serpico, The Reincarnation of Peter Proud, The Next Man*, more.

SHARPE, EDITH (Eng.) Character actress, in her 80s (b. 1894) and inactive in movies in the past decade. Onscreen from the '40s. IN: *The Guinea Pig, No Place for Jennifer, Brothers in Law, Happy Is the Bride, A French Mistress, Francis of Assisi, Satan Never Sleeps, Cash on Demand*, more.

SHARPE, DAVE (S. Cal.) Still wiry and handsome in his 60s (b. 1911), he has been in movies since he was 13, and in that time has been a man of all trades in Hollywood: juvenile lead, serial star, Western star, second-unit director, and famous stuntman (known as the "Crown Prince of Daredevils"). In the latter role he remains busy to date. Onscreen as an actor from 1924. IN: *The Thief of Bagdad, Scaramouche, Masked Emotions*, the "Young Friends" series (lead), *A Social Error, Front Money, Adventurous Knights, Hollywood Love, Melody of the Plains, Drums of Destiny, Daredevils of the Circus* (serial), the "Range Busters" Westerns (costarring with Ray Corrigan and Max Terhune), *Perils of Nyoka* (serial), *Silver Stallion, From Texas to Bataan, Trail Riders, Colorado Serenade, Covered Wagon Trails*, more.

SHARPE, KAREN (S. Cal.) Leading lady who married producer-director Stanley Kramer in 1966 and has been inactive in movies since. Onscreen from 1952. IN: *Bomba and the Jungle Girl, Strange Fascination, Mad at the World, The High and the Mighty, Man With the Gun, Tarawa Beachhead*, more, including 1964's *The Disorderly Orderly*, her most recent to date.

SHATNER, WILLIAM (S. Cal.) Leading man. Onscreen from 1958. IN: *The Brothers Karamazov, Judgment at Nuremberg, The Explosive Generation, The Intruder, The Outrage, Big Bad Mama, Dead of Night, The Devil's Rain*, more.

SHAUGHNESSY, MICKEY (S. Cal.) Comic character. Onscreen from 1952. IN: *The Marrying Kind, From Here to Eternity, Until They Sail, Slaughter on 10th Avenue, Don't Go Near the Water, The Sheepman, Don't Give Up the Ship, The Adventures of Huckleberry Finn, North to Alaska, A Pocketful of Miracles, How the West Was Won, A House Is Not a Home, Never a Dull Moment, The Boatniks*, more.

SHAVER, BOB (N.Y.) Singer-actor. Onscreen in 1957 in *The Pajama Game*.

SHAW, ANABEL (S. Cal.) Leading lady who mainly works in TV and commercials now. Former wife of actor Mark Stevens. Onscreen from the '40s. IN: *Shock, Home Sweet Homicide, Mother Wore Tights, Secret Beyond the Door, City Across the River, Gun Crazy*, more.

SHAW, ANTHONY (Eng.) Character. Onscreen from the '40s. IN: *Wings and the Woman, The Patient Vanishes, How to Murder a Rich Uncle*, more.

SHAW, ARTIE (N.Y.) Clarinet-playing bandleader, almost as famous for his marriages (8) to some of Hollywood's most beautiful women (Lana Turner, Ava Gardner, and presently Evelyn Keyes) as for his music. Onscreen in 1939 and 1941. IN: *Dancing Co-Ed* (with Lana Turner) and *Second Chorus*. (See Evelyn Keyes.)

SHAW, GLEN BYAM (Eng.) An illustrious stage character actor-director in England, only rarely in movies, Onscreen in 1959. IN: *Look Back in Anger*.

SHAW, PETER (Ire.) An agent now, he has long been married to Angela Lansbury and living much of the year on a farm in South Ireland. Onscreen from the '30s. IN: *Clive of India*, more.

SHAW, RALPH (N.Y.) Character. Onscreen from the '50s. IN: *The Thief, Act One, The Pawnbroker, Midnight Cowboy, Popi, The Hot Rock, The Gang That Couldn't Shoot Straight*, more.

SHAW, RETA (S. Cal.) Character. Onscreen from 1955. IN: *Picnic, Man Afraid, The Pajama Game, The Lady Takes a Flyer, Pollyanna, Sanctuary, Mary Poppins, The Ghost and Mr. Chicken, Made in Paris, Escape to Witch Mountain*, more.

SHAW, RICHARD (S. Cal.) Character. Onscreen from the '40s. IN: *The Caribbean Mystery, Attack on the Iron Coast*, more.

SHAW, ROBERT (Eng.) Costar. Nominated for Best Supporting Actor Oscar in *A Man for All Seasons*. Onscreen from 1951. IN: *The Lavender Hill Mob, The Dam Busters, Sea Fury, The Valiant, From Russia With Love, The Luck of Ginger Coffey, The Caretakers, Battle of the Bulge, The Royal Hunt of the Sun, Custer of the West, The Birthday Party, The Battle of Britain, Figures in a Landscape, Young Winston, The Hireling, The Sting, The Taking of Pelham One Two Three, Jaws, Robin and Marian, The Blarney Cock, Murder on the Bridge, Black Sunday,* more.

SHAW, SEBASTIAN (Eng.) The character actor—and former leading man—is in his 70s (b. 1905) and still professionally active. Onscreen from the '30s. IN: *Brewster's Millions, Men Are Not Gods, Murder on Diamond Row, Troopship, U-Boat 29, The Spy in Black, The Glass Mountain, Scotch on the Rocks, It Happened Here, A Midsummer Night's Dream,* more.

SHAW, SUSAN (Eng.) Leading lady. Onscreen from the '40s. IN: *London Town* (dancer), *The Upturned Glass, Dulcimer Street, It Always Rains on Sunday, Quartet* ("The Kite" episode), *Pool of London, Marry Me, Wall of Death, The Intruder, Carry On Nurse,* more.

SHAW, VICTORIA (S. Cal.) After several years offscreen, the leading lady—and onetime wife of actor Roger Smith—has lately resumed her career. Onscreen from 1956. IN: *The Eddy Duchin Story, Edge of Eternity, I Aim at the Stars, The Crimson Kimono, Alvarez Kelly, To Trap a Spy, Westworld,* more.

SHAW, WINI (WINIFRED) (N.Y.) Perhaps most famous for her big "Lullaby of Broadway" number in *Gold Diggers of 1935*, the dark-haired singer was spotlighted in more than a dozen Warner pix, including her exit movie, *Melody for Two* with James Melton in '37. A young widow (her husband was Leo Cummins) and the mother of three when she began her screen career, she is now the grandmother of ten. Later the wife of Frederick Vosberg, she has been married since '56 to William O'-Malley, assistant treasurer of Broadway's Mark Hellinger Theater. Occasionally, she too works in the box-office of another New York playhouse. Retired from performing, silver-haired and vivacious in her 60s (b. 1910), she lives with her husband in Sunnyside, Queens. At the time of Ruby Keeler's comeback in *No, No, Nanette* (they were together often during the dancing star's many months in New York), Wini Shaw wrote an article about her old friend, published in *Film Fan Monthly*. In it, briefly referring to herself, the singer said, "People have often asked me if I will ever make a comeback. I'm always flattered by this question, and I'm grateful that I made so many loyal fans . . . But I'm too happy being Mrs. Bill O'Malley, being with my kids and their kids, being active with such organizations as the Catholic Actors Guild and AGVA, being with my friends—well, just being." Onscreen from 1934. IN: *Million Dollar Ransom, Gift of Gab, Wake Up and Dream, Sweet Adeline, The Case of the Curious Bride, In Caliente, Front Page Woman, Broadway Hostess, The Singing Kid, Satan Met a Lady, Smart Blonde, Fugitive in the Sky; Ready, Willing and Able;* more.

SHAWLEE, JOAN (S. Cal.) Character who, first billed Joan Fulton, was one of Universal's "blonde bombshells" of the '40s. Onscreen from 1945. IN: *Men in Her Diary, I'll Be Yours, Casanova's Big Night, Prehistoric Women, The Marrying Kind, All Ashore, Francis Joins the Wacs, A Star Is Born, Bowery to Bagdad, A Farewell to Arms, Some Like It Hot* (leader of the all-girl band), *The Apartment, Irma la Douce, Tony Rome, The St. Valentine's Day Massacre; Live a Little, Love a Little; Willard, One More Train to Rob,* more. (See Joan Fulton.)

SHAWN, DICK (N.Y.) Comedian. Onscreen from the '50s. IN: *The Opposite Sex, The Wizard of Baghdad, Wake Me When It's Over; What Did You Do in the War, Daddy?; Penelope, Way Way Out, The Producers, The Happy Ending,* more.

SHAY, DOROTHY (S. Cal.) No longer the svelte "Park Avenue Hillbilly," the former singer is now a character actress on TV (*Police Story*) and in movies (*Mixed Company,* in which she played a social worker). First onscreen in 1951. IN: *Coming Round the Mountain.*

SHAYNE, KONSTANTIN (S. Cal.) Character actor who has been retired since 1958's *Vertigo*. Onscreen from 1939. IN: *Paris Honeymoon, Mission to Moscow, Five Graves to Cairo, For Whom the Bell Tolls, Passage to Marseille, None But the Lonely Heart, The Seventh Cross, Her Highness and the Bellboy, The Stranger, The Secret Life of Walter Mitty, Song of Love, To the Victor, Cry of the City, I Was a Communist for the F.B.I., Treasure of the Golden Condor,* more.

SHAYNE, ROBERT (S. Cal.) Living now in Reseda, not far from Hollywood, he still works in an occasional picture or TV segment. But, a member of the Boston Stock Exchange, he is primarily a business man today—head of the Robert Shayne Investors Financial Services, Inc. Onscreen from 1934. IN: *Wednesday's*

Child, The Shepherd of the Hills, Mr. Skeffington, Shine On Harvest Moon, Make Your Own Bed, Rhapsody in Blue, Christmas in Connecticut, I Ring Doorbells, My Reputation, Three Strangers, Smash-Up, Let's Live a Little, Experiment Alcatraz, Without Warning, Prince of Pirates, Murder Is My Beat, The Incredible Shrinking Man, North by Northwest, Cage of Evil, more.

SHAYNE, TAMARA (S. Cal.) Jolson's "mother," in The Jolson Story and Jolson Sings Again, she is the widow of great character actor Akim Tamiroff (d. 1972) and, childless, lives alone in Palm Springs. She was last onscreen in 1961's Romanoff and Juliet. In her late 70s now and a bit deaf, the actress remains an inveterate traveler. One recent journey was to Russia, her homeland, where a serious illness hospitalized her for some time. Fully recovered now, she makes plans for future journeys around the globe. Onscreen from 1943. IN: Mission to Moscow, Song of Russia, Pirates of Monterey, It Happened in Brooklyn, Northwest Outpost, The Snake Pit, Walk a Crooked Mile, Thieves' Highway, The Red Danube, Black Magic, Anastasia, more.

SHEA, MIKE (S. Cal.) Former juvenile (b. 1952). Onscreen from the '60s. IN: Namu the Killer Whale, Welcome to Hard Times, more.

SHEAFE, ALEX (N.Y.) Leading man. Onscreen from the '60s. IN: Target in the Sun, The Quick Colt, more.

SHEAR, PEARL (S. Cal.) Character. Onscreen from the '60s. IN: With Six You Get Egg Roll, The Harrad Summer, more.

SHEARER, MOIRA (Scot.) In her early 50s (b. 1926) the Red Shoes star still has it all—the same willowy ballerina's body, the flaming red hair, the blazing blue-gray eyes, the milk white skin, the long oval face. She also has a devoted husband (they married in '50), successful TV newsman and author Ludovic (Very Lovely People) Kennedy. And she has four fine children, three daughters and a son, who, in descending age order, are: Ailsa (b. 1952), Rachel, Fiona and Alastair (b. 1963). There's not a redhead among them; from the eldest, they are blonde, brunette, blonde, brunette. Nor is any of her children interested in dancing professionally. The Kennedys live in Scotland, where each was born, in the quaint border village of Makerstoun, in a small Georgian house that was once a Presbyterian parish house. She chose to bring up her children in Scotland, she says, because "the pace is slower there." She has no household help, and her husband says, "She's as great a cook as she was a dancer." She was

16 when, after a lifetime of dance training, she joined Sadler's Wells (The Royal Ballet now), and had only recently graduated from the corps de ballet when starred in the movie The Red Shoes. She says now, "I'm a bit embarrassed whenever I hear how many little girls were influenced by it. The dancing in it wasn't terribly good." She made Tales of Hoffman and, in '52, gave up ballet (onstage). After four other films, the last being 1962's Black Tights, she ceased dancing entirely. She did not perform again professionally until '74, when she starred onstage in London in Man and Wife, a play about Sir Winston Churchill's early career, in which she portrayed the young Lady Clementine Churchill. Her appearance then was proof that she had fully recovered after an automobile crash south of Edinburgh the previous year, in which she had suffered a broken hip. Onscreen from 1948. IN: The Red Shoes, Tales of Hoffman, The Story of Three Loves, The Man Who Loved Redheads, Peeping Tom, and Black Tights, her last, in 1962.

SHEARER, NORMA (S. Cal.) Star. Won Best Actress Oscar in The Divorcee. Nominated in the same category in Their Own Desire, A Free Soul, The Barretts of Wimpole Street, Romeo and Juliet, and Marie Antoinette. It has been well over three decades since this greatly admired star made her last movie. This was Her Cardboard Lover—not of the caliber of many earlier pictures—made in 1942. That year she became the wife of handsome ski-instructor Martin Arrouge, several years her junior, and she remains happily married to him. Encountered not long ago in Beverly Hills, they were observed holding hands like newlyweds. Once considered one of Hollywood's great patrician beauties, the actress, now in her 70s (b. 1904), looks neither younger nor older than her years. Reported to have been extremely ill for some time, she appeared on this occasion to be in excellent health, chatting pleasantly and striding vigorously from shop to shop. Slender, and in a stylish pantsuit, she wore her hair, gray-blonde now, in a modishly short cut. A wealthy woman, the widow of MGM production chief Irving Thalberg, the "boy genius" who died in 1936, aged 37, she lives with Arrouge in a beautiful home in Beverly Hills. She has two adult children by her first husband. Irving Jr., a slight, sandy-haired man in his 40s, served in the infantry during the Korean War and has been teaching Philosophy at Oberlin University in Ohio. Daughter Katherine, divorced from actor Richard Anderson (a lead in TV's The Six-Million Dollar Man), is the mother of three young girls, Ashley, Brooke, and Deva; at last report she and the children were living in Aspen, Colo., having moved there from Westwood. Norma Shearer's brother, Douglas, who founded MGM's sound department, died in '71, but her sister, Athole—former wife of director Howard Hawks—still lives near her. Several books about Irving Thalberg have appeared in recent years, some containing not altogether complimentary remarks about his actress-wife, but Miss Shearer has made public comments on none of them. The Arrouges mingle quietly with most of the socially elite of Beverly Hills, but it has been a number of years since they appeared at any publicized event. It was the star's hope to find privacy in her retirement and she has been successful in this. Onscreen from 1920. IN: *The Stealers, Lucretia Lombard, Broadway After Dark, Empty Hands, He Who Gets Slapped, Pretty Ladies, Slave of Fashion, The Devil's Circus, After Midnight, The Student Prince, The Actress, The Trial of Mary Dugan, The Last of Mrs. Cheyney, Let Us Be Gay, Private Lives, Smilin' Through, Strange Interlude, Riptide, Idiot's Delight, The Women, Escape, We Were Dancing*, more.

SHEARING, GEORGE (S. Cal.) Blind pianist. Onscreen in 1960 in *Jazz on a Summer's Day.*

SHEEN, FULTON J., REV. MSGR. (N.Y.) Living on Manhattan's East Side, he is in his 80s (b. 1895), and has been retired since 1969, after being designated Titular Archbishop of Newport, Wales, by Pope Paul VI. Onscreen in 1942. IN: *The Eternal Gift.* (He also, in '46, narrated *The Story of the Pope.*)

SHEEN, MARTIN (S. Cal.) Leading man. Onscreen from 1967. IN: *The Incident, The Subject Was Roses, Catch-22; No Drums, No Bugles; Badlands, The Little Girl Who Lives Down the Lane, The Cassandra Crossing*, more.

SHEFFIELD, JOHNNY (S. Cal.) Offscreen since 1956's *The Black Sheep*, the former movie youngster is in his 40s now (b. 1932) and, a big man in both size and real estate investments, lives with his wife and two sons in Malibu. Onscreen from 1939. IN: *Tarzan Finds a Son, Tarzan's Secret Treasure* (and six more "Tarzan" pix), *The Great Moment, Roughly Speaking; Bomba, the Jungle Boy* (and more "Bomba" pix); *The Lion Hunters, Africa Treasure, The Golden Idol, The Killer Leopard*, more, including 1956's *The Black Sheep*, his most recent to date.

SHEINER, DAVID (N.Y.) Character. Onscreen from 1965. IN: *The Greatest Story Ever Told, One Spy Too Many, The Odd Couple, Winning, A Man Called Gannon*, more.

SHELDON, GENE (S. Cal.) Support; inactive in movies lately. Onscreen from 1945. IN: *Where Do We Go From Here?, The Dolly Sisters, Golden Girl, Three Ring Circus, Toby Tyler, Babes in Toyland, The Sign of Zorro*, more.

SHELLE, LORI (N.Y.) Juvenile. Onscreen from 1969. IN: *Goodbye, Columbus; The Ski Bum*, more.

SHELLEY, BARBARA (It.) Leading lady who lives in Rome, making pictures there and in England. Onscreen from the '50s. IN: *The Camp on Blood Island, Village of the Damned, The Shadow of the Cat, Man in the Dark, Five Million Years to Earth*, more.

SHELLEY, CAROLE (N.Y.) Comic leading lady. Onscreen from 1942. IN: *Little Nell* (age 3), *The Man from Morocco, Cure for Love* (other child roles); *It's Great to be Young, Give Us This Day, The Odd Couple, The Boston Strangler*, more.

SHELLEY, JOSHUA (S. Cal.) Character and director (of 1967's *The Perils of Pauline*). Onscreen from 1949. IN: *City Across the River; Yes Sir, That's My Baby; The Front Page*, more.

SHELLY, NORMAN (N.Y.) Character. Onscreen from the '50s. IN: *The Great Adventure, Made for Each Other*, more.

SHELTON, ABIGAIL (S. Cal.) Support. Onscreen in the '70s. IN: *Zigzag*, more.

SHELTON, DON (S. Cal.) Supporting actor who, retired from movies, manages apartment houses now. Onscreen from 1948. IN: *You Gotta Stay Happy, Mystery Street, The Command, Then*, more. (Died 1976.)

SHELTON, JOY (Eng.) Leading lady. Onscreen from the '40s. IN: *Millions Like Us, Bees in Paradise, Waterloo Road, Send for Paul Temple, Uneasy Terms, No Room at the Inn, Hundred Hour Hunt, Emergency Call, Damn the Defiant*, more.

SHELTON, SLOANE (N.Y.) Supporting actress. Onscreen in the '70s. IN: *I Never Sang for My Father*, more.

SHENTALL, SUSAN (Eng.) Leading lady; married and retired. Onscreen in 1954. IN: *Romeo and Juliet* (as Juliet).

SHEPARD, ELAINE (S. Cal.) An elegant RKO blonde of the '40s, she turned roving correspondent and has published, in addition to her newspaper work, two books, *Forgive Us Our Press Passes* and *The Doom Pussy*. The latter was based on her firsthand observations as a war correspondent in Vietnam. She has lately formed her own production company, intending to bring it to the screen, saying, "I'm out to prove my point that the Vietnam story can be filmed with total honesty and still prove a box-office attraction." She has also announced her intention to use women in various production capacities on this movie. "The powers that be in Hollywood," she says, "have a complete lack of faith in the professionalism of women when it comes to movie production." In her 60s, she neither talks nor seems like a movie starlet, nor, actually, did she in her 20s. Onscreen from 1935. IN: *The Singing Vagabond, To Beat the Band, Darkest Africa* (serial), *Topper, You Can't Fool Your Wife, The Falcon in Danger, Seven Days Ashore,* more.

SHEPARD, JAN (S. Cal.) Leading lady; lately inactive in movies. Onscreen from the '50s. IN: *Sabre Jet, King Creole,* more.

SHEPARD, RICHARD (S. Cal.) Support. Onscreen in the '70s. IN: *Simon, King of Witches;* more.

SHEPHEARD, JEAN (Eng.) Former leading lady; inactive in movies now. Onscreen from the '40s. IN: *Thunder Rock, Inquest, A Canterbury Tale, Mr. Emmanuel, Adventures of Don Juan, Fame Is the Spur,* more.

SHEPHERD, CYBILL (S. Cal.) Leading lady who was a model and a discovery of director Peter Bogdanovich. Onscreen in the '70s. IN: *The Last Picture Show, Daisy Miller, At Long Last Love, Taxi Driver, Special Delivery,* more.

SHEPHERD, JACK (Eng.) Support. Onscreen from 1969. IN: *The Virgin Soldiers, The Bed Sitting Room,* more.

SHEPPERD, JOHN (N.Y.) During one phase of his career—as a young leading man under contract at 20th Century-Fox—actor Shepperd Strudwick used this screen name. Onscreen as John Shepperd (1941–47). IN: *Belle Starr, Remember the Day, Cadet Girl, The Men in Her Life, The Loves of Edgar Allan Poe* (his best-known role in this period), *Ten Gentlemen from West Point, Rings on Her Fingers, Dr. Renault's Secret, Chetniks, Home Sweet Homicide,* more. (See Shepperd Strudwick.)

SHERIDAN, DINAH (Eng.) Support; former leading lady. Onscreen from 1936. IN: *Irish and Proud of It, Murder in Reverse, The Facts of Love, Ivory Hunter, Breaking the Sound Barrier, Gilbert and Sullivan, Genevieve* (perhaps her best-recalled role), *The Railway Children,* more.

SHERMAN, GERALDINE (Eng.) Support. Onscreen from the '60s. IN: *Poor Cow, Interlude,* *There's a Girl in My Soup, Take a Girl Like You,* more.

SHERMAN, HIRAM (N.Y.) Character. Onscreen from 1938. IN: *One Third of a Nation, The Solid Gold Cadillac; Mary, Mary; Oh Dad, Poor Dad, Mamma's Hung You in the Closet and I'm Feeling So Sad;* more.

SHERMAN, JENNY (S. Cal.) Leading lady. Onscreen in the '70s. IN: *Mean Johnny Barrows,* more.

SHERMAN, ORVILLE (S. Cal.) Character. Onscreen from the '60s. IN: *Once You Kiss a Stranger, Pretty Maids All in a Row,* more.

SHERMAN, RANSOM (N.Y.) Character; inactive in movies for over two decades. Onscreen from 1943. IN: *Swing Your Partner, The Bachelor and the Bobby-Soxer, Gentleman's Agreement, Always Together, Winter Meeting, Are You With It?, Countess of Monte Cristo, One Last Fling, Always Leave Them Laughing,* more, including 1950's *Pretty Baby,* his last.

SHERMAN, SEAN (Hawaii) Juvenile lead. Son of actress Peggy Ryan. Onscreen from 1974. IN: *He Is My Brother.*

SHERMAN, SYLVAN ROBERT (N.Y.) Character. Onscreen from the '60s. IN: *Madigan, Lady in Cement, The Night They Raided Minsky's,* more.

SHERMAN, VINCENT (S. Cal.) After his acting career in movies, following one as a stage leading man, he became, in '38, a screenwriter (*Crime School*), and, in '39, a director. Among the many he has directed: *Old Acquaintance, Mr. Skeffington,* and *Goodbye, My Fancy.* He is now in his 70s (b. 1906) and a much-in-demand director for such TV shows as *Medical Center.* Onscreen from 1933. IN: *Counsellor-At-Law, Midnight Alibi, Speed Wings, The Crime of Helen Stanley, One Is Guilty, Girl in Danger, Hell Bent for Love,* more.

SHERMET, HAZEL (S. Cal.) Character. Onscreen from the '50s. IN: *A Star Is Born,* more.

SHERWOOD, GALE (S. Cal.) This singer-actress, for a long time Nelson Eddy's nightclub partner, still sings in clubs but has been inactive in movies for almost three decades. Onscreen in the '40s. IN: *Blonde Savage, Song of My Heart, Rocky,* more.

SHERWOOD, JAMES (N.Y.) Support. Onscreen in the '70s. IN: *The Only Game in Town,* more.

SHERWOOD, LYDIA (Eng.) Character. Onscreen from 1934. IN: *Little Friend, Don Quixote, Romeo and Juliet, The League of Gentlemen, Darling*, more.

SHERWOOD, MADELEINE (N.Y.) Character. Onscreen from 1956. IN: *Baby Doll, Cat on a Hot Tin Roof, Parrish, Sweet Bird of Youth, The 91st Day, Hurry Sundown, Pendulum*, more.

SHERWOOD, ROBERTA (Fla.) Singer-actress. In her 60s (b. 1912), she still plays club dates. Onscreen in 1963. IN: *The Courtship of Eddie's Father.*

SHEYBAL, VLADEK (WLADYSLAW) (Eng.) Character. Onscreen from the '50s. IN: *Kanal, Women in Love, The Music Lovers, S*P*Y*S*, more.

SHIGETA, JAMES (S. Cal.) Leading man. Onscreen from 1959. IN: *The Crimson Kimono, Walk Like a Dragon, Bridge to the Sun, Cry for Happy, Flower Drum Song; Paradise, Hawaiian Style; Nobody's Perfect, Lost Horizon*, more.

SHILLO, MICHAEL (S. Cal.) Character. Onscreen from the '50s. IN: *Hill 24 Doesn't Answer, Dunkirk, The Pillar of Fire, Cast a Giant Shadow, The Hell with Heroes*, more.

SHIMADA, TERU (S. Cal.) Character actor. Onscreen from 1932. IN: *The Night Club Lady, Four Frightened People, Revolt of the Zombies, The White Legion, Tokyo Joe, The Bridges at Toko-Ri, House of Bamboo, Battle Hymn, Tokyo After Dark, King Rat, You Only Live Twice*, more.

SHIMKUS, JOANNA (Bahamas) Leading lady. Married to actor Sidney Poitier. Onscreen from the '60s. IN: *Boom!, Zita, Six in Paris, The Lost Man* (opposite Poitier), *The Virgin and the Gypsy, Privilege, The Marriage of a Young Stockbroker*, more. (See Sidney Poitier.)

SHOMODA, YUKI (S. Cal.) Character actor. Onscreen from the '50s. IN: *Auntie Mame, A Majority of One, The Horizontal Lieutenant, Once a Thief*, more.

SHIMONO, SAB (N.Y.) Character actor. Onscreen from the '60s. IN: *Puzzle of a Downfall Child, Loving, The Hospital*, more.

SHINE, BILL (Eng.) Character. Onscreen from 1929. IN: *Under the Greenwood Tree, The Yellow Mask, Troop Ship, Champagne Charlie, Under Capricorn, The Caretaker's Daughter, Knave of Hearts, Raising a Riot, John and Julie, The Deep Blue Sea, Quentin Durward, Richard III*, more.

SHINGLER, HELEN (Eng.) Support; former leading lady. Onscreen from the '40s. IN: *Quiet Week-End, The Rossiter Case, The Lady with a Lamp, Laughing Anne, Edge of Divorce, Room in the House*, more.

SHIPMAN, NINA (S. Cal.) Leading lady. Onscreen from the '50s. IN: *Say One for Me, Blue Denim, The Oregon Trail, High Time*, more.

SHIRE, TALIA (N.Y.) Leading lady. Sister of director Francis Ford Coppola, and first in movies as Talia Coppola. Nominated for Best Supporting Actress Oscar in *The Godfather, Part II.* Onscreen as Talia Shire in the '70s. IN: *The Godfather*, more.

SHIRLEY, ANNE (S. Cal.) Leading lady. Nominated for Best Supporting Actress Oscar in *Stella Dallas.* Interviewed earlier in this decade, Anne Shirley said: "All's right with my world. We have a happy, quiet, peaceful existence and enjoy every minute of it." Her world changed, abruptly, early in 1976 when her husband of 26 years, the greatly admired screenwriter Charles Lederer, died suddenly. Her years with him, she says, were the happiest of her life. Up to the age of 26 when she retired from the screen, after 1945's *Murder, My Sweet*, the actress had known nothing but work. First put on the stage at 14 months by her widowed mother, she next was a child model, then, after they moved from New York to Hollywood, Anne (known variously as Dawn O'Day, Lenn Fondre, and Lindley Dawn though her real name was Dawn Evelyeen Paris) played small roles in movies—silents and talkies—for years. She was 15 in 1934 when RKO starred her in *Anne of Green Gables* as a schoolgirl named "Anne Shirley," which was from then on her screen name. She played top roles in another 37 pictures before retiring. Between 1937 and '43, she was married to actor John Payne, by whom she has a daughter, Julie, now an actress. This union particularly delighted fan magazine readers, for the stars, in their youth and success, were then the "ideal couple." Nostalgia buffs will be pleased to learn that through the years, Anne Shirley and John Payne have remained friends, with daughter Julie, of course, the connecting link. Today a small (5'2"), shapely woman with graying cinnamon-brown hair, a quiet smile, and a deeply suntanned face, Anne Shirley says: "By the time I was 18, I had discovered that I didn't want to be an actress forever. I've always been basically a shy person and it was hard being 'on' all the time. So, finally, I just walked away. I've never regretted that decision." She thought for a while about working behind the scenes in the movie industry as a dialogue coach. "Frankly," she says, in that familiar, low, mellifluous voice, "I thought I might be pretty good at it. A dialogue coach, you know, was someone who served as the director's right hand, guiding the cast through the rough parts prior to shooting so that they could come on set prepared to give the director the kind of performance he desired. But I never pursued this, and now they don't have them too much any more." She stayed with her acting career as long as she did, she says, for her mother's sake. "I realize," she explains, "how much she dedicated her life to making me a somebody. I suppose she could have gotten some kind of job, but she wanted so much more for the two of us. So she threw all her efforts behind me. Because of this, I'm very proud I did what I did. What I eventually became justified my mother's hard work, dedication and sacrifices. So, although I was propelled and pushed toward a life on camera, because of the pride and happiness my mother felt, I was happy too. For a while." After her divorce from John Payne, Anne Shirley starred, among other movies, in *Murder, My Sweet* (released in some areas as *Farewell, My Lovely*). This film introduced her to her second husband, Adrian Scott, who produced it. They were married in February 1945, and divorced in less than four years. They had no children. On December 26, 1972, the actress was saddened to pick up the Los Angeles papers and read that Scott, at 61, had died of cancer. The obituaries recounted once more that the producer-writer had been one of the "Hollywood 10" who were imprisoned during the McCarthy era for refusing to testify before the House Committee on Un-American Activities in 1947. It was after her divorce from Scott that the actress became the wife of Charles Lederer, nephew of Marion Davies, in a society wedding at the New York home of Bennett Cerf—and was launched upon the "quiet" life that brought her such lasting happiness. By him, she has a son in his 20s, Daniel Davies Lederer. "Danny," says his proud mother, "is a marvelous young man, very bright, very talented. He's a poet—yes, a working poet—which I suppose comes naturally to him because of his father's great literary gifts." As she has for years, the actress maintains two beautiful homes, only a few miles apart. In Bel Air she has a lavish establishment of rambling free-style decor and carpeted lawn bordered by orange and blue birds of paradise. The home in which she spends most of her time, though, is an ultramodern, oceanside place at Malibu. There, she paints, shops, keeps a beautiful house (always with a new batch of kittens underfoot), sees longtime Hollywood friends, cheers the accomplishments of her children—and misses her husband. On-

screen as Dawn O'Day from 1923. IN: *The Spanish Dancer, The Man Who Fights Alone, Riders of the Purple Sage, 4 Devils, So Big, The Life of Jimmy Dolan, The Key*, more. Onscreen as Anne Shirley from 1934. IN: *Steamboat Round the Bend, Make Way for a Lady, Law of the Underworld, Mother Carey's Chickens, A Man to Remember, Vigil in the Night, Anne of Windy Poplars, West Point Widow, All That Money Can Buy, Bombardier, The Powers Girl, Government Girl, Man from Frisco, Music in Manhattan*, more.

SHIRLEY, BILL (N.Y.) Singer-actor who not only played leading roles himself but dubbed the singing voices of others (Mark Stevens' in *I Wonder Who's Kissing Her Now*, "Freddie Eynsford-Hill" in *My Fair Lady*, etc.). Onscreen as an actor from 1941. IN: *Sailors on Leave, Rookies on Parade, Ice-Capades Revue, Flying Tigers; Hi, Neighbor!; Three Little Sisters, Abbott and Costello Meet Captain Kidd, I Dream of Jeanie* (as Stephen Foster), more, including 1953's *Sweethearts on Parade*, his most recent to date.

SHIRLEY, PEG(GY) (S. Cal.) Support. Onscreen from the '60s. IN: *The Thomas Crown Affair, The Return of Count Yorga*, more.

SHOCKLEY, MARIAN (Conn.) Popular as a leading lady in Westerns and Al Christie comedies, and later on radio in *Ellery Queen*, she was married for many years—until his death in '69 —to radio-TV star Bud Collyer. She has three grown children, is in her 60s now, still lives in the 14-room house in Greenwich that was the family's residence, and remains active in the nearby Presbyterian church where her late husband taught Sunday school. Onscreen from the '20s. IN: (besides the above) *Stage Door Canteen*.

SHOEMAKER, ANN (S. Cal.) Hepburn's mother in *Alice Adams*,—and the mother, in other movies, of Cary Grant, Judy Garland, Ginger Rogers, and Mickey Rooney—she is the mother in real life of one daughter, song lyricist Anne Hall. She is also, in her 80s (b. 1891), raring to act steadily again. Living now in Sun City, she says, "Things out here have been pretty dead but my agent thinks they will get a bit better, and of course I hope to do something —simply because I *enjoy* working—and miss it!" She had curtailed her long movie career after 1950's *The House by the River*. But when her husband, great character actor Henry Stephenson, died in '56, she returned to acting onstage. She created the role of Sara Delano Roosevelt in the play *Sunrise at Campobello*, repeating it later in the film. In the '60s, she also toured for more than a year in the musical *Half* a Sixpence, made brief appearances in one Mission: Impossible episode on TV and in the movie The Fortune Cookie, and, finally, in '69, played "Madame Roberta" in a Bob Hope television special of Roberta. Not content that this should be her swan song, the actress, in 1976, played the mother of President Harry Truman (portrayed by E. G. Marshall) on TV in the "ABC Theatre" special Collision Course. Onscreen from 1933. IN: Chance at Heaven, Dr. Monica, Shall We Dance, They Won't Forget, Stella Dallas, Romance of the Redwoods, Babes in Arms, Seventeen, My Favorite Wife, Strike Up the Band, You'll Never Get Rich, Above Suspicion, Thirty Seconds Over Tokyo, Conflict, Magic Town, Sitting Pretty, A Woman's Secret, Shockproof, House by the River, more.

SHOLDAR, MICKEY (S. Cal.) Support; former juvenile (b. 1949). Onscreen from the '60s. IN: Secrets of Animal Island, The Facts of Life, Boys' Night Out, One Man's Way, more.

SHOOP, PAMELA (S. Cal.) Leading lady. Daughter of actress Julie Bishop (Jacqueline Wells). Onscreen in the '70s. IN: Changes, more.

SHORE, DINAH (S. Cal.) Singer-actress-TV star. Onscreen from 1943. IN: Thank Your Lucky Stars, Up in Arms, Belle of the Yukon, Follow the Boys, Make Mine Music, Till the Clouds Roll By, Fun and Fancy Free, more, including 1952's Aaron Slick from Punkin Crick, her most recent.

SHORE, ELAINE (S. Cal.) Support. Onscreen from 1969. IN: Tell Me That You Love Me, Junie Moon; Move, more.

SHORE, JEAN (N.Y.) Support. Onscreen from the '50s. IN: Go, Man, Go, more.

SHORE, ROBERTA (S. Cal.) Former young leading lady, now married and retired. Onscreen from 1959. IN: The Shaggy Dog, The Young Savages, Because They're Young, Blue Denim, Strangers When We Meet, and Lolita.

SHOTTER, WINIFRED (Eng.) Leading lady who, in her 70s (b. 1904), is retired. Onscreen from 1930. IN: Rookery Nook, A Chance of a Night Time, Night and Day, Sorrell and Son, Petticoat Fever, High Treason, more.

SHOWALTER, MAX (N.Y.) Comic leading man, who lives and works in New York now. He has had two screen names: Max Showalter, his real name, and Casey Adams. Onscreen first under his real name in 1949 and 1952. IN: Always Leave Them Laughing and With a Song in My Heart. Onscreen as Casey Adams throughout the rest of the '50s. IN: What Price Glory, Niagara, Destination Gobi, Vickie, Night People, Naked Alibi, Bus Stop, Summer and Smoke, more. Reverted to Showalter (which he still uses) in 1963. IN: My Six Loves, Move Over Darling, How to Murder Your Wife, The Anderson Tapes, more.

SHRIMPTON, JEAN (Eng.) Model-leading lady. Onscreen in 1967 in Privilege.

SHROG, MAURICE (N.Y.) Character. Onscreen from the '50s. IN: The Mugger, more.

SHROPSHIRE, ANNE (N.Y.) Support. Onscreen in the '70s. IN: Pigeons, more.

SHULL, RICHARD B. (S. Cal.) Character. Onscreen in the '70s. IN: B.S. I Love You, The Anderson Tapes, Such Good Friends, Slither, Hail (lead), more.

SIBBALD, LAURIE (S. Cal.) Support. Onscreen from the '60s. IN: Taras Bulba, more.

SIBLEY, ANTOINETTE (Eng.) Ballerina. Onscreen in 1960 in The Royal Ballet.

SICARI, JOSEPH R. (N.Y.) Support. Onscreen in the '70s. IN: Who Is Harry Kellerman . . . ?, more.

SIDNEY, SYLVIA (N.Y.) Character actress (b. 1910); former star. Nominated for Best Supporting Actress Oscar in Summer Wishes, Winter Dreams, her first movie in 17 years. On Broadway in 1976 she starred in Me Jack, You Jill, which closed after 16 preview performances. Onscreen from 1929. IN: Thru Different Eyes, Crossroads, Street Scene, Bad Girl, An American Tragedy, Ladies of the Big House, Merrily We Go to Hell, The Miracle Man, If I Had a Million, Make Me a Star, Jennie Gerhardt, Good Dame, Thirty Day Princess; Mary Burns, Fugitive; The Trail of the Lonesome Pine, Fury, You Only Live Once, Dead End, You and Me, One Third of a Nation, Blood on the Sun, The Searching Wind, Love from a Stranger, Les Miserables, Violent Saturday, more, including 1956's Behind the High Wall, which until she made her comeback was her most recent.

SIEPI, CESARE (N.Y.) Opera baritone. Onscreen in 1956 in Don Giovanni.

SIGNORELLI, TOM (S. Cal.) Support. Onscreen in the '70s. IN: Kelly's Heroes, The Anderson Tapes, The Last Porno Flick, Big Bad Mama, more.

SIGNORET, SIMONE (Fr.) Star. Won Best Actress Oscar in *Room at the Top*. Nominated in the same category in *Ship of Fools*. Onscreen from 1938. IN: *Sacrifice d'Honneur, The Living Corpse, Bolero, Macadam, Symphonie d'Amour, Dedee, Four Days' Leave, The Cheat, Casque d'Or, La Ronde, Diabolique, Witches of Salem, Term of Trial, Sweet and Sour, The Sleeping Car Murder, Is Paris Burning?, The Deadly Affair, Games, The Sea Gull, Le Rose et le Noir, Le Chat,* more.

SIKKING, JAMES (S. Cal.) Support. Onscreen from the '60s. IN: *Charro!, Daddy's Gone A-Hunting, The Terminal Man,* more.

SILLIPHANT, TIANA (S. Cal.) Support. Wife of producer-writer Stirling Silliphant. Onscreen in the '70s. IN: *The Killer Elite,* more.

SILO, SUSAN (S. Cal.) Support. Onscreen from the '60s. IN: *Convicts 4,* more.

SILVA, HENRY (S. Cal.) Support. Onscreen from 1952. IN: *Viva Zapata!, Crowded Paradise, A Hatful of Rain, The Bravados, The Law and Jake Wade, Green Mansions, Ocean's Eleven, The Manchurian Candidate, Sergeants 3, Johnny Cool, The Reward, The Return of Mr. Moto, Matchless, The Hills Run Red, Never a Dull Moment, Shoot,* more.

SILVER, BORAH (S. Cal.) Character. Onscreen in the '70s. IN: *Calliope,* more.

SILVER, JOE (N.Y.) Character. Onscreen from the '60s. IN: *Klute, Move, Rhinoceros, The Apprenticeship of Duddy Kravitz,* more.

SILVER, JOHNNY (S. Cal.) Character. Onscreen from 1955. IN: *Guys and Dolls, The Thomas Crown Affair, Never a Dull Moment,* more.

SILVER, RONALD (N.Y.) Support. Onscreen in the '70s. IN: *The French Connection,* more.

SILVERHEELS, JAY (S. Cal.) The handsome Mohawk Indian who became most famous for playing "Tonto" in *The Lone Ranger* TV series still makes many movies—including 1973's *Santee* in which he and "Lone Ranger" John Hart (sans mask) teamed for the first time since the show went off the air. But he also has a new career. In 1974 he obtained a license to work as a harness racing driver, and since has raced competitively all over the country: Vernon Downs Racing Track near Syracuse, N.Y.; Churchill Downs, etc. Now in his 50s (b. 1920), he lives in Canoga Park, and has been married for almost three decades to Mari Di Roma, who is of course Italian. They have a grown daugh-

ter, Marilyn, a teacher, and three teenagers: Pamela, Karen, and Jay Anthony. Onscreen from 1947. IN: *Captain from Castile, Fury at Furnace Creek, Yellow Sky, Key Largo, Sand, Broken Arrow, Red Mountain, The Will Rogers Story, Saskatchewan, Drums Across the River, The Lone Ranger, Walk the Proud Land, The Lone Ranger and the City of Gold, Indian Paint, Smith!, True Grit, The Phynx, One Little Indian, The Man Who Loved Cat Dancing,* more.

SILVERS, PHIL (S. Cal.) Star comedian. Now in his 60s (b. 1911), he has recovered from a stroke that hospitalized him for months and threatened to end his career, though he still carries a collapsible cane that he uses in emergencies. And he is still going on all six cylinders. Since publishing his autobiography, *The Laugh's On Me*, in 1973, after his illness in '72, he has done numerous guest stints in TV dramatic series, starred in London in a revival of the play *A Funny Thing Happened on the Way to the Forum*, as well as in Disney's *The Strongest Man in the World*. He also, in '75, joined Rosalind Russell in a TV special saluting the 50th anniversary of Columbia Pictures, where many of his best pictures were made. Twice married and divorced—his wives were beauty queen Jo-Carroll Dennison and TV personality Evelyn Patrick—he is the father of five daughters. Divorced from his second wife since 1966, the comedian, financially well off, lives alone in a Los Angeles apartment and—doleful in private as opposed to his onscreen jollity—he says, "There really isn't much to laugh at in the world today." Onscreen from 1940. IN: *Hit Parade of 1941, You're in the Army Now, Lady Be Good, Roxie Hart, My Gal Sal, Footlight Parade, Coney Island, A Lady Takes a Chance, Cover Girl* (one of his finest performances and typical of his beaming "Hi ya, there!" characterizations), *Something for the Boys, Diamond Horseshoe, A Thousand and One Nights, If I'm Lucky, Summer Stock, Top Banana, Lucky Me, The Oscar, A Funny Thing Happened on the Way to the Forum, A Guide for the Married Man; Buona Sera, Mrs. Campbell;* more.

SILVESTRE, AMI (Ill.) Supporting actress, now on TV in Chicago. Onscreen in the '50s. IN: *The Harder They Fall, North by Northwest,* more.

SILVESTRE, ARMANDO (S. Cal.) Character. Onscreen from 1950. IN: *Wyoming Mail, Apache Drums, Hiawatha, Rosanna, The Scalphunters, Barquero, Two Mules for Sister Sara,* more.

SIM, ALASTAIR (Eng.) Character star. Onscreen from 1934. IN: *Riverside Murder, Gangway, Sailing Along, This Man Is News,*

Green for Danger, Captain Boycott, Stage Fright, The Happiest Days of Your Life, Hue and Cry, Laughter in Paradise, Folly to be Wise, An Inspector Calls, The Belles of St. Trinian's, Wee Geordie, School for Scoundrels, The Millionairess, Royal Flash, Escape from the Dark, more.

SIM, GERALD (Eng.) Support. Onscreen from the '60s. IN: *The L-Shaped Room, Seance on a Wet Afternoon, King Rat, The Murder Game, The Whisperers, The Madwoman of Chaillot; Long Ago, Tomorrow*; more.

SIM, SHEILA (Eng.) Leading lady. Onscreen from the '40s. IN: *A Canterbury Tale, Dear Mr. Prohack, Pandora and the Flying Dutchman, West of Zanzibar, The Night My Number Came Up*, more.

SIMMONDS, STANLEY (N.Y.) Stage character actor. Onscreen in 1959. IN: *Li'l Abner* (as "Dr. Finsdale").

SIMMONS, JEAN (S. Cal.) Costar. Nominated for Best Supporting Actress Oscar in *Hamlet*. Nominated for Best Actress Oscar in *The Happy Ending*. Onscreen from 1944. IN: *Give Us the Moon, The Way to the Stars, Caesar and Cleopatra, Great Expectations, Black Narcissus, The Blue Lagoon, So Long at the Fair, The Clouded Yellow, Androcles and the Lion* (her first in Hollywood in 1952), *Angel Face, Young Bess, Affair with a Stranger, The Actress* (in which she portrayed Oscar-winning actress Ruth Gordon), *The Robe, The Egyptian, Desiree, Guys and Dolls, Until They Sail, Home Before Dark, The Big Country, Spartacus, Elmer Gantry* (directed by Richard Brooks who became, and remains, her husband; she was first married to actor Stewart Granger), *The Grass Is Greener, All the Way Home, Life at the Top; Divorce—American Style; Say Hello to Yesterday, Mr. Sycamore*, more.

SIMMONS, RICHARD (S. Cal.) Onscreen over two decades, through 1964's *Robin and the 7 Hoods*, as well as being TV's *Sergeant Preston of the Yukon*, the former actor is now, in his white-haired late 50s (b. 1918), activities director of Rancho Carlsbad Mobile Home Park, in Carlsbad, Calif. Living with him in this multi-million-dollar complex is Jonni, his wife of more than three decades; their two children are grown and building careers of their own. He works with young people and old in his present occupation and says he enjoys "helping create a way of life for others to enjoy." A lifelong pilot, both privately and in the Air Force, he still flies his own plane and, a while back, had the pleasure of piloting Senator Barry Goldwater to various points in California. He does not

rule out a return to performing but doubts it will happen. Onscreen from 1942. IN: *Stand By for Action, Pilot No. 5, Love Laughs at Andy Hardy, Lady in the Lake, This Time for Keeps, On an Island with You, Look for the Silver Lining, Duchess of Idaho, The Well, Above and Beyond, Battle Circus, Men of the Fighting Lady, You're Never Too Young, Sergeants 3*, more.

SIMMS, HILDA (N.Y.) Black leading lady who acts mainly on TV and the Broadway stage. Onscreen 1953–54. IN: *The Joe Louis Story* and *Black Widow*. She also, in '43, narrated *Day After Day*.

SIMMS, LARRY (S. Cal.) "Baby Dumpling" is in his 40s now, slender and blond (but balding), has been an aeronautical engineer for over two decades, has had two wives (and two divorces), and is the father of three—one of them married. He was 3 when he made his first picture (*The Last Gangster Goes to Washington*) and 16 when he made his last (*Beware of Blondie*); he does not miss acting. Onscreen from 1937. IN: *Blondie* (and the many others in this series), *The Gay Sisters, It's a Wonderful Life, Footlight Glamour, Madame Bovary*, more.

SIMON, ROBERT F. (S. Cal.) Character. Onscreen from 1950. IN: *Where the Sidewalk Ends, Rogue Cop, Chief Crazy Horse, The Girl in the Red Velvet Swing, The Court-Martial of Billy Mitchell, The Benny Goodman Story, The Catered Affair, Spring Reunion, Compulsion, The Last Angry Man, Ada, The Spiral Road; Captain Newman, M.D.; Fate Is the Hunter, Blindfold, The Reluctant Astronaut*, more.

SIMON, SIMONE (Fr.) Beautifully preserved in her 60s (b. 1910), she continues to star in French films such as *The Woman in Blue* ('73). Never married, she has had a close gentleman friend for many years, and lives in a luxurious apartment in Paris overlooking L'Etoile. She regularly entertains Hollywood visitors such as Kurt Kreuger who was her costar in *Madamoiselle Fifi*. Onscreen from 1931. IN: *Les Yeux Noires, Le Roi des Palaces, Lac Aux Dames, Girls' Dormitory, Seventh Heaven* (her first in Hollywood), *Love and Hisses, Josette, The Human Beast, All That Money Can Buy, The Cat People* (her best-known role here), *Johnny Doesn't Live Here Anymore, Mademoiselle Fifi, Curse of the Cat People, Temptation Harbor, La Ronde, Pit of Loneliness, Le Plaisir, Double Destiny, The Extra Day*, more.

SIMPSON, O. J. (S. Cal.) Black leading man and pro football star. Onscreen in the '70s. IN: *The Klansman, The Towering Inferno, Killer Force, The Cassandra Crossing, Goldie and the Boxer*, more.

431

SIMS, JOAN (Eng.) Comedienne. Onscreen from the '50s. IN: *The Belles of St. Trinian's, Will Any Gentleman?, Trouble in Store, The Ship Was Loaded, Carry On Nurse, The Captain's Table, Doctor in Love, A Pair of Briefs, Carry On Cleo, Carry On Camping*, more.

SIMS, SYLVIA (Eng.) Leading lady. Onscreen in the '70s. IN: *The Tamarind Seed*, more.

SINATRA, FRANK (S. Cal.) Star. Won Best Supporting Actor Oscar in *From Here to Eternity*. Nominated for Best Actor Oscar in *The Man with the Golden Arm*, Onscreen from 1941. IN: *Las Vegas Nights, Ship Ahoy!, Reveille with Beverly* (all as a singer with bands), *Higher and Higher* (his first as a star), *Step Lively, Anchors Aweigh, Words and Music, It Happened in Brooklyn, The Kissing Bandit, On the Town, Meet Danny Wilson* (a failure; he was considered washed-up until he came back two years later in a straight acting role in *From Here to Eternity*), *Suddenly, Young at Heart, Not as a Stranger, Guys and Dolls, High Society, The Joker Is Wild, The Pride and the Passion, Pal Joey, Some Came Running, A Hole in the Head, Ocean's Eleven, Can-Can, The Devil at 4 O'-Clock, The Manchurian Candidate, Come Blow Your Horn, Robin and the 7 Hoods, None But the Brave, Marriage on the Rocks, Assault on a Queen, Tony Rome, The Detective, Lady in Cement, Dirty Dingus Magee*, more.

SINATRA, FRANK, JR. (S. Cal.) Singer-actor son of the above. Onscreen in 1968 in *A Man Called Adam*.

SINATRA, NANCY, JR. (S. Cal.) Singer-leading lady, daughter of Frank Sr., who is now married (second time), in her 30s (b. 1940), the mother of two, and retired from movies. Onscreen from 1964. IN: *For Those Who Think Young, Marriage on the Rocks, Get Yourself a College Girl, Last of the Secret Agents?, The Ghost in the Invisible Bikini, The Wild Angels, Speedway*, more.

SINCLAIR, BARRY (Eng.) Character. Onscreen from 1928. IN: *Young Woodley, The Tenth Man*, more.

SINCLAIR, BETTY (N.Y.) The actress who played "Pansy" in 1931's *City Streets*, her only movie, has long been—and continues to be—a prominent character actress on the Broadway stage.

SINCLAIR, MADGE (S. Cal.) Character. Onscreen in the '70s. IN: *Conrack; Cornbread, Earl and Me; I Will, I Will . . . For Now; Leadbelly*, more.

SINDEN, DONALD (Eng.) Leading man. Onscreen from 1953. IN: *The Cruel Sea, Mogambo, The Beachcomber, Doctor in the House* (and others in the "Doctor" series), *Above Us the Waves, Mad Little Island, The Captain's Table, Villain, The Day of the Jackal, The Island at the Top of the World*, more.

SINGER, CAMPBELL (Eng.) Character. Onscreen from 1931. IN: *Premiere, The Blue Lamp, Murder on Monday, Home at Seven, The Titfield Thunderbolt, The Yellow Balloon, Time Bomb, To Dorothy a Son, The Trials of Oscar Wilde*, more.

SINGER, IZZY (N.Y.) Character. Onscreen from the '60s. IN: *Little Murders, The Steagle, The Pursuit of Happiness, Husbands, Carnal Knowledge, Loving; Rachel, Rachel; The War Between Men and Women, Portnoy's Complaint, Made for Each Other, The Gang That Couldn't Shoot Straight*, more.

SINGLETON, DORIS (S. Cal.) Leading lady. Onscreen from 1957. IN: *Affair in Reno*, more.

SINGLETON, PENNY (S. Cal.) That charming movie brunette Dorothy McNulty begat, by dying her hair, "Blondie," who begat, by time and due process of evolution, a long, white-haired, sunburned tigress named Penny Singleton. If "Dagwood" ever found "Blondie" implacable, he should meet today's late 60-ish (b. 1908) Miss Singleton across a labor negotiations table. She somehow seems different from yesterday's Penny Singleton. For years the executive president of the American Guild of Variety Artists, she regularly goes to the mat with theater and nightclub owners, to get better deals for the singers and dancers she represents, and generally emerges victorious. Within her union there is a faction that tries regularly to unseat her, sometimes succeeding, but in short order she is usually to be found back in the driver's seat. Penny has not entirely stopped being an actress herself. The only movie role she has played since doing the last of the 28 "Blondies" was a supporting one in Henry Fonda's *The Best Man* in '64. But in the fall of '71 she was on Broadway in the star role in *No, No, Nanette*. Said *Variety* then: "Penny Singleton is fine as the substitute for the vacationing Ruby Keeler . . . Miss Singleton is no stranger to the footlights, having made her debut when she was eight years old in a vaudeville act. She has engaging warmth and charm, and although no hoofer, gives an excellent account of herself in her big number 'I Want to Be Happy.'!" She has since played the role many times on tour across the land, and in one midwestern engagement of *Nanette* costarred with Arthur

"Dagwood" Lake. Privately, the actress is the widow of movie producer Robert Sparks; at the time of his death in '63, they had been married 22 years. Her previous marriage ('37) to Dr. Lawrence Singleton ended in divorce ('39), lasting just long enough for her to acquire the moniker by which she is still famous. She has two daughters, DeeGee (Dorothy Grace) and Robin Susan, both in their 30s now. A girl who never got to college, Penny Singleton is understandably proud of the honorary degree of Doctor of Fine Arts she was accorded in '74 by the Staten Island branch of St. John's University. Onscreen as Dorothy McNulty from 1930. IN: *Love in the Rough, Good News, After the Thin Man, Vogues of 1938,* more. Onscreen as Penny Singleton from 1938. IN: *Swing Your Lady, Men Are Such Fools, Boy Meets Girl, Garden of the Moon, The Chump, The Mad Miss Manton, Blondie* (the first of the long series, in 1938); *Go West, Young Lady; Young Widow,* more.

SINNOTT, PATRICIA (N.Y.) Leading lady. Onscreen from the '50s. IN: *Happy Go Lovely, Where's Charley?, Melba, Stage Struck,* more.

SIROLA, JOSEPH (S. Cal.) Support. Onscreen from the '60s. IN: *Strange Bedfellows, The Super Cops, Seizure,* more.

SITKA, EMIL (S. Cal.) Character. Onscreen from the '60s. IN: *The Three Stooges in Orbit, Watermelon Man,* more.

SOJBERG, GUNNAR (Swe.) Leading man. Onscreen from the '40s. IN: *The Children, Wild Strawberries, Brink of Life,* more.

SKAFF, GEORGE (S. Cal.) Character. Onscreen from the '60s. IN: *The Champagne Murders,* more.

SKALA, LILIA (N.Y.) Character. Nominated for Best Supporting Actress Oscar in *Lilies of the Field.* Even after the fame this movie brought her, she sometimes worked in the boxoffice of New York's City Center—mainly because she dislikes inactivity and movie roles are too few and far between. Onscreen from the '50s. IN: *Call Me Madam, Ship of Fools, Caprice, Charly,* more.

SKELTON, RED (Nev.) In October 1973 he married Lothian Toland, daughter of great cinematographer Gregg Toland, at the First Unitarian Church in San Francisco. He was then 60, and she, his third wife, 35. Last onscreen in *Those Magnificent Men in Their Flying Machines* ('65), and generally inactive since then, the comedian has lately reactivated his career by appearing in Nevada nightclubs. He lives in Las Vegas. Onscreen from 1938. IN: *Having Wonderful Time* (billed Richard Skelton), *The Flight Command, Lady Be Good, Dr. Kildare's Wedding Day, Whistling in the Dark (. . . in Dixie, . . . in Brooklyn), Ship Ahoy!, Panama Hattie, DuBarry Was a Lady, I Dood It!, Bathing Beauty, Merton of the Movies, The Fuller Brush Man, A Southern Yankee, Three Little Words, Watch the Birdie, Excuse My Dust, Lovely to Look at, The Clown, Public Pigeon No. 1,* more.

SKERRITT, TOM (S. Cal.) Leading man. Onscreen from the '60s. IN: *War Hunt, M*A*S*H, Wild Rovers, Thieves Like Us, Big Bad Mama; Run, Joe!;* more.

SKINNER, CORNELIA OTIS (N.Y.) Actress and author (*Our Hearts Were Young and Gay*) who, living on Manhattan's East Side, remains forever young in her 70s (b. 1901) and busy—writing books, giving concert readings, and once in a while appearing on stage. Onscreen from 1943. IN: *Stage Door Canteen, The Uninvited* (a most memorable performance), *The Girl in the Red Velvet Swing, The Swimmer.*

SKYLAR, JOANNE ALEX (S. Cal.) Leading lady who received much press attention in 1976 when it was announced—erroneously—that she had married actor Al Pacino. Onscreen in 1976. IN: *Emma.*

SLADE, MARK (S. Cal.) Leading man. Onscreen from 1961. IN: *Splendor in the Grass* (bit), *Voyage to the Bottom of the Sea, Benji,* more.

SLATE, HENRY (S. Cal.) Character. Onscreen from 1944. IN: *Winged Victory, You're in the Navy Now, The Frogmen, Rhubarb, The Belle of New York, Somebody Loves Me, Miss Sadie Thompson, Hit the Deck, My Sister Eileen, Bus Stop, The Strongest Man in the World,* more.

SLATE, JEREMY (S. Cal.) Leading man. Once married to actress Tammy Grimes. Onscreen from the '60s. IN: *Girls! Girls! Girls!; Wives and Lovers, I'll Take Sweden, The Sons of Katie Elder, The Born Losers, The Mini-Skirt Mob, The Devil's Brigade, True Grit, Hell's Belles,* more.

SLATTERY, RICHARD X. (S. Cal.) Character. Onscreen from 1964. IN: *A Distant Trumpet, The Secret War of Harry Frigg, The Boston Strangler, Busting, Herbie Rides Again, Black Eye,* more.

SLEEPER, MARTHA (S.C.) This fine actress, onscreen almost 15 years through 1937's *Four*

Days' Wonder, had a splendid Broadway career thereafter, returned to Hollywood to act in just one more, 1945's *The Bells of St. Mary's*, and gave up her career the following year after appearing in New York in *Christopher Blake*. Ever since, she has been a highly successful costume designer (dresses, blouses, shawls, etc.) and shop owner, which she is today in Charleston. Previously, for many years, she had a similar enterprise on quaint Forteleza in Old San Juan, Puerto Rico. Still a small woman, in her 60s now (b. 1910), she has been married since '41 (no children) to construction engineer Harry Dresser Deutchbein. She was previously married to (1934–40) and divorced from the late actor Hardie Albright. Onscreen from 1923. IN: *The Mailman, Skinner's Big Idea, Danger Street, The Air Legion, Girls Demand Excitement, Ten Cents a Dance, A Tailor-Made Man, Confessions of a Co-Ed, Penthouse, Broken Dreams, Rasputin and the Empress, Midnight Mary, Lady of the Night, Spitfire, West of the Pecos, The Scoundrel, Two Sinners, Great God Gold, Rhythm on the Range*, more.

SLEZAK, WALTER (Switz.) Living in Lugano, Switzerland, for the past two decades, this grand character actor from Austria isn't publicized as he was during his years in Hollywood, but, in his 70s (b. 1902), he remains almost as professionally active. Besides making movies, he still sings in opera. In 1975 he flew to Philadelphia to star in *La Perichole*, remarking beforehand with that familiar Slezak chuckle: "I'm the only actor doing opera without a voice." The previous year, visiting his soap opera star-daughter, Erika Slezak, in New York, he appeared for two weeks with her in her series, *One Life to Live*, playing her godfather. It was the first time they had acted together since a summer stock production of *Rhinoceros* when she was 16. A sentimentalist, the actor observed then: "All I can say is that every time I look into her eyes, I remember how she looked when she was six months old. And now, here I am, exchanging dialogue with her on a show." He has another daughter, Ingrid, married, the mother of two, and living in Ottawa. And he has a son, Leo, in his late 20s, who is an assistant director in one of Vienna's biggest theaters and plans to become a movie director. Since they are alone now, the actor and his wife have sold their large house and moved into a smaller one beside a lake. It was in 1953 that Walter Slezak left Hollywood, though he would return on occasion, to go back to Broadway where he had made his American debut in 1930. He starred in *My Three Angels*, followed, in '54, by *Fanny*, which won him Broadway's Tony Award. After moving to Switzerland, he returned to New York in 1959, making his operatic debut—following in the footsteps of his famous father Leo—as Szupan in *The Gypsy Baron* at the Met. He has since starred in the San Francisco Opera Company's production of *Die Fledermaus*, among others. Onscreen in Hollywood and internationally from 1942. IN: *Once Upon a Honeymoon, This Land Is Mine, The Fallen Sparrow, And Now Tomorrow, Lifeboat, The Princess and the Pirate; Salome, Where She Danced; The Spanish Main, Cornered, Riffraff, Sinbad the Sailor, The Pirate, The Inspector General, The Yellow Cab Man, People Will Talk, Call Me Madam, The Steel Cage, Ten Thousand Bedrooms, The Miracle, The Gazebo, Come September, The Wonderful World of the Brothers Grimm, Emil and the Detectives, A Very Special Favor, The Caper of the Golden Bulls, Heidi* (TV), *Black Beauty*, more.

SMALL, RICHARD B. (S. Cal.) Support. Onscreen from the '70s. IN: *The Black Bird*, more.

SMILEY, RALPH (S.Cal.) Character. Onscreen from the '50s. IN: *My Favorite Spy, A Bullet for Joey*, more.

SMITH, ALEXIS (S. Cal.) After more than 15 years out of movies, her reputation both reinforced and enhanced, thanks to her Broadway triumphs in musicals (*Follies*) and dramas (*Summer Brave*), she has returned to the screen as a major star. Still beautiful in her 50s (b. 1921), she has been married—no children—to actor Craig Stevens since 1944. Onscreen from 1941. IN: *Dive Bomber, Flight from Destiny, Steel Against the Sky* (opposite Craig Stevens), *Gentleman Jim, Thank Your Lucky Stars, The Animal Kingdom, The Constant Nymph, The Adventures of Mark Twain, The Doughgirls, Rhapsody in Blue, Conflict, Night and Day, One More Tomorrow, Of Human Bondage, The Two Mrs. Carrolls, The Woman in White, South of St. Louis, Any Number Can Play, Montana, Here Comes the Groom, The Turning Point, Split Second, The Sleeping Tiger, Beau James, This Happy Feeling, The Young Philadelphians, Once Is Not Enough, The Little Girl Who Lives Down the Lane*, more.

SMITH, ARCHIE (N.Y.) Support. Onscreen from the '60s. IN: *Across the River*, more.

SMITH, CHARLES (N.Y.) In the "Henry Aldrich" movie series, he was Henry's pal, Basil "Dizzy" Stevens, who wiggled his ears to attract girls. Lately a Manhattan resident, he has specialized in TV commercials—sans ear-wiggling—and has appeared in many. Onscreen from 1938. IN: *Boys Town, The Shop Around the Corner, Tom Brown's School Days, Cheers for Miss Bishop, Henry Aldrich for President* (and many others in this series), *The Major and* the Minor, Wing and a Prayer, Lady in the Dark, God Is My Co-Pilot, Three Little Girls in Blue, Adventure in Baltimore, Two Weeks with Love, Rhythm Inn, The Gnome-Mobile, more.

SMITH, CHARLES MARTIN (S. Cal.) Support. Onscreen in the '70s. IN: *No Deposit No Return*, more.

SMITH, CONSTANCE (Eng.) Leading lady; retired for almost two decades. Onscreen from 1947. IN: *Brighton Rock, The Gay Lady, Murder at the Window, The Mudlark, Lucky Nick Cain, Red Skies of Montana, Lure of the Wilderness, Taxi, Treasure of the Golden Condor, The Man in the Attic*, more, including 1958's *Cross Up*, her most recent to date.

SMITH, DARWOOD K. (Mich.) "Our Gang's" Waldo, the studious lad in the horn rims, adored by Darla (and loathed by Alfalfa), is a studious man. Now an Elder in the Seventh-Day Adventist Church, he recently received his master's degree in theology at Michigan State. In features in addition to "Our Gang," he gave up his career as an actor (and, offscreen, as a concert pianist) to enlist in the Army in his teens. After his discharge, he married (he and wife, Jean, have four sons), studied for the ministry at U.C.L.A. and La Sierra College, and then served 12 years as a missionary in Thailand. Onscreen from the '30s. IN: *Quality Street, The Plot Thickens*, more.

SMITH, DEAN (S. Cal.) Support. Onscreen in the '70s. IN: *The Cheyenne Social Club, Rio Lobo, Big Jake*, more.

SMITH, DELOS V., JR. (N.Y.) Character. Onscreen from the '60s. IN: *Splendor in the Grass; Goodbye, Columbus; Stiletto*, more.

SMITH, DWAN (S. Cal.) Support. Onscreen in the '70s. IN: *Sparkle*, more.

SMITH, ELIZABETH (S. Cal.) Support. Onscreen in the '70s. IN: *The Hawaiians*, more.

SMITH, ETHEL (Fla.) The tiny redheaded "Empress of the Organ," as MGM flacks called her, is in her 60s now, has a fine house in Palm Beach where she always entertains the casts playing at the nearby Coconut Grove Playhouse ("That way I get to perform with some fine actors"), and is still—at clubs all over the globe —playing "Tico, Tico." She has not remarried since she was, three decades ago, Ralph Bellamy's third wife. Onscreen from 1944. IN: *Bathing Beauty, George White's Scandals, Twice Blessed, Easy to Wed, Cuban Pete, Melody Time; C'mon, Let's Live a Little; Pigeons*, more.

SMITH, FRANCESCA (N.Y.) Character. Onscreen in the '70s. IN: *Last Summer, The Gang That Couldn't Shoot Straight*, more.

SMITH, HAL (S. Cal.) Character. Onscreen from the '60s. IN: *The Great Race, Santa and the Three Bears* (cartoon voice), *$1,000,000 Duck*, more.

SMITH, JOE (N.J.) The great comedian, half of Smith & Dale (the late Charlie), is at this writing in his 90s (b.1884) and a resident at the Actors Fund Home in Englewood, N.J. But he frequently journeys across the Hudson River to attend showbiz functions in Manhattan. After he had participated in one in 1975, a Friars dinner, *Variety*'s Joe Cohen, noting his "keen mind" and "encyclopedic memory," then reported that he "has not lost his skill in the delineation of the line. Smith did his part and that of his late partner in the sketch about Bernard Schnapps. It was as funny today as when they recited this bit around the circuits. It brought a standing ovation at its conclusion, but he wasn't finished. He recited a poem about himself and his partner, which ended with the lines 'We were as close as two peas in a pod/And we could only have been separated by God.' The audience seemed beside itself." Smith & Dale were onscreen three times in features. IN: *Manhattan Parade* ('31), *The Heart of New York* ('32), and *Two Tickets to Broadway* ('51).

SMITH, JOHN (S. Cal.) Leading man. Onscreen from the '50s. IN: *The High and the Mighty, Seven Angry Men, Desert Sands, The Bold and the Brave, Wichita, Friendly Persuasion, Fury at Showdown, Tomahawk Trail, The Crooked Circle, Island of Lost Women, Circus World, Waco*, more.

SMITH, JUSTIN (S. Cal.) Character. Onscreen from the '50s. IN: *The Jazz Singer, How to Succeed in Business Without Really Trying*, more.

SMITH, KAREN (S. Cal.) Support. Onscreen in the '70s. IN: *Beyond the Valley of the Dolls*, more.

SMITH, KATE (N.Y.) In her 60s (b. 1909), slimmer than in years and still a bachelor girl, this greatly popular singer lives in New York, makes many records, and is often seen on TV. Onscreen in 1933 and 1943. IN: *Hello, Everybody!* and *This Is the Army*.

SMITH, KEELY (S. Cal.) Once the wife of Louis Prima, the singer-actress still appears in clubs. Onscreen 1958–59. IN: *Senior Prom; Thunder Road; Hey Boy! Hey Girl!*

435

SMITH, KENT (S. Cal.) Long a silver-haired character actor (b. 1907), the leading man of the '40s has been married since '62 to character actress Edith Atwater. They live in West Los Angeles, keep in shape by walking over three miles a day, and often appear together in movies or on TV. Onscreen from 1936. IN: *The Garden Murder Case, Back Door to Heaven, The Cat People* (the movie that made his reputation), *Hitler's Children, Forever and a Day, This Land Is Mine, The Curse of the Cat People, The Spiral Staircase, Nora Prentiss, Magic Town, The Voice of the Turtle, The Fountainhead, My Foolish Heart, The Damned Don't Cry, Sayonara, Party Girl, Strangers When We Meet, Susan Slade, Moon Pilot, The Trouble With Angels, Games, Death of a Gunfighter,* more.

SMITH, LANE (N.Y.) Support. Onscreen in the '70's. IN: *Man on a Swing,* more.

SMITH, LEONARD O. (S. Cal.) Character. Onscreen in the '70s. IN: *Tick Tick Tick,* more.

SMITH, LOIS (N.Y.) Support. Onscreen from 1955. IN: *East of Eden, Strange Lady in Town, Five Easy Pieces, The Way We Live Now, Brother John; Next Stop, Greenwich Village;* more.

SMITH, LORING (Conn.) In his 80s (b. 1895) and retired, the character actor lives in Norwalk and works on his golf. Onscreen from 1941. IN: *Shadow of the Thin Man, Keep 'Em Flying, Close-Up, Citizen Saint, Ma and Pa Kettle at Waikiki, Pat and Mike, The Clown, Happy Anniversary, The Cardinal,* more, including, 1967's *Hurry Sundown,* his latest.

SMITH, MADELINE (Eng.) Support. Onscreen in the '70s. IN: *Pussycat, Pussycat, I Love You; The Vampire Lovers, Up Pompeii,* more.

SMITH, MAGGIE (Eng.) Costar. Won Best Actress Oscar in *The Prime of Miss Jean Brodie.* Nominated in the same category in *Travels With My Aunt.* Nominated for Best Supporting Actress Oscar in *Othello.* Onscreen from 1957. IN: *Nowhere to Go, The V.I.P.s, The Pumpkin Eater, Young Cassidy, The Honey Pot, Hot Millions, Oh! What a Lovely War; Love, Pain and the Whole Damn Thing; Murder by Death,* more.

SMITH, MURIEL (N.Y.) Black singer-actress. Onscreen from 1952. IN: *Moulin Rouge, The Crowning Experience,* and *The Voice of the Hurricane.* (She also narrated 1948's *Strange Victory.)*

SMITH, NORWOOD (N.Y.) Support. Onscreen in the '70s. IN: *Huckleberry Finn,* more.

SMITH, PATRICIA (S. Cal.) Leading lady. Onscreen from the '50s. IN: *The Spirit of St. Louis* (as Anne Morrow Lindbergh), *The Bachelor Party, Save the Tiger,* more.

SMITH, PAUL (S. Cal.) Support. Onscreen from the '50s. IN: *Retreat, Hell!; Battle at Apache Pass, Madron,* more.

SMITH, PUTTER (S. Cal.) Character actor. Onscreen in the '70s. IN: *Diamonds Are Forever,* more.

SMITH, QUEENIE (S. Cal.) Well into her 70s (b. 1898), this fine character comedienne is still going strong. Onscreen from 1935. IN: *Mississippi, Show Boat, On Your Toes, The Killers, From This Day Forward, Nocturne, The Long Night, The Snake Pit, Sleep My Love, The Great Rupert, The First Legion, My Sister Eileen, You Can't Run Away from It, Hot Shots, Sweet Smell of Success, The Legend of Lylah Clare,* more.

SMITH, REBECCA DIANNA (S. Cal.) Leading lady. Onscreen in the '70s. IN: *Deadly Honeymoon,* more.

SMITH, REID (N.Y.) Support. Onscreen in the '70s. IN: *Dinah East, The Late Liz,* more.

SMITH, ROGER (S. Cal.) Married to star Ann-Margret, his second marriage, he has given up his career to manage hers. Onscreen from 1956. IN: *The Young Rebels, No Time to be Young, Operation Mad Ball, Man of a Thousand Faces, Auntie Mame, Never Steal Anything Small, Rogues' Gallery,* more.

SMITH, SAMMY (N.Y.) Character. Onscreen from 1963. IN: *Act One, How to Succeed in Business Without Really Trying,* more.

SMITH, SYDNEY (S. Cal.) Character. Onscreen from the '50s. IN: *The Frogmen, Fury at Showdown, No Time for Sergeants,* more.

SMITH, TRUMAN (N.Y.) Character. Onscreen from the '50s. IN: *The Phenix City Story, The Monte Carlo Story, One Plus One,* more.

SMITH, VINCENT (Eng.) Support. Onscreen in the '70s. IN: *Paddy, Underground.*

SMITH, WILLIAM (S. Cal.) Leading man. Onscreen from the '60s. IN: *Three Guns for Texas; Run, Angel, Run!; Darker Than Amber, C.C. and Company, The Losers, Angels Die Hard, Summertree, Chrome and Hot Leather, Tiger Cage,* more.

SMITH, WONDERFUL (S. Cal.) Black support. Onscreen from the '40s. IN: *Top Sergeant Mulligan, Over My Dead Body,* more.

SMITHERS, JAN (S. Cal.) Leading lady. On-screen in the '70s. IN: *Where the Lilies Bloom*, more.

SMITHERS, WILLIAM (S. Cal.) Leading man who was most popular as one of the stars of TV's *Peyton Place*. Onscreen from the '50s. IN: *Attack!*, more.

SMOTHERS, TOM AND DICK (S. Cal.) Comedians. Onscreen in the '70s. IN: *Get to Know Your Rabbit*.

SNODGRESS, CARRIE (S. Cal.) Leading lady. Nominated for Best Actress Oscar in *Diary of a Mad Housewife*. Onscreen in the '70s. IN: *Rabbit, Run*, more.

SNOWDEN, LEIGH (S. Cal.) A young Universal leading lady of the '50s, she is married to accordianist Dick Contino, has children, is retired. Onscreen from 1955. IN: *Francis in the Navy, All That Heaven Allows, Kiss Me Deadly, The Square Jungle, The Creature Walks Among Us, Outside the Law, I've Lived Before*, more.

SNOWDON, ROGER (Eng.) Character. On-screen from the '60s. IN: *Othello, Follow the Boys*, more.

SOBLE, RON (S. Cal.) Support. Onscreen from the '60s. IN: *True Grit, Chisum*, more.

SOBOLOFF, ARNOLD (N.Y.) Character. On-screen from the '60s. IN: *Popi*, more.

SOFAER, ABRAHAM (S. Cal.) Character who, in his 80s (b. 1896), remains active both in movies and TV. Onscreen from 1931. IN: *The Dreyfus Case, Rembrandt, Christopher Columbus, Quo Vadis, Pandora and the Flying Dutchman, His Majesty O'Keefe, Elephant Walk, Bhowani Junction, King of Kings, Omar Khayyam, Taras Bulba, The Greatest Story Ever Told, Head, Che!*, more.

SOKOL, MARILYN (N.Y.) Character. On-screen in the '70s. IN: *Zabriskie Point, The Hospital*, more.

SOLARI, RUDY (S. Cal.) Leading man. On-screen from the '60s. IN: *Judgment at Nuremberg, Kings of the Son*, more.

SOLOMON, TINA (Eng.) Character. Onscreen in the '70s. IN: *Leo the Last*, more.

SOLON, EWEN (Eng.) Character. Onscreen from 1954. IN: *Rob Roy, 1984, The Sundowners, The Hound of the Baskervilles, The Terror of the Tongs*, more.

SOMACK, JACK (S. Cal.) Character. On-screen from the '60s. IN: *Generation, Portnoy's Complaint, The Pursuit of Happiness*, more.

SOMBERT, CLAIRE (Fr.) Ballerina. Onscreen in 1956 in *Invitation to the Dance*.

SOMERS, BRETT (S. Cal.) Actress-TV panelist. Former wife of Jack Klugman. Onscreen from 1965. IN: *Bus Riley's Back in Town*, more.

SOMES, MICHAEL (Eng.) Ballet star. On-screen in 1960 and 1966. IN: *The Royal Ballet* and *Romeo and Juliet*.

SOMMARS, JULIE (S. Cal.) Leading lady married to Stuart Erwin Jr. Better known for her TV work than her movies. Onscreen from 1965. IN: *The Great Sioux Uprising, The Pad (And How to Use It)*, more.

SOMMER, ELKE (S. Cal.) Costar. Onscreen from the '50s. IN: *The Day It Rained, The Victors, The Prize, A Shot in the Dark, The Art of Love, Most Dangerous Game, The Oscar; Boy, Did I Get a Wrong Number!; The Money Trap, The Venetian Affair, Deadlier Than the Male, The Wicked Dreams of Paula Schultz, The Wrecking Crew, They Came to Rob Las Vegas, Zeppelin, Percy, Ten Little Indians, Carry On Behind, On a Dead Man's Chest*, more.

SOMMERS, JOANIE (S. Cal.) Singer-actress. Onscreen in the '60s. IN: *Everything's Ducky, The Lively Set*.

SONDERGAARD, GALE (S. Cal.) Winner of the first ('36) Supporting Actress Oscar, in *Anthony Adverse*, she is back in Hollywood after many years away—a "blacklist" victim—and extremely active again onstage (*The Crucible* with Charlton Heston in Los Angeles, *A Family and a Fortune* with Sylvia Sidney in Seattle, etc.), in TV series (*Medical Center*), and TV-movies (*The Cat Creature*). "As far as I'm concerned all the barriers are now down," the actress noted a while back, adding, "but I haven't done a major picture at a major studio—not since *East Side, West Side* in '49 at MGM." This was remedied in 1976 when she was signed for the top supporting role in *The Return of a Man Called Horse* with Richard Harris. Now in her 70s (b. 1900), she has two children—a daughter, Mrs. John Campos, and a son, Daniel Hans Biberman, who is one of her agents. And she is a widow; her husband, director Herbert J. Biberman, died of bone cancer in '71. As one of the "Hollywood 10," convicted for contempt of Congress in '50 for refusal to answer questions about possible Communist party affiliations, he received a six-month prison sentence and was blacklisted by Hollywood studios. At the time of his death he had completed a movie script about this experience, *Over the Carnage*, that Miss Sondergaard has lately shown to Hollywood producers. Her philosophy, which has helped her survive the upheavals in her life, the actress has said, is: "Follow the bends in the river." Onscreen from 1936. IN: *Anthony Adverse* (her first), *Maid of Salem, The Life of Emile Zola, Dramatic School, Lord Jeff, Juarez, The Cat and the Canary, The Mark of Zorro, The Blue Bird, The Letter, The Black Cat, My Favorite Blonde, A Night to Remember, Appointment in Berlin, Sherlock Holmes and the Spider Woman, The Climax, The Invisible Man's Revenge, Christmas Holiday, Anna and the King of Siam, The Time of Their Lives, The Spider Woman Strikes Back, The Road to Rio, The Slaves*, more.

SOO, JACK (S. Cal.) Character. Onscreen from the '60s. IN: *Flower Drum Song, Who's Been Sleeping in My Bed?, The Oscar, Thoroughly Modern Millie, The Green Berets*, more.

SORDI, ALBERTO (It.) Comedy star. Onscreen from the '40s. IN: *His Young Wife, The White Sheik, Vitelloni, A Farewell to Arms, The Best of Enemies; To Bed . . . Or Not to Bed; Mafioso, Made in Italy, While There's a Way There's a Hope*, more.

SOREL, GUY (N.Y.) Character. Primarily a stage-TV actor. Onscreen from 1951. IN: *The Thirteenth Letter, The Honeymoon Killers; Tell Me That You Love Me, Junie Moon*; more.

SOREL, JEAN (Fr.) Leading man. Onscreen from the '60s. IN: *From a Roman Balcony, A View from the Bridge, Adorable Julia, Sandra, Made in Italy, The Queens, Belle de Jour; Weekend, Italian Style; The Sweet Body of Deborah*, more.

SOREL, JEANNE (S. Cal.) Character. Onscreen from 1932. IN: *American Madness, Model Shop*, many more, including, in this decade, *B.S. I Love You*.

SOREL, LOUISE (N.Y.) Leading lady. Onscreen from the '60s. IN: *The Party's Over, Plaza Suite, B.S. I Love You*, more.

SORENSEN, LINDA (S. Cal.) Leading lady. Onscreen in the '70s. IN: *Breaking Point*, more.

SORENSEN, PAUL (S. Cal.) Character. Onscreen from the '60s. IN: *The Steel Claw, Hang 'Em High, Suppose They Gave a War and Nobody Came?*, more.

SORENY, EVA (S. Cal.) Character. Onscreen from the '60s. IN: *Assignment to Kill*, more.

SORIAN, JACK (N.Y.) Character. Onscreen from the '50s. IN: *The Joe Louis Story, Target U.S.A.* (lead), more.

SORRELLS, ROBERT (S. Cal.) Character. Onscreen from the '60s. IN: *A Man Called Gannon*, more.

SORVINO, PAUL (S. Cal.) Character star. Onscreen in the '70s. IN: *The Panic in Needle Park, Cry Uncle, Made for Each Other, The Gambler, A Touch of Class; Shoot It: Black, Shoot It: Blue; I Will, I Will . . . For Now*; more.

SOSA, GEO ANNE (S. Cal.) Support. Onscreen in the '70s. IN: *The Trial of Billy Jack*, more.

SOSA, SUSAN (S. Cal.) Support. Onscreen in the '70s. IN: *Billy Jack, The Trial of Billy Jack*, more.

SOTHERN, ANN (S. Cal.) She was one of MGM's great and shining stars, as well as one of TV's (*Private Secretary* and *The Ann Sothern Show*). But, during the '60s, when she appeared in just four movies, she seemed content to rest on her residuals in her Beverly Hills home and enjoy the success of her actress-daughter Tisha Sterling. Tisha, her only child, is by second husband, Robert Sterling (her first was late actor Roger Pryor); she has not remarried since she and Sterling were divorced in 1949. In recent years, the actress, now in her 60s (b. 1911) and far heavier than in more glamorous days, has reactivated her screen career—starring in such exploitation movies as *Golden Needles* and *Crazy Mama*. Regrettably, in such pictures, there is scant opportunity for the wry "Maisie" humor to shine through. Onscreen from 1929 as Harriet Lake (her real name). IN: *Show of Shows*, and *Dough Boys.* Onscreen as Ann Sothern from 1934: IN: *Melody in Spring, Let's Fall in Love, Kid Millions, The Girl Friend, Her Sacrifice, Don't Gamble with Love, My American Wife, Smartest Girl in Town, Fifty Roads to Town, There Goes My Gal, Trade Winds, Maisie* (first of the series of nine, in 1939); the last was 1947's *Undercover Maisie*), *Joe and Ethel Turp Call on the President, Dulcy, Lady Be Good, Panama Hattie, Cry Havoc, April Showers, A Letter to Three Wives, Words and Music, The Judge Steps Out, Nancy Goes to Rio, Blue Gardenia, Lady in a Cage, The Best Man, Sylvia, Chubasco*, more.

SOUL, DAVID (S. Cal.) Leading man. Onscreen in the '70s. IN: *Johnny Got His Gun*, more.

SOULE, OLAN (S. Cal.) Character. Famous three decades ago as the (final) romantic lead, opposite Barbara Luddy, of radio's *The First Nighter*. Preceding him in the role: Don Ameche and Les Tremayne. Onscreen from the '50s. IN: *Cuban Fireball, Call Me Madam, Dragnet, Prince of Players, Queen Bee, Daddy Long Legs, Girl Happy, The Destructors, The Seven Minutes, The Towering Inferno*, more.

SOULES, DALE (N.Y.) Leading lady. Onscreen in the '70s. IN: *Prism*, more.

SOUTHERN, RICHARD (S. Cal.) Support. Onscreen from the '60s. IN: *The Love Doctors*, more.

SPAAK, AGNES (Fr.) Support. Onscreen from the '60s. IN: *Better a Widow*, more.

SPAAK, CATHERINE (Fr.) Costar. Onscreen from 1960. IN: *La Trou, The Easy Life, Of Wayward Love, The Empty Canvas, Circle of Love, The Little Nuns, Hotel, Made in Italy, The Man with the Balloons, The Libertine; A Murder Is a Murder . . . Is a Murder; Take a Hard Ride, The Birds of Baden-Baden*, more.

SPACE, ARTHUR (S. Cal.) Character. Onscreen from 1941. IN: *Riot Squad, Tortilla Flat, Whistling in Brooklyn, Wilson, Leave Her to Heaven, The Guilt of Janet Ames, The Red House, Big Town After Dark, A Southern Yankee, Fighter Squadron, Mr. Belvedere Goes to College, The Fuller Brush Girl, Last of the Pony Riders, Yankee Pasha, The Spirit of St. Louis, Taggart!, The Shakiest Gun in the West, The Bat People, The Strongest Man in the World*, more.

SPACEK, SISSY (S. Cal.) Leading lady. Onscreen in the '70s. IN: *Badlands, Welcome to L.A.*, more.

SPAETH, MERRIE (N.Y.) The teenager-with-bangs who (with Tippy Walker) costarred and made such a splash in 1964's *The World of Henry Orient*, did a few TV dramas after it but never made another movie. Instead, she graduated from Smith College cum laude in '70, became politically active in her home town, Philadelphia, where, in '72, aged 23, she was the Republican candidate for the State Legislature from her home district. Asked then about her acting career, she shrugged and said, "That movie! People who have seen it on TV sometimes recognize me and are very friendly when I come around, but when they find out I'm after their vote, they suddenly become cautious. I guess they're still thinking of me as that 14-year-old." She lost the election. Lately, she has been the host of a radio talk show heard on Saturday mornings over local station WMCA. Still single, and a sophisticated-looking long-haired blonde, she insists that acting is no longer her first love. "Oh, I once thought I'd become another Gloria Swanson, but not any more." She continues to study drama, however, with a private teacher—"to improve my speaking voice," she says.

SPAIN, FAY (S. Cal.) Character; former leading lady. Onscreen from 1957. IN: *The Crooked Circle, Teenage Doll, God's Little Acre, Al Capone, The Beat Generation, Hercules and the Captive Women, Thunder Island, Flight to Fury, Welcome to Hard Times; The Godfather, Part II*; more.

SPARER, PAUL (N.Y.) Support. Onscreen in the '70s. IN: *Loving*, more.

SPARKS, RANDY (S. Cal.) Musician-supporting actor. Onscreen from the '50s. IN: *Thunder Road, College Confidential, The Big Night*, more.

SPARV, CAMILLA (It.) Leading lady. Onscreen from the '60s. IN: *Dead Heat on a Merry-Go-Round, The Trouble with Angels, Murderers' Row, Assignment K, The High Commissioner, Mackenna's Gold, Downhill Racer*, more.

SPEED, CAROL (S. Cal.) Black leading lady. Onscreen in the '70s. IN: *Black Samson, Abby* (title role), more.

SPELL, GEORGE (N.Y.) Character. Onscreen in the '70s. IN: *They Call Me Mr. Tibbs, The Organization*, more.

SPELL, WANDA (N.Y.) Character. Onscreen in the '70s. IN: *They Call Me Mr. Tibbs, The Organization*, more.

SPELLER, ROBERT (N.Y.) Support. Onscreen from 1969. IN: *Hello, Dolly!*, more.

SPELLING, AARON (S. Cal.) Screenwriter who was first an actor. Onscreen from 1953. IN: *Vickie, Three Young Texans, One Foot in Hell* (which he also wrote).

SPELVIN, GEORGINA (N.Y.) Porn star (*The Devil in Miss Jones*) who was originally a dancer in movies. Onscreen in the '60s. IN: *Ocean's Eleven, Sweet Charity*; since, besides her many X-rated films, she starred in the R-rated *Girls for Rent* ('74) with Kent Taylor and Robert Livingston.

SPENCER, BUD (It.) Character. Onscreen from the '60s. IN: *Ace High, The Five Man Army; Today We Kill . . . Tomorrow We Die!; A Reason to Live, A Reason to Die*; more.

SPENCER, MARIAN (Eng.) Character; former leading lady. Onscreen from 1937. IN: *The Life of David Livingstone* (as Mary Livingstone), *The Weaker Sex, Bond Street, Intimate Relations, Gulliver's Travels, The World of Suzie Wong, The Doctor of Seven Dials, Seance on a Wet Afternoon*, more.

SPENSER, JEREMY (Eng.) Leading man. Onscreen from 1948. IN: *Anna Karenina* (his debut at 11, first of many juvenile roles), *Prelude to Fame, Portrait of Clare, The Spider and the Fly, Outpost in Malaya, The Man Who Loved Redheads, Prince and the Showgirl, The Roman Spring of Mrs. Stone, Fahrenheit 451, King and Country, He Who Rides a Tiger*, more.

SPERLING, KAREN (N.Y.) Leading lady. Daughter of writer-producer Milton Sperling. Onscreen in 1971. IN: *Make a Face* (writing, producing, directing, and playing the leading role).

SPIELBERG, DAVID (N.Y.) Support. Onscreen in the '70s. IN: *The Effect of Gamma Rays on Man-in-the-Moon Marigolds, Newman, Law and Disorder, Hustle*, more.

SPILLANE, MICKEY (S. C.) The novelist, creator of "Mike Hammer," lives and fishes on the coast of South Carolina, and gives no thought to his days before the camera—which were, of course, only a by-product of his fame as a writer. Onscreen in 1954 in *Ring of Fear* and in 1964 in *The Girl Hunters*, in which he starred as Mike Hammer, no less.

SPINETTI, VICTOR (Eng.) Comedy star. Onscreen from 1964. IN: *A Hard Day's Night, Help!, The Taming of the Shrew, The Biggest Bundle of Them All; Unman, Wittering and Zigo; The Little Prince, The Return of the Pink Panther, Awareness of Emily*, more.

SPIVAK, ALICE (N.Y.) Support. Onscreen from the '60s. IN: *West Side Story, Something Wild, Lilith, The Miracle Worker, Requiem for a Heavyweight, The Angel Levine, Buck and the Preacher*, more.

SPRADLING, G. D. (S. Cal.) Support. Onscreen from the '60s. IN: *Will Penny, Zabriskie Point; Tora! Tora! Tora!; Number One, Monte Walsh, Hell's Angels, The Hunting Party; The Godfather, Part II*; more.

SPRATLEY, TOM (N.Y.) Character. Onscreen in the '70s. IN: *Going Home, Love Story, Bananas, The Panic in Needle Park, The Hospital, Where the Lilies Bloom*, more.

SPRIGGS, ELIZABETH (Eng.) Support. Onscreen from the '60s. IN: *Work Is a Four Letter Word, Three Into Two Won't Go*, more.

SPRING, HELEN (S. Cal.) Character. Onscreen from the '50s. IN: *To Please a Lady, Emergency Wedding, Something to Live For, Willard*, more.

SPRINGER, GARY (N.Y.) Support. Son of noted publicist-author John Springer, famous for his "Legendary Ladies" presentations—film-clips and personal appearances of stars such as Bette Davis. Onscreen in the '70s. IN: *Law and Disorder, Dog Day Afternoon*, more.

SQUIRE, KATHERINE (N.Y.) Character. Onscreen from 1959. IN: *Story on Page One, Song Without End, This Savage Land*, more.

SQUIRE, WILLIAM (Eng.) Character. Onscreen from the '50s. IN: *The Long Dark Hall, The Battle of the River Plate, Alexander the Great, Where Eagles Dare, Anne of the Thousand Days*, more.

STACK, ROBERT (S. Cal.) Costar. Nominated for Best Supporting Actor Oscar in *Written on the Wind*. Still a handsome man in his 50s (b. 1919), he has been married since '56 to actress Rosemarie Bowe—first marriage for each—and has two college-age children, Charles and Elizabeth; the latter, a student at Middleburg College in Vermont, made her acting debut in '75 in the leading role in the school's production of *Who's Afraid of Virginia Woolf*. The actor and his wife, who last acted in *The Peacemaker* the year they married, both were on hand to cheer. Onscreen from 1939. IN: *First Love, The Mortal Storm, Nice Girl?, To Be or Not to Be, Eagle Squadron, A Date with Judy, Miss Tatlock's Millions, The Bullfighter and the Lady, Bwana Devil, Sabre Jet, The High and the Mighty; Good Morning, Miss Dove; The Tarnished Angels, The Gift of Love, John Paul Jones, The Last Voyage, The Scarface Mob, The Caretakers, Is Paris Burning?, The Corrupt Ones*, more.

STACY, JAMES (S. Cal.) Leading man, married to and divorced from actresses Connie Stevens and Kim Darby, who, in this decade, lost an arm and a leg in a motorcycle accident in Los Angeles. *Posse*, in 1975, marked his return to acting. Onscreen from the '60s. IN: *Flareup*, more.

STAFFORD, FREDERICK (It.) Leading man from Austria. Onscreen from the '60s. IN: *OSS 117—Mission for a Killer; Topaz, The Dirty Heroes*, more.

STAFFORD, TIM/now **JEFFREY BYRON** (S. Cal.) Support. Son of actress Anna Lee. Onscreen in the '60s as Tim Stafford. IN: *Donovan's Reef, Hot Rods to Hell*, more. Onscreen in the '70s as Jeffrey Byron. IN: *At Long Last Love*, more.

STAIGER, LIBI (N.Y.) Singer-actress. On-screen in 1957. IN: *Undersea Girl* (nightclub singer).

STAINTON, PHILIP (Eng.) Character. On-screen from the '40s. IN: *The Spider and the Fly, The Blue Lagoon, Passport to Pimlico, Mogambo, Hobson's Choice, Ladykillers, Moby Dick, Reach for the Sky, Cast a Dark Shadow*, more.

STALEY, JOAN (S. Cal.) Leading lady. Lately inactive in movies, she is married to writer Dale Sheets and is the mother of twins, a son and daughter, born March 24, 1971. Onscreen from 1948. IN: *The Emperor Waltz* (specialty as a child prodigy on the violin, which she actually was), *Bells Are Ringing, Ocean's Eleven, Midnight Lace, All in a Night's Work, Dondi, Cape Fear, Breakfast at Tiffany's, Johnny Cool, Wives and Lovers, A New Kind of Love, Roustabout, The Ghost and Mr. Chicken, Gunpoint*, more.

STALMASTER, HAL (S. Cal.) The former Disney juvenile star, a business man now, is married and the father of a daughter born in 1970. Onscreen from the '50s. IN: *Johnny Tremain*, more.

STAMP, TERENCE (Eng.) Costar. Nominated for Best Supporting Actor Oscar in *Billy Budd*, his debut. Onscreen from 1962. IN: *Term of Trial, The Collector, Modesty Blaise, Far From the Madding Crowd, Poor Cow, Blue, The Mind of Mr. Soames, Teorema, Spirits of the Dead*, more.

STANDER, LIONEL (It.) As sardonic as ever in his graying 60s (b. 1908), the American character actor has lived in Rome for 15 years, on Appia Antica. He settled in Italy after being a Wall Street broker, after becoming a victim of Hollywood's blacklist in '49, after sending shivers down spines as a gravel-voiced movie thug for 15 years. He has returned to Hollywood just twice—for *The Loved One* ('65) and *The Black Bird* ('75). Abroad, he has played costar roles in more than 45 movies. Married to his sixth wife, Dutch starlet Stephane Van Hennick, who is in her 20s, he became the father of a daughter, Jennifer Stephane, in '72. With an earlier wife he has twin daughters, adopted in '46. Of his adopted country, Italy, he says, "It doesn't do anything like anybody else. It's crazy and I love it." Looking back on the '30s, when he was Hollywood's highest-paid character actor, he reflects, "Not many men of that era have been able to start a new and very lucrative career in another country in their 50s. I'm a very lucky man." Onscreen from 1935. IN: *The Scoundrel, Page Miss Glory, We're in the Money, Mr. Deeds Goes to Town, The Music Goes Round,* *More Than a Secretary, The Milky Way, Soak the Rich, League of Frightened Men, A Star Is Born, Professor Beware, Guadalcanal Diary, Hangmen Also Die, Spectre of the Rose, Gentleman Joe Palooka, Mad Wednesday* (a.k.a. *The Sin of Harold Diddlebock*), *Call Northside 777, St. Benny the Dip, Promise Her Anything, Cul de Sac, A Dandy in Aspic, Once Upon a Time in the West, Red Coat, Who's Afraid of Zorro?, The Black Hand, The Gang That Couldn't Shoot Straight, Your Pleasure Is My Business, Pulp*, more.

STANDING, JOHN (Eng.) Leading man. The son of Sir Ronald George Leon and former star Kay Hammond (real name Dorothy Katherine Standing), he uses his mother's family name, one of the most famous in the English theater. Onscreen from 1961. IN: *The Wild and the Willing, A Pair of Briefs, King Rat, All the Right Noises; Walk, Don't Run; The Psychopath; Thank You All Very Much; X, Y and Zee;* more.

STANG, ARNOLD (N.Y.) Comedian. Onscreen from 1942. IN: *Seven Days' Leave* (his debut, age 17), *So This Is New York* (costarred with Henry Morgan), *Two Gals and a Guy, The Man with the Golden Arm, Dondi, The Wonderful World of the Brothers Grimm, It's a Mad Mad Mad Mad World, Skidoo!, Hello Down There,* more.

STANHOPE, TED (S. Cal.) Character. Onscreen from the '40s. IN: *Teen Age, The Burning Cross, High Noon*, more.

STANHOPE, WARREN (S. Cal.) Character. Onscreen from the '60s. IN: *The Bedford Incident, The Revolutionary*, more.

STANLEY, FLORENCE (N.Y.) Character. Onscreen from the '60s. IN: *Up the Down Staircase, Jenny*, more.

STANLEY, JACK (S. Cal.) Character. Onscreen in the '70s. IN: *The Trial of Billy Jack*, more.

STANLEY, KEN (Eng.) Character. Onscreen from the '50s. IN: *The Mouse That Roared*, more.

STANLEY, KIM (N.M.) Costar. Nominated for Best Actress Oscar in *Seance on a Wet Afternoon*. A breakdown suffered after this 1964 movie forced her to give up her acting career. She retired to her native state, New Mexico, to recover. For a long while she lived in Taos, where she taught retarded children. In '72, tanned and considerably heavier than she had been onscreen, she made an attempt to resume her movie career. She flew to London to costar with Katharine Hepburn and Paul Scofield in *A Delicate Balance*. But, when it was time to leave for the studio, she decided it would be best if she withdrew from the assignment. After teaching a basic acting course during a summer session at the College of Santa Fe, the city in which she lives now, she became a full-time drama instructor there. She also directs campus plays presented at The Greer Garson Theater, one of which, in the '75–76 season, was William Inge's *Bus Stop*—the play in which she won the New York Drama Critics' Poll as Best Actress of 1955. Single now, as she enters her 50s (b. 1925), she has been married to and divorced from actor Bruce Franklin Hall, actor Curt Conway (d. 1974), by whom she has a grown son and daughter, and actor-director Alfred Ryder, by whom she has a teenage daughter. Onscreen first in 1958 in *The Goddess* (her debut and only other film).

STANLEY, PAT (N.Y.) Leading lady. Onscreen in 1961. IN: *The Ladies Man.*

STANLEY, RALPH (N.Y.) Character. Onscreen in the '70s. IN: *The Anderson Tapes,* more.

STANTON, BETTY (N.Y.) Support. Onscreen from 1960. IN: *Girl of the Night, The Troublemaker,* more.

STANTON, HARRY (S. Cal.) Character. Onscreen in the '70s. IN: *What's the Matter with Helen?,* more.

STANTON, HARRY DEAN/formerly **DEAN STANTON** (S. Cal.) Youngish character actor widely regarded as the logical successor to noted character actors of the past. He may be the most ubiquitous player in pictures today. Onscreen from 1958. IN: *The Proud Rebel, The Adventures of Huckleberry Finn, Pork Chop Hill, A Dog's Best Friend, Cool Hand Luke, Day of the Evil Gun, A Time for Killing, The Mini-Skirt Mob, Kelly's Heroes,* more (all as Dean Stanton); *Two-Lane Blacktop* (as H.D. Stanton), and (as Harry Dean Stanton) *Where the Lilies Bloom, Zandy's Bride; The Godfather, Part II; Face to the Wind, Cockfighter, 92 in the Shade, Rancho Deluxe; Farewell, My Lovely; Born to Kill, Rafferty and the Gold Dust Twins,* more.

STANWYCK, BARBARA (S. Cal.) Legendary star, the acknowledged favorite of directors Cecil B. DeMille and Frank Capra, as she has been of many thousands of moviegoers for decades. Nominated for Best Actress Oscar in *Stella Dallas, Ball of Fire, Double Indemnity,* and *Sorry, Wrong Number.* White-haired as she enters her 70s (b. 1907), and last onscreen in 1964's *The Night Walker* (with Robert Taylor, from whom she had been divorced for years), she lives alone in Beverly Hills in semiretirement, devoting herself to totally unpublicized charities. Onscreen from 1929. IN: *The Locked Door, Ladies of Leisure, Ten Cents a Dance, Night Nurse, So Big, Shopworn, The Bitter Tea of General Yen, Ladies They Talk About, A Lost Lady, The Woman in Red, A Message to Garcia, Internes Can't Take Money, This Is My Affair, The Mad Miss Manton, Union Pacific, Golden Boy, Remember the Night, The Lady Eve, Meet John Doe, The Gay Sisters, Lady of Burlesque, Christmas in Connecticut, My Reputation, The Strange Love of Martha Ivers, The Two Mrs. Carrolls, The Other Love, B.F.'s Daughter; East Side, West Side; Thelma Jordan, The Furies, Clash by Night, Titanic, Witness to Murder, Executive Suite, Cattle Queen of Montana, The Maverick Queen, Trooper Hook, Walk on the Wild Side, Roustabout,* more.

STAPLETON, JEAN (S. Cal.) Character. Co-star of TV's *All in the Family.* Onscreen from 1958. IN: *Damn Yankees, Bells Are Ringing, Something Wild, Up the Down Staircase,* more.

STAPLETON, MAUREEN (N.Y.) Character star. Nominated for Best Supporting Actress Oscar in *Lonelyhearts* and *Airport.* Onscreen from 1959. IN: *The Fugitive Kind, A View from the Bridge, Bye Bye Birdie, Trilogy,* more.

STAPLETON, VIVIAN (Eng.) Support. Onscreen from the '60s. IN: *The Young, the Evil and the Savage;* more.

STAPLEY, RICHARD/now **RICHARD WYLER** (S. Cal.) Leading man. Onscreen (as Richard Stapley) from 1948. IN: *The Three Musketeers, Little Women, The Strange Door, King of the Khyber Rifles, Target Zero; D-Day, the Sixth of June;* more; onscreen (as Richard Wyler) from 1968. IN: *The Ugly Ones,* more.

STAPP, MARJORIE (S. Cal.) Leading lady. Onscreen from the '50s. IN: *Gun for a Coward, Kronos, The Battle at Bloody Beach,* more.

STARENIOS, DIMOS (Greece) Character. Onscreen from the '40s. IN: *Anna of Rhodes, He Who Must Die, Never on Sunday, Oedipus the King, Thanos and Despina,* more.

STARK, DOUGLAS (N.Y.) Support. Onscreen from the '60s. IN: *Reflections in a Golden Eye, The French Connection, The Hot Rock, Hail,* more.

STARK, GRAHAM (Eng.) Character. Onscreen from the '60s. IN: *A Shot in the Dark,*

Alfie, Those Fantastic Flying Fools, Salt and Pepper, more.

STARKE, PAULINE (S. Cal.) The former leading lady is now in her 70s (b. 1900), lives in Santa Monica, has long been married to George Sherwood, and with him travels all over the globe. Onscreen from 1919. IN: *The Life Line, Soldiers of Fortune, A Connecticut Yankee in King Arthur's Court, Salvation Nell, In the Palace of the King, Dante's Inferno* (this silent may be her most famous role), *The Devil's Cargo, The Man Without a Country, Bright Lights, The Perfect Sap, Streets of Shanghai, The Viking, Royal Romance, What Men Want,* more, including 1935's *$20 a Week,* her last.

STARKE, TOD (S. Cal.) Former juvenile (b. 1961). Onscreen in the '60s. IN: *Angel in My Pocket,* more.

STARR, JACK (S. Cal.) Character. Onscreen in the '70s. IN: *The Peace Killers,* more.

STARR, RINGO (Eng.) Singer-actor; of the Beatles. Onscreen from 1964. IN: *A Hard Day's Night, Help!, The Magic Christian, Let It Be, Two Hundred Motels, Son of Dracula, This'll Be the Day,* more.

STARRETT, CHARLES (S. Cal.) During his first six years in movies, he was one of Hollywood's handsomest leading men. From '36 till his retirement in '52, at Columbia, he starred in a total of 115 Westerns (many of them "Durango Kids"), and was for 15 years one of the Top Ten Western Stars at the box-office. For many more years than that—since '28—the onetime Dartmouth gridiron star has been married to the former Mary McKinnon. "I think of Mary and myself as being fortunate after all our years of running together," Starrett said recently. "We enjoy the changes of seasons—our mountain home in the High Sierras, then migrating, for the winter, to our coastal home in Laguna. We both love to travel and have been able to since I left Columbia. Our sons [in their 40s now]—twins, not identical—are both happily married. Davis is an art teacher at Pasadena City College and Charles is successful in investment mutual funds. We have two grandchildren by the latter—both teenagers—David and Laura." In his 70s now (b. 1904), and very wealthy, Charles Starrett remains—silver hair or no—a rugged, healthy, handsome man. Onscreen from 1930. IN: *Fast and Loose, The Royal Family of Broadway, Damaged Love, Touchdown, The Mask of Fu Manchu, Our Betters, The Sweetheart of Sigma Chi, The Silver Streak, So Red the Rose, Along Came Love, Stampede, Call of the Rockies, The Man from Sundown, The Durango Kid, Down Rio Grande*

Way, Robin Hood of the Range, Sundown Valley, Cowboy from Lonesome River, West of Dodge City, Blazing Across the Pecos, Streets of Ghost Town, The Kid from Amarillo, Smoky Canyon, more, including *The Kid from Broken Gun,* his last.

STARRETT, CLAUDE E., JR. (S. Cal.) Support. Onscreen in the '70s. IN: *Blazing Saddles,* more.

STARRETT, JACK (S. Cal.) Support. Onscreen from the '60s. IN: *Angels from Hell, The Gay Deceivers, The Losers, Gravy Train,* more.

STARRETT, JENNIFER (S. Cal.) Support. Onscreen from the '60s. IN: *Run, Angel, Run!;* more.

STARRETT, VALERIE (S. Cal.) Support. Onscreen from the '60s. IN: *Run, Angel, Run!;* more.

STAUNTON, ANN (S. Cal.) Character. Onscreen from the '40s. IN: *Miracle on 34th Street, Hollow Triumph,* more.

STECK, HAZEL (N.Y.) Character. Onscreen in the '70s. IN: *Believe in Me,* more.

STEEL, ANTHONY (Fr.) For 20 years this handsome English actor—first husband of actress Anita Ekberg—was one of the screen's busiest leading men. Dropping out after 1968's *Anzio,* he reappeared in 1975—age 55—in, surprisingly, *The Story of O.* In this softcore porn film, which *Variety* termed "more kinky" than *Emmanuelle,* he played Sir Stephen, the older lover of the girl, Corinne Clery ("O"). Following an orgy of beatings, submissions, and, finally, her branding with the symbolic "O," the girl appears at a party nude with a bird headdress and a chain to show that she has accepted Steel as her lover completely. Certain audiences, recalling Steel in his youth—all brawn, dash, and clean-cut courage—found it hard to accept their hero in such a role, in such surroundings. Onscreen from 1948. IN: *Saraband* (extra), *The Blue Lamp* and *Don't Ever Leave Me* (bits), *The Wooden Horse* (first lead), *The Mudlark, Laughter in Paradise, Another Man's Poison, Ivory Hunter, Outpost in Malaya, The Master of Ballantrae, Hundred Hour Hunt, The Malta Story, The Sea Shall Not Have Them, West of Zanzibar, Storm over the Nile, Out of the Clouds, Checkpoint, The Black Tent, Valerie, Harry Black and the Tiger, A Question of Adultery, Hell Is Empty, Honeymoon,* more.

STEELE, BARBARA (It.) Leading lady from England who lives and works in Rome. Onscreen from 1958. IN: *Bachelor of Hearts, Sap-*

phire, *The Devil's Mask, 8½, The Horrible Dr. Hitchcock, The Castle of Terror, White Voices, The Hours of Love, Young Torless, Terror Creatures from the Grave, The Crimson Affair, Caged Heart,* more.

STEELE, BILL (N.Y.) Character. Onscreen from the '60s. IN: *The Pawnbroker, Hail,* more.

STEELE, BOB (S. Cal.) He would be grateful if someone would spread the word—Bob Steele, the Western star, is very much alive. Well over a decade ago, in Mississippi, a rodeo performer of the same name died and the event was widely reported. There has been considerable confusion ever since. But he was not *the* Bob Steele, the pint-sized dynamo so nimble with fists and lariat in more than 450 films from silent days till now. He was *not* the Bob Steele of "The Three Mesquiteers" and "The Trail Blazers" and the "Billy the Kid" movie series. The *real* Bob Steele, who, entering his 70th year in 1977, is a grizzled, gray, pocket-sized coiled spring of a man, still lives in Hollywood—the San Fernando Valley, actually—where he plies his trade, acting, when jobs come along. A while back, on the set of a Dean Martin Western, *Something Big,* in which he was playing a stagecoach driver, Bob Steele volunteered that there was really no stampede for his services these days. "I guess I'm just not suited to these modern movies," he said. Admittedly holding no high regard for the bold new liberality in films, he added: "I just don't think I'd like working with some of them mod directors and actors. I'm pretty careful what jobs I take even when they're offered, too. Everything is so professional nowadays. In my time, if you could ride and rope and say your lines, you were pretty good. Now, well, I get nervous. I make sure that there are always guys on these movies who I've worked with before, and I trust. I know they'd hire me because they'd know I could do the job. I'd hate to take a job and find out I wasn't good enough any more." It's a surprising statement from a seasoned, long-proven professional like Steele. Besides all his hardriding heroic roles, he's won his acting spurs repeatedly, in many kinds of parts. Such as the villainous Curly in *Of Mice and Men,* and the "heavy" roles in two Bogart films, *The Big Sleep* and *The Enforcer.* To say nothing of his work on TV—as the comic Duffy in the *F Troop* series (62 episodes), and other roles in *Gunsmoke, Cheyenne, Rawhide,* etc. A few oldtime moviegoers may go back to 1926 when he essayed juvenile leads in such Universal offerings as *The Collegians.* Fewer still, perhaps, recall him as a 12-year-old in a series of 1919 shorts titled *The Adventures of Bill and Bob.* (Bill was his twin brother who, at last report, according to friends, "is very ill and Bob is distraught

over it.") So Bob Steele, with this background, almost certainly has more to offer today's movies than either he or casting directors seem to realize. Interestingly, he has not always been "Bob Steele." He acquired this monicker at 21, when he played a character by that name in 1928's *The Mojave Kid.* He's used it professionally ever since, but his real name was, and remains, Robert North Bradbury Jr. (Dad was a well-known director of silents.) Always close, the Bradbury twins were born in Portland, Oregon, spent their early life on their grandmother's ranch in Washtukna, Wash., and went to high school (with John Wayne) in Glendale, Calif. After their dad starred them in the "Bill and Bob" shorts, they appeared in vaudeville in a comedy act that billed them as "The Murdock Brothers." At 21 Bob went into Western movies full-time. In 1937 and '38, he was one of the Top Ten Money-Making Western Stars, as a solo star. He then continued to hold that ranking, as one of Republic's "Three Mesquiteers," throughout the early '40s. As B Westerns were phased out, Bob, in the 1950s, began touring with the Clyde Beatty Circus and guesting at rodeos, finally turning to TV and character roles in high-budget Westerns. After working in 1971's *Something Big,* he did a personal appearance tour on behalf of the film. "I'm doing it because the studio asked me to," he said then. "It makes me nervous but I'm willing to do it if it'll help the picture." Little is on record about Bob Steele's private life, and he prefers it that way. All that is known is that in the autumn of 1935 he eloped to Reno with Alice Petty, a sweetheart from his school days. Any children? Friends answering for him, say no. An avid golfer, he also spends all time possible hunting and fishing at his cabin in California's High Sierras—with pals from "the good old days." Onscreen from 1919. IN: *The Adventures of Bill and Bob, Crooks Can't Win, Spirit of Youth, Captain Careless, Driftin' Sands, Come and Get It, Oklahoma Cyclone, Near the Rainbow's End, Sunrise Trail, South of Santa Fe, Breed of the Border, Mystery Squadron* (serial), *Powdersmoke Range, The Kid Ranger, The Colorado Kid, The Carson City Kid, Billy the Kid's Fighting Pals, Prairie Pioneers, Riders of the Rio Grande, Exposed, Killer McCoy, South of St. Louis, The Lion and the Horse, Column South, Island in the Sky, The Steel Jungle, Rio Bravo, Pork Chop Hill, The Comancheros, Taggart!, Requiem for a Gunfighter, Shenandoah, Major Dundee, Cheyenne Autumn, Hang 'Em High,* more.

STEELE, KAREN (S. Cal.) Leading lady. Onscreen from 1954. IN: *Man Crazy, Marty, Toward the Unknown, Bailout at 43,000, Ride Lonesome, The Rise and Fall of Legs Diamond, 40 Pounds of Trouble, The Happy Ending,* more.

STEELE, LEE (N.Y.) Character. Onscreen in the '70s. IN: *Shaft*, more.

STEELE, LOU (N.Y.) Support. Onscreen from the '50s. IN: *September Affair, Some of My Best Friends Are . . .*, more.

STEELE, MARJORIE (Eng.) Remarried since her divorce from Huntington Hartford, the A&P millionaire who produced her only movie, she lives in London, has children, and is a highly successful painter. Onscreen in 1953 in *Face to Face* (in "The Bride Comes to Yellow Sky" half of this two-part movie).

STEELE, PIPPA (Eng.) Leading lady. Onscreen from the '60s. IN: *Cop-Out, The Vampire Lovers*, more.

STEELE, TOMMY (Eng.) Singer-actor. Onscreen from 1956. IN: *Kill Me Tomorrow, Rock Around the World, The Tommy Steele Story, Missile Monsters, The Ghost of Zorro, It's All Happening, The Dream Maker, The Happiest Millionaire, Half a Sixpence, Finian's Rainbow, Where's Jack?*, more.

STEERE, CLIFTON (N.Y.) Character. Onscreen from the '60s. IN: *Rosemary's Baby, The Producers, Some of My Best Friends Are . . .*, more.

STEFFAN, GEARY (S. Cal.) Skater-actor, first husband of actress Jane Powell, who is now a Los Angeles business man. Onscreen in 1943 in *Wintertime*.

STEIGER, ROD (S. Cal.) Costar. Nominated for Best Supporting Actor Oscar in *On the Waterfront*. Nominated for Best Actor Oscar in *The Pawnbroker*. Won Best Actor Oscar in *In the Heat of the Night*. Onscreen from 1951. IN: *Teresa, The Big Knife, Oklahoma!, The Court-Martial of Billy Mitchell, The Harder They Fall, Run of the Arrow, Across the Bridge, Al Capone, The Mark, Convicts 4, The Loved One, Doctor Zhivago, No Way to Treat a Lady, The Sergeant, The Illustrated Man, Waterloo, Three Into Two Won't Go; Happy Birthday, Wanda June; Duck, You Sucker; Hennessy, W. C. Fields and Me*, more.

STEINBERG, DAVID (S. Cal.) Comedian-actor. Onscreen from the '60s. IN: *The Lost Man, Fearless Frank*, more.

STEN, ANNA (S. Cal.) Married since '32 to producer Eugene Frenke, the onetime Goldwyn star lives in Beverly Hills, paints professionally, has not been in a movie in many years. But, still a handsome woman at whatever her age (sources differ on her birth year: 1907, 1908, 1910), the Russian-born beauty looks fit to face the cameras on a moment's notice, and possibly might not even need makeup to do so. Onscreen in America (after European movies beginning in 1928) from 1934. IN: *Nana, We Live Again, The Wedding Night, Two Who Dared, Woman Alone, The Man I Married, So Ends Our Night, Chetniks, Three Russian Girls, Let's Live a Little* (produced by Frenke), *Soldier of Fortune, Runaway Daughters; Heaven Knows, Mr. Allison*; more.

STEPANEK, KAREL (Eng.) Character. Onscreen in Vienna from 1921. Onscreen in England and internationally from 1942. IN: *Our Film* (debut), *At Dawn We Die, The Captive Heart, The Fallen Idol, Walk East on Beacon, Affair in Trinidad, Never Let Me Go, Anastasia, Sink the Bismarck!, I Aim at the Stars, Operation Crossbow, The Frozen Dead, The Heroes of Telemark, Licensed to Kill*, more.

STEPHEN, SUSAN (Eng.) Leading lady; lately inactive in movies. Onscreen from 1951. IN: *His Excellency, Paratrooper, The Barretts of Wimpole Street, As Long As They're Happy, Value for Money, It's Never Too Late, Carry On Nurse, The Court Martial of Major Keller*, more.

STEPHENS, ANN (Eng.) Leading lady who began as a juvenile; lately inactive in movies. Onscreen from 1942. IN: *The Young Mr. Pitt* (debut, age 11), *In Which We Serve, Fanny by Gaslight, Dear Octopus, They Were Sisters, No Room at the Inn, Eye Witness, The Franchise Affair, Doublecross, Intent to Kill*, more.

STEPHENS, HELEN (KAY) (S. Cal.) Leading lady. Sister of Ann Stephens. Now lives and works—mainly in TV commercials—in Hollywood. Onscreen in 1946 in *They Were Sisters*.

STEPHENS, LARAINE (S. Cal.) Leading lady. Onscreen from 1965. IN: *None But the Brave* (debut), *Hellfighters*, more.

STEPHENS, MARVIN (Eng.) Former juvenile (b. 1949); lately inactive in movies. Onscreen from 1955. IN: *The Divided Heart, Another Time Another Place, Harry Black and the Tiger, Count Your Blessings, A Touch of Larceny, Village of the Damned, The Battle of the Villa Fiorita*, more.

STEPHENS, RACHEL (S. Cal.) Former leading lady; lately inactive in movies. Onscreen from 1956. IN: *Bigger Than Life; Oh Men! Oh Women!; The True Story of Jesse James, Desk Set*, more.

STEPHENS, ROBERT (Eng.) Leading man. Former husband of Oscar-winner Maggie Smith. Onscreen from 1960. IN: *Circle of De-*

ception, A Taste of Honey, Lisa, Cleopatra, Morgan!, Romeo and Juliet, The Prime of Miss Jean Brodie (in which Maggie Smith won her Best Actress Oscar), *The Private Life of Sherlock Holmes, Luther*, more.

STEPHENS, ROY (Eng.) Support. Onscreen from the '60s. IN: *Dr. Strangelove*, more.

STEPHENS, SHEILA (N.Y.) The name Sheila MacRae—former wife of Gordon—used in movies before becoming a TV and nightclub star. Onscreen in 1950. IN: *Caged, Backfire, Pretty Baby*.

STEPHENS, SOCORRO (N.Y.) Black juvenile actress. Onscreen in 1974. IN: *Claudine* (as Diahann Carroll's youngest daughter).

STEPIN FETCHIT (Ill.) (Listed under Fetchit.)

STERKE, JEANETTE (Eng.) Leading lady; inactive in movies in recent years. Onscreen from 1955. IN: *The Prisoner, The Final Column, Lust for Life*, more.

STERLING, DICK (S. Cal.) Support. Onscreen in the '70s. IN: *How Do I Love Thee*, more.

STERLING, JAN (Eng.) Costar. Nominated for Best Supporting Actress Oscar in *The High and the Mighty*. A close friendship with actor-director Sam Wanamaker has prompted her living in London for many years, but she returns home to America often for professional engagements. In '75 she starred in stock in *Hot L Baltimore*, and was previously seen onstage in eastern playhouses in *Come Back Little Sheba* and *Summer Brave*. In '74 in Hollywood, she did a guest stint in a *Kung Fu* episode. Though doubting she will ever have the chance to live there again, she says, "I adored Hollywood because I'd always wanted to be a movie star." And a movie star she was in more than 30 pictures. The actress is in her 50s (b. 1923), her hair is ash-blonde (rather than its former taffy shade), and she is plumper than in her starring days on the screen. Divorced from actor Jack Merivale, she was then married to actor Paul Douglas, who died in '59. By Douglas, she has a son, Adam (b. 1955), now launching his own acting career. In England she rarely acts. Instead, because as she has said, "I feel needed and useful," she works fulltime—without pay —for the Royal Voluntary Service. "In London," she says, "I'm just Mrs. Douglas, working at St. Pancras Hospital in my mulberry and green uniform and pork-pie hat, or at Brixton Prison. Sometimes at the prison, I feel as though I'm back in Hollywood making *Caged* or *Women's Prison* and that the girls and I will

take off our uniforms and go home. I do, but they can't." Onscreen from 1948. IN: *Johnny Belinda, Union Station, Mystery Street, The Mating Season, Ace in the Hole, The Vanquished, The Human Jungle, Female on the Beach, Man with a Gun, The Harder They Fall, Slaughter on 10th Avenue, The Female Animal, Love in a Goldfish Bowl, The Incident, The Minx*, more.

STERLING, PHIL (S. Cal.) Support. Onscreen from the '60s. IN: *Me, Natalie*; more.

STERLING, ROBERT (S. Cal.) The former leading man is a computer expert now in Los Angeles and, in his 50s (b. 1917), remains as handsome as in his starring days. Married first to Ann Sothern, he has been married for many years to Anne Jeffreys. Onscreen from 1938. IN: *Blondie Meets the Boss, Only Angels Have Wings, The Get-Away, Ringside Maisie* (with Ann Sothern), *Two Faced Woman, Johnny Eager, Dr. Kildare's Victory, This Time for Keeps, Somewhere I'll Find You, The Secret Heart, Roughshod, The Sundowners, Show Boat, Voyage to the Bottom of the Sea, Return to Peyton Place, A Global Affair*, more. (See Anne Jeffreys.)

STERLING, TISHA (S. Cal.) Leading lady. Daughter of Robert Sterling and Ann Sothern. Onscreen from 1968. IN: *The Name of the Game Is Kill, Coogan's Bluff, Journey to Shiloh, The Sandpit Generals, Crazy Mama* (with Ann Sothern), more.

STERN, ISAAC (N.Y.) The violin virtuoso lives in New York and in 1976 declared himself a year-long vacation from the concert stage, the first such sabbatical he has taken since making his debut in 1935 at 15. Onscreen from 1953. IN: *Tonight We Sing, A Journey to Jerusalem*, more. (He has also supplied the background violin solos "played" by many stars in movies.)

STERN, TOM (S. Cal.) Leading man. Formerly married to actress Samantha Eggar. Onscreen from the '60s. IN: *The Hallelujah Trail, Angels from Hell, Hell's Angels '69, The Devil's Brigade, Clay Pigeon*, more.

STERN, WES (S. Cal.) Support. Onscreen from 1969. IN: *The First Time, Three in the Cellar*, more.

STERNE, MORGAN (N.Y.) Support. Onscreen from 1960. IN: *Nine Miles to Noon, No Exit*, more.

STERNHAGEN, FRANCES (N.Y.) Character. Onscreen from 1967. IN: *Up the Down Staircase, The Tiger Makes Out*, more.

STEVEN, GARY (N.Y.) Juvenile. Onscreen in the '70s. IN: *The French Connection, Lovers and Other Strangers*, more.

STEVENS, ALEX (S. Cal.) Character. Onscreen from the '60s. IN: *Lady in Cement, The Projectionist*, more.

STEVENS, CONNIE (S. Cal.) Costar/singer. Formerly married to actor James Stacy and to singer Eddie Fisher by whom she has two daughters. Onscreen from 1957. IN: *Rock-a-Bye Baby, Dragstrip Riot, The Party Crashers, Parrish, Susan Slade, Palm Springs Weekend, Two on a Guillotine, Never Too Late, Way Way Out, Race With Death*, more.

STEVENS, CRAIG (S. Cal.) Costar. Long married to Alexis Smith. Onscreen from 1941. IN: *Memories of Melody Lane* (short; played Stephen Foster), *Dive Bomber* (supporting role in this movie in which Alexis Smith was the femme lead), *Steel Against the Sky* (they costarred), *Spy Ship, Secret Enemies, The Doughgirls, God Is My Co-Pilot, That Way with Women, Night Unto Day, Where the Sidewalk Ends, Drums in the Deep South, Phone Call from a Stranger, The French Line, Flashpoint, Trouble Zone, Gunn* (based on his successful TV series *Peter Gunn*), more. (See Alexis Smith.)

STEVENS, DODIE (S. Cal.) Ingenue singer-actress; now married and retired from movies. Onscreen from 1960. IN: *Hound-Dog Man, Convicts 4*, more.

STEVENS, FRAN (N.Y.) Character. Onscreen in the '70s. *Silent Night, Bloody Night; The Gang That Couldn't Shoot Straight*, more.

STEVENS, GEOFFREY (S. Cal.) Support. Onscreen from the '60s. IN: *Psych-Out*, more.

STEVENS, JULIE (Eng.) Support. Onscreen from 1940. IN: *Honeymoon Deferred, Tear Gas Squad, Carry On Cleo*, more.

STEVENS, K.T. (S. Cal.) In her 50s (b. 1919) and still blonde and slim, the former leading lady—retaining her striking, chiseled features—plays character roles in movies and does many TV commercials. Single since her long-ago divorce from actor Hugh Marlowe, by whom she has two grown children, she has often been seen lately in the company of millionaire Alfred Gwynne Vanderbilt—a beau from her teens. Onscreen from 1934. IN: *Peck's Bad Boy* (ingenue), *Kitty Foyle* (directed by her father, Sam Wood), *The Great Man's Lady, Nine Girls, Address Unknown, Harriet Craig, Vice Squad, Missile to the Moon*, more. including 1974's *Pets*. (See Hugh Marlowe.)

STEVENS, KAYE (S. Cal.) Singer-actress. Onscreen from 1964. IN: *The New Interns*, more.

STEVENS, LENORE (S. Cal.) Support. Onscreen in the '70s. IN: *Scandalous John*, more.

STEVENS, MARK (S. Cal.) In his 60s now (b. 1915), with a touch of silver in his hair, and after more than a decade of owning and operating a posh restaurant in Majorca, the actor has returned to Hollywood to resume his career—starting with a *Police Story* episode on TV. He is said to be a bit nonplussed to find that during his absence a porn star has come to the fore named Marc Stevens. But he isn't even considering returning to his first screen name, Stephen Richards. Onscreen as Stephen Richards from 1941. IN: *Two Faced Woman, Passage to Marseille, The Doughgirls, Objective Burma, Pride of the Marines*, more. Onscreen as Mark Stevens from 1945. IN: *Within These Walls, From This Day Forward, The Dark Corner, I Wonder Who's Kissing Her Now, The Street With No Name, The Snake Pit; Oh, You Beautiful Doll; Target Unknown, Little Egypt, Jack Slade, Torpedo Valley, Cry Vengeance* and *Timetable* (both of which he directed), *September Storm, Fate Is the Hunter, Escape from Hell Island*, more.

STEVENS, NAOMI (S. Cal.) Character. Onscreen from 1950. IN: *Caged, The Black Orchid, The Apartment, Convicts 4, Valley of the Dolls; Buona Sera, Mrs. Campbell; Superdad*, more.

STEVENS, ONSLOW (S. Cal.) First a leading man and later one of Hollywood's busiest, best character actors, he is now in his '70s (b. 1902), has been inactive in movies for more than a decade, and lives in nearby Eagle Rock. He is the son of the late character actor Houseley Stevenson (Stevenson being his real name), has been several times married and divorced, and has a businessman son. Onscreen from 1932. IN: *Radio Patrol* (serial), *Once in a Lifetime, Only Yesterday, Secret of the Blue Room, Counsellor-At-Law, Yellow Dust, The Vanishing Shadow* (serial), *This Side of Heaven, Affairs of a Gentleman, The Three Musketeers, Under Two Flags, Straight from the Shoulder, Easy Money, There Goes the Groom, When Tomorrow Comes, The Man Who Wouldn't Talk, Appointment in Berlin, O.S.S., Night Has a Thousand Eyes, Walk a Crooked Mile, Sirocco, A Lion Is in the Streets, Them, Tribute to a Bad Man, Lonelyhearts, All the Fine Young Cannibals, Geronimo's Revenge*, more.

STEVENS, OREN (S. Cal.) Support. Onscreen from the '60s. IN: *Downhill Racer*, more.

447

STEVENS, PAUL (S. Cal.) Support. Onscreen from 1960. IN: *Exodus, The Mark, Marlowe, Patton,* more.

STEVENS, RISE (N.Y.) The Metropolitan Opera mezzo-soprano gave up her singing career in '64, then for two seasons was co-general manager of the Metropolitan Opera National Company that toured the country and gave young singers needed experience. She was later a voice coach and tutor. In '75, aged 62, still a slender, enthusiastic woman with flashing, laughing eyes, she was named president of New York City's Mannes College of Music—a private conservatory with programs of study for singers, conductors, and composers. She has been married since '38 to Walter Surovy, then a Hungarian actor, later her manager, and now a real estate man. They live in a beautiful East Side apartment within walking distance of the college she now heads, located on East 74th Street. Their son, Nicholas, is an actor with the City Center Acting Company. The actress was injured in '74 when a car struck her at an intersection near her home. Though now sufficiently recovered to assume her new duties, she filed a $350,000 damage suit, early in '75, against the driver of the car. According to court papers, she sustained injuries to her "head, limbs and body; a severe shock to her nervous system; and internal injuries." Onscreen from 1941. IN: *The Chocolate Soldier* (costarring with Nelson Eddy at a time when MGM was "testing" him with a leading lady other than Jeanette MacDonald), *Going My Way, Carnegie Hall.*

STEVENS, RONNIE (Eng.) Comic support. Onscreen from the '50s. IN: *An Alligator Named Daisy; I'm All Right, Jack; A Pair of Briefs, A Home of Your Own; Goodbye, Mr. Chips; Some Girls Do,* more.

STEVENS, STELLA (S. Cal.) Costar. Onscreen from 1959. IN: *Say One for Me, Li'l Abner, Too Late Blues, The Nutty Professor, The Courtship of Eddie's Father, Synanon, The Silencers; Where Angels Go, Trouble Follows; How to Save a Marriage—And Ruin Your Life; Sol Madrid, The Ballad of Cable Hogue, Stand Up and Be Counted, The Poseidon Adventure, Slaughter, Cleopatra Jones and the Casino of Gold, Las Vegas Lady,* more.

STEVENS, WARREN (S. Cal.) One of Hollywood's busiest supporting actors, after a long leading-man career, he is, in his 50s (b. 1919), married to an English girl named Barbara, and by her has a young son, Adam (b. 1973). Also, by a previous marriage, he has a grown son who is a writer. Onscreen from 1951. IN: *The Frogmen, Mr. Belvedere Rings the Bell, Red Skies of Montana, Deadline U.S.A., Smoke Jumpers;*

Wait Till the Sun Shines, Nellie; The Barefoot Contessa, Women's Prison, Forbidden Planet, No Name on the Bullet, 40 Pounds of Trouble, Madame X, An American Dream, The Sweet Ride, Madigan, more.

STEVENSON, HOUSELEY, JR. (S. Cal.) Character. Brother of Onslow Stevens, son of Houseley Sr. Lately inactive in movies. Onscreen from the '50s. IN: *The Atomic City, The War of the Worlds, The Caddy,* more.

STEVENSON, MARGOT (N.Y.) Character; former leading lady. Onscreen from 1939. IN: *Smashing the Money Ring, Invisible Stripes, Castle on the Hudson, Calling Philo Vance, Flight Angels, Valley of the Dolls, The Brotherhood; Rabbit, Run;* more.

STEVENSON, McLEAN (S. Cal.) TV personality-supporting actor. Onscreen in the '70s. IN: *The Christian Licorice Store; Win, Place or Steal;* more.

STEVENSON, VENETIA (S. Cal.) Former leading lady. Daughter of director Robert Stevenson and actress Anna Lee. Twice divorced— from actor Russ Tamblyn and from singer Don Everly (of The Everly Brothers) by whom she has two daughters—she lives in Los Angeles and is retired from movies. Onscreen from 1958. IN: *Darby's Rangers, Island of Lost Women, Day of the Outlaw, The Big Night, Seven Ways to Sundown, Jet Over the Atlantic, Studs Lonigan,* more, including 1963's *Horror Hotel,* her most recent to date.

STEWART, ALEXANDRA (Eng.) Leading lady. Onscreen from 1960. IN: *Exodus, The Season of Love, Naked Autumn, The Fire Within, Sweet and Sour, And So to Bed, Only When I Larf, Waiting for Caroline, The Man Who Had Power Over Women, Zeppelin, Day for Night, Because of the Cats,* more.

STEWART, BARRY (Eng.) Support. Onscreen from the '60s. IN: *The Luck of Ginger Coffey,* more.

STEWART, CHARLOTTE (S. Cal.) Support. Onscreen in the '70s. IN: *The Cheyenne Social Club,* more.

STEWART, ELAINE (S. Cal.) Still a stunning redhead in her 40s (b. 1929), MGM's young star of the 1950s has lately been the regular "blackjack dealer" on the CBS-TV game show *Gambit.* Producer of the program is her husband (since '63), Merrill Heatter. "My partner, Bob Quigley, and I wanted some special glamour for this property," he says, "so the two of us sat down and told Elaine she had to do this for us.'' The actress had then been retired for a decade, enjoying their beautiful home in Beverly Hills and taking care of their two youngsters, Stewart and Gabrielle—the little girl named for her father's uncle, news commentator Gabriel Heatter. During her MGM years the actress was publicized as "the most beautiful girl in pictures." But in '59, a freak incident occurred that threatened to destroy her beauty. Visiting in the home of a friend, she was attacked and badly bitten on the jaw by the neighbor's German Shepherd. Miraculously, her face healed without plastic surgery, showing no trace now of the scars incurred that evening. Onscreen from 1951. IN: *Sailor Beware, Jeopardy, The Bad and the Beautiful, Rogue's March, You for Me, Everything I Have Is Yours, Young Bess, Code 2, Take the High Ground, Brigadoon, The Adventures of Hajii Baba, The Tattered Dress, Night Passage, The Rise and Fall of Legs Diamond, Most Dangerous Man Alive*, more, including 1963's *The Seven Revenges*, her most recent to date.

STEWART, JAMES (S. Cal.) Star. Won Best Actor Oscar in *The Philadelphia Story*. Nominated in the same category in *Mr. Smith Goes to Washington, It's A Wonderful Life, Harvey*, and *Anatomy of a Murder*. Onscreen from 1935. IN: *The Murder Men, Rose Marie, Wife vs. Secretary, Born to Dance, Navy Blue and Gold, Shopworn Angel, Of Human Hearts, You Can't Take It With You, Vivacious Lady, Made for Each Other, Destry Rides Again, The Mortal Storm, Come Live with Me, Ziegfeld Girl, Pot O' Gold, Call Northside 777, Rope, The Stratton Story, Winchester 73, Broken Arrow, No Highway in the Sky, The Greatest Show on Earth, Carbine Williams, Bend of the River, The Glenn Miller Story, Strategic Air Command, The Man Who Knew Too Much, The Spirit of St. Louis, Vertigo; Bell, Book and Candle; The Man Who Shot Liberty Valance, How the West Was Won, Cheyenne Autumn, Shenandoah, The Flight of the Phoenix, Firecreek, The Cheyenne Social Club, The Shootist*, more.

STEWART, JOHNNY (N.Y.) Yesterday's juvenile now does TV commercials, works in TV soap operas (*From These Roots*), has appeared on Broadway, and starred in touring productions of plays such as *Generation*. Onscreen from 1952. IN: *Boots Malone* (title role), more.

STEWART, KAY (S. Cal.) The pretty and practical teenage sister of "Henry Aldrich" (both Jackie Cooper and Jimmy Lydon) more than three decades ago, she still acts in an occasional movie but appears with great regularity in TV commercials. Onscreen from 1939. IN: *What A Life, Those Were the Days, Life With Henry,*

The Private War of Major Benson, The Square Jungle, more.

STEWART, LARRY (S. Cal.) Support. Onscreen from 1951. IN: *A Yank in Korea*, more, including, in this decade, *The Deserter*.

STEWART, LUCILLE LEE (S. Cal.) The actress-sister of silent star Anita Stewart, she lives in Beverly Hills, and is long married and retired. Onscreen from the teens. IN: *Our Mrs. McChesney, Bad Company*, more.

STEWART, MARIANNE (S. Cal.) Leading lady; inactive in movies for several years. Onscreen from 1950. IN: *Right Cross, Timetable, The Big Fisherman, The Facts of Life*, more.

STEWART, MARTHA (S. Cal.) The singer-actress, inactive in movies for more than two decades, lives in Los Angeles and still sings in clubs. For two years she was the wife (the only wife) of comedian Joe E. Lewis, until she divorced him in 1948. Shortly before his death in '71, according to an oft-told Hollywood story, she met him in a nightclub and said hello—and, after she had gone by, Lewis turned to a friend at the bar and said: "Who was that beautiful girl?" But there remain many movie fans of hers who do not have to be told. Onscreen from 1946. IN: *Doll Face, I Wonder Who's Kissing Her Now, Daisy Kenyon, Are You With It?, In a Lonely Place, Aaron Slick from Punkin Crick*, more.

STEWART, MEL (S. Cal.) Black character. Onscreen from the '60s. IN: *Odds Against Tomorrow, The Hustler, Shadows, Trick Baby, Summer Kill, Petulia, The Landlord, Newman, Halls of Anger, Nothing But a Man, The Conversation*, more.

STEWART, NICHOLAS (Eng.) Juvenile. Onscreen in the '70s. IN: *The Looking Glass War*, more.

STEWART, PATRICK (Eng.) Support. Onscreen in the '70s. IN: *Hedda*, more.

STEWART, PAUL (S. Cal.) This venerable character actor (b. 1908) suffered a heart attack in 1974 while on location in New Mexico in *Bite the Bullet*, but has since resumed his career at full throttle. He has done much TV (*Streets of San Francisco, Cannon*, etc.), as well as such movies as *The Day of the Locust* and *Live a Little, Steal a Lot*. Onscreen from 1941. IN: *Citizen Kane, Johnny Eager, Mr. Lucky, The Window, Champion, Easy Living, 12 O'Clock High; Walk Softly, Stranger; Deadline U.S.A., The Bad and the Beautiful, Carbine Williams, The Juggler, The Cobweb, Kiss Me Deadly,*

King Creole, A Child Is Waiting, The Greatest Story Ever Told, In Cold Blood, How to Commit Marriage, Suppose They Gave a War and Nobody Came?, Jigsaw, more.

STEWART, PAULA (S. Cal.) Singer-actress. Former wife of composer Burt Bacharach and comedian Jack Carter. Onscreen in the '70s. IN: Suppose They Gave a War and Nobody Came?, more.

STEWART, PEGGY (S. Cal.) For millions of adolescent boys in the years between '44 and '52—nearly all of whom would have died rather than admit it—the first love of their lives was Peggy Stewart, beautiful brunette heroine in more than 50 Allan "Rocky" Lane, Gene Autry, "Wild Bill" Elliott and Sunset Carson Westerns. When she quit movies she worked for a while as an associate casting director for NBC-TV in Hollywood. Divorced from cowboy star Don "Red" Barry, she became, in '53, the wife of actor Buck Young. They have a daughter, Abigail, in college, and a younger son, Greg, who does commercials and acted in the movie Pickup on Highway 101 with both his parents, playing their son. A character actress now, Peggy Stewart is busy in all media. Besides doing many TV commercials, she has lately been seen in a little theater production of John Brown's Body, in such TV series as Emergency and Mod Squad, the TV-movie The Cage, and theatrical films such as The Stranger and Terror in the Wax Museum. Of the latter, she says, "I played a Cockney charwoman, my first try at a dialect. The entire cast was British otherwise—Ray Milland, Louis Hayward, Elsa Lanchester—and no one knew I wasn't Cockney. I have to say that it was fun and satisfying." When not before the cameras, the actress says, "I have been a substitute teacher and fulltime attendee at a new Hollywood workshop, The Patio Playhouse." Reviewing her long career, which began at 14, she says, "I started in this business as a child actress, moved to ingenue [Girls in Chains, Back Street, etc.], to leading lady [The Vampire's Ghost], to older leading lady, and into character woman. I adore this business, and it has been extremely generous and rewarding to me. It has been what I can only call a 'rich life'!" A year or two ago, she flew to Tennessee to be an honored guest at the annually held Western Film Festival, attended by hundreds of middle-aging men who had adored her in their youth. When she stood before them, a slender, smiling woman in her early 50s, they cheered her to the rafters while she fought back happy tears. It mattered little to them that her dark hair is silvering now—their heroine, Peggy Stewart, had been returned to them for a while, and she was still beautiful.

Onscreen from 1937. IN: Wells Fargo, Little Tough Guy, That Certain Age, All This and Heaven Too, Stagecoach to Monterey, Cheyenne Wildcat, Tucson Raiders, Marshal of Laredo, Red River Renegades, California Gold Rush, Sheriff of Redwood Valley, The Phantom Rider (serial), Son of Zorro (serial), Stagecoach to Denver, Rustlers of Devil's Canyon, Tex Granger (serial), Dead Man's Gold; Ride, Ryder, Ride!; Cody of the Pony Express (serial), Kansas Territory, When the Clock Strikes, The Way West, more.

STEWART, ROBIN. (Eng.) Supporting actor. Onscreen in the '70s. IN: Cromwell, Horror House; Digby, the Biggest Dog in the World; more.

STEWART, SAM (S. Cal.) Character. Onscreen from the '60s. IN: The Taming, The Projectionist, more.

STEWART, SOPHIE (Eng.) Character; former leading lady (b. 1908). Onscreen from 1935. IN: Maria Marten, Things to Come, As You Like It, The Man Who Could Work Miracles, Under the Red Robe, Nurse Edith Cavell; My Son, My Son!; The Inheritance, Battle Hell, more.

STEWART, TOM (S. Cal.) Support. Onscreen from the '60s. IN: Marooned, more.

STEWART, YVONNE (S. Cal.) Support. Onscreen in the '70s. IN: Satan's Sadists, more.

STICH, PATRICIA (S. Cal.) Leading lady. Onscreen in the '70s. IN: Halls of Anger, more.

STICKNEY, DOROTHY (N.Y.) Character; former leading lady (b. 1900). Onscreen from 1931. IN: Working Girls, Wayward, Murder at the Vanities, The Little Minister, The Moon's Our Home, And So They Were Married, I Met My Love Again, What a Life, The Uninvited, Miss Tatlock's Millions, The Catered Affair, The Remarkable Mr. Pennypacker, I Never Sang for My Father, more.

STIPO, CARMINE (N.Y.) Support. Onscreen from the '60s. IN: What's So Bad About Feeling Good?, more.

STILLER, JERRY (N.Y.) Support. Half of the comedy team of Stiller & Meara (Anne Meara being his wife). Onscreen in the '70s. IN: The Taking of Pelham One Two Three, Airport 1975, The Ritz, more.

STIRLING, HELEN (Eng.) Support. Onscreen from the '60s. IN: Darling, more.

STIRLING, LINDA (S. Cal.) Panther-sleek, tall (5'7"), and sexy, Linda Stirling was to the talkies what Pearl White was to silents: Queen of the Serials. At Republic, besides doing leads in 15 B's, she headlined in six serials between '44 and '47: *Zorro's Black Whip, Manhunt of Mystery Island, The Purple Monster Strikes,* etc. In the late '50s, after a second career in television, she gave it all up to go to college. She got her B.A.—Phi Beta Kappa, too—and her Master's. So these days, when she wheels her car out of the family garage in North Hollywood, she heads, not for a movie studio, but for school— Glendale College. There, as an associate professor, she teaches—as she has for a decade— English and drama, including Shakespeare. On almost as many evenings she also attends school, UCLA, as a student working toward her Ph.D. Still a most attractive brunette, in her mid-50s, Linda says of her latest career, "Even though I've been teaching for years, there are still moments when I think I must be playing a 'teacher' part in a movie. I love teaching! It is different from acting in just about every way, yet there are similarities. In college the students pay and expect to get their money's worth. It's like being in the theater. You've got to give your best whether you feel like it or not and 'sell the part' even if the students don't think the play is very good—that is, convince them that Shakespeare really is terrific even if they do find him difficult to read. I'm having so much fun I seldom miss acting except once in a great while in a nostalgic moment." Outside the academic world, she coaches young professional actors in her spare time and has on occasion written and published magazine articles about her experiences in making serials. In one, published in *Movie Digest,* she confessed that, years ago, when moving to a new house, she made a bonfire of hundreds of serial stills and posters, never dreaming there would one day be a nostalgia craze. She has been married for over three decades to top Western screenwriter Sloan Nibley, who wrote, among scores of movies, Cooper's *Springfield Rifle.* They have two sons in their 20s, Chris, a Hollywood cameraman, and Tim, a fireman after studying Fire Science in college. Just as individual fans have their memories of her serials, so has Linda Stirling, who said recently, "I remember the hazards, the stunts, the runaway horses, the near-drownings, and the fun. But, most of all, I remember the bruises!" Onscreen from 1943. IN: *The Powers Girl* (debut), *San Antonio Kid, Vigilantes of Dodge City, The Tiger Woman* (her first serial, in 1944), *The Cherokee Flash, Santa Fe Saddlemates, The Topeka Terror, D-Day on Mars, The Crimson Ghost* (serial), *The Madonna's Secret, The Mysterious Mr. Valentine, Rio Grande Raiders, The Pretender,* more, including 1947's *Jesse James Rides Again* (her last serial and last appearance in movies).

STIRLING, PAMELA (Eng.) Leading lady; lately inactive in movies. Onscreen from 1944. IN: *Candlelight in Algeria, Madness of the Heart, To Paris With Love, The Divided Heart, Elephant Gun,* more.

STOCK, NIGEL (Eng.) Character. Onscreen from 1934. IN: *Lancashire Luck, Brighton Rock, It Always Rains on Sunday, Young Scarface, Malta Story, The Night My Number Came Up, Victim, Damn the Defiant!, Nothing But the Best, The Night of the Generals, The Lion in Winter, Week-End at Zoydcode, Cromwell,* more.

STOCKWELL, DEAN (S. Cal.) Leading man; former child star. Brother of Guy, son of Harry Stockwell and musical comedy star Betty Veronica, and former husband of actress Millie Perkins. He continues to costar in numerous movies such as the recent *The Pacific Connection* and appears often on TV—in *Streets of San Francisco, Police Story, Columbo,* etc. And, proof that time passes, he turned 40 on March 5, 1975. Onscreen from 1945. IN: *Anchors Aweigh, The Green Years, Home Sweet Homicide, The Romance of Rosy Ridge, Song of the Thin Man, Gentleman's Agreement, The Boy With Green Hair, Down to the Sea in Ships, The Secret Garden, Stars in My Crown, The Happy Years, Kim, Gun for a Coward, The Careless Years, Compulsion, Sons and Lovers, Long Day's Journey Into Night, Psych-Out, Dunwich Horrors; Win, Place or Steal;* more.

STOCKWELL, GUY (S. Cal.) Leading man. Older brother (by two years) of Dean Stockwell. He has been married—first marriage— since May 1975 to the former Olga Stulbaum, a nonprofessional. Onscreen from 1960. IN: *The Three Swords of Zorro, The War Lord, Blindfold, . . . And Now Miguel, Beau Geste, The Plainsman, Tobruk, Banning, In Enemy Country, The King's Pirate, King Gun, It's Alive, Airport 1975,* more.

STOCKWELL, HARRY (N.Y.) The father of the above two actors, he lives in Manhattan in the heart of the theater district, as befits an actor who has sung leading roles in such Broadway shows as *Oklahoma* and *As Thousands Cheer.* After his marriage to Betty Veronica, he was married to stage comedienne Nina Olivette —she had played the lead opposite Bert Lahr in *Hold Everything*—who died in 1971. Stockwell, in his 60s, remains professionally active. Onscreen from 1935. IN: *Broadway Melody of 1936, Snow White and the Seven Dwarfs* (the singing voice of Prince Charming), more.

STOCKWELL, JEREMY (N.Y.) Leading man. Onscreen in the '70s. IN: *Dinah East,* more.

STOKOWSKI, LEOPOLD (N.Y.) Symphonic conductor, in his 90s now, and still plying his trade. Onscreen from 1937. IN: *One Hundred Men and a Girl, Fantasia* (for which he received a special Oscar), *Carnegie Hall.*

STOLER, SHIRLEY (N.Y.) Hefty character lead. Onscreen from 1969. IN: *The Honeymoon Killers, Seven Beauties.*

STOLLERY, DAVID (S. Cal.) Former juvenile. Lately inactive in movies. Onscreen from 1951. IN: *Darling, How Could You!; Jack and the Beanstalk, Her Twelve Men, Storm Fear,* more.

STONE, CAROL (N.Y.) Former leading lady (b. 1915). Inactive both onstage and in movies for a number of years. Daughter of Fred Stone, sister of Paula and the late Dorothy. Onscreen from 1935. IN: *Freckles,* more.

STONE, CHRISTOPHER (S. Cal.) Leading man. Onscreen in the '70s. IN: *The Grasshopper,* more.

STONE, DANNY (S. Cal.) Support. Onscreen from the '60s. IN: *The Desperate Ones,* more.

STONE, EZRA (S. Cal.) Radio's famous "Henry Aldrich" who, in 1977, turns 60, and is now a portly character actor. He also, in 1975, produced a 60-minute documentary, *The Forty Million,* dealing with immigrants to the United States since the Revolution, which won a CINE Gold Eagle when screened in competition in Washington. Onscreen from 1940. IN: *Those Were the Days, This Is the Army,* more.

STONE, HAROLD J. (S. Cal.) Character. Onscreen from 1956. IN: *The Harder They Fall, Somebody Up There Likes Me, The Wrong Man, The Garment Jungle, These Thousand Hills, Spartacus, The Chapman Report, The Greatest Story Ever Told, The Big Mouth, The St. Valentine's Day Massacre, The McCullochs, Mitchell,* more.

STONE, JEFFREY (S. Cal.) Leading man. Once married to actress Corinne Calvet. Lately inactive in movies. Onscreen from the '50s. IN: *The Girl in the Kremlin, The Big Beat, The Thing That Couldn't Die,* more. (See Corinne Calvet.)

STONE, JOHN (Eng.) Character. Onscreen from 1949. IN: *The Weaker Sex, In the Devil's Garden,* more.

STONE, LEONARD (S. Cal.) Character. Onscreen from the '60s. IN: *The Big Mouth, Zigzag, Getting Straight, I Love My Wife, Willie Wonka and the Chocolate Factory,* more.

STONE, MARIANNE (Eng.) Character. Onscreen from the '40s. IN: *The Clouded Yellow, Tiger Bay, Lolita, Scrooge, Who Slew Auntie Roo?, In the Devil's Garden, Craze, Confessions of a Window Cleaner,* more.

STONE, MILBURN (N.M.) This veteran character actor, who is now in his 70s (b. 1904), didn't retire when TV's *Gunsmoke* did. Instead, he and wife Jane moved to Santa Fe, built a magnificent ranch house, and started a brand-new career—raising prize livestock. He took with him the Emmy award won in '68 for playing "Doc Adams" so splendidly and so long (20 seasons). Onscreen from 1936. IN: *The Milky Way, The Princess Comes Across, China Clipper, A Doctor's Diary, Federal Bullets, Mr. Boggs Steps Out, Crime School, Young Mr. Lincoln; Charlie McCarthy, Detective; Give Us Wings, Reap the Wild Wind, Sherlock Holmes Faces Death, Corvette K-225, The Mad Ghoul, Gung Ho!, Phantom Lady, Jungle Woman, The Master Key* (serial), *I'll Remember April, The Spider Woman Strikes Back, Calamity Jane and Sam Bass, No Man of Her Own, Branded, The Atomic City, Arrowhead, The Sun Shines Bright, The Long Gray Line, The Private War of Major Benson,* more.

STONE, PADDY (Eng.) Former principal male dancer with the Royal Ballet; Broadway and London stage actor-choreographer-director. Onscreen as an actor from the '50s. IN: *As Long As They're Happy, Value for Money, Invitation to the Dance* (dance role), *The Good Companions.* He later choreographed the movies *Great Catherine* and *Scrooge.*

STONE, PAULA (N.Y.) Former movie juvenile, dancer, Western leading lady, B-pic star, etc.; later a radio personality and Broadway producer. The daughter of Fred Stone, she has been married to producer Michael Sloane since 1946, has a grown son, is now in her 60s (b. 1916), lives in New York, and has been inactive in almost all areas of show business since the early 1950s. Onscreen from 1927. IN: *Slide, Kelly, Slide* (kid role), *Hopalong Cassidy, Two Against the World, Treachery Rides the Range, Colleen, The Case of the Velvet Claws, The Singing Kid, Trailin' West, Atlantic Flight; Swing It, Professor; The Girl Said No, In Old Chicago, Convicts at Large, Down in Arkansas, Laugh It Off,* more, including 1939's *Idiot's Delight,* her last.

STONE, SUZIE KAY/a.k.a. SUZIE KAY (S. Cal.) Singer-dancer-actress. Onscreen as Suzie Kay from 1961. IN: *West Side Story, Wild Wild Winter, C'mon Let's Live a Little,* more. Assumed her married name, Suzie Kay Stone, as her professional name in 1967. IN: *Clambake, Snowball, The Comic,* more.

STOPPA, PAOLO (It.) Character actor. Onscreen from the '40s. IN: *Rossini, Miracle in Milan, Beauty and the Devil; Rome, 11 O'-Clock; Time Gone By* ("The Idyll" episode), *Beauties of the Night, Where the Hot Wind Blows, Rocco and His Brothers, The Leopard, Becket, Behold a Pale Horse, The Visit, Male Companion, After the Fox,* more.

STORCH, ARTHUR (N.Y.) Support. Now a stage director. Onscreen from 1957. IN: *The Strange One, The Mugger, Girl of the Night.*

STORCH, LARRY (S. Cal.) Comic character. Onscreen from 1951. IN: *The Prince Who Was a Thief, The Last Blitzkrieg, Who Was That Lady?, 40 Pounds of Trouble; Captain Newman, M.D.; Sex and the Single Girl, The Great Race, That Funny Feeling, Bus Riley's Back in Town, The Great Bank Robbery,* more.

STORM, GALE (S. Cal.) Still pretty in her mid-50s (b. 1921), she acts constantly in summer stock now *(South Pacific, The Unsinkable Molly Brown, Cactus Flower, etc.),* recently formed Showtime Productions with her husband and a producer friend to develop a new TV series in which she would star, and she takes private tap-dancing lessons five times a week. The last, she says, is her own personal "secret of youth." She has been married since '41 to former actor Lee Bonnell. Under this, his real name, he was in *Lady Scarface, The Navy Comes Through,* and others of the early '40s; earlier, he was in several, including *Man Against the Sky,* as Terry Belmont. "Terry Belmont" and "Gale Storm" were the names they received as winners of Jesse L. Lasky's *Gateway to Hollywood* radio show, a talent-scouting program of the late '30s. Only Gale—real name Josephine Cottle—kept hers. Giving up acting long ago, Bonnell has since become an outstandingly successful insurance executive. The Bonnells have a daughter, Susanna, who is in college, and three grown sons, the two eldest in their 30s. Son Phillip, who is married, gave acting a try but is now with the United States Information Agency in Washington; Peter, also married and the father of two little girls, served three years in the Marines (including Vietnam duty), returned to college in Northern California to complete his interrupted education and is now a forest ranger; youngest son, Paul, a USC graduate, is in the insurance business with his father. At her rambling ranch house in Sherman Oaks, the actress admitted that, while movies hold little attraction for her now, she would like to return to TV. The hitch, she added, is that "the people who do the casting don't know I'm a draw, and when you've enjoyed success so long, you don't know how to be aggressive any more. But I'm more than available." Onscreen from 1940. IN: *Tom Brown's School Days* (debut), *Saddlemates, Red River Valley, City of Missing Girls, Lure of the Islands, The Man from Cheyenne, Campus Rhythm, Where Are Your Children?, Revenge of the Zombies, Forever Yours, Sunbonnet Sue, It Happened on 5th Avenue, The Tenderfoot, Stampede, The Kid from Texas, Between Midnight and Dawn, The Underworld Story, Al Jennings of Oklahoma,* more, including 1953's *Woman of the North,* her most recent to date—after which she became a TV star in three series: *My Little Margie, Oh, Susanna,* and *The Gale Storm Show.*

STRAIGHT, BEATRICE (N.Y.) Support. Onscreen from 1952. IN: *Phone Calls from a Stranger, Patterns, The Silken Affair, The Nun's Story, The Young Lawyers, Network,* more.

STRANGIS, JUDY (S. Cal.) Leading lady in movies and star of TV commercials ("Mean Mary Jean"). Onscreen from the '50s. IN: *Dragoon Wells Massacre, Like It Is,* more.

STRASBERG, LEE (N.Y.) Cofounder/director of Actors Studio. Character. Father of Susan Strasberg. Nominated for Best Supporting Actor in *The Godfather, Part II,* his screen debut. Onscreen from 1974. ALSO IN: *The Cassandra Crossing.*

STRASBERG, SUSAN (S. Cal.) Leading lady. Formerly married to actor Christopher Jones. Onscreen from 1955. IN: *The Cobweb, Picnic, Stage Struck, Hemingway's Adventures of a Young Man, Disorder, Kapo, The Trip, Psych-Out, Chubasco* (with Christopher Jones), *The Name of the Game Is Kill, The Brotherhood; So Evil, My Sister;* more.

STRASSER, ROBIN (N.Y.) Leading lady in TV soap operas. Onscreen from 1976. IN: *The Bride.*

STRATTON, JOHN (Eng.) Support. Onscreen from the '50s. IN: *Mr. Lord Says No!, No Cure for Love, The Cruel Sea, Appointment with Venus, Abandon Ship, The Third Key,* more.

STRAUSS, PETER (S. Cal.) Leading man. Onscreen from the '60s. IN: *Hail, Hero!; Soldier Blue, The Last Tycoon,* more.

STREISAND, BARBRA (S. Cal.) Star. Won Best Actress Oscar in *Funny Girl,* her debut movie. Nominated in the same category in *The Way We Were.* Onscreen from 1968. IN: *Hello, Dolly!; On a Clear Day You Can See Forever, The Owl and the Pussycat, What's Up, Doc?, Up the Sandbox, Funny Lady, A Star Is Born.*

STRIBLING, MELISSA (Eng.) Support. On-screen from the '50s. IN: *The First Gentleman, Out of the Clouds, Horror of Dracula, The League of Gentlemen, Only When I Larf, Confessions of a Window Cleaner,* more.

STRICKLAND, AMZIE (S. Cal.) Character actress. Onscreen from the '50s. IN: *Slaughter on Tenth Avenue, Penelope,* more.

STRICKLAND, CONNIE (S. Cal.) Leading lady. Onscreen in the '70s. IN: *Black Samson,* more.

STRICKLYN, RAY (S. Cal.) Leading man; lately inactive in movies. Onscreen from 1956. IN: *The Catered Affair, Crime in the Streets, Somebody Up There Likes Me, 10 North Frederick, The Remarkable Mr. Pennypacker, The Big Fisherman, The Plunderers, The Lost World, Track of Thunder,* more.

STRIDE, JOHN (Eng.) Support. Onscreen from 1959. IN: *Sink the Bismarck!* (debut), *Bitter Harvest, Macbeth, Something to Hide,* more.

STRIMPELL, STEPHEN (N.Y.) Comic support. Onscreen from the '60s. IN: *Fitzwilly, Jenny, Hester Street,* more.

STRINGER, MICHAEL (S. Cal.) Support. Onscreen in the '70s. IN: *The Hard Road, Angels Die Hard,* more.

STRITCH, ELAINE (Eng.) In 1973, age 48, the American character actress was married—her first—to English actor John Bay, and now makes her home in London. Onscreen from 1956. IN: *The Scarlet Hour, Three Violent People, A Farewell to Arms, The Perfect Furlough, Kiss Her Goodbye, Who Killed Teddy Bear?, Pigeons,* more.

STRODE, WOODY (WOODROW) (S. Cal.) Black support. Onscreen from 1941. IN: *Sundown* (debut), *The Lion Hunters, The City Beneath the Sea, The Gambler from Natchez, Tarzan's Fight for Life, Pork Chop Hill, The Last Voyage, Spartacus, Sergeant Rutledge* (a particularly outstanding performance), *Sins of Rachel Cade, The Man Who Shot Liberty Valance, 7 Women, The Professionals, Shalako, Che!, The Last Rebel, Black Jesus, The Revengers, Winterhawk,* more.

STROLL, EDSON (S. Cal.) Leading man. Onscreen from 1961. IN: *The Three Stooges in Orbit, Snow White and the Three Stooges, McHale's Navy, McHale's Navy Joins the Air Force,* more.

STRONG, DAVID (S. Cal.) Support. Onscreen in the '70s. IN: *The McMasters,* more.

STRONG, MICHAEL (S. Cal.) Support. Onscreen from 1951. IN: *Detective Story, Dead Heat on a Merry-Go-Round, Point Blank, Patton,* more.

STROOCK, GLORIA (N.Y.) Support. Sister of actress Geraldine Brooks. Onscreen in the '70s. IN: *The Day of the Locust,* more.

STROUD, CLAUDE (S. Cal.) Character. Onscreen from 1950. IN: *All About Eve, Love Me or Leave Me, Breakfast at Tiffany's; How to Save a Marriage—And Ruin Your Life;* more.

STROUD, DON (S. Cal.) Leading man. Onscreen from 1967. IN: *Banning, Games, Madigan, What's So Bad About Feeling Good?, Tick Tick Tick, Coogan's Bluff, Journey to Shiloh, Bloody Mama, Explosion, Angel Unchained, Von Richthofen and Brown; Live a Little, Steal a Lot;* more.

STROUD, SALLY ANN (S. Cal.) Support. Onscreen in the '70s. IN: *Foxy Brown,* more.

STROUP, DON (N.Y.) Support. Onscreen from the '60s. IN: *A Dream of Kings; Gaily, Gaily;* more.

STROZZI, KAY (N.Y.) Character. Now a stage and TV actress. Onscreen in 1933 in *Ex-Lady.*

STROYBERG, ANNETTE (Fr.) Leading lady. While married to director Roger Vadim (his second wife), she was billed Annette Vadim. Onscreen from the '60s. IN: *The Eye of the Needle,* more. (See Annette Vadim.)

STRUDWICK, SHEPPERD (N.Y.) Character. He began his career as a young leading man under this, his real name, using it during his first three years in Hollywood. From 1941–47 he was billed John Shepperd. In 1948 he reverted to Shepperd Strudwick and has used it since, both in many movies and stage plays. Onscreen as Shepperd Strudwick from 1938. IN: *Fast Company, That Mothers May Live, Congo Maisie, Flight Command, Dr. Kildare's Strange Case,* more; and, since 1948: *Enchantment, Joan of Arc, The Red Pony, Chicago Deadline, Reckless Moment, All the King's Men, A Place in the Sun, The Eddy Duchin Story, Autumn Leaves, Psychomania, Slaves,* more. (See John Shepperd for credits under that name.)

STRUS, GEORGE (N.J.) Support. Onscreen in the '70s. IN: *Once Upon a Day, Shaft, The Anderson Tapes,* more.

STRUTHERS, SALLY (S. Cal.) Leading lady. Known to TV audiences for the daughter role, "Gloria," in *All in the Family.* Onscreen from the '60s. IN: *The Phynx, Five Easy Pieces, The Getaway,* more.

STUART, AMY (S. Cal.) Support. Onscreen from the '60s. IN: *Hail, Hero!*, more.

STUART, ARLEN (S. Cal.) Character. Onscreen from the '60s. IN: *Kiss Me, Stupid; Pillow Talk, Kotch*, more.

STUART, BARBARA (S. Cal.) Leading lady. Onscreen from the '60s. IN: *Marines, Let's Go!; Hellfighters*, more.

STUART, BINKIE (Eng.) Once one of England's most famous moppets, she is now in her 40s (b. 1932) and has long since been retired from movies. Onscreen from 1938. IN: *Moonlight Sonata, My Irish Molly, Little Dolly Daydream*, more.

STUART, GIL (S. Cal.) Character. Onscreen from the '40s. IN: *A Yank in the R.A.F., The Sound of Music, Assault on a Queen*, more.

STUART, GINA (S. Cal.) Support. Onscreen in the '70s. IN: *The Big Doll House*, more.

STUART, GLORIA (S. Cal.) Still, in her 60s (b. 1911), a beautiful, slender blonde (but a darker shade now), she has been married to screenwriter Arthur Sheekman since '34, has traveled all over the globe, and is known as a gourmet cook. Last onscreen in 1946's *She Wrote the Book*, she lives in Beverly Hills, paints professionally, and spends every possible day at Malibu visiting her daughter. This daughter, Sylvia, who has said it was lonely growing up as an only child, has been happily married for many years to Vaughn Thompson and is the mother of four children—as well as the author of several published books. Onscreen from 1932. IN: *Street of Women* (debut), *The All-American, The Old Dark House, Sweepings, The Secret of the Blue Room, The Invisible Man, Roman Scandals, Beloved, I'll Tell the World, Gift of Gab, The Prisoner of Shark Island, Poor Little Rich Girl, The Girl on the Front Page, Rebecca of Sunnybrook Farm, Time Out for Murder, The Whistler, Enemy of Women*, more.

STUART, JOHN (S. Cal.) Character; former leading man. Now in his 70s (b. 1898), he has been inactive in movies in the past decade. Onscreen from 1920. IN: *Her Son, This Freedom, Kitty, Fanny Hawthorn, Atlantic, Children of Chance, Bella Donna, In a Monastery Garden, Flying Fortress, Courageous Mr. Penn, Madonna of the Seven Moons, Men of Sherwood Forest, John and Julie, Your Past Is Showing, Blood of the Vampire*, more.

STUART, MARGARET (Eng.) Support. Onscreen in the '70s. IN: *Digby, the Biggest Dog in the World;* more.

STUART, MARY (N.Y.) Support; former leading lady. For years one of the most popular actresses in TV soap operas. Onscreen from 1946. IN: *No Leave, No Love; This Time for Keeps, The Hucksters, Dark Delusion, Good News, Adventures of Don Juan, The Big Punch, The Girl from Jones Beach, Thunderhoof* (costar role), *Caribou Trail, Henry the Rainmaker, Father Makes Good*, more.

STUART, MAXINE (S. Cal.) Support. Onscreen from the '60s. IN: *Winning, Suppose They Gave a War and Nobody Came?*, more.

STUDY, LOMAX (S. Cal.) Character. Onscreen from the '60s. IN: *Boeing Boeing, The Caper of the Golden Bulls*, more.

STURGES, SOLOMON (S. Cal.) Support. Onscreen from the '60s. IN: *Charro!, The Working Girls*, more.

STYLES, EDWIN (Eng.) Character. Onscreen from the '30s. IN: *Hell Below, The Lady with a Lamp, Adam and Evelyn, Penny Princess, The Weak and the Wicked, The Dam Busters*, more.

SUBLETT, JOHN "BUBBLES" (S. Cal.) The famous black dancer, half of "Buck & Bubbles," lives in retirement now in Hollywood. Onscreen from 1937. IN: *Varsity Show, Cabin in the Sky, Atlantic City, A Song Is Born*, more.

SUCKSDORFF, ARNE (Swe.) Director-producer-writer. Onscreen in 1955 in *The Great Adventure*.

SULLIVAN, BARRY (S. Cal.) Character; former leading man. Onscreen from 1942. IN: *We Refuse to Die, Woman of the Town, High Explosives, Lady in the Dark, Rainbow Island, And Now Tomorrow, Suspense, The Gangster, Any Number Can Play, The Great Gatsby, A Life of Her Own, Payment on Demand, The Bad and the Beautiful, Jeopardy, Strategic Air Command, Julie, Light in the Piazza, A Gathering of Eagles, My Blood Runs Cold, An American Dream, Tell Them Willie Boy Is Here, Earthquake, The Human Factor, Take a Hard Ride*, more.

SULLIVAN, DAVID (S. Cal.) Support. Onscreen in the '70s. IN: *Adam at 6 A.M.*, more.

SULLIVAN, JEAN (N.Y.) Errol Flynn's lovely brunette leading lady in *Uncertain Glory*, she is today executive director of New York's South Street Seaport Museum. One of the museum's many activities is its Theater-on-the-Pier at Fulton Street and the East River. Two of its '75 productions were *Moby Dick* and *Spoon River Anthology*, in both of which the former Hollywood actress appeared. Now in her early 50s

(b. 1923), dark-haired still, slender and graceful, she has led a full life since leaving Warners. When first in New York she studied ballet and appeared with the Ballet Theatre, following this with TV commercials and acting on soap operas. For a long while she was also well known as the "weather girl" on a New York television station. From '55 to '68 she was married to actor Tom Poston; their daughter—only child—Francesca was born in '56. After the divorce, the actress and her daughter lived for almost two years in Italy, where, in Pisa, she still owns a house. Mother and daughter now share an apartment on New York's West Side. Francesca, a long-haired beauty looking not unlike her mother in her 20s, does TV commercials, has also acted at South Street theater, and in '75 appeared in *Romeo and Juliet* at several summer playhouses. As for Jean Sullivan herself, she still takes ballet lessons three times a week, and is working on her B.A. in theater at Empire State College. Onscreen 1944–45. IN: *Uncertain Glory, Hollywood Canteen, Escape in the Forest* (played the Bette Davis role in this '45 remake of *The Petrified Forest*).

SULLIVAN, JENNY (S. Cal.) Leading lady. Daughter of Barry Sullivan. Onscreen in the '70s. IN: *Getting Straight, Plaza Suite*, more.

SULLIVAN, JEREMIAH (N.Y.) Leading man. Onscreen from the '60s. IN: *Double-Stop*, more.

SULLIVAN, JOHN (Eng.) Support. Onscreen from the '60s. IN: *Nobody Waved Goodbye, The Tamarind Seed*, more.

SULLIVAN, LIAM (S. Cal.) Support. Onscreen from the '60s. IN: *The Magic Sword, One Man's Way, That Darn Cat*, more.

SULLIVAN, SEAN (Eng.) Support. Onscreen from the '60s. IN: *2001: A Space Odyssey; Pinocchio's Greatest Adventure*, more.

SUMAC, YMA (Peru) A resident of Lima these many years, well into her 50s (b. 1922) and a bit thicker of figure, "The Nightingale of the Andes" with the five-octave voice staged an American comeback in '75. She did a nightclub engagement at Chateau Madrid in New York, then gave two sellout performances in concert at Town Hall. She had not sung in this country since '68. Of her concerts, the *New York Times* critic said: "It would be lovely to say that the incredible purity of tone and impeccable technique that Miss Sumac displayed here in the nineteen-fifties are still as intact as her ability to negotiate multiple octaves." Then he added: "Her voice lacks resiliency now. It is grainier and far less controlled." She has been married since she was 14 to musician-promoter Moises Vivanco. Of Indian-Spanish descent, she has two names, both real: Yma Sumac (Indian) and Emperatria Chayarri (Spanish). Onscreen in 1954 and 1957. IN: *Secret of the Incas* and *Omar Khayyam*.

SUMMERFIELD, ELEANOR (Eng.) Character. Onscreen from the '40s. IN: *Dulcimer Street, Laughter in Paradise, The Story of Mandy, Both Sides of the Law, Tears for Simon, A Cry from the Streets, The Running Man, Operation Snafu*, more.

SUMMERLAND, AUGUSTA (S. Cal.) Support. Onscreen in the '70s. IN: *Airport 1975*, more.

SUMMERS, HOPE (S. Cal.) Character. Onscreen from 1960. IN: *Inherit the Wind, The Couch, The Shakiest Gun in the West, Rosemary's Baby, Our Time*, more.

SUMMERS, JERRY (S. Cal.) Support. Onscreen from the '60s. IN: *Surf Party, 99 44/100% Dead*, more.

SUMMERS, SHARI (S. Cal.) Support. Onscreen in the '70s. IN: *Harold and Maude*, more.

SUMNER, GEOFFREY (Eng.) Character. Onscreen from 1938. IN: *Premiere, While the Sun Shines, A Tale of Five Cities, Top Secret, Mr. Potts Goes to Moscow, Always a Bride, Cul de Sac*, more.

SUNDBERG, CLINTON (S. Cal.) Character. Onscreen from 1946. IN: *Undercurrent, Love Laughs at Andy Hardy, Song of Love, Undercover Maisie, Good News, Easter Parade, A Date with Judy, Words and Music, Command Decision, In the Good Old Summertime, The Barkleys of Broadway, Annie Get Your Gun, Two Weeks with Love, On the Riviera, The Caddy, The Birds and the Bees, Bachelor in Paradise, The Wonderful World of the Brothers Grimm, How the West Was Won, Hotel*, more.

SUNDSTROM, FLORENCE (S. Cal.) Character. Onscreen from the '50s. IN: *The Rose Tattoo, The Vagabond King, Spring Reunion, Bachelor in Paradise*, more.

SUNDSTROM, FRANK (S. Cal.) Character; former leading man from Sweden. Onscreen from the '40s. IN: *Song of My Heart, Katrina, Loving Couples, 491, Story of a Woman*, more.

SUROVY, NICK (NICOLAS) (N.Y.) Support. Son of opera star-actress Rise Stevens. Onscreen in the '70s. IN: *Initiation, For Pete's Sake, Nina*, more.

SUSMAN, TODD (S. Cal.) Support. Onscreen in the '70s. IN: *Star Spangled Girl,* more.

SUTHERIN, WAYNE (S. Cal.) Support. Onscreen in the '70s. IN: *Bless the Beasts & Children,* more.

SUTHERLAND, DONALD (S. Cal.) Costar. Onscreen from 1963. IN: *The World Ten Times Over; Die! Die! My Darling; The Bedford Incident, The Dirty Dozen, Interlude, The Split, Joanna, Start the Revolution without Me, M*A*S*H, Kelly's Heroes, Alex in Wonderland, Little Murders, Klute, Johnny Got His Gun, Steelyard Blues, The Day of the Locust,* more.

SUTTON, DOLORES (S. Cal.) Leading lady. Onscreen from the '60s. IN: *Where Angels Go, Trouble Follows;* more.

SUTTON, DUDLEY (Eng.) Support. Onscreen from the '60s. IN: *The Leather Boys, Rotten to the Core, Crossplot, One More Time, The Walking Stick, The Devils, A Town Called Hell,* more.

SUTTON, GRADY (S. Cal.) This comic character from Tennessee, who has never lost his accent and has endeared himself to generations of moviegoers, is in his late 60s (b. 1908), still a bachelor, and still providing laughs. Much in evidence in recent movies, he has appeared regularly on TV (*The Odd Couple, The Pruitts of Southampton,* etc.) and done many TV commercials, such as Chevrolet's "Mean Mary Jean" ads. Of the many hundreds of players he has worked with, he says his favorites—"two of the nicest people I've ever met"—remain Katharine Hepburn (they were together in *Alice Adams* and *Stage Door*) and W. C. Fields (together in *The Man on the Flying Trapeze, You Can't Cheat an Honest Man,* in which Sutton was the hapless carnival trainee, and *The Bank Dick*). Onscreen from 1925. IN: *The Mad Whirl, The Freshman, The Sophomore, Pack Up Your Troubles, College Humor, Only Yesterday, Pigskin Parade, Waikiki Wedding, Vivacious Lady, Alexander's Ragtime Band, In Name Only, Anne of Windy Poplars, Lucky Partners, Somewhere I'll Find You, The More the Merrier, A Lady Takes a Chance, Since You Went Away, A Royal Scandal, Anchors Aweigh, A Bell for Adano, Dragonwyck, Dead Reckoning, Air Hostess;* after this '49 movie, he went into another trade and was in just two pictures during the '50s (*Living It Up* and *A Star Is Born*) before resuming his acting career fulltime in '62; *The Chapman Report, Jumbo, Come Blow Your Horn, My Fair Lady; I Love You, Alice B. Toklas; Myra Breckinridge, Suppose They Gave a War and Nobody Came?,* *Dirty Dingus Magee, Support Your Local Gunfighter,* more.

SUTTON, JULIA (Eng.) Leading lady. Onscreen in 1968 in *Half a Sixpence.*

SUZMAN, JANET (Eng.) Leading lady. Nominated for Best Actress Oscar in *Nicholas and Alexandra.* Onscreen in the '70s. IN: *A Day in the Death of Joe Egg, The Black Windmill,* more.

SUZUKI, PAT (N.Y.) Singer-actress. Best known for her starring role on Broadway in *Flower Drum Song.* Onscreen in the '70s. IN: *Skullduggery,* more.

SVENSON, BO (S. Cal.) Leading man. Onscreen in the '70s. IN: *Walking Tall, Part II; Special Delivery, Death Weekend, Breaking Point,* more.

SWAN, ROBERT (S. Cal.) Character. Onscreen in the '70s. IN: *The Hard Ride,* more.

SWAN, WILLIAM (N.Y.) Leading man. Onscreen from the '60s. IN: *Hotel, Lady in Cement,* more.

SWANN, ELAINE (N.Y.) Character. Onscreen from the '60s. IN: *Goodbye, Columbus; The Producers,* more.

SWANN, LYNN (S. Cal.) Leading lady. Onscreen from the '60s. IN: *Coming Apart,* more.

SWANN, ROBERT (Eng.) Support. Onscreen from the '60s. IN: *Emil and the Detectives, If, Girly,* more.

SWANSON, GLORIA (N.Y.) Legendary star. Nominated for Best Actress Oscar in *The Trespasser, Sadie Thompson, Sunset Boulevard.* Early in 1976, age 77, she married her sixth husband, writer William Dufty, who is almost 20 years her junior. Her previous husbands were Wallace Beery, Herbert K. Somborn, the Marquis de la Falaise de la Coudray, Michael Farmer, and William Davey. She has two daughters (Gloria, by Somborn, founder of Hollywood's Brown Derby; and Michele Bridget, by Farmer), eight grandchildren, and one great-grandchild. When the latter was born she told the press: "There is no greater thrill than holding your great-grandchild in your arms for the first time." Her first child, adopted son Joseph P. Swanson, an electrical engineer, died suddenly in 1975 in Danvers, Mass., of internal hemorrhaging, leaving his widow and two daughters. It was long rumored in Hollywood that he was her illegitimate son by the late Joseph P. Kennedy, who financed some of her movies in the late 1920s. Shortly before her son's death, the actress, acknowledging these rumors, went on record, saying: "They called him Kennedy's child, they called him Mr. DeMille's child. Well, he was born in 1922, and I never laid eyes on Joseph Kennedy until 1928. The Joseph he is named after is my father. After my daughter, Gloria, was born, I never thought I'd get married again, and I wanted 12 children. So I went to an orphanage." The actress and her new husband—he's the author of the Billie Holiday book, *Lady Sings the Blues*—have lately been collaborating on her long-awaited autobiography. And, as the star promised when she first considered collecting and publishing her memories of 60-plus years in movies, "There are going to be a lot of bodies twirling in the ground." Onscreen from 1913. IN: *The Romance of an American Duchess, The Meal Ticket, Teddy at the Throttle, Shifting Sands; For Better, For Worse; Don't Change Your Husband, Male and Female, The Great Moment, The Affairs of Anatol, Bluebeard's 8th Wife, Zaza, Manhandled, Wages of Virtue, Madame Sans Gene, The Love of Sunya, What a Widow, Indiscreet, Tonight or Never, Perfect Understanding, Music in the Air;* after this '34 movie she was onscreen only in 1941's *Father Takes a Wife* before returning in 1950 for *Sunset Boulevard;* since, *3 for Bedroom C, Nero's Mistress, Airport 1975,* more.

SWANSON, MAUREEN (Eng.) The former leading lady is now in her 40s (b. 1932), married, and retired both from ballet (she had been with Sadler's Wells) and movies. Onscreen from the '50s. IN: *Moulin Rouge, Knights of the Round Table, Orders Are Orders, One Just Man, Jacqueline, A Town Like Alice, The Spanish Gardener,* more.

SWEENEY, BOB (S. Cal.) The former character actor is now half of the TV producing company Sweeney/Finnegan Productions, making TV movies and series. Onscreen from 1958. IN: *The Last Hurrah, Toby Tyler, Moon Pilot, Son of Flubber, Marnie,* more.

SWEET, BLANCHE (N.Y.) More than five decades ago, Vachel Lindsay wrote: "I am the one poet who has a right to claim for his muses Blanche Sweet, Mary Pickford, and Mae Marsh. I am the one poet who wrote them songs when they were Biograph heroines, before their names were put on the screen. . . ." Mae Marsh no longer lives, and illness has long forced Mary Pickford into a reclusive life. But his first-named muse, doing the late poet proud, charges ahead full-throttle. Not as an active performer, however. Her long movie career, which began when she was a teenager, continued with scarcely an interruption until '30 when she completed *The Silver Horde* (in which she had a secondary role) and retired from the screen. In the years since she has returned just once—to play the school headmistress in Danny Kaye's *The Five Pennies* ('59). For a decade after she gave up movie acting she continued to perform in all other media. Early in the '30s she toured in vaudeville with her *Sweet and Lovely* act, in which she sang, did comedy skits and a scene from *Anna Christie,* one of her great silent screen ('23) triumphs. She starred in a daily radio show in New York, was featured on Broadway in *The Petrified Forest,* and played leads on tour in numerous plays. Her frequent costar in these out-of-town plays was movie-stage actor Raymond Hackett, her second husband. (For seven years in the '20s she was the wife of Marshall Neilan, famous director of many of her best movies. They were divorced in '29.) She and Hackett—they had no children, nor did she and Neilan—were married from '36 until his death in '58, and she was later to say that their years together "were the happiest of my life." After his death, until she moved to New York to live, she worked as a saleswoman in a Los Angeles department store. Today, living in an apartment not far from where she lived as a child, newly in her 80s (b. 1896), she devotes her time to seeing friends, to her church (she has been a lifelong practicing Christian Scientist), and—though she had not planned it—to being a film-historian-by-accessory. She makes herself readily available to serious scholars of film and for appearances at movie retrospectives, far and near. Several times recently, she has been a principal attraction at Museum of Modern Art events (for Raoul Walsh, one of her directors, and D. W. Griffith, who was, of course, her mentor), and she has flown both to Paris and Los Angeles for film fetes (the latter also being in honor of Griffith). After her appearance in California, film historian Herbert G. Luft noted: "Blanche Sweet, unlike most of her contemporaries, has not changed her appearance much in almost 65 years: she looks as vibrant and youthful today as she did on the screen—a bit older and more mature, but still very beautiful, petite; also witty and frank in her response to questions." And, no recluse she, Blanche Sweet remains listed in the New York telephone book. Onscreen from 1909. IN: *The Rocky Road* (debut), *Was He a Coward?, A Smile of a Child, A Country Cupid, The Eternal Mother, The Making of a Man, The Goddess of Sagebrush Gulch, The Painted Lady, The Lesser Evil, Broken Ways, The Hero of Little Italy, The Battle of Elderberry Gulch, Judith of Bethulia, The Thousand-Dollar Husband, The Storm, Quincy Adams Sawyer, In the Palace of the King, Those Who Dance, Tess of the D'Urbervilles, His Supreme Moment, The Sporting Venus, Bluebeard's Seven Wives, The New*

Commandments, Diplomacy, Singed, Show Girl in Hollywood, more.

SWEET, DOLPH (N.Y.) Character actor. Onscreen from 1967. IN: *You're a Big Boy Now, Colossus, The Swimmer, Finian's Rainbow, The Lost Man, Fear Is the Key, The New Centurions, Sisters*, more.

SWEET, KATIE (S. Cal.) Former juvenile (b. 1957); inactive in movies now. Onscreen from 1959. IN: *Alias Jesse James, The Birds*, more.

SWEET, SHEILA (Eng.) Leading lady; retired from movies now. Onscreen in the '50s. IN: *Three's Company, Fuss Over Feathers, The Angel Who Pawned Her Harp, It's a Great Day*, more.

SWENSON, INGA (N.Y.) Leading lady; primarily a stage actress. Onscreen 1961–62. IN: *The Miracle Worker, Advise and Consent*.

SWENSON, KARL (S. Cal.) Character. Onscreen from 1957. IN: *Four Boys and a Gun, Kings Go Forth, The Hanging Tree, The Gallant Hours, North to Alaska, Judgment at Nuremberg, Lonely Are the Brave, Major Dundee, The Cincinnati Kid, Seconds, Tick Tick Tick*, more.

SWENSON, LINDA (N.Y.) Support. Onscreen in the '70s. IN: *Taking Off*, more.

SWENSON, SVEN (N.Y.) Dancer-actor. Onscreen from the '60s. IN: *Nez de Cuir, Monte Carlo Baby, What's the Matter with Helen?*, more.

SWIFT, CLIVE (Eng.) Support. Onscreen from the '60s. IN: *Catch Us If You Can, A Midsummer Night's Dream*, more.

SWINBURNE, NORA (Eng.) Character; former leading lady (b. 1902). Onscreen from 1921. Among her talkies: *Perfect Understanding, White Face, Dinner at the Ritz, The Citadel, Wings and the Woman, Jassy, Quartet* ("The Colonel's Lady" episode), *Christopher Columbus, The River, Quo Vadis, Landfall, The End of the Affair, Helen of Troy, Third Man on the Mountain, Interlude, A Man Could Get Killed, Anne of the Thousand Days*, more.

SWIT, LORETTA (S. Cal.) Leading lady. Popular as "Hot Lips Hoolihan" in TV's *M*A*S*H*. Onscreen in the '70s. IN: *Stand Up and Be Counted, Freebie and the Bean, Race with the Devil*, more.

SWOFFORD, KEN (S. Cal.) Leading man. Onscreen from the '60s. IN: *The Lawyer, Bless the Beasts & Children, The Black Bird*, more.

SWOPE, TOPO (S. Cal.) Leading lady. Daughter of actress Dorothy McGuire. Onscreen in the '70s. IN: *Pretty Maids All in a Row, Glory Boy, The Hot Rock*, more.

SYDNOR, EARL (N.Y.) Black character. Onscreen from the '60s. IN: *The Hustler, Up the Down Staircase, Funny Girl*, more.

SYKES, BRENDA (S. Cal.) Black leading lady. Onscreen in the '70s. IN: *The Liberation of Lord Byron Jones, Getting Straight, The Baby Maker, Skin Game, Pretty Maids All in a Row, Honky, Black Gunn, Mandingo, Drum*, more.

SYKES, ERIC (Eng.) Comic support. Onscreen from the '60s. IN: *Invasion Quartet, A Coming-Out Party, Heavens Above, One Way Pendulum, Rotten to the Core, The Liquidator, The Spy with a Cold Nose, Shalako, Those Daring Young Men in Their Jaunty Jalopies*, more.

SYLVESTER, WILLIAM (Eng.) Leading man. Onscreen from 1949. IN: *Give Us This Day* (as "Bill"), *The Yellow Balloon, Gorgo, Ring of Treason, Man in the Dark: 2001: A Space Odyssey; The Lawyer, Busting*, more.

SYMS, SYLVIA (Eng.) Leading lady. Onscreen from 1956. IN: *My Teenage Daughter, Woman in a Dressing Gown, Conspiracy of Hearts, Expresso Bongo, The World of Suzie Wong, Desert Attack, Ferry to Hong Kong, Victim, Quare Fellow, Operation Crossbow, Dangerous Route, Hostile Witness, Asylum*, more.

SZABO, SANDOR (N.Y.) Character; primarily a stage actor. Onscreen from 1936. IN: *Once in a Blue Moon*, more.

T

TABORI, KRISTOFFER (N.Y.) Leading man. Son of actress Viveca Lindfors and director Don Siegel; stepson of Broadway playwright George Tabori whose name he uses. Onscreen from 1960. IN: *Weddings and Babies* (with his mother; debut, age 5), *Making It, Journey Through Rosebud*, more.

TACKNEY, STANLEY (N.Y.) Character. Onscreen from the '40s. IN: *The House on 92nd Street*, more.

TAEGER, RALPH (S. Cal.) Leading man. Onscreen from 1958. IN: *It Started With a Kiss, Stage to Thunder Rock, X-15, The Carpetbaggers, A House Is Not a Home*, more.

TAFLER, SYDNEY (Eng.) Character. Onscreen from 1946. IN: *The Little Ballerina, No Room At the Inn, The Lavender Hill Mob, The Galloping Major, Hotel Sahara, The Cockleshell Heroes, Too Many Crooks, Make Mine Mink, Alfie, The Adventurers*, more.

TAFT, JERRY (S. Cal.) Support. Onscreen in the '70s. IN: *It's Alive*, more.

TAFUR, ROBERT (S. Cal.) Character. Onscreen from 1949. IN: *We Were Strangers, Secret of the Incas, Green Fire*, more.

TAKA, MIIKO (S. Cal.) When few roles came her way after *Sayonara*, she worked for a long while as a waitress at a Mexican restaurant, La Cantina, in Westwood. "Being around people is the best thing in the world. It's much better than sitting around the house and drinking that extra martini or taking pills," she exclaimed. After a minuscule role in the *Lost Horizon* remake, the Japanese actress worked in a supporting part in David Niven's *Paper Tiger*. She is married to TV director Lenny Blondheim. Onscreen from 1957. IN: *Cry for Happy, Hell to Eternity, A Girl Named Tamiko, Operation Bottleneck, A Global Affair, The Art of Love; Walk, Don't Run;* more.

TAKEI, GEORGE (S. Cal.) Support. Onscreen from 1960. IN: *Ice Palace, Red Line 7000; Walk, Don't Run; The Green Berets, Which Way to the Front?*, more.

TALBOT, LYLE (S. Cal.) He is a movie stalwart if ever there was one. Soft-spoken and still an attractive man in his 70s (b. 1904), he has been continuously onscreen for more than four decades, and in more than 100 movies. In recent years, frequently cast against type as a hood, he has been a character lead. But often, in his salad days, he was cast as a dashing man-about-town, which was actually the "real" Lyle Talbot if you recall the beauties he squired about Hollywood in the '30s; and, in truth, news about his romances made the gossip columns with great regularity back then. The blue-eyed, brown-haired gentleman from Pittsburgh —born Lysle Henderson, though columnists seemed to enjoy perpetuating the myth it was Lysle Hollywood—was catnip to the ladies. And he married three of them. New York society belle Marjorie Cramer was first ('37), then for five months in '46 he was married to actress Kevin McClure. But it was his third marriage, occurring in the late '40s, that most happily lasted. "We have four children," Talbot reports with pride. "Steve, the eldest, graduated from Wesleyan in 1970 and has been working for the University of New York as an administrative aide to the president of a new branch of the University at Old Westbury, Long Island. He majored in English but is also interested in film-making. He made a documentary his last year at Wesleyan—about the March on Washington in 1969. It won first prize at the Students' Film Festival at Lincoln Center in New York. He was an actor as a child of 8; was on the *Leave It to Beaver* show for about five years. Our next two, Cindy and David, are recent graduates of the University of California at Santa Cruz. Neither of them is interested in an acting career, and that's okay with me. Our youngest, Margaret Ann, who is a teenager, might be an actress, she says." Being the child of an actor, Margaret Ann surely holds no illusions that an actor's life is a soft one. There have been many years, though she wasn't around then, when her father appeared in as many as a dozen pictures a season. One of those years was 1933, and movie buffs still speak with admiration of several performances he gave in that period, notably in *20,000 Years in Sing Sing* and *The Life of Jimmy Dolan*. Though now he still works in an occasional movie, Lyle Talbot has lately been more active in other areas of show business. He was for 11 years on the *Ozzie & Harriet* TV show, and another five on *The Bob Cummings Show*. Since then, he says, "For the most part I've returned to the theater, which was my first love. I toured with the national road companies of *The Odd Couple, Never Too Late* and *There's a Girl in My Soup*. More recently, I've been doing shows at colleges with their drama classes. One of these was *The Little Foxes* at the University of Alabama with Mercedes McCambridge. I find these very satisfying, and of course they pay quite well. I've also done several musicals, *Camelot, My Fair Lady*, and *South Pacific* at Lincoln Center with Florence Henderson." And late in 1975 he was to be found playing editor Walter Burns in a revival of *The Front Page* at the Alley Theater in Houston. So it goes now with Lyle Talbot, ex-man-about-town, now man-about-the-nation—constantly, and all over the map, wherever an interesting job presents itself. Onscreen from 1932. IN: *Love Is a Racket, Three on a Match, No More Orchids, The 13th Guest, Ladies They Talk About, Parachute Jumper, A Lost Lady, Fog Over Frisco, Oil for the Lamps of China, Page Miss Glory, Our Little Girl, The Case of the Lucky Legs, The Singing Kid, Go West*

Young Man, Gateway, Second Fiddle, The Mexican Spitfire's Elephant, Up in Arms, The Falcon Out West, Mystery of the River Boat (serial), *Murder Is My Business, Danger Street, Joe Palooka in the Big Fight, Champagne for Caesar, Purple Heart Diary, The Sea Tiger, With a Song in My Heart, White Lightning, There's No Business Like Show Business, Trader Tom of the China Seas* (serial), *The Great Man, High School Confidential, City of Fear, Sunrise at Campobello, Adventures of Batman and Robin,* more.

TALBOT, NITA (S. Cal.) Support; former leading lady. Onscreen from 1956. IN: *Bundle of Joy, I Married a Woman, Who's Got the Action?, That Funny Feeling, A Very Special Favor, Girl Happy, The Cool Ones, The Manchu Eagle Murder Caper Mystery, The Day of the Locust,* more.

TALIAFERRO, MABEL (N.Y.) At last report the leading lady of early silents, who was born in 1887, was still living in New York where, in later years, she had been a dealer in fine antiques. The sister of actress Edith Taliaferro and the cousin of star Bessie Barriscale, she was married four times—last, and most lastingly (for 20 years), to playwright-actor Robert Ober who died in 1950. Her only child, a son, was by her second marriage (1913-19), to actor Thomas J. Carrigan. An actress on the stage before her movie career (from age 5), she returned to the stage in the '20s and remained highly active there through 1951—when she appeared in the Philadelphia tryout of the play *The Man That Corrupted Hadleyburg.* Onscreen from 1915. IN: *Cinderella, The Three of Us, The Dawn of Love, God's Half Acre, Her Great Price, The Sunbeam, The Jury of Fate, A Magdalen of the Hills, A Wife by Proxy, Peggy Leads the Way, The Barricade, Draft, The Battle for Billions,* more, including 1921's *Sentimental Tommy,* her last silent; she returned for a character role in one talkie, 1940's *My Love Came Back.*

TALLCHIEF, MARIA (Ill.) The prima ballerina —once the wife of George Balanchine (he has had five)—is happily married to her third husband, construction magnate Henry Paschen, has a teenage daughter, and lives in Chicago where she is artistic director of the Lyric Opera Ballet. In her 50s (b. 1925), she has not danced professionally since 1965, nor does she do ballet exercises ("It would depress me"), but her morning routine always includes an hour of calisthenics. Finally, she is an extraordinarily attractive woman still. Onscreen in 1952 in *Million Dollar Mermaid.*

TALLEY, MARION (S. Cal.) Entering her 70s (b. 1907), the Metropolitan Opera star who made just one movie lives in retirement in Southern California. She has been married twice (one annulment, one divorce) and is the mother of one child, now grown. Onscreen in 1936 in *Follow Your Heart.*

TALLICHET, MARGARET (S. Cal.) The protege of Lombard and for a while under contract to David O. Selznick, this actress from Texas left the screen in 1941. She has been happily married to Oscar-winning director William Wyler since '38 and is the mother of four grown children: Cathy (named for the heroine in *Wuthering Heights,* which Wyler directed), Judy, Melanie (named for Wyler's mother, not for the heroic lady in *Gone With The Wind*— though Miss Tallichet did test for this picture, but as Scarlett), and David. Onscreen from 1938. IN: *Girls' School, Stranger on the Third Floor, It Started With Eve,* more.

TALMA, ZOLYA (S. Cal.) Character actress. Onscreen from the '50s. IN: *The Rose Tattoo,* more.

TALMADGE, RICHARD (S. Cal.) Now in his 80s (b. 1892), the star of many action pix in silent days and talkie serials lives in retirement in Hollywood. Also a veteran stuntman, he was honored in '74—together with Yakima Canutt and Harvey Parry—at an awards dinner tendered by the Stuntmen's Association, which was taped as a TV special. Onscreen from the early '20s. IN: *American Manners, The Speed King, The Cavalier, Fighting Demon, Poor Millionaire, Bachelor's Club, Dancing Dynamite, Yankee Don, Speed Madness, Get That Girl, Pirate Treasure* (serial; lead), *The Speed Reporter, Black Eagle; What's New, Pussycat?; Never Too Late, Hawaii,* more.

TALTON, ALIX (S. Cal.) Supporting actress who began her career as Alice Talton. Onscreen from 1950. IN: *In a Lonely Place, The Great Jewel Robber, The Man Who Knew Too Much, Romanoff and Juliet,* more.

TAMBA, TETSURO (Japan) Character lead. Onscreen from the '60s. IN: *Bridge to the Sun, Harakiri, The Seventh Dawn, You Only Live Twice, The Five Man Army, Goyokin, The Scandalous Adventures of Buraikan, The Human Revolution,* more.

TAMBLYN, RUSS (S. Cal.) Costar. Nominated for Best Supporting Actor Oscar in *Peyton Place.* Playing leads again, though in movies more popular in small towns than large ones, he sports a great shock of curly hair now, and often a moustache, that is in high contrast to the boy-next-door look of his early years. But, of course, he is no longer a boy (b. 1935). After 1964's *The Long Ships* he quietly dropped out of movies and became a professional painter. Except for an accident—not tragedy, he insists —he might never have returned to acting. In 1971 his house in the Santa Monica mountains —representing his life's earnings but not, for some reason, covered by fire insurance— burned down. Since the blaze started in the garage, his automobile was his first loss. For a year he and his wife lived in a tent pitched in the yard, and the actor hitchhiked wherever he needed to go. His wife, to whom he has been married since 1960, is English-born Elizabeth Kempton, who was a chorus girl at the Dunes Hotel in Las Vegas—the city in which they married. They had met in England when she had a small part in his *The Wonderful World of the Brothers Grimm*. As a teenager, Tamblyn had been married briefly to former actress Venetia Stevenson. "As the result of the fire," the actor says, "I gained more than I lost. Many people wish they could get rid of everything and start fresh. So the fire represented a tremendous unburdening of possessions and material things. When you have had so much and eventually find yourself living in a tent, the thing that's gained is the most beautiful thing in life— the ability to live simply. The highest form of living is simplicity. I've been told that for years. But to discover for yourself that it is true is a different, and most rewarding thing." Today, less affluent than they once were, the Tamblyns live in a middle-class community, in which they own an unpretentious house, and drive an inexpensive car—and would trade places with no one. Onscreen—first as a child actor named Rusty Tamblyn—from 1948. IN: *The Boy With Green Hair, The Kid From Cleveland, Samson and Delilah, Father of the Bride, As Young As You Feel, The Winning Team*, more; then, from 1953, as Russ: *Take the High Ground, Seven Brides for Seven Brothers, Many Rivers to Cross, Hit the Deck, The Last Hunt, Don't Go Near the Water, High School Confidential, Tom Thumb, Cimarron, West Side Story, How the West Was Won, The Haunting*, more; and, since his comeback, *Satan's Sadists, The Last Movie, Another Day at the Races* (made for movie houses but sold to TV), *The World Through the Eyes of Children; Win, Place or Steal; Inside Straight*, more.

TAMU (N.Y.) Black leading lady. Onscreen in the '70s. IN: *Come Back Charleston Blue, Up the Sandbox, Claudine, The Super Cops*, more.

TANDY, DONALD (Eng.) Support. Onscreen in the '70s. IN: *11 Harrowhouse*, more.

TANDY, JESSICA (N.Y.) Character. Onscreen from 1932. IN: *This Is the Night, Murder in the Family, The Seventh Cross, The Valley of Decision, Dragonwyck, The Green Years, Forever Amber, A Woman's Vengeance, September Affair, The Light in the Forest, Hemingway's Adventures of a Young Man, The Birds*, more.

TANI, YOKO (Japan) Leading lady. Onscreen from the '50s. IN: *The Quiet American, The Wind Cannot Read, My Geisha, Who's Been Sleeping in My Bed?, Invasion, The Power*, more.

TANNER, CLAY (S. Cal.) Support. Onscreen in the '70s. IN: *How to Frame a Figg, Gravy Train*, more.

TANNER, GORDON (Eng.) Support. Onscreen from the '60s. IN: *Campbell's Kingdom, Dr. Strangelove, Return of Mr. Moto*, more.

TANNER, STELLA (Eng.) Support. Onscreen in the '70s. IN: *1000 Convicts and a Woman*, more.

TANNER, TONY (Eng.) Support. Onscreen from the '60s. IN: *The Pleasure Girls; Stop the World—I Want to Get Off*; more.

TANZY, JEANNE (N.Y.) Leading lady. Onscreen in the '70s. IN: *Rivals*, more.

TARITA (Tahiti) The wife (third) of Marlon Brando and the mother of his younger children, she lives with him on Tahiti, her native island. Onscreen in 1962. IN: *Mutiny on the Bounty*.

TARKINGTON, ROCKNE (S. Cal.) Black star. Onscreen in the '70s. IN: *Black Samson, Black Starlet*, more.

TARLOW, FLORENCE (N.Y.) Character. Onscreen in the '70s. IN: *Where's Poppa?, The Panic in Needle Park, Who Killed Mary What's-ername?, The Gang That Couldn't Shoot Straight*, more.

TARR, JUSTIN (S. Cal.) Leading man. Onscreen from the '60s. IN: *Bullitt*, more.

TATI, JACQUES (Fr.) Star comedian. Onscreen from 1952. IN: *Jour de Fete, Mr. Hulot's Holiday, My Uncle, Traffic* (all of which he wrote, directed, and—sans dialogue—starred in).

TAYBACK, VIC (S. Cal.) Character. Onscreen from the '60s. IN: *With Six You Get Egg Roll, Bullitt, Blood and Lace, Thunderbolt and Lightfoot, The Gambler*, more.

TAYLOR, BEVERLY (S. Cal.) Support. Onscreen in the '70s. IN: *Tick Tick Tick*, more.

TAYLOR, BRENDA (Eng.) Ballerina. Onscreen in 1960. IN: *The Royal Ballet.*

TAYLOR, BUCK (S. Cal.) Support. Son of Dub "Cannonball" Taylor. Onscreen from 1966. IN: *The Wild Angels, The Devil's Angels, Ensign Pulver,* more.

TAYLOR, CLARICE (S. Cal.) Support. Onscreen in the '70s. IN: *Tell Me That You Love Me, Junie Moon; Play Misty for Me,* more.

TAYLOR, DELORES (S. Cal.) The wife of Tom Laughlin, who costars with her. IN: *Billy Jack, The Trial of Billy Jack, Billy Jack Goes to Washington,* more.

TAYLOR, DON (S. Cal.) In '61, after almost two decades of leading roles, he chose to become a director. Friend Dick Powell gave him his first chance on TV's *Four Star Playhouse.* He has since been many times nominated for Emmys and has directed such movies as *Tom Sawyer* (in which, needing a character actor in a hurry on location and none being available, he was obliged to play the small role of a riverboat captain) and *The Last Castle.* He is now in his 50s (b. 1920), looks considerably younger, and has been married three times. By his first marriage, to former actress Phyllis Avery, he is the father of two grown daughters, Avery and Ann; by his second, of a college-age daughter named Sally. For years now, he has been happily married to the beautiful redheaded English actress (and now successful painter) Hazel Court. They live in a fine house in Santa Monica overlooking the Pacific and have a son, Jonathan David, who is in grammar school. Onscreen from 1943. IN: *Swing Shift Maisie, Girl Crazy, Salute to the Marines, Winged Victory* (the boy-next-door role of "Pinkie" made his reputation), *Song of the Thin Man, The Naked City, For the Love of Mary, Father of the Bride, Father's Little Dividend, Flying Leathernecks, The Blue Veil, Japanese War Bride, Stalag 17, Girls of Pleasure Island, I'll Cry Tomorrow, The Bold and the Brave, Men of Sherwood Forest,* more, including 1962's *The Savage Guns,* his most recent leading role to date.

TAYLOR, DUB "CANNONBALL" (S. Cal.) This veteran character actor is in his 70s now and his thick molasses drawl is still being heard from the screen—just as it was in the Saturday afternoon shoot-em-ups of Tex Ritter and Charles Starrett. Onscreen from 1938. IN: *You Can't Take It With You, What's Buzzin Cousin, Song of the Range, Moon Over Montana, Song of the Saddle, Riding High, No Time for Sergeants, A Hole in the Head, Sweet Bird of Youth, The Hallelujah Trail, Bonnie and Clyde, Support Your Local Gunfighter, Evel Knievel,* more.

TAYLOR, ELAINE (Eng.) Support. Onscreen from the '60s. IN: *Casino Royale, Half a Sixpence, The Anniversary,* more.

TAYLOR, ELIZABETH (Switz.) Star. Won Best Actress Oscar in *Butterfield 8* and *Who's Afraid of Virginia Woolf?* Nominated in the same category in *Raintree County, Cat on a Hot Tin Roof, Suddenly Last Summer.* Onscreen from 1940. IN: *Man or Mouse* (age 10), *Lassie Come Home, The White Cliffs of Dover, National Velvet, Life With Father, A Date With Judy, Little Women, Father of the Bride, A Place in the Sun, Ivanhoe, Beau Brummell, Giant, Cleopatra, The V.I.P.s, The Sandpiper, The Taming of the Shrew, Reflections in a Golden Eye, The Comedians, Doctor Faustus, Boom!, Secret Ceremony, The Only Game in Town, Under Milk Wood; X, Y and Zee; Hammersmith Is Out, Night Watch, The Blue Bird,* more.

TAYLOR, FRANKIE, JR. (N.Y.) Juvenile. Onscreen from 1968. IN: *The Detective,* more.

TAYLOR, HOWARD (Hawaii) Nephew of Elizabeth Taylor (son of her brother Howard, a scientist in Honolulu) who played a juvenile role in one picture of hers. Onscreen in 1968 in *Boom!*

TAYLOR, JACKIE LYNN (S. Cal.) Pre-Darla Hood, she was "Our Gang's" charming blonde "little leading lady"; later, as Jacqueline Taylor, or Jacquie Lyn, she was prominently cast in more than 70 pictures. Today, a most beautiful blonde still, and known professionally as Lynn Taylor, she is a successful TV news reporter. For years the Women's News Editor at KXTV in Sacramento, she now lives in Downey, south of Hollywood. Long and happily married to television producer-commentator John Louis Fries, she published, in 1970, a delightful book she had written on "Our Gang": *The Turned-On Hollywood 7.* The volume was an outgrowth of lectures she had given, and still gives, throughout California on the Gang and all its members. She was at last report preparing for a nationwide tour of the lecture circuit and preparing a revised, expanded edition of her book. Her research on "Our Gang" provides the surprising information that, over the years (1922–42), there were more than 300 kids in the series. Onscreen from the early '30s. IN: *Pack Up Your Troubles, Little Men, Prosperity,* more.

TAYLOR, JAMES (N.Y.) Singer-actor. Onscreen in 1971. IN: *Two Lane Blacktop.*

TAYLOR, JOAN (S. Cal.) The widow of TV producer (*Hawaii Five-O*) Leonard Freeman (as an actor, he had been known as Glen Roberts), she has young children and lives in retirement in Beverly Hills. Onscreen from 1949. IN: *Fighting Man of the Plains, The Savage, War Paint, Rose Marie, Fort Yuma, Earth vs. the Flying Saucers, Omar Khayyam, War Drums*, more, including 1957's *20,000 Miles to Earth*, her most recent to date.

TAYLOR, JOYCE (S. Cal.) Leading lady and recording star. Married to business man Edward Bellinson, she lives in Los Angeles and remains active in movies. Onscreen from 1959. IN: *The F.B.I. Story, Atlantis the Lost Continent, Ring of Fire, 13 Frightened Girls, Twice Told Tales, Santa and the Three Bears* (animated cartoon for which she sang the songs), *The Windsplitter*, more.

TAYLOR, KEITH (S. Cal.) Support; former juvenile. Onscreen from the '60s. IN: *Boy, Did I Get a Wrong Number!; Born Wild, The Young Animals*, more.

TAYLOR, KENT (S. Cal.) Handsome and dark-haired still, as he goes into his 70s (b. 1907), he still acts occasionally in movies and on TV, has been married to his one wife, the former Augusta Kulek, since his 20s, and is the father of three grown children, all still living nearby—Kay, Judy, and Bill. Onscreen from 1931. IN: *Road to Reno, Merrily We Go to Hell, The Devil and the Deep, Blonde Venus, I'm No Angel, Death Takes a Holiday, The Cradle Song, Mrs. Wiggs of the Cabbage Patch, David Harum, County Chairman, Sky Parade, Ramona, Wings Over Honolulu, Five Came Back, I Take This Woman, Men Against the Sky, Mississippi Gambler, Army Surgeon, Bomber's Moon; Roger Touhy—Gangster; Deadline for Murder, Young Widow, The Crimson Key, Payment on Demand, Track the Man Down, Fort Bowie, The Purple Hills, The Day Mars Invaded the Earth, The Crawling Hand, Brides of Blood*, more, including 1974's *Girls for Rent*, in which he and former cowboy star Robert Livingston play leads opposite Georgina Spelvin.

TAYLOR, KIT (Eng.) Character. Onscreen from the '50s. IN: *Long John Silver, In the Devil's Garden*, more.

TAYLOR, LARRY (Eng.) Character. Onscreen from the '50s. IN: *Alexander the Great, King and Country, Kaleidoscope, S*P*Y*S*, more.

TAYLOR, RENEE (N.Y.) Comic leading lady. Onscreen from 1968. IN: *The Detective, The Producers, A New Leaf, Jennifer on My Mind, Made for Each Other* (costarred with her husband, Joseph Bologna; they also wrote it), more.

TAYLOR, ROD (S. Cal.) Costar. Onscreen from 1955. IN: *Long John Silver, The Virgin Queen, The Catered Affair, Raintree County, Separate Tables, Ask Any Girl, The Time Machine, The Birds, The V.I.P.s, Sunday in New York, Fate Is the Hunter, Young Cassidy, Do Not Disturb, The Glass Bottom Boat, Hotel, Chuka, The Hell With Heroes, The High Commissioner, The Man Who Had Power Over Women, The Train Robbers, Trader Horn, Blondy, On a Dead Man's Chest* (which he wrote), more.

TAYLOR RUTH (S. Cal.) The grand (and beautiful) comedienne of silents, and a few talkies, left the screen in 1929 for marriage to a New York stockbroker. A widow since '65, she has moved back to Beverly Hills, and is retired. Her son, Buck Henry, wrote the screenplays of *Candy* and *The Graduate* (in which he appeared in the comedy role of the manager of the hotel where Dustin Hoffman rendezvoused with Mrs. Robinson). Onscreen from the late '20s. IN: *Gentlemen Prefer Blondes, Just Married, College Coquette, This Thing Called Love*, more.

TAYLOR, TROTTI TRUMAN (Eng.) Character actress. Onscreen from the '50s. IN: *Eight O'Clock Walk, The French They Are a Funny Race, Confessions of a Window Cleaner*, more.

TAYLOR, VALERIE (Eng.) The lovely leading lady of the '30s is in her 70s now (b. 1902) and still active on the stage in England—in this decade she played the Mother in *The Glass Menagerie*—and on TV. But her interest in movies waned years ago. Onscreen from 1933. IN: *Berkeley Square, 48 Hours*, more, including 1962's *No Place Like Homicide*, her most recent to date. (She also coauthored the screenplay of 1948's *Take My Life*.)

TAYLOR, VAUGHN (S. Cal.) The veteran character actor remains steadily busy. Onscreen from 1951. IN: *Up Front, Francis Goes to the Races, Meet Danny Wilson, Back at the Front, It Should Happen to You, Jailhouse Rock, Cowboy, Andy Hardy Comes Home, Cat on a Hot Tin Roof, Psycho, Diamond Head, The Unsinkable Molly Brown, Zebra in the Kitchen; The Russians Are Coming, The Russians Are Coming; In Cold Blood, The Shakiest Gun in the West, The Ballad of Cable Hogue, The Gumball Rally*, more.

TAYLOR, WALLY (S. Cal.) Black leading man. Onscreen in the '70s. IN: *Hangup, The Gumball Rally*, more.

TAYLOR, WAYNE (S. Cal.) Character. Onscreen from the '50s. IN: *Operation Secret, Untamed Youth*, more.

TAYLOR, WILDA (S. Cal.) Support. Onscreen from 1964. IN: *Roustabout*, more. (She has also choreographed movies such as *The Love God?* and *Angel, Angel, Down We Go*.)

TAYLOR, ZACK (S. Cal.) Leading man. Onscreen in the '70s. IN: *How to Succeed With Sex*, more.

TAYLOR-SMITH, JEAN (Eng.) Support. Onscreen from the '50s. IN: *Rob Roy, The Weak and the Wicked, Ring of Bright Water*, more.

TAYLOR-YOUNG, LEIGH (S. Cal.) This leading lady, second wife of actor Ryan O'Neal and mother of his youngest son, gave up her career for a while after their divorce but has since resumed it. Onscreen from 1969. IN: *I Love You, Alice B. Toklas!; The Big Bounce* (opposite Ryan O'Neal; they had also costarred in TV's *Peyton Place*), *The Adventurers, The Gang That Couldn't Shoot Straight, Soylent Green*, more.

TCHERINA, LUDMILLA (Fr.) Offscreen for a decade, the dancer-actress-writer-painter signed a contract in '75 to star in the French film *Nef*, in which she would play a modern version of the Egyptian Queen Nefertiti who becomes involved with contemporary politics. Onscreen from 1948. IN: *A Lover's Return, The Red Shoes, Sign of the Pagan, The Lovers of Teruel*, more.

TEAGUE, ANTHONY "SKOOTER" (S. Cal.) Support. Onscreen from the 60s. IN: *How to Succeed in Business Without Really Trying, The Trouble With Girls, The Barefoot Executive*, more.

TEASDALE, VERREE (S. Cal.) Offscreen since 1941's *Come Live With Me*, the widow of Adolphe Menjou (d. 1963) lives in retirement in Beverly Hills. A distinguished-looking woman in her 70s, she has a son, Peter Adolphe, whom she and her husband adopted in '37, and her lifelong interest in fashion has not abated. Onscreen from 1929. IN: *Syncopation, The Sap from Syracuse, Skyscraper Souls, Luxury Liner, They Just Had to Get Married, Roman Scandals, Fashions of 1934, Desirable, Madame Du Barry, A Midsummer Night's Dream, The Milky Way, Topper Takes a Trip, Fifth Avenue Girl, I Take This Woman, Turnabout, Love Thy Neighbor*, more.

TEBALDI, RENATA (It.) Metropolitan Opera star from Italy, where she still lives. Onscreen in 1954 and 1956. IN: *Aida* and *House of Ricordi*.

TEDROW, IRENE (S. Cal.) This noted character actress, now entering her 70s (b. 1907), remains active, doing commercials (recently for Koolaid) and TV shows. She has two children, Roger and Enid Kent. Her husband, entertainment insurance broker William E. Kent, died in '74. Onscreen from 1937. IN: *They Won't Forget, Cheers for Miss Bishop, Journey Into Fear, The Moon and Sixpence, The Strange Affair of Uncle Harry, They Won't Believe Me, Thieves' Highway, A Lion Is in the Streets, Not As a Stranger, The Ten Commandments, Never So Few, Please Don't Eat the Daisies, The Parent Trap, The Greatest Story Ever Told, The Cincinnati Kid, The Comic, Getting Straight*, more.

TELL, ARTHUR (N.Y.) Character. Onscreen in 1968 in *Funny Girl*.

TEMPLE, SHIRLEY (N. Cal.) The greatest child star of all, plump and dark-haired now in her late 40s (b. 1927), received much publicity in '74 when appointed U.S. Ambassador to Ghana. She took up residence in this West African nation with her eldest daughter, Susan (by actor John Agar), and her husband (since '50), Charles Black, president of an international marine-resources-development company. Their two children, Charlie and Lori, both in their early 20s, remained home in Northern California to complete their college educations. And, in October '75, daughter Susan returned there to become—in a formal wedding at the family church—the bride of Italian diplomat Roberto Falaschi. They had met in Ghana. Onscreen from 1932. IN: "Baby Burlesk" shorts ("Polly-Tax in Washington," "The Incomparable Miss Legs Sweetrick," etc.), *Red-Haired Alibi, Stand Up and Cheer, Little Miss Marker, Baby Take a Bow, Now and Forever, Bright Eyes, The Little Colonel, Our Little Girl, Curly Top, The Littlest Rebel, Captain January, Dimples, Stowaway, Wee Willie Winkie, Heidi, Rebecca of Sunnybrook Farm, Little Miss Broadway, The Little Princess, Susannah of the Mounties, The Blue Bird, Kathleen, Miss Annie Rooney* (an adolescent here and Dickie Moore gave her her first screen kiss), *Since You Went Away, I'll Be Seeing You, Kiss and Tell, The Bachelor and the Bobby-Soxer, That Hagen Girl* (opposite her was Ronald Reagan, then still a Democrat but their political affiliations soon would be the same), *Fort Apache* (with her then-new husband, John Agar), *Mr. Belvedere Goes to College, Adventure in Baltimore*, more, including *The Story of Seabiscuit*, her last, in 1949.

TERRANOVA, DAN (S. Cal.) Support. Onscreen from the '50s. IN: *The Blackboard Jungle, Crime in the Streets, Young Dillinger*, more.

TERRIS, NORMA (N.Y.) The singer-actress (star of Broadway's *Showboat*) is now in her 60s, and in '74 was one of the stars present when Luchow's, the famous restaurant, staged a salute to the famed beauties of the various Ziegfeld Follies. Onscreen 1929–30. IN: *Married in Hollywood* and *Cameo Kirby*.

TERRY, ALICE (S. Cal.) In her 70s (b. 1901), she remains what she was in her dozens of silents, a great beauty. The principal change in her looks is that her hair is silver now; occasionally onscreen her natural auburn locks were seen but most often she starred as a blonde—in a wig. For 29 years, until his death in '50, she was the wife of Rex Ingram, who directed most of her major films and was considered, in his prime, to be the handsomest man in Hollywood. She said once, referring not to his looks but to the man he was, "I would rather be Mr. Ingram's wife than the greatest star on the screen." She never changed her mind, nor has she remarried. Living quietly in Beverly Hills, she enjoys cooking and painting, and seeing friends—many from the "old days." Onscreen from 1916. IN: *Not My Sister, Wild Sinship's Widow, Old Wives for New, Hearts and Trumps, The Four Horsemen of the Apocalypse, The Conquering Power, The Prisoner of Zenda, Where the Pavement Ends, Scaramouche, The Arab, The Great Divide, Confessions of a Queen, Mare Nostrum, Lovers, The Garden of Allah*, more, including 1929's *The Three Passions*, her last.

TERRY, DON (S. Cal.) This popular leading man of serials (*Don Winslow of the Navy*, etc.) and B's is in his 70s (b. 1902), gave up movies more than three decades ago, was later in business, and is now retired. Onscreen from 1928. IN: *Me, Gangster; The Valiant, Untamed, Border Romance, A Fight to the Finish, When G-Men Step In, Mutiny in the Arctic, Unseen Enemy, Escape from Hong Kong, Moonlight in Havana, Danger in the Pacific*, more, including 1943's *Sherlock Holmes in Washington*, his most recent to date.

TERRY, NIGEL (Eng.) Support. Onscreen from the '60s. IN: *The Lion in Winter*, more.

TERRY, PHILLIP (S. Cal.) The leading man once married to Joan Crawford remains a most handsome man in his late 60s (b. 1909) and still plays an occasional character role in movies, but does many more TV commercials. In this decade he has also been active in such TV series as *The Name of the Game* and *Police Woman*. Well off from investments, he lives in Beverly Hills. Onscreen from 1937. IN: *Navy Blue and Gold, Mannequin* (with Crawford, long before their marriage), *Four Girls in White, Balalaika, The Parson of Panamint, Torpedo Boat, Wake Island, Here Comes the Bride, Ladies Courageous, George White's Scandals, The Lost Weekend, Seven Keys to Baldpate, Deadline U.S.A., Man from God's Country, The Leech Woman, The Navy vs. the Night Monsters*, more.

TERRY, ROBERT (S. Cal.) The dapper character actor, prominent in B's and serials, is in his 70s and still going strong. Onscreen from 1937. IN: *The Mysterious Pilot* (serial), *Renfrew of the Royal Mounted, Dick Tracy Returns* (serial), more.

TERRY-THOMAS (Eng.) Comedy star. Onscreen from 1956. IN: *Private's Progress, Brothers-in-Law, Lucky Jim, Too Many Crooks, I'm All Right Jack, Man in a Cocked Hat, Make Mine Mink, The Mouse on the Moon, How to Murder Your Wife, Those Magnificent Men in Their Flying Machines, A Guide for the Married Man, Those Fantastic Flying Fools; Don't Raise the Bridge, Lower the River; Where Were You When the Lights Went Out?, Danger Diabolik, How Sweet It Is!, The Abominable Dr. Phibes, Spanish Fly, Side by Side*, more.

TERZIEFF, LAURENT (Fr.) Costar. Onscreen from the '50s. IN: *The Cheaters, La Notte Brava, Kapo, The Seven Deadly Sins, Two Weeks in September, The Milky Way, La Prisonniere, Medea, Moses*, more.

TESSIER, ROBERT (S. Cal.) Character. Onscreen from the '60s. IN: *The Glory Stompers, The Jesus Trip, The Longest Yard*, more.

TETZEL, JOAN (Eng.) This actress, once a David O. Selznick leading lady, and in but one movie in the past two decades, is in her 50s (b. 1921), and lives in London with Oscar Homolka, her husband of many years. Recently in Hollywood on a visit, she played a character role in TV's *Police Woman*, the episode being shown in January 1976. Onscreen from 1947. IN: *Duel in the Sun, The Paradine Case, Thelma Jordan, Hell Below Zero, Joy in the Morning*.

THATCHER, HEATHER (Eng.) Character; former leading lady. Onscreen from 1929. IN: *The Plaything, It's a Boy, The Thirteenth Chair, Tovarich, Fools for Scandal, If I Were King, Girls' School, Man Hunt, Son of Fury, We Were Dancing, Journey for Margaret, Gaslight, The Gay Lady, Encore* ("Gigolo and Gigolette" episode), *Will Any Gentleman?, Duel in the Jungle*, more.

THATCHER, TORIN (S. Cal.) In movies more than four decades, this estimable character actor from England remains, in his 70s (b. 1905), one of Hollywood's most in-demand players.

Onscreen from 1934. IN: *General John Regan, The Man Who Could Work Miracles, Major Barbara, Frightened Lady, Saboteur, Bonnie Prince Charlie, The Black Rose, Affair in Trinidad, The Snows of Kilimanjaro, The Desert Rats, Knock on Wood, A Band of Angels, Seventh Voyage of Sinbad, Mutiny on the Bounty, Drums of Africa, The Sandpiper, Hawaii,* more.

THAW, JOHN (Eng.) Support. Onscreen from 1962. IN: *The Bofors Gun, The Last Grenade,* more.

THAXTER, PHYLLIS (Me.) MGM's "new girl" of '44, with the twinkly eyes that could so suddenly and touchingly brim with tears, is by no means finished with Hollywood. She flies there regularly to see her children—actress-daughter Skye Aubrey (wife of producer Ilya Salkind) and son Jim Watson Aubrey, who in '73 at age 20, became a groom. They are by her first husband, James Aubrey (married '44; divorced '62), who, coincidentally, was in recent years president of MGM. And she arrives in Hollywood almost as frequently to guest-star on TV in *Cannon, Medical Center, Barnaby Jones,* and "Movies of the Week" such as *The Longest Night* with David Janssen. Her roles are usually those of an attractive, well-groomed matron. Type-casting. The actress, in her 50s (b. 1921), has been remarried since '62. Her husband is Gilbert Lea, who owns and is president of Tower Publishing Company in Portland, not far from Cumberland Foreside where they live. She has three stepchildren—a married daughter living in Princeton, N.J., and two sons, both in Portland, Me., one working for his father's firm, the other for a bank. "When I am not working," she says, "my life is busy with community affairs. I am on the Women's Board of our Maine Medical Center and do volunteer work with the children at the hospital. I am enjoying my life here tremendously. It is happy, busy and full." Once, when at MGM, she told a reporter, "What is mine will come to me; I believe in Fate." It is interesting that Fate has brought her back to the homestate that she, daughter of a Maine Supreme Court justice, left in her teens to become a star—and did. Onscreen from 1944. IN: *Thirty Seconds Over Tokyo, Bewitched, Week-End at the Waldorf, The Sea of Grass, The Sign of the Ram, Blood on the Moon, Act of Violence, No Man of Her Own, The Breaking Point; Jim Thorpe—All-American; She's Working Her Way Through College, Springfield Rifle, Women's Prison, Man Afraid,* more, including 1964's *The World of Henry Orient,* her most recent movie to date.

THAYER, JULIA (Conn.) Jean Carmen was and is her real name; she sometimes acted un-

der it and uses it professionally now. But as Julia Thayer she was the heroine in Westerns such as Bob Livingstone's *Gunsmoke Ranch* and played the role—The Rider—that deep-dyed serial fans still cherish, in *The Painted Stallion.* Today, married, living in Greenwich, and in her late 50s, the actress is an independent film producer. Onscreen in the '30s in the above.

THAYER, LORNA (S. Cal.) Character; former leading lady. Onscreen from the '50s. IN: *The Lusty Men, Five Easy Pieces, The Traveling Executioner, Rhinoceros, Gravy Train, Gosh,* more.

THIESS, MANUELA (S. Cal.) Leading lady. Daughter of Ursula Thiess and stepdaughter of the late Robert Taylor. Onscreen from the '60s. IN: *Changes, Terror Circus,* more.

THIESS, URSULA (S. Cal.) The widow of Robert Taylor, this leading lady from Germany is retired, has not remarried, and devotes herself to her two children by the actor—Terrance, a college student now, and Tessa, who is of high school age. Onscreen from 1953. IN: *Monsoon, Bengal Brigade, The Iron Glove, The Americano,* and *Bandido.*

THIGPEN, LYNNE (N.Y.) Black singer-actress. Onscreen in the '70s. IN: *Godspell,* more.

THINNES, ROY (S. Cal.) Leading man. Onscreen from 1963. IN: *Toys in the Attic* (bit), *Journey to the Far Side of the Sun, Airport 1975, The Hindenburg,* more.

THOMAS, ANN (N.Y.) Character. She now lives in Pelham, N.Y. Onscreen from 1945. IN: *Duffy's Tavern, Walk East on Beacon; Me, Natalie;* more.

THOMAS, CHRISTINE (N.Y.) Character. Primarily a stage actress. Onscreen in 1960 in *Midnight Lace.*

THOMAS, DANNY (S. Cal.) Star comedian who is as famous for his TV series as his films. Onscreen from 1947. IN: *Unfinished Dance, Big City, Call Me Mister, I'll See You in My Dreams, The Jazz Singer, Rendezvous in Space; Don't Worry, We'll Think of a Title; Journey Back to Oz* (feature cartoon; voice), more.

THOMAS, DAVID (N.Y.) Character. Onscreen from the '60s. IN: *The Night They Raided Minsky's,* more.

THOMAS, DAXON (S. Cal.) Support. Onscreen from the '60s. IN: *Fever Heat,* more.

THOMAS, FRANK M. (S. Cal.) In '43, after *No Place for a Lady* and major roles in 75 in eight years onscreen, this actor, his wife, actress Mona Bruns, and son, Frankie Thomas, relocated in New York. They all enjoyed long careers in radio and, in the '50s, were known as the First Family of Television as they blanketed the networks in "live," though separate, shows. The head of the household played the editor in the soap opera *Love of Life* and in *Martin Kane* played Captain Burke through the successive reigns of William Gargan, Lee Tracy, and Lloyd Nolan. Mona Bruns headlined as Aunt Emily, the female lead, for years in both *The Brighter Day* and *Another World*. While Frankie Thomas starred in the title role of *Tom Corbett, Space Cadet*. These days, back in Hollywood again, while both Frank M. Thomas and Mona Bruns consider themselves semiretired, they hardly are. In the early '70s, they costarred in an experimental short, *The Cycle*, that rated showing at the Cannes Film Festival. And Mona has done much TV—*Adam-12, Mannix, Green Acres* (a recurring role). Also, in '73, she published her memoirs. The book was titled *By Emily Possessed*, a reference, of course, to Aunt Emily. Onscreen from 1936. IN: *The Ex-Mrs. Bradford, We Who Are About to Die, Don't Tell the Wife, Criminal Lawyer, China Passage, Meet the Missus, The Toast of New York, Breakfast for Two, Blind Alibi, A Man to Remember, Smashing the Rackets, Secret Service of the Air, Bachelor Mother, Geronimo; Brigham Young—Frontiersman; The Monster and the Girl, The Talk of the Town; Hello, Frisco, Hello; more.*

THOMAS, FRANKIE (S. Cal.) In his curly-haired teens, in the serial *Tim Tyler's Luck*, and as Bonita Granville's colead in all the "Nancy Drew" pix, he was one of the screen's most popular juveniles. And he was later famous on TV in *Tom Corbett, Space Cadet*. After Tom took his last flight on NBC in '56, Frankie forsook acting in favor of writing and producing. He wrote *My True Story* TV scripts, was a producer for *Four Star Theater* and a staff writer on ABC-Radio's *Theatre Five*. Today, a good-looking bachelor in his 50s (b. 1922) and back in Hollywood for years, he has—in a fashion—resumed his association with movies. A screenplay of his, *Five Keys to Death*, has been purchased for filming by London's Morglay Productions. But his principal career, these days, is in the field of bridge. As Frank Thomas Jr., he is editor of the *American Bridge Teachers Association Quarterly*, with offices in downtown Hollywood, and is one of the three most successful bridge teachers in the Southern California area. Each year he teaches the "inside" of the card game to more than 15,000 persons. "The large number," he explains, "is due to the fact that I specialize in department store teaching." Also, with another bridge expert, George Gooden, he has written and published a semifictional instruction book, *The Sherlock Holmes Bridge Book*. Onscreen from 1934. IN: *Wednesday's Child; Nancy Drew, Detective* (first of the series of four in which he played teenager Ted Nickerson); *Boys Town, Little Tough Guys in Society, Angels Wash Their Faces, Dress Parade, Invisible Stripes, Flying Cadets, One Foot in Heaven, Always in My Heart, The Major and the Minor,* more.

THOMAS, JOEL (N.Y.) Support. Onscreen from 1962. IN: *Dead to the World*, more.

THOMAS, LOWELL (N.Y.) The noted newscaster-narrator-scriptwriter-producer turned 84 in 1976 and remains as professionally active as ever. Still at the microphone, as he has been for more than four decades, he delivers his nightly newscast over the CBS radio network—speaking from his home in Pawling, N.Y. He has given this 600-acre Dutchess County estate to the University of Denver. It will eventually be sold, the proceeds being used to create a Lowell Thomas Law Center at his alma mater. In the autumn of 1975 he began for PBS a sizable undertaking titled *Lowell Thomas Remembers*—a 44-week recollection of American life and events from 1919 to 1963, using newsreel footage. Also, the author of 50 books, he is working on yet another. He has been a widower since the death of his wife, Frances, who was 81, in 1975. The movies he has narrated, often appearing on camera, date from 1932 and include: *The Blonde Captive, Borneo, Ski Champs, This Is Cinerama, Out of This World, Seven Wonders of the World, The Best of Cinerama,* more.

THOMAS, LOWELL, JR. (Alaska) The son—and only child—of the above, he has lately been Lieutenant Governor of Alaska. In 1964 he was producer-cinematographer-narrator of *Out of This World*, in which he also appeared.

THOMAS, MARIE (N.Y.) Black leading lady. Onscreen from the '60s. IN: *The Boston Strangler*, more.

THOMAS, MARLO (N.Y.) Leading lady. Daughter of Danny Thomas. Onscreen from 1965. IN: *The Knack . . . and how to get it* (billed Margot, an approximation of her real name, Margaret), *Jenny*, more.

THOMAS, PHILIP M. (S. Cal.) Black leading man. Onscreen in the '70s. IN: *Stigma, Mr. Ricco, Coonskin, Sparkle*, more.

THOMAS, RALPH (S. Cal.) Support. Onscreen from the '60s. IN: *The Lawyer*, more.

THOMAS, RICHARD (S. Cal.) Leading man. Famous for his TV role of "John Boy" in *The Waltons*. Onscreen from 1969. IN: *Winning, Last Summer, Cactus in the Snow, The Todd Killings, Red Sky at Morning, You'll Like My Mother, 9/30/55,* more.

THOMAS, SCOTT (S. Cal.) Support. Onscreen from the '60s. IN: *Kona Coast, Guns of the Magnificent Seven,* more.

THOMAS, TONY (ANTHONY) (S. Cal.) Support. Onscreen from the '60s. IN: *Wild Season,* more.

THOMAS, VILLESTA (VICKIE) (N.Y.) Black ingenue. Onscreen in the '70s. IN: *Cotton Comes to Harlem,* more.

THOMPSON, CARLOS (Switz.) From Argentina, of German descent (real name Carlos Mundanschaffter), he was greatly popular in South American movies before MGM picked him as a leading man "best bet" in the '50s. He later continued his screen career in Europe, finally tossing it over in 1967. Today, long and happily married to actress Lilli Palmer, with homes in Switzerland and on the Spanish coast, the still-handsome Thompson, wearing his silvering hair shoulder length and with bushy Edwardian sideburns, has two flourishing careers. He is the author of the best seller *The Assassination of Winston Churchill,* and he has written a series for British TV based on Emile Zola and his family. Secondly, after building their vacation home in Malaga, Spain, Thompson found his design for the house was so successful that others were asking him to design and build for them. So, in this decade, he has become one of the leading architects and builders on Spain's Costa del Sol. Onscreen in Hollywood and internationally from 1953. IN: *Fort Algiers, Flame and the Flesh, Valley of the Kings, Magic Fire, Raw Wind in Eden, Stefanie, Between Time and Eternity, The Spessart Inn, Our Man in the Caribbean, La Vie de Chateau,* more.

THOMPSON, DUANE (S. Cal.) The leading lady in many silent features and Westerns, she later had careers both onstage and in radio. A widow (her husband was a writer), she lives in retirement near Hollywood. Onscreen from 1926. IN: *Sweet Rosie O'Grady, Her Summer Hero, The Voice of the City,* more, including 1938's *Hollywood Hotel,* her last, in which she was the telephone operator of the famed hotel.

THOMPSON, EVAN (N.Y.) Support. Onscreen from the '60s. IN: *The Chapman Report, The Man Who Understood Women,* more.

THOMPSON, HILARIE (S. Cal.) Former ingenue. Onscreen from the '60s. IN: *Where Angels Go, Trouble Follows; How Sweet It Is!; If It's Tuesday, This Must Be Belgium;* more.

THOMPSON, JEFF (S. Cal.) Support. Onscreen from the '50s. IN: *Davy Crockett, King of the Wild Frontier; The Lawyer,* more.

THOMPSON, JIMMY (S. Cal.) Character. Onscreen from 1954. IN: *Brigadoon, Forbidden Planet, The Girl in Blue,* more.

THOMPSON, KAY (N.Y.) The cadaverous singer-actress-author no longer lives at the Plaza in New York, which acquired fame with the young set when she used it as the locale of her children's book *Eloise.* (She has lately designed and merchandised an "Eloise" doll.) Home, though she is in Manhattan as often as any place else, is wherever on the globe she happens to be—usually, in recent years, staging fashion shows with "pizazz" (she originated the word) for famous designers. Onscreen from 1937. IN: *Manhattan Merry-Go-Round, Funny Face; Tell Me That You Love Me, Junie Moon* (with her goddaughter, Liza Minnelli); more.

THOMPSON, MARSHALL (S. Cal.) Leading man. Onscreen from 1944. IN: *The Purple Heart, They Were Expendable, The Valley of Decision, Gallant Bess, Bad Bascomb, The Romance of Rosy Ridge, B. F.'s Daughter, Command Decision, Roseanna McCoy, Battleground, Mystery Street, My Six Convicts, To Hell and Back; Good Morning, Miss Dove; A Yank in Vietnam* (he also directed); *Clarence, the Cross-Eyed Lion* (he wrote the original story); *Around the World Under the Sea, George!* (besides starring, he wrote the original story and produced it), more.

THOMPSON, REX (N.Y.) He was one of Hollywood's most popular boy actors in the '50s. Now in his late 20s, he plays leads on Broadway (*Conduct Unbecoming, The Incomparable Max,* etc.) and stars in repertory companies across the nation—in *Romeo and Juliet, The Lion in Winter,* etc. Onscreen from 1953. IN: *Young Bess, Her Twelve Men, The Eddy Duchin Story, The King and I, All Mine to Give,* more.

THOMPSON, SADA (N.Y.) Support. Noted Broadway star. Onscreen from 1961. IN: *You Are Not Alone, The Pursuit of Happiness, Desperate Characters,* more.

THOMPSON, VICTORIA (N.Y.) Support. Onscreen from the '60s. IN: *Funny Girl, The Harrad Experiment,* more.

THOR, JEROME (S. Cal.) Support. Onscreen from 1959. IN: *Riot in a Juvenile Prison, 55 Days at Peking, Mr. Sycamore,* more.

THORDSEN, KELLY (S. Cal.) Character actor. Onscreen from the '60s. IN: *Desire in the Dust, Sweet Bird of Youth, The Ugly Dachshund; Boy, Did I Get a Wrong Number; Good Times, Blackbeard's Ghost, Did You Hear the One About the Traveling Saleslady?, The Boatniks, The Parallax View,* more.

THORLEY, VICTOR (N.Y.) Character. Primarily a stage actor. Onscreen from the '50s. IN: *The Young Don't Cry,* more.

THORNDIKE, DAME SYBIL (Eng.) Illustrious character star. Onscreen from 1921. IN: *Moth and Rust, Dawn, Nine Days a Queen, Major Barbara, The Forbidden Street, The Wild Heart, Prince and the Showgirl, Hand in Hand, The Big Gamble,* more. (Died 1976.)

THORNE, DYANNE (S. Cal.) Leading lady. Onscreen in the '70s. IN: *Like Me Like I Do, Pinocchio,* more.

THORNTON, FRANK (Eng.) Character. Onscreen from 1954. IN: *A Flea in Her Ear, The Bed Sitting Room, All the Way Up, The Private Life of Sherlock Holmes,* more.

THORPE, RICHARD (S. Cal.) After his career as leading man in silents, he became one of MGM's most noted directors—of *Night Must Fall, The Great Caruso, Ivanhoe,* etc.—and remained active until the late '60s. Retired now, he is entering his 80s (b. 1896), has long been married to the former Belva Kay, and devoted to his prize-winning hobby, candid camera photography. Onscreen in bits from the teens, then as a leading man from 1924. IN: *Three O'Clock in the Morning, Flame of Desire,* more.

THORPE-BATES, PEGGY (Eng.) Stage character actress. Onscreen from the '60s. IN: *Georgy Girl,* more.

THORSON, RUSSELL (S. Cal.) Character. Onscreen from the '50s. IN: *Zero Hour, I Want to Live!, My Blood Runs Cold, The Stalking Moon, The Learning Tree,* more.

THRING, FRANK (Eng.) Character. Onscreen from the '50s. IN: *The Vikings, Ben Hur, King of Kings, El Cid, Age of Consent, Ned Kelly,* more.

THRONE, MALACHI (S. Cal.) Character. Onscreen from the '60s. IN: *The Young Lovers, Beau Geste,* more.

THULIN, INGRID (Swe.) Costar. Onscreen from 1955. IN: *Foreign Intrigue, Wild Strawberries, The Magician, Brink of Life, The 4 Horsemen of the Apocalypse* (her first English-speaking film; after its completion her voice was dubbed by Anne Baxter), *Winter Light, The Silence, Return from the Ashes, La Guerre est Fini, Night Games, The Damned, Cries and Whispers, Moses, The Cassandra Crossing,* more.

THURMAN, BILL (S. Cal.) Support. Onscreen in the '70s. IN: *A Bullet for Pretty Boy, The Last Picture Show, The Sugarland Express, Gator Bait,* more.

THURSTON, TED (N.Y.) Character. Onscreen from the '50s. IN: *Li'l Abner,* more.

THYSSEN, GRETA (N.Y.) Leading lady; lately inactive in movies. Onscreen from the '50s. IN: *Bus Stop, Accused of Murder, The Beast of Budapest, Three Blondes in His Life, Shadows, Journey to the Seventh Planet,* more.

TIBBS, CASEY (S. Cal.) Rodeo champion once under contract to RKO. Onscreen in 1961 in *A Thunder of Drums* and in 1976 in *Breakheart Pass.*

TICE, STEVE (N.Y.) Young leading man in TV soap operas. Onscreen in the '70s. IN: *Hail,* more.

TIERNEY, GENE (Tex.) Star. Nominated for Best Actress Oscar in *Leave Her to Heaven.* Considerably heavier than in her screen prime, and with a Texas drawl that even Lady Bird Johnson would accept as authentic, the former 20th Century-Fox star—completely recovered from her mental illness—has been married for two decades to Houston millionaire-oil man W. Howard Lee. She was formerly married to (1941–52) and divorced from designer Oleg Cassini, and Lee to and from Hedy Lamarr. She is the mother of two daughters by Cassini, and, by their younger, Christina (Mrs. Giuliano Granata of Manhattan), the grandmother of a little girl. Their eldest daughter, Daria, brain damaged from birth, lives in a home in Massachusetts. In Houston, the actress, in her 50s now (b. 1920), takes an active role in charitable works close to her heart (such as Retarded Children), participates in local politics, and is the perfect hostess at frequent and enormous social affairs (usually wearing, still, the latest fashions of Cassini). With her husband, she travels much—every autumn to Connecticut, where she grew up, for the changing of the leaves; to New York in winter to see new shows and visit relatives; to France at least once a year. Her last movie was

1964's *The Pleasure Seekers*, after which, in '69, she costarred with Ray Milland in a memorable TV-film drama, *Daughter of the Mind*. In '74 she was a guest on *The Mike Douglas Show* on TV, revealing herself to be lovely, ample, and content with her life as it is now. Onscreen from 1940. IN: *The Return of Frank James, Hudson's Bay, Tobacco Road, Belle Starr, The Shanghai Gesture, China Girl, Thunder Birds, Heaven Can Wait, Laura, A Bell for Adano, Dragonwyck, The Razor's Edge, The Ghost and Mrs. Muir, Whirlpool, Night and the City, The Mating Season, On the Riviera, Close to My Heart, Plymouth Adventure, Never Let Me Go, The Egyptian, The Left Hand of God* (during the making of which, in 1955, she suffered a mental breakdown; did not return to the screen for seven years), *Advise and Consent, Toys in the Attic*, more.

TIERNEY, LAWRENCE (N.Y.) Trouble and tragedy, inevitably resulting in headlines, dog the steps of this onetime star—now a rapidly balding, gray-haired, chesty, and big-bellied character actor. His movie gangster image combined with a drinking problem managed to involve him in more than two dozen scrapes with the law—barroom brawls, drunken driving, disorderly conduct incidents—from the 1950s on. And the headlines always hark back to his most famous role, reading, as this one did in the *New York Post* in January 1973: "DILLINGER" STAR IS STABBED. In a street row outside a bar on Ninth Avenue, near the second-rate hotel where he had a room, the actor had required surgery for a "serious stab wound" in the abdomen. In June 1975 there was this stark news report: "Former movie actor Lawrence Tierney was questioned and then released by police in connection with the apparent suicide leap of a 24-year-old woman from the fourth-floor window of her midtown apartment." Tierney told police that he had come to visit the woman, Bonnie Jones, and "had just gotten there, and she just went out the window." In his 50s now, Tierney—the brother of actor Scott Brady—still gets occasional movie roles but not enough to support him. To get by, he has in this decade undertaken other endeavors. In 1971 he was a hard-hat construction worker on a West 57th Street skyscraper; in 1974 he was driving a horse-pulled hansom cab in Central Park and also starting up a drama workshop at 850 Seventh Avenue. Despite the enormous change in his looks, along Broadway, where he hangs out, tourists often recognize in him the 26-year-old who made an indelible impression, and ask: "Aren't you the man who played Dillinger?" He nods, smiles and signs, then—wondering if that's the only role anyone ever saw him play—goes his lonely way. Onscreen from 1943. IN:

The Falcon Out West, The Ghost Ship, Back to Bataan, Youth Runs Wild, Those Endearing Young Charms, Badman's Territory, San Quentin, Born to Kill, The Devil Thumbs a Ride, Bodyguard, Shakedown, Kill or Be Killed, The Hoodlum, Best of the Bad Men, The Greatest Show on Earth, The Bushwackers, The Steel Cage, A Child Is Waiting, Custer of the West, Such Good Friends (a bit, as a guard), more, including 1975's *Abduction*, patterned after the Patty Hearst kidnapping, in which he was—a switch—an F.B.I. agent.

TIFFIN, PAMELA (N.Y.) In the late 1960s when separated from *New York* magazine publisher, Clay Felker (divorced since '71), this leading lady made numerous movies in Rome. Also, determined to have an education—her formal learning ended at 16 when she became a model—she took courses at Loyola in history, art, and Irish and European literature. Lately, and having done no acting in this decade, the young (b. 1942) and still beautiful actress has been living in New York and working toward a degree in literature at Columbia University. Onscreen from 1961. IN: *Summer and Smoke; One, Two, Three; State Fair, Come Fly With Me, The Lively Set, For Those Who Think Young, The Pleasure Seekers, The Hallelujah Trail, Harper, The Protagonists, Torture Me But Kill Me With Kisses, Paranoia, Kiss the Other Sheik, Viva Max!*, more.

TIGERMAN, GARY (S. Cal.) Support. Onscreen from the '60s. IN: *Hello Down There, Halls of Anger, Pretty Maids All in a Row*, more.

TIGHE, KEVIN (S. Cal.) Support. Popular on TV as the costar of *Emergency!* Son of the late character actor Harry Shannon. Onscreen from the '60s. IN: *The Graduate*, more.

TILDEN, BEAU (N.Y.) Character. Onscreen from the '50s. IN: *Butterfield 8, A Fine Pair, The Swimmer; Harvey Middleman, Fireman*; more.

TILL, JENNY (Eng.) Leading lady. Onscreen from the '60s. IN: *A Story of David, Europe by Night, The Frightened City, Theatre of Death, A Challenge for Robin Hood*, more.

TILLER, NADIA (It.) Leading lady. Onscreen from the '50s. IN: *The Life and Loves of Mozart, Rosemary, Night Affair, Portrait of a Sinner, Riff Raff Girls, The World in My Pocket, The Burning Court, The Upper Hand, Tender Scoundrel, Tonio Kroger*, more.

TILTON, MARTHA (S. Cal.) The greatly popular Benny Goodman singer who still sings once in a while at a nostalgic event in Hollywood is married, retired, and living in the San Fernando Valley. Her favorite role now is that of "Aunt Martha"—cheering the success of her actress-model niece, Holly Hoffine. Onscreen from 1941. IN: *Sunny, Crime Incorporated, The Benny Goodman Story*, more.

TINGWELL, CHARLES (Eng.) Character. Onscreen from the '40s. IN: *Always Another Dawn, Kangaroo, The Desert Rats, Trouble in the Sky, Murder She Said (. . . at the Gallop, . . . Ahoy, . . . Most Foul*); *Dracula—Prince of Darkness*; more.

TINNE, ALEX (S. Cal.) Character. Onscreen in the '70s. IN: *Scandalous John*, more.

TINTI, GABRIELE (It.) Support. Onscreen from the '60s. IN: *Heaven on Earth, The Flight of the Phoenix, The Wild Eye, The Legend of Lylah Clare, The Oldest Profession, Seven Golden Men, The Mysterious Island of Captain Nemo*, more.

TINY TIM (N.Y.) Singer. Onscreen in 1968 in *You Are What You Eat.*

TIPPIT, WAYNE (N.Y.) Support. Onscreen in the '70s. IN: *Tell Me That You Love Me, Junie Moon*; more.

TOBEY, KEN (S. Cal.) Character. Onscreen from 1947. IN: *Dangerous Venture, I Was a Male War Bride, Twelve O'Clock High, My Friend Irma Goes West, Kiss Tomorrow Goodbye, The Thing, Rawhide, The Beast From 20,-000 Fathoms, Down Three Dark Streets, The Steel Cage, It Came From Beneath the Sea, The Steel Jungle, The Wings of Eagles, Gunfight at the O.K. Corral, Cry Terror, X-15, Marlowe, Billy Jack, Dirty Mary Crazy Larry, Homebodies*, more.

TOBIAS, GEORGE (S. Cal.) Each morning wherever he is, this greatly popular character actor jogs—to keep in shape to jog from TV assignments (*Medical Center*, etc.) to movies and back again. With his horses, he lives on an isolated 20-acre ranch in California's Lucerne Valley, where he is a volunteer member of the San Bernardino County Sheriff's Search and Rescue posse. He lives alone, as he always has, for in his 70s (b. 1901), bachelorhood is still his bag. "When you're married," he says, "you have no freedom. I see what's going on with married people. I feel I've been married thousands of times just watching them." Lady friends he has had, yes. But when any one of them seemed intent on marriage, he says, "I would introduce her to a friend and *he'd* marry her." How does he feel now, in the autumn of his life, without a mate? "I *like* it," he shouts.

Onscreen from 1939. IN: *Ninotchka, Maisie, Balalaika, City for Conquest, Torrid Zone, They Drive by Night, The Bride Came C.O.D., Sergeant York, Strawberry Blonde, My Sister Eileen, Captains of the Clouds, Yankee Doodle Dandy, Air Force, Mission to Moscow, The Mask of Dimitrios, Passage to Marseille, Objective Burma, Mildred Pierce, Her Kind of Man, My Wild Irish Rose* (in '47, the last under his 7-year contract at Warners where he had made 32 pictures), *The Set-Up, Everybody Does It, The Tanks Are Coming, Rawhide, Ten Tall Men, The Glenn Miller Story, The Seven Little Foys, Silk Stockings* (repeating the role he had just done on Broadway), *Marjorie Morningstar* (in '58; it took him back to Warners), *A New Kind of Love, Bullet for a Bad Man, The Glass Bottom Boat, The Phynx*, more.

TOBIN, DAN (S. Cal.) Character. Onscreen from 1938. IN: *The Stadium Murders, The Pittsburgh Kid, Woman of the Year, Undercurrent, The Bachelor and the Bobby-Soxer, Sealed Verdict, The Big Clock, Queen for a Day* (lead), *Dream Wife, The Catered Affair, The Last Angry Man, Who's Got the Action?, How to Succeed in Business Without Really Trying, Herbie Rides Again*, more.

TOBIN, DARRA LYN (S. Cal.) Support. Onscreen in the '70s. IN: *Bunny O'Hare*, more.

TOBIN, GENEVIEVE (N.Y.) The sophisticated blonde comedienne is in her 70s (b. 1901), still blonde, and still happily married (since '38) to William Keighley, former director at Warners where most of her screen career was spent. (1941's *Queen of Crime* was her last film.) After almost two decades in Paris, the actress and her husband moved to New York in '72. Today they live in a magnificent, art-filled, upper Fifth Avenue apartment not far from the Metropolitan Museum of Art, with which he is affiliated in an advisory capacity. Onscreen from 1930. IN: *A Lady Surrenders, Free Love, Seed, The Gay Diplomat, One Hour With You, Perfect Understanding, Infernal Machine, Goodbye Again, Dark Hazard, Kiss and Make-Up, The Woman in Red, The Goose and the Gander, The Case of the Lucky Legs, The Petrified Forest, The Great Gambini, Dramatic School, Zaza; Yes, My Darling Daughter; No Time for Comedy*, more.

TOBIN, MICHELE (S. Cal.) Support. Onscreen from the '60s. IN: *Yours, Mine and Ours; 80 Steps to Jonah*, more.

TODD, ANN (Eng.) Moviegoers who chanced upon a dreadful little British mystery of '72, *Beware of the Brethren*, received a rather nasty shock. Playing a pivotal role in it, the aging, fanatically religious mother of a girl-murdering son, and making her first screen appearance in six years was this actress: Ann Todd—the cool and classically beautiful blonde whom Selznick had brought from England to Hollywood in '47 to costar as Gregory Peck's wife in *The Paradine Case.* The inescapable fact is that time has not stood still. The actress is well on into her 60s (b. 1909), and is no longer even a blonde— her hair is brown now, and worn short and curly. She is a grandmother, the mother of a son, David, in young middle age (by her first husband, Victor Malcolm), and a daughter in her mid-30s, Francesca (by her second, composer Nigel Tangye). By her third marriage (1949–57), to famous British director David Lean, she has no children. The star's patrician face has aged, but, interestingly, the lines on it —about her mouth and eyes—give her something of the look that Gladys Cooper had when Hollywood's chief British aristocrat-in-residence. After leaving Hollywood, Ann Todd starred for another two decades in movies. And in her mid-40s she also became a Shakespearean actress. Joining the Old Vic, she played in —among others—*The Taming of the Shrew,* *Macbeth,* and *Love's Labour Lost.* After starring in the '66 movie *90 Degrees in the Shade,* she stopped acting. She loved moviemaking, however, and was a lifelong travel devotee. Combining these passions, no longer tied down by family or marital obligations, she embarked on an entirely new career as a documentary film maker. Her enthusiastic dedication to this art form has taken her to many faraway places and won her countless awards for her six (to date) documentaries. Perhaps the best-known of them is *Free in the Sun,* which she filmed in Australia on commission from New South Wales, and which—as with all her films—she produced, directed, and narrated. Among the locations where she has filmed are Jordan (*Thunder of Silence* was done there), Japan, and Russia, where she did a saga of the Trans-Siberian railway. It is assumed that her brief return to movie acting in the indescribably poor *Beware of the Brethren* was to raise capital for additional documentaries. It is hoped that she will return again—in a worthier vehicle. Onscreen from 1931. IN: *Keepers of Youth, The Ghost Train, Things to Come, South Riding, Ships With Wings, The Seventh Veil* (its success made her an international star), *Daybreak, So Evil My Love, The Passionate Friends, Madeleine, Breaking the Sound Barrier, The Green Scarf, Time Without Pity, Taste of Fear, Son of Captain Blood,* more.

TODD, BEVERLY (S. Cal.) Black leading lady. Onscreen from the '60s. IN: *The Lost Man, They Call Me Mr. Tibbs, Brother John,* more.

TODD, BOB (Eng.) Comic character. Onscreen from the '60s. IN: *The Intelligence Men, Hot Millions, Scars of Dracula; Digby, the Biggest Dog in the World;* more.

TODD, CHRISTINE (S. Cal.) Support. Onscreen from the '60s. IN: *Lady in Cement,* more.

TODD, LISA (S. Cal.) Leading lady. Popular on TV as the voluptuous brunette in *Hee Haw.* Onscreen in the '70s. IN: *Gaily Gaily* (bit), *The Doll Squad,* more.

TODD, LOLA (S. Cal.) The lovely brunette leading lady in Westerns and serials of the '20s (she also had secondary roles in other features) is in her 60s, lives in Hollywood, and is retired. Onscreen from 1925. IN: *The Harvester,* more.

TODD, RICHARD (Eng.) Costar. Nominated for Best Actor Oscar in *The Hasty Heart.* Still most active in movies, he also stars frequently on the stage, being recently on the boards in England in *Murder by Numbers* and *Death on Demand,* and on tour in Australia in *Sleuth.* For some time in the '60s, when there was a slack period in movies for him, he became a dairy farmer in England. He has since sold his farm and set up his own theater company in London. In 1969 the actor was divorced from his first wife, mother of his grown son and daughter, after 20 years of marriage. The following year he married model Virginia Mailer, who was named as corespondent in the divorce and is two decades his junior. (He was born in 1919.) They have a son who was born in '73. Onscreen from 1948. IN: *For Them That Trespass, Stage Fright, Lightning Strikes Twice, Interrupted Journey, The Story of Robin Hood, The Assassin, The Sword and the Rose, Rob Roy, A Man Called Peter, The Virgin Queen; D-Day, the Sixth of June; Battle Hell, Naked Earth, Jungle Fighters, The Longest Day, Never Let Go, Why Bother to Knock, Operation Crossbow, The Battle of the Fiorita, Coast of Skeletons, The Love-Ins, Subterfuge, Dorian Gray, Asylum, The Sky Is Falling,* more.

TOGNAZZI, UGO (It.) Leading man. Onscreen from the '50s. IN: *I Cadetti di Guascogna, The Conjugal Bed, Crazy Desire, The Ape Woman, Magnificent Cuckold, The Hours of Love, A Very Handy Man, The Climax, Barbarella,* more.

TOLAN, KATHLEEN (S. Cal.) Support. Onscreen in the '70s. IN: *Death Wish,* more.

TOLAN, MICHAEL (S. Cal.) Leading man. Onscreen from 1951. IN: *The Enforcer, Hiawatha, The Greatest Story Ever Told, Hour of the Gun, The Lost Man, John and Mary, Three Hundred Year Weekend,* more.

TOLKAN, JAMES (N.Y.) Character. Onscreen from the '60s. IN: *Stiletto, They Might Be Giants,* more.

TOLL, PAMELA (N.Y.) Ingenue. Onscreen from the '60s. IN: *Rascal*, more.

TOLSKY, SUSAN (S. Cal.) Support. Onscreen in the '70s. IN: *Pretty Maids All in a Row*, more.

TOMBES, ANDREW (S. Cal.) In his 80s now (b. 1891), this fine character actor is retired. Onscreen from 1933. IN: *Moulin Rouge, Charlie Chan at the Olympics, Wolf of New York, Captain Caution, Lady Scarface, Meet John Doe, Bedtime Story, My Gal Sal, They All Kissed the Bride, Coney Island, I Dood It, Can't Help Singing, Phantom Lady, You Came Along, Badman's Territory; Oh, You Beautiful Doll; Joe Palooka in Humphrey Takes a Chance, The Jackpot*, more, including 1955's *How to Be Very Very Popular*, his most recent to date.

TOMELTY, JOSEPH (Eng.) Character. Onscreen from 1947. IN: *Odd Man Out, Melba, The Horse's Mouth, Hobson's Choice, Hell Below Zero, Front Page Story, Moby Dick, John and Julie, The Day They Robbed the Bank of England, Upstairs and Downstairs*, more.

TOMKINS, DON (N.Y.) Broadway character. Onscreen in 1930 in *Follow Thru*.

TOMLAN, GWYNNE (N.Y.) Black support. Onscreen from the '60s. IN: *John and Mary, The Happening, Bananas*, more.

TOMLIN, LILY (S. Cal.) Actress-comedienne. Nominated for Best Supporting Actress Oscar in *Nashville*, her first picture. Onscreen from 1975.

TOMLIN, PINKY (S. Cal.) The shy comedy star-composer ("Object of My Affection," "The Love Bug Will Bite You," etc.) who, after his movie career, was greatly popular on TV is in his late 60s now (b. 1908) and retired. Onscreen from 1935. IN: *Times Square Lady, King Solomon of Broadway* (wrote its songs), *Paddy O'Day* (same), *Don't Get Personal, Down in Arkansas*, more, including 1943's *Here Comes Elmer*, his last.

TOMLINSON, DAVID (Eng.) Character lead. Onscreen from 1940. IN: *Quiet Wedding, Johnny in the Clouds, My Brother's Keeper, Fame Is the Spur, So Long at the Fair, The Wooden Horse, The Ship Was Loaded, Up the Creek, Tom Jones, Mary Poppins, War Gods of the Deep, The Love Bug, Bedknobs and Broomsticks, From Hong Kong with Love*, more.

TOMPKINS, ANGEL (S. Cal.) Leading lady. Onscreen in the '70s. IN: *I Love My Wife, How to Seduce a Woman, The Teacher; Walking Tall, Part II*; more.

TOMPKINS, DARLENE (S. Cal.) Support. Onscreen from 1962. IN: *Blue Hawaii*, more.

TOMPKINS, JOAN (S. Cal.) Character. Onscreen from the '60s. IN: *Popi, Zigzag, I Love My Wife, The Christine Jorgensen Story*, more.

TONER, TOM (S. Cal.) Character. Onscreen from the '60s. IN: *The Caper of the Golden Bulls, The Return of Count Yorga*, more.

TOOMEY, REGIS (S. Cal.) He was—he remains, in his 70s (b. 1902)—one of Hollywood's most popular actors. His picture record to date: 250-plus. And when not busy in a movie he is to be found all over the TV dials. For a long stretch in the '50s and '60s, he was on hand each week, being featured in four series: *Dante's Inferno, Hey Mulligan, Richard Diamond, Burke's Law*. On January 14, 1975, he and wife Kathryn marked their golden wedding anniversary, and celebrated by moving into a new home in Brentwood. A leader in Hollywood civic and charity affairs, the actor is past president of the Motion Picture Permanent Charities Committee, and a member of the governing body of the L.A. Community Chest. Toomey's career numbers many "firsts," including his costarring with Chester Morris in *Alibi*, the first all-talking gangster melodrama. In 1931 he appeared opposite Clara Bow in *Kick In*, her first talkie. Onscreen from 1929. IN: *Wheel of Life, Illusion, Shadow of the Law, Scandal Sheet, Other Men's Women, Murder by the Clock, Touchdown, Shopworn, She Had to Say Yes, Murder by the Blackboard, Redhead, G-Men, Shadows of the Orient, Submarine D-1, Wings of the Navy, Union Pacific, His Girl Friday, Northwest Passage, Arizona, Dive Bomber, They Died With Their Boots On, The Forest Rangers, Spellbound, The Big Sleep, The Bishop's Wife, The Boy with Green Hair, Show Boat, The High and the Mighty, Guys and Dolls, Warlock, Voyage to the Bottom of the Sea, Man's Favorite Sport?, Gunn, Change of Habit*, more.

TOONE, GEOFFREY (Eng.) Character. Onscreen from 1937. IN: *Sword of Honor, The Man Between, Diane, The King and I, Zero Hour; Once More, With Feeling; Dr. Crippen, The Entertainer, Terror of the Tongs, Kennwort Reiher*, more.

TOPART, JEAN (Eng.) Support. Onscreen in the '70s. IN: *Cold Sweat*, more.

TOPOL (Israel) Costar. Nominated for Best Actor Oscar in *Fiddler on the Roof*. Only now in his early 40s (b. 1935), despite numerous roles as an old man, he lives with his wife, Galia, and their two sons and daughter in Tel Aviv. There, besides starring, he produces films for the Israeli market, some of which are shown internationally. Onscreen from 1965. IN: *Sallah* (billed phonetically "Haym" though his name actually is Chaim Topol; he produced it), *Cast a Giant Shadow, A Talent for Loving, Before Winter Comes, The Public Eye, Follow Me, Galileo, The Boys Will Never Believe*, more.

TOPPER, BURT (S. Cal.) Director-producer-actor. Onscreen in 1964 in *War Is Hell*. (Besides this he has produced *Thunder Alley, Wild in the Streets*, etc.)

TORK, PETER (S. Cal.) The fortune he made as one of "The Monkees" dissipated, he later—in '72—served four months in federal prison after an arrest for hashish possession. In September 1975, long-haired, bearded, and in his 30s (b. 1942), the singer became a teacher—of math, English, and Eastern philosophy—at a private high school, Pacific Hills, in Santa Monica. He lives in nearby Venice in a three-room house with Barbara Iannoli, mother of his son Ivan (b. 1976), and with his young daughter, Hallie, by his marriage that ended in divorce. He has talked of a comeback in rock music. Meanwhile he is known to his students as Mr. Thorkelson, that being his real name. Onscreen in 1968 in *Head*.

TORME, MEL (S. Cal.) "The Velvet Fog," besides continuing to be a major nightclub attraction, is the author of one of the better books on Garland: *The Other Side of the Rainbow with Judy Garland on the Dawn Patrol*. He lives in Beverly Hills with wife, Janette Scott, and their children. Onscreen from 1943. IN: *Higher and Higher, Pardon My Rhythm, Let's Go Steady, Junior Miss, Janie Gets Married, Good News, Words and Music, Duchess of Idaho, Girls' Town, The Big Operator, Walk Like a Dragon, A Man Called Adam*, more.

TORN, RIP (N.Y.) Leading man. Husband of actress Geraldine Page. Onscreen from 1956. IN: *Baby Doll, Time Limit, A Face in the Crowd, Cat on a Hot Tin Roof, Pork Chop Hill, King of Kings, Sweet Bird of Youth* (with Geraldine Page), *The Cincinnati Kid, One Spy Too Many, You're a Big Boy Now, Beach Red, Sol Madrid, Beyond the Law, Tropic of Cancer, Maidstone, Crazy Joe, The Man Who Fell to Earth*, more.

TORNATORE, JOE (S. Cal.) Support. Onscreen in the '70s. IN: *Sweet Sweetback's Baadasssss Song, McQ, Black Samson*, more.

TORRES, JOSE (It.) Character. Onscreen from the '60s. IN: *Wild 90, Death Rides a Horse, The Five Man Army*, more.

TORRES, LIZ (S. Cal.) Singer-actress. Onscreen in the '70s. IN: *You've Got to Walk It Like You Talk It or You'll Lose That Beat*, more.

TORRES, RAQUEL (S. Cal.) Outrageously beautiful and raven-haired she was, and still is, in her late 60s (1908). Still slender and petite, she has been happily married to actor Jon Hall since St. Valentine's Day 1959. Newspaper reports of this event listed her age at the time as 40, an obvious misprint for no child of nine could have played the role she did in 1928's *White Shadows of the South Seas*. Content to be a housewife, she lives with Jon Hall in Santa Monica. She had given up her career for marriage to financier Stephen Ames, a successful marriage lasting until his death. Onscreen from 1928. IN: *The Bridge of San Luis Rey, Desert Rider, Under a Texas Moon, The Sea Bat, Free and Easy, Aloha, Tampico, So This Is Africa, The Woman I Stole, Duck Soup*, more, including 1936's *Red Wagon*, her last.

TORREY, ROGER (S. Cal.) Support. Onscreen from 1960. IN: *The Plunderers, The Nutty Professor, I'll Take Sweden, Town Tamer, The Fortune Cookie*, more.

TOTTER, AUDREY (S. Cal.) Revisiting one's past does not have to be sad affair, she says. In the summer of 1972 the actress went back to MGM for the first time in 23 years. Not since she had costarred with Clark Gable and Alexis Smith in *Any Number Can Play* had she been on the lot. She returned to do a guest role in TV's *Medical Center*, which quickly evolved into a recurring part, though on a "sometime" basis, as she wished. The role is that of Dr. Joe Gannon's (star Chad Everett) superefficient Nurse Wilcox. Going back to the studio, she says, "was like returning to an old, familiar home." MGM was indeed her first Hollywood home studio, for six years and 15 pictures. It was in her seventh picture that she became a recognized screen star, as she had been on radio, where she was famous as the "girl with a thousand voices." This picture was the experimental *Lady in the Lake*, directed by Robert Montgomery. Since the camera was the eyes of the never-seen hero (narrated by Montgomery), and mostly what it saw was a young actress giving the performance of her life, Audrey Totter's reputation was made. Also at MGM, offscreen, there were two serious romances—with Brian Donlevy (they had costarred in *The Beginning or the End*) and Clark Gable. The latter, promoted by mutual friends who felt she possessed the same gaiety as Carole Lombard, for whom Gable still grieved, developed finally into a long-lasting friendship. After leaving Metro, the actress played top roles in another 23 pictures. And, in 1952, age 33, she gave up her well-publicized "bachelor girl" status. A saleswoman at Saks Fifth Avenue introduced her to one of her preferred customers, Dr. Leo Fred. "The minute I met him," she says, "I knew I was going to marry him. He was gorgeous." These many years later, she says he still is. Also, she reports, as the wife of an M.D. she had been unwittingly rehearsing for her role in *Medical Center*. The actress and her husband have one child, Mary Elizabeth Anne, called Mia, a recent art history graduate of the University of California at Berkeley. It was to be with her youngster that she imposed a deliberate slowdown on her career after a short-lived comedy series on TV in 1962, *Our Man Higgins*. In that decade she worked in just three movies and did a mere handful of TV guest-star appearances. Her "retirement" years were spent, she says, sharpening her skills as a gourmet cook and at knitting. "The essence of the Women's Lib movement," she has said, "is that everyone should have the right to explore areas which bring them the most fulfillment. For me, happiness begins at home. I like having my husband make the decisions, and I derive great personal satisfaction from caring for him, as well as my daughter." It was after her husband retired from medicine—he had been Assistant Dean of U.C.L.A.'s School of Medicine and Chief of Staff at the Veterans Hospital in L.A. —that she decided to resume her career. Besides *Medical Center*, she has guested in *Hawaii Five-O*, and is looking for the right role for a movie comeback. Onscreen from 1944. IN: *Main Street After Dark, Her Highness and the Bellboy, Dangerous Partners, The Sailor Takes a Wife, The Postman Always Rings Twice, The Unsuspected, High Wall, Tenth Avenue Angel, The Saxon Charm, The Set-Up, The Blue Veil, The Woman They Almost Lynched, Man in the Dark, Mission Over Korea, Women's Prison, A Bullet for Joey, Jet Attack, The Carpetbaggers, Harlow* (the Magna version), *Chubasco*, more.

TOUMANOVA, TAMARA (S. Cal.) The legendary ballerina-actress from Russia has come a long way since her birth in a Siberian freight car somewhere between Toumen and Esternburg. Her mother, a Georgian princess married to a colonel of the Imperial Army, was en route during the Bolshevik Revolution, hoping to bear her child in her home at Tiflis—but did not arrive in time. At 7, Toumanova made her ballet debut with Pavlova, whose protegee she had become. (She later portrayed her mentor in the movie *Tonight We Sing*.) By age 12 she was a prima ballerina, and in her late 50s (b. 1917),

she remains one, as well as one of the world's most elegantly beautiful women. "I have to dance," she says. "I wear ballet shoes like a second skin. For me, dancing is life." She lives with her mother, Mrs. Khassidovitch-Boretcky, in Beverly Hills. Adjoining her house is a splendid dance studio. "I practice there for at least four hours every day, often to the Beatles' records," she says, "for they have such a marvelous rhythm." She continues to make frequent guest appearances with ballet companies in South America and Europe. It was during her (only) marriage to famous scriptwriter-producer Casey Robinson—now living in retirement in Australia—that he decided she should be a screen star as well as a ballerina. *Days of Glory*, though, a drama in which she was billed above her leading man, Gregory Peck (his debut too), was Robinson's showcase for her. Though she has been in numerous pictures since, it remains her only starring vehicle, and the only movie in which she did not dance. In 1974 she made her legitimate stage debut, costarring with Jean Stapleton at the Ahmanson Theatre in Los Angeles in *The Time of the Cuckoo*. This should make another chapter for the book, *Through Life With My Daughter*, that her mother is writing. Onscreen from 1944. IN: *Days of Glory, Tonight We Sing, Deep in My Heart, Invitation to the Dance, Torn Curtain, The Private Life of Sherlock Holmes*, more.

TOVAR, LUPITA (S. Cal.) Last onscreen in 1945's *The Crime Doctor's Courage*, she is still beautiful in her 60s (b. 1911), has long been the wife of agent Paul Kohner, and is the mother of former actress Susan Kohner and producer Pablo Kohner. Among the industry's most social, she and her husband live in Beverly Hills and travel widely. Onscreen from 1929. IN: *The Veiled Woman, Desire of Death, The Cat Creeps, East of Borneo, Yankee Don, Border Love, An Old Spanish Custom, Blockade, Maria, Tropic Fury, The Fighting Gringo, Two-Gun Sheriff*, more. (See Susan Kohner.)

TOWB, HARRY (Eng.) Character. Onscreen from the 50s. IN: *Quiet Woman, Gift Horse, Knave of Hearts, The Sleeping Tiger, A Prize of Gold, Doublecross, 30 Is a Dangerous Age, Cynthia, Prudence and the Pill*, more.

TOWERS, CONSTANCE (N.Y.) This beautiful actress, wife of actor John Gavin, no longer appears in movies, but stars instead in civic light opera (*The Sound of Music, South Pacific*, etc.) and at the most famous music fairs. Onscreen from 1955. IN: *Bring Your Smile Along, The Horse Soldiers, Sergeant Rutledge, Shock Corridor, Fate Is the Hunter, The Naked Kiss*, more.

TOWNE, ALINE (S. Cal.) Support; former leading lady. Onscreen from 1950. IN: *The Invisible Monster* (serial), *Zombies of the Stratosphere* (serial), *Trader Tom of the South Seas* (serial), *Julie, Send Me No Flowers, A Guide for the Married Man, Song of Norway*, more.

TOWNES, CHRISTOPHER (S. Cal.) Support. Onscreen in the '70s. IN: *Tough*, more.

TOWNES, HARRY (S. Cal.) Character. Onscreen from 1954. IN: *Operation Manhunt, The Mountain, The Brothers Karamazov, The Screaming Mimi, Cry Tough, Sanctuary, The Bedford Incident, Fitzwilly, Heaven With a Gun, In Enemy Country, Strategy of Terror*, more.

TOWNLEY, TOKE (Eng.) Character actor. Onscreen from the '50s. IN: *Time Gentlemen, Please; Innocents in Paris, The Runaway Bus, A Cry from the Streets, Men of Sherwood Forest, John and Julie, Doctor at Sea, Now and Forever, The Chalk Garden, Scars of Dracula*, more.

TOWNSEND, COLLEEN (D.C.) 20th Century-Fox, in the '40s, had plans to make her a star. But she had other plans. After *When Willie Comes Marching Home* ('50), her sixth film, this brunette beauty quit the screen to marry a young Presbyterian minister, Louis H. Evans Jr., to whom she remains most happily wed. In the first six years of their marriage (two of them in Edinburgh, Scotland, where her husband completed his ministerial studies at New College), four children were born to them: three sons—Dan, Tim, and Jim—and a daughter, Andie. Affiliated with the First Presbyterian Church of Bel Air for years, Colleen and her husband have now moved to the Washington, D.C., area where they have been called to serve the National Presbyterian Church. In '73 the former actress, now in her 40s (b. 1928), published an inspirational book, *A New Joy*, a modern woman's re-evaluation and rewriting of the Beatitudes. She explains that she chose the Beatitudes for special study "because in these words Jesus was speaking to believers like me —they weren't very pious and they were far from perfect, but they had decided *for* Jesus. Now they needed His help in trying to live the life to which He had called them." She says she was drawn to a study of the Scriptures at a time when the "glow had gone" from her life. Interestingly, her movie background was in large part responsible. "To me it didn't seem unusual that a spiritual rebirth should happen to someone in my profession—I have known, and still know, many dedicated Christians in the motion picture industry," she says. "But to many people the combination of my belief and my profession had a special attraction." Over the years, countless speaking invitations were extended—and accepted—for her to share her religious experiences. Eventually the pressure became intense. And, she adds, "I could see where the glow had gone. It had retreated to deep inside me. I was beginning to feel like an 'up front' Christian and obviously I was resisting the celebrity bit. It is one thing to talk about being a Christian in front of groups, but quite another to be a Christian in your home and in your community. I longed to be more deeply Christian where it really counted." It was then that she immersed herself in studies of the Scriptures. And, from them, for Colleen Townsend Evans, came *A New Joy*—both in print and in her personal life. Onscreen from 1944. IN: *Janie, Hollywood Canteen, The Very Thought of You, The Walls of Jericho, Chicken Every Sunday*, and *When Willie Comes Marching Home.*

TOWNSEND, JILL (Eng.) English leading lady, married to actor Nicol Williamson. Popular for a while in the United States in the TV series *Cimarron Strip*. Onscreen in the '70s. IN: *Oh, Alfie*, more.

TOWNSEND, K. C. (N.Y.) Supporting actress. Onscreen in the '70s. IN: *Husbands*, more.

TOY, NOEL (S. Cal.) Dancer-actress. Onscreen from the '50s. IN: *How to be Very, Very Popular;* more.

TOZZI, FAUSTO (It.) Character. Onscreen from the '50s. IN: *House of Ricordi, The Wonders of Aladdin, Constantine and the Cross, Crazy Joe*, more.

TRABERT, TONY (N.Y.) Tennis champion. Onscreen in 1974. IN: *The Outfit* (as himself).

TRACY, ARTHUR (N.Y.) The Famous "Street Singer," now in his 70s (b. 1903), lives in an apartment in Manhattan and is retired. Onscreen in the '30s. IN: *The Big Broadcast, Flirtation, Limelight, The Street Singer, Follow Your Star, Command Performance*, more.

TRAEGER, RICK (S. Cal.) Support. Onscreen in the '70s. IN: *Bedknobs and Broomsticks*, more.

TRAVERS, BILL (Eng.) Besides acting still, this leading man now produces nature films in England. He and Virginia McKenna, his frequent costar, have been married since 1957 and are the parents of four. Onscreen from 1951. IN: *The Browning Version, Romeo and Juliet, Bhowani Junction, Wee Geordie, The Barretts of Wimpole Street, The Seventh Sin, Gorgo, The*

Green Helmet, Invasion Quartet, Duel at Diablo, Born Free, The Lions Are Free, Ring of Bright Water, An Elephant Called Slowly, The Belstone Fox, more.

TRAVERS, LINDEN (Eng.) Character; former leading lady. Older sister of Bill Travers. Lately inactive in movies. Onscreen from the early '30s. IN: *Double Alibi, The Lady Vanishes, Jassy, Quartet* ("The Colonel's Lady" episode), *Master of Bankdam, Mr. Know-All, No Orchids for Miss Blandish, The Bad Lord Byron*, more.

TRAVERS, SUSAN (Eng.) Character. Onscreen in the '70s. IN: *The Statue, The Abominable Dr. Phibes*, more.

TRAVERS, SY (N.Y.) Character. Onscreen from the '60s. IN: *P.J., A New Leaf*, more.

TRAVIS, JUNE (Ill.) That lovely Warners leading lady of the '30s is a stunningly beautiful woman in her 60s (b. 1914), and looking 20 years younger. Also, living in Chicago and absent from movies since 1953, she has become a most accomplished stage actress. She has lately played Goneril opposite Morris Carnovsky in *King Lear* at Chicago's Goodman Theatre. She has also starred with Forrest Tucker in *Never Too Late* and *Life With Father*. In the latter, as wife Vinnie, she was nominated for both the Sarah Siddons Award and the Joseph Jefferson Award. Theatergoers around the country have seen her in *The Boy Friend, A View From the Bridge, I Found April* (with Jeanne Crain), *The Philadelphia Story* (with Lee Radziwill), and costarring with Douglas Fairbanks Jr. in *The Pleasure of His Company*. This play brought her back, for a while at least, to Hollywood, where countless Warner colleagues turned out to cheer her onstage at the Huntington Hartford Theatre. Onscreen from 1935. IN: *Stranded, Broadway Gondolier, Ceiling Zero, Earthworm Tractors, Times Square Playboy, Bengal Tiger, The Big Game, The Case of the Black Cat, Love Is on the Air, The Kid Comes Back, Over the Wall, Go Chase Yourself, The Gladiator, Mr. Doodle Kicks Off, Little Orphan Annie*, more, including 1939's *Federal Man-Hunt*, her last leading-lady role; she was then offscreen until returning for a supporting role in Bette Davis' *The Star* in 1953.

TRAVIS, RICHARD (S. Cal.) The rangy, rugged blond leading man from Arkansas reverted to his real name, William Justice, years ago, and as that has become one of the richest real estate entrepreneurs in Southern California. Now in his 60s (b. 1913) and a fine-looking man still, he was onscreen through *Missile to the Moon* in '58, appearing in exactly 32 mov-

ies. He does not anticipate there being a 33rd. Onscreen from 1941. IN: *The Man Who Came to Dinner, The Big Shot, The Postman Didn't Ring, Busses Roar, Mission to Moscow, Undercover Maisie, Big Town After Dark, Jewels of Brandenburg, Backlash, Waterfront at Midnight, Alaska Patrol, Sky Liner, Passage West, Mask of the Dragon, Fingerprints Don't Lie, The Annapolis Story, Blonde Bait*, more.

TRAYLOR, WILLIAM (S. Cal.) Character. Onscreen in the '70s. IN: *Who Fears the Devil*, more.

TREE, DAVID (Eng.) One of the most popular young leading men in British pictures of the '30s and early '40s, he lost an arm serving in the military during WW II. Back home, he never resumed his career, instead going into business. He is in his early 60s now (b. 1915). Onscreen from 1937. IN: *Knight Without Armor, The Gaiety Girls, The Return of the Scarlet Pimpernel, Drums, Pygmalion; Goodbye, Mr. Chips; Clouds Over Europe*, more, including *Major Barbara*, his last.

TREE, DOROTHY (N.Y.) In many meaty supporting roles in the '30s and '40s, this dark-haired actress from the stage made her presence felt. Today, a big silver-blonde of the name (Mrs.) Dorothy Uris, she still does; though in her late 60s (b. 1909) she no longer acts. She is a well-known voice teacher in Manhattan and the author of the recent book *A Woman's Voice* (Stein & Day), a handbook for successful public and private speaking. An ardent feminist, she believes that women's rights can be best served by "more resonance, clear speech and a better vocabulary." She notes with pleasure that American women have ceased imitating Jacqueline Kennedy Onassis' little-girl whisper—"an adopted mannerism," she says—and now "are studying assertiveness training . . . learning to speak out without sounding like a fishwife." Men, says this authority, "no longer want women who simper and whine. They like intelligent women who can level with them, can debate with them without becoming shrill." That's what she teaches, and why she wrote her book—to show them how. Onscreen from 1931. IN: *Husband's Holiday, Life Begins, Here Comes the Navy, The Dragon Murder Case, The Case of the Howling Dog, Madame Du Barry, The Woman in Red, The Great Garrick, Trade Winds, Confessions of a Nazi Spy, Abe Lincoln in Illinois; Knute Rockne—All-American; Edge of Darkness*, more, including 1943's *Crime Doctor*; she next —and last—returned to the screen in 1950 for character roles in three: *No Sad Songs for Me, The Asphalt Jungle*, and *The Men*.

TREEN, MARY (S. Cal.) Elder citizens at sanitariums and rest homes around Balboa Beach, Calif., count themselves fortunate for the live entertainment that's staged at regular intervals for them. One of their special favorites at these shows is a dancer-comedienne who seems far younger than her years (b. 1907). Best of all, she seems so very familiar, almost like family, like that humorous favorite cousin who, for some unexplained reason, never married. Some of these older people, grown forgetful in their years, may even suspect she is a cheerful nurse, or receptionist, that they encountered in some other place, some earlier time. It is small wonder that this dark-haired volunteer entertainer, Mary Treen, seems so immediately familiar to her audiences. For surely, whether they connect her with movies or not, she has brought them pleasure before, on the screen, for more than four decades. In more than 100 pictures, the plain, funny girls she played were a constant delight—shopgirls, waitresses, cashiers. But in later years those girls have been missing from the screen. And so, until her recent return, was Mary Treen. "I have owned a house at Balboa Beach for many years," she reports, "but could never live in it as my professional life kept me very busy in Hollywood, and it was too far for daily commuting. Now that the picture business has changed, and work for so many of us has slowed down, I'm living in my house, with my ex-vaudeville partner, whose husband died a few years ago." Born in St. Louis and reared in California, Mary Treen, as a teenager, danced with Fanchon and Marco revues before crashing the movies. Of dancing, she says, "It's still the thing I love most of all. I'm now studying Polynesian dancing." The shows she and her partner put on for senior citizens are enormously rewarding because, she says, "We enjoy sharing what we enjoy doing." The actress is single, her beloved mother died some years ago, and the only other living member of her family is a cousin, James W. Sullivan, a TV art director. She still keeps up her motion picture contacts, for she is determined to get her career into high gear once more. And she does enjoy living at Balboa Beach—"The air is so clear and fresh, and I have lovely neighbors." But—"I still like the smell of greasepaint *wherever* it is!" Onscreen from 1934. IN: *Happiness Ahead, Babbitt, Shipmates Forever, Page Miss Glory, G-Men, The Case of the Lucky Legs, I Live for Love, Colleen, Love Begins at 20, They Gave Him a Gun, Talent Scout, Second Honeymoon; Sally, Irene and Mary; Kentucky Moonshine, Kitty Foyle, The Great Man's Lady, They All Kissed the Bride, They Got Me Covered, So Proudly We Hail, I Love a Soldier, Casanova Brown, It's a Wonderful Life, The Stooge* (plus other Martin-Lewis comedies), *Room for One More,*

Bundle of Joy, All in a Night's Work; Paradise, Hawaiian Style; The Strongest Man in the World, more.

TREMAYNE, LES (S. Cal.) Character. Recalled by radio fans as the leading man, for seven years, of *The First Nighter.* (He was preceded in this show, which lasted 17½ years, by Don Ameche, and followed by Olan Soule.) Onscreen from 1951. IN: *The Racket, The Blue Veil, It Grows on Trees, Dream Wife, War of the Worlds, Susan Slept Here, A Man Called Peter, The Perfect Furlough, North by Northwest, The Gallant Hours, The Story of Ruth, The Fortune Cookie,* more.

TREVARTHEN, NOEL (Eng.) Support. Onscreen from the '60s. IN: *Corruption, The Abdication,* more.

TREVOR, AUSTIN (Eng.) Character who, in his late 70s (b. 1897), remains professionally busy onstage and in movies. Onscreen from 1930. IN: *Mystery at the Villa Rose, Escape, The Man from Chicago, Spy 77, As You Like It, Knight Without Armor; Goodbye, Mr. Chips; Night Train, Anna Karenina, The Red Shoes, So Long at the Fair, To Paris with Love, The Day the Earth Caught Fire,* more.

TREVOR, CLAIRE (S. Cal.) Costar. Won Best Supporting Actress Oscar in *Key Largo.* Nominated in the same category in *Dead End* and *The High and the Mighty.* The dynamic blonde —she remains both in her late 60s (b. 1909)— gave up her movie career after 1965's *How to Murder Your Wife.* A bit later she toured in the play *The Killing of Sister George.* Now, she says, she is completely retired and enjoying life at her two homes, in Newport Beach and Puerta Vallarta. Financially, there is no reason she should work. Wise real estate investments have made her quite wealthy. Additionally, she has been long (since '48) and happily married to producer Milton Bren, also now retired. Her two previous marriages, which ended in divorce, were to writer Clark Andrews (1938–42) and Navy Lt. Cyclos William Dunsmoore (1943 –47), by whom she has a son, Charles Cyclos (b. 1944). She and Bren also have a son, Peter, who has operated a well-known Hollywood discotheque. Of her many pictures, she recalls *Stagecoach* with particular pleasure. For it was her first picture after five dreary years of B's at Fox, and her first opportunity to work with director John Ford. She remembers vividly this prediction of Ford's, when he was editing the picture: "It's going to be great. And you're so good that they're not even going to notice it. It'll go right over their heads." And, she says now: "He was right. *Stagecoach* made Duke Wayne, but it didn't do much for me. There are certain parts that command attention like the one Jack Nicholson played in *Easy Rider*. I had mine in *Dead End* and *Key Largo*. But not *Stagecoach*. It was too subtle.'' Onscreen from 1933. IN: *The Last Trail, Baby Take a Bow, Dante's Inferno, Navy Wife, My Marriage, Star for a Night, Career Woman, One Mile from Heaven, Big Town Girl, The Amazing Dr. Clitterhouse, Five of a Kind, Valley of the Giants, Allegheny Uprising, Honky Tonk, The Adventures of Martin Eden, Crossroads, The Desperadoes, Woman of the Town, Murder My Sweet, Crack-Up, Born to Kill, The Babe Ruth Story, The Velvet Touch, Lucky Stiff, Best of the Badmen, My Man and I, Lucy Gallant, The Mountain, Marjorie Morningstar, Two Weeks in Another Town, The Stripper*, more.

TREVOR, HOWARD (Eng.) Young leading man. Onscreen in the '70s. IN: *Girly*, more.

TRIESAULT, IVAN (S. Cal.) In his 70s, sleek and smooth still, he continues doing what he has always done superbly—villainy. Onscreen from 1943. IN: *Mission to Moscow, In Our Time, The Hitler Gang, Days of Glory, Crime Doctor's Man Hunt, Counter-Attack, Notorious, Golden Earrings, To the Ends of the Earth, Five Fingers, The Bad and the Beautiful, Young Bess, Jet Pilot, The Amazing Transparent Man, The 300 Spartans, Barabbas, It Happened in Athens, Von Ryan's Express*, more.

TRIESTE, LEOPOLDO (It.) Character. Onscreen from the '50s. IN: *The White Sheik, Vitelloni, A Farewell to Arms; Divorce—Italian Style; White Voices, The Eye of the Needle, We Still Kill the Old Way; Weekend, Italian Style; The Sicilian Clan; Pussycat, Pussycat, I Love You; The Godfather, Part II*; more.

TRIGGER, IAN (Eng.) Character. Onscreen from the '60s. IN: *Pussycat, Pussycat, I Love You; Up Pompeii*, more.

TRIKONIS, GUS (S. Cal.) Actor-dancer, formerly married to actress Goldie Hawn, now a director. Onscreen in the '60s. IN: *West Side Story, The Unsinkable Molly Brown*, more.

TRINDER, TOMMY (Eng.) Comic character. Onscreen from 1931. IN: *Almost a Honeymoon, Save a Little Sunshine, She Couldn't Say No, Somewhere in France, Champagne Charlie, Fiddlers Three, You Lucky People*, more.

TRINTIGNANT, JEAN-LOUIS (Fr.) Star. Onscreen from the '50s. IN: *Race for Life, If All the Good Guys in the World, And God Created Woman, Violent Summer, Les Liaisons Dangereuses, The Easy Life, Castle in Switzerland,*

Il Successo, The Sleeping Car Murder, A Man and a Woman, Trans-Europ-Express, Les Biches, My Night at Maud's, Without Apparent Motive, Act of Aggression, It Is Raining on Santiago, Sunday Woman, more.

TRINTIGNANT, MARIE (Fr.) Small daughter of the above, who, in a screenplay written by her mother, Nadine Trintignant, based on a real-life tragedy (the loss of a previous child), was in 1971's *It Only Happens to Others*.

TRIOLA, ANNE (S. Cal.) Support; lately inactive in movies. Onscreen from the '40s. IN: *Without Reservations, Lullaby of Broadway*, more.

TRIPP, PAUL (N.Y.) Character. Onscreen in 1966. IN: *The Christmas That Almost Wasn't*.

TRISTAN, DOROTHY (S. Cal.) Support. Onscreen from the '60s. IN: *Klute, End of the Road, Scarecrow*, more.

TROOBNICK, GENE (N.Y.) Character. Onscreen from the '60s. IN: *Harvey Middleman, Fireman*; more.

TROUGHTON, PATRICK (Eng.) Character. Onscreen from the '40s. IN: *Hamlet, Treasure Island, Chance of a Lifetime, Richard III*, more.

TROUP, BOBBY (S. Cal.) Actor-musician. Husband of actress Julie London, with whom he has appeared in the long-running TV series *Emergency!* Onscreen from 1957. IN: *Bop Girl, The Five Pennies, The High Cost of Loving, The Gene Krupa Story, First to Fight, Number One, M*A*S*H*, more.

TROUPE, TOM (S. Cal.) Support. Onscreen from the '50s. IN: *The Big Fisherman, Sofi* (he wrote the screenplay), *The Devil's Brigade, Che!*, more.

TROY, HECTOR (N.Y.) Support. Onscreen in the '70s. IN: *The Super Cops*, more.

TROY, LOUISE (N.Y.) Support. Onscreen from 1968. IN: *The Swimmer; Yours, Mine and Ours*; more.

TRUBSHAWE, MICHAEL (Eng.) Character. Onscreen from the '50s. IN: *Dance Hall, The Lavender Hill Mob, Encore* (''The Ant and the Grasshopper'' episode), *Brandy for the Parson, The Titfield Thunderbolt, Gideon of Scotland Yard, Scent of Mystery, The Guns of Navarone, The Mouse on the Moon, Reach for Glory, A Dandy in Aspic, Salt and Pepper*, more.

TRUEMAN, PAULA (N.Y.) Character. Onscreen from 1934. IN: *Crime and Punishment, One Foot in Heaven, Paint Your Wagon, The Anderson Tapes, On a Clear Day You Can See Forever, Homebodies*, more.

TRUEX, PHILIP (N.Y.) The son of the late actor Ernest Truex, he gave up his acting career two decades ago when he and his wife converted his hobby—rooftop gardening—into a business. They still operate a unique shop, serving the special needs of New York City gardeners. Also, besides designing gardens for many prominent New Yorkers, he has done many articles for *The New York Times* and published a successful book—the title of which is also the name of his shop, *The City Gardener*. Onscreen from the '40s. IN: *The Trouble With Harry*, more.

TRUFFAUT, FRANCOIS (Fr.) Noted French director. Onscreen as an actor in 1963 in *Love at Twenty*.

TRUMAN, RALPH (Eng.) Character. Onscreen from 1931. IN: *City of Song, Mr. Cohen Takes a Walk, The Saint in London, Henry V, The Smugglers, Treasure Island, Massacre Hill, Oliver Twist, Quo Vadis, The Master of Ballantrae, Beau Brummell, The Man Who Knew Too Much, The Third Key, El Cid, Nicholas and Alexandra*, more.

TRUNDY, NATALIE (S. Cal.) A Park Avenue girl, this freckle-faced actress (b. 1942) was one of the most prominent starlets of the '50s. A teenage marriage—of five months—to young socialite Charles Hirshon ended in divorce. She gave up her career for several years after her back was broken in an automobile accident. Her second marriage, to movie producer Arthur Jacobs, lasted eight years, until his death in 1973 at 51. She had made her comeback in two of his productions—the "Apes" series—and was on location in Mississippi, playing a character role in *Huckleberry Finn*, another of his films, at the time of his sudden death. In May 1974 she was married to Robert Foggia, an Italian executive with Gucci's in Beverly Hills, who had been a friend of her late husband. Onscreen from 1957. IN: *The Careless Years, The Monte Carlo Story, Walk Like a Dragon, Mr. Hobbs Takes a Vacation, Beneath the Planet of the Apes, Conquest of the Planet of the Apes, Huckleberry Finn*, more.

TRUNNELLE, MABEL (S. Cal.) At last report this popular Edison Co. star of the early teens, who was married to leading man Herbert Prior, was living in retirement in the heart of Hollywood. Onscreen from 1911. IN: *How Mrs.*

Murray Saved the Army, The Message of the Sun-Dial, Ransom's Folly, more.

TRUSTMAN, SUSAN (N.Y.) Leading lady in TV soap operas. Onscreen from the '60s. IN: *Stay Away, Joe*, more.

TRYON, TOM (S. Cal.) He no longer acts, but is the author of such hugely successful novels as *The Other*, which was filmed, and *Harvest Home*. He turned 50 in '76 and remains both handsome and single. Onscreen from 1950. IN: *The Fall of the House of Usher, Three Violent People, Screaming Eagles, The Scarlet Hour, The Unholy Wife, I Married a Monster from Outer Space, The Story of Ruth; Marines, Let's Go; Moon Pilot, The Cardinal* (his best role), *In Harm's Way, Color Me Dead, Johnny Got His Gun*, more.

TSOPEL, CORINNA (S. Cal.) Leading lady. Onscreen from the '60s. IN: *The Sweet Ride, A Man Called Horse*, more.

TSU, IRENE (S. Cal.) Leading lady. Onscreen from 1943. IN: *China* (child role), *Flower Drum Song* (dancer), *Cleopatra* (handmaiden), *Caprice, How to Stuff a Wild Bikini, The Green Berets, Hot Potato*, more.

TUCKER, FORREST (S. Cal.) Character lead; former leading man. Onscreen from 1940. IN: *The Westerner, New Wine, Canal Zone, Shut My Big Mouth, Parachute Nurse, Keeper of the Flame, Never Say Goodbye, Renegades, The Yearling, Coroner Creek, Hellfire, Sands of Iwo Jima, Rock Island Trail, Warpath, Bugles in the Afternoon, Montana Belle, Trouble in the Glen, Three Violent People, Auntie Mame, The Crawling Eye, The Night They Raided Minsky's, Cancel My Reservation, The McCullochs*, more.

TUCKER, JOHN BARTHOLOMEW (N.Y.) TV personality-actor. Onscreen in 1975. IN: *Abduction*.

TUCKER, LARRY (S. Cal.) Former support; now a writer-producer. Onscreen in the '60s. IN: *Blast of Silence, Shock Corridor*, more.

TUCKER, TANYA (S. Cal.) C&W song star. Onscreen in the '70s. IN: *Jeremiah Johnson* (bit).

TULLY, TOM (S. Cal.) Character. Nominated for Best Supporting Actor Oscar in *The Caine Mutiny*. Newly into his 80s (b. 1896), he is still —whenever he feels a pall in his "semi-retirement"—giving corking performances in TV series (*The Rookies*), TV-movies (*Hijack* with David Janssen), and movies. Onscreen from

1943. IN: *Northern Pursuit, Destination Tokyo, I'll Be Seeing You, The Unseen, Till the End of Time, Adventure, Lady in the Lake; Scudda Hoo! Scudda Hay!; June Bride, Rachel and the Stranger, A Kiss for Corliss, Where the Sidewalk Ends, Ruby Gentry, The Turning Point, The Moon Is Blue, The Jazz Singer, Love Me or Leave Me, Ten North Frederick, The Wackiest Ship in the Army, The Carpetbaggers, Coogan's Bluff, Charley Varrick,* more.

TUNC, IRENE (Fr.) Support. Onscreen from the '60s. IN: *Live for Life, La Chamade,* more.

TUNE, TOMMY (N.Y.) Tall (6'7") dancer-actor. Onscreen from the '60s. IN: *Hello, Dolly!, The Boy Friend,* more.

TURGEON, PETER (N.Y.) Character. Onscreen from the '60s. IN: *Muscle Beach Party, Dear Heart, Some Kind of a Nut, Last Summer, Airport, The Possession of Joel Delaney,* more.

TURICH, FELIPE (S. Cal.) Character. Onscreen from the '30s. IN: *A Dangerous Man, To the Victor, The Lawless, Wyoming Mail, Short Grass; Hook, Line and Sinker;* more.

TURICH, ROSA (S. Cal.) Character. Onscreen from the '40s. IN: *Rose of the Rio Grande, Rangers of Fortune, The Kid from Texas,* more.

TURK, ARLENE M. (N.Y.) Support. Onscreen from the '60s. IN: *To Find a Man, The Panic in Needle Park, Who Is Harry Kellerman . . . ?, Mortadella, The Godfather, Made for Each Other; B.S., I Love You; The Anderson Tapes, Such Good Friends; Summer Wishes, Winter Dreams;* more.

TURKEL, ANN (S. Cal.) Leading lady. Wife of actor Richard Harris. Onscreen from the '60s. IN: *Paper Lion, 99 44/100% Dead,* more.

TURKEL, JOSEPH (S. Cal.) Character. Onscreen from the '40s. IN: *City Across the River, Duffy of San Quentin, Inside Detroit, The Killing, Paths of Glory, The Yellow Canary, The Sand Pebbles, The Devil's Eight, The Animals,* more.

TURLEIGH, VERONICA (Eng.) Support. Onscreen from the '50s. IN: *The Promoter, The Horse's Mouth,* more.

TURLEY, DIANNE (S. Cal.) Leading lady. Onscreen in the '70s. IN: *Angels Die Hard, End of August,* more.

TURMAN, GLYNN (S. Cal.) Black leading man. Onscreen in the '70s. IN: *Thomasine and Bushrod, Together Brothers, Cooley High, Minstrel Man, J.D.'s Revenge,* more.

TURNER, BARBARA (S. Cal.) Character. Onscreen from the '60s. IN: *Operation Eichmann, Soldier Blue,* more.

TURNER, BRIDGET (Eng.) Support. Onscreen in the '70s. IN: *The Walking Stick,* more.

TURNER, CHARLES (N.Y.) Black support. Onscreen in the '70s. IN: *The Super Cops,* more.

TURNER, CLARAMAE (N.Y.) Singer-character actress. Onscreen in 1956 in *Carousel.*

TURNER, DOUGLAS (N.Y.) Black support. He is also a director-playwright, using his full name, Douglas Turner Ward, for stage endeavors. Onscreen in the '70s. IN: *Man and Boy,* more.

TURNER, GEORGE (N.Y.) Under contract to Sir Alexander Korda in the 1930s as a leading man, he was later a popular character actor on Broadway, but now, in his 70s (b. 1902), is retired. Onscreen from 1925. In talkies from 1930. IN: *White Cargo, Fire Over England, The Well Groomed Bride, Race Street,* more.

TURNER, IKE (N.Y.) Rock star. Half of "Ike and Tina Turner." Onscreen in the '70s. IN: *Taking Off* (as himself), *Superstars in Film Concert.*

TURNER, LANA (S. Cal.) Star. Nominated for Best Actress Oscar in *Peyton Place.* Beautifully preserved in her 50s (b. 1920), she has, to date in this decade, made her stage debut (in out-of-town theaters) in *Forty Carats,* been presented in New York (one-night stand) as one of publicist-impresario John Springer's "Legendary Ladies," starred in a forgettable film, *Persecution* (written by her onetime beau, actor Robert Hutton), and costarred onstage in Chicago with Louis Jourdan in *The Pleasure of His Company.* Unmarried now, though she has been seven times divorced, she lives in splendor in an apartment building in Santa Monica. Her only child, Cheryl, who has never married (b. 1943), shares a house in the San Fernando Valley with her grandmother and works as general manager for the chain of restaurants owned by her father (former actor Steve Crane). A business woman herself, the actress has recently formed an international chain of franchised health spas—"Lana Turner Mini-Spas"—for women only. She is both a director and a major stockholder in the chain, the projected size of which is 2,000 spas. Retaining her sense of humor, always one of her more attractive screen attributes, she

482

laughs: "People say I must be at least 106 years old. But I've been working since I was 15." If she had a choice, would she relive her life the same way? "Yes, yes, yes. We all have ups and downs, but there's destiny." Onscreen from 1937. IN: *They Won't Forget, The Great Garrick, The Adventures of Marco Polo* (of this picture, she once told the author: "Sam Goldwyn had my eyebrows shaved off. They never grew back, and I've never forgiven him"), *Love Finds Andy Hardy, Dramatic School, These Glamour Girls, Dancing Coed* (Artie Shaw, who was in this with her, became her first husband; he was followed by Steve Crane, to whom she was married twice; millionaire Dan Topping; actor Lex Barker; store tycoon Fred May; writer Robert Eaton, who later wrote an expose novel about an actress much like Lana Turner; and nightclub hypnotist Ronald Dante), *Ziegfeld Girl, Dr. Jekyll and Mr. Hyde, Honky Tonk, Johnny Eager, Somewhere I'll Find You, Marriage Is a Private Affair, Weekend at the Waldorf, The Postman Always Rings Twice, Green Dolphin Street, Cass Timberlane, A Life of Her Own, The Merry Widow, Latin Lovers, The Sea Chase, Diane, Imitation of Life, Portrait in Black, Bachelor in Paradise, By Love Possessed, Who's Got the Action?, Madame X, The Big Cube*, more.

TURNER, MICHAEL (Eng.) Character. Onscreen from 1966. IN: *Othello, Battle of Britain*, more.

TURNER, TIM (Eng.) Leading man. Onscreen from the '40s. IN: *Gift Horse, Top Secret, Paratrooper, Companions in Crime, The Haunted Strangler, The Dam Busters, A Town Like Alice*, more.

TURNER, TINA (N.Y.) Black singer-actress. Half of "Ike and Tina Turner." Onscreen in the '70s. IN: *Taking Off* (as herself), *Superstars in Film Concert, Tommy*, more.

TURNER, TOM (N.Y.) Character. Onscreen in the '70s. IN: *Shoot It: Black, Shoot It: Blue*; more.

TURNER, VICKERY (S. Cal.) Supporting actress. Onscreen from the '60s. IN: *Prudence and the Pill, The Mind of Mr. Soames*, more.

TUSHINGHAM, RITA (Eng.) Leading lady. Onscreen from 1962. IN: *A Taste of Honey, The Leather Boys, Girl with Green Eyes, The Knack, Dr. Zhivago, Smashing Time, The Guru, The Bed-Sitting Room, The Human Factor*, more.

TUTIN, DOROTHY (Eng.) Leading lady. Onscreen from 1952. IN: *The Importance of Being Earnest, The Beggar's Opera, A Tale of Two Cities, Cromwell, Savage Messiah*.

TUTTLE, LURENE (S. Cal.) The character actress was bereaved in 1974 when her actress-daughter Barbara Ruick *(Carousel)* died suddenly. She was of her marriage, which ended in divorce, to late actor Melville Ruick, and was her only child. In 1975, Lurene Tuttle, known for many years as "First Lady of Radio," was cited as "L.A. Woman of the Year" by the American Federation of Radio & TV Artists. This was in recognition of her work before the microphone (in *Sam Spade*, etc.) and TV cameras (the series *Life With Father*, in which she was Vinnie Day, and *Julia*, as the nurse). Onscreen from 1947. IN: *Heaven Only Knows, Mr. Blandings Builds His Dream House; Goodbye, My Fancy; Don't Bother to Knock, Room for One More, Niagara, The Affairs of Dobie Gillis, The Glass Slipper, Sincerely Yours, Sweet Smell of Success, Psycho, Critic's Choice, The Fortune Cookie, The Ghost and Mr. Chicken, The Horse in the Gray Flannel Suit, Walking Tall; Walking Tall, Part II*; more.

TWIGGY (Eng.) Singer-leading lady. Onscreen from 1971. IN: *The Boy Friend, "W,"* more.

TWITTY, CONWAY (Tenn.) Singer-actor. Onscreen in 1960. IN: *College Confidential, Platinum High School, Sex Kittens Go to College*.

TYLER, BEVERLY (S. Cal.) It has been nearly two decades since this leading lady appeared in movies, but until recently her photograph appeared in the *Academy Players Directory* in Hollywood—meaning she was available for assignments. The photograph revealed her to be, in her 40s (b. 1928), still attractive and dark-haired. Onscreen from 1943. IN: *Best Foot Forward, The Green Years* (her best role), *My Brother Talks to Horses, The Beginning or the End, The Fireball, The Cimarron Kid, Chicago Confidential*, more, including 1958's *Hong Kong Confidential*, her most recent to date.

TYNE, GEORGE (S. Cal.) Character. Onscreen from the '40s. IN: *A Walk in the Sun, They Won't Believe Me, Sword in the Desert, Thieves' Highway, Sands of Iwo Jima, No Way Out; Not With My Wife, You Don't; The Counterfeit Killer, Marlowe, Mr. Ricco; I Will, I Will . . . For Now*; more.

TYNER, CHARLES (S. Cal.) Character. Onscreen from the '60s. IN: *The Stalking Moon, The Reivers, Lawman, Sometimes a Great Notion, Harold and Maude, The Longest Yard, The Midnight Man*, more.

TYRELL, SUSAN (S. Cal.) Leading lady. Nominated for Best Supporting Actress Oscar in *Fat*

City. Onscreen in the '70s. IN: *Shoot Out, The Steagle, Zandy's Bride, Catch My Soul, Islands in the Stream*, more.

TYSON, CICELY (S. Cal.) Black star. Nominated for Best Actress Oscar in *Sounder*. Onscreen from 1966. IN: *A Man Called Adam,*

The Comedians, The Heart Is a Lonely Hunter, The Blue Bird.

TYZACK, MARGARET (Eng.) Support. Onscreen from 1957. IN: *Ring of Treason, The Whisperers; 2001: A Space Odyssey; A Clockwork Orange, A Touch of Love*, more.

U

UGGAMS, LESLIE (S. Cal.) Black singer-actress. Onscreen from 1972. IN: *Skyjacked* (debut), *Black Girl.*

ULANOVA, GALINA (Rus.) Retired from dancing, the Soviet prima ballerina assoluta now coaches for the Russian Ballet in Moscow. Onscreen in the '50s. IN: *The Stars of the Russian Ballet* and *The Ballet of Romeo and Juliet.*

ULLMANN, LIV (Swe.) Star. Nominated for Best Actress Oscar in *The Emigrants*. Onscreen from 1959. IN: *The Wayward Girl, Persona, Hour of the Wolf, Shame, The Night Visitor, Pope Joan, Lost Horizon, Forty Carats, The Abdication, Cries and Whispers, Face to Face,* more.

ULTRA VIOLET (N.Y.) Leading lady. Graduate of Andy Warhol films. Onscreen from the '60s. IN: *Midnight Cowboy, Dinah East, Taking Off; Simon, King of the Witches; Believe in Me, Maidstone, The Telephone Book, Curse of the Headless Woman*, more.

UMEKI, MIYOSHI (S. Cal.) Character. Won Best Supporting Actress Oscar in *Sayonara*. Onscreen from 1957. IN: *Cry for Happy, Flower Drum Song, The Horizontal Lieutenant, A Girl Named Tamiku*, more.

UNDERDOWN, EDWARD (Eng.) Character. Onscreen from the early '30s. IN: *Wings of the Morning, Girls Please, Inspector Hornleigh, The Woman in the Hall, The Dark Man, Recoil, Beat the Devil, The Woman's Angle, The Two-Headed Spy, The Day the Earth Caught Fire,* more.

UNDERWOOD, IAN (Eng.) Support. Onscreen in the '70s. IN: *Two Hundred Motels*, more.

URQUHART, MOLLY (Eng.) Character. Onscreen from the '50s. IN: *Wee Geordie, The Sundowners, The Black Windmill; Digby, the Biggest Dog in the World;* more.

URQUHART, ROBERT (Eng.) Character. Onscreen from the early '50s. IN: *Knights of the Round Table, Tonight's the Night, The Warriors, Battle Hell, Golden Ivory, Foxhole in Cairo, Murder at the Gallop, The Looking Glass War, Brotherly Love*, more.

USTINOV, PETER (Eng.) Costar. Won Best Supporting Actor Oscar in *Spartacus*. Nominated in the same category in *Quo Vadis, Topkapi*. Onscreen from 1940. IN: *Mein Kampf, One of Our Aircraft Is Missing, The True Glory, Odette, Hotel Sahara, Beau Brummell, The Egyptian, We're No Angels, Lola Montes, The Sundowners, School for Scoundrels, Romanoff and Juliet, Billy Budd; John Goldfarb, Please Come Home; The Comedians, Blackbeard's Ghost, Hot Millions, Viva Max!, Hammersmith Is Out, One of Our Dinosaurs Is Missing*, more.

USTINOV, TAMARA (Eng.) Support. Daughter of Peter Ustinov. Onscreen in the '70s. IN: *The Blood on Satan's Claws*, more.

UYS, JAMIE (S. A.) South Africa's leading producer-director *(Dingaka)*, he also acts. Onscreen from the '60s. IN: *The Hellions; After You, Comrade;* more.

V

VACCARO, BRENDA (S. Cal.) Leading lady. Nominated for Best Supporting Actress Oscar in *Once Is Not Enough*. Onscreen from 1969. IN: *Where It's At, Midnight Cowboy, I Love My Wife, Summertree, Going Home, Death Weekend*, more.

VACIO, NATIVIDAD (S. Cal.) Character. Onscreen in the '50s. IN: *The Hitch-Hiker, Green Fire*, more.

VADIM, ANNETTE (Fr.) Leading lady Annette Stroyberg used this as her screen name when married to director Roger Vadim. Onscreen as Vadim in the early '60s. IN: *Blood and Lace, Les Liaisons Dangereuses*, more.

VADIM, ROGER (Fr.) French director. Onscreen as an actor in 1964 in *Sweet and Sour*.

VALBERG, BIRGITTA (Swe.) Character. Onscreen from 1960. IN: *The Virgin Spring, Story of a Woman, A Time in the Sun*, more.

VALDIS, SIGRID (S. Cal.) Support. Married to actor Bob Crane. Lately inactive in movies. Onscreen from 1965. IN: *Marriage on the Rocks, Our Man Flint, The Venetian Affair*, more.

VALENTA, VLADIMIR (Poland) One of Poland's top character leads. Onscreen from the '60s. IN: *Closely Watched Trains, End of a Priest*, more.

VALENTE, CATERINA (Switz.) The Italian singer-actress, living in Lugano, starred in 13 musical movies made in Germany in the '50s and '60s, but has not yet worked in American movies.

VALENTINE, ANTHONY (Eng.) Leading man. Onscreen in the '70s. IN: *Performance; To the Devil . . . A Daughter;* more.

VALENTINE, BARBARA (Fr.) Support. Onscreen from the '60s. IN: *Carmen Baby; Fear Eats the Soul—Ali;* more.

VALENTY, LILI (S. Cal.) Character. Onscreen from the '50s. IN: *Wild Is the Wind, In Love and War, The Story of Ruth, Rome Adventure, It Happened in Athens; Girls! Girls! Girls!; The Baby Maker, The Harrad Summer*, more.

VALERIE, JEANNE (It.) Support. Onscreen from the '60s. IN: *From a Roman Balcony, Les Liaisons Dangereuses, Adorable Julia, White Voices, The Hired Killer*, more.

VALERY, OLGA (Eng.) Character. Onscreen from the '50s. IN: *Love in the Afternoon, The Only Game in Town*, more.

VALLEE, RUDY (S. Cal.) "The Vagabond Lover" may be in his 70s (b. 1901), but no grass sprouts under his indefatigable feet. Consider the crooner's activities—some of them—in this decade alone. His only failure in the 1970s came at the beginning. He had sought to have the name of the street in the Hollywood Hills where he lives—in a veritable mansion with a 360° view —changed to Rue de Vallee. Rejecting the proposal, Los Angeles City Councilmen said they agreed with neighbors who wished the street's name to remain what it was. Never less than outspoken, the singer-actor was quoted as saying that his neighbors were "a bunch of disgruntled pukes who don't live on the street," and adding, "They are complaining because they are jealous." All after that was "heigh-ho" and smooth sailing. Almost. He completed his new autobiography—his third—titled *I Digress*, and which he himself wrote. He did a concert tour of the nation's campuses—a two-hour one-man show. He starred at the St. Louis Municipal Opera with Don Ameche and Dorothy Lamour. A deal to play a famous night spot in New York was called off before the opening because, he has informed the author, "that prick [nameless], in his megalomania as an IMPRESARIO, insisted on not only directing me as to what I should do BUT AS TO HOW TO DO IT!!!" In 1973, the man famous for his songs pulled a switch—by starring in summer theaters in a musical in which he neither sang nor spoke until the final scene. This was *Once Upon a Mattress*. One Ohio critic labeled his pantomime performance as King Septimus the Silent "terrific," adding that the actor brought forth "wild shrieks from his victims and wild laughter from his fans." Expert as always in his timing, Vallee saved an offstage fall, resulting in a broken nose and requiring 15 stitches in his forehead, until after the curtain had come down on the final performance of the tour. In 1975, onstage in Los Angeles, the star successfully reprised the role of J. B. Biggley in *How to Succeed in Business Without Really Trying*. He had previously triumphed for three years in the part on Broadway and in the movie version. That same year the University of Maine alumnus—class of 1925—who popularized the Maine "Stein Song" nearly 50 years before, returned to his alma mater where he played his one-man show to an SRO audience. Also in 1975, on September 3, he and his wife, Eleanor, celebrated their 26th wedding anniversary. His first marriage, to Leonie Cauchois, in 1928, was annulled the same year. He was later married to (1931–36) and divorced from Fay Webb, and actress Jane Greer (1943–44). He has no children by any of his marriages. For recreation and to stay in shape he plays tennis—often three sets daily. And he takes umbrage when journalists use the word "comeback" in connection with any of his professional work. A while back he made it plain that he had never been out of the show business spotlight, and added, "I'll be front page news until the day I die." Onscreen from 1929. IN: *Rudy Vallee and His Connecticut Yankees* (short), *The Vagabond Lover, George White's Scandals, Sweet Music, Gold Diggers in Paris, Second Fiddle, The Palm Beach Story* (an outstanding performance),

Happy Go Lucky, People Are Funny, The Bachelor and the Bobby-Soxer, I Remember Mama, Unfaithfully Yours, Mother Is a Freshman, Father Was a Fullback, Gentlemen Marry Brunettes, The Helen Morgan Story; Live a Little, Love a Little; The Phynx, more.

VALLI, ALIDA (It.) She is a handsome woman, though in her 50s (b. 1921) she is no longer the beauty she was when discovered by Selznick. She stars in film after film in Italy and France. Recently she has been in *Cher Victor (That Dear Victor)*, *The Anti-Christ*, *La Grande Trouille (The Big Scare)*, *The Spider's Stratagem*, etc. *Time* magazine hailed her performance in the last as "magnificently strong." She has done no American work since '65, when, in a three-part episode of TV's *Dr. Kildare*, she played an old sweetheart of "Dr. Gillespie," Raymond Massey. She has long been separated from musician-husband Oscar de Mejo (married 1941), by whom she has one son, Carlos (b. 1945). Onscreen from the '30s. IN: *Manon Lescaut*, *The Paradine Case*, *The Miracle of the Bells*, *Laugh Pagliacci*, *Weep No More*, *The Third Man*; *Walk Softly, Stranger*; *The White Tower*, *This Angry Age*, *The Night Heaven Fell*, *The Happy Thieves*, *Il Grido*, *The Long Absence*, *The Castilian*, *Disorder*, *Ophelia*, more.

VALLI, ROMOLO (It.) Support. Onscreen from the '60s. IN: *Girl With a Suitcase*, *The Leopard*, *Mandragola*, *Boom!*, more.

VALLIN, RICK (S. Cal.) Support; former leading man. Lately inactive in movies. Onscreen from 1942. IN: *Corregidor*, *The Panther's Claw*, *Isle of Forgotten Men*, *Army Wives*, *Northwest Outpost*, *Tuna Clipper*, *Jungle Jim*, *Killer Shark*, *King of the Congo* (serial), *Voodoo Tiger*, *Bowery to Bagdad*, *The Tijuana Story*, *Escape from Red Rock*; *Pier #5—Havana*; more.

VALLONE, RAF (It.) Costar. Onscreen from 1948. IN: *Bitter Rice*, *Vendetta*; *Rome, 11 O'-Clock*; *Anna, Passionate Summer*, *The Adulteress*, *Two Women*, *El Cid*, *A View from the Bridge*, *Phaedra*, *The Cardinal*, *Harlow* (the Paramount version starring Carroll Baker), *Nevada Smith*, *Kiss the Girls and Make Them Cry*, *The Desperate Ones*, *The Italian Job*, *A Gunfight*, *Rosebud*, *The Human Factor*, *That Lucky Touch*, more.

VAN, BOBBY (S. Cal.) Dancer-actor-singer whose career was revitalized when he costarred on Broadway with Ruby Keeler in *No, No, Nanette*. Onscreen from 1952. IN: *Because You're Mine*, *Small Town Girl*, *Kiss Me Kate*, *The Affairs of Dobie Gillis*, *The Navy vs. the Night Monsters*, *Lost Horizon*, more.

VAN ARK, JOAN (S. Cal.) Leading lady. Onscreen in the '70s. IN: *Frogs*, more.

VAN CLEEF, LEE (S. Cal.) Star. Onscreen from 1952. IN: *High Noon*, *The Beast from 20,000 Fathoms*, *Vice Raid*, *Rails Into Laramie*, *The Conqueror*, *Tribute to a Bad Man*, *Gunfight at the O.K. Corral*, *The Young Lions*, *The Man Who Shot Liberty Valance*, *For a Few Dollars More*, *The Big Gundown*; *The Good, the Bad and the Ugly*; *Death Rides a Horse*, *Day of Anger*, *Barquero*, *Sabata*, *El Condor*, *Bad Man's River*, *Take a Hard Ride*, *Power Kill*, *Grand Duel*, *Blood Money*, *Vendetta*, *God's Gun*, more.

VAN CLEVE, EDITH (N.Y.) She gave up her stage career, which preceded and followed her year in movies, after 1941 to become an actors' agent in New York. In her 70s now (b. 1903), she has lived for years at the Plaza and remains an avid member of various saddle and show horse organizations, this being an adjunct to her lifelong interest in riding, breeding, and showing saddlebred horses. Onscreen in 1934. IN: *The Age of Innocence* and *Hat, Coat and Glove*.

VAN DER VLIS, DIANA (N.Y.) Leading lady in TV soap operas. Onscreen from 1963. IN: *The Man With X-Ray Eyes*, *The Incident*, *The Swimmer*, more.

VAN DEVERE, TRISH (S. Cal.) Leading lady. Onscreen in the '70s. IN: *Where's Poppa?*, *The Last Run* (met George C. Scott while filming this and later became his wife), *One Is a Lovely Number*, *The Day of the Dolphin* (with Scott), *The Savage Is Loose* (again with Scott), *Fifty-Two Pickup*, more.

VAN DOREN, MAMIE (S. Cal.) In her 40s (b. 1931) the blonde sexpot—Universal's "answer" in the 1950s to Marilyn Monroe and Jayne Mansfield—still makes headlines and movies. In '73 Secretary of State Henry Kissinger had her come from Hollywood to be his dinner partner at a White House affair for (former) West German Chancellor Willy Brandt. Asked for her opinion of the foreign policy adviser, she replied: "Devastating." Kissinger turned to reporters and laughed: "Write that down for God's sake." In 1975 producer Matt Cimber, last husband of Jayne Mansfield, announced plans to film *That Girl From Boston*, with Mamie Van Doren in the starring role. And in '76 she did a guest role in the ABC soap opera *General Hospital*. The actress, single at present, has been married four times. First, at 16, the wife of a nonprofessional, she was next married for several years to bandleader Ray Anthony (they have a son, Peter, who was born in 1956). She also struck out on her third marriage, to Chicago Cubs pitcher (and winery heir) Lee Meyers; she was in her 30s and he 19 at the time of the marriage. Then, late in 1972 she was married for a while (the marriage eventually being annulled) to 51-year-old Ross McClintock, senior vice-president of a flour corporation. Onscreen from 1953. IN: *All-American, Forbidden, Yankee Pasha, Francis Joins the Wacs, The Second Greatest Sex, Running Wild, Star in the Dust, Untamed Youth, The Girl in Black Stockings, Teacher's Pet, High School Confidential, Born Reckless, The Beat Generation, Vice Raid, College Confidential, Four Nuts in Search of a Bolt, Las Vegas Hillbillies, You've Got to Be Smart*, more.

VAN DREELEN, JOHN (S. Cal.) Character. Onscreen from 1958. IN: *A Time to Live and a Time to Die, The Flying Fontaines, 13 Ghosts, Beyond the Time Barrier, The Enemy General, Von Ryan's Express, Madame X, I Deal in Danger, Topaz*, more.

VAN DUSEN, GRANVILLE (S. Cal.) Support. Onscreen in the '70s. IN: *The Statue*, more.

VAN DYKE, CONNY (S. Cal.) Singer-actress. Onscreen from the '60s. IN: *Hell's Angels '69, W. W. and the Dixie Dancekings, Framed*, more.

VAN DYKE, DICK (S. Cal.) Costar. Onscreen from 1963. IN: *Bye Bye Birdie, What a Way to Go!, Mary Poppins, The Art of Love; Lt. Robin Crusoe, USN; Divorce American Style, Fitzwilly, Chitty Chitty Bang Bang, Never a Dull Moment, Some Kind of a Nut, The Comic, Cold Turkey*, more.

VAN DYKE, JERRY (S. Cal.) Comic support. Brother of Dick Van Dyke. Onscreen from 1963. IN: *The Courtship of Eddie's Father, Palm Springs Weekend, McLintock!, Love and Kisses, Angel in My Pocket*, more.

VAN ESS, CONNIE (N.Y.) Support. Onscreen from the '50s. IN: *The Mugger*, more.

VAN EYSSEN, JOHN (Eng.) Former supporting actor. More recently a talent representative in London. Onscreen from the '50s. IN: *Four Sided Triangle, The Cockleshell Heroes, Horror of Dracula, Man in a Cocked Hat, Exodus*, more.

VAN FLEET, JO (N.Y.) Character. Won Best Supporting Actress Oscar in *East of Eden*, her first. Onscreen from 1955. IN: *The Rose Tattoo, I'll Cry Tomorrow, The King and Four Queens, Gunfight at the O.K. Corral, This Angry Age, Wild River, Cool Hand Luke; I Love You, Alice B. Toklas!; 80 Steps to Jonah, The Gang That Couldn't Shoot Straight*, more.

VAN NUTTER, RIK (Sp.) Leading man. Once the husband of actress Anita Ekberg. Onscreen from the '60s. IN: *Romanoff and Juliet, Thunderball*, more.

VAN PALLANDT, NINA (Sp.) Leading lady. She was also a figure in the Clifford Irving "Howard Hughes autobiography" case. Onscreen in the '70s. IN: *The Long Goodbye*.

VAN PATTEN, DICK (S. Cal.) Character. Onscreen from 1941. IN: *Regular Fellers* (teen role), *Psychomania, Joe Kidd, Making It, Dirty Little Billy, Westworld, Soylent Green, The Strongest Man in the World*, more.

VAN PATTEN, JOYCE (S. Cal.) Support. Sister of Dick Van Patten. Once the wife of character actor Martin Balsam, by whom she has a grown son and daughter, she is now married to singer Hal Lynch. Onscreen from 1951. IN: *Fourteen Hours* (teen role), *The Goddess; I Love You, Alice B. Toklas!; The Trouble With Girls; Pussycat, Pussycat, I Love You; Something Big, Thumb Tripping, The Manchu Eagle Murder Caper Mystery, Mame*, more.

VAN PATTEN, VINCENT (S. Cal.) Support. Son of Dick Van Patten. Onscreen in the '70s. IN: *Wild Horses*, more.

VAN PEEBLES, MELVIN (N.Y.) Black star-producer-director-composer. Onscreen in 1971. IN: *Sweet Sweetback's Baadasssss Song*.

VAN SICKLE, DALE (S. Cal.) Support. Onscreen from the '50s. IN: *Rogue Cop, Johnny Reno*, more.

VAN STRALEN, ANTON (S. Cal.) Character. Onscreen from the '60s. IN: *The Jailbreakers*, more.

VAN VOOREN, MONIQUE (N.Y.) Leading lady. Onscreen from 1952. IN: *Tomorrow Is Too Late, Tarzan and the She-Devil, Ten Thousand Bedrooms, Gigi, Happy Anniversary, Fearless Frank, Andy Warhol's Frankenstein*, more.

VANCE, VIVIAN (Conn.) Divorced from Philip Ober (they had no children), she has been married for years to book publisher John Dodds, and lives in Greenwich. Commuting from there, the actress—most famous for playing "Ethel Mertz" in TV's *I Love Lucy*—goes regularly to Hollywood for TV commercials and a running role in the *Rhoda* television series. Though she had a radical mastectomy earlier in this decade, her renewed professional activity seems evidence that, in her 60s (b. 1912), she again enjoys excellent health. Onscreen from 1950. IN: *The Secret Fury, The Blue Veil, The Great Race*, more.

VANDERS, WARREN (S. Cal.) Support. Onscreen from the '60s. IN: *Stay Away, Joe; The Split*, more.

VANDERVOORT, PHIL (S. Cal.) Support. Former husband of actress Lucie Arnaz, daughter of Desi Arnaz and Lucille Ball. Onscreen from the '60s. IN: *Maryjane*, more.

VANDEVER, MICHAEL (MIKE) (S. Cal.) Support. Onscreen from the '60s. IN: *Incident in an Alley, The New Interns*, more.

VANDIS, TITOS (N.Y.) Support. Onscreen from the '60s. IN: *Never on Sunday, It Happened in Athens, Island of Love, Topkapi, Stiletto, Newman's Law*, more.

VANECK, PIERRE (Fr.) Support. Onscreen from the '50s. IN: *He Who Must Die, The Season of Love, Is Paris Burning?*, more.

VANEL, CHARLES (Fr.) This noted French character, in more than 250 pictures, is now in his 80s (b. 1892) and still professionally active. Onscreen from the '20s. IN: *Waterloo, Les Miserables* (French talkie version released in the U.S. in 1936; costarred with Harry Baur), *They Were Five, Crossroads, The Woman Who Dared, The Wages of Fear* (as "Jo," the doomed middle-aged gangster who drove the second truck and had killed to get the job), *To Catch a Thief, Diabolique, Sinners of Paris, Symphony for a Massacre*, more, including 1976's *Seven Deaths by Prescription*.

VANNI, RENATA (S. Cal.) Character. Onscreen from the '50s. IN: *Westward the Women, Hell on Frisco Bay, Pay or Die*, more.

VANOCUR, SANDER (N.Y.) TV newsman. Onscreen in 1971. IN: *The Gang That Couldn't Shoot Straight* (as the Commentator).

VARDA, AGNES (Fr.) Famous director of *Cleo From 5 to 7*, etc. Onscreen in 1967 in *Far from Vietnam*.

VARDEN, NORMA (S. Cal.) As she approaches her 80s, this fine character actress—a specialist in roles as a *grande dame* or proprietress of exclusive shoppes—acts less often than before. But her photograph, meaning she is available still, appears in each edition of the *Academy Players Directory*. Onscreen in her native England from 1930. IN: *East Meets West, The Student's Romance, The Iron Duke, Fire Over England*, more. Onscreen in Hollywood from 1940. IN: *The Earl of Chicago, We Were Dancing, Random Harvest, The White Cliffs of Dover, National Velvet, The Green Years, The Searching Wind, Thunder in the Valley, Strangers on a Train, Thunder on the Hill, Gentlemen Prefer Blondes, Witness for the Prosecution, The Sound of Music, Doctor Dolittle*, more.

VARGA-DINICU, CAROLINA/a.k.a. MOROCCO (N.Y.) Support. Onscreen from the '60s. IN: *Song of Norway, The Projectionist*, more.

VARI, JOHN (N.Y.) Character. Onscreen from the '50s. IN: *The Last Mile*, more.

VARNEY, REG (Eng.) Comic support. Onscreen from the '50s. IN: *Miss Robin Hood, Mutiny on the Busses, The Best Pair of Legs in the Business*, more.

VARSI, DIANE (S. Cal.) Leading lady. Nominated for Best Supporting Actress Oscar in *Peyton Place*, her first picture. Onscreen from 1957. IN: *Ten North Frederick, From Hell to Texas, Compulsion; Sweet Love, Bitter; Wild in the Streets, Killers Three*, and, in 1971, *Johnny Got His Gun*.

VARTAN, SYLVIE (Fr.) Singer-actress. Married to singer Johnny Halladay, the French Elvis Presley. Onscreen in 1965 in *Friend of the Family*.

VASEK, MARISHA (N.Y.) Support. Onscreen from the '60s. IN: *Reflections in a Golden Eye*, more.

VAUGHAN, FRANKIE (Eng.) Singer-leading man. Onscreen from the '50s. IN: *These Dangerous Years, Wonderful Things, The Lady Is a Square, Let's Make Love, The Right Approach, It's All Over Town*, more.

VAUGHAN, GILLIAN (Eng.) Character. Onscreen from the '50s. IN: *The Horse's Mouth, A Cry from the Streets*, more.

VAUGHAN, PETER (Eng.) Character. Onscreen from the '50s. IN: *Sapphire, Village of the Damned; Die! Die! My Darling; The Naked Runner, Alfred the Great, Straw Dogs, Sudden Terror*, more.

VAUGHN, ALBERTA (S. Cal.) Last onscreen in 1934's *Randy Rides Alone*, she is in her 70s now (b. 1906) and lives in retirement in Pasadena. Onscreen from the mid-'20s. IN: *The Drop Kick, Skyscraper, Forbidden Hours, Working Girls, Wild Horse, Dancers in the*

Dark, Midnight Morals, Daring Danger, Love in High Gear, Alimony Madness, more.

VAUGHN, ROBERT (S. Cal.) Costar. Nominated for Best Supporting Actor Oscar in *The Young Philadelphians*. This scholarly actor, highly active still, has received his Ph.D. and is author of the book *The Victims* about the "Hollywood blacklist" during the McCarthy era. Onscreen from 1957. IN: *No Time to be Young, To Trap a Spy, A Good Day for a Hanging, The Magnificent Seven, The Big Show, One Spy Too Many, The Caretakers, The Venetian Affair, Bullitt, The Bridge at Remagen, The Statue, The Towering Inferno*, more.

VAUGHN, SAMMY (S. Cal.) Support. Onscreen from the '60s. IN: *Born Wild, The Young Animals*, more.

VAZ DIAS, SELMA (Eng.) Character actress. Onscreen from the '30s. IN: *The Lady Vanishes*, more. (Her billing was Zelma Vas Dias; she has since reverted to the above correct spelling of her name.)

VAZQUEZ, ROLAND (N.Y.) Ballet star. Onscreen in 1967 in *A Midsummer Night's Dream*.

VEAZIE, CAROL (S. Cal.) Character. Onscreen from the '50s. IN: *The Catered Affair, A Cry in the Night, Designing Woman, Auntie Mame; Baby, the Rain Must Fall*; more.

VEE, BOBBY (N.Y.) Singer. Onscreen in the '60s. IN: *Play It Cool, C'mon Let's Live a Little*.

VEGA, ISELA (Mex.) Leading lady. Onscreen in the '70s. IN: *Bring Me the Head of Alfredo Garcia, Drum, Tambores*, more.

VELASCO, JERRY (S. Cal.) Character. Onscreen from the '60s. IN: *Tell Them Willie Boy Is Here*, more.

VELOZ & YOLANDA (S. Cal.) The glorious ballroom dance team is no more. Its partners are separated, and Yolanda is retired and living in Los Angeles. Frank Veloz remains active behind the scenes and in '74 was Marge Champion's associate choreographer on the Maureen Stapleton TV drama special *Queen of the Stardust Ballroom*. The "product" of the dance team, their daughter, Yolanda Veloz, is an actress and married to young character actor Bernie Kopell. Veloz was onscreen as a solo artist in the '30s. IN: *Rumba, Under the Pampas Moon, Champagne Waltz*, more. Veloz & Yolanda were onscreen as a dance team in the '40s. IN: *The Pride of the Yankees, Brazil, The Thrill of Brazil*, more.

VENABLE, EVELYN (S. Cal.) It has been many a year since she and Kent Taylor, costarred in so many, were known as The Handsomest Lovers on the Screen. That was of course strictly an onscreen pairing. The actress, who was in movies exactly a decade, through 1943's *He Hired the Boss*, is now in her 60s (b. 1913) and remains a lovely woman. From '34 until his death in '74, she was most happily married to Hal Mohr, a noted cinematographer whose work won him countless nominations and two Oscars—for *A Midsummer Night's Dream* and 1943's *Phantom of the Opera*. Living in retirement in Santa Monica, the former star is hardly lonely. She has a son, Michael Mohr, four married daughters—Mrs. Carson Mitchell, Mrs. Donald Allen, Mrs. Charles Lofgren, and Mrs. Warren Woodson—seven grandchildren, and 17 great-grandchildren. Onscreen from 1933. IN: *Cradle Song, Death Takes a Holiday, David Harum, Mrs. Wiggs of the Cabbage Patch, The County Chairman, The Little Colonel, Alice Adams, Harmony Lane, Star for a Night, North of Nome, Racketeer in Exile, My Old Kentucky Home, The Stadium Murders, Heritage of the Desert, Lucky Cisco Kid*, more.

VENTURA, LENO (It.) Costar. Onscreen from the '50s. IN: *Marie Octobre, Razzi, Grisbi, Speaking of Murder, Frantic, Taxi for Tobruk, Greed in the Sun, Cloportes, The Great Spy Chase, The Last Adventure, The Wise Guys, Wild Horses, The Valachi Papers, A Pain in the A.., The Slap*, more.

VENTURA, VIVIANE (It.) Leading lady. Onscreen from the '60s. IN: *A High Wind in Jamaica, Battle Beneath the Earth*, more.

VENTURE, RICHARD (Conn.) Support. TV soap opera actor. Onscreen in the '70s. IN: *The Effect of Gamma Rays on Man-in-the-Moon Marigolds*, more.

VENUTA, BENAY (N.Y.) The singer-actress remains, in her slender, blonde 60s (b. 1912), as vivacious as at 16, which was her age when she entered movies. After starring on Broadway in 1963's *Dear Me, The Sky Is Falling*, she dropped out of show business for several years but has recently taken it up again on an on-and-off basis. In '72 she starred Off Broadway in a short-lived musical, *A Quarter for the Ladies Room*, and in '75 she appeared at the Poinciana Playhouse in Palm Beach with Joan Bennett and Jean-Pierre Aumont in *Janus*. She was also one of the New York friends who endeavored to assist Betty Hutton—they had been in *Annie Get Your Gun* together—when Betty left the Rhode Island rectory to try for a comeback. A wealthy woman, she lives in a sumptuous townhouse on East 79th Street, filled with original art works—a Picasso vase, paintings by Gauguin, line drawings by Modigliani and Miro, and pre-Columbian figures. An artist herself—her den is her studio—she works mostly in plastics now, doing commercial designs. One of her recent products, a Plexiglas easel—designed as a stand for photographs or decorative plates—has been mass-marketed, selling at New York's finest department stores as well as at the Metropolitan Museum Gift Shop. Single now, the actress has been married and divorced three times —first (1936–38) to Dr. Kenneth Kelly. By her second marriage, (1939–50) to movie producer Armand S. Deutsch, she has two daughters: Pat (wife of a Colgate executive), who has made her the grandmother of a young boy and girl, and Debbie (wife of a Macy's executive). She had no children by her third marriage (1951–63) to the late character actor Fred Clark. With rueful affection, she recently said of Clark: "He was always in a great poker game with people like John Hodiak and Frank Lovejoy. I think they're all up there playing poker now." Onscreen from 1928. IN: *Trail of 98, Kiki, Repeat Performance; I, Jane Doe; Annie Get Your Gun* (her best screen outing, as "Dolly Tate"), *Call Me Mister, Ricochet Romance, The Fuzzy Pink Nightgown.*

VERA-ELLEN (S. Cal.) As slender as ever, and in her 50s (b. 1920), she was married to millionaire Victor Rothschild in 1954, has been retired from the screen since 1959's *Web of Violence,* and lives a quiet social life in Beverly Hills. Onscreen from 1945. IN: *Wonder Man, The Kid from Brooklyn, Three Little Girls in Blue, Carnival in Costa Rica, Words and Music, On the Town, Love Happy, Three Little Words, Happy Go Lovely, The Belle of New York, Call Me Madam, White Christmas, Let's Be Happy,* more.

VERBIT, HELEN (N.Y.) Character. Onscreen in the '70s. IN: *Made for Each Other,* more.

VERDON, GWEN (N.Y.) Star dancer-actress. Married to (but legally separated from) dancer-director Bob Fosse, her second husband, by whom she has a daughter. She was first married to Hollywood columnist Jim Henaghan, father of her grown son. In 1975–76 she starred on Broadway—directed as usual by Fosse—in *Chicago,* the latest in a long string of hit musical comedies. Onscreen from 1951. IN: *On the Riviera* ("Popo the Puppet" number with Danny Kaye), *David and Bathsheba* (slave girl role), *Mississippi Gambler* (voodoo dance number), *Meet Me After the Show, The Farmer Takes a Wife, Damn Yankees* (repeating her Tony Award-winning Broadway role).

VERDUGO, ELENA (S. Cal.) Support; former leading lady. Popular on TV in the series *Meet Millie* (title role) and *Marcus Welby.* Onscreen from 1940. IN: *Down Argentine Way* (her debut, age 14), *The Moon and Sixpence, The Devil's Brood, Rainbow Island, The House of Frankenstein, The Frozen Ghost, Little Giant, Song of Scheherazade, The Big Sombrero, Tuna Clipper, El Dorado Pass, Cyrano de Bergerac, Gene Autry and the Mounties, Thief of Damascus, The Pathfinder, Panama Sal, How Sweet It Is!,* more.

VERDY, VIOLETTE (Fr.) Ballet star. Onscreen in 1951. IN: *Dream Ballerina.*

VEREEN, BEN (N.Y.) Black singer-dancer-actor. Onscreen in the '70s. IN: *Gas-sss, Funny Lady,* more.

VERLEY, BERNARD (Fr.) Character. Onscreen from the '60s. IN: *The Milky Way, Le Fantome de la Liberte,* more.

VERLEY, RENAUD (Fr.) Leading man. Onscreen from the '60s. IN: *How Not to Rob a Department Store, The Tender Moment,* more.

VERNO, JERRY (Eng.) Comic character who, in his 80s (b. 1895), remains busy. Onscreen from 1931. IN: *Two Crowded Hours, The 39 Steps, There Goes the Bride, Non-Stop New York, Troopship, A Clown Must Laugh, The Red Shoes, The Belles of St. Trinian's,* more.

VERNON, ANNE (Fr.) Former leading lady (b. 1925) who, in more recent years, has essayed mother roles. Onscreen from the late '40s. IN: *Warning to Wantons, Shakedown, Edward and Caroline, A Tale of Five Women, Time Bomb, Beautiful But Dangerous, General Della Rovere, The Umbrellas of Cherbourg, Friend of the Family, Therese and Isabelle,* more.

VERNON, GLEN (S. Cal.) A bit heavier now in his 50s (b. 1923) than in his starring years as an RKO juvenile in the '40s, he plays character roles on TV and in such movies as *Airport '75.* He and his wife (since '74), actress Joy Rogers, have a home in the Valley where, between film assignments, he composes popular songs (published). By his previous marriage, which ended in divorce, he has two teenage boys. Onscreen from 1944. IN: *Days of Glory, Youth Runs Wild, Those Endearing Young Charms, Bedlam, The Woman on the Beach, Hang 'Em High,* more.

VERNON, HOWARD (Fr.) Character. Onscreen from the '50s. IN: *Sins of the Borgias, The Girl in the Bikini, The Secret Ways, Alphaville, The Game Is Over, Succubus, The Blood Rose,* more.

VERNON, JACKIE (N.Y.) Support. Onscreen in the '70s. IN: *The Gang That Couldn't Shoot Straight*, more.

VERNON, JOHN (S. Cal.) Leading man. Onscreen from the '60s. IN: *Nobody Waved Goodbye, Point Blank, Justine, Tell Them Willie Boy Is Here, Topaz, Dirty Harry, One More Train to Rob, The Black Windmill, Brannigan, Drum,* more.

VERNON, RICHARD (Eng.) Character. Onscreen from the '60s. IN: *Cash on Demand, The Servant, A Hard Day's Night, Goldfinger, Song of Norway*, more.

VERONA, MICHAEL ROSS (S. Cal.) Support. Onscreen in the '70s. IN: *Candy Stripe Nurses*, more.

VERSOIS, ODILE (Fr.) Leading lady. Onscreen from the '40s. IN: *Les Dernieres Vacances, Man in the Dinghy, Paolo and Francesca, Chance Meeting, To Paris with Love, Checkpoint, Nude in a White Car, Cartouche, Benjamin*, more.

VERUSHKA (N.Y.) Exotic model-actress. Onscreen in 1966. IN: *Blow-Up.*

VESTOFF, VIRGINIA (N.Y.) Broadway leading lady. Onscreen in the '70s. IN: *1776.*

VICKERS, YVETTE (S. Cal.) Support. Onscreen from the '60s. IN: *Hud, What's the Matter with Helen?*, more.

VICTOR, JAMES (S. Cal.) Support. Onscreen from the '60s. IN: *A Global Affair, The President's Analyst, Faces, The Flip Side, Fuzz, Little Fauss and Big Halsy*, more.

VIDOR, FLORENCE (S. Cal.) This great beauty, who was onscreen well over a decade until '29 (that year's *Chinatown Nights* being her only talkie as she could not adjust to sound films), lives in solitary retirement—but with many close friends—in a beautiful big house in Pacific Palisades. She is in her 80s now (b. 1895) and there is still a trace of her native Texas in her talk. She has not remarried since her divorce in '45, after 17 years of marriage, from violinist Jascha Heifetz. By him she has two children, Robert and Josepha, both in their 40s now. By her first husband, whom she married in '15 as they set off together to make their fortunes in Hollywood, director King Vidor, she has an older daughter, Suzanne. Of her 58 movies, Florence Vidor says now she was totally pleased with just one, 1926's *The Grand Duchess and the Waiter* with Adolphe Menjou. Long ago she said, "Women must gain economic in-

dependence before they find contentment." Judging by her long, successful career, and the affluent surroundings of her life today, one might say Florence Vidor found it. Onscreen from 1916. IN: *Till I Come Back to You, Lying Lips, Hail the Woman, Main Street, The Marriage Circle, Welcome Stranger, Christine of the Hungry Heart, Husbands and Lovers, The Trouble with Wives, The Enchanted Hill, Sea Horses, The Eagle of the Sea, One Woman to Another, Honeymoon Hate, The Magnificent Flirt*, more.

VIGNON, JEAN-PAUL (N.Y.) Singer-actor. Once married to young leading lady Brigid Bazlen (retired). Onscreen from the '60s. IN: *The Devil's Brigade*, more.

VIGODA, ABE (N.Y.) Character. Onscreen in the '70s. IN: *The Godfather, Newman's Law; The Godfather, Part II*; more.

VIGRAN, HERB(ERT) (S. Cal.) Character. Onscreen from 1940. IN: *It All Came True, Murder by Invitation, Night Into Morning, Bedtime for Bonzo, Just for You, Susan Slept Here, The Midnight Story, Support Your Local Gunfighter, How to Seduce a Woman, Benji, Hawmps*, more.

VIHARO, ROBERT (S. Cal.) Support. Onscreen from the '60s. IN: *Valley of the Dolls, Villa Rides*, more.

VILBERT, HENRI (Fr.) Character. Onscreen from the '30s. IN: *Adieux les Beaux Jours, Sins of Paris, Letters From My Windmill, We Are All Murderers, The Easiest Profession, My Wife's Husband*, more.

VILLARD, FRANK (Fr.) Leading man. Onscreen from the '40s. IN: *Gigi* (French version; predated Hollywood's), *The Cheat, Savage Triangle, The Seven Deadly Sins* ("Lust" episode); *Money, Money, Money; Gigot, Mata Hari*, more.

VILLECHAIZE, HERVE (N.Y.) Diminutive (3'10") character. Onscreen in the '70s. IN: *The Gang That Couldn't Shoot Straight, Crazy Joe, Seizure, The Man With the Golden Gun*, more.

VILLELLA, EDWARD (N.Y.) Ballet star. Onscreen in 1967 in *A Midsummer Night's Dream*.

VILLIERS, JAMES (Eng.) Support. Onscreen from the '60s. IN: *Murder at the Gallop, Nothing But the Best, Eva, These Are the Damned, The Nanny, The Alphabet Murders, Half a Sixpence, The Ruling Class*, more.

VINCENT, JAN-MICHAEL (S. Cal.) Leading man. Onscreen—first billed as Michael Vincent

—from 1967. IN: *Bandido, Journey to Shiloh, The Undefeated, Going Home, The Mechanic, The World's Greatest Athlete, Buster and Billie, White Line Fever, Bite the Bullet, Shadow of the Hawk*, more.

VINCENT, JUNE (S. Cal.) Offscreen and in TV commercials, of which she does many, she remains attractively blonde in her 50s. In character roles in TV dramatic series (*Kung Fu*, etc.), she has frequently played plain older-women character roles. Onscreen from 1943. IN: *Honeymoon Lodge, Ladies Courageous, The Climax, Babes of Swing Street, Can't Help Singing, Black Angel* (perhaps her best-known starring role), *The Creeper, The Lone Wolf and His Lady; Mary Ryan, Detective; Night Without Sleep, Miracle of the Hills*, more.

VINCENT, LARRY (S. Cal.) Support. Onscreen in the '70s. IN: *The Incredible Two-Headed Transplant*, more.

VINCENT, ROMO (S. Cal.) Veteran character actor. Onscreen from 1937. IN: *Turn Off the Moon, Music for Madame, Start Cheering, Scene of the Crime, The Toast of New Orleans, Stars and Stripes Forever, The Caddy, The Naked Jungle, Female on the Beach, Blueprint for Robbery, Mister Buddwing, The Swinger, The Young Runaways; Won Ton Ton, the Dog Who Saved Hollywood*; more.

VINCENT, VIRGINIA (S. Cal.) Support. Onscreen from 1957. IN: *The Helen Morgan Story, I Want to Live!, Never Steal Anything Small, The Black Orchid, Love With the Proper Stranger, Tony Rome, Sweet November, Change of Habit, $1,000,000 Duck*, more.

VINCENT, YVES (Fr.) Leading man. Onscreen from the '50s. IN: *The Naked Woman, Babette Goes to War, Anatomy of a Marriage, Her and She and Him*, more.

VINSON, GARY (S. Cal.) Support. Onscreen from 1962. IN: *A Majority of One, McHale's Navy, Nobody's Perfect*, more.

VINSON, HELEN (N.Y.) The great "other woman" of the screen has been married for more than three decades to Donald Hardenbrook and has long been a leading figure on the New York social scene. Her two previous marriages—to business man Neilson Vickerman and tennis champion Fred Perry—both ended in divorce. Though no longer young (b. 1907), she still looks attractive enough to have stepped out of a frame of 1945's *The Thin Man Goes Home*, which was her last movie. Onscreen from 1932. IN: *Jewel Robbery, Two Against the World, I Am a Fugitive from a Chain Gang, The Power*

and the Glory, The Kennel Murder Case, Let's Try Again, Gift of Gab, Broadway Bill, Private Worlds, Vogues of 1938, In Name Only, Torrid Zone, Enemy Agent, Nothing But the Truth, Chip Off the Old Block, Are These Our Parents?, more.

VINT, ALAN (S. Cal.) Young leading man. Brother of Bill and Jesse Vint. Onscreen in the '70s. IN: *The McMasters, The Panic in Needle Park, Two-Lane Blacktop, Badlands, Earthquake*, more.

VINT, BILL (S. Cal.) Young leading man. Onscreen in the '70s. IN: *Summertree*, more.

VINT, JESSE (S. Cal.) Young leading man. Onscreen in the '70s. IN: *Two-Lane Blacktop, Earthquake, Chinatown, Welcome to Arrow Beach*, more.

VINTON, BOBBY (N.Y.) Singer-actor. Onscreen from the '60s. IN: *Surf Party, Big Jake, The Train Robbers*.

VIRGO, PETER (S. Cal.) Character. Onscreen from the '40s. IN: *Body and Soul, To the Ends of the Earth, Shakedown, The Narrow Margin, The San Francisco Story*, more.

VIRGO, PETER, JR. (S. Cal.) Support. Onscreen in the '70s. IN: *Johnny Got His Gun*, more.

VITALE, MARIO (It.) Leading man; inactive in movies for several years. Onscreen from 1950. IN: *Stromboli, The Island Sinner*, more.

VITALE, MILLY (It.) Leading lady; lately inactive in movies. Onscreen from 1950. IN: *Difficult Years, Revenge of the Pirates, The Juggler, The Seven Little Foys, Nero and the Burning of Rome, War and Peace, The Flesh Is Weak, Hannibal, A Breath of Scandal, The Lion of Amalfi*, more.

VITTI, MONICA (It.) Costar. Onscreen from 1961. IN: *L'Avventura, La Notte, Eclipse, Red Desert, Castle in Switzerland, Sweet and Sour, High Infidelity, Modesty Blaise, The Queens; On My Way to the Crusades, I Met a Girl Who . . . ; Midnight Pleasures, Duck in Orange Sauce*, more.

VIVA (N.Y.) Retired from movies, also divorced and the mother of a young daughter, the former Andy Warhol star lives on a farm in upstate New York, in the Thousand Islands area, and writes. She has published two novels: the barely disguised autobiography *Superstar* and *The Baby*. Onscreen from the '60s. IN: *Caio! Manhattan* (pre-Warhol); *The Loves of*

Ondine, The Nude Restaurant, Bike Boy, Tub Girl, Blue Movie (and others for Warhol); and *Lions Love* (for director Agnes Varda).

VIVYAN, JOHN (S. Cal.) Leading man from TV. Onscreen from 1959. IN: *Imitation of Life*, more.

VLADY, MARINA (Fr.) Leading lady. Onscreen from 1949. IN: *Orage d'Ete, La Sorciere, Sins of Casanova, Crime and Punishment, The Girl on the Third Floor, Nude in a White Car, The Conjugal Bed, Sweet and Sour; Falstaff: Chimes at Midnight; Run for Your Wife, Two or Three Things I Know About Her, Winter Wind, Seven Deaths by Prescription*, more.

VLASEK, JUNE (S. Cal.) The name—her real one—June Lang used onscreen in 1932–33. IN: *Chandu the Magician, The Man Who Dared*, more. (See June Lang.)

VOGEL, MITCH(ELL) (S. Cal.) Former juvenile (b. 1956). Onscreen from 1968. IN: *Yours, Mine and Ours; The Reivers*, more.

VOIGHT, JON (S. Cal.) Costar. Nominated for Best Actor Oscar in *Midnight Cowboy*. Onscreen from 1968. IN: *Out of It, The Hour of the Gun, Catch-22, The Revolutionary, Fearless Frank, Deliverance, The Hamster of Happiness* (or, *The All-American Boy*), *The Odessa File, Conrack, Murder on the Bridge; The Heretic: Exorcist II;* more.

VOGLER, KARL MICHAEL (Ger.) Character. Onscreen from the '60s. IN: *Those Magnificent Men in Their Flying Machines, The Blue Max, How I Won the War, Downhill Racer, Patton* (as Rommel), *Deep End*, more.

VOLAND, HERB (S. Cal.) Character. Onscreen from the '60s. IN: *With Six You Get Egg Roll, The Chase, The Love God?, The Shakiest Gun in the West, Don't Just Stand There*, more.

VOLONTE, GIAN MARIA (It.) Leading man. Onscreen from 1960. IN: *Under Ten Flags, A Fistful of Dollars, Magnificent Cuckold, For a Few Dollars More, We Still Kill the Same Old Way, The Violent Four, Investigation of a Citizen Above Suspicion, Sacco and Vanzetti; Re: Lucky Luciano;* more.

VON FURSTENBERG, BETSY (N.Y.) No longer in movies, the leading lady stars on Broadway (*Mary Mary, The Gingerbread Lady*) and, between plays, writes articles for *Viva* ("How to Stay Young Forever"), *Playbill*, and *The New York Times*. Onscreen from 1951. IN: *Women Without Names, Skirts Ahoy!*

VON KLAUSSEN, RONALD (Fla.) Character. He lives in the "other" Hollywood—Florida—and commutes. Onscreen from the '50s. IN: *Ben Hur, Hercules in New York, Gentle Ben, Every Man My Enemy, Thunderball, Don't Drink the Water, Hired Killer, The Gang That Couldn't Shoot Straight*, more.

VON REINHOLD, CALVIN (N.Y.) Dancer-singer-actor. Onscreen in the '50s. IN: *Gentlemen Marry Brunettes, The King's Rhapsody*, more.

VON SCHERLER, SASHA (N.Y.) Support. Primarily a stage actress. Onscreen from 1971. IN: *Women, Women, Women*.

VON SYDOW, CLAS and HENRIK (Swe.) Children of Max Von Sydow. Onscreen in 1966 in *Hawaii* (juvenile roles).

VON SYDOW, MAX (Swe.) Costar. Onscreen from the '50s. IN: *Miss Julie, The Seventh Seal, Wild Strawberries, The Magician, The Virgin Spring, Through a Glass Darkly, Winter Light, The Greatest Story Ever Told, The Reward, Hawaii, The Quiller Memorandum, Hour of the Wolf, Shame, The Touch, The Emigrants, The Exorcist, Three Days of the Condor, Facade (Trompe L'Oeil), Dog's Heart (Cuore di Cane), The Voyage of the Damned*, more.

VON ZELL, HARRY (S. Cal.) The famous radio announcer-actor is in his 70s (b. 1906) and retired, but he is prominently featured in many of Hollywood's nostalgic functions. Onscreen from 1945. IN: *Uncle Harry, How Do You Do?, Till the End of Time, The Guilt of Janet Ames, The Saxon Charm, Dear Wife, Where the Sidewalk Ends, Two Flags West, Call Me Mister, You're in the Navy Now, I Can Get It for You Wholesale*, more, including 1966's *Boy, Did I Get a Wrong Number!*, his most recent to date.

VON ZERNECK, PETER (S. Cal.) Character. Onscreen from the '40s. IN: *Notorious, 13 Rue Madeleine, Berlin Express, A Foreign Affair*, more.

VOSBURGH, DAVID (N.Y.) Support. Onscreen in the '70s. IN: *The Gang That Couldn't Shoot Straight*, more.

VOSKOVEC, GEORGE (N.Y.) Character. Onscreen in Europe from 1926. IN: *A Tale of May; Kate, the Mart Girl; Your Money or Your Life; The Golem, The World Is Ours*, more. Onscreen in American movies from 1951. IN: *Anything Can Happen, Affair in Trinidad, The Iron Mistress, 12 Angry Men, Uncle Vanya, The Bravados, Wind Across the Everglades, Butter-*

field 8, *Hamlet, The Spy Who Came in From the Cold, Mister Buddwing, The Desperate Ones, The Boston Strangler, Man on a Swing*, more.

VYE, MURVYN (N.Y.) Character; inactive in movies in the past decade. Onscreen from 1947. IN: *Golden Earrings, Whispering Smith, A Connecticut Yankee in King Arthur's Court,*

The Road to Bali, Pickup on South Street, River of No Return, Black Horse Canyon, The Best Things in Life Are Free, Voodoo Island, In Love and War, Al Capone, The Boy and the Pirates, more, including 1965's *Andy*, his most recent to date. (He later returned to Broadway and starred in *The Caucasian Chalk Circle*.)

W

WADDINGTON, PATRICK (Eng.) Singer-actor, now in his 70s (b. 1901), who was highly active up to this decade. Onscreen from 1926. IN: *Loyalties, The Black Tulip, I Give My Heart, The Loves of Madame DuBarry, Journey Together, School for Secrets, Esther Waters, The Wooden Horse, The Moonraker, Family Doctor, A Night to Remember*, more.

WADE, ADAM (N.Y.) Support. Onscreen in the '70s. IN: *Shaft, Claudine, Crazy Joe, Phantom of the Paradise*, more.

WAGENHEIM, CHARLES (S. Cal.) Character. Onscreen from 1940. IN: *Charlie Chan at the Wax Museum, Two Girls on Broadway, Meet Boston Blackie, Fingers at the Window, Summer Storm, Col. Effingham's Raid, The House on 92nd Street, The Dark Corner, Man-Eater of Kumaon, The House on Telegraph Hill, The Prodigal; Blackjack Ketchum—Desperado; Tunnel of Love, The Police Dog Story, The Baby Maker*, more.

WAGER, ANTHONY (Eng.) The juvenile lead in *Great Expectations* is now, entering his 40s, an English businessman, having given up acting in the early 1960s. Onscreen from 1947. IN: *Hungry Hill, The Guinea Pig, Fame Is the Spur, The Wind Cannot Read*, more.

WAGER, MICHAEL (N.Y.) Support. More active on the stage than in movies. Onscreen from 1955. IN: *Hill 24 Doesn't Answer, Exodus, King of Hearts*, more.

WAGNER, ED (N.Y.) Support. Onscreen from 1959. IN: *The F.B.I. Story, Murder Inc., Pretty Boy Floyd*, more.

WAGNER, ELSA (Ger.) Character; former leading lady. Onscreen from the '20s. IN: *Luther, Meistersinger, Hertha's Erwachen, City of Torment, Marriage of Figaro*, more, including 1974's *The Pedestrian*.

WAGNER, LEON (S. Cal.) Support. Onscreen in the '70s. IN: *A Woman Under the Influence*, more.

WAGNER, LINDSAY (S. Cal.) Leading lady. Star of TV's *The Bionic Woman*. Onscreen in the '70s. IN: *Paper Chase, Two People*, more.

WAGNER, LOU (S. Cal.) Character. Onscreen from the '60s. IN: *Planet of the Apes, Hello Down There, Airport, Beneath the Planet of the Apes*, more.

WAGNER, MIKE (S. Cal.) Character. Onscreen in the '70s. IN: *Support Your Local Gunfighter*, more.

WAGNER, ROBERT (S. Cal.) Costar. Onscreen from 1950. IN: *The Happy Years* (first role; a bit), *The Halls of Montezuma, The Frogmen, With a Song in My Heart, Stars and Stripes Forever, Titanic, Beneath the 12-Mile Reef, Prince Valiant, Broken Lance, The Mountain, Stopover Tokyo, All the Fine Young Cannibals* (with Natalie Wood, who became his first and, presently, his third wife; between, he was married to actress Marion Marshall), *Sail a Crooked Ship, The Longest Day, The Pink Panther, Harper, Banning, Don't Just Stand There, Winning, The Towering Inferno*, more.

WAGNER, WENDE (S. Cal.) Leading lady. Onscreen from 1964. IN: *Rio Conchos, A Covenant with Death, Rosemary's Baby, Guns of the Magnificent Seven*, more.

WAINWRIGHT, JAMES (S. Cal.) Leading man from TV. Onscreen in the '70s. IN: *Joe Kidd*, more.

WAITE, GENEVIEVE (S. Cal.) Leading lady. Married to composer-lyricist John Phillips. Onscreen from 1968. IN: *Joanna, Move*, more.

WAITE, RALPH (S. Cal.) Support. On TV as the father in *The Waltons*. Onscreen from 1968. IN: *A Lovely Way to Die, Five Easy Pieces, Lawman, The Grissom Gang, Dime Box, The Sporting Club*, more

WAKEFIELD, ANNE (N.Y.) Leading lady. Onscreen from 1962. IN: *The 300 Spartans*, more.

WAKELY, JIMMY (S. Cal.) It's been well over two decades since this singing cowpoke made his last movie, but on the rodeo circuit and in clubs across the land he remains a "rhinestone cowboy" of the first caliber. At the microphone, flanked in recent seasons by two other singers named Wakely—Linda Lee and Johnny, his grownup kids—he easily belies his years (b. 1914), remaining slender, dark-haired, and in good voice. Wakely and his wife, Inez, married since '36, have two other daughters, Carol and Deanna, both married. Adjoining their San Fernando Valley home is a modern recording studio, where the singer-actor makes commercial records, his and those of other C&W artists, some of whom sing songs owned by one of Wakely's two music publishing companies. Mrs. Wakely acts as business manager for this home-based enterprise. Truly a family-oriented man, the star says, "I guess the philosophy for the whole family would be that we have faith in God, a love for people and we like to use the talents we have." Oldtime fans flock to see him in his personal appearances. They wait expectantly, confident he will do it, for Jimmy Wakely to sing his first great hit, "Cimarron, Roll On." They smile as he begins to croon the first few bars, and the years roll away and it's Saturday afternoon at the Bijou again. You can almost smell the popcorn. Onscreen from 1939. IN: *Saga of Death Valley, The Tulsa Kid, Heart of the Rio Grande, Twilight on the Trail, Deep in the Heart of Texas, The Old Chisholm Trail, Song of the Range, Cowboy from Lonesome Valley, Sagebrush Heroes, Springtime in Texas, Moon over Montana, Song of the Sierras, Silver Trails, Cowboy Cavalier, Across the Rio Grande*, more, including 1955's *The Silver Star*, his most recent to date.

WALBERG, GARRY (S. Cal.) Character. Onscreen from the '60s. IN: *Charro!, Tell Them Willie Boy Is Here, The Organization*, more.

WALCOTT, GREGORY (S. Cal.) Character. Onscreen from 1955. IN: *Mister Roberts, The McConnell Story, The Lieutenant Wore Skirts, The Steel Jungle, The Outsider; Captain Newman, M.D.; The Sugarland Express, A Man from the East*, more.

WALD, JANE (S. Cal.) Leading lady. Onscreen from 1962. IN: *The Three Stooges in Orbit, Under the Yum-Yum Tree, What a Way to Go!, Dear Brigitte*, more.

WALDEN, ROBERT (S. Cal.) Support. Onscreen in the '70s. IN: *Bloody Mama, The Out-of-Towners, Pigeons, The Hospital, Our Time*, more.

WALDEN, SYLVIA (S. Cal.) Support. Onscreen in the '70s. IN: *The Harrad Summer*, more.

WALDER, ERNST (Eng.) Support. Onscreen from the '60s. IN: *Darling, Where Eagles Dare*, more.

WALDO, JANET (S. Cal.) A popular juvenile lead more than three decades ago, and later on radio as "Corliss Archer," she has been married since '48 to playwright Robert E. Lee, of *Inherit the Wind* fame. They live in Encino, travel widely, have a grown son and daughter—and in her early 50s the actress still looks like a college student. Onscreen from 1939. IN: *Zaza, The Star Maker, What a Life, Waterloo Bridge; Our Neighbors—The Carters; One Man's Law, Those Were the Days, The Silver Stallion, Land of the Open Range*, more, including 1941's *The Bandit Trail*, her most recent feature to date.

WALKEN, CHRISTOPHER (N.Y.) Leading man from TV soap operas and the New York stage. Onscreen in the '70s. IN: *The Anderson Tapes; Next Stop, Greenwich Village*; more.

WALKER, BETTY (N.Y.) Support. Onscreen from 1951. IN: *Molly, Middle of the Night, Exodus, Who Is Harry Kellerman . . . ?*, more.

WALKER, BILL (S. Cal.) Black character. Onscreen from 1946. IN: *The Killers, No Way Out, Night Without Sleep, Queen Bee, Wall of Noise, Kisses for My President, Riot, A Dream of Kings, The Great White Hope*, more.

WALKER, CLINT (S. Cal.) Muscular star of TV (*Cheyenne, Kodiak*) and movies. Onscreen from 1958. IN: *Fort Dobbs, Yellowstone Kelly, Gold of the Seven Saints, Send Me No Flowers, None But the Brave, The Night of the Grizzly, The Dirty Dozen, The Great Bank Robbery, More Dead Than Alive*, more.

WALKER, ELIZABETH "TIPPY" (S. Cal.) Leading lady. Onscreen from 1964. IN: *The World of Henry Orient, Jennifer on My Mind, The Jesus Trip*, more.

WALKER, FIONA (Eng.) Support. Onscreen from the '60s. IN: *Far From the Madding Crowd*, more.

WALKER, JIMMIE (S. Cal.) Black comedy star from TV (*Good Times*). Onscreen in the '70s. IN: *The Last Detail, Let's Do It Again*, more.

WALKER, JOYCE (S. Cal.) Black leading lady. Onscreen in the '70s. IN: *Willie Dynamite, The Education of Sonny Carson*, more.

WALKER, MICHAEL (S. Cal.) Support. One of Jennifer Jones' two actor sons by her first husband, late star Robert Walker, the other being Robert Jr. Onscreen from the '60s. IN: *Daring Games, Hell's Belles,* more.

WALKER, NANCY (S. Cal.) Comedy star, long offscreen, who staged a major comeback via TV's *Rhoda* and *McMillan & Wife,* and has also returned to moviemaking. Onscreen from 1943. IN: *Best Foot Forward, Girl Crazy, Broadway Rhythm, Lucky Me, The World's Greatest Athlete, Murder by Death,* more.

WALKER, PETER (S. Cal.) Character. Onscreen from the '50s. IN: *If All the Guys in the World, "W,"* more.

WALKER, ROBERT/formerly **ROBERT WALKER JR.** (S. Cal.) Leading man. Son of Jennifer Jones and Robert Walker. Onscreen from 1963. IN: *The Hook, The Ceremony, Ensign Pulver, The Happening, The War Wagon, The Savage Seven, Killers Three, Easy Rider, Young Billy Young, Road to Salina, The Spectre of Edgar Allan Poe, The Passover Plot,* more.

WALKER, SYDNEY (N.Y.) Character. Onscreen from the '60s. IN: *A Lovely Way to Die, Puzzle of a Downfall Child, Love Story, The Way We Live Now,* more.

WALKER, WILLIAM (S. Cal.) Character. Onscreen from 1950. IN: *Bright Leaf, Lydia Bailey; Wait Till the Sun Shines, Nellie; The Long, Hot Summer; Our Man Flint, Big Jake,* more.

WALKER, ZENA (Eng.) Leading lady. Onscreen from the '60s. IN: *The Hellions, The Traitors, The Model Murder Case, Sammy Going South, The Last Shot You Hear, The Reckoning, Cromwell,* more.

WALL, ANITA (Swe.) Character. Onscreen in the '70s. IN: *Scenes From a Marriage,* more.

WALLACE, ART (N.Y.) Character. Onscreen in the '70s. IN: *Welcome to the Club,* more.

WALLACE, GEORGE (S. Cal.) Support. Onscreen from the '60s. IN: *6 Black Horses, The Swinging Cheerleaders,* more.

WALLACE, JACK (S. Cal.) Support. Onscreen in the '70s. IN: *Death Wish,* more.

WALLACE, JEAN (S. Cal.) Long and happily married to Cornel Wilde, she remains a beautiful blonde and still acts. One of her two sons by the late Franchot Tone, Thomas Jefferson Tone, became a groom in '72, marrying Mallory Hathaway. Onscreen from 1941. IN: *Louisiana Purchase, You Can't Ration Love, It Shouldn't Happen to a Dog, Blaze of Noon, Jigsaw* (her

first opposite Tone), *The Man on the Eiffel Tower* (also with Tone), *The Good Humor Man, Native Son, The Big Combo* (in '55; first of several opposite Cornel Wilde), *Storm Fear, Star of India, The Devil's Hairpin, Sword of Lancelot, Beach Red, No Blade of Grass* (starred in this '70 film produced-directed by Wilde, who did not appear in it), more. (See Cornel Wilde.)

WALLACE, JUDY (S. Cal.) Support. Onscreen in the '70s. IN: *Darker Than Amber, How Do I Love Thee,* more.

WALLACE, LEE (N.Y.) Character actor. Onscreen in the '70s. IN: *The Taking of Pelham One Two Three,* more.

WALLACE, MARCIA (S. Cal.) Support. On TV in *The Bob Newhart Show.* Onscreen in the '70s. IN: *Lady Sings the Blues,* more.

WALLACE, PAUL (S. Cal.) Dancer-singer-actor. Lately inactive in movies, he lives in Encino and is a choreographer. Onscreen from 1956. IN: *Crime in the Streets, The Young Stranger, Johnny Trouble, Gypsy,* more.

WALLACE, RATCH (Can.) Character actor. Onscreen in the '60s. IN: *Isabel, Act of the Heart,* more.

WALLACE, REGINA (N.Y.) A character actress in movies of the 1940s, she returned to the New York stage where her career began in 1913 —she was a charter member of Actors Equity— and where, in the original *My Fair Lady,* she played Mrs. Eynsford-Hill. On Broadway, in her time, she has played four starring roles and countless leads. Today, in her late 70s (or early 80s; her exact age is her secret), she acts less often onstage but continues to do numerous "aristocratic lady-type" commercials for TV. Onscreen from 1942. IN: *Adventures of Martin Eden, The Male Animal* (repeating the "Myrtle Keller" role she did on Broadway), *Sherlock Holmes in Washington, The Crystal Ball, Mr. Skeffington, Pillow to Post, Because of Him, The Dark Corner, Avalanche, Welcome Stranger, Let's Live a Little, Rachel and the Stranger, Miracle of the Bells, B. F.'s Daughter, A Kiss for Corliss, My Foolish Heart,* more.

WALLACE, ROYCE (S. Cal.) Black character actress. Onscreen from 1961. IN: *Take a Giant Step; Goodbye, Columbus; Willie Dynamite,* more.

WALLACH, ELI (N.Y.) Costar. Onscreen from 1956. IN: *Baby Doll, The Magnificent Seven, The Misfits, How the West Was Won, The Victors, Act One, The Moonspinners, Lord Jim, How to Steal a Million, The Tiger Makes*

Out; How to Save a Marriage—And Ruin Your Life; The Good, the Bad and the Ugly; A Lovely Way to Die, Mackenna's Gold, Ace High, The People Next Door, The Angel Levine, Romance of a Horse Thief, Crazy Joe, Don't Turn the Other Cheek!; White, Yellow, Black; The Female is the Deadliest of the Species, more.

WALLACH, LEW (N.Y.) Support. Onscreen in 1967. IN: *Up the Down Staircase.*

WALLER, DAVID (Eng.) Character. Onscreen from the '60s. IN: *Love Is a Four-Letter Word, Perfect Friday,* more.

WALLER, EDDY (S. Cal.) This veteran character actor—especially popular as the sidekick in Allan "Rocky" Lane Westerns—has been retired for more than 15 years. Onscreen from 1937. IN: *Sweetheart of the Navy, Call the Mesquiteers, I'm from Missouri, Jesse James, The Grapes of Wrath, Hands Across the Rockies, Scattergood Survives a Murder, Home in Indiana, Renegades, Oklahoma Badlands, Black Bart, Death Valley Gunfighters, Frisco Tornado, El Paso Stampede, The Phantom Stagecoach,* more.

WALLEY, DEBORAH (S. Cal.) Leading lady. Onscreen from 1961. IN: *Gidget Goes Hawaiian, Bon Voyage!, Summer Magic, Ski Party, Beach Blanket Bingo, Spin-Out, It's a Bikini World, Benji,* more.

WALLIS, SHANI (Eng.) Singer-actress. Onscreen from 1967. IN: *Oliver!, Terror in the Wax Museum,* more.

WALMSLEY, JON (S. Cal.) Juvenile. On TV as "Jason" in *The Waltons.* Onscreen from 1968. IN: *The One and Only Genuine Original Family Band.*

WALPER, CICELY (S. Cal.) Character. Onscreen from the '60s. IN: *The Killing of Sister George, The Brotherhood of Satan,* more.

WALSH, ANTHONY (Eng.) Leading man. Onscreen from the '60s. IN: *Double-Stop,* more.

WALSH, ARTHUR (S. Cal.) Character. Onscreen from the '40s. IN: *This Man's Navy, They Were Expendable, My Darling Clementine, You Gotta Stay Happy, The Last Hurrah,* more.

WALSH, BRYAN (Eng.) Support. Onscreen from the '60s. IN: *The Touchables,* more.

WALSH, DERMOT (Eng.) Leading man. Onscreen from the '40s. IN: *Bedelia, Hungry Hill,* *Jassy, Desert Patrol, Ghost Ship, Counterspy, The Telltale Heart, It Takes a Thief,* more.

WALSH, EDWARD (S. Cal.) Support. Onscreen in the '70s. IN: *Count Yorga, Vampire, The Return of Count Yorga, California Split,* more.

WALSH, GEORGE (S. Cal.) Now in his 80s (b. 1892), the actor-brother of director Raoul Walsh ended his long screen career with minor roles in three in '36: *Rio Grande Romance, Put on the Spot,* and *Klondike Annie.* His screen forte from the beginning in early silents, had always been athletic heroics—he had easily one of the most perfect physiques in the movies—and he felt, rightfully, he was past his physical prime and it was time to get out. It had also been a decade since he'd had a starring role. For a while, then, he trained race horses for brother Raoul, but in more recent years has owned a lemon grove in Montclair. He has a grown daughter, Patricia, by his first wife, star Seena Owen; they met during *Intolerance,* married in '16 and divorced in '24. By his second wife he has two sons, both grown. While maintaining his California home, he travels extensively. As brother Raoul—they've always been close—noted in his recently published autobiography, *Each Man in His Time,* "Even as a kid, I suspected that the Walshes must have gypsy blood in them. The last I heard of brother George, he was somewhere in Africa . . ." Onscreen from 1914. IN: *Don Quixote, Intolerance, The Beast, The Island of Desire, I'll Say So, The Shark, Vanity Fair, Rosita, Slave of Desire, Reno, Out of Singapore, Black Beauty, Return of Casey Jones, The Bowery, Belle of the Nineties, Under Pressure,* more.

WALSH, JOEY (S. Cal.) Support. Began as a juvenile. Onscreen from 1952. IN: *Hans Christian Andersen, The Juggler, Anzio; Drive, He Said;* more.

WALSH, KAY (Eng.) Character; former leading lady (b. 1914). Onscreen from 1934. IN: *How's Chances?, The Luck of the Irish, The Secret of Stamboul, In Which We Serve, This Happy Breed, Stage Fright, The Last Holiday, The Magnet, Encore* ("Winter Cruise" episode), *The Stranger in Between, Young Bess, The Horse's Mouth, Tunes of Glory, Greyfriars' Bobby, Reach for Glory, The Devil's Own, The Ruling Class,* more.

WALSH, M. EMMET (S. Cal.) Support. Onscreen from the '60s. IN: *Midnight Cowboy, Stiletto, Alice's Restaurant, End of the Road, The Traveling Executioner, Little Big Man, Cold Turkey, Loving, Escape from the Planet of the Apes, They Might Be Giants,* more.

WALSH, RAOUL (S. Cal.) An actor before and for a while after he became one of Hollywood's most renowned action directors (*The Thief of Bagdad, What Price Glory, High Sierra*, etc.), he enters his 90th year in 1977. Retired from directing since 1964's *A Distant Trumpet*, he published his autobiography, a highly rewarding book about the movies, *Each Man in His Time*, in 1974. Onscreen from 1913. IN: *Life of Villa* (as Pancho Villa), *The Birth of a Nation* (as John Wilkes Booth), *Sadie Thompson* (he also directed), more. (Also, in 1928, he began playing the role of the Cisco Kid in *The Old Arizona*, which he directed, before an on-location accident cost him his right eye. He then assigned the role to Warner Baxter, who won an Oscar for it.)

WALSH, SEAN (S. Cal.) Support. Onscreen in the '70s. IN: *Cry Uncle*, more.

WALSH, WILLIAM (N.Y.) Character. Onscreen in the '70s. IN: *Diary of a Mad Housewife*, more.

WALSTON, RAY (S. Cal.) Comic character lead. Onscreen from 1957. IN: *Kiss Them for Me, South Pacific, Damn Yankees, Say One for Me, Tall Story, The Apartment, Portrait in Black, Wives and Lovers, Who's Minding the Store?; Kiss Me, Stupid; Caprice, Paint Your Wagon, Viva Max!*, more.

WALTER, JESSICA (S. Cal.) Leading lady. Onscreen from 1964. IN: *Lilith, The Group, Grand-Prix, Bye Bye Braverman, Number One, Play Misty for Me*, more.

WALTER-ELLIS, DESMOND (Eng.) Singer-character actor. Onscreen from the '50s. IN: *Maytime in Mayfair, Penny Princess, The Ship Was Loaded, The Statue*, more.

WALTERS, CASEY (N.Y.) Support. Onscreen from the '60s. IN: *Kathy O, The Other Life of Lynn Stuart*, more.

WALTERS, MARRIAN (S. Cal.) Support. Onscreen from the '60s. IN: *Medium Cool*, more.

WALTERS, THORLEY (Eng.) Character. Onscreen from the '30s. IN: *Gentleman of Adventure, It Happened to One Man, Waltz Time, Blue Murder at St. Trinian's, Man in a Cocked Hat, A French Mistress, Invasion Quartet, Murder She Said, The Phantom of the Opera, Ring of Treason, The Psychopath, The Last Shot You Hear*, more.

WALTHER, GRETCHEN (S. Cal.) Support. Onscreen in the '70s. IN: *The Landlord*, more.

WALTON, JESS (S. Cal.) Leading lady. Onscreen in the '70s. IN: *The Strawberry Statement, The Peace Killers*, more.

WALTON, PEGGY (S. Cal.) Ingenue. Onscreen in the '70s. IN: *What's the Matter with Helen?*, more.

WANAMAKER, SAM (Eng.) Leading man. A native of Chicago, and a product of Broadway, followed by Hollywood, he lives and works in London where, besides continuing in movies, he is a stage producer-director. Onscreen from 1948. IN: *My Girl Tisa, Cloak and Dagger, Mr. Denning Drives North, Taras Bulba, Those Magnificent Men in Their Flying Machines, The Spy Who Came in from the Cold, Warning Shot, The Day the Fish Came Out, Danger Route*, more. (See Jan Sterling.)

WANNER, HUGHES (Fr.) Character. Onscreen from the '50s. IN: *Four Bags Full, The Night of the Following Day*, more.

WARBURTON, JOHN (S. Cal.) Yesterday's handsome leading man from England is now, in his 70s (b. 1899), a handsome character actor, retaining a full head of hair plus, now, a moustache and neat beard. Onscreen from 1932. IN: *The Silver Lining, Cavalcade, Charlie Chan's Greatest Case, A Study in Scarlet, Love Is Dangerous, Becky Sharp, Let's Talk It Over, Partners of the Plains, The Sisters, Captain Fury, The White Cliffs of Dover, Dangerous Partners, Saratoga Trunk, The Valley of Decision, Tarzan and the Huntress, East of Sumatra, King Rat, Assault on a Queen*, more.

WARD, BURT (S. Cal.) Leading man. Onscreen in 1966. IN: *Batman* (as "Robin").

WARD, DAVE (S. Cal.) Character. Onscreen in the '70s. IN: *My Sweet Charlie*, more.

WARD, JAMES "SKIP" (S. Cal.) Leading man. Formerly married to Julie Payne, daughter of John Payne and Anne Shirley. Onscreen from 1961. IN: *Voyage to the Bottom of the Sea, The Night of the Iguana, Kitten with a Whip; Kiss Me, Stupid; Red Line 7000, Is Paris Burning?, Hombre; Easy Come, Easy Go; Myra Breckinridge*, more.

WARD, JANET (N.Y.) Support. Onscreen in the '70s. IN: *The Anderson Tapes*, more.

WARD, JOMARIE (S. Cal.) Support. Onscreen in the '70s. IN: *Pretty Maids All in a Row*, more.

WARD, LARRY (S. Cal.) Support. Onscreen from the '60s. IN: *A Distant Trumpet, Hombre*, more.

WARD, MARSHALL (S. Cal.) Character. Onscreen in the '70s. IN: *The Owl and the Pussycat*, more.

WARD, MICHAEL (Eng.) Character, Onscreen from the '40s. IN: *Lilli Marlene, Tom Brown's School Days, Sleeping Car to Trieste, Private's Progress, Trouble in Store, The Love Lottery, Carry On Cleo*, more.

WARD, PENELOPE DUDLEY (Eng.) Former leading lady; inactive in movies for two decades. Onscreen from the '30s. IN: *The Citadel, Hell's Cargo, Convoy, Frightened Lady, Adventure for Two, Her Man Gilbey*, more.

WARD, POLLY (Eng.) Comic leading lady. Now in her late 60s (b. 1908) and retired. Onscreen in the '20s. IN: *The Old Curiosity Shop* (a most memorable performance as the Marchioness), *Sidewalks of London, It's in the Air*, more.

WARD, RICHARD (N.Y.) Black character. On TV in 1975 as the chef in *Beacon Hill*. Onscreen from the '40s. IN: Various "Tarzan" pictures of Johnny Weissmuller, *Black Like Me, The Learning Tree, Brother John*, more.

WARD, RONALD (Eng.) Character. Onscreen from the '30s. IN: *The Passing of the Third Floor Back, East Meets West, Sidewalks of London, This England, Operation X, They Met in the Dark, My Daughter Joy, The Second Mrs. Tanqueray*, more.

WARD, SIMON (Eng.) Leading man. Onscreen from 1967. IN: *If, Frankenstein Must Be Destroyed, Young Winston* (title role as Churchill), *The Four Musketeers, Children of Rage*, more.

WARD, TREVOR (Eng.) Character. Onscreen from the '40s. IN: *The Fan, My Cousin Rachel*, more.

WARDE, HARLAN (S. Cal.) Character. Onscreen from the '40s. IN: *State Department—File 649; It's a Great Feeling, Task Force, No Sad Songs for Me, The Man Who Cheated Himself, Operation Secret, Julie, Hot Spell*, more.

WARDEN, JACK (S. Cal.) Character. Nominated for Best Supporting Actor Oscar in *Shampoo*. Onscreen from 1950. IN: *The Asphalt Jungle, You're in the Navy Now, From Here to Eternity, The Frogmen, The Bachelor Party, 12 Angry Men; Run Silent, Run Deep; The Sound and the Fury, That Kind of Woman, Donovan's Reef, Blindfold, Bye Bye Braverman, Welcome to the Club, Billy Two Hats, All the President's Men*, more.

WARE, MIDGE (S. Cal.) Leading lady; inactive in movies now. Onscreen from the '50s. IN: *The Prince Who Was a Thief, Door-to-Door Maniac*, more.

WARFIELD, CHRIS (S. Cal.) Support. Onscreen from the '50s. IN: *Take the High Ground, The Student Prince, Incident in an Alley, Diary of a Madman*, more.

WARFIELD, DON (N.Y.) Support. Onscreen in the '70s. IN: *Pigeons*, more.

WARFIELD, MARLENE (N.Y.) Black support. Onscreen in the '70s. IN: *Joe, The Great White Hope*, more.

WARFIELD, WILLIAM (Ill.) The great singer whose interpretation of "Old Man River" will not be forgotten is, in his 50s (b. 1920), professor of music at the University of Illinois in Urbana, where he teaches voice and a full-year graduate course in oratorio. In '75, he gave his 25th anniversary concert at Alice Tully Hall in New York—to ecstatic reviews. Onscreen in 1951 in *Show Boat*. (He also narrated 1960's *Masters of the Congo Jungle*.)

WARHOL, ANDY (N.Y.) Artist and producer-director-cinematographer of "underground" films. Onscreen from 1968. IN: *The Illiac Passion; Diaries, Notes and Sketches*; more.

WARIK, JOSEF (N.Y.) Support. Onscreen in the '70s. IN: *The Pursuit of Happiness*.

WARING, FRED (Pa.) Living in Shawnee-on-Delaware, Pa., the famous orchestra leader is in his 70s (b. 1900), and he and his "Pennsylvanians" maintain a full schedule of personal appearances and recording dates. Onscreen in 1937 in *Varsity Show*.

WARING, RICHARD (N.Y.) Warners planned to costar him with Davis in *The Corn Is Green*, in the Morgan Evans role he had created on Broadway; that plan, though was aborted by the U.S. Army. "How sad we all felt for Richard Waring—to have to give up this great part that he had originated on the stage," Bette Davis said recently. "His motion picture career never recovered from losing this opportunity." After military service, though, the actor's stage career—always his first love—flourished. He played, and continues to play, in many of the classics: Shakespeare, Ibsen, and Chekhov. His television appearances have been many and, to his pleasure (because of residuals), one *Alfred Hitchcock Presents* that he did ("Festive Season") is replayed constantly. He last appeared on Broadway with Dorothy Tutin in *Portrait of a Queen*, for which he also was associate producer. Lately, this still-handsome-in-his-60s actor (b. 1914) has done numerous TV commercials, for Air Jamaica, among others. Married for 18 years to actress Florida Friebus, he has not remarried since their divorce in '52, and lives in Greenwich Village. Onscreen in 1935 and 1944. IN: *The Perfect Gentleman* and *Mr. Skeffington*.

WARNER, ASTRID (S. Cal.) Leading lady. Onscreen from 1968. IN: *The Glory Stompers, Hell's Belles, A Bullet for Pretty Boy,* more.

WARNER, DAVID (Eng.) Costar. Onscreen from 1963. IN: *Tom Jones, Morgan!, Work Is a Four Letter Word, The Fixer, The Bofors Gun, The Sea Gull, The Ballad of Cable Hogue, Straw Dogs, A Doll's House, Tales from the Crypt, Mr. Quilp, From Beyond the Grave,* more.

WARNER, JACK (Eng.) The familiar British actor is in his 80s now (b. 1894) and retired from moviemaking. Onscreen from the '40s. IN: *The Captive Heart, Holiday Camp, Dear Murderer, My Brother's Keeper, Hue and Cry, The Blue Lamp, A Christmas Carol, Valley of the Eagles, Tonight at 8:30* ("Ways and Means" episode), *Hundred Hour Hunt, The Final Test, Ladykillers,* more.

WARNER, PAM (S. Cal.) Support. Onscreen in the '70s. IN: *Thieves Like Us,* more.

WARNER, RICHARD (Eng.) Character. Onscreen from the '60s. IN: *Othello, Village of the Damned; Mary, Queen of Scots;* more.

WARNER, ROBERT (S. Cal.) Leading man. Onscreen in the '70s. IN: *The Politician,* more.

WARNER, STEVEN (Eng.) Juvenile. Onscreen in 1974. IN: *The Little Prince* (title role).

WARRE, MICHAEL (Eng.) Character; primarily a stage actor. Onscreen from the '40s. IN: *Henry V, Reach for the Sky,* more.

WARREN, GARY (Eng.) Juvenile lead. Onscreen in the '70s. IN: *The Railway Children,* more.

WARREN, GLORIA (S. Cal.) The young lark who sang so magically is now in her late 40s, has been married since '46 to agent Peter Gold, has two children, lives in Beverly Hills, and hasn't sung professionally in decades. Onscreen from 1942. IN: *Always in My Heart, Cinderella Swings It, Dangerous Money,* more.

WARREN, JENNIFER (N.Y.) Leading lady. Onscreen in the '70s. IN: *Night Moves,* more.

WARREN, JOSEPH (N.Y.) Character. Onscreen in the '50s. IN: *The Long Gray Line; Me, Natalie; Bang the Drum Slowly,* more.

WARREN, KENNETH J. (Eng.) Support. Onscreen from the '60s. IN: *A High Wind in Jamaica, The Double Man, Leo the Last, The Revolutionary, S*P*Y*S; I, Monster; Demons of the Mind; Digby, the Biggest Dog in the World;* more.

WARREN, KENNY LEE (N.Y.) Support. Onscreen in the '70s. IN: *The Valachi Papers, Across 110th Street,* more.

WARREN, LESLEY (ANN) (S. Cal.) Singer-leading lady. Onscreen from 1967. IN: *The Happiest Millionaire, The One and Only Genuine Original Family Band,* more.

WARREN, MIKE (S. Cal.) Black leading man. Onscreen in the '70s. IN: *Drive, He Said;* more.

WARREN, WILSON (S. Cal.) Support. Onscreen in the '70s. IN: *The Longest Yard,* more.

WARRICK, RUTH (Conn.) Beautiful and still redhaired in her 60s (b. 1915), the actress remains busy and in the news. Consider her activities in this decade. *Professional*: She starred Off Broadway in the play *Conditions of Agreement*, on Broadway with Debbie Reynolds in *Irene*, her first musical comedy, costars regularly as "Phoebe Tyler" in the TV soap opera *All My Children*, and in 1976 became the hostess-singer at the new Manhattan club Top of the i (there to "meet, greet and entertain patrons," as *Variety* put it, adding, after her debut, that she possessed "a regal bearing and well-developed soprano pipes"). *Personal*: She has been a bride twice in the '70s. For a few months of 1972–73, before they were divorced, she was the wife of a younger playwright, Frank Freda. Previously she had been married to and divorced from actor Erik Rolf, interior decorator Carl Neubert, Bob McNamara, and Neubert, to whom she was married a second time. Her present husband, since March 1975, with whom she lives in Old Greenwich, is wealthy stockbroker L. Jarvis Cushing Jr. He has three children by his previous marriages, which ended in divorce. And she also has three. Her youngest, Tim McNamara, is a California college student; daughter Karen Rolf (divorced) has taught music in a high school in Cleveland; and her eldest son, Jon Rolf, and his wife, Ellie—parents of two—live in Vermont, where he teaches psychology at the State University. Explaining that she is a compulsive performer, the actress says she entertains no thought of ever giving up her career: "I can't stop being an actress. I'm not me if I'm not working." And she endeavors to live her life, she says, by this quotation from Rilke: "Celebrate the doing right, and do right with all your heart. Celebrate it confidently, even though external confusions and tribulations still surround one's inner world. The moment is an awakening, and a turning no longer seems out of reach." Onscreen from 1941. IN: *Citizen Kane* ("My kids used to tease me about *Citizen Kane*. It was my first movie, and they used to say, 'Mom, that picture is so old, it should be put on microfilm and placed in a museum.' But then *Citizen Kane* had a revival in movie houses and in colleges, and they all looked at me with new respect."), *The Corsican Brothers, Journey Into Fear, The Iron Major, Guest in the House, China Sky, Song of the South* (with husband Erik Rolf), *Perilous Holiday, Daisy Kenyon, The Great Dan Patch, Let's Dance, Three Husbands, Second Chance, Ride Beyond Vengeance,* more, including 1969's *The Great Bank Robbery,* her most recent to date.

WARSHAWSKY, RUTH (S. Cal.) Character. Onscreen from the '60s. IN: *Candy Stripe Nurses,* more.

WARWICK, JOHN (Eng.) Onscreen from the '30s. IN: *This Man Is News, The Saint's Vacation, The Avengers, Horrors of the Black Museum,* more.

WARWICK, RICHARD (Eng.) Support. Onscreen from the '60s. IN: *If, First Love, Nicholas and Alexandra,* more.

WASHBOURNE, MONA (Eng.) Character. Onscreen from the '40s. IN: *The Winslow Boy, Maytime in Mayfair, Cast a Dark Shadow, Count Your Blessings, Billy Liar, Night Must Fall, My Fair Lady, The Collector, The Third Day, Mr. Quilp,* more.

WASHBROOK, JOHN (N.Y.) Former juvenile star—as Johnny Washbrook—of TV's *My Friend Flicka.* Now a Broadway actor. Onscreen from the '60s. IN: *Lonelyhearts, The Fire Within, Space Children,* more.

WASHBURN, BEVERLY (S. Cal.) Leading lady; former juvenile. Onscreen from 1950. IN: *The Killer That Stalked New York, Here Comes the Groom, Hans Christian Andersen, The Juggler, The Lone Ranger, Old Yeller, Winner, Pit Stop,* more.

WASHINGTON, DINO (S. Cal.) Black support. Onscreen in the '70s. IN: *Tick Tick Tick, The Longest Yard,* more.

WASHINGTON, FREDI (Conn.) This superb and supremely beautiful actress made an indeli-bly poignant impression in the original *Imitation of Life* as Louise Beavers' daughter Peola who "passes" as white. She made just three other movies. In that Hollywood era there was no place for her to go. She was born to play romantic leads—with her delicate features, light skin, and green eyes. But this forerunner of Dorothy Dandridge, et al., was two decades ahead of her time. She returned to the stage, played Ethel Waters' rebellious daughter in *Mamba's Daughters,* and gave up her career. Today, still slender and beautiful in her 60s (b. 1913), and a widow (her husband died in '70), she lives—completely retired—in fashionable Stamford. Onscreen from 1933. IN: *The Emperor Jones, Drums of the Jungle,* and, last, 1937's *One Mile From Heaven.*

WASHINGTON, GENE (S. Cal.) Black leading man. Onscreen in the '70s. IN: *The Black Six,* more.

WASHINGTON, JUDY (S. Cal.) Support. Onscreen in the '70s. IN: *Phantom of the Paradise,* more.

WASHINGTON, KENNETH "KENNY" (S. Cal.) Black character. Onscreen from 1947. IN: *The Foxes of Harrow, Rogues' Regiment, Rope of Sand, Pinky, The Jackie Robinson Story,* and 1969's *Changes,* one of his more recent.

WASHINGTON, SHIRLEY (S. Cal.) Black leading lady. Onscreen in the '70s. IN: *Bamboo Gods and Iron Men,* more.

WASHINGTON, VERNON (N.Y.) Black character. Onscreen from the '50s. IN: *The Joe Louis Story, The Hustler,* more.

WATERMAN, DENIS (Eng.) Leading man. Onscreen from the '60s. IN: *Up the Junction; My Lover, My Son; Scars of Dracula, Man in The Wilderness, The Belstone Fox,* more.

WATERMAN, WILLARD (N.Y.) Radio and TV's "Great Gildersleeve," a Manhattan resident for more than a decade, still makes an occasional movie but acts mainly on the stage now. And, finding a good role, he hangs in there with it. Like that of pompous "Mr. Upson" in *Mame.* He first played it in the 1958 movie, *Auntie Mame,* with Rosalind Russell, followed by the West Coast stage production with Eve Arden. Then came the musical version, *Mame,* that he played onstage—on Broadway and on tour—for four years, with, successively, Angela Lansbury, Janis Paige, Jane Morgan, and Ann Miller. And for two years in the National Company of *How to Succeed in Business Without Really Trying,* he costarred as "J. B. Biggley." Happily married for many years,

"Gildy" has two daughters—Lynne, a young San Francisco matron with two daughters, and Susan, a postal employee in Beverly Hills. Onscreen from 1950. IN: *Riding High, Louisa, Mystery Street; Darling, How Could You; Rhubarb, It Happens Every Thursday, On the Sunny Side of the Street; How to be Very, Very Popular; Hollywood or Bust, The Apartment, Get Yourself a College Girl,* more, including 1973's *Hail! To the Chief* (an outstanding comedy role as the nincompoop Vice President).

WATERS, BUNNY (S. Cal.) One of MGM's "Glamazons," the beautiful blonde has been married to studio orchestra conductor-composer Johnny Green since '44, and has two grown children, Christopher and Kathe, a club singer and composer. Onscreen from the '40s. IN: *Broadway Rhythm, Maisie Goes to Reno, Dangerous When Wet, Pepe,* more.

WATERS, ETHEL (S. Cal.) Black character star. Nominated for Best Supporting Actress Oscar in *Pinky.* In her 70s (b. 1900), her religion is her life, and she is often to be found touring the revival circuit with evangelist Billy Graham, as one of his starred gospel singers. And in '74, after a cataract operation, it was at his home in Charlotte, N.C., that she recuperated. With no immediate family ties of her own, the singer-actress has been closely associated with Graham and his family since '57. She still maintains her home in Los Angeles but has not made a movie since 1959's *The Sound and the Fury,* her only picture in the past two decades. (She is also more slender than in decades, having trimmed down from 200 to 130 pounds.) In '72 she published the sequel to her autobiography *His Eye Is On the Sparrow;* titled *To Me It's Wonderful,* it was essentially an account of the paramount role religion has come to play in her life. That same year, she was also honored at— and attended—an "Ethel Waters Day" in her home town, Chester, Pa. A talk with the star invariably leads to the topic of religion. "When I had everything, I had nothing," she says. "Now I have nothing, but I have everything." Onscreen from 1929. IN: *On With the Show, New York Night, The Cotton Club, Gift of Gab, Tales of Manhattan, Cairo, Cabin in the Sky, Stage Door Canteen, Pinky, The Member of the Wedding,* more.

WATERS, JAN (Eng.) Supporting actress. Onscreen from 1962. IN: *Touch of Death, Corruption,* more.

WATERS, MIRA (N.Y.) Support. Onscreen from the '60s. IN: *The Learning Tree,* more.

WATERS, RUSSELL (Eng.) Character. Onscreen from the '40s. IN: *Street Corner, The*

Blue Lagoon, The Brave Don't Cry, Mr. Denning Drives North, Turn the Key Softly, Rob Roy, Yesterday's Enemy, more.

WATERSTON, SAM (N.Y.) Costar. Onscreen from the '60s. IN: *Generation, Three, The Great Gatsby, Rancho Deluxe, Mahoney's Last Stand,* more.

WATFORD, GWEN (Eng.) Support. Onscreen from 1961. IN: *Cleopatra, The Very Edge,* more.

WATKINS, JIM (S. Cal.) Black support. Onscreen in the '70s. IN: *Cool Breeze, Black Gunn,* more.

WATKINS, LINDA (S. Cal.) The lovely leading lady of the early '30s is, in her 60s (b. 1909), a character actress—and stunningly attractive. Onscreen from 1931. IN: *Sob Sister, Good Sport, Charlie Chan's Chance, The Gay Caballero, Cheaters at Play, Ten North Frederick, The Parent Trap, Good Neighbor Sam,* more.

WATKINS, PETER (Eng.) Support. Now a director (of *Privilege,* etc.). Onscreen in the '60s. IN: *The War Game,* more.

WATLING, JACK (Eng.) Character. Onscreen from 1938. IN: *Sixty Glorious Years, Easy Money, Quartet* ("The Facts of Life" episode), *Under Capricorn, The Naked Heart, Reach for the Sky, Gideon of Scotland Yard, Sink the Bismarck!, Mr. Arkadin, The Nanny,* more.

WATSON, BILLY (S. Cal.) Of the large family of acting Watson children who once had a monopoly on Hollywood juvenile roles—see Bobs Watson, below—he has long been a successful California business man. Onscreen in the '30s. IN: *The Little Minister, The Winning Ticket, In Old Chicago, Kidnapped,* more.

WATSON, BOBS (S. Cal.) A stocky, freckle-faced lad, with a winning little-man smile and tears that touched moviegoers' hearts, he was one of the most gifted child actors of his time. He was greatly affecting in *Boys Town,* as Rooney's young pal Pee Wee, and as the deaf youngster who learns to speak in *The Story of Alexander Graham Bell.* But the role for which he will always be recalled is that of Pud in *On Borrowed Time,* whose beloved Gramps (Lionel Barrymore) refuses to release Death's emissary, Mr. Brink (Cedric Hardwicke), from the tree where he has trapped him until some provision is made for Pud. Acting in fewer films in his teens—his total, though, being more than 125— Bobs Watson completed his education, receiving his bachelor's degree at Los Angeles State College. He served in the Infantry during the

Korean War, being stationed (1953–55) at Fort Ord, Calif., where he was assigned to Special Services and served voluntarily as assistant to the post chaplain. Returning to acting, he appeared regularly in the TV series *Hot Off the Wire* and played occasional supporting roles in movies—the last being 1967's *First to Fight*. Married in 1962 to an attractive girl from Iowa named Marilyn, he has since become the father of three sons, Christian, Timothy and Patrick. And he has become a minister—of Burbank's Magnolia Park United Methodist Church. "Religion has been a central part of my life always," he says. His father—the late Coy Watson, an actor, famous special-effects man, and the son of a Salvation Army chaplain—reared a large brood of boys (six) and girls (three), nearly all of whom as children acted in movies. "We grew up in them," Bobs says. "Mack Sennett's studio was a block from our home, across the vacant lot where we used to play. To work in a movie was no different to us than playing third base in a game in the lot." Today, with families of their own, the younger Watsons all still live in the Los Angeles area, but none act now. Recalling their childhood years, Bobs, who is the youngest, says: "We had very little, materially. Actually we were poor. But in family togetherness, love, and love of God, we were extremely wealthy. And we never wanted. Our father and our Father always provided." The one family member who did not work in pictures—"Her career was being a mother and housewife to the fullest"—was his "loving, patient" mother who, he relates, still lives and has derived great happiness from his becoming a minister. "We were not in any way the typical Hollywood family," Bobs explains. "Prayer was to us as natural as breath itself—prayer before each meal, prayer at bedtime, prayer if we needed special guidance. I remember times at the studio, such as before an especially difficult scene in *On Borrowed Time*, when my father took me to a quiet corner on the set and said, 'Let's pray.' He was a rare father, filled with tenderness and understanding. He taught me to act as I did—associating the parts I was playing to real life, and seeking out, always, the honesty to be found in the character. If there was sincerity and truth in any work I did, all credit must go to him." After the birth of his own first son, relates Bobs, as he is still called, "There was some quiet Voice that insistently asked, 'Isn't there something more you should be doing with your life?' Finally I knew I had to preach." His three-year ministerial course at Claremont Seminary extended to four when he suffered a broken back in an automobile accident. Incapacitated for a full year, he is now fully recovered. It was in 1968 that he was ordained as a minister. Today, in his 40s (b. 1930), Rev. Bobs Watson is a medium-sized, gray-haired (since his 20s) man with a high-pitched voice and boundless, youthful exuberance. And he still looks much as he did when he played Pud—which remains his favorite role. "Magnolia Park Church," he says, "has long been the core of my life. I was married here, ordained as a deacon here, two of my children were baptized here, and, alone, I conducted the services for my father's funeral here. I have been the church's minister since 1969 and, God willing, I would be happy to be the rest of my life." Still so near to Hollywood, yet so far away from it (except for many parishioners who are in the industry), Bobs Watson retains only one connection with his former profession. "I have written a Passion Play, covering the time from the Last Supper to the Crucifixion," he says. "It has a cast of 85 and I have produced it annually, each Easter, for seven years here at the church. The last time we did it we played to an audience of 1,400. That was one of the highlights of my life." Onscreen from 1930 (the year of his birth). IN: *Ride to Fame* (debut), *Follow the Leader, Manhattan Parade, In Old Chicago, Kentucky, Calling Dr. Kildare, Blackmail, Dodge City, Dr. Kildare's Crisis, Men of Boys Town, The Bold and the Brave*, more.

WATSON, DAVID (S. Cal.) Support. Not of the above-mentioned family. Onscreen in the '70s. IN: *Beneath the Planet of the Apes*, more.

WATSON, DEBBIE (S. Cal.) Former ingenue. Not of the above-mentioned family. Now married and retired. Onscreen in the '60s. IN: *Munster, Go Home; The Cool Ones, Tammy and the Millionaire*, more.

WATSON, DELMAR (S. Cal.) Former juvenile. Brother of Bobs, Billy, et al. Now a professional portrait photographer in Hollywood. Onscreen from 1930. IN: *Outside the Law, Compromised, The Right to Romance, Annie Oakley, Old Hutch, Heidi, Hunted Men, Kentucky*, more.

WATSON, DOUGLAS (N.Y.) Character. Onscreen from 1952. IN: *Julius Caesar, Sayonara*, more.

WATSON, JACK (Eng.) Character. Onscreen from the '60s. IN: *This Sporting Life, Master Spy, The Idol, Grand-Prix, Tobruk, The Devil's Brigade, The Strange Affair, Juggernaut, Eleven Harrowhouse*, more.

WATSON, JAMES A., JR. (S. Cal.) Black leading man. Onscreen in the '70s. IN: *Halls of Anger, The Organization*, more.

WATSON, MILLS (S. Cal.) Character. Onscreen in the '70s. IN: *Tick Tick Tick, The Wild Country, The Midnight Man*, more.

WATSON, MORAY (Eng.) Character. Onscreen from the '60s. IN: *The Grass Is Greener, Operation Crossbow*, more.

WATSON, THERESA (Eng.) Support. Onscreen in the '70s. IN: *Long Ago, Tomorrow;* more.

WATSON, VERNEE (N.Y.) Black supporting actress. Onscreen in the '70s. IN: *Cotton Comes to Harlem, Across 110th Street, Trick Baby, Come Back Charleston Blue*, more.

WATSON, WILLIAM (S. Cal.) Support. Onscreen in the '70s. IN: *Lawman, The Hunting Party*, more.

WATT, SPARKY (S. Cal.) Character actor. Onscreen in the '70s. IN: *The Trial of Billy Jack*, more.

WATT, STAN (N.Y.) Support. Onscreen from the '60s. IN: *Love With the Proper Stranger, The Possession of Joel Delaney*, more.

WATTERS, DON (S. Cal.) Support. Onscreen in the '70s. IN: *Truck Turner*, more.

WATTERS, WILLIAM (S. Cal.) Support. Onscreen in the '70s. IN: *Thieves Like Us*, more.

WATTS, GWENDOLYN (Eng.) Character. Onscreen from the '60s. IN: *Billy Liar; Die! Die! My Darling; The Games*, more.

WATTS, JEANNE (Eng.) Character lead. Onscreen in the '70s. IN: *Three Sisters* (costarred as "Olga").

WATTS, LITTLE JAMIE (S. Cal.) Support. Onscreen in the '70s. IN: *Solomon King*, more.

WATTS, QUEENIE (Eng.) Support. Onscreen from the '60s. IN: *Poor Cow*, more.

WATTS, SAL (S. Cal.) Leading man. Onscreen in the '70s. IN: *Solomon King* (besides starring he wrote, produced, codirected and coedited the film).

WAXMAN, STANLEY (S. Cal.) Character. Onscreen from the '40s. IN: *Slattery's Hurricane, Justine*, more.

WAYCOFF, LEON (S. Cal.) Leon Ames' real name, which he used in his early movies. (See Leon Ames.)

WAYNE, AISSA (S. Cal.) John Wayne's youngest daughter. Onscreen in 1960. IN: *The Alamo* (juvenile role).

WAYNE, CAROL (S. Cal.) Leading Lady. Onscreen from the '60s. IN: *The Party*, more.

WAYNE, DAVID (S. Cal.) Costar. Onscreen from 1949. IN: *Portrait of Jennie, Adam's Rib, My Blue Heaven, M., Up Front, With a Song in My Heart, We're Not Married, How to Marry a Millionaire, Tonight We Sing, Hell and High Water, The Tender Trap, The Three Faces of Eve, The Sad Sack, The Last Angry Man, The Big Gamble, The Andromeda Strain, The Front Page, The Apple Dumpling Gang*, more.

WAYNE, FRANK (N.Y.) Support. Onscreen in the '70s. IN: *Plaza Suite*, more.

WAYNE, FREDD (Eng.) Support. Onscreen from the '50s. IN: *Crest of the Wave, Torpedo Run, Hangup*, more.

WAYNE, JOHN (S. Cal.) Star. Won Best Actor Oscar in *True Grit*. Nominated in the same category in *Sands of Iwo Jima*. Onscreen from 1930. IN: *The Big Trail, Men Are Like That, I Cover the War, Idol of the Crowd, Stagecoach* (his career's turning point), *Allegheny Uprising, Dark Command, The Long Voyage Home, Seven Sinners, Reap the Wild Wind, The Spoilers, Pittsburgh, The Fighting Seabees, Back to Bataan, They Were Expendable, Fort Apache, Red River, Wake of the Red Witch, Three Godfathers, She Wore a Yellow Ribbon, Rio Grande, The Quiet Man, The High and the Mighty, The Searchers, Rio Bravo, The Man Who Shot Liberty Valance, The Sons of Katie Elder, El Dorado, The Green Berets, The Undefeated, Chisum, The Cowboys, The Train Robbers, McQ, Brannigan, Rooster Cogburn, The Shootist*, more.

WAYNE, JOHN ETHAN (S. Cal.) John Wayne's youngest son. Onscreen in 1971. IN: *Big Jake* (as his father's "grandson").

WAYNE, KEITH (S. Cal.) Support. Onscreen from the '60s. IN: *Night of the Living Dead*, more.

WAYNE, LLOYD (N.Y.) Support. Onscreen from the '60s. IN: *Love Story, Bananas, Lovers and Other Strangers, The Pursuit of Happiness, The French Connection*, more.

WAYNE, NINA (S. Cal.) Leading lady. Onscreen from the '60s. IN: *Dead Heat on a Merry-Go-Round, Luv, The Comic*, more.

WAYNE, PATRICK (S. Cal.) Leading man. John Wayne's son. Onscreen from 1950. IN: *Eye Witness, The Long Gray Line, Mister Roberts, The Searchers, Comanchero, McLintock!,*

Cheyenne Autumn, Shenandoah, The Green Berets, The Bears and I, Mustang Country, more.

WEAVER, DENNIS (S. Cal.) Costar. Onscreen from 1952. IN: *The Raiders, The Mississippi Gambler, Dangerous Mission, Seven Angry Men, Touch of Evil, The Gallant Hours, Duel at Diablo, Way . . . Way Out, Gentle Giant, What's the Matter with Helen?, A Man Called Sledge*, more.

WEAVER, DOODLES (S. Cal.) Comic character. Onscreen from 1937. IN: *Behind the Headlines, Topper; A Girl, a Guy and a Gob; The Great Imposter, Ring of Fire, Tammy and the Doctor, A Tiger Walks, Macon County Line, The McCullochs*, more.

WEAVER, FRANK & ELVIRY (S. Cal.) Of the comedy team "The Weaver Brothers & Elviry." Brother Leon died in 1950, and Frank and Jane, her real name, are retired. Onscreen from 1938. *Jeepers Creepers, Grand Ole Opry, In Old Missouri, Mountain Moonlight, Tuxedo Junction, Arkansas Judge, Mountain Rhythm, The Old Homestead, Shepherd of the Ozarks*, more.

WEAVER, FRITZ (N.Y.) Costar. Onscreen from 1964. IN: *Fail Safe, To Trap a Spy, The Maltese Bippy, A Walk in the Spring Rain, Black Sunday*, more.

WEAVER, LEE (S. Cal.) Black supporting actor. Onscreen in the '70s. IN: *The Lost Man, Vanishing Point*, more.

WEAVER, MARJORIE (S. Cal.) This delectably amusing brunette beauty from Dixie made her last movie—*We're Not Married* ('52)—by accident. Said the casting director: "We need a young Marjorie Weaver." Said his assistant, a friend of hers: "Get Marjorie Weaver, she still looks great. Here's her number." So for a few days she was back at the studio, 20th Century-Fox, where she had come within a whisker of stardom. Then she went right back into the retirement (from picture-making) she had chosen seven years before, after *Leave It to Blondie*, and has not faced a camera since. Not long ago, looking back on her 27-picture career, she laughed, "I had a fantastic career for a girl with no talent. I couldn't sing, I couldn't dance, but I did both. It was wonderful; nothing pressing, nothing urgent—just fun." It's possible she works twice as hard now as then, and enjoys it just as much. In Westwood there is a swank liquor store owned and operated by Mr. and Mrs. Don Briggs. He's a good-looking six-footer; she's a slender, friendly brunette with saucy brown eyes and long lashes, and—still—traces of a Southern accent. And she looks years younger than she is (b. 1913). The Briggses, Don and Marjorie, have been married since '43 and have a grown son and daughter, Joel and Leigh. To anyone mentioning the "big money" she must have made during her years onscreen, the actress laughs and says, "I never made big money. When I was costarring with Alice Faye in *Sally, Irene and Mary*, I was only making $100 a week!" But she always adds, of her decade in pictures, "It was a ball." Today she drives by 20th Century-Fox twice daily, going to and from the business that's made her far richer than the movies ever did. And, as she glides past the studio in her expensive car, she smiles. Some of her happiest memories were born just inside those gates. Onscreen from 1936. IN: *China Clipper, This Is My Affair, Life Begins in College, Second Honeymoon, Kentucky Moonshine, I'll Give a Million, Young Mr. Lincoln, The Cisco Kid and the Lady, Charlie Chan's Murder Cruise, Maryland, Murder Among Friends, The Man Who Wouldn't Die, Just Off Broadway, Let's Face It, You Can't Ration Love, The Great Alaskan Mystery, Fashion Model*, more.

WEBB, ALAN (Eng.) Character. Onscreen from the '50s. IN: *Challenge to Lassie, The Third Secret, The Pumpkin Eater, King Rat, The Taming of the Shrew, Interlude, Women in Love, Entertaining Mr. Sloane*, more.

WEBB, FRANK (S. Cal.) Support. Onscreen from the '60s. IN: *The Bridge at Remagen, The Computer Wore Tennis Shoes*, more.

WEBB, JACK (S. Cal.) Costar. His most recent movie was 1961's *The Last Time I Saw Archie*, which he also directed and produced. He is now primarily a producer of TV shows—*Emergency!*, etc. Onscreen from 1948. IN: *He Walked by Night, Dark City, The Men, Sunset Boulevard, You're in the Navy Now, Dragnet, Pete Kelly's Blues, The D.I., "30,"* more.

WEBB, JANET (Eng.) Support. Onscreen from the '60s. IN: *A Funny Thing Happened on the Way to the Forum*, more.

WEBB, RICHARD (S. Cal.) Still a rugged, good-looking guy in his 60s, the former movie leading man—and star of TV's *Captain Midnight* and *U.S. Border Patrol*—continues to play top character roles on TV (*Six Million Dollar Man, The Werewolf of Woodstock*, etc.) and in pictures (*Beware! The Blob*, more). He also has acquired the rights to *Captain Midnight*, planning to produce a revised TV series in which he would not appear. Also, an observer-investigator of psychic phenomena and the occult, he is an author and in this decade has had three books published pertaining to these subjects: *Great Ghosts of the West, These Came Back*, and *Flight Without Wings*, in addition to one on *Captain Midnight*. Privately, he has been happily married for many years—wife, Florence, being in real estate in the San Fernando Valley "selling everything that isn't nailed down—and in spite of earthquakes, people are buying like tomorrow *will* come and we won't all be shook loose." They have two daughters: Richelle, a housewife in New Haven, who has made them grandparents of a boy and a girl, and Patricia, a full Lieutenant Nurse, Marine Corps. (The actor himself is a Lt. Colonel, U.S. Army Reserve.) Onscreen from 1941. IN: *Sullivan's Travels, I Wanted Wings, Hold Back the Dawn, The Remarkable Andrew, O.S.S., Out of the Past, The Big Clock, Night Has a Thousand Eyes, My Own True Love, Sands of Iwo Jima, The Invisible Monster* (serial), *Distant Drums, This Woman Is Dangerous, Mara Maru, Carson City, Three Hours to Kill, On the Beach, Slaves of the Invisible Monster, The Gay Deceivers*, more.

WEBB, RITA (Eng.) Support. Onscreen from the '60s. IN: *The Idol; To Sir, With Love; Up Pompeii*, more.

WEBBER, PEGGY (S. Cal.) Support; former leading lady. Onscreen from 1950. IN: *Macbeth, Journey Into Light, Submarine Command*, more.

WEBBER, ROBERT (S. Cal.) Support. Onscreen from 1951. IN: *Highway 301, 12 Angry Men, The Stripper, The Sandpiper, The Third Day, Harper, Dead Heat on a Merry-Go-Round, The Dirty Dozen, Don't Make Waves, $, Bring Me the Head of Alfredo Garcia*, more.

WEBBER, PAUL (S. Cal.) Character. Onscreen from the '60s. IN: *Murderers' Row*, more.

WEBSTER, BYRON (N.Y.) Character. Onscreen from the '60s. IN: *The Killing of Sister George, On a Clear Day You Can See Forever*, more.

WEDGEWORTH, ANN (N.Y.) Leading lady. Onscreen from 1965. IN: *Andy, Scarecrow, Bang the Drum Slowly, Law and Disorder, Dragonfly, Birch Interval* (opposite, interestingly, first husband, Rip Torn, father of their teenage daughter; she is presently married to drama instructor Ernest Martin).

WEEKS, ALAN (S. Cal.) Black support. Onscreen in the '70s. IN: *Lost in the Stars, Black Belt Jones, Truck Turner*, more.

WEIL, ROBERT (N.Y.) Character. Onscreen in the '70s. IN: *The French Connection, The*

Hot Rock, The Gang That Couldn't Shoot Straight, Rhinoceros, more.

WEINER, ARN (N.Y.) Character. Onscreen from the '60s. IN: *All the Way Home, The Love Cage, Bye Bye Braverman*, more.

WEINRIB, LENNIE (S. Cal.) Supporting actor-director (of *Wild Wild Winter*). Onscreen from the '60s. IN: *Good Times, Bedknobs and Broomsticks* (voice), more.

WEIR, GREGG (N.Y.) Support. Onscreen from the '60s. IN: *A View from the Bridge, The Rat Race, A Fine Madness*, more.

WEIR, MOLLY (Eng.) Character. Onscreen from the '40s. IN: *Small Town Story, Life With the Lyons, John and Julie, The Silent Witness*, more.

WEISSMULLER, JOHNNY (Nev.) Though 14 others have played the role, they were only "acting"; he was *the* "Tarzan"—playing the Ape Man exactly 12 times before switching over to *Jungle Jim*, which he did as a series both in movies and on TV. His last acting was a cameo in *Go for Broke*; his last starring pix were *Jungle Moon* and *Devil Goddess* in '55. Now in his 70s (b. 1904), he lives in Las Vegas with his wife, German-born Maria Brock, to whom he has been married since '63; it is her fourth marriage, his sixth. He was previously married to Camille Louier, Bobbe Arnst, the late Lupe Velez, Beryle Scott, and golf champ Allene Gates. He has three grown children: Wendy, Heidi, and John. Johnny Weissmuller Jr. (b. 1939) lives in San Francisco, where he works on the waterfront as a longshoreman, acts on local stages (*One Flew Over the Cuckoo's Nest*), and in movies made there on location. Besides working as a greeter at Las Vegas' Caesars Palace, "Tarzan" has numerous business interests—a swimming pool concern in Florida, the "Johnny Weissmuller American Natural Foods" store in Hollywood, etc. Late in '73, at Caesars Palace, he fell, suffering a broken hip, and while hospitalized at Southern Nevada Memorial, it was discovered that he also had a cardiac condition. Recovered from the first, he has learned to live with the second. He keeps in shape by swimming a mile and a half daily in the pool at his home. As an Olympic swim champ, he set 67 world records and won five gold medals—three at Paris in '24 and two at Amsterdam in '28. On hand to observe Mark Spitz in the '72 Olympics in Munich, he said firmly, in the squeaky voice that never suited his 6'3" frame, "I was better than Mark Spitz is. I never lost a race. Never. Not even in the Y.M.C.A." He has donated all his memorabilia, including his Olympic medals, to the nation's retarded children. Subsequent Tarzans have often asked him for advice on playing the role and, always, he says, "I tell them the main thing is don't let go of the vine when you're swinging through the jungle." Onscreen from 1929. IN: *Glorifying the American Girl, Tarzan the Ape Man* (his first in this series in '32), *Tarzan and His Mate, Tarzan Escapes*, etc.; *Stage Door Canteen, Combat Correspondent, Swamp Fire, The Lost Tribe, Mark of the Gorilla, Pygmy Island, Captive Girl, Jungle Jim, Valley of the Headhunters, Savage Mutiny, Killer Ape, Cannibal Attack, Jungle Man-Eaters, The Phynx* (cameo), more.

WEISSMULLER, JOHNNY, JR. (N. Cal.) Support. Son of the above. Onscreen from 1958. IN: *Andy Hardy Comes Home, THX 1138, American Graffiti*, more.

WELCH, CHARLES C. (N.Y.) Character. Onscreen from 1953. IN: *City That Never Sleeps, Gone Are the Days!, A Fine Madness*, more.

WELCH, ELISABETH (Eng.) American-born black actress-singer, now in her 60s (b. 1908), who has lived and worked in England since 1933. Onscreen from 1934. IN: *Death at Broadcasting House, Big Fella, Song of Freedom, Over the Moon, Fiddlers Three, Dead of Night, Our Man in Havana*, more.

WELCH, NELSON (S. Cal.) Character. Onscreen from the '50s. IN: *Thunder in the East*, more.

WELCH, RAQUEL (S. Cal.) Star. Onscreen from 1964. IN: *Roustabout, A House Is Not a Home, Fantastic Voyage, Our Man Flint, One Million Years B.C., Bedazzled, Fathom, The Biggest Bundle of Them All, Bandolero, Lady in Cement, 100 Rifles, Flareup, Myra Breckinridge, Fuzz, Hannie Caulder, Kansas City Bomber, The Last of Sheila, The Three Musketeers, The Four Musketeers, The Wild Party; Mother, Jugs and Speed*; more.

WELD, TUESDAY (S. Cal.) Costar. Married to British comedy star Dudley Moore; her second marriage. Onscreen from 1956. IN: *Rock Pretty Baby, Rally Round the Flag Boys!, The Five Pennies, Sex Kittens Go to College, High Time, Because They're Young, Return to Peyton Place, Wild in the Country, Bachelor Flat, Soldier in the Rain, The Cincinnati Kid, Pretty Poison, I Walk the Line, A Safe Place, Play It As I Lays*, more.

WELDON, JOAN (N.Y.) A multi-talented Warners leading lady of the '50s, this chestnut-haired singer-actress came from the musical stage and returned to it after her screen career. In the early 1960s on Broadway she played leading roles in such musicals as *Kean* (opposite Alfred Drake) and a revival of *The Merry Widow*. Also at the gala opening of Lincoln Center's State Theater, she and John Raitt—in a *Carousel* duet—were the first performers to appear on its stage. Today, in her early 40s (b. 1933), and long married to a Manhattan M.D., Dr. David Podell, she is a slender, chic Park Avenue matron, and the mother of a young daughter, Melissa (b. 1968). No longer professionally active she assists behind the scenes in amateur theatricals at the Brick Presbyterian Church, of which she is an active member. Onscreen from 1953. IN: *The Command, The System, So This Is Love, The Stranger Wore a Gun, Them* (perhaps her best recalled lead), *Riding Shot Gun, Deep in My Heart, Gunsight Ridge, Day of the Bad Man*, and 1958's *Home Before Dark*, her most recent to date.

WELDON, TIM (S. Cal.) Support. Onscreen from the '60s. IN: *The Illustrated Man*, more.

WELKER, FRANK (S. Cal.) Support. Onscreen from the '60s. IN: *The Computer Wore Tennis Shoes*, more.

WELLES, BEATRICE (Sp.) Supporting actress. Daughter of Orson Welles by actress Paola Mori, his third wife. Onscreen in 1967. IN: *Falstaff: Chimes at Midnight* (her father's production).

WELLES, GWEN (S. Cal.) Leading lady. Daughter of former actress Rebecca Welles. No relation to Orson Welles. Onscreen in the '70s. IN: *A Safe Place, California Split, Nashville*, more.

WELLES, JESSE (S. Cal.) Supporting actress. Onscreen in the '70s. IN: *The Return of Count Yorga*, more.

WELLES, ORSON (Sp.) Legendary actor-writer-producer-director. Nominated for Best Actor Oscar in *Citizen Kane*, his first production. In 1970 he received a special Oscar "for superlative artistry and versatility in the creation of motion pictures." Onscreen from 1941. IN: *Journey Into Fear, Jane Eyre, Tomorrow Is Forever, The Stranger, The Lady from Shanghai, The Third Man, Macbeth, Trouble in the Glen, Othello, Moby Dick; The Long, Hot Summer; Touch of Evil, The Roots of Heaven, Compulsion, David and Goliath, Mr. Arkadin, The Trial, The V.I.P.s, Is Paris Burning?, A Man for All Seasons; Falstaff: Chimes at Midnight; The Sailor from Gibraltar, Casino Royale, I'll Never Forget What's 'Isname, Oedipus the King, The Immortal Story, The Kremlin Letter, Waterloo, Catch-22, A Safe Place, Necromancy, Treasure Island, The Voyage of the Damned*, more.

WELLES, REBECCA (S. Cal.) Former leading lady. No relation to Orson Welles, though he and first wife, Rita Hayworth, have a daughter by that name; this one's real name is Rebecca Tassell. Married to director Don Weis, she has lately become one of California's most famous fashion designers. Onscreen from the '50s. IN: *Desire Under the Elms*, plus numerous "motorcycle" pix.

WELLMAN, MICHAEL (S. Cal.) Former juvenile. No longer in movies. Son of late director William Wellman. Onscreen in 1954 in *The High and the Mighty*. (See Dorothy Coonan.)

WELLMAN, WILLIAM, JR. (S. Cal.) Leading man. Son of William Wellman. Onscreen from 1958. IN: *Lafayette Escadrille* and *Darby's Rangers* (both directed by his father), *Pork Chop Hill, Macumba Love, Dondi, Winter A-Go-Go, Young Fury, The Born Losers, The Happiest Millionaire, The Private Navy of Sgt. O'Farrell; Hook, Line and Sinker; The Trial of Billy Jack, It's Alive*, more. (See Dorothy Coonan.)

WELLS, CAROLE (S. Cal.) Leading lady. Onscreen from 1961. IN: *A Thunder of Drums, Come Blow Your Horn, The Lively Set, The House of Seven Corpses*, more.

WELLS, DAWN (S. Cal.) Leading lady. Onscreen from 1964. IN: *The New Interns, Winterhawk*, more.

WELLS, INGEBORG (Eng.) Former leading lady; lately inactive in movies. Onscreen from the '50s. IN: *Captain Horatio Hornblower, Death Is a Number, Secret People, Women of Twilight, House of Blackmail, Across the Bridge*, more.

WELLS, JACQUELINE (S. Cal.) (See Julie Bishop.)

WELLS, MARION (N.Y.) Character. Onscreen from the '60s. IN: *No Way to Treat a Lady, Last Summer, Jenny, Plaza Suite, A New Leaf, On a Clear Day You Can See Forever*, more.

WELLS, RICK (S. Cal.) Character. Onscreen in the '70s. IN: *The Last Rebel*, more.

WELLS, SHEILAH (S. Cal.) Support. Onscreen from the '60s. IN: *Love and Kisses*, more.

WELLS, VERONICA (Eng.) Support. Onscreen from the '60s. IN: *Boom!*, more.

WELSH, JOHN (Eng.) Character. Onscreen from the '50s. IN: *Lucky Jim, Room at the Top*, *Circle of Deception, Francis of Assisi, The Mark, The Playboy of the Western World, Attack on the Iron Coast, The Man Who Haunted Himself*, more.

WENCES, SENOR (Eng.) Ventriloquist. Onscreen in 1947 in *Mother Wore Tights*.

WENHAM, JANE (Eng.) Support. Onscreen from the '50s. IN: *An Inspector Calls, The Teckman Mystery, Make Me an Offer*, more.

WENZEL, ARTHUR J. (N.Y.) Character. Onscreen from the '60s. IN: *A Place Called Today, Mortadella*, more.

WERLE, BARBARA (S. Cal.) Leading lady. Onscreen from 1965. IN: *Battle of the Bulge, Harum Scarum, Seconds; Krakatoa—East of Java; Charro!*, more.

WERNER, OSKAR (Fr.) Star. Nominated for Best Actor Oscar in *Ship of Fools*. Onscreen from the '50s. IN: *Eroica, Decision Before Dawn, Wonder Boy, The Last Ten Days, Jules and Jim, The Spy Who Came in From the Cold, Fahrenheit 451, Interlude, Lola Montes, The Shoes of the Fisherman, The Voyage of the Damned*, more.

WERTIMER, NED (S. Cal.) Character. Onscreen from the '60s. IN: *The Impossible Years, Adam at 6 A.M.*, more.

WESCOURT, GORDON (Eng.) Support. Now a producer (of *The House That Dripped Blood*, etc.). Onscreen in the '60s. IN: *Finders Keepers, Lovers Weepers*; more.

WESSON, DICK (S. Cal.) Support. Onscreen from 1950. IN: *Destination Tokyo, Breakthrough, Inside the Walls of Folsom Prison, Force of Arms, About Face, The Desert Son, The Charge at Feather River, Calamity Jane, The Errand Boy*, more.

WESSON, EILEEN (S. Cal.) Support. Onscreen from the '60s. IN: *Journey to Shiloh, Did You Hear the One About the Traveling Saleslady?, Winning, Airport*, more.

WEST, ADAM (S. Cal.) Leading man. Popular in the TV series *Batman*. Onscreen from 1959. IN: *The Young Philadelphians, Geronimo, Tammy and the Doctor, Soldier in the Rain, That Darn Cat, Robinson Crusoe on Mars, Batman, The Marriage of a Young Stockbroker*, more.

WEST, BERNIE (N.Y.) Support; primarily a stage actor. Onscreen in 1960. IN: *Bells Are Ringing*.

WEST, BROOKS (S. Cal.) Character. The husband of Eve Arden with whom he often costars onstage. Onscreen from the '50s. IN: *Anatomy of a Murder*, more.

WEST, CHRISTOPHER (S. Cal.) Leading lady. Onscreen from the '60s. IN: *Speedway*, more.

WEST, H.E. (S. Cal.) Character. Onscreen from the '60s. IN: *Night Tide, The Best Man*, more.

WEST, JOHNNY (S. Cal.) Support. Onscreen in the '70s. IN: *The Trial of Billy Jack*, more.

WEST, JUDI (S. Cal.) Leading lady. Onscreen from 1966. IN: *The Fortune Cookie, A Man Called Gannon*, more.

WEST, LOCKWOOD (Eng.) Character. Onscreen from 1948. IN: *High Treason, The Horse's Mouth, The Leather Boys, A Dandy in Aspic, Life at the Top, Bedazzled, Jane Eyre*, more.

WEST, MAE (S. Cal.) In her 80s (b. 1892), retaining her original teeth (as she will proudly tell you) and sense of humor, she still dons her platinum wig and—with muscular escorts—attends various Hollywood social events. *Myra Breckinridge* ('70) was her most recent, and likely to be her last movie. Onscreen from 1932. IN: *Night After Night, She Done Him Wrong, I'm No Angel, Belle of the Nineties, Goin' to Town, Klondike Annie; Go West, Young Man; Every Day's a Holiday, My Little Chickadee*, and *The Heat's On.*

WEST, MARTIN (S. Cal.) Leading man. Costar of the TV soap opera *General Hospital*. Onscreen from 1960. IN: *Freckles* (debut; title role), *The Sergeant Was a Lady, The Man From Galveston; Captain Newman, M.D.; Lord Love a Duck, Sweet November, Soldier Blue, Family Plot*, more.

WEST, TIMOTHY (Eng.) Leading man. Onscreen from 1966. IN: *The Deadly Affair, The Looking Glass War, Nicholas and Alexandra*, more.

WEST, WALLY/a.k.a. TOM WYNN (S. Cal.) (See Tom Wynn.)

WESTBROOK, JOHN (Eng.) Character. Onscreen from the '50s. IN: *Room at the Top, Tomb of Ligeia*, more.

WESTCOTT, HELEN (S. Cal.) Support; former leading lady. Onscreen from 1935. IN: *A Midsummer Night's Dream* (age 7), *Smart Girls*

Don't Talk, 13 Lead Soldiers, Adventures of Don Juan, Mr. Belvedere Goes to College, Whirlpool, The Girl From Jones Beach, The Gunfighter, Take Care of My Little Girl, With a Song in My Heart, The Charge at Feather River, I Killed Wild Bill Hickok, God's Little Acre, The Last Hurrah, Studs Lonigan, I Love My Wife, more.

WESTMORELAND, JAMES (S. Cal.) Leading man. Originally billed Rad Fulton. Onscreen from 1961. IN: *The Last Sunset; No, My Darling Daughter*; more.

WESTON, BRAD (S. Cal.) Character. Onscreen in the '70s. IN: *Barquero*, more.

WESTON, DAVID (Eng.) Support. Onscreen from the '60s. IN: *Becket, The Masque of Red Death, The Heroes of Telemark, Von Richthofen and Brown*, more.

WESTON, JACK (S. Cal.) Character lead. Onscreen from 1958. IN: *Stage Struck, Please Don't Eat the Daisies, All in a Night's Work, The Honeymoon Machine, Palm Springs Weekend, The Incredible Mr. Limpet, Mirage, The Cincinnati Kid, Wait Until Dark, The Thomas Crown Affair, The Counterfeit Killer, Cactus Flower, The April Fools, Fuzz, The Ritz*, more.

WESTON, KIM (S. Cal.) Support. Onscreen from the '60s. IN: *Changes*, more.

WESTON, LESLIE (Eng.) Support. Onscreen from the '40s. IN: *Corridor of Mirrors, Sleeping Car to Trieste, Stowaway Girl*, more.

WESTON, MARK (N.Y.) Support. Onscreen in the '70s. IN: *Fuzz*, more.

WEVER, NED (S. Cal.) Character. Onscreen from the '50s. IN: *Some Came Running, These Thousand Hills, Anatomy of a Murder, The Prize*, more.

WEXLER, JODI (S. Cal.) Leading lady. Onscreen in the '70s. IN: *The Love Machine*, more.

WEXLER, PAUL (S. Cal.) Support. Onscreen from the '50s. IN: *Bloodhounds of Broadway, Suddenly, The Buccaneer, Day of the Outlaw, The Miracle of the Hills, The Busy Body, The Way West*, more.

WEXLER, YALE (S. Cal.) Leading man. Onscreen from the '50s. IN: *Time Limit, Stakeout on Dope Street*, more.

509

WEYAND, RONALD (N.Y.) Character. On-screen in the '70s. IN: *Alice's Restaurant, Child's Play, They Might Be Giants*, more.

WHEATLEY, ALAN (Eng.) Character. On-screen from 1937. IN: *Brighton Rock, Corridor of Mirrors, The End of the River, Sleeping Car to Trieste, Appointment with Crime, The Pickwick Papers, Simon and Laura, Master Spy*, more.

WHEELER, GENA (S. Cal.) Support. On-screen in the '70s. IN: *Husbands*, more.

WHEELER, JOHN (S. Cal.) Character. On-screen from the '60s. IN: *Tell Them Willie Boy Is Here, Move, Support Your Local Gunfighter*, more.

WHEELER, LOIS (N.Y.) The Broadway leading lady resumed her stage career after her brief movie period, and also starred in soap operas. Onscreen from 1950. IN: *My Foolish Heart, The Well*, more.

WHEELER, MARGARET (S. Cal.) Character. Onscreen in the '70s. IN: *The Brotherhood of Satan*, more.

WHELAN, ARLEEN (S. Cal.) A beautiful redhead still as she enters her 60s (b. 1916), she is quite social and quite retired. Her three marriages—to actor Alex D'Arcy, Paramount executive Hugh Owen, and Dr. Warren Cagney—all ended in divorce. She was last onscreen in two in '57: *Raiders of Old California* and *The Badge of Marshal Brennan*. Onscreen from 1938. IN: *Kidnapped, Gateway, Young Mr. Lincoln, Sabotage, Young People, Charter Pilot, Charley's Aunt, Sundown Jim, The Senator Was Indiscreet, Suddenly It's Spring, Ramrod, Dear Wife, Flaming Feather, Never Wave at a Wac, The Sun Shines Bright, San Antone, The Women of Pitcairn Island*, more.

WHILEY, MANNING (Eng.) Support; lately inactive in movies. Onscreen from the '30s. IN: *The Trunk Crime, The Saint's Vacation, The Seventh Veil, Conspiracy at Teheran, The Inheritance*, more.

WHITAKER, JOHNNY (S. Cal.) Juvenile. First popular on TV in *Family Affair*. Onscreen from 1966. IN: *The Russians Are Coming, The Russians Are Coming; The Biscuit Eater, Napoleon and Samantha, Snowball Express, Tom Sawyer*, more.

WHITBY, GWYNNE (Eng.) Character. On-screen from 1945. IN: *Quiet Week-End, Mine Own Executioner, The Blue Lamp, I Believe in You, Turn the Key Softly*, more.

WHITE, ALICE (S. Cal.) In the '20s Paramount had Clara Bow and First National had Alice White—the movies' sauciest, funniest, sexiest young flappers. There was such a sameness about the latter's pix that critics finally resorted to such blanket comments as "That White girl comes through with a snappy number every time and this is one of the snappiest." Though the zing went out of her stardom in the early '30s, she went steadily on in minor roles through *Annabel Takes a Tour* in '38—even coming back for a bit in 1941's *The Night of January 16th*. Odd coincidence: This pic starred Ellen Drew, who that same year married screenwriter Sy Bartlett, who not long before had been divorced by Alice White. Before movie fame, Alice had been a private secretary in a Hollywood real estate office. After stardom, too spirited to sit on the sidelines and not too proud to work at her earlier trade, she became one again—and continued as a secretary for many years. She tried marriage again, to John Roberts, filing for divorce in '49. And she tried movies once more, that same year, landing a bit in Crawford's *Flamingo Road*, which was her last time before the cameras. Essentially retired now as she heads into her 70s (b. 1907), she still lives where she grew up, in Hollywood. No one should conclude, though she does remain petite, that she is in any way a "little old lady." The sparkle, the sizzle, are still there—to say nothing of the mischief in those big brown eyes. Onscreen from 1927. IN: *The Satin Woman, American Beauty, The Private Life of Helen of Troy, Gentlemen Prefer Blondes, The Mad Hour, Harold Teen, Show Girl, Naughty Baby, Hot Stuff, The Girl From Woolworth's, Show Girl in Hollywood, The Naughty Flirt, Murder at Midnight, Luxury Liner, King for a Night, Jimmy the Gent, Gift of Gab, Coronado, Big City, King of the Newsboys*, more.

WHITE, BARBARA (Eng.) Former leading lady; no longer active in movies. Onscreen from the '40s. IN: *The Voice Within, Quiet Week-End, This Was a Woman, Mine Own Executioner, While the Sun Shines*, more.

WHITE, BARRY (S. Cal.) Support. Onscreen in the '70s. IN: *Coonskin*, more.

WHITE, BETTY (S. Cal.) Supporting actress. Lately featured in TV's *The Mary Tyler Moore Show*. Onscreen in 1962 in *Advise and Consent*.

WHITE, CAROL (Eng.) Leading lady. Onscreen from 1960. IN: *Never Let Go* (debut; age 16), *Bon Voyage!, A Matter of Who, The Playground, Prehistoric Women, Poor Cow, I'll Never Forget What's 'Isname, The Fixer, Daddy's Gone A-Hunting, Something Big*, more.

WHITE, CHARLES (N.Y.) Character. On-screen from the '60s. IN: *The Troublemaker, All the Way Home, Cold Turkey, The Hot Rock, Child's Play*, more.

WHITE, CHRISSIE (Eng.) This popular star of silents is in her 80s now (b. 1894) and has been retired from movies for more than four decades. Onscreen from the teens. IN: *David Garrick, Barnaby Rudge, Trelawny of the Wells, Broken Threads*, more.

WHITE, CHRISTINE (S. Cal.) Leading lady. Onscreen from the '50s. IN: *Macabre*, more.

WHITE, DAN (S. Cal.) Character. Onscreen from the '40s. IN: *The Yearling, Four Faces West, Unknown Island, Roseanna McCoy, Rawhide, Red Mountain*, more.

WHITE, DAVID (S. Cal.) Character. Onscreen from 1957. IN: *Sweet Smell of Success, Sunrise at Campobello, The Great Impostor, Madison Avenue*, more.

WHITE, FRANK (Eng.) Ballet star. Onscreen in 1960 in *The Royal Ballet*.

WHITE, JACQUELINE (S. Cal.) Long married to Dr. James Cyril Doyle, she is, in her mid-50s, a proper Beverly Hills society matron—and still regrets that MGM pulled her out of the mother role in *The Yearling* (in favor of Jane Wyman) after she had begun filming with Gregory Peck. It could have meant a great difference in her career. *The Narrow Margin*, in '52, was her movie swan song. Onscreen from 1943. IN: *Air Raid Wardens, Swing Shift Maisie, Song of Russia, Crossfire, Night Song, Return of the Badmen, The Capture*, more.

WHITE, JANE (N.Y.) Black support. Daughter of the late Walter White, Executive Secretary of the N.A.A.C.P. Primarily a stage actress and perhaps best known for the role of the Queen in *Once Upon a Mattress*, which she also did on TV. Onscreen from the '50s. *Le Dolce Signore* and *Non Scommettere con il Diavalo* (both Italian productions), *A Town Like Alice, Klute*, more.

WHITE, JENNIFER (Eng.) Support. Onscreen from the '60s. IN: *The L-Shaped Room*, more.

WHITE, JESSE (S. Cal.) Character. Besides his famous Maytag-repairman commercials, he still does many movies. Onscreen from 1950. IN: *Harvey, Francis Goes to the Races, Bedtime for Bonzo, Death of a Salesman, Million Dollar Mermaid, Witness to Murder, Not As a Stranger, The Bad Seed, Marjorie Morningstar, On the Double, Sail a Crooked Ship, A House Is Not a Home, The Reluctant Astronaut, Las Vegas Lady*, more.

WHITE, JOAN (Wash.) The English actress —principally on the stage—is in her 60s now (b. 1909), and in this decade has been a director of the School of Drama at the University of Washington in Seattle. Onscreen from the '30s. IN: *Admirals All, Second Bureau, As You Like It, A Girl Must Live, The Last of the Mohicans*, more.

WHITE, MYRNA (Eng.) Support. Onscreen from the '60s. IN: *A Funny Thing Happened on the Way to the Forum, Lost in the Stars*, more.

WHITE, NATHANIEL (N.Y.) Character. On-screen from the '50s. IN: *A Face in the Crowd, The Garment Jungle, North by Northwest, Sweet Smell of Success, The F.B.I. Story, Butterfield 8, Man on a String*, more.

WHITE, PATRICIA (S. Cal.) Actress Patricia Barry's original screen name—in *Cry Wolf, The Undercover Man*, more. (See Patricia Barry.)

WHITE, PETER (N.Y.) Support. Onscreen in the '70s. IN: *The Boys in the Band*, more.

WHITE, SHEILA (Eng.) Support. Onscreen from the '60s. IN: *Here We Go Around the Mulberry Bush, Oliver!, Goin' Down the Road*, more.

WHITE, SLAPPY (N.Y.) Black star comedian. Onscreen in the '70s. IN: *The Man from O.R.G.Y. and the Real Gone Girls, Amazing Grace*, more.

WHITE, THELMA (S. Cal.) The blonde comedienne with the upswept hairdo, who was in so many Edgar Kennedy and Leon Errol shorts plus "The Bowery Boys" pix (as the gal who was forever bugging Huntz Hall), has in recent years been a Hollywood actors' agent. Not by choice, though she admits loving it. Entertaining with the USO in Alaska in the mid-40s, she chanced to eat contaminated fish and contracted a rare disease that kept her bedridden for years, left her crippled, and ended her career as an actress. Twice married and divorced (her husbands were Claude Stroud, famous on radio as one of the Stroud Twins, and Max Hoffman Jr.), she has been single for years. Thelma is in her 60s now (b. 1911) and still going strong—at her "second" career. Onscreen from the '20s. IN: *Hectic Honeymoon, Wanted by the Police, Mary Lou, Song of the Open Road*, more.

WHITE, WARREN (N.Y.) Support. Onscreen from the '60s. IN: *Targets*, more.

WHITEHEAD, GEOFFREY (Eng.) Support. Onscreen in the '70s. IN: *Long Ago, Tomorrow; Kidnapped*, more.

WHITEHEAD, O. Z. (S. Cal.) Character. In recent years he has done more TV commercials than movies. Onscreen from 1935. IN: *The Scoundrel, The Grapes of Wrath, Romance of Rosy Ridge, A Song Is Born, Ma and Pa Kettle, The Hoodlum, We're Not Married, The San Francisco Story, Rally Round the Flag Boys!, The Last Hurrah, Two Rode Together, Summer Magic*, more.

WHITEHILL, WAYNE (N.Y.) Comic character. Onscreen from the '60s. IN: *Sweet Charity, John and Mary, Generation, Love Story, The Panic in Needle Park*, more.

WHITELAW, BILLIE (Eng.) Leading lady. Onscreen from the '50s. IN: *Make Mine Mink, Hell Is a City, No Love for Johnnie, I Like Money, Charlie Bubbles, Gumshoe, Frenzy, Leo the Last*, more.

WHITELEY, JON (Eng.) In 1954 he was awarded a special Oscar (miniature) "for his outstanding juvenile performance in *The Little Kidnappers*. Now in his 30s (b. 1945), he has rarely been active in movies for a decade. Onscreen from 1952. IN: *Hunted, The Stranger in Between, Moonfleet, The Spanish Gardener, Capetown Affair*, more.

WHITFIELD, ANNE (S. Cal.) Better known for her radio role of "Penelope" in *One Man's family*—played it between ages 7 and 21—than her movies, she is in her 30s, has been married since '58 to advertising executive Fred Schiller, has two youngsters, and continues to act regularly in pictures as well as on TV. Onscreen from 1950. IN: *The Gunfighter, White Christmas, Tick Tick Tick*, more.

WHITING, BARBARA (Mich.) Former ingenue. Sister of Margaret, daughter of the late composer Dick Whiting. Married, retired from movies for two decades, and living in Bloomfield Hills. Onscreen from 1945. IN: *Junior Miss, Centennial Summer, Home Sweet Homicide, Carnival in Costa Rica, City Across the River, I Can Get It for You Wholesale, Beware My Lovely, Dangerous When Wet*, more.

WHITING, GORDON (Eng.) Character. Onscreen in the '70s. IN: *The Railway Children*, more.

WHITING, LEONARD (Eng.) Leading man. Onscreen from 1968. IN: *Romeo and Juliet, The Royal Hunt of the Sun, Say Hello to Yesterday, Dr. Frankenstein*, more.

WHITING, MARGARET (S. Cal.) The singer remains popular in personal appearances across the land, lives in L.A., and has been three times married and divorced. Onscreen in 1955 and 1965. IN: *Fresh From Paris* (a.k.a. *Paris Follies of 1956*) and *Underworld Informer*.

WHITING, NAPOLEON (S. Cal.) Black character. Onscreen from the '60s. IN: *It Happened to Jane, Wall of Noise, Black Samson*, more.

WHITMAN, STUART (S. Cal.) Costar. Nominated for Best Actor Oscar in *The Mark*. Onscreen from 1951. IN: *The Day the Earth Stood Still, The Silver Lode, Rhapsody, Johnny Trouble, The Girl in Black Stockings, Darby's Rangers, Ten North Frederick, The Sound and the Fury, Francis of Assisi, The Comancheros, Shock Treatment, Sands of the Kalahari, Crazy Mama, Welcome to Arrow Beach, One Hour to Hell, Mean Johnny Barrows, Call Him Mr. Shatter, Las Vegas Lady*, more.

WHITMAN, WILLIAM (N. Cal.) Support. Onscreen from the '60s. IN: *The Great Man, The Clouded Crystal*, more.

WHITMORE, JAMES (S. Cal.) Costar. Nominated for Best Supporting Actor Oscar in *Battleground*. Nominated for Best Actor Oscar in *Give 'Em Hell, Harry!* Onscreen from 1949. IN: *The Undercover Man, The Asphalt Jungle, The Next Voice You Hear, It's a Big Country, Because You're Mine; Kiss Me, Kate; All the Brothers Were Valiant, Battle Cry, The McConnell Story, Oklahoma!, The Deep Six, Waterhole #3, Planet of the Apes, Madigan, Nobody's Perfect, The Split, Guns of the Magnificent Seven, The Harrad Experiment*, more.

WHITNEY, C. C./a.k.a. CE CE WHITNEY (S. Cal.) Character actress. Onscreen from the '60s. IN: *Twelve Hours to Kill; Happy Birthday, Wanda June*; more.

WHITNEY, ELEANORE (N.Y.) The gorgeous tap dancer so often teamed with Johnny Downs (*Blonde Trouble, Turn Off the Moon*, etc.) gave up her movie career after 1938's *Campus Confessions*. She has not acted since except once on Broadway, in '46, with the late comedian Bobby Clark in Moliere's *The Would-Be Gentleman*. In her 60s now (b. 1914), she lives on the East Side, and has been married since '39 to Frederick Backer, who was formerly an assistant U.S. Attorney. Onscreen from 1935. IN: *Millions in the Air, Timothy's Quest, Three Cheers for Love, Rose Bowl, College Holiday, Clarence, Thrill of a Lifetime*, more.

WHITNEY, MIKE (S. Cal.) Support. Onscreen in the '70s. IN: *Doc*, more.

WHITSUN-JONES, PAUL (Eng.) Character. Onscreen from the '50s. IN: *The Moonraker, Tunes of Glory, Bluebeard's Ten Honeymoons,* more.

WHITTINGHILL, DICK (S. Cal.) Support. Onscreen from the '50s. IN: *Will Success Spoil Rock Hunter?, Moon Pilot, Say One for Me,* more.

WHITTINGTON, GENE (S. Cal.) Black support. Onscreen in the '70s. IN: *Escape from the Planet of the Apes,* more.

WHITWAM, BARRY (Eng.) Support. Onscreen from the '60s. IN: *Hold On!, Mrs. Brown You've Got a Lovely Daughter,* more.

WHYTE, PATRICK (S. Cal.) Character. Onscreen from 1947. IN: *Forever Amber* (debut; bit), *Not Wanted, Beau Geste,* more.

WICK, BRUNO (S. Cal.) Character; inactive in movies now. Onscreen from the '40s. IN: *The House on 92nd Street, Deep Waters, Walk East on Beacon, Love Island,* more.

WICKES, MARY (S. Cal.) "Miss Bedpan!" roared the viperish Sheridan Whiteside (Monty Woolley) at his luckless nurse in 1941's *The Man Who Came to Dinner,* and a great movie character comedienne was born. Then not quite 30, and in her first movie—repeating her Broadway role—Mary Wickes looked much as she does today: hawk-nosed, lanky (though she's fleshed out a bit), gawky, and terribly funny. In the years since, though continuing to be a screen favorite, the actress has appeared in fewer than 40 pictures. There could have been many more but for her practice of putting her eggs in many baskets. One of TV's earliest "regulars" in "live" productions, she later guested in many series—from *Halls of Ivy* to *Colombo*—before becoming, in 1975, the costar of CBS-TV's *Doc.* As a stage actress, she has frequently returned to Broadway, and in recent years has devoted much time to stock and repertory companies. A sentimental favorite open-air theater with her is St. Louis' huge (13,000 seats) Municipal Opera, where, in 1972, she did her eighth annual summer appearance, costarring in *The Music Man,* playing always to SRO crowds. One of the youngest graduates ever—she received her B.A. at 18—at St. Louis' Washington University, she took a long sabbatical from her professional career to return there in 1968 as her alma mater's first artist-in-residence. The culmination of her months there was a fine production of *The Glass Menagerie.* In this, working with a student cast, she played to perfection a role such as Hollywood has never allowed her to do—the indomitable, maddening mother, Amanda Wingfield. The university conferred upon her, before she returned to the Coast, an honorary Doctor of Arts degree. More recently, the actress has written her thesis for a Master of Arts degree from U.C.L.A., after completing class requirements for it. Parts of her thesis were done during a seven-months engagement in 1972–73 with San Francisco's American Conservatory Theatre. There she starred in comedy *(You Can't Take It With You),* stark drama *(The Crucible),* and 13th-century mystery plays. A lifelong "bachelor girl," she lives in a posh apartment in Century City, just west of Beverly Hills. Between movie and TV assignments, she devotes one day each week to volunteer work at the Hospital of the Good Samaritan, and to date has logged more than 1,000 hours there. Currently she is also a volunteer aide to the Chaplain of the U.C.L.A. Hospital Center for the Health Sciences, besides working as a fundraiser for a local educational TV station. A long while back, pre-Hollywood, when she was still on Broadway (17 shows in a row), Mary Wickes appeared in a play based on the short stories of John Cheever. The author asserted in print about her that she "is first of all comical, yet also deeply human and admirable. She is no mere buffoon . . . but a woman with mind and heart." Onscreen from 1941. IN: *Now Voyager, Who Done It?, Private Buckaroo, Happy Land, My Kingdom for a Cook, Higher and Higher, June Bride, The Decision of Christopher Blake, Anna Lucasta, On Moonlight Bay, I'll See You in My Dreams, The Actress, White Christmas; Good Morning, Miss Dove; Don't Go Near the Water, The Music Man, How to Murder Your Wife, The Trouble With Angels, Napoleon and Samantha, Snowball Express,* more.

WICKI, BERNARD (Switz.) Former actor; now works only as a director. Onscreen from the '50s. IN: *The Last Bridge, Circus of Love, The Affairs of Julie, The Cat, La Notte,* more.

WIDDOES, KATHLEEN (N.Y.) Leading lady; primarily a stage actress. Onscreen from 1966. IN: *The Group, Petulia, The Sea Gull, The Mephisto Waltz,* more.

WIDMARK, RICHARD (S. Cal.) Star. Nominated for Best Supporting Actor Oscar in *Kiss of Death,* his first movie. Onscreen from 1947. IN: *Cry of the City, The Street with No Name, Yellow Sky, Down to the Sea in Ships, Panic in the Streets, No Way Out, The Halls of Montezuma, Don't Bother to Knock, Take the High Ground, Broken Lance, The Cobweb, Time Limit, Tunnel of Love, Two Rode Together,*

How the West Was Won, Cheyenne Autumn, The Bedford Incident, Alvarez Kelly, Madigan, Death of a Gunfighter, The Moonshine War, When the Legends Die, Murder on the Orient Express; To the Devil . . . A Daughter; Twilight's Last Gleaming, more.

WIECK, DOROTHY (Ger.) Erroneously reported killed in an air raid on Dresden in WW II, the actress lives in West Berlin, is now in her late 60s (b. 1908), and in the past 20 years has been in support in several films, including A Time to Love and a Time to Die, the German version (with Lilli Palmer) of Anastasia. Onscreen from 1932. IN: Maedchen in Uniform, Theodor Koerner, Anna and Elizabeth, Cradle Song, Miss Fane's Baby Is Stolen, Ein Toller Einfall, The Private Life of Louis XIV, Man on a Tightrope, Brainwashed, more.

WIENER, JULIA (N.J.) Support. Onscreen in the '70s. IN: The French Connection, The Hot Rock, more.

WIERE BROTHERS, THE (S. Cal.) Comedy team. Harry and Herbert have been inactive in movies since the death of brother Sylvester in 1970. Onscreen from 1941. IN: The Great American Broadcast, Swing Shift Maisie, Road to Rio, Double Trouble, more.

WILCOX, MARY (S. Cal.) Support. Onscreen from the '60s. IN: Flareup, The Lawyer, Willie Dynamite, more.

WILCOX-HORNE, COLLIN (S. Cal.) Leading lady. Early in her career, before her marriage to actor Geoffrey Horne, she was billed Collin Wilcox. Onscreen from 1963. IN: To Kill a Mockingbird, The Name of the Game Is Kill, The Baby Maker, The Revolutionary, Jump, more.

WILCOXON, HENRY (S. Cal.) Character; former star. Onscreen from 1931. IN: The Flying Squad, Lovelorn Lady, A Taxi to Paradise, Cleopatra, The Crusades, The Last of the Mohicans, The President's Mystery, Souls at Sea, Mysterious Mr. Moto of Devil's Island, If I Were King, Five of a Kind, Tarzan Finds a Son, Chasing Danger, Earthbound, Mystery Sea Raider, The Corsican Brothers, That Hamilton Woman, The Lone Wolf Takes a Chance, Mrs. Miniver, The Man Who Wouldn't Die, Unconquered, Dragnet, Samson and Delilah, The Miniver Story, Scaramouche, The Ten Commandments, The Private Navy of Sgt. O'Farrell, Man in the Wilderness, Against a Crooked Sky, more. (See Joan Woodbury.)

WILD, JACK (S. Cal.) Former juvenile (b. 1952). Nominated for Best Supporting Actor Oscar in Oliver!, his first movie. Onscreen from 1968. IN: Flight of the Doves, The Pied Piper, The Fourteen, Pufnstuf, more.

WILDE, BRIAN (Eng.) Support. Onscreen from the '60s. IN: Rattle of a Simple Man, The Jokers, more.

WILDE, CORNEL (S. Cal.) Star. Nominated for Best Actor Oscar in A Song to Remember. Now, besides starring, he usually writes-produces-directs his films. Onscreen from 1940. IN: Lady with Red Hair, High Sierra, The Perfect Snob, Life Begins at 8:30, Manila Calling, Wintertime, Guest in the House, A Thousand and One Nights, Leave Her to Heaven, The Bandit of Sherwood Forest, Forever Amber, I Had to Be You, Road House, Two Flags West, The Greatest Show on Earth, Treasure of the Golden Condor, The Scarlet Coat, Storm Fear (in '55; his first as producer-director-star), Star of India, Omar Khayyam, Sword of Lancelot, The Naked Prey, Beach Red, The Raging Sea, No Blade of Grass, Sharks' Treasure, more.

WIL-DEE, SPENCE (S. Cal.) Black support. Onscreen in the '70s. IN: The Klansman, more.

WILDER, ALEC (N.Y.) Composer. Onscreen in 1961 and 1964 in The Sand Castle and Open the Door and See All the People.

WILDER, GENE (S. Cal.) Co-star. Nominated for Best Supporting Actor Oscar in The Producers. Onscreen from 1967. IN: Bonnie and Clyde, Start the Revolution Without Me, Willy Wonka and the Chocolate Factory, Everything You Always Wanted to Know About Sex, The Little Prince, Rhinoceros, Blazing Saddles, Young Frankenstein, The Adventures of Sherlock Holmes' Smarter Brother, The Silver Streak, more.

WILDER, JOHN (S. Cal.) Support; lately inactive in movies. Onscreen from the '50s. IN: Until They Sail, Summer Love, Imitation General, more.

WILDER, JOHN DAVID (S. Cal.) Support. Onscreen in the '70s. IN: R.P.M., The Grasshopper, more.

WILDER, PATRICIA "HONEYCHILE" (Fr.) The Texas heiress, so beautiful and popular in pix of the '30s, has long been retired, is in her early 60s, and owns a splendid house in Paris on the Left Bank. Onscreen from 1936. IN: Speed, Bunker Bean; Wanted: Jane Turner; New Faces of 1937, That Girl from Paris, On Again-Off Again, The Big Broadcast of 1938, Little Miss Broadway, My Lucky Star, more.

WILDING, MICHAEL (Eng.) In his 60s (b. 1912), he is retired and a widower. His wife,

514

ctress Margaret Leighton, died early in 1976 of multiple sclerosis. He lives alone now in a country house outside London. The actor's previous wives were Kay Young (they divorced in '51) and Elizabeth Taylor (1952–57), by whom he has two sons, Michael Jr. and Christopher. Onscreen from 1935. IN: *Wedding Group, Convoy, Kipps, In Which We Serve, Ships With Wings, An Ideal Husband, Under Capricorn, Spring in Park Lane, Stage Fright, The Law and the Lady* (in 1951; his first in Hollywood), *Maytime in Mayfair, Torch Song, The Egyptian, The Glass Slipper, Zarak, The World of Suzie Wong, Naked Edge, A Girl Named Tamiku, Waterloo, The Sweet Ride, Lady Caroline Lamb*, more.

WILKE, ROBERT J. (S. Cal.) Western character. Onscreen from the '40s. IN: *Vigilantes of Dodge City, Santa Fe Saddlemates, Out California Way, Dick Tracy vs. Crime Inc., Carson City Raiders, Laramie, Cyclone Fury, The Las Vegas Story, Hellgate, High Noon, Arrowhead, The Magnificent Seven, Spartacus, The Gun Hawk, The Hallelujah Trail, Joaquin Murietta*, more.

WILLES, JEAN (S. Cal.) Support; former leading lady. Onscreen from the '40s. IN: *Chinatown at Midnight, A Woman of Distinction, From Here to Eternity, The King and Four Queens, No Time for Sergeants, The F.B.I. Story, Ocean's Eleven, By Love Possessed, Gypsy, The Cheyenne Social Club, Bite the Bullet*, more.

WILLIAMS, ADAM (S. Cal.) Support. Onscreen from 1950. IN: *Queen for a Day, Without Warning* (lead, as a sniper; made his screen reputation), *The Big Heat, The Proud and Profane, Fear Strikes Out, The Badlanders, North by Northwest, Convicts 4, The New Interns, The Horse in the Gray Flannel Suit*, more.

WILLIAMS, ALFONSO (S. Cal.) Black support. Onscreen in the '70s. IN: *The Hard Ride*, more.

WILLIAMS, ANDY (S. Cal.) Singer-actor. Onscreen from 1947. IN: *Something in the Wind* (as part of the singing "Williams Brothers"; his brothers later retired from show business but still live in Los Angeles), *I'd Rather Be Rich* (costar role).

WILLIAMS, ARNOLD (S. Cal.) Black support. Onscreen from the '60s. IN: *The Lost Man, The Panic in Needle Park*, more.

WILLIAMS, BARRY (S. Cal.) Former juvenile (b. 1954). On TV as "Greg" in *The Brady Bunch*. Onscreen from the '60s. IN: *Wild in the Streets*, more.

WILLIAMS, BERT (S. Cal.) Character. Onscreen from 1961. IN: *Angel Baby, The Nest of the Cuckoo Birds* (also produced-directed), *Around the World Under the Sea, The Klansman*, more.

WILLIAMS, BILL (S. Cal.) Character; former leading man. He and actress Barbara Hale—frequent costars at RKO—have been long and happily married. Onscreen from 1944. IN: *Those Endearing Young Charms, West of the Pecos, Deadline at Dawn, Till the End of Time, A Likely Story, The Stratton Story, The Great Missouri Raid, Son of Paleface, Legion of the Doomed, Hell to Eternity, Rio Lobo, Scandalous John*, more.

WILLIAMS, BILLY DEE (S. Cal.) Black star. Onscreen from 1959. IN: *The Last Angry Man, The Out-of-Towners, Lady Sings the Blues, The Take, Mahogany*, more.

WILLIAMS, BROOK (Eng.) Support. Onscreen from the '60s. IN: *Where Eagles Dare, Anne of the Thousand Days, Raid on Rommel; Long Ago, Tomorrow; Villain*, more.

WILLIAMS, CARA (S. Cal.) Support. Nominated for Best Supporting Actress Oscar in *The Defiant Ones*. She was once the wife of John Barrymore Jr. (now billed John Drew Barrymore), and is the mother of his son. Onscreen from 1943. IN: *Happy Land; In the Meantime, Darling; Something for the Boys, The Spider, It's a Wonderful Life, Heading for Heaven, Boomerang, Sitting Pretty, The Saxon Charm, Knock on Any Door, Meet Me in Las Vegas, Never Steal Anything Small, The Man From the Diner's Club, Doctors' Wives*, more.

WILLIAMS, CINDY (S. Cal.) Leading lady. Costar of TV's *Laverne & Shirley*. Onscreen in the '70s. IN: *Gas-sss, Return of the Blob, Travels With My Aunt, The Christian Licorice Store, American Graffiti, The Conversation, The Killing Kind, Mr. Ricco, The First Nudie Musical*, more.

WILLIAMS, CLARENCE, III (S. Cal.) Black leading man. Costar of TV's *The Mod Squad*. Onscreen from 1964. IN: *The Cool World*, more.

WILLIAMS, CURT (N.Y.) Support. Onscreen in the '70s. IN: *A Change in the Wind*, more.

WILLIAMS, DICK ANTHONY (S. Cal.) Black support. Onscreen from the '60s. IN: *Uptight, The Lost Man, The Anderson Tapes, Who Killed Mary What's 'Ername?*, more.

WILLIAMS, DONNIE (S. Cal.) Support. Onscreen in the '70s. IN: *Truck Turner*, more.

WILLIAMS, EDY (S. Cal.) Leading lady. Onscreen from 1966. IN: *The Pad (And How to Use It), Good Times, The Secret Life of an American Wife, A Guide for the Married Man, Where It's At, Beyond the Valley of the Dolls, The Seven Minutes*, more.

WILLIAMS, ELAINE (S. Cal.) Support. Onscreen from the '60s. IN: *The Subject Was Roses*, more.

WILLIAMS, EMLYN (Eng.) Costar. To date he has published two volumes of his autobiography (with more to come): *George* ('62) and *Emlyn: An Early Autobiography—1927–1935* ('74). Onscreen from 1932. IN: *The Case of the Frightened Lady, Roadhouse, Evensong, The Iron Duke, The Citadel, Jamaica Inn, Major Barbara, Hatter's Castle, Three Husbands, The Scarf, The Magic Box, Ivanhoe, The Deep Blue Sea, I Accuse!, The Wreck of the Mary Deare, The L-Shaped Room, The Walking Stick*, more.

WILLIAMS, ESTHER (S. Cal.) She is in her 50s (b. 1923) and that glorious athletic figure has filled out a bit. Reportedly she was one of the MGM luminaries who begged off attending the premiere of *That's Entertainment!*, saying, "I've changed." But, not surprisingly, portions of her old movies shown in it were the film's spectacular highlights, setting off a landslide of renewed interest in both the swim star and her movies. In revival houses and on TV, Esther Williams musicals are now among the most-booked pix of all. She has been offscreen since 1961's *The Big Show*, however, and says she will never act again. Actor-writer-director Fernando Lamas, to whom she has been happily married for many years, even wrote a script specifically for her, hoping to persuade her to return to the screen. She said no. Now Lamas concedes, "She's only one of two broads I know who really retired. The other is Jane Bryan." The actress has no children by Lamas, whom she has married in two separate ceremonies—in a civil ceremony in Europe in '67 and in one in church (the Founders' Church of Religious Science, near Hollywood) on December 31, 1969. By her marriage (1945–57) to Ben Gage, she has three, Benjamin, Kimball, and Susan. She had earlier been married (1940–44) to Leonard Kovner. She and Lamas live in a sprawling house (with pool) in the Valley and, she insists, she does all her own housework and cooking. Onscreen from 1942. IN: *Andy Hardy's Double Life, A Guy Named Joe, Bathing Beauty* (in '44; first of the type of Williams movie that later caused comedienne Fannie Brice to crack: "Wet she's a star, dry she ain't"), *Thrill of a Romance, The Hoodlum Saint, Ziegfeld Follies, Easy to Wed, This Time for Keeps, Fiesta, On An Island With You, Neptune's Daughter, Take Me Out to the Ball Game, Pagan Love Song, Duchess of Idaho, Texas Carnival, Skirts Ahoy!, Million Dollar Mermaid, Easy to Love, Dangerous When Wet, Jupiter's Darling* (in '55, her last swim pic), *The Unguarded Moment, Raw Wind in Eden*, more. (See Fernando Lamas.)

WILLIAMS, FRANCES (S. Cal.) Black leading lady. Onscreen in the '70s. IN: *Together Brothers, Baby Needs a New Pair of Shoes*, more.

WILLIAMS, FRED (Eng.) Support. Onscreen from the '60s. IN: *Sandra, Count Dracula*, more.

WILLIAMS, GENE (N.Y.) Character. Onscreen in the '70s. IN: *I Never Sang for My Father*, more.

WILLIAMS, GLORIA (S. Cal.) The widow of comic Walter Hiers, she lives in Beverly Hills, is retired, and in 1974 contributed to the University of Southern California's archives mementos from her career and that of her husband. Onscreen in the '30s. IN: *Cocoanut Grove, Prison Farm, Give Me a Sailor*, more.

WILLIAMS, GRANT (S. Cal.) Leading man. Onscreen from 1957. IN: *Written on the Wind, The Incredible Shrinking Man, The Monolith Monsters, Four Girls in Town, Lone Texan, The Leech Woman, Susan Slade, PT-109*, more.

WILLIAMS, GUY (S. Cal.) Leading man. Star of TV's *Lost in Space* and *Zorro*. Onscreen from 1952. IN: *Bonzo Goes to College, The Mississippi Gambler, Seven Angry Men, Sincerely Yours, The Last Frontier, The Sign of Zorro, Damon and Pythias* (made in Italy), *The Prince and the Pauper* (made in England), *Captain Sinbad* (made in Germany), more.

WILLIAMS, HANK, JR. (Tenn.) Country & Western star, son of the legendary Hank (whose life story was filmed as *Your Cheatin' Heart*, starring George Hamilton). Gravely injured in 1975 when he fell some 500 feet from a snowbank in Montana, while hiking, he underwent extensive plastic surgery in 1976, hoping to be able to resume his singing career. Onscreen from 1968. IN: *A Time to Sing*, more. (He also sang behind the credits of *Kelly's Heroes*.)

WILLIAMS, HOPE (N.Y.) The Broadway star *(Holiday)* made just one movie and has long been retired from the stage as well. Onscreen in 1935 in *The Scoundrel*.

WILLIAMS, HOWARD. (Eng.) Support. Onscreen from the '60s. IN: *Up the Junction*, more.

WILLIAMS, JACK (S. Cal.) Character. On-screen from 1943. IN: *Hit Parade of 1943, The Scalphunters*, more.

WILLIAMS, JASON (S. Cal.) Leading man. Onscreen in the '70s. IN: *Flesh Gordon* (title role), more.

WILLIAMS, JEFF (S. Cal.) Support. Onscreen in the '70s. IN: *The Brotherhood of Satan*, more.

WILLIAMS, JIMMY (S. Cal.) Support. On-screen in the '70s. IN: *Cockfighter*, more.

WILLIAMS, JOE (S. Cal.) Support. Onscreen in the '70s. IN: *The Moonshine War*, more.

WILLIAMS, JOHN (S. Cal.) Character. On-screen from the '30s. IN: *Emil, Somewhere in France, Kind Lady, Dial M for Murder* (highly impressive as Inspector Hubbard), *The Student Prince, Sabrina, The Solid Gold Cadillac, Island in the Sun, The Young Philadelphians, Midnight Lace, The Secret War of Harry Frigg, A Flea in Her Ear, Lost in the Stars, No Deposit No Return*, more.

WILLIAMS, JONATHAN (Eng.) Support. Onscreen in the '70s. IN: *Le Mans*, more.

WILLIAMS, JOYCE (S. Cal.) Support. Onscreen in the '70s. IN: *Pretty Maids All in a Row*, more.

WILLIAMS, KATE (Eng.) Character. On-screen from the '60s. IN: *Poor Cow, Melody*, more.

WILLIAMS, KATHERINE (S. Cal.) Long married to a college professor, she lives near Los Angeles and is retired. Onscreen in the '30s. IN: *Where Sinners Meet, Kiss and Make-Up*, more.

WILLIAMS, KAY (S. Cal.) Not remarried since Clark Gable's death, she now lives in Beverly Hills—having sold the Encino estate where she (and, previously, Carole Lombard) and Gable lived. Son John Clark Gable, a handsome teenager (b. 1961), attends Beverly Hills high. By her previous marriage she has a daughter, Joan Spreckles, who lives on the Riviera. The actress, in her 60s now and still beautiful, is one of the most popular figures in Hollywood society. Onscreen from the '40s. IN: *DuBarry Was a Lady* (and other musicals), *No Minor Vices, The Actress*, more.

WILLIAMS, KENNETH (Eng.) Character. On-screen from 1952. IN: *Trent's Last Case, The Beggar's Opera, Land of Fury, Carry On Sergeant, Make Mine Mink, Carry On Cleo*, more.

WILLIAMS, KENNY (S. Cal.) Former supporting actor, now an assistant director (*Shoot Out*, etc.). Onscreen from 1944. IN: *Irish Eyes Are Smiling, Mother Wore Tights, Slattery's Hurricane, When Willie Comes Marching Home, The Pride of St. Louis*, more.

WILLIAMS, LARRY (S. Cal.) Support. Not the late character actor. Onscreen in the '70s. IN: *The Klansman*, more.

WILLIAMS, PAUL (S. Cal.) Small (5') giant in the music world—a Grammy-winning and Oscar-nominated composer (for "You're So Nice to Be Around" in *Cinderella Liberty*). Onscreen in 1975. IN: *Phantom of the Paradise* (star role; he also wrote the music).

WILLIAMS, ROBERT B. (S. Cal.) Character. Onscreen from 1944. IN: *The Cry of the Werewolf, One Mysterious Night, The Dark Past, The Lawless, The Great Jewel Robbery, The Groom Wore Spurs, Revenge of the Creature, Pork Chop Hill*, more.

WILLIAMS, ROGER (S. Cal.) Western character; inactive in movies now. Onscreen from the '30s. IN: *Code of the Mounted, Trails of the Wild, The Arizona Wrangler, No Man's Range, Wildcat Trooper, Riders of the Whistling Skull, Heroes of the Alamo, Zorro Rides Again*, more.

WILLIAMS, SIMON (Eng.) Support. Onscreen in the '70s. IN: *The Blood on Satan's Claw*, more.

WILLIAMS, TED (S. Cal.) One of baseball's greats, with the Boston Red Sox, he was later—until 1972—manager of the Washington Senators. In more recent years he has been a sports consultant. Onscreen in 1941 and 1942. IN: *Untitled—Baseball Technique* and *The Ninth Inning*.

WILLIAMS, THAD (S. Cal.) Support. Onscreen in the '70s. IN: *Barquero*, more.

WILLIAMS, TIGER (S. Cal.) Juvenile actor. Onscreen in the '70s. IN: *Earthquake*, more.

WILLIAMS, VAN (S. Cal.) Former leading man. Star of TV's *The Green Hornet*. Now a successful banker in Burbank. Onscreen from the '60s. IN: *The Caretakers*, more.

WILLIAMSON, ALASTAIR (Eng.) Support. Onscreen from the '60s. IN: *The Oblong Box*, more.

WILLIAMSON, FRED (S. Cal.) Black star. Onscreen from 1970. IN: *M*A*S*H; Tell Me That You Love Me, Junie Moon; The Legend of Nigger Charley, Black Eye, Hammer* (capitalizing on the nickname that was his when a pro football star), *Black Caesar, The Soul of Nigger Charley, Three the Hard Way, Boss Nigger, Death Journey, Bucktown, Take a Hard Ride, Adios Amigo, Mean Johnny Barrows,* more.

WILLIAMSON, NICOL (Eng.) Costar. Onscreen from the '60s. IN: *Inadmissible Evidence, The Bofors Gun, Hamlet, The Reckoning, The Jerusalem File, The Wilby Conspiracy, Robin and Marian,* more.

WILLINGHAM, NOBLE (S. Cal.) Character. Onscreen in the '70s. IN: *My Sweet Charlie, The Last Picture Show, Chinatown, Big Bad Mama,* more.

WILLIS, AUSTIN (S. Cal.) Support. Onscreen from the '50s. IN: *The Mouse That Roared, Crack in the Mirror, Goldfinger, Eight on the Lam, Hour of the Gun, The Boston Strangler,* more.

WILLIS, JEROME (Eng.) Support. Onscreen from the '60s. IN: *Khartoum, The Magus,* more.

WILLIS, SUSAN (N.Y.) Support. Onscreen in the '70s. IN: *Puzzle of a Downfall Child,* more.

WILLMAN, NOEL (Eng.) Character. Onscreen from the '50s. IN: *The Pickwick Papers, Androcles and the Lion, Beau Brummell, The Man Who Knew Too Much, Across the Bridge, Never Let Go, Doctor Zhivago, The Vengeance of She, The Odessa File,* more.

WILLMER, CATHERINE (Eng.) Character. Onscreen from the '50s. IN: *An Inspector Calls, Women in Love, The Devils, Madhouse,* more.

WILLOCK, DAVE (S. Cal.) Character. He and Sinatra were look-alikes in early years. Onscreen from 1939. IN: *Legion of Lost Flyers, The Fleet's In, Lucky Jordan, Princess O'-Rourke, Pin-Up Girl, Pride of the Marines, Chicago Deadline, Call Me Mister, It Came From Outer Space, Wives and Lovers, Send Me No Flowers; Hush . . . Hush . . . Sweet Charlotte; The Legend of Lylah Clare, The Barefoot Executive, The Grissom Gang,* more.

WILLS, CHILL (S. Cal.) Character. Nominated for Best Supporting Actor Oscar in *The Alamo.* Hollywood friends of this fine actor grieved with him in '71 when his wife, the former Betty Chappelle, died. (They had been married since '28.) And near the end of '73 they rejoiced with him when he married the former Novadeen Googe; but his newfound happiness was not destined to run a smooth course—she

filed for divorce in December '74. The affable actor from Texas, now in his 70s (b. 1903), is the father of two grown children—Jill and Will He lives in Encino, travels the country promoting a grain company and chain of steak house in which he has an interest, and his movie ca reer is still booming. Also in '75, in that familiar bass-toned gravel voice, he recorded his firs album as a singer, *Everybody's Cousin.* The title, of course, derived from his robust, lifelong greeting to all, "Hey, Cousin!" Onscreen from 1935. IN: *Bar-20 Rides Again, Way Out West, Racketeers of the Range, Boom Town, The Westerner, Tugboat Annie Sails Again, Belle Starr, Honky Tonk; See Here, Private Hargrove; Leave Her to Heaven, The Harvey Girls, Rio Grande, The Sundowners, Francis Joins the Wacs* (the only one in the "Francis" series in which he actually appeared—as General Benjamin "Mustard Ben" Kaye; from 1949 to 1955, in this and five others, he was the "voice" of Francis, the Talking Mule; the "voice" in the seventh and final one was that of Paul Frees), *Giant, Gold of the Seven Saints, McLintock!, The Wheeler Dealers, The Cardinal, The Rounders, Fireball 500, Guns of a Stranger, Pat Garrett and Billy the Kid,* more.

WILLS, MAURY (S. Cal.) Black support. Former baseball star. Onscreen in the '70s. IN: *The Black Six,* more.

WILMER, DOUGLAS (Eng.) Character. Onscreen from the '50s. IN: *Richard III, Pursuit of the Graf Spee, Cleopatra, The Battle of the River Plate, A Shot in the Dark, Khartoum, The Vengeance of Fu Manchu, Patton, The Reckoning, The Golden Voyage of Sinbad,* more.

WILSON, ALEX (S. Cal.) Leading man. Onscreen in the '70s. IN: *Gas-s-s-s!,* more.

WILSON, BARON (S. Cal.) Character. Onscreen in the '70s. IN: *The Gambler,* more.

WILSON, BRUCE (S. Cal.) Support. Onscreen in the '70s. IN: *The Hawaiians,* more.

WILSON, CAL (S. Cal.) Support. Onscreen in the '70s. IN: *Halls of Anger,* more.

WILSON, CHRIS (S. Cal.) Character actress. Onscreen in the '70s. IN: *My Sweet Charlie, The Windsplitter,* more.

WILSON, CLAUDE (S. Cal.) Support. Onscreen from the '60s. IN: *Cry of Battle, The Walls of Hell, Warkill,* more.

WILSON, CYNTHIA (S. Cal.) Juvenile. Onscreen in the '70s. IN: *Johnny Got His Gun,* more.

WILSON, DANA (Eng.) Support; lately inactive in movies. Onscreen from the '50s. IN: *Once a Thief, A Cry from the Streets*, more.

WILSON, DEMOND (S. Cal.) Black leading man. Costar of TV's *Sanford and Son*. Onscreen in the '70s. IN: *The Organization*, more.

WILSON, DENNIS (S. Cal.) Support. Onscreen in the '70s. IN: *Two-Lane Blacktop*, more.

WILSON, DICK (S. Cal.) Character. Onscreen from the '60s. IN: *The Shakiest Gun in the West*, more.

WILSON, DON (S. Cal.) Character actor and Jack Benny's famous radio announcer for 33 years. He is in his 70s now and retired, but still participates in many of Hollywood's nostalgic events. Onscreen from 1934. IN: *Wharf Angel, Two Girls on Broadway, Thank Your Lucky Stars, Radio Stars on Parade, The Kid From Brooklyn, Sailor Beware, Niagara, The Stars Are Singing*, more.

WILSON, DOROTHY (S. Cal.) This dark-haired actress gave a number of quietly dynamic performances in the early '30s, then gave up her career to become the wife of director Lewis R. Foster. Remaining happily married to him until his death in 1974, she is the mother of grown children and has traveled widely. Particularly, she spent long periods in the British Isles where several of her husband's films were made. In her late 60s now (b. 1909), she is quite content to have been a part—but not in—the Hollywood scene. Onscreen from 1932. IN: *The Age of Consent, Lucky Devils, Eight Girls in a Boat, His Greatest Gamble, The White Parade, The Last Days of Pompeii, Bad Boy, In Old Kentucky, The Milky Way*, more, including 1936's *Craig's Wife*, her last.

WILSON, EARL (N.Y.) Noted show-biz columnist. Onscreen (as himself) from 1947. IN: *Copacabana, College Confidential, Where Were You When the Lights Went Out?*, more.

WILSON, ELEANOR (N.Y.) Character. Primarily a stage actress. Onscreen in the '70s. IN: *Alice's Restaurant*, more.

WILSON, ELIZABETH (N.Y.) Support. Onscreen from 1956. IN: *Picnic, Patterns, The Goddess, Tunnel of Love, Happy Anniversary, A Child Is Waiting, The Birds, The Tiger Makes Out, The Graduate, Jenny, Catch-22, Little Murders, Man on a Swing, The Happy Hooker*, more.

WILSON, FLIP (S. Cal.) Black star comedian. Onscreen in the '70s. IN: *Uptown Saturday Night*, more.

WILSON, IAN (Eng.) Character. Onscreen from the '50s. IN: *My Sister and I, Seven Days to Noon, Whispering Smith Hits London, The Brain Machine, See How They Run, How to Murder a Rich Uncle, Happy Is the Bride*, more.

WILSON, ILONA (S. Cal.) Support. Onscreen in the '70s. IN: *How to Seduce a Woman*, more.

WILSON, JEANNA (S. Cal.) Support. Onscreen in the '70s. IN: *Where the Red Fern Grows*, more.

WILSON, JUDY (Eng.) Support. Onscreen in the '70s. IN: *Three Sisters*, more.

WILSON, JULIE (N.Y.) Singer-actress. She remains a stellar attraction in the better supper clubs. Onscreen in 1957 in *The Strange One* and *This Could Be the Night*.

WILSON, LOIS (N.Y.) This vastly popular leading lady of silents continued her career—a total of more than 300 films—in talkies through 1949's *The Girl from Jones Beach*. Entering her 80s now (b. 1896), she lives near Beekman Place, has never married, acts occasionally on Broadway (*I Never Sang for My Father* is among her credits of late), tours in plays (was featured in *John Loves Mary* with James Garner), and does much character work in soap operas—*As the World Turns, Edge of Night, Guiding Light*, etc. She has donated all the memorabilia of her 60-year stage-movie-TV career to Kent State University which, in '70, declared a "Lois Wilson Day" in tribute to her. Onscreen from the teens. IN: *The Bells, Why Smith Left Home, Midsummer Madness, Miss Lulu Bett, Manslaughter, Bella Donna, Ruggles of Red Gap, The Covered Wagon, Pied Piper Malone, Icebound, Monsieur Beaucaire, The Vanishing American, Bluebeard's Seven Wives, The Great Gatsby, The Gingham Girl, Her Husband's Women, Lovin' the Ladies, Seed, Laughing at Life, No Greater Glory, Bright Eyes, Cappy Ricks Returns, The Return of Jimmy Valentine, Bad Little Angel, Nobody's Children*, more.

WILSON, MICHELLE (S. Cal.) Support. Onscreen in the '70s. IN: *The Trial of Billy Jack*, more.

WILSON, NEIL (Eng.) Support. Onscreen from the '60s. IN: *Staircase, A Clockwork Orange*, more.

WILSON, SARAH (S. Cal.) Support. Onscreen in the '70s. IN: *Pigeons*, more.

WILSON, SCOTT (S. Cal.) Leading man. Onscreen from the '60s. IN: *In the Heat of the*

Night, In Cold Blood, Castle Keep, The Gypsy Moths, The Grissom Gang, The Great Gatsby, The Passover Plot, more.

WILSON, SUE (Eng.) Character. Onscreen in the '70s. IN: Creatures the World Forgot, more.

WILSON, TERRY (S. Cal.) Character actor. Onscreen from the '60s. IN: The Plainsman, The War Wagon, A Man Called Gannon, The Shakiest Gun in the West, Dirty Dingus Magee, Support Your Local Gunfighter, more.

WILSON, THEODORE (S. Cal.) Black support. Onscreen in the '70s. IN: Cotton Comes to Harlem, Newman's Law, more.

WILTON, ANN (Eng.) Support; inactive in movies for many years. Onscreen from the '30s. IN: Dead Men Tell No Tales, The Man in Grey, Man of Evil, The Miniver Story, more.

WILTON, TERENCE (Eng.) Support. Onscreen from the '60s. IN: Anne of the Thousand Days, more.

WINCHELL, PAUL (S. Cal.) Character; formerly a headlined ventriloquist (with wise-cracking dummy "Jerry Mahoney"). He made news in 1975 when it was announced that he had invented a plastic heart pump with which the University of Utah's school of medicine is experimenting, first on animals. With the artificial heart, after its own was removed, a calf was once kept alive for 94 days. Except that the heart had to be powered externally, Winchell explains, the animal would have lived longer. Continuing to work with the school on perfecting the heart, he says: "We are attempting to power the heart with an atomic motor completely independent of external power sources. As soon as we can get a calf to live a year, we'll begin work on humans." Onscreen from 1961. IN: Stop! Look! and Laugh!; Which Way to the Front?, The Aristocats (cartoon voice), more.

WINDOM, WILLIAM (S. Cal.) Character; former leading man. And an Emmy-winner as the star of TV's My World and Welcome To It. Onscreen from the '60s. IN: To Kill a Mockingbird, Cattle King, One Man's Way, The Americanization of Emily, The Detective, The Gypsy Moths, Brewster McCloud; Now You See Him, Now You Don't; The Man, Echoes of a Summer, more.

WINDSOR, BARBARA (Eng.) Support. Onscreen from the '50s. IN: Lost, Sparrows Don't Sing, A Study in Terror, The Boy Friend, more.

WINDSOR, MARIE (S. Cal.) Support; former leading lady. Onscreen from 1941. IN: All-American Co-Ed, The Big Street, Pilot Number 5, Let's Face It, The Hucksters, The Kissing Bandit (all small roles), Outpost in Morocco (her first lead), Hellfire, Dakota Lil, Outlaw Woman, Japanese War Bride, The Narrow Margin, The Sniper, The Jungle, Trouble Along the Way, City That Never Sleeps, The Eddie Cantor Story, The Killing, The Unholy Wife, Mail Order Bride, The Good Guys and the Bad Guys, Support Your Local Gunfighter, The Outfit, more.

WINDUST, IRENE (N.Y.) Support. Onscreen from the '50s. IN: Four Girls in Town, Road Racers, Parrish, more.

WINFIELD, PAUL (S. Cal.) Black star. Nominated for Best Actor Oscar in Sounder. Onscreen from the '60s. IN: The Lost Man, Gordon's War, Conrack, Huckleberry Finn, Hustle, Twilight's Last Gleaming, more.

WING, TOBY (Fla.) "The most beautiful chorus girl in Hollywood," they called her in '34. The first part—"most beautiful"—applies still to the blonde, who is now in her 60s (b. 1913) and has been happily married to aviator Dick Merrill since '37. She gave up her career then, and has never performed since. They still live in Miami Beach and are faithful members of All Souls Episcopal Church where Toby—when their children were small—taught Sunday school. Onscreen from 1932. IN: The Kid from Spain, College Humor, Gold Diggers of 1933, 42nd Street, Too Much Harmony, Search for Beauty, Come On Marines, Murder at the Vanities, Kiss and Make-Up, Forced Landing, The Women Men Marry, Sing While You're Able, True Confession, Mr. Boggs Steps Out, more. (See Dick Merrill.)

WINGREEN, JASON (S. Cal.) Character. Onscreen from the '60s. IN: The Slender Thread, The Cheyenne Social Club, The Dunwich Horror, The Terminal Man, more.

WINKLER, HENRY (S. Cal.) Leading man. Became popular as "Fonzie" in TV's Happy Days. Onscreen in the '70s. IN: Crazy Joe, The Lords of Flatbush, more.

WINKLER, MARGO (S. Cal.) Support. Onscreen in the '70s. IN: The Strawberry Statement, more.

WINMILL, JOAN (S. Cal.) Leading lady. Onscreen in the '70s. IN: Time to Run, more.

WINN, KITTY (N.Y.) Leading lady. Onscreen in the '70s. IN: The Panic in Needle Park, They Might Be Giants, Peeper, more.

WINOGRADOFF, ANATOL (S. Cal.) Character. Onscreen from the '50s. IN: *Go, Man, Go; The Girl from Petrovka,* more.

WINSLOW, DICK (S. Cal.) Beginning as a juvenile in silents, then later a leading man, he is now a character actor in his 60s (b. 1915), and busy. Onscreen from 1924. IN: *Which Shall It Be?, Tom Sawyer, Seed, So Big, Laughter in Hell, Tom Brown of Culver, The Human Side, One Exciting Adventure, There's Always Tomorrow, Mutiny on the Bounty, Ten Gentlemen from West Point, Is Everybody Happy?, The Benny Goodman Story, Francis in the Haunted House, Do Not Disturb, Airport, The Wrecking Crew,* more.

WINSLOW, GEORGE "FOGHORN" (S. Cal.) The former kid star with the unique basso voice is in his 30s now (b. 1946), unmarried, and trying to make a career of photography, after having spent several years in the Navy. Onscreen from 1952. IN: *Room for One More, Monkey Business, My Pal Gus, Gentlemen Prefer Blondes, Mister Scoutmaster, Artists and Models, Rock Pretty Baby, Wild Heritage, Summer Love,* more.

WINSLOW, YVONNE (S. Cal.) Support. Onscreen in the '70s. IN: *The Touch of Satan,* more.

WINSTON, HELENE (S. Cal.) Character. Onscreen from the '60s. IN: *Send Me No Flowers, The Trouble With Girls, What's the Matter with Helen?, The Brotherhood of Satan, A Boy and His Dog,* more.

WINSTON, ROBERT (N.Y.) Support. Onscreen from the '60s. IN: *The Satan Bug, The Swingers, Horror from Beyond, Paradise of Terror,* more.

WINTER, LYNETTE (S. Cal.) Former juvenile. Onscreen from the '60s. IN: *The Parent Trap,* more.

WINTER, VINCENT (Australia) Former juvenile (b. 1947). In 1954 he was awarded a special Oscar (miniature) "for his outstanding juvenile performance in *The Little Kidnappers.*" He was, in this, the younger of the two boys. He continued his screen career for a number of years, well into the 1960s, but has more recently been a stage manager in Melbourne. Onscreen from the early '50s. IN: *The Witness, The Dark Avenger, Time-Lock, The Bridal Path, Gorgo, Greyfriars' Bobby, Born to Sing, The Three Lives of Thomasina, The Horse Without a Head,* more.

WINTERS, DAVID (S. Cal.) Actor-dancer. Now a choreographer. Onscreen from 1959.

IN: *The Last Angry Man, West Side Story,* more.

WINTERS, DEBORAH (S. Cal.) Leading lady; former juvenile. Daughter of retired actress Penny Edwards. Onscreen from the '60s. IN: *Me, Natalie; Hail, Hero!; The People Next Door, Kotch,* more. (See Penny Edwards.)

WINTERS, JONATHAN (S. Cal.) Star comedian. Onscreen from 1963. IN: *It's a Mad Mad Mad Mad World, The Loved One, Penelope; The Russians Are Coming, The Russians Are Coming; Eight on the Lam; Oh Dad, Poor Dad, Mama's Hung You in the Closet and I'm Feeling So Sad; Viva Max!,* more.

WINTERS, ROLAND (N.Y.) The movies' last "Charlie Chan" (starred in six between '47 and '49) is in his 70s now (b. 1904), continues to play character roles in many movies, and in this decade parlayed his "Chan" voice into a belated windfall. Starring in a series of radio commercials for Manhattan's House of Chan, he praised the Oriental delicacies to be found at his "cousin's" famous restaurant, ending each spiel with "tell 'em Charlie sent you." Onscreen from 1946. IN: *13 Rue Madeleine, The Chinese Ring* (first of his "Chans," followed by *Docks of New Orleans, The Shanghai Chest, The Mystery of the Golden Eye, The Feathered Serpent, Sky Dragon), Tuna Clipper, Once More My Darling, Malaya; Captain Carey, U.S.A.; To Please a Lady, Raton Pass, Follow the Sun, She's Working Her Way Through College, So Big, Never Steal Anything Small, Blue Hawaii, Follow That Dream, Loving,* more.

WINTERS, SHELLEY (N.Y.) Star. Won Best Supporting Actress Oscar in *The Diary of Anne Frank* and *A Patch of Blue.* Nominated in the same category in *The Poseidon Adventure.* Nominated for Best Actress Oscar in *A Place in the Sun.* She has been married and divorced three times. Her husbands: businessman Mack Meyer (1943–48), actor Vittorio Gassman (1952–54), and actor Anthony Franciosa (1957–60). By Gassman she has a daughter, Victoria, who in 1964 graduated magna cum laude from Radcliffe and lately has been a public school teacher in Boston. Onscreen from 1943. IN: *What a Woman, Sailor's Holiday, Knickerbocker Holiday, Tonight and Every Night* (plus many others in which she had bits or small roles and was billed Shelley Winter), *The Gangster* (in '47; her first as Winters), *A Double Life* (the role of the waitress strangled by Colman made her a star), *Larceny, Cry of the City, The Great Gatsby, Johnny Stool Pigeon, South Sea Sinner, Phone Call from a Stranger, Executive Suite, I Am a Camera, The Night of the Hunter, The Big Knife, Odds Against Tomorrow, Lolita, A*

House Is Not a Home, Harper, Alfie, Enter Laughing, Wild in the Streets, Bloody Mama, What's the Matter with Helen?, Who Slew Auntie Roo?, Blume in Love, That Lucky Touch; Next Stop, Greenwich Village; The Tenant, Something to Hide, more.

WINWOOD, ESTELLE (N.Y.) This fine character actress, in her 90s now (b. 1883), is said to be the oldest active member of the Screen Actors Guild. Onscreen from 1934. IN: *The House of Trent, Quality Street, The Glass Slipper, The Swan, 23 Paces to Baker Street, This Happy Feeling, Darby O'Gill and the Little People, The Misfits, The Cabinet of Dr. Caligari, The Notorious Landlady, Dead Ringer, Games, Camelot, The Producers*, more, including 1976's *Murder by Death*.

WISDOM, NORMAN (Eng.) Star comedian. Onscreen from the '50s. IN: *Trouble in Store, One Good Turn, As Long As They're Happy, Just My Luck, The Square Peg, Follow a Star, A Stitch in Time, The Early Bird, The Night They Raided Minsky's, What's Good for the Goose*, more.

WISEMAN, JOSEPH (N.Y.) Character. Onscreen from 1950. IN: *With These Hands, Detective Story, Viva Zapata!, Les Miserables, Three Brave Men, The Garment Jungle, The Unforgiven, The Happy Thieves, Dr. No, Bye Bye Braverman, The Night They Raided Minsky's, Stiletto, Lawman, The Valachi Papers, The Apprenticeship of Duddy Kravitz*, more.

WITHERS, GOOGIE (Australia) Directed by husband John McCallum, she has lately toured Australia, where they live now in Bayview, and New Zealand in a series of plays: *Plaza Suite, The First Four Hundred Years, Beekman Place*, etc. McCallum also directed her most recent movie, 1970's *The Nickel Queen*. Onscreen from 1934. IN: *Accused, Crime Over London, The Lady Vanishes, Haunted Honeymoon, One of Our Aircraft Is Missing, Jeannie, On Approval, The Silver Fleet, Dead of Night, Miranda* (delightful comedy performance as the seductive mermaid), *Night and the City, Pink String and Sealing Wax, White Corridors*, more. (See John McCallum.)

WITHERS, JANE (S. Cal.) In 1975 the once greatly popular moppet star retired as Comet Cleanser's TV spokeswoman, Josephine the Plumber, after a 12-year stint that made her a very rich woman. She costarred that same year in an ABC "Movie of the Week," *All Together Now*. It was her first acting assignment before the cameras since 1963's *Captain Newman, M.D.* She has since formed her own production company to make TV specials, one about an-

tique cars, the collection of which has been her hobby for many years. Yes, she laughs, she's still something of a tomboy. It was as a screen tomboy that she became America's "Beloved Rascal," a few pictures after *Bright Eyes*. This movie, in which she was so wretched to Shirley Temple, put Jane Withers on the map. Its casting director had asked the inexperienced youngster—she'd had a bit in one prior movie—if she could be mean enough for *Bright Eyes*. "Can I be mean? Can I be *mean?*" the eight-year-old came back. "Sah-ay, Just give me a chance!" After making the most of it she grew up before the world's eyes in the next 13 years—seguing from adorable tomboy *(Chicken Wagon Family)* to vivacious junior miss *(Small Town Deb)* to young leading lady *(Affairs of Geraldine)*. And in one golden year, 1938, was in the Top 10 Box-Office Stars. In 1947 she married millionaire William Moss and retired to Big Springs, Texas, his home town, where she bore him three children—Wendy, William III, and Randy. Her daughter, who is married, lives in Illinois now, but her sons have remained in Texas—her eldest, William, having become a Prestyberian minister and made the actress the grandmother, in '74, of William Paul Moss IV. After divorcing her first husband in 1954, she resumed her career for a while, as a character actress. From 1955 until his death in 1968, she was married to Kenneth Errair. Once a member of the Four Freshmen singing group, he had become a lawyer before he was killed in a plane crash. (With two other women whose husbands died in the same accident, the actress sued the California airport where the tragedy occurred. In 1974 she was awarded a settlement of $200,000.) By Errair, she has a son, Kenneth, in college now, and a daughter, Kendall, in high school. Jane Withers lives in a magnificent house in Hollywood—"built in 1926, just like me"—with her two youngsters and her mother, Mrs. Withers, a widow, who not only maneuvered her only child into a great career, but always managed it, still does this. She mans the telephones, the appointment book, and accompanies her daughter when she flies, for instance, to cities such as Pensacola, Fla., to participate in Cancerama telethons. The actress serves on the boards of the Hollywood Cancer Society and Chamber of Commerce. Also, a devoutly religious woman, a lifelong nonsmoking teetotaler who always says grace before meals, even silently before a business lunch at the Brown Derby, she is a trustee of Hollywood's Church of Religious Science. Her personal faith received its severest test in 1953 when her first marriage was breaking up and she, blaming herself for its failure, became desperately ill. "I began to suffer from rheumatoid arthritis," she relates. "I wound up in the hospital with such paralysis that it took five nurses just to turn me over. Then one day, I said to myself, 'You nincompoop! How dare you do this to yourself. You can't be a cripple. You don't have time. You're always telling your children that if you change your attitude you can change your life—why don't you practice what you preach?'!" She prayed and resolved to start a new life, having done all she could to save her marriage. She walked out of the hospital three months later under her own power. And she still attributes her miraculous recovery as much to her change in attitude and spiritual strength as to medical treatment. Before hitting the half-century mark on April 12, 1976, a healthy and happy Jane Withers said, "I always said I'd come back to my career full-time at 50, after my kids were grown. I'm right on schedule." Onscreen from 1933. IN: *Handle With Care, Ginger, Paddy O'Day, This Is the Life, Gentle Julia, Pepper, Little Miss Nobody, Wild and Wooly, The Holy Terror, Angel's Holiday, 45 Fathers, Checkers, Rascals, Keep Smiling, Pack Up Your Troubles, High School, Shooting High, Youth Will Be Served, Golden Hoofs, Her First Beau, Johnny Doughboy, The North Star, My Best Gal, Dangerous Partners,* more, including, as a character actress, *Giant* and *The Right Approach.*

WITNEY, MICHAEL (S. Cal.) Leading man. Married to Twiggy. Onscreen from the '60s. IN: *The Way West, Darling Lili, Head On, "W"* (costarred with Twiggy), more.

WITT, KATHY (S. Cal.) Support. Onscreen in the '70s. IN: *Freebie and the Bean,* more.

WIXTED, MICHAEL-JAMES (S. Cal.) Former juvenile (b. 1961). Onscreen in the '70s. IN: *The Cockeyed Cowboys of Calico County, Lost Flight, Lost in the Stars,* more.

WOLDERS, ROBERT (S. Cal.) Leading man. Husband of Merle Oberon. Onscreen from the '60s. IN: *El Greco, Von Ryan's Express, Juliet of the Spirits, Beau Geste, Tobruk, Interval,* more. (See Merle Oberon.)

WOLF, LAWRENCE (N.Y.) Character. Onscreen from the '60s. IN: *Chafed Elbows, No More Excuses, Deadhead Miles, Is There Sex After Death?, Putney Swope, Pound,* more.

WOLFE, DAVID (S. Cal.) Support; inactive in movies now. Onscreen from the '40s. IN: *The Undercover Man, The House of Strangers, Kansas Raiders, Appointment With Death, Salt of the Earth,* more.

WOLFE, IAN (S. Cal.) In 1935, already balding, this actor played Captain Bligh's cruel storekeeper and stool pigeon, Maggs, in *Mutiny on the Bounty,* and his reputation was made. Today, 200 movies and 125 TV shows later, as he enters his 80s (b. 1896), he remains one of Hollywood's busiest character actors. *Home Bodies* and Mike Nichols' *The Fortune* (as the dithery old Justice of the Peace) are among his recent films. Among earlier ones were the many in which the Illinois-born actor portrayed Englishmen ("I believe I have played more British parts than any other American actor," he says): *The Barretts of Wimpole Street, Random Harvest, Clive of India, Witness for the Prosecution,* etc. Besides the countless others in which he was a piercing-gazed, deep-dyed meanie, he has also been steadily employed as a movie priest or minister. Offscreen, married for over 50 years to Australian-born Elizabeth Schroder, and the father of two daughters, the actor is a scholar of Comparative Religions and Philosophies ("My favorites are Oriental ones though I was raised a Baptist!") and a devotee of the outdoors. "I have been and still am a trail-climbing addict," he reports. "I've climbed quite a few peaks alone—some by moonlight—including, in 1954, Mt. Whitney. I was utterly alone up there for some 36 hours due to a storm. I had fun singing 'The Lord's Prayer' and 'The Star Spangled Banner,' and reciting mantras toward global unity. In a lighter vein, I also stood on my head on the summit, 14,496 feet, thus establishing my personal 'Damphool Club'!" Onscreen from 1934. IN: *The Fountain, The Prince and the Pauper, The Emperor's Candlesticks, Conquest, Marie Antoinette, On Borrowed Time, Hudson's Bay, Holy Matrimony, The Song of Bernadette, The Moon Is Down, The Invisible Man's Revenge, Love Letters, Tomorrow Is Forever, Bedlam, The Searching Wind, Mr. Blandings Builds His Dream House, Johnny Belinda, The Magnificent Yankee, Julius Caesar, The Actress, Seven Brides for Seven Brothers, The Court-Martial of Billy Mitchell, Pollyanna, The Wonderful World of the Brothers Grimm, One Man's Way, Games, The Terminal Man, Mr. Sycamore,* more.

WOLFE, JOEL (N.Y.) Character. Onscreen in the '70s. IN: *On a Clear Day You Can See Forever, End of the Road, The Night They Raided Minsky's,* more.

WOLFINGTON, IGGIE (S. Cal.) Character actor. Onscreen from the '50s. IN: *Edge of the City, Penelope,* more.

WOLFMAN, JACK (S. Cal.) Radio personality. Real name: Bob Smith. Onscreen in the '70s. IN: *The Seven Minutes, American Graffiti,* more.

WONG, ARTHUR (S. Cal.) Character. On-screen from the '60s. IN: *One Spy Too Many*, more.

WONG, CHRIS (S. Cal.) Juvenile actor. On-screen in the '70s. IN: *The Grasshopper*, more.

WONG, JADINE (S. Cal.) Leading lady. On-screen from 1959. IN: *I Drink Your Blood*, more.

WONG, LINDA (S. Cal.) Leading lady. On-screen from 1959. IN: *Five Gates to Hell, The Horizontal Lieutenant, Paradise Hawaiian Style*, more.

WOOD, DAVID (Eng.) Support. Onscreen from 1968. IN: *If*, more.

WOOD, EUGENE (S. Cal.) Character. On-screen in the '70s. IN: *The Way We Live Now*, more.

WOOD, FORREST (S. Cal.) Character. On-screen from the '60s. IN: *Number One, The Hawaiians*, more.

WOOD, G. (Ga.) Character. He lives in Macon, Ga., and commutes to his movie assignments. Onscreen in the '70s. IN: *M*A*S*H, Brewster McCloud, Harold and Maude, Bank Shot*, more.

WOOD, GENE (S. Cal.) Character. Onscreen in the '70s. IN: *Dirtymouth*, more.

WOOD, GLORIA (S. Cal.) Singer-actress. On-screen from the '50s. IN: *Gaby*, more.

WOOD, HARRY (S. Cal.) Character. Onscreen in the '70s. IN: *Darker Than Amber*, more.

WOOD, JANE (Eng.) Character. Onscreen in the '70s. IN: *The Ragman's Daughter*, more.

WOOD, JANET (S. Cal.) Support. Onscreen in the '70s. IN: *Angels Hard As They Come*, more.

WOOD, JOHN (Eng.) Character. Onscreen from the '30s. IN: *The Last Days of Pompeii, Housemaster, Which Way to the Front?, Nicholas and Alexandra*, more.

WOOD, JUDITH (S. Cal.) Offscreen since the early '30s, she is a divorcee in her 60s and a costume designer in Los Angeles. She also made a number of movies earlier under the name Helen Johnson: *It Pays to Advertise, Sin Takes a Holiday, Women Love Once*, etc. On-screen from 1930. IN: *The Road to Reno, Girls About Town, Advice to the Lovelorn, Looking for Trouble, The Crime Doctor*, more.

WOOD, LANA (S. Cal.) Leading lady. Sister of Natalie Wood. Onscreen from 1956. IN: *The Silver Chalice, The Searchers, Five Finger Exercise, The Girls on the Beach, For Singles Only, A Dandy in Aspic, Diamonds Are Forever*, more.

WOOD, LEE (S. Cal.) Character. Onscreen in the '70s. IN: *The Castaway Cowboy*, more.

WOOD, LYNN (S. Cal.) Support. Onscreen from the '60s. IN: *Jumbo*, more.

WOOD, MARY LAURA (Eng.) Support; lately inactive in movies. Onscreen from the '50s. IN: *Valley of the Eagles, Raising a Riot, Scent of Mystery*, more.

WOOD, MICHAEL (S. Cal.) Support. On-screen from the '60s. IN: *The Young Animals, Born Wild*, more.

WOOD, MONTGOMERY (It.) This star of Ital-ian-made Westerns, genuinely Italian—unlike rival stars in the same genre, like Terence Hill, many of whom are German, began his career under his real name, Guiliano Giami. Switching to "Montgomery Wood," he became an over-night sensation. In time his billing read: Mont-gomery Wood (Guiliano Giami). Then: Guiliano Giami (Montgomery Wood). Now, having ditched "Montgomery Wood," he's back to Guiliano Giami. Onscreen from the '60s. IN: *A Pistol for Ringo, Adios Gringo*, more.

WOOD, NATALIE (S. Cal.) Star. Nominated for Best Supporting Actress Oscar in *Rebel Without a Cause*. Nominated for Best Actress Oscar in *Splendor in the Grass* and *Love With the Proper Stranger*. Onscreen from 1943. IN: *Happy Land* (age 5; a bit as a little girl who dropped an ice cream cone; before she became a professional—the movie was filmed on loca-tion in her home town near San Francisco), *To-morrow Is Forever* (in '46, her acting debut, ex-pert as a child with a German accent; *Happy Land* director Irving Pichel, recalling her, had her brought to Hollywood for the role), *Miracle on 34th Street, The Ghost and Mrs. Muir, Chicken Every Sunday, Father Was a Fullback, The Green Promise, Our Very Own, No Sad Songs for Me, Never a Dull Moment, Dear Brat, The Blue Veil, Just for You, The Star, One De-sire, Cry in the Night, The Searchers, The Girl He Left Behind, Bombers B-52, Marjorie Morn-ingstar, Kings Go Forth, All the Fine Young Cannibals, West Side Story, Gypsy, Sex and the Single Girl, The Great Race, Inside Daisy Clo-ver, This Property Is Condemned, Bob & Carol & Ted & Alice, Peeper*, more.

WOOD, PEGGY (Conn.) Character. Nomi-nated for Best Supporting Actress Oscar in *The*

Sound of Music. Retired now in her 80s (b. 1892) and living in Stamford, she has been a star in all media—TV (the title role in *Mama* from 1949 to 1957), radio, Broadway musicals (*Maytime,* etc.) and dramas (*The Merchant of Venice, Candida,* many more), and movies. In 1974, as a consequence of her stage work, this actress who founded the American College Theatre Festival received the American Theatre Association's "Distinguished Service to the Theatre" citation. She has been married since 1946 to retired insurance executive William Walling. She has a son, David, by her first husband, the late author John Van Alstyn Weaver (b. 1938), and several grandchildren. Onscreen from 1919. IN: *Almost a Husband* (opposite Will Rogers); she did not return to the screen until 1929 when she costarred in the part-talkie *Wonder of Women* (*Photoplay* said: "Strong, emotional drama of a misunderstood genius, a dutiful wife and the 'other woman,' played superlatively by Lewis Stone, Peggy Wood and Leila Hyams"), *Handy Andy, The Right to Live, Jalna, A Star Is Born, Call It a Day, The Housekeeper's Daughter, The Bride Wore Boots, Magnificent Doll, Dream Girl, The Story of Ruth,* more.

WOOD, SUSAN (Eng.) Support. Onscreen in the '70s. IN: *Waterloo,* more.

WOOD, VIRGINIA (S. Cal.) Support. Onscreen from the '60s. IN: *Lady in Cement,* more.

WOODBURN, ERIC (Eng.) Character. Onscreen from the '50s. IN: *The Little Kidnappers, The Battle of the Sexes, Trial and Error, Kidnapped,* more.

WOODBURY, JOAN (S. Cal.) Producing and directing for the stage always interested this volatile leading lady more than moviemaking. So in '49, after 70 pictures in 15 years, she closed out her screen career. In the years since she has been persuaded to play supporting roles in just two—*The Ten Commandments* ('56) and *The Time Travelers* ('64). For six years she was producer-stage director of all grand and light operas for the Redlands (Calif.) Bowl. She has since founded, with actor-husband Raymond Mitchell, Palm Springs' Valley Players Guild Theater. "During 30 weeks each year, October through May," she says, "we do six productions. As production manager I oversee and work on all sets and costumes, and handle publicity. Occasionally I direct, but rarely act—perhaps once a year." In addition, the former movie actress, now in her early 60s (b. 1915), writes feature articles for magazines—*Palm Springs Life, Mexican World*—and newspapers, principally Riverside County's *Press-Enterprise.* Each summer she and her husband re-

side at Chapala Lake in Jalisco, Mexico, where they plan eventually to retire. By former husband, Henry Wilcoxon, the actor, who continues to be quite active onscreen, she has three grown children. Of them, she says, "My daughter Wendy is a nurse in San Diego. Heather has caused no end of talk by having sailed, with her husband, from Honolulu to New Zealand in a 30-foot sloop without motor. Hopefully, a book will come out of it. And Cecilia [named for the wife of late director Cecil B. DeMille, with whom Henry Wilcoxon was associated for decades] runs her own boutique in Sausalito." Onscreen from 1935. IN: *The Eagle's Brood, Anthony Adverse, Song of the Gringo, There Goes My Girl, Forty Naughty Girls, Charlie Chan on Broadway, Algiers, Crashing Hollywood, Mystery of the White Room, King of the Zombies, Paper Bullets, Gangs Incorporated, Confessions of Boston Blackie, Dr. Broadway, The Hard Way, The Whistler; Brenda Starr, Reporter* (serial; title role); *The Arnelo Affair, Boston Blackie's Chinese Venture,* more.

WOODELL, BARBARA (S. Cal.) Character; lately inactive in movies. Onscreen from the '40s. IN: *Framed, Force of Evil, I Shot Jesse James, The Baron of Arizona, The Star,* more.

WOODELL, PAT (S. Cal.) Leading lady. First an ingenue in TV's *Petticoat Junction.* Onscreen in the '70s. IN: *The Big Doll House,* more.

WOODLEY, CHRIS (S. Cal.) Supporting actress. Onscreen in the '70s. IN: *Pretty Maids All in a Row, The Velvet Vampire,* more.

WOODS, AUBREY (Eng.) Character actor. Onscreen from 1947. IN: *Nicholas Nickleby, The Detective, School for Scoundrels, The Abominable Dr. Phibes, Willie Wonka and the Chocolate Factory, Up Pompeii,* more.

WOODS, DONALD (S. Cal.) During rehearsals for a play on the West Coast recently, this still-handsome-in-his-60s (b. 1909) actor said, "I try to do at least one play per year whatever else I'm doing—such as selling $300,000 worth of real estate in Palm Springs ten days before starting this show." Most of the properties he handles—all residential—are in and around Palm Springs, his home for more than 15 years. Most of the roles he has played in his 80-picture career, which began when he was 25, have been those of a "good guy" and solid citizen. Or, you might say, a reflection of the offscreen Donald Woods. He has been married since '33 to his college sweetheart, the former Josephine (Jo) Van der Horck, and is the father of two. Daughter, Linda, married to a Texas business man, lives in Dallas. Son, Conrad, is a Palm Springs tennis pro and an accomplished oil painter of the modern school. He is not the only tennis player in the family. The actor, an original member of Charles Farrell's Racquet Club, still plays there—doubles now—every day when he is home. Besides the stage work that commands most of his professional attention now—he hasn't worked in a picture since 1969's *True Grit*—he answers Hollywood's call regularly to guest-star in such TV shows as *Police Story*. The actor finds he is still most often cast, just as in so many movies, as a doctor. Onscreen from 1934. IN: *As the Earth Turns, Charlie Chan's Courage, The Case of the Curious Bride, The Florentine Dagger, A Tale of Two Cities, The Story of Louis Pasteur, Anthony Adverse, A Son Comes Home, The Black Doll, I Am the Law, Mexican Spitfire, Mexican Spitfire Out West, I Was a Prisoner on Devil's Island, The Gay Sisters, Watch on the Rhine, The Bridge of San Luis Rey, Roughly Speaking, Voice of the Whistler, Night and Day, Scene of the Crime, Mr. Music, The Beast from 20,000 Fathoms, Kissin' Cousins, The Satan Bug, Tammy and the Millionaire,* more.

WOODS, GRANT (S. Cal.) Character. Onscreen from the '60s. IN: *Warning Shot, Alvarez Kelly, The Horizontal Lieutenant,* more.

WOODS, JAMES (S. Cal.) Leading man. Onscreen from 1971. IN: *Home Free, The Gambler,* more.

WOODS, SUSAN (S. Cal.) Support; lately inactive in movies. Onscreen from the '60s. IN: *Cape Fear, Two for the Seesaw, Irma La Douce,* more.

WOODSON, WILLIAM (S. Cal.) Support. Onscreen from the '60s. IN: *The One and Only Genuine Original Family Band, Escape From the Planet of the Apes,* more.

WOODTHORPE, PETER (Eng.) Support; primarily a stage actor. Onscreen from the '60s. IN: *The Evil of Frankenstein,* more.

WOODVILLE, KATE/a.k.a. CATHERINE WOODVILLE (S. Cal.) Leading lady. Onscreen from the '60s. IN: *Young and Willing, Underworld Informers,* more.

WOODVINE, JOHN (Eng.) Support. Onscreen from 1964. IN: *Darling, The Walking Stick, The Devils,* more.

WOODWARD, EDWARD (Eng.) Leading man. Onscreen from the '50s. IN: *Where There's a Will, The File of the Golden Goose, Murders in the Rue Morgue, Julius Caesar, Young Winston, Sitting Target, Hunted,* more.

WOODWARD, JOANNE (Conn.) Star. Won Best Actress Oscar in *The Three Faces of Eve.* Nominated in the same category in *Rachel Rachel* and *Summer Wishes, Winter Dreams.* Married to Paul Newman, she lives in Westport. Onscreen from 1955. IN: *Count Three and Pray, A Kiss Before Dying, No Down Payment; The Long, Hot Summer* (first of many opposite Paul Newman); *Rally Round the Flag Boys!, The Sound and the Fury, The Fugitive Kind, From the Terrace, The Stripper, A Fine Madness, A Big Hand for the Little Lady, Winning, The Effect of Gamma Rays on Man-in-the-Moon Marigolds, The Drowning Pool,* more.

WOODWARD, MORGAN (S. Cal.) Character. Onscreen from the '60s. IN: *Cool Hand Luke, Firecreek, Death of a Gunfighter, The Wild Country, The Midnight Man, Ride in a Pink Car, The Killing of a Chinese Bookie,* more.

WOODWORTH, MARJORIE (S. Cal.) Hal Roach's lovely blonde discovery of the early '40s, hailed by *Life* magazine and others as a "new" Harlow, has long been married and retired, and still lives in Los Angeles. Onscreen from 1941. IN: *Road Show, Broadway Limited, The Devil With Hitler, Prairie Chickens; A Wave, a Wac and a Marine; Salty O'Rourke,* more.

WOOLAND, NORMAN (Eng.) Character. Onscreen from 1948. IN: *Escape, Hamlet, Madeleine, Quo Vadis, Ivanhoe, Romeo and Juliet, The Guns of Navarone, Barabbas, The Fall of the Roman Empire, Walk in the Shadow,* more.

WOOLEY, SHEB (S. Cal.) Character. Onscreen from 1950. IN: *Rocky Mountain, Inside the Walls of Folsom Prison, High Noon, Bugles in the Afternoon, The Boy From Oklahoma, Giant, Trooper Hook, Ride a Violent Mile, Terror in a Texas Town,* more.

WOOLF, HENRY (Eng.) Support. Onscreen from the '60s. IN: *Marat/Sade, Figures in a Landscape,* more.

WOOLF, LESLIE (N.Y.) Character actor. Onscreen from the '50s. IN: *The Trouble With Harry, That Kind of Woman, The Night They Raided Minsky's,* more.

WOOLEY, JAMES (Eng.) Support. Onscreen in the '70s. IN: *S*P*Y*S,* more.

WOOLMAN, CLAUDE (S. Cal.) Support. Onscreen from 1969. IN: *Heaven with a Gun, Three Faces of Love,* more.

WORDEN, HANK (S. Cal.) Character. Onscreen from the early '40s. IN: *Wild Horse*

Stampede (and other Bob Baker Westerns, as his sidekick), *The Sainted Sisters, Red River, Yellow Sky, Three Godfathers, Wagonmaster, The Indian Fighter, The Searchers, Good Times, Big Jake,* more.

WORDES, SMITTY (S. Cal.) Character. Onscreen from the '60s. IN: *The One and Only Genuine Orginal Family Band,* more.

WORDS, SIL (S. Cal.) Black support. Onscreen in the '70s. IN: *A Woman Under the Influence,* more.

WORDSWORTH, RICHARD (Eng.) Character. Onscreen from the '50s. IN: *Time Without Pity, The Camp on Blood Island, The Man Who Knew Too Much, The Quartermass Experiment, Song of Norway* (as "Hans Christian Andersen"), more.

WORLEY, JOANNE (S. Cal.) Comedienne-singer-actress. Onscreen from 1961. IN: *Moon Pilot,* more.

WORTH, BRIAN (Eng.) Character; former leading man. Onscreen from 1940: IN: *Arsenal Stadium Mystery, The Lion Has Wings, Pastor Hall, Last Holiday, A Christmas Carol, It Started in Paradise, An Inspector Calls, The Battle of River Plate, Sink the Bismarck!,* more.

WORTH, IRENE (Eng.) Character lead, from America, who has long lived and worked in England. Onscreen from 1949. IN: *One Night With You, Orders to Kill, The Scapegoat, King Lear, Nicholas and Alexandra, Thermidor* (voice only), more.

WRAY, FAY (S. Cal.) Though turning 70 on September 10, 1977, she still looks enormously like the girl everyone remembers screaming and thrashing in the hairy clutches of King Kong. (He was, incidentally, except in long shots of an actor in an ape suit, a rubbery studio-made model just 18 inches high, camera trickery producing that awesome 50-foot illusion.) Today, Fay Wray lives in a spacious house in Brentwood and has been the wife (since '71) of neurosurgeon Dr. Sanford Rothenberg. She was first married (1928–39) to screenwriter John Monk Saunders, by whom she has a daughter, Susan. Then, from '42 until his death in '55, she was the wife of Robert Riskin, who wrote such movies as *Mr. Deeds Goes to Town* and *Lost Horizon.* By him, she is the mother of Vicki and Robert Jr. Daughter Vicki, a young actress in Hollywood, is married to Alan Sachs, a Metromedia vice president. Also acting, in New York, is daughter Susan Riskin (she uses her stepfather's name). Besides acting Off Broadway, Susan did a series of TV commercials showing her climbing the Empire State Building with—King Kong. "The difference," she told her mother, "is that I'm not blonde, as you are." To which her mother replied, "I wasn't blonde, either, when I played the role." (Her naturally brown hair was capped by a blonde wig.) Fay Wray starred in more than 90 films before "retiring" after 1942's *Not a Ladies' Man,* and in the '50s played character roles (mothers usually) in another 11. But she is indelibly associated with *King Kong.* Good natured about it, she laughs, "When I'm in New York, I look at the Empire State Building and feel as though it belongs to me . . . or is it vice versa?" Over the years she has found film buffs insatiably curious about this movie's special effects, and particularly interested in knowing how the scenes of her in the animal's paw were done. She explains: "The hand and arm in which my close-up scenes were made was about eight feet in length. Inside the furry arm, there was a steel bar and the whole contraption (with me in the hand) could be raised or lowered like a crane. The fingers would be pressed around my waist while I was in a standing position. I would then be raised about ten feet into the air to be in line with an elevated camera. As I kicked and squirmed and struggled in the ape's hand, his fingers would gradually loosen and begin to open. My fear was real as I grabbed onto his wrist, his thumb, whatever I could, to keep from slipping out of that paw! When I could sense that the moment of minimum safety had arrived, I would call imploringly to the director and ask to be lowered to the floor of the stage. Happily, this was never denied for a second too long!" Onscreen from 1928. IN: *The Legion of the Condemned, The Wedding March, The Four Feathers, Behind the Makeup, The Sea God, The Finger Points, Dirigible, Captain Thunder, Doctor X, The Mystery of the Wax Museum, Ann Carver's Profession, One Sunday Afternoon, The Bowery, Madame Spy, The Countess of Monte Cristo, Viva Villa!, The Affairs of Cellini, The Richest Girl in the World, Alias Bulldog Drummond, Murder in Greenwich Village, Adam Had Four Sons,* more; then in the '50s as a character actress: *Small Town Girl, Treasure of the Golden Condor, The Cobweb, Queen Bee, Hell on Frisco Bay, Tammy and the Bachelor,* more, including 1958's *Summer Love,* her most recent to date. (See Julie Haydon.)

WRIGHT, BEN (S. Cal.) Character. Onscreen from the '50s. IN: *A Man Called Peter, Prince of Players, The Power and the Prize, On the Threshold of Space, Kiss Them for Me, Journey to the Center of the Earth, Judgment at Nuremberg, A Gathering of Eagles, The Sound of Mu-*

sic, *The Fortune Cookie, Raid on Rommel,* more.

WRIGHT, BOB (N.Y.) Character actor-announcer. Onscreen in 1960 in *Tall Story.*

WRIGHT, COBINA, JR. (S. Cal.) 20th Century-Fox's glamorous blonde debutante-actress of the '40s was tall and svelte. This year's Cobina Wright Jr. is tall and—not thin. She jokes about her weight but declines to give a figure. A guess would be 180 lbs. In her 50s now (b. 1921), still blonde and wearing her hair as she always did, shoulder-length and loose, she lives high on a hill in a small community (Santa Ynez Oaks) about 150 miles north of Hollywood. She is the mother of four children of whom she is enormously proud, and the grandmother of two on whom she dotes shamelessly. Her strappingly handsome grown sons, all in their late 20s or early 30s, live nearby. They are Oliver Joseph, William Wright, and Palmer Beaudette Jr. Her college-age daughter, Cobina III (but called Cee Cee), a gorgeous blonde look-alike for the actress, still lived at home as this was written. (She also reared a stepdaughter, Suzanne, who is as close to her as her own children; Suzanne is the mother of a beautiful toddler named Melissa.) Cobina's life after her screen career—she quit in 1943—contained considerable drama. In '41 she married a handsome young Army corporal, Palmer Beaudette, an heir to a fortune, whom her mother loathed. Her mother, Cobina Wright, was the famous society columnist, aggressive and ambitious, who had been singlehandedly responsible for her daughter's fame in society, as a singer in fashionable cafes, and in Hollywood. But the marriage—not an altogether happy one—lasted until Beaudette's death of a heart attack in '68. They lived then in a spacious ranch house in fashionable Carmel Valley. She learned after her husband died that the house was all that she possessed. Beaudette's share of the estate inherited from his father reverted, as per his father's will, to his brothers and sisters. Selling the big house, Cobina moved to the smaller one in which she lives now—on an inheritance from her mother and the profits from the sale of her mother's house in Beverly Hills. The actress devotes herself now, principally, to working as a volunteer for a program aiding alcoholics, Beacon House. She is also on the board of the National Council on Alcoholism. "I'm an arrested alcoholic," she says without dramatics. "My husband was an alcoholic, but he was sober for the last fifteen years of his life. When he stopped, I started." She stopped, finally, she says, with the help of the program for which she now works, which "has given me every reason I have for living." This program, she adds, has taught her "to take each day as it comes. You cannot afford self-pity or resentment." When she talks about her long-ago career—and she can be persuaded to with ease—it is with affection. She says it is "not just the singing and the acting that I miss—it's the people. I loved all the people I worked with." Her husband and her mother, lifelong enemies, are buried in the same plot—to the admitted shock of the actress' friends. "But I told them," she says, "that there was a space for me in the middle. That's where I've always been—in the middle . . . It's been the story of my life." Onscreen from 1941. IN: *Murder Among Friends, Moon Over Miami, Accent on Love, Charlie Chan in Rio, Week-End in Havana, Small Town Deb, Right to the Heart, Footlight Serenade, Something to Shout About,* more.

WRIGHT, HEATHER (Eng.) Leading lady. Onscreen in the '70s. IN: *The Belstone Fox,* more.

WRIGHT, JENNY LEE (Eng.) Support. Onscreen in the '70s. IN: *Husbands, Madhouse,* more.

WRIGHT, JOHN (S. Cal.) Support. Son of singer Kitty Wells, "Queen of Country Music." Onscreen from the '60s. IN: *McHale's Navy,* more.

WRIGHT, MAGGIE (Eng.) Support. Onscreen in the '70s. IN: *My Lover, My Son; One More Time,* more.

WRIGHT, PATRICK (PAT) (S. Cal.) Support. Onscreen from the '60s. IN: *Good Morning and Goodbye!, Project X, Caged Heat,* more.

WRIGHT, STEPHEN (N.Y.) Support. Onscreen from 1968. IN: *The Detective, The Pursuit of Happiness,* more.

WRIGHT, TERESA (N.Y.) Costar. Nominated for Best Supporting Actress Oscar in *The Little Foxes,* her first movie. The following year, 1942, she set an Academy Award record never equaled before or since: she was nominated in two categories. She won the Best Supporting Actress Oscar in *Mrs. Miniver,* but, also nominated for Best Actress Oscar in *The Pride of the Yankees,* she lost to her onscreen mother-in-law, Greer Garson, in *Mrs. Miniver.* After 1958's *The Restless Years,* the actress gave up her long Hollywood career and returned to the stage to star in *The Dark at the Top of the Stairs.* Divorced from novelist-screenwriter Niven Busch in '52, after 10 years of marriage, she is the mother of two children, Mary Kelly and Niven Terrence. Both are married now, and her son, who did graduate work in rhetoric at Berkeley, is launched on a career as a novelist. Married to playwright Robert *(Tea and Sympathy)* Anderson in '59, the actress worked only rarely in the following decade. Most notably, she starred on TV in two memorable dramas: *The Margaret Bourke-White Story* and, as Annie Sullivan, in *The Miracle Worker*, which won her an Emmy nomination. She finally returned to movies in '69, working in two—*Hail, Hero!* and *The Happy Ending* with Jean Simmons, who had played her daughter in 1953's *The Actress*. She has not acted onscreen since, though in '72 she costarred with Arthur Kennedy in the TV-movie *Crawlspace*. For much of her married life with Robert Anderson, when not traveling abroad (which they often did, to openings of his plays), she lived with him in Bridgewater, Conn., in a beautiful 1825 New England farmhouse. They also maintained a Park Avenue apartment where they spent several days each week. In her late 50s now (b. 1918) and separated from the playwright—as this is written—she lives alone in an East Side apartment and has resumed her career on the New York stage. In '75 she costarred with George C. Scott in *Death of a Salesman* and, on Broadway, with Geraldine Fitzgerald in *Ah, Wilderness!* Onscreen she smiled, but there always was something infinitely wistful and touching about the actress. And, if a relatively recent encounter on a Madison Avenue bus might be construed as indicative, life does sometimes imitate art. Onscreen from 1941. IN: *Shadow of a Doubt, Casanova Brown, The Best Years of Our Lives, Pursued, The Imperfect Lady, The Trouble With Women, Enchantment, The Capture, The Men, California Conquest, Something to Live For, The Steel Trap, Count the Hours, Track of the Cat, The Search for Bridey Murphy, Escapade in Japan*, more.

WRIGHT, TONY (Eng.) Leading man. Onscreen from the '50s. IN: *Broth of a Boy, In the Wake of a Stranger, Portrait of a Sinner, Jumping for Joy, Jacqueline, Tiger in the Smoke, Journey to Nowhere, The Liquidator*, more.

WRIGLEY, BEN (S. Cal.) Character. Onscreen in the '70s. IN: *Bedknobs and Broomsticks*, more.

WRIXON, MARIS (S. Cal.) She remains slender and blonde in her early 60s, has been long and happily married to executive producer Rudi Fehr, has not acted on the screen since 1951's *As You Were*, and in '72 acquired a son-in-law —when daughter Christine Yvonne married Dirk Toland Swanson. Onscreen from 1938. IN: *Broadway Musketeers, Jeepers Creepers, British Intelligence, The Ape, Flight Angels, The Man Who Talked Too Much, The Case of the Black Parrot, Million Dollar Baby, Bullets for O'Hara, Footsteps in the Dark, Sons of the* Pioneers, Spy Ship, The Master Key (serial), The Glass Alibi, Highway 13, more.

WYATT, JANE (S. Cal.) Character; former leading lady. Onscreen from 1934. IN: *One More River, Great Expectations, Lost Horizon, Girl From God's Country, Weekend for Three, Army Surgeon, The Navy Comes Through, None But the Lonely Heart, The Bachelor's Daughters, Boomerang, Gentleman's Agreement, Pitfall, No Minor Vices, Task Force, The Man Who Cheated Himself, Our Very Own, Criminal Lawyer, Never Too Late*, more.

WYENN, THAN (S. Cal.) Character actor. Onscreen from 1955. IN: *Good Morning, Miss Dove; Pete Kelly's Blues, Beginning of the End, The Invisible Boy, Imitation of Life, The Boy and the Pirates*, more.

WYETH, SANDY BROWN (N.Y.) Supporting actress. Onscreen from the '60s. IN: *The Stalking Moon, Easy Rider, Johnny Got His Gun*, more.

WYETH, KATYA (Eng.) Support. Onscreen in the '70s. IN: *A Clockwork Orange, Straight On Till Morning*, more.

WYLER, GRETCHEN (N.Y.) Broadway star of musicals. Onscreen in 1968 in *The Devil's Brigade.*

WYLER, RICHARD (S. Cal.) (See Richard Stapler.)

WYLER, SUSAN (N.Y.) Support. Onscreen from the '60s. IN: *Bye Bye Braverman*, more.

WYLIE, FRANK (Eng.) Support. Onscreen in the '70s. IN: *Macbeth, Three Sisters*, more.

WYLLIE, MEG (S. Cal.) Character. Onscreen in the '70s. IN: *Our Time*, more.

WYMAN, JANE (S. Cal.) Star. Won Best Actress Oscar in *Johnny Belinda*. Nominated in the same category in *The Yearling, The Blue Veil*, and *Magnificent Obsession*. Still a highly attractive woman, in her 60s (b. 1914), and still sporting the hairdo with bangs that became her trademark after 1949's *A Kiss in the Dark*, she lives alone in a posh apartment west of Beverly Hills. The only acting she has done since the '68 movie *How to Commit Marriage* has been, infrequently, on television. In '71 and '72 she starred in pilots (two) for a projected series titled *Amanda Fallon*, in which she played a pediatrician; the pilots were aired but the series did not sell. And in '74 she was a guest star in a single episode of *Owen Marshall, Counsellor at Law*. Now, she says, she has little interest in acting, adding: "My daughter's taken over for me." Daughter Maureen Reagan, a singer-actress, has guested in many TV shows (*The Partridge Family, The Girl with Something Extra*, etc.), and has starred on the road in legitimate productions of *Mame* and *Any Wednesday*. Instead of acting, Jane Wyman has devoted herself totally in recent years to the Arthritis Foundation—an organization she came to appreciate when a close friend was crippled by the disease —and was for a long while national chairman of the Foundation. She has also become a professional painter, her work enjoying a brisk sale at California galleries. Single now, she has been married and divorced four times. Her husbands were business man Myron Futterman (1937–38), Ronald Reagan (1940–48), and musician Fred Karger, to whom she was married twice (1952–54 and 1961–65). One subject she will not discuss is Ronald Reagan, who, after their marriage, became California Governor and Presidential candidate. The statement she made to reporter Rex Reed in 1968 still stands: "It's not because I'm bitter or because I disagree with him politically. I've always been a registered Republican. But it's bad taste to talk about ex-husbands or ex-wives, that's all. Also, I don't know a damn thing about politics." Onscreen from 1935. IN: *King of Burlesque, My Man Godfrey, Smart Blonde, The Singing Marine, Mr. Dodds Takes the Air, Wide Open Faces, The Crowd Roars, Brother Rat* (opposite Ronald Reagan), *Torchy Plays with Dynamite, Tugboat Annie Sails Again, Bad Men of Missouri, Princess O'Rourke, The Doughgirls, The Lost Weekend* (the role taking her out of the light leading-lady category and into that of star), *Magic Town, Cheyenne, The Lady Takes a Sailor, Stage Fright, The Glass Menagerie, Three Guys Named Mike, Here Comes the Groom, The Story of Will Rogers, So Big, All That Heaven Allows, Miracle in the Rain, Holiday for Lovers, Pollyanna, Bon Voyage!*, more.

WYMORE, PATRICE (Jamaica) At 24 this Warner Bros. song-dance star became the third and last Mrs. Errol Flynn, and, three years later, the mother of his youngest daughter, Arnella Roma (b. 1953), who is now a model in London. She and the star were separated before his death in 1959, his drug-addiction and drinking being the major contributing factors. In his recent book, *Bring on the Empty Horses*, actor David Niven wrote this of his last meeting with Flynn: "He brought me up to date about all his wives—he had just separated from Patrice Wymore, and he talked wistfully of how hard she had tried to help him and how impossible he must have been to live with." After Flynn's death, the actress, then living in Hollywood, resumed her career for a while—starring in a club act at Las Vegas' Desert Inn and, in

1966, in the soap opera *Never Too Young*. Today, still most attractive as she enters her 50s (b. 1926), and not remarried, Patrice Wymore lives in Jamaica in "Castle Comfort," the mansion built by Flynn and bequeathed to her, together with the adjoining 2,000-acre plantation. An expert business woman, she personally operates this cattle ranch and cocoanut plantation. She also owns and operates a boutique, Patrice Wymore Flynn Unlimited, in the swank Frenchman's Cove resort hotel, in addition to a wicker-furniture-manufacturing plant. Onscreen from 1950. IN: *Tea for Two, Rocky Mountain* (opposite Flynn), *I'll See You in My Dreams, The Big Trees, She's Working Her Way Through College, Man Behind the Gun, She's Back on Broadway, Ocean's Eleven*, more, including 1966's *Chamber of Horrors*, her last.

WYNANT, H. M. (S. Cal.) Support. Onscreen from the '50s. IN: *Decision at Sundown, Run of the Arrow; Run Silent, Run Deep; Tonka, It Happened at the World's Fair, The Slender Thread, Marlowe*, more.

WYNGARDE, PETER (Eng.) Support. Onscreen from the '50s. IN: *Alexander the Great, The Innocents; Burn, Witch, Burn;* more.

WYNKOOP, CHRISTOPHER (N.Y.) Support. Onscreen in the '70s. IN: *A Walk in the Spring Rain, The Landlord, The Pursuit of Happiness*, more.

WYNN, KEENAN (S. Cal.) Character star. Son of the late comedian Ed Wynn, father of Oscar-winning screenwriter Tracy Keenan Wynn. Onscreen from 1942. IN: *Northwest Rangers, For Me and My Gal, Somewhere I'll Find You, See Here Private Hargrove, Marriage Is a Private Affair, Without Love, The Clock, Easy to Wed; No Leave, No Love; The Hucksters, Neptune's Daughter, Annie Get Your Gun, Kiss Me Kate, The Great Man* (with his father), *Don't Go Near the Water, The Absent-Minded Professor, The Great Race, Welcome to Hard Times, Point Blank, Finian's Rainbow, The Internecine Project, The Devil's Rain, Nashville*, more.

WYNN, MAE (S. Cal.) Leading lady. Former wife of actor Jack Kelly. Inactive in movies now. Onscreen from 1954. IN: *The Caine Mutiny, They Rode West, The Violent Men, The White Squaw, The Unknown Terror*, more, including 1958's *The Hong Kong Affair*, her most recent to date.

WYNN, NED (S. Cal.) Support. Keenan Wynn's other son. No longer in movies. Onscreen in 1966 in *Stagecoach* (with his father).

WYNN, TOM/a.k.a. WALLY WEST (S. Cal.) In his 70s now (b. 1902), the cowboy star of the '30s—as Tom Wynn—is no longer active in movies. He began as a stuntman-bit-player-double in Westerns—as Wally West—and continued as this after his brief fame as a hero ended. As recently as the '60s he was doubling for Richard Egan in the TV series *Redigo*. Onscreen from the '20s. IN: *The General, Strawberry Roan, Roaming Wild, Phantom Empire, Desert Mesa, Ride Tenderfoot Ride, Starlight Over Texas, Fighting Texan, Straight Shooter, Westbound Stage,* more.

WYNTER, DANA (S. Cal.) Leading lady. Onscreen from 1951. IN: *White Corridors* and *The Crimson Pirate* (billed under her real name, Dagmar Wynter; became Dana in 1955), *The View From Pompey's Head, Invasion of the Body Snatchers, Something of Value, Fraulein, In Love and War, Sink the Bismarck!, The List of Adrian Messenger; If He Hollers, Let Him Go; Airport, The Savage,* more.

WYNTERS, CHARLOTTE (S. Cal.) Leading lady; lately inactive in movies. Onscreen from 1931. IN: *The Struggle, The Calling of Dan Matthews, Girl Overboard, Sunset Trail, Reformatory, City of Chance, The Falcon's Brother, A Woman of Distinction, Foxfire,* more.

Y

YACHIGUSA, KAORU (Japan) Costar. Onscreen from the '50s. IN: *Samurai, Madame Butterfly, Snow Country,* more.

YAFFEE, BEN (N.J.) Character. Onscreen from 1960. IN: *The Fugitive Kind, Some of My Best Friends Are . . .,* more.

YAMA, CONRAD (S. Cal.) Support. Onscreen from the '60s. IN: *The Chairman,* more.

YAMAGUCHI, SHIRLEY (S. Cal.) Leading lady; now retired from movies. Onscreen in the '50s. IN: *Japanese War Bride, House of Bamboo, Sword for Hire,* more.

YAMAMOTO, FUJIKO (Japan) Costar. Onscreen from the '50s. IN: *Golden Demon; Utamoro, Painter of Women; Buddha, The Great Wall, The Revenge of Okenojo,* more.

YAMAMOTO, KEI (Japan) Supporting actor. Onscreen in the '70s. IN: *Inn of Evil,* more.

YAMAMURA, SO (Japan) Costar. Onscreen from the '50s. IN: *Barbarian and the Geisha, The Human Condition, The Country Doctor, Tora! Tora! Tora!, The Emperor and the General,* more.

YANAI, MOSHE (It.) Character. Onscreen in the '70s. IN: *Every Bastard a King,* more.

YANCY, EMILY (N.Y.) Support. Onscreen in the '70s. IN: *Tell Me That You Love Me, Junie Moon; Cotton Comes to Harlem,* more.

YANG, C. K. (S. Cal.) Character. Onscreen in the '70s. IN: *There Was a Crooked Man, One More Train to Rob,* more.

YANNE, JEAN (Fr.) Leading man. Onscreen from the '60s. IN: *Inside Out, The Viscount, Weekend, This Man Must Die, Le Boucher,* more.

YANNI, ROSSANNA (It.) Leading lady. Onscreen in the '70s. IN: *Frankenstein's Bloody Terror, Dracula's Great Love,* more.

YARBROUGH, CAMILLE (N.Y.) Black support. Onscreen in the '70s. IN: *Shaft,* more.

YARNALL, CELESTE (S. Cal.) Leading lady. Onscreen from 1963. IN: *The Nutty Professor, Around the World Under the Sea; Live a Little, Love a Little; Bob & Carol & Ted & Alice, The Velvet Vampire, Beast of Blood,* more.

YARROW, PETER (N.Y.) Singer-actor. Part of the defunct singing team "Peter, Paul and Mary." Onscreen in 1968. IN: *You Are What You Eat* (also produced it).

YATES, LEO (S. Cal.) Character. Onscreen in the '70s. IN: *I Walk the Line,* more.

YNIGUEZ, RICHARD (S. Cal.) Support. Onscreen in the '70s. IN: *Together Brothers,* more.

YONG, SOO (S. Cal.) Character actress. Onscreen from 1934. IN: *The Painted Veil, China Seas, Klondike Annie, The Good Earth, China, Night Plane From Chunking, Big Jim McClain, Love Is a Many-Splendored Thing, Sayonara, The Hawaiians,* more.

YORK, DICK (S. Cal.) After-effects of a movie-incurred accident forced his retirement from acting in the '60s, during the *Bewitched* TV series. He now lives in the desert with his wife and children, and though still only in his 40s (b.

1928), it is doubtful he will resume his career. Onscreen from 1955. IN: *My Sister Eileen, Three Stripes in the Sun, Operation Mad Ball, Cowboy, The Last Blitzkrieg, They Came to Cordura*, and *Inherit the Wind*.

YORK, FRANCINE (S. Cal.) Leading lady. Onscreen in the '70s. IN: *Cannon for Cordoba, The Doll Squad, The Centerfold Girls*, more.

YORK, GERALD (S. Cal.) Support. Onscreen from the '60s. IN: *Chuka; Simon, King of the Witches; It's Alive*, more.

YORK, JAY (S. Cal.) Support. Onscreen from the '60s. IN: *Angels From Hell*, more.

YORK, JEFF (S. Cal.) Character. Onscreen from the '40s. IN: *They Were Expendable, Up Goes Maisie, The Postman Always Rings Twice, The Yearling, Blondie's Holiday, The Paleface, Davy Crockett and the River Pirates, Old Yeller, Savage Sam, Tammy and the Millionaire*, more.

YORK, LEONARD (S. Cal.) Support. Onscreen in the '70s. IN: *The Stoolie*, more.

YORK, MICHAEL (Eng.) Costar. Onscreen from 1967. IN: *The Taming of the Shrew, Accident, Smashing Time, The Strange Affair, Romeo and Juliet, Justine, The Guru, Alfred the Great, Zeppelin, Cabaret, Lost Horizon, The Three Musketeers, The Four Musketeers, Murder on the Orient Express, Conduct Unbecoming*, more.

YORK, SUSANNAH (Eng.) Costar. Nominated for Best Supporting Actress Oscar in *They Shoot Horses, Don't They?* Onscreen from 1960. IN: *Tunes of Glory, Loss of Innocence, Freud, Tom Jones, Sands of the Kalahari, Kaleidoscope, A Man for All Seasons, Lock Up Your Daughters, The Killing of Sister George, Battle of Britain; X, Y and Zee; Happy Birthday, Wanda June; Images, The Maids, Conduct Unbecoming, Sky Rider, Mrs. Eliza Fraser*, more.

YORK, TONY (S. Cal.) Support. Onscreen from the '60s. IN: *Killers Three*, more.

YORK, W. ALLEN (S. Cal.) Support. Onscreen in the '70s. IN: *It's Alive*, more.

YORSTON, DAVID (S. Cal.) Support. Onscreen from the '60s. IN: *The Green Slime*, more.

YOSHIMURA, JITSUKO (Japan) Character. Onscreen from the '60s. IN: *The Insect Woman, Onibaba, Dodes'ka-den*, more.

YOUNG, ALAN (S. Cal.) The comedian is back in Hollywood after six years as head of the Christian Science Church Film and Broadcasting Department. "I set up the department for the mother church in Boston," he says. "It's something I wanted to do for years." The English-born actor, now in his 50s (b. 1919), says Christian Science has been important to him since he was 16. "I was healed by Christian Science as a teenager," he says. "I had asthma. I was an invalid . . . bedridden a good deal of the time. My mother gave me a book to read. It taught me the principles of Christian Science and how to apply them. . . . It taught me that physical experience is subjective. From that time on I was aware of Christian Science." The father of two young adults and two teenagers—none, incidentally, of his religious persuasion—he is launching a movie-and-TV production company geared to children's programming. The shows, he says now, "may or may not include me as a performer." Onscreen from 1946. IN: *Margie, Chicken Every Sunday, Mr. Belvedere Goes to College, Aaron Slick From Punkin Crick, Androcles and the Lion, Gentlemen Marry Brunettes, Tom Thumb, The Time Machine, Never Too Young*.

YOUNG, AUDREY (S. Cal.) The actress and band singer (with Tommy Dorsey), retired for two decades, has been married since 1950 to Oscar-winning director Billy Wilder. Onscreen from the '40s. IN: *George White's Scandals, The Lost Weekend* (which Wilder directed), *The Wistful Widow of Wagon Gap, Love Me or Leave Me*, more.

YOUNG, BUCK (S. Cal.) Support. Onscreen from the '60s. IN: *Suppose They Gave a War and Nobody Came?, Mitchell*, more. (See Peggy Stewart.)

YOUNG, BURT (N.Y.) Support. Onscreen in the '70s. IN: *The Gang That Couldn't Shoot Straight, Chinatown, The Gambler, Twilight's Last Gleaming*, more.

YOUNG, CLINT (N.Y.) Support. Onscreen from the '60s. IN: *Odds Against Tomorrow; Murder, Inc.; Gypsy*, more.

YOUNG, DAVID (S. Cal.) Leading man. Onscreen in the '70s. IN: *Mary, Mary, Bloody Mary*, more.

YOUNG, DE DE (S. Cal.) Black dancer-actress. Onscreen from 1963. IN: *Irma La Douce* (billed Harriette Young, her real name), *Batman, Seconds*, more.

YOUNG, ERIC (Eng.) Support. Onscreen from the '60s. IN: *Lord Jim, A Matter of Innocence, The Chairman*, more.

YOUNG, FARON (Tenn.) C&W star. Onscreen from 1966. IN: *Nashville Rebel,* more.

YOUNG, GEORGIANA (S. Cal.) The youngest sister of Loretta, she acted in movies just once —as her sister. She has been married since '44 to Ricardo Montalban, and has four grown children, Laura, Mark, Anita, and Victor. Onscreen in 1939 in *The Story of Alexander Graham Bell.*

YOUNG, GIG (S. Cal.) Costar. Won Best Supporting Actor Oscar in *They Shoot Horses, Don't They?* Nominated in the same category in *Come Fill the Cup* and *Teacher's Pet.* Onscreen from 1941. IN: *Dive Bomber, Navy Blues, They Died With Their Boots On, The Man Who Came to Dinner* (in all of which he played bits under his real name, Byron Barr; after he changed it, another actor—now deceased—used the name Byron Barr throughout the '40s), *The Gay Sisters* (in '42, in which he played a character named "Gig Young"—his first leading man role —and took it for his screen name), *The Male Animal, Old Acquaintance, Air Force, Escape Me Never, The Woman in White, Wake of the Red Witch, You for Me, The Desperate Hours, Desk Set, Tunnel of Love, The Story on Page One, That Touch of Mink, For Love or Money, Strange Bedfellows, Lovers and Other Strangers, Bring Me the Head of Alfredo Garcia, The Hindenburg, The Killer Elite,* more.

YOUNG, HARRIETTE (S. Cal.) (See De De Young.)

YOUNG, HEATHER (S. Cal.) Singer-actress. Onscreen from the '60s. IN: *A Guide for the Married Man,* more.

YOUNG, J.D. (S. Cal.) Character. Onscreen in the '70s. IN: *Benji,* more.

YOUNG, JANIS (S. Cal.) Support. Onscreen in the '70s. IN: *Loving,* more.

YOUNG, JEREMY (Eng.) Support. Onscreen in the '70s. IN: *Sudden Terror,* more.

YOUNG, JOAN (Eng.) Character. Onscreen from 1943. IN: *The Lamp Still Burns, School for Secrets, Easy Money* (second episode), *The Fallen Idol; Time Gentlemen, Please; The Gay Lady, The Admirable Crichton; Suddenly, Last Summer;* more.

YOUNG, LORETTA (S. Cal.) Star. Won Best Actress Oscar in *The Farmer's Daughter.* Nominated in the same category in *Come to the Stable.* Still spectacularly beautiful in her 60s (b. 1911), and not remarried since her '69 divorce from TV exec Tom Lewis, she lives in splendor in Beverly Hills but spends most of her time working with the Loretta Young Youth Project ("a preventive program for youngsters") in Phoenix. Son Peter, a singer-guitar-player, records albums; son Chris is a disc jockey at a radio station in Ojai; daughter Judy, mother of a teenage daughter, Marie, won an annulment of her marriage to TV director Joseph Tinney Jr. and has returned to Hollywood where she acts on the stage and in TV shows. "The one vehicle that would make me return to the screen," Loretta says, "would be to play Claudia in Clare Booth Luce's *Pilate's Wife.* I've wanted to play it since the days when Howard Hughes was interested in starring me in it." Onscreen from 1928. IN: *Laugh, Clown, Laugh; The Squall, The Careless Age, The Man From Blankley's, Kismet, The Devil to Pay, Platinum Blonde, I Like Your Nerve, The Hatchet Man, Life Begins, Zoo in Budapest, The Life of Jimmy Dolan, Heroes for Sale, She Had to Say Yes, Man's Castle, The House of Rothschild, Bulldog Drummond Strikes Back, The White Parade, Clive of India, Call of the Wild, The Crusades, Ramona, Cafe Metropole; Wife, Doctor and Nurse; Four Men and a Prayer, Suez, Kentucky, Eternally Yours, The Doctor Takes a Wife, The Men in Her Life, Bedtime Story, China, And Now Tomorrow, Along Came Jones, The Stranger, The Bishop's Wife, Rachel and the Stranger, The Accused, Mother Is a Freshman, Key to the City, Half Angel, Because of You,* more, including 1953's *It Happens Every Thursday,* her most recent to date. (Following her movie career, before retiring in 1962, she starred in three television series: *A Letter to Loretta,* in '53, *The Loretta Young Show, 1954–60,* and *The New Loretta Young Show.*)

YOUNG, MICHELLE (S. Cal.) Support. Onscreen in the '70s. IN: *Lenny,* more.

YOUNG, NEIL (S. Cal.) Rock music star. Onscreen in the '70s. IN: *Celebration at Big Sur, Journey Through the Past* (he also produced), more.

YOUNG, OTIS (S. Cal.) Black leading man. Onscreen from the '60s. IN: *Don't Just Stand There, The Last Detail,* more.

YOUNG, PAUL (Eng.) Support. Onscreen from the '50s. IN: *Wee Geordie, Submarine X-1,* more.

YOUNG, POLLY ANN (S. Cal.) Loretta's eldest sister (b. 1908), she gave up her long (13-year) career as a leading lady after two in '41, *Road Show* and *The Invisible Ghost.* Happily married for many years to J. Carter Hermann, she is the mother of a daughter, Betty

Jane Royale. Betty Jane, once reported engaged to Glenn Ford's son, Peter, made a brief excursion into movies at 19 in *The Trouble with Angels* ('66), but decided against an acting career. Onscreen from 1928. IN: *The Masks of the Devil, Tanned Legs, The Bellamy Trial, Rich People, Stolen Secrets, The Man From Utah, Sons of Steel, Happiness C.O.D., The Crimson Trail, Hitchhike to Heaven, Border Patrolman, The Story of Alexander Graham Bell* (the only one in which all the Young sisters—Loretta, Georgiana, Polly Ann, and Sally Blane—appeared together, as sisters), *Mystery Plane, Turnabout, The Last Alarm,* more.

YOUNG, RAY (S. Cal.) Support. Onscreen in the '70s. IN: *Five Bloody Graves,* more.

YOUNG, RAYMOND (Eng.) Character. Onscreen from the '50s. IN: *Adam and Evelyn, Midnight Episode, The Silent Enemy; Arrivederci, Baby!;* more.

YOUNG, RICHARD (S. Cal.) Support. Onscreen in the '70s. IN: *Night Call Nurses,* more.

YOUNG, ROBERT (S. Cal.) Star. Popular on TV in recent years in *Marcus Welby, M.D.* Onscreen from 1931. IN: *Lullaby, The Black Camel, The Sin of Madelon Claudet, The Wet Parade, Strange Interlude, The Kid From Spain, Tugboat Annie, Carolina, Spitfire, The House of Rothschild, West Point of the Air, It's Love Again, Stowaway, I Met Him in Paris, Married Before Breakfast, The Bride Wore Red, Navy Blue and Gold, Three Comrades, The Toy Wife, The Shining Hour, Honolulu, Maisie, Northwest Passage, The Mortal Storm, Western Union, Lady Be Good; H.M. Pulham, Esq.* (perhaps his finest performance); *Joe Smith, American; Journey for Margaret, Claudia, The Enchanted Cottage, The Searching Wind, Crossfire, Sitting Pretty, Adventure in Baltimore, That Forsyte Woman; Goodbye, My Fancy; The Half Breed,* more, including 1954's *Secret of the Incas,* his most recent to date.

YOUNG, SKIP (S. Cal.) Support. Onscreen from 1961. IN: *A Cold Wind in August, WUSA,* more.

YOUNG, STEPHEN (S. Cal.) Leading man. Onscreen from 1963. IN: *Cleopatra, The Leopard, 55 Days at Peking, The Fall of the Roman Empire* (bits all), *The Thin Red Line, Patton, Soylent Green, Breaking Point,* more.

YOUNG, TONY (S. Cal.) Leading man. Son of late actor Carleton Young. Onscreen from 1960. IN: *He Rides Tall, Taggart, Charro!, Chrome and Hot Leather, A Man Called Sledge, The Outfit, Policewomen, Act of Vengeance,* more.

YOUNG, TRUDY (S. Cal.) Support. Onscreen in the '70s. IN: *Homer, The Grapedealer's Daughter,* more.

YOUNG, VICTORIA (S. Cal.) Leading lady. The wife of actor Brian Keith, with whom she starred in TV's *The Brian Keith Show.* Onscreen from the '60s. IN: *Blue Hawaii, The Ugly American, A Girl Named Tamiku; Lt. Robinson Crusoe, U.S.N.; Krakatoa—East of Java* (with Keith); more.

YOUNGBLOOD, BUTCH (S. Cal.) Support. Onscreen in the '70s. IN: *Adam at 6 A.M.,* more.

YOUNGER, BEVERLY (S. Cal.) Support. Onscreen from the '60s. IN: *Medium Cool,* more.

YOUNGER, JACK (S. Cal.) Character. Onscreen from the '60s. IN: *Dinosaurus!,* more.

YOUNGMAN, HENNY (N.Y.) Star comedian. Onscreen from 1944. IN: *A Wave, a Wac and a Marine; Nashville Rebel; Won Ton Ton, the Dog Who Saved Hollywood; The Silent Movie,* more.

YOUSKEVITCH, IGOR (N.Y.) The great ballet star is in his 60s now (b. 1912) and has long been retired from dancing. Onscreen in 1956. IN: *Invitation to the Dance* (the "Circus" and "Ring Around the Rosy" episodes).

YULIN, HARRIS (S. Cal.) Leading man. Onscreen in the '70s. IN: *End of the Road, Doc, Night Moves,* more.

YUNG, VICTOR SEN (S. Cal.) In the "Charlie Chan" movies, besides changing his own screen name in mid-course from Sen Yung to Victor Sen Yung, he played a variety of "sons." Entering the series in 1938 in *Charlie Chan in Honolulu* (the first starring Sidney Toler), he played #1 son "Lee" in just this one (replacing Keye Luke who had been "Lee" to the late Warner Oland). In his next, *Charlie Chan in Reno,* and in 10 subsequent Tolers, Lee disappeared from the scene and Victor Sen Yung appeared as #1 son "Jimmy Chan." Yet a third name change occurred. In the last "Chan" Sidney Toler made before his death in '47, *The Trap,* Victor Sen Yung was seen as usual as "Jimmy." But, a few weeks later, when Roland Winters assumed the title role, in *The Chinese Ring,* he was suddenly "Tommy," the only son in the series—until, in the fifth of them, Keye Luke came back to play his old role of "Lee"! Continuing his movie career to the present, Victor Sen Yung, turning 60 in 1976, has also had running roles in three TV series—*Bachelor Father, Kung Fu,* and *Bonanza,* as Hop Sing, the cook. Recently the San Francis-

534

co-born actor, who has never been to China, but has been an accomplished Chinese cook since he was 12, published a cookbook, *The Great Wok Cookbook*. He said at the time: "In the book I don't go on about China because I don't know anything about it." Onscreen from 1938. IN: *Shadows Over Shanghai, Charlie Chan at the Wax Museum* (etc.), *20,000 Men a Year, The Letter, A Yank on the Burma Road, Secret Agent of Japan, Moontide, Across the Pacific, China, Betrayal from the East, A Ticket to Tomahawk, The Breaking Point, The Left Hand of God, Blood Alley, Flower Drum Song*, more.

YURO, ROBERT (S. Cal.) Leading man. Onscreen from 1962. IN: *Satan in High Heels, The Shakiest Gun in the West, The Hell With Heroes*, more.

Z

ZABALA, ELSA (It.) Character. Onscreen in the '70s. IN: *Captain Apache*, more.

ZABOTKINA, OLGA (Rus.) Leading lady. Onscreen from the '60s. IN: *Song Over Moscow, The Sleeping Beauty*, more.

ZACHARIAS, STEPHEN/formerly **STEFFEN** (It.) Support. Onscreen from the '60s. IN: *Ace High, Machine Gun McCain, The Kremlin Letter*, more.

ZAHORSKY, BOHUZ (Pol.) Character. Onscreen from the '40s. IN: *Thunder in the Hills, The Emperor and the Golem, Happy End*, more.

ZANIN, BRUNO (It.) Adolescent lead. Onscreen in the '70s. IN: *Amarcord*, more.

ZANUCK, HARRISON (S. Cal.) Juvenile. Son of producer Richard D. Zanuck. Onscreen in 1974. IN: *The Sugarland Express*.

ZANVILLE, BERNARD (S. Cal.) The real name of actor Dane Clark, which he used in a few early movies including *Action in the North Atlantic*. (See Dane Clark.)

ZAPATA, CARMEN (S. Cal.) Character. Onscreen from the '60s. IN: *Hail, Hero!; "W"; I Will, I Will . . . For Now*; more.

ZAPATA, JOE (S. Cal.) Support. Onscreen in the '70s. IN: *Together Brothers*, more.

ZAPP, SYLVIA (N.Y.) Juvenile. Onscreen in the '70s. IN: *A Safe Place*, more.

ZAPPA, FRANK (S. Cal.) Rock star. Onscreen in the '70s. IN: *Two Hundred Motels*, more.

ZAREMBA, JOHN (S. Cal.) Character. Onscreen from the '50s. IN: *The Magnetic Monster, Chicago Syndicate, Earth vs. the Flying Saucers, R.P.M., Scandalous John*, more.

ZARZO, MANOLO (It.) Support. Onscreen in the '70s. IN: *A Drama of Jealousy (and Other Things)*, more.

ZEE, ELEANOR (S. Cal.) Support. Onscreen in the '70s. IN: *Husbands, Minnie and Moskowitz*, more.

ZEFFIRELLI, FRANCO (It.) Noted director—of *Romeo and Juliet, The Taming of the Shrew*, others. Onscreen in the '40s as an actor. IN: *Angelina*, more.

ZEITLIN, LOIS (S. Cal.) Support. Onscreen in the '70s. IN: *Cockfighter*, more.

ZELLER, BEN (S. Cal.) Support. Onscreen in the '70s. IN: *Thomasine and Bushrod*, more.

ZERBE, ANTHONY (S. Cal.) Costar. Onscreen from the '60s. IN: *Will Penny, The Omega Man, The Laughing Policeman, The Parallax View; Farewell, My Lovely; Rooster Cogburn*, more.

ZETTERLING, MAI (Eng.) The golden-haired glamour girl from Sweden is gone. Much in evidence for more than 15 years, she disappeared after 1963's *The Bay of St. Michel*. And she will not return. In her stead, living in a ramshackle house on the "wrong" side of the Thames, there is a dumpy, dark-haired, middle-aged woman (b. 1925) with solemn eyes, who, instead of acting in movies, makes them. Explicit sexuality is the keynote of most of those that she, as a director, has undertaken in the past decade. *Loving Couples* was hers, and *Night Games* (based on her own novel). *Night Games*, about the emotional obsession of a young boy for his swinging mother, is the film that caused Shirley Temple to quit the San Francisco Film Festival in a snit in '66; it was also banned for public showing that year at the Cannes Film Festival. In addition, she has made numerous other features, usually in Sweden, and documentaries. She also directed a 12-minute segment—the one about the weight lifters, "The Strongest"—for *Visions of Eight*, the documentary about the 1972 Munich Olympics. On most movies she makes now her coscriptwriter is novelist David Hughes, her second husband. (Her first was the Norwegian actor-writer-director Tutte Lemkow. By him she has a grown son and daughter.) In later years, she says, she has chosen total simplicity as her lifestyle. When not occupied in Britain, she and her husband spend time at their ancient house in the rough Arles area of France, which has no electricity. There she makes candles, grows her own organic food, has a medicinal herbal garden, cooks, plants trees—even creates her own makeup (elderberry water for an astringent, cucumber cream for the face). "All that I need is that place in the world where I can function excitingly and where I have land I can do something with," she has said, adding, "I don't really believe in having possessions." And what of all those accumulated during her years of glamorous stardom? "I've given almost everything away," she replies. Onscreen from 1947. IN: *Torment, Frieda, Quartet* ("The Facts of Life" episode), *The Girl in the Painting, The Lost People, The Bad Lord Byron, Hell Is Sold Out, Desperate Moment, Knock on Wood, A Prize of Gold, Abandon Ship, The Truth About Women, Only Two Can Play, Night Is My Future,* more.

ZIEMANN, SONJA (Ger.) Support. Onscreen from the '50s. IN: *The Merry Wives of Windsor, The Affairs of Julie, The Eighth Day of the Week, The Secret Ways, A Matter of Who, De Sade, The Bridge at Remagen,* more.

ZILZER, WOLFGANG/now **PAUL ANDOR** (N.Y.) (See Paul Andor.)

ZIMBALIST, EFREM, JR. (S. Cal.) Costar. Onscreen from 1949. IN: *House of Strangers, Bombers B-52, Band of Angels; Too Much, Too Soon; Home Before Dark, The Crowded Sky, Fever in the Blood, By Love Possessed, The Chapman Report, Wait Until Dark, Airport 1975,* more.

ZIMMER, LEE (N.Y.) Character actor. Onscreen from the '50s. IN: *Lonelyhearts,* more.

ZIMMER, PIERRE (Fr.) Support. Onscreen from the '60s. IN: *Secret World; Life, Love, Death; The Crook, Escape to Nowhere,* more.

ZIMMET, MARYA (N.Y.) Juvenile. Onscreen from the '60s. IN: *The Rain People,* more.

ZOLA, JEAN-PIERRE (Fr.) Character. Onscreen from the '50s. IN: *My Uncle, The Things of Life,* more.

ZORICH, LOUIS (N.J.) Character. Onscreen from the '60s. IN: *Coogan's Bluff, They Might*

Be Giants, Fiddler on the Roof, Made for Each Other, more.

ZORINA, VERA (N.Y.) She closed out her eight-year career as a movie star in 1946. Since then, except for the short-lived Broadway revival of *On Your Toes* ('54), the dancer-actress has directed her artistic energies to other areas. Particularly, in various opera houses, here and abroad, she has narrated—with symphony orchestras—such works as Stravinsky's *Persephone* and Honneger's *Joan of Arc at the Stake.* She has now ten or more such pieces in her repertoire, which she does in English, French, or German. (Berlin-born, German was her first language; her father was German, her mother Norwegian.) She has also directed operas. And, in '74, at the request of Norwegian television, she flew to Oslo where she directed the 12th-century drama *Herod.* The former ballerina has been married twice—first to choreographer George Balanchine (1938–46). Since '46 she has been the wife of Goddard Lieberson, who has twice served as president of Columbia Records and has recently retired. They have two sons in their 20s, Peter Goddard Crespian, who is a composer of serious music, and Jonathan, a bearded scholar who recently received his Ph.D. in philosophy at Columbia. The Liebersons have a spacious townhouse in Manhattan and, in Santa Fe, N.M., a modern adobe ranch house that is considerably more so. For several years they have divided their time between the two residences, but expect now, with her husband's retirement, to spend more time in the West than the East. The actress (b. 1917), who no longer dances, either professionally or privately, maintains her dancer's figure by playing tennis—a new recreation for her. Though her stage (and screen) name has been Vera Zorina since she joined the Monte Carlo Ballet Russe in the early '30s, she still dislikes it. To her it is no more than a name on a billboard. She was born Brigitta Hartwig, and her husband and friends have always called her Brigitta. Somewhere, every night, on some "Late Movie" on TV, in *Star-Spangled Rhythm,* ballerina Vera Zorina twirls gloriously through Paramount's ersatz snow to the sweeping strains of "That Old Black Magic"—finally twinkling out as a phantasmal sprite on the pillow of lovesick GI Johnny Johnston. But Brigitta Lieberson neither envies nor ever sees her. "I hated all of them," she says of Vera Zorina's movies, smiling, "making them—so boring." Onscreen from 1938. IN: *The Goldwyn Follies, On Your Toes, I Was an Adventuress, Louisiana Purchase, Follow the Boys, Lover Come Back.* (She also began as Maria in *For Whom the Bell Tolls* but, after a week's shooting, was replaced by Ingrid Bergman.)

ZOU ZOU (S. Cal.) Leading lady. Onscreen in the '70s. IN: *S*P*Y*S*, more.

ZUCKERT, BILL (S. Cal.) Character. Onscreen from the '60s. IN: *Ada, Shock Corridor, The Trouble with Girls, Scandalous John, How to Frame a Figg*, more.

ZUGSMITH, ALFRED (S. Cal.) Producer *(Touch of Evil)* and director *(College Confidential)*. Onscreen as a performer in 1965 in *Fanny Hill* (he also produced).

ZULU (Hawaii) Character actor. Perhaps best known for his role of "Kono" in TV's *Hawaii Five-O*. Onscreen from the '50s. IN: *Gidget, Rampage, Hawaii, Diamond Head*, more.

ZURICA, PAT (PATRICK J.) (S. Cal.) Support. Onscreen in the '70s. IN: *Patton, Bank Shot*, more.

ZURICA, ROBERT J. (S. Cal.) Support. Onscreen in the '70s. IN: *The Last Run*, more.

ZWERLING, DARRELL (N.Y.) Support. Onscreen in the '70s. IN: *Chinatown*, more.

LATE PLAYERS (1900-1974)

Each capsule biography includes year of death, age at death, and significant films.

A

AASEN, JOHN *(1938)* 51 ——The giant (real) in Harold Lloyd's *Why Worry?*, other silents.

ABBE, CHARLES *(1932)* 72 ——Played Alice Brady's socialite father in 1915's *The Boss;* at Paramount in the '20s, he was top support in numerous Thomas Meighan vehicles: *Homeward Bound, The Conquest of Canaan, Cappy Ricks*, others.

ABEL, ALFRED *(1937)* 72 ——Noted German star of many, but perhaps most famous as the authoritarian industrialist in *Metropolis* who, reconciled with labor at the fadeout, concludes: "The path to human dignity and happiness lies through the master of us all, the great Mediator, Love."

ABBOTT, BUD *(1974)* 78 ——Lou Costello's thin straight-man pal in all those Top Ten Universal comedies of the '40s and '50s: *Buck Privates, Hold That Ghost, In the Navy*, etc.; see Lou Costello for complete entry.

ABBOTT, DOROTHY *(1968)* ——Support in Rock Hudson's *A Gathering of Eagles.*

ABBOTT, FRANK *(1957)* 78 ——Supporting actor in silents, particularly in Westerns such as Fred Thomson's *The Wild Bull's Lair.*

ABBOTT, MARION *(1937)* 71 ——Support in 1923's *Backbone.*

ABELES, EDWARD *(1919)* 49 ——An early Lasky star who played the title role in 1914's *Brewster's Millions* and costarred with Bessie Barriscale in *Ready Money.*

ABINGDON, W. L. *(1918)* 59 ——Supported Lina Cavalieri in 1914's *Manon Lescaut.*

ACKERMAN, WALTER *(1938)* 57 ——Supporting actor long onscreen and particularly busy in action pix in the '20s: *Aflame in the Sky, Man of the Forest,* Renee Adoree's *Back to God's Country,* etc.

ACORD, ART *(1931)* 40 ——Famous black-suited cowboy star, noted for his trick riding and stunts; in many Universal pix in the '20s: *Lazy Lightning, Sky High Corral, Hard Fists,* etc.; also starred in numerous Western serials: *The Moon Riders, Winners of the West, The Oregon Trail, The White Horseman,* others; his early director, William Wyler, has summed him up: "He was not a great actor, but he had a kind of sincerity. He wasn't handsome but he looked good on a horse. Also, he was a nice fellow." Talkies—and a jail sentence for illegal bootlegging—ended his career.

ACOSTA, RUDOLFO *(1974)* 54 ——Mexican actor; featured roles in *One-Eyed Jacks* (leader of the Rurales), *One Way Street, Che,* etc.; was sometimes billed Rodolfo or Rudolph.

ACUFF, EDDIE *(1956)* 48 ——Postman (pratfall victim of Dagwood's wild, late dashes to the office) in the "Blondie" movies; genial comic support in dozens including *The Petrified*

Forest, Four Daughters, It Happened Tomorrow, and numerous Westerns and serials.

ADAIR, JACK *(1940)* 46 ——Small roles in *Peter Ibbetson, 52nd Street*, others.

ADAIR, JEAN *(1963)* 80 ——Thin, funny spinster in *Arsenic and Old Lace* whose elderberry wine delighted all but those who drank it.

ADAIR, JOHN *(1952)* 67 ——Support in a 1936 Preston Foster B, *Muss 'em Up*.

ADAIR, ROBERT *(1954)* 54 ——British character; Captain Hardy (instigator of the tedium-relieving cockroach race in the trenches) in *Journey's End;* English Chamberlain in *The Crusades;* sometimes billed A'Dair.

ADAMS, ERNIE *(1947)* 52 ——Support in many from 1919; was Miller Huggins in *The Pride of the Yankees*, the "stoolie" Fink in *San Quentin;* in B Westerns played outlaws or deputies in dozens.

ADAMS, FRANCES SALE *(1969)* 77 ——Featured in silents.

ADAMS, HOWARD *(1936)* 25 ——Few minor roles.

ADAMS, KATHRYN *(1959)* 65 ——Blonde star of silents: *Baby Mine, Forbidden Woman, Borrowed Husbands*, etc.; support in such talkies as *Bachelor Daddy, If I Had My Way, Saboteur*.

ADAMS, LESLIE *(1934)* 49 ——Played O'Brien in Claude Rains' *Crime Without Passion*.

ADAMS, LIONEL *(1952)* 86 ——Support in Metro's *Success* ('23).

ADAMS, MARY *(1973)* 60s ——Played Dean Jagger's wife in *Executive Suite*.

ADAMS, NICK *(1968)* 36 ——Smallish blond comic support in *No Time for Sergeants* (Andy Griffith's bespectacled pal, Ben), *Pillow Talk, Teacher's Pet*, etc.; nominee for Supporting Oscar in *Twilight of Honor;* star of TV's *The Rebel* series.

ADAMS, WILLIAM *(1972)* 85 ——Character (Customs Officer) in *The House on 92nd Street*.

ADLER, JACOB P. *(1926)* 71 ——A Yiddish-theater great, patriarch of the Adler theatrical dynasty (Luther, Stella, etc.), star of 1914's *Michael Strogoff*.

ADLON, LOUIS *(1947)* 40s ——Small roles in

Muni's *Counter-Attack* and Luise Rainer's *Dramatic School*, etc.

ADOREE, RENEE *(1933)* 35 ——French; most famous—and touching—as the girl John Gilbert leaves behind in *The Big Parade;* also in *The Bandolero, Back to God's Country*, other silents and early talkies; last in 1930's *Call of the Flesh*.

ADRIAN, MAX *(1973)* 69 ——British star; the Dauphin in *Henry V;* the seedy music hall impresario, Max, in *The Boy Friend;* in *Kipps, The Young Mr. Pitt, The Pickwick Papers*, others.

AFRIQUE *(1961)* 54 ——South African actor featured in Buddy Rogers' *Let's Make a Night of It*.

AGAR, JANE *(1948)* 59 ——Minor player in silents.

AGUGLIA, MIMI *(1970)* 85 ——Aunt Guadelupe in *The Outlaw;* old Assunta in *The Rose Tattoo;* in *That Midnight Kiss, Cry of the City*, etc.

AHEARNE, THOMAS *(1969)* 63 ——Character; in *Three in the Attic, The Window*, others.

AHERNE, PAT *(1970)* 63 ——Irish character actor; in *The Paradine Case, Bwana Devil, Green Dolphin Street, The Court Jester*.

AHLERS, ANNY *(1933)* 26 ——German leading lady: *Der Wahre Jakob, Die Marquise von Pompadour*, etc.

AINLEY, HENRY *(1945)* 66 ——English actor who starred for Famous Players in 1915; some of his silents: *The Prisoner of Zenda, The Manxman, The Royal Oak;* character in talkies: *The Good Companions, As You Like It* (the Duke), *The First Mrs. Fraser*, others.

AINLEY, RICHARD *(1967)* 56 ——Son of Henry; romantic lead opposite Miriam Hopkins in *Lady With Red Hair;* in *Shining Victory, Above Suspicion, White Cargo*, etc.

AINSLEY, NORMAN *(1948)* 66 ——Scottish support; character (Robbins) in *Captains Courageous;* minor roles in *A Tale of Two Cities* ('35), *Modern Times, Kitty, Adventure in Diamonds*.

AINSWORTH, SIDNEY *(1922)* 50 ——Hawk-nosed Essanay star; in *Madame X, The White Sister, A Man and His Money*, more silents.

AITKEN, SPOTTISWOODE *(1933)* 63 ——Dr.

Cameron (uncle of hero Henry Walthall) in *The Birth of a Nation;* featured in many other silents including *Nomads of the North, The Young Rajah, Monte Cristo, Captain Kidd Jr.*

AKED, MURIEL *(1955)* 68 ——Prim British character; in *The Happiest Days of Your Life, Rome Express, The Life and Death of Colonel Blimp, Gilbert and Sullivan,* etc.

ALBERNI, LUIS *(1962)* 75 ——Humorous accented roles (usually Italian) in scores; as representative as any, the derbied Alexander Petrovich Moscovich Voyda in *Roberta,* who hired "real Indians" to play in his Paris club, but instead got Fred Astaire and his Wabash Indianians.

ALBERS, HANS *(1960)* 67 ——Major German star; in Dietrich's *The Blue Angel* (Mazeppa), *Sergeant Berry, Monte Carlo Madness,* etc.

ALBERTSON, FRANK *(1964)* 55 ——In pix from the early '20s to *Bye Bye Birdie;* best in light comedy such as the role of Ginger Rogers' dimwitted boy friend in *Bachelor Mother;* in *Alice Adams* (the brother who's an embarrassment to Hepburn), *The Life of Vergie Winters,* many more.

ALBERTSON, LILLIAN *(1962)* 81 ——James Stewart's mom (seen in the bleachers) in *The Greatest Show on Earth;* more famous as RKO talent coach.

ALCAIDE, MARIO *(1971)* 40s ——Handsome guy; featured in the Hume Cronyn-Nancy Kelly pic *Crowded Paradise.*

ALCOCK, DOUGLAS *(1970)* 62 ——English character actor.

ALDEN, BETTY *(1948)* 50 ——Support (Richard Abbott's wife) in Ann Harding's *The Fountain;* in Will Rogers' *Lightnin',* others.

ALDEN, JOAN *(1968)* ——See Blanche Mehaffey.

ALDEN, MARY *(1946)* 63 ——Veteran character actress whose performances served D. W. Griffith well; the hateful mulatto mistress in *The Birth of a Nation;* the tragic fisher-village mother in *Home Sweet Home;* then was rich Mrs. Rhead in *Milestones;* also in *Babbitt, Brown of Harvard,* many more silents; last in *Strange Interlude,* one of her few talkies.

ALDERSON, ERVILLE *(1957)* 74 ——Played smalltown types; for Griffith, in silents, he was Judge Montague in *America,* Judge Foster in *Sally of the Sawdust,* the Professor in *Isn't Life*

Wonderful; rustic roles in dozens of talkies: *Cabin in the Cotton, Santa Fe Trail, Sergeant York, Along Came Jones,* etc.

ALDRIDGE, ALFRED *(1934)* 58 ——Featured in the silent *It Can Be Done.*

ALEXANDER, BEN *(1969)* 58 ——A most appealing child star in silents (Lillian Gish's *Hearts of the World, Penrod and Sam,* et al.); young leads in talkies (*Tom Brown of Culver, All Quiet on the Western Front, Are These Our Children?,* etc.); finally a fine character actor and Jack Webb's beefy partner in *Dragnet,* on TV and in the movie.

ALEXANDER, CLAIRE *(1927)* 29 ——Sennett beauty; featured in the silent serial *The Fatal Sign.*

ALEXANDER, EDWARD *(1964)* 76 ——Was Sinclaire in the 1913 version of *Uncle Tom's Cabin;* in *Curse of the Black Pearl,* other silents.

ALEXANDER, FRANK "FATTY" *(1937)* 58 ——Comic roles in silents: *Oh, What a Night!, Cyclone Jones,* etc.

ALEXANDER, JOHN ——Character actor most famous for role of Teddy Roosevelt in *Arsenic and Old Lace* and the ebullient cry of "Charge!"; year of death unreported.

ALEXANDER, ROSS *(1937)* 29 ——Busy, wavy-haired romantic lead at Warners; in *Shipmates Forever, Flirtation Walk, China Clipper, Boulder Dam,* etc.; married the late Anne Nagel shortly before his death.

ALEXANDER, SARA *(1926)* 87 ——Character actress in silents.

ALGIER, SIDNEY *(1945)* 55 ——Was in such silents as *Why Men Leave Home* and *Fine Clothes.*

ALLEN, ARTHUR *(1947)* 56 ——Character (Professor Willett) in *Our Town;* in *Ebb Tide* and *Rangers of Fortune.*

ALLEN, BARBARA JO *(1974)* 70 ——See Vera Vague.

ALLEN, DOROTHY *(1970)* 74 ——Featured in silents: *Over the Hill to the Poor House, The Hoosier Schoolmaster, School for Wives, If Winter Comes,* etc.

ALLEN, ETHAN *(1940)* 48 ——Was in such Westerns as *Trigger Pals* and *The Border Legion.*

ALLEN, FRED *(1957)* 62 ——Dry, nasal, great funnyman; starred in *Love Thy Neighbor; Sally, Irene and Mary; Thanks a Million*, etc., in addition to radio and TV, and "feuding" with Jack Benny.

ALLEN, GRACIE *(1964)* 62 ——Flighty, foolish and grand femme half of Burns and Allen; radio and TV plus movies: *The Big Broadcast of 1936* (and '37), *A Damsel in Distress, Honolulu, The Gracie Allen Murder Case*, others.

ALLEN, JANE MARIE *(1970)* 54 ——Featured dancer in musicals of the '40s.

ALLEN, JOE *(1955)* 66 ——Minor character actor.

ALLEN, JOSEPH, JR. *(1962)* 40 ——Romantic lead opposite Susan Hayward in *Our Leading Citizen;* in *The Night Before the Divorce, Who Is Hope Schuyler?, It Happened in Flatbush*, etc.

ALLEN, JOSEPH, SR. *(1952)* 80 ——Character actor-father of Joseph Jr.; many silents; in *Seven Keys to Baldpate* ('29), *Gambling*, and last in Robert Taylor's *Lucky Night* ('39).

ALLEN, LESTER *(1949)* 58 ——English comic; William Gaxton's sidekick, Mouse, in *The Heat's On;* also in *The Dolly Sisters, Ma and Pa Kettle* (as Geoduck), *The Pirate*, etc.

ALLEN, MAUDE *(1956)* 73 ——Support in *Whispering Smith Speaks*, Sybil Jason's *The Captain's Kid*, George O'Brien's *The Painted Desert*.

ALLEN, PHYLLIS *(1938)* 77 ——Sennett's wonderful, horsey character comedienne; often paired with Mack Swain (as in 1914's *Getting Acquainted* where she wallops him for—she thinks—getting fresh on a park bench); also in *Fatty's Jonah Day, Fickle Fatty's Fall*, others.

ALLEN, SAM *(1934)* 73 ——Featured in *The Virginian* ('23), *The Sea Beast, Midnight Limited*, and many silent Westerns.

ALLEN, VIOLA *(1948)* 80 ——Celebrated stage actress who starred in Essanay's *The White Sister* in 1915; Francis X. Bushman broke his contract with the company when asked to support her in this movie version of her stage success.

ALLENBY, THOMAS *(1933)* 72 ——Supporting player.

ALLERTON, HELEN *(1959)* 71 ——See Helen Kilduff.

ALLEY, BEN *(1970)* 69 ——Singer known as "The Golden Tenor."

ALLGOOD, SARA *(1950)* 66 ——Irish character actress who is never to be forgotten as the mother in *How Green Was My Valley* (Oscarnominated as Best Support); was also in *The Lodger, The Spiral Staircase, Lydia, This Above All, The Keys of the Kingdom*, etc.

ALLISON, STEVE *(1969)* 52 ——Support to Dan Duryea in *The Burglar;* also radio singer.

ALLISTER, CLAUD *(1970)* 75 ——Big-nosed English character; in *The Awful Truth* (Lord Fabian), *Lillian Russell* (Sullivan to Nigel Bruce's Gilbert), *The Private Life of Henry VIII* (Cornell), *Platinum Blonde, Dracula's Daughter*, etc.

ALONSO, JULIO *(1955)* 49 ——Actor-brother of Gilbert Roland.

ALTHOFF, CHARLES *(1962)* 72 ——Comedian in movies as well as on radio.

ALTHOUSE, EARL *(1971)* 76 ——In silent cowboy movies.

ALVARADO, DON *(1967)* 62 ——Handsome Latin; star of *Rio Rita* and *The Bridge of San Luis Rey* (both '29); in earlier silents: *Satan in Sables, The Wife Who Wasn't Wanted*, etc.; support in *Morning Glory, The Devil Is a Woman*, other talkies; last in a 1949 Mitchum pic, *The Big Steal*, playing a Mexican police officer, he was a lieutenant to Ramon Novarro's colonel, appropriately.

AMATO, PASQUALE *(1942)* 64 ——A Metropolitan Opera star from Italy, he played the supporting role of Napoleon in Dolores Costello's *Glorious Betsy* ('28).

AMAYA, CARMEN *(1963)* 50 ——Fiery Spanish dancer; in *Follow the Boys, See My Lawyer, Knickerbocker Holiday*, others.

AMBLER, JOSS *(1959)* 59 ——English character; often a police officer; in *The Citadel, Mine Own Executioner, Flying Fortress*, etc.

AMES, ADRIENNE *(1947)* 39 ——Lovely ex of the late Bruce Cabot; did society girls in Lombard's *Sinners in the Sun* and in *From Hell to Heaven*, etc.; starred in B's such as *The Death Kiss* and *Guilty As Hell*.

AMES, GERALD *(1933)* 42 ——British stage actor in a few movies.

AMES, JIMMY *(1965)* 50 ——Character (Rico Di Angelo) in Lamour's *The Lucky Stiff;* also in *Whistle Stop.*

AMES, MICHAEL *(1972)* ——See Tod Andrews.

AMES, PERCY *(1936)* 62 ——Character actor in silents (Barthelmess' *Soul Fire*) and talkies (*Gambling*).

AMES, ROBERT *(1931)* 42 ——Romantic lead in silents (*Three Faces East, Crown of Lies*) and talkies (*Rebound, A Lady to Love*, Ann Harding's *Holiday*, numerous others).

ANALLA, ISABEL *(1958)* 37 ——Minor support; *Vertigo, Pal Joey, Kiss Them for Me.*

ANDERSON, CLAIRE *(1964)* 68 ——Sennett beauty; in silent features: *She Loved a Sailor, The Road Demon, The Yellow Stain*, etc.

ANDERSON, G. M. "BRONCHO BILLY" *(1971)* 90 ——The movies' first great cowboy star; world-famous and vastly popular in scores of "Broncho Billy" pix between 1908 and 1918; earlier he had been in many pictures, including *The Great Train Robbery* ('03) as the passenger who tries to escape and is shot down; last seen in a cameo in Randolph Scott's *The Bounty Hunter* ('54).

ANDERSON, GENE *(1965)* 34 ——Dark-haired British beauty; she was with Jack Hawkins in *The Intruder;* in *The Day the Earth Caught Fire*, others.

ANDERSON, GEORGE *(1948)* 57 ——Support in *Murder, My Sweet* (detective), *Wilson* (Secretary Houston), *Nob Hill, The Palm Beach Story, King of Chinatown*, etc.

ANDERSON, JAMES *(1953)* 81 ——Scottish character; in *Tight Little Island, The College Boob, Fleetwing*, others.

ANDERSON, JAMES *(1969)* 48 ——Redneck husband of the girl (Collin Wilcox) who claimed to have been raped by the black in *To Kill a Mockingbird;* one of the stars of Arch Oboler's *Five;* in *Riot in Cell Block 11*, etc.

ANDRA, FERN *(1974)* 80 ——American-born actress who starred abroad; made over 80 pix in Germany; in *Eyes of the World*, etc.

ANDRE, GABY *(1972)* 35 ——French supporting actress; in Deborah Kerr's *Please Believe Me*, Glenn Ford's *The Green Glove, Hoboes in Paradise, The Cosmic Monster*, others.

ANDRE, GWILI *(1959)* 51 ——Norwegian beauty; New York fashion model; decorative, inanimate femme lead in B's: *Roar of the Dragon* (starring Richard Dix), *Secrets of the French Police;* last in 1942's *The Falcon's Brother.*

ANDREWS, ADORA *(1956)* 84 ——Character actress in *Smiling Faces* ('32).

ANDREWS, LA VERNE *(1967)* 52 ——Of the singing Andrews Sisters; in *What's Cookin'?, Hold That Ghost; Give Out, Sisters; Swingtime Johnny*, other WW II B musicals.

ANDREWS, LOIS *(1968)* 44 ——Stunning blonde ex-"child bride" of George Jessel; starred in title role in *Dixie Dugan;* featured in *Roger Touhy, Gangster; The Desert Hawk.*

ANDREWS, STANLEY *(1969)* 77 ——Tall, trim-moustached support in many: *Alexander's Ragtime Band, Kentucky, Meet John Doe*, etc.; in *The Lone Ranger* serial ('38) was chief outlaw villain Jeffries; was finally famous as The Old Ranger on TV's *Death Valley Days.*

ANDREWS, TOD *(1972)* 51 ——In movies from 1941; first known as Michael Ames (in *Murder in the Big House, Action in the North Atlantic; Now, Voyager;* other WB pix); as Tod Andrews was featured in *From Hell It Came, In Harm's Way*, etc., and starred in the TV series *The Gray Ghost.*

ANGELI, PIER *(1971)* 39 ——Delicate Italian beauty starred by MGM in *The Story of Three Loves, Sombrero, Teresa, Somebody Up There Likes Me*, others; was first wife of singer Vic Damone.

ANGELO, JEAN *(1933)* 45 ——A major French actor; star of silents *Nana* and *L'Atlantide* among others.

ANGOLD, EDIT *(1971)* 76 ——German character actress; the school principal in *Tomorrow the World.*

ANKRUM, MORRIS *(1964)* 68 ——Dependable character actor with handsome, weathered face; tweedy country-club types, seedy villains, ranchers, professional men; in *Roxie Hart, And Now Tomorrow, Lady in the Lake, The Harvey Girls*, and dozens more.

ANNABELLE *(1961)* 83——Lovely model for the original "Gibson Girl" who was known as "Peerless Annabelle" and featured in an 1897 Edison Kinetoscope, *Annabelle's Butterfly Dance;* later, as Annabelle Whitford, was one of the most famous Ziegfeld Girls.

ANSON, A. E. *(1936)* 57 ——Was Ronald Colman's teacher, Dr. Max Gottlieb, in *Arrowsmith*.

ANSON, LAURA *(1968)* 76 ——A "Fatty" Arbuckle leading lady; in *Bluebeard Jr.*, *Skid Proof*, *The Silent Partner*, others.

ANTHONY, JACK *(1962)* 61 ——Support in Noah Beery's *Hell-Ship Bronson* ('28).

ANTHONY, JOHN J. *(1970)* 60s ——Radio's famed Dr. Anthony; in a few movies.

ANTRIM, HARRY *(1967)* 72 ——Small, gray-haired character actor; Macy's department store owner in *Miracle on 34th Street*; Mr. Tubbs in *Intruder in the Dust*; in *The Solid Gold Cadillac*, *Teacher's Pet*, etc.

AOKI, TSURA *(1961)* 68 ——Costarred in silents; with husband Sessue Hayakawa in *The Typhoon*; with Earle Foxe in *Alien Souls*; in others.

APFEL, OSCAR *(1938)* 60s ——Director turned actor (with DeMille he codirected the 1913 *The Squaw Man*); bald support in scores of films from 1911; Secretary of War Stanton in Walter Huston's *Abraham Lincoln*; Margaret Sullavan's dad in *Only Yesterday*; in *The Bowery*, *I Am a Fugitive From a Chain Gang*, *Before Dawn*, etc.; the year before his death had character roles in eight films.

APOLLON, DAVE *(1972)* 74 ——He and his orchestra were featured in *Merry-Go-Round of 1938*.

APPEL, ANNA *(1963)* 70s ——Jewish mother in *Symphony of Six Million*; prominently featured in *Broken Hearts*, *Heart of New York*, *Green Fields*, etc.

APPLEGATE, HAZEL *(1959)* 73 ——Player in early Essanay films.

APPLEWHITE, ERIC LEON *(1973)* 76 —— Character actor.

ARBUCKLE, MACLYN *(1931)* 66 ——Starred in silents from 1915; in *The Country Chairman*, *The Prodigal Judge*, etc.; was Marion Davies' portly father in *Janice Meredith*.

ARBUCKLE, ROSCOE "FATTY" *(1933)* 46 — —One of the great comics of the silent screen, whose career was destroyed by the Virginia Rappe "wild party" scandal.

ARCHAINBAUD, GEORGE *(1959)* 68 ——A few screen roles; better known as director of *Her Jungle Love*, *Thanks for the Memory*, etc.

ARDEN, EDWIN *(1918)* 54 ——Curly-haired stage star; appeared in *Virtuous Wives* the year of his death.

ARLEDGE, JOHN *(1947)* 41 ——Second leads (often as the trim-moustached "other" man) or top support in many: *Devil Dogs of the Air*, *Shipmates Forever*, *Murder on a Bridle Path*, *City for Conquest*, *Cheers for Miss Bishop*, etc.

ARLEN, BETTY *(1966)* 61 ——Dark-haired Wampas Baby Star of 1925; in few films.

ARLEN, JUDITH *(1968)* 40s ——Dancer-actress; a Wampas Baby Star in '32; sister of Ann Rutherford.

ARLISS, FLORENCE *(1950)* 77 ——Acted on-screen only with husband George; in silents (*Disraeli*, *The Devil*) and talkies (*Disraeli*, *The King's Vacation*, *The House of Rothschild*, *The Millionaire*, etc.).

ARLISS, GEORGE *(1946)* 77 ——English stage actor who became an international screen star at 53; he remade some of his silent hits as talkies: *The Man Who Played God*; *Disraeli*, for which he became the first Britisher to win a Best Actor Oscar; was nominated also, that same year (1929–30) in another of his remakes, *The Green Goddess*; also starred in *Cardinal Richelieu*, *Voltaire*, *The House of Rothschild*; retired from the screen after 1937's *Dr. Syn*.

ARMENDARIZ, PEDRO *(1963)* 51 ——Virile, handsome Mexican star; in *Three Godfathers*, *Fort Apache*, *The Pearl*, *We Were Strangers*, others.

ARMETTA, HENRY *(1945)* 57 ——A comic Italian joy in more than 300 movies including *The Big Store*, *Ghost Chasers*, *Poor Little Rich Girl*, *Top of the Town*, *A Bell for Adano*, *Colonel Effingham's Raid* and *Princess O'Hara*.

ARMITAGE, WALTER *(1953)* 45 ——Appeared in *British Agent*, *Bombay Mail*, *Where Sinners Meet*.

ARMSTRONG, LOUIS *(1971)* 71 ——Beloved "Satchmo," Negro jazz star whose smile was as wondrous as his trumpet playing; in *High Society*, *Pennies from Heaven*, *Cabin in the Sky*, *Artists and Models*, *Here Comes the Groom*, more.

ARMSTRONG, ROBERT *(1973)* 82 —— Rugged star of adventure movies including *King Kong*, *The Lost Squadron*, *G Men*, *The Leatherneck*, *Panama Flo*, many more; then one of Hollywood's most durable character actors; retired after 1964's *For Those Who Think Young*.

ARMSTRONG, WILL *(1943)* 74 ——Support in silents such as *A Boy of the Streets* and *Clancy's Kosher Wedding*.

ARNA, LISSI *(1964)* 64 ——Beautiful German star of one American film, Pathe's *Beyond Victory* ('31), and many far better European productions.

ARNAUD, YVONNE *(1958)* 65 ——French star of charm and elegance seen in films of France (*My Uncle*, etc.) and England (*On Approval, Princess Charming, Canaries Sometimes Sing*, and *Tomorrow We Live*, released in the U.S. by Republic as *At Dawn We Die*).

ARNHEIM, GUS *(1955)* 56 ——Songwriter-bandleader; with his orchestra in musical shorts.

ARNOLD, CECILE *(1931)* 40s ——Chaplin's gorgeous leading lady in *The Face on the Barroom Floor, Dough and Dynamite*, etc.; also was featured in many Sennett comedies starring the late Fred Mace.

ARNOLD, EDWARD *(1966)* 66 ——Character star worth his weight (considerable) in sterling silver; his cool watchful eyes should have warned screen adversaries not to trust too readily his facile jovial laugh; an MGM mainstay (*Johnny Eager, Mrs. Parkington, Ziegfeld Follies, Design for Scandal*, etc.), he was especially memorable in roles undertaken elsewhere —political boss Jim Taylor in *Mr. Smith Goes to Washington*, Daniel Webster in *The Devil and Daniel Webster (All That Money Can Buy)*, and the title role in *Diamond Jim*.

ARNOLD, PHIL *(1968)* 59 ——Bald veteran screen comedian; Mayor Fiorello LaGuardia in *The Court-Martial of Billy Mitchell*; also in *Sis Hopkins, King of the Turf, G.I. Jane*, etc.

ARNOLD, SETH *(1955)* 69 ——Character (Clint Adams) in *Lost Boundaries*.

ARNOLD, WILLIAM *(1940)* 47 ——Support in *The Crowd Roars* ('32); *In Love With Life; Edison, the Man; Rich Man's Folly*, etc.

ARQUETTE, CLIFF *(1974)* 68 ——Pudgy rustic comic; "Charlie Weaver"; in *Comin' Round the Mountain*.

ARRAS, HARRY *(1942)* 60 ——Support in a Warners B, *Escape from Crime*, which starred Richard Travis.

ARTHUR, JOHNNY K. *(1951)* 68 ——Played prim, whiny-voiced little men; in dozens of shorts (including "Our Gang," in which he was sometimes Spanky's father, sometimes

Darla's); some of his features: *The King Steps Out, 20 Million Sweethearts, Road to Singapore;* was interestingly cast as chief villain Sakima in the serial *The Masked Marvel*.

ARTHUR, JULIA *(1950)* 81 ——Brunette star of Vitagraph's *Napoleon—The Man of Destiny* ('09), *The Woman the Germans Shot* (also shown as *The Cavell Case*), and *The Common Cause* ('18).

ARVIDSON, LINDA *(1949)* 65 ——D. W. Griffith's first wife (1906–36), she played femme leads in many very early silents including *Edgar Allan Poe, Enoch Arden*.

ASCHE, OSCAR *(1936)* 65 ——Screenwriter (*Chu Chin Chow*) who appeared in support in several British pix of the '30s: *Scrooge, Robber Symphony, Don Quixote*.

ASH, RUSSELL *(1974)* 62 ——Character actor.

ASH, SAM *(1951)* 67 ——Comic support (Frank) in *The Heat's On; Oh, You Beautiful Doll;* Laurel & Hardy's *The Dancing Masters;* character in the serial *Ace Drummond*.

ASHE, WARREN *(1944)* 44 —— Support; Lt. Morton in E. G. Robinson's *Destroyer;* in *Naval Academy, Harmon of Michigan, The Face Behind the Mask*.

ASHER, MAX *(1957)* 76 ——"The funniest Dutch comedian in pictures" was his label in silent comedies in which he starred (Universal's "Joker" series), though he was California-born; in silent features: *The Shooting of Dan McGrew, The Courtship of Myles Standish*, others; last in support in Margaret Sullavan's *Little Man, What Now?*

ASHTON, DORRIT *(1936)* 63 ——Was seen in silents; wife of Western actor Charles Newton.

ASHTON, SYLVIA *(1940)* 60 ——Plump character actress DeMille kept steadily occupied in silents: *Don't Change Your Husband* (as Mrs. Huckney), *For Better, For Worse* (Swanson's aunt), *Manslaughter* (prison matron), many others.

ASKAM, EARL *(1940)* 41 ——Handsome pirate in *Madam Satan's* dirigible party scene; in Hopalong Cassidy Westerns; Officer Torch in serial *Flash Gordon*.

ASKAN, PERRY *(1961)* 63 ——Top young support in a 1930 Technicolor pic, *Sweet Kitty Bellairs*, starring Claudia Dell.

ASTANGOV, MIKHAIL *(1965)* 64 ——A top Russian actor; in *Sadko, The First Front, Prisoners*, et al.

ASTOR, JUNIE *(1967)* 49 ——Prominently featured, when a teenager, in Renoir's *The Lower Depths.*

ATCHLEY, HOOPER *(1943)* 56 ——Dignified character; support in many features: *A Day at the Races* (race judge); *Hell's House; Rings on Her Fingers; Mr. Wong, Detective,* etc.; also in serials: *The Three Musketeers, Ace Drummond, Adventures of Red Ryder, Dick Tracy vs. Crime, Inc.*

ATES, ROSCOE *(1962)* 67 ——Got laughs in dozens with stutter, Dopey-like face, and pop eyes: *Chad Hanna, One Foot in Heaven, Those Redheads from Seattle, The Palm Beach Story,* etc.; had roles in countless Westerns including that of Eddie Dean's sidekick "Soapy."

ATKINSON, EVELYN *(1954)* 54 ——Featured in MGM's silent *Boy Friend* ('26).

ATKINSON, FRANK *(1963)* 69 ——British; Uncle Dick in *Cavalcade;* in *Three Men in a Boat, The Green Cockatoo, Ladies' Man,* etc.

ATWELL, ROY *(1962)* 82 ——Support in silents *(Grand Larceny, Souls for Sale,* etc.) and talkies *(Varsity Show, The Fleet's In,* others).

ATWILL, LIONEL *(1946)* 61 ——Smooth as any villain ever in the movies; was at his best worst in *The Hound of the Baskervilles, The Last Train from Madrid, The Ghost of Frankenstein, Sherlock Holmes and the Secret Weapon, Charlie Chan's Murder Cruise;* paid for his high crimes in serials such as *Junior G-Men of the Air* (The Baron), *Captain America* (Dr. Maldor), and *Lost City of the Jungle* (warmonger Sir Eric Hazarias).

AUDRAN, EDMOND *(1951)* 32 ——A featured dancer in *The Red Shoes* and *Tales of Hoffman.*

AUEN, SIGNE *(1966)* 70 ——See Seena Owen.

AUER, FLORENCE *(1962)* 82 ——A 1908 Biograph star; support in Griffith's *That Royle Girl* ('26); was dignified, elderly Grace Draper in *State of the Union* ('48), her last.

AUER, MISCHA *(1967)* 62 ——Comedies of the '30s and '40s wouldn't have been the same without this frenetic, pole-thin, language-mangling Russian; a few of his many: *One Hundred Men and a Girl, My Man Godfrey* (Oscar nomination as Best Support), *Destry Rides Again, East Side of Heaven,* and *You Can't Take It With You.*

AUGUST, EDWIN *(1964)* 81 ——Dashing, handsome star of silents from 1908; in *Smile of a Child* ('10), *The Revenue Man and the Girl, The Hand That Rocked the Cradle, In a Roman Garden, The Lesser Evil, The Yellow Passport, A Tale of Two Nations,* and many others including the 1918 serial *The Lion's Claw;* only a few talkies; last had a supporting role in a 1943 Milton Berle comedy, *Over My Dead Body.*

AULT, MARIE *(1951)* 81 ——Hilarious as freeloading Rummy Mitchens in *Major Barbara;* in other British pix: *Love on the Dole, Hobson's Choice* ('31), *Woman to Woman, Fanny Hawthorn.*

AUSTIN, ALBERT *(1953)* 71 ——Silent support; *My Boy, Keep Smiling, Suds, The Kid.*

AUSTIN, CHARLES *(1944)* 66 ——Played a yeoman in Flynn's *Another Dawn.*

AUSTIN, GENE *(1972)* 71 ——"My Blue Heaven" singer; in *Sadie McKee, Gift of Gab.*

AUSTIN, JERE *(1927)* 51 ——Support in Alice Joyce's *The School for Scandal* ('14), and in *Single Wives, A Regular Fellow,* and *Sundown.*

AUSTIN, JOHANNA *(1944)* 91 ——Performed in early silents for the Edison Co.

AVERY, PATRICIA *(1973)* 70 ——She went from studio secretary to featured roles in a few silents: *Annie Laurie* with Lillian Gish, *Alex the Great* with "Skeets" Gallagher, etc.; was once married to (then divorced from) late makeup wizard Merrill Pye.

AVERY, TOL *(1973)* 60s ——Character (Fat Man) in *I'll Cry Tomorrow;* also in *Hotel* and *Twist Around the Clock.*

AYE, MARION *(1951)* 48 ——A stunningly beautiful 1922 Wampas Baby Star; in *Montana Bill, Irene,* other silents.

AYLESWORTH, ARTHUR *(1945)* 60s —— Character (Renault) in Cooper's *Beau Geste;* in *Test Pilot* (Loy's farmer dad), *Drums Along the Mohawk, Jesse James, Dust Be My Destiny,* and a score more.

AYLMER, DAVID *(1964)* 31 ——Son of Felix; English support; in *Gideon of Scotland Yard, The Man Who Wouldn't Talk,* etc.

AYRES, AGNES *(1940)* 42 ——Shared those sizzling love scenes with Valentino in *The Sheik;* starred in many other silents: *The Affairs of Anatol, Forbidden Fruit, Clarence, The Ten Commandments, Cappy Ricks,* etc.

AYRES, MITCHELL *(1969)* 58 ——He and his orchestra were in 1943's *Swingtime Johnny.*

AYRES, ROBERT *(1968)* 54 ——American who played Cooper-type roles in English pix *(Night Without Stars, River Beat, A Prize of Gold, It's Never Too Late)* and American-produced films made abroad: *John Paul Jones, Battle Beneath the Earth* (Admiral Hillebrand), *The Road to Hong Kong.*

B

BACCALONI, SALVATORE *(1969)* 69 ——Opera star who played leading roles in *Fanny, Full of Life, The Merry Andrew, Rock-a-Bye Baby,* and *The Pigeon That Took Rome.*

BACKUS, GEORGE *(1939)* 81 ——Support in silents: *The Warrens of Virginia, The Exciters,* etc.

BACLANOVA, OLGA *(1974)* 74 ——Most famous as the star (beautiful, conniving trapeze artist who marries a midget) of *Freaks,* she was also in *The Docks of New York, Forgotten Faces, Three Sinners,* etc.; retiring in 1933, she made a one-performance "comeback" ten years later in a supporting role in *Claudia.*

BACON, DAVID *(1943)* 29 ——Starred in the title role in Republic's *The Masked Marvel* serial; also featured in *Ten Gentlemen from West Point* and *Crash Dive.*

BACON, FAITH *(1956)* 45 ——Famous stripper who claimed to have invented the fan dance; was featured in *Prison Train.*

BACON, FRANK *(1922)* 58 ——Gray-haired main support in Bushman's *The Silent Voice;* long a Broadway character star.

BACON, IRVING *(1965)* 72 ——Lanky, lugubrious comic character whose doleful demeanor brightened scores of movies: *State of the Union, Meet John Doe, It Happened One Night, The Bachelor and the Bobby-Soxer,* Garland's *A Star Is Born, The Amazing Dr. Clitterhouse,* etc.

BACON, LLOYD *(1955)* 65 ——In silents: *The Great Profit, The Road Demon, Hands Off.*

BAER, BUGS, *(1969)* 83 ——Humorist; featured in the silent *The Great White Way.*

BAER, MAX *(1959)* 50 ——Champion fighter, shared with Myrna Loy the title roles in *The Prizefighter and the Lady* ('33); ended acting career in support in another fight pic, *The Harder They Fall* ('56), with others *(The Navy Comes Through, Africa Screams,* etc.) in between.

BAGDASARIAN, ROSS *(1972)* 52 ——Actor-songwriter; character (the composer) in *Rear Window;* also in *Destination Gobi, The Proud and the Profane;* a.k.a. David Seville.

BAGGETT, LYNNE *(1960)* 42 ——WB starlet; in *Manpower, Adventures of Mark Twain,* etc.

BAGGOTT, KING *(1948)* 72 ——Major silents star; IMP's number one moneymaker; in *The Loan Shark, Science, Lady Audley's Secret, Ivanhoe* ('13), the first *Dr. Jekyll and Mr. Hyde,* etc.; became Universal's kingpin attraction via 1915's *The Corsican Brothers* (dual role), followed by many more; later a silver-haired character actor at MGM, he ended his career playing bits in *Come Live With Me* and others.

BAGLEY, SAM *(1968)* 65 ——Minor support in *The Lieutenant Wore Skirts.*

BAGNI, JOHN *(1954)* 42 ——Featured in *A Bell for Adano, Bombay Clipper, Captain China, The Pretender.*

BAILEY, ALBERT *(1952)* 61 ——Minor support in Westerns.

BAILEY, FRANKIE *(1953)* 94 ——Vaudeville's "Girl With the Million-Dollar Legs"; in *The Famous Mrs. Fair, The Crown of Lies,* etc.

BAILEY, WILLIAM NORTON *(1962)* 76 —— In features *(Charlie Chan's Secret, George White's Scandals, The Midnight Patrol,* etc.) plus many silent serials *(The Eagle's Eye, The Phantom Foe, House Without a Key,* others).

BAINES, BEULAH *(1930)* 25 ——Appeared in support in Wallace Reid's *The Charm School.*

BAINTER, FAY *(1968)* 76 ——Superb, warm character actress with one of the screen's most uniquely appealing speaking voices; won the Supporting Oscar as Aunt Belle in *Jezebel;* particularly memorable are her mother roles: *Our Town, White Banners* (Oscar-nominated as Best Actress), *The Human Comedy, State Fair* ('45), *Maryland,* and *Babes on Broadway;* her third Oscar nomination was as Best Support in 1961's *The Children's Hour,* one of her more chilling performances.

BAIRD, LEAH *(1971)* 80 ——Starred in silents for Universal and Vitagraph; in *The Heart Line, When the Devil Drives, Destroying Angel, Tried* *for His Own Murder*, etc.; later played minor supporting roles at WB for many years.

BAJOR, GIZI *(1951)* 55 ——Actress who had a top role in the Hungarian pic *Two Prisoners*.

BAKER, ART *(1966)* 68 ——Silver-haired character; in *Spellbound, Once Upon a Time, Daisy Kenyon, State of the Union, Task Force,* many more; eventually more famous as the genial host of TV's *You Asked for It*.

BAKER, BELLE *(1957)* 62 ——Vaudeville star; in *The Song of Love* ('29) and *Atlantic City*.

BAKER, EDDIE *(1968)* 70 ——A Keystone Kop; comic support in *Elmer and Elsie, Babes in Toyland* ('34), *City Lights*, more.

BAKER, LEE *(1948)* 71 ——Character actor in *Mourning Becomes Electra* and in silents.

BAKER, MARK *(1972)* ——Support in Steiger's *Across the Bridge*.

BAKER, PHIL *(1963)* 67 ——Comic radio star; onscreen in *The Goldwyn Follies, Take It or Leave It, The Gang's All Here, Gift of Gab*.

BALCH, SLIM *(1967)* ——Supporting player in *Hollywood Cowboy*, many others.

BALDRA, CHUCK *(1949)* 50 ——Support in *The Lawless Nineties;* also was in silents.

BALFOUR, LORNA *(1932)* 19 ——Supporting role in *Merely Mary Ann*, as daughter of Beryl Mercer, housekeeper of the boarding house where Janet Gaynor was a slavey.

BALIEFF, NIKITA *(1936)* 59 ——Moon-faced stage comedy star (*Chauve Souris*) who was prominently featured in Jimmy Savo's *Once in a Blue Moon* in '36.

BALIN, MIREILLE *(1968)* 59 ——Jean Gabin's beautiful costar in *Pepe le Moko*.

BALL, SUZAN *(1955)* 22 ——Dark-haired Universal starlet; in *War Arrow, City Beneath the Sea, Chief Crazy Horse, Yankee Buccaneer, East of Sumatra;* married late actor Richard Long after leg amputation to halt cancer caused by a fall during a movie dance number.

BALLANTINE, E. J. *(1968)* 80 ——One of the Norwegian hostages "shot" in *The Moon Is Down;* support in *Magic Town*, others.

BALLANTYNE, NELL *(1959)* ——Scottish character actress; in *Scotch on the Rocks*, etc.

BALLIN, MABEL *(1958)* 73 ——Lovely brunette star, of the liquid eyes and expressive brow, who was delightful in the title role of 1921's *Jane Eyre;* was in the silent *Vanity Fair,* others, including *Riders of the Purple Sage* as Tom Mix's love interest.

BALLOU, MARION *(1939)* 67 ——Support in *Night Work, Cradle Song, Portia on Trial*, etc.

BAMATTRE, MARTHA *(1970)* 78 ——Character (Mathilde Mattieu) in *An American in Paris*.

BANCROFT, CHARLES *(1969)* 58 ——Supporting roles.

BANCROFT, GEORGE *(1956)* 74 ——After 1927's *Underworld* he was a movie king, the #1 box-office attraction "whose infectious laughter was recognized and imitated all over the world"; his Paramount superstardom lasted till the mid-30s, through *Docks of New York, Thunderbolt,* (nominated for an Oscar as Best Actor), *The Drag Net*, etc.; replaced by Cagney, Robinson, and Muni as the nation's favorite gangster, he became one of Hollywood's ablest character actors: *Stagecoach, Young Tom Edison* (Rooney's father), *Little Men, Angels With Dirty Faces*, etc.

BANKHEAD, TALLULAH *(1968)* 65 ——Broadway's one-of-a-kind actress (best in *The Little Foxes*), the husky-voiced star scored indelibly onscreen in Hitchcock's *Lifeboat*, compensating for earlier movie disasters at Paramount.

BANKS, LESLIE *(1952)* 61 ——British; in *I am Suzanne, Jamaica Inn, Red Ensign*, etc.

BANKS, MONTY *(1950)* 52 ——Urbane British-American; in *Great Guns*, etc.; was husband of comedienne Gracie Fields.

BANNER, JOHN *(1973)* 63 ——An actor-refugee from Europe, he was a character in Hollywood pix from '39 (*The Fallen Sparrow, Tonight We Raid Calais, The Moon Is Down*, etc.), prior to greater popularity as paunchy Sgt. Schultz in TV's *Hogan's Heroes*.

BANNISTER, HARRY *(1961)* 72 ——In *The Girl of the Golden West* ('31), *Suicide Fleet*, others; once married to Ann Harding.

BARA, THEDA *(1955)* 65 ——"The prime dweller in the tents of wickedness" (as film historian Edward Wagenknecht has labeled her), she was the silents' unforgettable first "vamp"; seduced huge sections of the population in *A Fool There Was, Salome, Cleopatra*, et al.

BARBETTE *(1973)* 68 ——Noted French trapeze artist; was one of four members of the "Audience" in Cocteau's *The Blood of a Poet*.

BARBIER, GEORGE *(1945)* 80 ——One of the movies' best-loved characters, he played bespectacled dads and irascible old codgers; in *College Rhythm*, *Wife vs. Secretary*, *The Smiling Lieutenant*, *Sweethearts*, and a hundred more.

BARCROFT, ROY *(1969)* 67 ——Called "King of the Heavies" in B Westerns (200 in 31 years onscreen), he claimed he liked best the roles "where I could be the dirtiest, meanest unkempt individual possible"; besides stalking Roy Rogers, Allan Lane, et al. was in many serials: *The Purple Monster Strikes*, *Man Hunt of Mystery Island*, etc.

BARKER, BRADLEY *(1951)* 68 ——With Constance Binney in *Erstwhile Susan*, many other silents.

BARKER, LEX *(1973)* 54 ——Famous as the screen's tenth Tarzan, he also was seen in *La Dolce Vita*, *Away All Boats*, *Woman Times Seven*, etc.; ex of Lana Turner and Arlene Dahl.

BARLOW, REGINALD *(1943)* 76 ——In *Mata Hari*, *The Wet Parade*, *Horse Feathers*, more.

BARNARD, IVOR *(1953)* 66 ——British character; vicious killer (Major Ross) in *Beat the Devil*; Wemmick in *Great Expectations* ('47); in *The Stars Look Down*, *Pygmalion*, etc.

BARNELL, NORA ELY *(1933)* 51 ——Appeared in early Ince films.

BARNES, BARRY K. *(1965)* 59 ——British star of some charm (often boyish) in *The Return of the Scarlet Pimpernel* (title role), *Bedelia*, *The Man in Paris*, many more.

BARNES, FRANK *(1940)* 30s ——Brother of heroine "Annabelle Lee" in Keaton's *The General*.

BARNES, GEORGE *(1949)* 59 ——Lead bandit who fires at audience at end of *The Great Train Robbery*.

BARNES, JUSTUS D. *(1946)* 84—Gray character lead in 1915's *The Country Girl*.

BARNES, ROY T. *(1937)* 56 ——Marion Davies' handsome costar in the bucolic *Adam and Eva*, among other silents.

BARNES, V. L. *(1949)* 79 ——He was in silents: *Peggy of the Secret Service*, *The Fighting Cheat*, etc.

BARNETT, CHESTER *(1947)* 62 ——Vivian Martin's curly-haired costar in *The Wishing Ring*.

BARNETT, GRIFF *(1958)* 72 ——Character in *Possessed* ('47), *Cass Timberlane*, others; de Havilland's dad in *To Each His Own*.

BARR, BYRON *(1966)* 49 ——Young support; in *Pitfall*, *Tokyo Rose*, etc.; not Gig Young, whose real name is the same.

BARR, JEANNE *(1967)* 35 ——Was seen in *Lilith*, *The Fugitive Kind*, and on television.

BARRAT, ROBERT *(1970)* 78 ——Big, muscular, Roman-nosed character from New York who, in more than 100 pix (1933–51), was a master at dialects (a German officer in *The Florentine Dagger*, a Polish immigrant in *Stranded*, a Frenchman in *The Dressmaker*); the loudmouthed, smalltown doctor in *Dr. Socrates*, he was also in *Northwest Passage*, *Captain Blood*, *The Life of Emile Zola*, etc.

BARRETT, IVY RICE *(1962)* 64 ——One of Sennett's bathing beauties.

BARRETT, JANE *(1969)* 46 ——British; second leads; in Disney's *The Sword and the Rose*.

BARRETT, PAT *(1959)* 70 ——Radio's "Uncle Ezra"; in *Comin' Round the Mountain*.

BARRETT, TONY *(1974)* 58 ——In *Born to Kill*, *Dick Tracy's Dilemma*, *Impact*, *San Quentin*.

BARRI, MARIO *(1963)* 30s ——Philippine; top support in George Montgomery's *Samar*, *Huk*, *The Steel Claw*.

BARRIER, EDGAR *(1964)* 57 ——Suave, aquiline-nosed support (and frequent villain); best recalled for Universal pix of the '40s (*The Phantom of the Opera*, *Cobra Woman*, *Flesh and Fantasy*, *Arabian Nights*); last in *Irma la Douce*.

BARRIS, HARRY *(1962)* 57 ——Support in *The Spirit of Notre Dame*, *Birth of the Blues*.

BARRISCALE, BESSIE *(1965)* 81 ——A top silent star, this brunette beauty was in *Girl of the Golden West*, *Wooden Shoes*, *Not My Sister*, *Home*, and many more.

BARRON, MARCUS *(1944)* 75 ——Support in English films of the '30s: *Loyalties*, Hitchcock's *Strauss's Great Waltz* (a.k.a. *Waltzes from Vienna)*, in which he played Drexter.

BARROUX, LUCIEN *(1968)* 79 ——French star of the '39 version of *Moulin-Rouge, Naughty Martine*, etc.

BARROWS, JAMES O. *(1925)* 73 ——Character in silents: *The Sea Beast, Pawned*, etc.

BARRY, JOE *(1974)* 50s ——Character (Exterminator) in *Bell, Book and Candle*; in Mitchum's *The Man with the Gun* also.

BARRY, TOM *(1931)* 47 ——Support in Warner Baxter's *The Cisco Kid*, his only picture.

BARRY, VIOLA *(1964)* 70 ——Extraordinarily beautiful silent star who first (in '12) played femme fatales; later was in *The Mothering Heart, The Sea Wolf* ('20), numerous others.

BARRYE, EMILY *(1957)* 61 ——A reform-school inmate in DeMille's *The Godless Girl*, she also had a bit in his *The King of Kings*.

BARRYMORE, DIANA *(1960)* 38 ——John's daughter; Universal starred her, with scant success, in *Between Us Girls, Eagle Squadron, Nightmare, Ladies Courageous*, etc.

BARRYMORE, ETHEL *(1959)* 79 ——Cello voice, piercing gaze, impeccable acting style; dominated her every scene in *None But the Lonely Heart* (Supporting Oscar); others for which she was nominated *(The Spiral Staircase, The Paradine Case, Pinky);* and *The Farmer's Daughter, Portrait of Jennie, Rasputin and the Empress*, etc.

BARRYMORE, JOHN *(1942)* 60 ——Illustrious stage star whose screen performances often seemed too big for his frame; at his best in *Grand Hotel, The Great Man Votes, Dinner at Eight, A Bill of Divorcement;* at his worst, caricaturing his own past glory, in *The Great Profile;* portrayed by Jack Cassidy in *W. C. Fields and Me*.

BARRYMORE, LIONEL *(1954)* 76 ——MGM's beloved, crotchety, arthritic Dr. Gillespie in the "Dr. Kildare" series gave superlative performances before this casting *(The Copperhead, Sadie Thompson, Grand Hotel, Camille, Captains Courageous,* and *A Free Soul* which, his only nomination, won him a Best Actor Oscar); memorable later in *It's a Wonderful Life, Key Largo,* and *Duel in the Sun;* onscreen longer than any of the Barrymores, starting in 1908.

BARTELL, RICHARD *(1967)* 69 ——Character; in *Design for Scandal, My Sister Eileen*.

BARTELS, LOUIS JOHN *(1932)* 37 ——Support in *The Canary Murder Case, Broadway Nights*, others.

BARTH, BELLE *(1971)* 69 ——Longtime support.

BARTHELMESS, RICHARD *(1963)* 68 ——His gentleness and idealism in *Broken Blossoms* (not his debut) catapulted him to enormous popularity in silents, which later pix like *Way Down East* and *Tol'able David* augmented; retiring in '35, he came back later in support in *Only Angels Have Wings, The Spoilers* ('42), etc.; was Oscar-nominated as Best Actor in two in the same year (1927–28): *The Noose* and *The Patent Leather Kid*.

BARTHOLOMEW, AGNES *(1955)* ——Actress-wife of Holmes Herbert; in *A Man Called Peter*.

BARTLETT, CLIFFORD *(1936)* 33 ——British; minor roles.

BARTON, JAMES *(1962)* 71 ——Vigorous character; best as the garrulous Kit Carson in *The Time of Your Life*, he was fine too in *The Shepherd of the Hills, Yellow Sky, Here Comes the Groom,* and *Wabash Avenue*.

BARTON, JOE *(1937)* 54 ——Supported Chester Conklin in *McFadden's Flats*.

BARTY, JACK *(1943)* 52 ——English comic; support in Thelma Todd-Patsy Kelly shorts.

BARZELL, WOLFE *(1969)* 72 ——Heavy-faced, cleft-chinned character; in *Love With the Proper Stranger* (priest), *Sands of Beersheba, Frankenstein's Daughter*, other pix of '50s and '60s.

BASCH, FELIX *(1944)* 55 ——German roles in WW II pix: *Uncertain Glory, Desperate Journey, Chetniks*, etc.

BASFORD, MADALINE LEE *(1974)* 62 ——Movies, but most famous as *Amos 'n Andy's* "Miss Blue" on radio.

BASKETT, JAMES *(1948)* 44 ——Black who won a special Oscar as beaming "Uncle Remus" in Disney's *Song of the South*.

BASSERMAN, ALBERT *(1952)* 85 ——German emigre whose Hollywood performances were never less than distinguished; in *Foreign Corre-*

spondent (the assassinated Van Meer), *Dr. Ehrlich's Magic Bullet, The Searching Wind, Madame Curie*, etc.; nominated for Best Supporting Actor Oscar in *Foreign Correspondent*.

BASSERMAN, ELSE *(1961)* 83 ——Actress-wife of Albert who played his wife (Mme. Perot) in *Madame Curie;* also in *Escape.*

BASSETT, RUSSELL *(1918)* 72 ——Bald, stocky character who often played fathers, such as Dorothy Davenport's in *The Best Man Wins* ('11); was also in *Jim the Penman*, Pickford's *Hulda from Holland*, George M. Cohan's *Hit the Trail Holiday.*

BATEMAN, VICTORY *(1926)* 60 ——She was in *If I Were Queen, The Turmoil*, other silents.

BATES, BARBARA *(1969)* 43 ——Brunette ingenue; the girl in *All About Eve*'s final scene; earlier in *Cheaper By the Dozen, June Bride* (editor B. Davis planned to have her wedding photographed but she eloped instead), *This Love of Ours;* later in *Belles on Their Toes, Outcasts of Poker Flat*, etc.

BATES, BLANCHE *(1941)* 68 ——Famous Belasco stage star who, a bit past her prime, appeared on the screen in 1919's *The Border Legion.*

BATES, FLORENCE *(1954)* 65 ——Plump, smiling "meanie" who was at her best in *Rebecca* (Fontaine's employer who tried to entice Olivier); in *Saratoga Trunk, A Letter to Three Wives, The Devil and Miss Jones, Tonight and Every Night*, etc.

BATES, GRANVILLE *(1939)* 58 ——Character in *My Favorite Wife* (judge), *The Mortal Storm, Of Mice and Men, Green Light, Eternally Yours*, dozens more.

BATES, LES *(1930)* 53 ——In many action silents: *The Texas Streak, Belle of Alaska, Blues Blazes*, etc.

BATIE, FRANKLIN *(1949)* 69 ——Support in Jolson's *Big Boy.*

BATTIER, ROBERT *(1946)* 59 ——Support in Simone Simon's *Love and Hisses.*

BATTY, ARCHIBALD *(1961)* 74 ——British support; in *Drums* and *Four Feathers.*

BAUM, HARRY *(1974)* 58 ——actor-dancer-stuntman; in movies from age eight.

BAUR, HARRY *(1943)* 52 ——Bald, distinguished French star; *The Golem* (the emperor),

Un Carnet de Bal (the religious), Beethoven's *Great Love*, many more.

BAXTER, JIMMY *(1969)* 46 ——Was Fredric March as a child in *The Dark Angel;* others.

BAXTER, LORA *(1955)* 47 ——She played small roles in the '30s.

BAXTER, WARNER *(1951)* 59 ——Dependable, handsome, stolid leading man more popular with his fans (housewives mainly) than critics, except in such rarities as *In Old Arizona* (won him an Oscar) and *Adam Had Four Sons;* serviceable performances in *42nd Street* ("You're going out there a nobody . . ."); *Wife, Doctor and Nurse; The Prisoner of Shark Island; Lady in the Dark*, and dozens more dating from the early 1920s.

BAY, TOM *(1933)* 32 ——In silent Westerns: *The Devil's Gulch, The Valley of Bravery*, etc.

BEAL, FRANK *(1934)* 70 ——Support in silents: *The Best Bad Man, Soft Boiled*, etc.

BEAL, ROYAL *(1969)* 69 ——In *Lost Boundaries* (detective), *Anatomy of a Murder* (sheriff).

BEAMISH, FRANK *(1921)* 40 ——Appeared in *The Faithless Sex, The Blonde Vampire.*

BEATTY, CLYDE *(1965)* 62 ——Circus lion-tamer; starred in *The Big Cage, Ring of Fire*, and two serials.

BEATTY, GEORGE *(1971)* 76 ——Character; *Johnny Doesn't Live Here Anymore, Crazy House.*

BEATTY, MAY *(1945)* 63 ——English support; *Lloyds of London, Pride and Prejudice.*

BEAUBIEN, JULIEN *(1947)* 51 ——Support in Florence Vidor's *Main Street.*

BEAUDET, LOUISE *(1947)* 87 ——Brunette Vitagraph actress who costarred with Sidney Drew in 1913's *Jerry's Uncle's Namesake* and in '15 had top supporting roles in Norma Talmadge's *The Battle Cry of Peace* and three Antonio Moreno pix: *On Her Wedding Night, A "Model" Wife, The Price for Folly.*

BEAUMONT, DIANA *(1964)* 55 ——In *I Was Monty's Double* and many more British films.

BEAUMONT, HARRY *(1966)* 78 ——1916 Essanay star; in the serial *The Active Life of the Dailies.*

BEAUMONT, LUCY (*1937*) 54 ——Many silents (*Good Bad Boy, The Man Without a Country, The Crowd*, etc.) and talkies (*A Free Soul, The Devil Doll, Maid of Salem*).

BEAVERS, LOUISE (*1962*) 60 ——Joyous, large-sized black character; best as Colbert's cook and flapjack-making business partner in *Imitation of Life*; memorable too in *Make Way for Tomorrow, The Big Street, Virginia*, and scores more from '29.

BEBAN, GEORGE (*1928*) 55 ——A top character in *Pasquale, The Italian, Lost in Transit*, other silents.

BECHTEL, WILLIAM (*1930*) 63 ——Was in *Spite Marriage, Jazz Age, The Social Lion*.

BECK, DANNY (*1959*) 55 ——Bearded support in Cagney's *Man of a Thousand Faces*.

BECK, JAMES (*1973*) 41 ——British; support in Darren McGavin's *The Outsider*.

BECKETT, SCOTTY (*1968*) 38 ——Bright-faced, greatly appealing boy actor; in *Kings Row, My Favorite Wife, The Blue Bird*, and many others from the early '30s on; particularly impressive as Aherne's untrustworthy lad in *My Son, My Son*.

BECKWITH, REGINALD (*1965*) 57 ——English support in dozens: *Genevieve, Scott of the Antarctic*, etc.

BEDOYA, ALFONSO (*1957*) 53 ——Mexican actor; tops as the terrifying, laughing villain, Gold Hat, in *The Treasure of the Sierra Madre*.

BEECHER, JANET (*1955*) 71 ——Always perfect as a gray-haired aristocrat; in *The President Vanishes, The Thirteenth Chair, The Dark Angel, So Red the Rose, All This and Heaven Too*, and so many others.

BEERY, NOAH, SR. (*1946*) 63——Major support, usually a villain, in over 100 silents and talkies: *Beau Geste* ('26), *Main Street, She Done Him Wrong, David Harum*; last in 1945's *This Man's Navy* in support of his brother Wallace.

BEERY, WALLACE (*1949*) 68 ——Played the blackest of villains in early silents, became a menace with humor (late '20s), then evolved into MGM's burly tough-tender guy—and one of its greatest box-office hits; in his 19-year career there he starred in many of Metro's best: *The Big House* (was Oscar-nominated as Best Actor), *Min and Bill, The Champ* (he won the Oscar), *Grand Hotel, Dinner at Eight, Viva Villa!, Ah! Wilderness, China Seas*, etc.

BEGGS, MALCOLM LEE (*1956*) 49 ——Support in *Botany Bay, Houdini, Edge of Fury*.

BEGLEY, ED (*1970*) 69 ——Especially good as a snarling politico, as in *Sweet Bird of Youth* (Supporting Oscar); in *Boomerang; Sorry, Wrong Number; Patterns*, many others.

BEHRLE, FRED (*1941*) 50 ——In silents: *Through Thick and Thin, The Midnight Alarm*, etc.

BELA, NICHOLAS (*1963*) 63 ——Support in two Billie Dove pix: *Adoration* and *The Night Watch*.

BELASCO, GENEVIEVE (*1956*) 85 ——Support in silent *The Ten Commandments* and Valentino's *A Sainted Devil*.

BELCHER, ALICE (*1939*) 59 ——In silents: *Blondes by Choice, Second Hand Rose, Pals First*.

BELL, DIGBY (*1967*) 66 ——Stage comedian who starred, among others, in 1914's *The Education of Mr. Pipp*.

BELL, GASTON (*1963*) 86 ——Appeared in silents.

BELL, GENEVIEVE (*1951*) 50s ——In silents, then support in *Phone Call from a Stranger*.

BELL, GEORGE O. (*1969*) ——Character actor.

BELL, HANK (*1950*) 58 ——Mostly in silent Westerns: *Gold and Grit, Twin Triggers*, etc.

BELL, JAMES (*1973*) 83 ——Kind-faced, durable character; Red in *I am a Fugitive from a Chain Gang*, farmhand pal of young Roddy McDowall in *My Friend Flicka*, June Allyson's dad in *The Glenn Miller Story*; dozens more.

BELL, MONTA (*1958*) 67 ——In the silent *The Pilgrim*; more famous as director of *Broadway After Dark, Pretty Ladies*, etc.

BELL, RALPH (*1936*) 53 ——Support in *Cock o' the Walk* and Will Rogers' *A Connecticut Yankee*.

BELL, REX (*1962*) 58 —— Curly-haired redhead who starred in many early '30s Westerns, married Clara Bow, and became Lieutenant Governor of Nevada.

BELLAMY, GEORGE (*1944*) 78 ——Character actor in English pix including 1929's *Red Aces*.

BELLEW, COSMO KYRLE *(1948)* 61 ——Support in *Lummox*, Billie Dove's *The Lady Who Dared*, etc.

BELLEW, H. KYRLE *(1911)* 56 ——Noted British actor; filmed his stage hit, *A Gentleman of France*, in 1904.

BELMAR, HENRY *(1931)* 81 ——In early silents, then a Powers director; was husband of the late Laurel Love.

BELMORE, BERTHA *(1953)* 70 ——Bulky British comic character; support in *She Couldn't Say No, The Midas Touch, So You Won't Talk.*

BELMORE, DAISY *(1954)* 80 —— Onscreen from 1912; in *Fifty Million Frenchmen, My Past, Alias French Gertie*, etc.

BELMORE, LIONEL *(1953)* 85 ——Heavyset Englishman; character roles in *Moonlight Follies, Roaring Fires, Mary of Scotland, Tower of London, Cardinal Richelieu.*

BENADERET, BEA *(1968)* 62 ——Supporting role in *Tender Is the Night;* top radio actress and star of televison's *Petticoat Junction;* once married to cowboy actor Jim Bannon.

BEN-ARI, RAIKIN *(1968)* 63 ——Russian support; in Walter Matthau's *Gangster Story.*

BENASSI, MEMO *(1957)* 70 ——Italian; with Isa Miranda in *Scipio Africanus;* in *Rossini*, etc.

BENCHLEY, ROBERT *(1945)* 56 ——Humorous, bumbling sophisticate who always seemed to view life through a tilted cocktail glass; lent his fey charm (when not writing for *The New Yorker*) to *I Married a Witch, The Major and the Minor, Take a Letter Darling*, etc.

BENDER, RUSSELL *(1969)* 59 ——In *The Amazing Colossal Man, The Satan Bug, Born Wild.*

BENEDICT, BROOKS *(1968)* ——Many silents: *White Flannels, Orchids and Ermine, Speedy*, etc.

BENDIX, WILLIAM *(1964)* 58 ——Lovable (usually) Paramount "ugly" whose speech was right off the streets of New York; was Oscar-nominated for his second pic, 1942's *Wake Island;* memorable in several WW II movies: *Guadalcanal Diary, A Bell for Adano, Hostages*, etc.; many Alan Ladd pix benefitted by his costarring presence: *The Glass Key, China, Two Years Before the Mast, The Blue Dahlia,*

etc.; attempted heavy drama in O'Neill's *The Hairy Ape;* popular on TV as star of *Life With Riley.*

BENGE, WILSON *(1955)* 80 ——Support in many DeMille silents; in numerous talkies: *The Bat Whispers, The Ghost Walks, The Shadow Strikes, Trade Winds* (the butler).

BENNETT, ALMA *(1958)* 69 ——Beautiful vamp in *The Dawn of a Tomorrow* and other silents including *Why Men Leave Home* and *The Silent Lover.*

BENNETT, BARBARA *(1958)* 52 ——Brunette sister of Constance and Joan; in *Mother's Boy, Syncopation* ('29), *Love Among the Millionaires.*

BENNETT, BELLE *(1932)* 42 ——Memorable in the title role of the early ('25) *Stella Dallas;* also in *The Way of All Flesh* (27), *Mother Machree, Courage*, etc.

BENNETT, CHARLES, *(1943)* 51 ——Was in *The Adventures of Ruth* serial, *America* (William Pitt), *The Top of New York*, etc.

BENNETT, CONSTANCE *(1965)* 59 ——Brittle, sophisticated blonde (dark-haired when she entered pix in '22) whose sleek page-boy hairdo became her undeviating trademark; once Hollywood's highest-paid star; most delightful in *Topper;* also in *Our Betters, Ladies in Love, The Affairs of Cellini, Two Against the World, Paris Underground*, etc.; in only two movies in the '50s, she came back in a top supporting role in Lana Turner's *Madame X* (released posthumously); was sister of Joan, daughter of Richard.

BENNETT, ENID *(1969)* 71 ——Silent star; Fairbanks' fair Maid Marian in *Robin Hood;* also in *The Vamp, Stepping Out, Fuss and Feathers, The Courtship of Myles Standish, The Sea Hawk* ('24), etc.; came out of retirement for small roles in *Intermezzo* and *Strike Up the Band*, her last.

BENNETT, FRANK *(1957)* 66 ——He and wife, Billie West, costarred in early silents.

BENNETT, JOSEPH *(1931)* 35——In *The Shepherd of the Hills* ('28) and many other silents.

BENNETT, LEE *(1954)* 43 ——In *Spirit of West Point, Hold 'em Navy, Three Desperate Men*, etc.

BENNETT, MICKEY *(1950)* 35 ——Child star in "The Cohens and the Kellys" movies.

BENNETT, RAY (1957) 62 ——Support; *Canon City, Northwest Stampede, The Spoilers* ('42), *Ma and Pa Kettle*, etc.

BENNETT, RICHARD (1944) 71 ——Handsome dad of Joan and Constance; star of *Damaged Goods, The Eternal City, Lying Wives,* other silents; distinguished support in *Arrowsmith, If I Had a Million, The Magnificent Ambersons,* and numerous other talkies.

BENNETT, WILDA (1967) 73 ——A silent beauty; with Pickford in *A Good Little Devil,* etc.; character in *What a Life* and *Those Were the Days.*

BENNISON, LOUIS (1929) 45 ——Appeared in the silent *Lavender and Old Lace.*

BENNY, JACK (1974) 80 —It was always "Love in Bloom" between this comic great and his radio-TV-movie audience; in many 1930-45 movies: *Artists and Models, Buck Benny Rides Again, Man About Town, The Big Broadcast of 1937,* etc.; best as the cuckolded Hamlet in *To Be or Not to Be;* made a never-fail joke out of his biggest flop, *The Horn Blows at Midnight.*

BENTLEY, IRENE (1940) 70 ——Support in *My Weakness, Smoky, Frontier Marshal,* all 1933–34.

BENTLEY, ROBERT (1958) 63——In silents; *The New School Teacher, The Power Within.*

BERANGER, ANDRE (1973) 77——Character in many: *Grounds for Divorce, Surrender, Tiger Rose,* other silents, and such talkies as *Road House* and *Over My Dead Body.*

BEREGI, OSCAR (1965) 90 ——Hungarian; one of the supporting leads in *The Testament of Dr. Mabuse;* in Hollywood from 1952 in character roles in *Anything Can Happen, Call Me Madam* (Chamberlain), *Desert Legion.*

BERENDT, RACHEL (1957) ——French actress who played a lead in 1932's *Paris-Beguin.*

BERESFORD, HARRY (1944) 80 ——Character (Flavius) in *The Sign of the Cross;* also in *They Won't Forget* (Second Veteran), *Doctor X, Dinner at Eight, The Little Minister,* many more.

BERG, GERTRUDE (1966) 66 ——Her *The Goldbergs* (radio-TV) became the movie *Molly,* in which she also starred; did a cameo in *Main Street to Broadway* too.

BERGER, NICOLE (1967) 32 ——French actress; support (Marjori) in *He Who Must Die;* also in *Shoot the Piano Player, Girls of the Night,* and *Love is My Profession.*

BERGERE, OUIDA (1974) 88 ——Actress-scriptwriter; support in pix of the '20s such as *Kick In* and *Bella Donna;* wrote many scripts for silents (*On With the Dance, The Man From Home, The Cheat, To Have and to Hold,* etc.); the widow of Basil Rathbone, she was one of Hollywood's most famous party-givers; her memoirs of movietown life, completed shortly before her death, have not been published to date.

BERGERE, VALERIE (1938) 63 ——French support; in *It's Love I'm After, The Singing Marine.*

BERGMAN, HENRY (1946) 76 ——Chaplin stock actor; Hank in *The Gold Rush,* the janitor in *City Lights,* etc.

BERISTAIN, LEOPOLDO (1948) 64 ——Mexican actor; in *Mexico Lindo.*

BERISTAIN, LUIS, (1962) 44 ——Support in *This Strange Passion* and Bunuel's *The Exterminating Angel.*

BERKELEY, ARTHUR (1962) 66 ——Character actor; *I Was a Teenage Monster.*

BERKELEY, GERTRUDE (1946) 81 —— Played the old lady in Nazimova's *War Brides* ('16).

BERKES, JOHN (1951) 54 ——Character; Indian Geoduck in *The Egg and I* (same role played in later "Ma and Pa Kettle" pix by Oliver Blake and Lester Allen); also in *Branded, My Dream Is Yours, Ace in the Hole.*

BERLINER, MARTIN (1966) 70 ——German support in the Sammy Davis Jr. version of *The Three Penny Opera.*

BERNARD, BARNEY (1924) 47 ——Stage luminary who began with Vitagraph in 1916; featured in 1923's *Potash and Perlmutter.*

BERNARD, DICK (1925) 60 ——Support in Ben Lyon's *Bluebeard's Seven Wives.*

BERNARD, DOROTHY (1955) 65 ——Lovely brunette star who, for Griffith in his Biograph period, appeared in *The Cricket on the Hearth, The Girl and Her Trust,* etc.; later co-starred in *A Man of Sorrow, Little Women,* other silents.

BERNARD, HARRY *(1940)* 62 ——Keystone comic; then in *Sons of the Desert, The Bohemian Girl.*

BERNARD, PAUL *(1958)* ——French; costarred (as lover who abandoned Maria Casares) in *Les Dames du Bois de Boulogne;* in *Panic,* etc.

BERNARD, SAM, *(1927)* 54——Bald triangle character lead; *The Great Pearl Tangle,* etc.

BERNARD, SAM *(1950)* 61 ——Support; *When My Baby Smiles at Me, Prison Train,* others.

BERNES, MARK *(1969)* 57 ——Russian singer-actor; in *Far from Russia* ('51), *The Boys from Leningrad, School of Courage,* etc.

BERNHARDT, SARAH *(1923)* 78 ——Legendary stage star seen in such early films as *Queen Elizabeth, Jeanne Dore, Adrienne Lecouvreur, La Dame aux Camelias.*

BERNIE, BEN *(1943)* 52 ——Vaudeville-nightclub headliner; in *Wake Up and Live, Love and Hisses, Stolen Harmony,* etc.

BERNIE, DICK *(1971)* 60 ——Comedian; supporting roles.

BERRY, ALINE *(1967)* 62 ——Stage-radio actress in 1925's *Soul Fire.*

BERRY, JULES *(1951)* 67 ——French; costai in Carne's *Daybreak; Dreams of Love,* etc.

BERRY, W. H. *(1951)* 81 ——support in the 1936 English pic *The Student's Romance.*

BERTRAM, FRANK *(1941)* 70 ——Character in England's *The Amateur Gentleman* ('36).

BERTRAM, VEDAH *(1912)* 20 ——Leading lady in *Broncho Billy Outwitted* and 13 other "Broncho Billy" Westerns.

BESSER, JOE *(1972)* 71 ——Heavyset, bald-domed comic who was one of The Three Stooges (with Larry Fine and Moe Howard) 1955–59, after Shemp Howard's death; also in features: *Let's Make Love, Say One for Me,* others.

BESSERER, EUGENIE *(1934)* 64 ——Jolson's mother in *The Jazz Singer,* the mother in Lillian Gish's *The Greatest Question;* onscreen in many from 1910 through 1933's *To the Last Man.*

BEST, EDNA *(1974)* 74 ——The *Intermezzo* triangle was Bergman, Howard and Best; excel-lent also in *Swiss Family Robinson* ('40), *A Dispatch from Reuters,* and as Colman's wife in *The Late George Apley;* once was Mrs. Herbert Marshall.

BEST, WILLIE *(1962)* 46 ——Played shuffling, funny, "scared stiff" black in dozens: *The Ghost Breakers, The Littlest Rebel, Nothing but the Truth, Home in Indiana,* etc.

BETTON, GEORGE *(1969)* ——Support in British pix.

BETTS, WILLIAM *(1929)* 73 ——Support in the Naldi-Valentino pic *A Sainted Devil.*

BETZ, MATTHEW *(1938)* 56 ——Support; safari guide Nick in the Buster Crabbe serial *Tarzan the Fearless,* Prussian guard in *The House of Rothschild;* in *The Big House, Salvation Nell,* more.

BEVAN, BILLY *(1957)* 70 ——Aussie character actor; Hale in *The Lost Patrol;* the amusing cockney, Lt. Trotter, in *Journey's End;* Joe in *The Long Voyage Home;* in *Cavalcade, Cluny Brown, The Picture of Dorian Gray,* many more.

BEVANS, CLEM *(1963)* 83 ——Played ancient, shrewd hayseeds; in *Sergeant York* (Zeke), *The Yearling* (robust old Pa Forrester), *Abe Lincoln in Illinois, Of Human Hearts, Harvey,* etc.

BEVANS, PHILIPPA *(1968)* 55 ——Support in *The Group, The World of Henry Orient, The Notorious Landlady.*

BIBY, EDWARD *(1952)* 67 ——Character in Hedy Lamarr's *The Strange Woman.*

BICE, ROBERT *(1968)* 54 ——Western villain: *The Red Stallion, Bells of Coronado,* etc.

BICKEL, GEORGE *(1941)* 78 ——Supported Belle Bennett in *Recaptured Love;* in *One Heavenly Night, Soup to Nuts, The Man I Killed.*

BICKFORD, CHARLES *(1967)* 77 ——Rugged, two-fisted redhead; loved Garbo in *Anna Christie;* nominated for Supporting Oscars in *The Song of Bernadette, The Farmer's Daughter* (as Ethel Barrymore's politically influential butler), *Johnny Belinda* (Wyman's dad), but never won; starred in *East of Borneo, River's End, Dynamite,* many more; last famous as star of TV's *The Virginian.*

BILDT, PAUL *(1957)* 72 ——German actor; in *Razzia, As Long as You're Near Me,* etc.

BILLINGS, ELMO *(1964)* 51 ——Child actor; Freckles in "Our Gang" (after Mickey Daniels); in silent features (*Locked Doors*, etc.).

BILLINGS, GEORGE A. *(1934)* 63 ——Was a Los Angeles municipal employe who had never acted before trying out for and winning the starring role in 1924's *The Dramatic Life of Abraham Lincoln*; then in *The Man Without a Country, As the Earth Turns, The Adventures of Tom Sawyer* ('38), others.

BINDER, SYBILLE *(1962)* 62 ——Austrian character actress in many British pix: *Brighton Rock, Blanche Fury, The Man from Morocco, Broken Journey,* etc.

BING, GUS *(1967)* 74 ——Support; brother of character actor Herman Bing.

BING, HERMAN *(1947)* 48 ——Played funny, excitable Germans; grand as the bearded Passion Play actor in *Twentieth Century*; in *Dinner at Eight, Rose Marie, The Great Waltz, Dimples,* many more.

BIRCH, PAUL *(1964)* 30s ——Support; *War of the Worlds, The Man Who Shot Liberty Valance, Two Rode Together* (the caged wild white boy who had lived with the Comanches), *Portrait in Black.*

BIRELL, TALA *(1959)* 51 ——Viennese beauty who was expected to become "another Garbo"; in *The Doomed Battalion, Crime and Punishment, Let's Fall in Love, Bringing Up Baby, The Captain Hates the Sea,* and others through 1948's *Woman in the Night;* died behind the Iron Curtain.

BIRKETT, VIVA *(1934)* 47 ——Support in 1927's *The Prince of Lovers.*

BISHOP, CHESTER *(1937)* 79 ——Character in silents: *Missing Daughters, Lights Out,* etc.

BISHOP, RICHARD *(1956)* 58 ——Warden in *Call Northside 777;* in *The Long Gray Line, Teresa, Native Land,* etc.

BISHOP, WILLIAM *(1959)* 41 ——Handsome, dark-haired Columbia leading man; *Harriet Craig, The Killer That Stalked New York, Lorna Doone* ('51), *Gun Belt,* etc.; better known as costar (with Michael O'Shea and James Dunn) of the TV series *It's a Man's World.*

BJORNE, HUGH *(1966)* 80 ——Swedish; best known as support in *Torment.*

BLACK, MAURICE *(1938)* ——Character actor from Poland; in *I Cover the Waterfront, The*

Crusades (Amir), *Wake Up and Dream, The Front Page* ('31; Diamond Louie), *Little Caesar* (Little Arnie Lorch, the rival gang leader E. G. Robinson forces to leave town), numerous others.

BLACKFORD, MARY *(1937)* 23 ——Featured in *The Sweetheart of Sigma Chi* (Mary Carisle's pal Bunny).

BLACKMER, SIDNEY *(1973)* 78 ——Veteran of over 200 movies, first as a silent matinee idol, then as smooth, often villainous support; in *Little Caesar* (crime czar "Big Boy"), *Suez, Heidi* (Temple's adoptive father), *In Old Chicago;* played Teddy Roosevelt ten times on stage and in pix (*The Rough Rider, My Girl Tisa,* etc.); was back at his evil tricks in *Rosemary's Baby,* his last major role, as the chief, elderly Satanist.

BLACKWELL, CARLYLE *(1955)* 67 ——A major leading man in silents; starred in *His Royal Highness, The Restless Sex, Perils of the Sea, The Key to Yesterday, Sherlock Holmes* ('22), many others; retired from the screen when 42.

BLACKWELL, CARLYLE, JR. *(1974)* 61 —— Featured in *The Calling of Dan Matthews* and 30 other pix, but never achieved the fame of his father; left movies to become a noted portrait photographer of screen celebrities.

BLAGOI, GEORGE *(1971)* 73 ——Was young support in silents like Bushman's *Four Sons.*

BLAINE, ROSE *(1974)* 60s ——Singer in 1930s musical shorts and features with band of Abe Lyman, whom she married in '42.

BLAISDELL, CHARLES *(1930)* 56 ——Was seen in Christie comedies.

BLAKE, ANNE *(1973)* ——Character in *Orders to Kill, Scream of Fear,* etc.

BLAKE, MADGE *(1969)* 70 ——Beaming, plump little character; Aunt Harriet in *Batman* (movie and TV series); in *Singin' in the Rain* (the Parsons-like gossip columnist), *The Long Long Trailer,* others.

BLAKE, PAUL *(1960)* ——Minor British player; in *The Lilac Domino,* etc.

BLAKECLOCK, ALBAN *(1966)* ——British character; in *Murder in the Cathedral.*

BLAKENEY, OLIVE *(1959)* 56 ——Character actress fondly recalled as the mother of Jimmy Lydon in the final eight "Henry Aldrich" movies (*Henry and Dizzy; Henry Aldrich, Editor; Henry Aldrich's Little Secret,* etc.); she later became, in real life, the actor's mother-in-law; in movies from the early '30s, she was also in *Gangway, That Uncertain Feeling, Experiment Perilous, Sentimental Journey, The Strange Woman, Sealed Verdict,* many more including 1957's *The Green-Eyed Blonde,* her last.

BLANCHAR, PIERRE *(1963)* 67 ——Ascetically handsome, haunted-featured French star; superb as the Swiss pastor in *Symphonie Pastorale* whose love for the blind girl, Michele Morgan, brings tragedy; starred in *Un Carnet de Bal* (as the shady doctor), the French version of *Crime and Punishment* (Raskolnikov), many others.

BLANCHARD, MARI *(1970)* 43 ——Universal starred her in *Destry* ('54), *Black Horse Canyon, The Veils of Bagdad,* others.

BLANCHE, FRANCIS *(1974)* 52 ——French singer-actor-songwriter ("Besame Mucho"); in *Babette Goes to War, The Green Mare, The Seventh Juror,* others.

BLAND, JOYCE *(1963)* 57 ——British character actress; in *The Citadel* (Nurse Sharpe), *Sixty Glorious Years, Dreaming Lips,* etc.

BLAND, R. HENDERSON *(1941)* 60s ——English actor who portrayed Jesus Christ in Kalem's *From the Manger to the Cross* in 1912.

BLANDICK, CLARA *(1962)* 81 ——One of Hollywood's busiest and best-loved character actresses; Garland's Auntie Em in *The Wizard of Oz;* in *Huckleberry Finn* ('31 and '39), *Anne of Windy Poplars, Drums Along the Mohawk, Broadway Bill,* and 100 more.

BLANKMAN, GEORGE *(1925)* 47 ——Support in Fairbanks' *Don Q, Son of Zorro.*

BLATCHFORD, WILLIAM *(1936)* 50 ——Character in W. C. Fields' *The Old-Fashioned Way.*

BLEDSOE, JULES *(1943)* 44 ——Played Joe, and sang "Ol' Man River," in the 1929 *Show Boat;* also in *Drums of the Congo.*

BLEIBTREU, HEDWIG *(1958)* 90 ——Austrian character actress; in *The Third Man.*

BLICK, NEWTON *(1965)* 66 ——British character; the doctor in Peter O'Toole's *Lord Jim;* in *The Third Key,* others.

BLINN, BENJAMIN *(1941)* 69 ——Support in silents: *Quicker'n Lightning, Danger.*

BLINN, GENEVIEVE *(1956)* ——In silents: *Queen of Sheba, The Witching Hour, Crazy to Marry; Common Clay* was one of her few talkies.

BLINN, HOLBROOK *(1928)* 56 ——A major silent star; in *Rosita* (opposite Mary Pickford), *Janice Meredith* (as Lord Clowes who arrests Marion Davies), *Yolanda* and *Zander the Great* (also with Davies), *McTeague, The Bad Man,* and many more.

BLOCKER, DAN *(1972)* 43 ——Most famous as amiable, gigantic Hoss in the TV series *Bonanza;* had supporting roles in *Lady in Cement* and other films.

BLOMFIELD, DEREK *(1964)* 44 ——As a teenager was featured in Britain's *Turn of the Tide* and *Emil and the Detective;* later, support in Laughton's *Hobson's Choice.*

BLORE, ERIC *(1959)* 71 ——Movies' inimitable butler-valet with humor and quirky charm; Astaire and Rogers would have been lost without him in *The Gay Divorcee, Swing Time, Top Hat* and *Shall We Dance;* so would the later "Lone Wolf" movies; in others: *The Lady Eve, Sullivan's Travels, Road to Zanzibar,* and scores more.

BLUE, MONTE *(1963)* 73 ——After many early Griffith bits, he moved on to become a top silent star in rugged roles elsewhere; a huge moneymaker in *The Affairs of Anatol, Main Street, The Lover of Camille, The Black Swan,* many other silents; he acted again for Griffith as Danton (his best role) in *Orphans of the Storm* ('21); he always maintained that *White Shadows of the South Seas,* a silent with added sound (a high-pitched voice dubbed in for his), destroyed his starring career; later a character actor at WB for many years in: *Dodge City, Edge of Darkness, Key Largo,* etc.

BLUM, SAM *(1945)* 56 ——Character (Blanton) in *The Winning of Barbara Worth;* in *Night World, Iron Man, Rio Rita* ('29), many others.

BLUMENTHAL-TAMARINA, MARIA *(1938)* 79 ——Celebrated Russian actress who starred in 1923's *Kombrig Ivanov* and, in the '30s, was featured in such Russian films as *Three Women* and *A Greater Promise.*

BLYSTONE, STANLEY *(1956)* 61 ——Rugged, good-looking support in *Strike Me Pink, The Circus Ace* (villain), *Young Eagles, Boots and Saddles,* others; was in nine talkie serials: *King of the Texas Rangers* (main villain, Lynch), *Ace Drummond, The Sea Hound, Burn 'Em Up Barnes,* etc.

BLYTHE, BETTY *(1972)* 78 ——Statuesque vamp of silents; most famous role, *The Queen* of Sheba ('21), in which she succeeded Theda Bara as movies' "prime embodiment of sinful lure"; later in *The Breath of Scandal, Folly of Vanity*, etc.; support in *Honky Tonk, The Gorgeous Hussy*, and others.

BOARDMAN, TRUE *(1918)* 40s ——Good-looking star of Kalem's silent "Stingaree" Western series; also starred in *The Social Pirates*, and had a costar role in Elmo Lincoln's *Tarzan of the Apes*.

BOARDMAN, VIRGINIA TRUE *(1971)* 82 —— True Boardman's actress-wife; support in silents (*Penrod, Michael O'Halloran*) and talkies (*The Road to Ruin*, etc.); a.k.a. Virginia Eames.

BODEL, BURMAN *(1969)* 58 ——Comic support.

BOGART, HUMPHREY *(1957)* 56 ——Unflappable tough guy, Oscar winner (*The African Queen*), and one of the handful of stars whose very names are synonymous with Warner Bros.; acted there for 18 years in *Casablanca, The Treasure of the Sierra Madre, The Maltese Falcon, High Sierra*, and dozens more that made him a cult figure with college students of the '60s; received his first Oscar nomination for *Casablanca* and his third, and last, for *The Caine Mutiny*.

BOHNEN, ROMAN *(1949)* 50 ——Jennifer Jones' father in *The Song of Bernadette*, and Dana Andrews' in *The Best Years of Our Lives*, he was one of the screen's staunchest characters; also in *The Hard Way, The Hairy Ape, A Bell for Adano, Brute Force*, etc.

BOLAND, MARY *(1965)* 83 ——Feather-brained comic character-star; *Ruggles of Red Gap, If I Had a Million, Mama Loves Papa, The Women*, and *Six of a Kind* were all the better for her bosomy, bedizened presence.

BOLDER, ROBERT *(1937)* 78 —Supported Milton Sills in *The Sea Hawk;* other silents.

BOLES, JOHN *(1969)* 73 ——Busy, handsome matinee idol of the '30s, and the personification of the Arrow Collar man; most at ease in tux 'n tails (and sometimes artificially grayed sideburns) in heavy romantic dramas of the time: *Stella Dallas, The Life of Vergie Winters, Back Street* ('32); also looked splendid in uniform: *Only Yesterday, The Littlest Rebel, A Message to Garcia*, etc.; lifted his tenor voice in the first *Desert Song*, and, alongside Swarthout, in *Rose of the Rancho*.

BOLEY, MAY *(1963)* 81 ——Madam of the bawdy house in *The Informer*, she earlier had a comic burlesque turn in *The Dance of Life*, fol-lowing many silents; later in *Tovarich, The Women*, etc.

BONANOVA, FORTUNIO *(1969)* 73 ——Flamboyant character actor, big in size, voice, and gesture; in *Going My Way* (as rich Italian, Borzanni), *The Black Swan, For Whom the Bell Tolls* (the realist, Fernando), *Citizen Kane*, etc.

BOND, WARD *(1960)* 56 ——Leather-skinned tough guy, often with a soft core; in over 100 from 1930, he had a career-within-a-career as a John Ford stalwart: *Young Mr. Lincoln, The Long Voyage Home, Tobacco Road, They Were Expendable, My Darling Clementine, The Quiet Man*, and a dozen more; finally was top-billed in a long-running TV series, *Wagon Train*.

BONDHILL, GERTRUDE *(1960)* 80 ——In very early Essanay films.

BONIFACE, SYMONA *(1950)* 56 ——Dowager in "Three Stooges" shorts; almost always got a pie in the face.

BONILLAS, MYRNA *(1959)* 69——In silents: *The Claw, The Gingham Girl, Lummox*, etc.

BONN, FRANK *(1944)* 71 ——Support in Wallace Beery's *Old Ironsides*.

BONN, WALTER *(1953)* 64 ——Character; in *Cipher Bureau* and *International Crime*.

BONNER, ISABEL *(1955)* 47 ——Top support (psychiatrist) in *The Shrike*.

BONNER, JOE *(1959)* 77——In many silents.

BOOKER, HARRY *(1924)* 74 ——Irascible old charmer (judges, gamblers, dads) in Sennett comedies.

BOOT, GLADYS *(1964)* 74 ——British character; *Harry Black and the Tiger, The Blue Lagoon*, others.

BOOTH, HELEN *(1971)* ——British support seen in Hayley Mills' *The Family Way*.

BOOTH, NESDON *(1964)* 43 ——Squat character; henchman in *Pete Kelly's Blues*; in *Funny Face*, etc.

BORDEN, EDDIE *(1955)* 67 ——Support in silents (*The Dove*, etc.) and talkies (*A Chump at Oxford, The Devil Is a Woman, Give Me a Sailor*, others).

BORDEN, OLIVE *(1947)* 40 ——A 1925 Wampas Baby Star; starred as a brunette flapper in *Joy Girl, Fig Leaves, Pajamas*; in talkies was

Mary Brian's rival for Jack Oakie in *A Social Lion*, then in several forgettable B's.

BORDON, EUGENE *(1972)* 60 ——Support in Merle Oberon's *Dark Waters*.

BORDONI, IRENE *(1953)* 58 ——Black-banged comedienne captivated by Victor Moore in *Louisiana Purchase*; also in *Show of Shows* and *Paris*.

BORELL, LOUIS *(1973)* 67 ——Noted Dutch actor; character (Picard) in George Sanders' *Paris After Dark*, also in Tom Conway's *A Night of Adventure*.

BOREO, EMIL *(1951)* 66 ——In Hitchcock's *The Lady Vanishes* was the hotel manager.

BORG, VEDA ANN *(1973)* 58 ——Her face completely rebuilt by plastic surgery after an auto crash in '39 (and after a dozen pix at Warners as a dark-haired young sexpot), she spent the balance of her career—more than 80 films—in blonde tough-gal roles; in *Honky Tonk*, *The Corsican Brothers*, *Irish Eyes Are Smiling*, *Nob Hill*, etc.

BORGATO, AGOSTINO *(1939)* 68 ——Character; *The Maltese Falcon* ('31), *Not for Paris*, *Transgression*, etc.

BOROS, FERIKE *(1951)* 71 ——Cheerful gray-haired maids, housekeepers, mothers; in *Svengali*, *Bachelor Mother*, *Little Caesar*, *Make Way for Tomorrow* (Mrs. Rubens), more.

BORZAGE, FRANK *(1962)* 69 ——Handsome, curly-haired lead in such silents as *Immediate Lee*, but much more famous as the Oscar-winning director of *Seventh Heaven* and *Bad Girl*.

BORZAGE, RENA *(1966)* 60s ——Wife of Frank; acted in silents.

BOSWELL, MARTHA *(1958)* 53 ——Of the singing Boswell Sisters; in 1932's *The Big Broadcast*.

BOSWORTH, HOBART *(1943)* 76 ——Outstanding Hollywood character with an uninterrupted career from 1909 (he was in that year's *In the Sultan's Power*, the first movie produced on the West Coast) until his death; prominent in such silents as *Blood Ship*, *Behind the Door*, and *Bread*, he was in these talkies, among many others: Walter Huston's *Abraham Lincoln* (as Gen. Lee), *Lady for a Day*, *Steamboat Round the Bend*, *One Foot in Heaven*.

BOTELER, WADE *(1943)* 51 ——Jowly, mustachioed character in numerous silents (*While Satan Sleeps*), talkie features (*You Only Live Once*) and serials (*The Green Hornet*, and *The Green Hornet Strikes Again*, in both of which he was the Hornet's bodyguard, Michael Oxford).

BOTHWELL, JOHN *(1967)* 46 ——At one point was Freckles in "Our Gang."

BOTKIN, PERRY *(1973)* 66 ——Guitar player and popular composer; appeared in *Birth of the Blues*.

BOTTOMLEY, ROLAND *(1947)* 67 ——Dapper leading man in silents—curly-haired, with thin lips and a cleft chin—who was almost always to be found in a tux; was with Jackie Saunders in the serial *The Grip of Evil*; in features was with Arliss in (his first) *The Devil* and Mary Astor in *Enticement*.

BOUCICAULT, NINA *(1950)* 83 ——Character actress in England's *Juggernaut* ('37).

BOUCOT *(1949)* 59 ——French actor who rarely used his given name, Louis; in *Three Waltzes*, etc.

BOULTON, MATTHEW *(1962)* 69 ——British character in many Hollywood pix: 1937's *Night Must Fall* (as Belsize), *They Met in Bombay* (the police inspector pursuing jewel thief Gable), *Love Letters* (judge), *Bulldog Drummond in Africa*, etc.

BOURCHIER, ARTHUR *(1927)* 64 ——Starred in the title role in the 1913 German production of *Macbeth*.

BOURKE, FAN *(1959)* 72 ——Support in *Lummox* after long, minor silent career.

BOURVIL *(1970)* 57 ——French comedy star; gave Cannes Film Festival prize-winning performance as the petty black-marketeer in *Four Bags Full*; in *Those Daring Young Men in Their Jaunty Jalopies*, etc.

BOW, CLARA *(1965)* 60 ——Russet-haired "It" Girl, thus the flapper to end all screen flappers; set the silent screen afire with her joyous hi-jinks in *Dancing Mothers*, *Mantrap*, *Kid Boots*, *It*, *Red Hair*, and was greatly appealing in *Wings*, which of course was an entirely different kind of "high."

BOWERS, JOHN *(1936)* 36 ——Handsome male lead in many silents: *Lorna Doone*, *So Big*, *When a Man's a Man*, *Sis Hopkins*, etc.; ex-husband of Marguerite de la Motte; the on-screen suicide of the alcoholic ex-star in *A Star Is Born* was based on his—author Adela Rogers St. John having witnessed it.

BOWES, MAJOR *(1946)* 72 ——Radio's *Amateur Hour* major-domo; was seen onscreen as himself.

BOWMAN, PALMER *(1933)* 50 ——Worked in Essanay and Selig silents.

BOYD, WILLIAM *(1972)* 74——"Hopalong Cassidy" movies made this silver-haired, genial star—via television—a millionaire; in silents he'd starred in many A-budget films: *The Volga Boatman, The Road to Yesterday, The King of Kings, Two Arabian Knights;* in talkies, mostly B's: *The Road to Reno, Sky Devils,* etc.

BOYD, WILLIAM "STAGE" *(1935)* 45 —— Black-haired character with severe widow's peak who was often in serials: *The Lost City* (as maniacal chief villain, Zolok), *The Locked Door,* etc.

BOYNE, SUNNY *(1966)* 83 ——Character actress; *The Devil and Daniel Webster;* billed Eva Leonard Boyne in *None But the Lonely Heart* (Ma Chalmers).

BOZYK, MAX *(1970)* 71 ——Featured in Yiddish films: *The Dybbuk, Purim Spieler.*

BRACE, NORMAN *(1954)* 62 ——Acted in early silents, then was a director.

BRACEY, CLARA T. *(1941)* 94——Griffith's principal character actress in 1909; in *Eloping with Auntie,* many more silents.

BRACEY, SIDNEY *(1942)* 65——Good-looking actor who costarred (with James Cruze) in the serial *The Million Dollar Mystery* and its sequel, *Zudora;* later in many silent features (*The Courtship of Myles Standish, The Black Bird,* etc.) and talkies (*Anna Karenina,* as Fredric March's valet, *Dawn Patrol, My Bill,* more).

BRADBURY, JAMES, SR. *(1940)* 83 ——Character in many: *Tol'able David, Abraham Lincoln* ('30), *Hot Heels,* etc.

BRADFORD, LANE *(1973)* 50 ——Big, good-looking guy who led with his strong chin in dozens of Monogram and Republic Westerns, and in serials in which he was always one of the evil ones (*Zombies of the Stratosphere, The Invisible Monster,* etc.).

BRADFORD, MARSHALL *(1971)* 75 ——Western character; *Colorado Ambush, Hellgate,* etc.

BRADLEY, BETTY *(1973)* 57 ——Ingenue roles in a number of films.

BRADLEY, HARRY *(1947)* 78 ——Support; *It Happened One Night, The Big Store,* etc.

BRADLEY, TRUMAN *(1974)* 69 ——Burns and Allen's well-known radio announcer; onscreen in *Northwest Passage, Burma Convoy.*

BRADLEY, LOVYSS *(1969)* 63 ——Character; *Golden Girl, Outrage, The Blue Veil,* etc.

BRADSHAW, EUNICE *(1973)* 80 ——Support in silents.

BRADY, ALICE *(1939)* 47 ——Distinguished Broadway star who played giddy women in many of her films (*My Man Godfrey,* for which she was nominated for a Best Supporting Oscar as Lombard's dizzy rich mom, *100 Men and a Girl, Gold Diggers of 1935,* etc.); changing pace, she became the long-suffering mother of Ameche and Fonda in *In Old Chicago,* and won a Supporting Oscar; may be remembered longer for portrayal of the stoic mother in *Young Mr. Lincoln* whose sons are successfully defended by Fonda in a murder trial.

BRADY, EDWARD *(1942)* 53 ——In many silents: *Clancy's Kosher Wedding, Dressed to Kill, Lost at the Front, Three Faces West, To the Last Man,* etc.

BRADY, PAT *(1972)* 57 ——Roy Rogers' genial singer-comic sidekick, Sparrow Biffle, in dozens of Republic Westerns; earlier had been one of the Sons of the Pioneers and acted in Charles Starrett's Westerns.

BRAHAM, HARRY *(1923)* 49 ——Minor player in several Griffith films.

BRAHAM, HORACE *(1955)* 62 ——Was in silents: *Sinner or Saint, The Prodigal Judge.*

BRAHAM, LIONEL *(1947)* 68 ——English character in silents (*Skinner's Dress Suit, Don Juan,* etc.) and talkies (*Wee Willie Winkie, The Little Princess*).

BRAITHWAITE, LILIAN *(1948)* 77 ——English character; in *A Man About the House.*

BRANDON-THOMAS, AMY *(1974)* 84 —— Support in English pix: *Mystery at the Villa Rose* ('30), etc.

BRANDT, LOUISE *(1959)* 82 ——Was in silents.

BRASSEUR, PIERRE *(1972)* 66 ——French star; in *The Children of Paradise* (the actor, Lemaitre, who wins Arletty from the mime), *Port of Shadows, The Lovers of Verona,* more.

BRASWELL, CHARLES *(1974)* 49 ——Featured in *Pretty Boy Floyd, The Only Game in Town,* etc.

BRAVO, JAIME *(1970)* 38 ——Handsome matador; in Lana Turner's *Love Has Many Faces.*

BRAY, JOHN *(1955)* 49 ——Minor roles in *Viva Zapata!, The Paleface, Here Comes the Groom.*

BRAYFIELD, GEORGE *(1968)* ——Acted in silent Westerns.

BREAKSTON, GEORGE *(1973)* 53 ——Andy Hardy's pal Beezy in *Love Finds Andy Hardy,* etc.; earlier, as a lad, he'd starred in *No Greater Love,* played Pip in Universal's *Great Expectations* ('34), and been featured in Oberon's *The Dark Angel;* later he became a producer-director in South Africa.

BREAMER, SYLVIA *(1943)* 40 ——Sweet-faced brunette star of many silents: *Missing, The Devil, Flaming Youth, Doubling for Romeo* (with Will Rogers), *Sherlock Brown,* etc.

BRECHER, EGON *(1946)* 61 ——Support; in *Juarez* (Baron von Magnus), Shirley Temple's *Heidi* (innkeeper), *The Hairy Ape,* etc.

BREEN, MARGARET *(1960)* 60s ——Appeared in 1930's *Heads Up.*

BREESE, EDMUND *(1936)* 65 ——Forbidding, heavyset character actor; onscreen from 1914; many silents: *Wildfire, Womanhandled, The Brown Derby,* etc.; talkies: *All Quiet on the Western Front, Mata Hari* (warden), *Platinum Blonde, Broadway Bill,* many others.

BREEZE, LOU *(1969)* 68 ——Supporting roles.

BRENDEL, EL *(1964)* 73 ——Slang expression "Yumpin' yiminy" became a national byword, thanks to this Swedish-dialect comedian; best in *Just Imagine* ('31); also lent his crinkly-eyed charm to *If I Had My Way, Little Miss Broadway, Paris Model, Delicious* and *Happy Landing.*

BRENEMAN, TOM *(1948)* 45 ——Garrulous, chuckling radio emcee who starred when his network show, *Breakfast in Hollywood,* became a movie.

BRENNAN, WALTER *(1974)* 80 ——That "character of characters" who parlayed his characterizations of canny old men—long before he was one—into three Supporting Oscars (*Come and Get It, Kentucky, The Westerner*); also was nominated for *Sergeant York;* in 70 others including *The Story of Vernon and Irene Castle, Meet John Doe, To Have and Have Not,* and *My Darling Clementine.*

BRENON, HERBERT *(1958)* 78 ——Noted director who acted in silents: *Ivanhoe, Two Orphans,* etc.

BREON, EDMUND *(1951)* 68 ——Genial Britisher; in *Goodbye, Mr. Chips, Gaslight* (as General Huddleston), *Casanova Brown* (Teresa Wright's father), *Forever Amber* (Lord Redmond), *Devotion, Hills of Home,* etc.

BRERTON, TYRONE *(1939)* 45 ——Silents: *Secrets of the Night, The Canyon of Adventure,* etc.

BRESSART, FELIX *(1949)* 57 ——Long-nosed, twinkly-eyed German who spent most of his Hollywood career at Metro; in *Ninotchka* (one of the three Russian emissaries on whom Garbo rode herd in Paris), *The Shop Around the Corner, Blossoms in the Dust, Ziegfeld Girl, Comrade X,* etc.

BREWER, MONTE (SONNY) *(1942)* 8 ——Youngster featured in Lloyd Nolan's *Mr. Dynamite.*

BRIAN, DONALD *(1948)* 71 ——Dapper star of silents: *The Smugglers, The Voice in the Fog,* others.

BRICE, BETTY *(1935)* 38 ——In silents: *Beau Brummell, The Green Temptation, Heart's Haven,* etc.

BRICE, FANNY *(1951)* 59 ——All of Streisand's impersonations (*Funny Girl, Funny Lady*) cannot add one whit to the stature of this nonpareil comedienne; captivated millions in *The Great Ziegfeld, My Man, Everybody Sing,* and as radio's bratty Baby Snooks.

BRICKER, BETTY *(1954)* 63 ——Appeared in early silents.

BRICKERT, CARLTON *(1943)* 52 ——In silents: *You Are Guilty, The Rider of the King Log.*

BRIGGS, HARLAN *(1952)* 71 ——Hotel clerk in *My Little Chickadee;* in *The Bank Dick,* the pipe-smoking, whispery-voiced little doctor who helps W. C. Fields medicate bank examiner Franklin Pangborn with horse pills; in *Maisie, Having Wonderful Time,* many others.

BRIGGS, MATT *(1962)* 79 ——Character; *The Ox-Bow Incident* (Judge Tyler), *Coney Island* (Oscar Hammerstein), *Buffalo Bill* (General Blazier), *The Babe Ruth Story,* others.

BRIGGS, OSCAR *(1928)* 51 ——Support in silents.

BRISCOE, LOTTIE *(1950)* 68 ——Early Lubin star with long brunette curls, usually paired with handsome Arthur Johnson in comedies or serials (*The Beloved Adventurer*).

BRISSON, CARL *(1958)* 62 ——Dashing matinee-idol-type singer-leading man from Denmark; mesmerized the ladies in *All the King's Horses, Murder at the Vanities,* others.

BRISTER, ROBERT S. *(1945)* 56 ——Support in John Barrymore's *Dangerous to Know.*

BRITTON, ETHEL *(1972)* 57 ——Character actress in *Patterns.*

BRITTON, MILT *(1948)* 54 ——Led his band ("Mad Musical Maniacs") in Lamour's *Riding High.*

BRITTON, PAMELA *(1974)* 40s ——Usually played sweet daffy blondes; Sinatra's waitress-girlfriend, Brooklyn, in *Anchors Aweigh*; in a *Letter for Evie, Key to the City,* and was especially fine as Edmond O'Brien's costar in *D.O.A.*

BROCKWELL, GLADYS *(1929)* 35 ——Attractive leading lady in such silents as *Sins of the Parents*; support in others: *Seventh Heaven* (as wild-eyed, older, drunken sister Nana who flogged Janet Gaynor regularly), *The Hunchback of Notre Dame, So Big,* etc.; was in *The Drake Case* and a few other talkies.

BRODERICK, HELEN *(1959)* 68 ——Plainspoken, sharply funny femme with a crooked nose, bug eyes, and a worldly soul; *Top Hat* and *Swing Time,* in both of which she was Ginger Rogers' older pal, were her best but she was fun to have around in *Honeymoon in Bali, Virginia, Nice Girl,* and all the rest.

BRODIE, BUSTER *(1948)* 62 ——Was seen in the silent *All Aboard.*

BRODY, ANN *(1944)* 49 ——In silents (*A Sainted Devil, Clancy's Kosher Wedding,* etc.), talkies (*Drums of Jeopardy, The Heart of New York, Lawyer Man,* others).

BROMBERG, J. EDWARD *(1951)* 47 —— Usually cast as the wise, kind, bespectacled friend of the star; made 26 pix in a five-year career (1936–40) at 20th Century-Fox including *Hollywood Cavalcade, Jesse James, Second Honeymoon, Four Men and a Prayer;* under contract at Universal, he was in *Salome, Where She Danced; The Phantom of the Opera, Son of Dracula,* etc.; and, as a freelance, made numerous others elsewhere.

BRONSON, BETTY *(1971)* 64 ——Merry, tiny star of *Peter Pan* ('24), *A Kiss for Cinderella, Are Parents People?,* etc., she was also prominently cast in *Ben Hur* ('25), Jolson's *The Singing Fool, Sonny Boy,* others.

BROOK, CLIVE *(1974)* 87 ——Suave, handsome British star of *Cavalcade, Shanghai Express, The Devil Dancer, The Return of Sherlock Holmes, The Man From Yesteryear,* and many more from 1924 to '45; devoted his remaining years, after a minor supporting role "comeback" in 1963's *The List of Adrian Messenger,* to writing his memoirs (unpublished).

BROOKE, CLAUDE *(1933)* 80 ——Support in silents: *The Great Gatsby, The Sorrows of Satan, Pied Piper Malone,* others.

BROOKE, CLIFFORD *(1951)* 79 ——Lloyd George in *Wilson;* the watchman in *Hangover Square;* in *A Woman's Face, The Suspect,* etc.

BROOKE, TYLER *(1943)* 51 ——Actor-singer most often seen in musicals; portrayed the young composer in Chevalier's *Love Me Tonight* (sang reprise of "Isn't It Romantic" with two other actors); specialty numbers in *Tin Pan Alley, In Old Chicago,* and *Little Old New York.*

BROOK-JONES, ELWYN *(1962)* 51 —— Stocky British villain; *Beau Brummell, Odd Man Out, Lucky Nick Cain,* etc.

BROOKS, ALAN *(1936)* 48 ——Satan in De Mille's *The King of Kings;* others.

BROOKS, HANK *(1925)* ——Was in Sennett comedies.

BROOKS, JESS LEE *(1944)* 50 ——Impressive as the black minister Joel McCrea heard preach during his *Sullivan's Travels.*

BROOKS, PAULINE *(1967)* 54 ——Charming, dark-haired ingenue in *Alibi Ike, Beauty for Sale, Age of Indiscretion, Make a Million,* and other early '30s movies.

BROOKS, RANDY *(1967)* 49 ——Bandleader; in shorts; *not* actor Rand Brooks.

BROOKS, WILSON *(1967)* ——Supporting roles.

BROPHY, ED *(1960)* 65 ——Plump, bald, bushy-browed apoplectic comic character, often in bowler hat; perhaps best recalled as the valet in the *"Falcon"* pictures; sometimes a cop, sometimes a crook; in *A Slight Case of Murder, China Seas, The Thin Man,* more.

BROUGH, MARY *(1934)* 71 ——Character comedienne in British films: *Rookery Nook, On Approval,* etc.

BROWER, OTTO *(1946)* 50 ——Support in Billie Dove's *All the Brothers Were Valiant.*

BROWN, CHARLES D. *(1948)* 61 ——White-haired character who usually played politicos, cops, dads, and editors; in *The Strange Love of Martha Ivers* (Special Investigator), *The Big Sleep* (millionaire Sternwood's butler), *It Happened One Night* (reporter), various "Charlie Chan" and "Mr. Moto" programmers, many others.

BROWN, HARRY *(1966)* 74 ——Supporting player; *Marine Raiders*, etc.

BROWN, HELEN W. *(1974)* 59 ——Edgar Buchanan's wife in *Shane*; support in still others.

BROWN, JOE E. *(1973)* 80 ——Big mouth, big laughs, big heart; Warners made a mint on him via *Wide Open Faces, Bright Lights, Alibi Ike, Polo Joe, The Gladiator,* etc.; "officially retired" after 1944's *Hollywood Canteen,* he made four spaced-out return appearances on the screen: to play Cap'n Andy in *Show Boat* ('51); for a cameo in *Around the World in 80 Days* ('56); to do the aging pixilated playboy in *Some Like It Hot* ('59; spoke the now legendary final line, with a grin and shrug, after learning his "fiancee" is really Jack Lemmon in drag: "Nobody's perfect"); and for a fleeting part in *It's a Mad, Mad, Mad, Mad World* ('63).

BROWN, JOHNNY MACK *(1974)* 70 ——Millions of kids in the '30s and '40s wanted to be a Western hero just like him; earlier, when he was at Metro making screen love to Garbo (in *A Woman of Affairs*) and Crawford *(Our Dancing Daughters),* the kids' dads had just wanted to *be* him.

BROWN, PHIL *(1973)* 50s ——Played young Nick Adams in *The Killers* ('46), a G.I. in Colbert's *Without Reservations,* and youthful flyer Jimmy Masters in *I Wanted Wings.*

BROWN, RAYMOND *(1939)* 58 ——Character (Dr. Radisse) in *The Story of Louis Pasteur;* in many others: *King of the Underworld, The Magnificent Brute, Dr. Socrates* (Ben Suggs), etc.

BROWN, RUSS *(1964)* 72 ——In *Damn Yankees, Anatomy of a Murder, The Love Captive, South Pacific* (Capt. Brackett), etc.

BROWN, WALLY *(1961)* 57 ——Popular comedian given promotional push by RKO in the mid-40s; in *Seven Days Ashore* (top-billed), *Step Lively, Around the World,* etc.; later, elsewhere, was comic support in *The High and the Mighty, As Young as You Feel,* and *The Absent-Minded Professor.*

BROWNE, EARLE *(1944)* 72 ——Support in Pickford's *Sparrows, The Taming of the Shrew,* others.

BROWNE, IRENE *(1965)* 74 ——Elegant English actress; support in *Cavalcade, Berkeley Square* (Lady Anne Pettigrew), *Pygmalion* (Duchess), *Quartet* (in "The Alien Corn" episode, mother of the rich boy who longs to be a concert pianist).

BROWNE, W. GRAHAM *(1937)* 67 ——Dapper support in Marie Tempest's *Mrs. Plumb's Pudding* ('15) and Leslie Howard's *The Lady Is Willing* ('34), and many others in between.

BROWNING, WILLIAM E. *(1930)* ——Support in Helen Morgan's debut pic, *Applause.*

BRUCE, BELLE *(1960)* 70s ——In silents.

BRUCE, BETTY *(1974)* 54 ——"Tessie the Stripper" in *Gypsy,* the movie and Broadway show.

BRUCE, BEVERLY *(1925)* ——In one Photoplay Library release of '21, *Empty Arms.*

BRUCE, NIGEL *(1953)* 58 ——Sherlock Holmes' (Basil Rathbone's) inimitable Dr. Watson; his amiable, mumbling pixie English charm was an asset to *Lassie Come Home, Lillian Russell, Rebecca, Roxie Hart,* and a few dozen more too.

BRUCE, PAUL *(1971)* ——Support in *Born Losers,* a 1967 Hell's Angels pic.

BRUCE, TONY *(1937)* 27 ——Actor who had a top featured role in the '30 British pic *Tell England* with Fay Compton.

BRUGGERMAN, GEORGE *(1967)* 60s —— Character (Omnes) in Mae West's *I'm No Angel.*

BRUNDAGE, BERTHA *(1939)* 53 ——Character.

BRUNETTE, FRITZI *(1943)* 53 ——A Selig star in 1913, she was in *The Butterfly Girl, Discontented Wives, Driftwood,* others.

BRUNNS, JULIA *(1927)* 32 ——She played the love interest opposite Antonio Moreno in the 1913 Biograph pic *No Place for Father.*

BRUNOT, ANDRE *(1973)* 93 ——Character in French films: *The Red and the Black, Picnic on the Grass, The Virtuous Scoundrel,* etc.

BRYAN, ARTHUR Q. *(1959)* 59 ——Character (Fat Philistine Merchant) in *Samson and Delilah* ('49); in *Broken Lance, The Lieutenant Wore Skirts,* etc.

BRYAN, GEORGE *(1969)* 59 ——Narrator of *Lost Continent* and *Will It Happen Again?*

BRYANT, CHARLES *(1948)* 69 ——Nazimova's ex; in *Out of the Fog, Eye for Eye, The Brat,* other silents.

BRYANT, NANA *(1955)* 67 ——Played upper-class moms and haughty matrons; in Deanna Durbin's *Nice Girl* and *Mad About Music, The Unsuspected, Harvey, Theodora Goes Wild,* many more.

BUCHANAN, JACK *(1957)* 66 ——British musical star; headlined with Astaire and Fabray in *The Band Wagon* (remember the "Triplets" number?); in *Paris, Monte Carlo,* others.

BUCK, FORD *(1955)* ——Black radio comedian, also on the screen.

BUCK, FRANK *(1950)* 62 ——Famed pith-helmeted wild-game hunter; in *Bring 'Em Back Alive, Fang and Claw.*

BUCK, INEZ *(1957)* 67 ——Appeared in early Lubin films.

BUCKLER, HUGH *(1936)* 64 ——Lord Gainsford in *Lost Horizon* ('37); also in *Jungle Princess, Crash Donovan,* etc.

BUCKLER, JOHN *(1936)* 29 ——Young character (Ham) in *David Copperfield* ('35), in *Tarzan Escapes, The Unguarded Hour,* etc.; son of Hugh, they died in a highway accident.

BUCKLEY, FLOYD *(1956)* 82 ——In silent serials: *The Exploits of Elaine, Pearl of the Army,* others.

BUFFALO BILL, JR. *(1961)* 65 ——Popular in Action's Westerns of the 1920s; later, as character in cowboy movies, was billed Jay Wilsey.

BUHLER, RICHARD *(1925)* 48 ——A Lubin leading man in 1913.

BULGAKOV, LEO *(1948)* 59 ——Character in *For Whom the Bell Tolls* (Gen. Golz), *This Land Is Mine, The Country Doctor, Song of Russia.*

BUMPAS, BOB *(1959)* 48 ——The radio announcer at the scene of the cave-in tragedy in Billy Wilder's *Ace in the Hole.*

BUNCE, ALAN *(1965)* 62 ——Played Al Smith in *Sunrise at Campobello;* best known for comic parts on TV.

BUNKER, RALPH *(1966)* 67 ——Character in *The Hucksters* (Allison).

BUNNY, GEORGE *(1952)* 81 ——Character on-screen 1921–30; in *The Lost World, Lights of Old Broadway, The Locked Door,* etc.; less-famous brother of John.

BUNNY, JOHN *(1915)* 51 ——Vitagraph's great, plump comedy star; in *Pickwick Papers* ('13), *Pigs Is Pigs,* many comedies with scrawny Flora Finch—*Bunny's Dilemma,* etc.; summed up best by a London *Spectator* critic: "When Mr. Bunny laughs, people from San Francisco to Stepney Green laugh with him. When Mr. Bunny frowns, every kingdom of the earth is steeped in woe. When he smells a piece of Gorgonzola cheese there is no doubt whatever that his nose has been seriously offended."

BUNSTON, HERBERT *(1935)* 61 ——Bald character; Dr. Seward in *Dracula,* Lord Elton in *The Last of Mrs. Cheney;* in *Clive of India, Cardinal Richelieu,* etc.

BURANI, MICHELETTE *(1957)* 75 ——Opera star; in *The Gilded Lady* (Colbert's maid), *Everybody Sing,* etc.

BURCH, JOHN *(1969)* 72 ——Mr. Wopsle in David Lean's *Great Expectations;* in others.

BURGESS, DOROTHY *(1961)* 54 ——Warner Baxter's lovely leading lady, the faithless Tonia, in *In Old Arizona;* less important roles in later pix: *Swing High, Taxi, Orient Express, The Circus Clown,* etc.

BURGESS, HELEN *(1937)* 20 ——Made impressive debut as second femme lead in De Mille's *The Plainsman,* as the young wife of Buffalo Bill Cody (James Ellison); then in *A Doctor's Diary* and *King of Gamblers;* Paramount had planned a star buildup when she died of pneumonia.

BURKE, BILLIE *(1970)* 84 ——A feather-brained delight in *The Wizard of Oz* (Glinda, the good witch), *Topper, The Young in Heart, Merrily We Live,* for which she was Oscar-nominated as Best Support, etc.; was noteworthy too in heavier films: *A Bill of Divorcement* (Hepburn's mother), *Craig's Wife, In This Our Life, Only Yesterday,* and many others.

BURKE, JAMES *(1968)* 82 ——Curly-haired Irish character who was Sergeant Velie in all the "Ellery Queen" pix of Ralph Bellamy and William Gargan; also in *Ruggles of Red Gap; High, Wide and Handsome; On Borrowed Time, Dead End,* dozens more.

BURNABY, DAVY *(1949)* 68 ——Heavyset character in British pix: *Are You a Mason?, Three Men in a Boat,* etc.

BURNE, NANCY *(1954)* 41 ——In English films of the '30s: *Thunder in the City, Royal Eagle,* others.

BURNETTE, SMILEY *(1967)* 55 ——Gene Autry's roly-poly sidekick, Frog, of the bent-brimmed hat and the white horse with one black-ringed eye; besides hundreds of Westerns, was in *The Stadium Murders, Manhattan Merry-Go-Round,* etc.

BURNS, BOB *(1956)* 63 ——Paramount's homespun, Will Rogers-like *Arkansas Traveler,* with bazooka; starred in *Our Leading Citizen, I'm From Missouri, Alias the Deacon,* etc.; earlier was top comic support in *Rhythm on the Range, Waikiki Wedding, Wells Fargo,* others.

BURNS, DAVID *(1971)* 69 ——Gruff character comic; in *Knock on Wood, Let's Make Love,* etc.; more famous on Broadway in *Hello, Dolly!,* as Horace, the rich old widower snared by Dolly Levi.

BURNS, FRED *(1955)* 77 ——Often a gray-haired sheriff in Westerns; in *Flaming Guns, Parade of the West,* scores more.

BURNS, HARRY *(1939)* 55 ——Actor-dad of late star Bobby Vernon.

BURNS, HARRY *(1948)* 63 ——Character (The Crow) in *Northwest Mounted Police;* top support in *Kid Nightingale, Lady Scarface,* etc.

BURNS, IRVING *(1968)* 54 ——Supporting roles.

BURNS, NAT *(1962)* 75 ——Supporting roles.

BURNS, PAUL E. *(1967)* 78 ——Specialized in portraying professional men; in *Johnny Allegro, Hell Harbor, Storm Warning, The Mummy's Tomb, Seventeen,* etc.

BURNS, ROBERT E. *(1957)* 73 ——Long career; silent serials, dozens of Westerns *(Border Law, Guns and Guitars,* etc.), usually as a posse-leading deputy.

BURROUGHS, ERIC *(1960)* ——Support in *Odds Against Tomorrow.*

BURT, FREDERICK *(1943)* 67 ——Top support in Warner Baxter's *The Cisco Kid;* also in *The Royal Bed, Up for Murder, Eyes of the World.*

BURT, WILLIAM P. *(1955)* 82 ——Support in the silent serials *Pirate Gold* and *The Lightning Raider* (in which he was the gun-totin' old-timer, The Wasp, who abetted Pearl White); also in *The Leopard Lady, Danger Lights,* etc.

BURTON, CHARLOTTE *(1942)* 60 ——Dark-haired leading lady in silents: in 1915's *Man's Way* and the serial *The Diamond From the Sky* (second lead), etc.

BURTON, CLARENCE *(1933)* 51 ——A De Mille "regular"; in *The King of Kings* (the Repentant Thief), the silent *Ten Commandments* (the cruel Taskmaster), *The Road to Yesterday,* etc.

BURTON, GEORGE *(1955)* 55 ——Character (Hank) in McCarey's *Ruggles of Red Gap.*

BURTON, NED *(1922)* 72 ——In *Back Home and Broke,* and other silents.

BURTON, ROBERT *(1962)* 65 ——Top support in *A Man Called Peter* (Mr. Peyton), *Compulsion* (father of Artie Straus, the child-killer played by Bradford Dillman), *Broken Lance, The Big Heat,* etc.

BURTON, WILLIAM H. *(1926)* 81 ——In *Born Rich, Makers of Men,* other silents.

BUSCH, MAE *(1946)* 55 ——A now-legendary silent star, in scores of pix; in many von Stroheim films, was perhaps seen to best advantage in his *Foolish Wives* (as accomplice-cousin, who poses as a countess, of the contemptible phony Russian count); costarred with Lon Chaney in *The Unholy Three* and was featured in his *While the City Sleeps;* supporting roles in others, through 1940's *Women Without Names.*

BUSH, FRANCES CLEVELAND *(1967)* 78 —— Actress-widow of Lon Chaney.

BUSH, GEORGE *(1937)* 79 ——Rustic support in *The Adventures of Tom Sawyer.*

BUSHMAN, FRANCIS X. *(1966)* 83 ——1925's *Ben Hur,* in which he was a mighty Messala, was the capstone of the career of this king of the silent screen; the worldwide adulation that had been his from 1911 inexplicably (since he was only 42) diminished after this film; mostly thereafter he was seen in B's *(The Thirteenth Juror),* as support in Westerns *(The Dude Wrangler)* and serials *(Dick Tracy);* the year of his death he had a bit in a C-picture, *The Ghost in the Invisible Bikini.*

BUSLEY, JESSIE *(1950)* 80 ——Gray-haired character actress at Warners; played Priscilla Lane's grandmother in *Brother Rat, Brother Rat and a Baby;* also in *It All Came True, Personal Maid,* etc.

BUSTER, BUDD *(1965)* 74 ——An early leading man (1909–15), he returned in '34 and played Western villains and comics in scores of B's:

Covered Wagon Trails, The Old Chisholm Trail, etc.

BUTCHER, ERNEST *(1965)* 80 ——Meek British character; *The Tawny Pippit, My Brother Jonathan*, etc.

BUTLER, CHARLES *(1920)* 64 ——Top support in numerous silents including Pauline Frederick's *Zaza* ('15).

BUTLER, FRANK *(1967)* 76 ——Support in *The Sheik, A Tailor-Made Man, Satan in Sables*, other silents; later a top Paramount screenwriter (*Going My Way, Road to Singapore*, etc.).

BUTLER, JIMMIE *(1945)* 24 ——Margaret Sullavan's lad in *Only Yesterday*; in many other 1930s pix; killed in WW II.

BUTLER, JOHN *(1967)* 83 ——Character; in *Make Way for a Lady, Expensive Husbands, The Yellow Cab Man*, etc.

BUTLER, ROY *(1973)* 80 ——Support in many Johnny Mack Brown and Gene Autry Westerns.

BUTLER, WILLIAM J. *(1927)* 66 ——Supported Bushman and Bayne in the serial *The Great Secret*.

BUTTERFIELD, HERB *(1957)* 61 ——Character; in *A Blueprint for Murder, The House on Telegraph Hill, Shield for Murder*, etc.

BUTTERWORTH, CHARLES *(1946)* 49 —— Had a corner on the market as the screen's indecisive, often inebriated, confirmed-bachelor millionaire; in *The Cat and the Fiddle, Love Me Tonight, Thanks for the Memory, Second Chorus, Magnificent Obsession* ('35), etc.

BUTTERWORTH, WALTER *(1962)* 68 —— Screen actor-cousin of Charles.

BYFORD, ROY *(1939)* 66 ——In silents: *Love's Boomerang, The Spanish Jade*, etc.

BYINGTON, SPRING *(1971)* 77 ——Was a forever-young, gay, warm character; after an auspicious debut as Marmee in Hepburn's *Little Women*, she was a ray of sunshine in many of the best of the '30s and '40s: *You Can't Take It With You* (was Oscar-nominated as Best Support), *Dodsworth, Theodora Goes Wild, The Buccaneer; Ah, Wilderness!; The Story of Alexander Graham Bell, Heaven Can Wait, I'll Be Seeing You, The Enchanted Cottage, In the Good Old Summertime*, etc.; small-town fans retain fond memories of her, too, in the "Jones Family" pix, and TV audiences in her long-run *December Bride* series; last in movies in 1960's *Please Don't Eat the Daisies*.

BYLES, BOBBY *(1969)* 38 ——Minor roles in *War Is Hell* and *Onionhead*.

BYRD, RALPH *(1952)* 43 ——Starred in the "Dick Tracy" serials (*Dick Tracy's Return, Dick Tracy's G-Men*, etc.); in many other pix including *S O S Tidal Wave, The Howards of Virginia, Guadalcanal Diary*, and *Stallion Road*.

BYRON, ARTHUR *(1943)* 71 ——One of Hollywood's busiest and best character actors from '32; in *The Mummy, 20,000 Years in Sing Sing* (warden), *The House of Rothschild* (Baring), *The Man With Two Faces* (Dr. Kendall), *The Whole Town's Talking* (district attorney), *Oil for the Lamps of China*, etc.

BYRON, PAUL *(1959)* 68 ——In early Universal silents.

BYRON, ROY *(1943)* 56 ——Was in the silent *The Palm Beach Girl*.

BYRON, WALTER *(1972)* 80s ——Character in many from 1928's *The Awakening* to 1939's *Trade Winds*; in *Mary of Scotland* (Sir Francis Walsingham), *Charlie Chan's Greatest Case, British Agent*, others.

C

CABANNE, CHRISTY *(1950)* 62 ——Silent actor (*Judith of Bethulia*, etc.); better known as a director (many silents through 1940's *Drums of the Congo*).

CABOT, BRUCE *(1972)* 67 ——Ruggedly handsome hero who survived with style through four screen decades; rescuing Fay Wray in *King Kong* (his fifth movie) established his fame— and his future course; battled his way through the '30s in *Let 'Em Have It, Fury, Flying Devils, The Last of the Mohicans*, etc.; in the '40s was in *The Flame of New Orleans, Avalanche, Salty O'Rourke, Fallen Angel*, more; later was high-class support in many including *The Comancheros, Hatari!, The War Wagon* and, his last, a James Bond pic, *Diamonds Are Forever*.

CADELL, JEAN *(1967)* 83 ——Scottish character; W. C. Fields' missus in *David Copperfield;*

returned to England where she appeared in support in many: *I Know Where I'm Going, Pygmalion, Mad Little Island*, etc.

CAHILL, LILY *(1955)* 69 ——Support in *My Sin.*

CAHILL, MARIE *(1933)* 59 ——Plump silent star comedienne; *Judy Forgot, Gladys' Day Dreams.*

CAHN, DANA *(1973)* 17 ——Newcomer in several minor roles.

CAIN, ROBERT *(1954)* 67 ——Costarred with Hazel Dawn in *My Lady Incog;* many more silents.

CAINE, GEORGIA *(1964)* 87 ——Eddie Bracken's mom, Mrs. Truesmith, in *Hail the Conquering Hero,* one of several Preston Sturges comedies in which she appeared (others: *Christmas in July, The Miracle of Morgan's Creek,* and *The Beautiful Blonde From Bashful Bend).*

CAITS, JOE *(1957)* 67 ——Character ("No Nose Cohen") in *A Slight Case of Murder;* in many others.

CALDARA, ORME *(1925)* 50 ——Leading man who played opposite Jane Cowl in 1917's *The Spreading Dawn.*

CALDER, KING *(1964)* 64 ——Character; *The Rains of Ranchipur, Hong Kong Confidential.*

CALDWELL, MINNA *(1969)* ——Support.

CALDWELL, ORVILLE *(1967)* 71 ——Prominently featured in many silents: *The Harvester, The French Doll, The Scarlet Lily,* etc.; minor support in talkies such as Shirley Temple's *Just Around the Corner.*

CALHERN, LOUIS *(1956)* 61 ——Big, elegant, hawk-nosed star (as Justice Holmes) in *The Magnificent Yankee* for which he received an Oscar nomination as Best Actor; in *The Asphalt Jungle, Executive Suite, Julius Caesar* ('53), dozens more from 1932.

CALHOUN, ALICE *(1966)* 62 ——Charming brunette leading lady in *The Little Minister* ('21), *Pampered Youth, Hero of the Big Snows,* etc.

CALL, JOHN *(1973)* 64 ——Support; in *Hangman's Knot, Santa Claus Conquers the Martians,* etc.

CALLAHAN, BOBBY *(1938)* 42 ——Support in the '30s: *Battle of Greed, Wild Company.*

CALLAHAN, CHUCK *(1964)* 73 ——Vaudeville headliner featured in The Three Stooges wrestling short *Grips, Grunts and Groans.*

CALLIS, DAVID *(1934)* 46 ——Support in *What's Your Racket?* and *Sin Sister.*

CALTHROP, DAVID *(1940)* 52 ——Splendid British support; character (Tracy) in Hitchcock's *Blackmail;* in *Major Barbara, Fire Over England,* etc.; critic Graham Greene observed: "There is a concentrated venom in his acting, a soured malicious spirituality . . ."

CALVERT, CATHERINE *(1971)* 80 ——Dark-haired star of many silents: *The Heart of Maryland, Dead Men Tell No Tales, Fires of Faith,* etc.

CALVERT, E. H. *(1941)* 68 ——Character leads in dozens of silents: *Why Men Leave Home, A Daughter of the City, The Silent Partner,* etc.; in talkies, minor roles in *Horse Feathers, The Benson Murder Case,* others.

CAMELIA, MURIEL *(1925)* 13 ——Minor child player in Griffith pix.

CAMERON, DONALD *(1955)* 66 ——Lillian Walker's handsome costar in silent *Kitty MacKay;* others.

CAMERON, GENE *(1928)* ——Silent supporting actor; in *Circe, The Enchantress,* etc.

CAMERON, HUGH *(1941)* 62 ——Support in Thomas Meighan silents (*Cappy Ricks, Homeward Bound, Pied Piper Malone,* etc.), then in such talkies as *One Heavenly Night* and *One Third of a Nation,* in which he played Mr. Cassidy.

CAMP, SHEP *(1929)* 37 ——Supporting actor in *Song of the Flame, The Greene Murder Case.*

CAMPBELL, COLIN *(1966)* 83 ——Tall, thin, long-nosed Scotsman who played assorted British types (often servants or bobbies) in *Mrs. Miniver, This Above All, The Lodger, The Two Mrs. Carrolls,* etc., following a silent career dating back to 1915.

CAMPBELL, ERIC *(1917)* 39 ——Massive bearded "heavy" who tormented Chaplin in *The Cure, The Adventurer,* and most of those early two-reelers.

CAMPBELL, FRANK *(1934)* 87 ——Minor character.

CAMPBELL, MRS. PATRICK *(1940)* 75 ——After a glorious stage career (the orginal Eliza

Doolittle in *Pygmalion*, a role written for her by Shaw), she came to movies old, bulky and black-haired, to play women who were sinister (the pawnbroker in Peter Lorre's *Crime and Punishment)* or viper-tongued *(One More River, Riptide).*

CAMPBELL, VIOLET *(1970)* 76 ——Had small role in *Suspicion*, which featured husband, Nigel Bruce.

CAMPBELL, WEBSTER *(1972)* 79 ——Attractive silent leading man adept at both comedy *(Oh, Daddy,* '15) and drama *(The Clock Struck One,* '17); many other silents and talkies; was first husband of star Corinne Griffith.

CAMPEAU, FRANK *(1943)* 79 ——Prominent character in many: Walter Huston's *Abraham Lincoln* (gave a vigorous portryal as the almost-defeated General Sheridan, an indomitable figure on horseback, giving his troops the inspiration to fight on), Will Rogers' *Lightnin'*, *Captain Thunder*, etc.; in silents had crossed swords (onscreen) often with Fairbanks *(Bound in Morocco, Reaching for the Moon).*

CANE, CHARLES *(1973)* 76 ——Character; usually on the side of the law: *Dead Reckoning* (Lt. Kincaid), *All Through the Night, Hello, Frisco, Hello* (Irish cop), etc.

CANSINO, EDUARDO, JR. *(1974)* 54——Rita Hayworth's brother; played a native in a '53 Columbia serial, *The Great Adventures of Captain Kidd.*

CANTOR, CHARLES *(1966)* 68 ——Character (Finnegan) in *Duffy's Tavern;* also in *Stop, You're Killing Me.*

CANTOR, EDDIE *(1964)* 72 ——Great saucer-eyed comic star of radio, TV, and such movies as *Whoopee, Kid Boots, Roman Scandals, If You Knew Susie,* etc.; got a million laughs with jokes about Ida and their five daughters; of the latter, eldest, Margie, is dead; Natalie, Janet, and Edna have been married and divorced; and Marilyn is married to announcer Michael Baker, lives in New York where she has produced plays, and has a young daughter and son; Cantor was portrayed onscreen by Keefe Brasselle in *The Eddie Cantor Story.*

CAPRICE, JUNE *(1936)* 37 ——Portrayed Pickford-like youthful innocence in 1916-21 silents: *Caprice of the Mountains, A Modern Cinderella,* etc.

CARD, KATHRYN *(1964)* 71 ——Character roles in *Kiss and Tell, Home Before Dark,* etc.

CARDWELL, JAMES *(1954)* 33 ——One of the ill-fated sons (George) in *The Sullivans;* continued onscreen another six years in *A Walk in the Sun, Tokyo Joe, And Baby Makes Three,* etc.

CARELL, ANNETTE *(1967)* 60s ——English; character (Katherine von Bora) in *Martin Luther;* in *Our Mother's House,* etc.

CARETTE, *(1966)* 69 ——Polished French actor in scores of talkies; perhaps best known in America for roles in the Renoir films *Grand Illusion* and *The Rules of the Game* (was central figure of one of the pic's most famous sequences: Marceau the poacher, who's employed as a domestic at the Marquis' country chateau); sometimes was billed by full name, Julien Carette, sometimes not.

CAREW, ARTHUR EDMUND *(1937)* 43 ——Ruggedly built, handsome silent lead; in *Rio Grande* ('20), *Trilby* (as Svengali), *My Old Kentucky Home,* many more; support in such talkies as *Doctor X* and *The Mystery of the Wax Museum;* sometimes billed Carewe.

CAREW, JAMES, *(1938)* 62 ——Character in British movies: *Murder in the Stalls, Wings Over Africa,* etc.

CAREW, ORA *(1955)* 62 ——One of the most genuine of Mack Sennett's "beauties"; in *Oriental Love, Love Comet,* etc.

CAREWE, EDWIN *(1940)* 56 ——Handsome actor-director; costarred with Mabel Taliaferro in *The Snow Bird* ('16); directed *The Girl of the Golden West, Silver Wings,* and other silents.

CAREWE, RITA *(1955)* 47 ——Daughter of Edwin; featured roles in silents directed by him *(Ramona, Revenge, Joanna);* a.k.a. Rita Mason.

CAREY, HARRY *(1947)* 69 ——Great character star seen in hundreds, from the movies' earliest days; you knew he was kind and brave without his saying a word, and whenever he spoke it was always with authority; played every type of character—explorers, Senators, granddads, Old West settlers and lawmen, etc.; in *Trader Horn, Mr. Smith Goes to Washington* (Oscar-nominated as Best Support), *They Knew What They Wanted, The Shepherd of the Hills* ('41), *Barbary Coast, Red River,* etc.

CARLE, RICHARD *(1941)* 70 ——He looked rich—with his shiny bald head fringed with gray and pince-nez atop a strong-beaked nose—so he naturally played old millionaires (usually bankers); in *The Devil and Miss Jones, Ni-*

notchka, *True Confession, Seven Sinners, Love in Bloom*, more.

CARLETON, GEORGE *(1950)* 65 ——Character; in *And Now Tomorrow, A Tree Grows in Brooklyn, The Great Gildersleeve.*

CARLETON, LLOYD *(1933)* 61 ——Support in the silent *Tongues of Scandal.*

CARLETON, WILLIAM P. *(1947)* 74 ——Support in many silents (*Behind Masks, The Inside of the Cup, Homeward Bound,* etc.) and talkies to '38 (*Ann Vickers, The Bohemian Girl,* others).

CARLIE, EDWARD *(1938)* 60 ——Rustic support in Bob Burns' *I'm From Missouri.*

CARLISLE, ALEXANDRA *(1936)* 50 ——English; supported Constance Collier in *Half a Sinner.*

CARLYLE, HELEN *(1933)* 40 ——Support in Paramount's *Forgotten Commandments.*

CARLYLE, RICHARD *(1942)* 63 ——Character in silents: L. Barrymore's *The Copperhead, Hearts in Dixie, Guilty,* and talkies: *The Girl of the Golden West, Sons of Steel,* etc.

CARMICHAEL, MYRA *(1974)* 84 ——Support in silents.

CARMINATI, TULLIO *(1971)* 77 ——Romantic actor-singer star from Italy who shared top billing with Grace Moore in *One Night of Love* and gave that pic far more sparkle than did its celebrated diva; starred in the '30s in *Gallant Lady, Let's Live Tonight, Paris in Spring,* etc.; reduced to support in *Safari* ('40s), he retired to Italy; later popped up in small parts in movies filmed on European location: *Roman Scandal, El Cid, The Cardinal,* few others.

CARNAHAN, SUZANNE *(1952)* 31 ——See Susan Peters.

CARNERA, PRIMO *(1967)* 60 ——Outsized boxer from the Pampas who occasionally acted; in *The Prizefighter and the Lady, Prince Valiant.*

CARNEY, ALAN *(1973)* 63 ——RKO funnyman; teamed with Wally Brown in WW II "Rookie" comedy features; Cary Grant's dimwitted, loyal bodyguard in *Mr. Lucky;* in *Step Lively, Li'l Abner,* others.

CARNEY, GEORGE *(1948)* 60 ——English character; in *I Know Where I'm Going, Love on the Dole, Convoy, In Which We Serve,* etc.

CAROL, MARTINE *(1967)* 46 ——Voluptuous French star; a feast for the eyes in *Beauties of the Night* and *Lola Montes.*

CARPENTER, HORACE B. *(1945)* 70 ——Was Spanish Ed in DeMille's first ('14), *The Virginian,* following it with many Westerns, silent and talkie.

CARPENTER, PAUL *(1964)* 44 ——Handsome hero in many British B pix (*Night People, The Young Lovers, Black Glove,* etc.); support in English-made Hollywood pix (*I Aim at the Stars, The Iron Petticoat*).

CARR, ALEXANDER *(1946)* 68 ——In all the "Potash and Perlmutter" comedy features of the '20s, he was the second half of the team; comic support in such talkies as *Her Splendid Folly* and *Christmas in July.*

CARR, GEORGIA *(1971)* 46 ——Harry James band singer; in *Will Success Spoil Rock Hunter?*

CARR, GERALDINE *(1954)* 38 ——Character actress; in *The Sniper, The Company She Keeps.*

CARR, GERTRUDE *(1969)* 60 ——Character.

CARR, JACK *(1967)* 68 ——Support in 1938-43 pix: Bobby Breen's *Way Down South,* Bickford's *One Hour to Live, Flight for Freedom, Safari.*

CARR, JANE *(1957)* 48 ——British; femme lead in *The Triumph of Sherlock Holmes,* support in *36 Hours.*

CARR, LAWRENCE *(1969)* 51 ——Actor-producer.

CARR, MARY *(1973)* 99 ——Broke millions of hearts as the courageous mother in 1920's *Over the Hill to the Poor House;* never had a role to equal it though she was active through '39 in *Painted People, The Woman on the Jury, Lights of New York, Ladies in Love, East Side of Heaven,* many more; returned in '56 to play an old Quaker woman in *Friendly Persuasion.*

CARR, NAT *(1944)* 57 ——Support in many silents (*Kosher Kitty Kelly, The Jazz Singer, Private Izzy Murphy,* etc.) and talkies (*Portia on Trial, Next Time We Love, Union Depot,* others).

CARR, PERCY *(1926)* 61 ——Character (the butler) in Carol Dempster's *One Exciting Night;* in *The Ragged Edge,* other silents.

CARR, PHILIP *(1969)* 38 ——British player.

CARR, SADE *(1940)* 51 ——Was in early Essanay pictures.

CARR, WILLIAM *(1937)* 70 ——In many silents including *Get-Rich-Quick Wallingford.*

CARRE, BARTLETT *(1971)* 74 ——In silent Westerns: *Flying Hoofs, Behind Two Guns,* etc.

CARRIGAN, THOMAS J. *(1941)* 55 ——As the prince he costarred with wife, Mabel Taliaferro, in 1911's *Cinderella;* other silents: *Room and Board, Salomy Jane, Checkers,* and *Wings,* in which he had only a bit.

CARRILLO, LEO *(1961)* 80 ——There was laughter and joy in this star of many fractured accents (Spanish, Italian, etc., and all acquired, for he was a Californian), and audiences warmed to that in his dozens of movies; costarred as the little racketeer ruined for his love of Grace Moore in *Love Me Forever* (and gave one of the year's best performances); splendid, too, in *The Gay Desperado, History Is Made at Night, Lillian Russell;* later fans (and some old ones) found pleasure in his *Cisco Kid* TV series.

CARRINGTON, EVELYN *(1942)* 66 ——Support in silents: *Living on Love, Salvation Nell.*

CARRINGTON, HELEN *(1963)* 68 ——Support in the comedies *Queen High* and *Heads Up,* both in '30.

CARROLL, LEO G. *(1972)* 80 ——One of the most valued members of Hollywood's "British colony," he brought enormous dignity—and curiosity-provoking aloofness—to his every role; did splendid work for Hitchcock in several: *Rebecca* (Dr. Baker), *Suspicion, Spellbound* (doctor), *The Paradine Case, Strangers on a Train* (Senator), *North by Northwest* (professor); fine, too, in *Wuthering Heights, The House on 92nd Street* (as ace Nazi agent Col. Hammersohn), and *The Private Lives of Elizabeth and Essex.*

CARROLL, NANCY *(1965)* 58 ——Paramount, home studio of many great beauties, never had a star more piquantly lovely than this Valentine-faced charmer; introduced in making-merry flicks of the late '20s (*Sweetie; Easy Come, Easy Go,* etc.), she soon proved she could handle meatier material: *The Devil's Holiday* (Oscar-nominated as the nothing-can-stop-me manicurist, she lost to Shearer in *The Divorcee*), *Shopworn Angel, Child of Manhattan, The Dance of Life;* she was a star for nine years

(1927-35) but superpopular only in the mid-third of them.

CARROLL, WILLIAM A. *(1928)* 51 ——Support in silent serials: *The Screaming Shadow, The Branded Four.*

CARSEY, MARY *(1973)* 32 ——Small roles in *Elmer Gantry, A House Is Not a Home.*

CARSON, JACK *(1963)* 52 ——Beefy, funny "average guy" leading man at Warners, most popular in the '40s, especially when teamed with Dennis Morgan (*Shine On Harvest Moon, Two Guys From Texas, Two Guys From Milwaukee,* etc.); first hit his stride as a star—after lesser roles in 26 pix in the previous four years —as Cagney's rival for Rita Hayworth in 1941's *Strawberry Blonde;* got a crack at heavier drama in *The Hard Way, One More Tomorrow,* and *Cat on a Hot Tin Roof,* but fans still liked it best when, with that seesaw grin, he dished out the wisecracks.

CARSON, JAMES *(1958)* 73 ——Support in *Crime School, The Gracie Allen Murder Case, The Girl Downstairs.*

CARTER, BEN *(1947)* 36 ——Genial black character actor; Hattie McDaniel's love in *Maryland;* crusty old John-Henry in *The Harvey Girls;* in *Crash Dive,* the Navy messman, Oliver Cromwell Jones, who manned a machine gun during the Pearl Harbor attack, downing several enemy planes.

CARTER, CALVERT *(1932)* 73 ——In silents: *Slave of Desire, Lying Lips,* others.

CARTER, FRANK *(1920)* 32 ——Minor player in silents.

CARTER, LOUISE *(1957)* 81 ——Character actress in doleful roles in the '30s—e.g., the German mother (and wife of L. Barrymore) in *The Man I Killed,* whose forgiveness Phillips Holmes seeks for having killed her soldier-son in combat; also in *The Last Mile, Paddy O'Day,* etc.

CARTER, MONTE *(1950)* 64 ——Support in *Redhead, Million Dollar Racket,* etc.

CARTER, MRS. LESLIE *(1937)* 75 ——Famous stage actress who filmed two of her biggest hits, *The Heart of Maryland* and *Du Barry,* in '15; support in talkies (*Rocky Mountain Mystery, The Vanishing Pioneer*); was portrayed by Miriam Hopkins in *Lady With Red Hair,* which she also wrote.

CARTON, PAULINE *(1974)* 89 ——French character; the elderly governess in buttoned boots in Cocteau's *Blood of a Poet;* in *The Living Dead Man, Meet Miss Mozart,* etc.

CARUSO, ENRICO *(1921)* 48 ——Great operatic tenor; starred in 1918's *My Cousin,* which flopped.

CARVER, KATHRYN *(1947)* 41 ——Leading lady in silents: *The Yankee Senor, Service for Ladies, When Love Grows Cold,* etc; once married to Adolphe Menjou.

CARVER, LOUISE *(1956)* 87 ——The aunt, Mrs. Gilwattle, in *The Man from Blankleys;* support in other talkies *(The Big Trail; Hallelujah, I'm a Bum)* and silents *(Main Street, Scaramouche,* etc.).

CARVER, LYNNE *(1955)* 38 ——Promising blonde MGM leading lady in the '30s; was hometown love of Lew Ayres in *Young Dr. Kildare;* in *Maytime, Within the Law, Everybody Sing,* others.

CARVILL, HENRY *(1941)* 74 ——Support in William Farnum's *If I Were King* ('20) and Arliss talkie version of *Disraeli* ('29).

CASADESUS, MATHILDE *(1965)* 34 ——Support in French films: *Gervaise, Le Plaisir.*

CASEY, DOLORES *(1945)* 27 ——Paramount ingenue in the '30s; in *Artists and Models Abroad, Doctor Rhythm, Cocoanut Grove.*

CASEY, KENNETH *(1965)* 66 ——As a dark-haired lad of 12 with a Dutch Boy haircut, he starred as "Master Kenneth Casey" for Vitagraph.

CASEY, STUART *(1948)* 51 ——English; character (Capt. Hobart) in *Captain Blood;* also in *Reckless* and *Age of Indiscretion.*

CASH, WILLIAM F. *(1963)* 82 ——Character; nicknamed "Ardo the Frog."

CASS, MAURICE *(1954)* 70 ——Monocled little comedy character from Russia whose bushy gray hair always made him look as though he should be conducting a symphony orchestra; in *Thin Ice* (the Count), *Second Fiddle, Champagne Waltz, Gold Diggers in Paris,* more.

CASSEL, SID *(1960)* 63 ——Minor English actor.

CASSIDY, BILL *(1943)* 67 ——Minor Griffith player.

CASSIDY, ED *(1968)* 74 ——Stongly resembling Teddy Roosevelt, he frequently portrayed him; as sheriffs, ranchers, and bankers, was in dozens of B Westerns, 1935-52.

CASSON, SIR LEWIS *(1969)* 73 ——Distinguished British support; in *Rhodes, Victoria the Great, South Riding, Sixty Glorious Years,* more.

CASTIGLIONI, IPHIGENIA *(1963)* 61 —— Austrian actress of great beauty and regal bearing (Shaw saw her at 16 in *Caesar and Cleopatra* in Vienna and proclaimed: "The child is the reincarnation of my Cleopatra!"); twice in Hollywood she portrayed Empress Eugenie *(Maytime, The Story of Louis Pasteur);* also in *The Life of Emile Zola* (Madame Charpentier, and billed as Countess Iphigenia Castiglioni), *Rear Window* (the Bird Woman), *Funny Face,* etc.; was wife of actor Leonid Kinskey.

CASTLE, DON *(1966)* 47 ——Once a handsome young MGM lead *(These Glamour Girls, Out West With the Hardys,* etc.), hailed as a "new" Gable; later, tough guys in *The Big Land, Gunfight at the O.K. Corral,* others.

CASTLE, IRENE *(1969)* 75 ——Of the world-famed Vernon and Irene Castle dance team; in *Slim Shoulders* and other silents including the star role in the serial *Patria;* Astaire and Rogers portrayed the Castles onscreen.

CASTLE, LILLIAN *(1959)* 94 ——In *Confidential* ('35); a vaudeville headliner.

CASTLE, NICK *(1968)* 58 ——Well-known choreographer; was seen in *Artists and Models.*

CASTLE, PEGGY *(1973)* 45 ——Lovely blonde femme lead in *I, the Jury; 99 River Street, Air Cadet,* etc.

CASTLE, VERNON *(1918)* 32 ——Famed dancer; starred with wife Irene in 1915's *The Whirl of Life.*

CATLETT, WALTER *(1960)* 71 ——Long-nosed, google-eyed character comic in many of the best comedies and musicals from '24 through the '50s; *Bringing Up Baby* (the sheriff driven wild by Hepburn's and Grant's antics), *Mr. Deeds Goes to Town* (Morrow), *Platinum Blonde, My Gal Sal,* Durbin's *Spring Parade,* and *It Started With Eve, Lake Placid Serenade,* and several dozen others.

CAVALIERI, LINA *(1944)* 70 ——Italian opera star in silents: *The Rose of Granada, The Two Brides.*

CAVANAGH, PAUL *(1959)* 64 ——Crawford's suave older husband in *Humoresque;* polished top support in scores more: *A Bill of Divorcement* ('32), *I Take This Woman, The Hard Way, Night and Day, Secret Beyond the Door, Magnificent Obession* ('54), etc.

CAVANAUGH, HOBART *(1950)* 63 ——Famed in Milquetoast roles; henpecked husband of soap opera-scripting queen Florence Bates in *A Letter to Three Wives;* in over 100 more: *Good-Bye Again, A Lost Lady, Three Smart Girls, Rose of Washington Square, Margie, My Favorite Spy,* etc.

CAVANNA, ELISE *(1963)* 61 ——In silents *(Love 'Em and Leave 'Em)* and talkies *(I Met My Love Again,* billed Alice Cavenna; *Everybody Sing,* etc.).

CAVEN, ALLAN *(1941)* 60 ——Support in silents *(London After Dark,* the Allene Ray serial *The Terrible People,* etc.) and B talkies *(Old Louisiana, I Am a Criminal,* others).

CAVENDER, GLEN *(1962)* 78 ——Sennett comedian with upturned, painted-on moustache; "Fatty" Arbuckle demolished him with a test-your-weight hammer in *Fickle Fatty's Fall;* in Keaton's *The General* (Capt. Anderson), *Main Street,* many other silents.

CAVENDISH, DAVID *(1960)* 69 ——Character (Henry Chilcotte) in *Random Harvest,* his only film.

CAWTHORN, JOSEPH *(1949)* 81 ——Played distinguished old men: *Lillian Russell* (Leopold Damrosch), *Naughty Marietta* (Herr Schuman), *Love Me Tonight* (doctor), *The Great Ziegfeld* (Ziegfeld's father), 1929's *The Taming of the Shrew* (the timid priest, Gremio, who marries Pickford and Fairbanks), and dozens more.

CAZENUVE, PAUL *(1925)* 40s ——Support in Mae Murray's *The French Doll,* Betty Blythe's *The Queen of Sheba,* other silents.

CECIL, EDWARD *(1940)* 52 ——Support in many silents including *The Phantom of the Opera* (as Faust), *The Top of New York,* and Pathe's last serial, *The Black Book.*

CECIL, MARY *(1940)* 55 ——Shearer's wise-to-men cook in *The Women.*

CELLIER, FRANK *(1948)* 64 ——Unsympathetic Britisher; the Sheriff in *The 39 Steps;* in *Nine Days a Queen, The Magic Bow,* etc.

CERVI, GINO *(1974)* 72 ——Chunky Italian character; the mayor in *The Little World of Don Camillo, The Return of Don Camillo;* in *The Naked Maja, Becket* (Cardinal Zambelli), etc.

CESANA, RENZO *(1970)* 63 ——TV's The Continental; in *Francis of Assisi, The Naked Maja, Stromboli* (Italian priest unable to help bewildered Czech-bride Ingrid Bergman; he also collaborated on the script), others.

CHADWICK, HELENE *(1940)* 42 ——Blonde leading lady in silents from '16 *(Dancing Days, Modern Mothers, Gimmee),* and in support in talkies until '35 *(Hell Bound, Mary Burns, Fugitive);* first wife of director William Wellman.

CHAIRES, NESTOR *(1971)* 60 ——Known as "The Mexican Gypsy."

CHALIAPIN, FEODOR *(1938)* 65 ——Famed Russian basso; in 1933's *Don Quixote,* starring in both the French and English versions of this Pabst production, and billed Fedor Chaliapine; not to be confused with his son, of the same name, who acted in *For Whom the Bell Tolls.*

CHALMERS, THOMAS *(1966)* 76 ——In *All the Way Home* was old Joel; support in Paul Newman's *The Outrage;* had been in such silents as *Blind Alleys, Puritan Passions.*

CHALZEL, LEO *(1953)* 52 ——Support in Ida Lupino-starrer, *Come On Marines* and Gable's *Men in White.*

CHAMBERLIN, RILEY C. *(1917)* 62 ——Character actor who appeared in numerous Thanhouser films.

CHAMBERS, MARGARET *(1965)* 60s——Featured in the 1929 Tiffany B *Woman to Woman.*

CHAMBERS, MARIE *(1933)* 44 ——Support in Carol Dempster's *That Royle Girl.*

CHAMBERS, RALPH *(1968)* 76 ——Character (Charlie) in *The Pajama Game.*

CHAMBERS, WHEATON *(1958)* 69 ——Played mousey little men with bushy brows and a moustache; aided Garland's and Walker's hasty WW II marriage in *The Clock;* minor support in many *(They All Kissed the Bride, The Falcon Out West,* and various serials including *Adventures of Red Ryder).*

CHAN, OIE *(1967)* 81 ——Chinese actress in Anna May Wong's *Daughter of the Dragon.*

CHANCE, ANNA *(1943)* 58 ——With husband Charles Grapewin in Christie comedies.

CHANCE, NAOMI *(1964)* 30s ——Lovely British blonde; femme lead in 1954's *Saint's Girl Friday*; also in *The Trials of Oscar Wilde*.

CHANDLER, ANNA *(1957)* 70 ——Vaudeville entertainer who was in *The Big Broadcast* ('32).

CHANDLER, HELEN *(1965)* 59 ——Beautiful blonde target of vampire Lugosi in *Dracula*; delightful as the waif, Nikki, in Barthelmess' *The Last Flight*; in *Outward Bound, A House Divided, Salvation Nell*, more.

CHANDLER, JAMES ROBERT *(1950)* 89 —— Support in the Allene Ray serial *Hawk of the Hills* and other action silents.

CHANDLER, JEFF *(1961)* 42 ——Muscular, handsome star with premature steel-gray hair; clicked big as Cochise in *Broken Arrow*, for which he was Oscar-nominated as Best Support; starred afterward for 20th and Universal in *Two Flags West, Bird of Paradise, Yankee Pasha, Sign of the Pagan, Female on the Beach*, many more.

CHANDLER, LANE *(1972)* 73 ——Rugged, good-looking man who, in 40 years and over 400 pix, played everything from two-scene bits to leads; costarred with Clara Bow in *Red Hair*, starred in Warner's *Forward Pass*, was one of Garbo's leading men in *The Single Standard*, was featured in most DeMille talkies (*The Plainsman, Northwest Mounted Police*), starred in such serials as *The Lightning Express*, and had supporting parts in scores of Westerns.

CHANEY, CHUBBY *(1936)* 18 ——Was "Fatty" in "Our Gang" for eight years (1926-34).

CHANEY, LON *(1930)* 47 ——"The Man of a Thousand Faces"; set the screen's standard for the macabre as star of many: *The Hunchback of Notre Dame, The Phantom of the Opera, He Who Gets Slapped, The Tower of Lies, The Black Bird*, etc.; Cagney portrayed him later in *Man of a Thousand Faces*.

CHANEY, LON, JR. *(1973)* 67 ——Changed his name from Creighton (under which he'd played bits in *Lucky Devils*, etc.) to that of his more famous father, for his own career in horror epics: *The Wolf Man* (title role), the Mummy in *The Mummy's Tomb*, Dracula in *Son of Dracula*, etc.; was most impressive, though, as Lennie, the dim-witted, kind giant in *Of Mice and Men*.

CHAPIN, ALICE *(1934)* 76 ——Character actress in silents: *Manhattan* (Richard Dix's first

starring pic), Bebe Daniels' *Argentine Love* and *The Crowded Hour*.

CHAPLIN, CHARLES, JR. *(1968)* 42 ——Son of the comedian; minor roles in B's: *The Beat Generation, Girls' Town*, etc.

CHAPLIN, SYDNEY *(1965)* 80 ——Actor-brother of Charlie; talented but overshadowed; with Charles in *Shoulder Arms*; starred on his own in many silents: a 1915 Keystone Comedy series (replacing Charlie); *Charlie's Aunt* (title role); *King, Queen, Joker; Her Temporary Husband; The Rendezvous*, etc.

CHAPMAN, BLANCHE *(1941)* 90 ——Longtime minor character.

CHAPMAN, EDYTHE *(1948)* 84 ——One of De Mille's favorite character actresses; in many of his silents: *The Ten Commandments* (in the second, modern half, the Bible-reading mother of Richard Dix and Rod La Rocque), *Manslaughter, The Little American*, etc.; for other directors, in *Lightnin', My American Wife*, many more.

CHARLES, MICHAEL *(1967)* 50s ——Supporting player.

CHARLESWORTH, JOHN *(1960)* 25 ——British teen star; second lead in 1952's *Tom Brown's School Days*; in *The Horse's Mouth*, and *A Christmas Carol* ('51).

CHARSKY, BORIS *(1956)* 63 ——Russian; support in *Captain Lash* and Dolores Del Rio's *The Red Dance*.

CHARTERS, SPENCER *(1943)* 68 ——Played paunchy, bespectacled (and often foxy) rustics; in *Our Town* (Constable), *Jesse James* (Preacher), *Mr. Deeds Goes to Town*, 1931's *The Front Page* (Woodenshoe), *Young Mr. Lincoln* (Judge Bell, presiding at the trial of the unjustly accused boys), and more than 100 others.

CHASE, ARLINE *(1926)* 25 ——A Sennett bathing beauty.

CHASE, CHARLEY *(1940)* 46 ——A comic some rate alongside Chaplin; in dozens of silent comedies including *Tillie's Punctured Romance, Only a Farmer's Daughter, Long Live the King*, etc.; starred in a series of talkie two-reelers, and was in *The Sons of the Desert, Modern Love, Neighborhood House*, others.

CHASE, COLIN *(1937)* 51 ——Support in *The Iron Horse* (Tony), *The Godless Girl, Big News*, and many Westerns, both silent and talkie.

CHATTERTON, RUTH *(1961)* 67 ——Sophisticated, brittle blonde star of considerable popularity from '28; toplined *Madame X* and *Sarah and Son*, for both of which she was Oscar-nominated as Best Actress, *The Laughing Lady, Charming Sinners, The Rich Are Always With Us, Tomorrow and Tomorrow*, etc.; best as Walter Huston's spoiled, utterly selfish wife, who fears middle age, in *Dodsworth*.

CHATTERTON, THOMAS *(1952)* 71 —— Handsome, dimpled-chinned 1915 Kay-Bee star; in *The Secret of the Submarine*, other silents; support in talkie Westerns and Hayward's *Smash-Up*.

CHATTON, SYDNEY *(1966)* 48 ——English; support in Rowan and Martin's *Once Upon a Horse*.

CHAUTARD, EMILE *(1934)* 53 ——Distinguished support; in *Shanghai Express* (Major Lenard), Janet Gaynor's *Seventh Heaven* (Pere Chevillon), *Adoration, Lilac Time*, etc.; directed *Under the Greenwood Tree* and other silents.

CHECCHI, ANDREA *(1974)* 57 ——Italian actress; in *Times Gone By, The Walls of Malapaga*, etc.

CHEKHOV, MICHAEL *(1955)* 46 ——Bergman's teacher-friend in *Spellbound* (was Oscar-nominated as Best Support), the gentle androgyne in *Specter of the Rose*, Uncle Leopold in Lupino's *In Our Time*, the Jewish papa in *Abie's Irish Rose* ('46), others.

CHENE, ETHEL *(1972)* 72 ——In many Keystone comedies with Chaplin and Sennett.

CHERKASSOV, NIKOLAI *(1966)* 63 —— Starred in the title role of *Alexander Nevsky*; many Russian films.

CHERRY, CHARLES *(1931)* 59 ——A Famous Players 1915 leading man, with black patent-leather hair.

CHERRYMAN, REX *(1928)* 30 ——A most handsome Broadway actor featured in two Nazimova silents: *Camille* and *Madame Peacock*; was once engaged to Barbara Stanwyck.

CHESEBRO, GEORGE *(1959)* 71 ——Top henchman in dozens of Maynard, Autry, and Ritter Westerns.

CHESHIRE, HARRY "PAPPY" *(1968)* 76 —— Black-browed, jowly, gray-haired banker or townsman in *My Darling Clementine, Sand* ('49), and many more Westerns (mostly B's);

similar supporting roles in *Moonrise, If I'm Lucky, No Sad Songs for Me*, others.

CHESNEY, ARTHUR *(1949)* 67 ——Character in British films: *Sorrell and Son, French Leave, Girl in the Street*, etc.; Edmund Gwenn's brother.

CHESTER, ALMA *(1953)* 81 ——Support in George O'Brien's *The Dude Ranger*, and in *The Beloved Bachelor*.

CHEVALIER, MAURICE *(1972)* 83 ——Paris' inimitable boulevardier; most fondly recalled for his early '30s musicals (*The Love Parade* and *The Big Pond*, for both of which he was Oscar-nominated as Best Actor in the same year [1929-30], *The Smiling Lieutenant, One Hour with You, Love Me Tonight, The Merry Widow*, etc.), until he returned as a gay old roue in *Love in the Afternoon, Gigi*, and *Can-Can*; last in Disney's *Monkeys Go Home*.

CHIEF JACK *(1943)* 66 ——Indian in many B Westerns.

CHIEF JOHN BIG TREE *(1967)* 92 ——In *She Wore a Yellow Ribbon*, the weary old war chieftain Pony-That-Walks; in *Stagecoach*, the Cheyenne Scout; in *Drums Along the Mohawk*, Blue Back; in *Susannah of the Mounties*, the Chief; dozens more; his profile was on every Indian Head nickel minted, for which he posed in 1912.

CHIEF MANY TREATIES *(1948)* 73 ——A Blackfoot Indian (real name, William Hazlett) who almost always was dressed in cowboy garb in dozens of B Westerns including *King of the Stallions, Drums of Destiny*, etc.

CHIEF THUNDERCLOUD *(1955)* 56 ——Tonto in *The Lone Ranger* serial; in many other serials (*Black Arrow, Flaming Frontier*, etc.), numerous big-budget Westerns (*Union Pacific, The Plainsman, Buffalo Bill, Unconquered*), and scores of B's.

CHIEF THUNDERCLOUD *(1967)* 68 ——In many B Westerns in the '30s, but never enjoyed the prominence of the other Chief Thundercloud; interestingly, he also played Tonto in *The Lone Ranger*—on radio.

CHIEF YOWLACHIE *(1966)* 76 ——Huge Yakima Indian and a bad one—with a big sour face, shaven head with a fierce little black brush left on top, and great paws known to wield tomahawks and knives; in dozens: *Yellow Sky, Red River, A Ticket to Tomahawk, El Paso*, etc.

CHILDERS, NAOMI (1964) 71 ——Antonio Moreno's leading lady in 1915's *Anselmo Lee;* also in *Restless Wives, Mr. Barnes of New York, Lord and Lady Algy, Courage,* others.

CHILDS, GILBERT *(1931)* ——Support in 1930's *The Co-Optimists.*

CHIRELLO, GEORGE *(1963)* 65 ——Minor player in Welles' *Macbeth.*

CHISHOLM, ROBERT *(1960)* 62 ——Support in Jeanette MacDonald's *The Lottery Bride* and in a 1938 B, *Father O'Flynn.*

CHIVVIS, CHIC *(1963)* 79 ——Support in silents.

CHRISTIANS, GEORGE *(1921)* 52 ——Forceful in a major role in von Stroheim's *Foolish Wives,* as Hughes, the American envoy to Monaco whose "foolish wife," Miss Dupont, narrowly escapes von Stroheim's seduction; died of a heart attack during production—role was completed by Robert Edeson, filmed only from the back; credits for *Foolish Wives* give his name variously, as both George and Rudolph Christians.

CHRISTIANS, MADY *(1951)* 51 ——Gave several glowing performances as a mature character star (Edward G. Robinson's wife in *All My Sons,* the German refugee-housekeeper in *Tender Comrade,* Fontaine's mother in *Letter From an Unknown Woman*); had dismal roles in movies of the '30s: *A Wicked Woman* (Jean Parker's mother), *Heidi, Come and Get It, Escapade,* etc.

CHRISTY, BILL *(1946)* 29 ——Youth in Jane Powell's first, *Song of the Open Road.*

CHRISTY, IVAN *(1949)* 61 ——In silents: *Men of the Forest, Nevada, Rainbow,* etc.

CHRISTY, KEN *(1962)* 67 ——Supporting roles like the mailman in *Cheaper by the Dozen;* in *Burma Convoy, He Hired the Boss,* others.

CHURCHILL, BERTON *(1940)* 63 ——Bluff, portly, gray-haired character; crooked banker Gatewood in *Stagecoach;* in *Steamboat Round the Bend, Dimples, On Your Toes, Babbitt,* and 100 more.

CIANNELLI, ALMA *(1968)* 76 ——Character actress-wife of Eduardo.

CIANNELLI, EDUARDO *(1969)* 80 ——With those sinister eyes, as alarming a villain as any; in *Cairo, Passage to Marseille, Winterset* (perhaps his best, as cringing yet ruthless Trock Estrella), *Foreign Correspondent,* and many more; most surprising casting: the sympathetic bartender in *Kitty Foyle.*

CLAIRE, GERTRUDE *(1928)* 76 ——Character; *The Goose Hangs High, Widow by Proxy, Romance Road, Married Alive,* more.

CLAIRE, HELEN *(1974)* 68 ——Fox Movietone Newsreel's fashion commentator.

CLAPHAN, LEONARD *(1963)* 81 ——See Tom London.

CLARE, MARY *(1970)* 76 ——British character; starred in *Mrs. Pym of Scotland Yard;* featured in *The Lady Vanishes* (the Baroness), *The Citadel* (Mrs. Orlando), *The Black Rose, My Brother Jonathan,* etc.

CLARE, PHYLLIS *(1947)* 42 ——Appeared in a number of pix in the '30s: *Clive of India, Roadhouse Murder, His Brother's Wife, Along Came Sally,* etc.

CLARENCE, O. B. *(1955)* 85 ——Played elderly British gents, such as the Vicar in *Pygmalion;* also in *The Scarlet Pimpernel, Great Expectations* ('47), *Meet Me at Dawn,* others.

CLARGES, VERNER *(1911)* 40s ——Member of Griffith's first Biograph stock company; featured in his *Swords and Hearts* ('11).

CLARK, ANDY *(1960)* 57 ——As a child in silents, starred in a series of pix named after him (*Adventures of Andy Clark,* etc.); later, support in *Wings, Rio Rita* ('29), others.

CLARK, BOBBY *(1960)* 71 ——Great little Broadway comic—in painted on "spectacles"; costarred with partner Paul McCullough in three dozen 1928-35 shorts at Fox and RKO.

CLARK, BUDDY *(1949)* 38 ——Pop singer par excellence; besides dubbing for non-singing stars, he was onscreen in *Seven Days' Leave* ('42) and in Disney's *Melody Time,* in which he was the musical emcee and sang the title tune.

CLARK, CHARLES DOW *(1959)* 88 ——Character; *Ladies of the Jury, The Bat Whispers,* etc.

CLARK, CLIFF *(1953)* 59 ——Bartenders, honest cops: *Manpower, Mr. Moto's Gamble, Kentucky,* dozens more; a regular in all the Tom Conway "Falcon" pix, as Inspector Timothy Donovan.

CLARK, ED *(1954)* 65 ——Support in comedies, silent (*Private Izzy Murphy,* etc.) and talkie (*Rhubarb, Mr. Belvedere Rings the Bell, Bedtime for Bonzo*, others).

CLARK, ETHEL *(1964)* 48 ——At 22 had a supporting role in Evelyn Venable's *The Headleys at Home*.

CLARK, FRED *(1968)* 54 ——Slick-domed top comic support; *Auntie Mame, Bells Are Ringing, How to Marry a Millionaire, The Solid Gold Cadillac*; serious roles in *Sunset Boulevard, White Heat, Ride the Pink Horse*, many others.

CLARK, HARRY *(1956)* 45 ——Support in *Ice Capades* ('41) and *Taxi* ('53).

CLARK, HARVEY *(1938)* 52 ——Humorous support in several dozen: silents (*Ladies' Night in a Turkish Bath, In Old Kentucky*, etc.); talkies (*Red-Headed Woman, Alice in Wonderland*, in which he delighted Charlotte Henry by standing on his head, *Cracked Nuts, Going Wild*, others).

CLARK, JACK J. *(1947)* 70 ——Handsome early Kalem star; in *From the Manger to the Cross*, many more; support in such talkies as *Wells Fargo*.

CLARK, JIMMY *(1972)* 50s ——William Eythe's brother in *The Eve of St. Mark*.

CLARK, JOHNNY *(1967)* 50 ——Was young support in *The Locket; Las Vegas Nights; Hey, Rookie; Jive Junction*, etc.

CLARK, LES *(1959)* 52 ——Actor-dancer; in *White Christmas, When Willie Comes Marching Home*, etc.

CLARK, MARGUERITE *(1940)* 57 ——Tiny (under 5'), dark-haired beauty who was one of Famous Players' great and most charming silent stars; runner-up to Pickford as most popular actress in 1918; among her best: *Prunella, The Pretty Sister of Jose, Molly Make-Believe, Wildflower, Gretna Green, The Seven Swans*; married happily and retired after 1921's *Scrambled Wives*.

CLARK, PAUL *(1960)* 23 ——Was Marie Wilson's scene-stealing baby in *Boy Meets Girl*.

CLARK, WALLIS (1961) 71 ——Bald, funny English support in specs; in *It Happened One Night* (Lovington), *Lady for a Day, The Remarkable Andrew*, more; among his serious roles, the judge in the *Penny Serenade* scene in which Cary Grant begs him not to take away his and Dunne's adopted baby.

CLARKE, DOWNING *(1930)* 60s ——English character; in Griffith's *America* (Lord Chamberlain), Valentino's *Monsieur Beaucaire*, Edmund Lowe's *The Fool*, etc.

CLARKE, GORDON B. *(1972)* 65 ——Character (poolhall cashier) in *The Hustler*.

CLARKE-SMITH, D. A. *(1959)* 71 ——English character; in *The Man Who Never Was*, Disney's *The Sword and the Rose*, 1951's *Quo Vadis* (as Phaon), *The Ghoul, The Good Companions*, etc.

CLAUDIUS, DANE *(1946)* 72 ——Minor support.

CLAYTON, ETHEL *(1966)* 82 ——Beautiful silent actress who starred for Lubin (starting in 1909), World, and Paramount; noted for never giving a bad performance in usually forgettable pix: *The College Widow, Pettigrew's Girl, City Sparrow, The Cradle, If I Were Queen*, etc.; after starring career, she returned to Paramount for very minor roles in *Cocoanut Grove, The Buccaneer*, and Swarthout's *Ambush*, her last.

CLAYTON, HAZEL *(1963)* ——See Mrs. Mack Hilliard.

CLAYTON, LOU *(1950)* 63 ——One-third of Clayton, Jackson and Durante; in *Roadhouse Nights* ('30).

CLEARY, LEO *(1955)* 60 ——Support in *Johnny Holiday, The Human Jungle, The Red Menace, You Can't Fool Your Wife*.

CLEARY, PEGGY *(1972)* 80 ——Support in many silents.

CLEGG, VALCE *(1947)* 59 ——Support in the silent *Lucky Spurs*.

CLEMENT, CLAY *(1956)* 68 ——Character; except for *Rosalie, Tonight Is Ours, Each Dawn I Die* (Raft's attorney), mostly in B's: *Chinatown Squad, Passport to Alcatraz, Don't Bet on Blondes*, etc.

CLEMENT, DONALD *(1970)* 29 ——Support in *Tell Me That You Love Me, Junie Moon*.

CLEMENTS, DUDLEY *(1947)* 58 ——Support in many in the '30s: *New Faces of 1937, You Can't Buy Luck, The Toast of New York, Hideaway, The Big Shot*, etc.

CLEMONS, JAMES K. *(1950)* 67 ——Minor support.

CLERGET, PAUL *(1935)* 68 ——Supported Ethel Haller in *Woman* ('18), also in Paramount's *My Lady's Garter* two years later.

CLEVELAND, GEORGE *(1957)* 71 —— Grandpa in TV's *Lassie* series; similar roles in over 150: *Can't Help Singing, It Happened Tomorrow, Mother Wore Tights; A Girl, a Guy and a Gob*, etc.

CLIFF, LADDIE *(1937)* 46 ——British; in *Sleeping Car, The Co-Optimists*, etc.

CLIFFE, H. COOPER *(1939)* 77 ——Support in silents: *Monsieur Beaucaire, His Children's Children, Missing Millions*, etc.

CLIFFORD, JACK *(1956)* 76 ——Gruff Dogcatcher Nubbins in *Skippy* (how little Jackie Cooper did plead with him to give back "Sooky," Robert Coogan's dog!); kinder to Shirley Temple, as Uncle Tom in *Dimples*.

CLIFFORD, KATHLEEN *(1962)* 75 ——Brunette silent leading lady usually referred to as "Pretty Kitty Clifford"; in the 1917 serial *Who Is Number One?;* later in *Richard the Lion-Hearted, Excess Baggage, When Clouds Roll By*, etc.

CLIFFORD, WILLIAM *(1941)* 64 ——Early silent lead at Universal; later in *Ashes of Vengeance, Sowing the Wind, Three Miles Up*, etc.

CLIFT, MONTGOMERY *(1966)* 45 ——Star noted for portrayals of sensitive, often doomed young men; Oscar-nominated for *The Search* (his first), *A Place in the Sun, From Here to Eternity;* also memorable in *The Heiress; Red River; Suddenly, Last Summer; Freud; The Misfits.*

CLIFTON, ELMER *(1949)* 56 ——Star of *John Barleycorn* ('14); The Rhapsode in "The Babylonian Story" in *Intolerance;* was an assistant director for Griffith, besides being a member of his acting company, and doubled for Lillian Gish in certain (most dangerous) floating ice-floe scenes in *Way Down East.*

CLIFTON, HERBERT *(1947)* 63 ——English character; in *She's Got Everything*, Fontaine's *Ivy, False Pretenses*, others.

CLINE, EDDIE *(1961)* 68 ——In the silent *The Haunted House*, then as Edward F. Cline directed dozens, including *My Little Chickadee.*

CLIVE, COLIN *(1937)* 39 ——Splendid, strong-featured English who was at the top of his form as the star of *Journey's End;* also starred in *Frankenstein* and *The Bride of Frankenstein* (Baron Frankenstein in both), *Jane Eyre* ('34), *Clive of India, One More River*, others.

CLIVE, E. E. *(1940)* 60 ——Thin-faced, purse-lipped Welshman; featured as Tenny in all the 1937-39 "Bulldog Drummond" pix; fine support, too, in *Night Must Fall, Captain Blood, Kidnapped* ('38), *Pride and Prejudice, Lloyds of London*, many more.

CLIVE, HENRY *(1960)* 79 ——Costarred with Maxine Elliott in a 1917 Goldwyn picture, *The Fighting Odds;* also in *Obey the Law, Heedless Moths*, other silents.

CLONEBAUGH, G. BUTLER *(1943)* 80 —— See Gustav von Seyffertitz.

CLOUZOT, VERA *(1960)* 39 ——Brunette star of *Diabolique* and *Wages of Fear.*

CLOVELLY, CECIL *(1965)* 74 ——English character actor; in *The Forest Ring* and Anne Francis' *So Young, So Bad.*

CLUNES, ALEC *(1970)* 57 ——English character; in *Richard III, Melba, Quentin Durward.*

CLUTE, CHESTER *(1956)* 65 ——Bald, nervous, round little man with a tiny moustache, and often wearing a derby; in *Arsenic and Old Lace* (doctor), *My Favorite Spy, Guest Wife, Too Many Girls*, etc.

CLYDE, ANDY *(1967)* 75 ——William "Hopalong Cassidy" Boyd's sidekick Windy; support in *Abe Lincoln in Illinois, Million Dollar Legs, Cherokee Strip*, others.

CLYDE, DAVID *(1945)* 90 ——Brother of Andy, husband of Fay "Ma Hardy" Holden; in *The Lodger; The Gay Sisters; Now, Voyager;* etc.

CLYDE, JEAN *(1962)* 73 ——Character actress-sister of David and Andy.

COBB, EDMUND *(1974)* 82 ——Top star of silent Westerns for Universal; onscreen for 52 years.

COBB, IRVIN S. *(1944)* 67 ——Bushy-browed, paunchy, folksy humorist-actor; great support for Will Rogers in *Steamboat Round the Bend*, Jane Withers in *Pepper*, Bobby Breen in *Hawaii Calls*, Janet Gaynor in *The Young in Heart*, etc.

COBURN, CHARLES *(1961)* 82 ——Cigar-chomping, monocled "grand old man" of character actors; won a Supporting Academy Award by getting Jean Arthur to let him share her apartment in war-crowded Washington in *The More the Merrier*, and was nominated too for *The Devil and Miss Jones* (also with Arthur) and the grandpa role in *The Green Years;* and who can forget him in *The Lady Eve, Bachelor Mother, Kings Row,* and *In This Our Life?*

COCHRAN, STEVE *(1965)* 48 ——Muscular, dark, hint-of-menace star best in the Warners phase of his career: *White Heat, The Damned Don't Cry, Storm Warning, Dallas, The Tanks Are Coming, Jim Thorpe—All American,* etc.

COCHRANE, FRANK *(1962)* 80 ——English support; *Bulldog Drummond at Bay, Chu Chin Chow, Dark Sands,* others.

CODE, GRANT HYDE *(1974)* 78 ——Support in *The Miracle Worker, The Young Doctors, Serpico.*

CODEE, ANN *(1961)* 71 ——Elegant, accented (she was from Belgium) character actress in some of Hollywood's best: *Arise My Love, Old Acquaintance, Hangover Square, On the Riviera, Kiss Me Kate, The Clock,* many more.

CODY, BILL *(1948)* 57 ——Popular cowboy hero in the '20s and early '30s; was in *Six-Gun Justice, Lawless Border,* many more; no relation to "Buffalo Bill" Cody.

CODY, "BUFFALO BILL" *(1917)* 70 ——The genuine, original Colonel William "Buffalo Bill" Cody himself; portrayed himself for Edison Films before the turn of the century, again, in 1909, in a three-reeler, *Life of Buffalo Bill,* and then in a series in 1911.

CODY, ETHEL *(1957)* 62 ——Character roles.

CODY, HARRY *(1956)* 60 ——Minor support in *The People Against O'Hara, Singin' in the Rain.*

CODY, LEW *(1934)* 47 ——Dashing, debonair silent star best recalled for the lead in *Rupert of Hentzau* and as Swanson's costar in *Don't Change Your Husband* (the faithless playboy who stole her from and lost her back to her husband, Elliott Dexter); also *The Secrets of Paris, The Shooting of Dan McGrew, Adam and Evil,* many more silents; lesser roles in talkies: *Meet the Wife, X Marks the Spot, A Parisian Romance,* etc.; brief marriage to Mabel Normand, said to have been unconsummated.

COEDEL, LUCIEN *(1947)* 42 ——Gave one still-praised performance, as costar in the French *The Idiot,* released here in '48; previously in *Carmen* ('46), *The Bellman,* etc.

COFFIN, HANK *(1966)* 62 ——Support in aviation epics; *Hell's Angels, Dawn Patrol.*

COGAN, FANNY HAY *(1929)* 63 ——Support in many silents, usually cast as a mother.

COGDELL, JOSEPHINE *(1969)* 68 ——A Sennett bathing beauty.

COGHLAN, KATHERINE *(1965)* 76 ——Actress-mother of onetime juvenile Junior Coghlan.

COGHLAN, ROSE *(1932)* 81 ——A distinguished stage actress, she came to movies at 62 to star as Rosalind opposite the Orlando of Maurice Costello (then 35) in Vitagraph's three-reel production of *As You Like It;* went on to star in *The Sporting Duchess, Under the Red Robe,* and other silents; her last was a Sylvia Sidney pic, *Jennie Gerhardt* ('33), in which she had a supporting role as "Granddaughter of Old Weaver," Frank Reicher, who despite his makeup was 25 years younger.

COGLEY, NICK *(1936)* 67 ——Gray-haired character lead in *Toby's Bow* ('19), *Oriental Love,* more.

COHAN, AGNES MERRILL *(1972)* 89 ——Actress-wife of George M.

COHAN, GEORGE M. *(1942)* 64 ——Broadway's song-and-dance man who starred in pix in *The Phantom President, Gambling, Broadway Jones, Hit-the-Trail Holliday;* Cagney portrayed him, and Joan Leslie his wife, in *Yankee Doodle Dandy.*

COLBURN, CARRIE *(1932)* 73 ——Character in silents.

COLCORD, MABEL *(1952)* 80 ——Faithful old family servant in Hepburn's *Little Women;* also in *Sadie McKee, Reckless, David Copperfield,* etc.

COLE, ALONZO DEEN *(1971)* 74 ——Character.

COLE, FRED *(1964)* 63 ——In silents: *Daring Days, Two-Fisted Jones,* others.

COLE, JACK *(1974)* 60 ——Famous choreographer; danced with his company in *Moon Over Miami,* was also in *Designing Woman.*

COLE, LESTER *(1962)* 62 ——Singer-support in *Painted Faces, The Desert Song* (both '29).

COLE, NAT KING *(1965)* 46 ——Negro pianist-singer-actor; a headliner in *St. Louis Blues,* he also had prominent roles in *Small Town Girl, The Blue Gardenia, Istanbul, Cat Ballou,* etc.

COLEMAN, CHARLES *(1951)* 65 ——Mostly played butlers; *Little Miss Broadway, Merrily We Go to Hell, Poor Little Rich Girl, That Certain Age,* scores more.

COLEMAN, CLAUDIA *(1938)* 49 ——Myrna Loy's mother in *Test Pilot;* also in *Penrod and His Twin Brother, King of Burlesque,* others.

COLEMAN, EMIL *(1965)* 71 ——Led his famous dance orchestra in *Nob Hill.*

COLEMAN, WARREN *(1968)* 66 ——Black actor in movies, then Kingfish on TV's *Amos 'n Andy.*

COLLEANO, BONAR *(1958)* 35 ——American, first in British pix like *Stairway to Heaven* and *Sleeping Car to Trieste,* then in Hollywood's *Flame and the Flesh, Zarak, Fire Down Below.*

COLLIER, CONSTANCE *(1955)* 77 ——British grande dame; as the toothy old drama coach at the Footlights Club in *Stage Door,* she helped arrogant debutante Hepburn become a great success on stage—and as a human being: as drunken Lady Susan in *Kitty* she assisted guttersnipe Goddard in conniving her way to a titled marriage in 18th-century London; Crawford's new-found religion didn't rub off on her Lady Wigstaff in *Susan and God.*

COLLIER, SHERLEE *(1972)* 20s ——Played Jayne Meadows as a child in *Enchantment;* also in *Kind Lady.*

COLLIER, WILLIAM, SR. *(1944)* 77 —— Irene Dunne's father in *Invitation to Happiness,* Bogart's in *Up the River;* also in *Disputed Passage* (doctor), *Valiant Is the Word for Carrie, Give Us This Night,* more.

COLLINGE, PATRICIA *(1974)* 81 ——Unforgettable as Teresa Wright's tippling Aunt Birdie in *The Little Foxes,* and as her mother in *Shadow of a Doubt;* they were together again in *Casanova Brown;* also was in *Tender Comrade, The Nun's Story,* others; nominated for Best Supporting Actress Oscar in *The Little Foxes.*

COLLINGS, BLANCHE *(1968)* 58 ——Stage actress in occasional movies.

COLLINS, EDDIE *(1940)* 56 ——A 1938-40 20th Century-Fox "regular"; 17 good character roles (in many of their most lavish pix) in three years; Shirley Temple's Tylo, the Dog (to Son-dergaard's Tylette, the Cat), in *The Bluebird;* with Ameche in *Alexander's Ragtime Band, Hollywood Cavalcade* (played a Keystone Kop), *In Old Chicago,* with Fonda in *Young Mr. Lincoln, Drums Along the Mohawk,* and *The Return of Jesse James.*

COLLINS, GEORGE PAT *(1959)* 64 ——"Did time" in several prison pix: with Cagney in *White Heat* (inmate called The Reader), with Tracy in *20,000 Years in Sing Sing;* support in *Black Fury* (Lefty), *West Point of the Air,* etc.; sometimes billed Pat or G. Pat Collins.

COLLINS, JOSE *(1958)* 71 ——She starred as the beautiful guttersnipe in 1915's *The Light That Failed.*

COLLINS, MAY *(1955)* 49 ——Was Richard Dix's leading lady in 1921's *All's Fair in Love.*

COLLINS, MONTE *(1951)* 52 ——Prominently featured as a young man in silents: *The King of Kings* (A Rich Judean), *A Boy of Flanders, Our Hospitality, Long Live the King,* etc.

COLLINS, RAY *(1965)* 75 ——Superb character in over 60 pix, one of the best things Welles brought to the screen (in *Citizen Kane,* his debut, as Boss James Gettys); gave electrifying performances under Welles' direction in *The Magnificent Ambersons* (as Jack Amberson), and with him in *Touch of Evil,* his last; also in *Leave Her to Heaven, The Best Years of Our Lives, Roughly Speaking,* etc.; popular on TV as Lt. Tragg in *Perry Mason.*

COLLINS, RUSSELL *(1965)* 65 ——The stationmaster in *Bad Day at Black Rock,* the doctor in *The Enemy Below;* in *Niagara, Soldier of Fortune, Raintree County, Fail-Safe,* others.

COLLINS, S. D. J. *(1947)* 40 ——Minor role in *A Night at the Opera.*

COLLINS, TOM *(1973)* ——MGM support in 1939-40: *These Glamour Girls, Dr. Kildare's Strange Case, Fast and Loose, Tell No Tales.*

COLLUM, JOHN *(1962)* 36 ——Handsome British lead; in *Tom Brown's School Days* ('40).

COLLYER, JUNE *(1968)* 61 ——Leading lady in the '30s with a dimpled face of great sweetness; shared love scenes with Cooper (*The Man From Wyoming*), Buddy Rogers (*Illusion, River of Romance*), Dix (*The Love Doctor*); married comedian Stu Erwin and costarred with him, long after her movie career, in a popular TV series.

COLMAN, RONALD *(1958)* 67 ——Star of integrity, with outstanding (if saddened) good looks and a glorious speaking voice—perhaps the best ever heard on the screen; won Best Actor Academy Award for *A Double Life;* nominated also for *Bulldog Drummond* and *Condemned* (both same year), and *Random Harvest;* many unforgettable performances: *A Tale of Two Cities, The Prisoner of Zenda* and *Lost Horizon* (both '37), *The Light That Failed, The Talk of the Town,* and *The Late George Apley.*

COLUMBO, RUSS *(1934)* 26 ——Romantic, handsome singer; headlined in *Broadway Thru a Keyhole* (based on Fanny Brice's life), *Wake Up and Dream, Wolf Song,* etc.

COLVIG, VANCE *(1967)* 75 ——In many silent comedies, then Disney "voices": Pluto, Goofy, Grumpy.

COMINGORE, DOROTHY *(1971)* 53 —— Welles' alcoholic, failed-opera-singer-wife, who endlessly did jigsaw puzzles, in *Citizen Kane;* only minor opportunities later—*The Hairy Ape, Any Number Can Play* (a bit role), *The Big Night;* earlier had been a Columbia starlet named Linda Winters (*Blondie Meets the Boss*).

COMONT, MATHILDE *(1938)* 50 ——Buxom actress who played Italian/Spanish characters; in *Anthony Adverse* (cook Giusseppa), *Poor Little Rich Girl* (Henry Armetta's portly Italian wife), *Ceiling Zero,* etc., back to 1923.

COMPSON, BETTY *(1974)* 77 ——Blonde, beautiful, silent superstar (often earning over $5,000 a week) from 1919, whose career went up and down like a seesaw; several times labeled "washed up," when reduced to minor support or even bits, she often bounced back; nominated for a Best Actress Oscar in *The Barker,* she costarred with Barthelmess (*Weary River*), von Stroheim (*The Great Gabbo*), George Bancroft (*Docks of New York*), Lon Chaney (*The Miracle Man); after a bit in a 1948 B, *Here Comes Trouble,* she quit movies and became a successful California business woman.

COMPSON, JOHN *(1913)* 50s ——Plump, jolly member of the original (1908) Biograph stock company; costarred, as "Mr. Jones," with Florence Lawrence in the greatly popular "Jonesey" comedies: *Mr. Jones at the Ball, Mrs. Jones Entertains, Mr. Jones' Burglar,* etc.

COMPTON, BETTY *(1944)* 37 ——Beauty-singer of small talent once married to New York Mayor James J. Walker; in shorts and an English B pic.

COMPTON, FRANCIS *(1964)* 79 ——The trial judge in *Witness for the Prosecution;* support in Bergman's *Rage in Heaven.*

COMPTON, VIOLA *(1971)* 85 ——Aristocratic English character; sister of Fay; featured in *The Good Companions* and *The Last Journey,* both in the mid-30s.

CONE, MIKE "ZETS" *(1969)* 59 ——Musician in movies and on TV.

CONKLIN, CHESTER *(1971)* 83 ——Great walrus-moustached Sennett comic—"the epitome of Keystone comic villainy . . . the spiteful nuisance who made life miserable for everyone with whom he came in contact"; sometimes, too, the Chief of the Keystone Kops (but, famous as he was, he wasn't one of the original seven: Slim Summerville, Hank Mann, Mack Riley, Edgar Kennedy, Charles Avery, George Jeske, and Bobby Dunn; in literally hundreds from 1913, many with Chaplin, of course, including *The Great Dictator,* in which both he and Hank Mann had bit roles; bowed out with a tiny part in a 1966 Fonda pic, *A Big Hand for the Little Lady.*

CONKLIN, "HEINIE" *(1959)* 83 ——Famed comic in many silents (*The Cyclone Rider, A Fool and His Money, Seven Sinners, The Sap,* etc.) and talkies (*All Quiet on the Western Front, Little Miss Broadway, Abbott and Costello Meet the Keystone Kops*—but a Keystone Kop he'd never been, except a make-believe one in *Hollywood Cavalcade*).

CONKLIN, WILLIAM *(1935)* 60s ——First starred in the silent serial *Neal of the Navy* ('15), he was later Florence Lawrence's leading man in *The Enfoldment,* and one of Constance Talmadge's in *The Goldfish;* in many other silents: *Red Hot Dollars; Hay Foot, Straw Foot; Hairpins,* etc.

CONLAN, FRANK *(1955)* 81 ——In *Lydia,* was Old Ned, the family retainer; support in many: *All That Money Can Buy, The Scoundrel, Chad Hanna, Billy the Kid, The Crystal Ball,* etc.

CONLEY, LIGE *(1937)* 38 ——A Sennett comic, he later starred in his own series at both Mermaid and Educational; then was featured in such silent features as *The Charge of the Gauchos* ('28).

CONLIN, JIMMY *(1962)* 77 ——Rabbitty, chinless characters in Preston Sturges comedies (*Hail the Conquering Hero, The Palm Beach Story, The Great McGinty, Miracle of Morgan's Creek*); scores more including Harold Lloyd's

Mad Wednesday (The Sin of Harold Diddlebock), as the racetrack tout.

CONNELLY, BOBBY *(1922)* 13 ——Talented, handsome lad who costarred in the silent "Sonny Jim and Bobby Connelly" series; started at 4 with Clara Kimball Young in *Love's Sunset*; then in *A Prince in a Pawnshop*, *Intrigue* with Peggy Hyland, Earle Williams' *The Seal of Silence*, Blanche Sweet's *The Unpardonable Sin*, and finally was Vera Gordon's violin-playing youth in *Humoresque*.

CONNELLY, EDWARD *(1928)* 73 ——Support in Nance O'Neil's *The Fall of the Romanoffs* ('17), after having played an old man three years earlier in Pickford's *A Good Little Devil* (his debut); later, Viola Dana's Japanese father in *The Willow Tree*, in *Quincy Adams Sawyer*, *The Merry Widow*, *Scaramouche*, many others.

CONNELLY, ERWIN *(1931)* 57 ——He and wife Jane both had supporting roles in Houdini's *The Man from Beyond* and Keaton's *Sherlock Jr.*; alone, he had character parts in Colman's *The Winning of Barbara Worth* (as Pat), Keaton's *Seven Chances*, Pickford's *Kiki*, others.

CONNELLY, JANE *(1925)* 55 ——See immediately above.

CONNOLLY, WALTER *(1940)* 53 ——Droll character star with spluttery speech pattern; at his best when comically apoplectic—as Colbert's father in *It Happened One Night*, the newspaper publisher in *Nothing Sacred*, the theatrical moneyman in *Twentieth Century*; grand, too, in *Lady for a Day*, *Broadway Bill*, *Fifth Avenue Girl*, and in the title role in his last, *The Great Victor Herbert*.

CONNOR, EDRIC *(1968)* 43 ——British West Indian; Daggoo in Peck's *Moby Dick*.

CONNOR, EDWARD *(1932)* 50s ——Featured in *Anne of Little Smoky* ('22).

CONRAD, EDDIE *(1941)* 51 ——The Latvian diplomat in *Foreign Correspondent*; Temple's French tutor in *Just Around the Corner*; in *Down Argentine Way*, *Lucky Partners*, etc.

CONROY, FRANK *(1964)* 73 ——Topnotch character; the sadistic old major in Confederate uniform who led the lynch mob in *The Ox-Bow Incident*; lent his distinguished gray-haired presence to many: 1930's *The Royal Family of Broadway* (screen debut), *Grand Hotel* (hotel manager Rohna), *The Emperor's Candlesticks*, *Wells Fargo*, *The Snake Pit*, etc.

CONROY, THOM *(1971)* 60 ——In *Man With the Gun*, *The Young Savages*, others.

CONSTANDUROS, MABEL *(1957)* 77 ——Support in British pix: *The Gay Intruders*, *Bad Sister*, *Easy Money* (Episode I).

CONSTANT, MAX *(1943)* 20s ——Young support in Arthur Carewe's *Trilby* ('23).

CONTI, ALBERT *(1967)* 80 ——Austrian; star of Erich von Stroheim's *Merry-Go-Round*; prominent in many silents; *The Eagle*, *The Merry Widow*, *The Devil Dancer*, etc.; steady support in talkies through 1938's *Suez* and *Gateway*.

CONWAY, CURT *(1974)* 59 ——Support (The Writer) in *The Goddess*, starring his then wife, Kim Stanley; also in *Gentleman's Agreement*, *Singapore*, *Hud* (as Truman Peters who was cuckolded by Paul Newman), others.

CONWAY, JACK *(1951)* 70s ——Star of 1914's *The Valley of the Moon*; not the famous director.

CONWAY, JACK *(1952)* 65 ——Early silent star (*Restless Souls*, with Alma Rubens, *The Old Arm Chair*, etc.), then fine MGM director (*Boom Town*, *Viva Villa!*, *Too Hot to Handle*, others).

CONWAY, TOM *(1967)* 63 ——Suave, but less so than brother George Sanders, whom he followed as star of RKO's "The Falcon" series; in various Val Lewton horror pix: *I Walked With a Zombie*, *The Cat People*, *The Seventh Victim*, etc.; last had a bit (Lord Kensington) in Shirley MacLaine's *What a Way To Go*.

COOK, AL *(1935)* 53 ——In comedies: *The Sleeping Cutie*, *Love's Labor Found*, *The Telephone Girl*, *Cash and Merry*, others.

COOK, DONALD *(1961)* 60 ——A debonair actor, born to wear a tux (*The Casino Murder Case*, etc.), he was also effective in drama: *The Public Enemy* (Cagney's brother Mike), costarring with Sidney in *Jennie Gerhardt*, *The Man Who Played God*, etc.; last was Ann Blyth's loving adoptive father in *Our Very Own*.

COOK, JOE *(1959)* 69 ——Broadway star "of contagious good-naturedness" who headlined some of Educational's best shorts; grand, too, in talkie features: *Arizona Mahoney*, *Rain or Shine*.

COOK, MARY LOU *(1944)* 30s ——Support to Abbott and Costello's *Ride 'Em Cowboy*; former wife of Elisha Cook Jr.

COOKE, BEACH *(1948)* 50 ——Supporting actor in silents, played a West Point cadet in Barthelmess' *Classmates* ('24).

COOKE, SAM *(1964)* 32 ——Popular black recording star; in B musicals.

COOKE, WARREN *(1939)* 50 ——Popular support in silents: *Fog Bound, Slim Shoulders, Suspicious Wives*, Barthelmess' *Shore Leave*, others.

COOKSEY, CURTIS *(1962)* 57 ——Support in a few silents *(The Silver Horde*, etc.) and numerous talkies *(Scaramouche, Because You're Mine, Storm Center)*.

COOLEY, CHARLES *(1960)* 57 ——Character in Bob Hope comedies: *Son of Paleface, The Lemon Drop Kid* (as Goomba).

COOLEY, FRANK *(1941)* 71 ——Comic actor in silents: *Honor Bound, The First Year*.

COOLEY, JAMES *(1948)* 68 ——Handsome, cleft-chinned silent star of *A Tale of Two Nations* ('17), others.

COOLEY, SPADE *(1969)* 59 ——Western band leader; in *Chatterbox, Square Dance Jubilee*.

COOLIDGE, PHILIP *(1967)* 58 ——Character actor adept at both drama *(Inherit the Wind*, as the Mayor; *I Want to Live; Boomerang)* and comedy *(The Mating Game; The Russians are Coming, The Russians are Coming)*.

COOMBE, CAROL *(1966)* 55 ——Leading lady in 1933's *The Ghost Train*.

COOPER, ASHLEY *(1952)* 69 ——Support in Garbo's *The Torrent*, Betty Bronson's *Paradise*, plus *The Son of the Wolf, The Shadows of Conscience*, other silents.

COOPER, CLAUDE *(1932)* 51 ——Foppish star of 1915's *The Country Girl;* in *Daughters of the Night, A Heart to Let*, etc.

COOPER, EDWARD *(1956)* ——Support in many of the '30s: *Wife, Husband and Friend; Diplomaniacs; On the Avenue; Rascals; To Mary—With Love*, etc.

COOPER, FREDERICK *(1945)* 55 ——Support in British pix: *Dark Sands, Henry V* (as Corporal Nym), *The Great Mr. Handel*, others.

COOPER, GARY *(1961)* 60 ——That great, tall, silent, one-of-a-kind star; won Best Actor Oscars in *Sergeant York* and *High Noon*, was nominated too for *Mr. Deeds Goes to Town*, *The Pride of the Yankees, For Whom the Bell Tolls;* first an extra in Noah Beery's *The Thundering Herd* in '25 (and others), he leapt to fame in a secondary role in 1926's *The Winning of Barbara Worth* (nearly stealing the pic from star Ronald Colman), and from '27 on was an undisputed star—and frequently the movies' best-paid; a few of his most memorable films: *A Farewell to Arms, The Lives of a Bengal Lancer, Beau Geste, The Westerner, Ball of Fire, Saratoga Trunk, Unconquered,* and *Friendly Persuasion*.

COOPER, GEORGIE *(1968)* 86 ——Character actress in *Hollywood Hotel* and *Four Days' Wonder*.

COOPER, GLADYS *(1971)* 82 ——Superlative Britisher; Davis' mom in *Now, Voyager*, Fontaine's compassionate sister-in-law in *Rebecca*, Dennis Morgan's aristocratic mother in *Kitty Foyle;* an indispensable staple in all of Hollywood's "British" films of the '40s; *That Hamilton Woman, This Above All, Forever and a Day, Love Letters, The White Cliffs of Dover,* etc.; had two great roles near the end of her career, both in '64: the possessive grandmother in *The Chalk Garden* and Mrs. Higgins in *My Fair Lady*, which won her a third Best Supporting Actress nomination (the others: *Now, Voyager* and *The Song of Bernadette)*.

COOPER, MELVILLE *(1973)* 76 ——Droll, deadpan English character; often (but by no means always) a butler; in *Rebecca* (coroner), *The Lady Eve* (Stanwyck's card-sharp partner), *Pride and Prejudice* (pompous Mr. Collins whom Garson almost marries), *Random Harvest, Too Many Husbands, Immortal Sergeant*, and scores more.

COOPER, RICHARD *(1947)* 53 ——Support in British pix: *Mystery at the Villa Rose, Shipyard Sally*, etc.

COOPER, TEX *(1951)* 74 ——Gray-bearded character used as atmosphere in hundreds of B Westerns who, in stetson and boots, looked taller than the moon—and like everybody's conception of Buffalo Bill.

COPELAND, NICK *(1940)* 45 ——Support in Lyle Talbot's *Murder in the Clouds;* also in *The Main Event, Legion of Terror*, etc.

COQUELIN, BENOIT CONSTANT *(1909)* 68 ——Great French stage actor who appeared in a few very early silents.

COQUELIN, JEAN *(1944)* 79 ——In talkies of the '30s and character roles in *The Pearls of the*

Crown, The End of the Day, other European-made pictures.

CORBETT, BENNY *(1961)* 60 ——Costar in 1934's three-reel "Bud 'n Ben" Westerns; support in scores of other cowboy pix, silent and talkie.

CORBETT, JAMES J. *(1933)* 66 ——Heavyweight champ; starred in the silent serial *The Midnight Man.*

CORBETT, LEONORA *(1960)* 53 ——British lead; in *The Constant Nymph* ('34), *Farewell Again, Heart's Desire,* etc.

CORBIN, VIRGINIA LEE *(1942)* 31 ——Teenage star of many silents including *Aladdin and the Wonderful Lamp, Jack and the Beanstalk, Sinners in Silk, The Cloud Rider,* etc.

CORDING, HARRY *(1954)* 60 ——Support in dozens: *The Crusades* (Amir), *Cabin in the Cotton, The Adventures of Robin Hood* (Dicken Malbott), *The Prince and the Pauper,* etc.

CORDY, HENRY *(1965)* 57 ——Support in *The Great American Broadcast,* etc.

CORDY, RAYMOND *(1956)* 58 ——Gave a superb first performance as the top-billed star of *A Nous la Liberte* (of the two friends who escape from prison, he was the one who became the rich manufacturer of records); later in *Beauty and the Devil, Beauties of the Night,* etc.

COREY, JOSEPH *(1972)* 45 ——Was young support in *The Delicate Delinquent* and *Gaby.*

COREY, WENDELL *(1968)* 54 ——Versatile, but generally unexciting, leading man discovered by Hal Wallis, who costarred him with Lizabeth Scott *(Desert Fury, I Walk Alone),* Barbara Stanwyck *(Sorry, Wrong Number; Thelma Jordan, The Furies),* Hepburn *(The Thelma Jordan, The Furies),* Hepburn *(The Rainmaker,* in '64, his last good role though he remained active for another decade).

CORNELL, KATHARINE *(1974)* 81 ——A stage great who made one brief, memorable screen appearance in *Stage Door Canteen* in which she did an "impromptu" *Romeo and Juliet* scene with G.I. Lon McCallister.

CORNER, JAMES *(1944)* 25 ——Support in *What a Life* and *Winter Carnival;* killed in WW II.

CORNER, SALLY *(1959)* 65 ——Character; in *A Man Called Peter; The Robe* (Cornelia); *Two Flags West; Once More, My Darling.*

CORRELL, CHARLES *(1972)* 82 ——Andy of *Amos 'n Andy* radio fame; onscreen in *Check and Double Check.*

CORRIGAN, EMMETT *(1932)* 65—Character in *The Bitter Tea of General Yen, An American Tragedy* (Belknap), *The Night Mayor,* etc.

CORRIGAN, JAMES *(1929)* 58 ——Support in silents: *Peck's Bad Boy, Brewster's Millions, A Slave of Fashion,* others.

CORRIGAN, LLOYD *(1969)* 69 ——Plump, round-faced character with a born-smiling look; Jane Withers' pop in *High School;* smalltown doctors, bankers, etc., in many: *Young Tom Edison, The Great Man's Lady, Since You Went Away, Tennessee Johnson, The Lady in Question,* many more.

CORTEZ, LEON *(1970)* 72 ——British support in Garland's *I Could Go on Singing.*

CORTHELL, HERBERT *(1947)* 71 ——Support in many: *Sing You Sinners* (nightclub manager), *The Story of Louis Pasteur* (President Thiers), *Let's Talk It Over,* others.

COSGRAVE, LUKE *(1949)* 86 ——Character (Shanks) in *The Squaw Man* ('31); in *Lightnin'* ('30), *Gentlemen Prefer Blondes* ('28), *Merton of the Movies,* etc.

COSSAR, JOHN *(1935)* 70 ——Character (Justice of the Court) in Chaney's *The Hunchback of Notre Dame;* in silent serials *(Melting Millions, The Steel Trail)* and features (*Watch Your Step, The Poverty of Riches,* etc.).

COSSART, ERNEST *(1951)* 74 ——Roly-poly Englishman who almost always played butlers (Binns in both *Three Smart Girls* and *Three Smart Girls Grow Up;* Sidney in *The Great Ziegfeld,* Brassett in *Charley's Aunt,* etc.); also played Irish fathers: Ginger Rogers' in *Kitty Foyle,* Ann Sheridan's in *Kings Row.*

COSTELLO, DON *(1945)* 44 ——Played the prizefighter "Lefty" in *Here Comes Mr. Jordan;* other "big bruiser" roles in *Another Thin Man, Johnny Eager, The Blue Dahlia,* etc.

COSTELLO, HELENE *(1957)* 53 ——Leading lady, from 1925, in *The Man on the Box, Don Juan, Lights of New York, In Old Kentucky,* etc.; as children, she and sister Dolores had appeared in movies starring their father, Maurice.

COSTELLO, LOU *(1959)* 53 ——Round little comedian who was a giant at the box office with partner Bud Abbott in the 37 pix they did together; they were #1 in 1942 and in the Top 10 in 1941, '43, '44, '48, '49, '50, and '51; their early Universal entries remain their funniest: *Buck Privates, In the Navy, Hold That Ghost, Keep 'Em Flying, Ride 'Em Cowboy*, etc.; after the team broke up in '56, Costello made one additional comedy without Abbott, *The 30-Foot Bride of Candy Rock* ('59), which was not a success.

COSTELLO, MAURICE *(1950)* 73 ——The screen's first great matinee idol, noted for the "relaxed friendliness" of his enormous charm; starred in *A Tale of Two Cities* ('11), *The Closed Door, The Crimson Stain Mystery* (one of two serials he did), *Mr. Barnes of New York*, etc.; was fine support in later silents, particularly Norma Talmadge's *Camille* (as the elder Duval); minor roles in talkies (*Hollywood Boulevard, A Little Bit of Heaven, Lady from Louisiana*).

COSTELLO, WILLIAM *(1971)* 73 ——Character (a Babylonian Noble) in the silent *King of Kings*; Westerns (*Melody Trail*, etc.) and B's (*Wanted by the Police*) in talkies; far more famous as the screen voice of Popeye.

COTTON, BILLY *(1969)* 69 ——Support in Mary Alden's *The Old Nest* ('21).

COTTON, FRED *(1964)* 57 ——One of the many GIs in *Winged Victory*.

COTTON, LUCY *(1948)* 57 ——Lovely brunette star of silents (*The Devil, The Fugitive, Whispering Shadows*) who retired to become Princess Eristavi-Tchitecherine.

COURTENAY, WILLIAM *(1933)* 58 ——Second lead with Constance Bennett in 1930's *Three Faces East*; his real place in movie history may be that, at 19, he played the hero in *Miss Jerry* (1894), the first motion picture to have a "plot"; starred in 1917's *Kick In* with Mollie King; later in *The Way of All Men* and other talkies.

COURTLEIGH, WILLIAM, JR. *(1930)* 61 ——Popular silent lead; with Pickford in *Pollyanna*, Lillian Lorraine in the Pathe serial *Neal of the Navy*, Marguerite Clark in *Out of the Drifts*, Clara Kimball Young in *Eyes of Youth*.

COURTWRIGHT, WILLIAM *(1933)* 84 ——Character, usually in comic roles, in silents: *Some Punkins, The Rookie's Return, At the Sign of the Jack O' Lantern*, and Pickford's *My Best Girl*.

COWAN, JEROME *(1972)* 74 ——Dapper character lead with a ready quip, a trim moustache, and (often) a neatly tucked-in coat pocket handkerchief; a particular asset in "women's pictures," especially those of Davis: *The Old Maid, The Great Lie, Mr. Skeffington, June Bride* (her magazine publisher-boss); at his merriest in *Shall We Dance, Kiss the Boys Goodbye, Getting Gertie's Garter*; at his dramatic best as Bogart's slain detective buddy, Miles Archer, in *The Maltese Falcon*.

COWARD, NOEL *(1973)* 73 ——None was more sophisticated than this actor-composer-director-playwright; surprisingly, he was never more effective onscreen than in *The Scoundrel* (a maliciously destructive publisher—"the most odious man on earth") and *In Which We Serve* (as the gallant British naval commander); the gaiety he brought to his plays was but rarely in evidence on the screen.

COWL, JANE *(1950)* 65 ——After two silents in the teens (*The Garden of Lies, The Spreading Dawn*), this illustrious Broadway star delayed her return to the screen until it was almost too late; in 1949-50 she was top support in four: Robert Montgomery's *Once More, My Darling; No Man of Her Own* (Stanwyck's mother-in-law); Colbert's *The Secret Fury* (as her flighty aunt); and Davis' *Payment on Demand* (brittle, rich older divorcee addicted to young men and rum).

COWLES, JULES *(1943)* 65 ——Character in silents (*The Scarlet Letter*, as the Beadle, *The Lost World*, as Zambo; *Lord Jim*, etc.) and talkies (*Barbary Coast, Air Raid Wardens*, others).

COWLEY, ERIC *(1948)* 62 ——Support in 1933's *The Jewel*.

COX, ROBERT *(1974)* 79 ——In over 300 Sennett comedies, he's said to have been the last of the Keystone Kops (but was not one of the original seven); in *Little Men* ('35), etc.

COX, WALLY *(1973)* 48 ——Meek comic in glasses; in *The Yellow Rolls-Royce, A Guide for the Married Man, The One and Only Genuine Original Family Band*; not the success in movies that he was as TV's *Mr. Peepers*.

COXEN, ED *(1954)* 70 ——Wavy-haired, handsome young silent star: *The Profligate* ('15), *The Bells* and *A Man's Man*, both with Lois Wilson, *Foolish Mothers, Singer Jim McKee*, numerous others.

COY, JOHNNY *(1973)* 52 ——Young dancer-actor promoted to brief stardom by Paramount in the '40s; in *Bring on the Girls, Duffy's Tav-*

ern, That's the Spirit, Ladies' Man, and *Earl Carroll's Sketchbook.*

COY, WALTER *(1974)* 61 ——John Wayne's rancher-brother in *The Searchers,* whose two daughters were taken captive by the Comanches; support in many other Westerns (*Wichita, The Lusty Men,* etc.) and adventure pix (*Flat Top, On the Threshold of Space*).

CRADDOCK, CLAUDIA *(1945)* 56 ——Featured in one 1933 Paramount pic, *A Lady's Profession.*

CRAIG, ALEC *(1945)* 60 ——Small, pinch-faced Scot; the zookeeper in *The Cat People;* in *Winterset* (hobo), *Mary of Scotland, Vivacious Lady, Abe Lincoln in Illinois, Spider Woman,* etc.

CRAIG, EDITH *(1947)* 77 ——Character actress in *Smashing the Rackets, Behind the Headlines, Harmony Lane,* others in the '30s.

CRAIG, GODFREY *(1941)* 26 ——Minor member of "Our Gang."

CRAIG, GORDON *(1973)* ——Support in English pix.

CRAIG, JOHN *(1932)* 64 ——Character actor in 1931's *Silence.*

CRAIG, MAY *(1972)* 83 ——Famed Irish actress used by John Ford in *The Quiet Man* and *Rising of the Moon;* also in *Girl With Green Eyes.*

CRAIG, NELL *(1965)* 73 ——Nurse "Nosey" Parker in all 13 of the 1939-47 "Dr. Kildare" pix; at her best in combat with Dr. Gillespie (Lionel Barrymore); had been a beautiful Essanay star—acting with Rod La Rocque—as early as 1914; starred for them in *The Return of Richard Neal* (opposite Bushman), *In the Palace of the King, The Primitive Strain,* and for Fox in *The Queen of Sheba* ('21); when she was in 1924's *The Dramatic Life of Abraham Lincoln* one critic noted: "Nell Craig, who plays the role of Mrs. Lincoln, is extremely efficient in her grumbling"—a forecast of things to come.

CRAIG, RICHY, JR. *(1933)* 31 ——Featured in Vitaphone Big Star shorts.

CRAMER, EDD *(1963)* 39 ——Minor support in *On the Waterfront.*

CRAMER, RICHARD *(1960)* 71 ——Big-bellied with a heavy Irish face, he played desperadoes (and sometimes a bartender) in dozens of West-

erns: *Where the Trail Divides, Frontier Justice, O'Malley of the Mounted,* etc.; was often a hood in B features: *Night Club Scandal, Clipped Wings, Double Trouble.*

CRAMER, SUSANNE *(1969)* 31 ——Lovely German support in Brando's *Bedtime Story.*

CRANE, MAE *(1969)* 44 ——Small roles in *No Way to Treat a Lady* and *The Producers.*

CRANE, NORMA *(1973)* 42 ——Featured as Golde, wife of Tevye (star Topol), in *Fiddler on the Roof.*

CRANE, RICHARD *(1969)* 50 ——Dimpled, handsome blond who became a "bobby-soxer's dreamboat" in WW II after playing Ameche's ill-fated soldier son in *Happy Land;* also was in *Wing and a Prayer, None Shall Escape, Captain Eddie,* others.

CRANE, WARD *(1928)* 37 ——Suave lead in *The Lady in Ermine* with Corinne Griffith, following numerous other silents including *Sherlock Jr.* (Keaton's rival for The Girl, Kathryn McGuire), *Peacock Feathers, Boy Friend, The Blind Goddess,* etc.

CRANE, WILLIAM H. *(1928)* 82 ——Bald stage star who played the title role for Lasky in 1915's *David Harum:* shortest of the trio of elderly tuxedoed gents in Eleanor Boardman's *Three Wise Fools* ('23).

CRAVAT, NOEL *(1960)* 49 ——Beefy villain Ranga in the serial *G-Men vs. the Black Dragon;* also a meanie in *The Iron Curtain* and *The 5,000 Fingers of Dr. T.*

CRAVEN, FRANK *(1945)* 70 ——Folksy, pipe-smoking narrator of *Our Town;* earlier was in Will Rogers' *State Fair, The Harvester, Penrod and Sam,* etc.; later, father of Davis and de Havilland in *In This Our Life,* in *Keeper of the Flame, Colonel Effingham's Raid,* others.

CRAWFORD, ANNE *(1956)* 35 ——Elegant, charming British star; in *Tony Draws a Horse* (the boy's mother), *Bedelia, They Were Sisters, Caravan;* was the second femme lead in Robert Taylor's *Knights of the Round Table.*

CREGAR, LAIRD *(1944)* 28 ——20th Century-Fox's portly young star-villain; tops in *I Wake Up Screaming* (Hot Spot), *The Lodger, Hangover Square, The Black Swan,* and, among others, *Heaven Can Wait,* in which he was the Devil himself—but with such urbanity!

CREHAN, JOSEPH *(1966)* 82 ——Did officers of the law when not playing Ulysses S. Grant, which he did more than a few times in his 200 movies; in *Black Fury, Front Page Woman, The Case of the Lucky Legs, Babes in Arms, Phantom Lady, Murder in the Big House,* etc.

CREWS, KAY C. *(1959)* 58 ——Had minor supporting roles in silents.

CREWS, LAURA HOPE *(1942)* 62 ——Scarlett's rattled, twittery, curls-bouncing and bosom-heaving Aunt Pitty-pat; had roles not too dissimilar in *Camille* ('37), *Idiot's Delight,* and *The Flame of New Orleans;* but earlier, in *The Silver Cord,* her *la mere terrible* was *very* different.

CRICK, MONTE *(1969)* 63 ——English actor in a few minor roles.

CRINLEY, WILLIAM A. *(1927)* 50s ——Featured in Fox Company's *Big Town Round-Up* in 1921.

CRISP, DONALD *(1974)* 93 ——Never better than as the Welsh father in *How Green Was My Valley,* which won him a Supporting Oscar; had a career that was one of the screen's longest (from 1911) and most varied (early silent leads, in *Home Sweet Home,* etc.; D. W. Griffith assistant director on *The Birth of a Nation,* in which he portrayed Gen. U.S. Grant, and *Broken Blossoms,* in which, as Battling Burrows, he beat to death his daughter, Lillian Gish; then, in his own right, the director of Fairbanks' *Don Q, Son of Zorro* and John Barrymore's *Svengali;* top support in more than 70 talkies: *What Every Woman Knows, Mutiny on the Bounty* ('35), *Jezebel, Wuthering Heights, Lassie Come Home, National Velvet, The Long Gray Line,* etc.

CROKER-KING, C. H. *(1951)* 77 ——Character actor who played The Neighbor in Carol Dempster's *One Exciting Night.*

CROMWELL, RICHARD *(1960)* 50 ——With bland, blond "All American" good looks, he was destined for second-class fame—in uniform (*Annapolis Farewell, Tom Brown of Culver*), as romantic juvenile leads (*Poppy*), as everybody's brother (Fonda's in *Jezebel*) or son (Alice Brady's in *Young Mr. Lincoln,* wherein trial-lawyer Fonda wins his acquittal on a murder charge); was once married to Angela Lansbury.

CROSMAN, HENRIETTA *(1944)* 83 ——Like vintage wine, the performances this character star from the stage gave in 11 movies of the 1930s, made in rapid succession, linger deliciously in memory: the Dowager Queen of the theatrical tribe (the Barrymores) in *The Royal Family of Broadway,* the other mothers—tragic (*Pilgrimage*) and wise (*The Right to Live*)—and the grandmothers (particularly the mirthful one of volatile movie star Margaret Sullavan in *The Moon's Our Home*), and the proud old Southern woman in Janet Gaynor's *Carolina;* she had been in three silents previously, but her work in talkies remains her legacy.

CROSS, ALFRED *(1938)* 46 ——Support in Mary Astor's *Smart Woman.*

CROSSE, RUPERT *(1973)* 45 ——Black actor with Steve McQueen in *The Reivers* and nominated for a Supporting Oscar; also featured in Cassavetes' *Shadows.*

CROSSLEY, SID *(1960)* 75 ——Support in dozens of British pix: *Gay Love, Penny Paradise,* etc.

CROSTHWAITE, IVY *(1962)* 64 ——Sennett charmer who went to the beach with Roscoe Arbuckle in *Fickle Fatty's Fall.*

CRUSTER, AUD *(1938)* 49 ——Vaudeville actor in Eddie Cantor's *Kid Boots.*

CRUTE, SALLY *(1971)* 85 ——Dimpled star of Edison's *Helen of the Chorus* ('16); also in *His Children's Children, It Isn't Being Done This Season,* other silents.

CRUZE, JAMES *(1942)* 48 ——Star of the silent serial *The Million Dollar Mystery,* plus features; later, famed director of *The Covered Wagon.*

CRUZE, MAE *(1965)* 74 ——In silents and had minor roles in *Mary Poppins,* etc.

CUGAT, CARMEN *(1967)* 66 ——Singer, ex-wife of Xavier.

CULLEY, FREDERICK *(1942)* 63 ——British character actor who played the Duke of Norfolk in *The Private Life of Henry VIII;* was also in *Knight Without Armor, Drums, Four Feathers,* and *Talk of the Devil.*

CULLINGTON, MARGARET *(1925)* 34 ——Featured in *Wolves of the Border, The Son of Wallingford, The Breathless Moment,* etc.

CUMMINGS, IRVING *(1959)* 70 ——Silent matinee idol; Power Picture Plays' leading man in 1909; Armand Duval in 1912's *Camille,* Rochester in 1914's *Jane Eyre,* Lottie Pickford's leading man in the serial *The Diamond from the Sky;* at his romantic peak in 1917's *A Royal Romance,* and almost past it in 1922's *The Eternal Flame* with Norma Talmadge; later a famous director at 20th Century-Fox, specializing in musicals (*My Gal Sal*), comedies (*Hollywood Cavalcade*), and Temple pix (*Curly Top*).

CUMMINGS, RICHARD *(1938)* 80 ——Support in *The Social Lion* ('30), following long silent career (*Red Courage, Wolf Law*, etc.).

CUMMINGS, VICKI *(1969)* 50 ——Broadway star, of brittle, blase roles, featured in Susan Hayward's garment-district pic *I Can Get It for You Wholesale*.

CUNARD, GRACE *(1967)* 72 ——Was right up there behind Pearl White as star of silent serials, some of which she also wrote, directed, and edited; in *Lucille Love, Girl of Mystery; The Adventures of Peg O' the Ring, The Broken Coin, The Silent Mystery, Purple Mask, The Ace of Scotland*, and others between 1914 and 1929; famous for never needing the hero to bail her out of a tough spot; star of silent features too, she did character work in talkies through 1936's *The Rest Cure*.

CUNEO, LESTER *(1925)* 37 ——Tough, red-blooded, curly-haired hero of a series of minor, five-reel Westerns in the early '20s (*Blue Blazes, Masked Avenger, The Ranger and the Law*, etc.); earlier had been rugged support in Bushman's *Graustark* and in *Big Tremaine, Haunted Pajamas*, etc.

CUNNINGHAM, CECIL *(1959)* 70 ——Statuesque, with marcelled gray hair, she was like a duchess with humor—tongue in cheek; Irene Dunne could have been a dull girl indeed in *The Awful Truth* without this "aunt" to drag her off to nightclubs, find her a drab new beau (cow-rich Ralph Bellamy), thus propelling her back into the arms of almost-divorced hubby Cary Grant; a pleasure in dozens more: *If I Had a Million, Kitty Foyle, My Reputation, College Swing*, etc.

CUNNINGHAM, GEORGE *(1962)* 58 ——One of the handsome young swains in Crawford's *Our Modern Maidens*; in this, *The Broadway Melody, Thunder*, and *The Hollywood Revue of 1929*.

CUNNINGHAM, ZAMAH *(1967)* 74 ——Character (Mme. Kimmeloff) in *Dream Girl;* in *Baby, the Rain Must Fall; Key to the City*, etc.

CURRAN, THOMAS *(1941)* 60 ——Minor support; *Morocco, Dishonored, Charlie Chan's Chance*, etc.

CURRIE, CLIVE *(1935)* 58 ——Support in *Magic Night* ('32).

CURRIE, FINLAY *(1968)* 90 ——Magnificently ugly character star; the terrifying convict Pip encountered in the graveyard in *Great Expectations* ('47), who later, secretly, helped the boy become a gentleman; the hanged man who did not die in *People Will Talk;* memorable in scores more.

CURRIER, FRANK *(1928)* 71 ——The Roman nobleman who adopted Novarro in *Ben Hur;* in many previously (*The Lotus Eater, The Lights of New York, Desire*, etc.) and afterward (*La Boheme, Tell It to the Marines*, others).

CURTIS, ALAN *(1953)* 43 ——Good-looking, blue-eyed lead in B's (*Shady Lady, Remember Pearl Harbor, See My Lawyer*, etc.) and second lead in A's (*Hollywood Cavalcade, The Shopworn Angel, Good Girls Go to Paris*); once married to the late Ilona Massey.

CURTIS, ALLEN *(1961)* 84 ——Pioneer director who also acted in early silents.

CURTIS, BEATRICE *(1963)* 62 ——Featured in a Don Terry B, *Paid to Dance* ('37); earlier had been in shorts with husband Harry Fox.

CURTIS, DICK, *(1952)* 50 ——The coldest eyes, the meanest man in hundreds of B Westerns; was frequently up to his evil ways also in serials (*Mandrake the Magician, Terry and the Pirates*—chief heavy, Fang, *Overland with Kit Carson*) and A pix (*King Kong, Jack London, My Six Convicts*, etc.).

CURTIS, JACK *(1956)* 40s ——Pauline Frederick's little boy in *Lydia Gilmore* ('16); prominently featured as a youth in *Greed, Captain Blood* ('24), *Quicksands, The Wedding Song, Mammy*, etc.

CURTIS, KING *(1971)* 36 ——Minor support.

CURWEN, PATRIC *(1949)* 64 ——Support in *The Ringer* and *Loyalties* (both in the '30s) and *Don't Take It to Heart* ('48).

CUSTER, BOB *(1974)* 76 ——Rugged, handsome, hair center-parted star of 100 silent (from '24) and talkie Westerns; the lead in several talkie serials (*The Adventures of Rin Tin Tin*, with Rin Tin Tin Jr., and *Law of the Wild*, which featured Rex, King of the Wild Horses); pictures include: *Texas Bearcat, Flashing Spurs, Quick Trigger Lee*, etc.; acted under his real name, Raymond Glenn, in such silents as *Ladies at Ease* with Pauline Garon; retired in '38.

CUTLER, KATE *(1955)* 84 ——British character actress who played the Grand Old Lady at the ball in *Pygmalion*; was also in *I Stand Condemned* and *When Knights Were Bold*.

CUTTING, RICHARD *(1972)* 70s ——Character (Admiral Kester) in *South Pacific*; in *Chicago Syndicate*, other.

CUTTS, PATRICIA *(1974)* 47 ——Charming light British actress; Robert Montgomery's

leading lady in *Eye Witness*; second femme lead in Danny Kaye's *Merry Andrew* and in *The Man Who Loved Redheads*.

CYBULSKI, ZBIGNIEW *(1967)* 29 ——Cruelly handsome Brando-type Polish actor who became internationally famous in 1961's *Ashes and Diamonds*; also starred in *Love at Twenty*, *To Love*, and *La Poupee*.

D

DADE, FRANCES *(1968)* 58 ——In *Dracula*, young blonde beauty, Lucy (second femme lead), who herself turns into a vampire; in other 1930–31 movies: *Raffles, Grumpy, She-Wolf, Seed, Daughter of the Dragon*; a Wampas Baby Star.

DAI, LIN *(1964)* 33 ——Chinese lovely who starred in *The Last Woman of Shang* the year of her death.

DALBERT, SUZANNE *(1971)* 44 ——Charming French discovery of Hal Wallis; in *So Evil My Love, The Accused, Mark of the Gorilla*.

DALBY, AMY *(1969)* 81 ——Usually played spinsters in British pix; in *The Wicked Lady, The Haunting, The Man Upstairs*.

DALE, CHARLES *(1971)* 90 ——Dr. Kronkhite in the comedy team of (Joe) Smith & Dale of vaude-TV-radio-movie fame; they were in *Manhattan Parade, The Heart of New York*, and *Two Tickets to Broadway*.

DALE, DOROTHY *(1937)* 12 ——Was in a few short films.

DALE, DOROTHY *(1957)* 75 ——An Egyptian dancing girl in the silent *Ten Commandments*.

DALE, ESTHER *(1961)* 75 ——Played blunt-spoken, devoted housekeepers (Davis' indispensable Harriett in *Old Acquaintance*), dragonish mothers (Bellamy's in *The Awful Truth*), no-nonsense nurses (*Private Worlds*), prison matrons, and some of the screen's most viperish gossips.

DALE, MARGARET *(1972)* 96 ——Was mother of Carol Dempster in a 1922 melodramatic comedy, *One Exciting Night*; in *Disraeli, Second Youth* and other silents, and the talkie *The Man with Two Faces*.

DALE, PEGGY *(1967)* 63 ——Small role in John Boles' *The Desert Song*.

DALEY, JACK *(1967)* 84 ——Support in pix of the '30s: *The Sap From Syracuse, Mutiny in the Big House, O'Shaughnessy's Boy*, etc.

DALL, JOHN *(1971)* 50 ——Received a Supporting Actor Oscar nomination for *The Corn Is Green*, as Morgan Evans, the young Welsh coal miner who wins an Oxford scholarship under Davis' tutelage; fine, too, in Hitchcock's *Rope* and *Another Part of the Forest*.

DALLIMORE, MAURICE *(1973)* 70s ——Supporting actor, last in Wyler's *The Collector*.

DALROY, HARRY "RUBE" *(1954)* 75 —— Featured in an Associated Exhibitors' silent, *Stormy Seas*, then support in B's and Westerns.

DALTON, CHARLES *(1942)* 77 ——Supported Maxine Elliott and Henry Clive in 1917's *The Fighting Odds*.

DALTON, DOROTHY *(1972)* 78 ——Beautiful brunette starred by Triangle in *The Vagabond Prince* ('16), *The Flame of the Yukon*, many more; then by Paramount-Artcraft in *The Home Breaker, Moran of the Lady Letty* (with Valentino), etc.; her smile—one of the silent screen's most delectable—and dimples broke a million male hearts.

DALTON, IRENE *(1934)* 33 ——Featured in Swanson's *Bluebeard's Eighth Wife* ('23), and in *Children of Jazz*.

DALY, ARNOLD *(1927)* 51 ——Noted Broadway actor who supported Pearl White—portraying scientific detective Craig Kennedy—in three "Elaine" serials: *The Exploits of Elaine, The Romance of Elaine, The New Exploits of Elaine*; was also in silent features (*In Borrowed Plumes*, etc.).

DALY, JAMES L. *(1933)* 81——Character roles in silents.

DALY, MARK *(1957)* 70 ——Cheerful British character; in *Wings of the Morning, Break the*

News, Knight Without Armor, Bonnie Prince Charlie, etc.

DALY, PAT *(1947)* 56 ——Character (Champ's manager) in *A Slight Case of Murder.*

DALZELL, LYDA ST. CLAIR *(1974)* 70s —— Star of early silents at Essanay.

D'AMBRICOURT, ADRIENNE *(1957)* 69 —— Gallic character actress in many silents (*The Humming Bird, Wages of Virtue*, etc.) and talkies (*The Cat and the Fiddle, Design for Living* as the French cafe proprietress, *Saratoga Trunk* as Bergman's grandmother, others).

DAMEREL, DONNA *(1941)* 30 ——Marge in 1934's *Myrt and Marge*, with her mother as Myrt—the same roles they played in the radio serial.

DAMON, LES *(1962)* 53 ——In a few movies, but more noted as a radio actor.

DAMPIER, CLAUDE *(1955)* 69 ——Played rustics in British comedies: *She Shall Have Music, Boys Will Be Boys*, others.

DANDRIDGE, DOROTHY *(1965)* 41 ——Volatile, versatile beautiful black; a tigress as the star of *Carmen Jones* (nominated as Best Actress) and of *Porgy and Bess*, she played a back-country teacher with charm and restraint in *Bright Road*, and had other starring roles in *Island in the Sun, Tamango, The Decks Ran Red*, etc.; daughter of character actress Ruby Dandridge, she had been in movies as a child (*A Day at the Races*, as one of the youngsters following pied-piper Harpo, etc.) and as a very young woman (*Since You Went Away*, as the wife of a black military officer).

DANDY, JESS *(1923)* 52 ——Comedian in early Keystone comedies.

DANE, KARL *(1934)* 47 ——Great in *The Big Parade* as John Gilbert's tough, funny, blasphemous soldier-buddy Slim; equally fine as Giles in Gish's *The Scarlet Letter*, and in such George K. Arthur comedies as *China Bound* and *Brotherly Love.*

DANEGGER, THEODOR *(1959)* 68 —— Viennese star of *The Royal Waltz, Three Feathers for Anna*, etc.

DANFORTH, WILLIAM *(1941)* 73 ——Top support in numerous silents including Marguerite Clark's *The Seven Swans* and such talkies as *The Girl Said No* ('37).

DANIELL, HENRY *(1963)* 69 ——Austere, foxy-looking villain; in *The Body Snatchers, The Suspect* (became the second victim after trying to blackmail neighbor Laughton), *All This and Heaven Too, The Private Lives of Elizabeth and Essex, The Great Dictator* (wonderfully funny as Garbitsch, Minister of Propaganda), *Camille* (as Garbo's cold, but not entirely unsympathetic, lover, Baron de Varville), and many others.

DANIELS, BEBE *(1971)* 70 ——Vivacious, versatile, and gifted star of silents and talkies; first a luscious leading lady in Harold Lloyd comedies (the "Lonesome Luke" series), she next starred or was top-featured in many manners-and-morals pix for DeMille (*Male and Female, Why Change Your Wife?, The Affairs of Anatol, Feet of Clay*, etc.); was dynamic, too, for other directors in *The Glimpses of the Moon* and *Nice People;* 1929's *Rio Rita*, proving she had a beautiful voice, gave her a headstart in talkies, some of which were: *The Maltese Falcon* ('31), *Reaching for the Moon, My Past, 42nd Street, Love Comes Along;* in maturity in England (where husband Ben Lyons' studio-exec position caused them to relocate), she found success anew on radio, TV, and in movies, some featuring her entire family (*Life with the Lyons, The Lyons in Paris).*

DANIELS, FRANK *(1935)* 74 ——Comic stage actor, star of 1915's *Crooky Scruggs.*

DANIELS, HANK, JR. *(1973)* 50s——Was Lon, older brother of Garland and others, in *Meet Me in St. Louis;* also in *The Green Years, Bewitched* ('45), etc.

DANIELS, WALTER *(1928)* 53 ——Supported Norma Talmadge in *The Dove;* in *The Jazz Age,* etc.

D'ANNUNZIO, LOLA *(1956)* 26 ——Outstandingly promising New York stage actress who had a supporting role in just one, Hitchcock's *The Wrong Man;* Off Broadway's "Lola D'Annunzio" awards were established in her honor.

DANTE THE MAGICIAN *(1955)* 70 ——Laurel and Hardy's main support in *A-Haunting We Will Go.*

DANTE, LIONEL *(1974)* 67 ——Support in movies and on Broadway.

D'ARCY, ROY *(1969)* 75 ——Fine MGM near-star who was most often a nobleman in costume dramas of the '20s: Gish's *La Boheme* (Vicomte Paul who arouses John Gilbert's jealousy), *The*

Actress with Shearer, *Graustark, A Woman of Affairs, The Merry Widow* (the Crown Prince, a man with a "leer, a wicked-looking open mouth filled with perfect teeth, and a nasty stoop to his shoulders," who shoots his brother, Gilbert, in a duel over Mae Murray); ended his career in B's of the mid-30s: *Revolt of the Zombies*, etc.

DARE, DORRIS *(1927)* 28 ——Beauty featured in Francis Ford's 1919 serial *The Mystery of 13;* also in features: *Fighting Odds*, etc.

DARE, RICHARD *(1964)* 41 ——Featured in 1954's *World Dances.*

DARE, VIRGINIA *(1962)* 50s ——In a few minor roles in the '20s.

DARIEN, FRANK *(1955)* 70s ——Boyish-faced oldtimer; in *The Grapes of Wrath* (Uncle John); *Bad Girl; Magic Town; Cimarron* ('31); *Hello, Frisco, Hello; Claudia and David,* etc.

DARIN, BOBBY *(1973)* 37 ——Pop singer ("Mack the Knife") and actor; Oscar-nominated support in *Captain Newman, M.D.;* starred in *Too Late Blues, Hell Is for Heroes, That Funny Feeling* (one of three Universal comedies he did with his then wife, Sandra Dee).

DARK, CHRISTOPHER *(1971)* 40s ——In Sinatra's *Suddenly*, the would-be assassin who was accidentally electrocuted; in *Baby Face Nelson, None But the Brave, Platinum High School*, etc.

DARK CLOUD, BEULAH *(1946)* 60s ——Actress-wife of D. W. Griffith's Algonquin Indian actor-and-advisor, Dark Cloud; she was in many of the director's early Biograph movies and a 1922 Paramount pic, *The Crimson Challenge;* Dark Cloud himself starred in two fine Indian silents: *John Ermine of the Yellowstone* and *The Penitents.*

DARLING, CANDY *(1974)* 26 ——Female impersonator-star of Andy Warhol's *Flesh* and *Women in Revolt.*

DARLING, IDA *(1936)* 61 ——Corseted support in Ethel Barrymore's *The Nightingale* ('14), Colleen Moore's *Irene, Society Snobs,* other silents, plus talkies (*Lummox, The Girl Who Came Back*).

DARMOND, GRACE *(1963)* 65 ——A Selig star as early as 1915, she was in many serials for them and others: *The Shielding Shadow, The Hawk's Trail* (master crook "Iron" Dugan, posing as her uncle, tried to dispose of her in every chapter, but hero, King Baggot, of course

rescued her), *The Hope Diamond Mystery, A Dangerous Adventure*, etc.; also the leading lady in many silent features: *Daytime Wives, The Midnight Guest, Hour of Reckoning,* others.

DARNELL, JEAN *(1961)* 72 ——Starred in *The Poor Relation*, other silents.

DARNELL, LINDA *(1965)* 43 ——Brunette 20th Century-Fox star of the "photographically perfect" face; one of the studio's most versatile yet least appreciated luminaries; career divided neatly in two parts—angelic early roles (*Brigham Young, The Mark of Zorro, Blood and Sand, The Loves of Edgar Allan Poe,* and even appeared as the vision of the Virgin Mary in *The Song of Bernadette*), later roles had a touch (at least) of the whore (*Forever Amber, A Letter to Three Wives*, others).

DARRELL, STEVE *(1970)* 67 ——Villain in 100 Westerns: *Helldorado, Frontier Outpost, Treasure of the Ruby Hills*, etc.; in the serial *Ghost of Zorro* he was—surprise—the marshal.

DARVAS, LILI *(1974)* 72 ——Famous Hungarian actress; starred in the European film *The Affairs of Maupassant;* character actress in Hollywood's *Meet Me in Las Vegas* and *Cimarron* ('61); widow of playwright Ferenc (*Liliom*) Molnar.

DARVI, BELLA *(1971)* 44 ——Enormously untalented, beautiful Zanuck protegee; starred in several stupifyingly dull pix: *The Egyptian, Hell and High Water, The Racers.*

DARWELL, JANE *(1967)* 87 ——"They can't keep us down, we're the people," she told us as the indomitable Ma Joad in *The Grapes of Wrath*, and, heaven knows, she was "the people"—even as the monstrous old woman in *The Ox-Bow Incident* lynch mob; mostly, though, she was the archetypal ma or grandma (*Jesse James, All That Money Can Buy, Sunday Dinner for a Soldier, The Impatient Years,* etc.); after more than 90 movies, establishing her as perhaps the movies' most familiar character actress, the Supporting Oscar winner (as Ma Joad) faded out gracefully from the screen—in a one-scene cameo in *Mary Poppins* as the old lady in the "Feed the Birds" number.

DASH, PAULY *(1974)* 55 ——Stage-screen comedian in minor roles.

DASHIELL, WILLARD *(1943)* 66 ——Support in Bankhead's *The Cheat.*

DAUBE, HARDA *(1959)* 70 ——Character actress; minor roles.

DAUGHERTY, JACK *(1938)* 43 ——One of the handsomest light leads in silents; in '25 was in Cantor's *Special Delivery*, etc.; Universal's #2 serial king (*The Scarlet Streak*, others), second only to William Desmond; was married to Barbara La Marr and Virginia Brown Faire.

DAVENPORT, ALICE SHEPARD ——Wife of Harry Davenport, mother of Dorothy, Ann, and Kate; acted in Keystone comedies and was known to the company as "Mother Davenport"; year of death unreported.

DAVENPORT, ANN *(1968)* 60s ——Actress-daughter of Harry.

DAVENPORT, HARRY *(1949)* 83 ——Grand old character who was the doctor in *Gone With the Wind;* stole scenes from stars in many scores of films: *You Can't Take It With You* (Judge), *The Life of Emile Zola, Juarez, Kings Row, Meet Me in St. Louis* (Grandpa), *The Farmer's Daughter, Little Women* ('49), etc.

DAVENPORT, KATE *(1954)* 58 ——Harry's daughter; support in May McAvoy's *Sentimental Tommy.*

DAVENPORT, KENNETH *(1941)* 62 ——Support in a Douglas Fairbanks silent, *The Nut.*

DAVENPORT, MILLA *(1936)* 64 ——Popular leading lady in early silents (from 1912), then principal support in many (*The Girl from God's Country, Dulcy, The Road to Glory, Why Trust Your Husband*, etc.); finally, in talkies, played grandmothers (such as Cooper's in *The Wedding Night*) and housekeepers (*Merrily We Go to Hell*).

DAVID, WILLIAM *(1965)* 83 ——Support in Paramount pix of the '20s: *Fog Bound, Outcast.*

DAVIDSON, DORE *(1930)* 79 ——Character actor in silents: Vera Gordon's *Humoresque*, Anita Stewart's *The Great White Way*, Carol Dempster's *That Royle Girl*, etc.

DAVIDSON, JOHN *(1968)* 71 ——In shaved widow's peak or turbans, he set the sinister standard for Saturday serial villains of the '30s and '40s; made his evil, hollow-cheeked presence felt in 1934's *Perils of Pauline* (Dr. Bashan), *Tailspin Tommy* (Tiger Taggart), *King of the Royal Mounted*, many more; also served with wicked suavity in many features including *The Last Days of Pompeii, Dinner at Eight, Mr. Moto's Last Warning*, etc.

DAVIDSON, MAX *(1950)* 75 ——Jackie Coogan's lovable old partner in *Old Clothes;* in many other silent comedies (*Second Hand Rose, The Extra Girl, The Ghost Patrol*, etc.) and talkies (*The Cohens and the Kellys in Trouble, The Girl Said No, The World Gone Wrong*, others); numerous shorts for Hal Roach and The Masquers Club including *Oh! Oh! Cleopatra* (starring Wheeler and Woolsey), in which he was wonderfully funny as a royal musician.

DAVIDSON, WILLIAM B. *(1947)* 59 ——Handsome guy opposite Texas Guinan in *Queen of the Night Clubs*, and earlier, in '17, with Ethel Barrymore in *The Call of Her People;* long career (1914–47); after his career as a star (in *The Girl From Nowhere, Modern Cinderella, Ports of Call*, many more), he was one of the screen's busiest character actors, specializing in reporters, detectives, and judges, especially at Warners: *Bordertown, Devil Dogs of the Air, Gold Diggers of 1937, Dust Be My Destiny, Shine On Harvest Moon*, scores of others.

DAVIES, BETTY ANN *(1955)* 46 ——Principal support in many British pix: *Trio* (episode starring Jean Simmons), *The Belles of St. Trinian's, Tonight at 8:30, The History of Polly*, etc.

DAVIES, MARION *(1961)* 61 ——Blonde comedienne whose long starring career (1917–37) was under the personal sponsorship of publisher William Randolph Hearst, whose acknowledged mistress she was until his death; *Show People* and *The Patsy* were perhaps the best of her many silents (*When Knighthood Was in Flower, Janice Meredith, Enchantment*, etc.); among her talkies were *Cain and Mabel, Page Miss Glory, Polly of the Circus, Going Hollywood;* she was neither as good as Hearst believed nor as bad as many strident critics (not including Louella Parsons) insisted.

DAVIS, BOYD *(1963)* 77 ——Supporting actor in *You'll Never Get Rich* (Col. Schiller), *Captain Eddie* (Mr. Frost), *Ma and Pa Kettle* (Mr. Simpson), etc.

DAVIS, CONRAD *(1969)* 65 ——Farina in the "Our Gang" comedies.

DAVIS, EDWARD *(1936)* 65 ——Support in Milton Sills' *The Sea Hawk*, other silents (*The Best People; Tramp, Tramp, Tramp; Butterflies in the Rain*, etc.), and a few talkies (*Love in the Rough; Hello, Everybody*).

DAVIS, FREEMAN *(1974)* 71 ——Whistling entertainer; did specialty acts in movies.

DAVIS, GEORGE *(1965)* 76 ——Dutch character actor often seen as a waiter (*Thin Ice, I Met Him in Paris*, etc.); earlier, in silents, in *Sherlock Jr., He Who Gets Slapped, Four Devils, The Circus*, etc.

DAVIS, HARRY *(1929)* 55 ——Support in silents including *Burning Gold, Old Clothes,* Richard Arlen's *The Blood Ship,* others.

DAVIS, J. GUNNIS *(1937)* 63 ——Support in many silents: *Lilac Time, A Certain Rich Man, Lord Jim, The Secret of the Hills, Winds of Chance,* etc.; minor roles in such talkies as *One More River, Charlie Chan Carries On.*

DAVIS, JOAN *(1961)* 53 ——Knockabout, rubberlegged (and -faced) comedienne who starred in *If You Knew Susie, Show Business, Love That Brute,* etc., after long career as comic support (*My Lucky Star, Thin Ice, Wake Up and Live, Sun Valley Serenade,* others); star of the TV series *I Love Joan.*

DAVIS, MILDRED *(1969)* 68 ——Harold Lloyd's lovely leading lady in *Safety Last, Grandma's Boy, Doctor Jaek,* etc., who retired when she became his wife.

DAVIS, OWEN, JR. *(1949)* 42 ——Young support in *All Quiet on the Western Front* (Peter), *They Had to See Paris, Murder on the Bridle Path, These Glamour Girls, Touchdown Army, Knute Rockne: All-American.*

DAVIS, RUFE *(1974)* 66 ——"Lullaby" in Bob Steele's "Three Mesquiteers" Western series; support in *Doctor Rhythm, Mountain Music, The Big Broadcast of 1938, Cocoanut Grove,* etc.; one of the rustics in the long-running TV series *Petticoat Junction.*

DAW, EVELYN *(1970)* 58 ——Cagney's perky brunette singing leading lady in *Something to Sing About* ('37).

DAWSON, FRANK *(1953)* 83 ——Support in *A Day at the Races* (doctor), *Cafe Society, The Blue Bird* (Caller of the Roll), *The Woman in the Window* (steward), etc.

DAWSON, IVO *(1934)* 54 ——Supporting actor in *The Hate Ship* ('30).

DAY, EDITH *(1971)* 75 ——Beautiful brunette star of silents: *A Romance of the Air* and *The Grain of Dust* (both 1918).

DAY, JULIETTE *(1957)* 63 ——Stage actress who starred for Mutual in 1917.

DAY, MARIE L. *(1939)* 84 ——Gray-haired star of the 1922 comedy *Timothy's Quest.*

DAY, RICHARD *(1973)* 26 ——Actor-brother of television actress Lynda Day George.

DAZE, MERCEDES *(1945)* 53 ——Minor silent actress.

DEAN, BARNEY *(1954)* 50 ——Comic Russian support; in *Thanks for the Memory.*

DEAN, FABIAN *(1971)* 40 ——Support in Disney's *The Computer Wore Tennis Shoes* and Jack Lord's *Ride to Hangman's Tree.*

DEAN, IVOR *(1964)* 57 ——British character; *Where Eagles Dare, The Oblong Box,* etc.

DEAN, JACK *(1950)* 60s ——Husband of perennially youthful silent star Fannie Ward; co-starred with her in *Tennessee's Pardner* ('16), others.

DEAN, JAMES *(1955)* 24 ——Brilliant, eccentric young star of *Giant, East of Eden* (both of which won him Best Actor Oscar nominations), and *Rebel Without a Cause.*

DEAN, JULIA *(1952)* 74 ——The grandmother in *Curse of the Cat People;* similar roles in *People Will Talk, Magic Town, The Emperor Waltz,* etc.; few fans knew she had been a celebrated star—and beauty—in silents: *Judge Not* ('15); *Matrimony; Rasputin, the Black Monk;* others.

DEAN, MAN MOUNTAIN *(1953)* 62 ——Hairy wrestler-comic who enjoyed a vogue in the '30s; in Harlow's *Reckless,* Joe E. Brown's *The Gladiator, We're in the Money,* others; had a one-role "comeback" in a 1960 Mitzi Gaynor comedy, *Surprise Package.*

DEAN, MAY *(1937)* ——Support in Crosby's *Mississippi.*

DEANE, DORIS *(1974)* 73 ——Was the wife and frequent leading lady of Roscoe "Fatty" Arbuckle.

DEARING, EDGAR *(1974)* 81 ——In movies of the '30s, he played nice-looking, usually amiable, big-bruiser police sergeants; in *Swing Time* (suspicious of Astaire in tux at 8 a.m. in early scene, where he first meets Ginger Rogers), *Thanks for Everything, Miss Annie Rooney,* etc.

DEARLY, MAX *(1943)* 69 ——Starred in Renoir's *Madame Bovary,* Rene Clair's *Le Dernier Milliardaire,* etc.

DEASE, BOBBY *(1958)* 58 ——Support in Turner's *Dancing Co-Ed* and Shirley Ross' *Some Like It Hot.*

DE AUBRY, DIANE *(1969)* 79 ——Early, lovely silent leading lady; called "The Girl with the Million Dollar Eyes."

DE BECKER, HAROLD *(1947)* 48 ——Peg Leg in Rathbone's *Sherlock Holmes and the Secret*

Weapon; minor support (train conductor) in *This Above All*, etc.

DE BECKER, MARIE *(1946)* 65 ——Garson's cook, Ada, in *Mrs. Miniver;* in *None But the Lonely Heart, Random Harvest* (vicar's wife), etc.

DE BRAY, YVONNE *(1954)* 64 ——French star; hysterical mother in *Les Parents Terrible;* in *The Eternal Return, We Are All Murderers.*

DE BRULIER, NIGEL *(1948)* 60 ——Richelieu in the silent *The Three Musketeers;* in *Ben Hur* (Simonides), *Intolerance, The Hunchback of Notre Dame* (Dom Claude), *Don Juan,* many more silents; talkies: *The Man in the Iron Mask, I'm No Angel* (Rajah), *The Hound of the Baskervilles,* etc., plus several serials including *Adventures of Captain Marvel* in which, as graybearded Shazam, he gave Billy Batson (Frank Coghlan Jr.) the magical powers and the word that would become part of pop-art history.

DEBUCOURT, JEAN *(1958)* 64 ——French actor; top support in *Devil in the Flesh, Monsieur Vincent, Mayerling, Justice Is Done, The Golden Coach,* and many more of France's greatest films.

DE CASALIS, JEANNE *(1966)* 69 ——Character in numerous British pix: *Nell Gwyn, Mixed Doubles, They Met in the Dark,* etc.

DE CORDOBA, PEDRO *(1950)* 68 ——With his fine, strong face, this big man eventually became Hollywood's favorite priest (often Spanish, though he was New York-born): *The Song of Bernadette, Blood and Sand* ('41), *The Mark of Zorro, Keys of the Kingdom,* etc.; in several dozen, from 1915, when he was the savagely handsome Escamillo opposite Geraldine Farrar's *Carmen;* a most memorable role, the old Arab in Cagney's *The Time of Your Life* "with exquisite hands and a diagnosis of the world's ills: 'No foundation all down the line.' "

DE CORDOVA, ARTURO *(1973)* 66 ——Dashing, curly-haired Mexican star Paramount tried to popularize in the U.S. by teaming him with its biggest femme stars: Betty Hutton *(Incendiary Blonde)*, Joan Fontaine *(Frenchman's Creek)*, Lamour *(A Medal for Benny, Masquerade in Mexico)*, etc.

DE CORSIA, TED *(1973)* 69 ——Hooded eyes and saturnine expression doomed this big man to thug roles (or tough cops) in dozens: *The Naked City, The Lady from Shanghai, The Joker Is Wild, Gunfight at the O.K. Corral,* etc.

DEE, FREDDIE *(1958)* 34 ——Minor player.

DEELEY, BEN *(1924)* 46 ——Support in Chaney's *Victory,* Normand's *Molly O,* others; ex-husband of Barbara La Marr.

DEERING, JOHN *(1955)* 53 ——Support in one early talkie, *Forgotten Commandments.*

DEERING, MARDA *(1961)* 50s ——Beautiful supporting actress whose obituary asserted that she "was the model for Columbia Pictures' Statue of Liberty trademark"; was onscreen in the '30s, in *Night Life of the Gods,* etc.

DE FOE, ANNETTE *(1960)* 67 ——Was in silents.

DE FOREST, HAL *(1938)* 76 ——With Annette Kellerman in *The Daughter of the Gods* ('16).

DE GRASSE, JOSEPH *(1940)* 67 ——Support in early silents, then, in the '20s, in *The Cowboy Kid* and Colleen Moore's *So Big;* brother of Sam.

DE GRASSE, SAM *(1953)* 78 ——Major support or costar in dozens (1915–30); after *The Birth of a Nation* (as Sen. Charles Sumner), was in *Intolerance, Robin Hood* (sinister Prince John), *The Black Pirate* (pirate leader's lieutenant), *The King of Kings* (The Pharisee), many Colleen Moore pix *(Forsaking All Others, Slippy McGee,* etc.), and in the von Stroheim-directed *Blind Husbands* as the complacent mountain-climbing husband whose wife is seduced by army officer von Stroheim; retired in '30.

DE HAVEN, MRS. CARTER *(1950)* 67 ——Co-starred with her husband in such silent features as *Close to Nature, Why Divorce?, Twin Beds, A Ringer for Dad;* they also starred in two-reel marital comedies for both Paramount *(Hoodooed* and nine others) and R-C Pictures *(Their First Vacation,* etc.); her maiden name, Flora Parker, usually appeared in parentheses in her billing.

DE KEREKJARTO, DUCI *(1962)* 60 ——Supporting actor in Jane Powell's *Rich, Young and Pretty.*

DEKKER, ALBERT *(1968)* 62 ——Donned those thick specs and reduced everyone in sight to toy size as the star of *Dr. Cyclops,* and his future was evil-starred; was up to bad tricks earlier in *Marie Antoinette* (billed Albert Van Dekker), *Beau Geste, The Man in the Iron Mask,* etc., and later in *The Killers, Two Years Before the Mast, Suspense,* many more; once in a while had he-man leads, as when he co-starred with Trevor in *Woman of the Town.*

DE LA MOTTE, MARGUERITE *(1950)* 58 —— Fairbanks' brunette love in *The Mark of Zorro*

('20), *The Three Musketeers* and *The Nut* (both '21); was pretty and spirited in many other silents, too: *Desire, The Famous Mrs. Fair, Fifth Avenue, When a Man's a Man*, etc.; few minor roles in talkies including 1942's *Reg'lar Fellers* which headlined kid stars Billy Lee and Carl "Alfalfa" Switzer.

DE LANDA, JUAN *(1968)* 74 ——Spanish actor; character (Hispano-Suiza Driver) in Bogart's *Beat the Devil*.

DELANEY, CHARLES *(1959)* 57 ——Handsome co-lead, with Rin Tin Tin, in *The Man Hunter;* had almost a 40-year career; romantic young buck in silents (*College Days, Barbara Frietchie, Sporting Life*, etc.); then support in B's and Westerns (*Officer 13, Fighting Trooper, Kansas Raiders*, many more).

DELANEY, JERE *(1954)* 65 ——Support in a 1928 Helene Costello movie, *The Lights of New York*, the first all-talking picture, and in *Rubeville*.

DELANEY, MAUREEN *(1961)* 72 ——Irish support in *Odd Man Out, Under Capricorn*, etc.

DE LEON, RAOUL *(1972)* ——Minor support.

DELGADO, MARIA *(1969)* 65 ——Character actress.

DE LIGUORO, COUNTESS RINA *(1966)* 72 ——Support in silents (*Messalina, The Mystic Mirror*, and Garbo's *Romance*); long offscreen, she had a minor role in Burt Lancaster's *The Leopard*.

DELL, DOROTHY *(1934)* 19 ——Delectable blonde who, as Bangles Carson in *Little Miss Marker*, was Queen Guinevere in Shirley Temple's eyes; also in *Wharf Angel* and *Shoot the Works*, in which she introduced the song "With My Eyes Wide Open, I'm Dreaming."

DEL MAR, CLAIRE *(1959)* 58 ——Support in Valentino's *The Four Horsemen of the Apocalypse*, Jolson's *The Jazz Singer*, von Stroheim's *The Wedding March.*

DE MARCO, TONY *(1965)* 67 ——Of famous Tony and Sally De Marco dance team; specialty numbers in *Greenwich Village, The Gang's All Here, The Shining Hour, In Caliente, Crazy House.*

DEMAREST, RUBE *(1962)* 76 ——Actor-brother of William; in *The Gracie Allen Murder Case* and Lucille Ball's *A Girl, a Guy and a Gob.*

DE MARNEY, TERENCE *(1971)* 62 ——English supporting actor; in Cooper's *The Wreck of the Mary Deare, The Silver Chalice, 23 Paces to Baker Street, My Gun Is Quick*, etc.

DeMILLE, CECIL B. *(1959)* 77——Famed producer-director of Biblical (and other) epics; an early actor, he was frequently seen as himself in talkies: *Sunset Boulevard* ("I'm ready for my closeup, Mr. DeMille"), *Variety Girl, Star-Spangled Rhythm*, etc.

DE MILLE, WILLIAM C. *(1955)* 76—— Brother of Cecil; also an actor in early silents, he too became a director (of Lois Wilson in *Miss Lulu Bett*, Bebe Daniels in *Nice People*, etc.) and a considerably underrated one.

DEMPSEY, CLIFFORD *(1938)* 73 ——Character in comedies of the early '30s (*Soup to Nuts, Happy Days, Too Many Cooks*, etc.) as well as in Muni's *The Valiant.*

DEMPSEY, THOMAS *(1947)* 85 ——Support in *Elmer and Elsie* and Monte Blue's *The Bush Leaguer.*

DENNIS, CRYSTAL *(1973)* 80 ——Vaudeville headliner who was featured in silents.

DENNIS, RUSSELL *(1964)* 48 ——Support (Pvt. Fred Tyler) in Arthur Kennedy's *Bright Victory.*

DENNY, REGINALD *(1967)* 75 ——Polished handsome actor in literally hundreds of films from 1914 to '66; a few of the many silents in which he starred: *Footlights*, the "Leather Pusher" series, *39 East, The Abysmal Brute* (was frequently cast as a prizefighter to show off his superb physique), *Captain Fearless;* grand support in talkies: Davis' *Of Human Bondage*, Shearer's *Romeo and Juliet* (Benvolio), *Rebecca, The Lost Patrol*, the 1937-39 "Bulldog Drummond" series (as Algy), *The Macomber Affair*, etc.

DENT, VERNON *(1963)* 68 ——Beefy, funny man with moustache whose long career (though he did features too) was spent in two-reelers supporting all the comedy stars: Charley Chase (best in his classic "The Heckler"), Harry Langdon, Andy Clyde, The Three Stooges (in almost all), Vera Vague; played cops, husbands (irate and henpecked), bosses, etc.

DENTON, CRAHAN *(1966)* 42 ——Support in *Bird Man of Alcatraz* (Kramer), *To Kill a Mockingbird* (Walter Cunningham), *Hud* (Jesse), etc.

DEPP, HARRY *(1957)* 71 ——Support in *The Magnificent Dope, Blues in the Night; Swing It, Professor;* etc.

DE PUTTI, LYA *(1932)* 30——An exotic, animated, interesting and beautiful brunette star from Hungary imported by Paramount; the faithless trapeze-artist wife of Emil Jannings in *Variety*, a wide-eyed fraulein in *Buck Privates* ('28), in Griffith's *The Sorrows of Satan, The Scarlet Lady*, etc.

DE RAVENNE, CAROLINE MARIE *(1962)* 79 ——Supporting actress.

DE ROCHE, CHARLES *(1952)* 72 ——Barechested Rameses in DeMille's silent *The Ten Commandments;* earlier had been in French comedies starring Max Linder (and billed De-Rochefort); other silents: *The Cheat, Madame Sans Gene, The White Moth, The Marriage Broker*, etc.

DERWENT, CLARENCE *(1959)* 74 ——Character ("Papa Louis" Barraya) in *The Story of Vernon and Irene Castle;* also in *Stanley and Livingstone, The Night Angel*, others.

DES AUTELS, VAN *(1968)* 57 ——He had minor roles in *How to Marry a Millionaire, The Robe, Inside Detroit*, etc.

DE SEGUROLA, ANDRES *(1953)* 77 ——He was a Spanish opera star who had a supporting role (Caluppi) in Grace Moore's *One Night of Love;* earlier was in *The Loves of Sunya* (Paolo de Salvo), *My Man, The Red Dance*, others.

DESHON, FLORENCE——Dark-haired beauty who starred for Vitagraph in 1918; in *A Bachelor's Children, The Clutch of Circumstance;* born c. 1898, year of death unreported.

DE SICA, VITTORIO *(1974)* 72 ——One of Italy's great matinee idols in the '30s, he became a silver-haired international star in many fine films, most made abroad: *Miracle in Milan; Times Gone By; The Earrings of Madame de; Bread, Love and Dreams; Gold of Naples; General Della Rovere; The Shoes of the Fisherman*, and Selznick's *A Farewell to Arms*, for which he received an Oscar nomination as Best Support; directed numerous great films: *The Bicycle Thief, Shoe-Shine, Umberto D*, and *Two Women*, which won a Best Actress Academy Award for Sophia Loren, whom he directed in many others.

DESLYS, GABY *(1920)* 36 ——Notoriously beautiful French stage star who appeared for Famous Players in *Her Triumph* ('15) and Pathe in 1918's *Infatuation;* had remained amazingly youthful throughout her career, and the age given in her obituaries is believed incorrect by several years.

DESMOND, WILLIAM *(1949)* 71 ——One of the silent screen's handsomest, most heavily muscled men, and a star from the first (1915's *Peggy* opposite Billie Burke); in *Bullets and Brown Eyes, An Honest Man, Red Clay, The Captive God, Not My Sister, The Man from Make Believe, The Prince and Betty*, etc.; a paunchy 44 when he starred in his first serial, *Perils of the Yukon*, for Universal in 1922, he went on to make 10 more in the next seven years which, besides being among the best ever done by the studio, made him the company's serial king; then played minor roles in Westerns till 1940.

DESMONDE, JERRY *(1967)* 58 ——English character; in Chaplin's *A King in New York, The Malta Story*, others.

DESPRES, SUZANNE *(1951)* 76 ——French character actress in *Maria Chapdelaine, Flight Into Darkness*, and Grace Moore's *Louise*.

DESTE, LULI *(1951)* 49 ——Exotically lovely Viennese starred (1937-40) by Columbia *(Thunder in the City* with Edward G. Robinson, *She Married an Artist)* and Universal *(Ski Patrol, South to Karanga)*, each of whom hoped she would become "another Dietrich."

DE TELLIER, MARIETTE *(1957)* 66 ——Indian maiden roles in silent Westerns with Tom Mix and William S. Hart.

DEUTSCH, ERNEST, *(1969)* 77 ——Character (Dr. Behr) in Fredric March's *So Ends Our Night;* in *The Third Man, Nurse Edith Cavell*, etc.

DEUTSCH, LOU *(1968)* 70 ——Support in many Westerns.

DE VALDEZ, CARLOS *(1939)* 45 ——Handsome support in Margaret Sullavan's *Little Man, What Now?*, and in *Conquest, Lancer Spy, Blockade*, etc.

DE VAULL, WILLIAM *(1945)* 74 ——Character (Jake) in *The Birth of a Nation;* also support in *Kentucky Days, White Shoulders, Lights of Old Broadway*, other silents.

DEVERE, FRANCESCA *(1952)* 61 ——A Mack Sennett comedienne.

DEVEREAUX, JACK *(1958)* 75 ——Was in the silent *Superstition*.

DE VERNON, FRANK *(1923)* 78 ——Silent support; in Alma Rubens' *Under the Red Robe, The Black Panther's Cub, Yolande,* others.

DEVLIN, JOE *(1973)* 70s ——Played crooks such as Singapore Smith in the Tom Tyler serial *The Phantom;* support in many pix of the '40s: *They Got Me Covered, Body and Soul, Bringing Up Father.*

DEVOE, BERT *(1930)* 45 ——In Sennett comedies, then in *Shackles of Fear,* other silents.

DEWEY, EARL S. *(1950)* 68 ——Minor support in *Captain Eddie, Shadow of a Doubt, The Adventures of Mark Twain,* others.

DEWEY, ELMER *(1954)* 70 ——Support in silents: *Shadows of Chinatown, Taking Chances, The Million Dollar Mystery* (serial).

DEWHURST, WILLIAM *(1937)* 49 ——British support; *Bulldog Drummond at Bay, Dinner at the Ritz, Victoria the Great,* others.

DE WILDE, BRANDON *(1972)* 30 ——Was the towheaded lad who worshipped *Shane,* and whose sensitive performance won him a Best Supporting Oscar nomination; played Newman's kid brother in *Hud,* Beatty's in *All Fall Down;* was star-billed also in *The Member of the Wedding* (his debut), *Blue Denim, In Harm's Way, Those Calloways.*

DE WOLFE, BILLY *(1974)* 65 ——Fine, funny, prissy comic starred by Paramount in many in the '40s (*Dixie, Blue Skies, Our Hearts Were Growing Up, Dear Ruth, Miss Susie Slagle's,* etc.); then at Warners for two musicals (*Tea for Two, Lullaby of Broadway*), and 20th for *Call Me Madam;* later top-featured in a Doris Day TV series.

DEXTER, AUBREY *(1958)* 60 ——British character who was in *Angel Street* and Monroe's *The Prince and the Showgirl.*

DEXTER, ELLIOTT *(1941)* 71 ——A most handsome silent leading man; if ever there was a DeMille star it was he; between 1916 and '23, the director costarred him (with Swanson and all his great leading ladies) in many: *The Heart of Nora Flynn; Don't Change Your Husband; For Better, For Worse; The Squaw Man* ('19); *We Can't Have Everything; Something to Think About; The Affairs of Anatol; Adam's Rib* ('23); wound up his career with Pickford, one of his early costars, in 1930's *Stella Maris.*

DICENTA, MANUEL *(1974)* 70 ——Star of the U.S.-released Spanish pic *Morena Clara.*

DICKERSON, DUDLEY *(1968)* 60s ——Black character actor; "Ham" in *The Green Pastures* was perhaps his most memorable role; also in, among others, 1939's *Some Like It Hot.*

DICKEY, PAUL *(1933)* 47 ——Support in Fairbanks' *Robin Hood;* better known as a screenwriter (*The Ghost Breakers,* etc.).

DICKINSON, HAL *(1970)* 56 ——Singer with The Modernaires; onscreen in *The Glenn Miller Story.*

DICKSON, GLORIA *(1945)* 28 ——A combination of Lombard (in blonde looks) and Davis (in forceful acting style), she was so strong in a secondary role in *They Won't Forget*—wife of the lynching victim—that Warners built the pic's ad campaign around her; in *They Made Me a Criminal, Racket Busters, Gold Diggers in Paris, Secrets of an Actress,* etc., but never had the chance to fulfill her potential.

DICKSON, LAMONT *(1944)* ——Supporting actor who was in 1930's *Almost a Honeymoon.*

DICKSON, LYDIA *(1928)* 40 ——Comedienne in silents: *Don't Marry, Square Crooks.*

DIESSL, GUSTAV *(1948)* 48 ——Co-star of Pabst's *Westfront 1918,* other German films.

DIGGES, DUDLEY *(1947)* 68 ——Grand old Irish character; the ship's sawbones in Gable's *Mutiny on the Bounty;* in *The General Died at Dawn, Raffles, China Seas, The Emperor Jones* (co-starring with Paul Robeson), many more, including *The Searching Wind,* his last, in '46.

DIGGINS, PEGGY ——Lovely brunette starlet, one of Warners' famous "Navy Blues" sextette; in *Navy Blues, Lady Gangster, Truck Busters;* date of death unreported.

DILLON, DICK *(1961)* 65 ——Support in Pearl White's *The Perils of Pauline.*

DILLON, EDWARD *(1933)* 53 ——Member of Griffith's first movie stock company of actors; Chief Detective in "Modern" sequence in *Intolerance;* in *Judith of Bethulia; Fisher Folks; Home, Sweet Home* (The Musician); after Griffith he costarred with Fay Tincher in the 1915 comedy *Faithful to the Finish;* in other silents (*Lilac Time,* etc.) and early talkies (*The Broadway Melody* as the Stage Manager, *Sob Sister,* others).

DILLON, GEORGE *(1965)* 77 ——Character (jailer) in *The Mudlark.*

DILLON, JACK *(1934)* 47 ——One of the acting group Griffith first took with him to California in 1913; later starred in *Love, Dynamite and Baseballs*, acted for Keystone, and in such silents of the '20s as *Double Dealing, The Journey's End*, etc.; under his full name, John Francis Dillon, directed Mary Pickford in *Suds*, Jack Pickford in *Burglar by Proxy*, Colleen Moore in *The Perfect Flapper* and *We Moderns*, etc.

DILLON, JOHN *(1937)* 61 ——Support in *The Cisco Kid, In Old Arizona* (Second Soldier), after such silents as *Midnight Molly, The Family Closet*, others.

DILLON, JOHN WEBB *(1949)* 72 ——Was the fine-looking young actor who played Tybalt in Theda Bara's *Romeo and Juliet* ('16); in many other silents (*Jane Eyre, The Vanishing American, The Mohican's Daughter*, etc.) and early talkies (*Carolina, Girl of the Port*, others); also in many silent serials: *Speed, House Without a Key, Snowed In*, etc.

DILLON, JOSEPHINE *(1971)* 87 ——First of Gable's older wives; onscreen in Vera Hruba Ralston's *The Lady and the Mobster* ('44).

DILLON, TOM *(1962)* 66 ——Often played policemen; in *Going My Way* (Officer Patrick McCarthy), *The Search for Bridey Murphy, The Thin Man Goes Home*, etc.

DILLON, TOM *(1965)* 77 ——Of the Keystone Kops.

DILSON, JOHN *(1944)* 51 ——Support in *You Can't Escape Forever, They All Kissed the Bride, Naval Academy, Every Night at Eight*, others.

DINEHART, ALAN *(1944)* 54 ——Popular "heavy"—often a dyspeptic business man—so in demand he was once in 33 pix in 27 months; a favorite at 20th Century-Fox where he had top supporting roles in *Baby Take a Bow, Dante's Inferno, Charlie Chan at the Race Track, Second Fiddle, Hotel for Women, Sweet Rosie O'-Grady*, many more.

DINGLE, CHARLES *(1956)* 68 ——Played stinkers—great ones: Davis' conniving brother Ben in *The Little Foxes*, a Norwegian quisling in *Edge of Darkness*, the arsonist mill owner who persecuted Cary Grant in *Talk of the Town*, a fee-grubbing physician in *Calling Dr. Gillespie*; hadn't changed a bit by the time he played Senator Fullerton in *The Court-Martial of Billy Mitchell*, his last.

DIONNE, EMILIE *(1954)* 20 ——With the other famous Dionne Quintuplets in three features (*Reunion, The Country Doctor, Five of a Kind*), two shorts, and countless newsreels.

DIONNE, MARIE *(1970)* 35 ——Also one of the quints.

DISNEY, WALT *(1966)* 65 ——Cartoon genius, seen so often on TV and in trailers for his movies, his face was as familiar as Mickey Mouse's.

DIX, RICHARD *(1949)* 55 ——Stalwart, durable (from '21), strong-jawed star who was one of the screen's best representatives of rugged masculinity: the evidence: *Cimarron* ('31), for which he received his one Oscar nomination, *The Lost Squadron, The Vanishing American, Stingaree, Man of Conquest, Devil's Squadron*, dozens more; was active in movies until the end, last being in 1949's *The Fountainhead*.

DIXEY, HENRY E. *(1943)* 83 ——Star of 1908's *David Garrick;* later in many Universal silents.

DIXON, DENVER *(1972)* 71 ——Western star of the '20s and '30s known for his bullwhip skill; as a youth he appeared in cowboy pix as Art James; starred under the name Denver Dixon first (from 1920) and last—in 1938's *Mormon Conquest;* beginning in '23 he assumed the name Art Mix and wrote, produced, and directed the dozens of Westerns in which he starred; later hired other actors (George Kesterson, who became best known in the role, and Bob Roberts) to portray Art Mix; as Denver Dixon he continued to produce, direct, and star until he retired in his thirties.

DIXON, HARLAND *(1969)* 83 ——Famous vaudeville dancer in a few movies, then a dance director.

DIXON, LEE *(1953)* 42 ——He was a tall, dark-blond tap-dancer featured in Warners' 1930s musicals; in *Gold Diggers of 1937* (Boop Oglethorpe); *Ready, Willing and Able; Varsity Show; The Singing Marine*.

DOCKSON, EVELYN *(1952)* 64 ——Dowager (Mrs. Taylor) in Betty Hutton's *Let's Face It*.

DODD, CLAIRE *(1973)* 58 ——Moviegoers and leading ladies alike knew better than to trust this dimple-cheeked, chic blonde—one glance revealed she was The Other Woman; in *Roberta, The Glass Key* ('35), *Babbitt, Footlight Parade, The Case (. . . of The Curious Bride, . . . of the Velvet Claws, . . . of Mrs. Pembrook), The Black Cat*, etc.

DODD, JIMMY *(1964)* 54 ——Support in many *(Flying Tigers, Those Were the Days, You Gotta Stay Happy*, etc.), he was more famous as the curly-haried emcee of TV's *Mickey Mouse Club.*

DODD, REV. NEAL *(1969)* 87 ——A real-life Hollywood minister, he "married" the stars in many: *It Happened One Night, Here Comes the Groom, Merrily We Go to Hell*, etc.

DOLENZ, GEORGE *(1963)* 51 ——Darkly handsome leading man who had been in many from '41 *(Faculty Row, Hired Wife, Enter Arsene Lupin*, etc.) before Howard Hughes "discovered" him; the millionaire devoted several years to preparing *Vendetta* as a star-making showcase for Dolenz and Faith Domergue; after its failure the actor had supporting roles in many: *Sign of the Pagan, Timbuktu, The Racers*, etc.

DOLLY, JENNY *(1941)* 48 ——Half of the famous Dolly Sisters; she and twin sister Rosie starred in 1918's *The Million Dollar Dollies.*

DOLLY, ROSIE *(1970)* 77 ——Jenny and she were portrayed by Grable and Haver in *The Dolly Sisters.*

DOMINGUEZ, BEATRICE *(1921)* ——Support in Valentino's *The Four Horsemen of the Apocalypse.*

DOMINGUEZ, JOE *(1970)* 76 ——Doleful-faced Mexican in over 300 from 1913; in talkies: *One-Eyed Jacks* (Corral Keeper); *Viva, Villa!; Dallas, The Kissing Bandit*, and scores of B's.

DONAT, ROBERT *(1958)* 53 ——Was the essence of a British gentleman star; won an Oscar for *Goodbye Mr. Chips*, but was equally fine in comedy *(The Ghost Goes West)*, in costume *(The Count of Monte Cristo, The Private Life of Henry VIII)*, romantic vehicles *(Knight Without Armor)*, adventure stories *(The 39 Steps)*, contemporary dramas *(The Citadel, The Winslow Boy)*, or even at playing an aged Chinese mandarin *(The Inn of the Sixth Happiness*, his last; also nominated for Best Supporting Actor in *The Citadel.*

DONATH, LUDWIG *(1967)* 67 ——Proud father of Jolson (Larry Parks) in both *The Jolson Story* ("Oh, how we danced on the night we were wed . . .") and *Jolson Sings Again;* in many: *To the Ends of the Earth, The Great Caruso, Sealed Verdict, The Hitler Gang*, etc.

DONLAN, JAMES, *(1938)* 49 ——Support throughout the '30s: in Irene Dunne's *Back Street* (as Profhero), *Design for Living* (Fat Man), *The Bishop Murder Case, The Cat's Paw*, etc.

DONLEVY, BRIAN *(1972)* 69 ——Burly, barrel-chested star who could be heroic *(Wake Island, Stand By for Action)*, loathsomely evil *(Beau Geste* '39, which won him an Oscar nomination as Best Support), charmingly tough *(The Great McGinty)*, funny *(Miracle of Morgan's Creek)*, or a convincing empire-builder *(An American Romance)*; onscreen from 1929's *Mother's Boy* to 1968's *Rogues' Gallery.*

DONLIN, MIKE *(1933)* 43 ——Fine support in many comedies: Keaton's *The General* (Union General); *Ella Cinders; Slide, Kelly, Slide; Oh, Doctor*, etc.

DONNELLY, JAMES *(1937)* 72 ——Character in silents: *Black Beauty, A Girl's Desire, Bubbles of Trouble*, others.

DONNELLY, LEO *(1935)* 57 ——Comic in silents: *Roadhouse Nights, Potash and Perlmutter;* narrator of Ripley's "Believe It or Not" shorts.

DONNER, MAURICE *(1971)* 66 ——Minor support; *Torn Curtain, Congo Crossing*, others.

DONOHUE, JOE *(1921)* 37 ——Portly young character; in *Over the Hill*, Alice Joyce's *Within the Law*, etc.

DOOLEY, BILLY *(1938)* 45 ——Support in Richard Arlen's *Call of the Yukon;* in *Anything Goes, The Marines Are Here;* in 1927-28 he starred in 14 "Goofy Gob" two-reel comedies as a sailor-suited dimwit, made by Christie and released by Paramount.

DOOLEY, JOHNNY *(1928)* 41 ——Featured in Marion Davies' *When Knighthood Was in Flower* (the King's Jester) and *Yolanda* (the Dauphin); also in *East Side, West Side* and *Skinning Skinners.*

DOONAN, PATRIC *(1958)* 31 ——Support in Guinness' *The Man in the White Suit* and *The Lavender Hill Mob;* also in *The Cockleshell Heroes, John and Julie*, and MGM's *Crest of the Wave.*

DORALINDA, *(1936)* 47 ——Warner Oland's brunette leading lady in *The Naulahka* ('18); also in *Passion Fruit*, other silents.

DORETY, CHARLES *(1957)* 58 ——Support in Three Stooges comedies: *Ants in the Pantry, Men in Black, Movie Maniacs*, etc.; earlier had starred in a 1927-28 Universal two-reel series based on Rube Goldberg's comic strip *Ike and Mike,* appearing as a "pathetic type with a Stan Laurel style."

DORLEAC, FRANCOISE *(1967)* 25 ——Lovely brunette French star; in *That Man from Rio, The Young Girls of Rochefort, Where the Spies Are;* sister of Catherine Deneuve.

DORO, MARIE *(1956)* 74 ——Charming slender brunette who starred for Lasky in '16 in the title role of *Oliver Twist,* which she had played on Broadway, and for De Mille in *The Heart of Nora Flynn,* to high critical acclaim; star of other silents: *The White Pearl, The Wood Nymph, The Mysterious Princess,* etc.

D'ORSAY, LAWRENCE *(1931)* 71 ——Played the monocled title role in 1918's *Ruggles of Red Gap,* Lord Elton in Griffith's *The Sorrows of Satan;* others: *His Children's Children, Miss Bluebeard.*

DORSEY, EDMUND *(1959)* 62 ——Support in comedies for decades.

DORSEY, JIMMY *(1957)* 53 ——Famous saxophone-playing orchestra leader who, before starring with brother Tommy in *The Fabulous Dorseys,* had been featured with his band in *The Fleet's In* and *Four Jills in a Jeep.*

DORSEY, TOMMY *(1956)* 51 ——MGM's most glittering stars danced to this great trombonist and his band in *Du Barry Was a Lady, Presenting Lily Mars, Ship Ahoy, Girl Crazy,* and *Broadway Rhythm*—and so did Danny Kaye in Goldwyn's *A Song Is Born.*

DOSCHER, DORIS *(1970)* 88 ——Eve in *The Birth of a Nation;* other silents; was famous model (Miss Liberty on the 25¢ coin).

DOTY, WINSTON AND WESTON *(1934)* 18 ——The 10-year-old twins in Betty Bronson's *Peter Pan.*

DOUCET, CATHARINE *(1958)* 83——Blonde character actress who was flawless as the destructive aunt of Miriam Hopkins in *These Three,* and as the lady who crossed lances with W. C. Fields in *Poppy;* in several from '34 to '49: *Wake Up and Dream, It Started With Eve, As Husbands Go; Little Man, What Now?*

DOUCET, PAUL *(1928)* 42 ——Support in silents: *Polly of the Follies, Little French Girl,* Griffith's *America* (as Marquis de Lafayette), others.

DOUGLAS, BYRON *(1935)* 70 ——Character in silents: *Under the Red Robe, That Devil Quemado, The Perfect Sap, Red Clay,* etc.

DOUGLAS, DON *(1945)* 40 ——Lead in the Deadwood Dick serial; also in *Charlie Chan in Panama; Wings of the Navy; The Gladiator; Murder, My Sweet; Smashing the Rackets,* many more.

DOUGLAS, DORIS *(1970)* 52 ——Character roles.

DOUGLAS, KEITH *(1973)* 55 ——See Douglas Kennedy.

DOUGLAS, KENT *(1966)* 58 ——See Douglass Montgomery.

DOUGLAS, MILTON *(1970)* 64 ——Singer-actor who was the juvenile lead in the '31 Warner Technicolor musical *Viennese Nights.*

DOUGLAS, PAUL *(1959)* 52 ——Gravelly, gruff star who, the louder he bellowed at (or with) his leading lady, the better the show; worked best with Linda Darnell (*A Letter to Three Wives,* his first) and Judy Holliday (*Born Yesterday*), as junk dealer Harry Brock who, she insisted, "just ain't couth"); fine, too, in *Twelve O'Clock High, The Big Lift, Panic in the Streets, Clash by Night, Solid Gold Cadillac,* etc.

DOUGLAS, VALERIE *(1969)* 31 ——British actress in secondary pix.

DOUGLAS, WALLACE *(1958)* 36 ——Under this name was featured in British pix: Chevalier's *Break the News* (funny, periwigged assistant stage manager), Barry K. Barnes' *Spies of the Air;* also see Wallace J. Froes listing.

DOVEY, ALICE *(1969)* 84 ——Was a celebrated young Broadway musical star, and a dark-haired beauty, when she starred onscreen in 1915 for Famous Players in *The Commanding Officer* with Donald Crisp.

DOWLING, CONSTANCE *(1969)* 49 ——The dazzling, hazel-eyed blonde leading lady adored by Danny Kaye in *Up in Arms,* and by Nelson Eddy, who sang "September Song" to her in *Knickerbocker Holiday;* in others: *The Black Angel, The Well-Groomed Bride, Gog,* etc.; married producer Ivan Tors, retired to raise a family.

DOWLING, JOAN *(1954)* 26 ——Teen lead in England's *No Room at the Inn, Hue and Cry,* etc.

599

DOWLING, JOSEPH *(1928)* 80 ——Most impressive in 1919's *The Miracle Man* as the Patriarch, the old, blind, gray-haired faith healer who transmits the "miracle" of goodness and faith to the four crooks—one of them young Lon Chaney—who intend to victimize him; had many other major roles, such as the priest in Richard Dix's *The Christian*, in *The Kentucky Colonel*, *Little Lord Fauntleroy* ('21), and *Tess of the D'Urbervilles*.

DOWNING, HARRY *(1972)* 78 ——Supporting roles in silents.

DOWNING, WALTER *(1937)* 63 ——Featured in the silent *Pied Piper Malone*.

DOYLE, BUDDY *(1939)* 38 ——Portrayed Eddie Cantor in *The Great Ziegfeld*.

DOYLE, JOHN T. *(1935)* 62 ——Support in Morton Downey's *Mother's Boy*; was also in *His Woman* and *Gambling*.

DOYLE, MAXINE *(1973)* 50s ——Charming young actress at Warners in the early '30s; introduced in William Powell's *The Key*, she was then the feminine lead in Joe E. Brown's *6 Day Bike Rider*, and the ingenue in *Babbitt*; later had femme leads in serials: *SOS Coast Guard* and *G-Men vs. the Black Dragon*.

DRAINIE, JOHN *(1966)* 50 ——Was in Disney's live-action film *The Incredible Journey*.

DRAKE, JOSEPHINE *(1929)* 40s ——Dark-haired Broadway actress featured in silents: *The Palm Beach Girl*, *The Song and Dance Man*, etc.

DRANEM *(1935)* 66 ——Versatile French star comedian in many films exported to the U.S. in the early 1900s.

DRAYLIN, PAUL *(1970)* 56 ——Actor-magician; supporting roles.

DRAYTON, ALFRED *(1949)* 68 ——Bald British character; Squeers in *Nicholas Nickleby* ('47); many other English pix: *Don't Take It to Heart*, George Sanders' *So This Is London*, *The Halfway House*.

DRESSER, LOUISE *(1965)* 86 ——One of the screen's grandest, least sentimental mother-type characters; Will Rogers' pix especially would have been less without her: *State Fair*, *Doctor Bull*, *The County Chairman*, *Lightnin'*, *David Harum*; in silents: *Ruggles of Red Gap*, *The Eagle*, *A Ship Comes In* (Oscar-nominated as Best Actress), more; superb in many talkies: *Mother Knows Best* (title; talkie debut), *Maid of Salem*, *The Scarlet Empress* (as Empress Elizabeth), *Cradle Song* (Mother Superior), etc.

DRESSLER, MARIE *(1934)* 65 ——No beauty, this mugging, great rowdy, but when she and Wallace Beery squared off in *Min and Bill*, who did you watch?; won an Oscar for it, and was nominated the next year for *Emma*; incomparable in her many comedies with Polly Moran, in *Anna Christie* (as barfly Marthy), *Dinner at Eight*, *Tugboat Annie*, *Christopher Bean*, and, harking back to 1914, the hilarious "Tillie" pix (*Tillie's Punctured Romance*, *Tillie's Nightmare*, etc.).

DREW, ANN *(1974)* 83 ——Early silent leading lady, with Griffith and others, who specialized in bridal roles; with Pickford in *Hearts Adrift*; married and retired in '13.

DREW, SIDNEY *(1919)* 55 ——Starred with his wife (always billed Mr. and Mrs. Sidney Drew) in many early comedies; became Vitagraph's great money-makers when John Bunny left the company, and later starred for Metro; in *Good Gracious!*, *Childhood's Happy Days*, *The Patriot*, *Her First Game*, *Who's Who in Hogg's Hollow*, etc.; "the best of the comedians," said poet-critic Vachel Lindsay.

DREW, MRS. SIDNEY *(1925)* 35 ——Last on-screen in 1919 comedies with her husband (*Once a Mason*, *Harold and the Saxons*, etc.) she had acted earlier under two other names—Jane Morrow and Lucile McVey—and was one of the screen's earliest woman directors.

DREYFUSS, MICHAEL *(1960)* 32 ——Support in Rod Serling's *Patterns*.

DRIGGERS, DONALD *(1972)* 79 ——Veteran character actor.

DRISCOLL, BOBBY *(1968)* 31 ——Disney's most famous boy star; in *Song of the South*, *So Dear to My Heart*, *Melody Time*, *Treasure Island*; earlier in *Lost Angel*, *The Sullivans*, etc.; received a special Oscar in '49 (after *The Window*) as "outstanding juvenile actor of the year"; last had a minor role in a 1958 B, *The Party Crashers*.

DRUMIER, JACK *(1939)* 70 ——Character in silents: *Shadow of the Sea*, *Enemies of Youth*, *The Girl from Porcupine*, etc.

DUCHIN, EDDY *(1951)* 41 ——The Stork Club's inimitable society pianist (and father of Peter); in *Coronado*, *Mr. Broadway*, *The Hit Parade* ('37); was later portrayed by Tyrone Power in *The Eddy Duchin Story*.

DUDLEY, ROBERT *(1955)* 80 ——Long-eared, long-faced comic character in many from 1920 *(Flapper Wives, The Traveling Salesman,* etc.); talkies: *The Palm Beach Story* (the "Weenie King"), *Magic Town, It Happened Tomorrow,* others.

DUEL, PETER *(1972)* 29 ——Humorous, handsome star of two TV series *(Love on a Rooftop, Alias Smith and Jones)* who was in several movies; *Generation, The Hell With Heroes,* etc.); originally billed Deuel, the correct spelling of his name.

DUFFY, JACK *(1939)* 56 ——Comic support in silent features (Colleen Moore's *Sally* and *Ella Cinders,* plus *Harold Teen, Stop Flirting,* etc.); in 1927-28 costarred with Neal Burns and Anne Cornwall in 12 two-reel Christie comedies; in 1933's *Alice in Wonderland* (Leg of Mutton), others.

DUGAN, TOM *(1955)* 66 ——Funny, slow-witted Irish cop in over 100 from 1926; in *The Ghost Breakers, A Little Bit of Heaven, Wife vs. Secretary, Pennies From Heaven, Earl Carroll's Vanities, Four Daughters, Ellery Queen's Penthouse Mystery,* etc.

DUGGAN, TOM *(1969)* 53 ——Television personality featured in *Andy Hardy Comes Home,* Gable's *But Not for Me, Blueprint for Robbery,* others.

DULAC, ARTHUR *(1962)* 52 ——Character (French waiter) in Crosby's *Little Boy Lost.*

DULLIN, CHARLES *(1949)* 64 ——Character in many French films: *Volpone, Miracle of The Wolves, Les Miserables, Jenny Lamour, The Chess Player,* etc.

DU MAURIER, SIR GERALD *(1934)* 61 —— Noted British stage star who made his "official" movie debut in a leading role in 1930's *Escape,* an English film; actually, in '17, he had appeared with many other luminaries in a short British pic, *Masks and Faces,* for the benefit of the Royal Academy of Dramatic Arts; he also played major roles in *I Was a Spy* and *Catherine the Great,* just before his death; was the father of novelist Daphne Du Maurier.

DUMBRILLE, DOUGLASS *(1974)* 84 —— Stern-faced top character actor in over 250 from '31; played lawyers, senators, villains, judges, tycoons, and fathers; was in several Marx Brothers comedies *(A Day at the Races, The Big Store),* Jeanette MacDonald-Nelson Eddy musicals *(The Firefly, Naughty Marietta, I Married an Angel), The Lives of a Bengal Lan-*

cer (the turbaned Mohammed Khan), *Kentucky* (Richard Greene's unbending father), etc.; on TV was top cast in *The Phil Silvers Show* and *China Smith;* was last in 1958's *The Buccaneer,* 20 years after having appeared in the original version.

DUMKE, RALPH *(1964)* 64 ——Smallish, curly-haired support; character (Tiny Duffy) in *All the King's Men,* his first, and in many more: *We're Not Married, Daddy Long-Legs, They Rode West, Carbine Williams, Invasion of the Body Snatcher* (the sheriff).

DUMONT, GORDON *(1965)* 72 ——Support in numerous silents.

DUMONT, MARGARET *(1965)* 76 ——Where would the Marx Brothers (Groucho especially) have been without their slow-on-the uptake dowager foil?; with them in seven: *The Cocoanuts, Animal Crackers, A Night at the Opera, A Day at the Races, At the Circus, Duck Soup, The Big Store;* other comics "pilfered" her invaluable services, including W. C. Fields *(Never Give a Sucker an Even Break),* Laurel & Hardy *(The Dancing Masters),* Danny Kaye *(Up In Arms),* Jack Benny *(The Horn Blows at Midnight),* Abbott & Costello *(Little Giant);* last in 1964's *What a Way to Go!*

DUNBAR, DAVID *(1953)* 60 ——Support in silent Westerns *(The Cowboy Musketeer, Galloping Vengeance,* etc.) and serials *(Leatherstocking, The Fortieth Door),* and a few talkies *(The Return of Dr. Fu Manchu).*

DUNBAR, HELEN *(1933)* 65 ——Major character actress in many silents starting with Essanay in 1912; with Bushman and Bayne in *Graustark;* in *Three Weeks, The Little Clown, The Cheat; His Majesty, Bunker Bean;* etc.

DUNCAN, BOB *(1967)* 62 ——Support in *The Marshal's Daughter, The Fighting Redhead.*

DUNCAN, BUD *(1960)* 77 ——Diminutive half of the famous Kalem comedy team Ham and Bud, the other slapstick tramp being massive Lloyd Hamilton; they starred in *Don't Monkey with the Buzz Saw, Ham and the Villain Factory, The Tattered Duke,* many more; in '42 Bud starred for Monogram as the wise-cracking, sawed-off hillbilly Snuffy Smith in *Private Snuffy Smith* and *Hillbilly Blitzkrieg.*

DUNCAN, EVELYN *(1972)* 79 ——Sister of Vivian and Rosetta.

DUNCAN, KENNE *(1972)* 69 ——Henchman in over 400 B Westerns *(Hills of Utah, The Kid* *from Santa Fe*, etc.) and numerous talkie serials (*The Spider's Web* and *The Spider Returns*, as The Spider's Sikh servant Ram Singh; *Buck Rogers*, Lt. Lacy; *Adventures of Captain Marvel*, Barnett; *Perils of Nyoka*, Abou; etc.); was frequently billed Kenneth Duncan.

DUNCAN, ROSETTA *(1959)* 59 ——Costarred with sister Vivian in the silents *Topsy and Eva* (played Eva) and *Two Flaming Youths*, also in the early MGM talkie *It's a Great Life*.

DUNCAN, WILLIAM *(1945)* 71 ——Gray-haired support in B Westerns, often the heroine's rancher-dad; in "Hopalong Cassidy" pix (*Bar 20 Justice, Hopalong Rides Again*) and others; not the serial star William Duncan.

DUNCAN, WILLIAM *(1961)* 80 ——Athletic, handsome hero who was in the top rank of silent serial stars from 1917 till his retirement in '25; after 1920's *The Silent Avenger* he married his leading lady in it, Edith Johnson, and they appeared together in eight more: *Fighting Fate, The Steel Trail, The Fast Express, Wolves of the North*, etc.

DUNDEE, JIMMY *(1953)* 52 ——One of Bracken's Marine pals (Corporal) in *Hail, the Conquering Hero;* also in Jerry Lewis comedies (*At War with the Army, Sailor Beware*) and Marie Wilson's *My Friend Irma* and *My Friend Irma Goes West*.

DUNHAM, PHIL *(1972)* ——Character in Conrad Nagel's *Navy Spy* and Bob Burns' *Our Leading Citizen*.

DUNLAP, ETHEL MARGARET *(1968)* 70 —— Acted in silents.

DUNN, BOBBY *(1939)* 48 ——In 1920 starred for Arrow Co. in the two-reel Mirthquake comedy series.

DUNN, EDDIE *(1951)* 55 ——Veteran comic; support in many talkie two-reel comedies (Charley Chase, Edgar Kennedy, etc.), co-starred with Charles Parrott in MGM-Hal Roach shorts in '34, and was in dozens of features: *Give Me a Sailor, The Great Profile, The Fleet's In*, various "Falcon" pix (as Grimes), "Mexican Spitfire," "Saint," and Abbott and Costello comedies.

DUNN, EMMA *(1966)* 91 ——Fondly recalled as the mom of Lew Ayres in the "Dr. Kildare" series; similar roles from 1919 in scores: *Bad Sister, Letty Lynton, Mr. Deeds Goes to Town, Scattergood Baines, Each Dawn I Die*, etc.

DUNN, HARVEY B. *(1968)* ——Supporting roles.

DUNN, J. MALCOLM *(1946)* 70 ——Support in J. Barrymore's *Dr. Jekyll and Mr. Hyde* and other silents (*Sandy, The Magic Cup*, etc.).

DUNN, JAMES *(1967)* 61 ——Actor with enormously appealing Irish charm; got off to a smashing start as the star of 1931's *Bad Girl* first), following it with *Society Girl, Sailor's Luck, Handle with Care*, etc.; slid into B's and Shirley Temple pix (*Baby, Take a Bow, Bright Eyes*); came back strong in *A Tree Grows in Brooklyn*, winning and richly deserving the Best Supporting Actor Oscar as Johnny Nolan.

DUNN, JOHNNY *(1938)* 32 ——At 11 was in the silent serial *The Seven Pearls*.

DUNN, MICHAEL *(1973)* 39 ——Famous dwarf actor in dramatic roles; in *Ship of Fools* (nominated as Best Support), *No Way to Treat a Lady, Madigan, Boom!;* not leading man Michael Dunne who later changed his name to Steve.

DUNN, RALPH *(1968)* 66 ——Support in *Tenth Avenue Girl, Tail Spin, Return of the Cisco Kid, Laura* (as policeman Fred Callahan, which was typical of his roles).

DUNN, REV. ROBERT *(1960)* 64 ——Real-life Episcopal clergyman of Portsmouth, N.H., who acted in three De Rochemont films: *Lost Boundaries* (the minister who rallied the humanity of the townsfolk on behalf of the black family "passing" as white), *The Whistle at Eaton Falls, Walk East on Beacon*.

DUPONT, MISS (PATRICIA) *(1973)* 79 —— Billed simply Miss Dupont, she starred, as the main exponent of the title in von Stroheim's *Foolish Wives* ('22); also appeared with Clara Bow in *Hula* and *Man Trap*.

DUPREE, MINNIE *(1947)* 74 ——Old charmer; she took Janet Gaynor's *Young in Heart* card-sharp family in hand; earlier in *Night Club*, later in Anne Shirley's *Anne of Windy Poplars*.

DUPREZ, FRED *(1938)* 54 ——Supporting actor in such British pix of the '30s as *Dance Band, Head Over Heels in Love, Kathleen*, and *The Pearls of the Crown*.

DURAN, VAL *(1937)* 40 ——Chinese actor; in 1937's *Lost Horizon* (Talu), *The General Died at Dawn* (Wong).

DURAND, EDOUARD *(1926)* 55 ——Support in silents: *The King on Main Street, Potash and Perlmutter, The Sky Raider*, others.

DURIEUX, TILLA *(1971)* 79 ——Austrian character actress in Maria Schell's *The Last Bridge*.

DURKIN, ELEANOR ——Was in early talkie shorts with husband James Burke; year of death unreported.

DURKIN, JAMES *(1934)* 54 ——Support in talkies: *Shadow of the Law, The Secret of the Blue Room, Nice Women, The Big Cage,* others.

DURKIN, JUNIOR *(1935)* 19 ——One of the screen's most appealing juvenile stars; played Huck Finn in both *Tom Sawyer* ('30), *Huckleberry Finn* ('31); also in *Little Men* ('34), several others.

DURNING, BERNARD J. *(1923)* 33 ——Handsome actor-husband of Shirley Mason; in *Seeds of Vengeance, Devil Within;* directed *The Fast Mail* and *The Eleventh Hour.*

DURST, EDWARD L. *(1945)* 28 ——Supporting role (Petrov) in Gregory Peck's debut film, *Days of Glory.*

DURYEA, DAN *(1968)* 61 ——Real-life "nice guy" whose skinny frame and arrogant look helped make him one of the screen's best bad-guys; Davis' weakling, dangerous nephew Leo in *The Little Foxes* (his first); other cruel roles (*The Pride of the Yankees, The Woman in the Window, Ministry of Fear,* etc.) quickly led to stardom (*Black Bart, Winchester 73, Thunder Bay, 6 Black Horses,* etc.), and often change-of-pace good-guy parts.

DURYEA, GEORGE *(1963)* 64 ——See Tom Keene.

DUSE, ELEANORA *(1924)* 66 ——Italy's "Divine Duse"; starred onscreen in just two: 1916's *Cenere* and 1927's *Madre.*

DU VAL, JOE *(1966)* 59 ——Character actor; many small roles.

DUXBURY, ELSPETH *(1967)* 55 ——Support in the Terry-Thomas comedy *Make Mine Mink.*

DWIRE, EARL *(1940)* 56 ——Rugged-featured B-Western "heavy"; sometimes you saw him in black hair and moustache (natural), other times in gray, to play oldsters; equally threatening to Bob Steele, Johnny Mack Brown, and all, either way; in dozens.

DYALL, FRANKLIN *(1950)* 76 ——British character in many: *Atlantic, The Private Life of Henry VIII* (Thomas Cromwell), *The Iron Duke, The Yellow Canary, Bonnie Prince Charlie,* etc.

E

EAGELS, JEANNE *(1929)* 35 ——Beautiful, bedevilled Broadway star who triumphed onscreen in *Man, Woman and Sin* (with John Gilbert), but fared less well in the two that followed: *The Letter* and *Jealousy* (both '29); was portrayed later by Kim Novak in *Jeanne Eagels.*

EAGER, JOHNNY *(1963)* 33 ——Support in Sinatra's *4 for Texas.*

EAMES, CLARE *(1930)* 34 ——Ribald as Queen Elizabeth in Pickford's *Dorothy Vernon of Haddon Hall;* also in *The Three Passions;* engaged to Brian Aherne when she died.

EAMES, VIRGINIA *(1971)* 82 ——See Virginia True Boardman.

EARLE, BLANCHE *(1952)* 68 ——Supported Norma Talmadge in *Within the Law* and *The Battle Cry of Peace.*

EARLE, DOROTHY *(1958)* 60s ——Featured in the silent *Out All Night;* was wife of George "Gabby" Hayes.

EARLY, MARGOT *(1936)* ——Support in *Naughty Marietta, Operator 13,* others.

EARLY, PEARL *(1960)* 81 ——Minor support in Hope's *My Favorite Blonde.*

EASON, "BREEZY" *(1921)* 6 ——Talented, natural speaking, dimpled lad who appeared in Universal pix with his father, actor-director Reeves "Breezy" Eason, and with Harry Carey.

EAST, ED *(1952)* 55 ——Comic support to Sid Melton and Iris Adrian in *Stop That Cab;* also in shorts.

EAST, JOHN *(1924)* ——Support in 1914's *Little Lord Fauntleroy.*

EATON, JAY *(1970)* 70 ——Young support in silents of the '20s (Barthelmess' *The Noose,* Jack Mulhall's *Lady Be Good,* etc.), then roles such as "an aviator" in *A Night at the Opera.*

EATON, MARY *(1948)* 47 ——A Broadway beauty, she starred in silents (*Broadway After*

Dark, His Children's Children) and an early talkie, *Glorifying the American Girl;* also was in *The Cocoanuts.*

EBURNE, MAUDE *(1960)* 85 ——Sharp-tongued, sniffy old gal; taught Laughton a thing or two about the West in *Ruggles of Red Gap;* in all six of Jean Hersholt's "Dr. Christian" pix as his housekeeper, Mrs. Hastings; similar duties in *Valiant Is the Word for Carrie, The First Year, Sabotage, To Be or Not to Be,* dozens more.

ECCLES, JANE *(1966)* 70 ——English support; in Burton's *Look Back in Anger.*

ECKERLEIN, JOHN E. *(1926)* 42 ——Minor role in Marion Davies' *Little Old New York.*

ECKHARDT, OLIVER J. *(1952)* 79 ——Supported Constance Binney in *Sporting Life;* also in *The Cavalier, The Last Trail,* etc.

EDDY, DOROTHY *(1959)* 52 ——Of the famous singing Eddy Sisters; in occasional pix.

EDDY, NELSON *(1967)* 65 ——Stolid blond baritone who, with Jeanette MacDonald, made movie musical history in the '30s; *Naughty Marietta, Rose Marie, Maytime, Sweethearts,* etc., were catnip to the middle-aged matrons who were his devoted audience; worked with other sopranos too: Susannah Foster *(The Phantom of the Opera),* Ilona Massey *(Balalaika),* Rise Stevens *(The Chocolate Soldier),* but the magic wasn't there.

EDESON, ROBERT *(1931)* 62 ——Big man, big silent star; first was Winifred Kingston's unscrupulous lawyer-lover in 1914's *Where the Trail Divides;* then was top-billed in many: *The Light That Failed* ('16), *How Molly Made Good, Extravagance,* etc.; from '23, in addition to others, he played major character roles in numerous DeMille pix; *The Ten Commandments, Feet of Clay, The Golden Bed, The Volga Boatman* (father of the Princess, leading lady Elinor Fair), *The King of Kings* (Matthew the Apostle), and *Dynamite;* the title of his last, in 1931, was significant: *Aloha.*

EDGAR-BRUCE, TONI *(1966)* 73 ——British supporting actress; in *The Citadel, The Private Life of Henry VIII, Captain Bill,* etc.

EDLER, CHARLES *(1942)* 65 ——Supporting roles in silents: *The Sign of the Rose, That Girl Montana,* and *The Magnificent Brute,* etc.

EDWARDS, ALAN *(1954)* 61 ——Minor roles in silents, then support in many talkies: Gish's *The White Sister, If You Could Only Cook, Junior Miss, Mr. District Attorney,* etc.

EDWARDS, CLIFF *(1971)* 76 ——Ever-smiling "Ukelele Ike"; in dozens of talkies: *George White's Scandals, What Price Glory?, Saratoga, Maisie,* etc.: Charles Starrett's sidekick, Harmony, in many Westerns; voice of Jiminy Cricket ("When You Wish Upon a Star") in *Pinocchio.*

EDWARDS, EDNA PARK *(1967)* 72 ——Once Tom Mix's leading lady in silents.

EDWARDS, ELEANOR *(1968)* 86 ——Actress-wife of Snitz Edwards; was in silents.

EDWARDS, GUS *(1945)* 48 ——Vaudeville star internationally famous for his school-kids act; onscreen in *The Hollywood Revue of 1929* and *Mr. Broadway,* plus shorts; Crosby portrayed him in *The Star Maker.*

EDWARDS, JAMES *(1970)* 48 ——First black to crash through to fame in post-WW II era, in *Home of the Brave;* also strong in *The Steel Helmet, The Set-Up, Bright Victory, The Joe Louis Story, Anna Lucasta,* etc., in which he mostly played sensitive, intelligent, potentially explosive men; last in a most minor role (George C. Scott's aide) in *Patton.*

EDWARDS, MATTIE *(1944)* 58 ——Character in Jan Kiepura's *Give Us This Night.*

EDWARDS, NEELY *(1965)* 75 ——Gray-haired support in many silents *(The Princess on Broadway, Brewster's Millions, The Little Clown)* and talkies *(Dynamite, Gold Diggers of Broadway,* etc.).

EDWARDS, SARAH *(1955)* 72 ——Small, gray character with pince-nez; sometimes a grandmother *(It's a Wonderful Life),* but more often a crabbed spinster; in *The Dark Angel, Meet John Doe, Strike Up the Band, The Bishop's Wife, It's Love I'm After,* others.

EDWARDS, SNITZ *(1937)* 75 ——Fairbanks' large-nosed Evil Associate in *The Thief of Bagdad;* Florine Papillon in Chaney's *The Phantom of the Opera;* in *The Red Mill, Inez From Hollywood, College,* more.

EDWARDS, TED *(1945)* 62 ——A Keystone Kop; in *Fires of Youth,* other silents.

EDWARDS, VIRGINIA *(1964)* 70s ——Minor character (Emma Abbott) in Robinson's *Silver Dollar.*

EGGENTON, JOSEPH *(1946)* 75 ——Character in Loretta Young's *The Doctor Takes a Wife* (elderly doctor) and Kay Kyser's *You'll Find Out.*

EKMAN, GOESTA *(1938)* 50 ——Swedish actor; costarred (title role) with Emil Jannings in Murnau's *Faust* ('26); others.

ELDREDGE, JOHN *(1961)* 56 ——Busy secondary leading man, with high forehead and moustache, at Warners in the '30s: *Flirtation Walk, The Man With Two Faces, Dangerous, The Woman in Red*, etc.; later in B's *(The Mad Doctor at Market Street, Bermuda Mystery)*, serials *(Lost City of the Jungle*, heroine's father), and on TV (father in *Meet Corliss Archer)*.

ELDRIDGE, CHARLES *(1922)* 68 ——Grandfather in Constance Binney's *Sporting Life;* other silents: *Made in Heaven, Hearts and Spurs*, etc.

ELLINGFORD, WILLIAM *(1936)* 62 ——Character in one Universal silent, *Hands Off* ('27).

ELLINGTON, DUKE *(1974)* 75 ——Jazz great; composer ("Mood Indigo" and 5,000 more); pianist (unforgettable at the keyboard on "Take the 'A' Train"), band leader (joyous, finger-snapping); onscreen with his great orchestra in *The Hit Parade* ('37), *Reveille With Beverly.*

ELLINGWOOD, HELMERT *(1971)* 64 —— Supporting roles.

ELLIOT, CASS *(1974)* 33 ——Plump, mellow pop songstress; lead voice in The Mamas and the Papas group; played Witch Hazel in Universal's *Pufnstuf.*

ELLIOTT, DICK *(1961)* 75 ——Casting directors called him (1934–58) when they needed a small, full-bellied blowhard—of Texas or any variety; mile-a-minute patter and roof-raising laughter were his trademarks; politicians (Carl Cook in *Mr. Smith Goes to Washington),* judges *(Christmas in Connecticut),* Texas oilmen and ranchers *(Annie Oakley, Fort Defiance*, etc.), Santa Claus (TV shows of Skelton, Benny, etc.)

ELLIOTT, GERTRUDE *(1950)* 76 ——Starred as Ophelia opposite husband J. Forbes-Robertson in 1915's *Hamlet.*

ELLIOTT, GORDON *(1965)* 61 ——See "Wild Bill" Elliott.

ELLIOTT, LILLIAN *(1959)* 84 ——Character actress in silents and talkies who often played snobs (the mother who didn't want Crawford to marry her Wall Street broker-son, Alan Forrest, in *Old Clothes);* other silents: *Sally, Irene and Mary; The Chorus Lady; One Glorious Night*, etc.; talkies: *Polly of the Circus, The Man I Killed, Her Wedding Night*, others.

ELLIOTT, MAXINE *(1940)* 67 ——Dramatic, aristocratically beautiful Broadway actress who starred, a bit too late at 44, for Goldwyn in *The Fighting Odds* ('17); dropped out after 1919's *The Eternal Magdalene* to return to the stage.

ELLIOTT, ROBERT *(1951)* ——Supporting player.

ELLIOTT, ROBERT *(1963)* 84 ——Starred (as the American diplomat who jilted the Chinese viceroy's daughter) in 1918's *For the Freedom of the East;* other silents; *A Virgin Paradise, Checkers, Man Wife*, many more; support in numerous talkies: *Gone With the Wind* (Rhett Butler's Yankee Major-jailer), *Trade Winds, The Roaring Twenties* (police officer), *I Stole a Million*, etc.

ELLIOTT, "WILD BILL" *(1965)* 61 ——As Gordon Elliott, after having been a silents dress extra, he was a popular light lead between 1927's *The Private Life of Helen of Troy* and '38's *The Devil's Party;* in many: *The Case of the Velvet Claws, Polo Joe*, etc.; after starring in a 1938 serial, *The Great Adventures of Wild Bill Hickok*, became Bill Elliott in the following year's *Overland with Kit Carson*, and thereafter "Wild Bill"; as star of dozens of Republic Westerns *(In Old Sacramento*, etc.) was among the Top Ten Cowboy Money-makers each year from '40 to '54.

ELLIOTT, WILLIAM *(1932)* 46 ——Dark-haired leading man who was with Ethel Clayton in *The Fortune Hunter* (Lubin: '14); starred for Famous Players after that.

ELLIS, DIANE *(1930)* 20 ——Delectable blonde; co-femme lead (Lombard was the other) in *High Voltage;* opposite George O'-Brien in *Is Zat So?;* also in *Happiness Ahead, Chain Lightning, Laughter*, etc.

ELLIS, EDWARD *(1952)* 79 ——Fine-faced oldster and a magnificent actor; had a chance to shine as the star (the old horse-and-buggy doctor) in Garson Kanin's *A Man to Remember* ('38); superb too in *Fury* (sheriff beaten by lynch mob after jailee Tracy), *I Am a Fugitive from a Chain Gang* (old prisoner Bomber Wells), *Winterset* (as the mentally overwrought Judge Gaunt), and dozens more through 1942's *The Omaha Trail.*

ELLIS, EVELYN *(1958)* 64 ——Eleanor Parker's dignified black maid in *Interrupted Melody;* also in *The Joe Louis Story, The Lady from Shanghai.*

ELLIS, FRANK *(1969)* 72 ——Sour-faced, checker-shirted outlaw in scores of B Westerns *(Law of the Saddle, Riders of the Whistling Skull*, etc.).

ELLIS, PATRICIA *(1970)* 54 ——Pretty-as-a-picture blonde leading lady at Warners in the '30s; among the 42 pix in her eight-year (1932–39) career: *Elmer the Great, Three on a Match, The Case of the Lucky Legs, The Circus Clown, The King's Vacation, Boulder Dam.*

ELLIS, ROBERT *(1935)* 40 ——Society-type leading man with cleft chin, extremely popular in silents: *Upstairs and Down, The Woman Who Fooled Herself, Dark Secrets, Louisiana,* many others; last in 1934's *The Girl of the Limberlost.*

ELLIS, ROBERT *(1973)* 40 ——Juvenile, then GI roles; Ann Sothern's vaudeville song-and-dance youngster in *April Showers;* then in *The Green Promise, Retreat Hell!, The McConnell Story, Gidget;* billed Bobby Ellis as a child.

ELLSLER, EFFIE *(1942)* 87 ——Edward G. Robinson's kidnapped Aunt Agatha in *The Whole Town's Talking;* many more: *The Front Page* ('31; mother of leading lady Mary Brian), *Song O' My Heart, Black Fury,* etc.; often played a landlady.

ELMAN, ZIGGY *(1968)* 54 ——Famous bandleader; in *The Benny Goodman Story.*

ELMER, BILLY *(1945)* 74 ——Rugged, moustachioed cowpoke in Dustin Farnum's *The Virginian* ('14), his first; other silents: *The Road Demon, The Whipping Boss, Pawned,* etc.

ELTINGE, JULIAN *(1940)* 58 ——Famed female impersonator; star of many silents: *Widows Might, Madame Behave, How Molly Made Good, The Clever Mrs. Carfax,* etc.

ELVIDGE, JUNE *(1965)* 72 ——Lovely brunette star of silents; in *La Boheme* (with Alice Brady in '16), *Fine Feathers, The Man Who Saw Tomorrow, Beauty's Worth, Painted People, Forsaking All Others,* etc.; retired from the screen in '24.

EMERICK, BESSE *(1939)* 64 ——Support in silents: *Welcome to Our City, The Black Stork,* others.

EMERSON, HOPE *(1960)* 62 ——Hatchet-faced, oversized meanie; prison matron in *Caged* (nominated for Best Supporting Actress); in *House of Strangers, Cry of the City, Westward the Women, Thieves' Highway,* etc.; could be funny (circus strong woman in *Adam's Rib* who hoists Spencer Tracy to prove her prowess); was a pussycat in later pix and on TV's *Peter Gunn* as the nightclub owner.

EMERSON, JOHN *(1956)* 81 ——Flamboyant actor *(Bachelor's Romance, The Flying Torpedo,* Harold Lockwood's *The Conspiracy:* all 1914–16), director (Pickford's *Less Than the Dust,* Fairbanks' *His Picture in the Papers,* of the Talmadges), writer, and producer; husband of writer Anita Loos; less than a hero in her book *Kiss Hollywood Goodbye.*

EMERTON, ROY *(1944)* 52 ——Long-nosed English villain; in 1935's *Lorna Doone* (Carver), *Drums, Dr. Syn, Henry V* (Lt. Bardolph), etc.

EMERY, GILBERT *(1945)* 70 ——Character actor of distinguished mien; *The House of Rothschild* (Prime Minister), *The Life of Emile Zola* (Minister of War), *Magnificent Obsession, A Woman's Face* (Associate Judge), *That Hamilton Woman* (Lord Spenser), *Dracula's Daughter,* and scores more between '21 and '45.

EMERY, JOHN *(1964)* 59 ——John Barrymore look-alike once married to Bankhead; the supersmooth Broadway producer who tries to beat GI Ronald Reagan's time with Eleanor Parker in *The Voice of the Turtle;* oily in *The Woman in White, The Corsican Brothers, Here Comes Mr. Jordan, Spellbound, The Spanish Main,* more.

EMERY, POLLY *(1958)* 83 ——Support in Anna Neagle's *Peg of Old Drury.*

EMMETT, CATHERINE *(1960)* 78 ——Character (Countess de Linieres) in *Orphans of the Storm;* also *Hole in the Wall, Paying the Piper.*

EMMETT, FERN *(1946)* 50 ——Thin-faced and in grandma specs she almost always played country women: *Trail of the Lonesome Pine* ('36), *Made for Each Other* (farmer's wife), *Scattergood Baines, A Song to Remember* (Madame Lambert, a most unusual casting for her), etc.

EMMONS, LOUISE *(1935)* 82 ——Character in silents from the earliest; last in 1931's *Heaven on Earth.*

EMPEY, GUY *(1963)* 79 ——Stocky, handsome young man who starred as the soldier-hero in 1918's *Over the Top,* which he also directed, basing it on his best-selling book about his experiences as an American fighting in the British Army in the Great War; battle scars seen on-screen were authentic; also starred in *Millionaire for a Day* and *The Undercurrent;* left the screen, wrote books and pulp fiction; died—appropriately—in a veterans' hospital, leaving his medals to the men in the ward.

ENGEL, ALEXANDER *(1968)* 62 ——German star of many European films; character in Universal's *A Time to Love and a Time to Die* ('58), his only American film.

ENGEL, MARIE *(1971)* 69 ——Actress-widow of character actor Tom Dugan.

ENGLE, BILLY *(1966)* 77 ——Pint-sized Christie and Hal Roach comic; in silents (*The Cat and the Canary, Red Hot Leather*, etc.), talkies (*It's a Gift, Big Broadcast of 1936, Wistful Widow of Wagon Gap*), and shorts.

ENGLISCH, LUCIE *(1956)* 68 ——German star; in *Our Little Wife, My Heart Belongs to Thee*, etc.

ENNIS, SKINNAY *(1963)* 56 ——Bob Hope's longtime bandleader; in *College Swing*.

ENRIGHT, FLORENCE *(1961)* 70s ——Support in Crawford's first, *Possessed*, ('31) Sidney's *Street Scene*, Fields' *Six of a Kind*, etc.; later a famous Hollywood drama coach.

ENTWISTLE, HAROLD *(1944)* 78 ——English; character (Capt. Colpoys) in Gable's *Mutiny on the Bounty*; in *Our Betters* (butler); *Vanessa, Her Love Story; Paris in Spring*, etc.

ENTWISTLE, PEG *(1932)* 24 ——Blonde English actress now considered camp for having leapt to her death from the thirteenth letter of the "Hollywoodland" sign above the movie capital—after playing a secondary role in Selznick's *Thirteen Women*; no routine "starlet," she had that year played leads in two Broadway plays: *Alice Sit-By-The Fire* and *Getting Married*.

ERICKSON, KNUTE *(1946)* 74 ——Swedish-born character; in *The Bitter Tea of General Yen*, Gary Cooper's *The Spoilers* (ship captain), *Waterfront*, other talkies, plus silents (*Gasoline Gus, Johnny Get Your Hair Cut*, etc.).

ERMELLI, CLAUDIO *(1964)* 72 ——Italian supporting actor in American pix made in Italy: *Roman Holiday* (Giovanni), *It Started in Naples, A Farewell to Arms* ('57).

ERROL, LEON *(1951)* 70 ——Sly little baldie who gave big laughs—and headaches to stars unable to compete with his scene-stealing; grand as Uncle Matt in all the "Mexican Spitfire" comedies, in which he often also played bumbling, bowlegged, featherbrained Lord Epping, and in one (*Mexican Spitfire*) had a slapstick bonanza as Uncle Matt, Lord Epping, and Uncle Matt *pretending* to be Lord Epping; among his other 50 pix (besides all those two-reelers): *Her Majesty Love, Never Give a Sucker an Even Break, The Captain Hates the Sea*, and *Joe Palooka, Champ*.

ERSKINE, WALLACE *(1943)* 80 ——Supported Alfred Lunt in *The Ragged Edge* ('23); other silents.

ERWIN, JUNE *(1965)* 47 ——In "Our Gang" in the '20s.

ERWIN, MADGE *(1967)* ——Supporting actress.

ERWIN, STUART *(1967)* 64 ——Folksy character star; had principal billing in many pix of the '30s: *Make Me a Star* (remake of *Merton of the Movies* in which he was the hayseed Merton who becomes a movie headliner), *Palooka* (was Joe), *Up Pops the Devil*, etc.; then played stars' brothers (Garland's in *Pigskin Parade*, receiving an Oscar nomination as Best Support), buddies (McCrea's in *Three Blind Mice*, Gable's in *After Office Hours*, Cagney's in *The Bride Came C.O.D.*), amiable smalltowners (milkman Howie Newsome in *Our Town*); finally starred on TV, with his family, in the long-run *Stu Erwin Show*.

ESMOND, ANNIE *(1945)* 71 ——Support in many British talkies: *The Iron Duke, Bulldog Drummond at Bay, Men of Tomorrow, Thunder in the City, Reserved for Ladies*.

ESSEN, VIOLA ——The lovely ballerina who starred in *The Spectre of the Rose;* later was married to and divorced from Gabriel Dell; year of death unreported.

ESSLER, FRED *(1973)* 77 ——Played men of great distinction in *The Unsinkable Molly Brown* (Baron von Ettenberg), *Where Do We Go from Here?* (Dutch Councilman), *Saratoga Trunk* (Monsieur Begue), many others.

ESTELITA *(1966)* 50 ——Tiny, perfect-figured, musical Mexican sexpot, easily the most luscious girl ever starred by Republic; there a decade, often top-billed (*Belle of Old Mexico*, etc.), or with the studio's singing cowboy stars; was in many: *The Gay Ranchero, On the Spanish Trail*, etc.; was sometimes billed under her full name, Estelita Rodriguez.

ETHIER, ALPHONSE *(1943)* 67 ——Support in Warner Baxter's *In Old Arizona* (sheriff), *The Crusades* (priest), Temple's *Rebecca of Sunnybrook Farm*, etc.; he had starred in 1910's *Thelma*, then had secondary roles in many silents: *Contraband, The Lone Wolf Returns, The Alaskan*, etc.

EVANS, BRANDON *(1958)* 60s ——Top support in *The Emperor Jones;* was the husband of character actress Elizabeth Risdon.

EVANS, CECILIA *(1960)* 58 ——Famed as "The Girl With the $100,000 Legs," she was featured in silents: *The Goose Hangs High, Whispering Wires, Worldly Goods*, others.

EVANS, CHARLES E. *(1945)* 88 ——Name any Arliss pic, he was in it: *Disraeli* (Potter), *The Man Who Played God* (doctor), *The King's Vacation, The House of Rothschild* (Nesselrode), *The Working Man, Cardinal Richelieu*.

EVANS, DOUGLAS *(1968)* 64 ——Support in many Jerry Lewis pix: *The Errand Boy, The Birds and the Bees, The Family Jewels*, etc.; in over 90 other movies including many Westerns, most often as distinguished-looking townsman or heroine's rancher-father: *South Pacific Trail, The Golden Stallion*, etc.

EVANS, EDITH *(1962)* 68 ——Featured in silents; not the English character actress.

EVANS, EVAN S. *(1954)* 52 ——One of the handsome sons (Gwilym) in *How Green Was My Valley*, the only American film for this English actor.

EVANS, HELENA PHILLIPS *(1955)* 80 —— Support in many: *Design for Living* (Mrs. Egelbauer), *My Favorite Brunette, My Bill, Elmer and Elsie*, etc., including two Arliss pix (*Voltaire, The King's Vacation*) with husband Chares E. Evans; sometimes billed Helena Evans or Helena Phillips.

EVANS, HERBERT *(1952)* 69 ——Tall, imposing English character; in Peck's *The Great Sinner*, Turner's *The Prodigal, Pardon My Past, Bringing Up Father, The Corn Is Green*, etc.

EVANS, JACK *(1950)* 57 ——Featured in the silent *The Hidden Woman*.

EVANS, NANCY *(1963)* 50s ——Played comedy characters: Baby Hawks in Stanwyck's *My Reputation*, the short-termed Irish cook in *Life With Father*.

EVANS, REX *(1969)* 66 ——You would find this large, worldly looking Englishman around Hollywood's best tables as either a butler (Hepburn's in *The Philadelphia Story*, fearful that reporter Stewart might pilfer an ashtray) or distinguished guest; in many from '33: *The Thin Man Goes Home, The Shanghai Gesture*, Garland's *A Star Is Born* (emcee at the theater benefit), *Zaza*, etc.

EVELYN, JUDITH *(1967)* 54 ——Broadway star in hypertense roles (*Angel Street*), who had similar parts onscreen: *Rear Window* (Miss Lonely Hearts), *The Brothers Karamazov, Giant, Female on the Beach, Hilda Crane*, others.

EVEREST, BARBARA *(1968)* 77 ——Heavyset, fine English character who was in ten Hollywood pix during WW II years; except for *Mission to Moscow* (wife of Oscar Homolka as Litvinov), was nearly always cast as a housekeeper (*Jane Eyre, Gaslight, The Uninvited, The Valley of Decision*); returned to England and was active for years (*Tony Draws a Horse, Frieda*, others).

EVERTON, PAUL *(1948)* 79 ——After supporting King Baggot in the 1916 serial *The Eagle's Eye*, was in many silents: *That Royle Girl, The Conquest of Canaan, Cappy Ricks*, etc.; talkies: *Topper Takes a Trip* (Defender), *Merrily We Live* (Senator), *The Great Man Votes, Leave Her to Heaven* (Judge), others.

EYTHE, WILLIAM *(1957)* 38 ——20th Century-Fox star in the Tyrone Power mold, popular 1943–46; Bankhead's dashing Russian soldier-lover in *A Royal Scandal*, Linda Darnell's beau in *Centennial Summer*, Anne Baxter's GI guy in *The Eve of St. Mark* (perhaps his most memorable performance); also starred in *A Wing and a Prayer, The House on 92nd Street*, others.

F

FABER, LESLIE *(1929)* 50 ——Supporting player in *White Cargo*, made in England.

FABRE, SATURNIN *(1961)* 77 ——French character actor; in *Pepe le Moko, Holiday for Henrietta*, others.

FABRIZI, MARIO *(1963)* 38 ——Featured in English pix: *On the Beat, Postman's Knock*.

FADDEN, GENEVIEVE *(1959)* 60s ——Actress-wife of character actor Tom Fadden.

FAHEY, MYRNA *(1973)* 34 ——All American girl-type brunette beauty; featured at 20th Century-Fox in the '60s in *The Story on Page One, The House of Usher* (femme lead); had the Elizabeth Taylor role on TV in the series *Father of the Bride*.

FAHRNEY, "MADCAP" MERRY *(1974)* 64 ——Headline "cafe society" girl; one small role, in DeMille's *Cleopatra*.

FAHRNEY, MILTON *(1941)* 70 ——Support in

silents: *Chasing Trouble, Yankee Speed, In the First Degree*, etc.

FAIN, JOHN *(1970)* 54 ——Support in teeny-bopper "Beach" pix of the '60s.

FAIR, ELINOR *(1957)* 50s ——Stunningly beautiful brunette DeMille starred as the Russian Princess in *The Volga Boatman* ('26) opposite William Boyd, whom she subsequently married; earlier she had been featured in Universal's *Driven* and Goodman Co.'s *Has the World Gone Mad!*; later in the '20s in *The Yankee Clipper* and *Let 'Er Go, Gallegher*; in the '30s mostly famous for marrying the same man three times, an aviator.

FAIRBANKS, DOUGLAS *(1939)* 56 ——Movies' first (and genuinely unforgettable) great swashbuckler; his derring-do, gaiety of smile, and perfect physique made him a prince with moviegoers everywhere; some of his best: *Robin Hood; The Thief of Bagdad; The Black Pirate; Don Q. Son of Zorro; The Three Musketeers; The Mark of Zorro*; says one critic, Edward Wagenknecht: "His feeling for rhythm and movement was flawless, and he was ideally adapted to the film medium. . . . He was the Yankee Doodle Boy whom George M. Cohan had put on the stage when the eagle screamed more lightheartedly than he does today, but he performed on a larger stage than was ever available to Cohan"; says Mary Pickford, his wife 1920–35: "He was a little boy who never grew up."

FAIRBROTHER, SIDNEY *(1941)* 68 ——British character; Gagool in Sir Cedric Hardwicke's *King Solomon's Mines* ('37); many British silents (*Nell Gwyn, Iron Justice*, etc.) and talkies (*Chu Chin Chow, Dreaming Lips*, others).

FAIRE, VIRGINIA BROWN *(1948)* 48 —— Lovely, dark-haired young star in many silents: with Guy Bates Post in *Omar the Tentmaker*, Weber and Fields in *Friendly Enemies*, Richard Arlen in *Vengeance of the Deep*, etc.; ended her career in B Westerns and was John Wayne's leading lady in her last, a 1934 Monogram pic, *West of the Divide*.

FAIRFAX, JAMES *(1961)* 64 ——English character; in *Mrs. Mike, Fortunes of Captain Blood, White Goddess*, etc.

FAIRMAN, AUSTIN *(1964)* 72 ——English support in John Barrymore's *Bulldog Drummond's Peril* ('38), *Her Hired Husband*, etc.

FALCONETTI *(1946)* 45 ——French stage actress (full name: Marie Falconetti) who gave one of the screen's great performances as the star of Dreyer's *The Passion of Jeanne d'Arc*, her one and only film.

FALCONI, ARTURO *(1934)* ——Featured in Italy's *La Vecchia Signora*, etc.

FALLON, CHARLES *(1936)* 51 ——Belgian character; in *The Man Who Broke the Bank at Monte Carlo* and Margaret Sullavan's *Next Time We Love*.

FANNING, FRANK *(1934)* 53 ——Support in Cesar Romero's *Dance Hall*, after a few silents.

FAREBROTHER, VIOLET *(1969)* 81 —— Gray, aristocratic, heavy-faced English character; costar of *Mr. Cohen Takes a Walk* ('36); in *Mystery at the Villa Rose, The Woman for Joe, Man of the Moment*, many more British pix.

FARLEY, JAMES *(1947)* 65 ——Versatile character in dozens of silents and talkies: *Dynamite* (police officer), the silent *King of Kings* (executioner), *The Devil and Daniel Webster, Captain January* (sheriff), *This Gun for Hire*, countless Westerns.

FARMER, FRANCES *(1970)* 56 ——Troubled, exceptionally beautiful and talented blonde star of the '30s and early '40s; highest critical praise in Goldwyn's *Come and Get It* (dual role: saloon singer in the Northwest and her society belle daughter); also in *Ebb Tide, The Toast of the Town, Rhythm on the Range, South of Pago-Pago, Flowing Gold*, etc.; declared insane, was seven years in a Washington State asylum; comeback attempts in the '50s came to little— on TV (folksinger on one *Ed Sullivan Show*), the stage (*The Chalk Garden* in stock), in movies (a mother role in a 1958 B, *The Party Crashers*, at Paramount, where once it had been expected she would become their greatest star).

FARNUM, DUSTIN *(1929)* 55 ——Muscular, handsome man who starred in his first picture (DeMille's too), 1914's *The Squaw Man*, setting the course for his great career in Westerns and action pix; offered one-fourth of the De Mille company to do the role, or $250 a week, he opted for the cash; one critic, noting Farnum's "masterly characterization" in *The Squaw Man*, added: "His performance is so manly, so apparently devoid of stale artifice, that I could only regret that he was not representing a typical American"; was splendid too in *The Virginian* ('14), *The Iron Strain, Light of the Western Stars, The Corsican Brothers*, etc.; brother of William.

FARNUM, FRANKLYN *(1961)* 83 ——No relation to Dustin or William; star of many silent Westerns including the 1920 serial *Vanishing*

Trails (Silent Joe); played henchmen in dozens of B Westerns (*Powdersmoke Range*, *The Texas Bad Man*, etc.); acted in one talkie serial, *The Clutching Hand*, with William Farnum, but was billed far below him.

FARNUM, WILLIAM *(1953)* 76 ——Legendary Westerns *(The Painted Desert, Kit Carson)*, brother Dustin; as star of 1914's *The Spoilers* he participated in a fight, with Tom Santschi, that's firmly entrenched in screen folklore; silents that solidified his fame: *A Man of Sorrow*, *A Tale of Two Cities, If I Were King, The Conqueror, The Plunderer, Les Miserables, The Nigger, The Heart of a Lion*, etc.; in talkies, as a top character actor, was in dozens of A-grade Westerns *(The Painted Desert, Kit Carson)*, B's *(Santa Fe Stampede, The Silver Bullet*, etc.), and big-budget pix: DeMille's *Cleopatra* and *The Crusades* (Duke of Burgundy), *Maid of Salem* (Crown Justice Sewall), *Cheers for Miss Bishop*, more; one of his last ('52) was a Western, Gable's *Lone Star*.

FARQUHARSON, ROBERT *(1966)* 85 ——Support in English pix: *The Man They Couldn't Arrest*, others.

FARR, PATRICIA *(1948)* 32 ——Femme lead in the 1934 serial *Tailspin Tommy*; smaller roles in *Mr. and Mrs. Smith, I Am Suzanne, All American Sweetheart*, etc.

FARRAR, GERALDINE *(1967)* 85 ——Most famous opera prima donna of her time and the first to enter movies; in 14 pix in six years (1915-21), she was as great a screen star—without music, of course—as she had been in opera; some of her best: *The World and Its Woman, The Woman and the Puppet, The Stronger Vow, Joan the Woman* (Joan of Arc), *The Woman God Forgot*.

FARRAR, GWEN *(1944)* 45 ——Was in Imperial's *She Shall Have Music* ('42).

FARRELL, GLENDA *(1971)* 66 ——No other blonde star ever dished out the wisecracks in such a "good Joe" tough way as she, especially in all those "Torchy Blane" pix at Warners; earlier she had been simply gangland-tough, in *I Am a Fugitive from a Chain Gang, Little Caesar*, etc.; grand with the put-down in many: *Hi, Nellie, Lady for a Day, Gold Diggers of 1935, Go Into Your Dance*, etc.; infrequently onscreen in the '50s and '60s, she had a character role in an Elvis Presley pic (*Kissin' Cousins*), was Kim Novak's mother in *Middle of the Night*, and, last, supported Tippi Hedren in *Tiger by the Tail* ('69); ended her career costarring on Broadway, as Julie Harris' sophisticated, wisecracking mom, in *Forty Carats*.

FARRELL, JOHN W. *(1953)* 68 ——Character (policeman) in *Portrait of Jennie*.

FARRELL, SKIP *(1962)* 42 ——Actor-singer; in Dean Martin's *The Girl Hunters*.

FARRELL, VESSIE *(1935)* 45 ——Support in one Monogram pic, *The Healer* ('35), starring Ralph Bellamy.

FARRINGTON, ADELE *(1936)* 69 ——Starred with husband Hobart Bosworth in *The Country Mouse* ('14); in many other silents: *Bobbed Hair, Black Beauty, Little Wildcat*, etc.

FARRINGTON, FRANK *(1924)* 60 ——Support in serials *(The Million Dollar Mystery, Zudora: The Twenty Million Dollar Mystery)* and such features as *The Courtship of Myles Standish*.

FAUST, HAZEL LEE *(1973)* 63 ——Was an MGM contract actress for years; minor roles.

FAUST, MARTIN *(1943)* 57 ——Star of 1910's *A Winter's Tale*; support in silents of the '20s: Davies' *Yolanda* (Count Galli), *Under the Red Robe, Chain Lightning*, etc.; in the last of his few talkies, a minor role in *Ali Baba and the Forty Thieves*.

FAVERSHAM, WILLIAM *(1940)* 72 ——Dark, handsome star who, in 1915, was second only to Francis X. Bushman as Metro's biggest box-office attraction; some of his great silent hits: *The Sin That Was His, The Silver King, The Man Who Lost Himself*; support in a few talkies: *Becky Sharp* (as the Duke of Wellington), *Mystery Woman, Lady by Choice*, etc.

FAWCETT, GEORGE *(1939)* 79 ——One of the silent screen's most admirable character stars; Griffith used him advantageously in many, often as Robert Harron's father (in *A Romance of Happy Valley, The Greatest Question, The Girl Who Stayed at Home*); in other Griffith pix: *Intolerance* (Babylonian Judge), *Hearts of the World* (village carpenter), *The Great Love* (Lillian Gish's father), *True Heart Susie* (The Stranger), *Scarlet Days* (sheriff), etc.; dozens more for many directors; in 25 early talkies, often being seen as a statesman or other dignitary: *Lady of the Pavements, Men Are Like That, Once a Gentleman*, etc.

FAWCETT, MRS. GEORGE *(1945)* 64 —— Billed under her married name, she (alongside her husband) supported Chevalier in *Innocents of Paris*; also acted under the name Percy Haswell.

FAWCETT, WILLIAM *(1974)* 80 —— Best known as Pete, the sunken-cheeked costar of the long-running TV series *Fury*, who so humorously mangled the English language; entered movies in his 50s, after other careers, and was in dozens of B Westerns (*Ride, Ryder, Ride; The Tioga Kid*, etc.) and a few A's (*Springfield Rifle*, as an old cavalry corporal, *Seminole Uprising*, etc.).

FAY, FRANK *(1961)* 63 ——Freckled Irishman whose charm (cloaking a certain irascibility) never worked as powerfully onscreen as on the stage *(Harvey)*; among his pix: *Under a Texas Moon, Bright Lights, The Matrimonial Bed, They Knew What They Wanted, Nothing Sacred*; was once married to Barbara Stanwyck.

FAY, W. G. *(1947)* 74 ——Fine as the old Irish priest who tried to save James Mason in *Odd Man Out*; also in *Storm in a Teacup, The Patient Vanishes*, etc.

FAYE, JULIA *(1966)* 70 ——In DeMille's 1923 *Ten Commandments*—when she was 27—she was one of his top-billed stars, The Wife of Pharaoh; in his '56 version—when she was 60—she was far down the cast list, as Elixsheba; in between (and besides having been in six of his very earliest), in roles major—as Martha in *The King of Kings* ('27)—and minor, she appeared in more than a dozen DeMille epics; some of them: *Feet of Clay, Triumph, The Golden Bed, Union Pacific, Northwest Mounted Police*; her last was a bit in a 1958 remake (by Anthony Quinn) of *The Buccaneer*, one DeMille original in which she did not appear.

FAYLAUER, ADOLPH *(1961)* 74 ——In Excellent Pictures' *The Dream Melody* ('29).

FAZENDA, LOUISE *(1962)* 67 ——The silent screen's "country bumpkin" *par excellence*; she and Polly Moran were Sennett's only real comedienne stars; no one who saw her in *Down on the Farm* (or others like it) will ever forget her—in her checkered calico, with her spitcurl and those four tight pigtails flying to the wind; among her many: *The Summer Girls, Main Street, Bombs and Brides, Maggie's First False Step, Maid Mad, Her Fame and Shame*; supporting roles in the '30s—some antic, some straight; married producer Hal Wallis and, after playing a house servant in his production of *The Old Maid*, retired; her philanthropies in later years are legendary.

FEALY, MAUDE *(1971)* 90 ——A dark, handsome-faced star of Broadway, she was a 1915 Thanhauser Co. headliner, starring in *Little Dorrit, King Rene's Daughter*, and other silents for several years; in talkies she was a character actress, in *Laugh and Get Rich* and various "also in the cast" bits in DeMille pix: *The Buc-*

caneer ('38), *Union Pacific, The Ten Commandments*.

FEILER, HERTA *(1970)* 54 ——German leading lady; in *Men Are That Way*, others.

FELDARY, ERIC *(1968)* 48 ——Handsome young Loyalist guerrilla (Andres) in *For Whom the Bell Tolls*; Rosemary DeCamp's son (Josef Kurz) in *Hold Back the Dawn*; in *The Master Race* (Altmeter), *Hostages, Sealed Cargo*, etc.

FELDMAN, ANDREA *(1972)* 20s ——In Andy Warhol's skin flicks.

FELDMAN, EDYTHE *(1971)* 58 ——Minor support in *Midnight Cowboy*.

FELDMAN, GLADYS *(1974)* 82 ——One of Ziegfeld's most famous brunette Girls, she vamped Glenn Hunter in 1924's *West of the Water Tower*, and had another small role in his *Merton of the Movies*.

FELIX, GEORGE *(1949)* 83 ——Support in the 1916 silent *Haystacks and Steeples*.

FELLOWES, ROCKLIFFE *(1950)* 64 —— Ruggedly handsome, curly-haired star often found (onscreen) with gun in hand; costarred with Clara Kimball Young in his first, *The Easiest Way* ('17), with Crawford in *The Understanding Heart*; starred in *Trifling with Honor* (ex-crook who becomes a star baseball player), and a score more silents; support in *20,000 Years in Sing Sing, Ladies of the Big House*, and 15 other talkies to 1934.

FELTON, HAPPY *(1964)* 56 ——Big, hearty guy who had humorous roles in *Whistling in Brooklyn, Swing Shift Maisie*; in vaudeville and on radio; became an executive with Fawcett Publishing Co. in New York.

FELTON, VERNA *(1966)* 76 ——Hearty old charmer with gray upswept, wavy hairdo; most famous as Spring Byington's buddy, Hilda, in TV's *December Bride*; most memorable for that poignant scene in *Picnic* as she and Betty Field, in a park swing at dusk near the end of the annual town picnic, discuss life; in many: *Buccaneer's Girl, If I Had My Way, Belles on Their Toes, The Gunfighter*, etc.

FENTON, FRANK *(1957)* 51 ——Leathery-faced guy, handsome in a tough Gregory Peck way, in many Westerns: *Red River, Buffalo Bill, Silver City, The Doolins of Oklahoma*, etc.; also in war and adventure pix: *The Navy Comes Through, This Man's Navy, Tripoli, Island in the Sky*, others.

FENTON, LUCILE *(1966)* 50 ——English actress; in *Citizen Saint*, etc.

FENTON, MABEL *(1931)* 63 ——Featured in the 1915 comedy *How Molly Made Good*.

FENTON, MARK *(1925)* 55 ——Support in the Grace Cunard serial *The Adventures of Peg o' the Ring*; many silents: *The Village Blacksmith, The Yellow Stain, The Mystery of 13, Speed King*, etc.

FENWICK, IRENE *(1936)* 49 ——Lionel Barrymore's beautiful brunette wife; leading lady in one silent, *A Coney Island Princess*.

FEODOROFF, LEO *(1949)* 82 ——Russian actor; support in *Laugh, Clown, Laugh* (personal favorite pic of its star, Lon Chaney), and *The Music Master* and *God Gave Me Twenty Cents*, both starring Lois Moran.

FERGUSON, CASSON *(1929)* 78 ——Silent star; handsome barrister in Pauline Frederick's *Madame X;* The Scribe in *The King of Kings;* also in *The Road to Yesterday, The Wedding March, Manslaughter*, many others.

FERGUSON, ELSIE *(1961)* 78 ——Lovely, patrician actress from the stage who starred in 16 pix in her first three years onscreen (from '17); *Barbary Sheep, The Song of Songs, The Rise of Jenny Cushing, A Doll's House, Under the Greenwood Tree, Peter Ibbetson, Forever*, etc.; played an attorney in 1930's *Scarlet Pages*, her starring talkie debut and screen swansong.

FERGUSON, GEORGE S. *(1944)* 60 ——Supporting roles in silents.

FERGUSON, HILDA *(1933)* 30 ——A Mack Sennett bathing beauty.

FERGUSON, W. J. *(1930)* 85 ——Was Carol Dempster's father in *Dream Street;* support in Mae Murray's *Peacock Alley;* other silents: *The World's Champion, To Have and to Hold, John Smith;* had been in the cast of *Our American Cousin* (playing Lieutenant Vernon) the night Lincoln was killed.

FERN, FRITZIE *(1932)* 30 ——Had supporting roles in a few early talkies: Reginald Denny's *Clear the Decks*, Margaret Livingston's *The Charlatan*, etc.

FERNANDEL *(1971)* 67 ——Great French comedy star with the toothy, horsey face; perhaps best loved as the humorously indomitable priest in the ''Don Camillo'' films; starred in *The Well Digger's Daughter, The Sheep Has Five Legs, Hoboes in Paradise, Un Carnet de Bal*, many more; *Around the World in 80 Days* (as Niven's coachman) was one of his rare American pix.

FERNANDEZ, BIJOU *(1961)* 84 ——She had supporting roles in two Richard Barthelmess silents: *Just Suppose* and *New Toys*.

FETHERSTONE, EDDIE *(1965)* 60s ——Star Kane Richmond's buddy, Jerry, in the serial *The Lost City;* first in silent serials (Herbert Rawlinson's *The Flame Fighter*), had supporting roles in various features, silent (Beery's *Old Ironsides*) and talkie (*The Lone Wolf in Paris, Homicide Bureau*, etc.).

FEUSIER, NORMAN *(1945)* 60 ——Supporting roles: *The Diamond Trail*, etc.

FIELD, BEN *(1939)* 61 ——Support in *The Silver King, Michael and Mary, Reserved for Ladies, Loyalties, The Clairvoyant*, other English pix.

FIELD, BETTY *(1973)* 55 ——Fine Broadway actress who starred in many—with an inimitable flat vocal tone—and never repeated a characterization: the trampish Lola in *Of Mice and Men*, demented Cassandra in *Kings Row*, the ugly girl transformed by love into a beauty in *Flesh and Fantasy*, Daisy in *The Great Gatsby* ('49), the girl of the Ozarks in *The Shepherd of the Hills* ('41), the mirthful society beauty in *Are Husbands Necessary?*, the downtrodden sharecropper wife in *The Southerner*, etc.; later, major supporting roles: Novak's mother in *Picnic*, Hope Lange's in *Peyton Place*, and in *Butterfield 8, Bus Stop* (bawdy cafe proprietress, Grace), *Birdman of Alcatraz*, and *Coogan's Bluff*.

FIELD, NORMAN *(1956)* 77 ——Minor support in *Mister 880, Crazylegs, Street Bandits*, etc.

FIELD, SID *(1950)* 45 ——British music hall star of *London Town, Cardboard Cavalier*, etc.

FIELDING, EDWARD *(1945)* 64 ——Elegant British support; in *Rebecca* (Frith, the butler), *Mr. Lucky, Kitty Foyle* (Ginger Rogers' Uncle Edgar), *All This and Heaven Too* (Dr. Louis), *In This Our Life, Pride of the Yankees, Lady in the Dark*, and a score more.

FIELDING, MARJORIE *(1956)* 64 ——Thin-faced, gray-haired English actress who always played high-born, usually kind, ladies; in *The Lavender Hill Mob, The Mudlark* (Lady Margaret Prior), *The Franchise Affair, Mandy, Rob Roy*, more.

FIELDING, ROMAINE *(1927)* 45 ——Handsome, dapper star who in 1913 was the #1 most

612

popular movie actor; main money-maker for Lubin for some years; secondary roles in the '20s in Gilbert Roland's *Rose of the Golden West*, Barthelmess's *The Noose*, Esther Ralston's *Ten Modern Commandments*, etc.

FIELDS, BENNY *(1959)* 65 ——Great vaudeville headliner with wife Blossom Seeley; onscreen in *The Big Broadcast of 1937*, *Minstrel Man*, and *Mr. Broadway*; Paramount produced a movie, *Somebody Loves Me* ('52), based on Seeley and Fields with Betty Hutton playing her, and Ralph Meeker him.

FIELDS, DOROTHY *(1974)* 69 ——Oscar-winning lyricist ("The Way You Look Tonight"— her words, Jerome Kern's music); collaborating with many famous composers, she had contributed lyrics to 400 songs heard in pix such as *Up in Central Park*, *Annie Get Your Gun*, *Lovely To Look At*, etc.; was onscreen, as herself, in *Stage Door Canteen*.

FIELDS, LEW *(1941)* 74 ——Bald half of Weber & Fields comedy team; they starred in *Friendly Enemies*, *Two of the Finest*, *The Best of Enemies*, *The Worst of Friends*, etc. (all silents); in talkies they appeared as themselves in *Lillian Russell* and *The Story of Vernon and Irene Castle*; Fields also starred in shorts without Weber.

FIELDS, STANLEY *(1941)* 61 ——Versatile support in more than 90 in 11 years (1930–41); played hoods (Sam Vettori in *Little Caesar*), hicks (in Dunne's *Show Boat*), British sailors (Muspratt in Gable's *Mutiny on the Bounty*), Orientals (Bayan in *The Adventures of Marco Polo*); was also in *Souls at Sea*, *Kid Millions*, *Cracked Nuts*, *Algiers*, etc.

FIELDS, W. C. *(1946)* 67 ——Bibulous, irascible, strawberry-nosed star comedian who hated kids (especially Baby LeRoy), dogs, politicians, preachers, the WCTU, and Christmas; steadily onscreen from 1924's *Janice Meredith*, he was at his cantankerous best in *The Bank Dick*, *My Little Chickadee*, *Never Give a Sucker an Even Break*, *David Copperfield* (as Micawber, of course), *You Can't Cheat an Honest Man*, *If I Had a Million*, *Poppy*, and, particularly, *It's a Gift*; it was no gift to the world when he left it— on Christmas Day; Rod Steiger, first actor brave enough to try to fill his spats, portrayed him in the recent *W. C. Fields and Me*.

FIGMAN, MAX *(1952)* 85 ——Dapper Lasky star of 1914; was in *The Adventures of Wallingford*, *What's His Name*, etc.; was later a director.

FIGMAN, OSCAR *(1930)* 48 ——Support in Richard Dix's *Manhattan* ('24).

FILLMORE, CLYDE *(1948)* 72 ——Handsome, strapping, cleft-chinned actor who starred in his first, 1920's *The Devil's Passkey* (von Stroheim directed), cutting a fine figure as the Army Captain hero; other silents: *Nurse Marjorie*, *Moonlight Follies*, etc.; support in many talkies, his commanding presence causing him to be cast as Senators (Noonan in *The More the Merrier*, Boyd in *The Talk of the Town*), doctors *(Margin for Error)*, police commissioners (Bullitt in *Laura)*, etc.

FINCH, FLORA *(1940)* 71 ——Scrawny, skinny comedienne who, at Biograph from 1908, hit her stride in 1910 when she and fat John Bunny joined forces and became the screen's first great comedy team—he as the erring husband, she as the shrewish wife—in more than 250 one- and two-reelers; movie theater managers packed houses simply by posting signs "Today! John Bunny & Flora Finch!"—no title necessary; after his death in 1915 she starred awhile alone *(War Prides*, *The Starring of Flora Finchurch)*, less successfully; rest of her life supported others: Laura La Plante in *The Cat and the Canary*, Marion Davies in *When Knighthood Was in Flower* (a French lady-in-waiting) and *Quality Street*, Bronson in *A Kiss for Cinderella*, etc.

FINDLAY, RUTH *(1949)* 45 ——Lane Chandler's leading lady in *Heroes of the Alamo*.

FINDLEY, THOMAS *(1941)* 65 ——Support in the silents of Richard Dix *(Let's Get Married*, *Lucky Devil)* and Marion Davies *(Little Old New York*, *Yolanda*, *Buried Treasure)*.

FINLAY, BOB *(1929)* 41 ——Featured in *The Winning Punch* ('17).

FINLAYSON, JAMES *(1953)* 66 ——A Keystone Kop from 1915 on, he was comic support in many silent features too: *The Crossroads of New York*, *Lady Be Good*, *Hollywood*, *Show Girl*, *A Small Town Idol*, etc.; beginning with 1927's *With Love and Hisses*, this bald master of the double-take was *the* top support in any Laurel and Hardy pic you might name, two-reelers (such as *Big Business* in which he furiously demolishes their Model T with an ax) and features: *Pack Up Your Troubles* (General who sends them to the guardhouse), *Way Out West* (saloonkeeper), *Blockheads*, *The Bohemian Girl*, *Saps at Sea*, etc.

FINNERTY, LOUIS *(1937)* 54 ——Minor support in *Saratoga*.

FINNERTY, WALTER *(1974)* 49 ——The rancher with the young family who befriended hippies Fonda and Hopper in *Easy Rider*; also in *The Pawnbroker*.

FIO RITO, TED *(1971)* 70 ——Famous band-leader-discoverer of Grable and June Haver; with his orchestra in *Twenty Million Sweethearts* and Belita's *Silver Skates*.

FISHER, ALFRED *(1933)* 84 ——Character actor particularly popular at Universal in the '20s: *The Breathless Moment, The Storm Daughter* (with Priscilla Dean), *The Home Maker* (with Alice Joyce), *Railroaded, Burning Words, Fighting American.*

FISHER, FREDERICK "SCHNICKELFRITZ" *(1967)* 63 ——Led his famous Schnickelfritz Band in *Gold Diggers in Paris*.

FISHER, GEORGE *(1960)* 66 ——Rugged, wavy-haired handsome man who, at 19, starred in his first, as the Yankee soldier in 1913's *The Man Who Went Out*; then in *Civilization, Environment, Midnight Follies*, many more silents.

FISHER, HARRY *(1923)* 55 ——Support in, among others, two Constance Talmadge pix: *Bertie's Stratagem* and *Polly of the Follies.*

FISHER, SALLIE *(1950)* 66 ——Was an Essanay star (from vaudeville) in 1916.

FISHER, WILLIAM *(1933)* 65 ——Featured in silents: *The Broken Silence* (as a Mountie), *The Keeper of the Bees*, etc.

FISKE, MINNIE MADDERN *(1932)* 66 ——One of the great actresses of the stage; starred in such silents as 1913's *Tess of the D'Urbervilles* and 1915's *Vanity Fair.*

FITZGERALD, BARRY *(1961)* 72 ——A little bit of Ireland; his priestly blarney—and a tear-jerking reunion with his ancient mother, Adeline DeWalt Reynolds—in *Going My Way* won him a Supporting Oscar; previously in 20 Hollywood pix (*The Plough and the Stars, Bringing Up Baby, The Sea Wolf*, etc.), and was not always so lovable—e.g., the viperish steward, Cocky, in *The Long Voyage Home*; exercised his whimsical charm in a score later: *None But the Lonely Heart, Welcome Stranger, Top o' the Morning, Two Years Before the Mast, And Then There Were None, The Quiet Man*; last in the English *Broth of a Boy* ('59), after he'd returned home to Ireland where he died.

FITZGERALD, CISSY *(1941)* 66 ——Entered movies a buxom 40 (after long success on the English stage) as the star of 1914's *A Win(k)some Widow*; in the '20s and '30s, a gray-haired tower of strength in many: Chaney's *Laugh, Clown, Laugh* (as Giacinta), *Babbitt, Only Yesterday, Lilies of the Field, Transgression*, etc.

FITZGERALD, EDWARD *(1942)* 59 ——In Sennett silent comedies.

FITZGERALD, FLORENCE IRENE DIMON *(1962)* 72 ——In very early silents.

FITZGERALD, LILLIAN *(1947)* ——Support in the Gene Krupa-Shirley Ross *Some Like It Hot* ('39).

FITZHARRIS, EDWARD *(1974)* 84 ——Featured in early Vitagraph pix.

FITZMAURICE, GEORGE *(1940)* 55 ——Starred in *The Avalanche* ('19), he later was more famous as director of Colleen Moore in *Lilac Time* and Vilma Banky in *The Dark Angel*.

FITZMAURICE, MICHAEL *(1967)* 59 ——Character (TV announcer) in Basehart's *Fourteen Hours*; earlier: *Reported Missing, The House of a Thousand Candles*.

FITZROY, EMILY *(1954)* 89 ——So stern, so rigid, so good; her sharp nose sniffed disapprovingly at some of the biggest stars—Lombard in *Vigil in the Night* (as nurse Sister Gilson), fat millionaire hubby Mack Swain making an ass of himself in *Gentlemen Prefer Blondes* ('28). Loretta Young in *The Man from Blankley's* (the vulgar middle-class woman for whose children Young was governess); so it went from 1920's *Way Down East* to 1943's *Forever and a Day*.

FLAGSTAD, KIRSTEN *(1962)* 67 ——Large, great Wagnerian soprano from Norway and the Met; onscreen in *The Big Broadcast of 1938*; labeled a Nazi sympathizer during the War.

FLAHERTY, PAT *(1970)* 67 ——Good-looking guy who played lean youngish men usually named Mike; flew in the Andes with Grant (*Only Angels Have Wings*), was in the Argonne trenches with Cooper and Tobias (*Sergeant York*), played detectives (*Twentieth Century*); in many: *Meet John Doe, Navy Blue and Gold, Gentleman Jim, Pigskin Parade*, etc.

FLANAGAN, BUD *(1968)* 72 ——Fine British comic; in "Crazy Gang" pix: *OK for Sound, Gasbags*, etc.

FLANAGAN, EDWARD J. *(1925)* 45 ——Vaudeville comic, featured in Gareth Hughes' *The Hunch*, others.

FLATEAU, GEORGES *(1953)* 70 ——French support; in Darrieux's *Katia*.

FLEISCHMANN, HARRY *(1943)* 44 ——Support in William Powell's *Crossroads*, Robert Taylor's *Stand By for Action*, others.

FLEMING, ALICE *(1952)* 70 ——Funny dowager; in Fontaine's *The Affairs of Susan*, Kay Kyser's *Playmates* (Mrs. Pennypacker), *Who Done It?*; earlier in silents such as Thomas Meighan's *The Conquest of Canaan*.

FLEMING, ERIC *(1966)* 41 ——Lean, rugged hero; star of B's *(Queen of Outer Space, Conquest of Space)*, one of Doris Day's leading men in *The Glass-Bottom Boat*, and costar of TV's *Rawhide* (played Gil Favor).

FLEMING, IAN *(1969)* 80 ——Was Dr. Watson in the British "Sherlock Holmes" pix of the '30s; also in *Quartet, The Trials of Oscar Wilde, Murder Will Out*, etc.; not the "James Bond" creator.

FLETCHER, LAWRENCE *(1970)* 70 ——Support in Teresa Wright's *The Search for Bridey Murphy*; busier on Broadway (33 plays).

FLEU, DORRIS BELL *(1955)* 33 ——Singer with Harry James and Woody Herman; in musical shorts.

FLICK, PAT C. *(1955)* 56 ——Support in Bogart's *The Black Legion*, Pat O'Brien's *Stars Over Broadway* (billed Patsy Flick), Paul Kelly's *Missing Guest*, etc.; a screenwriter too *(The Singing Kid, Nobody's Baby*, others).

FLIEGEL, MRS. ERNIE *(1966)* 70s ——Comic support in Charles Ruggles' *Turn Off the Moon*; was one of vaudeville's Albee Sisters.

FLINT, HAZEL *(1959)* 66 ——Was in the Realarts silent *Modern Daughters*, and was the sickly sister of the working-girl heroine in 1922's *The Bootleggers*.

FLINT, HELEN *(1967)* 68 ——Played prostitutes with the best of them in the '30s in *The Black Legion, Ah! Wilderness, Fury*; and lower-class working girls (Harlow's cannery factory colleague in *Riffraff*); also in *Broadway Bill; Handy Andy; Step Lively, Jeeves*, etc.

FLIPPEN, JAY C. *(1971)* 70 ——Craggy featured character whose visage was once described as "a cross between a tomato and a Pekinese"; was raspy-voiced tough—and terrific—in dozens from '47: *Brute Force* (prison warden), many James Stewart pix *(Winchester 73, Bend of the River, Strategic Air Command,* etc.), *The Wild One, Oh, You Beautiful Doll*, others; had starred, during his 56-year-career, in minstrel shows, vaudeville, on Broadway

(Padlocks of 1927, etc.), radio *(Colonel Flippen's Amateur Hour)*, TV (costar, as comical chief petty officer, in *Ensign O'Toole)*.

FLOWERTON, CONSUELO *(1965)* 65 —— Beauty who supported Nazimova in *Camille*; actress Nina Foch is her daughter.

FLYNN, ERROL *(1959)* 50 ——Warners' gallant, handsome, devil-may-care swashbuckler —by far the best of the talkies; was dashing (and most often triumphant) in all the great combats of history—medieval *(The Adventures of Robin Hood)*, Elizabethan *(The Private Lives of Elizabeth and Essex* and *The Sea Hawk)*, the Spanish pirates era of James II *(Captain Blood)*, the Civil War (Jeb Stuart in *Santa Fe Trail)* and the American Indian wars following it *(They Died with Their Boots On)*, the Victorian Indian wars *(The Charge of the Light Brigade)*, World War I *(Dawn Patrol)*, and of course WW II—in Norway *(Edge of Darkness)*, Burma *(Objective, Burma!)*, Canada *(Northern Pursuit)*, in the RAF over Germany *(Desperate Journey)*, on land in France *(Uncertain Glory)*; and in the prizefight ring, as James J. Corbett in *Gentleman Jim*, he defeated John L. Sullivan (Ward Bond) to become heavyweight champ of the world; as a star, and in his genre, he truly was.

FLYNN, HAZEL *(1964)* 65 ——Was in early Essanay films.

FLYNN, JOE *(1974)* 49 ——Bespectacled comic star; in *This Happy Feeling, Lover Come Back, The Last Time I Saw Archie, Divorce American Style*, various Disney comedies; in *McHale's Navy*, the film and the TV series, was the long-suffering Commander.

FLYNN, MAURICE "LEFTY" *(1959)* 66 —— Tall, handsome, athletic and poker-faced star of action pix in the '20s: *Bucking the Line, Omar the Tentmaker, Drums of Fate, The Snow Bride, Open All Night, Breed of the Border*, etc.

FOLEY, JOE *(1955)* 45—Support in *The Whistle at Eaton Falls*.

FOLEY, RED *(1968)* 58 ——C&W song star; in an occasional musical Western.

FOLWELL, DENIS *(1971)* 66 ——British support.

FONTAINE, TONY *(1974)* 40s ——Rock-gospel singer; starred in the autobiographical *The Tony Fontaine Story*.

FOO, WING *(1953)* 43 ——Character in *Wonder Man, God Is My Co-Pilot, Hotel Berlin, The Purple Heart*, etc.

FORBES, MARY *(1974)* 91 ——English actress who was perhaps Hollywood's queen of the dowagers; onscreen from '29, in Janet Gaynor's *Sunny Side Up* (Charles Farrell's haughty mom), *Cavalcade* (Duchess of Churt), *A Farewell to Arms* ('32), Garbo's *Anna Karenina* (Princess Sorokino), *The Awful Truth, You Can't Take It With You* (James Stewart's snobbish mother), etc.

FORBES, MARY ELIZABETH *(1964)* 84 —— Support in James K. Hackett's *The Prisoner of Zenda* ('13), the silent serial *Zudora: The Twenty Million Dollar Mystery*, etc.; no relation to Mary Forbes.

FORBES, RALPH *(1951)* 55 ——Handsome Britisher who costarred with Colman in 1926's *Beau Geste* (as brother John), his first American pic; opposite Lillian Gish in *The Enemy*; in 50 more through the mid-40s: *Christopher Strong, Mamba, Smilin' Through* ('31), *The Lady of Scandal*, The *Thirteenth Chair, If I Were King*, etc.; was married to Ruth Chatterton and Heather Angel; son of Mary Forbes, brother of character actress Brenda.

FORBES-ROBERTSON, SIR J. *(1937)* 84 —— Ascetic English stage star, hailed as the greatest Hamlet of his time, who starred in two silents: a three-reel version of *Hamlet* in '15, and two years later, *The Passing of the Third Floor Back*, another of his great stage successes; last supported Sally O'Neil in the European-made *Kathleen*, released in '38.

FORCE, FLOYD CHARLES *(1947)* 71 —— Comic support in silents: Dolores Costello's *The Heart of Maryland, The Love Pirate, Hearts and Spangles*, etc.; earlier was in Sennett comedies.

FORD, FRANCIS *(1953)* 71 ——Toward the end of his career was a specialist at playing old codgers in pix directed by brother John (*Wagonmaster, The Quiet Man, The Sun Shines Bright, My Darling Clementine*, many more); earlier, from '14, had been one of the screen's handsomest leading men, costarring with Grace Cunard in four serials: *Lucille Love—Girl of Mystery, The Adventures of Peg o' the Ring, The Mystery of 13, The Purple Mask*; they also costarred in several features (*In the Fall of '64, The Campbells Are Coming*, etc.); in Westerns throughout the '20s as his fame waned; thereafter a character in perhaps 200 more pix.

FORD, HARRISON *(1957)* 73 ——Major femme stars of silents, from 1916, who would have been less without the charm of this handsome costar include: Mary MacLaren (*The Mysterious Mrs. Musselwhite*), Constance Talmadge (*A Pair of Silk Stockings*), Norma Talmadge (four in a row: *Passion Flower, The Wonderful Thing, Love's Redemption, Smilin' Through*), Lila Lee (*Such a Little Pirate*), Justine Johnstone (*A Heart to Let*), Mabel Ballin (*Vanity Fair*), Marion Davies (*Little Old New York*), Marie Prevost (*Up in Mabel's Room*); long past being one of the Top Ten male stars, he retired after 1932's *Love in High Gear*.

FORD, WALLACE *(1966)* 68 ——His freckled, friendly Irish mug was seen in dozens: *The Lost Patrol, Three-Cornered Moon, Men in White, The Mummy's Hand, Blues in the Night, The Set-Up, The Rainmaker, The Last Hurrah*, etc.; his unforgettable performance: the Irish rebel, Frankie, in *The Informer*, who "came in from the hills, to slip home in the fog and be sold to his death," by betrayer Gypo Nolan, Victor McLaglen.

FORDE, HAL *(1955)* 78 ——Was featured in 1924's *The Great White Way*; was chiefly famous for his Broadway musical roles.

FORDE, VICTORIA *(1964)* 60s ——One of Tom Mix's several wives, and often his Western leading lady, she earlier had been the beauty in such Christie comedies as *When the Mummy Cried for Help* ('15).

FORMAN, TOM *(1938)* 34 ——Had many "decent young men" silent leads: 1915's *The Wild Goose Chase* (Ina Claire was his sweetheart), *Sweet Kitty Bellairs* (with Belle Bennett), *The Evil Eye* (fought for Blanche Sweet), *For Better, For Worse* (with Swanson), *Louisiana* (with Vivian Martin), *The Sea Wolf* (with Noah Beery), *Kosher Kitty Kelly*, etc.; last in support in a Smith Ballew Western, *Rawhide*, the year of his death.

FORMBY, GEORGE *(1961)* 56 ——Toothy Top Ten English comic; in *Let George Do It, Keep Fit, Bell-Bottom George*, a score more.

FORREST, ALAN *(1941)* 51 ——Dark-haired silent star; opposite Pickford in *Dorothy Vernon of Haddon Hall*, Mary Miles Minter in *Rosemary Climbs the Heights*; costarred with J. Warren Kerrigan in *Captain Blood*; in a score more: *Long Live the King, Very Truly Yours, The Man From Lost River*, etc.; last in 1930's *Dangerous Nan McGrew*.

FORREST, ARTHUR *(1933)* 74 ——Character actor who portrayed Cardinal Wolsey in Marion Davies' *When Knighthood Was in Flower*.

FORREST, BELFORD *(1938)* 60 ——An early Hal Roach silent comic.

FORSTER, RUDOLF *(1968)* 84 ——Noted German actor who starred in *The Threepenny Op-*

era ('31), *The White Horse Inn, Tonio Kroger,* and *Hohe Schule* (reviewing it critic Graham Greene said: "I have a fondness for Herr Rudolf Forster's middle-aged and unresilient charm, his heavy period moustaches, his well-bred voice, but . . ." proceeding to blast the film).

FORSYTHE, MIMI *(1952)* 30 ——Dark-haired beauty who, with Anna Sten, was one of the *Three Russian Girls* ('44); also in Eleanor Powell's *Sensations of 1945.*

FORTE, JOE *(1967)* 70 ——The last chapter of the '46 serial *The Crimson Ghost* revealed him as the titled villain; also in Westerns (*Fury at Gunsight Pass*), prison pix (*Cell 2455: Death Row*), comedies (*The Buster Keaton Story*).

FORTIER, HERBERT *(1949)* 72 ——Support in silents of the '20s: *Children of Night,* Ethel Clayton's *Beyond,* Gareth Hughes' *Garments of Truth,* Florence Vidor's *Dusk to Dawn,* Milton Sills' *Legally Dead,* Jack Hoxie's *Ridgeway of Montana,* etc.

FOSHAY, HAROLD *(1953)* 68 ——In silents of the '20s: *The Brown Derby, The Fair Cheat, The Devil's Confession,* etc.; support in one talkie, Myrna Loy's *To Mary—With Love* ('36).

FOSTER, DONALD *(1969)* 80 ——Support in *Please Don't Eat the Daisies* (Justin Withers), *Scaramouche* ('52), *Al Capone,* others.

FOSTER, DUDLEY *(1973)* 48 ——British character who played villains and comic roles; in *Term of Trial, The Little Ones,* etc.

FOSTER, J. MORRIS *(1966)* 84 ——Support in silents.

FOSTER, PRESTON *(1970)* 67 ——Virile, blue-eyed star who never looked handsomer than in the scarlet tunic of a Mountie in DeMille's *North West Mounted Police,* or was more valiant than in *Guadalcanal Diary,* or meaner than as Killer Mears in *The Last Mile;* in more than 100 from 1930: *The Informer* (rebel leader, the role of which he was proudest); *My Friend Flicka; The Last Days of Pompeii; Roger Touhy, Gangster; The Big Cat,* etc.; vastly popular later on TV as the star of *Waterfront.*

FOULGER, BYRON *(1970)* 70 ——Played smalltowners, either meek or mean-tempered little men, with high receding hairline (center-parted), moustache, and granny glasses; in hundreds: *The Human Comedy, Edison the Man, Arizona, Sullivan's Travels, Ministry of Fear, Since You Went Away,* etc.

FOWLER, BRENDA *(1942)* 59 ——Character actress who played country women; in *Stage-coach* (wife of bank-embezzler Gatewood), *Judge Priest, Dust Be My Destiny, Ruggles of Red Gap* ('35), *Coming Round the Mountain, The Cowboy and the Lady,* others.

FOX, FRANKLYN *(1967)* 83 ——Doris Day's dad in *The Pajama Game;* also in *First Man Into Space, High Tide at Noon;* as Frank Fox had been in the British *Clouds Over Europe* ('39).

FOX, HARRY *(1959)* 70 ——Was the hero in the 1916 serial *Beatrice Fairfax,* with Grace Darling; support in Olsen & Johnson's *Fifty Million Frenchmen* ('31), Alice Faye's *365 Nights in Hollywood;* in early talkie shorts with wife Beatrice Curtis; had been married to Evelyn Brent and Jenny Dolly.

FOX, ROSE *(1966)* 67 ——Was in silents.

FOX, SIDNEY *(1942)* 31 ——Diminutive brunette who starred, in title role, in *Bad Sister* (Bette Davis, billed below her, was the plain "good" sister); she also played another lead role, in *Murders in the Rue Morgue,* for which the director had wanted Davis; had a brief (four years), busy (13 pix) career; had major billing in *Once in a Lifetime* (as the ungifted, aspiring actress forever reciting Kipling's "Boots"), *Strictly Dishonorable, The Mouthpiece, Six Cylinder Love, Nice Women, Down to Their Last Yacht;* made two abroad: *The Merry Monarch* (with Jannings), *Don Quixote* (with Chaliapin); last in 1935's *School for Girls.*

FOY, EDDIE *(1928)* 74 ——Famous star-dad of vaudeville's Seven Little Foys; starred on-screen in just one feature, with his children, 1915's *A Favorite Fool;* later was portrayed by Bob Hope in *The Seven Little Foys.*

FOYER, EDDIE *(1934)* 51 ——Character (Dopey) in Wallace Beery's *The Big House,* his only film.

FRALICK, FREDDIE *(1958)* 69 ——Was seen in early Biograph films.

FRANCE, C. V. *(1949)* 80 ——English; one of the leads in an early Hitchcock, *The Skin Game* ('31); then support in many: *Victoria the Great, A Yank at Oxford, If I Were King, Night Train to Munich, The Yellow Canary, Secret Agent,* etc.

FRANCIS, ALEC B. *(1934)* 65 ——He wasn't really born with that nice-old-man face—just acquired it early on; entered movies in 1911 (after being a successful English barrister and stage actor); starred in *Vanity Fair* ('11), as *Robin Hood* ('12), as Christ in *The Crimson Cross* ('13); by 1934 had been in more than 70, usually

617

as father or grandfather, and most often with star or costar billing; a sampling: *Lola* (with Clara Kimball Young), *Flame of the Desert* (Geraldine Farrar), *Earthbound*, 1927's *The Music Master* (starred in title role), Norma Talmadge's *Smilin' Through* and *Camille*, *Three Wise Fools*, *The Return of Peter Grimm*, and *Arrowsmith*.

FRANCIS, KAY *(1968)* 63 ——Sophisticated brunette star celebrated for her lisp, best-dressed reputation, deep voice and easy laughter (tears, too), astronomical salaries, and unusual attitude about her roles—quantity, not quality, counted, especially when she freelanced; onscreen from 1929's *Gentlemen of the Press*, she was memorable in *One Way Passage*, *Trouble in Paradise*, *Girls About Town*; enjoyable in *It's a Date*, *Charley's Aunt*, *Little Men*; admirable (as Florence Nightingale) in *The White Angel*; despicable in *In Name Only* (had Cary Grant and was hanging onto him); and, in all the rest until '45, gay and weepy pix alike, forever fashionable.

FRANCIS, ROBERT *(1955)* 25 ——Muscular, handsome, curly-haired blond neophyte star in *The Caine Mutiny* (Ensign Willie Keith), *The Long Gray Line*, and *Two Rode West*.

FRANCISCO, BETTY *(1950)* 50 ——A Wampas Baby Star of '23, she had brunette "pretty girl" roles in many silents (*Her Night of Nights*, *Straight from Paris*, *East of Broadway*, *Fifth Avenue Models*, etc.), and a few talkies (*Street of Chance*, *Charlie Chan Carries On*, others).

FRANEY, BILLY *(1940)* 55 ——In 23 Edgar Kennedy two-reel comedies between '37 and '40, he was the father-in-law old "Slow Burn" suffered and several times tried to marry off; from 1915 had been in shorts (*Jokers* at Universal), silent feature comedies (*An Honest Man*) and Westerns (*Moran of the Mounted*, *Kit Carson over the Great Divide*, etc.), and talkie features (*Joy of Living*, *Having Wonderful Time*, others).

FRANK, CARL *(1972)* 63 ——Character (District Attorney) in *The Lady from Shanghai*.

FRANK, WILL *(1925)* 45 ——Support in the Ralph Lewis silent-starrer *The Last Edition*; also in Roach comedies.

FRANKAU, RONALD *(1951)* 57 ——English comedian typed in "idle rich" roles; in *His Brother's Keeper*, *The Ghosts of Berkeley Square*, *The Skin Game*, *Radio Parade of 1935*, etc.

FRANKEL, FRANCHON *(1937)* 63 ——She was in such silents of the '20s as *Sensation*

Seekers, *Desperate Courage* and *Jake the Plumber*.

FRANKEUR, PAUL *(1974)* 69 ——French; a principal in *Children of Paradise, Jour de Fete, Monkey in Winter, We Are All Murderers*.

FRANKLIN, IRENE *(1941)* 65 ——Support in many talkies: *The President Vanishes, Saratoga* (a train passenger), *Ladies Crave Excitement, Lazy River*, etc.

FRANKLIN, RUPERT *(1939)* 77 ——Character roles; in Metro-Goldwyn's *The Prairie Wife*, other silents.

FRANKLIN, SIDNEY *(1931)* 61 ——Character actor in many of the '20s: Fairbanks' *The Three Musketeers*, Mae Murray's *Fashion Row*, Coogan's *A Boy of Flanders*, Barthelmess' *The Wheel of Chance*; also in *Somebody's Mother, King of Kings, Dusk to Dawn, Rose of the Tenements, The Vermilion Pencil, In Hollywood with Potash and Perlmutter*, etc.; not the Oscar-winning producer *(Mrs. Miniver)* -director *(The Good Earth)* of the same name who died in 1972; not the famous "Bullfighter from Brooklyn" of the same name who appeared in a few pix (*The Kid From Spain*) and died in 1976.

FRANKLYN, IRWIN *(1966)* 62 ——Had been a child actor in silents, then a screenwriter.

FRANTZ, DALIES *(1965)* 57 ——Blond pianist-actor who had been one of MGM's star hopefuls in the late '30s; Ilona Massey's brother in *Balalaika*; also in *Sweethearts* and *I Take This Woman*.

FRASER, CONSTANCE *(1973)* 63 ——British character actress; minor roles.

FRASER, RICHARD *(1971)* 58 ——Young actor from Scotland who had important roles in many Hollywood movies of the '40s: *A Yank in the R.A.F., How Green Was My Valley* (as one of the sons, Davy), *Joan of Paris, Desperate Journey, The Gorilla Man, Edge of Darkness, Holy Matrimony, Ladies Courageous, The Picture of Dorian Gray, Bedlam, The Private Affairs of Bel Ami*, etc.; married Hollywood actress Ann Gillis (later divorced) and returned to Great Britain where he gave up acting and became a corporation executive.

FRAWLEY, WILLIAM *(1966)* 79 ——Before making a career of being Fred Mertz in TV's *I Love Lucy*, this chuckling baldie had been among Hollywood's busiest (scores of pix from '29), best-loved characters; in *Gentleman Jim, Miracle on 34th Street, Mad About Music, Rhythm on the River, Mother Wore Tights*, etc.; last in 1962's *Safe at Home* (his first pic in a decade), in support of Yankee baseball heroes Mickey Mantle and Roger Maris.

FRAZER, ALEX *(1958)* 58 ——Character (Dr. James) in *War of the Worlds;* also in *Gentlemen Prefer Blondes, The Blonde Bandit, Bigger Than Life,* etc.

FRAZER, ROBERT *(1944)* 53 ——Handsome actor onscreen from 1912's *Robin Hood* (he starred); opposite Clara Kimball Young in *The Feast of Life,* Pola Negri in *Men,* Jacqueline Logan in *One Hour of Love,* dozens more silents; rest of his career, usually as a "heavie," was in scores of B's (*Gambling Souls*), B Westerns (*Pals of the Pecos*), and serials (*The Miracle Rider,* as Indian Chief Black Wing, *The Clutching Hand, The Black Coin,* others).

FRAZIN, GLADYS *(1939)* 38 ——Small roles in *Let Not Man Put Asunder* (among the worst pix of the '20s, said critics), Garbo's *Inspiration,* etc.

FREDERICI, BLANCHE *(1933)* 60s ——Pickle-puss who endangered clocks everywhere; stern Head Nurse in Cooper's *A Farewell to Arms,* a nun in Garbo's *Mata Hari,* vinegary wife of Reverend (Lionel Barrymore) Davidson in *Sadie Thompson,* a country woman (Zeke's wife) in *It Happened One Night,* Madame Si-Si in *The Hatchet Man;* battle-axe roles in another 40.

FREDERICK, PAULINE *(1938)* 53 ——Sleek, dramatic, major brunette star of silents, starting with Famous Players in '15; at her peak in *Bella Donna* ('15) and *Madame X* ('20); memorable also in *The Eternal City; Zaza; Her Honor, the Governor;* starred in a few early talkies (*The Sacred Flame, On Trial, Evidence,* etc.), after which she had supporting roles, usually as a snobbish society woman (Colleen Moore's *Social Register,* Nancy Carroll's *Wayward,* etc.).

FREDERICKS, CHARLES *(1970)* 51 ——Character (Court Clerk) in *To Kill a Mockingbird;* also in *Tender Is the Night* (as the husband of Bea Benaderet), *A House Is Not a Home,* etc.

FREEMAN, AL *(1956)* 71 ——Black character actor; father of Al Jr.

FREEMAN, HOWARD *(1967)* 65 ——Played fuddy-duddies, pussyfooting or pompous-ass businessmen, plump smalltime crooks with a weak smile; in *Once Upon a Time* (Cary Grant's production aide), *The Time of Your Life* (Society Gentleman), *You Came Along, The Blue Dahlia, The Snake Pit,* and, in *Hitler's Madmen,* played Himmler; many more.

FREEMAN, MAURICE *(1953)* 81 ——Comical character actor in English pix: *Strangers on a Honeymoon,* etc.

FREEMAN-MITFORD, RUPERT *(1939)* 44 ——Minor role in *Goodbye Mr. Chips* the year he died.

FRENCH, CHARLES K. *(1952)* 92 ——Had the lead in Bison Films' first production, *A True Indian's Heart* ('09), then in Pathe's *The Prisoner of the Mohicans* ('11); supported Charles Ray in 1915's *The Coward* and, mostly in Westerns or action pix, many stars afterward in *The Yosemite Trail; The Saddle Hawk; Oh, You Tony; The Charge of the Gauchos,* other silents; a few Western talkies (*Overland Bound,* etc.); last in a 1935 Johnny Mack Brown serial, *Rustlers of Red Dog,* as father of heroine Joyce Compton.

FRENCH, GEORGE *(1961)* 78 ——Support in Elmo Lincoln's *Tarzan of the Apes* and many other silents; Lila Lee's *Wandering Husbands, Cupid's Knockout,* Esther Ralston's *Sawdust Paradise, Grinning Guns,* etc.; William Powell's *Street of Chance* was his only talkie.

FREY, ARNO *(1961)* 61 ——German support in Hollywood pix since '34; in *Hangmen Also Die* (Camp Officer), *Chetniks, Appointment in Berlin, Jungle Siren,* others; was main villain, renegade German general Carl Engler, in the Bill Elliott serial *The Valley of Vanishing Men.*

FREY, NATHANIEL *(1970)* 57 ——Genial, white-haired manager of baseball's Washington Senators in *Damn Yankees* (stage and screen); also in *Kiss Them for Me.*

FRIEDMANN, SHRAGA *(1970)* 47 ——He supported Topol in the Israeli film *Sallah;* also in Sophia Loren's *Judith.*

FRIGANZA, TRIXIE *(1955)* 84 ——Beefy, gray-haired old gal who played society dames (usually funny) such as in the Edward Everett Horton silent *The Whole Town's Talking;* mother of flapper Vera Reynolds in *The Road to Yesterday;* other silents: *Mind Over Motor,* Rod La Rocque's *The Coming of Amos, Gentlemen Prefer Blondes,* Laura La Plante's *Thanks for the Buggy Ride,* etc.; few talkies, the last being a bit in Crosby's *If I Had My Way.*

FRINTON, FREDDIE *(1968)* 56 ——British comedian; support in Terry-Thomas's *Make Mine Mink.*

FRISBY, MILDRED *(1939)* 40s ——Silent actress in minor roles who later wrote movie reviews as Mildred Spain for New York *Daily News.*

FRISCO, JOE *(1958)* 68 ——Famous stuttering comic; in *Mr. Broadway, Shady Lady, Atlantic City, The Gorilla, Riding High,* others.

FRITH, LESLIE *(1961)* 71 ——Support in English pix: *The Dreyfus Case, Murder in the Old Red Barn*, etc.

FRITH, TOM *(1945)* 62 ——Support in Westerns of the '20s and '30s.

FRITSCH, WILLY *(1973)* 72 ——A top German star; in *Congress Dances* (German version only) was the romantic Tsar Alexander opposite Lilian Harvey; starred in *The Waltz Dream, Hungarian Rhapsody, The Last Waltz*, Fritz Lang's *Spies*, etc.

FROES, WALTER J. *(1958)* 36 ——Under this name he was radio's "Froggie Froes," and in musical shorts with Fred Waring; acted in features as Wallace Douglas; see Wallace Douglas.

FRYE, DWIGHT *(1943)* 44 ——No hunchback he, nor dwarf, but he was terrifying (to audiences and Dr. Frankenstein's monster alike) as the crazed creature who was *both* in *Frankenstein, Bride of Frankenstein, Frankenstein Meets the Wolf Man*, etc.; you saw him upright in *The Maltese Falcon* ('31), Cagney's *Something to Sing About*, Paul Kelly's *Mystery Ship*, Richard Arlen's *Submarine Alert*, etc.

FULLER, CLEM *(1961)* 52 ——Support in Westerns (*High Lonesome, The Great Sioux Uprising, They Came to Cordura*, etc.) and, until '60, the bartender in TV's *Gunsmoke*.

FULLER, IRENE, *(1945)* 47 ——Had secondary roles in silents.

FULLER, LESLIE *(1948)* 59 ——Plump comic in British pix: *Captain Bill, Two Smart Men, Nice Work Sailor, Front Line Kids*, many more.

FULLER, MARGARET *(1952)* 46 ——Actress-wife of supporting actor Robert Griffin.

FULTON, MAUDE *(1950)* 69 ——Comic support in silents (Madge Bellamy's *Silk Legs*, Lois Wilson's *The Gingham Girl*, Virginia Lee Corbin's *Bare Knees*) and a few talkies (*The Cohens and the Kellys in Trouble*, etc.); also wrote 1929's *Nix on Dames*, in which she appeared, Claire Trevor's *Song and Dance Man*, others.

FUQUA, CHARLIE *(1971)* 60 ——Baritone-guitarist with the original Ink Spots; in *Pardon My Sarong.*

FUSIER-GIR, JEANNE *(1974)* 88 ——French character actress in many from the early '30s to 1960: *Crainquebille, Claudine, Parole Fixer, Pop Always Pays, The Honorable Catherine, Fire in the Straw, Fruits of Summer, Witches of Salem, Marie Octobre*, etc.

FYFFE, WILL *(1947)* 63 ——Cunning Scots comedian; many British pix: *The Brothers, Owd Bob, Sez O'Reilly to MacNab, The Prime Minister*, etc.

G

GAAL, FRANCISKA *(1972)* 68 ——Lovely blonde Hungarian DeMille costarred with Fredric March in *The Buccaneer* and called—an overstatement—"a combination of Helen Hayes, the early Mary Pickford, Elisabeth Bergner and Clara Bow"; costarred in just two more before retiring—*The Girl Downstairs* with Franchot Tone and *Paris Honeymoon* with Bing Crosby.

GABLE, CLARK *(1960)* 59 ——The screen's irreplaceable he-man and King; his Rhett Butler in *Gone With the Wind* ensures eternal fame, but he was great too in *Test Pilot, San Francisco, Boom Town, It Happened One Night* (won him an Oscar), *Mutiny on the Bounty* (nominated for this and *GWTW*, his only other times as a contender), *Strange Cargo, Command Decision, Honky Tonk*, etc.; an MGM stalwart for 25 years, and in the box-office Top Ten 1932–43, 1947–49 and in 1955 (surprisingly, never higher than #2, which he was six times); portrayed onscreen in '76 by actor James Brolin.

GABY, FRANK *(1945)* 48 ——Support in a Lloyd Nolan B, *Mr. Dynamite.*

GAIGE, RUSSELL, *(1974)* 70s ——Character (Theatrical Producer) in Ginger Rogers' *Forever Female.*

GALE, MRS. MARGUERITE H. *(1948)* 63 —— —A heroine (there were two) in the 1916 Edwin Stevens serial *The Yellow Menace*; also in *How Molly Made Good.*

GALINDO, NACHO *(1973)* 60s ——Mexican character; in *South of St. Louis, Lightning Strikes Twice, Green Fire, Lone Star*, etc.

GALLAGHER, SKEETS *(1955)* 53 —— Smooth, slick, generally amusing silent star; in *Stocks and Blondes* with Jacqueline Logan, *Three-Ring Marriage, The Daring Years*, etc.; top support in talkies: *Fast Company* (Oakie's deceitful baseball club manager), *Merrily We Go to Hell* (March's pal Buck), *Polo Joe, Alice*

620

in Wonderland (White Rabbit), *Idiot's Delight,* many others.

GALLANT, ANN *(1973)* 90 ——Veteran supporting player.

GALLI, ROSINA *(1940)* 45 ——Support in *Blockade, The Housekeeper's Daughter, Fisherman's Wharf, You Can't Fool Your Wife,* etc.

GALLIAN, KETTI *(1972)* 59 ——Beautiful French actress who starred in *Marie Galante* ('34), costarred with Warner Baxter in *Under the Pampas Moon* ('35), supported Edmund Lowe and Madge Evans in *Espionage,* and Astaire and Rogers in *Shall We Dance* (both '37), then vanished from the screen.

GALVANI, DINO *(1960)* 70 ——Italian character in many British pix: *Atlantic,* Hitchcock's *Secret Agent, Four Feathers, Sleeping Car to Trieste, It's That Man Again, Father Brown,* more.

GAMBLE, FRED *(1939)* 69 ——Stocky star of American Co.'s early social comedy-dramas ('14); support in many other silents: the Ben Wilson-Neva Gerber serial *The Screaming Shadow, The Red Mill* (as the Innkeeper, billed, oddly, Fred Gambold), Corinne Griffith's *Black Oxen,* William S. Hart's *Tumbleweeds,* etc.

GAMBLE, RALPH *(1966)* 64 ——Support in *Mr. Scoutmaster, In the Money, Sudden Danger,* etc.

GAMBLE, WARBURTON *(1945)* 62 ——Character actor in silents (*The Silver King, The Paliser Case, A Society Exile*) and talkies (*As You Desire Me,* in which he was the Baron, *Tonight Is Ours, Child of Manhattan,* etc.).

GAN, CHESTER *(1959)* 50 ——Portly Chinese character; in *The Good Earth* (Singer in Teahouse), *Victory* (Wang), *Across the Pacific* (Captain Higoto), *Blood Alley,* the serial *Ace Drummond* (as Chinese sword-wielding "good guy" Kai-Chek), more.

GANZHORN, JACK *(1956)* 75 ——Support in silent serials (Allene Ray's *Hawk of the Hills*), action pix (*The Iron Horse*), Westerns (*Fightin' Odds, The Apache Raider,* etc.).

GARAT, HENRY *(1959)* 57 ——French support; in *Congress Dances, Adorable, The Charm School,* more.

GARDEN, MARY *(1967)* 92 ——Opera prima donna who followed diva Geraldine Farrar onto the screen but came a cropper in both her pix: *Thais* ('17) and *The Splendid Sinner* ('18).

GARDNER, ED *(1963)* 62 ——Radio-TV comic who transferred his *Duffy's Tavern* to Paramount screens in '45.

GARDNER, HELEN *(1968)* 80s ——Often called the screen's first "vamp," she starred as Becky Sharp in *Vanity Fair* ('11), in *Cleopatra* (produced by her own company in '12), *The Wife of Cain, A Princess of Bagdad, A Sister to Carmen, The Still Small Voice,* more early silents; supported others in the '20s: Barbara La Marr in *Sandra,* etc.

GARDNER, HUNTER *(1952)* 52 ——Support in George M. Cohan's *Gambling.*

GARDNER, JACK *(1929)* 63 ——Co-starred with Helen Ferguson in *Gift O' Gab* ('17); support in William S. Hart's *Wild Bill Hickok,* Agnes Ayres' *Bluff,* in *Wild Geese,* Barthelmess' *Scarlet Seas,* Claire Windsor's *Blondes by Choice,* etc.

GARDNER, JACK *(1955)* 40 ——Played young reporters in *The Glass Key* ('42), *It Happened Tomorrow, The Pride of the Yankees.*

GARDNER, RICHARD *(1972)* 40s ——Character (Pvt. Cowley) in *The Young Lions.*

GARDNER, SHAYLE *(1945)* 55 ——Featured in *Three Live Ghosts* ('29), *The Return of Dr. Fu Manchu, Phantom Fiend,* etc.

GARFIELD, JOHN *(1952)* 39 ——Warners' great gentle little tough guy; suddenly famous for the way he smoked a cigarette, composed music and loved Priscilla Lane—to say nothing of his performance—in *Four Daughters* (Oscar-nominated as Best Support); tops in *Destination Tokyo, Air Force, Humoresque, The Postman Always Rings Twice, They Made Me a Criminal, Body and Soul* (his only Oscar nomination as Best Actor), *Gentleman's Agreement,* etc.

GARGAN, EDWARD *(1964)* 62 ——Curly-haired brother of William who played dozens of good-natured detectives such as the forever-wrong Bates in many of the "Falcon" pix of both George Sanders and Tom Conway; also in *My Gal Sal, My Man Godfrey, Ceiling Zero, Hands Across the Table,* dozens more.

GARLAND, JUDY *(1969)* 47 ——She will be remembered as long as there are movies, for *The Wizard of Oz* and other musicals of incomparable quality (*Meet Me in St. Louis, The Harvey Girls, Babes in Arms, Easter Parade,* etc.); for such musical-dramas as *Ziegfeld Girl* and *A Star Is Born* (was nominated for Best Actress); for her dramatic performances (*The Clock* and *Judgment at Nuremberg,* for which she was nominated as Best Support); but perhaps most of all—and particularly from her early films—for her exuberant youthful gaiety.

GARLAND, RICHARD *(1969)* 40s ——Featured actor; once the husband of actress Beverly Garland.

GARON, PAULINE *(1965)* 64 ——Doll-faced blonde who starred as a flapper for DeMille in 1923's *Adam's Rib* (after a few earlier efforts) and kept right on being one—in dozens—throughout the '20s; in *Compromise, The Painted Flapper, Temptations of a Shop Girl, Satan in Sables, Passionate Youth,* etc.; a handful of talkies, including, near the end of her career, a bit in Hopkins' *Becky Sharp.*

GARR, EDDIE *(1956)* 56 ——Second male lead in the now-famous Marilyn Monroe B at Columbia, *Ladies of the Chorus* (played Billy Mackay); also in *Obey the Law,* etc.

GARRICK, RICHARD *(1962)* 83 ——Support in several Kazan pix: *Boomerang* (Mr. Rogers), *Viva Zapata!* (Old General), *A Streetcar Named Desire* (Strange Man); others: *High Society* (Bing Crosby's butler), *Call Me Madam* (Supreme Court Justice), *A Man Called Peter,* etc.

GARRY, CLAUDE *(1918)* 41 ——Co-starred in the 1911 French film *Notre Dame de Paris.*

GARTH, OTIS (1955) 54 ——Support in Clifton Webb's *Mr. Scoutmaster.*

GAUGE, ALEXANDER *(1960)* 46 ——Tiny-nosed, roly-poly Pickwick Club pal of roly-poly James Hayter (star) in *The Pickwick Papers;* Tetzel in *Martin Luther;* dozens more British films: *Murder In the Cathedral, Penny Princess,* etc.

GAUTIER, GENE *(1966)* 86 ——Dramatic, beautiful, and gifted brunette who was Kalem's leading lady for years, starting in 1907; starred in over 500, including *The Kalem Girl,* most of which she wrote; most famous was the five-reel *From the Manger to the Cross,* in which she played Mary; shot in Egypt and Palestine in 1912, it was still playing in theaters a decade later.

GAWTHORNE, PETER *(1962)* 78 ——Stiff-necked British support; in several early Hollywood talkies: *His Glorious Night* (John Gilbert's first talkie), Janet Gaynor's *Sunny Side Up, Charlie Chan Carries On* (as Inspector Duff); from '35 in English pix: *The Iron Duke, East Meets West,* etc.

GAXTON, WILLIAM *(1963)* 69 ——Aggressive, bombastic Broadway comedian who

starred in *Fifty Million Frenchmen,* co-starred with West in *The Heat's On,* and in several Technicolor musicals of the '40s: *Best Foot Forward, Something to Shout About, Diamond Horseshoe,* etc.

GAYE, ALBIE *(1965)* 30s ——Singer-actress in *The Miami Story.*

GAYER, ECHLIN *(1926)* 48 ——In *Her Love Story* he was the older king with whom youthful princess Swanson was forced into marriage.

GEARY, BUD *(1946)* 47 ——Did tough guys in Laurel and Hardy comedies (*Great Guns, Saps at Sea, A-Haunting We Will Go*), and even thuggier ones in serials (*The Purple Monster Strikes, Haunted Harbor, Jungle Girl*), often as top villain Roy Barcroft's #1 aide and with names like Snell.

GEE, GEORGE *(1959)* 64 ——Support in British pix: *Leave It to Me, Weekend Wives,* etc.

GELDART, CLARENCE *(1935)* 67 ——Dignified character with long (1915–36) career; silents: Swanson's *The Great Moment* and *Why Change Your Wife?* (the doctor who treated injured Thomas Meighan), *Adam's Rib,* etc.; talkies: *The Bishop Murder Case, Emma,* others.

GEMIER, FIRMIN *(1933)* 68 ——He had a top supporting role in Alice Terry's *The Magician;* was also in, among others, the French film *Grandeur et Decadence.*

GEMORA, CHARLIE *(1961)* 58 ——In *King Kong* shots where a replica was not used, he was inside the gorilla suit; same applies to *White Witch Doctor, At the Circus, The Gorilla;* out of uniform had minor supports in *One-Eyed Jacks, Swiss Miss,* etc.

GENDRON, PIERRE *(1956)* 60 ——Evelyn Brent's lean, lanky lover in *The Dangerous Flirt* ('25); youthful leads in other silents: *The Man Who Played God,* Hope Hampton's *Does It Pay?,* Pauline Frederick's *Three Women,* etc.

GENIAT, MARCELLE *(1959)* 80 ——Support in such talkies as *The Man of the Hour, They Were Five,* and *Les Mysteres de Paris.*

GENTLE, ALICE *(1958)* 68 ——Opera star who had top supporting roles in two all-Technicolor operettas at Warners in '30: Bernice Claire's *Song of the Flame,* Vivienne Segal's *Golden Dawn.*

GENTRY, BOB *(1962)* 44 ——Supporting roles.

GEORGE, GLADYS *(1954)* 50 ——Husky-voiced, hardbitten, heart-of-gold blonde by whom Hollywood should have done better; starred (after forgettable silents) with Tone in 1934's *Straight Is the Way;* next had solo star billing in *Valiant Is the Word for Carrie,* her finest (Oscar-nominated as Best Actress), and in *Madame X* (fifth actress to do this tearjerker); then came the tough-gal—co-star at first—roles: *They Gave Him a Gun, The Roaring Twenties* (almost stole it as nightclub hostess Panama Smith who, cradling the gunned-down Cagney in her arms at the fadeout, tells the world, "He was Somebody"); and so was she—in every one of the 32 talkies in which, sometimes all too briefly, she was seen.

GEORGE, GRACE *(1961)* 81 ——The fragile little old lady who, after a great stage career, starred onscreen just once—with touching elegance—in *Johnny Come Lately,* as the lady newspaper publisher to whom vagrant Cagney is paroled.

GEORGE, HEINRICH *(1946)* 53 ——German star; one of the leads (the labor foreman) in Fritz Lang's *Metropolis;* also in *Bondage, The Dreyfus Case,* many other European films.

GEORGE, MURIEL *(1965)* 82 ——Plump British character; in *Dear Octopus, Simon and Laura, Vacation from Marriage,* more.

GEORGE, VOYA *(1951)* 56 ——Rumanian actor who had top supporting roles in many silents of the '20s: *The Life and Death of 9413—A Hollywood Extra,* Gary Cooper's *The Legion of the Condemned* (as the gambler), etc.

GERAGHTY, CARMELITA *(1966)* 65 —— Black-haired beauty who, starring at Selznick in '24, had good roles in many: *Black Oxen, The Great Gatsby* ('26), *The Last Trail, High Speed,* etc.; lesser roles in talkies until '35: *Night Life in Reno, Malay, Forgotten Women,* etc.

GERALD, ARA *(1957)* 63 ——Opera singer; minor support in Kay Francis' *The White Angel.*

GERALD, JIM *(1958)* 69 ——French supporting actor; in *The Barefoot Contessa* (Mr. Blue), *Moulin Rouge* (Pere Cotelle), *French Without Tears* (the professor), *Father Brown,* etc.; earlier had been in Rene Clair's *The Italian Straw Hat,* other silents.

GERARD, TEDDIE *(1942)* 52 ——She had solo star billing in First National's *Cave Girl* ('21) and was with Barthelmess in the following year's *The Seventh Day.*

GERAY, STEVEN *(1973)* 69 ——Polished Continental (from Czechoslovakia) whose smile and bland face sometimes, but not always, cloaked a treacherous heart; in *Gilda* (bar-

tender, Uncle Pio), *Cornered, The Moon and Sixpence, Spellbound* (Dr. Graff), *Call Me Madam,* numerous spy pix (*The Mask of Dimitrios,* as Bulic, *The Seventh Cross, Hotel Berlin*), Rains' *The Phantom of the Opera;* had the lead in one, a '46 Columbia B, *So Dark the Night.*

GERMI, PIETRO *(1974)* 60 ——Italian character actor and Oscar-winning director (*Divorce Italian Style*); appeared in movies from the 1940s: in *Flight Into France, La Viaccia,* and—both of which he wrote and directed—*The Facts of Murder* and *The Railroad Man.*

GERRARD, GENE *(1971)* 78 ——Light comic in British films: *My Wife's Family, Her Radio Romeo, Mister Hobo,* others.

GERRON, KURT *(1943)* 50s ——Portly German actor; the magician-impresario in Dietrich's *The Blue Angel;* in *Berlin After Dark, You Don't Need Any Money,* other German films.

GERSON, EVA *(1959)* 56 ——Minor support in *North by Northwest* and Muni's *The Last Angry Man.*

GERSON, PAUL *(1957)* 86 ——Starred in (and produced) 1923's *The Cricket on the Hearth.*

GERSTEN, BERTA *(1972)* 79 ——Was seen as star Steve Allen's mom in *The Benny Goodman Story.*

GERSTLE, FRANK *(1970)* 53 ——Usually a professional man or officer of the law; in *Autumn Leaves, Tight Spot, Vicki, I Was a Communist for the FBI, Vice Raid,* more.

GEST, INNA *(1965)* 43 ——Was the young femme lead (19) in a 1940 East Side Kids pic, *The Ghost Creeps* (or *Boys of the City*), then both a Busby Berkeley beauty (MGM musicals) and a Goldwyn Girl (*Up In Arms*), and a B Westerns heroine.

GETTINGER, WILLIAM *(1966)* 77 ——See William Steele.

GIACHETTI, FOSCO *(1974)* 70 ——Italian character; in *Scipio Africanus, Life of Giuseppe Verdi,* Louis Jourdan's *Fear No Evil,* Vittorio Gassman's *Love and Larceny,* etc.

GIBBONS, ROSE *(1964)* 78 ——Supporting actress; minor roles.

GIBSON, HOOT *(1962)* 70 ——The cowboy idol of almost every kid in America in the '20s and well into the '30s; had been in Westerns from 1911's *Shotgun Jones,* and competing in rodeos in '12 had won the title "World's Champion Cowboy"; that decade, many cowboy two-reelers; rocketed to fame in his first full-length feature, 1921's *Action;* in the '20s he was Universal's #1 cowboy star—earning $14,000 a week as star and producer—and was the only real rival to Fox's Tom Mix; made scores: *Kid from Powder River, The Saddle Hawk, King of the Rodeo,* etc.; exact index to the year of his popularity decline—in the '36 Ten Top Money-Making Western stars list, the poll's first year, he was #9; Autry was #3, and next year #1, and the Western tune had changed; except for a '37 serial, was offscreen till '40; came back to co-star (until '44) with Ken Maynard and Bob Steele in Monogram's low-budget "Trail Blazers" series; last did a supporting role in John Ford's *The Horse Soldiers* (a Yankee sergeant) and a bit (roadblock guard) in Sinatra's *Ocean's 11.*

GIBSON, JAMES *(1938)* 72 ——Western-type support; in *Greed* (deputy sheriff), Lefty Flynn's *Glenister of the Mounted,* Oakie's *The Social Lion,* Warner Baxter's *The Arizona Kid.*

GIGLI, BENIAMINO *(1958)* 67 ——Great Italian opera star; top-billed in many: *Forever Yours, Ave Maria, Laugh Pagliacci, Singing Taxi Driver,* more.

GILBERT, BILLY *(1971)* 78 ——Rotund, well-loved, sneezing comic support; was voice for Sneezy, of course, in *Snow White and the Seven Dwarfs,* just one of his 300 pix: *Anchors Aweigh, Destry Rides Again, Seven Sinners, His Girl Friday, On the Avenue, The Great Dictator* (the hilarious Herring), etc.; despite all his accented roles, he was American—from Kentucky.

GILBERT, BOB *(1973)* 75 ——Comedian featured in MGM's *Never the Twain Shall Meet* ('31).

GILBERT, JOHN *(1936)* 38 ——Handsome matinee idol of the '20s who rose from screen extra with Ince to William S. Hart Westerns (*Hell's Hinges*), to Pickford's leading man (*Heart o' the Hills*), to stardom (in *His Hour, The Snob, He Who Gets Slapped, The Merry Widow*), to superstardom (in *The Big Parade* and the many silents that followed); sound, though he made 15 talkies, destroyed his career; offscreen this great lover was married to a non-pro ("Miss Burwell"), Leatrice Joy (still uses his name), Ina Claire and Virginia Bruce (both of whom do not)—and loved Garbo, just as he did in *Flesh and the Devil* and *Queen Christina.*

GILBERT, WALTER *(1947)* 80 ——Support in *Gambling* ('34).

GILES, ANNA *(1973)* 99 ——Veteran silent screen actress.

GILL, BASIL *(1955)* 78 ——Support in British pix: *Knight Without Armour* (as Alexstein), *Rembrandt, The Citadel* (doctor), more.

GILLETTE, WILLIAM *(1937)* 81 ——Starred for Essanay in the 1916 film version of his great stage hit *Sherlock Holmes,* his only screen work.

GILLIE, JEAN *(1949)* 34 ——Charming British actress; femme lead in *The Tawny Pipit* and Monogram's *Decoy* ('46) with Edward Norris; also in *The Macomber Affair, The Spider,* etc.

GILLINGWATER, CLAUDE *(1939)* 69 ——Played irascible old men—skinny, with bald pate and gray fringe—from the beginning, in Pickford's *Little Lord Fauntleroy* in '21, to Shirley Temple's *Poor Little Rich Girl, Little Miss Marker,* and *Just Around the Corner;* in between were dozens: Constance Talmadge's *Dulcy, Three Wise Fools,* Mae Marsh's *Daddies,* Colman's *A Tale of Two Cities, The Prisoner of Shark Island, Broadway Bill,* etc.

GILLIS, WILLIAM *(1946)* 60s ——Support in the Ruth Roland serial *Ruth of the Rockies.*

GILMORE, DOUGLAS *(1950)* 47 ——Dark-haired leading man who was in many from 1925: *Sally, Irene and Mary* (as playboy Glen Nester), *Cameo Kirby* (young villain with Loy as his mistress), *The Naughty Flirt, Hell's Angels* (Captain Redfield), *Paris, The Taxi Dancer, Dance Madness,* etc.

GILMORE, FRANK *(1943)* 75 ——Had a leading role in Ethel Barrymore's *The Lifted Veil* ('17).

GILMORE, LOWELL *(1960)* 53 ——Suave, wavy-haired support who seemed British (actually was a Minnesotan), was always cool, and could be cruel; at his lip-pursing best in 1950's *King Solomon's Mines* (as Eric Masters), *Calcutta, Dream Girl, Plymouth Adventure* (as Pilgrim Edward Winslow), *The Prince of Thieves,* more.

GILPIN, CHARLES S. *(1930)* 51 ——Support in the last silent version of *Ten Nights in a Barroom* ('26).

GILSON, TOM *(1962)* 28 ——Saturnine blond newcomer who had a supporting role in Newman's *Rally Round the Flag, Boys.*

GIM, H. W. *(1973)* 70s ——Veteran supporting actor.

GIRARD, JOSEPH *(1949)* 68 ——Support in silent comedies (*Fireman, Save My Child*; *In Hollywood with Potash and Perlmutter*, etc.) and suspense pix in the '30s (*The Gang Buster, The Sky Spider, The Mystery of the Hooded Horseman*, others).

GIRARDOT, ETIENNE *(1939)* 83 ——He was daffy and delightful as the old Jesus-freak-before-his-time, pasting those religious stickers on every window in *Twentieth Century*; laughter was not his "music" in his first, 1914's *The Violin of M'sieur* with Clara Kimball Young— "A violinist and his daughter are reunited after a long separation, when she recognizes the strains of his instrument from a distance"; in many other dramas (*Hearts Divided; Little Man, What Now?*, etc.), comedies (*There Goes My Heart*), and musicals (*The Story of Vernon and Irene Castle*, as Aubel, the French producer who thought he was hiring Castle as a comedian).

GISH, DOROTHY *(1968)* 70 —— A silent immortal like sister Lillian, and like her a blonde, though she had dark hair (a wig) in her most famous roles; *Orphans of the Storm* remains the most notable of her over-100 films, but her outstanding gift was always for comedy; some of the best of her silents (dating from her debut in '12): *Hearts of the World, Remodeling Her Husband* (first of many romantic comedies), *The Bright Shawl, Night Life of New York, Romola, Fury*; leaving the screen in 1930, for a highly successful stage career, she was seen in just four later movies; she played mothers (Gail Russell's in *Our Hearts Were Young and Gay*; Jeanne Crain's and Linda Darnell's in *Centennial Summer*; Tom Tryon's in *The Cardinal*) and starred as the widow-owner of the New England factory in *The Whistle at Eaton Falls*.

GLASER, LILLIAN *(1969)* 78 ——Actress-widow of De Wolf Hopper; in 1915's *How Molly Made Good*.

GLASER, LULU *(1958)* 84 ——Lillian's sister who was also in *How Molly Made Good*.

GLASER, VAUGHN *(1958)* 76 ——Sour-tempered school principal, Mr. Bradley, in Jimmy Lydon's "Henry Aldrich" pix; support in *Saboteur* and *Arsenic and Old Lace* (the judge).

GLASS, EVERETT *(1966)* 75 ——Character who played a Quaker Elder in *Friendly Persuasion* and Reverend Brown in *Elmer Gantry*; was also in *The Petty Girl, Demetrius and the Gladiators, Inferno, Two Flags West*, etc.

GLASS, GASTON *(1965)* 66 ——Starred in 1920's *Humoresque* as the young concert violinist; in *Daughters of the Rich, The Hero, Rich Men's Wives, Little Miss Smiles, After the Ball*, numerous other silents; support in talkies: *The Princess Comes Across* (photographer), *Desire* (employed his native-born French accent as a French policeman), *Sylvia Scarlett* (purser), *Sutter's Gold*, etc.; retired in '37.

GLASSMIRE, GUS *(1946)* 67 ——Minor support; in *Scarlet Street, Fallen Angel, Wilson, My Gal Sal*, etc. and in the 1943 *Batman* serial.

GLAUM, LOUISE *(1970)* 70 ——Greatly popular Ince-Triangle star who was, playwright Robert E. Sherwood once ventured, "in her time, the best actress of all the screen vamps"; at her brunette seductive best in *The Lure of Woman, The Iron Strain, Sex, I Am Guilty!, The Leopard Woman*, other silent sizzlers; was William S. Hart's leading lady in *Hell's Hinges, The Aryan, The Last Card*; never appeared in talkies.

GLEASON, JAMES *(1959)* 72 ——Jaundiced, heart-of-gold little guy; his side-of-the-mouth—cabbies, detectives, reporters, marine sergeants, pals—made stars look good in every one of the 150 pix he did, from Constance Talmadge's *Polly of the Follies*; perhaps his best: Robert Montgomery's fight manager in *Here Comes Mr. Jordan* (Oscar-nominated as Best Support); great, too, in *The Bishop's Wife* (the cabbie who found he could ice-skate like a champ—with the aid of Angel Dudley, Cary Grant), *A Tree Grows in Brooklyn, Meet John Doe, Arsenic and Old Lace*; last was Tracy's politician crony in *The Last Hurrah*; let's hear it for the tough-talking little Irishman!

GLEASON, LUCILLE *(1947)* 59 ——James' wife who, with her gray bangs, played gruff gals in many—*Klondike Annie, Rhythm on the Range*, etc.—and was with him in several (*The Shannons of Broadway, The Ex Mrs. Bradford, The Clock*).

GLEASON, RUSSELL *(1945)* 36 ——Son of James and Lucille; entering pix in Marie Prevost's *The Flying Fool* ('29), he had young supporting roles (or romantic juvenile leads) in many in the next 15 years: *Hitchhike to Heaven, The Higgins Family* (with both parents), *Money to Burn, Grandpa Goes to Town, Off to the Races*, etc.

GLECKLER, ROBERT *(1939)* 49 ——Tough-guy support, such as "Dirty Eddie" in *Alexander's Ragtime Band*; a bruiser, too, in *The Case of the Curious Bride, Show Them No Mercy, Bulldog Drummond's Revenge*, many more.

GLENDINNING, ERNEST *(1936)* 52 ——Fine as Sir Edwin Caskoden in the silent *When*

Knighthood Was in Flower, after which this Englishman returned to the legitimate stage.

GLENDON, FRANK *(1937)* 50 ——Handsome leading man in silents; in *The Wooing of Princess Pat*, *What Do Men Want?* (opposite Claire Windsor), *Mid-Channel* (with Clara Kimball Young), *Kissed* (with Marie Prevost), Marion Davies' *Lights of Old Broadway* (in which he played Thomas A. Edison), etc.; in talkies, in Westerns *(King of the Pecos)* and serials *(The Lost Special*, as #1 villain, and Gene Autry's *Phantom Empire)*; sometimes billed J. Frank Glendon.

GLENN, RAYMOND *(1974)* 76 ——See Bob Custer.

GLENN, ROY *(1971)* 56 ——Played Poitier's father with dignity in *Guess Who's Coming to Dinner;* first in *Lydia Bailey* and *Carmen Jones*, last in James Earl Jones' *The Great White Hope.*

GLYNNE, MARY *(1954)* 57 ——Upper-class English character; in *The Good Companions* (Miss Trant), *The Heirloom Mystery*, *Scrooge*, etc.

GODERIS, ALBERT *(1971)* 89 ——Veteran supporting actor.

GODFREY, PETER *(1970)* 70 ——Gray-haired support in Tracy's *Edison the Man* and Dr. Jekyll and Mr. Hyde (his butler), *Raffles* and *The Two Mrs. Carrolls;* directed the last as he did many other WB pix: *Christmas in Connecticut*, *The Woman in White*, *Hotel Berlin*, etc.

GODFREY, RENEE *(1964)* 44 ——Lovely leading lady in a Rathbone-Sherlock Holmes pic, *Terror by Night*, and gave a charming performance in an Anne Shirley comedy, *Unexpected Uncle*, directed by her husband, Peter; early in her career had been billed Renee Haal.

GODFREY, SAM *(1935)* 43 ——Support in Colbert's *Private Worlds*, E. G. Robinson's *I Loved a Woman*, *Washington Merry-Go-Round*, others.

GOLD, JIMMY *(1967)* 71 ——Co-starred with Charlie Naughton in England's "Crazy Gang" comedies.

GOLDENBERG, SAM *(1945)* 59 ——Character (Prince de Namur) in *The Fallen Sparrow.*

GOLDIE, WYNDHAM *(1957)* 60 ——Character actor in British pix: *Sixty Glorious Years*, *Night Train*, *Under the Red Robe*, *The Girl in the News*, etc.

GOLDNER, CHARLES *(1955)* 55 ——Austrian character; top supporting role in Guinness' *The Captain's Paradise;* also in *Brighton Rock*, *The Rocking Horse Winner*, and many American pix: *Secret People*, *Flame and the Flesh*, *The Racers*, *Duel in the Jungle.*

GOLDSTEIN, JENNIE *(1960)* 63 ——Featured in the '38 Yiddish film *Two Sisters.*

GOLUBEFF, GREGORY *(1958)* 60s ——The orchestra leader in Lombard and Raft's *Bolero.*

GOMBELL, MINNA *(1973)* 81 ——Of the scores in which she appeared (stole?) one was *Strictly Dynamite*—and she invariably was, whether dishing out the one-liner wisecracks (as *Stepping Sisters'* aging burlesque queen), gripes *(Babbitt)*, common sense (as James Dunn's "friendly enemy," his wife's chum, in *Bad Girl)*, or callous cruelty (agreeing to her elderly parents' spending their final years a continent apart, as in those heartbreaking closing scenes in *Make Way for Tomorrow);* bowed out, and was missed, after 1951's *I'll See You in My Dreams.*

GOMEZ, THOMAS *(1971)* 65 ——Porcine character who well understood the meaning of "to smile and smile, yet be a villain"; Maria Montez suffered often at his hands *(Arabian Nights*, *White Savage)*, as did other stars of Universal's *The Climax*, *Phantom Lady*, *Singapore*, etc.; nominated as Best Support as the Mexican in *Ride the Pink Horse;* at his menacing, perspiry best as Robinson's chief henchman in *Key Largo.*

GONZALES, GILBERTO *(1954)* 48 ——Supported Armendariz in *The Pearl* and *The Littlest Outlaw.*

GONZALES, JIMMY *(1971)* 59 ——Actor, dancer, singer; minor roles.

GOOD, KIP *(1964)* 45 ——One of the young supporting soldiers in *Stage Door Canteen.*

GOODE, JACK *(1971)* 63 ——One of the three dancing Yankee Clippers—on the wing span—in *Flying Down to Rio;* other Astaire pix.

GOODRICH, EDNA *(1974)* 90 ——Lovely brunette Mutual star (from Broadway) who had silent leads from 1915; in *A Daughter of Maryland*, *Reputation*, others.

GOODRICH, G. W. *(1931)* 70 ——The father in Louise Brooks' *The Show-Off*, his only film; Broadway character actor.

GOODRICH, LOUIS *(1945)* 79 ——Support in English pix: Arthur Wontner's *Sherlock*

Holmes' Fatal Hour, The Thirteenth Candle, The Captain's Table, etc.

GOODWIN, BILL *(1959)* 49 ——With the face, permanent smile, and glibness of a traveling salesman, this famous radio announcer was a natural for blustery good-guy roles in *Incendiary Blonde, Bathing Beauty, Riding High, The Jolson Story*, many more.

GOODWIN, NAT C. *(1920)* 63 ——Fagin in 1912's *Oliver Twist*, based on his great stage success; also top-billed in *The Master Hand* with moppet Katherine Lee.

GOODWIN, RUBY (1961) 50s ——Black character actress; did maids in Lupino's *Strange Intruder* and in *The View from Pompey's Head*.

GOODWINS, LESLIE *(1969)* 69 ——Christie comic who later directed most of the Edgar "Slow Burn" Kennedy shorts.

GORCEY, BERNARD *(1955)* 67 ——Leo's comedian dad; played Louie in 29 "Bowery Boys" pix *(Trouble Makers, Fighting Fools, Crazy Over Horses*, etc.); had been the original Isaac Cohen, father of Abie, in *Abie's Irish Rose*, both on Broadway and in the Nancy Carroll silent movie; character roles in *The Great Dictator* (Mr. Mann), *Joan of Paris*, etc.

GORCEY, LEO *(1969)* 52 ——"Dead End Kids'" immortal, monkey-faced Spit; with them in *Dead End, Angels with Dirty Faces, Crime School*, etc.; without them in *Maisie Gets Her Man, Destroyer, Mr. Wise Guy*, many others; top-billed as Slip Mahoney in 41 of the 48 "Bowery Boys" pix at Monogram (1946–58); this B series featured (not always at the same time) four of the original "Dead End Kids": Leo, Huntz Hall (all 48), Bobby Jordan (the first 8), Gabriel Dell (came in on #4, *Spook Busters*, and was in 17 from 1946–50); Billy Halop never appeared, nor did Bernard (Milty) Punsley, who had become a physician; retiring to ranch life in the late '50s, Gorcey came back in the '60s for cameos in two: *It's a Mad, Mad, Mad, Mad World* and *The Phynx*, an all-star WB flop never generally released.

GORDON, BERT *(1974)* 76 ——The inimitable little "Mad Russian," of radio fame and comedy antics in *She Gets Her Man, Sing for Your Supper, New Faces of 1937*, etc.

GORDON, C. HENRY *(1940)* 57 ——Specialized in satanic scoundrels—cultivated, mockingly suave; in dozens from '30 and some of the screen's best: *Scarface* (as Angelo), *The Crusades* (Philip of France), *Mata Hari* (Dubois), *Conquest, The Charge of the Light Brigade* (evil Surat Kahn, skewered on a spike by Flynn); Charlie Chan tripped him up, too, in *Charlie Chan in City in Darkness, Charlie Chan at the Wax Museum*, others.

GORDON, COLIN *(1972)* 61—Comedy character in many British pix; best in *Folly to Be Wise*, wherein Army entertainment officer Alistair Sim stages a quiz show for the troops and asks the wrong question ("Is marriage a good idea?" of the wrong panel of "experts"—Elizabeth Allan (wife), Roland Culver (husband), and Gordon (lover).

GORDON, EDWARD R. *(1938)* 52 ——Support in Westerns in the '20s: *Ridin' Luck, Gun-Hand Garrison*, etc.

GORDON, GAVIN *(1970)* 69 ——Garbo's smooth lover in *Romance* (her second talkie), who lost her because she felt unworthy of him, a bishop's grandson; co-starred in *The Great Meadow*; quickly slipped into supporting roles and had many major ones; in *The Scarlet Empress, The Bitter Tea of General Yen, They Gave Him a Gun, White Christmas* (Gen. Carlton in the big party finale), many others.

GORDON, GLORIA *(1962)* 81 ——Gale's mother; Mrs. O'Reilly in *My Friend Irma*; others.

GORDON, HAL *(1946)* 52 ——Jovial English support in comedies: *Old Mother Riley, Captain Bill, Adam's Apple*, etc.

GORDON, HAROLD *(1959)* 39 ——Support in Kazan's *East of Eden* (Mr. Albrecht) and *Viva Zapata!* (Madero); in Danny Thomas' *The Jazz Singer, The Iron Mistress*, etc.

GORDON, HARRIS *(1947)* 60 ——Memorable as the unemployed cigar salesman who joins the collectivist farm in King Vidor's classic, *Our Daily Bread*; previously in silents: *Burning Sands*, Dorothy Dalton's *The Woman Who Walked Alone, The Dawn of Tomorrow*, others.

GORDON, HUNTLEY *(1956)* 69 ——Before playing Crawford's father in *Our Dancing Daughters*, he had been a vastly popular star in many silents: *Beyond the Rainbow* (with Billie Dove), *Our Mrs. McChesney* (Ethel Barrymore), *Bluebeard's Eighth Wife* (Swanson), *The Famous Mrs. Fair*, etc.; support in a score of talkies: *Stage Door* (onstage in the play Hepburn did), *Only Yesterday, Portia on Trial*, others.

GORDON, JAMES *(1941)* 60 ——Star of 1914's *The Oath of a Viking*, George O'Brien's dad in *The Iron Horse*; many in between (*Nancy from*

Nowhere, The Man from Lost River, etc.) and later (*Babe Comes Home, Tongues of Scandal,* 1931's *The Front Page*, as the mayor, others).

GORDON, JULIA SWAYNE *(1933)* 54 ——Dignified, dour character actress in a score of talkies (*Gold Diggers of Broadway, Scandal, Broken Lullaby*, etc.); in silents, from age 20 and almost always playing older women, a major star; in *Rock of Ages, Napoleon Bonaparte and the Empress Josephine of France, The Battle Hymn of the Republic* (as Julia Ward Howe), *King Lear* (Goneril), *Lady Godiva*, etc.; support in many later silents, such as the mother of Richard Arlen in *Wings*; very early in her career had been billed Julia Swayne.

GORDON, KITTY *(1974)* 96 ——Brunette actress from England famed for the beauty of her back; starred in America in such silents as *As In a Looking Glass* (the lovely double agent in WW I), *Mandarin's Gold, The Interloper Adele* (Army nurse captured and raped by Huns), etc.

GORDON, LEON *(1960)* 64 ——Support in Barbara La Marr's *Sandra*; later a well-known producer (*Mrs. Parkington*) and writer (*Balalaika*).

GORDON, MACK *(1959)* 54 ——Famous composer ("Once in a Blue Moon," dozens more songs) who was onscreen in *Collegiate* and *You're My Everything.*

GORDON, MARY *(1963)* 81 ——Apple-cheeked, gray-haired little dear with a touch of Ireland (sometimes Scotland) in her speech; well recalled as the housekeeper, Mrs. Hudson, in six of Rathbone's 14 "Sherlock Holmes" pix (*Sherlock Holmes and the Spider Woman*, etc.); often played moms, such as Cagney's and O'Brien's in *The Irish in Us*; active, in dozens, through 1950's *West of Wyoming.*

GORDON, NORA *(1970)* 76 ——Plump, gray, coronet-braided English character; often a cook, as in *The Fallen Idol*; in *Horrors of the Black Museum, Blackmailed*, etc.

GORDON, RICHARD *(1956)* 63 ——The psychiatrist in *13 Rue Madeleine*, he had been handsome young support in early talkies (Colleen Moore's *Synthetic Sin*, etc.), silent features (*Romance Road*) and serials (Herbert Rawlinson's *The Flame Fighter*).

GORDON, ROBERT *(1971)* 76 ——Popular youth in silents; was Huck Finn in Jack Pickford's *Tom Sawyer* ('17) and the later *Huck and Tom*; starred, as the young soldier, in a 1918 Paramount tearjerker, *Missing*; in *The Rosary, Main Street, The Wildcat*, others.

GORDON, VERA *(1948)* 61 ——Best and most endearing of all Yiddish mamas; touched the world's heart as the mother in *Humoresque* ('20) who inspired her son to become a noted violinist; later, heavier, she tickled the world's funnybone as the battling Mrs. Cohen in *The Cohens and the Kellys* and this comedy hit's several sequels; after '31 onscreen only seven times including her last, *Abie's Irish Rose*, in '46.

GORE, ROSA *(1941)* 64 ——Silent support in George Walsh's *Vanity Fair*, Nazimova's *Madonna of the Streets*, Matt Moore's *Three Weeks in Paris*, Monte Banks' *Play Safe*, many more.

GORGEOUS GEORGE *(1963)* 47 ——Bedizened, beefy wrestler-actor; in a few B's.

GORMAN, ERIC *(1971)* 85 ——Irish actor; Castletown Engineer in *The Quiet Man*; in *Saints and Sinners, The Rising of the Moon*, others.

GORMAN, TOM *(1971)* 63 ——Support in *12 Angry Men, Edge of the City.*

GORSS, SAUL *(1966)* 58 ——Character (Police Captain) in *Unchained*; similar-type roles in *Murderer's Row, Legion of the Doomed*, etc.

GOSFIELD, MAURICE *(1964)* 51 ——Support in *The Naked City, Kiss of Death, The Thrill of It All*, etc.

GOTTSCHALK, FERDINAND *(1944)* 75 —— Garbo's impresario, Pimenov, in *Grand Hotel*; the Duke, deBrissac, in Swanson's *Zaza*, Glabrio in *The Sign of the Cross*, Clubman in *Gold Diggers of 1933*; one of Hollywood's busiest characters, this bald-pated Englishman was also in *Les Miserables, Clive of India, Cafe Metropole, The Garden of Allah*, and 50 more.

GOUGH, JOHN *(1968)* 70 ——Support in silents: John Gilbert's *Gleam O' Dawn*, Evelyn Brent's *The Broadway Lady* and *Midnight Molly*, Charlie Murray's *The Gorilla*, many more.

GOULD, BILLY *(1950)* 81 ——From Broadway; featured in 1924's *The Great White Way.*

GOWLAND, GIBSON *(1951)* 79 ——Part of film history because of his star role of the boorish dentist McTeague, "the human Beast," in von Stroheim's *Greed*; earlier the director had featured this huge English actor as the hulking Tyrolean mountain guide in *Blind Husbands*; without his *Greed*-bleached hair and eyebrows, Gowland had major supporting roles in many more silents: *The Phantom of the Opera* (Simon), *Rose Marie, The Prairie Wife,* etc.; most of his talkies were made in England: *The Mystery of the Mary Celeste, Cotton Queen, Secret of the Loch;* retired in '38.

GRABLE, BETTY *(1973)* 56 ——One thinks of her in colors—pink, blonde, blue (eyes and ribbons on period-costume bonnets)—because, once a star, she was almost always seen in Technicolor; went from chorus girl at Fox *(Let's Go Places,* '30) to undisputed Queen of the 20th Century-Fox lot; was #1 in the hearts of WW II GIs and at the box-office (1943, and in the Top 10 each year from '42 to '51); some of the musicals that kept her there: *Springtime in the Rockies, Coney Island, Sweet Rosie O'-Grady, Pin-Up Girl, The Dolly Sisters;* did creditable acting jobs, sans songs or dances or color, in *I Wake Up Screaming* (*Hot Spot*) and *A Yank in the R.A.F.;* her last was 1955's *How to Be Very Very Popular*—that secret she surely knew.

GRAETZ, PAUL *(1937)* 46 ——Support in British pix of the '30s: *Bulldog Jack, Mr. Cohen Takes a Walk, Alias Bulldog Drummond, Bengal Tiger,* etc.

GRAFF, WILTON *(1969)* 64 ——Durable, versatile solid supporting actor in more than 60 from 1945's *Pillow to Post;* equally at home in heavy drama (*Compulsion,* as father of child-murderer Dean Stockwell), musicals (*Million Dollar Mermaid, So This Is Love*), Westerns (*Springfield Rifle*), swashbucklers (*Rogues of Sherwood Forest, King Richard and the Crusaders*), comedies (*Once More, My Darling*).

GRAHAM, CHARLIE *(1943)* 46 ——Supported Houdini in the silent serial *The Master Mystery;* in many silent features: Pearl White's *The Mountain Woman,* Will Rogers' *The Headless Horseman,* Swanson's *The Untamed Lady* (as Shorty), etc.

GRAHAM, FRANK *(1950)* 35 ——Famous radio announcer who was seen in Disney's *The Three Caballeros.*

GRAHAM, JULIA ANN *(1935)* 20 ——Starlet in Burns and Allen's *Love In Bloom.*

GRAHAM, MORLAND *(1949)* 57 ——Chunky actor in British pix; Sir Thomas Erpingham in *Henry V,* Old Bill in *Old Bill and Son;* also in *Night Train, Jamaica Inn, The Scarlet Pimpernel, Bonnie Prince Charlie,* more.

GRAHAM, RONALD *(1950)* 38 ——Handsome young man from Scotland who co-starred with Trudy Marshall in a 20th Century-Fox B, *La-dies of Washington* ('44); earlier in *Old Man Rhythm;* not the comedian Ronnie Graham.

GRAHAME, BERT *(1971)* 78 ——Silent support.

GRAMATICA, EMMA *(1965)* 80 ——Legendary Italian actress; the old-lady angel in De Sica's *Miracle in Milan;* also in *Marcella, Jeanne d'Ore,* many others.

GRAN, ALBERT *(1932)* 70 ——Old Boul in Gaynor's *Seventh Heaven;* earlier in Norma Talmadge's *Graustark,* Davies' *Beverly of Graustark,* etc.; later in *Four Sons, The Blue Danube,* followed by numerous talkies (*The Man from Blankley's,* as Uncle Gabriel, *Kiss Me Again,* others).

GRANACH, ALEXANDER *(1945)* 55 ——With Sig Rumann and Felix Bressart was one of *Ninotchka's* three bumbling jewel-selling emissaries from Russia (he was Kopalski); had been in silents (*Warning Shadows,* etc.); later this Polish actor was in *The Hitler Gang, Hangmen Also Die, For Whom The Bell Tolls* (as Paco).

GRANBY, JOSEPH *(1965)* 80 ——Handsome actor who co-starred with Valeska Surratt in 1916's *Jealousy;* support in pix of the '40s: Richard Arlen's *The Phantom Speaks,* von Stroheim's *The Great Flamarion,* Dietrich's *Kismet,* etc.

GRANGER, WILLIAM *(1938)* 84 ——Character in Billie Dove's *The Other Tomorrow,* Joe E. Brown's *6-Day Bike Rider.*

GRANT, EARL *(1970)* 39 ——Black musician; in *Tender Is the Night,* Turner's *Imitation of Life.*

GRANT, LAWRENCE *(1952)* 82 ——English actor who came to America in 1918 to star, as the Kaiser, in Metro's *To Hell with the Kaiser* and stayed—to play the Kaiser in others and become one of Hollywood's busiest, best characters; in Clara Bow's *Red Hair* (judge-father of her beau), *Shanghai Express* (Reverend Carmichael), 1931's *The Squaw Man* (General Stafford), *A Tale of Two Cities* (Prosecuting Attorney in Old Bailey), many others through Boyer's *Confidential Agent* in '45.

GRANT, SYDNEY *(1953)* 80 ——Tuxedoed comic support in Charlotte Greenwood's *Jane* ('16); primarily a stage actor.

GRANVILLE, AUDREY *(1972)* 62 ——Popular child actress in silents.

GRANVILLE, LOUISE *(1969)* 73 ——Leading lady in early John Ford pix; in his *The Scrapper* ('17), others.

GRAPEWIN, CHARLES *(1956)* 81 ——The screen's great irascible old man—Jeeter Lester in *Tobacco Road*, Grandpa in *The Grapes of Wrath*, Old Father in *The Good Earth*; in dozens more from 1929's *The Shannons of Broadway* (with James and Lucille Gleason): *Alice Adams, Three Comrades, Dust Be My Destiny, Of Human Hearts*, etc.; shaved off his stubbly gray whiskers and became Inspector Queen, father of Ralph Bellamy and then William Gargan, in seven "Ellery Queen" pix; active through 1951's *When I Grow Up*, starring Bobby Driscoll.

GRAUMAN, SID *(1950)* 71 ——Famous Hollywood theater impresario (Grauman's Chinese Theater, of the star footprints); occasionally onscreen as himself, in *Star Dust*, etc.

GRAVES, GEORGE *(1949)* 73 ——Support in England's *Robber Symphony* and *The Tenth Man* ('37).

GRAVET, FERNAND *(1970)* 65 ——Belgian actor whose name Warners changed from Gravey and tried to make a star here in *The King and the Chorus Girl* and *Fools for Scandal*; MGM starred him as unsuccessfully as Johann Strauss in *The Great Waltz*; failed in Hollywood, discoverer Mervyn LeRoy has said, because "his wife ruined him. . . . At the time, he was somewhere around thirty-five, and his wife must have been at least thirty years his senior. She controlled him completely, and she wanted to keep him all to herself"; became a popular star in France (*La Ronde, Symphonie d'Amour*, etc.), and had supporting roles in U.S. pix made abroad: Audrey Hepburn's *How To Steal a Million*, Katharine Hepburn's *The Madwoman of Chaillot* (as a police sergeant and back to Gravey).

GRAY, EDDIE *(1969)* 71 ——English comedian in several "Crazy Gang" pix.

GRAY, GENE *(1950)* 50 ——Westerns; called "Silver King of the Cowboys."

GRAY, GEORGE *(1967)* 78 ——Support in Three Stooges comedies: *Goofs and Saddles, Uncivil Warriors*, etc.; had been a Sennett comic.

GRAY, GILDA *(1959)* 58 ——Silent star most famous, of course, for originating the "shimmy"; shook it in *Aloma of the South Seas, The Devil Dancer, Piccadilly, Cabaret*, etc.; more restrained in her last, Jeanette MacDonald's *Rose Marie*.

GRAY, GLEN *(1963)* 63 ——Led his famous Casa Loma orchestra in musicals of the '40s: *Jam Session, Time Out for Rhythm*, etc.

GRAY, JACK *(1956)* 75 ——Moon-faced top support to Robert Montgomery and Madge Evans in *Fugitive Lovers*, etc.

GRAY, LAWRENCE *(1970)* 71 ——Handsome leading man with slicked-back black hair whose career lasted a bit more than a decade (1925–36); with Swanson in *Coast of Folly*, Colleen Moore in *Oh Kay!* (she, a titled English lady, pretended to be a maid to win him, the penniless hero), Louise Brooks in *Love 'Em and Leave 'Em*, Dorothy Mackaill in *Convoy*, Shearer in *After Midnight*, and Marilyn Miller in *Sunny*, which was preceded and followed by other talkies; last in support in a 1936 B, *Timber War*.

GRAY, LINDA *(1963)* 50 ——James Dunn's lovely newcomer leading lady in a 1938 B, *Shadows over Shanghai*; in *Holiday Inn* (credited as a Dancing Girl and billed Lynda Grey), *Happy Go Lucky*, and Westerns.

GRAYBILL, JOSEPH *(1913)* ——One of Griffith's earliest character actors, he is perhaps best recalled as the sinister stranger in *The Painted Lady* ('12), his last picture; earlier, from 1910, he had been in *The Italian Barber, A Victim of Jealousy, A Romany Tragedy, Love in the Hills, The Voice of the Child, Saved from Himself*, etc.

GREAZA, WALTER *(1973)* 76 ——Well-known as the grandfather in the TV soap opera *The Edge of Night*; character in pix: *Boomerang*, (Mayor Swayze), Doris Day's *It Happened to Jane, The Street With No Name, Larceny* (Caulfield's dad).

GREEN, DENIS *(1954)* 49 ——English character; in *Northwest Passage* (Capt. Williams), *This Above All* (Dr. Ferris), Tracy's *Dr. Jekyll and Mr. Hyde, A Yank in the R.A.F., Mighty Joe Young*, etc.

GREEN, DOROTHY *(1963)* 71 ——Appropriately regal as brunette Princess Naia in Marion Davies' *The Dark Star*; in silents earlier *(The American Way, A Parisian Romance*, Irene Castle's serial *Patria)* and later *(The Good Bad Wife*, etc.).

GREEN, FRED E. *(1940)* 50 ——Supported the Duncan Sisters in *Topsy and Eva*.

GREEN, HARRY *(1958)* 66 ——Comedian who had supporting roles in Nancy Carroll's *Close Harmony* (and later her *Honey*), *She Learned About Sailors*, Mack & Moran's *Why Bring That Up?*, others through 1940's *Star Dust*; moved to England and was in Chaplin's *A King in New York, Joe Macbeth*, etc.

GREEN, KENNETH *(1969)* 61 ——"Fatso" in "Our Gang" comedies; supported juvenile star Wesley Barry in the silent *Penrod.*

GREEN, MITZI *(1969)* 48 ——Famous child star often referred to as "Little Mitzi"—or, as critics hailed her in 1930's *Honey,* "amazing little Mitzi Green"; hit her starring stride that same year as Becky Thatcher in Coogan's *Tom Sawyer* and soon played the title role in *Little Orphan Annie* (interestingly, another little actress, Ann Gillis, later played both these roles too); some of Mitzi's other pix: *Skippy, Huckleberry Finn* ('31), *Finn and Hattie, Newly Rich, Dude Ranch;* leaving the screen in her late teens, she starred on Broadway in *Billion Dollar Baby,* and returned in top supporting roles in two 1952 comedies: Abbott & Costello's *Lost in Alaska* and Mitzi Gaynor's *Bloodhounds of Broadway.*

GREEN, NIGEL *(1972)* 48 ——Polished English actor; in *The Ipcress File,* the British Intelligence chief who turns out to be a double agent; other costar roles in *Khartoum, Deadlier Than the Male, Tobruk,* and *The Face of Fu Manchu.*

GREEN, SUE *(1939)* 37 ——Adult support in Hal Roach comedies of the '30s.

GREENE, BILLY *(1973)* 76 ——Screen veteran; last in support in *Papillon.*

GREENE, BILLY M. *(1970)* 43 ——Night clerk, Swine, at hotel in *Lolita* where Humbert and Lolita spent their first night; also in *Never Steal Anything Small, The Shrike,* etc.

GREENE, HARRISON *(1945)* 51 ——Comic support in Three Stooges shorts (*Ants in the Pantry*), etc.; plus many feature comedies: *You Can't Fool Your Wife, Blondie for Victory, Kentucky Kernels, Mr. Boggs Steps Out,* etc.

GREENLEAF, RAYMOND *(1963)* 70 ——Dignified white-haired actor who played fathers and professional men, often a judge (*Pinky, Birdman of Alcatraz, All the King's Men*), lawyer, or doctor; in *From the Terrace, Harriet Craig, Deep Waters, Storm Warning,* many more.

GREENSTREET, SYDNEY *(1954)* 74 ——Warners' bulky, sly, great scoundrel whose chuckle was as terrifying as his cold, hooded eyes; first onscreen at 61, after a stage career dating back to 1902, in *The Maltese Falcon,* which rated him his one and only Best Supporting Oscar nomination; was no less worthy, or evil, in many of his other 23 movies: *Casablanca, The Mask of Dimitrios, The Woman in White, Ruthless,* etc.; often overlooked is that he could do comedy (*Pillow to Post*) and frequently was on the "right" side of the law (*Conflict, The Conspirators, The Verdict, The Velvet Touch*).

GREENWOOD, WINNIFRED *(1961)* 70 ——From 1911 she starred for Selig in *The Two Orphans* (with Kathlyn Williams), *Under Suspicion, The Prosecuting Attorney, The Last Dance,* etc.; then, for others, in *The Profligate, The Derelict, The High Cost of Flirting,* more.

GREER, JULIAN *(1928)* 57 ——Supporting actor in *Sunshine Harbor* and Norma Talmadge's *The Passion Flower.*

GREET, CLARE *(1939)* 67 ——English character who acted for Hitchcock in four of his early films: *The Manxman, The Ring, The Man Who Knew Too Much, Jamaica Inn;* also in *Sidewalks of London, Little Friend, Emil,* others.

GREGG, EVERLEY *(1959)* 80s ——Mrs. Eynsford Hill (playboy Freddie's mother) in *Pygmalion;* also in many of the rest of England's best: *The Ghost Goes West* (Jean Parker's mother), *The Private Life of Henry VIII* (Catherine Parr), *The Scoundrel, Brief Encounter, Great Expectations* (Sarah Pocket).

GREGOR, NORA *(1949)* 50s ——Beautiful Austrian actress imported by MGM to costar, with Robert Montgomery, in just one, *But the Flesh Is Weak;* in Hollywood, played the leads in German-language versions of three Metro hits: *The Trial of Mary Dugan, His Glorious Night, The Hollywood Revue;* returned to Europe to great success as the feminine lead (Christine, philandering wife of the rich, party-giving Marquis) in Renoir's masterpiece, *The Rules of the Game;* this, reputedly, was her last film.

GREGORY, DORA *(1954)* 81 ——Was old Mrs. Lemmon in Noel Coward's *In Which We Serve;* also in Hitchcock's *The Skin Game, Star of the Circus,* other British pix.

GREGORY, WILL *(1926)* ——Support in the silent *Sensation Seekers.*

GREIG, ROBERT *(1958)* 78 ——Played towering, fish-eyed, penguin-shaped, hair-parted-in-the-middle butlers; opened doors for (or closed them on) the biggest stars in *Lloyds of London, The Moon and Sixpence, Theodora Goes Wild, Animal Crackers, The Lady Eve,* many more; did it for 19 years—1930-49.

GREY, GLORIA *(1947)* 44 ——A 1924 Wampas Baby Star, this brunette beauty was in a score of silents: *Girl of the Limberlost, Dante's Inferno, The Millionaire Cowboy, The Ghetto*

Shamrock, etc., and as the leading lady in the '27 serial *Blake of Scotland Yard,* was saved from "The Spider" by supporting actress, former serial queen, Grace Cunard.

GREY, JANE *(1944)* 61 ——Starred for Triangle in 1914's *The Little Gray Lady* and others, and in '17 for Paramount in several; in the '20s in such tearjerkers as *The Governor's Lady* and *The Love Wager.*

GREY, MADELINE *(1950)* 63 ——With Richard Dix in *Nothing But the Truth.*

GRIBBON, EDDIE *(1965)* 75 ——One of Sennett's busiest utilitarian comics in the teens, he went on to co-star (or top supporting) roles in dozens in the '20s: *Buck Privates, The Victor* (with Herbert Rawlinson), *The Fourth Musketeer, Bachelor Brides,* plus many Westerns *(Code of the West, Desert Gold,* etc.); support in comedy features, Westerns, action pix *(I Cover Chinatown,* others), and Leon Errol two-reelers in the '30s; from 1946 on, he was one of Joe Kirkwood Jr.'s ringside team in all the "Joe Palooka" pix.

GRIBBON, HARRY *(1960)* 74 ——Eddie's comedian brother: began at Sennett's fun factory as "Silk Hat," the tall thief in evening clothes in the Keystone Kops pix; also in many Mabel Normand comedies there *(Mabel, Fatty and the Law,* etc.); supported many in the '20s; William Russell in *A Self-Made Man,* Richard Dix in *Knockout Reilly,* Marion Davies in *Show People,* etc.; in B's in the '30s *(You Said a Mouthful, Ride Him, Cowboy,* others), plus Andy Clyde two-reelers.

GRIFFIN, CARLTON *(1940)* 47 ——Comic support to many in the '20s: Harry Langdon in *Tramp, Tramp, Tramp,* Harold Lloyd in *Girl Shy,* William Farnum in *Shackles of Gold,* etc.; in the '30s was in some of the best Charley Chase shorts *(The Pip from Pittsburgh, Rough Seas,* etc.).

GRIFFITH, D. W. *(1948)* 73 ——Immortal director, rightfully called "the father of Hollywood"; had acted in very early silents, such as *Rescue from an Eagle's Nest,* under various names (Lawrence Carter, Lawrence Griffith, Larry Griffith); as long as any kind of screen exists, they will be reflecting his finest films: *The Birth of a Nation, Intolerance, Broken Blossoms, Way Down East,* etc.

GRIFFITH, GORDON *(1958)* 51 ——Juvenile star of silents; Tom Sawyer in 1920's *Huckleberry Finn;* pal of Wesley Barry in *Penrod;* in the serial *Son of Tarzan* (title role), *Main Street, Little Annie Rooney, The Village Blacksmith,* etc.

GRIFFITH, KATHERINE *(1934)* 76 ——Character actress in many silents; the rich old lady in Pickford's *Pollyanna.*

GRIFFITH, RAYMOND *(1957)* 70 ——A great, now neglected star of silent comedies; how great?—reviewing a new Keaton pic in '27, critic Robert E. Sherwood ventured: "In spite of its pretentious proportions, *The General* is not nearly so good as Raymond Griffith's Civil War comedy, *Hands Up.* "; at his comedic peak in 1925–26, he was actually grand in *Wet Paint;* did a complete turnabout in his last, *All Quiet on the Western Front,* and, said the *New York Times:* "Raymond Griffith, the erstwhile comedian who, years before acting in film comedies, lost his voice through shrieking in a stage melodrama, gives a marvelous performance as the dying Frenchman."

GRIFFITH, ROBERT *(1961)* 54 ——Was in *The Night Club, The Girl in the Canal,* etc.

GRIFFITH, WILLIAM *(1960)* 63 ——Supported Claire Trevor in *Time Out for Romance,* etc.

GRIGGS, JOHN *(1967)* 58 ——Played a young naval officer in James Ellison's *Annapolis Salute;* other supporting roles in the '30s.

GRIMWOOD, HERBERT *(1929)* 54 ——Supported the Gish sisters in *Romola* and Barthelmess in *The Amateur Gentleman.*

GRISEL, LOUIS *(1928)* 80 ——Character actor in the '20s; in *The Black Panther's Cub* and the Mabel Ballin version of *Jane Eyre.*

GRISWOLD, GRACE *(1927)* 55 ——Character actress who played Auntie Fairfax in Carol Dempster's *One Exciting Night.*

GROSS, WILLIAM J. *(1924)* 87 ——Character in Marguerite Clark's very best film, *Prunella* ('18); later in *Ashamed of Parents,* etc.

GROSSMITH, GEORGE *(1935)* 60 ——Lanky English stage actor with center-parted hair; in several British-made pix: Fifi D'Orsay's *Women Everywhere* and *Those Three French Girls,* Bea Lillie's *Are You There?,* *Princess Charming,* other comedies.

GROSSMITH, LAWRENCE *(1944)* 66 —— George's brother; after numerous British pix (Fairbanks' *The Private Life of Don Juan,* Bergner's *Catherine the Great,* etc.), came to Hollywood as support in several: *Captain Fury, Gaslight* (as Lord Dalroy), *I'm From Missouri.*

GUARD, KIT *(1961)* 67 ——Danish comic in dozens of two-reelers in the '20s (the "Pacemaker," "Beauty Parlor," "Go-Getters" series); in talkies played gangsters, usually, in dramas (You and Me, Prison Train), comedies (It Ain't Hay and other Abbott & Costello pix), and serials (The Green Archer).

GUDGEON, BERTRAND *(1948)* 70s ——Support in various silent serials: Pearl White's *The Perils of Pauline* and *The Iron Claw*, etc.

GUENTHER, RUTH *(1974)* 64 ——Supporting roles in talkies.

GUHL, GEORGE *(1943)* 40s ——Played the Police Sergeant in all the Glenda Farrell "Torchy Blane" pix; similar roles in comedies (Scattergood Solves a Murder) and mysteries (Night Club Scandal, Crime by Night).

GUILBERT, YVETTE *(1944)* 79 ——One of France's greatest, she was in *Faust* ('26), *L'Argent*, *Pecheurs d'Islande*, etc.

GUILFOYLE, PAUL *(1961)* 58 ——Superb foxy-faced character; onscreen from '35, he got his best notices in his sixth, *Winterset*, containing one of his few sympathetic roles—Esdras, the unwilling youth forced (by Ciannelli) to drive the murder car; said the *New York Times:* "His portrayal of the despairing violinist with the weight of remorse on his heart is one of the film's finer things"; after that—in scores—played sly hoods doomed to bad ends, e.g., Cagney stuffing him into a car trunk in *White Heat*; was last seen in '60 in, of all things, a kiddie pic, *The Boy and the Pirates*.

GUINAN, TEXAS *(1934)* 50s ——Lusty real-life Broadway nightclub owner-hostess ("Hello, Sucker!") who starred as herself in *Queen of the Night Clubs* ('29), Eddie Cantor's *Glorifying the American Girl* ('30), and *Broadway Thru a Keyhole* ('33); earlier, this Canadian (despite her adopted nickname) starred in pistol-totin' Westerns: *Little Miss Deputy, The Gun Woman*, etc.; in '45 Betty Hutton portrayed her in *Incendiary Blonde*.

GUITRY, SACHA *(1957)* 72 ——"The old master of casual, ironic wit," who was one of France's immortals; *merveilleux* in *Bonne Chance, The Story of a Cheat, Royal Affairs in Versailles, Nine Bachelors, Champs-Elysses* (played five roles including both Napoleons); directed most of his own films; critic Graham Greene, noting his "sagacious hollow voice, that swinging monocle and the conqueror's

gait," added that "he might be described as the Montaigne of the screen."

GUITTY, MADELEINE *(1936)* 82 ——French actress who was top support (La Rousette) in Swanson's made-in-France silent *Madame Sans-Gene*; in many French films: *Le Roi des Champs-Elysees, Barcarolle*, etc.

GULLAN, CAMPBELL *(1939)* ——British support in one Fox talkie; 1929's *Pleasure Crazed*; otherwise in English pix: *The Iron Duke, Power, Song of the Road*, etc.

GURIE, SIGRID *(1969)* 58 ——Goldwyn wagered—and lost—a fortune on his conviction that this classic-featured, but frozen-faced, beauty from Norway (and Brooklyn) would be a major star; in *The Adventures of Marco Polo* (the public preferred Cooper), *Algiers* (Lamarr got the notices), starred in *Rio* and was with Wayne in *Three Faces West;* the title of her third pic, though, had been prophetic: *Forgotten Woman;* was in B's the rest of the '40s: *Enemy of Women, Dark Streets of Cairo, Sword of the Avenger*, but in one of them—a minor classic now, *Voice In the Wind*—she gave a glorious performance, as the wife of Czech refugee-pianist Francis Lederer; after 1948's *Sofia*, happily married, and a weight problem threatening her beauty, she left the screen.

GURIN, ELLEN *(1972)* 24 ——Young support in *Who Killed Mary Whats'ername?*

GURNEY, EDMUND *(1925)* 73 ——The father of Barthelmess in *Tol'able David*, the only film of this noted Broadway character player.

GUTHRIE, SIR TYRONE *(1971)* 70 ——Tall and distinguished English stage director who also acted in two Laughton films, *Sidewalks of London* and *The Beachcomber.*

GWENN, EDMUND *(1959)* 83 ——Twinkly-eyed old elf who made us believe he really was Santa in *The Miracle on 34th Street* and a counterfeiting innocent in *Mister 880;* convinced the Motion Picture Academy too—got a Supporting Oscar for the first-mentioned and a nomination, his only other, for the second; was no less plumply glorious in scores of Hollywood pix from 1936's *Sylvia Scarlett* (had been in British films from '20); a few: *Pride and Prejudice, Lassie Come Home, Foreign Correspondent, Apartment for Peggy, The Keys of the Kingdom, Anthony Adverse, Green Dolphin Street*, and *The Trouble with Harry.*

H

HAADE, WILLIAM *(1966)* 63 ——Character actor who played roles similar to those of Guinn "Big Boy" Williams and from '37 was in hundreds of Westerns: *My Pal Trigger, Union Pacific, Carson City,* etc.; was also in *Juke Girl, Rise and Shine, Pittsburgh,* others, as hoods or "dumb" good-looking cops.

HAAL, RENEE *(1964)* 44 ——See Renee Godfrey.

HAAS, HUGH *(1968)* 67 ——Heavy, and heavy-handed, Czechoslovakian actor-writer-producer-director; did all these chores on various Columbia B's of "European-style" in the '50s: *Bait, Pickup, One Girl's Confession, Thy Neighbor's Wife,* etc.; as an actor, at his mittel-Europe best in *My Girl Tisa, Mrs. Parkington, Summer Storm, Holiday in Mexico, A Bell for Adano,* more.

HACK, SIGNE *(1973)* 74 ——Character actress who was seen in horror pix, *The Viking Women,* and frequently on TV in *Range Riders, Petticoat Junction,* and *The Beverly Hillbillies.*

HACKATHORNE, GEORGE *(1940)* 44 —— Popular young star of silents of the '20s; in *The Little Minister* (title role), *The Last of the Mohicans* ('20), von Stroheim's *Merry-Go-Round* (as the Hunchback), *The Human Wreckage, Notoriety,* etc.; support in B's (*I Cover Chinatown*) and Westerns (*Flaming Guns*) in talkies, except for his last two: Irene Dunne's *Magnificent Obsession* (former hospital patient), *Gone With the Wind* (at the Atlanta hospital, Wounded Soldier in Pain).

HACKETT, FLORENCE *(1954)* 72 ——Fleshy brunette star of 1915's *Siren of Corsica* and the serial *The Beloved Adventurer;* actors Albert (in *Mickey* with Mabel Normand) and Raymond were her sons.

HACKETT, HAL *(1967)* 44 ——Juvenile at MGM in the '40s; in Skelton's *The Show-Off,* two Rooney pix (*Summer Holiday* and *Love Laughs at Andy Hardy,* as his pal Duke); and, at Republic, *Campus Honeymoon* with the Wilde Twins.

HACKETT, JAMES K. *(1926)* 67 ——Handsome hero of 1913's *The Prisoner of Zenda,* the stage star's only film.

HACKETT, KARL *(1948)* 55 ——Check-shirted henchman in scores of B Westerns: *Song and Bullets, Sons of the Pioneers, Thundering Trails,* and numerous "Three Mesquiteers" pix.

HACKETT, LILLIAN *(1973)* 70s ——Support in silents: *In Hollywood with Potash and Perlmutter, Ladies at Ease,* etc.

HACKETT, RAYMOND *(1958)* 55 ——A most popular young leading man in silents (he and brother Alfred fought over Dorothy Gish in *The Country Flapper*); was in *The Loves of Sunya* (Swanson's brother), *The Cruise of the Make-Believe, Faithless Lover,* etc., and a few early talkies: *Our Blushing Brides, The Cat Creeps, Seed,* others.

HADDON, PETER *(1962)* 64 ——British comic with a light touch; was Lord Peter Wimsey in 1935's *The Silent Passenger;* also in *The Beloved Vagabond, The Secret of Stamboul, The Second Mrs. Tanqueray,* etc.

HADLEY, REED *(1974)* 63 ——Sleek, handsome, black-haired second lead in dozens (*Dallas, Captain from Castile, A Southern Yankee, Wing and a Prayer, Guadalcanal Diary,* etc.); later starred on TV in *Racket Squad.*

HAEFELI, CHARLES *(1955)* 65 ——Character (Brevet) in *Les Miserables;* in silents had been in *The Hunchback of Notre Dame,* others.

HAGEN, CHARLES *(1958)* 86 ——Support in early Biograph pix.

HAGER, CLYDE *(1944)* 57 ——Comic support in Cantor's *Strike Me Pink.*

HAGGARD, STEPHEN *(1943)* 31 ——Minor British support in *Jamaica Inn, The Young Mr. Pitt,* etc.

HAGNEY, FRANK *(1973)* 89 ——Character actor in silent action pix (*Roaring Rails, The Last Trail,* etc.) and talkies (*The Squaw Man,* as the English clerk, *The Glass Key, It's a Wonderful Life,* others).

HAINE, HORACE J. *(1940)* 72 ——Support in silents: *The Fifth Horseman, The Moonshiners,* etc.

HAINES, RHEA *(1964)* 69 ——Young beauty in silents; in Wallace Reid's *Always Audacious, Smiling All the Way, Mary Ellen Comes to Town,* etc.

HAINES, WILLIAM *(1973)* 73 ——Light-hearted star of silents who several times played the wisecracking, penniless young man —or salesman—who won the millionaire's daughter in the final reel; in real life, though, he never married; at his best in *Slide, Kelly, Slide;*

Mike with Sally O'Neil; *Brown of Harvard; Tell It to the Marines; Sally, Irene and Mary; Alias Jimmy Valentine;* retired from movies after 1935's *The Marines Are Coming* and became an interior decorator.

HALE, ALAN *(1950)* 57 ——At the end he was known as Warners' grand, garrulous (isn't this really why Lupino murdered him in *They Drive by Night?*) character actor; wonderfully gregarious in *The Adventures of Robin Hood, Dodge City, The Fighting 69th, Gentleman Jim, Strawberry Blonde, Destination Tokyo,* and on for another 150; in silents of the teens he was one of the screen's handsomest young leads in: *The Cricket on the Hearth, Martin Chuzzlewit, Masks and Faces,* etc.; in later silents, he was star or co-star in dozens: *The Four Horsemen of the Apocalypse, Black Oxen, Long Live the King, Babbitt,* others.

HALE, BARNABY *(1964)* 37 ——Minor roles in a few.

HALE, CREIGHTON *(1965)* 83 ——One of the silent screen's most popular and versatile actors; first the hero in 1915's *The New Exploits of Elaine* and other serials, he was at the top of the cast—or near—in numerous features: *The Idol Dancer* (the lovesick youth), *Broken Hearts of Broadway* with Colleen Moore, *Way Down East* (bespectacled young Professor Sterling who watched helplessly as stern Burr McIntosh sent Lillian Gish out into the snow), *Trilby,* Lubitsch's *The Marriage Circle* (suave Dr. Muller who adores married woman Florence Vidor), *The Cat and the Canary* (back in spectacles, but comically), *Annie Laurie* (back with Gish, but in kilts now), etc.; a character actor in a score of talkies, he was fleetingly in view in several Bette Davis pix: *The Bride Came C.O.D., Watch on the Rhine* (her mother's, Lucille Watson's, chauffeur), and *Beyond the Forest,* a most minor role, and his last.

HALE, DOROTHY *(1938)* 33 ——Support in England's *Catherine the Great.*

HALE, JOHN *(1947)* 88 ——Support in *The Singing Kid.*

HALE, JONATHAN *(1966)* 74 ——Mr. Dithers, scourge of Dagwood in 18 "Blondie" comedies, he was also a regular in two other series— "Charlie Chan" (playing different roles in four), "The Saint" (Inspector Fernack to both Louis Hayward and George Sanders); managed to squeeze in (1934–56) another 125 movies: *Boys Town, Yellow Jack, The Story of Alexander Graham Bell, Johnny Belinda, Riot in Cell Block 11,* and *Jaguar,* his last.

HALE, LOUISE CLOSSER *(1933)* 60 ——Soon after her screen debut in Colbert's talkie (first for each actress) *A Hole in the Wall,* this Broadway *doyenne* gave a magazine interview professing to have suffered greatly from mike fright; one believes it reluctantly; in 28 talkies in five years, every gray, marcelled wave rigidly in place, she was the movies' domineering *grande dame* of all time—in *Another World* (tyrannical mom who won every family argument by feigning a heart attack), *Dinner at Eight, Letty Lynton* (Crawford's cranky traveling companion), *Shanghai Express* (quirky old lady), *Platinum Blonde, The White Sister,* etc.; one wishes she had been around when Supporting Oscars were instituted in 1936.

HALE, ROBERT *(1940)* 66 ——English character: *Storm in a Teacup, It's Love Again,* etc.

HALE, SONNIE *(1959)* 57 ——Famous debonair British comedian who co-starred with his wife, Jessie Matthews, in the still delightful *Evergreen;* many others: *Fiddlers Three, Sailing Along, Be Mine Tonight, My Heart Is Calling,* etc.

HALL, ALEXANDER *(1968)* 74 ——Acted in the silent serial *The Million Dollar Mystery,* then directed many (*Little Miss Marker, My Sister Eileen,* more).

HALL, CHARLIE *(1959)* 60 ——If this plump little comedian hadn't existed, producer Hal Roach would have had to invent him—to serve as the nemesis and sometime patsy, in the two-reelers of Laurel & Hardy, "The Boy Friends," etc.; he did time, too, with the Three Stooges and Edgar Kennedy; in many features including *Kentucky Kernels, One Night in the Tropics,* and *Hangover Square.*

HALL, CLIFF *(1972)* 78 ——Straight man for Jack (Baron Munchhausen) Pearl on radio and in movies; in *Meet the Baron, Hollywood Party.*

HALL, DOROTHY *(1953)* 46 ——Featured in silents (*The Winning Oar, Back to Liberty*) and early talkies (Chatterton's *The Laughing Lady,* Richard Dix's *Nothing But the Truth*).

HALL, DUDLEY *(1960)* 79 ——Character in silents.

HALL, ETHEL MAY *(1967)* 85 ——Supporting actress.

HALL, GEORGE M. *(1930)* 40 ——Featured in one silent, *West of Broadway.*

HALL, GERALDINE *(1970)* 65 ——Support, as was husband Porter, in *Ace in the Hole;* also in

The Proud and the Profane, The Captive City, many more.

HALL, HALLENE (1966) ——Supporting roles.

HALL, HENRY (1954) 70s ——Character actor in many; a judge in Hopkins' The Story of Temple Drake, the carpenter who comes to Tom Keene's collective farm in Our Daily Bread, in Jail Break, The Ape, etc.

HALL, JAMES (1940) 39 ——Handsome Hell's Angels co-star—cowardly brother Ben Lyon seduced his fiancee, Harlow's in 25 others (1923–32): Four Sons, The Fleet's In, The Canary Murder Case, Let's Go Native, Sporting Chance, etc.

HALL, JOHN (1936) 57 ——Support in silents: The Wild West Show, Men of Daring, others; not Jon.

HALL, JUANITA (1968) 66 ——Black actress-singer who was Bloody Mary in South Pacific; also in The Flower Drum Song and Miracle in Harlem.

HALL, PAULINE (1974) 83 ——Character roles.

HALL, PORTER (1953) 65 ——Anyone who would shoot Gary Cooper—and he did in The Plainsman—has got to be a nasty; he was, in dozens, from 1934's The Thin Man to 1954's Return to Treasure Island; spelled trouble in Arizona, Mr. Smith Goes to Washington, His Girl Friday, The Desperadoes, Double Indemnity, Unconquered, etc.; in real life?—a Hollywood First Presbyterian Church deacon.

HALL, THURSTON (1958) 75 ——Once a crooked politician (or banker), always one—and this big, fine-dressed, gray-haired one was especially not to be trusted when he gave a weak, cold-eyed smile or harrumphed over that cigar; this he did in The Secret Life of Walter Mitty, You Can't Cheat an Honest Man, The Great Man, The Farmer's Daughter, The Hard Way, dozens more; this fine actor dated back to 1917's Cleopatra, when he was—believe it!—Theda Bara's Anthony.

HALLARD, C. W. (1942) 76 ——Character in British pix: Jack of All Trades, Jubilee Cavalcade, The Battle of Gallipoli, more.

HALLATT, HENRY 1952) 64 ——Support in British pix: Gangway, Victoria the Great, Sixty Glorious Years.

HALL-DAVIES, LILLIAN (1933) 20s ——Appealing, plain-faced young English star of an early ('28) Hitchcock, The Farmer's Wife; also in 1929's White Sheik.

HALLETT, ALBERT (1935) 65 ——Silent support in action pix and Westerns: Ken Maynard's The Haunted Range, The Passing of Wolf McLean, etc.

HALLIDAY, JOHN (1947) 67 ——Hepburn's millionaire dad in The Philadelphia Story; roles similarly aristocratic in Lydia, Desire (only in looks here; he was Dietrich's jewel-thief confederate, "Prince" Margoli), The Dark Angel, Intermezzo, three dozen more.

HALLIGAN, WILLIAM (1957) 63 ——Character (Brunton) in The Leopard Man; support in many: Boom Town, Lucky Jordan, Coney Island, etc.

HALLOR, EDITH (1971) 75 ——Featured in 1921's The Inside of the Cup and other silents, Human Hearts, etc.; support in A Tree Grows in Brooklyn, other talkies.

HALLOR, RAY (1944) 44 ——Top young support in silents: Charles Ray's The Courtship of Miles Standish, Constance Talmadge's A Dangerous Maid, Colleen Moore's Sally, Buck Jones' The Circus Cowboy, more; last in an early ('30) Loretta Young talkie, The Truth about Youth.

HALLS, ETHEL MAY (1967) 85 ——Support in Bickford's Thou Shalt Not Kill, Bob Burns' Our Leading Citizen; onscreen from early Biograph days.

HALTON, CHARLES (1959) 83 ——Prim, uptight, indignant little man who, glaring through gold-rimmed glasses, always looked as though he'd had a lemon for breakfast; the Marx Bros. were his nemesis when he was Dr. Glass in Room Service; choleric in dozens: Gold Diggers of 1937, They Drive by Night, To Be or Not to Be (producer Dubosh), Mr. and Mrs. Smith, Friendly Persuasion, his last; and, in Dr. Cyclops, Albert Dekker reduced him in size—without diminishing his wrath one whit.

HAMER, GERALD (1972) 86 ——In Swing Time, the elegantly tuxedoed lush, Eric Facannistrom, who took Astaire for everything, pants included, at a game of piquet; also in Enter Arsene Lupin, Bulldog Drummond's Bride, Sherlock Holmes Faces Death, etc.

HAMILTON, GORDON GEORGE (1939) 60s ——Support in Pearl White's The Perils of Pauline.

HAMILTON, HALE *(1942)* 62 ——Onscreen from '15, he became one of Metro's biggest stars in 1918's *The Winning of Beatrice, Opportunity,* and *Five Thousand an Hour;* next year co-starred with wife Grace LaRue in *That's Good;* starred also in *The Manicure Girl, His Children's Children;* segued into character roles in *The Great Gatsby* ('26) and continued in them in many talkies: *Grand Hotel, The Adventures of Marco Polo* (Cooper's brother, Maffeo Polo), *Dr. Monica, Three on a Match,* etc.

HAMILTON, JOHN *(1958)* 71 ——Did iron-gray, pipe-smoking execs, lawyers, judges; judge in *The Roaring Twenties, Rose of Washington Square;* district attorney in Bogart's *The Maltese Falcon,* inspector in *In This Our Life;* business men in *The Great Flamarion, Tugboat Annie Sails Again,* etc.; Eva Marie Saint's father, "Pop" Doyle, in *On the Waterfront.*

HAMILTON, JOHN "SHORTY" *(1967)* 73 — —Pint-sized star of Westerns from the teens to the late '20s; a slapstick vaudeville comedian, from 1912, he introduced these routines into his Westerns to his detriment; most famous star role was in the '27 Pathe serial *The Masked Menace;* supporting roles (frequently comic) in many talkie features (*Gold Rush Maisie, The Saint's Double Trouble,* etc.) and serials.

HAMILTON, LAUREL *(1955)* 62 ——She was in Sennett comedies.

HAMILTON, LLOYD *(1935)* 43 ——Massive, hilarious Ham in the "Ham and Bud" comedy team; in dozens of memorable shorts from 1914 to 1933; starred in features in the '20s: *His Darker Self, A Self-Made Failure;* support in early talkies of others: *Black Waters,* Ann Pennington's *Tanned Legs,* Beatrice Lillie's *Are You There?*

HAMILTON, MAHLON *(1960)* 77 ——The handsome, wealthy guardian Pickford grew up to marry in *Daddy Long Legs,* he was one of the movies' top leading men from 1916's *The Eternal Question;* was with Olga Petrova; was with Louise Glaum in *I Am Guilty!,* Mae Busch in *The Christian,* Davies in *Little Old New York,* Agnes Ayres in *The Heart Raider;* support in talkies: *The Single Standard, Strangers of the Evening,* Crosby's *Mississippi,* others.

HAMMERSTEIN, ELAINE *(1948)* 51 ——Brunette beauty of the Broadway theatrical family who entered movies in '15 and quickly became a major star; in *The Co-respondent* and *The Mad Lover* (both '17), *Wanted for Murder, Accidental Honeymoon, The Country Cousin;* in 1921 was #14 in the Top 15 movie actresses (the Talmadges topped the list); was at the pinnacle of her beauty and stardom in a 1923 Selznick (Myron) film, *Rupert of Hentzau,* as Princess Flavia, the role played two decades later by Madeleine Carroll in another Selznick (David O.) production, *The Prisoner of Zenda.*

HAMMOND, VIRGINIA *(1972)* 78 ——Character (Lady Montague) in Shearer's *Romeo and Juliet;* numerous others: *Cabin in the Cotton, Rumba, Chandu the Magician, Newly Rich, Come on Marines,* etc.

HAMPDEN, WALTER *(1955)* 75 ——Aristocratic, hawk-nosed gentleman who presented Anne Baxter her Sarah Siddons award in *All About Eve;* his other hand-picked screen roles were as distinguished (as his stage roles were too) as his bearing; first in talkies in Laughton's *The Hunchback of Notre Dame,* he was then in *All This and Heaven Too* (Pasquier), *Northwest Mounted Police* (Big Bear), *They Died With Their Boots On, Reap the Wild Wind* (Commodore Devereaux), *Five Fingers* (Sir Frederic), *Sabrina* (Larrabee, father of Bogart and Holden), more.

HAMPER, GENEVIEVE *(1971)* 81 ——Lovely brunette star of 1916's *A Woman's Sacrifice* and 1923's *Under the Red Robe.*

HAMPTON, FAITH *(1949)* 39 ——Featured roles in the '20s.

HAMPTON, LOUISE *(1954)* 73 ——Character (Mrs. Wickett) in Donat's *Goodbye, Mr. Chips;* many other English films: *The Horse's Mouth, Bedelia, Haunted Honeymoon,* etc.; in one Hugh Sinclair "Saint" pic, *The Saint Meets the Tiger,* was Aunt Agatha.

HAMPTON, MYRA *(1945)* 44 ——Support in Shearer's *The Trial of Mary Dugan* and in *Once a Sinner* ('31).

HAMRICK, BURWELL *(1970)* 64 ——Child actor in early silents, later a set designer.

HANCOCK, TONY *(1968)* 44 ——British comic; Popperwell in *Those Magnificent Men in Their Flying Machines;* in *Call Me Genius, The Wrong Box,* others.

HANDLEY, TOMMY *(1949)* 46 ——British comedian, best in *It's That Man Again;* also in *Time Flies, Two Men in a Box,* more.

HANDYSIDES, CLARENCE *(1931)* 77 ——Top support in silents: Pauline Frederick's *The Woman in the Case* and *Double-Crossed,* Geraldine Farrar's *The Turn of the Wheel,* Fairbanks' *His Picture in the Papers.*

HANEY, CAROL *(1964)* 39 ——Comic dancing star with boyish haircut; famed for her sizzling "Steam Heat" number in *The Pajama Game;* also in *Invitation to the Dance* and *Kiss Me, Kate.*

HANLEY, JIMMY *(1970)* 52 ——English juvenile actor (*Little Friend, Red Wagon, Brown on Revolution, Boys Will Be Boys,* other 1930s pix); support in others later: *The Deep Blue Sea, Angel Street, The Blue Lamp,* etc.

HANLEY, WILLIAM B., JR. *(1959)* 59 ——Actor-husband of Madge Kennedy.

HANLON, BERT *(1972)* 77 ——Humorous support in many of the '30s: *A Slight Case of Murder* (Sad Sam), *The Amazing Dr. Clitterhouse* (Pal), *Boy Meets Girl* (one of the antic songwriters), *Society Girl,* etc.

HANNEFORD, POODLES *(1967)* 75 ——Main circus clown in Temple's *Our Little Girl;* same in a Virginia Brown Faire silent, *The Circus Kid;* support (Cpl. Hammel) in *Springfield Rifle.*

HANRAY, LAURENCE *(1947)* 73 ——British character who played Archbishop Cranmer in *The Private Life of Henry VIII;* was also in *The Scarlet Pimpernel, The Man Who Could Work Miracles, Hatter's Castle,* more.

HANSEN, EINAR *(1927)* 27 ——Handsome Swede imported by Universal for 1926's *Her Big Night;* at Paramount in '27 to co-star with Negri in *Barbed Wire* and *The Woman on Trial,* Clara Bow in *Children of Divorce,* Corinne Griffith in *The Lady in Ermine,* Esther Ralston in *Fashions for Women.*

HANSEN, HANS *(1962)* 76 ——Minor role in *The House on 92nd Street.*

HANSEN, JUANITA *(1961)* 66 ——Beautiful blonde who succeeded Pearl White as queen of silent serials (*The Lost City, The Phantom Foe, The Yellow Arm, The Secret of the Submarine*); starred in silent features also: *The Brass Bullet, Girl from the West, The Broadway Madonna,* others; offscreen after '21, and a narcotics addict (until cured in '34), she was tragically disfigured in a scalding accident in '28; in her last years was a train order-clerk for the Southern Pacific Railroad in Los Angeles.

HANSON, GLADYS *(1973)* 89 ——Lewis Stone's leading lady in 1916's *The Havoc.*

HANSON, LARS *(1965)* 78 ——Swedish actor; Lillian Gish's lover, Reverend Dimmesdale, in *The Scarlet Letter;* had been a minister-lover (and star) in the earlier Swedish pic *The Story of*

Gosta Berling, which launched Garbo; reunited with Garbo in two later MGM silents, *Flesh and the Devil* (dueled with John Gilbert over her) and *The Divine Woman* (the soldier who saves her from a life of wickedness and destruction); after other Hollywood pix, returned to Sweden in 1930 for other films; last in a '64 Swedish sexploitation film—about homosexuality—*491.*

HARBAUGH, CARL *(1960)* 74 ——Support in silents: Mae Murray's *Jazzmania, The Silent Command, Lost and Found,* Keaton's *College* (boat crew trainer); is also credited with the screenplay of Keaton's *Steamboat Bill Jr.;* last in support in *The Tall Men* (salesman) and *The Revolt of Mamie Stover.*

HARBEN, HUBERT *(1941)* 63 ——Character in British films: *The Battle of Gallipoli, Mozart, Victoria the Great,* more.

HARBEN, JOAN *(1953)* 44 ——English support in the "Winter Cruise" segment of *Encore.*

HARCOURT, JAMES *(1951)* 77 ——Support in many British pix: *I Met a Murderer, Night Train, The Old Curiosity Shop, Laburnum Grove, Meet Me at Dawn, The Hidden Room,* etc.

HARDIE, RUSSELL *(1973)* 69 ——Handsome young romantic lead in many in the 30's: *Sequoia* with Jean Parker, *The Harvester, West Point of the Air, As the Earth Turns, Christopher Bean, Meet Nero Wolfe, Operator 13,* etc.; finally old men roles in *The Whistle at Eaton Falls* and 1958's *Cop Hater.*

HARDING, GILBERT *(1960)* 53 ——Dignified, mustachioed Britisher who was often a constable; in *An Alligator Named Daisy, Expresso Bongo,* etc.

HARDING, LYN *(1952)* 85 ——British character; Moriarty to Arthur Wontner's Holmes in *The Triumph of Sherlock Holmes,* etc.; in Hollywood for two Marion Davies pix in the '20s: *When Knighthood Was in Flower* (Davies' brother, bemused King Henry VIII) and *Yolanda* (her father, Charles, Duke of Burgundy); thereafter in English-made films: *Fire over England, Spy of Napoleon, Knight Without Armor, Goodbye, Mr. Chips* (Wetherby), others.

HARDTMUTH, PAUL *(1962)* 72 ——German support in British pix: *Doctor Blood's Coffin, The Wonder Kid, Desperate Moment,* etc.

HARDWICKE, SIR CEDRIC *(1964)* 71 —— Calmly electric British character star, and wise, with pipe in hand; particularly memorable as Death's representative, Mr. Brink, kept up an apple tree by young Pud in *On Borrowed Time;* splendid, too, in another 60 of Hollywood's best: *Suspicion, Victory, Les Miserables, The Keys of the Kingdom, The Lodger, The Moon Is Down, Rope, Forever and a Day, I Remember Mama,* etc.

HARDY, OLIVER *(1957)* 65 ——Georgia's great roly-poly gift to the world, the beloved, short-tempered Ollie who endured cry-baby Stan Laurel from 1926 to 1951; together in dozens of Hal Roach-MGM two-reelers and 27 features, many of them masterpieces of slapstick art (*Sons of the Desert, Block-Heads, Flying Deuces, A Chump at Oxford, Saps at Sea, Way Out West,* etc.); Hardy also did numerous pix without Laurel: *Zenobia, The Fighting Kentuckian, Riding High,* others; each of the comics had been onscreen from the teens, Hardy having begun in 1913; he always credited Stan Laurel, whom he seldom saw off the set, with being the "genius" of the team; it still took the two of them to become screen immortals.

HARDY, SAM *(1935)* 52 ——Featured in scores of silents and talkies; silents of the '20s: *Little Old New York* (as Cornelius Vanderbilt), Natacha Rambova's *When Love Grows Cold,* May McEvoy's *The Savage,* Lya de Putti's *The Prince of Tempters,* Lois Wilson's *Broadway Nights,* etc.; in the '30s was seen in: *King Kong* (Weston), *Little Miss Marker* (Benny the Gouge), *Ann Vickers,* etc.

HARE, LUMSDEN *(1964)* 89 ——Irish, but when Hollywood needed a most distinguished "Britisher," he was among the first called; on American screens from 1923's *On the Banks of the Wabash,* he was in more than 70 big-budget pix: *The Lives of a Bengal Lancer* (Maj. Gen. Woodley), *Suspicion* (Inspector Hodgson), *Svengali, Rebecca* (Tabbs), *The Little Minister* (Thammas), *The House of Rothschild* (Prince Regent), *The Charge of the Light Brigade* (Col. Woodward), *Love Letters* (Joseph Cotten's father, Mr. Quinton), etc.; acted in three, including Kerr's *Count Your Blessings,* when 84, his last year in movies.

HARKER, GORDON *(1967)* 82 ——Strong-jawed Cockney comic who, after playing a riotously greedy farmhand in an early Hitchcock, *The Farmer's Wife* (the actor's fourth pic), found himself a mainstay of the British film industry; starred in *Inspector Hornleigh* and two sequels; otherwise, top support in many: *Derby Day, Her Favorite Husband, The Frog, Elstree Calling,* etc.

HARKINS, DIXIE *(1963)* 57 ——Support in silents: Dolores Del Rio's *Resurrection,* Craw-

ford's *Sally, Irene and Mary,* Garbo's *The Temptress.*

HARLAM, MACEY *(1923)* 50s ——Rugged top support in 14 (mostly costumers) in his four years (1920–23) on the screen; in Negri's *Bella Donna,* Geraldine Farrar's *The Woman and the Puppet,* Davies' *When Knighthood Was in Flower, The Tents of Allah, Fair Lady,* etc.

HARLAN, KENNETH *(1967)* 71 ——Big, handsome, vastly popular leading man in silents from '17; best as the pipsqueak male secretary who comes back from war a hero and sweeps Constance Talmadge off her feet in *Dangerous Business,* and as Colleen Moore's boastful boxer-love in *Twinkletoes;* in *Cheerful Givers* (with Bessie Love), *The Hoodlum* (Pickford), *The Beautiful and the Damned* (Marie Prevost), *The Virginian* (Florence Vidor), *Butterfly* (Laura La Plante), more; from the mid-30s to '43, when he retired, was support in B's (*Duke of West Point, The Shadow Strikes,* etc.), Westerns, many of them "Hopalong Cassidys" (*Trail Dust, Sunset Trail, Pride of the West*), and serials (*Dick Tracy's G-Men, Daredevils of the West, The Masked Marvel*).

HARLAN, OTIS *(1940)* 74 ——Round little gray-haired mischief-maker in dozens from '21 to '38; in silents: Reginald Denny's *What Happened to Jones,* Edward Everett Horton's *The Whole Town's Talking,* Nazimova's *The Redeeming Sin,* 1925 version of *Lightnin',* etc.; talkies: comedies (*The Old-Fashioned Way*), Westerns (*Rider of Death Valley, The Texans*), action pix (*King Kelly of the U.S.A.*), Shakespeare (*A Midsummer Night's Dream,* as Starveling), Disney voices (Happy's in *Snow White and the Seven Dwarfs*).

HARLAN, VIET *(1964)* 64 ——Acted in Germany's *Meistersinger* and *Hungarian Nights;* better known as a producer and director (*Kreutzer Sonata, The Ruler,* etc.).

HARLEIN, LILLIAN *(1971)* 70 ——Character actress.

HARLOW, JEAN *(1937)* 26 ——MGM's glorious *Platinum Blonde;* onscreen almost a decade (first in walk-ons in Hal Roach two-reelers), she underwent a subtle metamorphosis from expensive trollop (*Hell's Angels*), gangster's moll (*The Secret Six, The Public Enemy*) and good-natured prostitutes (*Red Dust*), to comedienne-cum-vulgarity (*Dinner at Eight*), to good-girl comedienne (*Wife vs. Secretary*), to lovable, humorous, utterly bewitching star of the first magnitude (*Suzy, Libeled Lady, Personal Property, Saratoga*); later actresses—Carroll Baker, Carol Lynley—who attempted to portray her in cheap exploitation pics were foolish to try.

HARMER, LILLIAN *(1946)* 60 ——Pickle-faced character; in *Huckleberry Finn* ('31), *Alice in Wonderland* (Cook), *Jennie Gerhardt* (midwife; delivered Sylvia Sidney's illegitimate baby by Edward Arnold), *Riffraff, The Great O'Malley, Little Miss Nobody*, etc.

HARMON, PAT *(1958)* 70 ——Supporting actor in dozens of silents: Westerns (*The Back Trail, Ridgeway of Montana*), serials (*Ruth of the Range*), action pix (*Surging Seas*), comedies (*The Freshman*); a few talkies: *The Gang Buster, Hell's Angels.*

HAROLDE, RALF *(1974)* 75 ——The good-looking tough, pickpocket Slick Wiley, Mae West lived with in *I'm No Angel*; in 50 others from late silents through '47; in *Murder, My Sweet* (Dr. Sonderberg), Evelyn Brent's *Framed, Baby, Take a Bow* (hood Trigger Stone), E.G. Robinson's *The Sea Wolf* (agent), *A Tale of Two Cities* (Prosecutor), etc.

HARRIGAN, WILLIAM *(1966)* 71 ——The Federal Agent Barton MacLane captured and tormented in *G-Men*; the middle-aged lawyer Claude Rains forced to do his evil bidding in *The Invisible Man*; the Judge in Lizabeth Scott's *Desert Fury*; like roles in many for 30 years (1927-57).

HARRINGTON, PAT, SR. *(1965)* 64 ——Comic support.

HARRIS, AVERELL *(1966)* 60s ——Top support in two early Colbert pix: *His Woman* (ship's mate knocked overboard by Gary Cooper for making a pass at Colbert) and *Secrets of a Secretary.*

HARRIS, JOSEPH *(1953)* 83 ——Top support in numerous silent Westerns: Hoot Gibson's *Red Courage* and *Sure Fire*, Harry Carey's *The Wallop* and *Crashing Through*, others.

HARRIS, KAY *(1972)* 52 ——Charming brunette who starred in the "Tillie, the Toiler" series in the '40s; also in *Sabotage Squad, Parachute Nurse.*

HARRIS, LENORE *(1953)* 74 ——Black-haired top support in silents: Dorothy Gish's *Betty of Graystone*, Florence Reed's *Today*, etc.

HARRIS, MILDRED *(1944)* 43 ——The first youthful Mrs. Charles Chaplin; conceding, in his book, *My Autobiography*, that she was young and pretty but "no mental heavy-weight," the comedian added: "After we were married Mildred's pregnancy turned out to be a false alarm"; in movies from age 10, she grew up to star in many Jewel pix (*Borrowed Clothes*, etc.); she became a Metro leading lady in '18, immediately after their marriage and on the basis of it; was steadily busy onscreen through '31 in: *The Daring Years, Fool's Paradise, The Desert Hawk, Flaming Love, Rose of the Bowery, The Cruise of the Jasper B*, etc.; in seven after 1930, including a bit in Betty Hutton's *Here Comes the Waves*, her last.

HARRIS, MITCHELL *(1948)* 65 ——In *A Connecticut Yankee*, Will Rogers triumphed over this actor's sinister Merlin, whose magic wasn't sufficient to make a cigarette lighter work; was in many: *The Sea Wolf* ('30), *Peach O'Reno, Scandal for Sale, Hypnotized*, etc.

HARRIS, MORRIS O. *(1974)* 59 ——Member of the original Ink Spots; in *The Great American Broadcast.*

HARRIS, STACY *(1973)* 54 ——Character (Max Troy) in the pic *Dragnet*; also in *The Great Sioux Uprising, Appointment With Danger, Good Day for a Hanging, The Brass Legend*, others.

HARRIS, WADSWORTH *(1942)* 77 ——Character in silent B's (*Rich Girl, Poor Girl*) and serials (*The Dragon's Net*).

HARRISON, CAREY *(1957)* 67 ——Support in Norma Terris' *Married in Hollywood* ('29), Jane Withers' *Pepper.*

HARRISON, JUNE *(1974)* 48 ——Juvenile; then played Maggie and Jiggs' daughter, Nora, in *Bringing Up Father* ('46); also in *Citizen Saint.*

HARRON, JOHN *(1939)* 36 ——Robert Harron's less famous brother; sometimes billed Johnny; in 25 silents from 1921: *Dulcy* with Constance Talmadge, 1922's *Penrod* (Marjorie Daw's young sweetheart), *Closed Gates* (youthful millionaire and wartime amnesiac, rehabilitated by Jane Novak), *The Painted Flapper*, etc.; minor support in talkies including four "Torchy Blane" pix (. . . *In Panama*, . . . *Gets Her Man*, . . . *Runs for Mayor*, . . . *Plays with Dynamite*).

HARRON, ROBERT *(1920)* 26 ——Griffith's enormously talented and popular star portrayer of sensitive youths; with the director from the beginning, he was in *The Battle of the Sexes, The Escape, The Birth of a Nation* (Gish's brother Tod), *Intolerance* (in the Modern Story, The Boy, saved from the gallows), *Hearts of the World* (again, The Boy), *A Romance of Happy*

Valley, *The Greatest Thing in Life, The Girl Who Stayed Home, True Heart Susie, The Greatest Question,* many others; allegedly a suicide, he actually accidentally shot himself while unpacking a revolver; Billy Bitzer, Griffith's legendary cameraman, writes touchingly of Harron in his book, *Billy Bitzer—His Story:* "He lived . . . long enough to make his confession and receive the sacraments from Father William Humphrey . . . the priest who had brought him as a boy to the old Biograph studio. . . . Bobby would not have lied to him. . . . His death marked the end of an era. With Bobby's passing, some thread of unity seemed to leave us. . . . We felt that Bobby had brought us luck when he came to us so young and eager. I can still see his face as I photographed *Bobby's Kodak* early in 1908. . . . After Bobby's death in 1920, it was never the same again."

HARRON, TESSIE *(1920)* 16 ——Sister of John and Robert; in 1918's *Hearts of the World,* in which Robert starred, she played the Refugee Girl; also in the cast were their mother (Woman with Daughter) and sister Mary (Wounded Girl), as well as Johnny (Boy with Barrel).

HART, ALBERT *(1940)* 65 ——Sylvia Sidney's father in *An American Tragedy;* character in dozens of Westerns (1921-34): *Diane of Star Hollow, Spawn of the Desert, Home on the Range,* etc.; also serials (*The Firefighters* and Louise Lorraine's *The Diamond Master).*

HART, "INDIAN JACK" *(1974)* 102 ——Support in many B Westerns.

HART, NEAL *(1949)* 70 ——Billed "America's Pal" in dozens of starring Westerns (mainly at Universal) in the '20s: *Butterfly Range, South of the Northern Lights, Left Hand Brand,* etc.; was also the husky hero of several silent serials: *The Scarlet Brand, The Wolf and His Mate,* others; unable to make it as a star beyond a few class C Westerns in talkies; support in many till the end.

HART, RICHARD *(1951)* 35 ——Garson's handsome leading man in *Desire Me,* Turner's in *Green Dolphin Street;* with Stanwyck in *B.F.'s Daughter,* Robert Cummings in *Reign of Terror.*

HART, TEDDY *(1971)* 73 ——Derbied little comedian who, with Sam Levene and Allen Jenkins, was one of the *Three Men on a Horse;* in other comedies of the '30s and '40s: *Million Dollar Legs; Ready, Willing and Able; Lady Luck; My Favorite Spy,* etc.; last, alternated with three other actors at playing the Indian Crowbar in the "Ma and Pa Kettle" pix; was in

. . . *at the Fair,* . . . *at Waikiki,* . . . *on the Farm,* . . . *on Vacation.*

HART, WILLIAM S. *(1946)* 83 ——Great, stone-faced Western star who, in his prime, was one of the screen's most widely idolized and remains now its most authentic representative of the "real" Old West; first a stage actor (created the role of Messala in *Ben Hur,* supported Modjeska in *Camille,* and she termed him "the best Armand Duval she had ever had"), he became a Western film star in '13; during the teens he, Chaplin, and Fairbanks were the screen's three most famous males; certain of his movies are still regarded as classics of their genre: *Hell's Hinges, Tumbleweeds, The Narrow Trail, The Toll Gate, The Dawn Maker, The Aryan, Wagon Tracks, Wild Bill Hickok;* so ingrained was his Western integrity that he even denounced one of his own, 1923's *The Covered Wagon,* as "a falsification"; still popular, he closed out his Western career in 1925, at 63; did a cameo appearance three years later, in a Davies comedy, *Show People.*

HARTE, BETTY *(1965)* 82 ——Lovely young brunette who co-starred with Hobart Bosworth in *The Roman* ('08) and *The Profligate* ('11), and with House Peters in 1914's *The Pride of Jennico;* also starred in *Kings of the Forest* ('12), *A Woman's Triumph,* and *The Oath of a Viking* (both '14).

HARTFORD, DAVID *(1932)* 56 ——Support in *Dame Chance* ('26) and an early George O'Brien lumberjack talkie, *Rough Romance.*

HARTLEY, CHARLES *(1930)* 78 ——Character actor; in Marguerite Clark's best pic, *Prunella* ('18), and Thomas Meighan's *The Conquest of Canaan.*

HARTMAN, GRACE *(1955)* 48 ——She and dance partner-husband Paul were a most famous nightclub act; were together onscreen in Jane Withers' *Forty-five Fathers,* Anna Neagle's *Sunny,* and Sinatra's *Higher and Higher.*

HARTMAN, PAUL *(1973)* 69 ——After the pix he did with wife Grace, and various stage successes, he returned to the screen as a top character actor; in *Man on a Tightrope* (Jaromir, member of Fredric March's circus troupe), *Inherit the Wind, The Longest Day* (German Field Marshal von Rundstedt), *How to Succeed in Business Without Really Trying, Luv.*

HARVEY, DON *(1963)* 52 ——Slender, darkly handsome guy with Germanic mien who played villains in many serials from '49, including the last two ever made, in '56 (*Blazing the Overland*

Trail, as chief outlaw Rance Devlin, and *Perils of the Wilderness*); similar chores in Westerns: *Blackjack Ketchum, Desperado, Forth Worth, The Outlaw Stallion*, etc.; a young policeman in *Picnic*, one of his few A's; sometimes billed Don C.

HARVEY, FORRESTER *(1945)* 55 ——A top character actor, from Ireland, in many from '29: *Tarzan the Ape Man* (Beamish), *The Invisible Man, Captain Blood* (Honesty Nuthall), *The Gilded Lily* (Proprietor of English Inn), *This Above All, None But the Lonely Heart*, etc.

HARVEY, GEORGETTE *(1952)* 69 ——Support in Aline MacMahon's *Back Door to Heaven*.

HARVEY, JACK *(1954)* 73 ——Curly-haired screen cowboy who, with Pickford, was one of Imp's original ('11) stars.

HARVEY, JEAN *(1966)* 66 ——Character actress in a Tommy Steele musical, *The Dream Maker*.

HARVEY, JOHN *(1970)* 53 ——20th Century-Fox's handsome WW II "fill-in" male lead; Grable's romantic interest in *Pin-Up Girl*, Carole Landis' in *Four Jills in a Jeep*; later had supporting roles in *The Man with My Face, High Treason, The Psychopath*.

HARVEY, LAURENCE *(1973)* 45 ——Star who played cads with charm in both English and American pix; most notable performance (Oscar-nominated as Best Actor) was as the young social-climber who married for money in *Room at the Top*; excellent also in *The Manchurian Candidate, Summer and Smoke, Expresso Bongo, Darling, The Spy with the Cold Nose, I Am a Camera*, and *Walk on the Wild Side*.

HARVEY, LILIAN *(1968)* 61 ——Petite English star of fey charm, at her best in German-made musicals, and particularly as the lead in *The Congress Dances*; in many including Hollywood's *My Lips Betray, My Weakness, Let's Live Tonight*, and perhaps the best of those she did at Fox, *I Am Suzanne* with Gene Raymond; returned to Germany and starred until 1960.

HARVEY, MORRIS *(1944)* 66 ——Support in British pix: *21 Days Together, Office Girl, Scrooge* ('35), *The Great Mr. Handel*, etc.

HARVEY, PAUL *(1955)* 71 ——Played lawyers, doctors, fathers, and executives—usually domineering—in many from '29; was Jed Prouty's boss in the "Jones Family" comedies; in *The Petrified Forest* (millionaire Chisholm), *Spellbound* (Dr. Hanish), *Call Northside 777, Father of the Bride* (as Rev. Galsworthy performed Elizabeth Taylor's wedding ceremony), *Father's Little Dividend* (same character, baptized her baby), *Maryland*, and over 100 more.

HASHIM, EDMUND *(1974)* 42 ——Support in Ray Danton's *The Outsider*.

HASKELL, AL *(1969)* 60s ——Classy villain in B Westerns, with saturnine face, tiny moustache, flyaway brows, and usually found in white hat and long jacket; in hundreds: *In Old California, Mexicali Rose, Vigilante Terror*, etc.

HASSELL, GEORGE *(1937)* 65 ——Heavyset character; first onscreen in America (he was English) in Lew Fields' *Old Dutch* ('15); a decade later, support in Lillian Gish's *La Boheme*; in the '30s in *Becky Sharp* (Sir Pitt Crawley), *Captain Blood* (Governor Steed), *Girls' Dormitory, The King Steps Out*, others.

HASWELL, PERCY *(1945)* 64 ——See Mrs. George Fawcett.

HATCH, IKE *(1961)* 69 ——Support in England's *Dark Sands*.

HATHAWAY, JEAN *(1938)* 62 ——She had supporting roles in Houdini's *The Master Key* serial, Grace Cunard's serial *The Purple Mask*, and in the '20s flapper pix of Gladys Walton (*Short Skirts*, etc.).

HATHAWAY, ROD (RHODY) *(1944)* 74 ——Support in silents of the '20s: Neva Gerber-Ben Wilson's *A Daughter of the Sioux, The Old Code, The Phantom of the Forest, Bigger Than Barnum's*, etc.

HATTON, DICK *(1931)* 40 ——Cowboy star in the '20s; in *Rip Snorter, Roving Bill Atwood, Come On Cowboys, Whirlwind Ranger*, etc.

HATTON, FRANCES *(1971)* 83 ——Raymond's actress-wife; supported Leatrice Joy in *Java Head*, Buck Jones in *Straight from the Shoulder*, Alice Terry and Lewis Stone in *Confessions of a Queen*, others.

HATTON, RAYMOND *(1971)* 84 ——Great Western favorite; for most of '40s the "Three Mesquiteers" were Robert Livingston, Duncan Renaldo, and tobacco-chewin', rip-snortin' Raymond Hatton as Rusty Joslin; co-starred next with Tim McCoy and Buck Jones in the "Rough Riders" pix; then was Johnny Mack Brown's sidekick in many, which is where he had started in Westerns in the early '30s; one of the screen's most durable actors (around from 1911 and in more than 300), he was top support in various Geraldine Farrar pix in the teens (*Joan the Woman*, as the Dauphin, *The Woman God Forgot*), was top-cast with Leatrice Joy in *Bunty Pulls the Strings*, became a full-fledged star in '25 when teamed with Wallace Beery in a series of first-rate comedies (*We're in the Navy Now*, etc.) at Paramount; then came the cowboy pix by which he is best known now; the last Western in which he had a supporting role was *Requiem for a Gunfighter*—a most fitting title.

HATTON, RONDO *(1946)* 44 ——Born with a facial deformity rendering his features those of a Neanderthal Man, he starred in the title role of 1946's *The Brute Man*; in many other horror pix (*The Spider Woman Strikes Back, The Creeper, House of Horrors*, etc.), as well as *The Ox-Bow Incident, In Old Chicago, Hell Harbor*.

HAUPT, ULRICH *(1931)* 43 ——Slender, suave, cool character who played the Adjutant Caesar, who released Dietrich in *Morocco*; support in silents (Barrymore's *Tempest*, as the aristocratic Russian officer who stubbed out his cigarette on the back of Louis Wolheim's neck; Rod La Rocque's *Captain Swagger*, etc.) and other early talkies (Chatterton's *Madame X*, Gaynor's *The Man Who Came Back*, more).

HAVEL, JOE *(1932)* 62 ——Support in silents of the '20s.

HAVEN, CHARNA *(1971)* 46 ——Supporting actress.

HAVER, PHYLLIS *(1961)* 60 ——Perhaps the loveliest of all Sennett Bathing Beauties, she was a charming fixture for four years (1917-21) in comedies such as *A Small Town Idol* with Ben Turpin; graduated to top support in Colleen Moore's *So Big*, then to stardom in *The Temple of Venus, The Shady Lady, Thunder, Chicago*, Griffith's *The Battle of the Sexes*, etc.; retired in '29.

HAVIER, ALEX J. *(1945)* 36 ——Support; Yankee Salazar in *Bataan*, Sgt. Biernesa in *Back to Bataan*, Benny Lecoco in *They Were Expendable*.

HAWKINS, JACK *(1973)* 62 ——Husky-voiced, ruggedly handsome British star of the first magnitude; at the top of his form as courageous Major Warden in *The Bridge on the River Kwai*; excellent also in *The Fallen Idol, The Cruel Sea, The Prisoner, The Third Key, Lawrence of Arabia* (as General Allenby); *The Poppy Is Also a Flower* ('68) was his last with his natural voice, after which cancer of the throat was diagnosed and his larynx removed; learned to speak again through his esophagus ten consecutive words at a time—and came back to do sev-

eral: *Shalako, Oh, What a Lovely War!, Nicholas and Alexandra, Young Winston*.

HAWLEY, ALLEN BURTON *(1925)* 30 ——Actor-husband of Wanda Hawley.

HAWLEY, H. DUDLEY *(1941)* 62 ——English character actor in two American pix: Ethel Barrymore's *An American Widow* ('17) and Colbert's *Young Man of Manhattan* (played a doctor).

HAWORTH, MARTHA *(1966)* 50s ——Actress-wife of Wallace Ford; he died four months after she did.

HAWTHORNE, DAVID *(1942)* ——Support in English pix: *The Prince of Lovers, Escape* ('30), *Laburnum Grove*.

HAWTREY, ANTHONY *(1954)* 45 ——English support in Aumont's *The Affairs of a Rogue*; otherwise on the British stage.

HAY, GEORGE D. *(1968)* 72 ——Radio's "Solemn Old Judge"; in rustic B's.

HAY, MARY *(1957)* 56 ——Young dancer chosen by Griffith to complete the role of Kate Brewster in *Way Down East* started by actress Clarine Seymour (died after filming the winter scenes); married the film's male star, Richard Barthelmess, and in '25 co-starred with him in a comedy of married life, *New Toys*.

HAY, WILL *(1949)* 61 ——Incomparable comedian-star of British pix, usually seen as a wildly inept schoolmaster; at his best in *Oh Mr. Porter, Good Morning Boys, The Ghost of St. Michael's*.

HAYAKAWA, SESSUE *(1973)* 87 ——Oscar-nominated as Best Support as Japanese camp commander Colonel Saito in *The Bridge on the River Kwai*; a Japanese-American, he had starred on U.S.A. screens (often with wife Tsuru Aoki) from 1914's *The Typhoon* and *Wrath of the Gods*; many other silents (over 120): *The Bottle Imp, Forbidden Paths, The Cheat* ('15), *The First Born*, etc., in which he alternated as lover and villain; anti-Japanese sentiments drove him from Hollywood screens after 1931's *Daughter of the Dragon*; lived in France in the '30s (co-starred in two: *Yoshiwara, Macao*) and during WW II (painted to earn an income during the occupation); from '49-'60, in several Hollywood films: *Tokyo Joe, Three Came Home, Green Mansions, Hell to Eternity*, etc.; left the screen in '60, returned to Japan, became an ordained Zen Priest and, he who had earned and lost millions, taught acting.

HAYDEN, HARRY *(1955)* 71 ——Smiling, round-faced character actor in steelrimmed specs; lawyers, judges, doctors, fathers, etc., from '36; in *Hail the Conquering Hero* (Dr. Bissell), *The Palm Beach Story, Intruder in the Dust* (Claude Jarman Jr.'s dad), *Tales of Manhattan* (Judge in the E. G. Robinson segment), *Springtime in the Rockies,* several dozen more.

HAYE, HELEN *(1957)* 83 ——White-haired British dowager; in Vivien Leigh's *Anna Karenina* and *The Deep Blue Sea,* also *The 39 Steps* (wife of chief villain, Godfrey Tearle), *Kipps,* Laughton's *Hobson's Choice, The Man in Grey, Lilacs in the Spring,* more.

HAYES, CATHERINE *(1941)* 54 ——Support in Loretta Young's *Zoo in Budapest* and Elissa Landi's *The Warrior's Husband.*

HAYES, FRANK *(1923)* 48 ——Dour, angular Keystone Kop, hailed by Sennett historian Kalton C. Lahue as "the most accomplished in a long line of comic policemen who wore the Keystone badge and uniform"; also in *Fatty and Mabel at the San Diego Exposition; Mabel, Fatty and the Law* (he was "the law"), etc.; in nine years onscreen, played just one serious role, Old Grannis in *Greed,* which he did not live to see.

HAYES, GEORGE *(1967)* 78 ——Support in British pix; character (Compeyson) in *Great Expectations;* in *Emil,* etc.

HAYES, GEORGE "GABBY" *(1969)* 83 —— Grand toothless, swearing, bearded sidekick to "Hopalong Cassidy" and Roy Rogers; in scores from 1929, which marked his comedy debut onscreen in Eddie Dowling's *The Rainbow Man;* in program Westerns mostly, he occasionally followed the trail to big-budget oaters: *The Plainsman, Tall in the Saddle, Return of the Badmen.*

HAYES, LAURENCE C. *(1974)* 71 ——Character actor.

HAYLE, GRACE *(1963)* 74 ——Overstuffed Madame Napaloni, with whom Hynkel (Chaplin) endured one dance at the Embassy ball in *The Great Dictator;* support in a score from '34; in *Tovarich* (Madame Van Hemert), *Let's Face It* (Mrs. Wigglesworth), *Crossroads,* etc.

HAYNES, ARTHUR *(1966)* 52 ——Character in British pix: *Doctor in Clover,* etc.; also in Rock Hudson's *Strange Bedfellows.*

HAYNES, DANIEL L. *(1954)* 50s ——Starred with virile authority as Zeke, the killer-preacher, in King Vidor's all-black classic, *Hallelujah!;* also in *So Red the Rose, The Last Mile, Escape from Devil's Island, The Invisible Ray;* was sometimes billed Donald Haines in these later films.

HAYS, WILL *(1937)* 50 ——Character (Patch Dugan) in the serial *Terry of the Times;* earlier, support in silents: *Lena Rivers, Cupid's Knockout, Get-Rich-Quick Wallingford,* etc.

HAYWORTH, VINTON *(1970)* 64 ——Classy support in Jose Ferrer's *The Great Man* and Tab Hunter's *The Girl He Left Behind.*

HAZELL, HY *(1970)* 50 ——British supporting actress; in many: *Meet Me at Dawn, The Key Man, The Yellow Balloon, Anastasia* (Blonde Lady), etc.

HEALY, DAN *(1969)* 80 ——Song-dance vaudeville headliner featured in the early all-star talkie *Glorifying the American Girl;* also in Chatterton's *The Laughing Lady;* widower of Helen "Boop-a-Doop" Kane.

HEALY, TED *(1937)* 41 ——Stage-radio-vaudeville star prominently billed in many in the '30s: *Sing, Baby, Sing; Hollywood Hotel; Soup to Nuts; Reckless; Bombshell; San Francisco; Lazy River,* more.

HEARN, EDWARD *(1963)* 74 ——Handsome silent star; title role in 1925's *The Man Without a Country;* other silents: *When a Man's a Man, Daughters of Today, The Harvester, Ned McCobb's Daughter;* support in a few talkies: *Young and Beautiful, The Rainbow Trail,* etc.; occasionally, as in a Charles (Buck) Jones prizefight pic, *Winner Take All,* was billed Eddie Hearn.

HEARN, SAM *(1964)* 75 ——Jack Benny's "Schlepperman"; with him in *The Big Broadcast of 1937;* without him in *The Man in the Trunk, Florida Special,* Danny Kaye's *The Inspector General,* etc.

HEATH, TED *(1969)* 67 ——Famed English orchestra leader; in *It's a Wonderful World.*

HEATHERLEY, CLIFFORD *(1937)* 49 —— Support in many English pix: *The Private Life of Don Juan, Glamour, After the Ball, Catherine the Great,* etc.

HECHT, JENNY *(1971)* 29 ——Great fun in dad Ben's pic *Actors and Sin* ('52), as Daisy Marcher, the precocious moppet of nine who had written a most lascivious book.

HECHT, TED *(1969)* 61 ——Support in many from '42; in *So Proudly We Hail* (Dr. Jose Bardia), *Dragon Seed* (Major Yohagi), *The Lost Weekend* (at Bellevue, Man with Bandage on Ear), *Corregidor* (Filipino Lieutenant), *Man-Eater of Kumaon*, etc.

HEDRICK, CLARENCE *(1969)* ——Supporting roles.

HEFLIN, VAN *(1971)* 60 ——Actors sharing scenes with him never stood a chance against his soft words, keen, bemused eyes and coiled-spring performances; onscreen from 1936's *A Woman Rebels*, he won a Supporting Oscar in *Johnny Eager* (surprisingly, his only nomination); superb in many: *Shane, The Strange Love of Martha Ivers, Patterns, Madame Bovary, Tennessee Johnson, My Son John*, etc.

HEGGIE, O.P. *(1936)* 56 ——Most impressive as the bearded blind hermit in *The Bride of Frankenstein*, who befriends the monster (Karloff) and teaches him to speak; in many from a '28 Norma Shearer pic, *The Actress: The Prisoner of Shark Island, Anne of Green Gables* (the farmer who expected to adopt a boy but got Anne Shirley instead; she was also his ward in a later pic, *Chasing Yesterday*), *East Lynne* (as Ann Harding's discarded husband), etc.

HEIGHT, JEAN *(1967)* 65 ——Famous radio announcer who also acted.

HEINZ, GERARD *(1972)* 69 ——German character in *The Dirty Dozen, Thunder Rock, The Guns of Navarone*, etc.

HELD, ANNA *(1918)* 45 ——Ziegfeld star whose "milk baths" made good publicity fodder; starred in the 1916 Morosco pic *Madame la Presidente;* Luise Rainer portrayed her (winning an Oscar) in *The Great Ziegfeld*.

HELMS, RUTH *(1961)* 60s ——Gorgeous girl who had a top supporting role in 1920's *The Fighting Chance*, starring husband, Conrad Nagel.

HELTON, PERCY *(1971)* 77 ——Gnomish character (usually fun but sometimes slyly evil) with whispery voice; in scores: *Miracle on 34th Street* (a Macy's Santa but *not* Kris Kringle), *Chicken Every Sunday, Call Northside 777* (mailman), *The Set-Up, My Friend Irma, Kiss Me Deadly, How to Marry a Millionaire; Hush, Hush, Sweet Charlotte;* etc.

HEMINGWAY, MARIE *(1939)* 46 ——English actress who was the first Mrs. Claude Rains.

HEMSLEY, ESTELLE *(1968)* 81 ——Black actress who was superb as young Johnny Nash's grandmother in *Take a Giant Step;* also in *Harvey; Green Mansions; Baby, the Rain Must Fall; Edge of the City*, etc.

HENDERSON, DEL *(1956)* 73 ——Memorable, in one of his least representative roles, as the kindly, plump auto salesman in *Make Way for Tomorrow*, who gives oldsters Beulah Bondi and Victor Moore a spin—in their last happy hour together; onscreen from 1909, as a Griffith stalwart, he is generally recalled as a comedy actor (director, too, for Sennett and others); support in *It's a Gift, The Old Fashioned Way, Poppy, Ruggles of Red Gap*, many more.

HENDERSON, GEORGE A. *(1923)* ——Supporting role in Metro's *The Fog* in the year of his death.

HENDERSON, GRACE *(1944)* 84 ——Leading lady in many 1909-12 Biograph pix directed by Griffith: *Lucky Jim, A Corner in Wheat, A Midnight Cupid, His Trust Fulfilled, The Marked Time-Table, Enoch Arden* (Part I), *A String of Pearls, Sunshine Through the Dark, The Old Confectioner's Mistake, An Unseen Enemy*, more.

HENDERSON, IVO *(1968)* 70s ——Support in John Barrymore's *Bulldog Drummond Comes Back*, others.

HENDERSON, LUCIUS *(1947)* 86 ——Character in silents of the '20s: Aileen Pringle's *The Great Deception*, Richard Dix's *A Man Must Live, The New Commandment*, more.

HENDERSON, TALBOT V. *(1946)* 67 ——Support in one Parthenon Pictures B of 1929, *The Bachelor's Club*.

HENDERSON, TED *(1962)* 74 ——Reportedly had supporting roles in over 300 silents.

HENDERSON-BLAND, R. *(1941)* 50s ——British actor who gave a moving performance as the Christ in 1912's *From the Manger to the Cross*, his only film, about which he later wrote a book, *From Manger to Cross: The Story of the World-Famous Film of the Life of Jesus*.

HENDRICKS, BEN, JR. *(1938)* 44 ——Handsome romantic lead in a score of silents: Will Rogers' *The Headless Horseman, Room and Board, Just Off Broadway, Against All Odds, A Racing Romeo*, etc.; support in talkies: *Rain* (Griggs), Clara Bow's *The Wild Party* (Ed), *The Public Enemy* (Bugs Moran), *Slim*, more.

HENDRICKS, BEN, SR. *(1930)* 68 ——Character actor in silents of the '20s: Virginia Lee Corbin's *The City That Never Sleeps*, Luke Cosgrave's *Welcome Home*, Mae Marsh's *Tides of Passion*, etc.

HENDRICKS, LOUIS *(1923)* 60s ——Support in Norma Talmadge's *The Sign on the Door*, Thomas Meighan's *The Conquest of Canaan*, others of the early '20s.

HENDRIX, JIMI *(1970)* 31 ——Black rock star; onscreen in *Woodstock*.

HENIE, SONJA *(1969)* 57 ——Dimpled, blonde Olympic skate champion from Norway who proved herself a box-office champ for 20th Century-Fox; was in the Top Ten 1937-39 via her ice-with-music pix: *One in a Million, Thin Ice, Happy Landing, My Lucky Star, Second Fiddle, Everything Happens at Night;* after *Sun Valley Serenade, Iceland,* and *Wintertime,* the studio closed the rink; she took the show to RKO (*It's a Pleasure*) and Universal (*The Countess of Monte Cristo*), but the going proved slushier there.

HENLEY, HOBART *(1964)* 72 ——Dark-haired star of *Graft* ('15); later a well-known director (*Bad Sister, The Big Pond,* etc.).

HENNECKE, CLARENCE R. *(1969)* 74 ——Comic support from the Keystone Kops to "Joe Palooka's" *Humphrey Takes a Chance.*

HENNING, PAT *(1973)* 62 ——Was longshoreman "Kayo" Dugan in *On the Waterfront;* major character roles in others: *Man on a Tightrope* (Konradin, member of March's circus troupe), *Wind Across the Everglades,* etc.

HENNINGS, JOHN *(1933)* ——Featured in one early talkie, *The Poor Millionaires.*

HENRY, JAY *(1951)* 41 ——Milland's brother, Prince Alexander Stofani, aboard Lombard's yacht in *We're Not Dressing;* his only movie role.

HENRY, JOHN *(1958)* 72 ——Character in silents of the '20s: *Yankee Speed, Poison.*

HENRY, ROBERT "BUZZ" *(1971)* 39 ——As a teenager had top roles in three serials: *Hop Harrigan* (hero's young pal Jackie), *Son of the Guardsman, Tex Granger;* then handsome support in *Rocky Mountain* (a Confederate soldier, Kip Waterson, who went West with Flynn), *The Indian Fighter* (Lt. Shaefer), *Cowboy, In Like Flint,* etc.

HENSON, LESLIE *(1957)* 66 ——Pop-eyed English comedian; *It's a Boy, Sport of Kings.*

HEPBURN, BARTON *(1955)* 49 ——Billed with Leslie Fenton as "Young Vultures" in De Mille's *Dynamite;* in Joe E. Brown's *Painted Faces, The Bridge of San Luis Rey, Hi Diddle Diddle,* etc.

HERBERT, HANS *(1957)* 82 ——Minor roles in *Mr. Skeffington, Under My Skin,* etc.

HERBERT, HENRY *(1947)* 68 ——Character in silents of the '20s: *Captain Blood, The Day of Faith,* Colleen Moore's *So Big,* etc.

HERBERT, HOLMES *(1956)* 76 ——Tall, dignified English actor who, in his early Hollywood years (from '18), was a most handsome co-star; silents: *The Enchanted Cottage* (Barthelmess' blind friend), *Her Lord and Master* with Alice Joyce, *A Stage Romance* with William Farnum, *Gentlemen Prefer Blondes,* dozens more; support in just as many talkies: *Dr. Jekyll and Mr. Hyde* (Fredric March's colleague, Dr. Lanyan), *The Thirteenth Chair, The Invisible Man, Johnny Belinda* (Judge), various Rathbone "Sherlock Holmes" pix; onscreen through '52.

HERBERT, HUGH *(1952)* 66 ——Butterbrained comedian whose "Woo-Woo" had moviegoers rolling in the aisles for decades; in *Gold Diggers of 1935, Dames, Wonder Bar, The Great Waltz, Hellzapoppin, Million Dollar Legs,* etc., right through a '51 co-star stint (with Estelita Rodriguez) in Republic's *Havana Rose;* little known is that he was co-author of the first all-talkie, *The Lights of New York.*

HERBERT, LEW *(1968)* 65 ——Brooklyn-style, heavyset hoods in many: *Jigsaw, Young Man with a Horn, Kiss of Death, Guilty Bystander,* etc.

HERBERT, TOM *(1946)* 57 ——Comedian-brother of Hugh; character (Gilbert) in Mae West's *Belle of the Nineties;* minor roles in *Topper, Banjo on My Knee,* etc.

HERLEIN, LILLIAN *(1971)* 75 ——Was one of several marriageable daughters in a '23 comedy, *Solomon in Society.*

HERMAN, AL *(1967)* 80 ——Comic support in several in the '30s: *Talent Scout, Paid to Dance, Torchy Blane, the Adventurous Blonde,* etc.; also a director (the "Mickey McGuire" comedies, *Renfrew of the Royal Mounted,* others).

HERMAN, TOMMY *(1972)* 68 ——Boxer who played one, named Tommy, in Bogart's *The Harder They Fall.*

HERNANDEZ, JUANO *(1970)* 72 ——Puerto Rico's most noted actor, acclaimed for his portrayal of the proud, stoic black in *Intruder in the Dust*, his first; in many later: *Stars in My Crown, The Pawnbroker, Trial, Sergeant Rutledge, The Breaking Point*, etc.

HERRING, AGGIE *(1938)* ——Character actress who specialized in "shanty Irish" roles in *Clancy in Wall Street, She Done Him Wrong, Don't Tell the Wife, Green Eyes*, etc.

HERSHOLT, JEAN *(1956)* 69 ——One thinks of this Danish actor first, for it was type-casting of the finest sort, as wise and kind "Dr. Christian" (of radio and six RKO pix), or as Dr. DaFoe in the Dionnne Quintuplet movies; actually, in his 450 pix (80 of them one-reelers in his first year onscreen, 1915), he ran the gamut —leading man, villain, comedian; some of his memorable silent performances: *Stella Dallas, Greed, So Big, The Four Horsemen of the Apocalypse;* a few of his talkies: *Grand Hotel, Dinner at Eight, Heidi, Emma, The Sin of Madelon Claudet, Reunion, Alexander's Ragtime Band;* one of Hollywood's most involved citizens; he was a prime mover behind the Motion Picture Relief Fund; never nominated for an Oscar, he received a special statuette in '49 for distinguished service to the motion picture industry, and the infrequently awarded "Jean Hersholt Humanitarian Award" is, of course, named for him.

HESLOP, CHARLES *(1966)* 82 ——British character comic; in *Flying Fortress, Lambeth Walk, Waltzes from Vienna*, etc.

HESSE, BARON VON *(1936)* 51 ——Top support in a Corinne Griffith part-talkie, *Prisoners*.

HESTER, HARVEY *(1967)* ——Character actor.

HEYBURN, WELDON *(1951)* 46 ——Dimpled-chin, wavy-haired romantic lead in the early '30s; in *Convention Girl, Careless Lady, West of Singapore, Chandu the Magician*, etc.; later, support in crime pix *(Murder in the Fun House)* and Westerns *(Code of the Prairie, Yellow Rose of Texas*, others).

HEYDT, LOUIS JEAN *(1961)* 54 ——Strong-faced blond character with tight blue eyes; support (villain, hero's buddy, etc.) in 150: *Test Pilot, Thirty Seconds Over Tokyo, Come to the Stable, Dive Bomber, Each Dawn I Die, They Were Expendable*, etc.

HEYES, HERBERT *(1958)* 68 ——Theda Bara's handsome leading man in *Under Two Flags, The Vixen, The Darling of Paris* (all 1916 –17); many other silents including two Ruth Roland serials and Betty Blythe's *The Queen of Sheba;* returning to Broadway in '24 for various

star roles, he reentered movies in the '40s, specializing in military officers *(Only the Valiant, Tripoli)* and sympathetic executives (most notably Elizabeth Taylor's millionaire-father in *A Place in the Sun);* in *Ruby Gentry, Miracle on 34th Street*, many others.

HIBBARD, EDNA *(1942)* 47 ——Support in Corinne Griffith's *Island Wives*.

HIBBERT, GEOFFREY *(1969)* 47 ——Starred as a young man in England's *Love on the Dole*, others; then support in many: *Secret People, Orders to Kill, The Great Van Robbery*, etc.

HICKMAN, ALFRED *(1931)* 69 ——Elegant English actor who co-starred with Nance O'-Neil in both *The Mad Woman* and *The Fall of the Romanoffs;* in other U.S.A. silents (*The Enchanted Cottage*, the Ella Hall serial *The Master Key*, etc.) and talkies (Colman's *The Rescue*, ZaSu Pitts' *A Woman of Experience*, others).

HICKMAN, HOWARD *(1949)* 69 ——As esthetic-type young man starred in several silents of the teens *(Matrimony* with Julia Dean, etc.); after a long Broadway career, went to Hollywood in '28 for a long career as a slender, distinguished-looking character; in *Watch on the Rhine* (wealthy Cyrus Penfield), *Gone With the Wind* (Leslie Howard's father, John Wilkes), *Cheers for Miss Bishop, Strike Up the Band, Blossoms in the Dust*, many more.

HICKOK, RODNEY *(1942)* 49 ——Featured in Westerns of the '20s: *The Rawhide Kid, The Bandolero*, etc.

HICKS, RUSSELL *(1957)* 62 ——One of his movies (about the 30th in a career of 200) was titled *Laughing Irish Eyes*, and, above his slim-line moustache, this dapper, gray character lead almost always had them; occupied executive suites, admiral's unforms, and rich-dad roles as if to the manor-born; in *To the Shores of Tripoli* (John Payne's Major Wilson), *The Little Foxes; The Sea of Grass; Kentucky; Johnny Apollo; Joe Smith, American; The Blue Bird* (Temple's dad); *The Great Lie*, etc.

HICKS, SIR SEYMOUR *(1949)* 78 ——Starred in the title role in England's *Scrooge* ('35); top support in many: *Busman's Holiday, Fame Is the Spur, Haunted Honeymoon*, etc.

HIERS, WALTER *(1933)* 39 ——Roly-poly comedy star in a score of silents; in *It Pays to Advertise* with Lois Wilson, *So Long Letty* with Colleen Moore, *Mr. Billings Spends His Dime, The Ghost Breaker, Sham*, etc.; *Dancers in the Dark* and *Private Scandal* were among his few talkies.

HIGBY, WILBUR *(1934)* 68 ——Character actor in many silents: *Lights of Old Broadway, Live Wires, The Ladder Jinx, Confessions of a Queen*, others.

HIGGINS, DAVID *(1936)* 78 ——Support in Thomas Meighan's *The Confidence Man*.

HIGNETT, H. R. *(1959)* 89——Character in British pix: *Caravan, Spring in Park Lane*.

HILDEBRAND, RODNEY *(1962)* 69 ——In the silent *Mother Machree* with Belle Bennett, and (billed Hildebrandt) in a John Wayne talkie serial, *The Three Musketeers*.

HILDEBRAND, LO *(1936)* 42 ——Cowboy actor, mostly in silents.

HILL, BEN *(1969)* 75 ——In silent Westerns: *The Border Raiders, On the High Card*.

HILL, GEORGE *(1934)* 77 ——Character actor.

HILL, THELMA *(1938)* 31 ——Beauty in Sennett comedies of the late '20s; then in Marion Davies' *The Fair Co-ed* (was co-ed Rose), Virginia Browne Faire's *The Chorus Kid*, Madge Bellamy's *The Play Girl*, etc.

HILL, TINY *(1971)* 60 ——Bandleader seen onscreen in the '40s.

HILL, VIRGINIA *(1966)* 49 ——Atmosphere player in MGM musicals of the '30s, more famous as mobster Bugsy Siegel's girl friend.

HILLIARD, ERNEST *(1947)* 57 ——Support in dozens of silents (Evelyn Brent's *The Broadway Lady*, Pauline Frederick's *Evidence*, Bushman's *Modern Marriage*, etc.) and talkies *(The Magnificent Dope, Life of the Party*, others).

HILLIARD, HARRY *(1966)* 70s ——Theda Bara's handsome Romeo in 1916's *Romeo and Juliet*, the only movie made by this Broadway star.

HILLIARD, HAZEL *(1971)* 83 ——Actress-mother of Harriet.

HILLIARD, MRS. MACK *(1963)* 77 ——Leads in many early silents; a.k.a. Hazel Clayton.

HILLIAS, PEG *(1961)* 50s ——Stanley Kowalski's upstairs neighbor in *A Streetcar Named Desire;* it was to her that pregnant Kim Hunter went, in the final scene, leaving Brando crying "Stella!"

HINDS, SAMUEL S. *(1948)* 73 ——Character actor who had perhaps the wisest, kindest face

(and manner) ever on the screen; best known as Lew Ayres' doctor-dad in the "Dr. Kildare" pix, he was in more than 150 others, from 1932's *If I Had a Million: Little Women* (father of Hepburn and the other March girls), *You Can't Take It with You* (Jean Arthur's dad), *Stage Door, The Shepherd of the Hills, Destry Rides Again, Seven Sinners*, etc.

HINES, HARRY *(1967)* 78 ——Rustic support; in *The Kettles in the Ozarks, Last of the Pony Riders, Texas Across the River*, others.

HINES, JOHNNY *(1970)* 72 ——Slender, good-looking, dark-haired comedy star who was one of First National's (Warners') top box-office hits in the '20s; at his funniest and most dashing in *The Crackerjack;* this former Broadway dance star was tops, too, in *Burn 'Em Up Barnes, Surefire Flint, Little Johnny Jones, Stepping Along*, etc.; in talkies, top support through *Too Hot to Handle*.

HINES, SAMUEL E. *(1939)* 58 ——Johnny's less famous brother; support in *The Lost Chord*, Barthelmess' *Shore Leave*, other silents; in talkies, the comic character "Gassy" in Cagney's *He Was Her Man*, etc.

HINTON, ED *(1958)* 30 ——Youth roles in many: *Cry Terror, Three Girls and a Sailor, River of No Return* (gambler), *The Decks Ran Red*, etc.

HITCHCOCK, KEITH *(1966)* ——Character who played the Major-Domo in *The Black Swan;* was also in *The Blue Bird, Raffles, Man Hunt;* earlier, had acted in many under the name Keith Kenneth: *Limehouse Blues, Clive of India, Paris Honeymoon, The Little Princess*, others.

HITCHCOCK, RAYMOND *(1929)* 64 ——Great stage comedian who termed movies (especially movie-making) "an eternal monstrosity" after doing three in '15 for Sennett: *Stolen Magic* (with Mabel Normand), *The Valet, The Village Scandal;* in the '20s he came back and hit his stride as a tails 'n top hat comic in *Broadway After Dark, The Monkey Talks, The Beauty Shop, Red Heads Preferred*, etc.

HITCHCOCK, REX *(1950)* 58 ——See Rex Ingram.

HIX, DON *(1964)* 70s ——In early Universal silents, later a well-known radio personality, he was last a character actor in *Diary of a High School Bride*.

HOBBES, HALLIWELL *(1962)* 84 ——Distinguished-looking, heavyset Englishman, of serious mien, who in more than 100 pix was often a butler for the best: Davis in *Mr. Skeffington,* Bergman in *Gaslight,* Cooper in *Casanova Brown,* Robert Montgomery in *Here Comes Mr. Jordan;* non-butler roles in *Charlie Chan in Shanghai* (Chief of Police), *Maid of Salem, The Story of Louis Pasteur* (Dr. Lister), *To Be or Not to Be* (English General Armstrong); last in 1956's *Miracle in the Rain.*

HOBBES, NANCY MARSLAND *(1968)* 71 —— Actress-wife of Halliwell.

HODGES, HORACE *(1951)* 86 ——Character in British pix: *Escape, Jamaica Inn, Girl in the Street,* etc.

HODGES, RUSS *(1971)* 61—Famous bandleader; in musical shorts.

HODGES, WILLIAM C. *(1961)* 85 ——Support in silents.

HODGINS, EARL *(1964)* 64 ——An amusing fixture in B Westerns—as con man, medicine show spieler, etc.—from the early '30s; in *Hills of Old Wyoming, Hoppy Serves a Writ, Guns and Guitars,* scores more; occasionally applied his rustic antics to the "Scattergood Baines" series, and more rarely was in A's (*The Southerner,* as the Wedding Guest, *Bitter Creek).*

HODGSON, LEYLAND *(1949)* 56 ——English actor in Hollywood movies from 1930's *The Case of Sergeant Grischa* with Richard Dix; usually typecast as police official (*Hangover Square, International Lady, Scotland Yard, Mr. Moto's Last Warning, Susannah of the Mounties,* as a Mountie, etc.), he gave perhaps his most stirring performance as John Wilkes in *Bedlam.*

HODIAK, JOHN *(1955)* 41 ——MGM diamond-in-the-rough star, at his best pitted against a strong femme (Bankhead in *Lifeboat,* made on loanout) or as a military leader (*Command Decision, A Bell for Adano, Battleground,* etc.); effective in musicals (*Ziegfeld Girl, The Harvey Girls),* Westerns (*Across the Wide Missouri, Ambush at Tomahawk),* crime pix (*The Arnelo Affair, Somewhere in the Night),* comedies (*Maisie Goes to Reno, I Dood It);* turned on the rugged charm most persuasively in *Sunday Dinner for a Soldier* with Anne Baxter, who subsequently became his wife.

HOEY, DENNIS *(1961)* 67 ——British character actor in Hollywood (after many English pix of the '30s) from *How Green Was My Valley;* perhaps best known as the none-too-bright Inspector Lestrade (with the mod hairstyle) in six of Rathbone's "Sherlock Holmes" movies (. . .

and the Secret Weapon, . . . Faces Death, . . . and the Spider Woman, etc.); in many top-budget pix: *Kitty, Golden Earrings, Anna and the King of Siam* (Sir Edward), *Joan of Arc, National Velvet,* others.

HOFFE, MONCKTON *(1951)* 70 ——Irish support in the English-made *Lady with a Lamp;* better known as a screenwriter *(The Lady Eve, The Last of Mrs. Cheney,* etc.).

HOFFMAN, EBERHARD *(1957)* 74 ——Played character roles in silents.

HOFFMAN, GERTRUDE W. *(1966)* 95 —— German character actress in Hollywood pix: old Mrs. Benson in *Foreign Correspondent, A Guy Named Joe* (credited simply Old Woman), *Lydia, The Ape, The Moon Is Down, The Commandos Strike at Dawn,* etc.

HOFFMAN, HOWARD *(1969)* 75 ——Support in B's: *Macabre, The House on Haunted Hill.*

HOFFMAN, MAX, JR. *(1945)* 42 ——Support in two dozen: *The Great Waltz; Topper Takes a Trip; Wings of the Navy; Sailor, Be Good; Virginia City,* etc.

HOFLICH, LUCIE *(1956)* 73 ——The star of such German silents as *The Wild Duck* ('26), she later had character roles in *Sky Without Stars,* etc.

HOGAN, PAT *(1966)* 35 ——Handsome young support in a score from *Fixed Bayonets* ('51); in *Gun Fury, Arrowhead, Pony Express, Kiss of Fire, Sign of the Pagan,* more.

HOGAN, "SOCIETY KID" *(1962)* 63 —— Played himself in Hope's *The Lemon Drop Kid.*

HOGG, CURLY *(1974)* 57 ——Famous banjo king; an original member of the Sons of the Pioneers; in 150 Autry-Rogers-Ritter Westerns.

HOLDEN, FAY *(1973)* 79 ——Andy Hardy's wise and loving mom; a character actress from England, via the Pasadena Playhouse stage, she was in several others before the "Hardy Family" films *(Polo Joe, Wives Never Know, Love Is a Headache,* etc.), during it (*H. M. Pulham, Esq.; Blossoms in the Dust; Bitter Sweet),* and after the series had presumably run its course in the late '40s (*Samson and Delilah, The Big Hangover, Whispering Smith);* appropriately, her very last was the reunion pic, *Andy Hardy Comes Home* in '58, which brought her together again with Andy, Marian, and, in a flashback, the late Judge Hardy himself.

HOLDEN, HARRY *(1944)* 75 ——Character in silents: William Boyd's *The Yankee Clipper*, Richard Dix's *The Gay Defender*, etc.

HOLDEN, VIOLA *(1967)* ——Character in Abbott & Costello's *Mexican Hayride*.

HOLDEN, WILLIAM *(1932)* 60 ——Support in late silents (Clara Bow's *Three Week-Ends*, Cooper's *The First Kiss*, etc.) and early talkies (Davies' *Not So Dumb*, as Julia Faye's husband, *Dynamite*, as one of the "Three Wise Fools," *The Man Who Came Back*, etc.); no relation to William *(Golden Boy)* Holden.

HOLDREN, JUDD *(1974)* 50s ——With black wavy hair and a widow's peak, he was easily the handsomest hero of serials in the '50s; did three: *Captain Video, Zombies of the Stratosphere, The Lost Planet*; support in such features as *Lady in the Iron Mask*.

HOLIDAY, BILLIE *(1959)* 44 ——Great black jazz singer who was featured in *New Orleans* ('47); Diana Ross won an Oscar nomination portraying her in *Lady Sings the Blues*.

HOLLES, ANTONY *(1950)* 49 ——Character in British pix: *The Rocking Horse Winner, Caesar and Cleopatra, The Magic Bow, Jassy*, many more.

HOLLIDAY, JUDY *(1965)* 41 ——Oscar-winning *(Born Yesterday)* comedienne who played Brooklyn-accented, sweet-dumb broads (albeit nobody's fool) better than any; first did comedy bits at 20th Century-Fox in Carmen Miranda pix *(Greenwich Village, Something for the Boys)* and *Winged Victory*; then, in a featured comedy role in *Adam's Rib*, the husband-shooter defended by lawyer Hepburn, she almost stole the picture from both Tracy and Hepburn; as a star at Columbia, where she was not in favor with studio boss Harry Cohn because she was never slender enough, she top-lined six: besides *Born Yesterday, The Marrying Kind, Phffft, It Should Happen to You, The Solid Gold Cadillac, Full of Life*; last in a Metro musical, *Bells Are Ringing*.

HOLLIDAY, MARJORIE *(1969)* 49 ——Starlet at 20th Century-Fox who had small roles in several Grable musicals; wife of actor Michael St. Angel.

HOLLINGSWORTH, ALFRED *(1926)* 52 —— Villainous Silk Miller in William S. Hart's *Hell's Hinges;* equally evil in the silent serial *The Mystery Box;* also in Hoot Gibson's *Trimmed, The Bearcat*, etc.

HOLLINGSWORTH, HARRY *(1947)* 59 —— Support in James Melton's *Sing Me a Love Song*, Hope's *My Favorite Blonde*, others.

HOLMAN, HARRY *(1947)* 73 ——Mayor Hawkins in Capra's *Meet John Doe;* also in *Gentle Julia, It Happened One Night* (manager of the tourist cabin where Gable and Colbert erected the "Walls of Jericho"), *Roman Scandals, Seven Days Leave*, more.

HOLMAN, LIBBY *(1971)* 65 ——Broadway's famous "Moanin' Low" torch singer; narrated *The Russian Story* ('43).

HOLMES, BEN *(1943)* 53 ——Was in one early talkie, *The Expert*, then a director *(The Saint in New York*, etc.).

HOLMES, BURTON *(1958)* 88 ——Famed as the "sun sinks slowly in the West" travelog headliner.

HOLMES, HELEN *(1950)* 58 ——Fearless miss with long black curls who hitched her star to a locomotive and never switched tracks in her entire career; top featured in Kalem railroad dramas of '13 *(The Operator at Black Rock, The Car of Death)*, she then became a world-famous serial queen—surpassed only by Pearl White and Ruth Roland—in *The Hazards of Helen* (48 chapters of chasing villains atop moving trains); eight more serials followed, three of which had railroad backgrounds: *A Lass of the Lumberlands, The Lost Express, The Railroad Raiders;* plus such features as *The Train Wreckers, Crossed Signals, The Open Switch, Peril of the Rail*, etc.; in talkies, when no longer so young and athletic, a few minor roles, in *Poppy* and, her last, 1941's *Dude Cowboy*.

HOLMES, PHILLIPS *(1942)* 33 ——Blond, this son of actor Taylor Holmes had the face and physique of a Greek god; was discovered at Princeton in '28 by Paramount, which brought him along slowly for three years, from bits (Clara Bow's *The Wild Party*) to leading man (best in three with Nancy Carroll: *Devil's Holiday, Stolen Heaven, The Man I Killed*) to dramatic star (doomed Clyde Griffiths in *An American Tragedy;* same role played later by Clift in *A Place in the Sun);* his star rose no higher though he was in many more (1933's *State Fair, Dinner at Eight, The Criminal Code*, etc.) before his last, 1939's *Housemaster;* killed while serving in the Royal Canadian Air Force.

HOLMES, RALPH *(1945)* 56 ——Actor-brother of Phillips; character (Martos of the White Robes) in the serial *Undersea Kingdom*.

HOLMES, ROBERT *(1945)* 81 ——Character in 1931's *Jaws of Hell.*

HOLMES, STUART *(1971)* 84 ——Long nose, moustache and high forehead—and one of the silent screen's busiest actors; first in 1911's *How Mrs. Murray Saved the Army;* had the top role in the first Fox venture, 1914's *Life's Shop Window;* other silents: *A Daughter of the Gods* with Annette Kellerman, 1917's *The Scarlet Letter* (not the Gish version), *The New Moon* with Norma Talmadge, *The Prisoner of Zenda* with Alice Terry, *Tess of the D'Urbervilles* with Blanche Sweet, *The Four Horsemen of the Apocalypse,* etc.; starred in one serial—1920's *Trailed by Three;* support in talkies from John Boles' *Captain of the Guard* ('30) to John Wayne's *The Man Who Shot Liberty Valance* ('62).

HOLMES, TAYLOR *(1959)* 81 ——Briefly on-screen in the teens (starred in the title role of *Ruggles of Red Gap),* the '20s (with Priscilla Dean in *The Crimson Runner)* and '30s *(Make Way for a Lady,* etc.), he returned permanently to Hollywood in '47 to become a top character actor; was best in *Kiss of Death* (Victor Mature's crooked lawyer) and *Nightmare Alley* (the industrialist who is skeptical of Tyrone Power's mentalist abilities, yet vulnerable); many others: *Mr. Belvedere Goes to College, Joan of Arc,* etc.

HOLMES, WENDELL *(1962)* 47 ——Support in *Elmer Gantry* (Rev. Ulrich), *Lost Boundaries, Good Day for a Hanging,* etc.; had starred on radio as "Scattergood Baines."

HOLMES, WILLIAM J. *(1946)* 69 ——Support in an Edward Everett Horton comedy, *Once a Gentleman* ('30).

HOLT, JACK *(1951)* 62 ——Great Western star who, from '13, could ride, shoot, and fight with the best; homely handsome, hard-boiled, and tough; for years was Paramount's #1 box-office attraction; at his most vigorous in *Wanderer of the Wasteland, The Squaw Man* ('19), *The Thundering Herd, North of 36;* heroic figure in many major silents out of Western garb: *The Cheat, The Little American* (with Pickford), *The Claw, Held by the Enemy,* etc.; star of many talkies: *Dirigible, Hell's Island, Fifty Fathoms Deep,* more; costar or top support in: *The Littlest Rebel, Thunderbirds, They Were Expendable, The Cat People, Task Force,* and last *Across the Wide Missouri,* the year he died.

HOLT, TIM *(1973)* 54 ——Handsome son of Jack; in B Westerns, a Top Ten box-office star 1941–43, 1948–52; entered pix at 10, playing his father as a lad in *The Vanishing Pioneer;* played earnest teenagers in *Stella Dallas, History Is Made at Night, Spirit of Culver, Swiss Family Robinson;* vivid as the young cavalry lieutenant in *Stagecoach,* he became, fleetingly, and oddly, a bobby-soxer's delight after playing the Nazi youth in *Hitler's Children,* then had a top role in *My Darling Clementine;* the two roles for which he will be longest remembered: Curtin in *The Treasure of Sierra Madre,* and the arrogant aristocrat George Amberson, obsessed by mother Dolores Costello, in Welles' *The Magnificent Ambersons.*

HOMANS, ROBERT *(1947)* 72 ——Usually a uniformed, white-haired cop; in *Black Legion, The Amazing Dr. Clitterhouse, Jack London, Out of the Fog,* etc.

HONDA, FRANK *(1924)* 39 ——Japanese support in pix of the '20s; *Lawful Larceny,* Constance Talmadge's *Wedding Bells,* etc.

HOPE, DIANA *(1942)* 60 ——English character; Mrs. Bodfish in John Barrymore's *The Man from Blankley's,* etc.

HOPE, MAIDIE *(1937)* 56 ——Support in the British pic *This'll Make You Whistle.*

HOPE, VIDA *(1962)* 44 ——English character; in *The Man in the White Suit, Nicholas Nickleby* (as one of the revolting Squeers family members), *Johnny in the Clouds, Interrupted Journey,* etc.

HOPKINS, BOB *(1962)* 44 ——Support in *Autumn Leaves, The Kid from Left Field,* more.

HOPKINS, MIRIAM *(1972)* 69 ——Blonde spitfire from Dixie who was one of Paramount's most glamorous stars in the '30s; was tempestuously alluring for them in 12: *The Smiling Lieutenant, Trouble in Paradise, Design for Living,* etc.; made screen history at RKO as star of the first full-length Technicolor pic, *Becky Sharp* (her only Oscar nomination), and for Goldwyn in *These Three* with Merle Oberon, as the are-they-or-aren't they (Lesbians?); at her bitchy best word-dueling with Bette Davis in two at Warners: *The Old Maid* and *Old Acquaintance* ('43); came back to the screen in '49 as a top character star in *The Heiress, Carrie, The Mating Season, The Chase,* and *The Children's Hour* (remake of *These Three,* under its original stage title, with Shirley MacLaine in her original role and Hopkins as Mrs. Mortar, played previously by character actress Catharine Doucet); starred at the end in a still-unreleased B, perversely titled *Comeback.*

HOPPER, DE WOLF *(1935)* 77 ——Imposing star of silents: *Don Quixote, Casey at the Bat,* after the poem he recited professionally thousands of times; Hedda's ex, and only, husband.

HOPPER, HEDDA *(1966)* 75 ——Support in many talkies *(Rebound, West of Broadway, Men Must Fight,* etc.), usually as a clotheshorse, years before she became a famous gossip columnist; in silents she'd had a long career, specializing in "vampire" roles *(Virtuous Wives; Her Excellence, the Governor; The Third Degree,* etc.); certain victims of her later columns might have called it type-casting.

HOPPER, WILLIAM *(1970)* 54 ——Hedda's and De Wolf's gray-haired son; first billed De Wolf Hopper Jr. (real name), he made his screen debut at one in his father's *Sunshine Dad;* as William, in the late '30s, he costarred in numerous B's at Warners *(Public Wedding* with Jane Wyman, etc.); a movie dropout for over a decade (became an auto salesman), he came back as a character actor in the '50s to play the Texas beau of tart Jan Sterling in *The High and the Mighty,* Natalie Wood's dad in *Rebel Without a Cause,* etc.; became most famous as imperturbable detective Paul Drake in TV's *Perry Mason.*

HOPTON, RUSSELL *(1945)* 45 ——Character actor with black wavy, center-parted hair who specialized in hoods; was a prime one in *G-Men, Mutiny in the Big House, Crime Takes a Holiday,* etc.; played many other low-lifes, such as the barker for sideshow vamp Mae West in *I'm No Angel.*

HORNE, DAVID *(1970)* 72 ——Pompous, bald, well-upholstered British character; the minister in *Lust for Life;* also in *The Prince and the Showgirl, Beau Brummell, Martin Luther* (Duke Frederick of Saxony), etc.

HORTON, EDWARD EVERETT *(1970)* 84 —— It's impossible to think of the comedies of the '20s *(Ruggles of Red Gap, The Whole Town's Talking,* etc.), '30s *(The King and the Chorus Girl, Holiday,* etc.), '40s *(Arsenic and Old Lace, The Magnificent Dope,* etc.), or later decades *(Pocketful of Miracles, Cold Turkey),* without thinking of this lanky, bushy-browed Nervous Nellie; at his peak in the '30s when he reportedly made a picture a month; highlights of that era: *Lost Horizon,* the Astaire-Rogers musicals *(The Gay Divorcee, Top Hat, Shall We Dance),* Lubitsch's *Design for Living;* in the '40s he gave his two very best performances— in *Here Comes Mr. Jordan* (as heavenly Messenger 7013) and Russian-localed *Summer Storm* in which as Count Volsky, a dramatic role with comic overtones, he vied, seriously, with George Sanders over 21-year-old Linda Darnell.

HOTALING, ARTHUR *(1938)* 63 ——Support, in the '20s, in Westerns *(Kit Carson over the Great Divide, King of the Herd),* and B's (Lila Lee's *The Little Wild Girl).*

HOUDINI, HARRY *(1926)* 52 ——Escape artist-magician who starred in silent serials *(The Master Mystery)* and features *(The Man from Beyond, Terror Island, Haldane of the Secret Service,* etc.); later portrayed, in *Houdini,* by Tony Curtis.

HOUSE, BILLY *(1961)* 71 ——Heavyweight baldie with many chins who could be funny *(The Egg and I,* as Billy Reed, *People Will Talk)* or frightening *(Where Danger Lives, Bedlam,* the gross Lord Mortimer).

HOUSE, JACK *(1963)* 76 ——In silent Westerns: *Fightin' Odds, The Smoking Trail.*

HOUSMAN, ARTHUR *(1942)* 52 ——An Edison Co. comedy star from '15, he had humorous top supporting roles in countless comedies of the '20s: *The Bat; Nellie, the Cloakroom Model;* Clara Bow's *Rough House Rosie,* etc.; in the '30s he made a career of the perpetual funny drunk, in shorts (Patsy Kelly-Thelma Todd, his own series at Pathe co-starring with Edgar Kennedy) and features *(She Done Him Wrong,* as Barfly, *Step Lively, Jeeves,* etc.).

HOUSTON, CISCO *(1961)* 42 ——He was a singer in Westerns.

HOUSTON, GEORGE *(1945)* 47 ——Handsome hero who starred in the musical "Lone Rider" Western series at P.R.C. 1943–45: *Return of the Lone Rider, Riders of the Plains,* etc.; opera-trained (once sang *Faust* before President Coolidge), he was first featured in big-budget musicals: *The Melody Lingers On, The Great Waltz,* etc.

HOVICK, LOUISE *(1970)* 56 ——See Gypsy Rose Lee.

HOWARD, BOOTHE *(1936)* 47 ——A principal villain, Ditmar, in the serial *Underworld Kingdom;* a thug in many: *Charlie Chan at the Circus; Mary Burns, Fugitive; Every Night at Eight; Mystery Liner,* etc.

HOWARD, CURLY *(1952)* 45 ——Grunting, squealing burrhead comedian; he, brother Moe, and Larry Fine were The Three Stooges 1932–46; suffering a stroke, he was replaced by brother Shemp; Curly was seen just once when not a Stooge, as a clown, with Moe, in MGM's *Broadway to Hollywood.*

HOWARD, EDDY *(1963)* 54 ——Orchestra leader; in musical shorts.

HOWARD, ESTHER *(1965)* 72 ——Always played tough broads like Mrs. Florian in *Murder, My Sweet;* in *Ladies of the Big House, Merrily We Go to Hell,* and many Sturges comedies: *The Great McGinty, Sullivan's Travels* (Miz Zeffie), *The Miracle of Morgan's Creek, Hail the Conquering Hero* (comedian Raymond Walburn's wife), and *The Beautiful Blonde from Bashful Bend* (Mrs. Smidlap).

HOWARD, EUGENE *(1965)* 84 ——Starred with brother Willie in comedy shorts of the late '20s: *The Music Makers, Between the Acts of the Opera,* etc.

HOWARD, GERTRUDE *(1934)* 43 ——Black character actress; was the maid who received Mae West's immortal line: "Beulah, peel me a grape"; onscreen from 1914, she was in such later silents as Anna Q. Nilsson's *Easy Pickings* and such early talkies as *Show Boat* ('29) and *The Wet Parade.*

HOWARD, KATHLEEN *(1956)* 77 ——Sweet-faced character actress who frequently played housekeepers or maids, as she did in *Ball of Fire, Laura, Centennial Summer,* and *The Late George Apley;* that is, when not portraying W. C. Fields' nagging wife, as she did in *It's a Gift, You're Telling Me, Man on the Flying Trapeze.*

HOWARD, LESLIE *(1943)* 50 ——Besides the role of Ashley Wilkes in *Gone With the Wind,* other portrayals of this English gentleman (and he played only men of quality) give him a permanent niche in motion picture annals: *Pygmalion* and *Berkeley Square* (both rating him Oscar nominations), *The Petrified Forest, Of Human Bondage,* ('34), *Outward Bound, The Animal Kingdom, The Scarlet Pimpernel, Romeo and Juliet* ('36), *Intermezzo;* entering movies at 37, after a stage career, his body of work is relatively small—only 27 films in 13 years.

HOWARD, LEWIS *(1956)* 38 ——Shaggy-haired young man who competed with Robert Stack for Deanna Durbin in *First Love;* next in her *It's a Date,* he was then Marsha Hunt's beau in *Seven Sweethearts;* in other pix of the '40s (*Hellzapoppin, Up Goes Maisie, I've Always Loved You,* etc.), he last had a supporting role in Bogart's *In a Lonely Place.*

HOWARD, LISA *(1965)* 35 ——Femme lead in two B's of the early '50s: *The Man Who Cheated Himself* and *Donovan's Brain;* became a TV newscaster.

HOWARD, PETER *(1968)* 34 ——Socialite-actor; support in B's and on TV.

HOWARD, RUTH *(1944)* 50 ——Support in one Columbia B, *My Woman* ('33).

HOWARD, SHEMP *(1955)* 60 ——One of the Three Stooges in vaudeville, he was not one of them in movie shorts until succeeded ailing younger brother Curly in '46; as a solo he had been a comic character in many: *Hellzapoppin, Blondie Knows Best,* Westerns (*San Antonio Rose,* etc.), numerous Abbott & Costello pix (*Buck Privates, It Ain't Hay*), and perhaps most notably as the bartender in Fields' *The Bank Dick.*

HOWARD, SYDNEY *(1946)* 62 ——Rotund comedian in English pix: *When We Are Married, Tilly of Bloomsbury,* many others.

HOWARD, TOM *(1955)* 69 ——Skinny, cigar-smoking comedian; first onscreen with Joe Cook in 1930's *Rain or Shine* (was in it on Broadway too), and last in *Where Is Wall Street* ('36), he was featured in a score of two-reel comedies in between.

HOWARD, WENDY *(1972)* 40s ——Pretty redhead who had small roles in numerous B's and Encyclopaedia Britannica short features.

HOWARD, WILLIAM *(1944)* 59 ——Supporting roles in two Edward Arnold pix: *Diamond Jim* and *Come and Get It.*

HOWARD, WILLIE *(1949)* 61 ——Thin half of the famous Eugene & Willie Howard comedy team; together in Vitaphone shorts in the '20s, he soloed in *Rose of the Rancho, Broadway Melody of 1938,* and *Millions in the Air.*

HOWES, BOBBY *(1972)* 76 ——British comedian, father of Sally Ann; in Vera-Ellen's *Happy Go Lovely;* also in *Yes Madam, Over the Garden Wall,* more.

HOWES, REED *(1964)* 63 ——For two good reasons—fine face and perfect physique—this world-famous "Arrow-Collar Man" was deemed in '24 to be America's handsomest man; co-starred in many silents: *Bobbed Hair* with Marie Prevost, *Rough House Rosie* with Clara Bow, *Ladies' Night in a Turkish Bath* with Dorothy Mackaill, and numerous other "flaming youth" pix; after starring in one of the first talkie serials, *Terry of the Times,* he became a Western star (*Kentucky Handicap, The High Flyer,* etc.); by '36 he was playing villains in serials (*The Clutching Hand, Custer's Last Stand*), and then gray-haired, black-hatted desperadoes in B Westerns (*Under Arizona Skies,*

Wild Horse Stampede, etc.), until illness forced him to lay down his guns in the '50s.

HOWLAND, JOBYNA *(1936)* 45 ——Tall, slender, blonde-gray character comedienne who specialized in overpowering matrons; in *Honey, Once in a Lifetime* (domineering mother of movie-hopeful Sidney Fox), *Dixiana, The Cuckoos, Rockabye;* especially grand as the exburlesque queen Shakespearean actress in *Stepping Sisters;* last feature: 1933's *The Story of Temple Drake;* last role: a two-reel comedy, *Ye Old Saw Mill,* in '35.

HOWLAND, OLIN *(1959)* 63 ——Sometimes spelled Howlin; brother of Jobyna; played nasal rustics in hundreds, as in *Nothing Sacred,* the train station baggage man in Lombard's hometown, Warsaw, Vermont; in *Brother Rat, Chad Hanna, The Wistful Widow of Wagon Gap, Home Sweet Homicide,* etc.

HOXIE, JACK *(1965)* 76 ——Legendary cowboy star of the silent screen; winning the National Riding Championship in '14, he became a Hollywood stuntman, and in '19, as Hartford Hoxie (real name), starred in the serial *Lightning Bryce,* then in Western features as Art Hoxie; in '21 Universal changed his name to Jack and starred him in action (*Red Warning, Galloping Ace,* etc.), on which his fame rests; ill-suited to talkies (couldn't handle the dialogue), he quit after 1934's *Outlaw Justice* and retired to his native Oklahoma.

HOYT, ARTHUR *(1953)* 79 ——Onscreen from '16 to '47, this character actor was in perhaps 200; silents: *The Lost World, Camille, Sundown, When a Man's a Man,* etc.; talkies: *20,000 Years in Sing Sing, Only Yesterday, It Happened One Night* (Zeke), *Mr. Deeds Goes to Town* (Budington), *Hail the Conquering Hero* (Reverend Upperman); active through 1947's *My Favorite Brunette.*

HOYT, CLEGG *(1967)* 56 ——Support in *The Young Savages, Santiago, Gun Fever,* etc.

HOYT, JULIA *(1955)* 58 ——Young support in silents of the '20s: Thomas Meighan's *The Man Who Found Himself,* Norma Talmadge's *The Wonderful Thing* (second lead).

HUBER, HAROLD *(1959)* 49 ——Played scarfaced gangsters, Mongolians, Arabs, petty thieves, leering bodyguards, con-men; up to evil, from '32, in *G-Men, The Thin Man, The Adventures of Marco Polo, The Bowery, San Francisco,* many "Charlie Chan" pix, and another 60; was miscast as a Leo Carrillo type in Beery's *Viva Villa,* but it was an interesting switch.

HUBERT, GEORGE *(1963)* 82 ——Onscreen from the mid-teens, he was support in many; last in Mitchum's *Foreign Intrigue.*

HUDD, WALTER *(1963)* 64 ——Big, lean, reserved English character; in *I Know Where I'm Going, The Importance of Being Earnest, Major Barbara, Look Back in Anger,* many more.

HUDMAN, WES *(1964)* 48 ——Slim guy who played Western desperadoes in many: *Blackjack Ketchum, The Sheepman, Fort Defiance, Pack Train,* etc.

HUDSON, LARRY *(1961)* 40 ——Chauffeur in *The Solid Gold Cadillac;* also in *Tank Commandos, The Redhead from Wyoming, Jubal,* others.

HUDSON, ROCHELLE *(1972)* 58 ——Few would complain if it were argued that she was the prettiest ingenue onscreen in the '30s, in *Poppy, Les Miserables, Curly Top, Imitation of Life* (fine as Colbert's daughter), *Judge Priest, The Mighty Barnum,* etc.; in the '40s she starred in action B's (*Meet Boston Blackie, Island of Doomed Men, Men Without Souls,* etc.), but none could hold a candle to the real-life role she played for the U.S. during WW II —as a spy in Mexico; on TV in the '50s (*That's My Boy* series) and Natalie Wood's mother in *Rebel Without a Cause;* in the '60s, alas, hardfaced support in two: Crawford's *Strait-Jacket* and Stanwyck's *The Night Walker.*

HUDSON, WILLIAM *(1974)* 49 ——Handsome guy; major support in *Objective Burma* (Fred Hollis); *Hard, Fast and Beautiful; The Amazing Colossal Man; Mister Roberts* (Olson), etc.

HUFF, FORREST *(1947)* 71 ——Musical stage star with twirled moustache; in Swanson's *The Loves of Sunya.*

HUFF, LOUISE *(1973)* 77 ——Exquisitely beautiful girl, from the stage, who co-starred with young Jack Pickford in three: *Seventeen* ('16), *Jack and Jill,* and *Great Expectations*—as the strange young Estella (played later by Jean Simmons), adored by him as Pip; later, opposite Ernest Truex in *Oh, You Women,* with Arliss in the silent *Disraeli,* etc.

HUGHES, DAVID *(1974)* 70s ——Character in many: *The Grapes of Wrath* (as Frank), *The Long Voyage Home* (Scotty), etc.

HUGHES, GARETH *(1965)* 71 ——Silent star particularly adept at portraying sensitive youths; first in 1919's *Mrs. Wiggs of the Cabbage Patch* and Clara Kimball Young's *Eyes of Youth;* starred in many, including *Sentimental*

Tommy (in which he gave his most glowing performance), *The Hunch, Kick In, The Spanish Dancer,* and *The Christian* (as a young priest).

HUGHES, J. ANTHONY *(1970)* 70s ——Support in many in the '30s and '40s: *Tail Spin, In Old Chicago, Call of the Yukon, The Cisco Kid and the Lady,* etc.

HUGHES, LLOYD *(1958)* 60 ——Popular silent star who generally played upstanding young men, from 1915's *Turn of a Road;* often the hero opposite Colleen Moore: *The Huntress, Sally, The Desert Flower, Irene, Ella Cinders;* in many others of the '20s: *The Sea Hawk, Three-Ring Marriage* (with Mary Astor), *Tess of the Storm Country* (Mary Pickford), *Scars of Jealousy, The Lost World, American Beauty* (Billie Dove), more; starred or co-starred in talkies (*Kelly of the Secret Service, Clipped Wings,* etc.) through a 1940 B, *Vengeance of the Deep,* in which he was top-billed.

HUGHES, THOMAS ARTHUR *(1953)* 66—— Western support when not portraying Churchill.

HUGO, MAURITZ *(1974)* 65 ——Slender, dark-haired support in many (*The Iron Curtain, Wanted by the Police, A Ticket to Tomahawk,* etc.), plus serials of the '50s: *Government Agents vs. Phantom Legion, Man with the Steel Whip* (chief villain, saloon-keeper Barnet), *King of the Carnival.*

HULBERT, CLAUDE *(1964)* 63 ——Pompous comic roles in British pix: *Bulldog Jack, Sailors Three, Alias Bulldog Drummond, The Ghost of St. Michael's,* more.

HULEY, PETE *(1973)* 80 ——Support in silents.

HULL, JOSEPHINE *(1957)* 71 ——Pixilated little partridge who co-starred in *Arsenic and Old Lace* with Cary Grant as one of his aunts (humorously, diabolically concerned about lonely old men), and won a Supporting Oscar as James Stewart's sister in *Harvey;* earlier she'd had supporting roles in *Careless Lady* and *After Tomorrow,* and later, and last, in Howard Duff's *The Lady from Texas.*

HULL, WARREN *(1974)* 71 ——Handsome, smiling, curly-haired star of B's in the '30s and early '40s (*Bengal Tiger, The Lone Wolf Meets a Lady, Her Husband's Secretary, Fugitive in the Sky,* etc.), and of serials (*The Spider's Web, The Spider Returns, Mandrake the Magician, The Green Hornet Strikes Again*); later famous as emcee of TV's you-suffer-we-pay show, *Strike It Rich.*

HUME, BENITA *(1967)* 60 ——Dark-haired English leading lady of warmth and charm; on Hollywood screens in *Flying Fool, Reserved for Ladies, Clear All Wires, Suzy, Tarzan Escapes, Rainbow on the River,* many others; wife of Ronald Colman (co-starred with him on radio and TV in *Halls of Ivy*), and after his death, George Sanders.

HUMPHREYS, CECIL *(1947)* 64 ——English supporting actor in many American silents (*The Glorious Adventure,* Thomas Meighan's *Irish Luck,* etc.) and talkies (*Wuthering Heights,* as Judge Linton, *The Razor's Edge,* as the Holy Man, *A Woman's Vengeance,* many others).

HUNT, JAY *(1932)* 75 ——Had old-man leads in 1925's *Lightnin'* and 1927's *The Harvester,* plus major roles in many other silents: Buck Jones' *The Gentle Cyclone* and *A Man Four-Square, The Phantom of the Opera,* Betty Compson's *Counsel for the Defense,* etc.

HUNT, MARTITA *(1969)* 69 ——British character actress guaranteed movie immortality for her eccentric Miss Havisham in 1947's *Great Expectations;* in dozens (1932–69): *Prison Without Bars, The Man in Grey, So Evil My Love, Anastasia, Becket,* etc.

HUNT, REA M. *(1961)* 68 ——One of the Keystone Kops.

HUNTER, GLENN *(1945)* 52 ——No star of the '20s was so fine as he at playing handsome, humorous country bumpkins, which he did in *Merton of the Movies* (had created the stage role too), *The Scarecrow, The Pinch Hitter, The Broadway Boob, The Country Flapper,* etc.; also in *Smilin' Through* with Norma Talmadge, *West of the Water Tower, The Cradle Buster,* more; retired after 1926's *A Romance of a Million Dollars.*

HUNTER, JEFFREY *(1969)* 42 ——Handsome, blue-eyed 20th Century-Fox star: *Sailor of the King, No Down Payment, A Kiss Before Dying, Fourteen Hours, Belles on Their Toes;* starred elsewhere in *King of Kings* (as Jesus), *Sergeant Rutledge, The Searchers, Custer of the West,* more.

HUNTER, RICHARD *(1962)* 87 ——Oldtimer who had supporting roles in many Westerns.

HUNTLEY, CHET *(1974)* 62 ——Prize-winning NBC newscaster; onscreen in 1949's *Arctic Manhunt.*

HUNTLEY, FRED *(1931)* 69 ——Character actor in silent features (*What Every Woman Knows, A Prince There Was, Bronze Bell, Peg*

O'My Heart, etc.) and Westerns (*North of the Rio Grande, Thundering Hoofs, Call of the Canyon,* more).

HURST, BRANDON *(1947)* 81 ——British character actor who set a high-water mark of villainy in his first American pic, Chaney's *The Hunchback of Notre Dame,* as the slimy Jehan who betrayed Quasimodo; redeemed himself by playing a clown in Chaney's next, *He Who Gets Slapped;* many silents: *The Thief of Bagdad, Seventh Heaven* (Uncle George), *Cytherea, Lover of Camille,* etc.; among his talkies: *The Little Minister, Mary of Scotland, The Remarkable Andrew* (Justice Marshall), *House of Frankenstein, The Corn Is Green.*

HURST, PAUL *(1953)* 65 ——In hundreds (1926 –53), this fine character actor made perhaps his most vivid impression in one of his briefest roles—in *Gone With the Wind,* as the thieving Yankee soldier Scarlett shot on the stairs at Tara; perhaps his longest-running role, the sidekick, Doc Meadowlark, in dozens of Monte Hale Westerns at Republic (*Outcasts of the Trail,* etc.); played comics or heavies—often Irish—in *Topper Takes a Trip* (bartender), *Each Dawn I Die, Alexander's Ragtime Band, In Old Chicago, The Ox-Bow Incident, Big Jim McLain,* etc.

HUSING, TED *(1962)* 70 ——Famed radio sportscaster; in Gable's *To Please a Lady.*

HUSSEY, JIMMY *(1930)* 39 ——Dapper Broadway musical comedy lead who starred in Vitaphone shorts.

HUSTON, WALTER *(1950)* 66 ——An irreplaceable actor, considered by some the finest American actor ever on the screen; magnificent as an old irascible—Scratch in *All That Money Can Buy (The Devil and Daniel Webster)*—for which he was nominated as Best Actor, and Howard in *The Treasure of the Sierra Madre,* which won him a Best Supporting Oscar; he was also nominated as Best Actor in *Dodsworth* and Best Support in *Yankee Doodle Dandy;* from 1929's *Gentlemen of the Press* through 1950's *The Furies,* he remains vividly memorable in every role he undertook: *Abraham Lincoln, Rain, Gabriel Over the White House, Mission to Moscow, Dragon Seed, Duel in the Sun, The Outlaw, Edge of Darkness,* etc.

HUTH, HAROLD *(1967)* 76 ——Leading man in British silents and early talkies: *Balaclava, The Triumph of the Scarlet Pimpernel, The Outsider, The Ghoul, Jaws of Hell,* more.

HUTTON, JUNE *(1973)* 50s ——Charlie Spivak band singer; in musical shorts.

HUXHAN, KENDRICK *(1967)* 75 ——Support in Signoret's *Games;* also in *Pirates of Tortuga,* etc.

HYAMS, JOHN *(1940)* 63 ——Wispy, sly character; in *The Mighty Barnum,* he "sold" Beery the "160-year-old nurse of George Washington"; support in many: *The Virginia Judge, A Day at the Races, Swell People,* etc.; father of Leila.

HYLTON, RICHARD *(1962)* 41 ——Made his strongest impression in his first, as Mel Ferrer's teenage son in *Lost Boundaries;* then in *Fixed Bayonets!, Halls of Montezuma, The Pride of St. Louis, Secrets of Convict Lake.*

HYMER, WARREN *(1948)* 42 ——In one of his earliest, *Up the River,* as Dannemora Dan, Tracy's hardboiled, humorous (and paper doily-making) fellow-convict pal, he established the two personality facets he would bank on for two decades in over 100 pix; was dangerously tough in *Show Them No Mercy, You Only Live Once, 36 Hours to Kill,* many others; was strong, funny support in *George White's Scandals; Destry Rides Again; Birth of the Blues; Charlie McCarthy, Detective,* more.

HYTTEN, OLAF *(1955)* 56 ——Scottish supporting actor in many Hollywood pix from '24; in *Berkeley Square* (Sir Joshua Reynolds), *The Good Earth* (Grain Merchant Liu), *Becky Sharp* (Prince Regent), *Sherlock and the Voice of Terror* (Fabian Prentiss), *My Name Is Julia Ross, The Black Swan,* etc.

I

IHNAT, STEVE *(1972)* 37 ——Handsome Czech-Canadian support in many: *Dragstrip Riot, Madigan, The Chase, In Like Flint, Fuzz,* etc., plus more than 30 TV shows; last starred in *Do Not Throw Cushions Into the Ring,* which he also produced, directed, and wrote.

ILLING, PETER *(1966)* 61 ——Austrian support in dozens: *Bhowani Junction, Fire Down Below, The V.I.P.s* (as Mr. Damer), *The Wreck of the Mary Deare* (Gunderson), *Whirlpool, I Accuse!,* many more.

ILLINGTON, MARGARET *(1934)* 53 ——Brunette stage actress who starred for Zukor in *The Inner Shrine* and *Sacrifice* (both '17); was the wife of radio's Major Bowes.

IMBODEN, DAVID *(1974)* 87 ——Was St. Andrew the Apostle in DeMille's *The King of Kings*; in many others.

IMBODEN, HAZEL *(1956)* 70s ——Actress-wife of David; in silents from the mid-teens.

IMHOF, ROGER *(1958)* 83 ——Stern-faced, bushy-browed character who specialized in country men, American pioneers, and rugged tycoons; in *Drums Along the Mohawk* (General Nicholas Herkimer), *The Grapes of Wrath* (Thomas), *Young Mr. Lincoln, Home in Indiana* (Old Timer), *Little Old New York* (John Jacob Astor), and many Will Rogers movies: *Steamboat 'Round the Bend, Judge Priest, David Harum, Handy Andy*, etc.

INCE, JOHN *(1947)* 68 ——A popular leading man, first with Lubin in '14, he later co-starred in *Madame Sphinx* ('18) with Alma Rubens; supported others in the '20s (Conrad Nagel in *Hate*, etc.), the '30s (*In Old Kentucky, Way Out West, Mr. Smith Goes to Washington*, etc.), and the '40s (*Wilson*, as Senator Watson, *The Paradine Case, Pride of the Yankees*, others); also directed silents (*Old Lady 31, If Marriage Fails*, etc.); brother of Ralph and Thomas.

INCE, RALPH *(1937)* 50 ——First of the famous Ince family to enter movies, he rose from property man to star at Vitagraph; first seen impersonating Lincoln in a series in 1906, then appeared in another 500 and directed some 150 for the same company, prior to '14; throughout the '20s alternated acting (*Yellow Fingers*), acting-directing (*The Sea Wolf, Chicago After Midnight, Shanghaied*), and directing (*A Man's Home, Success*, etc.); in the '30s he was a supporting actor in many (*The Hatchet Man, So You Won't Talk*, and, perhaps most notably, *Little Caesar*, in which he was Diamond Pete Montana).

INCE, THOMAS H. *(1924)* 42 ——An early screen actor, he doffed the mantle of performer in '11 when he directed his first picture, *Across the Plains*; then quickly outdistanced both brothers, historically, as producer-director and creator of the Ince film empire, devoted primarily to spectacles (*Civilization, The Wrath of the Gods*) and the Westerns of William S. Hart.

INCLAN, MIGUEL *(1956)* 56 ——Mexican actor who was Cochise in John Ford's *Fort Apache*; also in *The Fugitive, Seven Cities of Gold, The Young and the Damned*, etc.

INDRISANO, JOHN *(1968)* 62 ——Played boxers and thugs; in *Ringside Maisie, Callaway Went Thattaway, Joe Palooka in the Counterpunch, Chicago Confidential, The Yellow Cab Man*, more.

INGERSOLL, WILLIAM *(1936)* 76 ——Character actor from the stage, in silents (*Partners of the Night*) and talkies (*Mary Burns, Fugitive*, in which he was the Judge, *The Cheat*, etc.).

INGRAHAM, LLOYD *(1956)* 81 ——In later years, a fine-faced, gray-haired man who played ranchers, dads of heroines, and sheriffs in dozens of Westerns (*Twenty-Mule Team, Riders of the Dawn, Painted Desert, Frontier Gal*, etc.); had been a most handsome leading man in very early silents, a director (of Fairbanks, Pickford, others), a major supporting player in silents of the '20s (*Scaramouche, A Front Page Story*) and non-Western talkies (*Sixteen Fathoms Deep, In Love with Life*, etc.).

INGRAM, JACK *(1969)* 66 ——In hundreds of B Westerns (*Under Texas Skies, The Strawberry Roan*, etc.), this lean-faced guy shot to kill—good guys, who always won; was at this trade from '29, when he first became a Paramount contract player, through 1957's *Utah Blaine*; villain in 33 serials too (more even than bad-guy Roy Barcroft), including *Terry and the Pirates, Dick Tracy Returns, White Eagle, King of the Texas Rangers*, etc.

INGRAM, REX *(1950)* 58 ——Billed Rex Hitchcock, he was the lanky, handsome, top support of many Vitagraph stars in '13 (Lillian Walker in *The Artist's Madonna*; Helen Gardner, Clara Kimball Young, Maurice Costello in others); soon this black-haired Irishman became one of the silents' most famous directors (*The Four Horsemen of the Apocalypse, The Prisoner of Zenda*, etc.), and married star Alice Terry.

INGRAM, REX *(1969)* 73 ——Black star who was huge and fine as the genie with the thunderous laughter in Sabu's *The Thief of Bagdad*, and as De Lawd (plus Adam and Hezdrel) in *The Green Pastures*; in another 35, from 1918's *Tarzan of the Apes: The Big Parade, The King of Kings, The Emperor Jones, King Kong, A Thousand and One Nights* (again, the genie), *Sahara, Cabin in the Sky*, etc.

IRELAND, ANTHONY *(1957)* 55 ——Support in English pix: *The Water Gypsies, Juggernaut, The Prime Minister, Sweet Devil*, more.

IRVINE, ROBIN *(1933)* 31 ——English actor who played young leads in two early Hitchcocks (*When Boys Leave Home*, a.k.a. *Downhill*, and *East Virtue*), plus *Eine Nacht in London* with Lilian Harvey.

IRVING, GEORGE *(1961)* 87 ——Splendid, gray-haired character of distinguished appearance in over 100: *Wings* (Buddy Rogers' father), *Bright Eyes* (Judge), *Captain January* (millionaire Mason), *Bringing Up Baby, Christmas Holiday, New Moon, Son of Dracula.*

IRVING, PAUL *(1959)* 82 ——Character in several in the '30s: *The Great Ziegfeld* (as producer Erlanger), *The Silver Cord, Hollywood Hotel, Gold Diggers of 1937, Balalaika,* etc.

IRVING, WILLIAM *(1943)* 50 ——Support in silents (*Ham and Eggs, Love Letters,* Clara Bow's *Red Hair,* etc.) and talkies (*All Quiet on the Western Front,* as soldier Ginger, *Orient Express; Her Majesty, Love;* others).

IRWIN, BOYD, *(1957)* 76 ——English actor who was top support in many silents (Fairbanks' *The Three Musketeers, Captain Blood,* etc.) and talkies (*The Prisoner of Zenda,* as Master of Ceremonies, *The Major and the Minor, Devil's Squadron, The Man in the Iron Mask,* others).

IRWIN, CHARLES *(1969)* 81 ——Irish support in more than 50 from Paul Whiteman's *King of Jazz;* in *The Foxes of Harrow* (Rex Harrison's father), *The Black Swan, Hangover Square,* *The Light That Failed, Mrs. Miniver, Lord Jeff,* etc.

IRWIN, MAY *(1958)* 96 ——John C. Rice gave her *The Kiss* (1896) that gave them both a permanent pictorial place in screen history books; she starred in only one other, *Mrs. Black Is Back,* for Zukor in 1914.

ITURBI, AMPARO *(1969)* 70 ——Pianist-sister of Jose; onscreen with him, in duo piano stints, in *Holiday in Mexico* and *That Midnight Kiss.*

IVAN, ROSALIND *(1959)* 77 ——Laughton did her in when she was his acid-tongued spouse in *The Suspect;* Bette Davis must have felt like it when she was the religious hypocrite-mom ("I've bin si-ved, I have") of Bessie Watting (Joan Lorring) in *The Corn Is Green;* a harridan in others: *The Verdict, Scarlet Street, Three Strangers, Johnny Belinda,* etc.

IVES, DOUGLAS *(1969)* 60s ——Support in English pix: *Doctor in the House, What Every Woman Wants, Miracle in Soho, The Big Chance,* more.

J

JACK, T. C. *(1954)* 72 ——Supporting actor, from silents of the mid-teens.

JACKIE, BILL *(1954)* 64 ——Comic support in Guy Kibbee's *Don't Tell the Wife;* had been in silents also.

JACKSON, COLETTE *(1969)* 30s ——Bar girl in *Seven Days in May.*

JACKSON, JOE *(1942)* 62 ——Famed stage comedian from Vienna; starred in Keystone comedies in the mid-teens: *Gypsy Joe, A Modern Enoch Arden,* etc.

JACKSON, MAHALIA *(1972)* 62 ——Noted black gospel singer; onscreen in *St. Louis Blues, Imitation of Life* ('59), *The Best Man.*

JACKSON, SELMER *(1971)* 70s ——One of the screen's busiest and best portrayers of gray-haired substantial citizens—dads, doctors, lawyers, etc.—in scores from 1929's *Thru Different Eyes;* in *Black Fury, Stand Up and Fight, The Grapes of Wrath* (inspection officer at California state line), *They Died With Their Boots On, Johnny Apollo* (warden), *Magic Town, Autumn Leaves,* etc.

JACKSON, THOMAS E. *(1967)* 72 ——Character actor with a lean, hard, jaundiced Irish face, and a well-dented cocked brim hat, that made him the very model of a police lieutenant (*Little Caesar,* as soft-voiced Lt. Flaherty) or crime reporter ("Torchy Blane's" *Blondes at Work, The Thin Man*); in more than 250 from 1929's *Broadway* including: *The Mystery of the Wax Museum, Manhattan Melodrama, The Woman in the Window, Shady Lady, Phone Call from a Stranger,* etc.

JACKSON, WARREN *(1950)* 57 ——Character (Curly) in Flynn's *Montana;* also in *Oh, You Beautiful Doll, Hollywood Round-up,* more.

JACOBS, ANGELA *(1951)* 58 ——Created the role of Goldie Rindskops in *Counsellor-at-Law* onstage and repeated in the John Barrymore movie, her only screen appearance.

JAFFE, CARL *(1974)* 72 ——Polished (and monocled in modern pix) German-born British character actor; in *Ivanhoe* (Austrian Monk), *The Roman Spring of Mrs. Stone, Mad Little Island, The Saint in London, Lili Marlene, The Life and Death of Colonel Blimp, Operation Crossbow,* etc.

JAMES, ALFRED P. *(1946)* 81 ——Comic support in Charles Ruggles' *Six of a Kind,* Wheeler & Woolsey's *Cockeyed Cavaliers,* others of the '30s.

JAMES, ART *(1972)* 71 ——See Denver Dixon.

JAMES, CLIFTON *(1963)* 65 ——Title role in *I Was Monty's Double*, based on his book and real-life adventures as the English government-chosen look-alike for Field Marshal Montgomery.

JAMES, EDDIE *(1944)* 64 ——Support in silents: Viola Dana's *Wild Oats Lane*, Richard Dix's *The Lucky Devil*, others.

JAMES, GLADDEN *(1948)* 56 ——Handsome curly-haired guy who flew with Barthelmess and Fairbanks Jr. in *The Dawn Patrol* ('30); started with Vitagraph in 1912; Mollie King's leading man in the 1917 serial *The Mystery of the Double Cross;* was the young engineer-lover who spurned half-breed Norma Talmadge in *The Heart of Wetona* ('18), and the chauffeur who attempted to seduce her in *Yes or No?* ('20); many other silents (*Adorable Cheat, The Faithless Sex, Wise Husbands*, etc.) and talkies (support in *Lucky Devils, For Me and My Gal*, others).

JAMES, HORACE D. *(1925)* 52 ——Character in pix of the '20s; in Davies' *Adam and Eva*, Mary Alden's *A Woman's Woman, Get-Rich-Quick-Wallingford*, etc.

JAMES, JOHN *(1960)* 40s ——Played young servicemen in the '40s: *Flying Tigers* (pilot Selby), *Gung Ho!* (Buddy Andrews), *Bedside Manner* (Dick Smith); later in Westerns (*Topeka, Saddle Pals*, etc.).

JAMES, RUTH *(1970)* ——Character actress.

JAMES, WALTER *(1946)* 60 ——Character; last a Marshal in *Street Scene*, he had played similar law-officer roles in silents: *Glenister of the Mounted, Patent Leather Kid, The Seventh Bandit*, more.

JAMESON, HOUSE *(1971)* 68 ——Gray-haired wealthy suburbanite Halloran, whose pool was one Burt Lancaster stroked through as *The Swimmer;* earlier was Dr. Stoneman in *The Naked City;* famous on radio as the father in *The Aldrich Family.*

JAMISON, ANNE *(1961)* 51 ——Singer; minor roles in musicals.

JAMISON, BUD *(1943)* 49 ——Big, threatening support—cops, irate husbands, etc.—in literally hundreds of two-reel comedies; in Chaplin's Essanay period (1915-18), was present in almost all: *A Night Out, The Champion, In the Park* (furious, portly beau of the nursemaid Chaplin flirts with), *The Tramp* (one of the hoboes who steal Chaplin's lunch), *By the Sea, Shanghaied*, etc.; more of the same in talkies with Leon Errol, Andy Clyde, Edgar Kennedy, Harry Langdon, et al.; support in many features: *Her Cardboard Lover, Topper Takes a Trip, See My Lawyer*, etc.

JANIS, ELSIE *(1956)* 66 ——Sweetheart of every World War I doughboy for entertaining troops in the trenches in France, this dark-haired beauty starred in many silents from '14: *The Caprices of Kitty, Betty in Search of a Thrill, Everybody's Sweetheart, Nearly a Lady, 'Twas Ever Thus, A Regular Girl, The Imp*, etc.; offscreen for years (as scriptwriter and lyricist), she returned to star last in Republic's *Women in War* in 1940.

JANNINGS, EMIL *(1950)* 63 ——American-born (Brooklyn) German star perhaps better known now for *The Blue Angel*, in which cabaret singer Dietrich proved the downfall of this old professor of English Lit, than for the two roles which won him the first Best Actor Oscar presented: *The Last Command* and *The Way of All Flesh;* though he continued to act—ponderously—in talkies (almost all German-language), through 1941's *Ohm Kruger*, his fame rests most securely on *The Blue Angel*, his first sound film, and several silents that led up to it: *The Last Laugh, Variety, Faust*, etc.

JANS, HARRY *(1962)* 62 ——Comic support in several of the mid-1930s: *Don't Tell the Wife, Charlie Chan at the Race Track, That Girl from Paris, Don't Turn 'Em Loose*, etc.

JANSON, VICTOR *(1960)* 75 ——German star; in *1914: The Last Days Before the War*, etc.

JARRETT, ARTHUR *(1960)* 72 ——Handsome sport in those jalopy love scenes with Crawford in *Dancing Lady;* also in *Riptide, Ace of Aces, Let's Fall in Love*, etc.

JARRETT, DAN *(1938)* 44 ——Support in George O'Brien's *The Cowboy Millionaire;* better known as a screenwriter (*Let's Sing Again, Hollywood Cowboy*, etc.); brother of Arthur.

JARVIS, AL *(1970)* 60 ——TV-radio disc jockey; onscreen in *The Phantom Planet, The Twonky.*

JARVIS, JEAN *(1933)* 30 ——Beautiful supporting actress in Glenn Hunter's *The Little Giant*, other pix of the '20s.

JARVIS, ROBERT *(1971)* 79 ——Minor support at Warners in the '30s; in *Torchy Gets Her Man, Gold Diggers of 1933*, others.

JARVIS, SYDNEY *(1939)* 58 ——Support in De Wolf Hopper's *Casey at the Bat*, Karl Dane's *Circus Rookies*, Roland Young's *The Unholy Night*, others of the '20s, and in the '30s: *The Count of Monte Cristo, Movie Crazy*, etc.

JAVOR, PAUL *(1959)* 57 ——Hungarian actor; in *The Great Caruso* (as Antonio Scotti), after long career in European pix.

JAY, ERNEST *(1957)* 63 ——Character in English pix (*The Franchise Affair, Blanche Fury*, etc.) and such made-in-England American movies as *Edward, My Son* and *The Sword and the Rose*.

JEANS, URSULA *(1973)* 66 ——A most beautiful and talented English star who had just one co-lead in an American film, *Cavalcade*, as the pub-owner's daughter, Fanny Bridges, who becomes a torch singer; in many in England: *Storm in a Teacup, The Life and Death of Colonel Blimp, The Night My Number Came Up*, and *The Battle of the Villa Fiorita*.

JEAYES, ALLAN *(1963)* 78 ——Dignified character in many of England's best: *Four Feathers, Elephant Boy, Rembrandt, The Thief of Bagdad, Sanders of the River, The Scarlet Pimpernel*, more.

JEFFERIES, DOUGLAS *(1959)* 75 ——Character in British pix: *Channel Crossing, Frieda*, etc.

JEFFERS, WILLIAM *(1959)* 61 ——Featured roles in silents.

JEFFERSON, DAISY *(1967)* 78 ——Character in silents.

JEFFERSON, JOSEPH *(1905)* 76 ——First major stage actor to face motion picture cameras; in 1896 he filmed, for Biograph, scenes from his perennial stage hit *Rip Van Winkle*.

JEFFERSON, HILTON *(1968)* 66 ——Black actor; support in Lena Horne's *Stormy Weather*.

JEFFERSON, THOMAS *(1932)* 73 ——With Griffith from early Biograph days, as support in his *Judith of Bethulia* and others, this already-gray actor stepped out to star (two silent versions of *Rip Van Winkle*, '14 and '21) or co-star in many: *Ghosts, A Hoosier Romance, The Beloved Liar, Sis Hopkins*, etc.; onscreen in *Forbidden* the last year of his life.

JEFFREY, MICHAEL *(1960)* 65 ——Support in B's: *Mr. Boggs Steps Out, Dangerous Holiday*, etc.

JEFFREYS, ELLIS *(1943)* 64 ——English actress featured in Korda's *Lilies of the Field*; also in *Eliza Comes to Stay, The Perfect Alibi*, others.

JENKINS, ALLEN *(1974)* 74 ——Droll, funny, long-faced WB stalwart (over 100 there), often a stogie-smoking hood in snap-brim hat, straight out of a Damon Runyon yarn; in *I Am a Fugitive from a Chain Gang, Dead End, The Amazing Dr. Clitterhouse, The Case of the Howling Dog, Marked Woman, 42nd Street, 20 Million Sweethearts*, etc.; in '74 had supporting roles in *The Front Page, Stone*, and TV's *Police Story*.

JENKINS, ELIZABETH *(1965)* 86 ——Support in silents.

JENKS, FRANK *(1962)* 59 ——Wavy-haired, easygoing, humorous character in scores from 1933's *College Humor*; long at Universal, he first attracted critical attention as a funny cabbie (played such many times) in *100 Men and a Girl*; an occasional co-star (with Preston Foster in *Lady in the Morgue*, etc.), he generally headed the supporting cast in *His Girl Friday, Follow the Fleet, The Under-Pup, Christmas in Connecticut, A Little Bit of Heaven*, 100 more; last in 1957's *The Amazing Colossal Man*, just after co-starring in the TV series *Colonel Flack*.

JENKS, SI *(1970)* 93 ——Bewhiskered, funny old codger in scores of Westerns—frequently as sheriff—from '22; in *Girl from God's Country, Kentucky Jubilee, Outcasts of Poker Flat* ('37), *Gallopin' Thru*, etc.; rustic support in non-Westerns: *Topper, Captain January, Pigskin Parade, The President's Mystery*, more.

JENNINGS, AL *(1961)* 95 ——Real-life Old West outlaw; acted in support in silent features (*The Sea Hawk, The Ridin' Rascal*, others), and played himself—whitewashed—in two-reelers of the '20s.

JENNINGS, DE WITT *(1937)* 57 ——The sheriff in William Boyd's *The Squaw Man*; major support in 150, starting in Bert Lytell's *Ladyfingers* in '22; in *Merton of the Movies* (the director who gives hayseed Glenn Hunter his first "big break"), Muni's *The Valiant* (prison warden), *Min and Bill, Arrowsmith, The President Vanishes, Murder on a Honeymoon*, etc.

JEROME, EDWIN *(1959)* 75 ——Dignified character (Major General) in *The House on 92nd Street*; also in Jeanne Crain's *The Tattered Dress* (judge), *The Three Faces of Eve*, etc.

JERROLD, MARY *(1955)* 78 ——Kind-faced British elder; in *The Way Ahead, The Queen of Spades, The Magic Bow, Transatlantic Tunnel,* more.

JESKE, GEORGE *(1951)* 60 ——One of the seven original Keystone Kops; at Sennett for years; support in such later silents as *Heart of the Yukon,* he became a scriptwriter (*The Day the Bookies Wept*).

JESSEL, PATRICIA *(1968)* 47 ——Major English support; Domina in *A Funny Thing Happened on the Way to the Forum,* in *The Man Upstairs, Quo Vadis,* more; created onstage the role Dietrich played in *Witness for the Prosecution.*

JETT, SHELDON *(1960)* 59 ——Minor roles in *Yolanda and the Thief, The Robe,* etc.

JEWELL, ISABEL *(1972)* 62 ——Great blonde actress—curious career; began as a star (often loaned-out) at MGM earning $3,000 a week in Lee Tracy's *Blessed Event;* superlative in two with Colman—*Lost Horizon* and *A Tale of Two Cities* (the girl he comforted on the guillotine scaffold); co-starred in an occasional romantic comedy such as *He Wanted to Marry* with Wallace Ford; quickly degenerated into tough-blonde (often trollop) roles: *Marked Woman, High Sierra, Gone With the Wind* (Scarlett threw the red dirt of Tara into the face of her white-trash Emmy Slattery), 100 others; long offscreen, she last had principal roles in two unreleased B's of the '70s: *Ciao, Manhattan* and Tab Hunter's *A Kiss from Eddie.*

JIMINEZ, SOLEDAD *(1966)* 92 ——Plump Spanish actress who played cooks (*In Old Arizona*) and mamas—Italian (Robinson's in *Kid Galahad*) and Mexican (Muni's in *Bordertown*); in 50: *The Arizona Kid, The Robin Hood of El Dorado, Black Bart,* etc., through 1950's *Red Light* with George Raft, as supporting player Philip Pine's mamecita.

JINGU, MIYOSHI *(1969)* 75 ——Japanese support.

JOBY, HANS *(1943)* 59 ——Von Schlieben in *Hell's Angels;* character in several of the '30s: *I Met Him in Paris* (Lower Tower Man), *Beasts of Berlin, Suicide Fleet,* etc.

JOHN, ALICE *(1956)* 75 ——Character actress who was in England's *These Thirty Years.*

JOHNSON, ARTHUR *(1916)* 40 ——Fine young stage actor with an extraordinarily handsome, disenchanted face, who, discovered by D. W.

Griffith, had a short, distinguished screen career; starred in the director's first, 1908's *The Adventures of Dolly;* according to film historian Edward Wagenknecht, "as late as 1926, Griffith was still remembering him as the finest of all screen actors"; starred often with Florence Lawrence (*The Song of the Shirt, Resurrection, Her Two Sons,* etc.) and Lottie Briscoe (*The Beloved Adventurer,* etc.); also starred in *The Sealed Room, In Old California,* others; death attributed to tuberculosis and alcoholism.

JOHNSON, BILL *(1957)* 41 ——Romantic lead in Lana Turner's *Keep Your Powder Dry* and Sonja Henie's *It's a Pleasure.*

JOHNSON, CHIC *(1962)* 66 ——Roly-poly half of the famous Olsen & Johnson comedy team; most famous for their four 1941–45 Universal comedies: *Hellzapoppin, Crazy House, Ghost Catchers, See My Lawyer;* had two earlier screen careers, at Warners (1930–31) in *Oh Sailor Behave!, Fifty Million Frenchmen, Gold Dust Gertie,* at Republic ('37) in *Country Gentlemen* and *All Over Town.*

JOHNSON, CHUBBY *(1974)* 71 ——Plump, kindly sidekick in the Republic Westerns of Allan "Rocky" Lane (*Fort Dodge Stampede,* etc.); also in A Westerns: *Rocky Mountain, Bend of the River, Calamity Jane, Tribute to a Bad Man,* many more.

JOHNSON, EDWARD *(1925)* 63 ——Minor support in silents: *The Hunchback of Notre Dame, The Egg Crate Wallop,* etc.

JOHNSON, EMORY *(1960)* 66 ——Tall, wavy-haired Goldwyn star in silents; opposite Betty Compson in *Prisoners of Love,* Ruth Clifford in *A Kentucky Cinderella;* also in *In the Name of the Law* (which he directed), *Always the Woman;* directed many silents and, last, wrote-directed 1932's *The Phantom Express.*

JOHNSON, HALL *(1970)* 82 ——Led his famous all-black Hall Johnson Choir in *The Green Pastures, Swanee River, Hearts Divided.*

JOHNSON, JAY *(1954)* 26 ——Stan Kenton band singer; in Garland's *A Star Is Born.*

JOHNSON, KATIE *(1957)* 79 ——Cheerful old lady who triumphed over Alec Guinness in *The Ladykillers;* in other British pix: *Meet Me at Dawn, How to Murder a Rich Uncle, Jeannie,* etc.

JOHNSON, KENNETH, II *(1974)* 62 ——Moppet in silents including early "Our Gang" pix

JOHNSON, LORIMER GEORGE *(1941)* 81 — —Character actor in such silent features as *Dante's Inferno, A Fool's Enticement,* Mary Astor's *Enticement;* support in serials of the '20s: *Tarzan, the Mighty; Ruth of the Range.*

JOHNSON, RITA *(1965)* 52 ——Blonde MGM discovery whose glinty eyes, brittle style, and overly precise speech restricted her to "other woman," usually bitchy, roles; in *Stronger Than Desire, Here Comes Mr. Jordan, The Major and the Minor, They Won't Believe Me, The Big Clock,* etc.; rare exceptions: Tracy's wife in *Edison, the Man,* Roddy McDowall's mother in *My Friend Flicka* and *Thunderhead.*

JOHNSON, TOR *(1971)* 50s ——Supporting actor in comedies: *The Man on the Flying Trapeze, Abbott and Costello in the Foreign Legion, The Lemon Drop Kid* (as a wrestler), etc.

JOHNSTON, EDITH *(1969)* 70s ——Lovely brunette who costarred with William Duncan in the 1918–20 silent serials *A Fight for Millions, Man of Might, Smashing Barriers,* and *The Silent Avenger,* before becoming his wife; till the middle of the '20s there was no more popular serial team; together in *Fighting Fate, The Steel Trail, Wolves of the North, The Fast Express,* plus features *(Where Men Are Men, The Silent Vow,* etc.); both retired in '25 and they remained married until his death in '61.

JOHNSTON, J. W. *(1946)* 70 ——Virile silent star, from Ireland; started at Reliance in '12; was hero Dustin Farnum's best pal, Steve (hanged as a cattle thief), in 1914's *The Virginian;* in *Where the Trail Divides, Runaway June,* a '15 serial in which he costarred with "Our Mutual Girl" Norma Phillips, *The Valley of Silent Men,* etc.; support in the '20s through Bebe Daniels' *Take Me Home* ('28).

JOHNSTON, OLIVER *(1966)* 78 ——British character; top support in Chaplin's *Countess of Hong Kong* and *A King in New York;* also in *Indiscreet, Waltz of the Toreadors, Cleopatra,* others.

JOHNSTONE, BERYL *(1969)* 54 ——British support.

JOLSON, AL *(1950)* 64 ——Great stage-screen song ("Mammy") star; blackface (he first used it in 1906) was his trademark; used it in key scenes when he starred in WB's historic talkie *The Jazz Singer,* and at some point in almost all subsequent pix: *The Singing Fool; Say It With Songs; Mammy; Big Boy; Hallelujah, I'm a Bum; Sonny Boy,* etc.; in a career decline, he supported Alice Faye in *Rose of Washington Square* and *Hollywood Cavalcade* (as himself),

Don Ameche in *Swanee River,* and Robert Alda in *Rhapsody in Blue* (as himself); came back strong—records, radio, TV, but not in movies —when Larry Parks portrayed him (Jolson supplying the vocals) in *The Jolson Story,* which won Parks a Best Actor nomination, and *Jolson Sings Again.*

JONES, BUCK *(1942)* 53 ——One cowboy who had it all—good looks, great physique, superior riding skill (Oklahoma ranch background), fighting fists, legions of fans (was #1 Western Money-Maker in '36, the poll's first year, and in the Top Ten 1937–39), and a horse named Silver; in Westerns from '17, he first starred in 1920's *The Last Straw,* for Fox, where he made another 57 in the next seven years, surpassing Tom Mix and William S. Hart as King of the Cowboys; some of those for Fox were boxing pix *(The Big Punch,* designed to exploit his build) and car-race yarns *(Skid Proof),* for which he was given a more "dignified" screen name—Charles Jones (real name: Charles Frederick Gebhard, but he later had Buck Jones made his legal name); leaving Fox, he made Buck Jones Westerns exclusively, over 100 more at Columbia and Monogram, his popularity remaining strong through the final six made the year he died—in a nightclub fire in Boston.

JONES, ELIZABETH *(1952)* 60s ——See Tiny Jones.

JONES, EMRYS *(1972)* 56 ——Slender-faced, wavy-haired English support; as a youth, in his debut, he was bomber crew member Bob Ashley in *One of Our Aircraft Is Missing;* then in *The Wicked Lady, Nicholas Nickleby, Miss Pilgrim's Progress, The Trials of Oscar Wilde.*

JONES, GORDON *(1963)* 52 ——Was the muscular football player "Rambling Wreck," always seen in his shorts, in Rosalind Russell's *My Sister Eileen;* support in many: *Flying Tigers* (humorous pilot Alabama), *They All Kissed the Bride, Out West with the Hardys, The Doctor Takes a Wife,* etc.; last in 1963's *McLintock!*

JONES, HAZEL *(1974)* 79 ——British support; in 1933's *Strictly Personal.*

JONES, JOAN GRANVILLE *(1974)* ——TV actress also in minor movie roles.

JONES, JOHNNY *(1962)* 54 ——Under this name he was a teen star of silents: *Edgar and the Teacher's Pet, Edgar's Little Saw,* etc.; for those made as an adult under his real name, see the Edward Peil Jr. listing.

JONES, MORGAN *(1951)* 72 ——One of the bandit gang in *The Great Trail Robbery;* in later silents including a 1928 serial, *Mark of the Frog.*

JONES, SPIKE *(1965)* 53 ——Leader of the zany "City Slickers" band; with it in several: *Variety Girl, Bring on the Girls, Meet the People, Breakfast in Hollywood,* others.

JONES, STAN *(1963)* 49 ——Was General U. S. Grant in Ford's *The Horse Soldiers;* support in Westerns: *Invitation to a Gunfighter, Rio Grande* (for which he also wrote the screenplay), *The Great Locomotive Chase,* more; famous also as a songwriter ("Ghost Riders in the Sky," many others).

JONES, T. C. *(1971)* 50 ——Well-known female impersonator; onscreen in *The President's Analyst; Head; Promises, Promises; The Name of the Game Is Kill; Three Nuts in Search of a Bolt,* etc.

JONES, TINY *(1952)* 85 ——Diminutive character actress; in *Greed* ('23), as Mrs. Heise, in the wedding scene; support in many, including John Barrymore's *The Man from Blankley's* (humorous character labeled "Miss Bugle"), *Drums Along the Mohawk* (as Eddie Quillan's mother and billed, as she rarely was, Elizabeth "Tiny" Jones).

JONES, WALLACE *(1936)* 53 ——British support; in *Red Love.*

JOPLIN, JANIS *(1970)* 27 ——Major rock star ("Me and Bobby McGee," etc.); onscreen posthumously in the documentary of her life and career, *Janis.*

JORDAN, BOBBY *(1965)* 42 ——In the Dead End Kids, he was Angel, the youngest; with the group in *Dead End, Angels With Dirty Faces, Angels Wash Their Faces, Crime School,* others of the '30s; on his own, starred in *Military Academy* and was featured in *Young Tom Edison,* more in the early '40s; in '46–47, as a character named Bobby, was reunited with Leo Gorcy, Huntz Hall, and sometimes Gabriel Dell in the first eight of "The Bowery Boys" pix: *In Fast Company* through *News Hounds;* in the '50s, one supporting role, his last, in Dane Clark's *The Man Is Armed.*

JORDAN, MARIAN *(1961)* 62 ——Fondly recalled Molly ("T'aint funny, McGee") of radio and movie comedy team Fibber McGee and Molly, in which she shared billing with husband Jim Jordan; made their screen debut in a Betty Grable-Buddy Rogers pic, *This Way, Please* ('38), starred for RKO in three comedies in the '40s: *Look Who's Laughing, Here We Go Again,* and *Heavenly Days,* the titles all being based on catch-phrases from their radio show.

JORGE, PAUL *(1939)* 79 ——French support;

in France's 1925 version of *Les Miserables,* still hailed by critics as the best made.

JOUVET, LOUIS *(1951)* 63 ——Of the "ugly, humorous and tragic face," he was one of France's greatest actors, perhaps *the* greatest; few would argue with critic Otis Ferguson's estimation that "he is among the blessed of histrionic types—an arresting awkward figure, infinitely capable of shaping all odd motions into a grotesque central dignity that becomes beautiful as it mounts"; his art was at its zenith in *Carnival in Flanders, The Lower Depths, Carnet de Bal, Volpone, Topaze,* so many more.

JOY, NICHOLAS *(1964)* 80 ——Big, gray-haired Broadway character actor who first took his bushy gray moustache and incisive acting style to Hollywood for *Daisy Kenyon,* and remained for 20 more; in *Gentleman's Agreement* (Dr. Craigie), *Joan of Arc* (Archbishop of Thiems), *The Iron Curtain* (Dr. Norman), *And Baby Makes Three* (Robert Hutton's father), *Here Comes the Groom* (Uncle Prentiss), etc.

JOYCE, ALICE *(1955)* 65 ——Serenely beautiful actress who was (1909–15) Kalem's most beloved star; in *The Cabaret Dancer, The Shadow, A Celebrated Case,* many more; in '13 was voted the most popular actress in America and remained so until '17, when she was #2 to Mary Pickford; with Vitagraph from '16, she starred in *Within the Law, A Woman Between Friends, Cap'n Abe's Niece, The Third Degree, The Sporting Dutchess, Cousin Kate;* for Goldwyn she costarred with George Arliss in 1923's *The Green Goddess* (seven years later she supported him in his talkie remake), then eased gracefully into supporting roles, as Colman's wife in *Stella Dallas;* elsewhere, played mothers (flapper Clara Bow's in *Dancing Mothers,* etc.), aristocratic aunts (Colman's, alas, one year after playing his wife); in '30, still beautiful in maturity, in her last year onscreen, she was top support in Irish singer John McCormack's *Song O' My Heart* and in two other films.

JOYCE, PEGGY HOPKINS *(1957)* 63 —— When this blonde, diamond-studded divorcee from Manhattan's cafe society arrived in Hollywood to star in *Skyrocket* ('26), they called her "A Circe of the Cinema"; failing to live up to that, she was seen in just one more, seven years later, supporting W. C. Fields in *International House.*

JUDGE, ARLINE *(1974)* 61 ——Dark-haired second-rank star of innate gaiety, a husky "little girl" voice, and a pertness that made her seem as though she had stepped off the cover of *College Humor*—and whose marriages and divorces (seven) eventually overshadowed all that she had done on the screen; at her breezy best in *Pigskin Parade, King of Burlesque, College Scandal, Shoot the Works,* other '30s comedies; good in others a bit heavier: *The Age of Consent* and *Are These Our Children?,* in both of which she was a junior-league vamp, and *Valiant Is the Word for Carrie;* offscreen from '37, she made unsuccessful comeback attempts in three in the '40s (Dietrich's *The Lady Is Willing,* Fontaine's *From This Day Forward,* Harold Lloyd's *Mad Wednesday)* and in a role in *Perry Mason* on TV in the '60s.

JULIAN, RUPERT *(1943)* 54 ——Handsome dark-haired actor who costarred (as Antonio) with Lois Weber in 1914's *The Merchant of Venice,* with Pavlova in the next year's *The Dumb Girl of Portici,* Ella Hall in *The Bugler of Algiers* ('16); character roles after '17 in Ruth Clifford's *A Kentucky Cinderella, The Kaiser, the Beast of Berlin,* etc.; in '22, replaced Erich von Stroheim as director of *Merry-Go-Round,* then directed several other excellent movies *(The Phantom of the Opera,* both the '24 and the '30 versions, *Three Faces West, The Cat Creeps,* etc.).

JUNE, MILDRED *(1940)* 34 ——Beauty who costarred with Billy Bevan in the Sennett feature comedy *Ma and Pa;* in others of the '20s: *Rich Man's Wives,* Lewis Stone's *The Rosary,* Hoot Gibson's *Hook and Ladder, The Crossroads of New York,* etc.

JUSTIN, MORGAN *(1974)* 47 ——Famous baseball player who subsequently had supporting roles in movies: *The Court Jester, Dirty Dingus Magee,* etc.

K

KACHALOV, VASSILLI IVANOVICH *(1948)* 73 ——He played a lead in Russia's *The Lower Depths* ('47).

KAHANAMOKU, DUKE *(1968)* 77 ——Hawaiian Olympic swimming champion; onscreen in supporting roles, almost always as the Native Chief *(Mister Roberts);* in other talkies *(Wake of the Red Witch, Girl of the Port,* etc.) and silents *(Old Ironsides, Lord Jim,* others).

KAHN, FLORENCE *(1951)* 72 ——Supporting actress in Hitchcock's *Secret Agent.*

KAHN, RICHARD *(1960)* 62 ——Support in silents; directed 1935's *A Dangerous Man.*

KAHN, WILLIAM *(1959)* 77 ——Character in two Hugo Haas B's of the '50s: *Edge of Hell, Girl on the Bridge.*

KALICH, BERTHA *(1939)* 64 ——Black-haired opera and stage actress from Poland who starred first for Famous Players in 1914's *Marta of the Lowlands,* then, two years later, in three for Fox: *Slander, Ambition,* and, with Stuart Holmes, *Love and Hate.*

KALIONZES, JANET *(1961)* 39 ——Support in Colman's *A Double Life.*

KALIZ, ARMAND, *(1941)* 48 ——French support in Hollywood; good roles in many silents including Garbo's *The Temptress,* Reginald Denny's *Fast and Furious,* Betty Compson's *Temptations of a Shop Girl;* more minor roles in talkies: *Skylark* (the jeweler), *Flying Down to Rio* (one of the three Greeks), *Algiers,* more.

KALKHURST, ERIC *(1957)* 55 ——Handsome young support in Paul Lukas' *Unfaithful,* Kay Francis' *The Virtuous Sin,* others of the early '30s.

KALSER, ERWIN *(1958)* 65 ——Distinguished character from Germany; in *Stalag 17* (Geneva Man), *Watch on the Rhine* (Dr. Klauber), *Kings Row* (Mr. Sandor, father of Robert Cummings' new love, Kaaren Verne, in the final scenes), *Berlin Correspondent* (Virginia Gilmore's father), *Hotel Berlin* (Dr. Dorf), more.

KANE, EDDIE *(1969)* 81 ——When in his 40s and 50s was comic support in dozens: *The Broadway Melody* (as Dillon), *Swiss Miss, The Mummy, Once in a Lifetime, Give Me a Sailor, Up in Arms, Mexican Hayride,* etc.

KANE, GAIL *(1966)* 81 ——Lovely brunette from the stage who, from '13, starred in many: *Arizona, The Great Diamond Robbery, The Jungle* (based on Upton Sinclair's novel), *Via Wireless, The Labyrinth;* became especially popular in movies about World War I: *Soul in Pawn* (became a spy against the Germans to avenge the death of her soldier-husband), *On Dangerous Ground* (was a French girl who, tortured by Germans, helped an American soldier to escape from occupied France); last in support in Lillian Gish's *The White Sister* and Lowell Sherman's *Convoy.*

KANE, HELEN *(1966)* 62 ——Famous "Boop-oop-a-doop" singer; starred in *Sweetie, Nothing But the Truth, Pointed Heels, Dangerous Nan McGrew, Heads Up* (all 1929–30); impersonated by Debbie Reynolds later in *Three Little Words* (Kane supplying her own musical voice).

KANE, JOHN *(1969)* 60s ——Support in *Act One, Fail-Safe, The Man with My Face.*

KANE, LIDA *(1955)* 50s ——Young support in two early talkies: Colbert's *Secrets of a Secretary* and Ed Wynn's *Follow the Leader.*

KANE, WHITFORD *(1956)* 75 ——Dignified character in several in the '40s: *The Walls of Jericho* (Judge), *The Ghost and Mrs. Muir* (Gene Tierney's Lawyer Sproule), *The Adventures of Mark Twain,* etc.

KANNON, JACKIE *(1974)* 54 ——Comedian.

KARLIN, BO-PEEP *(1969)* 60s ——Comedienne; mother of starlet Trudi Ames in *Bye Bye Birdie;* in movies from early talkies: *Happy Days* and the futuristic *Just Imagine.*

KARLOFF, BORIS *(1969)* 81 ——*Frankenstein*'s immortal monster; he played the role just three times—in *Frankenstein* ('31), *The Bride of Frankenstein,* ('35), *Son of Frankenstein* ('39)—but it severely limited the career of a splendid actor; some of his other monsters were those in: *The Mummy, The Ghoul, The Walking Dead, Abbott and Costello Meet Dr. Jekyll and Mr. Hyde,* etc.; from England (and then Canada), he entered movies in '19 via the friendship of monster-master Lon Chaney; had supporting roles in 49 silents, 18 talkie features, and two talkie serials before becoming a full-fledged star in *Frankenstein;* in the 100 that followed he occasionally had the chance to prove his versatility: *The House of Rothschild* (bigoted, scheming Baron Ledratz), *The Lost Patrol* (pathetic soldier Sanders), *The Mask of Fu Manchu* (ruthless Chinese), the "Mr. Wong" series (Chinese detective), *Devil's Island* (pathetically wronged political revolutionary), *You'll Find Out* and *The Secret Life of Walter Mitty* (comic villainy), *Unconquered* (savage Indian Chief Guyasuta), *Targets* (aging horror-movie star who captures a teenage sniper); remained appreciative of the success horror films brought him, saying near the end, "I just had the luck to stumble into that field."

KARLSTADT, LIESL *(1960)* 67 ——Character actress in German-made films: *Aren't We Wonderful,* etc.

KARNS, ROSCOE *(1970)* 77 ——Gently funny guy who was the perfect "newspaper reporter-type"—and often a bit tippled—in at least 30 of his 100 pix; from 1920's *The Life of the Party* he was near the top of the cast in: *Twentieth Century, Front Page Woman, His Girl Friday, Scandal Sheet, If I Had a Million, They Drive by Night, Thanks for the Memory, Woman of the Year,* etc.; co-starred in TV's *Hennessy.*

KARLWEIS, OSCAR *(1956)* 61 ——Balding, splendid German actor who scored resoundingly in *Five Fingers,* his first American film, as Mayzisch; then in *Anything Can Happen, The Juggler, Meet Me in Las Vegas,* others.

KATCH, KURT *(1958)* 62 ——How Maria Montez suffered at the hands of this bald, big-nosed Lithuanian in *Ali Baba and the Forty Thieves!;* so did almost every star who crossed his sinister path in *The Purple Heart, Watch on the Rhine, The Mask of Dimitrios, The Seventh Cross, Berlin Correspondent,* and 40 more.

KAUFMAN, RITA *(1968)* 60 ——Actress once married to Edmund Lowe.

KAUFMAN, WILLY *(1967)* ——German actor who played Gruetzwald in *Confessions of a Nazi Spy;* was also in *Beasts of Berlin, The Man I Married, Nurse Edith Cavell, Mystery Sea Raider,* etc.

KAYE, PHIL *(1959)* 47 ——Minor support in two John Huston pix: *The Asphalt Jungle* and *Red Badge of Courage.*

KAYE, SPARKY *(1971)* 65 ——Featured as the Sands Hotel manager in Sinatra's *Ocean's 11.*

KEAN, RICHARD *(1959)* 67 ——Minor support in *The Story of Will Rogers, The Court Jester,* and a Tim Holt Western, *Storm over Wyoming.*

KEANE, DORIS *(1945)* 60 ——Attractive brunette who starred in '20 in the film version of her great Broadway success *Romance;* in '17 she had been one of 30 stage luminaries in the all-star English-made *Masks and Faces.*

KEANE, ROBERT EMMETT ——Character who played stuffy execs, actors, managers, theatrical impresarios, and salesmen in many; in *When My Baby Smiles at Me* (was producer Sam Harris), *Tin Pan Alley, Boys Town, Fifth Avenue Girl, He Hired the Boss, Jolson Sings Again, The Devil and Miss Jones,* etc.; last in 1954's *The Atomic Kid;* born 1883, year of death unreported.

KEARNS, ALLEN *(1956)* 60 ——Had the comic-romantic lead opposite Doris Eaton in 1929's *The Very Idea;* top support in Ann Pennington's *Tanned Legs* and Richard Dix's *Lovin' the Ladies.*

KEARNS, JOSEPH *(1962)* 55 ——Best known as the long-suffering neighbor Mr. Wilson on TV's *Dennis the Menace,* he was in numerous movies in the '50s: *Anatomy of a Murder, Our Miss Brooks, Daddy Long Legs,* etc.

KEATING, FRED *(1961)* 64 ——Supporting actor and magician; in *Eternally Yours* (master of ceremonies for Niven's magic act), *Tin Pan Alley*, *The Nitwit*, *Dr. Rhythm*, *Melody for Two*, more.

KEATING, LARRY *(1963)* 67 ——Had the "look of respectability" required to be a screen doctor, lawyer, tycoon or high-rank military man; in 50 including *When Worlds Collide*, *Whirlpool*, *Monkey Business*, *A Lion Is in the Streets*, *Daddy Long Legs* (the American ambassador to France who is suspicious of Astaire's motives in sponsoring Leslie Caron's education in the U.S.A.), etc.; on TV's *Mister Ed* was Alan Young's explosive neighbor, and was also on *The George Burns and Gracie Allen Show*, as Harry Morton.

KEATON, BUSTER *(1966)* 70 ——Future generations may rate this poker-faced comedian above Chaplin, as some already do; his body of work is formidable: *The General*, *Steamboat Bill Jr.*, *Sherlock Junior*, *The Navigator*, *Seven Chances*, *Go West*, *Battling Butler*, *College*, *Our Hospitality*, not to mention his dozens of two-reelers, the numerous silent features (from '17) leading up to his major films, or the 75 talkies in which he was so often hilarious top support to others (*Hollywood Cavalcade*, *Limelight*, with Chaplin, *In the Good Old Summertime*, *Bathing Beauty*, etc); Donald O'Connor, portraying him in 1957's *The Buster Keaton Story*, tried but failed to capture his antic genius; once, and only once, did he smile on camera—and audiences were not appreciative; they preferred him as he always had been—ever turning a granite face to objects, people, and events that, hilariously, picked on him.

KEATON, HARRY *(1966)* 69 ——Comedian who was Buster's younger brother; in numerous two-reel comedies including 1937's *Love Nest on Wheels* with Buster (and their sister Louise).

KEATON, JOE *(1946)* 68 ——Character comedian-father of Buster, Harry, and Louise; uproarious support in many of Buster's pix: *Sherlock Jr.* (the girl's father), *The General* (Union General), *Our Hospitality* (engineer), *Steamboat Bill Jr.* (barber), the two-reel *Neighbors* (Buster's father).

KEATON, MYRA *(1955)* 70s ——She, son Buster and husband Joe were together in several silent two-reelers (*The Electric House*, *Convict 13*, etc.) and the talkie short *Palooka from Paducah*, which also included her daughter Myra—both women appearing as comic hillbillies; mother and daughter then repeated the characterizations in a Joan Davis two-reeler, *Way Up Thar*.

KEEN, MALCOLM *(1970)* 82 ——Illustrious British stage actor who was onscreen in no more than ten in 35 years; starred first in 1929's *The Manxman*, Hitchcock's last silent; other major roles, widely spaced, in *Sixty Glorious Years*, *The Great Mr. Handel*, Gene Tierney's *The Mating Season* (his only Hollywood film; as Cora Witherspoon's husband), *Francis of Assisi*, *Walk in the Shadow*.

KEENAN, FRANCES *(1950)* 63 ——Actress-daughter of Frank.

KEENAN, FRANK *(1929)* 70 ——Noted stage actor recruited by Ince as a character star in 1915; played fathers generally; in *The Coward* with Charles Ray, *The Bells* with Lois Wilson, *Hearts Aflame* with Anna Q. Nilsson, and with Alma Rubens, *East Lynne* and *The Gilded Butterfly* (both '26), which were his last.

KEENE, DAY *(1969)* 65 ——Actor and screenwriter (wrote original story of *Joy House*).

KEENE, RICHARD *(1971)* 60s ——Popular wavy-haired light lead at Fox in 1929–30 in such abandoned youth pix as Frank Albertson's *Wild Company*; also in *Happy Days*, *Why Leave Home*, *Her Golden Calf*.

KEENE, TOM *(1963)* 63 ——Rugged, handsome star of dozens of Westerns throughout the '30s and into the '40s, who—college-educated and Broadway trained—played his cowboy hero as a thinking man who fought only as a last resort; some of his best: *Dude Wrangler*, *Sunset Pass*, *In Old California*; already a well-established Western favorite, he starred in '34 in King Vidor's Great Depression classic, *Our Daily Bread*, his best screen opportunity ("His performance is an expression of the undying optimism of youth," said the *Times*); had separate acting careers under two other names; entered pix as George Duryea (real name), starring in DeMille's *The Godless Girl*; used this name for *Honky Tonk* (also '29), *Thunder*, *Tol'able David*; in '44, after being cowboy star Tom Keene for 13 years at five different studios, he ditched the name and became Richard Powers; as this, he had supporting roles in many (from 1944's *Up In Arms* through 1959's *Plan 9 For Outer Space*) and starred in the '50 serial *Desperadoes of the West*.

KEITH, IAN *(1960)* 61 ——Lean, with a strong handsome face, he was a greatly popular leading man in the '20s: in *Christine of the Hungry Heart*, *Manhandled* with Swanson, *My Son* with Nazimova; career as major supporting actor began in '30 when he played John Wilkes Booth in Walter Huston's *Abraham Lincoln*; in many other talkies: *The Big Trail*, *The Sign of the Cross* (as Tigellinus), *The Crusades* (infidel ruler Saladin who allows the Christians to enter

666

Jerusalem), DeMille's *Cleopatra* (Octavius), *Mary of Scotland, The Spanish Main, Prince of Players, Nightmare Alley,* (Blondell's rummy husband), and last, 1956's *The Ten Commandments* (Rameses I).

KEITH, ROBERT *(1966)* 68 ——Bald Broadway actor, in a few in the '20s and '30s, who became one of Hollywood's busiest character actors after *Boomerang* ('47); in another 30, often as the star's father: *My Foolish Heart* (Susan Hayward's), *Small Town Girl* (Debbie Reynolds'), *Young at Heart* (Doris Day's), *Fourteen Hours* (dad of would-be suicide Basehart); other types of roles in *Guys and Dolls* (Lt. Brannigan), *They Came to Cordura* (U.S. Cavalry Col. Rogers), etc.

KELCEY, HERBERT *(1917)* 61 ——The star of 1914's *After the Ball*.

KELLARD, RALPH *(1955)* 70 ——In 1920's *The Restless Sex* he co-starred with Davies as the husband who committed suicide so that she might marry her foster brother, Carlyle Blackwell.

KELLAWAY, CECIL *(1973)* 82 ——It was not for nothing that he was cast as a leprechaun in *The Luck of the Irish*, which rated him his first Best Supporting Actor Oscar nomination; from Australia (where, in the '30s, he was a bigger box-office draw than Gable), he was a genial, witty, gray-haired pixie in dozens in Hollywood; first in *Wuthering Heights*, then *I Married a Witch, Mrs. Parkington, Love Letters, Kitty* (as Gainsborough), *Portrait of Jennie, Harvey*, etc., and last, 1967's *Guess Who's Coming to Dinner,* as Tracy's charming priest-friend, which won him his only other Supporting Actor Oscar nomination.

KELLER, HELEN *(1968)* 87 ——Inspiration to the world's blind and deaf, she played the lead in 1919's *Deliverance*, the story of her life and triumph over her handicaps.

KELLER, NELL CLARK *(1965)* 89 ——Character actress in pix of the '20s: *Lightnin', The Virgin*, 1922 version of *Ten Nights in a Barroom*, etc.

KELLOGG, CORNELIA *(1934)* 57 ——Character in Alice White's *Lingerie* ('28), others.

KELLY, AL *(1966)* 67 ——Double-talk comedian; minor support for 50 years.

KELLY, DOROTHY *(1966)* 72 ——Dark-haired early ('12) Vitagraph star; in *The Troublesome Daughters* and many others.

KELLY, DOROTHY HELEN *(1969)* 51 ——Minor ingenue in the '40s.

KELLY, MRS. FANNIE *(1925)* 48 ——Comedienne in Sennett two-reelers.

KELLY, GREGORY *(1927)* 35 ——Louise Brooks' dashing leading man in *The Show-Off*; with Richard Dix in *Manhattan.*

KELLY, KITTY *(1968)* 66 ——Perky little dark-eyed blonde, from the Ziegfeld Follies, first on-screen in Adolphe Menjou's *A Kiss in the Dark* ('25); delightful in many comedy roles in the '30s: Wheeler & Woolsey's *Girl Crazy* (ingenue lead opposite Eddie Quillan), *Ladies of the Jury, Too Much Harmony,* etc.; minor support as she grew older, in *So Proudly We Hail* (one of the Army lieutenant nurses), *The Lady Is Willing, The Mad Doctor*, etc.

KELLY, LEW *(1944)* 65 ——Comedian from burlesque who had supporting roles in many comedies in the '30s: Laurel & Hardy's *Pack Up Your Troubles,* Wheeler & Woolsey's *The Nitwits,* Fields' *The Old-Fashioned Way, Six of a Kind, The Man on the Flying Trapeze,* etc.

KELLY, MARY *(1941)* 46 ——Support in Jack Benny's *Love Thy Neighbor* and Blondell's *Model Wife.*

KELLY, MAURICE *(1974)* 59 ——Angela Lansbury's handsome dance partner in *Till the Clouds Roll By*; later support in Jerry Lewis pix.

KELLY, PAUL *(1956)* 57——Lean, tough redheaded star whose career was interrupted for two years in the late '20s, as he served a San Quentin prison term for the murder of the husband of actress Dorothy Mackaye, whom he later married; came back to star, two-fistedly, in scores of B's in the '30s and '40s: *Silk Hat Kid, Murder With Pictures, Parole Racket, Mystery Ship, Within the Law, Call Out the Marines,* etc.; later, top support in *Thelma Jordan, Springfield Rifle, The High and the Mighty,* and, ironically, *Duffy of San Quentin,* in which he was reform-minded Warden Duffy.

KELLY, WALTER C. *(1939)* 66 ——Character star of 1935's *The Virginia Judge,* which had long been his nickname, as he had played the role onstage for years in most English-speaking countries; also in *Laughing Irish Eyes, McFadden's Flats, Seas Beneath*; uncle of Grace.

KELLY, WILLIAM J. *(1949)* 74 ——Support in silents (*Parisian Nights,* Harrison Ford's *Proud Flesh,* Anna Q. Nilsson's *Her Second Chance*) and talkies (*Woman Accused,* as captain of the cruise ship on which Cary Grant and Nancy Carroll sailed, *Six of a Kind,* etc.).

KELSEY, FRED *(1961)* 77 ——First onscreen in the silent *Four Horsemen of the Apocalypse*, he came to play cops (often humorous)—heavy-faced, gray-haired with a fierce little black moustache—in scores; perhaps best recalled as Officer Dickens in six of Warren William's "Lone Wolf" pix, he also was in *Diamond Jim, The Crime Doctor, She Got What She Wanted, Donovan's Kid, Gentleman Jim*, etc., plus dozens of two-reel comedies.

KELT, JOHN *(1935)* 70 ——Was featured in England's *The Tell-Tale Heart* ('34).

KELTON, PERT *(1968)* 61 ——Delightful little comedienne who, in earlier pix, lived up to her name (in Marilyn Miller's *Sunny, The Bowery, Bed of Roses, Sing and Like It, Kelly the Second*, others); in *Mary Burns, Fugitive*, she was the prison "stoolie" who betrayed Sylvia Sidney after helping her escape; in maturity, a humorous harridan usually (in *The Music Man*, as Mrs. Paroo, mother of little boy Ronny Howard, and Ozzie Nelson's *Love and Kisses*).

KEMBLE-COOPER, VIOLET *(1961)* 62 —— British character actress in Hollywood pix; in *Romeo and Juliet* was Shearer's mother, Lady Capulet; in *The Fountain*, Ann Harding's stern Dutch mother; in *The Invisible Ray* was almost murdered by mad-doctor-son Karloff ("Radium-X"-exposed, before destroying the antidote he needed to live, sending him up in a ball of fire); forbidding as Miss Jane Murdstone in *David Copperfield* and as the Duchess in Constance Bennett's *Our Betters*.

KEMP, EVERETT *(1958)* 84 ——Supported Mr. and Mrs. Sidney Drew in early silent comedies.

KEMP, HAL *(1940)* 36 ——Famous band leader; in *Radio City Revels*.

KEMP, PAUL *(1953)* 54 ——Lead in German pix: *Our Little Wife, The Song of Happiness*, others; support in the Sammy Davis-Hildegard Knef *The Threepenny Opera*, made in Germany in '60.

KEMPER, CHARLES *(1950)* 49 ——Character actor who, in *Intruder in the Dust*, was described by critic Bosley Crowther as "porcine and brutal as the stubborn leader of the mob"; support in many from 1929's *Beach Babies: The Southerner, Yellow Sky* (as Walrus), *Scarlet Street* (Patcheye), *Sister Kenny, Wagonmaster* (evil Uncle Shiloh Clegg), etc.

KENDALL, CY *(1953)* 72 ——Stabbing, poisoning or just plain torture—in more than 100 pix it was all in a day's work for this beefy, cold-eyed villain; rarely did the dirty work himself for he was usually The Boss; in *White Bondage, They*

Won't Forget, Crime School, Laura, Johnny Eager, Mystery Ship, etc.; frequently a "baddie" in serials too (*The Green Hornet, Junior G-Men*, as gang leader Brand, *Jungle Queen*), he was, in his last chapter-play, *The Scarlet Horseman*, a good guy—named Amigo.

KENDALL, HENRY *(1962)* 65 ——Suave British character; in many: *French Leave, An Alligator Named Daisy, School for Husbands, The Flying Fool*, etc.

KENDALL, KAY *(1959)* 33 ——Delicious, and beautiful, rail-thin British star-comedienne; at her classy funniest in *Genevieve, Les Girls, Doctor in the House, The Reluctant Debutante, The Constant Husband*; husband Rex Harrison paid an affecting tribute to her in his autobiography *Rex* ('75).

KENNEDY, CHARLES *(1950)* 79 ——Character (Lt. Norton) in *Crime Without Passion*; earlier in the Marion Davies silent *Little Old New York*, as Reilly.

KENNEDY, DOUGLAS *(1973)* 55 ——Famous as TV's curly-haired *Steve Donovan*, he was lean, rugged major support in many films from '41; in *Possessed* (Assistant D.A.), *The Unfaithful, South of St. Louis, Montana, I Was an American Spy, Indian Uprising, Sitting Bull, Cry Vengeance*, etc.

KENNEDY, EDGAR *(1948)* 58 ——Bald master of the "slow burn"; onscreen from '11, he became (in '13) one of the seven original Keystone Kops; in scores of silent two-reelers and features (*Golden Princess, Oh! What a Nurse!*, etc.); starred in 103 shorts at RKO 1931-48; comic support in more than 200 talkie features: *San Francisco, Three Men on a Horse, Heaven Only Knows, Anchors Aweigh, Sandy Is a Lady, Crazy House*, etc.; last in *My Dream Is Yours*, released posthumously.

KENNEDY, FRED *(1958)* 48 ——Western support; in *She Wore a Yellow Ribbon* (as Badger), *Rio Grande* (Heinze), *The Charge at Feather River*, etc.

KENNEDY, JOHN F. *(1960)* 70s ——Support in Keystone Kop comedies.

KENNEDY, JOYCE *(1943)* 44 ——British; featured in Ralph Richardson's *The Return of Bulldog Drummond*; also in *Doomed Cargo, Black Mask*, etc.

KENNEDY, KING *(1974)* 70 ——Featured in *Seven Days' Leave*; was once Louella Parsons' son-in-law.

KENNEDY, MERNA *(1944)* 36 ——Chaplin's lovely brunette leading lady, the circus equestrienne, in 1928's *The Circus*; did well the next year in her first talkie, *Broadway*, and in *Skinner Steps Out* with Glenn Tryon; after that it was mostly downhill in *Red-Haired Alibi, Arizona to Broadway, Laughter in Hell*; last in 1934's *I Like It That Way*.

KENNEDY, TOM *(1965)* 80 ——With his Irish face, beefy body, floppy ears and squashed nose (had been an amateur heavyweight fight champ), this character was a natural for dumdum cabbies, bartenders, and, especially, cops; was lovable, birdbrained, poetry-quoting Sergeant Gahagan (in vest and bowler hat) in all nine of the "Torchy Blane" pix—where much of his dialogue was "If it's who I think it is, throw her out"; onscreen from '15, he was in some 175: *She Done Him Wrong, Remember the Night, Married Before Breakfast, The Day the Bookies Wept*, etc.; last in 1963's *It's a Mad, Mad, Mad, Mad World*.

KENNETH, KEITH *(1966)* ——See Keith Hitchcock.

KENNEDY, JACK *(1964)* 76 ——Western support: *Cattle Town, The Tin Star, Gun Fight, Walking Target*; first onscreen in Louise Dresser's *Not Quite Decent* ('29), he also had character roles in *Atlantic City, Vice Raid, Chicago Confidential*.

KENNY, LEOLA *(1956)* 64 ——Support in the early talkie sci-fi comedy *Just Imagine*, others; was sometimes billed Lee Kenny.

KENT, ARNOLD *(1928)* 29 ——Handsome silent leading man from Italy (real name Lido Manetti); in Norma Talmadge's *The Woman Disputed* ('28), her last silent, he was the Russian officer she spurned for Gilbert Roland—but he got her by default as his mistress at the fadeout; the year before, his first onscreen, he had made love to Negri in *The Woman on Trial*, Clara Bow in *Hula*; in '28 he was in Evelyn Brent's *Beau Sabreur*, Richard Dix's *Easy Come, Easy Go*, and George Bancroft's *The Showdown*.

KENT, CHARLES *(1923)* 69 ——White-haired Vitagraph actor who starred as St. Clare in 1910's *Uncle Tom's Cabin* and *Twelfth Night* with Julia Swayne Gordon; was also in *Kennedy Square* and *Daniel*; directed *Vanity Fair* ('11) and *Rip Van Winkle* ('12).

KENT, CRAUFORD *(1952)* 72 ——Good-looking, black-haired actor from England who, from '15, starred in dozens of silents: *Jane Eyre, Silas Marner, Shadows of the Sea, The Song of Songs, The Eagle's Feather*, etc.; major support in scores of talkies: *The Constant Nymph; Vanessa, Her Love Story; Foreign Correspondent; We Are Not Alone; International Squadron*, more.

KENT, ETHEL *(1952)* 68 ——Actress-widow of movie mogul John Ince; onscreen from very early silents; character role in Yvonne De Carlo's *Buccaneer's Girl*.

KENT, GERALD *(1944)* 22 ——Promising British actor who appeared in just one film, *Four Corners*; died in a German POW camp.

KENT, KENNETH *(1963)* 71 ——British character; in *Night Train, Suicide Squad*, etc.

KENT, MARSHA *(1971)* 50 ——Beautiful dancer, minor roles; in *The Prisoner of Zenda, The Great Ziegfeld*, etc.

KENT, ROBERT *(1954)* 40s ——One of the handsomest young romantic leads at 20th Century-Fox in the '30s, he was in two dozen: *Dimples, King of the Royal Mounted, Mr. Moto Takes a Chance, The Country Beyond, The Crime of Dr. Forbes, Charlie Chan at Monte Carlo*; after service in WW II there were few calls for his services; was in such B's as *Joe Palooka, Champ* and *For Heaven's Sake*; last had a minor supporting role in *The Country Girl*.

KENT, WILLIAM *(1945)* 59 ——Character (The King's Tailor) in Marion Davies' *When Knighthood Was in Flower*; support in such talkies as *Saturday's Millions* and Colleen Moore's last film, *The Scarlet Letter* ('34).

KEROUAC, JACK *(1969)* 47 ——Legend-in-his-time hippie novelist (*On the Road*); narrated the underground film *Pull My Daisy*.

KERR, FREDERICK *(1933)* 75 ——The old Baron Frankenstein in *Frankenstein*, this English elder was in another dozen: Colman's *Raffles*, Chatterton's *The Lady of Scandal*, Douglass Montgomery's *Waterloo Bridge*, Warren William's *Beauty and the Boss*, etc.

KERR, JANE *(1954)* 83 ——Character in March's *Les Miserables* (Frances Drake's mother) and in *The Garden of Allah* (the madam, Ouled Nails).

KERRICK, THOMAS *(1927)* 50s ——Support in the silent Jack Hoxie Western *Men in the Raw*.

KERRIGAN, J. M. *(1964)* 76 ——Great character actor, from Dublin's Abbey Theater, on

Hollywood screens from '34; in many of the best: *The Long Voyage Home* (Crimp/Nick), *The Lost Patrol* (doomed British cavalryman Quincannon, to whom the Arabian desert is the "devil's backyard"), *The Plough and the Stars*, *The Great Man Votes*, *Gone With the Wind*, *Union Pacific*, *Lloyds of London*, and dozens more.

KERRIGAN, J. WARREN *(1947)* 58 ——A magazine article title of 1916, "The Great God Kerrigan," gives clear indication of this matinee idol's status in silents, which he maintained from '12 (after entering movies in '09) to '24; for the first three and a half years of his popularity he starred in two pictures a week; was in *For the Flag, The Stranger at Coyote, The Wishing Seat, Samson, The Adventures of Terence O'Rourke, Landon's Legacy, A Man's Man, A White Man's Chance*, etc.; at most studios where he starred—American, Universal, Hodgkinson—he was the company's #1 attraction, and nationwide, in '14, was second only to Francis X. Bushman; his greatest role came in '23—that of hero Will Banion in the first epic Western ever made, *The Covered Wagon*, a classic, and a box-office bonanza; a couple of minor (comparatively) films followed before he climaxed his career in a blaze of glory, in the 1924 swashbuckler, *Captain Blood*, and retired.

KERRIGAN, KATHLEEN *(1957)* 88 ——Sister of J. Warren; support in numerous silents including the early *Samson and Delilah* and Alec B. Francis' *The Music Maker* ('27); in talkies was in Victor McLaglen's *Wicked* ('31).

KERRY, NORMAN *(1956)* 67 ——Best known now as the handsome hero in two of Chaney's best—*The Hunchback of Notre Dame* (Phoebus) and *The Phantom of the Opera* (Raoul de Chagny); onscreen from '16 in *The Black Butterfly* with Olga Petrova; in many silents: Marion Davies' *The Black Star, Soldiers of Fortune, Brothers Under the Skin, Three Live Ghosts, Merry-Go-Round, Cytherea, Butterfly, Annie Laurie* with Lillian Gish, *The Unknown* (again with Chaney), more; after seven early talkies, he retired after playing the second male lead in Irene Dunne's 1931 *Bachelor Apartment;* came back, inexplicably, one decade later for a supporting role in a forgotten William Tracy-Elyse Knox B, *Tanks a Million;* footnote: began his career under his real name, Norman Kaiser—in '18, for obvious reasons, changed it to Kerry.

KERSHAW, WILLETTE *(1960)* 78 ——Brunette actress who was an Artcraft star in 1918.

KEY, KATHLEEN *(1954)* 51 ——Lovely brunette, a '23 Wampas Baby Star, whose best screen break was the role of the sister (Tirzah) in the silent *Ben-Hur;* minor roles in such other A's as *The Sea Hawk;* femme leads in silent Westerns *(The Flaming Frontier, Bells of San Juan,* etc.) and comedies *(Money Talks, A Lover's Oath,* others); last in a '29 silent Northwest epic, *Phantoms of the North;* career ended after a row, never fully explained, in Buster Keaton's dressing room.

KEYS, NELSON *(1939)* 52 ——British support; in *The Triumph of the Scarlet Pimpernel, Madame Pompadour*, etc.

KIBBEE, GUY *(1956)* 70 ——Kind-hearted and foxy, pot-bellied and bald, he was the small-towner (editor, doctor, civic leader) par excellence, and everybody's favorite uncle or grandpop; was "Scattergood Baines" (starred in the 1941–42 RKO series of five); onscreen from Nancy Carroll's *Stolen Heaven* ('31) and in more than 100: *Mr. Smith Goes to Washington, Gold Diggers of 1933, Captain January, Our Town, Babes in Arms, Of Human Hearts*, etc.; last in *Three Godfathers* ('48), as the town judge.

KIDD, KATHLEEN *(1961)* 61 ——One of the belles in the silent *What Price Glory*.

KIDDER, HUGH *(1952)* 72 ——Support in *His Private Secretary*.

KIEPURA, JAN *(1966)* 60 ——Famous singing star from Poland noted for his tenor and temperament; starred handsomely in many musicals in the '30s: *Be Mine Tonight, My Heart Is Calling, Farewell to Love, Give Us This Night, My Song for You; Thank You, Madame;* etc.; last in 1950's *Her Wonderful Lie;* world popular, he was a national idol—a day of mourning was declared for him in his homeland and the memorial in central Warsaw was attended by tens of thousands.

KILBRIDE, PERCY *(1964)* 76 ——Twangy, hawk-nosed, hilarious Pa Kettle—the role he played eight times; first in a Carole Lombard jungle drama, *White Woman* ('33), as a humorous character named Jakey, he soon fell into his homely philosopher-handyman specialty—usually a Down Easter; in *George Washington Slept Here, You Gotta Stay Happy, Guest in the House, State Fair* ('45), *Crazy House, You Were Meant for Me*, many more.

KILBRIDE, RICHARD *(1967)* 48 ——In 1965's *The Playground*, an experimental filmusical.

KILDUFF, HELEN *(1959)* 71 ——Support in numerous silents; sometimes acted under the name Helen Allerton.

670

KILGALLEN, DOROTHY *(1965)* 52 —— Famed gossip columnist and TV panelist *(What's My Line)*; played a young reporter in Bruce Cabot's *Sinner Take All* ('37).

KILGOUR, JOSEPH *(1933)* 69 ——Portrayed George Washington in *Janice Meredith* ('24); was also in *The Battle Cry for Peace, Ponjola, The Top of the World, The King of Main Street,* other silents.

KILPACK, BENNETT *(1962)* 79 ——Featured in RKO's *Way Back Home;* better known on radio as star of *Mr. Keen, Tracer of Lost Persons.*

KIMBALL, EDWARD M. *(1938)* 78 ——Portly, bearded character in daughter Clara Kimball Young's *Lola* ('15); in others of hers: *Magda, Mid-Channel, Charge It, The Woman of Bronze;* gray support in Will Rogers' *Boys Will Be Boys, An Unwilling Hero,* Reginald Denny's *I'll Show You the Town,* Ethel Clayton's *The Remittance Woman,* Negri's *The Cheat,* other silents.

KIMMINS, ARTHUR *(1963)* 62 ——Top featured in early English talkie comedies; *White Ensign, The Golden Cage,* etc.

KING, ANITA *(1963)* 74 ——Small, busty brunette who played top character leads in many of DeMille's early silents: *The Virginian* (Mrs. Ogden), *The Man from Home* (Helene, Countess de Champigney), *The Girl of the Golden West* (card-cheating Wowkle), *Chimmie Fadden* (millionaire's daughter, Fanny Van Cortlandt), *Carmen* (gypsy girl), *Maria Rosa;* starred, for other directors, in numerous silents: *Snobs* ('15) with Victor Moore, *The Squaw Man's Son* ('17), as the Indian maiden Wallace Reid loved, etc.

KING, CHARLES *(1944)* 50 ——Dapper, top-hatted song-dance star who came in with the first big talkie musicals: *The Broadway Melody, Orange Blossom Time, Road Show, The Girl in the Show, Climbing the Golden Stairs,* etc., after which he returned to the musical stage.

KING, CHARLES *(1957)* 58 ——No relation to above; moustachioed, Spanish-looking mean rascal in scores of Westerns, silent *(Hearts of the West, Triple Action,* etc.) and talkie *(Riders of the West, West of Carson City,* etc.), and serials (in which he was often a good guy): *The Painted Stallion, Zorro's Fighting Legion, White Eagle, Jungle Raiders* (trading post-owner Jake Rayne), *Brick Bradford,* etc.

KING, CLAUDE *(1941)* 62 ——Distinguished support from England in many silents: Negri's *Bella Donna,* Alice Joyce's *The Scarab Ring,* Milton Sills' *Paradise,* etc.; numerous talkies: *The Gilded Lily* (captain of ocean liner on which Colbert fled Milland), *Arrowsmith, Beloved Enemy, Love Under Fire, New Moon,* etc.

KING, DENNIS *(1971)* 73 ——Broadway musical headliner who costarred with Jeanette MacDonald in *The Vagabond King;* when he was the light opera lead in Laurel & Hardy's *The Devil's Brother,* critic Pare Lorentz said of him: "I know of none who is less offensive when called upon to make love in E-flat"; later had supporting roles in Garfield's *Between Two Worlds* and, in Italy, *The Miracle;* son John Michael King appeared on Broadway as Freddie in *My Fair Lady;* his other son, Dennis King Jr., was in Marilyn Monroe's *Let's Make Love.*

KING, EMMETT *(1953)* 87 ——Last the Lord High Chamberlain in Colman's *The Prisoner of Zenda,* he had previously played many supporting roles in silents *(Laugh, Clown, Laugh, The Air Hawk, The Mistress of Shenshone,* etc.) and talkies *(Reno, The Shopworn Angel,* as the gray chaplain in pince-nez who married soldier Gary Cooper and Nancy Carroll, *Mata Hari,* etc.).

KING, EUGENE *(1950)* ——Support in Grant Withers' *Bill Cracks Down.*

KING, JACK *(1943)* 60 ——Character (Herman) in DeMille's *Madam Satan.*

KING, WILL *(1953)* 71 ——Support in several early talkies: *Weak But Willing, The Fatal Forceps,* etc.

KINGDON, DOROTHY *(1939)* 45 ——Support in a few in the '20s: the sobbing melodrama *The Lost Chord,* Lionel Barrymore's *A Man of Iron,* etc.

KINGDON, FRANK *(1937)* 72 ——Supported Dorothy Gish and James Rennie in *Remodelling Her Husband* ('20).

KINGSFORD, WALTER *(1958)* 73 ——When not playing hospital chief Dr. Carew in Lew Ayres' "Dr. Kildare" films, this gray-moustached, always perfectly tailored character from England was busy (1934–58) in scores of others: *Mr. Skeffington* (Dr. Melton), *Juarez* (Prince Metternich), *The Life of Emile Zola* (Colonel Sandherr), *The Story of Louis Pasteur* (Napoleon III), *Little Lord Fauntleroy, Kitty Foyle, Mr. Lucky,* etc.; last in Danny Kaye's *Merry Andrew.*

KINGSTON, WINIFRED *(1967)* 72 ——After co-starring (as Diana, Countess of Kerhill) with husband Dustin Farnum in 1914's *The Squaw*

Man, this beautiful brunette was seen in numerous silents: *The Virginian* (later in '14 and again with Farnum), *The Call of the North, Where the Trail Divides, The Scarlet Pimpernel, David Garrick, The Corsican Brothers*, etc.

KINNELL, MURRAY *(1954)* 65 ——Character (Schweimann) in *Grand Hotel;* one of the most active English supporting players in Hollywood in the '30s, he was in numerous Arliss pix: *The House of Rothschild, Voltaire, The Man Who Played God* (his recommendation to Arliss got Bette Davis her star-making role in this); many others: *Charlie Chan in London* (English inspector), *Charlie Chan in Paris* (French inspector), *Kind Lady, Ann Vickers, The Witness Chair*, etc.

KINSELLA, KATHLEEN *(1961)* 83 ——Biograph actress; many early silents.

KINSOLVING, LEE *(1974)* 36 ——Briefly a teen idol after playing the juvenile lead in *The Dark at the Top of the Stairs;* also in *All the Young Men* and *The Explosive Generation.*

KIPPEN, MANART *(1947)* 60s ——Best known for playing Stalin in *Mission to Moscow;* also in *Mildred Pierce* (Dr. Gale), *The Song of Bernadette* (Charles Bouhouhoris), *Roughly Speaking, The Wife Takes a Flyer*, others of the '40s.

KIRBY, DAVID *(1954)* 74 ——In the '20s supported Blanche Sweet in *In The Palace of the King*, George O'Brien in *The Man Who Came Back*, Ralph Lewis in *The Last Edition;* also in *Shield of Honor, The Spirit of the U.S.A.*, etc.

KIRBY, JOHN *(1973)* 41 ——When in his 20s had a featured role (Macklin) in John Derek's *An Annapolis Story.*

KIRKE, DONALD *(1971)* 69 ——In the serial *G-Men vs. the Black Dragon*, was the thug Muller; in *The Ghost Walks, Hawaii Calls*, others of the '30s.

KIRKLAND, HARDEE, *(1929)* 65 ——Character actor in numerous silents from '18: Thomas Meighan's *Woman Proof*, Monte Blue's *The Perfect Crime*, Pauline Frederick's *Road of Destiny;* also in *Quicksands, Sherlock Brown, The Lure of Jade*, others.

KIRKLAND, MURIEL *(1971)* 68 ——Fine Broadway actress whose half-dozen film roles in 1933–34 were minor: *Little Man, What Now; Nana, The Cocktail Hour, The White Parade, Secret of the Blue Room, Hold Your Man.*

KIRKWOOD, GERTRUDE ROBINSON *(1962)* 71 ——See Gertrude Robinson.

KIRKWOOD, JACK *(1964)* 69 ——Scottish character; in *Fancy Pants* (Lucille Ball's father), *Chicken Every Sunday, Never a Dull Moment*, etc.

KIRKWOOD, JAMES *(1963)* 80 ——Flamboyant, life-loving actor of distinguished good looks who began as a D. W. Griffith leading man in '09; starred first opposite Florence Lawrence in *The Mended Lute* and Marion Leonard in *Comato the Sioux* (two of his several Indian hero roles); in 1914-15 he directed Mary Pickford in nine (*Rags, Cinderella, Fanchon the Cricket, Esmeralda*, etc., and, in two of them, *The Eagle's Mate* and *Behind the Scenes*, was her leading man); co-starred with juvenile Jack Pickford in *Home Sweet Home*, then directed him in two (*In Wrong* and *Bill Apperson's Son*); in the '20s he starred in *Man, Woman and Marriage; Bob Hampton of Placer, The Branding Iron, The Sin Flood, The Great Impersonation* (in a then-famous dual role, with both characters in the same scenes), *The Man from Home*, etc.; support in programmers in the '30s (*Careless Lady, Charlie Chan's Chance*, etc.), Westerns in the next two decades (*Red Stallion in the Rockies, The Last Posse*, etc.).

KIRKWOOD-HACKETT, EVE *(1968)* 91 —— English character actress.

KITZMILLER, JOHN *(1965)* 52 ——American black who had a distinguished career in foreign-made films; after minor roles in *Paisan* and *To Live in Peace*, in Italy, he starred in Yugoslavia's *The Valley of Peace*, as the American parachutist who dies saving two children from being deported in WW II (in '57, won the Cannes Film Festival Award as Best Actor); had top roles in Juliette Greco's *The Naked Earth* and the first directed by Fellini, *Variety Lights.*

KLEIN, AL *(1951)* 66 ——Support; in *365 Nights in Hollywood, Oh, You Beautiful Doll, Opportunity Night*, etc.

KLEINAU, WILLY A. *(1957)* ——Character; in Germany's *The Captain from Koepenick* ('58).

KLEIN-ROGGE, RUDOLF *(1955)* 66 ——Fine German actor who, in disguises that masked his youthful good looks, starred in numerous crime classics; in the silent *Dr. Mabuse* and, ten years later, *The Testament of Dr. Mabuse*, he was the greatest criminal mastermind of them all—in the latter, ruling a world organization of evil from a lunatic asylum; evil, too, in *Spies, Metropolis* (the mad inventor of the robot doll looking exactly like Brigitte Helm), *Siegfried* ('24), as Attila the Hun, etc.; last in 1937's *Truxa.*

KNAGGS, SKELTON *(1955)* 42 ———Most memorable as the mute, gnomelike Finn in Val Lewton's *The Ghost Ship*, foretelling tragedies of the ship and its crew; in the same producer's *Isle of the Dead*, plus *None But the Lonely Heart* (Slush), *Dick Tracy vs. Cueball, House of Dracula, Blackbeard the Pirate*, more.

KNIGHT, PERCIVAL *(1923)* 50 ———Support in England's series of 15 two-reel "Sherlock Holmes" pix released in '22.

KNOTT, CLARA *(1926)* 44 ———Had the title role, wearing Pickford-like curls, in a '20 Metro pic, *Old Lady 31*.

KOERBER, HILDE *(1969)* 63 ———Featured in Germany's *The Third Sex, Hot Harvest*, etc.

KOHLER, FRED, SR. *(1938)* 50 ———Film historian William K. Everson hails him appropriately in his book *The Bad Guys* as the "best Western badman of all," adding: "Fred was a badman of the old school—crafty, ugly, brawny. . . . When displeased, which was frequently, he would grind his teeth audibly and glower. . . . His meanest crime was probably hacking an old man to death with a tomahawk— and blaming the Indians"; onscreen from 1911's *Code of Honor*—something his contemptible screen self never recognized—he hurled his 6'2" frame and trademarked evil sneer into literally hundreds of pix; in a few major Westerns (*The Iron Horse*, as main villain Deroux, *The Plainsman*, others), even fewer non-Western A's (*The Buccaneer, Blockade, The Way of All Flesh*), countless B Westerns (*West of the Pecos, Under the Tonto Rim, The Texas Bad Man*, etc.), and even managed to squeeze in three serials: *The Wolf Dog, The Vigilantes Are Coming*, and the silent *The Tiger's Trail;* today son Fred Jr., brawny and illtempered, carries on the family name in screen villainy.

KOHLMAR, LEE *(1946)* 68 ———Comic character in dozens: *Twentieth Century* (one of the two Bearded Men on the train), *She Done Him Wrong* (Jacobson), *Roman Scandals, The Big Store, The Strange Case of Clara Deane*, etc.

KOLB, CLARENCE *(1964)* 90 ———Played gray, bushy-browed execs full of bombast, and often as not, sentimentality; spluttered his way grandly, and always tycoon-dressed, through more than 60 from 1937's *The Toast of New York;* in *Carefree* (pompous Judge Joe Travers, put down by Ginger Rogers when he asks her for a dance: "Joe, you know I don't dance at your age"), *No Time for Comedy, Adam's Rib* (again the Judge), *His Girl Friday* (crooked mayor), *Hellzapoppin, Caught in the Draft,*

etc.; on TV as boss Mr. Honeywell in *My Little Margie*.

KOLKER, HENRY *(1947)* 73 ———Fine character actor in more than 100 in his 28 years in movies; first in *How Molly Made Good* ('15), last in *Sarong Girl* ('43); in *Holiday* (Hepburn's millionaire father), Shearer's *Romeo and Juliet* (Friar Laurence), *A Woman's Face* (Judge), Colbert's *Imitation of Life* (Dr. Preston), *Maid of Salem* (Crown Chief Justice), *Theodora Goes Wild* (Melvyn Douglas' father), etc.

KOLLMAR, RICHARD *(1971)* 60 ———Support in 1948's *Close-Up;* radio-TV talk show star, husband of the late Dorothy Kilgallen.

KOOY, PETE *(1963)* ———Support in a low-budget film, *Death in Small Doses*, starring Mala Powers.

KORFF, ARNOLD *(1944)* 73 ———Character actor in many in the '30s: *Magnificent Obsession* (a doctor), *An American Tragedy* (judge presiding at Phillips Holmes' trial), *Ambassador Bill, Scarlet Dawn, Shanghai, The Jazz King*, etc.

KORNMAN, MARY *(1973)* 56 ———In "Our Gang," the very first ('23) little leading lady, with Farina, Wheezer, Pineapple, Mickey Daniels, et al. for years; in '30, when she was an irresistibly cute blonde pixie of 13, producer Hal Roach co-starred her with freckle-faced Daniels (and two other couples) in "The Boy Friends" series—15 comedy shorts in the next two years; in numerous features in the '30s: *Are These Our Children, College Humor, Flying Down to Rio* (jealous of friend Dolores Del Rio's success with men, delivered the movie's best line: "What have these South Americans got below the equator that we haven't?"), *Desert Trail* (John Wayne's leading lady), etc.; retired for marriage after 1938's *King of the Newsboys*.

KORTNER, FRITZ *(1970)* 78 ———Austrian character in Hollywood from 1943's *The Strange Death of Adolf Hitler* (after years on English and European screens); in *The Hitler Gang, Somewhere in the Night, The Brasher Doubloon, The Razor's Edge, The High Window, Berlin Express*, etc.

KOSHETZ, NINA *(1965)* 73 ———Actress-singer-singing coach from Russia; in *Our Hearts Were Young and Gay* (played herself), *Algiers, Captain Pirate, It's a Small World*, etc.; MGM singer-actress Marina is her daughter.

KOSLOFF, THEODORE *(1956)* 74 ———Muscular, dark young Russian star from the ballet world who, in exotic roles, was a DeMille regular from '17; in *The Woman God Forgot* (Spanish warrior-lover Guatemoco), *Why Change Your Wife?*, *The Affairs of Anatol* (turbaned Nazzer Singh), *The Golden Bed*, *The King of Kings*, and six other DeMille pix, including *Madam Satan*, his last; in another dozen in the '20s for other directors.

KOVACS, ERNIE *(1962)* 43 ——Black-haired star comedian with an offbeat view, bushy moustache and ever-present giant stogie; at his mad funniest in *Operation Mad Ball*, his first; also in *It Happened to Jane; Bell, Book and Candle; Strangers When We Meet; Pepe; Sail a Crooked Ship*, etc.

KOWAL, MITCHELL *(1971)* 55 ——Support (an American Marine) in *55 Days at Peking*; also in *John Paul Jones, Violated, Abbott and Costello Meet the Mummy*.

KRAH, MARC *(1973)* ——Character (Nicco) in Raft's *Intrigue*; also in *Criss Cross*, Pat O'-Brien's *Riff-Raff*, *The Black Hand*, etc.

KRAMER, WRIGHT *(1941)* 71 ——Character; in *Anne of Windy Populars* was Grandpa Pringle ("owned" Pringleton, where Anne Shirley came to teach); also in *Mr. Smith Goes to Washington, Professor Beware, The Gladiator*, etc.

KRAUSS, WERNER *(1959)* 75 ——Great German character star; in top hat and sinister spectacles in *The Cabinet of Dr. Caligari*, he was the insane Caligari who sent hypnotized Conrad Veidt on a murder spree; also starred in *Waxworks* (Jack the Ripper), *Tartuffe, Three Wax Men*, and other European films through 1940's *Jew Suess*.

KRIEGER, LEE *(1967)* 48 ——Supporting actor in *Period of Adjustment, The Horizontal Lieutenant, Bachelor in Paradise*, others of the '60s.

KRUEGER, BUM *(1971)* 65 ——Character actor in Zbigniew Cybulski's *The Eighth Day of the Week*, other German-made films.

KRUGER, ALMA *(1960)* 88 ——Character actress, with an inimitable viola speaking voice, best recalled now as the no-nonsense head nurse, Molly Byrd, in the "Dr. Kildare" and "Dr. Gillespie" movie series; creating the role in the third Lew Ayres episode, *The Secret of Dr. Kildare* in '39, she played it in all 12 that followed, through 1947's *Dark Delusion*, when Lionel Barrymore, as Dr. Gillespie, had long since been the series' mainstay; her best screen role was her first—in *These Three* (the grandmother who, told and believing a vicious lie about Hopkins-Oberon-McCrea, wrecked their

lives, to her later regret); next best— *Craig's Wife* (Russell's aunt, who correctly informed her "people who live to themselves are generally left to themselves"); star of radio's *Those We Love*, she was featured in many more pix: *100 Men and a Girl, His Girl Friday, Saboteur*, etc.; last in Priscilla Lane's *Fun on a Weekend* ('48).

KRUGER, FRED *(1961)* 48 ——Support in a Mara Corday B, *Girls on the Loose*.

KRUGER, OTTO *(1974)* 89 ——For 32 years in talkies (1933's *The Intruder* through *Sex and the Single Girl*), in 82 pix, there was none more suave; starred in several, he was more generally an ace silver-haired character lead making his presence—elegantly, vitally (sometimes villainously)—felt in *Cover Girl; Dr. Ehrlich's Magic Bullet; Saboteur; Hitler's Children; Murder My Sweet; Men in White; They Won't Forget; The Man I Married; Another Thin Man*, etc.; a severe stroke, rendering him unable to remember lines (he mainly surmounted its paralysis), forced his retirement in '64.

KRUGER, STUBBY *(1965)* 68 ——Hawaiian character actor who played Schlemmer in *Mister Roberts*; was also the double for Douglas Fairbanks, who seldom used one, in the more dangerous stunts in *The Black Pirate*.

KRUMSCHMIDT, EBERHARD *(1956)* 51 —— One of Claude Rains' villainous colleagues in Rio in *Notorious*.

KRUPA, GENE *(1973)* 64 ——Frenetic curly-haired jazz drummer, greatest of his time, who, with his famous band and volatile sticks, was in *Ball of Fire* and *George White's Scandals*; as himself, was in *The Glenn Miller Story* and *The Benny Goodman Story*; Sal Mineo portrayed him in *The Gene Krupa Story*, which emphasized his triumph over drugs.

KULKA, HENRY *(1965)* 53 ——Professional wrestler, Bomber Kulkavich, turned actor, who often played bartenders (as in *Call Northside 777*), thugs, and servicemen; in *Fixed Bayonets, Up Periscope, Wabash Avenue, South Sea Sinner, Bodyhold*, etc.

KUN, MAGDA *(1945)* 34 ——Hungarian actress; support in England's *Dance Band*.

KUNDE, ANNA *(1960)* 64 ——Support in *One-Eyed Jacks, Li'l Abner*, etc.

KUNKEL, GEORGE *(1937)* 70 ——Character actor in numerous silents: Madge Kennedy's *Leave It to Susan*, Will Rogers' *An Unwilling Hero*, others.

KUPCINET, KAREN *(1963)* 22 ——Brunette starlet featured in Jerry Lewis' *The Ladies Man;* victim in one of Hollywood's more famous murders.

KUZNETZOFF, ADIA *(1954)* 64 ——Actor from Russia who several times played supporting characters named Boris; in *Second Chorus, Devil's Island, Bulldog Drummond's Bride, Arabian Nights, For Whom the Bell Tolls* (as Gustavo), *The Princess and the Pirate*, etc.

L

LA BADIE, FLORENCE *(1917)* 23 ——Ravishingly beautiful model who became, in 1909, through an introduction by Mary Pickford to D. W. Griffith, one of the director's first leading ladies at Biograph; most famous as star of the 1914 serial *The Million Dollar Mystery*, she was also in features: *The Country Girl, Cymbeline, The Merchant of Venice* ('12), *Enoch Arden* ('11), *Lucile, Undine, The Star of Bethlehem* ('12), etc.

LACKAYE, WILTON *(1932)* 70 ——A heavyweight, walrus-moustached leading character actor in silents; Constance Bennett's father in *What's Wrong With Women?* ('22); also in *The Sky Raider, God's Crucible*, etc.

LACKTEEN, FRANK *(1968)* 74 ——In the serial *Jungle Girl*, he was the crease-faced witch doctor in the horned Viking headdress who yearned to sacrifice Frances Gifford to the gods; had been up to evil in serials since '16, soon after his arrival from his native land (now Lebanon); first a villainous Chinese in *The Yellow Menace*, then in *The Veiled Mystery*, Ruth Roland's *The Avenging Arrow* (wicked Pablo) and *White Eagle, Leatherstocking* (ruthless Indian Briarthorn), and many other silent serials plus features; just a few of the talking serials in which his savage-eyed, bony visage leered menacingly: Buster Crabbe's *Tarzan the Fearless* (as Abdul), *Perils of Pauline* ('34; as Fang), *The Mysterious Pilot* (Yoroslaf), *Don Winslow of the Navy, The Desert Hawk;* in features, best in (silent) *Hawk of the Hills* and (talkie) *Escape from Devil's Island;* last in 1965's *Requiem for a Gunfighter*—a terror to the end.

LADD, ALAN *(1964)* 51 ——Short star, tall at the box-office for Paramount—in the Top 10 in '47, '53, '54; onscreen in small roles for a full decade before becoming the rage, in trenchcoat and monotone, as conscienceless killer Phillip Raven in *This Gun for Hire;* thereafter, his tough blond handsomeness was on display (his height, about 5'5", well camouflaged) in dozens for 20 years, in which there were always two obligatory scenes—a big fist-fight and a torso baring (capitalizing on his perfectly proportioned muscular shoulders and chest); in *The Glass Key, The Blue Dahlia* and *Saigon*, all with Veronica Lake, and *Two Years Before the Mast, China, Lucky Jordan, Calcutta, Red Mountain, The McConnell Story, The Great Gatsby*, etc.; gave his finest performance in *Shane;* in only one movie, after he became a star, did his name not appear above the title—his last, *The Carpetbaggers*, in which he played a supporting role, made at his old home studio.

LADMIRAL, NICOLE *(1958)* 27 ——Leading lady in France's *The Diary of a Country Priest*.

LAFAYETTE, RUBY *(1935)* 89 ——Last in a minor supporting role in an early Marion Davies talkie, she had played character roles in many in the '20s: *Idle Tongues, The Coming of Amos, Mother O' Mine, Hollywood*, etc.

LA FLEUR, JOY *(1957)* 43 ——Support in Robert Taylor's *D-Day, The Sixth of June* and Helmut Dantine's *Whispering City*.

LAHR, BERT *(1967)* 72 ——Great Broadway comedian though he was, he could never shake the moviegoer's image of him as the Cowardly Lion in *The Wizard of Oz;* when, after his death, his son John wrote a book about the star's life (apparently not a happy one), the title was *Notes on a Cowardly Lion;* was in several before *Oz (Mr. Broadway, Flying High, Love and Hisses, Just Around the Corner)* and after it *(DuBarry Was a Lady, Ship Ahoy, Rose Marie, Meet the People);* last in *The Night They Raided Minsky's*, released the year after his death.

LAIDLAW, ETHAN *(1963)* 63 ——A checkered-shirted rustler in scores of Westerns from 1925's *No Man's Law* starring Rex, the Wild Horse, through 1953's *Powder River* starring Rory Calhoun; in between: *The Lone Star Vigilantes, Western Caravans, Stage to Chino, The Desperadoes*, etc.; serials: *Pirate Treasure, Gordon of Ghost City;* very few non-Westerns: *The Marines Fly High, I'm from the City, Joan of Arc* (played Jean D'Aulon).

LAKE, ALICE *(1967)* 71 ——Pretty brunette who from '16 to '19 was a Sennett comedy star often teamed with "Fatty" Arbuckle (in *The Cook, The Waiter's Ball*) and in many other two-reelers; beginning in '20 was a Metro star; in *Shore Acres, Body and Soul, Should a Woman Talk?*, many more; was seldom a favorite with critics (*Over the Wire:* "Alice Lake is pleasing but overshadowed by George Stewart"; *The Greater Claim:* "If you have any greater claim on your time, don't waste it by seeing Alice Lake's latest"; *The Infamous Miss Revell:* "Alice Lake is her usual self, playing a dual role by changing her hair-dress"); onscreen through a '34 Paul Lukas pic, *Glamour,* in which she played a secretary.

LAKE, FRANK *(1936)* 87 ——Character in Lawrence Tibbett's *The Rogue Song.*

LAKE, VERONICA *(1973)* 53 ——Paramount's tiny, sultry blonde star with the "peekaboo" hair; occasionally evidenced wit and substance in her acting *(Sullivan's Travels, I Married a Witch);* revealed herself a genuine actress as the courageous nurse in *So Proudly We Hail;* more often had somnolent roles, in *The Hour Before the Dawn, Miss Susie Slagle's, Bring on the Girls, The Sainted Sisters, Slattery's Hurricane;* made first big splash in 1941's *I Wanted Wings* after several years in bits; often teamed with Alan Ladd—her size and equally sleepy-eyed; off Hollywood screens after a '52 B pic, *Stronghold* —alcoholism and other problems—she lived a hand-to-mouth existence in New York; made occasional minor stage comebacks and, in '66, a battered bantamweight by now, starred for a Canadian company in her last movie, *Footsteps in the Snow,* which records indicate has never been released.

LALOR, FRANK *(1932)* 63 ——Support in Constance Talmadge's *Polly of the Follies.*

LA MARR, BARBARA *(1925)* 28 ——Brunette star considered by many (Louella Parsons included) the most beautiful woman in world, and by one California judge "too beautiful for her own good" (he advised her to leave Los Angeles since, by 25, she had already figured in four marriages); onscreen in 22 movies, she first attracted fans' admiration as Milady in Fairbanks' *The Three Musketeers;* made with ease the transition to sympathetic star from sultry femme fatale (said one critic after 1922's *The Prisoner of Zenda,* "The beauty of the lady villainess, Barbara La Marr, makes the blonde loveliness of Alice Terry seem almost weak at times"); starred in *Arabian Love, The Eternal City, Mary of the Movies, The White Moth, Sandra,* etc.

LAMBERTI, PROFESSOR *(1950)* 58 ——Was spotlighted with his hilarious vaudeville dog act in *Tonight and Every Night, Linda Be Good,* etc.

LA MONT, HARRY *(1957)* 69 ——Character actor in *China Girl, The Black Swan,* etc., who had been in movies since the silents (*Blood and Sand, Robin Hood Jr., Fazil,* others).

LAMONT, JACK *(1956)* 62 ——Minor comic in "Keystone Kops" pix.

LANCASTER, ANN *(1970)* 50 ——English support; in the David McCallum pic *Three Bites of the Apple,* etc.

LANDAU, DAVID *(1935)* 57 ——Character actor in 32 in four years onscreen (1931-34); in *I Am a Fugitive from a Chain Gang* (sadistic, club-wielding warden), *Street Scene* (Sylvia Sidney's father), *Polly of the Circus* (Beef), *She Done Him Wrong* (Dan Flynn), *Death on the Diamond,* etc.

LANDI, ELISSA *(1948)* 43 ——Patrician, greatly talented red-haired star—and authentic Austrian countess; after numerous roles in English pix, she was given her best early break in Hollywood in *The Sign of the Cross* (co-star role of the Christian girl, Poppaea) by DeMille, who said, "She has a white, radiant sort of glamour that will carry her far"; numerous subsequent pix did not make her a major box-office attraction: *The Masquerader* with Colman, *The Warrior's Husband, I Loved You Wednesday, The Count of Monte Cristo,* etc.; recognizing her as a woman of charm who photographed "cold," MGM's Irving Thalberg used her in secondary roles in *After the Thin Man* and *The Thirteenth Chair* while planning a campaign to establish the "new" Elissa Landi—but he died before it was effected; after one more, a Poverty Row wartime B, *Corregidor,* she retired and became the author of five successful novels.

LANDIN, HOPE *(1973)* 80—Bulky, gray-haired Aunt Jenny in the movie *I Remember Mama;* also in *The Walls of Jericho, The Great John L, The Sun Comes Up, Sugarfoot,* etc.

LANDIS, CAROLE *(1948)* 29 ——Beautiful blonde star who started as a Busby Berkeley dancer at 15 and had the same outspokenness and wacky humor as Lombard; had earliest starring opportunities at Roach: *One Million B.C., Turnabout* (a delectable comedy performance—and only 19); 20th Century-Fox co-starred her, with admirable results, in many in the '40s: *Moon Over Miami, I Wake Up Screaming, My Gal Sal, Orchestra Wives, It Happened in Flatbush, A Gentleman at Heart,* etc.; brainy but uneducated, she wrote a book about her wartime experiences while entertaining troops with the U.S.O., *Four Jills in a Jeep,* and co-starred in the pic based on it; after *Having a Wonderful Crime* in '45, only B's came her way, then Hollywood doors were closed to her

—Rex Harrison, a friend then, attributing it, in his book, *Rex*, to her being a liberated woman ahead of her time; she made two in England, *The Brass Monkey* and *The Silk Noose*, the year of her death.

LANDIS, JESSIE ROYCE *(1972)* 68 ——Red-haired character actress particularly adept at portraying aristocrats or well-bred women of wealth: *North by Northwest* (Cary Grant's mother), *To Catch a Thief* and *The Swan* (Grace Kelly's mother in each), *My Foolish Heart* (Susan Hayward's mother); also in *Mr. Belvedere Goes to College, It Happens Every Spring, Bon Voyage!, Critic's Choice*, more.

LANDRETH, GERTRUDE GRIFFITH *(1969)* 72 ——Actress in silents, mainly Sennett two-reelers.

LANE, ALLAN "ROCKY" *(1973)* 64 ——One of the handsomest of Republic's Western stars in the '40s and early '50s; two years in the Top Ten Western Money-Makers: '51, '53; a model with Broadway experience, he entered movies in '29, playing the romantic lead in a Louise Dresser-starrer, *Not Quite Decent*; through the '30s, billed simply Allan Lane, he had similar roles in 25 (*Charlie Chan at the Olympics, Maid's Night Out* with Joan Fontaine, *Twelve Crowded Hours, Panama Lady*, etc.) at WB, 20th, MGM and RKO, where he was under contract for several years; at Republic from '40, he first starred in several serials: *King of the Royal Mounted, The Tiger Woman, King of the Mounties*; made his first starring Western, *Silver City Kid* in '44, followed by *Trail of Kit Carson, Stagecoach to Monterey*, etc.; after portraying "Red Ryder" in eight, he became Allan "Rocky" Lane in 1947's *The Wild Frontier*; tough times followed the demise of B Westerns in '53; had supporting roles in just three more pix, the last being *Posse from Hell*; ended his career as the voice of *Mr. Ed*, in TV's "talking horse" series.

LANE, HARRY *(1960)* 50 ——Character in British pix: *Fire Over Africa, Old Mother Riley's Jungle Treasure*, more.

LANE, LEOTA *(1963)* 50s ——Older sister of Lola, Rosemary, and Priscilla; singer-comedienne in occasional pix (minor roles), but never with them.

LANE, LUPINO *(1959)* 67 ——Small, youthful-looking, acrobatic, rubber-jointed comedian from England who took pratfalls galore in a starring series of two-reelers (1925-29); famous for one expression—"that of an empty-headed child"; also in features: Griffith's *Isn't Life Wonderful?* (in this story of the struggle of Ger-

many's poor for food in 1923, he was a cheerful note as one of the sons in the family), *The Love Parade* (Chevalier's mirthful singing valet), Vivienne Segal's Technicolor operetta, *The Golden Dawn* ('30), etc.; returned to England, was last seen in 1939's *The Lambeth Walk*.

LANE, ROSEMARY *(1974)* 61 ——Of the Lane Sisters, she was middle one, overshadowed by Lola (who entered pix far earlier) and Priscilla (blonde, all-American-girl type then much in vogue), but possibly the most talented of all; first onscreen in '37, with Priscilla as singers with Fred Waring's band in *Varsity Show*, in which she also was Dick Powell's leading lady; best known for costarring with Lola and Priscilla in *Four Daughters, Four Wives, Four Mothers*; also played romantic leads in *The Boys from Syracuse, The Return of Doctor X, The Oklahoma Kid*, etc.; a great success on Broadway as the singing-dancing lead in the musical comedy *Best Foot Forward* ('41), she returned to movies for *Chatterbox, All by Myself*, and *The Fortune Hunter*, then in '45 became the first of the Lane Sisters to retire from show business—and became a realtor.

LANE, WALLACE *(1961)* 63 ——See Wallace Lupino.

LANG, HAROLD *(1971)* 48 ——Rugged blond British support; in Davis' *The Nanny, The Saint's Girl Friday, The Franchise Affair*, more.

LANG, HARRY *(1953)* 58 ——Supporting actor in Stewart Granger's *Soldiers Three*.

LANG, HOWARD *(1941)* 64 ——Support in silents (*Peacock Alley*) and talkies (*Cradle Song*, "Hopalong Cassidy's" *Bar 20 Rides Again, Navy Spy*, Colman's *The Prisoner of Zenda*, as Josef, etc.).

LANG, MATHESON *(1948)* 69 ——A tall, most handsome star of silents: *Carnival, Dick Turpin's Ride to York, Mr. Wu, The Wandering Jew*, others; starred in the title role in 1929's *The Triumph of the Scarlet Pimpernel*; many English pix in the '30s: *Little Friend, The Passing of the Third Floor Back, Drake of England*, etc.

LANG, PETER *(1932)* 65 ——Character in 1924's *Dangerous Money*, starring Bebe Daniels.

LANGDON, HARRY *(1944)* 60 ——Sad-faced star comedian with an owlish blink, whose innocent trust in the world's goodness brought him successfully through onscreen woes from '23 to the end; best in the 23 silent two-reelers he did for Sennett: *His Marriage Vow, Smile Please, Picking Peaches, Boobs in the Woods,* etc.; was excellent also in his first features: *Tramp, Tramp, Tramp* and *The Strong Man* (both '26); starred in dozens of talkie shorts for various companies (Roach, Educational, Columbia, Monogram), but never duplicated his silent success; supported others in numerous features: *There Goes My Heart; Zenobia; Hallelujah, I'm a Bum,* etc.; last had a minor role in a Jane Frazee musical, *Swingin' on a Rainbow.*

LANGDON, LILLIAN *(1943)* 70s ——Top support in many silents, frequently as a dowager such as Lady Mary in William Desmond's *Society for Sale;* played Swanson's domineering mother—driving her husband to suicide—in *Everywoman's Husband* ('18), and was the aristocratic mother of leading man Joe King in Swanson's next, *Shifting Sands;* also in Fairbanks' *His Majesty, the American,* plus *The Mother Heart, Cobra, Fools of Fortune,* etc.

LANGFORD, WILLIAM *(1955)* 35 ——Handsome Canadian in Sweden's *The True and the False.*

LANGLEY, HERBERT *(1967)* 79 ——Support in the Metro silent *Chu Chin Chow.*

LANGLEY, STUART *(1970)* 60 ——Actor-singer; in *Winged Victory.*

LANGTRY, LILY *(1929)* 75 ——"The Jersey Lily," noted for her brunette beauty; starred for Famous Players at 60, and, still lovely, in *His Neighbor's Wife;* Walter Brennan's "Judge Roy Bean" in *The Westerner* idolized her, named his town (Langtry, Texas) for her, and "died" on the day he finally got to see her on stage.

LANPHIER, FAY *(1959)* 53 ——Miss America of 1926 who was featured in an Esther Ralston pic that year, *The American Venus,* about the Atlantic City beauty pageant; also was the beautiful girl in a few Laurel & Hardy silents.

LANPHIER, JAMES *(1969)* 48 ——Character (Saloud) in *The Pink Panther;* also in *The Perfect Furlough, Darling Lili, Flight of the Lost Balloon.*

LANSING, JOI *(1972)* 44 ——Busty, dazzling, and humorous blonde; prominently featured in many from the late '40s on; in *A Hole in the Head, Who Was That Lady?, Marriage on the Rocks,* etc.; also popular and busy on TV, especially in the role of Shirley Swanson in Robert Cummings' series *Love That Bob.*

LANZA, MARIO *(1959)* 38 ——Metro's *Great Caruso;* a heavyweight—at the box-office, vocally, and physically; the last, because of a bizarre reducing diet undertaken in Rome, contributed greatly to his early death; starred for MGM (1949-52) in four: *That Midnight Kiss, Toast of New Orleans, The Great Caruso, Because You're Mine;* did the music soundtrack for 1954's *The Student Prince* which starred Edmund Purdom; starred in one at Warners: *Serenade;* made two more in Italy, *Seven Hills of Rome* and *For the First Time,* which were released by MGM.

LA RENO, DICK *(1945)* 71 ——Top support (Big Bill) in Dustin Farnum's *The Squaw Man;* supported the star also in *Cameo Kirby* and *The Virginian* (as Balaam); DeMille, director of the first and third of these, featured him often: *The Man from Home* (as heroine Mabel Van Buren's millionaire father, Old Man Simpson), *Rose of the Rancho* (landjumper Kincaid), *The Warrens of Virginia* (General Kincaid); in dozens of silent Westerns through 1928's *The Apache Raider* starring Leo Maloney.

LARGAY, RAYMOND *(1974)* 88 ——Character actor in many from 1930: *Soldiers and Women, She Wrote the Book, The Shocking Miss Pilgrim, Four Faces West, Force of Evil, The Petty Girl, The Second Woman, April in Paris,* etc.

LARIMORE, EARLE *(1947)* 48 ——Was seen as a football player in George Walsh's *The Kickoff* ('26); minor roles in a few other silents.

LARKIN, JOHN *(1936)* 62 ——Black actor featured in Marion Davies' *Hearts Divided* (as Isham), E. G. Robinson's *Smart Money* (gambler Snake Eyes), *Mississippi, The Great Jasper,* etc.

LARKIN, JOHN *(1965)* 52 ——Handsome actor who had co-star roles in several: *The Satan Bug, Those Calloways,* etc.; top support in others: *Seven Days in May* (Col. Broderick); most popular on TV as star of the *12 O'Clock High* series (the Peck role) and the soap opera *The Edge of Night* (criminal lawyer Mike Karr).

LA ROCQUE, ROD *(1969)* 70 ——One of the silents' biggest stars, in popularity and size (6'3"); onscreen from Essanay days ('14), when directors never guessed he was only 16; at 19, in New York, was Goldwyn's principal leading man, playing in tragedies with Mae Marsh (*Hidden Fires, Money Mad*) and comedies with Mabel Normand (*The Venus Model*); 1923, his first year in Hollywood, put him on the superstar roster—appeared opposite Mae Murray in *Jazzmania* (as a gigolo) and in *The French Doll,* and co-starred as the young "heavy" in De-Mille's *The Ten Commandments* (Robert E. Sherwood, then a critic, wrote: "Of the many stars who appear, Rod La Rocque stands out vividly. His performance of an unregenerate youth who flouts the Ten Commandments is one to be remembered as long as we old cronies sit around the fire and discuss the movies of yesterday"); starred in many: *Resurrection, Feet of Clay, Forbidden Paradise, The Coming of Amos, Strong Heart*, etc.; in '27 married (and stayed married to) Vilma Banky; in talkies, long since wealthy, he acted—in some leads, some supporting roles—only when he wished; in *The Delightful Rogue, The Gay Bandit, The Shadow Strikes*, etc.; onscreen in four in '41-42: *Beyond Tomorrow, Dr. Christian Meets the Women, Dark Streets of Cairo*, and *Meet John Doe.*

LARQUEY, PIERRE *(1962)* 78 ——Support in French pix: *Diabolique, Witches of Salem, Second Bureau*, in which he gave an outstanding performance as a silly, pathetic French officer ruined by his love of a beautiful spy, and many others.

LA RUE, FRANK *(1960)* 81 ——Support in *Once in a Lifetime, Sidewalks of New York, Flying Devils*, etc., then was in B Westerns—usually as the sheriff—for the rest of his career; in *Under the Pampas Moon, Song of the Buckaroo, Overland Stage Raiders*, etc., through Johnny Mack Brown's *The Sheriff of Medicine Bow* in '48.

LA RUE, GRACE *(1956)* 74 ——Reviewing *She Done Him Wrong*, in which this once-famous musical comedy and vaudeville star, made her debut in talkie features, *Variety* said: "Grace LaRue . . . who headlined when Miss West was chasing acrobats in the No. 2 spot, has a bit"; much later she had one other supporting role, in Crosby's *If I Had My Way;* her only silent screen appearance was in 1919's *That's Good*, appearing opposite star-husband Hale Hamilton.

LA RUE, JEAN *(1956)* 55 ——He had a minor supporting role in Ramon Novarro's *Where the Pavement Ends* ('23).

LASCOE, HENRY *(1964)* 50 ——Support in a Barry Nelson B, *The Man With My Face.*

LATELL, LYLE *(1967)* 62 ——Featured in a running role (Pat Patton) in the "Dick Tracy" series (*Dick Tracy vs. Cueball, Dick Tracy's Dilemma*, etc.); also in Abbott & Costello pix (*In the Navy, Buck Privates Come Home, The Noose Hangs High*, others).

LATHROP, DONALD *(1940)* 52 ——Support in Vivien Leigh's *Fire over England*, other British pix.

LAUDER, SIR HARRY *(1950)* 79 ——Celebrated music hall star from Scotland; in five British pix: *Auld Lang Syne, Huntingtower, The End of the Road, Happy Days, Song of the Road.*

LAUGHLIN, ANNA *(1937)* 52 ——Featured in Vitagraph's *Crooky Scruggs* ('15).

LAUGHTON, CHARLES *(1962)* 63 ——Fat and fabulous character star, cherished by critics and fans, regarded warily by directors (could be difficult) and co-players (could act most right off the screen); on Hollywood screens (after British pix) from 1931's *Devil and the Deep*, he began to win his loyal following the next year, as Nero in *The Sign of the Cross*, consolidating it one year later in *The Private Life of Henry VIII* (won his only Best Actor Oscar in this); 1935 offered proof in spades of his versatility: comedy—brilliant in *Ruggles of Red Gap*, drama—superb as Captain Bligh in *Mutiny on the Bounty* (another Best Actor nomination) and as Javert in *Les Miserables;* then came *Rembrandt, Jamaica Inn, They Knew What They Wanted, This Land Is Mine, The Suspect, The Paradine Case, The Big Clock, Witness for the Prosecution* (yet another Oscar nomination), and a score more, all enriching the moviegoing lives of everyone who saw them.

LAUGHTON, EDDIE *(1952)* 48 ——A seedy look-alike for Warner Baxter, he was support—usually villainous—in many: *Men without Souls, I Was a Prisoner on Devil's Island, Atlantic Convoy, The Lost Weekend* (Mr. Brophy), etc.; in numerous B Westerns—frequently a bartender: *Bullets for Rustlers, West of Abilene, Outlaws of the Panhandle*, others.

LAUNDERS, PERC *(1952)* 47 ——Played a band member, Tom, in *The Stork Club;* also in *The Falcon Out West, For Heaven's Sake*, etc.

LAUREL, STAN *(1965)* 74 ——Skinny, crybaby half of the great Laurel & Hardy team, and, behind the scenes, the more enterprising half—conceiving many of their best gags and overseeing the editing of their films; from England, he was on American screens in two-reelers for various companies (Universal, Vitagraph) before becoming a Hal Roach contractee in '26—primarily as director and gagman, but also, of course, acting in comedies; Laurel & Hardy were first starred as a comedy team—though they had already appeared in many of the same movies—in *Hats Off* and 13 other 1927 two-reel comedies; once the L & H "comedy machine" was turned on, there was no turning it off before they had been seen in more than 100 films together; their '32 three-reeler *The Music Box* (delivering that piano up the steps to the house at the top of the hill) won the Oscar as Best Short; in '60 Laurel was awarded a special Oscar "for his creative pioneering in the field of cinema comedy."

LAURENZE, JOHN *(1958)* 49 ——Character (Benji) in Weissmuller's *Tarzan and the Mermaids*; also in *Apache Rose, Border Outlaws*, etc.

LAURIER, JAY *(1969)* 89 ——Character in British pix: *Hobson's Choice* ('32), *Waltz Time*, others.

LA VERNE, LUCILLE *(1945)* 74 ——Was the old hag, La Vengeance, in Colman's *A Tale of Two Cities* who, ring-side at the guillotine, relished the beheadings; in *Little Caesar*, was the rooming house old crone with the walking stick, Ma Magdelena; did other old witches in the '30s (including the voice of wicked Queen in *Snow White and the Seven Dwarfs*); in silents, sympathetic roles: the mulatto in Mae Marsh's *Polly of the Circus*, a refugee mother in *America*, etc.

LA VERNIE, LAURA *(1939)* 86 ——Character actress in Nancy Carroll's *The Devil's Holiday*, Pickford's *Kiki*, others.

LAW, DON "FATS" *(1959)* 38 ——In "Our Gang" in the late '20s, played the fat lad, after Joe Cobb and before Chubby Chaney.

LAW, WALTER *(1940)* 64 ——Character; silents: *Janice Meredith* (as Gen. Charles Lee), *If I Were King, Flying Dutchman*, etc.; talkies: *Whoopee* (dad of leading lady Eleanor Hunt), the serial *The Adventures of Frank Merriwell*, etc.

LAWFORD, BETTY *(1960)* 50 ——English actress in Hollywood who, in her 20s, expertly played aristocratic or rich young women: Marjorie Frant in *Berkeley Square*, the daughter of Mary Boland in *Secrets of a Secretary;* in *Lucky in Love, Stolen Holiday, Love Before Breakfast*.

LAWRENCE, EDWARD *(1931)* ——Had the top supporting role in a '25 Milton Sills pic, *The Knockout*.

LAWRENCE, FLORENCE *(1938)* 50 —— Around 1910 no star was more famous or worshipped than the radiantly attractive "Biograph Girl"; often teamed with Arthur Johnson and, in the "Mr. and Mrs. Jones" series, with John Compson; starred (1906-14) for several companies (Edison, Vitagraph, Biograph, and Imp, where she also was known as the "Imp Girl"); in dozens: *Redemption, The Slave, Resurrection, The Road to the Heart, Her Two Sons*, etc.; starring career ended in '15 when, in a studio fire, she saved another's life and was herself tragically burned; paralyzed, and an invalid for some years, she came back, unsuccessfully, in '20 in *The Enfoldment;* later silents were failures also: *Gambling Wives, Satin Girl;* at the time of her death was playing bits as a member of the MGM stock company.

LAWRENCE, GERALD *(1957)* 84 ——Support in England's *The Iron Duke* and *As You Like It*.

LAWRENCE, GERTRUDE *(1952)* 54 ——Brilliantly sophisticated star-comedienne of the stage who, not being highly photogenic, made only a handful of movies: *Men Are Not Gods, Mimi, Aren't We All, Rembrandt, No Funny Business*, etc.; later co-starred as the voluble mother (Amanda) of Jane Wyman in *The Glass Menagerie;* in the '60s Julie Andrews, missing both the diamond-hard dazzle and the skylarking humor, portrayed her in *Star!*

LAWRENCE, JOHN *(1974)* 30s ——In *The Goddess* played one of the two GI's who flirted with Kim Stanley: also in Rock Hudson's *Seconds*.

LAWRENCE, LILLIAN *(1926)* 56 ——Character actress in Norma Talmadge's *Graustark*, Constance Talmadge's *East Is West*, Florence Vidor's *Christine of the Hungry Heart*, Pickford's *Stella Maris*, other silents.

LAWRENCE, WILLIAM *(1947)* 51 ——In the '20s, support in serials (*Bride 13*), Westerns (William Desmond's *Fightin' Mad*, Buck Jones' *Get Your Man*), action pix (*They Like 'Em Rough, The Thrill Chaser*, etc.).

LAWSON, MARY *(1941)* 30 ——Was prominently featured in British pix of the '30s: *Things Are Looking Up, Scrooge, Trouble Ahead*.

LAWSON, WILFRID *(1966)* 66 ——Topnotch English character actor; Eliza Dolittle's shiftless father in *Pygmalion*, Black George in *Tom Jones*, Prince Bolkonsky in Audrey Hepburn's *War and Peace;* in many others: *The Great Mr. Handel, The Wrong Box, The Prisoner*, etc.; briefly in America in 1939-40 for *The Long Voyage Home* (ship's captain) and John Wayne's *Allegheny Uprising*.

LAWTON, FRANK *(1969)* 64 ——In his 20s, he became a screen star overnight in England in the title role of *Young Woodley* (had played it onstage too); in Hollywood's *Cavalcade* he was splendid as Joe Marryot, the young soldier-son of Clive Brook and Diana Wynyard killed in WW I; was no less fine in *David Copperfield* as Freddie Bartholomew grown up; in *The Invisible Ray*, *The Devil Doll*, *One More River*, etc.; a top character actor in England in later years, in *Gideon of Scotland Yard*, *A Night to Remember* (as the cowardly chairman of the ship line owning the Titanic), *The Winslow Boy*, others.

LAWTON, THAIS *(1956)* 75 ——Brunette character actress from Broadway who had a supporting role in Norma Talmadge's *The Battle Cry of Peace* ('15).

LEAHY, MARGARET *(1967)* 64 ——Brunette actress who won a beauty contest in England (sponsored by the Talmadge sisters) and a trip to Hollywood; Buster Keaton gave her the femme lead in his first ('23) full-length comedy feature, *The Three Ages*; in a few other silents, she retired to become an interior decorator.

LEASE, REX *(1966)* 65 ——Handsome actor, who, after years as an extra, became a star opposite Sharon Lynn in 1927's *Clancy's Kosher Wedding*; many more pre-talkies: *The College Hero, Broadway Daddies, Making the Varsity, Queen of the Chorus*, etc.; after 1929's *The Younger Generation*, his best serious role, in numerous mysteries *(Chinatown After Dark)* and drawing-room dramas *(When Dreams Come True)*; experienced in Westerns, too, he next went into them full-time, starring in many *(The Utah Kid, The Lone Trail*, etc.); his last stint as a star was in the '36 serial *Custer's Last Stand*, after which he played the hero's buddy, and then the worst of villains, in dozens of B Westerns and serials *(The Lone Ranger Rides Again, Daredevils of the West, The Crimson Ghost*, and the last serial made, 1956's *Perils of the Wilderness*—as a good guy, a Canadian Mountie).

LEAVITT, DOUGLAS *(1960)* 73 ——Character in Columbia pix of the '40s: *You Were Never Lovelier* (as actress Isobel Elsom's Argentinian husband, Juan Castro); *Reveille with Beverly, Two Senoritas from Chicago*, etc.

LE BARGY, CHARLES *(1936)* 77 ——In early French silents, he starred *(La Tosca,* '09) and directed *(The Return of Ulysses,* '08).

LEBEDEFF, IVAN *(1953)* 54 ——From Lithuania, he was black-haired, cultured, dapper, and dangerous; early in his Hollywood career, it was expected that he would become the "new" Valentino, after playing the gigolo who seduced Swanson in *The Loves of Sunya*; instead, he became one of the screen's smoothest

bad guys; in *China Seas* (Ngah), *The Shanghai Gesture* (The Gambler), *Conquest, Passport to Alcatraz, History Is Made at Night*, etc.

LE BLANC, GEORGETTE *(1941)* 65 ——Star of France's *L'Inhumaine* ('23).

LE BRANDT, GERTRUDE *(1955)* 92 ——Dowager in Constance Talmadge's *Mama's Affair* ('21).

LE BRUN, MINON *(1941)* 53 ——Actress-wife of Cullen Landis; few minor roles.

LEDERER, GRETCHEN *(1955)* 64 ——Buxom brunette who starred in many for Vitagraph, from 1909, and later was in several for Universal including *A Kentucky Cinderella*.

LEDUC, CLAUDINE *(1969)* ——Minor support in *The Song of Bernadette*, others.

LEE, AURIOL *(1941)* 50s ——English actress who, in her only screen appearance, contributed vividly to the suspense in Hitchcock's *Suspicion* as Isobel Sedbusk, a lady mystery-story writer.

LEE, BELINDA *(1961)* 26 ——Lovely, busty, ash-blonde English star; in many: *The Belles of St. Trinian's, Eye-Witness, Joseph and His Brethren, The Devil's Choice, The Secret Place*, etc.

LEE, BRUCE *(1973)* 32 ——Chinese-American actor, on TV as Kato in *The Green Hornet* series, who became a cult figure in the '70s as the Kung Fu king-pin in *Enter the Dragon*, etc., with a movie being made about him after his death.

LEE, CANADA *(1952)* 45 ——Black actor from Broadway who gave superlative screen performances in four: *Lifeboat* (dignified, courageous steward, Joe), *Body and Soul* (inarticulate boxing champion, defeated by Garfield, who finally dies slugging in a deserted ring), *Lost Boundaries* (Lt. Thompson) and *Cry, the Beloved Country* (profoundly moving in the leading role, as the old African Anglican priest whose cherished son commits murder and is doomed).

LEE, DIXIE *(1952)* 41 ——Perky blonde singer-actress with sparkling brown eyes who had ingenue leads in many early talkies: *Let's Go Places, Cheer Up and Smile, Happy Days, Harmony at Home*, etc.; married Bing Crosby in '30 and temporarily retired for childbirth; came back in '34 for *Love in Bloom, Redheads on Parade*, and *Manhattan Love Song*, then retired permanently.

LEE, DUKE R. *(1959)* 78 ——Support in many silent Westerns *(Just Tony, The Western Wallop, The White Outlaw,* etc.) and serials *(In the Days of Buffalo Bill,* in which he was the title character, *Vanishing Trails,* where he did memorable work as the criminal mastermind, others).

LEE, EARL *(1955)* 69 ——Was the oldest of the radiation-attack survivors in Arch Oboler's sci-fi pic *Five;* also in *Geraldine, The Story of Will Rogers,* etc.

LEE, ETTA *(1956)* 50 ——In Fairbanks' *The Thief of Bagdad,* was the #2 beauty (after Princess Julanne Johnston); also in Leatrice Joy's *A Tale of Two Worlds, The Sheik,* Colman's *A Thief in Paradise,* Monte Blue's *Recompense,* others of the '20s.

LEE, FLORENCE *(1962)* 74 ——The principal supporting actress in *City Lights,* she had previously been in many in the '20s: *Mary of the Movies, The Little Buckaroo, Luck and Sand,* etc.

LEE, GWEN *(1961)* 50s ——A Wampas Baby Star of '28, she arrived at MGM simultaneously with Shearer and Crawford, but, while in two dozen *(His Secretary, Orchids and Ermine, Show Girl,* etc.), never got her colleagues' breaks; as film historian Richard Griffith noted in *The Movie Stars:* "Gwen Lee must indeed have been heartsick when she was let out after six years at Metro-Goldwyn-Mayer. Her wisecracking chorines brightened up many a dull picture, and everyone agreed that she was a natural to play Lorelei Lee in *Gentlemen Prefer Blondes.* But she could play neither that part nor any other lead. She was too tall for romantic roles, and no amount of camera trickery could alter or disguise the fact"; last in 1933's *Corruption*—still the hard-boiled dame.

LEE, GYPSY ROSE *(1970)* 56 ——A multi-talented brunette beauty; the stage's #1 stripper, she had movie careers under two different names; as Louise Hovick (real name), she was a comedienne in many in the '30s: *Ali Baby Goes to Town; Sally, Irene and Mary; My Lucky Star,* etc.; as Gypsy Rose Lee, had star roles, from 1944's *Belle of the Yukon,* in *Doll Face, Babes in Bagdad, Wind Across the Everglades,* then top support in *The Stripper* and *The Trouble with Angels* (as a nun); wrote *The G-String Murders* (Stanwyck starred in it as *Lady of Burlesque)* and the autobiographical *Gypsy,* basis of the musical and the movie, in which Natalie Wood played Gypsy Rose Lee; was last the hostess of a TV talk show.

LEE, HARRY *(1932)* 60 ——Support in action pix of the '20s: *Channing of the Northwest, Men*

of Steel, Boomerang Bill, Bucking the Tiger, etc.

LEE, HENRY *(1910)* 53 ——Produced and appeared in early travelogs.

LEE, JANE *(1957)* 45 ——Dark-haired child star, with younger blonde sister Katherine, in Fox silents; were billed "Two Little Imps"; on-screen from 1914's *Neptune's Daughter,* they were in *Soul of Broadway* with Valeska Suratt, *Doing Our Bit,* in which they shamed the grownups into making sacrifices during WW I, *Smiles,* another wartime drama, others.

LEE, JENNIE *(1925)* 75 ——A 1917 magazine article hailed this trouping elder as "Mother of Many," for she had been in many *(The Birth of a Nation, His Mother's Son, Her Mother's Oath,* etc.) and continued to be in the '20s (in Tom Mix's *North of Hudson Bay,* Buck Jones' *The Big Punch, Hearts of Oak,* and T. Roy Barnes' *Young Ideas).*

LEE, JOHN *(1965)* 67 ——Support in Donald Pleasence's *Dr. Crippen.*

LEE, LILA *(1973)* 68 ——Demure black-eyed brunette who began with Famous Players-Lasky in the teens and starred in many; in *Blood and Sand* with Valentino, *Such a Little Pirate* with Harrison Ford, *The Dictator* with Wallace Reid, *Male and Female* opposite Thomas Meighan, *The Heart of Youth,* more silents; in talkies, was the pickpocket reformed by love in *The Unholy Three* with Lon Chaney, and in *Drag* with Barthelmess, *The Gorilla, The Sacred Flame, Faces in the Sky,* etc., through 1936's *The Ex-Mrs. Bradford,* in which—by then blonde—she was support to Jean Arthur; starred onstage in '25 in *Edgar Allan Poe* (a flop into which she and star-husband James Kirkwood had put $100,000 of their own money) and, successfully, in the '30s (in *Lady Jane)* and '40s *(Kiss and Tell);* last appeared in TV soap operas; son James Kirkwood Jr. wrote the '75 hit Broadway musical *A Chorus Line.*

LEE, MARGO *(1951)* ——Was featured in Paul Henreid's *So Young, So Bad.*

LEE, RAYMOND *(1974)* 64 ——Jackie Coogan (with an assist from Chaplin) gave this little movie bully a black eye in *The Kid;* Chaplin also used him—one of his favorite child actors —in *A Day's Pleasure* (Coogan made his debut in this 1919 pic) and *The Pilgrim* (was the little boy in church who applauded at the end of the David-and-Goliath sermon delivered by escaped con Chaplin, thought by the townspeople to be their new minister); became a movie historian, writing *The Films of Mary Pickford,* among other books.

LEE, SAMMY *(1968)* 77 ——Comic support in *The Gracie Allen Murder Mystery;* was the choreographer of *The Hollywood Revue of 1929* and *New Faces of 1937.*

LEE, SYLVAN *(1962)* 56 ——Support in the Marx Brothers' *The Cocoanuts.*

LE GUERE, GEORGE *(1947)* 76 ——Curly-haired leading man in silents at Metro, Famous Players, Universal, etc.; starred in *The Seven Deadly Sins, The Soul of a Woman,* many more.

LEHR, LEW *(1950)* 64 ——Fox Movietone's cockeyed comic narrator ("Monkies is the kwaziest people").

LEHRMAN, HENRY *(1946)* 60 ——An early movie comedian, for Sennett and others, in *A Beast at Bay, As the Bells Rang Out, A Busted Johnny;* quickly became a director (of Chaplin in his first four Keystone comedies; *Kid Auto Races at Venice, Between Showers, Making a Living, Mabel's Strange Predicament),* and producer of two-reel comedies.

LEIBER, FRITZ *(1949)* 57 ——Of the ascetic visage and shock of snow-white hair, this distinguished Shakespearean actor appeared in many of Hollywood's most distinguished films from Theda Bara's *Cleopatra* in '17 (as Julius Caesar, and, that early, still dark-haired); in talkies was capital support in: *A Tale of Two Cities* (Gaspard), *The Story of Louis Pasteur* (Dr. Charbonnet), *All This and Heaven Too* (Abbe), *The Sea Hawk, The Hunchback of Notre Dame* (Old Nobleman), *The Phantom of the Opera, The Spanish Main* (Bishop), *Humoresque, Another Part of the Forest,* more.

LEIGH, FRANK *(1948)* 60s ——English actor; support in American movies from the teens: in Tom Moore's *Lord and Lady Algy,* Norma Talmadge's *Ashes of Vengeance,* Jack Pickford's *The Hill Billy,* Matt Moore's *His Majesty Bunker Bean;* onscreen through 1942's *The Black Swan,* in which he was a sea captain.

LEIGH, GEORGE *(1957)* 69 ——Support in *Champagne for Caesar* and *Dial M for Murder,* in which he portrayed William.

LEIGH, NELSON *(1967)* 53 ——Supporting actor in many between '44 and '63: *Follow the Boys, Louisiana Hayride, Thief of Damascus, The Saracen Blade, Bombers B-52, These Thousand Hills,* etc.; offscreen in Hollywood, he was well known for his moving portrayal— many seasons in succession—of Christ in the annual Pilgrimage Play.

LEIGH, VIVIEN *(1967)* 52 ——So rare—such artistry encased in the most exquisite Dresden;

from England, she won her first Best Actress Academy Award as Scarlett O'Hara, ensuring everlasting screen fame, in *Gone With the Wind;* it is little noted that in the English film preceding this, *Sidewalks of London,* her spitfire role was a direct antecedent to Scarlett; won her second Oscar (her only other nomination), again playing a Southern woman, for 1951's *A Streetcar Named Desire;* was first introduced to American audiences in Robert Taylor's made-in-England *A Yank at Oxford* (as the vivacious, flirtatious wife of an Oxford bookstore owner); onscreen in just eight after GWTW: *Waterloo Bridge* (fine performance, generally underrated, as Taylor's tragic ballerina-to-prostitute love), *That Hamilton Woman* (her only "American" film opposite husband Laurence Olivier; they had met while making 1937's *Fire Over England), Caesar and Cleopatra, Anna Karenina* (pallid in comparison with Garbo's), *A Streetcar Named Desire* (in which she had starred on the London stage), *The Deep Blue Sea, The Roman Spring of Mrs. Stone, Ship of Fools;* was offscreen for long periods because of stage work (thought of herself as primarily a stage actress) and illness—tuberculosis, a major contributing factor to her death.

LEIGHTON, LILLIAN *(1956)* 81 ——A major character actress from 1911's *The Two Orphans* (driving poor "orphan" Kathlyn Williams into the snowy streets, this old hag shrieked—silently—"You must sing, I'll do the begging"); in many silents: *Cinderella* (mean stepmother to star Mabel Taliaferro), Jackie Coogan's *Peck's Bad Boy,* Edward Everett Horton's *Ruggles of Red Gap,* etc.; in talkies was onscreen through a '36 Tracy-Loy pic, *Whipsaw.*

LEISEN, MITCHELL *(1972)* 74 ——Famous director of many including *Hold Back the Dawn,* in which he played the supporting role of Mr. Saxon.

LEISTER, FREDERICK *(1970)* 85 ——British character actor; Masham in the original *Goodbye, Mr. Chips;* also in *Quartet* ("The Kite" segment), *So Well Remembered, The Prime Minister, The Captive Heart, Dear Octopus,* etc.

LE MAIRE, GEORGE *(1930)* 45 ——Support in Virginia Browne Faire's *The Circus Kid;* also starred in numerous early talkie shorts.

LE MAIRE, WILLIAM *(1933)* 40 ——Brother of George; supporting roles: convicts (*I Am a Fugitive from a Chain Gang*), rustics (*Cabin in the Cotton*), cowboys (Richard Arlen's *The Light of the Western Stars, The Painted Desert,* etc.).

LE MOYNE, CHARLES *(1956)* 76 ——Western support in the '20s; in Harry Carey's *Desert*

Driven, Hoot Gibson's *Headin' West*, Buck Jones' *The Rough Shod*, many more.

LEMUELS, WILLIAM *(1953)* 62 ——After numerous shorts with James Barton, support in one RKO comedy, *His Family Tree*.

LENGLEN, SUZANNE *(1938)* 39 ——Tennis champion from France who was in occasional sports shorts.

LENIHAN, WINIFRED *(1964)* 65 ——Broadway star (of 1923's *Saint Joan* and others) who was onscreen just once, in a supporting role in Franchot Tone's *Jigsaw*.

LENROW, BERNARD *(1963)* 60 ——Character in *The Violators* starring Arthur O'Connell.

LEON, CONNIE *(1955)* 74 ——Character actress who had small roles in many of Hollywood's "English" pix; in *Mrs. Miniver* was Lady Beldon's (Dame May Whitty's) maid Simpson; similar roles in *Love Letters, This Above All, Anna and the King of Siam, The Little Princess, Hangover Square*, etc.

LEONARD, ARCHIE *(1959)* 42 ——Support in Dick Powell's *Mrs. Mike*, others.

LEONARD, DAVID *(1967)* 75 ——Character (Emile Bernard) in *Lust for Life;* earlier in 1933's *Victims of Persecution* (which he wrote), *Captain Carey U.S.A., Song of My Heart*, etc.

LEONARD, EDDIE *(1941)* 70 ——Minstrel actor who starred in one for Universal, a '29 talkie, *Melody Lane*, receiving a harsh critical reception ("The world seems full of clowns with breaking hearts. Eddie Leonard brings no vitality to a dead yarn"); later he had a supporting role in the same studio's *If I Had My Way*.

LEONARD, GUS *(1939)* 83 ——Comic support from France, on American screens from the teens; in Harold Lloyd's *The Lonesome Luke,* Charles Ray's *The Deuce of Spades,* William Powell's *Times Have Changed*, Laurel & Hardy's *Babes in Toyland*, more.

LEONARD, JACK E. *(1973)* 61 ——Big (300 lbs.), bald Broadway comedian who got big laughs with his insult jokes; onscreen in Jane Powell's *Three Sailors and a Girl*.

LEONARD, JAMES *(1930)* 62 ——Support in silents: Ralph Graves' *The Cheer Leader,* Johnny Hines' *All Aboard*, etc.

LEONARD, MARION *(1956)* 75 ——Beautiful actress noted for her strong resemblance to Sarah Bernhardt, who, with Florence Auer, was one of Biograph's first leading ladies; starred in many early silents—often directed by Griffith: *At the Crossroads of Life, The Sealed Room, The Seed of the Fathers, Comato the Sioux, In Old California, Carmen* ('13), *The Dragon's Claw, The Lonely Villa* (Pickford played her daughter in this in her first week at Biograph), etc.

LEONARD, MURRAY *(1970)* 72 ——Burlesque comedian featured in *A Thousand and One Nights*, Frankie Laine's *Bring Your Smile Along*, others.

LEONARD, ROBERT Z. *(1968)* 78 ——Without the "Z" he starred in many early silents *(Robinson Crusoe, The Primeval Test*, etc.); later a famous MGM director (*Ziegfeld Girl, Week-End at the Waldorf*, others); was married to stars Gertrude Olmstead and Mae Murray.

LEONE, HENRY *(1922)* 64 ——Starred in 1914's *A Passover Miracle* (billed Henri), had supporting roles in Enrico Caruso's *My Cousin* and Alice Brady's *The Ordeal of Rosetta*.

LEONIDOV, LEONID *(1941)* ——Noted actor who starred and gave an excellent portrayal as Ivan IV in Russia's *Ivan the Terrible,* a.k.a. *Wings of a Serf* ('26); the following year, he starred in a dual role—the governor and the rabbi—in the Soviet film *Seeds of Freedom*.

LE PAUL, PAUL *(1958)* 57 ——Magician-actor; in Loretta Young's *Eternally Yours*.

LE SAINT, EDWARD *(1940)* 69 ——Versatile gray-haired character; usually dignified: Judge Rankin in *Jesse James,* the ship-captain father of heroine Cecilia Parker in the serial *The Lost Jungle,* and rancher-dads of leading ladies in dozens of B Westerns; could be pompously funny too, as when, in round specs and graduation gown, he was a Huxley College colleague of Groucho Marx in *Horse Feathers;* also a director (of Wallace Reid in *The Squaw Man's Son*, others); was billed variously: Edward J., Ed, and E. J.

LE SAINT, STELLA *(1948)* 67 ——Featured in a George O'Brien silent, *Three Bad Men*.

LESLEY, CAROLE *(1974)* 38 ——Lovely femme lead in many British pix: *Doctor in Love, Three on a Spree, Those Dangerous Years*, etc.

LESLIE, EDITH *(1973)* 70s ——Six-foot-two character actress; in *Green Dolphin Street* (Sister Angelique), *Pufnstuf, Bedknobs and Broomsticks*, more.

684

LESLIE, GENE *(1953)* 48 ——Minor supporting actor; in *Holiday in Mexico, Duel in the Sun, The Gay Senorita, The Spanish Main,* etc.

LESLIE, NOEL *(1974)* 85 ——Character actor; minor roles.

LESTER, LOUISE *(1952)* 85 ——Beginning in '11, this character star—reminiscent of Marjorie Main—headlined in the American ("Flying A") Film Company's "Calamity Anne" comedy series; in the '20s was support in *Gallopin' On,* May McAvoy's *Her Reputation,* etc.

LE STRANGE, DICK *(1963)* 73 ——Major support in several early DeMille silent features; in 1914's *The Squaw Man* (was Grouchy), *What's His Name* (Best Man at the runaway lovers' wedding), *The Girl of the Golden West* (Senor Slim); support in many Westerns of the '20s: Hoot Gibson's *The Silent Rider, Desert Dust, Thunder Riders,* etc.; sometimes billed La Strange; became, as L'Estrange, the assistant producer of *The Cisco Kid Returns,* others.

L'ESTRANGE, JULIAN *(1918)* 40 ——Dark-haired actor who co-starred with Pauline Frederick in three in a row in '15: *Sold, Bella Donna,* and *Zaza.*

LE SUEUR, HAL *(1963)* 59 ——Handsome actor-brother of Joan Crawford; minor roles such as Millard in Gable's *Mutiny on the Bounty.*

LETONDAL, HENRI *(1955)* 52 ——Character in dignified roles: *Come to the Stable* (Father Barraud), *Apartment for Peggy* (Professor Pavin), *Monkey Business* (Siegfried Kitzel), *On the Riviera* (Louis Foral), many others.

LEVANT, OSCAR *(1972)* 65 ——Famous pianist and scathing wit; was found around the keyboard, with saturnine look and dangling cigarette, in many: *An American in Paris, Rhapsody in Blue, Kiss the Boys Goodbye, Humoresque, The Band Wagon, The Barkleys of Broadway,* etc.

LE VINESS, CARL *(1964)* 79 ——Character in Patsy Ruth Miller's *Twin Beds.*

LEWIS, CATHY *(1968)* 50 ——Dark-haired, top-caliber radio actress, best known as Marie Wilson's pal in *My Friend Irma;* early in her career, as Catherine, had a supporting role in Van Heflin's *Kid Glove Killer;* later, as Cathy, was in *The Devil at 4 O'Clock* and June Havoc's *The Story of Molly X.*

LEWIS, FRED *(1927)* 67 ——Support in E. H. Sothern's *An Enemy to the King* ('16).

LEWIS, FREDERICK *(1946)* 73 ——Support in *The Moral Sinner* ('24); earlier ('16), he wrote the story of the Henry B. Walthall serial *The Strange Case of Mary Page.*

LEWIS, HARRY *(1950)* 64 ——Was thug Toots Bass in *Key Largo;* also support in *The Unsuspected, Gun Crazy, Deadly Is the Female,* others; had been onscreen in the '20s in Jack Mulhall's *God Gave Me Twenty Cents,* etc.

LEWIS, IDA *(1935)* 86 ——Bulky character actress first in Lois Wilson's *The Bells* (the domineering mother), then in many in the '20s: Charles Ray's *Some Punkins* and *Sweet Adeline, A Man's Man,* etc.; last played Lombard's grandmother in 1932's *Sinners in the Sun.*

LEWIS, JAMES *(1928)* 70s ——Character in the silent *The Broken Violin.*

LEWIS, JOE *(1938)* 40 ——Support in several at 20th Century-Fox: Loretta Young's *Private Number* (as Smiley Watson), Jane Withers' *The Holy Terror,* etc.; not the prizefight champ.

LEWIS, JOE E. *(1971)* 69 ——Famous nightclub star whose run-in with real-life gangsters almost cost him his life, as was detailed when Sinatra portrayed him in *The Joker Is Wild;* was onscreen himself in 1942's *Private Buckaroo.*

LEWIS, MARY *(1941)* 41 ——Metropolitan Opera singer who was in Christie comedies in the '20s and a Vitagraph short (Mary Lewis in *Way Down South*).

LEWIS, MEADE LUX *(1964)* 58 ——Famous boogie-woogie jazz pianist; onscreen in *New Orleans.*

LEWIS, MITCHELL *(1956)* 76 ——Ruggedly handsome silent star; in *The Barrier* ('17), the serial *The Million Dollar Mystery, Safe for Democracy, The Siren Call, The Spoilers, The Bar Sinister,* 1922's *Salome* (co-starred with Nazimova), many more leads; became a major character actor, in silents (*Ben-Hur,* as Ilderim, *The Sea Wolf, Old Ironsides,* etc.) and talkies (1931's *The Squaw Man,* as Indian Tabywanna, *A Tale of Two Cities,* as Ernest Defarge, *The Bohemian Girl,* etc.); an MGM contract character actor from '37 and was in dozens: *Waikiki Wedding, Rio Rita, Billy the Kid, Courage of Lassie,* etc., through 1953's *All the Brothers Were Valiant;* one of Hollywood's more distinguished citizens, he was a founder and chairman of the executive board of the Motion Picture Relief Fund.

LEWIS, RALPH *(1937)* 65 ——Noted character actor onscreen from '12; in many early Griffith films: 1914's *The Escape* (as the Senator), *The Avenging Conscience* (the detective), *The Birth of a Nation* (Lillian Gish's father, Stoneman), *Intolerance* (in the Modern Story was the Governor who reprieved Bobby Harron at the last minute); two dozen more silents; in talkies: *Abraham Lincoln, The Lost City, Sucker Money, Mystery Liner,* etc.

LEWIS, RICHARD *(1935)* 66 ——Character in such silents of the '20s as *Stick to Your Story* and *Yankee Speed.*

LEWIS, SHELDON *(1958)* 89 ——Was as good as they come when it comes to being bad; one of the movies' first full-fledged major villains; was evil Pierre Frochard, who kidnapped blind Dorothy Gish and forced her to beg, in *Orphans of the Storm;* was the tall slim menace who threatened Pearl White in two serials *(The Exploits of Elaine,* as her lawyer, and *The Iron Claw),* Leah Baird in *Wolves of Kultur,* and Ruth Hiatt in *The Chinatown Mystery;* starred in *The Ticket of Leave Man* ('14), in the title role(s) in *Dr. Jekyll and Mr. Hyde* ('16); in dozens more silents; continued to be villainously active in talkies: horror films *(The Monster Walks),* Westerns *(Tombstone Canyon),* and serials *(Terry of the Times,* but here, in his last serial, in a dual role, he was the good guy *and* the bad guy; last onscreen in a '36 Western, *The Cattle Thief.*

LEWIS, TED *(1971)* 80 ——Famous "Me and My Shadow" song-dance man; with cane and crushed top hat in *Is Everybody Happy?* (his catch-phrase), *Manhattan Merry-Go-Round, Show of Shows, Hold That Ghost, Here Comes the Band.*

LEWIS, TOM *(1927)* 63 ——Character; Marion Davies' father in both *Enchantment* and *Adam and Eva;* Keaton's Mate in *Steamboat Bill Jr.;* in others of the '20s: *The Great White Way, Passers By,* etc.

LEWIS, VERA *(1956)* 80s ——Hatchet-faced character actress, wife of actor Ralph Lewis; was with him in her first, *Intolerance* (in the Modern Story was Mary T. Jenkins); in dozens of silents: *Peg o' My Heart, Long Live the King, Resurrection, Ramona, Ella Cinders, Stella Dallas,* etc.; in even more talkies: *The Iron Mask* (was Mme. Perrone), *The Home Towners* (Mrs. Calhoun), *Way Down East, Four Daughters* and its sequels (Mrs. Ridgefield in each), *The Cat Creeps,* etc.

LEYSSAC, PAUL *(1946)* 60s ——Danish character in one Hollywood pic, Elisabeth Bergner's *Paris Calling* ('42), after several in England: *Victoria the Great, Head Over Heels in Love,* others.

LIBBEY, J. ALDRICH *(1925)* 53 ——Supporting actor in *Greed.*

LICHO, EDGAR *(1944)* 68——Actor from Russia; minor support (Anton) in *Days of Glory* and in *The Seventh Cross;* more prominent in the German silent *Loves of Jeanne Ney.*

LIEBMANN, HANS *(1960)* 64 ——Half of the dance team of "Harold and Lola," featured in *Variety Time, Pan-Americana,* etc.

LIEDTKE, HARRY *(1945)* 60s ——Handsome German actor who played the romantic lead (Ramphis) in Lubitsch's 1922 Ufa spectacle *The Loves of Pharaoh;* star of many others including *Gypsy Blood, Forbidden Love,* and *I Kiss Your Hand, Madame* with Dietrich as his young leading lady; died in Germany in an air raid.

LIEVEN, ALBERT *(1971)* 65 ——Prussian-born character actor; in *The Guns of Navarone* (Commandant, Capt. Muesel), *The Victors,* and numerous English movies: *Sleeping Car to Trieste, The Seventh Veil, Jeannie, The Life and Death of Colonel Blimp,* etc.

LIGHTNER, WINNIE *(1971)* 71 ——Warners' raucous star-comedienne, of the modified Betty Boop hairstyle, famous for the uninhibited vulgarity of her clowning; starred first in 1929's *The Gold Diggers of Broadway,* the first all-color, all-talkie musical; many others: *She Couldn't Say No, Show of Shows, Sit Tight, The Life of the Party* (she always was), *Gold Dust Gertie,* etc.; short career: last had a supporting role in Crawford's *Dancing Lady* ('33).

LIGON, GROVER *(1965)* 80 ——Character-comedian; last onscreen in Lewis Stone's *Father's Son* ('30), after a long career that began with Biograph in '11 and included such silents as *A Maiden's Trust.*

LILLARD, CHARLOTTE *(1946)* 102 ——Minor roles in *Marie Antoinette,* Edmund Lowe's *The Great Impersonation,* etc., after a career that began with Edison Films in '10.

LINCOLN, ELMO *(1952)* 63 ——Part of screen history for being the first Tarzan *(Tarzan of the Apes,* '18); played the role twice more: *The Romance of Tarzan, The Adventures of Tarzan;* a professional strong-man, he'd earlier had a small role in *The Birth of a Nation* and a more arresting one in *Intolerance* (in the "Babylonian Story," was The Mighty Man of Valor, the Chaldean warrior who lopped off heads); from '19 was one of Universal's great serial stars: *Elmo the Mighty, Elmo the Fearless, The Flaming Disc,* etc.; also in many features in the '20s: *Rupert of Hentzau, Whom Shall I Marry, Un-*

der Crimson Skies, others; in retirement for almost two decades, he returned for a minor role in 1949's *Tarzan's Magic Fountain*, then had bits in three more: *The Iron Man*, *The Hollywood Story* (as himself), and *Carrie*.

LINDER, ALFRED *(1957)* 50s ——Was a German villain (Klaen) in *The House on 92nd Street*, and another (Hans Feinkl) in *13 Rue Madeleine*; also in *I Was a Male War Bride* (bartender), *Canon City*, others.

LINDER, MAX *(1925)* 42 ——Dapper, enormously popular French comedian whose style greatly influenced Chaplin; French comedies such as *Max*, *Toreador* and *Max and His Mother-in-Law* (both '11), plus his fame as an ace pilot in WW I, made him an idol in his homeland; when Chaplin departed Essanay the company brought Linder to America to replace him; starred for Essanay in *Max Comes Across*, *Max Wants a Divorce*, then for other companies in *Be My Wife*, *Seven Years Bad Luck*, and *The Three Must-Get-Theres* (all of which he also wrote and directed), after which he returned to France.

LINDO, OLGA *(1968)* 69 ——English-Norwegian character; dowager type; had the top femme role in *An Inspector Calls*; also in *Sapphire*, *Bedelia*, others.

LINDSAY, HOWARD *(1968)* 78 ——Broadway playwright-star (*Life with Father*) who was onscreen in *The Big Broadcast of 1938*.

LINDSAY, LEX *(1971)* 70 ——Featured in an early Fox talkie, *Sob Sister*.

LINGHAM, THOMAS *(1950)* 75 ——Entire supporting career, from '13, was in serials (*The Adventures of Ruth*, *The Vanishing Dagger*, *The Lost Express*, etc.) and Westerns (*Sky High Corral*, *The Desert Pirate*, and many more through *Pals of the Prairie* in '29).

LINLEY, BETTY *(1951)* 61 ——English; character (Mrs. Montgomery) in *The Heiress*.

LINN, BUD *(1968)* 59 ——Of Ken Darby's King's Men quartet; group (as G.I.s) harmonized with "Fibber McGee" in a troop train scene in *Heavenly Days*, and impersonated the Marx Bros. in *Honolulu*.

LINN, MARGARET *(1973)* 39 ——Brunette who had small roles in *Klute* and *Puzzle of a Downfall Child*.

LION, LEON M. *(1947)* 68 ——British actor who played the leading role (Ben) in Hitchcock's *Number Seventeen* ('32); was also in *Man With 100 Faces*.

LISTER, FRANCIS *(1951)* 52 ——Smooth English character actor who played Captain Nelson in Gable's *Mutiny on the Bounty* and the Duke of Orleans in *Henry V*; many British pix: *Atlantic*, *Clive of India*, *The Wicked Lady*, etc.

LITEL, JOHN *(1972)* 77 ——The screen's legal profession would not have been the same without this stalwart character; was the attorney dad of Jimmy Lydon in all nine of his "Henry Aldrich" pix, and lawyers in many more; of his 150 roles, he was outstanding in *The Life of Emile Zola* (as Charpentier), *Jezebel*, *Black Legion*, *Marked Woman*, *Dodge City*, *My Bill*, *The Amazing Dr. Clitterhouse*, *Cass Timberlane*, etc.; last onscreen in *Nevada Smith* ('66), he also made guest appearances in TV series (*The Virginian*, *I Love Lucy*) in his later years.

LITTLE, BILLY *(1967)* 72 ——One of the leads in Sol Lesser's one-of-a-kind all-midget Western, *Terror of Tiny Town* ('38); also in *Men in Black*, *The Side Show*, other features, plus shorts.

LITTLE, JAMES *(1969)* 62 ——Comedian-support in Dan Dailey's *Taxi*.

LITTLE, LITTLE JACK *(1956)* 55 ——Bandleader-singer who wasn't, but was in musical shorts.

LITTLE BOZO *(1952)* 45 ——The clown in the Marx Brothers' *At the Circus*; also in *The Sign of the Cross*, Johnny Hines' *White Pants Willie*, *Freaks*.

LITTLEFIELD, LUCIEN *(1960)* 64 ——Moustachioed, high-domed character (with the rest of his hair plastered firmly down) who made an excellent grouchy high school teacher in the "Henry Aldrich" movies (both Cooper's and Lydon's); in scores from '21, most often as a meek, wizened little man; in *Babbitt*, *The Man I Killed*, *Shopworn*, *Ruggles of Red Gap*, *If I Had a Million*, *The Gladiator*, *The Little Foxes*, *Mr. and Mrs. North*, etc., through '58.

LIVESEY, JACK *(1961)* 60 ——Starred in England's *The Passing of the Third Floor Back* ('35); many British pix: *Penny Paradise*, *The Wandering Jew*, *Rembrandt*, etc.; support in two American comedies: Doris Day's *That Touch of Mink* (as Dr. Richardson) and Kim Novak's *The Notorious Landlady*.

LIVESEY, SAM *(1936)* 63 ——Character actor-father of Jack (and Roger); numerous English films: *The Private Life of Henry VIII* (the English executioner), *Young Woodley*, *Elizabeth of England*, *The Dreyfus Case*, *Wings of the Morning*, etc.

LLEWELLYN, FEWLASS *(1941)* 75 ——Supported Fay Compton in 1923's *This Freedom.*

LLOYD, DORIS *(1968)* 68 ——Fine supporting actress from England, in dozens from the mid-'20s: *Sarah and Son* (took Chatterton's child away from her), 1930's *Disraeli* (Mrs. Travers, the spy) and *Charley's Aunt* (Donna Lucia), 1932's *Back Street* (John Boles' upper-crust wife), 1933's *Oliver Twist* (Nancy Sykes), *Tovarich, The Plough and the Stars, The Letter, The Constant Nymph, The Lodger, Journey for Margaret, My Name Is Julia Ross*, etc., through Rosalind Russell's *Rosie* in '67.

LLOYD, FRANK *(1960)* 71 ——Oscar-winning director (*Cavalcade*) who had first starred in silents: *Damon and Pythias*, the serial *The Black Box*, etc.

LLOYD, FREDERICK *(1949)* 69 ——Character in English pix: *April Romance, The Battle of Gallipoli, Sleepless Nights*, etc.

LLOYD, GLADYS *(1971)* 75 ——Minor roles in the films of Edward G. Robinson, then her husband: *Smart Money* (cigar stand clerk), *Five Star Final* (secretary), *The Hatchet Man* (a Chinese girl, Fan Yi).

LLOYD, HAROLD *(1971)* 77 ——Silent comedies made him immortal and, deservedly, a multimillionaire—if for nothing else (and there was much else), for the hair-raisingly hilarious times he dangled from the hands of a clock ten stories above earth; his finest rib-ticklers in the '20s: *Safety Last, The Freshman, Grandma's Boy, The Kid Brother*; was no less grand in such early talkies as *Movie Crazy* and *Feet First*; made his screen debut—as a Yaqui Indian—in a now-forgotten Edison Films pic of '12, then had minor roles (as animals) in '13 in Frank L. Baum's "Wizard of Oz" films; his earliest comedy character was "Willie Work," succeeded by "Lonesome Luke" (moustache copied from Chaplin), whom he played in many dozens of one-reelers; then came the character that captivated the world—the smalltown innocent in the horn-rimmed (lensless) specs, endlessly chased by tigers, locomotives, cops, and natural disasters, but just as endlessly triumphant (and surprised to be) over them; retired after 1938's *Professor Beware*, one of his least successful comedies; came back in the '40s to make an ill-received comedy that was released twice, in '47 and '51, under two titles, *Mad Wednesday* and *The Sin of Harold Diddlebock*; a philanthropist of note, he was awarded in '52 a special Academy Award for being a "master comedian and good citizen."

LLOYD, HAROLD, JR. *(1971)* 39 ——Son of Harold and his "Lonesome Luke" leading lady, Mildred Harris, whom Lloyd Sr. married in '23; in 13 films from age 16, including *Our Very Own* and *Frankenstein's Daughter*; died of natural causes three months after his father.

LLOYD, JOHN *(1944)* 74 ——British actor who had a leading role in 1936's *The Last Journey.*

LLOYD, PATRICIA *(1969)* 34 ——Minor roles.

LLOYD, ROLLO *(1938)* 55 ——Character actor; was Napoleon Bonaparte in *Anthony Adverse*, the Ghazi in *The Lives of a Bengal Lancer*; onscreen only in the '30s, he was in many: *Private Scandal, Barbary Coast, The Devil Doll, Today We Live, Come and Get It*, etc.

LOBACK, MARVIN *(1938)* 42 ——Support in the Tom Mix silent *Hands Off.*

LOCHER, FELIX *(1969)* 87 ——The dad of Jon Hall, he had minor character roles in several from the late '50s on: *Frankenstein's Daughter, Thunder in the Sun, Curse of the Faceless Man*, etc.

LOCKERBEE, BETH *(1968)* 53 ——Canadian actress; was in *The Incredible Journey.*

LOCKHART, GENE *(1957)* 65 ——A sterling character actor whose jowly countenance often gave the impression of an angry pug; but he could play any role—doctors, lawyers, dads, guys as good as Santa or wicked as Satan; onscreen from 1934's *By Your Leave*, he was in more than 80: *Algiers* (as conniving Regis he received his only Oscar nomination as Best Supporting Actor), *Miracle on 34th Street* (Judge Harper who is finally convinced Edmund Gwenn is Kris Kringle), *Something to Sing About* (as Cagney's movie producer), *Abe Lincoln in Illinois* (as Stephen Douglas, and grand in the big debate sequence), *Meet John Doe* (Mayor Lovett), *The Sea Wolf* (Dr. Prescott), *His Girl Friday* (sheriff), etc., and, last, *Jeanne Eagles*, made in his final year.

LOCKLEAR, LIEUTENANT *(1920)* 28 —— Billed thusly, this actor-stunt pilot was in three: *The Great Air Robbery, The Skywayman, Cassidy of the Air Lanes.*

LOCKWOOD, HAROLD *(1918)* 31 ——Rugged and handsome, blond and blue-eyed, tanned and dimple-chinned, and engagingly extroverted, he was the all-American dream of every girl in America; a star from his first day before Rex Company cameras, as the valiant trapper in 1911's *A White Redman*, he was an ever-more-popular one through another 120 films; starred for many companies: Nestor, Ince, Selig, Famous Players, and finally Metro; was Mary Pickford's leading man in three: *Tess of the*

Storm Country, Hearts Adrift, and Such a Little Queen; achieved his greatest fame in 1916-17 when teamed with the lovely May Allison in a series of romantic dramas—22 in succession: The Secretary of Frivolous Affairs, The Great Question, The House of a Thousand Scandals, Pardoned, The End of the Road, etc.; so great was the popularity of this perfectly matched pair of screen lovers that they outdistanced Francis X. Bushman and Beverly Bayne at the box-office; died of influenza at the height of fame, his last three movies, without May Allison, and released posthumously (The Great Romance, Shadows of Suspicion, A Man of Honor), attracting vast audiences.

LOCKWOOD, KING (1971) 73 ——Minor support in The Man in the Gray Flannel Suit.

LOEB, PHILIP (1955) 61 ——Was Jake, husband of Molly Goldberg (Gertrude Berg), in the movie Molly; earlier in Room Service, A Double Life.

LOESSER, FRANK (1969) 58 ——Famous Broadway show composer (A Most Happy Fella); portrayed a character, Hair-Do Lempke, in Betty Hutton's Red, Hot and Blue.

LOFF, JEANETTE (1942) 36 ——Ingenue, with heart-shaped faced and long blonde hair worn Ann Harding style, popular in late silents and early talkies, particularly in "youth" pix: Hold 'Em Yale, The Sophomore, Annapolis, Party Girl; also in King of Jazz, the serial The Man Without a Face, etc.

LOFTUS, CECILIA (1943) 66 ——Stage actress from Scotland who was an early star in America (in 1913's A Lady of Quality for Famous Players, and in other silents), and in talkies was one of Hollywood's finer characters; in East Lynne, as Cornelia Carlyle, was the meanest of all to heroine Ann Harding; was the grandmother of Davis and Hopkins in The Old Maid, and of Shirley Temple (Granny Tyl) in The Blue Bird; also in The Black Cat, It's a Date; billed Cissie (her nickname) once, in 1939's Dress Parade.

LOGAN, ELLA (1969) 56 ——Short brunette singer with the most caressing Scottish burr in musical memory; most famous as a stage star (Finian's Rainbow) but memorable too in five screen appearances: The Goldwyn Follies (sang "I Was Doing Alright"), 52nd Street, Flying Hostess, Woman Chases Man, Top of the Town.

LOGAN, MAY (1969) 68 ——Actress-sister of Ella.

LOGAN, STANLEY (1953) 67 ——Polished English support in many Hollywood films: We

Are Not Alone (barrister Sir Guy Lockwood); With a Song in My Heart (diplomat); Wilson (Secretary Lansing); My Son, My Son; Three Strangers; Escape to Glory, many more.

LOHMAN, ZALLA (1967) 62 ——She did minor roles in silents.

LOMAS, HERBERT (1961) 74 ——Tall, haggard-faced character in "Hollywood" movies made in England: The Ghost Goes West (one of Donat's creditors), Knight Without Armour (Dietrich's father, Russian Minister of the Interior), Jamaica Inn; also in Rembrandt, Bonnie Prince Charlie, South Riding, more.

LOMAS, JACK (1959) 48 ——Support in Copper Sky, April in Paris, That Certain Feeling, Cattle Empire, etc.

LOMBARD, CAROLE (1942) 32 ——Wacky, wonderful blonde comedienne loved by Gable and all America—for her lack of inhibition, inspired zaniness, and, long before perishing on a War Bond-selling tour, unabashed patriotism; nominated for a Best Actress Oscar in My Man Godfrey, she deserved to be in still others: Nothing Sacred, Twentieth Century, comedies in which her nonpareil free-swinging style was at its zenith, and Vigil in the Night and They Knew What They Wanted, where she had vastly different "straight" roles and was superlative in each; onscreen from childhood (a bit in Monte Blue's A Perfect Crime when 12), she understood better than most every nuance of acting for the camera; this mastery of expression and voice, and the proper technique of the throwaway line, was in evidence in her every performance as a star; was portrayed in '76 by actress Jill Clayburgh in Universal's Lombard and Gable.

LOMBARDO, CARMEN (1971) 67 ——Guy's brother; was in Ray Milland's Many Happy Returns ('34), and composed the music for Johnny Downs' Thrill of a Lifetime.

LONDON, TOM (1963) 81 ——Western actor who had the longest career and, most sources agree, acted in more movies than any other player; was first in 1903's The Great Train Robbery (locomotive engineer, which he had been in real life) and last in Willard Parker's The Lone Texan in 1959; in between, many hundreds of cowboy pix; after numerous featured roles, he starred for Universal under his real name, Leonard Clapham, in dozens of 1919-23 Westerns; changed his name to Tom London in '24 and was an in-demand supporting actor in Westerns for the next four years; in '29 he again starred, in a series of cowboy pix for Pathe; thereafter was support—alternately sheriff, ranchers, or badmen—to every known cowboy star, and in almost every cowboy pic and more than a dozen serials; *High Noon,* in which he was a good guy, Sam, was his last major Western.

LONERGAN, LESTER *(1931)* 62 ——Was the judge in an early Muni pic, *Seven Faces.*

LONERGAN, LESTER, JR. *(1959)* 65 ——A Broadway leading man who had a supporting role (Cary) in Kazan's *Boomerang.*

LONG, FREDERIC *(1941)* 84 ——Character role in the silent ('29) *Lost Patrol.*

LONG, JOHNNY *(1972)* 58 ——Bandleader (of "Shanty Town" fame); onscreen with his orchestra in Abbott & Costello's *Hit the Ice.*

LONG, MERVYN HARRY *(1940)* 45 ——Minor support; in Bickford's *Queen of the Yukon.*

LONG, NICK, JR. *(1949)* 43 ——Dancer-son of Nick (who was in a Barthelmess silent, *Shore Leave*); was prominently featured in two: *Broadway Melody of 1936* (as young Basil Newcombe) and Warner Baxter's *King of Burlesque* (Anthony Lamb).

LONG, RICHARD *(1974)* 47 ——Dark-haired leading man, most of whose career was at Universal; was introduced, as Colbert's teenage son, in *Tomorrow Is Forever;* received major billing in many thereafter: *The Egg and I* and the first three "Ma and Pa Kettle" comedies (in which he was eldest Kettle son, Tom), *Willie & Joe Back at the Front, Tap Roots, Criss Cross, The Dark Mirror, All I Desire, Saskatchewan, Home from the Hill,* etc.; starred in four TV series: *Bourbon Street Beat, 77 Sunset Strip, The Big Valley,* and, at the time of his death, *Nanny and the Professor.*

LONG, WALTER *(1952)* 68 ——His evil, Roman-nosed face—frequently fitted out with a scraggly moustache or beard—carried him far, from '09; for years was Griffith's best badman in *The Birth of a Nation* (Gus, the renegade Negro, which of course he wasn't, who lusted after Little Sister, Mae Marsh, driving her to suicide), *Intolerance* (Musketeer of the Slums in "The Modern Story"), *Scarlet Days* (dance hall proprietor); twirled his moustache at Gish in *Sold for Marriage,* treated her despicably as the bull-necked Hun in *The Little American,* brawled with Valentino in *Moran of the Letty,* as bald Iron Head Joe tried to kill little Junior Coghlan aboard *The Yankee Clipper;* continued to be a bad guy in many in the '30s: *Naughty Marietta,* numerous B Westerns (*Bar 20 Justice, North of the Rio Grande,* etc.), comedies (Fields' *Six of a Kind, Pardon Us*—burly jailbird 31752 who terrified cellmates Laurel &

Hardy); in just two in the '40s, *City of Missing Girls* and a Monogram Western, *Silver Stallion.*

LONSDALE, H. G. *(1923)* ——Portrayed Lincoln in 1912's *The Fall of Black Hawk.*

LONTOC, LEON *(1974)* 50s ——Chinese actor with upsweep hairdo; usually villainous; in *Panic in the City, I Was an American Spy, The Gallant Hours.*

LOOS, THEODOR *(1954)* 71 ——One of the stars (King Gunther) of German *Siegfried* ('25); in *Manon Lescaut, The Weavers,* many other European films, including *Circus Girl,* released in America by Republic in '56.

LOPER, DON *(1972)* 66 ——Famous Hollywood choreographer; onscreen as the dancing partner of Rogers in *Lady in the Dark* and Henie in *It's a Pleasure,* and, as himself, in *Thousands Cheer.*

LORCH, THEODORE *(1947)* 74 ——Big bald character, with big nose, big chin, who was a big bad guy in many serials: Red Grange's *The Galloping Ghost* (as Mystery Man), Rin-Tin-Tin's *The Lightning Warrior* (La Farge), *Flash Gordon* (Ming's High Priest), *Dick Tracy;* in dozens of B Westerns (*Texas Bad Man,* etc.), when not a henchman, was the doting dad of heroines like Lucile Brown in *Cheyenne Rides Again.*

LORD, MARION *(1942)* 59 ——Support in two early talkies: Glenn Tryon's *Broadway* and John Boles' *One Heavenly Night* (also released as *The Queen of Scandal*).

LORD, PAULINE *(1950)* 60 ——Noted Broadway actress who starred—magnificently—in just two movies, neither worthy of her glory: *Mrs. Wiggs of the Cabbage Patch* ('34) and the tearjerking *A Feather in Her Hat.*

LORDE, ATHENA *(1973)* 57 ——Support in *Marjorie Morningstar, How to Frame a Figg, Fuzz,* many others.

LORNE, MARION *(1968)* 83 ——A dithery delight on TV (*The Garry Moore Show*), she was a character actress of restraint in *Strangers on a Train* (as the well-to-do mother of villainous Robert Walker, who wants Farley Granger to murder his dad); also in *The Graduate* and *The Girl Rush.*

LORRAINE, LILLIAN *(1955)* 63 ——A *Follies* beauty who played the femme lead in 1915's *Neal of the Navy.*

LORRE, PETER *(1964)* 59 ——Gentle-voiced little master villain whose girth in later years expanded to approximate his talent; made his masterpiece, *M,* portraying the child-molester, in Germany before coming to America; for a decade was Warners' quietly insidious menace; in *The Maltese Falcon* ('41), *Casablanca, The Mask of Dimitrios, Hotel Berlin, Passage to Marseille, The Beast With Five Fingers,* etc.; starred, most sympathetically, in 1941's *The Face Behind the Mask,* and, in a series of eight, as "Mr. Moto"; came, eventually, to caricature his frog-eyed, evil screen self in such pix as *Beat the Devil, The Big Circus, Voyage to Bottom of the Sea, The Patsy, Muscle Beach Party,* etc.; last did a walk-on in *Torn Curtain,* for whose director, Hitchcock, he had starred so menacingly in 1935's *The Man Who Knew Too Much.*

LOSEE, FRANK *(1937)* 81 ——Heavyset, gray, major character in many silents; in *Orphans of the Storm* (the Count), Marguerite Clark's *Uncle Tom's Cabin* (as Uncle Tom, in blackface), *Disraeli, Such a Little Queen, Hulda from Holland,* etc.; in few talkies: *Annapolis Farewell,* Barthelmess' *Four Hours to Kill,* etc.

LOTHAR, HANS *(1967)* 50s ——German character actor, Cagney's nervous aide (Schlemmer) in *One, Two, Three,* wildly funny in drag in the big-boobed polka-dot dress; in *Buddenbrooks,* others.

LOTINGA, ERNEST *(1951)* 56 ——Slapstick British comic in the "Josser" series in the '30s: *Josser Joins the Navy, Josser in the Army,* etc.

LOUDEN, THOMAS *(1948)* 74 ——Character; in *The Corn Is Green* (Old Tom), *Tomorrow Is Forever* (Englishman on Ship), *Safari,* 1938's *Kidnapped,* etc.

LOUIS, WILLARD *(1926)* 40 ——Few were his equal at playing the heavyweight dandy, as in Fairbanks' *Don Juan,* Eleanor Boardman's *Vanity Fair,* and John Barrymore's *Beau Brummel,* as the arrogant Prince with the Georgian pouting lips; also in *Madame X, The Lover of Camille, The French Doll,* and others of quality in the '20s.

LOUISE, ANITA *(1970)* 55 ——Blonde second-drawer star of the aristocratic face whose porcelain beauty, even when young, bordered alarmingly on fragility; onscreen from childhood (first in 1920's *The Sixth Commandment*), she was the leading lady in numerous B's (*Nine Girls, Main Street Lawyer, Harmon of Michigan,* etc.), more rarely the romantic lead opposite a more famous male (Flynn in *Green Light,* Cornel Wilde in *The Bandit of Sherwood Forest*), and more usually had "With" billing in the vehicles of big-name stars (*Marie Antoinette, The Story of Louis Pasteur, The Sisters, The Little Princess, Tovarich, Anthony Adverse, Love Letters,* etc.); married wealthily, twice; retired and became Hollywood's most noted party-giver.

LOVE, MONTAGU *(1943)* 66 ——One of those English character actors whose performances were like burnished gold; first played romantic leads (with Ethel Clayton in 1916's *A Woman's Way,* etc.), but almost immediately segued into starring character roles, as when, in '17, he was *Rasputin, the Black Monk;* in dozens in the '20s: *Don Juan* with Barrymore (forecasting all the talkie costume epics to come), *The Wind* with Gish, *Little Old New York* with Davies, *The Son of the Sheik* (desert chieftain who lashed tied-up Valentino); a few of the 90 talkies in which he shone: *The Prince and the Pauper* (Henry VIII), *The Crusades, Clive of India, Parnell, The Life of Emile Zola* (Cavaignac), *Gunga Din* (commander, Col. Weed), *The Man in the Iron Mask, Juarez, North West Mounted Police;* in three his last year: *The Constant Nymph* (as the father of Fontaine and the other "Sangers"), *Holy Matrimony,* and *Forever and a Day.*

LOVE, ROBERT *(1948)* 34 ——Supporting role in Muni's *Counter-Attack.*

LOVEJOY, FRANK *(1962)* 50 ——Husky-voiced, ruggedly handsome "man's man"; co-starred in many from '48; particularly effective in tough-talking military men roles (*Home of the Brave, Strategic Air Command, Retreat, Hell!, Beachhead*), Westerns (*Black Bart, The Charge at Feather River*), and as officials of the law (*I Was a Communist for the F.B.I., In a Lonely Place*); romantic roles with Crawford in *Goodbye, My Fancy,* Shelley Winters in *South Sea Sinner.*

LOVELL, RAYMOND *(1953)* 53 ——Jowly British character; in many: *Caesar and Cleopatra* (Lucius Septimius), *The Mudlark* (Sergeant Footman Naseby), *Quartet* (in the "Alien Corn" segment), *So Evil My Love,* etc.; starred in one, as crystal ball-gazing Dr. Winkler in the '41 English thriller *Alibi.*

LOVERIDGE, MARGUERITE *(1925)* 36 —— See Marguerite Marsh.

LOW, JACK *(1958)* 59 ——Support in Robert Ryan's *The Proud Ones.*

LOWE, EDMUND *(1971)* 81 ——They said he —the screen's suave, dinner-jacketed bachelor of the gleaming black hair and manicured moustache—couldn't play it: *What Price Glory's* Sergeant Quirt; Quirt who, according to adversary Captain Flagg (Victor McLaglen), was "the lousiest, filthiest bum who ever wore a uniform," and was, per company clerk Lipinsky, "a top with two glass eyes, a slit across his face for a mouth, and a piece out of his ear"; he did it, magnificently, and of the 100 roles he played, it was Quirt that brought him lasting renown; Lowe and McLaglen extended their hilarious non-com vs. officer warfare—"Sez you"– "Yeah! Sez me!"—through a long series of Marines comedies; in the '30s and '40s the actor also continued to be a drawing-room Romeo (as he had been since '17) in many: *Dinner at Eight, The Misleading Lady, I Love That Man*, etc.; also starred as Philo Vance in one (1936's *The Garden Murder Case*) and in a '52 TV series (*Front Page Detective*); offscreen almost a decade after 1948's *Good Sam*, he came back in '56 for a cameo in *Around the World in 80 Days*, then did once-a-year supporting roles in *The Wings of Eagles* ('57), *The Last Hurrah* ('58), *Plunderers of Painted Flats* ('59), and, last, *Heller in Pink Tights* ('60); in the end, though, the image that remained was of Quirt shouting, "Hey, Flagg, wait for baby!," and Flagg wrapping a comradely arm around his scrappy noncom as they trudged off to new battles just over the horizon.

LOWE, JAMES B. *(1963)* 83 ——Handsome black actor who was arrestingly effective as star of the last American version of *Uncle Tom's Cabin* ('27); historically important because he was the first black to be publicized by a studio; sending him to England to ballyhoo the picture, Universal not only declared that the company regarded him "as a living black god," but predicted "a most marvelous future and worldwide reputation for James B. Lowe"; strangely, though he had appeared in two earlier films, both Westerns (*Demon River* and *Blue Blazes* starring Pete Morrison), Lowe never made another movie after *Uncle Tom's Cabin*.

LOWE, K. ELMO *(1971)* ——Support in George Brent's *The Kid from Cleveland.*

LOWELL, HELEN *(1937)* 71 ——Thin, big-eyed little character actress from Broadway, she played old ladies in dozens; in *Isn't Life Wonderful?* (the poverty-stricken grandmother), *Page Miss Glory* (Davies' mother), *High, Wide and Handsome, Valiant Is the Word for Carrie, Dr. Socrates*, etc.

LOWELL, JOAN *(1967)* 67 ——Author of an "autobiographical" (but it wasn't) seafaring book, *Cradle in the Deep*; acted in two silents (Monte Blue's *Loving Lies, Cold Nerve*) and one talkie, RKO's *Adventure Girl*, which she also wrote and narrated.

LOWELL, JOHN *(1937)* ——Support in B's of the '20s: *The Big Show, Lost in a Big City, Bad Men's Money, Floodgates*, others.

LOWERY, ROBERT *(1971)* 57 ——Ruggedly handsome, dimple-chinned look-alike for Gable, and just as ready with his fists; 20th Century-Fox kept him busy (1937-40) in romantic leads in many: *Charlie Chan in Reno; Mr. Moto in Danger Island; Tail Spin; Star Dust; Free, Blonde and 21*, etc.; most effective there as one of Eugenie Leontovich's *Four Sons;* was dauntlessly courageous in the '40s as the star of Pine-Thomas adventure pix: *Dark Mountain, High Powered, Dangerous Passage, Big Town, They Made Me a Killer*, etc., in several of which Jean Parker, who became his wife, was his leading lady; in dozens more—usually Westerns and most often in support—through Doris Day's *The Ballad of Josie* in '68.

LOYD, ALISON *(1935)* 30 ——See Thelma Todd.

LUBITSCH, ERNST *(1947)* 55 ——His directorial "Lubitsch touch" meant sophisticated comedies (*Ninotchka*, etc.); acted in Negri's *One Arabian Night*, Barbara La Marr's *Souls for Sale*, others.

LUCAN, ARTHUR *(1954)* 67 ——His comic impersonation of "Old Mother Riley" in 14 British comedies made him a Top Ten star in England in '42.

LUCAS, JIMMY *(1949)* 61 ——Support in *My Heart Belongs to Daddy*, Ozzie Nelson's *Strictly in the Groove*, etc.

LUCAS, WILFRED *(1940)* 69 ——Onscreen from early Biograph days, this large-sized actor often starred for Griffith; in his *The Lonedale Operator, Man's Genesis* (as villain Brute-force), *Enoch Arden, The Girl and Her Trust, Under Burning Skies*, etc.; for others he starred in *The Acquitted, The Fighting Breed*, and dozens more silents; top support in many talkies: *Cock o' the Walk, Dishonored, I Cover the Waterfront, The Count of Monte Cristo, Pardon Us* (so good as the warden that he was cast in other Laurel & Hardy comedies: *The Devil's Brother, A Chump at Oxford);* last in Robinson's *The Sea Wolf*, as a helmsman—rugged still.

LUCHAIRE, CORINNE *(1950)* 28 ——Blonde and French, she was a momentary sensation after starring in 1939's *Prison Without Bars;* records indicate she made only two other French films: *The Affair Lafont* (also '39) and 1944's *Three Hours*, after which she was convicted as a Nazi collaborator and denied acting assignments.

LUCKETT, KEITH *(1973)* 12 —Small roles in several films.

LUCY, ARNOLD *(1945)* ——Support in many silents including three with Constance Talmadge *(In Search of a Sinner, The Love Expert,* in which he had a major role, and *Good References),* and in numerous talkies *(All Quiet on the Western Front,* as Kantorek, March's *Dr. Jekyll and Mr. Hyde,* as Utterson, *Merely Mary Ann, Manslaughter, The Princess and the Plumber, Alias the Doctor,* etc.).

LUGOSI, BELA *(1956)* 74 ——Tall and handsome (yes) as a youth, he was for ten years a matinee idol at the Royal National Theatre in Budapest, playing romantic leads *(Camille, Romeo and Juliet,* etc.); in America in '23, he starred in many silents *(The Silent Command, The Midnight Girl,* others); then was on Broadway ('27) in a long run in *Dracula,* followed inevitably ('31) by the movie version; the die was cast: *White Zombie, Island of Lost Souls, Chandu the Magician, Mark of the Vampire, Son of Frankenstein, The Human Monster, The Wolf Man, The Body Snatcher, Bela Lugosi Meets the Brooklyn Gorilla,* etc., right to the horrifying end; in '74, his heirs (son Bela Jr. is a noted Los Angeles attorney) were awarded $53,000 in royalties from the sale of Count Dracula masks, costumes, etc., the court ruling that property rights to the character had passed on to them; among his heirs, three grandchildren who never knew him but are fascinated by his old movies on TV.

LUKAS, PAUL *(1971)* 76 ——Unbending dignity was the hallmark of this star from Hungary, even when up to evil *(Confessions of a Nazi Spy, The Lady Vanishes,* etc.); won '43 Best Actor Oscar as the besieged anti-Nazi in *Watch on the Rhine;* suavely romantic in many *(Manhattan Cocktail, Two Lovers,* etc.), bashfully romantic in others *(Little Women,* as older man, Prof. Bhaer, beloved of Hepburn), he went through a "German" period in the '40s: *Hostages, Uncertain Glory, Address Unknown,* etc.; came, finally, to play distinguished older men: *Kim, The Roots of Heaven, Tender Is the Night, Lord Jim, 55 Days at Peking;* last in a top supporting role in 1968's *Sol Madrid.*

LULLI, FOLCO *(1970)* 58 ——In *Wages of Fear,* was Luigi, the cheerful Italian bricklayer, driver of the first oil truck, which exploded; also in *Times Gone By, Variety Lights, Under Ten Flags,* many more European films.

LUNG, CHARLES *(1974)* 60s ——Oriental roles in William Gargan's *Destination Unknown,* Rosalind Russell's *Flight for Freedom,* Alan Ladd's *Thunder in the East,* etc.; most often villainous.

LUPINO, STANLEY *(1942)* 46 ——Ida's comedian-dad; a headliner in many British musical comedies in the '30s: *Sleepless Nights, You Made Me Love You, Cheer Up, Lucky to Me,* etc.

LUPINO, WALLACE *(1961)* 63 ——Ida's uncle (also the brother of comedian Lupino Lane); starred, as Wallace Lane, in a series of polite domestic two-reel comedies for Cameo (released by Educational), 1923-33; as Lupino, was in *The Man Who Could Work Miracles, The Lambeth Walk,* other British pix.

LUTHER, ANNA *(1960)* 67 ——Silent actress who starred first as Anna (for Lubin in *The Changeling,* '14, and others, and for Fox in *The Beast,* '16, etc.); then starred as Anne in two very popular serials in '19: *The Lurking Peril* and *The Great Gamble;* continued onscreen into the '20s, in, among others, *Sinners in Silk.*

LUTHER, JOHNNY *(1960)* 51 ——Support in many cowboy pix.

LUTHER, LESTER *(1962)* 74 ——Character in Republic's *The Red Menace.*

LYEL, VIOLA *(1972)* 72 ——British comedy character who played the leading role in 1930's *Hobson's Choice;* on the screen from 1928 she was featured in many, through 1957's *The Little Hut;* in *Channel Crossing, The Patient Vanishes, The Farmer's Wife, Quiet Wedding, Wanted for Murder, This Man Is Dangerous, Mr. Perrin and Mr. Traill, It's Not Cricket, No Place for Jennifer, Isn't Life Wonderful, Fabian of the Yard, See How They Run,* etc.

LYMAN, ABE *(1957)* 60 ——Famous bandleader; featured with his orchestra in *Broadway Thru a Keyhole* and *Mr. Broadway;* later produced a Vaughn Monroe Western, *Singing Guns.*

LYNDON, ALICE *(1949)* 75 ——Was an early Sennett comedienne.

LYNCH, HELEN *(1965)* 64 ——A '23 Wampas Baby Star; featured in many of the '20s: *Fifth Avenue Models, My Own Pal, Underworld, Ladies of the Mob,* etc.; *Elmer and Elsie* was among her few in the '30s; last in 1940's *Women Without Names;* sometimes billed Helene.

LYNN, DIANA *(1971)* 45 ——Paramount's most delightful young comedienne in the '40s; in *The Miracle of Morgan's Creek, And the Angels Sing, Henry Aldrich Gets Glamour, Our Hearts Were Young and Gay* (her best starring entry), *Out of This World,* etc.; had minor roles under her real name, Dolly Loehr, in two earlier pix: *They Shall Have Music* and *There's Magic in Music,* in both of which she played the piano; was particularly fine in her first as Diana Lynn,

The Major and the Minor, as the precocious real teenager who "saw through" phony teenager Ginger Rogers; her perennial brainychild's face worked against her when she starred as an adult in *Ruthless, Paid in Full, Plunder of the Sun, The Kentuckian,* etc.; was making a comeback in *Play It As It Lays* when stricken by a brain hemorrhage—the role then assumed by Tammy Grimes.

LYNN, EMMETT *(1958)* 61 ——When not playing character roles such as Nathan in *The Robe,* he was the grizzle-bearded, stogie-chomping, funnily cantankerous sidekick in all the "Red Ryder" pix of Allan (Rocky) Lane, Bill Elliott, and Jim Bannon; in scores more B Westerns; onscreen from '13.

LYNN, GEORGE *(1967)* ——Support in many: *To Be or Not to Be* (as the Actor-Adjutant), *Charlie Chan at Monte Carlo, Sudan, Grand Central Murder, Sinner Take All, City Girl,* etc.

LYNN, RALPH *(1962)* 81 ——Brilliant, dithery British comedian; he, his monocle, and fluttery hands provoked hilarity in *A Cuckoo in the West, Rookery Nook, A Chance of a Night Time,* many more.

LYNN, ROBERT *(1969)* 72 ——Character in *Good Morning, Miss Dove; The Barefoot Mailman,* etc.

LYNN, SHARON *(1963)* 53 ——One of Fox's most promising blonde starlets in the late '20s and early '30s; in *Sunny Side Up,* was rich Jane Worth, so snippy to Janet Gaynor; also in *Lightnin', Wild Company, Let's Go Places;* altering her name to Sharon Lynne, she was in *Enter Madame* (losing Cary Grant to his divawife, Elissa Landi), *The Big Broadcast, Way Out West* (ticklish Stan Laurel had a fit of giggling hysteria when she, pretending to be the mine heiress, tried to extricate the land deed from his shirt, where he hid it); onscreen through 1941's *West Point Widow.*

LYNN, WILLIAM *(1952)* 62 —— In *Harvey,* he was the judge who "understood" Elwood P. Dowd; also in *Mr. Belvedere Rings the Bell, Katie Did It,* etc.

LYON, FRANK *(1961)* 59 ——In *The Big Pond* was the suitor Colbert almost married before

Chevalier kidnapped her; also in *Paris After Dark* (Nazi Agent), *I Met My Love Again, Night Must Fall,* more.

LYONS, CANDY *(1966)* 21 ——One of the beauties in Troy Donahue's *Palm Springs Weekend.*

LYONS, CLIFF *(1974)* 72 ——Big, heavy-faced character, often with walrus moustache, frequently in John Ford Westerns: *Wagonmaster* (the sheriff who invited hero Ben Johnson to get out of town), *She Wore a Yellow Ribbon* (Trooper Cliff); also in *Bend of the River, The Lawless Nineties,* etc.

LYONS, GENE *(1974)* 40s ——Splendid Broadway lead (had, in *Witness for the Prosecution,* the role Tyrone Power played in the movie); support in Sal Mineo's *The Young Don't Cry.*

LYTELL, BERT *(1954)* 69 ——Silent star whose thin-lipped, cleft-chinned face, and piercing gaze had the ladies swooning, making him one of Hollywood's brightest luminaries; *Rupert of Hentzau* ('23), in particular, gave femme fans romantically thrilling, lingering memories; first onscreen in '17, after a career onstage, in *The Lone Wolf,* a role he played four more times in the next 13 years (*The Lone Wolf Returns, Alias the Lone Wolf,* etc.); starred in *The Trail to Yesterday; Lombardi, Ltd.; Alias Jimmy Valentine, To Have and to Hold, The Eternal City, Born Rich*—big moneymakers all; closed out his screen career after 1931's *The Single Sin;* continued as a major star on radio and Broadway (last toplining 1946's *I Like It Here*); returned to movies just once, to appear as himself in *Stage Door Canteen.*

LYTELL, JIMMY *(1972)* 67 ——Clarinetistbandleader on Morton Downey's radio show; in musical shorts.

LYTELL, WILFRED *(1954)* 62 ——Handsome, Arrow Collar-type leading man in silents; with Pearl White in *Know Your Man,* Anita Stewart in *The Combat,* Ethel Barrymore in *Our Mrs. McChesney;* also in *Heliotrope, The Man Who Paid,* etc.; being a look-alike of more-famous older brother Bert hindered his career, which ended after a secondary role in Ben Lyon's *Bluebeard's Seven Wives* in '26.

M

MacARTHUR, CHARLES *(1956)* 60 —— Famed playwright (*The Front Page*); played a reporter in *Crime Without Punishment,* of which he was co-author and co-director.

MACAULAY, JOSEPH *(1967)* 76 ——Support in Jeanette MacDonald's *The Lottery Bride;* better known as gray-haired Ben Fraser on TV soap opera *From These Roots.*

694

MacBRIDE, DONALD *(1957)* 63 ——In *Room Service*, at the beginning of his character career, he was the hotel manager driven to the edge of lunacy in his efforts to evict the Marx Brothers; cynical detectives, though, were a specialty; in *The Great Man Votes, My Favorite Wife, Topper Returns, Here Comes Mr. Jordan, You'll Never Get Rich, Love Crazy, They Got Me Covered*, many more.

MACCHIA, JOHN *(1967)* 35 ——Support in Jerry Lewis pix: *The Disorderly Orderly, Three on a Couch, The Nutty Professor.*

MacCOLL, JAMES *(1956)* 56 ——As Corporal MacColl was with the Allon Trio in *This Is the Army*; later a TV actor.

MacCORMACK, FRANK *(1941)* 65 ——Support in Constance Binney's *The Case of Becky* ('21), and, later, in *The Case of Sergeant Grischa* and *Brothers.*

MacCORMACK, FRANKLYN *(1971)* 63 —— Minor support in many.

MacDERMOTT, MARC *(1929)* 47 ——An early (from '08) Edison Films headliner, he starred in *What Happened to Mary*, serial with Mary Fuller, his own series, *The Man Who Disappeared, Mary Stuart* and *Aida* with his wife, Miriam Nesbitt, *Ranson's Folly*, etc.; in the '20s, co-star and top supporting roles: in *The New Moon, While New York Sleeps, The Sea Hawk* (dueled admirably with star Milton Sills), *Blind Wives, Flesh and the Devil* (Garbo's Count-husband, killed in a duel with John Gilbert); last in Dolores Costello's *Glorious Betsy* ('28).

MacDONALD, DONALD *(1959)* 61 ——Young support in pix of the '20s: Charles Ray's *The Midnight Bell*, Madge Bellamy's *Lorna Doone*, Clive Brook's *If Marriage Fails?*, etc.; few talkies: *These Thirty Years*, etc.

MacDONALD, EDMUND *(1951)* 40 ——Thug type, especially active in WW II pix: *To the Shores of Tripoli* (a Marine, Butch), *Flying Tigers* (pilot Blackie Bales), *Corvette K-225;* in mysteries (*Black Friday, Strange Case of Dr. Rx, Sherlock Holmes in Washington*, as Lt. Grogan) and serials (villain, Waldron, in *The Mysterious Mr. M.*).

MacDONALD, J. FARRELL *(1952)* 77 —— Fine wrinkled and bald character; in more than 300 pix; both he (good-looking and dark-haired then) and his wife (billed Mrs. MacDonald) began as leads with Imp Co. in '11; he starred in many, including *The Heart of Maryland* with Mrs. Leslie Carter; from the '20s, in supporting roles; for John Ford in '24, in *The Iron Horse*, he played the role that remains his most famous —jocular transcontinental railroad worker, Corporal Casey; worked for Ford next in a top supporting role (Mike Costigan) in *Three Bad Men*, becoming a Ford "reliable" in many, including, later, *My Darling Clementine* (the barman, Mac); active through 1951's *Elopement*, starring Clifton Webb, he was also in *Topper* (the policeman), *In Old Arizona* (Tad), Dunne's *Show Boat* (Windy), *Meet John Doe* (Sourpuss Smithers), *The Miracle of Morgan's Creek* (sheriff), etc.

MacDONALD, JEANETTE *(1965)* 60 ——Russet-haired soprano who for two decades (from 1929's *The Love Parade* to 1949's *The Sun Comes Up*) was operatic catnip to millions and pure gold at the box-office, particularly for MGM, where she starred after '34; often teamed with baritone Nelson Eddy (*Rose Marie, Naughty Marietta, Maytime, The Girl of the Golden West*, etc.), she made the Top Ten once ('36), but he never did; pre-Eddy, she was paired with Maurice Chevalier (*Love Me Tonight, The Love Parade, The Merry Widow*), Ramon Novarro (*The Cat and the Fiddle*), Jack Buchanan (*Monte Carlo*); during the MacDonald-Eddy period, she also co-starred with Lew Ayres (*Broadway Serenade*), Allan Jones (*The Firefly*), real-life husband Gene Raymond (*Smilin' Through*), Robert Young (*Cairo*); went solo in her final three: *Three Daring Daughters, The Birds and the Bees, The Sun Comes Up.*

MacDONALD, KATHERINE *(1956)* 62 —— Stunningly lovely (in fact called the "American Beauty"), she was a popular leading lady from her first two in '18 (*Riddle Gawne* with William S. Hart and *Headin' South* with Fairbanks) to her last in '26 (*Old Loves for New* with Lewis Stone); teamed with Jack Holt in *The Woman Thou Gavest Me* and Elliott Dexter in *The Squaw Man* (perhaps her peak, as Lady Diana), Charles Meredith in *The Beautiful Liar*, others; critics often were harsh ("her acting ability is not to be classed with her beauty").

MacDONALD, KENNETH *(1972)* 70 ——TV viewers seeing him almost weekly as the judge on Raymond Burr's *Perry Mason* series may not have guessed it, but for years, previously, he had been on the other side of the law; in dozens of Westerns (often Charles Starrett's), he was the suave, black-suited crook who hired henchmen to do his dirty work—and, with black curly hair and manicured moustache, a look-alike for Fredric March in *The Buccaneer;* sly in a dozen serials too: *Mandrake the Magician, Overland with Kit Carson, Perils of the Royal Mounted*, etc.

MacDOUGALL, ALLAN ROSS *(1956)* 62 —— Support in Walter Connolly's *Soak the Rich.*

MacDOWELL, MELBOURNE *(1941)* 84 —— Support in Westerns and adventure pix in the '20s: *The Golden Snare, Nomads of the North, Richard the Lion-Hearted, Outside the Law, The Outlaw Express, Code of the Cow Country,* etc.

MACE, FRED *(1917)* 38 ——Moon-faced comedian with querulous black eyebrows, which always caught your eye first, who was one of Sennett's early greats; his popularity in '13 was almost equal to John Bunny's; played comic villains, the Keystone Chief of Police (*The Bangville Police*), irate husbands (*Toplitsky and Company*), inept fire department chief, punchdrunk boxers (*"One-Round" O'Brien* and the subsequent series), and frequently had a custard pie heaved into his unsuspecting face by Mabel Normand; was at his best in *At Twelve O'Clock* and *My Valet.*

MacFARLANE, BRUCE *(1967)* 57 ——Handsome black-haired Broadway lead (*Sailor, Beware*) featured in two at Republic in '38: *Come On, Rangers* and *Come On, Leathernecks.*

MacFARLANE, GEORGE *(1932)* 55 ——Character (Jessup) in Tracy's *Up the River;* also in *Frozen Justice, Happy Days, Union Depot, Cameo Kirby,* etc.

MacGOWRAN, JACK *(1973)* 54 ——Wiry, sharp-featured, superb Abbey Theatre actor; featured in many: *Young Cassidy, The Quiet Man* (Feeney), *The Titfield Thunderbolt, Doctor Zhivago* (Petya), *Tom Jones* (Partridge), *The Exorcist,* more.

MacGREGOR, LEE *(1961)* 34 ——Darkly handsome 20th Century-Fox contract player; in *Slattery's Hurricane* (Navigator), *Twelve O'-Clock High* (Lt. Zimmerman), *Scudda-Hoo! Scudda-Hay!* (Ches).

MacINTOSH, LOUISE *(1933)* 68 ——Bogart's proper smalltown New England mom in *Up the River.*

MACK, ANDREW *(1931)* 40s ——Virile handsome star of 1914's *The Ragged Earl;* also had a supporting role in 1926's *Bluebeard's Seven Wives.*

MACK, ARTHUR *(1942)* 55 ——Support in Clive Brook's *The Return of Sherlock Holmes.*

MACK, BILLY *(1961)* 70s ——Minor support in Chaney's *The Black Bird,* Elyse Knox's *A Wave, a Wac, and a Marine,* etc.

MACK, CACTUS *(1962)* 62 ——Leathery-faced B Westerns villain with a strong resemblance to Peck as he was in *The Gunfighter;* in *Racketeers of the Range, Six Gun Serenade, Twilight in the Sierras,* etc.; first had been a cowboy musician, playing guitar in Fred Scott's *The Cimarron Cowboys.*

MACK, CHARLES *(1956)* 78 ——Support in several in the '20s: the sobby *Lost Chord, The Trunk Mystery,* Barbara La Marr's *The White Monkey,* etc.

MACK, CHARLES E. *(1934)* 46 ——Shorter, slow-and-easy half of the blackface Moran & Mack ("The Two Black Crows") comedy team; they supported Fields in one silent (*Two Flaming Youths*), starred in three talkies, the moderately good *Why Bring That Up?* (their catchphrase), the poor *Anybody's War,* and the dreadful *Hypnotized,* followed by a series of abysmal two-reelers for Educational.

MACK, CHARLES EMMETT *(1927)* 27 —— Slender handsome youth discovered and used by Griffith in major roles in three starring Carol Dempster: *Dream Street* (as Billy, brother of lead Ralph Graves), *One Exciting Night* (A Guest), *America* (as Charles Philip Edward Montague); then starred in *Driven, The Unknown Soldier, Old San Francisco, The Sixth Commandment,* others; had two released posthumously: *The Rough Riders,* in which he was particularly fine, and *The First Auto,* in which he was working when he was killed while en route to location in—ironically—an auto crash.

MACK, GEORGE E. *(1948)* 82 ——Support in Lillian Russell's *Wildfire* ('15).

MACK, GERTRUDE *(1967)* 70 ——Supporting player in many.

MACK, HUGHIE *(1927)* 43——Tremendously popular young comedian who, in Vitagraph pix of the early teens, was a guaranteed laugh-getter just by entering a scene—all 318 pounds (later more) of him; he and his benevolent smile became a national institution in *The Win(k)some Widow, John Tobin's Sweetheart, The New Secretary, Roughing the Cub, Mr. Bingle's Melodrama, The Lion Tamer;* starred in his own series in '16 with Patsy de Forest, and later worked for Sennett; finally was gross comedy relief in serials (*The Silent Flyer, The Riddle Rider*), features (*Going Up, Reno, Greed*—walrus-moustached Heise at the wedding, *The Merry Widow,* as the innkeeper, *The Wedding March,* as the wine-garden keeper), and Westerns (*The Arizona Whirlwind,* etc.).

MACK, JAMES T. *(1948)* 77 ——In *Anna Christie,* was Johnny the Priest; also in *Fools of*

Fashion; Queen of the Night Clubs; Women's Wares; Mary Burns, Fugitive, others.

MACK, JOE *(1946)* 67 ——From Italy, he usually played comic-Italian bits, as in Hepburn's *A Woman Rebels;* also in silents: Laura La Plante's *Finders Keepers*, and *Driftwood, The Man from Headquarters*, etc.

MACK, LESTER *(1972)* 66 ——Plump, smiling, gray support in *The Parisienne*, others; best known in Broadway comedy support.

MACK, WILBUR *(1964)* 70s ——Support in a '30 Louise Lorraine serial, *The Jade Box, Up the River, Dixie, A Day at the Races* (a racing judge), *A Night at the Opera, Atlantic City*, other talkies, plus numerous silent Westerns.

MACK, WILLARD *(1934)* 56 ——The year before his death, this heavyset, multitalented man wrote, directed, and starred in *What Price Innocence?* (playing Dr. Dan Davidge) and was also in *Broadway to Hollywood*, which, essentially, was his real-life route; besides headlining in and writing many plays (*The Dove, Kick In*), he starred onscreen in '16, with Enid Markey, in *Aloha-ee*, and was top-featured in Metro's *Your Friend and Mine* ('23) and *The Voice of the City* ('29), which he also directed; found time, too, to marry (and be divorced by) three well-known actresses: Maude Leone, Pauline Frederick, and Marjorie Rambeau.

MACK, WILLIAM B. *(1955)* 83 ——Support in pix of the '20s: Alice Brady's *Missing Millions*, Bessie Love's *The Song and Dance Man*, Esther Ralston's *The American Venus*, plus *Heliotrope, The Steadfast Heart, Missing Millions*, etc.

MACKAY, CHARLES *(1935)* 68 ——Support in the '20s: Pearl White's *Without Fear*, Alice Calhoun's *The Matrimonial Web*, plus *The Inner Man, Lost in a Big City*, and such Westerns as *Diane of Star Hollow* and *Peggy Puts It Across*.

MACKAYE, DOROTHY *(1940)* 40s ——Actress-wife of Paul Kelly, of whom Adela Rogers St. John once wrote: ". . . a *real* good actress. From Broadway. Good-looking, dark, never going to make it to the top . . . Something harsh about her"; didn't make it; became a screenwriter—of *Lady Gangster*—after serving time in San Quentin (as did Kelly) for the murder of her first husband.

MacKAYE, NORMAN *(1968)* 62 ——Character actor in several: *The Hoodlum Priest* (as Father Dunne), *You're in the Navy Now* (first released as *U.S.S. Teakettle*; as Aide to Admiral Ray Collins), *Call Northside 777* (a detective), *Kiss of Death*, etc.

MACKEN, WALTER *(1967)* 51 ——Irish actor who starred in *Home Is the Hero*, based on his own play; also in *Quare Fellow*.

MacKENNA, KATE *(1957)* 79 ——Character actress in minor roles: *Bus Stop* (elderly bus passenger), Colbert's *The Bride Comes Home* (maid Emma), *The Wife Takes a Flyer* (one of the elderly twins), others.

MacKENNA, KENNETH *(1962)* 63 ——As a slender dark-haired youth from Broadway, he had leads in many silents from the mid-'20s (*Miss Bluebeard, A Kiss in the Dark, The American Venus*, etc.) and talkies to '32 (*Secrets* with Pickford, *Those We Love* with Mary Astor, *Crazy That Way* with Joan Bennett, others); long offscreen, for stage roles, he came back as a character actor in *Judgment at Nuremberg* (Judge Kenneth Norris), *High Time, 13 West Street*.

MACKENZIE, ALEX *(1966)* 79 ——Irascible Scottish ship captain who was in humorous conflict with Paul Douglas in *High and Dry* (a.k.a. *The Maggie*); also in *Greyfriars' Bobby, Mad Little Island*, etc.

MacKENZIE, MARY *(1966)* 44 ——English actress; was the unregenerate crook in *Stolen Face* whose face was remolded by plastic surgeon Henreid into Lizabeth Scott's likeness (rest of role being played by Miss Scott); used her "old" face herself in *Duel in the Jungle, Trouble in the Glen, Scotland Yard Inspector*, others.

MacLANE, BARTON *(1969)* 66 ——Tough-talking semi-star in more than 300 films; Bogart battled him over his oil-driller wages in the casino in *The Treasure of Sierra Madre*, and "Torchy Blane" (Glenda Farrell) fought with him (albeit adoringly), as Detective Lieutenant Steve McBride, in seven pix; some others in which his (frequently friendly) Irish mug was prominently in the midst of the action: *San Quentin, You Only Live Once*, Bogart's *The Maltese Falcon, Western Union, The Big Street* (crook who knocked nightclub queen Lucille Ball down a flight of stairs, crippling her for life), *Bullets or Ballots, High Sierra;* starred in the TV series *The Outlaws* and was in pictures through 1968's *Arizona Bushwackers*.

MacLAREN, IVOR *(1962)* 58 ——Support in English pix: *Evergreen, Princess Charming, Radio Parade of 1935*, more.

MacLEAN, DOUGLAS *(1967)* 70 ——Onscreen 1917–29, he was a leading man of breezy charm, particularly delightful in comedies such as 1923's *Going Up;* starred in many: *Souls in*

Pawn, Captain Kidd Junior with Pickford, in several Paramount-Artcraft comedies with Doris May (Mary's Ankle, etc.), The Home Breaker with Dorothy Dalton, Introduce Me, Soft Cushions with Sue Carol; also starred in WW I comedy, 23½ Hours Leave (young private goes A.W.O.L., captures spy ring, wins the general's daughter), which, two decades later, when a successful Hollywood producer (of So Red the Rose, etc.), he remade, starring James Ellison.

MacLEAN, R. D. (1948) 89 ——Character actor in Cradle Song, Don't Neglect Your Wife, The Bishop of the Ozarks, numerous others.

MacMILLIAN, VIOLET (1953) 66 ——Was in the 1920 serial The Master Mind.

MACOWAN, NORMAN (1961) 84 ——Scottish character; in Whisky Galore, Valley of the Eagles, City of the Dead, Tread Softly Stranger, etc.

MACPHERSON, JEANIE (1946) 60s ——Became the scriptwriter of many of DeMille's biggest (The Buccaneer, The King of Kings, The Affairs of Anatol, etc.), after leading roles—as a very pretty young brunette—in numerous early silents (Winning Back His Love, Enoch Arden, The Last Drop of Water, Fisher Folks, Mrs. Jones Entertains).

MacPHERSON, QUINTON (1940) 69 ——Support in The Ghost Goes West (a creditor), Murder in the Old Red Barn, Talk of the Devil, etc.

MacQUARRIE, MURDOCK (1942) 64 —— Dark-haired leading man at Universal in the mid-teens (after more than a dozen years in minor roles); was especially popular in the 1914 serial The Oubliette, based on the life and adventures of Francois Villon; support in many in the '20s: Ethel Clayton's If I Were Queen, Hoot Gibson's Sure Fire, Norma Talmadge's The Only Woman and Ashes of Vengeance, etc.; in minor roles in talkies, such as a doctor in March's Dr. Jekyll and Mr. Hyde, he was onscreen through 1938's Blockade.

MacRAE, DUNCAN (1967) 61 ——Scottish actor who was most effective as the stern but loving grandfather of the lads in The Little Kidnappers; also in Tunes of Glory, The Brothers, Mad Little Island, Wee Geordie, Grayfriars' Bobby, many others.

MACREADY, GEORGE (1973) 73 ——Gilda, as Hayworth's sinister husband, put him on the movie map—tall, cold, Germanic-looking (despite his Scottish name), with silver-blond hair, and, on his right cheek, the perfect finishing touch for a classy villain, a most aristocratic scar (rapier wound?; auto accident?); onscreen then four years (from Commandos Strike at Dawn), with 20 years more to come, bringing icy roles in another 40: The Big Clock, Knock on Any Door, The Desert Fox, Detective Story, Seven Days in May, and, best of all, Paths of Glory, as heartless General Mireau who ordered artillery fire on his own men and the execution of three innocent soldiers—a superlative performance; cold-hearted to the end, on TV, as patriarch Martin Peyton in Peyton Place.

MACY, CARLETON (1946) 85 ——Comic old-timer in Richard Dix's Seven Keys to Baldpate, other early talkies.

MACY, JACK (1956) 70 ——Support in Tyrone Power's Untamed.

MADEIRA, HUMBERTO (1971) 50 ——Character (Tio) in Milland's Lisbon; also wrote the screenplay.

MADISON, CLEO (1964) 81 ——Boyish brunette (later buxom) best recalled for starring in two serials: 1914's Trey O' Hearts (played twins, good and evil) and 1919's The Great Radium Mystery; also starred in The Heart of a Cracksman with Wallace Reid, Damon and Pythias with Herbert Rawlinson, The Severed Hand, The Dangerous Age with Lewis Stone; last in a '25 George O'Brien Western, The Roughneck.

MADISON, HARRY (1936) 59 ——Featured in an Eddie Polo silent serial, King of the Circus.

MADRIGUERA, ENRIC (1973) 71 ——Appeared with his dance orchestra in Evelyn Keyes' Thrill of Brazil, for which he also composed the title tune.

MAE, JIMSEY (1968) 74 ——She was young support in a '15 Richard Bennett pic, Damaged Goods.

MAGEE, HARRIETT (1954) 76 ——Supporting roles in silents.

MAGNANI, ANNA (1973) 65 ——Italy's fiery, scraggly-haired, greatest movie actress; won the Best Actress Oscar as the neurotic Sicilian-born seamstress in 1955's The Rose Tattoo; had made her screen reputation a decade before as the earthy heroine of Open City, consolidating it with Bellissima, The Miracle, The Golden Coach, etc.; later American pix were disappointing: Wild Is the Wind, The Fugitive Kind with Brando; last starred in 1967's Made in Italy; last seen in a cameo in Fellini's Roma ('72).

MAGRILL, GEORGE *(1952)* 52 ——Tough character who frequently played thugs and cops; in serials, silent (*Hawk of the Hills*) and talkie (*G-Men Never Forget*); features, silent (*Stolen Secrets*) and talkie (*Meet Boston Blackie* as Georgie, *The Flying Irishman*, etc.).

MAGUIRE, TOM *(1934)* 64 ——Silent support; in Ben Lyon's *The Savage*, Richard Dix's *Shanghai Bound*, Barthelmess' *The Bond Boy*, others.

MAHER, WALLY *(1951)* 43 ——Minor support in several Dick Powell pix: *Hollywood Hotel, Right Cross, The Reformer and the Redhead; also in Submarine D-1, Murder in the Fleet, Mystery Street*, etc.

MAHONEY, WILL *(1967)* 73 ——Co-star of the '38 British pic *Sez O'Reilly to MacNab;* also in the silent *Lost in the Arctic.*

MAIGNE, CHARLES *(1929)* 50 ——Actor in early silents who, in the '20s, was one of Hollywood's leading directors (*The Copperhead, The Silent Partner, The Firing Line*, etc.).

MAILES, CHARLES H. *(1937)* 66 ——Stalwart, frequently bearded character actor—sometimes good, more often evil (the lecherous seducer in *Two Paths*)—who was a member of D. W. Griffith's earliest screen stock company; first onscreen in 1909's *The Lonely Villa* with Mary Pickford (was with her later in *The New York Hat, Home Folks*, others); major roles in dozens: *Judith of Bethulia* (General of the Jews), *A Girl and Her Trust* (abducted telegraph operator Dorothy Bernard on a railroad handcar), *The Billionaire, Drums of Love* (Duke of Granada), *Old Ironsides* (fine as the Constitution's Commodore Preble), many more silents; continued on in talkies through a '33 Jane Darwell starrer, *Women Won't Tell;* sometimes billed C. H. or Charles Hill Mailes.

MAINES, DON *(1934)* 64 ——Support in the silent *The Man Who Waited.*

MAISON, EDNA *(1946)* 52 ——Brunette Broadway musical comedy actress; starred for three companies: Bison, Rex (*In Slavery Days*, '13), Universal (*The Merchant of Venice*, '14).

MAJERONI, MARIO *(1931)* 61 ——Support in many in the '20s: Swanson's *Her Love Story* (Prime Minister), Ed Wynn's *Rubber Heels*, Babe Daniels' *Argentine Love*, Alice Brady's *The Snow Bride*, etc.

MAKEHAM, ELIOT *(1956)* 73 ——Small British character who often portrayed timid clerks in specs; in *Night Train to Munich, Scrooge,* *Peg of Old Drury, Storm in a Teacup, The Verger*, more.

MALA *(1952)* 46 ——An attractive half-Jewish Eskimo (r.n. Ray Wise) with a rugged physique, he was popular for a decade after starring in 1932's *Igloo* and the following year's *Eskimo;* "Mala the Magnificent" he was billboarded; starred in two serials (*Robinson Crusoe of Clipper Island* and *Hawk of the Wilderness*), was support in another (*The Great Adventures of Wild Bill Hickok*), plus numerous features (*The Tuttles of Tahiti, Coast Guard, The Jungle Princess*, etc.); ten years offscreen, he came back in '52 to co-star with Guy Madison in *Red Snow*, being billed, as he rarely was, under the name Ray Mala.

MALAN, WILLIAM *(1941)* 73 ——In the '20s, was comic support in Westerns (*Flashing Spurs, Red Hot Leather, The Broncho Buster*, etc.) and "youth" pix (Lefty Flynn's *The College Boob*, etc.); had been with Sennett.

MALATESTA, FRED *(1952)* 62 ——From Italy, in American movies from the mid-teens; was particularly impressive in two in the '30s: *A Farewell to Arms* (Cooper's soldier-colleague Manera) and *The Crusades* (William, King of Sicily); many silents: *The Girl Who Came Back, Forbidden Paradise, The Lullaby*, etc.; last in Nan Grey's *The Black Doll* in '38.

MALLALIEU, AUBREY *(1948)* 74 ——Support in British silents, then talkies: *Haunted Honeymoon, Courageous Mr. Penn, Meet Me at Dawn, Bedelia*, more.

MALLESON, MILES *(1969)* 80 ——In the very best British films, this plump, gray-haired elf with the perpetually surprised eyebrows, beaky nose, and long quirky mouth, was forever there —acting the stars right off the screen; in *Dead of Night* (coachman who delivered the terrifying line "Room for one more"), *The Captain's Paradise, Folly to be Wise, Kind Hearts and Coronets* (the contemptuous executioner), *Laughter in Paradise, The Importance of Being Earnest* (the clergyman), *I'm All Right, Jack, The Man in the White Suit*, many more.

MALLORY, BOOTS *(1958)* 45 ——From the Broadway musical stage, she was the pretty femme lead in several minor pix of the '30s: *Handle with Care, Humanity, Hello Sister!* with James Dunn, *Sing Sing Nights*, the serial *The Wolf Dog*, the Western *Powdersmoke Range*, and, last, 1938's *Here's Flash Casey* opposite Eric Linden; perhaps best recalled as a Hollywood society figure because of her marriages to producer William Cagney and actor Herbert Marshall.

MALLOY, JOHN J. *(1968)* 70 ——Support in silents.

MALO, GINA *(1963)* 54 ——American-born wife of actor Romney Brent, who played spitfire roles for a decade in England; first in 1932's *Magic Night*, then in *Waltz Time, In a Monastery Garden, My Song for You, Over She Goes*, more.

MALONE, DUDLEY FIELD *(1950)* 68 —— President Wilson's real-life Assistant Secretary of State, he portrayed Churchill in *Mission to Moscow*.

MALONE, FLORENCE *(1956)* 60s ——Heroine in the silent serial *The Yellow Menace*.

MALONE, MOLLY *(1952)* 50s ——Brunette leading lady in the 1927 serial *The Golden Stallion* and the femme lead in many features at Universal in the '20s; in *Just Out of College, Little Johnny Jones, The Freshie, Bucking the Line, The Bandit Buster*, more.

MALONEY, LEO *(1929)* 41 ——Vastly popular, rugged, dapper star of Pathe Westerns in the '20s; in *Arizona Catclaw, The Lost Express, Whispering Smith*, dozens more; onscreen from '14, he was first Helen Holmes' leading man (Tom) in the serials *Hazards of Helen* and *A Lass of the Lumberlands*, and starred in many Mutual adventure pix; at Pathe he wrote, produced, and directed most of the Westerns in which he starred; was at his zenith in a '28 Mascot serial, *The Vanishing West*; his only talkie, *Overland Bound*, was released shortly after his death.

MALTBY, H. F. *(1963)* 82 ——British support (and playwright); in *Caesar and Cleopatra, To the Victor, Trouble Ahead, Pygmalion*, etc.

MALYON, EILY *(1961)* 82 ——Father Fitzgibbon's (Barry Fitzgerald's) hatchet-faced housekeeper in *Going My Way*; from England and the New York stage, was in 50 in 15 years (from '31); kind-lady roles at first then many bony, mean-spirited spinsters; in *On Borrowed Time* ("Aunt Demetria is a pismire!" said Pud properly), *Young Tom Edison, The Little Princess, Foreign Correspondent, Night Must Fall, She Wolf of London*, etc.; last in Colbert's *The Secret Heart* in '46—retired crabbing.

MANDEL, FRANCES WAKEFIELD *(1943)* 52 ——A famous beauty (modeled often for James Montgomery Flagg) in very early silents.

MANDER, MILES *(1946)* 58 ——Suave, elegant-faced top character from England, com-

mandingly present in more than 75; Hollywood snared him for 1935's *The Three Musketeers* (was Richelieu); then in *The Little Princess; Wuthering Heights* (flawless as Mr. Lockwood); *The Man in the Iron Mask; Stanley and Livingstone; Primrose Path* (comic change of pace; Rogers' shiftless, drunken stepfather); *That Hamilton Woman; This Above All; Murder, My Sweet* (superbly villainous Mr. Grayle); *Confidential Agent*; last in Teresa Wright's *The Imperfect Lady*, released posthumously.

MANDY, JERRY *(1945)* 52 ——Comic support in many: Evelyn Brent's *Underworld*, Bobby Breen's *Hawaii Calls*, Colbert's *The Bride Comes Home*, Fields' *It's a Gift*, others.

MANLEY, DAVE *(1943)* 60 ——Support (Mill Worker) in the Griffith talkie *The Struggle*.

MANN, HANK *(1971)* 84 ——Great walrus-moustached, original Keystone Kop who looked like a soulful basset hound—and was Sennett's personal favorite; a roll call of his movies (from '12) would be a potted history of screen comedy; his comic character, Sennett historian Kalton C. Lahue has noted, "always stood out as an impossible creature; surely no one could really be as much a victim of circumstance as was the ubiquitous Mr. Mann," and he adds that "he might just have been the funniest of them all"; after scores with Sennett, he starred in his own series, then switched (in the '20s) to features: *The Patent Leather Kid, Broadway After Midnight, When Danger Calls, Garden of Eden, Hollywood Cavalcade*, etc.; bald (and with no moustache) was with Chaplin in *City Lights* (the tough boxer Chaplin fought in the prizefight ring), *Modern Times*, and *The Great Dictator* (a bit); in the '40s, between his seven minor screen roles, he became Edward Everett Horton's makeup man; busy in the '50s as comic support in the pix of Jerry Lewis, "Joe Palooka," Abbott & Costello, and he and old silent-comedy pal Snub Pollard played waiters in Cagney's *Man of a Thousand Faces*.

MANN, LOUIS *(1931)* 65 ——Distinguished Broadway actor who starred—always as a father—in several 1929–30 films: MGM's *The Richest Man in the World, Sins of the Children, Father's Day*, etc.

MANN, STANLEY *(1953)* 69 ——In several silents, and, last, a small role in *The Robe*.

MANNING, AILEEN *(1945)* 60 ——Support—usually "society" roles—in many in the '20s: *Main Street, The Tailor-Made Man, Beauty's Worth, The Snob, Stella Maris, Home James*, etc.

MANNING, JOSEPH *(1946)* ——Character; in the 1920 Ben Wilson serial *The Screaming Shadow.*

MANNING, TOM *(1936)* 56 ——Support in Jolson's *The Singing Kid.*

MANSFIELD, JAYNE *(1967)* 34 ——Blonde star more famous for her big bosom than her limited comedy talent; during its difficulties with Marilyn Monroe, 20th Century-Fox promoted her heavily as Monroe's successor in *Will Success Spoil Rock Hunter?* (she had starred in it on Broadway), *The Wayward Bus,* and *Kiss Them for Me;* after these, except for *The Sheriff of Fractured Jaw* and *The Loved One,* most of her starring films were poor: *The Fat Spy, Panic Button, Country Music, The George Raft Story,* etc.

MANSFIELD, JOHN *(1956)* 37 ——Support in adventure pix (*The Naked Jungle, Man-Eater of Kumaon*) and big-budget Westerns (*Pony Express, Warpath, Denver and the Rio Grande,* etc.).

MANSFIELD, MARTHA *(1923)* 23 ——John Barrymore's leading lady in *Dr. Jekyll and Mr. Hyde;* from the Broadway musical stage, she entered movies in '17 as French comedian Max Linder's romantic interest in *Max and His Taxi;* in a dozen more pix: *Broadway Bill, Man of Stone, Fog Bound, Youthful Cheaters, Queen of the Moulin,* etc.; died of fire burns sustained on the Texas location of *The Warrens of Virginia.*

MANTELL, ROBERT B. *(1928)* 74 ——Famed stage actor; starred (1915–16) in *A Woman's Sacrifice, The Green-Eyed Monster, The Blindness of Devotion;* in 1924's *Under the Red Robe,* was the Cardinal.

MANTZ, PAUL *(1965)* 61 ——Famous movie stunt flyer onscreen in *Test Pilot, Hell's Angels, Flying Leathernecks,* etc.

MANX, KATE *(1964)* 34 ——Offbeat, sexy-looking blonde who starred in one, *Private Property,* directed by husband Leslie Stevens.

MAPLE, AUDREY *(1971)* 72 ——Featured in the '34 sexploitation pic *Enlighten Thy Daughter.*

MARCH, EVE *(1974)* 50s ——Teacher of the little girl (Ann Carter) in *Curse of the Cat People;* first stand-in of Katharine Hepburn, was in many of her pix including *Adam's Rib,* as secretary Grace; also in *How Green Was My Valley, The Sun Shines Bright,* etc.

MARCH, HAL *(1970)* 49 ——Most famous as the nice-guy emcee of TV's *The $64,000 Question,* he played comedy leads in several pix: *My Sister Eileen* ('55), *It's Always Fair Weather, Send Me No Flowers, A Guide for the Married Man,* etc.

MARCH, NADINE *(1944)* 46 ——Support in Ruth Chatterton's *The Rat* ('38).

MARCHAT, JEAN *(1966)* 64 ——French actor; in Bresson's *Les Dames du Bois de Boulogne, Tomorrow Is My Turn, Stormy Waters,* others.

MARCUS, JAMES *(1937)* 69 ——Was the paunchy boozer-trader, Joe Horn, in Swanson's *Sadie Thompson;* support in *The Iron Horse* (saloon-keeping Judge Haller, whose bar was one of "justice and likker"), *Beau Brummel, The King of Kings, The Scarlet Letter, In Old Arizona, Arrowsmith* (the Old Doctor), others through '36.

MARCUSE, THEODORE *(1967)* 47 ——Bald bad buy in *The Cincinnati Kid;* also in *The Glass Bottom Boat, The Last of the Secret Agents?, A Tiger Walks, Sands of Beersheba,* others.

MARGETSON, ARTHUR *(1951)* 54 ——English support in *Sherlock Holmes Faces Death* (Dr. Sexton), *Random Harvest* (Chetwynd), *Commandos Strike at Dawn* (German Colonel); earlier in British pix: *Little Friend, Juggernaut, I Give My Heart,* others.

MARGOLIS, CHARLES *(1926)* 52 ——Minor support in Mae Murray's *The Merry Widow.*

MARGULIES, VIRGINIA *(1969)* 53 ——Actress-daughter of silent star Edward Peil.

MARIANO, LUIS *(1970)* 50 ——Spanish singer; in the European-made *Candide* ('62).

MARINOFF, FANIA *(1971)* 81 ——Slender, raven-haired, Russian-born actress famous on Broadway; co-starred for World in 1915's *McTeague* with Holbrook Blinn and for Artcraft in 1917's *The Rise of Jennie Cushing* with Elliott Dexter.

MARION, EDNA *(1957)* 48 ——Lovely young comedienne and perhaps the unluckiest of the 1926 Wampas Baby Stars (Crawford, Astor, Del Rio, Gaynor, etc.); she was active mainly in Hal Roach comedies such as Laurel & Hardy's golf-links two-reeler *Should Married Men Go Home?* ('28); a few features: *The Call of the Wilderness, The Desert's Price, Skinner Steps Out,* etc.

MARION, GEORGE *(1945)* 85 ——Magnificent character actor who all but made a career of playing the seafaring father, who shook his fist at that "Ole Devil Sea," in *Anna Christie;* created the role on Broadway opposite Pauline Lord, played it in the silent movie version ('23) with Blanche Sweet, and did it again, better than ever, in Garbo's first talkie; onscreen from '14, he was also in *Clothes Make the Pirate, The White Monkey, The King of Kings, Evangeline, The Big House;* last in 1935's *Metropolitan* with Jane Darwell.

MARION, SID *(1965)* 65 ——Comic support in *Call Me Madam* (cafe proprietor), Dunne's *Magnificent Obsession* (sword swallower), *Lady of Burlesque, Love That Brute,* etc.; sometimes billed Sidney.

MARION-CRAWFORD, HOWARD *(1969)* 55 ——Hearty, well-upholstered English character; in many: *Lawrence of Arabia* (Medical Officer), *The Hasty Heart, Where's Charley?, Gideon of Scotland Yard, The Man in the White Suit,* etc.

MARKS, JOE E. *(1973)* 82 ——Was Pappy Yokum in *Li'l Abner* on Broadway and in the '59 movie; character roles in 20 others.

MARKS, SIDNEY *(1974)* 51 ——Support in many.

MARLE, ARNOLD *(1970)* 81 ——Czech-born character who looked like the soured twin brother of Marie Dressler and was in scores of British films: *One of Our Aircraft Is Missing* (played Dutchman Pieter Sluys), *The Glass Mountain, Mr. Emmanuel, The Red Monkey,* etc.

MARLO, MARY *(1960)* 62 ——Played Jeanne Crain's mother in *The Second Greatest Sex.*

MARLOWE, ANTHONY *(1962)* 52 ——Support in Dietrich's *The Flame of New Orleans* (as the Opera Singer, which he actually was), John Beal's *The Great Commandment,* Cornel Wilde's *Saadia.*

MARLOWE, FRANK *(1964)* 60 ——Support; first in Tracy's *Now I'll Tell* (Gambler Curtis), then in *Murder in the Blue Room, Barricade, Lucy Gallant, The Man with the Golden Arm* (Piggy), *Chicago Confidential,* etc.

MARR, WILLIAM *(1960)* 67 ——Support in a Milton Sills silent, *Men of Steel,* others.

MARRIOTT, MOORE *(1949)* 64 ——English character actor, usually a humorous old country man; on British screens from 1908 and in hundreds: *Peg of Old Drury, Green for Danger, As You Like It, Nell Gwyn, The History of Mr. Polly,* and many Will Hay comedies (always as scrappy old Harbottle).

MARRIOTT, SANDEE *(1962)* 60 ——He played a character role in Jean Simmons' *Hilda Crane.*

MARSH, CHARLES *(1953)* 50s ——Minor support in *My Wild Irish Rose, Atlantic City, Christmas in Connecticut,* etc.; usually a business man.

MARSH, MAE *(1968)* 72 ——Poet Vachel Lindsay once claimed as his muses three early stars —Blanche Sweet, Mary Pickford, Mae Marsh (with whom he was not so secretly in love); arguably, of these and others (just possibly Gish too), Mae Marsh was the greatest silent actress on the screen; she could convey with economy every known emotion, being particularly adept at tragedy; friend Lillian Gish has said: "She had a quality of pathos in her acting that has never been equaled . . . she was the only actress of whom I was ever jealous"; a slight, freckled Irish redheaded schoolgirl of 15, she was discovered by D. W. Griffith, who used her in small roles (first in Pickford's *Ramona*) in 1910–12; had her first lead in 1912's *Man's Genesis,* then many major roles with Griffith in the next five years: *The Lesser Evil, The Sands of Dee, Judith of Bethulia, The Birth of a Nation* (*Little Sister,* whose suicide still breaks hearts whenever this masterpiece is shown), *Home Sweet Home, Intolerance* (in The Modern Story, the Dear One who saves her young husband from the gallows), *Avenging Conscience,* etc.; for two years (1917–19), was Goldwyn's first star ("The Goldwyn Girl"), in *Polly of the Circus, The Cinderella Man,* etc., at $2,500 a week; became one of the first international stars, filming in England (*Flames of Passion, Paddy-the-Next-Best-Thing*) and Germany (*Arabella*); returned to star for Griffith one last time, in 1923's *The White Rose;* except for *Racing Through* ('28), was offscreen from '25 to '31, when she returned as a character actress in *Over the Hill;* but in talkies, she once confessed, she found it "hard for me to learn lines"; did bits at 20th Century-Fox for 13 years (1940–53) in *Jane Eyre, Apartment for Peggy, The Snake Pit,* etc.; and, because of a lifelong friendship with John Ford, she was in virtually all his movies—but barely, for he well knew that, turned loose, Mae Marsh could still act rings around all his stars.

MARSH, MARGUERITE *(1925)* 36 ——Helped younger sister Mae crash the movies; began with Sennett, Goldwyn, and Griffith; she and Mae co-starred, as French girls, in 1918's *Fields*

702

of Honor; in the '20s was in *Women Men Love, The Idol of the North, Iron to Gold, Boomerang Bill,* etc.; began onscreen as Marguerite Loveridge and also was sometimes billed Margaret Marsh.

MARSHAL, ALAN *(1961)* 52 ——Exceedingly handsome Colman-type star (charm, moustache, English accent), onscreen from '36 (*The Garden of Allah*); for a decade was a "Selznick star" who never made a Selznick movie, being loaned out instead to co-star: with Merle Oberon in *Lydia,* Ginger Rogers in *Tom, Dick and Harry,* Anna Neagle in *Irene,* Loretta Young in *He Stayed for Breakfast,* and, most impressively, Irene Dunne in *The White Cliffs of Dover;* illness (a nervous condition) kept him offscreen for long periods (1942–43 and 1945–48); when he returned he was in just four more: *The Barkeleys of Broadway* ('49), *The Opposite Sex* ('56), *House on Haunted Hill* ('58), *Day of the Outlaw* ('59); resumed his stage career then and was co-starring with Mae West in Chicago in *Sextette* when fatally stricken.

MARSHALL, BOYD *(1950)* 65 ——A handsome silent lead, one of the stars of 1915's *King Lear.*

MARSHALL, CHARLES "RED" *(1974)* 50s ——Elyse Knox's handsome leading man, "Red," in *A Wave, a Wac and a Marine;* also in *Specter of the Rose,* others; sometimes billed Chet.

MARSHALL, HERBERT *(1966)* 75 ——Polished English star who, in the '30s, was a matinee idol, playing well-bred (and often a bit world-weary) lovers opposite all the famous Hollywood femme stars; in *Blonde Venus, Trouble in Paradise, The Painted Veil, Michael and Mary, The Dark Angel, The Good Fairy, Angel,* etc.; from '40 it was often top-billed roles as fathers (*Foreign Correspondent, Kathleen, A Bill of Divorcement, The Secret Garden*) or friends (*The Enchanted Cottage*); gave one of his finer character performances in *The Little Foxes* as the husband Davis dispatches by withholding his pills: a couple of "repeats" in his career: co-starred twice in *The Letter* (first with Jeanne Eagels, then with Davis), and twice portrayed Somerset Maugham (*The Moon and Sixpence, The Razor's Edge*); last in 1965's *The Third Day* with George Peppard.

MARSHALL, TULLY *(1943)* 78 ——One of the finest of character actors, onscreen from '14, who had a genius for landing good roles in memorable movies: *Intolerance* (The Babylonian Story: High Priest of Bel), 1916's *Oliver Twist* (Fagin), *The Covered Wagon* (Indian scout Jim Bridger), *He Who Gets Slapped*

(Count Mancini), the silent *Hunchback of Notre Dame* (King Louis XI), Mae Murray's *The Merry Widow* (Baron Sadoja), the silent *Cat and the Canary* (crooked lawyer Crosby), *Black Fury* (labor leader Tommy Poole), *This Gun for Hire* (corrupt syndicate chief Brewster), Colman's *A Tale of Two Cities* (Woodcutter), *Ball of Fire* (white-suited Professor Robinson, one of the old scholars Stanwyck taught the Conga), and 100 more; was last in 1943's *Behind Prison Walls,* which is where many stars would long since have sent him—for theft of scenes.

MARSON, AILEEN *(1939)* 26 ——British leading lady; with John Lodge in *The Tenth Man;* also in *My Song for You, Honeymoon for Three, Waves of Desire,* others.

MARSTINI, ROSITA *(1948)* 53 ——Support in *The Big Parade* (as the French mother) and numerous others of the '20s: *The Lover of Camille, Enter Madame, Hot for Paris, Shadows of Paris,* etc.; fewer talkies: *In Love with Life, I Cover the Waterfront, Holiday in Mexico.*

MARSTON, ANN *(1971)* 32 ——Child actress who had a few minor roles in the '50s.

MARSTON, JOHN *(1962)* 72 ——Character actor who usually played men of principle; in *Cabin in the Cotton, The Little Giant* (the D.A. who gives beer baron Edward G. Robinson a "break"), *Silver Dollar* (also with Robinson), *Love Is a Racket, Mayor of Hell,* etc.

MARTIN, CHRIS-PIN *(1953)* 59 ——Fine fun as big-bellied, wall-eyed Pancho in all six of the "Cisco Kid" pix starring Cesar Romero (1939–41), and two of Gilbert Roland's ('47); earlier, in two of Warner Baxter's, had portrayed his sidekick Gordito; an extra in movies from '11, he became a featured player in talkies in which he could wrap his exaggerated Mexican accent around the straightest lines and make them hilarious; actually was a Yaqui Indian born in Tucson; in hundreds of Westerns, small and big (*The Mark of Zorro, The Ox-Bow Incident, San Antonio*), he was also in many musicals (*Week-End in Havana, Down Argentine Way*); last in 1953's *Ride the Man Down;* and his name was real—almost: Ysabel Poinciana Chris-Pin Martin Piaz.

MARTIN, EDIE *(1964)* 84 ——Tiny English ramrod who always looked as though she should be wearing high-button shoes; in many Guinness comedies: *The Lavender Hill Mob* (the landlady whose garage he uses to make pure-gold miniature Eiffel Towers), *The Man in the White Suit, The Ladykillers;* also in *Sparrows Can't Sing, The Titfield Thunderbolt,* many more.

MARTIN, LEWIS *(1969)* 60s ——Dignified character, especially active at Paramount in the '50s: *The War of the Worlds* (Pastor Collins), *Arrowhead, Ace in the Hole, The Caddy, Knock on Wood, Houdini, The Man Who Knew Too Much* (detective), others.

MARTIN, OWEN *(1960)* 70 ——Character (Max) in *The Pajama Game.*

MARTIN, VIRGINIA *(1971)* 45 ——A Paramount starlet in the late '40s.

MARTINDEL, EDWARD *(1955)* 79 ——Support in dozens of silents (*Clarence, The Dangerous Little Demon, The Dixie Handicap, Ducks and Drakes, Children of Divorce,* etc.) and talkies (*The Gay Diplomat, Divorce Among Friends, Champagne for Breakfast,* others).

MARTYN, PETER *(1955)* 27 ——British support; in *Folly to Be Wise, You Know What Sailors Are,* other comedies.

MARUM, MARILYN HARVEY *(1973)* 44 —— Minor support in *Rosemary's Baby,* others.

MARX, CHICO *(1961)* 70 ——The "Italian" Marx Brother, the sly "illiterate" forever swindling (or unwittingly wrecking the best-laid schemes of) con-artist Groucho; was the first-born of the brothers; co-starred with Groucho, Harpo and Zeppo in their first five: *The Cocoanuts, Animal Crackers, Monkey Business, Horse Feathers,* and *Duck Soup* (some call this their best); then with Groucho and Harpo in another eight in which they were the starring attraction: *A Night at the Opera* (others opt for this as the best), *A Day at the Races, Room Service, At the Circus, Go West, The Big Store, A Night in Casablanca, Love Happy;* in '57, all three did individual cameos—Chico playing a monk—in an all-star, all-time flop, Warners' *The Story of Mankind;* was on movie screens just once without any of his brothers, in a '33 Paramount short, *Hollywood on Parade,* with W. C. Fields and Buster Crabbe; on TV he starred once alone, in a straight role, in a '50 *Silver Theatre* episode, *Papa Romani.*

MARX, HARPO *(1964)* 70 ——Bewigged blond, top-hatted, harp-playing, girl-chasing (with the ever-present honker) Marx Brother; second eldest; was the first of the brothers to appear onscreen—in a bit in a '25 Richard Dix pic, *Too Many Kisses;* superb pantomimist and, some argue, the most comically inventive of the Marxes; besides being in all the above movies with his brothers, he appeared—as himself—in one feature, *Stage Door Canteen,* and two screen shorts: *La Fiesta de Santa Barbara* ('36) and *All-Star Bond Rally* ('45); on TV several

times in the '50s: an *I Love Lucy* episode (May 1955), *G.E. Theatre*'s "The Incredible Jewel Robbery" (March 1959; the last time Harpo, Groucho and Chico ever appeared together), the *Dupont Show of the Month*'s "The Red Mill" (April 1958; perhaps the only time his voice was heard—he narrated it); his very last appearance was as the star in a dramatic non-speaking role, in *The June Allyson Show*'s "Silent Panic" (December 1960).

MARX, MAX *(1925)* 30s ——No relation to above; actor-stuntman in the William Desmond serial *Strings of Steel.*

MASKELL, VIRGINIA *(1968)* 31 ——Dark-haired English actress who co-starred (as the wife) with Oskar Werner in *Interlude;* also in *Only Two Can Play, Doctor in Love, The Man Upstairs,* others.

MASON, BILLY *(1941)* 52 ——See William Mason.

MASON, DAN *(1929)* 76 ——Starred as the Skipper in the "Toonerville Trolley" series: *Skipper Has His Fling,* etc.; long onscreen, he was in dozens of features in the '20s: *A Self-Made Failure, Sally, The Fire Brigade, Seven Sinners, The Chinese Parrot,* etc.

MASON, ELLIOTT *(1949)* 52 ——Scottish character actress; was Mrs. MacNiff in *The Ghost Goes West;* in many British pix: *The Citadel, On Approval, The Captive Heart, O'wd Bob, The Ware Case,* etc.

MASON, EVELYN *(1926)* 34 ——Black actress in minor roles.

MASON, JAMES *(1959)* 69 ——Not the English star; onscreen from '14 (a bit in *The Squaw Man*), he was support—usually a villain—in dozens of Westerns, silent (*Lights of the Desert, Wanderer of the Wasteland,* etc.) and talkie (*Hopalong Cassidy, The Dude Ranger,* others); in occasional non-Westerns: *The King of Kings* (Gestas, the Repentant Thief), *The Story of Temple Drake,* etc.

MASON, JOHN *(1919)* 61 ——Co-starred in 1915's *Jim the Penman.*

MASON, LE ROY *(1947)* 44 ——Swarthy, muscular, with raven-black hair (curly) and a fine set of teeth, he seemed a sure bet for stardom—especially after romantic leads with such as Pauline Starke in *The Viking* ('29); but, in Westerns first (Tom Mix's *Tom and His Pals,* etc.), he returned to them; became the lithe, slick, "big boss" villain in scores of B Westerns (*Wyoming Outlaw, Silver Stallion*) and serials

(11 including *The Painted Stallion, The Tiger Woman*, and *Daughter of Don Q*).

MASON, LOUIS *(1959)* 71 ——The sheriff in *Stagecoach*, he played rustics in dozens: *Judge Priest, Kentucky Kernels, Banjo on My Knee, The Return of Frank James, Gold Rush Maisie*, etc.

MASON, MARJORIE *(1968)*——Minor roles in silents.

MASON, REGINALD *(1962)* 80 ——Dignified support, often a doctor, active in the '30s; in Loretta Young's *Life Begins*, Harlow's *Suzy*, Loy's *Topaze*, Lukas' *The Kiss Before the Mirror*, others.

MASON, SULLY *(1970)* 64 ——Kay Kyser's comic saxophonist; with Kyser in *That's Right, You're Wrong*, etc.

MASON, WILLIAM *(1941)* 52 ——Essanay's dimpled handsome juvenile lead, "Smiling Billy," from '13; in *Dizzy Heights and Daring Hearts, A Dash of Courage* (in which Wallace Beery supported him); starred for Universal in '16 in the slapstick "Baseball Bill" shorts, then in Foxfilm comedies (two-reelers) in '17; and offscreen several years, he came back, unsuccessfully, in '22 for a series with an independent company.

MASSEY, ILONA *(1974)* 62 ——MGM's gloriously blonde Hungarian soprano with the delectable beauty mark (real); introduced in *Rosalie*, she starred for Metro in two: *Balalaika* (with Nelson Eddy) and *Holiday in Mexico*; elsewhere, was in *New Wine* (with Alan Curtis, whom she married), *International Lady, Invisible Agent, Northwest Outpost* (again with Eddy), *Love Happy*, and last, *Jet Over the Atlantic* ('59); final professional engagement was 1960 singing tour in South Africa; happily remarried, retired to a Virginia manor house, devoted herself to such causes as Hungarian Co-ordinated Relief and fighting pollution.

MASTERS, DARRYL *(1961)* 48 ——Support in two Jim Davis pix: *Wolf Dog, The Flaming Frontier*.

MASTERS, RUTH *(1969)* 75 ——Gray-haired character (Aunt Peggy) in Carroll Baker's *Bridge to the Sun*; popular on TV as Mrs. Muldoon in the series *Car 54, Where Are You?*

MATHER, AUBREY *(1958)* 72 ——Bald, round little character from England on Hollywood screens 1937-50, usually as a twinkly-eyed butler; in *No, No, Nanette, Rage in Heaven, Night Must Fall, Ball of Fire, Random Harvest, Keys*

of the Kingdom, many more; returned to England, where he had been a screen favorite since '09, for *The Importance of Being Earnest, Cash on Delivery, The Golden Mask*.

MATHER, JACK *(1966)* 58 ——Played roles such as the bartender in *The Revolt of Mamie Stover*; also in *Broken Lance, The Bravados, The View from Pompey's Head*, etc.

MATHOT, LEON *(1968)* 72 ——Star of French silents: *Appassionata, A Daughter of Israel*; became a director later.

MATHEWS, CARL *(1959)* 59 ——Lanky Cooper type who played sheriffs in numerous B Westerns: *Wild Horse Range, West of Wyoming, Frontier Scout*, etc.

MATIESEN, OTTO *(1932)* 59 ——Handsome Scandinavian actor who starred in many in Hollywood in the '20s: *The Dawn of Tomorrow* with Jacqueline Logan, *The Last Moment, The Salvation Hunters, Scaramouche, Vanity Fair, Parisian Love, The Beloved Rogue*, etc.; last had a supporting role in 1931's *The Maltese Falcon*.

MATTERSTOCK, ALBERT *(1960)* 48 ——German leading man; in *Our Little Wife*, others.

MATTHEWS, A. E. *(1960)* 90 ——Distinguished, charming Britisher; in many comedies: *Laughter in Paradise, Man With a Million, Carry On Admiral, Doctor at Large, Penny Princess, The Galloping Major*, etc.; had played romantic leads in English pix of the '20s.

MATTHEWS, JEAN *(1961)* 60s ——Minor roles in early silents.

MATTHISON, EDITH WYNNE *(1955)* 79 —— Brunette Lasky star of '15; wife of character actor Charles Rann Kennedy.

MATTOX, MARTHA *(1933)* 54 ——Of the harsh visage, she played housekeepers (the sinister one in Laura La Plante's *The Cat and the Canary*) and country women from the '20s to the end; in *Huckleberry Finn* ('20), *Beauty's Worth* (Aunt Elizabeth), *Penrod and Sam* ('23), *East Lynne* ('25), *The Keeper of the Bees, The Little Shepherd of Kingdom Come, Kentucky Courage*, etc.

MATTRAW, SCOTT *(1946)* 61 ——In the '20s, support in serials (*Haunted Island, The Return of the Riddle Rider*), Westerns (*Quick Triggers, Captain Cowboy*), adventure pix (*The Thief of Bagdad*).

MATZENAUER, MARGARET *(1963)* 81 ——A real-life opera star, she played one, Madame Pomponi, in *Mr. Deeds Goes to Town*.

MAUDE, CHARLES *(1943)* 61 ——Played a lead in England's *The House of Temperley* ('14).

MAUDE, CYRIL *(1951)* 88 ——As an older man, he recreated for Paramount in '30 his famous lovable-crab stage role in *Grumpy;* earlier, this English actor had starred in the title role in 1915's *Peer Gynt;* last in 1950's *While the Sun Shines.*

MAURICE, MARY *(1918)* ——Vitagraph actress, known as "Mother" Mary Maurice, who had major roles in *Saving an Audience* ('11), *The Battle Cry of Peace, My Old Dutch,* etc.

MAURUS, GERDA *(1968)* 59 ——German actress featured in Fritz Lang's *Spies,* etc.

MAWDESLEY, ROBERT *(1953)* 53 ——Support in the British pic *Loyalties.*

MAWSON, EDWARD *(1917)* 55 ——Bearded, he played a lead in 1916's *Return of Eve.*

MAXAM, LOUELLA *(1970)* 74 ——Pretty, dimple-cheeked, blonde Sennett comedienne; in Chester Conklin's *Bucking Society,* Edgar Kennedy's *His Bitter Pill,* others in '16.

MAXEY, PAUL *(1963)* 55 ——Heavyset, gray support in dozens from '40: *With a Song in My Heart* (the General), *The Narrow Margin* (a hood), *South of St. Louis, Kid Monk Baroni, Stars and Stripes Forever, The Reformer and the Redhead,* etc.

MAXTED, STANLEY *(1963)* 62 ——English support; in *I Am a Camera, Never Let Me Go, Across the Bridge, The Weapon,* etc.

MAXWELL, EDWIN *(1948)* 58 ——Jovial (usually), gray and well-rounded, he lent his Irish charm to character roles in dozens: *All Quiet on the Western Front* (Lew Ayres' father), two Pickford talkies (*The Taming of the Shrew* and *Kiki*), *Scarface* (Chief of Detectives), *Grand Hotel* (Dr. Waitz), *Duck Soup, The Crusades* (Ship's Master), *Come and Get It, Ninotchka, The Jolson Story,* and on, through *The Set-Up* and *Thieves' Highway.*

MAXWELL, ELSA *(1963)* 80 ——Famous roly-poly cafe society party-giver of the '30s, given to calling herself—with some small cause then —"a legend in my own lifetime"; 20th Century-Fox top-featured her in 1939's *Hotel for Women,* based on a story she wrote, and in 1940's *Public Deb. No. 1;* appeared as herself in *Stage Door Canteen.*

MAXWELL, MARILYN *(1972)* 49 ——Vivacious, long-lashed, brown-eyed blonde leading lady, popular at Metro in the '40s: *Stand By for Action, Salute to the Marines, Three Men in White, Lost in a Harem, High Barbaree, Summer Holiday* (as the sensuous Belle), etc.; was excellent love interest with Kirk Douglas in *Champion;* later was fine comedy foil for comedians Bob Hope (*The Lemon Drop Kid, Off Limits, Critic's Choice*) and Jerry Lewis (*Rock-a-Bye Baby*); starred on TV in a '61 series, *Bus Stop;* later, her career at a standstill, and having played a bubble dancer in *Key to the City,* she did a burlesque-type stage stint in Brooklyn; servicemen, whom she entertained all over the globe in both WW II and the Korean War, retain fond memories of her.

MAY, EDNA *(1948)* 58 ——Celebrated Broadway beauty who starred for Vitagraph in 1916's *Salvation Nell.*

MAY, HAROLD R. *(1973)* 70 ——Said to have been the "youngest" of the Keystone Kops; came in as replacement for one of the originals.

MAYALL, HERSCHEL *(1941)* 78 ——Handsome support in Theda Bara's *Cleopatra* (the Messenger), Betty Blythe's *The Queen of Sheba,* John Gilbert's *Arabian Love,* many more in the '20s; played a doctor in March's *The Royal Family of Broadway,* one of his last.

MAYFIELD, CLEO *(1954)* 57 ——Brunette Broadway musical comedy star; headlined in MGM musical shorts in '30.

MAYHEW, KATE *(1944)* 91 ——Character actress in silents: Thomas Meighan's *Tongues of Flame,* Pearl White's *Hazel Kirke,* etc.

MAYHEW, STELLA *(1934)* 59 ——In several, but more famous as one of the stars of Broadway's *Hit the Deck* ('27).

MAYNARD, CLAIRE *(1941)* 29 ——One of Fox's promising starlets of '31 when she was featured in *Good Sport* and Mae Marsh's *Over the Hill.*

MAYNARD, KEN *(1973)* 77 ——Super-cowboy hero of more than 300 Saturday afternoon Westerns, who survived his three great rivals, Tom Mix, Buck Jones, and Hoot Gibson; rangy, square-jawed and a superb trick rider, he —with horse Tarzan—packed movie houses for 21 years (1924-45); this Palomino (actually, there were two) was such a drawing card that one '32 action pic capitalized on his name, *Come On, Tarzan!;* in '36 and '37, the first two years of the poll, Ken Maynard was in the Top Ten Western Money-Makers at the box-office; a few of the pix that put him there: *Tombstone Canyon, Smoking Guns, Phantom Thunderbolt,*

Whirlwind Horseman; offscreen after '38, he came back in '43 to co-star with Hoot Gibson and Bob Steele in five "Trail Blazer" pix: Wild Horse Stampede, Blazing Guns, Arizona Whirlwind, etc.; as an oldtimer, played a few widely spaced cameo roles in B Westerns as late as '71, when in two made in Kentucky by former cowboy Sunset Carson.

MAYNARD, KERMIT (1971) 69 ——Never a legendary figure like older brother Ken, this 1933 World's Champion Trick and Fancy Rider did star (1931-35) in many B Westerns: Prince of the Plains, The Fighting Trooper, Red Blood of Courage, etc.; in the '40s, besides doubling hazardous stunts for big-name stars, he was chiefly a villain in the Westerns of Johnny Mack Brown, Bob Livingston, and Gene Autry; later had small roles in How the West Was Won, The Fighting Texan, etc.

MAYNE, ERIC (1947) 74 ——Character actor from Ireland; in many silents: My American Wife, Cameo Kirby, Garments of Truth, Black Oxen, The Black Bird, etc.; fewer talkies: Duck Soup (as The Third Judge), East Lynne (doctor), All the King's Horses, others.

MAYO, FRANK (1963) 74 ——Dapper, very popular leading man in silents from the teens through the '20s; co-starred in many with his then real-life wife, Dagmar Godowsky, as well as other femme stars: Colleen Moore in The Perfect Flapper (the old-fashioned young lawyer she married at the fadeout), Kitty Gordon in The Interloper, Mae Busch in Souls for Sale; was star-billed in numerous others: Dr. Jim, The Brute Breaker, Afraid to Fight, etc.; until retirement in '47, had supporting roles in dozens: Confessions of a Nazi Spy, The Male Animal, Gentleman Jim, Buck Privates Come Home, The Gorilla Man, etc.

MAYO, GEORGE (1950) 59 ——Support in a '34 Monogram pic, A Woman's Man.

MAYO, HARRY (1964) 65 ——Minor roles in many pix from The Birth of a Nation on; organized and was president of the bit-role actors Screen Players Union.

MAYOR, AUGUSTIN (1968) 33 ——Minor role in Requiem for a Heavyweight.

McATEE, CLYDE (1947) 66 ——Support in several of the '20s including Charles Ray's Percy.

McCABE, HARRY (1925) 45 ——Support in silent cowboy pix: Lefty Flynn's The No-Gun Man, many others.

McCALL, WILLIAM (1938) 58 ——Support in Westerns of the '20s and early '30s: Sell 'Em Cowboy, The Phantom Horseman, Rounding Up the Law, Under Texas Skies, etc.; in such silent serials as William Duncan's Fighting Fate.

McCANN, CHARLES ANDREW (1927) 30s ——Minor support in Theda Bara's The Tiger Woman.

McCARROLL, FRANK (1954) 61 ——Lantern-jawed actor who rode with the gang in cowboy pix: Silver City Kid, Twilight on the Rio Grande, more.

McCARTHY, MYLES (1928) 50s ——Support in the '20s; in George A. Billings' The Dramatic Life of Abraham Lincoln, Milton Sills' Captain Blood, Tom Mix's Oh, You Tony!, others.

McCLAIN, BILLY (1950) 92 ——Black support; in Dimples (Rufus), Gone With the Wind (Old Levi, at the Atlanta Bazaar), others.

McCLUNG, ROBERT (1945) 23 ——At 16 had minor parts in The Toast of the Town (bellhop), Polly Moran's Two Wise Maids, a few others.

McCLURE, BUD (1942) 56 ——Support in cowboy pix.

McCLURE, FRANK (1960) 65 ——Character actor; many minor roles.

McCOMAS, CARROLL (1962) 76 ——Dark-haired Paramount leading lady of '19; later a character actress in Dennis O'Keefe's Chicago Syndicate, Ray Milland's Jamaica Run, others.

McCONNELL, LULU (1962) 70 ——Radio comic-panelist (It Pays to Be Ignorant); support in Blondell's Stage Struck.

McCONNELL, MOLLIE (1920) 70s ——Support in several: James Morrison's Black Beauty, the Ruth Roland serial Who Pays?, others.

McCORMACK, JOHN (1945) 61 ——Famed Irish operatic tenor; starred in one in Hollywood, Song O' My Heart with Maureen O'Sullivan, and had a top supporting role in another in England, Wings of the Morning with Annabella.

McCORMICK, ALYCE (1932) ——Support in Bad Girl, Frankenstein, Madge Bellamy's Mother Knows Best, Ruth Roland's comeback talkie, Reno, etc.

McCORMICK, F. J. (1948) 54 ——Great Dublin actor; best as Shell in Odd Man Out; in Hun-

gry Hill that same year and, earlier, *The Plough and the Stars.*

McCORMICK, MERRILL *(1953)* 62 ——— Usually, during his 42-year career, he was an unshaven Western villain looking like a seedy Douglas Fairbanks Jr.; in *Romance of the Rio Grande* (Warner Baxter version), *Deadwood Pass, Outlaws of Sonora,* etc.; also in such serials as *The New Adventures of Tarzan* ('35).

McCORMICK, MYRON *(1962)* 54 ———Hilarious as gravel-voiced Sgt. King, the topkick in (and reason for title of) *No Time for Sergeants,* and pathetic as Newman's tin-horn manager in *The Hustler;* one of the movies' ablest characters, he was first in *Winterset* (as Carr), then in *One-Third of a Nation* (Sam Moon), *China Girl, Not As a Stranger* (Dr. Snider), *Jolson Sings Again,* others.

McCOY, GERTRUDE *(1967)* 70s ———A soulful-eyed, ash-blonde beauty, and a fine comedienne, she was one of Edison Films' biggest stars in 1914, after appearing in *The Stenographer;* later starred in *The Blue Bird* ('18), *On the Stroke of 12, Out of the Darkness,* etc.; filming in England, she met and married character actor Duncan (*The Little Kidnappers*) MacRae, and, a Tennessean, lived the rest of her life in the British Isles.

McCOY, HARRY *(1937)* 43 ———Wavy-haired, moustachioed young Sennett comic; did many with Chaplin (*The Masquerader,* etc.) and Mabel Normand (*Mabel's Busy Day,* among others); supported Max Asher in the "Joker" comedy series and, in '20, starred in the two-reel "Hallroom Boys" comedies; in the '20s, supported Buddy Rogers in *Heads Up,* Syd Chaplin in *Skirts,* etc.; last in 1928's *Hearts of Men.*

McCRACKEN, JOAN *(1961)* 38 ———Pixie-faced Broadway comic dance star ("The Girl Who Falls Down"); was a mirthful addition to *Hollywood Canteen, Good News.*

McCULLOUGH, PAUL *(1936)* 52 ———In raccoon coat and derby, or other outlandish attire, he was perennially (from 1902) the straight man to comedian Bobby Clark; they starred first for Fox (1928–29) in a series of 14 comedies, one-reel to five (*In Holland, The Diplomats, Hired and Fired,* etc.); then were at RKO (1931–35) in a series of 22 two-reelers, the best of which may have been *Hokus Focus* and *Snug in the Jug.*

McCUTCHEON, WALLACE *(1928)* 45 ——— Handsome and versatile, he played leads in silent serials opposite Juanita Hansen (*The Phantom Foe*) and his wife, Pearl White (*The Black*

Secret); he and Miss White also were together in a 1920 feature, *The Thief;* in 1908, as a director at Biograph, he had been the first to buy stories from a would-be scriptwriter, D. W. Griffith, and it was his illness (temporary) which furnished Griffith his first opportunity to direct.

McDANIEL, GEORGE *(1944)* 58 ———Support in the Helen Holmes silent serial *The Girl and the Game;* in the '20s, was in *The Barefoot Boy, Silent Years, Burning Words,* etc.

McDANIEL, HATTIE *(1952)* 57 ———Of this splendid character actress it could be said that black was bountifully beautiful; huge and grand as Scarlett's Mammy in *Gone With the Wind,* she was the first black ever to win an Oscar (Support); onscreen from '32 (*Blonde Venus*), she was first merely a bossy domestic (making lazy Stepin Fetchit really step in *Judge Priest*) or a cantankerous one (the disdainful hired-for-the-night maid in Hepburn's *Alice Adams*); subtly, her maids became protective, outspoken mother-surrogates for heroines (Stanwyck in *The Mad Miss Manton,* Harlow in *Saratoga*); a few of her many: *Nothing Sacred,* 1936's *Showboat* (in which she sang "Ah Suits Me"), *Shopworn Angel, Since You Went Away, The Male Animal, Song of the South, Maryland;* later starred on radio and TV in *Beulah;* twice divorced and once widowed, she—who had "mothered" dozens—died childless.

McDANIEL, SAM *(1962)* 66 ———A gleamingly bald look-alike for sister Hattie, and often playing characters named Deacon (his own nickname), he was onscreen in dozens from '35: *Captains Courageous, Mr. and Mrs. North, Birth of the Blues, Home in Indiana,* the "Joe Palooka" series, *The Foxes of Harrow,* etc.; he and Hattie were together in *Hearts Divided* and *The Great Lie.*

McDERMOTT, HUGH *(1972)* 63 ———Wavy-haired, jovial character in British pix: *No Orchids for Miss Blandish, The Seventh Veil, Trent's Last Case, Night People,* etc.

McDERMOTT, JOHN *(1946)* 53 ———Had a supporting role in 1923's *Mary of the Movies,* which he directed (as he had many earlier Christie comedies); later a scriptwriter (*College Rhythm, Three Wise Fools,* etc.).

McDONALD, CHARLES *(1964)* 78 ———In '14 was support in Jacob P. Adler's *Michael Strogoff;* in the '20s was in Thomas Meighan's *Irish Luck,* Pauline Starke's *Salvation Nell,* etc.

McDONALD, FRANCIS *(1968)* 77 ———One thinks of him as hard-faced and moustachioed, frequently a villain (and many times an Indian one) but often a sheriff or banker, in scores of B Westerns (*Gun Law*), A-grade Westerns (*The Plainsman, Rancho Notorious*), and such features as *Prisoner of Shark Island* and *North West Mounted Police;* actually, onscreen from 1912, he was one of the most ruggedly handsome (albeit short: 5'9") leading man in silents; so good-looking was he that, in '23, magazine editors voted him Hollywood's "prettiest" man —and that's when he decided to become a villain; was active in movies through 1959's *The Big Fisherman.*

McDONALD, MARIE *(1965)* 52 ——Tall, beautiful blonde publicized as "The Body"; onscreen from '41, first in B's (*Melody Lane, You're Telling Me*) and bits (*Lucky Jordan, I Love a Soldier*); made a resounding impression first in 1944's *Guest in the House,* as the leggy pin-up model with whom artist Ralph Bellamy goes on a toot; her comedy flair was then used to advantage in *Getting Gertie's Garter, It's a Pleasure, Living in a Big Way, Tell It to the Judge, The Geisha Boy,* etc.

McDONALD, RAY *(1959)* 35 ——MGM's song-and-dance lad with the beaming Pinocchio-like face; in *Babes on Broadway, Presenting Lily Mars, Born to Sing, Good News, Till the Clouds Roll By;* later, elsewhere, in *Shamrock Hill, There's a Girl in My Heart,* and *All Ashore* ('53), supporting Mickey Rooney just as he had in his second pic at Metro, 1941's *Life Begins for Andy Hardy;* brother of actress-dancer Grace McDonald.

McDOWELL, CLAIRE *(1967)* 78 ——As a strong-faced brunette, she was one of Biograph's earliest ('10) stars—in D. W. Griffith's *The Female of the Species* (the long-suffering Western wife who takes a hatchet to philandering Dorothy Bernard); from the '20s and to the end of her career (1944's *Are These Our Parents?*), she was the "mother" of them all, in *Ben-Hur* (Ramon Novarro's), *The Big Parade* (John Gilbert's), *Mother O' Mine, Black Oxen, The Show-Off* (Louise Brooks'), *The Big House* (Robert Montgomery's), *An American Tragedy* (Phillips Holmes'), etc.

McDOWELL, NELSON *(1947)* 72 ——Was a tall, string-tied townsman in many Westerns, silent (*The Phantom Bullet, The Frontier Trail,* etc.) and talkie (*Wilderness Mail, Feud of the West,* others); also support in *Uncle Tom's Cabin* ('27), Dickie Moore's *Oliver Twist, College Swing,* and such serials as *The Vanishing Rider.*

McELROY, JACK *(1959)* 44 ——Comic support in Martin & Lewis' *Hollywood or Bust.*

McFARLANE, GEORGE *(1932)* 55 ——Support in many early talkies: *Up the River* (as Jessup), *Nix on Dames, South Sea Rose, Happy Days, Half Shot at Sunrise, Union Depot,* etc.

McGAUGH, WILBUR *(1965)* 70 ——Top support—the would-be evil influence on hero Charles Brinley—in the 1924 serial *Days of '49;* in many Westerns in the '20s: *The Sheriff of Hope Eternal, At Devil's Gorge, Bad Man's Bluff,* etc.

McGEEHEE, GLORIA *(1964)* 42 ——Support (with Garland at the clinic for mentally retarded children) in *A Child Is Waiting.*

McGIVENEY, OWEN *(1967)* 83 ——Fine character actor from the stage; on movie screens from the late '40s in: *Show Boat* (as Windy McClain), *Brigadoon* (Old Angus), *Pat and Mike* (Harry MacWade), *Scaramouche, If Winter Comes,* etc.

McGLYNN, FRANK *(1951)* 84 ——Every director's idea of Lincoln (after portraying him on Broadway), he played the President in more than a dozen movies (*Union Pacific, Prisoner of Shark Island, The Littlest Rebel,* etc.) and one serial (1938's *The Lone Ranger*); he doffed the stove-pipe hat for *Boom Town,* Sylvia Sidney's *The Trail of the Lonesome Pine* (Preacher), *The Mad Empress, Little Miss Marker,* etc.; after his namesake son entered movies, playing such roles as Patrick Henry in Griffith's *America,* he was billed Sr.

McGOWAN, J. P. *(1952)* 72 ——Helen Holmes' husband, director, and frequent leading man in silent serials (*The Hazards of Helen,* etc.); a popular player in very early silents, he co-starred with Gene Gautier for Kalem in *The Colleen Bawn* ('11) and *From the Manger to the Cross* ('12); a director most of the rest of that decade, in the '20s and '30s was a supporting player in many dozens of Westerns (*Moran of the Mounted, Arizona Days,* etc.).

McGOWAN, OLIVER *(1971)* 64 ——Support in Robert Wagner's *Banning,* Anita Ekberg's *Screaming Mimi;* earlier, in '33, billed Shirling Oliver, he had appeared in *Victims of Persecution.*

McGRAIL, WALTER *(1970)* 80 ——The handsome black-haired hero who saved Pearl White in the serial *The Black Secret* ('19), he starred in many Vitagraph pix from '16: *Within the Law* with Alice Joyce, the serial *The Scarlet Runner,* etc.; in the '20s starred or co-starred in even more for First National and Columbia; was in *Playthings of Destiny* with Anita Stewart, *The Bad Man* with Jack Mulhall, *Old San Fran-*

cisco, *American Beauty, Man Crazy,* etc.; support in the '30s: *Calling All Marines, All The King's Horses, Stagecoach* (Captain Sickels); after *My Little Chickadee,* and two B Westerns in '42, retired.

McGRANARY, AL *(1971)* 70s ——Portrayed Senator Walsh in *Sunrise at Campobello.*

McGRATH, FRANK *(1967)* 64 ——Popular on TV as the cantankerous trail cook in *Wagon Train,* he was in *She Wore a Yellow Ribbon* (as Bugler/Indian); *The Tin Star; They Were Expendable; Ride, Vaquero; The Reluctant Astronaut; Tammy and the Millionaire,* others.

McGRATH, LARRY *(1960)* 70 ——Support in Richard Dix's *Knockout Reilly,* Warner Baxter's *The Arizona Kid, The Milky Way, The Jackie Robinson Story,* etc.

McGREGOR, HARMON *(1948)* 60 ——Support in silents such as Richard Arlen's *Vengeance of the Deep,* Bessie Love's *Slave of Desire,* and *The Dancing Cheat.*

McGREGOR, MALCOLM *(1945)* 52 ——Dashing, dark-haired, cleft-chinned leading man in dozens in the '20s: *The Prisoner of Zenda* (played Rupert of Hentzau), *Smouldering Fires* with Pauline Frederick, *Broken Chains* with Colleen Moore (the weak youth frontier lad Moore made a man of), *The Dancer of the Nile* with Carmel Myers, *Buck Privates,* a comedy in which he co-starred with Eddie Gribbon, *Headlines* with Virginia Lee Corbin, etc.; retired after a '35 B, *Happiness C.O.D.*

McGUINN, JOE *(1971)* 67 ——A brawny, handsome guy, in the Rod Cameron vein, he started as a B-Western heavy in such 1939–40 pix as *Wagons Westward* and *Marshal of Mesa City;* during the War, played military men (*Two Yanks in Trinidad, Flight Lieutenant*) and reporters (*The Glass Key*); back in Westerns, was a sheriff in many (*The Gambler Wore a Gun; Jack McCall, Desperado*), occasionally breaking out to play a character part such as Dr. English in *Ten North Frederick.*

McGUIRE, BENJAMIN *(1925)* 50 ——Acted in early Famous Players pix.

McGUIRE, TOM *(1954)* 80 ——Gray-haired character actor in many father roles (often stern) in the '20s: *Cinderella of the Hills* with Barbara La Marr, *Steamboat Bill Jr.* (father of heroine Marion Byron), *The Married Flapper* with Marie Prevost, *Red Hot Tires* with Patsy Ruth Miller, etc.

McGURK, ROBERT *(1959)* 52 ——Minor support; onscreen for three decades.

McHUGH, CATHERINE *(1944)* 75 ——Character actress-mother of Frank and Matt.

McHUGH, CHARLES *(1931)* 60s ——Character actor who was Shamus O'Tandy, the luckless immigrant father of Marion Davies in *Lights of Old Broadway;* in many others in the '20s: *Smiling Irish Eyes, The Girl of the Golden West* (the J. Warren Kerrigan version), *Finnegan's Ball, Smilin' at Trouble,* etc.

McHUGH, JIMMY *(1969)* 74 ——Famous songwriter ("Lovely to Look At"); onscreen in *The Helen Morgan Story.*

McHUGH, MATT *(1971)* 77 ——Comedian-brother of Frank; from late silents to '50, in more than 150 pix: *Jones Family in Hollywood; It Happened in Flatbush; Street Scene; Flight for Freedom; Salome, Where She Danced; Dark Corner,* etc., plus several "Three Stooges" shorts.

McILLWAIN, WILLIAM *(1933)* 50 ——Support in the '20s in Bryant Washburn's *Passionate Youth; The Dramatic Life of Abraham Lincoln,* etc.

McINTOSH, BURR *(1942)* 80 ——Hefty, bald character who will always be remembered as stern Squire Bartlett who sent Lillian Gish out into the snow in *Way Down East;* Miss Gish later recalled: "Mr. McIntosh had once been the editor of a magazine, and he remembered that as children Dorothy and I had posed for photographs for him. He was always apologizing for having to treat me so cruelly in the film"; onscreen from '13 to 1934's *The Richest Girl in the World,* he was most active in the '20s; was in *Lilac Time, The Adorable Cheat, Reckless Wives, Skinner Steps Out,* and two score more.

McINTYRE, FRANK *(1949)* 71 ——A popular Paramount comedian in '17, he starred in *Too Fat to Fight* (which he was) and co-starred with Doris Kenyon in *The Traveling Salesman.*

McINTYRE, LEILA *(1953)* 71 ——Character (Mary Todd Lincoln) in *The Prisoner of Shark Island;* in others of the '30s: *Topper, Zenobia, Murder in the Fleet, Three Smart Girls Grow Up,* etc.; was the mother of star Leila Hyams.

McIVOR, MARY *(1941)* 40 ——Lovely Ince leading lady of the '20s (*The Burning Trail,* etc.), and the wife of serial star William Desmond.

McKAY, GEORGE *(1945)* 65 ——Character (Mr. Van Heusen) in *Going My Way;* in many from '30: *The Case of the Missing Man, The Devil's Playground, Duke of West Point, The Face Behind the Mask, Babes in Arms,* etc.

McKEE, DONALD *(1968)* 69 ——Character (R. M. Lukas) in *The Goddess;* also in *The Whistle at Eaton Falls.*

McKEE, LAFE *(1959)* 87 ——Played the moustachioed father of the heroine in countless Westerns from 1912 well into the '40s; in *Mark of the Spur, Melody of the Plains, Pioneers of the Frontier, The Ivory-Handled Gun,* etc.; at the beginning, still billed Lafayette McKee (real name), was the father of Kathlyn Williams in the serial *The Adventures of Kathlyn.*

McKEE, TOM *(1960)* 43 ——Played Captain Eddie Rickenbacker in *The Court-Martial of Billy Mitchell;* also in *Vice Raid, Three Came to Kill, The Search for Bridey Murphy,* etc.

McKEEN, SUNNY *(1933)* 8 ——As a tyke, he was the delightful Baby Snookums in the two-reel silent comedy series "The Newlyweds and Their Baby," with Ethlyne Clair and Syd Saylor as his bungling young parents; then starred in his own series and by age 4 was earning over $15,000 a year.

McKENZIE, BOB *(1949)* 65 ——A small man with (in later years) a big belly, he was a gold-watch-chained banker in many dozens of Westerns; in silents (from Essanay days of 1915); *The Sheriff of Sun-Dog, The Devil's Dooryard, The Desert Hawk,* etc.; talkies: *Tall in the Saddle, Sing Cowboy Sing, The Sombrero Kid, Cimarron* ('31), *Duel in the Sun* (a bartender there), others; usually billed Robert in big-budget pix.

McKENZIE, EVA *(1967)* 78 ——An early ('15) ingenue, later a character actress (1931's *Virtuous Husband,* others); mother of actress Fay.

McKIM, ROBERT *(1927)* 40 ——Dashingly handsome as the Army officer who dueled Fairbanks over Marguerite de la Motte in *The Mark of Zorro,* he was in more than 40 in his 12 years (1915–27) onscreen: *The Edge of the Abyss* with Mary Boland, *The Primal Lure* with William S. Hart, *The Stepping Stone, All the Brothers Were Valiant, Monte Cristo, Her Kingdom of Dreams,* etc.

McKINNELL, NORMAN *(1932)* 62 —— Holmes' nemesis Moriarty in Arthur Wontner's *Sherlock Holmes' Fatal Hour* ('31); also in *Criminal at Large, White Face,* others.

McKINNEY, NINA MAE *(1967)* 58 ——Greatly talented star of King Vidor's *Hallelujah* ('29), who was the screen's first black love goddess; MGM, impressed by her, as the sassy, hands-on-hips vamp, Chick, signed her to a five-year contract but used her in just two—*Safe in Hell* ('31) and Jean Harlow's *Reckless* ('35), in which she had a very small role and also dubbed Harlow's songs; after singing in cafes in Paris, Athens, and Budapest, as "the Black Garbo," went to England to co-star with Paul Robeson in *Sanders of the River;* then, in America, came many all-black pix for black audiences; Hollywood brought her back for supporting roles in several in the '40s: *Together Again, Dark Waters, Night Train to Memphis, Danger Street,* and *Pinky;* in the last, was a "razor-totin', high-strung, high-yeller girl," and, black-movie historian Donald Bogle has noted, "it was hard to believe that the stocky, bleary-eyed harridan on screen had once been the bright-eyed carefree Chick."

McLAGLEN, VICTOR *(1959)* 73 ——A laughing stallion of a man—a great, garrulous (even in silents), brawling, and fun-loving star for almost 40 years (1920-59); won the Best Actor Oscar for *The Informer* and perhaps deserved one (but it came before Oscars were invented) for Captain Flagg in *What Price Glory?* (its director, Raoul Walsh, has said: "McLaglen had the qualities that his declared rival [Sgt. Quirt] listed in the play: 'Straight as a mast, muscled like a gorilla, and Christian as hell.' "); co-starred in many other Flagg-Quirt comedies *(Sez You—Sez Me,* etc.); top roles in many notable movies: *The Lost Patrol, Gunga Din, Dishonored, Mary of Scotland, Under Two Flags, The Princess and the Pirate, Forever and a Day,* etc.; 1949–52 worked exclusively in John Ford pix: *Fort Apache, She Wore a Yellow Ribbon, Rio Grande,* and *The Quiet Man,* which won him a Best Supporting Actor nomination; starred last in 1959's *Sea Fury.*

McMAHON, DAVID *(1972)* 63 ——In *I Was a Male War Bride,* was the Army chaplain who married Grant and Sheridan; also in *Operation Mad Ball, Eight Iron Men.*

McMAHON, HORACE *(1971)* 64 ——Lean-faced, frog-voiced, beatle-browed top character actor who played both sides of the law; in more than 135 pix, he was a hood for his first seven years in Hollywood, often named Blackie, bumping off scores of victims before being bumped off himself; among those pix (from '37): *When G-Men Step In, Big Town Czar, King of the Newsboys, Gangs of Chicago, Roger Touhy, Gangster;* his "reformation" came with the play *Detective Story;* played a hard-nosed, scrupulously honest cop (Lieutenant Monaghan) in it, repeated the role in the movie version, then played variations of it in *Susan Slept Here, Duffy of San Quentin, Blackboard Jungle, The Detective,* and the TV series *Naked City* (as Lieutenant Mike Parker); early in his career was billed MacMahon.

McNAMARA, EDWARD *(1944)* 60 ——Usually played cops *(Arsenic and Old Lace)* and wardens (*I Am a Fugitive from a Chain Gang*); began as a singing actor in Morton Downey's *Lucky in Love;* also in *Strawberry Blonde, The Devil and Miss Jones,* etc.

McNAMARA, TED *(1928)* 20s ——Made a comic name for himself in *What Price Glory?* as Private Kiper, who gave the razzberry to Captain Flagg; he and his long-nosed teammate in this, Sammy Cohen (Private Lipinsky), made later comedies together; was also in *Shore Leave, Colleen, Why Sailors Go Wrong, The Gay Retreat,* etc.

McNAMEE, DONALD *(1940)* 43 ——Support in von Stroheim's *The Great Gabbo* and Claire Windsor's *Fashion Madness.*

McNAUGHTON, GUS *(1969)* 85 ——Comic character in British pix: *Sidewalks of London, The Thirty-Nine Steps, Storm in a Teacup, Keep Your Seats Please, Jeanie, Busman's Holiday,* more.

McNAUGHTON, HARRY "BOTTLE" *(1967)* 70 ——British comedian who starred in such shorts (all 1930) as *Sixteen Sweeties, Tom Thumbs Down, All Stuck Up.*

McNEAR, HOWARD *(1969)* 63 ——Most famous as Floyd the Barber on TV's *The Andy Griffith Show,* he was comic support in many pix: *Bell, Book and Candle; Kiss Me, Stupid; Bundle of Joy; The Errand Boy,* etc.

McPHAIL, DOUGLAS *(1942)* 32 ——Handsome young baritone who was being groomed for stardom by MGM; under contract there 1936–42, he was seen, and most enjoyably heard, in *Maytime, Born to Dance, Babes in Arms, Little Nellie Kelly, Honolulu, Born to Sing, Broadway Melody of 1940,* etc.; the recent *That's Entertainment,* featuring him in several old clips, made young audiences curious about his career and life; like several young Metro musical contemporaries, he died a suicide.

McPHERSON, QUINTON *(1940)* 68 ——Minor British support, such as a Creditor in *The Ghost Goes West;* also in *Annie Laurie, Murder in the Old Barn, Talk of the Devil,* etc.

McQUOID, ROSE LEE *(1962)* 75 ——Support in many silents (from '11) and early talkies such as *Just Imagine!*

McREA, BRUCE *(1927)* 60 ——Pearl White loved him in 1916's *Hazel Kirke;* he later supported Elinor Glyn in *The World's a Stage.*

McSHANE, KITTY *(1964)* 66 ——The daughter in England's wildly funny "Old Mother Riley"

pix, she actually was the wife of Arthur Lucan who starred as OMR.

McTURK, JOE *(1967)* 62 ——A Runyon character to his massive fingertips, he was Angie the Ox in *Guys and Dolls;* had facsimile roles in *Pocketful of Miracles, The Man With the Golden Arm,* etc.

McVEY, PATRICK *(1973)* 63 ——Starred in Kazan's *The Visitors* ('72), and was in several earlier: *The Big Caper, Party Girl, Two Guys from Milwaukee, Pierre of the Plains;* was best known for starring as Steve Wilson in the *Big Town* TV series.

McVICKER, JULIUS *(1940)* 64 ——Was Senator Melrose in the Colbert-Cohan comedy *The Phantom President.*

McWADE, EDWARD *(1943)* 70s ——The old man Cary Grant saved from drinking his dippy aunt's fatal elderberry wine in *Arsenic and Old Lace;* was in dozens: *They Won't Forget* (the old Third Veteran), *The Return of Frank James* (Col. Jackson), *A Lost Lady,* etc.

McWADE, MARGARET *(1956)* 73 ——One of the "pixilated" sisters—the dark-haired one— in *Mr. Deeds Goes to Town;* had similar roles (sometimes with, sometimes without "sister" Margaret Seddon) in *Theodora Goes Wild* (as Dunne's Aunt Elsie), *Wings Over Honolulu, The Bishop's Wife,* etc.

McWADE, ROBERT *(1913)* 78 ——Played the title role in Vitagraph's 1913 production of *Rip Van Winkle;* was also in *There's Music in the Hair* with John Bunny and Flora Finch.

McWADE, ROBERT *(1938)* 56 ——Janet Gaynor's screen dad in *The First Year* and bald little Meierheim in *Grand Hotel;* onscreen from 1924's *Second Youth,* he was in many: *Ladies of the Jury, Madame Racketeer,* Irene Dunne's *Back Street* (Uncle Felix), *Once in a Lifetime, 42nd Street, Of Human Hearts,* others.

MEADE, CLAIRE *(1968)* 84 ——Dignified character actress who, in *Mother Is a Freshman,* was the wife of college dean Griff Barnett; was also in *The Unfaithful.*

MEADER, GEORGE *(1963)* 73 ——Character actor, onscreen from 1940, who played such roles as the Railroad Clerk in *Spellbound,* the Professor in *On the Town,* and a smalltown businessman in *The Courageous Dr. Christian;* also in *Father Takes a Wife, Bachelor Daddy, The Glass Key, Roughly Speaking, For the Love of Rusty, That Midnight Kiss, The Groom Wore Spurs,* and, last, 1952's *She's Working Her Way Through College.*

MEAKIN, CHARLES *(1961)* 81 ——Fine support in many in the '20s: Billie Dove's *The Marriage Clause*, Shearer's *Upstage*, Wesley Barry's *Penrod*, others.

MEEHAN, LEW *(1951)* 60 ——Character with a sharp flat nose who was a henchman in many dozens of Westerns: *Arizona Gunfighter, Fighting Pioneers, Roaring Frontiers, The Gun Ranger*, etc.

MEEK, DONALD *(1946)* 66 ——His name no lie, he played mousey, bald little men to quavering-voiced perfection in more than 100 from 1928: *Stagecoach* (whiskey-drummer Mr. Peacock, in the Sherlock Holmes cap), *You Can't Take It With You* (Poppins), *Young Mr. Lincoln, My Little Chickadee, Hollywood Cavalcade, Babes on Broadway, Maisie Goes to Reno*, etc., right through *Magic Town*, released a full year after his death; his screen characterization was a misrepresentation—privately, he was a forceful, erudite gentleman.

MEEKER, GEORGE *(1963)* 60 ——Tall, cool, gray-blond and balding, and, often as not, menacing; in the first of his 120 pix, in '28, he was a good guy with a fine shock of flaxen hair—as one of Margaret Mann's *Four Sons;* Germanic (or Austrian) roles thereafter were often his lot, though he was Brooklyn-born; was in Irene Dunne's *Back Street* (Kurt Shendler), *Only Yesterday, Spy Ship, Secret Enemies, History Is Made at Night, Up in Arms, Marie Antoinette* (one of his better opportunities, as Robespierre), etc.

MEHAFFEY, BLANCHE *(1968)* 60s —— Lovely leading lady with dark curls in generally secondary pix of the '20s and early '30s; was in *The White Sheep* with Glenn Tryon, *The Battling Orioles, Proud Heart* with Rudolph Schildkraut (excellent Jewish immigrant pic; may have been her peak), *A Woman of the World*, which starred Negri, etc.; changed name to Joan Alden, with no improvement in her roles; in '48 sued Paramount—unsuccessfully—to keep her old movies off TV.

MEHRMANN, HELEN ALICE *(1934)* ——Supported the Gleasons, James and Lucille, in a very bright 1930 comedy, *The Shannons of Broadway.*

MEIGHAN, JAMES, JR. *(1970)* 66 ——Supporting player; nephew of Thomas; best known as one of several actors who starred as "The Falcon" on radio.

MEIGHAN, THOMAS *(1936)* 57 ——Little known to the current generation, he was for 13 years (1915–28) Paramount's most consistently successful and popular male star; a big man of virility and charm, he represented to men and women alike the utmost in dependability; in leads from the beginning (*The Fighting Hope*), he starred in another 32 before 1919's *The Miracle Man* made him a superstar; headlined in five for Cecil B. DeMille: *Kindling, The Trail of the Lonesome Pine, Male and Female, Why Change Your Wife?, Manslaughter;* in a total of 80 starring vehicles, he was frequently seen opposite particular femme stars: Lila Lee (11 times); Blanche Sweet, Lois Wilson, Billie Burke, and Pauline Frederick (5 times each); Leatrice Joy, Norma Talmadge, and Charlotte Walker (3 each), etc.; among his many pix: *A Prince There Was, The Man Who Saw Tomorrow, Woman-Proof, The Racket* (next to *The Miracle Man*, his best); went to Warners in '29 for his (successful) starring debut in talkies, *The Argyle Case;* thereafter, played "The Lone Wolf" in *Cheaters at Play*, a top supporting role in *Madison Square Garden*, and fathers in three: *Young Sinners, Skyline*, and *Peck's Bad Boy* ('34), after which he retired.

MEISTER, OTTO *(1944)* 75 ——Comic in 1914's *Droppington's Family Tree.*

MELCHIOR, LAURITZ *(1973)* 82 ——Going from the Met to Metro, this great gray tenor twinkled his roly-poly way through three Technicolor musicals in the '40s (*Thrill of a Romance, This Time for Keeps, Luxury Liner*) and one black-and-white (*Two Sisters from Boston*); later co-starred with Rosemary Clooney, at Paramount, in *The Stars Are Singing.*

MELESH, ALEX *(1949)* 58 ——Bald Russian character; often a waiter, as in Ginger Rogers' *Once Upon a Honeymoon;* also in *On Your Toes, The Big Broadcast, Golden Boy, The Lady Takes a Chance*, etc.

MELFORD, GEORGE *(1961)* 80s ——Was usually to be found behind a badge; in *My Little Chickadee* (sheriff), *The Miracle of Morgan's Creek* (U.S. Marshal), *Hail the Conquering Hero* (sheriff); also in *A Tree Grows in Brooklyn* (Mr. Spencer), *Prince of Players, Dixie Dugan*, etc.; a noted director in the '20s and early '30s (*The Sheik*, the silent *The Light That Failed, East of Borneo*, etc.), he had been, in 1911, a most handsome Kalem leading man.

MELFORD, LOUISE *(1942)* 62 ——Frequently a supporting actress in pix directed by husband George.

MELLER, HARRO *(1963)* 56 ——Always played Germans, usually bad; in *The House on 92nd Street* (spy Conrad Arnulf), *Counter-Attack* (Ernemann, the German officer in the bombed-out cellar whom Muni was forced to shoot), the Marx Brothers' *A Night in Casablanca*, in which his billing was Mellor.

MELLER, RAQUEL *(1962)* 74 ——Spanish singer most famous for the '26 French version of *Carmen*, a superproduction directed by Jacques Feyder and designed as a vehicle for her; was brought to Hollywood amid much fanfare to star in 1929's *The Oppressed*, but impressed neither moviegoers nor critics ("This ought to be renamed *The Depressed*—meaning the audience. Raquel Meller disappoints"); made more pix abroad.

MELLINGER, MAX *(1968)* ——Character roles.

MELLISH, FULLER *(1936)* 71 ——Character; the judge in *Crime Without Passion;* father of Mellish Jr.

MELLISH, FULLER, JR. *(1930)* 34 ——Dark-haired, long-nosed and usually up to no good, he was shiftless husband who took Chatterton's son away from her in *Sarah and Son*, the seedy burlesque actor who lived with Helen Morgan —and made her pay—in *Applause;* also in *Roadhouse Nights, Two Shall Be Born*, etc.

MELTON, FRANK *(1951)* 43 ——Popular youth in many at Fox in the early '30s: Will Rogers pix (*David Harum, State Fair, Judge Priest, Handy Andy*), *Stand Up and Cheer, 365 Nights in Hollywood*, etc.; later in several Goddard movies: *The Cat and the Canary* (reporter), *Second Chorus* (Stu), *Pot O' Gold* (Jasper).

MELTON, JAMES *(1961)* 57 ——Famous radio tenor who starred in three at Warners in the mid-'30s: *Stars Over Broadway* (with Pat O'-Brien), *Sing Me a Love Song* and *Melody for Two* (both with Patricia Ellis); became a Metropolitan Opera star and returned to Hollywood for 1945's *Ziegfeld Follies*, in which he and Marion Bell sang a love duet from *La Traviata*.

MELVILLE, EMILIE *(1932)* 82 ——Supported Buddy Rogers and Nancy Carroll in *Illusion*.

MELVILLE, ROSE *(1946)* 73 ——Comedienne who starred for Kalem in '16 as pigtailed Sis Hopkins in *She Came, She Saw, She Conquered; Leap Year Wooing;* others in the same series of shorts; in '19, she appeared for Goldwyn in the feature *Sis Hopkins*, based on her own original story.

MENDELSSOHN, ELEANORA *(1951)* 50 —— Played Gene Kelly's Italian mother in the anti-Mafia pic *Black Hand*.

MENDES, JOHN P. *(1955)* 36 ——Was on-screen as himself, Sgt. John P. Mendes, in *This Is the Army*.

MENJOU, ADOLPHE *(1963)* 73 ——Being debonair, sophisticated, and moustachioed in 1923's *A Woman of Paris* (the movie Chaplin wrote-produced-directed to launch longtime leading lady Edna Purviance as a headliner) made him a star; had already been in many— *The Sheik, Kiss*, etc.—in seven years onscreen, usually as a villain; 1924's *Broadway After Dark* decidedly made him a matinee idol; thereafter was one of the movies' stalwarts, starring or co-starring—and almost always dapper—in more than 100: *The Front Page* (his only Oscar nomination as Best Actor), *One in a Million, A Farewell to Arms, Little Miss Marker, A Star Is Born* ('37), *Stage Door, Golden Boy* (seedy here as Holden's fight manager), *Roxie Hart, The Hucksters, State of the Union, Paths of Glory* (never better than as General Broulard who allows three innocent soldiers to be executed), and, last, *Pollyanna* ('60).

MENKEN, HELEN *(1966)* 64 ——Famous star of Broadway (*The Old Maid*) who appeared as herself in *Stage Door Canteen*.

MERA, EDITH *(1935)* ——A lead in France's *The Three Musketeers* ('33), others.

MERCER, BERYL *(1939)* 57 ——Mother-love never had such a staunch screen representative as this little dumpling; was "Mom" or "Ma" from the beginning (Colleen Moore's *Broken Chains* and Richard Dix's *The Christian*, when she was barely 40), and kept right on in *Seven Days' Leave* (Cooper's), *All Quiet on the Western Front* (Ayres'), *The Public Enemy* (Cagney's), etc.; was also in *Outward Bound* (Mrs. Midget), *Three Live Ghosts* (greedy Mrs. Gubbins), *Night Must Fall* (saleslady), *A Little Princess*, many others, including Frieda Inescort's *A Woman Is the Judge* ('39), her last.

MEREDITH, CHARLES *(1964)* 70 ——Leading man, tall, good-looking, with high-parted hair, who was quite popular in the last decade of silents; was in *Luck in Pawn* with Marguerite Clark, *Simple Souls* with Blanche Sweet, *The Beautiful Liar* with Katherine MacDonald, *Hail the Woman* with Florence Vidor, etc.; long offscreen, he returned as a character actor (the judge in 1947's *Daisy Kenyon*), remaining a busy, distinguished one to the end in *A Foreign Affair, The Boy with Green Hair, The Miracle of the Bells, Chicago Confidential*, etc.

MEREDITH, CHEERIO *(1964)* 74 ——Character actress; *I Married a Woman, The Wonderful World of the Brothers Grimm, The Legend of Tom Dooley*, etc.

MEREDITH, MELBA MELSING *(1967)* 71 — —Supporting roles.

MEREDYTH, BESS *(1969)* 70s ——In 1914's *The Desert's Sting* she was the curly-haired white woman with whom Indian girl Jeanie Macpherson's white husband fell in love—and, after his death, both women went off together to do missionary work among the Apaches; in real life, both Miss Macpherson and Miss Meredyth went off the acting reservation to become legendary scriptwriters; Miss Meredyth's credits include *Don Juan, The Mighty Barnum, Metropolitan, The Unsuspected*, others.

MERIVALE, PHILIP *(1946)* 59 ——Distinguished character actor from England, and as ascetically handsome as they come; on Hollywood screens in *Give Us This Night, Rage in Heaven, Mr. and Mrs. Smith, This Above All* (appearing alongside real-life wife Gladys Cooper), *Crossroads, This Land Is Mine, The Hour Before the Dawn, Tonight and Every Night, Sister Kenny*, etc.

MERRALL, MARY *(1973)* 83 ——Character in many British pix: *Dead of Night, The Pickwick Papers, Love on the Dole, The Belles of St. Trinian's*, etc.

MERRILL, FRANK *(1966)* 71 ——Serial strong-man Joe Bonomo, who had been set to star, broke a leg, so this muscular stuntman-actor became the screen's (fifth) Tarzan in two serials: *Tarzan the Mighty* ('28) and *Tarzan the Tiger* ('29); there is no record he ever acted again; earlier, he had minor roles in George O'Brien's *The Fighting Heart*, Lila Lee's *The Little Wild Girl*, which was one of several he did for—believe it—Hercules Films.

MERRILL, LOUIS *(1963)* 52 ——Character (Jake) in *The Lady from Shanghai;* also in *The Devil at 4 O'Clock, Kit Carson, The Crooked Web*, others.

MERTON, COLETTE *(1968)* 61 ——Vivacious young support in Colleen Moore's *Why Be Good?*, Lina Basquette's *The Godless Girl, King of the Campus*, Reginald Denny's *Clear the Decks*, and several "Collegians" comedies.

MERTON, JOHN *(1959)* 58 ——Was a henchman in B Westerns for almost 40 years, as was son Lane Bradford after him; in *The Mysterious Rider, Flame of the West, Man from Sonora*, etc.; also was in 13 talkie serials: *Dick Tracy Returns* (as villainous Champ), *The Lone Ranger, Zorro's Fighting Legion*, etc.

MESSINGER, BUDDY *(1965)* 58 ——One of the most popular of all kid stars in silents; at 7 he (and little sister Gertrude) starred in *Aladdin and His Wonderful Lamp;* then was in *The Old Nest, The Flirt, When Love Comes, Penrod and Sam* (a chubby 14-year-old by then), several "Buddy Messinger Comedies" (in '24), *Hot Stuff*, etc.; last in 1936's *College Holiday*.

MESSINGER, JOSEPHINE *(1968)* 83 ——Supporting roles in silents.

MESSITER, ERIC *(1960)* 68 ——English; minor support in *The Mudlark* (Ash, Lieutenant of Police), *Kind Hearts and Coronets*, others.

METAXA, GEORGES *(1950)* 51 ——In the finale of *Swing Time*, Astaire stole the pants of this sleek, oily bandleader so he couldn't marry Ginger Rogers; also in *The Mask of Dimitrios, Secrets of a Secretary* (the gigolo who married wealthy deb Colbert), *Paris Calling*, others.

METCALF, EARLE *(1928)* 38 ——A most handsome leading man, onscreen from '12, he was opposite Anna Q. Nilsson in *What Women Will Do*, Estelle Taylor in *While New York Sleeps*, Doris May in *Eden and Return*, Corinne Griffith in *The Garter Girl;* later in the '20s, slid into supporting roles in lesser features and Westerns (*Buffalo Bill on the U.P. Trail*, etc.).

METCALFE, JAMES *(1960)* 59 ——The first murder victim in the 1941 serial *The Iron Claw*, he also had supporting roles in Berle's *A Gentleman at Heart, The Hard Way*, etc.

METHOT, MAYO *(1951)* 47 ——The real-life wife who lost Bogart (they were famed as "the Battling Bogarts") to Bacall, she was a plain-faced toughie in many: *Marked Woman* (as Davis' prostitute pal, Estelle), *Lilly Turner, Women in Prison, Dr. Socrates, The Case of the Curious Bride, The Night Club Lady* (lead role), etc.; last in *Brother Rat and a Baby*.

METZETTI, VICTOR *(1949)* 54 ——Support in several in the '20s: *Bulldog Pluck, Putting It Over, Stepping Lively*, etc.

MEYER, HYMAN *(1945)* 70 ——In 1929's *The Saturday Night Kid* Clara Bow sold gym appliances at Ginsberg's Department Store—he was Ginsberg; also was in Will Rogers' *Judge Priest*.

MEYERKHOLD, VSEVOLOD *(1942)* 68 —— Featured in Russia's *The Lash of the Czar* ('29).

MEYN, ROBERT *(1972)* 76 ——German character actor; in Maria Schell's *The Last Bridge;* also in *Sunderin*, etc.

MICHAEL, GERTRUDE *(1964)* 53 ——Sophisticated, elegantly tall blonde from Dixie whose screen fame is based most solidly on her starring role in *The Notorious Sophie Lang* and its sequels (*The Return of Sophie Lang, Sophie*

Lang Goes West); a Wampas Baby Star of '34, she also was in DeMille's *Cleopatra* (as Calpurnia), *Murder at the Vanities, I'm No Angel, Menace, It Happened in New York,* etc.; in the '40s she began to play tough broads—good supporting roles—in B's: *Behind Prison Walls, Women in Bondage,* others; continued to play them—bit roles finally, but in better pix—in *Flamingo Road* (a waitress), *Caged* (an inmate), *Bugles in the Afternoon;* last in 1962's *Twist All Night.*

MICHAELS, SULLY *(1966)* 38 ——Character in Mickey Rooney's *The Last Mile* ('59).

MICHALESCO, MICHAEL *(1957)* 72 ——Support in Yiddish films: *Power of Life; God, Man and Devil;* and *Catskill Honeymoon.*

MICHELENA, BEATRIZ *(1942)* 52 ——Brunette star in 1914's *Salomy Jane* and 1915's *Mignon.*

MICHELENA, VERA *(1961)* 76 ——Less famous actress-sister of Beatriz.

MIDDLETON, CHARLES *(1949)* 70 —— "Ming, the Merciless"—three words speak volumes to anyone who ever saw him as the bald (he really wasn't) demonic Ruler of the Universe in the serials *Flash Gordon, Flash Gordon's Trip to Mars,* and *Flash Gordon Conquers the Universe;* the man who put a capital S in Sinister was in just one serial before these (Tom Mix's *The Miracle Rider,* as evil Zaroff), but many afterwards (*Perils of Nyoka, Batman, The Desert Hawk, Jack Armstrong,* as Grood); onscreen from '27 to '49 (*The Black Arrow*), he was in more than 100 features: *The Grapes of Wrath, David Harum,* Dunne's *Show Boat* (Vallon), *Jesse James* (doctor), *Abe Lincoln in Illinois, Charlie Chan's Murder Cruise,* etc.

MIDDLETON, GUY *(1973)* 65 ——Specialized in cads, with high forehead and manicured moustache, in British films: *Suicide Squadron, Doctor at Large, Laughter in Paradise, Notorious Gentleman, The Captive Heart,* etc. *Gentlemen Marry Brunettes* (in which he was the Earl of Wickenware) was one of his few Hollywood movies.

MIDDLETON, JOSEPHINE *(1971)* 87 ——British support; in *The Browning Version, A Lady Surrenders, Woman in Question,* others.

MIDGLEY, FLORENCE *(1949)* 59 ——In *Sadie Thompson,* was the wife of Dr. McPhail (played by Charles Lane); in others in the '20s: James Kirkwood's *The Great Impersonation,* Joe E. Brown's *Painted Faces,* Harry Carey's *Burning Bridges,* etc.

MIDGLEY, RICHARD *(1956)* 46 ——Supporting roles.

MIKHOELS, SOLOMON *(1948)* ——Featured in *The Return of Nathan Becker* and *The Oppenheim Family,* both Russian films.

MILAM, PAULINE *(1965)* 53 ——One of the 12 "Goldwyn Girls" (Lucille Ball was another) in *Roman Scandals;* later an MGM dancer.

MILASH, ROBERT *(1954)* 69 ——Support in Jan Kiepura's *Give Us This Night,* Patsy Ruth Miller's *A Hero for a Night,* Helen Kane's *Dangerous Nan McGrew,* etc.; sometimes billed Bob, and sometimes as Robert Milasch.

MILCREST, HOWARD *(1920)* 28 ——Minor support in Griffith's earliest Biograph pix.

MILES, ART *(1955)* 56 ——Character (sheriff) in the Dietrich-Wayne version of *The Spoilers;* also in the Ritz Brothers' *The Gorilla, Paris Underground,* others.

MILES, JACKIE *(1968)* 54 ——Comic support.

MILES, LOTTA *(1937)* 38 ——Famous Broadway comedienne (was with the Marx Brothers in 1924's *I'll Say She Is*) who was featured in one Mascot B pic, *Waterfront Lady* ('35).

MILJAN, JOHN *(1960)* 67 ——More often than not the suave, black-haired baddie, he was in more than 100 from '23: *The Yankee Clipper* (plotted the mutiny), *Three Kids and a Queen* with May Robson, *Sutter's Gold, The Plainsman* (General Custer here), *The Kid from Spain, Belle of the Nineties, The Ghost Walks, If I Were King, Juarez* (Escobedo), *The Fallen Sparrow* (one of several, including 1931's *Paid,* in which he was on the right side of the law as a police inspector), *Samson and Delilah* (Lesh Lakish), etc.; last in 1958's *The Lone Ranger and the City of Gold.*

MILLAR, LEE *(1941)* 53 ——The voice of Disney's Pluto.

MILLAR, MARJIE *(1970)* 36 ——Fresh-faced, All-American-girl type with long blonde pageboy hairdo; a discovery of Hal Wallis', she was featured by him in *About Mrs. Leslie* and *Money from Home;* on Ray Bolger's TV series, was his dance partner; auto accident crippled her, its lingering after-affects finally causing her death.

MILLARD, HARRY *(1969)* 41 ——Rugged, handsome support in Rooney's *The Last Mile.*

MILLARDE, HARRY ——Kalem leading man who co-starred with Alice Hollister in 1914's

716

The Scorpion's Sting and 1915's Don Caesar de Barzan; later directed Mary Carr in Over the Hill, Edmund Lowe in The Fool, Percy Marmont in If Winter Comes, etc.; year of death unreported.

MILLER, ALICE DUER (1942) 68 ——The author of The White Cliffs of Dover, she had a small role in Soak the Rich.

MILLER, ASHLEY (1949) 82 ——Member of the acting stock company at Biograph which D. W. Griffith "inherited" when he began directing there.

MILLER, CHARLES (1955) 64 ——Character (Senator Bromfield) in Wilson; support in many Westerns (South of Santa Fe, Days of Old Cheyenne), mysteries (The Caribbean Mystery), comedies (They All Kissed the Bride, Caught in the Act), horror pix (House of Frankenstein).

MILLER, EDDIE (1971) 80 ——Of Eddie Miller & His Bob Cats; they were featured in Donald O'Connor's Mister Big.

MILLER, FLOURNOY (1971) 84 ——Black comedian prominently featured in Stormy Weather and Yes Sir, Mr. Bones.

MILLER, GLENN (1944) 40 ——On the trombone, he led his smooth dance band through Orchestra Wives and Sun Valley Serenade, and today, bearing his name, the band goes successfully on; was portrayed onscreen by James Stewart in The Glenn Miller Story.

MILLER, HAROLD (1972) 78 ——Acted in silents as a member of the MGM stock company.

MILLER, HUGH (1956) 54 ——Support in Thomas Meighan's Blind Alleys; also in Bulldog Drummond at Bay, The Return of the Scarlet Pimpernel, I Give My Heart, etc.

MILLER, LU (1941) 35 ——Supporting actress in a fine Lloyd Nolan B pic, Hunted Men.

MILLER, MARILYN (1936) 37 ——One of Ziegfeld's great star discoveries, this scintillating blonde dancer (singer too) was introduced to the screen with most gratifying results in a '29 Technicolor talkie, Sally, based on the Broadway show in which she had starred nine years earlier; the following year she was even more radiant in Sunny, but in '31 came a rather flat romantic comedy, Her Majesty Love with Ben Lyon, canceling out her movie career; coming in a bit later, and a bit younger, she could easily have been the queen of musical movies; was portrayed onscreen by Garland (Till the Clouds Roll By), and Haver (Look for the Silver Lining).

MILLER, MARTIN (1969) 70 ——Bespectacled Czech character; in many: Where's Charley?, 55 Days at Peking (played Hugo Bergmann), Encore (the "Gigolo and Gigolette" episode), Exodus (Dr. Odenheim), etc.

MILLER, MAX (1963) 68 ——Rather bawdy comedian in English pix: Get Off My Foot, The Good Companions, Educated Evans, Channel Crossing, more.

MILLER, MORRIS (1957) 20s ——One of the three young stars of Stakeout on Dope Street; support in Alan Ladd's The Deep Six.

MILLER, RANGER BILL (1939) 61 ——Support in minor pix in the '20s: A Pair of Hellions, The Web of the Law, etc.

MILLER, SETON I. (1974) 71 ——An actor in silents from 1926 (Brown of Harvard, etc.), he became a screenwriter (The Adventures of Robin Hood, The Black Swan, and others, including Here Comes Mr. Jordan, which won him an Oscar); from the '40s he was a producer (Ministry of Fear, Calcutta, Fighter Squadron, etc.); was married to former actress Ann Evers.

MILLER, THOMAS (1942) 70 ——Comic support in Fields' The Old-Fashioned Way, etc.

MILLER, WALTER (1940) 48 ——He and Allene Ray were the most famous team in silent serials; they co-starred, romantically, in ten 1925-29 Pathe chapter plays: Sunken Silver, Play Ball, The Green Archer, Hawk of the Hills, Man Without a Face, etc.; an early Biograph leading man, he had played, in '11, Lillian Gish's young husband in The Musketeers of Pig Alley; besides Allene Ray, he co-starred heroically in serials with Jacqueline Logan (King of the Kongo) and Ethlyne Clair (Queen of the Northwoods); in the '30s, was an arch-villain in many serials (Secret of Treasure Island), played Sylvia Sidney's boss in Street Scene, and was one of the worst of badmen in dozens of B Westerns (Wild Horse Rodeo, Smoking Guns, etc.).

MILLICAN, JAMES (1955) 45 ——Well-built, good-looking man who in 22 screen years was seen in more than 350 movies; wore chaps well in many big-budget Westerns: Springfield Rifle (as Matthew Quint), Carson City, Warpath, The Man from Laramie, Top Gun, etc.; also was an impressive figure in military uniform in Command Decision (as Major Davenport), Strategic Air Command (General Castle), The Story of Dr. Wassell, more.

MILLMAN, WILLIAM (1937) 54 ——Support in The Lost City, Richard Arlen's Silent Barriers, other B's.

MILLS, BILLY *(1971)* 77 ——Support in many.

MILLS, FLORENCE *(1927)* 32 ——Gifted black Broadway star; few screen appearances.

MILLS, FRANK *(1921)* 51 ——Popular silent leading man; was with Florence Reed in *Today* ('17), Norma Talmadge in *Deluxe Annie*, Ethel Barrymore in *The Eternal Mother*, etc.

MILLS, FREDDIE *(1965)* 46 ——Champion boxer turned actor; was featured in 1953's *Hundred Hour Hunt*.

MILLS, GRANT *(1973)* 70s ——Support in Harold Lloyd's *Professor Beware*, etc.

MILLS, JOE *(1935)* 60 ——Support in James Kirkwood's *Love's Whirlpool*, Fields' *The Old-Fashioned Way*, *The Dramatic Life of Abraham Lincoln*, etc.

MILLS, THOMAS R. *(1953)* 75 ——Character (L'Estrange) in March's *Les Miserables*, after support in numerous silents: John Gilbert's *A Man's Mate*, Mae Marsh's *Tides of Passion*, Edmund Lowe's *The Kiss Barrier*, etc.

MILTERN, JOHN *(1937)* 67 ——With his fine, lean older-man's face, he was the picture of respectability in many: DeMille's *Manslaughter* (Gov. Albee), *The Dark Angel* (Oberon's father), *Lost Horizon* (Carstairs), *Give Us This Night*, *Murder on the Bridle Path*, etc.

MILTON, ERNEST *(1974)* 84 ——English support; in *It's Love Again, The Scarlet Pimpernel, A Wisp in the Woods*, etc.

MILTON, GEORGES *(1970)* 82 ——The star of France's *The Queen and the Cardinal* ('44), and other European films.

MILTON, HARRY *(1965)* 64 ——Support in British pix of the '30s: *King of the Ritz, The King's Cup*, others.

MILTON, LOUETTE *(1930)* 23 ——Minor role in Vivienne Segal's *Bride of the Regiment*.

MILTON, MAUD *(1945)* 86 ——Character actress in silents; had a top supporting role in Antonio Moreno's *The Old Flute Player* ('14), among others.

MINCIOTTI, ESTHER *(1962)* 74 ——Most famous as the Italian mama of Borgnine in *Marty*, she also was the mother of all Edward G. Robinson's "sons" in *House of Strangers*; in others: *Strictly Dishonorable, The Undercover Man, Shockproof*, etc.

MINCIOTTI, SILVIO *(1961)* 78 ——His best role that of Papa in Monroe's *Clash by Night*, he had smaller parts in many (*Up Front, The Great Caruso*, etc.), including several with wife Esther (*Full of Life, The Wrong Man, Marty*, etc.).

MINEVITCH, BORRAH *(1955)* 52 ——He and his harmonica-playing "Rascals" were in several: *Always in My Heart, Love under Fire, One in a Million, Rascals* with Jane Withers, etc.

MINNER, KATHRYN *(1969)* 77 ——Played little old ladies in several: *Miracle in My Pocket, The Love Bug, Blackbeard's Ghost*, others.

MINZEY, FRANK *(1949)* 70 ——Co-starred with rustic comedienne-wife Rose Melville in all the silent "Sis Hopkins" comedies (*Leap Year Wooing*, etc.).

MIRANDA, CARMEN *(1955)* 41 ——The little "Brazilian Bombshell" who, in tutti-frutti costumes (always with bared midriff) and wedgies, was musical dynamite for 20th Century-Fox in the '40s in *Down Argentine Way, Weekend in Havana, That Night in Rio, The Gang's All Here, Springtime in the Rockies*, etc.; was almost as riveting at Metro in *A Date with Judy* and *Nancy Goes to Rio*, and at Paramount in *Scared Stiff*; "super-puritanical pressure groups" caused 20th to drop her option, said studio boss Darryl F. Zanuck in his book *Don't Say Yes Until I Finish Talking*: "There was a big scandal when Carmen danced and didn't have any pants on under her skirt. I don't think she ever wore pants when she danced. She was not a tart by any means. A real lady . . . It was a matter of her freedom of body movement. But one time a free lance still photographer had a camera set at a low angle as she danced. It revealed *everything*. Millions of her pictures were suddenly being sold . . . It was the finish of her . . . It was one of those Hollywood periods where the women's organizations ganged up on us . . ."

MIRANDY *(1974)* 84 ——Rustic comedienne (r.n. Mrs. Marjorie Bauersfeld) who was featured in *Comin' Round the Mountain*.

MIROSLAVA *(1955)* 25 ——Anthony Quinn's lovely blonde leading lady in *The Brave Bulls*; earlier had a small part in Arturo de Cordova's *Adventures of Casanova*, later co-starred with McCrea in *Stranger on Horseback*; a Greek-American who lived most of her life in Mexico, she also starred in numerous Mexican films.

MISTRAL, JORGE *(1972)* 49 ——A most famous Spanish actor, he had a supporting role in Sophia Loren's *Boy on a Dolphin*.

MITCHELL, BRUCE *(1952)* 68 ——In silents he often played lead in pix he directed (e.g., Norma Talmadge's *Captivating Mary Carstairs*); in talkies, played supporting roles in Westerns: *Bar 20 Justice, Riders of the Frontier,* etc.

MITCHELL, DODSON *(1939)* 71 ——A Famous Players character lead in the teens; was in —among many—Harold Lockwood's *The Conspiracy.*

MITCHELL, GEORGE *(1972)* 67 ——Character (Monsignor Ryan) in *The Unsinkable Molly Brown;* also in *The Phenix City Story, 3:10 to Yuma,* others.

MITCHELL, GRANT *(1957)* 82 ——Hollywood comedies from '30 would have been less without this dapper little gentleman who talked a lot and well (especially when an exec or politican), and frequently wore a perplexed smile; in more than 80 pix: *Mr. Smith Goes to Washington* (Senator MacPherson), *The Man Who Came to Dinner* (at his house acerbic Monty Woolley broke his leg), *Skylark, Gold Diggers of 1935, Seven Keys to Baldpate, My Sister Eileen* ('42), etc.; more serious roles in *The Life of Emile Zola* (Georges Clemenceau), *The Grapes of Wrath, The Great Lie, On Borrowed Time.*

MITCHELL, HELEN *(1945)* ——Featured in Artclass Pictures' *Unmasked* ('29).

MITCHELL, HOWARD *(1958)* 70 ——Support in such early (1914-15) serials as Lottie Briscoe's *The Beloved Adventurer* and *Road O' Strife,* and such 1938-41 pix as *Queen of the Mob; Tom Sawyer, Detective;* and *The Mad Doctor.*

MITCHELL, JOHNNY *(1951)* 31 ——One of Warners' best bets for stardom, he was the very tall and dark young man who paid court to Davis in *Mr. Skeffington,* the film from which he took his screen name; had been on radio as Douglas Drake; also was featured in *Pillow to Post* with Lupino.

MITCHELL, JULIEN *(1954)* 65 ——Dignified British character in several Hollywood movies: *Vigil in the Night* (wealthy hospital patron, Matthew Bowley), *The Sea Hawk,* etc.; in more British pix: *Bedelia, The Last Journey* (train engineer who went mad), *The Galloping Major,* others.

MITCHELL, LES *(1965)* 80 ——A Keystone Kop at one time; not the musician.

MITCHELL, MILLARD *(1953)* 50 ——Saturnine, with a slit for a mouth and a tough bark (cloaking, usually, a heart of mush), he seemed born to wear a uniform—military or detective— of high rank; did so in *A Foreign Affair* (Col. Rufus John Plummer), *Twelve O'Clock High, You're in the Navy, A Double Life, Kiss of Death, My Six Convicts,* etc.; comes as a shock to find that he began with a bit role in Colbert's *Secrets of a Secretary*—as a drunk.

MITCHELL, NORMA *(1967)* ——Nearly always played maids—Nancy Carroll's in *The Woman Accused,* Crawford's in *Susan and God,* etc.

MITCHELL, RHEA *(1957)* 52 ——Attractive brunette who starred for Mutual in '16 (*On the Night Stage*), then played star Grace Darmond's sister in the serial *The Hawk's Trail* ('20), and was the heroine in the Westerns of William S. Hart and others.

MITCHELL, THOMAS *(1962)* 70 ——Unforgettable in almost every role he played: rummy Dr. Josiah Boone in *Stagecoach* (won him the Best Supporting Actor Oscar), *Hurricane* (his only other nomination), Scarlett O'Hara's father in *Gone With the Wind, The Long Voyage Home, Craig's Wife, Only Angels Have Wings, Make Way for Tomorrow* (the son with whom aged Beulah Bondi finally must live), *Our Town, The Sullivans, The Keys of the Kingdom, It's a Wonderful Life,* etc.; last in 1961's *Pocketful of Miracles;* probably the only *forgettable* movie he ever made was 1934's *Cloudy with Showers,* his first.

MIX, ART *(1972)* 71 ——See Denver Dixon.

MIX, TOM *(1940)* 60 ——As legendary a hero as any cowboy star ever was or is likely to be; onscreen from 1910 in many kinds of roles (sometimes even wearing a tux), he made his first starring Westerns in '17 and by '20 had replaced William S. Hart as King of the Cowboys; Fox Studios became a major company almost exclusively on the basis of his worldwide success; his movies—over 350—were characterized by his reckless, devil-may-care spirit, his fancy garb, his breathtaking stunts and expert horsemanship—aboard the internationally famous Tony (there were several over the years); some of his action-filled best: *The Untamed, The Daredevil, The Heart Buster, Just Tony, Ranch Life in the Great Southwest;* reigned supreme throughout the '20s and fared well in talkies, his last series of pix (*The Fourth Horseman, Flaming Guns, Rider of Death Valley,* etc.) being made for Universal (1932-34); his final screen appearance was as the star of a 1935 Mascot serial, *The Miracle Rider,* after which he—and the fabulous Tony—thrilled audiences in Mexico, Canada, and the U.S. with "The Tom Mix Circus"; the only time this great six-shooter hero ever "bit the dust" (almost) occurred offscreen in 1924—when fourth wife, Victoria Forde, shot and seriously wounded him during a domestic argument.

MOEHRING, KANSAS *(1968)* 71 ——Gray-haired actor who played ranchers or sheriffs in many Westerns: *Trailing Danger, Down Texas Way, The Cariboo Trail,* etc.

MOFFAT, MARGARET *(1942)* 52 ——Character actress from England who played Victor Mature's mother in *My Gal Sal,* her last film; earlier, had been in *Ringside Maisie, Troopship, Farewell Again, Song of the Road.*

MOFFATT, GRAHAM *(1965)* 46 ——Portly young character actor in British pix: *I Know Where I'm Going, Dr. Syn, Where There's a Will* (one of many Will Hay comedies in which he was featured), *I Thank You,* etc.

MOHAN, EARL *(1928)* 40s——Minor Hal Roach comedian; later at Fox in such comedies as *Love Makes 'Em Wild,* on which critics pounced: "Yes, and pictures like this make 'em wild, too."

MOHR, GERALD *(1968)* 54 ——Fine, sleek, and dark, with a headful of curly hair, he was both an excellent villain (such as Slick Latimer in 1941's *Jungle Girl* serial, his first screen role) and convincing hero (*The Lone Wolf in London, The Lone Wolf in Mexico,* and TV's *Foreign Intrigue*); among his 50 movies: *Gilda, Lady of Burlesque, Detective Story, Ten Tall Men, Murder in Times Square, The Eddie Cantor Story;* was last in *Funny Girl.*

MOISSI, ALEXANDER *(1935)* 55 ——Co-starred with Camilla Horn in the German-made *The Royal Box* ('30), historically important as the first full-length talkie in German to be released in the U.S. by a major company, Warners.

MOJA, HELLA *(1937)* 38 ——Femme lead in Germany's *U-Boat 9.*

MOJAVE, KING *(1973)* ——Support in numerous serials.

MOJICA, JOSE *(1974)* 78 ——Of the golden tenor voice and handsome profile, and already Mexico's most famous singer, he co-starred with Mona Maris for Fox in 1930's *One Mad Kiss*—billed Don Jose Mojica; thereafter made many more pix in Mexico: *The Forbidden Melody, The Adventurous Captain, The Miracle Song,* etc.; starred on many operatic stages—

the Metropolitan, Chicago Civic Opera, Mexico City's Ideal Theater; at 46 and at the height of his fame he gave up his career to enter a Franciscan order in Peru, becoming, six years later, an ordained priest, Fray Jose; last sang in public in eight '49 radio concerts in Buenos Aires, to raise money for church seminaries; when older, he reflected: "All the world's gold, fame, power, applause and pleasure are not equal to one hour in the service of Christ."

MOLNAR, LILLY *(1950)* ——British character actress who appeared in *No Orchids for Miss Blandish, The Long Dark Hall,* etc.

MOLONEY, JOHN *(1969)* 58 ——Minor support in *Gypsy.*

MOMO, ALESSANDRO *(1974)* 20 ——Italian actor who became a star overnight in *Malizia,* as the adolescent Don Juan who seduces the maid before she marries his father; also in *Honey and Darkness* with Vittorio Gassman.

MONCRIES, EDWARD *(1938)* 79 ——Comic support in many in the '20s including Charles Ray's *The Girl I Loved.*

MONG, WILLIAM V. *(1940)* 65 ——In scores from 1910's *A Connecticut Yankee* to 1938's *Painted Desert,* he remains especially memorable as Cognac Pete in *What Price Glory?*—the innkeeper so determined that Sgt. Quirt (Edmund Lowe) marry his daughter (Dolores Del Rio); earlier had been the handsome star of many, including 1916's *A Severed Hand;* supporting roles in the '20s in *Monte Cristo, In The Palace of the King, Fine Clothes,* etc., and in the '30s in *The Sign of the Cross* (as Licinius), *I Loved a Woman, The Last Days of Pompeii, Stand-In,* others.

MONROE, MARILYN *(1962)* 36 ——Blonde 20th Century-Fox star who, projecting availability and naivete, was Hollywood's last great Sex Queen; gave her most delightful performance as ukelele-playing Sugar Kane in Billy Wilder's *Some Like It Hot;* was charming, too, in *Gentlemen Prefer Blondes, How to Marry a Millionaire, The Seven Year Itch, The Prince and the Showgirl;* played vulnerable young women in highly effective fashion in both *Bus Stop* and *The Misfits,* her final film; onscreen in minor roles from the late '40s, she first attracted major attention as the gangster's moll in *The Asphalt Jungle* ('50) and the hopelessly inept Broadway "starlet," Miss Caswell, in *All About Eve;* countless authors in recent years, as did several while she lived, have found accounts of her life both highly exploitable and financially rewarding—including onetime husband-playwright Arthur Miller whose unsparing play *After the Fall* is apparently based on her decline.

MONROE, VAUGHN *(1973)* 62 ——Famous monotone-baritone bandleader whom Republic attempted to pass off as a Western musical star in 1950's *Singing Guns*, which backfired; earlier, had been with his orchestra in two: *Carnegie Hall* and *Meet the People*.

MONTAGUE, FRED ——Barrel-chested Broadway actor who played the villain in Dustin Farnum's *Cameo Kirby* ('15); year of death unreported.

MONTAGUE, RITA *(1962)* 78 ——Actress-wife of Fred; also in silents.

MONTAGUE, MONTE *(1959)* 67 ——An early saddle pal of Buck Jones and Tom Mix, he later played sheriffs in many: *Song of the Saddle, The Apache Kid, The Vigilante's Return*, etc.

MONTANA, BULL *(1950)* 62 ——From Italy, he was a burly brute with cauliflower ears (had been a professional wrestler) who was especially active onscreen in the '20s; was well cast in Pat O'Malley's *Go and Get It* ('20) as the ape given a murderer's brain, and, since it was a comedy, as an esthetic Cardinal Richelieu in French comedian Max Linder's *The Three Must-Get-Theres* ('22); also was in *The Son of the Sheik, The Four Horsemen of the Apocalypse, Dick Turpin*, etc., plus two silent serials: *Vanishing Millions, The Timber Queen;* last in Dennis O'Keefe's *Good Morning, Judge* ('43).

MONTEZ, MARIA *(1951)* 43 ——Camp now, and perhaps even then, Universal's "in house" exotic from the Dominican Republic was ready-made to be the raven-haired, English-garbling queen of Technicolor adventure fantasies: *Arabian Nights, Cobra Woman, Ali Baba and the Forty Thieves, White Savage, Sudan*, etc., in many of which barechested Jon Hall was her brawny playmate.

MONTGOMERY, DOUGLASS *(1966)* 58 —— Was a big young man with a strong, handsome face who might have become a more important star but for a profusion of screen names; MGM signed him from the stage, changing his real name (Robert Douglas Montgomery) to Kent Douglas in '31, and cast him as a leading man under that name in four: *Paid* (with Crawford), *Daybreak, Five and Ten, A House Divided*, plus loaning him to Universal for *Waterloo Bridge;* leaving Metro, he changed it to Douglass Montgomery, appearing in *Little Women* (as Hepburn's beloved Laurie), *Little Man, What Now?* with Sullavan, *The Mystery of Edwin Drood*, etc.; his career visibly in decline by

WW II, he enlisted in the Canadian infantry, serving four years; at war's end he starred in two in England (*The Way to the Stars, Woman to Woman*), had a supporting role in another (*Johnny in the Clouds*); returned to Hollywood as a character actor in Tony Curtis' *Forbidden* ('48) and Van Johnson's *When in Rome* ('52), his last.

MONTGOMERY, EARL *(1966)* 73 ——Comic roles in many.

MONTGOMERY, JACK *(1962)* 69 ——Support —usually a rustler—in many Westerns (*Pursued, Border Wolves, Colorado Territory, Black Bandit*, etc.); father of moppet star "Baby Peggy" Montgomery.

MONTOYA, ALEX *(1970)* 50s ——Droopy-moustached character, Squint-Eye, in Brando's *The Appaloosa;* also in *The Golden Hawk* and *The Flight of the Phoenix* (as Carlos who, after the cargo plane crash, goes into the Sahara with English captain Peter Finch in search of help).

MONTROSE, BELLE *(1964)* 78 ——Steve Allen's vaudeville star-mother; character (Mrs. Chatsworth) in *The Absent-Minded Professor*.

MONTT, CHRISTINA *(1969)* 72 ——Support in several in the '20s: *The Sea Hawk*, Gilbert Roland's *Rose of the Golden West*, etc.

MOODY, RALPH *(1971)* 83 ——Character actor in Westerns (*Red Mountain, Seminole*), comedies, (*Road to Bali, Going Steady*), horror pix (*The Monster That Challenged the World*), "Biblical" epics (*The Story of Ruth, The Big Fisherman*).

MOOERS, DE SACIA *(1960)* 72 ——Dark blonde and rather buxom, she was featured in many melodramas and comedies of the '20s: *Potash and Perlmutter*, Pauline Garon's *The Average Woman, Restless Wives*, Alice Terry's *Any Woman, Broadway Daddies*, etc.

MOON, GEORGE *(1961)* 75 ——Comic support in British pix: *Carry On Admiral, An Alligator Named Daisy*, etc.

MOORE, ALICE *(1960)* 44 ——As a pretty girl of 18 she had a small role in Laurel & Hardy's *Babes in Toyland;* the daughter of Alice Joyce and Tom Moore.

MOORE, CLEO *(1973)* 44 ——Busty blonde starred by Hugo Haas in several heavy-handed Mittel-European/Hollywood B melodramas: *Thy Neighbor's Wife, Strange Fascination, Bait, One Girl's Confession*, etc.; after her movie career, and having once been married to

Huey Long's youngest son, she ran—unsuccessfully—for Governor of Louisiana.

MOORE, CLEVE *(1961)* 57 ——Handsome young man with a shy smile, and the younger brother of Colleen Moore, he was in several in the '20s: *The Stolen Bride, It Must Be Love, Her Summer Hero,* and, with Colleen, *Lilac Time* and *We Moderns.*

MOORE, DEL *(1970)* 53 ——Best known as the co-star of TV's *Life with Elizabeth,* this one-time radio announcer had supporting roles in several Jerry Lewis comedies: *The Errand Boy, The Big Mouth, The Patsy, The Nutty Professor,* others.

MOORE, DENNIS *(1964)* 56 ——Good-looking, tight-lipped, and dark-haired, he played dramatic roles in *China Clipper, Sing Me a Love Song, Mutiny in the Big House,* etc., before turning to Westerns and serials; was a cowboy hero in many: *The Man from Tascosa* ('40), the "Range Busters" series with "Crash" Corrigan and Max Terhune, etc.; in serials, starred in *The Purple Monster Strikes* and *The Master Key* (both '45), and, in '56, in the last two serials made, *Blazing the Overland Trail* and *Perils of the Wilderness;* thereafter played villains in numerous B Westerns.

MOORE, EULABELLE *(1964)* 61 ——Character in *The Horror of Party Beach.*

MOORE, EVA *(1955)* 85 ——British character; the ancient gargoyle in *The Old Dark House* ('32), she also was in *Just Smith, Scotland Yard Investigates, Jew Suess,* other English pix; was in Hollywood for *Of Human Bondage* (Eleanor Parker version) and *The Bandit of Sherwood Forest.*

MOORE, FLORENCE *(1935)* 49 ——Support in Adolphe Menjou's *Broadway After Dark,* etc.

MOORE, GRACE *(1947)* 45 ——Golden of hair and voice, this glamorous diva from the Met did more for popularizing opera on the screen than any of her '30s colleagues; particularly glowing in *One Night of Love* (Oscar-nominated as Best Actress) and *Love Me Tonight,* she was also enchanting—if occasionally a bit formidable— in *When You're in Love, The King Steps Out,* and *I'll Take Romance;* last starred in *Louise,* made abroad; was portrayed by Kathryn Grayson in *So This Is Love.*

MOORE, HENRIETTA *(1973)* 50 ——Supporting actress; numerous minor roles.

MOORE, HILDA *(1929)* 42 ——Support in Jeanne Eagles' *Jealousy.*

MOORE, IDA *(1964)* 82 ——Dried-apple "Granny" dolls, pixie-faced with quirky smiles, might have been patterned after this charming mite; the little old lady in *The Egg and I* with the "invisible" husband, she was in many from Mae Murray's *The Merry Widow: Good Sam, Johnny Belinda, To Each His Own, Harvey, Mr. Music,* etc.

MOORE, MARY *(1931)* 69 ——Actress-mother of three handsome Irish sons, Matt, Tom, Owen, all of whom became famous leading men, and of a fourth, Joe, who acted a while at Universal in '14 but dropped out; she had featured roles in several, including Clara Kimball Young's *Lola* ('15); quit pictures, returned to the British Isles, became Lady Wyndham.

MOORE, MATT *(1960)* 72 ——Youngest of the Moore brothers, his career lasted longest—1913 (*Traffic in Souls*) to 1958 (*I Bury the Living*); at the beginning they were called "the hero brothers" because of their roles; he was in *A Singular Cynic* with Florence Lawrence, *The Pride of the Clan* and *Coquette* with Pickford, *Everybody's Sweetheart* with Elsie Janis, *Strangers of the Night* with Barbara La Marr, *Tillie the Toiler* with Marion Davies, *Heart of the Wilds* with Elsie Ferguson; assumed supporting roles from the mid-'30s in *Anything Goes, Wilson* (Secretary Burleson), *Spellbound* (railroad station policeman), *Seven Brides for Seven Brothers* (uncle of one bride), *An Affair to Remember* (Irish priest), etc.

MOORE, MONETTE *(1962)* 50 ——Featured in the all-star minstrel movie *Yes Sir, Mr. Bones* ('51).

MOORE, OWEN *(1939)* 52 ——More famous than star-brothers Matt and Tom, perhaps, because he was Mary Pickford's first husband; also because he had extraordinary good looks and charm; "the nice guy who drank too much" reputation pinned on him at the time of their divorce ('20) surprised fans but did not decelerate his career; made as many movies in the '20s (*Made in Heaven, Manhandled,* etc.) as he had in the teens; made his screen debut opposite, fatefully, Mary Pickford in 1908's *In a Lonely Villa;* followed it with *The Cricket on the Hearth, Flo's Disciple* with Florence Lawrence, numerous Griffith films including *The Battle of the Sexes* with Gish and *Home Sweet Home* and *The Escape* with Blanche Sweet, *Nearly a Lady* with Elsie Janis, *My Valet* with Mabel Normand, *Under Cover* with Hazel Dawn; in the '20s was in *Her Temporary Husband, The Skyrocket, The Red Mill* with Davies, *East of Broadway,* etc.; in the '30s, had supporting roles in such as *She Done Him Wrong* (as Chick Clark) and *A Star Is Born* (reporter Casey Burke), which was his last.

MOORE, PERCY *(1945)* 67 ——Support in Richard Dix's *The Shock Punch.*

MOORE, RUTH *(1952)* 70s ——Support in Blanche Sweet's *Judith of Bethulia,* Betty Bronson's *The Companionate Marriage,* etc.

MOORE, SCOTT *(1967)* 78 ——Was the handsome gigolo in Zita Johann's *The Struggle.*

MOORE, TOM *(1955)* 71 ——Strappingly handsome, and eldest of the Moore brothers, he began as a star the same year ('13) as Matt; like Owen, in his first pic, *Nina of the Theatre,* he co-starred with his future wife, gentle and gloriously beautiful Alice Joyce; they later did many together including *The Mystery of the Sleeping Death;* he starred in *Who's Guilty?* with Anna Q. Nilsson, *The Cinderella Man* with Mae Marsh, *Thirty a Week* (in this '18 pic, his leading lady was a teenager who had never acted before on stage or screen—Tallulah Bankhead), *A Kiss for Cinderella, Lord and Lady Algy, Toby's Bow, Stop Thief, The Song and Dance Man* with Bessie Love, etc.; in '21 was one of the Top Ten box-office male stars; his popularity lasted well into the '30s in *The Last Parade, Vanishing Men,* etc., but all were less than major movies; offscreen 1936–46, he came back as a character actor in *Moss Rose, Forever Amber* (small role, Killigrew), *The Fighting O'Flynn;* was last in Rhonda Fleming's *The Redhead and the Cowboy* ('50), at Paramount where two decades before he had been one of their biggest stars.

MOORE, VICTOR *(1962)* 86 ——Great, stubby little namby-pamby comedian who remained the same through 30 movies in 40 years and six separate screen careers—except that at the beginning he wasn't bald; between pic careers he would disappear for long periods to star in Broadway musical comedies; some recall him best in his 1940s period—in *Louisiana Purchase* (comedienne Irene Bordoni pursued him relentlessly here), *Star-Spangled Rhythm* (the studio gateman thought by sailor-son Eddie Bracken to be a studio chief), *The Heat's On* with Mae West, etc.; that was career #5; #1 was 1912–16 when he starred in *Snobs,* two "Chimmie Fadden" comedies, *The Clown, Home Defense,* etc.; in the '20s (#2) he came back for just one, to co-star with Thomas Meighan in *The Man Who Found Himself;* returned (#3) for two in 1930: *Heads Up, Dangerous Nan McGrew;* 1934–38 (#4) was a busy period—*Swing Time, Gold Diggers of 1937, Gift of Gab,* others, including *Make Way for Tomorrow,* in which, as the devoted old husband forcibly separated from wife Beulah Bondi, he gave one of the great starring performances of all time; was back onscreen again in many in the '40s—*Rid-*

ing High, Duffy's Tavern, It Happened on Fifth Avenue, etc.; wrapped it up (#6) with two in the '50s: as the Justice of the Peace in *We're Not Married* and the hilarious plumber in *The Seven Year Itch.*

MOORE, VIN *(1949)* 71 ——Support in such pix of the '20s as *The Man from the West* and *Lazy Lightning;* better known as a director at Universal of *The Cohens and the Kellys in Africa, Many a Slip,* etc.

MOOREHEAD, AGNES *(1974)* 67 ——Superlative character star who entered movies as a member of Orson Welles' Mercury Players in *Citizen Kane* (the mother); was four times nominated, without ever winning, as Best Supporting Actress—*The Magnificent Ambersons; Mrs. Parkington; Johnny Belinda; Hush . . . Hush . . . Sweet Charlotte;* best at playing authoritative or soured women, she was in more than 60 films: *Journey Into Fear* and *Jane Eyre* with Welles, *The Big Street, The Seventh Cross, Keep Your Powder Dry, Our Vines Have Tender Grapes, Caged, Show Boat, The Stratton Story, Raintree County,* etc.; on TV she was Endora, the witch, in *Bewitched;* last onscreen in *The Singing Nun,* her last professional engagement was in the Broadway musical *Gigi,* as the grandmother.

MOORHOUSE, BERT *(1954)* 58 ——In *Sunset Boulevard,* played Gordon Cole, the studio man who wanted to rent Swanson's ancient limousine; earlier had supporting roles in *The Girl from Woolworth's, Hey, Rube!, The Woman I Love,* others.

MORALES, ESY *(1950)* 33 ——Leader of the famous Copacabana Orchestra, he was in Burt Lancaster's *Criss Cross.*

MORAN, GEORGE *(1949)* 61 ——Taller half of the Moran & Mack comedy team ("The Two Black Crows"); they starred in *Why Bring That Up?, Hypnotized;* Moran was the wonderfully funny, stolid Indian in *My Little Chickadee* later; also was in *The Bank Dick.*

MORAN, LEE *(1961)* 70 ——Half of the early great comedy team of (Eddie) Lyons & Moran which, 1914–20, starred in dozens of shorts for both Christie and Universal (*War Bridegrooms, Eddie's Little Love Affair,* etc.); after the team broke up Moran was a steadily employed character actor until retirement after 1936's *The Calling of Dan Matthews;* in silents: Shearer's *The Actress, Once a Plumber, Fifth Avenue Models, Her Big Night,* etc.; talkies: *Stowaway, Circus Clown, Dance Hall,* many more.

MORAN, PAT *(1965)* 64 ——Husband of Patsy; support in the Bowery Boys' *Trouble Makers*, etc.

MORAN, PATSY *(1968)* 63 ——Fine gawky comedienne featured in many in the late '30s and '40s: *Blockheads, Foreign Agent, The Golden Trail, Come Out Fighting*, etc., plus numerous two-reel comedies in which she frequently was a maid.

MORAN, POLLY *(1952)* 68 ——Buck-toothed comedienne always at her best when teamed with Marie Dressler; they were a raucous pair in many silent comedies plus such talkies as *Caught Short, Politics, Reducing, Prosperity*, etc.; earlier ('15) she was, perhaps second only to Louise Fazenda, Sennett's best comedienne; was unsurpassed at broad burlesque, particularly when a grinning husband-hunter—which she was often; Sennett publicity had her from South Africa, but it was really Chicago; onscreen through 1941's *Petticoat Politics*, she dropped out for eight years, coming back for just two: *Adam's Rib* and *The Yellow Cab Man*.

MORANTE, MILBURN *(1964)* 77 ——Played gray-haired crooks in several dozen B Westerns: *Gold Mine in the Sky, The Ghost Rider, Wild Mustang*, etc.

MORDANT, EDWIN *(1942)* 74 ——A distinguished-looking oldtimer in his first, 1915's *The Prince and the Pauper* (as the bishop), he remained on through such movies of the '30s as *County Fair* and *I'll Tell the World*.

MORDANT, GRACE *(1952)* 80 ——Actress-wife of character actor Edwin.

MORELAND, MANTAN *(1973)* 72 ——Grand black comic—moon-faced and startled eyed—whose style of comedy ("Feets! Do your stuff!") would not be tolerated today but was great fun then; best known as "Charlie Chan's" forever-terrified chauffeur Birmingham, which he played in 15 (1944-49), for both Sidney Toler and Roland Winters; in *Charlie Chan in Secret Service, Charlie Chan in Black Magic, The Feathered Serpent*, etc.; was in dozens of others from '38: *Next Time I Marry, Cabin in the Sky, Sarong Girl, Footlight Serenade, Eyes in the Night*, others; was last in 1970's *Watermelon Man;* his photo last appeared in a Hollywood paper in '72 when, after a serious illness, he placed an ad in *Daily Variety* specifically to "thank the Motion Picture Convalescent Home for their wonderful care."

MORENCY, ROBERT "BUSTER" *(1937)* 5 — —Lad who had a few minor roles.

MORENO, ANTONIO *(1967)* 80 ——Before Valentino, this extraordinarily handsome man (whose looks only improved with age) was *the* Latin lover, setting femme hearts afire in *The Mark of Cain, The Naulahka, The Supreme Temptation*, etc.; made screen love to every great woman star: Garbo (*The Temptress*), Negri (*The Spanish Dancer*), Swanson (*My American Wife*), Mary Miles Minter (*The Trail of the Lonesome Pine*), Pickford, Alice Terry, Davies, Dove, Gish, et al; onscreen from 1912's *The Voice of the Million*, he starred—on American screens—in more than 80 features, plus numerous serials (*The Perils of Thunder Mountain, The Veiled Mystery*, etc.), plus several made in Spain and Mexico, plus a dozen Spanish-language versions of Hollywood pix, most of which starred others in English; turned character actor in '30 and was active in another 30 including *Captain from Castile* (Tyrone Power's father), *The Bohemian Girl, Seven Sinners* (had a romantic interlude with Dietrich), *Fiesta, Crisis, The Spanish Main* (Commandante), *Dallas* (Ruth Roman's father), *Thunder Bay*, and last, in '56, *The Searchers* (as a Spanish-American trader).

MORENO, DARIO *(1968)* 47 ——Turkish actor who had supporting roles in *Wages of Fear*, Guinness' *The Prisoner* and *Hotel Paradiso*, and numerous French films.

MORENO, PACO *(1941)* 55 ——Minor support in *The Devil Is a Woman, Storm Over the Andes*, etc.

MOREY, HARRY T. *(1936)* 62 ——Handsome silent star who played heroes first (1911's *The Deerslayer*), regarded himself as an unlikely romantic candidate, and turned villain (in 1914's *A Million Bid* and *The Battle of the Weak*); fans' demands drove him back into the arms of Alice Joyce in several, Clara Kimball Young in *My Official Wife*, Edna May in *Salvation Joan*, etc.; onscreen through the '20s—often in father roles—in *The Green Goddess, The Painted Lady, Under the Tonto Rim, Twin Flappers*, etc.

MOREY, HENRY A. *(1929)* 80 ——Support in 1921's *The Inside of the Cup*.

MORGAN, CLAUDIA *(1974)* 62 ——Blonde daughter of Ralph; femme leads in many B's (*That's My Story*, etc.) and second leads in bigger films (*Stand Up and Fight, Vanity Street*, others); perhaps better known for her Broadway roles (*The Man Who Came to Dinner*, as Maggie Cutler, played in the movie by Davis) and radio's *The Thin Man* (the role Loy had played onscreen).

MORGAN, FRANK *(1949)* 59 ——If this fine, bumbling chortler—giggler, sometimes—had not existed MGM would have had to invent him; under contract there 20 years, he was a plus in every movie in which he appeared; among his dozens: *The Wizard of Oz* (the inept Wizard himself, of course), *Bombshell, A Lost Lady, When Ladies Meet, The Good Fairy, Naughty Marietta, Saratoga, Boom Town, Tortilla Flat* (his only Oscar nomination as Best Support), *Affairs of Cellini* (his one nomination as Best Actor), *Summer Holiday, Green Dolphin Street,* and last, *Key to the City;* no "absent-minded professor" of comparable affability has been seen since.

MORGAN, GENE *(1950)* 48 ——Minor support —such as a waiter in *Mr. Deeds Goes to Town* —in many in the '30s including *Blonde Venus, Elmer the Great, Make Way for Tomorrow* (Carlton Gorman), *The Housekeeper's Daughter,* etc.

MORGAN, HELEN *(1941)* 41 ——Tragedy-ridden singer forever associated with "My Bill," which she was the first to sing in *Show Boat,* both on Broadway and in the first ('29) movie version; she repeated the role of Julie (singing it again) in the second ('36) version; made a brilliant screen debut early in 1929 in *Applause,* but most of her later films were poor: *Roadhouse Nights, Sweet Music, Frankie and Johnnie,* etc.; was portrayed by Ann Blyth in *The Helen Morgan Story.*

MORGAN, JOAN *(1962)* 43 ——Played a secondary role in 1928's *The Woman Tempted.*

MORGAN, JANE *(1972)* 90 ——Eve Arden's landlady on radio and TV in *Our Miss Brooks,* she also had featured roles in several pix.

MORGAN, LEE *(1967)* 65 ——An outlaw in countless Westerns: *Shadow Valley, Rio Grande, The Younger Brothers, Black Hills,* etc.

MORGAN, MARGO *(1962)* 65 ——Singer in early MGM musical talkies.

MORGAN, RALPH *(1956)* 72 ——Slimmer, older, perhaps more versatile, but less famous, brother of Frank; came in later (1930 to Frank's 1917), made more movies (over 100) but frequently in smaller roles; most famous for his roles in *The Power and the Glory* and *Rasputin and the Empress* (as Czar Nicholas II); alternatedly played bad guys and good, e.g., his four serials: *Dick Tracy vs. Crime, Inc.* (villain Morton), *Gang Busters* (villain Professor Mortis), *The Great Alaskan Mystery* and *The Monster and the Ape* (heroine's upstanding dad in each);

a few of his features: *Wells Fargo, The Life of Emile Zolo* (Commander of Paris), *Anthony Adverse* (De Bruille), *Sleep My Love, I'll Be Seeing You, Forty Little Mothers.*

MORGAN, RUSS *(1969)* 65 ——Famous orchestra leader; with his band in *The Great Man, The Big Beat, Disc Jockey,* others.

MORGAN, SIDNEY *(1931)* 46 ——He portrayed Joxer in Hitchcock's *Juno and the Paycock* ('30).

MORIARTY, JOANNE *(1964)* 25 ——Pretty blonde who had a supporting role in Brando's *Bedtime Story;* was wife of actor Michael Parks.

MORLAY, GABY *(1964)* 67 ——Noted character actress in many famous French films: *Royal Affairs in Versailles, Mitsou, Life of Giuseppe Verdi,* etc.; starred in one *Le Plaisir* episode ("Le Masque") as the wife whose ancient husband went to dance halls in a mask to hide his wrinkled visage.

MORRELL, GEORGE *(1955)* 82 ——Was a townsman in dozens of Westerns, silent (*The Heart of the North*) and talkie (*The Whispering Skull, Two Fisted Sheriff, Buckskin Frontier,* etc.).

MORRIS, ADRIAN *(1940)* 38 ——In *The Grapes of Wrath* he was the heartless, beefy, plainclothes police official who harassed the Okies after they arrived in California; as callous in others: *Angels With Dirty Faces, The Petrified Forest* (the hood Ruby), *Dr. Socrates,* etc.; brother of Chester.

MORRIS, CHESTER *(1970)* 69 ——Fine actor with slicked-back patent-leather hair who will forever be associated with "Boston Blackie"; played the wise-cracking, girl-chasing sleuth in all 13 of the 1941-49 movies (*Meet Boston Blackie, Alias Boston Blackie,* etc.) and on radio; made a sensational screen debut in, and was Oscar-nominated as Best Actor for, 1929's *Alibi*—about a young gunman who married a cop's daughter; thereafter was seldom seen without gun in hand: *The Big House, Red Headed Woman, Blind Alley, Aerial Gunner, Smashing the Rackets,* etc.; returning to the stage after the final "Boston Blackie" pic, he came back as a character actor in three: *Unchained, The She-Creature,* and 1970's *The Great White Hope,* as the black prizefight champion's manager.

MORRIS, CLARA *(1925)* 28 ——Support in several: Jean Hersholt's *When Romance Rides,* Mr. and Mrs. Carter De Haven's *My Lady Friends,* etc.

MORRIS, DENISE *(1969)* ——Supporting roles.

MORRIS, DIANA *(1961)* 54 ——Young beauty in silents; minor roles.

MORRIS, GLENN *(1974)* 62 ——The 1936 Olympic decathlon champion who played Tarzan onscreen just once—rather dully—in 1938's *Tarzan's Revenge;* his only other movie was that same year's *Hold That Co-ed* with Marjorie Weaver; then played pro football with the Detroit Lions, was a naval hero in WW II, and was a California construction exec until retirement in '62.

MORRIS, GORDON *(1940)* 41 ——Actor-brother of Chester and Adrian; minor roles; better known as a screen writer (*Under the Pampas Moon, Six Hours to Live*, etc.).

MORRIS, MARGARET *(1968)* 60s ——A Wampas Baby Star of '24, this attractive brunette had featured roles at Paramount in Jack Holt's *Wild Horse Mesa*, Richard Dix's *Womanhandled*, Douglas MacLean's *That's My Baby, The Best People*, etc., all 1925-26.

MORRIS, MARY *(1970)* 73 ——Famous Broadway actress who repeated her stage role of the wicked oldtimer in 1934's *Double Door;* not the English character actress.

MORRIS, PHILIP *(1949)* 56 ——Support in Westerns (*Whirlwind Raiders, Home on the Range*, etc.) and a few bigger pix (*Cluny Brown, Home Sweet Homicide*).

MORRIS, WAYNE *(1959)* 45 ——Blond, friendly, open-faced Warners star who made a big hit as the fighter in 1937's *Kid Galahad* (had been in several before it); co-starred in dozens after it, never going beyond the nice-guy-but-not-too-bright characterization, but was always pleasant to have around; was in *I Wanted Wings, Brother Rat, John Loves Mary, Task Force, The Time of Your Life, The Younger Brothers*, etc.; was last in *Paths of Glory*.

MORRIS, WILLIAM *(1936)* 74 ——Actor-father of Chester, Adrian and Gordon; support in *Behind Office Doors, The Convict's Code, The Washington Masquerade*, others.

MORRISON, ANNA MARIE *(1972)* 88 ——Supporting actress in many silents.

MORRISON, ARTHUR *(1950)* 70 ——Character actor; played Limpy in the 1930 Rin-Tin-Tin serial *The Lone Defender;* in dozens of Westerns in the '20s: *Riders of the Purple Sage, Tony Runs Wild, Singing River*, etc.

MORRISON, CHIT *(1968)* 80s ——Character in silent Westerns: *Hair Trigger Casey*, etc.

MORRISON, JACK *(1948)* 61 ——Support in *There Goes the Bride.*

MORRISON, JAMES *(1974)* 86 ——Good-looking actor who starred for Vitagraph perhaps longer than any other—from 1911's *Saving an Audience* and *A Tale of Two Cities* to 1924's *Captain Blood;* also was in *The Battle Cry of Peace* (one of several opposite Norma Talmadge), *The Hero of Submarine D-2, The Enemy, The Little Minister, The Nth Commandment* with Colleen Moore, etc.; retiring from the screen, he taught drama for 17 years at Brooklyn's Packer Collegiate Institute; never married, he died in a nursing home on November 15, his birthday.

MORRISON, PETE *(1973)* 82 ——A cowboy star (as were brothers Charlie and Carl) as early as 1912's *The Stranger at Coyote*, he starred for Universal and others in dozens of Westerns (always featuring daredevil riding stunts) and several serials until the late '20s; also made Westerns in Brazil, Mexico, and Argentina; a few of his features: *Rainbow Rangers, The Better Man Wins, Bucking the Truth;* turning character actor, he was in Beery's *Chinatown Nights* (billed Peter) plus many more Westerns before retirement in '35.

MORRISSEY, BETTY *(1944)* 40s ——Charming ingenue featured by Chaplin in three in a row: *A Woman of Paris, The Gold Rush* (dance hall girl second-billed to Georgia Hale), *The Circus* (second femme lead); danced the Charleston with Reginald Denny in *Skinner's Dress Suit* and was a bright spot in several others of the '20s.

MORRISSEY, WILL *(1957)* 72 ——Co-starred with vaudeville partner Midgie Miller in two-reel comedies in the '20s: *The Morrissey and Miller Night Club*, etc.

MORROW, DORETTA *(1968)* 41 ——Brunette star of Broadway musicals (*Kismet*) who co-starred with Mario Lanza in *Because You're Mine*, her only film.

MORROW, JANE *(1925)* 35 ——See Mrs. Sidney Drew.

MORSE, LEE *(1954)* 50 ——A popular recording star, she was onscreen in the short *The Music Racket.*

MORSE, ROBIN *(1958)* 43 ——One of the buddies (Joe) in *Marty*, he also was in *Pal Joey*, as a bartender, *Abbott and Costello Meet the Mummy*, etc.

MORTIMER, CHARLES *(1964)* 79 ——Character actor in British pix: *The Return of Bulldog Drummond*, Arthur Wontner's *The Triumph of Sherlock Holmes, Rhodes, Living Dangerously*, others.

MORTIMER, ED *(1944)* 69 ——Minor support in Bette Davis' *It's Love I'm After*.

MORTIMER, HENRY *(1952)* 77 ——Colbert's millionaire father in *La Grande Mare*, the French version of her *The Big Pond* (she played the lead in both versions, made simultaneously; George Barbier did the father role in English); was a character actor in silents also.

MORTON, JAMES C. *(1942)* 58 ——Chunky little bald comic with a moon face and a tiny fierce black moustache who was a Hal Roach stock actor; in dozens of shorts (Charley Chase, Laurel & Hardy, "Our Gang," etc.); was in many Laurel & Hardy features (*Our Relations, The Bohemian Girl, Way Out West*), *My Little Chickadee, Never Give a Sucker an Even Break, Topper Takes a Trip* (as the bailiff), *Yokel Boy*, etc.

MOSCOVITCH, MAURICE *(1940)* 68 ——Superb Russian-born actor; in *Winterset*, his first, was Esdras (father of Margo and the youth, Paul Guilfoyle, forced to be a car thief); was the tragic Mr. Jaeckel in *The Great Dictator*, Max Rubens in *Make Way for Tomorrow*, Indian Big Eagle in *Susannah of the Mounties*, Dr. Muller in *In Name Only*.

MOSER, HANS *(1964)* 83 ——Excellent Austrian character actor in many European films, perhaps best recalled as the despairing guardian of the morals of leading man Leo Slezak in 1935's *Liebesmelodie*.

MOSICK, MARIAN PERRY *(1973)* 67 ——Support in many Crosby-Hope "Road" pix and Jerry Lewis comedies.

MOSJOUKINE, IVAN *(1939)* 49 ——Franco-Russian actor who starred, as the aristocratic Russian officer, in Universal's *Surrender* ('27); a star from 1911 (*The Defense of Sebastopo*), he was especially popular in French films: *Michel Strogoff, Sergeant X, Tempest*, others; was sometimes billed Moskine.

MOULAN, FRANK *(1939)* 63 ——Character actor in Irene Hervey's *The Girl Said No*.

MOULDER, WALTER *(1967)* 34 ——Attractive young actor from Broadway (*Take Her*,

She's Mine) who had small roles in *North by Northwest* and Loren's *That Kind of Woman* (as a G.I.).

MOUNET-SULLY, JEAN *(1916)* 75 ——Great French stage actor who starred in (and directed) 1912's *Oedipus Rex* in France; with Bernhardt and Rejane, was among the first stage luminaries to make films.

MOVAR, DUNJA *(1963)* 22 ——German actress much acclaimed for her leading role in *The Angel That Pawned a Harp*.

MOWBRAY, ALAN *(1969)* 72 ——Yes, this fine character actor from England did play George Washington (in 1931's *Alexander Hamilton*), but he was more likely to be found—in some 200 movies—in tux (*Marry the Girl*) or the monkey suit of a butler (*His Butler's Sister, Topper, My Man Godfrey*, etc.); many other roles, though, proved his versatility: Major Clinton in *Berkeley Square*, the absent-minded professor in *Touchdown*, Captain Crawley in *Becky Sharp*, Metternich in *The House of Rothschild*, Sir William Hamilton in *That Hamilton Woman* (Vivien Leigh deserted him for Olivier as Lord Nelson), etc.; eventually comedies claimed his talents almost exclusively: *The Doughgirls, Panama Hattie, The Powers Girl, Holy Matrimony, Earl Carroll's Vanities*, others, including his last, *A Majority of One*.

MOWER, JACK *(1965)* 74 ——In the '20s this big handsome Hawaiian—running the gamut from pirate leader to cowboy—starred in eight serials: *The Third Eye* with Eileen Percy, *In the Days of Daniel Boone* with Eileen Sedgwick, *Over the Cliff* (again as Daniel Boone), *Ten Score Make a Man* with Allene Ray, *Perils of the Wild*, etc.; he also toplined many Western features (*Riding with Death, Rustlers of the Night*, etc.); in talkies, had supporting roles, often as a cop, in several dozen pix: *Missing Witness, Confessions of a Nazi Spy, Crime School, Torrid Zone*, etc., through 1950's *County Fair*.

MOZART, GEORGE *(1947)* 83 ——Minor British support; in *Pygmalion, Mystery of the Mary Deare*, others.

MUDIE, LEONARD *(1965)* 81 ——Ascetic-faced British character in many of Hollywood's best: *Dark Victory* (Dr. Driscoll), *Captain Blood* (Parliament member Lord Jeffries), *Anthony Adverse, They Won't Forget* (Judge Moore who presided over the trial of the innocent black man accused of murdering Lana Turner), *Devil's Island, Lloyds of London*, plus 50 more, including last, *The Greatest Story Ever Told*.

MUELLER, WOLFGANG *(1960)* 37 ——German star; in *Aren't We Wonderful?*, *The Spessart Inn*, others.

MUIR, GAVIN *(1972)* 62 ——Polished sandy-haired actor with British accent (born in Chicago, educated in London) who alternated between semiheroic roles and deep-eyed villains; at 20th Century-Fox from the mid-'30s in *Half Angel*, *Wee Willie Winkie*, *Lloyds of London*, etc.; at Universal in the early '40s in *Salome, Where She Danced; Nightmare; Patrick the Great*, etc.; then at Paramount in *O.S.S.*, *California*, *Calcutta*, *Unconquered*, *Ivy*, and *Chicago Deadline*.

MUIR, HELEN *(1934)* 70 ——Character actress in silent Westerns *(The Mistress of Shenshone)* and others *(Live and Let Live)*.

MULCASTER, G. H. *(1964)* 73 ——British support in *Under Capricorn*, *Spring in Park Lane*, *The Naked Heart*, *Bonnie Prince Charlie*, many others; thin-faced and long-nosed, with a perpetually surprised look on his face, he often played clerks.

MULCAY, JIMMY *(1968)* 68 ——Support in several "Road" pix with Crosby & Hope.

MULHAUSER, JAMES *(1939)* 48 ——Support in such silent comedies as Charlie Murray's *The Head Man* and Karl Dane's *China Bound*, and such talkie two-reelers as those of Slim Summerville.

MULLER, RENATE *(1937)* 30 ——German actress who starred in *Waltz Time in Vienna*, *Sunshine Susie*, *For Her Country's Sake*, etc.

MULLIGAN, MOON *(1967)* 57 ——Many minor roles, including 1931's *The Spirit of Notre Dame*.

MUMBY, DIANA *(1974)* 51 ——Statuesque blonde "Goldwyn Girl" who was in Kaye's *Up In Arms*.

MUNDIN, HERBERT *(1939)* 40 ——Small Englishman with a kewpie-doll kisser whose every appearance was a signal for laughter: Much, the Miller in *The Adventures of Robin Hood*, Barkis in *David Copperfield* ('35), bibulous pub-owner Alfred Bridges in *Cavalcade*, mess boy Smith in *Mutiny on the Bounty*, and some 40 more.

MUNI, PAUL *(1967)* 71 ——A master of makeup and at playing old men (almost his entire background in the Yiddish theater), this retiring actor genius "hid" behind beards or other heavy makeup in most of his 22 films: *The Story of Louis Pasteur* (won the Best Actor Oscar), *The Life of Emile Zola* (nominated, just as he had been earlier for both *The Valiant*, his debut movie, and *I Am a Fugitive from a Chain Gang*), *Juarez*, *The Good Earth*, *A Song to Remember*, *Seven Faces*, *Hudson's Bay*; wore his "own face," more or less, in *Commandos Strike at Dawn*, *Bordertown*, *Black Fury*, *We Are Not Alone*; made his farewell screen appearance in 1959's *The Last Angry Man*.

MUNIER, FERDINAND *(1945)* 55 ——Brought comic distinction to supporting roles in many: *Hands Across the Table* (butler), *Tovarich*, *Midnight*, *The Gilded Lily*, *Roberta* (Lord Delves), *Ambassador Bill*, *Everything Happens at Night*, *Claudia*, etc.

MUNRO, JANET *(1972)* 38 ——A Disney discovery, this freckle-faced little charmer from England starred for him in three: *Darby O'Gill and the Little People* ('59), *Third Man on the Mountain*, *Swiss Family Robinson*; elsewhere was in *The Day the Earth Caught Fire*, *Walk in the Shadow*, *Sebastian*, others.

MUNSHIN, JULES *(1970)* 54 ——Sinatra's and Kelly's wacky, homely sailor pal, Ozzie, in *On the Town*, he was one of the best things that ever happened to—or in—MGM musicals; was in *Easter Parade*, *Take Me Out to the Ball Game*, *That Midnight Kiss*, *Silk Stockings*, *Ten Thousand Bedrooms*, etc.

MUNSON, ONA *(1955)* 48 ——Created, out of whole cloth, the classic characterization of *Gone With the Wind*'s Belle Watling, buxom and redhaired—but she was neither, being tiny, thin, and blonde; later played variations of Belle in several: *Lady from Louisiana* with John Wayne, *The Shanghai Gesture* (Mother Gin Sling), *The Cheaters*; a star of Broadway musical comedies, she never made a musical but did do several comedy leads in her early movies: *The Head of the Family* ('29), *The Hot Heiress*, *Going Wild*, etc.; last played Lon McCallister's mother in *The Red House*.

MURA, CORINNA *(1965)* 55 ——In *Casablanca*, at Rick's, she was the club singer with the guitar who first struck up "Le Marseillaise" in challenge to the German patrons singing their national anthem; also was in *Passage to Marseille*, *Call Out the Marines*, *The Gay Senorita*.

MURAT, JEAN *(1968)* 80 ——French actor who starred in *The Night Is Ours*, *Carnival in Flanders*, *The Eternal Return*, etc., all European-made; in Hollywood, had supporting roles in *On the Riviera* (as Periton) and *Rich, Young and Pretty*; was the first husband of Annabella.

MURPHY, ADA *(1961)* 73 ——Actress who played supporting roles from the mid-teens.

MURPHY, AUDIE *(1971)* 46 ——Small only in size, this wavy-haired Texan who was the #1 hero of WW II started in movies with a bit in Alan Ladd's *Beyond Glory;* he quickly rose to stardom in Technicolor Westerns at Universal: *Sierra, The Kid from Texas, Kansas Raiders, 6 Black Horses,* etc.; starred in other kinds of roles—less successfully—in *The Quiet American, Joe Butterfly,* and *Red Badge of Courage;* portrayed himself in *To Hell and Back,* based on his book about his wartime experiences.

MURPHY, BOB *(1948)* 46 ——In Jeanette MacDonald's *Girl of the Golden West,* he was Sonora Slim; in Alice Faye's *You're a Sweetheart,* the bailiff; other supporting roles in *Shine On Harvest Moon, Portia on Trial, Nancy Steele Is Missing,* etc.

MURPHY, CHARLES B. *(1942)* 58 ——Support in the '20s in many: Raymond Griffith's *Red Lights,* Hoot Gibson's *Single Handed, The Rowdy,* etc.; in the '30s he was in Hope Hampton's *Road to Reno, County Fair,* others.

MURPHY, JOE *(1961)* 84 ——Starred hilariously as "chinless" Andy Gump in the many two-reel comedies based on the comic strip "The Gumps" which Universal produced 1923-28.

MURPHY, JOHN DALY *(1934)* 61 ——Support in silent comedy features (Ethel Barrymore's *Our Mrs. McChesney,* Constance Talmadge's *Polly of the Follies, The Truth about Wives*) and dramas (*Icebound, Thunderclap,* etc.).

MURRAY, CHARLIE *(1941)* 69 ——In the famous "Cohens and the Kellys" comedy features (1926-33), he was always-ready-for-a-fight Kelly; long before that he had been one of the nation's favorite comedians; for 20 years prior to his screen debut in '12, he had been teamed in vaudeville with partner Ollie Mack ("Murray & Mack"); then, via dozens of Sennett comedies, teamed with Louise Fazenda and Slim Summerville, and particularly through his "Hogan" series, he won vast new audiences that never seemed to tire of the "average little man" with the funny set of chin whiskers; was in numerous features in the '20s (*The Girl in the Limousine, Who Cares, Fool's Highway,* etc.) and '30s (*Circus Girl, Caught Cheating, Breaking the Ice,* more).

MURRAY, DAVID MITCHELL *(1923)* 70 —— Character actor in the Glenn Hunter-Bessie Love pic *The Silent Watcher.*

MURRAY, ELIZABETH *(1946)* 75 ——In Marion Davies' *Little Old New York,* she played the mother of the fighter, Bully Boy Brewster, then did another mother role in Morton Downey's *Lucky in Love.*

MURRAY, J. HAROLD *(1940)* 49 ——Handsome Broadway musical comedy star (*Rio Rita*) who cut quite a princely figure in 1929's *Married in Hollywood,* the screen's very first all-talkie Viennese operetta; then was in *Happy Days, Cameo Kirby, Women Everywhere;* returned to the stage.

MURRAY, JAMES *(1936)* 35 ——His name was on everyone's lips in '28 for his extraordinary performance of "average man" Johnny Sims, insurance clerk, in King Vidor's *The Crowd;* before that, had been for years one of Hollywood's faceless extras; in the seven years after *The Crowd,* it was a continual slide downward, though he was in numerous others: *The Big City, The Little Wildcat, Shanghai Lady, Bright Lights, Frisco Jenny,* etc.; finally, as he became a hopeless alcoholic, had small roles in 1935's *Ship Cafe* and *$20 a Week.*

MURRAY, JOHN T. *(1936)* 71 ——Supporting actor in many silents from Nazimova's *Madonna of the Streets: Sonny Boy, Stop Flirting, High Steppers,* etc.; also many talkies: *Lost Horizon* (as Meeker), *True Confession, Ever Since Eve, Sweetheart of the Navy,* etc.; made numerous early talkie two-reel comedies with wife, Vivian Oakland.

MURRAY, MAE *(1965)* 75 ——Of the frizzed blonde hair and bee-stung lips, this dancer-actress was one of Metro's most valuable, albeit outré, stars in the '20s; her greatest talent was perhaps a sense of movement which, even in non-musical scenes, was fluid poetry; *The Merry Widow* ('25) is her movie everyone recalls; she starred—always in gauzy soft focus—in just six following it (*Altars of Desire, Valencia, Show People, High Stakes,* etc.); one of the few Ziegfeld star-dancers to succeed in transferring her popularity from stage to screen, she was in many from 1916's *To Have and To Hold,* including *Delicious Little Devil, On With the Dance, Peacock Alley, Jazzmania,* more; after her starring days, never succeeded in making a comeback but never stopped hoping; film historian Richard Griffith has reported of her later years, "Her appearance eventually became an outlandish caricature of the superstar. . . . At charity balls, which she attended all the time, she would command the orchestra to play the theme tune from *The Merry Widow* and waltz to it solo. . . ."

729

MURRAY, MARION *(1951)* 66 ——Character (Eloise) in Garland's *The Pirate*, others; the wife of Jed (*Jones Family*) Prouty.

MURRAY, TOM *(1935)* 60 ——In *The Gold Rush*, was outlaw Black Larson who unwillingly accepted Chaplin and Mack Swain as his cabin guests; also was in Chaplin's *The Pilgrim*, plus other comedies of the '20s: Harry Langdon's *Tramp, Tramp, Tramp*, George Jessel's *Private Izzy Murphy*, Edward Everett Horton's *Too Much Business*, etc.

MURRAY-HILL, PETER *(1957)* 49 ——Popular co-star in many English films: *Madonna of the Seven Moons, House of the Arrow, The Ghost Train, They Were Sisters* (with wife, Phyllis Calvert), others.

MURROW, EDWARD R. *(1965)* 57 ——Irreplaceable CBS (radio and TV) newsman, most noted for wartime reporting from London and *See It Now;* was onscreen in *Sink the Bismarck* and *Around the World in 80 Days.*

MURTH, FLORENCE *(1934)* 32 ——Cowboy Fred Thomson's lovely leading lady in *Thundering Hoofs;* had become a Sennett Bathing Beauty.

MUSIDORA *(1957)* 68 ——Was the heroine—in molded black silk tights—in the classic French serial *Les Vampires* (1915–16); starred, as a lady crook, in a followup serial, *Judex.*

MUSSON, BENNET *(1946)* 79 ——Support in a Paramount Western of '21, *White Oak.*

MUZQUIZ, CARLOS *(1960)* 53 ——Character (Montoya) in *The Sun Also Rises;* also in several Westerns: *My Outlaw Brother, Hidden River*, etc.

MYERS, HARRY *(1938)* 52 ——Made an invaluable contribution to *City Lights*—as the millionaire who is Chaplin's bosom buddy only when intoxicated; was just one of his 50 films; onscreen from 1908, he began as a handsome, wavy-haired comic leading man; in 1916–17 teamed with star-wife in more than 40 (one a week) short domestic comedies, *Housekeeping* being the first; was with Florence Lawrence in *Her Two Sons,* starred in *A Connecticut Yankee in King Arthur's Court* ('21), was with Marie Prevost in *The Beautiful and the Damned,* etc.; in all of these was billed Harry C. Myers; career continued through 1937's *Dangerous Lives.*

MYERS, PETER *(1968)* 40 ——Had a top supporting role in *The Reluctant Debutante.*

N

NAGEL, ANNE *(1966)* 54 ——Attractive and talented dark-haired leading lady, long at Universal, especially popular as love interest in serials: *Don Winslow of the Navy, The Green Hornet Strikes Again, Winners of the West*, etc.; much of her career (1933-49) was spent in pix in which she had to look terrified and scream often: *Black Friday, The Invisible Woman, Legion of the Lost Flyers, Mystery House,* many others.

NAGEL, CONRAD *(1970)* 72 ——Among the most suave of the matinee-idol stars, he made the first of his 225 movies, *Little Women,* in '18, and was perhaps at his romantic best in two with Garbo in the late '20s, *The Mysterious Lady* and *The Kiss;* some of the silents that made his reputation: *Three Weeks* (then considered shockingly sexy), *Tess of the D'Urbervilles, Pretty Ladies, Lights of Old Broadway, Quality Street;* was fortuitously cast, since he possessed a rich stage-trained speaking voice, in 1928's *Glorious Betsy* with Dolores Costello, the first feature-length talkie with dialogue (*The Jazz Singer,* just before it, only had songs in sound); a lucky accident—Metro mogul Louis B. Mayer, angry with him, had loaned him out to Warners as "punishment"; thereafter it was

"Get Nagel, he can talk"; among the many in which he starred: *Dynamite, The Divorcee, A Lady Surrenders, Ann Vickers;* became a star on radio (longtime host of *Silver Theater*) and Broadway (*Goodbye My Fancy, State of the Union*); later, a top Hollywood character actor in such as Wyman's *All That Heaven Allows,* playing not untypically, as he once said, "a fussy old guy with aches and pains."

NAGY, BILL *(1973)* 40s ——Character (Midnight) in *Goldfinger;* also in *Across the Bridge* and *A Countess from Hong Kong.*

NAINBY, ROBERT *(1948)* 78 ——Support in British pix: *We're Going to Be Rich, The Student's Romance, Forbidden Music.*

NAISH, J. CARROL *(1973)* 73 ——Hollywood's most versatile character actor and master dialectician, he could and did play men of almost every nationality; in movies from 1926, his first major role was in *The Hatchet Man* ('32), as an aging Chinese businessman (and he much later starred in the *Charlie Chan* TV series); was twice nominated as Best Support: *Sahara,* in which he was Italian (later starred in the radio series *Life With Luigi*), and *A Medal* for Benny, as an illiterate Mexican-American; some of the best of his 150 pix: *The Lives of a Bengal Lancer, Captain Blood, Sitting Bull, The Beast with Five Fingers, Beau Geste, Black Fury, Blood and Sand, Voice in the Wind, The Southerner.*

NALDI, NITA *(1961)* 63 ——In the '20s, her only screen decade, this raven-haired vamp was right up there with Bara and Negri, but while they could and did play romantic roles, she was forever the villainess; perhaps her best role was opposite Valentino in *A Sainted Devil;* was vivid, too, in *Blood and Sand, Dr. Jekyll and Mr. Hyde, Cobra, The Ten Commandments, The Woman Who Lied;* her last pic was 1928's *What Price Beauty?;* later starred on Broadway and even did a few TV shows; never stopped yearning for a screen comeback, admitting once on a radio program in the '50s, "Oh Gawd, just one more chance."

NANOOK *(1923)* 30s ——The real-life Eskimo hunter who was the hero focal point of Robert J. Flaherty's *Nanook of the North.*

NANSEN, BETTY *(1943)* 67 ——Danish actress who, because of her interpretation of Ibsen heroines onstage, was called "The Idol of Europe"; then came to America in 1915 to star in several for Fox; had earlier starred in the Danish film *Princess Elena's Prisoner* ('13).

NARES, OWEN *(1943)* 55 ——A matinee idol in England in the '20s (*Young Lochinvar, Milestones,* etc.), he had a featured role in Griffith's *The Sorrows of Satan;* top support in later British pix: *Sunshine Susie, The Prime Minister, The Loves of Madame DuBarry,* etc.

NASH, FLORENCE *(1950)* 61 ——Was one of Shearer's society friends (Nancy Blake) in *The Women;* was sister of Mary.

NASH, GEORGE *(1944)* 71 ——Dignified, large-sized character actor who was in several Marion Davies pix: *Janice Meredith* (as Lord Howe), *When Knighthood Was in Flower* (an adventurer); also was in *The Great Gatsby* (silent), *Under the Red Robe,* and a few talkies including *Oliver Twist* ('33), *Mystery Liner,* etc.

NASH, MARY *(1965)* 76 ——A most excellent character actress—even if she was mean to Shirley Temple in *Heidi* (as Fraulein Rottermeier) and *The Little Princess* (Miss Minchin); was on her aristocratic best behavior as Hepburn's mother in *The Philadelphia Story;* also was in *The Human Comedy, The Rains Came, Come and Get It, Wells Fargo, Till the Clouds Roll By,* etc.

NATHEAUX, LOUIS *(1942)* 44 ——Support in *Modern Times* (one of the burglars with whom Chaplin got involved, landing him back in jail); also in *Street Scene* (as Henry Easter), *Ned McCobb's Daughter, Transatlantic,* etc., in addition to many silents: *Stand and Deliver, Dress Parade, Risky Business,* others.

NAVARRO, CARLOS *(1969)* 47 ——Popular Mexican actor best known here for his top supporting role in *The Brave One.*

NAVARRO, JESUS *(1960)* 47 ——Support in Bunuel's *Los Olvidados (The Young and the Damned).*

NAZARRO, CLIFF *(1961)* 57 ——Comedian noted for his double-take; was featured in *Arise My Love* (as Botzelberg), *Rookies on Parade* (Joe Martin), *Dive Bomber* (Corps Man), *St. Louis Blues,* etc.

NAZIMOVA, ALLA *(1945)* 66 ——A great screen artist, from Russia, this small, dark actress brought Metro considerable prestige through her many starring vehicles: *Revelation* and *Toys of Fate* (her first, in '18), *An Eye for an Eye, Out of the Fog, The Red Lantern, Camille, The Brat,* many more silents; was noted, in these, for her pantomime (incomparable in tragic roles), mobility of movement, and the restless boldness of her acting style; offscreen 15 years, she came back in '40 as an incandescent character actress in *Blood and Sand* (Tyrone Power's Spanish mother), *Escape* (German Emmy Ritter), *In Our Time* and *Since You Went Away* (Polish women in both; in the latter, was welder Koslowska whose love of America was an inspiration to war wife Colbert), *The Bridge of San Luis Rey.*

NEAL, FRANK *(1955)* 38 ——Black actor-dancer featured in *Stormy Weather.*

NEAL, TOM *(1972)* 58 ——Muscular handsome guy who looked great in boxer trunks and military uniform (*Flying Tigers, First Yank into Tokyo, Behind the Rising Sun, Top Sergeant Mulligan,* etc.); MGM had groomed him for stardom, as "another" Gable, in many in the '30s: *Burn 'Em Up O'Connor, 6000 Enemies, No Greater Love* (starred as famous "leper priest" Father Damien), etc.; in the early '50s made shocking headlines when he and Franchot Tone fought over actress Barbara Payton (she subsequently married Tone, divorced him, resumed her association with Neal); his 180-pic career ended by the scandal, Neal became a professional gardener; made more shocking news in '65 when convicted of the involuntary manslaughter of his third wife; served seven years at the California Institution for Men at Chino and died eight months after parole.

NEDELL, ALICE BLAKENEY *(1959)* 60s —— Actress-sister of Olive Blakeney.

NEDELL, BERNARD *(1972)* 79 ——Character actor-husband of Alice; good-looking and polished, he mostly played bad guys (*Call of the Sea, They All Come Out, Strange Cargo, Angels Wash Their Faces, Mr. Moto's Gamble,* etc.).

NEGRETE, JORGE *(1953)* 42 ——Mexico's #1 matinee idol, he was in dozens of films (*Silk, Blood and Sun,* etc.), all made south of the border.

NEHER, JOHN *(1972)* 61 ——Singer-actor; minor roles.

NEILAN, MARSHALL *(1958)* 67 ——Best known now for his directing career, he began as an actor and starred in many; worked for both Universal and American (*The Stranger at Coyote,* '12) before becoming Kalem's top leading man; co-starred with Pickford in *Madam Butterfly* ('15), starred in *The Crisis,* etc.; directed Pickford in several of her greatest hits: *Daddy Long Legs* (also played the male lead), *Rebecca of Sunnybrook Farm, The Little Princess;* also directed *Dinty, Penrod* ('22), and Colleen Moore in several including *Mickey;* last played leading roles in 1923's *Souls for Sale* and *Broadway Gold;* acted in just one talkie, *A Face in the Crowd,* in which he played a Senator.

NEILL, JAMES *(1931)* 70 ——A character actor from the first (the old man in a '17 Sessue Hayakawa pic, *The Bottle Imp*), he continued to be one in many silents; acted often for DeMille: *The King of Kings* (as James), *The Ten Commandments* (Aaron, Brother of Moses), *Manslaughter* (Butler); was also in *Our Leading Citizen* with Thomas Meighan, *Salomy Jane* with Jacqueline Logan, etc.

NEILL, RICHARD *(1970)* 94 ——Supporting actor in silent serials (*Go Get 'Em Hutch, The Great Gamble*) and Westerns (*Wanderer of the Wasteland, Whispering Smith, Born to the West*).

NEILSEN-TERRY, DENNIS *(1932)* 37 ——Onscreen in British silents.

NELSON, GORDON *(1956)* 58 ——Support in *The Groom Wore Spurs, The Iron Mistress.*

NELSON, HAROLD *(1937)* ——Featured in a '28 Rayart mystery, *Sisters of Eve,* and the serial *The Lost Special* ('32; as Prof. Wilson).

NELSON, LOTTIE *(1966)* 91 ——Character actress in silents.

NELSON, VIRGINIA TALLENT *(1968)* 57 —— Comedienne in supporting roles.

NESBIT, EVELYN *(1967)* 81 ——Celebrated (later notorious) Broadway beauty who starred in three: *Threads of Destiny* ('14), *Redemption* ('17), and *The Hidden Woman* ('22); known to tabloid readers as Evelyn Nesbit Thaw, central figure in a famous love scandal in which her millionaire husband, Harry K. Thaw, shot and killed noted architect Stanford White in jealousy; scandal was rehashed when Joan Collins portrayed her in *The Girl in the Red Velvet Swing,* as she was known onstage; Nesbit, Thaw, and White appeared as characters, under their own names, in a best-selling novel of '75, *Ragtime.*

NESBITT, JOHN *(1960)* 49 ——The brain behind MGM's splendid "Passing Parade" shorts.

NESBITT, MIRIAM ——Lovely brunette who was one of the most talented and charming of all early (from '11) stars; most often co-starred with husband Marc McDermott; were together in *Lady Clare, Aida, Mary Stuart, When John Bolt Slept, Lena, The Colonel of the Red Hussars,* and the '14 serial *The Man Who Disappeared;* she also was in *The Three Musketeers* ('11; as the queen) and *The Foreman's Treachery;* year of death unreported.

NESMITH, OTTOLA *(1972)* 83 ——Character actress of the beautiful aristocratic face; was in *Becky Sharp* (as Lady Jane Crawley), *Fools for Scandal* (socialite Agnes), *My Name Is Julia Ross, Three Men on a Horse,* in which she was billed as Tola Nesmith; was last in *Witness for the Prosecution* (Miss Johnson).

NESS, OLE M. *(1953)* 65 ——Support in many FBO pix of the late '20s: Sally O'Neil's *Hardboiled,* Ralph Ince's *Chicago After Midnight,* Bryant Washburn's *Skinner's Big Idea,* etc.; talkies: *The Last Days of Pompeii, The Sin of Madelon Claudet,* others.

NESTELL, BILL *(1966)* 71 ——Character in Westerns of the '20s: Hoot Gibson's *The Thrill Chaser,* Tom Tyler's *The Trail of the Horse Thieves,* Ken Maynard's *The Fighting Legion,* etc.

NEWALL, GUY *(1937)* 50 ——Popular lead in British silents: *The Duke's Son, The Ghost Train, The Marriage Bond,* etc.

NEWBURG, FRANK *(1969)* 82 ——Youthful lead in Vitagraph's *Saving an Audience* ('11);

support in silents of the '20s: *The Dramatic Life of Abraham Lincoln*, the Jack Hoxie Western *The Sign of the Cactus*, Patsy Ruth Miller's *Lorraine of the Lions*, others.

NEWCOMB, MARY *(1967)* 72 ——Support in Matt Moore's *The Passionate Pilgrim* ('21), and in a few talkies: *Women Who Play, Frail Women*, etc.

NEWELL, WILLIAM *(1967)* 72 ——Character whose smiling "average guy" countenance lit up many a screen; in the serial *Robinson Crusoe of Clipper Island* he was hero Mala's jovial dog-keeper (heroic dog Buck) and man Friday, Hank; in the serial *Mysterious Dr. Satan*, was hero Robert Wilcox's pal Speed Martin; in *Riff-raff*, was Una Merkel's blue-collar beau; also was in *The Voice of Bugle Ann, Mr. Smith Goes to Washington, Libeled Lady*, etc.; was last in 1960's *Who Was That Lady?*

NEWHALL, MAYO *(1958)* 68 ——In *Meet Me in St. Louis*, he was the frightening neighbor, Mr. Braukoff, that Tootie (Margaret O'Brien) dared to insult on Halloween; in other MGM pix: *Yolanda and the Thief, Her Highness and the Bellboy*, etc.

NEWMAN, ALFRED *(1970)* 68 ——Noted 20th Century-Fox composer-conductor; was on-screen in *They Shall Have Music*.

NEWMAN, JOHN K. *(1927)* 63 ——Support in a 1924 George Beban comedy, *The Greatest Love of All*.

NEWTON, CHARLES *(1926)* 30s ——Support in many Westerns of the '20s: *The Iron Horse* (as Collis P. Harrington), the Art Acord serial *The Moon Rider*, Tom Mix's *Riders of the Purple Sage*, etc.

NEWTON, ROBERT *(1956)* 51 ——English character star given to scraggly characters and florid, bug-eyed performances; roles representative of his style were in *Odd Man Out* (deranged painter Lukey), *Jamaica Inn* (naval officer who pretended to be a spy), 1948's *Oliver Twist* (Bill Sikes), *The Beachcomber, Major Barbara* (too-tough-for-salvation bully, Bill Walker), *Blackbeard the Pirate, Long John Silver*.

NEWTON, THEODORE *(1963)* 58 ——Character who early played cops (*Gambling, The House on 56th Street*) and later military officers: *Friendly Persuasion* (Army Major), *What Next, Corporal Hargrove?* (Captain Parkson), *The Proud and the Profane*, etc.

NIBLO, FRED *(1948)* 74 ——Most famous as director of many great silents: *Ben-Hur, Blood and Sand, The Mark of Zorro*, etc.; an early movie actor, he resumed acting in Buster Keaton's *Free and Easy* ('30); played Marsha Hunt's dad in *Ellery Queen, Master Detective* and Jackie Cooper's in *Life With Henry*.

NICHOLLS, GEORGE *(1927)* 62 ——Beefy, gray-haired character in many important silents; was a member of the acting stock company D.W. Griffith took with him to California from New York in 1910; in Griffith's *A Romance of Happy Valley* (as Lillian Gish's father), *The Greatest Question* (Martin Cain), *Hearts of the World* (a German Sergeant); also was in *The Eagle, The Queen of Sheba, The Wedding March* (the Magnate, Schweisser), many others; also directed many, including 1912's *A Celebrated Case*.

NICHOLLS, GEORGE, JR. *(1939)* 42 ——As a youth had acted in several Griffith pix with his father; better known as a director in the '30s: *Anne of Green Gables, Portia on Trial, Man of Conquest*, others.

NICHOLS, MARGARET *(1941)* 41 ——Pretty girl in minor silent roles; wife of producer Hal Roach, mother of starlet Margaret Roach.

NICHOLS, MARJORIE *(1970)* 50s ——Stage actress who had minor roles in *Splendor in the Grass, North by Northwest*, etc.

NICHOLS, NELLIE V. *(1971)* 86 ——Character actress in a few in the '30s; Clara Kimball Young's *Women Go on Forever*, Chester Morris' *Playing Around*, Phil Regan's *Manhattan Merry-Go-Round*.

NICHOLS, RED *(1965)* 60 ——Led his famous "Five Pennies" band in several musical shorts; Danny Kaye portrayed him in *The Five Pennies*.

NICHOLSON, NORA *(1973)* 86 ——Fey British character actress in *A Town Like Alice, The Blue Lagoon, Upstairs and Downstairs*, more.

NICHOLSON, PAUL *(1935)* 57 ——Specialized in executive and father roles in the '20s: Marie Prevost's *Up in Mabel's Room*, Pauline Frederick's *Married Flirts*, Milton Sills' *I Want My Man*, Madge Bellamy's *Bertha, the Sewing Machine Girl*, many others; onscreen from before the turn of the century, was last in ZaSu Pitts' *Two Alone* ('34).

NIELSEN, ASTA *(1972)* 90 ——Great Danish silent actress who, before Garbo and Dietrich, was unrivalled as Europe's #1 femme star; had the leading woman's role in the German-made

The Street of Sorrow (The Joyless Street) which made a star of second lead Garbo and took her immediately to Hollywood; Nielsen played the destitute woman who became a prostitute and eventually committed murder; earlier, had been a sensation when she starred in Hamlet ('21); after a '34 German talkie, Crown of Thorns, returned to the stage.

NILSSON, ANNA Q. (1974) 85 ——From Sweden, she was one of the silent screen's great blonde beauties, with dimples, and enormously popular from her debut in 1911's Mollie Pitcher; among her many successes: Seven Keys to Baldpate ('17), The Silent Master, Heart of the Sunset, The Way of the Strong, Miss Nobody, The Spoilers ('23), Ponjola (her personal favorite), Painted People, Inez from Hollywood, Sorrell and Son, The Whip ('28); a broken hip (fall from a horse), keeping her off-screen five years, ended her starring career; thereafter, character roles, all small and emphasizing her Swedish accent; was Loretta Young's mother in The Farmer's Daughter; also was in Magic Town, Fighting Father Dunne, and, as herself—part of Norma Desmond's "waxworks"—in Sunset Boulevard; when old, another fall invalided her permanently, requiring a craniotomy, but she retained her sweet smile to the very end.

NINCHI, CARLO (1974) 78 ——Italian character, perhaps best as the Prince in Beauty and the Devil; also in Cavalleria Rusticana, Scipio Africanus, 1958's The Ten Commandments, others.

NOBLES, DOLLIE (1930) 67 ——Played the heroine in 1910's The Phoenix, in which Wallace Reid made his screen debut.

NOBLES, MILTON (1924) 80 ——Was the Old Patriot in Griffith's America ('24).

NOBLES, MILTON, JR. (1925) 32 ——Screen actor son of the above.

NOEMI, LEA (1973) 90 ——She was featured in two Yiddish films in the '30s: Green Fields and The Singing Blacksmith.

NOLAN, MARY (1948) 42 ——At 22, this blonde beauty, newly named Mary Nolan, embarked on a 20-picture Hollywood career (1927–32); her first, Sorrell and Son, was best; among the forgettable others: Shanghai Lady, Outside the Law, X Marks the Spot, Docks of San Francisco; by then she had already run through three professional names; as a Ziegfeld Girl on Broadway, was Imogene "Bubbles" Wilson—until involvement in a scandal; pre-Hollywood, as Mary Robertson, she starred in a few German movies, but made more (The Adventures of a Ten Mark Note, Armored Vault, etc.) as Imogene Robertson; real name: Mary Imogene Robertson, but never used it all together.

NOMIS, LEO (1932) 30s ——Stunt pilot who also acted; was "Loop the Loop" Murphy in Hell's Angels and had a supporting role (Jim) in Cagney's auto-race pic The Crowd Roars.

NOON, PAISLEY (1932) 36 ——Support in a Universal B, Night World, and, earlier, several silents.

NOONAN, PATRICK (1962) 64 ——Support in many British pix: Vivien Leigh's Anna Karenina, Captain Boycott, Arms and the Man, Over the Moon, etc.

NOONAN, TOMMY (1968) 46 ——Breezy young comic in specs, and many important roles: Gentlemen Prefer Blondes (Monroe's love interest, Gus), The Best Things in Life Are Free, How to be Very Very Popular (Sheree North's beau), A Star Is Born (played Danny McGuire), Bundle of Joy, The Ambassador's Daughter; had a nightclub act with straight man Peter Marshall and they co-starred in several pix: The Rookie, Swingin' Along, etc.; onscreen from 1945's George White's Scandals, was last in 1963's Promises! Promises!

NORCROSS, FRANK (1926) 70 ——Character actor in several in the '20s: Gareth Hughes' Garments of Truth, Virginia Valli's The Escape, Gladys Walton's All Dolled Up, Harry Carey's The Man from Red Gulch, etc.

NORDSTROM, CLARENCE (1968) 75 ——In his 30s he had featured roles in several at Warners: 42nd Street (credited as The Actor), Gold Diggers of 1933 (Gordon), David Manners' Crooner, etc.

NORMAN, GERTRUDE (1943) 93 ——Character actress from England who played sharp-featured old ladies for two decades, from the first, 1914's The Unwelcome Mrs. Hatch with Harold Lockwood, to the last, 1934's The Trumpet Blows with George Raft; also was in Widow by Proxy, The Age of Innocence, The Greene Murder Case, Cradle Song.

NORMAN, JOSEPHINE (1951) 46 ——Lovely young actress onscreen in the '20s whose best opportunities were in two DeMille pix: The King of Kings (as Mary of Bethany) and The Road to Yesterday (as Anne Vener); also was in The Forbidden Woman, Chicago, Prince of Pilsen, etc.

NORMAND, MABEL (1930) 35 ——Delicious, beautiful, and the very creme de la creme of silent comediennes; her very last picture, in '24, was titled *The Extra Girl*, and in 1910 that is what she had been—in a D.W. Griffith one-reeler; but then, after acquiring comedy experience in John Bunny comedies, she quickly became Mack Sennett's star comedienne and rose to dizzying heights of popularity; starred in literally hundreds of comedies, her name figuring in the titles of almost half of them: *Mabel's Lovers, Mabel's New Hero, Fatty and Mabel's Married Life* (just one of many she made with Roscoe "Fatty" Arbuckle), *Mabel at the Wheel, Mabel's Nerve*, etc.; after her long association with Sennett she starred for Goldwyn in many: *The Jinx, What Happened to Rosa, When Doctors Disagree, Pinto, Sis Hopkins*; returned to Sennett for *Molly O, Oh, Mabel Behave* and, fittingly, her swansong, *The Extra Girl*; tried Broadway in '25, unsuccessfully, in *The Little Mouse*; in '74 she and Mack Sennett —they had once set a wedding date in 1915 but never married—were portrayed on Broadway, by Bernadette Peters and Robert Preston, in *Mack and Mabel*.

NORRIE, ANNA *(1957)* 97 ——One of the stars of Sweden's *Ett Hemligt Giftermal* ('12).

NORRIS, WILLIAM *(1929)* 57 ——Droll character; was feeble old King Louis II in *When Knighthood Was in Flower;* others in the '20s: Anita Stewart's *The Love Piker*, Dustin Farnum's *My Man*, Olive Borden's *The Joy Girl*, etc.

NORTH, JOE *(1945)* 70 ——English character who was the butler in Cary Grant's *Ladies Should Listen;* similar roles in Elissa Landi's *Without Regret*, Ida Lupino's *Paris in Spring;* sometimes billed Joseph.

NORTH, WILFRED *(1935)* 82 ——English character; in many in the '20s: Wally Van's *The Drivin' Fool*, Shearer's *The Trial of Mary Dugan, Captain Blood*, Tom Moore's *On Thin Ice*, Rin-Tin-Tin's *Tracked by the Police*, etc.; earlier, had directed *The Mind-the-Paint Girl*.

NORTON, BARRY *(1956)* 51 ——Gave several affecting performances as a youth in the '20s; particularly memorable in *What Price Glory?* as Private Lewisohn, the "mother's boy" killed in battle; was Belle Bennett's son in *The Lily*, and was in Janet Gaynor's *Sunrise* and *Four Devils*, etc.; in the '30s was in *Only Yesterday* (as Jerry), *Nana, History Is Made at Night*, others; bi-lingual (from Argentina), he starred in Spanish-language versions of many Hollywood pix (*The Benson Murder Case*, etc.); in the late '30s, except for minor roles in *The Buccaneer* and a James Gleason B, *Should Husbands Work?*, he worked exclusively in Mexican

films; came back only to do a cameo in *Around the World in 80 Days*.

NORTON, FLETCHER *(1941)* 64 ——Character (inmate Oliver) in *The Big House;* also was in silents (*Exclusive Rights, Davy Crockett at the Fall of the Alamo*, etc.) and other talkies (*The Bowery, The Star Witness*, others).

NORTON, JACK *(1958)* 69 ——Balding, pie-eyed, inimitable movie "drunk"; did his always hilarious bit in many dozens: *Marked Woman, The Fleet's In, Cockeyed Cavaliers, The Bank Dick, The Palm Beach Story*, etc.; sidelight: in real life, a teetotaler.

NORWOOD, EILLE *(1948)* 70 ——Actor who starred as Sherlock Holmes in England's *The Hound of the Baskervilles* ('22), a feature-length film, then was Holmes in almost 50 two-reelers.

NORWORTH, JACK *(1959)* 80 ——Actor-husband of singer Nora Bayes (wrote "Shine On Harvest Moon" for her); was onscreen, besides his many "Nagger" two-reel comedies, in *Queen of the Night Clubs* and *The Southerner* (as Doc White); in *Shine on Harvest Moon*, was portrayed by Dennis Morgan, with Ann Sheridan as Nora Bayes.

NOTARI, GUIDO *(1957)* 62 ——Minor support in Warners' *Helen of Troy.*

NOVARRO, RAMON *(1968)* 69 ——Ben-Hur— bulging biceps lashing fleet steeds around the chariot-strewn Colosseum; this is the immediate mental picture whenever his name is read or spoken; many more films, though, made and kept him Metro's great Latin lover throughout the '20s; *The Prisoner of Zenda* ('22) catapulted him from extra to star overnight, and it was followed by *Scaramouche, The Arab, Thy Name Is Woman, The Red Lily, The Student Prince, Across to Singapore*, and many more silents; making an easy transition into talkies with 1929's *The Flying Fleet*, he starred in a dozen more to the mid-'30s, including *The Pagan, In Gay Madrid, Daybreak, The Son-Daughter*, and, most notably, *Mata Hari* with Garbo; then he did two for Republic, *The Sheik Steps Out* and *A Desperate Adventure* ('38), and his career as a star was ended; came back a decade later as a most-distinguished-looking, Spanish-accented (he was born in Durango) police official in *We Were Strangers;* had similar roles in just four more: *Crisis, The Big Steal, The Outriders*, and *Heller in Pink Tights*.

NOVELLI, ANTONIO *(1919)* 67 ——Major Italian star of silents: *For Napoleon and Country* ('14), *The Lion Tamer's Revenge, Michael Perrine, Anthony and Cleopatra, Julius Caesar*, etc.; was also billed as both Amleto and Ermete Novelli.

NOVELLO, IVOR *(1951)* 59 ——Black-haired Welshman, handsome and multitalented (playwright and popular-music composer) who began his screen starring career here in the '20s; was in *Carnival, The White Rose* with Mae Marsh; continued, to even greater acclaim, in British pix until the mid '30s: *The Lodger, The Man Without Desire, Sleeping Car, The Constant Nymph, The Rat* (based on his own play), *Autumn Crocus*, others; thereafter was a musical comedy star onstage and a producer.

NOVIS, DONALD *(1966)* 59 ——Irish tenor who, in the '30s, starred in musical shorts for Sennett (*The Singing Boxer*, for which W. C. Fields wrote the script), Vitaphone, and RKO; also sang in *New York Nights* with Norma Talmadge, *Monte Carlo* and *One Hour with You* with Jeanette MacDonald, *The Big Broadcast*, Leon Errol's *Slightly Terrific*; last had a supporting role in a '50 C pic, *Mr. Universe*.

NOWELL, WEDGWOOD *(1957)* 79 ——Fine figure of a man who always played top supporting roles; in 1916's *The Deserter*, one of his first, he dashingly competed with Charles Ray for the hand of the heroine; in the '20s was in Norma Talmadge's *The Eternal Flame*, Viola Dana's *The Match-Breaker*, Nazimova's *A Doll's House*, Clara Kimball Young's *Enter Madame*, etc.; was last in *Calling Philo Vance* ('40), as the character Brisbane Coe.

NUGENT, J. C. *(1947)* 72 ——Character actor-father of Elliott; often played fathers: Leila Hyams' in *The Big House*, Martha Raye's in *Give Me a Sailor*, Janet Gaynor's in *A Star Is Born*; also in *Love in the Rough, They Learned About Women, This Is My Affair, Love in Bloom*, etc.

NYE, CARROLL *(1974)* 72 ——In *Gone With the Wind*, was Scarlett's second husband, lumberyard owner Frank Kennedy; in few movies after *GWTW*, he was in many before it; started as a handsome young leading man in '25 with Corinne Griffith in *Classified*, then was with Anita Page in *While the City Sleeps*, in Monte Blue's *The Brute, Kosher Kitty Kelly*, etc.; in talkies, was in Irene Rich's *Craig's Wife, Rebecca of Sunnybrook Farm*, others; after his career in movies, was radio editor for the Los Angeles *Times*, a Hollywood newscaster, and a publicity man for other screen personalities.

O

OAKLAND, VIVIAN *(1958)* 63 ——Blonde who played middle-aged battle-axe wives in dozens of two-reel comedies; made life hell for "husbands" Andy Clyde, Leon Errol, Edgar Kennedy; in '29–'30 had co-starred with her real husband in many "John T. Murray and Vivian Oakland" shorts; in the '20s had serious supporting roles in several: *Uncle Tom's Cabin*, Nazimova's *Madonna of the Streets*, etc.; in the '30s and '40s was rowdy in support in many features: *Cock of the Air, Neighbors' Wives, Way Out West, The Man in the Trunk*, etc.; last had a bit in Robert Sterling's *Bunco Squad* ('50).

OAKLAND, WILL *(1956)* 73 ——In the '20s starred in shorts such as *Dreamy Melody*.

OAKLEY, ANNIE *(1926)* 87 ——Western bullseye queen; made pix for Edison before 1900; was portrayed by Stanwyck in *Annie Oakley*, Betty Hutton in *Annie Get Your Gun*.

OAKLEY, FLORENCE *(1956)* 65 ——Was young support in Leatrice Joy's *A Most Immoral Lady*.

OAKMAN, WHEELER *(1949)* 58 ——Handsome actor of humor and charm who rose from extra to star in early silents; created his first big splash as Broncho Kid in 1914's *The Spoilers*; had already played dozens of juveniles and heavies; starred in *The Ne'er-Do-Well, The Virgin of Stamboul, In the Long Ago, The Story of the Blood Red Rose, The Salvation of Nance O'Shaughnessy, The Cycle of Fate*, etc., prior to '20; made a few with wife Priscilla Dean, more with Bessie Eyton; in the '20s was in many: *Other Men's Daughters, Slippery McGee, Masked Angel*, etc.; dozens of supporting roles afterward in Westerns (*Texas Cyclone, Frontier Days*, etc.), B's (*Murder in the Clouds, Mutiny in the Big House*, others), and many serials (*Darkest Africa; The Airmail Mystery*, as villain Black Hawk; *The Lost Jungle; Brick Bradford; Brenda Starr, Reporter*, as gangster Joe Heller; *Jack Armstrong*).

OATES, CICELY *(1934)* 45 ——Supporting actress in Hitchcock's first *The Man Who Knew Too Much*.

OBECK, FRED *(1929)* 47 ——Support in several at First National in 1927–28: Thelma Todd's *Vamping Venus*, Barthelmess' *The Patent Leather Kid*, Colleen Moore's *Oh, Kay!*, etc.

OBER, ROBERT *(1950)* 68 ——Character (Harry) in *The Big Parade;* in many others of the '20s: *Black Butterflies, The Idle Rich, The Young Rajah, Introduce Me, The Little Adventuress,* etc.

OBERLE, FLORENCE *(1943)* 73 ——Top character actress (usually played smalltown mothers) in several Charles Ray comedies in the '20s: *Smudge, The Barnstormer, R.S.V.P.,* etc.

O'BRIEN, BARRY *(1961)* 69 ——Starred as Irish hero Robert Emmett in 1914's *Ireland, a Nation,* made in the U.S.

O'BRIEN, DAVE *(1969)* 57 ——The handsome "falling down" patsy in dozens of Pete Smith shorts; starred heroically in one serial, *Captain Midnight,* and was near the top of the cast list in others—*The Black Coin, The Secret of Treasure Island, The Spider Returns;* onscreen from 1933's *Jennie Gerhardt,* he had small roles in many that decade before, in the early '40s, co-starring with James Newill in two outdoor-pix series: "Renfrew of the Mounted" and "The Texas Rangers," in which he was Dave "Tex" O'Brien; top roles in countless B's: *The Ghost Creeps, The Yanks Are Coming, Prisoner of Japan, Flying Wild,* etc.; in the '50s starred in his own TV series, *Meet the O'Briens,* had featured roles in three, including *Kiss Me Kate* (as Ralph); became a comedy writer for Red Skelton.

O'BRIEN, DONNELL *(1970)* ——Vaude vet who had small roles in *The Pawnbroker, On the Waterfront, The Last Angry Man,* etc.

O'BRIEN, EUGENE *(1966)* 85 ——Became a romantic idol in silents when he was Norma Talmadge's leading man in ten: *Poppy, The Moth, Ghosts of Yesterday, By Right of Purchase, Deluxe Annie, The Safety Curtain,* and *Her Only Way* (all 1917–18), then (1924–25) *Secrets, The Only Woman, Graustark;* onscreen from 1915's *The Moonstone,* this most handsome man made screen love to every top woman star: Swanson, Anna Q. Nilsson, Shearer, Mary Astor, Marguerite Clark, Claire Windsor, numerous others; among his memorable films: *Channing of the Northwest, Under the Greenwood Tree, The Wonderful Chance, Chivalrous Charley;* retired (rich) in '28 after one of his worst, *The Faithless Lover.*

O'BRIEN, TOM *(1947)* 55 ——Was great in a top supporting role, the rough and blasphemous doughboy, Bull, in *The Big Parade,* perhaps his best role in a long (1913–34) movie career; also was in *Twelve Miles Out* (again with John Gilbert; as Irish), *The Bugle Call, White Fang, San Francisco Nights, Phantom Express, The Night Mayor,* etc.

O'BRYNE, PATSY *(1968)* 82 ——Comedienne; in a 1926 Billy Bevan comedy, *A Sea Dog's Tale,* was the landlady who tried to force in-arrears tenant Billy to marry her; in many Sennett pix (particularly Charlie Chase comedies), she also was in such features as Lenore Ulric's *South Sea Rose,* Loretta Young's *Loose Ankles, Doctor Bull, Saps at Sea.*

O'CONNELL, HUGH *(1943)* 44 ——Secondary roles for over a decade—reporters, detectives, young millionaires, etc.; was in *Secrets of a Secretary, The Smiling Lieutenant* (military orderly), *Torchy Blane in Panama, Diamond Jim, The Good Fairy, My Favorite Wife,* etc.

O'CONNOR, FRANK *(1959)* 71 ——Dignified, gray-haired support (fathers, ranchers, parsons) in dozens of Westerns: *Riders of the Black Hills, Gun Law,* etc.; also (as doctors and government officials) in serials: *G-Men Never Forget, Ghost of Zorro, Dangers of the Canadian Mounted,* others; co-directed (with Marshall Neilan) the silent *Penrod* and wrote many, including *Devil's Island.*

O'CONNOR, HARRY *(1971)* 98 ——Support in many Westerns from the earliest days through the '20s: Tom Tyler's *Red Hot Hoofs, When the Law Rides, The Trail of the Horse Thieves,* plus *Cyclone of the Range, Flashing Steeds,* etc.

O'CONNOR, JOHN *(1941)* 67 ——Character actor in 1921's *The Barricade.*

O'CONNOR, KATHLEEN *(1957)* 60 ——Pretty blonde girl who played the romantic interest in Sennett two-reelers (comedian Toto's *The One Night Stand,* etc.), was in serials such as *The Lion Man* and *The Midnight Man,* and had secondary roles in Marie Prevost's *The Married Flapper, Come On Over* (as the lovely Fifth Avenue model who almost won Ralph Graves from Colleen Moore), *The Old Homestead,* William S. Hart's *Wild Bill Hickok,* etc., all in the early '20s.

O'CONNOR, KATHRYN *(1965)* 76 ——Character roles.

O'CONNOR, L. J. *(1959)* 79 ——Character actor in many in the '20s: *Four Sons,* Cullen Landis' *Watch Your Step,* Herbert Rawlinson's *Don't Shoot,* Reginald Denny's *Sporting Youth,* Gaston Glass' *The Midnight Limited,* etc.

O'CONNOR, ROBERT EMMETT *(1962)* 77 ——Big, bull-necked guy who was forever a detective (*A Night at the Opera*) or other police official—often brutal (*Up the River,* as the warden, *The Big House, Lady for a Day, Framed, The Frame Up, Boy of the Streets, The Big Shakedown,* etc.).

O'CONNOR, UNA *(1959)* 78 ——Pinch-faced and pursed-lipped, this Irish gnome was at her keening best as Wallace Ford's mother in *The Informer;* begân her character-actress career in America as the mourning maid, Ellen Bridges, in *Cavalcade* (after earlier pix in England); was a maid again in *The Barretts of Wimpole Street, Cluny Brown,* etc.; was the gossiping old crone who caused Muni's destruction in *We Are Not Alone,* the old lady sot in *The Plough and the Stars,* the pathetic old Mrs. Gammidge in *David Copperfield,* de Havilland's coy maid, Bess, in *The Adventures of Robin Hood,* and a terrified screamer par excellence in *The Bride of Frankenstein* and *The Invisible Man; Witness for the Prosecution* was her last.

O'DAY, PEGGY *(1964)* 64 ——A lesser Pearl White, she starred in the '25 serial *Peggy of the Secret Service* and had top supporting roles in others: *The Chinatown Mystery, The Fighting Skipper,* etc.; also was in many silent Westerns: *Riders of the Sand Storm, Battlin' Buckaroo, Hoof Marks, Trail's End,* more.

O'DEA, JIMMY *(1965)* 64 ——Irish support in *Darby O'Gill and the Little People,* John Ford's *The Rising of the Moon,* etc.

O'DEA, JOSEPH *(1968)* 65 ——Irish character (a guard) in Ford's *The Quiet Man;* also in his *The Rising of the Moon.*

O'DELL, DIGGER *(1957)* 53 ——Character in a few movies; more famous on radio and TV.

O'DONNELL, CATHY *(1970)* 45 ——Sweet-faced Goldwyn discovery who was one of the screen's best representatives of the idealized girl-next-door; in *The Best Years of Our Lives,* was Wilma, who gently persuaded handless Harold Russell they should marry; after this first film, was in *They Live By Night* with Farley Granger, *The Miniver Story* (Garson's daughter), *Detective Story, Your Red Wagon, Eight O'Clock Walk,* and several lesser films; was last in two in '59; *Terror in the Haunted House (My World Dies Screaming)* and *Ben Hur* (as Tirzah), directed by William Wyler, who had guided her through her screen debut and was by this time her brother-in-law.

O'DONOVAN, FRANK *(1974)* 74 ——Character actor from Ireland.

O'DONOVAN, FRED *(1952)* 62 ——Support in *Another Shore* ('51), made abroad.

O'FARRELL, MARY *(1968)* 75 ——Character actress in British pix.

OFFERMAN, GEORGE *(1938)* 58 ——Character actor who had minor roles in many, includ-

ing Sally O'Neil's *The Girl on the Barge;* father of George Jr.

OFFERMAN, GEORGE, JR. *(1963)* 46 —— Was briefly of considerable interest to audiences after playing one of the five tragic sons (Joe) in *The Sullivans;* had then been onscreen 14 years, since *The Broadway Drifter,* in minor roles in many: *The Mayor of Hell, Black Fury, Jalna, Action in the North Atlantic,* etc., later had servicemen roles in several: *See Here, Corporal Hargrove* (Pvt. Orrin Esty), *A Walk in the Sun* (Tinker), *Purple Heart Diary,* and, his last, *With a Song in My Heart* (Muleface).

OFFERMAN, MARIE *(1950)* 56 ——Character actress-mother of George Jr.; minor roles.

OGLE, CHARLES *(1940)* 75 ——Hero in early Edison Kinetoscopes, one of which, *How Mrs. Murray Saved the American Army* ('11), made him a "new" discovery with young audiences during the Bicentennial celebration; this movie about the Revolutionary War tells of the daring (and imaginary) American Captain Barb (Ogle), who, with Mrs. Murray, steals British plans that contribute to Washington's victory; found in 1975 in a vault at the Edison National Historic Site (his original laboratory) in New Jersey, this film and eight relevant others were dusted off, reproduced in new 16-mm prints and made available to schools; Ogle, onscreen from '07, played many other leading roles in *Martin Chuzzlewit, Hard Cash,* the serial *Dolly of the Dailies* with Mary Fuller (his frequent co-star), etc.; in the '20s was an in-demand character actor; played Lois Wilson's gray-bearded father in *The Covered Wagon* ('23), was featured in *The Ten Commandments* (Part II: the doctor), *Conrad in Quest of His Youth, Grumpy, Secrets, Ruggles of Red Gap,* and many others before retiring in the late '20s.

O'HARA, FISKE *(1945)* 67 ——Irish-born actor who was dignified support in two Janet Gaynor pix: *Paddy, the Next Best Thing* (the millionaire she worked for as a servant girl) and *Change of Heart.*

O'HARA, GEORGE *(1966)* 67 ——Muscular, handsome actor with cleft chin who, in the '20s, starred in FBO's "Fighting Blood" (boxing) movie series.

OHARDIENO, ROGER *(1959)* 30 ——Black dancer featured in *Stormy Weather.*

O'KEEFE, DENNIS *(1968)* 60 ——Sandy-haired leading man with blithe, brash Irish charm; played his first lead in 1938's *Bad Man of Brimstone* on the recommendation of Gable, who had spotted his potential in a bit in *Saratoga;* had earlier done bits in more than 50 from

1931's *Reaching for the Moon,* in almost all being billed Edward (Bud) Flanagan; hit his starring stride in comedies in the '40s (*Up in Mabel's Room, Hi Diddle Diddle, Getting Gertie's Garter, Brewster's Millions, Abroad with Two Yanks,* etc.), and in comedy roles in service dramas (*The Story of Dr. Wassell, The Fighting Seabees*); proved his dramatic mettle in *Hangmen Also Die;* later turned to tough-guy roles—often a crime-busting Federal agent—in *T-Men, Raw Deal, Chicago Syndicate, Inside Detroit, Las Vegas Shakedown;* starred on TV in 1959's *The Dennis O'Keefe Show;* last movie was 1961's *All Hands on Deck.*

OLAND, WARNER *(1938)* 57 ——Actor from Sweden who (1931–38) starred 16 times as Charlie Chan: *Charlie Chan Carries On, Charlie Chan in London,* etc.; previously, in silents, Chan had been portrayed by Japanese actors George Kuwa (a serial: *The House Without a Key*) and Sojin (the feature *The Chinese Parrot*), and in a minor role in a talkie, *Behind That Curtain,* English actor E. L. Parks had played the sleuth; Oland, then, was the first to star in a talkie Chan series; onscreen from '09, this intellectual actor (translator of Strindberg plays) had played Oriental villains in dozens, including Pearl White serials; had also played Jolson's cantor father in *The Jazz Singer;* during the Chan period, he had outside top character roles in *Shanghai Express, The Son-Daughter, Before Dawn, Mandalay, The Painted Veil, Shanghai,* and others.

OLCOTT, SIDNEY *(1949)* 76 ——Dapper early (from '07) Kalem leading man (*Arrah-Na-Pogue, The Colleen Bawn,* etc.) who turned director (*From the Manger to the Cross*) and became an increasingly important one in silents through the '20s ((*Little Old New York, The Green Goddess, Monsieur Beaucaire,* others).

OLDFIELD, BARNEY *(1946)* 68 ——Indianapolis Speedway champ race driver who starred as himself in 1913's *Barney Oldfield's Race for Life,* and, in the '20s, was prominently cast in *The First Auto* and *The Speed Demon.*

OLDHAM, DEREK *(1968)* 75 ——Character actor in British pix: *Charing Cross Road, The Broken Rosary,* others.

O'LEARY, BYRON *(1970)* 36 ——Light leading man in British pix; was husband of actress Nyree Dawn Porter.

OLIVER, EDNA MAY *(1942)* 57 ——Tall, thin professional spinster with long, aristocratic horse-face and equally high-born sniff; "They always hand me an old hyena role, and I keep right on barking," said the actress, Oscar-nominated (Best Support) in *Drums Along the Mo-*

hawk as the "warlike Widow McKlennar with a tongue sharper than a tomahawk"; onscreen from 1924's *Three O'Clock in the Morning,* she made her ramrod way through another 45; in the '30s was in *David Copperfield* (Aunt Betsey Trotwood, who beat those luckless donkey-boys, but hid a soft heart under a cranky demeanor), *Little Women* (Aunt March), *A Tale of Two Cities* (Miss Pross), *Alice in Wonderland* (the Red Queen), *Romeo and Juliet* (the Nurse), *Little Miss Broadway, The Story of Vernon and Irene Castle* (manager Maggie Sutton); starred in *Fanny Foley Herself* ('31), *Ladies of the Jury* ('32), and three times as spinster-sleuth Miss Hildegarde Withers, in *The Penguin Pool Murder, Murder on the Blackboard, Murder on a Honeymoon;* in the '40s was in two: *Pride and Prejudice* and *Lydia* (Oberon's grandmother); sidelight: the sniff that became her famous trademark was an accident—at the end of a scene in a '30 Wheeler and Woolsey comedy, *Half Shot at Sunrise,* she sniffed in disgust at their antics and it was kept in.

OLIVER, GUY *(1932)* 57 ——Dour character onscreen from 1912's *Robin Hood* (Friar Tuck); secondary roles in many famous pix of the '20s: *The Covered Wagon* (as Dunston), *Manslaughter* (Musician), *Fool's Paradise* (Briggs), *Ruggles of Red Gap, What Every Woman Knows, Old Ironsides,* etc.; also numerous Westerns.

OLIVER, LARRY *(1973)* 93 ——Character (Norval Hedges) in *Born Yesterday.*

OLIVER, SHIRLING *(1971)* 64 ——See Oliver McGowan.

OLIVER, TED *(1957)* 62 ——Support such as ship's officer in Crosby's *We're Not Dressing;* onscreen from the mid-'20s, was also in *The Return of Sophie Lang, Yellow Dust, Geronimo,* etc.

OLIVER, VIC *(1964)* 66 ——Comic character with Viennese accent in many British pix: *Give Us the Moon; Hi, Gang; Rhythm in the Air,* etc.; once married to Sarah Churchill.

OLIVETTE, MARIE *(1959)* 67 ——Minor roles in silents.

OLIVETTE, NINA *(1971)* 63 ——Attractive young comedienne featured in the Paramount musical comedy *Queen High* ('30) after co-starring on Broadway with Bert Lahr in *Hold Everything!;* wife of actor Harry Stockwell.

OLSEN, GEORGE *(1971)* 78 ——He and his famous orchestra were in Will Rogers' *Happy Days.*

OLSEN, MORONI *(1954)* 65 ——Big, powerful character actor who often played politicians and slick lawyers and who, in 75 pix from 1935's *The Three Musketeers* (Porthos), was always billed right behind the stars; was in *Kentucky* (Richard Greene's father), *Call Northside 777* (parole board chairman), *Notorious, Invisible Stripes, One Foot in Heaven, Air Force, The Fountainhead,* etc.

OLSEN, OLE *(1963)* 70 ——Thinner half of the famous Olsen & Johnson comedy team; after their last movie, 1945's *See My Lawyer,* the two zanies toured in a revival of *Hellzapoppin,* headlined in two TV series, starred on Broadway in the revue *Pardon Our French,* did nightclubs, spent long periods onstage in Australia, entertained for the U.S.O.; see Chic Johnson.

O'MADIGAN, ISABEL *(1951)* 78 ——In *The Egg and I* and *Ma and Pa Kettle* she played the ancient mother of character actress Esther Dale, who was Mrs. Hicks.

O'MALLEY, JOHN *(1945)* 41 ——Handsome lead in Republic's *A Sporting Chance,* his only pic, the year of his death.

O'MALLEY, JOHN P. *(1959)* 43 ——Australian character actor in several Hollywood pix: *Julius Caesar* (as a Citizen of Rome), *The Desert Rats, Diane, Kind Lady,* others.

O'MALLEY, PAT *(1966)* 75 ——Not to be confused with bald character comedian J. Pat O'-Malley; this athletic, handsome black-haired actor began onscreen as a leading man with the Edison Stock Company in '07; starred first in 1911's *The Papered Door* for Essanay, then in many for Kalem, First National, Vitagraph, others; most popular in the '20s, he co-starred with Pauline Starke in *My Wild Irish Rose,* J. Warren Kerrigan in *The Man from Brodney's,* Marion Nixon in *Spangles,* Claire Windsor in *Brothers Under the Skin,* Agnes Ayres in *Go and Get It,* Jack Kirkwood in *Bob Hampton of Placer,* etc.; played character roles to the end in *Frisco Jenny, Behind the Evidence, Wanderer of the Wasteland,* etc.

O'MALLEY, THOMAS *(1926)* 70 ——Character actor in Thomas Meighan's *Cappy Ricks,* Lloyd Hamilton's *His Darker Self,* a few others in the '20s.

O'MOORE, BARRY *(1945)* 65 ——Under this name he starred in many for Edison Films in 1913-14 (*Hard Cash,* etc., plus an Edison "series"); Herbert Yost was his real name, which he used in many more films; see Herbert Yost.

O'NEIL, NANCE *(1965)* 90 ——A legendary and beautiful stage actress who entered movies in her 40s and starred in several 1915-20 pix: *The Kreutzer Sonata, The Fall of the Romanoffs, Hedda Gabler, Greed* (not von Stroheim's), *The Mad Woman;* after spending the next decade on Broadway, she returned to do splendid character work—still slender, dark-haired, and fine-boned—in 20 1929-35 movies: John Gilbert's *His Glorious Night* (his first, disastrous talkie), *The Rogue Song, Cimarron* (playing Felice Venable), *Ladies of Leisure, The Royal Bed, False Faces,* etc.; retired at 60.

O'NEIL, SALLY *(1968)* 57 ——Pert, lovely gamine who became an overnight star in her first pic, *Sally, Irene and Mary,* in '25 ("Sally O'Neil is a knockout!" said *Photoplay,* ignoring both Crawford and Constance Bennett); played charming urchins in many more: *Mike, Frisco Sally Levy, The Lovelorn, The Auction Block, On With the Show, The Sophomore,* etc.; in decline by '30, she starred onstage in *The Brat,* repeated in the film version, and won a new five-year contract leading nowhere; secondary roles in *Ladies Must Love, Too Tough to Kill,* etc.; tried unsuccessfully to make a comeback in 1938's *Kathleen,* made in Ireland; a decade later, still trying and still beautiful, co-starred with Lenore Ulric in a single Pasadena Playhouse production; married, retired.

O'NEILL, HENRY *(1961)* 69 ——Suave, grayhaired character actor in 150 who usually played distinguished fathers, clerics, lawyers, judges, doctors; most of his career was spent at two studios, Warners and MGM; at WB was in *Anthony Adverse* (Father Xavier), *The Story of Louis Pasteur, The Life of Emile Zola* (Colonel Picquart), *Jezebel, Juarez, Dodge City, The Fighting 69th,* etc.; at Metro was in *Blossoms in the Dust, Best Foot Forward, Tortilla Flat, The Human Comedy, The Green Years, A Guy Named Joe,* many more; was last in John Wayne's *The Wings of Eagles* ('57).

O'NEILL, JAMES *(1938)* 89 ——Father of playwright Eugene O'Neill; starred in 1913's *The Count of Monte Cristo,* film version of the play which he did, year in and year out, all over the globe; was depicted as James Tyrone in his son's play *Long Day's Journey Into Night* and portrayed in the '62 film version by Sir Ralph Richardson.

O'NEILL, JAMES, JR. *(1923)* 44 ——Stage actor-son of above; no ascertainable picture credits; portrayed onstage and onscreen in *Long Day's Journey Into Night* by Jason Robards Jr.

O'NEILL, MAIRE *(1952)* 67 ——Fine Irish actress who had character roles in *Saints and Sinners, Juno and the Paycock, Peg of Old Drury, Love on the Dole,* many other British pix including *The Horse's Mouth*, her last; was Sara Allgood's sister.

O'NEILL, PEGGY *(1945)* 21 ——Lovely girl who had a supporting role, Cricket, in Henie's *It's a Pleasure;* also was in Jane Powell's debut film, *Song of the Open Road.*

O'NEILL, ROBERT *(1951)* 40 ——Supporting roles in two the year he died: James Craig's *Drums in the Deep South,* Richard Conte's *The Raging Tide.*

ONODERA, SHO *(1974)* 59 ——Japanese support in *The Taking of Pelham One Two Three.*

OPPENHEIM, MENASHA *(1973)* ——Featured in a 1938 Yiddish film, *The Vow.*

ORDE, BERYL *(1966)* 54 ——At 23 was featured in England's *Radio Parade of 1935.*

ORMAN, FELIX *(1933)* 48 ——Was featured in Victor McLaglen's *The Glorious Adventure* ('22), "the first photoplay in colors" (two-tone Kinemacolor), filmed in England.

O'ROURKE, BREFNI *(1946)* 57 ——Irish actor usually seen as a short-fused character in British pix: *I See a Dark Stranger, They Were Sisters, The Tawny Pipit, Hatter's Castle,* etc.

O'ROURKE, J. A. *(1937)* 55 ——Featured in England's *The Blarney Kiss.*

ORR, FORREST *(1963)* 63 ——Support who appeared in—among others—Lamour's *Rainbow Island,* in which he played Dr. Curtis.

ORTH, FRANK *(1962)* 82 ——The friendly little bartender, Mike Ryan, in six "Dr. Kildare" movies (*Dr. Kildare's Strange Case, . . . Crisis, . . . Wedding Day,* etc.) and in *Dr. Gillespie's New Assistant;* earlier had played Inspector Milligan in three of Bonita Granville's "Nancy Drew" pix (*Nancy Drew, Detective, . . . Reporter, . . . and the Hidden Staircase*); had begun in '29 in a two-reel series with wife Ann Codee; among his dozens of non-series movies, in which he was often a cop and forever Irish: *Strawberry Blonde, My Gal Sal, I Wake Up Screaming, The Dolly Sisters,* etc.; last onscreen in 1953's *Houdini,* he wound up his career as Inspector Farraday on Kent Taylor's '54 TV series *Boston Blackie.*

ORY, EDWARD "KID" *(1973)* 86 ——Jazz great; onscreen in *New Orleans* and *The Benny Goodman Story.*

OSBORN, LYN *(1958)* 36 ——Small, ski-nosed comedian most famous as Cadet Happy on the TV series *Space Patrol;* among his pix: *Invasion of the Saucer Men, The Amazing Colossal Man, Torpedo Run,* etc.

OSBORNE, BUD *(1964)* 79 ——Western actor who, 1916-18 at the Ince-Nestor Company, was one of the better-known cowboy heroes; for most of the rest of his career, through 1958's *Escape from Red Rock,* he was one of the best of the really bad guys opposite every Western star; besides several hundred B Westerns, he was a lowdown crook in 10 talkie serials: *Gordon of Ghost City, Tailspin Tommy, The Adventures of Frank Merriwell, Battling with Buffalo Bill,* etc.; by his 60s was playing good oldtimers, stagecoach drivers, and sheriffs.

OSBORNE, VIVIENNE *(1961)* 60 ——After playing the brunette beauty (billed second only to star Mary Carr) in 1920's *Over the Hill,* she starred on Broadway (*Aloma of the South Sea,* etc.) for a decade; onscreen in the '30s she usually played the "other woman"; was in *The Beloved Bachelor, Husband's Holiday, The Famous Ferguson Case, Wives Never Know,* many others, including *Sailor Be Good,* in which she vamped Jack Oakie; last had a supporting role (Johanna) in *Dragonwyck.*

OSCAR, HENRY *(1969)* 78 ——English support in a few Hollywood movies (*The Black Rose, Beau Brummell*) and many British ones: *Four Feathers, Private's Progress, The Return of the Scarlet Pimpernel* (played Robespierre), *Oscar Wilde, Murder Ahoy,* etc.

O'SHEA, "BLACK JACK" *(1967)* 61 ——The black-hatted, black-suited, black-moustachioed villain in more Westerns than the King Ranch has cows; from the early '30s he was "The Man You Love to Hate" in *The San Antonio Kid; Wyoming; Ride, Ryder, Ride; Overland Riders,* etc.; amplified his villainy in serials: *Son of Zorro, G-Men Never Forget, Ghost of Zorro,* etc.; in real life was honorary sheriff of his California community, Paradise, where he was the most cordial proprietor of an antique shop.

O'SHEA, MICHAEL *(1973)* 67 ——Cocky, toothy, and redheaded, this star came on strong with the Irish charm and, at the beginning (*Lady of Burlesque*), was predicted to become the "new" Tracy; starred in the title role of *Jack London,* then in *The Eve of St. Mark, Something for the Boys, It's a Pleasure, Man from Frisco, Mr. District Attorney,* etc.; after starring in the TV series *It's a Great Life* in the mid-'50s, and guesting in others in the '60s, gave up acting and became a plainclothes detective with the sheriff's department of Ventura County, Calif.; was married to Virginia Mayo.

O'SHEA, OSCAR *(1960)* 78 ——Dignified character in many: *Captains Courageous* (Cushman), *Mannequin* (Crawford's father, "Pa" Cassidy), *The Shining Hour, Invitation to Happiness* (Judge), *Man-Proof, Corvette K-225, My Wild Irish Rose*, etc.

OSHINS, JULIE *(1956)* 50 ——Comedian; when an Army sergeant, played Ollie in *This Is the Army;* later in *I'll See You in My Dreams.*

OSTERMAN, JACK *(1939)* 37 ——Support in 1936's *Wanted Men.*

O'SULLIVAN, MICHAEL *(1971)* 37 ——Blond supporting actor who played Kurt Doughty in Geraldine Page's *You're a Big Boy Now.*

O'SULLIVAN, TONY *(1920)* 40s ——Plump support in many of Griffith's early Biograph pix; was in many 1908-10 "Jonesy" comedies, in several of which he sported a huge moustache; in *A Convict's Sacrifice, The Honor of His Family, What Drink Did*, etc.; became a director.

OTT, FRED *(1936)* 76 ——This walrus-moustached man, then an assistant in the Edison West Orange (N.J.) Laboratory, is of historical importance as the first "actor" ever to face a motion picture camera; was in an 1893 "movie," the first recorded film, called *Sneeze* —and that is what he did.

OTTIANO, RAFAELA *(1942)* 48 ——Small black-haired, black-eyed character actress who in her single decade onscreen (1932-42) created many vividly recalled roles; *Grand Hotel* (Garbo's adoring maid), *She Done Him Wrong* (Russian Rosie, the villainous white slaver bumped off by West; had played the same role onstage), *Bondage* (evil woman who ran the home for unwed mothers), *The Devil Doll, Curly Top* (mean Mrs. Higgins), *The Long Voyage Home* (Tropical Woman), *Maytime, The Adventures of Martin Eden*, etc.

OTTO, HENRY *(1952)* 74 ——Support in Fairbanks' *The Iron Mask*, Leo Maloney's *The Outlaw Express*, Reginald Denny's *One Hysterical Night;* earlier had directed *Dante's Inferno, The Willow Tree*, others.

OUSPENSKAYA, MARIA *(1949)* 73 ——Great wrinkled little treasure from Russia; was a sensation (and a Best Supporting Oscar nominee) in her debut film, *Dodsworth*, as the Austrian mother (of Gregory Gaye) who forbids Chatterton to marry her son; was no less splendid in her other 20: *Conquest, Love Affair* (Boyer's aged grandmother; her only other Oscar nomination), *The Rains Came, Dr. Ehrlich's Magic Bullet, Waterloo Bridge* (the imperious ballet mistress), *Kings Row* (grandmother of Scotty Beckett as young Parris Mitchell), *The Shanghai Gesture, I've Always Loved You*, etc.; she even made one horror pic, *Frankenstein Meets the Wolf Man*, perhaps for the same reason she gave for making a Western, *Wyoming*—"I'd never tried it."

OVERBECK, BUD *(1970)* 61 ——Singer-actor in minor roles.

OVERMAN, JACK *(1950)* 34 ——Young toughguy support in many: *The Lone Wolf and His Lady* (as Bill Slovak), *Brute Force, T-Men, Force of Evil, The Brasher Doubloon, Flaxy Martin*, etc.

OVERMAN, LYNNE *(1943)* 55 ——Rangy character who was like chablis—the drier the better; always played men, with a uniquely hoarse voice and drawling tone, who were low-key, dour, and kindly; first in 1934's *Girl in Pawn*, except for most-rare loan-outs (*Roxie Hart, Edison the Man*), he was exclusivly Paramount's droll gold-mine; was in *Little Miss Marker* (a Runyonesque character, as he generally was, named Regret), *Broadway Bill, Jungle Princess, Spawn of the North, Men with Wings, Union Pacific, North West Mounted Police* (the Scottish scout), *Reap the Wild Wind, The Forest Rangers, Star Spangled Rhythm*, etc.

OVERTON, FRANK *(1967)* 49 ——A "typical" American onscreen, this fine actor was the sheriff in *To Kill a Mockingbird*, a military officer in *Fail Safe*, a small-towner in *The Dark at the Top of the Stairs;* also was in *Lonelyhearts, Desire Under the Elms, Wild River*, others; in the TV series *12 O'Clock High*, co-starred in specs as Major Stovall, the role Dean Jagger played in the film.

OWEN, CATHERINE DALE *(1965)* 62 ——In movies only in her 20s (1927-31), she was a beautiful, but aloof, blonde co-star; introduced in Jetta Goudal's *The Forbidden Woman*, she was John Gilbert's leading lady in *His Glorious Night*, Lawrence Tibbett's in *The Rogue Song*, Warner Baxter's in *Such Men Are Dangerous* (one of her better outings), Conrad Nagel's in *Today*, Edmund Lowe's in *Born Reckless*, etc.

OWEN, GARRY *(1951)* 49 ——In 16 years in movies he almost always played cops when not a Runyon type (Grinder in *Little Miss Marker*); was in *The Thin Man, San Quentin, Arsenic and Old Lace, Mildred Pierce, Dark Mirror, The Killers*, etc.; not Gary Owen, a comedian in TV's *Laugh-In.*

OWEN, MILTON *(1969)* 78 ——Support in *The Great Garrick, The Exile*, etc.

OWEN, REGINALD *(1972)* 85 ——Big, genial, often pipe-smoking Britisher who for almost two decades was one of MGM's most cherished players; was highly visible (6'3" and an effortless scene-stealer) in more than 100 absolutely Grade-A films: *Random Harvest, Woman of the Year, I Married an Angel, Somewhere I'll Find You, The Good Fairy, National Velvet, Rose Marie, A Woman's Face, Mrs. Miniver,* etc.; was first onscreen in 1929's *The Letter* and last in 1971's *Bedknobs and Broomsticks;* in his last year he supported Phil Silvers in a Broadway revival of *A Funny Thing Happened on the Way to the Forum;* when "between roles" he wrote several books, plays, and screenplays, and was co-author of the original story of Mickey Rooney's *Stablemates.*

OWEN, SEENA *(1966)* 70 ——At the end of that unprecedented "boom shot" that opens the Babylonian Story in *Intolerance,* and once past the closeup of the two white turtledoves, you find yourself confronted by the lush blonde beauty of Princess Beloved—Seena Owen; she was, in the words of Billy Bitzer, Griffith's legendary cameraman, "a truly beautiful girl, who needed no help from the camera"; much earlier, even when still billed Signe Auen, she made many films for Griffith which were, his other cameraman, Karl Brown, has claimed, greatly responsible for the director's reputation; among her prior non-Griffith films: *The Fox Woman, A Yankee from the West, The Lamb,* with Fairbanks; during *Intolerance,* Griffith played matchmaker for her and George Walsh, the handsome Bridegroom at the Feast of Cana in the Judean Story—they married; during the '20s she starred in many: *The Woman God Changed, The Go-Getter,* with T. Roy Barnes, *The Face in the Fog, The Hunted Woman,* etc.; last had a minor supporting role in Fredric March's *The Marriage Playground* ('29).

OWENS, WILLIAM *(1926)* 73 ——Character roles.

OWSLEY, MONROE *(1937)* 36 ——Perhaps he parted his hair wrong—high near the center—but whatever, from his first he was doomed to play the "other man" (*The First Kiss,* vying with Cooper for Fay Wray), charming drunks (Ned, the brother in Ann Harding's *Holiday*), or cads (the stockbroker Colbert married in haste in *Honor Among Lovers*); such was his lot in the rest: *Hat Check Girl; Ex-Lady; Little Man, What Now?; Twin Husbands,* etc., right through the last, *The Hit Parade.*

OYSHER, MOISHE *(1958)* 51 ——Cantor who starred in several Yiddish musical films: *The Singing Blacksmith, Singing in the Dark,* others.

P

PACKARD, CLAYTON *(1931)* 43 ——Played Bartholomew in *The King of Kings,* his only film.

PACKER, NETTA *(1962)* 65 ——Character (Mrs. Butler) in Cooper's *Good Sam;* other minor roles in *Condemned Woman* and Debbie Reynolds' *It Started with a Kiss.*

PADDEN, SARAH *(1967)* 70 ——Character actress often seen as a grim prison matron (*A Woman's Face, Women in Prison*) or country woman (*The Great Meadow, Spitfire, David Harum, Chad Hanna, Rebecca of Sunnybrook Farm,* etc.).

PADEREWSKI, IGNACE *(1941)* 81 ——Noted Polish pianist; featured in England's *Moonlight Sonata* ('37).

PADOVANO, JOHN *(1973)* 57 ——Featured role in Mitchum's *Foreign Intrigue.*

PAGE, LUCILLE *(1964)* 93 ——She and vaudeville partner-husband, Art Wellington, made educational comedy shorts in the '30s.

PAGE, PAUL *(1974)* 70 ——Handsome actor who played second leads in early talkie melodramas at Fox: *Speakeasy, The Girl from Havana, Men Without Women, Born Reckless;* later was in *Palmy Days, The Road to Ruin, Kentucky Kernels,* others.

PAGE, RITA *(1954)* 48 ——English actress who played a nurse (Glennie) in *Vigil in the Night;* other small roles in *Little Nellie Kelly, Aren't We All?,* etc.

PAGET, ALFRED *(1925)* 40s ——A famous Griffith character lead, he played the gang leader in *The Musketeers of Pig Alley* and Belshazzar in *Intolerance;* onscreen from 1910, he was in many other Griffith productions: *The Primal Call, A Mohawk's Way, The Spanish Gypsy, The Old Bookkeeper, The Girl and Her Trust, The Inner Circle, The Battle of Elderberry Gulch,* etc.; later in his career, he was seen in *The Fall of Babylon* and *Big Timber* with Wallace Reid and Kathlyn Williams.

PAIGE, MABEL *(1954)* 74 ——The vinegary-sharp little old joy in Ladd's *Lucky Jordan*——

the Times Square lush that he, racketeer and reluctant draftee, hired to pretend to be his needy mother and get him sprung from the Army; did other humorous, sharp-tongued ladies at Paramount in the '40s: *True to Life; The Crystal Ball; Murder, He Says; Happy Go Lucky; Out of This World*, etc.; Republic borrowed and starred her in *Someone to Remember*, the best tearjerker that studio ever made; long before coming to Hollywood, back in teens at the Lubin Studio in Florida, she and her husband (actor Charles Ritchie) made 15 one-reel comedies with a very young Oliver Hardy; as one of Hollywood's best-loved character actresses she worked in 36 pix, through 1953's *Houdini*.

PAIVA, NESTOR *(1966)* 61 ——Bull-chested, bald, and with a dark complexion, this character actor could and did play anything—cops, crooks, editors, and, especially, ethnic roles of every nationality and accent; was onscreen almost three decades, from 1938's *Prison Trail*, and in more than 120: *Hold Back the Dawn* (a Mexican, Flores), *The Crystal Ball* (Russian villain, Stukov), *Pittsburgh, The Purple Heart, A Thousand and One Nights, Shoot to Kill, Mara Maru, The Great Caruso* (Barretto), *Can-Can* (bailiff), etc.; was last in Sid Caesar's *The Spirit Is Willing*, released in '67.

PALLETTE, EUGENE *(1954)* 65 ——His big belly entered a scene first, followed by that gravel voice that seemed to come up from his heels; whether in a millionaire's tux (the Deanna Durbin pix and *My Man Godfrey*), the seersucker of a country squire (*Steamboat Round the Bend*), or a monk's garb (*The Adventures of Robin Hood*, as Friar Tuck), he was a bushy-browed squareshooter, and often the best thing in a picture; onscreen from 1910, he was one of the slimmest, handsomest leading men in silents: *Parlor, Bedroom and Bath* with Ruth Stonehouse, *Going Straight* with Norma Talmadge (crook, ex-pal, who blackmails her), *The World Apart, Fine Feathers* with Claire Whitney, *The Three Musketeers* ('21), etc.; later, when of ample girth (over 300 pounds), came the dozens that made him an almost weekly delight at the movies: *The Ghost Goes West, Topper, Mr. Smith Goes to Washington, The Lady Eve, Swamp Water, Tales of Manhattan, Heaven Can Wait*, etc.; 1948's *Silver River*, with old WB pals Flynn and Sheridan, was his last, after which he retired because of a throat ailment of which he later died.

PALMER, DAWSON *(1972)* 35 ——Secondary roles in several; often on TV in *Lost in Space* and *Voyage to the Bottom of the Sea*.

PALMER, EFFIE *(1942)* 50s ——Radio actress who recreated her role of Ma Parker in *Way*

Back Home, movie version of the hit radio series *Seth Parker*.

PANGBORN, FRANKLIN *(1958)* 65 ——Built his entire 30-year career (from 1927's *Exit Smiling* with Bea Lillie) on playing prissy, fluttery clerks, bank tellers, assistant hotel managers, etc.; among the 150 in which he hilariously flitted: *My Man Godfrey, The Bank Dick, Vivacious Lady, Mad About Music, Christmas in July, Turnabout, The Palm Beach Story; Oh, Men! Oh, Women!* was his last.

PANZER, PAUL *(1958)* 86 ——The "villains' villain"—and in that particular pantheon he sits forever at the head of the class, firmly, cunningly, craftily, ruthlessly; "born to kill," he employed, as dastardly Koerner, every devious device to dispatch desperate Pearl White in *The Perils of Pauline* (his first serial outing as a menace); it was also to be "Curses! Foiled again!" in many other silent serials: *Exploits of Elaine, The House of Hate, Alias the Grey Seal, Hawk of the Hills, The Mystery Mind, The Black Book*, etc.; was in numerous features in the '20s (*The Johnstown Flood, Under the Red Robe, The Best Bad Man*, etc.); just a passable actor, ill-suited to talkies, he was only rarely active in the '30s; was in demand once more, for very small roles, when the "Nazi" vogue began: *Beasts of Berlin* (villain Brahm, far down the cast list), *Casablanca, Action in the North Atlantic, Hotel Berlin* (a bit, Kurt); in Betty Hutton's *The Perils of Pauline* ('47), was right back where he started—but with a difference, for instead of menacing her, his bit was one listed as "Gent—Interior Drawing Room"; he never acted again.

PAPE, LIONEL *(1944)* 77 ——Dignified, gray-haired character who, in 20 Hollywood pix after 1935's *The Man Who Broke the Bank at Monte Carlo*, played lords (*Arise, My Love*), high-rank military officers (*Drums Along the Mohawk, Wee Willie Winkie*), wealthy men (*Fifth Avenue Girl, Raffles*).

PARKE, MacDONALD *(1960)* 68 ——Bull-necked and fierce-looking tourist, Mr. McIlhenny, in early scenes of Hepburn's *Summertime*; support in many British pix: *The Mouse That Roared, Candlelight in Algeria, No Orchids for Miss Blandish*, etc.

PARKE, WILLIAM, SR. *(1941)* 68 ——Character (Josephus) in Chaney's *The Hunchback of Notre Dame*; also was in Charles Ray's *The Tailor Made Man*.

PARKER, BARNETT *(1941)* 70s ——Character (Prince DeRohan) in *Marie Antoinette*; this was high on the social scale for him for he usually was a butler—in *Babes in Arms, He Married*

His Wife, The Last of Mrs. Cheney, The Girl Downstairs, etc.

PARKER, CECIL *(1971)* 73 ——Stuffy (but usually nice) upper-crust English character actor; the Colonel in "The Colonel and His Lady" segment of *Quartet;* in scores, but among his best were several Guinness pix: *The Detective* (as the bishop), *The Ladykillers, The Man in the White Suit;* notable also in *Tony Draws a Horse, Indiscreet, The Lady Vanishes, The Stars Look Down, Oh, What a Lovely War.*

PARKER, FLORA *(1950)* 67 ——See Mrs. Carter DeHaven.

PARKER, FRANKLIN *(1962)* 71 ——Actor-singer in Jack Benny's *Transatlantic Merry-Go-Round.*

PARKER, LEW *(1972)* 65 ——Broadway comedian who was Donald O'Connor's top support in *Are You With It?*

PARKER, MARY *(1966)* 50 ——In *Lady in the Dark,* was one of Ginger Rogers' attractive secretaries (Miss Parker); had a small role earlier in *Artists and Models* and later in *Music for Millions.*

PARKER, "UNCLE MURRAY" *(1965)* 69 —— From TV; few minor roles in movies.

PARKER, VIVIAN *(1974)* 77 ——Supporting roles in silents.

PARKHURST, FRANCES *(1969)* ——Minor support in one of Milton Sills' best, *Men of Steel.*

PARKINGTON, BEULAH *(1958)* ——Usually an extra, she had a minor role in Grable's *My Blue Heaven.*

PARKYAKARKUS *(1958)* 65 ——Comic who carried his famous radio routines into a dozen movies: *New Faces of 1937, Strike Me Pink, Earl Carroll's Vanities, The Life of the Party, Glamour Boy,* etc.

PARLO, DITA *(1972)* 66 ——German star whose 1932–33 Hollywood movies (*Mr. Broadway,* etc.) amounted to little, but whose reputation was considerable in European films; she was in German movies from 1928 (*Heimkehr, Hungarian Rhapsody, Die Dame mit der Maske, Honor of the Family, Melody of the Heart,* etc.); from 1934 she starred in France (in *L'Atalante, The Mystic Mountain, The Courier of Lyons, Mademoiselle Docteur, Grand Illusion,* others); after 1940's *L'Or du 'Cristobal,'* she was arrested as a German and returned to Germany; she was in France again after the war, playing supporting roles in just a few: *Justice Is Done, Quand le Soleil Montera,* and 1965's *La Dame de Pique,* her last.

PARNELL, JAMES *(1961)* 38 ——Good-looking guy who was in several at Paramount in the '50s: *White Christmas* (as the young sheriff), *The Birds and the Bees, You're Never Too Young* (train conductor); in even more at Universal: *Yankee Buccaneer, No Room for the Groom, The Looters,* etc.; son of character actor Emory Parnell.

PARRISH, HELEN *(1959)* 35 ——Sweet-faced brunette ingenue with a devastating smile whose entire life (from age 2) was spent in movies and in large part at Universal; in *Three Smart Girls Grow Up* she was Durbin's sister Kay (the late Barbara Read had played this role in *Three Smart Girls*), but in that same year's *First Love,* was the socialite-cousin so snippy to Durbin; others of that period: *Mad About Music* (Deanna's jealous roommate), *Too Many Blondes, Little Tough Guy, Where Did You Get That Girl?;* as a child, often played the daughter of a star—Babe Ruth (*Babe Comes Home,* her first), Irene Dunne (*Cimarron*), John Boles, Frank Morgan; portrayed Davis as a child in *Seed;* was often a star's sister (Crawford's in *They All Kissed the Bride,* Sheridan's spoiled one in *Winter Carnival*); after numerous leads in B's in the '40s (*The Mystery of the 13th Guest, X Marks the Spot,* etc.), she left the screen after 1949's *The Wolf Hunters* but was a frequent guest star on TV for the next decade.

PARROTT, PAUL "POLL" *(1939)* 47 —— Starred in two-reel comedies in the '20s, then as James (his real name) became writer-director for brother Charlie (Parrott) Chase and Laurel & Hardy.

PARRY, PAUL *(1966)* 58 ——Supporting actor; minor roles.

PARSONS, LOUELLA *(1972)* 91 ——Legendary gossip columnist ("And now for my first exclusive"); onscreen as herself in *Hollywood Hotel* and *Without Reservations.*

PARSONS, PERCY *(1944)* 66 ——Character in many British pix: *The Citadel* (Mr. Stillman), *Suicide Squadron, King of the Damned, Criminal at Large, Flying Fortress,* etc.

PASHA, KALLA *(1933)* 56 ——Played the title role (villain) in the Ben Turpin comedy *Yukon Jake;* had supporting roles in many in the '20s: *A Small Town Idol, Breaking into Society, West of Zanzibar,* etc.; was last in 1929's *The Show of Shows* (a soldier in the "Mexican Moonshine" segment).

PASTOR, TONY *(1969)* 62 ——Orchestra leader; in musical shorts.

PATCH, WALLY *(1970)* 83 ——Played laugh-a-minute Cockney characters in British pix: *I'm All Right, Jack, The Millionairess, In Which We Serve, Sparrows Can't Sing, Get Off My Foot,* etc.

PATRICK, JEROME *(1923)* 49 ——Good-looking actor with dark wavy hair who was Barthelmess' rival for Marguerite Clark in *Three Men and a Girl;* also was in *Officer 666* with Tom Moore, *Forever* with Elsie Ferguson, *School Days* with Wesley Barry, etc.

PATRICOLA, TOM *(1950)* 55 ——Featured as himself in *Rhapsody in Blue,* this vaude headliner starred in many Educational comedy shorts.

PATSTON, DORIS *(1957)* 53 ——Featured in the early British talkie *Smiling Faces.*

PATTERSON, ELIZABETH *(1966)* 90 —— Fragile darling who, in aprons and fresh from the jam pots, was everyone's favorite spinster aunt and always seemed to have about her a touch of the smalltown South; once in a while she was a mother (Crosby's in *Sing, You Sinners*), and sometimes she crabbed or even suffered *(Tobacco Road),* but usually she smiled—sweetly; in movies from 1926, she was in more than 100: *Kiss the Boys Goodbye; Remember the Night; High, Wide and Handsome; Together Again; Intruder in the Dust; So Red the Rose; The Adventures of Tom Sawyer,* etc.; offscreen —a single, genteel urban sophisticate (no rose-covered cottage for her), given to dressmaker-original fashions, keeping her hair an attractive red, a swank apartment in one of the best hotels on Hollywood Boulevard, and a limousine ever ready to whisk her off to the latest play or art gallery.

PATTERSON, JAMES *(1972)* 40 ——Gave an unforgettable performance as the psychopathic killer in *In The Heat of the Night;* also in *Lilith.*

PATTERSON, JOY *(1959)* 53 ——One of the pretty girls in Universal's long-popular (1926–29) series "The Collegians" *(College Love,* etc.).

PAULSEN, ARNO *(1969)* 69 ——Starred, as a Nazi criminal, in *Murderers Are Among Us,* the first post-WW II German film; also in *Wozzeck, Razzia,* etc.

PAVLOVA, ANNA *(1931)* 36 ——Celebrated Russian prima ballerina; starred in Universal's *The Dumb Girl of Portici* ('16); 1935 saw the release of *The Immortal Swan,* a composite movie made up of short films of several of her dances made years earlier.

PAWLE, LENNOX *(1936)* 64 ——Chubby, smiley blond who was Mr. Dick in *David Copperfield;* from England, he also was in *Sylvia Scarlet, The Sin of Madelon Claudet, The Gay Deception,* etc.

PAWLEY, WILLIAM *(1952)* 46 ——Sally Eilers' brother (Jim Haley) in *Bad Girl,* he was often a bad boy: e.g., the thin, derbied, tuxedoed hood, Danny Leggett, who gave Cagney such a rough time in *G-Men;* in many: *Bullets or Ballots; Mary Burns, Fugitive; White Banners; Crime Takes a Holiday; Union Pacific,* etc.

PAXINOU, KATINA *(1973)* 72 ——Greek character actress who won the Best Supporting Oscar as Spanish guerrilla Pilar in *For Whom the Bell Tolls;* in just four more in Hollywood: *Hostages, Confidential Agent, Mourning Becomes Electra, Prince of Foxes;* then made several in Europe: *The Miracle, The Inheritance, Rocco and His Brothers, Mr. Arkadin,* etc.; returned to Athens to establish a stage company in which she played Ibsen, Strindberg, O'Neill; retained fond feelings for Hollywood, saying two years before her death, "It's 18 years since I was last in Hollywood, and I don't want to die without seeing that wonderful city again, and working there. I had an offer last year, for *A Man Called Horse,* but had to turn it down because of my commitments in Athens. It nearly broke my heart"; she never made it back.

PAXTON, SIDNEY *(1930)* 69 ——Character actor in several in the '20s: Thomas Meighan's *Old Home Week, The Midnight Girl,* and one of Pathe's poorer serials, *The Mark of the Frog,* etc.

PAYNE, DOUGLAS *(1965)* 90 ——Support in British pix: *The Triumph of the Scarlet Pimpernel, The Scarlet Devil,* etc.

PAYNE, LOUIS *(1953)* 80 ——Popular support in the '20s: *We Moderns* with Colleen Moore, *The Lady Who Lied* with Nita Naldi, *The Last Edition* with Ralph Lewis, many others; offscreen 15 years, he came back to play the aristocratic Raymond Soule in *Saratoga Trunk.*

PAYSON, BLANCHE *(1964)* 83 ——Character actress, tall, with a battle-axe face and short black bob; often in comedy parts, in many silents: Lillian Gish's *La Boheme,* Richard Arlen's *Figures Don't Lie,* Colleen Moore's *We Moderns, Oh, Doctor!,* etc.

PAYTON, BARBARA *(1967)* 39 ——Big-busted, and not untalented, blonde who was

Peck's leading lady in *Only the Valiant* and Cagney's in *Kiss Tomorrow Goodbye;* numerous others: *Drums in the Deep South, Run for the Hills, The Great Jesse James Raid, Bride of the Gorilla,* etc.; see Tom Neal.

PAYTON, CORSE *(1934)* 66 ——Stage actor in a few early silents who was given to a florid, melodramatic style of histrionics.

PEABODY, EDDIE *(1970)* 58 ——A C&W great, the "King of the Banjo," who, besides one feature, Lee Tracy's *The Lemon Drop Kid,* starred in numerous musical shorts at Paramount.

PEACOCK, KEITH *(1966)* 35 ——Minor role in *Casino Royale.*

PEACOCK, KIM *(1966)* 65 ——Supporting actor in many British pix: *Things to Come, Hell's Cargo, Waltz Time, The Manxman, Mad Hatters,* etc.

PEARCE, AL *(1961)* 62 ——Famous radio comedian (*Al Pearce and His Gang;* played shy door-to-door salesman Elmer Blurt: "Nobody home, I hope, I hope, I hope"); was featured in 1937's *The Hit Parade.*

PEARCE, ALICE *(1966)* 47 ——Plain-faced comedienne who, between sinus attacks and sneezes, chased Sinatra in *On the Town;* funny in many: *That Darn Cat; The Belle of New York; Kiss Me, Stupid; How to Be Very Very Popular,* etc.; was last on TV's *Bewitched,* as neighbor Gladys Kravitz.

PEARCE, GEORGE *(1940)* 75 ——Character actor in many comedies in the '20s: *Hold That Lion, The Traveling Salesman, Watch Your Step, Quarantined Rivals, Home James,* etc.; in fewer talkies, *Six of a Kind, Men in Her Life, The Singing Cowboy,* others.

PEARCE, VERA *(1966)* 69 ——Character actress in British pix: *Nicholas Nickleby, That's a Good Girl, Make Mine a Double, Men of Sherwood Forest,* etc.

PEARSON, LLOYD *(1966)* 69 ——Portly character actor in many British pix: *Under Capricorn, Three Weird Sisters, When We Are Married, Kipps, Good Companions,* others.

PEARSON, MOLLY *(1959)* 83 ——Pretty Broadway leading lady who was in the silent comedy *The Patsy of the Third Floor Back.*

PEARSON, VIRGINIA *(1958)* 70 ——Lovely brunette who began in starring roles (*The Vital Question, The Kiss of a Vampire, The Stain*) in

1914; by '17 was one of Fox's two leading vamps (the other, Valeska Surratt); starred in *A Royal Romance, The Bishop's Emeralds* (with husband Sheldon Lewis), *Blazing Love,* etc.; a character actress in the '20s, she was in Shearer's *The Actress, The Phantom of the Opera* (Carlotta), *Red Kimona, What Price Beauty,* etc., plus the serial *Lightning Hutch;* last had a very minor role in Dunne's *Back Street* ('32).

PEER, HELEN *(1942)* 44 ——As a youngster, appeared in Edison Company pix.

PEGG, VESTER *(1951)* 61 ——Character in B Westerns—usually as a townsman—for 30 years: *The Phantom Riders* ('18), *The Dawn Trail, Colorado,* etc.

PEIL, EDWARD *(1958)* 76 ——Onscreen from 1908, this sterling character could play villains with the best of them (Evil Eye in *Broken Blossoms*); more often was a good guy, rancher or sheriff, in hundreds of B Westerns (*The Lone Ranger in Ghost Town, The Man from Sundown, Colorado Trail,* etc.); perhaps his most unusual role was that of the Old Chinaman in *The Iron Horse.*

PEIL, EDWARD, JR. *(1962)* 54 ——Son of Edward, he was a handsome young lead in several in the '20s: Patsy Ruth Miller's *Rose of the World, The Family Upstairs, The Goose Hangs High, The College Coquette,* etc.; for his credits as a teen star under another name, see Johnny Jones.

PELLICER, PINA *(1964)* 24 ——Young Mexican actress who was Brando's leading lady in *One-Eyed Jacks;* otherwise in Mexican movies.

PELLY, FARRELL *(1963)* 72 ——Irish character actor; in *Darby O'Gill and the Little People.*

PEMBERTON, BROCK *(1950)* 64——Famous Broadway producer-director who was seen as himself in *Stage Door Canteen.*

PEMBERTON, HENRY *(1952)* 77 ——Support in an Arrow Productions silent, *Luxury.*

PEMBROKE, GEORGE *(1972)* 71 ——As a youngish character actor in the late '30s and early '40s, he played doctors in two serials (*Adventures of Captain Marvel, Captain Midnight*); supporting in B features: *The Invisible Ghost, Spooks Run Wild, Gangs Incorporated, Flying Wild,* etc.; a.k.a. George Prud'homme.

PENBROOK, HENRY *(1952)* 73 ——Played minor roles for many years.

PENDLETON, NAT *(1967)* 72 ——Producers (ignoring that he held an economics degree from Columbia) saw him as big, good-natured, and dumb—and fans found him most agreeable in such type-casting; typical of his roles at MGM (1934-44) was that of ambulance driver Joe Wayman in eight of the "Dr. Kildare-Dr. Gillespie" pix, in which his flirting with switchboard operator Marie Blake never got him much; also was in *The Crowd Roars, The Shopworn Angel, On Borrowed Time, Northwest Passage*, etc.; exceptional casting for him was the role of Detective Guild, William Powell's skeptical buddy, in both *The Thin Man* and *Another Thin Man*; a silver-medal winner in wrestling in the 1920 Olympics, he had opportunity to show off his muscles in *The Great Ziegfeld* (as Sandor the Great) and *At the Circus*; was at his comedic best in *Buck Privates* and *Buck Privates Come Home*, as Abbott & Costello's hometown cop who was also their top-kick in the Army; not so dumb, he had starred in 1933's *Deception* in a role (wrestler) he wrote for himself; besides which he was a linguist—reading and speaking five languages; retired after 1949's *Death Valley*.

PENMAN, LEA *(1962)* 67 ——Character actress who played Lucille Ball's mother, Effie Floud, in *Fancy Pants*, and Madame Parole in *We're No Angels*; in '26 had a leading role in the comedy *The Romance of a Million Dollars*.

PENNELL, R. O. *(1934)* 73 ——English character actor long onscreen and particularly busy in the '20s; was in Edmund Lowe's *Dressed to Kill*, Eve Southern's *Clothes Make the Woman, The Olympic Hero*, etc.

PENNER, JOE *(1941)* 36 ——Famous "Wanna buy a duck?" comedian; starred in many 1934-40 pix: *College Rhythm, Collegiate, The Life of the Party, Mr. Doodle Kicks Off, Go Chase Yourself, The Day the Bookies Wept, The Boys from Syracuse*, etc.

PENNICK, JACK *(1964)* 68 ——Toothy, freckled Westerner who was in every John Ford movie—or so it certainly seemed: *Fort Apache* (Sgt. Shattuck), *Stagecoach* (bartender), *She Wore a Yellow Ribbon* (Sergeant Major), *The Grapes of Wrath, Young Mr. Lincoln, The Horse Soldiers*, and at least 20 more, including his last, *The Man Who Shot Liberty Valance*; DeMille also kept him busy in *The Buccaneer, Union Pacific, North West Mounted Police, Unconquered*.

PENNINGTON, ANN *(1971)* 77 ——Spectacularly beautiful dance star (with dimpled knees) of the Ziegfeld Follies; starred onscreen, from 1916's *Susie Snowflakes* through 1930's *Happy Days*, in almost 20: *The Antics of Ann, The Rainbow Princess, The Mad Dancer, The Gold*

Diggers of Broadway, Tanned Legs, etc.; came back just once, still looking great, to do a cameo—cast-listed as The Entertainer—in Tierney's *China Girl*.

PENNINGTON, EDITH MAE *(1974)* 70s ——"The Most Beautiful Girl in America" in 1921, she was decorative in a few minor silents.

PENNY, FRANK *(1946)* 51 ——Burlesque headliner who was in *Hold That Ghost, Pardon My Sarong*, many other Abbott & Costello pix.

PENROSE, CHARLES *(1952)* 76 ——Comedian; featured in Lugosi's *The Human Monster*.

PEPPER, BARBARA *(1969)* 57 ——First a blonde sexpot compared favorably with Harlow (when in *Roman Scandals, Portia on Trial, Forty Naughty Girls*, others of the '30s); a bit heavier in the '40s, played loud-mouthed tough broads (*Manpower; Murder, He Says; Prison Ship; Cover Girl; Brewster's Millions*, etc.); rarely onscreen in the '50s, she was last in *Kiss Me, Stupid* and *My Fair Lady* (the Grosvenor Square scene with Stanley Holloway) and seemed—to early admirers—shockingly gross.

PERCIVAL, WALTER *(1934)* 46 ——Secondary roles in silents (*The Flying Horseman, The Moral Sinner*, etc.) and talkies (*Lights of New York, Cabin in the Cotton, The Champ, Blonde Crazy*, others).

PERCY, EILEEN *(1973)* 72 ——Pretty, dark-blonde, and Irish, she was Fairbanks' leading lady in three in '17: *Reaching for the Moon, Down to Earth*, and *The Man from Painted Post*; was the femme lead in 1919's *Brass Buttons* and *In Mizzoura* and the 1920 serial *The Third Eye*; secondary roles in many in the '20s: Menjou's *The Fast Mail*, Norma Talmadge's *Within the Law*, John Gilbert's *Twelve Miles Out*, etc.; 1932's *The Cohens and the Kellys in Hollywood*, in which she had a minor role, was her last.

PERCY, ESME *(1957)* 69 ——English character actor best known for playing Count Karpathy, the charlatan speech expert who pronounced Eliza Doolittle "a princess," in *Pygmalion*; in many other British pix: *Nell Gwyn, Bitter Sweet, 21 Days Together, The Frog*, etc.

PERIOLOT, GEORGE *(1940)* 64 ——Heavy-faced top support who, onscreen from '11, first appeared for Essanay, American, and Universal; Governor Alvarado in Fairbanks' *The Mark of Zorro*, he had fine roles in many in the '20s: *Blood and Sand, The Young Rajah, Black Butterflies, The Kiss, The Red Lily*, etc.

PERKINS, JEAN *(1923)* 24 ——Actor-stuntman in serials (*Do or Die, The Eagle's Talons*, etc.), he often doubled in dangerous stunts for—perish the thought—both Eddie Polo and Helen Holmes.

PERKINS, OSGOOD *(1937)* 45 ——In *Scarface* Muni was triggerman for this thin, black-haired mobster, Johnny Lovo, before Lovo ordered his assassination (unsuccessful) and was, in turn, executed by George Raft; it was perhaps his finest hour in a score of movies: *The President Vanishes, Tarnished Lady, Gold Diggers of 1937, Madame Du Barry, I Dream Too Much*, etc.; father of Anthony.

PERKINS, WALTER *(1925)* 55 ——Character in several after 1918: *When Romance Rides, Peaceful Valley, Bill Henry, Golden Dreams*, etc.

PERLEY, CHARLES *(1933)* 46 ——Acted in minor roles for Griffith in the early days.

PERRIN, JACK *(1967)* 71 ——Big, rangy, black-haired, and good-looking, he had what it takes to be a major leading man; 1920's *Pink Tights*, in which he was a handsome priest, proved it; instead, having first headlined in an action pic, *Toton the Apache* ('17), he chose to star in serials (*The Lion Man, The Santa Fe Trail, Riders of the Plains, The Jade Box*, etc.) and Westerns; he and his famous trick horse, Starlight, a white stallion, traveled to fame in dozens of cowboy pix (*Beyond the Rio Grande, Romance of the West, Loser's End*, etc.); his last starring series filmed in '36, he then played characters in Westerns into the '50s.

PERRINS, LESLIE *(1962)* 60 ——Supporting actor, usually a smooth villain, in scores of British pix: *The Scotland Yard Mystery, Bulldog Drummond at Bay, I Killed the Count, Nine Days a Queen, Guilty*, etc.

PERRY, ANTOINETTE *(1946)* 58 ——Was featured in a film in the '20s: *After Marriage*, then was a noted stage director; Broadway's Tony Awards are named after her.

PERRY, CHARLES EMMETT *(1967)* 60 —— Many minor supporting roles.

PERRY, MARY *(1971)* 83 ——Was plump, gray-haired great-aunt Sadie in *All the Way Home*; also was in *Uncle Vanya* and *The Fugitive Kind*.

PERRY, ROBERT *(1962)* 82 ——A hobo in *My Man Godfrey*, he had supporting roles in many: *Jaws of Steel; Me, Gangster; Carnival Boat; Riffraff*, etc.

PERRY, SARA *(1959)* 86 ——Played Crawford's mother in *The Damned Don't Cry*.

PERRY, VICTOR *(1974)* 54 ——Support in Widmark's *Pickup on South Street*; also was in *Julius Caesar* (Popilius Lena).

PERSSE, THOMAS *(1920)*——Support in one Goldwyn production, *It's a Great Life*, the year of his death.

PETERS, FRED *(1963)* 78 ——Support in the '20s in Nazimova's *Salome, Tarzan and the Golden Lion*, John Gilbert's *Twelve Miles Out*, Renee Adoree's *The Spieler*, etc.

PETERS, HOUSE *(1967)* 87 ——An elegant, most handsome actor, onscreen from 1913's *In the Bishop's Carriage* as Pickford's leading man, his early expressed wish was to play villains; the closest he ever came was playing reformed villain-hero Ramerrez in DeMille's *The Girl of the Golden West* in '15 (irony: his son, House Jr., became and is one of the best Western villains ever in pictures); otherwise he played rugged gallants—in *Lady of Quality, The Pride of Jennico, Salomy Jane, The Great Divide, Mignon, The Storm, Held to Answer*, etc., through 1928's *Rose Marie*, after which he retired.

PETERS, JOHN *(1940)* 50s ——Character (Kruger) in 1939's *Beasts of Berlin*, this German actor had been onscreen, from Barthelmess' *Ranson's Folly*, in *The Student Prince* ('27), *The Enemy, White Zombie*, etc.

PETERS, RALPH *(1959)* 56 ——In Westerns was a comic sidekick, such as "Scrubby" in Kermit Maynard's *Rough Ridin' Rhythm*; in many: *Six-Gun Rhythm, Across the Sierras, Beyond the Purple Hills*, etc.

PETERS, SUSAN *(1952)* 31 ——MGM gave the fragile beauty this new name, the coveted role of Kitty in *Random Harvest* (the aristocratic young woman who woos Colman in the amnesiac period when he has "forgotten" Garson), and she won a Best Supporting Oscar nomination; she next proved herself a delightful comedienne in *Tish*, co-starred with Jean-Pierre Aumont in *Assignment in Brittany*, Robert Taylor in *Song of Russia*, Lana Turner in *Keep Your Powder Dry*; was shot and permanently paralyzed from the waist down in a '45 hunting accident; starred just once more, in 1948's *The Sign of the Ram*, from her wheelchair; at the beginning, under real name Suzanne Carnahan, had ingenue roles in a half dozen: *Scattergood Pulls the Strings, Santa Fe Trail*, etc.

PETERS, WERNER *(1971)* 50 ——German actor; villain Bruno Ulrich in Holden's *The Coun-*

terfeit Traitor; also in *Battle of the Bulge*; (General Kohler), *A Fine Madness, The Secret War of Harry Frigg*, others.

PETERSEN, ELSA *(1974)* 77 ——In DeMille's *Madame Satan*, was Martha, the maid, on whose advice star Kay Johnson became the mysterious, alluring "Madame Satan" and won back husband Reginald Denny's love; also in *The Expert, Guilty as Hell*, etc.

PETERSON, MARJORIE *(1974)* 60s —— Played second femme leads—in Helen Twelvetrees' *Panama Flo* and Fairbanks Jr.'s *Love Is a Racket*, both in '32.

PETLEY, FRANK E. *(1945)* 72 ——British support.

PETRIE, HAY *(1948)* 53 ——Brilliant English character star who specialized in bizarre characters, e.g., the grotesque, malicious dwarf Quilp in *The Old Curiosity Shop* ('34); also was in *Jamaica Inn, The Thief of Bagdad, Great Expectations, Knight Without Armour* (weird stationmaster who repeatedly cries "Train No. 671—All aboard for Petrograd"—beside an imaginary express), *Twenty-one Days* (outcast curate), *The Fallen Idol*, many more.

PETRIE, HOWARD *(1968)* 61 ——Famous radio announcer (*Blondie, The Jimmy Durante Show*, etc.) who played supports in *Pony Express, Fair Wind to Java, Bounty Hunters, Bend of the River*, many others.

PETTINGILL, FRANK *(1966)* 75 ——Double-chinned, good-humored Britisher; was Mossop in *Hobson's Choice* ('31); also in *When We Are Married, The Good Companions, Tonight at 8:30, Becket*, dozens more.

PHELPS, FANCHER, SR., *(1972)* 74 ——Support in numerous silents.

PHELPS, LEE *(1952)* 59 ——Played Larry in *Anna Christie*; his nice, Irish-looking face was then seen (often as a plainclothes cop) in dozens more: *Trade Winds, Kid Nightingale, The Gladiator, Parole Girl, Crash Donovan*, etc., and several serials (*Desperadoes of the West, Don Daredevil Rides Again*), plus B Westerns.

PHILIPE, GERARD *(1959)* 36 ——Handsome, versatile French star whose films made him internationally admired: *The Devil in the Flesh, La Ronde, Fanfan the Tulip, Les Liaisons Dangereuses, Lovers of Paris, The Proud and the Beautiful, The Red and the Black, The Beauty of the Devil, Beauties of the Night, Seven Deadly Sins*, more

PHILLIBER, JOHN *(1944)* 72 ——In *It Happened Tomorrow*, was Pop Benson, the old city-desk editor who gave cub reporter Dick Powell the three one-day-ahead newspapers; also was in *Double Indemnity, Summer Storm, A Lady Takes a Chance*, etc.

PHILLIPS, EDWARD "EDDIE" *(1965)* 66 —— In *The Collegians*, Universal's two-reel comedies of the '20s, he co-starred as the cocky, wavy-haired "big man on campus"; onscreen from a '21 Pickford pic, *The Love Light*, he was top support in scores for three decades: *The Bells* with Lionel Barrymore, *College Love, Big Boy, Wild Boys of the Road, Champagne Charlie*, etc.

PHILLIPS, HELENA *(1955)* 80 ——See Helena Phillips Evans.

PHILLIPS, MINNA *(1963)* 91 ——English-accented actress who played dignified characters such as a professor's wife in *The Male Animal*; also in *Sherlock Holmes Faces Death, A Yank at Eton, My Sister Eileen*, etc.

PHILLIPS, NORMA *(1931)* 38 ——First onscreen as the star of 1913's *Ashes*, she became nationally famous the following year as "Our Mutual Girl," appearing weekly in the lead in the *Mutual Girl* one-reel series; starred in '15 in the same company's feature *Runaway June*.

PHILLIPS, WILLIAM "BILL" *(1957)* 50s —— First won recognition as rugged youthful support in *See Here, Private Hargrove* (as "The New Jersey Toughie"); earlier was in *City for Conquest, Action in the North Atlantic*, etc.; besides other service pix (*Thirty Seconds over Tokyo, What Next, Corporal Hargrove?*, etc.), was in many gangster movies (*Johnny Allegro, Prison Warden*) and major Westerns (*Bugles in the Afternoon, High Noon, Man from Colorado*, others).

PIAF, EDITH *(1963)* 47 ——Bedraggled "French sparrow," singer of sad cabaret songs; onscreen in *French Can-Can, Royal Affairs in Versailles*, etc.

PICA, TINA *(1968)* 80 ——Italian character actress in *Bread, Love and Dreams; Yesterday, Today and Tomorrow*, others.

PICHEL, IRVING *(1954)* 63 ——Smooth support in dozens from '31: *An American Tragedy*; 1933's *Oliver Twist* (Fagin); *Cleopatra; High, Wide and Handsome; Jezebel; Juarez; There Goes My Heart*, etc.; concurrently a director, he helmed *The Man I Married, Hudson's Bay, A Medal for Benny, Destination Moon*, etc., and several times played character roles in films he directed (*The Moon Is Down*, as the Innkeeper; *Martin Luther*, others).

PICK, LUPU (1931) 35 ——German actor whose last role, in '28, as the star of Fritz Lang's *The Spy* (*Spione*), was perhaps his most famous; had previously starred in several and directed *Shattered, New Year's Eve, The Wild Duck*, other German films.

PICKARD, HELENA (1959) 59 ——English support in *Nell Gwyn* (with then-husband Sir Cedric Hardwicke), *Let George Do It*, other British pix; in one American film, *The Lodger*.

PICKETT, INGRAM (1963) 64 ——One of Sennett's lesser comedians.

PICKFORD, JACK (1933) 36 ——Mary's devil-may-care younger brother, a talented actor, whose handicap was he did not grow tall enough to be a convincing leading man; was at his peak in the teens when he starred in *Seventeen, Tom Sawyer, Huck and Tom, Great Expectations, Sandy*, etc., and in the early '20s in *The Little Shepherd of Kingdom Come, Little Lord Fauntleroy* (had been in his sister's pix as far back as 1910's *White Roses*), *Just Out of College*, etc.; 1928's *Gang War* was his last.

PICKFORD, LOTTIE (1936) 36 ——In curls like sister Mary's (only brunette), she starred in the 1915 serial *The Diamond from the Sky* (the producers wanted Mary, settled for her); she also starred in *Mile-a-Minute Kendall*, supported Mary in *Dorothy Vernon of Haddon Hall*, and had a minor role in Fairbanks' (then Mary's husband) *Don Q*; Smith was real family name but they all acted under the name Pickford after Mary assumed it in '07.

PIERCE, EVELYN (1960) 53 ——Heart-faced brunette, a '25 Wampas Baby Star, who had featured roles in several 1925–31 pix: *The Border Cavalier, Sonia*, Dolores Costello's *Tenderloin*, Edward Everett Horton's *Once a Gentleman*, etc.; married actor-singer Robert Allen, became a realtor.

PIERLOT, FRANCIS (1955) 79 ——Was almost always a dignified oldtimer and frequently wore a black-ribboned pince-nez; was in dozens: *Our Vines Have Tender Grapes* (old minister), *The Robe* (Dodinius), *Remember the Day, Dragonwyck, Roughly Speaking, A Tree Grows in Brooklyn, Chicken Every Sunday*, etc.

PIGOTT, TEMPE (1962) 78 ——In Cooper's *Seven Days' Leave* ('30), she was a delight as the gin-guzzling old Cockney charwoman; played Cockneys in many in the '30s: *Cavalcade, One More River, Limehouse Blues, Becky Sharp, The Devil Is a Woman*, etc.

PIKE, NITA (1954) 41 ——She had a very small role in *The Great Dictator*.

PINCHOT, ROSAMOND (1936) 30 ——A legendary beauty, famous on Broadway as the Nun in *The Miracle* when just 18; she was stunningly lovely as the Queen in 1935's *The Three Musketeers*, her only screen role.

PINZA, EZIO (1957) 65 ——Baritone heart-throb of the Met and Broadway (*South Pacific*), he starred for Metro in the '50s in two (*Mr. Imperium, Strictly Dishonorable*), and for 20th Century-Fox in *Tonight We Sing*; had earlier made a guest appearance in *Carnegie Hall*.

PITT, ARCHIE (1940) 45 ——British comic in *Barnacle Bill, Excuse My Glove*, etc.

PITTMAN, TOM (1958) 25 ——Secondary roles in *Bernardine* (as Olsen), *The Young Stranger, The Way to the Gold, The Proud Rebel*, etc.

PITTS, ZASU (1963) 65 ——One of the funniest women on the screen for over four decades—with her fluttery hands, flustered manner, doleful face and voice; was in more than 100 films (from 1917's *A Little Princess* to 1963's *It's a Mad, Mad, Mad, Mad World*) and, with Thelma Todd, 17 comedy shorts (1931–33); was at her comedic best in *Ruggles of Red Gap* (Laughton adored her), *Mrs. Wiggs of the Cabbage Patch* (W.C. Fields romanced her as the wacky Mrs. Hazy), *The Dummy, Once in a Lifetime* (the so-"refeeed" receptionist), *Make Me a Star, Dames, Life With Father*, etc.; was a superlative tragedienne—two von Stroheim films are evidence: *Greed* and *The Wedding March*—but audiences, accustomed to her zaniness, could not accept her as this; greatly in demand in movies through the '40s, she was most active on TV in the '50s—still doing her "Oh dear me" bit as co-star of Gale Storm's *Oh Susanna*.

PLATT, ED (1974) 58 ——Best known as The Chief on TV's *Get Smart*, he was rugged, bald-topped support—often a police official or military officer—in many pix: *Rebel Without a Cause, North by Northwest, They Came to Cordura, Written on the Wind, The Lieutenant Wore Skirts*, etc.

PLAYFAIR, SIR NIGEL (1934) 60 ——Support in such British pix as *Perfect Understanding* and *The Lady Is Willing*.

PLOWDEN, ROGER *(1960)* 58 ——Character (Macfadden) in *Five Fingers*.

PLUES, GEORGE *(1953)* 58 ——Played henchmen in many dozens of Westerns in 35 years onscreen: Bob Livingston's *Come On, Cowboys*, John Wayne's *Overland Stage Riders*, *Ragtime Cowboy Joe*, etc.

PLUMMER, LINCOLN *(1928)* 52 ——Support in many in the '20s: *Back Stage*, Norma Talmadge's *Within the Law*, Constance Talmadge's *A Dangerous Maid*, Raymond Griffith's *A Regular Fellow*, Jean Hersholt's *Alias the Deacon*, etc.

PLUMMER, ROSE LINCOLN *(1955)* 70s —— Minor roles in *Knock on Any Door, Jack London, The Girl in the Case*, etc.

POGUE, THOMAS *(1941)* 65 ——Was Benjamin Franklin in *Lloyds of London*; also was in *Citizen Kane, The Letter, Foreign Correspondent*, etc.

POINTER, SIDNEY *(1955)* ——Support in England's *The Blue Lamp*.

POLK, GORDON *(1960)* 36 ——Character (Sillers) in *Inherit the Wind*.

POLLA, PAULINE *(1940)* 72 ——Support in silents.

POLLACK, BEN *(1971)* 67——Famous bandleader (Park Central Orchestra) who was seen as himself in *The Benny Goodman Story* and *The Glenn Miller Story*; also did musical shorts.

POLLAR, GENE ——Actor who played Tarzan in *The Revenge of Tarzan* ('20); death (no date given) reported in the *New York Times* (8-29-75), as per—stated the newspaper—the advisement of the family of "Tarzan" creator Edgar Rice Burroughs; Pollar had been living in retirement in Florida.

POLLARD, BUD *(1952)* 65 ——Was featured in 1933's *Victims of Persecution*, which he both produced and directed; also directed the all-black *The Black King* ('32) and *Alice in Wonderland* ('31).

POLLARD, HARRY *(1934)* 51 ——An early screen idol, he starred in many in the teens, usually with star-wife Margarita Fischer, as in *The Peacock Feather Fan* and *Susie's New Shoes*; also directed Miss Fischer in two versions of *Uncle Tom's Cabin*—in '13 (in which, in blackface, he played Uncle Tom) and again in '27 (in which he did not); also directed the first ('29) version of *Show Boat* plus many others.

POLLARD, SNUB *(1962)* 72 ——Actually named Harry also, but no relation; one of the screen's best-loved, droopy-moustached comedians, he was onscreen in literally hundreds of films (shorts and features) from 1912 to 1962's *Pocketful of Miracles*; first became greatly famous in 1919 via a series (more than 100) of one-reel comedies for Hal Roach (*Start Something*, etc.); from '22 became more famous in his dozens of two-reelers (*The Courtship of Miles Sandwich, The Dumb Bell, The Bow Wows, Years to Come*, etc.), with kids all over the nation imitating his frenetic manner and roly-poly eyes; in talkies, he supported others in many: *Cockeyed Cavaliers, Make Me a Star, Starlight Over Texas* (one of numerous Westerns), *Just My Luck, Man of a Thousand Faces*, etc.

POLO, EDDIE *(1961)* 86 ——As lithe and dangerous as a little black whip, he was early a circus aerialist and daredevil horseback rider, and these athletic talents were used to spellbinding effect in the many silent serials in which he starred: *Bull's Eye, The Lure of the Circus, The Vanishing Dagger, Do or Die, King of the Circus, Captain Kidd, The Secret Four*, etc.; also starred, in 1919, in numerous two-reel "Cyclone Smith" Westerns (*Cyclone Smith's Partner, Cyclone Smith's Vow*, etc.); had earlier supported other stars in such serials as *The Broken Coin* and *The Gray Ghost*; at the height of his fame he was, to Hollywood's astonishment, England's Dowager Queen Alexandra's favorite movie star; played bits in several talkies, long afterward, including *Hers to Hold* and *Between Us Girls* at Universal, where he had once been one of the biggest drawing cards.

POLO, SAM *(1966)* 93 ——Eddie's actor-brother; support in many silent serials including Joe Bonomo's *The Great Circus Mystery*.

PONCIN, MARCEL *(1953)* ——Support in British (or filmed-in-England) pix: *So Long at the Fair, The Lost People, Melba, Saadia, One Woman's Story*, etc.

PONTO, ERICH *(1957)* ——German actor; support in *The Third Man*.

PORCASI, PAUL *(1946)* 66 ——Beefy, gray-haired character actor from Italy, with an arrogant little black moustache, who was called on to play dignified (or pompous) men in dozens: *Flying Down to Rio* (Mayor of Rio), *The Gay Divorcee* (French headwaiter), *Maytime* (composer Trintini), *Devil and the Deep* (Hassan), *Footlight Parade* (stage producer Appolinaris for whom dance director Cagney slaved), *Hail the Conquering Hero, Torrid Zone*, etc.

PORTEN, HENNY *(1960)* 70 ——One of the great German actresses, whose starring career lasted from 1907 to 1933, after which, being married to a Jew, she was rarely allowed to work; outstanding among her 40 films: *The Colonel's Wife* ('14), *Kohihiesel's Daughter*, Lubitsch's *Anna Boleyn* (a.k.a. *Deception*) with Jannings, *Backstairs* (which she also produced), *INRI* (played the Virgin Mary); during the Nazi regime was seen only in *Mother Love, Trouble Back Stairs, Comedians*; tried unsuccessfully to come back as a star in two in the '50s, the last being *Carola Lamberti* ('55).

PORTER, EDWARD *(1939)* 58 ——Support in Weber & Fields' *Friendly Enemies* ('25).

PORTERFIELD, ROBERT *(1971)* 66 ——Founder of Virginia's famous Abingdon Barter Theater, he played country types in several: *Sergeant York* (hillbilly Zeb Andrews), *The Yearling* (riverboat captain's mate), others.

PORTMAN, ERIC *(1969)* 66 ——British star who often played aloof aristocrats with a sharp-cutting edge; was in scores including *One of Our Aircraft Is Missing* (gruff Yorkshireman Tom Earnshaw), *The Deep Blue Sea, The Colditz Story, Freud, The Spy With a Cold Nose, The Invaders, The Naked Edge*, etc.

POST, GUY BATES *(1968)* 92 ——From the stage, he starred with considerable distinction in two in the '20s: *Omar, the Tentmaker; The Masquerader* (an early famous dual role); his only other in that decade, *Gold Madness*, was a critical disaster; later, from '36 to '42, was one of Hollywood's busiest character actors: *Camille* (auctioneer), *Crossroads, Maytime* (Emperor Louis Napoleon), *Champagne Waltz, Fatal Lady*, etc.; came back in '47 for a small role in *A Double Life*.

POST, WILEY *(1935)* 50s ——Famous pioneer pilot; died in the plane crash with Will Rogers; had been featured onscreen that year in *Air Hawks*.

POTEL, VICTOR *(1947)* 58 ——An extravagantly tall (and, early on, skinny) comedian, he was a funny fixture onscreen from 1910's *Joyriding* through 1947's *The Egg and I* (the first of several to play wacky Indian Crowbar); in between he was in dozens of "Snakeville" shorts (from 1911, in which he was famous as "Slippery Slim"), countless Keystone comedies, plus Harry Carey's *The Outcasts of Poker Flat, Quincy Adams Sawyer, A Self-Made Failure, Marianne*, and a hundred more features in the '20s and '30s; in his last decade, was a sterling member of Preston Sturges' "stock company" in *Christmas in July, Sullivan's Travels* (as a Hollywood cameraman), *The Miracle of Morgan's Creek* (newspaper editor who broke the news of Betty Hutton's sextuplets), *The Great Moment, Hail the Conquering Hero* (antic leader of the band welcoming Marine "hero" Bracken home to Progressive).

POWELL, DAVID *(1925)* 50s ——They labeled this handsome English actor, who could not have looked more like young Tyrone Power, "the military heartburglar"; on American screens from 1916, he frequently wore uniform in films where, usually to their ultimate regret, he captivated Pickford (*Less Than the Dust*), Billie Burke (the serial *Gloria's Romance*), Ann Murdock (*The Beautiful Adventure*), Olive Tell (*The Unforeseen*), etc.; in the '20s was one of Paramount's most popular leading men, opposite Mae Murray in both *Idols of Clay* and *Right to Love*, Bebe Daniels in *The Glimpses of the Moon*, others.

POWELL, DICK *(1948)* 50s ——Actor-pilot featured in 1925's *The Air Hawk* and *The Cloud Rider*, others.

POWELL, DICK *(1963)* 58 ——Curly-haired tenor who, more than any other star, *was* the Warner musical of the '30s; most often, between her taps, he sang June-moon lyrics into the ear of Ruby Keeler: *42nd Street, Gold Diggers of 1933, Footlight Parade, Dames, Flirtation Walk, Shipmates Forever*; other femme stars received his musical attentions in *20 Million Sweethearts*, other "Gold Diggers" pix, *The Singing Marine, Varsity Show*, etc.; essayed straight comedy in 1940–41, in *Christmas in July* and two with then-wife Joan Blondell, *Model Wife* and *I Want a Divorce*; was briefly back in musicals at Paramount with Mary Martin in both *Happy Go Lucky* and *True to Life*, and Lamour in *Riding High*; broke the mold completely in '45 by starring as tough private-eye Philip Marlowe in *Murder, My Sweet* (a.k.a. *Farewell, My Lovely*); followed it with other rugged roles in *Cornered, Johnny O'Clock, Pitfall, Right Cross, Cry Danger*, etc.; his last movie (though many TV roles came later) was 1954's *Susan Slept Here* in which he sang, for the first time in a decade, to Debbie Reynolds; Joan Blondell's seemingly autobiographical novel, *Center Door Fancy* ('72), delineates a character not unlike him, and not altogether flatteringly; was portrayed by his son (by June Allyson), Dick Powell Jr., in 1975's *Day of the Locust*.

POWELL, LEE *(1944)* 32 ——Handsome actor who starred in the title role in the 1938 serial

The Lone Ranger (first to portray the part in movies); starred that same year in the serial *Fighting Devil Dogs* but, two years later, was a supporting character (Roka) in *Flash Gordon Conquers the Universe*; in Westerns he co-starred with Art Jarrett in *Trigger Pals*, supported Roy Rogers in *Come On, Rangers*.

POWELL, RICHARD *(1937)* 39 ——Minor roles such as a truck driver in Cooper's *The Wedding Night*; also was in *Another Dawn, Yours for the Asking*, etc.

POWER, HARTLEY *(1966)* 72 ——Bald, imposing character who had the principal supporting role (Mr. Hennessy, bureau chief of Peck's news agency) in *Roman Holiday*; in many others: *Dead of Night* (rival of schizophrenic ventriloquist Michael Redgrave), *Man with a Million, Island in the Sun, Evergreen*, etc.

POWER, PAUL *(1968)* 66 ——Support in such pix of the '20s as Glenn Tryon's *Hot Heels*, then, later, in *Underwater City, Jet Attack*, etc.

POWER, TYRONE *(1958)* 45——For 17 years (1936-53) exclusively a 20th Century-Fox star, he was regarded by studio chief, Darryl F. Zanuck, as "the truest, the handsomest, the best of the lot"; was suitable in any type of film—swashbuckler (*The Black Swan, Captain from Castile*), Western (*Jesse James, Pony Soldier*), period drama (*Lloyds of London, Suez*), modern comedy (*The Luck of the Irish, Second Honeymoon*), contemporary drama (*Nightmare Alley, The Razor's Edge, Johnny Apollo*), musical drama (*Rose of Washington Square, Alexander's Ragtime Band*), war films (*Crash Dive, A Yank in the R.A.F.*), etc.; among the Top 10 Box-Office Stars 1938-40; one of his best films, *Witness for the Prosecution* ('58), was his last.

POWER, TYRONE, SR. *(1931)* 62 ——Noted stage actor, from whom his later-famous son inherited his dark Irish looks; starred in many from 1914: *Aristocracy, Where Are My Children?, John Needham's Double, Dream Street, Bright Lights of Broadway, The Lone Wolf, Braveheart*, etc., through 1930's *The Big Trail*, his last, which made a star of John Wayne, but in which he received top billing.

POWERS, JOHN *(1941)* 55 ——Minor support in Marion Davies' *Adam and Eva*, later in *Zaza* (train conductor).

POWERS, LEONA *(1970)* 73 ——Radio actress famous as Homer's mother in *The Aldrich Family*; support in a few pix: *Sweet Surrender* ('35), *Deep Waters* ('48), etc.

POWERS, MARIE *(1973)* 60s ——Well-upholstered singer who starred in the title role of Menotti's opera movie, *The Medium*.

POWERS, MARY GARE *(1961)* ——Acted in silents.

POWERS, RICHARD *(1963)* 63 ——See Tom Keene.

POWERS, TOM *(1955)* 65 ——Forceful, smooth, and tough-talking, he was one of Hollywood's top character actors after *Double Indemnity* (it was to collect on his insurance that "wife" Stanwyck and Fred MacMurray bumped him off); many pix: *Two Years Before the Mast; East Side, West Side; They Won't Believe Me; Destination Moon; The Blue Dahlia*, etc.; previously, besides being a major Broadway actor (*Strange Interlude*, etc.), had been one of the leads in 1911's *Saving an Audience*, starred in several for Vitagraph, and for Goldwyn in 1917's *The Auction Block*.

PRAGER, STANLEY *(1972)* 55 ——Curly-haired, roly-poly comedian with a Brooklyn Kewpie-doll kisser who was a bright spot in many in the '40s: *The Eve of St. Mark* (as Glinka), *Junior Miss, A Bell for Adano* (Sgt. Trampani), *Do You Love Me, A Foreign Affair* (Mike), *The Lady Takes a Sailor*, etc.; offbeat for him was the killer role in *Force of Evil*; became a top TV and Broadway director (*Don't Drink the Water*), as well as starring (again) on stage (*70—Girls—70*).

PRATHER, LEE *(1958)* 67 ——Besides playing the heroine's father in many Westerns in his 30 years onscreen (*Texas Stampede, Two-Gun Law, Bullets for Rustlers*, etc.), he was dignified support in *Women in Prison*, Bruce Cabot's *Homicide Bureau*, etc.

PRATT, LYNN *(1930)* 66 ——Character actor in Pearl White's *A Virgin Paradise* ('21).

PRATT, PURNELL *(1941)* 54 ——Slender, classy, gray-haired support; was the millionaire dad of Kent Douglas (Douglass Montgomery) in *Paid*; in scores from '25 including *Grand Hotel* (as Zinnowitz), *Scarface* (Garston), *A Night at the Opera* (Mayor), *Emma, The Plainsman, High, Wide and Handsome*, etc.

PREER, EVALYN *(1932)* 36 ——Black actress; maid Iola in *Blonde Venus*; earlier had supporting roles in many in the '20s: Monte Blue's *The Brute, Melancholy Dame, The Spider's Web, The Homesteader*, etc.

PREISSER, CHERRY *(1964)* 46 ——Dancer-sister of blonde "baby vamp" June; in the early

'30s, doing their musical vaudeville numbers, they co-starred in several Vitaphone shorts.

PREVOST, MARIE *(1937)* 44 ——As deliciously wicked as any comedienne on the screen, this brunette beauty was at her peak in such frothy items of the '20s as *Getting Gertie's Garter, Up in Mabel's Room,* and particularly Lubitsch's *The Marriage Circle* (the ironic, mischievous smile she gave "happily" married man Monte Blue, at its lingering fadeout, was as talked about then as was Chaplin's in the later *City Lights*); earlier, 1917–22, had been one of Sennett's most toothsome Bathing Beauties; in the '30s, grown heavier, looking a bit blowzy, she played the good-natured pal of other stars—Stanwyck (*Ladies of Leisure*), Lombard (*Hands Across the Table*), Crawford (*Paid*), etc.; in her last screen year, '36, had supporting roles in three: *Cain and Mabel, 13 Hours by Air, Tango.*

PRICE, ALONZO *(1962)* 74 ——Support in several in the mid-30s: *Forgotten Faces, Black Legion, Slim,* etc.

PRICE, DENNIS *(1973)* 58 ——Aristocratically handsome British star who was at his best in *Kind Hearts and Coronets* as he eliminated the eight heirs (all played by Guinness) who stood between him and the dukedom; onscreen from the '40s, he also starred as the blackmailing publisher in *Laughter in Paradise* and was in many more: *Hungry Hill, Jassy, The Bad Lord Byron, Tunes of Glory,* etc.

PRICE, GEORGIE *(1964)* 64 ——Funny vaudeville star who was in such shorts as *Don't Get Nervous.*

PRICE, HAL *(1964)* 79 ——Bald, with a drooping moustache, he played ranchers for years in B Westerns: *Arizona Frontier, Prairie Gunsmoke,* etc.; also was in the '41 serial *The Iron Claw.*

PRICE, KATE *(1942)* 69 ——Stout, black-haired Mrs. Kelly in all "The Cohens and the Kellys" comedies of the '20s; had started as a comedienne, ever portly, in '11, first being John Bunny's wife in *Stenographers Wanted;* in dozens in the '20s, she was outstanding support in many Colleen Moore pix (*Dinty, Come On Over, Broken Hearts of Broadway,* etc.); was seen in the early '30s in *Have a Heart, Ladies of the Jury,* still the big, funny Irish woman.

PRICE, NANCY *(1970)* 90 ——Compelling English character who always played strong-minded old women; *Whiteoaks* (the grandmother), *I Know Where I'm Going, Mandy, The Stars Look Down, Madonna of the Seven Moons,* etc.

PRICE, STANLEY *(1955)* 55 ——The original Abie in Broadway's *Abie's Irish Rose,* he had a long villainous career in features (*Crime, Inc., Power of the Whistler,* etc.), but especially in serials: *The Invisible Monster* (diabolical Phantom Ruler), *The Tiger Woman, G-Men Never Forget* (the plastic surgeon), etc.

PRINCE, JOHN T. *(1937)* 66 ——Thaddeus in DeMille's *The King of Kings,* he had supporting roles in many silents: *Over There, Dame Chance, Little Eva Ascends, Heartless Husbands,* others.

PRINGLE, JOHN *(1929)* 60s ——Father of star John Gilbert (who used his stepfather's name), he had featured roles in several in the '20s: *Travelin' Fast, Black Lightning,* etc.

PRIOR, HERBERT ——Distinguished actor from England, onscreen from 1909; he and Mabel Trunnelle were one of the first husband-and-wife teams in domestic comedy, starring in *On the Lazy Line* ('14) and dozens more; was starred in Griffith's *The Cricket on the Hearth* ('09), *Why Girls Leave Home, The Battle of Trafalgar* ('11), *Christian and Moor* ('11), etc.; in the '20s was in *Stranger Than Death,* Bessie Love's *Slave of Desire,* Nazimova's *Madonna of the Streets,* Shearer's *Waking up the Town,* etc.; was last with Marie Dressler and Polly Moran in 1930's *Caught Short;* date of death unreported.

PROSSER, HUGH *(1952)* 46 ——Smooth B-Western villain; in *Border Patrol, Western Renegades, West of Cimarron,* etc.; also in such non-Westerns as *Pardon My Past.*

PROUTY, JED *(1956)* 77 ——If he had made no other movies, he would always be remembered by fans of the "Jones Family" movies as the bespectacled father, whose wife's (Spring Byington's) antics kept him in a state of round-eyed astonishment; he was genially present, though, in over 100 more, from 1921's *Room and Board* to 1950's *Guilty Bystander: The Broadway Melody, Annabelle's Affairs, 100 Men and a Girl, Hollywood Cavalcade, Pot O'Gold, The Duke of West Point,* etc.

PRUD'HOMME, CAMERON *(1967)* 75 ——A hugely virile, vigorous character, he was Hepburn's rancher-dad in *The Rainmaker;* also was strong old Din in *The Cardinal;* principally a Broadway actor, he had been in several 1930–31 films: *Half Shot at Sunrise, Abraham Lincoln, Doorway to Hell, I Like Your Nerve, Honor of the Family,* etc.

PRUD'HOMME, GEORGE *(1972)* 71 ——See George Pembroke.

PRYOR, AINSLIE *(1958)* 37 ——He was leathery-faced support in a dozen in the '50s: *Ransom!, The Girl in the Red Velvet Swing, The Left Handed Gun, Walk the Proud Land*, etc.

PRYOR, ROGER *(1974)* 72 ——Dapper, with marcelled waves and trim moustache, he always seemed a bit too slick to win the girl—and usually didn't (except, in real life, Ann Sothern, after playing opposite her in 1935's *The Girl Friend);* onscreen from '30, the bandleader-actor was in many—usually B's—in that decade and the early '40s: *Moonlight and Pretzels, Belle of the Nineties, The Man With Nine Lives, Power Dive, She Couldn't Say No, Bullets for O'Hara,* etc.

PRYSE, HUGH *(1955)* 44 ——Support in *Botany Bay* and *Three Cases of Murder* (the "In the Picture" episode).

PUDOVKIN, VSEVOLOD *(1953)* 60 ——Famous Russian actor-director, most famous here as the director of *Mother* and *Admiral Nakhimov* (in which he acted), and for portraying the mystic beggar who led the peasant insurrection in *Ivan the Terrible, Part I.*

PULLY, B. S. *(1972)* 61 ——As Big Julie in *Guys and Dolls* he was every Runyon character rolled into one great bundle; was fun, too, in *Four Jills in a Jeep, Greenwich Village, Wing and a Prayer, Nob Hill, A Hole in the Head,* etc.

PURCELL, DICK *(1944)* 36 ——In the '30s at Warners, this good-looking, curly-haired guy was the busiest second lead (and, in B's, lead) on the lot; was in dozens: *Navy Blues, Ceiling Zero, Bullets or Ballots, King of Hockey, Alcatraz Island,* etc.; continued in B's in the '40s:

High Explosives, Torpedo Boat, Aerial Gunner. Reveille with Beverly, others; last starred (title role) in the '44 serial *Captain America.*

PURCELL, IRENE *(1972)* 70 ——Pretty darkblonde with a charming tip-tilted nose, she had a brief career in the early '30s as a leading lady —Robert Montgomery's in *The Man in Possession,* Keaton's in *The Passionate Plumber,* William Haines' in *Just a Gigolo;* also was in *Westward Passage* and *Bachelor's Affairs,* and that was about it.

PURDELL, REGINALD *(1953)* 57 ——Leading man in British pix: *Haunted Honeymoon,* 1935's *The Old Curiosity Shop* (as Dick Swiveller), *We Dive at Dawn, Captain Boycott,* many others.

PURVIANCE, EDNA *(1958)* 62 ——For nearly a decade (1915–23), this "star soubrette," as she was called, was Chaplin's one-and-only leading lady; starting with *A Night Out,* she was the lovely girl of his dreams in *The Champion, The Tramp, A Night in the Show, The Floorwalker, Shoulder Arms, The Kid,* etc.; he then wrote-produced-directed (even played a bit) 1923's *A Woman of Paris,* a drama, to launch her as a star; the picture succeeded but she did not, nor did she three years later in a French-made film, *The Education of a Prince* (never released here), or in *The Sea Gull* (a.k.a. *A Woman of the Sea),* which Chaplin produced, hired Josef von Sternberg to direct, and partially redirected himself—and never released; offscreen from '26, she made a token, nonspeaking appearance in his *Limelight* in '52; but she had continued to be under contract to Chaplin, and on salary, all those years—and remained so until the day of her death.

PYNE, JOE *(1970)* 45 ——Acidulous, hard-hitting TV talk-show host; in one pic, *The Love-Ins.*

***

Q

QUALTERS, TOT *(1974)* 79 ——Broadway musical comedy actress often with Eddie Cantor (nicknamed him "Banjo Eyes"); supported Bebe Daniels and Fairbanks in *Reaching for the Moon.*

QUARTERMAINE, CHARLES *(1958)* 80 —— English actor who had a character role (John Pardee) in William Powell's *The Bishop Murder Case,* and in John Gilbert's first talkie, *Redemption.*

QUARTERMAINE, LEON *(1967)* 91 ——English actor who had supporting roles in two Elis-

abeth Bergner films: *Escape Me Never, As You Like It.*

QUILLAN, SARAH *(1969)* 90 ——Character actress-mother of Eddie.

QUILLIAN, JOSEPH *(1962)* 78 ——Character actor from Scotland; support in Alberta Vaughn's *Noisy Neighbors.*

QUINLIVAN, CHARLES *(1974)* 50 ——Support in *All the Young Men, Airport 75,* etc.; many TV roles.

QUINN, ALLEN *(1944)* 54 ——Rose Coghlan's handsome leading man in 1915's *The Sporting Duchess;* other silents of the period.

QUINN, JIMMY *(1940)* 55 ——Support in many in the '20s: George Jessel's *The Broadway Kid* (a.k.a. *Ginsberg the Great),* Charles Ray's *Second-Hand Love,* Crawford's *Pretty Ladies* (in which he portrayed Eddie Cantor), Thomas Meighan's *The Argyle Case,* others.

QUINN, JOE *(1974)* 75 ——Irish, this veteran character actor played the rabbi in the original Broadway production of *Abie's Irish Rose;* support in many pix.

QUINN, TONY *(1967)* 60s ——Not Anthony; Irish actor who had a supporting role in a British-made Anna Lee pic, *Non-Stop, New York.*

QUIRK, BILLY *(1926)* 45 ——Debonair, good-looking comic who, from 1908, starred for most companies of the day: Solax, Gem, Pathe, Vitagraph; was initially famous as the character Muggsy in a Biograph comedy series (*The Russian Hessians,* etc.) in which Mary Pickford often was his leading lady; starred in dramas, *Fra Diavolo, The Mended Lute,* that were critical but not popular successes; then made a series of comedies, several of which carried his name (*Billy, the Bear Tamer, Billy's Troubles,* etc.), in which Constance Talmadge was generally the femme interest; geared to blithely youthful comedy roles for which he was no longer suited by the mid-teens, he found his star falling fast; supported others in the '20s in *Broadway Broke* (with Mary Carr), *The Dixie Handicap, Success, My Old Kentucky Home,* etc.

R

RABAGLIATI, ALBERTO *(1974)* 67 ——Italian singer-actor; played a policeman in Janet Gaynor's *Street Angel,* a nightclub proprietor in *The Barefoot Contessa;* in others.

RADCLIFF, JACK *(1967)* 67——Character in the British comedy *Wee Geordie.*

RADFORD, BASIL *(1952)* 55 ——Fine British character star; in *Dead of Night* was in the golfers' story with Naunton Wayne, his frequent companion in comedy; they were together in *The Lady Vanishes,* as stereotyped "hip hip" Britishers abroad, and again in *Passport to Pimlico,* as red-tape-harried bureaucrats; he was also in *The Winslow Boy, Night Train, Flying Fortress,* others.

RAE, CLAIRE *(1938)* 49 ——Minor actress in silents.

RAFFERTY, CHIPS *(1971)* 62 ——Lanky star of the Australian "Western" *The Overlanders* ('46), hailed as the "new" Gary Cooper; didn't become that but had supporting roles in many: *The Desert Rats, Kangaroo, The Sundowners, The Rats of Tobruk, The Wackiest Ship in the Army, King of the Coral Sea,* etc.

RAGLAN, JAMES *(1961)* 60 ——English actor who had a supporting role in Richard Carlson's *Whispering Smith vs. Scotland Yard.*

RAGLAND, RAGS *(1946)* 41 ——MGM comedian of the '40s with a long nose and a tall, droll talent; was with Skelton in the "Whistling" pix: *Whistling in the Dark, . . . in Dixie, . . . in Brooklyn;* also was in several musicals: *Girl Crazy, DuBarry Was a Lady, Anchors Aweigh;* plus a couple of wartime dramas: *Somewhere I'll Find You, The War Against Mrs. Hadley.*

RAIMU *(1946)* 62 ——Starred as the father, Cesar, in the great French trilogy: *Marius, Fanny, Cesar;* also in *The Baker's Wife, Un Carnet de Bal,* many more.

RAINS, CLAUDE *(1967)* 77 ——An actor among actors, this small man with a unique, quietly commanding voice and a piercing intelligence came across on the screen like a giant; never won an Oscar but was four times nominated as Best Support: *Mr. Smith Goes to Washington, Casablanca, Mr. Skeffington, Notorious;* was at the top of his form in many others: *Here Comes Mr. Jordan, The Adventures of Robin Hood, Kings Row, Lawrence of Arabia, The Phantom of the Opera,* even *Four Daughters* and its sequels; always brought out the best in Bette Davis—in *Mr. Skeffington; Juarez; Now, Voyager; Deception;* last was Herod the Great in *The Greatest Story Ever Told;* the title of a film containing one of his most perfect performances was prophetic— *They Won't Forget;* they won't.

RALLI, PAUL *(1953)* 47 ——Had a top supporting role in Marion Davies' *Show People;* was also in other 1928–29 movies: Jack Holt's *The Water Hole,* J. Harold Murray's *Married in Hollywood,* etc.

RALPH, JESSIE *(1944)* 79 ——A generous dollop of twinkly-eyed benevolence, this fine character actress was often on hand to comfort a troubled star—Freddie Bartholomew in *David Copperfield* (she was old Nurse Peggoty), Garbo in *Camille* (maid Nanine), Shirley Temple in *The Blue Bird* (Fairy Berylune); onscreen nine years, after a stage career, she was first Nancy Carroll's Aunt Minnie in *Child of Manhattan* ('33) and last the Duchess of Beltravers in *They Met in Bombay*, owner of the diamond pendant coveted by jewel thieves Gable and Russell; among her 50 other pix: *San Francisco, Jalna, Cafe Society, The Good Earth, Drums Along the Mohawk.*

RALSTON, JOBYNA *(1967)* 66 ——Delightful brunette who was so frequently Harold Lloyd's leading lady in the '20s (*The Freshman, Why Worry?, The Kid Brother, Girl Shy, Grandma's Boy, Hot Water, For Heaven's Sake*, etc.); quit the screen in '30 after being the leading lady in *Rough Waters*, a Rin-Tin-Tin pic; was Richard Arlen's wife.

RAMBEAU, MARJORIE *(1970)* 80 ——Character actress with a strong lusty voice and acting attack; could be anything—raucous (*Primrose Path*; Oscar-nominated as Best Support), raucous-plus (*Tobacco Road*; hymn-singing revivalist Sister Bessie), *grande* as in *dame* (*Torch Song*; her only other nomination), vicious (the waterfront tramp Marie Dressler killed in *Min and Bill*), heartbreaking (the derelict in *A Man's Castle*), commanding (Queen of the Amazons in *The Warrior's Husband*); in more than 50 talkies from 1930's *Her Man*, she last had a top supporting role (Gert) in Cagney's *Man of a Thousand Faces* ('57); earlier, when one of Broadway's great beauties, had starred in a half dozen silents: *The Dazzling Miss Davison* ('16), *The Debt, The Greater Woman*, etc.

RAMBO, DIRK *(1967)* 25 ——Handsome twin brother of actor Dack; minor movie roles; best known on TV as one of the (twin) sons in *The New Loretta Young Show* ('62).

RAMBOVA, NATACHA *(1966)* 69 ——A self-made exotic and Mrs. Rudolph Valentino, she co-starred with Clive Brook in 1925's *When Love Grows Cold.*

RAMSEY, NELSON *(1929)* 66 ——Support in *A Romance of Seville* ('29).

RANALDI, FRANK *(1933)* 27 ——Child actor in silents.

RANALOW, FREDERICK *(1953)* 80 ——Support in England's *Autumn Crocus* and *The Inheritance.*

RAND, JOHN *(1940)* 67 ——For years a Chaplin supporting comic—in *City Lights, The Circus, Modern Times, Pay Day, The Immigrant, Easy Street* (the hymn-singing bum next to Chaplin in the opening mission service scene).

RANDALL, ADDISON "JACK" *(1945)* 38 —— After romantic leads at RKO (*Navy Born, His Family Tree*), he became, in '37 at Monogram, a

quite popular singing cowboy; starred—with Al St. John as his sidekick—in 22 Westerns: *Stars over Arizona, Wild Horse Canyon, Down the Wyoming Trail*, etc.; was Bob Livingston's brother, Joan Bennett's brother-in-law.

RANDALL, BERNARD *(1954)* 70 ——Supporting roles in many in the '20s: ZaSu Pitts' *Pretty Ladies* (as Aaron Savage), Constance Talmadge's *Polly of the Follies*, Anna Q. Nilsson's *Ponjola*, Betty Compson's *Counsel for the Defense*, etc.

RANDALL, RAE *(1934)* 25 ——She had minor roles in several DeMille pix: *The Godless Girl, The King of Kings*, etc.

RANDLE, FRANK *(1957)* 56 ——Raucous comedian who starred in England's "Somewhere" pix: *Somewhere in England, . . . in Camp, . . . in Civvies*, etc.

RANDOLPH, AMANDA *(1967)* 65 ——Black actress who usually played comic servants with dignity; in *Mr. Scoutmaster, At the Circus, She's Working Her Way Through College*, etc.; was radio's first Aunt Jemima.

RANDOLPH, ANDERS *(1930)* 53 ——Big, burly, and mean, under any name, and he used several—Rudolf Amendt, Robert O. Davis, Anders Randolf, Rudolph Anders; was the pirate leader in Fairbanks' *The Black Pirate*, Garbo's violent husband in *The Kiss*, the treacherous duke in Pickford's *Dorothy Vernon of Haddon Hall*; onscreen from 1916's *The Hero of Submarine D2* with Zena Keefe, he was top support in another 40: *Within the Law* with Alice Joyce, *The Splendid Sinner* with Mary Garden, *Erstwhile Susan* with Constance Binney, *Me Gangster* with Don Terry, etc.

RANDOLPH, ISABEL *(1973)* 83 ——Was "Fibber McGee & Molly's" Mrs. Uppington, both on radio and in their movies, *Look Who's Laughing, Here We Go Again*; was also in *Our Hearts Were Growing Up, Practically Yours, Standing Room Only, If You Knew Susie.*

RANGEL, ARTURO SOTO *(1965)* 83——Mexican actor who was in several made-in-Mexico Hollywood pix: *Treasure of Sierra Madre* (Presidente), *Garden of Evil* (priest), etc.

RANKIN, ARTHUR *(1947)* 46 ——Good-looking secondary leading man who was in many throughout the '20s and well into the '30s: *Little Miss Smiles* with Shirley Mason, *Broken Laws, Fearless Lover, Dearie, Glad Rag Doll, The Wild Party*, etc.; was the son of character actor Harry Davenport.

RANKIN, DORIS *(1946)* ——Character actress who played the jail matron in Nancy Carroll's *The Night Angel;* had earlier been in *The Copperhead* with Lionel Barrymore, as his leading lady.

RANKIN, PHYLLIS *(1934)* 60 ——Screen actress-wife of Harry Davenport; was a major stage "name" at the time of their marriage.

RAPPE, VIRGINIA *(1921)* 20s ——Brunette minor actress in two-reel comedies whose sex-party death provoked the trials that destroyed the career of comedian Roscoe "Fatty" Arbuckle, though three separate juries acquitted him.

RASUMNY, MIKHAIL *(1956)* 66 ——Big talent in a small package from Russia; in Hollywood for 16 years from 1940's *Comrade X,* he was most of that time a Paramount stalwart: *For Whom the Bell Tolls* (wryly impish Rafael), *Hold Back the Dawn, This Gun for Hire, Wake Island, And the Angels Sing, Saigon, Anything Can Happen,* etc.; elsewhere was in *Anna and the King of Siam* (Alak), *The Kissing Bandit, Holiday in Mexico, A Royal Scandal,* others; last played a gypsy in Jane Russell's *Hot Blood.*

RATHBONE, BASIL *(1967)* 75 ——Suave, sophisticated, and lean as a wolfhound, he had three sets of admirers: those who recalled him as a sleek matinee idol of the '20s (*The Great Deception* with Aileen Pringle, *The Masked Bride* with Mae Murray, etc.), the fans of all those double-dyed villains (Sir Guy of Gisborne in *The Adventures of Robin Hood,* heartless Mr. Murdstone in *David Copperfield,* pirate Captain Levasseur in *Captain Blood,* etc.), and devotees of his "Sherlock Holmes" (played him 14 times, with Nigel Bruce as Dr. Watson in each, from 1939's *The Hound of the Baskervilles* to 1946's *Dressed to Kill);* was Oscar-nominated as Best Support in two: *Romeo and Juliet* (as Tybalt) and *If I Were King;* had a few straight character roles in the '50s (*The Last Hurrah, We're No Angels*), went into horror pix in the '60s (*Tales of Terror, The Comedy of Terrors*); the one role he coveted and fought to get, to no avail—Rhett Butler.

RATNER, ANNA *(1967)* 75 ——Was featured in early Essanay films.

RATOFF, GREGORY *(1960)* 67 ——Russian character actor who mangled the English language hilariously, usually as a producer, in more than 50: *What Price Hollywood; Once in a Lifetime; I'm No Angel; King of Burlesque; Sally, Irene and Mary; All About Eve,* etc.; was concurrently a top Hollywood director: *Adam Had Four Sons, The Heat's On, Moss Rose, Lancer Spy, Intermezzo,* more.

RATTENBERRY, HARRY *(1925)* 65 ——Character in numerous pix of the '20s: Wesley Barry's *The Printer's Devil,* Cullen Landis' *Watch Your Step, His Pajama Girl, Daring Days,* etc.

RAUCOURT, JULES *(1967)* 76 ——Dashing and black-haired, this French actor was one of the silent screen's handsomest leading men; was in *Prunella* with Marguerite Clark, *La Tosca* with Pauline Frederick, others; starred last here in a critically acclaimed avant-garde film of 1928, *The Life and Death of 9413—A Hollywood Extra;* returned to France where, among others, he starred in *Le Spectre Vert.*

RAVEL, SANDRA *(1954)* 50s ——Actress popular in French and Italian films of the '30s: *The Single Sin, Those Three French Girls, L'Enigmatique Monsieur Parkes,* etc.

RAWLINS, JUDY *(1974)* 36 ——Minor roles; ex-wife of Vic Damone.

RAWLINSON, HERBERT *(1953)* 67 ——Tall, handsome actor from England whose screen career spanned exactly 50 years, from 1911's *The Novice* to 1951's *Gene Autry and the Mounties,* and who was a star for at least one-third of that time; early, he starred for Universal in *The Sea Wolf* ('13), *On the Verge of War, Won in the Clouds;* a bit later came *Damon and Pythias, The High Sign, Come Through, The Millionaire, The Jack O'Clubs, Playthings of Destiny,* dozens more; starred also in numerous silent serials: *The Carter Case; The Flame Fighter; Sanford Quest, Criminologist; The Black Box,* etc.; in talkies, besides supporting roles in seven serials (*Robinson Crusoe of Clipper Island, SOS Coast Guard, Blake of Scotland Yard,* etc.), he was in scores of features: *Dark Victory* (Dr. Carter; typical of his always dignified roles), *Seven Sinners, Bullets or Ballots, Hawaii Calls,* and more B Westerns than even he could count.

RAY, BARBARA *(1955)* 41 ——Supporting actress-wife of Roscoe Ates.

RAY, CHARLES *(1943)* 52 ——Ince's great (and good-looking) country-boy-come-to-town star, who went from bits ('12) to superstardom (1915–25) to second-rate pix (1926–27) and back to bits in talkies; it is as the yokel boy, lovable, "real," not outrageously comic, in gingham shirts and faded overalls, that his fans will always think of him; played this boy in nearly all his 118 starring pictures: *The Coward, The Hired Man, The Busher, Alarmclock Andy, The Old Swimin' Hole, The Girl I Loved,* etc.; poet Vachel Lindsay captured the essence of his screen personality when he noted: "Many of the pictures of Charles Ray make the hero quite a bronze-looking sculpturesque person, despite his yokel raiment"; attempting to change that image into a more sophisticated one, when he was no longer a youth, bankrupted the actor; the last time he starred was in a '32 two-reeler, *Snake in the Grass;* between 1932's *The Bride's Bereavement* and 1942's *The Magnificent Dope,* had bits in 13 (typical: a uniformed hotel doorman in *Ladies Should Listen*), and was glad to get the work.

RAY, EMMA *(1935)* 63 ——Vaudeville comedienne who had a small role in Fields' *The Old-Fashioned Way.*

RAY, HELEN *(1965)* 86 ——Supporting role in Barthelmess' *Experience.*

RAY, JOHNNY *(1927)* 68 ——Vaudeville star-husband of Emma; had a supporting role in Dressler's *Bringing up Father.*

RAY, MARJORIE *(1924)* 23 ——Minor roles in the '20s.

RAYMOND, CYRIL *(1973)* 76 ——Polished supporting actor in numerous British movies from the early 1930s; was notable in *Brief Encounter* as the middle-class husband whose wife, Celia Johnson, had an affair with Trevor Howard; was also in *The Ghost Train, It's Love Again, Dreaming Lips, U-Boat 29, Quartet* ("The Colonel's Lady" episode), *Rough Shoot, The Heart of the Matter, Dunkirk, Night Train to Paris, Charley Moon,* and many more.

RAYMOND, FORD *(1960)* 60 ——Character actor in Alan Ladd's *One Foot in Hell.*

RAYMOND, FRANCES *(1961)* 92 ——Aristocratic-looking character actress in pix of the '20s: Colleen Moore's *Flirting with Love,* Lowell Sherman's *Satan in Sables,* Clara Bow's *Get Your Man* (as her mother), Dix's *The Gay Defender,* many others; in Keaton's *Seven Chances,* in which she was the mother of heroine Ruth Dwyer, was billed Frankie Raymond.

RAYMOND, HELEN *(1965)* 80 ——Character actress active in the '20s in Anita Stewart's *Her Mad Bargain,* Katherine MacDonald's *Her Social Value,* Colleen Moore's *The Huntress,* Mr. and Mrs. Carter De Haven's *Twin Beds,* etc.

RAYMOND, JACK *(1951)* 49 ——Minor roles in many in the '20s: Clara Bow's *The Wild Party* (as Balaam), *Sally of the Scandals, Three Week Ends, Lover's Island, Synthetic Sin,* etc.

RAYNER, MINNIE *(1941)* 72 ——Support in several English-made Sherlock Holmes pix: *Sherlock Holmes' Fatal Hour, The Missing Rembrandt, The Triumph of Sherlock Holmes;* played his housekeeper.

REA, MABEL LILLIAN *(1968)* 36 ——Minor roles in *I Married a Woman, Pal Joey,* etc.

READ, BARBARA *(1963)* 46 ——When she was one of *Three Smart Girls* (was Kay to "sisters" Deanna Durbin and Nan Grey), this dark-haired beauty was one of Universal's most promising ingenues; had a few other opportunities: *The Mighty Treve, The Road Back, Make Way for Tomorrow* (Fay Bainter's rebellious daughter), *The Crime of Dr. Hallet,* etc.; last had a small role in John Beal's *Key Witness* ('47).

REAL, BETTY *(1969)* ——Minor role in *Crime Without Passion.*

RED WING *(1974)* 90 ——Beautiful girl who was Dustin Farnum's love in 1913's *The Squaw Man;* the screen's first Indian star (she was of the Winnebago tribe; real name Princess Lillian Red Wing St. Cyr), she had played leading roles from 1907's *The Falling Arrow,* in *Red Wing's Gratitude, Red Wing's Loyalty, The White Squaw, The Flight of Red Wing,* etc.; after *The Squaw Man* (usually, erroneously, referred to as her movie debut), she starred (with husband James Young Deer) in a series of Indian Westerns: was with Donald Crisp in *Ramona* ('16), and opposite Tom Mix in *In the Days of the Thundering Herd;* retired to devote herself to Indian affairs in New York State and Washington.

REDWING, RODD *(1971)* 66 ——Perhaps the handsomest Indian onscreen, this Chickasaw was usually in big-budget Westerns and almost always as the chief: *Copper Sky, Sergeants Three, Cattle Queen of Montana, The Cowboy, Shalako,* etc.; was often in non-Westerns: *Lives of a Bengal Lancer, Elephant Walk, Gunga Din, The Naked Jungle.*

REECE, BRIAN *(1962)* 48 ——Comic character actor in British pix who wore a suspicious look well; in *Carry On Admiral, Wee Geordie, Orders Are Orders,* others.

REED, DONALD *(1973)* 68 ——Colleen Moore's handsome leading man in *Naughty But Nice* ('27), he had leads in many others at First National in the late '20s: *Convoy, Mad Hour* with Sally O'Neil, *The Night Watch* with Billie Dove, *Show Girl* with Alice White; in the '30s, was in *Little Johnny Jones* with George M. Cohan, *The Texan* with Cooper, *Crusade Against Rackets,* and *Renfrew of the Mounted* ('37), his last.

REED, FLORENCE *(1967)* 84 ——Large-sized and formidable Broadway star who had two careers in movies; first, 1915-1921, the star of *The Dancing Girl, New York, Today, The Eternal Sin, The Eternal Mother, Indiscretion,* etc.; in talkies, as a character actress, was in 1934's *Great Expectations* (played Miss Havisham, badly), *Frankie and Johnnie, The Shanghai Gesture.*

REED, GEORGE *(1952)* 85 ——Black character actor who was fine as the caretaker, Old Ben, in *Kentucky;* also was in *Swanee River, Home in Indiana, Sporting Blood,* and *The Green Pastures,* as the kindly Reverend Deshee; was on-screen from 1920's *Huckleberry Finn,* in which he was Jim.

REED, GEORGE E. *(1952)* ——Supporting actor in the '20s; was in Raymond Griffith's *Red Lights,* Baby Peggy's *Helen's Babies,* Lloyd Hughes' *Scars of Jealousy,* Mary Astor's *Three-Ring Marriage,* etc.

REED, MAXWELL *(1974)* 54 ——Leading man from Ireland; onscreen from 1946; in *The Brothers, The Dark Man, Daybreak, Notorious Landlady, The Years Between, Picture Mommy Dead, The Square Ring,* more.

REESE, JAMES *(1960)* 62 ——Character role in Sal Mineo's *The Young Don't Cry.*

REEVE, ADA *(1966)* 92 ——British character actress who had a featured role (Molly) in Gene Tierney's *Night and the City;* was also in *Meet Me at Dawn, Eye Witness, They Came to a City,* etc.

REEVES, BILLY *(1943)* 79 ——English comedian who starred in the title role of 1915's *The New Butler;* a member of the Fred Karno touring company that introduced Chaplin to American audiences, he was the acknowledged creator of the Little Tramp character Chaplin made famous.

REEVES, BOB *(1960)* 68 ——A now-forgotten second-rank cowboy hero of the '20s; starred then in *The Iron Fist, Fighting Luck, Cyclone Bob,* many others, plus the serial *The Great Radium Mystery* ('19); in talkies had small roles in features such as *Our Daily Bread* (was Hannibal) and played villains in the Westerns of others, like Johnny Mack Brown's *The Son of Roaring Dan* ('39), the last pic in which Reeves acted.

REEVES, GEORGE *(1959)* 45 ——Last famous as the star of TV's *Superman* series, he earlier played leads in many B's: *Ladies Must Live, Dead Men Tell, Man at Large, Tear Gas Squad,* etc.; also had excellent second leads in numerous A's: *Lydia, So Proudly We Hail, Torrid Zone, Strawberry Blonde,* others; made his debut in movies as one of the Tarleton Twins (but he and the other actor, Fred Crane, were not) in *Gone With the Wind.*

REEVES, JIM *(1964)* 40 ——C&W star known as "Gentleman Jim"; starred in Embassy's *Kimberly Jim,* released posthumously.

REEVES, KYNASTON *(1971)* 78 ——Long-nosed, professorial British character actor; was in *The Mudlark* (as Gen. Sir Henry Ponsonby), *Captain Horatio Hornblower, The Winslow Boy, Anne of the Thousand Days,* more.

REEVES, RICHARD *(1967)* 54 ——Played the Rebel Chief in the '54 serial *Trader Tom of the China Seas.*

REEVES-SMITH, H. *(1938)* 74 ——Was Watson in Clive Brook's *The Return of Sherlock Holmes;* had supporting roles in others of the '20s: Conrad Nagel's *Three Weeks, No More Women,* etc.

REEVES-SMITH, OLIVE *(1972)* 77 ——Small roles in many.

REGAN, JOSEPH *(1931)* 35 ——Starred in the '28 short *America's Foremost Irish Tenor.*

REGAS, GEORGE *(1940)* 50 ——Tall, handsome Greek actor who played romantic villains in many in the '20s: *The Wanderer* with Greta Nissen, *Beau Geste* and *The Rescue* with Colman, *That Royle Girl* with Carol Dempster, etc.; in the next decade was in *Viva Villa!, Rose Marie* (Boniface), *Lives of a Bengal Lancer* (Kushal Khan), *The Charge of the Light Brigade* (Wazir), *The Mark of Zorro* (Sgt. Gonzales), *The Light That Failed,* etc.; was just as often billed Rigas, and sometimes Rigos.

REGAS, PEDRO *(1974)* 82 ——Strong-faced actor, discovered on Broadway and brought to Hollywood by Mary Pickford, who for 53 years —in scores of pix—played characters of many nationalities; a few of his many: *Bulldog Drummond Strikes Back* with Colman, *Only Angels Have Wings* (as Pancho), *Perilous Holiday,* and, more recently, *Pocket Full of Money, Flapping Eagle, High Plains Drifter.*

REHAN, MARY *(1963)* 76 ——Featured in a '22 Lee-Bradford B pic, *Flesh and Spirit;* was also a practicing lawyer.

REICHER, FRANK *(1965)* 90 ——Distinguished by his Roman nose (though German-born) and half-moon, baggy eyes, this sterling actor was in more than 150 from 1921's *Behind Masks,* which he also directed; often was a smooth villain, as in *Sutter's Gold;* among his many: *King Kong* (Captain Englehorn), *Anthony Adverse, Mata Hari* (The Cook-Spy), *The Story of Louis Pasteur* (Dr. Pfeiffer), *Stage Door* (Stage Director), *Lancer Spy, The Gay Sisters, The Mummy's Ghost,* etc.; was last in

Louis Hayward's *The Lady and the Bandit* ('51).

REICHOW, WERNER *(1973)* 51 ——Was typecast in German character roles for years.

REID, CARL BENTON *(1973)* 79 ——Memorable in *The Little Foxes* ('41) as Oscar Hubbard, conniving brother of Davis and father of Dan Duryea, this strong character actor was active in the next 25 years; often played fathers: Will Rogers' in *The Will Rogers Story*, Ann Blyth's in *The Great Caruso*, etc.; also was in *The North Star, In a Lonely Place, Carbine Williams, The Left Hand of God, Broken Lance*, etc., including *Madame X* ('66) with Lana Turner, his last; on TV in the 60s, had a continuing role in *Burke's Law*.

REID, HAL *(1920)* 60 ——Handsome actor-father of Wallace; starred in 1911's *The Deerslayer* (in which his son had a top supporting role as a muscular Indian), 1912's *Cardinal Wolsey*, other Vitagraph pix of the day.

REID, TREVOR *(1965)* 45 ——Support in several: *How to Murder a Rich Uncle, Satellite in the Sky, Mary Had a Little*, etc.

REID, WALLACE *(1923)* 31 ——An idol, of handsome face, abundant charm and perfect physique, he was catapulted to overnight stardom in '15 by the small role of Jeff, the blacksmith, in *The Birth of a Nation;* "Seeing him was just like finding a 180-pound diamond," said producer Jesse L. Lasky, for whom he starred exclusively the rest of his life; at that point, having started in '10, had already (often in character parts) been in more than 100 films, many of them one- or two-reelers, which he sometimes also wrote and directed; starred in more than 60, among the best of which were five with Geraldine Farrar (*Joan the Woman, The Devil Stone, Carmen, The Woman God Forgot, Maria Rosa*), *To Have and to Hold* with Mae Murray, *The Golden Chance* with Cleo Ridgely, *Across the Continent* (one of his several auto-racing pix), *Forever* with Elsie Ferguson, *Clarence* with Kathlyn Williams, etc.; a 1921 poll revealed him to be the #1 male star at the box-office; his last film was 1922's *Thirty Days*.

REIMERS, GEORG *(1936)* 76 ——Character actor who had the bad luck to be in 1923's *Queen of Sin* ("Not sinful but awful," said one critic of the day).

REINHARDT, JOHN *(1953)* 52 ——Actor from Germany who was featured in *The Prince of Hearts* ('29), which was a pale copy of the earlier *Merry Widow; Love, Live and Laugh* with Jessel; *The Climax* with Jean Hersholt, etc.

REJANE, MME. GABRIELLE *(1920)* 63 —— Great French stage actress who starred onscreen in the title role in *Madame Sans-Gene* ('11), and, that same year, in *Miarka, the Daughter of the Bear;* her only other film, *Gypsy Passion*, was released two years after her death.

RELPH, GEORGE *(1960)* 72 ——English character actor who had the leading role, the vicar, in *The Titfield Thunderbolt;* also was in *Nicholas Nickleby*, 1960's *Ben Hur* (as Tiberius), *Doctor at Large*, etc.

REMLEY, RALPH M. *(1939)* 54 ——In *Make Way for Tomorrow* was the decent son-in-law of Beulah Bondi and Victor Moore (husband of their sharp-tongued daughter, Elizabeth Risdon); was in many others: *Princess O'Hara, King of the Underworld, Let Them Live, The Story of Alexander Graham Bell*, etc.

REMY, ALBERT *(1967)* 55 ——French actor; played the father of the boy in *The 400 Blows;* also in *French Can-Can, Children of Paradise, The Train, Shoot the Piano Player*, etc.

REMY, DICK, SR. *(1947)* 72 ——Character actor in silents.

RENARD, DAVID *(1973)* 52 ——Character actor who played the Woodcarver in *Ship of Fools;* also in *Hang-Up*, others; played a variety of types—peasants, priests, etc.

RENAVENT, GEORGE *(1969)* 74 ——First a leading man—Constance Binney's in *Erstwhile Susan* ('17)—this good-looking actor from France let a decade go by before returning as one of Hollywood's best and busiest character actors; was in *Rio Rita* (as General Ravenoff), *Lloyds of London* (French Lieutenant), *The House of Rothschild* (Talleyrand), *Cafe Metropole* (maitre d'), *Jezebel* (De Lautrec), *Sullivan's Travels* (Old Tramp), *The Foxes of Harrow*, etc., through 1952's *Mara Maru*, in which he was Ortega.

RENFRO, RENNIE *(1962)* 68 ——He was in Sennett comedies; later was a famous trainer of movie dogs.

RENNIE, JAMES *(1965)* 76 ——Dorothy Gish picked this handsome Broadway actor to play opposite her in 1920's *Remodeling Her Husband* (directed by sister Lillian) and soon married him; was a charming light lead in many in the '20s: *Star Dust* with Hope Hampton, *Mighty Lak a Rose* with Dorothy Mackaill, *Argentine Love* with Bebe Daniels, *Clothes Make the Pirate*, again with Dorothy Gish, etc.; rarely onscreen in the '30s, he had character roles in several of the '40s: *A Bell for Adano, Now,*

Voyager (as Lee Patrick's husband), *Wilson, Tales of Manhattan*, others.

RENNIE, MICHAEL *(1971)* 62 ——Debonair English star with a handsome, cadaverous face who, after a long career in Britain, came to America and co-starred in many, particularly at 20th Century-Fox: *The Day the Earth Stood Still, Five Fingers, Phone Call from a Stranger, The Robe, King of the Khyber Rifles, Demetrius and the Gladiators, The Rains of Ranchipur,* etc.; later was in *Mary, Mary; Ride Beyond Vengeance, Hotel,* others; *Krakatoa, East of Java* ('69) was his last.

RENOIR, PIERRE *(1952)* 67 ——French character actor; in *Children of Paradise, Dr. Knock, Sirocco,* etc.

REPP, STAFFORD *(1974)* 56 ——A policeman, as he often was, in *I Want to Live!*, he also was in *Hot Spell, A Very Special Favor,* etc.; in TV's *Batman* series, was Captain O'Hara.

REVELLE, HAMILTON *(1958)* 85 ——A Metro leading man of 1917; co-starred with Mary Garden in *Thais.*

REY, ROSA *(1969)* ——Character actress in *The Secret Beyond the Door, The Rose Tattoo* (as Mariella), etc.

REYES, EVA *(1970)* 55 ——Half of the Paul & Eva Reyes dance team that had a specialty dance number in *Copacabana.*

REYNOLDS, ABE *(1955)* 71 ——Schmidt, the tailor, who reluctantly put the cuffs on groom-to-be Astaire's morning-suit trousers in *Swing Time;* a comic cab driver in *My Dear Secretary,* etc.

REYNOLDS, ADELINE DE WALT *(1961)* 98 ——Wrinkled little dear who was James Stewart's mom in *Come Live with Me,* her movie debut at 79, after which she was in an additional 21: *Lydia, Tuttles of Tahiti, Going My Way* (greatly moving as the mother Irish priest Barry Fitzgerald had not seen in many years), *Happy Land, Since You Went Away,* etc.; one of her personal favorites was *Pony Soldier,* in which she played an old Indian woman.

REYNOLDS, CRAIG *(1949)* 42 ——Handsome second lead at Warners before the war; was in *Ceiling Zero, The Case of the Stuttering Bishop, Jailbreak, Times Square Cowboy, Making Headlines,* and another 40; after the war, minor roles in just a few (while he worked as a cab-driver): *Queen of Burlesque, Just Before Dawn, My Dog Shep,* etc.; a Marine hero in WW II, a Purple Heart winner, he sustained multiple injuries which contributed to his death; was married to Barbara Pepper.

REYNOLDS, VERA *(1962)* 61 ——Lovely brunette who, in 1924–25, starred for DeMille in three back to back: *Feet of Clay, The Golden Bed, The Road to Yesterday,* in which she was most effective; was excellent also with H. B. Warner in *Silence;* others of the '20s in which she starred: *The Prodigal Daughters, Flapper Wives, Shadow of Paris, Broken Barriers;* played bits in a few in the early '30s: *Dragnet Patrol, Lawless Woman, The Gorilla Ship,* etc.

RIANO, RENIE *(1971)* 72 ——Comedienne who was Maggie in Monogram's "Maggie and Jiggs" series; her rubbery hatchet-face was also humorously in view (in the role of Effie Schneider) in all the "Nancy Drew" pix; was in another 150 from 1937's *Tovarich: Adam Had Four Sons, You Belong to Me, Winter Wonderland, The Time of Your Life,* etc.; left the screen after 1966's *Three on a Couch* to do stage work (began as a kid star on stage, "Little Baby Renie," age 4) and TV (*The Partridge Family, Mayberry R.F.D.,* etc.).

RICE, FLORENCE *(1974)* 67 ——MGM's refreshingly natural, page-boy-blonde leading lady in almost 30 in five years, from 1936; most often cast opposite Robert Young (*Sworn Enemy, The Longest Night, Navy Blue and Gold, Married Before Breakfast,* others), she was Robert Taylor's love interest in *Stand Up and Fight,* Melvyn Douglas' in *Fast Company,* and Walter Pidgeon's in *Phantom Raiders; Four Girls in White* was one of the few in which she received top billing; 1943's *Stand By, All Networks* was her last, after which she did radio-TV publicity, married, retired to Hawaii.

RICE, FRANK *(1936)* 44 ——A comic rustic, Buck, in Laughton's *Ruggles of Red Gap,* and the humorous Grouchy in Warner Baxter's *The Squaw Man,* he had similar supporting roles in the Westerns of Ken Maynard, Buck Jones, George O'Brien: *King of the Arena, Hound of Silver Creek, Somewhere in Sonora,* others.

RICE, GRANTLAND *(1954)* 73 ——Famed sportscaster-writer and father of Florence; did many *Grantland Rice Sportslights* shorts in the '20s and '30s, and won a best short subject Oscar in '43 for *Amphibious Fighters.*

RICE, NORMAN *(1957)* 47 ——Was featured in *The Miracle of Our Lady of Fatima.*

RICE, SAM *(1946)* 72 ——Once called "The King of Burlesque," he was the actor-dad of "Behind the 8-Ball" comedian George O'Hanlon; had small roles in many.

RICH, DICK *(1967)* 58 ——Support in many: *The Ox-Bow Incident* (as Mapes), 1952's *Outcasts of Poker Flat* (Drunk), *Seven Brides for*

Seven Brothers (father of "bride" Julie Newmar), *Oh, You Beautiful Doll* (Burly Man), *Rise and Shine* (Gogo), etc.

RICH, DORIS *(1971)* 52 ——Actress who was one of John Carradine's wives.

RICH, FREDDIE *(1956)* 58 ——He and his famous dance band were featured in *A Wave, a Wac and a Marine* and *Rambling 'Round Radio Row.*

RICH, HELEN *(1963)* 66 ——Was in silents.

RICH, LILLIAN *(1954)* 54 ——Dark-haired beauty from England who starred for DeMille in one (and in a blonde wig), 1925's *The Golden Bed;* was in many, for other directors, in the '20s: *Whispering Smith* with H.B. Warner, *Man to Man* with Harry Carey, *The Ship of Souls* with Bert Lytell, *The Isle of Retribution* with Robert Frazer, etc.; by '30 was getting secondary billing in two-reel comedies (*Northern Exposure, The Eternal Triangle,* etc.) and playing bits in such features as *The Devil Plays* and *Once a Lady.*

RICHARD, FRIEDA *(1946)* 73 ——Austrian character actress in many 1925-35 pix: *The Peak of Fate, Faust, Cinderella, New Year's Eve,* etc., all filmed in Germany or Switzerland.

RICHARDS, ADDISON *(1964)* 61 ——You felt you could trust him (his was that kind of face) to command a battleship, run the police force, keep the bank from failing, get you through an emergency operation; any man who could be the father of Polly Benedict (Ann Rutherford) in the "Andy Hardy" pix had to be upstanding; onscreen from 1933's *Riot,* he was in more than 200: *The Pride of the Yankees* (Coach), *Spellbound* (Police Captain), *Air Force* (Major Daniels), *Boys Town* (Judge), *The Great Lie, Arizona, Flying Tigers,* etc.; when he was bad (as in *The Black Doll* and a few others), the shock was great.

RICHARDS, CHARLES *(1948)* 48 ——Supporting roles in several in the '20s, including the highly praised semi-Western *The Call of the Canyon* ('23).

RICHARDS, GORDON *(1964)* 70 ——Dignified English character who several times played butlers—Crosby's in *High Society,* Garson's in *Mrs. Parkington,* etc.; had perhaps his best chance to shine as Sir Joshua Reynolds in *Kitty;* also was in *Slightly Dangerous, The Wife Takes a Flyer, The Canterville Ghost,* others.

RICHARDS, GRANT *(1963)* 47 ——Handsome young man who, 1937-42, played romantic leads in numerous B's: *My Old Kentucky Home* (with Evelyn Venable), *A Night of Mystery, On Such a Night* (opposite Karen Morley), *Under the Big Top* (with Anne Nagel), *Isle of Destiny, Risky Business,* etc.; offscreen until '59 (the war, radio and stage work), he returned as support in more B's: *Inside the Mafia, Twelve Hours to Kill,* etc.

RICHARDS, PAUL *(1974)* 50 ——Good-looking, suave (sometimes icy-cold) top support: *Beneath the Planet of the Apes* (Mendez), *The Black Whip, Blood Arrow, Apache War Paint, Tall Man Riding, Fixed Bayonets, The Strange One,* etc.; perhaps best known as the star (psychiatrist Dr. McKinley Thompson) of the TV series *Breaking Point.*

RICHARDSON, FRANK *(1962)* 63 ——Between '25 and '30, was youthful support in almost a dozen: Leila Hyams' *Masquerade,* Janet Gaynor's *Sunny Side Up* (as Eddie Rafferty), Clive Brook's *Seven Sinners, Let's Go Places,* plus *Happy Days, Fox Movietone Follies of 1929* (and *of 1930*), in which he sang.

RICHMAN, CHARLES *(1940)* 70 ——He costarred with Norma Talmadge in 1915's *The Battle Cry of Peace* and starred in the 1917 serial *The Secret Kingdom;* in the '20s was support, to Talmadge in *The Sign on the Door,* and other stars in *Trust Your Wife, Has the World Gone Mad?,* etc.; character roles in the next decade in Griffith's last film, *The Struggle* (as Mr. Craig), *George White's Scandals of 1935, The Life of Emile Zola* (M. Delagorgue), *The Adventures of Tom Sawyer* (Judge Thatcher, father of Ann Gillis as Becky), *Dark Victory,* more.

RICHMAN, HARRY *(1972)* 77 ——Debonair and colorful Broadway song-and-dance star *(Ziegfeld Follies)* who strutted splendidly—top hat, tails, and cane—onscreen in the '30s in *Puttin' on the Ritz* (based on his theme song, which he wrote) and *The Music Goes 'Round.*

RICHMOND, KANE *(1973)* 67 ——Except possibly for Buster Crabbe, he was easily the handsomest and best hero in talkie serials; starred gallantly in seven: *The Adventures of Rex and Rinty* ('35); *The Lost City; Spy Smasher; Haunted Harbor; Brenda Starr, Reporter; Jungle Raiders;* and *Brick Bradford* ('47); the leading man in many B's (*Sailor's Lady, Three Russian Girls, Black Market Babies,* etc.), he had his best romantic roles in Alice Faye's *Tail Spin* and Loretta Young's *Ladies Courageous;* left the screen in the late '40s, established a distributing company for ladies' fashions.

RICHMOND, WARNER *(1948)* 53 ——In Barthelmess' *Tol'able David* ('21), he was the handsome older brother beaten and crippled for life by the moronic outlaw; from 1916's *Betty of Graystone* with Owen Moore and Dorothy Gish, had romantic (sometimes second) leads in many silents: *The Heart of Maryland* (both versions), *Sporting Life* with Constance Binney, *The Crowded Hour* with Bebe Daniels, *The Making of O'Malley* with Dorothy Mackaill, etc.; in talkies was classy support (often a crooked smoothie with a Southern accent) in *Hearts in Bondage, So Red the Rose, Happy Landing, This Day and Age,* etc., plus serials (*The Lost Jungle, Phantom Empire, The Secret of Treasure Island*), and many B Westerns.

RICHTER, PAUL *(1961)* 65 ——German star who played the title role in *Siegfried* ('24); also was in *Peter the Pirate, Forbidden Love* (an English pic with Lily Damita), many others.

RICKETTS, TOM *(1939)* 85 ——Character actor from England, bald with a fringe of white and often a disapproving countenance, who was in 50 between '21 and '38: *Bobbed Hair* with Kenneth Harlan, *Within the Law* with Norma Talmadge, *The Cat's Pajamas* with Betty Bronson, *Ambassador Bill, A Farewell to Arms* (as Count Greffi), *The Young in Heart* (Andre), *Bluebeard's Eighth Wife* (Uncle Andre), etc.

RICKSEN, LUCILLE *(1925)* 17 ——Meltingly beautiful girl who was the heroine in the serial *The Social Buccaneer* and, from '21, was in 20 features: *The Old Nest, The Hill Billy* with Jack Pickford, *Those Who Dance* with Blanche Sweet, *The Denial* with Claire Windsor, etc.

RIDGELY, CLEO *(1962)* 59 ——Lovely blonde Lasky star first in 1914's *The Spoilers,* then in *The Love Mask* and *The Yellow Pawn,* in both of which she was billed above her co-star, Wallace Reid; played virtuous women and villainesses, and sometimes directed; in the early '20s had supporting roles in Betty Compson's *The Law and the Woman, The Forgotten Law,* Marie Prevost's *The Beautiful and Damned.*

RIDGELY, JOHN *(1968)* 59 ——A "real Joe," homely handsome with a most engaging grin; Warners used his Main Street naturalness in more than 75 from 1937's *Submarine D-1;* played reporters (*Torchy Gets Her Man*), truck drivers (*They Drive by Night*) and unlucky racing car drivers (*Indianapolis Speedway*), but was most in his element in military uniform: *Air Force* (his best role; starred as intrepid Capt. Quincannon, pilot of the Mary Ann), *Destination Tokyo, God Is My Co-Pilot, Pride of the Marines,* etc.; also was in *Possessed, The Big Sleep, Cry Wolf, Nora Prentiss;* in the '50s, elsewhere, had supporting roles in many: *A Place in the Sun* (Coroner), *The Greatest Show on Earth, Room for One More;* left the screen

after 1953's *Off Limits,* in which he again was in an Army uniform.

RIDGES, STANLEY *(1951)* 59 ——Audiences were flattered to think of this sterling character —fine face, intelligent eyes, small, easy smile, graying-at-the-temples hair—as "typically American"; seemed it—as lawyer, medic, father, military officer; onscreen from '32, he was in more than 60: *The Story of Dr. Wassell* (Commander Bill Goggins), *The Scoundrel, Sergeant York* (Major Buxton), *Wilson* (Admiral Grayton), *The Lady Is Willing, The Mad Miss Manton,* 1947's *Possessed* (compassionate Dr. Williard), *Thelma Jordan,* etc.; was thoroughly dastardly as Shadow in *Winterset* and understatedly fascinating in *The Suspect,* as the Scotland Yard man who played a cat-and-mouse game with murderer Laughton's conscience; was last in Ginger Rogers' *The Groom Wore Spurs;* note: he was English-born.

RIDGEWAY, FRITZI *(1961)* 62 ——Attractive brunette who starred in a few quickies in the '20s (*Face Value,* etc.) but more often supported others: Mary Miles Minter in *Judy of Rogue's Harbor,* Marie Prevost in *Getting Gertie's Garter,* Edward Everett Horton in *Ruggles of Red Gap,* Leatrice Joy in *Nobody's Widow,* etc.; played bits in talkies to '35: *Ladies of the Big House, The Mad Parade,* a few others.

RIESNER, CHUCK *(1962)* 75 ——In *The Kid* he was the rooming-house owner who stole little Jackie Coogan for the reward, and in Another Chaplin film, *The Pilgrim,* on which he was associate director, played the crook who stole the mortgage money from Edna Purviance's mother; in the same pic, his son, Dinky Dean, was the obnoxious kid kicked across the room by Chaplin; in still other Chaplin films, such as *A Dog's Life,* Riesner was also comic support in Owen Moore's *Her Temporary Husband,* Syd Chaplin's *The Man on the Box,* Lloyd Hamilton's *A Self-Made Failure,* etc.; directed many while an actor (*Steamboat Bill Jr., The Missing Link,* others), and when he stopped acting (after 1936's *Everybody Dance*), directed fulltime: *The Big Store, Meet the People, Manhattan Merry-Go-Round, The Traveling Saleswoman;* the last, a Joan Davis pic, featured an actor named Dean Riesner—the former "obnoxious" Dinky Dean—who went on to become the well-known screenwriter of *The Helen Morgan Story, Coogan's Bluff,* etc.

RIETTI, VICTOR *(1963)* 75 ——Italian-born supporting actor whose entire career was in English movies (*Juggernaut, Yellow Canary, Escape Me Never,* etc.) and such made-in-England "Hollywood" movies as *The Story of Esther Costello* (as Signor Gatti), and *The Ghost Goes West.*

RIGA, NADINE *(1968)* 59 ——Support in Dolores Del Rio's *Ramona, For Whom the Bell Tolls,* etc.

RIGBY, ARTHUR *(1971)* 70 ——English support; in *The Third Key,* others.

RIGBY, EDWARD *(1951)* 72 ——Splendid as the father in *The Stars Look Down,* this English character actor was in dozens more: *The Mudlark* (Watchman), *A Yank at Oxford, Kipps, Flying Fortress, I Live in Grosvenor Square, The Ware Case,* etc.

RIGGS, RALPH *(1951)* 66 ——Had a supporting role (Loren Tucker) in *Lost Boundaries.*

RIGGS, TOMMY *(1967)* 57 ——Famous radio ventriloquist who, with his "Betty Lou," was featured in Charles Winninger's *Goodbye Broadway* ('38).

RILEY, GEORGE *(1972)* 72 ——Comic support in Berle's *Over My Dead Body.*

RILEY, JACK *(1933)* 38 ——Was young support in Monte Blue's *A Broken Doll* ('21).

RING, BLANCHE *(1961)* 84 ——Lovely, languid-eyed, dark-haired stage star whose screen appearances were rare: starred in the title role of 1915's *The Yankee Girl,* supported W. C. Fields eleven years later in his first starring vehicle, *It's the Old Army Game,* and in '40 had a small role in Crosby's *If I Had My Way;* was sister of Cyril and stage actress Frances Ring (Mrs. Thomas Meighan), and was for years the wife of Charles Winninger.

RING, CYRIL *(1967)* 74 ——Was Betty Blythe's handsome Lothario in *In Hollywood with Potash and Perlmutter;* in the '20s had supporting roles—besides in the films of others—in many pix starring brother-in-law Thomas Meighan: *Back Home and Broke, The Ne'er-Do-Well, Pied Piper Malone, Homeward Bound,* etc.; active until '47, he had secondary roles in *I Wake Up Screaming,* Abbott & Costello's *One Night in the Tropics* and *In Society,* the Marx Brothers' *Cocoanuts,* Laurel & Hardy's *Great Guns* and *The Bullfighters,* etc.

RIN-TIN-TIN *(1932)* 16 ——German shepherd who, between 1922's *The Man from Hell's River* and a '31 serial, *Lightning Warrior,* was Hollywood's most famous dog star (12,000 fan letters a week); starred courageously—mainly at Warners—in 26 other films: *Rinty of the Desert, Jaws of Steel, A Dog of the Regiment,* etc.; a German attack dog, actually found in a dugout in France in WW I, he was beloved by moviegoers but hated by his colleagues; in the book

Warner Brothers, film historian Charles Higham has noted: "Everyone who worked with this celebrated quadruped is agreed that he was a monster: ill-tempered, vicious, dangerous. He would attack members of the cast without warning, savage his directors, and answer a friendly pat with a menacing growl and perhaps a serious bite."

RIORDAN, ROBERT *(1968)* 54 ——Support in a Steve Brodie B, *Arson for Hire.*

RIOS, LALO *(1973)* 46 ——As the second male lead in Joseph Losey's *The Lawless,* he gave a sensational performance as the young Mexican immigrant wrongly accused of attacking an American girl; was also in *City Beneath the Sea.*

RIPLEY, RAY *(1938)* 47 ——Support in the '20s in action pix (Lefty Flynn's *Smilin' at Trouble*), Westerns (*The Blazing Trail*), serials (Eddie Polo's *The Vanishing Dagger*), comedies (*Why Trust Your Husband?*), etc.

RIPLEY, ROBERT L. *(1949)* 55 ——Headlined in many shorts based on his *Believe It or Not.*

RISCOE, ARTHUR *(1954)* 57 ——Comedian prominently cast in several British films of the '30s and early '40s: *Kipps* (as Chitterlow), *For Love of You, For the Love of Mike, Going Gay,* etc.; was not everyone's cup of tea, including critic Graham Greene, who wrote after one film that he had to bear "with patience Mr. Riscoe's contorted music-hall face which thrust every joke down one's gullet with the relentless energy of the machine that corks the bottles in a lemonade factory."

RISDON, ELIZABETH *(1958)* 71 ——Fine gray-haired character actress whose English speech fell musically on the ear whether she played a country woman (Rooney's *Huckleberry Finn*), a Southern aristocrat (Goddard's mother in *Reap the Wild Wind*), a city woman with charm and bite (Aunt Mary in *Theodora Goes Wild*) or one with ice water in her veins (daughter Cora Payne in *Make Way for Tomorrow*), "typical" American mothers (Priscilla Lane's in *The Roaring Twenties*), or well-bred Englishwomen (*Random Harvest*); on American screens from 1935's *Guard That Girl* through 1952's *Scaramouche,* she was in more than 60 top movies; in 1913–17 English movies, had been a star—and a great beauty.

RISING, WILLIAM S. *(1930)* 79 ——Played Edmund Burke in Griffith's *America.*

RISS, DAN *(1970)* 60 ——Character who almost always played representatives of the law: the District Attorney in *Kiss Tomorrow Goodbye,*

Neff in *Panic in the Streets*, Lt. Imlay in *Vice Squad*, Stanley in *Pinky*, etc.

RISSO, ATTILIO *(1967)* 54 ——Member of the musical group The Vagabonds which was featured in Abbott & Costello's *It Ain't Hay*.

RITCHIE, BILLIE *(1921)* 42 ——A comedian patterned after Chaplin who starred in many L-KO comedies (released by Universal in '14) and in 1916 one- and two-reelers for Fox.

RITTER, ESTHER *(1925)* 23 ——Minor roles in silents.

RITTER, TEX *(1974)* 67 ——Singing cowboy star right up there behind Autry and Rogers; was a Western mainstay from 1936's *Song of the Gringo* through 1955's *Apache Ambush*, making the Top Ten Western Stars list 1937–41 and again in '44 and '45; a few of the 85 in which he and his pony White Flash (several of the same name, really) starred: *Swing, Cowboy, Swing; Starlight Over Texas; Rhythm of the Rio Grande; The Whispering Skull*, etc.; remained active in show business after his starring days in pix: narrated a Glenn Ford movie (*Cowboy*), sang the title songs behind the credits of five others (*High Noon, Trooper Hook, Wichita, The Marshal's Daughter, Down Liberty Road*), acted in one *Zane Grey Theater* episode on TV, and—after relocating in Nashville—sang each week on *Grand Ole Opry*; in '66, besides running his franchise restaurant empire ("Tex Ritter's Chuck Wagons"), attempted a comeback as the star of a low-budget Western, *Girl from Tobacco Row*, and, that same year, appeared as himself in two others—*Nashville Rebel* and *What Am I Bid?*; ran for U.S. Senator in Tennessee in '70 and lost; in the summer of '73 made a highly successful personal appearance tour in the United Kingdom; son John is now a Hollywood actor—not in Westerns; his last record album, released Dec. '73, was titled *Tex Ritter—An American Legend*, and perhaps he was.

RITTER, THELMA *(1969)* 63 ——Knowing *All About Eve*—and this sardonically funny character did—got her no Supporting Oscar, though she was nominated; neither did *The Mating Season, With a Song in My Heart, Pickup on South Street, Pillow Talk*, or *Bird Man of Alcatraz*, and she was nominated for each; was wonderfully wry in many other memorable pix: *Miracle on 34th Street* (and she seemed one, bursting fullblown as a star comedienne in her debut movie), *A Letter to Three Wives, Titanic, Rear Window, A Hole in the Head, The Misfits, The Model and the Marriage Broker*; no other actress ever made so much of being salty and sassy, Brooklyn and bitter.

RITZ, AL *(1965)* 62 ——The Ritz Brothers' Harry is the one critics most often single out for praise, but his antics would not have been so funny without look-alike older brothers Jimmy and Al—and if there was a "best looking" one in the trio, it was Al; Al entered movies before his brothers, playing a bit in a 1918 Harold Lockwood Western, *The Avenging Trail*; as a team in Hollywood, they were featured in several 20th Century-Fox musicals (*Sing, Baby, Sing; On the Avenue*, etc.) before the studio promoted them to full stardom in 1937's *Life Begins at College*; starred there in five more: *Kentucky Moonshine; Straight, Place and Show; Pack Up Your Troubles; The Gorilla; The Three Musketeers*; then starred at Universal in four: *Argentine Nights, Behind the Eight-Ball, Never a Dull Moment, Hi'Ya Chum*; returned to night clubs and did a few TV guestings.

RIVIERE, FRED "CURLY" *(1935)* 60 —— Support in silent Westerns such as Buddy Roosevelt's *The Dangerous Dub*.

ROACH, BERT *(1971)* 79 ——Large-sized, funny man-character actor who was prominently featured in dozens from 1925's *Excuse Me* to 1947's *Perils of Pauline;* was in Marion Davies' *Tillie the Toiler, The Crowd, Arrowsmith* (Beulah Bondi's son), *No, No, Nanette* ('30), *Love Me Tonight, San Francisco, The Great Waltz, Algiers, The Man in the Iron Mask*, etc.

ROACH, MARGARET *(1964)* 43 ——Blonde, busty daughter of producer Hal Roach who, in her late teens, had small roles in several of her father's films: *Turnabout, Captain Fury, Road Show*, etc.; married cowboy Bob Livingston, left the screen.

ROACHE, VIOLA *(1961)* 75 ——Plump, gray, fine character actress from Broadway who was onscreen in just three: two Crawford pix, *Harriet Craig* (housekeeper Mrs. Harold) and *Goodbye, My Fancy*, and Astaire's *Royal Wedding* (as Sarah Churchill's mother).

ROBARDS, JASON, SR. *(1963)* 70 ——On-screen from 1921's *The Gilded Lily* through a '61 Presley pic, *Wild in the Country*, he was in more than 100, almost always as an arch villain; among his films: *Polly of the Movies, Paris, Streets of Shanghai, Abraham Lincoln* (as Herndon), *The Crusades* (Slave/Amir), *I Stole a Million, The Master Race, Isle of the Dead, The Falcon's Alibi;* except for *The Second Woman* ('51), was inactive in movies in the '50s due to an eye infection; recovered, he appeared on Broadway in '58 in *The Disenchanted* with his namesake son.

ROBBINS, MARC *(1931)* 63 ——Character actor in several in the '20s: *The Gray Dawn*, Bert Lytell's *Alias Jimmy Valentine*, Gladys Walton's *The Girl Who Ran Wild*, etc.

ROBBINS, RICHARD *(1969)* 50 ——In *The Wrong Man*, he was the "right" man—the thief for whose crime look-alike Fonda was jailed.

ROBER, RICHARD *(1952)* 46 ——Big, thick-skinned, pockmarked tough guy whose best opportunities were starring roles in *Kid Monk Baroni* and *The Well*; played hoods, cops, military men; was in *Call Northside 777, Task Force, Larceny, Any Number Can Play, The Rose Bowl Story*, etc.; also was in *Jet Pilot*, made in '51 but released five years after his death.

ROBERTI, LYDA *(1938)* 31 ——Raucous, sexy, blonde comedienne-singer who was with Patsy Kelly in *Nobody's Baby* and a couple of two-reelers (*At Sea Ashore, Hill Tillies*); may be best recalled for the hilarious takeoff she did on Garbo—as Continental spy Mata Machree—in *Million Dollar Legs*; Polish-born, European-educated, Broadway-starred (*You Said It*), she first exhibited her bombastic humor in Oakie's *Dancers in the Dark* and Cantor's *The Kid from Spain*, both in '32; also was in *College Rhythm, George White's 1935 Scandals, Wide Open Faces*, others.

ROBERTS, ALBERT *(1941)* 39 ——Actor-husband of starlet Peggy Shannon, who killed himself two weeks after her death.

ROBERTS, CLEDGE *(1957)* 52 ——Wavy-haired light Broadway lead; in an occasional movie.

ROBERTS, DICK *(1966)* 69 ——Banjo player who was in *Banjo on My Knee*.

ROBERTS, EDITH *(1935)* 36 ——Brunette beauty who became a Universal star at 18; there, she was in *The Unknown Wife, The Adorable Savage, Thunder Island, Bill Henry*, etc.; elsewhere, sometimes with lighter hair, was in *Age of Innocence* with Beverly Bayne, *Seven Keys to Baldpate* opposite Douglas Mac-Lean, *On Thin Ice* opposite Tom Moore, etc.; was last onscreen in 1929's *The Wagon Master*, a talkie Western, with Ken Maynard—back at Universal.

ROBERTS, FLORENCE *(1927)* 56 ——Dark-haired star of 1913's *Sappho*.

ROBERTS, FLORENCE *(1940)* 78 ——The loving grandmother in all "The Jones Family" comedies with Spring Byington; character roles in many others in the '30s: *The Life of Emile Zola* (as Muni's mother, Madame Zola), *Miss Fane's Baby Is Stolen, Next Time We Love, Les Miserables* (as Toussaint), *Personal Secretary*, etc.

ROBERTS, GLEN *(1974)* 53 ——Had a supporting role, as a tenement youth, in 1953's *Girls in the Night;* resumed his real name, Leonard Freeman, became a producer, created TV's *Hawaii Five-O;* was married to former actress Joan Taylor.

ROBERTS, J. H. *(1961)* 76 ——Support in many British talkies: *Accused, White Face, Juggernaut, The Divorce of Lady X, Troopship, The Agitator*, etc.

ROBERTS, LEONA *(1954)* 74 ——Character actress most memorable as the wife of old Dr. Meade (Harry Davenport) in *Gone With the Wind* and as the aged country woman in *Of Human Hearts;* in many: *Kentucky, The Blue Bird* (as Sybil Jason's grandmother), *Bringing Up Baby* (Barry Fitzgerald's wife), etc.; last in 1947's *Boomerang*, as the mother of Philip Coolidge.

ROBERTS, NANCY *(1962)* 70 ——Support in English pix: *Prison Without Bars, Black Narcissus*, etc.

ROBERTS, SARA JANE *(1968)* 44 ——One of the little girls in "Our Gang" around 1930.

ROBERTS, THAYER *(1968)* 65 ——Support in a '51 Sid Melton B, *Sky High*.

ROBERTS, THEODORE *(1928)* 67 ——Was called "The Grand Duke of Hollywood," for no character star in silents was more highly esteemed than he; usually played an oldster with a flinty exterior who, inside, was pure gold; on-screen from 1910's *Uncle Tom* (as Simon Legree; no heart of mush there), then in 1913's *Arizona*, he signed in '14 a contract with producer Jesse L. Lasky highly publicized as being "for life"; Lasky's company went through several name changes, finally becoming Paramount, but except for three loanouts to Realart and one to Ince, Roberts never worked for another studio until the last year of his life; had top roles at this one company in 96 features—23 directed by Cecil B. DeMille and many others by William C. de Mille; after 1914's *The Call of the North* he was in *The Circus Man, The Girl of the Golden West* (sheriff Jack Rance), *Pudd'n Head Wilson* (title role), *Joan the Woman* (Bishop Cauchon), *The Girl Who Came Back, Grumpy* (apotheosis of his lovable-old-codger starring roles), *M'liss* with Pickford, *The Roaring Road* with Wallace Reid, 1923's *The Ten Commandments* (as Moses), *The Affairs of An-*

atol, etc.; in '28 was in one at MGM (as the portrait painter in John Gilbert's *The Masks of the Devil*) and two at Pathe *(Ned McCobb's Daughter*, as star Irene Rich's father, and *Noisy Neighbors* with Eddie Quillan).

ROBERTSHAW, JERROLD *(1941)* 75 —— Emaciated-looking actor in English pix; starred in the title role of 1923's *Don Quixote;* in other silent films: *The Arab, Dombey and Son, The Bonnie Briar Bush*, etc.

ROBERTSON, IMOGENE *(1948)* 42 ——See Mary Nolan.

ROBERTSON, JAMES "SCOTTY" *(1936)* 77 ——Character roles in silents.

ROBERTSON, JEAN *(1967)* 73 ——She was featured in a '22 Lee-Bradford pic, *Flesh and Spirit.*

ROBERTSON, JOHN S. *(1964)* 86 ——Starred in one—1916's *An Enemy to the King*—before becoming known as "the best-liked director in Hollywood"; directed Pickford in 1922's *Tess of the Storm Country* (the only remake she ever did; superior to her '14 version), John Barrymore in *Dr. Jekyll and Mr. Hyde*, Barthelmess in *The Enchanted Cottage*, etc.

ROBERTSON, ORIE O. *(1964)* 83 ——Support in silent Westerns including Pete Morrison's *Bucking the Truth.*

ROBERTSON, STUART *(1958)* 57 ——Actor-brother of British star Anna Neagle; in many of her pix: *Bitter Sweet, Irene, No, No, Nanette, etc.;* also in *A Yank in the R.A.F., This Above All, Forever and a Day, The Black Swan.*

ROBERTSON, WILLARD *(1948)* 62 ——Jovial, prosperous-looking character from Texas, a real-life lawyer once publicized as having turned down the chance of being a United States Attorney to become a screen actor; had been on stage as a youth; generally played vested, gold-watch-chained lawyers—in *Renegades, Jesse James, My Little Chickadee*, etc.; often was a doctor (*If I Had a Million*) or policeman (*Winterset*); in more than 100 from 1930: *Skippy, Tugboat Annie, The Gorgeous Hussy, To Each His Own, Deep Valley*, etc.

ROBEY, GEORGE *(1954)* 85 ——Comedian who starred, as Sancho Panza, in 1923's *Don Quixote;* among his other British pix: *Chu Chin Chow, Henry V* (as Sir John Falstaff), *The Pickwick Papers, Waltz Time*, etc.; long billed "the prime minister of mirth," he was knighted by the Crown.

ROBINS, EDWARD H. *(1955)* 74 ——Support in *Meet the Missus* and *Music for Madame.*

ROBINSON, BILL *(1949)* 71 ——The beloved "Bojangles" whose dancing feet and eyes—and beatific smile—were a screen joy from 1930's *Dixiana;* taught Shirley Temple to dance up and down that staircase in *The Little Colonel* and tapped alongside her in five others: *Dimples, The Littlest Rebel, Curly Top, Rebecca of Sunnybrook Farm, Just Around the Corner;* was also in *Hooray for Love, In Old Kentucky* with Will Rogers, *The Big Broadcast of 1936;* had a straight role in Claire Trevor's *One Mile from Heaven; Stormy Weather* was his last.

ROBINSON, DEWEY *(1950)* 52 ——Big bruiser with black eyebrows and the neck of an ox who played gangsters and funny prizefighters; was in more than 70 from 1931's *Enemies of the Law: Blonde Venus, She Done Him Wrong* (as Spider Kane), *A Midsummer Night's Dream* (Snug), *The Big Street, Dillinger, Pardon My Past, The Big Store, My Friend Irma*, etc.

ROBINSON, EDWARD G. *(1973)* 79 ——An irreplaceable star, a "little giant" of the screen who, in zesty performances in 101 films, was, incredibly, never nominated for an Oscar; on-screen in a supporting role in one silent, 1923's *The Bright Shawl*, he was a star from his first talkie, 1929's *The Hole in the Wall* with Colbert; his eighth talkie, *Little Caesar*, put him on the movie map; among those that kept him there: *A Slight Case of Murder, The Amazing Dr. Clitterhouse, Confessions of a Nazi Spy, The Sea Wolf, Tales of Manhattan, Double Indemnity, The Woman in the Window, Scarlet Street, Our Vines Have Tender Grapes, Key Largo, All My Sons, The Ten Commandments* ('56), *The Cincinnati Kid;* his personal favorite: *Dr. Ehrlich's Magic Bullet* ("This character obsessed me"); his last was *Soylent Green*, released in '73 shortly before his autobiography, *All My Yesterdays*, was published (posthumously); early in January 1973, when terminally ill, he was notified the Academy of Motion Picture Arts and Sciences would present him a special Oscar "for his outstanding contribution to motion pictures"; the award was duly made on March 27 but he was not alive to receive it.

ROBINSON, EDWARD G., JR. *(1974)* 40 —— E.G.'s only child, known to magazine readers of the '30s, via his father's publicity, as Manny; had minor supporting roles in a few, including *Screaming Eagles.*

ROBINSON, FORREST *(1924)* 64 ——Memorable as the Judge in Pickford's '22 version of *Tess of the Storm Country;* in Barthelmess' *Tol'able David* was leading lady Gladys Hulette's Grandpa Hatburn; also was in *When a Man's a Man, Ashes of Vengeance, Good Bad Boy,* others.

ROBINSON, FRANCES *(1971)* 55 ——Blonde with a page-boy hairdo and a resemblance to Lupino who had leading lady roles in many B's of the '30s and '40s (*Secret of a Nurse, Risky Business, The Invisible Man Returns, The Lone Wolf Keeps a Date,* etc.) and two serials (*Tim Tyler's Luck* and *Red Barry*).

ROBINSON, GERTRUDE *(1962)* 71 ——Dark-curled beauty starred by Griffith when having difficulty with Mary Pickford—as in 1909's *Pippa Passes* (role originally intended for Pickford) and *The Open Gate;* in many of his early Biograph films including, in a supporting role, *Judith of Bethulia;* starred for other directors in *The Faith Healer* ('12) and *The Bells* ('13), and for DeMille in *The Arab* ('15); in support in the '20s, she retired after 1925's *On Thin Ice* starring Tom Moore.

ROBINSON, JACKIE *(1972)* 53 ——First black major-league baseball star; played himself in *The Jackie Robinson Story.*

ROBINSON, RUTH *(1966)* 78 ——Character actress onscreen in the '30s and '40s; played little Dickie Moore's mother in *The Story of Louis Pasteur,* was the Queen Regent in Francis Lederer's *The Lone Wolf in Paris;* also was in *China Clipper, The Case of the Velvet Claws, The Spider Woman Strikes,* etc.

ROBINSON, "SPIKE" *(1942)* 58 ——Support in several in the '20s: the Jack Dempsey serial *Daredevil Jack, The Fear Fighter, The Foolish Age,* etc.; earlier, this real-life boxer had been hired as D.W. Griffith's athletic trainer and on-set sparring partner and had a featured role in the director's *The Musketeers of Pig Alley* ('12).

ROBLES, RICHARD *(1940)* 38 ——Minor support in *Union Pacific.*

ROBLES, RUDY *(1970)* 60 ——Supporting actor from the Philippines who was in many from 1939's *The Real Glory,* in which he was Lt. Yabo; among his pix: *Wake Island* (Triunfo), *Across the Pacific, South of Pago Pago, Nocturne,* the "Rusty" series, *Okinawa,* etc.

ROBSON, ANDREW *(1921)* 54 ——Character actor in several 1918–21 movies: the Douglas MacLean comedy *One a Minute, Mother O'-Mine, Alarm Clock Andy, Scratch My Back, Black Roses,* etc.

ROBSON, MAY *(1942)* 77 ——Crusty, twinkly-eyed, no-nonsense old darling who was onscreen steadily from 1926's *Pals in Paradise,* in

more than 60; had starred earlier ('15) in one: *How Molly Made Good;* starred most memorably in one talkie, Capra's *Lady for a Day,* as Apple Annie (nominated for an Oscar as Best Actress); was also at the top of her warm-gruff form in *The Adventures of Tom Sawyer* (as Aunt Polly), *Bringing Up Baby* (Hepburn's Aunt Elizabeth), *Dinner at Eight, If I Had a Million,* Garbo's *Anna Karenina, Yes, My Darling Daughter, Irene,* and in her many grandmother roles (Gaynor's *A Star Is Born, They Made Me a Criminal, Four Daughters* and its sequels); the latter roles were typecasting—in real life was several times a grandmother; *Joan of Paris,* with Michele Morgan, was her last.

ROBSON, MRS. STUART *(1924)* 56——Support in Alice Brady's *His Bridal Night.*

ROBYNS, WILLIAM *(1936)* 80 ——Character in several in the '20s and early '30s: *The Fair Cheat, Get-Rich-Quick Wallingford, The Expert, Elmer and Elsie,* etc.

ROCHE, FRANK *(1963)* 59 ——Starred in a 1960 B, *The Prime Time.*

ROCHE, JOHN *(1952)* 56 ——In 1926's *The Return of Peter Grimm,* ghostly Alec B. Francis returned to earth and prevented Janet Gaynor from a disastrous marriage to him; in many other silents: *Lucretia Lombard, A Lost Lady, The Man Upstairs,* etc.; in talkies to '35, he had supporting roles in *The Cohens and the Kellys in Hollywood, Monte Carlo, Winner Take All, Just My Luck,* etc.

ROCK, CHARLES *(1919)* 53 ——Starred in the '14 English pic *A Christmas Carol* and in 1918's *The Better 'Ole.*

ROCKWELL, JACK *(1947)* 60s ——A regular in Charles Starrett Westerns, he usually played the sheriff, but was sometimes a villain or rancher; was in *The Stranger from Texas, The Lawless Nineties, Cherokee Strip, Under Western Skies,* many more; also played sheriffs in two serials: Rin-Tin-Tin Jr.'s *The Law of the Wild,* Allan Lane's *Daredevils of the West.*

RODE, WALTER *(1973)* ——Support in George Raft's *Johnny Allegro.*

RODGERS, WALTER *(1951)* 64 ——Was young support in silent serials starring William Duncan (*The Fighting Trail, Vengeance and the Woman*), and in action pix of the '20s: Earle Williams' *The Silver Car,* Antonio Moreno's *The Secret of the Hills, Rugged Waters,* etc.

RODILAK, CHARLES *(1972)* 65 ——Supporting actor from Czechoslovakia; many minor roles.

RODNEY, EARLE *(1932)* 41 ——Muscular, good-looking Christie Comedies star who was opposite Colleen Moore in *A Roman Scandal* and Dorothy Devore in *Winter Has Come;* a few of his others: *Secrets of a Beauty Parlor, Crooked to the End, The Nick of Time Baby.*

RODNEY, JACK *(1967)* 51 ——Support in British pix: *The Criminal, The Horse Without a Head,* etc.

RODRIGUEZ, ESTELITA *(1966)* 50 ——See Estelita.

ROGERS, CARL D. *(1965)* 66 ——Comic support in early "Our Gang" comedies.

ROGERS, MILDRED *(1973)* 74 ——Singer-actress first under contract to MGM in '25; in numerous musicals, Westerns, and B's, one of the last being a featured role in Irene Hervey's *The Girl Said No* ('37).

ROGERS, RENE *(1966)* 65 ——Lovely brunette who starred in 1916's *Where Are My Children?*

ROGERS, WILL *(1935)* 55 ——Folksy, beloved humorist-star from Oklahoma who radiated love for all mankind; most fondly recalled for his many country-brand comedies at Fox in the '30s: *Lightnin', State Fair, A Connecticut Yankee, David Harum, Ambassador Bill, Judge Priest, Handy Andy, Steamboat Round the Bend, The County Chairman,* etc.; earlier, a lariat-twirling *Ziegfeld Follies* comedian on Broadway, he starred in many silents; after 1918's *Laughing Bill Hyde,* was in *Cupid, the Cowpoke; Jes' Call Me Jim; The Headless Horseman; Honest Hutch; Boys Will Be Boys,* etc.; was portrayed onscreen by his look-alike son, Will Rogers Jr., in *The Will Rogers Story* ('52), *Look for the Silver Lining,* and *The Eddie Cantor Story,* and onstage by James Whitmore; his syndicated humorous columns on politics, widely popular in the '30s, have been re-syndicated in recent years.

ROGNAN, LORRAINE *(1969)* 57 ——Tiny comic dancer; she and her husband-partner (Lorraine & Rognan) were a funny highlight in 1942's *The Fleet's In.*

ROLAND, FREDRIC *(1936)* 50 ——Support in a '35 RKO comedy, *The Rainmakers.*

ROLAND, RUTH *(1937)* 44 ——Blonde (a wig) Pearl White was #1 serial queen of silent days, auburn-haired Ruth was #2; turned to serials after a four-year (1911–14), 200-movie (one- and two-reel) apprenticeship at Kalem, playing leads in Westerns, comedies, melodramas; between 1915's *The Red Circle* and 1923's *Haunted Valley,* she starred precariously (though she did have numerous doubles—usually men—for dangerous stunts) in nine other serials: *The Neglected Wife, The Tiger's Trail, The Adventures of Ruth, Ruth of the Rockies, The Avenging Arrow, White Eagle, Timber Queen, Ruth of the Range, Hands Up;* starred in several features between serials (*Love and the Law, Would You Do It?,* etc.); starred in two after her serial days, both poorly received by critics and the public alike: *Where the Worst Begins* and *Down Dollar* with Henry B. Walthall; had a secondary role in one more, her last, silent—Anna Q. Nilsson's *The Masked Woman;* made a quickie talkie, *Reno,* in '30 ("Ruth Roland's screen comeback. She looks beautiful but her acting is hopelessly old-fashioned," wrote *Photoplay's* critic); starred in just one more movie, in Canada and almost unknown in the U.S., *From Nine to Nine* ('36).

ROLLETT, RAYMOND *(1961)* 54 ——Portly character, with many chins and center-parted hair, who played cops, solicitors, doctors in British pix: *Gone to Earth, A Kid for Two Farthings, Men of Sherwood Forest, The Elusive Pimpernel, Pastor Hall,* etc.

ROLLINS, DAVID *(1952)* 44 ——Handsome, dark-haired young leading man onscreen 1927–33; starred opposite Sue Carol in his first, *Win That Girl;* also was in *The High School Hero, Prep and Pep, The Air Circus, The Big Trail* (as heroine Marguerite Churchill's brother); last starred for Hal Roach in "The Boy Friends," series of two-reel comedies.

ROLLOW, PRESTON *(1947)* 76 ——Character actor in silents.

ROMANOFF, MIKE *(1971)* 81 ——Owner of "Romanoff's," a celebrated Beverly Hills restaurant, this famous phony Russian "Prince" played minor roles in several: *Goodbye, Charlie; Arch of Triumph, Tony Rome, A Guide for the Married Man,* etc.

ROME, STEWART *(1965)* 78 ——One of England's earliest movie stars (1906's *Justice*), this matinee idol of the stage starred in many in the '20s: *The Prodigal Son, The Desert Sheik, Gentleman Rider, Sweet Lavender,* etc.; was a character actor later in *One of Our Aircraft Is Missing, Wings of the Morning, Dinner at the Ritz,* etc.

ROMER, LEILA *(1944)* 66 ——Character in Mary Miles Minter's *Anne of Green Gables.*

ROMER, TOMI *(1969)* 45 ——On TV in *The Phil Silvers Show,* she was in one minor film, *It Took a Miracle.*

ROONER, CHARLES *(1954)* 53 ——Character actor from Austria who lived in Mexico and appeared in Hollywood pix made there: Glenn Ford's *Plunder of the Sun* (as Captain Bergman), John Ford's *The Pearl*, etc.

ROONEY, PAT *(1933)* 41 ——Actor in Essanay silents.

ROONEY, PAT *(1962)* 82 ——Famous stage comic-dancer who starred in 1924's *Show Business;* later did several Universal shorts, and was last onscreen in the all-star *Variety Time* ('48).

ROOPE, FAY *(1961)* 68 ——Stern-faced, gray-haired character actor who gave many strong performances in the '50s: *Viva Zapata!* (as Diaz), *You're in the Navy Now* (Battleship Admiral), *Carbine Williams, The F.B.I. Story* (as MacCutcheon), *Deadline U.S.A., Washington Story,* etc.

ROPER, JACK *(1966)* 62 ——Supporting actor onscreen from 1928's *The Red Mark* who often played villains in Westerns: *West of Carson City, Heroes of the Saddle, Ridin' the Cherokee Trail,* etc.; was also in *Angels Over Broadway, Swing Fever, Gentleman Joe Palooka,* etc.

ROQUEMORE, HENRY *(1943)* 55 ——Played country types for 15 years in Westerns (*The Wagon Show, Romance of the West, The Parting of the Trails,* etc.) and others (*The Arkansas Traveler, Hearts in Bondage, Barefoot Boy,* many more).

ROQUEVERT, NOEL *(1973)* 81 ——Noted French actor; in *Fanfan the Tulip* was third-billed as the recruiting sergeant who signed up star Gerard Philipe for the Seven Years War; was also in *Justice Is Done, Diabolique, The Sheep Has Five Legs,* many others.

RORKE, MARGARET HAYDEN *(1969)* 85 ——Character actress-mother of Hayden Rorke.

ROSAR, ANNIE *(1963)* 75 ——Austrian actress who, after a few starring silents, had character roles in many European films: *Marika, Embezzled Heaven, The Devil Makes Three, The Mozart Story,* etc.

ROSAY, FRANCOISE *(1974)* 82 ——White-haired (for many later years) French character star who acted with distinction in many in France, England, and the U.S.; in France: *Carnival in Flanders* (the burgomaster's wife), *Un Carnet de Bal, The Seven Deadly Sins* (Michele Morgan's mother in the "Pride" episode), *The Devil Is an Empress,* etc.; in England: *Quartet* (in "The Alien Corn" episode was the music expert who informed the aristocratic youth he would never make a concert pianist, inadvert-

ently provoking his suicide), *Saraband, Johnny Frenchman,* others; for American companies she acted in *September Affair, That Lady, The Sound and the Fury, Me and the Colonel,* etc.; last played a cameo role in the Maximilian Schell production *The Pedestrian* ('74).

ROSCOE, ALAN *(1933)* 44 ——Support in many in the '20s and early '30s: Colleen Moore's *Flirting With Love,* Harry Langdon's *Long Pants,* Esther Ralston's *The Sawdust Paradise,* Rudy Vallee's *The Vagabond Lover, Dirigible, Hell Divers, The Last Mile, The Death Kiss,* etc.

ROSE, BLANCHE *(1953)* 74 ——Character actress who several times played rural women in Charles Ray comedies: *The Barnstormer, The Old Swimmin' Hole, Smudge;* last had a small role in *The Paradine Case.*

ROSE, JEWEL *(1970)* ——Supporting roles.

ROSELEIGH, JACK *(1940)* 54 ——Support in several '20s melodramas: *That Girl Montana, Singing River, Bare Knuckles,* etc.

ROSELLE, WILLIAM *(1945)* 67 ——Support in silents: the Billie Burke serial *Gloria's Romance,* Constance Talmadge's *Wedding Bells,* Elsie Ferguson's *The Avalanche,* etc.

ROSEMOND, CLINTON *(1966)* 82 ——Black actor who, in his 50s, gave a most memorable performance in *They Won't Forget,* as Tump Redwine, the janitor wrongfully accused of murdering Lana Turner—a portrayal still spoken of with admiration by the film's director, Mervyn LeRoy; previously in *The Green Pastures* (as the Prophet), he later had small roles in many (*The Toy Wife, Calling Dr. Kildare, Blossoms in the Dust, Safari,* the serial *Jungle Queen,* etc.), but there was never to be another *They Won't Forget.*

ROSENBERG, SARAH *(1964)* 90 ——Character actress in early silents.

ROSENTHAL, HARRY *(1953)* 52 ——Big, bluff character in several Preston Sturges films: *The Miracle of Morgan's Creek* (Mr. Schwartz), *The Great McGinty* (Louie), *Christmas in July, The Great Moment;* also was in *Johnny Apollo* (as the Pianist; was a real-life pianist-orchestra leader), *Unfinished Business* (again the Pianist), *Wife, Husband and Friend,* etc.

ROSING, BODIL *(1942)* 63 ——Danish-accented character actress who almost always played maids, nursemaids, or Teutonic mothers; had small parts from a '25 ZaSu Pitts pic, *Pretty Ladies,* in dozens: *Lights of Old New*

York, Sunrise, The Bishop Murder Case, Conquest, The Painted Veil, Roberta, You Can't Take It With You, Beasts of Berlin, etc.

ROSLEY, ADRIAN (1937) 47 ——Character actor from France who was in 25 from 1933: The Garden of Allah (Mustapha), Roberta (the Professor), Gaynor's A Star Is Born (Makeup Man who tried out "Crawford lips," etc., on the aspiring actress), Viva Villa! (with Henry Armetta, one of the Mendoza Brothers), Alibi Ike, etc.

ROSMER, MILTON (1971) 90 ——Character actor in British (or English-made) pix: The Stars Look Down (friendly Member of Parliament), Donat's Goodbye Mr. Chips (Chatteris), Fame Is the Spur, The Monkey's Paw, etc.; onscreen from '13.

ROSS, ANTHONY (1955) 49 ——Played the heartless stage producer, Phil Cook, in Crosby's The Country Girl, his last film; previously in Kiss of Death, The Gunfighter, Perfect Strangers, Rogue Cop, Taxi, etc.; perhaps most famous for creating the role of The Gentleman Caller on Broadway in The Glass Menagerie.

ROSS, BARNEY (1967) 57 ——Boxing champ; onscreen in Requiem for a Heavyweight.

ROSS, BETTY (1947) 66 ——Often in Tom Mix's silent Westerns.

ROSS, CHRIS (1970) 24 ——He had supporting roles in Ustinov's Viva Max! (as Gomez), How Sweet It Is; a member of the San Francisco improvisational comedy group, The Committee, he was with them in Petulia and their own feature, A Session with the Committee; sometimes billed Christopher.

ROSS, CHURCHILL (1962) 61 ——A "campus type," a comic blond lad in round specs, he was at Universal in the late '20s in its "The Collegians" two-reel comedies and the features in which the "gang" appeared: The College Hero, College Love; also was with Marion Nixon in the youth comedy The Fourflusher.

ROSS, HERBERT (1934) 68 ——Support in English pix: Hitchcock's The Skin Game, etc.

ROSS, MARION (1966) 68 ——Supporting actress in The Proud and the Profane (as a Red Cross Worker), The Glenn Miller Story (Polly Haynes), Operation Petticoat (Lt. Colfax), Forever Female (secretary Patty), etc.; was first onscreen in 1920's Over the Hill.

ROSS, THOMAS W. (1959) 86 ——Co-starred with Jane Darwell in 1914's The Only Son; supporting roles in later silents: Fine Feathers with Eugene Pallette, Without Limit; in talkies was in The Mortal Storm (Professor Werner), Remember the Night, The Remarkable Andrew (Judge Krebbs, before whom the "ghosts" of Andrew Jackson and George Washington plead to prevent Holden's being committed as a lunatic), etc.

ROSSON, ARTHUR (1960) 70 ——Acted in a few silents before directing Raymond Griffith in Wet Paint, Madge Bellamy in Silk Legs, etc.

ROTH, SANDY (1943) 54 ——A Sennett comedian who later had supporting roles in Loretta Young's Midnight Mary, Harlow's The Beast of the City, Hell's Highway, etc.

ROUGHWOOD, OWEN (1947) 70 ——Supporting actor.

ROUNSEVILLE, ROBERT (1974) 60 ——Famous operatic tenor who starred in Tales of Hoffman and was also in Carousel as the straitlaced beau, Mr. Snow, of Barbara Ruick as Carrie.

ROUSE, HALLOCK (1930) 32 ——Minor role in Warner Baxter's "Charlie Chan" pic, Behind That Curtain.

ROWAN, DON (1966) 60 ——In the serial Flash Gordon Conquers the Universe, he was the pilot of Ming the Merciless' spaceship; often a bad guy, he was also in Brother Orchid, The Devil's Playground, Racket Busters, The Return of Sophie Lang, etc.

ROWLANDS, ART (1944) 46 ——Support in several early talkies: Mystery Valley, Lightnin' Shot, The Black Pearl, Colleen Moore's Synthetic Sin, etc.; later in "Three Stooges" two-reelers.

ROY, HARRY (1971) 67 ——Famous English bandleader who starred in 1936's Everything Is Rhythm.

ROYCE, BRIGHAM (1933) 69 ——Support in Marguerite Clark's Helene of the North.

ROYCE, JULIAN (1946) 76 ——Support in Criminal at Large ('33).

ROYCE, LIONEL (1946) 55 ——With his strong, handsome Teutonic face (he actually was Polish), it was inevitable he should almost always play Nazis; did so in Confessions of a Nazi Spy (as Hentze), So Ends Our Night, The Man I Married, My Favorite Spy, Cross of Lorraine, The Hitler Gang, etc.; in the serial Secret Service in Darkest Africa had the dual role of the Sultan and the villainous Nazi baron who kidnapped him; played Germans who were not Nazis in *Four Sons, Nurse Edith Cavell, Victory,* and *Gilda,* his last.

ROYCE, VIRGINIA *(1962)* 30 ——Support in Crawford's *The Caretakers.*

ROYER, HARRY *(1951)* 62 ——Support in the '20s: *Sky High Corral, The Block Signal,* other action pix.

ROYTON, VERNA *(1974)* 81 ——Character actress in minor roles.

RUB, CHRISTIAN *(1956)* 69 ——Gaunt-faced character actor from Austria, with a bushy moustache and often in pince-nez or other spectacles, who usually played comic or sympathetic Germans; was in more than 50 from '32: *Little Man, What Now?* (the Jewish antiques dealer), *Four Sons, You Can't Take It With You* (Schmidt), *Mr. Deeds Goes to Town* (Swenson), *Heidi, One Hundred Men and a Girl, Berlin Correspondent, Everything Happens at Night,* etc.; was the voice of woodcarver Geppetto in *Pinocchio.*

RUBEN, JOSE *(1969)* 80 ——Support in Dorothy Dalton's *Dark Secrets,* Anna Q. Nilsson's *The Man from Home,* Jetta Goudal's *Salome of the Tenements,* others in the '20s.

RUBENS, ALMA *(1931)* 32 ——Dark and classically beautiful, she became a major star soon after playing one of the Girls of the Marriage Market in "The Babylonian Story" of *Intolerance;* starred first in 1917's *The Firefly of Tough Luck,* then in *Madame Sphinx, Restless Souls, Humoresque, Under the Red Robe, Enemies of Women, Cytherea, Fine Clothes,* after which, for the rest of the '20s, it was downhill in such second-rate pix as *The Gilded Butterfly;* last had a secondary role in Eleanor Boardman's *She Goes to War* ('29); was once married to Ricardo Cortez.

RUDANI, ROSA *(1966)* 66 ——Support in several in the '20s: *A Poor Girl's Romance,* Leatrice Joy's *The Wedding Song,* Belle Bennett's *The Lily,* etc.

RUFFO, TITO *(1953)* 76 ——Italian opera star who appeared in musical shorts at MGM in the early '30s.

RUGGERI, RUGGERO *(1953)* 81 ——Support in Italian pix: *La Donna D'una Notte, The Spirit and the Flesh,* etc.

RUGGLES, CHARLES *(1970)* 84 ——Great low-key comic character star who never

seemed to age a day in almost 40 years of screen fame; brought his dimples and charm to dozens of Hollywood's best: *Ruggles of Red Gap* (Egbert Floud who won perfect English valet Laughton in a poker game), *The Smiling Lieutenant, One Hour with You, Love Me Tonight, If I Had a Million, Anything Goes, Bringing Up Baby, Our Hearts Were Young and Gay, The Doughgirls, A Stolen Life,* etc.; toward the end was a Disney "regular"—in *The Parent Trap, The Ugly Dachshund, Son of Flubber,* others; he claimed his favorite role was that of the millionaire in a Monogram pic, *It Happened on Fifth Avenue,* in which he co-starred with Ann Harding.

RUGGLES, WESLEY *(1972)* 82 ——An actor in early silents, he became much more famous later as the director of *Cimarron* ('31), *I'm No Angel,* etc.

RUICK, BARBARA *(1974)* 42 ——Lovely blonde singer-actress who was one of Metro's most promising young stars in the '50s; had leads in *I Love Melvin, Invitation, Above and Beyond, You and Me,* etc.; had perhaps her best opportunity a bit later in *Carousel* as Shirley Jones' friend Carrie who sang "When I Marry Mr. Snow"; retired for marriage (to Oscar-winning composer John Williams) and motherhood, she was making a comeback in *California Split* at the time of her death; was the daughter of Lurene Tuttle and Melville Ruick.

RUICK, MELVILLE *(1972)* 74 ——One of the best actors on radio (announced *Lux Radio Theater* and acted in dramas) and TV (a lead in the *City Hospital* series), and a prominent Broadway actor, he had featured roles in several films: *The President's Mystery, Moon Over Miami,* etc.

RUMANN, SIG *(1967)* 82 ——Blustery, popeyed, bushy-browed German-accented comic (usually, but could be mean) who was at his best in *Ninotchka,* as Iranoff, one of the bumbling Russian trio Garbo went to Paris to keep tabs on; onscreen from 1929's *The Royal Box,* was in more than 100: *A Night at the Opera, The Princess Comes Across, Dr. Ehrlich's Magic Bullet* (Dr. Hans Wolfert), *Confessions of a Nazi Spy, Suez, Only Angels Have Wings, Remember Pearl Harbor, To Be or Not to Be, The Hitler Gang, Stalag 17,* etc.; final role was in 1966's *The Last of the Secret Agents;* little known is that he was a scientist who, in the first decade of his career, worked concurrently in the department of bacteriology at the University of Southern California.

RUNYON, DAMON *(1946)* 62 ——Broadway's famous "Guys and Dolls" journalist-playwright-author; was husband of actress Gladys Glad; onscreen in 1924 in *The Great White Way*.

RUSSELL, BYRON *(1963)* 79 ——Supporting roles; in the '20s in *Janice Meredith, It Is the Law, The Family Closet*, etc.; in the '30s in *Mutiny on the Bounty* (as Quintal), *Parnell, One-Third of a Nation* (Inspector Castle).

RUSSELL, GAIL *(1961)* 36 ——Small-talented but beautiful young brunette starred by Paramount, as a junior-league Lamarr, in numerous pix in the '40s: *Salty O'Rourke* with Alan Ladd, *Our Hearts Were Young and Gay* (as young Cornelia Otis Skinner), *The Unseen, Calcutta, The Night Has a Thousand Eyes*, etc.; her best dramatic outing was as the terrified girl in *The Uninvited* (in which, coincidentally, the real Cornelia Otis Skinner had a supporting role); in fewer in the '50s, because of personal problems: *The Lawless, Seven Men from Now, The Tattered Dress*, and, finally *The Silent Call*.

RUSSELL, J. GORDON *(1935)* 52 ——Support in Westerns and action melodramas of the '20s: William S. Hart's *Singer Jim McKee* and *Tumbleweeds*, Buck Jones' *Hearts and Spurs*, Jack Hoxie's *The Sign of the Cactus*, Norman Kerry's *The Claw*, Wally Wales' *Saddle Mates*, etc.

RUSSELL, LEWIS *(1961)* 76 ——Character actor; played Jane Wyman's father in *The Lost Weekend;* was in the Marx Brothers' *A Night in Casabalanca* (as Galoux), *Molly and Me, Kiss the Blood Off My Hands, Cross My Heart, She Wouldn't Say Yes*, etc.

RUSSELL, LILLIAN *(1922)* 62 ——Buxom legendary singer adored by Diamond Jim Brady and portrayed by Alice Faye in *Lillian Russell*, Binnie Barnes in *Diamond Jim*, Ruth Gillette in *The Great Ziegfeld*, Andrea King in *My Wild Irish Rose*, Ann Blyth in *Bowery to Broadway*, and other actresses; starred onscreen once, in 1915's *Wildfire*.

RUSSELL, PEE WEE *(1969)* 62 ——Famous bandleader who was in *Jazz Dance*.

RUSSELL, WILLIAM *(1929)* 45 ——Athletic, handsome actor who went from Shakespeare onscreen (1912's *The Merchant of Venice*, 1913's *Cymbeline*) to serials; starred—doing breathtakingly dangerous stunts—in one truly classic silent serial, the 60-episode *The Diamond from the Sky*, followed by *The Sequel to the Diamond from the Sky* and numerous lesser ones made by five different companies, several of which he also directed; in the '20s, became a top leading man in features (*Anna Christie* opposite Blanche Sweet, *Mixed Faces, Children of*

Night, etc., in many of which his muscular chest was bared) and a daredevil star of Westerns (*The Big Brute* with Victor McLaglen, *The Passing of Wolf McLean, Blue Eagle, Singing River*, etc.); *Girls Gone Wild* in '29 was his last ("Plenty hot and plenty fast," said *Photoplay*—and that was the keynote of his entire career).

RUTH, BABE *(1948)* 53 ——Baseball's home-run king; starred in silents *(Headin' Home, Babe Comes Home)* and, as himself, was in Harold Lloyd's last silent, *Speedy*, and again in *Pride of the Yankees;* was portrayed by William Bendix in *The Babe Ruth Story*.

RUTH, MARSHALL *(1953)* 55 ——Supporting actor who often played characters with catchy nicknames like "Stew"; was featured in silents *(Virgin Lips* with Olive Borden, *Joy Street* with Lois Moran, *Wild Born, Nix on Dames*, etc.) and talkies (*The Broadway Melody, False Pretenses, Wedding Present*, others).

RUTHERFORD, MARGARET *(1972)* 80 —— Bulky British comedy star with chin(s); won a Best Supporting Oscar in *The V.I.P.s;* was most joyful as sleuthing Miss Marple in *Murder at the Gallop, Murder Most Foul, Murder Ahoy;* dominated her every scene in *Blithe Spirit, The Importance of Being Earnest, Passport to Pimlico, I'm All Right Jack, The Happiest Days of Your Life*, many more.

RUTHERFURD, TOM *(1973)* ——Character (King Ferdinand) in *The Firefly;* was also in *Rosalie, Those Were the Days, Virginia, Beg, Borrow or Steal*.

RUYSDAEL, BASIL *(1960)* 72 ——Dignity and severity (often with kindliness underneath) marked all 30 screen portrayals of this famous radio announcer (*Your Hit Parade*); in *Pinky* was Judge Walker, who ruled that Jeanne Crain should inherit Ethel Barrymore's estate; also was in *People Will Talk* (Dean Brockwell), *Come to the Stable* (Bishop), *Half Angel* (Dr. Jackson), *Broken Arrow* (General Howard), *The Blackboard Jungle* (Professor Kraal), *Carrie, The Horse Soldiers*, etc.; *The Story of Ruth* was his last.

RYAN, ANNIE *(1943)* 78 ——Character actress in Norman Kerry's *The Claw*.

RYAN, DICK *(1969)* 72 ——Character actor who, in Fontaine's *The Constant Nymph*, portrayed Trigorin, and in her *Born to Be Bad* was Arthur; was in several comedies: *Mr. Peabody and the Mermaid, Chicken Every Sunday, Top of the Morning, The Buster Keaton Story*, etc.

RYAN, IRENE *(1973)* 70 ——Comedienne most famous as Granny in the TV series *The Beverly*

Hillbillies; had wisecracking secondary roles in dozens of movies: *My Dear Secretary; Meet Me After the Show; Sarong Girl; San Diego, I Love You; That Night With You,* etc.; scored sensationally on Broadway as the star of *Pippin,* her last engagement; was once the wife of Tim Ryan.

RYAN, MARY *(1948)* 62 ——Co-starred with Harry Mestayer in 1915 Kleine productions.

RYAN, ROBERT *(1973)* 63 ——Rangy, ruggedly handsome and versatile star who was introduced as a straight leading man almost always in uniform *(Tender Comrade, Bombardier, Behind the Rising Sun, Marine Raiders);* made several memorable Westerns *(Trail Street, Return of the Badmen);* his best role—and his personal favorite—was in 1949's *The Set-Up* as the washed-up boxer who wins that last big fight, and pays; *Crossfire,* in '47, in which he was a murderous psychotic, set the stage for count-

less roles to come in which he would be dastardly in the extreme: *Bad Day at Black Rock, Caught, Billy Budd, Clash by Night, Act of Violence, Odds Against Tomorrow, The Tall Men,* etc.; many retain fond memories of his comedy playing as the grizzled redneck father in *God's Little Acre;* in '73 he starred in three: *The Iceman Cometh, The Outfit,* and *Executive Action,* bringing his credits to 81.

RYAN, TIM *(1956)* 57 ——Bald on top and wisecracking, this vaudeville comedian had supporting roles—reporters, street-wise cops, politicos—in more than 70 after 1940's *Brother Orchid;* had a running role in the "Jiggs and Maggie" comedies *(Jiggs and Maggie in Court,* etc.); he and then wife Irene often had supporting roles in the same pic *(Hot Rhythm,* etc.); among his many: *Hit Parade of 1943, Bedtime Story, Body and Soul, Stand By for Action, The Petty Girl, Reveille with Beverly.*

S

SABIN, MRS. CATHERINE JEROME *(1943)* 64 ——Character actress in Barthelmess' *New Toys.*

SABOURET, MARIE *(1960)* 30s ——French actress; in *Rififi* was the girl friend of one of the jewel thieves and was killed by the rival gang.

SABU *(1963)* 39 ——Discovered as a youngster in India, he was starred in *Elephant Boy, Drums,* and *The Thief of Bagdad* before coming to Hollywood; after *The Jungle Book,* co-starred with Maria Montez in sex-and-sand epics at Universal: *Arabian Nights, Cobra Woman, White Savage, Tangier;* then, except for *Black Narcissus,* was in adventure pix exclusively: *Man-Eater of Kumaon, Song of India, Savage Drums, Sabu and the Magic Ring, Jaguar,* etc.

SACKVILLE, GORDON *(1926)* 50s ——Big bruiser who played the cowboy lead in Dorothy Davenport's *The Best Man Wins* ('11); in others, including two serials, *With Stanley in Africa, The Red Circle;* support in Westerns in the '20s: *Cowboy Courage, Slow as Lightning,* etc.; also in John Gilbert's *The Snob.*

SADLER, DUDLEY *(1951)* 60s ——Character (Dr. Rainsford) in *Boomerang;* also in Gable's *Lone Star* and Shelley Winters' *Behave Yourself.*

SADLER, IAN *(1971)* 69 ——Minor support in British pix.

SAGE, BYRON *(1974)* 59 ——Boy actor who had featured roles in Corinne Griffith's *Into Her Kingdom* ('26), Eve Southern's *Clothes Make the Woman,* and, in '30, in Belle Bennett's *Courage* and Lillian Gish's first talkie, *One Romantic Night.*

SAGE, WILLARD *(1974)* 51 ——Handsome support in *Dragnet* (Chester Davitt), *That Touch of Mink* (Hodges), *It's a Dog's Life,* etc.

ST. AUDRIE, STELLA *(1925)* 49 ——Was featured in England's 1914 *Little Lord Fauntleroy.*

ST. CLAIR, LYDIA *(1970)* 60s ——Memorable as the brunette Nazi spy in *The House on 92nd Street,* her only film.

ST. CLAIR, MAURICE *(1970)* 67 ——Had a character role in Dan Duryea's *Black Angel.*

ST. CLAIR, YVONNE *(1971)* 57 ——Starlet who had minor roles in *A Midsummer Night's Dream, The Great Ziegfeld,* etc.

ST. DENIS, JOE *(1968)* 40 ——Minor support.

ST. DENIS, RUTH *(1968)* 80 ——Celebrated modern dancer; was the Solo Dancer in "The Babylonian Story" in *Intolerance;* had a character role (the Duchess) in Goddard's *Kitty.*

ST. HELIER, IVY *(1971)* 70s ——In *Henry V,* was Alice, Lady-in-Waiting, to the French Princess, Renee Asherson; also in *Bitter Sweet, Dulcimer Street,* other British pix.

ST. JOHN, AL "FUZZY" *(1963)* 69 ——Best known to later generations as the antic, bewhiskered sidekick "Fuzzy Q. Jones" of Western stars Bob Steele, Fred Scott, Jack Randall, Lash LaRue, several others; a few of his Westerns: *Songs and Bullets, Western Trail, Frontier Scout, Return of the Lone Rider;* in hundreds of pix, he began as a slapstick comedian at Sennett in 1914; in hayseed roles, for years, he supported his uncle, star Roscoe "Fatty" Arbuckle, in dozens of comedies *(Fickle Fatty's Fall, Fatty and Mabel Adrift,* etc.), before being starred at Warners, Fox, Paramount, and Educational in his own series, which always featured his pop-eyed stare, acrobatic talents, and bicycle stunts; for a while in the '20s, was to be seen in tux and silk hat—but funny—in such as Betty Compson's *The Garden of Weeks,* Billie Dove's *American Beauty,* etc.; went into Westerns in '28, eventually becoming so popular as a sidekick (his comedy often dominating the action) that one Buster Crabbe pic was even titled after him, 1944's *Fuzzy Settles Down;* among his few non-Western talkies: *His Private Secretary, I'm from Arkansas, Marked Man, Fame Street.*

ST. JOHN, HOWARD *(1974)* 69 ——Broderick Crawford's drunken attorney, Devery, in *Born Yesterday,* this big sandy-haired character actor had prominent roles in more than 30 from '47: *The Men* (Teresa Wright's father), *Mister 880, Li'l Abner* (General Bullmoose), *Strangers on a Train* (Police Captain Turley), *Saturday's Hero, Lover Come Back,* etc.

ST. JOHN, MARGUERITE *(1940)* 79 ——Support in Ruth Chatterton's *The Laughing Lady.*

ST. MAUR, ADELE *(1959)* 71 ——The nurse in Crosby's *Little Boy Lost,* she had supporting roles in many: *The Invisible Ray, The Melody Lingers On, The Gay Deception, History Is Made at Night,* etc.

ST. POLIS, JOHN *(1946)* 59 ——In Chaney's *The Phantom of the Opera* was good-looking Philippe de Chegny, ill-fated brother of romantic lead Norman Kerry; support in many memorable movies of the '20s (*The Four Horsemen of the Apocalypse, Coquette, Three Weeks, Why Be Good?, Three Wise Fools,* etc.); except for *Kismet,* was in less good pix in the '30s (*King of the Arena, Symphony of Six Million, Mr. Wong —Detective,* many more); early, was occasionally billed Sainpolis.

SAKALL, S. Z. *(1955)* 67 ——"Cuddles," he was called (and often billed in parentheses), and this chubby, curly-blond kewpie-doll character from Hungary was indeed cuddly, offscreen as well as on; was first on American screens, as the confused producer, in a 1940 Durbin pic, *It's a Date* (learned his role phonetically; did not then speak English); 40 more followed: *Ball of Fire, Casablanca, Shine On Harvest Moon, Christmas in Connecticut, The Dolly Sisters, In the Good Old Summertime,* etc., and last, *The Student Prince;* as Szocke Szakall, he had (from '16) starred in comedy films in Germany, Hungary, and England, where he was in *Smile, Please,* and *The Lilac Domino* with June Knight.

SALE, CHARLES "CHIC" *(1936)* 51 —— When *His Nibs* was released in '22, *Photoplay* said: "Charles 'Chic' Sale brings a new face and a new personality to the screen . . . suggests his ever-popular vaudeville act in that he assumes seven distinct roles"; they quickly dwindled to one—the lovable, crusty old codger with the corncob pipe; he was on display in *Marching On, When a Feller Needs a Friend* with Jackie Cooper, *Lucky Dog, Stranger in Town,* etc.

SALE, FRANCES *(1969)* 77 ——Supporting roles in silents.

SALISBURY, MONROE *(1935)* 59 ——Darkly handsome actor who became an early matinee idol through his romantic Indian roles in *The Rose of the Rancho* ('14), *Ramona* ('16), *The Savage, The Barbarian,* etc.; made a most attractive Englishman of Sir Henry in DeMille's first ('14), *The Squaw Man,* and was a charming leading man opposite Marguerite Clark in *The Goose Girl;* last played the father of hero Jack Perrin in the '30 serial *The Jade Box.*

SALTER, HARRY "HAL" *(1928)* 50s ——Actor-friend who helped D.W. Griffith enter movies as a writer; Griffith then starred him in *The Redman and the Child* ('08), *What Drink Did* with Florence Lawrence, *The Slave;* in many for other directors; last in two Ken Maynard Westerns in '28: *The Code of the Scarlet, The Canyon of Adventure.*

SALTER, THELMA *(1953)* 48 ——Child actress who starred as Becky Thatcher in 1920's *Tom Sawyer.*

SAMSON, IVAN *(1963)* 68 ——Support in British pix: *The Browning Version, That Winslow Boy, The Life of Handel, Libel, Waltz Time,* more.

SANBORN, FRED *(1961)* 62 ——*Soup to Nuts* in '30 featured "Ted Healy and His Racketeers," the latter being comedians Larry Fine,

Moe and Shemp Howard (soon to be The Three Stooges) and Sanborn; he and Shemp were later reunited in Olsen & Johnson's *Crazy House.*

SANDE, WALTER *(1972)* 65 ——A top character actor for 35 years, this flattened-nose guy caught the public's eye in 1944's *I Love a Soldier;* played G.I. Stiff Banks, blinded in combat and being shipped home—and the courage with humor displayed by himself and screen wife Ann Doran was so affecting that many critics praised them to exclusion of stars Goddard and Tufts; in most of his other 250 roles was merely strong support, a law man usually; was in *A Place in the Sun, Dark City, To Have and Have Not, Bad Day at Black Rock, Sunrise at Campobello,* etc.; had continuing roles in several TV series: *Dragnet, The Farmer's Daughter, Wild, Wild West,* etc.

SANDERS, GEORGE *(1972)* 65 ——Suave, icy-cold English snob—he rarely deviated from this characterization in more than 50 in 36 years in Hollywood movies, from *Lloyds of London* (as Lord Stacy); won a Supporting Oscar as acidulous critic Addison De Witt in *All About Eve,* his only nomination; was also outstandingly good in *Rebecca, The Moon and Sixpence, Foreign Correspondent, Confessions of a Nazi Spy, Forever Amber, Call Me Madam, The Picture of Dorian Gray, Summer Storm;* starred in two film series: "The Saint" (five pictures 1939–41; *The Saint Strikes Back, The Saint in London,* etc.) and "The Falcon" (four in 1941–42; *The Gay Falcon, A Date with the Falcon,* etc., after which brother Tom Conway assumed the role); his last role, in 1970's *The Kremlin Letter,* was a shocker—an ancient drag queen who became the darling of Moscow's homosexual literary set; among his wives: Zsa Zsa Gabor, Benita Hume, Magda Gabor.

SANDERS, HUGH *(1966)* 54 ——Character actor onscreen from '50 who alternately played cops, sheriffs, detectives, and bad guys; was in *The Damned Don't Cry, The Wild One, Mister 880, I Was a Communist for the F.B.I., The Glass Web,* plus such A-grade Westerns as *Montana Territory, Cattle Queen of Montana,* and *Along the Great Divide.*

SANDERS, SCOTT *(1956)* 68 ——English support who played Old George in the Errol Flynn-Anna Neagle pic *Lilacs in the Spring,* a.k.a. *Let's Make Up.*

SANDROCK, ADELE *(1937)* 73 ——Co-starred with Hans Albers in *Liebe Und Heimat* and with Rudolf Forster in *Morgenrot.*

SANDS, DIANA *(1973)* 39 ——Dynamic, beautiful black actress; gave a compelling perform-ance as the sister in *A Raisin in the Sun,* later starred in *An Affair of the Skin* and *Honey Baby, Honey Baby.*

SANFORD, ALBERT, JR. *(1953)* 60 ——Supporting roles in early Biograph films.

SANFORD, ERSKINE *(1950)* 70 ——Strong-featured character who had important roles in several Welles pix: *Citizen Kane* (rattled newspaper editor Carter), *Macbeth* (Duncan), *The Magnificent Ambersons* (Benson), *The Lady from Shanghai;* was also in 1947's *Possessed* (Dr. Max Sherman), *The Best Years of Our Lives, Crack-Up,* many more.

SANFORD, RALPH *(1963)* 64 ——Heavy-faced character with a can't-be-conned look who played well-upholstered, spiffily dressed show-biz types (*Copacabana, Hit Parade of 1947, The Bull Fighters*), country sheriffs (arrested Bogart robbing the drugstore in *High Sierra*), city police officials (*Union Station*), comedy roles (*Give Me a Sailor, It Shouldn't Happen to a Dog*); in more than 50 from the late '30s.

SANGER, BERT *(1969)* 75 ——One of Sennett's lesser comedians.

SANTLEY, FRED *(1953)* 82 ——First billed Frederic, he was a leading Kalem actor in '11, then played many dozens of supporting roles for the rest of his life; among his talkies: *Morning Glory* (producer Menjou's stage director, Will Seymour), *If I Had a Million* (one of ailing millionaire Richard Bennett's doctors), *George White's 1935 Scandals, This Is My Affair,* and last, Betty Grable's *The Farmer Takes a Wife.*

SANTLEY, JOSEPH *(1971)* 82 ——In early silents, this stage actor later directed many; among his talkies: *Million Dollar Baby* and *Harmony Lane* (both of which he also wrote), *Walking on Air, Spirit of Culver, Brazil.*

SANTSCHI, TOM *(1931)* 53 ——Curly-haired, ruggedly handsome star who, with William Farnum, has made every film history book for his participation in that great brawling, clawing, endless fight in 1914's *The Spoilers;* then onscreen for five years, having played the male lead in the serial *The Adventures of Kathlyn,* etc., he starred in many more: *The Crisis, The Garden of Allah, The Country That God Forgot, Little Orphan Annie* with Colleen Moore, *Shadows, The Hell Cat,* and *The Stranger Vow,* all prior to '20; in the early '20s, starred in many features (*Two Kinds of Women, Brass Commandments, Is Divorce a Failure?,* etc.), numerous Westerns (*The Plunderer, The Desert's Toll*), and sea dramas (*The Storm Daughter, Thundering Dawn*); last played fathers (the ex-baseball star in *Life's Greatest Game*) and other supporting roles (in *The Shannons of Broadway, In Old Arizona*, in which he was listed simply as a Cowpuncher, *Isle of Lost Men*, etc., plus the serials *Vultures of the Sea, King of the Wild*, and *The Phantom of the West*).

SARGENT, KENNY *(1969)* 63 ——Famous crooner with Glen Gray's Casa Loma Band; with it in musical shorts.

SARNER, ALEXANDER *(1948)* 55 ——Support in English pix: *The Dreyfus Case, The Passing of the Third Floor Back* ('36), etc.

SARNO, HECTOR V. *(1953)* 73 ——The Galilean Carpenter in DeMille's *The King of Kings*, this character actor, in movies from '09, was prominently present in many of the best in the '20s: Norma Talmadge's *Ashes of Vengeance* and *The Song of Love*, Milton Sills' *The Sea Hawk*, Garbo's *The Temptress*, Gaynor and Farrell's *Lucky Star* (as Pop Fry), etc.; in the '30s was support in *Death Takes a Holiday* (Pietro), *Wee Willie Winkie* (Coach Driver), and Jack Holt's *Flight Into Nowhere*.

SATZ, LUDWIG *(1944)* 53 ——Was in *His Wife's Lover*, first Yiddish musical talkie.

SAUM, CLIFF *(1943)* 60 ——Support in many silents (Dorothy Mackaill's *Bridge of Sighs*, Dorothy Revier's *The Tigress*, Marguerite de la Motte's *Wandering Daughters*) and talkies (Louise Dresser's *The 3 Sisters, Torchy Gets Her Man*, Wayne Morris' *Ladies Must Live*).

SAUNDERS, JACKIE *(1954)* 56 ——Gorgeous dark-blonde star famous for her perfect nose and limpid gray eyes; starred first for the Balboa Company in '13; was the heroine of the '16 serial *The Grip of Evil*, and was William Farnum's leading lady in *Drag Harlan* (by which time she was billed Jacquelin); in the '20s supported others: Alice Lake in *The Infamous Miss Ravell*, Irene Rich in *Defying Destiny*, Dorothy Davenport Reid in *Broken Laws*, etc.

SAUNDERS, NELLIE *(1942)* 73 ——Character actress in the '20s; was in Ann Pennington's *The Mad Dancer*, Charles Ray's *A Tailor-Made Man, A Little Girl in a Big City*, etc.

SAVILLE, GUS *(1934)* 77 ——In the '20s was a character in Westerns (*The High Hand, Fighting Courage, The Wolverine*), Western serials (*Wild West, Idaho*), and Pickford's *Tess of the Storm Country;* last in Richard Arlen's *The Light of Western Stars* in '30.

SAVO, JIMMY *(1960)* 64 ——Leprechaun-like comedian (with bangs) from Broadway who had

star roles in several in the '30s (*Once in a Blue Moon, Merry-Go-Round of 1938, Reckless Living*) and one silent (*Exclusive Rights* in '26).

SAWYER, LAURA *(1970)* 85 ——Dark-haired beauty who starred in Edison's *The Lighthouse Keeper's Daughter* in '12 and *Die Lorelei* in '13; then for Famous Players in *Port of Doom, The Daughter of the Hills, A Woman's Triumph*, and last, for World in *One of Millions* in '14.

SAXE, TEMPLAR *(1935)* 69 ——Fine, gray support in dozens of silents: *Intrigue, Beau Brummell, Captain Blood, The White Black Sheep, The Dancers, Her Night of Romance, When a Man Loves*, etc.

SAXON, HUGH *(1945)* 76 ——Character actor who played Irene Rich's butler in *Cytherea*, but usually in that decade (the '20s) was to be found in action pix: William S. Hart's *Sand!*, Rex Lease's *Phantom of the Turf, Hair Trigger Baxter, Fightin' Odds*, etc.

SAYLES, FRANCIS *(1944)* 53 ——Played the sheriff, heroine's dad, or decent townsman in many B Westerns (*Riders of Black River, Home on the Range, The Texas Bad Man*, etc.); minor roles in *Blonde Venus, Black Fury*, others.

SAYLOR, SYD *(1962)* 67 ——Skinny comedian whose bobbing Adam's apple co-starred with him in several dozen "Syd Saylor" two-reelers in the '20s; with talkies, he added a stubbly beard and a slight stutter and was set as the sidekick in the Westerns of Buster Crabbe, Bob Livingston, et al.; a few of his many: *Wyoming Wildcat, Forlorn River, Wilderness Mail, Mule Train;* was comic relief in numerous big Westerns (*Arizona, Union Pacific*, Joel McCrea's *The Virginian*) and many A-grade features (*Abe Lincoln in Illinois, There Goes My Heart, Gentleman Jim, The Spirit of St. Louis*, etc.)

SAYRE, JEFFREY *(1974)* 73 ——Support in Bickford's *Mutiny in the Big House* and many others, he was the founder of the Screen Extras Guild.

SCADUTO, JOSEPH *(1943)* 45 ——Featured in one of the funniest comedies of the '20s, *Racing Luck*.

SCALA, GIA *(1972)* 38 ——Tall, dark-haired Irish-Italian beauty from Liverpool whose best role was one of her last—Anna in *The Guns of Navarone;* was the femme lead in many in the '50s: *Tip on a Dead Jockey, Don't Go Near the Water, The Garment Jungle, Tunnel of Love, I Aim at the Stars*, etc.

SCARDON, PAUL *(1954)* 75 ——Athletic, curly-haired, and handsome, he starred in many for Majestic from 1911; was Anita Stewart's courageous hero in the '15 serial *The Goddess;* then for years a director (*Partners of the Night*, etc.) and the husband of Betty Blythe, he returned to acting—most dignified in his 60s—in John Wayne's *Lady from Louisiana;* was then in *Mrs. Miniver* (Nobby), *My Favorite Blonde* (Dr. Higby), *Magic Town, A Yank at Eton,* etc.

SCHABLE, ROBERT, *(1947)* 74 ——Character in many in the '20s: *The Loves of Sunya* (was Henri Picard), Negri's *The Cheat* and *Bella Donna,* John Barrymore's *Sherlock Holmes,* Agnes Ayres' *A Daughter of Luxury,* etc.

SCHAEFER, ALBERT *(1942)* 26 ——At age 10 he had a featured role in the Art Acord Western *The Set Up.*

SCHAEFER, CHARLES *(1939)* 75 ——Character in action melodramas and Westerns of the '20s: Hoot Gibson's *The Winged Horseman,* Richard Dix's *Man Power, Gun-Hand Garrison.*

SCHARF, HERMAN *(1963)* 62 ——Character in Heston's *The Far Horizons.*

SCHEFF, FRITZI *(1954)* 65 ——Beautiful brunette star of the musical stage (*Kiss Me Again* was written for her); starred onscreen in 1915's *Pretty Mrs. Smith* with Owen Moore.

SCHENCK, JOE *(1930)* 39 ——Half of the dapper (Gus) Van & Schenck song duo from the *Ziegfeld Follies* who sang better than they starred in 1930's *They Learned About Women;* also in MGM musical shorts.

SCHIESKE, ALFRED *(1970)* 61 ——German actor who was in *Odette, Tomorrow Is My Turn,* etc.

SCHILDKRAUT, JOSEPH *(1964)* 68 ——Won the '37 Best Supporting Oscar in *The Life of Emile Zola* in a most sympathetic role—Captain Dreyfus, victim of French anti-Semitism; next year, in *Marie Antoinette,* was the dastardly dandy Duke of Orleans, and type-casting made him Hollywood's handsomest villain for years (*The Man in the Iron Mask, The Phantom Raiders, Lady of the Tropics,* etc.); in 1945's *Flame of the Barbary Coast* with Ann Dvorak, he returned briefly to the suave romantic-type role that had made him such a matinee idol ("the handsomest actor in motion pictures") after playing Chevalier de Vaudry in *Orphans of the Storm;* a few of his best in the '20s: *Young April* with Bessie Love, *The Heart Thief, Tenth Avenue* with Phyllis Haver, *Meet the Prince, Show Boat* with Laura LaPlante; his later vil-lainous career was certainly presaged by one role in the '20s—Judas Iscariot in *The King of Kings*—and another in '34—traitorous General Pascal in *Viva Villa!;* finally, after many years on Broadway, came back to give a superb character performance as the father in *The Diary of Anne Frank; The Greatest Story Ever Told,* as Nicodemus, was his last.

SCHILDKRAUT, RUDOLPH *(1930)* 65 ——Joseph's magnificent tragedian-father; came to the screen in the '20s after a long, illustrious stage career; gave several still-talked-about performances—in *Proud Heart* (a.k.a. *His People*), his best, *Pals in Paradise, Turkish Delight, A Harp in Hock, The Main Event, His Country,* etc.; was in two with his son: *The King of Kings* (as Caiaphas, High Priest of Israel) and *Young April; Christina* ('29) with Janet Gaynor was his last.

SCHILLING, GUS *(1957)* 49 ——Nervous, "chinless" funny character; in *It Started With Eve, You Were Never Lovelier, Mexican Spitfire Out West, Hers to Hold, Chatterbox, It's a Pleasure, See My Lawyer,* more.

SCHIPA, TITO *(1965)* 76 ——Italian opera star in many pix shown in the U.S.: *Tito Schipa, Tito Schipa Concert No. 2, The Life of Donizetti,* etc.

SCHNEIDER, JAMES *(1967)* 85 ——A Keystone Kop; not one of the seven originals.

SCHOENBERG, ALEX *(1945)* 59 ——Played German characters; in *Nothing Sacred* (Dr. Kerchinwisser), *They Shall Have Music, Romance in the Dark,* etc.; sometimes billed Alexander and sometimes his last name was spelled Schonberg.

SCHONBERG, IB *(1955)* 53 ——Danish actor in Lippert Prods.' *We Want a Child.*

SCHRECK, MAX *(1936)* 57 ——German character star, in movies from the '20s, and most famous for playing the title role in *Nosferatu the Vampire;* also in *The Strange Case of Dr. Ramper, At the Edge of the World; Rasputin: The Holy Devil; Roman Einer Nacht,* etc.

SCHULTZ, HARRY *(1935)* 52 ——Character actor from Germany in J. Farrell MacDonald's *Riley the Cop, I'm No Angel, The Big House, Little Man, What Now?,* etc.

SCHUMANN-HEINK, ERNESTINE *(1936)* 75 ——One of the greatest international opera stars (her career span on the stage: 1878-1930) who appeared in one movie, 1935's *Here's to Romance*—as Nino Martini's singing coach and revealing, said the *New York Times*, "a gruff gift for comedy."

SCHUMANN-HEINK, FERDINAND *(1958)* 65 ——Ernestine's character actor-son; was First Officer of the zeppelin in *Hell's Angels*; also in 1928's *Four Sons*, Eddie Dowling's *Blaze O'Glory*, *My Pal the King*, *Orient Express*, *The King and the Chorus Girl*, etc.; was the author of the Jean Hersholt pic *Mamba*.

SCHUMM, HARRY *(1953)* 75 ——With his coldly aristocratic face, he was the star of *The Broken Coin*, a 44-chapter Universal serial of '15.

SCHUNZEL, REINHOLD *(1954)* 70 ——Character actor from Germany who, in the '40s, played Nazis in *First Comes Courage* (Col. Kurt von Elser), *Hangmen Also Die* (Ritter), *The Hitler Gang*, *Notorious* ("Dr. Anderson"), etc.; also was in *Golden Earrings* (Professor Korsigk), *Dragonwyck* (Count de Grenier), *Berlin Express*, others; also directed while in Hollywood (*Balalaika*, *New Wine*, etc.); returned to Germany in the '50s.

SCHWARTZ, MAURICE *(1960)* 68 ——Character actor from the Yiddish stage who had a role in one silent, Lila Lee's *Broken Hearts*, and several of the '50s: Debra Paget's *Bird of Paradise*, Richard Conte's *Slaves of Babylon* (as Nebuchadnezzar), Hayworth's *Salome* (as Ezra).

SCOTT, CYRIL *(1945)* 79 ——An early Famous Players lead who starred in *The Day of Days* ('13), *How Molly Made Good* ('15), etc.

SCOTT, FREDERICK T. *(1942)* 70s ——Long career as a supporting actor; after a small role in *The Great Train Robbery*, was in *Over There* ('17), many others in the teens.

SCOTT, HAROLD *(1964)* 73 ——Character (Taylor) in *The Yellow Rolls-Royce*; in many British pix: *The Spanish Gardener*, *The Man in Grey*, *Brides of Dracula*, etc.

SCOTT, IVY *(1947)* 61 ——Support in *Too Many Girls*, *Higher and Higher*, etc.

SCOTT, JAMES *(1964)* 25 ——Minor roles as a child actor in movies; best known on radio for playing, in *Blondie and Dagwood*, Baby Dumpling grown older and called Alexander.

SCOTT, KAY *(1971)* 44 ——At 19 she played the femme lead in a Paul Kelly chiller, *Fear in the Night*, her only picture.

SCOTT, LESLIE *(1969)* 48 ——Huge black actor-singer who played Jake in *Porgy and Bess*; also was in *Island Women*.

SCOTT, MARK *(1960)* 45 ——Was featured in John Ireland's *Hell's Horizon*, Brian Keith's *Chicago Confidential*, etc.

SCOTT, MARKIE *(1958)* 85 ——Had character roles in dozens of silent cowboy pix.

SCOTT, ZACHARY *(1965)* 51 ——Lean, handsome actor who proved his versatility in his first two starring pix—the exotic *The Mask of Dimitrios* and *The Southerner* (as the trouble-beset young farmer); was quickly type-cast as a cad—often a playboy in tux or tweeds—and played that in many: *Mildred Pierce*, *The Unfaithful*, *Cass Timberlane*, *Ruthless*, *Whiplash*, *Flamingo Road*, *Born to be Bad*; worked rarely when the type went out of vogue; in just three in the '60s: *Natchez Trace*, *The Young One*, and a Jerry Lewis comedy, *It's Only Money*.

SEABURY, YNEZ *(1973)* 65 ——Nationally famous around 1910 as the "Biograph Baby," in the '20s she had featured roles in Reginald Denny's *The Leather Pushers*, the Slim Summerville two-reelers, etc., and in the '30s in *Dynamite* (cast-listed as "a neighbor"), *The Sign of the Cross*, *The Girl of the Golden West* (Wowkle), others; long a radio actress, she was last onscreen in a small role in *Samson and Delilah*, after which she became an actors' business manager.

SEARLE, KAMUELA *(1920)* 20s ——Starred in the title role of the 1920 serial *The Son of Tarzan*; was fatally injured during the filming.

SEARS, ALLAN *(1942)* 65 ——Big, handsome male lead in 1920's *Rio Grande* with Rosemary Theby and *Judy of Rogues Harbor* with Mary Miles Minter; during that decade was also in *Long Live the King* with Jackie Coogan, *The Scarlet Honeymoon*, *Into Her Kingdom* with Corinne Griffith, etc.; in the '30s was in Pickford's *Secrets*, *The Singing Vagabond*, others.

SEARS, FRED F. *(1957)* 44 ——Played generals and other officials in B Westerns from '47: *Fort Savage Raiders*, *West of Dodge City*, *Texas Dynamo*, *Laramie*, etc.

SEARS, ZELDA *(1935)* 61 ——Character actress in *The Bishop Murder Case* (played Mrs. Drukker, wife of character actor George Marion), Shearer's *The Divorcee*, Garbo's *Inspiration*, others.

SEASTROM, VICTOR *(1960)* 80 ——Swedish actor-director who, as the old father in *Wild*

Strawberries, gave one of the screen's immortal performances; in Hollywood for a decade (1920 –30), he directed Chaney in *He Who Gets Slapped,* Gish in *The Scarlet Letter* and *The Wind,* Garbo in *The Divine Woman,* John Gilbert in *Mask of the Devil;* he also starred in and directed *A Man There Was* and *The Stroke of Midnight* (wrote this too); a.k.a. Victor Sjostrom.

SEATON, SCOTT *(1968)* 90 ——Supporting actor in the late '20s and early '30s (in Monte Blue's *The Greyhound Limited,* Billie Dove's *The Other Tomorrow,* William Boyd's *The Leatherneck,* etc.), and later in *Father of the Bride, Donovan's Reef, Twilight of Honor.*

SEBASTIAN, DOROTHY *(1957)* 54 ——Dark-haired beauty who was one of the almost-stars of the '20s; first at Paramount and Warners (in *Winds of Chance, Sackcloth and Scarlet,* etc.), after '27 she was at MGM—almost always the second femme lead—in many: *Our Dancing Daughters, Our Blushing Brides, A Woman of Affairs, Show People, Montana Moon,* etc.; after '30 was starring in B's at smaller companies (*The Deceiver, Contraband, Ship of Wanted Men,* etc.), serials (1937's *The Mysterious Pilot*), and playing the love interest in Westerns (*The Arizona Kid, Kansas Cyclone*); last ('42) had an unbilled bit in Judy Canova's *True to the Army* and an even smaller one—but billed "also in the cast"—in *Reap the Wild Wind;* was once married to William Boyd, whose leading lady she was in 1930's *Officer O'Brien.*

SEDDON, MARGARET *(1968)* 95 ——One of the "pixilated sisters"—the gray-haired one— in *Mr. Deeds Goes to Town;* played old lady roles in many silents (*Little Johnny Jones, New Lives for One, The Snob,* etc.) and talkies (*Lilly Turner, Midshipman Jack, A Woman Rebels, Dr. Kildare's Strange Case,* etc., through 1950's *House by the River*).

SEDGWICK, EDIE *(1971)* 28 ——Uninhibited star of Andy Warhol movies: *Vinyl, Prison,* etc.

SEDGWICK, EDWARD *(1953)* 61 ——After being a boy stage star he played young leading man roles in several—such as 1919's *Checkers* —before becoming the director of *The Flaming Frontier; Slide, Kelly, Slide; Circus Rookies, I'll Tell the World, The Gladiator, Air Raid Wardens,* etc.

SEDGWICK, JOSIE *(1973)* 75 ——Often the blonde leading lady in Hoot Gibson's silent Westerns, she was also in Jackie Coogan's *Daddy,* Barbara La Marr's *The White Moth,* and the heroine in the Charles Hutchinson se-rial *Double Adventure;* sometimes billed Josephine; sister of Eileen and Ed.

SEELEY, BLOSSOM *(1974)* 82 ——Great vaudeville headliner ("Melancholy Baby") who had a top role in 1933's *Broadway Thru a Keyhold* and was later portrayed by Betty Hutton in *Somebody Loves Me;* husband Benny Fields was her partner from 1921 to '59.

SEELEY, JAMES *(1943)* 76 ——Support in Eugene O'Brien's *Channing of the Northwest.*

SEFTON, ERNEST *(1954)* 71 ——Support in Imperial's 1937 *Broken Blossoms.*

SEGAL, BERNARD *(1940)* 72 ——Character role in *Wells Fargo.*

SEGAR, LUCIA *(1962)* 88 ——Character actress in silents (Barthelmess' *Fury* and *The Bond Boy,* Richard Dix's *Knockout Reilly, The Wild Goose,* etc.); last in *Boomerang* (as Mrs. Lukash).

SEITZ, GEORGE B. *(1944)* 56 ——Handsome, multitalented man who was the dean of silent serials—as writer-producer-director of many of the best of Pearl White and Charles Hutchinson; starred in many serials (*The Sky Ranger, Velvet Fingers, Bound and Gagged, Pirate Gold,* etc.) and played the lead opposite June Caprice in *Rogues and Romance,* which he also wrote; then directed dozens (*Society Doctor, Lazy River,* etc.) including most of the "Andy Hardy" pix.

SEKELY, IRENE *(1950)* 36 ——Hungarian actress who was featured in Barbara Britton's *The Fabulous Suzanne,* directed by husband Steve Sekely.

SELBIE, EVELYN *(1950)* 68 ——From 1912 she was so frequently "Broncho Billy" Anderson's leading lady in Westerns, she was called "The Broncho Billy Girl"; supporting roles in dozens of silents: *Omar, the Tentmaker; Camille; The Half Breed; Snowdrift; The Prairie Pirate,* etc.; in numerous talkies: *The Mysterious Dr. Fu Manchu, The Return of Dr. Fu Manchu, The Hatchet Man* (as Wah Li), etc.

SELBY, NORMAN *(1940)* 66 ——Support in the '20s in Maurice "Lefty" Flynn's *Bucking the Line,* Colleen Moore's *April Showers,* Billie Dove's *The Painted Angel,* others.

SELK, GEORGE *(1967)* 73 ——Character in *It Came from Outer Space,* the '54 serial *Trader Tom of the South Seas,* etc.

SELLON, CHARLES *(1937)* 58 ——Shirley Temple's sour-puss Uncle Ned Smith in *Bright Eyes*, he was one of the busiest of character actors; silents: *The Bad Man, Merton of the Movies, Lucky Devil, The Speeding Venus,* many more; talkies: *The Social Lion, Honey, Let's Go Native, The Devil Is a Woman, Diamond Jim,* and especially W.C. Fields' *It's a Gift,* as the crotchety old, cane-waving blind man, Mr. Muckle.

SELTEN, MORTON *(1939)* 79 ——British actor who was superb as the ancient, ghostly head of Robert Donat's Scottish clan in *The Ghost Goes West;* was a distinguished old man in many: *A Yank at Oxford, Fire over England, The Thief of Bagdad, Juggernaut,* etc.

SELWYN, RUTH *(1954)* 49 ——Onscreen in the early '30s, her best break was as Keaton's leading lady in *Speak Easily* (made at MGM, the parent company of which, Loew's, was controlled by her sister's husband, Nicholas Schenck); had a supporting role (Mitzi) in *Polly of the Circus,* starring close friend Marion Davies, *New Morals for Old, Fugitive Lovers,* etc.; wife of director Edgar Selwyn.

SEMON, LARRY *(1928)* 39 ——Vitagraph's great little whey-faced country bumpkin comedian, with his bowler hat and baggy trousers held by suspenders close to his chin; in dozens of one- and two-reelers loaded with sight gags, he was the simpleton who drew violence like a magnet—resulting in the inevitable chase; among the best of his short films: *The Sawmill* (the lovely heroine was wife, Dorothy Dwan), *Bathing Beauties and Big Boobs, The Sportsman, The Grocery Clerk, Chumps and Chances;* made numerous longer films from the mid-'20s on: *The Girl in the Limousine; The Wizard of Oz; Spuds; Stop, Look and Listen; The Perfect Clown*—and he was, just one step behind Chaplin and Keaton.

SENNETT, MACK *(1960)* 80 ——The father of motion picture comedy at whose "fun factory" was to be found every great screen comic, and at his or her hilarious best: Roscoe "Fatty" Arbuckle, Mabel Normand, Chaplin, Ben Turpin, Louise Fazenda, Hank Mann, et al.; and in scores of their pictures their mentor—producer-director-boss—was to be clowning alongside them, in the "Mabel" pix, the "Fatty" pix, the "Tillie" pix, etc.; once onscreen, moviegoers had the opportunity to see, as himself, the genius whose "Keystone Kops" had brought them pleasure for so many years—in *Hollywood Cavalcade;* two years earlier, the Academy of Motion Picture Arts and Sciences had honored him with an honorary Oscar "for his lasting contribution to the comedy technique of the screen, the basic principles of which are as important today as when they were first put into practice"; was last seen onscreen in '55 in a token appearance in one scene of *Abbott and Costello Meet the Keystone Kops,* in which one "original" Kop, Hank Mann, also appeared; was portrayed on Broadway in '74 by Robert Preston in the musical comedy *Mack and Mabel*—Mabel being, of course, Mabel Normand.

SERRANO, VINCENT *(1935)* 68 ——Stage actor who brought dignity to top supporting roles in just three: *Eyes of Youth* with Clara Kimball Young and Milton Sills ('19), *The Branded Woman* ('20), and *Convoy* with Lowell Sherman ('27).

SERVOSS, MARY *(1968)* 80 ——Fine character actress from Broadway who entered movies in her 50s; was in *So Proudly We Hail* (Capt. "Ma" McGregory), *In This Our Life* (as the wife of Bette Davis' "uncle," Charles Coburn), *Mrs. Parkington* (Mrs. Graham), *Summer Storm* (Mrs. Kalenin), *Conflict, Experiment Perilous, Beyond the Forest,* etc.

SESSIONS, ALMIRA *(1974)* 85 ——Played skinny, beaky, eagle-eyed gossips—usually spinsters or widows—in more than 200 after *Little Nellie Kelly: The Miracle of Morgan's Creek* (wife of Justice of the Peace Porter Hall), *Apartment for Peggy* (Mrs. Landon), *Sullivan's Travels* (Ursula), *The Diary of a Chambermaid* (Marianne), *Rosemary's Baby* (oldest member of the witches' coven), etc.; last in Woody Allen's *Everything You Wanted to Know About Sex But Were Afraid to Ask.*

SETON, BRUCE *(1969)* 60 ——Tall, lean, good-looking character (after being a leading man) in dozens of British pix; often was a law official: *The Green Cockatoo, Fabian of the Yard, Love from a Stranger, Tight Little Island,* etc.

SEVER, ALBERT *(1953)* 62 ——Support in the '20s.

SEVERIN-MARS, M. *(1921)* 20s ——Starred as doomed soldier Francois in the French epic war drama *J'Accuse* ('19), which was a "cry against the German militarism that destroyed civilized Europe"; was also in *La Roue* and *La Dixieme Symphonie.*

SEWELL, ALLEN *(1954)* 70 ——Support in silent Westerns: *Between Dangers,* the first versions of both *The Spoilers* and *The Squaw Man,* etc.

SEYFERTH, WILFRIED *(1954)* 46 ——Support in German movies and two American ones: Gene Kelly's *The Devil Makes Three* (Nazi Hansig), Basehart's *Decision Before Dawn*.

SEYMOUR, CLARINE *(1920)* 20 ——Vivacious brunette dancing beauty who seemed destined to become one of Griffith's greatest discoveries; a sensation in his *The Girl Who Stayed at Home*, she supported Gish in *True Heart Susie* and Barthelmess in *Scarlet Days*, before achieving stardom opposite him in *The Idol Dancer*; Griffith had scheduled her for the *Way Down East* role eventually played by Mary Hay.

SEYMOUR, HARRY *(1967)* 77 ——Character comedian who spent the '30s at Warners: *Boy Meets Girl* (one of the screwball songwriters), *A Slight Case of Murder* (The Singer), *Shipmates Forever, Six Day Bike Rider*, more; and the '40s and '50s at 20th Century-Fox: *A Ticket to Tomahawk* (as Velvet Fingers), *I Wonder Who's Kissing Her Now, Daddy Long Legs*, etc.

SEYMOUR, JANE *(1956)* 57 ——Ma in Ginger Rogers' *Tom, Dick and Harry;* Mrs. Roberts in Colbert's *Remember the Day;* also played the Mother on radio's *Claudia*.

SHACKLETON, ROBERT *(1956)* 42 ——Romantic lead in Ray Bolger's *Where's Charley?;* sang "My Darling, My Darling" and, with Bolger, the title song.

SHADE, JAMESSON *(1956)* 61 ——Character actor in several in the '40s: *Wilson* (Secretary Baker), *Cover-Up, The Woman of the Town, The Utah Kid*, etc.

SHAFER, MOLLIE *(1940)* 68 ——In the '20s was support at Fox (*While the Devil Laughs*) and Universal (*The Big Adventure*).

SHAIFFER, "TINY" *(1967)* 49 ——An "Our Gang" kid in the '20s; r.n. Howard Charles Shaiffer.

SHANKLAND, RICHARD *(1953)* 48 ——Support in Eva Gabor's *Love Island*.

SHANLEY, ROBERT *(1968)* 50s——Singing U.S. Army Sergeant who played Ted Nelson in *This Is the Army*.

SHANNON, MRS. DALE *(1923)* 60s ——Was in early silents.

SHANNON, EFFIE *(1954)* 87 ——Regal stage star who first appeared in '14 in the film version of her Broadway hit *After the Ball*, which had featured that popular song; top supporting roles in many in the '20s: Constance Talmadge's *Mamma's Affair, The Man Who Played God, The Secrets of Paris, Roulette*, Blanche Sweet's *The New Commandment, Sally of the Sawdust* (wife of the Judge, Erville Alderson), others.

SHANNON, ELIZABETH *(1959)* 45 ——Minor actress once married to Alan Curtis.

SHANNON, ETHEL *(1951)* 53 ——Dark-haired beauty who was Syd Chaplin's leading lady in *Charley's Aunt;* in others of the '20s: *The Hero* with Barbara La Marr, *Babe Comes Home* with Babe Ruth, *Oh, Baby!, Daughters of the Rich, Stop Flirting*, etc.; became an extra.

SHANNON, FRANK *(1959)* 84 ——As brilliant scientist Dr. Zarkov, in the "Flash Gordon" serials, he built the rocket ships that launched pals Flash Gordon and Dale Arden and himself to planet Mongo (*Flash Gordon*), Mars (*Flash Gordon's Trip to Mars*), and the frozen land of Frigia (*Flash Gordon Conquers the Universe*); besides being in such silents as *Monsieur Beaucaire* and such talkies as *The Prisoner of Shark Island*, was a regular (McTavish) in the "Torchy Blane" pix.

SHANNON, HARRY *(1964)* 74 ——Casting directors most often called on this gray-haired character when they needed a decent strong-faced smalltown or country type—such as the farmer-father of young *Citizen Kane;* among his 100: *Young Tom Edison, Tugboat Annie Sails Again, The Sullivans*, Fay Bainter's *Mrs. Wiggs of the Cabbage Patch, The Eve of St. Mark* (Chaplain who married Anne Baxter and William Eythe), *Come Next Spring;* sometimes, in Westerns such as Tim Holt's *Rustlers*, was a crooked banker; onscreen from '40, he was last in *Gypsy*, as Rosalind Russell's father.

SHANNON, JACK *(1968)* 76 ——Actor-stuntman who was married to serial queen Grace Cunard for 42 years, surviving her by one; had supporting roles in Westerns.

SHANNON, PEGGY *(1941)* 34 ——A red-headed knockout from the *Follies*, she was chosen by Paramount to succeed Clara Bow and, in her first two years (1931-32), was rushed through nine pix: *The Secret Call* (role intended for Bow, who had quit the studio), *Touchdown, Society Girl, The Road to Reno*, etc.; didn't succeed in making fans forget the Brooklyn Bonfire; secondary roles in another 15 (*Turn Back the Clock, Night Life of the Gods, Blackwell's Island*, etc.); one of her last was 1940's *Street of Missing Women*, in which onetime admirers had to look fast or miss her altogether.

SHANOR, PEGGY *(1935)* 30s ——Beautiful blonde ingenue in several silent serials: *The House of Hate* ('18), *The Sky Ranger* with June

Caprice and George B. Seitz, *The Mystery Mind*, *The Lurking Peril* with George Larkin and Anne Luther.

SHARLAND, REGINALD *(1944)* 57 ——Supporting actor from England; after appearing with John Barrymore in the *Richard III* episode in *The Show of Shows* ('29), was in *Inside the Lines* with Betty Compson, *The Girl of the Port*, with Sally O'Neil, *Scotland Yard*, *Long Lost Father*, *Born to Love*, etc.

SHARP, HENRY *(1964)* 77 ——Pioneer character actor who later played Abe Steiner in *A Face in the Crowd* and the Russian Count in *A Song to Remember*.

SHARP, LEONARD *(1958)* 68 ——British supporting actor; was in *The Mudlark* (as Ben Fox), *The Lady Killers*, *At the Stroke of Nine*, etc.

SHATTUCK, TRULY *(1954)* 78 ——Character actress in Ed Wynn's *Rubber Heels*, James Kirkwood's *The Great Impersonation*, Pauline Frederick's *The Glory of Clementina*, Marion Davies' *Beauty's Worth* (as rich Mrs. Garrison), others of the '20s.

SHAVERS, CHARLIE *(1971)* 53 ——Famous black trumpet player; musical shorts.

SHAW, JACK *(1970)* 88 ——Character in British pix.

SHAW, MONTAGUE *(1968)* 85 ——English-accented, dignified character in many memorable films of the '30s and '40s: *David Copperfield; Rasputin and the Empress; Four Men and a Prayer; My Son, My Son; Tonight and Every Night*, etc.; had bigger roles—often the heroine's brilliant scientist-dad—in almost a dozen serials: *Ace Drummond*, *Undersea Kingdom*, *Flash Gordon's Trip to Mars* (as King of the Clay People), *Buck Rogers*, *The Green Hornet Strikes Again*, etc.; sometimes billed C. Montague Shaw.

SHAW, OSCAR *(1967)* 76 ——Curly-haired, handsome actor who played a boxer in *The Great White Way* ('24) opposite Anita Stewart; also was in *The King on Main Street* and *Going Crooked* with Bessie Love, co-starred with Shearer in *Upstage*, and played the romantic lead opposite Mary Eaton in *The Cocoanuts;* in '29 was involved in one of the screen's historic curiosities—played the doughboy lover of Marion Davies in a silent version of *Marianne;* sound came in, the pic was immediately remade with Davies playing her same role opposite Lawrence Gray—with the silent version being shown in small towns, the talkie in cities; last had a supporting role in Crosby's *Rhythm on the River.*

SHAWN, PHILIP *(1972)* 48 ——Starred in 1951's *The Sun Sets at Dawn;* later was support (billed under real name Pat Waltz) in Gary Merrill's *The Human Jungle.*

SHAWN, TED *(1972)* 80 ——World-famous modern dancer who was co-founder, with wife Ruth St. Denis, of the Denishawn Dancers; portrayed Faun in Swanson's *Don't Change Your Husband* and starred in a dance film, *Arabian Duet* ('22).

SHCHUKIN, BORIS *(1939)* 45 ——Starred as Lenin in a '38 Russian film, *Lenin in October;* was honored as "People's Artist of the U.S.S.R."

SHEA, BIRD *(1925)* ——Support in Norma Talmadge's *The Lady.*

SHEA, JACK *(1970)* 70 ——Support in Wyman's *Lucy Gallant*, two Republic B's, *Satan's Satellites* and *Million Dollar Pursuit*, and the serial *Zombies of the Stratosphere* (a cop).

SHEAN, AL *(1949)* 81 ——Of Mr. Gallagher and Mr. Shean, the legendary comedy team that starred in *Around the Town* ('23) after Broadway success in the *Follies;* Shean played gently comic characters in many in the '30s and '40s: *Page Miss Glory* (Mr. Hansburger), *San Francisco* (MacDonald's Music Professor), *The Blue Bird* (Grandpa Tyl), *Joe and Ethel Turp Call on the President, Ziegfeld Girl* (himself), etc.; ventured into drama by playing a priest in *Hitler's Madman.*

SHEARN, EDITH *(1968)* 98 ——Actress-widow of Warner Oland.

SHEEHAN, JOHN *(1952)* 61 ——Runyonesque supporting actor who was in more than 60 after 1930: *Little Miss Marker* (Sun Rise), *Wake Up and Live, Marked Woman, The Case of the Black Cat, Wake Island, I Wouldn't Be in Your Shoes, King for a Night*, etc.; sometimes billed Jack.

SHEFFIELD, LEO *(1951)* 77 ——Support in British pix.

SHEFFIELD, REGINALD *(1957)* 56 ——English actor of slight build who, in the '30s, was in several Arliss films: *Old English* (ingenue Betty Lawford's love interest), *The Green Goddess, Cardinal Richelieu, The House of Rothschild;* also in *Of Human Bondage* (a young doctor who treated Davis in her final illness), *Gunga Din, Suspicion*, many WW II pix in which he was an English officer (*Tonight We Raid Calais, Bomber's Moon, Eagle Squadron*, etc.); last of his 50 roles was in 1958's *The Buccaneer.*

SHELDON, JERRY *(1962)* 61 ——Minor roles such as a train conductor in Presley's *Love Me Tender.*

SHELDON, MRS. MARION *(1944)* 58 ——Support in silents.

SHELTON, GEORGE *(1971)* 86 ——He and comedy partner, Tom Howard, starred in Educational two-reelers; alone, he was in *The House on 92nd Street* (as Frank Jackson), and a few more.

SHELTON, JOHN *(1972)* 55 ——Thin-faced, with black wavy hair and an easy grin, he was a promising MGM lead in the '40s; was in *We Who Are Young* (with his to-be wife Kathryn Grayson), *Dr. Kildare Goes Home, Whispering Ghosts, A-Haunting We Will Go, The Time of Their Lives,* etc.; became a businessman and would-be producer—was in Ceylon setting up a multiple picture deal at the end.

SHEPARD, ALICE ——See Alice Shepard Davenport.

SHEPLEY, MICHAEL *(1961)* 54 ——Stocky support with moustache and thrust-out chin in many British pix: *Henry V* (Captain Gower); *Goodbye, Mr. Chips; Maytime in Mayfair; Crackerjack; Gideon of Scotland Yard; A Place of One's Own,* etc.

SHEPLEY, RUTH *(1951)* 62 ——Brunette beauty who was Lady Jane Bolingbroke in Marion Davies' *When Knighthood Was in Flower.*

SHERIDAN, ANN *(1967)* 51 ——Warners publicized her with sexy stills and pinned the Oomph Girl label on her, but what she was, really, red-haired beauty or no, was a "good Joe"—the role of Randy best revealing that in *Kings Row;* dished out down-to-earth humor with charm in scores: *They Drive by Night, Angels With Dirty Faces, Navy Blues, Torrid Zone, Good Sam, The Doughgirls,* etc.; was at her most glamorous in *Shine On Harvest Moon, The Man Who Came to Dinner, Honeymoon for Three;* proved her dramatic abilities in *Nora Prentiss, The Unfaithful, Come Next Spring;* offscreen after 1956's *Woman and the Hunger,* she starred on TV in a soap opera (*Another World*), guested on such TV dramatic shows as *Playhouse 90,* toured in a play (*Odd Man In*), and, finally, starred in the television series *Pistols 'n Petticoats.*

SHERIDAN, FRANK *(1943)* 74 ——Character, in many after '21, who most often played lawyers and doctors; was in *A Free Soul* (Prosecuting Attorney), *The Life of Emile Zola* (Van Cassell), *The Last Mile, Woman Accused, Donovan's Kid, Washington Merry-Go-Round,* etc.

SHERMAN, FRED *(1969)* 64 ——Character (Jeb Farley) in Bogart's *Chain Lightning;* also in *Lady in the Lake, Some Like It Hot,* etc.

SHERMAN, LOWELL *(1934)* 49 ——Introduced in 1920's *Way Down East* as the handsome scoundrel who deceived Lillian Gish in a mock marriage, this star played many more smoothies (sometimes not bad, just rich) in silents and talkies: *Convoy* with Dorothy Mackaill, *Yes or No?* with Norma Talmadge, *The Divine Woman* with Garbo, *Bright Lights of Broadway, The Heart of a Follies Girl;* in 1930-32 he directed five in which he also starred: *The Pay-Off, Lawful Larceny, The Royal Bed, The Greeks Had a Word for Them, Bachelor Apartment;* also directed *Morning Glory,* which won Hepburn her first Academy Award.

SHERRY, J. BARNEY *(1944)* 72 ——Prematurely white-haired and strong-featured, this actor was starred from his first short film, 1905's *Raffles, the Amateur Cracksman,* with 1910-20 being his most popular decade; starred then in numerous Westerns, often as an Indian chief (*The Heart of an Indian, The Secret Code, Flying Colors, High Stakes*), religious motif films (*Civilization*), serials (*The Lion Man*); in the '20s had character roles—frequently a millionaire in tux—in two dozen features (*Dinty, The White Sister, What Fools Men Are, Born Rich, The Secrets of Paris,* etc.) and numerous serials (*Casey of the Coast Guard, The Crimson Flash,* Allene Ray's *Play Ball,* others); *Jazz Heaven,* with John Mack Brown and Sally O'-Neil, was his last.

SHERWOOD, HENRY *(1967)* 83 ——Character in minor roles for years.

SHERWOOD, YORKE *(1958)* 85 ——Large-sized character actor who, before playing Dr. Samuel Johnson in *Lloyds of London,* was one of the old millionaires in the first *Gentlemen Prefer Blondes,* Mr. Bodfish in *The Man from Blankley's,* a taxi driver in *The Eagle and the Hawk;* later, he was Beadle in Fontaine's *Jane Eyre.*

SHIELD, FRED *(1974)* 70 ——Was top-billed in Disney's *The Three Caballeros.*

SHIELDS, ARTHUR *(1970)* 73 ——Character from Ireland whose brogue and face were reminiscent of more-famous brother Barry Fitzgerald's, but whose acting style was less elfin; on Hollywood screens from *The Plough and the Stars* ('37), he was to be found, in strong, small roles, in the best: *Drums Along the Mohawk* (Reverend), *The Long Voyage Home* (Donkey Man), *How Green Was My Valley* (Mr. Parry), *National Velvet* (Mr. Hallam, at whose shop was held the horse raffle won by Taylor), *The White Cliffs of Dover*, dozens more; last in 1962's *The Pigeon That Took Rome.*

SHIELDS, HELEN *(1963)* 60s ——One of radio's most famous actresses (star of the soap opera *I Love Linda Dale*, etc.), she had minor supporting roles in *The Wrong Man* and *The Whistle at Eaton Falls.*

SHIELDS, SYDNEY *(1960)* 72 ——She had supporting roles in silents.

SHINE, JOHN L. *(1930)* 76 ——Support in silents: *Little Lady Eileen*, Pauline Frederick's *Mrs. Dane's Defense*, others.

SHINER, RONALD *(1966)* 63 ——Comedy star in English pix, with a long nose, long face, and long-lasting smile; in two score: *Reluctant Heroes*, *The Ship Was Loaded*, *The Way to the Stars*, *The Night We Got the Bird*, *Worm's Eye View*, *The Smugglers*, etc.

SHIPMAN, NELL *(1970)* 77 ——Lovely dark-haired Vitagraph leading lady of 1919, who, in '35, was the original author of the movie *Wings in the Dark.*

SHIRART, GEORGIA *(1929)* 67 ——Character actress in one of 1923's poorer films, *The Girl Who Came Back.*

SHIRLEY, BOBBIE *(1970)* ——Supporting actress in silents.

SHIRLEY, FLORENCE *(1967)* 74 ——Dignified support in Shearer's last movies, *Her Cardboard Lover* and *We Were Dancing*, *A Yank at Eton*, *Stars and Stripes Forever*, etc.

SHIRLEY, TOM *(1962)* 62 ——In his 20s had supporting roles in many Universal Westerns such as Jack Hoxie's *Red Hot Leather;* started as a kid actor with Essanay.

SHOOTING STAR *(1966)* 76 ——Sioux Indian featured in many Westerns, including *Laramie.*

SHORES, BYRON *(1957)* 50 ——Played officers —police and military—in *Johnny Eager* (cop), *The Major and the Minor* (military school's Captain Durand), *Too Many Girls* (Sheriff Andaluz), etc.

SHORT, ANTRIM *(1972)* 72 ——"All-American" boy type who was one of the silent screen's most popular juveniles; in 1917's *Tom Sawyer* with Jack Pickford, *Pride and the Man* with William Russell, *O'Malley of the Mounted* with William S. Hart, *Classmates* with Barthelmess, *Wild-Fire* with Aileen Pringle, and co-starred with Viola Dana in *Please Get Married;*

became a casting director for Goldwyn and Universal and finally a top Hollywood agent.

SHORT, FLORENCE *(1946)* 57 ——Support in silents: the King Baggot serial *The Eagle's Eye*, Barthelmess' *The Enchanted Cottage*, Constance Talmadge's *Lessons in Love*, Hope Hampton's *Does It Pay?*, etc.; she and Gertrude were the daughters of Lew.

SHORT, GERTRUDE *(1968)* 66 ——Funny, cute little fat girl who starred in '24 in RKO's "The Telephone Girl" comedy series (*Sherlock's Home*, *Julius Sees Her*, etc.); onscreen from 1913's *Uncle Tom's Cabin* (was Little Eva), she had supporting roles in dozens in the '20s and '30s: *Tillie the Toiler* (Davies' Pal Bubbles), *Crinoline and Romance*, *The People vs. Nancy Preston*, *Broadway Hoofer*, *Affairs of Susan*, *Tip-Off Girls*, *Son of Kong*, etc.

SHORT, HASSARD *(1956)* 78 ——Geraldine Farrar's tuxedoed leading man in *Turn of the Wheel;* was also in *Woman's Place* with Constance Talmadge, *The Stronger Vow*, *The Way of a Woman.*

SHORT, LEW *(1958)* 83 ——Onscreen from early Biograph days, this character actor was especially popular in the '20s; was in Chaney's *The Big City* (as O'Hara), Dolores Costello's *The Heart of Maryland*, Ted Lewis' *Is Everybody Happy?*, *The Black Pearl*, *Blue Eagle*, etc.

SHOTWELL, MARIE *(1934)* 54 ——Character actress who, after 1916's *The Witching Hour*, was in many silents: *The Manicure Girl*, *Shore Leave*, *Lovers in Quarantine*, *Running Wild*, *One Woman to Another*, etc.

SHRINER, HERB *(1970)* 51 ——Folksy TV-radio humorist who was featured in *Main Street to Broadway.*

SHUBERT, EDDIE *(1937)* 38 ——Comic support in many at Warners in the '30s: *Alibi Ike*, *The Goose and the Gander*, *6-Day Bike Rider*, *The Case of the Velvet Claws*, *Don't Bet on Blondes*, more.

SHUMAN, ROY *(1973)* 48 ——Supporting actor —popular in TV soap operas—who appeared in *The Goddess*, *The Gang That Couldn't Shoot Straight* (as the Mayor), others.

SHUTTA, JACK (1957) 58 ——Supporting comic in *Abbott and Costello Go to Mars* and their *The Wistful Widow of Wagon Gap;* also in *Whoopee* (with wife Ethel), *The Burning Cross*, etc.

SHY, GUS *(1945)* 51 ——Collegiate type who was one of the stars of MGM's 1930 version of

Good News; also in that year's *New Moon* and *A Lady's Morals* (Grace Moore's first), then in *I Sell Anything, The Captain's Kid, Once a Doctor;* became a dialogue director.

SIDNEY, GEORGE *(1945)* 67 ——Pugnacious little Cohen in all "The Cohens and the Kellys" comedies and Potash in the "Potash and Perlmutter" movies; was also in *Manhattan Melodrama, The Good Old Soak, Diamond Jim, We Americans,* many others.

SIDNEY, SCOTT *(1928)* 56 ——A supporting actor for Ince in the teens, he became a director of comedy features—Syd Chaplin's *Charley's Aunt,* Phyllis Haver's *The Nervous Wreck,* etc.

SIERRA, MARGARITA *(1963)* 26 ——Spanish beauty who starred on TV in *Surfside 6* and had a few minor movie roles.

SIEGMANN, GEORGE *(1928)* 45 ——Big-bodied, brutal-faced actor who was prominently cast in most of the epics of the silent screen: *The Birth of a Nation* (mulatto politician Silas Lynch), *Intolerance* (Cyprus the Persian in "The Babylonian Story"), *The King of Kings* (Barabbas), *The Queen of Sheba, The Three Musketeers,* and many more.

SIGNORET, GABRIEL *(1937)* 63 ——Sharpnosed French character actor who supported Sarah Bernhardt in 1916's *Mothers of France;* in other silents.

SILBERT, LISA *(1965)* 85 ——Support in Lila Lee's *Broken Hearts.*

SILETTI, MARIO *(1964)* 60 ——Jovial, fleshy Italian actor who was Papa Caruso in *The Great Caruso;* was also in *East of Eden* (Piscora) and many at 20th Century-Fox in the '50s: *Three Coins in the Fountain, Under My Skin, My Cousin Rachel, Taxi, Anne of the Indies,* etc.

SILLS, MILTON *(1930)* 48 ——Few silent stars loomed larger than this "strong silent type" who—onscreen from 1914's *The Pit*—starred in more than six dozen; made many with Doris Kenyon, who became his wife (*Men of Steel, The Rack, I Want My Man, The Hawk's Nest,* etc.), and had romantic roles opposite most other femme stars of the time (Gloria Swanson in *The Great Moment,* Viola Dana in *Satan Jr.,* Ethel Clayton in *Souls Adrift,* Pauline Frederick in *The Fear Woman,* etc.); was particularly effective in swashbucklers (*The Sea Hawk*) and other action dramas (1923's *The Spoilers, The Sea Wolf, At the End of the World,* etc.); at Warners when talkies came in, he made an easy transition to sound in *The Barker.*

SILVA, SIMONE *(1957)* 29 ——Voluptuous leading lady in *Duel in the Jungle, The Dynamiters, The Weak and the Wicked,* etc.; made newspaper headlines via a wayward bikini at a Cannes Film Festival in the '50s.

SILVANI, ALDO *(1964)* 73 ——In *The Nights of Cabiria* was the jowly old movie-house fortune teller who predicted Giulietta Masina's future; was Colombaini in *La Strada,* the Man in Nazareth in *Ben Hur;* in many others: *To Live in Peace, Beat the Devil, Sodom and Gomorrah,* etc.

SILVER, CHRISTINE *(1960)* 75 ——Character actress in such British pix as Emlyn Williams' *Dead Men Tell No Tales.*

SILVER, PAULINE *(1969)* 80 ——Support in silents.

SILVERA, FRANK *(1970)* 56 ——Small, dynamic black actor from Jamaica who almost always played Spaniards and was particularly fine as Huerta in *Viva Zapata!;* was in another 25: *Che!, The Bravados, The Mountain, The Appaloosa, Guns of the Magnificent Seven, Hombre,* and *The Greatest Story Ever Told,* in which he was Caspar; co-starred on TV in *High Chaparral.*

SIMANEK, OTTO *(1967)* 66 ——Minor support in Hitchcock's *The Wrong Man.*

SIMMONDS, ANNETTE *(1959)* 41 ——British support in *No Orchids for Miss Blandish,* Dane Clark's *Blackout,* etc.

SIMON, SOL *(1940)* 76 ——Minor support in Milton Sills' *The Barker, Greed,* Westerns such as *Headin' North.*

SIMPSON, IVAN *(1951)* 76 ——Scottish character actor who played Limmiter in Bartholomew's *David Copperfield,* Reverend Parris in *Maid of Salem,* Battle in both the silent and talkie versions of *The Green Goddess* (a member of Arliss' "stock company," he also was in *Disraeli, The House of Rothschild,* and both versions of his *The Man Who Played God*); one of Hollywood's busiest for three decades—in more than 100—he last played Mr. Woods in Fontaine's *Jane Eyre* and the Magistrate in Veronica Lake's *The Hour Before the Dawn.*

SIMPSON, RONALD *(1957)* 61 ——Support in the English pic *The Long Dark Hall.*

SIMPSON, RUSSELL *(1959)* 81 ——One thinks of him first, this veteran of 500 films, for the fine-faced, grizzled rustics he portrayed for John Ford: *The Grapes of Wrath* (splendid as

Pa Joad), *Drums Along the Mohawk* (Dr. Petry), *Young Mr. Lincoln, Tobacco Road* (Chief of Police), *My Darling Clementine, The Sun Shines Bright,* more; memorable movies he did for other directors: *Mr. Smith Goes to Washington, Romance of Rosy Ridge, Meet John Doe, San Francisco, Tennessee Johnson,* etc.; onscreen from the first ('14) *The Virginian,* in a small role, he soon starred, most handsomely, in many Westerns: *The Brand, The Barrier, The Branding Iron, Blue Jeans,* etc.; became a top character actor in the '20s and remained one; last played the Sheriff in *The Horse Soldiers,* directed by—appropriately—John Ford.

SINCLAIR, ARTHUR *(1951)* 68 ——Support in numerous British pix: Ann Neagle's *Peg of Old Drury,* Margaret Lockwood's *Hungry Hill,* etc.

SINCLAIR, HORACE *(1949)* 64 ——English actor who played the butler in *One-Third of a Nation.*

SINCLAIR, HUGH *(1962)* 59 ——Tall, curly-haired, and handsome, this Englishman had his first screen opportunity in Hollywood, as Lord Henry Blayne, in Constance Bennett's *Our Betters;* returned to England to star in many in the '30s: *The Marriage of Corbal, Escape Me Never, Strangers on a Honeymoon,* etc.; had top supporting roles in many later: *The Rocking Horse Winner, Circle of Danger, Three Steps in the Dark,* more.

SINGLETON, CATHERINE *(1969)* 65 ——Miss Universe of 1926 who was featured in more than a dozen silents and the *Ziegfeld Follies.*

SINOEL *(1949)* 81 ——French character actor; in *Francis the First, The Last Millionaire,* etc.

SIPPERLY, RALPH *(1928)* 38 ——Played the Barber in Janet Gaynor's *Sunrise.*

SISSON, VERA *(1954)* 63 ——Dark-haired, dark-eyed beauty who became an "overnight star" at Universal in 1914—after being an extra—and was J. Warren Kerrigan's leading lady in *Landon's Legacy* and others; support in the '20s in Louise Brooks' *Love 'Em and Leave 'Em,* etc.

SJOSTROM, VICTOR (VIKTOR) *(1960)* 80 ——See Victor Seastrom.

SKELLY, HAL *(1934)* 43 ——Starred sensationally opposite Nancy Carroll in the '29 talkie *The Dance of Life,* based on the Broadway play *Burlesque,* in which he had created the role of Skid; was just as dynamic in his other six: *Woman Trap* with Chester Morris, *Behind the Make-Up* with Fay Wray, *Men Are Like That,*

The Struggle (Griffith's disastrous last, but this star won raves), *Hotel Variety, Shadow Laughs;* all but forgotten now, he could have been an alltime great.

SKELLY, JAMES *(1969)* 33 ——Minor supporting roles.

SKINNER, GLADYS *(1968)* ——Supporting actress.

SKINNER, OTIS *(1942)* 84 ——*Kismet* has become synonymous with this distinguished actor's name; played it on the world's stages for years and starred in a silent movie version of it ('20) and a talkie ('30); also starred onscreen in *Romance* with Doris Keane and *Mister Antonio* with Leo Carrillo; father of character actress Cornelia Otis Skinner.

SKIPWORTH, ALISON *(1952)* 88 ——Grand old comedienne from England and the stage—big and broad, like her acting; W.C. Fields several times met his nemesis in her (*Six of a Kind, If I Had a Million, Tillie and Gus*); on Hollywood screens just eight years, from '30, she was authoritatively present in more than 60 movies: *Outward Bound, Night After Night* (imposing Miss Jellyman who gave Raft elocution lessons), *Madame Racketeer, Song of Songs, The Gorgeous Hussy, The Casino Murder Case, Becky Sharp, Wide Open Faces,* etc.; returned to Broadway, retiring after 1942's *Lady of the Valley.*

SLACK, FREDDIE *(1965)* 55 ——He and his dance orchestra ("Cow Cow Boogie") were in *The Sky's the Limit, Reveille with Beverly, Follow the Boys, High School Hero,* etc., almost always with Ella May Morse upfront winging the lyrics.

SLADE, OLGA *(1949)* ——British actress who had a supporting role in Hitchcock's *The Farmer's Wife* ('28).

SLAUGHTER, TOD *(1956)* 71 ——Melodramatic English star, black of hair and heart, who, the more movie fans hissed, the more he hammed; was at his evil best in *The Face at the Window, The Hooded Terror, Crimes at the Dark House, Murder in the Red Barn.*

SLEZAK, LEO *(1946)* 71 ——Opera star-father of Walter; featured in many European films: *Love in Waltz Time, Immortal Melodies, La Paloma,* etc.

SLEZAK, MARGARETE *(1953)* 51 ——Daughter of Leo; played Paul Hartman's wife, Mrs. Jaromir, in *Man on a Tightrope;* otherwise in European films.

SLOANE, EVERETT *(1965)* 55 ——Superlative, sandy-haired character actor who came to Hollywood as a member of Welles' Mercury Players and was with him in *Citizen Kane* (lawyer Bernstein), *The Lady from Shanghai* (Hayworth's husband, Arthur Bannister), *Journey Into Fear, The Prince of Foxes;* other pix in which he was outstanding: *Patterns, The Big Knife* (as Palance's cowed-by-Hollywood agent), *The Men, Marjorie Morningstar* (Natalie Wood's father), *Somebody Up There Likes Me.*

SLOANE, OLIVE *(1963)* 67 ——British character actress (a look-alike for Ilona Massey) who was at her prime as the boozy old show girl scientist Barry Jones forces to help him with his mad-bomber scheme in *Seven Days to Noon;* also in *A Prize of Gold, The Weak and the Wicked, Meet Mr. Lucifer, Under Capricorn,* etc.

SMALL, DICK *(1972)* 58 ——Popular band singer in the '30s who was in musical shorts.

SMALLEY, PHILLIPS *(1939)* 63 ——Fine-looking actor, onscreen from 1909, who starred as Shylock in 1914's *The Merchant of Venice* with wife Lois Weber as Portia; they also co-starred in *The Jew's Christmas, False Colors;* she went on to become, almost immediately, the "highest salaried woman director in the world," helming 1916's *Where Are My Children?*, many more; and he—also a director—played top roles in dozens to the end of his life: *A Cigarette—That's All* with Jack Holt, *Daughters of Today, Charley's Aunt* with Syd Chaplin, *Stella Maris* with Mary Philbin, *Stage Kisses, Bolero, Night Life of the Gods, A Night at the Opera,* etc.

SMART, J. SCOTT *(1960)* 57 ——Starred in *The Fat Man* both on radio and in the movie; had a character role in *Kiss of Death.*

SMILEY, COL. JOSEPH *(1945)* 64 ——Solidly built gray-haired character who, with all the Pickfords and others, was a member of the original Imp Company in 1910; was in and directed (1913's *The Battle of Shiloh,* etc.) many early silents; in the '20s was one of Hollywood's most stalwart character actors in Alice Joyce's *The Scarab Ring,* Barthelmess' *Experience,* Gilda Gray's *Aloma of the South Seas,* Thomas Meighan's *Old Home Week,* etc.

SMITH, ALBERT J. *(1939)* 45 ——Young support in the '20s in many serials (*The Fast Express, Strings of Steel, In the Days of Daniel Boone,* etc.) and Westerns (Buck Jones' *Whispering Sage,* Hoot Gibson's *Taming the West,* Art Acord's *Hard Fists* and *The Circus Cyclone,* more); last played a con in Preston Foster's *The Last Mile.*

SMITH, ART *(1973)* 73 ——Top character actor with a distinctive shock of white hair who was in 30 from 1942: *Native Land, Brute Force, Edge of Darkness, T-Men, None Shall Escape, Letter From an Unknown Woman, South Sea Sinner, A Tree Grows in Brooklyn, In a Lonely Place,* etc,; retired after starring on TV in the play *Do Not Go Gentle Into That Good Night* in '67.

SMITH, C. AUBREY *(1948)* 85 ——Hollywood's "resident Britisher," this big, blustery man with the bushy brows and mustache, and ever present pipe, was the Union Jack personified; Shirley Temple doted on him in *Wee Willie Winkie,* as did movie audiences in that and over 100 others in which he was incisively present from 1915's *Builder of Bridges* on; among his most representative talkies: *The Lives of a Bengal Lancer, Little Lord Fauntleroy, The Prisoner of Zenda* ('37), *Four Feathers, The Sun Never Sets, Rebecca, Waterloo Bridge, Forever and a Day, The White Cliffs of Dover;* last in *Little Women* with Taylor and Allyson.

SMITH, CHARLES H. *(1942)* 76 ——Was the father of heroine Annabelle Lee (Marian Mack) in Keaton's *The General;* was also in *Naughty Nanette, The Silver Lining* with Jewel Carmen, *Clear the Decks* with Reginald Denny, *The Girl on the Barge* with Sally O'Neil, etc.

SMITH, CYRIL *(1963)* 71 ——Character in British pix, reminiscent of Arthur Treacher except that he played milder men—when not a bobbie; in more than 100: *Sailor Beware, John and Julie, So Well Remembered, Sidewalks of London, Mother Riley Meets the Vampire,* etc.

SMITH, G. ALBERT *(1959)* 61 ——Young support in Nancy Carroll's *Stolen Heaven.*

SMITH, GEORGE W. *(1946)* 48 ——Actor from Broadway who had a supporting role in the Robert Benchley comedy *Snafu.*

SMITH, GERALD OLIVER *(1974)* 81 —— Played butlers in *100 Men and a Girl, That Forsyte Woman,* and many of the others in which he appeared: *Top of the Town, The Man I Marry, When You're in Love,* etc.

SMITH, HOWARD I. *(1968)* 75 ——Uncle Charlie in *Death of a Salesman* was the best screen outing of king-sized character who was generally typecast as a politico (*State of the Union*) or military officer (Admiral Boatwright in *Don't Go Near the Water*); was also in *Kiss of Death, Street With No Name, A Face in the Crowd, Murder, Inc.,* others.

SMITH, JACK C. *(1944)* 47 ——Was Monk, the ex-convict cohort of mad scientist Lugosi, in the serial *The Phantom Creeps;* was often in Westerns (*Frontier Scout, Heroes of the Alamo*) and prison pix (*Paroled to Die*).

SMITH, JOE *(1952)* 52 ——Supporting role (Harry) in Tony Martin's *Two Tickets to Broadway;* also in Gordon MacRae's *The Desert Song.*

SMITH, MARGARET *(1960)* 79 ——Character actress in silent Westerns such as Jack Hoxie's *Roaring Adventure.*

SMITH, MATTHEW *(1953)* 47 ——Played one of Shearer's brothers, George Barrett, in *The Barretts of Wimpole Street.*

SMITH, SID (SIDNEY) *(1928)* 36 ——Knockabout comedian who starred with a partner (alternately Harry McCoy, George Monberg, Jimmy Adams), as Percy and Ferdy, in many "Hall Room Boys" two-reelers in the early '20s; later was featured in comedy spoofs of WW I: *Dugan of the Dugouts* and *Top Sergeant Mulligan.*

SMITH, STANLEY *(1974)* 69 ——Handsome and greatly popular leading man who was on-screen from 1929; among his pictures: *The Sophomore* (his debut), *Sweetie, Honey, King of Jazz, Good News, Queen High, Love Among the Millionaires, Stepping Sisters,* and *Flight Command;* had been retired from movies for more than three decades.

SMITH, THOMAS C. *(1950)* 58 ——Featured in Syndicate Films' *The Invaders* ('29).

SMYTHE, FLORENCE *(1925)* 47 ——Character actress in several Lasky silents including *The Wild Goose Chase* (as hero Tom Forman's mother), in which her character star-husband, Theodore Roberts, also appeared; sometimes billed Smith.

SNELLING, MINNETTE *(1945)* 67 ——Character comedienne in Sennett two-reelers.

SNOW, MARGUERITE *(1958)* 69 ——Radiantly beautiful brunette who starred in several major silent serials; played Princess Olga in *The Million Dollar Mystery* (her leading man, playing Jimmy Norton, the Reporter, was husband James Cruze, later the famous director of *The Covered Wagon*); starred in the title role in *Zudora—The Twenty Dollar Mystery* and was King Baggot's leading lady in *The Eagle's Eye;* among her features: *Broadway Jones* with George M. Cohan, *The Silent Voice* with Francis X. Bushman; onscreen from 1912's *Lucille* through 1925's *Kit Carson over the Great Divide.*

SNOW, MORTIMER, *(1935)* 66 ——Minor support in *When Knighthood Was in Flower,* others.

SODERLING, WALTER *(1968)* 76 ——Distinguished character whose wise old face suggested he had studied the world closely and found it sad; was in *Maid of Salem, Penny Serenade* (as Gillings), *Mr. Smith Goes to Washington* (Senator Pickett), *Meet John Doe* (Barrington), *Rhapsody in Blue* (Muscatel); *So Dear to My Heart* was his last.

SOJIN *(1954)* 70 ——Japanese actor who had top supporting (sometimes co-star) roles in many in the '20s; most memorable for his vindictive malice as Fairbanks' chief rival, the Mongol Prince, in *The Thief of Bagdad* ("remarkable for his undemonstrative countenance, cruel and comfortable, with just a scintillation of a smile when dirty work is to be done," said the *New York Times*); also in *The Chinese Parrot, East of Suez, The Crimson City, Streets of Shanghai,* others; name sometimes spelled So-Jin; returned to Japan after 1930, made more films there.

SOKOLOFF, VLADIMIR *(1962)* 72 ——Great small-size actor from Russia, his face so wonderfully wrinkled it could have been painted on him by the Epstein Brothers; played Anselmo in *For Whom the Bell Tolls,* President Kalinin in *Mission to Moscow,* the priest in *Mr. Lucky,* the Portuguese fisherman in *The Conspirators,* and, in *Passage to Marseilles,* the old butterfly-catcher convict on Devil's Island who buys the boat but may not escape with Bogart and others; made many movies in France (*L'Atalantide,* etc.) before making his Hollywood debut, as Cezanne, in *The Life of Emile Zola,* which was followed by 60; *Taras Bulba* was his last.

SOLAR, WILLIE *(1956)* 65 ——Vaudevillian who was seen as himself in *Billy Rose's Diamond Horseshoe.*

SOMERS, FRED *(1970)* ——Supporting actor in many.

SOMERSET, PAT *(1974)* 77 ——English actor who entered Hollywood movies in his 20s and played important supporting roles for a decade; was in Belle Bennett's *Mother Machree,* Kenneth McKenna's *Men Without Women,* Edmund Lowe's *Born Reckless, Hell's Angels* (as Marryat), *Clive of India, Wee Willie Winkie* (Capt. Stuart), etc.; became, and remained until retirement, an executive of the Screen Actors Guild.

SONNEMANN, EMMY *(1974)* 80 ——German leading lady who married Hermann Goering and retired; was in such talkies as *The Legend of William Tell, Oberwachtmeister Schwenke,* etc.

SONNEVELD, WIM *(1974)* 56 ——Dutch actor who, in *Silk Stockings,* was Peter Ilyitch Boroff, the composer-musician the three Russian emissaries came to Paris to persuade to return to the homeland; after this, his only Hollywood film, returned to Holland where he was a legendary screen star (*Going Dutch,* etc.) and played Professor Higgins onstage in *My Fair Lady.*

SOREL, CECILE *(1966)* 92 ——Character actress in such French films as *The Pearls of the Crown;* much earlier ('09) had starred in *La Tosca.*

SOREL, GEORGE *(1948)* 48 ——Comic support in *Swiss Miss,* The Ritz Brothers' *The Three Musketeers, Hitler—Dead or Alive, Once Upon a Honeymoon,* etc.

SORIN, LOUIS *(1961)* 67 ——In *Animal Crackers* was the ritzy art dealer, Roscoe W. Chandler—nee Abie the Fish Peddler—who was so hilariously disrobed by Chico and Harpo; also in two Morton Downey pix: *Mother's Boy* and *Lucky in Love.*

SOTHERN, E. H. *(1933)* 74——One of the most distinguished names in the American theater; starred in two in '16: *An Enemy to the King* and *The Chattel.*

SOTHERN, HARRY *(1957)* 73 ——Featured in such silents as *How Women Love, The Secrets of Paris,* and *A Tragedy of the East Side.*

SOTHERN, HUGH *(1947)* 66 ——Played Andrew Jackson in *The Buccaneer* ('38), and, the same year, the chief villain (The Lightning) in the serial *Fighting Devil Dogs;* also top support in *Northwest Passage* (Jesse Beacham), *A Dispatch from Reuters* (American Ambassador), etc.

SOTHERN, JEAN *(1924)* 28 ——Classically beautiful co-star in 1915's *The Two Orphans;* she and Theda Bara played the French children —Sothern as the blind sister, Louise—later portrayed by the Gish sisters in the remake, *Orphans of the Storm;* was also the leading lady in the 1916 serial *The Mysteries of Myra.*

SOTHERN, SAM *(1920)* 60s ——Played a millionaire in Milton Sills' *Eyes of Youth.*

SOTO, ROBERTO *(1960)* 72 ——Plump Mexican actor who played comic characters such as Roberto in Lamour's *Tropic Holiday.*

SOUPER, KAY *(1947)* ——Support in England's *The Dreyfus Case.*

SOUTHARD, HARRY *(1939)* 58 ——Character in several minor silents: *Wildness of Youth, The Winning Oar, The Broadway Peacock,* etc.

SOUTHWICK, DALE *(1968)* 55 ——One of the "Our Gang" boys in the '20s.

SOVERN, CLARENCE *(1929)* 28 ——Support in cowboy pix in the '20s.

SPACEY, JOHN G. *(1940)* 44 ——Played Henry Fonda's secretary in *The Moon's Our Home;* was also in *I'm from Missouri; Thank You, Jeeves; Who Killed Gale Preston?,* others.

SPANIER, MUGGSY *(1967)* 64 ——Famous jazz artist on the cornet; was on view in Ted Lewis' *Is Everybody Happy?, Here Comes the Band,* etc.

SPARKS, NED *(1957)* 73 ——Sour-faced, sour-voiced comedian; he, his cigar and nasal tones were great fun in *The Star Maker, 42nd Street, Gold Diggers of 1933, Wake Up and Live, Collegiate, Hawaii Calls,* and a few dozen more including *One in a Million,* which he was.

SPAULDING, GEORGE *(1959)* 77 ——Character actor in Dan Dailey's *When Willie Comes Marching Home,* Heston's *The President's Lady,* etc.

SPEAR, HARRY *(1969)* 56 ——Child player in Mack Sennett's 1926–28 "Smith Family" two-reelers: *Smith's Baby, Smith Baby's Birthday, Smith's Pony,* etc.

SPELLMAN, LEORA *(1945)* 54 ——Support in Walter Huston's *Kongo, Wise Girl;* was the wife of serial villain Charles (Ming the Merciless) Middleton.

SPENCE, RALPH *(1949)* 59 ——One of Sennett's comedy stars in the "Sunshine Comedies" and in two-reelers bearing his name.

SPENCER, DOUGLAS *(1960)* 69 ——Versatile character in many from 1948's *The Big Clock: A Place in the Sun* (Boatkeeper), *Monkey Business* (Dr. Brunner), *Mr Friend Irma* (Interior Decorator), *Shane* (Nordic farmer Mr. Shipstead), *The Diary of Anne Frank* (Kraler), *The Gunfighter, The Thing,* etc.

SPENCER, KENNETH *(1964)* 51 ——Black actor who was superb—and tragically heroic—as demolitions expert Wesley Epps in the doomed Marine patrol in *Bataan;* was also impressive— resplendent in white uniform and gold braid—

as Heaven's General in *Cabin in the Sky;* a singer reminiscent of Robeson, he relocated in Germany after the war and starred in several films.

SPENCER, TIM *(1974)* 65 ——Originator of the musical Sons of the Pioneers, he sang with them in more than 75 Roy Rogers Westerns (the cowboy began as a member of the group); he also appeared in Crosby's *Rhythm on the Range* and Autry's *The Old Corral;* retired from singing and acting in '50 but managed the group for five more years.

SPIKER, RAY *(1964)* 62 ——Played the young ex-con in Vidor's *Our Daily Bread* and lantern-jawed big badmen in many Westerns—Johnson in *Shane*, Rebel White in *San Antonio*—and epics like *Prince Valiant* and *Demetrius and the Gladiators.*

SPINGLER, HARRY *(1953)* 62 ——Support in the Goldwyn silent *Perfect Lady.*

SPITALNY, PHIL *(1970)* 80 ——Led his famous "Hour of Charm" all-girl radio orchestra in numerous musical shorts as well as in Abbott & Costello's *Here Come the Co-eds.*

SPIVY *(1971)* 63 ——She was the bartender in *Requiem for a Heavyweight*, also in *Studs Lonigan* and *All Fall Down;* Ruby Lightfoot in *The Fugitive Kind;* was primarily, offscreen, an owner of nightclubs in which she entertained.

SPONG, HILDA *(1966)* 80 ——Appeared in a 1919 Universal two-reeler, *A Star Over Night.*

SPOONER, EDNA MAY *(1953)* 78 ——Character in *Man and Wife* ('23), other silents.

SPOTTSWOOD, JAMES *(1940)* 58 ——Support in Richard Arlen's *Thunderbolt* and Neil Hamilton's *Hollywood Stadium Mystery.*

SQUIRE, RONALD *(1958)* 72 ——English character with a face of kind refinement who had strong roles in many: *Man With a Million, The Rocking Horse Winner, My Cousin Rachel, Encore, No Highway in the Sky* (Sir John), *Island in the Sun* (Island Governor), *Scotch on the Rocks*, etc.

STAFFORD, HANLEY *(1968)* 69 ——"Daddy" who was with his "Baby Snooks" (Fanny Brice) in *The Great Ziegfeld* and without her in several others: *Francis Covers the Big Town, Lullaby of Broadway, Just This Once*, etc.

STAHL, WALTER *(1943)* 59 ——German-accented character who was Col. Hess in *Beasts of Berlin*, the guest of the Baron (Walter Sle-

zak) in *Once Upon a Honeymoon;* was also in *Woman of the Year*, Grace Moore's *I'll Take Romance*, etc.

STAHL-NACHBAUR, ERNEST *(1960)* 74 —— A lead in *mother Love* and other German films of the early '30s.

STAMP-TAYLOR, ENID *(1946)* 42 ——Support in many English pix: *Hatter's Castle, The Wicked Lady, Caravan, The Lambeth Walk, Candlelight in Algeria*, etc.

STANFORD, HENRY *(1921)* 49 ——Support in Marguerite Clark's *Uncle Tom's Cabin* ('18).

STANDING, GORDON *(1927)* ——Support in the '20s in *Skedaddle Gold, Are Children to Blame?*, Selznick's *Outlaws of the Sea*, and the serial *King of the Jungle.*

STANDING, SIR GUY *(1937)* 53 ——Stalwart English actor who performed with distinction in many Hollywood pix of the '30s: *Death Takes a Holiday* (Duke Lambert at whose Italian villa the drama took place), *The Eagle and the Hawk* (Major Dunham), *Lives of a Bengal Lancer* (Colonel Stone), *Bulldog Drummond Escapes, Now and Forever, The Cradle Song*, etc.; father of Guy Jr. and English star Kay Hammond.

STANDING, GUY, JR. *(1954)* 40s ——Played Widener in *Titanic;* essentially a stage actor.

STANDING, HERBERT *(1955)* 71 ——Support in many in the '20s: Alice Lake's *The Infamous Miss Revell*, Chaney's *The Trap* (as the Priest), Guy Bates Post's *The Masquerader*, Swanson's *The Impossible Mrs. Bellow* (Rev. Dr. Helstan), etc.; brother of Sir Guy.

STANLEY, EDWIN *(1944)* 64 ——Character who played police officers (Detective Casey in *Marked Woman*), doctors *(Buffalo Bill)*, lawyers *(Ninotchka);* in more than 50: *The Life of Vergie Winters, The Man Who Came to Dinner, The Loves of Edgar Allan Poe, You Belong to Me*, etc.; sometimes billed Ed.

STANMORE, FRANK *(1943)* 65 ——British actor who had a top supporting role in Pauline Frederick's *Mumsie* and in 1934's *Don Quixote.*

STANTLEY, RALPH *(1972)* 58 ——Character who specialized in tough-guy roles—in *The Joe Lewis Story*, Marlo Thomas' *Jenny*, etc.

STANTON, FRED *(1925)* 44 ——Support in serials (William Desmond's *Perils of the Yukon*, Bushman and Bayne's *The Great Secret*) and features (John Bowers' *When a Man's a Man*, Claire Windsor's *The Little Church Around the*

Corner, Rockliffe Fellowes' *Trifling with Honor,* etc.).

STARK, MABEL *(1968)* 79 ——Female counterpart to lion-tamer Clyde Beatty; onscreen in 1922's *A Dangerous Adventure.*

STARKEY, BERT *(1939)* 59 ——Support in a few talkies such as *Scarface* (played Epstein) but mostly in silents: Russell Simpson's *Wild Geese,* Cornelius Keefe's *You Can't Beat the Law, Put 'Em Up,* others.

STARR, FRANCES *(1973)* 86 ——Splendid blonde stage actress of whose three movie roles the one in *Five Star Final* was best—the ex-society woman driven to suicide when reporter Edward G. Robinson rehashes a 20-year-old murder in which she was involved; also was in *The Star Witness* and played Frances Dee's mother in *This Reckless Age;* returned to the stage for the memorable role of Dorothy McGuire's dying mother in *Claudia,* remaining active through '53.

STARR, FREDERICK *(1921)* 43 ——Featured in serials (Jack Dempsey's *Daredevil Jack,* Elmo Lincoln's *Elmo the Mighty)* and such Westerns as *The Mysterious Rider.*

STAUB, RALPH *(1969)* 70 ——Famous for his "Screen Snapshots" shorts.

STEADMAN, VERA *(1966)* 66 ——Lovely girl who, after Sennett Bathing Beauty days, was Charles Ray's leading lady in *Scrap Iron;* was also in *The Nervous Wreck, Meet the Prince, Stop Flirting;* support in such talkies as *Ring Around the Moon.*

STEDMAN, LINCOLN *(1948)* 41 ——Roly-poly young man who was Baby Peggy's friend in *Captain January* ('24); good-natured support in many silents: *The Freshie, The Homespun Vamp, Old Swimmin' Hole, One Minute to Play, Harold Teen, Dame Chance,* etc.; among his talkies: *The Wild Party, Sailor Be Good, The Woman Between;* son of star Myrtle Stedman.

STEDMAN, MARSHALL *(1943)* 69 ——Supporting actor; Myrtle's husband, Lincoln's father.

STEDMAN, MYRTLE *(1938)* 48 ——Seeing her in the bit role of a nurse in *Green Lights* in '37, her last year in movies, only those with long memories knew she had been a Selig Polyscope Co. leading lady as far back as 1910—her heart-shaped face, enormous eyes, and dark-blonde beauty being familiar to fans long before they learned her name; in the teens starred in *The*

Valley of the Moon (and numerous others based on Jack London stories), *Peer Gynt,* etc.; in the '20s was in *The Silver Horde, Flaming Youth* with Colleen Moore, *The Famous Mrs. Fair* with Marguerite de la Motte, *Alias the Deacon, Black Roses, Rich Men's Wives,* and two dozen more.

STEELE, MINNIE *(1949)* 67 ——Support in *The Darling of New York* and others that starred Baby Peggy.

STEELE, VERNON *(1955)* 72 ——Silent lead with classically handsome features who was with Mae Marsh in *Polly of the Circus,* Clara Kimball Young in *Hearts in Exile,* Ethel Clayton in *For the Defense,* etc.; support in talkies: *Design for Living* (First Manager), *They Were Expendable* (Corregidor Army Doctor), *Madam Bovary,* etc.

STEELE, WILLIAM *(1966)* 77 ——Top support in several dozen Westerns and action pix in the '20s: Adolphe Menjou's *The Fast Mail,* Hoot Gibson's *The Saddle Hawk,* Jack Hoxie's *A Six-Shootin' Romance,* Jack Donovan's *Hoof Marks,* Buck Jones' *Whispering Sage,* etc.; support in such talkies as Keaton's *Dough Boys* and George O'Brien's *The Lone Star Ranger;* also acted under the name William Gettinger.

STEERS, LARRY *(1951)* 70 ——Character actor in many from the early '20s who several times played lawyers (not always honest), such as the one in pince-nez in *If I Had a Million;* in silents: *New Brooms, The Girl in the Limousine, Bride of the Storm,* etc.; talkies: *Navy Born, Atlantic City, The Gangster,* more.

STEFAN, VIRGINIA *(1964)* 38 ——Supporting roles.

STEHLI, EDGAR *(1973)* 89 ——Veteran radio and stage actor who came to movies late and usually played cantankerous old men: *Executive Suite* (Julius Steigel), *The Brothers Karamazov* (Grigory), *The Cobweb, Seconds* (shop presser Taylor), *The Spiral Road,* etc.

STEIN, SAMMY *(1966)* 60 ——Memorable as the gallant Jew, Abelson, in *The Lost Patrol,* he was also in *Sing Your Worries Away, Remember Pearl Harbor,* others.

STEINKE, HANS *(1971)* 78 ——Character actor from Germany who played Tarsus in 1938's *The Buccaneer;* was also in Lugosi's *Island of Lost Souls* and Charles Ruggles' *People Will Talk.*

STEINRUECK, ALBERT *(1929)* 54 ——Noted star of German films who portrayed Rabbi Loew in the '20 (and best) version of *The Go-*

lem; *Asphalt, Decameron Nights, At the Edge of the World* were other of his successes.

STEPHENSON, HENRY *(1956)* 85 ——One look at his strong-featured English face with its compassionate eyes and you felt you could trust him with your life—if you were on the side of right; was often in Flynn epics: *The Prince and the Pauper* (Duke of Norfolk), *The Charge of the Light Brigade* (Sir Charles Macefield), *Captain Blood* (Lord Willoughby), *The Private Lives of Elizabeth and Essex* (Lord Burghley); among his other 100: Hepburn's *Little Women* (Mr. Laurence), *Marie Antoinette* (Count Mercy), *This Above All* (General Cathaway), *The Green Years,* and *The Locket.*

STEPHENSON, JAMES *(1941)* 52 ——Handsome English actor who was Davis' defending lawyer in *The Letter;* long at Warners *(The Old Maid, We Are Not Alone, White Banners, A Dispatch from Reuters,* etc.), he was finally—too late—starred in four: *Shining Victory, South of Suez, Flight from Destiny, International Squadron;* nominated for Best Supporting Actor Oscar in *The Letter.*

STEPHENSON, JOHN *(1963)* 74 ——Support in *Teenage Rebel* and *The Careless Years.*

STEPHENSON, ROBERT *(1970)* 69 ——Played the Executioner in *David and Bathsheba;* was also in *Hotel Berlin.*

STEPPAT, ILSE *(1969)* 42 ——Memorable as evil Fraulein Irma Bunt—Blofeld's assistant—who was finally daunted by James Bond in *On Her Majesty's Secret Service;* this German actress was in many others: *The Bridge, The Eighth Day of the Week, The Confessions of Felix Krull,* etc.

STEPPLING, JOHN *(1932)* 63 ——Stocky, prominent character in two dozen in the '20s: *The Dramatic Life of Abraham Lincoln, Madame Peacock, Garments of Truth, Nobody's Kid, The Reckless Age,* etc.; earlier, at Essanay, was the star of the many "Billy" comedies.

STERLING, EDYTHE *(1962)* 75 ——Leading lady in Westerns of the '20s: *The Stranger in Canyon Valley, Crimson Gold,* etc.

STERLING, FORD *(1939)* 55 ——For several years in the early teens he was the most famous of all Sennett comedians, with Mabel Normand in dozens and getting equal footage—as the hissable, boo-able, hysterically laughable villain; a few of his countless pix: *Cohen Saves the Flag, Barney Oldfield's Race for a Life, Professor Bean's Removal, The Mistaken Masher;* af-

ter a half-dozen years of stardom, supported others in comedy features in the '20s: *Stranded in Paris, Miss Brewster's Millions, Sporting Goods,* many more; in the '30s, after losing a leg in an accident, was in but a few: *Alice in Wonderland, Headline Woman, Behind Green Lights, Sally,* etc.

STERLING, LARRY *(1958)* 33 ——Support in *The Naked and the Dead.*

STERLING, MERTA *(1944)* 81 ——Character actress in the '20s in *Paid to Love,* Shirley Mason's *The Star Dust Trail,* others.

STERN, BILL *(1971)* 64 ——Famous staccato-voiced sportscaster; did sports shorts and, as himself, appeared in *The Pride of the Yankees, Spirit of West Point, Stage Door Canteen,* etc.

STERN, LOUIS *(1941)* 81 ——Character in the Louise Lorraine serial *The Diamond Master* and such '20s features as Chaney's *Where East Is East* (as the Padre), Vera Gordon's *Humoresque,* Milton Sills' *I Want My Man.*

STEVEN, BOYD *(1967)* 92 ——Scottish oldtimer who was in *I Know Where I'm Going.*

STEVENS, BYRON *(1964)* 60 ——Dapper actor-brother of Barbara Stanwyck; small roles; was married to Wampas Baby Star Caryl Lincoln.

STEVENS, CHARLES *(1964)* 71 ——Diminutive Apache Indian (Geronimo's real grandson) who nearly always played sneaky redskins; onscreen from *The Birth of a Nation* to 1961's *The Outsider* (story of Indian Ira Hayes, of Iwo Jima flag-raising fame); was in several Fairbanks pix including *The Black Pirate* (the Powder Man), countless B-Westerns *(Frontier Marshal, Marked Trails),* horror pix *(The Mummy's Curse),* serials (was Snake Eye in *Winners of the West),* scores of A-pix *(My Darling Clementine,* as Indian Charlie; *Warpath; Ride, Vaquero; Fury at Furnace Creek; Blood and Sand,* etc.).

STEVENS, CY *(1974)* 60s ——Small-sized baldie who was support in many including William Lundigan's *Follow Me Quietly.*

STEVENS, EMILY *(1928)* 45 ——Aristocratic-looking young star who was one of Metro's 1915–17 luminaries; starred in *The Soul of a Woman* with George La Guere, *The Slacker* with Walter Miller, etc.

STEVENS, EVELYN *(1938)* 45 ——One of Griffith's early leading ladies.

STEVENS, INGER *(1970)* 35 ——Lovely blonde from Sweden whose dozen co-starring roles were generally unworthy of her talent: *Man on Fire; Madigan; The World, the Flesh and the Devil; A Dream of Kings; Cry Terror,* etc.; starred in the TV series *The Farmer's Daughter.*

STEVENS, LANDER *(1940)* 62 ——In *Swing Time* was Betty Furness' father, Judge Watson; in various other talkies (*The Gorilla, We Who Are About to Die, The Trial of Mary Dugan,* etc.) and silents (*Wild Honey, The Veiled Woman, Battling Bunyon*).

STEVENS, LYNN *(1950)* 52 ——Supporting actor in the '20s in Eve Southern's *Clothes Make the Woman,* Milton Sills' *Men of Steel,* etc.

STEVENS, MORTON *(1959)* 69 ——Character actor whose supporting career spanned from *The Perils of Pauline* to *Lost Boundaries,* in which he was Dr. Brackett.

STEVENS, ROBERT *(1963)* 81 ——Minor support in movies; better known on stage.

STEVENS, VI *(1967)* 75 ——British character actress who was Mrs. Dawkins in *The Mudlark;* also in *Lisa, A Cry from the Streets,* etc.

STEVENSON, CHARLES *(1943)* 55 ——Support in *The Mysterous Dr. Fu Manchu,* etc.

STEVENSON, CHARLES A. *(1929)* 78 ——Character who, in the '20s, often played distinguished-looking, white-haired millionaires, as in Barthelmess' *Experience;* was also in *The Spanish Dancer, The Bolted Door, The Wise Virgin,* etc.

STEVENSON, DOUGLAS *(1934)* 52 ——Had a supporting role (Charles Mobray) in *Janice Meredith.*

STEVENSON, HOUSELEY *(1953)* 74 —— Played grizzled oldtimers, usually with humor, in many from the mid-'30s: *Moonrise, You Gotta Stay Happy, The Brasher Doubloon, All the King's Men, Sierra,* etc.

STEWART, ANITA *(1961)* 66 —— "*Virtuous Wives* starring Anita Stewart" proclaimed the posters announcing Louis B. Mayer's first production, in 1918; he had lured the stunning young beauty from Vitagraph where she had starred for six years—in *The Wood Violet, My Lady's Slipper, A Million Bid, The Girl Philippa, The Combat,* and the serial *The Goddess;* starred for Mayer in 15 others (*Her Kingdom of Dreams, Sowing the Wind, In Old Kentucky,* etc.) and in 1921 was #4 at the box-office behind the Talmadges and Pickford; starred in many through the '20s: *Playthings of Destiny; The Great White Way; Baree, Son of Kazan* (which took her back to Vitagraph in '25); *Go Straight; Whispering Wires; Never the Twain Shall Meet,* etc.; married, retired, wrote a novel *(The Devil's Toy),* devoted herself to such philanthropies as the Film Welfare League.

STEWART, ATHOLE *(1940)* 61 ——Character actor in British pix: *The Constant Nymph* ('33), *Dr. Syn, The Amateur Gentleman,* more.

STEWART, DANNY *(1962)* 52 ——Hawaiian actor who had supporting roles in *White Shadows of the South Seas* and many more made on South Pacific locations.

STEWART, DAVID J. *(1966)* 52 ——Youngish, strong-faced character actor in *The Young Savages; Murder, Inc.; The Silver Chalice.*

STEWART, DONALD. *(1966)* 55 ——Support in *Wild Horse Stampede, Flying Fortress, Arizona Whirlwind,* etc.

STEWART, FRED *(1970)* 63 ——Played Natalie Wood's father in *Splendor in the Grass;* was also in *The World of Henry Orient;* played leads in TV soap operas (*Edge of Night, Secret Storm*).

STEWART, GEORGE *(1945)* 57 ——Actor who was Anita's younger brother; an early Vitagraph lead, he had major roles in many in the '20s: *The Seventh Day, Gilded Lies, Back to Life, Over the Wire,* etc.; ill health forced his early retirement.

STEWART, JACK *(1966)* 51 ——Scottish character who played Dominie in *The Little Kidnappers;* was also in *High and Dry, The Stranger in Between, The Three Lives of Thomasina,* etc.

STEWART, RICHARD *(1939)* 40s ——Featured in the 1922 pic *Face to Face.*

STEWART, ROY *(1933)* 49 ——Triangle's handsome cowboy star (from '17) with dimples and an engaging grin; was first a leading man in *The House Built Upon Sand* with Lillian Gish, *Daughter of the Poor* with Bessie Love, etc.; then starred in *Boss of the Lazy Y, Faith Enduring, The Fighting Gringo, Cactus Crandall, Wolves of the Border,* etc.; several times in the '20s donned a tux to co-star in social melodramas such as *Just a Wife* with Kathlyn Williams; later played supporting roles—in Ken Maynard's *Come On, Tarzan!, Zoo in Budapest,* etc.

STIRLING, EDWARD *(1948)* 56 ——Support in *Eagle with Two Heads.*

STOCKDALE, CARL *(1953)* 79 ——Played smalltowners—often a judge or lawyer—in many: *A Regular Fellow, The Shepherd of the Hills* ('28), *Along the Rio Grande, The Carnation Kid, Hide Out*, etc.

STOCKFIELD, BETTY *(1966)* 61 ——Support in British pix: *Edward and Caroline, Flying Fortress, The Beloved Vagabond, Nine Bachelors*, etc.

STODDARD, BELLE *(1950)* 81 ——Character actress who, in the '20s, was in two John Ford horse race pix, *Kentucky Pride* and (his last silent) *Hangman's House* with Victor McLaglen; was also in a cheapie musical comedy, *Anne Against the World*.

STOKER, H. G. *(1966)* 81 ——Character actor who was last in Bolger's *Where's Charley?* and earlier in many British pix: *Rhodes, Moonlight Sonata, Channel Crossing*, etc.

STONE, ARTHUR *(1940)* 56 ——His comical face and accents—often Mexican—gave laughs galore in scores: *The Bad Man* (Walter Huston's scraggly colleague), *Charlie Chan in Egypt* (Dragonman), *Arizona Kid, I'll Tell the World, The Vagabond King* ('30), *Go Chase Yourself*, etc.; had been in many silents: *The Patent Leather Kid, An Affair of the Follies, Babe Comes Home*, more.

STONE, DOROTHY *(1974)* 69 ——Broadway actress prominently featured in *Smiling Faces, Revolt of the Zombies*, and, between them, in a '34 two-reel musical short with Bob Hope, *Paree, Paree*, in which they sang "You Do Something to Me"; was Fred's daughter.

STONE, FRED *(1959)* 85 ——Famous stage headliner (*The Red Mill*) who starred in numerous silents: *Under the Top, The Duke of Chimney Butte, Broadway After Dark, The Goat*, etc.; his best role in talkies was as Hepburn's long-suffering dad in *Alice Adams;* was also in *My American Wife, Life Begins in College, Quick Money*, and played still other fathers in *The Trail of the Lonesome Pine* (Sylvia Sidney's) and *The Westerner* (heroine Doris Davenport's), his last film; was the father of actresses Dorothy, Carol, and Paula.

STONE, GEORGE E. *(1967)* 64 ——His name had the ring of a comedian's but his hard-faced little gangsters—always gripping a gat or a tommygun—were no laughing matter; when not gunned down (as Otero in *Little Caesar*), he went to the electric chair (*The Last Mile*); in the '40s, midway in his 200-pic career, he compensated for his "bad record" by playing The Runt, crime-busting Chester Morris' amiable, dim-witted crony, in 11 "Boston Blackie" mov-

ies: *Alias Boston Blackie, Boston Blackie Goes Hollywood*, etc.; backslid in *The Miami Story, The Man with the Golden Arm*, etc., but finally played comic caricatures of his old bad self in *Guys and Dolls, Some Like It Hot*, and *Pocketful of Miracles*, departing the screen after this last—smiling.

STONE, JAMES *(1969)* 68 ——Was featured as the comic delivery man in *Barefoot in the Park*.

STONE, LEWIS *(1953)* 73 ——Was Andy (always Andrew to him) Hardy's distinguished father, Judge Hardy, in 14—from 1938's *You're Only Young Once* through 1946's *Love Laughs at Andy Hardy;* was in the last one too, 1958's *Andy Hardy Comes Home*, in a flashback of one of his and Rooney's famous "father-and-son" talks; during his "Hardy" reign was in several others: *Joe and Ethel Turp Call on the President, The Bugle Sounds, Ice Follies of 1939, The Hoodlum Saint*, etc.; after it was in many: *State of the Union, The Sun Comes Up, Stars in My Crown, It's a Big Country*, etc., through 1953's *All the Brothers Were Valiant;* had been a major silent star, beginning in 1915's *Honor Altar* opposite Bessie Barriscale; some of his outstanding silents: *Scaramouche, The Private Life of Helen of Troy, The Girl from Montmartre, Three in Love;* received his only Oscar nomination, as Best Actor, in the 1928–29 competition, as the star of Paramount's *The Patriot;* became an MGM stalwart shortly prior to sound and was a commanding presence in many: *Mata Hari, The Big House, The Sin of Madelon Claudet, Grand Hotel, The White Sister*, and 100 more.

STONE, MAXINE *(1964)* 54 ——Was in Cinerama's *South Seas Adventure*.

STONEHOUSE, RUTH *(1941)* 48 ——Versatile, dark-haired Essanay and Universal actress who was a star from her first pic, 1911's *The Papered Door;* was in *The Spy's Defeat* with Bushman; *Parlor, Bedroom and Bath; Flames of Passion; Don't Call Me Little Girl;* the serial *The Adventures of Peg O' the Ring*, many more; toward the end of her career, 1927–28, was supporting others—Dorothy Davenport Reid in *The Satin Woman, The Ape*, etc.

STOSSEL, LUDWIG *(1973)* 89 ——A delight as Cooper's (Lou Gehrig's) father in *The Pride of the Yankees*, he was equally so in many others: *Lake Placid Serenade, A Song Is Born, Iceland, Call Me Madam*, etc.; hit his "intellectual" peak as Albert Einstein in *The Beginning or the End?;* like all other characters with German accents, he was pressed into "service" in "Nazi" pix both before the war (*Man Hunt, Underground, The Man I Married*) and during it (*Hitler's Madman*, as Mayor Bauer, and *The*

Strange Death of Adolf Hitler, as Graub); was famous at the end as the pixeyish "little ol' winemaker" in TV commercials.

STOWELL, C. W. *(1940)* 62 ——Was in "The March of Time's" feature-length pic, *The Ramparts We Watch.*

STRADNER, ROSE *(1958)* 45 ——Lovely actress from Austria who starred in many European films, and was long the wife of Joseph L. Mankiewicz; was seen in just three American pix: Chester Morris' *Blind Alley, The Last Gangster,* as the long-suffering European bride of gangster Edward G. Robinson, and *The Keys of the Kingdom,* as the principal nun, Mother Maria Veronica.

STRANG, HARRY *(1972)* 70s ——In the Linda Stirling serial *Manhunt of Mystery Island,* he was chief villain, Mephisto, and in *Buck Privates,* Sgt. Callahan; was also in *My Gal Sal, Calling Philo Vance, Kit Carson, Mr. Moto Takes a Vacation,* etc.

STRANGE, GLENN *(1973)* 74 ——Last famous as Sam the Bartender in TV's *Gunsmoke,* he had earlier succeeded Karloff as Frankenstein's monster in *House of Frankenstein, House of Dracula,* and *Abbott and Costello Meet Frankenstein;* was also in *Comin' Round the Mountain* and *Texas Carnival.*

STRANGE, ROBERT *(1952)* 71 ——Popular in serials, this strong-featured character was in *Perils of Nyoka* (the good Professor-father of heroine Kay Aldridge—a switch); in *King of the Royal Mounted* had been chief villain, saboteur Kettler, and in *Adventures of Captain Marvel,* suspect Scientist Malcolm (but he wasn't the Scorpion!); onscreen only in the first decade of sound, he was in more than 50: *The Story of Vernon and Irene Castle* (Dr. Hubert Foote), *The Smiling Lieutenant* (Adjutant von Rockoff), *Marked Woman, I Found Stella Parish, They Made Me a Criminal, High Sierra, All That Money Can Buy,* etc.

STRASSBERG, MORRIS *(1974)* 76 ——In *Klute* he was the old, sexually warped dress manufacturer, Mr. Goldfarb; a top Broadway character actor and long a luminary in New York's Yiddish theater, he was onscreen in only a few others: a Lila Lee silent, *Broken Hearts,* and such talkies as *Power of Life, Tevya,* and Gertrude Berg's *Molly.*

STRATTON, CHET *(1970)* 57 ——In *The Greatest Story Ever Told* this handsome actor was Theophilus, and in *Julius Caesar* (castlisted as Chester), was Caesar's servant; also featured in *Advise and Consent, In Harm's Way, Bus Riley's Back in Town,* etc.

STRAUSS, WILLIAM *(1943)* 58 ——Played Mr. Carp in *Golden Boy* and the Messenger in *The House of Rothschild;* in a few other talkies: *Beloved, Lucky Boy, Smiling Irish Eyes,* etc.; many silents: Jessel's *Private Izzy Murphy,* Madge Bellamy's *Ankles Preferred, Solomon in Society, The Shamrock and the Rose,* etc.

STREET, DAVID *(1971)* 54 ——Actor-singer, once married to Mary Beth Hughes and Debra Paget, who was in *Holiday Rhythm, Moonrise,* etc.

STRICKLAND, HELEN *(1938)* 75 ——Had a character role (Mrs. Rollinson) in *The Scoundrel.*

STRIKER, JOSEPH *(1974)* 74 ——Played John the Baptist in DeMille's *The King of Kings;* was in others of the '20s: *Silver Wings, The Steadfast Heart,* Colleen Moore's *Painted People, The Best People,* Lillian Gish's *Annie Laurie,* Louise Fazenda's *Cradle Snatchers,* etc.

STRONG, JAY *(1953)* 57 ——Featured in the silent *The Moonshine Trail;* became a TV and stage producer.

STRONG, PORTER *(1923)* ——Character actor whose brief career (1919-23) was spent almost exclusively in D. W. Griffith films and generally in black-face comedy roles; his credits include *One Exciting Night* (in black-face), *Way Down East* (not), *A Romance of Happy Valley, The White Rose,* etc.

STRONGHEART, NIPO *(1966)* 75 ——Rather the "Claude Rains" of Indian actors, he played the wise Cree medicine man (actually was Yakima) in Tyrone Power's *Pony Soldier;* was also in *Across the Wide Missouri, Lone Star, Westward the Women,* etc.

STUART, DONALD *(1944)* 46 ——Attractive British actor who played Buddy in Colman's *Beau Geste,* Scotland Yard Inspector Lane in *The Invisible Man,* Harry Baker in *A Yank in the R.A.F.;* was also in *The Hour Before the Dawn, Eagle Squadron, The Canterville Ghost,* others.

STUART, IRIS *(1936)* 33 ——Pretty leading lady of the '20s who was in Wallace Beery's *Casey at the Bat,* Bebe Daniels' *Stranded in Paris,* Raymond Griffith's *Wedding Bills,* then retired for marriage.

STUART, JEAN *(1926)* 22 ——Delightful girl in Bebe Daniels' *The Campus Flirt.*

STUART, NICK *(1973)* 69 ——Handsome bandleader-actor who, in collegiate pix, often with then-wife Sue Carol, was emphatically the

BMOC; was in *Swing High, High School Hero, Girls Gone Wild, Why Leave Home, Why Sailors Go Wrong,* others between '27 and '33; after movies, played campus dance-dates billed "The Man with the Band from Movie Land," then became a businessman in his native Biloxi, Miss.; in '66 was persuaded to play a cameo, a railroad conductor, in Natalie Wood's *This Property Is Condemned*—white-haired, but still lean and good-looking.

STUART, RALPH *(1952)* 62 ——Supported Mollie King in the '17 Pathe serial *The Mystery of the Double Cross.*

STYLES, EDWIN *(1960)* 61 ——Support in English pix: *Hell Below, Adam and Evalyn, Penny Princess,* etc.

SUDLOW, JOAN *(1970)* 78 ——Character actress in *Pride of St. Louis, A Fine Madness, Queen for a Day.*

SUES, LEONARD *(1971)* 50 ——A juvenile in *What a Life,* he was later in *Manhattan Angel,* and, still later, Milton Berle's music director.

SUESSENGUTH, WALTHER *(1964)* 64 —— Support in *City of Secrets.*

SULLAVAN, MARGARET *(1960)* 48 ——Everything about this star was original: fluffy hairdo with soft bangs, not-quite-beautiful features, throaty-voiced charm; her greatest Broadway triumph was a gay comedy, *The Voice of the Turtle;* in movies she shed—or caused audiences to shed—tears enough to flood the Los Angeles River; cases in point: *Three Comrades* (was Oscar-nominated as Best Actress); *Only Yesterday; Little Man, What Now?; The Good Fairy; The Mortal Storm; Back Street, So Ends Our Night;* only rarely— in *The Shop Around the Corner, The Moon's Our Home* (with ex-husband Henry Fonda)— was she allowed to be blithely charming; her last screen appearance, in '50, unleashed a veritable Johnstown Flood as she, a dying wife, taught another, Viveca Lindfors, how to care for her husband and child in *No Sad Songs for Me;* continued to act onstage until deafness forced her retirement.

SULLIVAN, BRIAN *(1969)* 50 ——An MGM stock player at 25, he appeared in Wallace Beery's *This Man's Navy* and *Courage of Lassie;* later starred handsomely on Broadway in musicals such as *Street Scene* with Anne Jeffreys.

SULLIVAN, ED *(1974)* 73 ——Famous TV host and newspaper columnist; was onscreen in *Big Town Czar* and *Mr. Broadway.*

SULLIVAN, ELLIOTT *(1974)* 66 ——First on-screen as the brother of the murdered girl, Lana Turner, in *They Won't Forget,* he was in 80 more: *Gangs of New York, Racket Busters, Smashing the Money Ring, The Saint's Double Trouble,* etc.; invoking the Fifth Amendment before the House Un-American Activities Committee hobbled his career in movies; lived his last decade in England; was back onscreen in small roles in *The Sergeant* and 1974's *The Great Gatsby,* in which he played a gas-station operator.

SULLIVAN, FRANCIS L. *(1956)* 53 ——Blimpish and English, he was splendid in many: 1947's *Great Expectations* (as Pip's lawyer-friend), *Joan of Arc* (Pierre Cauchon), *Drums, Caesar and Cleopatra, The Winslow Boy, Night and the City, My Favorite Spy, The Prodigal,* etc.

SULLIVAN, FRED *(1937)* 65 ——Support in *Duck Soup, If I Had a Million, Beggar on Horseback, Murder by the Clock, You're Telling Me,* etc.

SULLIVAN, JAMES E. *(1931)* 67 ——Played the college dean in the silent comedy *The Pinch Hitter* starring Constance Bennett and Glenn Hunter.

SULLIVAN, JAMES MAURICE *(1949)* 73 —— In Crosby's *Blue Skies* was a Sugar Daddy; also in *You're Telling Me, Walking on Air, Strangers in Love,* etc.

SUL-TE-WAN, MME. *(1959)* 86 ——Black actress who, in *Maid of Salem,* was Tituba, the old slave accused of witchcraft; onscreen from *The Birth of a Nation* (numerous small parts in different costumes); was in many dozens of pix including *Kentucky,* in which she was Old Lily, etc., and, at the end, Quinn's production of *The Buccaneer;* also remained one of D.W. Griffith's most intimate friends until the day he died.

SUMMERS, ANN *(1974)* 54 ——Once an RKO contract player, she later became a Broadway and TV actress and was last onscreen in 1970's *The Glass House.*

SUMMERS, DOROTHY *(1964)* 70 ——British character actress.

SUMMERVILLE, AMELIA *(1934)* 72 —— Character actress in Ben Lyon's *The Great Deception,* the Gish sisters' *Romola,* etc.

SUMMERVILLE, SLIM *(1946)* 54 ——Long, mournful-looking comedian, onscreen from 1914's *Mabel's Busy Day* to 1946's *The Hoodlum Saint,* who was ever a joy to behold—in dozens of silent shorts and features in which he starred and scores of talkies in which he supported others; shuffled amiably through (always in ill-fitting clothes and frequently in overalls) *Anne of Windy Poplars, Tobacco Road, Way Down East, The Farmer Takes a Wife, Life Begins at 40, Captain January, Pepper, Five of a Kind, Jesse James, The Country Doctor*, etc.; the memory of him makes one smile, especially to think of that funny thing he did with his upper lip.

SUNDERLAND, NAN *(1973)* 70s ——Actress-wife of Walter Huston; appeared in support of Lionel Barrymore in *Sweepings* and in a small character role (Mrs. Pratt) in *Unconquered*.

SUNDHOLM, BILL *(1971)* ——Support in a '32 Columbia B, *The Last Man*.

SUNSHINE, MARION *(1963)* 65 ——Child actress who appeared in Biograph pix under Griffith's direction from 1908; was in numerous Pickford movies: *Three Sisters, A Decree of Destiny, Her First Biscuits*, etc., plus *Sunshine Sue* with Violet Mesereau, *The Tavern Keeper's Daughter* with Marion Leonard, others; retired young, but in her 40s had a supporting role in Slim Summerville's *I'm from Arkansas*.

SURATT, VALESKA *(1962)* 80 ——Fox already had one great vamp, Theda Bara, but felt it needed two, so this dark beauty joined the company in 1915; had starred the previous year for Lasky in *The Immigrant*; drove men mad in *Jealousy* and a few others, but not enough so to make them forget Bara—or even Virginia Pearson.

SUSANN, JACQUELINE *(1974)* 53 ——Best-selling novelist who wrote and played a small part (First Reporter) in *Valley of the Dolls*.

SUTHERLAND, ANNE *(1942)* 75 ——Had a character role (Mrs. Gordon) in Fredric March's *My Sin*.

SUTHERLAND, DICK *(1934)* 52 ——Villains—the one with the terrifying visage in Harold Lloyd's *Grandma's Boy*, the apelike one who pursued Carol Dempster through the grove of trees in *Isn't Life Wonderful?*; was in many in the '20s: *The Magnificent Brute, The Mask of Lopez, Quicksands, The Road to Yesterday, Uncle Tom's Cabin*, etc.

SUTHERLAND, EDWARD *(1974)* 77 ——Beginning his career in support in a Helen Holmes serial in '15, he was next a Keystone comedian before graduating to leading man roles in such silents as *Conrad in Quest of His Youth*; later was a highly successful movie director (*June*

Moon, Diamond Jim, The Invisible Woman, Dixie, etc.).

SUTHERLAND, VICTOR *(1968)* 79 ——Support in the '20s in *The Love Bandit, The Valley of Lost Souls*, etc.; later had character roles in *The Pride of St. Louis, The Whistle at Eaton Falls, Powder River*, others; once married to Pearl White (1907–14).

SUTTON, FRANK *(1974)* 51 ——Best known as Sgt. Carter in the *Gomer Pyle* TV series, this crewcut actor had supporting roles in *The Satan Bug, Marty, Town Without Pity*, etc.

SUTTON, JOHN *(1963)* 51 ——Suave and British, he was one of 20th Century-Fox's handsomest co-stars but his charm and neat moustache were never enough to keep the girls from capitulating to Tyrone Power (Grable in *A Yank in the R.A.F.*, Tierney in *Thunder Birds*) or Victor Mature (Hayworth in *My Gal Sal*) or even Orson Welles (Fontaine in *Jane Eyre*); onscreen from 1937's *Bulldog Drummond's Revenge* (did several of this series) through the Kim Novak version of *Of Human Bondage*, he was in 70 others: *Hudson's Bay, Ten Gentlemen from West Point, Tonight We Raid Calais, Claudia and David, My Cousin Rachel*, etc.

SUTTON, PAUL *(1970)* 58 ——Character (Wolf) in Alice Faye's *Little Old New York*; was in other A's (*Balalaika, Wild Geese Calling*), B's (*Air Devils*), Westerns (*Bar 20 Justice, In Old California*); starred on radio as *Sergeant Preston of the Yukon*.

SWAIN, MACK *(1935)* 58 ——A Keystone great—with the spit curl in the middle of his forehead and bushy moustache growing up each side of his long nose almost to his eyes; bulky, lecherous Ambrose was his most famous comic creation; played him (1914–17) in countless comedies: *Ambrose's Lofty Perch, Madcap Ambrose, Ambrose's Day Off*, etc.; in '25 he gave an immortal comedy performance as "Big Jim" McKay in *The Gold Rush*; followed it with supporting roles in many: *Kiki, Tillie's Punctured Romance, Gentlemen Prefer Blondes, Marianne, My Best Girl, Midnight Patrol*, etc.

SWAN, PAUL *(1972)* 88 ——Dancer-actor who was in 1916's *Diana the Huntress*.

SWARTHOUT, GLADYS *(1969)* 64 ——Brunette mezzo-soprano from the Met who was easily the most beautiful opera star ever seen in talkies; Paramount starred her—however unrewardingly—in four musicals: *Rose of the Rancho, Give Us This Night, Champagne Waltz, Romance in the Dark*; for her last ('39), there was a disastrous, tuneless melodrama, *Ambush;* the fault (and loss) was Paramount's, both in the pix and its misguided publicity attempts (ripe tomatoes in the kisser) to "humanize" her.

SWARTS, SARA *(1949)* 50 ——Support in silents.

SWAYNE, JULIA *(1933)* 54 ——See Julia Swayne Gordon.

SWEENEY, JACK *(1950)* 61 ——Support in Sennett comedies.

SWEENEY, JOSEPH *(1963)* 70s ——Thin-faced, gray-haired veteran of Broadway and TV who had supporting roles in several: *Twelve Angry Men* (Juror #9, seated next to Fonda), *The Man in the Gray Flannel Suit, The Fastest Gun Alive, Soak the Rich,* etc.

SWEET, TOM *(1967)* 34 ——Support in *Sniper's Ridge;* more famous on TV for his "White Knight" commercials.

SWENSON, ALFRED *(1941)* 58 ——Featured in a '29 FWA film, *The Great Power.*

SWICKARD, CHARLES *(1929)* 68 ——Actor-brother of Joseph (Josef); support in a few silents.

SWICKARD, JOSEPH (JOSEF) *(1940)* 73 —— Gray-haired great character star in many silents; was in *The Four Horsemen of the Apocalypse* (as old Don Marcelo), *Dante's Inferno* (he ran the establishment), *Men* with Pola Negri, *A Boy of Flanders, Maytime, The Keeper of the Bees, Old San Francisco, Fifth Avenue Models,* etc.; continued through the '30s in *Mamba, Return of Chandu, The Crusades* (as the Buyer), the serial *The Lost City* (genius Dr. Manyus), *The Girl Said No,* and last, *You Can't Take It With You,* in which he was the Professor.

SWINLEY, ION *(1937)* 45 ——Was in 1929's *The Unwritten Law.*

SWITZER, CARL "ALFALFA" *(1959)* 33 —— No "Our Gang" kid was more beloved than the squeaky-voiced freckleface with the twist of hair that pointed heavenward; and only Spanky and Buckwheat appeared in more of the shorts than he—89 times each for them, 60 for him; outgrowing "Our Gang," he was seen in many features as a teenager: *I Love You Again, Johnny Doughboy, Going My Way, Rosie the Riveter, Courage of Lassie,* several "Gas House Kids" pix, *State of the Union,* etc.; in the '50s tried to make it as a young character actor in *The High and the Mighty* (Ensign Keim), *Pat and Mike* (Bus Boy), *Island in the Sky, Track of the Cat,* etc., and finally, *The Defiant Ones* (a rustic named Angus); trouble was—he never stopped looking like "Alfalfa."

SWOR, BERT *(1943)* 65 ——Supporting role in the Moran & Mack (Two Black Crows) comedy *Why Bring That Up?;* then co-starred with Mack (as "Moran," when George Moran temporarily left the act) in *Anybody's War,* his last film.

SWOR, JOHN *(1965)* 83 ——Played the comic character Elmer Benbow in *Charlie Chan Carries On;* supporting roles in Spencer Tracy's first two pix: *Up the River* and *Quick Millions* (the Contractor); brother of Bert.

SYDNEY, BASIL *(1968)* 73 ——British actor well known to American audiences at two different stages of his career, first, in the '20s, was familiar as the dashingly handsome co-star of *Romance* (with beautiful wife, Doris Keane) and *Red Hot Romance* (with Olive Valerie); then, in the late '40s, as a superb character star who was particularly vivid as the stepfather-king in Olivier's *Hamlet;* followed this with *Treasure Island, Salome* (as Pontius Pilate), *Hell Below Zero, Island in the Sun* (as James Mason's father), *John Paul Jones,* and last ('60), *The Three Worlds of Gulliver;* his career between these two chapters had been entirely in English pix: *Transatlantic Tunnel, Rhodes, Next of Kin,* many others.

SYDNEY, BRUCE *(1942)* 53 ——Support in Freddie Bartholomew's *Kidnapped.*

SYLVIA, MARGUERITA *(1957)* 81 ——Noted Belgian-English opera singer who starred (from 1910) with the Chicago-Philadelphia Opera Company; starred onscreen in a '16 European-made version of *Carmen* (her famous role) and in 1920's *The Honey Bee;* had character roles in two in the '40s: *The Seventh Victim* with Kim Hunter (as Mrs. Romari) and *The Gay Senorita* with Jinx Falkenburg.

SYLVANI, GLADYS *(1953)* 67 ——A pioneer film star in England.

SYLVIE *(1970)* 87 ——Top French character actress who specialized in mean, obsessive old-lady roles; was in *Un Carnet de Bal,* Signoret's *The Adulterers* (as the paralyzed mother), *We Are All Murderers, Devil in the Flesh,* etc.; capped her long career by starring as the elderly woman who discovers the modern world in 1966's *The Shameless Old Lady.*

SZIGETI, JOSEPH *(1973)* 80 ——Famed violinist; made a cameo appearance in *Hollywood Canteen.*

SZOLD, BERNARD *(1960)* 66 ——Played a Runyon character, Honest Harry, in Bob Hope's *The Lemon Drop Kid;* was also in *M,* *Flying Leathernecks, The Tanks Are Coming,* etc.

T

TABER, RICHARD *(1957)* 72 ——Big, handsome Broadway actor who had a lead in Morton Downey's *Lucky in Love* ('29); later had character roles in two Richard Conte pix: *The Sleeping City* and *Under the Gun.*

TABLER, P. DEMPSEY ——Actor who played Tarzan in *The Son of Tarzan* ('20); death (no date given) reported in the *New York Times* (8-29-75), as per—stated the newspaper—the advisement of the family of "Tarzan" creator Edgar Rice Burroughs.

TABOR, JOAN *(1968)* 35 ——Beautiful, busty blonde who was in *Teenage Millionaire* and Jerry Lewis' *The Bellboy;* once married to Broderick Crawford.

TACKOVA, JARMILA *(1971)* 59 ——Supporting actress.

TAGGART, HAL *(1971)* 78 ——Support in Tim Holt's *The Monster That Challenged the World.*

TAILLON, GUS *(1953)* 65 ——Had a small role in *Top O' the Morning* with Barry Fitzgerald, whose stand-in he was.

TALBOT, SLIM *(1973)* 77 ——Minor roles in the pix of Gary Cooper, whose lifelong stand-in he was.

TALIAFERRO, EDITH *(1958)* 63 ——Winsome brunette who was the younger sister of Mabel; minor roles in early DeMille silents.

TALMADGE, CONSTANCE, *(1973)* 74 ——Vivacious blonde star who rode fame's highest crest as a comedienne from 1914's *Buddy's Last Call* to 1929's *Venus,* with 74 others in between; a few of the best: *Her Sister from Paris, Two Weeks, The Perfect Woman, The Love Expert, East Is West, Woman's Place, Venus of Venice, Breakfast at Sunrise, Dulcy;* also memorable is her role of The Mountain Girl, played comically, in "The Babylonian Story" in *Intolerance;* was in a few 1915-16 pix with older sister Norma: *Captivating Mary Carstairs, The Missing Links,* etc.; tied with Norma in '21 in #2 femme star at the box-office; never made a talkie nor ever considered a comeback, saying always, "Why on earth would I ever do a thing like that?"; a Manhattan society matron in the years after leaving the screen, she worked regularly as a volunteer nurse in New York hospitals; generous in death as in life, she left a multi-million-dollar estate to be divided among relatives (stepchildren of her fourth marriage, their children, and the sons of sister Natalie) and numerous charities.

TALMADGE, NATALIE *(1969)* 70 ——Brunette sister of Constance and Norma, and less famous; had major roles in three of Norma's pix *(Isle of Conquest, Yes or No?, Passion Flower)* and was the leading lady of husband (1921-32) Buster Keaton in *Our Hospitality*—in which the firstborn of their two sons, Joseph Keaton, also appeared as The Baby; after the divorce, which was bitter, she had the son's name legally changed from Keaton to Talmadge; did not remarry.

TALMADGE, NORMA *(1957)* 60 ——Onscreen from 1910's *A Dixie Mother* to 1930's *DuBarry—Woman of Passion,* this great favorite starred in more than 60 full-length features, preceded by over 250 shorter ones; drama—almost always tearful through smiles—was her forte, and in her long, enormously successful career, as has been noted by film historian Jack Spears, "she never ceased to be the woman who gave and paid, brave and defiant against the world"; her first major hit was 1911's *A Tale of Two Cities;* among the many later ones: *Secrets, Smilin' Through, The Voice from the Minaret, Within the Law, The Only Woman, Panthea, Graustark, Ashes of Vengeance;* poorly equipped vocally for talkies, she starred in two truly dreadful ones: *New York Nights* and *DuBarry—Woman of Passion* (said *Photoplay,* kinder to the star than most of the movie's critics, "Norma Talmadge gives a hint of her old fire, but loses in the fight against the long, artificial speeches"); "Get out now—and be thankful for the trust funds Mama set up," wired already retired sister Constance; her only later professional endeavor was a syndicated radio show in the mid-'30s with husband (#2) George Jessel; after that marriage, she was the wife, from '46 to the end, of a Las Vegas physician.

TALMAN, WILLIAM *(1968)* 51 ——Most famous as the District Attorney who forever lost to *Perry Mason* on TV, he had tough-guy supporting roles in two dozen pix: *The Hitch-Hiker, The Racket, One Minute to Zero, The City That Never Sleeps, The Woman on Pier 13,* etc.

TAMARA *(1943)* ——After playing a beautiful adventuress in Garbo's *The Joyless Street,* she was in *A Midsummer Night's Dream* and Anna Neagle's *No, No, Nanette.*

TAMBLYN, EDDIE *(1957)* 50 ——Actor-dad of Russ; humorous support in *Harold Teen,* Frances Langford's *Palm Springs, The Sweetheart of Sigma Chi,* etc.

TAMIROFF, AKIM *(1972)* 72 ——Bearlike character actor from Russia who from 1934's *Sadie McKee* was one of Hollywood's greatest; was twice nominated for Best Support Oscars —as Spanish guerrilla leader Pablo in *For Whom the Bell Tolls* and as the Chinese general in *The General Dies at Dawn;* other memorable movie portraits of his: the Tartar rebel in *The Soldier and the Lady,* the shady Russian banker in *Anastasia,* the terrified Grandi in *Touch of Evil,* friendly prince Emir in *The Lives of a Bengal Lancer,* many unfriendly (petulant and dangerous) gangster bosses (*King of Chinatown, King of Alcatraz, King of Gamblers,* etc.), the Cuban host in *Anthony Adverse,* the mangy Duroc in *North West Mounted Police,* and the marvelous magician in a model B pic, *The Great Gambini.*

TANGUAY, EVA *(1947)* 68 ——The stage's famous "I Don't Care Girl" who starred for the Selznick Co. in the mid-teens; was portrayed by Mitzi Gaynor in 1953's *I Don't Care Girl.*

TANNEN, JULIUS *(1965)* 84 ——Many supporting roles at 20th Century-Fox: Hawkins in *Dimples,* Ship's First Mate in *Stowaway,* a lieutenant in *The Road to Glory,* the tailor in *Unfaithfully Yours,* etc.

TANSEY, EMMA *(1942)* 60 ——Character (Mrs. Delaney) in *Meet John Doe;* support in Westerns: *Beyond the Rio Grande, Fast Fightin',* Fred Scott's *Knight of the Plains,* etc.

TAPLEY, ROSE *(1956)* 72 ——Handsome, dark-haired actress, onscreen from near the turn of the century, who starred in the Vitagraph comedy series "The Jarr Family" ('15); in that decade also starred in *As You Like It, The Christian, Vanity Fair,* etc.; in the '20s, supported Nazimova in *The Redeeming Sin,* Wallace Beery in *The Pony Express,* Clara Bow in *It* (played a Welfare Worker), etc.; last in 1931's *Resurrection.*

TARASAVA, ALLA *(1973)* 75 ——She had leading roles in Russia's *Peter the First* and *The Conquests of Peter the Great.*

TASHMAN, LILYAN *(1934)* 35 ——Beautifully blonde and beautifully dressed second-caliber star who was in dozens of silents: *Bright Lights, I'll Show You the Town, So This Is Paris, For Alimony Only,* etc.; in many talkies —and better—in aciculous, sophisticated, husky-voiced second leads: *Gold Diggers of Broadway; Queen of Scandal; No, No, Nanette; Girls About Town; One Heavenly Night,* etc.; *Riptide,* with Shearer, was her last; was married to Edmund Lowe.

TATA, PAUL M., SR. *(1962)* 79 ——Was in Edison's *The Three Musketeers* ('11).

TATE, HARRY *(1940)* 67 ——Support in English pix: *I Spy, Keep Your Seats Please, Wings of the Morning, Look Up and Laugh,* etc.

TATE, REGINALD *(1955)* 58 ——Played the Commanding Officer of the Infantrymen in *The Way Ahead;* in many other English pix: *The Life and Death of Colonel Blimp, So Well Remembered, Madonna of the Seven Moons,* etc.

TATE, SHARON *(1969)* 26 ——Stunningly beautiful, blonde, hazel-eyed leading lady in *The Wrecking Crew, House of Seven Joys, Thirteen Chairs,* others of the '60s; made her first strong impression as doomed sexpot Jennifer North in *Valley of the Dolls;* famous victim in the Manson murders in California.

TATUM, BUCK *(1941)* 43 ——Support in cowboy pix.

TAUBER, RICHARD *(1948)* 56 ——Famous Austrian opera star who was in many: *Blossom Time, Pagliacci, The Lisbon Story, Heart's Desire, Forbidden Music,* etc.

TAYLOR, AL *(1940)* 69 ——Most active in serials and as a lawman: *The Vanishing Legion* (Sheriff of Slocum), *The Lone Ranger Rides Again, Zorro's Fighting Legion, Mysterious Dr. Satan, Jungle Girl;* minor roles in such features as *The Good Fairy* and *Reckless.*

TAYLOR, ALMA *(1974)* 79 ——British silent star; was the young mother in 1913's *David Copperfield;* starred in *The Heart of Midlothian* ('14), etc.

TAYLOR, ESTELLE *(1958)* 58 ——Meltingly beautiful brunette whose leading roles in 30 in the 1920s left strong men panting; was in *The Ten Commandments* (as Miriam), *The Lights of New York, Desire, Don Juan* (Lucrezia Borgia), *Where East Is East, Dorothy Vernon of Haddon Hall* (Mary, Queen of Scots), *Manhattan Madness* with Jack Dempsey, whom she married, others; in fewer in the '30s: *The Unholy Garden* with Colman, *Cimarron* (Western prostitute Dixie Lee), *Street Scene* (adulterous ghetto mother, Mrs. Maurrant), *Liliom* (vampish carousel woman), etc.; *The Southerner*, in which she was the trampish Lizzie, was her only credit in the '40s.

TAYLOR, FERRIS *(1961)* 73 ——Folksy type who was in many Westerns (*Santa Fe Stampede, Two Flags West, Diamond Frontier*), comedies (*You Can't Cheat an Honest Man, Mr. Dodds Takes the Air, She Couldn't Say No*), and smalltown pix (*Happy Land, Main Street Lawyer, Hoosier Holiday*).

TAYLOR, FORREST *(1965)* 81 ——Strong-faced, stalwart character, with a curly shock of hair reminiscent of William Farnum's, who played good guys, bad guys, bankers, judges, and dads in more than 150, many of them Westerns: *Rockin' in the Rockies, Bullets for Bandits, Chip of the Flying U, Four Faces West, Silver Spurs*, etc.

TAYLOR, GEORGE *(1939)* 50 ——Supported Victor McLaglen in *Nancy Steele Is Missing.*

TAYLOR, HENRY *(1969)* 61 ——Comedian with The Radio Rogues who appeared as themselves in Raft's *Every Night at Eight;* also had a character role (Kozderonas) in *You Only Live Once.*

TAYLOR, JACK *(1932)* 36 ——Actor-bandleader who was in shorts at Warners.

TAYLOR, JOSEPHINE *(1964)* 73 ——An early leading lady at Essanay.

TAYLOR, LAURETTE *(1946)* 62 ——One of Broadway's immortals, she starred in three in the '20s: *Peg O' My Heart* (her famous stage role), *One Night in Rome, Happiness;* was the screen's loss that she did not live to recreate on film her last great performance as the mother in *The Glass Menagerie.*

TAYLOR, ROBERT *(1969)* 57 ——Few stars ever made femme hearts beat faster than this black-haired man with the widow's peak and perfect features; one of MGM's greatest for 25 years—much spent combating the "pretty boy" label—he starred most effectively in *A Yank at Oxford, Three Comrades, Camille, Waterloo Bridge, Johnny Eager, Billy the Kid, Bataan, Stand By for Action*, etc.; was among the Top Ten Box-Office Stars 1936-38; at his peak in handsome maturity, was a tower of strength in various epics: *Ben Hur, Ivanhoe, Knights of the Round Table;* his final screen decade was mostly spent in Westerns: *The Hangman, Return of the Gunfighter, Guns of Wyoming, Hondo and the Apaches;* intermixed were several melodramas (*The Glass Sphinx, A House Is Not a Home*), including *The Night Stalker* which reunited him with *This Is My Affair* co-star Barbara Stanwyck, who was his former wife; director William Wellman, in his recent autobiography, saluted him as "the finest man I ever knew."

TAYLOR, WILLIAM DESMOND *(1922)* 45 ——Handsome man who starred in the title role of Vitagraph's *Captain Alvarez* ('17), then directed *Judy of Rogue's Harbor, Nurse Marjorie*, etc., and became far better known as the victim in one of Hollywood's still-talked-about unsolved murders.

TEAGARDEN, JACK *(1964)* 57 ——Famous trombone-playing bandleader who was in *Birth of the Blues, The Glass Wall, Glory Alley*, etc.

TEAGUE, GUY *(1970)* 60s ——Support in B Westerns (*The Outlaw Stallion, Vigilante Hideout*, etc.) and serials (*Desperadoes of the West* and *Don Daredevil Rides Again*, in which he was the crooked sheriff).

TEARE, ETHEL *(1959)* 65 ——Leading lady in Kalem's 1915 "Ham and Bud" comedies (replacing Ruth Roland); the following year starred in her own one-reel comedy series; was a zany espionage agent, with Chester Conklin, in *An International Sneak* ('18); in the '20s was in *A Woman Who Sinned, The Tomboy, Skirts,* etc.

TEARLE, CONWAY *(1938)* 60 ——Suave sex was the keynote in the long (from '14) silent career of this tall, handsome star from England; "virtuous" was used several times in the titles of his pix (*Virtuous Wives, A Virtuous Vamp*), but other titles were tipoff enough that virtue was not uppermost in the minds of the man he played: *The Rustle of Silk, Flirting with Love, After Midnight, Altars of Desire, One Week of Love*, and yes, *Three Weeks* with Constance Talmadge; sex took a back seat in the '30s when he was in *Sing Sing Nights, The Lost Zeppelin, The Preview Murder Case*, and *Romeo and Juliet*, in which he was the Prince of Verona.

TEARLE, SIR GODFREY *(1953)* 78 ——On-screen even longer (from '06) than half-brother Conway, this stalwart character actor proved his versatility in two highlight performances; in Hitchcock's *The 39 Steps* he was the chief enemy agent, Professor Jordan—of the telltale missing finger; a dozen years later, in *The Beginning or the End*, he played President Franklin D. Roosevelt; among his others: *One of Our Aircraft Is Missing* (star role: Sir George Corbett), *At Dawn We Die, The Titfield Thunderbolt, The Story of Mandy*, etc.

TEEGE, JOACHIM *(1969)* 44 ——Featured in the Austrian operatic film *The Merry Wives of Windsor* ('52).

TELL, ALMA *(1937)* 45 ——Pensive, sweet, and soothing, this dark-haired beauty was a femme lead (usually second) in a dozen in the '20s: *Paying the Piper* with Reginald Denny, *Broadway Rose* with Mae Murray, *San Francisco Nights* with Percy Marmont, *Saturday's Children* with Corinne Griffith, etc.

TELL, OLIVE *(1951)* 57 ——Younger sister of Alma who starred first for Mutual in 1918's *The Unforseen* with David Powell; in the '20s she was in *Wings of Pride, Worlds Apart, Chickie* with Dorothy Mackaill, *Slaves of Beauty* (and her beauty secrets were catnip to fan magazine readers), *Sailors' Wives* with Mary Astor, etc.; onscreen through the '30s, she was usually a socialite—*Private Scandal, Strictly Personal, Polo Joe*, others.

TELLEGEN, LOU *(1934)* 50 ——"When he appears and smiles, we know that he is not only the greatest of lovers, the greatest of actors, but the most handsome of them all as well," wrote one enraptured critic after a '15 film of his; sculptor Rodin would not have disagreed, having used him as the model for "The Kiss"; great tragedienne Sarah Bernhardt would not, having shared quarters with him (when she was in her 60s and he in his 20s) and had him as her screen lover in three in 1912: *Adrienne Lecouvreur, La Dame au Camelias, Queen Elizabeth*; nor (at first) would opera star Geraldine Farrar, who married him after he played the handsome villain in her *Maria Rosa* ('16), but, five years later, ditched him in a name-calling divorce; they had played lovers in three: *The World and Its Woman, The Woman and the Puppet, Flame of the Desert*; some others of his that caused palpitations: *The Explorer, Parisian Nights, The Long Trail, Single Wives, Between Friends, The Breath of Scandal*; in '31, fame's bubble having long since burst, he appeared (in a supporting role) in his last movie, *Enemies of the Law*, and, having been four times married, published his braggadacian autobiography, *Women Have Been Kind*.

TEMPEST, DAME MARIE *(1942)* 78 ——English stage star of regal bearing who starred in 1915's *Mrs. Plum's Pudding* and, in the '30s, was in *Yellow Sands* and *Moonlight Sonata*, as Paderewski's leading lady.

TEMPLETON, ALEC *(1963)* 53 ——Blind pianist, famous on radio, who was in *A Date with Judy*.

TEMPLETON, FAY *(1939)* 72 ——Celebrated Broadway musical star for decades; was on-screen in Frank Morgan's *Broadway to Hollywood*; Irene Manning portrayed her in *Yankee Doodle Dandy*.

TERHUNE, MAX *(1973)* 82 ——Ventriloquist-comic who, with dummy Elmer Sneezeweed, played Lullaby Joslin in 21 "Three Mesquiteers" Westerns, then was the sidekick of ex-"Mesquiteer" Ray "Crash" Corrigan in 24 "Range Busters" Westerns at Monogram, followed by another eight alongside Johnny Mack Brown; between Westerns he was in *The 1937 Hit Parade, Manhattan Merry-Go-Round, Rawhide*, and *Giant*, in which he was Dr. Walker.

TERRANOVA, DINO *(1969)* 65 ——Support in *The Brotherhood, The Wrong Man*, etc.

TERRIS, ELLALINE *(1971)* 100 ——Character actress in British pix: *Atlantic, The Secret Four, Blighty*, others.

TERRY, DAME ELLEN *(1928)* 80 ——One of English stage's greatest actresses; American companies released the films she made in Britain in her maturity: *Her Greatest Performance, Pillars of Society, The Bohemian Girl, Potter's Clay*—all 1916–23.

TERRY, ETHEL *(1931)* 40s ——Dark-haired leading lady of 1917's *Arsene Lupin*; in the '20s had major roles in *Peg O'My Heart, The Crossroads of New York, Under Two Flags* with Priscilla Dean, *Garrison's Finish* with Jack Pickford, *The Fast Worker* with Reginald Denny, etc.

TERRY, FRED *(1933)* 69 ——Was in 1922's *With Wings Outspread*.

TERRY, HAZEL *(1974)* 56 ——British stage actress who had supporting roles in several.

TERRY, SHEILA *(1957)* 46 ——Blonde and beautiful, she was one of Warners' busiest second-string leading ladies in the '30s: *20,000 Years in Sing Sing, Lawyer Man, Parachute Jumper, The House on 56th Street, The Great Radio Mystery, Murder on a Bridle Path, Three on a Match*, etc.; then was a popular heroine in such Westerns as *Lawless Frontier* and *'Neath Arizona Skies*.

TERRY-LEWIS, MABEL *(1957)* 85 ——Support in British pix: *The Scarlet Pimpernel, Murder on Diamond Row, They Came to a City*.

THATCHER, EVA *(1942)* 80 ——Character comedienne in many silent comedies; in the Sennett comedy *A Bedroom Blunder*, was the browbeating wife of star Charlie Murray left standing in her bloomers when her dress got caught in an errant window shade; was also in *Ranchers and Rascals, Haystacks and Needles, Thirst*, etc.

THAW, EVELYN NESBIT *(1967)* 81 ——See Evelyn Nesbit.

THESIGER, ERNEST *(1961)* 81 ——Bony British character, proud of carriage with a long nose jauntily tipped; top comic support in various Guinness pix: *Last Holiday, The Detective* (as the librarian), *The Horse's Mouth* (Hickson), *The Man in the White Suit* (ancient industrialist); was also in *Man With a Million, The Old Dark House* ('32), *Henry V* (Duke of Beri), *Laughter in Paradise, Three Men in a Boat*, dozens more.

THIGPEN, HELEN *(1966)* 60s ——She appeared as the Strawberry Woman in *Porgy and Bess*.

THIMIG, HELENE *(1974)* 85 ——Austrian character actress with deep-set eyes who could be frightening (black-robed Kyra in *Isle of the Dead)*, humorously taciturn (the cook in *The Gay Sisters* with the little boy presumably hers but actually Stanwyck's), or, in war pix, deadly grim (*The Moon Is Down, Edge of Darkness, The Hitler Gang, Hotel Berlin, Cloak and Dagger*, in which she was the Austrian scientist Katerina Lodor, murdered by Nazi agents after her rendezvous with OSS man Cooper); the widow of Max Reinhardt, she returned home to Vienna in the late '40s where, in '51, she acted in her last film, *Decision Before Dawn*.

THOMAS, EDNA *(1974)* 88 ——Support (Mexican Woman) in *A Streetcar Named Desire;* was also in *Take a Giant Step* and *The Enforcer*.

THOMAS, GRETCHEN *(1964)* 67 ——Support in the Alexander Gray-Bernice Claire musical *Spring Is Here* ('30); also in Mary Nolan's *Young Desire*, Pedro de Cordoba's *Damaged Goods*, etc.

THOMAS, JAMESON *(1939)* 47 ——British actor who in *It Happened One Night* was the man Colbert almost married; was also in *100 Men and a Girl, Now and Forever* (Carstairs, aristocratic brother-in-law to whom Gary Cooper tries to "sell" his little girl, Shirley Temple, for $75,000), *The Lives of a Bengal Lancer* (Hendrickson), *Three Wise Girls, Charlie Chan in Egypt, Bombay Mail*, etc.

THOMAS, JOHN CHARLES *(1960)* 68 ——Famous operatic baritone who starred—heavily and awkwardly—in 1923's *Under the Red Robe;* in '27 made Vitaphone shorts in which he sang "In the Gloaming," "Will You Remember?," "Danny Deever," etc.

THOMAS, OLIVE *(1920)* 25 ——Dimpled-chin beauty who went from a yard-goods counter in McKees Rocks, Pa. to the front line of the *Ziegfeld Follies*, to brief (1916–20) stardom in *Beatrice Follies, Limousine Life, The Glorious Lady, The Flapper*, and to an even briefer marriage to Jack Pickford.

THOMPSON, BILL *(1971)* 58 ——Was "Wally Wimple" and "Oldtimer" on "Fibber McGee and Molly's" radio show and in their movie *Here We Go Again;* was also in *Comin' Round the Mountain*.

THOMPSON, DAVID H. *(1957)* 71 ——Support in 1910–14 pix at Thanhauser and Edison.

THOMPSON, FREDERICK *(1925)* 54 ——Support in the '20s in *Heart Line* and Charles Ray's *A Tailor-Made Man;* earlier ('11) had directed Earle Williams in *War*.

THOMPSON, GEORGE *(1929)* 61 ——Support in Moran & Mack's *Why Bring That Up?*

THOMPSON, MOLLY *(1928)* 49 ——Was seen in support in many of Harold Lloyd's short comedies.

THOMPSON, ULU *(1957)* 83 ——Character actress.

THOMPSON, WILLIAM H. *(1923)* 70 ——Support in Alma Rubens' *Enemies of Women* and John Gilbert's *The Eye of the Night*.

THOMSON, FRED *(1928)* 38 ——One of the handsomest of all movie cowboy stars, he left the Presbyterian ministry to become one; starred athletically (he and pony, Silver King, were noted for their daredevil stunts) in dozens from 1923 on; among his pix: *Thundering Hooves, Riding the Wind, Galloping Gallagher, The Mask of Lopez;* was among the Top Five cowboys of the decade; also starred in the serial *The Eagle's Talons* and was Pickford's leading man in *The Love Light*.

THOMSON, KENNETH *(1967)* 68 ——Good looking man who played the second lead (Jack Warriner) in *The Broadway Melody;* had earlier been in *The Secret Hour* with Negri, *Corporal Kate* with Vera Reynolds, *The King of Kings* (as Lazarus), others; later was in dozens: *Change of Heart, Murder at Midnight, Behold My Wife*, etc.

THORBURN, JUNE *(1967)* 34 ——Blonde, beautiful English actress who was star Kerwin Mathews' love interest, Elizabeth, in *The Three Worlds of Gulliver;* in *The Pickwick Papers*, her first, was the charming ingenue over whom love-smitten Mr. Winkle (James Donald) mooned; was also in *Tom Thumb, The Cruel Sea, Broth of a Boy*, others.

THORNDIKE, LUCILLE *(1935)* 40 ——Support in the '20s in Betty Compson's *The Garden of Weeds*, a few others.

THORNDIKE, OLIVER *(1954)* 35 ——In *The Story of Dr. Wassell* was good-looking, humorous young Navy man Alabam.

THORNDIKE, RUSSELL *(1972)* 87 ——Character in English pix; was the Duke of Bourbon in *Henry V*, the Priest in *Hamlet* (billed Thorndyke); also wrote *Dr. Syn* and was the brother of Dame Sybil.

THORNE, ROBERT *(1965)* 84 ——Made a handsome Patrick Henry—receiving third billing—in Marion Davies' *Janice Meredith* ('24), his only film.

THORNHILL, CLAUDE *(1965)* 57 ——Led his dance band in musical shorts.

THORNTON, GLADYS *(1964)* 65 ——Longtime radio actress (Ella in *When a Girl Marries*) who had a supporting role in a Sandra Dee comedy, *If a Man Answers*.

THORPE, JIM *(1953)* 65 ——Famed Indian athlete, winner of the pentathlon and decathlon in the '12 Olympics; played chiefs and (more often) renegades in dozens of B Westerns from '31: *Wanderer of the Wasteland, Prairie Schooners, Wild Horse Mesa*, etc.; in one serial: Tom Tyler's *Battling with Buffalo Bill*, in which he was Swift Arrow; Burt Lancaster portrayed him in *Jim Thorpe—All-American*.

THURMAN, MARY *(1925)* 31 ——Beauty who was often in Sennett's Charlie Murray comedies (*Watch Your Neighbor*, etc.); in the '20s had supporting roles in many: Monte Blue's *The Broken Doll*, Barthelmess' *The Bond Boy*, Swanson's *Zaza* (soubrette Florianne with whom the star battled in the music hall scenes), Edmund Lowe's *The Fool*, Aileen Pringle's *Wild-Fire*, etc.

THURSTON, CAROL *(1969)* 48 ——Sloe-eyed beauty who created much excitement as charmingly unconventional native nurse Tremartini ("Three-Martini") in *The Story of Dr. Wassell*; the best having come first, she was then in *The Conspirators, China Sky, Swamp Fire, Rogues' Regiment*, and last, a supporting role in 63's *Showdown*.

THURSTON, CHARLES *(1940)* 71 ——Character in the '20s and early '30s in Reginald Denny's *Rolling Home*, Harry Langdon's *The Chaser*, Will Rogers' *Boys Will Be Boys*, Jack

Hoxie's *Ridgeway of Montana*, numerous others.

TIAZZA, DARIO *(1974)* 70 ——He played secondary roles for 25 years before becoming a costume designer in the '50s; won an Emmy in this category for *Bonanza*.

TIBBETT, LAWRENCE *(1960)* 63 ——Dashing Metropolitan baritone who, in 1930's *The Rogue Song*, became the first and only opera star ever nominated for a Best Actor Oscar; followed up with five other films: *New Moon* with Grace Moore, *The Prodigal* (a.k.a. *The Southerner*) with Esther Ralston, *Cuban Love Song* with Lupe Velez, *Metropolitan* with Jane Darwell, *Under Your Spell* with Wendy Barrie; continued on at the Met, on radio and Broadway.

TICKLE, FRANK *(1955)* 62 ——Support in British pix: Vivien Leigh's *Anna Karenina, Escape, Brandy for the Parson*.

TIEDTKE, JACOB *(1960)* 85 ——Noted German actor who was in several dozen European films after his debut in 1926's *The Waltz Dream*; last worked in a pic, *Leave on Parole*, when 80.

TIGHE, HARRY *(1935)* 50s ——Featured in one Selznick silent, *A Wide-Open Town*.

TILBURY, ZEFFIE *(1950)* 87 ——Unforgettable as "Gramma" in *The Grapes of Wrath*, who didn't make it to California, and as the Grandma in *Tobacco Road*, she had similar old-lady roles in many: *The Story of Alexander Graham Bell, The Gorgeous Hussy, Maid of Salem, Alice Adams, The Werewolf of London*, etc.; in movies two decades, she retired in '41.

TILDEN, BILL *(1953)* 60 ——Great tennis champ; had a featured role in Alec B. Francis' *The Music Master* ('27) and was seen in sports shorts.

TILTON, EDWIN BOOTH *(1926)* 65 ——Character in many thrillers and Westerns in the '20s: *The Midnight Express, Thundergate, The Primal Law, The Lone Chance*, etc.

TIMBERG, HERMAN *(1952)* 60 ——Vaudeville comic in several talkie shorts.

TINDALL, LOREN *(1973)* 52 ——Handsome youth who, as Jeff Donnell's G.I. husband in *Over 21*, in '45, was briefly a bobby-soxers' dreamboat and gave promise of becoming a star; was also in *Till the End of Time, Good News, Miss Grant Takes Richmond*; later built and operated Hollywood's McLoren Playhouse; early femme fans will perhaps be interested—he never married.

TINNEY, FRANK *(1940)* 62 ——Broadway star who was seen onscreen in a brief interpolated scene in 1924's *Broadway After Dark.*

TISSIER, JEAN *(1973)* 77 ——Character actor in French films: *And God Created Woman; Children of Paradise; Mama, Papa, The Maid and I,* etc.

TISSOT, ALICE *(1971)* 81 ——Played matronly roles in French films for four decades; was in *La Maternelle, Gates of Paris, Last Desire,* others.

TITHERADGE, MADGE *(1961)* 74 ——Starred as Queen Victoria in 1913's *Sixty Years a Queen;* was in such later English silents as *David and Jonathan* and *Her Story.*

TITUS, LYDIA YEAMANS *(1929)* 95 ——Major character actress who played little old ladies from the first, 1918's *All Night* with Carmel Myers and Rudolph Valentino; in numerous Christie comedies (*Winter Has Come*); was in more than 50 features in the '20s: Chic Sale's *His Nibs,* Shirley Mason's *Queenie,* Colleen Moore's *Irene,* Ramon Novarro's *Scaramouche,* Belle Bennett's *The Lily,* etc.; *Lummox,* released in '30, was her last.

TODD, HARRY *(1935)* 70 ——Pixeyish, clodkicker-type comedian who co-starred with plump Margaret Joslin in two different comedy series in the teens—first in Essanay's "Snakeville" pix and then in a series for Hal Roach; was comic support in many Westerns in the '20s and '30s: *Rawhide Kid, Lucky Larkin, Under Montana Skies, Under the Tonto Rim,* etc.; last had supporting roles in *It Happened One Night* (the Flag Man) and *Broadway Bill* (Pop).

TODD, JAMES *(1968)* 70s ——Had supporting roles in many from the early '30s on: *Charlie Chan's Chance* (as Kenneth Dunwood), *Careless Lady, Francis* (Col. Saunders), *Titanic* (Sandy Comstock), *Torch Song, The Wings of Eagles,* etc.

TODD, THELMA *(1935)* 30 ——Vivacious comedienne who was one of the loveliest blondes ever seen on the screen; in movies from the mid '20s (*Nevada* with Gary Cooper, etc.), she achieved her greatest popularity at Hal Roach Studios in 17 two-reelers with ZaSu Pitts and another 21 with Patsy Kelly; in features she was with the Marx Bros. in both *Horsefeathers* and *Monkey Business,* Keaton in *Speak Easily,* Joe E. Brown in *Son of a Sailor,* and Laurel & Hardy in *The Bohemian Girl,* last of her more than 60 talkies; for one, *Corsair,* in which she had a straight leading-lady role that she hoped

would change her image, she changed her name to Alison Loyd; her death remains one of Hollywood's unsolved mysteries.

TOLER, HOOPER *(1922)* 31 ——Minor roles.

TOLER, SIDNEY *(1947)* 72 ——Between Warner Oland and Roland Winters, and between '38 and '47, he was Charlie Chan in 22 pix: *Charlie Chan in Honolulu* being first and *The Trap* coming last; a few others: *Charlie Chan at the Wax Museum, . . . in Rio, . . . in Secret Service, . . . in Reno;* a native of Missouri, he entered movies in Ruth Chatterton's *Madame X* ('29), in which he played an Englishman, Merivel; had supporting roles in 50 before playing Chan: *Blondie of the Follies, Spitfire* (a rustic named Mr. Sawyer), *The Gorgeous Hussy* (as Daniel Webster), *If I Were King,* etc.; during the Chan period he was also in Maria Montez' *White Savage,* Loretta Young's *A Night to Remember* (Inspector Hankins), Jack Benny's *It's in the Bag,* others.

TOMACK, SID *(1962)* 55 ——Slight and bald, he frequently played Brooklyn-accented characters, usually funny; onscreen nearly two decades, from *A Wave, a Wac, and a Marine,* he was in more than 40: *The Fuller Brush Girl* (as Bangs), *The Thrill of Brazil, My Girl Tisa, Somebody Loves Me, Joe Palooka in Triple Cross, Sail a Crooked Ship, That Certain Feeling,* etc.

TONE, FRANCHOT *(1968)* 63 ——No star ever wore a tux so perfectly or was such a debonair to-the-mansion-born playboy; he was authentically a blueblood and it showed—in *Suzy, Bombshell, No More Ladies, Nice Girl, His Butler's Sister,* etc.; there was more to him, as was proved by *Mutiny on the Bounty* (Oscar-nominated for Best Actor as Byam), *Five Graves to Cairo, Phantom Lady, Uncle Vanya, Three Comrades, Advise and Consent* (as the President), *The Man on the Eiffel Tower,* etc.; his natural gift for urbane comedy was demonstrated often, in *She Knew All the Answers* with Joan Bennett, *True to Life* with Mary Martin, *Between Two Women* with Virginia Bruce, *Dancing Lady* with then-wife Joan Crawford, *The Girl from Missouri* with Harlow, and many others; on TV's *Ben Casey* in 1965–66, it disconcerted many to see him as gray-bearded neurosurgeon Dr. David Niles Freeland; 1968's *The High Commissioner* was his last.

TONG, KAM *(1969)* 62 ——In *The Flower Drum Song* was bespectacled Dr. Li, father of Miyoshi Umeki, and in *Love Is a Many-Splendored Thing,* Dr. Sen; later in *Mister Buddwing* and *Kill a Dragon;* was onscreen from 1942's *Across the Pacific* and *China Girl.*

TONG, SAMMEE *(1964)* 63 ——More recently famous as the houseboy in the John Forsythe TV series *Bachelor Father,* this small actor had been onscreen since 1934's *Happiness Ahead;* was in *The Good Earth, Only Angels Have Wings, Oil for the Lamps of China, Shanghai,* others.

TONGE, PHILIP *(1959)* 66 ——Polished character actor who played Inspector Hearne in *Witness for the Prosecution,* the Associate Judge in *Les Girls;* in many others: *Miracle on 34th Street, House of Wax, Track of the Cat, The Prodigal,* etc.

TOOKER, WILLIAM H. *(1936)* 62 ——Fine gray-haired character who was in dozens in the '20s; played the Governor in Gish's *The Scarlet Letter,* the father in a Barthelmess comedy, *The White Black Sheep,* and was also in Gilda Gray's *The Devil Dancer,* Mae Murray's *Peacock Alley,* Madge Bellamy's *The Purple Highway,* etc.; *It's a Gift* was his last.

TOREN, MARTA *(1957)* 30 Universal imported this green-eyed beauty from Sweden in '48, cast her in the Lamarr role in the *Algiers* remake, *Casbah,* and publicized her as its #1 Star of Tomorrow; had top roles in *Sword in the Sand, Illegal Entry, Rogues' Regiment, Sirocco, One-Way Street,* others; settled permanently in Italy in '52 and made a few European pix: *The Man Who Watched the Trains Go By, The House of Riccordi,* and best, as well as last, 1955's *Maddelena,* in which she was a woman who was both saint and devil.

TORRENCE, DAVID *(1942)* 62 ——For two decades, and in many of the best, this tall, aristocratic-looking man was one of Hollywood's most dependable character actors; in *Tess of the Storm Country,* the talkie version of *Disraeli,* Ann Harding's *East Lynne* (as Sir Richard Hare), Shearer's *Smilin' Through* (gardener), *Berkeley Square* (Lord Stanley), *Queen Christina, Captain Blood,* others.

TORRENCE, ERNEST *(1933)* 54 ——Character actor who, in films of the '20s, gave several performances of such excellence they will never be forgotten: *The Covered Wagon* (old frontier scout Jackson, perennially drunk, who does hero J. Warren Kerrigan the unrequested favor of dispatching loutish villain Alan Hale), *Tol'able David* (lecherous, murderous, feeble-minded villain Luke Hatburn), *The Side Show of Life* (starred here as the English circus clown who became a WW I General and later could not adjust to being laughed at), *Broken Chains* (sadistic prospector), *The Hunchback of Notre Dame* (beggar king, Clopin), *Steamboat Bill Jr.* (owner of the riverboat Stonewall Jackson),

The King of Kings (Disciple Peter), many more; a giant among actors.

TORRIANI, AIMEE *(1963)* 73 ——In *To Catch a Thief,* was the peasant-type Woman in Kitchen, gifted at making Quiche Lorraine and, reputedly, at having dispatched Nazis with her bare hands.

TORRUCO, MIGUEL *(1956)* 36 ——Mexican actor who had a top supporting role in Dane Clark's *Massacre.*

TOSO, OTELLO *(1966)* ——Italian supporting actor who was in *Death of a Cyclist, What Price Innocence?, Casanova,* other European films.

TOTO *(1967)* 70 ——Great Italian comedian of the weary eyes that had seen everything; superlative in *The Gold of Naples, Big Deal on Madonna Street, Toto Le Moko, The Law Is the Law,* more; in real life was Antonio, Prince de Curtis-Gagliardi, bearer of many titles: Prince of Byzantium, Duke of Cyprus, Noble Knight of the Holy Roman Empire, Count of Drivasto; calling him "a world unto himself . . . a stylized image of age, sadness, and decadence," critic Pauline Kael has noted that, while usually labeled a clown, he was a "clown the way champagne is a wine."

TOUREL, JENNIE *(1973)* 63 ——Metropolitan Opera star who was featured in 1968's *A Journey to Jerusalem.*

TOVER, MAY *(1949)* 38 ——Wild-animal trainer seen in *The Reformer and the Redhead.*

TOWNSEND, ANNA *(1923)* 70s ——Memorable as the Grandma in Harold Lloyd's *Grandma's Boy, Safety Last,* and *Doctor Jack;* was also in Jackie Coogan's *Daddy.*

TOYNE, GABRIEL *(1963)* 58 ——British actor-producer; husband of actress Diana Beaumont.

TOZERE, FREDERIC *(1972)* 71 ——Character actor who was in *Confessions of a Nazi Spy* (as Phillips), *The Iron Curtain* (Col. Trigorin), *Hell's Kitchen, The Return of October, Live Today for Tomorrow,* etc.; sometimes billed Fred.

TRACY, LEE *(1968)* 70 ——Star who had no equal at playing a fast-talking, scoop-chasing newspaper reporter; was at his brightest and breeziest in *I'll Tell the World, Bombshell, Big Time, Love Is a Racket, Washington Merry-Go-Round, The Night Mayor, Clear All Wires, Millionaires in Prison;* was promoted to the ex-President of the U.S. in his last, 1964's *The Best Man* (repeating his great stage role), and was still straight-shooting, nasal, and terrific, being nominated as Best Supporting Actor.

TRACY, SPENCER *(1967)* 67 ——Perhaps MGM's finest actor (from 1935's *Whipsaw* through 1955's *Bad Day at Black Rock*), he was unique at portraying characters who "lived" without ever seeming to have been created by an actor; had previously been at Fox for five years and 25 pix (several made on loanout), the best of which were *Quick Millions, The Power and the Glory, 20,000 Years in Sing Sing* (loanout), *Man's Castle, The Show Off;* at Metro, won Best Actor Oscars in *Captains Courageous* ('37) and *Boys Town* ('38), and was nominated in *San Francisco* ('36), *Father of the Bride* ('50), *Bad Day at Black Rock* ('55); was later nominated in Warner's *The Old Man and the Sea* ('58) and Stanley Kramer's *Inherit the Wind* ('60), *Judgment at Nuremberg* ('61), and *Guess Who's Coming to Dinner* ('67), the last of his 76 starring movies; gave other notable performances in *Test Pilot, Boom Town, Northwest Passage, Edison the Man, Dr. Jekyll and Mr. Hyde, A Guy Named Joe, Thirty Seconds Over Tokyo, The Actress, The Last Hurrah,* and nine with Katharine Hepburn (*Woman of the Year, Keeper of the Flame, Without Love, State of the Union, Adam's Rib, Pat and Mike, The Sea of Grass, The Desk Set,* and the previously mentioned *Guess Who's Coming to Dinner*); was among the Top Ten Box-Office Stars in these years: 1938–42, 1944, '45, '48, '50, '51; was exceptional among all his contemporaries in that he never played a character appreciably younger or older than his age at any given time, and that he matured naturally before the eyes of his public from a young Irish redhead brooking no nonsense to a white-haired older man of similar disposition.

TRACY, WILLIAM *(1967)* 48 ——Curly-haired, squeaky-voiced comic who made his first impression as the nervous young military school plebe in *Brother Rat;* then was browbeaten little messenger Pepi in *The Shop Around the Corner,* auto-crazy young hillbilly Dude Lester in *Tobacco Road,* Mac in Kay Harris' *Tillie the Toiler;* starred first in the '40 serial *Terry and the Pirates,* then in a series of Hal Roach comic features, as Dudo Doubleday, whose photographic memory landed him in hot water in *Tanks a Million, About Face, Hayfoot, Fall In,* etc.; was comic support in the '50s in *On the Sunny Side of the Street, The Wings of Eagles,* others.

TRAIN, JACK *(1966)* 64 ——Comic in England's *Showtime.*

TRAINOR, LEONARD *(1940)* 61 ——Support in Westerns in the '20s: Bob Steele's *Headin' for Danger,* Jack Hoxie's *The Border Sheriff,* others.

TRAUBEL, HELEN *(1972)* 69 ——One of the Metropolitan Opera's greatest Wagnerian sopranos, who was onscreen in *Deep in My Heart, Gunn,* and *The Ladies Man* with Jerry Lewis.

TRAVERS, HENRY *(1965)* 91 ——Lovable, bushy-browed oldtimer, onscreen from 1933's *Reunion in Vienna,* who was a special delight as angel Clarence in *It's a Wonderful Life* and as prize-winning rose grower Mr. Ballard in *Mrs. Miniver,* for which he was Oscar-nominated as Best Support; was grand too in *Shadow of a Doubt, On Borrowed Time, The Invisible Man, The Rains Came, The Primrose Path, Ball of Fire, Madame Curie, The Moon Is Down,* etc.; he rarely played a grouch, but loved it—*The Bells of St. Mary's;* retired at 75, after *The Girl from Jones Beach.*

TRAVERS, RICHARD *(1935)* 45 ——Handsome Essanay leading man who first appeared, opposite Swanson, in 1914's *The Romance of an American Duchess;* then was in *The White Sister* with Viola Allen, *The Snowman, In the Palace of the King* with Nell Craig, *Captain Jinks of the Horse Marines, The Mountain Woman* with Pearl White, many others.

TRAVERS, TONY *(1959)* 39 ——Accordian-playing actor who was in several.

TRAVERSE, MADALINE *(1964)* 88 ——Lovely brunette who had star roles in Famous Players' *Leah Kleschna* ('13), Reliable's *Three Weeks* ('14), and the Pathe serial *The Shielding Shadow* ('16).

TREACY, EMERSON *(1967)* 61 ——Began as humorous support in Edward Everett Horton's *Once a Gentleman* ('30) and continued to be in many: *Give Me a Sailor* (Meryl), *Invitation to Happiness* (photographer), *Adam's Rib* (Jules Frikke), *Lover Come Back,* etc., and played Spanky's harried dad in two "Our Gang" comedies: *Wild Poses* and *Bedtime Worries.*

TREADWAY, CHARLOTTE *(1963)* 67 ——Character roles in Ramon Novarro's *The Sheik Steps Out* and Evelyn Venable's *Female Fugitive.*

TREADWELL, LAURA *(1960)* 81 ——Usually played dowagers: Mrs. Galloway (Holmes Herbert's wife) in *Accent on Youth,* Mrs. Taylor (Edward Arnold's wife) in *Mr. Smith Goes to Washington,* Mrs. Anderson in *Strangers on a Train,* etc.

TREE, SIR HERBERT BEERBOHM *(1917)* 63 ——Noted British stage actor who starred for D. W. Griffith in 1916's *Macbeth.*

TREE, LADY *(1937)* 73 ——British actress who played Laughton's Old Nurse in *The Private Life of Henry VIII;* was also in *The Man Who Could Work Miracles, Wedding Rehearsal,* numerous other English films.

TREE, VIOLA *(1938)* 54 ——Support in England's *Heart Desire.*

TRENHOLME, HELEN *(1962)* 50 ——Played ingenue leads in two at Warners in '34: *The Case of the Howling Dog* and *The Firebird.*

TRENT, JOHN *(1966)* 59 ——Actor-pilot who was in many: *The Chinese Parrot, The Great Gambini, I Wanted Wings, A Doctor's Diary, John Meade's Woman, The Spider Monkey,* etc.

TRESKOFF, OLGA *(1938)* 35 ——Minor roles in a few silents.

TREVELYAN, HILDA *(1959)* 79 ——Support in British pix: *Trans-Atlantic Tunnel,* etc.

TREVOR, ANN *(1970)* ——Support in England's *Murder in the Old Red Barn.*

TREVOR, HUGH *(1933)* 30 ——Handsome second lead with widow's peak who was in a dozen: *Beau Broadway* with Sue Carol; *Skinner's Big Idea* with Bryant Washburn; *The Pinto Kid* with Buzz Barton; *Her Summer Hero; Dry Martini; Hey, Rube; Conspiracy* with Bessie Love, etc.

TREVOR, NORMAN *(1929)* 52 ——A now-neglected Cooper-type star of silents; starred in 1917's *The Runaway,* was with Doris Keane in *Romance,* played Rochester in *Jane Eyre* in '21, was Swanson's leading man in *Wages of Virtue,* and, as the dancing husband of Alice Joyce (and father of Clara Bow) in *Dancing Mothers,* was an impeccable figure in white tie and tails.

TREVOR, SPENCER *(1945)* 70 ——Support in *Congress Dances* and *April Romance.*

TROTSKY, LEON *(1940)* 61 ——Famous Russian revolutionary; played a secondary role in Clara Kimball Young's *My Official Wife* ('14), made on various locations, including Switzerland where he then lived.

TROUNCER, CECIL *(1953)* 55 ——Character in numerous British pix: *The Pickwick Papers, Pygmalion, Saraband, The Lady with a Lamp,* etc.

TROUT, FRANCIS *(1950)* 48 ——He was comic support in *Up in Arms, Scattergood Baines, Gildersleeve's Bad Day,* etc.

TROW, WILLIAM *(1973)* 82 ——Supporting roles in silents.

TROWBRIDGE, CHARLES *(1967)* 85 —— Character actor with piercing blue eyes (color wasn't required to reveal this) and a supremely intellectual face which signaled at once he was a man of prestige; played doctors (*Captains Courageous*), governors (the serial *Mysterious Dr. Satan*), presidents (Martin Van Buren in *The Gorgeous Hussy*), other political figures (Cordell Hull—inspired casting—in both *Sergeant York* and *Mission to Moscow*); plus many ranking military officers (*Ten Gentlemen from West Point, The Fighting 69th, They Were Expendable,* etc., including his last, 1957's *The Wings of Eagles,* in which he was Admiral Crown); had been onscreen, in more than 150, from 1917's *Thais,* in which he acted opposite diva Mary Garden.

TROY, HELEN *(1942)* 37 ——Radio's hilarious "telephone girl," she was in several in the '30s: *Born to Dance, Everybody Sing, Broadway Melody of 1938, Song and Dance Man,* etc.

TRUESDELL, FREDERICK *(1937)* 64 ——Top support in many silents: *Pleasure Mad,* Geraldine Farrar's *Shadows,* Alice Brady's *The Boss,* Anita Stewart's *The Love Piker;* sometimes billed Fred C.

TRUEX, ERNEST *(1973)* 83 ——Sweet-natured, "ageless" actor who spent most of his movie life as a timid (or henpecked) soul; his career was of such duration that at 17 he appeared on Broadway with (the real) Lillian Russell in *Wildfire* and in 1940's *Lillian Russell* played her (Alice Faye's) father; in between had been in dozens: 1918's *Good Little Devil* with Mary Pickford, numerous two-reelers with Shirley Mason, *Artie,* and such talkies as *The Warrior's Husband, Bachelor Mother, The Under-Pup, His Girl Friday;* later was in *Christmas in July, The Crystal Ball, Star Spangled Rhythm, Men in Her Diary,* and, last, 1965's *Fluffy;* an outstanding Broadway star throughout his screen career, he was also greatly successful in TV's *Mr. Peepers* and *The Truex Family* with wife, Sylvia Field; last acted professionally in a '66 episode of *Petticoat Junction.*

TRUJILLO, LORENZO "CHEL" *(1962)* 56 — —Character in Bunuel's *The Exterminating Angel* and many more Mexican films.

TRYON, GLENN *(1970)* 76 ——Handsome, wavy-haired actor who starred, usually as an "all-American boy," in many comedy features in the '20s and early '30s: *The White Sheep, The*

Battling Orioles, How to Handle Women, Painting the Town, A Hero for a Night, Dames Ahoy, Skinner Steps Out, etc.; in the mid '30s became a director (*Beauty for the Asking, Two in Revolt*), and in the '40s a producer (*The Devil With Hitler, That Nazty Nuisance, Calaboose*—all for Hal Roach, who had originally discovered and starred him); made several brief screen appearances in the '40s, in *George White's Scandals, Variety Girl,* and such Universal comedies as *Hellzapoppin'*, which featured wife Jane Frazee, *Hold That Ghost,* and *Keep 'em Flying.*

TSIANG, H. T. *(1971)* 72 ——Played Hosannah Wang in *The Keys of the Kingdom;* was also in *Panic in the Streets* (cook), *The Purple Heart, Chicken Every Sunday.*

TUBBS, BILL *(1953)* 44 ——In the one comic episode in *Paisan,* he played the Catholic U.S. Army chaplain who comes to the monastery where the monks feel compelled to do penance for his "lost soul" companions—a Protestant chaplain and a Jewish one; played Anaxander in *Quo Vadis?* (billed William) and was also in *Three Steps North,* etc.

TUCKER, GEORGE LOANE *(1921)* 49 —— Handsome actor who was one of the stars of the Original Imp Company in 1911; later starred for Majestic, and still later ('19) wrote and directed *The Miracle Man* which made a star of Lon Chaney.

TUCKER, RICHARD *(1942)* 73 ——An Edison star from '15, this big, good-looking actor was in *While the Tide Was Rising, Vanity Fair* with Minnie Maddern Fiske, *Roads of Destiny, Branding Iron,* etc., before launching the character-actor career that would occupy him, in more than 100, for the next two decades; was top support in *Hearts Aflame* with Anna Q. Nilsson, *The Broken Wing* with Miss Du Pont, *The Blind Goddess, Broken Dishes, Only Yesterday, Handy Andy, Diamond Jim, The Great Victor Herbert, The River of Missing Men,* etc.

TUCKER, SOPHIE *(1966)* 82 ——Lusty, buxom, and blondined song star of Broadway, vaudeville, and radio fame, known the world over as "The Last of the Red-Hot Mamas"; starred onscreen in *Honky Tonk* ('29), *Thoroughbreds Don't Cry, Broadway Melody of 1938, Sensations of 1945,* and made a guest appearance in *Follow the Boys.*

TUFTS, SONNY *(1970)* 59 ——Big, grinning, shaggy-haired blond who, in the '40s, was Paramount's grown-up juvenile; introduced shirtless in *So Proudly We Hail,* he became the Pin-up King, with excuses found to show off his rangy torso in many other pix in which he co-

starred: *Here Come the Waves, I Love a Soldier, Bring on the Girls, The Well Groomed Bride,* etc.; older, paunchier, he frequently played smiling villains; among his later credits: *The Crooked Way, Easy Living, Cat-Women of the Moon, Run for the Hills, The Parson and the Outlaw,* and last, *Town Tamer* ('65).

TULLEY, ETHEL *(1968)* 70 ——Acted for Vitagraph in the teens.

TUNIS, FAY *(1967)* 77 ——Support in silents.

TURNBULL, JOHN *(1956)* 75 ——British character actor who played Holbein in *The Private Life of Henry VIII;* in many English pix: *The Scarlet Pimpernel, Rembrandt, Nine Days a Queen, So Well Remembered,* etc.

TURNER, FLORENCE *(1946)* 61 ——Vitagraph's great first dramatic star, known nationally as "The Vitagraph Girl" long before her name was disclosed; 1907–13 was her period of enormous popularity, when she starred in *A Tale of Two Cities, Jealousy, The New Stenographer, Lancelot and Elaine, A Dixie Mother, My Old Dutch,* others; then made several in England (*East Is East,* etc.), returning home to find her fame dissipated; supported others in the '20s: Gladys Walton in *All Dolled Up,* Vilmy Banky in *The Dark Angel,* Anita Stewart in *Never the Twain Shall Meet,* Sojin in *The Chinese Parrot,* etc.; *The Rampant Age* in '30, one of several unimportant talkies in which she appeared, was her swan song.

TURNER, MAIDEL *(1953)* 72 ——The plump character lead in 1933's *Another Language,* this stage actress had supporting roles in many others of the '30s: *It Happened One Night* (Auto Camp Manager's Wife), *The Life of Vergie Winters, Diamond Jim, The Raven,* etc.; came back later to play the overblown wife of Raymond Walburn, the Judge, in *State of the Union,* and Aunt Abby in *Here Comes the Groom.*

TURNER, COL. ROSCOE *(1970)* 74 —— Famed real-life pilot who played one in *Hell's Angels* and starred in 1939's *Flight at Midnight.*

TURNER, WILLIAM H. *(1942)* 81 ——Character (Boot Maker) in Chevalier's *Love Me Tonight;* had supporting roles in several prior to this: Baby Peggy's *The Darling of New York,* Betty Compson's *The Enemy Sex* and *The Garden of Weeds,* Wallace Beery's *The Pony Express.*

TURPIN, BEN *(1940)* 66 ——Immortal cross-eyed comedy star for Essanay, Vogue and Keystone; onscreen from 1907 to *Saps at Sea* in his last year, he caused howls of laughter in hundreds; his trademarks were his backward somersaults and, of course, those eyes, which did not become permanently crossed until he was in his 30s; a few of his best comedies: *A Small Town Idol, Bright Eyes* ('22), *A Clever Dummy, The Shriek of Araby, A Harem Knight, Yukon Jake, A Blonde's Revenge, The Wife's Relations,* which brought him up to talkies; was in just five features in the '30s: *Cracked Nuts, Swing High, Million Dollar Legs, Make Me a Star,* and in the decade's last year, *Hollywood Cavalcade.*

TURPIN, CARRIE *(1925)* 30s ——Comedienne-wife of Ben, who appeared with him in several short comedies in 1915–16.

TWEDDELL, FRITZ *(1971)* 76 ——In both *Claudia* and *Claudia and David,* played Fritz, the handyman; was also in *Carousel* (as Captain Watson), *I'd Climb the Highest Mountain, The Undercover Man,* etc.

TWEED, TOMMY *(1971)* 64 ——Featured in *The Incredible Journey.*

TWELVETREES, HELEN *(1958)* 50 ——Beautiful blonde star of the woeful countenance, and of the '30s, whose three dozen roles rarely provided the opportunity to prove her excellence as an actress; typical of the sturm-and-drang: *Panama Flo, A Woman of Experience, Bad Company, True Heart;* her best by far were *Now I'll Tell* opposite Spencer Tracy, *A Bedtime Story* with Chevalier, *Millie, State's Attorney* with John Barrymore; she and Buck Jones made an attractive twosome in both *Hollywood Roundup* and *Unmarried,* neither a Western; later a stage actress, she eventually played Blanche in *A Streetcar Named Desire* in stock—superbly.

TWITCHELL, ARCHIE *(1957)* 50 ——Dark-haired and attractive, with a widow's peak, he played secondary roles for years at Paramount: *I Wanted Wings* (Lt. Clankton), *Spawn of the North* (fisherman), *Her Jungle Love* (Roy Atkins), *Cocoanut Grove, Ambush,* etc.; later in *The Arnelo Affair, Follow Me Quietly, The French Key,* others.

TYLER, GLADYS *(1972)* 79 ——Supporting roles.

TYLER, HARRY *(1961)* 73 ——Busy, dour-pussed character actor—in more than 100 after 1929's *The Shannons of Broadway*—who was often to be found in country garb in John Ford movies: *The Grapes of Wrath* (Bert), *Young Mr. Lincoln* (barber), *Tobacco Road* (auto dealer who sold Sister Bessie the new convertible for her loony young lover, Dude Lester), *The Quiet Man* (Pat Cohan); also in *A Night at the Opera* (sign painter), *Remember the Day, Jesse James, Bedtime for Bonzo,* etc.

TYLER, JUDY *(1957)* 24 ——Vivacious brunette from Broadway who had the femme lead opposite Presley in *Jailhouse Rock.*

TYLER, TOM *(1954)* 51 ——Huge cowboy and serial star with a poker face, kettledrum voice, and magnificent physique (was a weight-lifting champ for a dozen years); in movies from the mid-'20s, he starred in *Lone Horseman, Law of the Plains, Powdersmoke Range, Pride of Pawnee,* many more, including "The Three Mesquiteers" series in which he played hero Stony Brooke 13 times; starred unforgettably in several serials: 1931's *Battling with Buffalo Bill* and *The Phantom of the West,* 1932's *The Jungle Mystery,* 1933's *Clancy of the Mounted* and *The Phantom of the Air,* 1941's—and best of all for he looked like the comic-strip hero come to life—*Adventures of Captain Marvel,* and 1943's *The Phantom;* in classier pix often played steely-eyed villains, such as Luke Plummer in *Stagecoach;* crippled by arthritis in the mid-'40s, he played bits in *The Great Missouri Raid, Marshal of Heldorado, Best of the Badmen,* etc., to the end.

TYNAN, BRANDON *(1967)* 87 ——Character actor from Ireland; in *Nancy Drew, Detective* was Dr. Spires whose kidnapping was solved by juvenile sleuth Bonita Granville; was also in *The Girl of the Golden West* (the Professor), *Parnell, The Great Man Votes, Lucky Partners,* etc.

U

ULLMAN, GRETA *(1972)* ——Minor supporting roles for many years.

ULRIC, LENORE *(1970)* 78 ——Raven-haired dynamo from Broadway, often cast as a half-breed, who began (her name still spelled Ulrich) as a rose-clenched-between-teeth star for Essanay in 1912; starred in *Kilmeny, The Better Woman, Intrigue, Tiger Rose, Capital Punishment,* other silents: *South Sea Rose* and *Frozen Justice,* both in '29, were her only starring talkies; later was splendid support in *Camille* (as bitchy Olympe, courtesan rival-colleague of Garbo), Lucille Ball's *Two Smart People* (Senora Maria Ynez), Nelson Eddy's *Northwest Outpost.*

813

UNDERWOOD, FRANKLIN *(1940)* 63 —— Support in Nick Stuart's *The News Parade* ('28).

UNDERWOOD, LAWRENCE *(1939)* 67 —— Lincolnesque leading man in Metro's *Old Lady 31* ('20); later in *Passionate Youth* and such silent Westerns as *Thundering Through* and *Twisted Triggers.*

URBAN, DOROTHY *(1961)* 92 ——Played the grandmother in Pare Lorentz' 1940 semi-documentary *The Fight for Life.*

URECAL, MINERVA *(1966)* 70 ——Hawknosed character who was often a spiteful gossip; onscreen three decades in more than 100, usually comedies: *You Can't Fool Your Wife, Men in Her Diary, Her Husband's Secretary,* *My Favorite Blonde, Good Sam, Sitting Pretty, Aaron Slick from Punkin Crick,* etc., and last, Tony Randall's *Seven Faces of Dr. Lao* ('64); actually named Holzer, her screen name was an amalgam of her birthplace, Eureka, California.

URQUHART, ALASDAIR *(1954)* 40 ——Scottish actor who had a supporting role in Richard Todd's *Rob Roy.*

USHER, GUY *(1944)* 69 ——Support for a decade, he played many policemen (*Charlie Chan at the Opera,* as Inspector Regan, *Marked Woman, Sophie Lang Goes West*), fathers (Dunne's in *Invitation to Happiness*), serial villains (Aldar in *Buck Rogers*), miscellaneous characters (Grey Beard in *The Crusades*), and businessmen in B Westerns (*Under Western Skies, Boots and Saddles,* etc.).

V

VAGUE, VERA *(1974)* 70 ——Raven-haired comedienne who played a dizzy man-chaser on Bob Hope's radio show and in movies: *Melody Ranch, Rosie the Riveter, Lake Placid Serenade, Earl Carroll's Sketchbook, Snafu,* etc.; was sometimes billed under her real name, Barbara Jo Allen, with Vera Vague inserted in parentheses.

VAIL, LESTER *(1959)* 59 ——Popular light lead in the early '30s in *Dance, Fools, Dance; Beau Ideal; Murder by the Clock; Consolation Marriage;* later a top radio director.

VAIL, OLIVE *(1951)* 47 ——Supporting actress.

VALENTINE, DICKIE *(1971)* 41 ——Supporting actor.

VALENTINO, RUDOLPH *(1926)* 31 ——The silent screen's greatest "Latin Lover," who became that after starring in 1921's *The Four Horsemen of the Apocalypse;* had then been onscreen seven years, in *All Night* with Carmel Myers, *Eyes of Youth* with Clara Kimball Young, *The Delicious Little Devil* with Mae Murray, etc.; among the later films that kept him an international superstar were *Blood and Sand* and *The Young Rajah* (on both of which his studio, Paramount, did a curious thing— billed him as Rodolph), *The Sheik, Monsieur Beaucaire, The Eagle,* and last, *Son of the Sheik;* was portrayed in '51 by Anthony Dexter in *Valentino.*

VALERIO, ALBANO *(1961)* 72 ——Featured in 1928's *The Loves of Ricardo.*

VALK, FREDERICK *(1956)* 55 ——Was the analyst of schizophrenic ventriloquist Michael Redgrave in *Dead of Night;* support in many other British pix: *Night Train, Outcast of the Islands, Brighton Rock, The Colditz Story, Suicide Squadron,* etc.

VALKYRIEN, VALDA *(1953)* 59 ——A Brunhilde from Denmark, this actress with flowing blonde hair starred in American movies in the teens for Vitagraph (*Youth*), Pathe (*Hidden Valley*), and Fox; sometimes billed simply Valkyrien, she was in real life Baroness DeWitz.

VALLI, VALLI *(1927)* 45 ——Comedienne from Germany who starred for Metro in '16 in *The Turmoil;* married, retired to England.

VALLI, VIRGINIA *(1968)* 70 ——Incredibly lovely actress who went from bits in '15 (*In the Palace of the King*) to leads (*Uneasy Money, The Golden Idiot,* etc.) to stardom in the '20s (*A Lady of Quality, Flames, Wild Oranges, Up the Ladder, Siege, The Signal Tower,* many others); was in just four quickies in 1930–31: *The Lost Zeppelin, Storm, Night Life in Reno, Guilty?;* left the screen for a long and happy marriage to Charles Farrell.

VAN, BILLY *(1973)* 61 ——Minor support in several.

VAN, BILLY B. *(1950)* 72 ——Vaudeville actor featured in a '22 Paramount pic, *The Beauty Shop,* which was, claimed one critic, the "greatest aggregation of old puns ever assembled."

VAN, GUS *(1968)* 80 ——Of the famous Van & Schenck comedy team which appeared in *The Pennant* and *They Learned About Women* plus several musical shorts; alone, he made other shorts and had a supporting role in *Atlantic City* with Constance Moore.

VAN, WALLY *(1974)* 94 ——An early ('13) athletic and romantic comedian who starred for Vitagraph and was popularly known as "Cutie"; was in *Love, Luck and Gasoline* (involving, appropriately, a motorboat chase; a trained engineer, he had first been employed by the president of Vitagraph to look after the engines of his speed boats), *The Win(k)some Widow, The New Secretary*, etc.; in the '20s he starred in *The Drivin' Fool, The Common Law, Slave of Desire, Barriers Burned Away.*

VAN AUKER, C. K. *(1938)* 50s ——Support in the '20s in Barbara La Marr's *Cinderella of the Hills*, Nell Shipman's *The Girl from God's Country*, Tom Mix's *Trailin'*, Shirley Mason's *The Ragged Heiress*, etc.

VAN BEERS, STANLEY *(1961)* 50 ——Balding, villainous-looking support in many British films: *Cry, the Beloved Country; The Dam Busters; So Little Time; Brandy for the Parson; Terror Ship*, etc.

VANBRUGH, IRENE *(1949)* 77 ——Played the Duchess in Dietrich's *Knight Without Armor;* in many British pix: *Catherine the Great, Wings of the Morning, Escape Me Never, Moonlight Sonata*, etc.

VANBRUGH, VIOLET *(1942)* 75 ——English actress who played the Ambassadress in *Pygmalion;* was also in *Captivation* ('31), and, in '13, played Lady Macbeth in the German-made *Macbeth.*

VAN BUREN, MABEL *(1947)* 69 ——Limpideyed brunette beauty who in the teens starred for DeMille in *The Man from Home* and *The Girl of the Golden West;* starred in the same period in numerous other Lasky-produced pix: *The Victoria Cross, The Man on the Box, The Circus Man*, etc.; in the '20s, supported others (Lois Wilson in *Miss Lulu Bett*, Evelyn Brent in *Smooth as Satin*, James Kirkwood in *The Top of the World*, etc.) and played bits for DeMille in *Manslaughter* (a prisoner), *The King of Kings* (crowd scenes); last had a small role in William Boyd's *His First Command* ('30).

VANCE, LUCILE *(1974)* 81 ——Character roles in several in the '40s: Lugosi's *Bowery at Midnight*, a Dave O'Brien Western, *Boss of Rawhide, Thundergap Outlaws*, etc.

VANCE, VIRGINIA *(1942)* 40 ——Had leads in several minor pix in the '20s (*Undressed, New Year's Eve*, etc.) and in the Gene Tunney serial *The Fighting Marine.*

VANDERGRIFT, MONTE *(1939)* 46 ——Supporting roles in the '30s in *Woman Chases Man* (process server), Gene Raymond's *Seven Keys to Baldpate, Private Worlds, Easy Money, Miracles for Sale*, others.

VANE, DENTON *(1940)* 50 ——Featured in several minor pix in the '20s (*Flesh and Spirit, Women Men Love*, etc.).

VAN EYCK, PETER *(1969)* 56 ——Handsome blond German actor in *The Moon Is Down* whose romantic liaison with the young Norwegian widow, Dorris Bowdon, leads to her stabbing him to death with scissors; played many other rugged (and ruthless) Nazis: *Five Graves to Cairo, The Hitler Gang, The Desert Fox, Address Unknown*, etc.; starred in numerous European pix, the best being *Wages of Fear, Rosemary, The Glass Tower;* was also in *The Longest Day, The Spy Who Came in from the Cold, Station Six-Sahara, Shalako, The 1,000 Eyes of Dr. Mabuse*, etc.

VAN HADEN, ANDERS *(1936)* 60 ——Support in several in the '30s: Edward G. Robinson's *Barbary Coast* (as Second Mate), Lionel Atwill's *Secret of the Blue Room*, Paul Lukas' *Passport to Hell*, etc.

VAN HORN, JIMMY *(1966)* 49 ——Support in Westerns: *Marshal of Heldorado, Hostile Country*, and *Fast on the Draw* (all starring James Ellison), and Macdonald Carey's *The Cave of the Outlaws.*

VANNE, MARDA *(1970)* 70s ——South African character actress featured, as Granny, in Calvin Lockhart's *Joanna.*

VAN ROOTEN, LUIS *(1973)* 66 ——Fine slickdomed character who specialized in dialects and villainous roles; was in *The Hitler Gang* (as Himmler), *Two Years Before the Mast* (Foster), *Night Has a Thousand Eyes, City Across the River, The Big Clock, My Favorite Spy, Fraulein, Detective Story* (a switch—a plainclothes cop), etc.; did much TV before retiring to become an author on horticultural subjects.

VAN SAHER, LILLA *(1968)* 56 ——Hungarian actress who was in *Grain au Vent.*

VAN SLOAN, EDWARD *(1964)* 82 ——Gray, hawk-nosed character who several times played professors in horror movies: *The Mummy* (occult authority, Dr. Muller, who tried to break Im-Ho-Tep's—Karloff's—evil spell over Zita Johann), *Frankenstein* (old teacher of Dr. Frankenstein, Colin Clive), *Dracula, Dracula's Daughter;* was also in the serial *The Phantom Creeps* and more than 60 other features, including *Death Takes a Holiday* (Dr. Valle), *The Scarlet Empress, The Doctor Takes a Wife,* and *The Conspirators.*

VAN TRESS, MABEL *(1962)* 89 ——Character roles in silents.

VAN TRUMP, JESSALYN *(1939)* 63 ——Brunette actress who, between '12 and '15, played many leads (sometimes character parts) for several companies—Flying "A," Universal, Majestic, etc.

VAN TUYI, HELLEN *(1964)* 63 ——Character actress who always played aristocrats such as, in *Titanic,* wealthy victim Mrs. Straus; was also in *Stars and Stripes Forever,* Astaire's *Daddy Long Legs,* others.

VAN UPP, VIRGINIA *(1970)* 67 ——Child actress in silents who was later Columbia's famous woman producer (*Gilda, Together Again,* etc.).

VAN VOORHIS, WESTBROOK *(1968)* 64 —— The voice of "March of Time."

VAN ZANDT, PHILIP *(1951)* 54 ——In more than 200 he played oily little villains, often city types in cheap suits and flashy ties; was in *The Big Clock, Somewhere in the Night, Air Raid Wardens, The Lady Gambles,* etc.; was also in such costume pics as *The Loves of Carmen, Yankee Pasha, Sudan, Cyrano de Bergerac.*

VARCONI, VICTOR *(1976)* 80 ——A most handsome man, with widow's peak, who was onscreen from the early '20s and played opposite Phyllis Haver in *Chicago;* had second leads or was top support in dozens more: *Feet of Clay* (the Bookkeeper), *The Volga Boatman* (Prince Dimitri Orlaff who lost Elinor Fair to peasant William Boyd), *The King of Kings* (Pontius Pilate), *Roberta* (dress salon doorman—actually a Russian prince; told by Astaire he was fired, he replied, "No, no. I am not fired. I am perfectly cool"), *The Hitler Gang, Unconquered* (Captain Ecuyer), etc., through the late '40s.

VARDEN, EVELYN *(1958)* 63 ——Was several times a talkative, middle-aged Southern woman (*Pinky,* as bigot Melba Wooley; *Cheaper by the Dozen,* as the school principal); was also in *The Bad Seed* (Monica), *Phone Call from a Stranger, Desiree, Athena,* etc.

VARLEY, BEATRICE *(1969)* 73 ——Played timorous old ladies in many British pix: *My Brother Jonathan, Jassy, So Well Remembered, Gone to Earth,* etc.

VASSAR, QUEENIE *(1960)* 89 ——Stole the show as Ginger Rogers' salty old Grandma in *Primrose Path;* was in just two others: Dunne's *Lady in a Jam* (Cactus Kate) and *None But the Lonely Heart* (Ma Snowden).

VAUGHAN, DOROTHY *(1955)* 66 ——Sweet-faced character actress, onscreen from '35, who often played moms or housekeepers; among her dozens: *Gentleman Jim* (Flynn's mother), *Sweet Rosie O'Grady, Henry Aldrich's Little Secret, Square Dance Katy, The Iron Major, Unexpected Father,* etc.

VAUGHN, ADAMAE *(1943)* 37 ——Pretty girl was was Tom Tyler's leading lady in *The Arizona Streak,* had second leads in Ralph Lewis' *The Last Edition* and Sue Carol's *Dancing Sweeties,* and did a routine with more famous sister Alberta in 1929's *Show of Shows.*

VAUGHN, HILDA *(1957)* 59 ——Skinny and tough; at her best as Harlow's blackmailing personal maid in *Dinner at Eight* and as Beryl Mercer's Cockney crony in *Three Live Ghosts* (her first, in '29); was also in *Ladies of the Big House, Anne of Green Gables* (Mrs. Blewett), *Charlie Chan at the Wax Museum, Banjo on my Knee,* etc.

VAUGHN, WILLIAM *(1946)* 64 ——See Wilhelm Von Bricken.

VAVERKA, ANTON *(1937)* 60s ——Character actor from Czechoslovakia who twice played Emperor Franz-Joseph for von Stroheim—in *Merry-Go-Round* and *The Wedding March* (being billed, in both instances, Wawerka); was also in Chaney's *The Phantom of the Opera* (the Prompter), Norman Kerry's *The Love Thief,* William Collier Jr.'s *The Melody Man,* etc.

VEDDER, WILLIAM H. *(1961)* 88 ——In the Marilyn Monroe episode of *O. Henry's Full House,* he was the Judge; was also in *The Wild One* (Simmy), *Paula, Boots Malone, Leave It to Henry,* etc.

VEIDT, CONRAD *(1943)* 50 ——Star from Germany whose face should have been painted by the masters—aristocratic, lean, sensuous, sinister, commanding, and most of all, enigmatic; in the '40s in his second Hollywood career (had starred here in several in the '20s), he gave several performances that will not be forgotten: *A Woman's Face* (the cruel nobleman, Torsten

Barring, that Crawford loves), *Casablanca* (Major Strasser), *Escape* (Gen. Kurt von Kolb who loves Shearer), *Above Suspicion*, etc.; immediately prior to this came his English period in which he starred in *The Thief of Bagdad, Storm over Asia, The Passing of the Third Floor Back, U-Boat 29*, others; still earlier, the German period: *The Congress Dances, Ich und die Kaiserin*, and a score more, all the way back to 1921's *The Cabinet of Dr. Caligari* that made him an international name; and even earlier, to now-forgotten films of 1916 in which he first played the cool, dangerous man on whom he built an illustrious career.

VEJAR, HARRY J. *(1968)* 77 ——Played Louie Costillo in *Scarface*, the bartender in *Treasure of Sierra Madre;* in the '20s had supporting roles in *The Sheik*, Stanwyck's *Mexicali Rose*, etc.

VEKROFF, PERRY *(1937)* 45 ——Support in silents.

VELEZ, LUPE *(1944)* 36 ——Funny-sexy pepperpot from South of the Border who starred in RKO's eight "Mexican Spitfire" comedies: *Mexican Spitfire Out West, Mexican Spitfire at Sea, Mexican Spitfire Sees a Ghost*, etc.; the titles of two were ironic, *Mexican Spitfire's Baby* and *Mexican Spitfire's Blessed Event* (her last film), for it was because she was unwed and expecting a child that she committed suicide; onscreen from '27, she had been Fairbanks' leading lady in *The Gaucho*, co-starred with Monte Blue in *Tiger Rose*, William Boyd in *Lady of the Pavements*, and, in the '30s, been in many others; *The Squaw Man, Palooka, Hot Pepper, Strictly Dynamite, Gypsy Melody*, etc.; was once married to Johnny Weissmuller.

VENABLE, REGINALD *(1974)* 48 ——Actor-son of Fay Bainter; supporting roles.

VENESS, AMY *(1960)* 84 ——Plump, cheerful character actress (often a housekeeper) in dozens of British pix: *Doctor in the House, The Astonished Heart, Tom Brown's School Days* ('52), *Madeleine*, and *The Old Curiosity Shop*, in which she was Mrs. Jarley and splendid.

VERDI, JOE *(1957)* 72 ——Supported von Stroheim in *The Crime of Dr. Crespi*, Mel Ferrer in *The Vintage*, others.

VERMILYEA, HAROLD *(1958)* 68 ——Short, stocky, sandy-haired, and pleasant, this character actor was in many in the '40s and early '50s: *The Emperor Waltz* (Chamberlain); *O.S.S.; Sorry, Wrong Number; The Big Clock; Chicago Deadline*, etc.

VERNE, KAAREN *(1967)* 49 ——A most attractive and intriguing blonde from Germany, she had her best opportunity as Bogart's leading lady in *All Through the Night;* was also appealing in the last reel of *Kings Row* as Elise Sandor, Robert Cummings' new love, reminiscent of his lost Cassandra (Betty Field); had other femme leads in the same period in *Sky Murder, Sherlock Holmes and the Secret Weapon, Underground;* a character actress when older, she was in *Ship of Fools* (Frau Lutz), *Torn Curtain, A Bullet for Joey*, etc.; was once married to Peter Lorre.

VERNEY, GUY *(1970)* 60s ——British character actor who played Melanchthon in *Martin Luther;* was also in *This Happy Breed, Fame Is the Spur, Cage of Gold*, other English films.

VERNON, BOBBY *(1939)* 42 ——Boyish, effervescent little comedian who co-starred with Swanson in dozens of romantic comedies for Sennett in the late teens; along for laughs in many was also a famous Great Dane named Teddy; a few of their many: *Haystacks and Steeples, Dangers of a Bride, Teddy at the Throttle;* in the '20s was greatly popular and prankish in the "Bobby Vernon Comedies" for Al Christie and then Educational; rarely in features, he did support Jacqueline Logan in 1926's *Footloose Widows;* last had minor roles in two 1931–32 shorts: *Stout Hearts and Willing Hands* and *Ship A Hooey*.

VERNON, WALLY *(1970)* 64 ——Hawk-nosed comedian who got laughs in dozens in his 33-year career: *Kentucky Moonshine, Tail Spin, The Gorilla, Sandy Gets Her Man, Reveille with Beverly, Pistol Packin' Mama*, etc.: for years in the '40s was comic foil for Roy Rogers and Don Barry in such as *Outlaws of Santa Fe, Stagecoach to Monterey, Silver City Kid*, etc.; later was in *Bloodhounds of Broadway, What a Way to Go!, Everybody's Dancing*, other comedies.

VICKERS, MARTHA *(1971)* 46 ——Best known for portraying the retarded heiress, Carmen Sternwood, in *The Big Sleep*, this beautiful honey-blonde was prominently featured in others at Warners: *The Man I Love; The Time, the Place and the Girl; That Way with Women*, etc.; was also in *Ruthless, The Burglar, The Falcon in Mexico*, and, last, *Four Fast Guns* ('60); was one of Mickey Rooney's wives.

VICTOR, CHARLES *(1965)* 69 ——Doleful-faced character who usually played Cockneys in such British pix as *Meet Mr. Lucifer, Charley Moon, The Love Lottery, An Alligator Named Daisy*, many more.

VICTOR, HENRY (1945) 47 ——In Freaks was Hercules the Strong Man who assisted his cold-blooded sweetheart, trapeze artist Cleopatra (Olga Baclanova), in poisoning her midget-husband for his inheritance; was equally villainous in Confessions of a Nazi Spy (as Helldorf); The Mummy; The Hate Ship; Desperate Journey; Nick Carter, Master Detective; etc.

VIDACOVICH, IRVINE (1966) 61 ——Played Johnston in Panic in the Streets.

VIDAL, HENRI (1959) 40 ——Handsome French star whose incredibly muscular physique made Fabiola a smash hit; was also in Gates of Paris (the gangster), The Seven Deadly Sins (in the Gluttony segment), The Damned, Naughty Martine, Attila, etc.; was married to Michele Morgan.

VIGNOLA, ROBERT (1953) 71 ——Good-looking, dimpled-chin actor who was in early Kalem silents; later directed Davies in several: Yolanda, When Knighthood Was in Flower, Beauty's Worth.

VILAR, JEAN (1971) 58 ——Featured in such French films as The Thirst of Men and Gates of the Night.

VILLARREAL, JULIO (1958) 73 ——Mexican character actor who played Senor Mendoza in Shirley Temple's Honeymoon and Navarro in Glenn Ford's Plunder of the Sun; was also in Seven Cities of Gold and The Beast of Hollow Mountain, plus many Mexican films.

VINCENOT, LOUIS (1967) 83 ——Character in Limehouse Blues, others.

VINCENT, GENE (1971) 36 ——Rock 'n roller who was in Ring-a-Ding Rhythm, Sing and Swing, other youth musicals of the '60s.

VINCENT, JAMES (1957) 74 ——Supporting roles.

VINCENT, ROBBIE (1968) 72 ——Comedian in British pix.

VINE, BILLY (1958) 42 ——Played Joe Di Angelo in Lamour's The Lucky Stiff and a supporting role in Oreste's The Vagabond King.

VINTON, ARTHUR (1963) 50s ——Had secondary roles in many between '30 and '35: Dames (the Bugler), Washington Merry-Go-Round, Blondie Johnson, Little Big Shot, Lilly Turner, etc.; went into radio, became famous as "The Shadow."

VISAROFF, MICHAEL (1951) 58 ——Character actor from Russia who played Jean, the caretaker, in Freaks; the circus director in Janet Gaynor's Four Devils; a butler in Angel; and the Russian Governor in A Song to Remember; in dozens of Hollywood pix from the mid '20s on.

VIVIAN, PERCIVAL (1961) 70 ——Support in Prince Valiant, Jane Wyman's A Kiss in the Dark, and Astaire's Daddy Long Legs.

VIVIAN, ROBERT (1944) 85 ——Support in Elsie Ferguson's Under the Greenwood Tree, Alice MacMahon's Back Door to Heaven, etc.

VIVIAN, RUTH (1949) 66 ——In The Man Who Came to Dinner she played Russell Arms' mother, Harriett Stanley, and in A Letter to Three Wives was Miss Hawkins.

VODEDING, FREDRIK (1942) 52 ——Stern-visaged character actor from the Netherlands who, often playing Germans, worked both sides of the law in movies; was villainous in Confessions of a Nazi Spy (as Captain Richter), Man Hunt, Mysterious Mr. Moto, the serial Ace Drummond; often played police officials in "Charlie Chan" pix (Charlie Chan at the Olympics, . . . in City of Darkness).

VOGAN, EMMETT (1969) 76 ——Gray and strong-featured, he played sheriffs or ranchers in many B Westerns: Smoky River Serenade, The Denver Kid, Utah, Along the Navajo Trail, etc.; played cops in other features: Murder in the Blue Room, Whistling in Dixie, Sorrowful Jones, others.

VOGEL, HENRY (1925) 60 ——Support in silents.

VOGLER, WALTER (1955) 58 ——Minor support in All Quiet on the Western Front.

VOKES, MAY (1957) 72 ——Character actress who played Marion Davies' maid, Susie, in Janice Meredith.

VOLPE, FREDERICK (1932) 66 ——Support in English pix: The Middle Watch, Captivation, etc.

VON ALTEN, FERDINAND (1933) 48 ——Featured in several German silents of the late '20s released here: The Man Who Cheated Life, Small Town Sinners, etc.

VON BLOCK, BELA (1962) 72 ——Support in silents.

VON BRINCKEN, WILHELM (1946) 64 ——Character actor from Germany who was in three dozen Hollywood films; was perhaps most noted for playing Von Richthofen in

Hell's Angels; was Kraftstein in Colman's *The Prisoner of Zenda*, Captain von Eichen in *Confessions of a Nazi Spy* (billed as William Vaughn, which he sometimes used, in addition to Roger Beckwith); was also in *Dracula's Daughter, They Gave Him a Gun, I'll Tell the World, Four Sons*, etc.

VON ELTZ, THEODORE *(1964)* 70 ——Fine-looking leading man in many in the '20s: *Tiger Rose, The Four Feathers, The Red Kimona, The Sporting Chance*, etc.; then became, in more than 100, one of the screen's most dependable character actors; was in *Private Worlds; Susan Lennox, Her Fall and Rise; The Midnight Lady; Suzy; The Road to Glory; Topper*, etc.; was especially noteworthy in *The Big Sleep*, as pornography king-blackmailer Arthur Gwynne Geiger whose actions set into motion this *film noir;* he was finally Father Barbour in the TV version of *One Man's Family*.

VON MEYERINCK, HUBERT *(1971)* 74 —— German character actor who played Count von Droste-Schattenburg in Cagney's *One, Two, Three;* in many European films.

VON SEYFFERTITZ, GUSTAV *(1943)* 80 —— Unforgettable as the evil swampland farmer in Pickford's *Sparrows* and as Moriarty in John Barrymore's *Sherlock Holmes* ('22), he was for almost three decades—with his sharp-featured, gray face—one of the classic villains of the screen; of course, in WW I Liberty Bond films he did play Uncle Sam, but he also played the Kaiser too; in these, and in that period of great antipathy to all things German, he temporarily changed his billing to G. Butler Clonebaugh; was so credited in *Till I Come Back to You;* back to von Seyffertitz, he was in such pix of the '20s as *Dead Men Tell No Tales; The Bandolero; The Wizard; Me, Gangster;* and *The Docks of New York;* in the '30s, was in *The Bat Whispers, Queen Christina, The Doomed Battalion, Mad Holiday, She*, and last, *Nurse Edith Cavell*.

VON STROHEIM, ERICH *(1957)* 71 ——Bald, monocled, stiff-necked Prussian meanie—"The Man You Love to Hate"; moviegoers, enthralled by his fearsome arrogance, went along with that, but behind the scenes, alas, so did several producers whose money he spent in lavish abundance when directing such epics for them as *The Merry Widow, Foolish Wives*, and *Greed;* as an actor—onscreen in America from 1914—his reputation rests most solidly on *The Wedding March, The Lost Squadron, As You Desire Me, Grand Illusion* (French-made), *So Ends Our Night, Five Graves to Cairo*, and *Sunset Boulevard* (as Max, Swanson's chauffeur, ex-husband, ex-director), his last Hollywood film and first to bring him an Oscar nomination as Best Supporting Actor; was later in numerous French films, the last, *L'homme aux Cent Visages*, released here posthumously.

VON STROHEIM, ERICH, JR. *(1968)* 52 —— American-born son of Erich; played Ravinski in Kirk Douglas' *Two Weeks in Another Town,* and was also in Jackie Gleason's *Skidoo*.

VON TWARDOWSKI, HANS *(1958)* 60 —— Character actor from Germany in numerous Hollywood pix of the '30s and early '40s; played Heydrich in *Hangmen Also Die;* Nicholas, Count of Hungary, in *The Crusades;* Ivan Shuvolov in *The Scarlet Empress;* a German officer in *Casablanca;* Wildebrandt in *Confessions of a Nazi Spy*, etc.

VON WINTERSTEIN, EDUARD *(1961)* 89 —— Support in Erich von Stroheim's *Three East,* Richard Dix's *The Lost Squadron*, etc.

VOSPER, JOHN *(1954)* 50s ——Support in *The Magnetic Monster, The Perfect Marriage, The Desert Fox, Counter-Attack, A Stolen Life*.

VROOM, FREDERICK *(1942)* 84 ——Especially memorable for roles in Buster Keaton comedies—*The Navigator* (the girl's father and owner of "The Navigator"), *The General* (a Southern General); support in many additional silents: *The Glorious Fool, The Lane That Had No Turning, The Great Impersonation, The Faith Healer*, etc.

VUOLO, TITO *(1962)* 69 ——Squat and bald, he played Italians—sometimes tough, sometimes comic—in many: *House of Strangers* (as Lucca), *Mr. Blandings Builds His Dream House* (Mr. Zucca), *The Bishop's Wife* (Maggenti), *Flamingo Road* (Pete Ladas), *Up Front, Cry of the City, The Racket*, others.

VYVYAN, JENNIFER *(1974)* 49 ——English opera star who was in Olivier's *The Beggar's Opera*.

W

WADE, BESSIE *(1966)* 81——Supporting actress in silents.

WADE, JOHN *(1949)* 73 ——Character in B Westerns such as the Three Mesquiteers' *Heroes of the Hills.*

WADHAMS, GOLDEN *(1929)* 60 ——Support in *Laughing at Death*, a Bob Steele attempt at a swashbuckler, Negri's *Hotel Imperial*, other silents.

WADSWORTH, HENRY *(1974)* 72 ——Introduced as a young sailor on leave in New York in Helen Morgan's *Applause*, this handsome second lead was later to be found in a tux in many: *Slightly Scarlet* with Evelyn Brent, *The Thin Man* (as playboy Andrew), *Fast and Loose*, *Evelyn Prentiss*, etc.; was also in *Ceiling Zero* (as Tay Lawson), *Operator 13*, *This Side of Heaven*, *West Point of the Air*, *The Voice of Bugle Ann*; after 1943's *Silver Skates*—no longer the "perennial juvenile"—he returned to Broadway, where he last had a supporting role in *The Happy Time*, in '50, with Eva Gabor.

WADSWORTH, WILLIAM *(1950)* 77 ——Prematurely bald, a bit chubby, and an early exponent of restraint in movie acting, he starred for Edison in the 1913–15 "Mr. Wood B. Wedd" comedy series (*Wood B. Wedd Goes Snipe Hunting*, *Wood B. Wedd and the Microbes*, etc.); in '12 had played the villain, Billy Peart, in the first serial, *What Happened to Mary?*; onscreen through 1926's *White Mice.*

WAGNER, JACK *(1965)* 67 ——Minor support in Tullio Carminati's *Paris In Spring.*

WAGNER, WILLIAM *(1964)* 78 ——Actor who played Boswell in *Lloyds of London* and had other supporting roles in Virginia Bruce's *Jane Eyre* and Temple's *Rebecca of Sunnybrook Farm.*

WAHL, WALTER DARE *(1974)* 78 ——Support in Phil Silvers' *Top Banana.*

WAINWRIGHT, HOPE *(1972)* 30 ——Support in *The Graduate*, *What Ever Happened to Baby Jane?*

WAINWRIGHT, MARIE *(1923)* 67 ——Old lady in Ina Claire's *Polly with a Past.*

WAKEFIELD, DUGGIE *(1951)* 50 ——Comedian in English pix: *Look Up and Laugh*, *Calling All Crooks*, *Spy for a Day*, etc.

WAKEFIELD, HUGH *(1971)* 83 ——Character in English pix; in Hitchcock's first version of *The Man Who Knew Too Much*, he was Clive, the amateur sleuth, friend of the kidnapped girl's father; sported his monocle in others: *Blithe Spirit*, *Man with a Million*, *The Fortunate Fool*, *It's You I Want*, etc.

WAKEFIELD, OLIVER *(1956)* 47 ——Support in Gracie Fields' *Shipyard Sally.*

WALBROOK, ANTON *(1967)* 66 ——Imperious, cloaked in suavity, this handsome world-weary Austrian was at the top of his form as the impresario in *The Red Shoes* and *La Ronde*; was excellent also, as Albert, Prince Consort of Queen Victoria, in both *Victoria the Great* and *Sixty Glorious Years*, and in *Lola Montez*, *Angel Street*, *Suicide Squadron*, *The Life and Death of Colonel Blimp*, *The Queen of Spades*; came to Hollywood for just one, 1936's *Michael Strogoff.*

WALBURN, RAYMOND *(1969)* 81 ——Hollywood's perennial Kentucky Colonel—blustering, round-eyed, and looking like *Esquire's* famous "Esky" come-to-life—this character made fine, funny contributions to many of the screen's best comedies: *Broadway Bill* (had the same mint-julep-swilling role in the '50 remake, *Riding High*); *Mr. Deeds Goes to Town*, (Cooper's "prairie oyster"-serving valet); *Christmas in July*; *Kiss the Boys Goodbye*; *Third Finger, Left Hand*; *Hail the Conquering Hero*; *State of the Union*; starred for Monogram in the modest "Henry, the Rainmaker" comedies in the late '40s; was onscreen, ever the cheeky braggart, in 87 from 1930's *The Laughing Lady* with Ruth Chatterton to 1955's *The Spoilers*; returned to Broadway, where he last appeared in *A Very Rich Woman* with Ruth Gordon in '65.

WALDIS, OTTO *(1974)* 68 ——Character actor from Germany who was in many from the late '40s: *Letter From an Unknown Woman* (as the concierge), *Berlin Express*, *The Fighting O'-Flynn*, *Knock on Wood* (Brodnik), *Judgment at Nuremberg* (Pohl), etc.

WALDRIDGE, HERBERT *(1957)* 50 —— Played office boys several times in the '30s; was in *Sob Sister*, *Private Scandal*, *June Moon*, *The Heart of New York*, *Three Men on a Horse*, etc.

WALDRON, CHARLES *(1946)* 69 ——Character actor of great dignity who played the Bishop of Tarbes in *The Song of Bernadette*; a few of his 75 others: Loretta Young's *Ramona* (doctor), *The Big Sleep* (General Sternwood, millionaire husband of Bacall and father of Vickers), *On Borrowed Time, Random Harvest, The Gay Sisters.*

WALDRON, CHARLES K. *(1952)* 36 ——Actor-son of Charles; minor roles.

WALDRON, JACK *(1967)* 76 ——Played the Salesman in *The Pajama Game;* had similar aggressive roles in *Blindfold* and *Say, Darling.*

WALES, ETHEL *(1952)* 70 ——The mother in *The Covered Wagon,* this dark-haired character actress was one of the best and busiest in the '20s; was in *Merton of the Movies, Miss Lulu Bett, The Wreck of the Hesperus, Craig's Wife, The Unknown Soldier,* many others; in talkies, always a specialist in smalltown or country women, she was in Coogan's *Tom Sawyer, Klondike, The Gladiator,* and numerous Westerns (*Bar 20 Rides Again, Days of Jesse James,* etc.); retired after '41, she came back for old-lady roles in William Boyd's *Lumber Jack* ('44) and a Republic B starring Arthur Franz, *Tarnished* ('50).

WALKER, CHARLOTTE *(1958)* 80 ——DeMille starred this most beautiful woman, a great stage favorite, opposite Thomas Meighan in 1915's *Kindling* and the following year's *The Trail of the Lonesome Pine;* in the '20s she was in *The Midnight Girl, The Clown, Classmates, The Sixth Commandment,* others; then, through 1941's *Scattergood Meets Broadway,* she had minor roles in *Salvation Nell, Three Faces East, Millie, Lightnin',* etc.; was the mother of character actress Sara Haden.

WALKER, CHERYL *(1971)* 49 ——Many thousands of WW II moviegoers—G.I.s in particular—after seeing *Stage Door Canteen,* her debut, left their hearts with the girl who played Eileen; a blonde whose "naturalness" before the camera was most winning, she had femme leads in numerous others: *A Song for Miss Julie, Three Little Sisters, Identity Unknown, Larceny in Her Heart, Three Is a Family,* etc.—all totally forgettable except for her; retired after 1948's *Waterfront at Midnight* to her home town, Pasadena, Calif., devoting herself to rearing her daughter (became the grandmother of a boy before her demise) and to community service.

WALKER, HELEN *(1968)* 47 ——Blonde leading lady of the '40s with a distinctive gift for sophisticated, but good-natured, comedy; introduced opposite Ladd in *Lucky Jordan,* she displayed wit and vivacity in several more: *Mur-der, He Says; Brewster's Millions; Abroad with Two Yanks; Her Adventurous Night,* etc.; later played second leads in *Cluny Brown, My Dear Secretary, Nancy Goes to Rio,* etc.; a long-term illness forced her retirement after 1955's *The Big Combo.*

WALKER, JOHNNIE *(1949)* 53 ——Lean, rugged, handsome, this black-haired actor co-starred in many in the '20s (*The Matinee Idol* with Bessie Love, *Captain Fly-By-Night, The Third Alarm, Wine of Youth,* etc.) and had second leads in numerous others (*The Spirit of the U.S.A., Lena Rivers, The Earth Woman,* etc.); was most effective in *Old Ironsides* as young Lt. Decatur who conceived and carried out the daring scheme to sink the Philadelphia; left acting in the early '30s to become a stage and movie director (*Mr. Broadway*); sometimes billed Johnny.

WALKER, JUNE *(1966)* 61 ——One of Broadway's best and prettiest who only sporadically worked in movies; in '21 she was Robert Harron's leading lady in *Coincidence,* in '30 she co-starred with Robert Montgomery in *War Nurse,* in '42 she supported Frank Craven in a B, *Thru Different Eyes,* and, missing the '50s, supported Burt Lancaster in two in the '60s: *The Unforgiven* and *A Child Is Waiting;* was the mother of John Kerr.

WALKER, MARTIN *(1955)* 54 ——Support in English pix: *Drums, Sanders of the River, Love on the Dole, This England, The Woman in the Hall,* etc.

WALKER, ROBERT *(1951)* 32 ——MGM's fine, introverted, curly-haired star who became an overnight hit via the role of the heroic young Marine in *Bataan;* was not his first—had previously had small roles in a Jack Randall Western, *Pioneer Days,* and Sheridan's *Winter Carnival;* consolidated his fame by playing other servicemen roles in *See Here, Private Hargrove; What Next, Corporal Hargrove?; Thirty Seconds Over Tokyo; The Clock; Since You Went Away* with (almost-divorced) wife, Jennifer Jones; *The Sailor Takes a Wife,* etc.; proved himself adept at drama (*Madame Curie, The Sea of Grass*), musicals (*Till the Clouds Roll By*), and comedy (*Her Highness and the Bellboy*); last played neurotics—splendidly—in *Strangers on a Train* and *My Son John.*

WALKER, SYD *(1945)* 57 ——Star of English comedies: *What Would You Do, Chums?* (phrase he used in his radio and stage monologs), *Over She Goes, Hold My Hand,* etc.

WALKER, VIRGINIA *(1946)* 30 ——In *Bringing Up Baby* was Grant's secretary and fiancee, pre-Hepburn; this pic, her only credit, was directed by her then-husband, Howard Hawks.

WALL, DAVID *(1938)* 68 ——Support in Thomas Meighan's *Pied Piper Malone* and a few more in the '20s.

WALL, GERALDINE *(1970)* 57 ——Versatile character actress who was in many at 20th Century-Fox: *Scudda Hoo! Scudda Hay!* (as June Haver's mother), *Winged Victory* (as Jo-Carroll Dennison's), *Green Grass of Wyoming, Mister 880, An Affair to Remember;* in numerous others at Paramount: *Beyond Glory, Alias Nick Beal, Thelma Jordan,* etc.

WALLACE, BERYL *(1948)* 38 ——Pneumatic brunette beauty, a famous showgirl, who had leads in *Air Devils* opposite Dick Purcell, *Murder at the Vanities, Enemy of Women, Sunset of the Desert,* etc.

WALLACE, ETHEL LEE *(1956)* 68 ——Support in silents.

WALLACE, GEORGE *(1960)* 66 ——Played supporting roles during the '30s in British comedies (*Let George Do It, His Royal Highness,* etc.) and in the '50s in Hollywood Westerns (*Destry, Drums Across the River, Six Black Horses,* others).

WALLACE, INEZ *(1966)* 60s ——Support in silents; later wrote the story on which *I Walked with a Zombie* was based.

WALLACE, LOUISE CHAPMAN *(1962)* 80 ——Character actress.

WALLACE, MAUDE *(1952)* 58 ——Character actress at 20th Century-Fox in *Love Nest* (as Mrs. Arnold), *Stars and Stripes Forever, Elopement, People Will Talk* (hospital night-matron), etc.

WALLACE, MAY *(1938)* 61 ——Character in various "Our Gang" comedies: *Love Business* (mom of Jackie Cooper, who rented a room to his teacher, Miss Crabtree), *Beginner's Luck* (Spanky's grandmother); was in many silent features (*Oh, You Tony!, The Cup of Life*) and talkies (*The Sky Parade,* Warren William's *Midnight Madonna,* etc.).

WALLACE, MILTON *(1956)* 68 ——Minor support in *None But the Lonely Heart* (as Ike Lesser), *The Lost Weekend, Kiss of Death,* others.

WALLACE, MORGAN *(1953)* 72 ——Stocky, durable character actor, onscreen 25 years, who, in his first, Griffith's *Dream Street,* played

the key figure of The Masked Violinist—symbol of evil; was doubly evil in his next, *Orphans of the Storm,* as Jacques Frochard, which set the keynote for much of his 100-movie career; a few "bad" examples: *Charlie Chan at the Olympics* (as Zaraka); *Mr. Moto Takes a Vacation* (Perez); *Ellery Queen, Master Detective* (Zachary); Roy Rogers' *Billy the Kid Returns* (outlaw); *Hell's House; The Lady in the Morgue,* etc.

WALLER, FATS *(1943)* 39 ——Great black jazz pianist who was onscreen in *King of Burlesque, Stormy Weather, Hooray for Love,* etc.

WALLINGTON, JIMMY *(1972)* 64 ——Famous radio announcer (*The Eddie Cantor Show, Burns and Allen*); had roles in *Start Cheering, The Stadium Murders,* etc.

WALLIS, BERTRAM *(1952)* 78 ——Support in the '35 version of *The Wandering Jew.*

WALLS, TOM *(1949)* 66 ——Character star in many British pix: *Half-Way House, Pot Luck, Johnny Frenchman, Spring in Park Lane, Maytime in Mayfair, The Blarney Kiss,* etc.

WALLY, GUS *(1966)* 62 ——Supporting roles for years.

WALPOLE, HUGH *(1941)* 57 ——Famous British novelist who played the Vicar in MGM's *David Copperfield.*

WALSH, BLANCHE *(1915)* 42 ——One of early stage notables to make movies, she starred in 1912's *Resurrection* with a supporting cast comprised chiefly of Russian actors.

WALSH, THOMAS H. *(1925)* 62 ——Support in the Cleo Madison serial *The Trey O' Hearts* ('14).

WALTERS, JACK *(1944)* 58 ——Handsome, black-haired actor who had top supporting roles in many silent Westerns: Hoot Gibson's *Sure Fire* and *The Galloping Kid,* Rex Bell's *Wild West Romance,* Richard Talmadge's *The Better Man,* etc.

WALTERS, PATRICIA *(1967)* 30s ——Lovely actress who had the central role in Renoir's *The River*—played the English girl, Harriet, in love with American ex-soldier Captain John, who, finding him in the arms of her best friend and rival, Adrienne Corri, attempts suicide; was the daughter of comedian Bert Wheeler.

WALTHALL, HENRY B. *(1936)* 60 ——A Griffith star who would rank high in the pantheon of film if he had played but one role—the Little

Colonel in *The Birth of a Nation;* as late as the 1940s Griffith still spoke of this as the greatest male performance in the history of films; a man of small stature, with an expressive, sensitive face, he gave many dozens of towering portrayals from 1906 on; acted for Griffith in many: *Judith of Bethulia* (as Assyrian general Holofernes), *The Battle of Elderberry Gulch, Home Sweet Home* (composer John Howard Payne), *The Avenging Conscience, Abraham Lincoln* (Colonel Marshall), numerous others; a star until the '20s, his acting philosophy of "Think it, feel it, do it" and the fine performances resulting therefrom, kept him in great demand as a character actor as long as he lived; among his 50 performances in talkies, outstanding was that of President Madero in *Viva Villa!*; in the last year of his life he was in six: *The Devil Doll, China Clipper, Hearts in Bondage, The Garden Murder Case, The Mine with the Iron Door,* and *The Last Outlaw;* Lillian Gish, his frequent co-star and lifelong friend, has recently said of him: "'Wally,' as he was affectionately called, was everything in life that his 'Little Colonel' was on the screen: dear, patient, lovable."

WALTON, DOUGLAS *(1961)* 64 ——British "type" (actually Canadian) character in more than 60 from 1931's *Over the Hill: Cavalcade, The Lost Patrol* (Pearson), *Mary of Scotland* (weak Lord Darnley whom Hepburn marries), *Kitty, Northwest Passage* (Lt. Avery), *The Long Voyage Home* (Second Mate), *Charlie Chan in London,* etc.

WALTON, FRED *(1936)* 71 ——Character from England who was often cast as a doctor, as in *Dynamite;* in many silents (*New Brooms, The City, The Wise Wife,* etc.) and talkies (*Kiki, Little Lord Fauntleroy, Dracula's Daughter, Sin Takes a Holiday,* others).

WALTON, HERBERT C. *(1954)* 74 ——Support in British pix: *The Titfield Thunderbolt, Hobson's Choice* ('54), *The Little Ballerina,* etc.

WALTON, VERA *(1965)* 74 ——Minor support in *A Face in the Crowd.*

WALTZ, PAT *(1972)* 48 ——See Philip Shawn.

WANGEL, HEDWIG *(1961)* 83 ——German actress who was in 1929's *Rasputin,* others.

WANZER, ARTHUR *(1949)* 60s ——Support in B's: *Soldiers of the Storm, The Gentleman from Louisiana, Unknown Valley,* etc.

WARAM, PERCY *(1961)* 80 ——Bald with a gray fringe, this character actor was perhaps best in *A Face in the Crowd* as the straw-hatted

Colonel, wily promoter of hick deejay Andy Griffith; was also in *Ministry of Fear, The Late George Apley* (father of groom, Richard Ney), *It Had to Be You* (Ginger Rogers' father), others.

WARD, BEATRICE *(1964)* 74 ——Character actress in silents.

WARD, CARRIE CLARK *(1926)* 63 ——Character actress in many in the '20s: *The Eagle, Scaramouche, Old Lady 31, Ashes,* Wesley Barry's *Penrod,* etc.

WARD, FANNIE *(1952)* 80-plus ——Famous as an "ageless" beauty (only she knew the date of her birth and she carried that secret to the grave), she starred in DeMille's *The Cheat* in '15, then, provably in her 40s, she looked to be in her early 20s; starred in numerous others up to 1922: *Betty to the Rescue* (opposite much younger husband Jack Dean), *The Gutter Magdalene, Common Clay, She Played and Paid, The Hardest Way, The Winning of Sally Temple* (typical of many of hers, being a tense melodrama played in period costume), etc.; returned to Broadway, where she had started in 1890, ever portraying youthful women; made one talkie, a short, *The Miracle Woman* ('29)—and indeed she was, small (always an exact 100 pounds), unlined, and perfect of feature and figure; retired from the stage in 1938.

WARD, HAP, JR. *(1940)* 41 ——Support in several.

WARD, HAP, SR. *(1944)* 75 ——Character in *Fugitives* ('29).

WARD, KATHERINE CLARE *(1938)* 66 —— Character in *Lilly Turner, Beyond London's Lights, Three Wise Girls, The Conquering Horde,* Bickford's *Vanity Street,* a dozen others.

WARD, LUCILLE *(1952)* 72 ——Character actress who played Ellen Drew's mother in *Christmas in July,* her last; earlier, from the '20s, had been in many: *Skinner's Dress Suit; His Majesty, Bunker Bean;* Mitzi Green's *Rebecca of Sunnybrook Farm; Zoo in Budapest; Little Miss Marker; Mother Carey's Chickens,* etc.

WARD, SAM *(1952)* 63 ——One of Hal Roach's supporting comics.

WARD, SOLLY *(1942)* 51 ——Support in Joan Fontaine's *Maid's Night Out* (as comic Mischa), Sally Eilers' *Everybody's Doing It,* Richard Dix's *Blind Alibi,* others in the '30s.

WARD, VICTORIA *(1957)* 43 ——Support in Robert Taylor's *D-Day, the Sixth of June.*

WARDE, ERNEST C. *(1923)* 49 ——Acted in and directed the Ruth Roland serial *Ruth of the Range*, played the star's father.

WARDE, FREDERICK *(1935)* 64 ——Noted English Shakespearean actor who brought to the screen several classics in which he starred: *Richard III* ('13), *King Lear* ('16), *Vicar of Wakefield* ('17), *Silas Marner* ('21); also co-starred with Jeanne Eagels in *Under False Colors.*

WARDWELL, GEOFFREY *(1955)* 55 ——As a young man he had a top supporting role in the Pickford-Fairbanks *The Taming of the Shrew;* was later in *The Challenge.*

WARE, HELEN *(1939)* 61 ——Fine character actress who is especially memorable for playing "Ma" Taylor in Cooper's *The Virginian;* was in 25 others: *Sadie McKee* (Crawford's mother), *Abraham Lincoln* (Mrs. Edwards), *The Warrior's Husband, New Year's Eve, The Raven, She Had to Say Yes*, etc.

WARE, WALTER *(1936)* 55 ——Minor support in Aline MacMahon's *Kind Lady, Captain Blood*, etc.

WARING, MARY *(1964)* 72 ——Character roles in the '20s.

WARMINGTON, S. J. *(1941)* 56 ——Support in such English pix as *Escape, The Woman Alone*, and *Murder.*

WARNER, H. B. *(1958)* 82 ——Tall actor of ascetic visage whose name will be forever associated with two roles—the Christ in DeMille's *The King of Kings* and the wise Chang in Capra's *Lost Horizon*, which brought his only Oscar nomination as Best Support; onscreen from 1915, he starred most handsomely in many before '30: *The Vagabond Prince* with Dorothy Dalton, *The Danger Trail, Seven Deadly Sins, The Man Who Turned White, One Our Before Dawn* with Anna Q. Nilsson (they would reappear together many years later as members of Swanson's "waxworks" in *Sunset Boulevard*), *Zaza* opposite Swanson herself, *The Temptress* with Garbo, *Sorrell and Son* (a role in which he starred splendidly twice—in '27 and '34), etc.; a few of his many superlative character performances were those in *A Tale of Two Cities* (Gabelle), *Mr. Deeds Goes to Town* (Judge Walker), *You Can't Take It With You* (Ramsey), *Mr. Smith Goes to Washington* (Senator Fuller), *All That Money Can Buy/The Devil and Daniel Webster* (Justice Haythorne),

Hitler's Children (the Bishop), *It's a Wonderful Life* (Mr. Gower), *Here Comes the Groom* (Uncle Elihu); offscreen after '51, he came back in '56 for DeMille's last, *The Ten Commandments* (as Amminadab), and in '58 for *Darby's Rangers*, his last.

WARNER, J. B. *(1924)* 29 ——Leads in cowboy movies.

WARREN, C. DERNIER *(1971)* 82 ——Roly-poly comic character who played Potts in *Lolita;* an American long in England, he also appeared in *Old Mother Riley, Spy of Napoleon, It's in the Air, The Great Defender*, other British pix.

WARREN, E. ALYN *(1940)* 64 ——Versatile character; played Stephen Douglas in *Abraham Lincoln*, Buxton (head of the business college where Lana Turner was murdered) in *They Won't Forget*, the kidnapped father of the heroine in the Buster Crabbe serial *Tarzan the Fearless*, and Gable's Chinese servant in *A Free Soul* (one of many Chinese roles he played—in *The Hatchet Man, Limehouse Blues*, etc.).

WARREN, EDWARD *(1930)* ——Support in *The Belle of Broadway*, other silents.

WARREN, ELIZA *(1935)* 69 ——Support in very early Griffith films.

WARRENDER, HAROLD *(1953)* 55 ——Character who played Locksley in *Ivanhoe* and is well recalled for playing the mock hero in the classic short *Day Dreams;* in many British pix:*Catherine the Great, Scott of the Antarctic, Convoy, The Ivory Hunter*, etc.

WARRENTON, LULU *(1932)* 69 ——Character actress in a dozen in the '20s: *Ladies Must Live, The Sin That Was His*, Carmel Myers' *The Dangerous Moment, Strength of the Pines*, etc.

WARWICK, ROBERT *(1964)* 85 ——More recently, he was one of Hollywood's truly sterling character actors in several score major films: 1958's *The Buccaneer, Salome, In a Lonely Place, Sullivan's Travels* (studio exec Lebrand who wanted director McCrea only to make movies "with a little sex"), *The Private Lives of Elizabeth and Essex* (Lord Mountjoy), *The Adventures of Robin Hood* (Sir Geoffrey), *Romeo and Juliet* (Lord Montague), etc.; earlier, from '15, after being a stage matinee idol, had been one of the movies' handsomest, starring in *Human Driftwood, The Silent Master, Hunting Trouble, The Mad Lover*, many more.

WASHBURN, ALICE *(1929)* 68 ——Featured in 1912–14 Edison comedies such as *On the Lazy*

Line, in which she was the woman walking beside the railroad track, traveling as fast as the slowpoke locomotive.

WASHBURN, BRYANT *(1963)* 74 ——At first ('14) he played Essanay villains, but with dark eyes, black wavy hair, and a dimple in his chin —plus charm—he was fated to be a star; became one the next year in *The Little Straw Wife* and remained one, in romantic dramas and comedies, until late in the '20s; among his pix: *The Blindness of Virtue, The Havoc, Till I Come Back to You* with Florence Vidor, *Skinner's Dress Suit* ('17), *It Pays to Advertise, The Six Best Cellars, Rupert of Hentzau, Passionate Youth;* in talkies, now jowly, had minor roles in B's (*Paper Bullets*), B-Westerns (*West of the Pecos*), A's (*Stagecoach,* as Cavalry Captain Simmons), and was most active in serials: *The Return of Chandu* (Prince Andre), *Tailspin Tommy in the Great Air Mystery, The Black Coin, Jungle Jim* (co-chief Redmond), *King of the Royal Mounted* (villain Crandall), *Adventures of Captain Marvel,* etc.; onscreen through 1947's *Sweet Genevieve.*

WASHINGTON, DINAH *(1963)* 40s ——Noted black singer of blues and jazz; onscreen in *Jazz on a Summer's Day.*

WATERMAN, IDA *(1941)* 89 ——Character in silents; in *A Society Scandal* was the bitter, aristocratic mother-in-law who tried to ruin Swanson; also in Colleen Moore's *The Lotus Eater,* Carol Dempster's *That Royle Girl,* Barthelmess' *The Enchanted Cottage,* more.

WATKIN, PIERRE *(1960)* 66 ——Tall, well-built character with a neat moustache, fine shock of wavy gray hair, and a well-worn air of success and authority; onscreen in 200 after his debut in *Dangerous;* typical roles: Senator Barnes in *Mr. Smith Goes to Washington,* millionaire Carmichael in *Stage Door,* Senator Lauterback in *State of the Union,* Teresa Wright's father in *The Pride of the Yankees;* was also in *Claudia and David, Swing Time, Tulsa, About Mrs. Leslie,* etc.

WATSON, ADELE *(1933)* 42 ——Supporting actress who played John Qualen's wife, Mrs. Novak, in *Arrowsmith,* and again—as Mrs. Olsen—in *Street Scene;* in many earlier: *Tower of Lies, The Black Pearl, Reno, Don't Doubt Your Husband,* etc.

WATSON, BOBBY *(1965)* 77 ——Character who, because of his resemblance, made a career during WW II of playing Hitler: *The Hitler Gang, The Devil With Hitler, That Nazty Nuisance, Hitler—Dead or Alive;* before and after, played mild-mannered little men in many: *That Royle Girl, Society Doctor, The Paleface, Copper Canyon,* etc.; in his last, *The Story of Mankind* ('57)—back to Hitler.

WATSON, CAVEN *(1953)* 49 ——British support; in Donat's *Vacation from Marriage,* etc.

WATSON, COY *(1968)* 78 ——Actor, special-effects man, and father of Billy, Delmar, and Bobs Watson, and six other movie children who, together, appeared in 1,000 pictures; besides being the wizard who made Fairbanks' carpet "fly" in *The Thief of Bagdad,* he played supporting roles in many including *The Smart Set* and *Restless Youth;* in 1958 he and his wife (who still lives) were subjects of a *This Is Your Life* segment on TV.

WATSON, FANNY *(1970)* 83 ——See Kitty Watson.

WATSON, JOSEPH *(1942)* 55 ——Support in several Westerns (*Echo Mountain,* Dick Foran's *Cherokee Strip,* etc.) and in James Melton's *Melody for Two.*

WATSON, KITTY *(1967)* 79 ——She and Fanny were vaudeville's famous Watson Sisters; starred in one talkie short, *Bigger and Better.*

WATSON, LUCILE *(1962)* 83 ——Queen of the dowagers—tart, forceful, compassionate, and ever spellbinding as an actress; best of all her roles was that of Bette Davis' mother in *Watch on the Rhine,* for which she received her only Oscar nomination as Best Support; was splendid too in another 40: *What Every Woman Knows* (the Contesse), *The Young in Heart, Three Smart Girls, Waterloo Bridge* (as Robert Taylor's mother), *The Great Lie, Tomorrow Is Forever, Song of the South, Little Women* ('49), and last, 1951's *My Forbidden Past* with Ava Gardner.

WATSON, MINOR *(1965)* 75 ——One of the screen's busiest and best characters, he had a face, often smiling, that bore the stamp of success; was onscreen from 1931's *24 Hours* in more than 150; frequently played professional men (they were often stars' fathers) and high-rank military officers; typical roles were in *Woman of the Year* (Hepburn's dad, William J. Harding), *Boys Town* (Bishop), *To the Shores of Tripoli* (John Payne's Marine Captain father), *Guadalcanal Diary* (Colonel Grayson), *The Story of Dr. Wassell* (Navy Admiral); atypical was lodge caretaker Moose, murdered by Bette Davis, in *Beyond the Forest;* his last, 1956's *The Ambassador's Daughter,* found him back in his genial, worldly, high-position style.

WATSON, ROY *(1937)* 61 ——Support in silent serials (Helen Holmes' *The Hazards of Helen*, Elmo Lincoln's *Elmo the Fearless*) and Westerns (Pete Morrison's *Blue Blazes, Cactus Trails, The Loser's End*).

WATSON, WYLIE *(1966)* 77 ——In *The 39 Steps*, this character actor was the pivotal vaudeville star Mr. Memory; then in many more British films: *Jamaica Inn, Tawny Pipit, Tight Little Island, The Years Between*, etc.

WATTS, CHARLES *(1966)* 60s ——Support in dozens: *Million Dollar Mermaid* (policeman), *Giant* (Whiteside), *The Spirit of St. Louis* (O. W. Schultz), *Don't Go Near the Water* (Smithfield), *Jumbo* (Ellis), etc.; during WW II, in recognition of his many tours overseas, the USO designated him "Mr. Hollywood."

WATTS, CHARLES "COTTON" *(1968)* 66 ——Musical headliner who was in the all-star minstrel pic *Yes Sir, Mr. Bones* ('51).

WATTS, GEORGE *(1942)* 65 ——In *The Talk of the Town*, he played Judge Granstadt, before whose bench Ronald Colman saved Cary Grant from jail; played Benjamin Franklin in *The Remarkable Andrew* and had supporting roles in numerous others: *Soak the Rich, Angels Over Broadway, Wild Geese Calling, Mr. District Attorney*, etc.

WAWERKA, ANTON *(1937)* 60s ——See Anton Vaverka.

WAYNE, NAUNTON *(1970)* 69 ——In *Dead of Night* this English comic was one of the two golfers (the other being perennial partner Basil Redford) who fought a phantom; a few of his many British pix: *The Lady Vanishes* (vague sporting toff, Caldicott), *The Titfield Thunderbolt, Night Train to Munich, Passport to Pimlico*, etc.

WAYNE, RICHARD *(1958)* ——Support in the '20s in Negri's *The Cheat, Reno*, Louise Fazenda's *Cheaper to Marry, Broadway Gold, The Unknown Purple*, others.

WEAVER, LEON *(1950)* 60s ——Was Abner in the team of The Weaver Bros. and Elviry; onscreen in *Mountain Rhythm, Swing Your Lady*, etc.

WEBB, CLIFTON *(1966)* 72 ——His viper's tongue and old-maid ways were pure gold for 20th Century-Fox and moviegoers; starred in the "Mr. Belvedere" series (*Sitting Pretty*, which rated him a Best Actor Oscar nomination, *Mr. Belvedere Goes to College, Mr. Belvedere*

Rings the Bell); co-starred caustically in *Laura* and *The Razor's Edge* (both of which rated him Oscar nominations as Best Support), *Cheaper by the Dozen, The Dark Corner, Elopement, Three Coins in the Fountain*, etc.; did less one-sided characterizations in *Titanic* and *Stars and Stripes Forever*; had been, of course, one of Broadway's most sophisticated musical comedy stars; few later fans knew anything of the movies of the '20s in which he was a most dapper co-star: *Polly With a Past* with Ina Claire, *New Toys* with Barthelmess, *The Heart of a Siren* with Barbara La Marr.

WEBB, FAY *(1936)* 30 ——Actress and #2 wife of Rudy Vallee.

WEBB, MILLARD *(1935)* 41 ——Support in early silents; later a famous director: *The Sea Beast, The Black Swan* ('24), *Her Golden Calf*, etc.

WEBER, JOE *(1942)* 75 ——Tall half of the famous Weber & Fields comedy team that starred in numerous silents: *Old Dutch, The Best of Enemies, The Worst of Friends*, etc.; they last appeared, as themselves, in *Lillian Russell*.

WEBER, LOIS *(1939)* 56 ——In 1914, more than a decade after her screen debut, she starred as Portia in *The Merchant of Venice*, and later in *False Colors, A Midnight Romance*, etc.; in '16, at Universal, became the screen's first major woman producer; produced Mary MacLaren's *The Mysterious Mrs. Musslewhite*, Mildred Harris' *For Husbands Only*, others; and, as the "highest salaried woman director in the world," directed many, including *Angel of Broadway* and Tyrone Power Sr.'s *Where Are My Children?*

WEBSTER, BEN *(1947)* 82 ——Dame May Whitty's distinguished actor-husband who acted on both sides of the Atlantic; in England's *The Old Curiosity Shop* ('35), starred as Little Nell's old Grandfather; in Hollywood was the British Ambassador in Colman's *The Prisoner of Zenda* and Dan'l Fadden in *Lassie Come Come* (in which Dame May was one of the costars); was the father of late stage director Margaret Webster.

WEEKS, ANSON *(1969)* 72 ——Famous band leader; musical shorts.

WEEKS, MARION *(1968)* 81 ——Starred for Edison in several 1912–13 films (*The Office Boy's Birthday*, etc.); in one, she talked and sang on a record which was synchronized to the film, and this is generally agreed to be the first "talkie"; remained active as a singer and actress—and as a beautiful blonde—on Broadway (*Strange Bedfellows*) and TV (*The Phil Silvers Show*, etc.) throughout her lifetime.

WEEMS, TED *(1963)* 62 ——He and his famous band were featured in Ken Murray's *Swing, Sister, Swing*.

WEGENER, PAUL *(1948)* 74 ——Great German star of *The Golem, Lucrezia Borgia, Svengali*, etc.

WEIDLER, VIRGINIA *(1968)* 41 ——Beloved, enormously talented, pigtailed kid star; stole scenes from many a big name—Hepburn in *The Philadelphia Story*, Rooney in *Young Tom Lincoln*, even John Barrymore (aware of it, he tried forcibly but unsuccessfully to halt it) in *The Great Man Votes;* was a delightful little presence in Pauline Lord's *Mrs. Wiggs of the Cabbage Patch* (her first), *Freckles, Mother Carey's Chickens, Out West with the Hardys;* starred charmingly in *Bad Little Angel* and, a bit later, as a teenager, as the dauntless autograph-collecting fan in *The Youngest Profession;* also had top roles in many MGM "youth" pix: *Babies on Broadway, Born to Sing, Best Foot Forward;* retired in '43 for marriage—her two sons, Ronnie and Gary Krisel, now in their 20s, became actors; died of cancer.

WEINBERG, GUS *(1952)* 86 ——Support in Barthelmess' *Soul-Fire* and several Thomas Meighan pix (*The Ne-er-Do-Well, Coming Through, Homeward Bound*).

WEISER, GRETE *(1970)* 67 ——Character actress in many German films: *Our Little Wife, City of Secrets, The Divine Jetta*, etc.

WEISSE, HANNI *(1967)* 75 ——Femme star (later a character) in German films from early silents to WW II; *Berlin After Dark* was one of her many.

WEISSMAN, DORA *(1974)* 70s ——Well known as Mrs. Herman on *The Goldbergs* (radio and TV) for ten years, she was onscreen in two: *Middle of the Night* (as Albert Dekker's wife, Mrs. Lockman) and Helmut Dantine's *Guerrilla Girl*.

WELCH, EDDIE *(1963)* 62 ——Support in Constance Moore's *Las Vegas Nights*.

WELCH, HARRY *(1973)* 74 ——Supporting comic who played Spud La Rue in Warner Baxter's *King of Burlesque;* was one of several actors who did "Popeye's" cartoon voice.

WELCH, JAMES *(1949)* 80 ——Character actor who played Private Schultz in *The Iron Horse;*

was also in *The Dramatic Life of Abraham Lincoln* and Dolores Costello's *The Heart of Maryland*, but was mostly in B Westerns in the '20s: *The Sheriff of Sun-Dog, West of the Rainbow's End, Rough Ridin' Red*, etc.

WELCH, JOSEPH L. *(1960)* 69 ——Famous real-life lawyer (a hero in the McCarthy hearings) who portrayed the judge in *Anatomy of a Murder*.

WELCH, MARY *(1958)* 35 ——Blonde Broadway dramatic actress who starred in one film, 1952's *Park Row*.

WELCHMAN, HARRY *(1966)* 79 ——Character in British pix: *Waltz Time, A Southern Maid, Eight O'Clock Walk*, etc.

WELFORD, DALLAS *(1946)* 74——Supporting actor in Constance Talmadge's *Wedding Bells*.

WELLESLEY, CHARLES *(1946)* 71 ——Played Alma Rubens' husband in *Cytherea;* top support in many others in the '20s: *The Perfect Flapper, Don't Marry for Money, College Days, Traffic in Hearts*, etc.

WELLINGTON, BABE *(1954)* 57 ——Child actress in early silents.

WELLS, BILLY *(1967)* 79 ——In J. Arthur Rank Films' trademark, he was the bronzed muscleman striking the gong; had been the English heavyweight champion, as "Bombardier" Billy.

WELLS, DEERING *(1961)* 65 ——Support in Olivier's *Richard III*.

WELLS, H. G. *(1946)* 80 ——Famous British author (*Things to Come*) who played a featured role in a 1922 serial, *The Jungle Goddess*, starring Elinor Field.

WELLS, MAI *(1941)* 79 ——Character actress in several of the '20s: Chaplin's *The Pilgrim*, Claire Windsor's *Blondes by Choice, Opened Shutters*, etc.

WELLS, MARIE *(1949)* 55 ——Played Dietrich's maid, Marie, in *The Scarlet Empress;* had supporting roles in several earlier: John Boles' *Song of the West* and *The Desert Song, The Man from New York*, etc.

WENGRAF, JOHN *(1974)* 77 ——Distinguished, dour-faced character actor who played Von Papen in *Five Fingers;* was also in *Ship of Fools* (played Graf), *Call Me Madam* (Ronchin), *Tomorrow Is Forever* (Dr. Ludwig), *Sa-*

hara (Major von Falken), *Judgment at Nuremberg* (Dr. Weick), many others.

WENMAN, HENRY *(1953)* 78 ——Character actor in British pix: *The Middle Watch, Brewster's Millions* ('35), etc.

WENTWORTH, MARTHA *(1974)* 80s —— Plump character actress who wore her hair in a distinctive, circular, off-the-face bun; played Sara in Orson Welles' *The Stranger;* was also in *Good Morning, Miss Dove; A Tree Grows in Brooklyn; Waterloo Bridge,* etc.

WERBISECK, GISELA *(1956)* 80 ——She played Mrs. Schmidt in Danny Kaye's *Wonder Man;* was also in *The Hairy Ape* and George Sanders' *A Scandal in Paris;* always played heavily accented European character types.

WERTZ, CLARENCE *(1935)* ——Support in Marion Nixon's *Spangles.*

WESSEL, DICK *(1965)* 52 ——Big-chinned character whose scowls could be hilarious or deadly serious; was in more than 100 from 1935: *Beasts of Berlin* (as Buchman), *They Made Me a Criminal, Action in the North Atlantic* (cherub), *Pitfall* (desk sergeant), *Thieves' Highway, The Caddy, The Ugly Dachshund* (dog catcher), etc.; not Dick Wesson.

WESSELHOEFT, ELEANOR *(1945)* 72 —— Played immigrant types in *Street Scene* (Greta Fiorentino), *Thirty Day Princess* (Mrs. Schmidt), *The Wedding Night* (Mrs. Sobieski), many others.

WEST, BASIL *(1934)* 75 ——Character roles.

WEST, BUSTER *(1966)* 64 ——Comic support in Bob Burns' *Radio City Revels* and Ray Bolger's *Make Mine Laughs;* had earlier starred in Christie and Educational two-reelers.

WEST, EDNA *(1963)* 74 ——Support in Jean Arthur's *Half Way to Heaven.*

WEST, HENRY ST. BARBE *(1935)* 55 ——Support in *Jaws of Hell, Condemned to Death,* others.

WEST, PAT *(1944)* 55 ——Character actor often in Howard Hawks pix: *His Girl Friday* (Warden Cooley), *Only Angels Have Wings* (Baldy), *To Have and Have Not* (bartender); was also in *Geronimo, Turn Off the Moon, Ceiling Zero,* etc.

WEST, THOMAS *(1932)* 73 ——Was nicknamed "Chinese Tommy" for the many oriental roles he played in silents.

WESTCOTT, GORDON *(1935)* 32 ——Handsome, popular second lead; played Lt. Toll in *Devil and the Deep,* Roger in Loretta Young's *Heroes for Sale,* young Wellington in *Bright Lights,* Thompson in *Footlight Parade;* was also in *Front Page Woman, Lilly Turner, Go Into Your Dance.*

WESTERFIELD, JAMES *(1971)* 58 ——Rugged character who played Big Mac in *On the Waterfront,* Jess Younger in *Birdman of Alcatraz,* Lee Remick's father in *Wild River;* among his other 50, from 1941: *Undercurrent, The Whistle at Eaton Falls, The Cobweb, Three Brave Men, The Sons of Katie Elder.*

WESTERTON, FRANK H. *(1923)* ——Supported opera star Lina Cavalieri in 1914's *Manon Lescaut.*

WESTLEY, HELEN *(1942)* 63 ——Fine character actress who played eagle-eyed grandmas in *Lillian Russell* and several Temple pix: *Stowaway, Dimples, Rebecca of Sunnybrook Farm, Heidi;* was also great imperious fun in two Dunne vehicles: *Show Boat* (Parthy Ann Hawks) and *Roberta* (Aunt Minnie); among her many others: *Death Takes a Holiday, The House of Rothschild* (the matriarch), *All This and Heaven Too, Anne of Green Gables* (spinster Marilla Cuthbert).

WESTMAN, NYDIA *(1970)* 68 ——In dozens in the '30s and '40s she played giggly, giddy little women and smalltown gossips; was in Hepburn's *Little Women* (Mamie), *The Cradle Song* (shy, sweet nun), *One Night of Love, Sweet Adeline, Forty Little Mothers, They All Kissed the Bride, The Remarkable Andrew, The Late George Apley,* etc.; offscreen for Broadway roles in the '50s, came back—just the same—in the '60s for *Nobody Loves Flapping Eagle, For Love or Money, The Reluctant Astronaut,* others.

WESTMORE, PERC *(1970)* 65 ——Of the famous makeup Westmores, he was onscreen in *Hollywood Hotel.*

WESTON, DORIS *(1960)* 42 ——Pretty actress-singer who had two femme leads at Warners in the late '30s—*Submarine D-1* and *The Singing Marine* opposite Dick Powell—then was at Republic for *Born to Be Wild,* Columbia for the femme lead (Betty) in the Warren Hull serial *Mandrake the Magician,* and Universal for *Chip of the Flying "U,"* a Western with Johnny Mack Brown, after which she quit.

WESTON, RUTH *(1955)* 49 ——In the '30s had secondary roles in several: Ann Harding's *Devotion* (as Margaret), Durbin's *That Certain*

Age, Hopkins' *Splendor, Made for Each Other, The Public Defender*, etc.

WETHERELL, M. A. *(1939)* 52 ——Featured in Amer-Anglo Corp.'s *Livingstone in Africa.*

WHALEN, MICHAEL *(1974)* 72 ——Virile, handsome, curly-haired King of the B's in the '30s and '40s; long at 20th Century-Fox, he played opposite Gloria Stuart in many, as well as Rochelle Hudson, Claire Trevor, Lynn Bari, et al.; headed the cast in *Island in the Sky, Time Out for Murder, Sign of the Wolf, While New York Sleeps, Walking Down Broadway*, etc.; was Alice Faye's leading man in *Sing, Baby, Sing* and in Temple's *Poor Little Rich Girl*, after which he was Shirley's pal Coppy in *Wee Willie Winkie*; offscreen—for the stage—after 1943's *Tahiti Honey*, he came back for minor roles in *She Shoulda Said No* ('57) and, last, *Elmer Gantry* ('60); his only other role in the '60s was a guest appearance in one *My Three Sons* episode on TV; of interest to femme fans—he never married.

WHEATCROFT, ADELINE STANHOPE *(1935)* 82 ——Character actress.

WHEATCROFT, STANHOPE *(1966)* ——Character actor who played John Hay in *The Iron Horse;* had a comedy role in *Madame Behave* with female impersonator Julian Eltinge and was in many other silents: *Women's Wares, The Breath of the Gods, The Yankee Consul,* etc.

WHEELER, BERT *(1968)* 73 ——Wavy-haired half of the Wheeler & Woolsey comedy team which, between '29 and '37, starred in almost two dozen: *Kentucky Kernels, Cracked Nuts, Cockeyed Cavaliers, Mummy's Boys, High Flyers, So This Is Africa*, etc.; starred in two after Woolsey's death: *Cowboy Quarterback* ('39) and *Las Vegas Nights* ('41); later did nightclubs, stock, Broadway (*Laugh Time, All For Love*), TV—had a running role in the series *Brave Eagle.*

WHELAN, RON *(1965)* 61 ——British character who played Annas in *The Greatest Story Ever Told*, Fenner in Maureen O'Hara's *Kangaroo;* was also in *Gun Hawk, Massacre Hill*, others.

WHELAN, TIM *(1957)* 63 ——Hollywood director of many (*Higher and Higher, Step Lively,* etc.), who played small roles in the '20s.

WHIFFEN, BLANCHE (MRS. THOMAS) *(1936)* 91 ——Played the title role in 1915's *Barbara Frietchie*, which starred Mary Miles Minter as her romantic young niece.

WHITAKER, CHARLES "SLIM" *(1960)* 67 — —Paunchy and hook-nosed, he was, for three decades in Westerns, one of the most lowdown of all henchmen; often "rode" for smooth Big Boss Harry Woods; was in *Phantom Gold, In Early Arizona, The Mysterious Rider*, etc.

WHITE, BILL *(1933)* 76 ——Support in Westerns in the '20s: *The Devil's Dooryard, Western Feuds, The Sheriff of Sun-Dog*, others.

WHITE, FISHER *(1945)* 79 ——Support in many English pix: *Loose Ends, The Dreyfus Case, Jaws of Hell, As You Like It, Dreaming Lips*, etc.

WHITE, FRANCES *(1969)* 70 ——Ziegfeld Girl who starred in Associated Exhibitors' *Face to Face* ('22); was Frank Fay's first wife.

WHITE, GEORGE *(1968)* 78 ——The stage and screen "Scandals" produced by him remain a synonym for showgirl glamour; was seen as himself in several movie editions of his shows, including *George White's (1935) Scandals*, as well as in *Rhapsody in Blue.*

WHITE, HUEY *(1938)* 42 ——Tough-guy support in such B's as *Crash Donovan, When G-Men Step In, The Hell Cat.*

WHITE, IRVING *(1944)* 79 ——Minor support in Cooper's *The Spoilers*, Ann Harding's *The Girl of the Golden West*, etc.

WHITE, LEE "LASSES" *(1949)* 64 ——Out of minstrels, he was for years the pixeyish, comically strutting sidekick of Western heroes Jimmy Wakely and Tim Holt; among his scores of cowboy pix: *Moon over Montana, Indian Agent, Song of the Sierras, Rovin' Tumbleweeds;* had a regular role in the "Scattergood Baines" comedies and was in such A's as *Sergeant York* (Luke, the Target Keeper), *The Adventures of Mark Twain, Something to Shout About.*

WHITE, LEO *(1948)* 68 ——English comedian who, 1915–16, was a mainstay in Chaplin comedies—usually in top hat, goatee, and upturned moustache, and often the wild-eyed, bomb-throwing French count; was in his *A Night Out* (the man-about-town victim of Charlie's drunkenness), *The Champion, The Tramp, The Vagabond*, etc.; had supporting roles in the '20s in *Blood and Sand, Vanity Fair, Ben Hur* (as Sanballat), many others; minor roles in the '30s and '40s in numerous B Westerns (*Smilin' Guns*, etc.), *A Night at the Opera* (one of the comic aviators), *Only Yesterday, My Wild Irish Rose*, Chaplin's *The Great Dictator* (a bit); was last in *The Fountainhead.*

WHITE, MARJORIE *(1935)* 27 ——Energetic blonde comedienne who was always a delight in Fox musicals: *Sunny Side Up* (played Bee Nichols), *Movietone Follies of 1930, Just Imagine, Happy Days;* also had second leads in two "Charlie Chan" pix: *The Black Camel, Charlie Chan Carries On.*

WHITE, PEARL *(1938)* 49 ——"The Fearless Peerless Pearl White" who was not only Queen of Silent Serials, but whose name has itself become synonymous with "cliff-hangers"; 1914's *The Perils of Pauline* made her world famous; had then been onscreen almost five years playing leads in dramas (*The Lost Necklace, The New Magdalene,* etc.) and numerous slapstick comedies (*Pearl's Dilemma, Pearl's Adventure,* others); did more than any other star to make the serial a legitimate form of movie entertainment; by 1919, she had triumphed over diabolically clever master-villains in eight more Pathé serials: *The Exploits of Elaine, The New Exploits of Elaine, The Iron Claw, Pearl of the Army, The Fatal Ring, The House of Hate, The Lightning Raider, The Black Secret;* her only other serial, *Plunder* ('23), was also for Pathé; in between, had starred in 10 lacklustre features for Fox: *A Virgin Paradise* ("Pearl White's followers will not be disappointed in her . . . She has never seen a man nor anything as modern as an electric light, nevertheless in a few weeks she is handling a gun like Bill Hart and wallops the villain with Jack Dempsey skill," said *Photoplay*), *The Tiger's Cub, Know Your Man, The Broadway Peacock,* etc.; her last movie was made in France—titled *Terror* there, it was released here in '25 as *Perils of Paris;* appeared in revues in music halls in both France and England before retiring in '25; was portrayed by Betty Hutton in *The Perils of Pauline* ('47); added note #1: producers permitted her to do all her own stunts except the most extremely hazardous, e.g., in *Plunder* the leap from the bus top to elevated railroad platform done by a stunt man—who fell to his death; added note #2: her famous blonde hair was a wig—underneath her hair was red, dyed from its natural brown.

WHITE, RUTH *(1969)* 55 ——Character actress whose best role was perhaps that of Jon Voight's wanton grandmother in *Midnight Cowboy;* was excellent also in *To Kill a Mockingbird* (neighbor woman Mrs. Dubose), *The Nun's Story* (Mother Marcella), *No Way to Treat a Lady, Up the Down Staircase, Charly,* others.

WHITE, SAMMY *(1960)* 65 ——Broadway comedian onscreen in the '30s, first recreating his stage role of Frank Schultz in *Show Boat*, then doing specialties in *Cain and Mabel, Swing Your Lady, The Hit Parade;* came back, after stage and TV work, as a character comic in several of the '50s: *Somebody Up There Likes Me* (Whitey Bimstein), *Pat and Mike* (Barney Grau, Tracy's wry partner in the athletic agency), *The Bad and the Beautiful,* etc., including last *The Helen Morgan Story,* which took him right back to *Show Boat.*

WHITEFORD, JOHN P. "BLACKIE" *(1962)* 73 ——Stocky, stubbly, wild-eyed henchman in many Westerns: *The Old Wyoming Trail, Mark of the Spur, Toll of the Desert,* etc.

WHITEHEAD, JOHN *(1962)* 89 ——Support in many, including *Escape from Zahrain.*

WHITEMAN, PAUL *(1967)* 77 ——Famous band leader, of considerable girth, who lifted his smiling moon face and baton in a half-dozen talkies: *King of Jazz* (his trademark), *Strike Up the Band, Thanks a Million, Rhapsody in Blue* (recreated his historic first playing of Gershwin's rhapsody, which he had commissioned), *Atlantic City, The Fabulous Dorseys;* had earlier appeared in one silent, 1924's *Broadway after Dark.*

WHITESIDE, WALKER *(1942)* 73 ——Star of the 1915 comedy *The Melting Pot* and of the 1917 drama *The Belgian.*

WHITFIELD, ROBERT "SMOKY" *(1967)* 50 ——Played Fredric March's black servant in *Another Part of the Forest* and the fighter, Nassau, in *Right Cross;* was also in *You Can't Take It With You; Bomba, the Jungle Boy; Three Little Girls in Blue.*

WHITFORD, ANNABELLE *(1961)* 83 ——See Annabelle.

WHITING, JACK *(1961)* 59 ——Broadway's "perennial juvenile" song-and-dance man (unmatched record of leads in 24 musicals), this breezy guy with the dazzling smile and blond waves starred for Warners in three in 1930: *College Lovers, The Life of the Party, Top Speed;* was top support at Paramount in *Give Me a Sailor* and then, while in England starring in three successive stage shows, in the Jessie Matthews musical *Sailing Along,* his last pic; continued nimbly on Broadway.

WHITLOCK, LLOYD *(1966)* ——Supporting actor in many silents.

WHITMAN, ERNEST *(1954)* 61 ——Black actor who scored sensationally as the cantankerous, loud-mouthed Pharaoh in *The Green Pastures;* also played Buck in *The Prisoner of Shark Island* and Pinky in *Jesse James;* in many others: *Congo Maisie, Cabin in the Sky, My Brother Talks to Horses*, etc.

WHITMAN, ESTELLE *(1970)* 80s ——Support in early silents.

WHITMAN, GAYNE *(1958)* 67 ——Tough-guy support in many in the '20s: *The Wife Who Wasn't Wanted, Hell-Bent for Heaven, His Jazz Bride*, etc.; after the '30 serial *Finger Prints*, as the blackmailing principal villain, dropped out for a decade; a radio headliner, he was, late in the '30s, the *Strange As It Seems* narrator (and still later, the star of *Chandu the Magician*); came back for another 10 pix: *Parachute Battalion* (Staff Officer), *Big Jim McLain* (psychiatrist-terrorist who killed special investigator James Arness with a truth serum overdose), *Phantom Killer*, etc.

WHITMAN, WALT *(1928)* 60 ——Character who played Frey Felipe in Fairbanks' *The Mark of Zorro*; in many more in the '20s: Coogan's *Long Live the King*, Chic Sale's *His Nibs*, Anita Stewart's *A Question of Honor*, Anna Q. Nilsson's *Hearts Aflame*, etc.; not the poet, of course.

WHITNEY, CLAIRE *(1969)* 79 ——A beauty, she co-starred with Stuart Holmes in the first Fox film, *Life's Shop Window*, in '14; then starred in *The Nigger* with William Farnum, *The Isle of Conquest*, etc.; in the '20s had major supporting roles in Eugene Pallette's *Fine Feathers*, Matt Moore's *The Passionate Pilgrim*, Warner Baxter's *The Great Gatsby*, others; in talkies, played country women in Westerns (*Chip of the Flying "U," Frontier Investigator*) and had minor roles in B's (*An Old-Fashioned Girl, She Gets Her Man*, etc.) until 1950.

WHITNEY, PETER *(1972)* 55 ——Big, burly guy who scored hilariously as the whacked-out hillbilly twins in *Murder, He Says*, a '45 MacMurray comedy; previously, a WB contractee for four years, had been in many: *Blues in the Night, Action in the North Atlantic* (Whitey Lara), *Destination Tokyo* (Dakota), *Mr. Skeffington* (Forbish), etc.; was later in another 25 including *The Iron Curtain, The Big Heat, All the Brothers Were Valiant*, and *In the Heat of the Night*.

WHITNEY, RENEE *(1971)* 63 ——Young beauty who played flappers and chorines; onscreen five years, from Clara Bow's *The Wild Party* ('29), in which she played Janice, she was in *Play Girl, Baby Face, I've Got Your Number, Side Streets*, etc.

WHITNEY, ROBERT, II *(1969)* 24 ——Several juvenile roles.

WHITTELL, JOSEPHINE *(1961)* 70s —— Blonde character actress who was manager of the canteen where Dorothy McGuire worked in *The Enchanted Cottage*, and, in *It's a Gift*, Baby LeRoy's catty mother, Mrs. Dunk; in many more: *Standing Room Only, Molly, The Magnificent Dope, Follow Your Heart*, etc.

WHITTY, DAME MAY *(1948)* 82 ——English character star whose smallest gesture was as eloquently magnificent as her regal presence; was twice nominated for Oscars as Best Support—in *Night Must Fall* as Mrs. Bramson and for *Mrs. Miniver* as Lady Beldon; was equally glorious in many more: *The Lady Vanishes, Suspicion, Forever and a Day, The Constant Nymph, Lassie Come Home, Gaslight, The White Cliffs of Dover, Madame Curie, Devotion, My Name Is Julia Ross*.

WHORF, RICHARD *(1966)* 60 ——Forceful, unpretty, black-haired lead who scored strongly as the piano player in *Blues in the Night*, Clive Kerndon in *Keeper of the Flame*, Kerenor in *Assignment in Brittany*, Francois in *The Cross of Lorraine*; also in *Juke Girl, Christmas Holiday, Chain Lightning*, etc.; concurrently directed many: *Till the Clouds Roll By, It Happened in Brooklyn, The Groom Wore Spurs*, others.

WICKLAND, LARRY *(1938)* 39 ——Had a small role when a teenager in Thomas Meighan's *The Trail of the Lonesome Pine*; in a few other silents.

WIDDECOMB, WALLACE *(1969)* 100 ——Minor support.

WIERE, SYLVESTER *(1970)* 60 ——Chubby-cheeked, youngest of The Wiere Brothers comedy team which was in *The Road to Rio, The Great American Broadcast, Swing Shift Maisie*, etc.

WIETH, MOGENS *(1962)* 42 ——British character actor who played the Ambassador in Hitchcock's remake of *The Man Who Knew Too Much*; was also in *Tales of Hoffman, A Matter of Morals, The Invisible Army*.

WILBUR, CRANE *(1973)* 83 ——In Pearl White's *The Perils of Pauline*, he was the hero, Handsome Harry; handsome, indeed, with a shock of black curly hair and strong "trustworthy" features, he was a greatly popular star in the teens and '20s; starred in *Road O' Strife* (serial), *The Corsair, The Heart of Maryland, The Compact, A Nation's Peril*, etc.; last had a supporting role in 1935's *High School Girl*, which he directed (as he did many others —*Canon City, He Walked by Night, The Bat*, etc.); one of Hollywood's most successful writers, he last did the screenplays for *The George Raft Story* and *House of Women*, both in '62.

WILCOX, FRANK *(1974)* 66 ——Well known for playing Mr. Brewster in the TV series *The Beverly Hillbillies*, and Elliot Ness's boss in *The Untouchables*, this slender, professorial-type character had major supporting roles in 166 pix from '40: *The Fighting 69th* (Lt. Norman), *They Died With Their Boots On*, *Across the Pacific* (Captain Morrison), *Conflict*, *Gentleman's Agreement*, *The Voice of the Turtle*, *The Greatest Show on Earth* (Circus Doctor), *Ruby Gentry*, etc.

WILCOX, ROBERT *(1955)* 44 ——Handsome lead in many B's in the '30s: *Let Them Live*, *City Girl*, *The Man in Blue*, *Little Tough Guy*, *Armored Car*, *Gambling Ship*, etc.; played villains in such Westerns of the '40s as *The Vigilantes Return*; married Diana Barrymore in '50, with whom he acted onstage, after which they made several explosive headlines; a '54 B, *Day of Triumph*, was his only screen credit in his last years.

WILDHACK, ROBERT *(1940)* 48 ——Radio comedian who, as Hornblow, did his inimitable "Sneezes and Snores" routine in *Broadway Melody of 1936* and *... of 1938;* was also in Aline MacMahon's *Back Door to Heaven*.

WILEY, JOHN *(1962)* 78 ——Minor support in *The Winning of Barbara Worth*, *The Covered Wagon*, *The Great Locomotive Chase*, etc.

WILHELM, THEODORE *(1971)* 62 ——Character from Germany who had supporting roles in *The Crawling Eye*, Bradford Dillman's *Circle of Deception*, etc.

WILKE, HUBERT *(1940)* ——Supported Ben Lyon and Aileen Pringle in *The Great Deception*.

WILKERSON, BILL *(1966)* 62 ——Indian actor who played Tomas Mejia in *Juarez*, Juan in *Broken Arrow*, and was prominent in support in *Dr. Cyclops*, *Davy Crockett*, *Indian Scout*, *Rock Island Trail*, etc.

WILKERSON, GUY *(1971)* 73 ——Lean, lanky Western support (frequently villainous) who looked much like Fonda and, from the late '30s, was in dozens: *Paradise Express*, *Mountain Justice*, *The Whispering Skull*, *The Big Sky*, *The Great Missouri Raid*, etc., including, last, *True Grit;* in the serial *Captain Midnight*, played Ichabod Mudd.

WILKINS, JUNE *(1972)* 50 ——Pretty girl, once a contract player at MGM and 20th Century-Fox; played the supporting role of Louise King in *Bachelor Mother* and of the teenager Louise in Garbo's *Camille;* was also in *When the Daltons Rode*, etc.

WILLARD, EDMUND *(1956)* 71 ——Support in many British pix: *Pastor Hall*, *The Iron Duke*, *I Stand Condemned*, *Love Storm*, *Troopship*, *Courageous Mr. Penn*, etc.

WILLENZ, MAX *(1954)* 66 ——Character who played Colletti in *The Pride of the Yankees*, the Court Clerk in *Gentlemen Prefer Blondes;* was also in *I Married an Angel*, *Yolanda and the Thief*, etc.

WILLIAM, WARREN *(1948)* 53 ——Starred, as he did in all else from the '20s, with great savoir-faire in eight "Lone Wolf" pix from '39 to '43 (*The Lone Wolf Strikes*, *The Lone Wolf Meets a Lady*, *... Takes a Chance*, etc.); had been Pearl White's leading man in her last serial, *Plunder*, Colbert's co-star in both *Cleopatra* (Julius Caesar) and *Imitation of Life*, Davis' in *Three on a Match*, starred in *The Case of the Curious Bride* (*... Lucky Legs*, *... Velvet Claws*), many more; had top supporting roles in *Lillian Russell*, *The Firefly*, *Arizona*, and, last, *The Private Affairs of Bel Ami;* a victim of multiple myeloma, he had been able to work in just three after 1943.

WILLIAMS, BERT *(1922)* 55 ——Legendary black stage comedian who starred in Biograph's final two-reelers in '16, one of which was *A Natural Born Gambler;* had earlier, in '14, headlined in *Darktown Jubilee*—historically of note because it was the first attempt to star a black in a movie; at its opening, white audiences —accustomed only to seeing a black in a tom role and rejecting this star, dapper in top hat and zoot suit—jeered the film off the screen, precipitating a race riot.

WILLIAMS, BRANSBY *(1961)* 91 ——Polished support in British pix, silents (*Troublesome Wives*, *The Gold Cure*) and talkies (*Song of the Road*, *At Dawn We Die*, *The Woman in Command*, etc.).

WILLIAMS, CHARLES *(1958)* 60 ——Baby-faced, small and humorous character, with bushy brows and often in specs, who was in several dozen from the '20s on; was especially active at 20th Century-Fox after the mid-'30s in *Alexander's Ragtime Band* (an agent), *Wake Up and Live* (Alberts), *Charlie Chan on Broadway*, *Mr. Moto's Gamble*, *Just Around the Corner* (candid cameraman), etc.; was later in *Our Hearts Were Growing Up*, *It's a Wonderful Life* (cousin Eustace), *Doll Face*, others.

WILLIAMS, CLARA *(1928)* 30s ——William S. Hart's lovely leading lady, Faith Henly, in

Hell's Hinges; played heroines in other action pix: *Carmen of the Klondike, Paws of the Bear,* etc.

WILLIAMS, CORA *(1927)* 56 ——Character actress active in the '20s in Richard Dix's *Womanhandled,* Betty Compson's *Temptations of a Shop Girl,* Glenn Hunter's *His Buddy's Wife,* others.

WILLIAMS, EARLE *(1927)* 46 ——Handsome major star, onscreen from 1910, who in 1914 was the most popular actor on the screen, as per a *Motion Picture* magazine poll; 1915's *The Juggernaut* was perhaps his greatest triumph, but there were many others: *The Highest Trump* (dual role), *The Stolen Treaty, Happy-Go-Lucky* (one of many in which he and Clara Kimball Young—Vitagraph's most popular players—co-starred), *The Artist's Madonna, My Official Wife, My Lady's Slipper, Arsene Lupin, The Seal of Silence, The Fortune Hunter, The Man from Downing Street, Lena Rivers, The Sky Rocket;* starred in three in his last year: *Say It with Diamonds, She's My Baby, Red Signals.*

WILLIAMS, FRANCES *(1959)* 56 ——Blonde headliner from the stage who, in top hat and tails, was a standout in *Broadway Thru a Keyhole;* was also prominently featured in *Hollywood Party, Magnificent Doll, Her Sister's Secret, The Reckless Moment;* last played Queenie in Grayson's *Show Boat.*

WILLIAMS, FRED J. *(1942)* 67 ——Support in 1925's *A Modern Cain.*

WILLIAMS, GEORGE *(1936)* 81 ——Character in several in the '20s: Shirley Mason's *Little Miss Smiles, The Silent Stranger, The Rattler, Geared to Go,* etc.

WILLIAMS, GEORGE B. *(1931)* 65 ——Distinguished-looking character who played opera manager Monsieur Richard in Chaney's *The Phantom of the Opera;* was also in Marie Prevost's *Her Night of Nights,* J. Warren Kerrigan's *Captain Blood,* Mary Philbin's *Fifth Avenue Models,* etc.

WILLIAMS, GUINN "BIG BOY" *(1962)* 62 ——*Palooka,* one of his in '34, is a title that describes his every (100-plus) movie role—none-too-bright-but-good-natured, fun to have around; first played many curly-haired, big-kid football players: *Forward Pass, College Lovers, College Coach,* etc.; wore military uniforms of several different wars: *The Littlest Rebel, The Fighting 69th, The Bugle Sounds, Thirty Seconds over Tokyo;* was no stranger to comedy: *Professor Beware, Dulcy, Six Lessons from Madame La Zonga, Between Us Girls;* finally

was most agreeably at home in big-league Westerns: *Rocky Mountain, The Alamo, Hangman's Knot,* and, last, *The Comancheros.*

WILLIAMS, HANK *(1953)* 29 ——Drug-bedeviled C&W star who was portrayed by George Hamilton in *Your Cheatin' Heart.*

WILLIAMS, HARCOURT *(1957)* 77 ——Distinguished British character who played the Ambassador in *Roman Holiday,* Charles VI of France in *Henry V,* the First Player in the drama staged at the King of Denmark's court in *Hamlet;* in many English pix (*Brighton Rock, Cage of Gold, No Room at the Inn,* etc.) and various "Hollywood" pix made in England (*Under Capricorn, Quentin Durward*).

WILLIAMS, HERB *(1936)* 62 ——Character in Swarthout's *Rose of the Rancho.*

WILLIAMS, HUGH *(1969)* 65 ——Dapper, and one of England's handsomest leading men, he was in several Hollywood films in the '30s: *David Copperfield* (as Steerforth), *Wuthering Heights* (Hindley), *Sorrell and Son;* his major opportunities, though, came in English pix: *The Holly and the Ivy, One of Our Aircraft Is Missing* (crew member Frank Skelley), *Glory at Sea, The Intruder, The Avengers,* etc.; was last onscreen in *Khartoum.*

WILLIAMS, IRENE *(1970)* 38 ——Singer-actress; minor roles.

WILLIAMS, JEFFREY *(1938)* 78 ——Comic character who played Hutchins in Keaton's *The Saphead* ('20).

WILLIAMS, JULIA (1936) 56 ——Was in early Biographs.

WILLIAMS, KATHLYN *(1960)* 72? ——Early actress who had the misfortune to star in one serial, and that her name figured in the title—1913's *The Adventures of Kathlyn*—thus going into many movie histories as a serial queen; actually, a major dramatic star for both Selig (was known as The Selig Girl) and Paramount, she was at one time known as the Bernhardt of the screen; onscreen from 1908, she was particularly effective in the teens in *The Rosary, Hearts and Masks* with Harold Lockwood (he was again with her in *The Tide of Destiny*), the first version of *The Spoilers* (as Cherry Malotte), *The Carpet from Bagdad, The Ne'er-Do-Well,* etc.; lost her beauty "overnight," leading to speculation she was much older than her admitted years; shocking indeed is a comparison between the radiant woman who starred for De-Mille in 1918's *We Can't Have Everything* and the grim-lipped actress who, three years later, had the top supporting role in his *Forbidden*

Fruit; (note: the death of her only child occurred soon after this film's release, thus could not have been the contributing factor); played important character roles in two dozen more in the '20s: *The Wanderer* (mother of The Prodigal), *The World's Applause* with Menjou, *Locked Doors* with Betty Compson, *Our Dancing Daughters, The Spanish Dancer,* etc.; had minor character roles in a mere half-dozen after '30 (*Unholy Love, Road to Paradise*), including, last, Stanwyck's *The Other Love* ('47); lost a leg in an auto accident in '49, was confined to a wheelchair the remainder of her life.

WILLIAMS, LARRY *(1956)* 66 ——Busy support at WB 1938–40 in *Garden of the Moon* (as Trent), *Brother Rat, Brother Rat and a Baby, Wings of the Navy, Torchy Blane in Panama,* etc.

WILLIAMS, MACK *(1965)* 58 ——Played Lt. Col. Virgil Jackson in *Command Decision,* Whorton in *Whirlpool;* was also in *Call Me Mister, The Blue Veil, Cape Fear, No Way Out,* etc.

WILLIAMS, MALCOLM *(1937)* 67 ——In *The First Kiss* he played Cooper's lawyer-brother, "Pap," who successfully defended him against a charge of theft.

WILLIAMS, MARIE *(1967)* 46 ——Was featured as a tyke in Renee Adoree's *The Eternal Struggle.*

WILLIAMS, MOLLY *(1967)* ——English support.

WILLIAMS, RHYS *(1969)* 76 ——Bald, splendid character who was in many of Hollywood's best; was in *How Green Was My Valley* (prizefighter Dai Bando), *The Bells of St. Mary's* (Dr. McKay), *The Farmer's Daughter* (Adolph), *The Corn Is Green* (Mr. Jones), *Mrs. Miniver* (Horace), dozens more; born in Wales, he came to the States at four, but often used a Welsh accent onscreen.

WILLIAMS, ROBERT *(1931)* 32 ——Leading man who was great as the handsome, wise-cracking reporter in *Platinum Blonde;* that same year ('31), his only one in movies, had leads in three others: *The Common Law, Devotion, Rebound;* as recently as 1975 director Frank Capra cited Williams (in *Platinum Blonde*), Gable (in *It Happened One Night*), and Cooper (in *Mr. Deeds Goes to Town*) as best representations of a Capra hero—in that each was "not so much chasing the woman as he was chasing ideas."

WILLIAMS, SPENCER *(1969)* 76 ——Black actor featured in Walter C. Kelly's *The Virginia*

Judge; for black audiences he wrote, directed, and co-starred in *Go Down Earth* and directed *The Blood of Jesus;* was later famous on TV as Andy in *Amos 'n Andy.*

WILLIAMS, WILLIAM *(1942)* 72 ——In *La Grande Mare* (the French version of *The Big Pond;* both versions starring Colbert and Chevalier in '30), he played Ronnie, the suitor Colbert almost married before Chevalier kidnapped her; Frank Lyon played the role in the domestic version.

WILLINGHAM, HARRY G. *(1943)* 62 ——Support in silents.

WILLS, BEVERLY *(1963)* 29 ——Blonde comedienne with a raucous style who was most amusing as all-girl-band member Dolores in *Some Like It Hot;* later was in *Son of Flubber* and *The Ladies' Man;* started at 11 with a bit in *George White's Scandals* starring her mother, comedienne Joan Davis; as a teenager was in *Skirts Ahoy, Mickey, Small Town Girl.*

WILLS, BREMBER *(1948)* 65 ——Support in many British pix, including *The Old Dark House* and *Unfinished Symphony.*

WILLS, DRUSILLA *(1951)* 65 ——Support in English pix: *The Lodger* (the Ivor Novello version), *The Queen of Spades, The Man in Grey, Champagne Charlie,* many others.

WILLS, LOU *(1968)* 88 ——Veteran character actor in small roles.

WILLS, NAT *(1917)* 44 ——Stage actor who, in 1911, starred in the "King of Kazam" series of comic tramp pix.

WILLS, WALTER *(1967)* 86 ——Support in Viola Dana's *In Search of a Thrill* and in many B Westerns, as well as such talkie serials as *The Great Adventures of Wild Bill Hickok.*

WILMER-BROWN, MAISIE *(1973)* 80 —— Character actress in silents.

WILSEY, JAY *(1961)* 65 ——See Buffalo Bill Jr.

WILSON, BEN *(1930)* 54 ——Rugged, wavy-haired, handsome hero of numerous silent serials (in which he most often rescued Neva Gerber): *The Mystery Ship, What Happened to Mary, Screaming Shadow, Trail of the Octopus,* etc.; before and after his final serial, 1926's *Officer 444,* he starred in many features, usually Westerns: *Tonio, Son of the Sierras; The Mystery Brand; Shadow Ranch; Wolves of the Desert,* etc.

WILSON, CHARLES *(1948)* 53 ——Heavy-faced character with slicked-back gray hair parted just off-center who was most at home as a politico, city editor, or detective; was in dozens: *Pennies from Heaven, The Glass Key* ('35); *Torchy Blane, the Adventurous Blonde; Blues in the Night; Lady Gangster; Sandy Is a Lady*, etc.

WILSON, CLARENCE H. *(1941)* 64 ——Small and bald, with a little black moustache, he often played crabby characters and was generally to be found, neatly dressed as a clerk or banker, in Westerns: *The Texans, The Mysterious Rider, Melody Ranch, Flaming Guns*, many more; was at his very best, though, as hissable little shyster lawyer Phineas Pratt in W.C. Fields' *Tillie and Gus*.

WILSON, DOOLEY *(1953)* 59 ——"Play it, Sam"—*Casablanca*, of course; it was the first for the black pianist-singer-actor but a dozen more followed it: *My Favorite Blonde* (a porter), *Stormy Weather* (breezy, smooth-talking Gabriel), *Cairo, Higher and Higher* (bankrupt millionaire Leon Errol's piano-playing servant), *Come to the Stable, Take a Letter, Darling*, etc.; came from Broadway, where he was one of the stars of *Cabin in the Sky*, after having been a well-known band leader.

WILSON, EDNA *(1960)* 80 ——A onetime "Gibson Girl" who was in a few silents.

WILSON, FRANCIS *(1935)* 81 ——One of Sennett's comics in the teens.

WILSON, FRANK *(1956)* 69 ——Black actor who played Moses with splendid irony in *The Green Pastures*; was also in *Watch on the Rhine* (as Joseph, a servant of Lucile Watson), *Emperor Jones, All-American Sweetheart*, etc.

WILSON, GEORGE *(1954)* 100 ——Support in England's *Caesar and Cleopatra, Henry V, The Life and Death of Colonel Blimp*, others.

WILSON, HAL *(1933)* 46 ——Support in silent serials (Ann Little's *Nan of the North*, Eddie Polo's last one, *The Secret Four*) and features (*Main Street; Don Q, Son of Zorro; The Iron Mask*, etc.).

WILSON, JACK *(1966)* 49 ——Character who played the Second Mug in *Francis Goes to the Races* and was in a number of Westerns.

WILSON, M. K. *(1933)* 43 ——Supporting actor in Lola Lane's *The Costello Case*.

WILSON, MARIE *(1972)* 56 ——Lovable, long-lashed "dumb" (she wasn't) blonde who had two high points in her long (41 years) career; the first was the femme lead in 1938's *Boy Meets Girl*; had then already been in a dozen: *China Clipper, Satan Met a Lady, Miss Pacific Fleet*, etc.; the second, a decade later, was starring in *My Friend Irma* and *My Friend Irma Goes West* (derived from her hit radio show which also became a TV series); in between and later, she was a busty, giggly, daffy "plus" in scores: *Virginia, Music for Millions, Shine on Harvest Moon, The Private Affairs of Bel Ami, A Girl in Every Port, Never Wave at a Wac, Mr. Hobbs Takes a Vacation*, etc.; offscreen, starred in *Ken Murray's Blackouts*, onstage in Hollywood, during the '40s and was famous for never missing a performance in her seven-year run.

WILSON, WHIP *(1964)* 49 ——Dimpled, pudgy-faced star of Monogram Westerns between '48 and '52; a rodeo champ and skilled at stunts with a bullwhip, he—aboard trusty white steed Silver Bullet—rode excitingly through three dozen pix: *Riders of the Dusk, Range Land, Shadows of the West, Guns Roar at Rock Hill*, etc.; retired from the movies to do circuses and rodeos.

WILSON, WILLIAM F. *(1956)* 61 ——Support in the Monte Blue silent *The Bush Leaguer*.

WILTON, ROBB *(1957)* 75 ——Support in *It's Love Again, Break the News*, other British pix.

WINANT, FORREST *(1928)* 39 ——Florence Reed's leading man in 1916's *New York*.

WINCHELL, WALTER *(1972)* 74 ——Staccato-voiced gossip king of newspapers and radio; starred onscreen in *Wake Up and Live* and *Love and Hisses*; was seen as himself in *College Confidential* and *The Helen Morgan Story* and narrated others; additionally, was the original author of the pic *Broadway Thru a Keyhole*, based on the life of Fanny Brice.

WINCHESTER, BARBARA *(1968)* 70 ——Support in *The Connection*.

WINDHEIM, MAREK *(1960)* 65 ——Small (about 5') Polish character actor-operatic tenor who, for a decade after 1937's *Something to Sing About*, was in two dozen: *Ninotchka* (hotel manager), *Mission to Moscow, I'll Take Romance, On Your Toes, Dramatic School, Holiday Inn* (headwaiter Francois), etc.

WINDSOR, CLAIRE *(1972)* 74 ——Silent star who was one of the great blonde beauties (and remained stunningly attractive until the end); discovered by director Lois Wilson in '20, she starred—for Goldwyn, Tiffany-Stahl and Metro—in 45 silents in which she generally evinced a zest for life; among her best: *Rich Men's Wives* (her personal favorite), *Captain Lash* with Victor McLaglen, *What Wives Want, Sister to Judas, Barefoot Boy, Cross Streets, Dance Madness, The Little Journey*, and *Rupert of Hentzau* opposite Bert Lytell whom she married in '25 and divorced two years later (never remarried); at the end of her MGM contract in '33 she co-starred with Jolson on tour in *Wonder Bar*; played an occasional secondary role in pix until '52; remained wealthy via owning and managing a fishing fleet and a Beverly Hills apartment house; a few weeks before the end, this great-grandmother of four wrote a friend from the past: "You want to know how my life has changed from the glamour days of the twenties . . . I spend a lot of my time painting in oil [past president of the American Fine Arts Institute and an accomplished artist, she refused exhibits as she could not bear to sell her pictures], and," added the star who more than once played a princess, "sometimes I get the old roller out and paint the walls in my home. I even enjoy that . . . "

WING, DAN *(1969)* 46 ——Supporting roles.

WINN, GODFREY *(1971)* 62 ——Played character roles in a few British films (*Billy Liar, Very Important Person*, etc.), but this ever-boyish man with thinning hair was primarily a popular journalist on London's *Daily Mirror;* starred, in '37, in *Personality Parade*, a self-serving documentary about a "typical" day in his life, beginning with his setting out for the office ("some flowers and a kiss from his mother"), etc., and leaving himself open to considerable negative criticism—particularly from other journalists.

WINNINGER, CHARLES *(1969)* 85 ——Captain Andy in *Show Boat* ('36) is the one role everyone associates with this genial, ample-bellied character, but there were dozens more in which he was equally grand; among his best talkies: *Babes in Arms, Three Smart Girls, Nothing Sacred, Destry Rides Again, Fifth Avenue Girl, Sunday Dinner for a Soldier, State Fair* ('45), *The Sun Shines Bright;* was first on-screen in pie-in-the-face comedies at Universal in '15, followed by several features in the '20s (*Summer Bachelors, Pied Piper Malone*); he was last—a joy to the end—in 1960's *Raymie* with David Ladd.

WINSTON, BRUCE *(1946)* 67 ——British character actor who played The Merchant in 1940's *The Thief of Bagdad;* was also in *Children of Dreams, The Private Life of Henry VIII, The Man Who Worked Miracles*, etc.

WINSTON, IRENE *(1964)* 44 ——In *Rear Window* she played the pivotal character Mrs.

Thorwald, whose murder by husband Raymond Burr set off the movie's plot; also played Ruth Carlin in *My Son John* and was in Jerry Lewis' *The Delicate Delinquent.*

WINSTON, JACKIE *(1971)* 56 ——Tough-guy support in Anthony Quinn's *The Happening.*

WINTHROP, JOY *(1950)* 95 ——Character actress in the '20s; in Viola Dana's *Her Fatal Millions, Stolen Love, The Blazing Trail*, etc.

WINTON, JANE *(1959)* 51 ——Lovely secondary leading lady of the '20s and early '30s whose publicity tag—"The Green-Eyed Goddess of Hollywood"—was a bit overwhelming; appeared, however, in many: *Why Girls Go Back Home* with Clive Brook, *Don Juan* (as Beatrice, just one of Barrymore's loves), *The Beloved Rogue, Sunrise* (the Manicure Girl), *My Old Dutch, The Monkey Talks*, etc.; was last in 1934's *The Hired Wife.*

WISE, JACK *(1954)* 51 ——Humorous support in Kay Francis' *Comet Over Broadway*, Joe E. Brown's *Bright Lights*, etc.

WISE, TOM *(1928)* 43 ——Was the gray, derbied fight manager of leading man Oscar Shaw in *The Great White Way* starring Anita Stewart; was in a few others.

WISMER, HARRY *(1967)* 56 ——Famous radio sportscaster who was seen in *Spirit of West Point, Somebody Up There Likes Me*, etc.

WITHERS, CHARLES *(1947)* 58 ——Support in *Hideaway* ('37).

WITHERS, GRANT *(1959)* 55 ——For years, from the mid-'20s, he was a ruggedly handsome, curly-haired leading man—in *Tiger Rose, Hold 'Em Yale, Red-Haired Alibi, Soldiers and Women*, etc.; in the mid-'30s was vastly popular as the star of such serials as *Jungle Jim, Radio Patrol*, and *Fighting Marines;* by the late '30s his face had weathered into that of a journeyman (often villainous) character actor, which he was for the remainder of his long (over 200 movies) career; was especially active in John Ford and/or John Wayne pix: *A Lady Takes a Chance, The Fighting Seabees, My Darling Clementine, Fort Apache, Tycoon, Rio Grande, Fair Wind to Java, The Sun Shines Bright;* was last in 1958's *I, Mobster;* Loretta Young's first husband, he was later married to Estelita.

WITHERSPOON, CORA *(1957)* 67 ——Her face was made for gossiping, and that is how it and her acid-dripping tongue were used in dozens for 25 years; played society bitches in *Dark Victory, Libeled Lady, On the Avenue, Charlie*

Chan's Murder Cruise, Three Loves Has Nancy, Piccadilly Jim, etc.

WIX, FLORENCE (1956) 73 ——Character actress who was busy in the '20s in Mary Astor's Enticement, Norma Talmadge's Secrets, Eleanor Boardman's She Goes to War, etc.; Paul Kelly's The Missing Guest was one of her few talkies.

WOEGERER, OTTO (1966) 59 ——German support in Oskar Werner's The Last Ten Days.

WOLBERT, DOROTHEA (1958) 84 ——Dour-faced character who was particularly active in the '20s in The Flirt, Reginald Denny's The Abysmal Brute, Hoot Gibson's Action, Virginia Valli's A Lady of Quality, etc.; among her many talkies: Hallelujah, I'm a Bum; Paris in Spring; The Medicine Man; Borrowed Wives; and, last, Rhonda Fleming's Little Egypt.

WOLFF, FRANK (1971) 43 ——In Kazan's America, America, he was second-billed, in the role of Vartan Damadian, and he starred, as The Man, in his last, 1970's The Lickerish Quartet; also had top supporting roles in Judith, The Four Days of Naples, A Stranger in Town, Villa Rides, etc.; an American, he worked exclusively in pix made abroad, and particularly in Italy.

WOLFIT, SIR DONALD (1968) 65 ——A noted English actor of the "old school," given to the broad gesture and a bit of scenery-chewing, he gave generally baroque performances in many: Lawrence of Arabia (as General Murray), The Pickwick Papers, Svengali, Room at the Top, Becket (Bishop Folliot), Knight without Armour, etc.

WOLFSON, MARTIN (1973) 69 ——Played the father of Moss Hart (George Hamilton) in Act One.

WOLHEIM, LOUIS (1931) 50 ——Tough, amiable war veteran Katczinsky, in All Quiet on the Western Front, was the role for the great movie "ugly"; before this supremely sympatic part, though, he had been one of the screen's most horrifying brutes—in Orphans of the Storm (the executioner), John Barrymore's Dr. Jekyll and Mr. Hyde, Lionel Barrymore's The Face in the Fog, and especially as sadistic Captain Hare in America (who can forget him in warpaint, joining the Indians in their tortures, savagely, gleefully gouging out the eyes of one victim?); in his next-to-last, 1931's The Sin Ship, this short, squat man with the prognathous jaw was back at it—choking the screams out of poor Mary Astor; of course, being both the star and the director, he did win the lady at the fadeout—and Freudians had a field day.

WONG, ANNA MAY (1961) 54 ——The first (and only) Chinese actress to become a major box-office star; at the outset, as fragilely lovely as a silk-screen figure, she scored sensationally as the Mongol slave in Fairbanks' The Thief of Bagdad, then starred in many silents (Piccadilly being best); in the '30s, after doing movies and stage musicals abroad, she starred in a long string of hits: Daughter of the Dragon, Chu Chin Chow, The Flame of Love, Daughter of Shanghai, Java Head, Limehouse Blues, King of Chinatown, etc., several of which were also made in England; after using her in a few B's in the '40s (Bombs Over Burma, Ellery Queen's Penthouse Mystery, Impact), Hollywood dropped her; was last—far down the cast list—in Portrait in Black ('60) and close friend Anthony Quinn's The Savage Innocents ('61), in which, inexplicably, her voice was dubbed by another actress; offscreen, a proud, aloof woman who never married.

WONG, BRUCE (1953) 47 ——Chinese actor featured in a Lloyd Nolan B, Time to Kill.

WONTNER, ARTHUR (1960) 85 ——Many contend, not without reason, that in Sherlock Holmes' Fatal Hour ('31) and The Triumph of Sherlock Holmes ('32), this English actor was the best of all possible Holmeses; his fine, ascetic face was seen onscreen from the mid-teens, but he was most active in top character roles in British pix from '30; among his many: The Sign of Four, Storm in a Teacup, Brandy for the Parson, Genevieve, Lady Windermere's Fan, others.

WOOD, BRITT (1965) 70 ——Big-nosed, amiable guy who played the comic role of Speedy in several "Hopalong Cassidy" pix (Trail Dust, etc.); was funny in many Westerns: Down Rio Grande Way, Knights of the Range (played Laigs in it), Pirates on Horseback, Riders of the Whistling Pines, etc.

WOOD, DONNA (1947) 29 ——Singer with Kay Kyser's band who played Paulette Goddard's sister in Pot O' Gold.

WOOD, DOUGLAS (1966) 85 ——Dignified, jowly character who was often found in judicial robes, or as a middle-class father or granddad; was in more than 70: Love in Bloom, The President Vanishes, On the Avenue, This Is My Affair, The Prisoner of Shark Island, My Wild Irish Rose, Boston Blackie Booked on Suspicion, H.M. Pulham, Esq., Harriet Craig, etc.

WOOD, ERNEST (1942) 50 ——Supporting actor who played Will Whitney in Jennie Gerhardt; was also in W.C. Fields' International House, Will Rogers' Ambassador Bill, June Moon, and a dozen more.

WOOD, EUGENE *(1971)* 66 ——Dignified, gray support—primarily on Broadway—who played Mr. Aldridge in *The Way We Love Now;* was also in *Diary of a Mad Housewife.*

WOOD, FRANKER *(1931)* 48 ——Was seen in RKO's *Hit the Deck.*

WOOD, FREEMAN *(1956)* 59 ——Suave, he had top supporting roles in 50 in the '20s: Reginald Denny's *Raffles*, Gladys Walton's *Gossip*, Pauline Frederick's *Josselyn's Wife*, Corinne Griffith's *Garden of Eden*, etc.; in fewer in the '30s: *Lady with a Past, Ladies in Love, Kept Husbands*, etc.

WOOD, MARJORIE *(1955)* 67 ——Character actress who, in *The Women*, played Sadie, the Old Maid in the Powder Room, and, in *Seven Brides for Seven Brothers*, was Mrs. Bixby, wife of Russell Simpson; in many others: *Pride and Prejudice* (Lady Lucas), *Excuse My Dust, They Shall Have Music, Texas Carnival*, etc.

WOOD, MICKEY *(1963)* 65 ——Support in Bradford Dillman's *Circle of Deception.*

WOOD, PHILIP *(1940)* 44 ——Played Simon Stimson in *Our Town* and Simon Jenkins in *Room Service.*

WOOD, ROLAND *(1967)* 70 ——Wry-faced, beetle-browed character from Broadway who was in support in *The Tiger Makes Out.*

WOOD, SAM *(1949)* 66 ——Famous director (*Kitty Foyle*) who played minor roles for DeMille pre-*The Squaw Man*, while working as his assistant director.

WOOD, VICTOR *(1958)* 44 ——Character actor from England who played Captain Class in *The Iron Curtain*, Nicholas Midi in *Joan of Arc*, Charles in *The Snows of Kilimanjaro;* was also in *Moss Rose, Hills of Home, The Desert Fox*, etc.

WOODBRIDGE, GEORGE *(1973)* 66 ——Rotund character in British pix; played the Lord Mayor of London in *Richard III*, a police sergeant (often played bobbies) in *The Fallen Idol;* was also in *The Naked Heart, Blanche Fury, Murder in the Cathedral, Heavens Above!*, etc.

WOODBURN, JAMES *(1948)* 60 ——Support in English pix: *Tight Little Island, The Brothers, Chinese Den.*

WOODBURY, DOREEN *(1957)* 29 ——Beautiful support in a Phil Carey B, *The Shadow on the Window.*

WOODFORD, JOHN *(1927)* 65 ——Character in several in the '20s: Ann Pennington's *The Mad Dancer, Success, Get-Rich-Quick Wallingford*, etc.

WOODRUFF, BERT *(1934)* 78 ——Support in a dozen following 1919's *Greased Lightning:* Milton Sills' *The Sea Hawk, The Fire Brigade* (one of several Charles Ray comedies he was in), Jason Robards' *The Isle of Lost Ships*, George Sidney and Charlie Murray's *The Life of Riley*, etc.

WOODS, AL *(1946)* 51 ——Support in a '36 B, *Easy Money.*

WOODS, HARRY *(1968)* 75 ——They told you —the black suit and string tie, the dustless black hat, and, in the shadow of its brim, those satanic black brows, cobra eyes, and downward-tilted little black moustache: he was the Western villains' Big Boss; had good training— started in Ruth Roland's silent serials; threw his demoniacal weight around in literally hundreds of Westerns: *Call of the Rockies, West of the Law, Riders of the West, West of Carson City*, ad infinitum; often made Saturday afternoons a pleasurable double chill by turning up, too, as the chief villain in the serial (such as Buck Jones' *The Phantom Rider*, in which he was lowdown rancher, big boss of the outlaws, Harvey Delaney); bigtime directors knew his value as a baddie and used him often: DeMille (*The Plainsman, Union Pacific, The Buccaneer, Reap the Wild Wind*), Ford (*My Darling Clementine, She Wore a Yellow Ribbon*), Wellman (*Beau Geste*), Vidor (*The Fountainhead*); quit the screen in '56, retiring as the champ, the best of the Black Hats, easily the most-imitated boss villain in B-Western history.

WOODTHORPE, GEORGIA *(1927)* 68 —— Character actress who, after the James J. Corbett serial *The Midnight Man* ('19), was in several other silents: *The Four Horsemen of the Apocalypse*, Helene Chadwick's *Gimme*, Viola Dana's *Rouged Lips*, Raymond Hatton's *Bunty Pulls the Strings*, etc.

WOODWARD, ROBERT *(1972)* 63 ——Besides doubling for Buck Jones and Dick Foran, he rode hard—usually as a baddie—in dozens of B Westerns.

WOOLLCOTT, ALEXANDER *(1943)* 56 —— Porcine, viperish theater critic who was the inspiration for Sheridan Whiteside in *The Man Who Came to Dinner;* played a famous writer ("perishing languidly in a sea of tired epigrams," said the *Times*) in Noel Coward's *The Scoundrel* and was seen as himself in *Babes on Broadway.*

WOOLLEY, MONTY *(1963)* 74 ——He starred as Sheridan Whiteside in *The Man Who Came to Dinner*, and what he lacked in heft, as compared to Woollcott, he made up for in beard and bile; it didn't get him an Oscar nomination as Best Actor, but a picture he made the next year, *The Pied Piper*, did, and there was a Best Supporting nomination two years later ('44) for *Since You Went Away;* earlier, after a career as an Ivy League professor, he had played supporting roles in 15: *Nothing Sacred* (Dr. Vunch), *The Girl of the Golden West* (Governor), *Zaza* (interviewer Fouget), *Midnight* (Judge), etc.; as a star he was in *Holy Matrimony* and *Molly and Me* (both with Gracie Fields), *Life Begins at 8:30* with Lupino, *Irish Eyes Are Smiling* with June Haver, *Night and Day* (as himself, composer Cole Porter's real-life Yale professor), *The Bishop's Wife*, etc.; Ann Blyth's *Kismet* ('55) was his last; his lifelong dream was to play George Bernard Shaw—could have been fun.

WOOLSEY, ROBERT *(1944)* 55 ——Cigar-smoking, bespectacled half of the Wheeler & Woolsey comedy team that made a mint for RKO in the '30s; see Bert Wheeler for their combined credits; starred without his partner in a '28 Broadway show, *Rio Rita*, and onscreen in *Everything's Rosie* with Anita Louise in '31; odd note from a 1936 issue of *Picturegoer* magazine: "During the past six years he has smoked 20,000 cigars for screen and publicity work. Offscreen he is a non-smoker."

WORLOCK, FREDERICK *(1973)* 87 ——Distinguished, bald British character in several dozen Hollywood pix: *How Green Was My Valley* (Dr. Richards, who treated young Roddy McDowall for paralysis), *Spartacus* (Laelius), *Hangover Square* (Superintendent Clay), *Strange Cargo* (Grideau), *Johnny Belinda*, *The Black Swan*, *Man Hunt*, *Hills of Home*, *The Notorious Landlady*, etc.

WORTH, CONSTANCE *(1963)* 51 ——Beautiful blonde who, besides being known as one of George Brent's ex-wives, was most enterprising as the British-agent heroine (in black wig) of the '43 serial *G-Men vs. the Black Dragon;* was the leading lady in numerous B's: *China Passage*, *Meet Boston Blackie*, *Boston Blackie Goes Hollywood*, *Crime Doctor*, *Why Girls Leave Home*, etc.

WORTH, PEGGY *(1956)* 65 ——At 20 she played the lead, a young piano tuner, in the B pic *You Find It Everywhere.*

WORTHING, HELEN LEE *(1948)* 43 —— Played the young, beautiful Mrs. Loring in *Jan-ice Meredith;* had supporting roles in still other silents: *Don Juan*, Leatrice Joy's *Vanity*, Adolphe Menjou's *The Swan*, George Walsh's *The Count of Luxembourg*, etc.

WORTHINGTON, WILLIAM *(1941)* 68 —— Co-starred with Herbert Rawlinson in Universal's 1915 spectacle, *Damon and Pythias;* had supporting roles in several in the '20s: *Kid Boots; Her Honor, the Governor; The Green Goddess; Red Lights*, etc.; in the '30s was in *Duck Soup* (First Minister of Finance); *Susan Lenox, Her Fall and Rise; No More Orchids*, etc.; was also in two serials: Kenneth Harlan's *Finger Prints* (as father of the heroine) and Evelyn Knapp's *Perils of Pauline* (American consul).

WRAY, ALOHA *(1968)* 40 ——Dancer who was in *George White's (1935) Scandals;* was once married to Frankie Darro.

WRAY, JOHN *(1940)* 42 ——Sharp-nosed young supporting actor whose role of Himmelstross (his second) in *All Quiet on the Western Front* was one of his best; was in 70 more in one decade, often playing a proletarian: *The Miracle Man* (The Frog), *You Only Live Once* (Warden), *I Am a Fugitive from a Chain Gang* (Nordine), *Poor Little Rich Girl* (Flagin), *We Who Are About to Die*, *A Man to Remember*, *Blackmail*, *Each Dawn I Die*, etc.

WREN, SAM *(1962)* 65 ——Tough support in *Marked Woman*, *I Married a Doctor*, *Dr. Socrates*, etc.

WRIGHT, FRED, JR. *(1928)* 57 ——Supported Victor McLaglen in *The Glorious Adventure*, the first feature made completely in full color, filmed in England in '22.

WRIGHT, HAIDEE *(1943)* 45 ——One of the two femme stars—Benita Hume was the other—of Great Britain's *Jew Suss* (released in the U.S. as *Power*); was also in *The Blarney Kiss*, *Tomorrow We Live*, etc.

WRIGHT, HUGH E. *(1940)* 60 ——Support in Hollywood silents (Sydney Chaplin's *The Better 'Ole*, etc.) and then in many British talkies: *The Good Companions*, *Radio Parade of 1935*, *On the Air*, others.

WRIGHT, HUNTLEY *(1941)* 71 ——Character in England's *Look Up and Laugh*, *Heart Song*, others.

WRIGHT, MARIE *(1949)* 87 ——Character actress in British pix: *Angel Street*, *Sixty Glorious Years*, *Day Dreams.*

WRIGHT, WILL *(1962)* 71 ——With his long, pointy noise, long, pointy ears, and a frazzled cigar clamped tightly in the corner of his mouth, this wry old grayhead was a gaunt smalltown or rustic fixture in Hollywood pix for 30 years; seemed old even in the first of his 100 movies; was in *Blondie Plays Cupid; Tennessee Johnson; Shut My Big Mouth; Salome, Where She Danced; Uncle Harry; Blaze of Noon; All the King's Men; A Ticket to Tomahawk,* etc.

WRIGHT, WILLIAM *(1949)* 47 ——Black-haired routine leading man who often worked in B's at Republic, PRC, and Columbia; was in *Rookies on Parade, Down Missouri Way, Sweetheart of the Fleet, One Mysterious Night, Escape in the Fog, A Night to Remember,* more.

WRIGHTMAN, ERIC *(1968)* 65 ——Scottish actor in supporting roles.

WU, HONORABLE *(1945)* 42 ——Played Latchee Lee in *Stowaway,* Wong in *Mr. Moto Takes a Vacation,* Lee in *Ellery Queen and the Perfect Crime,* etc.

WUEST, IDA *(1958)* 74 ——Actress in many German films: *The Merry Widow's Ball, The Burning Heart, The Last Waltz,* etc.

WUNDERLEE, FRANK *(1925)* 50 ——Portly, moustachioed villain in serials: *Sunken Silver, The Fatal Fortune, The Carter Case;* was also in features: Carol Dempster's *One Exciting Night, No Mother to Guide Her, A Divorce of Convenience,* etc.

WYCHERLY, MARGARET *(1956)* 74 —— "Top of the world, Ma!"; Cagney blew sky-high with the gasworks with his loony old mother on his mind in *White Heat;* this great English stage actress played a mother of quite another sort, the humble hillbilly Ma of Cooper, in *Sergeant York,* and won a Best Supporting Actress nomination; gave excellent performances in many others of the '40s: *Keeper of the Flame, The Enchanted Cottage, Crossroads, The Moon Is Down, The Yearling, Random Harvest,* etc.; was in four in the '50s: *The President's Lady* (Andrew Jackson's corncob-pipe-smoking mother), *That Man from Tangier, The*

Man with a Cloak, and, last, Olivier's *Richard III.*

WYMARK, PATRICK *(1970)* 44 ——British character actor with small features and a round-ish face who was in *Repulsion* (the landlord who made advances to Catherine Deneuve and was killed by her), *Where Eagles Dare, Cromwell, Operation Crossbow, Woman Times Seven,* others.

WYNN, DORIS *(1925)* 15 ——Youngster who was featured in Christie comedies.

WYNN, ED *(1966)* 79 ——One of the great clowns of the century in vaudeville (opened the bill on the opening night of the Palace in 1913), on Broadway (many musicals that he wrote, produced, and starred in), radio (Texaco's never-to-be-forgotten "Fire Chief"), silent movies (*Rubber Heels*), talkies in the '30s (*The Chief, Follow the Leader, Manhattan Mary*), television (won two Emmys in his starring series); finally, in his last decade, a masterful character actor in movies; was in *The Diary of Anne Frank* (won a Best Supporting Oscar nomination as the tremulous old performer, Mr. Dussell), *Marjorie Morningstar, The Great Man, Mary Poppins* ("I Love to Laugh") and five other Disney pix (*The Absent-Minded Professor, Son of Flubber,* etc.), *Warning Shot, The Greatest Story Ever Told* (Old Aram); was the father of Keenan.

WYNN, NAN *(1971)* 55 ——Beautiful brunette singer who was featured in Abbott & Costello's *Pardon My Sarong,* de Havilland's *Princess O'Rourke, Jam Session,* etc.; also dubbed Rita Hayworth's singing voice in both *My Gal Sal* and *You Were Never Lovelier.*

WYNYARD, DIANA *(1964)* 58 ——Superb, elegantly beautiful British star who was no stranger to Hollywood; starred here in *Cavalcade* (was Oscar-nominated as Best Actress), *Rasputin and the Empress, Reunion in Vienna, Men Must Fight, Let's Try Again,* and, near the end of her movie career, *Island in the Sun* (as James Mason's mother); pix she made in England include *Angel Street, Tom Brown's School Days* ('52), *Kipps, An Ideal Husband.*

Y

YACONELLI, FRANK *(1965)* 67 ——Played chubby, gap-toothed, funny Mexican sidekicks —of Ken Maynard, Jack Randall, Tom Keene, et al.—for 35 years; was in *Riding the Sunset Trail, Wild Horse Canyon, Blazing Justice, South of Monterey,* scores more Western features; was Johnny Mack Brown's buddy, Mike,

in the '37 serial *Wild West Days;* in *Death Takes a Holiday,* played the Italian vendor whose cart was hit by Evelyn Venable's auto in the early scenes.

YAKOLEV, YURI *(1970)* 58 ——Actor who starred as the epileptic Prince Myshkin in the

1960 Russian film *The Idiot* and, in the same period, in *The Ballad of a Hussar* and *No Ordinary Summer*.

YARBOROUGH, BARTON *(1951)* 51 —— Tough-guy support in many B's in the '40s: *I Love a Mystery, The Ghost of Frankenstein, Kilroy Was Here, The Unknown, Captain Tugboat Annie*, etc.

YARDE, MARGARET *(1944)* 65 ——Character actress in numerous British pix: *Scrooge, Tiger Bay* ('33), *Prison without Bars, The Good Companions, Broken Rosary*, etc.

YARNELL, BRUCE *(1973)* 35 ——Big, curly-haired, and handsome actor-singer who co-starred on Broadway (with Merman in the *Annie Get Your Gun* revival), and TV (as Deputy Marshal Chalk Bresson in the series *The Outlaw*); in *Irma La Douce* played Hippolyte, the cruel pimp who was Jack Lemmon's predecessor in managing the career of prostitute Shirley MacLaine.

YASSINE, ISMALI *(1972)* 60 ——Egyptian actor who starred in the 1951 Oriental Film Company release *Little Miss Devil*.

YBARRA, VENTURA "ROCKY" *(1965)* 65 — —He had supporting roles in Laraine Day's *The Third Voice*, Randolph Scott's *Frontier Marshal*, other Westerns; was sometimes billed Roque.

YEARSLEY, RALPH *(1928)* 31 ——Was the youngest of the three outlaws, the Hatburns, who beat Richard Barthelmess in *Tol'able David*; was in many others in the '20s: *The Village Blacksmith*, Jack Pickford's *The Hill Billy*, Harold Lloyd's *Kid Brother* (essentially a comedy version of *Tol'able David*), Crawford's *Rose-Marie* (played Jean), *The Little Shepherd of Kingdom Come*, etc.

YORK, DUKE, JR. *(1952)* 50 ——In the *Flash Gordon* serial he played King Kala, ruler of the underwater kingdom; played supporting roles in many Westerns (*Stampede, Rogue River*), comedies (*Strike Me Pink, Topper Takes a Trip*, as cop Grogan), and Three Stooges shorts (*Three Little Twerps*, etc.).

YORK, ELIZABETH *(1969)* 46 ——Actress-dancer; minor roles.

YORKE, CAROL *(1967)* 38 ——At 19 played Marie, one of Louis Jourdan's loves, in *Letter from an Unknown Woman*.

YORKE, OSWALD *(1943)* 76 ——Support in Valentino's *Monsieur Beaucaire*.

YOST, HERBERT *(1945)* 65 ——Starred for D. W. Griffith in 1909's *Edgar Allan Poe* (opposite Mrs. Griffith, Linda Arvidson); then played leads in such features as *Every Rose Has Its Stem* and such serials as *What Happened to Mary* and *The Man Who Disappeared*; later played character roles, including, in '34, that of Laura Hope Crews' husband in *The Age of Innocence*; for his credits under an assumed name, see Barry O'Moore.

YOUNG, ARTHUR *(1959)* 61 ——Benign, plump character who played diplomats and other upper-crust gentlemen in many English pix: *Victoria the Great, My Brother Jonathan, An Inspector Calls, The Twenty Questions Murder Mystery, The Lady with a Lamp*, etc.

YOUNG, CARLETON *(1971)* 64 ——Midway in his career, in Esther Williams' *Thrill of a Romance*, this handsome, wavy-haired actor played the second lead, a playboy, with such suave elegance there was promise—never fulfilled—he would become a major leading man; previously he had played leads in B's (*Join the Marines, Pride of the Bowery*, etc.), support in many serials (*Dick Tracy*, as Ralph Byrd's brother, *Buck Rogers, SOS Coast Guard, Adventures of Captain Marvel*, others), Westerns (*Cassidy of Bar 20, Heroes of the Hills*), and A's (*In the Meantime, Darling*); later became a journeyman actor in military pix (*Flying Leathernecks, American Guerrilla in the Philippines, Battle Cry*), swashbucklers (*Anne of the Indies, Prince Valiant*), crime movies (*Riot in Cell Block 11, A Blueprint for Murder*), and numerous big-league Westerns (*The Horse Soldiers, Sergeant Rutledge, Bitter Creek, Red Mountain, The Man Who Shot Liberty Valance*), in which he was ever a captain or a colonel—and always elegant.

YOUNG, CLIFTON *(1951)* 34 ——At seven he was Toughie in the "Our Gang" comedies; in his early 20s played the petty crook who attempted to blackmail Bogart (and was killed) in *Dark Passage* and was an interne in *Possessed*; mostly he was a villain in such Westerns as *Blood on the Moon, Bells of Coronado, Pursued*, and Allan "Rocky" Lane's *Salt Lake Raiders*.

YOUNG, CLARA KIMBALL *(1960)* 70 ——In more than 60 movies in 13 years (1912–25) she was a star of great consequence—a "dark madonna," a tall and beautiful (and beautifully dressed) socialite who, in a dignified manner, dallied with romance, rarely getting burned though she played with fire; among the men she "played with," to the envy of millions of femme fans, were Maurice Costello, Milton Sills, Rudolph Valentino, Elliott Dexter, Conway Tearle; Vitagraph's *My Official Wife* ('14) made this dark-haired beauty a major star; those she made for Lewis J. Selznick (1916–19) made her a superstar: *Camille, Magda, Trilby, The Easiest Way, The Common Law, Marionettes*, others; so great was her popularity that, to book her films, exhibitors were obliged also to take the movies of the young Talmadge sisters; was one of the first women stars to have her own producing company, for which she made *Straight from Paris, Mid-Channel, Hush, Charge It*, etc.; her last starring vehicle was 1925's *Lying Wives* ("Lots of intense domestic trouble enjoyed by a batch of characters who seem to be half-witted," said *Photoplay*); the rest of her life was a series of thwarted comeback dreams; offscreen for a vaudeville try, she returned in '31 and played minor roles, mostly in B pix, for the next four years: *Probation, Romance in the Rain, Women Go on Forever*, etc.; received eighth billing in her one A pic, Colbert's *She Married Her Boss*, playing an officious character named Parsons; then came three "Hopalong Cassidy" Westerns, in the last of which, 1938's *The Frontiersman*, she played a camp cook—heavyset and graying—and a million hearts broke.

YOUNG, DESMOND *(1966)* 74 ——Author who played himself in *The Desert Fox*.

YOUNG, LUCILLE *(1934)* 42 ——Had a very small role in Will Rogers' *Lightnin'*, after years of secondary parts.

YOUNG, MARY *(1934)* 77 ——Character in minor pix in the '20s: *The Ninety and Nine, The Angel of Crooked Street*, others.

YOUNG, MARY *(1971)* 92 ——Character actress who played society women with high-arched brows; was in *Watch on the Rhine* (Mrs. Mellie Sewell), *The Lost Weekend* (Mrs. Deveridge), *The Mating Season* (spinster socialite), *The Stork Club* (sister-in-law of millionaire Barry Fitzgerald), *The Bride Wore Boots, This Is My Affair*, etc.

YOUNG, NED *(1968)* 54 ——First played GI's (*Bombs Over Burma*), then was in Larry Parks swashbucklers (*The Gallant Blade, The Swordsman*), followed by Westerns (*The Iron Mistress*) and crime pix (*Gun Crazy*); last had a very minor role, Henry Bushman, in Rock Hudson's *Seconds*; was also a screenwriter (*Decoy, Jailhouse Rock*); was sometimes billed Nedrick.

YOUNG, OLIVE *(1940)* 33 ——Played the heroine in two 1930 Westerns: *Ridin' Law* and *Trailing Trouble*.

YOUNG, ROLAND *(1953)* 65 ——Droll, whimsical Cosmo Topper, in *Topper*, of course, which

got him an Oscar nomination as Best Support—and *Topper Takes a Trip*, which didn't; restrained humor was his trademark—the wispy smile and unchuckled chuckle, bemused gray eyes that twitched at the corners, faint, unfinished gestures; a lifelong free-lance, he generally picked the best of comedies in which to work: *Ruggles of Red Gap* (the Earl of Burnstead whose three treys in poker lost him his perfect valet, Laughton, to Cousin Egbert, Charles Ruggles), *One Hour with You, The Guardsman, The Young in Heart, The Philadelphia Story, The Lady Has Plans, They All Kissed the Bride, Standing Room Only*, many more; only once did he play a thoroughly disagreeable character—the unctuous Uriah Heep in *David Copperfield*—and always pegged it as his favorite role; from England, and Broadway, he appeared in several silents in the '20s: John Barrymore's *Sherlock Holmes* (played Watson), its sequel, *Moriarty*, Glenn Hunter's *Grit*, etc.; in '29 he starred in his first talkie, a mystery, *The Unholy Night* (directed by Lionel Barrymore), then came all the fine comedies that constituted his "real" screen career.

YOUNG, TAMMANY *(1936)* 49 ——Hair-in-the-face, ski-nosed little character who was so often a W. C. Fields comedy stooge; in *It's a Gift* he was Fields' slow-witted grocery assistant who sent Baby LeRoy sailing gleefully through the air in that old-fashioned high-wire package carrier; was also in *The Old-Fashioned Way, Six of a Kind, Poppy, The Man on the Flying Trapeze*, etc.; onscreen from the teens, he was in dozens without Fields: *She Done Him Wrong* (played Chuck Connors), *Little Miss Marker* (Buggs), *Tugboat Annie, Gold Diggers of 1933*, etc.

YOUNG, WALTER *(1957)* 79 ——Had character roles in John Litel's *Alcatraz Island* and Glenda Farrell's *Torchy Blane, the Adventurous Blonde*, both in '37.

YULE, JOE *(1950)* 61 ——Short, round little character best known for being Mickey Rooney's father and/or starring as Jiggs in the Monogram series—*Jiggs and Maggie in Jackpot Jitters, Bringing Up Father, Jiggs and Maggie Out West*; was six years at MGM and in many (*Idiot's Delight, Broadway Melody of 1940, Boom Town, New Moon*, etc.), including one with Mickey—*Judge Hardy and Son*—but not as his father; that role was taken.

YURKA, BLANCHE *(1974)* 86 ——Great, gaunt Broadway actress (the Queen in Barrymore's *Hamlet*) whose best screen role was that of the maniacal Madame DeFarge in Colman's *A Tale of Two Cities*; was in many others: *The Bridge of San Luis Rey, The Southerner, The Song of Bernadette, The Furies, 13 Rue Madeleine*, etc., including, last, *Thunder in the Sun* ('59); starred on Broadway until she was 82, appearing then in *The Mad Woman of Chaillot;* was once married to Ian Keith.

Z

ZABELLE, FLORA *(1968)* 88 ——Brunette actress who was John Barrymore's leading lady in 1916's *The Red Widow*, and was in others; was the widow of Raymond Hitchcock.

ZACCONI, ERMETE *(1948)* 91 ——One of the great early names in Italian cinema, he starred in *The Palace of Flames* ('12), *The Dread of Doom* ('13), etc.

ZANETTE, GUY *(1962)* 55 ——Support in Garfield's *Under My Skin*, Kirby Grant's *Snow Dog*, etc.

ZANY, KING *(1939)* 60s ——Support in many in the '20s: George K. Arthur's *Hollywood*, Warner Baxter's *The Garden of Weeds*, Hoot Gibson's *Broadway or Bust*, Thomas Meighan's *The City Gone Wild*, etc.

ZELAYA, DON *(1951)* 57 ——Nicaraguan actor who was featured in Chester Morris' *Girl from God's Country*, Mitchum's *Macao* (as Gimpy), *The Hairy Ape*, others.

ZIMINA, VALENTINA *(1928)* 29 ——Russian-born actress who played supporting roles in the '20s: Pola Negri's *The Woman on Trial*, Lillian Gish's *La Boheme*, Shirley Mason's *Rose of the Tenements;* was last in *The Scarlet Lady*, in which she played a lead.

ZIMMERMANN, ED *(1972)* 39 ——Played the supporting role of Halloran in *Who Is Harry Kellerman and Why Is He Saying Those Terrible Things About Me?;* was best known as a star of TV soap operas (*The Guiding Light, As the World Turns, Love of Live*).

ZUCCO, FRANCES *(1962)* 29 ——Support in *Never Wave at a Wac;* was the daughter of George.

ZUCCO, GEORGE *(1960)* 74 ——When this smooth, quiet-spoken Englishman appeared on the scene—in any one of the 100 he was in after 1934's *Autumn Crocus*—you automatically knew treachery was both afoot and ahead; this was most obvious in scores of horror flicks: *The Mad Monster, The Mummy's Hand, The Mad Ghoul, House of Frankenstein, The Monster and the Girl*, etc.; was more slyly sinister in *Marie Antoinette* (Governor of Conciergerie), *The Adventures of Sherlock Holmes* (as Moriarty, stole the picture from Rathbone), *A Woman's Face, Conquest, The Cat and the Canary* ('39), *The Seventh Cross, Captain from Castile;* and, in *Sudan*, containing one of his more florid performances, when he cocked that evil eye and plotted the death of rightful ruler Maria Montez, he was, positively, the last word in movie villainy.

PLAYERS WHO DIED IN 1975 AND 1976

(Note: Future editions will contain more detailed information on these performers. Deaths occuring after April 1, 1976 are not included.)

AKAR, JOHN J. 48—Stage-screen actor from Sierra Leone; in *Something of Value. (1975)*

ALBRIGHT, HARDIE 71—Youthful lead in *So Big* ('32), *Young Sinners*, many more. *(1975)*

ALEXANDER, MURIEL 91—British character actress. *(1975)*

ALEXANDER, SUZANNE 40s—Was featured in *Cat-Women of the Moon. (1975)*

ALLYN, ALYCE 50s—Blonde character; *The Manchurian Candidate, The Wild Bunch. (1976)*

ALSEN, ELSA 94—Operatic soprano; with Lawrence Tibbett in *The Rogue Song. (1975)*

ARLEN, RICHARD 75—Rugged star of 250, from '23, including Oscar-winning *Wings. (1976)*

ARNO, SIG 79—German comic support in scores: *Up in Arms, Tales of Manhattan. (1975)*

AUBREY, GEORGES 47—Belgian comedian; in 1975's *On the Tip of the Lips. (1975)*

BADDELEY, ANGELA 71—British character; in *The Speckled Band, Tom Jones*, etc. *(1976)*

BAGDAD, WILLIAM —Was "Igor" in *The Astro-Zombies;* in others. *(1975)*

BAKER, BOB 74—A 1937-44 cowboy star who, in '39, was one of the Top Ten. *(1975)*

BAKER, JOSEPHINE 68—Exotic black singer; in *Moulin Rouge* ('44), *The French Way. (1975)*

BARAGREY, JOHN 57—Smooth villain in *The Loves of Carmen, The Saxon Charm*, etc. *(1975)*

BARCLAY, DON 83—Support in *Man Hunt, The Falcon's Brother, Navy Spy*, many more. *(1975)*

BARNES, FLORENCE 73—Hollywood's first woman stunt pilot, in *Hell's Angels*, etc. *(1975)*

BARRINGER, NED 87—Actor-writer; in silents prior to 1915. *(1976)*

BATES, LAWSON —Supporting actor. *(1975)*

BELMONTE, HERMAN 84—Character actor and featured dancer. *(1975)*

BERK, SARA 76—Character actress. *(1975)*

BERKELEY, BUSBY 80—Legendary dance director; famed for kaleidoscope patterns. *(1976)*

BLAIR, DAVID 43—Starred in ballet pix: *An Evening With the Royal Ballet*, etc. *(1976)*

BLAISE, PIERRE 24—French; starred as peasant youth Lucien in *Lacombe, Lucien. (1975)*

BLUE, BEN 73—Sad-faced comic in many: *Panama Hattie, Thousands Cheer*, etc. *(1975)*

BLYDEN, LARRY 49—Bespectacled support in *The Bachelor Party, Kiss Them for Me. (1975)*

BORZAGE, DAN 78—Veteran support; in *Mister Roberts, The Wings of Eagles*, etc. *(1975)*

BRENT, EVELYN 74—Starred memorably in *Underworld, Queen of Diamonds*, many more. *(1975)*

BROKAW, CHARLES 77—Support from '26; in *Fascinating Youth, I Cover the War. (1975)*

BROWN, BARBARA 70s—Played mothers; in *Janie, That Hagen Girl*, dozens more. *(1975)*

BROWN, PAMELA 58—Major British support; *I Know Where I'm Going, Cleopatra*, etc. *(1975)*

BRUNTON, GARLAND LEWIS 72—Character actor. *(1975)*

BRYANT, ROBIN 50—Supporting actress; in *Boomerang, Portrait of Jennie*, etc. *(1976)*

BURNS, JAMES —Supporting actor. *(1975)*

BURNSIDE, WILLIAM W., JR. 49—Support; in *Donovan's Reef, The Ugly American. (1976)*

BURR, EDMUND —Supporting actor. *(1975)*

CAIRNS, ANGUS 65—Character actor. *(1975)*

CALLEIA, JOSEPH 78—Suave bad guy from '31; *My Little Chickadee, Juarez*, more. *(1975)*

CALVIN, HENRY 57—Plump Disney support; *Sign of Zorro* (as Garcia), *Toby Tyler*. *(1975)*

CARPENTIER, GEORGES 81—Handsome boxer; in *The Wonder Man, Show of Shows*, etc. *(1975)*

CARRINGTON, FRANK 73—Support in a few; best known as stage actor-director. *(1975)*

CHARON, JACQUES 55—French; in *The Paris Waltz, Cartouche, In the French Style*. *(1975)*

CHEFE, JACK 81—Character; in *It's a Pleasure*, more. *(1975)*

CHIEF BLACK HAWK —Indian character actor. *(1975)*

CLARE, MADELYN 81—Silent actress; widow of *The Clansman* author, Thomas Dixon. *(1975)*

COBB, LEE J. 64—Oscar nominee (Support) in *On the Waterfront, The Brothers Karamazov*. *(1976)*

COHN, JULIA 73—Support in *The Producers*. *(1975)*

COLBY, BARBARA 36—Brunette support in *California Split, Memory of Us*. *(1975)*

COLE, MARIE KEITH 61—Singer-actress. *(1975)*

CONTE, RICHARD 65—Actor of intensity who starred in 75 after *A Walk in the Sun*. *(1975)*

COOPER, CLANCY 68—Support in *The Sainted Sisters, Lulu Belle*, and 60 more. *(1975)*

COUGHLIN, KEVIN 30—Juvenile lead; *Storm Center, Happy Anniversary*, etc. *(1976)*

COURTNEY, INEZ 67—Harlow's pal in *Suzy*, Rogers' in *Having Wonderful Time*, etc. *(1975)*

"COUSIN JODY" 61—Baggy-pants rustic comic in Westerns of Roy Rogers and others. *(1975)*

CRAWFORD, NAN 82—Veteran character actress. *(1975)*

CROSBY, WADE 70—Support in dozens: *Arizona, Ride a Crooked Mile, Airport 1975*. *(1975)*

DAGET, ROBERT TRUE —Support in *The Hustler*; veteran Broadway actor. *(1975)*

DALEY, CASS 59—Raucous, buck-toothed Paramount comedienne; *The Fleet's In*, etc. *(1975)*

DANSON, LINDA —Supporting actress. *(1975)*

DARE, PHYLLIS 84—British musical star; featured in 1923's *The Common Law*. *(1975)*

DARE, ZENA 88—British character actress; sister of Phyllis Dare. *(1975)*

DAVENPORT, HAVIS 42—TV's "White Rain Girl"; the newlywed in *Rear Window*. *(1975)*

DEEN, NEDRA (ELIZABETH) —Support in movies; also on stage and T-V. *(1975)*

DELEVANTI, CYRIL 86—Was the grandfather, Nonno, in *The Night of the Iguana*. *(1975)*

DELIGHT, JUNE 77—Stage dancer in silents: *Adventures of Huckleberry Finn*, etc. *(1975)*

DEL VAL, JEAN 83—French support in many silents (*A Sainted Devil*) and talkies. *(1975)*

DE MOTT, JOHN A. 63—Child actor in early "Our Gang" comedies and features. *(1975)*

DE TOLLY, DEENA —Actress-dancer, small roles in many DeMille epics. *(1976)*

DIERKES, JOHN 69—Veteran support; the Tall Soldier in *The Red Badge of Courage*. *(1975)*

DONAHUE, VINCENT J. 51—Actor and Actors Equity exec; in *Beyond Glory*. *(1976)*

DONALDSON, JACK 65—Young MGM contractee just prior to WW II. *(1975)*

DORN, PHILIP 75—Handsome, deep-voiced star; in *Chetniks, Ziegfeld Girl*, more. *(1975)*

DOWLING, EDDIE 81—B'way star; in early talkies: *Rainbow Man, Honeymoon Lane*. *(1976)*

DOWNING, JOSEPH 72—Support in gangster pix: *Racket Busters, Each Dawn I Die*. *(1975)*

DOWNING, ROBERT 61—Support in *On the Waterfront, Splendor in the Grass*. *(1975)*

DOYLE, PATRICIA 60—Minor roles prior to '42, in *The Grapes of Wrath*, etc. *(1975)*

DRESDEL, SONIA 67—British character; diabolic as butler's wife in *The Fallen Idol*. *(1976)*

DURFEE, MINTA 85—Early Chaplin leading lady; first wife of "Fatty" Arbuckle. *(1975)*

ECKLES, ROBERT 55—Supporting actor. *(1975)*

EMERSON, EDWARD 65—Supporting actor. *(1975)*

ENRIGHT, JOSEPHINE 72—Character actress in many from 1942. *(1976)*

FAX, JESSLYN 70s—Character actress; in *Rear Window, An Affair to Remember*, etc. *(1975)*

FAY, BRENDAN 54—Support in *The Hustler, Juke Box Racket*, etc. *(1975)*

FEE, VICKIE 28—Once under contract at Universal; daughter of Astrid Allwyn. *(1975)*

FIELDS, SIDNEY 77—Vet comic; in *Strike Me Pink, Mexican Hayride*, etc. *(1975)*

FINE, LARRY 73—Frizzy-haired comic; one of "The Three Stooges," first to last. *(1975)*

FLANDERS, MICHAEL 53—Wheelchair-bound British actor; in *Long Ago, Tomorrow*. *(1975)*

FONTAINE, LILIAN 88—Mother of de Havilland, J. Fontaine; played moms onscreen. *(1975)*

FORD, PHILIP 75—Director-son of late Francis Ford; began as child in silents. *(1976)*

FRANKLIN, ALBERTA 79—In silents: *Dance of the Seven Veils, Devil's Trail*, etc. *(1976)*

FRANKLYN, LEO 78—Often played comic drunks in British pix. *(1975)*

FRECHETTE, MARK 27—James Dean type who starred in Antonioni's *Zabriskie Point*. *(1975)*

FRESNAY, PIERRE 77—French star of *Grand Illusion, Marius, Fanny, Cesar*, etc. *(1975)*

GAINES, RICHARD 71—Did bald prigs in dozens: *The More the Merrier*, etc. *(1975)*

GARON, NORMAN 20s—Supporting actor; primarily on stage and TV. *(1975)*

GAY, INEZ —Support in *Father's Son* ('41), starring John Litel. *(1975)*

GIEHSE, THERESE 76—Character in *La-combe, Lucien*, Duvivier's *Anna Karenina*, etc. *(1975)*

GILBERT, PAUL 58—Co-star comedian-dancer; *So This Is Paris, The Second Greatest Sex*. *(1975)*

GIOI, VIVI 58—Played leads in Italy's *The Earth Cries Out, Women Without Names*. *(1975)*

GLYN, NEVA CARR 70s—Famed Australian character; in Disney's *Ride a Wild Pony*. *(1975)*

GODOWSKY, DAGMAR 78—"Vamp" star of many silents: *A Sainted Devil, Red Lights*. *(1975)*

GOODLIFFE, MICHAEL 61—British character; in *Rob Roy, Von Ryan's Express*, etc. *(1976)*

GREEN, MARTYN 75—D'Oyly Carte star of *The Mikado*; in Gilbert and Sullivan, etc. *(1975)*

GREGSON, JOHN 55—Handsome British star of *Genevieve, Tight Little Island*, etc. *(1975)*

GRIFFIES, ETHEL 97—Old-lady roles in 100: *Love Me Tonight, Vigil in the Night*. *(1975)*

GROSSKURTH, KURT 66—Funny character; in *Willy Wonka and the Chocolate Factory*. *(1975)*

HABERFIELD, GRAHAM 34—In British pix; was "Jerry" in TV's *Coronation Street*. *(1975)*

HANSEN, WILLIAM 64—Character; walked with limp in *Pinky, The Bramble Bush*, etc. *(1975)*

HARTNELL, WILLIAM 67—Support in *Odd Man Out, The Pickwick Papers*, more. *(1975)*

HARVEY, EDWARD 82—Veteran character actor. *(1975)*

HAYWARD, SUSAN 55—Redhaired star; won Oscar (5th nomination) in *I Want to Live*. *(1975)*

HENABERY, JOSEPH 88—Was Lincoln in *The Birth of a Nation*; later a director. *(1976)*

HERMINE, HILDA —Supporting actress. *(1975)*

HILL, HOWARD 76—Champ archer-star of shorts; stand-in bowman for Errol Flynn. *(1975)*

HOWARD, MOE 78—Black-banged last surviving member of original "Three Stooges." *(1975)*

HOWERTON, CLARENCE "MAJOR MITE" 62—Midget; in *The Wizard of Oz*, "Our Gang." *(1975)*

HUSTED, BEVERLY 49—Shep Fields and Sammy Kaye vocalist; with them in pix. *(1975)*

HUTCHISON, MURIEL 60—Played Jane in *The Women*; in *Another Thin Man*, more. *(1975)*

INESCORT, FRIEDA 75—Did "cold" femmes like no other; *The Letter, Pride and Prejudice*, etc. *(1976)*

ISHAM, SIR GYLES 72—Character in *The Iron Duke*, Garbo's *Anna Karenina*, etc. *(1976)*

JACKSON, JENNIE 54—Singer-supporting actress; in *Imago*, more. *(1976)*

JOHNSON, CLINT 60—Supporting actor; also a producer-writer. *(1975)*

JOHNSON, KAY 70—Blonde leading lady in DeMille's *Dynamite, Madame Satan. (1975)*

JONES, CHESTER 60s—Black character; in *Legend of Hillbilly John*, more. *(1975)*

JORDAN, LOUIS 66—Famed sax-playing bandleader; in *Follow the Boys. (1975)*

JOSLIN, HOWARD 67 ——Played "Gus Keogh" in *Detective Story*; also in *Quebec*, etc. *(1975)*

JUSTICE, JAMES ROBERTSON 70—Beefy bearded surgeon in England's "Doctor" pix. *(1975)*

KALICH, JACOB 83—Yiddish theater veteran; was Yankel in *Fiddler on the Roof.(1975)*

KELLERMAN, ANNETTE 87—Swimmer, star of silents: *A Daughter of the Gods*, etc. *(1975)*

KINSELLA, WALTER 74—TV-radio-stage actor; was in The *Tatooed Stranger. (1975)*

KIRK, JOE 71—Comic support in *Margin for Error, Pistol Packin' Mama*, etc. *(1975)*

KNIGHT, FUZZY 74—Comic saddle pal of Johnny Mack Brown; was a Top 10 Cowboy in '46. *(1976)*

KNOTT, ELSE 63—A principal player with Germany's Ufa; in *Morgenrot*, etc. *(1975)*

LA MARR, RICHARD 79—Support in Pearl White serials; with Pathe from 1917. *(1975)*

LANDIS, CULLEN 79—He starred in silents and 1st all-talkie, *Lights of New York. (1975)*

LARRIMORE, FRANCINE 77—Starred in '37 in *John Meade's Woman* with Edward Arnold. *(1975)*

LAX, FRANCES 80—Character; in Jerry Lewis' *The Family Jewels*, etc. *(1975)*

LEAL, MILAGROS 73—Spanish character actress; in *The Nail* ('49), etc. *(1975)*

LEE, LEONA —Supporting actress. *(1975)*

LEE, RUTH 79—Support in *Sensations of 1945, Whirlpool*, etc. *(1975)*

LEIGHTON, MARGARET 53—English star; nominated for Supporting Oscar in *The Go-Between. (1976)*

LETTIERI, AL 47—Played burly hoods in *The Godfather* (Sollozzo), *The Getaway*, etc. *(1975)*

LINDSAY, KEVIN 51—Support in British pix. *(1975)*

LIVESEY, ROGER 69—English star; in *I Know Where I'm Going, Drums*, many more. *(1976)*

LOHR, MARIE 84—British dowager; "Mrs. Higgins" in *Pygmalion*; in *Major Barbara. (1975)*

LORD, PHILLIPS H. 73—Created and played "Seth Parker" in *Way Back Home. (1975)*

LORRAINE, LEOTA 80s—Was "Mrs. Belknap-Jackson" in *Ruggles of Red Gap* ('35). *(1975)*

LOSCH, TILLY 70s—Exotic dancer-actress; *The Good Earth, Duel in the Sun*, etc. *(1975)*

LUEDERS, GUENTHER 70—Top character in Germany's *Fraulein Liselott*, many more. *(1975)*

LUNDIGAN, WILLIAM 61—Leading man in 125 in 38 years. *Pinky, Dishonored Lady*, etc. *(1975)*

LYON, THERESE —Character; in *A Letter for Evie, Half Angel*, more. *(1975)*

MABLEY, JACKIE "MOMS" 78—Black comedienne; starred in 1974's *Amazing Grace. (1975)*

MacGILL, MOYNA 80—A. Lansbury's character actress-mom; in many of the '40s. *(1975)*

MacKENZIE, GEORGE 74—British magician; in several movies. *(1975)*

MADISON, C. J. 67—Circus elephant trainer; was onscreen in *Jumbo*. *(1975)*

MADISON, NOEL 77—Played criminals in *Little Caesar, Manhattan Melodrama,* etc. *(1975)*

MAIN, MARJORIE 85—Raucous-voiced character; in 100; starred as "Ma Kettle." *(1975)*

MARCH, FREDRIC 77—Won Oscars in *Dr. Jekyll and Mr. Hyde, The Best Years of Our Lives*. *(1975)*

MARK, MICHAEL 88—Horror pix vet: *Frankenstein, The Mummy's Hand,* many more. *(1975)*

MARLOWE, MARILYN 48—Actress and look-alike stand-in for Marilyn Monroe. *(1975)*

MARSHALL, GEORGE 83—Famed director (*Destry Rides Again*); began as actor in '12. *(1975)*

MASON, BUDDY —Supporting actor. *(1975)*

MATHIESON, MUIR 64—British music director; onscreen in *The Seventh Veil*. *(1975)*

McCOY, BILL 75—Supporting player. *(1975)*

McEVOY, DOROTHEA 79—Onscreen from 1915; in many Universal silents. *(1976)*

McGIVER, JOHN 62—Big, bald, slow-talking; *Breakfast at Tiffany's, Fitzwilly*. *(1975)*

McGRATH, MICHAEL —Stage actor; support in a few pix. *(1976)*

McGUIRK, HARRIET 72—Roller skate champ; was in a few pix. *(1975)*

McINTYRE, MARION 90—Support at Paramount and MGM from '37 until '61. *(1975)*

MEDWICK, JOE 63—Support in *The Ninth Inning* ('42), etc. *(1975)*

MERANDE, DORO 70s—Thin, humorous character; *Our Town; Kiss Me, Stupid;* etc. *(1975)*

MEYER, TORBEN 90—Big-nosed Sturges "regular"; *Hail the Conquering Hero,* etc. *(1975)*

MILLER, RUBY 86—England's music hall "Gaiety Girl"; in *Sorrell and Son,* etc. *(1976)*

MINEO, SAL 37—Oscar-nominated (Support) in *Rebel Without a Cause* and *Exodus*. *(1976)*

MITCHELL, LESLIE 70—Commentator for British Movietone News. *(1975)*

MOORE, REX 75—Support in numerous Buster Crabbe pix. *(1975)*

MORGAN, DAN —Character; in *Charly,* etc. *(1975)*

MORGAN, RAY —Radio-TV actor-announcer; narrated 1950's *Congolaise*. *(1975)*

MORRIS, BARBOURA 43—Appeared in *The Helen Keller Story*. *(1975)*

MORRISON, CHESTER —Was in "Our Gang." *(1975)*

MORTON, CLIVE 71—Character in 60 British pix: *The Lavender Hill Mob, Jassy,* etc. *(1975)*

MYLONG, JOHN 82—Austrian; in 100; was Power's dad in *The Eddy Duchin Story*. *(1975)*

NELSON, OZZIE 68—Genial TV "family man"; onscreen in *The Impossible Years,* etc. *(1975)*

NERVO, JIMMY 85—Teamed with Teddy Knox in England's "Crazy Gang" comedies. *(1975)*

NIELSEN, INGVARD —Supporting actress. *(1975)*

NIESEN, GERTRUDE 62—Sultry song star; in *Rookies on Parade, Start Cheering,* etc. *(1975)*

ODIN, SUSAN —Support; in *The Eddie Cantor Story, Girls in the Night,* etc. *(1975)*

OLIVER, EDDIE 69—Bandleader; onscreen in '53 in *Easy to Love*. *(1976)*

OLMSTED, GERTRUDE 70—Star of silents; *Babbitt, Empty Hands, Puppets,* etc. *(1975)*

O'NIEL, COLETTE 80—British character actress. *(1975)*

ORLOVA, LYUBOV —Russian actress; in *Petersburg Nights, Moscow Laughs,* more. *(1975)*

ORNELLAS, NORMAN 36—Support in *Serpico*. *(1975)*

PALMER, CHARLES "CHUCK" 46—Support; in movies 21 years. *(1976)*

PARDEE, "DOC" 90—Support in Tom Mix pix: *Wild Horse Mesa, The Vanishing American. (1975)*

PARKER, SETH 73—See Phillips H. Lord, above. *(1975)*

PARKS, LARRY 60—Starred in *The Jolson Story* (Oscar-nominated), many more. *(1975)*

PATTEN, DOROTHY 70—Character in many, including *Botany Bay. (1975)*

PATTERSON, ALBERT —Supporting actor. *(1975)*

PATTERSON, HANK 86—Support in Westerns: *Relentless, Abilene Town*, many more. *(1975)*

PATTERSON, TROY 49—Hollywood actor who worked mainly in made-in-Italy pix. *(1975)*

PEERS, JOAN 65—Winsome leading lady in R. Cromwell's *Tol'able David*; many more. *(1975)*

PENN, LEONARD 68—Support. In *The Firefly, Marie Antoinette, Bachelor Mother*, etc. *(1975)*

PEPITO 79—"The Spanish Clown"; in *Annabel Takes a Tour, Tropic Holiday*, etc. *(1975)*

PHILIPS, MARY 74—J. Caulfield's mother in *Dear Ruth, Dear Wife*; in many more. *(1975)*

PIERSEN, ARTHUR 73—Support in *You Belong to Me, Air Hostess, Rackety Rax*, etc. *(1975)*

POLAN, LOU 71—B'way veteran; character role in *Across the River. (1976)*

PONS, LILY 71—Met coloratura; starred in *I Dream Too Much, That Girl From Paris*, etc. *(1976)*

PUGLIA, FRANK 86—Great support from *Orphans of the Storm* to *Cry Tough* ('59). *(1975)*

PUTNAM, GEORGE —Supporting actor. *(1975)*

RATHBUN, JANET 70s—Support; sister-in-law of the late Charles Winninger. *(1975)*

RAY, JACK 58—Played "Freckles" in "Our Gang" in silents. *(1975)*

REES, EDWARD RANDOLPH 57—Supporting actor in movies. *(1976)*

RENN, KATHARINA 62—French character; in *The Rise of Louis XIV*, others. *(1975)*

RICHTER, HANS 87—Director (*Dreams That Money Can Buy*); in many German films. *(1976)*

RIVERO, JULIAN 85—Character in many: *Dancing Pirate, The Outlaw, The Reward*, etc. *(1976)*

ROBBINS, ARCHIE 62—Comic master of ceremonies (Army Cpl.) in *Winged Victory. (1975)*

ROBERTS, ROY 69—Stalwart character; 900 pix in 40 years; *Guadalcanal Diary*, etc. *(1975)*

ROBESON, PAUL 77—Black singer-actor; starred in *The Emperor Jones, Show Boat*, more. *(1976)*

ROCCO, MAURICE 56—Black boogie-woogie pianist; in *Incendiary Blonde. (1976)*

ROSE, HARRY 57—Minor roles in dozens in a 30-year career in movies. *(1975)*

ROSENBLOOM, "SLAPSIE" MAXIE 71—Did funny dimwits for three decades in dozens. *(1976)*

ROSENTHAL, MARA 81—Russian; starred in Eisenstein short *Romance Sentimentale. (1975)*

ROSS, DAVID 84—In the '30s narrated *The Fight for Peace, Isle of Paradise. (1975)*

ROSS, MYRNA 36—Support; in *The Swinger*, more. *(1975)*

ROSS, SHIRLEY 62—Blonde Paramount song star; *Thanks for the Memory, Waikiki Wedding*, etc. *(1975)*

RUSSELL, EVELYN 49—Supporting actress from Broadway; in *92 in the Shade*, etc. *(1976)*

RYAN, SHEILA 54—Brunette lead in 20th B's: *Dressed to Kill, Dead Men Tell*, etc. *(1975)*

SAYRE, BIGELOW 60s—Character; "Detective Ross" in Holden's *Union Station. (1975)*

SCHIOTZ, AKSEL 68—Famed Danish tenor; starred abroad in *I Have Lived and Loved. (1975)*

SERVAIS, JEAN 65—French star; in *He Who Must Die* (Pope Fotis), *Rififi* (gang leader), etc. *(1976)*

SHELTON, JAMES 62—Was youthful support in silents: *Over the Hill, City Lights. (1975)*

SHIELDS, FRANK 66—Tennis champ; acted in

Murder in the Fleet, Come and Get It. (1975)

SHIPSTAD, ROY 64—Ice show star-producer; in *Ice Follies of 1939. (1975)*

SHUTTA, ETHEL 79—Song star; featured in Cantor's *Whoopee!* (in her B'way role). *(1976)*

SIMON, MICHEL 80—Portly, homely French star; *Beauty and the Devil*, dozens more. *(1975)*

SINGLETON, ZUTTY 77—Black jazz drummer; in *Stormy Weather* and *New Orleans. (1975)*

SLATER, JOHN 58—In many British pix: *Passport to Pimlico, 48 Hours*, etc. *(1975)*

SMITH, TOM 84—Veteran character; in dozens of Westerns from 1930. *(1976)*

SOUSSANIN, NICHOLAS 86—Support in silents (*A Gentleman of Paris*), many talkies. *(1975)*

SPAAK, CHARLES 71—Belgian scriptwriter (*Panic*, etc.); narrated *Man to Men. (1975)*

STENGEL, CASEY 85—Colorful baseball manager; onscreen in *Safe at Home* ('41). *(1975)*

STEVENSON, ROBERT 60—Support; in *White Heat* ('34), *I Was a Male War Bride*, etc. *(1975)*

STRAUSS, ROBERT 61—Comic; nominated for Supporting Oscar as "Stosh" in *Stalag 17. (1975)*

STRONG, STEVE —Supporting actor. *(1975)*

SUBJECT, EVELYN 80s—Played supporting roles in Essanay and Vitagraph silents. *(1975)*

SULLY, FRANK 67—Small, beaming character; in 1,200: *The More the Merrier*, etc. *(1975)*

SZATHMARY, ALBERT —Supporting actor. *(1975)*

TANNY, MARK —Supporting actor. *(1975)*

TEAL, RAY 74—Character in 200 (*Ramrod, No Way Out, Ace in the Hole*, etc.). *(1976)*

TETLEY, WALTER 60—Was young support in *Lord Jeff, Spirit of Culver*, more. *(1975)*

THOR, LARRY 59—Character; in *The Amazing Colossal Man, Let's Make Love*, more. *(1976)*

TIDBLAD, INGA 73—Swedish character actress; in *The Pistol, For Her Sake*, etc. *(1975)*

TREACHER, ARTHUR 81—Movies' grand English butler; viewed world with icy disdain. *(1975)*

TROTTER, JOHN SCOTT 67—Crosby's music conductor; in *Rhythm on the River*, etc. *(1975)*

UPTON, FRANCES 71—Comedienne; in movies and on the stage. *(1975)*

URE, MARY 42—Blonde British star; nominated for Supporting Oscar in *Sons and Lovers. (1975)*

WAGNER, MAX 74—Character in many: *The Roaring Twenties, Dancing Pirate*, etc. *(1975)*

WALKER, LILLIAN 88—Lovely, dimpled Vitagraph star from '11; *Kitty Mackaye*, etc. *(1975)*

WALKER, WALLY 74—Support in many from 1920 to 1963. *(1975)*

WARDE, ANTHONY 66—A heavy in serials (*Buck Rogers*) and many features from '38. *(1975)*

WATTIS, RICHARD 62—Thin, bald, bespectacled support in 100 British pix. *(1975)*

WELLMAN, WILLIAM A. 79—Director of *Wings*, etc.; acted in silents of the '20s. *(1975)*

WENDELL, HOWARD 67—Support in *Affair in Trinidad, The Big Heat*, many more. *(1975)*

WERY, CARL 77—German actor; support in European pix: *Heidi, Angelika*, etc. *(1975)*

WESSON, GENE 54—Half of the comedy team The Wesson Brothers, with Dick. *(1975)*

WEST, BILLY 82—He starred in "Billy West Comedies," silent two-reelers. *(1975)*

WHIPPER, LEIGH 98—Fine black character; *Of Mice and Men, The Ox-Bow Incident. (1975)*

WHITE, VALERIE 59—Leading lady in England's *Hue and Cry, Half-Way House*, etc. *(1975)*

WILLIAMS, O. T. "CHALKY" 68—Support in Westerns. *(1976)*

WILLS, BOB 70—C&W song star; in *Go West, Young Lady*; wrote "San Antonio Rose." *(1975)*

WRIGHT, ED —Supporting actor. *(1975)*

YEATS, MURRAY 65—Support in a few pix; primarily a stage actor. *(1975)*

"LOST" PLAYERS

Among the following performers you will find stars, starlets, serial players, character actors, bit players, ingenues, leading ladies of Westerns, specialty performers, one-movie "sensations," and, in a separate list, yesterday's children of the screen. The best efforts on the part of the author have failed to pinpoint their present whereabouts. The author would appreciate hearing from readers who might know where they are today—or from the players themselves. Letters should be addressed to the author, c/o the publisher: Arlington House, New Rochelle, N.Y. 10801.

ADAIR, ALICE (The Wild Party)
ADAMS, CAROL (Ridin' on a Rainbow)
ADAMS, JANE (Lost City of the Jungle: serial)
AGNEW, ROBERT (Gold Diggers of 1933)
AINSLEE, MARY (The Spider Returns: serial)
AINSWORTH, CUPID (Cafe Society)
ALDRICH, KAY (Navy Blues)
ALEXANDER, KATHARINE (Kiss and Tell)
ALEXANDER, RICHARD (Donovan's Kid)
ALLAN, RICHARD (The Egyptian)
ALLEN, DREW (Aerial Gunner)
ALLEN, FLORENCE (The Ace of Scotland Yard: serial)
AMANN, BETTY (The White Devil)
AMES, ROSEMARY (I Believed in You)
ANDERS, CAROL (The Bullfighters)
ANDERSON, AGNES (Vanessa: Her Love Story)
ANDERSON, EVE (Perils of the Wilderness: serial)
ANDERSON, ROBERT (The Hun Within)
ANDREWS, SLIM ("Tex Ritter" Westerns)
ANDROIT, POUPEE (All Quiet on the Western Front)
ARDELL, ALICE (Go West, Young Man)
ARGYLE, PEARL (Chu Chin Chow)
ARMIDA (La Conga Nights)
ARTHUR, LOUISE (Lucy Gallant)
AUBERT, LENORE (They Got Me Covered)
AUBREY, JIMMY (China Slaver)
AUSTIN, CHARLOTTE (Pawnee)
AUSTIN, WILLIAM (The Man from Blankley's)
AVERY, TED (Kid Monk Baroni)
BAILEY, RICHARD (Manhunt of Mystery Island: serial)
BALDWIN, ROBERT (Meet Doctor Christian)
BALENDA, CARLA (Sealed Cargo)
BANNISTER, MONICA (The Mystery of the Wax Museum)
BARCENA, CATALINA (Mama)
BARCLAY, JOAN (Shadow of Chinatown: serial)
BARRETT, CLAUDIA (Taggart)
BARRETT, EDITH (Ladies in Retirement)
BARRIE, MONA (I Met Him in Paris)

BARRINGTON, PHYLLIS (Ten Nights in a Barroom)
BARRY, PHYLLIS (Affairs of Cappy Ricks)
BARTLETT, MICHAEL (Follow Your Heart)
BARTON, "BUZZ" (The Boy Rider)
BARTON, CHARLES (Rose Bowl)
BARTON, FINIS (My Pal the King)
BARTON, JOAN (Lone Star Midnight)
BARY, JEAN (June Moon)
BEATTY, LAURI (Libelled Lady)
BECK, ALFRED F. (Trailed by Three)
BECK, THOMAS (Charlie Chan in Paris)
BEDFORD, BARBARA (The Last of the Mohicans: '22)
BEEBE, MARJORIE (Rackety Rax)
BEECHER, SYLVIA (Innocents of Paris)
BEKASSY, STEPHEN (A Song to Remember)
BELFORD, BARBARA (silents)
BELMONT, VIRGINIA (Dangers of the Canadian Mounted: serial)
BENEDICT, JEAN (Blondes at Work)
BENEDICT, RICHARD (Race Street)
BENNETT, EDNA (Ladies of the Big House)
BENNETT, FRAN (King of the Carnival: serial)
BENNETT, LEILA (Fury)
BENTON, DEAN (Hard Rock Harrigan)
BERGEN, CONSTANCE (Turn Off the Moon)
BERGER, HARRIS (Little Tough Guys in Society)
BESTAR, BARBARA (Man with the Steel Whip: serial)
BILBROOK, LYDIA (Mexican Spitfire at Sea)
BILLER, IRENE (The Man Who Dared)
BILLINGTON, FRANCELLA (Blind Husbands)
BLACKLEY, DOUGLAS (Shoot to Kill)
BLACKWOOD, GEORGE (I Loved a Woman)
BLAKE, GLADYS (Andy Hardy Meets Debutante)
BLAKE, PAMELA/a.k.a. ADELE PEARCE (The Omaha Trail)
BLAKEWELL, WILLIAM (Hop Harrigan: serial)
BLINN, BEATRICE (Born to Dance)
BOLES, GLEN (The Quitter)
BOND, RICHARD (Condemned Women)
BONDERESS, BARBARA (Queen Christina)

BONNER, PRISCILLA *(The Strong Man)*
BOOTH, KARIN *(Unfinished Dance)*
BORLAND, CAROL *(Mark of the Vampire)*
BOURNE, WHITNEY *(The Mad Miss Manton)*
BOWERS, KENNY *(Best Foot Forward)*
BOWKER, ALDRICH *(Angels Wash Their Faces)*
BOYD, MILDRED *(Merrily We Go to Hell)*
BRADFORD, JOHN *(365 Nights in Hollywood)*
BRADFORD, VIRGINIA *(Craig's Wife)*
BRAGGIOTTI, HERBERT *(Flying High)*
BRASNO, OLIVE *(Charlie Chan at the Circus)*
BREEDEN, JOHN *(Madame Racketeer)*
BRESLAU, JOAN *(Amateur Daddy)*
BREWSTER, CAROL *(The Belle of New York)*
BREWSTER, DIANE *(Torpedo Run)*
BREWSTER, JUNE *(Bombshell)*
BRIDGES, LORRAINE (Paramount player of '35)
BRINCKMAN, NAN *(Mr. Muggs Rides Again)*
BRINKLEY, JOHN *(Hot Rod Girl)*
BRITTON, FLORENCE *(Confessions of a Co-ed)*
BRODELET, ESTHER *(Young As You Feel)*
BRODIE, STEVE *(Home of the Brave)*
BROOKS, JEAN *(Youth Runs Wild)*
BROOKS, NORMA *(Blazing the Overland Trail:* serial)
BROWN, EVERETT *(Gone With the Wind)*
BROWN, STANLEY *(Blind Alley)*
BROX SISTERS, THE *(Singing in the Rain:* '29)
BRUCE, KATE *(Way Down East)*
BRYAN, ELLA (starlet of '40)
BUCKLAND, VEDA *(Doctor Bull)*
BUCKLAND, VERA *(The Mystery of Edwin Drood)*
BUCKLER, JOHN *(David Copperfield)*
BUCKLEY, JOHN *(Tarzan Escapes)*
BURGESS, BETTY *(Coronado)*
BURKE, FRANKIE *(Hell's Kitchen)*
BURKE, KATHLEEN *(Bulldog Drummond Strikes Back)*
BURNS, MARION *(Devil Tiger)*
BURR, EUGENE *(The Painted Lily)*
BUSHMAN, FRANCIS X., JR. *(Sins of the Children)*
BUSHMAN, LENORE *(Just a Gigolo)*
BUSHMAN, RALPH E. *(It's a Great Life)*
BUSHMAN, VIRGINIA
BUTLER, ROSITA *(Cradle Song)*
BYRON, MARION *(The Matrimonial Bed)*
CAHOON, WYN *(Who Killed Gail Preston?)*
CALLAHAN, BILL *(Chicken Every Sunday)*
CALLAHAN, MARGARET *(Seven Keys to Baldpate:* '35)
CALLEJO, CECILIA *(The Cisco Kid Returns)*
CALVERT, JOHN *(Appointment with Murder)*
CAMPAGNO, NINA *(South of Pago Pago)*
CAMPBELL, FLO (Columbia player of '39)
CANTY, MARIETTA *(Sunday Dinner for a Soldier)*
CARDENAS, ELSA *(The Brave One)*

CARLON, FRANCES (Fox player of '35)
CARLSON, JUNE *("The Jones Family" series)*
CARLYLE, AILEEN *(Too Young to Marry)*
CARMEN, JEWELL *(The Bat)*
CARPENTER, VIRGINIA *(The Lone Star Vigilantes)*
CARROLL, PEGGY (RKO player of '39)
CARROLL, VIRGINIA *(The Black Widow:* serial)
CARTER, HELENA *(River Lady)*
CARTER, JULIE *(Stagecoach War)*
CARTER, WILLIAM *(I've Always Loved You)*
CARUSO, ENRICO, JR. (Warner player of '35)
CARVER, TINA *(Hell on Frisco Bay)*
CASSINELLI, DOLORES *(Peter Ibbetson:* '21)
CASTELLO, WILLY (Universal player of '35)
CASTLE, JOAN *(Young Sinners)*
CATTELL, IRENE *(Another Language)*
CECIL, NORA *(Design for Living)*
CELLIER, ANTOINETTE *(The Great Barrier)*
CHAMBERS, JANICE (MGM player of '39)
CHAMBERS, SHIRLEY *(Melody Cruise)*
CHAMPTON, JOHN *(Panhandle)*
CHANCE, LARRY *(War Drums)*
CHANDLER, JOAN *(Humoresque)*
CHANDLER, TANIS *(Spirit of West Point)*
CHANNING, RUTH *(Broadway to Hollywood)*
CHATBURN, JEAN *(Bad Guy)*
CHESTER, HALLY *(Little Tough Guy)*
CHEVRET, LITA *(Ladies of the Jury)*
CHRISTIAN, HELEN *(Zorro Rides Again:* serial)
CHRISTOPHER, ROBERT *(The Decks Ran Red)*
CHRISTY, DOROTHY *(Playboy of Paris)*
CHRISTY, EILEEN *(I Dream of Jeannie)*
CHURCH, FRED *(The Vanishing West:* serial)
CLAIR, BERNICE *(No, No, Nanette:* '30)
CLAIRE, MARION *(Make a Wish)*
CLANCY, ELLEN/a.k.a. JANET SHAW *(Prairie Thunder)*
CLARK, JUDY *(Bruce Gentry, Daredevil of the Skies:* serial)
CLARK, KEN *(Away All Boats)*
CLARKE, BETSY ROSS *(Judge Hardy's Children)*
CLAYTON, MARGUERITE ("Broncho Billy" Westerns)
CLIFTON, DORINDA *(The Marauders)*
COLEMAN, DON *(Rough Riding Country)*
COLES, MILDRED *(Here Comes Happiness)*
COLLIER, WILLIAM, JR. *(The Fighting Gentleman)*
COLTON, SCOTT *(Women in Prison)*
COMPTON, JULIETTE *(Berkeley Square)*
CONDON, DAVID *(Tell It to the Marines)*
CONLON, TOM *(Only Yesterday)*
CONNORS, BUCK (early Western star)
CONOVER, THERESA MAXWELL *(Night Life of the Gods)*
CONWAY, LITA *(King of the Royal Mounted:* serial)

COOK, CLYDE (Blondie of the Follies)
COOLEY, HALLAM (Little Wildcat)
COOLEY, MARJORIE (The Great
Commandment)
COOPER, GEORGE (She Devils)
COOPER, INEZ (I Married an Angel)
CORAL, TITO (Marie Galante)
CORDAY, MARCELLE (Hands Across the
Table)
CORRADO, GINO (Enter Madame)
CORRELL, MADY (Midnight Madonna)
COTTON, CAROLINA (Hoedown)
COURTOT, MARGUERITE (The Cradle
Busters)
COWLING, BRUCE (The Painted Hills)
COX, JOHN (Car 99)
COX TWINS, THE (Seed)
CRANDALL, SUZI (Station West)
CRANE, FRED (Gone With the Wind)
CRANE, PHYLLIS (Ten Cents a Dance)
CRAVEN, EDDIE (The Invisible Menace)
CRAVEN, JAMES (Flying Disc Man from
Mars: serial)
CRAVEN, JOHN (Someone to Remember)
CRAWFORD, KATHRYN (New Morals for
Old)
CUMMINGS, DOROTHY (Divine Lady)
CURTIS, ROXANNE (Fox player of '32)
CURWOOD, BOB (Brand of Courage)
D'ALBROOK, SIDNEY (The Bat Whispers)
DALE, JEAN (Missing Witness)
DALE, VIRGINIA (Holiday Inn)
DAMIER, JOHN (Last of the Badmen)
DANE, PAT(RICIA) (Life Begins for Andy
Hardy)
DANN, ROGER (Crime Doctor's Gamble)
DARE, DOROTHY (Sweet Adeline)
DARLING, ANNE (The Bride of Frankenstein)
DARR, VONDELL (Scouts to the Rescue:
serial)
DAVID, MICHAEL (Let's Make Love)
DAVIS, KARL "KILLER" (Fingerprints Don't
Lie)
DAVIS, JOHNNIE (Varsity Show)
DAVIS, TYRELL (Let Us Be Gay)
D'AVRIL, YOLA (Scarlet Dawn)
DAW, MARJORIE (The Dangerous Maid)
DAY, DORIS/not the singer (Thou Shalt Not
Kill)
DAYTON, DOROTHY (Paramount player of
'39)
DEAN, JEAN (Radar Patrol vs. Spy King:
serial)
DEANE, SHIRLEY (Charlie Chan at the Races)
DE BERGH, JOANNE (Call Northside 777)
DE CARLO, PAULA (Paramount player of '39)
DEE, GLORIA (King of the Congo: serial)
DEERING, PATRICIA (The Lady Lies)
DELCAMBRE, ALFRED (So Red the Rose)
DELL, CLAUDIA (Scandal for Sale)
DELROY, IRENE (The Life of the Party)
DEMETRIO, ANNA (McFadden's Flats)

DENNETT, JILL (The Devil Is a Woman)
DE NOVARA, MEDEA/a.k.a. MEDEA
NOVARA (The Mad Empress)
DESMOND, MARY JO (The Last Frontier:
serial)
DEVEREAUX, HELEN (The Scarlet Clue)
DE VORSKA, JESSIE (The Last Parade)
DEW, EDDIE (Army Surgeon)
DEXTER, ANTHONY (Valentino)
DILLAWAY, DONALD (Mr. Lemon of Orange)
DIONE, ROSE (Bringing Up Father)
DIX, DOROTHY (Guns and Guitars)
DIX, TOMMY (Best Foot Forward)
DIXON, JOAN (The Law of the Badlands)
DORAN, MARY (The Divorcee)
DORE, ADRIENNE (The Famous Ferguson
Case)
DOUGLAS, SUSAN (Lost Boundaries)
DOUGLAS, TOM (Road to Reno)
DOUGLAS, WARREN (God Is My Co-Pilot)
DOVER, NANCY (Dynamite)
DOWNS, CATHY (My Darling Clementine)
DOYLE, ADALYN (Advice to the Lovelorn)
DOYLE, MARY (Beloved Brat)
DRAKE, ALLYN (Columbia player of '35)
DRAKE, CLAUDIA (Border Patrol)
DRAKE, PEGGY (King of the Mounties: serial)
DREW, ROLAND (Evangeline)
DREXEL, NANCY (Four Devils)
DRURY, NORMA (The Mystery of Marie
Roget)
DUDGEON, ELSPETH (Sh! The Octopus)
DUDLEY, FLORENCE (Party Girl)
DUFF, AMANDA (Mr. Moto in Danger Island)
DUGAY, YVETTE (Hiawatha)
DUGGAN, JAN (Thanks for Everything)
DUNCAN, ARLETTA (Marriage Forbidden)
DUNCAN, CHARLES (Newsboys' Home)
DUNCAN, JOHN (Batman and Robin: serial)
DUNSTEAD, SHIRLEY (Wild Boys of the
Road)
DURANT, JACK (The Singing Kid)
D'USE, MARGO (The Lost City: serial)
DUVAL, DIANE (The Phantom of the West:
serial)
DWAN, DOROTHY (Fighting Legion)
EARL, ELIZABETH (River's End)
EARLE, EDWARD (Spite Marriage)
EARLY, MARGARET (Stage Door Canteen)
EATON, DORIS (The Very Idea)
EDDY, HELEN JEROME (The Great Meadow)
EDEN, ALICE (Career)
EDWARDS, BRUCE (The Black Widow: serial)
ELDER, RUTH (Moran of the Mounties)
ELLIOTT, EDYTHE (Show Them No Mercy)
ELLIOTT, LORRAINE (a 1940 starlet)
EMORY, RICHARD (Perils of the Wilderness:
serial)
ENGELS, WERA (The Great Jasper)
ERICSON, HELEN (Wife, Husband and
Friend)
ERNST, LEILA (Life with Henry)

ESTABROOK, HOWARD *(The Mysteries of Myra:* serial)
ESTRELLA, ESTHER *(Prairie Pioneers)*
EVANS, MURIEL *(The Prizefighter and the Lady)*
EYTON, BESSIE *(The Crisis)*
FAIR, FLORENCE *(The Florentine Dagger)*
FAIRBANKS, BILL *(Devil's Door Yard)*
FAIRBANKS, LUCILLE *(Klondike Fury)*
FARLEY, DOT *(Should a Girl Marry)*
FARLEY, PATRICIA *(King of the Jungle)*
FARRINGTON, BETTY *(Anybody's War)*
FAY, VIVIEN *(A Day at the Races)*
FENTON, LESLIE *(Marie Galante)*
FENWICK, JEAN *(Ellery Queen and the Murder Ring)*
FIELD, CHARLOTTE *(Pride of the West)*
FIELDING, MARGARET *(Nancy Steele Is Missing)*
FILMER, JUNE *(One Man's Journey)*
FISCHER, MARGARITA *(Uncle Tom's Cabin)*
FISKE, RICHARD *(Homicide Bureau)*
FLEMING, ALICE *(Sheriff of Redwood Valley)*
FLETCHER, TEX *(Six-Gun Rhythm)*
FLINT, SAM *(Florida Special)*
FORBES, HAZEL *(Down to Their Last Yacht)*
FORBES, MADELINE *(Wilson)*
FORD, DOROTHY *(Let's Go Navy)*
FORD, GRACE *(The Devil Doll)*
FORMAN, CAROL *(The Black Widow:* serial)
FORREST, ANN *(Love's Boomerang)*
FORREST, MABEL *(Hollywood Boulevard)*
FOSTER, PHOEBE *(Our Betters)*
FOWLER, ALMEDA *(Damaged Lives)*
FOXE, EARLE *(Dance, Fools, Dance)*
FOY, GLORIA *(Dancing Lady)*
FRANCIS, NOEL *(Ladies of the Big House)*
FRANCIS, WILMA *(Lady, Be Careful)*
FRANKLIN, GLORIA *(Drums of Fu Manchu)*
FRANQUELLI, FELY *(The Leopard Man)*
FREEMAN, HELEN *(Symphony of Six Million)*
FROOS, SYLVIA *(Stand Up and Cheer)*
FULLER, DALE *(The Glad Rag Doll)*
FULLER, MARY *(What Happened to Mary)*
FUNG, WILLY *(Maisie)*
GABRIEL, LYNN *(Heart of the West)*
GALE, ROBERTA *(Girl of the Rio)*
GALLAUDET, JOHN *(Sing, You Sinners)*
GALLAGHER, CAROLE *(The Falcon Out West)*
GALLOWAY, MORGAN *(Lena Rivers)*
GARVIN, ANITA *(The Play Girl)*
GARWOOD, WILLIAM *(Cymbeline:* '13)
GAZE, GWEN *(The Secret of Treasure Island:* serial)
GENTRY, RACE *(Black Horse Canyon)*
GEORGE, FLORENCE *(College Swing)*
GEORGE, JOHN *(Island of Lost Souls)*
GEORGE, SUE *(Undersea Girl)*
GERBER, NEVA *(The Trail of the Octopus:* serial)

GERRARD, CHARLES *(Dracula)*
GERRARD, DOUGLAS *(General Crank)*
GERRITS, PAUL *(Stolen Harmony)*
GIBSON, DIANA *(The Phantom Rider:* serial)
GILBERT, HELEN *(Florian)*
GILBERT, LYNN *(Wild West Days)*
GILMAN, FRED *(The Outlaw and the Lady)*
GITTLESON, JUNE *(Mark of the Vampire)*
GIVOT, GEORGE *(Riffraff)*
GOLM, LISA *(Journey for Margaret)*
GOODALL, GRACE *(Handy Andy)*
GORCEY, DAVID *(Little Tough Guys in Society)*
GORDON, KITTY *(The Interloper)*
GORDON, MAUDE TURNER *(Living on Velvet)*
GOVER, MILDRED *(Daytime Wife)*
GRAHAM, BETTY JANE *(Night Nurse)*
GRAHAM, RONALD *(Ladies of Washington)*
GRANDSTEDT, GRETA *(Manhattan Parade)*
GRANT, FRANCES *(Red River Valley)*
GRANT, HELENA *(Quality Street)*
GRAVES, RALPH *(Ladies of Leisure)*
GRAY, ALEXANDER *(Song of the Flame)*
GRAY, DOROTHY *(Princess O'Hara)*
GREENWAY, TOM *(Last of the Badmen)*
GREENWOOD, WINIFRED *(To the Last Man)*
GREGORY, ELEANOR (MGM player of '32)
GREY, ANNE *(Break of Hearts)*
GREY, OLGA *(Intolerance)*
GREY, SHIRLEY *(The Life of Jimmy Dolan)*
GRIFFITH, ELEANOR *(Alibi)*
GUY, EULA *(The Spider Woman Strikes Back)*
HAGMAN, HARRIET *(Thirteen Women)*
HALE, GRACE *(Front Page Woman)*
HALL, EVELYN *(Lovers Courageous)*
HALL, MARIAN *(The Gorilla Man)*
HAMPTON, GRACE *(Gigolette)*
HANSEN, ELEANOR *(Flaming Frontiers:* serial)
HARDING, KAY *(The Mummy's Curse)*
HARDING, TEX (in Paramount Westerns)
HARE, MARILYN *(Angels With Broken Wings)*
HARRIS, BRAD *(It Happened in Athens)*
HARRIS, EDNA MAY *(The Green Pastures)*
HARRIS, MARCIA *(So's Your Old Man)*
HARRIS, MARION *(Devil May Care)*
HARRIS, TERESA *(Baby Face)*
HARRIS, WINIFRED *(The Kid from Kokomo)*
HARRISON, IRMA *(One Exciting Night)*
HARTLEY, JOHN *(Million Dollar Legs)*
HARTMAN, GRETCHEN *(The College Coquette)*
HARVEY, GRISELDA *(The Informer)*
HASWELL, ARA *(Second Hand Wife)*
HATCHER, MARY *(Variety Girl)*
HAWKS, FRANK *(The Mysterious Pilot:* serial)
HAWORTH, ETHYL (RKO player of '39)
HAYES, BERNADENE *(Prison Nurse)*
HAYES, LINDA *(Mexican Spitfire out West)*
HAZARD, JAYNE *(The Powers Girl)*
HEALY, EUNICE *(Follow Your Heart)*

HEATHER, JEAN *(Double Indemnity)*
HENDERSON, MARCIA *(All I Desire)*
HENRY, GALE *(Merton of the Movies)*
HENRY, LOUISE *(The Casino Murder Case)*
HERRICK, VIRGINIA *(Roar of the Iron Horse:* serial*)*
HILLIE, VERNA *(Under the Tonto Rim)*
HILLS, BEVERLY *(Young Dillinger)*
HOCTOR, HARRIET *(The Great Ziegfeld)*
HOFFMAN, OTTO *(Death Takes a Holiday)*
HOHL, ARTHUR *(Bad Man of Brimstone)*
HOLDEN, GLORIA *(Behind the Rising Sun)*
HOLMES, PEE WEE *(Double Cinched)*
HOLT, ULA *(The New Adventures of Tarzan:* serial*)*
HOPE, GLORIA *(The Law of the North)*
HOTELEY, MAE *(Mountain Mother)*
HOUSE, NEWTON *(The Final Reckoning:* serial*)*
HOUSTON, JOSEPHINE *(On With the Show)*
HOWARD, ANNE *(Princess O'Hara)*
HOWARD, JUNE *(Adventures of Captain Africa:* serial*)*
HOWE, DOROTHY/a.k.a. VIRGINIA VALE *(King of Alcatraz)*
HOWELL, KENNETH *("The Jones Family"* series)
HOWELL, LOTTICE *(In Gay Madrid)*
HOWELL, VIRGINIA *(They Just Had to Get Married)*
HOXIE, AL (Western star)
HUGHES, KAY *(Every Saturday Night)*
HUGHES, ROY (Western star)
HUGHES, STANLEY *(Secrets of a Nurse)*
HULETTE, GLADYS *(Tol'able David)*
HUMES, FRED *(Hurricane Kid)*
HUNT, ROGER (RKO player of '39)
HUNTLEY, G.P., JR. *(Little Man, What Now?)*
HURLBURT, GLADYS *(A Man Called Peter)*
HUTCHINSON, CHARLES (early serial star)
HUTTON, BEULAH *(Danger Island:* serial*)*
HYLAND, PEGGY (Fox star of '17)
INCE, ADA *(The Vanishing Shadow:* serial*)*
IRVING, MARGARET *(Thanks a Million)*
IRVING, MARY JANE *(Lovey Mary)*
IVERS, ROBERT *(G.I. Blues)*
IVO, TOMMY *(Earl Carroll's Vanities)*
JAMES, GARDNER *(The Studio Murder Mystery)*
JANIS, DOROTHY *(The Pagan)*
JANNEY, WILLIAM *(Cimarron: '31)*
JARRETT, JANICE (a starlet of '36)
JAYNES, BETTY *(Babes in Arms)*
JENSEN, EULALIE *(Up Pops the Devil)*
JOHNSON, EMORY *(In the Name of the Law)*
JOHNSON, JUNE *(Lone Star Raiders)*
JOHNSON, LINDA *(Brick Bradford:* serial*)*
JOHNSON, NOBLE *(Mamba)*
JOHNSON, WALTER *(Bright Eyes)*
JONES, OLIVE *(The Goose and the Gander)*
JORDAN, MIRIAM *(I Loved You Yesterday)*
JOYCE, JEAN *(Outlaws of Sonora)*

JOYNER, JOYZELLE *(Just Imagine)*
JUDELS, CHARLES *(Captain Thunder)*
KAISER, HELEN *(Rio Rita: '29)*
KANE, KATHRYN *(Spirit of Culver)*
KAY, KAROL *(Second Hand Wife)*
KAY, MARY ELLEN *(Government Agents vs. Phantom Legion:* serial*)*
KAYE, CLAUDELLE *(Manhattan Melodrama)*
KEANE, EDWARD *(Charlie Chan in Panama)*
KEANE, RAYMOND *(The Lone Eagle)*
KECKLEY, JANE *(The Quitter)*
KEENE, RICHARD *(Her Golden Calf)*
KEITH, DONALD *(Just Off Broadway)*
KEITH, JANE *(The Sea Wolf: '30)*
KEITH, ROSALIND *(Poppy)*
KELLARD, ROBERT *(Time Out for Murder)*
KELLY, JEANNE *(Riders of Death Valley:* serial*)*
KENNEDY, BILL *(The Royal Mounted Rides Again:* serial*)*
KENNEDY, DAUN *(The Royal Mounted Rides Again:* serial*)*
KENNEDY, PHYLLIS *(Vivacious Lady)*
KENT, DOROTHEA *(Having Wonderful Time)*
KENT, LARRY *(The Heart of a Follies Girl)*
KENYON, GWEN *(The Cisco Kid in Old New Mexico)*
KIBBEE, MILTON *(California Mail)*
KING, CARLOTTA *(The Desert Song: '29)*
KING, JOSEPH *(Satan Met a Lady)*
KING, JUDY *(Our Neighbors, the Carters)*
KINGDON, EDITH *(Once a Lady)*
KIRBY, MICHAEL *(The Countess of Monte Cristo)*
KIRBY, OLLIE *(Social Pirates)*
KIROV, IVAN *(Specter of the Rose)*
KNAPP, ROBERT *(Gunmen from Laredo)*
KNIGHT, FELIX *(The Bohemian Girl)*
KNIGHT, JUNE *(Broadway Melody of 1935)*
KOLK, SCOTT *(All Quiet on the Western Front)*
KOMAI, TETSU *(Chinatown Nights)*
KOSHETZ, MARINA *(Two Sisters from Boston)*
KOSTANT, ANNA *(Street Scene)*
LA FRACONI, TERRY *(The Singer of Naples)*
LAING, JOHN *(Conspiracy)*
LAMBERT, JACK *(Bend of the River)*
LAMONG, MARTEN *(Federal Operator 99:* serial*)*
LAMONT, MOLLY *(Nora O'Neale)*
LANDRY, MARGARET *(The Leopard Man)*
LANE, NORA *(Careless Lady)*
LANE, VICKI *(The Cisco Kid Returns)*
LANG, CHARLES *(Tampico)*
LATIMER, LOUISE *(Murder on a Bridle Path)*
LAURENT, JACQUELINE *(Daybreak)*
LAWRANCE, JODY *(Ten Tall Men)*
LAWRENCE, BARBARA *(Margie)*
LAWRENCE, ROSINA *(Way Out West)*
LAWSON, PRISCILLA *(Flash Gordon:* serial*)*
LAWTON, EDDIE (Columbia player of '39)

LAYSON, LORENA (*I Loved a Woman*)
LE BRETON, FLORA (*The White Monkey*)
LE CLAIR, BLANCHE (*Jealousy*)
LEE, DORIS (*The Girl Dodger*)
LEE, JOCELYN (*The Marriage Playground*)
LEIGHTON, DONRUE (*Oh, Doctor*)
LENDER, MARY LOU (*Professor Beware*)
LEONARD, ADA (*Forty Naughty Girls*)
LEONARD, BARBARA (*Ladies of the Night Club*)
LESLIE, GLADYS (Vitagraph player of '18)
LESLIE, KAY (a starlet of '40)
LESLIE, MAXINE (*Raiders of Red Rock*)
LESSING, MARION (*Red-Haired Alibi*)
LESTER, BRUCE (*The Mysterious Doctor*)
LESTER, VICKI (*Tall, Dark and Handsome*)
LEWIS, GEORGE J. (*The Falcon in Mexico*)
LEWIS, JARMA (*The Prodigal*)
LIBAIRE, DOROTHY (*Murder on a Honeymoon*)
LIGHT, ROBERT (*Murder in the Clouds*)
LINAKER, KAY (*Charlie Chan in Reno*)
LINDEN, MARTA (*Andy Hardy's Blonde Trouble*)
LINDLEY, VIRGINIA (*The Black Widow:* serial)
LINOW, IVAN (*The Cockeyed World*)
LITTLE, ANN (*The Cradle of Courage*)
LLOYD, ALMA (*Song of the Saddle*)
LLOYD, JIMMY (*The Sea Hound:* serial)
LODER, LOTTIE (*A Soldier's Plaything*)
LOGAN, GWENDOLEN (*Christopher Strong*)
LOGAN, JANICE (*Dr. Cyclops*)
LONG, AUDREY (*Pan-Americana*)
LONG, LOTUS (*Think Fast, Mr. Moto*)
LORD, GAYLE (*Colt Comrades*)
LORING, TEALA (*The Arizona Cowboy*)
LOVETT, DOROTHY (*The Courageous Dr. Christian*)
LOWE, ELLEN (*Dancing Pirate*)
LOWRY, MORTON (*Immortal Sergeant*)
LOYD, BEVERLY (*Utah*)
LUDEN, JACK (*Shootin' Irons*)
LUEZ, LAURETTE (*Siren of Bagdad*)
LUSK, FREEMAN (*The Caddy*)
LYNN, ELEANOR (*You're Only Young Once*)
LYNN, GEORGE (*Charlie Chan at Monte Carlo*)
LYNN, LORNA (RKO player of '39)
LYONS, COLLETTE (*52nd Street*)
LYONS, EDDIE (*Declasse*)
LYS, LYA (*Confessions of a Nazi Spy*)
MacCLOY, JUNE (*Reaching for the Moon*)
MacDONALD, WALLACE (*Fifty Fathoms Deep*)
MacKELLAR, HELEN (*The Past of Mary Holmes*)
MACKINTOSH, LOUISE (*The Phantom President*)
MacLAREN, IAN (*Little Orphan Annie*)
MACE, PATSY (Paramount player of '39)
MACK, MARION (*The General*)

MACREADY, RENEE (*Lovin' the Ladies*)
MADDEN, JEANNE (*Talent Scout*)
MADISON, HELENE (*The Warrior's Husband*)
MADISON, JULIAN (*A Shot in the Dark:* '35)
MADISON, MAE (*Expensive Woman*)
MAGUIRE, MARY (*Alcatraz Island*)
MALLINSON, RORY (*Nora Prentiss*)
MANN, FRANKIE (*Trailed by Three*)
MANN, HELEN (*Ladies They Talk About*)
MANN, MARGARET (*Four Sons:* '28)
MANNING, AILEEN (*Home James*)
MANNING, KNOX (*Cheers for Miss Bishop*)
MANNING, ROBERT (*The Sign of the Cross*)
MANON, MARCIA (*They Had to See Paris*)
MANSFIELD, MARIAN (*Love in Bloom*)
MAPLE, CHRISTINE (*Roarin' Lead*)
MARDEN, ADRIENNE (*The Sound and the Fury*)
MARION, JOAN (*Black Limelight*)
MARITZA, SARI (*A Lady's Profession*)
MARLOW, LUCY (*Tight Spot*)
MARLOWE, FAYE (*The Spider*)
MARLOWE, JERRY (*Legion of Lost Flyers*)
MARQUIS, ROSALIND (*Marked Woman*)
MARSHALL, EVERETT (*Dixiana*)
MARSTON, JOEL (*The Last Voyage*)
MARTEL, JUNE (*Arizona Mahoney*)
MARTELL, GREGG (*Tonka*)
MARTIN, JILL (*Hawk of the Wilderness:* serial)
MARTIN, LOIS (*Outlaw Valley*)
MARTIN, RICHARD (*The Mysterious Mr. M.:* serial)
MARTIN, VIVIAN (*The Wishing Ring*)
MASON, VIVIAN (*The Lost Planet:* serial)
MASSEN, OSA (*A Woman's Face*)
MATTHEWS, DOROTHY (*The Doorway to Hell*)
MAXWELL, JOHN (*Murder in the Big House*)
MAY, ADA (*Dance, Girl, Dance:* '33)
MAYBELL, LOIS (Paramount player of '35)
MAYFAIR, MITZI (*Four Jills in a Jeep*)
MAYNARD, CLAIRE (*Over the Hill*)
MAYO, EDNA (*The Strange Case of Mary Page*)
McCLURE, GREGG (*The Great John L.*)
McCONNELL, MARGARET (MGM player in '38)
McDANIEL, ETTA (*The Magnificent Brute*)
McDONALD, GRACE (*Strictly in the Groove*)
McDONALD, IAN (*Ramrod*)
McGUIRE, MARCY (*Seven Days Leave*)
McHUGH, KITTY (*On Again-Off Again*)
McINTIRE, CHRISTINE (*Wanted, Dead or Alive*)
McKAY, WANDA (*The Monster Maker*)
McKEE, RAYMOND (*Babbitt*)
McKENZIE, ROBERT (*The Sombrero Kid*)
McKINNEY, FLORINE (*Horse Feathers*)
McNAMARA, MAGGIE (*The Moon Is Blue*)

McPHAIL, ADDIE (Corsair)
McVEY, PAUL (One Mile from Heaven)
MEI, TSEN (For the Freedom of the East)
MENDEZ, LUCILA (Coney Island: '28)
MERSEREAU, VIOLET (The Shepherd King)
MEREDITH, IRIS (Those High Grey Walls)
MEREDITH, MADGE (The Falcon's Adventure)
MERRIAM, CHARLOTTE (Dumbbells in Ermine)
MERRICK, DORIS (The Big Noise)
MESSENGER, GERTRUDE (Love Past Thirty)
MEYER, GRETA (Jennie Gerhardt)
MICHAELS, DOLORES (Warlock)
MILAN, LITA (The Violent Men)
MILLARD, HELENE (Broadway Bill)
MILLER, EVE (The Big Trees)
MILLER, KRISTINE (Young Daniel Boone)
MILLER, MARY LOUISE (Sparrows)
MILLS, SHIRLEY (Henry Aldrich Gets Glamour)
MITCHELL, FRANK (Double Alibi)
MITCHELL, GENEVA (False Faces)
MITROVICH, MARTA (The Dark Mirror)
MIX, RUTH (The Black Coin: serial)
MOFFETT, FRANCES (Sinners in the Sun)
MONTELL, LISA (Tomahawk Trail)
MONTI, MILLI (The Girl from Scotland Yard)
MONTGOMERY, GOODEE (Charlie Chan Carries On)
MOORE, CARLYLE, JR. (Road Gang)
MOORE, DENNIS (The Purple Monster Strikes: serial)
MOORE, DOROTHY (Blondie Meets the Boss)
MOORE, PAULINE (Young Mr. Lincoln)
MOOREHEAD, NATALIE (The Benson Murder Case)
MORALES, CARMEN (The Valley of Vanishing Men: serial)
MORRISON, JOE (Four Hours to Kill)
MORRISS, ANN (The Women)
MORTIMER, JOAN (Henry Aldrich Haunts a House)
MORTON, TOM (Main Street to Broadway)
MOULTON, ZITA (Employees' Entrance)
MOWING, HELEN (The Fighting Frontiersman)
MOYLAN, CATHERINE (Love in the Rough)
MUIR, ESTHER (The Bowery)
MURPHY, EDNA (Little Johnny Jones)
MURPHY, HORACE (Frontier Town)
MURPHY, MAURICE (Tailspin Tommy: serial)
NAMARA, MARGUERITE (Thirty Day Princess)
NASH, JACQUELINE (They Shall Have Music)
NASH, JUNE (Two Kinds of Woman)
NEAL, ELLA (Mysterious Dr. Satan: serial)
NELSON, BILLY (Hal Roach player of '35)
NEWELL, DAVID (Polo Joe)
NISSEN, GRETA (Transatlantic)
NOEL, HATTIE (Lady for a Night)
NORMAN, LUCILLE (Painting the Clouds with Sunshine)
NORRIS, RICHARD (Abie's Irish Rose: '46)
O'CONNOR, MAUREEN (Boy of the Streets)
O'DAY, NELL (The Road to Ruin)
O'HEARN, EILEEN (Thunder Over the Prairie)
OLIVER, DAVID (The Girl on the Front Page)
OLIVER, GORDON (The Spiral Staircase)
O'NEAL, ZELMA (Peach O'Reno)
O'SHEA, DANNY (The Plough and the Stars)
O'SHEA, KEVIN (The Purple Heart)
O'SULLIVAN, LAWRENCE (Delicious)
OWEN, GRANVILLE (Lil'l Abner: '40)
OWEN, TUDOR (Yankee Pasha)
PADGEON, JACK (silent Western star)
PADULA, MARGUERITA (Hit the Deck: '30)
PAGE, BRADLEY (Against the Law)
PAGE, DOROTHY (King Solomon of Broadway)
PAGE, PAUL (The Naughty Flirt)
PALANGE, INEZ (The Melody Lingers On)
PALEY, NATALIE (Sylvia Scarlett)
PALMER, SHIRLEY (This Sporting Age)
PARERA, VALENTIN (Fox player of '35)
PARKER, RAYMOND (Swing That Cheer)
PARKES, GAY (a starlet of '40)
PARMA, TULA (The Leopard Man)
PARSONS, PATSY LEE (Meet Doctor Christian)
PATRICK, DOROTHY (Till the Clouds Roll By)
PATTERSON, SHIRLEY (Batman: '43 serial)
PATTON, BILL (Lucky Spurs)
PATTON, VIRGINIA (Janie)
PAWLEY, EDWARD (White Banners)
PAYNE, SALLY (La Conga Nights)
PELLETIER, YVONNE (Cradle Song)
PEREDA, RAMON (Paramount player of '32)
PERRY, KATHRYN (Side Street)
PERRY, LINDA (California Mail)
PETERS SISTERS, THE (Ali Baba Goes to Town)
PETERSON, ELSA (Madame Satan)
PETERSON, RUTH (Charlie Chan in Paris)
PHILLIPS, DOROTHY (Jazz Cinderella)
PHILLIPS, EDDIE (Soak the Rich)
PHILLIPS, EDWARD (Sob Sister)
POGGI, GRACE (Roman Scandals)
POLK, OSCAR (Gone With the Wind)
POLLARD, DAPHNE (South Sea Rose)
POWERS, LUCILLE (Man to Man)
PREISSER, JUNE (Babes in Arms)
PRESTON, ANN (Parole)
BABA, PRINCESS (You Can't Cheat an Honest Man)
PRIOR, ALLAN (Bride of the Regiment)
PRIVAL, LUCIEN (Hell's Angels)
QUARTARO, NENA (Monsieur le Fox)
QUIGLEY, CHARLES (King of Burlesque)
QUIMBY, MARGARET (Sally of the Scandals)
RALSTON, MARCIA (The Singing Marine)
RAMSDEN, FRANCES (Mad Wednesday)
RANDALL, MEG (Ma & Pa Kettle)

RANDALL, REBEL (Happy Go Lucky)
RANDALL, STEVE (20th Century-Fox player of '39)
RANDLE, KAREN (Mysterious Island: serial)
RANSON, LOIS (Angels with Broken Wings)
RATCLIFFE, E. J. (The Jazz Age)
RAY, ALLENE (The Fortieth Floor: serial)
RAY, TERRANCE (Life Begins)
REID, VIRGINIA (RKO Player of '35)
REGAN, JAYNE (Silver Bullet)
REYNOLDS, JOYCE (Janie)
RHODES, BETTY JANE (Oh Johnny, How You Can Love)
REICHER, HEDWIGA (The Leopard Lady)
RICE, MARY ALICE (Flying Hostess)
RICH, VIVIAN (The Adventures of Jacques)
RICHARDS, JEFF (Crest of the Wave)
RICHARDSON, JACK (In the Days of Trajan)
RILEY, ELAINE (Hills of Utah)
RIO, JOANNE (Riding with Buffalo Bill: serial)
RIORDAN, MARJORIE (Stage Door Canteen)
ROBBINS, BARBARA (Hat, Coat and Glove)
ROBERTI, MAYNA (The Spider)
ROBERTS, ADELLE (Just Before Dawn)
ROBERTS, ALLENE (The Red House)
ROBERTS, BEATRICE (The Devil's Party)
ROBERTS, LEE (Blazing the Overland Trail: serial)
ROBERTSON, GUY (King Kelly of the U.S.A.)
ROCHELLE, CLAIRE (The Kid from Santa Fe)
ROGERS, JIMMY (Forty Thieves)
ROGERS, RUTH (Hidden Gold)
ROLF, TUTTA (Dressed to Thrill)
ROONEY, ANN (Henry Aldrich Gets Glamour)
RORK, ANN (Old Loves and New)
ROSS, PEGGY (Business and Pleasure)
ROY, GLORIA (Charlie Chan's Secret)
RUPPERT, CHARLES (RKO player of '39)
RUSSELL, GILBERT (Everybody Does It)
RUSSELL, MARY (Riders of the Whistling Skull)
RUTH, PHYLLIS (Louisiana Purchase)
RYAN, EDDIE (The Sullivans)
SABIN, CHARLES (Columbia player of '35)
SARGENT, ANNE (Naked City)
SAUNDERS, NANCY (Arizona Territory)
SAYERS, LORETTA (Men Are Like That)
SAYERS, MARION (Whoopee)
SCHILLING, MARGARET (Children of Dreams)
SCHUBERT, MARINA (British Agent)
SCOTT, ROBERT (The Black Arrow: serial)
SEABROOK, GAY (Half a Sinner)
SEDAN, ROLFE (Ruggles of Red Gap)
SEDGWICK, EDNA (You're a Sweetheart)
SELF, WILLIAM (The Thing)
SELWYNNE, CLARISSA (The Heart of a Follies Girl)
SEMELS, HARRY (King of the Turf)
SERGAVA, KATHRYN (Bedside)
SEVEN, TONI (a '43 starlet)

SEWARD, BILLIE (Once to Every Woman)
SHARON, JEAN (A Child Is Born)
SHEA, GLORIA (Last Days of Pompeii)
SHEFFIELD, FLORA (Charlie's Aunt: '30)
SHELDON, KATHERINE (Gold Rush Maisie)
SHELLEY, GEORGE (Wild West Days: serial)
SHELTON, MARIA (The Phantom Rider: serial)
SHELTON, MARLA (Stand-In)
SHERIDAN, GAIL (Hopalong Cassidy Returns)
SHERIDAN, MARGARET (The Thing)
SHIPMAN, GWYNNE (Trail Dust)
SHIPMAN, HELEN (Men Without Names)
SHORT, DOROTHY (The Call of the Savage: serial)
SHUMWAY, LEE (The Leathernecks)
SILVERS, SID (Transatlantic Merry-Go-Round)
SIMMS, GINNY (Shady Lady)
SINCLAIR, DIANE (Washington Masquerade)
SINGERMAN, BERTA (Fox player of '35)
"SNOWFLAKE" (FRED TOONES) (The Biscuit Eater: '40)
SOUTHERN, EVE (Fighting Caravans)
SPINDOLA, ROBERT (The Firefly)
STAFFORD, GRACE (Confessions of a Nazi Spy)
STANDING, JOAN (The Campus Flirt)
STANLEY, FORREST (The Cat and the Canary: '27)
STANLEY, KATHRYN (The Girl from Everywhere)
STANLEY, LOUISE (The Oregon Trail: serial)
STANTON, PAUL (The Road to Glory)
STAPP, MARJORIE (The Blazing Trail)
STARR, SALLY (The Sweetheart of Sigma Chi)
STEELE, MICHAEL (Command Decision)
STENGEL, LENI (The Animal Kingdom)
STEPHENS, HARVEY (The Lady Is Willing)
STEVENS, ANGELA (Without Warning)
STEVENS, ROBERT (Perils of the Royal Mounted: serial)
STEVENS, RUTHELMA (Circus Queen Murder)
STEWART, ELEANOR (Fighting Devil Dogs: serial)
STEWART, FREDDIE (Freddie Steps Out)
STEWART, LARRY (Captain Video: serial)
STOREY, EDITH (The Lady of the Lake)
STOREY, JUNE (The Lone Wolf Takes a Chance)
STRATTON, GIL, JR. (Girl Crazy)
STRICKLAND, ROBERT (Good News)
STROTHER, BILL (Safety Last)
STUART, RANDY (Sitting Pretty)
SUTTON, GERTRUDE (Sailor Be Good)
SUTTON, KAY (Carefree)
SWEET, SALLY (Universal player of '32)
TABOR, BILL (Warner player of '39)
TALBOT, HELEN (King of the Forest Rangers: serial)

TALBOTT, GLORIA (We're No Angels)
TALIAFERRO, HAL/a.k.a. WALLY WALES
(Vanishing Hooves)
TANNEN, WILLIAM (Flight Command)
TAPLEY, COLIN (Becky Sharp)
TATTERSALL, VIVA (Whispering Shadows:
serial)
TAYLOR, AVONNE (Honor Among Thieves)
TAYLOR, BRAD (Atlantic City)
TAYLOR, MARY (Soak the Rich)
TAYLOR, NORMA (The Adventures of Rex
and Rinty: serial)
TERRY, ETHELIND (Lord Byron of
Broadway)
TERRY, LINDA (Parents on Trial)
TERRY, RUTH (Rookies on Parade)
TEVIS, CAROL (Once in a Lifetime)
THAYER, TINA (A Yank at Eton)
THEBY, ROSEMARY (The Girl of the Golden
West: '23)
THEILADE, NINI (A Midsummer Night's
Dream)
THIELE, HERTHA (Maedchen in Uniform)
THOMPSON, LARRY (King of the Forest
Rangers: serial)
THOMPSON, LOTUS (Terry of the Times:
serial)
TIBBETTS, MARTHA (Ceiling Zero)
TIDBURY, ELDRED (Paramount player of '35)
TINCHER, FAY (Sally's Blighted Career)
TOBEY, RUTH (Janie)
TOBIN, VIVIAN (Bordertown)
TODD, JAMES (Charlie Chan's Chance)
TOWNE, ROSELLA (Adventures of Jane
Arden)
TRENKER, LUIS (The Doomed Battalion)
TRUAX, MAUDE (Two Against the World)
TURNELL, DEE (The Pirate)
TYRRELL, JOHN (Criminals of the Air)
VAIL, LESTER (Dance, Fools, Dance)
VAIL, MYRTLE (Myrt and Marge)
VALE, VIRGINIA/a.k.a. DOROTHY HOWE
(Three Sons)
VALENTINE, PAUL (Out of the Past)
VALERIE, JOAN (Charlie Chan at the Wax
Museum)
VALKIS, HELEN (The Old Barn Dance)
VAN DORN, MILDRED (Liliom)
VAN DYKE, MARCIA (In the Good Old
Summer Time)
VAN DYKE, TRUMAN (The Jungle Goddess:
serial)
VARNO, ROLAND (Quality Street)
VAVITCH, MICHAEL (Wolf Song)
VERRILL, VIRGINIA (Vogues)
VINCENT, ALLEN (No More Orchids)
VINCENTI, PAUL (Die Csikos Baroness)
VISCHER, BLANCA (A Message to Garcia)
VOGAN, EMMETT (Horror Island)
VOKEL, ELDA (The First Year)
VOHS, JOAN (Fort Ti)
VOLUSIA, EROS (Rio Rita: '42)

VONN, VYOLA (Burma Convoy)
VOSELLI, JUDITH (Kiss Me Again)
VYNER, MARGARET (Sailing Along)
WALCAMP, MARIE (Liberty, A Daughter of
the U.S.A.)
WALKER, NELLA (Three Smart Girls)
WALKER, POLLY (Sleepless Nights)
WALKER, RAY (Swingtime Johnny)
WALLACE, IRENE (Bleeding Hearts)
WALSH, DALE (The New Adventures of
Tarzan: serial)
WALTERS, LUANA (The Durango Kid)
WALTERS, POLLY (Union Depot)
WALTHALL, PATRICIA (Empty Holsters)
WALTON, GLADYS (Top O' the Morning)
WARD, ALICE (Skyline)
WARD, AMELITA (Who's Guilty?: serial)
WARD, DOROTHY (Courage)
WARE, IRENE (You Belong to Me)
WARREN, JAMES (Three for Bedroom C)
WARREN, JANE (Goldwyn player of '39)
WARREN, JANET (Jade Mask)
WARREN, KATHARINE (Harriet Craig)
WARREN, PHILIP (Give Me a Sailor)
WASHINGTON, MILDRED (Hearts in Dixie)
WAYNE, CAROLE (The Great Adventures of
Wild Bill Hickok: serial)
WEAVER, LORETTA (Heroes of the Saddle)
WEEKS, BARBARA (Soldiers of the Storm)
WELCH, NILES (McKenna of the Mounted)
WELCH, PHYLLIS (Professor Beware)
WELDEN, BEN (Hollywood Cavalcade)
WELFORD, NANCY (The Gold Diggers of
Broadway)
WELLES, VIRGINIA (Kiss and Tell)
WELLS, TED (Born to the Saddle)
WESTOVER, WINIFRED (The Lummox)
WHITLEY, RAY (Cyclone on Horseback)
WHITNEY, EVE (Radar Patrol vs. Spy King:
serial)
WHITNEY, HELENE (The Saint's Double
Trouble)
WHITNEY, ROBERT (Judge Hardy's Children)
WIDRIN, TANYA (a starlet of '40)
WILDE, LEE & LYN (Andy Hardy's Blonde
Trouble)
WILDE, LOIS (Undersea Kingdom: serial)
WILEY, JAN (Dick Tracy vs. Crime, Inc.:
serial)
WILLIAMS, ADA (Common Clay)
WILLIAMS, CHILI (Copacabana)
WILLIAMS, CLARK (The Werewolf of
London)
WILLIAMS, HOPE (The Scoundrel)
WILLIAMS, LOTTIE (Murder by an
Aristocrat)
WILSON, HOWARD (The Lost Patrol)
WILSON, MARGERY (The Clodhopper)
WINFIELD, JOAN (The Adventures of Mark
Twain)
WINSLOW, LEAH (She-Wolf)
WINTER, LASKA (Frozen Justice)

WITHERS, ISABEL *(Paid)*
WOLFE, BILL *(Poppy)*
WOOD, HELEN *(Charlie Chan at the Race Track)*
WOODS, EDWARD *(The Public Enemy)*
WOODWARD, FRANCES *(Riders of the Deadline)*
WOODWORTH, JANE *(Powder Town)*

WORTH, BARBARA *(Plunging Hoofs)*
WORTH, LILLIAN *(Tarzan the Tiger:* serial*)*
WRIGHT, HELEN *(Dames Ahoy)*
YARBO, LILLIAN *(You Can't Take It With You)*
YOUNG, ELIZABETH *(There's Always Tomorrow)*
YOUNGBLOOD, GLORIA *(Trade Winds)*

"LOST" CHILD PLAYERS

ALEXANDER, TAD *(Rasputin and the Empress)*
BABY BROCK *(The Woman on Trial)*
BABY CHARLIE SPAFFORD (a child star of '17)
BABY DORIS *(Little Orphan Annie)*
BABY HELEN *(The Baby and the Boss)*
BABY MARIE ELINE (a "Thanhouser Kid")
BADGLEY, HELEN (a "Thanhouser Kid")
BELLE, TULA *(The Blue Bird: '18)*
BENHAM, LELAND (a "Thanhouser Kid")
BEULAH, BODDY & THELMA BURNS (in "The Fox Kiddies")
BORENE, JACKIE *(Once in a Blue Moon)*
BORENE, SALLY
BOSS, YALE (Edison Co. child star of '14)
BREWER, BETTY *(Rangers of Fortune)*
BUPP, TOMMY ("Our Gang")
BUTCH & BUDDY *(A Little Bit of Heaven)*
BUTLER, LOIS *(Mickey)*
CALKINS, JOHNNY *(Life with Father)*
CARPENTER, FRANCIS (in "The Fox Kiddies")
CARROLL, JOAN *(Primrose Path)*
CARTER, ANN *(The Cat People)*
CHALDECOTT, FAY *(David Copperfield)*
CHAPMAN, JANET *(Little Miss Thoroughbred)*
CHAPIN, BILLY *(The Kid from Left Field)*
CHAPIN, MICHAEL *(The Dakota Kid)*
CLANCY, KITTY *(Midnight Madonna)*
COAD, JOYCE *(The Scarlet Letter)*
COLLINS, CORA SUE *(The Dark Angel)*
CONDON, JACKIE ("Our Gang")
COOK, BILLY *(The Blue Bird: '40)*
COSBY, RONNIE *(King of the Jungle)*
COX, BOBBIE *(Young Eagles: serial)*
DANTE, JEANNE *(Four Days' Wonder)*
DARE, IRENE *(Breaking the Ice)*
DAWSON, BILLY *(Father's Son)*
DE BORA, DOROTHY ("Our Gang")
DE GARDE, ADELE (Biograph child star of '08)
DE RUE, CARMEN (in "The Fox Kiddies")
DONALDSON, TED *(Once Upon a Time)*
DURAND, DAVID *(Cradle Song)*
EGAN, GLADYS (Biograph child star of '08)
ERNEST, GEORGE ("The Jones Family" series)
EVERETT, CHARLES NEVILLE (a child star of '13)
EYER, RICHARD *(Friendly Persuasion)*
FAIRBANKS, MADELEINE & MARION *(On With the Show)*
FOSTER, EDNA (in early silents)
GEBERT, GORDON *(Holiday Affair)*
GIBSON, MIMI *(Everything I Have Is Yours)*

GIFFT, DON *(The Yearling)*
GRIFFITH, NONA *(The Uninvited)*
HALE, PATTY (DIANA) *(My Friend Flicka)*
HARRIS, MARILYN *(Frankenstein)*
HODGES, RALPH *(The Sea Hound: serial)*
HOLT, DAVID *(The Adventures of Tom Sawyer)*
HORNER, JACKIE *(Panama Hattie)*
HUNT, JIMMIE *(High Barbaree)*
INFUHR, TEDDY *(The Tuttles of Tahiti)*
JACKSON, MARY ANN ("Our Gang")
JACOBS, BILLIE (a child actor of '16)
JACOBS, PAUL (in Sennett comedies)
JANSSEN, EILEEN *(About Mrs. Leslie)*
JOHNSON, CARMENCITA *(Mrs. Wiggs of the Cabbage Patch: '34)*
JOHNSON, OLIVE (Reliance star of '15)
KENT, MARJORIE (the "Blondie" series)
KIM, SUZANNA *(The Good Earth)*
KNOWLDEN, MARILYN *(Les Miserables)*
KUHN, MICKEY *(Juarez)*
LEE, BILLY *(The Biscuit Eater: '40)*
LEE, DAVEY *(Sonny Boy)*
LEE, KATHERINE *(Two Little Imps)*
MacDOUGALL, ROBIN *(The Blue Bird: '18)*
MARLOWE, JO ANN *(Mildred Pierce)*
MARSHALL, CONNIE *(Sentimental Journey)*
McCASKILL, RODDY *(Sitting Pretty)*
McINTIRE, PEGGY *(I Remember Mama)*
McKIM, SAMMY *(The Painted Stallion: serial)*
McMANUS, SHARON *(Anchors Aweigh)*
MESSINGER, MARIE (in "The Fox Kiddies")
MOFFETT, SHARYN *(The Locket)*
MORAN, JACKIE *(Valiant Is the Word for Carrie)*
MUMMERT, DANNY (the "Blondie" series)
MUTCHIE, MARJORIE JANE (the "Blondie" series)
NELSON, BOBBY *(Partners)*
NICHOLS, RICHARD *(A Woman's Face)*
NUNN, LARRY *(Men of Boys Town)*
O'CONNOR, PATSY *(It Ain't Hay)*
PERL, LLOYD (in "The Fox Kiddies")
PHELPS, BUSTER *(Three on a Match)*
PRESTON, JANE *(Anne of Green Gables)*
PROFITT, DONALD ("Our Gang")
QUILLAN, BOBBY *(Swiss Family Robinson: '40)*
RENTSCHLER, MICKEY *(Radio Patrol: serial)*
ROBERTS, ERIC *(Watch on the Rhine)*
ROUBERT, MATTY (Universal star of '14)
SCOTT, DOUGLAS *(Cavalcade)*
SEESE, DOROTHY ANN ("Five Little Peppers" series)
SEVERN, CHRISTOPHER *(Mrs. Miniver)*

SIMMONS, BETTY SUE *(Frontier Gal)*
SINCLAIR, RONALD/a.k.a. RA HOULD
   (Thoroughbreds Don't Cry)
STARK, AUDAINE (Ramo Productions star of
   '14)
STEWART, JOHNNY *(Boots Malone)*
TANSY, JOHNNY (Biograph child of '08)
THOMAS, MARY *(Mrs. Wiggs of the Cabbage
   Patch: '42)*
TODD, ANN *(Three Daring Daughters)*
TRINN, MARVIN ("Our Gang")
TUCKER, JERRY ("Our Gang")

TYLER, RICHARD *(The Bells of St. Mary's)*
VANCE, JIM *(Young Eagles:* serial *)*
WARE, LINDA *(The Star Maker)*
WATTS, TWINKLE *(Lake Placid Serenade)*
WILCOX, CLAIRE *(40 Pounds of Trouble)*
WILSON, JANIS *(Now, Voyager)*
WONACOTT, EDNA MAY *(Shadow of a
   Doubt)*
WOOTEN, SARITA *(Wuthering Heights)*
WYATT, CHARLENE *(Valiant Is the Word for
   Carrie)*